TELECOMMUNICATIONS LAW HANDBOOK

To our new born sons Daniel and Ben

TELECOMMUNICATIONS LAW HANDBOOK

Edited by

John Angel

and

Ian Walden

BLACKSTONE
PRESS LIMITED

First published in Great Britain 1997 by Blackstone Press Limited,
9–15 Aldine Street, London W12 8AW.
Telephone 0181-740 2277 (00 + 44-181-740 2277)

© John Angel, Ian Walden 1997

ISBN: 1 85431 595 1

British Library Cataloguing in Publication Data
A CIP catalogue record for this book is available from the British Library

Typeset by Style Photosetting Ltd, Mayfield, East Sussex
Printed by Bell and Bain Limited, Glasgow

CONTENTS

PREFACE

The changes that are currently underway in the global telecommunications industry can best be described as monumental. The old state monopolies are giving way to a multitude of new players of all sizes and from many different commercial origins. Convergence with related industries, such as broadcasting and computing, is already well advanced.

Liberalisation has been the key political objective that has underpinned this sea-change, complemented by the rapid pace of technological development. Such liberalisation has meant a process of both de-regulation and re-regulation within jurisdictions, as traditional controls on the ability to provide services have been removed and new anti-competitive mechanisms have been established. Such change is set to continue for the foreseeable future.

The main objective of this *Telecommunications Law Handbook* is to provide in a convenient and easily accessible form some of the main regulatory texts within telecommunications law. The Handbook concentrates on telephony rather than broadcasting which has historically operated under a separate regulatory regime (although it is recognised that technological convergence is diminishing such regulatory distinctions).

The main problem faced by us as editors was the volume of material that could have been included. We were required on a number of occasions to rethink the contents, arguing our respective corners over particular items which felt dear to our hearts, but for which no room could be found. In some cases it was decided only to include extracts of a document, while in other cases only a reference in a footnote was possible.

The telecommunications industry is undergoing rapid change which has created its own set of problems. However, we do feel that the book represents a period of relative stability in the area of regulation. Where useful we have provided World Wide Web site references to enable the reader to follow-up the latest developments in each area.

The book arose out of our involvement in the University of London's LLM course in Telecommunications Law offered by the Centre for Commercial Law Studies (CCLS), Queen Mary & Westfield College. The course was established in 1992–93 by Christopher Millard, a Senior Visiting Fellow in the Centre and partner in Clifford Chance. Since its inception, the course has prospered, attracting increasing numbers of students (both full-time and occasional students working for law firms), and continues to be the only such course offered by a UK law school. The course is supported by a Web site which will be kept updated with regard to recent developments; the reader is invited to visit the site.

Finally, we would like to acknowledge the following organisations for their invaluable assistance in the preparation of the book: BT, for permission to reproduce their Interconnect agreement, the Department of Trade and Industry, the European Commission, OFTEL, HMSO, for permission to reproduce the licences within the licensing section and the librarians at Theodore Goddard.

John Angel   Ian Walden
Consultant, Theodore Goddard   Tarlo Lyons Senior Research Fellow
Visiting Fellow   CCLS, QMW
CCLS, QMW

February 1997   http://www.ccls.edu/ ccls/itlaw

PART I
UNITED KINGDOM

INTRODUCTION

The recent liberalisation of the telecommunications market has led to extensive and complicated new legislation in the UK which has been further complicated by the privatisation of British Telecommunications (BT).

The first part of the Handbook covers UK law. The starting point is 'radio' which significantly expanded the scope of telecommunications activities in the early 20th century. Legislation regulating radio was consolidated in the Wireless Telegraphy Act 1949. This statute is reproduced in the Handbook, to the extent relevant to telecoms, and annotated with subsequent amendments for ease of reference. This means that amending statutes like the Wireless Telegraphy Act 1967 are not reproduced as such, but where relevant incorporated into the principal legislation. There is a similar approach with other secondary amending legislation.

BT was created and split from the Post Office in 1981 by the British Telecommunications Act which started the process of competition. The 1981 Act also gave the Government power to dispose of its shares in Cable & Wireless. However, the inadequacies of the 1981 Act to achieve liberalisation plus the subsequent decision to privatise BT, resulted in the passing of the Telecommunications Act 1984 which introduced a regulator, the Director General of Telecommunications (DGT) with an Office of Telecommunications (OFTEL).[1] Because the Handbook mainly concentrates on the liberalisation of the market and operation of the industry, rather than its privatisation, only the 1984 Act is reproduced as amended in the Handbook. The 1984 Act gave the DGT powers to deal with anti-competitive practices which included powers under general competition law. As a result relevant extracts of the Fair Trading Act 1973 and the Competition Act 1980 are included.

Part II of the Handbook covers European Union legislation. Although Europe is introducing liberalisation measures later than the UK, it has been necessary, through a number of statutory instruments (SIs), to comply with rather detailed measures on public procurement, leased lines, terminal equipment, electromagnetic compatibility and satellite communications. These SIs are reproduced in the text to the extent relevant to a non-technical handbook either as annotations to other reproduced legislation or in their own right.

Part III of the Handbook covers international treaties. As a result the Outer Space Act 1986 is reproduced in Part I, and completes the legislation covering the licensing of telecoms — radio, wire/cable/fibre (fixed) and space.

---

1 Web site - http://www.open.gov.uk/oftel/oftelhm.htm.

The final UK statute covered under Part I is the Interception of Communications Act 1985, which is the main provision designed to protect the privacy of users of telephony.

Telecommunications systems cannot be run without a licence granted by the Department of Trade and Industry.[2] Therefore, the conditions under which these licences are operated are a crucial part of telecoms law. A large section of Part I is devoted to BT's licence upon which most other licences are based. BT's licence has been fully annotated in the text to take into account the numerous amendments over the years and includes the important new fair trading condition which had only just been introduced at the time of publication. Also the principal class licences are reproduced — Telecommunication Services[3] and Satellite Services, and extracts from examples of other types of operators' licences — Cable, Mobile, International Simple Resale and International Facilities-Based Services (IFL). The IFL completes the principal liberalisation process of the UK market well ahead of the EU objective of the full opening of the European Market by 1 January 1998.

Finally in this part of the Handbook we have reproduced a draft of BT's standard interconnect agreement which is so important to a liberalised and fully competitive marketplace. We would have included OFTEL's Fair Trading Competition Guidelines which although having no legal effect, as such, will have important regulatory influences now that the new fair trading condition is becoming incorporated into most telecom's licenses. Unfortunately, it had not been finalised at the date of publication, but we would hope to include the guidelines in any future edition.

Part I of the Handbook starts with a chronology of the liberalisation of the UK's telecoms market.

CHRONOLOGY OF THE LIBERALISATION OF THE UK'S TELECOMMUNICATIONS MARKET

1981   British Telecommunications Act: formation of British Telecommunications Corporation (BT) and separation from the Post Office. British Electrotechnical Approvals Board (BABT) set up to facilitate relaxation of terminal equipment monopoly.

1982   Government award licence to Mercury Communications (Mercury), and announce that BT would get half the available mobile frequencies but only in partnership with another company (i.e. Securicor to create Cellnet). The second operator licensed was Racal Vodafone. General licence issued for value added network services.

1983   Mercury allowed to compete in the international services market. The government announces 'Duopoly Policy' — the right to provide basic telecom services over fixed links (cable, radio or satellite), domestic and international — shall be limited to BT and Mercury. Mobile licences are granted to Cellnet and Vodaphone.

---

2 Web site - http://www.dti.gov.uk/.
3 The Self-Provision Class Licence (SPL) is not reproduced in this Handbook because it is very similar to the TSL. The latest version of the SPL at the date of publication was 9 September 1996 and copies can be obtained from OFTEL.

1984   Telecommunications Act: privatisation of BT, with the public sale of 51% of the equity. The Office of Telecommunications (OFTEL) established to regulate the market. Class licences for cellular radio issued.

1985   Mercury request OFTEL to determine interconnection terms and conditions with BT. Mobile licencees commence operations.

1989   Simple inland resale permitted.

1990   Government publishes consultative document on the duopoly. Broadcasting Act: regulates cable operators. Class licences published for satellite services and self-provision (SPL).

1991   Government White Paper 'Competition and Choice: Telecommunications Policy for the 1990s' announces results of the duopoly review. Offer for sale of further Government shares in BT, reducing the Government's holding to 25.8%. Cable operators permitted to offer voice telephony in their own right, rather than as agents for BT or Mercury; and interconnect directly with neighbouring franchises.

1992   Introduction of Class Licences for Telecommunication Services (TSL) and revised SPL.

1993   Sale of last of Government's shares in BT. Ionica awarded operator's licence (Fixed Radio Access). BT required to publish terms of interconnection agreements. Energis granted a licence.

1994   OFTEL takes over responsibility from BT for number allocation. Orange launches its personal communications network (PCN) services, Energis launches its services.

1995   OFTEL referral to the MMC of who pays for number portability. BT required to have separate accounts for its businesses.

1996   Government opens up international facilities-based telecommunications services to all operators. OFTEL increases its powers to handle anti-competitive practices, and starts the de-regulation of pricing. Introduction of number portability. Ionica commences operation. TSL and SPL revised.

GLOSSARY OF TERMS TO NOTES IN PART I

1949 Act	Wireless Telegraphy Act 1949
1984 Act	Telecommunications Act 1984
BABT	British Electrotechnical Approvals Board
BBC	British Broadcasting Corporation
BT	British Telecommunications plc or British Telecom
CA	Court of Appeal
DGT	Director General of Telecommunications
Director General	Director General of Telecommunication
DTI	Department of Trade and Industry
EC	European Commission
EU	European Union
HL	House of Lords
IFL	International Facilities-Based Services Licence
ISPA	Information Service Providers Association
ISR	International Simple Resale
Leased Lines Regulations	The Telecommunications (Leased Lines) Regulations (SI 1993/2330 as amended by SI 1994/2251)
Mercury	Mercury Communications Limited
MMC	Monopolies and Mergers Commission
OFTEL	Office of Telecommunications
PTO	Public telecommunications operator
QBD	Queen's Bench Division
SPL	Self-Provision Licence
TSL	Telecommunication Services Licence

WIRELESS TELEGRAPHY ACT 1949
(1949, c. 54)

ARRANGEMENT OF SECTIONS
PART I
REGULATION OF WIRELESS TELEGRAPHY

PART II
SPECIAL PROVISIONS AS TO INTERFERENCE

PART III
SUPPLEMENTAL

SCHEDULES:

An Act to amend the law relating to Wireless Telegraphy

[30 July 1949]

Note

The Wireless Telegraphy Act 1967 has been incorporated into this annotated version of the 1949 Act so far as it is relevant to this Handbook.

PART I
REGULATION OF WIRELESS TELEGRAPHY

1. Licensing of wireless telegraphy

(1)   No person shall establish or use any station for wireless telegraphy or instal or use any apparatus for wireless telegraphy except under the authority of a licence in that behalf [granted under this section—
  (a)   by the Secretary of State (unless it is a television licence), or
  (b)   if it is a television licence, by the BBC;
and any person] who establishes or uses any station for wireless telegraphy or instals or uses any apparatus for wireless telegraphy except under and in accordance with such a licence shall be guilty of an offence under this Act:

Provided that the [Secretary of State] may by regulations exempt from the provisions of this subsection the establishment, installation or use of stations for wireless telegraphy or wireless telegraphy apparatus of such classes or descriptions as may be specified in the regulations, either absolutely or subject to such terms, provisions and limitations as may be so specified.

(2)   A licence granted under this section (hereafter in this Act referred to as a wireless telegraphy licence) may be issued subject to such terms, provisions and [limitations—
  (a)   as the Secretary of State may think fit; or
  (b)   in the case of a television licence, as the Secretary of State may direct or (subject to any such direction) the BBC may think fit,
including] in particular in the case of a licence to establish a station, limitations as to the position and nature of the station, the purpose for which, the circumstances in which, and the persons by whom the station may be used, and the apparatus which may be installed or used therein, and, in the case of any other licence, limitations as to the apparatus which may be installed or used, and the places where, the purposes for which, the circumstances in which and the persons by whom the apparatus may be used.

(3)   A wireless telegraphy licence shall, unless previously revoked by the [Secretary of State] [or (if it is a television licence) by the BBC], continue in force for such period as may be specified in the licence.

(4)   A wireless telegraphy licence [other than a television licence] may be revoked, or the terms, provisions or limitations thereof varied, by a notice in writing of the [Secretary of State] served on the holder of the licence or by a general notice applicable to licences of the class to which the licence in question belongs published in such manner as may be specified in the licence [; and a television licence may be revoked, or the terms, provisions or limitations thereof varied, by the BBC (either of their own motion or to give effect to any direction of the Secretary of State under subsection (2)(b) of this section)—
  (a)   by a notice in writing served on the holder of the licence; or
  (b)   by a general notice published as mentioned above].

(5)   Where a wireless telegraphy licence has expired or has been revoked, it shall be the duty of the person to whom the licence was issued, and of every other person in whose possession or under whose control the licence may be,

to cause the licence to be surrendered to the [Secretary of State] if required by the [Secretary of State] so to do, and any person who without reasonable excuse fails or refuses to comply with the provisions of this subsection shall be guilty of an offence under this Act:

Provided that this subsection shall not apply to a licence relating solely to apparatus not designed or adapted for emission (as opposed to reception).

(6)   Nothing in this section shall authorise the inclusion, in any wireless telegraphy licence relating solely to apparatus not designed or adapted for emission (as opposed to reception), of any term or provision requiring any person to concede any form of right of entry into any private dwelling-house.

(7)   In this Act—

'television licence' means a wireless telegraphy licence authorising the installation and use of a television receiver; and

'television receiver' means television receiving apparatus of any class or description specified in regulations made by the Secretary of State under section 2 of this Act.

Notes

1.   The words in the first pair of square brackets in s. 1(1) and the words in square brackets in s. 1(2) were substituted, the words in the second pair of square brackets in s. 1(3) and the words in the first pair of square brackets in s. 1(4) were inserted, and the words in the third pair of square brackets in s. 1(4) and the whole of s. 1(7) were added by the Broadcasting Act 1990.

2.   The words in the second pair of square brackets in s. 1(1). the words in the first pair of square brackets in s.1 (3), the words in the second pair of square brackets in s. 1(4) and the words in square brackets in s. 1(5) were substituted by the Post Office Act 1969 and the Ministry of Posts and Telecommunications (Dissolution) Order 1974 (SI 1974/691).

3.   A relevant case includes: *Rudd* v *Secretary of State for Trade and Industry* [1987] 1 WLR 786, HL.

4.   Relevant regulations include: The Wireless Telegraphy (Exemption) Regulations 1980, SI 1980/1848, as amended by SI 1987/776; the Wireless Telegraphy (Exemption) Regulations 1982, SI 1982/1697, as amended by SI 1987/775, SI 1992/2009; the Wireless Telegraphy (Cordless Telephone Apparatus) (Exemption) Regulations 1988, SI 1988/1648; the Wireless Telegraphy (Cordless Telephone Apparatus) (Exemption) Regulations 1992, SI 1992/2009 as amended by SI 1996/316, the Wireless Telegraphy Apparatus (Land Mobile-Satellite Service) (Low Bit Rate Data) (Exemption) Regulations 1993, SI 1993/21; the Wireless Telegraphy (Short Range Devices) (Exemption) Regulations 1993, SI 1993/1591, as amended by SI 1995/1081.

1A   Offence of keeping wireless telegraphy station or apparatus available for unauthorised use

Any person who has any station for wireless telegraphy or apparatus for wireless telegraphy in his possession or under his control and either—

(a)   intends to use it in contravention of section 1 of this Act; or

(b)   knows, or has reasonable cause to believe, that another person intends to use it in contravention of that section,

shall be guilty of an offence.

Note

Section 1A was inserted by the Broadcasting Act 1990.

Sections 1B–1C relate to broadcasting and are not reproduced.

2.   Fees and charges for telegraphy licences

(1)   On the issue or renewal of a wireless telegraphy licence, and, where the regulations under this section so provide, at such times thereafter as may be prescribed by the regulations, there shall be [paid—

(a)   to the Secretary of State; or

(b)   in the case of a television licence, to the BBC,

by the person] to whom the licence is issued such sums as may be prescribed by regulations to be made by the [Secretary of State] with the consent of the Treasury, and different provision may be made in relation to different licences, according to the nature, terms, provisions, limitations and duration thereof:

Provided that the regulations made may contain provisions authorising, in such cases as are not otherwise dealt with by the regulations, the charge by the [Secretary of State] of such sums, whether on the issue or renewal of the licence or subsequently, as may in the particular case appear to him to be proper, but this proviso shall not apply to licences of any type wholly or mainly intended to meet the needs of persons desiring to use, in a private dwelling-house and without making any charge to other persons, apparatus not designed or adapted for emission (as opposed to reception).

(2)   [Notwithstanding anything in subsection (1) of this section, where—

(a)   an application for the issue or renewal of a television licence is made to the BBC by a person ordinarily resident in the United Kingdom, and

(b)   the BBC are satisfied, by means of a certificate issued by the local authority and produced to them by the applicant, that the applicant is a blind person not resident in a public or charitable institution or in a school,

the BBC shall, to such extent as the Secretary of State may determine, dispense with the payment of any sum which would otherwise be payable on the issue or renewal of the licence.]

In this subsection, the expression 'blind person' means a person so blind as to be unable to perform any work for which eyesight is essential, and the expression 'the local authority' means—

(a)   in relation to any person ordinarily resident in England and Wales, the council of the county or county borough in which he is ordinarily resident;

(b)   in relation to a person ordinarily resident in a large burgh in Scotland, the town council of that burgh;

(c)   in relation to a person ordinarily resident elsewhere in Scotland, the council of the county in which he is ordinarily resident;

(d)   in relation to a person ordinarily resident in Northern Ireland, the [Health and Social Services Board established under the Health and Personal Social Services (Northern Ireland) Order 1972], for the area in which he is ordinarily resident.

(3)   Where sums will or may become payable under subsection (1) of this section subsequently to the issue or renewal of a licence, the [Secretary of State] may, on the issue or renewal thereof, require such security to be given, by way of deposit or otherwise, for the payment of the sums which will or may become payable as he thinks fit.

Notes

1.   The words in the first pair of square brackets in s. 2(1) and the words in the first pair of square brackets in s. 2(2) were substituted by the Broadcasting Act 1990.

2. The words in the second and third pairs of square brackets in s. 2(1) and the words in square brackets in s. 2(3) are substituted by the Post Office Act 1969 and the Ministry of Posts and Telecommunications (Dissolution) Order 1974, SI 1974/691.

3. The words in the second pair of square brackets in s. 2(2) were substituted by the Transfer of Functions (Local Government, etc) (Northern Ireland) Order 1973, SR & O (NI) 1973/256.

4. Relevant regulations include: The Wireless Telegraphy (Exemption) Regulations 1980, SI 1980/1848, as amended by SI 1987/776; and the Wireless Telegraphy (Licence Charges) Regulations 1995, SI 1995/1331 (revoking and replacing SI 1991/542), as amended by SI 1996/1464.

3. Regulations as to wireless telegraphy

(1)   The [Secretary of State] may make regulations—

(a)   prescribing the things which are to be done or are not to be done in connection with the use of any station for wireless telegraphy or wireless telegraphy apparatus, and, in particular, requiring the use of any such station or apparatus to cease on the demand in that behalf of any such persons as may be prescribed by or under the regulations;

(b)   imposing on the person to whom a wireless telegraphy licence is issued with respect to any station for wireless telegraphy or wireless telegraphy apparatus, or who is in possession or control of any station for wireless telegraphy or wireless telegraphy apparatus, obligations as to permitting and facilitating the inspection of the station and apparatus, as to the condition in which the station and apparatus are to be kept and, in the case of a station or apparatus for the establishment, installation or use of which a wireless telegraphy licence is necessary, as to the production of the licence, or of such other evidence of the licensing of the station or apparatus as may be prescribed by the regulations;

(c)   where sums are or may become due from the person to whom a wireless telegraphy licence is issued after the issue or renewal thereof, requiring that person to keep and produce such accounts and records as may be specified in the regulations; and

(d)   requiring the person to whom a wireless telegraphy licence authorising the establishment or use of a station has been issued to exhibit at the station such notices as may be specified in the regulations,

and different provision may be made by any such regulations for different classes of case:

Provided that nothing in any such regulations shall require any person to concede any form of right of entry into a private dwellinghouse for the purpose of permitting or facilitating the inspection of any apparatus not designed or adapted for emission (as opposed to reception).

(2)   Any person who contravenes any regulations made under this section, or causes or permits any station for wireless telegraphy or wireless telegraphy apparatus to be used in contravention of any such regulations, shall be guilty of an offence under this Act.

Notes
1. The words in square brackets in s. 3(1) were substituted by the Post Office Act 1969 and the Ministry of Posts and Telecommunications (Dissolution) Order 1974, SI 1974/691.

2.   Relevant regulations include: The Wireless Telegraphy (Content of Transmission) Regulations 1988, SI 1988/47; The Wireless Telegraphy (Testing and Development Under Suppressed Radiation Conditions) (Exemption) Regulations 1989, SI 1989/1842; the Wireless Telegraphy (Cordless Telephone Apparatus) (Exemption) Regulations 1992, SI 1992/2009; the Wireless Telegraphy Apparatus (Land Mobile-Satellite Service) (Low Bit Rate Data) (Exemption) Regulations 1993, SI 1993/21; the Wireless Telegraphy (Short Range Devices) (Exemption) Regulations 1993, SI 1993/159/1591 as amended by SI 1995/1081.

3A.   Restriction on revocation or variation of certain wireless telegraphy licences

(1)   Subject to subsection (2) below, this section applies in any case where a wireless telegraphy licence is granted to any person who holds a licence granted under section 7 of the Telecommunications Act 1984 ('the telecommunications licence') authorising the running of a telecommunication system ('the system'), and the wireless telegraphy licence authorises all or any of the following, that is to say—

(a)   the establishment of stations for wireless telegraphy or the installation of apparatus for wireless telegraphy, being stations or apparatus forming or intended to form part of the system;

(b)   the use of any such stations or apparatus in running the system; and

(c)   the installation and use for the purposes of the system (whether by the holder of the licence or by any other person) of any such apparatus connected or intended to be connected to the system.

(2)   This section does not apply unless the telecommunications licence is one to which section 8 of that Act applies (licences including conditions imposing certain obligations with respect to the provision of telecommunications services or other matters).

(3)   In any case to which this section applies the wireless telegraphy licence may include terms restricting the exercise by the Secretary of State of his power under section 1(4) of this Act to revoke or vary the licence.

(4)   Without prejudice to the generality of subsection (3) above, the terms that may be included in a wireless telegraphy licence by virtue of that subsection include, in particular, terms providing that the licence may not be revoked or varied except with the consent of the holder of the licence or (as the case may be) in such other circumstances and on such grounds as may be specified in the licence.

(5)   Any such circumstances or grounds may relate to matters relevant for the purposes of the Telecommunications Act 1984 as well as to matters relevant for the purposes of this Act (and may, in particular, be dependent upon action taken under that Act in relation to the telecommunications licence).

(6)   A wireless telegraphy licence containing any terms included in the licence by virtue of subsection (3) above may also provide that regulations made under section 3 of this Act—

(a)   shall not apply in relation to any station or apparatus to which the licence relates; or

(b)   shall apply in relation to any such station or apparatus to such an extent only, or subject to such modifications, as may be specified in the licence.

(7)   Notwithstanding any terms or provisions included in a wireless telegraphy licence in accordance with this section the Secretary of State may at any time, by a notice in writing served on the holder of the licence, revoke the licence or vary its terms, provisions or limitations, if it appears to him to be requisite or expedient to do so in the interests of national security or relations with the government of a country or territory outside the United Kingdom.

(8)   Expressions used in this section to which a meaning is given for the purposes of the Telecommunications Act 1984 have the same meaning in this section; and section 106(4) of that Act (interpretation of power of Secretary of State to give a direction if it appears to him to be requisite or expedient to do so as mentioned in subsection (7) above) shall apply in relation to the power of the Secretary of State under subsection (7) above to revoke or vary a wireless telegraphy licence as it applies to any power of the Secretary of State under that Act to give such a direction.

Note
This section was inserted by the Telecommunications Act 1984.

4.   Experimental licences

(1)   Subject to the provisions of this section, where an application for the grant or renewal of a wireless telegraphy licence is made to the [Secretary of State] by a British subject and the [Secretary of State] is satisfied that the only purpose for which the applicant requires the licence is to enable him to conduct experiments in wireless telegraphy for the purpose of scientific research, the [Secretary of State] shall not refuse to grant or renew the licence and shall not revoke the licence when granted, and no sum shall be payable under the regulations under section two of this Act otherwise than on the issue or renewal of the licence.

(2)   Nothing in subsection (1) of this section shall limit the discretion of the [Secretary of State] as to the terms, provisions or limitations which he attaches to any licence or his power to vary the terms, provisions or limitations of any licence.

(3)   Nothing in subsection (1) of this section shall prevent the [Secretary of State] from refusing to grant or renew, or from revoking, any licence if, whether before or after the grant or last renewal of the licence, the applicant has been convicted of any offence under this Part of this Act, whether in relation to the same or any other apparatus, or has contravened any of the terms, provisions or limitations of that or any other wireless telegraphy licence granted to him, or has been convicted under Part II of this Act of using any apparatus for the purpose of interfering with any wireless telegraphy.

(4)   If it appears to the [Secretary of State] that, by reason of the existence of a national emergency, it is expedient so to do, he may, by a notice in writing served on the holder of any licence granted in pursuance of this section, revoke that licence, or by a general notice published in the London, Edinburgh and Belfast Gazettes, revoke all licences granted in pursuance of this section which are for the time being in force, and the [Secretary of State] shall not be obliged by virtue of this section to grant or renew any licence, if it appears to him, by reason of the existence of such an emergency, inexpedient so to do.

Note
The words in square brackets were substituted by the Post Office Act 1969 and the Ministry of Posts and Telecommunications (Dissolution) Order 1974, SI 1974/691.

5. Misleading messages and interception and disclosure of messages

Any person who—

(a) by means of wireless telegraphy, sends or attempts to send, any message which, to his knowledge, is false or misleading and is, to his knowledge, likely to prejudice the efficiency of any safety of life service or endanger the safety of any person or of any vessel, aircraft or vehicle, and, in particular, any message which, to his knowledge, falsely suggests that a vessel or aircraft is in distress or in need of assistance or is not in distress or not in need of assistance; or

(b) otherwise than under the authority of the [Secretary of State] or in the course of his duty as a servant of the Crown, either—

(i) uses any wireless telegraphy apparatus with intent to obtain information as to the contents, sender or addressee of any message (whether sent by means of wireless telegraphy or not) which neither the person using the apparatus nor any person on whose behalf he is acting is authorised by the [Secretary of State] to receive; or

(ii) except in the course of legal proceedings or for the purpose of any report thereof, discloses any information as to the contents, sender or addressee of any such message, being information which would not have come to his knowledge but for the use of wireless telegraphy apparatus by him or by another person,

shall be guilty of an offence under this Act.

Notes
1. The words in square brackets were substituted by the Post Office Act 1969 and the Ministry of Posts and Telecommunications (Dissolution) Order 1974, SI 1974/691.
2. Relevant cases include: *Malone* v *Commissioner of Police* [1979] 2 WLR 700; *DPP* v *Waite, The Times,* 17 May 1996; and *Francome* v *Mirror Group Newspapers* [1984] 1 WLR 892.

6. Territorial extent of preceding provisions

(1) Subject to the provisions of this section, the preceding provisions of this Part of this Act shall apply—

(a) to all stations and apparatus in or over, or for the time being in or over, the United Kingdom or the territorial waters adjacent thereto; and

(b) subject to any limitations which the [Secretary of State] may by regulations determine, to all stations and apparatus on board any . . . ship or . . . aircraft which is registered in the United Kingdom but is not for the time being in or over the United Kingdom or the said territorial waters; and

(c) subject to any limitations which the [Secretary of State] may by regulations determine, to all apparatus which is not in or over the United Kingdom or the said territorial waters but was released from within the United Kingdom or the said territorial waters, or from any . . . ship or . . . aircraft which is registered in the United Kingdom, and, without prejudice to the liability of any other person, in the event of any contravention of the said preceding provisions or of any regulations made thereunder occurring in relation to any station or apparatus on board or released from any vessel or aircraft, the captain or person for the time being in charge of the vessel or aircraft shall be guilty of an offence under this Act:

Provided that the captain or person for the time being in charge of a vessel or aircraft shall not be guilty of any offence under this Act by reason of any contravention of the said provisions or regulations occurring in relation to apparatus on board the vessel or aircraft if the contravention consists of the use by a passenger on board the ship or aircraft of apparatus not designed or adapted for emission (as opposed to reception) which is not part of the wireless telegraphy apparatus, if any, of the ship or aircraft.

(2)   The [Secretary of State] may make regulations for regulating the use, on board any [ship or aircraft which, not being registered in the United Kingdom, is registered in a country other than the United Kingdom, the Isle of Man or any of the Channel Islands while that ship or aircraft is] within the limits of the United Kingdom and the territorial waters adjacent thereto, of wireless telegraphy apparatus on board the ship or aircraft, and such regulations may provide for the punishment of persons contravening the regulations by [a maximum fine for each offence of an amount not exceeding level 5 on the standard scale, . . . or of a lesser amount] and for the forfeiture of any wireless telegraphy apparatus in respect of which an offence under such regulations is committed; but, save as aforesaid [or by virtue of an Order in Council under subsection (3) of this section], nothing in this Part of this Act shall operate so as to impose any prohibition or restriction on persons using wireless telegraphy apparatus on board any [such ship or aircraft as aforesaid].

(3)   His Majesty may by Order in Council direct that any reference in this section to any . . . ship or aircraft registered in the United Kingdom shall be construed as including a reference to any . . . ship or aircraft registered in the Isle of Man, in any of the Channel Islands, or in any colony, British protectorate or British protected state, or registered under the law of any other country or territory outside the United Kingdom which is for the time being administered by His Majesty's Government in the United Kingdom.

[(4)   . . .]

Notes
1.   The words 'Secretary of State' in s. 6(1) and (2) were substituted by the Post Office Act 1969 and the Ministry of Posts and Telecommunications (Dissolution) Order 1974, SI 1974/691.
2.   The words omitted from s. 6(1) and (3) were repealed by the Wireless Telegraphy Act 1967.
3.   The words in the second, fourth and fifth pairs of square brackets in s. 6(2) were substituted or inserted by the Wireless Telegraphy Act 1967, the words in the third pair of square brackets in that subsection were substituted by the Criminal Justice Act 1982, and the words omitted from that subsection were repealed by the SL(R) Act 1993.
4.   Section 6(4) was added by the Criminal Justice Act 1982, and repealed by the Fines and Penalties (Northern Ireland) Order 1984, SI 1984/703 (NI 3).
5.   Relevant cases include: *Post Office* v *Estuary Radio Ltd* [1967] 1 WLR 1369; *R* v *Kent Justices, ex parte Lye and others* [1967] 2 QB 153.

7. Powers of [Secretary of State] as to wireless personnel

(1)   The [Secretary of State] may hold examinations to determine the competence of the persons examined to fill positions in connection with the operation of stations for wireless telegraphy or wireless telegraphy apparatus and may issue to persons successful at such examinations certificates of competence of such types as he may from time to time determine.

(2)   The [Secretary of State] may issue to such persons as he thinks fit authorities in writing authorising the persons to whom the authorities are issued to fill such positions in connection with the operation of stations for wireless telegraphy or wireless telegraphy apparatus as may be specified in the respective authorities, being positions for the holding of which the possession of such an authority is, under wireless telegraphy licences granted under this Act or under any licences granted under any corresponding law of any part of His Majesty's dominions, a necessity or a qualification.

(3)   The [Secretary of State], if it appears to him that there are sufficient grounds so to do, may at any time suspend any authority granted under the last preceding subsection with a view to the revocation thereof, and where he so suspends an authority, the provisions of the First Schedule to this Act shall have effect.

(4)   Where any authority granted under subsection (2) of this section has ceased to be in force or has been suspended, it shall be the duty of the person to whom the authority was issued, and of every other person in whose possession or under whose control the authority may be, to cause the authority to be surrendered to the [Secretary of State] if required by the [Secretary of State] so to do, and any person who without reasonable excuse fails or refuses to comply with the provisions of this subsection shall be guilty of an offence under this Act.

(5)   The [Secretary of State] may charge to persons applying to take part in any examination under this section, and to applicants for, or for copies of, any certificate or authority issued under this section, such fees, if any, as he may determine.

Notes
The words 'Secretary of State' in square brackets were substituted by the Post Office Act 1969 and the Ministry of Posts and Telecommunications (Dissolution) Order 1974, SI 1974/691.

PART II
SPECIAL PROVISIONS AS TO INTERFERENCE

9. Advisory committee and appeal tribunal

(1)   For the purposes specified in this Part of this Act there shall be established—
      (a)   . . .
      (b)   a tribunal (in this Part of this Act referred to as 'the appeal tribunal').
(2)   . . .
(3)   Subject to the provisions of this section, the appeal tribunal shall consist of—

(a) one person to be appointed by the Lord Chancellor who shall be a [person who has a 7 year general qualification, within the meaning of section 71 of the Courts and Legal Services Act 1990,] or a person who has held judicial office, and who shall act only as respects proceedings in England and Wales and shall as respects such proceedings be the president of the tribunal;

(b) one person to be appointed by the Lord President of the Court of Session who shall be an advocate of not less than seven years' standing or a solicitor of not less than seven years' standing or a person who has held judicial office, and who shall act only as respects proceedings in Scotland and shall as respects such proceedings be the president of the tribunal;

(c) one person to be appointed by the Lord Chief Justice of Northern Ireland who shall be a barrister of not less than seven years' standing or a solicitor of not less than seven years' standing or a person who has held judicial office, and who shall act only as respects proceedings in Northern Ireland and shall as respects such proceedings be the president of the tribunal; and

(d) two assessors, to assist the president of the tribunal, to be appointed by the President of the Institution of Electrical Engineers with the approval of the Council thereof, being persons who, in the opinion of the President of the said Institution, possess expert knowledge of the matters likely to come before the tribunal and are not members of the advisory committee.

(4) If, within such time, if any, as may be limited in that behalf by the rules regulating the procedure of the appeal tribunal, the parties to any particular case before the tribunal other than the [Secretary of State] request the President of the Institution of Electrical Engineers to appoint either one or two specially qualified assessors under this subsection, the President of the Institution of Electrical Engineers shall, with the approval of the Council thereof, select and appoint one or, as the case may be, two such assessors to act for that case, and the assessor or assessors so appointed shall act therefore accordingly in lieu of the assessors appointed under paragraph (d) of subsection (3) of this section, or, if the request is for the appointment of one specially qualified assessor and expresses a specific desire that he shall act in lieu of one only of the assessors appointed under the said paragraph (d), in lieu of such one of the assessors appointed under the said paragraph (d) as the President of the said Institution may select.

(5) If, in the case of any reference or application to the appeal tribunal under section eleven of this Act, any of the parties or the president of the tribunal, within such time, if any, as may be limited in that behalf by the rules regulating the procedure of the tribunal, request the Lord Chancellor, if the proceedings are in England and Wales, or the Secretary of State, if the proceedings are in Scotland or Northern Ireland, to appoint two additional members of the tribunal to act for that case, the Lord Chancellor or Secretary of State, as the case may be, shall select and appoint two persons, who need not possess any legal qualifications or expert knowledge, to act as additional members of the tribunal for that case, and the additional members so appointed shall act therefore accordingly in addition to the president and the assessors or assessor.

(6) The provisions of the Second Schedule to this Act shall have effect with respect to the period for which members of the appeal tribunal are to hold office, the appointment of deputies in case of illness or inability to act,

the incidental powers of the tribunal, their procedure and the enforcement and proof of their orders.

(7) The expenses incurred by . . . the appeal tribunal, to such extent as may be determined by the [Secretary of State] with the consent of the Treasury, (including, . . . such sums by way of fees to, and in respect of the expenses of, the members or persons acting as members thereof, as may be so determined) shall be [paid by the [Secretary of State]].

Notes
1. Section 9(1)(a) and (2), and the words omitted from s. 9(7), were repealed by the Telecommunications Act 1984.
2. The words in brackets in s. 9(3)(a) were substituted by the Courts and Legal Services Act 1990.
3. The words 'Secretary of State' in square brackets in s. 9(4) and (7) were substituted by the Post Office Act 1969 and the Ministry of Posts and Telecommunications (Dissolution) Order 1974, SI 1974/691.
4. The words in the second (outer) pair of square brackets in s. 9(7) were substituted by the Post Office Act 1961.

10. Regulations as to radiation of electro-magnetic energy, etc

(1) The [Secretary of State] may, . . . make regulations for both or either of the following purposes, that is to say—
(a) for prescribing the requirements to be complied with in the case of any apparatus to which this section applies if the apparatus is to be used;
(b) for prescribing the requirements to be complied with in the case of any apparatus to which this section applies if the apparatus is to be sold otherwise than for export, or offered or advertised for sale otherwise than for export, or let on hire or offered or advertised for letting on hire, by any person who in the course of business manufactures, assembles or imports such apparatus.

(2) The said requirements shall be such requirements as the [Secretary of State] thinks fit for the purpose of ensuring that the use of the apparatus does not cause undue interference with wireless telegraphy, and may in particular include—
(a) requirements as to the maximum intensity of electro-magnetic energy of any specified frequencies which may be radiated in any direction from the apparatus while it is being used; and
(b) in the case of an apparatus the power for which is supplied from electric lines, requirements as to the maximum electro-magnetic energy of any specified frequencies which may be injected into those lines by the apparatus,
and, in so far as appears to the [Secretary of State] necessary or expedient in the case of the regulations in question, different requirements may be prescribed for different circumstances and in relation to different classes or descriptions of apparatus, different districts or places and different times of use.

(3) The apparatus to which this section applies shall be such apparatus as may be specified in the regulations made thereunder, being apparatus generating, or designed to generate, or liable to generate fortuitously, electro-

magnetic energy at frequencies of not more than three million megacycles per second . . .

The references in this subsection to apparatus include references to any form of electric line, and other references in this Act to apparatus shall be construed accordingly.

(4) It shall not be unlawful for any person to use any apparatus to which this section applies or to sell any such apparatus or offer or advertise it for sale or let it on hire or offer or advertise it for letting on hire by reason only that it does not comply with the requirements applicable under any regulations made under this section, but the non-compliance shall be a ground for the giving of a notice under the next succeeding section or under section twelve of this Act, as the case may be.

Notes

1. The words in square brackets in s. 10(1) and (2) were substituted by the Post Office Act 1969 and the Ministry of Posts and Telecommunications (Dissolution) Order 1974, SI 1974/691.

2. The words omitted from s. 10(1) were repealed by the Telecommunications Act 1984.

3. The words omitted from s. 10(3) were repealed by the Wireless Telegraphy Act 1967.

4. Relevant regulations include: the Electromagnetic Compatability Regulations 1992, SI 1992/2372 amended by SI 1994/3080 which implement EC Council Directive 89/336; OJ L139 23/5/1989.

11.   Enforcement of regulations as to use of apparatus

(1) If the [Secretary of State] is of opinion—

(a)   that any apparatus does not comply with the requirements applicable to it under regulations made for the purpose specified in paragraph (a) of subsection (1) of the last preceding section; and

(b)   that either—

(i)   the use of the apparatus is likely to cause undue interference with any wireless telegraphy used for the purposes of any safety of life service or for any purpose on which the safety of any person or of any vessel, aircraft or vehicle may depend; or

(ii)   the use of the apparatus is likely to cause undue interference with any other wireless telegraphy and in fact has caused or is causing such interference in a case where he considers that all reasonable steps to minimise interference have been taken in relation to the station or apparatus receiving the telegraphy,

he may serve on the person in whose possession the apparatus is a notice in writing requiring that, after a date fixed by the notice, not being less than twenty-eight days from the date of the service thereof, the apparatus shall not be used, whether by the person to whom the notice is given or otherwise, or, if the [Secretary of State] thinks fit so to frame the notice, shall only be used in such manner, at such times and in such circumstances as may be specified in the notice:

Provided that—

(i)   if before the date fixed by the notice, a notice is given under subsection (3) of this section requiring the [Secretary of State] to refer the matter to the appeal tribunal, the [Secretary of State's] notice shall not operate until the termination of the proceedings before the tribunal, and any notice given under this subsection by the [Secretary of State] (other than a notice to which paragraph (ii) of this proviso applies) shall be framed accordingly;

(ii)   if the [Secretary of State] is satisfied that the use of the apparatus in question is likely to cause undue interference with any wireless telegraphy used for the purposes of any safety of life service or for any purpose on which the safety of any person or of any vessel, aircraft or vehicle may depend, the date to be fixed by the notice may be the date of the service thereof, and paragraph (i) of this proviso shall not apply.

(2)   A notice under subsection (1) of this section may be revoked or varied by a subsequent notice in writing by the [Secretary of State] served on the person in whose possession the apparatus then is:

Provided that where a notice under this subsection has the effect of imposing any additional restrictions on the use of the apparatus, the provisions of subsection (1) of this section relating to the coming into force of notices shall apply in relation to the notice as if it had been a notice served under the said subsection (1).

(3)   Where notice has been given under subsection (1) of this section, any person having possession of or any interest in the apparatus to which the notice relates may at any time (whether before or after the date fixed by the said notice), by notice in writing served on the [Secretary of State], require the [Secretary of State] to refer the matter to the appeal tribunal, and the [Secretary of State], unless he revokes his notice or modifies it to the satisfaction of the said person, shall refer the matter to the tribunal accordingly.

This subsection applies in relation to a notice under subsection (1) of this section which has been varied by a subsequent notice as it applies in relation to a notice which has not been so varied.

(4)   On any such reference, the tribunal shall hear the [Secretary of State] and the person at whose instance the reference was made and any other person appearing to them to be interested who desires to be heard, and has, in accordance with the rules regulating the procedure of the tribunal, procured himself to be made a party to the reference, and—

(a)   if they are satisfied that the apparatus in question complies with requirements applicable to it under the regulations, shall direct the [Secretary of State] to revoke the notice;

(b)   if they are satisfied that the said requirements ought properly to be relaxed in relation to the apparatus, may direct the [Secretary of State] to revoke the notice or to vary it in such manner as may be specified in the direction,

and the [Secretary of State] shall revoke or vary the notice accordingly:

Provided that the making by the tribunal of a direction under this subsection or the refusal by the tribunal to make a direction under this subsection shall not prevent any such person as is mentioned in subsection (3) of this section from giving a further notice under subsection (3) of this section and shall not, where the [Secretary of State] is of opinion that there has been a relevant change in the circumstances, prevent the [Secretary of State] from giving a further notice under subsection (1) or subsection (2) of this section.

(5) A direction given under subsection (4) of this section may be absolute, or may be conditional on such steps being taken in relation to the apparatus, or on the apparatus being made to comply with such requirements, as may be specified in the direction, and any question whether or not those steps have been taken or, as the case may be, whether or not the apparatus has been made to comply with those requirements, shall, on the application of the [Secretary of State] or of any person having possession of or any interest in the apparatus, be determined by the tribunal.

(6) Where any matter is referred to the tribunal under subsection (3) of this section or any application is made to the tribunal under the last preceding subsection, the tribunal shall, unless the parties otherwise agree, sit in England and Wales, in Scotland or in Northern Ireland, according to the place where the apparatus was at the date of the reference or application, and in some place which in the judgment of the tribunal is reasonably near to the place where the apparatus was as aforesaid.

(7) Any person who, knowing that a notice of the [Secretary of State] under this section is in force with respect to any apparatus, uses that apparatus, or causes or permits it to be used, in contravention of the notice, shall be guilty of an offence under this Act.

Note
The words 'Secretary of State' in square brackets are substituted by the Post Office Act 1969 and the Ministry of Posts and Telecommunications (Dissolution) Order 1974, SI 1974/691.

12. Enforcement of regulations as to sales, etc., by manufacturers and others

(1) If the [Secretary of State] is of opinion that any apparatus does not comply with the requirements applicable to it under regulations made for the purpose specified in paragraph (b) of subsection (1) of section ten of this Act, he may serve on any person who has manufactured, assembled or imported the apparatus in the course of business a notice in writing prohibiting him from selling the apparatus, otherwise than for export, or offering or advertising it for sale, otherwise than for export, or letting it on hire or offering or advertising it for letting on hire.

(2) Where a notice has been served under subsection (1) of this section, the person on whom the notice has been served may, by notice in writing served on the [Secretary of State], require the [Secretary of State] to refer the matter to the appeal tribunal and the [Secretary of State], unless he revokes the notice, shall refer the matter to the tribunal accordingly.

(3) On any such reference, the tribunal shall hear the [Secretary of State] and the person at whose instance the reference was made and any other person appearing to them to be interested who desires to be heard and has, in accordance with the rules regulating the procedure of the tribunal, procured himself to be made a party to the reference, and, if they are satisfied that the apparatus in question complies with the requirements applicable to it under the regulations, shall direct the [Secretary of State] to revoke the notice and he shall revoke it accordingly:
Provided that the making by the tribunal of a direction under this subsection shall not, where the apparatus is subsequently altered, prevent the

[Secretary of State] from serving a fresh notice under subsection (1) of this section with respect to the apparatus and the refusal by the tribunal to make a direction under this subsection shall not, where the apparatus is subsequently altered, prevent the [Secretary of State] from revoking the notice or the person on whom the notice was served from giving a further notice under subsection (2) of this section.

(4) The provisions of subsection (6) of section eleven of this Act shall apply in relation to any reference under this section as they apply in relation to any reference under subsection (3) of that section.

(5) Where a notice has been served under subsection (1) of this section, the person on whom the notice has been served shall, if he contravenes the provisions of the notice without the notice having been previously revoked by the [Secretary of State], be guilty of an offence under this Act.

Note
The words 'Secretary of State' in square brackets are substituted by the Post Office Act 1969 and the Ministry of Posts and Telecommunications (Dissolution) Order 1974, SI 1974/691.

13. Deliberate interference

(1) Any person who uses any apparatus for the purpose of interfering with any wireless telegraphy shall be guilty of an offence under this Act.

(2) This section shall apply whether or not the apparatus in question is wireless telegraphy apparatus or apparatus to which any of the preceding provisions of this Part of this Act apply, and whether or not any notice under section eleven or section twelve of this Act has been given with respect to the apparatus, or, if given, has been varied or revoked.

PART III
SUPPLEMENTAL

14. Penalties and legal proceedings

(1) Any person committing—

(aa) any offence under section 1(1) of this Act other than one falling within subsection (1A)(a) of this section;

(ab) any offence under section 1A of this Act other than one falling within subsection (1A)(aa) of this section;

(ac) any offence under section 1B or 1C of this Act;

(a) any offence under section 5(a) of this Act; or

(b) any offence under section 13 of this Act;

shall be liable on summary conviction to imprisonment for a term not exceeding six months or a fine not exceeding the statutory maximum or both, or on conviction on indictment to imprisonment for a term not exceeding two years or a fine or both.

(1A) Any person committing—

(a) any offence under section 1(1) of this Act consisting in the installation or use, otherwise than under and in accordance with a wireless telegraphy licence, of any apparatus not designed or adapted for emission (as opposed to reception); or (aa) any offence under section 1A of this Act committed in relation to any wireless telegraphy apparatus not designed or adapted for emission (as opposed to reception);

(b) any offence under section 3(2) of this Act consisting in a contravention, in relation to any such apparatus, of any regulations made under that section; or

(c) any offence under section 11(7) or 12(5) of this Act involving or consisting in a contravention of a notice of the Secretary of State in relation to any apparatus, not being apparatus the use of which is likely to cause undue interference with any wireless telegraphy used for the purpose of any safety of life service or any purpose on which the safety of any person or of any vessel, aircraft or vehicle may depend; or

(d) any offence under section 1(5) or 7(4) of this Act; or

(e) any offence under section 12A of this Act; or

(f) any offence under this Act which is an offence under section 5 or 8(2) of the Wireless Telegraphy Act 1967 (failure to comply with notices under Part I of that Act, giving false information, etc.);

shall be liable on summary conviction to a fine not exceeding level 3 on the standard scale.

(1B) Any person committing—

(a) . . .

(b) any offence under section 11(7) of this Act other than one within subsection (1A) (c) of this section;

shall be liable on summary conviction to imprisonment for a term not exceeding three months or to a fine not exceeding level 5 on the standard scale, or both.

(1C) Any person committing any other offence under this Act shall be liable on summary conviction to a fine not exceeding level 5 on the standard scale.

(2) Where any offence under this Act has been committed by a body corporate, every person who at the time of the commission of the offence was a director, general manager, secretary or other similar officer of the body corporate, or was purporting to act in any such capacity, shall be deemed to be guilty of that offence unless he proves that the offence was committed without his consent or connivance, and that he exercised all such diligence to prevent the commission of the offence as he ought to have exercised having regard to the nature of his functions in that capacity and in all the circumstances.

In this subsection, the expression 'director', in relation to any body corporate established by or under any enactment for the purpose of carrying on under national ownership any industry or part of an industry or undertaking, being a body corporate whose affairs are managed by the members thereof, means a member of that body.

(3) Where a person is convicted of—

(a) an offence under this Act consisting in any contravention of any of the provisions of Part I of this Act in relation to any station for wireless telegraphy or any wireless telegraphy apparatus (including an offence under section 1B or 1C of this Act) or in the use of any apparatus for the purpose of interfering with any wireless telegraphy;

(b)   any offence under section 12A of this Act;

(c)   any offence under the Marine, &c, Broadcasting (Offences) Act 1967; or

(d)   any offence under this Act which is an offence under section 7 of the Wireless Telegraphy Act 1967 (whether as originally enacted or as substituted by section 77 of the Telecommunications Act 1984),

the court may, in addition to any other penalty, order such of the following things to be forfeited to the Secretary of State as the court considers appropriate, that is to say—

(i)   any vehicle, vessel or aircraft, or any structure or other object, which was used in connection with the commission of the offence;

(ii)   any wireless telegraphy apparatus or other apparatus in relation to which the offence was committed or which was used in connection with the commission of it;

(iii)   any wireless telegraphy apparatus or other apparatus not falling within paragraph (ii) above which was, at the time of the commission of the offence, in the possession or under the control of the person convicted of the offence and was intended to be used (whether or not by that person) in connection with the making of any broadcast or other transmission that would contravene section I of this Act or any provision of the Marine, &c, Broadcasting (Offences) Act 1967.

(3AA)   The power conferred by virtue of subsection (3)(a) above does not apply in a case where the offence is any such offence as is mentioned in subsection (1A)(a) or (aa) above.

(3AB)   References in subsection (3)(ii) or (iii) above to apparatus other than wireless telegraphy apparatus include references to—

(a)   recordings;

(b)   equipment designed or adapted for use—

(i)   in making recordings; or

(ii)   in reproducing from recordings any sounds or visual images; and

(c)   equipment not falling within paragraphs (a) and (b) above but connected, directly or indirectly, to wireless telegraphy apparatus.

(3A)   Without prejudice to the operation of subsection (3) of this section in relation to any other apparatus, where a person is convicted of an offence under this Act involving restricted apparatus, the court shall order the apparatus to be forfeited to the Secretary of State unless the accused or any person claiming to be the owner of or otherwise interested in the apparatus shows cause why the apparatus should not be forfeited.

Apparatus is restricted apparatus for the purposes of this subsection if custody or control of apparatus of any class or description to which it belongs is for the time being restricted by an order under section 7 of the Wireless Telegraphy Act 1967.

(3B)   Apparatus may be ordered to be forfeited under this section notwithstanding that it is not the property of the person by whom the offence giving rise to the forfeiture was committed, and any apparatus ordered to be forfeited under this section may be disposed of by the Secretary of State in such manner as he thinks fit.

(3C)   Subsections (3) to (3B) of this section have effect notwithstanding anything in section 140 of the Magistrates' Courts Act 1980 or Article 58 of the Magistrates' Courts (Northern Ireland) Order 1981.

(3D)   The court by whom any apparatus is ordered to be forfeited under this section may also order the person by whom the offence giving rise to the forfeiture was committed not to dispose of that apparatus except by delivering it up to the Secretary of State within forty-eight hours of being so required by him.

(3E)   If a person against whom an order is made under subsection (3D) of this section contravenes that order or fails to deliver up the apparatus to the Secretary of State as required he shall be guilty of a further offence under this Act which, for the purpose of determining the appropriate penalty in accordance with the provisions of this section relating to penalties, shall be treated as an offence committed under the same provision, and at the same time, as the offence for which the forfeiture was ordered.

(4), (5) . . .

(6)   Without prejudice to the right to bring separate proceedings for contraventions of this Act taking place on separate occasions, a person who is convicted of an offence under this Act consisting in the use of any station or apparatus, or in a failure or refusal to cause any licence or authority to be surrendered, shall, where the use, or failure or refusal continues after the conviction, be deemed to commit a separate offence in respect of every day on which the use, failure or refusal so continues.

(7)   Nothing in the preceding provisions of this section shall limit any right of any person to bring civil proceedings in respect of the doing or apprehended doing of anything rendered unlawful by any provision of this Act, and, without prejudice to the generality of the preceding words, compliance with the provisions of this Act contraventions of which are declared to be offences under this Act shall be enforceable by civil proceedings by the Crown for an injunction or for any other appropriate relief.

In the application of this subsection to Scotland, for the words 'civil proceedings by the Crown for an injunction' there shall be substituted the words 'civil proceedings by the Lord Advocate for an interdict'.

(8), (9) . . .

Notes

1.   Sections 14(1), (1A)–(1C) were substituted for the original s. 14(1) by the Telecommunications Act 1984.

2.   Section 14(1)(aa)–(ac), (1A)(aa) were inserted, s. 14(1B)(a) was repealed, and the words in square brackets in s. 14(3E) were substituted, by the Broadcasting Act 1990.

3.   A new s. 14(3) and (3A)–(3E) were substituted for the original s. 14(3) by the 1984 Act and the current s. 14(3), (3AA), (3AB) were substituted for the new s. 14(3) by the 1990 Act.

4.   Section 14(4), (5) were repealed by the Post Office Act 1969.

5.   Section 14(8)(9) were added by the 1984 Act and repealed by the SL(R) Act 1993.

6.   Relevant cases include: *Post Office v Estuary Radio Ltd* [1967] 1 WLR 1396.

15.   Entry and search of premises, etc.

(1)   If, in England, Wales or Northern Ireland, a justice of the peace, or, in Scotland, the sheriff, is satisfied by information on oath that there is reasonable ground for suspecting that an offence under this Act [or under the

Marine, &c, Broadcasting (Offences) Act 1967] has been or is being committed, and that evidence of the commission of the offence is to be found on any premises specified in the information, or in any vehicle, vessel or aircraft so specified, he may grant a search warrant [authorising—

(a)   any person or persons authorised in that behalf by the Secretary of State; or

(b)   where the offence relates to the installation or use of a television receiver, any person or persons authorised in that behalf by the BBC or the Secretary of State,]
. . ., with or without any constables, to enter, at any time within one month from the date of the warrant, the premises specified in the information or, as the case may be, the vehicle, vessel or aircraft so specified and any premises upon which it may be, and to search the premises, or, as the case may be, the vehicle, vessel or aircraft, and to examine and test any apparatus found on the premises, vessel, vehicle or aircraft.

(2)   If, in England, Wales or Northern Ireland, a justice of the peace, or, in Scotland, the sheriff, is satisfied upon an application supported by sworn evidence—

(a)   that there is reasonable ground for believing that, on any specified premises or in any specified vessel, aircraft or vehicle, apparatus to which section ten of this Act applies is to be found which does not comply with the requirements applicable to it under regulations made under that section; and

(b)   that it is necessary to enter those premises, or that vessel, aircraft or vehicle, for the purpose of obtaining such information as will enable the [Secretary of State] to decide whether or not to serve a notice under section eleven or section twelve of this Act; and

(c)   that access to the premises, vessel, aircraft or vehicle for the purpose of obtaining such information as aforesaid has, within fourteen days before the date of the application to the justice or sheriff, been demanded by a person authorised in that behalf by the [Secretary of State] and producing sufficient documentary evidence of his identity and authority, but has been refused,
the justice or sheriff may issue a written authorisation under his hand empowering any person or persons authorised in that behalf by the [Secretary of State] . . ., with or without any constables, to enter the premises or, as the case may be, the vessel, aircraft or vehicle and any premises on which it may be and to search the premises, vessel, aircraft or vehicle with a view to discovering whether any such apparatus as aforesaid is situate thereon or therein, and, if he finds or they find any such apparatus thereon, or therein, to examine and test it with a view to obtaining such information as aforesaid:

Provided that an authorisation shall not be issued under this subsection unless either—

(i)   it is shown to the justice or sheriff that the [Secretary of State] is satisfied that there is reasonable ground for believing that the use of the apparatus in question is likely to cause undue interference with any wireless telegraphy used for the purposes of any safety of life service or any purpose on which the safety of any person or of any vessel, aircraft or vehicle may depend; or

(ii)   it is shown to the justice or sheriff that not less than seven days' notice of the demand for access was served on the occupier of the premises, or, as the case may be, the person in possession or the person in charge of the vessel, aircraft or vehicle, and that the demand was made at a reasonable hour and was unreasonably refused.

(2A)   Without prejudice to any power exercisable by him apart from this subsection, a person authorised by the Secretary of State or (as the case may be) by the BBC to exercise any power conferred by this section may use reasonable force, if necessary, in the exercise of that power.

(3)   Where under this section a person has a right to examine and test any apparatus on any premises or in any vessel, aircraft or vehicle, it shall be the duty of any person who is on the premises, or is in charge of, or in or in attendance on, the vessel, aircraft or vehicle, to give him any such assistance as he may reasonably require in the examination or testing of the apparatus.

(4)   Any person who—

(a)   [intentionally] obstructs any person in the exercise of the powers conferred on him under this section; or

(b)   [without reasonable excuse] fails or refuses to give to any such person any assistance which he is under this section under a duty to give to him; or

(c)   discloses, otherwise than for the purposes of this Act or of any report of proceedings thereunder, any information obtained by means of the exercise of powers under this Act, being information with regard to any manufacturing process or trade secret,

shall be guilty of an offence under this Act . . .

Notes
1.   The words in the first pair of square brackets in s. 15(1) and the whole of s. 15(2A) were inserted, the words in the second pair of square brackets in s. 15(1) were substituted, and the words omitted from s. 15(1) and (2) were repealed, by the Broadcasting Act 1990.
2.   The words in square brackets in s. 15(2) were substituted by the Post Office Act 1969 and the Ministry of Posts and Telecommunications (Dissolution) Order 1974, SI 1974/691.
3.   The words in square brackets in s. 15(4) were inserted by the Telecommunications Act 1984, and the words omitted from that subsection were repealed by the Post Office Act 1969.

16.   Regulations and orders

(1)   Any Order in Council under this Act may be revoked or varied by a subsequent Order in Council.

(2)   The power to make orders conferred on the [Secretary of State] by section eight of this Act and any power conferred on him by any of the provisions of this Act to make regulations shall be exercisable by statutory instrument, and any statutory instrument made in the exercise of any of the said powers shall be subject to annulment in pursuance of a resolution of either House of Parliament.

Notes
1.   Section 16(2) was repealed so far as it related to the power conferred by s. 8 of this Act which itself has been repealed by the Post Office Act 1969.
2.   The words in square brackets in s. 16(2) were substituted by the Post Office Act 1969 and the Ministry of Posts and Telecommunications (Dissolution) Order 1974, SI 1974/691.

17. Financial provisions

(1) . . . any fines imposed for offences under this Act, shall be paid into the Exchequer.

(2) . . .

Notes
1. The words omitted from s. 17(1) were repealed by the Post Office Act 1961.
2. Section 17(2) was repealed by the Transfer of Functions (Local Government, etc) (Northern Ireland) Order 1973, SR & O 1973/256.

19. Interpretation

(1) In this Act, except where the context otherwise requires, the expression 'wireless telegraphy' means the emitting or receiving, over paths which are not provided by any material substance constructed or arranged for that purpose, of electro-magnetic energy of a frequency not exceeding three million megacycles a second, being energy which either—

(a) serves for the conveying of messages, sound or visual images (whether the messages, sound or images are actually received by any person or not), or for the actuation or control of machinery or apparatus; or

(b) is used in connection with the determination of position, bearing, or distance, or for the gaining of information as to the presence, absence, position or motion of any object or of any objects of any class,

and references to stations for wireless telegraphy and apparatus for wireless telegraphy or wireless telegraphy apparatus shall be construed as references to stations and apparatus for the emitting or receiving as aforesaid of such electro-magnetic energy as aforesaid:

. . .

(2) In this Act, the expression 'station for wireless telegraphy' includes the wireless telegraphy apparatus of a ship or aircraft, and the expression 'electric line' has the same meaning as in [the Electricity Act 1989].

(2A) In this Act—

'the BBC' means the British Broadcasting Corporation; and

'television licence' and 'television receiver' have the meaning given by section 1(7) of this Act.

(3) Any reference in this Act to the emission of electro-magnetic energy, or to emission (as opposed to reception), shall be construed as including a reference to the deliberate reflection of electro-magnetic energy by means of any apparatus designed or specially adapted for that purpose, whether the reflection is continuous or intermittent.

(4) In this Act, the expression 'interference,' in relation to wireless telegraphy, means the prejudicing by any emission or reflection of electro-magnetic energy of the fulfilment of the purposes of the telegraphy (either generally or in part, and, without prejudice to the generality of the preceding words, as respects all, or as respects any, of the recipients or intended recipients of any message, sound or visual image intended to be conveyed by the telegraphy), and the expression 'interfere' shall be construed accordingly.

(5) In considering for any of the purposes of this Act, whether, in any particular case, any interference with any wireless telegraphy caused or likely to be caused by the use of any apparatus, is or is not undue interference,

regard shall be had to all the known circumstances of the case and the interference shall not be regarded as undue interference if so to regard it would unreasonably cause hardship to the person using or desiring to use the apparatus.

(6)   Any reference in this Act to the sending or the conveying of messages includes a reference to the making of any signal or the sending or conveying of any warning or information, and any reference to the reception of messages shall be construed accordingly.

(7)   In this Act, the expressions 'ship' and 'vessel' have the [same meaning as 'ship' in the Merchant Shipping Act 1995].

(8)   References in this Act to apparatus on board a ship or vessel include references to apparatus on a kite or captive balloon flown from a ship or vessel.

(9)   Any notice required or authorised by any provision of this Act to be served on any person may be served by registered post.

(10)   Any reference in this Act to any enactment shall, except so far as the context otherwise requires, be construed as a reference to that enactment as amended by or under any other enactment, including this Act.

Notes
1.   The words omitted from s. 19(1) were repealed by the Cable and Broadcasting Act 1984.
2.   The words in square brackets in s. 19(2) were substituted by the Electricity Act 1989.
3.   Section 19(2A) was inserted by the Broadcasting Act 1990.
4.   The words in square brackets in s. 19(7) were substituted by the Merchant Shipping Act 1995.

20.   Short title and extent

(1)   This Act may be cited as the Wireless Telegraphy Act 1949.

(2)   It is hereby declared that this Act extends to Northern Ireland.

(3)   His Majesty may by Order in Council direct that all or any of the provisions of this Act shall extend to the Isle of Man or any of the Channel Islands with such adaptations and modifications, if any, as may be specified in the Order.

FAIR TRADING ACT 1973
(1973, c. 41)

ARRANGEMENT OF SECTIONS

PART IV
FUNCTIONS OF DIRECTOR AND COMMISSION IN RELATION TO
MONOPOLY SITUATIONS AND UNCOMPETITIVE PRACTICES

Powers for Director to require information

Monopoly references

PART VIII
ADDITIONAL PROVISIONS RELATING TO REFERENCES TO COMMISSION

PART XII
MISCELLANEOUS AND SUPPLEMENTARY PROVISIONS

An Act to provide for the appointment of a Director General of Fair Trading and of a Consumer Protection Advisory Committee, and to confer on the Director General and the Committee so appointed, on the Secretary of State, on the Restrictive Practices Court and on certain other courts new functions for the protection of consumers; to make provision, in substitution for the Monopolies and Restrictive Practices (Inquiry and Control) Act 1948 and the Monopolies and Mergers Act 1965, for the matters dealt with in those Acts and related matters, including restrictive labour practices; to amend the Restrictive Trade Practices Act 1956 and the Restrictive Trade Practices Act 1968, to make provision for extending the said Act of 1956 to agreements relating to services, and to transfer to the Director General of Fair Trading the functions of the Registrar of Restrictive Trading Agreements; to make provision with respect to pyramid selling and similar trading schemes; to make new provision in place of section 30(2) to (4) of the Trade Descriptions Act 1968; and for purposes connected with those matters. [25 July 1973]

Note
The draft Competition Bill published by the DTI as part of a consultative document 'Tackling Cartels and the Abuse of Market Power' in August 1996 would substantially increase the Director General's powers under ss. 44 and 45 of this Act.

Powers for Director to require information

44.   General power for Director to require information

(1)   Where it appears to the Director that there are grounds for believing—

(a)   that a monopoly situation may exist in relation to the supply of goods or services of any description, or in relation to exports of goods of any description from the United Kingdom, and

(b)   that in accordance with the following provisions of this Part of this Act he would not be precluded from making a monopoly reference to the Commission with respect to the existence or possible existence of that situation,

the Director, for the purpose of assisting him in determining whether to make a monopoly reference with respect to the existence or possible existence of that situation, may exercise the powers conferred by the next following subsection.

(2)   In the circumstances and for the purpose mentioned in the preceding subsection the Director may require any person who supplies or produces goods of the description in question in the United Kingdom, or to whom any such goods are supplied in the United Kingdom, or (as the case may be) any person who supplies services of that description in the United Kingdom, or for whom any such services are so supplied, to furnish to the Director such information as the Director may consider necessary with regard to—

(a)   the value, cost, price or quantity of goods of that description supplied or produced by that person, or of goods of that description supplied to him, or (as the case may be) the value, cost, price or extent of the services of that description supplied by that person or of the services of that description supplied for him, or

(b)   the capacity of any undertaking carried on by that person to supply, produce or make use of goods of that description, or (as the case may be) to supply or make use of services of that description, or

(c)   the number of persons employed by that person wholly or partly on work related to the supply, production or use of goods of that description, or (as the case may be) the supply or use of services of that description.

Note
The functions under this section and ss. 45, 50, 52, 53, 86 and 88 of this Act so far as they relate to the telecommunications sector are exercisable by the Director General of Telecommunications under s. 50(2), Telecommunications Act 1984.

45.   Special power to require information with respect to complex monopoly situations

(1)   Where it appears to the Director that there are grounds for believing—

(a)   that a complex monopoly situation may exist in relation to the supply of goods or services of any description, or in relation to exports of goods of any description from the United Kingdom, and

(b)   that in accordance with the following provisions of this Part of this Act he would not be precluded from making a monopoly reference to the Commission with respect to the existence or possible existence of that situation,

the Director may formulate proposals for requiring specified persons to furnish information to him in accordance with the proposals for the purpose of assisting him in determining whether to make a monopoly reference with respect to the existence or possible existence of that situation.

(2)   The persons specified in any such proposals shall be persons appearing to the Director to be, or to be included among, those who, in relation to

the production or supply of goods or to the supply of services of the description in question, or in relation to exports from the United Kingdom of goods of the description in question,—

(a)   may be parties to any such agreement as is mentioned in paragraph (d) of section 6(1) or paragraph (d) of section 7(1) of this Act (or mentioned in either of those paragraphs as modified by section 9(2) of this Act) or may be parties to any such agreement as is mentioned in subsection (2) or subsection (3) of section 8 of this Act, or

(b)   may be conducting their respective affairs as mentioned in section 6(2) or in section 7(2) of this Act.

(3)   Any such proposals shall also specify the description of goods or services in question, and—

(a)   in a case falling within paragraph (a) of subsection (2) of this section, shall indicate the particular respects in which it appears to the Director that any agreement in question may be such an agreement as is referred to in that paragraph, or

(b)   in a case falling within paragraph (b) of that subsection, shall indicate the particular respects in which it appears to the Director that the persons specified in the proposals may be conducting their respective affairs in a manner referred to in that paragraph,

and shall state what information the Director proposes that the persons specified in the proposals should be required to furnish for the purpose of indicating whether, in those respects, they are parties to such an agreement, or are so conducting their respective affairs, and, if so, of indicating in what circumstances they are parties to such an agreement or are so conducting their affairs.

(4)   Where the Director has formulated proposals under this section, he may submit those proposals to the Secretary of State for approval; and if the Secretary of State approves the proposals, with or without modifications, the Director may require any person specified in the proposals to furnish to the Director such information as the Director may specify in accordance with the proposals, or, if the proposals have been approved with modifications, in accordance with the proposals as so modified.

Monopoly References

50.   Monopoly references by Director

(1)   [Subject to subsection (2A) of this section] Where it appears to the Director that a monopoly situation exists or may exist in relation to—

(a)   the supply of goods of any description, or

(b)   the supply of services of any description, or

(c)   exports of goods of any description from the United Kingdom, either generally or to any particular market,

the Director, subject to section 12 of this Act and to the following provisions of this section, may if he thinks fit make a monopoly reference to the Commission with respect to the existence or possible existence of such a monopoly situation.

(2)   No monopoly reference shall be made by the Director with respect to the existence or possible existence of a monopoly situation in relation to the supply of goods or services of any description specified in Part I of Schedule 5 or in Part I of Schedule 7 to this Act.

(2A) Subsection (2) of this section shall not preclude the making of a monopoly reference by the Director with respect to the existence or possible existence of a monopoly situation in relation to the supply of such services as are specified in paragraph 5 of Schedule 5 to this Act in Great Britain, except in relation to the supply of any such services by—

(a) a body corporate to which section 16 of this Act applies;

(b) a subsidiary, within the meaning of section 736 of the Companies Act 1985, of any such body corporate; or

(c) a publicly owned railway company, within the meaning of the Railways Act 1993.

(3) Notwithstanding anything in subsections (3) and (4) of section 10 of this Act—

(a) for the purposes of any monopoly reference made by the Director the supply of goods or services of any description specified in the first column . . . of Part II of Schedule 7 to this Act in any manner specified in relation to that description of goods or services in the second column of Part II of the relevant Schedule shall be taken to be a separate form of supply, and

(b) any monopoly reference made by the Director in relation to the supply of goods or services of any such description shall be limited so as to exclude that form of supply.

(4) For the purposes of any monopoly reference made by the Director in relation to goods of any description specified in the first column of Part III of Schedule 7 to this Act—

(a) the supply of goods of that description in Northern Ireland in any manner specified in relation to that description of goods in the second column of that Part of that Schedule shall be taken to be a separate form of supply, and, notwithstanding anything in section 10(3) and (4) of this Act, any monopoly reference so made in relation to the supply of goods of any such description in Northern Ireland shall be limited so as to exclude that form of supply, and

(b) for the purposes of any such monopoly reference the Director shall so exercise his powers under section 9 of this Act as to comply with the requirements of the preceding paragraph.

(5) The Secretary of State may by order made by statutory instrument vary any of the provisions of Schedule 7 to this Act, either by adding one or more further entries or by altering or deleting any entry for the time being contained in it; and any reference in this Act to that Schedule shall be construed as a reference to that Schedule as for the time being in force.

(6) On making a monopoly reference to the Commission, the Director shall send a copy of it to the Secretary of State; and if, before the end of the period of fourteen days from the day on which the reference is first published in the Gazette in accordance with section 53 of this Act, the Secretary of State directs the Commission not to proceed with the reference,—

(a) the Commission shall not proceed with that reference, but

(b) nothing in the preceding paragraph shall prevent the Commission from proceeding with any subsequent monopoly reference, notwithstanding that it relates wholly or partly to the same matters.

Notes
1. The words in square brackets in s. 50(2) were inserted, and s. 50(2A) was inserted, by the Railways Act 1993.

2. The words omitted from s. 50(3)(a) were repealed by the Telecommunications Act 1984.

52 Variation of monopoly reference

(1) Subject to the following provisions of this section, the Director may at any time vary a monopoly reference made by him, and the Secretary of State (or, in the case of a monopoly reference made by the Secretary of State jointly with one or more other Ministers, the Secretary of State and that Minister or those Ministers acting jointly) may vary a monopoly reference made by him or them.

(2) A monopoly reference not limited to the facts shall not be varied so as to become a monopoly reference limited to the facts; but (subject to the following provisions of this section) a monopoly reference limited to the facts may be varied so as to become a monopoly reference not limited to the facts, whether the Commission have already reported on the reference as originally made or not.

(3) A monopoly reference made by the Director shall not be varied so as to become a reference which he is precluded from making by any provisions of section 50 of this Act.

(4) On varying a monopoly reference made by him, the Director shall send a copy of the variation to the Secretary of State; and if, before the end of the period of fourteen days from the day on which the variation is first published in the Gazette in accordance with the next following section, the Secretary of State directs the Commission not to give effect to the variation,—

(a) the Commission shall proceed with the reference as if that variation had not been made, but

(b) nothing in the preceding paragraph shall prevent the Commission from proceeding with any subsequent monopoly reference, or from giving effect to any subsequent variation, notwithstanding that it relates wholly or partly to the matters to which that variation related.

(5) In this section and in sections 53 to 55 of this Act 'Minister' includes the Minister of Agriculture for Northern Ireland and the Minister of Commerce for Northern Ireland.

53. Publication of monopoly references and variations, and of directions relating to them

(1) On making a monopoly reference, or a variation of a monopoly reference, the Director or, as the case may be, the Secretary of State (or, in the case of a monopoly reference or variation made by the Secretary of State acting jointly with one or more other Ministers, the Secretary of State and that Minister or those Ministers acting jointly) shall arrange for the reference or variation to be published in fun in the Gazette, and shall arrange for the reference or variation to be published in such other manner as he or they may think most suitable for bringing it to the attention of persons who, in his or their opinion, would be affected by it.

(2) Where the Secretary of State gives a direction under section 50(6) of this Act with respect to a monopoly reference, or gives a direction under section 52(4) of this Act with respect to a variation of a monopoly reference, the Secretary of State shall arrange for the direction to be published in the Gazette and otherwise in the same manner as the monopoly reference or variation was published in accordance with the preceding subsection.

(3) In this section 'the Gazette' means the London, Edinburgh and Belfast Gazettes, except that, in relation to a monopoly reference under which consideration is limited to a particular part of the United Kingdom in accordance with section 9 of this Act (including a reference under which consideration is required to be so limited by section 50(4)(b) of this Act), it means such one or more of those Gazettes as are appropriate to that part of the United Kingdom.

(4) In sections 50 and 52 of this Act any reference to publication in the Gazette is a reference to publication in the London Gazette, the Edinburgh Gazette or the Belfast Gazette, whichever first occurs.

PART VIII

ADDITIONAL PROVISIONS RELATING TO REFERENCES
TO COMMISSION

86. Director to receive copies of reports

(1) Subject to the next following subsection, a copy of every report of the Commission on a monopoly reference, or on a merger reference other than a newspaper merger reference, shall be transmitted by the Commission to the Director; and the Minister or Ministers to whom any such report is made shall take account of any advice given to him or them by the Director with respect to a report of which a copy is transmitted to the Director under this section.

(2) The preceding subsection shall not apply to a report made on a monopoly reference, where the reference was made by a Minister or Ministers and (by virtue of any of the provisions of section 50 of this Act) could not have been made by the Director.

(3) In this section 'Minister' includes the Minister of Agriculture for Northern Ireland and the Minister of Commerce for Northern Ireland.

88. Action by Director in consequence of report of Commission on monopoly or merger reference

(1) Where a report of the Commission on a monopoly reference, or on a merger reference other than a newspaper merger reference, as laid before Parliament,—

(a) in the case of a monopoly reference, sets out such conclusions as are mentioned in section 56(1) of this Act, or

(b) in the case of a merger reference, sets out such conclusions as are mentioned in section 73(1) or in section 75(4)(e) of this Act,

and a copy of the report is transmitted to the Director under section 86 of this Act, it shall be the duty of the Director, [to comply with any request of the appropriate Minister or Ministers to consult with any persons mentioned in the request (referred to below in this section as 'the relevant parties')] with a view to obtaining from them undertakings to take action indicated in the request made to the Director as being action requisite, in the opinion of the appropriate Minister or Ministers, for the purpose of remedying or preventing the adverse effects specified in the report.

(2) The Director shall report to the appropriate Minister or Ministers the outcome of his consultations under the preceding subsection; and if any

undertaking is given by any of the relevant parties to take action indicated in
the request made to the Director as mentioned in that subsection (in this
section referred to as an 'appropriate undertaking') the Minister to whom the
undertaking is given shall furnish particulars of it to the Director.

(2A)   Where—

(a)   an undertaking is given under this section after the commencement
of this subsection, or

(b)   an undertaking given under this section is varied or released after
that time,

the Minister to whom the undertaking is or was given shall cause the
undertaking or, as the case may be, the variation or release to be published
in such manner as the Minister may consider appropriate.

(3)   Where in his consultations under subsection (1) of this section the
Director seeks to obtain an appropriate undertaking from any of the relevant
parties, and either—

(a)   he is satisfied that no such undertaking is likely to be given by that
party within a reasonable time, or

(b)   having allowed such time as in his opinion is reasonable for the
purpose, he is satisfied that no such undertaking has been given by that party,

the Director shall give such advice to the appropriate Minister or Ministers
as he may think proper in the circumstances (including, if the Director thinks
fit, advice with respect to the exercise by the appropriate Minister or
Ministers of his or their powers under section 56 or section 73 of this Act, as
the case may be).

(4)   Where the Director has made a report under subsection (2) of this
section, and particulars of an undertaking given by any of the relevant parties
have been furnished to the Director in accordance with that subsection, it
shall be the duty of the Director—

(a)   to keep under review the carrying out of that undertaking, and from
time to time to consider whether, by reason of any change of circumstances,
[the undertaking is no longer appropriate and either the relevant parties (or
any of them) can be released from the undertaking or the undertaking] needs
to be varied or to be superseded by a new undertaking, and

(b)   if it appears to him [that any person can be so released or that an
undertaking] has not been or is not being fulfilled, or needs to be varied or
superseded, to give such advice to the appropriate Minister or Ministers as
he may think proper in the circumstances.

(5)   Where, in consequence of a report of which a copy is transmitted to
the Director under section 86 of this Act, an order is made under section 56
or section 73 of this Act in relation to any of the matters to which the report
relates, it shall be the duty of the Director to keep under review the action (if
any) taken in compliance with that order, and from time to time to consider
whether, by reason of any change of circumstances, the order should be
varied [or revoked] or should be superseded by a new order, and—

(a)   if it appears to him that the order has in any respect not been
complied with, to consider whether any action (by way of proceedings in
accordance with section 93 of this Act or otherwise) should be taken for the
purpose of securing compliance with the order, and (where in his opinion it
is appropriate to do so) to take such action himself or give advice to any
Minister or other person by whom such action might be taken, or

(b)   if it appears to him that the order needs to be varied [or revoked], or to be superseded by a new order, to give such advice to the appropriate Minister or Ministers as he may think proper in the circumstances.

(6)   In this section . . . in relation to a report of the Commission, 'the appropriate Minister or Ministers' means the Minister or Ministers to whom the report is made, 'undertaking' means an undertaking given to that Minister or to one of those Ministers, as the case may be, and, in subsections (3) and (5) of this section, the references to section 73 of this Act shall be construed as including references to that section as applied by section 75(4) of this Act.

Note
The words in square brackets in s. 88(1) were substituted and the words omitted from s. 88(6) were repealed by the Companies Act 1989, except in relation to any report made before 16 November 1989. Section 88(2A) and the words in square brackets in s. 88(5) were inserted, and the words in square brackets in s. 88(4) were substituted, by the 1989 Act.

PART XII
MISCELLANEOUS AND SUPPLEMENTARY PROVISIONS

133.   General restrictions on disclosure of information

(1)   Subject to subsections (2) to (4) of this section, no information with respect to any particular business which has been obtained under or by virtue of the provisions (other than Part II) of this Act . . . shall, so long as that business continues to be carried on, be disclosed without the consent of the person for the time being carrying on that business.

(2)   The preceding subsection does not apply to any disclosure of information which is made—

(a)   for the purposes of facilitating the performance of any functions of the . . . [the Director General of Telecommunications,] . . . [the Competition Act 1980] [or the Telecommunications Act 1984] . . .

(b)   . . .

(3)   . . .

Notes
1.   The words omitted from s. 133(1) were repealed by the Restrictive Trade Practices Act 1976.
2.   The words in square brackets in s. 133(2)(a) were added by the Telecommunications Act 1984.
3.   Only parts of the section relevant to telecommunications are reproduced.

COMPETITION ACT 1980
(1980, c. 21)

ARRANGEMENT OF SECTIONS

Control of anti-competitive practices
Section
2   Anti-competitive practices
3   Preliminary investigation by Director of possible anti-competitive practice
4   Undertakings in consequence of Director's reports

General provisions about references and investigations

An Act to abolish the Price Commission; to make provision for the control of anti-competitive practices in the supply and acquisition of goods and the supply and securing of services; to provide for references of certain public bodies and other persons to the Monopolies and Mergers Commission; to provide for the investigation of prices and charges by the Director General of Fair Trading; to provide for the making of grants to certain bodies; to amend and provide for the amendment of the Fair Trading Act 1973; to make amendments with respect to the Restrictive Trade Practices Act 1976, to repeal the remaining provisions of the Counter-Inflation Act 1973; and for purposes connected therewith. [3 April 1980]

Note
The draft Competition Bill published by the DTI as part of a consultative document 'Tackling Cartels and the Abuse of Market Power' in August 1996 would increase the Director General's powers under ss. 2, 3 and 4 of this Act.

Control of anti-competitive practices

2. Anti-competitive practices

(1)   The provisions of sections 3 to 10 below have effect with a view to the control of anti-competitive practices, and for the purposes of this Act a person engages in an anti-competitive practice if, in the course of business, that person pursues a course of conduct which, of itself or when taken together with a course of conduct pursued by persons associated with him, has or is intended to have or is likely to have the effect of restricting, distorting or preventing competition in connection with the production, supply or acqui- sition of goods in the United Kingdom or any part of it or the supply or securing of services in the United Kingdom or any part of it.

(2)   To the extent that a course of conduct is required or envisaged by a material provision of, or a material recommendation in, an agreement which is registered or subject to registration under the Restrictive Trade Practices Act 1976, that course of conduct shall not be regarded as constituting an anti-competitive practice for the purposes of this Act; and for the purposes of this subsection—

(a)   a provision of an agreement is a material provision if, by virtue of the existence of the provision (taken alone or together with other provisions) the agreement is one to which that Act applies; and

(b)   a recommendation is a material recommendation in an agreement if it is one to which a term implied into the agreement by any provision of section 8 or section 16 of that Act (terms implied into trade association agreements and services supply association agreements) applies.

(3) For the purposes of this Act, a course of conduct does not constitute an anti-competitive practice if it is excluded for those purposes by an order made by the Secretary of State; and any such order may limit the exclusion conferred by it by reference to a particular class of persons or to particular circumstances.

(4) Without prejudice to the generality of subsection (3) above, an order under that subsection may exclude the conduct of any person by reference to the size of his business, whether expressed by reference to turnover, as defined in the order, or to his share of a market, as so defined, or in any other manner.

(5) . . .

(6) For the purposes of this section any two persons are to be treated as associated—

(a) if one is a body corporate of which the other directly or indirectly has control either alone or with other members of a group of interconnected bodies corporate of which he is a member, or

(b) if both are bodies corporate of which one and the same person or group of persons directly or indirectly has control;

and for the purposes of this subsection a person or group of persons able directly or indirectly to control or materially to influence the policy of a body corporate, but without having a controlling interest in that body corporate, may be treated as having control of it.

(7) In this section 'the supply or securing of services' includes providing a place or securing that a place is provided other than on a highway, or in Scotland a public right of way, for the parking of a motor vehicle (within the meaning of [the Road Traffic Act 1988]).

(8) For the purposes of this Act any question whether, by pursuing any course of conduct in connection with the acquisition of goods or the securing of services by it, a local authority is engaging in an anti-competitive practice shall be determined as if the words 'in the course of business' were omitted from subsection (1) above; and in this subsection 'local authority' means—

(a) in England and Wales, a local authority within the meaning of the Local Government Act 1972, the Common Council of the City of London or the Council of the Isles of Scilly,

(b) in Scotland, a local authority within the meaning of the Local Government (Scotland) Act 1973, and

(c) in Northern Ireland, a district council established under the Local Government Act (Northern Ireland) 1972.

Notes

1. Section 2(5) was repealed by the Deregulation and Contracting Out Act 1994.

2. The words in square brackets in s. 2(7) were substituted by the Road Traffic (Consequential Provisions) Act 1988.

3. Functions of the Director General of Fair Trading: the functions under this section and ss. 3–10 and 16 of this Act, so far as relating to courses of conduct which have or are intended to have or are likely to have the effect of restricting, distorting or preventing competition in connection with the production, supply or acquisition of telecommunication apparatus and the supply or securing of telecommunication services, are exercisable concurrently by the Director General of Telecommunications under the Telecommunications Act 1984.

3. Preliminary investigation by Director of possible anti-competitive practice

(1) If it appears to the Director that any person has been or is pursuing a course of conduct which may amount to an anti-competitive practice, the Director may in accordance with this section carry out an investigation with a view to establishing whether that person has been or is pursuing a course of conduct which does amount to such a practice.

. . .

(7) For the purposes of an investigation under this section the Director may, by notice in writing signed by him—

(a) require any person to produce, at a time and place specified in the notice, to the Director or to any person appointed by him for the purpose, any documents which are specified or described in the notice and which are documents in his custody or under his control and relating to any matter relevant to the investigation; or

(b) require any person carrying on any business to furnish to the Director such estimates, returns or other information as may be specified or described in the notice, and specify the time, the manner and the form in which any such estimates, returns or information are to be furnished;

but no person shall be compelled for the purpose of any such investigation to produce any document which he could not be compelled to produce in civil proceedings before the High Court or, in Scotland, the Court of Session or, in complying with any requirement for the furnishing of information, to give any information which he could not be compelled to give in evidence in such proceedings.

(8) Subsections [(6)] to (8) of section 85 of the Fair Trading Act 1973 (enforcement provisions relating to notices under subsection (1) of that section requiring production of documents etc) shall apply in relation to a notice under subsection (7) above as they apply in relation to a notice under subsection (1) of that section [but as if, in subsection (7) of that section, for the words from 'any one' to 'the Commission' there were substituted 'the Director'].

. . .

Notes

1. Sections 3(2)–(6), (9), (10) were repealed by the Deregulation and Contracting Out Act 1994.

2. Section 3(8) the figure in the first pair of square brackets was substituted and the words in the second pair of square brackets were added by the Companies Act 1989.

4. Undertakings in consequence of Director's reports

(1) Where it appears to the Director—

(a) that there are reasonable grounds for believing that any person is pursuing, or has pursued, a course of conduct which constitutes an anti-competitive practice,

(b) that the practice may operate, now or in future, or have operated, against the public interest, and

(c) that an undertaking offered to be given to the Director by that person, or by a person associated with that person, would remedy or prevent effects adverse to the public interest which the practice may now or in future have,

he may, at any time before making a reference under section 5(1)(a) below in relation to the course of conduct in question, accept the undertaking by giving notice to the person by whom it is offered.

(2) The Director may not accept an undertaking under subsection (1) above unless he has—

(a) arranged for the publication of an appropriate notice, and

(b) considered any representations made to him in accordance with the notice.

(3) Publication under subsection (2)(a) above shall be in such manner as the Director considers most suitable for bringing the notice to the attention of persons who, in his opinion, would, if the course of conduct in question were the subject of a reference under section 5(1)(a) below, be affected by the reference or be likely to have an interest in it.

(3A) In subsection (2)(a) above, the reference to an appropriate notice is to a notice which—

(a) states that the Director is proposing to exercise his power under subsection (1) above,

(b) identifies the course of conduct whose pursuit prompts the exercise of that power,

(c) identifies the person who the Director believes is pursuing, or has pursued, that course of conduct,

(d) identifies the goods or services in relation to which the Director believes that person is pursuing, or has pursued, that course of conduct,

(e) specifies the effects which the Director has identified as effects adverse to the public interest which that course of conduct may now or in future have,

(f) sets out the terms of the undertaking which the Director is proposing to accept,

(g) identifies the person by whom the undertaking is to be given, and

(h) specifies a deadline for the making to the Director of representations about what he proposes to do.

(3B) Once the Director has considered any representations made to him in accordance with a notice under paragraph (a) of subsection (2) above, that subsection shall not apply to the acceptance of a modified version of the undertaking set out in the notice.

(4) It shall be the duty of the Director—

(a) to arrange for—

(i) any undertaking accepted by him under this section, and

(ii) any variation or release of such an undertaking after the passing of the Companies Act 1989,

to be published in such manner as appears to him to be appropriate.

(b) to keep under review the carrying out of any such undertaking and from time to time to consider whether, by reason of any change of circumstances, the undertaking is no longer appropriate and either the person concerned can be released from the undertaking or the undertaking needs to be varied or superseded by a new undertaking, and

(c)   if it appears to him that the person by whom an undertaking was given has failed to carry it out, to give that person notice of that fact.

(5)   If at any time the Director concludes under subsection (4)(b) above—

(a)   that any person can be released from an undertaking, or

(b)   that an undertaking needs to be varied or superseded by a new undertaking,

he shall give notice to that person stating that he is so released, or specifying the variation or, as the case may be, the new undertaking which in his opinion is required.

(6)   Where a notice is served on any person under subsection (5) above specifying a variation or new undertaking, the notice shall state the change of circumstances by virtue of which the notice is served.

(7)   Subject to subsection (8) below, the Director may at any time, by notice given to the person concerned—

(a)   agree to the continuation of an undertaking in relation to which he has given notice under subsection (5) above specifying a variation or new undertaking, or

(b)   accept a new or varied undertaking which is offered by that person as a result of such a notice.

(8)   If the Director makes a reference under section 5 below in relation to a notice under subsection (5) above, he shall not, after the reference has been made, agree to the continuation of the undertaking in relation to which that notice was given or accept a new or varied undertaking which is offered as a result of that notice.

(9)   The Secretary of State may by regulations prescribe the manner in which any notice is to be given under this section, and the evidence which is to be sufficient evidence of its having been given, and of its contents and authenticity.

(10)   Subsection (6) of section 2 above shall apply for the purposes of this section as it applies for the purposes of that.

Notes
1.   Section 4(1)–(3), (3A), (3B) were substituted for section 4(1)–(3) as originally enacted and s. 4(10) was inserted by the Deregulation and Contracting Out Act 1994.
2.   Section 4(4)(a) was substituted by the Companies Act 1989.

5.   Competition references

(1)   In any case where—
(a)   there are reasonable grounds for believing that any person is pursuing, or has pursued, a course of conduct which constitutes an anti-competitive practice,

(b)   the Director has given notice to any person under section 4(4)(c) above with respect to an undertaking given by that person, or

(c)   the Director has given notice to any person under section 4(5) above specifying either a variation of an undertaking or a new undertaking which is required and has neither accepted a new or varied undertaking from that person nor agreed upon the continuation of the original undertaking, then, subject to the following provisions of this section, the Director may make a reference under this section to the Monopolies and Mergers Commission (in the following provisions of this Act referred to as a 'competition reference').

(2) . . .

(3) No competition reference may be made [by virtue of subsection (1)(b) or (c) above] within the period of four weeks beginning with the relevant date nor, subject to subsection (4) below, may such a reference be [so] made after the expiry of the period of eight weeks beginning on that date; and in this subsection 'the relevant date' means . . . the date on which notice was given as mentioned in subsection (1)(b) or, as the case may be, subsection (1)(c) above.

(4) If the Secretary of State so directs, subsection (3) above shall have effect in relation to a competition reference of a description specified in the direction as if for the period of eight weeks specified in that subsection there were substituted such longer period not exceeding twelve weeks as may be specified in the direction; but the Secretary of State shall not give a direction under this subsection unless, upon representations made to him by the Director, it appears to the Secretary of State that it would be appropriate in the case in question to allow the Director a longer period in which to negotiate one or more undertakings under section 4 above.

(5) . . .

Note
Section 5(1)(a) and the words in the first and second pairs of square brackets in s. 5(3) were substituted, and s. 5(2), (5) and the words omitted from s. 5(3) were repealed by the Deregulation and Contracting Out Act 1994.

6. Scope of competition references

(1) In a competition reference the Director shall specify—

(a) the person or persons whose activities are to be investigated by the Commission (in this section referred to as the person or persons 'subject to the reference'),

(b) the goods or services to which the investigation is to extend, and

(c) the course or courses of conduct to be investigated.

(2) . . .

(3) Where the Director has accepted an undertaking under section 4 above with respect to the pursuit by any person of a course of conduct in relation to any goods or services, the Director may not, while the undertaking is in force, make a competition reference by virtue of section 5(1)(a) above with respect to the pursuit by that person of that course of conduct in relation to those goods or services.

(5) Subject to subsection (6) below, on a competition reference the Commission shall investigate and report on the following questions, namely—

(a) whether any person subject to the reference was at any time during the period of twelve months ending on the date of the reference pursuing, in relation to goods or services specified in the reference, a course of conduct so specified or any other course of conduct which appears to be similar in form and effect to the one so specified; and

(b)   whether, by pursuing any such course of conduct, a person subject to the reference was at any time during that period engaging in an anti-competitive practice; and

(c)   whether, if any person was so engaging in an anti-competitive practice, the practice operated or might be expected to operate against the public interest.

(6)   The Director may at any time, by notice given to the Commission, restrict the scope of a competition reference by excluding from the reference—

(a)   some or all of the activities of any person subject to the reference,

(b)   any goods or services specified in the reference, or

(c)   any course of conduct so specified,

and, subject to section 7 below, on the receipt of such notice the Commission shall discontinue their investigation so far as it relates to any matter so excluded and shall make no reference to any such matter in their report.

Note

Section 6(2) was repealed, and s. 6(3) was substituted for s. 6(3), (4) as originally enacted, by the Deregulation and Contracting Out Act 1994.

7.   Supplementary provisions as to competition references

(1)   On making a competition reference or on varying such a reference under section 6(6) above the Director shall send a copy of the reference or, as the case may be, the variation to the Secretary of State.

(2)   If, before the end of the period of two weeks beginning with the day on which the Secretary of State receives a copy of a competition reference under subsection (1) above, the Secretary of State directs the Commission not to proceed with the reference—

(a)   the Commission shall not proceed with that reference, but

(b)   nothing in paragraph (a) above shall prevent the Commission from proceeding with a subsequent competition reference, notwithstanding that it relates wholly or partly to the same matters.

(3)   If, before the end of the period of two weeks beginning with the day on which the Secretary of State receives a copy of a variation of a competition reference under subsection (1) above, the Secretary of State directs the Commission not to give effect to the variation—

(a)   the Commission shall proceed with the reference as if that variation had not been made, but

(b)   nothing in paragraph (a) above shall prevent the Commission from giving effect to any subsequent variation, notwithstanding that it relates wholly or partly to the matters to which that variation related.

(4)   On making a competition reference or on varying such a reference under section 6(6) above the Director shall arrange for the reference or, as the case may be, the variation to be published in such manner as he considers most suitable for bringing it to the attention of persons who, in his opinion, would be affected by it or be likely to have an interest in it.

(5)   Where the Secretary of State gives a direction under subsection (2) or subsection (3) above, the Secretary of State shall arrange for the direction to be published in such manner as he considers most suitable for bringing it to the attention of persons who, in his opinion, would have been affected by, or

likely to have had an interest in, the reference or variation to which the direction relates.

(6)   Sections 70 (time limit for report on merger reference), 84 (public interest) and 85 (attendance of witnesses and production of documents) of the Fair Trading Act 1973 and Part II of Schedule 3 to that Act (performance of functions of Commission) shall apply in relation to competition references as if—

(a)   the functions of the Commission in relation to those references were functions under that Act;

(b)   the expression 'merger reference' included a competition reference;

(c)   in paragraph 11 of that Schedule the reference to section 71 of that Act were a reference to section 6(6) above; and

(d)   in paragraph 16(2) of that Schedule the reference to section 56 of that Act were a reference to sections 9 and 10 below.

8.   Conclusions and reports of the Commission

(1)   A report of the Commission on a competition reference shall be made to the Secretary of State.

(2)   Subject to section 6(6) above and subsection (3) below, a report on a competition reference shall state, with reasons, the conclusions of the Commission with respect to the following matters—

(a)   whether any person whose activities were investigated was at any time during the period of twelve months referred to in paragraph (a) of subsection (5) of section 6 above pursuing any such course of conduct as is referred to in that paragraph; and

(b)   if so, whether by pursuing such a course of conduct any such person was at any time during that period engaging in an anti-competitive practice; and

(c)   if so, whether that anti-competitive practice operated or might be expected to operate against the public interest; and

(d)   if so, what are, or are likely to be, the effects adverse to the public interest.

(3)   If, on a competition reference, the Commission conclude that any person was pursuing such a course of conduct as is referred to in section 6(5)(a) above but that, by virtue of section 2(2) above, that course of conduct does not, in whole or in part, constitute an anti-competitive practice, the Commission shall state their conclusion in their report and shall not make any recommendation under subsection (4) below with respect to things done as mentioned in section 2(2) above.

(4)   If, on a competition reference, the Commission conclude that any person was at any time during the period of twelve months referred to in section 6(5)(a) above engaging in an anti-competitive practice which operated or might be expected to operate against the public interest, the Commission—

(a)   shall, as part of their investigations, consider what action (if any) should be taken for the purpose of remedying or preventing the adverse effects of that practice; and

(b)   may, if they think fit, include in their report recommendations as to such action including, where appropriate, action by one or more Ministers (including Northern Ireland departments) or other public authorities.

(5)   A copy of every report of the Commission on a competition reference shall be transmitted by the Commission to the Director; and the Secretary of State shall take account of any advice given to him by the Director with respect to any such report.

9.   Undertakings following report on competition reference

(1)   In any case where—

(a)   the report of the Commission on a competition reference concludes that any person specified in the report was engaging in an anti-competitive practice which operated or might be expected to operate against the public interest, and

(b)   it appears to the Secretary of State that the effects of that practice which are adverse to the public interest might be remedied or prevented if that person or any other person specified in the report took or refrained from taking any action,

the Secretary of State may by notice in writing request the Director to seek to obtain from the person or, as the case may be, each of the persons specified in the notice an undertaking to take or refrain from taking any action with a view to remedying or preventing those adverse effects.

(2)   Where the Secretary of State makes a request under subsection (1) above—

(a)   he shall at the same time send a copy of the notice by which the request is made to the person or, as the case may be, each of the persons from whom an undertaking is to be sought; and

(b)   it shall be the duty of the Director to seek to obtain an undertaking or undertakings of the description requested.

(3)   In any case where—

(a)   the Director is satisfied that a person from whom he has been requested to seek to obtain an undertaking is unlikely to give a suitable undertaking within a reasonable time, or

(b)   having allowed such time as in his opinion is reasonable for the purpose, he is satisfied that a suitable undertaking has not been given by the person in question,

the Director shall give such advice to the Secretary of State as he may think proper in the circumstances.

(4)   Where, following a request under subsection (1) above, an undertaking has been accepted by the Director, it shall be his duty—

(a)   to give a copy of the undertaking [and of any variation of it after the passing of the Companies Act 1989] to the Secretary of State;

(b)   to arrange for the undertaking [and any variation or release of it after that time] to be published in such manner as appears to him to be appropriate;

(c)   to keep under review the carrying out of the undertaking and from time to time to consider whether, by reason of any change of circumstances, the undertaking is no longer appropriate and either the person concerned can be released from the undertaking or the undertaking needs to be varied or to be superseded by a new undertaking; and

(d)   if it appears to him that any person can be so released or that an undertaking has not been or is not being fulfilled, or needs to be varied or superseded, to give such advice to the Secretary of State as he may think proper in the circumstances.

(5) If, following advice from the Director that a person can be released from an undertaking, the Secretary of State considers that it is appropriate for the Director to release him from it—

(a) the Secretary of State shall request the Director to do so, and

(b) the Director shall give the person concerned notice that he is released from the undertaking;

and regulations under subsection (9) of section 4 above shall apply in relation to such a notice as they apply to a notice under subsection (5) of that section.

(6) The Secretary of State shall take account of any advice given to him by the Director under this section (including advice as to the exercise by the Secretary of State of any of his powers under this Act).

Note
The words in square brackets in s. 9(4) were inserted by the Companies Act 1989.

10. Orders following report on competition reference

(1) If, in any case where the report of the Commission on a competition reference concludes that any person specified in the report was engaged in an anti-competitive practice which operated or might be expected to operate against the public interest—

(a) the Secretary of State has not under section 9(1) above requested the Director to seek to obtain undertakings from one or more of the persons so specified, or

(b) following a request under subsection (1) of section 9 above, the Director has informed the Secretary of State that he is satisfied as mentioned in paragraph (a) or paragraph (b) of subsection (3) of that section, or

(c) the Director has informed the Secretary of State that an undertaking accepted by him under section 9 above from a person specified in the report has not been or is not being fulfilled,

the Secretary of State may, if he thinks fit, make an order under this section.

(2) Subject to the following provisions of this section, an order under this section may do either or both of the following, that is to say—

(a) prohibit a person named in the order from engaging in any anti-competitive practice which was specified in the report or from pursuing any other course of conduct which is similar in form and effect to that practice; and

(b) for the purpose of remedying or preventing any adverse effects which are specified in the report as mentioned in section 8(2)(d) above, exercise one or more of the powers specified in Part I of Schedule 8 to the Fair Trading Act 1973 to such extent and in such manner as the Secretary of State considers necessary for that purpose.

(3) No order may be made by virtue of paragraph (a) of subsection (2) above in respect of any person unless he is a person specified in the Commission's report and either—

(a) he has not given an undertaking which the Director sought to obtain from him in pursuance of a request under section 9(1) above; or

(b) the Director was not requested under section 9(1) above to seek to obtain an undertaking from him; or

(c)   the Director has informed the Secretary of State that an undertaking given by him and accepted by the Director under section 9 above has not been or is not being fulfilled.

(4)   In the Fair Trading Act 1973—

(a)   section 90 (general provisions as to orders under section 56 etc) except subsection (2),

(b)   section 91(2) (publication of proposals to make an order),

(c)   section 93 (enforcement of certain orders), and

(d)   Part I of Schedule 8 (powers exercisable by orders under section 56 etc),

shall have effect as if any reference in those provisions to an order under section 56 of that Act included a reference to an order under this section.

General provisions about references and investigations

16.   General provisions as to reports

(1)   In making any report under this Act the Commission or the Director shall have regard to the need for excluding, so far as that is practicable—

(a)   any matter which relates to the private affairs of an individual, where the publication of that matter would or might, in the opinion of the Commission or the Director, as the case may be, seriously and prejudicially affect the interests of that individual, and

(b)   any matter which relates specifically to the affairs of a body of persons, whether corporate or unincorporate, where publication of that matter would or might, in the opinion of the Commission or the Director, as the case may be, seriously and prejudicially affect the interests of that body, unless in the opinion of the Commission or the Director, as the case may be, the inclusion of that matter relating specifically to that body is necessary for the purposes of the report.

(2)   For the purposes of the law relating to defamation, absolute privilege shall attach to any report of the Commission or of the Director under this Act.

(3)   For the purposes of this section, the publication by the Director of a notice under section 4(2)(a) above shall be treated as the making by him of a report under this Act.

Note
Section 16(3) was inserted by the Deregulation and Contracting Out Act 1994.

19.   Restriction on disclosure of information

(1)   Subject to subsection (2) below, no information obtained under or by virtue of the preceding provisions of this Act about any business shall, so long as the business continues to be carried on, be disclosed without the consent of the person for the time being carrying it on.

(2)   Subsection (1) above does not apply to any disclosure of information made—

(a)   for the purposes of facilitating the performance of any functions under this Act or any of the enactments or subordinate legislation specified in subsection (3) below of any Minister, . . . the Director General of Telecommunications . . .

(3)   The enactments and subordinate legislation referred to in subsection (2) above are—

. . .

(g)   the Telecommunications Act 1984

(5)   Nothing in subsection (1) above shall be construed—

(a)   as limiting the matters which may be included in any report of the Director or of the Commission made under this Act or in anything published under section 4(2)(a) above; or

(b)   as applying to any information which has been made public as part of such a report or as part of the register kept for the purposes of the Act of 1976.

(6)   Any person who discloses information in contravention of this section shall be liable on summary conviction to a fine not exceeding the statutory maximum and, on conviction on indictment, to imprisonment for a term not exceeding two years or to a fine or both.

Note
Only the parts of the section relevant to telecommunications are reproduced.

TELECOMMUNICATIONS ACT 1984
(1984, c. 12)

ARRANGEMENT OF SECTIONS

PART I
INTRODUCTORY

Section

PART II
PROVISION OF TELECOMMUNICATION SERVICES

Licensing etc. of telecommunication systems

Modification of licences

PART III
OTHER FUNCTIONS OF DIRECTOR

PART VI
PROVISIONS RELATING TO WIRELESS TELEGRAPHY

Amendment and enforcement of Wireless Telegraphy Acts

(Sections 75 to 92 have been incorporated where relevant into the Wireless
Telegraphy Act 1949).

PART VII
MISCELLANEOUS AND SUPPLEMENTAL

Miscellaneous

An Act to provide for the appointment and functions of a Director General of Telecommunications; to abolish British Telecommunications' exclusive privilege with respect to telecommunications and to make new provision with respect to the provision of telecommunication services and certain related services; to make provision, in substitution for the Telegraph Acts 1863 to 1916 and Part IV of the Post Office Act 1969, for the matters there dealt with and related matters; to provide for the vesting of property, rights and liabilities of British Telecommunications in a company nominated by the Secretary of State and the subsequent dissolution of British Telecommunications; to make provision with respect to the finances of that company; to amend the Wireless Telegraphy Acts 1949 to 1967, to make further provision for facilitating enforcement of those Acts and otherwise to make provision with respect to wireless telegraphy apparatus and certain related apparatus; to give statutory authority for the payment out of money provided by Parliament of expenses incurred by the Secretary of State in providing a radio interference service; to increase the maximum number of members of British Telecommunications pending its dissolution; and for connected purposes.   [12 April 1984]

PART I
INTRODUCTORY

1. The Director General of Telecommunications

(1) The Secretary of State shall appoint an officer to be known as the Director General of Telecommunications (in this Act referred to as 'the Director' for the purpose of performing the functions assigned or transferred to the Director by or under this Act.

(2) An appointment of a person to hold office as the Director shall not be for a term exceeding five years; but previous appointment to that office shall not affect eligibility for re-appointment.

(3) The Director may at any time resign his office as the Director by notice in writing addressed to the Secretary of State; and the Secretary of

State may remove any person from that office on the ground of incapacity or misbehaviour.

(4) Subject to subsections (2) and (3) above, the Director shall hold and vacate office as such in accordance with the terms of his appointment.

(5) The Director may appoint such staff as he may think fit, subject to the approval of the Treasury as to numbers and as to terms and conditions of service.

(6) There shall be paid out of money provided by Parliament the remuneration of, and any travelling or other allowances payable under this Act to, the Director and any staff of the Director, any sums payable under this Act to or in respect of the Director and any expenses duly incurred by the Director or by any of his staff in consequence of the provisions of this Act.

(7) The provisions of Schedule 1 to this Act shall have effect with respect to the Director.

2. Abolition of British Telecommunications' exclusive privilege

As from such day as the Secretary of State may by order appoint for the purposes of Parts II to IV of this Act (in this Act referred to as 'the appointed day'), the exclusive privilege of running telecommunication systems conferred on British Telecommunications by section 12 of the British Telecommunications Act 1981 (in this Act referred to as 'the 1981 Act') shall cease to exist.

3. General duties of Secretary of State and Director

(1) The Secretary of State and the Director shall each have a duty to exercise the functions assigned or transferred to him by or under Part II or Part III of this Act in the manner which he considers is best calculated—

(a) to secure that there are provided throughout the United Kingdom, save in so far as the provision thereof is impracticable or not reasonably practicable, such telecommunication services as satisfy all reasonable demands for them including, in particular, emergency services, public call services, directory information services, maritime services and services in rural areas; and

(b) without prejudice to the generality of paragraph (a) above, to secure that any person by whom any such services fall to be provided is able to finance the provision of those services.

(2) Subject to subsection (1) above, the Secretary of State and the Director shall each have a duty to exercise the functions assigned or transferred to him by or under Part II or Part III of this Act in the manner which he considers is best calculated—

(a) to promote the interests of consumers, purchasers and other users in the United Kingdom (including, in particular, those who are disabled or of pensionable age) in respect of the prices charged for, and the quality and variety of, telecommunication services provided and telecommunication apparatus supplied;

(b) to maintain and promote effective competition between persons engaged in commercial activities connected with telecommunications in the United Kingdom;

(c) to promote efficiency and economy on the part of such persons;

(d) to promote research into and the development and use of new techniques by such persons;

(e) to encourage major users of telecommunication services whose places of business are outside the United Kingdom to establish places of business in the United Kingdom;

(f) to promote the provision of international transit services by persons providing telecommunication services in the United Kingdom;

(g) to enable persons providing telecommunications services in the United Kingdom to compete effectively in the provision of such services outside the United Kingdom;

(h) to enable persons producing telecommunication apparatus in the United Kingdom to compete effectively in the supply of such apparatus both in and outside the United Kingdom.

(3) Subsections (1) and (2) above do not apply in relation to anything done—

(a) by the Secretary of State in the interests of national security or relations with the government of a country or territory outside the United Kingdom; or

(b) in the exercise of functions assigned or transferred by or under section 50 below;

and subsection (2) above does not apply in relation to anything done in the exercise of functions assigned by section 10(3) or (8) or 52 below.

(3A) Subsections (1) and (2) above do not apply in relation to the determination of disputes by the Director under or by virtue of section 27A, 27F, 27G or 27I below.

(4) In this section 'international transit service' means a telecommunication service consisting in the conveyance of sounds, visual images or signals which have been conveyed from, and are to be conveyed to, places outside the United Kingdom.

Note
Section 3(3A) was inserted by the Competition and Service (Utilities) Act 1992.

4. Meaning of 'telecommunication system' and related expressions

(1) In this Act 'telecommunication system' means a system for the conveyance, through the agency of electric, magnetic, electro-magnetic, electro-chemical or electro-mechanical energy, of—

(a) speech, music and other sounds;

(b) visual images;

(c) signals serving for the impartation (whether as between persons and persons, things and things or persons and things) of any matter otherwise than in the form of sounds or visual images; or

(d) signals serving for the actuation or control of machinery or apparatus.

(2) For the purposes of this Act telecommunication apparatus which is situated in the United Kingdom and—

(a) is connected to but not comprised in a telecommunication system; or

(b) is connected to and comprised in a telecommunication system which extends beyond the United Kingdom, shall be regarded as a telecommunication system and any person who controls the apparatus shall be regarded as running the system.

(3)   In this Act—

'commercial activities connected with telecommunications' means any of the following, that is to say, the provision of telecommunication services, the supply or export of telecommunication apparatus and the production or acquisition of such apparatus for supply or export;

'telecommunication apparatus' means (except where the extended definition in Schedule 2 to this Act applies) apparatus constructed or adapted for use—

(a)   in transmitting or receiving anything falling within paragraphs (a) to (d) of subsection (1) above which is to be or has been conveyed by means of a telecommunication system; or

(b)   in conveying, for the purposes of such a system, anything falling within those paragraphs;

'telecommunication service' means any of the following, that is to say—

(a)   a service consisting in the conveyance by means of a telecommunication system of anything falling within paragraphs (a) to (d) of subsection (1) above;

(b)   a directory information service, that is to say, a service consisting in the provision by means of a telecommunication system of directory information for the purpose of facilitating the use of a service falling within paragraph (a) above and provided by means of that system; and

(c)   a service consisting in the installation, maintenance, adjustment, repair, alteration, moving, removal or replacement of apparatus which is or is to be connected to a telecommunication system.

(4)   Subject to subsection (6) below, a telecommunication system is connected to another telecommunication system for the purposes of this Act if it is being used, or is installed or connected for use, in conveying anything falling within paragraphs (a) to (d) of subsection (1) above which is to be or has been conveyed by means of that other system.

(5)   Subject to subsection (6) below, apparatus is connected to a telecommunication system for the purposes of this Act if it is being used, or is installed or connected for use—

(a)   in transmitting or receiving anything falling within paragraphs (a) to (d) of subsection (1) above which is to be or has been conveyed by means of that system; or

(b)   in conveying, for the purposes of that system, anything falling within those paragraphs;

and references in this subsection to anything falling within those paragraphs shall include references to energy of any kind mentioned in that subsection.

(6)   The connection to a telecommunication system of any other telecommunication system or any apparatus shall not be regarded as a connection for the purposes of this Act if that other telecommunication system or that apparatus would not be so connected but for its connection to another telecommunication system.

(7)   In this section, except subsection (1) above, 'convey' includes transmit, switch and receive and cognate expressions shall be construed accordingly.

PART II
PROVISION OF TELECOMMUNICATION SERVICES

Licensing etc. of telecommunication systems

5. Prohibition on running unlicensed systems

(1) Subject to the provisions of this section and section 6 below, a person who runs a telecommunication system within the United Kingdom shall be guilty of an offence unless he is authorised to run the system by a licence granted under section 7 below.

(2) Subject to the provisions of this section, a person who runs within the United Kingdom a telecommunication system which he is authorised to run by a licence granted under section 7 below shall be guilty of an offence if—

    (a) there is connected to the system—

        (i) any other telecommunication system; or

        (ii) any apparatus,

which is not authorised by the licence to be so connected; or

    (b) there are provided by means of the system any telecommunication services which are not authorised by the licence to be so provided.

(3) A person guilty of an offence under this section shall be liable—

    (a) on summary conviction, to a fine not exceeding the statutory maximum;

    (b) on conviction on indictment, to a fine.

(4) Where the commission by any person of an offence under this section is due to the act or default of some other person, that other person shall be guilty of the offence; and a person may be charged with and convicted of the offence by virtue of this subsection whether or not proceedings are taken against the first-mentioned person.

(5) In any proceedings for an offence under this section it shall, subject to subsection (6) below, be a defence for the person charged to prove that he took all reasonable steps and exercised all due diligence to avoid committing the offence.

(6) Where the defence provided by subsection (5) above involves an allegation that the commission of the offence was due to the act or default of another person, the person charged shall not, without leave of the court, be entitled to rely on that defence unless, within a period ending seven clear days before the hearing, he has served on the prosecutor a notice in writing giving such information identifying or assisting in the identification of that other person as was then in his possession.

(7) No proceedings shall be instituted in England and Wales or Northern Ireland in respect of an offence under this section except by or on behalf of the Secretary of State or the Director.

6. Exceptions to section 5

(1) . . .

(2) Section 5(1) above is not contravened by—

    (a) the running of a telecommunication system in the case of which the only agency involved in the conveyance of things thereby conveyed is light and the things thereby conveyed are so conveyed as to be capable of being received or perceived by the eye and without more;

(b)   the running by a person of a telecommunication system which is not connected to another telecommunication system and in the case of which all the apparatus comprised therein is situated either—

(i)   on a single set of premises in single occupation; or

(ii)   in a vehicle, vessel, aircraft or hovercraft or in two or more vehicles, vessels, aircraft or hovercraft mechanically coupled together; or

(c)   the running by a single individual of a telecommunication system which is not connected to another telecommunication system and in the case of which—

(i)   all the apparatus comprised therein is under his control; and

(ii)   everything conveyed by it that falls within paragraphs (a) to (d) of section 4(1) above is conveyed solely for domestic purposes of his;

and references in paragraphs (b) and (c) above to another telecommunication system do not include references to [a telecommunication system to which subsection (2A) below applies] (whether run by a broadcasting authority or by any other person).

(2A)   This subsection applies to a telecommunication system in the case of which every conveyance made by it is either—

(a)   a transmission, by wireless telegraphy, from a transmitting station for general reception of sounds, visual images or such signals as are mentioned in paragraph (c) of section 4(1) above; or

(b)   a conveyance within a single set of premises of sounds, visual images or such signals which are to be or have been so transmitted.

(3)   In the case of a business carried on by a person, section 5(1) above is not contravened by the running, for the purposes of that business, of a telecommunication system which is not connected to another telecommunication system and with respect to which the conditions specified in subsection (4) below are satisfied.

(4)   The said conditions are—

(a)   that no person except the person carrying on the business is concerned in the control of the apparatus comprised in the system;

(b)   that nothing falling within paragraphs (a) to (d) of section 4(1) above is conveyed by the system by way of rendering a service to another;

(c)   that, in so far as sounds or visual images are conveyed by the system, they are not conveyed for the purpose of their being heard or seen by persons other than the person carrying on the business or any employees of his engaged in the conduct thereof;

(d)   that in so far as such signals as are mentioned in paragraph (c) of section 4(1) above are conveyed by the system, they are not conveyed for the purpose of imparting matter otherwise than to the person carrying on the business, any employees of his engaged in the conduct thereof or things used in the course of the business and controlled by him; and

(e)   that, in so far as such signals as are mentioned in paragraph (d) of section 4(1) above are conveyed by the system, they are not conveyed for the purpose of actuating or controlling machinery or apparatus used otherwise than in the course of the business.

(5)   In this section—

'broadcasting authority' means a person licensed under the Wireless Telegraphy Act 1949 to broadcast programmes for general reception;
'business' includes a trade, profession or employment and includes any activity carried on by a body of persons, whether corporate or unincorporate;
'vessel' means a vessel of any description used in navigation;
'wireless telegraphy' has the same meaning as in the said Act of 1949.

Note
Section 6(1) was repealed, the words in square brackets in s. 6(2) were substituted, and s. 6(2A) was inserted, by the Broadcasting Act 1990.

7. Power to license systems

(1)   A licence may be granted—
   (a)   by the Secretary of State after consultation with the Director; or
   (b)   with the consent of, or in accordance with a general authorisation given by, the Secretary of State, by the Director,
for the running of any such telecommunication system as is specified in the licence or is of a description so specified.

(2)   A licence granted under this section shall be in writing and, unless previously revoked in accordance with any term in that behalf contained in the licence, shall continue in force for such period as may be specified in or determined by or under the licence.

(3)   A licence granted under this section may be granted either to all persons, to persons of a class or to a particular person.

(4)   A licence granted under this section may authorise—
   (a)   the connection to any telecommunication system to which the licence relates of—
      (i)   any other telecommunication system specified in the licence or of a description so specified; and
      (ii)   any apparatus so specified or of a description so specified; and
   (b)   the provision by means of any telecommunication system to which the licence relates of any telecommunication services specified in the licence or of a description so specified.

(5)   A licence granted under this section may include—
   (a)   such conditions (whether relating to the running of a telecommunication system to which the licence relates or otherwise) as appear to the Secretary of State or the Director to be requisite or expedient having regard to the duties imposed on him by section 3 above;
   (b)   conditions requiring the rendering to the Secretary of State of a payment on the grant of the licence or payments during the currency of the licence or both of such amount or amounts as may be determined by or under the licence; and
   (c)   conditions requiring any person who is authorised by the licence to run a telecommunication system to furnish to the Director, in such manner and at such times as he may reasonably require, such documents, accounts, estimates, returns or other information as he may require for the purpose of exercising the functions assigned or transferred to him by or under this Part or Part III of this Act.

(6)   Without prejudice to the generality of paragraph (a) of subsection (5) above, conditions included by virtue of that paragraph in a licence granted under this section to a particular person may require that person—

(a)   to comply with any direction given by the Director as to such matters as are specified in the licence or are of a description so specified;

(b)   except in so far as the Director consents to his doing or not doing them, not to do or to do such things as are specified in the licence or are of a description so specified; and

(c)   to refer for determination by the Director such questions arising under the licence as are specified in the licence or are of a description so specified.

(7)   A licence granted under this section specified otherwise than to a particular person shall be published in such manner as the Secretary of State or the Director considers appropriate for bringing it to the attention of the persons for whose benefit it will enure.

(8)   A copy of every licence granted under this section by the Secretary of State shall be sent to the Director.

(9)   Any sums received by the Secretary of State under this section shall be paid into the Consolidated Fund.

(10)   Neither the requirement to consult with the Director imposed by subsection (1)(a) above nor sections 8(5) and 10(6) below shall apply to the granting by the Secretary of State of the licence or licences which, having regard to the provisions of this Act, require to be granted (whether to British Telecommunications or to any other person) before the appointed day.

(10A) Before the Secretary of State or the Director decides whether to grant or revoke a licence under this section which authorises the running of a telecommunication system to which subsection (10B) below applies, he shall consult with the [Independent Television Commission].

(10B)   A telecommunication system is one to which this subsection applies if—

(a)   any person proposes to provide or is providing, by means of the system, a local delivery service (within the meaning of Part II of the Broadcasting Act 1990); and

(b)   notice of that fact has been given to the Secretary of State or the Director.

(11)   Where a licence granted under this section to a particular person includes a provision requiring that person to run any telecommunication system to which the licence relates through the agency of some other person, that other person, as well as the first mentioned person, shall be taken for the purposes of this section and the following provisions of this Part to be authorised by that licence to run that system.

Notes
1.   Section 7(10A), (10B) were inserted by the Cable and Broadcasting Act 1984 and saved by the Broadcasting Act 1990.
2.   The words in square brackets in s. 7(10A), (10B) were substituted by the Broadcasting Act 1990.
3.   Relevant cases include: *Mercury Communications* v *Director General of Telecommunications and and another* [1996] 1 WLR 48, HL.

8. Special provisions applicable to certain licences

(1)   This section applies to any licence granted under section 7 above to a particular person which includes conditions requiring that person—

(a)   to provide such telecommunication services as are specified in the licence or are of a description so specified;

(b)   to connect to any telecommunication system to which the licence relates, or permit the connection to any such system of, such other telecommunication systems and such apparatus as are specified in the licence or are of a description so specified;

(c)   to permit the provision by means of any telecommunication system to which the licence relates of such services as are specified in the licence or are of a description so specified;

(d)   not to show undue preference to, or to exercise undue discrimination against, particular persons or persons of any class or description (including, in particular, persons in rural areas) as respects any service provided, connection made or permission given in pursuance of such conditions as are mentioned in the foregoing paragraphs (whether in respect of the charges or other terms or conditions applied or otherwise); and

(e)   to publish, in such manner and at such times as are specified in the licence, a notice specifying, or specifying the method that is to be adopted for determining, the charges and other terms and conditions that are to be applicable to such services so provided, such connections so made and such permissions so given as are specified in the licence or are of a description so specified.

(2)   Where a licence granted under section 7 above to a particular person includes a condition requiring that person to provide such directory information services to which this subsection applies as are specified in the licence or are of a description so specified, subsection (1) above shall have effect as if the conditions there mentioned included a condition requiring that person to provide without charge for subscribers who are blind or otherwise disabled such directory information services to which this subsection applies as are appropriate to meet the needs of those subscribers and are specified in the licence or are of a description so specified.

(3)   Subsection (2) above applies to any directory information service which is provided for the purpose of facilitating the use of a voice telephony service and in that subsection 'blind or otherwise disabled' means so blind or otherwise disabled as to be unable to use a telephone directory.

(4)   It is immaterial for the purposes of subsections (1) and (2) above whether the person to whom the licence is granted is required to refer for determination by the Director such questions arising under the conditions mentioned in those subsections as are specified in the licence or are of a description so specified.

(5)   Before granting a licence to which this section applies, the Secretary of State or the Director shall give notice—

(a)   stating that he proposes to grant the licence and setting out its effect;

(b)   stating the reasons why he proposes to grant the licence; and

(c)   specifying the time (not being less than 28 days from the date of publication of the notice) within which representations or objections with respect to the proposed licence may be made,

and shall consider any representations or objections which are duly made and not withdrawn.

(6)   A notice under subsection (5) above shall be given by publication in such manner as the Secretary of State or the Director considers appropriate for bringing the matters to which the notice relates to the attention of persons likely to be affected by them.

9.   Public telecommunication systems

(1)   The Secretary of State may by order designate as a public telecommunication system any telecommunication system the running of which is authorised by a licence to which section 8 above applies; and any reference in this Act to a public telecommunication system is a reference to a telecommunication system which is so designated and the running of which is so authorised.

(2)   An order under subsection (1) above shall not come into operation until after the end of the period of 28 days beginning with—

(a)   the day on which copies of the order, and of the licence to which section 8 above applies, are laid before each House of Parliament; or

(b)   if such copies are so laid on different days, the last of those days.

(3)   In this Act 'public telecommunications operator' means a person authorised by a licence to which section 8 above applies to run a public telecommunication system.

(4)   In any case where it appears to the Secretary of State that it is expedient for transitional provision to be made in connection with a telecommunication system ceasing to be a public telecommunications operator, the Secretary of State may make a scheme giving effect to such transitional provision as he thinks fit.

10.   The telecommunications code

(1)   Subject to the following provisions of this section, the code (to be known as 'the telecommunications code') which is contained in Schedule 2 to this Act shall have effect—

(a)   where it is applied to a particular person by a licence granted by the Secretary of State under section 7 above authorising that person to run a telecommunication system; and

(b)   where the Secretary of State or a Northern Ireland department is running or is proposing to run a telecommunication system.

(2)   The telecommunications code shall not be applied to a person authorised by a licence under section 7 above to run a telecommunication system unless—

(a)   that licence is a licence to which section 8 above applies; or

(b)   it appears to the Secretary of State—

(i)   that the running of the system will benefit the public; and

(ii)   that it is not practicable for the system to be run without the application of that code to that person.

(3)   Where the telecommunications code is applied to any person by a licence under section 7 above it shall have effect subject to such exceptions and conditions as may be included in the licence for the purpose of qualifying the rights exercisable by that person by virtue of the code.

(4) Without prejudice to the generality of subsection (3) above, the exceptions and conditions there mentioned shall include such exceptions and conditions as appear to the Secretary of State to be requisite or expedient for the purpose of securing—

(a) that the physical environment is protected and, in particular, that the natural beauty and amenity of the countryside is conserved;

(b) that there is no greater damage to streets or interference with traffic than is reasonably necessary;

(c) that funds are available for meeting any liabilities which may arise from the exercise of rights conferred by or in accordance with the code;

and any condition falling within this subsection may impose on the person to whom the code is applied a requirement to comply with directions given in a manner specified in the condition and by a person so specified or of a description so specified.

(5) A licence under section 7 above which applies the telecommunications code to any person in relation to any part or locality of the United Kingdom shall include a condition requiring that person to cause copies of—

(a) the exceptions and conditions subject to which the telecommunications code has effect as so applied; and

(b) every direction given in a manner specified in any such condition by a person so specified or of a description so specified,

to be open for inspection by members of the public free of charge at such premises in that part or locality as are specified in the licence or are of a description so specified.

(6) Before granting under section 7 above a licence which applies the telecommunications code to a particular person in relation to any part or locality of the United Kingdom, the Secretary of State shall publish a notice—

(a) stating that he proposes to apply the code to that person in relation to that part or locality and setting out the effect of the exceptions and conditions subject to which he proposes that the code should have effect as so applied;

(b) stating the reasons why he proposes to apply the code to that person in relation to that part or locality and why he proposes that the code as so applied should have effect subject to those exceptions and conditions; and

(c) specifying the time (not being less than 28 days from the date of publication of the notice) within which representations or objections with respect to the proposed application of the code to that person in relation to that part or locality and with respect to the proposed exceptions and conditions may be made,

and shall reconsider his proposals in the light of any representations or objections which are duly made and not withdrawn.

(7) If the Secretary of State, on reconsidering in pursuance of subsection (6) above any proposals specified in a notice under that subsection, grants a licence under section 7 above applying the telecommunications code to any person in relation to any part or locality of the United Kingdom, he shall on granting that licence publish a further notice—

(a) stating that the code has been applied to that person in relation to that part or locality and setting out the effect of the exceptions and conditions subject to which the code has effect as so applied; and

(b)   stating the reasons why the code has been applied to that person in relation to that part or locality and why the code as so applied has effect subject to those exceptions and conditions.

(8)   Where the Secretary of State has granted a licence under section 7 above which applies the telecommunications code to a particular person in relation to any part or locality of the United Kingdom, he may—

(a)   with the consent of that person; or

(b)   if it appears to him requisite or expedient to do so for the purpose mentioned in subsection (4) above,

modify the exceptions and conditions subject to which the code has effect as so applied.

(9)   Before modifying the exceptions and conditions subject to which the telecommunications code has effect as applied to any person in relation to any part or locality of the United Kingdom by a licence granted under section 7 above, the Secretary of State shall publish a notice—

(a)   stating that he proposes to make the modifications and setting out their effect;

(b)   stating the reasons why he proposes to make the modifications; and

(c)   specifying the time (not being less than 28 days from the date of publication of this notice) within which representations or objections with respect to the proposed modifications may be made.

and shall reconsider his proposals in the light of any representations or objections which are duly made and not withdrawn.

(10)   If the Secretary of State, on reconsidering in pursuance of subsection (9) above any proposals specified in a notice under that subsection, modifies the exceptions and conditions subject to which the telecommunications code has effect as applied to any person in relation to any part or locality of the United Kingdom by a licence granted under section 7 above, he shall on making the modifications publish a further notice—

(a)   stating that the modifications have been made and setting out their effect; and

(b)   stating the reasons why the modifications have been made.

(11)   A notice under this section shall be published in such manner as the Secretary of State considers appropriate for bringing the matters to which the notice relates to the attention of persons likely to be affected by them.

11.   Provisions supplementary to section 10

(1)   . . . the Secretary of State may by order apply paragraphs 1 to 6 of Schedule 3 to the Electricity Supply (Northern Ireland) Order 1972 (execution of works affecting roads, bridges, sewers and pipes), with such modifications as may be specified in the order, to the exercise in Northern Ireland of any right conferred by or in accordance with that code to do one or more of the things mentioned in that sub-paragraph.

(2)   Without prejudice to the generality of subsection (1) above, an order under that subsection may contain provisions creating an offence punishable on summary conviction with a fine not exceeding level 3 on the standard scale.

(3)   The Secretary of State may from time to time by order provide that the telecommunications code shall have effect for all purposes as if an amount

specified in the order were substituted for the amount specified, or for the time being having effect as if specified, in sub-paragraph (3) of paragraph 16 of the code as the minimum amount of compensation payable under that paragraph; and an order under this section may contain such transitional provisions as the Secretary of State considers appropriate.

(4)   In any case where it appears to the Secretary of State that it is expedient for transitional provision to be made in connection with the telecommunications code ceasing to apply to any person by reason of the expiry or revocation of a person's licence under section 7 above, the Secretary of State may make a scheme giving effect to such transitional provision as the Secretary of State thinks fit.

(5)   Without prejudice to the generality of subsection (4) above, a scheme under that subsection may—

(a)   impose obligations on a person to whom the telecommunications code has ceased to apply as mentioned in subsection (4) above to remove anything installed in pursuance of any right conferred by or in accordance with the telecommunications code, to restore land to its condition before anything was done in pursuance of any such right or to pay the expenses of any such removal or restoration;

(b)   provide for those obligations to be enforceable in such manner (otherwise than by criminal penalties) and by such persons as may be specified in the scheme;

(c)   authorise the retention of apparatus on any land pending the grant of a licence under section 7 above authorising the running by any person of a telecommunication system for the purposes of which that apparatus may be used;

(d)   provide for the purposes of any provision contained in the scheme by virtue of paragraph (a), (b) or (c) above for such questions arising under the scheme as are specified in the scheme, or are of a description so specified, to be referred to, and determined by, the Director.

Note

The words omitted from s. 11(1) were repealed by the New Roads and Street Works Act 1991.

Modification of licences

12.   Modification of licence conditions by agreement

(1)   Subject to the following provisions of this section, the Director may modify the condition of a licence granted under section 7 above.

(2)   Before making modifications under this section, the Director shall give notice—

(a)   stating that he proposes to make the modifications and setting out their effect;

(b)   stating the reasons why he proposes to make the modifications; and

(c)   specifying the time (not being less than 28 days from the date of publication of the notice) within which representations or objections with respect to the proposed modifications may be made,

and shall consider any representations or objections which are duly made and not withdrawn.

(3) A notice under subsection (2) above shall be given by publication in such manner as the Director considers appropriate for the purpose of bringing the matters to which the notice relates to the attention of persons likely to be affected by them and, in the case of a licence granted to a particular person, by sending a copy of the notice to that person.

(4) In the case of a licence granted to a particular person, the Director shall not make the modifications except with the consent of that person; and, in the case of a licence granted to all persons or to persons of a class, the Director shall not make the modifications unless either—

(a) no representations or objections are duly made by persons authorised by that licence to run telecommunication systems; or

(b) any representations or objections duly made by such persons are withdrawn.

(5) The Director shall also send a copy of a notice under subsection (2) above to the Secretary of State; and if, within the time specified in the notice, the Secretary of State directs the Director not to make any modification, the Director shall comply with the direction.

(6) The Secretary of State shall not give a direction under subsection (5) above unless—

(a) it appears to him that the modification should be made, if at all, under section 15 below; or

(b) it appears to him to be requisite or expedient to do so in the interests of national security or relations with the government of a country or territory outside the United Kingdom.

(7) References in this section and in sections 13 to 15 below to modifications of the conditions of a licence do not include references to modifications of conditions relating to the application of the telecommunications code.

13. Licence modification references to Commission

(1) The Director may make to the Monopolies and Mergers Commission (in this Act referred to as 'the Commission') a reference which is so framed as to require the Commission to investigate and report on the questions—

(a) whether any matters which relate to the provision of telecommunication services or the supply of telecommunication apparatus by a person authorised by a licence under section 7 above to run a telecommunication system and which are specified in the reference operate, or may be expected to operate, against the public interest; and

(b) if so, whether the effects adverse to the public interest which those matters have or may be expected to have could be remedied or prevented by modifications of the conditions of that licence.

(2) The Director may, at any time, by notice given to the Commission vary a reference under this section by adding to the matters specified in the reference or by excluding from the reference some or all of the matters so specified; and, subject to subsection (5) below, on receipt of such notice the Commission shall give effect to the variation.

(3) The Director may specify in a reference under this section, or a variation of such a reference, for the purpose of assisting the Commission in carrying out the investigation on the reference—

(a) any effects adverse to the public interest which, in his opinion, the matters specified in the reference or variation have or may be expected to have; and

(b) any modifications of the conditions of the licence by which, in his opinion, those effects could be remedied or prevented.

(4) The Director shall publish particulars of a reference under this section, or of a variation of such a reference, in such manner as he considers appropriate for the purpose of bringing the reference or variation to the attention of persons likely to be affected by it and, in the case of a licence granted to a particular person, shall send a copy of the reference or variation to that person.

(5) The Director shall also send a copy of a reference under this section, or a variation of such a reference, to the Secretary of State; and if, before the end of the period of 14 days beginning with the day on which the Secretary of State receives the copy of the reference or variation, the Secretary of State directs the Commission not to proceed with the reference or, as the case may require, not to give effect to the variation, the Commission shall comply with the direction.

(6) The Secretary of State shall not give a direction under subsection (5) above unless it appears to him to be requisite or expedient to do so in the interests of national security or relations with the government of a country or territory outside the United Kingdom.

(7) It shall be the duty of the Director, for the purpose of assisting the Commission in carrying out an investigation on a reference under this section, to give to the Commission—

(a) any information which is in his possession and which relates to matters falling within the scope of the investigation, and which is either requested by the Commission for that purpose or is information which in his opinion it would be appropriate for that purpose to give to the Commission without any such request; and

(b) any other assistance which the Commission may require, and which it is within his power to give, in relation to any such matters,

and the Commission, for the purpose of carrying out any such investigation, shall take account of any information given to them for that purpose under this subsection.

(8) In determining for the purposes of this section whether any particular matter operates, or may be expected to operate, against the public interest, the Commission shall have regard to the matters as respects which duties are imposed on the Secretary of State and the Director by section 3 above.

(9) Sections 70 (time limit for report on merger reference) and 85 (attendance of witnesses and production of documents) of the Fair Trading Act 1973 (in this Act referred to as 'the 1973 Act') and Part II of Schedule 3 to that Act (performance of functions of the Commission) [together with section 24 of the Competition Act 1980 (modification of provisions about performance of Commission's functions)] shall apply in relation to references under this section as if—

(a) the functions of the Commission in relation to those references were functions under that Act;

(b) the expression 'merger reference' included a reference under this section;

(c)   in the said section 70 references to the Secretary of State were references to the Director and the reference to three months were a reference to six months;

(d)   in paragraph 11 of the said Schedule 3 the reference to section 71 of that Act were a reference to subsection (2) above; and

(e)   paragraph 16(2) of that Schedule were omitted.

(10)   For the purposes of references under this section the Secretary of State shall appoint not less than three additional members of the Commission; and if any functions of the Commission in relation to any such reference are performed through a group, the chairman of the Commission shall select one, two or three of those additional members to be members of the group and the number of regular members to be selected by him under paragraph 10 of Schedule 3 to the 1973 Act shall be reduced accordingly.

Notes
1.   The words in square brackets in s. 13(9) were inserted by the Companies Act 1989.
2.   There have been two references to the MMC: Telephone Number Portability presented to the DGT in November 1995 and Chatline and Message Services presented to the DGT in January 1989.

14.   Reports on licence modification references

(1)   In making a report on a reference under section 13 above, the Commission—

(a)   shall include in the report definite conclusions on the questions comprised in the reference together with such an account of their reasons for those conclusions as in their opinion is expedient for facilitating proper understanding of those questions and of their conclusions;

(b)   where they conclude that any of the matters specified in the reference operate, or may be expected to operate, against the public interest, shall specify in the report the effects adverse to the public interest which those matters have or may be expected to have; and

(c)   where they conclude that any adverse effects so specified could be remedied or prevented by modifications of the conditions of the licence, shall specify in the report modifications by which those effects could be remedied or prevented.

(2)   Where, on a reference under this section, the Commission conclude that any person who is authorised by the licence to run a telecommunication system is a party to an agreement to which the Restrictive Trade Practices Act 1976 applies, the Commission in making their report on that reference, shall exclude from their consideration the question whether the provisions of that agreement, in so far as they are provisions by virtue of which it is an agreement to which that Act applies, operate, or may be expected to operate, against the public interest; and paragraph (b) of subsection (1) above shall have effect subject to the provisions of this subsection.

(3)   Section 82 of the 1973 Act (general provisions as to reports) shall apply in relation to reports of the Commission on references under section 13 above as it applies to reports of the Commission under that Act.

(4)   A report of the Commission on a reference under section 16 above shall be made to the Director.

(5)   On receiving such a report, the Director—

(a)   shall send a copy of the report to the Secretary of State and, in the case of a licence granted to a particular person, to that person; and

(b)   subject to any direction given under subsection (6) below, shall publish the report in such manner as he considers appropriate for bringing the report to the attention of persons likely to be affected by it.

(6)   If it appears to the Secretary of State that the publication of any matter in such a report would be against the public interest or the commercial interests of any person, he may, before the end of the period of 14 days beginning with the day on which he receives the copy of the report, direct the Director to exclude that matter from the report as published under subsection (5) above.

15.   Modification of licence conditions following report

(1)   Where a report of the Commission on a reference under section 13 above—

(a)   includes conclusions to the effect that any of the matters specified in the reference operate, or may be expected to operate, against the public interest;

(b)   specifies effects adverse to the public interest which those matters have or may be expected to have;

(c)   includes conclusions to the effect that those effects could be remedied or prevented by modifications of the conditions of the licence; and

(d)   specifies modifications by which those effects could be remedied or prevented,

the Director shall, subject to the following provisions of this section, make such modifications of the conditions of the licence as appear to him requisite for the purpose of remedying or preventing the adverse effects specified in the report.

(2)   Before making modifications under this section, the Director shall have regard to the modifications specified in the report.

(3)   Before making modifications under this section, the Director shall give notice—

(a)   stating that he proposes to make the modifications and setting out their effect;

(b)   stating the reasons why he proposes to make the modifications; and

(c)   specifying the time (not being less than 28 days from the date of publication of the notice) within which representations or objections with respect to the proposed modifications may be made,

and shall consider any representations or objections which are duly made and not withdrawn.

(4)   A notice under subsection (3) above shall be given by publication in such manner as the Director considers appropriate for the purpose of bringing the matters to which the notice relates to the attention of persons likely to be affected by them and, in the case of a licence granted to a particular person, by sending a copy of the notice to that person.

(5)   The Director shall also send a copy of a notice under subsection (3) above to the Secretary of State; and if, within the time specified in the notice, the Secretary of State directs the Director not to make any modification the Director shall comply with the direction.

(6)   The Secretary of State shall not give a direction under subsection (5) above unless it appears to him requisite or expedient to do so in the interests of national security or relations with the government of a country or territory outside the United Kingdom.

Enforcement of licences

16.   Securing compliance with licence conditions

(1)   Subject to subsections (2) and (5) and section 17 below, where the Director is satisfied that a person who is authorised by a licence granted under section 7 above to run a telecommunication system (in this Act referred to as a 'telecommunications operator') is contravening, or has contravened and is likely again to contravene, any of the conditions of his licence, the Director shall by a final order make such provision as is requisite for the purpose of securing compliance with that condition.

(2)   Subject to subsection (5) below, where it appears to the Director—

(a)   that a telecommunications operator is contravening, or has contravened and is likely again to contravene, any of the conditions of his licence; and

(b)   that it is requisite that a provisional order be made,

the Director shall (instead of taking steps towards the making of a final order) by a provisional order make such provision as appears to him requisite for the purpose of securing compliance with that condition.

(3)   In determining for the purposes of subsection (2)(b) above whether it is requisite that a provisional order be made, the Director shall have regard, in particular, to the extent to which any person is likely to sustain loss or damage in consequence of anything which, in contravention of the relevant condition, is likely to be done, or omitted to be done, before a final order may be made.

(4)   Subject to subsection (5) and section 17 below, the Director shall confirm a provisional order with or without modifications if—

(a)   he is satisfied that the telecommunications operator is contravening, or has contravened and is likely again to contravene, any of the conditions of his licence; and

(b)   the provision made by the order (with any modifications) is requisite for the purpose of securing compliance with that condition.

(5)   The duties imposed by subsections (1) to (4) above shall not apply where the Director gives notice that he is satisfied—

(a)   that the duties imposed on him by section 3 above preclude the making of a final or provisional order or, as the case may be, the confirmation of the provisional order; or

(b)   that the contraventions or apprehended contraventions are of a trivial nature;

and a notice under this subsection shall be given by publication in such manner as the Director considers appropriate for the purpose of bringing the matters to which the notice relates to the attention of persons likely to be affected by them and by sending a copy of the notice to the telecommunications operator.

(6)   A final or provisional order—

    (a)　shall require the telecommunications operator (according to the circumstances of the case) to do, or not to do, such things as are specified in the order or are of a description so specified;

    (b)　shall take effect at such time, being the earliest practicable time, as is determined by or under the order; and

    (c)　may be revoked at any time by the Director.

  (7)　In this section and sections 17 to 19 below—

'contravention', in relation to any condition of a licence, includes any failure to comply with that condition and 'contravene' shall be construed accordingly;

'final order' means an order under this section other than a provisional order;

'provisional order' means an order under this section which, if not previously confirmed under subsection (4) above, will cease to have effect at the end of such period (not exceeding three months) as is determined by or under the order.

  (8)　References in this section to conditions of a licence do not include references to conditions relating to the application of the telecommunications code.

17.　Procedural requirements

  (1)　Before making a final order or confirming a provisional order, the Director shall give notice—

    (a)　stating that he proposes to make or confirm the order and setting out its effect;

    (b)　stating the relevant condition of the licence and the acts or omissions which, in his opinion, constitute or would constitute contraventions of it; and

    (c)　specifying the time (not being less than 28 days from the date of publication of the notice) within which representations or objections to the proposed order or confirmation of the order may be made,

and shall consider any representations or objections which are duly made and not withdrawn.

  (2)　The Director shall not make a final order, or confirm a provisional order, with modifications except with the consent of the telecommunications operator or after complying with the requirements of subsection (3) below.

  (3)　The said requirements are that the Director shall—

    (a)　give to the telecommunications operator such notice as appears to him requisite of his proposal to make or confirm the order with modifications;

    (b)　specify the time (not being less than 28 days from the date of the service of the notice) within which representations or objections to the proposed modifications may be made; and

    (c)　consider any representations or objections which are duly made and not withdrawn.

  (4)　Before revoking a final order or a provisional order which has been confirmed, the Director shall give notice—

    (a)　stating that he proposes to revoke the order and setting out its effect; and

    (b)　specifying the time (not being less than 28 days from the date of publication of the notice) within which representations or objections to the proposed revocation may be made,

and shall consider any representations or objections which are duly made and not withdrawn.

(5)   A notice under subsection (1) or (4) above shall be given by publication in such manner as the Director considers appropriate for the purpose of bringing the matters to which the notice relates to the attention of persons likely to be affected by them and by sending a copy of the notice to the telecommunications operator.

(6)   As soon as practicable after a final order is made or a provisional order is made or confirmed, the Director shall—

(a)   publish the order in such manner as he considers appropriate for the purpose of bringing the order to the attention of persons likely to be affected by it; and

(b)   serve a copy of the order on the telecommunications operator.

18.   Validity and effect of orders

(1)   If the telecommunications operator is aggrieved by a final or provisional order and desires to question its validity on the ground that the making or confirmation of it was not within the powers of section 16 above or that any of the requirements of section 17 above have not been complied with in relation to it, he may within 42 days from the date of service on him of a copy of the order make an application to the court under this section.

(2)   On any such application the court may, if satisfied that the making or confirmation of the order was not within those powers or that the interests of the telecommunications operator have been substantially prejudiced by a failure to comply with those requirements, quash the order or any provision of the order.

(3)   Except as provided by this section, the validity of a final or provisional order shall not be questioned by any legal proceedings whatever.

(4)   No criminal proceedings shall, by virtue of the making of a final order or the making or confirmation of a provisional order, lie against any person on the ground that he has committed, or aided, abetted, counselled or procured the commission of, or conspired or attempted to commit, or incited others to commit, any contravention of the order.

(5)   The obligation to comply with a final or provisional order is a duty owed to any person who may be affected by a contravention of it.

(6)   Where a duty is owed by virtue of subsection (5) above to any person—

(a)   any breach of the duty which causes that person to sustain loss or damage; and

(b)   any act which, by inducing a breach of that duty or interfering with its performance, causes that person to sustain loss or damage and which is done wholly or partly for the purpose of achieving that result,
shall be actionable at the suit or instance of that person.

(7)   In any proceedings brought against any person in pursuance of subsection (6)(a) above, it shall be a defence for him to prove that he took all reasonable steps and exercised all due diligence to avoid contravening the order.

(8)   Without prejudice to any right which any person may have by virtue of subsection (6)(a) above to bring civil proceedings in respect of any

contravention or apprehended contravention of a final or provisional order, compliance with any such order shall be enforceable by civil proceedings by the Director for an injunction or interdict or for any other appropriate relief.

(9) In this section—

'act', in relation to any person, includes any failure to do an act which he is under a duty to do and 'done' shall be construed accordingly;

'contravention', in relation to a final or provisional order, includes any failure to comply with it;

'the court'—

(a) in relation to England and Wales and Northern Ireland, means the High Court; and

(b) (*applicable only to Scotland*).

19. Register of licences and orders

(1) The Director shall keep a register of licences granted under section 7 above and final and provisional orders at such premises and in such form as he may determine.

(2) Subject to any direction given under subsection (3) below, the Director shall cause to be entered in the register the provisions of—

(a) every licence granted under section 7 above and every modification or revocation of, and every direction or consent given or determination made under, such a licence; and

(b) every final or provisional order, every revocation of such an order and every notice under section 16(5) above.

(3) If it appears to the Secretary of State that the entry of any provision in the register would be against the public interest or the commercial interests of any person, he may direct the Director not to enter that provision in the register.

(4) The register shall be open to public inspection during such hours and subject to payment of such fee as may be prescribed by an order made by the Secretary of State.

(5) Any person may, on payment of such fee as may be prescribed by an order so made, require the Director to supply to him a copy of or extract from any part of the register, certified by the Director to be a true copy or extract.

(6) Any sums received by the Director under this section shall be paid into the Consolidated Fund.

Note
Orders under this section inlude: the Telecommunications (Registers) Order 1995, SI 1995/232.

Approvals etc. for the purposes of licences

20. Approval of contractors

(1) Where licences granted under section 7 above include provisions which are framed by reference to the carrying out of relevant operations by persons for the time being approved under this section then, for the purposes of those provisions, persons may be approved under this section in relation to such operations—

    (a) by the Secretary of State; or

    (b) with the consent of, or in accordance with a general authorisation given by, the Secretary of State, by the Director.

(2) A person applying for an approval under this section may be required by the person to whom the application is made to comply with such requirements as the person to whom the application is made may think appropriate; and those requirements may include a requirement to satisfy some other person with respect to any matter.

(3) An approval under this section may apply either to a particular person or to persons of a description specified in the approval, and may so apply either in relation to particular relevant operations or in relation to relevant operations of a description so specified.

(4) An approval under this section may specify conditions which must be complied with if the approval is to apply, for any purposes specified in the approval, to any person who is so specified or is of a description so specified; and any such condition may impose on the person to whom the approval is given a requirement from time to time to satisfy any person with respect to any matter.

(5) Nothing in this section shall preclude a person (not being the Secretary of State or the Director) by whom any matter falls to be determined for the purposes of any requirement imposed in pursuance of subsection (2) or (4) above from charging any fee in respect of the carrying out of any test or other assessment made by him.

(6) Any power conferred by this section to give an approval includes power to vary or withdraw an approval given in exercise of that power.

(7) The Secretary of State shall send to the Director—

    (a) a copy of every approval given by him under this section; and

    (b) particulars of every variation or withdrawal of an approval so given.

(8) The Secretary of State may by order provide for the charging of fees in respect of the exercise of any functions conferred by or under this section.

(9) Any sums received by the Secretary of State or the Director under this section shall be paid into the Consolidated Fund.

(10) In this section 'relevant operations' means the installation, maintenance, adjustment, repair, alteration, moving, removal or replacement of apparatus which is or is to be connected to any telecommunication system to which a licence under section 7 above relates.

21. Register of approved contractors

(1) The Director shall keep a register of approvals given under section 20 above at such premises and in such form as he may determine.

(2) The Director shall cause particulars of every such approval, and of every variation or withdrawal of such an approval, to be entered in the register.

(3) Subsections (4) to (6) of section 19 above shall apply for the purposes of this section as they apply for the purposes of that section.

22. Approval etc. of apparatus

(1) Where licences granted under section 7 above include provisions which are framed by reference to apparatus for the time being approved

under this section for connection to telecommunications systems to which the licences relate, then, for the purposes of those provisions, apparatus may be approved for connection to those systems—

    (a)   by the Secretary of State; or

    (b)   with the consent of, or in accordance with a general authorisation given by, the Secretary of State, by the Director.

    (2)   A person applying for an approval under this section may be required by the person to whom the application is made to comply with such requirements as the person to whom the application is made may think appropriate; and those requirements may include a requirement to satisfy some other person with respect to any matter.

    (3)   An approval under this section may apply either to particular apparatus or to any apparatus of a description specified in the approval, and may so apply either for the purposes of a particular telecommunication system or for the purposes of any telecommunication system of a description so specified.

    (4)   An approval under this section may specify conditions which must be complied with if the approval is to apply, for any purposes specified in the approval, to any apparatus which is so specified or is of a description so specified; and any such conditon may impose on the person to whom the approval is given a requirement from time to time to satisfy any person with respect to any matter.

    (5)   Nothing in this section shall preclude a person (not being the Secretary of State or the Director) by whom any matter falls to be determined for the purposes of any requirement imposed in pursuance of subsection (2) or (4) above from charging any fee in respect of the carrying out of any test or other assessment made by him.

    (6)   Standards to which apparatus of a description specified in the designation must conform if it is to be approved for connection to a telecommunication system so specified or of a description so specified may be designated—

    (a)   by the Secretary of State; or

    (b)   with the consent of, or in accordance with a general authorisation given by, the Secretary of State, by the Director;

and the standard so designated may apply subject to such exceptions as may be determined by or under the designation.

    (7)   A designation under this section may specify conditions which must be complied with if any apparatus of a description specified in the designation is to be regarded, for any purposes so specified, as conforming to the standard to which the designation relates.

    (8)   Before designating a standard under this section, the Secretary of State or the Director shall give notice—

    (a)   stating that he proposes to make the designation and setting out its effect;

    (b)   stating any conditions which he proposes to specify in the designation; and

    (c)   specifying the time (not being less than 28 days from the date of publication of the notice) within which representations or objections with respect to the proposed designation may be made,

and shall consider any representations or objections which are duly made and not withdrawn.

(9)   A notice under subsection (8) above shall be given by sending a copy of the notice to the person running the system and such other persons (if any) as the Secretary of State or the Director considers appropriate.

(10)   Any power conferred by this section to give an approval or designate a standard includes power to vary or withdraw an approval given or designation made in the exercise of that power.

(11)   The Secretary of State shall send to the Director—

(a)   a copy of every approval given or designation made by him under this section; and

(b)   particulars of every variation or withdrawal of an approval so given or a designation so made,

except where it appears to him requisite or expedient not to do so in the interests of national security.

(12)   The Secretary of State may by order provide for the charging of fees in respect of the exercise of any functions conferred by or under this section.

(13)   Any sums received by the Secretary of State or the Director under this section shall be paid into the Consolidated Fund.

Notes

1.   Terminal equipment: this section is disapplied in relation to applicable equipment, and modified in its application to exempt terminal equipment, by the Telecommunications Terminal Equipment Regulations 1992, SI 1992/2423, as amended by SI 1994/3129 and SI 1995/144.

2.   Orders under this section include: the Telecommunications Apparatus (Approval Fees) (British Approvals Board for Telecommunications) Order 1992, SI 1992/1875.

23.   Register of approved apparatus etc.

(1)   The Director shall keep a register of approvals given and designations made under section 22 above at such premises and in such form as he may determine.

(2)   Subject to subsection (3) below and to any direction given under subsection (4) below, the Director shall cause particulars of every such approval or designation, and of every variation or withdrawal of such an approval or designation, to be entered in the register.

(3)   The Director shall not enter in the register particulars of—

(a)   any approval given or designation made by the Secretary of State under section 22 above a copy of which is not sent to the Director under subsection (11) of that section; or

(b)   any variation or withdrawal of an approval so given or a designation so made particulars of which are not so sent.

(4)   Subsections (3) to (6) of section 19 above shall apply for the purposes of this section as they apply for the purposes of that section.

24.   Approval etc. of meters

(1)   Where licences granted under section 7 above include provisions which are framed by reference to meters for the time being approved under this section for use in connection with telecommunication systems to which the licences relate, then, for the purposes of those provisions, meters may be approved for use in connection with those systems—

(a)   by the Secretary of State; or

(b)   with the consent of, or in accordance with a general authorisation given by, the Secretary of State, by the Director.

(2)   A person applying for an approval under this section may be required by the person to whom the application is made to comply with such requirements as the person to whom the application is made may think appropriate; and those requirements may include a requirement to satisfy some other person with respect to any matter.

(3)   An approval under this section may apply either to a particular meter or to any meter of a description specified in the approval, and may so apply either for the purposes of a particular telecommunication system or for the purposes of any telecommunication system of a description so specified.

(4)   An approval under this section may specify conditions which must be complied with if the approval is to apply, for any purpose specified in the approval, to any meter which is so specified or is of a description so specified; and any such condition may impose on the person to whom the approval is given a requirement from time to time to satisfy any person with respect to any matter.

(5)   Nothing in this section shall preclude a person (not being the Secretary of State or the Director) by whom any matter falls to be determined for the purposes of any requirement imposed in pursuance of subsection (2) or (4) above from charging any fee in respect of the carrying out of any test or other assessment made by him.

(6)   Standards to which any meter of a description specified in the designation must conform if it is to be approved for use in connection with a telecommunication system so specified or of a description so specified may be designated—

(a)   by the Secretary of State; or

(b)   with the consent of, or in accordance with a general authorisation given by, the Secretary of State, by the Director;

and a standard so designated may apply subject to such exceptions as may be determined by or under the designation.

(7)   A designation under this section may specify conditions which must be complied with if any meter of a description specified in the designation is to be regarded, for any purposes so specified, as conforming to the standard to which the designation relates.

(8)   A meter shall not be approved under this section for use in connection with any telecommunication system unless either—

(a)   the meter conforms to a standard designated under this section which applies to it for the purposes of that system; or

(b)   the Secretary of State or the Director is satisfied that, if used in connection with that system in accordance with the approval, the meter would be sufficiently accurate and reliable.

(9)   Before giving an approval under this section by virtue of subsection (8)(b) above or designating a standard under this section, the Secretary of State or the Director shall give notice—

(a)   stating that he proposes to give the approval or make the designation and setting out its effect;

(b)   stating any conditions which he proposes to specify in the approval or designation; and

(c) specifying the time (not being less than 28 days from the date of publication of the notice) within which representations or objections with respect to the proposed approval or designation may be made,
and shall consider any representations or objections which are duly made and not withdrawn.

(10) A notice under subsection (9) above shall be given by sending a copy of the notice—

(a) in the case of an approval, to the person applying for the approval;

(b) in the case of a designation, to the person running the system,
and (in either case) to such other persons (if any) as the Secretary of State or the Director considers appropriate.

(11) Any power conferred by this section to give an approval or designate a standard includes power to vary or withdraw an approval given or designation made in the exercise of that power.

(12) The Secretary of State shall send to the Director—

(a) a copy of every approval given or designation made by him under this section; and

(b) particulars of every variation or withdrawal of an approval so given or a designation so made.

(13) The Secretary of State may by order provide for the charging of fees in respect of the exercise of any functions conferred by or under this section.

(14) Any sums received by the Secretary of State or the Director under this section shall be paid into the Consolidated Fund.

(15) In this section 'meter' means any system or apparatus constructed or adapted for use in ascertaining the extent of telecommunication services provided by means of a telecommunication system.

25. Delegation of functions under sections 22 and 24

(1) The functions conferred on the Secretary of State by sections 22 and 24 above (other than the powers to make orders) shall be exercisable by any person appointed by the Secretary of State for the purpose to such extent and subject to such conditions as may be specified in the appointment; and an appointment under this section may authorise the person appointed to retain any fees received by him.

(2) Before appointing any person under this section, the Secretary of State shall consult with the persons running the telecommunication systems concerned, or with such organisations as appear to the Secretary of State to be representative of those persons.

26. Grants and loans to persons exercising certain functions

(1) The Secretary of State may, with the approval of the Treasury, make grants or loans—

(a) to persons by whom any matter falls to be determined for the purposes of any requirement imposed in pursuance of subsection (2) or (4) of section 20, 22 or 24 above; or

(b) to persons appointed under section 25 above.

(2) Any loans under this section shall be repaid to the Secretary of State at such times and by such methods and interest thereon shall be paid to him

at such rates and at such times as he may, with the approval of the Treasury, from time to time direct.

(3)   There shall be paid out of money provided by Parliament any sums required by the Secretary of State for making grants or loans under this section.

(4)   Any sums received by the Secretary of State under subsection (2) above shall be paid into the Consolidated Fund.

27.   Recognition of bodies representing consumers etc.

(1)   Where licences granted under section 7 above include provisions which are framed by reference to bodies for the time being recognised under this section to be representing the interests of consumers, purchasers and other users of telecommunication services provided by means of, or telecommunications apparatus connected to, telecommunication systems to which the licences relate, then, for the purposes of those provisions, bodies may be so recognised by the Secretary of State.

(2)   A recognition under this section may apply either to a particular body or to bodies of a description specified in the recognition, and may so apply either for the purposes of a particular telecommunication system or for the purposes of any telecommunication system of a description so specified.

(3)   The Secretary of State may pay such allowances as he may determine to members of a body recognised by him under this section, and may pay such expenses of a body so recognised as he may determine.

(4)   Any power conferred by this section to give a recognition includes power to withdraw a recognition given in the exercise of that power.

(5)   There shall be paid out of money provided by Parliament any sums required by the Secretary of State for making payments under this section.

Standards of performance

27A.   Standards of performance in individual cases

(1)   The Director may make regulations prescribing, for any designated operator, such standards of performance in connection with the provision of relevant services by that operator as, in his opinion, ought to be achieved in individual cases.

(2)   Regulations under subsection (1) above may only be made—
    (a)   with the consent of the Secretary of State;
    (b)   after consulting—
        (i)   the designated operator; and
        (ii)   persons or bodies appearing to the Director to be representative of persons likely to be affected by the regulations; and
    (c)   after arranging for such research as the Director considers appropriate with a view to discovering the views of a representative sample of persons likely to be so affected and considering the results.

(3)   Regulations under this section may—
    (a)   prescribe circumstances in which the designated operator is to inform persons of their rights under this section;
    (b)   prescribe such standards of performance in relation to any duty arising under paragraph (a) above as, in the Director's opinion, ought to be achieved in all cases;

(c) prescribe circumstances in which the designated operator is to be exempted from any requirements of the regulations or this section.

(4) If the designated operator fails to meet a prescribed standard, he shall make to any person who is affected by the failure such compensation as may be determined by or under the regulations.

(5) The making of compensation under this section in respect of any failure to meet a prescribed standard shall not prejudice any other remedy which may be available in respect of the act or omission which constituted that failure.

(6) Any dispute arising under this section or regulations made under this section—

(a) may be referred to the Director by either party; and

(b) on such a reference, shall be determined by order made—

(i) by the Director; or

(ii) by such other person as may be prescribed.

(7) Any person making an order under subsection (6) above shall include in the order his reasons for reaching his decision with respect to the dispute.

(8) The practice and procedure to be followed in connection with any such determination shall be such as may be prescribed.

(9) An order under subsection (6) above shall be final and shall be enforceable—

(a) in England and Wales and in Northern Ireland, as if it were a judgment of a county court; and

(b) *(applicable only to Scotland).*

(10) In this section 'prescribed' means prescribed by regulations under this section.

Note
This section was inserted by the Competition and Service (Utilities) Act 1992.

27B. Overall standards of performance

(1) The Director may from time to time—

(a) determine such standards of overall performance in connection with the provision of relevant services by the designated operator as, in his opinion, ought to be achieved by that operator; and

(b) arrange for the publication, in such form and in such manner as he considers appropriate, of the standards so determined.

(2) The Director may only make a determination under subsection (1)(a) above after—

(a) consulting the designated operator concerned and persons or bodies appearing to the Director to be representative of persons likely to be affected; and

(b) arranging for such research as the Director considers appropriate with a view to discovering the views of a representative sample of persons likely to be affected and considering the results.

Note
This section was inserted by the Competition and Service (Utilities) Act 1992.

27C. Information with respect to levels of performance

(1) The Director shall from time to time collect information with respect to—

(a)   the compensation made by designated operators under section 27A above; and

(b)   the levels of overall performance achieved by designated operators in connection with the provision of relevant services.

(2)   At such times as the Director may direct, each designated operator shall give the following information to the Director—

(a)   as respects each standard prescribed by regulations under section 27A above, the number of cases in which compensation was made and the aggregate amount or value of that compensation; and

(b)   as respects each standard determined under section 27B above, such information with respect to the level of performance achieved by the operator as may be so specified.

(3)   A designated operator who, without reasonable excuse, fails to do anything required of him by subsection (2) above shall be liable on summary conviction to a fine not exceeding level 5 on the standard scale.

(4)   The Director shall, at least once in every year, arrange for the publication, in such form and in such manner as he considers appropriate, of such of the information collected by or furnished to him under this section as it may appear to him expedient to give to users or potential users of any relevant services provided by designated operators.

(5)   In arranging for the publication of any such information the Director shall have regard to the need for excluding, so far as practicable—

(a)   any matter which relates to the affairs of an individual, where publication of that matter would or might, in the opinion of the Director, seriously and prejudicially affect the interests of that individual; and

(b)   any matter which relates specifically to the affairs of a particular body of persons, whether corporate or unincorporate, where publication of that matter would or might, in the opinion of the Director, seriously and prejudicially affect the interests of that body.

Note
This section was inserted by the Competition and Service (Utilities) Act 1992.

27D.   Information to be given to customers about overall performance

(1)   Each designated operator shall, in such form and manner and with such frequency as the Director may direct, take steps to inform those of his customers to whom he supplies relevant services of—

(a)   the standards of overall performance determined under section 27B above which are applicable to that operator; and

(b)   that operator's level of performance as respects each of those standards.

(2)   In giving any such direction, the Director shall not specify a frequency of less than once in every period of twelve months.

Note
This section was inserted by the Competition and Service (Utilities) Act 1992.

27E. Procedures for dealing with complaints

(1)   Each designated operator shall establish a procedure for dealing with complaints made by his customers or potential customers in connection with the provision by the designated operator of relevant services.

(2)   No such procedure shall be established, and no modification of such a procedure shall be made, unless—

(a)   the designated operator has consulted persons or bodies appearing to him to be representative of customers for whom he provides relevant services; and

(b)   the proposed procedure or modification has been approved by the Director.

(3)   The designated operator shall—

(a)   publicise the procedure in such manner as may be approved by the Director; and

(b)   send a description of the procedure, free of charge, to any person who asks for one.

(4)   The Director may give a direction to a designated operator requiring the operator to review his procedure or the manner in which it operates.

(5)   A direction under subsection (4) above—

(a)   may specify the manner in which the review is to be conducted; and

(b)   shall require a written report of the review to be made to the Director.

(6)   Where the Director receives a report under subsection (5)(b) above, he may, after consulting the designated operator, direct him to make such modifications of—

(a)   the procedure; or

(b)   the manner in which the procedure operates,

as may be specified in the direction.

(7)   Subsection (2) above does not apply to any modification made in compliance with a direction under subsection (6) above.

Notes
This section was inserted by the Competition and Service (Utilities) Act 1992.

27F. Disputes about discrimination etc. in fixing charges

(1)   Any dispute, of a kind to which this section applies, between—

(a)   a person ('the customer') who is, or wishes to be, provided with any relevant service by a designated operator, and

(b)   that designated operator,

may be referred to the Director by either party.

(2)   This section applies to any dispute as to whether the designated operator—

(a)   has exercised undue discrimination against the customer in respect of charges applied, or to be applied, in connection with the provision of the service in question;

(b)   has shown undue preference to any other person in respect of such charges, to the detriment of the customer; or

(c)   has applied, or proposes to apply, any charge in connection with the provision of the service in question to the customer which is neither specified in, nor determined in accordance with a method specified in, a notice required by a condition of a kind mentioned in section 8(1)(e) above.

(3)   Where a dispute is referred to him under this section, the Director, or an arbitrator (or in Scotland an arbiter) appointed by him, shall determine whether the customer's allegation is well founded and, if it is, make such order as he considers appropriate.

(4)   Any person making an order under subsection (3) above shall include in the order his reasons for reaching his decision with respect to the dispute.

(5)   No act or omission of a designated operator which is permitted by any condition—

(a)   relating to any of the matters referred to in section 8(1)(d) above, and

(b)   included in the licence granted to him under section 7 above, shall be taken to constitute undue discrimination or undue preference for the purposes of this section.

(6)   The practice and procedure to be followed in connection with a reference under this section shall be determined by the Director.

(7)   An order under this section—

(a)   may include such incidental, supplemental and consequential provision (including provision requiring either party to pay a sum in respect of the costs or expenses incurred by the person making the order) as that person considers appropriate; and

(b)   shall be final and—

(i)   in England and Wales and in Northern Ireland enforceable, in so far as it includes such provision as to costs or expenses, as if it were a judgment of a county court; and

(ii)   (applicable only to Scotland).

(8)   In including in an order under this section any such provision as to costs or expenses, the person making the order shall have regard to the conduct and means of the parties and any other relevant circumstances.

Note
This section was inserted by the Competition and Service (Utilities) Act 1992.

27G.   Billing disputes

(1)   The Secretary of State may by regulations make provision for billing disputes to be referred to the Director for determination in accordance with the regulations.

(2)   In this section 'billing dispute' means a dispute between a designated operator and a customer concerning the amount of the charge which the operator is entitled to recover from the customer in connection with the provision of any relevant service.

(3)   Regulations under this section may only be made after consulting—

(a)   the Director; and

(b)   persons or bodies appearing to the Secretary of State to be representative of persons likely to be affected by the regulations.

(4)   Regulations under this section may provide that, where a billing dispute is referred to the Director, he may either—

(a)   determine the dispute, or

(b)   appoint an arbitrator (or in Scotland an arbiter) to determine it.

(5)   Any person determining any billing dispute in accordance with regulations under this section shall, in such manner as may be specified in the regulations, give his reasons for reaching his decision with respect to the dispute.

(6)   Regulations under this section may provide—

(a)   that disputes may be referred to the Director under this section only by prescribed persons; and

(b)   for any determination to be final and enforceable—

(i)   in England and Wales and in Northern Ireland, as if it were a judgment of a county court; and

(ii)   *(applicable only to Scotland)*.

(7)   Except in such circumstances (if any) as may be prescribed by regulations under this section—

(a)   the Director or an arbitrator (or in Scotland an arbiter) appointed by him shall not determine any billing dispute which is the subject of proceedings before, or with respect to which judgment has been given by, any court; and

(b)   neither party to any billing dispute which has been referred to the Director for determination in accordance with regulations under this section shall commence proceedings before any court in respect of that dispute pending its determination in accordance with the regulations.

(8)   No designated operator may commence proceedings before any court in respect of any charge in connection with the provision by him of any relevant service unless, not less than 28 days before doing so, the customer concerned was informed by him, in such form and manner as may be prescribed by regulations under this section, of—

(a)   his intention to commence proceedings;

(b)   the customer's rights by virtue of this section; and

(c)   such other matters (if any) as may be so prescribed.

Note
This section was inserted by the Competition and Service (Utilities) Act 1992.

27H.   Deposits

(1)   Each designated operator shall, with the agreement of the Director, settle criteria by reference to which the operator will determine—

(a)   whether a customer is required to pay a deposit before being provided with any relevant service; and

(b)   if so, the amount which he is required to pay.

(2)   The criteria may be varied by the designated operator with the consent of the Director.

(3)   Before settling, or varying, the criteria the designated operator shall consult persons or bodies appearing to him to be representative of persons likely to be affected.

(4)   Except in such circumstances as may be specified in the criteria, no person who is disabled (as defined by the criteria) shall be required to pay a deposit before being provided with any relevant service by the designated operator.

(5) The designated operator shall—

(a) prepare a summary of the criteria, with the agreement of the Director;

(b) publicise it in such manner as may be approved by the Director; and

(c) send a copy of it, free of charge, to any person who asks for one.

(6) The Director may, after consulting the designated operator, direct him to vary the criteria as specified in the direction.

(7) Subsection (3) above does not apply to any variation made in compliance with a direction under subsection (6) above.

Note
This section was inserted by the Competition and Service (Utilities) Act 1992.

27I. Complaints about deposits

(1) Any person who is aggrieved by—

(a) the decision of a designated operator to require him to pay a deposit before he is provided with a relevant service, or

(b) by the amount which he is so required to pay,
may refer the matter to the Director.

(2) On any such reference the Director, or an arbitrator (or in Scotland an arbiter) appointed by him, shall consider whether the criteria settled under section 27H above—

(a) have been applied correctly, or

(b) are inappropriate in the particular case.

(3) If the Director or arbitrator (or arbiter) considers that the criteria have not been correctly applied, or that they are inappropriate in the particular case, he shall, unless the complaint has been withdrawn or it is otherwise inappropriate to proceed, determine—

(a) whether the person concerned is to be required to pay a deposit, and

(b) if so, the amount which he is to be required to pay,
and give the appropriate direction to the designated operator.

(4) Any person giving a direction under subsection (3) above shall include in the direction his reasons for reaching his decision with respect to the complaint.

(5) The practice and procedure to be followed in connection with a complaint under subsection (1) above shall be determined by the Director.

(6) A direction under this section—

(a) may include such incidental, supplemental and consequential provision (including provision requiring either party to pay a sum in respect of the costs or expenses incurred by the person giving the direction) as that person considers appropriate; and

(b) shall be final and—

(i) in England and Wales and in Northern Ireland enforceable, in so far as it includes such provision as to costs or expenses, as if it were a judgment of a county court; and

(ii) *(applicable only to Scotland).*

(7) In including in a direction under this section any such provision as to costs or expenses, the person giving the direction shall have regard to the conduct and means of the parties and any other relevant circumstances.

Note
This section was inserted by the Competition and Service (Utilities) Act 1992.

27J. Disconnections

Where any person has falled to pay any charges in connection with the provision of any relevant service by a designated operator, no power of that designated operator to discontinue the provision of that service shall be exercised against him as respects any amount which is genuinely in dispute.

Note
This section was inserted by the Competition and Service (Utilities) Act 1992.

27K. Enforcement of standards of performance, etc.

(1) Sections 16 to 18 above shall apply in relation to a designated operator as if it were a condition of the licence granted to him under section 7 above that he shall—

(a) achieve the standards of overall performance determined in relation to him under section 27B above;

(b) take steps to inform those of his customers to whom he supplies relevant services about—

(i) those standards, and

(ii) the levels of performance which he has achieved as respects those standards,

in accordance with section 27D above;

(c) comply with—

(i) the requirements of section 27E above, and

(ii) any direction given by the Director under subsection (4) or (6) of that section;

(d) comply with any order made under section 27F(3) above;

(e) comply with any direction given by the Director under section 27H(6) above;

(f) comply with any direction given under section 27I(3) above; and

(g) comply with the requirements of section 27J above.

(2) For the purposes of the application by this section of sections 16 to 18 above, any term of a licence granted under section 7 above which has or which might have the effect—

(a) of excepting a designated operator from liability for a contravention of a condition of that licence, or

(b) otherwise restricting any such liability,

shall not apply in relation to any contravention of the condition mentioned in subsection (1) above.

Note
This section was inserted by the Competition and Service (Utilities) Act 1992.

27L. Definitions for sections 27A to 27K

(1) For the purposes of sections 27A to 27K above—

'designated operator' means any public telecommunications operator designated for the purposes of those sections by order made by the Secretary of State; and

'relevant services' means—

(a)   any voice telephony service, telephone rental service, directory service, directory information service or facsimile transmission service provided for occupiers of residential or single line premises; and

(b)   any public call box service.

(2)   The Secretary of State shall not exercise his power under subsection (1) above to designate a telecommunications operator unless he is satisfied that the operator provides at least 25 per cent of the voice telephony services supplied within the area in relation to which he is a public telecommunications operator.

(3)   For the purposes of this section—

'public call box service' means a service which is provided by a designated operator and which consists of the provision of telecommunication apparatus which—

(a)   is owned and operated by the designated operator;

(b)   gives access to a voice telephony service; and

(c)   is intended for use by members of the public generally;

'directory service' means a service which consists of the preparation and provision of a list (which may be made available in separate parts and through different media) of customers of a designated operator which is not arranged by reference to a description of the trades, professions or businesses carried on by those customers;

'directory information service' has the same meaning as in section 4(3) above;

'facsimile transmission service' means a telecommunication service for the transmission of electronic signals by a designated operator, over exchange lines provided by him, for the purposes of making a facsimile of a document;

'hard wired telephone' means a telephone of a kind which can only be connected to a public telecommunication system by means other than—

(a)   the insertion of a plug into a socket; or

(b)   wireless telegraphy;

'single line premises' means premises which are not residential premises but which are served by a single exchange line provided by the designated operator;

'telephone rental service' means a service consisting in the hiring out of any hard wired telephone which is capable of emitting or receiving signals which have been, or are to be, conveyed by means of a public telecommunication system run by a designated operator;

'voice telephony service' means a telecommunication service for the conveyance of speech over exchange lines provided by the designated operator.

Notes

1.   This section was inserted by the Competition and Service (Utilities) Act 1992.

2.   The designated operators for the purposes of ss. 27A to 27K from 1 July 1992 were BT and Kingston Communications (Hull) plc under the Competition and Services (Utilities) Act 1992 Designated Order 1992, SI 1992/1360.

Marking etc. of telecommunication apparatus

28. Information etc. to be marked on or to accompany telecommunication apparatus

(1)   Where it appears to the Secretary of State expedient that any description of telecommunication apparatus should be marked with or accompanied by any information or instruction relating to the apparatus or its connection or use, the Secretary of State may by order impose requirements for securing that apparatus of that description is so marked or accompanied, and regulate or prohibit the supply of any such apparatus with respect to which the requirements are not complied with; and the requirements may extend to the form and manner in which the information or instruction is to be given.

(2)   Where an order under this section is in force with respect to telecommunication apparatus of any description, any person who, in the course of any trade or business, supplies or offers to supply telecommunication apparatus of that description in contravention of the order shall, subject to subsection (3) below, be guilty of an offence and liable—

(a)   on summary conviction, to a fine not exceeding the statutory maximum;

(b)   on conviction on indictment, to a fine.

(3)   Subsections (4) to (6) of section 5 above shall apply for the purposes of that section.

(4)   An order under this section may, in the case of telecommunication apparatus supplied in circumstances where the information or instruction required by the order would not be conveyed until after delivery, require the whole or part thereof to be also displayed near the apparatus.

(5)   For the purposes of this section a person exposing telecommunication apparatus for supply or having telecommuncation apparatus in his possession for supply shall be deemed to offer to supply it.

(6)   In this section and section 29 below 'supply' shall [have the same meaning as it has in Part 11 of the Consumer Protection Act 1987].

Notes
1.   The words in square brackets in s. 28(6) were substituted by the Consumer Protection Act 1987.
2.   Orders under this section include: the Telecommunication Apparatus (Marking and Labelling) Order 1985, SI 1985/717, as amended by SI 1985/1031; the Telecommunication Apparatus (Bell Noise-Labelling) Order 1985, SI 1985/718. These orders were disapplied in respect of applicable terminal equipment, connection-capable equipment and radio connection-capable equipment by the Telecommunications Terminal Equipment Regulations 1992, SI 1992/2423 as amended by SI 1995/144.

29. Information etc. to be given in advertisements

(1)   Where it appears to the Secretary of State expedient that any description of advertisements of telecommunication apparatus should contain or refer to any information relating to the apparatus or its connection or use, the Secretary of State may by order impose requirements as to the inclusion of that information, or an indication of the means by which it may be obtained, in advertisements of that description.

(2) Where an advertisement of any telecommunication apparatus to be supplied in the course of any trade or business fails to comply with any requirement imposed under this section, any person who publishes the advertisement shall, subject to subsections (3) and (4) below, be guilty of an offence and liable—

(a) on summary conviction, to a fine not exceeding the statutory maximum;

(b) on conviction on indictment, to a fine.

(3) Subsections (4) to (6) of section 5 above shall apply for the purposes of this section as they apply for the purposes of that section.

(4) In any proceedings for an offence under this section it shall be a defence for the person charged to prove that he is a person whose business it is to publish or arrange for the publication of advertisements and that he received the advertisement for publication in the ordinary course of business and did not know and had no reason to suspect that its publication would amount to an offence under this section.

(5) An order under this section may specify the form and manner in which any information or indication required by the order is to be included in advertisements of any description.

(6) In this section 'advertisement' includes a catalogue, a circular and a price list.

Note

Orders under this section include: the Telecommunication Apparatus (Advertisement) Order 1985, SI 1985/719, as amended by SI 1985/1030. This order was disapplied in respect of applicable terminal equipment, connection-capable equipment and radio connection-capable equipment by the Telecommunications Terminal Equipment Regulations 1992, SI 1992/2423, as amended by SI 1995/144.

30. Enforcement provisions

(1) The Director or a relevant authority shall have power to purchase telecommunication apparatus, and to authorise any of his or their officers to purchase telecommunication apparatus on his or their behalf, for the purpose of ascertaining whether sections 28 and 29 above and orders made under those sections (in this section referred to as 'the relevant provisions') are being complied with.

(2) The Director shall have power to enforce the relevant provisions and every local weights and measures authority in Great Britain shall have power to enforce those provisions within their area; but nothing in this subsection shall be construed as authorising the Director or a local weights and measures authority to institute proceedings in Scotland for an offence.

(3) In this section 'relevant authority' means—

(a) in relation to Great Britain, the Secretary of State or a local weights and measures authority on whom a power to enforce the relevant provisions is conferred by subsection (2) above;

(b) in relation to Northern Ireland, the Department of Economic Development for Northern Ireland.

Rating of telecommunications operators

31, 32. (*Section 31 repealed, with savings, by the Local Government Finance (Repeals, Savings and Consequential Amendments) Order 1990 SI 1990/776. Section 32 applicable only to Scotland.*)

33. (*Applicable only to Northern Ireland.*)

Acquisition etc. of land by public telecommunications operators

34. Compulsory purchase of land in England and Wales

(1)   Subject to subsection (2) below, the Secretary of State may authorise a public telecommunications operator to purchase compulsorily any land in England and Wales which is required by the operator for, or in connection with, the establishment or running of the operator's system or as to which it can reasonably be foreseen that it will be so required; and the Acquisition of Land Act 1981 shall apply to any compulsory purchase under this section as if the operator were a local authority within the meaning of that Act.

(2)   No order shall be made authorising a compulsory purchase under this section except with the consent of the Director.

(3)   The power of purchasing land compulsorily under this section includes power to acquire an easement or other right over land by the creation of a new right.

(4)   The following provisions of [the Town and Country Planning Act 1990] shall have effect in relation to land acquired compulsorily by a public telecommunications operator under this section as they have effect in relation to land acquired compulsorily by statutory undertakers under any other enactment, namely—

(a)   [sections 238 to 240] (use and development of consecrated land and burial grounds);

(b)   [section 241] (use and development of land for open spaces); and

(c)   [sections 271 to 274] (extinguishment of rights of way, and rights as to apparatus, of statutory undertakers).

(5)   Where a public telecommunications operator has acquired any land under this section, he shall not dispose of that land or of any interest or right in or over it except with the consent of the Director.

Note
The words in square brackets in s. 34(4) were substituted by the Planning (Consequential Provisions) Act 1990.

35. (*Applicable only to Scotland*).

36. (*Applicable only to Northern Ireland.*)

37. Entry, for exploratory purposes, on land in England and Wales

(1)   A person nominated by a public telecommunications operator and duly authorised in writing by the Secretary of State may, at any reasonable

time, enter upon and survey any land in England and Wales, other than land covered by buildings or used as a garden or pleasure ground, for the purpose of ascertaining whether the land would be suitable for use by the operator for, or in connection with, the establishment or running of the operator's system.

(2)　[Sections 324(8), 325(1) to (5), (8) and (9) of the Town and Country Planning Act 1990] (which contain supplementary provisions relating to the powers of entry conferred by [section 324(1) to (7)] thereof) shall have effect in relation to the powers conferred by [the said section 324], subject however to the following modifications, namely—

(a)　that [section 324(8)] (which relates to power to search and bore for the purpose of ascertaining the nature of the subsoil or the presence of minerals therein) shall so have effect as if the words 'or the presence of minerals therein' were omitted; and

(b)　that [section 325(1)] (which requires twenty-four hours' notice to be given of an intended entry upon occupied land) shall so have effect as if for the words 'twenty-four hours' there were substituted the words 'twenty-eight days'.

(3)　Where, in an exercise of the power conferred by this section, any damage is caused to land or to chattels, the operator shall make good the damage or pay to every person interested in the land or chattels compensation in respect of the damage; and where, in consequence of an exercise of that power, any person is disturbed in his enjoyment of any land or chattels, the operator shall pay to that person compensation in respect of the disturbance.

(4)　[Section 118 of the said Act of 1990] (which provides for the determination of disputes as to compensation under [Part IV of that Act]) shall apply to any question of disputed compensation under this section.

Note
The words in square brackets in s. 37(2), (4) were substituted by the Planning (Consequential Provisions) Act 1990.

38.　*(Applicable only to Scotland.)*

39.　*(Applicable only to Northern Ireland.)*

40.　Acquisition of land by agreement

(1)　For the purpose of the acquisition by agreement by a public telecommunications operator of land in England and Wales the provisions of Part I of the Compulsory Purchase Act 1965 (so far as applicable) other than sections 4 to 8, section 27 and section 31 shall apply.

(2)　*(Applicable only to Scotland.)*
(3)　*(Applicable only to Northern Ireland.)*

41.　Purchase of Duchy of Lancaster land

The Chancellor and Council of the Duchy of Lancaster may, if they think fit, agree with a public telecommunications operator for the sale, and absolutely make sale, for such sum of money as appears to them to be sufficient consideration for the same, of any land belonging to Her Majesty in right of the Duchy of Lancaster which the operator seeks to acquire for, or in connection with, the establishment or running of his system.

Offences

42. Fraudulent use of telecommunication system

(1) A person who dishonestly obtains a [service to which this subsection applies] with intent to avoid payment of any charge applicable to the provision of that service shall be guilty of an offence and liable—

(a) on summary conviction, to imprisonment for a term not exceeding six months or to a fine not exceeding the statutory maximum or to both;

(b) on conviction on indictment, to imprisonment for a term not exceeding two years or to a fine or to both.

(2) [Subsection (1) above applies to any service (other than a service [such as is mentioned in section 297(1) of the Copyright, Designs and Patents Act 1988)] which is provided by means of] a telecommunication system the running of which is authorised by a licence granted under section 7 above.

Notes
1. The words in square brackets in s. 42(1) and the words in the first (outer) pair of square brackets in s. 42(2) were substituted by the Cable and Broadcasting Act 1984 (and saved by the Broadcasting Act 1990), and the words in the second (inner) pair of square brackets in s. 42(2) were substituted by the Broadcasting Act 1990.
2. It is proposed to amend this section by the Telecommunications (Fraud) Act 1997 in relation to dishonest use obtaining and supply of mobile phone services.

43. Improper use of public telecommunication system

(1) A person who—

(a) sends, by means of a public telecommunication system, a message or other matter that is grossly offensive or of an indecent, obscene or menacing character; or

(b) sends by those means, for the purpose of causing annoyance, inconvenience or needless anxiety to another, a message that he knows to be false or persistently makes use for that purpose of a public telecommunication system,

shall be guilty of an offence and liable on summary conviction to a fine not exceeding level 3 on the standard scale.

(2) Subsection (1) above does not apply to anything done in the course of providing a [programme service (within the meaning of the Broadcasting Act 1990)] . . .

Notes
1. The words in square brackets in s. 43(2) were substituted by the Broadcasting Act 1990.
2. The words omitted from s. 43(2) were repealed by the Cable and Broadcasting Act 1984 and saved by the Broadcasting Act 1990.
3. Relevant cases include: *Armhouse Lee Ltd* v *Chappell and another,* 23 July 1996, CA (unreported); *R* v *Johnson, The Times,* 22 May 1996.

44. Modification etc. of messages

(1) A person engaged in the running of a public telecommunication system who otherwise than in the course of his duty intentionally modifies or interferes with the contents of a message sent by means of that system shall be guilty of an offence.

(2) A person guilty of an offence under subsection (1) above shall be liable—

(a) on summary conviction, to imprisonment for a term not exceeding six months or to a fine not exceeding the statutory maximum or to both;

(b) on conviction on indictment, to imprisonment for a term not exceeding two years or to a fine or to both.

45. Interception and disclosure of messages etc.

(1) A person engaged in the running of a public telecommunication system who otherwise than in the course of his duty intentionally discloses to any person—

(a) the contents of any message which has been intercepted in the course of its transmission by means of that system; or

(b) any information concerning the use made of telecommunication services provided for any other person by means of that system, shall be guilty of an offence.

(2) Subsection (1) above does not apply to—

(a) any disclosure which is made for the prevention or detection of crime or for the purposes of any criminal proceedings;

(b) any disclosure of matter falling within paragraph (a) of that subsection which is made in obedience to a warrant issued by the Secretary of State under section 2 of the Interception of Communications Act 1985 or in pursuance of a requirement imposed by the Commissioner under section 8(3) of that Act; or

(c) any disclosure of matter falling within paragraph (b) of that subsection which is made in the interests of national security or in pursuance of the order of a court.

(3) For the purposes of subsection (2)(c) above a certificate signed by a Minister of the Crown who is a Member of the Cabinet, or by the Attorney General or the Lord Advocate, certifying that a disclosure was made in the interests of national security shall be conclusive evidence of that fact; and a document purporting to be such a certificate shall be received in evidence and deemed to be such a certificate unless the contrary is proved.

(4) A person guilty of an offence under this section shall be liable—

(a) on summary conviction, to a fine not exceeding the statutory maximum;

(b) on conviction on indictment, to a fine.

Note
This section was substituted by the Interception of Communications Act 1985.

46. Assaults etc. on persons engaged in the business of public telecommunications operators

(1) A person who—

(a)   assaults or intentionally obstructs a person engaged in the business of a public telecommunications operator; or

(b)   whilst in any premises used for the purposes of the business of such an operator, intentionally obstructs the course of business of the operator,

shall be guilty of an offence and liable on summary conviction to a fine not exceeding level 3 on the standard scale.

(2)   Any person engaged in the business of a public telecommunications operator may require any person guilty of an offence under subsection (1) above to leave premises used for the purposes of that business and, if any such offender who is so required refuses or fails to comply with the requirement, he shall be liable on summary conviction to a further fine not exceeding level 3 on the standard scale and may be removed by a person engaged in that business; and any constable shall on demand remove or assist in removing any such offender.

Regulations

46A.   Powers to make regulations

(1)   Any power under this Part of this Act to make regulations shall be exercisable by statutory instrument.

(2)   Any statutory instrument containing regulations made by the Secretary of State under this Part of this Act shall be subject to annulment in pursuance of a resolution of either House of Parliament.

(3)   Any such regulations may—

(a)   provide for the determination of questions of fact or of law which may arise in giving effect to the regulations;

(b)   make provision regulating (otherwise than in relation to any court proceedings) any matters relating to the practice and procedure to be followed in connection with the determination of such questions;

(c)   make provision as to the mode of proof of any matter;

(d)   make provision as to parties and their representation;

(e)   provide for the right to appear before and be heard by the Secretary of State, the Director and other authorities;

(f)   make provision as to awarding costs or expenses of proceedings for the determination of such questions, including the amount of the costs or expenses and the enforcement of the awards;

(g)   provide for anything falling to be determined under the regulations to be determined by such persons, in accordance with such procedure and by reference to such matters and to the opinion of such persons, as may be prescribed by the regulations;

(h)   make different provision for different cases, including different provision in relation to different persons, circumstances or localities; and

(i)   make such supplemental, consequential and transitional provision as the Secretary of State or, as the case may be, the Director considers appropriate.

(4)   Any such regulations which prescribe a period within which things are to be done may provide for extending the period so prescribed.

Note
This section and the cross-heading preceding it were inserted by the Competition and Service (Utilities) Act 1992.

PART III
OTHER FUNCTIONS OF DIRECTOR

47. General functions

(1) It shall be the duty of the Director, so far as it appears to him practicable from time to time, to keep under review the carrying on both within and outside the United Kingdom of activities connected with telecommunications.

(2) It shall also be the duty of the Director, so far as it appears to him practicable from time to time, to collect information with respect to commercial activities connected with telecommunications carried on, with a view to his becoming aware of, and ascertaining the circumstances relating to, matters with respect to which his functions are exercisable.

(3) The Secretary of State may give general directions indicating—

(a) considerations to which the Director should have particular regard in determining the order of priority in which matters are to be brought under review in the performance of his duty under subsection (1) or (2) above; and

(b) considerations to which, in cases where it appears to the Director that any of his functions are exercisable, he should have particular regard in determining whether to exercise those functions.

(4) It shall be the duty of the Director, where either he considers it expedient or he is requested by the Secretary of State or the Director General of Fair Trading to do so, to give information, advice and assistance to the Secretary of State or that Director with respect to any matter in respect of which any function of the Director is exercisable.

48. Publication of information and advice

(1) The Director may arrange for the publication, in such form and in such manner as he may consider appropriate, of such information and advice as it may appear to him to be expedient to give to consumers, purchasers and other users of telecommunication services or telecommunication apparatus in the United Kingdom.

(2) In arranging for the publication of any such information or advice, the Director shall have regard to the need for excluding, so far as that is practicable,—

(a) any matter which relates to the private affairs of an individual, where the publication of that matter would or might, in the opinion of the Director, seriously and prejudicially affect the interests of that individual; and

(b) any matter which relates specifically to the affairs of a particular body of persons, whether corporate or unincorporate, where publication of that matter would or might, in the opinion of the Director, seriously and prejudicially affect the interests of that body.

(3) Without prejudice to the exercise of his powers under subsection (1) of this section, it shall be the duty of the Director to encourage relevant associations to prepare, and to disseminate to their members, codes of practice for guidance in safeguarding and promoting the interests of consumers, purchasers and other users of telecommunication services or telecommunication apparatus in the United Kingdom.

(4)   In this section 'relevant association' means any association (whether incorporated or not) whose membership consists wholly or mainly of persons engaged in the provision of telecommunication services or the supply of telecommunication apparatus or of persons employed by or representing persons so engaged and whose objects or activities include the promotion of the interests of persons so engaged.

49.   Investigation of complaints

(1)   It shall be the duty of the Director to consider any matter which—
(a)   relates to telecommunication services provided or telecommunication apparatus supplied in the United Kingdom; and
(b)   is the subject of a representation (other than one appearing to the Director to be frivolous) made to the Director by or on behalf of a person appearing to the Director to have an interest in that matter.
(2)   . . .
(3)   Where any matter considered by the Director under subsection (1) above is one in respect of which any of his functions is exercisable, the Director shall, if he is required to do so or if he thinks fit, exercise that function with respect to that matter.
(4)   Section 9 of the 1981 Act (users' councils), which is superseded by this section and section 54 below, shall cease to have effect.

Note
Section 49(2) was repealed by the Broadcasting Act 1990.

50.   Functions under 1973 and 1980 Acts

(1)   If and to the extent that he is requested by the Director General of Fair Trading to do so, it shall be the duty of the Director to exercise the functions of that Director under Part III of the Fair Trading Act 1973 (in this Act referred to as 'the 1973 Act') so far as relating to courses of conduct which are or may be detrimental to the interests of consumers of telecommunication services or telecommunication apparatus, whether those interests are economic or interests in respect of health, safety or other matters; and references in that Part to that Director shall be construed accordingly.
(2)   There are hereby transferred to the Director (so as to be exercisable concurrently with the Director General of Fair Trading)—
(a)   the functions of that Director under sections 44 and 45 of the 1973 Act; and
(b)   the functions of that Director under sections 50, 52, 53, 86 and 88 of that Act,
so far as relating to monopoly situations which exist or may exist in relation to commercial activities connected with telecommunications; and references in Part IV and sections 86, 88 and 133 of that Act to that Director shall be construed accordingly.
(3)   There are hereby transferred to the Director (so as to be exercisable concurrently with the Director General of Fair Trading) the functions of that Director under sections 2 to 10 and 16 of the Competition Act 1980 (in this Act referred to as 'the 1980 Act') so far as relating to courses of conduct

which have or are intended to have or are likely to have the effect of restricting, distorting or preventing competition in connection with the production, supply or acquisition of telecommunication apparatus or the supply or securing of telecommunication services; and references in those sections and in section 19 of that Act to that Director shall be construed accordingly.

(4) Before either Director first exercises in relation to any matter functions transferred by any of the following provisions, namely—

  (a) paragraph (a) of subsection (2) above;

  (b) paragraph (b) of that subsection; and

  (c) subsection (3) above,

he shall consult with the other Director; and neither Director shall exercise in relation to any matter functions transferred by any of those provisions if functions transferred by that provision have been exercised in relation to that matter by the other Director.

(5) It shall be the duty of the Director, for the purpose of assisting the Commission in carrying out an investigation on a reference made to them by the Director by virtue of subsection (2) or (3) above, to give to the Commission—

  (a) any information which is in his possession and which relates to matters falling within the scope of the investigation, and which is either requested by the Commission for that purpose or is information which in his opinion it would be appropriate for that purpose to give to the Commission without any such request; and

  (b) any other assistance which the Commission may require, and which it is within his power to give, in relation to any such matters,

and the Commission, for the purposes of carrying out any such investigation, shall take into account any information given to them for that purpose under this subsection.

(6) If any question arises as to whether subsection (2) or (3) above applies to any particular case, that question shall be referred to and determined by the Secretary of State; and no objection shall be taken to anything done under—

  (a) Part IV or section 86 or 88 of the 1973 Act; or

  (b) sections 2 to 10 of the 1980 Act,

by or in relation to the Director on the ground that it should have been done by or in relation to the Director General of Fair Trading.

(7) Expressions used in this section which are also used in the 1973 Act or the 1980 Act have the same meanings as in that Act.

51. Co-ordination of functions under Part II and wireless telegraphy functions

(1) With a view to co-ordinating the exercise of functions under Part II of this Act and the Secretary of State's licensing powers under section 1 of the Wireless Telegraphy Act 1949 (licensing of wireless telegraphy), it shall be the duty of the Director, where either he considers it expedient or he is requested by the Secretary of State to do so, to give to the Secretary of State—

  (a) advice with respect to the exercise of those powers in cases where the running of a telecommunication system is involved; and

(b) information with respect to any matters appearing to him to be relevant to the exercise of those powers in such cases.

(2) The Director shall, in exercising his functions under Part II or Part III of this Act, have regard to such of the principles applied by the Secretary of State in exercising his licensing powers under section 1 of the said Act of 1949 as may from time to time be notified to the Director by the Secretary of State for the purposes of this subsection.

(3) For the purposes of this section—

(a) references to the licensing powers of the Secretary of State under section 1 of the said Act of 1949 are references to the powers of the Secretary of State with respect to the grant, variation or revocation of licences authorising the establishment, installation or use of stations for wireless telegraphy or wireless telegraphy apparatus; and

(b) the running of a telecommunication system is involved in cases where those powers are exercisable in relation to any station or apparatus which is in use or intended for use in running a telecommunication system.

(4) In this section 'station for wireless telegraphy' and 'wireless telegraphy apparatus' have the same meanings as in the said Act of 1949.

52. Power to give assistance in relation to certain proceedings

(1) Where, in relation to any proceedings or prospective proceedings to which this section applies, any actual or prospective party to the proceedings (other than the telecommunications operator) applies to the Director for assistance under this section, the Director may grant the application if he thinks fit to do so—

(a) on the ground that the case raises a question of principle; or

(b) on the ground that it is unreasonable, having regard to the complexity of the case or to any other matter, to expect the applicant to deal with the case without any assistance under this section; or

(c) by reason of any other special consideration.

(2) This section applies to any proceedings in which there falls to be determined any question arising under or in connection with—

(a) the telecommunications code as applied to a telecommunications operator in relation to any part or locality of the United Kingdom; or

(b) any exception or condition subject to which that code has effect as so applied.

(3) Assistance by the Director under this section may include—

(a) giving advice;

(b) procuring or attempting to procure the settlement of the matter in dispute;

(c) arranging for the giving of advice or assistance by a solicitor or counsel;

(d) arranging for representation by a solicitor or counsel, including such assistance as is usually given by a solicitor or counsel in the steps preliminary or incidental to any proceedings, or in arriving at or giving effect to a compromise to avoid or bring to an end any proceedings;

(e) any other form of assistance which the Director may consider appropriate,

but paragraph (d) above shall not affect the law and practice regulating the descriptions of persons who may appear in, conduct, defend, and address the court in, any proceedings.

(4)   In so far as expenses are incurred by the Director in providing the applicant with assistance under this section, the recovery of those expenses (as taxed or assessed in such manner as may be prescribed by rules of court) shall constitute a first charge for the benefit of the Director—

(a)   on any costs or expenses which (whether by virtue of a judgment or order of a court or agreement or otherwise) are payable to the applicant by any other person in respect of the matter in connection with which the assistance is given; and

(b)   so far as relates to any costs or expenses, on his rights under any compromise or settlement arrived at in connection with that matter to avoid or bring to an end any proceedings.

(5)   A charge conferred by subsection (4) above is subject to—

(a)   any charge under the Legal Aid Act 1988 and any provision of that Act for payment of any sum to the Legal Aid Board;

(b)   *(applicable only to Scotland)*; or

(c)   *(applicable only to Northern Ireland)*.

(6)   Any expenses incurred by the Director in providing assistance under this section shall be paid out of money provided by Parliament; and any sums received by the Director by virtue of any charge conferred by subsection (4) above shall be paid into the Consolidated Fund.

Note
Section 52(5) was substituted by the Legal Aid Act 1988.

53.   Power to require information etc.

(1)   The Director may, for any relevant purpose, by notice in writing signed by him—

(a)   require any person to produce, at a time and place specified in the notice, to the Director or to any person appointed by him for the purpose, any documents which are specified or described in the notice and are in that person's custody or under his control; or

(b)   require any person carrying on any business to furnish to the Director such estimates, returns or other information as may be specified or described in the notice, and specify the time, the manner and the form in which any such estimates, returns or information are to be furnished;
but no person shall be compelled for any such purpose to produce any documents which he could not be compelled to produce in civil proceedings before the court or, in complying with any requirement for the furnishing of information, to give any information which he could not be compelled to give in evidence in such proceedings.

(2)   A person who refuses or, without reasonable excuse, fails to do anything duly required of him by a notice under subsection (1) above shall be guilty of an offence and liable on summary conviction to a fine not exceeding level 5 on the standard scale.

(3)   A person who—

(a)   intentionally alters, suppresses or destroys any document which he has been required by any such notice to produce; or

(b)   in furnishing any estimate, return or other information required of him under any such notice, makes any statement which he knows to be false in a material particular, or recklessly makes any statement which is false in a material particular,

shall be guilty of an offence.

(4) A person guilty of an offence under subsection (3) above shall be liable—

(a) on summary conviction, to a fine not exceeding the statutory maximum;

(b) on conviction on indictment, to a fine.

(5) If a person makes default in complying with a notice under subsection (1) of this section, the court may, on the application of the Director, make such order as the court thinks fit for requiring the default to be made good; and any such order may provide that all the costs or expenses of and incidental to the application shall be borne by the person in default or by any officers of a company or other association who are responsible for its default.

(6) In this section—

'the court' has the same meaning as in section 18 above;

'relevant purpose' means any purpose connected with—

(a) the investigation of any offence under section 5, 28 or 29 above or any proceedings for any such offence;

(aa) the determination of any dispute referred to the Director under section 27F above;

(ab) the determination of any dispute referred to the Director in accordance with regulations made under section 27G above; or

(b) the exercise of the Director's functions under section 16 [27E, 27H, 27I] or 49 above.

Note

Section 53(6)(aa), (ab) and the words in square brackets in s. 53(6)(b) were inserted by the Competition and Service (Utilities) Act 1992.

54. Power to establish advisory bodies

(1) The Secretary of State shall, as soon as practicable after the appointed day, establish advisory bodies for matters affecting England, Scotland, Wales and Northern Ireland respectively; and each body so established shall consist of such members as he may from time to time appoint.

(2) In establishing a body under subsection (1) above, the Secretary of State shall have regard to the desirability of having members who are familiar with the special requirements and circumstances of the part of the United Kingdom concerned (including, in particular, the special requirements and circumstances of consumers, purchasers and other users in that part of telecommunication services and telecommunication apparatus).

(3) Subject to subsection (1) above, the Director may establish such advisory bodies as he thinks fit consisting in each case of such members as he may from time to time appoint.

(4) Without prejudice to his power under subsection (3) above, the Director shall, as soon as practicable after the appointed day and after consultation with the Secretary of State, establish—

(a) an advisory body for matters affecting small businesses; and

(b) an advisory body for matters affecting persons who are disabled or of pensionable age.

(5)   In establishing an advisory body under subsection (4) above, the Director shall have regard to the desirability of having members who are familiar with the special requirements and circumstances of small businesses or persons who are disabled or of pensionable age, as the case may require.

(6)   It shall be the duty of an advisory body established under this section to advise the Director on any matter—

(a)   in respect of which any of the Director's functions is exercisable; and

(b)   which is referred to it by the Director or is a matter on which it considers it should offer its advice.

(7)   Each of the advisory bodies established under subsection (1) or (4) above shall, as soon as practicable after the end of the year of 1984 and of each subsequent calendar year, make to the Director a report on its activities during that year.

(8)   The Secretary of State or the Director may, to such extent as may be approved by the Treasury, defray or contribute towards the expenses of an advisory body established under this section.

55.   Annual and other reports

(1)   The Director shall, as soon as practicable after the end of the year 1984 and of each subsequent calendar year, make to the Secretary of State a report on—

(a)   his activities during that year; and

(b)   the Commission's activities during that year so far as relating to references made by him.

(2)   Every such report shall include—

(a)   a general survey of developments, during the year to which it relates, in respect of matters falling within the scope of the Director's functions (including, in particular, those affecting small businesses or persons who are disabled or of pensionable age); and

(b)   the reports which the advisory bodies established under section 54(1) or (4) above make to him on their activities during that year.

(3)   The Secretary of State shall lay a copy of every report made by the Director under subsection (1) above before each House of Parliament, and shall arrange for every such report to be published in such manner as he may consider appropriate.

(4)   The Director may also prepare such other reports as appear to him to be expedient with respect to such matters as are mentioned in subsection (2) above and may arrange for any such report to be published in such manner as he may consider appropriate.

(5)   In making any report under this section the Director shall have regard to the need for excluding, so far as that is practicable, the matters specified in section 48(2)(a) and (b) above.

PART VII

MISCELLANEOUS AND SUPPLEMENTAL

Miscellaneous

93.   Grants to promote interests of disabled persons

(1)   The Secretary of State may, with the approval of the Treasury, make grants for the purpose of defraying or contributing towards—

(a)   any expenses which may be incurred by any person in supporting research into or the development of apparatus to which this section applies; or

(b)   any fees incurred by any person in respect of the exercise in relation to apparatus to which this section applies of any function conferred by or under section 22 above.

(2)   This section applies to—

(a)   telecommunication apparatus which is constructed for use by disabled persons;

(b)   telecommunication apparatus which is so constructed as to be capable of being adapted for such use; and

(c)   apparatus by means of which telecommunication apparatus falling within paragraph (b) above may be so adapted.

3)   In making a grant under this section, the Secretary of State may impose such conditions as he thinks fit and may, in particular, impose a condition requiring the repayment of all or any part of the grant—

(a)   if any other condition is not complied with; or

(b)   in such other circumstances as he may specify.

(4)   There shall be paid out of money provided by Parliament any sums required by the Secretary of State for making grants under this section.

(5)   Any sums received by the Secretary of State under subsection (3) above shall be paid into the Consolidated Fund.

94.   Directions in the interests of national security etc.

(1)   The Secretary of State may, after consultation with a person to whom this section applies, give to that person such directions of a general character as appear to the Secretary of State to be requisite or expedient in the interests of national security or relations with the government of a country or territory outside the United Kingdom.

(2)   If it appears to the Secretary of State to be requisite or expedient to do so in the interests of national security or relations with the government of a country or territory outside the United Kingdom, he may, after consultation with a person to whom this section applies, give to that person a direction requiring him (according to the circumstances of the case) to do, or not to do, a particular thing specified in the direction.

(3)   A person to whom this section applies shall give effect to any direction given to him by the Secretary of State under this section notwithstanding any other duty imposed on him by or under this Act.

(4)   The Secretary of State shall lay before each House of Parliament a copy of every direction given under this section unless he is of opinion that disclosure of the direction is against the interests of national security or relations with the government of a country or territory outside the United Kingdom, or the commercial interests of any person.

(5)   A person shall not disclose, or be required by virtue of any enactment or otherwise to disclose, anything done by virtue of this section if the Secretary of State has notified him that the Secretary of State is of the opinion that disclosure of that thing is against the interests of national security or relations with the government of a country or territory outside the United Kingdom, or the commercial interests of some other person.

(6) The Secretary of State may, with the approval of the Treasury, make grants to public telecommunications operators for the purpose of defraying or contributing towards any losses they may sustain by reason of compliance with the directions given under this section.

(7) There shall be paid out of money provided by Parliament any sums required by the Secretary of State for making grants under this section.

(8) This section applies to the Director and to any person who is a public telecommunications operator or approved contractor (whether in his capacity as such or otherwise); and in this subsection 'approved contractor' means a person approved under section 20 above.

95. Orders under the 1973 and 1980 Acts

(1) Where in the circumstances mentioned in subsection (2) below the Secretary of State by order exercises any of the powers specified in Parts I and II of Schedule 8 to the 1973 Act or section 10(2)(a) of the 1980 Act, the order may also provide for the revocation or modification of licences granted under section 7 above to such extent as may be requisite to give effect to or to take account of any provision made by the order.

(2) Subsection (1) above shall have effect where—

(a) the circumstances are as mentioned in section 56(1) of the 1973 Act (order on report on monopoly reference) and the monopoly situation exists in relation to a commercial activity connected with telecommunications;

(b) the circumstances are as mentioned in section 73(1) of that Act (order on report on merger reference) and the two or more enterprises which ceased to be distinct enterprises were engaged in such an activity; or

(c) the circumstances are as mentioned in section 10(1) of the 1980 Act (order on report on competition reference) and the anti-competitive practice relates to the production, supply or acquisition of telecommunication apparatus or the supply or securing of telecommunication services.

(3) Expressions used in this section which are also used in the 1973 Act or the 1980 Act have the same meanings as in that Act.

96. Prohibitions and restrictions applying to lessees with respect to telecommunications

(1) Subject to subsection (4) below, where any provision contained in a lease to which this section applies, or in any agreement made with respect to premises to which such a lease relates, has the effect of imposing on the lessee any prohibition or restriction with respect to any of the matters falling within subsection (3) below, that provision shall have effect in relation to things which are done—

(a) inside a building, or part of a building, occupied by the lessee under the lease, or

(b) for purposes connected with the provision to the lessee by any telecommunications operator of any telecommunication services,

as if the prohibition or restriction applied only where the lessor has not given his consent in relation to the matter in question and as if the lessor were required not to withhold that consent unreasonably.

(2)   Where a provision of a lease or agreement imposes (whether by virtue of this section or otherwise) a requirement on the lessor under a lease not to withhold his consent unreasonably in relation to any matter falling within subsection (3) below, the question whether that consent is unreasonably withheld shall be determined having regard to all the circumstances and to the principle that no person should unreasonably be denied access to a telecommunication system.

(3)   The matters falling within this subsection are—
     (a)   the running of relevant telecommunication systems;
     (b)   the connection of any telecommunication apparatus to a relevant telecommunication system or of relevant telecommunication systems to each other; and
     (c)   the installation, maintenance, adjustment, repair, alteration or use, for purposes connected with the running of a relevant telecommunication system, of any telecommunication apparatus.

(4)   The Secretary of State may by order provide, in relation to such cases, prohibitions or restrictions as are specified in the order, or are of a description so specified, that subsection (1) above shall not apply.

(5)   This section applies to any lease for a term of a year or more granted on or after the day on which this section comes into force; but the Secretary of State may by order provide that this section shall apply, subject to such transitional provisions as may be contained in the order, to leases granted before that day.

(6)   This section is without prejudice to paragraph 2(3) of the telecommunications code.

(7)   In this section—
     'alteration' and 'telecommunication apparatus' have the same meanings as in Schedule 2 to this Act;
     'lease' includes any leasehold tenancy (whether in the nature of a head lease, sub-lease or under lease) and any agreement to grant such a tenancy, and cognate expressions, and references to the grant of a lease, shall be construed accordingly;
     'relevant telecommunication system' means a public telecommunication system or a telecommunication system specified for the purposes of this section in an order made by the Secretary of State, or a telecommunication system which is, or is to be, connected to a public telecommunication system or to a system so specified.

97.   Contributions by local authorities towards provision of facilities

(1)   Where a local authority consider that it would be for the benefit of the whole or any part of their area that—
     (a)   any additional telecommunication facilities should be provided; or
     (b)   any existing telecommunication facilities should continue to be provided,
by a public telecommunications operator, whether within or outside the area to be benefited, the authority may undertake to pay to that operator any loss he may sustain by reason of the provision or continued provision of those facilities.

(2)   (applicable only to Scotland.)

(3) In this section 'local authority'—
(a) in relation to England and Wales, means a county council, . . . a district council, a London borough council, the Common Council of the City of London, a parish council or a community council;
(b) (*applicable only to Scotland*);
(c) in relation to Northern Ireland, means a district council.

Note
The words omitted from s. 97(3)(a) were repealed by the Local Government Act 1985.

98. Use of certain conduits for telecommunication purposes

(1) The functions of an authority with control of a relevant conduit shall include the power—
(a) to carry out, or to authorise another person to carry out, any works in relation to that conduit for or in connection with the installation, maintenance, adjustment, repair or alteration of telecommunication apparatus;
(b) to keep telecommunication apparatus installed in that conduit or to authorise any other person to keep telecommunication apparatus so installed;
(c) to authorise any person to enter that conduit to inspect telecommunication apparatus kept installed there;
(d) to enter into agreements, on such terms (including terms as to the payments to be made to the authority) as it thinks fit, in connection with the doing of anything authorised by or under this section; and
(e) to carry on an ancillary business consisting in the making and carrying out of such agreements.
(2) Where any enactment or subordinate legislation expressly or impliedly imposes any limitation on the use to which a relevant conduit may be put, that limitation shall not have effect so as to prohibit the doing of anything authorised by or under this section.
(3) Where the doing by an authority with control of a public sewer of anything authorised by this section would, apart from this subsection, constitute a contravention of any obligation imposed (whether by virtue of any conveyance or agreement or otherwise) on the authority, the doing of that thing shall not constitute such a contravention to the extent that it consists in, or in authorising, the carrying out of works or inspections, or keeping of apparatus, wholly inside a public sewer.
(4) Subject to subsections (2) and (3) above, subsection (1) above is without prejudice to the rights of any person with an interest in land on, under or over which a relevant conduit is situated.
(5) Without prejudice to subsections (1) to (4) above, the Secretary of State may by order provide for any local Act under or in accordance with which any conduits (whether or not relevant conduits) are kept installed in streets to be amended in such manner as appears to him requisite or expedient for securing—
(a) that there is power for those conduits to be used for telecommunication purposes;
(b) that the terms (including terms as to payment) on which those conduits are used for those purposes are reasonable; and

(c) that the use of those conduits for those purposes is not unreasonably inhibited (whether directly or indirectly) by reason of the terms of any consent, licence or agreement which has been given, granted or made in relation to any of those conduits for the purposes of that Act.

(6) In this section 'relevant conduit' means—

(a) any conduit which, whether or not it is itself an electric line, is maintained by an electricity authority for the purpose of enclosing, surrounding or supporting such a line, including where such a conduit is connected to any box, chamber or other structure (including a building) maintained by an electricity authority for purposes connected with the conveyance, transmission or distribution of electricity, that box, chamber or structure; or

(b) a water main or any other conduit maintained by a water authority for the purpose of conveying water from one place to another; or

(c) a public sewer; or

(d) a culvert which is a designated watercourse within the meaning of the Drainage (Northern Ireland) Order 1973.

(7) In this section a reference to the authority with control of a relevant conduit—

(a) in relation to a conduit or structure falling within paragraph (a) or (b) of subsection (6) above, shall be construed as a reference to the authority by whom the conduit or structure is maintained;

(b) in relation to a public sewer, shall be construed, subject to subsection (8) below, as a reference to the [person] in whom the sewer is vested; and

(c) in relation to a culvert falling within paragraph (d) of subsection (6) above, shall be construed as a reference to the Department of Agriculture for Northern Ireland.

(8) Where—

(a) the functions of an authority with control of a public sewer are, in pursuance of any enactment, discharged on its behalf by [another person], and

(b) the [other person] is authorised by the authority with control of the sewer to act on its behalf for the purposes of the matters referred to in subsection (1) above,

this section shall have effect in relation to that sewer as if any reference to the authority with control of the sewer included, to such extent as may be necessary for the [other person] so to act, a reference to the [other person].

(9) In this section—

'alteration', 'street' and 'telecommunication apparatus' have the same meanings as in Schedule 2 to this Act;

'conduit' includes a tunnel or subway;

'electric line'—

(a) in Great Britain, has the same meaning as in [the Electricity Act 1989]; and

(b) in Northern Ireland, has the same meaning as in the [Electricity (Northern Ireland) Order 1992];

'electricity authority' means [a person authorised by a licence under Part I of the Electricity Act 1989 to transmit or supply electricity] or [a person authorised by a licence under Part II of the Electricity (Northern Ireland) Order 1992 to transmit or supply electricity];

'public sewer'—

(a)   in England and Wales, has the same meaning as in the Public Health Act 1936;

(b)   *(applicable only to Scotland)*; and

(c)   in Northern Ireland, means a sewer as defined in the Water and Sewerage Services (Northern Ireland) Order 1973;

'subordinate legislation' means any subordinate legislation within the meaning of the Interpretation Act 1979 or any instrument, as defined in section 1 of the Interpretation Act (Northern Ireland) 1954;

'water authority'—

[(a)   in England and Wales, means the National Rivers Authority or a water undertaker;]

(b)   *(applicable only to Scotland)*; and

(c)   in Northern Ireland, means the Department of the Environment for Northern Ireland;

'water main'—

[(a)   in England and Wales, means a water main [or resource main within the meaning of the Water Industry Act 1991];]

(b)   *(applicable only to Scotland)*; and

(c)   in Northern Ireland, means a main within the meaning of the Water and Sewerage Services (Northern Ireland) Order 1973.

Notes

1.   The words in square brackets in s. 98 (7), (8), and, in s. 98 (9), para. (a) of the definition 'water authority' and para. (a) of the definition 'water main', were substituted by the Water Act 1989. The words in square brackets in para (a) of the latter definition were further substituted by the Water Consolidation (Consequential Provisions) Act 1991.

2.   In s. 98(9), the words in the first and third pairs of square brackets were substituted by the Electricity Act 1989, and the words in the second and fourth pairs of square brackets were substituted by the Electricity (Northern Ireland) Order 1992, SI 1992/231.

Supplemental

101.   General restrictions on disclosure of information

(1)   Subject to the following provisions of this section, no information with respect to any particular business which—

(a)   has been obtained under or by virtue of the provisions of this Act; and

(b)   relates to the private affairs of any individual or to any particular business,

shall during the lifetime of that individual or so long as that business continues to be carried on, be disclosed without the consent of that individual or the person for the time being carrying on that business.

(2)   Subsection (1) above does not apply to any disclosure of information which is made—

(a)   for the purpose of facilitating the performance of any functions assigned or transferred to the Secretary of State, the Director or the Commission by or under this Act;

(b) for the purpose of facilitating the performance of any functions of any Minister, any Northern Ireland department, the head of any such department, the Director General of Fair Trading [the Director General of Water Services] [the Director General of Electricity Supply] [the Director General of Electricity Supply for Northern Ireland] [the Rail Regulator] or a local weights and measures authority in Great Britain under any of the enactments or subordinate legislation specified in subsection (3) below;

(bb) for the purpose of facilitating the carrying out by the Comptroller and Auditor General of any of his functions under any enactment;

(c) in connection with the investigation of any criminal offence or for the purposes of any criminal proceedings;

(d) for the purpose of any civil proceedings brought under or by virtue of this Act or any of the enactments or subordinate legislation specified in subsection (3) below; or

(e) in pursuance of a Community obligation.

(3) The enactments or subordinate legislation referred to in subsection (2) above are—

(a) the Trade Descriptions Act 1968;

(b) the 1973 Act;

(c) the Consumer Credit Act 1974;

(d) the Restrictive Trade Practices Act 1976;

(e) the Resale Prices Act 1976;

(f) the Estate Agents Act 1979; . . .

(g) the 1980 Act;

(h) the Consumer Protection Act 1987

[(i) the Consumer Protection (Northern Ireland) Order 1987

(i) the Control of Misleading Advertisements Regulations 1988

(j) the Water Act 1989] [the Water Industry Act 1991 or any of the other consolidation Acts (within the meaning of section 206 of that Act of 1991)]

(k) the Electricity Act 1989

(l) the Electricity (Northern Ireland) Order 1992

(m) the Railways Act 1993.

(4) Nothing in subsection (1) above shall be construed—

(a) as limiting the matters which may be published under section [27C or] 48 above or may be included in, or made public as part of, a report of the Director or of the Commission under this Act; or

(b) as applying to any information which has been so published or has been made public as part of such a report.

(5) Any person who discloses any information in contravention of this section shall be guilty of an offence and liable—

(a) on summary conviction, to a fine not exceeding the statutory maximum;

(b) on conviction on indictment, to imprisonment for a term not exceeding two years or to a fine or to both.

Notes

1. The words in the first pair of square brackets in s. 101(2)(b) were inserted and s. 101(3)(j) was added by the Water Act 1989.

2. The words in the second pair of square brackets in s. 101(2)(b) were inserted and s. 101(3)(k) was added by the Electricity Act 1989.

3. The words in the third pair of square brackets in s. 101(2)(b) were inserted and s. 101(3)(l) was added by the Electricity (Northern Ireland) Order 1992, SI 1992/231 (NI 1).
4. The words in the fourth pair of square brackets in s. 101(2)(b), were inserted and s. 101(3)(m) was added by the Railways Act 1993.
5. The words 'or subordinate legislation' in s. 101(2)(b), (d), (3) were inserted and the second s. 101(3)(i) was added by the Control of Misleading Advertisements Regulations 1988, SI 1988/915.
6. Section 101(2)(bb) and the words in square brackets in s. 101(4)(a) were inserted by the Competition and Service (Utilities) Act 1992.
7. The word 'and' at the end of s. 101(3)(f) was repealed by the Consumer Protection Act 1987 and s. 101(3)(h) was added by that Act.
8. The first s. 101(3)(i) was added by the Consumer Protection (Northern Ireland) Order 1987, SI 1987/2049.
9. The words in square brackets in s. 101(3)(j) were added by the Water Consolidation (Consequential Provisions) Act 1991.
10. Sections 101(3)(k), (l) and (m) were added by the statutes referred to in the sub-sections.

102. Offences by bodies corporate

(1) Where a body corporate is guilty of an offence under this Act and that offence is proved to have been commited with the consent or connivance of, or to be attributable to any neglect on the part of, any director, manager, secretary or other similar officer of the body corporate or any person who was purporting to act in any such capacity he, as well as the body corporate, shall be guilty of that offence and shall be liable to be proceeded against and punished accordingly.

(2) Where the affairs of a body corporate are managed by its members, subsection (1) above shall apply in relation to the acts and defaults of a member in connection with his functions of management as if he were a director of the body corporate.

103. Summary proceedings

Proceedings for any offence under this Act which is punishable on summary conviction may be commenced at any time within twelve months next after the commission of the offence.

104. Orders and schemes

(1) Any power of the Secretary of State to make an order or a scheme under this Act shall be exercisable by statutory instrument subject, except in the case of an order under section 2, [27L] 60(1) or (3), 69(2) or 110(5), or paragraph 1 of Schedule 5, to annulment in pursuance of a resolution of either House of Parliament.

(2) Any order or scheme under this Act may make different provision with respect to different cases or descriptions of case.

(3) This section does not apply to the power of the Secretary of State to make vesting orders under section 36 above.

Note
The section number in square brackets in s. 104(1) was inserted by the Competition and Service (Utilities) Act 1992.

105. Financial provisions

There shall be paid out of money provided by Parliament any administrative expenses incurred by the Secretary of State in consequence of the provisions of this Act and any increase attributable to this Act in the sums payable out of money so provided under any other Act.

106. General interpretation

   (1)   In this Act, unless the context otherwise requires—

'the 1973 Act' means the Fair Trading Act 1973;

'the 1980 Act' means the Competition Act 1980;

'the 1981 Act' means the British Telecommunications Act 1981;

'the appointed day' has the meaning given by section 2 above;

'commercial activities connected with telecommunications' has the meaning given by section 4(3) above;

'the Commission' means the Monopolies and Mergers Commission;

'consumer', 'monopoly situation', 'practice' and 'supply' have the meanings given by section 137 of the 1973 Act;

'the Director' means the Director General of Telecommunications;

'directory information service' has the meaning given by section 4(3) above;

'disabled person' means any person who is blind, deaf or dumb or who is substantially and permanently handicapped by illness, injury, congenital deformity or any other disability and 'disabled' shall be construed accordingly;

'the excepted liabilities' has the meaning given by section 60(2) above;

'modifications' includes additions, alterations and omissions and cognate expressions shall be construed accordingly;

'public telecommunications operator' has the meaning given by section 9(3) above;

'public telecommunication system' has the meaning given by section 9(1) above;

'public telecommunication system' has the meaning given by section 9(1) above;

'the successor company' and 'the transfer date' have the meanings given by section 60(1) above;

'telecommunication apparatus' (except where the extended definition in Schedule 2 to this Act applies) has the meaning given by section 4(3) above;

'telecommunication service' has the meaning given by section 4(3) above;

'telecommunications operator' has the meaning given by section 16(1) above;

'telecommunication system' has the meaning given by subsection (1) of section 4 above (read with subsection (2) of that section);

'transitional period' has the meaning given by section 69(1) above.

   (2), (3)   ...

   (4)   Any power conferred on the Secretary of State by this Act to give a direction if it appears to him to be requisite or expedient to do so in the

interests of national security or relations with the government of a country or territory outside the United Kingdom includes power to give the direction if it appears to him to be requisite or expedient to do so in order—

(a)   to discharge, or facilitate the discharge of, an obligation binding on Her Majesty's Government in the United Kingdom by virtue of it being a member of an international organisation or a party to an international agreement;

(b)   to attain, or facilitate the attainment of, any other objects the attainment of which is, in the Secretary of State's opinion, requisite or expedient in view of Her Majesty's Government in the United Kingdom being a member of such an organisation or a party to such an agreement; or

(c)   to enable Her Majesty's Government in the United Kingdom to become a member of such an organisation or a party to such an agreement.

(5)   For the purposes of any licence granted, approval given or order made under this Act any description or class may be framed by reference to any circumstances whatsoever.

Note
Section 106(2) and (3) was repealed by the SL(R) Act 1993.

SCHEDULES

SCHEDULE 1

Section 1
DIRECTOR GENERAL OF TELECOMMUNICATIONS

1.   There shall be paid to the Director such remuneration, and such travelling and other allowances, as the Secretary of State with the approval of the Treasury may determine.

2.   In the case of any such holder of the office of the Director as may be determined by the Secretary of State with the approval of the Treasury, there shall be paid such pension, allowance or gratuity to or in respect of him on his retirement or death, or such contributions or payments towards provision for such a pension, allowance or gratuity as may be so determined.

3.   If, when any person ceases to hold office as the Director, it appears to the Secretary of State with the approval of the Treasury that there are special circumstances which make it right that he should receive compensation, there may be paid to him a sum by way of compensation of such amount as may be so determined.

4, 5.   . . .

6.   The Director shall have an official seal for the authentication of documents required for the purposes of his functions.

7.   The Documentary Evidence Act 1868 shall have effect as if the Director were included in the first column of the Schedule to that Act, as if the Director and any person authorised to act on behalf of the Director were mentioned in the second column of that Schedule, and as if the regulations referred to in that Act included any document issued by the Director or by any such person.

8.   Anything authorised or required by or under this Act or any other enactment to be done by the Director, other than the making of a statutory

instrument, may be done by any member of the staff of the Director who is
authorised generally or specially in that behalf by the Director.

Notes
1. Paragraph 4 was repealed by the Parliamentary and Health Service Commissioners Act 1987.
2. Paragraph 5 amends the House of Commons Disqualification Act 1975 and the
Northern Ireland Assembly Disqualification Act 1975.

SCHEDULE 2

Section 10

THE TELECOMMUNICATIONS CODE

Arrangement of paragraphs

Interpretation of code

1.—(1)   In this code, except in so far as the context otherwise requires—
'agriculture' and 'agricultural'—
    (a)   in England and Wales, have the same meanings as in the
Highways Act 1980;

(b)   (*applicable only to Scotland*); and

(c)   in Northern Ireland, have the same meanings as in the Agriculture Act (Northern Ireland) 1949;

'alter', 'alteration' and 'altered' shall be construed in accordance with sub-paragraph (2) below;

'bridleway' and 'footpath'—

(a)   in England and Wales, have the same meanings as in the Highways Act 1980;

(b)   (*applicable only to Scotland*); and

(c)   in Northern Ireland, mean a way over which the public have, by virtue of the Access to the Countryside (Northern Ireland) Order 1983, a right of way on horseback and on foot, respectively;

'the court' means, without prejudice to any right of appeal conferred by virtue of paragraph 25 below or otherwise—

(a)   in relation to England and Wales and Northern Ireland, the county court; and

(b)   (*applicable only to Scotland*);

'emergency works' in relation to the operator or a relevant undertaker for the purposes of paragraph 23 below, means works the execution of which at the time it is proposed to execute them is requisite in order to put an end to, or prevent, the arising of circumstances then existing or imminent which are likely to cause—

(a)   danger to persons or property,

(b)   the interruption of any service provided by the operator's system or, as the case may be, interference with the exercise of any functions conferred or imposed on the undertaker by or under any enactment; or

(c)   substantial loss to the operator or, as the case may be, the undertaker, and such other works as in all the circumstances it is reasonable to execute with those works;

'line' shall be construed in accordance with the definition in this paragraph of telecommunication apparatus;

'maintainable highway'—

(a)   [in England and Wales, means a maintainable highway within the meaning of Part III of the New Roads and Street Works Act 1991] other than one which is a footpath or bridleway that crosses, and forms part of, any agricultural land or any land which is being brought into use for agriculture; and

(b)   in Northern Ireland, means a highway maintainable by the Department of the Environment for Northern Ireland.

'the operator' means—

(a)   where this code has effect by virtue of paragraph (a) of subsection (1) of section 10 of this Act, the person to whom this code is applied by the licence mentioned in that paragraph; and

(b)   where this code has effect by virtue of paragraph (b) of that subsection, the Secretary of State or the Northern Ireland department in question;

'the operator's system' means the telecommunication system the running of which is for the time being authorised by the licence mentioned in paragraph (a) of section 10(1) of this Act or, as the case may require, the telecommunication system which the Secretary of State or the

Northern Ireland department in question is running or proposing to run;

'railway' includes a light railway;

'the statutory purposes' means the purposes of establishing and running the operator's system;

'street' has [the same meaning as in Part III of the New Roads and Street Works Act 1991];

'structure' does not include a building;

'telecommunications apparatus' includes any apparatus falling within the definition in section 4(3) of this Act and any apparatus not so falling which is designed or adapted for use in connection with the running of a telecommunication system and, in particular—

(a) any line, that is to say, any wire, cable, tube, pipe or other similar thing (including its casing or coating) which is so designed or adapted; and

(b) any structure, pole or other thing in, on, by or from which any telecommunication apparatus is or may be installed, supported, carried or suspended;

and references to the installation of telecommunication apparatus shall be construed accordingly.

(2) In this code, references to the alteration of any apparatus include references to the moving, removal or replacement of the apparatus.

(3) In relation to any land which, otherwise than in connection with a street on that land, is divided horizontally into different parcels, the references in this code to a place over or under the land shall have effect in relation to each parcel as not including references to any place in a different parcel.

(4) . . .

(5) For the purposes of the definition in this paragraph of 'street' [Part III of the New Roads and Street Works Act 1991] shall be deemed to extend to Northern Ireland.

Note

The words in square brackets in sub-paras (1), (5) were substituted, and sub-para. (4) was repealed, by the New Roads and Street Works Act 1991.

Agreement required to confer right to execute works etc.

2.—(1) The agreement in writing of the occupier for the time being of any land shall be required for conferring on the operator a right for the statutory purposes—

(a) to execute any works on that land for or in connection with the installation, maintenance, adjustment, repair or alteration of telecommunication apparatus; or

(b) to keep telecommunication apparatus installed on, under or over that land; or

(c) to enter that land to inspect any apparatus kept installed (whether on, under or over that land or elsewhere) for the purposes of the operator's system.

(2) A person who is the owner of the freehold estate in any land or is a lessee of any land shall not be bound by a right conferred in accordance with sub-paragraph (1) above by the occupier of that land unless—

(a)   he conferred the right himself as occupier of the land; or

(b)   he has agreed in writing to be bound by the right; or

(c)   he is for the time being treated by virtue of sub-paragraph (3) below as having so agreed; or

(d)   he is bound by the right by virtue of sub-paragraph (4) below.

(3)   If a right falling within sub-paragraph (1) above has been conferred by the occupier of any land for purposes connected with the provision, to the occupier from time to time of that land, of any telecommunication services and—

(a)   the person conferring the right is also the owner of the freehold estate in that land or is a lessee of the land under a lease for a term of a year or more, or

(b)   in a case not falling within paragraph (a) above, a person owning the freehold estate in the land or a lessee of the land under a lease for a term of a year or more has agreed in writing that his interest in the land should be bound by the right,

then, subject to paragraph 4 below, that right shall (as well as binding the person who conferred it) have effect, at any time when the person who conferred it or a person bound by it under sub-paragraph (2)(b) or (4) of this paragraph is the occupier of the land, as if every person for the time being owning an interest in that land had agreed in writing to the right being conferred for the said purposes and, subject to its being exercised solely for those purposes, to be bound by it.

(4)   In any case where a person owning an interest in land agrees in writing (whether when agreeing to the right as occupier or for the purposes of sub-paragraph (3)(b) above or otherwise) that his interest should be bound by a right falling within sub-paragraph (1) above, that right shall (except in so far as the contrary intention appears) bind the owner from time to time of that interest and also—

(a)   the owner from time to time of any other interest in the land, being an interest created after the right is conferred and not having priority over the interest to which the agreement relates; and

(b)   any other person who is at any time in occupation of the land and whose right to occupation of the land derives (by contract or otherwise) from a person who at the time the right to occupation was granted was bound by virtue of this sub-paragraph.

(5)   A right falling within sub-paragraph (1) above shall not be exercisable except in accordance with the terms (whether as to payment or otherwise) subject to which it is conferred; and, accordingly, every person for the time being bound by such a right shall have the benefit of those terms.

(6)   A variation of a right falling within sub-paragraph (1) above or of the terms on which such a right is exercisable shall be capable of binding persons who are not parties to the variation in the same way as, under sub-paragraphs (2), (3) and (4) above, such a right is capable of binding persons who are not parties to the conferring of the right.

(7)   It is hereby declared that a right falling within sub-paragraph (1) above is not subject to the provisions of any enactment requiring the registration of interests in, charges on or other obligations affecting land.

(8)   In this paragraph and paragraphs 3 and 4 below—

(a)   references to the occupier of any land shall have effect—

(i)   in relation to any footpath or bridleway that crosses and forms part of any agricultural land or any land which is being brought into use for agriculture, as references to the occupier of that land;

(ii)   in relation to any [street or, in Scotland, road] (not being such a footpath or bridleway), [as references—

in England and Wales or Northern Ireland, to the street managers within the meaning of Part III of the New Roads and Street Works Act 1991 (which for this purpose shall be deemed to extend to Northern Ireland), and

in Scotland, to the road managers within the meaning of Part IV of that Act; and]

(iii)   in relation to any land (not being a [street or, in Scotland, road]) which is unoccupied, as references to the person (if any) who for the time being exercises powers of management or control over the land or, if there is no such person, to every person whose interest in the land would be prejudicially affected by the exercise of the right in question;

(b)   'lease' includes any leasehold tenancy (whether in the nature of a head lease, sub-lease or underlease) and any agreement to grant such a tenancy but not a mortgage by demise or sub-demise and 'lessee' shall be construed accordingly; and

(c)   (applicable only to Scotland).

(9)   Subject to paragraphs 9(2) and 11(2) below, this paragraph shall not require any person to give his agreement to the exercise of any right conferred by any of paragraphs 9 to 12 below.

Note
The words in square brackets in sub-para. (8)(a) were substituted by the New Roads and Street Works Act 1991.

Agreement required for obstructing access etc.

3.—(1)   A right conferred in accordance with paragraph 2 above or by paragraph 9, 10 or 11 below to execute any works on any land, to keep telecommunication apparatus installed on, under or over any land or to enter any land shall not be exercisable so as to interfere with or obstruct any means of entering or leaving any other land unless the occupier for the time being of the other land conferred, or is otherwise bound by, a right to interfere with or obstruct that means of entering or leaving the other land.

(2)   The agreement in writing of the occupier for the time being of the other land shall be required for conferring any right for the purposes of sub-paragraph (1) above on the operator.

(3)   The references in sub-paragraph (1) above to a means of entering or leaving any land include references to any means of entering or leaving the land provided for use in emergencies.

(4)   Sub-paragraphs (2) to (7) of paragraph 2 above except sub-paragraph (3) shall apply (subject to the following provisions of this code) in relation to a right falling within sub-paragraph (1) above as they apply in relation to a right falling within paragraph 2(1) above.

(5)   Nothing in this paragraph shall require the person who is the occupier of, or owns any interest in, any land which is a street or to which paragraph 11 below applies to agree to the exercise of any right on any other land.

Effect of rights and compensation

4.—(1) Anything done by the operator in exercise of a right conferred in relation to any land in accordance with paragraph 2 or 3 above shall be deemed to be done in exercise of a statutory power except as against—

(a)   a person who, being the owner of the freehold estate in that land or a lessee of the land, is not for the time being bound by the right; or

(b)   a person having the benefit of any covenant or agreement which has been entered into as respects the land under any enactment and which, by virtue of that enactment, binds or will bind persons deriving title or otherwise claiming under the covenantor or, as the case may be, a person who was a party to the agreement.

(2)   Where a right has been conferred in relation to any land in accordance with paragraph 2 or 3 above and anything has been done in exercise of that right, any person who, being the occupier of the land, the owner of the freehold estate in the land or a lessee of the land, is not for the time being bound by the right shall have the right to require the operator to restore the land to its condition before that thing was done.

(3)   Any duty imposed by virtue of sub-paragraph (2) above shall, to the extent that its performance involves the removal of any telecommunication apparatus from any land, be enforceable only in accordance with paragraph 21 below.

(4)   Where—

(a)   on a right in relation to any land being conferred or varied in accordance with paragraph 2 above, there is a depreciation in the value of any relevant interest in the land, and

(b)   that depreciation is attributable to the fact that paragraph 21 below will apply to the removal from the land, when the owner for the time being of that interest becomes the occupier of the land, of any telecommunication apparatus installed in pursuance of that right,

the operator shall pay compensation to the person who, at the time the right is conferred or, as the case may be, varied, is the owner of that relevant interest; and the amount of that compensation shall be equal (subject to sub-paragraph (9) below) to the amount of the depreciation.

(5)   In sub-paragraph (4) above 'relevant interest', in relation to land subject to a right conferred or varied in accordance with paragraph 2 above, means any interest in respect of which the following two conditions are satisfied at the time the right is conferred or varied, namely—

(a)   the owner of the interest is not the occupier of the land but may become the occupier of the land by virtue of that interest; and

(b)   the owner of the interest becomes bound by the right or variation by virtue only of paragraph 2(3) above.

(6)   Any question as to a person's entitlement to compensation under sub-paragraph (4) above, or as to the amount of any compensation under that sub-paragraph, shall, in default of agreement, be referred to and determined by the Lands Tribunal; and sections 2 and 4 of the Land Compensation Act 1961 (procedure and costs before Lands Tribunal) shall apply, with the necessary modifications, in relation to any such determination.

(7)   A claim to compensation under sub-paragraph (4) above shall be made by giving the operator notice of the claim and specifying in that notice

particulars of—
    (a)   the land in respect of which the claim is made;
    (b)   the claimant's interest in the land and, so far as known to the
claimant, any other interests in the land;
    (c)   the right or variation in respect of which the claim is made and
    (d)   the amount of the compensation claimed;
and such a claim shall be capable of being made at any time before the
claimant becomes the occupier of the land in question, or at any time in the
period of three years beginning with that time.

    (8)   For the purposes of assessing any compensation under sub-paragraph
(4) above, rules (2) to (4) set out in section 5 of the Land Compensation Act
1961 shall, subject to any necessary modifications, have effect as they have
effect for the purposes of assessing compensation for the compulsory acquisition of any interest in land.

    (9)   Without prejudice to the powers of the Lands Tribunal in respect of
the costs of any proceedings before the Tribunal by virtue of this paragraph,
where compensation is payable under sub-paragraph (4) above there shall
also be payable, by the operator to the claimant, any reasonable valuation or
legal expenses incurred by the claimant for the purposes of the preparation
and prosecution of his claim for that compensation.

    (10)   Subsections (1) to (3) of section 10 of the Land Compensation Act
1973 (compensation in respect of mortgages, trusts for sale and settled land)
shall apply in relation to compensation under sub-paragraph (4) above as they
apply in relation to compensation under Part I of that Act.

    (11)   (*Applicable only to Scotland.*)

    (12)   In the application of this paragraph to Northern Ireland—
    (a)   for any reference to the Lands Tribunal there is substituted a
reference to the Lands Tribunal for Northern Ireland;
    (b)   for the references in sub-paragraphs (6) and (8) above to sections
2, 4 and 5 of the Land Compensation Act 1961 there are substituted
references to Articles 4, 5 and 6 of the Land Compensation (Northern
Ireland) Order 1982, respectively;
    (c)   for the references in sub-paragraph (10) above to subsections (1) to
(3) of section 10 of the Land Compensation Act 1973 and to Part I of that
Act there are substituted references to paragraphs (1) to (3) of Article 13 of
the Land Acquisition and Compensation (Northern Ireland) Order 1973 and
to Part II of that Order, respectively.

Power to dispense with the need for required agreement

    5.—(1)   Where the operator requires any person to agree for the purposes
of paragraph 2 or 3 above that any right should be conferred on the operator, or
that any right should bind that person or any interest in land, the operator may
give a notice to that person of the right and of the agreement that he requires.

    (2)   Where the period of 28 days beginning with the giving of a notice
under sub-paragraph (1) above has expired without the giving of the required
agreement, the operator may apply to the court for an order conferring the
proposed right, or providing for it to bind any person or any interest in land,
and (in either case) dispensing with the need for the agreement of the person
to whom the notice was given.

(3)   The court shall make an order under this paragraph if, but only if, it is satisfied that any prejudice caused by the order—

(a)   is capable of being adequately compensated for by money; or

(b)   is outweighed by the benefit accruing from the order to the persons whose access to a telecommunication system will be secured by the order;

and in determining the extent of the prejudice, and the weight of that benefit, the court shall have regard to all the circumstances and to the principle that no person should unreasonably be denied access to a telecommunication system.

(4)   An order under this paragraph made in respect of a proposed right may, in conferring that right or providing for it to bind any person or any interest in land and in dispensing with the need for any person's agreement, direct that the right shall have effect with such modifications, be exercisable on such terms and be subject to such conditions as may be specified in the order.

(5)   The terms and conditions specified by virtue of sub-paragraph (4) above in an order under this paragraph, shall include such terms and conditions as appear to the court appropriate for ensuring that the least possible loss and damage is caused by the exercise of the right in respect of which the order is made to persons who occupy, own interests in or are from time to time on the land in question.

(6)   For the purposes of proceedings under this paragraph in a county court in England and Wales or Northern Ireland, section 63(1) of the County Courts Act 1984 and Article 33(1) of the County Courts (Northern Ireland) Order 1980 (assessors) shall have effect as if the words 'on the application of any party' were omitted; and where an assessor is summoned, or, in Northern Ireland, appointed, by virtue of this sub-paragraph—

(a)   he may, if so directed by the judge, inspect the land to which the proceedings relate without the judge and report on the land to the judge in writing; and

(b)   the judge may take the report into account in determining whether to make an order under this paragraph and what order to make.

(7)   Where an order under this paragraph, for the purpose of conferring any right or making provision for a right to bind any person or any interest in land, dispenses with the need for the agreement of any person, the order shall have the same effect and incidents as the agreement of the person the need for whose agreement is dispensed with and accordingly (without prejudice to the foregoing) shall be capable of variation or release by a subsequent agreement.

Note

The words omitted from sub-para. 5(6) are spent.

Acquisition of rights in respect of apparatus already installed

6.—(1)   The following provisions of this paragraph apply where the operator gives notice under paragraph 5(1) above to any person and—

(a)   that notice requires that person's agreement in respect of a right which is to be exercisable (in whole or in part) in relation to telecommunication apparatus already kept installed on, under or over the land in question, and

(b)   that person is entitled to require the removal of that apparatus but, by virtue of paragraph 21 below, is not entitled to enforce its removal.

(2)   The court may, on the application of the operator, confer on the operator such temporary rights as appear to the court reasonably necessary for securing that, pending the determination of any proceedings under paragraph 5 above or paragraph 21 below, the service provided by the operator's system is maintained and the apparatus properly adjusted and kept in repair.

(3)   In any case where it is shown that a person with an interest in the land was entitled to require the removal of the apparatus immediately after it was installed, the court shall, in determining for the purposes of paragraph 5 above whether the apparatus should continue to be kept installed on, under or over the land, disregard the fact that the apparatus has already been installed there.

Court to fix financial terms where agreement dispensed with

7.—(1)   The terms and conditions specified by virtue of sub-paragraph (4) of paragraph 5 above in an order under that paragraph dispensing with the need for a person's agreement, shall include—

(a)   such terms with respect to the payment of consideration in respect of the giving of the agreement, or the exercise of the rights to which the order relates, as it appears to the court would have been fair and reasonable if the agreement had been given willingly and subject to the other provisions of the order; and

(b)   such terms as appear to the court appropriate for ensuring that that person and persons from time to time bound by virtue of paragraph 2(4) above by the rights to which the order relates are adequately compensated (whether by the payment of such consideration or otherwise) for any loss or damage sustained by them in consequence of the exercise of those rights.

(2)   In determining what terms should be specified in an order under paragraph 5 above for requiring an amount to be paid to any person in respect of—

(a)   the provisions of that order conferring any right or providing for any right to bind any person or any interest in land, or

(b)   the exercise of any right to which the order relates,
the court shall take into account the prejudicial effect (if any) of the order or, as the case may be, of the exercise of the right on that person's enjoyment of, or on any interest of his in, land other than the land in relation to which the right is conferred.

(3)   In determining what terms should be specified in an order under paragraph 5 above for requiring an amount to be paid to any person, the court shall, in a case where the order is made in consequence of an application made in connection with proceedings under paragraph 21 below, take into account, to such extent as it thinks fit, any period during which that person—

(a)   was entitled to require the removal of any telecommunication apparatus from the land in question, but

(b)   by virtue of paragraph 21 below, was not entitled to enforce its removal;

but where the court takes any such period into account, it may also take into account any compensation paid under paragraph 4(4) above.

(4)   The terms specified by virtue of sub-paragraph (1) above in an order under paragraph 5 above may provide—

(a)   for the making of payments from time to time to such persons as may be determined under those terms; and

(b)   for questions arising in consequence of those terms (whether as to the amount of any loss or damage caused by the exercise of a right or otherwise) to be referred to arbitration or to be determined in such other manner as may be specified in the order.

(5)   The court may, if it thinks fit—

(a)   where the amount of any sum required to be paid by virtue of terms specified in an order under paragraph 5 above has been determined, require the whole or any part of any such sum to be paid into court;

(b)   pending the determination of the amount of any such sum, order the payment into court of such amount on account as the court thinks fit.

(6)   Where terms specified in an order under paragraph 5 above require the payment of any sum to a person who cannot be found or ascertained, that sum shall be paid into court.

Notices and applications by potential subscribers

8.—(1)   Where—

(a)   it is reasonably necessary for the agreement of any person to the conferring of any right, or to any right's binding any person or any interest in land, to be obtained by the operator before another person ('the potential subscriber') may be afforded access to the operator's system, and

(b)   the operator has not given a notice or (if he has given a notice) has not made an application in respect of that right under paragraph 5 above, the potential subscriber may at any time give a notice to the operator requiring him to give a notice or make an application under paragraph 5 above in respect of that right.

(2)   At any time after notice has been given to the operator under sub-paragraph (1) above, the operator may apply to the court to have the notice set aside on the ground that the conditions mentioned in that sub-paragraph are not satisfied on the ground that, even if the agreement were obtained, the operator would not afford the potential subscriber access to the operator's system and could not be required to afford him access to that system.

(3)   Subject to any order of the court made in or pending any proceedings under sub-paragraph (2) above, if at any time after the expiration of the period of 28 days beginning with the giving to the operator of a notice under sub-paragraph (1) above the operator has not complied with the notice, the potential subscriber may himself, on the operator's behalf, give the required notice and (if necessary) make an application under paragraph 5 above or, as the case may be, make the required application.

(4)   The court may, on an application made by virtue of sub-paragraph (3) above, give such directions as it thinks fit—

(a)   with respect to the separate participation of the operator in the proceedings to which the application gives rise, and

(b)   requiring the operator to provide information to the court.

(5)   A covenant, condition or agreement which would have the effect of preventing or restricting the taking by any person as a potential subscriber of any step under this paragraph shall be void to the extent that it would have that effect.

(6)   Nothing in this paragraph shall be construed as requiring the operator to reimburse the potential subscriber for any costs incurred by the potential subscriber in or in connection with the taking of any step under this paragraph on the operator's behalf.

Street works

9.—(1)   The operator shall, for the statutory purposes, have the right to do any of the following things, that is to say—

(a)   install telecommunication apparatus, or keep telecommunication apparatus installed, under, over, [in, on,] along or across [a street or, in Scotland, a road];

(b)   inspect, maintain, adjust, repair or alter any telecommunication apparatus so installed; and

(c)   execute any works requisite for or incidental to the purposes of any works falling within paragraph (a) or (b) above, including for those purposes the following kinds of works, that is to say—

(i)   breaking up or opening [a street or, in Scotland, a road];

(ii)   tunnelling or boring under [a street or, in Scotland, a road]; and

(iii)   breaking up or opening a sewer, drain or tunnel;

(2)   This paragraph has effect subject to section 11(1) of this Act, paragraph 3 above and the following provisions of this code, and the rights conferred by this paragraph shall not be exercisable [in a street which is not a maintainable highway or, in Scotland, a road which is not a public road] without either the agreement requiring by paragraph 2 above or an order of the court under paragraph 5 above dispensing with the need for that agreement.

(3)   The rights conferred by this paragraph shall not be exercisable on any land comprised in the route of [a special road within the meaning of the Roads (Northern Ireland) [Order 1993]].

Notes
1.   The words in square brackets in sub-paras (1), (2) were inserted or substituted and the words omitted from sub-para. (1) were repealed by the New Roads and Street Works Act 1991.
2.   The words in the first (outer) pair of square brackets in sub-para. (3) were substituted by the 1991 Act and the words in the second (inner) pair of square brackets in that sub-paragraph were substituted by the Roads (Northern Ireland) Order 1993, SI 1993/3160.

Power to fly lines

10.—(1)   Subject to paragraph 3 above and the following provisions of this code, where any telecommunication apparatus is kept installed on or over any land for the purposes of the operator's system, the operator shall, for the statutory purposes, have the right to install and keep installed lines which—

(a)   pass over other land adjacent to or in the vicinity of the land on or over which that apparatus is so kept; and

(b)   are connected to that apparatus; and

(c)   are not at any point in the course of passing over the other land less than 3 metres above the ground or within 2 metres of any building over which they pass.

(2)   Nothing in sub-paragraph (1) above shall authorise the installation or keeping on or over any land of—

(a)   any telecommunication apparatus used to support, carry or suspend a line installed in pursuance of that sub-paragraph; or

(b)   any line which by reason of its position interferes with the carrying on of any business (within the meaning of section 6 of this Act) carried on on that land.

Tidal waters etc.

11.—(1)   Subject to paragraph 3 above and the following provisions of this code, the operator shall have the right for the statutory purposes—

(a)   to execute any works (including placing any buoy or seamark) on any tidal water or lands for or in connection with the installation, maintenance, adjustment, repair or alteration of telecommunication apparatus;

(b)   to keep telecommunication apparatus installed on, under or over tidal water or lands; and

(c)   to enter any tidal water or lands to inspect any telecommunication apparatus so installed.

(2)   A right conferred by this paragraph shall not be exercised in relation to any land in which a Crown interest, within the meaning of paragraph 26 below, subsists unless agreement to the exercise of the right in relation to that land has been given, in accordance with sub-paragraph (3) of that paragraph, in respect of that interest.

(3)   Before executing any works in exercise of a right conferred by this paragraph the operator (not being the Secretary of State) shall submit a plan of the proposed works to the Secretary of State for the Secretary of State's approval.

(4)   Sub-paragraph (3) above shall not apply to the execution of any emergency works, but as soon as practicable after commencing any emergency works on any tidal water or lands the operator (not being the Secretary of State) shall submit a plan of those works to the Secretary of State for the Secretary of State's approval.

(5)   As soon as reasonably practicable after a plan is submitted to him under sub-paragraph (3) or (4) above the Secretary of State shall, after consulting such authorities exercising functions in relation to the tidal water or lands in question as it appears to him appropriate to consult, consider whether to approve it; and, if he does approve it, he may do so subject to such modifications and conditions and on such terms as he thinks fit.

(6)   The Secretary of State shall not approve a plan submitted to him under sub-paragraph (3) or (4) above unless he is satisfied that adequate arrangements have been made for compensating any persons appearing to him to be owners of interests in the tidal water or lands in question for any loss or damage sustained by those persons in consequence of the execution of the works to which the plan relates.

(7)   If—

(a)   the operator (not being the Secretary of State) executes any works in exercise of a right conferred by this paragraph, but

(b)   those works are executed otherwise than in accordance with a plan approved by the Secretary of State (including, in the case of emergency works, where works already commenced are not approved) or a condition on which any approval of the Secretary of State is given is or has been contravened,

the Secretary of State may by notice require the operator to execute such remedial works as the Secretary of State thinks appropriate having regard to the terms and conditions of any approval that he has given and, if those works are not executed in accordance with the notice, may execute them himself at the operator's expense.

(8)   Where, as the result—

(a)   of the failure of the operator (not being the Secretary of State) reasonably to maintain any telecommunication apparatus kept installed for the purposes of the operator's system on, under or over any tidal water or lands, or

(b)   of the abandonment by the operator of any such apparatus,

it appears to the Secretary of State that any remedial works should be executed, he may by notice require the operator to execute those works and, if those works are not executed in accordance with the notice, may execute them himself at the operator's expense.

(9)   The Secretary of State shall have power for the purposes of exercising his functions (other than as the operator) under this paragraph, and of determining whether to exercise those functions, to cause a survey or examination to be carried out, at the operator's expense, of any works or apparatus or of the site or proposed site of any works or apparatus.

(10)   Where the Secretary of State is authorised by this paragraph to do any thing at the operator's expense, the expenses incurred by the Secretary of State in or in connection with the doing of that thing shall be recoverable by the Secretary of State from the operator in any court of competent jurisdiction.

(11)   In this paragraph—

'remedial works' includes any works of repair or restoration, the alteration of any apparatus and any works to restore the site of any apparatus to its original condition;

'tidal water or lands' includes any estuary or branch of the sea, the shore below mean high water springs and the bed of any tidal water.

Linear obstacles

12.—(1)   Subject to the following provisions of this code, the operator shall, for the statutory purposes, have the right in order to cross any relevant land with a line, to install and keep the line and other telecommunication apparatus on, under or over that land and—

(a)   to execute any works on that land for or in connection with the installation, maintenance, adjustment, repair or alteration of that line or the other telecommunication apparatus; and

(b)   to enter on that land to inspect the line or the other apparatus.

(2)   A line installed in pursuance of any right conferred by this paragraph need not cross the relevant land in question by a direct route or by the shortest route from the point at which the line enters that land, but it shall not cross that land by any route which, in the horizontal plane, exceeds the said shortest route by more than 400 metres.

(3)   Telecommunication apparatus shall not be installed in pursuance of any right conferred by this paragraph in any position on the relevant land in which it interferes with traffic on the railway, canal or tramway on that land.

(4)   The operator shall not execute any works on any land in pursuance of any right conferred by this paragraph unless—

(a)   he has given the person with control of the land 28 days' notice of his intention to do so; or

(b)   the works are emergency works.

(5)   A notice under sub-paragraph (4) above shall contain a plan and section of the proposed works or (in lieu of a plan and section) any description of the proposed works (whether or not in the form of a diagram) which the person with control of the land has agreed to accept for the purposes of this sub-paragraph.

(6)   If, at any time before a notice under sub-paragraph (4) above expires, the person with control of the land gives the operator notice of objection to the works, the operator shall be entitled to execute the works only—

(a)   if, within the period of 28 days beginning with the giving of the notice of objection, neither the operator nor that person has given notice to the other requiring him to agree to an arbitrator to whom the objection may be referred under paragraph 13 below; or

(b)   in accordance with an award made on such a reference; or

(c)   to the extent that the works have at any time become emergency works.

(7)   If the operator exercises any power conferred by this paragraph to execute emergency works on any land, he shall, as soon as reasonably practicable after commencing those works, give the person with control of the land a notice identifying the works and containing—

(a)   a statement of the reason why the works are emergency works; and

(b)   either the matters which would be required to be contained in a notice under sub-paragraph (4) above with respect to those works or, as the case may require, a reference to an earlier notice under that sub-paragraph with respect to those works.

(8)   If within the period of 28 days beginning with the giving of a notice under sub-paragraph (7) above the person to whom that notice was given gives a notice to the operator requiring him to pay compensation, the operator shall be liable to pay that person compensation in respect of loss or damage sustained in consequence of the carrying out of the emergency works in question; and any question as to the amount of that compensation shall, in default of agreement, be referred to arbitration under paragraph 13 below.

(9)   If the operator commences the execution of any works in contravention of any provision of this paragraph, he shall be guilty of an offence and liable on summary conviction to a fine not exceeding level 3 on the standard scale.

(10)   In this paragraph 'relevant land' means land which is used wholly or mainly either as a railway, canal or tramway or in connection with a railway,

canal or tramway on that land, and a reference to the person with control of any such land is a reference to the person carrying on the railway, canal or tramway undertaking in question.

Arbitration in relation to linear obstacles

13.—(1) Any objection or question which, in accordance with paragraph 12 above, is referred to arbitration under this paragraph shall be referred to the arbitration of a single arbitrator appointed by agreement between the parties concerned or, in default of agreement, by the President of the Institution of Civil Engineers.

(2) Where an objection under paragraph 12 above is referred to arbitration under this paragraph the arbitrator shall have the power—

(a) to require the operator to submit to the arbitrator a plan and section in such form as the arbitrator may think requisite for those purposes.

(b) to require the observations on any such plan or section of the person who objects to the works to be submitted to the arbitrator in such form as the arbitrator may think requisite for those purposes.

(c) to direct the operator or that person to furnish him with such information and to comply with such other requirements as the arbitrator may think requisite for those purposes;

(d) to make an award requiring modifications to the proposed works and specifying the terms on which and the conditions subject to which the works may be executed; and

(e) to award such sum as the arbitrator may determine in respect of one or both of the following matters, that is to say—

(i) compensation to the person who objects to the works in respect of loss or damage sustained by that person in consequence of the carrying out of the works, and

(ii) consideration payable to that person for the right to carry out the works.

(3) Where a question as to compensation in respect of emergency works is referred to arbitration under this paragraph, the arbitrator—

(a) shall have the power to direct the operator or the person who requires the payment of compensation to furnish him with such information and to comply with such other requirements as the arbitrator may think requisite for the purposes of the arbitration; and

(b) shall award to the person requiring the payment of compensation such sum (if any) as the arbitrator may determine in respect of the loss or damage sustained by that person in consequence of the carrying out of the emergency works in question.

(4) The arbitrator may treat compliance with any requirement made in pursuance of sub-paragraph (2)(a) to (c) or (3)(a) above as a condition of his making an award.

(5) In determining what award to make on a reference under this paragraph, the arbitrator shall have regard to all the circumstances and to the principle that no person should unreasonably be denied access to a telecommunication system.

(6) For the purposes of the making of an award under this paragraph—

(a)   the references in sub-paragraphs (2)(e) and (3)(b) above to loss shall, in relation to a person carrying on a railway, canal or tramway undertaking, include references to any increase in the expenses of carrying on that undertaking; and

(b)   the consideration mentioned in sub-paragraph (2)(e) above shall be determined on the basis of what would have been fair and reasonable if the person who objects to the works had given his authority willingly for the works to be executed on the same terms and subject to the same conditions (if any) as are contained in the award.

(7)   (*Applicable only to Scotland.*)

(8)   In the application of this paragraph to Northern Ireland, the Arbitration Act (Northern Ireland) 1937 shall apply in relation to an arbitration under this paragraph as if this code related exclusively to matters in respect of which the Parliament of Northern Ireland had power to make laws.

Alteration of apparatus crossing a linear obstacle

14.—(1)   Without prejudice to the following provisions of this code, the person with control of any relevant land may, on the ground that any telecommunication apparatus kept installed on, under or over that land for the purposes of the operator's system interferes, or is likely to interfere, with—

(a)   the carrying on of the railway, canal, or tramway undertaking carried on by that person, or

(b)   anything done or to be done for the purposes of that undertaking, give notice to the operator requiring him to alter that apparatus.

(2)   The operator shall within a reasonable time and to the reasonable satisfaction of the person giving the notice comply with a notice under sub-paragraph (1) above unless before the expiration of the period of 28 days beginning with the giving of the notice he gives a counter-notice to the person with control of the land in question specifying the respects in which he is not prepared to comply with the original notice.

(3)   Where a counter-notice has been given under sub-paragraph (2) above the operator shall not be required to comply with the original notice but the person with control of the relevant land may apply to the court for an order requiring the alteration of any telecommunication apparatus to which the notice relates.

(4)   The court shall not make an order under this paragraph unless it is satisfied that the order is necessary on one of the grounds mentioned in sub-paragraph (1) above and in determining whether to make such an order the court shall also have regard to all the circumstances and to the principle that no person should unreasonably be denied access to a telecommunication system.

(5)   An order under this paragraph may take such form and be on such terms as the court thinks fit and may impose such conditions and may contain such directions to the operator or the person with control of the land in question as the court thinks necessary for resolving any difference between the operator and that person and for protecting their respective interests.

(6)   In this paragraph references to relevant land and to the person with control of such land have the same meaning as in paragraph 12 above.

Use of certain conduits

15.—(1) Nothing in the preceding provisions of this code shall authorise the doing of anything inside a relevant conduit without the agreement of the authority with control of that conduit.

(2) The agreement of the authority with control of a public sewer shall be sufficient in all cases to confer a right falling within any of the preceding provisions of this code where the right is to be exercised wholly inside that sewer.

(3) In this paragraph—

(a) 'relevant conduit' and 'public sewer' have the same meanings as in section 98 of this Act; and

(b) a reference to the authority with control of a relevant conduit shall be construed in accordance with subsections (7) and (8) of that section.

Compensation for injurious affection to neighbouring land etc.

16.—(1) Where a right conferred by or in accordance with any of the preceding provisions of this code is exercised, compensation shall be payable by the operator under section 10 of the Compulsory Purchase Act 1965 (compensation for injurious affection to neighbouring land etc) as if that section had effect in relation to injury caused by the exercise of such a right as it has effect in relation to injury caused by the execution of works on land that has been compulsorily purchased.

(2) Sub-paragraph (1) above shall not confer any entitlement to compensation on any person in respect of the exercise of a right conferred in accordance with paragraph 2 or 3 above, if that person conferred the right or is bound by it by virtue of paragraph 2(2)(b) or (d) above, but, save as aforesaid, the entitlement of any person to compensation under this paragraph shall be determined irrespective of his ownership of any interest in the land where the right is exercised.

(3) Compensation shall not be payable on any claim for compensation under this paragraph unless the amount of the compensation exceeds £50.

(4) *(Applicable only to Scotland.)*

(5) In the application of this paragraph to Northern Ireland—

(a) for any reference in sub-paragraph (1) to section 10 of the Compulsory Purchase Act 1965 there is substituted a reference to Article 18 of the Land Compensation (Northern Ireland) Order 1982;

(b) any question as to a person's entitlement to compensation by virtue of sub-paragraph (1) above, or as to the amount of that compensation, shall, in default of agreement, be determined by the Lands Tribunal for Northern Ireland.

Objections to overhead apparatus

17.—(1) This paragraph applies where the operator has completed the installation for the purposes of the operator's system of any telecommunication apparatus the whole or part of which is at a height of 3 metres or more above the ground.

(2) At any time before the expiration of the period of 3 months beginning with the completion of the installation of the apparatus a person who is the occupier of or owns an interest in—

(a)   any land over or on which the apparatus has been installed, or

(b)   any land the enjoyment of which, or any interest in which, is, because of the nearness of the land to the land on or over which the apparatus has been installed, capable of being prejudiced by the apparatus, may give the operator notice of objection in respect of that apparatus.

(3)   No notice of objection may be given in respect of any apparatus if the apparatus—

(a)   replaces any telecommunication apparatus which is not substantially different from the new apparatus; and

(b)   is not in a significantly different position.

(4)   Where a person has both given a notice under this paragraph and applied for compensation under any of the preceding provisions of this code, the court—

(a)   may give such directions as it thinks fit for ensuring that no compensation is paid until any proceedings under this paragraph have been disposed of, and

(b)   if the court makes an order under this paragraph, may provide in that order for some or all of the compensation otherwise payable under this code to that person not to be so payable, or, if the case so requires, for some or all of any compensation paid under this code to that person to be repaid to the operator.

(5)   At any time after the expiration of the period of 2 months beginning with the giving of a notice of objection but before the expiration of the period of 4 months beginning with the giving of that notice, the person who gave the notice may apply to the court to have the objection upheld.

(6)   Subject to sub-paragraph (7) below, the court shall uphold the objection if the apparatus appears materially to prejudice the applicant's enjoyment of, or interest in, the land in right of which the objection is made and the court is not satisfied that the only possible alterations of the apparatus will—

(a)   substantially increase the cost or diminish the quality of the service provided by the operator's system to persons who have, or may in future have, access to it, or

(b)   involve the operator in substantial additional expenditure (disregarding any expenditure occasioned solely by the fact that any proposed alteration was not adopted originally or, as the case may be, that the apparatus has been unnecessarily installed), or

(c)   give to any person a case at least as good as the applicant has to have an objection under this paragraph upheld.

(7)   The court shall not uphold the objection if the applicant is bound by a right of the operator falling within paragraph 2 or 3(1) above to install the apparatus and it appears to the court unreasonable, having regard to the fact that the applicant is so bound and the circumstances in which he became so bound, for the applicant to have given notice of objection.

(8)   In considering the matters specified in sub-paragraph (6) above the court shall have regard to all the circumstances and to the principle that no person should unreasonably be denied access to a telecommunication system.

(9)   If it upholds an objection under this paragraph the court may by order—

(a)   direct the alteration of the apparatus to which the objection relates;

(b) authorise the installation (instead of the apparatus to which the objection relates), in a manner and position specified in the order, of any apparatus so specified;

(c) direct that no objection may be made under this paragraph in respect of any apparatus the installation of which is authorised by the court.

(10) The court shall not make any order under this paragraph directing the alteration of any apparatus or authorising the installation of any apparatus unless it is satisfied either—

(a) that the operator has all such rights as it appears to the court appropriate that he should have for the purpose of making the alteration or, as the case may be, installing the apparatus, or

(b) that—

(i) he would have all those rights if the court, on an application under paragraph 5 above, dispensed with the need for the agreement of any person, and

(ii) it would be appropriate for the court, on such an application, to dispense with the need for that agreement;

and, accordingly, for the purposes of dispensing with the need for the agreement of any person to the alteration or installation of any apparatus, the court shall have the same powers as it would have if an application had been duly made under paragraph 5 above for an order dispensing with the need for that person's agreement.

(11) For the purposes of sub-paragraphs (6)(c) and (10) above, the court shall have power on an application under this paragraph to give the applicant directions for bringing the application to the notice of such other interested persons as it thinks fit.

Obligation to affix notices to overhead apparatus

18.—(1) Where the operator has for the purposes of the operator's system installed any telecommunication apparatus the whole or part of which is at a height of 3 metres or more above the ground, the operator shall, before the expiration of the period of 3 days beginning with the completion of the installation, in a secure and durable manner affix a notice—

(a) to every major item of apparatus installed; or

(b) if no major item of apparatus is installed, to the nearest major item of telecommunication apparatus to which the apparatus that is installed is directly or indirectly connected.

(2) A notice affixed under sub-paragraph (1) above shall be affixed in a position where it is reasonably legible and shall give the name of the operator and an address in the United Kingdom at which any notice of objection may be given under paragraph 17 above in respect of the apparatus in question; and any person giving such a notice at that address in respect of that apparatus shall be deemed to have been furnished with that address for the purposes of paragraph 24(4)(a) below.

(3) If the operator contravenes the requirements of this paragraph he shall be guilty of an offence and liable on summary conviction to a fine not exceeding level 2 on the standard scale.

(4) In any proceedings for an offence under this paragraph it shall be a defence for the person charged to prove that he took all reasonable steps and exercised all due diligence to avoid committing the offence.

Tree lopping

19.—(1) Where any tree overhangs any street and, in doing so, either—

(a) obstructs or interferes with the working of any telecommunication apparatus used for the purposes of the operator's system, or

(b) will obstruct or interfere with the working of any telecommunication apparatus which is about to be installed for those purposes, the operator may by notice to the occupier of the land on which the tree is growing require the tree to be lopped so as to prevent the obstruction or interference.

(2) If within the period of 28 days beginning with the giving of the notice by the operator, the occupier of the land on which the tree is growing gives the operator a counter-notice objecting to the lopping of the tree, the notice shall have effect only if confirmed by an order of the court.

(3) If at any time a notice under sub-paragraph (1) above has not been complied with and either—

(a) a period of 28 days beginning with the giving of the notice has expired without a counter-notice having been given, or

(b) an order of the court confirming the notice has come into force, the operator may himself cause the tree to be lopped as mentioned in sub-paragraph (1) above.

(4) Where the operator lops a tree in exercise of the power conferred by sub-paragraph (3) above he shall do so in a husband-like manner and in such a way as to cause the minimum damage to the tree.

(5) Where—

(a) a notice under sub-paragraph (1) above is complied with either without a counter-notice having been given or after the notice has been confirmed, or

(b) the operator exercises the power conferred by sub-paragraph (3) above,

the court shall, on an application made by a person who has sustained loss or damage in consequence of the lopping of the tree or who has incurred expenses in complying with the notice, order the operator to pay that person such compensation in respect of the loss, damage or expenses as it thinks fit.

Power to require alteration of apparatus

20.—(1) Where any telecommunication apparatus is kept installed on, under or over any land for the purposes of the operator's system, any person with an interest in that land or adjacent land may (notwithstanding the terms of any agreement binding that person) by notice given to the operator require the alteration of the apparatus on the ground that the alteration is necessary to enable that person to carry out a proposed improvement of the land in which he has an interest.

(2) Where a notice is given under sub-paragraph (1) above by any person to the operator, the operator shall comply with it unless he gives a counter-notice under this sub-paragraph within the period of 28 days beginning with the giving of the notice.

(3) Where a counter-notice is given under sub-paragraph (2) above to any person, the operator shall make the required alteration only if the court on an application by that person makes an order requiring the alteration to be made.

(4)   The court shall make an order under this paragraph for an alteration to be made only if, having regard to all the circumstances and the principle that no person should unreasonably be denied access to a telecommunication system, it is satisfied—

(a)   that the alteration is necessary as mentioned in sub-paragraph (1) above; and

(b)   that the alteration will not substantially interfere with any service provided by the operator's system.

(5)   The court shall not make an order under this paragraph for the alteration of any apparatus unless it is satisfied either—

(a)   that the operator has all such rights as it appears to the court appropiate that he should have for the purpose of making the alteration, or

(b)   that—

(i)   he would have all those rights if the court, on an application under paragraph 5 above, dispensed with the need for the agreement of any person, and

(ii)   it would be appropriate for the court, on such an application, to dispense with the need for that agreement;

and, accordingly, for the purposes of dispensing with the need for the agreement of any person to the alteration of any apparatus, the court shall have the same powers as it would have if an application had been duly made under paragraph 5 above for an order dispensing with the need for that person's agreement.

(6)   For the purposes of sub-paragraph (5) above, the court shall have power on an application under this paragraph to give the applicant directions for bringing the application to the notice of such other interested persons as it thinks fit.

(7)   An order under this paragraph may provide for the alteration to be carried out with such modifications, on such terms and subject to such conditions as the court thinks fit, but the court shall not include any such modifications, terms or conditions in its order without the consent of the applicant, and if such consent is not given may refuse to make an order under this paragraph.

(8)   An order made under this paragraph on the application of any person shall, unless the court otherwise thinks fit, require that person to reimburse the operator in respect of any expenses which the operator incurs in or in connection with the execution of any works in compliance with the order.

(9)   In sub-paragraph (1) above 'improvement' includes development and change of use.

Restriction on right to require the removal of apparatus

21.—(1)   Where any person is for the time being entitled to require the removal of any of the operator's telecommunication apparatus from any land (whether under any enactment or because that apparatus is kept on, under or over that land otherwise than in pursuance of a right binding that person or for any other reason) that person shall not be entitled to enforce the removal of the apparatus except, subject to sub-paragraph (12) below, in accordance with the following provisions of this paragraph.

(2)   The person entitled to require the removal of any of the operator's telecommunication apparatus shall give a notice to the operator requiring the removal of the apparatus.

(3)   Where a person gives a notice under sub-paragraph (2) above and the operator does not give that person a counter-notice within the period of 28 days beginning with the giving of the notice, that person shall be entitled to enforce the removal of the apparatus.

(4)   A counter-notice given under sub-paragraph (3) above to any person by the operator shall do one or both of the following, that is to say—

(a)   state that that person is not entitled to require the removal of the apparatus;

(b)   specify the steps which the operator proposes to take for the purpose of securing a right as against that person to keep the apparatus on the land.

(5)   Those steps may include any steps which the operator could take for the purpose of enabling him, if the apparatus is removed, to re-install the apparatus; and the fact that by reason of the following provisions of this paragraph any proposed re-installation is only hypothetical shall not prevent the operator from taking those steps or any court or person from exercising any function in consequence of those steps having been taken.

(6)   Where a counter-notice is given under sub-paragraph (3) above to any person, that person may only enforce the removal of the apparatus in pursuance of an order of the court; and, where the counter-notice specifies steps which the operator is proposing to take to secure a right to keep the apparatus on the land, the court shall not make such an order unless it is satisfied—

(a)   that the operator is not intending to take those steps or is being unreasonably dilatory in the taking of those steps; or

(b)   that the taking of those steps has not secured, or will not secure, for the operator as against that person any right to keep the apparatus installed on, under or over the land or, as the case may be, to re-install it if it is removed.

(7)   Where any person is entitled to enforce the removal of any apparatus under this paragraph (whether by virtue of sub-paragraph (3) above or an order of the court under sub-paragraph (6) above), that person may, without prejudice to any method available to him apart from this sub-paragraph for enforcing the removal of that apparatus, apply to the court for authority to remove it himself; and, on such an application, the court may, if it thinks fit, give that authority.

(8)   Where any apparatus is removed by any person under an authority given by the court under sub-paragraph (7) above, any expenses incurred by him in or in connection with the removal of the apparatus shall be recoverable by him from the operator in any court of competent jurisdiction; and in so giving an authority to any person the court may also authorise him, in accordance with the directions of the court, to sell any apparatus removed under the authority and to retain the whole or a part of the proceeds of sale on account of those expenses.

(9)   Any telecommunication apparatus kept installed on, under or over any land shall (except for the purposes of this paragraph and without prejudice to paragraphs 6(3) and 7(3) above) be deemed, as against any person who was at any time entitled to require the removal of the apparatus, but by virtue of this paragraph not entitled to enforce its removal, to have been lawfully so kept at that time.

(10)   Where this paragraph applies (whether in pursuance of an enactment amended by Schedule 4 to this Act or otherwise) in relation to telecommunication apparatus the alteration of which some person ('the relevant person') is entitled to require in consequence of the stopping up, closure, change or diversion of any street or the extinguishment or alteration of any public right of way—

(a)   the removal of the apparatus shall constitute compliance with a requirement to make any other alteration;

(b)   a counter-notice under sub-paragraph (3) above may state (in addition to, or instead of, any of the matters mentioned in sub-paragraph (4) above) that the operator requires the relevant person to reimburse him in respect of any expenses which he incurs in or in connection with the making of any alteration in compliance with the requirements of the relevant person;

(c)   an order made under this paragraph on an application by the relevant person in respect of a counter-notice containing such a statement shall, unless the court otherwise thinks fit, require the relevant person to reimburse the operator in respect of any expenses which he so incurs; and

(d)   sub-paragraph (8) above shall not apply.

(11)   References in this paragraph to the operator's telecommunication apparatus include references to telecommunication apparatus which (whether or not vested in the operator) is being, is to be or has been used for the purposes of the operator's system.

(12)   A person shall not, under this paragraph, be entitled to enforce the removal of any apparatus on the ground only that he is entitled to give a notice under paragraph 11, 14, 17 or 20 above; and this paragraph is without prejudice to paragraph 23 below and to the power to enforce an order of the court under the said paragraph 11, 14, 17 or 20.

Abandonment of apparatus

22.   Without prejudice to the preceding provisions of this code, where the operator has a right conferred by or in accordance with this code for the statutory purposes to keep telecommunication apparatus installed on, under or over any land, he is not entitled to keep that apparatus so installed if, at a time when the apparatus is not, or is no longer, used for the purposes of the operator's system, there is no reasonable likelihood that it will be so used.

Undertaker's works

23.—(1)   The following provisions of this paragraph apply where a relevant undertaker is proposing to execute any undertaker's works which involve or are likely to involve a temporary or permanent alteration of any telecommunication apparatus kept installed on, under or over any land for the purposes of the operator's system.

(2)   The relevant undertaker shall, not less than 10 days before the works are commenced, give the operator a notice specifying the nature of the undertaker's works, the alteration or likely alteration involved and the time and place at which the works will be commenced.

(3)   Sub-paragraph (2) above shall not apply in relation to any emergency works of which the relevant undertaker gives the operator notice as soon as practicable after commencing the works.

(4)   Where a notice has been given under sub-paragraph (2) above by a relevant undertaker to the operator, the operator may within the period of 10 days beginning with the giving of the notice give the relevant undertaker a counter-notice which may state either—

(a)   that the operator intends himself to make any alteration made necessary or expedient by the proposed undertaker's works; or

(b)   that he requires the undertaker in making any such alteration to do so under the supervision and to the satisfaction of the operator.

(5)   Where a counter-notice given under sub-paragraph (4) above states that the operator intends himself to make any alteration—

(a)   the operator shall (subject to sub-paragraph (7) below) have the right, instead of the relevant undertaker, to execute any works for the purpose of making that alteration; and

(b)   any expenses incurred by the operator in or in connection with the execution of those works and the amount of any loss or damage sustained by the operator in consequence of the alteration shall be recoverable by the operator from the undertaker in any court of competent jurisdiction.

(6)   Where a counter-notice given under sub-paragraph (4) above states that any alteration is to be made under the supervision and to the satisfaction of the operator—

(a)   the relevant undertaker shall not make the alteration except as required by the notice or under sub-paragraph (7) below; and

(b)   any expenses incurred by the operator in or in connection with the provision of that supervision and the amount of any loss or damage sustained by the operator in consequence of the alteration shall be recoverable by the operator from the undertaker in any court of competent jurisdiction.

(7)   Where—

(a)   no counter-notice is given under sub-paragraph (4) above, or

(b)   the operator, having given a counter-notice falling within that sub-paragraph, fails within a reasonable time to make any alteration made necessary or expedient by the proposed undertaker's works or, as the case may be, unreasonably fails to provide the required supervision,

the relevant undertaker may himself execute works for the purpose of making the alteration or, as the case may be, may execute such works without the supervision of the operator; but in either case the undertaker shall execute the works to the satisfaction of the operator.

(8)   If the relevant undertaker or any of his agents—

(a)   executes any works without the notice required by sub-paragraph (2) above having been given, or

(b)   unreasonably fails to comply with any reasonable requirement of the operator under this paragraph,

he shall, subject to sub-paragraph (9) below, be guilty of an offence and liable on summary conviction to a fine which—

(i)   if the service provided by the operator's system is interrupted by the works or failure, shall not exceed level 4 on the standard scale; and

(ii)   if that service is not so interrupted, shall not exceed level 3 on the standard scale.

(9)   Sub-paragraph (8) above does not apply to a Northern Ireland department.

(10)   In this paragraph—

'relevant undertaker' means—

(a)   any person (including a local authority) authorised by any Act (whether public general or local) or by any order or scheme made under or confirmed by any Act to carry on—

(i)   any railway, tramway, road transport, water transport, canal, inland navigation, dock, harbour, pier or lighthouse undertaking; [or]

(ii), (iii) . . .

(b)   any person (apart from the operator) to whom this code is applied by a licence under section 7 of this Act; and

(c)   any person to whom this paragraph is applied by any Act amended by or under or passed after this Act;

'undertaker's works' means—

(a)   in relation to a relevant undertaker falling within paragraph (a) of the preceding definition, any works which that undertaker is authorised to execute for the purposes of, or in connection with, the carrying on by him of the undertaking mentioned in that paragraph;

(b)   in relation to a relevant undertaker falling within paragraph (b) of that definition, any works which that undertaker is authorised to execute by or in accordance with any provision of this code; and

(c)   in relation to a relevant undertaker falling within paragraph (c) of that definition, the works for the purposes of which this paragraph is applied to that undertaker.

(11)   The application of this paragraph by virtue of paragraph (c) of each of the definitions in sub-paragraph (10) above to any person for the purposes of any works shall be without prejudice to its application by virtue of paragraph (a) of each of those definitions to that person for the purposes of any other works.

Notes
1.   The word in square brackets in sub-para. (10)(a)(i) was inserted, and sub-para. (10)(a)(iii) and the word 'or' preceding it were repealed, by the Water Act 1989.
2.   Sub-para. (10)(a)(ii) was repealed by the Electricity Act 1989.

Notices under code

24.—(1)   Any notice required to be given by the operator to any person for the purposes of any provision of this code must be in a form approved by the Director as adequate for indicating to that person the effect of the notice and of so much of this code as is relevant to the notice and to the steps that may be taken by that person under this code in respect of that notice.

(2)   Any notice required to be given to any person for the purposes of any provision of this code may be given to him either by delivering it to him or by leaving it at his proper address or by post, but a notice shall not be given by post unless it is sent by registered letter or by the recorded delivery service.

(3)   Any notice required to be given under this code may be given to an incorporated company or body by giving it to the secretary or clerk of the company or body.

(4)   For the purposes of this paragraph and of the application in relation to this code of section 7 of the Interpretation Act 1978 (service by post), the proper address of any person shall be—

(a) if the person to whom the notice is to be given has furnished the person giving the notice with an address for service under this code, that address;

(b) in a case not falling within paragraph (a) abovea where the person to whom the notice is to be given is an incorporated company or body, the registered or principal office of the company or body; and

(c) in any other case, the last known address of the person to whom the notice is to be given.

(5) If it is not practicable, for the purposes of giving any notice under this code, after reasonable inquiries to ascertain the name and address—

(a) of the person who is for the purposes of any provision of this code the occupier of any land, or

(b) of the owner of any interest in any land,

a notice may be given under this code by addressing it to a person by the description of 'occupier' of the land (describing it) or, as the case may be, 'owner' of the interest (describing both the interest and the land) and by delivering it to some person on the land or, if there is no person on the land to whom it can be delivered, by affixing it, or a copy of it, to some conspicuous object on the land.

(6) In any proceedings under this code a certificate purporting to be signed by the Director and stating that a particular form of notice has been approved by him as mentioned in sub-paragraph (1) above shall be conclusive evidence of the matter certified.

Appeals in Northern Ireland

25. Article 60 of the County Courts (Northern Ireland) Order 1980 (ordinary appeals from the county court in civil cases) shall apply in relation to any determination of the court in Northern Ireland under this code in like manner as it applies in relation to any decree of the court made in the exercise of the jurisdiction conferred by Part III of that Order.

Application to the Crown

26.—(1) This code shall apply in relation to land in which there subsists, or at any material time subsisted, a Crown interest as it applies in relation to land in which no such interest subsists.

(2) In this paragraph 'Crown interest' means an interest which belongs to Her Majesty in right of the Crown or of the Duchy of Lancaster or to the Duchy of Cornwall or to a Government department or which is held in trust for Her Majesty for the purposes of a Government department and, without prejudice to the foregoing, includes any interest which belongs to Her Majesty's Government in Northern Ireland or to a Northern Ireland department or which is held in trust for Her Majesty for the purposes of a Northern Ireland department.

(3) An agreement required by this code to be given in respect of any Crown interest subsisting in any land shall be given by the appropriate authority, that is to say—

(a) in the case of land belonging to Her Majesty in right of the Crown, the Crown Estate Commissioners or, as the case may require, the government department having the management of the land in question;

(b)   in the case of land belonging to Her Majesty in right of the Duchy of Lancaster, the Chancellor of that Duchy;

(c)   in the case of land belonging to the Duchy of Cornwall, such person as the Duke of Cornwall, or the possessor for the time being of the Duchy of Cornwall, appoints;

(d)   in the case of land belonging to Her Majesty in right of Her Majesty's Government in Northern Ireland, the Northern Ireland department having the management of the land in question;

(e)   in the case of land belonging to a government department or a Northern Ireland department or held in trust for Her Majesty for the purposes of a government department or a Northern Ireland department, that department; and if any question arises as to what authority is the appropriate authority in relation to any land that question shall be referred to the Treasury, whose decision shall be final.

(4)   Paragraphs 12(9) and 18(3) above shall not apply where this code has effect by virtue of section 10(1)(b) of this Act.

Savings for and exclusion of certain remedies etc.

27.—(1)   Except in so far as provision is otherwise made by virtue of section 109(2) or (3) of or Schedule 4 to this Act, this code shall not authorise the contravention of any provision made by or under any enactment passed before this Act.

(2)   The provisions of this code, except paragraphs 8(5) and 21 and sub-paragraph (1) above, shall be without prejudice to any rights or liabilities arising under any agreement to which the operator is a party.

(3)   Except as provided under the preceeding provisions of this code, the operator shall not be liable to compensate any person for, or be subject to any other liability in respect of, any loss or damage caused by the lawful exercise of any right conferred by or in accordance with this code.

(4)   The ownership of any property shall not be affected by the fact that it is installed on or under, or affixed to, any land by any person in exercise of a right conferred by or in accordance with this code.

Application of code to existing systems

28.—(1)   Subject to the following provisions of this paragraph, references in this code to telecommunication apparatus installed on, under or over any land include references to telecommunication apparatus so installed before this code comes into force.

(2)   Without prejudice to sub-paragraph (1) above, any line or other apparatus lawfully installed before this code comes into force which if this code had come into force could have been installed under paragraph 12 of this code shall (subject to sub-paragraph (6) below) be treated for the purposes of this code as if it had been so installed.

(3)   Any consent given (or deemed to have been given) for the purposes of any provision of the Telegraph Acts 1863 to 1916 before this code comes into force shall—

(a)   have effect after this code comes into force as an agreement given for the purposes of this code, and

(b)   so have effect, to any extent that is necessary for ensuring that the same persons are bound under this code as were bound by the consent, as if it were an agreement to confer a right or, as the case may require, to bind any interest in land of the person who gave (or is deemed to have given) the consent.

(4)   Where by virtue of sub-paragraph (3) above any person is bound by any right, that right shall not be exercisable except on the same terms and subject to the same conditions as the right which, by virtue of the giving of the consent, was exercisable before this code comes into force; and where under any enactment repealed by this Act those terms or conditions included a requirement for the payment of compensation or required the determination of any matter by any court or person, the amount of the compensation or, as the case may be, that matter shall be determined after the coming into force of this code in like manner as if this Act had not been passed.

(5)   A person shall not be entitled to compensation under any provision of this code if he is entitled to compensation in respect of the same matter by virtue of sub-paragraph (4) above.

(6)   Neither this code nor the repeal by this Act of any provision of the Telegraph Acts 1863 to 1916 (which contain provision confirming or continuing in force certain agreements) shall prejudice any rights or liabilities (including any rights or liabilities transferred by virtue of section 60 of this Act) which arise at any time under any agreement which was entered into before this code comes into force and relates to the installation, maintenance, adjustment, repair, alteration or inspection of any telecommunication apparatus or to keeping any such apparatus installed on, under or over any land.

(7)   Any person who before the coming into force of this code has—

(a)   given a notice ('the Telegraph Acts notice') under or for the purposes of any provision of the Telegraph Acts 1863 to 1916 to any person, or

(b)   made an application under or for the purposes of any such provision (including, in particular, an application for any matter to be referred to any court or person),

may give a notice to the person to whom the Telegraph Acts notice was given or, as the case may be, to every person who is or may be a party to the proceedings resulting from the application stating that a specified step required to be taken under or for the purposes of this code, being a step equivalent to the giving of the Telegraph Acts notice or the making of the application, and any steps required to be so taken before the taking of that step should be treated as having been so taken.

(8)   A notice may be given under sub-paragraph (7) above with respect to an application notwithstanding that proceedings resulting from the application have been commenced.

(9)   Where a notice has been given to any person under sub-paragraph (7) above, that person may apply to the court for an order setting aside the notice on the ground that it is unreasonable in all the circumstances to treat the giving of the Telegraph Acts notice or the making of the application in question as equivalent to the steps specified in the notice under that sub-paragraph; but unless the court sets aside the notice under that sub-paragraph, the steps specified in the notice shall be treated as having been taken and any proceedings already commenced shall be continued accordingly.

(10) Where before this code comes into force anything has, in connection with the exercise by the operator of any power conferred on him by the Telegraph Acts 1863 to 1916, been done under or for the purposes of the street works code contained in the Public Utilities Street Works Act 1950, that thing shall, in so far as it could have been done in connection with the exercise of any power conferred by this code, have effect under sub-paragraph (7) above, as if it had been done in connection with the power conferred by this code.

(11) In relation to anything done under section 5 of Schedule 3 to the Water Act 1945 or section 5 of Schedule 4 to the Water (Scotland) Act 1980 before the coming into force of this code, the preceding provisions of this paragraph shall have effect, so far as the context permits, as if references to the Telegraph Acts 1863 to 1916 included references to that section.

(12) References in this paragraph to the coming into force of this code shall have effect as references to the time at which the code comes into force in relation to the operator.

INTERCEPTION OF COMMUNICATIONS ACT 1985
(1985, c. 56)

ARRANGEMENT OF SECTIONS

Section

SCHEDULES:

An Act to make new provision for and in connection with the interception of communications sent by post or by means of public telecommunication systems and to amend section 45 of the Telecommunications Act 1984.   [25 July 1985]

Note
See Council Resolution of 17 January 1995 on the lawful interception of telecommunications OJ 96/C 329/01.

1. Prohibition on interception

(1) Subject to the following provisions of this section, a person who intentionally intercepts a communication in the course of its transmission by

post or by means of a public telecommunication system shall be guilty of an offence and liable—

(a) on summary convicion, to a fine not exceeding the statutory maximum;

(b) conviction on indictment, to imprisonment for a term not exceeding two years or to a fine or to both.

(2) A person shall not be guilty of an offence under this section if—

(a) the communication is intercepted in obedience to a warrant issued by the Secretary of State under section 2 below; or

(b) that person has reasonable grounds for believing that the person to whom, or the person by whom, the communication is sent has consented to the interception.

(3) A person shall not be guilty of an offence under this section if—

(a) the communication is intercepted for purposes connected with the provision of postal or public telecommunication services or with the enforcement of any enactment relating to the use of those services; or

(b) the communication is being transmitted by wireless telegraphy and is intercepted, with the authority of the Secretary of State, for purposes connected with the issue of licences under the Wireless Telegraphy Act 1949 or the prevention or detection of interference with wireless telegraphy.

(4) No proceedings in respect of an offence under this section shall be instituted—

(a) in England and Wales, except by or with the consent of the Director of Public Prosecutions;

(b) in Northern Ireland, except by or with the consent of the Director of Public Prosecutions for Northern Ireland.

Note

The background to this Act is considered in *R* v *Preston* [1993] 3 WLR 891, HL. This section does not create an offence triable in the UK in respect of an act committed outside the UK by a non-resident: see *R* v *Governor of Belmarsh Prison, ex parte Martin* [1995] 1 WLR 412; *R* v *Khan (Sultan)* [1996] 3 All ER 289, HL; and *R* v *Ahmed and others* [1995] Crim LR 246, CA.

2. Warrants for interception

(1) Subject to the provisions of this section and section 3 below, the Secretary of State may issue a warrant requiring the person to whom it is addressed to intercept, in the course of their transmission by post or by means of a public telecommunication system, such communications as are described in the warrant; and such a warrant may also require the person to whom it is addressed to disclose the intercepted material to such persons and in such manner as are described in the warrant.

(2) The Secretary of State shall not issue a warrant under this section unless he considers that the warrant is necesary—

(a) in the interests of national security;

(b) for the purpose of preventing or detecting serious crime; or

(c) for the purpose of safeguarding the economic well-being of the United Kingdom.

(3) The matters to be taken into account in considering whether a warrant is necessary as mentioned in subsection (2) above shall include

whether the information which it is considered necessary to acquire could reasonably be acquired by other means.

(4)   A warrant shall not be considered necessary as mentioned in subsection (2)(c) above unless the information which it is considered necessary to acquire is information relating to the acts or intentions of persons outside the British Islands.

(5)   References in the following provisions of this Act to a warrant are references to a warrant under this section.

Note
See *R v Preston and others* [1995] 3 WLR 891, HL for a case where a telephone interception warrant was issued pursuant to s. 2(2)(b).

3.   Scope of warrants

(1)   Subject to subsection (2) below, the interception required by a warrant shall be the interception of—

(a)   such communications as are sent to or from one or more addresses specified in the warrant, being an address or addresses likely to be used for the transmission of communications to or from—

(i)   one particular person specified or described in the warrant; or

(ii)   one particular set of premises so specified or described; and

(b)   such other communications (if any) as it is necessary to intercept in order to intercept communications falling within paragraph (a) above.

(2)   Subsection (1) above shall not apply to a warrant if—

(a)   the interception required by the warrant is the interception, in the course of their transmission by means of a public telecommunication system, of—

(i)   such external communications as are described in the warrant; and

(ii)   such other communications (if any) as it is necessary to intercept in order to intercept such external communications as are so described; and

(b)   at the time when the warrant is issued, the Secretary of State issues a certificate certifying the descriptions of intercepted material the examination of which he considers necessary as mentioned in section 2(2) above.

(3)   A certificate such as is mentioned in subsection (2) above shall not specify an address in the British Islands for the purpose of including communications sent to or from that address in the certified material unless—

(a)   the Secretary of State considers that the examination of communications sent to or from that address is necessary for the purpose of preventing or detecting acts of terrorism; and

(b)   communications sent to or from that address are included in the certified material only in so far as they are sent within such a period, not exceeding three months, as is specified in the certificate.

(4)   A certificate such as is mentioned in subsection (2) above shall not be issued except under the hand of the Secretary of State.

(5)   References in the following provisions of this Act to a certificate are references to a certificate such as is mentioned in subsection (2) above.

4.   Issue and duration of warrants

(1)   A warrant shall not be issued except—

(a)   under the hand of the Secretary of State; or

(b)   in an urgent case where the Secretary of State has expressly authorised its issue and a statement of that fact is endorsed thereon, under the hand of an official of his department of or above the rank of Assistant Under Secretary of State.

(2)   A warrant shall, unless renewed under subsection (3) below, cease to have effect at the end of the relevant period.

(3)   The Secretary of State may, at any time before the end of the relevant period, renew a warrant if he considers that the warrant continues to be necessary as mentioned in section 2(2) above.

(4)   If, at any time before the end of the relevant period, the Secretary of State considers that a warrant is no longer necessary as mentioned in section 2(2) above, he shall cancel the warrant.

(5)   A warrant shall not be renewed except by an instrument under the hand of the Secretary of State.

(6)   In this section 'the relevant period'—

(a)   in relation to a warrant which has not been renewed, means—

(i)   if the warrant was issued under subsection (1)(a) above, the period of two months beginning with the day on which it was issued; and

(ii)   if the warrant was issued under subsection (1)(b) above, the period ending with the second working day following that day;

(b)   in relation to a warrant which was last renewed within the period mentioned in paragraph (a)(ii) above, means the period of two months beginning with the day on which it was so renewed; and

(c)   in relation to a warrant which was last renewed at any other time, means—

(i)   if the instrument by which it was so rendered is endorsed with a statement that the renewal is considered necessary as mentioned in section 2(2)(a) or (c) above, the period of six months beginning with the day on which it was so renewed, and

(ii)   if that instrument is not so endorsed, the period of one month beginning with that day.

5.   Modification of warrants etc.

(1)   The Secretary of State may at any time—

(a)   modify a warrant by the insertion of any address which he considers likely to be used as mentioned in section 3(1)(a) above; or

(b)   modify a certificate so as to include in the certified material any material the examination of which he considers necessary as mentioned in section 2(2) above.

(2)   If at any time the Secretary of State considers that any address specified in a warrant is no longer likely to be used as mentioned in section 3(1)(a) above, he shall modify the warrant by the deletion of that address.

(3)   If at any time the Secretary of State considers that the material certified by a certificate includes any material the examination of which is no longer necessary as mentioned in section 2(2) above, he shall modify the certificate so as to exclude that material from the certified material.

(4)   A warrant or certificate shall not be modified under subsection (1) above except by an instrument under the hand of the Secretary of State or, in an urgent case—

(a)   under the hand of a person holding office under the Crown who is expressly authorised by the warrant or certificate to modify it on the Secretary of State's behalf; or

(b)   where the Secretary of State has expressly authorised the modification and a statement of that fact is endorsed on the instrument, under the hand of such an officer as is mentioned in section 4(1)(b) above.

(5)   An instrument made under subsection (4)(a) or (b) above shall cease to have effect at the end of the fifth working day following the day on which it was issued.

6. Safeguards

(1)   Where the Secretary of State issues a warrant he shall, unless such arrangements have already been made, make such arrangements as he considers necessary for the purposes of securing—

(a)   that the requirements of subsections (2) and (3) below are satisfied in relation to the intercepted material; and

(b)   where a certificate is issued in relation to the warrant, that so much of the intercepted material as is not certified by the certificate is not read, looked at or listened to by any person.

(2)   The requirements of this subsection are satisfied in relation to any intercepted material if each of the following, namely—

(a)   the extent to which the material is disclosed;

(b)   the number of persons to whom any of the material is disclosed;

(c)   the extent to which the material is copied; and

(d)   the number of copies made of any of the material;

is limited to the minimum that is necessary as mentioned in section 2(2) above.

(3)   The requirements of this subsection are satisfied in relation to any intercepted material if each copy made of any of that material is destroyed as soon as its retention is no longer necessary as mentioned in section 2(2) above.

7. The Tribunal

(1)   There shall be a tribunal (in this Act referred to as 'the Tribunal') in relation to which the provisions of Schedule 1 to this Act shall apply.

(2)   Any person who believes that communications sent to or by him have been intercepted in the course of their transmission by post or by means of a public telecommunication system may apply to the Tribunal for an investigation under this section.

(3)   On such an application (other than one appearing to the Tribunal to be frivolous or vexatious), the Tribunal shall investigate—

(a)   whether there is or has been a relevant warrant or a relevant certificate; and

(b)   where there is or has been such a warrant or certificate, whether there has been any contravention of sections 2 to 5 above in relation to that warrant or certificate.

(4)   If, on an investigation, the Tribunal, applying the principles applicable on an application for judicial review, conclude that there has been a

contravention of sections 2 to 5 above in relation to a relevant warrant or a relevant certificate, they shall—

    (a)   give notice to the applicant stating that conclusion;

    (b)   make a report of their findings to the Prime Minister; and

    (c)   if they think fit, make an order under subsection (5) below.

    (5)   An order under this subsection may do one or more of the following, namely—

    (a)   quash the relevant warrant or the relevant certificate;

    (b)   direct the destruction of copies of the intercepted material or, as the case may be, so much of it as is certified by the relevant certificate;

    (c)   direct the Secretary of State to pay to the applicant such sum by way of compensation as may be specified in the order.

    (6)   A notice given or report made under subsection (4) above shall state the effect of any order under subsection (5) above made in the case in question.

    (7)   If, on an investigation, the Tribunal come to any conclusion other than that mentioned in subsection (4) above, they shall give notice to the applicant stating that there has been no contravention of sections 2 to 5 above in relation to a relevant warrant or a relevant certificate.

    (8)   The decisions of the Tribunal (including any decisions as to their jurisdiction) shall not be subject to appeal or liable to be questioned in any court.

    (9)   For the purposes of this section —

    (a)   a warrant is a relevant warrant in relation to an applicant if —

        (i)   the applicant is specified or described in the warrant; or

        (ii)   an address used for the transmission of communications to or from a set of premises in the British Islands where the applicant resides or works is so specified;

    (b)   a certificate is a relevant certificate in relation to an applicant if and to the extent that an address used as mentioned in paragraph (a)(ii) above is specified in the certificate for the purpose of including communications sent to or from that address in the certified material.

Note

An example of a case heard by the Tribunal under this section is *Griffin* v *Interceptions of Communications Tribunal (ICT)*, 6 July 1993, CA (unreported).

8. The Commissioner

    (1)   The Prime Minister shall appoint a person who holds or has held a high judicial office (in this section referred to as 'the Commissioner') to carry out the following functions, namely—

    (a)   to keep under review the carrying out by the Secretary of State of the functions conferred on him by sections 2 to 5 above and the adequacy of any arrangements made for the purposes of section 6 above; and

    (b)   to give to the Tribunal all such assistance as the Tribunal may require for the purpose of enabling them to carry out their functions under this Act.

    (2)   The Commissioner shall hold office in accordance with the terms of

his appointment and there shall be paid to him out of money provided by Parliament such allowances as the Treasury may determine.

(3)   It shall be the duty of every person holding office under the Crown or engaged in the business of the Post Office or in the running of a public telecommunication system to disclose or to give to the Commissioner such documents or information as he may require for the purpose of enabling him to carry out his functions under this section.

(4)   It shall be the duty of the Tribunal to send to the Commissioner a copy of every report made by them under section 7(4) above.

(5)   If at any time it appears to the Commissioner—

(a)   that there has been a contravention of sections 2 to 5 above which has not been the subject of a report made by the Tribunal under section 7(4) above; or

(b)   that any arrangements made for the purposes of section 6 above have proved inadequate,

he shall make a report to the Prime Minister with respect to that contravention or those arrangements.

(6)   As soon as practicable after the end of each calendar year, the Commissioner shall make a report to the Prime Minister with respect to the carrying out of his functions under this section.

(7)   The Prime Minister shall lay before each House of Parliament a copy of every annual report made by the Commissioner under subsection (6) above together with a statement as to whether any matter has been excluded from that copy in pursuance of subsection (8) below.

(8)   If it appears to the Prime Minister, after consultation with the Commissioner, that the publication of any matter in an annual report would be prejudicial to national security, to the prevention or detection of serious crime or to the economic well-being of the United Kingdom, the Prime Minister may exclude that matter from the copy of the report as laid before each House of Parliament.

9.   Exclusion of evidence

(1)   In any proceedings before any court or tribunal no evidence shall be adduced and no question in cross-examination shall be asked which (in either case) tends to suggest—

(a)   that an offence under section 1 above has been or is to be committed by any of the persons mentioned in subsection (2) below; or

(b)   that a warrant has been or is to be issued to any of those persons.

(2)   The persons referred to in subsection (1) above are—

(a)   any person holding office under the Crown;

(b)   the Post Office and any person engaged in the business of the Post Office; and

(c)   any public telecommunications operator and any person engaged in the running of a public telecommunication system.

(3)   Subsection (1) above does not apply—

(a)   in relation to proceedings for a relevant offence or proceedings before the Tribunal; or

(b)   where the evidence is adduced or the question in cross-examination is asked for the purpose of establishing the fairness or unfairness of a dismissal on grounds of an offence under section 1 above or of conduct from which such an offence might be inferred;

and paragraph (a) of that subsection does not apply where a person has been convicted of the offence under that section.

(4)   In this section 'relevant offence' means—

(a)   an offence under section 1 above or under section 45 of the Telegraph Act 1863, section 20 of the Telegraph Act 1868, section 58 of the Post Office Act 1953 or section 45 of the 1984 Act;

(b)   an offence under section 1 . . . of the Official Secrets Act 1911 relating to any sketch, plan, model, article, note, document or information which tends to suggest as mentioned in subsection (1) above;

(bb)   an offence under section 4 of the Official Secrets Act 1989 relating to any such information, document or article as is mentioned in subsection (3)(a) of that section;

(c)   perjury committed in the course of proceedings for a relevant offence;

(d)   attempting or conspiring to commit, or aiding, abetting counselling or procuring the commission of, an offence falling within any of the preceding paragraphs; and

(e)   contempt of court committed in the course of, or in relation to, proceedings for a relevant offence.

Note

The words omitted from s. 9(4)(b) were repealed and s. 9(4)(bb) was inserted by the Official Secrets Act 1989. See *R* v *Effik* [1994] 3 WLR 583, HL.

10.   Interpretation

(1)   In this Act, unless the context otherwise requires—

'the 1984 Act' means the Telecommunications Act 1984;

'address' means any postal or telecommunication address;

'copy'. in relation to intercepted material, means any of the following, whether or not in documentary form—

(a)   any copy, extract or summary of the material; and

(b)   any record of the identities of the persons to or by whom the material was sent,

and cognate expressions shall be construed accordingly;

'external communication' means a communication sent or received outside the British Islands;

'high judicial office' has the same meaning as in the Appellate Jurisdiction Act 1876;

'intercepted material', in relation to a warrant, means the communications intercepted in obedience to the warrant;

'person' includes any organisation and any association or combination of persons;

'public telecommunications operator' and 'public telecommunication system' have the same meanings as in the 1984 Act;

'public telecommunication service' means a telecommunication service provided by means of a public telecommunication system;

. . .

'telecommunication service' has the same meaning as in the 1984 Act;

'the Tribunal' means the tribunal established under section 7 above;

'wireless telegraphy' has the same meaning as in the Wireless Telegraphy Act 1949;

'working day' means any day other than a Saturday, a Sunday, Christmas Day, Good Friday or a day which is a bank holiday under the Banking and Financial Dealings Act 1971 in any part of the United Kingdom.

(2)   For the purposes of this Act a communication which is in the course of its transmission otherwise than by means of a public telecommunication system shall be deemed to be in the course of its transmission by means of such a system if its mode of trnasmission identifies it as a communication which—

(a)   is to be or has been transmitted by means of such a system; and

(b)   has been sent from, or is to be sent to, a country or territory outside the British Islands.

(3)   For the purposes of this Act conduct which constitutes or, if it took place in the United Kingdom, would constitute one or more offences shall be regarded as serious crime if, and only if—

(a)   it involves the use of violence, results in substantial financial gain or is conduct by a large number of persons in pursuit of a common purpose; or

(b)   the offence or one of the offences is an offence for which a person who has attained the age of twenty-one and has no previous convictions could reasonably be expected to be sentenced to imprisonment for a term of three years or more.

Note
The definition 'statutory maximum' was repealed by the SL(R) Act 1993.

11.   Amendments, saving and repeal

(1)   For section 45 of the 1984 Act (interception and disclosure of messages etc) there shall be substituted the section set out in Schedule 2 to this Act.

Note
See the annotated s. 45 of the Telecommunications Act 1984

12.   Short title, commencement and extent

(1)   This Act may be cited as the Interpretation of Communication Act 1985.

(2)   This Act shall come into force on such day as the Secretary of State may by order made by statutory instrument appoint.

(3)   This Act extends to Northern Ireland.

(4)   Her Majesty may by Order in Council direct that any of the provisions of this Act specified in the Order shall extend to the Isle of Man or any of the Channel Islands with such exceptions, adaptations and modifications as may be so specified.

SCHEDULES

SCHEDULE 1

Section 7

THE TRIBUNAL

Constitution of Tribunal

1.—(1)   The Tribunal shall consist of five members each of whom shall be
[(a)   a person who has a 10 year general qualification, within the
meaning of section 71 of the Courts and Legal Services Act 1990;
(b)   an advocate or solicitor in Scotland of at least 10 years' standing;
(c)   a member of the Bar of Northern Ireland or solicitor of the
Supreme Court of Northern Ireland of at least 10 years' standing].
(2)   The members of the Tribunal shall be such persons as Her Majesty
may by Letters Patent appoint and shall, subject to the following sub-
paragraphs, hold office during good behaviour.
(3)   A member of the Tribunal shall vacate office at the end of the period
of five years beginning with the day of his appointment but shall be eligible
for reappointment.
(4)   A member of the Tribunal may be relieved of office by Her Majesty
at his own request.
(5)   A member of the Tribunal may be removed from office by Her
Majesty on an Address presented to Her by both Houses of Parliament.

The President and Vice-President

2.—(1)   Her Majesty may by Letters patent appoint as President or
Vice-President of the Tribunal a person who is, or by virtue of those Letters
will be, a member of the Tribunal.
(2)   If at any time the President of the Tribunal is temporarily unable to
carry out the functions of the President under this Schedule, the Vice-
President shall carry out those functions.
(3)   A person shall cease to be President or Vice-President of the Tribunal
if he ceases to be a member of the Tribunal.

Procedure of Tribunal

3.   The functions of the Tribunal in relation to any application made to
them shall be capable of being carried out, in any place in the United
Kingdom, by any two or more members of the Tribunal designated for the
purpose by their President; and different members of the Tribunal may carry
out functions in relation to different applications at the same time.
4.—(1)   It shall be the duty of every person holding office under the
Crown or engaged in the business of the Post Office or in the running of a
public telecommunications system to disclose or give to the Tribunal such
documents or information as they may require for the purpose of enabling
them to carry out their functions under this Act.

(2)   Subject to paragraph 6(2) below, the Tribunal shall carry out their functions under this Act (except their functions in relation to reports under section 7(4) of this Act) in such a way as to secure that no document or information which is disclosed or given to the Tribunal is disclosed or given to any person (including an applicant to the Tribunal or a person holding office under the Crown) without the consent of the person who disclosed or gave it to the Tribunal; and accordingly the Tribunal shall not, except in reports under section 7(4) of this Act, give reasons for any decision made by them.

(3)   Subject to sub-paragraph (2) above, the Tribunal may determine their own procedure.

Salaries and expenses

5.—(1)   The Secretary of State shall pay to the members of the Tribunal out of money provided by Parliament such remuneration and allowances as he may with the approval of the Treasury determine.

(2)   Such expenses of the Tribunal as the Secretary of State may with the approval of the Treasury determine shall be defrayed by him out of money provided by Parliament.

Officers

6.—(1)   The Secretary of State may, after consultation with the Tribunal and with the approval of the Treasury as to numbers, provide the Tribunal with such officers as he thinks necessary for the proper discharge of their functions.

(2)   The Tribunal may authorise any officer provided under this paragraph to obtain any documents or information on the Tribunal's behalf.

Note
Paragraphs 1(1)(a)–(c) were substituted by the Courts and Legal Services Act 1990.

OUTER SPACE ACT 1986
(1986, c. 38)

ARRANGEMENT OF SECTIONS

Application of Act

Licensing of activities

An Act to confer licensing and other powers on the Secretary of State to secure compliance with the international obligations of the United Kingdom with respect to the launching and operation of space objects and the carrying on of other activities in outer space by persons connected with this country.   [18 July 1986]

Application of Act

1.   Activities to which this Act applies

This Act applies to the following activities whether carried on in the United Kingdom or elsewhee—
   (a)   launching or procuring the launch of a space object;
   (b)   operating a space object;
   (c)   any activity in outer space.

2.   Persons to whom this Act applies

   (1)   This Act applies to United Kingdom nationals, Scottish firms, and bodies incorporated under the law of any part of the United Kingdom.
   (2)   For this purpose 'United Kingdom national' means an individual who is—
   (a)   a British citizen, a British Dependent Territories citizen, a British National (Overseas), or a British Overseas citizen,
   (b)   a person who under the British Nationality Act 1981 is a British subject, or
   (c)   a British protected person within the meaning of that Act.
   (3)   Her Majesty may by Order in Council extend the application of this Act to bodies incorporated under the law of any of the Channel Islands, the Isle of Man or any dependent territory.

Licensing of activities

3.   Prohibition of unlicensed activities

   (1)   A person to whom this Act applies shall not, subject to the following provisions, carry on an activity to which this Act applies except under the authority of a licence granted by the Secretary of State.

(2)   A licence is not required—
  (a)   by a person acting as employee or agent of another; or
  (b)   for activities in respect of which it is certified by Order in Council that arrangements have been made between the United Kingdom and another country to secure compliance with the international obligations of the United Kingdom.
(3)   The Secretary of State may by order except other person or activities from the requirements of a licence if he is satisfied that the requirement is not necessary to secure compliance with the international obligations of the United Kingdom.
(4)   An order shall be made by statutory instrument which shall be subject to annulment in pursuance of a resolution of either House of Parliament.

Note
This section and ss. 4–6 are designed to fulfil certain obligations to 'authorise and supervise' activities in space which arise under the United Nations Treaty on Principles Governing the Activities of States in the Exploration and Use of Outer Space including the Moon and Other Celestial Bodies (1967).

4.   Grant of licence

(1)   The Secretary of State may grant a licence if he thinks fit.
(2)   He shall not grant a licence unless he is satisfied that the activities authorised by the licence—
  (a)   will not jeopardise public health or the safety of persons or property,
  (b)   will be consistent with the international obligations of the United Kingdom, and
  (c)   will not impair the national security of the United Kingdom.
(3)   The Secretary of State may make regulations—
  (a)   prescribing the form and contents of applications for licences and other documents to be filed in connection with applications;
  (b)   regulating the procedure to be followed in connection with applications and authorising the rectification of procedural irregularities;
  (c)   prescribing time limits for doing anything required to be done in connection with an application and providing for the extension of any period so prescribed;
  (d)   requiring the payment to the Secretary of State of such fees as may be prescribed.

Note
Relevant regulations under this section include the Outer Space Act 1986 (Fees) Regulations 1989, SI 1989/1306, as amended by SI 1993/406.

5.   Terms of licence

(1)   A licence shall describe the activities authorised by it and shall be granted for such period, and may be granted subject to such conditions, as the Secretary of State thinks fit.
(2)   A licence may in particular contain conditions—
  (a)   permitting inspection by the Secretary of State of the licensee's facilities, and inspection and testing by him of the licensee's equipment;

(b)   requiring the licensee to provide the Secretary of State as soon as possible with information as to—

(i)   the date and territory or location of launch, and

(ii)   the basic orbital parameters, including nodal period, inclination, apogee and perigee,

and with such other information as the Secretary of State thinks fit concerning the nature, conduct, location and results of the licensee's activities;

(c)   permitting the Secretary of State to inspect and take copies of documents relating to the information required to be given to him;

(d)   requiring the licensee to obtain advance approval from the Secretary of State for any intended deviation from the orbital parameters, and to inform the Secretary of State immediately of any unintended deviation;

(e)   requiring the licensee to conduct his operations in such a way as to—

(i)   prevent the contamination of outer space or adverse changes in the environment of the earth,

(ii)   avoid interference with the activities of others in the peaceful exploration and use of outer space,

(iii) avoid any breach of the United Kingdom's international obligations, and

(iv)   preserve the national security of the United Kingdom;

(f)   requiring the licensee to insure himself against liability incurred in respect of damage or loss suffered by third parties, in the United Kingdom or elsewhere, as a result of the activities authorised by the licence;

(g)   governing the disposal of the payload in outer space on the termination of operations under the licence and requiring the licensee to notify the Secretary of State as soon as practicable of its final disposal; and

(h)   providing for the termination of the licence on a specified event.

6.   Transfer, variation, suspension or termination of licence

(1)   A licence may be transferred with the written consent of the Secretary of State and in such other cases as may be prescribed.

(2)   The Secretary of State may revoke, vary or suspend a licence with the consent of the licensee or where it appears to him—

(a)   that a condition of the licence or any regulation made under this Act has not been complied with, or

(b)   that revocation, variation or suspension of the licence is required in the interests of public health or national security, or to comply with any international obligation of the United Kingdom.

(3)   The suspension, revocation or expiry of a licence does not affect the obligations of the licensee under the conditions of the licence.

Other controls

7.   Register of space objects

(1)   The Secretary of State shall maintain a register of space objects.

(2)   There shall be entered in the register such particulars of such space objects as the Secretary of State considers appropriate to comply with the international obligations of the United Kingdom.

(3)   Any person may inspect a copy of the register on payment of such fee as the Secretary of State may prescribe.

Note
This section fulfils the UK's obligations under the 1974 United Nations Convention on Registration of Objects Launched into Outer Space requiring the keeping of a register of space objects (which replaces a register which has been kept on a voluntary basis) so as to enable the furnishing of certain information to the United Nations Secretary General.

8.   Power to give directions

(1)   If it appears to the Secretary of State that an activity is being carried on by a person to whom this Act applies—
    (a)   in contravention of section 3 (licensing requirment), or
    (b)   in contravention of the conditions of a licence,
he may give such directions to that person as appear to him necessary to secure compliance with the international obligations of the United Kingdom or with the conditions of the licence.
(2)   He may, in particular, give such directions as appear to him necessary to secure the cessation of the activity or the disposal of any space object.
(3)   Compliance with a direction may, without prejudice to other means of enforcement, be enforced on the application of the Secretary of State by injunction or, in Scotland, by interdict or by order under section 91 of the Court of Session Act 1868.

9.   Warrant authorising direct action

(1)   If a justice of the peace is satisfied by information on oath that there are reasonable grounds for believing—
    (a)   that an activity is being carried on by a person to whom this Act applies in contravention of section 3 (licensing requirement) or in contravention of the conditions of a licence, and
    (b)   that a direction under section 8 has not been complied with, or a refusal to comply with such a direction is apprehended, or the case is one of urgency,
he may issue a warrant authorising a named person acting on behalf of the Secretary of State to do anything necessary to secure compliance with the international obligations of the United Kingdom or with the conditions of the licence.
(2)   The warrant shall specify the action so authorised.
(3)   The warrant may authorise entry onto specified premises at any reasonable hour and on production, if so required, of the warrant.
(4)   The powers conferred by the warrant include power to use reasonable force, if necessary, and may be exercised by the named person together with other persons.
(5)   A warrant remains in force for a period of one month from the date of its issue.
(6)   (*Applicable only to Scotland.*)

10. Obligation to indemnify government against claims

(1) A person to whom this Act applies shall indemnify Her Majesty's government in the United Kingdom against any claims brought against the government in respect of damage or loss arising out of activities carried on by him to which this Act applies.

(2) This section does not apply—

(a) to a person acting as employee or agent of another; or

(b) to damage or loss resulting from anything done on the instructions of the Secretary of State.

Note

Under the 1972 United Nations Convention on International Liability for Damage Caused by Space Objects the UK is absolutely liable to pay compensation if an activity for which the UK is internationally responsible causes damage to another State, its nationals or its companies. This section enables the UK to recover any amount the country may have to pay as a result of any activities in outer space to which this Act applies. Licence conditions may be required to ensure that relevant persons have sufficient funds to reimburse the UK Government by way of appropriate liability insurance.

General

11. Regulations

(1) The Secretary of State may make regulations—

(a) prescribing anything required or authorised to be prescribed under this Act, and

(b) generally for carrying this Act into effect.

(2) Regulations under this Act shall be made by statutory instrument which shall be subject to annulment in pursuance of a resolution of either House of Parliament.

12. Offences

(1) A person commits an offence who—

(a) carries on an activity in contravention of section 3 (licensing requirement);

(b) for the purpose of obtaining a licence (for himself or for another) knowingly or recklessly makes a statement which is false in a material particular;

(c) being the holder of a licence, fails to comply with the conditions of the licence;

(d) fails to comply with a direction under section 8;

(e) intentionally obstructs a person in the exercise of powers conferred by a warrant under section 9; or

(f) fails to comply with such of the regulations under this Act as may be prescribed.

(2) A person committing an offence is liable on conviction on indictment to a fine and on summary conviction to a fine not exceeding the statutory maximum.

(3)   Where an offence committed by a body corporate is proved to have been committed with the consent or connivance of, or to be attributable to neglect on the part of, a director, secretary or other similar officer of the body corporate, or a person purporting to act in any such capacity, he as well as the body corporate is guilty of the offence and liable to be proceeded against and punished accordingly.

In this subsection 'director', in relation to a body corporate whose affairs are managed by its members, means a member of the body corporate.

(4)   Proceedings for an offence committed outside the United Kingdom may be taken, and the offence may for incidental purposes be treated as having been committed, in any place in the United Kingdom.

(5)   In proceedings for an offence under paragraph (a), (c), (d) or (f) of subsection (1) it is a defence for the accused to show that he used all due diligence and took all reasonable precautions to avoid the commission of the offence.

(6)   A person other than a person to whom this Act applies is not guilty of an offence under this Act in respect of things done by him outside the United Kingdom, except—

(a)   an offence of aiding, abetting, counselling or procuring, conspiracy or incitement in relation to the commission of an offence under this Act in the United Kingdom; or

(b)   an offence under subsection (3) (liability of directors, officers, &c) in connection with an offence committed by a body corporate which is a person to whom this Act appies.

(7)   Section 2 (person to whom this Act applies) shall not be construed as restricting the persons against whom proceedings for an offence may be brought.

13.   Minor definitions

(1)   In this Act—
'dependent territory' means—
(a)   a colony, or
(b)   a country outside Her Majesty's dominions in which her Majesty has jurisdiction in right of Her Government in the United Kingdom;
'outer space' includes the moon and other celestial bodies; and
'space object' includes the component parts of a space object, its launch vehicle and the component parts of that.

(2)   For the purposes of this Act a person carries on an activity if he causes it to occur or is responsible for its continuing.

14.   Index of defined expressions

The following Table shows provisions defining or otherwise explaining expressions used in this Act (other than provisions defining or explaining an expression used in the same section)—

activities to which this Act applies	section 1
carrying on an activity	section 13(2)

dependent territory	section 13(1)
outer space	section 13(1)
person to whom this Act applies	section 2
prescribed	section 11(1)(a)
space object	section 13(1)

15. Short title, commencement and extent

(1)   This Act may be cited as the Outer Space Act 1986.

(2)   This Act comes into force on such day as the Secretary of State may appoint by order made by statutory instrument.

(3)   The Secretary of State may appoint a later day for the commencement of so much of section 2(2)(a) as refers to the status of a British National (Overseas).

(4)   Activities to which this Act applies begun before the commencement of this Act may be carried on without a licence under section 3 for six months after commencement;

but sections 8 and 9 (directions and action to secure compliance with international obligations) apply to such activities as they apply to activities carried on in contravention of that section.

(5)   This Act extends to England and Wales, Scotland and Northern Ireland.

(6)   Her Majesty may by Order in Council direct that this Act shall apply, subject to such exceptions and modifications as may be specified in the Order, to the Channel Islands, the Isle of Man or any dependent territory.

STATUTORY INSTRUMENTS

THE TELECOMMUNICATIONS (LEASED LINES) REGULATIONS 1993

SI 1993/2330

Made	24th September 1993
Laid before Parliament	29th September 1993
Coming into force	20th October 1993

Note: Where relevant, this SI has been amended by SI 1994/2251.

The Secretary of State, being a Minister designated[a] for the purposes of section 2(2) of the European Communities Act 1972[b] in respect of measures relating to access to public telecommunication systems, in exercise of the powers conferred on him by that section and of all other powers enabling him in that behalf, hereby makes the following Regulations:—

1. Citation and commencement

These Regulations may be cited as the Telecommunications (Leased Lines) Regulations 1993 and shall come into force on 20th October 1993.

2. Interpretation

(1)   In these Regulations—
'the 1972 Act' means the European Communities Act 1972;
'the 1984 Act' means the Telecommunications Act 1984[c]
'the approvals register' means the register of approvals given and designations made under section 22 of the 1984 Act which the Director keeps pursuant to section 23 of that Act;
'BT' means British Telecommunications plc;
'the BT licence' means the licence granted by the Secretary of State under section 7 of the 1984 Act to British Telecommunications on 22nd June 1984 to run the telecommunication systems referred to in Annex A thereof, in relation to which BT became the licensee as the nominated successor company on the transfer date[d];

---

[a] SI 1992/2870 (as amended by SI 1994/2251).
[b] 1972, c. 68.
[c] 1984, c. 12.
[d] The transfer date appointed under s. 60 of 1984, c. 12 was 6 August 1984; SI 1984/876, art. 5.

'the Commission' means the Commission of the European Communities;
'common ordering procedure' means an ordering procedure for the
procurement of intra-Community private circuits which ensure that
there is commonality across the telecommunications organisations in the
information that has to be supplied by the user and the telecommunications organisations, and in the format in which the information is
presented;

'the EEA' means the European Economic Area, and an 'EEA State'
means a State which is a Contracting Party to the EEA Agreement, but

(a)   until the EEA Agreement comes into force in relation to
Liechtenstein—

(i)   the EEA shall not include Liechtenstein; and

(ii)   Liechtenstein shall not be taken to be an EEA State; and

(b)   for the purposes of the definition of 'EEA State', the Aland
Islands (being not part of the EEA) shall not be taken to be part of
Finland,

and in this definition, 'the EEA Agreement' means the Agreement on the
European Economic Area signed at Oporto on 2nd May 1992 as
adjusted by the Protocol signed at Brussels on 17th March 1993;

'The Directive' means Council Directive 92/44/EEC on the application
of open network provision to leased lines[c];

'Hull' means Kingston upon Hull City Council and Kingston Communications (Hull) PLC;

'the Hull licence' means the licence granted by the Secretary of State
under section 7 of the 1984 Act to Hull on 30th November 1987 to run
the telecommunication systems referred to in Annex A thereof;

'Mercury' means Mercury Communications Limited;

'the Mercury licence' means the licence granted by the Secretary of State
under section 7 of the 1984 Act to Mercury on 5th November 1984 to
run the telecommunication systems referred to in Annex A thereof;

'one-stop-ordering' is a system whereby all transactions involving a user,
required for the procurement of private circuits with network termination points in more than one member State, supplied by more than one
telecommunications organisation to a single user, can be completed at
one location between the user and a single telecommunications organisation;

'one-stop-billing' is a system whereby the billing and payment transaction for private circuits with network termination points in more than
one member State supplied by more than one telecommunications
organisation to a single user can be completed at one location between
the user and a single telecommunications organisation;

'private circuit' means a telecommunications facility provided in the
context of the establishment, development and operation of the public
telecommunications network, which provides for transparent transmission capacity between network termination points where both or all
such points are situated within the Community and which does not
include on-demand switching (that is to say, switching functions which
the user can control as part of the private circuit provision); and

---

[c] OJ No. L165, 19.6.92, p. 27.

'users' means end users and service providers, including telecommunications organisations where the latter are engaged in providing services which are or may be provided also by others.

(2)   References in these Regulations to the BT licence, the Hull licence and the Mercury licence are references to such licences as modified from time to time pursuant to sections 12 and 15 of the 1984 Act and regulations made under section 2(2) of the 1972 Act.

(3)   Any word or expression used in these Regulations shall, unless the context otherwise requires, have the same meaning as it has in the 1984 Act.

3.   Effect

(1)   These Regulations shall have effect for the purposes of the implementation of the Directive, and accordingly—

(a)   Schedule 1 shall have effect for the purposes of providing for the presentation of the information required to be published pursuant to Article 3 of the Directive; and

(b)   Schedule 2 shall have effect for the purposes of providing for the definition of a minimum set of private circuits with harmonised technical characteristics which the United Kingdom is required by Article 7 of the Directive to ensure is provided by telecommunications organisations separately or jointly.

(2)   For the purposes of the 1984 Act, the modifications to the conditions of the BT licence, the Hull licence and the Mercury licence made by regulations 4, 5 and 6 below respectively shall have effect as if they were made under section 12 of that Act by the Director.

[Modification of the BT licence is annotated in the licence itself contained in this Handbook. The other modifications relate to the Hull and Mercury licences.]

7.   Functions of the Director and the Secretary of State

(1)   The Director shall—

(a)   from time to time publish in an appropriate manner so as to provide easy access thereto for users information on the licensing and declaration requirements for private circuits in accordance with the presentation given in paragraph D of Schedule 1 to these Regulations; and

(b)   in keeping the approvals register, in causing particulars to be entered in that register regarding the information in respect of the conditions for the attachment of terminal equipment to private circuits, enter that information in accordance with the presentation given in paragraph E of the said Schedule 1.

(2)   The Director shall from time to time by notice published in the London, Edinburgh and Belfast Gazettes provide references to the publication of information in respect of private circuits—

(a)   by—

(i)   BT pursuant to paragraph 16.3B of the conditions of the BT licence;

(ii)   Hull pursuant to paragraph 15.4A of the conditions of the Hull licence; and

(iii)   Mercury pursuant to paragraph 15.3A of the conditions of the Mercury licence;
regarding the information in respect of offerings and technical characteristics, tariffs and supply and usage conditions; and

(b)   by himself—

(i)   regarding the information in respect of licensing and declaration requirements which he is required to publish pursuant to paragraph (1) of this regulation; and

(ii)   in the approvals register, regarding the information in respect of the conditions for the attachment of terminal equipment.

(3)   The Director shall, in relation to any application for consent to the taking of any measure pursuant to paragraph 46A.3(b) of conditions of the BT licence, paragraph 48A.3(b) of the conditions of the Hull licence, or paragraph 1A.2(b) of the conditions of the Mercury licence adopt a procedure providing for a transparent decision-making process in which due respect is given to the rights of the parties, and without prejudice to the generality of the foregoing, the Director shall—

(a)   give both parties the opportunity to state their case; and

(b)   notify to the parties in writing the decision and the reasons therefor within one week of its adoption.

(4)   The Director shall encourage the establishment, in accordance with the procedural and substantive rules of competition in the EEC Treaty and in consultation with BT, Hull and Mercury and with users, of—

(a)   a common ordering procedure for private circuits throughout the Community;

(b)   a one-stop-ordering procedure for private circuits, to be applied where requested by the user; and

(c)   a one-stop-billing procedure for private circuits, to be applied where requested by the user, which envisages that all price elements resulting from the national private circuits and the respective parts of international private circuits provided by the telecommunications organisations involved are identified separately in the bill for the user.

(5)   The Director shall—

(a)   where he approves a cost accounting system pursuant to paragraph 46A.5 of the conditions of the BT licence or paragraph 48A.5 of the conditions of the Hull licence, inform the Secretary of State, who shall thereupon inform the Commission before the system is applied;

(b)   keep available, with an adequate level of detail, information on the cost accounting systems applied by BT and Hull pursuant to the said conditions, and, upon receipt by the Secretary of State of a request from the Commission for this information, he shall submit it to the Secretary of State, who shall thereupon submit it to the Commission.

(6)   The Director shall—

(a)   at least for each calendar year, make available to the Secretary of State statistical reports showing the performance in relation to the supply conditions, in particular (but without prejudice to the generality of the foregoing) with respect to delivery time and repair time, published by BT in accordance with paragraph 16.3B of the conditions of the BT licence, by Hull in accordance with paragraph 15.4A of the conditions of the Hull licence and by Mercury in accordance with paragraph 15.3A of the conditions of the

Mercury licence, and the Secretary of State shall send such reports to the Commission no later than five months after the end of the relevant calendar year; and

(b)   keep available the data on cases where the access to or use of leased lines has been restricted, in particular (but without prejudice to the generality of the foregoing) because of alleged infringements of special or exclusive rights or the prohibition of simple resale of capacity, as well as details of the measures taken, including the reasons therefor, and upon receipt by the Secretary of State of a request from the Commission for this data, he shall submit it to the Secretary of State, who shall thereupon submit it to the Commission.

Patrick McLoughlin
Parliamentary Under-Secretary of State,
24th September 1993   Department of Trade and Industry

Regulations 3(1)(a) and 7(1)

SCHEDULE 1
PRESENTATION OF THE INFORMATION TO BE PROVIDED IN RESPECT OF PRIVATE CIRCUITS

The information in respect of private circuits shall follow the presentation given below—

A.   Technical characteristics

The technical characteristics include the physical and electrical characteristics a well as the detailed technical and performance specifications which apply at the network termination point. Clear reference shall be made to the standards implemented.

B.   Tariffs

The tariffs include the initial connection charges, the periodic rental charges, and other charges. Where tariffs are differentiated, for example, for reasons of different levels of quality of service or the number of private circuits provided to a user (bulk provision), this must be indicated.

C.   Supply conditions

The supply conditions include at least the elements defined below—

(a)   information concerning the ordering procedure;

(b)   the typical delivery period, which is the period, counted from the date when the user has made a firm request for a private circuit, in which 80% of all private circuits of the same type have been put through to the customers. This period will be established on the basis of the actual delivery periods of private circuits during a recent time interval of reasonable duration. The calculation must not include cases where late delivery periods were requested by users. For new types of private circuits a target delivery period shall be published instead of the typical delivery period;

(c)   the contractual period, which includes the period which is in general foreseen for the contract and the minimum contractual period which the user is obliged to accept;

(d)   the typical repair time which is the period, counted from the time when a failure message has been given to the Licensee's responsible unit up to the moment in which 80% of all private circuits of the same type have been re-established and in appropriate cases notified back in operation to the users. For new types of private circuits a target repair time period shall be published instead of the typical repair time. Where different classes of quality of repair are offered for the same type of private circuit, the different typical repair times shall be published; and

(e)   any refund procedure.

D.   Licensing requirements

The information on licensing requirements, licensing procedures and licensing conditions provides a complete overview of all factors which have an impact on the usage conditions set out for private circuits. It shall include the following information, where applicable—

(a)   a clear description of the service categories for which the licensing procedures have to be followed and for which the licensing conditions have to be met by the user of the private circuit or by his customers;

(b)   information on the character of the licensing conditions, and, without prejudice to the generality of the foregoing, in particular whether such licence is a class or general licence which does not require individual registration or authorisation, or whether the licensing conditions require registration or authorisation on an individual basis;

(c)   a clear indication of the duration of the licence, including a review date, where applicable;

(d)   the conditions resulting from the application of the essential requirements in conformity with Article 6 of the Directive;

(e)   other obligations which may be imposed in the licence conditions on the users of private circuits in accordance with Council Directive 90/388/EEC of 28th June 1990 on competition in the markets for telecommunications services[f] as regards packet-switched or circuit-switched data services, requiring the adherence to conditions of permanence, availability or quality of service;

(f)   a clear reference to conditions aiming at the enforcement of the prohibition to provide services for which exclusive or special rights have been maintained in conformity with Community law; and

(g)   a list referring to all documents containing licensing conditions imposed on the users of private circuits when these are using private circuits for the provision of services to others.

E.   Conditions for the attachment of terminal equipment

The information on the attachment conditions includes a complete overview of the requirements which terminal equipment to be attached to the relevant

---

[f] OJ No. L192, 24.7.1990, p. 10. [BT unsuccessfully challenged the implementation of the Directive in the UK: *R v Secretary for Trade and Industry, ex parte British Telecommunications plc* C-302/94 ECJ 12 December 1996.]

leased line has to fulfil in accordance with Council Directive 91/263/EEC of 29th April 1991 on the approximation of the laws of the Member States concerning telecommunications terminal equipment[g].

Regulation 3(1)(b)   SCHEDULE 2

Note: These technical characteristics are not reproduced in this Handbook. The latest version can be found in SI 1994/2251.

EXPLANATORY NOTE
(This note is not part of the Regulations)

Council Directive 92/44/EEC on the application of open network provision to leased lines ('the Leased Lines Directive') harmonises the technical characteristics for leased lines on the public telecommunication network, and provides for certain requirements in relation to access to leased lines and to the availability of information about the conditions of supply of such lines.

These Regulations modify the licences granted under section 7 of the Telecommunications Act 1984 to British Telecommunications plc (regulation 4), Kingston upon Hull City Council and Kingston Communications (Hull) PLC (regulation 5) and Mercury Communications Limited (regulation 6) to insert appropriate new conditions implementing the Leased Lines Directive. The Secretary of State and the Director General of Telecommunications are given appropriate powers and duties as the national regulatory authorities for the purposes of the Leased Lines Directive (regulation 7).

Copies of the relevant licences, and the register of approvals given and designations made under section 22 of the 1984 Act referred to in regulations 2 and 7, may be inspected at the office of Telecommunications, Export House, 50 Ludgate Hill, London EC4M 7JJ. Copies of the TSS specifications and recommendations referred to in Schedule 2 may be obtained from the Director of the Telecommunications Standardisation Bureau, International Telecommunication Union, Place de Nations, CH–1211, Geneva 20, Switzerland.

THE SATELLITE COMMUNICATIONS SERVICES REGULATIONS 1995

SI 1995/1947

Made	24th July 1995
Laid before Parliament	24th July 1995
Coming into force	14th August 1995

The Secretary of State, being a Minister designated[a] for the purposes of section 2(2) of the European Communities Act 1972[b] in respect of measures

---

[g] Council Directive 90/387/EEC on the establishment of the internal market for telecommunications services through the implementation of open network provision (OJ No. L192, 24.7.90, p. 1).

[a] SI 1995/751.

[b] 1972, c. 68.

relating to competition in the markets for satellite communications and telecommunications services other than public voice telephony, mobile and telex services, and satellite communications and telecommunications terminal equipment in exercise of the power conferred by the said section 2(2), and of all other powers enabling him in that behalf, hereby makes the following Regulations:

1. Citation and commencement

(1) These Regulations may be cited as the Satellite Communications services Regulations 1995 and shall come into force on 14th August 1995.

2. Interpretation and effect

(1)   In these Regulations—
'the Act' means the Telecommunications Act 1984[c];
'the Directives' means Commission Directive 94/46/EC[d] amending Directive 88/301/EEC[e] and Directive 90/388/EEC[f] in particular with regard to satellite communications;
'EEA State' means a State, not being a member State[g], which is a Contracting Party to the European Economic Area Agreement;
'licence' means, save in paragraph (3) of this regulation, a licence to run a telecommunications system granted pursuant to section 7 of the Act;
'network termination point' means all physical connections and their technical access specifications which form part of the public telecommunications network and are necessary for access to and efficient communication through that public network;
'public voice telephony' means the commercial provision for the public of the direct transport and switching of speech in real-time between public switched network (or the equivalent in such other State) termination points, enabling any user to use equipment connected to such a network termination point in order to communicate with any other network termination point;
'satellite earth station' means a station for wireless telegraphy established for the purposes of providing uplinks and downlinks between itself and space segment; and
'satellite services' means the provision of satellite communications services or the provision of satellite network services or both; and in this definition—
(a)   'satellite communication services' means any service other than radio or television broadcasting to the public whose provision makes use, wholly or partly, of satellite network services; and

---

[c] 1984, c. 12.
[d] OJ No. L268, 19.10.94, p. 15.
[e] OJ No. L131, 27.5.88, p. 73.
[f] OJ No. L192, 24.7.90, p. 10.
[g] On 1 January 1995, Finland, Sweden and Austria became members of the European Community. Whilst the Aland Islands were not regarded as part of Finland for the purposes of the EEA Agreement, they are part of the European Community for the purposes of these Regulations.

   (b) 'satellite network services' means the establishment and oper-ation of satellite earth station networks; these services consist, as a minimum, in the establishment, by satellite earth stations, of radiocom-munications to space segment ('uplinks'), and in the establishment of radiocommunications between space segment and satellite earth stations ('downlinks').

   (2) Words and expressions used in these Regulations shall, unless the context otherwise requires, have the same meaning as in the Act.

   (3) Nothing in these Regulations shall be taken as dispensing with the requirement for a licence granted under section 1 of the Wireless Telegraphy Act 1949 for the establishment and use of any satellite earth station.

3. Licensees authorised to provide full range of satellite services in traffic between the United Kingdom, and the European Community and European Economic Area

The Schedule hereto shall have effect for the purposes of amending licences specified therein to permit the provision of all satellite services, other than those consisting in public voice telephony, between a network termination point in the United Kingdom and a network termination point in another member State or EEA State, to comply with the requirements of the Directive.

Ian Taylor
Minister for Science and Technology,
Department of Trade and Industry

24th July 1995

SCHEDULE

PART I

LICENCES GRANTED TO PUBLIC TELECOMMUNICATIONS OP-ERATORS

   1. In the licences the titles and dates of grant of which are listed in the table below, there shall be substituted for paragraph 3(e) of the Service Authorisation in Schedule 3 to each such licence the following sub-para-graph—

   'any service consisting in the transmission of Messages to or the recep-tion of Messages from earth orbiting apparatus where such Messages consist in live speech and have been or are to be conveyed both:

      (i) by means of a Public Switched Network in the United Kingdom; and

      (ii) by means of the equivalent of a Public Switched Network in another country or territory;

provided that, in relation to such services provided between a network termination point in the United Kingdom and a network termination point in another member State of the European Community or an EEA State, this sub-paragraph shall have effect as if it provided as follows:

   'any service consisting in public voice telephony involving the trans-mission of Messages to or the reception of Messages from earth orbiting apparatus where such messages have been or are to be conveyed both:

(i)   by means of a Public Switched Network in the United Kingdom; and

(ii)   by means of the equivalent of a Public Switched Network in another member State of the European Community or EEA State,' and in this sub-paragraph—

(aa)   'public voice telephony' means the commercial provision for the public of the direct transport and switching of speech in real-time between public switched network (or the equivalent in such other State) termination points, enabling any user to use equipment connected to such a network termination point in order to communicate with any other network termination point; and

(bb)   'EEA State' means a State, not being a member State of the European Community, which is a Contracting Party to the European Economic Area Agreement.'

TABLE

Title of licence	Date of grant
LICENCE GRANTED BY THE SECRETARY OF STATE FOR TRADE AND INDUSTRY TO CITY OF LONDON TELECOMMUNICATIONS LTD UNDER SECTION 7 OF THE TELECOMMUNICATIONS ACT 1984	30th April 1993
LICENCE GRANTED BY THE SECRETARY OF STATE FOR TRADE AND INDUSTRY TO ENERGIS COMMUNICATIONS LIMITED UNDER SECTION 7 OF THE TELECOMMUNICATIONS ACT 1984	24th May 1993
LICENCE GRANTED BY THE SECRETARY OF STATE FOR TRADE AND INDUSTRY TO SCOTTISH HYDRO-ELECTRIC PLC UNDER SECTION 7 OF THE TELECOMMUNICATIONS ACT 1984	24th May 1993
LICENCE GRANTED BY THE SECRETARY OF STATE FOR TRADE AND INDUSTRY TO MFS COMMUNICATIONS LIMITED UNDER SECTION 7 OF THE TELECOMMUNICATIONS ACT 1984	24th September 1993
LICENCE GRANTED BY THE SECRETARY OF STATE FOR TRADE AND INDUSTRY TO SCOTTISHPOWER TELECOMMUNICATIONS LIMITED UNDER SECTION 7 OF THE TELECOMMUNICATIONS ACT 1984	24th September 1993
LICENCE GRANTED BY THE SECRETARY OF STATE FOR TRADE AND INDUSTRY TO TORCH COMMUNICATIONS LIMITED UNDER SECTION 7 OF THE TELECOMMUNICATIONS ACT 1984	24th September 1993

LICENCE GRANTED BY THE SECRETARY OF STATE FOR TRADE AND INDUSTRY TO NORWEB PLC UNDER SECTION 7 OF THE TELECOMMUNICATIONS ACT 1984	3rd March 1994
LICENCE GRANTED BY THE SECRETARY OF STATE FOR TRADE AND INDUSTRY TO VIDEOTRON CITY AND WESTMINSTER LIMITED UNDER SECTION 7 OF THE TELE-COMMUNICATIONS ACT 1984	3rd March 1994
LICENCE GRANTED BY THE SECRETARY OF STATE FOR TRADE AND INDUSTRY TO SPRINT HOLDING (UK) LIMITED UNDER SECTION 7 OF THE TELECOMMUNICA-TIONS ACT 1984	31st March 1994
LICENCE GRANTED BY THE SECRETARY OF STATE FOR TRADE AND INDUSTRY TO TELSTRA (UK) LIMITED UNDER SECTION 7 OF THE TELECOMMUNICATIONS ACT 1984	31st March 1994
LICENCE GRANTED BY THE SECRETARY OF STATE FOR TRADE AND INDUSTRY TO WORLDCOM INTERNATIONAL, INC UNDER SECTION 7 OF THE TELECOMMUNICA-TIONS ACT 1984	31st March 1994
LICENCE GRANTED BY THE SECRETARY OF STATE FOR TRADE AND INDUSTRY TO RACAL NETWORK SERVICES LIMITED UN-DER SECTION 7 OF THE TELECOMMUNI-CATIONS ACT 1984	2nd September 1994
LICENCE GRANTED BY THE SECRETARY OF STATE FOR TRADE AND INDUSTRY TO AT&T COMMUNICATIONS (UK) LTD UN-DER SECTION 7 OF THE TELECOMMUNI-CATIONS ACT 1984	20th December 1994

PART II

SATELLITE LICENCES GRANTED TO PERSONS OTHER THAN PUBLIC TELECOMMUNICATIONS OPERATORS EXCEPT FOR MAXAT LIMITED, NATIONAL TRANSCOMMUNICATIONS LIMITED, SATELLITE FINANCIAL SERVICES LTD AND TELE-PORT LONDON INTERNATIONAL LTD

2.   In each of the licences the titles and dates of grant of which are listed in the table below, there shall be substituted for paragraph 3(ii) of the Service Authorisation in Schedule 3 to each such licence the following sub-para-graph—

'Messages which consist in live speech and have been or are to be conveyed both:

(i)   by means of a Public Switched Network in the United Kingdom; and

(ii)   by means of the equivalent of a Public Switched Network in another country or territory outside the United Kingdom;
provided that, in relation to services provided between a network termination point in the United Kingdom and a network termination point in another member State of the European Community or an EEA State, this sub-paragraph shall have effect as if it provided as follows:
"Messages which consist in public voice telephony and which have been or are to be conveyed both:
(i)   by means of a Public Switched Network in the United Kingdom; and
(ii)   by means of the equivalent of a Public Switched Network in another member State or EEA State,"
in this sub-paragraph—

(aa)   "public voice telephony" means the commercial provision for the public of the direct transport and switching of speech in real-time between public switched network (or the equivalent in such other State) termination points, enabling any user to use equipment connected to such a network termination point in order to communicate with any other network termination point; and

(bb)   "EEA State" means a State, not being a member State of the European Community, which is a Contracting Party to the European Economic Area Agreement.'.

TABLE

Title of licence	Date of grant
LICENCE GRANTED UNDER SECTION 7 OF THE TELECOMMUNICATIONS ACT 1984 TO PANAMSAT L.P. TO RUN TELECOMMUNICATION SYSTEMS FOR THE PROVISION OF SATELLITE TELECOMMUNICATION SERVICES	19th April 1993
LICENCE GRANTED UNDER SECTION 7 OF THE TELECOMMUNICATIONS ACT 1984 TO E-SAT TELECOMMUNICATIONS LTD TO RUN TELECOMMUNICATION SYSTEMS FOR THE PROVISION OF SATELLITE TELECOMMUNICATION SERVICES	2nd April 1993
LICENCE GRANTED UNDER SECTION 7 OF THE TELECOMMUNICATIONS ACT 1984 TO INCOM (UK) LTD TO RUN TELECOMMUNICATION SYSTEMS FOR THE PROVISION OF SATELLITE TELECOMMUNICATION SERVICES	11th November 1993
LICENCE GRANTED UNDER SECTION 7 OF THE TELECOMMUNICATIONS ACT 1984 TO KINGSTON COMMUNICATIONS (HULL) PLC TO RUN TELECOMMUNICATION SYSTEMS FOR THE PROVISION OF SATELLITE TELECOMMUNICATION SERVICES	26th October 1993

PART III

OTHER LICENCES

3. In the licence entitled 'LICENCE GRANTED UNDER SECTION 7 OF THE TELECOMMUNICATIONS ACT 1984 TO SATELLITE FINANCIAL SERVICES LIMITED TO RUN TELECOMMUNICATION SYSTEMS FOR THE PROVISION OF SATELLITE TELECOMMUNICATION SERVICES' granted on 30th September 1993, there shall be substituted for paragraph 3(b) of the Service Authorisation in Schedule 3 to such licence the following sub-paragraph—
'Messages which have been or are to be conveyed also by both of:
    (i)   a Public Switched Network in the United Kingdom; and
    (ii)   the equivalent of a Public Switched Network in another country or territory outside the United Kingdom;
provided that, in relation to services provided between a network termination point in the United Kingdom and a network termination point in another member State of the European Community or an EEA State, this sub-paragraph shall have effect as if it provided as follows:
"Messages which consist in public voice telephony and which have been or are to be conveyed also by both of:
    (i)   a Public Switched Network in the United Kingdom; and
    (ii)   the equivalent of a Public Switched Network in another member State of the European Community or EEA State,"
and in this sub-paragraph—
    (aa)   "public voice telephony" means the commercial provision for the public of the direct transport and switching of speech in real-time between public switched network (or the equivalent in such other State) termination points, enabling any user to use equipment connected to such a network termination point in order to communicate with any other network termination point; and
    (bb)   "EEA State" means a State, not being a member State of the European Community, which is a Contracting Party to the European Economic Area Agreement.'.
4. In the licence entitled 'LICENCE GRANTED UNDER SECTION 7 OF THE TELECOMMUNICATIONS ACT 1984 TO TELEPORT LONDON INTERNATIONAL LIMITED TO RUN TELECOMMUNICATION SYSTEMS FOR THE PROVISION OF SATELLITE TELECOMMUNICATION SERVICES' granted on 13th January 1995, there shall be substituted for paragraph 3(a)(ii) of the Service Authorisation in Schedule 3 to such licence the following sub-paragraph—
'Messages comprising live speech which have been or are to be conveyed also by both of:
    (i)   a Public Switched Network in the United Kingdom; and
    (ii)   the equivalent of a Public Switched Network in another country or territory outside the United Kingdom;
provided that, in relation to services provided between a network termination point in the United Kingdom and a network termination point in another member State of the European Community or an EEA State, this sub-paragraph shall have effect as if it provided as follows:

"Messages comprising public voice telephony which have been or are to be conveyed also by both of:
    (i)   a Public Switched Network in the United Kingdom; and
    (ii)   the equivalent of a Public Switched Network in another member State of the European Community or EEA State,"
and in this sub-paragraph—
    (aa) "public voice telephony" means the commercial provision for the public of the direct transport and switching of speech in real-time between public switched network (or the equivalent in such other State) termination points, enabling any user to use equipment connected to such a network termination point in order to communicate with any other network termination point; and
    (bb) "EEA State" means a State, not being a member State of the European Community, which is a Contracting Party to the European Economic Area Agreement.'.

5.   In the licence entitled 'LICENCE GRANTED UNDER SECTION 7 OF THE TELECOMMUNICATIONS ACT 1984 TO MAXAT LIMITED TO RUN TELECOMMUNICATION SYSTEMS FOR THE PROVISION OF SATELLITE TELECOMMUNICATION SERVICES' granted on 1st October 1993, there shall be substituted for paragraph 3(b) of the Service Authorisation in Schedule 3 to such licence the following sub-paragraph—
'Messages comprising live speech which have been or are to be conveyed also by both of:
    (i)   a Public Switched Network in the United Kingdom; and
    (ii)   the equivalent of a Public Switched Network in another country or territory outside the United Kingdom;
provided that, in relation to services provided between a network termination point in the United Kingdom and a network termination point in another member State of the European Community or an EEA State, this sub-paragraph shall have effect as if it provided as follows:
"Messages comprising public voice telephony which have been or are to be conveyed also by both of:
    (i)   a Public Switched Network in the United Kingdom; and
    (ii)   the equivalent of a Public Switched Network in another member State of the European Community or EEA State,"
and in this sub-paragraph—
    (aa) "public voice telephony" means the commercial provision for the public of the direct transport and switching of speech in real-time between public switched network (or the equivalent in such other State) termination points, enabling any user to use equipment connected to such a network termination point in order to communicate with any other network termination point; and
    (bb) "EEA State" means a State, not being a member State of the European Community which is a Contracting Party to the European Economic Area Agreement.'.

6.   In the licence entitled 'LICENCE GRANTED TO NATIONAL TRANSCOMMUNICATIONS LIMITED TO RUN TELECOMMUNICATION SYSTEMS UNDER SECTION 7 OF THE TELECOMMUNICATIONS ACT 1984' granted on 30th December 1992, there shall be

substituted for paragraph 3(e) of the Service Authorisation in Schedule 3 to such licence the following sub-paragraph—

'any service consisting in the transmission of Messages to or the reception of Messages from earth orbiting apparatus where such Messages consist in live speech and have been or are to be conveyed both:

(i)   by means of a Public Switched Network in the United Kingdom; and

(ii) by means of the equivalent of a Public Switched Network outside the United Kingdom;

provided that, in relation to such services provided between a network termination point in the United Kingdom and a network termination point in another member State of the European Community or an EEA State, this sub-paragraph shall have effect as if it provided as follows:

"any service consisting in public voice telephony involving the transmission of Messages to or the reception of Messages from earth orbiting apparatus where such messages have been or are to be conveyed both:

(i)   by means of a Public Switched Network in the United Kingdom; and

(ii) by means of the equivalent of a Public Switched Network in another member State of the European Community or EEA State,"

and in this sub-paragraph—

(aa) "public voice telephony" means the commercial provision for the public of the direct transport and switching of speech in real-time between public switched network (or the equivalent in such other State) termination points, enabling any user to use equipment connected to such a network termination point in order to communicate with any other network termination point; and

(bb) "EEA State" means a State, not being a member State of the European Community, which is a Contracting Party to the European Economic Area Agreement.'.

EXPLANATORY NOTE

(This note is not part of the Regulations)

These Regulations implement Commission Directive 94/46/EC which provides for the removal of special and exclusive rights in respect of fixed satellite communication services, other than public voice telephony, between the United Kingdom and other member States and members of the EEA and of the market for satellite earth station equipment by amending Directives 88/301/EEC and 90/388/EEC. There are no special or exclusive rights in respect of satellite earth station equipment in the United Kingdom. The obligations in respect of satellite communication services are given effect to by detailed amendment of the service authorisations in each of the individual licences granted under the Telecommunications Act 1984 and authorising the provision of telecommunication services by means of satellites, so as to authorise the provision of all telecommunication services, other than public voice telephony and mobile services, by means of satellites between a network termination point in the United Kingdom and another such point elsewhere in the European Community or the EEA.

LICENCES

LICENCE GRANTED BY THE SECRETARY OF STATE FOR TRADE AND INDUSTRY TO BRITISH TELECOMMUNICATIONS UNDER SECTION 7 OF THE TELECOMMUNICATIONS ACT 1984

TABLE OF CONTENTS

Note

This licence incorporates the amendments made by the Director General of Telecommunications up to 1 October 1996 and the Telecommunications (Leased Lines)
Regulations 1993, SI 1993/2330 made 24 September 1993 as amended by SI
1994/2251 (the Leased Lines Regulations).

LICENCE GRANTED TO BRITISH TELECOMMUNICATIONS TO RUN TELECOMMUNICATION SYSTEMS UNDER SECTION 7 OF THE TELECOMMUNICATIONS ACT 1984

THE LICENCE

1.   The Secretary of State, in exercise of the powers conferred on him by
section 7 of the Telecommunications Act 1984 (hereinafter referred to as 'the
Act') and of all other powers exercisable by him for that purpose, hereby
grants to British Telecommunications (hereinafter referred to as 'the Licensee') a licence, for the period specified in paragraph 3, subject to the
Conditions set out in Schedule 1 and to revocation as provided for in
paragraph 3 and in Schedule 2, to run the telecommunication systems
specified in Annex A (hereinafter referred to as 'the Applicable Systems') and
authorises the Licensee to do all or any of the acts specified in Schedule 3.

2.   The telecommunications code contained in Schedule 2 to the Act shall
apply to British Telecommunications for all purposes except those not
relating to the Applicable Systems and subject to the other exceptions and
Conditions set out in Schedule 4 for so long as this Licence is one to which
section 8 of the Act applies.

3.   This Licence shall enter into force on the day appointed under section 2
of the Act for the purposes of Part II of the Act and shall be of 25 years
duration in the first instance but, without prejudice to Schedule 2 to this
Licence, shall be subject to revocation thereafter on ten years notice in writing
of such revocation and such notice shall accordingly not be given before the
end of the fifteenth year after the granting of this Licence.

RT Hon Norman Tebbit MP
Secretary of State for Trade and Industry
22 June 1984

Note
The Licence came into force on 5 August 1984 and has been subject to a number of Licence Amendments since that date which are fully annotated in the text so that the version in this Handbook is up-to-date at the date of publication. These Licence Amendments are identified by date of implementation and are listed below with a brief description of the areas of modification concerned:

23 March 1987	payment of fees
1 May 1987	alteration to the applicable systems, number arrangements in respect of relevant services
2 June 1987	priority fault repair services in favour of disadvantaged groups
23 April 1987	restrictions on prices for certain services
23 April 1989	restrictions on prices for certain services
27 July 1989	controlled services; provision of special facilities
24 November 1989	restrictions on prices
24 September 1991	directory information; interconnection; equal access; essential interfaces; service providers; price notifications; differential charging; price control; billing; number arrangements; private circuits; financial statements — the start of transparency provisions
9 March 1993	public call box services; interconnection; price notifications; interconnect agreements; differential charging; access charges; bases and publication of accounts; control of general prices; charges for the installation of certain exchange lines; provision of relay service for textphone — continuation of transparency provisions
14 December 1993	control of private circuit prices
15 September 1994	control of general prices
31 March 1995	connection of systems providing connection services; publication of charges, terms and conditions to be applied; prohibition on undue preference and undue discrimination — quality of service; separate accounts; further provisions relating to general prices; confidential information — introduction of accounts separation and the basis for establishing costs
2 November 1995	separate accounts
13 February 1996	connection of systems providing connection services; standard services; control of general prices; treatment of certain packages and standard prices for price control purposes; residential low user scheme — abolition of Access Deficit Contribution — start of deregulation
29 July 1996	number portability introduced
1 October 1996	price control provisions; fair trading — special powers given to DGT to deal with anti-competitive behaviour

SCHEDULE 1   CONDITIONS INCLUDED UNDER SECTION 7 OF THE ACT

PART 1   DEFINITIONS, INTERPRETATIONS AND TRANSITIONAL PROVISIONS RELATING TO THE CONDITIONS IN SCHEDULE 1

1   In these Conditions unless the context otherwise requires:

(a) 'Apparatus Production Company' has the meaning given to it in Condition 21;

(*b*) 'Apparatus Supply Business' has the meaning given to it in Condition 18;

(*c*) 'Authorised Overseas System' means any telecommunication system outside the United Kingdom which is authorised to be connected to the Applicable Systems under Schedule 3;

(*d*) 'Bringing into Service' means the process of connecting by means requiring the use of a tool telecommunication apparatus (including apparatus comprised in a telecommunication system) or a telecommunication system to another telecommunication system, or the process of disconnecting by such means such apparatus or such system from another such system; and includes such testing or inspection of that apparatus or system and any other apparatus or system to which it is or is to be connected as is necessary for the purpose of ensuring that the apparatus or the system in which it is or is to be comprised, or the system, is authorised to be connected to any of the Applicable Systems; and expressions cognate with 'Bringing into Service' shall be construed accordingly;

(*e*) 'Call Box Services' and 'Public Call Box' have the meanings given to them in Condition 11;

(*f*) 'Connectable System' and 'Connection Service' have the meanings given to them in Condition 13;

(*g*) 'cost' includes a reasonable profit;

(*h*) 'to dial' includes any equivalent operation;

(*i*) 'Emergency' means an emergency of any kind including any circumstance whatever resulting from major accidents, natural disasters and incidents involving toxic or radio-active materials;

(*j*) 'Emergency Organisations' has the meaning given to it in Condition 6;

(*k*) 'Exchange Line' means telecommunication apparatus (within the meaning of Schedule 2 to the Act) comprised in the Applicable Systems and installed for the purpose of connecting a telephone exchange run by the Licensee to a Network Termination Point comprised in Network Termination and Testing Apparatus installed by the Licensee on premises within the Licensed Area for the purpose of providing voice telephony services at those premises;

(*l*) 'International Connection Service' means a telecommunication service consisting in the conveyance of any Message which has been conveyed or which is to be conveyed by means of any telecommunication system outside the United Kingdom the connection of which to the system by means of which that service is provided is authorised by a Licence;

(*m*) 'Licence' means a licence granted or having effect as if granted under section 7 of the Act;

(*n*) 'Licensed Area' means the United Kingdom other than the area in which the City of Kingston upon Hull is licensed to run telecommunication systems under a Licence coming into force on the date on which this Licence enters into force;

(*o*) 'Licensee's Group' means the Licensee and all of its Subsidiaries taken together;

(*p*) 'Limited Maintenance Telecommunication System' and 'Limited Maintenance Telecommunication Apparatus' mean any telecommunication system or telecommunication apparatus as the case may be which is, or is to be, run under a Licence which requires Maintenance Services to be provided in respect of it, if it is, or is to be, connected to any of the Applicable Systems, by either the Licensee or the person running any other public telecommunication system to which it is, or is to be, connected;

(q) 'Local Authority' has the same meaning as in section 97 of the Act;

(r) 'Maintenance Services' means in relation to any apparatus which has been installed:

(a) Pre-Maintenance Inspection;

(b) carrying out repairs;

(c) verifying or ensuring that:

(i) the apparatus performs in accordance with its specification or as may be required by the operator of the Connectable System in which such apparatus is incorporated;

(ii) the apparatus continues to comply with any condition contained in an approval of that apparatus under section 22 of the Act or in the designation of a standard under that section;

(iii) any terms or conditions regarding the apparatus or its connection or use that may be stipulated by the Licensee and which must be observed if the Connectable System is or is to remain connected to the Applicable Systems are observed;

(d) any activity involving the removal of the outer cover of the apparatus or alteration of the apparatus including alterations of any stored commands capable of affecting the compliance of the apparatus with the technical requirements and conditions mentioned in (c) above; or

(e) any activity involving the use of any test apparatus or other equipment not forming a permanent part of the apparatus;
but shall not include operations incidental to the installation, Bringing into Service or routine use of the apparatus to convey Messages;

(s) 'Message' means anything falling within paragraphs (a) to (d) of section 4 (1) of the Act;

(t) 'Network Connecting Apparatus', 'Network Termination Point' and 'Network Termination and Testing Apparatus' have the meanings given to them in Annex A;

(u) 'Operator' has the meaning given to it in Condition 13;

(v) 'Pre-Maintenance Inspection' means any inspection reasonably necessary to ensure that apparatus has been properly installed in a manner rendering it fit to be maintained by the person making the inspection, but does not include any inspection for the purpose of Bringing into Service;

(w) 'Private Circuit' means a circuit which is:

(a) provided by means of a telecommunication system comprised in the Applicable Systems;

(b) made available to a particular person or particular persons for the conveyance of Messages between fixed points within that system; and

(c) installed in such a way that persons sending Messages by means of that circuit are not able to select the destination within that system to which Messages are conveyed;

[and a 'Relevant Private Circuit' means a Private Circuit, not being a Private Circuit provided by the Licensee for another public telecommunications operator, where:

(i) at least one Network Termination Point of which is located within the United Kingdom and all the network termination points of that circuit, and of any half circuit to which it is connected, are located within the European Economic Community; and

      (ii)   the agreement between the Licensee and the user to provide the Private Circuit does not provide for messages to be conveyed thereby to be routed via a satellite link (notwithstanding that they may be so conveyed);]

    (x) 'Public Emergency Call Service' has the meaning given to it in Condition 6;

    (y) 'Relevant Connectable System' has the meaning given to it in Condition 13;

    (yA) 'Relevant Service' means any service which is provided in whole or in part by means of any of the Applicable Systems and which could have been provided on 30 April 1987 under and in accordance with the Class Licence for the running of telecommunication systems providing value added and data services granted by the Secretary of State on 30 April 1987 in whole or in part by means of a telecommunication system the running of which was authorised by that Licence;

    (z) 'Relevant Terminal Apparatus' has the meaning given to it in Annex A;

    (aa) 'Served Premises' has the meaning given to it in Annex A;

    (bb) 'Subsidiary' has the same meaning as in section 154 of the Companies Act 1948;

    (bbA) 'Supplemental Services Business' has the meaning given to it in Condition 18;

    (cc) 'Systems Business' has the meaning given to it in Condition 18;

    (dd) 'Telephone' means an item of telecommunication apparatus capable when connected to the Licensee's public switched telephone network of transmitting and receiving uninterrupted simultaneous two way speech conveyed, or as the case may be to be conveyed, by means of that network;

    (ee) 'United Kingdom' includes any area to which the provisions of the Act apply by virtue of section 107;

    [(eeA) 'users' means end users and service providers, including telecommunications organisations where the latter are engaged in providing services which are or may be provided also by others;]

    (ff) 'Wholly Owned Subsidiary' means a body corporate all the issued shares in which are held by or on behalf of the Licensee.

2   The Interpretation Act 1978 shall apply for the purpose of interpreting these Conditions as if they were an Act of Parliament.

3   Any word or expression used in these Conditions shall unless the context otherwise requires have the same meaning as it has in the Act.

4   For the avoidance of doubt it is hereby declared that for the purposes of these Conditions references to the supply of telecommunication apparatus do not include the making available of apparatus comprised or to be comprised in any of the Applicable Systems.

5   For the purposes of interpreting these Conditions headings and titles to any Condition shall be disregarded.

6   Nothing which the Licensee may do, or omit to do, after the date on which any provision of these Conditions enters into force shall be held to constitute a failure to comply with an obligation imposed on the Licensee by or under these Conditions to the extent that the Licensee is obliged to do or to omit to do (as the case may be) that thing by the terms of any contract subsisting immediately before that date; but any contract which takes effect

as from the appointed day by virtue of paragraph 12 of Schedule 5 to the Act shall not be treated for the purposes of these Conditions as a contract subsisting immediately before the date on which these Conditions enter into force.

7   Without prejudice to the generality of paragraph 6 above, nothing which the Licensee may do, or omit to do after 1 May 1987 shall be held to constitute a failure to comply with an obligation imposed on the Licensee by virtue of any of the amendments made to these Conditions on that date to the extent that the Licensee is obliged to do or to omit to do (as the case may be) that thing by the terms of any contract subsisting immediately before 14 November 1986.

8   Any reference in any of these Conditions, however expressed, to the Director notifying the Licensee of any matter, consulting the Licensee about any matter, affording the Licensee an opportunity to make representations, taking representations made by the Licensee into account, or explaining, or giving reasons for, any matter to the Licensee, shall be without prejudice to any obligation of due process or similar obligation which the Director is or may be under by virtue of any rule or principle of law or otherwise.

Notes
1.   The words in square brackets were added by the Leased Lines Regulations.
2.   Paragraphs (yA) (bbA) and 7 were inserted by licence amendments dated 1 May 1987.
3.   Paragraph 8 was inserted by a licence amendment dated 24 September 1991.

SCHEDULE 1

PART 2: SPECIAL CONDITIONS REFERRED TO IN SECTION 8 OF THE ACT

Condition 1   Universal Provision of Telecommunication Services

1.1   The Licensee shall provide to every person who requests the provision of such services at any place in the Licensed Area:
   (*a*)   voice telephony services; and
   (*b*)   other telecommunication services consisting in the conveyance of Messages;
by means of the Applicable Systems, except to the extent that the Director is satisfied that any reasonable demand is or is to be met by other means and that accordingly it would not be reasonable in the circumstances to require the licensee to provide the services requested; and the Licensee shall ensure that Applicable Systems are installed, kept installed and run for those purposes.

Notes
1.   In the PanAmSat determination on 22 March 1988 the Director General was called upon to interpret and apply Condition 1 for the first time. The would-be independent satellite operator claimed that BT was in breach of its licence Conditions 1, 5, 17 and 35 in refusing to agree to provide service linking customers in the UK to PanAmSat's satellite. The Director General gave his view that 'reasonable demand is primarily demonstrated in the market: reasonable demand exists if one or more customers will pay a fair price for the service'. The Director General concluded that BT had not breached its licence and so the determination is not on public record.

2. See OFTEL consultative document 'Universal Telecommunication Services' for proposed arrangements for universal service in the UK from 1997, dated February 1997.

Condition 2   Provision of Telecommunication Services in Rural Areas

2.1   The Licensee shall provide to every person who requests the provision of such services in a rural area within the Licensed Area:
   (*a*)   voice telephony services; and
   (*b*)   other telecommunication services consisting in the conveyance of Messages;
by means of the Applicable Systems, except to the extent that the Director is satisfied that any reasonable demand is or is to be met by other means and that accordingly it would not be reasonable in the circumstances to require the Licensee to provide the services requested; and the Licensee shall ensure Applicable Systems are installed, kept installed and run for those purposes.

Note
Other social obligations are provided for the blind (Condition 3.5 directory information), for the disabled (Condition 3.11 telecommunications apparatus) and for those with hearing impairments (Conditions 32.1 and 33 special telephones and apparatus in public call boxes).

Condition 3   Directory Information

3.1   The Licensee shall:
   (*a*)   on request by any person in the United Kingdom (other than a public telecommunications operator) to whom it provides voice telephony services by means of any of the switched Applicable Systems, provide to that person by means of any such System used to provide such services to that person a directory information service relating to the switched voice telephony services it provides to any other person by means of either the same Applicable System or any other Applicable System to which it is connected and which is a switched voice telephony system; and
   (*b*)   on the written request of any person in the United Kingdom supply to that person such directories as the Licensee, for the purpose of facilitating the use by others of any switched telecommunication service it provides by means of any of the Applicable Systems, publishes and makes available generally to persons to whom it provides those services.
3.2   Where the Licensee provides switched voice telephony services by means of any Applicable System which is connected to another public telecommunication system in the United Kingdom (the 'Other System') by means of which switched voice telephony services are provided it shall:
   (*a*)   to the extent that the operator of the Other System makes available directory information to the Licensee and to those to whom that other operator provides voice telephony services, ensure that those to whom the Licensee provides voice telephony services can obtain by using the Applicable System by means of which those services are provided (whether together with some other system or not) such directory information as is so available about

persons to whom such services are provided by means of that Other System; and

(b) supply to the operator of that Other System, whether by providing on-line access to the Licensee's electronic database referred to in paragraph 3.2 (c) or by providing directories of the kind referred to in paragraph 3.1 (b) or by providing the totality of the contents of that database in machine readable form, directory information about persons to whom the Licensee provides switched voice telephony services and do so for the purpose of enabling that operator to provide directory information about such services provided by means of the Applicable Systems and that Other System when connected together and to route calls, and do so in a form which is sufficient to meet any reasonable request of that operator for those purposes having regard in particular to the cost to, and the reasonable convenience of, the Licensee and that operator and to the desirability of that operator being able to use complete and up to date directory information; and

(c) where the operator of that Other System requests the Licensee pursuant to and in accordance with paragraph 3.2 (b) to provide access including on-line access or including the provision of an appropriate storage medium containing the data in machine readable form, to all the names, addresses and telephone numbers on the electronic database which is used by the Licensee to provide by means of the Applicable Systems directory information services to persons to whom the Licensee provides switched voice telephony services then the Licensee shall grant such access on reasonable terms (which may include recovery of fully allocated costs and a reasonable return on capital employed) provided that:

(i) the operator of that Other System undertakes to use the directory information only for the purpose of providing directory information services or to route calls;

(ii) the Licensee may lawfully provide such information to the operator of the Other System; and

(iii) the Licensee shall not be required to do anything in contravention of the Data Protection Act 1984.

3.3 Where the Licensee provides switched voice telephony services by means of any of the Applicable Systems which is connected to an Authorised Overseas System by means of which such services are provided, then, if a directory information service is provided by means of that Authorised Overseas System in respect of that Authorised Overseas System, the Licensee shall provide to any person to whom it provides switched voice telephony services by means of that Applicable System information as to how that person may avail himself by means of that Applicable System and that Authorised Overseas System when connected together of the directory information service provided in respect of that Authorised Overseas System and shall take all reasonable steps to secure that that can be done.

3.4 Where the Licensee provides switched voice telephony services by means of any of the Applicable Systems which is connected to both:

(a) an Authorised Overseas System by means of which such services are provided; and

(b) a Connectable System in the United Kingdom by means of which such services are provided which is run under a Licence which does not authorise the connection of that system to a system outside the United

Kingdom so as to convey Messages from the United Kingdom to a place outside the United Kingdom;

it shall not unreasonably refuse to provide to the operator of that Connectable System access to such directory information services relating to the Authorised Overseas System as the Licensee makes available to those to whom it provides voice telephony services.

3.5   The directory information service provided by the Licensee under Condition 3.1 (a) and 3.3 and the information made available under Condition 3.2 (a) shall include a service or information as the case may be satisfactory to the Director whereby directory information is made available in a form which is appropriate to meet their needs to persons in the Licensed Area who are so blind or otherwise disabled as to be unable to use a telephone directory in a form in which it is generally available to persons to whom the Licensee provides services; and the service so provided to such persons shall from the date on which this Licence enters into force be provided free of charge or, if the Director is satisfied that that is not practicable, the Licensee shall provide, in accordance with arrangements agreed with the Director, appropriate reasonable compensation in respect of charges that are paid.

3.6   The obligations in Conditions 3.1, 3.2 (a) and 3.3 shall not apply when the directory information requested relates to a person who has requested the Licensee or the operator of the connected telecommunication system not to provide such information in relation to him.

3.7   This Condition operates without prejudice to Condition 13.

Notes

1. Condition 3.2(b) was deleted and replaced by a licence amendment dated 24 September 1991. Condition 3.2(c) was inserted by the same licence amendment.

2. Condition 3.6 was amended by the same licence amendment.

3. See OFTEL's consultative document 'Use of Directory Information' October 1995.

Condition 4   Maintenance Services

4.1   If so required by any person to whom it provides telecommunication services in accordance with Condition 1 or 2, the Licensee shall also provide Maintenance Services in respect of any telecommunication system or telecommunication apparatus in that person's control which is or is to be lawfully connected to any of the Applicable Systems, except:

(*a*) where the Licensee has notified that person that the system or apparatus is beyond economic repair or the components or tools necessary to effect the repair are no longer available and the Director has not determined to the contrary;

(*b*) where the system or apparatus has been supplied by a person who is not a member of the Licensee's Group and is neither a Limited Maintenance Telecommunication System nor Limited Maintenance Telecommunication Apparatus; or

(*c*) where the approval under section 22 of the Act of the apparatus for connection to any of the Applicable Systems or to any system which is itself connected to or to be connected to any of the Applicable Systems does not require it to be maintained, while it is so connected, by either the Licensee or the person running any other public telecommunication system to which it is or is to be connected.

Note
Also see priority fault repairs for emergency services (Condition 10) and publication of charges and other terms and conditions of maintenance services (Condition 44).

Condition 5   International Services

5.1   The Licensee shall take all reasonable steps to provide by means of the Applicable Systems to any person to whom it provides telecommunication services by means of those Systems and who so requests International Connection Services to the extent necessary to satisfy all reasonable demands for such Services by such a person.

Note
Also see Conditions 47 and 48 in relation to International Services.

Condition 6   Public Emergency Call Services

6.1   The Licensee shall provide a Public Emergency Call Service, that is to say a telecommunication service by means of which any member of the public may, at any time and without incurring any charge, by means of any item of telecommunication apparatus which is lawfully connected to any of the Applicable Systems at any place in the Licensed Area and which is capable of transmitting and receiving unrestricted two way voice telephony services, communicate as swiftly as practicable with any of the Emergency Organisations for the purpose of notifying them of an Emergency.

6.2   For the purposes of this Condition:

(a)   'Emergency Organisations' means in respect of any locality:

(i)   the relevant public police, fire, ambulance and coastguard services for that locality; and

(ii)   any other similar organisation providing assistance to the public in Emergencies in respect of which the Licensee is providing a Public Emergency Call Service on the day on which this Licence enters into force;

(b)   telecommunication apparatus shall only be regarded as capable of transmitting and receiving unrestricted two way voice telephony services if it is capable of both:

(i)   transmitting for conveyance by means of an Applicable System specific signals designated by the Licensee for the purpose of establishing communication with voice telephony apparatus controlled by the Emergency Organisations; and

(ii)   transmitting and receiving uninterrupted simultaneous two way speech conveyed, or as the case may be to be conveyed, by means of that Applicable System.

6.3   The Licensee may restrict the telecommunication services provided under this Condition in respect of any of the Emergency Organisations mentioned in paragraph 6.2(a)(ii) to the extent to which such restriction is agreed by the authority responsible for that Organisation or, in the absence of such agreement, to such extent as may be authorised by the Director.

6.4   In this Condition, the 'Licensed Area' does not include any area to which the Act is extended under section 107.

Note

This Condition was deleted on 31 December 1996 when new Condition 18A came into effect.

Condition 7   Calls Made by Emergency Organisations

7.1   The Licensee shall, for the purpose of facilitating the provision of services by Emergency Organisations in circumstances where telephone numbers cannot be dialled direct, provide operator-assisted voice telephony services with a view to enabling officials of any authority designated by the Secretary of State for the purposes of this Condition to send messages for conveyance by means of any of the Applicable Systems to any Network Termination Point for switched voice telephony within the Applicable Systems either:

(*a*)   with the least possible delay if such officials send specific signals designated by the Licensee for the purpose and proffer evidence of identity sufficient to establish to the Licensee's satisfaction that they are such officials; or

(*b*)   with priority over all communications except emergency calls and those covered by (a) above if such persons send specific signals designated by the Licensee for the purpose and proffer such evidence of identity.

Condition 8   Maritime Emergency Services

8.1   The Licensee shall enter into an agreement with the Secretary of State for the provision of distress, urgency and safety services for shipping in accordance with the Radio Regulations of the International Telecommunication Union to the extent that the Secretary of State pays the costs of such services, except costs which the Director determines to be unjustifiable.

Condition 9   Planning and Implementation of Special Arrangements for Emergencies:

9.1   The Licensee shall, after consultation with the authorities responsible for Emergency Organisations and such departments of central and local government as the Director may from time to time determine and whose names are notified to the Licensee by him for the purpose, make plans or other arrangements for the provision or, as the case may be, the rapid restoration of such telecommunication services as are practicable and may reasonably be required in Emergencies.

9.2   The Licensee shall, on request by any such person as is designated for the purpose in the relevant plans or arrangements, implement those plans or arrangements insofar as it is reasonable and practicable to do so.

9.3   Nothing in this Condition precludes the Licensee from:

(*a*) ₁ recovering the costs which it incurs in making or implementing any such plans or arrangements from those on behalf of or in consultation with whom the plans or arrangements are made; or

(*b*)   making implementation of any plan or arrangement conditional upon the person or persons for whom or on whose behalf that plan or arrangement is to be implemented indemnifying the Licensee for all costs incurred as a consequence of the implementation.

Condition 10   Priority Fault Repair Service

10.1   Without prejudice to any other obligation under these Conditions the Licensee shall, when notified of any fault or failure of any of the Applicable Systems or of a Relevant System which causes any interruption, suspension or restriction of the telecommunication services provided by means of that Applicable System or that Relevant System, provide:

(*a*)   to any person described in paragraph 10.2;

(*b*)   to any person described in paragraph 10.3; and

(*c*)   in respect of any Exchange Line or Private Circuit described in paragraph 10.3;

a priority Fault Repair Service with a view to restoring those services as swiftly as practicable and with priority so far as is reasonably practicable over Fault Repair Services provided by the Licensee to other persons.

10.2   The persons to whom paragraph 10.1 (a) applies are those:

(*a*)   who are engaged in the provision of an emergency service to the public, the provision of any essential services, the supply of any essential goods or in public administration; and

(*b*)   (i)   (A)   whom the Licensee reasonably believes are within any class or description included in a list prepared by the Director in consultation with the Licensee and notified to the Licensee by the Director; and

(B)   who apply, or on behalf of whom an application is made, to the Licensee for priority Fault Repair Service; or

(ii)   whose names and other particulars are notified to the Licensee by the Director; and

(*c*)   who pay the Licensee's charges for the priority Fault Repair Service or in respect of whom those charges are paid; and

(*d*)   who have a bona fide need for an urgent repair.

10.3   Subject to paragraph 10.4, the persons to whom paragraph 10.1(b) applies and the Exchange Lines or Private Circuits to which paragraph 10.1(c) applies, are those:

(*a*)   whom or which the Licensee reasonably believes are within any class or description contained in a determination made and notified to the Licensee by the Director; and

(*b*)   who apply, or in respect of whom or which an application is made, for priority Fault Repair Service; and

(*c*)   who pay, or in respect of whom or which are paid, the Licensee's charges for the priority Fault Repair Service; and

(*d*)   who have or in respect of which there is a bona fide need for an urgent repair.

10.4(*a*)   The Director shall not make a determination under paragraph 10.3 (a) without the consent of the Licensee.

(*b*)   A determination made under paragraph 10.3 (a) may require the Licensee to provide the priority Fault Repair Service free of charge or on charges which are less than those which are payable by the persons described in paragraph 10.2.

(*c*)   Where the Director has made a determination under paragraph 10.3 (a) and:

(i)   the Licensee gives notice to the Director that it wishes the determination to cease to have effect; or

(ii)   the Director notifies the Licensee that he wishes the determination to cease to have effect;
the determination shall cease to have effect at the end of the period of six months beginning on the day when the notification was given.

10.5   The priority Fault Repair Service shall be available for 24 hours a day or for such lesser periods of each day as may be agreed between the Licensee and the person paying for its provision.

10.6   In this Condition:

'Fault Repair Service' means a service consisting in such repair, maintenance, adjustment or replacement of any of the Applicable Systems or such repair or adjustment of any Relevant System as is necessary to restore and maintain a sufficient service; and

'Relevant System' means any:

(i)   telecommunication system not comprised in any of the Applicable Systems; or

(ii)   telecommunication apparatus which is or is to be connected to any of the Applicable Systems and in respect of which the Licensee is contractually bound to provide Maintenance Services.

10.7   Where on the date on which this Licence enters into force, the Licensee is unable to comply with this Condition, it shall do so as soon as reasonably practicable thereafter and meanwhile shall provide a priority Fault Repair Service as like to that required under this Condition as is reasonably practicable.

Note

This Condition was deleted and replaced by a licence amendment dated 2 June 1987.

Condition 11   Public Call Box Services

11.   The Licensee shall secure that Call Box Services are provided at all its Public Call Boxes and Temporary Call Boxes in the Licensed Area whether installed before, on or after the date on which this Licence enters into force.

11.2   The Licensee may cease to provide Call Box Services at any Temporary Call Box at any time but may cease to provide such services at any Public Call Box only if:

(a)   their continued provision is impracticable;

(b)   the Revenue from the services provided at that Call Box in any period of twelve months ending not more than six months before the cessation has fallen below the Minimum Figure applying to that Call Box or Call Boxes of that description and the Licensee is not entitled to receive the difference between the Revenue and that Figure from any other person;

(c)   the Call Box in question is located near another Public Call Box at which such Services continue to be provided and which is readily accessible from the place where the Call Box at which Services will cease to be provided is situated;

(d)   the Licensee has, before the cessation, agreed with the Director that it will provide such Services at another Public Call Box to be installed near to, and readily accessible from, the place where the Call Box at which they are no longer to be provided is situated;

(*e*)   such Services are available to the public at a Private Call Box:

(i)   which is near to, and readily accessible from, the place where the Public Call Box at which Services will cease to be provided is situated; and

(ii)   the person controlling that Private Call Box has entered into a contract with the Licensee undertaking to give the public unrestricted access to the Private Call Box at all times (or for such periods of each day as the Director determines in relation to that Call Box or all Call Boxes of that description) for the purpose of obtaining such Services and that that Private Call Box has installed in it apparatus enabling persons using hearing aids designed for use in conjunction with Telephones to use such hearing aids when voice telephony services are provided to them, and the Licensee takes all reasonable steps necessary to ensure that the terms of all such contracts are observed;

(*f*)   any person with power to require the removal of the Call Box in question requests the Licensee to remove it;

(*g*)   the Director is satisfied that all reasonable demands for Call Box Services in any particular area are being met at Public Call Boxes installed there by another public telecommunications operator or under arrangements made by such an operator similar to those in paragraph 11.2 (e); or

(*h*)   the Director agrees that such Services need no longer be provided at the Call Box in question for any other reason.

11.3   Where the Licensee ceases to provide Call Box Services at any Public Call Box on the ground that their continued provision there is impracticable, it shall use its best endeavours to provide such Services at another Public Call Box near to, and readily accessible from, the place where the first mentioned Call Box was situated, failing which it shall send by registered post or recorded delivery or by hand to the Director and to the Relevant Local Authorities and Relevant Consumer Bodies for the area in which the Public Call Box is situated a notice specifying the reasons why it considers that the continued provision of Call Box Services at that Public Call Box is no longer practicable and inviting those Authorities and Bodies to make representations in regard to the proposed cessation to the Director within a period of 42 days from the giving of notice. The Licensee shall as soon as reasonably practicable resume the provision of Services at a Public Call Box installed in the same place as, or in a place which is near to, and readily accessible from, the place where the Public Call Box at which Services are no longer provided was situated, if the Director, after considering the terms of the notice and any representations and objections received by him in connection with it, concludes that the provision of Call Box Services either in the place where the first mentioned Call Box was situated or in a place near to, and readily accessible therefrom, is practicable and within 70 days of the giving of the notice requires the Licensee to do so.

11.4   Where the Licensee proposes to cease to provide Call Box Services at any Public Call Box on the ground set out in paragraph 11.2 (b) of this Condition, it may cease to provide those Services at that Call Box only if it has:

(*a*)   posted prominently in or on that Call Box a notice specifying:

(i)   that the Licensee is proposing to cease to provide Services there;

(ii)   the reasons for the proposal;

(iii)   the Minimum Figure;

(iv)   the steps (whether in the form of financial contributions or the provision of services) which if taken by others would oblige the Licensee to continue to provide Services at that Call Box;

(v)   the address of the Licensee's office to which representations and objections with respect to the proposal may be made;

(vi)   the period (not being less than 28 days commencing with the date when the notice is first posted in or on that Call Box) within which representations and objections with respect to the proposal may be made;

(b)   sent by registered post or recorded delivery or by hand a copy of that notice to the Relevant Local Authority and Relevant Consumer Bodies for the area in which that Call Box is situated;

(c)   considered any representation or objection duly made with respect to the proposal within the period specified in sub-paragraph (a) (vi) above; and

(d)   sent to the Director by registered post or recorded delivery or by hand a copy of the notice described in sub-paragraph (a) together with copies of any representations and objections that the Licensee has received with respect to the proposal and its comments and conclusions thereon;

and 28 days have elapsed after the material specified in paragraph 11.4 (d) has been sent to the Director.

11.5   The Licensee shall, after consultation with the Director, publish from time to time in accordance with Condition 16.3 guidelines for determining when:

(a)   Public Call Boxes should be installed in new locations; and

(b)   Temporary Call Boxes should be installed in locations where major events of national or international standing take place;

and shall install Call Boxes on request in accordance with those guidelines unless there are special circumstances which make it unreasonable to require the Licensee to do so.

11.6   Without prejudice to paragraph 11.5, the Licensee shall provide Call Box Services at Public Call Boxes or Temporary Call Boxes installed or to be installed in locations specified by any person who undertakes to pay to the Licensee its costs incurred in providing such Services and to comply with the Licensee's terms and conditions.

11.6A   Except in so far as the Director may otherwise consent in writing, the Licensee shall secure that any Prepayment Apparatus which the Licensee installs in a Public Call Box or Temporary Call Box is for the time being approved for connection to any of the Applicable Systems under section 22 of the Act.

11.7   In this Condition:

(a)   'Call Box' means any kiosk, booth, acoustic hood, shelter or similar structure at which apparatus is installed for the provision of voice telephony services to the public or a class of the public together with such apparatus;

(b)   'Call Box Services' means the installation, repair and maintenance of Call Boxes, the service of conveying by means of the Applicable Systems voice telephony messages to and from such Boxes, directory information services relating to switched voice telephony services available at such Boxes and Public Emergency Call Services so available;

(c)   'Minimum Figure' means £185 per annum or such other amount as the Director and the Licensee may agree for the time being in respect of any Call Box or any description of Call Boxes, after consultation with the advisory bodies established by the Secretary of State under section 54 (1) of the Act;

(*cc*) 'Prepayment Apparatus' means telecommunication apparatus which has as its function, or one of its functions, the automatic enabling of Messages to be transmitted or received on the prior provision of consideration by means of the insertion in the apparatus of cash, or tokens, or cards, or by similar means;

(*d*) 'Private Call Box' means a Call Box owned by or supplied to a person other than the Licensee or another public telecommunications operator at which Call Box Services are or may be provided;

(*e*) 'Public Call Box' means a Call Box to which the public has access at all times which is neither a Private Call Box nor a Temporary Call Box and at which Call Box Services are or may be provided;

(*f*) 'Relevant Consumer Body' means the bodies referred to in Condition 29;

(*g*) 'Relevant Local Authority' means the smallest unit of Local Authority for the area where the Public Call Box is located;

(*h*) 'Revenue', in relation to services provided at any Public Call Box, means the actual amounts received by the Licensee in respect thereof, together with a notional sum equal to 25 per cent. (or such other percentage as the Director and the Licensee may agree for the time being) of the aggregate of such amounts representing revenue earned in respect of transfer charge, credit and similar facilities provided at that Call Box and of services provided and paid for elsewhere which involve conveyance of messages to that Call Box; and

(*i*) 'Temporary Call Box' means a Call Box run by the Licensee which is mobile or is installed for a limited period or is permanently installed but at which Call Box Services are provided to the public or a class of the public for limited periods of time.

Notes
1. Conditions 11.6A and 11.7(cc) were inserted by a licence amendment dated 9 March 1993.
2. Under OFTEL's consultative document 'Universal Telecommunication Services' February 1997, this Condition would be deleted and replaced with a new Condition set out in Annex 3 to the Consultative document. Also public guidelines would be introduced from August 1997.

Condition 12   Maritime Services

12.1   The Licensee shall provide two way telecommunication services (including voice telephony and data transmission services) consisting in the transmission and reception of Messages conveyed or to be conveyed between seagoing vessels and hovercraft and any Network Termination Point in any of the Applicable Systems. Such services shall comply with any relevant requirements of the Radio Regulations of the International Telecommunication Union.

12.2   In this Condition 'seagoing vessel' includes any floating structure for the exploration for, or exploitation of, oil or gas, or similar structure, while it is not maintained on a station.

Condition 13   Connection of Systems Providing Connection Services

13.1   Without prejudice to Condition 3 and subject to the provisions of this Condition the Licensee shall, unless it is impracticable to do so, enter into an agreement with the Operator, that is to say any person who is authorised by a Licence to run a Relevant Connectable System, if the Operator requires it to do so:

(*a*)   to connect, and keep connected, to any of the Applicable Systems, or to permit to be so connected and kept connected that Relevant Connectable System and accordingly to establish and maintain such one or more Points of Connection as are reasonably required and are of sufficient capacity and in sufficient number to enable Messages conveyed or to be conveyed by means of the Operator's system to be conveyed by means of any of the Applicable Systems in such a way as conveniently to meet all reasonable demands for the conveyance of Messages between the Relevant Connectable System and any of the Applicable Systems;

(*b*)   without prejudice to paragraph 13.1 (a), where the Operator is a Long Line Public Telecommunications Operator to establish and maintain such Points of Connection as will enable persons running telecommunication systems connected to the Operator's system and persons running telecommunication systems connected to any of the Applicable Systems to exercise freedom of choice as to the extent to which Messages are conveyed by means of the Applicable Systems and in routing Messages so conveyed;

(*c*)   to provide such other telecommunication services (including the conveyance of Messages which have been, or are to be, transmitted or received at such Points of Connection), information and other services as the Director determines are reasonably required (but no more than reasonably required) to secure that Points of Connection are established and maintained and to enable the Operator effectively to provide the Connection Services which he provides or proposes to provide; and

(*d*)   to provide any other telecommunication service which is either an Initial Standard Service or a service which the Director and the Licensee agree should be a service for the purposes of this sub-paragraph.

13.2   The Licensee shall not be obliged under paragraph 13.1 to enter into an agreement to do anything if:

(*a*)   in the opinion of the Licensee it would be liable to cause the death of or personal injury to, or damage to the property of, the Licensee or any person engaged in the Licensee's business, or materially to impair the quality of any telecommunication service provided by means of any of the Applicable Systems or any telecommunication system (other than the Operator's system) connected thereto and the Director has not expressed a contrary opinion; or

(*b*)   in the opinion of the Licensee:

(i)   it would require an adjustment to, or modification of any of the Applicable Systems whether by incorporation of apparatus or otherwise or the provision by the Licensee of services or information which in any particular case would not be reasonably required; or

(ii)   it would not be reasonably practicable to require the Licensee to do that thing, or permit it to be done, at the time or in the manner required by the Operator, having regard to the state of technical development of the Applicable Systems or any other matter which appears to the Director to be relevant;

and the Director has not expressed a contrary opinion.

13.3   The Licensee may require that an agreement to be entered into under paragraph 13.1 should be subject to terms and conditions, but only such terms and conditions as are permitted in relation to that agreement in accordance with paragraphs 13.4, 13.5 and 13.6.

13.4   Subject to paragraphs 13.5 and 13.6 and Condition 16B terms and conditions are permitted if they are agreed between the Operator and the Licensee and relate to all or any of the following matters:

(*a*)   the charges to be paid by the Operator for anything done under an agreement of the kind described in paragraph 13.1 or as a result of such agreement;

(*aa*)   the charges to be paid by the Operator for the provision by the Licensee to the Operator of telecommunication services and other services to enable the Operator to provide a Public Emergency Call Service where those services are to be provided;

(*b*)   the method adopted or to be adopted to make or maintain the connection;

(*c*)   the Points of Connection in the Applicable Systems at which the connection is or is to be made (including arrangements for determining the point at which Messages will be transferred from one system to another and arrangements for conveying, routing and rerouting Messages);

(*d*)   any restrictions on the telecommunication services to be provided by the Licensee or the Operator being restrictions needed to satisfy international obligations or recommendations applying to and accepted by Her Majesty's Government or to which the Director consents from time to time;

(*e*)   the time when and period from which the Licensee or the Operator is to be obliged to do anything or to permit anything to be done and any arrangements for reviewing the terms and conditions of the agreement;

(*f*)   the form and manner in which Messages are to be transmitted or received at the Points of Connection including arrangements for numbering and the use of appropriate call progress tones and announcements;

(*ff*)   arrangements whereby each of the Licensee and the Operator agree to keep confidential Confidential Information relating to the other;

(*g*)   the means of securing that any Message will be received by means of the connection with a signal quality which is in accordance with any obligations and recommendations of the International Telecommunication Union which apply to Her Majesty's Government and are accepted by them or with any other standard to which the Director consents for the purpose from time to time;

(*h*)   arrangements for charging customers and others in respect of Messages conveyed by virtue of the agreement;

(i)   arrangements for Messages conveyed or to be conveyed outside the United Kingdom;

(ii)   arrangements for the Quality of Standard Services;

(*j*)   provision by the Operator of a reasonable indemnity against any loss or damage sustained by the Licensee in consequence of the agreement in circumstances where the Licensee provides to the Operator an equivalent indemnity; and

(*k*)   any other matter of which the Director is satisfied that account should be taken in the special circumstances of any particular case or which is agreed between the Licensee and the Operator.

13.5   Where:

(*l*)   after a period which appears to the Director to be reasonable for the purpose either:

(i)   the Licensee has failed to enter into an agreement as required by the Operator under paragraph 13.1 or as requested by the Operator to enable it to provide a Public Emergency Call Service; or

(ii)   the Licensee and the Operator, having undertaken, pursuant to provisions for the purpose contained in an agreement entered into under paragraph 13.1, a review of the terms and conditions of the agreement or any of them, have failed to agree whether any of the terms and conditions subject to the review should be amended or if so, what amendments should be made; or

(2)   the Licensee refers for determination the charge (or the means of calculating that charge) to be paid by an Operator to the Licensee:

(i)   pursuant to Condition 16B.1 for each Initial Standard Service during the financial year ending 31 March 1996; and

(ii)   pursuant to Condition 16B.2 for each Standard Service (other than a Competitive Standard Service) the charge for which has been previously determined by the Director pursuant to this Condition;
then the Director shall:

(*aa*)   in the case of sub-paragraph (1)(i) on the application of the Operator or the Licensee, determine with effect from the date of the application the permitted terms and conditions for the purpose of that agreement;

(*bb*)   in the case of sub-paragraph (1)(ii), on the application of the Operator or the Licensee requesting him to do so, and provided he is satisfied that the application was made pursuant to, and in accordance with, any provision in the agreement permiting such application and that any modifications sought to the agreement are material, determine, consistent with the provisions in the agreement relating to such determination, whether any terms and conditions referred to in the application should be amended and if so the amendments to those terms and conditions, (and so that any charge to be paid under the agreement shall take effect in accordance with the agreement); or

(*cc*)   in the case of sub-paragraph (2), determine the charge (or the means of calculating that charge); being

(*A*)   in the case of sub-paragraph (aa), terms and conditions relating to the matters mentioned in paragraph 13.4;

(*B*)   in the case of sub-paragraph (bb), amendments so relating; and

(*C*)   in the case of sub-paragraph (cc), a charge (or the means of calculating that charge);
which appear or appears to the Director reasonably necessary (but no more than reasonably necessary) to secure:

(*a*)   that the Operator pays to the Licensee the cost of anything done pursuant to or in connection with the agreement including fully allocated costs attributable to the services to be provided and taking into account relevant overheads and a reasonable rate of return on attributable assets (provided that the Director may determine whether those fully allocated costs including those relevant overheads and relevant costs of capital incurred in prior years and the current year should be wholly attributed in the current year or deferred and carried forward, in whole or in part, to be attributed in future years);

(*b*)   that the Licensee is properly indemnified against any liabilities to third parties or damage to the Applicable Systems or loss arising from such damage which may result from the performance of the agreement;

(c)   that the Licensee is reasonably able in all the circumstances (including its obligations and reasonably foreseeable obligations to permit other Operators to provide services by means of Points of Connection under this Condition) to finance the other services which it is required by this Licence to provide and to recover costs which are incurred for the provision of those other services or are necessarily incidental thereto;

(d)   that the quality of any telecommunication services provided by means of the Applicable Systems and any systems (other than the Operator's system) connected thereto is maintained;

(e)   that the requirements of fair competition are satisfied;

(f)   that proper account is taken of any other matter reasonably required for the protection of the interests of the Licensee to the extent that no interest of the Operator is unduly prejudiced, including the need to ensure:

(i)   that arrangements for connection accord with good engineering principles and practice;

(ii)   that the commercial development of the Applicable Systems is not unduly impeded;

(iii)   that charging arrangements take account of the overall pattern of the Licensee's costs;

(iv)   that Messages which originate on one system and are conveyed by another should pass through a Point of Connection as near as reasonably practicable to the place from which they are initially sent or at which they are ultimately received;

(v)   that the Operator does not rely unduly upon services provided by the Licensee as a means of satisfying his own obligations under his Licence;

(vi)   that the Licensee's obligations to the Operator are determined having due regard to its obligations and reasonably foreseeable obligations to establish Points of Connection for others;

(vii)   that arrangements made under this Condition are so far as circumstances allow in as similar a form as practicable notwithstanding the variety of Operators entitled to such arrangements under this Condition;

(viii)   that commercial and confidential information of the Licensee is properly protected; and

(ix)   that the technical evolution and numbering arrangements of the Applicable Systems are not unreasonably constrained.

(g)   that without prejudice to paragraph 13.5C the Licensee may be required to carry out any work which the agreement requires it to carry out within an appropriate period of time having regard to all the circumstances which would be reasonable for an efficient telecommunications operator who was not required to give the particular work priority over work for the Licensee's customers generally.

13.5A   Where in pursuance of such an application as is referred to in paragraph 13.5 the Director determines any charge, or the means of calculating any charge, payable to the Licensee by the Operator, he shall do so in accordance with the following provisions:

13.5A.1   Where the customer for any call would reasonably be expected to be billed by the Operator in relation to the conveyance of calls of the type concerned, or where the revenue attributable to that call would reasonably be expected to be collected by the Operator from the operator of another system (other than the Applicable Systems) over which the call was conveyed, the Operator shall pay a charge to the Licensee in respect of that call.

13.5A.2   Subject to paragraphs 13.5A.5 and 13.5D and Condition 16B the Operator shall pay the Licensee charges calculated as set out in paragraph 13.5A.3, which charges will differ according to:

(*a*)   whether the call is a local, national or international call and, if the Director considers it appropriate in the interests of fair and effective competition, according to any Sub-Categories of any of those categories of call;

(*b*)   the portion or portions of the Applicable Systems by means of which the Message is conveyed; and

(*c*)   the time of day at which the call is made, fixed by reference to the times for peak, standard and cheap rate calls published from time to time by the Licensee.

13.5A.3   Each of the charges referred to in paragraph 13.5A.2 payable to the Licensee by the Operator in respect of the conveyance of any Message shall cover:

(*a*)   the Licensee's fully allocated costs of the conveyance calculated on an historic cost basis, including a full contribution to relevant overheads, calculated on the basis of information supplied by the Licensee drawn from:

(i)   to the extent that a period in respect of which the charge is payable falls within a financial year ending on or before 31 March 1995, its audited FRBS figures for the financial year preceding that financial year; and

(ii)   in any other case, the audited information appearing by virtue of Condition 20B.4 (b) (i) in the Licensee's Financial Statement for the relevant Business for the financial year ending on 31 March in respect of which the charge is payable (the 'financial year in question');

(provided that the Director may determine whether those fully allocated costs including those relevant overheads and relevant costs of capital incurred in prior years and the current year should be wholly attributed in the current year or deferred and carried forward, in whole or in part, to be attributed in future years);

(*b*)   the Applicable Rate of Return applied to the relevant capital employed; and

(*c*)   until the expiry of the period during which the Licensee is subject to such restrictions on increases in residential and single line business rental charges as are referred to in Condition 17A.2 (a) or (b) (whether or not that Condition remains in force in that form) or any similar restrictions, a contribution ('the Contribution'), assessed in accordance with paragraph 13.5A.4 below, towards the Licensee's Access Deficit.

'Access Deficit' means, in relation to any financial year, the difference between:

(*a*)   the Licensee's aggregate revenue by way of connection charges and periodic charges in respect of the provision, use and Ordinary Maintenance of Exchange Lines; and

(*b*)   the aggregate of:

(i)   the Licensee's fully allocated costs incurred in respect of those services (including a full contribution to relevant overheads) as assessed by the Director on the basis of:

(*aa*)   to the extent that a period for which the charge is payable falls within a financial year ending on or before 31 March 1995, the Licensee's audited FRBS figures in respect of the financial year preceding that financial year; and

(*bb*)   in any other case, the audited information appearing by virtue of Condition 20B.4 (b) (i) in the Licensee's Financial Statement for the relevant Business for the financial year in question;

(provided that the Director may determine whether those fully allocated costs including those relevant overheads and relevant costs of capital incurred in prior years and the current year should be wholly attributed in the current year or deferred and carried forward, in whole or in part, to be attributed in future years); and

(ii)   the return on capital employed in providing such services, calculated at the Applicable Rate of Return.

The Licensee's fully allocated costs as specified in the audited FRBS figures or, as appropriate, the audited information appearing by virtue of Condition 20B.4 (b)(i) in the Licensee's Financial Statement for the relevant Business for the financial year in question will be used for the purposes of calculating the Access Deficit unless:

(*a*)   the Director, following consultation with the Licensee, has notified the Licensee that in his view a cost has been improperly allocated and should be allocated to some other service, having regard to the causality criterion where it is applicable, and has notified the Licensee of the service to which he considers the cost should be reallocated and his reasons for taking that view; and

(*b*)   The Licensee has had a reasonable opportunity of making representations about those reasons.

13.5A.3A   For the purposes of calculating the charge (or the means of calculating that charge) for a Standard Service (other than a Competitive Standard Service) or Contribution in accordance with paragraph 13.5A, subject to paragraph 13.5A.3C (a)(ii), the Licensee shall submit to the Director not later than two months before the commencement of the financial year in question:

(*a*)   in respect of that Standard Service, a forecast of the Licensee's fully allocated costs (including the relevant capital employed) of the conveyance calculated on an historic cost basis including a full contribution to relevant overheads for the financial year in question (provided that the Director may determine whether those fully allocated costs including those relevant overheads and relevant costs of capital incurred in prior years and the current year should be wholly attributed in the current year or deferred and carried forward, in whole or in part, to be attributed in future years); and

(*b*)   a forecast of the Contribution for the financial year in question assessed in accordance with paragraph 13.5A.4;

(each the 'Forecast') based on:

(i)   the audited information appearing by virtue of Condition 20B.4 (b) (i) in the Licensee's Financial Statement for the relevant Business for the financial year two years immediately preceding the financial year in question;

(ii)   the audited information appearing by virtue of Condition 20B.4 (b) (i) in the Licensee's interim Financial Statement for the relevant Business for the first six months of the financial year immediately preceding the financial year in question; and

(iii)   any other relevant information available at that time;

and, pending the determination of the Final Charge (as defined in paragraph 13.5A.3B (a)) for the financial year in question, the charge for that Standard Service shall be calculated using the Forecast (each an 'Interim Charge').

13.5A.3B   (a)   As soon as reasonably practicable after the end of the financial year in question, the Director shall recalculate and redetermine the charge (or the means of calculating that charge) for the relevant Standard Service or the Contribution (each a 'Final Charge') in accordance with paragraph 13.5A. That recalculation and redetermination shall include a provision that where the Interim Charge and the Final Charge differ, the Licensee shall offer to include in the agreement with the Operator for the provision of that Standard Service terms (that offer not to be conditional on the acceptance by that Operator of the inclusion in that agreement of any other terms and conditions whether relating to the charge (or the means of calculating that charge for that Standard Service)) which provide that:

(i)   if the Interim Charge is greater than the Final Charge, the Licensee shall pay to the Operator the amount of the difference together with interest calculated in accordance with sub-paragraph (b); and

(ii)   if the Interim Charge is less than the Final Charge, the Operator shall pay to the Licensee the amount of the difference together with interest calculated in accordance with sub-paragraph (b);
provided that:

(aa)   where the charge for that Standard Service paid by an Operator to the Licensee pending the recalculation and redetermination of the charge in accordance with this paragraph (the 'Actual Charge') is less than the Interim Charge (whether as a result of the operation of Condition 24F or in circumstances where the Director has consented to that lesser charge pursuant to Condition 16B.5), the Final Charge shall be whichever is the lower of the Actual Charge and what would have been the Final Charge but for the operation of this proviso;

(bb)   where a Contribution is payable by an Operator, any payment to be made in accordance with this paragraph shall be adjusted to take account of any reassessment of the Contribution calculated using any revised Contributions pursuant to either of Conditions 24F.10 and 24F.13 for the period the revised Contributions were paid; and

(cc)   any payment to be made in accordance with this paragraph shall be adjusted to take account of any revision of the charge calculated using any revised charge (or the means of calculating that charge) pursuant to either of Conditions 24F.11 and 24F.14 for the period the revised charge was paid.

(b)   A recalculation and redetermination of charges as described in sub-paragraph (a) shall include a provision requiring the Licensee to offer to include in the agreement with the Operator for the provision of that Standard Service terms which provide for interest to be added to any payment to be made in accordance with sub-paragraph (a), calculated from the date on which the relevant payment was due to the date on which payment is made, both dates inclusive. The applicable annual percentage rate shall be the London Inter Bank Offered Rate plus 3/8 per cent. For the purposes of this paragraph the 'London Inter Bank Offered Rate' means the rate of interest which is the rate per annum of the offered quotation for deposits of sterling for delivery on the due date for payment for a period of three months which appears on the display designated as 'Page 3750' on the Telerate Service (or any other page as may replace 'Page 3750' on that Service) at or about 11 am London time on the due date of payment; if that rate does not appear on 'Page 3750' on the Telerate Service (or any replacement page) 'London Inter Bank Offered Rate' shall mean the rate quoted by National Westminster Bank PLC to leading banks in the London interbank market at or about 11 am London time on the due date of payment for the offering of sterling deposits of a comparable amount for a period of three months.

(c) The Licensee shall, without prejudice to Condition 52, submit to the Director in the manner and at the times as the Director specifies, any information in addition to any Forecast which it is required to submit in accordance with paragraphs 13.5A.3A and 13.5A.3C which he may reasonably require for the purposes of calculating the charge (or the means of calculating that charge) for a Standard Service (whether the Interim Charge or the Final Charge or both).

(d) The Director shall be entitled to amend any Forecast which the Licensee is required to submit in accordance with paragraphs 13.5A.3A and 13.5A.3C in any manner which he considers to be necessary to render it a more accurate forecast of the Licensee's fully allocated costs (including the relevant capital employed) of the conveyance calculated on an historic cost basis including a full contribution to relevant overheads and the Contribution to be assessed in accordance with paragraph 13.5A.4 (provided that the Director may determine whether those fully allocated costs including those relevant overheads and relevant costs of capital incurred in prior years and the current year should be wholly attributed in the current year or deferred and carried forward, in whole or in part, to be attributed in future years).

13.5A.3C (a) Notwithstanding paragraph 13.5A.3A:

(i) in relation to a new Standard Service (other than an Initial Standard Service and a Competitive Standard Service) the charge for which the Licensee or the Operator, as the case may be, refers to the Director for determination in accordance with this Condition, the Licensee shall in respect of that Standard Service submit to the Director, as soon as reasonably practicable after the reference of that charge for determination, a Forecast based on the information specified in paragraph 13.5A.3A (i), (ii) and (iii), the Financial Statement of the relevant Business for the financial year immediately preceding the financial year in question (if available) and the Interim Financial Statement of the relevant Business for the financial year in question (if available); and

(ii) for the purposes of the financial year ending 31 March 1996, the Licensee shall submit the Forecast for each Initial Standard Service to the Director not later than seven working days after the date on which this Condition comes into force based on the audited FRBS Statement for the financial year ended 31 March 1994 together with any other relevant information available at that time.

(b) For the purposes of sub-paragraph (a) 'FRBS Statement' means an accounting statement the purposes of which are to set out and fairly present the costs (including capital costs), revenue and financial position of the Licensee's relevant services including a reasonable assessment of the assets employed in and liabilities attributable to those services.

13.5A.4 The Contribution shall be assessed according to the following formulae on the basis of figures for the financial year in question. It shall (subject to the following proviso) be assessed separately in relation to each of the following categories of call, namely local, national and international calls, carried solely (within the United Kingdom) over the Applicable Systems (the category of international calls comprising both incoming and outgoing international calls). The Contribution per minute of traffic in respect of each category will (subject to the following proviso) be:

(a)   in respect of local calls:

$$\dfrac{A_1 \times \dfrac{Access\ Deficit}{A_1 + A_2 + A_3 + A_4}}{2D_1}$$

(b)   in respect of national calls:

$$\dfrac{A_1 \times \dfrac{Access\ Deficit}{A_1 + A_2 + A_3 + A_4}}{2D_2}$$

(c)   in respect of international calls:

$$\dfrac{A_1 \times \dfrac{Access\ Deficit}{A_1 + A_2 + A_3 + A_4}}{2D_3}$$

Where:

A_1, A_2, A_3 and A_4 are respectively, in respect of each such category and a fourth category (comprising calls conveyed within the United Kingdom by means of the Applicable Systems and the Systems of one or more Operator and calls used to provide other telecommunication services not comprised in A_1, A_2, or A_3) the profit for the financial year in question, calculated by reference to the Licensee's fully allocated costs, assessed on the basis set out in paragraph 13.5A.3 (a), after meeting the cost of capital at the Applicable Rate of Return on the capital employed;

D_1, D_2 and D_3 are respectively, in respect of each such category (but not the fourth category) the total duration in conversation minutes of all Messages conveyed, during the financial year in question;

provided that:

(i)   without prejudice to paragraph 13.5A.2 (c), any determination of charges in pursuance of the provsions of paragraphs 13.5A.3 or 5 which cover the Contribution shall take into account the different rates according to time of day (referred to in paragraph 13.5A.2 (c)) charged by the Licensee so that the relationship between those rates is reflected as nearly as possible in the charges so determined, the times of day being those applied by the Licensee on the coming into force of this paragraph 13.5A, provided that if the Licensee changes the times of day, appropriate adjustments approved by the Director shall be made to take account of the changes, for the purpose of this paragraph 13.5A.4;

(ii)   each of the categories of call specified in paragraphs 13.5A.4 (a), (b) and (c) may be divided by the Director into Sub-Categories for the purpose of assessing the Contribution separately in relation to each such Sub-Category on the basis of the formula for that category applied, *mutatis mutandis*, to that Sub-Category; and

(iii) the Contribution shall be paid in respect of each portion of the Applicable Systems by means of which the call is conveyed, where 'portion' means a part of the Applicable Systems between a Network Termination Point interfacing with a customer and a point at which the Applicable Systems are connected to the Operator's system.

13.5A.5 (*a*) Where and to the extent that the Director considers that it is necessary, in order to enable a person wishing to enter a particular market for the provision of telecommunication services to do so, or to enable a person engaged in such a market to establish or maintain a presence in that market, to reduce the contribution that person makes to the Access Deficit, in determining charges payable to the Licensee by the Operator, the Director may, if he considers it appropriate to do so, make a determination under this paragraph. Such determination may provide that the Operator shall before 1 July 1997 make no or only a partial contribution to the Access Deficit in respect of its first 10 per cent. of market share, provided that such a determination shall secure that the Licensee receives a full contribution to its Access Deficit:

(i) in respect of all calls conveyed by the Operator's system by virtue of a choice made by a customer of the Licensee using equal access either by pre-selection or on a call-by-call basis (as described in paragraphs (i) and (ii) of Condition 13A.5 (a)); or

(ii) if the Licensee's market share is less than 85 per cent., on the market share of the Operator and other Operators (taken together) which is in excess of 15 per cent. of the total market.

In calculating the contribution to the Access Deficit payable in respect of an Operator's international calls, it shall be assumed that the proportions in which incoming international calls conveyed by that Operator's system are distributed between those on which a full contribution is to be paid pursuant to paragraph 13.5A.5 (a) (i) and those in respect of which no or only a partial contribution is to be paid is the same as the distribution of outgoing international calls between those two classes.

(*b*) Where the Director makes a determination in accordance with paragraph 13.5A.5 (a) he may also determine that the Operator shall pay to the Licensee such additional contributions to the Access Deficit in relation to any part of the Operator's market share which is in excess of 10 per cent. as he considers appropriate (provided that the total contribution payable by the Operator shall not exceed the amount which would represent a full contribution on the whole of the Operator's market share) and he shall determine that, in the event that the Operator achieves a market share of 25 per cent. or more, the Operator shall thereafter pay to the Licensee in such manner as the Director may determine full contributions to the Access Deficit on the basis set out in paragraph 13.5A.4 and thereafter the Director's determination under paragraph 13.5A.5 (a) shall cease to apply.

(*c*) For the purposes of paragraph 13.5A.5 (a) and (b):

(i) in calculating whether an Operator's market share is in excess of 10 per cent., no account shall be taken of:

(A) calls which have originated with the customer of another system (other than the Applicable Systems) using that system before being conveyed by the Operator's system; or

(B) calls of the type referred to in paragraph 13.5A.5 (a) (i);

but such calls shall be brought into account in calculating whether that Operator's market share exceeds 25 per cent. or whether its market share, when taken with the market shares of any other Operators, exceeds 15 per cent.;

(ii) in relation to calls of the kind referred to in paragraph 13.5A.5 (c) (i) (A) the Director may exercise the power conferred on him by paragraph 13.5A.5 (a) (whether or not the Operator's market share is in excess of 10 per cent.) unless the operator of the system on which the call originated is an operator (not being a person of the kind referred to in paragraph 13.5A.5 (f)) who has a market share in excess of 10 per cent.; and

(iii) in calculating the contribution to the Access Deficit payable on an Operator's market share which is in excess of 10 per cent. the proportions of calls assumed to be conveyed over one and two portions respectively of the Applicable Systems (as defined in proviso (iii) to paragraph 13.5A.4) or to possess any other attribute relevant to the calculation of the contribution to the Access Deficit shall be the same as the respective proportions of the total calls possessing that attribute.

(d) For the purposes of this paragraph 13.5A.5 the Director shall be entitled to define the market segments (whether by reference to geographical area, category of call or otherwise) by reference to which the market shares referred to in this paragraph are to be calculated and different market segments may be defined for the purposes of the charges payable by different Operators but in respect of any Operator the Director shall define markets:

(i)   so that the maximum size of that Operator's market is the geographical area in which the Operator is authorised by a Licence to run the Relevant Connectable System concerned; and

(ii)   by reference only to those services which that Operator may lawfully provide by virtue of that Licence.

Shares of markets shall be determined by reference to retail call revenues. In determining shares of markets, revenues of service providers shall be attributed to the Operator who bills, or would reasonably be expected to bill, the service providers.

(e) A determination may be made under paragraph 13.5A.5 (a), if, and to the extent that, the Director concludes it is necessary to do so in view of:

(i)   the extent to which the Operator's average volume of call minutes per line differs, or is expected to differ, from that of the Licensee;

(ii)   the need to ensure that any such determination does not reduce the incentive on the Operator to exercise diligence in developing the services which he is authorised to provide;

(iii) the availability of number portability;

(iv)   the extent of economies of scale achieved and, in the opinion of the Director, to be expected to be achieved, by the Operator and other Operators;

(v)   the effect of the telecommunications activities of the Operators referred to in paragraph 13.5A.5 (e) (iv) on the economies of scale of the Licensee; and

(vi)   the provisions concerning the charges payable to the Licensee of any existing determinations by the Director, or agreements to which the Licensee is a party, (whether or not the Operator in respect of whom the determination under Condition 13.5A.5 (a) is to be made is also a party to any of the first mentioned determinations or to any of the agreements) for the conveyance by the Licensee of calls originating on systems run by other Operators and the existence of profitable Operators of such systems.

(*f*) Notwithstanding any other provision of this Licence the Director shall be entitled to determine that any persons to whom cellular licences (including personal communication network licences) were granted under section 7 and 8 of the Act on or before 31 July 1991 (but including any such licences granted to the same licensee in substitution for those licences after that date) shall, in relation to Land Mobile Radio Services (as defined in Condition 18) provided under that licence, make no or only a partial contribution to the Access Deficit, and in making any determination pursuant to this paragraph 13.5A.5 (f) the Director shall have regard in particular to:

(i)   the relationship between the charges and costs of such cellular licensees;

(ii)   the considerations of fair competition based on the relationship between the respective call charges of cellular and fixed link operators including the Licensee.

For the avoidance of doubt, the Director shall be entitled to make a determination under this paragraph 13.5A.5 (f) irrespective of the market share achieved by the cellular licensee concerned.

(*g*) Notwithstanding any other provision of this Licence the Director may determine that any contribution from any Operator to the Access Deficit shall be modified or further modified to the extent that the Director considers appropriate to reflect the extent, if any, to which the Licensee has not availed itself, at any time after 31 July 1991, of its freedom to rebalance charges in a way which would reduce the amount of the Access Deficit.

(*h*) Where the Licensee has entered into an agreement with any other Operator under paragraph 13.1 which was entered into or remains in force on or after the date on which this paragraph 13.5A comes into force, which does not in the opinion of the Director provide for a full contribution to the Access Deficit, and the Director determines that in consequence the total amount of the Access Deficit in respect of which other Operators are or may be required to make contributions is proportionately greater, the Director may, notwithstanding any other provision of this Licence, if he considers it appropriate to do so, modify the contribution to the Access Deficit payable by an Operator to the extent necessary to ensure that that Operator does not pay a greater contribution than he otherwise would as a result of that agreement.

(*i*) Before making a determination pursuant to paragraph 13.5A.5, the Director will consult with the Licensee and the Operator. If he concludes that a determination is appropriate he shall notify the Licensee and the Operator of the proposed determination and, if any, the proposed contribution and his reasons for making it and give them a reasonable opportunity to make representations.

(*j*) On request from time to time by the Licensee or the Operator the Director may, if he considers it appropriate, determine to review any determination made under paragraph 13.5A.5 and determine whether the nil or partial contribution payable by the Operator should be varied, and the provisions of paragraph 13.5A.5 shall apply *mutatis mutandis* to such review. Any agreement entered into pursuant to a determination under paragraph

13.5A.5 shall include provision for revision pursuant to a determination under this paragraph 13.5A.5 (j).

13.5A.6 Any determination under paragraph 13.5A.5 shall require arrangements to be made between the Licensee and the Operator so that the Licensee receives, without undue delay, such information as is necessary for the purpose of calculating the charges payable by the Operator to the Licensee.

13.5A.7.1 If the Director is satisfied in respect of either of the periods of 12 months ending 31 March 1992 and 31 March 1993 (an 'Efficiency Year') that the Licensee will not meet the Efficiency Standard in the Efficiency Period (one of the periods of twelve months commencing respectively on 1 August 1991 and 1 August 1992) commencing in either of those respective Years, he may require the Licensee for the purposes of this paragraph to reduce the costs on which the Access Deficit is calculated in the relevant Efficiency Period by the Efficiency Margin.

13.5A.7.2 The Efficiency Margin shall be the lesser of:

(a) an amount by which the Director considers that the costs should be reduced in the particular Efficiency Period in order reasonably to compensate for the shortfall of actual performance compared with the Efficiency Standard which the Director considers likely to occur; and

(b) (i) for the first Efficiency Period, 5 per cent. of the costs of the Access Business for the year ended 31 March 1991; and

(ii) for the second Efficiency Period, 10 per cent. of such costs for the year ended 31 March 1992 less the percentage gain in efficiency which the Director determines the Licensee has achieved in that year.

13.5A.7.3 The Efficiency Standard will be calculated in accordance with Guidelines to be issued by the Director as agreed with the Licensee on or before the coming into force of this paragraph 13.5A.7, which will also cover other related matters. Such Guidelines may only be revoked or amended by agreement with the Licensee.

13.5A.8 In this paragraph 13.5A:

'Applicable Rate of Return' means the single rate of return which is notified by the Director from time to time to the Licensee as reasonable for the Systems Business;

'audited FRBS figures' and 'FRBS figures' mean figures in the FRBS Statement furnished and, in respect of the financial year ending on 31 March 1992 and thereafter, reported on by the Licensee's auditors, in accordance with Condition 52.3;

'Message' and 'call' refer respectively to Messages and calls the conveyance of which involves the provision of voice frequency switched services including (without limitation) voice and data Messages and calls (or equivalent digital services);

'Ordinary Maintenance' has the meaning given to it in Condition 24A.14;

'Sub-Category' means a sub-category which corresponds to one or more items contained in the Licensee's price list that specify prices for calls; and the definition of 'cost' set out in paragraph (g) of Part 1 of Schedule 1 shall not apply.

13.5B.1 Where in pursuance of such an application as is referred to in paragraph 13.5 the Director determines any charge or the means of calculating any charge, the determination shall include terms and conditions which appear to the Director reasonably necessary (but no more than reasonably necessary) to secure that any charge payable by the Licensee to the Operator in respect of the conveyance of any message shall cover:

(*a*)   the Operator's fully allocated costs of the conveyance calculated on a historic cost basis, including a full contribution to relevant overheads, calculated on the basis of information supplied by the Operator drawn from audited figures relating to the relevant services for the latest financial year ending before the period in relation to which the charge is to be payable (provided that the Director may determine whether those fully allocated costs including those relevant overheads and relevant costs of capital incurred in prior years and the current year should be wholly attributed in the current year or deferred and carried forward, in whole or in part, to be attributed in future years); and

(*b*)   a reasonable rate of return on attributable assets applied to the relevant capital employed.

13.5B.1A   (*a*)   For the purposes of calculating the charge (or the means of calculating that charge) for a service provided by the Operator to the Licensee referred to in paragraph 13.5B.1 for a financial year in respect of which the charge is payable which commences on or after 1 April 1995 ('the relevant financial year'), the calculations shall be made on the basis of the audited figures relating to that service for the financial year immediately preceding the relevant financial year or, if those figures are not available, the most recent audited figures which are available or, if no audited figures are available the best information available to the Director (the 'Interim Charge'). As soon as reasonably practicable after the end of the relevant financial year the calculations of the charge for that service shall be recalculated and redetermined on the basis of the audited figures relating to that service for the relevant financial year or, if those figures are not available, the most recent audited figures which are available or, if no audited figures are available, the best information available to the Director (the 'Final Charge'). That recalculation and redetermination shall include a provision that where the Interim Charge and the Final Charge differ, the Operator shall offer to include in the agreement with the Licensee for the provision of that service terms (that offer not to be conditional on the acceptance by the Licensee of the inclusion in that agreement of any other terms and conditions whether relating to the charge (or the means of calculating that charge for that service)) which provide that:

(i)   if the Interim Charge is greater than the Final Charge, the Operator shall pay to the Licensee the amount of the difference together with interest calculated in accordance with sub-paragraph (b); and

(ii)   if the Interim Charge is less than the Final Charge, the Licensee shall pay to the Operator the amount of the difference together with interest calculated in accordance with sub-paragraph (b).

(*b*)   A recalculation and redetermination of charges as described in sub-paragraph (a) shall include a provision requiring the Operator to offer to include in the agreement with the Licensee for the provision of that service terms which provide for interest to be added to any payment to be made in accordance with sub-paragraph (a), calculated from the date on which the relevant payment was due to the date on which payment is made, both dates inclusive. The applicable annual percentage rate shall be the rate specified in paragraph 13.5A.3B (b).

13.5B.2   The following provisions of paragraph 13.5B apply in respect of any period in which a Contribution is payable by the Operator (being a Local Fixed Link Public Telecommunications Operator) by virtue of a determination made under paragraph 13.5A.

13.5B.3   A determination made in accordance with paragraph 13.5B.1 may provide that in addition to any charge referred to in that paragraph, the Licensee shall pay a contribution towards the access deficit of the Operator ('the Payment'). The Payment shall be expressed as an amount per minute and calculated in accordance with paragraphs 13.5B.5 and 6.

13.5B.4   When determining the amount of any Payment in accordance with paragraphs 13.5B.5 and 6 the Director shall have full regard to the objective that competition from the Operator should only be established and sustained as a result of such Payment if the Operator's business is carried on with reasonable efficiency.

13.5B.5   In respect of any period which is more than three years after the date on which the Operator first provided voice telephony services in pursuance of an authorisation contained in or made under his licence, the amount of the Payment shall not exceed the weighted arithmetical average amount per minute by way of Contribution (excluding any Contribution made pursuant to paragraph 13.5A.5 (a) (i)) payable to the Licensee by the Operator by virtue of a determination made under paragraph 13.5A. That amount shall be reduced in inverse proportion according to the relationship which the respective volumes of different categories of calls originated on lines forming part of the Operator's system bear to the volumes of those respective categories of calls originated on Exchange Lines in the financial year the figures for which are used for the purposes of the calculations specified in paragraph 13.5A.4. The Payment shall be calculated according to the following formula, and in the event of any conflict between the formula and the preceding sentence of this paragraph 13.5B.5, the formula shall prevail:

$$P = C \times \frac{V_L}{V_O}$$

Where

P	= one of P_1, P_2 and P_3;
P_1, P_2, P_3	= the Payment per minute in respect of each of the categories (local, national and international) of call referred to in paragraph 13.5A, but not the fourth category;
C	= the Contribution for each such category of call as calculated pursuant to paragraph 13.5A (as qualified by paragraph 13.5B.5);
V_L	= the weighted average total annual minutes of calls per Exchange Line calculated as set out below; and
V_O	= the weighted average total annual minutes of calls per line of the Operator system, calculated as set out below;

provided that where the Director has divided a category of call used for the purposes of assessing the Contribution under paragraph 13.5A.4 into Sub-Categories, the Payment under this paragraph 13.5B.5 shall be calculated separately for each such Sub-Category on the basis of the formula for that category applied, *mutatis mutandis*, to that Sub-Category.

The weighted average total annual minutes of calls shall be calculated as follows:

(a)   in respect of the Applicable Systems:

$$V_L = \frac{M_1 C_1 + M_2 C_2 + M_3 C_3}{X_L}$$

(b)   in respect of the Operator's systems:

$$V_O = \frac{N_1 C_1 + N_2 C_2 + N_3 C_3}{X_O}$$

Where:

M_1, M_2, M_3 = the total annual minutes for each category of call originated on Exchange Lines;

N_1, N_2, N_3 = the total annual minutes for each category of call originated on lines of the Operator's System;

C_1, C_2, C_3 = the Contribution in respect of each category of call as defined above;

X_L = the average number of lines forming part of the Applicable Systems during the financial year the figures for which are used for the purpose of the calculations made under paragraph 13.5A.4;

X_O = the average number of lines forming part of the Operator's systems during the relevant financial year, being the financial year the figures for which are used for the purposes of the calculations made under paragraph 13.5A.4.

13.5B.6   In respect of any period which is less than three years after the date on which the Operator first provided voice telephony services, as referred to in paragraph 13.5B.5, the Payment shall be such amount per minute (subject to the following provisions) as the Director considers appropriate, but:

(a)   the amount in respect of any category of call shall, before sub-paragraph (b) below is applied, be no greater than the Contribution payable to the Licensee by the Operator in respect of calls of that category by virtue of a determination made under paragraph 13.5A; and

(b)   the amount shall be proportionately reduced, where appropriate, to take account of the likely average volume per line of minutes of calls in each category which is likely to be generated by or otherwise attributable to the Operator's customers and prospective customers compared with the average volume per line of minutes of calls in each category likely to be generated by or otherwise attributable to the Licensee's customers for the whole of the Licensed Area.

13.5B.7   Where the Director proposes to make a determination under this paragraph 13.5B he shall notify the Licensee, the Operator and any other person the Director considers appropriate ('the Interested Parties') of his proposed determination and invite each Interested Party within a reasonable time, being at least 28 days, to present its views to the Director. In relation to each of the views expressed by an Interested Party, he shall notify that Interested Party of his conclusions.

13.5B.8   In this paragraph 13.5B:

'access deficit', in relation to an Operator, means the excess of costs over revenues equivalent to those referred to in relation to the Access Deficit;

'Local Fixed Link Public Telecommunications Operator' means a Public Telecommunications Operator who:

(a)   is authorised by or under his licence (however expressed and whether or not limited in any way) to provide voice telephony services to any person;

(b)   provides such services by means of a line; and

(c)   is not authorised to provide a Land Mobile Radio Service;

'Land Mobile Radio Service' means any telecommunication service provided by means of wireless telegraphy where every Message that is conveyed has been, or is to be, conveyed by means of apparatus which is or is to be used while in motion;

'line' means:

(a)   in the case of the Applicable Systems, an Exchange Line;

(b)   in the case of the systems of Mercury Communications Limited a Direct Service Line as defined in its licence dated 5 November 1984; and

(c)   in the case of any other Operator, telecommunication apparatus forming part of the Operator's system which is equivalent to an Exchange Line;

'Message' and 'call' have the meanings given to them in paragraph 13.5A.8; and

'Sub-Category' has the meaning given in paragraph 13.5A.8.

13.5C   Where in pursuance of such an application as is referred to in paragraph 13.5 the Director determines any charge (or the means of calculating any charge) payable in respect of the establishment of a connection between the Applicable Systems and the system of the Operator he shall do so in accordance with the following provisions.

13.5C.1   Any costs incurred in the establishment of such a connection, including (without limitation) the provision of dedicated capacity at a point (a 'point of connection') at which the Applicable Systems and the Operator's system are connected, but not transmission capacity, shall be shared between the parties according to the proportions in which each of them will bill the customers originating calls which are to be conveyed over the point of connection. The proportions shall be derived from forecasts by each party of the capacity required to convey those calls for which the respective parties will bill customers originating them. These costs shall be assessed on the basis of:

(a)   the Licensee's or the Operator's respective fully allocated costs of the establishment of the connection including a reasonable contribution to relevant overheads (provided that the Director may determine whether those fully allocated costs including those relevant overheads and relevant costs of capital incurred in prior years and the current year should be wholly attributed in the current year or deferred and carried forward, in whole or in part, to be attributed in future years); and

(*b*)   the application to relevant capital employed of (in the case of the Licensee's costs) the Applicable Rate of Return or (in the case of the Operator's costs) a reasonable rate of return on attributable assets;

Provided that where the charge is payable in respect of a financial year which commences on or after 1 April 1995 ('the relevant financial year') the costs shall be assessed on the basis of:

(*aa*)   in the case of the Licensee:

(i)   the fully allocated costs of the establishment of the connection including a reasonable contribution to relevant overheads calculated on the basis of information supplied by the Licensee drawn from the audited information appearing by virtue of Condition 20B.4 (b) (i) in the Licensee's Financial Statement for the relevant Business for the relevant financial year (provided that the Director may determine whether those fully allocated costs including those relevant overheads and relevant costs of capital incurred in prior years and the current year should be wholly attributed in the current year or deferred and carried forward, in whole or in part, to be attributed in future years); and

(ii)   the Applicable Rate of Return applied to the relevant capital employed; and

(*bb*)   in the case of the Operator:

(i)   the fully allocated costs of the establishment of the connection including a reasonable contribution to relevant overheads calculated on the basis of information supplied by the Operator drawn from audited figures relating to the relevant service for the relevant financial year or, if those figures are not available, the most recent audited figures which are available or, if no audited figures are available, the best information available to the Director (provided that the Director may determine whether those fully allocated costs including those relevant overheads and relevant costs of capital incurred in prior years and the current year should be wholly attributed in the current year or deferred and carried forward, in whole or in part, to be attributed in future years); and

(ii)   a reasonable rate of return on attributable assets applied to the relevant capital employed.

13.5C.2   Any determination of any charge (or the means of calculating the same) to be payable under paragraph 1 above may include a provision that no such charge shall be payable where the party imposing the charge fails to provide the connection within six months (or such longer period as the Licensee and the Operator may agree) of the date of the request therefor, provided that this provision shall not apply in any particular case unless it is reasonable in all the circumstances for it to apply. It shall be deemed not to be reasonable if:

(*a*)   it was not reasonably practicable for any reason for the first party to provide the connection in time;

(*b*)   the other party's request for the connection was unreasonable in quantum having regard to its current and future needs; or

(*c*)   in order to comply with the time period the Licensee would have had to give priority to making the connection beyond that given to its own customers generally.

13.5C.3   The period referred to in paragraph 2 shall be extended by such period as equates to or, if there is no period that equates, as is reasonably commensurate with, delays attributable to any default or lack of co-operation by the Operator, or to force majeure of any kind.

13.5C.4   Where one party has in pursuance of a provision in the agreement required the other party to provide a connection and subsequently cancels the order, it shall reimburse the other party for all costs (assessed on the basis of that party's fully allocated costs together with, in the case of the Licensee's costs, the Applicable Rate of Return and, in the case of the Operator's costs, a reasonable rate of return on attributable assets) incurred by the other party in the provision of the connection up to the date of cancellation.

13.5C.5   In this paragraph, 'Applicable Rate of Return' has the meaning given to it in paragraph 13.5A.

13.5C.6   (a)   For the purposes of calculating the charge (or the means of calculating that charge) for a Standard Service (other than a Competitive Standard Service) payable in respect of the financial year ending on 31 March 1996 or any subsequent financial year in accordance with paragraph 13.5C.1 or 13.5E, the calculations shall be made on the basis of:

(i)   in the case of the financial year ending on 31 March 1996, the Financial Statement for the relevant Business for the financial year ending on 31 March 1995; and

(ii)   in the case of subsequent financial years the audited information appearing by virtue of Condition 20B.4 (b) (i) in the Licensee's Financial Statement for the relevant Business for the financial year immediately preceding the financial year in question;

or if, at any time when this paragraph is to be applied, that Financial Statement is not available, on the basis of the Financial Statement of the relevant Business for the financial year two years immediately preceding the financial year in respect of which the charge is payable or, if that is not available, on the best information available to the Director (the 'Interim Charge'). As soon as reasonably practicable after the end of the financial year in respect of which the charge is payable commencing with the financial year ending 31 March 1996 the Director shall recalculate and redetermine the charge on the basis of the audited information appearing by virtue of Condition 20B.4 (b) (i) in the Licensee's Financial Statement for the relevant Business for the financial year in respect of which the charge is payable (the 'Final Charge'). That recalculation and redetermination shall include a provision that where the Interim Charge and the Final Charge differ, the Licensee shall offer to include in the agreement with the Operator for the provision of that Standard Service terms (that offer not to be conditional on the acceptance by that Operator of the inclusion in that agreement of any other terms and conditions whether relating to the charge (or the means of calculating that charge for that Standard Service)) which provide that:

(i)   if the Interim Charge is greater than the Final Charge, the Licensee shall pay to the Operator the amount of the difference together with interest calculated in accordance with sub-paragraph (b); and

(ii)   if the Interim Charge is less than the Final Charge, the Operator shall pay to the Licensee the amount of the difference together with interest calculated in accordance with sub-paragraph (b);

provided that:

(aa)   where the charge for that Standard Service paid by an Operator to the Licensee pending the recalculation and redetermination of the charge in accordance with this paragraph (the 'Actual Charge') is less than the Interim Charge (whether as a result of the operation of Condition 24F or in circumstances where the Director has consented to that lesser charge pursuant to Condition 16B.5), the Final Charge shall be whichever is the lower of the Actual Charge and what would have been the Final Charge but for the operation of this proviso; and

(bb)   any payment to be made in accordance with this paragraph shall be adjusted to take account of any revision of the charge (or the means of calculating that charge) pursuant to either of Conditions 24F.11 and 24F.14.

(b)   A recalculation and redetermination of charges as described in sub-paragraph (a) shall include a provision requiring the Licensee to offer to include in the agreement with the Operator for the provision of that Standard Service terms which provide for interest to be added to any payment calculated in accordance with paragraph 13.5A.3B (b).

(c)   For the purposes of calculating the charge (or the means of calculating that charge) for a service provided by the Operator to the Licensee referred to in paragraph 13.5C.1, the calculations shall be made in the same manner as the calculations made in accordance with paragraph 13.5B.1A.

13.5D   Where the Director determines any charges or the means of calculating any charges, he may, in addition to the other powers conferred on him by this Condition 13:

(a)   adjust the Contribution (which apart from such adjustment would be payable by the Operator to the Licensee towards the latter's Access Deficit) so that the Operator pays, in relation to any category of call, a Contribution to the financing of the Licensee's Access Deficit no greater than the average amount the Licensee would charge as a contribution to the financing of the Licensee's Access Deficit if the Operator's customers for such calls had made them (so far as conveyance by any public telecommunication system is concerned) wholly by means of the Applicable Systems taking advantage of all appropriate discounts which the Licensee makes available to its customers; and

(b)   incoming international calls which are first conveyed within the United Kingdom on the Operator's System (as distinct from any of the Applicable Systems), adjust the Contribution (as described in sub-paragraph (a) above) so as to take account of any discounts (or matters having the effect of such discounts) made available by the Licensee in charging certain of its customers for outgoing international calls, where such discounts (or such other matters) have the effect that any losses the Licensee may make on outgoing international calls made by customers qualifying for the discount are funded by profits on incoming international calls. Any such adjustment made by the Director shall be for the purpose set out in sub-paragraph (a), that is to say, for the purpose of ensuring that the Operator pays in relation to any incoming international calls, a Contribution no greater than the average of the amounts which the Licensee might appropriately apply as contributions to the financing of its Access Deficit if the Operator's customers had made all their outgoing international calls (so far as conveyance by any public telecommunication system is concerned) wholly by means of the Applicable Systems taking advantage of all appropriate discounts which the Licensee makes available to its customers and if the corresponding incoming international calls had been first conveyed within the United Kingdom on any of the Applicable Systems (as distinct from the Operator's system).

The discounts (or other matters) referred to in sub-paragraphs (a) and (b) above are those which fall within the publication requirements of Condition 16.

13.5E   Where in pursuance of such an application as is referred to in paragraph 13.5 the Director determines any charge (or means of calculating that charge) payable in respect of the provision of a service other than a service the charge (or the means of calculating that charge) payable in respect of which falls to be determined in accordance with paragraph 13.5A or paragraph 13.5C he shall do so in accordance with paragraph 13.5C.6.

13.5F   Before making an adjustment pursuant to paragraph 13.5D, the Director shall consult with the Licensee and the Operator. If he concludes that an adjustment is appropriate, he shall notify the Licensee and Operator of the proposed adjustment and his reasons for making it and give them a reasonable opportunity to make representations. For the avoidance of doubt, in deciding whether and to what extent to exercise the power conferred on him by paragraph 13.5A.5 the Director shall take account of the extent (if any) to which adjustments provided for paragraphs 13.5D or 13.5E have been made at that time or are appropriate to be made.

13.5G   Without prejudice to paragraph 13.5A.3B or Condition 16B, with effect from 8 February 1996 and notwithstanding any agreement entered into by the Licensee or determination made under Condition 13, the Licensee shall not recover from an Operator (nor will any determination made before that date oblige an Operator to pay) any Contribution in relation to any period commencing on or after 8 February 1996 and if an Operator has, immediately before that date, been under an obligation to pay a Contribution, the Licensee shall reduce the relevant charge or charges payable by the Operator to the Licensee by the amount of the Contribution.

13.6   Where the Licensee is required to enter into an agreement to do anything under paragraph 13.1 (b) the permitted terms and conditions may relate to all or any of the matters mentioned in paragraph 13.4 but in determining the terms and conditions, in the event of a failure to agree, under paragraph 13.5 the Director shall have regard to (in addition to the matters specified in paragraph 13.5) the need to ensure:

(a)   that, insofar as any freedom of choice is conferred upon persons running telecommunication systems connected to the Operator's system as to the extent to which Messages are conveyed by means of the Applicable Systems and in routing messages so conveyed, a corresponding freedom of choice is conferred so far as reasonably practicable on persons running telecommunication systems connected to the Licensee's system;

(b)   that the requirements of fair competition, including the need for those to whom telecommunication services are provided to have a reasonable means of learning by whom the Messages sent by them are conveyed, are satisfied;

but paragraph 13.5 shall have effect for this purpose with the omission of sub-paragraph (f) (iv).

13.7 The Licensee shall not be obliged to enter into any agreement under paragraph 13.1 if he refuses to do so, giving his reasons in writing to the Operator and to the Director, and the Director determines that those reasons are proper ones having regard to the matters mentioned in paragraphs 13.5 and 13.6.

13.8 Where:

(*a*) an agreement has been entered into under paragraph 13.1 but for any reason (whether breach of that agreement or otherwise) anything which the Licensee is required to do under the agreement is not being done;

(*b*) the Director considers that the thing ought to be done in order to ensure that a connection made pursuant to that agreement is maintained or that a connection is established pursuant to that agreement and that Messages are conveyed by means of the connection in accordance with the agreement; and

(*c*) the Director is satisfied that the Operator is not able satisfactorily to enforce the agreement so that that thing is done within such time as the Director considers necessary;

then, if the Director so directs, the Licensee shall do that thing subject to such conditions as the Director determines to be reasonable in the circumstances, having regard, in particular, to the permitted terms and conditions which apply and to any thing which he may reasonably require the Operator to do in order to mitigate the effects of the Licensee's failure to do the thing which he is required to do.

13.8A.1 This paragraph 13.8A applies where:

(*a*) an Operator establishes a prima facie case that the Licensee is unreasonably not performing an obligation which he is required to perform under an agreement entered into under paragraph 13.1;

(*b*) the Director considers that:

(i) the obligation ought to be performed in order to achieve the purposes of paragraph 13.1;

(ii) the Operator is not able satisfactorily to enforce the agreement so that the obligation is performed within such time as the Director considers necessary and the balance of convenience requires the Director to take action under this paragraph rather than leave it to the Courts; and

(iii) the Operator has performed all its obligations which are relevant to the Licensee's obligation that is allegedly not being performed; and

(*c*) paragraph 13.8 does not apply.

13.8A.2 Where this paragraph 13.8A applies the Director may require the Licensee to perform the obligation subject to such conditions as are reasonable in the circumstances having regard, in particular, to the permitted terms and conditions which apply and to anything which the Operator may reasonably be expected to do in order to mitigate the effects of the Licensee's failure to perform its obligation.

13.8A.3 Before making a requirement under paragraph 13.8A.2 the Director shall notify the Licensee of the prima facie case established by the Operator, his conclusions thereon, and on the matters referred to in paragraph 13.8A.1 (b) and the direction he proposes to make. The Licensee shall be afforded adequate time in which to make representations.

13.8B.1 Notwithstanding, and without prejudice to, any of the foregoing provisions of this Condition, if the Director considers that there is likely to be a category comprising a sufficient number of Operators seeking determinations under paragraph 13.5 for whom standard terms and conditions would be appropriate, he may require the Licensee to publish standard provisions (including, without limitation, charges or the method for calculating them) which set out the terms on which the Licensee will enter into an agreement under paragraph 13.1 with Operators of that particular category.

13.8B.2   If on an application by an Operator in that category the Director is satisfied that the Operator has established a prima facie case that any such standard term or condition proposed by the Licensee is unreasonable and that the Licensee has acted unreasonably in relation to negotiations on that term or condition, the Director may, if he considers it necessary to do so, either determine that the Licensee shall modify that standard provision in such a way as to make the term reasonable in the agreement with the Operator, or modify that standard provision in such a way in the provisions published under paragraph 13.8B.1:

In applying this paragraph 13.8B.2:

(a)   any such standard provision shall be confined to the subject matter of the term or condition proposed by the Licensee except that, where the Director considers that a term or condition is essential in relation to subject matter not covered by any term or condition proposed by the Licensee, he may determine a term or condition to cover the subject matter;

(b)   the Licensee shall not be deemed to have acted unreasonably merely by virtue of having proposed the term or condition in question; and

(c)   no determination may be made in relation to any provision which would be subject to the Unfair Contract Terms Act 1977.

13.8B.3   Before making a determination under paragraph 13.8B.2 the Director shall notify to the Licensee and the Operator the grounds of the Operator's application and his conclusions thereon and the modification he proposes to make or require the Licensee to make, and shall afford the Licensee and the Operator adequate time, being not less than 28 days, in which to make representations.

13.8B.4   Where an Operator makes an application to the Director under paragraph 13.5, the Director may treat the application as an application under paragraph 13.8B.2 above and act accordingly.

13.8B.5   For the avoidance of doubt the provisions of paragraphs 13.5, 13.5A, 13.5B and 13.5C shall apply in respect of any determination made under this paragraph as they apply in relation to a determination made under paragraph 13.5.

13.9   In this Condition:

'Business' has the meaning given to it in Condition 20B;

'Competitive Standard Service' has the meaning given to it in Condition 16B;

'Confidential Information' has the meaning given to it in Condition 41A;

'Connectable System' means a telecommunication system which is authorised to be run under a Licence which authorises connection of that system to any of the Applicable Systems;

'Connection Service' means a telecommunication service consisting in the conveyance of any Message which has been, or is to be, conveyed by means of any of the Applicable Systems;

'Financial Statement' has the meaning given to it in Condition 20B;

'Initial Standard Service' has the meaning given to it in Condition 16B;
'Long Line Public Telecommunications Operator' means a public tele-communications operator who is authorised by a Licence to provide telecommunication services consisting in the conveyance of Messages by fixed links run by him over distances greater than 50 linear kilometres;
'Quality' has the meaning given to it in Condition 17B;
'Relevant Connectable System' means a Connectable System which is authorised to be run under the Licence which authorises the provision by means of that System of Connection Services for reward to the public, or any class of the public, not being a system:

(i)   authorised to be run under a Licence granted to all persons or persons of any class; and

(ii)   for the connection of which, and for the provision of matters necessary for such connection, the Licensee offers standard terms and conditions which satisfy the requirements of Condition 16;
and not being a system which the Director has determined ought not to be deemed to be a Relevant Connectable System for the purposes of this Condition; and
'Standard Service' has the meaning given to it in Condition 16B.

13.10   This Condition operates without prejudice to Condition 19 (access charges) but due account shall be taken for the purposes of this Condition of any charge imposed on the Operator for the purposes of that Condition.

13.11   An agreement made pursuant to this Condition shall not contain any restrictive provision unless, before the agreement is made, the Director has expressly consented to the inclusion of such a provision or has determined that that provision should be included under paragraph 13.5 or 13.6 and, for the purposes of this paragraph, a provision in an agreement is a restrictive provision if by virtue of the existence of such a provision (taken alone or with other provisions) the agreement is one to which the Restrictive Trade Practices Act 1976 would apply but for paragraph 1(1) of Schedule 3 of that Act.

13.2   Where the Director so directs the Crown shall be treated for the purposes of this Condition as a person authorised to run a Relevant Connect-able System and where he does so he may also direct that the Crown is to be treated as a Long Line Public Telecommunications Operator for those purposes.

Condition 13A   Equal Access

13A.1   This Condition applies in respect of any Long Line Public Tele-communications Operator (the term 'Operator' referring in this Condition 13A to such an Operator) with whom the Licensee has entered into an agreement as required by Condition 13.1 and where the Director has made a direction under paragraph 13A.2.

13A.2   (a)   At any time after 31 December 1992 the Director may, subject to the provisions of paragraph 13A.3, make a direction that whenever an Operator so requests after a date specified in the direction the Licensee shall make Equal Access available in respect of that Operator on the basis set out in this Condition 13A.

(b)   The direction shall contain a functional specification of exchange software for the provision of Equal Access. The specification shall be that submitted to the Director by the Licensee (following receipt of a request from the Director) or, if the Director, having carried out such consultation as appears to him appropriate, considers that specification to be unsatisfactory, in a form determined by the Director. Before making such a determination the Director shall notify the Licensee as to why the Licensee's specification is unsatisfactory and give the Licensee the opportunity to make representations.

13A.3   The Director shall not make a direction under paragraph 13A.2 unless;

(a)   he has carried out a cost-benefit analysis comparing the likely benefits to telecommunications customers to be gained from the introduction of Equal Access with all costs likely to be incurred, including opportunity costs, which analysis indicates that the gains outweigh the likely costs; and

(b)   in his opinion sufficient arrangements in relation to the pricing of telecommunication services provided by the Licensee have been made in relation to the following matters to achieve fair competition:

(i)   the extent to which the Licensee has been able to rebalance its charges to align them more appropriately with costs;

(ii)   the extent to which regulatory controls, whether imposed by this Licence or otherwise and including voluntary commitments, affect the balance referred to in paragraph 13A.3(b)(i);

(iii)   the amount and structure of charges payable to the Licensee by virtue of agreements with Operators entered into by the Licensee under Condition 13; and

(iv)   the extent to which charges are payable to the Licensee by virtue of Condition 19.

13A.4   When carrying out the cost-benefit analysis referred to in paragraph 13A.3(a), the Director shall consult the Licensee and such other persons as appear to him appropriate, affording them a reasonable period, being not less than 28 days, in which to make representations, and he shall take their representations into account when reaching his conclusions. On conclusion of the analysis he shall make it available to the Licensee and such other persons.

13A.5   (a)   In this Condition 'Equal Access' means a facility provided to an Operator whereby he can arrange with a customer of the Licensee that, following a request by that customer to the Licensee, the customer may choose over which public telecommunications system, being a system run by a Long Line Public Telecommunications Operator, to route National and International calls made by means of an Exchange Line provided to him by the Licensee. The choice shall be exercisable in either of the following ways, at the option of the customer.

(i)   by pre-selection, that is to say that the customer may, by registering a preference with the Licensee, name a particular such Operator for the conveyance of all such calls. The Licensee may offer to provide a facility to override the preference in the case of any particular call; or

(ii)   on a call-by-call basis, that is to say that the customer must, for each call, exercise his choice by dialling a short initial code designated for the particular such Operator (or the Licensee) chosen by the customer for the call in question. The respective initial codes for the Licensee and for all Operators shall be of equal length.

'National' and 'International' calls shall be defined by reference to the Licensee's charges and other terms and conditions published in accordance with Condition 16.

(*b*) The Licensee shall not require the customer to acquire any special equipment or to pay any fee as a prerequisite to his being able to obtain the Equal Access facility. For the avoidance of doubt the Licensee may impose a charge if a customer who has registered a preference changes that preference in any way.

13A.6 Where a Long Line Public Telecommunications Operator requires the Licensee to provide Equal Access, and specifies exchanges forming part of the Applicable Systems at which it is to be provided, and the Licensee has not, after a reasonable period, entered into an agreement with that Operator for the provision of Equal Access, the Director may, on the application of either the Licensee or the Operator, determine the terms and conditions of the agreement, being terms and conditions necessary for the provision of Equal Access, or such terms and conditions which the Licensee and the Operator have failed to agree.

13A.7 Before making a determination under paragraph 13A.6, the Director shall:

(*a*) carry out in relation to the Operator concerned an analysis taking into account the results of the analysis referred to in paragraph 13A.3(a) comparing the benefits likely to be gained with all the costs incurred and likely to be incurred, including opportunity costs. The provisions of paragraph 13A.4 shall apply to the analysis. The purpose shall be to decide whether, in relation to that Operator's request for Equal Access, the costs will outweigh the benefits; and

(i) if the Director concludes that the costs will outweigh the benefits, his determination shall secure that no part of those costs shall be borne by the Licensee;

(ii) if the Director concludes that the benefits will outweigh the costs, his determination shall secure that the costs are apportioned as provided in paragraph 13A.10; and

(*b*) notify the Licensee and that Operator in respect of which terms and conditions he proposes to make a determination, and why, and shall afford the Licensee and that Operator adequate time, being not less than 28 days, in which to make representations.

13A.8 In making a determination under paragraph 13A.6, the Director shall:

(*a*) subject to paragraph 13A.10, secure that the principles set out in Condition 13.5 (a) to (g), so far as applicable, are achieved; and

(*b*) secure that the Licensee's obligation in relation to the provision of Equal Access is limited to:

(i) the acceptance of registrations of such preference as is referred to in sub-paragraph 13A.5(a)(i);

(ii) the delivering of calls to the Operator's system in accordance with the choice of the Licensee's customers as described in paragraph 13A.5; and

(iii) the provision of facilities contained in the specification referred to in paragraph 13A.2(b).

13A.9 (*a*) Where the Director makes a determination under paragraph 13A.6 he shall secure that any development of the Applicable Systems made necessary thereby is consistent with the Licensee's then planned programme of network modernisation and development and in particular that the Licensee is not required to introduce Equal Access at any exchange if to do so would involve either:

(i)   modernising the exchange in a case where, but for the proposed introduction of Equal Access, the exchange would not have been modernised at that time; or

(ii)   a significant risk of impairment to the quality of telecommunication services provided by means of the Applicable Systems.

(b)   Subject to paragraph 13A.9(a), where the Director makes a determination under paragraph 13A.6 the following shall apply in relation to the preparation of exchanges for Equal Access:

(i)   The determination may require the Licensee to introduce Equal Access within a reasonable period. At a digital exchange to which the determination relates which does not require conversion for the introduction of Equal Access, a reasonable period for adapting the exchange to provide Equal Access shall be six months. In relation to such an exchange which does require conversion, or any other exchange of an exchange type which is capable of conversion to provide Equal Access, a reasonable period for conversion and adaptation shall, subject to paragraph 13A.9(a), be eighteen months. Different periods may be specified for different exchanges;

(ii)   Where at the date of the determination an exchange to which it relates is not digital, and is of an exchange type which is not capable of conversion to provide Equal Access, the Licensee shall ensure (subject to paragraph 13A.9(a)) that, when modernisation to digital is planned, the specification therefore provides for Equal Access.

13A.10   Where, in an analysis carried out under paragraph 13A.7(a), the Director concludes that the benefits will outweigh the costs, any determination under paragraph 13A.6 shall secure that the Licensee's costs of introducing Equal Access are apportioned according to the following provisions:

(a)   The following costs of introducing Equal Access, among any others which the Director may consider relevant, shall be included among those brought into account:

(i)   costs incurred by the Licensee which are not related to any particular locality consisting of initial development and set-up costs including, without limitation, the costs of hardware design and production, the costs of software development and the costs of planning and training;

(ii)   costs incurred by the Licensee in relation to a particular locality where an Operator has requested the introduction of Equal Access, consisting of initial development and set-up costs in relation to that locality including, without limitation, the costs of installation of hardware and software and the costs of distribution of necessary documentation and instructions and of training;

(iii)   the incremental costs of providing at any particular locality Equal Access to any further Operator after the first Operator at that locality;

(iv)   the costs per customer of registering preferences and of implementing arrangements for the initial code referred to in paragraph 13A.5(a)(ii); and

(v)   the costs per customer of changing registered preferences or removing, in relation to any particular exchange line, arrangements for the initial code.

(*b*)   Subject to paragraph 13A.10(c) and (d):

(i)   the costs referred to in paragraph 13A.10(a)(i) shall be apportioned between the Licensee and Operators who make requirements under paragraph 13A.6. The costs shall initially be apportioned between the Licensee and the first such Operator. Procedures will be established for subsequent Operators to make a proportionate contribution to the costs in such manner as the Director shall determine from time to time;

(ii)   the costs referred to in paragraph 13A.10(a)(ii) shall be apportioned between the Licensee and Operators who make requirements under paragraph 13A.6 in relation to the particular locality. The apportionment rules set out in paragraph 13A.10(b)(i) shall apply *mutatis mutandis*;

(iii)   where the addition of an Operator at a locality reduces the contribution to the costs of Equal Access at that locality of the Licensee and the other Operators, the procedures in paragraph 13A.10(b)(i) shall apply *mutatis mutandis* to the costs referred to in paragraph 13A.10(a)(iii). In any other case that Operator shall pay such costs;

(iv)   the costs referred to in paragraph 13A.10(a)(iv) and (v) above shall be met by the Long Line Public Telecommunications Operator, whether the Licensee or an Operator, to whom the customer chooses to route calls by registering a preference or, where the customer exercises choice on a call-by-call basis, apportioned equitably among the Long Line Public Telecommunications Operators (including, where appropriate, the Licensee) to whom the customer has the option of routing calls from time to time.

(*c*)   The apportionment of the costs referred to in paragraph 13A.10(a)(i),(ii) and (iii) shall reflect equitably the benefit to the Operator and his customers, actual and potential, of the implementation of Equal Access in relation to that Operator.

(*d*)   Before determining the apportionment of any costs referred to in paragraph 13A.10(a), the Director shall inform the Licensee and the Operator of his proposed determination, together with a full explanation of how it is calculated, and shall allow the Licensee and the Operator a reasonable period, being not less than 28 days, in which to make representations.

13A.11   In this Condition 13A, 'potential' customers include those customers of the Licensee who it is reasonable to expect will apply for the Equal Access facility.

13A.12   The provisions of this Condition form part of Condition 13 and accordingly shall be treated for all purposes as contained and laid down in Condition 13.

Condition 13B   Essential Interfaces

13B.1   This Condition is without prejudice to Condition 13.

13B.2   (*a*)   The Director may, having first notified the Licensee of his proposal, affording the Licensee adequate time, being not less than 28 days, in which to make representations, specify an Essential Interface.

(*b*)   'Essential Interface' means in respect of a point of connection, as defined in Condition 13.5C, an interface at which in the opinion of the Director it is essential that interoperability between the Applicable Systems and the respective Operator's system is available.

13B.3   (a)   Where in pursuance of paragraph 13B.2 the Director specifies an interface as an Essential Interface, and the Licensee thereafter makes
that interface available to an Operator in relation to its Applicable Systems,
it shall do so in such a manner as it considers appropriate, but shall ensure
such availability in compliance with the Relevant Standard if the Operator so
requires.

   (b)   'Relevant Standard' means:
      (i)   an appropriate European or other international standard; or
      (ii)   in the absence of such a standard, any other standard specified
by the Director after notifying the Licensee of his proposal and allowing the
Licensee adequate time, being not less than 28 days, in which to make
representations, provided that the Director shall not specify a standard if an
appropriate European or other international standard is expected to be
promulgated within a reasonable time, including, by way of example, if the
European Telecommunications Standards Institute have published a work
programme for the development of such a standard;
to the extent that such a standard is necessary to ensure interoperability.

   (c)   Where in pursuance of paragraph 13B.3 (b)(ii) the Director specifies a standard as a Relevant Standard, he shall include in that Standard a
technical specification. The Director shall use all reasonable endeavours to
obtain the agreement of the Licensee and other relevant licensees to a
technical specification applicable to the Standard, being a specification
defined by reference to:
      (i)   an appropriate European or other international specification; or
      (ii)   in the absence of such a specification, a specification defined by
reference to any other standard having currency within the European Community at the time.
Where after a reasonable time the Director has been unable to secure the
agreement of the Licensee and other relevant licensees to a technical specification, the Director shall adopt for inclusion in the Relevant Standard an
appropriate technical specification selected by him which has been promulgated by a recognised standards body, including, by way of example, the
European Telecommunications Standards Institute, or the British Standards
Institution, or other such body as is recognised by the Director as representative of all relevant telecommunications interests.

   (d)   In any event the Director shall specify a Relevant Standard in
pursuance of paragraph 13B.3(b) only if the owners of relevant intellectual
property rights have agreed to grant any necessary licences in respect thereof
to the Licensee on reasonable terms.

13B.4   For the avoidance of doubt this Condition shall not:
   (a)   without prejudice to paragraph 13B.3, prevent the Licensee using
such interfaces as it considers appropriate in relation to the Applicable
Systems; or
   (b)   where it makes available to an Operator an interface which the
Director has specified as an Essential Interface, require the Licensee to
comply with the Relevant Standard if the Operator does not require it to do
so.

13B.5   When implementing an Essential Interface, the Licensee shall not
be obliged to conform with the Relevant Standard:
   (a)   if to do so would necessitate the Licensee:

(i) acquiring apparatus, software or other goods or supplies of any kind, or implementing any operation, incompatible with, as the case may be, apparatus, software or such other goods or supplies already at the time in use, or the subject at the time of contracts for their procurement for use, in connection with any of the Applicable Systems, or, in the case of an operation, incompatible with any other operation being carried out at the time in connection therewith; or

(ii) incurring any cost, or having to resolve technical difficulties, disproportionate to the benefits to be gained from the implementation of the Relevant Standard;

provided that the Licensee shall take reasonable steps to incorporate the Relevant Standard in its plans for network development, with a view to implementation of that Standard in connection with the Applicable Systems, but without the Licensee incurring any incremental expenditure disproportionate to the benefits to be gained from the implementation of the Relevant Standard which, but for the implementation of the Relevant Standard, would not have been incurred;

(b) if the Relevant Standard is inappropriate for the particular application for any reason, including, without limitation:

(i) that it does not afford the Licensee adequate protection for the security of the Applicable Systems;

(ii) that its implementation would be liable to cause material impairment in the quality of any telecommunications service provided by means of any of the Applicable Systems;

(iii) that it does not cater adequately for billing, metering or other customer administration systems; or

(iv) that it is technically inadequate in the light of technical developments which have taken place since it was originally created;

(c) if the Essential Interface concerned is of a genuinely innovative nature and accordingly the use in connection with it of the Relevant Standard would not be appropriate;

(d) if compliance with the Relevant Standard would involve the infringement by the Licensee of any intellectual property right vested in any person; or

(e) if the Director so agrees.

13B.6 Where paragraph 13B.5(b) or (c) applies the Licensee shall notify the Director thereof, with an explanation why.

13B.7 It is a precondition of any obligation on the Licensee under this Condition that equivalent obligations as are contained in this Condition are included in the respective licences of all Operators.

13B.8 In this Condition 'Operator' has the meaning given to it in Condition 13.1.

Notes to Condition 13
1. Conditions 13.1(b), 13.1(c), 13.1(d), 13.4 (header), 13.4(c), 13.5 (header), 13.5(a), 13.5A.3 (part only), 13.5B.1(a), 13.5C.1(a), 13.5D (header), 13.5D(a) were amended by a licence amendment dated 31 March 1995.
2. Conditions 13.4(aa), 13.4(ff), 13.4(ii), 13.5A.3(b)(i), 13.5A.3A, 13.5A.3B, 13.5A.3C, 13.5B.1A, 13.5C.1 (proviso), 13.5C.6, 13.5E, 13.9 (some definitions) were inserted by a licence amendment dated 31 March 1995.

3.   Conditions 13.5(g), 13.5A, 13.5A.1, 13.5A.2, 13.5A.4, 13.5A.5, 13.5A.6, 13.5A.7.1, 13.5A.7.2, 13.5A.7.3, 13.5A.8, 13.5A.9, 13.5B.1, 13.5B.2, 13.5B.3, 13.5B.4, 13.5B.5, 13.5B.6, 13.5B.7, 13.5B.8, 13.5C, 13.5C.1, 13.5C.2, 13.5C.3, 13.5C.4, 13.5C.5, 13.8A.1, 13.8A.2, 13.8A.3, 13.8B.1, 13.8B.2, 13.8B.3, 13.8B.4, 13.8B.5, 13.A, 13.A.1–12, 13.B, 13.8.1–8 were inserted by a licence amendment dated 24 September 1991.

4.   Condition 13.5A.2 (header) was amended by a licence amendment dated 9 March 1993 and again by a licence amendment dated 31 March 1995.

5.   Conditions 13.5A.3(a), 13.5A.3(b)(ii), 13.5A.9 (deleted only), 13.5E were deleted and replaced by a licence amendment dated 31 March 1995.

6.   Conditions 13.5A3(c), 13.5A.3A (header), 13.5A.3A (part only), 13.5B.3, 13.5F were amended by a licence amendment dated 13 February 1996.

7.   Conditions 13.5A.3A(b), 13.5A.7.1, 13.5A.7.2, 13.5A.7.3 were deleted by a licence amendment dated 13 February 1996.

8.   Conditions 13.5D, 13.5E, 13.5F were inserted by a licence amendment dated 9 March 1993.

9.   Condition 13.5G was inserted by a licence condition dated 13 February 1996.

10.   Condition 13.5A.5(g) was amended by a licence amendment dated 1 October 1996.

11.   In May 1995 BT produced a standard interconnection agreement which is reproduced in its latest draft version in this Handbook, at p. 525. Under Condition 16A BT must publish information in relation to such agreement.

12.   The Director General has made a number of determinations under Condition 13, two of the most important of which related to the terms and conditions of the interconnection of the systems of Mercury Communications Ltd to those of BT on 11 October 1985 and 2 December 1993. Such determinations are by virtue of s. 19(2), Telecommunications Act 1984 on the public record, although the Director General has powers under s. 19(3) to keep such determinations off the record under certain circumstances.

13.   See the OFTEL Consultative Document 'The Future Pricing of IPLCs in a Liberalised International Facilities Market' July 1996.

14.   Condition 13.5A was added as part of the post-duopoly review modifications following the 1991 White Paper 'Competition and Choice; Telecommunications Policy of the 1990s'.

15.   See OFTEL's policy on indirect access, equal access and direct connection to the access network, July 1996.

16.   Further changes are envisaged to Condition 13 as a result of an OFTEL Statement 'Pricing of Telecommunications Services from 1997' produced in June 1996 and a Consultative Document 'Network Charges for 1997' published in December 1996 in order to supplement network charge caps from August 1997.

Condition 14   Connection of Other Systems and Apparatus

14.1   Subject to the provisions of this Condition the Licensee:

(*a*)   shall connect, at a Network Termination Point within Network Termination and Testing Apparatus situated on Served Premises, any of the Applicable Systems to:

(i)   any item of telecommunication apparatus which is approved for the time being for connection to that Applicable System under section 22 of the Act; or

(ii)   any other telecommunication system to which this Condition applies which is or is to be run by the Crown or which is composed of apparatus which is approved for connection to that system;

which is owned by or supplied to another person, at the written request of such person, where such connection is or is to be made of by means requiring the use of a tool;

(b) shall not discontinue such connection of any such apparatus or system lawfully made; and

(c) shall permit any person to connect, or to keep connected, at a Network Termination Point within Network Termination and Testing Apparatus comprised in any Applicable System any such apparatus or other such system where such connection is or is to be made by means that do not require the use of a tool.

14.2 Apparatus shall not be regarded as approved for connection to any system for the purposes of paragraph 14.1 unless that apparatus has been so approved:

(a) by the Secretary of State; or

(b) by some other person by virtue of an authorisation given by the Secretary of State being an authorisation which required the person authorised, before approving any apparatus or designating any standard to which apparatus must conform if it is to be approved, to be satisfied that connection of the apparatus to the system would not be liable:

(i) to cause the death of, or personal injury to, or damage to the property of the Licensee or any person engaged in the running of that system; or

(ii) materially to impair the quality of any telecommunication service provided by means of that system or any system connected to it (other than the system being connected).

14.3 No apparatus or system is required under paragraph 14.1 to be, or to be permitted to be, kept connected to any of the Applicable Systems if that apparatus, or any apparatus comprised in that system, as the case may be:

(a) conformed to the relevant standard or standards at the time when the connection to the Applicable System was made but no longer does so and does not conform to the relevant standard or standards (if any) for the time being designated under section 22 (6) of the Act; or

(b) while continuing to conform to the relevant standard is in the opinion of the Licensee liable to cause the death of, or personal injury to, or damage to the property of, the Licensee, or any person engaged in the running of any of the Applicable Systems or materially to impair the quality of any telecommunication service provided by means of any Applicable System and the Director has not expressed a contrary opinion.

14.4 For the purposes of this Condition apparatus shall not be regarded as constituting a system if it would not, but for its connection to any of the Applicable Systems, constitute such a system, and this Condition applies to any apparatus or system which is not a Relevant Connectable System within the meaning of Condition 13.

Condition 15 Provision by Others of Services by Means of the Applicable Systems

15.1 The Licensee shall permit any person, who is licensed to run a Connectable System under a Licence which authorises him to provide telecommunication services to others, including Connection Services, to provide such services whilst that Connectable System is connected to the relevant Applicable System.

15.2   The Licensee shall permit any person:

(*a*)   using telecommunication apparatus which is lawfully connected to any of the Applicable Systems or which is connected to another telecommunication system which itself is lawfully connected to any of the Applicable Systems; or

(*b*)   running a telecommunication system which is so connected; to provide by means of the Applicable Systems any service other than the installation, maintenance, adjustment, repair, alteration, moving, removal or replacement of telecommunication apparatus comprised in any of the Applicable Systems.

15.3   The Licensee shall, following a request by any Service Provider to do so, provide to that Service Provider any description of telecommunication service which the Licensee at the time the request is made offers to its customers generally and which is specified in the request, on terms which would not prohibit the Service Provider from contracting with another person to provide that person with that description of service.

15.4   (*a*)   If on an application by a Service Provider the Director is satisfied that the Service Provider has established a prima facie case that any charge, term or condition proposed by the Licensee is unreasonable and that the Licensee has acted unreasonably in relation to negotiations on it, the Director may, if he considers it necessary to do so, determine that the Licensee shall modify that provision in such a way as to make it reasonable, in the agreement with the Service Provider.

In applying this paragraph 15.4:

(i)   no determination made shall affect any exclusion or restriction equivalent to one which is, at the relevant time, included in the Licensee's current usual terms and conditions upon which the Licensee provides the same description of service to the generality of the Licensee's customers in a way which would or might have the effect of rendering the position of the Licensee in relation to the provision of the service the subject of the determination worse than the position of the Licensee in relation to the provision of the same description of service to the generality of the Licensee's customers;

(ii)   any such modified provision shall be confined to the subject matter of the term or condition proposed by the Licensee except that, where the Director considers that a term or condition is essential in relation to subject matter not covered by any term or condition proposed by the Licensee, he may determine a term or condition to cover that subject matter;

(iii)   the Licensee shall not be deemed to have acted unreasonably merely by virtue of having proposed the term or condition in question; and

(iv)   no determination may be made in relation to any provision which would be subject to the Unfair Contract Terms Act 1977.

(*b*)   Before making a determination under paragraph 15.4(a) the Director shall notify to the Licensee and the Service Provider the grounds of the Service Provider's application and his conclusions thereon and the modification he proposes to make or require the Licensee to make, and shall afford the Licensee and the Service Provider adequate time, being not less than 28 days, in which to make representations.

15.5 (a) Subject to the terms of this paragraph 15.5, any charge determined under paragraph 15.4 by the Director shall be determined by reference to the Licensee's usual charge ('the usual charge') for the provision to its customers generally of the service of the description in question ('the Service').

(b) Any charge determined under paragraph 15.4 by the Director shall not be:

(i) less than the usual charge for the Service by an amount which exceeds any cost savings of the Licensee which are shown to be likely; or

(ii) less than the usual charge for the Service plus any additional costs of the Licensee which are shown to be likely.

(c) Where the cost to the Licensee of the provision of a service to a Service Provider exceeds the usual charge no charge determined under paragraph 15.4 shall be less than the usual charge.

(d) In this paragraph 15.5 'costs' means fully allocated costs and a reasonable rate of return on capital employed.

15.6 If at any time it appears to the Director that the Service Provider no longer satisfies the criteria within paragraph 15.8 (a), the Director may, on giving not less than three months notice to both the Licensee and the Service Provider of his intention to do so, direct the Licensee to cease providing that description of telecommunication service to the Service Provider.

15.7 Where a direction given by the Director under paragraph 15.6 contains a statement that it appears to him that the need to protect the customers of the Service Provider or to protect any other person requires that the direction should be made without delay, the Director shall not be required to give the notice required to be given by paragraph 15.6 or any notice.

15.8 In this Condition 'Service Provider' means:

(a) any person proposing to carry on the business of reselling any description of telecommunication service proposed to be provided to that person by the Licensee and in respect of whom the Licensee has no reason to believe that such person will be unable to carry on that business effectively, economically and efficiently; or

(b) any person actually carrying on that business from time to time; or

(c) where, on the application of any person proposing to carry on that business to whom the Licensee has refused to provide any telecommunication service, the Director is satisfied that such service has been refused and has determined that such service should be provided by the Licensee to such person, that person;

but does not in any case mentioned in paragraph 15.8(a),(b) or (c) include any person who carries on or would carry on that business by means which necessarily involve the running of a telecommunication system by him or on his behalf.

15.9 Nothing in this Condition affects any need for a Service Provider to have any licence in respect of the service which is the subject of a request referred to in paragraph 15.3.

Note

Condition 15.2 (footer) was amended by and Conditions 15.3–9 were inserted by a licence amendment dated 24 September 1991.

Condition 16   Publication of Charges, Terms and Conditions to be Applied

16.1   Subject to the provisions of Condition 24F, [in relation to services other than the provision of Relevant Private Circuits the Licensee] shall, except in so far as the Director may otherwise consent in writing and except in respect of terms and conditions under Condition 13:

(*a*)   publish in the manner and at the times specified in paragraph 16.3 a notice specifying, or specifying the method that is to be adopted for determining, the charges and other terms and conditions on which it offers;

(i)   to provide each description of telecommunication service by means of any of the Applicable Systems in accordance with an obligation imposed by or under this Licence;

(ii)   to maintain, adjust or repair any apparatus comprised in any of the Applicable Systems in accordance with an obligation imposed by or under this Licence;

(iii)   to connect to any of the Applicable Systems any apparatus or any other system which, in either case, is not and is not to be comprised in any of the Applicable Systems in accordance with an obligation imposed by or under this Licence;

(iv)   to grant permission to connect such systems or apparatus to, or to provide services by means of, any of the Applicable Systems in accordance with an obligation imposed by or under this Licence; or

(v)   to Bring into Service any apparatus or system which, in either case, is or is to be connected to but not comprised or to be comprised in any of the Applicable Systems, where only the Licensee is permitted to provide such service; and

(*b*)   where it does any of the things mentioned in paragraph 16.1(a)(i) to (v), do those things at the charges and on the other terms and conditions so published and not depart therefrom.

16.2   The requirement to publish under paragraph 16.1 shall not apply in respect of any service which is materially different from any service already provided by the Licensee by means of any of the Applicable Systems until such time as it is provided.

16.3   Publication of the notice [referred to in paragraph 16.1(a)] shall be effected by:

(*a*)   sending a copy thereof to the Director not more than 28 days after the date on which this Licence enters into force and thereafter not less than 28 days before any proposal to amend any charge, term or condition or the method of determining the same is to become effective, provided however that if the Director consents in writing to any variation in a proposal to amend those charges, terms, conditions or methods in the said period of 28 days the Licensee shall not be prevented from making the amendments with variations 28 days after the date when the notice was first sent to the Director in accordance with this sub-paragraph: Provided that in its application to any Relevant Service, this sub-paragraph shall have effect as if the words 'one day' were substituted for the words '28 days' wherever they appear. In respect of a service to which paragraph 16.2 applies a copy of the notice shall be sent to the Director at the time the service is first provided;

(*b*) placing as soon as practicable thereafter a copy thereof in a publicly accessible part of every Major Office of the Licensee in such manner and in such place that it is readily available for inspection free of charge by members of the general public during the hours of 10am to 4pm Mondays to Fridays inclusive, except where any such day is a bank holiday (being a day which is, or is to be observed as, a bank holiday, or a holiday, under the Banking and Financial Dealings Act 1971) in that part of the United Kingdom where the Major Office in question is situate, Christmas Day or Good Friday or during such shorter hours as the Director may direct; and

(*c*) sending a copy thereof or such part or parts thereof as are appropriate to any person who may request such a copy.

Where the Licensee publishes a notice of an amendment to a charge in the form of an extract from the Licensee's price list the new price shall be clearly identifiable and the operative date specified.

16.3A The Licensee shall take reasonable measures to ensure that persons who receive any of the things charged for at Main Prices may have the opportunity to inform the Licensee from time to time that they require in advance details of increases to the Main Prices. The Licensee shall in advance of increases in Main Prices send any such persons details of such increases.

[16.3B The Licensee shall publish by notice in accordance with the presentation given in paragraphs A to C of Schedule 1 to the Telecommunications (Leased Lines) Regulations 1993 information on offerings on technical characteristics, tariffs and supply and usage conditions in respect of Relevant Private Circuits. The information shall be published in the manner provided for in paragraph 16.3 above. Where the information concerns new types of Relevant Private Circuit offerings, it shall be published as soon as possible, and no later than two months before the implementation of the offering. Changes in existing offerings shall be published as soon as possible and, unless the Director agrees otherwise, no later than two months before the implementation. The supply conditions published pursuant to this paragraph shall include at least the elements defined in paragraph C of Schedule 1 to the Telecommunications (Leased Lines) Regulations 1993.]

16.4 In this Condition:

'Major Office' means the office of the General Manager of each telephone area established on the day on which this Licence enters into force or such other offices as the Director may agree from time to time;

'Main Prices' means:

(*a*) all periodic charges for the ordinary use and Ordinary Maintenance of an Exchange Line;

(*b*) all charges based on duration for the conveyance by means of such Exchange Lines of voice telephony messages; and

(*c*) all charges for the provision of a directory information service.

16.5 Where the Licensee offers to provide a Relevant Service paragraph 16.1(a)(i) shall be deemed to be satisfied in respect of each telecommunication service comprised in that Relevant Service if the Licensee publishes, in the manner and at the times specified in paragraph 16.3, a notice specifying, or specifying the method that is to be adopted for determining, the aggregate charge and other terms and conditions on which it offers to provide the Relevant Service.

16.6   The things mentioned in paragraph 16.1(a)(i) do not include the provision of any telecommunication service comprised in a Relevant Service provided by the Licensee in so far as that telecommunication service is provided by means of a telecommunication system which is of such a description and run in such a way that if it was run by any person other than a public telecommunications operator it could be run under and in accordance with the Class Licence for the running of branch telecommunication systems granted by the Secretary of State.

Condition 16A   Publication Requirements Relating to Condition 13.1 Agreements (Interconnect Agreements)

16A.1   Not later than 28 days after entering into an agreement under Condition 13.1, the Licensee shall publish either:

(a)   an adequate description of the interconnection arrangements provided for by the agreement and the precise method of calculation of the charges referred to in Conditions 13.4 (a) and (aa) together with any provisions of the agreement which relate to particular circumstances which would materially affect those charges; or

(b)   the agreement;

in either case subject to the exclusion of any matter to the exclusion of which the Director shall have consented following representations to him on the matter by the Licensee, the Operator or any other person appearing to him to have an interest in it, prior to publication by the Licensee. Where the Director notifies the Licensee that he is considering such representations, the Licensee shall refrain from publication until such time as the Director notifies it of his decision to consent or to refuse his consent. The 28 day period mentioned above shall cease to run on the first notification and shall run once more on the second notification.

The description of the method of calculation referred to in sub-paragraph (a) above shall be such as to enable those charges readily to be calculated by a third party. Any description of such method shall be taken to comply with the requirements of this paragraph 16A.1 if the Director has indicated to the Licensee in advance of its publishing the description that the description does so comply. Where the Director receives, from persons appearing to have a reasonable interest in the matter, representations to the effect that the description is in need of clarification, he may, where such representations appear reasonable, require the Licensee to amend the description so as to provide such clarification as the Director may specify.

16A.2   For the purposes of paragraph 16A.1 publication shall be effected by:

(a)   sending to the Director either a document setting out what is required by paragraph 16A.1(a) or (as the case may require) the agreement; and

(b)   keeping a list of all such documents or agreements (together with a note of the address and telephone number of the person or persons to whom any request for a copy of any or all of such list or documents or agreements or any part of parts of them may be made).

16A.3   The Licensee shall send a copy or copies of such list or such document or documents or of such agreement or agreements or part or parts of them to any person who may (after the expiry of the 28 day period mentioned in paragraph 16A.1) request, on the basis of paying a reasonable charge for it, such a copy or copies. The Licensee shall send any documents and so forth so requested within 7 working days of receiving the request.

16A.4   The Licensee shall make available and continue to make available in a publicly accessible part of every Major Office of the Licensee in such place as is required by Condition 16.3(b) a notice of the address and telephone number referred to in paragraph 16A.2 above.

16A.5   Not less than seven days prior to publishing any description of the kind referred to in paragraph 16A.2(a) above, the Licensee shall send a draft of the proposed description to the Operator.

16A.6   For the purposes of paragraphs 16A.1–16A.3 above, 'agreement' includes any variation (whether provided for by the agreement or otherwise) of any agreement entered into under Condition 13.1.

16A.7   Where, but for this paragraph, the obligation imposed on the Licensee by paragraph 16A.1 could be satisfied by publishing a variation of an agreement in existence at the time of the coming into force of this Condition, the Licensee shall, instead of publishing the variation, publish an adequate description of the effect of the variation.

Condition 16B   Standard Services

16B.1   Within seven working days after the date on which this Condition comes into force, the Licensee shall refer to the Director for determination under Condition 13.5(2) the charge to be paid by any Operator to the Licensee for each Initial Standard Service.

16B.2   Not later than two months before the commencement of each financial year of the Licensee, commencing with the financial year ending 31 March 1997, the Licensee shall refer to the Director for determination under Condition 13.5(2) the charge for each Standard Service (other than a Competitive Standard Service) which shall be payable by an Operator in that financial year, the charge for which has been previously determined by the Director pursuant to Condition 13.

16B.3   Where the Director has determined the charge payable by an Operator to the Licensee for any Standard Service, following a reference by the Licensee under this Condition, that charge shall, subject to paragraphs 16B.2, 16B.6(b) and 16B.9, be payable by all Operators which may have requested, or may request in the future, that Standard Service from the Licensee and the Director shall not be required to determine the charge payable by any other Operator to the Licensee, for that Standard Service.

16B.4   Without prejudice to paragraph 16B.3, the Licensee shall, subject to the ability of an Operator to whom an offer is made pursuant to paragraph 16B.9 to decline that offer, ensure that:

(*a*)   the same charge for the same Standard Service is payable by all Operators (whether or not that charge has been determined by the Director);

(*b*)   where a Network Component or combination of Network Components is provided by the Licensee from one Business to another Business, the unit cost charged by way of Transfer Charge in respect of that provision is equal to the amount applied to that Network Component or combination of Network Components in the charge payable by an Operator to the Licensee for a Conveyance Standard Service which the Licensee is required to include in the Standard List in accordance with paragraph 16B.8 (a)(iii) (aa); and

(*c*)   where a Network Part or combination of Network Parts is provided by the Licensee from one Business to another Business, the unit cost charged by way of Transfer Charge in respect of that provision is equal to the amount applied to that Network Part or combination of Network Parts in the charge payable by an Operator to the Licensee for a Non-conveyance Standard Service which the Licensee is required to include in the Standard List in accordance with paragraph 16B.8 (a)(iii)(bb).

16B.5   (a)   Subject to sub-paragraph (b), the Licensee may offer to provide a Standard Service to an Operator at a charge (the 'New Charge') less than the charge payable for that Standard Service as determined by the Director pursuant to Condition 13.

(*b*)   The Licensee shall, before it makes an offer pursuant to sub-paragraph (a), send to the Director a written notice (an 'Offer Notice') specifying:

(i)   the existing charge payable for the Standard Service;

(ii)   the proposed New Charge and effective date of the Charge (which may pre-date the Offer Notice);

(iii)   in the case of a Conveyance Standard Service, the existing amount applied to each Network Component comprised in that Conveyance Standard Service and, in the case of a Non-conveyance Standard Service, the existing amount applied to each Network Part comprised in that Non-conveyance Standard Service, reconciled in each case with the existing charge payable for the relevant Standard Service; and

(iv)   in the case of a Conveyance Standard Service, the new amount applied to each Network Component comprised in that Conveyance Standard Service and, in the case of a Non-conveyance Standard Service, the new amount applied to each Network Part comprised in that Non-conveyance Standard Service, reconciled in each case with the New Charge payable for the relevant Standard Service.

(*c*)   If the Director consents to the proposed New Charge, the Licensee shall be entitled to offer the New Charge with effect from any date on or after the proposed effective date (subject to the terms of the consent).

(*d*)   Notwithstanding sub-paragraph (b), if, in the opinion of the Director, the information provided in an Offer Notice does not contain all the information specified in that sub-paragraph or is inaccurate in any way, the Licensee shall, without prejudice to Condition 52, furnish to the Director, in the manner and at the times as the Director may request, any further information which the Director may reasonably require. For the avoidance of doubt, pending the receipt and consideration of that further information by the Director, the Licensee shall not offer the proposed New Charge to any Operator.

16B.6   (a)   The Director shall, following a representation by the Licensee or an Operator or both that the market for a Standard Service is competitive, determine whether or not that market is competitive.

(*b*)   If the Director determines that the market for a Standard Service is competitive, then that Standard Service shall be a Competitive Standard Service. If the charge for that Standard Service:

(i)   has been determined by the Director, that charge shall no longer be the charge at which the Licensee is obliged to provide that Standard Service; or

(ii)   has not been determined by the Director, he shall not be required to determine the charge payable by an Operator; and
in each case, the Licensee shall be entitled to set the charge for that Standard Service.

(c)   The Director may, following a representation by the Licensee or an Operator or both that the market for a Competitive Standard Service has ceased to be competitive, determine that the market has ceased to be competitive. If the Director determines that the market for a Competitive Standard Service has ceased to be competitive, that Standard Service shall cease to be a Competitive Standard Service and, pursuant to an application by the Licensee or an Operator under Condition 13, the Director shall determine the charge for that Standard Service payable by an Operator to the Licensee pursuant to Condition 13.

16B.7   (a)   Before making a determination or giving consent under this Condition, the Director shall consult with the Licensee and Interested Parties. If he concludes that a determination or consent is appropriate, or that a consent is not appropriate, he shall notify the Licensee and Interested Parties of the proposed determination or consent or refusal of consent, as the case may be, and his reasons for proposing to make or give it or refuse to give consent and give each of them a reasonable opportunity to make representations. On making a determination or giving consent or refusing to give consent, he shall notify the Licensee and Interested Parties of the determination or consent or refusal, as the case may be, and his reasons for making or giving it or refusing consent.

(b)   Each notification of reasons shall, as appropriate, set out the Director's reasons:

(i)   for proposing to make the determination, or to give or refuse consent, as the case may be; or

(ii)   for making the determination or giving or refusing consent, as the case may be;
those reasons being sufficient to give the Licensee and Interested Parties a reasonable understanding of the proposed decision or decision, as the case may be.

16B.8   (a)   Except to the extent that the Director otherwise consents, the Licensee shall maintain a full list of Standard Services (the 'Standard List') as updated to take account of all changes to it identifying:

(i)   the charge to be paid by an Operator for each Standard Service determined by the Director pursuant to Condition 13;

(ii)   the charge to be paid by an Operator for each Standard Service:

(aa)   where that charge is less than the charge mentioned in sub-paragraph (a)(i) (whether as a result of the operation of Condition 24F or in circumstances where the Director has consented to that lesser charge pursuant to paragraph 16B.5);

(bb)   where the charge to be paid by an Operator has not been determined by the Director; and

(cc)   where the charge to be paid by an Operator which has been determined by the Director has ceased to be applicable;

(iii)   the amount applied to:

(aa)   each Network Component or combination of Network Components used in providing each Conveyance Standard Service and the unit cost charged by way of Transfer Charge for each Network Component or combination of Network Components provided by one Business to another Business; and

(bb)   each Network Part or combination of Network Parts used in providing each Non-conveyance Standard Service and the unit cost charged by way of Transfer Charge for each Network Part or combination of Network Parts provided by the Licensee from one Business to another Business reconciled;

in each case, with the relevant charge mentioned in paragraph (a)(i) or (ii): Provided that in the case of any Network Component, combination of Network Components or a Network Part or combination of Network Parts that is used in the provision of one or more Competitive Standard Services but is not also used in the provision of any other Standard Service that is not a Competitive Standard Service the Licensee shall not be required to include in the Standard List the amount applied to that Network Component, combination of Network Components, Network Part or combination of Network Parts or the unit cost charged by way of Transfer Charge applied in respect of any of those matters;

(iv)   The Transfer Charge for each Network Component which is not used in providing a Conveyance Standard Service;

(v)   The Transfer Charge for each Network Part which is not used in providing a Non-conveyance Standard Service; and

(vi)   each Competitive Standard Service.

(b)   As soon as reasonably practicable following a determination by the Director of a charge for a Standard Service the Licensee shall amend the Standard List to take account of that determination and shall publish the amendments made by sending a copy of them to the Director.

(c)   The Licensee shall send a copy of the most up to date Standard List to any person who may request it on payment of a reasonable charge for it. The Licensee shall send the copy within seven working days after receiving payment of that charge.

(d)   The Licensee shall make available and continue to make available in a publicly accessible part of every Major Office of the Licensee in the place required by Condition 16.3(b) a notice of the address and telephone number of the person to whom any request for a copy of the most up to date Standard List may be made.

16B.9   (a)   Subject to sub-paragraph (b) and notwithstanding paragraph 6 of Part 1 of Schedule 1, the Licensee shall offer to include in each agreement between the Licensee and an Operator for the provision of any Standard Service, whether subsisting before the date on which this Condition comes into force or otherwise an obligation on the Licensee to provide that Standard Service to that Operator at the charge determined from time to time by the Director pursuant to Condition 13 or any charge less than that charge to which the Director has consented pursuant to paragraph 16B.5, which the Licensee is obliged to apply as a result of the operation of Condition 24F or, in the case of a Competitive Standard Service, which the Licensee has set pursuant to paragraph 16B.6, as the case may be;

Provided that where the agreement provides for the provision by the Licensee to the Operator of more than one Standard Service, the offer shall be made in respect of all the Standard Services for which that agreement provides and the Licensee shall not be in breach of this paragraph if the Operator declines to accept the offer in its entirety.

(*b*) Subject to sub-paragraph (a), an offer for the purposes of that sub-paragraph shall not be conditional on the acceptance by the Operator of the inclusion in the agreement of any other terms and conditions except for terms and conditions which are necessarily incidental to the performance of the Standard Service in question.

16B.10 In this Condition:

(*a*) 'Business' has the meaning given to it in Condition 20B;

'Competitive Standard Service' means a Standard Service the market for which is determined by the Director to be competitive pursuant to paragraph 16B.6;

'Conveyance Standard Service' means a Standard Service the charge for which falls to be determined in accordance with Condition 13.5A;

'Initial Standard Service' means a service which appears on the list of services as agreed between the Director and the Licensee on or before the date on which this Condition comes into force;

'Interested Parties' means those persons (if any), other than the Licensee, with whom, in any particular case, the Director considers it appropriate to consult;

'Major Office' has the meaning given to it in Condition 16;

'Network Components' means the network components specified on the list of network components as agreed between the Director and the Licensee on or before the date on which this Condition comes into force;

'Network Parts' means the network parts specified on the list of network parts as agreed between the Director and the Licensee on or before the date on which this Condition comes into force;

'Non-conveyance Standard Service' means a Standard Service which is not a Conveyance Standard Service;

'Operator' means in relation to each Standard Service any person who has required, and with whom the Licensee is obliged to enter into an agreement to provide, that Standard Service under Condition 13;

'Standard Service' means a service, including, without limitation, a Competitive Standard Service, which an Operator has required from the Licensee and which the Licensee is obliged to provide, or to enter into an agreement to provide, under Condition 13; and

'Transfer Charge' means the charge which is applied by the Licensee to a Business for the provision by the Licensee from another Business to that Business of a Network Component or combination of Network Components or a Network Part or combination of Network Parts;

(*b*) references to a charge for a Standard Service shall include (as well as such charge itself) the means of calculating that charge; and

(*c*) references to a charge being payable are references to a charge being payable in accordance with an agreement made in pursuance of Condition 13.

Notes to Condition 16
1. The words in square brackets were added by the Leased Lines Regulations.
2. Condition 16.1 (header), 16B, 16B1–4, 16B5–10 were inserted by a licence amendment dated 31 March 1995.

3. Condition 16.3(a) (part) was inserted by licence amendments dated 1 May 1987 and 24 September 1991.
4. Condition 16.3(b) was amended by a licence amendment dated 9 March 1993.
5. Conditions 16.3 (last sentence) 16.3A, 16.4 were inserted by a licence amendment dated 24 September 1991.
6. Conditions 16.5, 16.6 were inserted by a licence amendment dated 1 May 1987.
7. Condition 16.A, 16A.1–7 were inserted by a licence amendment dated 9 March 1993.
8. Condition 16A.1(a) was amended by a licence amendment dated 31 March 1995.
9. Condition 16B.5(b)(ii), 16B.5(c), 16B.8 (header), 16B.10(a) and (b) were amended by a licence amendment dated 13 February 1996.
10. See DGT determination on Interim Charges for BT's Initial Standard Services for year ending 31 March 1996, published in January 1996.
11. Further changes are envisaged to Condition 16 as a result of OFTEL's statement on 'Privacy of Telecommunications Services from 1997' published in June 1996 and a Consultative Document 'Network Charges for 1997' published in December 1996.

Condition 17   Prohibition on Undue Preference and Undue Discrimination

17.1   The Licensee shall not (whether in respect of the charges or other terms or conditions applied or otherwise) show undue preference to, or exercise undue discrimination against, particular persons or persons of any class or description (including, in particular, persons in rural areas) as respects:

(*a*)   the provision by means of any of the Applicable Systems of any telecommunication service (other than a telecommunication service comprised in a Relevant Service) in accordance with an obligation imposed by or under this Licence;

(*aa*)   the provision of any Relevant Service;

(*b*)   the provision of Maintenance Services in respect of any Limited Maintenance Telecommunication Apparatus or Limited Maintenance Telecommunication System or the maintenance, adjustment or repair of any apparatus in accordance with an obligation imposed by or under this Licence;

(*c*)   the connection to any of the Applicable Systems of any telecommunication apparatus or any other system which, in either case, is not and is not to be comprised in any of the Applicable Systems in accordance with an obligation imposed by or under this Licence;

(*d*)   the granting of permission to connect such systems or apparatus to, or to provide services by means of, any of the Applicable Systems in accordance with an obligation imposed by or under this Licence; or

(*e*)   the Bringing into Service of any apparatus or system which, in either case, is or is to be connected to but not comprised or to be comprised in any of the Applicable Systems, where only the Licensee is permitted to provide such service.

17.2   The Licensee may be deemed to have shown such undue preference or to have exercised such undue discrimination if it unfairly favours to a material extent a business carried on by it in relation to the doing of any of the things mentioned in paragraph 17.1 so as to place at a significant competitive disadvantage persons competing with that business.

17.3 Any question relating to whether any act done or course of conduct pursued by the Licensee amounts to such undue preference or such undue discrimination shall be determined by the Director, but nothing done in any manner by the Licensee shall be regarded as undue preference or undue discrimination if and to the extent that the Licensee is required to do that thing in that manner by or under any provision of this Licence.

17.3A (a) The introduction by the Licensee of tariff changes which result in different percentage increases or decreases for different Relevant Prices shall not be regarded as the showing of undue preference or the exercise of undue discrimination by the Licensee where the requirements set out below are satisfied. Requirements (i) and (ii) shall apply separately to the following classes of services:

provision of services by means of the Licensee's public switched telecommunications network;

provision of services by means of Private Circuits or International Private Circuits.

The requirements are that:

(i) the effect of tariff changes shall, taken together by class of customer, achieve greater uniformity of the ratios of revenues accruing from different classes of customers for the class of service to the long run incremental costs (or, where those costs cannot be ascertained, the fully allocated costs) of providing the service to those classes of customer;

(ii) the revenue accruing in respect of such service shall, for any class of customer, not decrease to an extent which brings it below the incremental cost (as qualified in paragraph 17.3A (a) (i)) to the Licensee of providing that service to that class of customer; and

(iii) any combination of charges required to be paid by any class of customer in respect of a service shall not include any call charges in respect of any category of call which, after the date of the coming into force of this paragraph 17.3A, have been decreased so as to be below the cost to the Licensee of conveying the category of call in question.

(b) In this paragraph 17.3A, 'Relevant Price' means any price within any of the definitions of that term contained in Condition 24A.

17.4 For the purposes of paragraph 17.1, the things mentioned in paragraph 17.1 (aa) do not include:

(a) a service consisting only in the reception by a Relevant Applicable System of information from a person other than the Licensee for the purpose of storing that information and making it available as part of a Relevant Service to the generality of customers who have contracted with the Licensee for that Relevant Service, who request access to that information and who pay the Licensee's charges for it; or

(b) the provision of any Relevant Service by the Licensee in so far as that Relevant Service is provided by means of a telecommunication system which is of such a description and run in such a way that if it was run by any person other than a public telecommunications operator it could be run under and in accordance with the Class Licence for the running of branch telecommunication systems granted by the Secretary of State.

17.5 For the purposes of paragraph 17.2, the things mentioned in paragraph 17.1 shall include the things mentioned in paragraph 17.4.

17.6 In this Condition, 'Relevant Applicable System' has the same meaning as in Condition 18.

Notes
1. Conditions 17.1(a) and 17.1(aa) were amended by a licence amendment dated 1 May 1987.
2. Condition 17.3A was amended by a licence amendment dated 24 September 1991.
3. Condition 17.4–6 was inserted by a licence amendment dated 1 May 1987.

Condition 17A   Differential Charging

17A.1 This Condition applies to the Licensee's charges for doing any of the things mentioned in Condition 16.1 (a) (i) to (v) when those charges vary or may vary:

(a) according to whether the Licensee does any other thing so mentioned for the customer in question; or

(b) according to the extent to which it does any of those things for that customer.

17A.2 In relation to any charge to which this Condition applies the Licensee will be deemed not to show undue discrimination or undue preference for the purposes of Condition 17 if in respect of that charge, the Licensee complies with guidelines to be issued by the Director as agreed with the Licensee on or before the coming into effect of this Condition. Such guidelines shall specify the levels above or below which any such charge or combination of charges may be set, and may only be varied or revoked by agreement with the Licensee.

Notes
1. Conditions 17A.1–3 were inserted by a licence amendment dated 24 September 1991.
2. Conditions 17A.2 (proviso) and 17A.3 were deleted by a licence amendment dated 9 March 1993.
3. This Condition was deleted on 31 December 1996 when the new fair trading Condition 18A came into effect.

Condition 17B   Prohibition on Undue Preference and Undue Discrimination—Quality of Service

17B.1 Without prejudice to Condition 17 the Licensee shall not show undue preference to, or exercise undue discrimination against, an Operator in respect of the Quality of any Standard Service or any Private Circuit provided by the Licensee to that Operator under any agreement between them.

17B.2 The Licensee may be deemed to have shown such undue preference or to have exercised such undue discrimination if it unfairly favours a Business in relation to the Quality of:

(i) Network Service compared with the provision to an Operator of a Standard Service which is the same as that Network Service, or comprises the same combination of Network Components or Network Parts, as the case may be, as are used in the provision of, that Network Service; or

(ii)   a Private Circuit Service compared with the provision to an Operator of a Private Circuit; or

(iii)   a Standard Service comprising, inter alia, the establishment, maintenance or alteration of Network Connecting Apparatus if the performance of any such establishment, maintenance or alteration activity is materially different from the performance of a comparable activity elsewhere in the Licensee's System Business;

so as to place an Operator competing with that Business at a significant competitive disadvantage.

17B.3   Any question relating to whether any act done or course of conduct pursued by the Licensee amounts to such undue preference or such undue discrimination shall be considered by, and, if appropriate, be determined by the Director, but nothing done in any manner by the Licensee shall be considered or determined to be undue preference or undue discrimination if and to the extent that the Licensee is required to do that thing in that manner by or under any provision of this Licence.

17B.4   (a)   before making a determination under this Condition, the Director shall consult with the Licensee and Interested Parties. If he considers that a determination is appropriate he shall notify the Licensee and Interested Parties of the proposed determination and his reasons for proposing to make it and give each of them a reasonable opportunity to make representations. On making a determination he shall notify the Licensee and Interested Parties of the determination and his reasons for making it.

(b)   Each notification of reasons shall, as appropriate, set out the Director's reasons:

(i)   for proposing to make the determination; or

(ii)   for making the determination;

those reasons being sufficient to give the Licensee and Interested Parties a reasonable understanding of the proposed decision or decision, as the case may be.

17B.5   In this Condition:

'Business' has the meaning given to it in Condition 20B;

'Interested Parties' has the meaning given to it in Condition 16B;

'Network Components' has the meaning given to it in Condition 16B;

'Network Parts' has the meaning given to it in Condition 16B;

'Network Service' means a service which the Licensee is providing to a Business which is the same as or comprises the same combination of Network Components or Network Parts, as the case may be, as a Standard Service;

'Operator' means:

(a)   in relation to a Standard Service, any person who has required, and with whom the Licensee is obliged to enter into an agreement to provide, that Standard Service under Condition 13; or

(b)   in relation to a Private Circuit, any person who has required, and with whom the Licensee is obliged to enter into an agreement to provide, that Private Circuit;

'Private Circuit' means a Private Circuit to which Condition 46 relates;

'Private Circuit Service' means a service which the Licensee is providing to a Business which provides the same functionality and has the same characteristics as a Private Circuit;

'Quality' means the effect of the performance of the relevant service in a manner which, given the purpose for which it was provided, determines the degree of satisfaction of a user of that service, and, for the avoidance of doubt, does not include the charge for that service; and

'Standard Service' has the meaning given to it in Condition 16B.

Note

Conditions 17B.1–5 were inserted by a licence amendment dated 31 March 1995, and Condition 17B.1 was later amended by a licence amendment dated 1 October 1996.

Condition 17C   Quality of Service—Quality Schedule

17C.1   The Licensee shall publish the results of the measurements of actual performance against the Target Performance specified in the Quality Schedule which it has achieved in providing the Standard Services and Private Circuits specified in the Quality Schedule to the Operators specified in that Schedule.

17C.2   For the purposes of paragraph 17C.1:

(a)   the Licensee shall publish the results of those measurements at regular intervals, being not less than once in each financial year of the Licensee, the first publication to take place in the financial year of the Licensee ending 31 March 1996; and

(b)   publication shall be effected by sending to the Director a document setting out the results referred to in paragraph 17C.1 (the 'Quality of Service Report').

17C.3   Following publication pursuant to paragraph 17C.2:

(a)   subject to sub-paragraph (c), the Licensee shall send a copy of the most recent Quality of Service Report to any person who may request it on payment of a reasonable charge for it, within seven working days after receiving payment of that charge provided that such person agrees in writing with the Licensee to use the Quality of Service Report and its contents for the purpose only of noting the extent to which the Licensee has achieved its Target Performance;

(b)   the Licensee shall make available and continue to make available in a publicly accessible part of every Major Office of the Licensee in the place as is required by Condition 16.3 (b) a notice of the address and telephone number of the person to whom any request for a copy of the most recent Quality of Service Report may be made; and

(c)   the Licensee shall:

(i)   be entitled to exclude from any Quality of Service Report which it is obliged to send to any person who may request one pursuant to sub-paragraph (a) any matter to the exclusion of which the Director shall have consented following representations to him on the matter by the Licensee on the basis that if the matter were made available in accordance with sub-paragraph (a) it would or might, in the opinion of the Director, seriously and prejudicially affect the interests of the Licensee; and

(ii)   shall extract from that Quality of Service Report any matter which the Director directs should be excluded.

17C.4   Notwithstanding paragraph 6 of Part 1 of Schedule 1, the Licensee shall offer to include, as a minimum, in each agreement between the Licensee and an Operator for the provision of any Standard Service or any Private Circuit, or both, which is or are included in the Quality Schedule whether subsisting before the date on which this Condition comes into force or otherwise:

(a)   a description of the Target Performance specified from time to time in the Quality Schedule in relation to each such Standard Service and Private Circuit; and

(b)   an obligation on the Licensee to that Operator to use reasonable endeavours to achieve that Target Performance in relation to each such Standard Service or Private Circuit provided to that Operator pursuant to the relevant agreement;

provided that such offer shall not be conditional on the acceptance by that Operator of the inclusion in that agreement of any other terms and conditions whether relating to that Target Performance or otherwise, except for terms or conditions which are necessarily incidental to the attaining of the Target Performance.

17C.5   Subject to paragraph 17C.6, the Quality Schedule may be amended as the Director and the Licensee agree from time to time. In addition, the Licensee shall ensure that the Quality Schedule is kept under review and shall prepare and submit to the Director any amendments which it proposes from time to time to make to the Schedule to take account of technological progress or other relevant considerations provided that the Licensee shall not be obliged to review the Schedule more than once in each financial year, the first such review to take place in the financial year ending 31 March 1996. The Director shall then, if he considers it appropriate to do so, consult with Interested Parties as to the proposed amendments and give them a reasonable opportunity to make representations. If the Director, following any period of consultation, consents to the Licensee's proposed amendments the Licensee shall adopt them, but if the Director does not consent to the proposed amendments, the Licensee may, subject to its obligations contained in this paragraph, withdraw them.

17C.6   (a)   Where the Director has reasonable grounds to believe that the Licensee:

(i)   has, within the previous three years (excluding any period falling before the date on which this Condition comes into force), shown undue preference to, or exercised undue discrimination against, any Operator in respect of the Quality of a Standard Service or Private Circuit or both, contrary to the provisions of Condition 17 or Condition 17B or both, and has ceased to do so but is likely to repeat that undue preference or undue discrimination at any time in the future; or

(ii)   is showing undue preference or undue discrimination as described in sub-paragraph (a) (i);

or both, and has notified the Licensee of those reasonable grounds, the Licensee shall, without prejudice to Condition 52, extend to the Director, his representatives and members of his staff such prompt co-operation as the Director may reasonably request in order to investigate the matter and, in particular, on request by the Director shall:

(aa)   furnish to the Director in accordance with his reasonable requirements any information, documents, accounts, estimates, returns, reports or other relevant information (including, without limitation, any facility enabling him to read data not held in readable form);

(bb)   on reasonable notice by him allow at all reasonable times the Director, his representatives and any member of his staff on production of his special authority, access to any relevant premises of the Licensee to investigate, assess, examine, review or verify any of its relevant records, systems or processes; and

(cc)   for the purpose of sub-paragraph (bb), allow the Director, his representatives and any member of his staff to be accompanied by any person whom the Director may specify, and to whom the Licensee has raised no reasonable objection, whose assistance he might reasonably require provided that the Director has given the Licensee notice (save in exceptional circumstances) of at least 5 working days of the identity of that person.

(b) If, as a result of any investigation, assessment, examination or review referred to in sub-paragraph (a), the Director is satisfied that the Licensee has done or is doing any of the things referred to in sub-paragraph (a) (i) and (ii) or he has insufficient information to conclude whether or not the Licensee has done or is doing any of the things referred to in sub-paragraph (a) (i) and (ii), he may direct with effect from the date specified in the direction (not being a date earlier than the date of the direction), without prejudice to his other powers under this Licence, that the Quality Schedule shall be amended, provided that any direction given pursuant to this paragraph shall relate to the results of the relevant investigation, assessment, examination or review referred to in sub-paragraph (a) in respect of which the direction is given and shall not require any change to the Quality Schedule beyond that reasonably required to remedy or prevent the undue preference or undue discrimination, or to remedy any defect in the procedures set out in the Quality Schedule, which shall have given rise to the lack of information revealed by the relevant investigation.

17C.7   (a)   before giving a direction or consent under this Condition, the Director shall consult with the Licensee and Interested Parties. If he concludes that a direction or consent is appropriate he shall notify the Licensee and Interested Parties of the proposed direction or consent, as the case may be, and his reasons for proposing to give it and give each of them a reasonable opportunity to make representations. On giving a direction or consent, he shall notify the Licensee and Interested Parties of the direction or consent, as the case may be, and his reasons for giving it.

(b) Each notification of reasons shall, as appropriate, set out the Director's reasons:

(i)   for proposing to give the direction or consent as the case may be; or

(ii)   for giving the direction or consent as the case may be; those reasons being sufficient to give the Licensee and Interested Parties a reasonable understanding of the proposed decision or decision, as the case may be.

17C.8   In this Condition:

'Interested Parties' has the meaning given to it in Condition 16B;

'Major Office' has the meaning given to it in Condition 16;

'Operator' has the meaning given to it in Condition 17B;

'Private Circuit' means a Private Circuit to which Condition 46 relates;

'Quality' has the meaning given to it in Condition 17B;
'Quality Schedule' means the schedule specifying:
> (a)   quality measures and Target Performance;
> (b)   certain Standard Services;
> (c)   certain Private Circuits defined in accordance with Condition 46; and
> (d)   certain Operators or groups of Operators;

in each case as agreed between the Director and the Licensee on or before the date on which this Condition comes into force as amended from time to time in accordance with this Condition;
'Standard Service' has the meaning given to it in Condition 16B; and
'Target Performance' means the minimum level of performance which the Licensee intends to provide.

Notes

1. Conditions 17C.1–8 were inserted by a licence amendment dated 31 March 1995.
2. This condition is one of the special category of conditions required to be included in licences granted to PTOs under s. 8, Telecommunications Act 1984.
3. The Director General has made a number of determinations under this condition. If the Director General establishes discrimination or preference he should consider whether or not to take action in accordance with his duties under s. 3 of the 1984 Act.
4. The condition only applies to those services provided in accordance with an obligation imposed by or under BT's licence — see *Maystart Ltd* v *Director General of Telecommunications*, 17 February 1994, CA (unreported).

SCHEDULE 1

PART 3: OTHER CONDITIONS INCLUDED UNDER SECTION 7 OF THE ACT

Condition 18   Prohibition on Cross-Subsidies

18.1   Where it appears to the Director that the Licensee is unfairly cross-subsidising or unfairly subsidising:
> (i)   the Apparatus Supply Business, insofar as that Business is carried on in the United Kingdom;
> (ii)   the production of telecommunication apparatus by the Apparatus Production Company insofar as that apparatus is produced for supply in the United Kingdom and the supply of such apparatus by that Company in the United Kingdom;
> (iii)   the provision in the United Kingdom of Land Mobile Radio Services; or
> (iv)   the Supplemental Services Business;

it shall take such steps as the Director may direct for the purpose of remedying the situation.

18.2   The Licensee shall record, except where the Director agrees otherwise, at full cost in its accounting records, any material transfer between any part of the Licensee's business and:
> (a)   any of the businesses mentioned in paragraph 18.1 (i) to (iii) as soon as reasonably practicable and in any event not later than 1 April 1987; and

(*b*) the Supplemental Services Business as soon as reasonably practicable and in any event not later than 1 April 1988.

18.3   In this Condition:

'Apparatus Production Company' has the same meaning as in Condition 21;

'Apparatus Supply Business' means the following activities of the Licensee or of any Wholly Owned Subsidiary taken together:

    (*a*)   the supply of any telecommunication apparatus neither comprised nor to be comprised in any of the Applicable Systems; and

    (*b*)   the installation, maintenance, adjustment, repair, alteration, moving, removal or replacement of any telecommunication apparatus where those activities are not part of the Systems Business nor part of the Supplemental Services Business;

but does not include the supply by the Apparatus Production Company of telecommunication apparatus produced by it;

'Land Mobile Radio Service' means any telecommunication service provided by wireless telegraphy for reception by means of apparatus which is or is to be used while in motion, but does not include services of a kind provided under Conditions 8 and 12;

'Relevant Applicable System' means that part of any of the Applicable Systems (other than a fixed link) which is used for the purpose of providing a Relevant Service provided by the Licensee, but only to the extent that it is so used;

'Supplemental Services Business' means the following activities of the Licensee taken together:

    (*a*)   the provision in the United Kingdom by the Licensee of Relevant Services;

    (*b*)   the running of any Relevant Applicable System;

    (*c*)   the installation, maintenance, adjustment, repair, alteration, moving, removal or replacement of any apparatus comprised or to be comprised in a Relevant Applicable System; and

    (*d*)   the conveyance of Messages by means of any Relevant Applicable System or by means of any fixed link which has been made available by the Systems Business to the Supplemental Services Business for the purpose of providing a Relevant Service;

'Systems Business' means the following activities of the Licensee or of any Wholly Owned Subsidiary to the extent that they are undertaken in the United Kingdom taken together:

    (*a*)   the running of the Applicable Systems except where it is part of the Supplemental Services Business;

    (*b*)   the installation, maintenance, adjustment, repair, alteration, moving, removal or replacement of any apparatus comprised or to be comprised in any of those Systems where those activities are not part of the Supplemental Services Business;

    (*c*)   without prejudice to the generality of sub-paragraph (a) or (b) the Bringing into Service of any item of telecommunication apparatus or telecommunication system connected or to be connected to any of the Applicable Systems whether comprised in any of those Systems or not; and

    (*d*)   without prejudice to the generality of sub-paragraph (a) the conveyance of Messages (not including switching) by means of any of the

Applicable Systems and switching incidental to such conveyance where such conveyance is not part of the Supplemental Services Business.

18.4   For the purposes of this Condition:

(*a*) 'supply' and 'provision' include supply or provision in the course of one business of the Licensee for the purposes of another such business notwithstanding that there is no supply or provision to any other person;

(*b*) a transfer from one business to another business or a company takes place when any thing (including any service or money) produced or acquired by, normally used in, or otherwise at the disposal of, the first mentioned business is made available for the purposes of the other business or the company; and

(*c*) 'full cost' in the case of money transferred includes the market rate of interest for that money.

18.5   This Condition shall apply with the omission of paragraph 18.1 (i) if and for so long as the supply of telecommunication apparatus by the Licensee does not constitute a monopoly situation within the meaning of section 6 of the Fair Trading Act 1973.

18.6   In considering whether any cross-subsidy of the Supplemental Services Business is unfair, the Director shall have regard to the extent to which the Licensee cross-subsidised that Business for the purpose of satisfying any obligation imposed on it by Condition 1, 2, 3 or 12.

Notes

1.   Condition 18.1 (header) was amended by a licence amendment dated 31 March 1995.

2.   Conditions 18.1(iv), 18.2, 18.3 (definitions of 'Value Added Service' deleted only) were deleted and replaced by a licence amendment dated 1 May 1987.

3.   Conditions 18.2, 18.3 (definitions of 'Relevant Applicable System'; 'Supplementary Services Business') were inserted by a licence amendment dated 1 May 1987. Condition 18.3 (definitions of 'Apparatus Supply Business', para. (b); 'Systems Business', paras (a) and (d)) were amended by a licence amendment dated 1 May 1987.

Condition 18A   Fair Trading

18A.1   The Licensee shall not do any thing, whether by act or omission, which has or is intended to have or is likely to have the effect of preventing, restricting or distorting competition where such act or omission is done in the course of, as a result of or in connection with, providing telecommunication services, or any particular description of telecommunication service, or running a telecommunication system.

For the purpose of this Condition such an act or omission will take the form of:

(*a*) any abuse by the Licensee, either alone or with other undertakings, of a dominant position within the United Kingdom or a substantial part of it. Such abuse may, in particular, consist in:

—   directly or indirectly imposing unfair purchase or selling prices or other unfair trading conditions;

—   limiting production, markets or technical development to the prejudice of consumers;

— applying dissimilar conditions to equivalent transactions with other parties, thereby placing them at a competitive disadvantage; or

— making the conclusion of contracts subject to acceptance by the other parties of supplementary obligations which, by their nature or according to commercial usage, have no connection with the subject of such contracts; or

(b) the making (including the implementation) of any agreement, the compliance with any decision of any association of undertakings or the carrying on of any concerted practice with any other undertaking which has the object or effect of preventing, restricting or distorting competition within the United Kingdom.

18A.2 (a) An act or omission of a kind.described in paragraph 18A.1 is not prohibited where:

(i)   it has or would have no appreciable effect on competition; or

(ii)   it has or would have no effect on competition between persons engaged in commercial activities connected with telecommunications and it would have no effect on users of telecommunication services.

(b) An act or omission of a kind described in paragraph 18A.1(b) is not prohibited by this Condition if the agreement decision or concerted practice contributes to improving the provision of any goods or services or to promoting technical or economic progress, while allowing consumers a fair share of the resulting benefit and does not:

(i)   impose on the parties concerned restrictions which are not indispensable to attaining those objectives; and

(ii)   afford such parties the possibility of eliminating competition in respect of a substantial part of the goods or services in question.

(c)   This Condition shall not apply to any provision of an agreement insofar as it is a provision by virtue of which the Restrictive Trade Practices Act 1976 applies to that agreement.

(d)   This Condition shall not apply to a merger situation qualifying for investigation under the Fair Trading Act 1973.

18A.3 Whether any act or omission is prohibited by this Condition shall be determined :-

(a)   with a view to securing that there is no inconsistency with the general principles having application to similar questions of directly applicable competition law, in particular those laid down by the Court of Justice of the European Communities on the scope of the competition rules contained in the EC Treaty and block exemptions adopted by the European Commission under Article 85(3); and

(b)   having regard to—

(i)   any decision taken, or notice issued, by the European Commission in applying the competition rules contained in the EC Treaty and any relevant pronouncement of the Director General of Fair Trading or report of the Monopolies and Mergers Commission; and

(ii)   any guidelines on the application of this Condition issued from time to time by the Director.

18A.4 (a) If it appears to the Director that an act or omission of the Licensee is or was prohibited by this Condition he may make an initial determination to that effect (an 'Initial Determination').

(b) Before making an Initial Determination the Director shall give a notice to the Licensee:

(i)   stating that he is investigating a possible contravention of this Condition;

(ii)   setting out the reasons why it appears to him that this Condition may be being, or may have been, breached, including any matters of fact or law which he thinks relevant;

(iii)   requesting within a reasonable period laid down by the Director such further information as he may require from the Licensee in order to complete his Determination; and

(iv)   where appropriate, setting out the steps he believes the Licensee would have to take in order to remedy the alleged breach.

18A.5   (a)   Within 28 days of the Director—

(i)   making an Initial Determination;

(ii)   making a provisional order; or

(iii)   giving notice of his proposal to make a final order under section 17(1) of the Act

in respect of the contravention in question, the Licensee may notify the Director that it—

(iv)   requires him to make a final determination (a 'Final Determination') of the matter;

(v)   requires that in making the Final Determination he take into account a report of a body of experts appointed by him to consider the matter ('the Advisory Body').

(b)   Before making a Final Determination the Director shall—

(i)   give a notice to the Licensee setting out the matters referred to in paragraph 18.A.4(b); and

(ii)   if the Licensee has given notice under sub-paragraph (a)(v) above, take into account the report of the Advisory Body on the matter.

(c)   The Director shall then determine whether he is satisfied that the act or omission in respect of which the Initial Determination was made is or was prohibited by this Condition.

18A.6   (a)   Before making his Initial Determination or Final Determination the Director shall give the Licensee, and any other person whom he considers it appropriate to consult, such period within which to make representations (both orally and in writing) in response to the notice as he considers reasonable in all the circumstances.

(b)   The Director shall notify the Licensee and any other person whom he considers it appropriate to notify of every Initial Determination and Final Determination made by him and of his reasons for making it; and he shall, if so requested by the Licensee, publish any report of the Advisory Body on the matter, subject to such exclusions as he may consider it appropriate to make of matters of a kind mentioned in section 48 (2) of the Act.

18A.7   The Director shall publish a description of his office's procedures for the enforcement of this Condition including the steps taken to ensure that he has access to appropriate independent advice in enforcing this Condition.

18A.8   This Condition shall not limit or affect in any way the Licensee's obligations arising under any other Condition of this Licence nor limit the Director's powers of enforcement under sections 16 to 18 of the Act.

18.A.9   (a)   On the coming into force of any Act or subordinate legislation which—

(i)   contains a prohibition enforceable by the Director, or gives to the Director the power to enforce an existing prohibition, of any behaviour prohibited under paragraph 18A.1;

(ii)   gives to third parties in respect of a breach of that prohibition at least the rights they have under section 18 of the Act in respect of a breach of a provisional or final order; and

(iii)   permits the imposition on the Licensee of monetary penalties in respect of the breach of that prohibition
this Condition shall cease to apply to the behaviour prohibited by or the prohibition enforceable by such Act or subordinate legislation.

(b)   If this Condition still has effect on 31st July 2001, it shall cease to have effect after that date.

18A.10   (a)   This Condition shall come into force on 31st December 1996.

(b)   The prohibition in paragraph 18A.1(b) shall not apply to acts or omissions done before 31 March 1997 in pursuance of agreements entered into before 1 October 1996.

Notes to Condition 18A

1.   Condition 18A was added by a licence amendment dated 1 October 1996 and came into effect on 31 December 1996. Also OFTEL is in the process of producing 'Guidelines on the Operation of the Fair Trading Condition' — first draft was produced in the OFTEL Statement 'Pricing of Telecommunications Services from 1997' June 1996, final draft 22 January 1997.

2.   BT has unsuccessfully challenged the Director General's power to introduce Condition 18A by judicial review. High Court ruling dated 20 December 1996.

3.   A transitional period until 31 March 1997 will allow any interconnect agreements made before 1 October 1996 which may be prohibited by the new condition to be changed to comply with the condition.

4.   The following Conditions were deleted from BT's licence when Condition 18A came into effect:

Condition 7 — Calls made by emergency organisations.
Condition 17A — Differential charging.
Condition 22 — Prohibition of preferential treatment.
Condition 25 — Charges for maintenance of certain exchange lines.
Condition 28 — Arbitration of disputes with consumers.
Condition 35 — Prohibition of linked sales.
Condition 36 — Prohibition of certain exclusive dealing arrangements.
Condition 37 — Requirement to provide itemised information.
Condition 40 — Prohibition of non-statutory testing requirements.
Condition 40A — Requirement to provide means of access to the applicable systems.
Condition 41 — Statutory testing.
Condition 42 — Limitations on integrated wiring situated on served premises.
Condition 44 — Limitations on certain maintenance arrangements.
Condition 49 — Pre-notification of joint ventures.

5.   These licence modifications for fair trading followed extensive consultation by OFTEL — see 'A Framework for Effective Competition' December 1994, 'Effective Competition: Framework for Action' July 1995, 'Pricing of Telecommunications Services from 1997' June 1996.

6.   Where the Director General is satisfied BT is unfairly subsidising or cross-subsidising he may direct BT to remedy the situation under Condition 20B.15.

Condition 19   Access Charges

19.1   Notwithstanding the prohibitions made in or under Conditions 17 and 18 and without prejudice to the Licensee's other powers to impose charges in any circumstances or to organise its internal finances in any way, the Licensee may impose upon a person running a Relevant Connectable System who provides Connection Services to others a charge for the provision of telecommunication services by means of a connection to one of the Applicable Systems (an 'Access Charge') provided that all the conditions set out in paragraph 19.2 are fulfilled.

19.2   The said conditions are that:

(*a*)   the Access Charge, or the method adopted for determining it, is the same for all such persons;

(*b*)   the Licensee has furnished to the Director particulars of the Access Charge or the method adopted for determining it and either:

(i)   the Director has approved that Charge or that method; or

(ii)   he has failed to give written notice of his disapproval within a period of 6 months; and

(*c*)   the Licensee has made arrangements which as nearly as practicable secure that:

(i)   all persons to whom there are provided by means of an Applicable System services, for which Access Charges would have been levied on a person under paragraph 19.1 if they had been provided by means of a Relevant Connectable System, are required to pay charges at least equal to the Access Charges which would have been so payable; and

(ii)   the estimated proceeds of the charges referred to in paragraphs 19.1 and 19.2 (c) (i) are used exclusively to defray:

(a)   costs (less any revenue received) incurred in providing services or supplying apparatus in accordance with Conditions 3, 5, 6, 11, 31, 32 and 33;

(b)   losses which the Director is satisfied are reasonably incurred as a consequence of fulfilling an obligation imposed under Condition 1 or 2 in any area which the Director is satisfied is a proper one to be taken into account for the purposes of this Condition; and

(c)   payments made by the Licensee in discharge of its obligations under Condition 31A and any arrangement entered into thereunder with a Relay Service Provider.

19.3   In this Condition, 'Relay Service Provider' has the same meaning as in Condition 31A.

Notes
1.   Condition 19.2(c) was deleted and replaced by a licence amendment dated 9 March 1993.
2.   Conditions 19.2(c)(ii) and 19.3 were inserted by a licence amendment dated 9 March 1993.

Condition 20   Separate Accounts for Certain Activities

20.1   This Condition applies for the purpose of ensuring that the Licensee establishes as soon as reasonably practicable and in any event not later than

1 April 1987 accounting and reporting arrangements sufficient to enable the Licensee's finances in relation to the Systems Business and the Apparatus Supply Business to be assessed and reported on separately both from each other and from the other activities of the Licensee and for the purposes of ensuring that the Licensee establishes as soon as reasonably practicable and in any event not later than 1 April 1988 accounting arrangements sufficient to enable the Licensee's finances in relation to the Supplemental Services Business to be assessed separately from the other activities of the Licensee.

20.2   The Licensee shall:

(*a*)   maintain accounting records in such a form that the activities of the Supplemental Services Business, the Systems Business and the Apparatus Supply Business are separately identifiable or separately attributable in the books of the Licensee, being records sufficient to show and explain the transactions of each of those Businesses;

(*b*)   prepare in respect of each complete financial year of the Licensee, or of such lesser periods as the Director may specify but not more frequently than quarterly, accounting statements setting out, and, in the case of yearly statements, fairly presenting, the costs (including capital costs), revenue and financial position of each of the Systems Business and the Apparatus Supply Business and including a reasonable assessment of the assets employed in and liabilities attributable to each of them and showing separately, in the case of yearly accounting statements, the amount of any material item of revenue, cost, asset or liability which has been either:

(i)   charged from or to any other business of the Licensee together with a description of the basis of the value on which the charge was made; or

(ii)   determined by apportionment or attribution from an activity common to the Business and any other business of the Licensee and, if not otherwise disclosed, the basis of the apportionment or attribution;

(*c*)   procure in respect of each of those accounting statements prepared in respect of a complete financial year of the Licensee a report by the Licensee's Auditor stating whether in his opinion that statement is adequate for the purposes of this Condition; and

(*d*)   deliver to the Director a copy of each of the accounting statements and of the reports relating thereto required under sub-paragraphs (b) and (c) above as soon as reasonably practicable and in any event not later than six months after the end of the period to which they relate.

20.3   Accounting statements prepared under paragraph 20.2 (b) in respect of each financial year shall, so far as reasonably practicable, be prepared in the formats and in accordance with the accounting principles and rules which apply to the annual accounts of the Licensee and shall state the accounting policies used.

20.4   For the purposes of this Condition the Licensee shall be free to treat the Apparatus Supply Business as not including any business relating to the supply of apparatus outside the United Kingdom but when it does so it shall inform the Director.

20.5   Subject to paragraph 20.4, in this Condition:

'the Applicable Systems' include any systems which the Director agrees should be treated as Applicable Systems for the purposes of this Condition; 'the Auditor' means the Licensee's auditor for the time being appointed in accordance with the requirements of the Companies Act 1948 to 1963; and references to the costs of any business do not include profits of that business.

Note
Conditions 20.1, 20.2(a) and (b) were amended by a licence amendment dated 1 May 1987.

Condition 20A   Bases and Publication of Accounts

20A.1   The Licensee shall publish accounts for the Licensee's Group on a current cost basis relating to its 1993-94 financial year and each succeeding complete financial year. If the Licensee so requests, the Director may determine that the accounts required by this paragraph may be for other than the Group.

20A.2   The Licensee shall procure in respect of the accounts required by paragraph 20A.1 a report by the Licensee's Auditor stating that the auditor has examined the accounts and stating whether in his opinion the accounts have been properly prepared in accordance with the current cost principles, accounting policies and methods as described in the notes to the accounts.

20A.3   Paragraph 20A.1 is without prejudice to the manner in which the Licensee discharges the obligations relating to the preparation of accounts imposed on it by the Companies Act 1985.

20A.4   The Licensee shall prepare in respect of each complete financial year accounting statements on a current cost basis setting out and fairly presenting the costs (including capital costs), revenue and financial position of the Systems Business, and including a reasonable assessment of the assets employed in, and liabilities attributable to, that Business, and showing separately the amount of any material item of revenue, cost, asset or liability which has been either:

(i)   charged from or to any other business of the Licensee together with a description of the basis of the value on which the charge was made; or

(ii)   determined by apportionment or attribution from an activity common to the Business and any other business of the Licensee and, if not otherwise disclosed, the basis of the apportionment or attribution;
and shall:

(*a*)   for the 1994–95 financial year and each succeeding complete financial year procure a report by the Licensee's Auditor stating that the Auditor has examined the accounting statements and stating whether in his opinion those statements have been properly prepared in accordance with the current cost principles, accounting policies and methods as described in the notes to the accounting statements and are consistent with the accounts published under paragraph 20A.1; and

(*b*)   deliver to the Director a copy of those accounting statements and of the report relating thereto, when applicable, as soon as reasonably practicable and in any event not later than six months after the end of the period to which they relate.

Note
Conditions 20A, 20A.1–4 were inserted by a licence amendment dated 9 March 1993.

Condition 20B   Separate Accounts

20B.1   The whole purpose of this Condition is:

(*a*)   to ensure that the Licensee does not unfairly subsidise or unfairly cross-subsidise or show undue preference or exercise undue discrimination; and

(*b*)   to assist the Director, in pursuance of his functions in that respect under this Licence, to determine charges to be payable to the Licensee by an Operator which are properly and transparently derived from relevant costs.

20B.1   (*a*)   Subject to paragraph 20B.18:

(i)   the composition of each Business in terms of any or all of the revenues, costs or assets it comprises may be amended; and

(ii)   each Business may be divided to create one or more additional Businesses or aggregated to create one or more fewer Businesses;

as the Director and the Licensee agree from time to time in writing.

(*b*)   Each Business shall be disaggregated in terms of the activities of the Business on the basis agreed between the Licensee and the Director on or before the date on which this Condition comes into force. Subject to paragraph 20B.18, that disaggregation may be amended by agreement in writing between the Licensee and the Director.

20B.2   The Licensee shall establish sufficient accounting and reporting arrangements to comply with its obligations under this Condition.

20B.3   (*a*)   The Licensee shall maintain accounting records in a form:

(i)   which enables each Business and, insofar as it has been disaggregated in terms of activities of the Business, each of the activities of that Business, to be separately identified or the costs, revenues and assets of each Business and, insofar as it has been disaggregated in terms of activities of the Business, the costs, revenues and assets of each of those activities, to be separately attributable, on an historic cost basis;

(ii)   which enables each Business, or one or more Businesses taken together as agreed between the Director and the Licensee in writing from time to time, to be separately identified or the costs, revenues and assets of each Business, or one or more Businesses taken together as agreed between the Director and the Licensee in writing from time to time, to be separately attributable, on a current cost basis; and

(iii)   which shows and explains the transactions of each Business and, insofar as it has been disaggregated in terms of activities of the Business, the transactions of each of the activities of that Business.

(*b*)   the accounting records referred to in sub-paragraph (a) shall be kept in a form which enables the Licensee to prepare the Financial Statements, the Restated Financial Statements (both as defined in paragraph 20B.4) and the Interim Financial Statements (as defined in paragraph 20B.8):

(i)   in the case of each Business, on an historic cost basis; and

(ii)   in the case of each Business, or one or more Businesses taken together as agreed between the Director and Licensee in writing from time to time, on a current cost basis;

which comply, in each case, with the requirements of this Condition.

(*c*)   Records sufficient to provide an adequate explanation of each Financial Statement, each Restated Financial Statement and each Interim Financial Statement shall be preserved by the Licensee for a period of six years from the date on which they were made.

20B.4   (*a*)   The Licensee shall prepare in accordance with paragraph 20B.5, in respect of each of its financial years, beginning with the financial year ending 31 March 1995, a financial statement:

(i)   on an historic cost basis, in respect of each Business and, insofar as it has been disaggregated in terms of activities of the Business, each activity of that Business; and

(ii)   on a current cost basis, in respect of each Business or, if the Director and the Licensee so agree from time to time, one or more Businesses taken together;

(each a 'Financial Statement' and together the 'Financial Statements').

(b)   Each Financial Statement prepared for the purposes of sub-paragraph (a) (i) above shall comprise:

(i)   a statement of fully allocated costs calculated on a basis which is not inconsistent with the Licensee's statutory accounts for the relevant financial year;

(ii)   a profit and loss account, a statement of mean capital employed, statements of costs (if applicable) and additional information to be provided by way of notes for the relevant financial year; and

(iii)   an explanation and reconciliation of any differences between the statement mentioned in sub-paragraph (i) above and the matters mentioned in sub-paragraph (ii) above.

(c)   Each Financial Statement prepared for the purposes of sub-paragraph (a) (ii) above shall comprise a profit and loss account, a statement of mean capital employed, statements of costs (if applicable) and additional information to be provided by way of notes for the relevant financial year.

(d)   Following the recalculation and redetermination of the charge (or the means of calculating that charge) for or in respect of each Standard Service (other than a Competitive Standard Service) payable in a financial year after the end of that financial year pursuant to Condition 13, the Licensee shall prepare a restatement of each Financial Statement for that financial year to take account of that recalculation and redetermination (each a 'Restated Financial Statement' and together the 'Restated Financial Statements').

20B.5   (a)   The Licensee shall ensure that each Financial Statement and Restated Financial Statement shall:

(i)   be prepared as to the form and content of:

(aa)   the profit and loss account;

(bb)   the statement of mean capital employed; and

(cc)   the statements of costs (if applicable);

as the Licensee and the Director shall have agreed, on or before the date on which this Condition comes into force together with such additional information to be provided by way of notes as the Licensee and the Director shall from time to time agree;

(ii)   be prepared, except in the case of those parts of each Financial Statement prepared in accordance with paragraph 20B.4 (b) (i) and (iii), in accordance with the Accounting Documents and insofar as there is any inconsistency between any or all of the Accounting Documents, the Licensee shall ensure that each Financial Statement shall be prepared in accordance with the Accounting Documents in the following order of priority:

(aa)   the Regulatory Accounting Principles;

(bb)   the Attribution Methods;

(cc)   the Transfer Charging System; and

(dd)   the Accounting Policies; and

(iii)   subject to sub-paragraph (ii), in the case of the Financial Statements prepared on:

(aa)   an historic cost basis, be reconciled with the annual statutory financial statements and that reconciliation shall be demonstrated and explained;

(bb)   on a current cost basis, be:

(A)   reconciled with the accounts which the Licensee is required to publish under Condition 20A and that reconciliation shall be demonstrated and explained; and

(B)   reconciled with the Financial Statements prepared on an historic cost basis for the corresponding financial year and that reconciliation shall be demonstrated and explained.

(b)   Subject to paragraph 20B.18, the form and content referred to in sub-paragraph (a) (i) may be amended as the Director and the Licensee agree from time to time in writing.

20B.6   The Licensee shall procure in respect of each Financial Statement and Restated Financial Statement for each Business an audit report by the Auditor which shall conform to Auditing Standards in which he shall state whether in his opinion:

(a)   the Financial Statement or the Restated Financial Statement, as the case may be, complies with the requirements of paragraph 20B.5;

(b)   the Financial Statement or the Restated Financial Statement, as the case may be, prepared on an historic cost basis fairly presents in accordance with the Accounting Documents:

(i)   in the case of the profit and loss account, the results of the relevant Business or, insofar as it has been disaggregated in terms of activities of the Business, of the relevant activity of that Business, for the relevant financial year;

(ii)   in the case of the statement of mean capital employed, the mean capital employed of the relevant Business or, insofar as the Business has been disaggregated in terms of activities of the Business, of the relevant activity of that Business, for the relevant financial year; and

(iii)   in the case of the statements of costs (if any), the costs incurred by the relevant Business or, insofar as the Business has been disaggregated in terms of the activities of the Business, by the relevant activities of that Business, for the relevant financial year;

(c)   the Financial Statement or the Restated Financial Statement, as the case may be, prepared on a current cost basis is properly prepared in accordance with the Accounting Documents.

20B.7   (a)   The Licensee shall, except in so far as the Director may consent:

(i)   publish the 1994 Financial Statements as soon as practicable, and, in any event, not later than four months after the date on which this Condition comes into force;

(ii)   publish the Financial Statements prepared on an historic cost basis:

(aa)   for the financial year ending 31 March 1995, as soon as practicable, and, in any event, not later than six months, after the end of the period to which they relate;

(bb)   for each subsequent financial year, within two months after the date on which the licensee's annual statutory financial statements are published and, in any event, within four months after the end of the period to which they relate;

    (iii)   publish the Financial Statements prepared on a current cost basis:

        (aa)   for the financial year ending 31 March 1995, as soon as practicable and, in any event, not later than eight months after the end of the period to which they relate; and

        (bb)   for each subsequent financial year, as soon as practicable, and, in any event, not later than two months, after the date on which the Financial Statements for the same financial year prepared on an historic cost base are published; and

    (iv)   publish the Restated Financial Statements as soon as practicable, and, in any event, not later than two months after the date on which the Director recalculates and redetermines the charge (or the means of calculating that charge) for each Standard Service (other than a Competitive Standard Service) payable in a financial year after the end of that financial year pursuant to Condition 13 provided that the requirements of this paragraph shall be suspended pending the final disposal of any proceedings seeking to have any such recalculations and redeterminations quashed, set aside, modified or varied;

together, in each case, with the relevant Auditor's report as required under paragraph 20B.6.

    (b)   For the purposes of sub-paragraph (a), publication shall be effected by making the relevant Financial Statements and Restated Financial Statements together with the relevant Auditor's reports (if applicable) publicly available and by sending copies to the Director.

    (c)   The Licensee shall send a copy of the Financial Statements and Restated Financial Statements together with the relevant Auditor's report (if applicable) to any person who may (after they have been published pursuant to sub-paragraph (a)) request them, on the basis of that person paying a reasonable charge for them. The Licensee shall send the copies within seven working days after receiving payment of that charge.

    (d)   The Licensee shall make available and continue to make available in a publicly accessible part of every Major Office of the Licensee in the place as is required by Condition 16.3 (b) a notice of the address and telephone number of the person to whom any request for a copy of any or all of the Financial Statements and Restated Financial Statements together with the relevant Auditor's reports or any part of them may be made.

20B.8   In addition to the requirements of paragraph 20B.4, the Licensee shall, in respect of each of its financial years, prepare on an historic cost basis a financial statement for each six month period ending 30 September, beginning with the six months ending 30 September 1995, in respect of each Business and, insofar as it has been disaggregated in terms of activities of the Business, each activity of that Business (each an 'Interim Financial Statement' and together the 'Interim Financial Statements'). Each Interim Financial Statement shall comprise a profit and loss account, a statement of mean capital employed, statements of costs (if applicable) and additional information to be provided by way of notes for the relevant period.

20B.9   The provisions of paragraphs 20B.4 (b) (i), (ii) and (iii) and 20B.5 (a) (i) and (ii) shall apply to Interim Financial Statements as they apply to

Financial Statements and Restated Financial Statements with the substitution for references to Financial Statements and Restated Financial Statements of references to Interim Financial Statements. In addition, the Licensee shall ensure that the Interim Financial Statements shall be reconciled with the interim results of the Licensee for the same period and that reconciliation shall be demonstrated and explained.

20B.10   The Licensee shall procure in respect of each Interim Financial Statement for each Business an interim report by the Auditor in which he shall:

(a)   have regard to the Bulletin 'Review of Interim Financial Information' issued by the Auditing Practices Board (or any body which replaces the Auditing Practices Board from time to time) or any other bulletin or notice issued by the Auditing Practices Board (or any replacement body) from time to time which replaces that Bulletin; and

(b)   state whether in his opinion on the basis of his review he is aware of any material modifications which should be made to that Interim Financial Statement as presented.

20B.11   (a)   The Licensee shall publish the Interim Financial Statements as soon as reasonably practicable and, in any event, within four months after the end of the period to which they relate, together with the relevant Auditor's report required under paragraph 20B.10.

(b)   For the purposes of sub-paragraph (a), the provisions of paragraph 20B.7 (b) to (d) inclusive shall apply to Interim Financial Statements as they apply to Financial Statements and Restated Financial Statements with the substitution for references to Financial Statements and Restated Financial Statements of references to Interim Financial Statements.

20B.12   (a)   Subject to paragraphs 20B.16 and 20B.18, the Accounting Documents may be amended as the Director and the Licensee agree from time to time in writing.

(b)   The Licensee shall not make any change to the way in which it attributes costs, revenues, assets and liabilities if that change would cause a change in the total costs attributed to one or more Standard Services of 5 per cent. or more without the prior written consent of the Director, such consent not to be unreasonably withheld.

20B.13   The Licensee shall use its best endeavours to obtain from the Auditor any further explanation and clarification of the reports required under paragraphs 20B.6 and 20B.10 and any other information in respect of the matters which are the subject of the reports as the Director shall reasonably require.

20B.14   (a)   The Licensee shall publish details of the definitions of the Businesses as soon as practicable after the coming into force of this Condition and shall publish details of any amendment to the composition, or any division or aggregation, of a Business as soon as practicable, and in any event within 28 days, after the making of the amendment.

(b)   The Licensee shall publish details as the Director may direct of the Accounting Documents, as soon as practicable after the Director's direction to do so, and, in any event, within 28 days after that direction, together with any further descriptions of the costs, revenues, assets and liabilities attribution systems used by the Licensee to prepare the Financial Statements, the Restated Financial Statements and the Interim Financial Statements the level of detail of which shall be agreed in writing between the Director and the Licensee from time to time. Provided that the Licensee shall be entitled to exclude from any details, further descriptions or amendments, as the case may be, which it is obliged to publish in accordance with this paragraph any matter to the exclusion of which the Director shall have consented following representations to him on the matter by the Licensee on the basis that if the matter were made available in accordance with this paragraph it would or might, in the opinion of the Director, seriously and prejudicially affect the interests of the Licensee.

(c)   The Licensee shall publish details of any amendment to the details of the Accounting Documents published in accordance with paragraph 20B.14 (b), as soon as practicable, and in any event within 28 days, after the making of the amendment.

(d)   For the purposes of sub-paragraphs (a) to (c) publication shall be effected by making the required details, further descriptions or amendments, as the case may be, publicly available and by sending copies to the Director.

(e)   The Licensee shall send a copy of each of the required details, further descriptions or amendments, as the case may be, or any of them to any person who may (after the expiry of the period specified in each of sub-paragraphs (a) to (c)) request them, on the basis of that person paying a reasonable charge for them. The Licensee shall send the copies within seven working days after receiving payment of that charge.

(f)   The Licensee shall make available and continue to make available in a publicly accessible part of every Major Office of the Licensee in the place as is required by Condition 16.3 (b) a notice of the address and telephone number of the person to whom any request for a copy of any or all of the required details or amendments may be made.

20B.15   Without prejudice to Condition 18, where the Director is satisfied, on the basis of the most up to date information which has been made available to him at the relevant time, that the Licensee:

(a)   has within the previous six years (excluding any period before the date on which this Condition comes into force) unfairly subsidised or unfairly cross subsidised and has ceased to unfairly subsidise or unfairly cross subsidise but is likely to repeat that unfair subsidy or unfair cross subsidy at any time in the future; or

(b)   is unfairly subsidising or unfairly cross subsidising;
either:

(i)   any or all of the Businesses other than the Residual Business; or

(ii)   any part or parts of any of the Businesses other than the Residual Business where the Director is satisfied that unfair subsidy or unfair cross subsidy, as the case may be, has or could have a material effect on competition in the United Kingdom in relation to the activity to which the unfair subsidy or unfair cross subsidy relates;

or both, it shall take such steps as the Director may direct for the purpose of remedying the situation.

20B.16   The Licensee shall, with the consent of the Director, make such amendments as are from time to time required to:

(a)   the definition of each Business in terms of the revenues, costs and assets comprised in it;

(b)   the number of Businesses for the purposes of this Condition;

(c)   the manner in which each Business may be disaggregated;

(d)   the form and content of:

(i)   the profit and loss account;

(ii)   the statement of mean capital employed;

(iii)   the statements of costs (if any); and

(iv)   the additional information to be provided by way of notes;

comprised in each Financial Statement; or

(e)   the Accounting Documents;

to ensure that they are consistent with, and give effect fully to:

(aa)   modifications of any of the Conditions in Schedule 1 of this Licence;

(bb)   final Orders made under section 16 of the Act;

(cc)   formal undertakings given by the Licensee to the Director following investigations by him into possible contraventions by the Licensee of any of the Conditions in Schedule 1 to this Licence; and

(dd)   directions, consents and determinations given or made by the Director from time to time under any of the Conditions in Schedule 1 of this Licence;

made or given on or after the date on which this Condition comes into force together with, in each case, any published explanations and reasons given by the Director in connection with any of the matters specified in sub-paragraphs (aa) to (dd) provided that the requirements of this paragraph shall be suspended pending the final disposal of any proceedings seeking to have any such final Orders, directions, consents, or determinations, quashed, set aside, modified or varied.

20B.17   (a)   Before giving a direction or consent under this Condition, the Director shall consult with the Licensee and, except in the case of a consent or refusal to consent for the purposes of paragraph 20B.14 (b) or a direction referred to in paragraph 20B. 15 (each an 'excluded case') Interested Parties. If he concludes that a direction or consent is appropriate, or that a consent is not appropriate, he shall notify the Licensee and (except in an excluded case) Interested Parties of the proposed direction or consent or refusal of consent, as the case may be, and his reasons for proposing to give it or refuse to give consent and give each of them a reasonable opportunity to make representations. On giving a direction or consent or refusing to give consent, he shall notify the Licensee and (except in an excluded case) Interested Parties of the direction or consent or refusal, as the case may be, and his reasons for giving it or refusing consent.

(b)   Each notification of reasons shall, as appropriate, set out the Director's reasons:

(i)   for proposing to give the direction or give or refuse consent, as the case may be; or

(ii)   for giving the direction or giving or refusing consent, as the case may be;

those reasons being sufficient to give the Licensee and Interested Parties a reasonable understanding of the proposed decision or decision, as the case may be.

20B.18   (a)   Where the Director has reasonable grounds to believe that:

(i)   the Licensee has done or is doing any of the things specified in paragraph 20B. 15 or Condition 18 or both; or

(ii)   the Licensee:

(aa)   has within the previous six years (excluding any period before the date on which this Condition comes into force) shown undue preference to, or exercised undue discrimination against, any Operator in respect of the provision or Quality of a Standard Service or Private Circuit or both contrary to the provisions of Condition 17 or Condition 17B or both and has ceased to do so but is likely to repeat that undue preference or undue discrimination at any time in the future; or

(bb)   is showing undue preference or undue discrimination as described in sub-paragraph (a) (ii) (aa); or

(iii)   the Licensee is in breach of this Condition; or

(iv)   any or all of the Accounting Documents, the Financial Statements, the Restated Financial Statements and the Interim Financial Statements are deficient;

the Licensee shall, without prejudice to Condition 52, extend its prompt co-operation to the Director, his representatives and members of his staff and, in particular, on the Director's reasonable request shall:

(A)   furnish the Director in accordance with his reasonable requirements with any information, documents, accounts, estimates, returns, reports or other information (including, without limitation, any facility enabling him to read data not held in readable form);

(B)   on reasonable notice by him allow at all reasonable times the Director, his representatives and any member of his staff on production of his special authority access to any relevant premises of the Licensee to investigate, assess, examine, review or verify any of its accounting records or accounting and reporting arrangements, systems or processes; and

(C)   for the purpose of sub-paragraph (B), allow the Director, his representatives and any member of his staff to be accompanied by any person whom the Director may specify, being a person to whom the Licensee has raised no reasonable objection, whose assistance the Director might reasonably require: Provided that the Director has given the Licensee notice (which save in exceptional circumstances shall be of at least 5 working days) of the identity of that person.

(*b*)   If, as a result of any investigation, assessment, examination or review referred to in sub-paragraph (a), the Director is satisfied that:

(i)   the Licensee has done or is doing any of the things referred to in sub-paragraph (a) (i) to (iii);

(ii)   any or all of the Accounting Documents, the Financial Statements, the Restated Financial Statements and the Interim Financial Statements are deficient; or

(iii)   he has insufficient information to conclude whether or not the Licensee has done or is doing any of the things referred to in sub-paragraph (a) (i) to (iii);

he may direct with effect from the date specified in the direction, without prejudice to his other powers under this Licence, that:

(i)   the Licensee shall amend any or all of:

(aa)   the composition of any or all of the Businesses in terms of any or all of the revenues, costs and assets they respectively comprise;

(bb)   the manner in which any or all of the Businesses are disaggregated in terms of activities of the relevant Business;

(cc) the form and content of any or all of the profit and loss account, the statement of mean capital employed and the additional information to be provided by way of notes comprised in the Financial Statements, the Restated Financial Statements or the Interim Financial Statements of any or all of the Businesses; and

(dd) any or all of the Accounting Documents; or

(ii) the Licensee shall divide any or all of the Businesses to create additional Businesses, or aggregate them to create fewer Businesses;

or both: Provided that any direction given pursuant to this sub-paragraph shall relate to the results of the relevant investigation, assessment, examination or review referred to in sub-paragraph (a) in respect of which the direction is given.

20B.19   This Condition operates without prejudice to Conditions 20 and 20A.

20B.20   In this Condition:

'Accounting Documents' means together the Accounting Policies, the Attribution Methods, the Regulatory Accounting Principles and the Transfer Charging System;

'Accounting Policies' means the manner in which the requirements of the Companies Act 1985, the Accounting Standards and the accounting policies applied by the Licensee in the preparation of its annual statutory financial statements, where relevant and appropriate, are applied in each of the Financial Statements, the Restated Financial Statements and the Interim Financial Statements as agreed in writing between the Director and the Licensee on or before the date on which this Condition comes into force, as amended from time to time in accordance with this Condition;

'Accounting Standards' has the meaning given to it in the Companies Act 1985;

'attributable' includes allocatable and apportionable, 'attribute' includes allocate and apportion and 'attribution' includes allocation and apportionment;

'Attribution Methods' means the practices used to attribute revenue (including appropriate transfer charges), costs (including appropriate transfer charges), assets and liabilities to a Business or, insofar as that Business has been disaggregated in terms of activities of that Business, to each activity of that Business as agreed in writing between the Director and the Licensee on or before the date on which this Condition comes into force, as amended from time to time in accordance with this Condition;

'Auditing Standards' means United Kingdom auditing standards and guidelines issued from time to time by the Auditing Practices Board and its predecessor body, the Auditing Standards Board;

'Auditor' has the meaning given to it in Condition 20;

'Businesses' means the businesses comprising the revenues, costs and assets as agreed in writing between the Director and the Licensee on or before the date on which this Condition comes into force, as amended in accordance with this Condition and 'Business' means any one of them;

'1994 Financial Statements' means together the profit and loss account, the statement of mean capital employed, and the additional information to be provided by way of notes prepared on an historic cost basis for each Business for the financial year ended 31 March 1994, the form and content of which have been agreed between the Director and the Licensee on or before the date on which this Condition comes into force; 'Interested Parties' has the meaning given to it in Condition 16B; 'Major Office' has the meaning given to it in Condition 16; 'Operator' has the meaning given to it in Condition 16B; 'Private Circuit' means a Private Circuit to which Condition 46 relates; 'Quality' has the meaning given to it in Condition 17B; 'Regulatory Accounting Principles' means the principles agreed in writing between the Director and the Licensee on or before the date on which this Condition comes into force, as amended from time to time in accordance with this Condition; 'Residual Business' means the business or businesses of which the revenues, costs and assets are not comprised in any Business as agreed between the Director and the Licensee in accordance with this Condition, as amended from time to time in accordance with this Condition; 'Standard Service' has the meaning given to it in Condition 16B; and 'Transfer Charging System' means the system which enables a Business to use a service or good from another Business and to account for it as though it had purchased that service or good, as agreed in writing between the Director and the Licensee on or before the date on which this Condition comes into force, as amended from time to time in accordance with this Condition.

Notes to Condition 20B
1. Conditions 20B and 20.B.1–20 were inserted by a licence amendment dated 31 March 1995.
2. Condition 20B.1 was inserted and renumbered 20B.1A by a licence amendment dated 2 November 1995.
3. See OFTEL statement 'Interconnection and Accountancy Separation: The Next Step' March 1994.

Condition 21   Apparatus Production

21.1   If the Licensee is, or before 1 July 1986 becomes, engaged in the business of production of telecommunication apparatus, that business shall, as soon as reasonably practicable and in any event not later than 1 July 1986, be transferred to a Subsidiary of its ('the Apparatus Production Company'), unless it has previously been transferred to some other person; and the Licensee shall not after that date engage in any such business.
21.2   The Licensee shall secure that the Apparatus Production Company does not engage in the business of running telecommunications systems.
21.3   The Licensee shall secure that the Apparatus Production Company furnishes to the Director as soon as reasonably practicable and in any case not later than six months after the end of each financial year a copy of its annual accounts together with a statement showing the matters which are required to be shown in respect of the Systems Business and the Apparatus Supply Business in equivalent statements under Condition 20.
21.4   Unless the Director otherwise agrees, where for the time being:

(*a*)   the Director determines that the Licensee is a Monopoly Purchaser in the United Kingdom in relation to telecommunication apparatus of any particular description;

(*b*)   the Director is of the opinion, after considering any representations from the Licensee, that in the interests of promoting fair competition the Licensee ought not to acquire apparatus of that particular description from the Apparatus Production Company unless it has complied with the open tender procedures specified in paragraph 21.5; and

(*c*)   the Director so notifies the Licensee;

then the Licensee shall not acquire any such apparatus from the Apparatus Production Company for the purpose of its business in the United Kingdom unless it has complied with those procedures in relation to that apparatus.

21.5   Compliance with the open tender procedures requires the Licensee, in accordance with a procedure adopted after consultation with the Director from time to time:

(*a*)   to publish a notice giving particulars of the proposed acquisition of apparatus sufficient for the purposes of this Condition and the date by which it is required and inviting any person to offer to supply that apparatus accordingly; and

(*b*)   to give due consideration to any offers made.

21.6   Paragraphs 21.4 and 21.5 shall not apply to the acquisition of telecommunication apparatus:

(*a*)   for supply outside the United Kingdom;

(*b*)   which is intended for use by any member of the Licensee's Group other than in the provision of telecommunication services to others;

(*c*)   which in the opinion of the Director is apparatus which is not normally regarded as telecommunication equipment;

(*d*)   such that there is no producer in the United Kingdom other than the Apparatus Production company capable of supplying apparatus of that particular kind in the quantities and at the times required;

(*e*)   of a particular kind which is so different from other apparatus produced in the United Kingdom that compliance with the open tender procedures would place the Licensee or the Apparatus Production Company at an unfair competitive disadvantage; or

(*f*)   the acquisition of which from the Apparatus Production Company is not in material quantities.

21.7   The Director shall, when exercising his powers under this Condition, have regard insofar as he may do so to the interests of the Licensee, the shareholders in the Licensee and the Licensee's employees, without prejudice to his duties under section 3 of the Act (including his duties towards other persons engaged in the production of telecommunication apparatus).

21.8   Where the Licensee:

(*a*)   is under an obligation to comply with the open tender procedures in respect of telecommunication apparatus of a particular description; and

(*b*)   furnishes evidence to the Director that it has ceased to be a Monopoly Purchaser of apparatus of that description;

the Licensee shall at the end of a period of six months after it has furnished that evidence cease to be required to comply with the open tender procedures in respect of that description of apparatus unless the Director has given notice to the Licensee in that period that he is satisfied that the Licensee continues to be a Monopoly Purchaser of apparatus of that description.

21.9 Notwithstanding the provisions of this Condition, the Licensee may engage in:

(a)   research and development;

(b)   production of prototypes or samples;

(c)   production of apparatus exclusively for the purpose of being tested; or

(d)   production of apparatus in quantities which are not substantial or which do not significantly affect competition in commercial activities connected with telecommunications in the United Kingdom;

but where the Licensee is engaged in production of the kind mentioned in sub-paragraphs (b), (c) or (d) above in any financial year it shall as soon as reasonably practicable after the end of that year furnish to the Director a general description of that production sufficient for the purposes of this Condition.

21.10   In this Condition:

'production' in relation to apparatus includes, unless in any case the Director determines otherwise:

(a)   assembly or reassembly of apparatus; and

(b)   refurbishment of apparatus;

at a place where it is not normally connected to a telecommunication system;

'Monopoly Purchaser' in relation to telecommunication apparatus of any description means a person in relation to whom there exists a monopoly situation within the meaning of any of the provisions of section 6 of the Fair Trading Act 1973 in respect of the supply to him of apparatus of that description; and

'telecommunication apparatus of any particular description' means items of telecommunication apparatus, or sets of such items used together, which perform the same or substantially similar functions.

Condition 22   Prohibition of Preferential Treatment

22.1   If the Licensee habitually provides any service or makes any arrangement in any Area whereby:

(a)   a person normally engaged in the Systems Business incidentally to the carrying on of that Business:

(i)   delivers to Served Premises telecommunication apparatus for connection to any of the Applicable Systems; or

(ii)   connects such apparatus to Network Termination and Testing Apparatus forming part of the Applicable Systems; or

(b)   a person normally engaged in the Apparatus Supply Business incidentally to the carrying on of that Business:

(i)   arranges for the installation by the Systems Business of any telecommunication apparatus comprised or to be comprised in any of the Applicable Systems;

(ii)   arranges for the provision of telecommunication services by the Systems Business by means of or in relation to such apparatus so installed; or

(iii)   arranges for the provision of Maintenance Services in respect of Limited Maintenance Telecommunication Systems or Limited Maintenance Telecommunication Apparatus supplied by the Licensee or to be so supplied;

then the Licensee shall take all reasonable steps to ensure to the satisfaction of the Director, if required by him to do so, that a person carrying on a business similar to the Apparatus Supply Business in that Area has a reasonable opportunity to avail himself of that service or to make such arrangements on equivalent charges and terms for the purpose of that person's business.

22.2   Where the Licensee is required to do anything under paragraph 22.1 it may impose such additional terms and conditions as are reasonably necessary to protect it in the circumstances of any particular case.

22.3   In this Condition 'Area' means any of the Licensee's telephone areas for the time being or any other equivalent management unit.

Note
This Condition was deleted on 31 December 1996 when new Condition 18A came into effect.

Condition 23   Alterations to the Applicable Systems

23.1   The Licensee shall:

(*a*)   from time to time inform the Director and provide him with such additional information as he may reasonably require about any proposals for changes to the Applicable Systems or to any apparatus comprised therein or to any stored commands or protocol; and

(*b*)   inform the Director of any proposals for changes to the means of access to a Relevant Service provided by the Licensee, which Service was previously capable of being accessed by means of an OSI Standard or by any other means, not less than six months before the coming into effect of such proposals;

being in either case changes of which the Director has not already been informed under this Condition and which the Licensee might reasonably anticipate from the facts known to it would or might when made have the effect of requiring any person:

(i)   running any Connectable System which is or is to be connected to the Applicable Systems;

(ii)   connecting telecommunication apparatus to the Applicable Systems; or

(iii)   producing or supplying telecommunication apparatus or telecommunication systems for connection to the Applicable Systems without becoming comprised in them;

materially to modify, or, as the case may be, to replace or cease to produce or supply, any item of telecommunication apparatus connected or to be connected to any of the Applicable Systems or, where the change is of a kind described in sub-paragraph (b), to cease to provide or obtain any service by means of the Applicable Systems.

23.2   The Licensee shall prepare and publish in consultation with the Director a statement of its procedures for consulting, and giving advance notice to, those persons likely to be affected by such changes (including in particular in the case of changes of a kind described in paragraph 23.1 (a) the British Standards Institution and any person appointed by the Secretary of State under section 25 of the Act) and shall adhere to those procedures, and, in the case of changes of a kind described in paragraph 23.1 (b), the statement shall be published by 31 October 1987.

23.3   For the purposes of changes of a kind described in paragraph 23.1 (b), any telecommunication system, and any apparatus comprised in a telecommunication system, which is not connected to an Applicable System shall be treated as being so connected if it is connected to or comprised in a telecommunication system which is so connected or treated as so connected.

23.4   In this Condition:

'to modify' in relation to any Other Apparatus or System means to make any alteration to that Apparatus or System which may be necessary to ensure that any Message which has been or is to be conveyed by means of any of the Applicable Systems connected or to be connected to that Other Apparatus or System is capable of being properly conveyed by that Other Apparatus or System or by that Applicable System as the case may be;

'Other Apparatus or System' means any telecommunication apparatus or telecommunication system together with any protocol, message format or stored command in such apparatus or system connected or to be connected to but not comprised in any of the Applicable Systems; and

'OSI Standard' means any standard or rule which supports capabilities described in the International Standards Organisation's — Open Systems Interconnection — Basic Reference Model and which is specified by the Director for the purposes of this Licence and described in a list kept for the purpose by him and made available by him for inspection by the general public, and is not removed by him from that list.

Notes

1.   Conditions 23.1–3 were deleted and replaced by and Condition 23.4 was inserted by a licence amendment dated 1 May 1987.

2.   The definition of OSI Standard in Condition 23.4 was changed by a licence amendment dated 31 October 1996.

Condition 24A   Control of General Prices

[24A.1   The Licensee shall take all reasonable steps to secure that, during any Relevant Year, the amount of General Prices remains such that:

(*a*)   if the Controlling Percentage for that Year (determined in accordance with paragraphs 24A.3 to 24A.5 and, if appropriate, adjusted in accordance with paragraphs 24A.10 and 24A.11) is zero or positive, any Percentage Change which has taken place in the aggregate of all General Prices (determined and calculated, on a weighted basis, in accordance with paragraphs 24A.6 and 24A.7) at the end of each Period does not constitute an increase by more than the Controlling Percentage; or

(*b*)   if that Percentage is negative, there is no Percentage Change in General Prices by way of increase and before the end of that year there is such a Change by way of reduction of not less than that percentage.

24A.1A   Where, for the purpose of complying with this Condition 24A, the Licensee is required to reduce its General Prices in any Relevant Year (not being the Relevant Year beginning on 1 August 1993 and ending on 31 July 1994) the Licensee shall take all reasonable steps to ensure that the combined effect on accrued income of the Licensee of all individual changes in General Prices shall be not less than that which would have been produced had all of those changes been made at exactly the same time and no later than on 1

November in that Year, and accordingly 1 November in that year shall be the latest weighted average date (within the meaning of paragraph 24A.1B below) in that Year for the purposes of the making of reductions in General Prices. For the purpose of establishing whether or not the Licensee has complied with the obligation imposed on it by this paragraph 24A.1A a calculation shall be carried out by employing the formula set out in paragraph 24A.1B below.

24A.1B   The formula mentioned in paragraph 24A.1A above is:

$$\text{WAD} = \sum_{i=1}^{n} \frac{R_i}{RC} \times D_i \leq 0$$

Where:
WAD   = the weighted average date.
R_i = the revenue change associated with the ith price change made in the Relevant Year.
RC   = the total revenue change required in the Relevant Year to achieve compliance with this Condition 24A.1.
D_i = the date on which the ith price change takes effect expressed as a numeric entity on a scale ranging from 1 August = -92 to 31 July = 272, except in a Leap Year when 31 July = 273.

24A.1C   To the extent that the licensee has made, during any Relevant Year, any reductions in General Prices beyond those necessary for compliance with this Condition 24A, those reductions shall be relevant in applying paragraph 24A.1A and paragraph 24A.1B to price changes in the Relevant Year immediately following the Relevant Year in which those reductions are made. In applying the formula referred to in paragraph 24A.1B to such changes, subject to paragraph 24A.1D, that formula shall apply with the meaning of D_i amended as follows:

D_i = the date on which the ith price change takes effect expressed as a numeric entity on a scale ranging from 1 August = -457 to 31 July = -93, except in a leap year, when 1 August = -458

24A.1D   If, in relation to any reduction in General Prices to which paragraph 24A.1C applies, the Director is of the opinion that D_i should not equal the date on which that price change takes effect as described in that paragraph, but should equal I August in the immediately following Relevant Year (expressed as a numeric entity where 1 August = -92), he shall so notify the Licensee as soon as practicable after receipt by the Director of notification by the Licensee of the price change and the Director shall include in his notification the reasons for his opinion. Where the Director has given such a notification the formula referred to in paragraph 24A.1B shall apply with D_i = -92 to any reduction in General Prices to which that notification applies.

24A.2   Where, notwithstanding the obligation imposed on the Licensee by paragraph 24A.1, (or paragraph 24A.1 of the Condition 24A having effect on 31 July 1993) there has taken place a change in General Prices (or 'Relevant Prices' as defined in that Condition 24A which are also General Prices) of a kind not permitted under paragraph 24A.1 (a) or (b) (or paragraph 24A.1 (a) or (b) of the Condition 24A having effect on 31 July 1993), the Licensee shall make adjustments in General Prices sufficient to satisfy the Director that the matter has been remedied.

24A.2A   Where notwithstanding the obligation imposed on the Licensee by paragraph 24A.1A the effect on accrued income of the changes in General

Prices referred to in that paragraph fails, in the opinion of the Director, to meet the requirements of that paragraph, the Licensee shall make such further reductions in General Prices as may be reasonably required to satisfy the Director that the matter has been remedied.

24A.3   Subject to paragraphs 24A.4, 24A.5, 24A.10 and 24A.11 the Controlling Percentage in relation to any Relevant Year is the amount of the change in the Retail Prices Index in the period of 12 months ending on 30 June immediately before the beginning of that Year, expressed as a percentage (rounded to two decimal places) of that Index as at the beginning of that period, reduced by 7.5.

24A.4   If the difference between General Prices charged at the beginning and at the end of any Relevant Year is such that the relevant Percentage Change in General Prices is less (in the case of a permitted increase), or greater (in the case of a required reduction), than the change permitted, or required, in accordance with paragraph 24A.1, then the Controlling Percentage for the following Relevant Year shall be determined in accordance with paragraph 24A.3 but increased subject to paragraph 24A.5 by the amount of such deficiency or excess (as the case may be).

24A.5   The Controlling Percentage for the Fourth Relevant Year shall only be increased by virtue of paragraph 24A.4 to the extent that such an increase would have been permitted if that paragraph had not applied to increase the Controlling Percentage for the second such year.

24A.6   The amount of a Percentage Change in General Prices which has taken place at any time during a Relevant Year is determined by taking the amount of the change in each General Price which has taken place between the beginning of the Relevant Year and that time, multiplying that amount by the amount of the revenue reasonably believed by the Licensee to have accrued during the Relevant Financial Year in respect of the service for which that Price is charged, dividing in each case the amounts so produced by the price charged at the beginning of the Relevant Year for the service to which each such amount relates, and taking the aggregate of the results, expressed as a percentage of all the revenue reasonably believed to have accrued for such services during the Relevant Financial Year.

24A.7   Notwithstanding paragraph 24A.6, if the Licensee has notified the Director in writing both of its intention to increase during a Period one or more General Prices and of its intention within three months of the first such increase to reduce one or more General Prices then, unless:

(a)   the Director dissents within 28 days of such notification on the ground that undue advantage is being taken of this paragraph; or

(b)   the reduction as so notified is not introduced;

for the purposes of paragraph 24A.6 when determining the amount of a Percentage Change which has taken place at the end of the said Period and each subsequent Period it shall be assumed that any such reduction had taken place during the first mentioned Period.

24A.8   Where the Licensee makes a material change (other than as to the amount of a General Price) in any service for which a General Price is charged or in the date on which its financial year ends or there is a material change in the basis of the Retail Prices Index, this Condition shall have effect subject to such reasonable adjustment to take account of the change as the Director may, after consultation with the Licensee, determine to be appropriate in the circumstances; and for the purposes of this paragraph a material change in any service includes the introduction of a new service wholly or substantially in substitution for that existing service.

24A.9   Subject to this paragraph this Condition shall not have effect in relation to a new service, the charges for which would otherwise be General Prices, other than a new service to which paragraph 24A.8 applies. In relation to a new service other than one to which paragraph 24A.8 applies the Director may, after consultation with the Licensee, in any Relevant Year during which it is first possible, from the Relevant Financial Year accounts, to ascertain 12 months actual revenue in respect of that service accrued in relation to that Relevant Financial Year, determine that the charges for that service shall in the subsequent year be General Prices and this Condition shall, from that subsequent Relevant Year, apply accordingly.

24A.10   If the Licensee imposes a specific charge or an increased charge in relation to any goods or service which up to the time when the charge or increased charge is first imposed had been provided without charge or at a lower charge and the Director determines after consultation with the Licensee that some or all the costs properly attributable to that service had previously been attributed to services to which General Prices apply and that it would be proper in the circumstances for the newly introduced or increased charge to be controlled, that charge shall, unless the Director determines otherwise, be a General Price and this Condition shall have effect subject to the following provisions:

(*a*)   the Licensee shall produce a forecast of the revenue expected to accrue as a result of the charge or increased charge for the goods or service over a period of twelve months from the date of introduction or increase of the charge;

(*b*)   the forecast shall be expressed as a percentage of the total amount of revenue reasonably believed by the Licensee to have accrued in respect of General Prices during the Relevant Financial Year which relates to the Relevant Year during which the charge is introduced or increased;

(*c*)   the Controlling Percentage for that Relevant Year shall be reduced by that percentage;

(*d*)   an adjustment shall be made to the Controlling Percentage for that Relevant Year in respect of which it is first possible, from the Relevant Financial Year accounts, to take into account a comparison between the first 12 months actual accrued revenue from the charge and the forecast referred to in sub-paragraph (a) above, whereby the Controlling Percentage for that Relevant Year shall be increased or reduced (as the case may be) by the difference between the forecast amount referred to in sub-paragraph (a) and the amount of actual accrued revenue (the difference to be expressed as a percentage of the total amount of revenue accrued in respect of General Prices during the Relevant Financial Year which relates to that Relevant Year);

(*e*)   further adjustments shall be made to the Controlling Percentage referred to in sub-paragraph (d) and adjusted as specified therein:

(i)   where there is any difference between the forecast referred to in sub-paragraph (a) and the actual accrued revenue referred to in sub-paragraph (d), in order to compensate for the extent to which, by virtue of that difference, General Prices in previous Relevant Years have been too high or too low (as the case may be); and

(ii)   where there has been any variation in the charge for the service between the Relevant Year referred to in sub-paragraph (b) and the Relevant Year referred to in sub-paragraph (d) which the Director, after consultation with the Licensee, determines should be taken into account for the purposes of calculating the Controlling Percentage;

(f)   The adjustments referred to in sub-paragraphs (d) and (e) shall be made in the precise manner which the Director determines to be appropriate in the circumstances, after consultation with the Licensee.

24A.11   If the charge or increased charge for any goods or service covered by paragraph 24A.10 is altered following its introduction but before the adjustment referred to in paragraph 24A.10 (d) can be made then, in respect of that charge, in calculating the amount of a Percentage Change in General Prices in paragraph 24A.6, the forecast set out in paragraph 24A.10 (a) shall be substituted for the amount referred to in paragraph 24A.12 (a).

24A.12   The Licensee shall no later than the time at which it notifies or should have notified under Condition 16 the Director of any amendment of any charge which is a General Price inform the Director in writing of:

(a)   the amount of revenue which the Licensee reasonably believes to have accrued in the Relevant Financial Year for each service in respect of which a General Price is charged; and

(b)   the amount of each General Price at the beginning of the Relevant Year.

24A.13   Without prejudice to its obligations under Condition 16 in relation to General Prices, the Licensee shall as soon as practicable after the end of each Period in which there has been a change in a General Price inform the Director in writing of:

(a)   the changes made or new charges imposed in relation to any General Price during the Period specifying its nature and amount and the service for which the Price is charged; and

(b)   the amount of the Percentage Change in General Prices which has taken place during the Period and whether by way of increase or reduction.

24A.14   Notwithstanding any of the earlier paragraphs of this Condition the Licensee shall take all reasonable steps to secure that no individual General Price increases during any Relevant Year by more than the amount of the change in the Retail Prices Index in the period of 12 months ending on 30 June immediately before the beginning of that Year, expressed as a percentage (rounded to two decimal places) of that Index as at the beginning of that period, except that Exchange Line rentals may be increased subject to a maximum of the amount of that change increased by, in the case of Exchange Lines generally, 2, and, in the case of Wholesale Exchange Lines, 5. In this paragraph 'Wholesale Exchange Line' means an Exchange Line which is used by the Licensee's customer for that Line for the conveyance, on the payment of money or money's worth to that customer, of the Messages of third parties (an example of a Wholesale Exchange Line being an Exchange Line connected for the purpose of serving a Public Call Box or a Private Call Box as defined in Condition 11.7). The obligation imposed by this paragraph 24A.14 does not apply to:

(a)   call units chargeable in accordance with Condition 24D (Residential Low User Scheme); or

(b)   charges for International Calls over routes determined, after consultation with the Licensee, by the Director. Where such a determination is made the Licensee shall ensure that the charges in question do not increase during any Relevant Year by more than the amount of the change in the Retail Prices Index in the period of 12 months ending on 30 June immediately before the beginning of that year, expressed as a percentage (rounded to two decimal places) of that Index as at the beginning of that period, increased by 5; or

(c)   charges for calls to be conveyed by a Relevant Connectable System, the operator of which is entitled to receive from the Licensee charges for the conveyance of those calls or for any other service provided by means of that System, of an amount which is greater than the amount which the Licensee would be entitled to receive (in the absence of the exercise by the Director of the power conferred on him by Condition 13.5A.5 (Access Deficit Contribution 'waiver') pursuant to the relevant provisions of Condition 13 if the conveyance or the provision of other services to which the operator's charge relates had been by means of the Applicable Systems, in which case the Licensee shall be entitled to increase its charges to its customers in respect of such calls so as to recover the difference between those two amounts.

24A.15   In this Condition:

'Discounted General Prices' means prices which are charged as part of a Package (as defined in Condition 24C.8) and which, if they were not so charged, would be General Prices;

'General Prices' means (being in all cases the Licensee's Standard Prices):

Any reference to 'service' which is not part of the expression 'goods or service' shall be taken to include a reference to goods for the purposes of paragraphs 24A.10 and 24A.11.

References to accrued revenue are references to the revenue attributable to General Prices but with the addition of the revenue attributable to Discounted General Prices where those prices are grossed up so as to leave the discount out of account, and cognate expressions shall be construed accordingly.

24A.16   This Condition shall not apply to such extent as the Director may determine upon request by the Licensee]

New Condition 24A in italics will be substituted for the words in square brackets from 1 August 1997 by a licence amendment dated 1 October 1996.

Condition 24A   Control of General Prices

24A.1   The Licensee shall take all reasonable steps to secure that, during any Relevant Year, the amount of General Prices remains such that:

(a)   if the Controlling Percentage for that Year (determined in accordance with paragraph 24A.9) is zero or positive, any Percentage Change which has taken place in the aggregate of all General Prices (determined in accordance with paragraphs 24A.11 and 24A.12) at the end of each Period does not constitute an increase by more than the Controlling Percentage;

(b)   if that Percentage is negative, there is no Percentage Change in General Prices by way of increase and, before the end of that Year, there is such a Change by way of reduction of not less than that Percentage.

24A.2   Where, for the purpose of complying with this Condition, the Licensee is required to reduce, or to limit any increase in, its General Prices in any Relevant

Year the Licensee shall take all reasonable steps to ensure that the combined effect on accrued revenue of the Licensee of all individual changes in General Prices shall be no less than, in the case of a required reduction, that which would have been produced had all of those changes been made at exactly the same time and no later than on 1 February in that Year, or more than, in the case of a limited increase, that which would have been produced had all of those changes been made at exactly the same time and no earlier than on 1 February in that Year, and accordingly 1 February in that Year shall be the latest or, as the case may be, earliest weighted average date (within the meaning of paragraph 24A.3) in that Year for the purposes of the making of reductions of increases in General Prices. For the purpose of establishing whether or not the Licensee has complied with the obligation imposed on it by this paragraph, a calculation shall be carried out by employing the formula set out in paragraph 24A.3.

24A.3   The formula mentioned in paragraph 24A.2 is—

$$\text{WAD} = \sum_{i=1}^{n} \frac{R_i}{RC} \times D_i \leq 0$$

Where:

WAD = the weighted average date

R_i = *the revenue change associated with the ith price change made in the Relevant Year*

RC = *the total revenue change required in the Relevant Year to achieve compliance with paragraph 24A.1*

D_i = *the date on which the ith price change takes effect expressed as a numeric entity on a scale ranging from 1 August = − 184 to 31 July = 180, except in a leap year when 31 July = 181.*

24A.4   To the extent that the Licensee has made, during any Relevant Year, any reductions in General Prices beyond those necessary for compliance with this Condition, or, as the case may be, any increases in such Prices less than those permitted, those changes shall be relevant in applying paragraphs 24A.2 and 24A.3 to price changes in the Relevant Year immediately following the Relevant Year in which those changes were made. In applying the formula referred to in paragraph 24A.3 to such changes, subject to paragraph 24A.5, that formula shall apply with the meaning of Di amended as follows:

D_i = *the date on which the ith price change takes effect expressed as a numeric entity on a scale ranging from 1 August = − 549 to 31 July = − 185, except in a leap year, when 1 August = − 550.*

24A.5   If, in relation to any change in General Prices to which paragraph 24A.4 applies, the Director is of the opinion that D_i should not equal the date on which that price change takes effect as described in that paragraph, but should equal 1 August in the immediately following Relevant Year (expressed as a numeric entity where 1 August = − 184), he shall so direct the Licensee as soon as practicable after receipt by the Director of notification by the Licensee of the price change and the Director shall include in his direction the reasons for his opinion. Where the Director has given such a direction the formula referred to in paragraph 24A.3 shall apply with D_i = − 184 to any change in General Prices to which that direction applies.

24A.6   Where the Licensee decides that a charge (or group of charges) for any of the things included within the definition of General Prices is to be offered only:

(a)   *in combination with another such charge (or group of charges) or with an additional periodic fee; and*

(b)   *in two or more such combinations.*

the Licensee shall nominate one charge (or group of charges) in such combinations (including the fee, if any) to be the General Price for the purposes of this Condition (The 'Reference Price'). The Licensee shall offer the Reference Price for the conveyance of Messages to residential customers in combination with the Reference Price for the use and Ordinary Maintenance of residential Exchange Lines.

24A.7   *Where, notwithstanding the obligation imposed on the Licensee by paragraph 24A.1 (or paragraph 24A.1 of Condition 24A having effect on 31 July 1997), there has taken place a change in General Prices (or General Prices as defined in that Condition 24A) of a kind not permitted under paragraph 24A.1(a) or (b) (or paragraph 24A.1(a) or (b) of Condition 24A having effect on 31 July 1997), the Licensee shall make such adjustments in General Prices (or leave them unchanged), for such period, whether in the year in question or the following year (and whether or not that year is a Relevant Year), as may be reasonably required to satisfy the Director that the matter has been remedied. Such adjustments shall not be relevant for the purposes of establishing compliance with paragraph 24A.1 in a following Relevant Year.*

24A.8   *Where, notwithstanding the obligation imposed on the Licensee by paragraph 24A.2 (or paragraph 24A.1A of Condition 24A having effect on 31 July 1997), the effect on accrued revenue of the changes in General Prices (or General Prices as defined in that Condition 24A) fails, in the opinion of the Director, to meet the requirements of that paragraph, the Licensee shall make such adjustments in General Prices (or leave them unchanged), for such period, whether in the year in question or the following year (and whether or not that year is a Relevant Year), as may be reasonably required to satisfy the Director that the matter has been remedied.*

24A.9   *Subject to paragraphs 24A.10, 24A.14 and 24A.15 and Conditions 24C.4 and 24C.5, the Controlling Percentage in relation to any Relevant Year is the amount of the change in the Retail Prices Index in the period of 12 months ending on 30 June immediately before the beginning of that Year, expressed as a percentage (rounded to two decimal places) of that Index as at the beginning of that period ('RPI'), reduced by 4.5.*

24A.10   *If the difference between General Prices charged at the beginning and at the end of any Relevant Year is such that the relevant Percentage Change in General Prices is less (in the case of a permitted increase), or greater (in the case of a required reduction), than the change permitted, or required, in accordance with paragraph 24A.1, then the Controlling Percentage for the following Relevant Year shall be determined in accordance with paragraph 24A.9 but increased by the amount of such deficiency or excess (as the case may be).*

24.11   *The amount of a Percentage Change in General Prices which has taken place at any time during a Relevant Year is determined by taking the amount of the change in each General Price which has taken place between the beginning of the Relevant Year and that time, multiplying that amount by the amount of the revenue reasonably believed by the Licensee to have accrued during the Relevant Financial Year in respect of the service for which that Price is charged from customers whose bills from the Licensee are equal to or less than the Threshold, dividing in each case the amounts so produced by the Price charged at the beginning of the Relevant Year for the service to which each such amount relates, and taking the aggregate of the* results, expressed as a percentage of all the revenue reasonably believed to have accrued for such services from such customers during the Relevant Financial Year. The Threshold is the highest bill of residential customers in the eighth decile of all residential customers (ranked on the basis of the amount billed by the Licensee to all residential customers for the services for which General Prices are charged, the highest bill being at the top of the tenth decile) in the Relevant Financial Year.

24A.12 Notwithstanding paragraph 24A.11, if the Licensee has notified the Director in writing both of its intention to increase during a Period one or more General Prices and of its intention within three months of the first such increase to reduce one or more General Prices then, unless:

(a)   the Director dissents within 28 days of such notification on the ground that undue advantage is being taken of this paragraph; or

(b)   the reduction as so notified is not introduced,
for the purposes of paragraph 24A.11, when determining the amount of a Percentage Change which has taken place at the end of the said Period and each subsequent Period, it shall be assumed that any such reduction had taken place during the first mentioned Period.

24A.13 Where the Licensee makes a material change (other than to the amount of a General Price) to any service for which a General Price is charged or to the date on which its financial year ends or there is a material change in the basis of the Retail Prices Index, this Condition shall have effect subject to such reasonable adjustment to take account of the change as the Director may, after consultation with the Licensee determine to be appropriate in the circumstances; and for the purposes of this paragraph a material change to any service includes the introduction of a new service wholly or substantially in substitution for that existing service.

24A.14 If the Licensee imposes a specific charge or an increased charge in relation to any goods or service which up to the time when the charge or increased charge is first imposed had been provided without charge or at a lower charge and the Director determines, after consultation with the Licensee, that some or all the costs properly attributable to that service had previously been attributed to services to which General Prices apply and that it would be proper in the circumstances for the newly introduced or increased charge to be controlled, that charge shall, unless the Director determines otherwise, be a General Price and this Condition shall have effect subject to the following provisions:

(a)   the Licensee shall produce a forecast of the revenue expected to accrue as a result of the charge or increased charge for the goods or service over a period of twelve months from the date of introduction or increase of the charge;

(b)   the forecast shall be expressed as a percentage of the total amount of revenue reasonably believed by the Licensee to have accrued in respect of General Prices during the Relevant Financial Year which relates to the Relevant Year during which the charge is introduced or increased;

(c)   the Controlling Percentage for that Relevant Year shall be reduced by that percentage;

(d)   an adjustment shall be made to the Controlling Percentage for that Relevant Year in respect of which it is first possible, from the Relevant Financial Year accounts, to take into account a comparison between the first 12 months' actual accrued revenue from the charge and the forecast referred to in sub-paragraph (a), whereby the Controlling Percentage for that Relevant Year shall be increased or reduced (as the case may be) by the difference between the forecast amount referred to in sub-paragraph (a) and the amount of actual accrued revenue (the *difference to be expressed as a percentage of the total amount of revenue accrued in respect of General Prices during the Relevant Financial Year which relates to that Relevant Year);*

(e)   *further adjustments shall be made to the Controlling Percentage referred to in sub-paragraph (d) and adjusted as specified therein:*

(i)   *where there is any difference between the forecast referred to in sub-paragraph (a) and the actual accrued revenue referred to in sub-paragraph (d), in order to compensate for the extent to which, by virtue of that difference, General Prices in previous Relevant Years have been too high or too low (as the case may be); and*

(ii)   *where there has been any variation in the charge for the service between the Relevant Year referred to in sub-paragraph (b) and the Relevant Year referred to in sub-paragraph (d) which the Director, after consultation with the Licensee, determines should be taken into account for the purposes of calculating the Controlling Percentage; and*

(f)   *the adjustments referred to in sub-paragraphs (d) and (e) shall be made in the manner which the Director determines to be appropriate in the circumstances, after consultation with the Licensee.*

24A.15   *If the charge or increased charge for any goods or service covered by paragraph 24A.14 is altered following its introduction but before the adjustment referred to in paragraph 24A.14 (d) can be made then, in respect of that charge, in calculating the amount of a Percentage Change in General Prices in paragraph 24A.11, the forecast set out in paragraph 24A.14 (a) shall be substituted for the amount referred to in paragraph 24A.16(a).*

24A.16   *The Licensee shall no later than the time at which it notifies or should have notified the Director under Condition 16 of any amendment of any charge which is a General Price inform the Director in writing of:*

(a)   *the amount of revenue which the Licensee reasonably believes to have accrued in the Relevant Financial Year for each service in respect of which a General Price is charged; and*

(b)   *the amount of each General Price at the beginning of the Relevant Year.*

24A.17   *Without prejudice to its obligations under Condition 16 in relation to General Prices, the Licensee shall as soon as practicable after the end of each Period in which there has been a change in a General Price inform the Director in writing of:*

(a)   *the changes made or new charges imposed in relation to any General Price during the Period specifying its nature and amount and the service for which the Price is charged; and*

(b)   *the amount of the Percentage Change in General Prices which has taken place during the Period and whether by way of increase or reduction.*

24A.18   *In this Condition:*

'Discounted General Prices' *means prices which are charged as part of a Package (not including Reference Prices) and which, if they were not so charged, would be General Prices;*

'General Prices' *means (being the Licensee's Standard Prices or Reference Prices nominated under paragraph 24A.6):*

(a)   *charges for the use and Ordinary Maintenance of a residential Exchange Line;*

(b)   *charges for the connection or taking over of a residential Exchange Line;*

(c) *charges for the conveyance by means of such Exchange Lines of voice telephony Messages from a place within the Licensed Area to any other place (whether or not within the Licensed Area); and*

(d) *charges for the facility of transferring, with assistance from a human operator, charges for the conveyance of the voice telephony Messages referred to in sub-paragraph (c),*

other than:

(i) *charges payable by Operators;*

(ii) *charges for Private Circuits or International Private Circuits (as defined in Condition 24B);*

(iii) *charges for special, emergency or priority Fault Repair Services, as defined in Condition 10, whether required to be provided under that Condition or not;*

(iv) *charges for the conveyance of voice telephony Messages in relation to any services provided by means of the Licensee's Applicable Systems which form part of its Supplemental Services Business;*

(v) *charges for the conveyance of voice telephony Messages which are to be conveyed to customers of an Operator which is not a Fixed Link Operator;*

(vi) *charges for Specially Tariffed Voice Services;*

(vii) *charges for directory information services;*

(viii) *charges, whether paid in cash or by credit card or debit card or token or otherwise, in respect of calls from Public Call Boxes, and calls from Private Call Boxes where the charge to the renter is based on charges for calls from Public Call Boxes published by the Licensee in accordance with Condition 16, and transferred charges in respect of calls from Call Boxes; and*

(ix) *charges for any service of a kind provided under Condition 12, and each discrete charge of any such description shall be treated as a separate General Price;*

'Fixed Link Operator' means a public telecommunications operator which runs a public telecommunication system and whose Licence does not authorise the provision of a Land Mobile Radio Service (as defined in Condition 18);

'Operator' has the meaning given to it in Condition 13;

'Ordinary Maintenance' means maintenance which is part of the service provided by the Licensee in consideration of the charge for an Exchange Line and includes normal fault repair, as defined in the Licensee's standard terms and conditions;

'Package' has the meaning given to it in Condition 24C.8;

'Percentage Change' has the meaning given to it in paragraph 24A.6;

'Period' means a calendar month or such longer period as the Director may determine;

'RPI' is the amount of the change in the Retail Prices Index in relation to any Relevant Year as specified in paragraph 24A.9;

'Reference Price' has the meaning given to it in paragraph 24A.6;

'Relevant Year' means any of the four periods of 12 months beginning on 1 August starting with 1 August 1997 and ending on 31 July 2001;

'Relevant Financial Year' means in relation to a Relevant Year the financial year of the Licensee ending last before the beginning of the Relevant Year, being a financial year in respect of which annual accounts have been prepared and audited in accordance with the requirements of the Companies Act 1985;

'Retail Prices Index' means the index of retail prices compiled by Her Majesty's Government in respect of all items;

'Specially Tariffed Voice Services' means calls to access premium rate services, number translation services (including local call services, freephone services, and national call services) and other services where the charge to a customer is determined at least in part by an agreement between the Licensee and the person called;

'Standard Price' means any price charged or offered by the Licensee otherwise than in relation to a Package; and

'Threshold' has the meaning given to it in paragraph 24A.11.

Any reference to 'service' which is not part of the expression 'goods or service' shall be taken to include a reference to goods for the purposes of paragraphs 24A.14 and 24A.15.

References to accrued revenue are references to the revenue attributable to General Prices but with the addition of the revenue attributable to Discounted General Prices where the revenue is grossed up so as to leave the discount out of account (or grossed down where the revenue is greater than that attributable to the relevant General Price), and cognate expressions shall be construed accordingly.

24.A.19   *This Condition shall not apply to such extent as the Director may determine on request by the Licensee.*

Notes

1.   Conditions 24, 24.1–14 were deleted and replaced by licence amendment dated 9 March 1993.

2.   Conditions 24A, 24A.1–9, 24A.10–14 were inserted by a licence amendment dated 23 April 1989.

3.   Conditions 24A, 24A.1–9, 24A.9A, 24A.10–14, 24A.14A–D were deleted and replaced by a licence amendment dated 9 March 1993.

4.   Conditions 24A.9A, 24A.14A and B were inserted by a licence amendment dated 24 November 1989.

5.   Conditions 24A.14C and D were inserted by a licence amendment dated 24 September 1991.

6.   Conditions 24A.1A–D, 24A.2A were inserted by a licence amendment dated 15 September 1994.

7.   Conditions 24A.1E, 24A.14(d) was inserted by a licence amendment dated 13 February 1996.

8.   Condition 24A.14 (header), 24A.14(a)–(c), 24A.15 (definition of 'Discounted General Prices') amended by a licence amendment dated 13 February 1996.

Condition 24B   Control of Private Circuit Prices

[24B.1   The Licensee shall take all reasonable steps to ensure that, during any Relevant Year, the amount of Private Circuit Prices remains such that:

(a)   if the Controlling Percentage for that Year (determined in accordance with paragraphs 24B.3 to 24B.5 and, if appropriate, adjusted in accordance with paragraphs 24B.10 and 24B.11) is zero or positive, and Percentage Change which has taken place in the aggregate of all the Private Circuit Prices to which paragraph 24B.3 (a), (b) or (c) respectively apply (determined and calculated, on a weighted basis, in accordance with paragraphs 24B.6 and 24B.7) at the end of each Period does not constitute an increase by more than the Controlling Percentage applicable to the Private Circuit Price or Prices in question; or

(*b*) if that Percentage is negative, there is no Percentage Change in Private Circuit Prices by way of increase and before the end of that Year there is such a Change by way of reduction of not less than that percentage.

24B.2 Where, notwithstanding the obligation imposed on the Licensee by paragraph 24B.1 there has taken place a change in Private Circuit Prices of a kind not permitted under paragraph 24B.1 (a) or (b), the Licensee shall make adjustments in Private Circuit Prices sufficient to satisfy the Director that the matter has been remedied.

24B.3 Subject to paragraphs 24B.4, 24B.5, 24B.10 and 24B.11 the Controlling Percentage in relation to any Relevant Year is as follows:

(*a*) as regards the aggregate of Private Circuit Prices (except Prices in respect of International Private Circuits) where the circuit involved is presented on an analogue basis, the amount of the change in the Retail Prices Index in the period of 12 months ending on 30 June, immediately before the beginning of that Year, expressed as a percentage (rounded to two decimal places) of that Index as at the beginning of that period and, as regards any individual such Private Circuit Price, the amount of such change, increased by 2;

(*b*) as regards the aggregate of Private Circuit Prices (except Prices in respect of International Private Circuits) where the circuit involved is presented on a digital basis, the amount of the change in the Retail Prices Index in the period of 12 months ending on 30 June immediately before the beginning of that Year expressed as a percentage (rounded to two decimal places) of that Index as at the beginning of that period and, as regards any individual such Private Circuit Price, the amount of such change, increased by 1;

(*c*) as regards the aggregate of Private Circuit Prices in respect of International Private Circuits only, the amount of the change in the Retail Prices Index in the period of 12 months ending on 30 June immediately before the beginning of that Year, expressed as a percentage (rounded to two decimal places) of that Index as at the beginning of that period and, as regards any individual such Private Circuit Price, where the circuit involved is presented on an analogue basis, the amount of such change, increased by 2 and, where the circuit involved is presented on a digital basis, the amount of such change, increased by 1.

24B.4 If the difference between Private Circuit Prices charged at the beginning and at the end of any Relevant Year is such that the relevant Percentage Change in Private Circuit Prices is less (in the case of a permitted increase), or greater (in the case of a required reduction), then the change permitted, or required, in accordance with paragraph 24B.1, then the Controlling Percentage for the following Relevant Year shall be determined in accordance with paragraph 24B.3 but increased subject to paragraph 24B.5 by the amount of such deficiency or excess (as the case may be).

24B.5 The Controlling Percentage for the Fourth Relevant Year shall only be increased by virtue of paragraph 24B.4 to the extent that such an increase would have been permitted if that paragraph had not applied to increase the Controlling Percentage for the second such Year.

24B.6 The amount of a Percentage Change in the relevant set of Private Circuit Prices which has taken place at any time during a Relevant Year is determined by taking the amount of the change in each relevant Private Circuit Price which has taken place between the beginning of the Relevant Year and that time, multiplying that amount by the amount of the revenue reasonably believed by the Licensee to have accrued during the Relevant Financial Year in respect of the service for which that Price is charged, dividing in each case the amounts so produced by the price charged at the beginning of the Relevant Year for the service to which each such amount relates, and taking the aggregate of the results, expressed as a percentage of all the revenue reasonably believed to have accrued for such services during the Relevant Financial Year.

24B.7 Notwithstanding paragraph 24B.6, if the Licensee has notified the Director in writing both of its intention to increase during a Period one or more Private Circuit Prices and of its intention within three months of the first such increase to reduce one or more Private Circuit Prices then, unless:

(a) the Director dissents within 28 days of such notification on the ground that undue advantage is being taken of this paragraph; or

(b) the reduction as so notified is not introduced;

for the purposes of paragraph 24B.6 when determining the amount of a Percentage Change which has taken place at the end of the said Period and each subsequent Period it shall be assumed that any such reduction had taken place during the first mentioned Period.

24B.8 Where the Licensee makes a material change (other than as to the amount of a Private Circuit Price) in any service for which Private Circuit Price is charged or in the date on which its financial year ends or there is a material change in the basis of the Retail Prices Index, this Condition shall have effect subject to such reasonable adjustment to take account of the change as the Director may, after consultation with the Licensee, determine to be appropriate in the circumstances; and for the purposes of this paragraph a material change in any service includes the introduction of a new service wholly or substantially in substitution for that existing service.

24B.9 Subject to this paragraph this Condition shall not have effect in relation to a new service, the charges for which would otherwise be Private Circuit Prices, other than a new service to which paragraph 24B.8 applies. In relation to a new service other than one to which paragraph 24B.8 applies the Director may, after consultation with the Licensee, in any Relevant Year during which it is first possible, from the Relevant Financial Year accounts, to ascertain 12 months actual revenue in respect of that service accrued in relation to that Relevant Financial Year, determine that the charges for that service shall in the subsequent Year be Private Circuit Prices and this Condition shall, from that subsequent Relevant Year, apply accordingly.

24B.10 If the Licensee imposes a specific charge or an increased charge in relation to any goods or service which up to the time when the charge or increased charge is first imposed had been provided without charge or at a lower charge and the Director determines after consultation with the Licensee that previously Private Circuit Prices were wholly or substantially financing those goods or services, that charge shall, unless the Director determines otherwise, be a Private Circuit Price and this Condition shall have effect subject to the following provisions:

(a) the Licensee shall produce a forecast of the revenue expected to accrue as a result of the charge or increased charge for the goods or service over a period of twelve months from the date of introduction or increase of the charge;

(*b*) the forecast shall be expressed as a percentage of the total amount of revenue reasonably believed by the Licensee to have accrued in respect of Private Circuit Prices during the Relevant Financial Year which relates to the Relevant Year during which the charge is introduced or increased;

(*c*) the Controlling Percentage for that Relevant Year shall be reduced by that percentage;

(*d*) an adjustment shall be made to the Controlling Percentage for that Relevant Year in respect of which it is first possible, from the Relevant Financial Year accounts, to take into account a comparison between the first 12 months actual accrued revenue from the charge and the forecast referred to in sub-paragraph (a) above, whereby the Controlling Percentage for that Relevant Year shall be increased or reduced (as the case be) by the difference between the forecast amount referred to in sub-paragraph (a) and the amount of actual accrued revenue (the difference to be expressed as a percentage of the total amount of revenue accrued in respect of Private Circuit Prices during the Relevant Financial Year which relates to that Relevant Year);

(*e*) further adjustments shall be made to the Controlling Percentage referred to in sub-paragraph (d) and adjusted as specified therein:

(i) where there is any difference between the forecast referred to in sub-paragraph (a) and the actual accrued revenue referred to in sub-paragraph (d), in order to compensate for the extent to which, by virtue of that difference, Private Circuit Prices in previous Relevant Years have been too high or too low (as the case may be); and

(ii) where there has been any variation in the charge for the service between the Relevant Year referred to in sub-paragraph (b) and the Relevant Year referred to in sub-paragraph (d) which the Director, after consultation with the Licensee, determines should be taken into account for the purposes of calculating the Controlling Percentage;

(*f*) The adjustments referred to in sub-paragraphs (d) and (e) shall be made in the precise manner which the Director determines to be appropriate in the circumstances, after consultation with the Licensee.

24B.11 If the charge or increased charge for any goods or service covered by paragraph 24B.10 is altered following its introduction but before the adjustment referred to in paragraph 24B.10(d) can be made then, in respect of that charge, in calculating the amount of a Percentage Change in Private Circuit Prices in paragraph 24B.6, the forecast set out in paragraph 24B.10 (a) shall be substituted for the amount referred to in paragraph 24B.12 (a).

24B.12 The Licensee shall no later than the time at which it notifies or should have notified under Condition 16 the Director of any amendment of any charge which is a Private Circuit Price inform the Director in writing of:

(*a*) the amount of revenue which the Licensee reasonably believes to have accrued in the Relevant Financial Year for each service in respect of which a Private Circuit Price is charged; and

(*b*) the amount of each Private Circuit Price at the beginning of the Relevant Year.

24B.13 Without prejudice to its obligations under Condition 16 in relation to Private Circuit Prices, the Licensee shall as soon as practicable after the end of each Period in which there has been a change in a Private Circuit Price inform the Director in writing of:

(a) the changes made or new charges imposed in relation to any Private Circuit Price during the Period specifying its nature and amount and the service for which the Price is charged; and

(b) the amount of the Percentage Change in the relevant set of Private Circuit Prices which has taken place during the Period and whether by way of increase or reduction.

24B.14   In this Condition:

'International Private Circuit' means a communication facility:

(i)   which is provided by means of both a telecommunication system comprised in the Applicable Systems and a telecommunication system in a country or territory other than the United Kingdom;

(ii)   for the conveyance of Messages between points, all of which are points of connection between telecommunication systems referred to in (i) and other telecommunication systems;

(iii)   which is made available to a particular person or particular persons;

(iv)   which is such that all of the Messages transmitted at any of the points mentioned in (ii) above are received at every other such point; and

(v)   which is such that the points mentioned in (ii) above are fixed by the way in which the facility is installed and cannot be selected by persons or apparatus sending Messages by means of that facility;

'International Videoconferencing' means a communication facility consisting in the simultaneous point to point conveyance by means including the Applicable Systems between a place or places in the Licensed Area and a place or places outside the United Kingdom of voice telephony Messages and associated visual images (an 'International Videoconferencing Service') whether or not on any particular occasion the International Videoconferencing Service includes a service between two places in the Licensed Area or between a place in the Licensed Area and a place in the United Kingdom;

'Land Mobile Radio Service' has the same meaning as in Condition 18;

'Ordinary Maintenance' means maintenance which is part of the service provided by the Licensee in consideration of the periodic Private Circuit rental and International Private Circuit rental for any particular category of Private Circuit or International Private Circuit and includes normal fault repair as defined in the Licensee's standard terms and conditions;

'Offshore Private Circuit' means a communication system which is:

(i)   provided by means of both a telecommunication system comprised in the Applicable Systems and a telecommunication system which is on any installation which is maintained in waters to which the Mineral Workings (Offshore Installations) Act 1971 applies;

(ii)   for the conveyance of Messages between points, all of which are points of connection between a public telecommunication system and a telecommunication system which is not a public telecommunication system;

(iii)   which is made available to a particular person or particular persons;

(iv)   which is such that all Messages transmitted at any of the points mentioned in (ii) above are received at every other such point; and

(v)   which is such that the points mentioned in (ii) above are fixed by the way in which the facility is installed and cannot otherwise be selected by persons or apparatus sending Messages by means of that facility;

'Period' means a calendar month or such longer period as the Director may determine

'Private Circuit Prices' means all periodic and other charges imposed by the Licensee by way of any Standard Price for the provision use and Ordinary Maintenance of:

(a)   a terrestrial Private Circuit, provided by the Licensee which is wholly situated within the Licensed Area other than:

(i)   a Private Circuit used to provide analogue presented broadcast sound and vision services and a Private Circuit used to provide closed circuit television services;

(ii)   a Fixed Link provided to any person authorised by a Licence to provide Land Mobile Radio Services where such Link is provided solely for the purpose of facilitating the provision by that person of such Services;

(b)   that part of an International Private Circuit provided by the Licensee by means of the Applicable Systems, other than:

(i)   an International Private Circuit used to provide broadcast quality sound and vision services;

(ii)   an Offshore Private Circuit;

(iii)   a VSAT Service;

(iv)   a circuit used in the provision of International Videoconferencing services by the Licensee;

(c)   Virtual Private Networks;

provided that:

(i)   each discrete charge of any such description shall be treated as a separate Private Circuit Price (any reference in this Condition to an individual Private Circuit Price being a reference to the total charge imposed by the Licensee in respect of the periodic rental or the connection charge, as the case may be, for the circuit in question and not to any element comprised in that total charge); and

(ii)   such charges so imposed in respect of Virtual Private Networks shall not be treated as Private Circuit Prices unless the Director has determined after consultation with the Licensee (and not revoked such determination but without prejudice to his power to make a further determination) that those charges (or any of them) shall be so treated for any period commencing after 31 July 1994;

'Relevant Year' means any of the four periods of 12 months beginning on 1 August starting with 1 August 1993 and ending on 31 July 1997;

'the Relevant Financial Year' means in relation to a Relevant Year the financial year of the Licensee ending last before the beginning of the Relevant Year, being a financial year in respect of which annual accounts have been prepared and audited in accordance with the requirements of the Companies Act 1985;

'Retail Prices Index' means the index of retail prices compiled by Her Majesty's Government in respect of all items;

'Standard Price' means any price charged or offered by the Licensee:

(*a*)   before the application to it of any discount; and

(*b*)   in relation to a contract for a fixed term, before the application to it of any discount or premium;

'VSAT Service' means a telecommunication service consisting in the conveyance by means including the Applicable Systems, earth orbiting apparatus and a terrestrial telecommunication system outside the United Kingdom between a point in the Licensed Area and more than one point outside the United Kingdom of Messages whether or not on any particular occasion the conveyance includes a transmission between points in the Licensed Area or between points in the Licensed Area and points in the United Kingdom;

'Virtual Private Network' means an assembly of transmission, switching and network control apparatus and functions, embedded within a public telecommunication system, as used to provide services at least equivalent to those capable of being provided by a network of Private Circuits;

Any reference to 'service' which is not part of the expression 'goods or service' shall be taken to include a reference to goods for the purposes of paragraphs 24B.10 and 24B.11.

References to accrued revenue are references to the amount of revenue which would be produced if all prices were Standard Prices.

24B.15   This Condition shall not apply to such extent as the Director may determine upon request by the Licensee.

25B.16   The Director may, after consulting the Licensee, determine that any periodic or other charge imposed by the Licensee by way of any Standard Price for the provision use and Ordinary Maintenance of a Virtual Private Network shall, instead of falling within the definition of Private Circuit Prices in paragraph 24B.14, fall within the definition of General Prices in Condition 24A.15. The Director may revoke any such determination and, where he does so, the charge which was the subject of it shall once more fall within the definition of Private Circuit Prices.

New Condition 24B in italics will be substituted for the words in square brackets from 1 August 1997 by a licence amendment dated 13 February 1996.

Condition 24B   'Control of Private Circuit Prices

24B.1   The provisions of Condition 24A (except Conditions 24A.2 to 24A.6, 24A.8 and 24A.11) shall apply separately to:

(a)   *the aggregate of Private Circuit Prices for analogue Private Circuits; and*

(b)   *the aggregate of Private Circuit Prices for digital Private Circuits of a capacity less than or equal to 64 kbits,*

respectively as though the Prices in each such aggregate group of Prices are General Prices except that the Controlling Percentage applicable to each such group (described in Condition 24A.9) shall (subject only to Conditions 24A.10, 24A.14, and 24A.15) be RPI.

24B.2   The amount of a Percentage Change in Private Circuit Prices which has taken place at any time during a Relevant Year is determined by taking the amount of the change in each Private Circuit Price which has taken place between the beginning of the Relevant Year and that time, multiplying that amount by the amount of the revenue reasonably believed by the Licensee to have accrued during the Relevant Financial Year in respect of the service for which that Price is charged, dividing in each case the amounts so produced by the Price charged at the beginning of the Relevant Year for the service to which each such amount relates, and taking the aggregate of the results, expressed as a percentage of all the revenue reasonably believed to have accrued for such services during the Relevant Financial Year.

24B.3   The Licensee shall take all reasonable steps to secure that no discrete International Private Circuit Price increases during any Relevant Year by more than RPI.

24B.4   In this Condition:

'International Private Circuit' means a communication facility:

(a)   which is provided by means of both a telecommunication system comprised in the Applicable Systems and a telecommunication system in a country or territory other than the United Kingdom;

(b)   made available to a person for the conveyance of Messages between points, all of which are points of connection between telecommunication systems referred to in sub-paragraph (a) and other telecommunication systems;

(c)   which is such that all of the Messages transmitted at any of the points mentioned in sub-paragraph (b) are received at every other such point; and

(d)   which is such that the points mentioned in sub-paragraph (b) are fixed by the way in which the facility is installed and cannot be selected by persons or apparatus sending Messages by means of that facility;

'International Private Circuit Prices' means all charges imposed by way of a Standard Price for the connection, use and Ordinary Maintenance of the parts of International Private Circuits provided by means of the Applicable Systems, other than:

(a)   charges for a Circuit used in the provision of broadcast quality sound and vision services, VSAT Services or International Videoconferencing Services;

(b)   charges for an Offshore Private Circuit; and

(c)   charges payable by Operators under Condition 13,

and each discrete charge of any such description shall be treated as a separate International Private Circuit Price;

'International Videoconferencing' means a communication facility consisting in the simultaneous point to point conveyance by means including the Applicable Systems between a place or places in the Licensed Area and a place or places outside the United Kingdom of voice telephony Messages and associated visual images (an 'International Videoconferencing Service') whether or not on any particular occasion the International Videoconferencing Service includes a service between two places in the Licensed Area or between a place in the Licensed Area and a place in the United Kingdom;

'Land Mobile Radio Service' has the meaning given to it in Condition 18;

Offshore Private Circuit' means a communication system which is:

(a)   provided by means of both a telecommunication system comprised in the Applicable Systems and a telecommunication system which is on any installation which is maintained in waters to which the Mineral Workings (Offshore Installations) Act 1971 applies;

(b)   made available to a person for the conveyance of Messages between points, all of which are points of connection between a public telecommunication system and a telecommunication system which is not a public telecommunication system;

(c) which is such that all Messages transmitted at any of the points mentioned in sub-paragraph (b) above are received at every other such point; and

(d) which is such that the points mentioned in sub-paragraph (b) above are fixed by the way in which the facility is installed and cannot otherwise be selected by persons or apparatus sending Messages by means of that facility;

'Ordinary Maintenance' means maintenance which is part of the service provided by the Licensee in consideration of the periodic Private Circuit charge for any particular category of Private Circuit and includes normal fault repair, as defined in the Licensee's standard terms and conditions;

'Private Circuit Prices' means all charges imposed by way of a Standard Price for the connection, use and Ordinary Maintenance of terrestrial Private Circuits which are wholly situated within the Licensed Area other than:

(a) charges for a Private Circuit used to provide analogue presented broadcast sound and vision services;

(b) charges for a Private Circuit used to provide closed circuit television services;

(c) charges for a fixed link provided to any person authorised by a Licence to provide Land Mobile Radio Services where such link is provided solely for the purpose of facilitating the provision by that person of such Services; and

(d) charges payable by Operators under Condition 13,

and each discrete charge of any such description shall be treated as a separate Private Circuit Price;

'Standard Price' means any price charged or offered by the Licensee:

(a) before the application to it of any discount; and

(b) in relation to a contract for a fixed term, before the application to it of any discount or premium; and

'VSAT Service' means a telecommunication service consisting in the conveyance by means including the Applicable Systems, earth orbiting apparatus and a terrestrial telecommunication system outside the United Kingdom between a point in the Licensed Area and more than one point outside the United Kingdom of Messages whether or not on any particular occasion the conveyance includes a transmission between points in the Licensed Area or between points in the Licensed Area and points in the United Kingdom.

References to accrued revenue in Condition 24A are, for the purposes of this Condition, references to the amount of revenue which would be produced before the application of any discounts to the relevant Private Circuit Prices.

24B.5 This Condition shall not apply to such extent as the Director may determine upon request by the Licensee.'

Note

Conditions 24B.1–16 were inserted by a licence amendment dated 14 December 1993.

Condition 24C Treatment of Condition 17A 'Packages' For Price Control Purposes

[24C.1 This Condition shall have effect for the purpose of securing in accordance with the following paragraphs that:

(a) no new benefits to the Licensee's customers arising from variations in its charges or manner of charging for Packages are brought into account for the purpose of ascertaining whether the obligation imposed on the Licensee by Condition 24A.1 has been satisfied; and

(b) the Licensee, where benefits (including discounts) in existence on 31 July 1993 are withdrawn, makes compensating reductions in its other prices which are subject to the controls imposed by Condition 24A.

24C.2   The Licensee shall estimate as at 31 July in each Relevant Year the numbers of its customers who take:

(a)   Packages; or

(b)   Standard Price combinations of the type described in Condition 24A.1E (with the addition of combinations which include a non-periodic fee),

which it has offered in that Year. On the basis of that estimate the Licensee shall calculate, on a weighted average basis, the amounts of accrued revenue which it would have forgone (or gained) in respect of each such Package or Standard Price combination in the associated Relevant Financial Year (except any revenue attributable to Reference Prices as defined in Condition 24A.1E) on the assumption that those Packages or Standard Price combinations had been offered to its customers in that Financial Year. The aggregate of those amounts plus any increase in revenue forgone pursuant to Condition 24D.2A shall be the estimated Discount Yield for the Relevant Year.

24C.3   The Licensee shall send the Director a forecast of the Score attributable to Packages as at 31 July 1993 and of the Percentage Discount Yield as at 31 July immediately preceding each Relevant Year thereafter. The Score and the Percentage Discount Yield shall be calculated in the precise manner and provided at times determined by the Director after consultation with the Licensee.

24C.4   If in respect of any Relevant Year it transpires that the Percentage Discount Yield is less than the Score, the difference between the Score and the Percentage Discount Yield shall, at the option of the Licensee be either deducted from the Controlling Percentage or added to the Score, or partly the one and partly the other, for the next following Relevant Year, but for that Year only.

24C.5   If in respect of any Relevant Year the Licensee elects to reduce the Percentage Discount Yield below the Score, the difference between the Score and the Percentage Discount Yield shall be deducted from the Controlling Percentage for that Year (and that Year only) and deducted from the Score for that Year and each succeeding Relevant Year.

24C.6   The Licensee shall furnish to the Director, at such times and in such manner as the Director may request, sufficient accounts, information, estimates, forecasts and returns to enable the Director properly to assess the operation of this Condition 24C and in particular to establish whether:

(a)   any reductions in the Controlling Percentage or additions to the Score which are required by paragraph 24C.4 above have been properly made; and

(b)   any reductions in the Controlling Percentage and the Score which are required by paragraph 24C.5 above have been properly made.

24C.7   When it proposes to amend or substitute a Package or a Standard Price combination of the type described in paragraph 24C.2(b) or to offer a new Package or Standard Price combination of that type or there is (or will be) a material increase in the revenue forgone under the Residential Low User Scheme which may be brought into account under Condition 24D.2A for the purpose of calculating the Discount Yield, the Licensee shall:

(a)   no later than the time at which it notifies or should have notified the Director under Condition 16 of any such amendment, substitution or offer; or

(b)   when it becomes aware that there is or will be such a material increase,

as the case may be, inform the Director in writing of any necessary adjustment to the forecast Percentage Discount Yield created by such amendment, substitution or offer or such increase.

24C.8   In this Condition:

'Controlled Revenue' is the revenue accruing (grossed up so as to leave all discounts out of account) to the Licensee in respect of those Services (other than terrestrial Private Circuits and International Private Circuits) the prices of which are subject to the price control provisions of the Condition numbered 24A of this Licence immediately before the coming into effect of this Condition;

'Controlling Percentage' has the same meaning as in Condition 24A.3 (but for any Relevant Year for which a reduction is required to be made pursuant to paragraph 24C.4 or 24C.5 adjusted accordingly);

'Discount Yield' has the meaning given to it in paragraph 24C.2;

'Packages' means charges or combinations of charges to which Condition 17A applies, but does not include any scheme made available by the Licensee for the purpose of complying with the obligations imposed on it by Condition 24D (Residential Low User Scheme);

'Percentage Discount Yield' is the Discount Yield for a Relevant Year expressed as a percentage of the Controlled Revenue in the Relevant Financial Year;

'Relevant Financial Year' has the same meaning as in Condition 24A.15;

'Relevant Year' has the same meaning as in Condition 24A.15, but includes the period 1 August 1992 to 31 July 1993;

'Score' is the Percentage Discount Yield for the Relevant Year ended 31 July 1993, subject to any adjustments made under paragraphs 24C.3, 24C.4 and 24C.5.]

New Condition 24C in italics will be substituted for the words in square brackets from 1 August 1997 by a licence amendment dated 13 February 1996.

Condition 24C   Treatment of Certain Packages and Standard Prices for Price Control Purposes

24C.1   This Condition shall have effect for the purpose of securing in accordance with the following paragraphs that:

(a)   no new benefits to the Licensee's customers arising from variations in its charges or manner of charging for Packages are brought into account for the purpose of ascertaining whether the obligation imposed on the Licensee by Condition 24A.1 has been satisfied; and

(b) the Licensee, where benefits (including discounts) in existence on 31 July 1993 are withdrawn, makes compensating reductions in its other prices which are subject to the controls imposed by Condition 24A.

24C.2 The Licensee shall estimate as at 31 July in each Relevant Year the numbers of its residential customers who take Packages which it has offered in that Year. On the basis of that estimate the Licensee shall calculate, on a weighted average basis, the amounts of accrued revenue which it would have forgone (or gained) in respect of each such Package in the associated Relevant Financial Year (except any revenue attributable to Reference Prices as defined in Condition 24A.6) on the assumption that those Packages had been offered to its residential customers in that Financial Year. The aggregate of those amounts plus any increase in revenue forgone pursuant to Condition 24D.2A shall be the Discount Yield for the Relevant Year.

24C.3 The Licensee shall send to the Director a forecast of the Percentage Discount Yield as at 31 July immediately preceding each Relevant Year. The Score and the Percentage Discount Yield shall be calculated in the precise manner and provided at times determined by the Director after consultation with the Licensee.

24C.4 If in respect of the year ending on 31 July 1997 and any Relevant Year, it transpires (or, in the case of the year ending on 31 July 1997, has transpired) that the Percentage Discount Yield is less than the Score (in the case of the year ending on 31 July 1997, as calculated under Condition 24C having effect on that date), the difference between the Score and the Percentage Discount Yield shall, at the option of the Licensee (except in the case of the fourth Relevant Year), be either deducted from the Controlling Percentage or added to the Score, or partly the one and partly the other, for the next following Relevant Year, but for that Year only. In the case of the fourth Relevant Year, the difference shall be deducted from the Controlling Percentage for that Year.

24C.5 If in respect of the year ending on 31 July 1997 and any Relevant Year, the Licensee elects (or, in the case of the year ending on 31 July 1997, has elected) to reduce the Percentage Discount Yield below the Score (in the case of the year ending on 31 July 1997, as calculated under Condition 24C having effect on that date), the difference between the Score and the Percentage Discount Yield shall (except in the case of the fourth Relevant Year), if it has not already been deducted, be deducted from the Controlling Percentage for that year (and that year only) and deducted from the Score for that year and each succeeding Relevant Year. In the case of the fourth Relevant Year, the difference shall be deducted from the Controlling Percentage for that Year.

24C.6 The Licensee shall furnish to the Director, at such times and in such manner as the Director may request, sufficient accounts, information, estimates, forecasts and returns to enable the Director properly to assess the operation of this Condition and in particular to establish whether:

(a) any reductions in the Controlling Percentage or additions to the Score which are required by paragraph 24C.4 have veen properly made; and

(b) any reductions in the Controlling Percentage and the Score which are required by paragraph 24C.5 have been properly made.

24C.7 When it proposes to amend or substitute a Package or to offer a new Package or there is (or will be) a material increase in the revenue forgone under the Residential Low User Scheme which may be brought into account under Condition 24D.2A for the purpose of calculating the Discount Yield, the Licensee shall:

(a) no later than the time at which it notifies or should have notified the Director under Condition 16 of any such amendment, substitution or offer; or

(b)   *when it becomes aware that there is or will be such a material increase, as the case may be, inform the Director in writing of any necessary adjustment to the forecast Percentage Discount Yield created by such amendment, substitution or offer or such increase.*

24C.8   *In this Condition:*

'*Controlled Revenue' means accrued revenue as described in Condition 24A.18;*

'*Controlling Percentage' has the meaning given to it in Condition 24A.9;*

'*Discount Yield' has the meaning given to it in paragraph 24C.2;*

'*Packages' means charges or combinations of charges for any of the things included within the definition of General Prices (in Condition 24A.18) which vary or may vary:*

(a)   *according to whether the Licensee does any other thing so mentioned for the customer in question; or*

(b)   *according to the extent to which it does any of those things for that customer,*

and combinations of the type described in Condition 24A.6 (with the addition of combinations which include a non-periodic fee), but does not include any scheme made available by the Licensee for the purpose of complying with the obligations imposed on it by condition 24D (Residential Low User Scheme);

'*Percentage Discount Yield' means the Discount Yield for a Relevant Year expressed as a percentage of the Controlled Revenue in the Relevant Financial Year;*

'*Relevant Financial Year' has the meaning given to it in Condition 24A.18;*

'*Relevant Year' has the meaning given to it in Condition 24A.18; and*

'*Score' means the Percentage Discount Yield for the year ending on 31 July 1996 (calculated under Condition 24C having effect on that date and subject to any adjustments under paragraphs 24C.3, 24C.4 and 24C.5, but taking into account only residential customers and revenue from such customers).*

Notes

1.   Conditions 24C.1-8 were inserted by a licence amendment dated 9 March 1993.

2.   Conditions 24C.2, 24C.7 and 24C.8 (definition of 'Packages' amended only) were deleted and replaced by a licence amendment dated 13 February 1996.

Condition 24D   Residential Low User Scheme

24D.1   As soon as reasonably practicable after 1 August 1993 and in any event no later than 1 January 1994 the Licensee shall introduce and within three months of that date make generally available and thereafter continue to make generally available during the whole of any period which falls within any Relevant Year a scheme ('the Scheme') the effect of which would be to reduce (as compared with the Licensee's standard charges published in accordance with Condition 16.1 (a)) the aggregate of charges for line rentals and for calls payable to the Licensee by those of its residential customers who make, as compared with the generality of such customers, relatively few telephone calls which immediately after passing across the Network Termination Points interfacing with them are conveyed by any of the Applicable Systems.

24D.2   The Licensee's administrative costs in deciding, and notifying the relevant customers of, entitlement to be charged on the basis of the Scheme shall not be brought into account for the purposes of Condition 24A.

24D.2A   No increase in the revenue forgone by the Licensee as a result of the operation of the Scheme (above the amount of the change in the Retail Prices Index as calculated under Condition 24A) shall be brought into account for the purposes of Condition 24A, but any such increase (as measured from 1 August 1995) may be brought into account for the purpose of calculating the Discount Yield under Condition 24C.

24D.3   The Scheme shall comply with guidelines to be agreed between the Director and the Licensee.

24D.4   Those guidelines:

(a)   shall specify the requirements to be met by the Scheme including the criteria to be applied by the Licensee in deciding which of its residential customers are entitled to be charged on the basis of the Scheme; and

(b)   may not be revoked or varied save with the prior written agreement of the Licensee.

24D.5   In this Condition:

'Network Termination Point' has the same meaning as in Annex A to this Licence;

'Relevant year' has the same meaning as in Condition 24A.15.

Notes

1.   Conditions 24D.1–5 were inserted by a licence amendment dated 9 March 1995.

2.   Condition 24D.2A was inserted by a licence amendment dated 13 February 1996 and the words 'Condition 24A.14' shall be replaced with the words 'Condition 24A.9' with effect from 1 August 1997 by a licence amendment dated 1 October 1996.

Condition 24E   Control of 'Hard-Wired' and Other Telephone Rentals

24E.1   The Licensee shall ensure that no periodic or other charge in respect of renting from the Licensee telephone apparatus to which paragraph 24E.2 applies increases during any Relevant Year (as defined in Condition 24A.15) by more than the amount of the change in the Retail Prices Index (as so defined) in the period of 12 months ending on 30 June immediately before the beginning of that Year.

24E.2   This paragraph applies to telephones, other than telephones described in paragraph 24E.3 below ('the excepted telephones'), which are not capable of being connected to the Licensee's Applicable Systems at a Network Termination Point by means of a fitted plug which complies with British Standard number 6312 : 1985 as published on 28 February 1985, for example, telephones which are only capable of being connected to those Systems by means of hard-wiring or round-pin plugs.

24E.3   The excepted telephones are:

(a)   ISDN telephones;

(b)   telephones which are connected to the Applicable Systems by means of a single line PBX; and

(c)   telephones which are connected by a means other than a plug of the kind described in paragraph 24E.2 above for the puposes of ensuring safety in a hazardous environment.

Notes

1.   Conditions 24E.1–3 were inserted by a licence amendment dated 9 March 1993.

2. In Condition 24E.1 for the words 'Condition 24A.15' shall be substituted the words 'Condition 24A' as from 1 August 1997 as a result of a licence amendment dated 1 October 1996.

Condition 24F   Further Provisions Relating to General Prices

24F.1   In this Condition:

(a)   a 'General Price (Type A)' means a proposed General Price which is less than the aggregate (the 'Aggregate Cost') of the Retail Cost, the Delivery Outpayment Cost (if applicable), the Conveyance Outpayment Cost (if applicable) and the Network Cost which are attributable in each case to the provision of the relevant Retail Service before the implementation of the proposed change in General Price;
other than a proposed General Price which is less than the Aggregate Cost:

(i)   as a result of the application of any law (including a regulatory control, which includes a voluntary commitment in the nature of a regulatory control) other than the provisions of paragraphs 24A.1 to 24A.13 or as a result of any regulatory or other action by Government, by the Director or by any other regulatory agent but is set at the highest level to which the Licensee is permitted to raise that General Price; or

(ii)   for any reason, but which would be greater than the General Price before the implementation of the proposed change in General Price; and

(b)   a 'General Price (Type B)' means a proposed General Price which is not a General Price (Type A).

24F.2   The Licensee shall, as soon as practicable after the coming into force of this Condition, publish in accordance with paragraphs 24F.7 and 24F.8 details of the matters which it and the Director have agreed, on or before the date on which this Condition comes into force, should be excluded from the definition of 'General Price' in paragraph 24F.21.

24F.3   Where the Licensee proposes a change to a General Price, whether through the introduction of a Special Offer or otherwise, it shall send to the Director, in the manner and at the time specified in paragraph 24F.4 or 24F.5, as the case may be, a written notice (a 'Price Change Notice') specifying:

(a)   the General Price before the implementation of the proposed change in that General Price;

(b)   the General Price after the implementation of the proposed change in that General Price;

(c)   the following elements attributable to the provision of the relevant Retail Service both before the implementation of the proposed change in that General Price and after the implementation of that proposed change identifying separately:

(i)   the Retail Cost;

(ii)   the Delivery Outpayment Cost (if applicable);

(iii) the Conveyance Outpayment Cost (if applicable);

(iv) the Network cost showing separately the Transfer Charge for each Network Component and each Network Part used for the provision of the relevant Retail Service;

(e)   in the case of a change in a proposed General Price through the introduction of a Special Offer, the period of time not exceeding three months for which the Licensee proposes to offer the new General Price; and

(f) any charge for a Standard Service which the Licensee is required to notify to an Operator in accordance with paragraph 24F.11 (b) or 24F.14 (b).

24F.4 In the case of a General Price (Type A) the Licensee shall send the Price Change Notice to the Director before the publication of any notice required under Condition 16 of a change in a General Price. The Licensee shall not publish a notice pursuant to Condition 16 relating to the proposed new General Price or make that new General Price available to any customer unless the Director has given his prior written consent, which shall not be unreasonably withheld.

24F.5 In the case of a General Price (Type B) the Licensee shall send the Price Change Notice to the Director as soon as reasonably practicable before it publishes any notice required under Condition 16 of the change in the General Price.

24F.6 As soon as the Licensee becomes aware that the Delivery Outpayment Cost attributable to the provision of a Retail Service, assessed in the manner notified by the Director to the Licensee from time to time as an average over a period of three months, has for any reason been at a level such that had the General Price for that Retail Service been a proposed General Price it would have been a General Price (Type A), the Licensee shall, as soon as practicable after it has become so aware, send to the Director a Price Change Notice. Following receipt of the Price Change Notice, the Director may direct the Licensee to increase that General Price to a level not above the level at which, had that General Price been a proposed General Price it would have been a General Price (Type B) and, notwithstanding Condition 24A, the Licensee shall increase that General Price accordingly.

24F.7 Subject to paragraph 24F.9, the Licensee shall send a copy of the Price Change Notice to any person who may (after the publication of the notice in accordance with Condition 16 of a change in a General Price) request one, on payment of a reasonable charge. The Licensee shall, subject to paragraph 24F.9, send a copy of the Price Change Notice so requested within seven working days after receiving payment of that charge.

24F.8 At the same time as the Licensee publishes a notice in accordance with Condition 16 of a change in General Price, it shall make available and continue to make available in a publicly accessible part of every Major Office of the Licensee in the place as is required by Condition 16.3 (b) a notice of the address and telephone number of the person to whom any request for a copy of the Price Change Notice may be made.

24F.9 The Licensee shall be entitled to exclude from any Price Change Notice which it is obliged to send to any person who may require one pursuant to paragraph 24F.7 any matter to the exclusion of which the Director shall have consented following representations to him on the matter by the Licensee on the basis that if the matter were made available in accordance with paragraph 24F.7 it would or might, in the opinion of the Director, seriously and prejudicially affect the interests of the Licensee.

24F.11 In the case of a change to a General Price, otherwise than through the introduction of a Special Offer, if the Network Cost attributable to the provision of the relevant Retail Service after the implementation of the proposed change in a General Price is different from the Network Cost attributable to the provision of the relevant Retail Service before the implementation of the proposed change in a General Price, at the same time as the

Licensee publishes any notice in accordance with Condition 16 of a change in a General Price:

(*a*) the charge payable by each relevant Operator for any relevant Standard Service shall be revised by the Licensee as necessary to take account of the difference; and

(*b*) the Licensee shall notify each relevant Operator of any revised charges which shall have effect from the date on which the proposed General Price takes effect.

24F.14   In the case of a change to a General Price through the introduction of a Special Offer, if the Network Cost attributable to the provision of the relevant Retail Service after the implementation of the proposed change in a General Price is different from the Network cost attributable to the provision of the relevant Retail Service before the implementation of the proposed change in a General Price, at the same time as the Licensee publishes any notice in accordance with Condition 16 of a change in a General Price:

(*a*) the charge payable by each relevant Operator for any relevant Standard Service shall be revised by the Licensee as necessary for the duration of the Special Offer to take account of the defference; and

(*b*) the Licensee shall notify each Operator of any revised charges which shall have effect from the date on which the proposed General Price takes effect for the duration of the Special Offer.

24F.15   Notwithstanding paragraphs 24F.11 and 24F.14, where the Director gives his written consent pursuant to paragraph 24F.4, he shall, following a representation by the Licensee at the same time that it sends a Price Change Notice to the Director pursuant to paragraph 24F.3, consider whether the charges specified in each of sub-paragraphs (a) in paragraphs 24F.11 and 24F.14 should not be revised in the case of any Standard Service which is not comprised within the same category of services as the relevant Retail Service. If he concludes that those charges should not be revised in the case of any Standard Service, he shall consent thereto and notify the Licensee at the same time as he gives his consent pursuant to paragraph 24F.4 and paragraphs 24F.11 and 24F.14 shall be applied accordingly.

24F.16   The Licensee shall not be entitled to introduce a Special Offer which the Director determines to be the same as or similar to a previous Special Offer in relation to the same Retail Service unless a period of three months has elapsed from the expiry of that previous Special Offer in relation to that Retail Service.

24F.19   (*a*)   Before giving a direction under paragraph 24F.6 or a consent under paragraph 24F.4, 24F.9 or 24F.15, or before making a determination under paragraph 24F.16, the Director shall consult with the Licensee and (except in the case of paragraph 24F.4) Interested Parties. If he concludes that a direction, determination or consent is appropriate or that consent is not appropriate he shall notify the Licensee and (except in the case of paragraph 24F.4) Interested Parties of the proposed direction, determination, or consent or proposed refusal to give consent, as the case may be, and his reasons for proposing to give it or refuse to give consent, and give each of them a reasonable opportunity to make representations. On giving a direction, determination or consent, or refusing to give consent, he shall notify the Licensee and (except in the case of paragraph 24F.4) Interested Parties of the direction, determination or consent, or refusal to give consent, as the case may be, and his reasons for giving it or refusing to give consent.

(*b*) Each notification of reasons shall, as appropriate, set out the Director's reasons:

(i)　for proposing to give the direction, determination or consent or refusing to give consent, as the case may be; or

(ii)　for giving the direction, determination or consent or refusing to give consent, as the case may be;

those reasons being sufficient to give the Licensee a reasonable understanding of the proposed decision or desision, as the case may be.

24F.20　This Condition is without prejudice to Conditions 16, 16A, 17, 17A and 24A.

24F.21　In this Condition:

'Conveyance Outpayment Cost' means any payment made to any person by the Licensee in respect of the conveyance of a call which is not a Delivery Outpayment Cost;

'Delivery Outpayment Cost' means either:

(i)　the payment made by the Licensee to an International Operator for the delivery of an outgoing international call passed on to it by the Licensee assessed on the basis of the net settlement after taking account of receipts under the system of settlement provided for by the ITTCC and the cost incurred by the Licensee of the delivery of an incoming international call passed on to it by an International Operator; or

(ii)　the average payment made by the Licensee to Operators in the United Kingdom or to operators in the Isle of Man or the Channel Islands for the delivery of calls to or within any of those respective places; or

(iii)　the payment made by the Licensee to an Operator for the conveyance of an international call to a destination outside the United Kingdom, Isle of Man and Channel Islands;

'Exchange Line Price' means a General Price imposed by the Licensee for:

(*a*)　the use and Ordinary Maintenance; and

(*b*)　the connection or taking over;

of an Exchange Line;

['General Price' has the meaning given to it in Condition 24A except that it shall not include those General Prices agreed between the Director and the Licensee on or before the date on which this Condition comes into force but, subject to that exception, shall include charges (or groups of charges) (including the fee, if any) for services offered in combination with charges (or groups of charges) for other services (or groups of services) or with a periodic or non-periodic fee and which, if the relevant service (or group of services) was charged for separately or a fee was not payable, would be General Prices;]

'General Price' has the meaning given to it in Condition 24A.18 except that it shall not include those General Prices agreed between the Director and the Licensee on or before the date on which this Condition comes into force and, subject to that exception, shall include:

Condition 24F.21 definition of 'General Price' in square brackets will be deleted and replaced by the words in italics with effect from 1 August 1997 by a licence amendment dated 1 October 1996.

(a) charges (or groups of charges) (including the fee, if any) for services offered in combination with charges (or groups of charges) for other services (or groups of services) or with a periodic or non-periodic fee and which, if the relevant service (or group of services) was charged for separately or a fee was not payable, would be General Prices; and

(b) charges for services which, if offered to residential customers, would be General Prices;

'Financial Statement' has the meaning given to it in Condition 20B;

'International Operator' means an operator recognised as such by the ITTCC;

'ITTCC' means the International Telegraph and Telephone Consultation Committee;

'Major Office' has the meaning given to it in Condition 16.4;

'Network Component' has the meaning given to it in Condition 16B;

'Network Cost' means:

(a) in the case of a General Price which is not an Exchange Line Price, the aggregate of the Transfer Charges for each Network Component and each Network Part, as the case may be, applied to the provision of a Retail Service; and

(b) in the case of an Exchange Line Price, the fully allocated costs of providing the service for which the Exchange Line Price is charged as shown in the Financial Statement of the relevant Businesss for the financial year in respect of which the charge is payable or, if that Financial Statement is not available, based on the latest available information;

'Network Part' has the meaning given to it in Condition 16B;

'Operator' means a person to whom the Licensee is obliged to provide a Standard Service pursuant to Condition 13;

'Ordinary Maintenance' has the meaning given to it in Condition 24A;

'Retail Cost' means the retail cost that is in the opinion of the Director appropriately allocated by the Licensee to the provision of a Retail Service;

'Retail Service' means a service provided by the Licensee to any person for which a General Price is charged;

'Special Offer' means a General Price offered by the Licensee for a limited period of time not exceeding three months specified by the Licensee at the time the General Price is first offered;

'Standard Service' has the meaning given to it in Condition 16B; and

'Transfer Charge' has the meaning given to it in Condition 16B.

Notes

1. Conditions 24F.1–21 were inserted by a licence amendment dated 31 March 1995.

2. Conditions 24F.3 (c)(v), 24F.3(d), 24F.10, 24F.12, 24F.13, 24F.17, 24F.18, 24F.21 (definitions of 'Access Deficit', 'Access Deficit Contributions', 'Contributions') were deleted by a licence amendment dated 13 February 1996.

3. Conditions 24F.11(a), 24F.14(a), 24F.15, 24F.21 (definitions of 'General Price') were amended by a licence amendment dated 13 February 1996.

4. In Condition 24F.1(a)(i) for the words 'paragraphs 24A.1 to 24A.13' shall be substituted the words 'Condition 24A' and in Condition 24F.20, the word ',17A' shall

be deleted as a result of a licence amendment dated 1 October 1996 and will come into effect as from 1 August 1997.
5.   See OFTEL statement 'Pricing of Telecommunications Services' from 1997 with annexes June 1996.
6.   This condition enables the Director General to 'cap' or control BT's retail prices. A cap of RPI - 7.5% was set for the period 1 August 1993 to 31 July 1997. A cap of RPI - 4.5% has been set for the period 1 August 1997 to 31 July 2001 but excludes business and high spending residential customers.

Condition 25   Charges for the Maintenance of Certain Exchange Lines

25.1   Subject to paragraph 25.2, the Licensee shall from time to time during every Relevant Year (as defined in Condition 24A.15) publish in accordance with Condition 16.3 its charges for the provision of services consisting of the maintenance and adjustment of any Exchange Line to which this Condition relates and the charge for maintenance and the charge for adjustment shall be uniform throughout the Licensed Area.

25.2   Nothing in this Condition shall preclude the Licensee from charging different amounts from those charged in respect of the generality of Exchange Lines to which this Condition relates where a customer contracts with the Licensee for the provision of service of a different quality than is provided in respect of the generality of Exchange Lines to which this Condition relates, provided always that the different quality service is available throughout those parts of the Licensed Area where there is a reasonable demand for it.

25.3   The Exchange Lines to which this Condition relates are those Exchange Lines (other than those installed in pursuance of Condition 42.2) used to provide simple voice telephony services in circumstances where only one Exchange Line is connected to the Served Premises at which those services are provided.

25.4   In this Condition 'maintenance' includes repair.

Notes
1.   Condition 25.1 was amended by licence amendments dated 23 April 1989 and 9 March 1993.
2.   This Condition was deleted on 31 December 1996 when new Condition 18A came into effect.

Condition 26   Charges for the Installation of Certain Exchange Lines

26.1   The Licensee shall until 1 August 1997 publish in accordance with Condition 16.3 the charges or the method to be adopted for determining the charges for the installation of any Exchange Line to which this Condition relates ('Installation') and shall apply the charges or method so published uniformly throughout the Licensed Area.

25.2   Subject to paragraph 26.3, where any such Exchange Line is brought into service after 31 July 1993 and before 1 August 1994 the Licensee shall not charge more than £99 (excluding VAT) in total (being a flat rate) in respect of the cost of the Installation.

26.3   Where the man-hours of work involved in any Installation exceed 100 (or such lower number as the Director may determine for the purpose of this paragraph in relation to all Installations), the Licensee may charge the reasonable cost of those excess man-hours of work (in addition to the charge referred to in paragraph 26.2) and any other of its reasonable costs provided that the charge (or the method to be adopted for determining the charge) in respect of any such man-hour of work and any such cost has been published in accordance with Condition 16.3 save where the Director agrees with the Licensee as provided for by paragraph 26.4, in which case paragraph 26.5 shall apply instead of this paragraph 26.3.

26.4   On request by the Licensee, the Director may, if he considers it appropriate to do so and after consulting such organisations as appear to him to be representative of persons likely to be substantially affected agree with the Licensee that paragraph 26.3 is to have effect in relation to any Installation where the reasonable costs to the Licensee exceed such figure as may be agreed between the Director and the Licensee in relation to all Installations. If such agreement is made, paragraph 26.5 shall apply.

26.5   Where the Licensee's reasonable costs in respect of an Installation exceed such figure as may from time to time be agreed between the Licensee and the Director in relation to all Installations, the Licensee may charge, in addition to any charge referred to in paragraph 26.2, the amount by which those costs exceed that figure, provided that the method to be adopted for determining the Licensee's charges in respect of such costs shall have been published in accordance with Condition 16.3.

26.6   The Licensee shall ensure that a person eligible for an installation to which paragraph 26.7 applies is notified that he may, should he so wish, pay the charge for it by an initial payment, which shall not exceed 25 per cent. of the total charge, followed by not less than four equal quarterly instalments (in respect of which the Licensee may charge a reasonable rate of interest and a reasonable administration fee) and, where that person indicates his wish so to pay, the Licensee shall bill him accordingly, subject to the Licensee's right to refuse such an instalment facility where it reasonably considers that there is a substantial risk that the person concerned would not make repayment in accordance with his agreement with the Licensee relating to the installation. On request by the Licensee, the Director may, if he considers it appropriate to do so and after consulting such organisations as appear to him to be representative of persons likely to be substantially affected, consent to the Licensee's charging a different initial payment and different instalments from those referred to above in this paragraph 26.6.

26.7   This paragraph applies to the installation of an Exchange Line to which this Condition relates at residential premises where the Exchange Line is to be used for private (as distinct from business) purposes, not being an Exchange Line:

(a)   which, if provided (whether or not together with any other Excange Line), would mean that the customer concerned would have more than one Exchange Line (whether or not at the same premises);

(b)   additional to a similar facility obtained by the customer concerned (whether or not at the same premises) from a person or body other than the Licensee;

(c)   for a customer who runs a switched telecommunications system (whether or not at the same premises); or

(d)   of a class falling within those classes of line listed in sub-paragraph 2.2 of the Guidelines relating to the residential Low User Scheme agreed between the Director and the Licensee under paragraph 24D.3 of Condition 24D.

26.8 The Exchange Lines to which this Condition relates are those Exchange Lines to which Condition 25 relates.

Notes
1. Conditions 26.1, 26.2 were deleted and replaced by a licence amendment dated 9 March 1993.
2. Conditions 26.3–8 were inserted by a licence amendment dated 9 March 1993.

Condition 27 Code of Practice for Consumer Affairs

27.1 The Licensee shall, in consultation with the Director, prepare and not later than three months after the date on which this Licence enters into force publish in accordance with Condition 16.3 a Code of Practice giving guidance to the Licensee's customers and employees in respect of any disputes and complaints relating to the provision by the Licensee of telecommunication services by means of, or in relation to, any of the Applicable Systems.

27.2 The Licensee shall consult the Director not less frequently than once every three years about the operation of the Code of Practice.

Condition 28 Arbitration of Disputes with Customers

28.1. The Licensee shall include in the standard terms and conditions on which it provides telecommunication services provisions giving persons who have entered into contracts with it for the provision of telecommunication services by the Licensee by means of, or in relation to, any of the Applicable Systems the opportunity to refer to an inexpensive independent arbitration procedure, instead of to a court of law, any dispute relating to the provision of those services which does not involve a complicated issue of law or a sum greater than such sum as the Director may from time to time determine. The arbitration procedures and the method of appointment of the arbitrators shall be subject to consultation with the Director and the Licensee shall consult the Director not less frequently than once every five years about the operation of the arbitration procedures.

Condition 29 Bodies Recognised to be Representing the Interests of Consumers

29.1 The Licensee shall give due consideration to any matter which relates to:

(*a*) telecommunication services provided by means of or in relation to any of the Applicable Systems;

(*b*) telecommunication apparatus supplied by the Licensee; or

(*c*) the connection to any of the Applicable Systems:

(i) of any telecommunication system run by any person other than the Licensee; or

(ii) any telecommunication apparatus;

and which is the subject of a representation made to the Licensee by either:

(*aa*)   a body recognised by the Secretary of State under section 27 of the Act, after consultation with the Licensee, as representing the interests of consumers and other users of such telecommunication services or apparatus;

(*bb*)   an advisory body established by the Secretary of State under section 54(1) of the Act.

29.2.   The Licensee shall, if requested by the Director or if it sees fit, furnish to the Director particulars of any matter considered by the Licensee under this Condition or a digest of activities undertaken in any period in pursuance of this Condition.

Condition 30   Metering, Billing, etc.

30.1   As regards any description of meter in use on a date specified by the Director in connection with any of the Applicable Systems and so specified, the Licensee shall apply for approval as soon as practicable and in any case not later than such date as the Director may determine in relation to that description of meter.

30.2   As regards any description of meter specified by the Director and not in use in connection with the Applicable Systems on the date specified under paragraph 30.1, the Licensee shall, unless the Director consents otherwise, apply for approval no later than such date as further specified by the Director or not less than six months before the date on which the Licensee intends to bring that meter into such use, whichever shall be later.

30.3   The Licensee shall not after such date as the Director may determine in relation to any description of meter specified by him, keep in or bring into use in connection with any of the Applicable Systems, any description of meter so specified which is not approved or for which the Licensee has not made an application for approval.

30.4   Where approval is not granted to or is withdrawn from a particular description of meter the Licensee shall, as soon as is reasonably practicable, either:

(*a*)   inform the Director of the action to be taken by the Licensee to remedy the absence of approval in relation to that description of meter and the anticipated date of such approval; or

(*b*)   inform the Director that the Licensee intends to cease use of that description of meter in connection with any of the Applicable Systems within a time reasonably practicable to the Licensee. On request of the Director, the Licensee shall provide the Director with a timetable for the withdrawal of that description of meter.

30.5   The Licensee shall not render any bill in respect of any description of telecommunication service provided by means of any of the Applicable Systems unless every amount (other than an indication of unit charge) stated in that bill is no higher than an amount which represents the true extent of any such service actually provided by the Licensee to the customer in question. In this paragraph 30.5 'customer' does not include an Operator within the meaning of Condition 13.

30.6   Without prejudice to the generality of paragraph 30.5, the Licensee shall at all times maintain in operation such a billing process as facilitates compliance by the Licensee with, and is calculated to prevent contravention by it of, that paragraph.

30.7   The Licensee shall not be regarded as being in contravention of its obligation under paragraph 30.5 except where the failure is in relation to the billing process and the Licensee has failed to take all reasonable steps to prevent a contravention of that obligation.

30.8   The Licensee shall keep such records as may be necessary or as may be determined by the Director to be necessary for the purpose of satisfying him that the billing process has the characteristics specified in relation to it by paragraph 30.6, provided that nothing in this paragraph shall require the Licensee to retain any records for more than 2 years from the date on which they came into being.

30.9   For the purpose of giving the Director an independent quality assurance from time to time that the billing process has the characteristics specified in relation to it by paragraph 30.6, the Licensee shall where the Director has prima facie grounds to believe the billing process does not have those characteristics and has so notified the Licensee, extend its prompt co-operation to the Director and, in particular, on request by the Director shall:

(*a*)   furnish the Director in accordance with his reasonable requirements with any information, document (including any facility enabling him to read data not held in readable form) or other thing;

(*b*)   carry out (or cause to be carried out by such person having such special expertise as the Director may specify and to whom the Director has raised no reasonable objection) in such manner as the Director may specify an examination of the whole or any part of the billing process and as soon as practicable after the conclusion of such examination furnish the Director with a written report by the Licensee or such specified person, as the case may be, of the results of such examination;

(*c*)   on reasonable notice by him allow at all reasonable times the Director and, in the case of any member of his staff, on production of his special authority in that behalf, access to any relevant premises, plant or equipment of the Licensee;

(*d*)   on reasonable notice by him allow at all reasonable times the Director and, in the case of any member of his staff, on production of his special authority in that behalf, to examine or test the whole or any part of the billing process including any plant or equipment whether or not forming part of any of the Applicable Systems;

(*e*)   for the purpose of paragraph 30.9 (c) and (d), allow the Director to be accompanied by any person as the Director may specify and to whom the Licensee has raised no reasonable objection whose assistance he might reasonably require for the purpose mentioned at the beginning of this paragraph provided that the Director shall have given the Licensee notice (save in exceptional circumstances of at least 5 working days) of the identity of that person; and

(*f*)   install and keep installed any equipment (whether or not supplied by the Director) for the purpose of verifying:

(i)   the accuracy and reliability of any equipment or apparatus (including any meter) of the Licensee; and

(ii)   in the case of any meter which is or is required to be approved and is in use in connection with any of the Applicable Systems, compliance with any conditions or other matters which may be required as regards such use of that meter.

30.10   When this Condition first comes into force paragraphs 30.1, 30.2 and 30.4 above shall only apply to any description of meter for voice frequency switched telecommunication services.

30.11   In this Condition:

'approved' means approved under section 24 of the Act;

'billing process' means metering systems and billing systems taken together, where 'billing system' means the totality of all equipment, data, procedures and activities which the Licensee employs to determine the charges to be sought for service usage recorded by a metering system based on published or previously negotiated pricing structure and to present these charges on customers' bills; and 'metering system' means the totality of all equipment, data, procedures and activities which the Licensee employs to determine the extent of any telecommunication services provided by means of any of the Applicable Systems;

'information' includes account, estimates and returns;

'meter' means any system or apparatus installed or maintained, or to be installed or to be maintained, at the Licensee's premises, constructed or adapted for use in ascertaining the extent of telecommunication services provided by means of a telecommunication system and cognate expressions shall be construed accordingly; and

'service' includes any service provided by any person to whom the Licensee is bound to account for any part of the amount charged by the Licensee.

Note
Conditions 30.1–11 were inserted by a licence amendment dated 24 September 1991.

Condition 31   Supply and Connection of Apparatus for the Disabled

31.1   The Licensee shall consult the Director from time to time about the arrangements made, or to be made, by the Licensee for:

(*a*)   the supply of telecommunication apparatus designed or adapted to meet the reasonable demands of the disabled; and

(*b*)   the connection to the Applicable Systems and the provision of Maintenance Services in respect of telecommunication apparatus designed or adapted to assist the disabled to obtain telecommunication services;

and shall, if requested by the Director to do so, participate in the work of the advisory body for matters affecting persons who are disabled or of pensionable age established by him under section 54(4) of the Act.

Condition 31A   Provision of Relay Service for Textphone Users

31A.1   Subject to the financial limits set out below and from 1 August 1993, the Licensee shall provide the funds for the operation by a person or body ('the Relay Service Provider') agreed from time to time by the Director, the Licensee and any other person contributing to its funding of a telephone relay service for people, whether customers of the Licensee or of another operator, who need to use textphones because of their disabilities. Such service shall consist of the provision of facilities for the receipt and translation of voice messages into text and the conveyance of that text to such textphones and vice versa ('the Service').

31A.2 The Licensee shall discharge its obligations under this Condition 31A by complying with guidelines issued from time to time and agreed by the Director, by the Licensee, by the Relay Service Provider and by any other person contributing to the funding of the Service. The Guidelines shall describe the Service and its provision by the Relay Service Provider. The Licensee shall enter into an arrangement with the Relay Service Provider on such terms and conditions as they both consider to be appropriate provided that any such arrangement is in accordance with the Guidelines. Failure of the Relay Service Provider to comply with the Guidelines shall not constitute a breach of the Guidelines by the Licensee.

31A.3 Users of the Service who are customers of the Licensee shall be charged for the conveyance of such voice messages and text to which the Service applies at no more than the Licensee's prevailing standard prices or such other charges as are, so far as reasonably practicable, equivalent to such prices as if that conveyance had been made directly between the caller's Network Termination Point and the Network Termination Point of the called person, except that the calling customer may be charged at the Licensee's standard local call prices for the element of the Service which consists of calls made to the Relay Service Provider in order to make a call to a called person irrespective of whether the call to the called person is successful.

31A.4 The Licensee's obligations under this Condition 31A consist solely of an obligation to provide funds for the Service and do not extend to either the provision of or funds for any textphones or other apparatus on the customer's side of the Network Termination Point.

31A.5 The financial limits referred to in paragraph 31A.1 above are that:

(a) the Licensee shall not be obliged to provide funds:

(i) in the year 1 August 1993 to 31 July 1994 in excess of £10 million;

(ii) in the year 1 August 1994 to 31 July 1995 in excess of £10 million or such larger sum (if any) as has been calculated by increasing £10 million by the percentage equal to the amount of any increase in the Retail Prices Index in the period of 12 months ending on 30 June 1994;

(iii) in the years 1 August 1995 to 31 July 1996 and 1 August 1996 to 31 July 1997 the sum applicable in the preceding year or such larger sum (if any) as has been calculated by increasing the sum applicable in the preceding year by the percentage equal to the amount of the charge in the Retail Prices Index in the period of 12 months ending on 30 June immediately before the beginning of that year;

(b) notwithstanding sub-paragraph (a) above the Licensee shall not be obliged to provide funds in excess of a total of £14 million in the period commencing on 1 April 1993 and ending on 31 March 1996 indexed on the basis of the Retail Prices Index up to the latter date.

31A.6 The financial limits referred to in paragraph 31A.1 above for years subsequent to the year 1 August 1996 to 31 July 1997 shall be reviewed by the Director in consultation with the Licensee at the same time as the Director reviews the price control provisions contained in Condition 24A, the Director first having given written notice to the Licensee of his intention to review those financial limits. In the absence of contrary agreement between the Director and the Licensee, the financial limit applicable to each of those subsequent years shall be the successive amounts produced by increasing the sum of £10 million year by year (that is to say, cumulatively) on 30 June 1994 and each anniversary of that date by the percentage equal to the amount of the change in the Retail Prices Index during each previous yearly period.

31A.7   In this Condition:

'customer of the Licensee' means a person who rents an exchange line from the Licensee or a person using such an exchange line with the authority of a person who does so rent one;

'people who need to use textphones because of their disabilities' means people who are deaf, deaf-blind or speech-impaired;

'textphone' means a text terminal connected to the public switched telephone network;

'Retail Prices Index' has the same meaning as in Condition 24A.

Note

Conditions 31A.1–7 were inserted by a licence amendment dated 9 March 1993.

Condition 32   Special Telephones for the Hearing Impaired

32.1   The Licensee shall ensure that there are available for supply in such a way as to meet all reasonable demands for them Telephones of the following descriptions:

(a)   Telephones capable of being inductively coupled to hearing aids which have been designed to be so coupled to Telephones; and

(b)   Telephones incorporating sound amplification facilities.

32.2   This Condition shall be deemed to be satisfied if the Licensee ensures that there is available for supply either one type of Telephone which meets both descriptions or two types of Telephone each of which meets one description.

Condition 33   Special Facilities for the Hearing-Impaired Using Public Call Boxes

33.1   As from the date on which this Licence enters into force the Licensee shall take all reasonable steps to install and keep installed in all Public Call Boxes at which it provides Call Box Services apparatus enabling persons using hearing aids designed for use in conjunction with Telephones of the kind installed in Public Call Boxes on the said date to use such hearing aids when voice telephony services are provided at Public Call Boxes.

Condition 33A   Controlled Services

33A.1   The Licensee may only provide a Controlled Service in whole or part by means of the Applicable Systems (whether or not Messages comprised in, or resulting from the provision of, such Services have previously been or are subsequently conveyed by any other public telecommunication system) where the Relevant Condition is satisfied.

33A.2   The Licensee may only provide a telecommunication service to another person by means of the Applicable Systems by means of which that person, to the knowledge of the Licensee, provides a Controlled Service (whether or not Messages comprised in, or resulting from the provision of, such services have previously been or are subsequently conveyed by any other public telecommunication system) where the Relevant Condition is satisfied.

33A.3   The Relevant Condition is that there is in effect at the time the Controlled Service concerned is provided, a Code of Practice governing the provision of such a Service, which has been recognised by the Director for the purposes of this Condition after consultation with the Licensee and with any body which he considers to be representative of those wishing to provide such Services.

33A.4   A Code of Practice shall only be recognised for the purposes of Paragraph 33A.3 if the Director is satisfied that:

(a)   its provisions are capable of properly regulating the provision of the Controlled Services to which it relates and, without prejudice to the generality of the foregoing, make adequate provision for compensating those who suffer as a result of the provision of such Services; and

(b)   adequate arrangements have been made for the constitution of a body of persons to apply and administer the Code.

33A.5   A Code of Practice is recognised for the purposes of this Condition where it is specified as such in a determination made by the Director, and the Director may, at any time after such a Code is recognised and after giving not less than one month's notice in writing of his intention to the body of persons applying and administering the Code, determine that its recognition be revoked if he is satisfied that its provisions are not capable of properly regulating the provision of the Controlled Services to which it relates or that it is not being properly applied and administered.

33A.6   For the purposes of this Condition the Director may recognise a Code of Practice in relation to any description of Controlled Service or to all Controlled Services and the provisions of this Condition shall apply accordingly.

33A.7   If a recommendation is made to the Director by the body of persons applying and administering a Code of Practice recognised under paragraph 33A.3 that any person (including the Licensee) should no longer be permitted or should not be permitted to provide a particular Controlled Service or any Controlled Services (whether or not he is providing it or them when the recommendation is made) and the Director considers it appropriate, he may direct the Licensee to cease to provide, or, as the case may be, not to provide that person or any other person with any service facilitating or enabling the provision of the relevant Controlled Service or Services or, as the case may be, itself cease to provide, or, as the case may be, not to provide the relevant Controlled Service or Services.

33A.8   The Director may determine, subject to such conditions as he thinks fit, that:

(a)   any Controlled Service of any description, or any individually specified such Service provided by a person named in the determination, is not to be treated as a Controlled Service for the purposes of this Condition; and

(b)   any individually specified Controlled Service in respect of which a determination under sub-paragraph (a) above has been made or which is within a description of Controlled Services in respect of which such a determination has been made, is to be treated as a Controlled Service for those purposes notwithstanding such determination;

and where a determination of the kind specified in sub-paragraph (b) above is made the provisions of this Condition shall apply to such a Service from the date specified in the determination.

33A.9   Subject to paragraph 33A.8, the provisions of this Condition only apply to a Controlled Service in respect of which;

(a)   the person providing the Service obtains the whole or any part of his revenue from the Licensee (or, where that person is the Licensee, that part of the Licensee's business which provides the Service is credited with revenue from the part of its business which conveys the Messages comprised in, or resulting from the provision of, the Service); and

(b)   the person responsible for paying the charges for the telephone calls by means of which the Service is obtained is billed by means of his telephone bill for any amount in respect of the provision of the Service.

33A.10   In this Condition:

(a)   'Controlled Service' means any service of the following descriptions:

(i)   a Chatline Service; or

(ii)   [. . .]

(iii)   a Live Conversation Message Service.

(b)   'Chatline Service' means, subject to paragraph 33A.11 below, a service which consists of or includes:

(i)   the enabling of more than two persons ('the participants') simultaneously to conduct a telephone conversation with one another without either:

(A)   each of them having agreed with each other; or

(B)   one or more of them having agreed with the person enabling such a telephone conversation to be conducted;

in advance of making the call enabling them to engage in the conversation the respective identities of the other intended Participants or the telephone numbers on which they can be called.

(c)   [. . .]

(d)   'Live Conversation Message Service' means a Message Service (other than a directory information service) which consists of the provision of live telephone conversation for any purpose, whether or not including the provision of information of any kind;

(i)   between the person providing the service (or a person acting on his behalf) and a person who obtains the service, or

(ii)   between a person who has independently called the service for the purpose of conducting a telephone conversation with one other such person, and such other person;

and, for the avoidance of doubt, it does not include a service provided by a human operator of the Licensee which is incidental to the conveyance of a voice telephony message.

(e)   'Message Service' means a service which consists of, or includes, the sending of speech, music or other sounds or signals to any person who obtains access to that service by means of a Public Switched Telephone Network.

(f)   'Public Switched Telephone Network' means any public telecommunication system which is used to provide switched voice telephony services to the general public.

33A.11 A service by which one or more additional persons who are known (by name or telephone number) to one or more of the parties conducting an established telephone conversation can be added to that conversation by means of being called by one or more of such parties is not on that account a Chatline Service if it would not otherwise be regarded as such a service.

33A.12 The provisions of this Condition shall cease to have effect on the making of a direction by the Director under Condition 33B to the extent specified in the direction.

33A.13 The provisions of this Condition and Condition 33B shall come into force on such day as the Director may determine and different days may be so determined for different provisions or different purposes.

Notes

1. Conditions 33A.1–13 were inserted by a licence amendment dated 27 July 1989 following an MMC report on Premium Rate Services.
2. Conditions 33A.10(a)(ii) and 33A.10(c) were quashed by the High Court in *R v Director General of Telecommunications, ex parte Computerdial Limited* on 1 February 1990.
3. There are more determinations under Condition 33A.8 than any other in this Licence. Recent examples include Broker Hotline 14 June 1996, Legal Helpline 8 May 1996, AutoCheck Technical Helpline 2 May 1996 and Computer Home Link 25 July 1996.
4. The Code of Practice referred to in this Condition is in its 7th edition and is produced by The Independent Committee for the Supervision of Standards of Telephone Information Services (ICSTIS). The Code will be changed as a result of a statement issued by OFTEL in October 1996 on 'The Future Regulation of Premium Rate Services'.
5. See *R v Director General of Telecommunications ex parte Let's Talk (UK) Ltd* CO/757/92 6 April 1992, QBD.

Condition 33B Provision of Special Facilities

33B.1 The Licensee shall comply with any direction made under this paragraph which requires the Licensee to make available such of the facilities listed in paragraph 33B.2 as are specified in the direction. A direction under this paragraph shall be made by the Director after consultation with the Licensee and shall specify only facilities which the Director considers it will be technically and economically practicable for the Licensee to provide. The direction shall specify the date by which each facility is to be provided and the class or description of customer (whether described by reference to area or otherwise) to whom it is to be provided and shall be subject to such conditions as the Director thinks fit.

33B.2 The facilities referred to in paragraph 33B.1 are:

(*a*) The provision to any customer of the Licensee for voice telephony services who requests it of a bill or invoice showing, by reference to the number used to access the service, and the date and time on which access was obtained, the amount of any charge imposed by the Licensee for a telephone call to any service to which this Condition applies;

(*b*) The notification to such a customer who requests it, as soon as reasonably practicable, of:

(i)   the date on which the total charges accrued within the standard billing period of the Licensee for voice telephony services and any other service to be included in the bill or invoice for such services exceed an amount specified by that customer being an amount, or one of a number of amounts, from time to time specified by the Licensee as being suitable for the purpose; or

(ii)   the date on which the aggregate charges accrued in any such period in respect of Chatline Services and Message Services to which this Condition applies exceed an amount determined from time to time by the Director; and

(c)   the barring, by means of apparatus forming part of the Applicable Systems, on request by any such customer, of access from any Exchange Line specified by that customer and in respect of which that customer is the customer of the Licensee, to all Chatline Services and Messages Services to which this Condition applies.

33B.3   The services to which this Condition applies are those Chatline Services and Message Services in respect of which:

(a)   the person providing the service obtains the whole or any part of his revenue from the Licensee (or, where that person is the Licensee, that part of the Licensee's business which provides the Service is credited with revenue from that part of its business which conveys the Messages comprised in, or resulting from the provision of, the Service); and

(b)   the person responsible for paying the charges for the telephone calls by means of which the Service is obtained is billed by means of his telephone bill for any amount in respect of the provision of the Service.

33B.4   In this Condition 'Chatline Service' and 'Message Service' have the respective meanings given to those terms in Condition 33A.

Note
Conditions 33B.1–4 were inserted by a licence amendment dated 27 July 1989.

Condition 34   Numbering Arrangements

34.1   The Licensee shall from the date on which this Licence enters into force adopt a Numbering Plan and shall not later than three months thereafter furnish details thereof to the Director and on request to any other person having a reasonable interest.

34.2   The Numbering Plan shall describe the method adopted and to be adopted for allocating and re-allocating in respect of each Network Termination Point such numbers as may be necessary for each item of Relevant Apparatus or each Relevant System that is or is to be connected by means of that Network Termination Point to any of the switched Applicable Systems.

34.3   The Licensee shall install, maintain or adjust its switched Applicable Systems so that those Systems convey Messages to Network Termination Points in respect of which numbers have been allocated in accordance with the Numbering Plan.

34.4   The Numbering Plan on the date on which this Licence enters into force shall be the numbering arrrangements applied immediately before that date but the Licensee shall from time to time thereafter consult:

(a)   the Director about the arrangements for the allocation and reallocation of numbers within the Numbering Plan; and

(b)   in one body approved by the Director for the purpose and represen-tative of public telecommunications operators and other persons whom the Director considers appropriate about any developments of, additions to or replacements of, the Numbering Plan.

34.5   The Licensee shall from time to time (but in the case of proposals for a Numbering Plan based on more than nine digits not before 1 January 1987) prepare, taking into account the consultations in paragraph 34.4(b), and furnish to the Director proposals for developing, adding to or replacing the Numbering Plan and changing the switched Applicable Systems to the extent necessary to secure that:

(a)   sufficient numbers are made available, having regard to the antici-pated growth in demand for telecommunication services, for a number or numbers to be allocated without undue delay;

(b)   numbers include as few digits as practicable and their allocation does not confer any undue advantage on the Licensee or undue disadvantage on persons running Relevant Systems;

(c)   the cost of changing any of the switched Applicable Systems or any Relevant Apparatus or Relevant System in order to accommodate the revised Numbering Plan is reasonable; and

(d)   inconvenience caused by the alteration of the Numbering Plan to the Licensee and to persons using Relevant Apparatus or Relevant Systems in respect of which numbers have previously been allocated is minimised.

34.6   If the Director determines that the Numbering Plan with any developments, additions and replacements submitted in accordance with paragraph 34.5 is sufficient to provide compatibility with the numbering arrangements applied or to be applied by other public telecommunications operators and to meet the objectives specified in paragraph 34.5, the Licensee shall adopt the Numbering Plan but, if the Director determines that it is not compatible with numbering arrangements applied or to applied by another public telecommunications operator or will not be sufficient to achieve the objectives specified in paragraph 34.5, then the Licensee shall adopt the Numbering Plan with such developments, additions or replacements as the Director may determine are best calculated to secure the objectives specified in paragraph 34.5.

34.7   The Director shall not exercise his powers under paragraph 34.6 before 1 April 1990 so as to require the Licensee to change the Applicable Systems provided that it does not develop, add to or replace the Numbering Plan before that date except with the consent of the Director.

34.8   Before making a determination under paragraph 34.6 above the Director shall take account of:

(a)   the state of technical development of the Applicable Systems and the Licensee's plans for their commercial development;

(b)   the balance of advantage between:

(i)   making developments of, additions to or replacements of numb-ering arrangements applied or to be applied, or making changes to systems run, by others; and

(ii)   making any requirement of the Licensee;

(c)   the cost to the Licensee and to those to whom the Licensee provides telecommunication services arising from any determination;

(*d*)   any obligations and recommendations of the International Telecommunication Union which apply to Her Majesty's Government and are accepted by them and any other standard to which the Director consents for the purpose from time to time; and

(*e*)   the views of the Licensee and such other persons (including operators of public telecommunication systems, those to whom telecommunication services are provided or telecommunication apparatus is supplied and producers of telecommunication apparatus) as appear to the Director to have an interest in the matter.

34.9   If the Director determines that the Numbering Plan shall be developed, added to or replaced in accordance with paragraph 34.6, nothing in paragraph 34.6 shall preclude the Licensee from submitting to the Director proposals for further developments of, additions to or replacements of the Numbering Plan or from subsequently changing the Applicable Systems if the Director does not object to the further developments, additions or replacements proposed by the Licensee.

34.10   The Licensee shall not charge any person for a number which is allocated to him (other than a coveted number allocated to a person who is not a public telecommunications operator at the request of such a person) but nothing in this Condition shall preclude the Licensee from recovering from the operator of a Relevant System the reasonable cost of allocating a number and of carrying out any change to any of the Applicable Systems necessary for the purpose of permitting Messages to be sent to a number allocated to that person and any reasonable continuing costs arising from such a change.

34.11   For the purposes of this Condition:

'to change' includes to make any alteration to the telecommunication apparatus or telecommunication systems or to the protocols (including message formats) or stored commands in such apparatus or systems:

'Relevant System' means a Connectable System which is, or is to be, connected to any of the switched Applicable Systems; and

'Relevant Apparatus' means any apparatus which is, or is to be, so connected.

34.12   For the avoidance of doubt, it is hereby declared that this Condition applies notwithstanding any arrangements for numbering under Condition 13.

34.13   The numbers to which this Condition applies are numbers:

(*a*)   of a class described in CCITT Recommendations E160, E163, E164 or F69 or their functional successors; or

(*b*)   which are of a class described in CCITT Recommendation X121 and which include any Data Network Identification Code which has been:

(i)   allocated before 14 November 1986 in accordance with the Numbering Plan furnished to the Director in accordance with paragraph 34.1; or

(ii)   specified by the Director for the purposes of this Licence and described in a list kept for that purpose by the Director and made available by him for inspection by the general public.

Note
Condition 34.13 was inserted by a licence amendment dated 1 May 1987.

Condition 34A   Numbering Arrangements in Respect of Relevant Services

34A.1   The Licensee shall from the date on which it first provides a Relevant Service adopt a numbering plan ('the Relevant Services Numbering Plan'), in respect of Relevant Services provided or to be provided by means of an Applicable System, for the allocation of any Numbers which:

(*a*)   are not allocated in accordance with a Specified Numbering Scheme; and

(*b*)   are used or are intended to be used:

(i)   by any licensee, other than a public telecommunications operator, under a Licence who provides a service of a description which the Licensee could provide as a Relevant Service under and in accordance with the provisions of this Licence; or

(ii)   by any other public telecommunications operator; and

(*c*)   are necessary for access to each separately distinguishable element of each Relevant Service.

34A.2   The Relevant Services Numbering Plan shall describe the method adopted and to be adopted for allocating and re-allocating Numbers of a kind described in paragraph 34A.1. That method shall allow for sufficient Numbers to be available in relation to all telecommunication services, having regard to the reasonably foreseeable growth in demand for such services.

34A.3   The Licensee shall:

(*a*)   within three months of 30 April 1987; or

(*b*)   on or before the date on which he first provides a Relevant Service or as soon as practicable thereafter;

whichever is the later, furnish details of the Relevant Services Numbering Plan to the Director and on request to any other person having a reasonable interest.

34A.4   The Licensee shall furnish to the Director details of any proposals the Licensee may have from time to time to change the arrangements for allocating or re-allocating Numbers within, or to develop, add to or replace, the Relevant Services Numbering Plan adopted and funished in accordance with paragraphs 34A.1, 34A.2 and 34A.3.

34A.5   Where any arrangements for allocating or re-allocating Numbers within the Relevant Services Numbering Plan or any developments, additions or replacements submitted in accordance with paragraph 34A.4:

(*a*)   are insufficient to provide Compatibility with the numbering arrangements applied or to be applied by any other public telecommunications operator or by any licensee, other than a public telecommunications operator, under a Licence who provides a service of a description which the licensee could provide as a Relevant Service under and in accordance with the provisions of this Licence;

(*b*)   do not allow for sufficient Numbers to be available in relation to all telecommunication services, having regard to the reasonably foreseeable growth in demand for such services; or

(*c*)   are not consistent with any obligations and recommendations of the International Telecommunication Union which apply to Her Majesty's Government and are accepted by them;

the Licensee shall adopt the Relevant Services Numbering Plan with such developments, additions or replacements as are best calculated to secure such Compatibility, availability or consistency.

34A.6 The Licensee shall allocate and re-allocate Numbers in accordance with the Relevant Services Numbering Plan it has adopted.

34A.7 In this Condition:

'Compatibility' means that between the parties concerned there is no reasonably foreseeable risk of:

(*a*) duplication of any Number; or

(*b*) any other related effect;

such as would introduce ambiguity or errors or impose undue restrictions on any user or group of users;

'Number' means any identifier (including any name or address) of any user, telecommunication apparatus or service element; and

'Specified Numbering Scheme' means a scheme for the allocation and re-allocation of Numbers which is specified by the Director for the purpose of this Licence and described in a list kept for that purpose by him and made available by him for inspection by the general public.

34A.8 The Numbers to which this Condition applies do not include Numbers which:

(*a*) are of a class described in CCITT Recommendations E160, E163, E164, or F69 or their functional successors; or

(*b*) are of a class described in CCITT Recommendation X121 and which include a Data Network Identification Code which has been:

(i) allocated before 14 November 1986 in accordance with the Numbering Plan furnished to the Director in accordance with Condition 34.1; or

(ii) specified by the Director for the purposes of Condition 34 or the equivalent Condition in any Licence granted to a public telecommunications operator and described in a list kept for that purpose by the Director and made available by him for inspection by the general public.

Note
Conditions 34A.1–8 were inserted by a licence amendment dated 1 May 1987

Condition 34B Numbering Arrangements

34B.1 Subject to the provisions of this Condition, Condition 34 shall cease to have effect on the coming into force of this Condition.

34B.2 Any Numbering Plan in force immediately before the coming into effect of this Condition by virtue of paragraphs 34.1 to 34.4 shall remain in force until the adoption of any Numbering Plan amending or replacing the same under any of the following provisions of this Condition.

34B.3 Where before the coming into force of this Condition the Licensee has furnished to the Director proposals in accordance with paragraph 34.5, the Director shall, notwithstanding paragraph 34B.1, make a determination in relation to those proposals in accordance with paragraph 34.6 and the Licensee shall adopt the Numbering Plan referred to in that paragraph as provided therein.

34B.4   Where before the coming into force of this Condition the Licensee has adopted a Numbering Plan in accordance with paragraph 34.6, or the Director has made a determination under that paragraph (by virtue of which the Licensee shall adopt the Numbering Plan), the Numbering Plan so adopted shall be the Licensee's Numbering Plan until the Licensee adopts a Numbering Plan pursuant to the following provisions of this Condition. The Numbering Plan referred to in the following provisions of this Condition is the Numbering Plan adopted pursuant to those provisions.

34B.5   The Director may determine a Specified Numbering Scheme (the 'Scheme') in accordance with the National Numbering Conventions (the 'Conventions') published in accordance with paragraph 34B.9 and he will allocate Numbers from this Scheme to the Licensee in accordance with the Conventions. The initial allocation of Numbers to the Licensee shall be of those Numbers to which the Numbering Plan referred to in paragraphs 34B.3 and 34B.4 relates and of any other Numbers to which any other Numbering Plan in force immediately before such allocation relates, provided that, at such time of initial allocation, those Numbers are currently in use by the Licensee, and where not so in use, the Director shall have due regard to the Licensee's plans and future requirements for its use and allocation of additional Numbers. The Director shall, at the request from time to time of the Licensee, allocate to it:

(a)   such quantity of additional Numbers as it may require; and

(b)   in accordance with the Conventions, such specific Numbers as it may request and which the Director is satisfied are not required for other purposes.

34B.6   The Licensee shall adopt a Numbering Plan for such Numbers as the Director may allocate to it from time to time in accordance with the Conventions. It shall within three months of being notified of such allocation furnish details of the Numbering Plan to the Director, and keep him informed of material changes to the Numbering Plan as they occur. The Licensee shall also furnish details of the Numbering Plan together with any material changes to that Numbering Plan on request to any other person having a reasonable interest. Except where the Director agrees otherwise, the Numbering Plan shall be consistent with the Conventions published in accordance with paragraph 34B.9. If the Numbering Plan is not consistent with those Conventions, the Director may direct the Licensee to adopt and furnish him with a new Numbering Plan or to take such other reasonable remedial action which does not cause undue inconvenience to the Licensee's customers, as may be necessary to ensure consistency.

34B.7   The Licensee shall install, maintain and adjust its switched Applicable Systems so that those Systems route Messages and otherwise operate in accordance with the Numbering Plan, including any requirement relating to Portability contained in paragraph 34C. The Licensee shall not use Numbers other than those allocated to it from the Scheme except:

(a)   with the written consent of the Director; or

(b)   where the use of those Numbers is the subject of an agreement to which Condition 13 applies.

34B.8   (a)   The Licensee shall provide to the Director on request, such information about its operations under its Numbering Plan as he may reasonably require to administer the Scheme and in particular on:

(i)   the percentages of Numbers in significant ranges which have already been allocated to end-users or which for other reasons are unavailable for further allocation;

(ii)   any allocation of blocks of Numbers to any person for purposes other than end use;

(iii)   Numbers whose use has been transferred at an end-user's request to another Operator; and

(iv)   the Licensee's current forecasts of all of the above matters.

(b) The Licensee shall not be required to provide information about individual end-user customers.

(c) In making any such request the Director shall ensure that no undue burden is imposed on the Licensee in procuring and furnishing such information and, in particular, that the Licensee is not required to procure or furnish information which would not normally be available to it, unless the Director is satisfied that such information is essential to the administration of the Scheme.

34B.9 (a) The Conventions referred to in this Condition will be a set of principles and rules published from time to time by the Director after consultation with interested parties who are members of the Telecommunications Numbering and Addressing Body and, if deemed appropriate, with end-users.

(b) In consulting the said interested parties, the Director shall afford a reasonable period, not being less than 28 days, for them to make representations, and he shall take the said representations into account when publishing the Conventions. The Conventions shall govern the specification and application of the Scheme and the Numbering Plan of the Licensee and may also include such other matters relating to the use and management of Numbers as (but not limited to):

(i)   criteria and procedures relating to the application for, allocation of and withdrawal of numbers;

(ii)   dialling plans;

(iii)   access codes;

(iv)   prefixes;

(v)   standard ways of recording Numbers for convenience or ease of use, such as the grouping of digits in Numbers of particular lengths;

(vi)   methods of enabling end-users to understand the meaning implicit in Numbers or other dialled digits, and in particular the rate at which a call to a particular Number will be chargeable;

(vii)   arrangements for the transfer of Numbers between Operators as a result of Portability.

(c) the Director may from time to time amend or withdraw a Convention already published, after consultation with interested parties who are members of the Telecommunications Numbering and Addressing Body. The Licensee shall not be required to comply with any such amendment or withdrawal unless the Licensee has been given a reasonable period of notice, such notice not being less than three months. Numbers allocated to the Licensee may only be withdrawn after similar consultation and notice, and the Director shall consult end-users affected by such withdrawal. Subject to overriding national interests, or where there is no alternative solution available, the power to withdraw Numbers shall not apply to any Numbers which the Director has approved from time to time as part of a specific service of the Licensee, which as a result of investment by the Licensee, has a recognised identity and quality associated with that particular Number and which the Licensee is using and plans to continue to use.

34B.10   In deciding on the details of and any subsequent changes to the Scheme and the Conventions, and when making or changing Number allocations within the Scheme or making determinations under this Condition, the Director shall ensure that the Scheme complies with the Conventions and shall have regard to:

(a)   the need for sufficient Numbers to be made available, having regard to the anticipated growth in demand for telecommunication services, together with the need for good husbandry of that supply at any time;

(b)   the need to ensure Compatibility with the Numbering Plans adopted or to be adopted by other public telecommunications operators;

(c)   the convenience and preferences of end-users;

(d)   the requirements of effective competition;

(e)   the practicability of implementing the Conventions in licensed systems by the date when the Conventions are intended to apply;

(f)   any costs or inconvenience imposed on the Licensee, other network operators, end-users and other interested parties (including those overseas);

(g)   any relevant international agreements, recommendations or standards;

(h)   the views of the Licensee and other interested parties; and

(i)   any other matters he regards as relevant.

34B.11   The Licensee shall not, unless the Director consents otherwise, charge any person for a Number which is allocated to him (other than a coveted Number allocated to a person who is not a public telecommunications operator at the request of such a person).

34B.12   For the purposes of this Condition:

'Compatibility' means the absence between the parties concerned of any reasonably foreseeable risk of:

(a)   duplication of any Number; or

(b)   any other related or like effect;

which would be liable to introduce ambiguity or errors or to impose undue restrictions on any user or group of users;

'Number' means any identifier which would need to be used in conjunction with any public switched service for the purposes of establishing a connection with any Network Termination Point, user, telecommunications apparatus connected to any public switched network or service element, but not including any identifier which is not accessible to the generality of users of a public switched service;

'Numbering Plan' means a plan describing the method adopted or to be adopted for allocating and re-allocating a Number to any Network Termination Point or to any user, telecommunications apparatus or service element;

'Relevant System' means a Connectable System which is, or is to be, connected to any of the switched Applicable Systems;

'Relevant Apparatus' means any apparatus which is, or is to be, so connected;

'Specified Numbering Scheme' means a scheme for the allocation and re-allocation of Numbers for the purposes of any of the switched

Applicable Systems and the systems of other licensed Operators which is specified by the Director for the purposes of this Licence and described in a list kept for the purpose by him and made available by him for public inspection; and

'Telecommunications Numbering and Addressing Body' means a body approved by the Director as representative of the Licensee, other public telecommunications operators and other persons whom the Director considers it appropriate to include in consultations about the content of the Conventions and the Scheme.

34B.13   For the avoidance of doubt, it is hereby declared that this Condition applies notwithstanding any arrangements for numbering arising by virtue of any agreement to which Condition 13 applies. But nothing in this paragraph shall affect the operation of any such agreements entered into before the coming into force of this Condition.

34B.14   The Numbers to which this Condition applies are Numbers:

(a)   of a class described in CCITT Recommendation E.160, E.164 or F.69 or their functional successors; or

(b)   which are of a class described in CCITT Recommendation X.121 and which include any Data Network Identification Code which has been:

(i)   allocated before 14 November 1986 in accordance with the Numbering Plan furnished to the Director in accordance with paragraph 34.1; or

(ii)   specified by the Director for the purposes of this Licence and described in a list kept for that purpose by the Director and made available by him for inspection to the general public.

Notes

1.   Conditions 34B.1–18 were inserted by a licence amendment dated 24 September 1991.

2.   On 22 February 1995 the Director General issued a notice to modify Condition 34.B so as to introduce a power for the Director General to determine the charges to be levied by BT or other operators to provide number portability. BT would not agree to such a modification and on 27 April 1995 the matter was referred to the MMC. In November 1995 the MMC presented their recommendations to the Director General and these have been introduced as modifications to this Condition by a licence amendment dated 29 July 1996.

3.   Conditions 34B.11–14 were deleted and Conditions 34B.15–18 were renumbered accordingly by a licence amendment dated 29 July 1996.

4.   In 1994 OFTEL assumed management of the UK numbering scheme and has now adopted a numbering plan. See OFTEL publications 'Numbering Conventions', June 1994; 'Telephone number portability', November 1995; and 'The National Numbering Scheme', August 1996.

Condition 34C   Number Portability

34C.1   (a)   If directed to do so by the Director, the Licensee shall provide Portability from the date specified in such direction to any Qualifying Operator in accordance with the Functional Specification and with the following provisions.

(b)   'Qualifying Operator' means an Operator which has notified the Licensee in writing that throughout an area which is specified in such notification and is within the licensed area referred to in its licence granted under section 7 of the Act, it is able and willing to provide on reasonable terms Reciprocal Portability in conformity with the Functional Specification, and wishes the Licensee to provide Portability throughout the same specified area.

(c)   The Licensee or the Operator may refer in writing to the Director for his determination any question as to the reasonableness of—

(i)   the extent of the area notified in accordance with sub-paragraph (b);

(ii)   the terms upon which an Operator is prepared to offer Reciprocal Portability

provided that no application shall be made under this sub-paragraph with respect to charges otherwise determinable by the Director under the provisions of this Condition.

34C.2   (a)   Having given a direction under paragraph 34C. 1, the Director may determine, subject to the following provisions, the reasonable costs of the Licensee in providing Portability and the Standard Portability Charges, allowing the recovery of such costs, to be paid by each Qualifying Operator—

(i)   in relation to the period from the date specified in accordance with paragraph 34C.1 to 31 March 1997;

(ii)   annually thereafter in relation to each financial year ending on 31 March.

(b)   Any determination of costs made under sub-paragraph (a) shall:

(i)   be based upon the Licensee's fully allocated costs of providing Portability, calculated on the basis of information provided by the Licensee to the Director by virtue of its obligations under Condition 13 and related provisions of this Licence, and in response to any written request by the Director made under this paragraph for the purposes of this Condition which shall be responded to within the reasonable time limits specified in the request, unless some other cost-basis shall have been substituted in relation to the charges determined by the Director or otherwise provided for under the provisions of Condition 13 of this Licence, in which case the Director may determine appropriate arrangements for altering the cost-base in order to conform with those provisions which shall accordingly apply to any determination made under sub-paragraph (a) of this paragraph on or after the date on which such alteration takes effect;

(ii)   subject to sub-paragraph (d)(ii), categorise the Licensee's reasonable costs incurred in providing Portability as System Set-Up Costs, Per Line Set-Up Costs, Administrative Costs and, for the purposes of sub-paragraph (c)(ii) of this paragraph, Additional Conveyance Costs.

(c)   Any determination of Standard Portability Charges made under sub-paragraph (a) shall be subject to the following provisions:

(i)   the Licensee's System Set-Up Costs shall not be recovered;

(ii)   subject to sub-paragraph (iii), the Licensee's Additional Conveyance Costs shall not be recovered by way of a charge determined under this Condition after 31 October 1997, provided that until that date the Licensee may by means of a Standard Portability Charge, recover an amount representing half the difference between —

(aa)   its Additional Conveyance Costs during the period between commencing the provision of Portability and 31 October 1997; and (bb) such Additional Conveyance Costs as the Director determines that it would have incurred if Call Drop-Back had been in operation for the whole of that period;

(iii) any Additional Conveyance Costs other than the amount recoverable by virtue of sub-paragraph (ii) above shall be treated in the same manner as costs recoverable by charges for interconnection made and determined under and in accordance with Condition 13 of this Licence.

(*d*) The following provisions shall also apply with respect to any determination made under sub-paragraph (a):

(i) the director may determine that a cost is not reasonable if he considers that the Licensee could at the relevant time have used lower cost methods in implementing the relevant aspect of Portability and in that event the Director may disallow the item of cost in question in whole or in part as appropriate;

(ii) in respect of any individual item of cost the Director may determine into which category of cost it falls, and if he considers that any such item of cost cannot reasonably be categorised as System Set-Up Costs, Per Line Set-Up Costs, Administrative Costs or Additional Conveyance Costs, the Director may determine whether and to what extent the Licensee may reasonably recover such costs;

(iii) in the event that, in making any determination under sub-paragraph (a), the Director considers that the cost basis of any Standard Portability Charge in any preceding period has been inaccurately estimated, he shall make such adjustment to such Charge determined by him as he considers is appropriate for rectifying the matter.

34C.3 Before making any determination under paragraph 34C.2, the Director shall consult with Interested Parties and take into account any representations made by them.

34C.4 For the purposes of this Condition:

'Additional Conveyance Costs' means any costs associated with resources used in

(*a*) effecting the switch-processing required to set up each ported call, and

(*b*) providing the switch and transmission capacity whether in the local or trunk exchange for any part of the duration of each ported call additional to the costs of conveyance of non-ported calls from the Applicable Systems to the Operator's system;

'Administrative Costs' means those costs, similar in nature to Per Line Set Up Costs, which are incurred by the Licensee when a Customer, retaining a Number allocated by the Licensee, moves from one location to another, whether at the same time as that Customer takes a Directly Provided Telecommunication Service from a Qualifying Operator or thereafter;

'Call Drop-Back' means the process whereby signals passing between the Licensee's local exchange serving the Porting Customer and the Licensee's trunk exchange enable Messages conveyed by the Applicable Systems to be routed to the system of the relevant Qualifying Operator and thence to the Porting Customer's system, releasing the call path between the local and trunk exchanges once signalling is completed;

'Customer' means a person provided with a Directly Provided Telecommunication Service by the Licensee or an Operator as the case may be;

'Directly Provided Telecommunication Service' means a telecommunication service provided directly to any Customer by the Licensee (or the Operator) by means of the connection at the Network Termination Point in the case of the Licensee (or the equivalent point in the Operator's system) between the Customer's system and the Licensee's Applicable Systems (or the Operator's system);

'Functional Specification' means a document published from time to time by the Director following consultation with the Licensee and Interested Parties which specifies technical and other principles which are intended to enable the efficient implementation and utilisation of Portability;

'Interested Parties' has the same meaning as in Condition 16B;

'Number' has the same meaning as in Condition 34B;

'Operator' has the same meaning as in Condition 13;

'Per Line Set-Up Costs' means the costs of the Licensee in providing switching and administration with respect to each Number ported;

'Portability' means a facility which may be provided by the Licensee to an Operator and which enables

(a) a Customer to whom Directly Provided Telecommunication Services are provided by reference to a Number allocated by or on behalf of the Licensee to retain that Number irrespective of the identity of the person providing such Services; and

(b) the resumption of the provision of such Services by the Operator to a Customer

(i) to whom Directly Provided Telecommunication Services have been provided by reference to a Number allocated by or on behalf of that Operator and

(ii) who has as a result of the provision of Reciprocal Portability obtained such Services from the Licensee by reference to that Number;

'Porting Customer' means a former Customer of the Licensee who has been allocated a Number by or on behalf of the Licensee and who receives Directly Provided Telecommunication Services from any Qualifying Operator by means of the same Number;

'Reciprocal Portability' means a facility provided by an Operator to the Licensee and which enables

(a) a Customer to whom Directly Provided Telecommunication Services are provided by reference to a Number allocated by or on behalf of the Operator to retain that Number irrespective of the identity of the person providing such Services; and

(b) the resumption of the provision of such Services by the Licensee to a Customer—

(i) to whom Directly Provided Telecommunication Services have been provided by reference to a Number allocated by or on behalf of the Licensee; and

(ii) who has as a result of the provision of Portability obtained such services from an Operator by reference to that Number;

'Standard Portability Charges' means the charges payable to the Licensee by each Qualifying Operator for the provision of Portability to it by the Licensee, each such Operator paying the same charge as determined by the Director under this Condition with respect to each category of cost;

'System Set-Up Costs' means costs of the Licensee incurred—

(i)   in the course of making network and system modifications, configurations or reconfigurations, including adapting or replacing software;

(ii)   in the course of testing functionality within the Applicable Systems and in conjunction with any Qualifying Operator's systems; anywhere within the Licensed Area thereby establishing the technical and administrative capability to provide Portability.

Notes
1.   See Note 2 to Condition 34B.
2.   Condition 34C was inserted by a licence amendment dated 29 July 1996.
3.   The Functional Specification referred to in Condition 34C.1(a) was issued at the same time as the licence amendment. It is not reproduced in this Handbook but may be obtained from OFTEL.
4.   In January 1997 the Director General made his first determination under this Condition in relation to BT's cost charges for geographic number portability.

Condition 35   Prohibition of Linked Sales

35.1   *The Licensee shall not make it a condition of:*

(a)   providing any telecommunication service (other than a telecommunication service comprised in a Relevant Service) by means of or in relation to any of the Applicable Systems;

(aa)   providing any Relevant Service;

(b)   supplying any telecommunication apparatus for connection to any of the Applicable Systems; or

(c)   connecting any other system or apparatus to any of the Applicable Systems;
that any Relevant Person should acquire from the Licensee or from any other person specified or described by the Licensee:

(i)   any telecommunication service other than the telecommunication service requested save where that service cannot be provided without the provision of that other telecommunication service; or

(ii)   any telecommunication apparatus not incorporated in the Applicable Systems save where the telecommunication service requested cannot otherwise be provided or the telecommunication apparatus requested cannot otherwise be used.

35.2   *Except where the Director has agreed otherwise, the Licensee shall not do any one or more of the things described in sub-paragraphs (a), (aa), (b) and (c) of paragraph 35.1 together with any other of those things in a manner or for charges or on terms or conditions more favourable than would be available for doing that thing or those things without that other thing or those other things.*

35.3   *Notwithstanding paragraphs 35.1 and 35.2 the Licensee may:*

(a)   impose such terms and conditions as are permitted terms and conditions under Condition 13;

(b)   where it supplies as part of the same transaction or interconnected series of transactions two or more items of telecommunication apparatus for connection to any of the Applicable Systems, offer quantity discounts or more favourable terms and conditions in respect of quantity in relation to such apparatus which it so supplies whether those items of apparatus are of the same or different descriptions;

(c) where it provides by means of or in relation to any of the Applicable Systems and as part of the same transaction or an interconnected series of transactions, two or more telecommunication services which are of the same description or which are so related as to permit economies of scale when they are provided together, offer such quantity discounts or such more favourable terms and conditions in respect of quantity for those services as have been published in accordance with Condition 16.3;

(d) where prior to 1 January 1985 it provides to any person telecommunication services by means of:

(i) a single direct Exchange Line forming part of the public switched telephone network; or

(ii) more than one such Line each terminating on a separate item of Network Termination and Testing Apparatus;

make it a condition of the provision, before that date but not thereafter, of those services that that person should acquire one Instrument supplied, installed and Brought into Service by the Licensee and in respect of which Maintenance Services are provided by the Licensee (the prime instrument) and may require that at all times when any such direct Exchange Line is used for conveying messages to or from the Served Premises occupied by that person the prime instrument is and continues to be connected to that Line by means of apparatus supplied, installed, and Brought into Service by the Licensee and that Maintenance Services are provided in respect of it by the Licensee;

(e) where a telecommunication system is a Limited Maintenance Telecommunication System or contains any item of Limited Maintenance Telecommunication Apparatus impose such reasonable terms and conditions as are necessary in connection with the provision of Maintenance Services in respect of it by the Licensee; or

(f) where the Director consents, impose such other conditions of the kind referred to in paragraph 35.1 as are incidental to the provision of the telecommunication service or the supply of the apparatus requested by the Relevant Person.

35.4 In this Condition:

'Instrument' means either:

(a) where no switching apparatus is connected to the Line, a Telephone; or

(b) where switching apparatus is connected to the Line, that switching apparatus together with a Telephone whether included in that apparatus or not and any other Telephone comprised in such apparatus; and

'Relevant Person' means a person:

(a) who requests that a telecommunication service be provided by means of or in relation to any of the Applicable Systems, or for whom or on whose behalf such a telecommunication service is provided; or

(b) who requests that telecommunication apparatus be supplied or to whom or on whose behalf such apparatus is supplied; or

(c) who requests that any telecommunication system or telecommunication apparatus be connected to any of the Applicable Systems or for whom or on whose behalf such a system or such apparatus is so connected.

Notes

1. Conditions 35.1(a). 35.2 were amended by a licence amendment dated 1 May 1987.

2. Condition 35.1(aa) was inserted by the same licence amendment.
3. This Condition was deleted on 31 December 1996 when the new Condition 18A came into effect.

Condition 36   Prohibition of Certain Exclusive Dealing Arrangements

36.1   The Licensee shall not, except with the written consent of the Director, make the acquisition from any person in the United Kingdom by the Licensee or any of its Wholly Owned Subsidiaries or the installation or servicing by any person in the United Kingdom for it or any such Subsidiary of any telecommunication apparatus of any description conditional upon agreement:

(a)   to supply to the Licensee or to supply or not to supply to any other person apparatus of a different description;

(b)   to provide to the Licensee or to provide or not to provide to any other person any telecommunication service of a different description; or

(c)   to transfer to the Licensee or to any other person any interest in Industrial or Intellectual Property with a view to restricting unreasonably the freedom of the supplier of the apparatus or the provider of the service in question to exploit his Industrial or Intellectual Property in order to confer on the Licensee or some other person an unfair competitive advantage.

36.2   If the Director is satisfied that persons in the United Kingdom, who are not genuinely willing to give to the Licensee or to any of its Wholly Owned Subsidiaries the sole right to supply to customers telecommunication apparatus supplied by those persons, are being so required by the Licensee then the Director may direct the Licensee to comply with the condition in paragraph 36.3.

36.3   The said condition is that the Licensee shall not, except with the written consent of the Director, make the acquisition of telecommunication apparatus, or of telecommunication apparatus specified by the Director or of a description so specified, by the Licensee or any of its Wholly Owned Subsidiaries from any person in the United Kingdom or any such person specified by the Director or such persons of a description specified by the Director conditional upon the agreement of the supplier not to supply to any other person apparatus of the same description as that to be supplied to the Licensee or to a Wholly Owned Subsidiary.

36.4   Notwithstanding paragraph 36.1 or any direction under paragraph 36.2, the Licensee shall be free:

(a)   to agree with any person that that person will supply to the Licensee, or one of its Wholly Owned Subsidiaries, alone telecommunication apparatus of any description which is distinguishable (by any means other than ones which account for a disproportionate share of the cost of that apparatus) by its external appearance, or by any marking or similar attribute, from other apparatus of the same description, and which is or is intended to be thereby associated with the Licensee or that Subsidiary;

(b)   to require that other telecommunication apparatus should be supplied or another telecommunication service should be provided with or in connection with any apparatus or service where the supply of that other apparatus or the provision of that other service is reasonably related to that supply or provision;

(c) to require the transfer to the Licensee or any of its Wholly Owned Subsidiaries of any interest in Industrial or Intellectual Property which the Director agrees is necessary or desirable to facilitate the running of any of the Applicable Systems;

(d) to dispose of any interest in Industrial or Intellectual Property owned by the Licensee or any of its Wholly Owned Subsidiaries free from all encumbrances and restrictions of whatsoever nature arising out of or under this Licence;

(e) to require the transfer to the Licensee or any of its Wholly Owned Subsidiaries by any person of any interest in Industrial or Intellectual Property arising out of any work done in pursuance of any agreement made between the Licensee or any of its Wholly Owned Subsidiaries and that person for any research or development to be carried out by him, unless the Director otherwise directs;

(f) to require the transfer to the Licensee or any of its Wholly Owned Subsidiaries or any other person of any interest in Industrial or Intellectual Property to the extent that that is reasonably necessary for the purpose of enabling the Licensee to secure alternative sources of supply of telecommunication apparatus; or

(g) to require any person who supplies telecommunication apparatus or who provides telecommunication services to enter into an agreement of the kind referred to in paragraph 36.1, 36.2 or 36.3 where the Licensee or any of its Wholly Owned Subsidiaries makes available research, design or development work or where the Licensee or such Subsidiary agrees to finance such work on terms that an agreement of that kind will be entered into.

36.5 In this Condition 'Industrial or Intellectual Property' has the same meaning as in Condition 39.

Condition 37 Requirement to Provide Itemised Information

37.1 If the Licensee provides to any person by means of any part of the Applicable Systems any telecommunication service as part of a transaction involving:

(a) the supply to that person of any telecommunication apparatus; or

(b) the provision to that person of any other telecommunication service (including the Bringing into Service of any apparatus or system) provided otherwise than by means of any of the Applicable Systems;

then it shall specify in any quotation or any invoice relating to that transaction the charge or charges for each such service separately from the charge or charges for apparatus.

37.2 The Licensee shall not be obliged under paragraph 37.1 to specify charges for telecommunication services separately in invoices until 1 July 1987 or it has installed the necessary billing system in the area in which the service to which the invoice relates is provided whichever is the sooner.

37.3 Where the Licensee provides to any person a Relevant Service, paragraph 37.1 shall be deemed to be satisfied in respect of each telecommunication service comprised in that Relevant Service if the Licensee specifies in any quotation or any invoice relating to that Relevant Service the aggregate charge for that Relevant Service.

Notes
1. Condition 37.3 was inserted by a licence amendment dated 1 May 1987.

2.   This Condition was deleted on 31 December 1996 when new Condition 18A came into effect.

Condition 38   Code of Practice on the Confidentiality of Customer Information

38.1   The Licensee shall take all reasonable steps to ensure that those of its employees who are engaged in the Systems Business observe the provisions of a Code of Practice which:
(a)   specifies the persons to whom they may not disclose information about a customer of the Licensee which has been acquired in the course of the Systems Business without the prior consent of that customer;
(b)   regulates the information about any such customer which may be disclosed without his consent; and
(c)   restricts disclosure of information relating to the testing of apparatus referred to in Condition 41.
38.2   The Licensee shall within three months of the date on which this Licence enters into force submit a draft of the Code of Practice to the Director for his approval and if the Licensee and the Director fail to agree on the provisions of the Code they shall be determined by the Director.
38.3   This Condition is without prejudice to the duties at law of the Licensee towards its customers.

Note
See BT's Code of Practice on the Disclosure of Customer Information for Systems Business which has been approved by DGT.

Condition 38A   Code of Practice on the Confidentiality of Customer Information Relating to Supplemental Services Business

38A.1   The Licensee shall take all reasonable steps to ensure that those of its employees who are engaged in the Supplemental Services Business observe the provisions of a Code of Practice which:
(a)   specifies the persons to whom they may not disclose information about a customer of the Licensee or that customer's business which has been acquired in the course of the Licensee's business of providing telecommunication services comprised in Relevant Services without the prior consent of that customer; and
(b)   regulates the information about any such customer or his business which may be disclosed without his consent.
38A.2   The Licensee shall within three months of 30 April 1987 confirm in writing to the Director that it has taken all reasonable steps to ensure that those of its employees who are engaged in the Supplemental Services Business are observing the provisions of a Code of Practice.
38A.3   In this Condition, 'Code of Practice' means:
(a)   any Model Code of Practice issued by the Director; or
(b)   where the Director so agrees, any Code of Practice submitted by the Licensee to the Director.
38A.4   This Condition is without prejudice to the duties at law of the Licensee towards its customers.

38A.5   Notwithstanding anything contained in Condition 38, any incidental amendments to the Code of Practice previously approved by the Director under Condition 38.2 which may be requisite in consequence of the Code of Practice referred to in this Condition may be made by the Licensee without obtaining the Director's approval, but the Licensee shall not otherwise make any amendments to that Code of Practice without the Director's approval.

Notes
1.   Conditions 38A.1–5 were inserted by a licence amendment dated 1 May 1987.
2.   See BT's Code of Practice on the Disclosure of Customer Information for Supplemental Services Business which has been approved by DGT.

Condition 39   Intellectual Property

39.1   Where it appears to the Director that any Relevant Intellectual Property Right has been, is being or is likely to be exercised (whether by the Licensee or by any other person in pursuance of an agreement, arrangement or concerted practice to which the Licensee is a party) so as to prevent:

(*a*)   any telecommunication system or telecommunication apparatus, which may lawfully be connected to any of the Applicable Systems, from being so connected either at all or on reasonable charges, terms and conditions; or

(*b*)   any service, which may lawfully be provided by means of any of the Applicable Systems, from being so provided or obtained either at all or on reasonable charges, terms and conditions;
he may direct the Licensee in writing in accordance with paragraph 39.2 or 39.3.

39.2   Where the exercise of the Relevant Intellectual Property Right prevents a product from being made available either at all or on reasonable charges, terms and conditions to the person wishing to make such a connection or to provide or obtain such a service, the Director may direct the Licensee to take such steps as are within the power of the Licensee and are, in the opinion of the Director, reasonable and necessary in all the circumstances to secure that the product is made available to that person on charges, terms and conditions acceptable to that person or which (in default of agreement) are, in the opinion of the Director, reasonable to enable such connection to be made or such service to be provided or obtained.

39.3   Where paragraph 39.1 applies in circumstances other than those described in paragraph 39.2, the Director may direct the Licensee to take such steps as are within the power of the Licensee and are, in the opinion of the Director, reasonable and necessary in all the circumstances to secure that the person wishing to make such a connection or to provide or obtain such a service is enabled to make use of the Relevant Intellectual Property Right, for the purpose of making the connection or of providing or obtaining the service, upon charges, terms and conditions acceptable to that person or which (in default of agreement) are, in the opinion of the Director, reasonable for such purpose.

39.4   In this Condition:
'Relevant Intellectual Property Right' means any right, which is wholly or partly controlled by a member of the Licensee's Group, in Industrial

320 BRITISH TELECOMMUNICATIONS

or Intellectual Property or is subject to an agreement, an arrangement or concerted practice to which a member of the Licensee's Group is a party; and

'Industrial or Intellectual Property' includes, without prejudice to its generality, patents, designs, know-how and copyright.

39.5 Nothing in this Condition shall require the Licensee to do anything which would contravene the terms of or would result in revocation of a licence or assignment of a Relevant Intellectual Property Right granted or made to a member of the Licensee's Group on or before the date on which this Licence enters into force or which would result in a member of the Licensee's Group incurring any liability under such a licence or assignment.

Note

This condition gives powers to the Director General of Telecommunications to require BT to compulsory licence its intellectual property rights in certain circumstances. See Article 86 of the Treaty of Rome, and the Competition Act 1980. Also see *Volvo* v *Veng* [1988] ECR 6211 and *Magill* joined cases C–241/91P and C242/91E judgment of 6 April 1995.

Condition 40 Prohibition of Non-Statutory Testing Requirements

40.1 Where the Director notifies the Licensee in writing that this Condition applies in circumstances specified or described in the notification, the Licensee shall not in such circumstances (whether in pursuance of any agreement, arrangement, concerted practice or otherwise) make it a condition of any telecommunication system or telecommunication apparatus being connected or kept connected to any of the Applicable Systems or of any telecommunication service being provided by means of any of the Applicable Systems that any such system, apparatus or service shall obtain the approval of, comply with any standard designated by, or pass any test set by, any person other than the Secretary of State or the Director or by a person appointed under section 25 of the Act, except insofar as the Director otherwise agrees.

40.2 Nothing in this Condition shall prevent the Licensee from requiring the passing of any test which the Director agrees is reasonably necessary or desirable for the purpose of determining whether:

(*a*) any telecommunication apparatus or telecommunication system which is, or is to be, connected to any of the Applicable Systems is authorised to be so connected; or

(*b*) notwithstanding such authorisation, the Licensee is obliged to connect it or permit its connection to the Applicable Systems.

Condition 40A Requirement to Provide Means of Access to the Applicable Systems

40A.1 Subject to paragraph 40A.2 the Licensee shall ensure within 12 months from the date on which an OSI Standard is specified by the Director, where the Licensee provides a Relevant Service means of access to which are capable, in whole or in part, of being provided in conformance with that OSI Standard, that the Relevant Applicable System is so run that it provides means of access, which conform to that OSI Standard, to that Relevant Service.

40A.2   Notwithstanding paragraph 40A.1, where the Licensee provides a Relevant Service means of access to which conform to an OSI Standard and that OSI Standard is subsequently replaced by another OSI Standard, the Licensee shall ensure that the Relevant Applicable System is run so as to provide within 3 years means of access to the Relevant Service which conform to that other OSI Standard.

40A.3   If the Director so requests, the Licensee shall furnish to the Director, in such manner and at such times as the Director may request, at any time after the expiry of:

(a)   the period of 90 days beginning on the date on which the Licensee first provides a Relevant Service; or

(b)   the period described in paragraph 40A.1;

whichever is the later, such information as is reasonably necessary to show whether the Relevant Applicable System providing means of access to the Relevant Service adequately conforms to an appropriate OSI Standard and, where means of access do not conform to an appropriate OSI Standard, the reason why those means of access cannot at that time so conform.

40A.4   Where access to a Relevant Service is provided by means which do not conform to an OSI Standard the Licensee shall ensure that access to that Service is provided on terms which are not an undue or unfair inducement to any person who wishes to obtain such access in conformance to an OSI Standard to obtain such access by other means.

40A.5   Nothing done in any manner by the Licensee shall be regarded as undue or unfair inducement if and to the extent that the Licensee is required to do that thing in that manner by or under any provision of this Licence.

40A.6   For the purposes of this Condition, means of access shall be deemed to conform to an OSI Standard when those parts of the means of access to which the OSI Standard applies conform to that OSI Standard.

40A.7   In this Condition:

'OSI Standard' means any standard or rule which supports capabilities described in the International Standards Organisation's—Open Systems Interconnection—Basic Reference Model and which is specified by the Director for the purposes of this Licence and described in a list kept for the purpose by him and made available by him for inspection by the general public, and is not removed by him from that list; and

'Relevant Applicable System' means that part of any of the Applicable Systems (other than a fixed link) which is used for the purpose of providing the Relevant Service concerned, but only to the extent that it is so used.

Notes
1.   Condition 40A.1–7 was inserted by a licence amendment dated 1 May 1987.
2.   This condition was deleted on 31 December 1996 when new Condition 18A came into effect.

Condition 41   Statutory Testing

41.1   If the Licensee carries out any test or assessment of any telecommunication apparatus for any person for the time being appointed under section 25 (1) of the Act, then unless the Director agrees otherwise it shall take all reasonable steps to ensure that no information with respect to any telecommunication apparatus which has been obtained in the course of or for the purpose of any such test or assessment shall be disclosed to any person including the Licensee's employees and agents except:

(a)   with the consent of:

(i)   the Director;

(ii)   the producer or supplier of that apparatus; or

(iii)   the person who requested the Licensee to carry out that test or assessment;

(b)   to the extent necessary to enable the Licensee to carry out any such test or assessment and report on it to the person for whom it was carried out; or

(c)   to the extent necessary for the purpose of managing persons conducting any such test or assessment.

41.2   *No person engaged in any such test or assessment shall (except to the extent agreed by the Director) be answerable in a way which requires disclosure of information of the kind referred to in paragraph 41.1, to anyone engaged in the activities of running telecommunication systems or the production or supply of telecommunication apparatus other than the Licensee's board of directors or a member of it or a person answerable directly to that board or a member of it.*

Notes

1.   See BT's Code of Practice on the Disclosure of Customer Information for Systems Business in Part I of this Handbook.

2.   This Condition was deleted on 31 December 1996 when new Condition 18A came into effect.

Condition 41A   Confidential Information

41A.1   The Licensee shall:

(i)   as soon as it enters into discussions with an Operator with a view to entering into an Agreement with that Operator, offer to enter into a confidentiality agreement (the 'Confidentiality Agreement') with that Operator which contains the minimum provisions specified in paragraph 41A.2; and

(ii)   as soon as it offers to enter into an Agreement, offer to include such minimum provisions in that Agreement.

41A.2   The minimum provisions referred to in paragraph 41A.1 are provisions which achieve the following objectives:

(*a*)   that each Party keeps (and uses its reasonable endeavours to ensure that its officers, employees, servants, agents, professional advisers and Associates keep) all Confidential Information relating to the other Party confidential, takes all practicable steps to prevent that Confidential Information from being disclosed or made public to any third party, and uses that Confidential Information solely for the purposes for which it was disclosed;

(*b*)   that each Party exercises no lesser degree of care of the Confidential Information relating to the other Party than would a reasonable person with the knowledge of the confidential nature of that Confidential Information, and exercises no lesser degree of care or security in relation to that Confidential Information than it applies to its own Confidential Information which is of an equivalent nature;

(*c*)   that each Party restricts disclosure of Confidential Information relating to the other Party solely to those persons to whom disclosure is necessary and limits use of that Confidential Information to the purpose for which it was disclosed; and

(*d*)   that neither Party shall be in breach of the Confidentiality Agreement or Agreement, as the case may be, to the extent that disclosure of Confidential Information relating to the other Party is:

(i)   authorised in writing by that other Party, and disclosure is within the scope of that authority;

(ii)   made to a contractor, Associate or agent subject to the contractor, Associate or agent undertaking to comply with obligations of confidence equivalent to those contained in the Confidentiality Agreement or Agreement, as the case may be;

(iii)   made to an Emergency Organisation in connection with an Emergency; or

(iv)   properly made pursuant to this Licence or the relevant Operator's Licence or a statutory or other regulatory obligation (including, without limitation, any obligation imposed by the rules of any recognised stock exchange) or pursuant to any order of a competent court or tribunal.

41A.3   An offer pursuant to paragraph 41A.1 (i) or (ii) ('a relevant offer') shall not be conditional on the acceptance by the Operator of the inclusion in that Confidentiality Agreement or Agreement, as the case may be, of any other terms and conditions whether relating to Confidential Information or otherwise. For the avoidance of doubt, it is hereby declared that provided the Licensee has made a relevant offer, the Licensee shall be entitled to agree terms in a Confidentiality Agreement or Agreement, as the case may be, which are additional to, or differ from, the terms of the relevant offer.

41A.4   In this Condition:

'Agreement' means any agreement entered into between the Licensee and the Operator under Condition 13 for the provision of one or more Standard Services;

'Associate' has the meaning given to it in Condition 50;

'Confidential Information' means any information, in whatever form, which, in the case of written or electronic information, is clearly designated as confidential, and which, in the case of information disclosed orally, is identified at the time of disclosure as being confidential or is by its nature confidential, but excluding any information which:

(a)   enters the public domain otherwise than by reason of breach of the relevant Confidentiality Agreement or Agreement, as the case may be;

(b)   is previously known to the relevant one of the Licensee or the Operator at the time of its receipt;

(c)   is independently generated or discovered at any time by the relevant one of the Licensee or the Operator; or

(d)   is subsequently received from a third party without any restriction on disclosure;

'Operator' has the meaning given to it in Condition 16B;

'Interested Parties' has the meaning given to it in Condition 16B; and

'Party' means a party to an Agreement or a Confidentiality Agreement.

Note
Conditions 41A.1–4 were inserted by a licence amendment dated 31 March 1995.

Condition 42   Limitations on Integrated Wiring Situated on Served Premises

42.1   The Licensee shall not after 31 December 1985 except:

(a)   in accordance with guidelines determined by the Director; or

(b)   in accordance with a contract or arrangement made on or before that date; or

(c)   where the structure in which the line is to be installed has been designed before that date in a way which envisages the installation of lines otherwise than in accordance with this paragraph; or

(d)   where the Director agrees;

install on any Served Premises any line comprised or to be comprised in any of the Applicable Systems in such a manner that relevant operations (within the meaning of section 20 of the Act) cannot be carried out in relation to wires or cables comprised in any other system (whether because that line is installed within a shared casing or coating or otherwise) situated on the same Served Premises independently of any such operations carried out in relation to any of the Applicable Systems on those Premises.

42.2   Subject to any guidelines determined by the Director for the purpose, where the Licensee has at any time installed any apparatus in a manner which would, if it had been installed at a time when paragraph 42.1 was in force, have contravened paragraph 42.1, it shall (except if the Director agrees otherwise) if requested by the person occupying the Served Premises in question who wishes the other system to be run by a person other than the Licensee and to whom the Licensee supplies telecommunication services by means of any of the Applicable Systems so installed install such additional apparatus comprised in the Applicable Systems as will permit relevant operations to be carried out in relation to so much of the previously installed apparatus as does not form a part of any Applicable System by such a person.

42.3   Paragraph 42.2 shall take effect on 31 March 1985 or such other date as the Director may determine.

42.4   In this Condition 'line' has the same meaning as in Condition 43.3 (a).

Note

This Condition was deleted on 31 December 1996 when new Condition 18A came into effect.

Condition 43   Wiring etc. Not Forming Part of the Applicable Systems

43.1   The Licensee shall make any telecommunication apparatus to which this Condition applies but which is not part of any of the Applicable Systems available to any person ('the User') wishing to use it in the running of any telecommunication system:

(a)   in the case where the Licensee retains ownership or control of that apparatus, upon charges, terms and conditions no less favourable to the user than would apply for the use of the apparatus if:

(i)   the Licensee ran the system in which it is comprised;

(ii)   the Licensee or any of its Wholly Owned Subsidiaries provided Maintenance Services in respect of such system; or

(iii)   the Licensee or any of its Wholly Owned Subsidiaries had supplied all or any of the other telecommunication apparatus so comprised; or

(b)   in the case where the Licensee does not retain ownership or control of that apparatus, at a reasonable capital charge having regard to the charges,

terms and conditions which would have applied if it had retained ownership or control of that apparatus;
but, if it is impossible to establish a reasonable estimate of the charges, terms and conditions in accordance with sub-paragraph (a) or (b), on such reasonable charges, terms and conditions as may be agreed between the Licensee and the User.

43.2   The Licensee shall on reasonable charges, terms and conditions permit the User of any telecommunications apparatus to which this Condition applies and which remains in the Licensee's ownership or control to carry out, or have carried out on his behalf, any operation in relation to it which is reasonably necessary to enable him to use it for the purpose of running the telecommunication system in which it is comprised; but this paragraph shall not apply to any apparatus which is installed together with apparatus comprised in the Applicable Systems in such a manner that Maintenance Services cannot be carried out in relation to it independently of such operations carried out in relation to the Applicable Systems (whether because it is installed in a shared casing or coating or otherwise).

43.3   The telecommunication apparatus to which this Condition applies is:

(a)   any line, that is to say, any wire, cable, tube, pipe or other similar thing (including its casing or coating) which is designed or adapted for use in connection with the running of a telecommunication system together with any plug, socket or any other connecting apparatus; and

(b)   any structure, pole or other thing in, on, by or from which any such line is installed, supported, carried or suspended:
installed on premises occupied by the User.

Condition 44   Limitations on Certain Maintenance Arrangements

44.1   If any Limited Maintenance Telecommunication System or Limited Maintenance Telecommunication Apparatus is or is to be supplied by the Licensee or any of its Wholly Owned Subsidiaries it shall take all reasonable steps to ensure that customers are notified that the Licensee will provide Maintenance Services at charges and on terms and conditions on the same basis irrespective of who supplies the System or Apparatus.

44.2   Except insofar as the Director may otherwise agree in writing and without prejudice to Condition 37, the Licensee shall in respect of any Limited Maintenance Telecommunication System or any Limited Maintenance Telecommunication Apparatus which the Licensee is obliged under Condition 4 to maintain:

(a)   publish in the manner and at the time specified in Condition 16.3 a notice specifying, or specifying the method that is to be adopted for determining, the charges and other terms and conditions on which it offers to provide Maintenance Services in relation to each description of it separately identifying the charges for Pre-Maintenance Inspection; and

(b)   where it provides Maintenance Services in respect of any such System or Apparatus, supply those Services at the charges and on the other terms and conditions so published and not depart therefrom.

44.3   Nothing in this Condition prevents the Licensee or any of its Wholly Owned Subsidiaries from reimbursing a person to whom any telecommunication system or apparatus is supplied by it for the charges for any Maintenance Services which the Licensee or such Subsidiary is obliged, or reasonably believes that it is obliged, to provide in its capacity as supplier of that system or apparatus, including work undertaken pursuant to or arising out of the contract for its supply, notwithstanding that it does not provide such reimbursement to a person to whom a system or apparatus is supplied by another person.

Note
This Condition was deleted on 31 December 1996 when new Condition 18A came into effect.

Condition 45   Connection Arrangements

45.1   Except with the consent of the Director the Licensee shall not connect nor permit to be connected any Relevant Terminal Apparatus to any of the Applicable Systems on Served Premises except by means of Network Termination and Testing Apparatus.

Condition 46   Private Circuits

46.1   Following the application of any public telecommunications operator for Private Circuits of a description which that operator is authorised by a licence to provide the Licensee shall, in accordance with Condition 1, provide Private Circuits to that operator, unless the Director is satisfied:
  (*a*)   as to the matters described in Condition 1.1; or
  (*b*)   that the public telecommunications operator in question would be unduly reliant upon services provided by the Licensee as a means of satisfying his obligations under his licence;
and Condition 13 shall not apply in respect of any such application as is mentioned in this paragraph.

46.2   Nothing in this Condition shall require the Licensee to:
  (*a*)   deal with applications from public telecommunications operators in priority to other applications or otherwise discriminate in favour of public telecommunications operators; or
  (*b*)   act in a way which is likely seriously to reduce the quality of service provided by the Licensee to the generality of its customers, in respect of any telecommunication service.

Notes
1.   Conditions 46.1–3 were deleted and replaced by a licence amendment dated 24 September 1991.
2.   Condition 46.3 (definitions of 'Associate' and 'Basic Services') was inserted by a licence amendment dated 1 May 1987.
3.   Conditions 46.4–6 were inserted by a licence amendment dated 24 September 1991.
4.   Conditions 46.2–5 were deleted by a licence amendment dated 31 October 1996 and Condition 46.6 was renumbered 46.2.

Condition 46A   Relevant Private Circuits

46A.1   The Licensee shall provide a minimum set of Relevant Private Circuits in accordance with Schedule 2 to the Telecommunications (Leased Lines) Regulations 1993. The Licensee must ensure, if it provides other

Relevant Private Circuits beyond the minimum set, that such provision does not impede the provision of the minimum set.

46A.2   The Licensee shall not terminate an existing offering of a Relevant Private Circuit unless:

(a)   the offering has continued for a reasonable period of time; and

(b)   the Licensee has consulted with the users affected.

Without prejudice to any other remedy or right of appeal which the user may have in law or pursuant to contract or these conditions, where the user does not agree with the termination date as envisaged by the Licensee, he may bring the case before the Director.

46A.3   The Licensee shall not take for reasons of the alleged failure of the user of a Relevant Private Circuit to comply with the usage conditions any measure (including, without prejudice to the generality of the foregoing, the refusal to provide a Relevant Private Circuit, the interruption of the provision of Relevant Private Circuits or the reduction of the availability of Relevant Private Circuit features) unless:

(a)   the measure is a specified measure authorised by the Director in the case of a defined infringement of usage conditions; or

(b)   the Licensee has been notified pursuant to regulation 7 (3) of the Telecommunications (Leased Lines) Regulations 1993 that the Director consents to the taking of the measure.

46A.4   The Licensee shall ensure that tariffs for Relevant Private Circuits follow the basic principles of cost orientation and transparency in accordance with the following rules:

(a)   tariffs for Relevant Private Circuits shall be independent of the type of application which the users of the Relevant Private Circuits implement;

(b)   tariffs for Relevant Private Circuits shall normally contain the following elements:

(i)   an initial connection charge; and

(ii)   a periodic rental charge, that is to say, a flat-rate element;

and when other tariff elements are applied, these must be transparent and based on objective criteria;

(c)   tariffs for Relevant Private Circuits apply to the facilities provided between Network Termination Points at which the user has access to the Relevant Private Circuits.

For Relevant Private Circuits provided by more than one telecommunications organisation, half-circuit tariffs, that is to say, from one Network Termination Point to a hypothetical mid-circuit point, can be applied.

46A.5   The Licensee shall formulate and put in practice, by 31st December 1993 at the latest, a cost accounting system suitable for the implementation of paragraph 46A.4. Without prejudice to the generality of the foregoing, that system shall include the following elements:

(a)   the cost of Relevant Private Circuits shall in particular include the direct costs incurred by the Licensee for setting up, operating and maintaining them, and for marketing and billing them; and

(b)   common costs, that is to say, costs which can neither be directly assigned to Relevant Private Circuits nor to other activities, are allocated as follows:

(i)   whenever possible, common cost categories shall be allocated based upon direct analysis of the origin of the costs themselves;

(ii)   when direct analysis is not possible, common cost categories shall be allocated based upon an indirect linkage to another cost category or group of cost categories for which a direct assignment or allocation is possible, and such indirect linkage shall be based on comparable cost structures;

(iii)   when neither direct nor indirect measures of cost allocation can be found, the cost category shall be allocated based upon a general allocator computed by using the ratio of all expenses directly or indirectly assigned or allocated, on the one hand, to Relevant Private Circuits and, on the other hand, to other services.

After 31st December 1993, other cost accounting systems may be applied only if they are suitable for the implementation of paragraph 46A.4 and have as such been approved by the Director for application by the Licensee.

Note
Condition 46A was inserted by the Leased Lines Regulations.

Condition 47   Prohibition of Exclusive Dealing in International Services

47.1   The Licensee shall not enter into any agreement or arrangement with any person running an Authorised Overseas System on terms or conditions which unfairly preclude or restrict the provision by another public telecommunications operator of International Connection Services.

47.2   The Licensee shall not unreasonably exclude any other public telecommunications operator who is authorised by a Licence to connect his system to another telecommunication system situated outside the United Kingdom so as to convey Messages to that other system from a reasonable opportunity to participate in any international arrangements into which it proposes to enter after the date on which this Licence enters into force for the installation and operation of any submarine cable linking any of the Applicable Systems to any telecommunication system outside the United Kingdom.

Condition 48   Other Arrangements for International Services

48.1   Subject to paragraph 48.2 the Licensee shall consult from time to time with the Director and with other persons authorised to provide International Connection Services with a view to agreeing with them a Code of Practice in respect of international accounting arrangements which are to apply in respect of such Services provided by the Licensee and those persons and shall abide by the terms of that Code of Practice as agreed for the time being. If no such Code of Practice is agreed on 30 September 1984 or at any time thereafter its terms shall be such as the Director may determine.

48.2   Where the Director is of the opinion that the Licensee proposes to enter into or vary an agreement or arrangement with a person running a telecommunication system outside the United Kingdom with a view to the provision of International Connection Services, being an agreement or arrangement establishing international accounting methods, rates and divisions, which would prejudice the interests of providers and users of International Connection Services in the United Kingdom, and where the Director, within 28 days of the matter being brought to his notice, and after consultation with the Licensee and any other public telecommunications operator authorised to provide such Services, and after taking account of the provisions of the Code of Practice, directs the Licensee that it should not enter into or so vary that agreement or arrangement, then the Licensee shall refrain from doing so.

Note
A Code of Practice was introduced on 4 March 1987 as a result of a determination by DGT.

Condition 49 Pre-Notification of Joint Ventures

49.1 Unless the Director otherwise agrees the Licensee shall notify the Director not later than 30 days before the taking effect of any of the agreements or arrangements to which this Condition applies giving particulars of those agreements or arrangements.

49.2 Those agreements and arrangements are:

(a) an agreement with any person for the establishment or control of any body corporate for the purpose of:

(i) the running of a telecommunication system which requires a Licence; or

(ii) providing telecommunication services in the United Kingdom which necessarily involve the running of such a system; or

(iii) the production of telecommunication apparatus for supply in the United Kingdom where that production would lead to a monopoly situation which would not otherwise exist in relation to the supply of telecommunication apparatus of any description in the United Kingdom;

(b) an agreement for the establishment of a partnership for any of those purposes and in those circumstances;

(c) any other agreement or arrangement in the nature of a joint venture for the purpose of running a telecommunication system which requires a Licence or for the purpose of providing telecommunication services in the United Kingdom which necessarily involve the running of such a system.

49.3 Paragraphs 49.2 (a) and (b) apply in relation to an agreement or arrangement for the establishment or control of any body corporate or partnership where the Licensee has or is to have not less than 20 per cent. of the voting power in any organ controlling that body.

49.4 For the purposes of this Condition a monopoly situation shall be taken to exist where such a situation would be taken to exist for the purpose of any of the provisions of section 6 of the Fair Trading Act 1973 but with the substitution of the words 'one fifth' for the words 'one quarter' whenever they appear in that section.

49.5 In any case where circumstances beyond the Licensee's control require him to enter into an agreement or arrangement, if he is to enter into it at all, without having made a notification in accordance with paragraph 49.1 he shall notify the Director as soon as reasonably practicable but otherwise in accordance with the provisions of this Condition.

Note
This Condition was deleted on 31 December 1996 when new Condition 18A came into effect.

Condition 50   Associates

50.1   Without prejudice to the Licensee's obligations under these Conditions in respect, in particular, of anything done on its behalf, where:

(*a*)   any Associate of the Licensee does anything which the Licensee is prohibited from doing under these Conditions or fails to do anything which the Licensee is in the circumstances required to do; and

(*b*)   the Director is of the opinion:

(i)   that in consequence the Licensee is seeking to or is in a material and substantial way avoiding obligations which would apply under these Conditions if the thing had been done or not done by the Licensee; and

(ii)   that, having regard to the duties imposed on him by section 3 of the Act he ought to make a direction under this Condition;

then the Licensee shall take such reasonable steps to ensure that the Associate ceases to do that thing or otherwise to remedy the matter as the Director directs him to take.

50.2   Where these Conditions apply in respect of the Applicable Systems they do not apply in respect of any other telecommunication system, whether run by the Licensee or another.

50.3   Where any person becomes an Associate of the Licensee, then the Licensee shall not be subject to paragraph 50.1 before that is reasonably practicable but shall be so not later than one year after that person becomes such an Associate or such later date as the Director may determine.

50.4   This Condition shall not apply to any particular Associate if and to the extent that the Director so determines.

50.5   For the purposes of this Condition a person is an Associate of the Licensee if he is a Subsidiary of, or another body corporate controlled by, it.

Condition 51   Payment of Fees

51.1   The Licensee shall pay the following amounts to the Secretary of State at the times stated:

(*a*)   on the grant of this Licence the sum of £2.75 million; and

(*b*)   on 1 April 1985 and annually thereafter a renewal fee which shall represent a fair proportion, to be determined each year by the Director according to a method that has been disclosed to the Licensee, of the estimated costs to be incurred in that fiscal year by the Director in the regulation and enforcement of telecommunication licences and in the exercise of his other functions under the Act; and

(*c*)   where the Director so determines, on 1 January 1988 and annually thereafter a special fee which shall represent a fair proportion, to be determined each year by the Director according to a method that has been disclosed to the Licensee, of that amount, if any, by which the aggregate of:

(i)   the costs estimated to have been already incurred in that fiscal year by the director in the regulation and enforcement of telecommunication licences and in the exercise of his other functions under the Act; and

(ii)   the costs estimated to have been already incurred in that fiscal year by the Monopolies and Mergers Commission following licence modification references under section 13 of the Act; and

(iii)   the estimated costs to be incurred in the remainder of that fiscal year:

(A)   by the Director in the regulation and enforcement of telecommunication licences and in the exercise of his other functions under the Act; and

(B)   by the Monopolies and Mergers Commission following licence modification references under section 13 of the Act;

exceeds the renewal fee for that year;

save always that the aggregate of the renewal fee and the special fee for any fiscal year shall not exceed 0.08 per cent. of the annual turnover of the Licensee's Systems Business in the financial year before the last complete financial year of the Licensee before the renewal fee is payable.

Note

Condition 51.1 was inserted by a licence amendment dated 23 March 1987.

Condition 52   Requirement to Furnish Information to the Director

52.1   The Licensee shall furnish to the Director, in such manner and at such times as the Director may request, such documents, accounts, estimates, returns or other information and procure and furnish to him such reports as he may reasonably require for the purpose of exercising the functions assigned or transferred to him by or under Parts II and III of the Act.

52.2   In making any such request the Director shall ensure that no undue burden is imposed on the Licensee in procuring and furnishing such information and, in particular, that the Licensee is not required to procure or furnish a report which would not normally be available to it unless the Director considers the particular report essential to enable him to exercise his functions.

Notes

1.   Conditions 52.3 and 4 were deleted by a licence amendment dated 31 March 1995.

2.   Condition 52.3, referred to in Condition 13.5A.8 provides as follows:

'52.3   Without prejudice to the generality of paragraph 52.1 the Licensee shall furnish to the Director within 6 months of its financial year end, an FRBS statement which, unless otherwise agreed by the Director, shall be in a form substantially similar to that previously supplied to the Director. For the FRBS statement in respect of the financial year ending on 31 March 92 and thereafter the Licensee shall procure a report by the Licensee's auditor stating whether in his opinion the methods of allocation of costs, assets and liabilities are reasonable and whether the statement has been properly prepared applying those methods and is adequate for the purposes specified in paragraph 52.4 and Condition 13.5A.

52.4   In this Condition 'FRBS statement' means an accounting statement the purposes of which are to set out and fairly present the cost (including capital costs), revenue and financial position of the Licensee's services including a reasonable assessment of the assets employed in and liabilities attributable to those services. The level of desegregation as between services specified in, and in relation to the financial information contained in, the statement shall be substantially similar to that contained in the figures supplied to the Director for the financial year ended 31 March 1990 or such other level as the Licensee and the Director may agree from time to time.'

Condition 53   Exceptions and Limitations on Obligations in Schedule I

53.1   Unless the context otherwise requires and subject to paragraph 53.12, the Licensee's obligations under these Conditions have effect subject to the following exceptions and limitations.

53.2   The Licensee is not obliged to do anything which is not practicable.

53.3   [Subject to paragraph 53.3A] the Licensee shall not be held to have failed to comply with an obligation imposed upon it by or under these Conditions if and to the extent that the Licensee is prevented from complying with that obligation by any physical, topographical or other natural obstacle, by the malfunction or failure of any apparatus or equipment, by the act of any national authority, Local Authority or international organisation or as the result of fire, flood, explosion, accident, Emergency, riot or war.

[53.3A   In relation to Relevant Private Circuits, the Licensee shall not be held to have failed to comply with these Conditions if the Licensee takes the following measures in order to safeguard the security of network operations during the period when an emergency situation prevails:

(*a*)   the interruption of the service;

(*b*)   the limitation of service features; or

(*c*)   the denial of access to the service;

provided that the following conditions are satisfied:

(i)   the Licensee makes every reasonable endeavour to ensure that service is maintained to all users; and

(ii)   the Licensee takes as soon as reasonably possible all reasonable steps to notify the users and the Director of the beginning and the end of the emergency as well as the nature and extent of temporary service restrictions; and in this paragraph, an emergency situation means an exceptional case of force majeure, which, without prejudice to the generality thereof, includes extreme weather, flood, lightning or fire, industrial action or lockouts, war, military operations, or civil disorder.]

53.4   The obligation to provide any voice telephony service shall not apply:

(*a*)   where there is no reasonable demand for it;

(*b*)   where provision of the service requested would expose any person engaged in its provision to undue risk to health or safety;

(*c*)   where the Licensee is unable to obtain (either because it has not been developed or for some other reason beyond the Licensee's control) anything necessary to provide a service of the quality or standard required by the person who requests the provision of the service and, in the event of dispute, the Director's decision as to whether anything is necessary shall be final;

(*d*)   where the person to whom the Licensee would otherwise be under an obligation to provide any service requests a service at a place in which the apparatus necessary to provide that service in that area has not been installed (or in which the installation of such apparatus has not been completed) or as the case may be such apparatus has not been adapted or modified to make it capable of providing the service of the kind requested or the trained manpower necessary to provide the service is not available in that area, provided that in every case where the Licensee declines to provide a service to which this sub-paragraph relates it shall have published, or furnished to the Director, or within 28 days (or such longer period as the Director considers reasonable) following receipt by it of the request that service be provided shall have furnished to the Director, proposals for:

(i)   progressively installing or completing the installation or for the adaptation or the modification of the apparatus; or

(ii)   the allocation of the trained manpower necessary for the provision of that service in that area and the Director has not determined that those proposals are unreasonable or are not being effectively carried out; or

(e)   where in the opinion of the Director it is not reasonably practicable in all the circumstances for the Licensee to provide the service requested at the time or place demanded.

53.5   The obligation to provide any telecommunication service other than a voice telephony service shall not apply:

(a)   where any of the circumstances described in paragraph 53.4 (a) to (e) apply; or

(b)   where the person to whom the Licensee would otherwise be under an obligation to provide any service requests a service at a place in an area in which the demand or the prospective demand for the service is not sufficient, having regard to the revenue likely to be earned from the provision of the service in that area, to meet all the costs reasonably to be incurred by the Licensee in providing the service there, including:

(i)   the cost of apparatus necessary for the provision of the service there;

(ii)   the cost of installing, maintaining and operating such apparatus for the purpose of providing the service there; and

(iii)   the cost of the trained manpower necessary to provide the service there.

53.5A   (a)   The obligation to provide means of access to a Relevant Service in conformance with an OSI Standard shall not apply where:

(i)   the Licensee is unable to obtain (either because it has not been developed or for some other reason beyond the Licensee's control) anything necessary to provide such means of access; or

(ii)   the Licensee is unable, for any reason beyond its control, to install apparatus necessary to provide such means of access or to adapt or modify that apparatus for the purpose; or

(iii)   the Director so agrees, having regard to the extent to which the provision of the means of access would not for the time being promote the interests of consumers of telecommunication services provided by the Licensee (including consumers of such services where the Licensee is not obliged to provide means of access which conform to an OSI Standard to those services).

(b)   The exception in sub-paragraph 53.5A (a) (ii) shall not apply where the Licensee has declined to provide means of access to a Relevant Service for any reason given in that sub-paragraph unless:

(i)   within 28 days of first receiving a request to provide such means of access, (or such longer period as the Director considers reasonable) it submits proposals for installing, adapting or modifying the apparatus so as to provide such means of access within a reasonable time; and

(ii)   those proposals are reasonable and are being effectively carried out.

[53.5B Nothing in these conditions shall prevent the Licensee, where it considers it unreasonable to provide a Relevant Private Circuit in response to a particular request under its tariffs and supply conditions published pursuant to paragraph 16.3B, from varying those conditions in that case with the consent of the Director.]

53.6 The Licensee shall not be obliged to supply, connect, or to keep connected to any of the Applicable Systems, or to permit to be so connected or kept connected any telecommunication system or telecommunication apparatus or to provide telecommunication services if the person to or for whom that is or is to be done:

(a) has not entered or will not enter into a contract for the purpose with the Licensee for reasons other than the unreasonable refusal of the Licensee to agree terms for the purpose but this paragraph does not apply in a case where the Director is satisfied that:

(i) the Licensee has not published standard terms and conditions which it proposes to apply for the purpose in question, or the transaction is not fit to be governed by such terms and conditions; and

(ii) the Licensee has unreasonably refused to agree terms and conditions for the purpose;

(b) is, or in the Director's opinion has given reasonable cause to believe that he may become:

(i) in breach of a contract with the Licensee for the provision of telecommunication services or for the supply of telecommunication apparatus or a telecommunication system supplied by the Licensee; or

(ii) in default in regard to any debt or liability owed to the Licensee in respect of any such contract;

(c) is using, or permitting the use of, apparatus so supplied for any illegal purpose or has done so in the past and is likely to do so again; or

(d) has obtained, or attempted to obtain, any telecommunication apparatus or telecommunication service from the Licensee by corrupt, dishonest or illegal means at any time.

53.7 Nothing in these Conditions shall prevent the Licensee from withdrawing from, or declining to provide to, any person any telecommunication service which the Licensee has notified the Director that it is providing in a limited area, or to a limited class of customers, for the purpose of evaluating the technical feasibility of, or the commercial prospects for, that service.

53.8 Nothing in these Conditions shall require the Licensee to supply any telecommunication apparatus or to provide any telecommunication service, or to supply or to provide any telecommunication apparatus or service of any particular class or description, if he supplies or provides instead apparatus or a service, or apparatus or a service of a class or description, which satisfies the purposes of that requirement at least to the same extent.

53.9 This Condition shall apply without prejudice to any limitation or qualification of the requirements imposed by or under any other Condition.

53.10 Nothing in these Conditions shall prevent the Licensee from withdrawing or restricting any service requiring the attendance of any of its employees:

(a) on Bank Holidays and other public or statutory holidays (but so that, where any such holiday is observed only in a part of the Licensed Area, this sub-paragraph shall apply in respect of that holiday to that part only); or (*b*) on any other day on which the Director determines it is unreasonable to require the relevant employees of the Licensee to attend for the purpose of providing those services.

53.11 The Licensee shall be relieved of any obligation under these Conditions by virtue of a combination of any of the events and circumstances set out in the preceding paragraphs of this Condition, insofar as those paragraphs apply to the obligation in question; or a combination of any such events and circumstances and any limitation or exception contained in the Condition in question.

53.12 This Condition does not apply to Conditions 13, 15.6, 17, 18A, 19, 22, 24, 24A, 28, 29.1, 30.1, 35, 36, 38.1, 38A.1, 39, 40, [46A.3 to 46A.5] and 47 and:

(i) only paragraphs 53.1, 53.2, 53.3, 53.9 and 53.11 apply to Conditions 16, 16B, 17B, 17C, 18, 20, 20B, 21, 23, 24F, 25, 26, 27, 29.2, 30.2 and 30.3, 31, 32, 37, 38.2, 41, 41A, 44, 45, 48, 49, 51 and 52;

(ii) only paragraphs 53.1, 53.6 (a), 53.9 and 53.11 apply to Condition 9.2;

(iii) only paragraphs 53.1, 53.2, 53.3, 53.6, 53.9 and 53.11 apply to Conditions 11.6 and 34;

(iv) only paragraphs 53.1, 53.2, 53.3, 53.9 and 53.11 apply to Condition 50;

(ivA) only paragraphs 53.1, 53.2, 53.3, 53.5A, 53.9 and 53.11 apply to Condition 40A;

(v) only paragraphs 53.1, 53.2, 53.3, 53.4 (b), 53.6 (a), 53.9 and 53.11 apply to Conditions 6 and 7; and

(vi) only paragraphs 53.1, 53.2, 53.3, 53.4 (b), 53.9 and 53.11 apply to Conditions 8, 11 (except 11.6) and 33;

but paragraphs 53.4 (a), 53.4 (d) and 53.5 (b) do not apply to Condition 10 and paragraphs 53.6 and 53.8 do not apply to Condition 9.1.

53.13 Notwithstanding paragraph 53.12, Conditions 22, 41 and 43 shall not come into operation until 1 November 1984; and Conditions 16.1 (a) (v) and 17.1 (e) and 44 shall not come into operation until 1 October 1984.

Notes

1. The words in square brackets were inserted by the Leased Lines Regulations.

2. Condition 53.5A was inserted by a licence amendment dated 1 May 1987. Conditions 53.12 (header) was amended by the same licence amendment and then deleted and replaced by a licence amendment dated 24 September 1991 and subsequently amended by the above Leased Lines Regulations and a licence amendment dated 31 October 1996.

3. Condition 53.12(i) was amended by a licence amendment dated 31 March 1995.

4. Condition 53.12(ivA) was inserted by a licence amendment dated 1 May 1987.

SCHEDULE 2

REVOCATION

1 Notwithstanding paragraph 3 of the Licence the Secretary of State may at any time revoke this Licence by 30 days notice in writing given to the Licensee at its registered office in any of the following circumstances:

(*a*) if the Licensee agrees in writing with the Secretary of State that this Licence should be revoked;

(*b*) if any amount payable under Condition 51 of Schedule 1 is unpaid 30 days after it becomes due and remains unpaid for a period of 14 days after the Secretary of State notifies the Licensee that the payment is overdue, such notification not to be given earlier than the sixteenth day after the day on which the payment became due;

(*c*) if the Licensee fails to comply with a final order (within the meaning of section 16 of the Act) or a provisional order (within the meaning of that section) which has been confirmed under that section and that order is not subject to proceedings for review and such failure is not rectified within 3 months after the Secretary of State has given notice in writing of such failure to the Licensee such notice being given after the conclusion of any such proceedings;

(*d*) if, pursuant to section 60 of the Act the property, rights and liabilities of the Licensee become property rights and liabilities of a company nominated for the purposes of that section by the Secretary of State ('the Successor Company') and the Successor Company;

(i) is unable to pay its debts (within the meaning of section 223 of the Companies Act 1948), convenes any meeting with its creditors generally with a view to the general readjustment or re-scheduling of its indebtedness or makes a general assignment for the benefit of its creditors generally;

(ii) enters into receivership or liquidation;

(iii) ceases to carry on its business; or

(*e*) if the Successor Company or any other person takes any action for voluntary winding-up or dissolution of the Successor Company, or if the Successor Company enters into any scheme of arrangement (other than in any such case for the purpose of reconstruction or amalgamation upon terms and within such period as may previously have been approved in writing by the Secretary of State) or if a receiver, trustee or similar Officer of the Successor Company, or of all or any material part of the revenues and assets of it, is appointed, or if any order is made for the compulsory winding-up or dissolution of it.

2 For the purposes of sub-paragraph (1) (d) (i) of this Schedule, in construing the terms of paragraph (a) of section 223 of the Companies Act 1948 the figure of '£200' therein shall be deemed to be replaced by '£250,000' or such higher figure as the Director may determine and the said paragraph (a) shall not apply if the demand therein referred to is being contested in good faith by the Successor Company with recourse to all appropriate measures and procedures, whether legal or otherwise, or if the demand is satisfied prior to the expiry of the notice from the Secretary of State.

3 The Interpretation Act 1978 shall apply for the purpose of interpreting this Schedule as if it were an Act of Parliament.

4 Any word or expression used in this Schedule shall unless the context otherwise requires have the same meaning as it has in the Act.

SCHEDULE 3

AUTHORISATION TO CONNECT OTHER SYSTEMS AND APPARATUS TO THE APPLICABLE SYSTEMS AND TO PROVIDE TELECOMMUNICATION SERVICES BY MEANS OF THE APPLICABLE SYSTEMS

1   Nothing in this Licence removes any need to obtain any other licence that may be required under any other enactment but, subject to that limitation, this Licence authorises:

(*a*)   the connection to any Applicable System of:

(i)   any other Applicable System;

(ii)   any telecommunication system outside the United Kingdom except a telecommunication system which the Secretary of State has notified the Licensee should not, or as the case may be should cease to, be connected to the Applicable System;

(iii)   any telecommunication system run by the Crown;

(iv)   any telecommunication system in the Licensed Area the Licence for which authorises it to be connected to one or more of the Applicable Systems;

(v)   any telecommunication system in the Hull Area situated in an aircraft, seagoing vessel or hovercraft or run by the Kingston upon Hull City Council or by another public telecommunications operator;

(vi)   any telecommunication system of the kind mentioned in section 6 (1) of the Act;

(vii)   telecommunication apparatus of every description which is comprised in an Applicable System;

(viii)   telecommunication apparatus comprised in a telecommunication system mentioned in sub-paragraphs (i) to (vi) above;

(ix)   any telecommunication apparatus not comprised in any of the Applicable Systems which is for the time being approved for connection to any of the Applicable Systems in accordance with section 22 of the Act; and

(x)   any hearing aid;

(*b*)   the provision by means of the Applicable Systems of telecommunication services consisting in:

(i)   the conveyance (not including switching) of Messages (not including cable programme services sent under a licence granted under section 58 of the Act) and switching incidental to such conveyance; and

(ii)   directory information services;

but not any Land Mobile Radio Service.

2   In this Schedule:

(*a*)   'Hull Area' has the meaning given to it in Annex A;

(*b*)   'Land Mobile Radio Service' means any telecommunication service provided by wireless telegraphy for reception by means of apparatus which is or is to be used while in motion, but does not include services of a kind provided under Conditions 8 and 12 of Schedule 1;

(*c*)   'Licensed Area' means the United Kingdom other than the area in which the City of Kingston upon Hull is licensed to run telecommunication systems under a Licence coming into force on the date on which this Licence enters into force;

(*d*) 'Message' means anything falling within paragraphs (a) to (d) of section 4 (1) of the Act;

(*e*) 'seagoing vessel' includes any floating structure for the exploration for, or exploitation of, oil or gas, or similar structure, while it is not maintained on a station; and

(*f*) 'United Kingdom' includes any area to which the provisions of the Act apply by virtue of section 107.

3   The Interpretation Act 1978 shall apply for the purpose of interpreting this Schedule as if it were an Act of Parliament.

4   Any word or expression used in this Schedule shall unless the context otherwise requires have the same meaning as it has in the Act.

SCHEDULE 4

OTHER EXCEPTIONS AND CONDITIONS RELATING TO THE APPLICATION OF THE TELECOMMUNICATIONS CODE

Definitions and Interpretation

1   In this Schedule unless the context otherwise requires:

(*a*) 'Duct' means a structure or apparatus (with appropriate entry points) installed underground in such a way that lines can be installed in it without having to break up the surface of the highway;

(*b*) the expressions 'emergency works', 'maintainable highway', 'street' and 'telecommunication apparatus' shall have the meanings given to them by paragraph 1 of Schedule 2 to the Act;

(*c*) 'Highway Authority' means, in England and Wales, the highway authority as defined in section 1 of the Highways Act 1980, in Scotland, the highway authority as defined in section 50 of the Roads (Scotland) Act 1970 and, in Northern Ireland, the Department of the Environment for Northern Ireland;

(*d*) 'line' shall have the meaning given to it by sub-paragraph (a) of the definition of 'telecommunication apparatus' in paragraph 1 of Schedule 2 to the Act and 'Service Line' shall mean any line placed or intended to be placed for the purpose of providing any telecommunication service to the occupier from time to time of any land, as distinct from lines placed or intended to be placed for the general purposes of any telecommunication system;

(*e*) 'Planning Authority' means:

(i)   in relation to England and Wales, the local planning authority for the area in question within the meaning of section 1 of the Town and Country Planning Act 1971;

(ii)   in relation to Scotland, the general planning authority or the district planning authority for the area in question within the meaning of section 172 of the Local Government (Scotland) Act 1973;

(iii)   in relation to Northern Ireland, the Department of the Environment for Northern Ireland.

2   The Interpretation Act 1978 shall apply for the purpose of interpreting this Schedule as if it was an Act of Parliament.

3   Any word or expression used in this Schedule shall unless the context otherwise requires have the same meaning as it has in the Act.

4   For the purposes of interpreting this Schedule headings and titles shall be disregarded.

Condition 1   Conservation Areas

1.1   Subject to paragraph 1.2 and except in the case of emergency works, any line installed by the Licensee after the date on which this Licence enters into force in any Relevant Area shall be installed underground and no pole shall be installed in any such area after that date.

1.2   Notwithstanding paragraph 1.1, nothing in this paragraph shall prevent the installation on or above the ground of:

(a)   a line or pole required temporarily for the purpose of emergency works;

(b)   an overhead Service Line flown from a pole installed:
   (i)   before the date on which this Licence enters into force;
   (ii)   before the area was designated a conservation area; or
   (iii)   under sub-paragraphs (e) or (f) below;
provided that the line is of a not noticeably larger diameter than that of the majority of the Licensee's overhead Service Lines in the same locality;

(c)   an overhead Service Line flown from a building in a locality where overhead Service Lines attached to poles or buildings are already installed in adjacent streets or on neighbouring land by the Licensee for the purpose of providing telecommunication services, provided that the line is of a not noticeably larger diameter than that of the majority of such other overhead Service Lines;

(d)   any other line replacing an existing line provided that the replacement line is of a not noticeably larger diameter than that of the line it replaces;

(e)   a replacement pole in a position not substantially different from the pole it replaces;

(f)   subject to paragraph 1.3, a pole (other than one mentioned in sub-paragraph (e) above) in a street or on neighbouring land where overhead Service Lines attached to poles are already installed by the Licensee in that street or on that neighbouring land for the purpose of providing telecommunication services;

(g)   a Service Line affixed to and lying on the surface of the exterior structure of a building provided that the line is of a not noticeably larger diameter than the majority of service lines affixed to and lying on the surface of the exterior structures of buildings in the same locality.

1.3   Before installing a pole under paragraph 1.2 (f) the Licensee shall give the Planning Authority written notice of its intention to do so describing the proposed works and shall consider any written representations made by the Planning Authority within 28 days of the giving of the notice.

1.4   In this Condition 'Relevant Area' means:

(a)   in relation to England and Wales, the City of London or any area designated as a conservation area under section 277 of the Town and Country Planning Act 1971;

(b)   in relation to Scotland, any area designated as a conservation area under section 262 of the Town and Country Planning (Scotland) Act 1972; and

(c)   in relation to Northern Ireland, any area designated as a conservation area under Article 37 of the Planning (Northern Ireland) Order 1972.

Condition 2   Listed Buildings and Ancient Monuments

2.1   Except in the case of emergency works, the Licensee shall before installing lines, poles or other telecommunication apparatus in proximity to a building shown as Grade 1 in the statutory list of buildings of special architectural or historic interest compiled by the Secretary of State under section 54 of the Town and Country Planning Act 1971 (or under section 52 of the Town and Country Planning (Scotland) Act 1972, or Article 31 of the Planning (Northern Ireland) Order 1972) give written notice to the Planning Authority. Where the installation would detrimentally affect the character and appearance of the building and the Planning Authority indicates within 28 days of the giving of the notice that the installation should not take place, the Licensee may install the apparatus only if the Secretary of State so directs in writing, or with the agreement of the Planning Authority.

2.2   For the avoidance of doubt it is hereby declared that nothing in this Licence affects:

(a)   the statutory requirement that the consent of the Secretary of State shall be obtained before any work is carried out which will affect the site of an ancient monument scheduled under sections 1 and 2 of the Ancient Monuments and Archaeological Areas Act 1979 or section 7 of the Historic Monuments (Northern Ireland) Act 1971; or

(b)   the obligation imposed on the Licensee by virtue of section 55 of the Town and Country Planning Act 1971 (or by section 53 of the Town and Country Planning (Scotland) Act 1972 or by Article 32 of the Planning (Northern Ireland) Order 1972) to obtain listed building consent for any works which affect the character of a listed building, or involve the demolition of any part of such a building.

Condition 3   Overhead Lines

3.1   Without prejudice to Condition 1.1, the Licensee shall take steps to ensure that, wherever practicable, taking into account the need to provide telecommunication services at the lowest reasonable cost, new lines (other than overhead Service Lines flown from poles) installed after the date on which this Licence enters into force are installed underground.

3.2   The Licensee shall consider carefully a request by any person that any of its existing lines be resited underground. If the Licensee is satisfied that the person making the request will pay the costs of placing the lines underground, the Licensee shall, wherever it is reasonable and practicable, so place the line. In other cases, except where the request is frivolous, the Licensee shall be obliged within 28 days of receiving it, to give notice of its decision whether or not to accede to the request in writing to the person making the request giving, where it decides to refuse, reasons.

3.3   Where telecommunication services are to be provided to a person occupying or proposing to occupy a new development the Licensee shall consider in conjunction with those responsible for the development and any other statutory undertaker providing or proposing to provide a service to persons occupying that development whether lines can be installed underground on a shared cost basis.

Condition 4   National Parks etc.

4.1   Subject to paragraph 4.2, and except in the case of emergency works, before installing overhead telecommunication apparatus in any National Park, Area of Outstanding Natural Beauty, National Scenic Area, or the area administered by the Broads Authority, and before installing any apparatus in any Limestone Pavement Area, Site of Special Scientific Interest or Area of Scientific Interest, the Licensee shall give the Relevant Authority written notice of its intention to do so describing the proposed works.

4.2   Where:

(a)   the Licensee has given notice of proposed works in accordance with paragraph 4.1; and

(b)   the Relevant Authority has, within 28 days of the giving of the notice, made written representations to the Licensee about the proposed works;

the Licensee shall consider those representations and if it considers that, notwithstanding those representations, the proposed works which are the subject of that notice should be carried out in the form proposed in that notice or with modifications to take account of those representations it shall, before carrying out the proposed works, give written notice to the Relevant Authority of its intention to carry out the proposed works and of the modifications if any of the proposed works and the reasons for its decision to do so.

4.3   The Licensee shall also comply with any direction given to it in writing by the Secretary of State relating to giving notice to and considering representations made by any other authority exercising statutory functions in relation to any of the areas specified in paragraph 4.1 or such other environmentally sensitive areas as may be specified in the direction.

4.4   The Licensee shall not be required to give notice pursuant to paragraph 4.1 where the apparatus installed consists solely of:

(a)   an overhead Service Line affixed to and lying on the surface of the exterior structure of a building or flown from a pole provided that the line is of a not noticeably larger diameter than that of the majority of such overhead Service Lines in the same locality; or

(b)   a replacement pole installed in a position not substantially different from the pole it replaces.

4.5   In this Condition:

(a)   in relation to England and Wales and Scotland:

(i)   'National Park' and 'Area of Outstanding Natural Beauty' respectively mean any area notified as such under section 5 or section 87 of the National Parks and Access to the Countryside Act 1949 and the Relevant Authority in relation thereto shall be the Planning Authority;

(ii)   'Site of Special Scientific Interest' means an area designated as such under section 28 of the Wildlife and Countryside Act 1981 or an area in respect of which the Secretary of State has made an order under section 29 of that Act; and in both cases the Nature Conservancy Council established under the Nature Conservancy Council Act 1973 shall be the Relevant Authority in respect of any such area;

(iii) 'Limestone Pavement Area' means an area designated by the Secretary of State or relevant authority under section 34 of the Wildlife and Countryside Act 1981; and the Relevant Authority in England and Wales is the Planning Authority and in Scotland is the Planning Authority exercising district planning functions; and

(iv) 'National Scenic Area' means any area in Scotland designated as such under the Town and Country (Planning) Scotland Act 1972; and the Relevant Authority in relation thereto is the Planning Authority;

(b) in relation to Northern Ireland:

(i) 'Area of Outstanding Natural Beauty' means any area designated as such under section 10 of the Amenity Lands Act (Northern Ireland) 1965; and the Relevant Authority in relation thereto shall be the Department of the Environment for Northern Ireland; and

(ii) 'Area of Scientific Interest' means an area designated under section 15 of the Amenity Lands Act (Northern Ireland) 1965; and the Relevant Authority in relation thereto means the Department of the Environment for Northern Ireland.

Condition 5   National Trust and National Trust for Scotland

5.1   Except in the case of emergency works, before installing any telecommunication apparatus for the purpose of providing a service to the occupier of any land which the National Trust or the National Trust for Scotland has notified the Licensee that it owns, or holds any interest in, the Licensee shall give the relevant regional office of whichever of those bodies is concerned written notice of its intention to do so, describing the proposed works; and shall consider any written representations made within 28 days of the giving of such notice to it by either of those bodies.

Condition 6   Maintainable Highways

6.1   For the avoidance of doubt it is hereby declared that paragraph 6.2 applies in addition to any obligations of the Licensee under the Public Utilities Street Works Act 1950 and any order made under section 11 (1) of the Act.

6.2   Except in the case of emergency works, before executing any works involving the breaking up of a maintainable highway in connection with the installation of any telecommunication apparatus in that highway the Licensee shall give to the Highway Authority written notice of its intention to do so describing the proposed works and shall consider any written representations made by that Highway Authority within 8 days of the giving of the notice by the Licensee in the case of an overhead line or any underground Service Line and within 29 days of the giving of the notice by the Licensee in other cases.

Note
Two statutory instruments made under the New Roads and Street Works Act 1991 — Street Works (Notices) Order 1992, SI 1992/3053 and SI 1992/3063 (for Scotland) means that a notice given under the 1991 Act satisfies the requirement to give a notice under this Condition.

Condition 7 Placing of Underground Apparatus in Ducts.

7.1 All lines installed underground after the date on which this Licence enters into force, in a part of a maintainable highway which is paved, shall, whenever practicable, be installed in Ducts.

Condition 8 Height of Overhead Lines

8.1 Lines installed over the carriageway of a maintainable highway shall be placed at a height of not less than 5.5 metres above the carriageway (or in the case of a designated high load route not less than 6.5 metres), except where the Highway Authority has previously otherwise agreed in writing.

Condition 9 Maintenance and the Safety of Apparatus

9.1 The Licensee shall from time to time inspect its telecommunication apparatus which is not inside a building and which is on or above the surface of the ground with a view to ensuring that it will not cause harm to other persons or property; and the Licensee shall notify the Director of its arrangements for inspecting such apparatus.

9.2 In addition to carrying out inspections of its own apparatus on or above the surface of the ground the Licensee shall take such steps as are appropriate in the circumstances to investigate any report (other than a frivolous one) of any of its apparatus (wherever situated) being in a dangerous state and to remove any danger.

Condition 10 Arrangements with Electricity Boards

10.1 Subject to any modifications agreed between the Licensee and the Relevant Board, the Licensee shall:

(a) where it installs and keeps installed telecommunication apparatus in proximity to previously installed plant which is the responsibility of a relevant Board, continue to observe the terms of the 1928 Agreement between the Postmaster General and the Electricity Commissioners and subsequent agreements or arrangements concerning the engineering principles to be adopted and the allocation and apportionment of costs which arise; and

(b) where a Relevant Board gives notice that it proposes to install its plant in proximity to any of the Licensee's installed apparatus, continue to observe the relevant terms of the agreements and arrangements referred to in sub-paragraph (a) above.

10.2 In this Condition 'Relevant Board' means an Electricity Board as defined in section 26 of the Energy Act 1983, or the Northern Ireland Electricity Service.

Condition 11 Instructions for the Installation of Apparatus

11.1 Without prejudice to any of its statutory obligations the Licensee shall give instructions to its employees and agents with a view to securing that:

(*a*)   where apparatus is to be installed underground in a maintainable highway, the normal practice will be to place it in the verge or footway if any rather than the carriageway;

(*b*)   provision is made for any new ducts installed after the date on which this Licence comes into effect to contain sufficient spare capacity to meet demand which is reasonably foreseeable by the Licensee for telecommunication services provided by it;

(*c*)   attention is drawn to the need wherever practicable to place lines at minimum depths of cover appropriate for the locality (varying between 350mm and 600mm in footways and between 600mm and 900mm in the carriageway);

(*d*)   regular liaison is maintained with Highway Authorities with a view to ensuring that, as far as possible, telecommunication code works which entail breaking up the surface of the highway are carried out in advance of scheduled resurfacing works or together with other schemes affecting the highway;

(*e*)   regular liaison is maintained with statutory undertakers and other operators to whom the telecommunications code is applied with a view to reducing the disruption of the services provided by those persons;

(*f*)   where apparatus is installed in a manner which involves the breaking up or opening of the highway and the licensee is to do the reinstatement and making good at upper levels under section 7 (2) (c) of the Public Utilities Street Works Act 1950, all reasonable steps are taken to reinstate the surface of the highway in its previous form, unless the Highway Authority agrees otherwise;

(*g*)   with a view to reducing to a minimum the need for the erection of new poles or the construction of new Ducts, before installing any such poles or Ducts steps will be taken to investigate the possibility of using existing poles, Ducts or other conduits;

(*h*)   attention is drawn to the desirability of:

(i)   installing the minimum practicable number of poles and other items of apparatus, allowing for estimated growth in demand for telecommunication services; and

(ii)   protecting the visual amenity of properties in proximity to which poles or other items of apparatus are installed; and

(*i*)   lines and other items of apparatus are placed so that they do not present safety hazards.

11.2   The Licensee shall within three months of the date on which this Licence enters into force furnish details to the Director of the steps taken to implement paragraph 11.1.

Condition 12   Records of Apparatus

12.1   The Licensee shall keep records of any of its apparatus installed underground after the date on which this Licence enters into force which can be made available in the form of route plans drawn on an Ordnance Survey map background of one of the following scales (1:625, 1:1,250, 1:2,500, 1:10,000) according to the density of development in the area concerned.

12.2   The Licensee shall provide by means of a telecommunication system free of charge, to any Highway Authority or other person who is intending to undertake works in the vicinity of any telecommunication apparatus it has installed underground, a service furnishing information about the location of that apparatus and shall whenever practicable:

(*a*) respond to bona fide enquiries; and

(*b*) where necessary confirm its advice in diagrammatic form and make trained staff available to give on-site advice about such apparatus so installed; and shall also respond to any other reasonable request from a Highway Authority for information about the location of the Licensee's apparatus installed underground.

12.3 The Licensee shall co-operate in any joint projects involving persons who are statutory undertakers under any enactment or to whom the powers of the telecommunications code have been applied which have as their purpose the recording and making available of information about underground apparatus, unless the Director agrees that it would be inappropriate having regard to its existing practice in the area concerned for it to do so.

Condition 13 Emergency Works

13.1 Where the Licensee executes emergency works which would otherwise require prior notice under Condition 1, 2, 4, 5 or 6, it shall, as soon a practicable after the commencement of the works, give to any body to whom notice is required to be given under that Condition written notice describing the works.

Condition 14 Public Events and Construction Sites

14.1 Where the Licensee is to provide telecommunication services for a limited period at the site of a public event or a construction site, it may install overhead lines and associated poles to provide that service notwithstanding Conditions 1, 2, 4, and 5, provided that the lines or poles are removed at the end of the event or after the work at the construction site is complete.

Condition 15 Emergency Organisations

15.1 Where the Licensee is to provide any telecommunication service for a limited period to an Emergency Organisation in an Emergency it may, notwithstanding Conditions 1, 2, 4, 5, 6 and 8, install overhead lines and associated poles for the purposes of providing such services as are made necessary by the Emergency provided that any such line or pole is removed after such services cease to be required.

15.2 In this Condition 'Emergency Organisation' and 'Emergency' have the same meaning as in Schedule 1 to this Licence.

Condition 16 Public Inspection of Code Related Licence Conditions

16.1 The Licensee shall place a copy of this Schedule and of every direction given to the Licensee under section 10 (4) of the Act in a publicly accessible part of every Major Office of the Licensee in such a manner and in such a place that it is readily available for inspection free of charge by the general public during such hours as the Secretary of State may prescribe under section 19(4) of the Act for the register of licences and orders to be open for public inspection.

16.2 'Major Office' has the same meaning as in Condition 16.4 of Schedule 1 to this Licence.

ANNEX A

The Applicable Systems

1   The Applicable Systems are telecommunication systems of every description within the United Kingdom provided that a system ('the System') is an Applicable System only to the extent that it satisfies each of the following conditions:

(*a*)   the System is one by means of which Messages are conveyed or are to be conveyed:

(i)   from one Network Termination Point to another such Point;

(ii)   from a Network Termination Point to another place which is neither a Network Termination Point nor a Call Office or from such a place to such a Point;

(iii)   between a place which is neither a Network Termination Point nor a Call Office and another such place where their conveyance is not by way of provision of a service to another person; or

(iv)   between a Call Office and any other place;
but in any case not beyond a Network Termination Point;

(*b*)   none of the apparatus comprised in the System is Relevant Terminal Apparatus installed on premises occupied by a person to whom there are provided telecommunication services by means of the System;

(*c*)   the System is not, insofar as it is within the Hull Area, connected to any Network Termination Point other than one in an item of Network Connecting Apparatus which Point exists for the purpose of connecting the System to an aircraft, a seagoing vessel or hovercraft or to another public telecommunication system run by either the Kingston upon Hull City Council or any other person running a public telecommunication system within the Hull Area; and

(*d*)   the System is not a telecommunication system which conveys messages by means of wireless telegraphy, except where every Station for Wireless Telegraphy and every item of Wireless Telegraphy Apparatus comprised within the system constitutes a permanent or temporary Fixed Wireless Telegraphy Station.

2   In this Annex:

(*a*)   'Approved Apparatus' means in relation to any system apparatus approved under section 22 of the Act for connection to that system;

(*b*)   'Call Office' means telecommunication apparatus not supplied by the Licensee to any particular person but made available for use by the public or a class of the public;

(*c*)   'Fixed Wireless Telegraphy Station' means any Station for Wireless Telegraphy or Wireless Telegraphy Apparatus which is not used while in motion and which is operated for the purpose of being connected by wireless telegraphy solely to:

(i)   a Station for Wireless Telegraphy or Wireless Telegraphy Apparatus comprised in the System or any other system which but for this paragraph would be an Applicable System and which is not used while in motion;

(ii) other Wireless Telegraphy Apparatus or another Station for Wireless Telegraphy which is itself neither designed nor adapted for use while in motion;

(iii) earth orbiting apparatus or apparatus outside the United Kingdom; or

(iv) apparatus on an aircraft or seagoing vessel or hovercraft;

(d) 'the Hull Area' means the area within which the Kingston upon Hull City Council is authorised to run telecommunication systems under a Licence coming into force on the date on which this Licence enters into force;

(e) 'Licence' means a licence granted or having effect as if so granted under section 7 of the Act;

(f) 'Message' means anything falling within paragraphs (a) to (d) of section 4(1) of the Act;

(g) 'Relevant Terminal Apparatus' means:

(i) 'Terminal Apparatus' that is to say any telecommunication apparatus installed on Served Premises by means of which Messages are initially transmitted or ultimately received except a Call Office; and

(ii) any other telecommunication apparatus directly connected to Terminal Apparatus (including apparatus which is Terminal Apparatus by virtue of this sub-paragraph) which would, if it were run with such Terminal Apparatus and any other apparatus by means of which it is so connected, constitute a system authorised to be run by the person running that Terminal Apparatus under a Licence;

(h) 'Network Connecting Apparatus' means telecommunication apparatus comprised in the System which is not Network Termination and Testing Apparatus and is connected to another telecommunication system;

(i) 'Network Termination Point' means any point:

(i) within an item of Network Connecting Apparatus at which energy of any of the forms specified in section 4(1) of the Act is conveyed directly to or from apparatus comprised in a telecommunication system other than the one in which that Network Connecting Apparatus is comprised; or

(ii) within an item of Network Termination and Testing Apparatus at which such energy is conveyed directly to any Relevant Terminal Apparatus;

(j) 'Network Termination and Testing Apparatus' means an item of telecommunication apparatus comprised in the System installed in a fixed position on Served Premises which enables:

(i) Approved Apparatus to be readily connected to, and disconnected from, the System; and

(ii) the conveyance of Messages between such Apparatus and the System; and

(iii) the due functioning of the System to be tested;
but the only other functions of which, if any, are:

(aa) to supply energy between such Apparatus and the System;

(bb) to protect the safety or security of operation of the System; or

(cc) to enable other operations exclusively related to the running of any Applicable System to be performed or the due functioning of any system to which the System is or is to be connected to be tested (separately or together with the System);

(*k*) 'seagoing vessel' includes any floating structure for the exploration for, or exploitation of, oil or gas, or similar structure, while it is not maintained on a station;

(*l*) 'Served Premises' means a single set of premises in single occupation where apparatus has been installed for the purpose of the provision of telecommunication services by means of the System at those premises;

(*m*) 'Subsidiary' has the same meaning as in section 154 of the Companies Act 1948;

(*n*) 'United Kingdom' includes any area to which the provisions of the Act apply by virtue of section 107; and

(*o*) 'Station for Wireless Telegraphy' and 'Wireless Telegraphy Apparatus' have the same meaning as in the Wireless Telegraphy Acts 1949 to 1967.

3   In determining whether any telecommunication system is an Applicable System for the purposes of this Annex:

(i)   any point at which any two systems run by the Licensee neither of which is a system authorised to be run and which is run under another Licence are connected shall be deemed not to be a Network Termination Point;

(ii)   in determining whether Messages are conveyed by way of provision of a service all members of the Licensee's Group (that is to say the Licensee and its Subsidiaries taken together) shall be treated as one person; and

(iii)   apparatus shall be deemed to remain installed in a fixed position notwithstanding that it has been moved without authority.

4   The Interpretation Act 1978 shall apply for the purposes of interpreting this Annex as if it were an Act of Parliament.

5   Any word or expression used in this Annex shall unless the context otherwise requires have the same meaning as it has in the Act.

CLASS LICENCE TO RUN BRANCH SYSTEMS TO PROVIDE TELECOMMUNICATION SERVICES GRANTED BY THE SECRETARY OF STATE UNDER SECTION 7 OF THE TELECOMMUNICATIONS ACT 1984

9 SEPTEMBER 1996

TABLE OF CONTENTS

The Licence

1   The Secretary of State, in exercise of the powers conferred on him by section 7 of the Telecommunications Act 1984 (hereinafter referred to as 'the Act') and having consulted the Director, hereby grants to all persons of the class defined in paragraph 2 (each such person being hereinafter referred to as 'the Licensee') a Licence, subject to the Conditions set out in Schedule 1 and to revocation as provided for in Schedule 2, to run the telecommunication systems specified in Annex A ('the Applicable Systems') and authorises the Licensee to do all or any of the acts specified in Schedule 3.

Coverage

2   This Licence is granted to all persons except:
(*a*)   any person in respect of whom the Secretary of State or the Director has revoked this Licence in relation to all Applicable Systems in accordance with Schedule 2 and whose name and particulars are for the time being included in a list kept for the purpose by the Director and made available by him for inspection by the general public;
(*b*)   any Specified Public Telecommunications Operator in respect of the geographical area in which that Operator is authorised to run a public telecommunication system; and
(*c*)   any person who, but for this sub-paragraph, would be running the telecommunication system in question under this Licence to provide only the telecommunication services which are authorised to be provided under the licence granted on 9 September 1996 entitled Class licence for the running of self provided telecommunication systems granted by the Secretary of State for Trade and Industry under Section 7 of the Telecommunications Act 1984 or any successor thereto.

Duration

3   This Licence shall enter into force on the date of signature and shall be of 25 years' duration unless previously revoked in accordance with Schedule 2.

Interpretation

4 The Interpretation Act 1978 shall apply for the purposes of interpreting this Licence as if it were an Act of Parliament. In this Licence, except as hereinafter provided or unless the context otherwise requires, words or expressions shall have the meaning there assigned to them and otherwise any word or expression shall have the same meaning as it has in the Act. For the purposes of interpreting this Licence, headings and titles shall be disregarded.

5 For the purposes of this Licence:

(a) references to the 'Applicable Systems' are references to any or all of the telecommunication systems run by the Licensee under this Licence unless the context otherwise requires it; and

(b) 'Specified Public Telecommunication Operator' means British Telecommunications plc, Kingston Communications (Hull) plc and such other public telecommunication operator as may be specified by the Secretary of State from time to time and described in a list kept by the Director and made available by him for inspection by the general public.

Specifications, Determinations and Consents

6 Any specification, determination or consent made by the Secretary of State or the Director under powers contained in the class licence to run Branch Systems to provide Telecommunication Services dated 4 November 1994 shall, in the absence of any revocation of that specification, determination or consent, be deemed to be made under the equivalent powers contained in this Licence.

7 Where this Licence provides for any power of the Secretary of State or the Director to give any direction or consent or make any specification, designation, or determination, it implies, unless the contrary intention appears, a power, exercisable in the same manner and subject to the same conditions or limitations, to revoke, amend or give or make again any such direction, consent, specification, designation or determination.

8 Any notification which is required to be given under this Licence by the Secretary of State or the Director shall be satisfied by serving the document by post on the Licensee at the Licensee's registered office.

Ian Taylor MP
Parliamentary Under Secretary of State
for Science and Technology
9 September 1996

SPECIFICATION BY THE SECRETARY OF STATE FOR THE PURPOSES OF THE CLASS LICENCE TO RUN BRANCH SYSTEMS TO PROVIDE TELECOMMUNICATIONS SERVICES GRANTED ON 9 SEPTEMBER 1996 ('THE LICENCE')

The Secretary of State hereby revokes the specification dated 17 February 1995 made by him under paragraph 3(b) of Schedule 3 of the Class Licence to Run Branch Systems to Provide Telecommunications Services granted by him on 4 November 1994 and for the purposes of the Licence hereby specifies under paragraph 3 (b) of Schedule 3 thereof as services which may be provided International Simple Data Resale Services of all descriptions to and from all countries and territories in the world.

In this specification words and phrases shall have the same meaning as in the Licence.

Ian Taylor MP
Parliamentary Under Secretary of State
for Science and Technology
9 September 1996

Notes
1. This class licence revokes and replaces the previous TSL dated 4 November 1994 and came into force on 9 September 1996, and applies to businesses generally.
2. The Self-Protection Licence (SPL) applies to consumers and is similar to the TSL and is not reproduced in this Handbook. The latest version of the SPL came into force on 9 September 1996 and copies may be obtained from OFTEL.

SCHEDULE 1

CONDITIONS INCLUDED UNDER SECTION 7 OF THE ACT

PART 1   DEFINITIONS AND INTERPRETATION RELATING TO THE CONDITIONS IN SCHEDULE 1

1   In this Schedule unless the context otherwise requires:

(*a*) 'Apparatus' means telecommunication apparatus within the extended definition in Schedule 2 to the Act;

(*b*) 'Appeal' includes further appeal and application for leave to appeal or further to appeal;

(*c*) 'Appeal Period' means:

(i) where the Licensee appeals against neither conviction nor sentence, the period within which such an Appeal might have been brought; or

(ii) where the Licensee appeals against conviction or sentence or both, the period ending on the date on which such an Appeal is finally disposed of;

(*d*) 'Applicable Terminal Equipment' means apparatus which is applicable terminal equipment within the meaning of regulation 4 of the Telecommunications Terminal Equipment Regulations 1992;

(*e*) 'Call Routing Apparatus' means Apparatus capable of switching Messages consisting in two-way live speech telephone calls between two or more items of Extension Telephone Apparatus and two or more circuits forming part of one or more Public Switched Networks.

For the purposes of this definition a basic access Integrated Services Digital Network connection constitutes one circuit;

(*f*) 'Compatibility' means the absence between the parties concerned of any reasonably foreseeable risk of:

(i) duplication of any Number; or

(ii) any other related effect,

which would be liable to introduce ambiguity or errors or to impose undue restrictions on any user or group of users;

(g) 'Compliant Terminal Equipment' means Applicable Terminal Equipment which satisfies the requirements of regulation 8 of the Telecommunications Terminal Equipment Regulations 1992;

(h) 'Conventions' means a set of principles and rules governing the use and management of Numbers and related matters published from time to time by the Director after consultation with interested parties who are members of the Telecommunications Numbering and Addressing Body and, if the Director deems it appropriate, end users;

(i) 'Emergency' means an emergency of any kind including any circumstances whatever resulting from major accidents, natural disasters and incidents involving toxic or radioactive materials.

(j) 'Emergency Organisation' means in respect of any locality the relevant public police, fire, ambulance and coastguard service for that locality and any other similar organisation providing assistance to the public in Emergencies.

(k) 'Extension Telephone Apparatus' means any item of Apparatus which is not itself Call Routing Apparatus and which is constructed or adapted for use in enabling the sending or hearing of two-way live speech where such speech may be conveyed by means of Call Routing Apparatus to which that Apparatus is connected;

(l) 'Group' means a parent undertaking and its subsidiary undertaking or undertakings within the meaning of section 258 of the Companies Act 1985 as substituted by section 21 of the Companies Act 1989; and 'Licensee's Group' means a Group in respect of which the Licensee is either a parent undertaking or a subsidiary undertaking, except that a company which was a member of a Group at any time within a period of nine months preceding the date in question shall be regarded as being a member of that Group if it elects to be treated as a member of that Group rather than as a member of any Group of which it has become a member;

(m) 'International Private Leased Circuit' means a communication facility which is:

(i) comprised both in a public telecommunication system and in an equivalent telecommunication system in a country or territory other than the United Kingdom;

(ii) for the conveyance of Messages between points, all of which are points of connection between telecommunication systems referred to in paragraph 1(m)(i) and other telecommunication systems;

(iii) made available to a particular person or particular persons;

(iv) such that all of the Messages transmitted at any of the points mentioned in paragraph 1(m)(ii) are received at every other such point; and

(v) such that the points mentioned in paragraph 1(m)(ii) are fixed by the way in which the facility is installed and cannot otherwise be selected by persons or Apparatus sending Messages by means of that facility;

(n) 'Live Speech Telephone Call' means a series of communications which involve the conveyance of Messages comprising two-way live speech.

(o) 'Major Office' means:

(i) in the case of a company incorporated under the Companies Act 1985, its registered office; or

(ii) in the case of any other person, its principal place of business in the United Kingdom;

(*p*) 'Message' means anything falling within paragraphs (a) to (d) of section 4(1) of the Act;

(*q*) 'Metering System' means the totality of all equipment, data, procedures and activities which the Licensee employs to determine the extent of any telecommunication services provided by means of the Applicable Systems;

(*r*) 'Network Termination and Testing Apparatus' means an item of Apparatus comprised in a public telecommunication system, which enables Apparatus not comprised in that system to be connected to and disconnected from that system;

(*s*) 'Number' means any identifier (including any name or address) of any user, Apparatus, or telecommunication service-related element;

(*t*) 'Private Leased Circuit' means a communication facility which is:

(i)   provided by means of one or more public telecommunication systems;

(ii)   for the conveyance of Messages between points, all of which are points of connection between telecommunication systems referred to in paragraph 1(t)(i) and other telecommunication systems;

(iii)   made available to a particular person or particular persons;

(iv)   such that all of the Messages transmitted at any of the points mentioned in paragraph 1(t)(ii) are received at every other such point; and

(v)   such that the points mentioned in paragraph 1(t)(ii) are fixed by the way in which the facility is installed and cannot otherwise be selected by Persons or Apparatus sending Messages by means of that facility;

(*u*) 'Public Switched Network' means a public telecommunication system by means of which two-way telecommunication services are provided whereby Messages are switched incidentally to their conveyance, and, for the avoidance of doubt, a Public Switched Network does not mean that part of a public telecommunication system involving the provision of Private Leased Circuits or International Private Leased Circuits;

(*v*) 'Relevant Service' means any telecommunication service which is provided by means of the Applicable Systems;

(*w*) 'Specified Numbering Scheme' means a scheme for the allocation and re-allocation of Numbers for the purposes of the switched Applicable Systems and the systems of other licensed operators which is specified by the Director for the purpose of this Licence and described in a list kept for that purpose by him and made available by him for public inspection;

(*x*) 'Specified Person' means a person specified for the time being by the Director (and who has consented to be so specified) for the purpose of keeping and making available for inspection by the general public a list such as is referred to in Condition 6.2(b);

(*y*) 'Telecommunications Numbering and Addressing Body' means a body approved by the Director as representative of the Licensee, other telecommunications operators and other persons whom the Director considers it appropriate to include in consultations about the content of the Conventions and the Specified Numbering Scheme; and

(*z*) 'Wireless Telegraphy' has the same meaning as in the Wireless Telegraphy Act 1949.

2   Expressions cognate with those referred to in this Schedule shall be construed accordingly.

PART 2

CONDITIONS INCLUDED UNDER SECTION 7 OF THE ACT

Condition 1 Approval of Equipment

1.1 Where Apparatus comprised in the Applicable Systems is connected to a public telecommunication system, it shall either be approved for such connection under section 22 of the Act or be Compliant Terminal Equipment.

1.2 Where the Applicable Systems are capable of conveying Messages which have been or are to be conveyed also by a public telecommunication system, any Apparatus comprised in the Applicable Systems which interworks with the public telecommunication system at any time:

(a) in the case of Apparatus to which the Telecommunications Terminal Equipment Regulations 1992 apply, shall be Compliant Terminal Equipment; or

(b) in other cases, shall unless the Director has consented otherwise and has not withdrawn that consent, be Apparatus which is approved for the time being under section 22 of the Act for connection to the Applicable Systems.

1.3 For the purposes of this Condition, approvals framed by reference to branch systems should be regarded as approvals for connection to the Applicable Systems.

Notes

1. Condition 1.1 has been amended by the Telecommunications Terminal Equipment Regulations 1992, SI 1992/2423, as amended and extended by the Telecommunications Terminal Equipment (Amendment and Extensions) Regulations 1994, SI 1994/3129 and the Telecommunications Terminal Equipment (Amendment) Regulations 1995, SI 1995/144, which revokes s. 22, Telecommunications Act 1984 with regard to applicable terminal equipment. This is equipment to which a Common Technical Regulation (CTR) applies. A CTR is a measure adopted by the EC under Article 6.2 of the Telecommunications Terminal Equipment Directive — see Part II of this Handbook. Compliant Terminal Equipment is equipment which satisfies the requirements of Regulation 8 of the above Regulations.

2. Condition 1.2 has been amended so that only apparatus comprised in the Applicable Systems which is capable of interworking with the public telecommunication system requires to be approved, either under s. 22 of the 1984 Act or, if it is applicable terminal equipment, under the Telecommunications Terminal Equipment Regulations. Apparatus interworks with the public telecommunication system by establishing, modifying, charging for, holding and clearing real or virtual connection.

The amendment aligns the approval requirements of the Self-Provision Licence (SPL) and Telecommunication Services Licence (TSL) with those of the Telecommunications Terminal Equipment Directive and has the virtue of excluding much 'indirectly' connected equipment, caught by the present condition, from having to be approved. In consequence, equipment comprised in the Applicable Systems that is not directly connected to a public telecommunication system, such as personal computers, television receivers and VHS recorders will no longer require approval.

Condition 2 Connection Arrangements

2.1 The Applicable Systems (with the exception of hearing aids) may be connected to any public telecommunication system only:

(*a*)   by means of Network Termination and Testing Apparatus which is installed on premises on which the Applicable Systems are situated; or

(*b*)   by means of Wireless Telegraphy provided that the Licensee shall secure that every such connection complies with such reasonable conditions as the operator of that public telecommunication system may from time to time lay down; or

(*c*)   by a means which has been specified by the Director for the purpose of this Condition and which is described in a list kept for the purpose by the Director and made available by him for inspection by the general public.

Notes
1.   Conditions 2.2 and 2.3 have been deleted. Hitherto, the authority to connect apparatus to a public network, other than by means of plug-and-socket, has been restricted to network operators, registered installers and registered maintainers. Given the continuing requirement that only approved apparatus may be connected to a public network and the resilience of modern networks, the existing conditions are excessive. These restrictions have now been relaxed.
2.   The accreditation scheme for installers and maintainers who wish to carry out network connection procedures will continue in operation without OFTEL's direct involvement, on a voluntary basis. Although OFTEL will no longer be registering accredited installers and maintainers, any restrictions imposed on their connection rights by network operators will be viewed as having anti-competitive implications.

Condition 3   Technical Requirements

3.1   The Applicable Systems shall, unless the Director agrees otherwise, be connected to a public telecommunication system only if:

(*a*)   such relevant technical requirements, if any, for connection to that public telecommunication system, as the Director may from time to time specify, and which are described in a list kept for the purpose by the Director and made available by him for inspection by the general public, are complied with; or

(*b*)   the connection is a temporary connection made solely for the purpose of commissioning Call Routing Apparatus comprised in or to be comprised in the Applicable Systems.

Condition 4   Emergency Telephones for the Hearing Impaired

4.1   Where the Applicable Systems, or any Apparatus comprised in them, are installed in a lift to which members of the public have access in circumstances where it may be necessary for them to use the Applicable Systems to summon assistance in Emergencies, the Licensee shall take reasonable steps to ensure that:

(*a*)   any telephone installed in such a lift is capable of coupling inductively to hearing aids which have been designed to be so coupled to such a telephone; and

(*b*)   a notice which indicates that the facility for coupling inductively to a hearing aid is available together with instructions on the use of that facility is affixed on or adjacent to the telephone.

Note
This Condition was formerly Condition 6 of the 1994 TSL. Old Condition 4 has been deleted.

Condition 5   Use of Automatic Calling Equipment

5.1   This Condition applies if the Applicable Systems are capable of conveying Messages which have been or are to be conveyed also by a Public Switched Network and if the Applicable Systems, or any Apparatus comprised in them, are capable:

(*a*)   of automatically initiating a sequence of calls to each of more than one destination in accordance with instructions stored in the Applicable Systems or Apparatus comprised in them; and

(*b*)   of transmitting, for reception by persons at some or all of the destinations so called, sounds other than:

(i)   live speech; or

(ii)   sounds for the purpose of the transmission or reception of facsimile messages.

5.2   The Licensee shall, except in so far as the Director consents otherwise:

(*a*)   secure that the Applicable Systems are used to initiate calls to transmit the Messages of the description referred to in paragraph 5.1(b) only to telecommunication systems which are run by the Licensee or by persons who have consented in writing to receive such calls and which are identified by reference to Numbers which are used to make calls to those telecommunication systems; and

(*b*)   maintain, or secure that there is maintained, a record giving particulars of the persons and the Numbers referred to in paragraph 5.2(a), and shall make that record available for inspection on reasonable notice by the Director.

Notes

1.   This Condition was formerly Condition 7 of the 1994 TSL

2.   Old Condition 5 (maintenance, inspection and bringing into service of certain apparatus) has been deleted in its entirety. Its removal has abolished the 'designated maintainer' (DM) regime. The DM regime required the user to have a written contract with a designated maintainer if a telecommunications system contained Call Routing Apparatus connected to two or more public exchange lines in such a way as to be capable of switching messages of live speech between two or more telephone extensions. In addition any Serially Connected Equipment used in conjunction with Call Routing Apparatus was required to be covered by such a contract.

3.   The reliability of modern equipment is such that routine maintenance is now seldom necessary, and it can no longer be reasonably argued that the DM regime is required to protect the safety and integrity of the public network. The abolition of the mandatory maintenance requirement will produce a more competitive environment for the provision of maintenance services and promises better value for money for the end user. Maintainers who have achieved accreditation by an approved body against the recognised quality standard will no longer require the additional approval of OFTEL. Users will now have the choice of either entering into a contract for the provision of maintenance services or paying for them as and when such services are needed.

Condition 6   Restrictions on Advertising and Supply Activities

6.1   Where the Licensee sends and conveys Messages on its own behalf, or on behalf of any member of the Licensee's Group, by means of the

Applicable Systems which are to be conveyed by means of a public telecommunication system for the purposes of the advertising, the offering for supply or provision or the supply or provision of goods, services or any other thing, and receives from any person who runs a telecommunication system by means of which that person receives such Messages a request to cease so sending them to a telecommunication system run by that person, then:

(a)   the Licensee and every member of the Licensee's Group shall cease sending such Messages to any telecommunication system run by that person and identified for the purpose to the Licensee by reference to a Number which is used to make calls to that telecommunication system; and

(b)   the Licensee or a member of the Licensee's Group shall maintain, or secure that there is maintained, a record giving particulars of the persons and the Numbers referred to in paragraph 6.1 (a) and shall make that record available for inspection on reasonable notice by the Director.

6.2   Where:

(a)   in respect of a telecommunication system run by him or on his behalf, a person has notified a Specified Person that he does not wish to receive unsolicited calls (whether of a general or a particular kind) made for the purpose of the advertising, the offering for supply or provision or the supply or provision of goods, services or any other thing; and

(b)   a Specified Person keeps a list of such notifications in a form specified by the Director and made available for inspection by the general public,
neither the Licensee nor any member of the Licensee's Group nor their agent, subcontractor or employee shall make such unsolicited calls by means of the Applicable Systems to the telecommunication systems so listed.

6.3   Paragraph 6.2 shall have effect only where the Director has determined for the time being:

(a)   the description of unsolicited call to which that paragraph shall apply; and

(b)   the description or descriptions of persons who shall be entitled to notify a Specified Person under that paragraph in relation to any such description of unsolicited call,
and such determinations are described in a list kept for the purpose by the Director and made available by him for inspection by the general public.

Note
This Condition was formerly Condition 8 of the 1994 TSL.

Condition 7   Privacy of Messages

7.1   The Licensee shall not use or allow to be used any Apparatus comprised in or connected to the Applicable Systems (except for Apparatus connected to or comprised in the Applicable Systems for the purpose of law enforcement or in the interests of national security) which is capable of recording, silently monitoring (except for monitoring where the meaningful content of the Message is not monitored) or intruding into Live Speech Telephone Calls, unless he complies with paragraphs 7.3 and 7.4. This paragraph shall not apply if the Licensee is an Emergency Organisation or if the Director has consented to the Licensee not complying with any or all of paragraphs 7.3, and 7.4 and has not withdrawn that consent.

7.2   The provisions of each consent given under paragraph 7.1 shall be entered in the register kept by the Director for the purpose of section 19 of the Act.

7.3   The Licensee shall make every reasonable effort to inform parties to whom or by whom a Live Speech Telephone Call is transmitted before recording, silent monitoring or intrusion into such Call has begun that the Live Speech Telephone Call is to be or may be recorded, silently monitored or intruded into.

7.4   The Licensee shall maintain a record of the means by which parties to whom or by whom a Live Speech Telephone Call is transmitted have been informed that such Call is to be or may be recorded, silently monitored or intruded into. The Licensee shall furnish to the Director such information on request.

Notes

1.   Condition 7 is a new condition in the TSL and SPL which applies in circumstances where you wish to use telecommunications apparatus comprised in or connected to your system to record, silently monitor or intrude into live speech telephone calls. (It does not apply where the apparatus in question is not telecommunications apparatus, i.e., is not apparatus that has been constructed or adapted for use in transmitting or receiving telecommunications messages.) Silent monitoring is the establishment of a receive only transmission path to a third terminal, enabling a third party to hear the call. Intrusion is the establishment of a bothway speech transmission to another terminal enabling a third party to hear and be heard by at least one of the other parties to the call. The Condition does not apply to the monitoring of telephone calls for systems control or diagnostic purposes where the meaningful content of the call itself is not monitored.

2.   The Condition provides that you should make every reasonable effort to inform all parties to a call that it may or will be recorded, silently monitored or intruded into. The particular means by which you choose to do this are not specified in the condition. Acceptable options, depending on circumstances, might include warning tones, pre-recorded messages, spoken warnings by the operator or written warnings included in publicity material, telephone directories, contracts, terms of business, staff notices, etc. It may not always be possible to warn first-time callers with whom you have had no previous contact but what is important is that you have a systematic procedure in place which provides the necessary information wherever this is a realistic possibility.

3.   It is necessary also to maintain a record of the means by which callers have been warned which the Director may request sight of. This does not mean that you have to log each telephone call; rather that should a dispute arise it will be possible for you to show from records how callers were being made aware at that time.

4.   The Condition does not apply where apparatus is being used for the purpose of law enforcement or in the interests of national security or to calls involving the national Emergency Organisations. It also provides that other licensees may be excluded, by means of a Director's consent, where there are compelling factors that outweigh the normal expectation of privacy. Such factors might apply where security is a consideration or in the case of specialised users such as helplines. In accordance with s. 19, Telecommunications Act 1984 these consents will be entered on a register open to public inspection.

5.   This Condition attempts to secure objectives similar to those which were previously achieved through an approval requirement that equipment capable of recording, silently monitoring or intruding into telephone conversations should emit warning tones as these operations took place, The removal of warning tones was permitted by an OFTEL General Variation provided that an alternative form of warning was given. The expectation is that procedures complying with the General Variation should, generally, also meet the requirements of this Condition.

Condition 8   Privacy, Confidentiality and Metering Systems

8.1   Subject to the other provisions of this Licence, the Licensee shall take all reasonable steps to safeguard the privacy and confidentiality of:
(a)   any Message conveyed for a consideration by means of the Applicable Systems; and
(b)   any information acquired by the Licensee in relation to such conveyance.
8.2   The Licensee shall take all reasonable steps to ensure the accuracy and reliability of any Metering System used in connection with the Applicable Systems and shall, in relation to any Metering System, keep such records as the Director has specified and notified to the Licensee.

Note
This Condition was formerly Condition 11 of the 1994 TSL.

Condition 9   Numbering Arrangements

9.1   Subject to paragraph 9.7, the Licensee shall, from the date on which it first provides a Relevant Service, adopt a numbering plan, in respect of Relevant Services provided or to be provided, for the allocation of any Numbers which:
(a)   are not allocated in accordance with a Specified Numbering Scheme;
(b)   are used or are intended to be used:
(i)   by one or more other licensees under this Licence; or
(ii)   by any person running a telecommunication system, other than a public telecommunication system under a Licence, who provides a telecommunication service of a description which the Licensee could provide in accordance with the provisions of this Licence; or
(iii)   by any public telecommunications operator, and
(c)   are necessary for access to each separately distinguishable element of each Relevant Service.
9.2   The numbering plan shall describe the method adopted or to be adopted for allocating and re-allocating Numbers of a kind described in paragraph 9.1. That method shall allow for sufficient Numbers to be available in relation to all telecommunication services, having regard to the reasonably foreseeable growth in demand for such services.
9.3   The Licensee shall, on or before the date on which it first provides a Relevant Service or as soon as practicable thereafter, furnish details of the numbering plan to the Director and, on request, to any other person having a reasonable interest.
9.4   The Licensee shall furnish to the Director details of any proposals which the Licensee may have from time to time to change the arrangements for allocating or re-allocating Numbers within, or to develop, add to or

replace, the numbering plan adopted and furnished in accordance with paragraphs 9.1, 9.2 and 9.3.

9.5   Where any arrangements for allocating or re-allocating Numbers within the numbering plan or any developments, additions or replacements furnished in accordance with paragraph 9.4:

(*a*)   are insufficient to provide Compatibility with the numbering arrangements applied or to be applied by any public telecommunications operator or other person naming a telecommunication system under a Licence who provides a service of a description which the Licensee could provide in accordance with the provisions of this Licence; or

(*b*)   do not allow for sufficient Numbers to be available in relation to all telecommunication services, having regard to the reasonably foreseeable growth in demand for such services; or

(*c*)   are not consistent with any obligations and recommendations of the International Telecommunication Union which apply to Her Majesty's Government and are binding on or are accepted by it;

the Licensee shall adopt the numbering plan with such developments, additions or replacements as are best calculated to secure such Compatibility or availability or consistency.

9.6   The Licensee shall allocate and re-allocate Numbers in accordance with the numbering plan it has adopted.

9.7   Numbers which are of a class described in CCITT Recommendations E160, E164 or F69 (relating to public switched telephone and telex networks) and are assigned to the Licensee shall be allocated only in accordance with a Specified Numbering Scheme. In relation to such Numbers, the Licensee shall also comply with any Conventions which are published from time to time by the Director.

Note
This Condition was formerly Condition 10 of the 1994 TSL.

Condition 10   Display of Tariff Information

10.1   This Condition applies where:

(*a*)   the Applicable Systems are capable of conveying Messages which have been or are to be conveyed also by one or more Public Switched Networks;

(*b*)   a person, on payment of a charge, however levied, may initiate and make a call by means of such Systems over one or more Public Switched Networks; and

(*c*)   the Licensee belongs to a class of persons specified from time to time for the purpose of this Condition by the Director.

10.2   The Licensee shall display such notice, in such form and in such place as the Director may from time to time specify.

10.3   The specifications referred to in this Condition shall be described in a list kept for the purpose by the Director and made available by him for inspection by the general public.

Note
This Condition was formerly Condition 9 of the 1994 TSL.

Condition 11   Provision of Telecommunications Services in Shared Premises

11.1   This Condition shall apply if the Licensee is running the Applicable Systems within premises occupied by any other person ('the Occupier') whether or not those premises are occupied also by the Licensee.

Prohibition on refusal to provide telecommunication services

11.2   The Licensee shall not refuse to provide Relevant Services to an Occupier who requests the provision of such Services, unless:

(*a*)   the provision of those Services is impracticable, whether because the Applicable Systems cannot be modified or adjusted to provide those Services or otherwise; or

(*b*)   the provision of those Services requires a material modification of the Applicable Systems and it is possible for the Occupier to obtain those telecommunication services otherwise than from the Licensee; or

(*c*)   the Occupier gives the Licensee reasonable cause to believe that Apparatus or a telecommunication system which the Occupier wishes to connect to the Applicable Systems would, if so connected, render the Licensee in breach of any of the provisions of this Licence; or

(*d*)   the Occupier will not (for reasons other than the unreasonable refusal of the Licensee to agree terms for the purpose) enter into a contract with the Licensee for the provision of those Services; or

(*e*)   the Occupier is (or gives the Licensee reasonable cause to believe that he will be) in breach of a contract with the Licensee for the provision of telecommunication services or for the supply of Apparatus by the Licensee or is in default in regard to any debt or liability owed to the Licensee in respect of any such contract; or

(*f*)   the provision of any telecommunication services requested would expose the Licensee or the Licensee's servants or agents to undue risk to health or safety; or

(*g*)   the Occupier is using any Apparatus connected to the Applicable Systems for any illegal purpose or has done so in the past and is likely to do so again; or

(*h*)   the Director determines that it is not reasonably practicable to provide the services requested at the time or place demanded.

Prohibition on certain exclusive dealing arrangements

11.3   The Licensee shall not require an Occupier to obtain telecommunication services from the Licensee or prevent or restrict the Occupier from obtaining telecommunication services from any other person.

Prohibition on linked sales

11.4   The Licensee shall not, except with the consent of the Director, and subject to paragraph 11.5, make the provision to an Occupier of any Relevant Services conditional on the acquisition of:

(*a*)   any other telecommunication services, except where those Relevant Services cannot be provided without the provision of those other services; or (*b*) any Apparatus forming part of a telecommunication system run by the Occupier.

11.5 The obligation in paragraph 11.4(b) shall not apply where the telecommunication services requested cannot otherwise be provided, whether because the design of the Applicable Systems requires the connection of Apparatus of a particular description or for any other reason.

Note
This Condition was formerly Condition 12 of the 1994 TSL.

Condition 12   Wiring no Longer forming Part of the Applicable Systems

12.1   This Condition applies to:
    (*a*)   any line;
    (*b*)   any structure, pole or other thing in, on, by or from which any such line is installed, supported, carried or suspended; and
    (*c*)   any plug, socket or other connection apparatus
owned by the Licensee or under the Licensee's control and installed on premises occupied by any person ('the User') wishing to use it in the naming of any telecommunication system and which was, but is no longer, comprised in an Applicable System run by the Licensee.

12.2   The Licensee shall (unless the Director otherwise agrees) secure that any Apparatus to which this Condition applies is made available upon reasonable terms to the User.

12.3   Subject to paragraph 12.4, the Licensee shall on reasonable charges, terms and conditions permit the User to carry out, or have carried out on his behalf, any operation in relation to Apparatus to which this Condition applies which is reasonably necessary to enable the User to use such Apparatus for the purpose of running the telecommunication system in which such Apparatus is comprised.

12.4   Paragraph 12.3 shall not apply to any Apparatus which is installed, together with Apparatus comprised in any other telecommunication system, in such a manner that maintenance services cannot be carried out in relation to it independently of operations carried out in relation to the other Apparatus (whether because it is installed in a shared casing or coating or otherwise).

Note
This Condition was formerly Condition 13 of the 1994 TSL.

Condition 13   Requirement to Furnish Information to the Director

13.1   The Licensee shall furnish or procure and furnish to the Director, in such manner and at such times as the Director may request, such documents, accounts, estimates, returns or other information as he may reasonably require for the purpose of exercising the functions assigned or transferred to him by or under Parts II and III of the Act.

13.2   In making any such request the Director shall ensure that no undue burden is imposed on the Licensee in procuring and furnishing such information and that the Licensee is not required to procure or furnish information which would not normally be available, unless the Director considers such information essential to enable him to exercise his functions.

13.3 The Licensee shall maintain (or secure that there is maintained) a record of the information described in Annex B and make it available (or secure that it is made available) for inspection on reasonable notice by the Director or the operator of any public telecommunication system to which the Applicable Systems are connected.

13.4 The Licensee shall permit the Director and any person authorised by him in writing to inspect the Applicable Systems at any reasonable time for the purpose of verifying whether:

(a) the Licensee is naming the Applicable Systems in accordance with this Licence; or

(b) the connection or the proposed connection of any other telecommunication system to the Applicable Systems causes or would cause any contravention of the Licence under which that other system is run.

13.5 If the Licensee is convicted of an offence under section 5(2) of the Act relating to the Applicable Systems, the Licensee shall, not later than fourteen days after the expiry of the Appeal Period, notify the Director of such conviction, specifying the offence, the date of such conviction, the name and address of the Court concerned and the penalty imposed.

Note
This Condition was formerly Condition 14 of the 1994 TSL.

Condition 14   Exceptions and Limitations on Obligations in Schedule 1

14.1 Unless the context otherwise requires, the Licensee's obligations under these Conditions have effect subject to the following exceptions and limitations.

14.2 The Licensee is not obliged to do anything which is not practicable.

14.3 The Licensee shall not be held to have failed to comply with an obligation imposed upon it by or under these Conditions if and to the extent that the Licensee is prevented from complying with that obligation by any physical, topographical or other natural obstacle, by the malfunction or failure of any Apparatus or equipment owing to circumstances beyond the control of the Licensee, by the act of any national authority, local authority or international organisation or as the result of fire, flood, explosion, accident, emergency, riot or war.

Note
This Condition was formerly Condition 15 of the 1994 TSL.

SCHEDULE 2

REVOCATION

1 The Secretary of State may revoke this Licence at any time by giving not less than 30 days' notice published in such a manner as the Secretary of State considers appropriate.

2   The Secretary of State or the Director (as the case may be) may at any time revoke this Licence in respect of any particular Licensee or in respect of all or any part of the Applicable Systems run by a particular Licensee in any of the following circumstances:

(*a*)   where the Licensee has failed to comply with a final order (or a provisional order confirmed) under section 16 of the Act and the Secretary of State or the Director, as the case may be, has given the Licensee not less than 30 days' notice in writing that, if the Licensee fails to comply with the order within that period of 30 days, he intends to revoke the Licence in respect of that Licensee or in respect of all or any part of the Applicable Systems run by that Licensee; no such notice of intention shall be given where the question of the validity of the order is the subject of any court proceedings, and where that question becomes so subject during the 30 day notice period, that period shall cease to run until the final disposal of those proceedings (including any Appeal); or

(*b*)   if the Licensee has been convicted of an offence under section 5(2) of the Act relating to the Applicable Systems, not later than three months after the Director first having had actual notice of the conviction, or the expiry of the Appeal Period, whichever is the later; or

(*c*)   where:

(i)   the Secretary of State or the Director considers that the Licensee is relying, has relied, or is likely to rely on this Licence in circumstances in which the effect of such actions is, was or may be such that the Licensee or any member of the Licensee's Group is relieved wholly or in part of any obligation, limitation or restriction imposed on that person in respect of any telecommunication services, the provision of which is authorised under a Licence granted to that person individually; and

(ii)   the Secretary of State or the Director, as the case may be, has given to the Licensee written notice of his intention to do so and has given the Licensee not less than 28 days in which to make representations in relation to such revocation; or

(*d*)   if the Secretary of State, having consulted the Director, or the Director:

(i)   is of the opinion that competition in the provision of any Relevant Service is, or is likely to become, adversely affected by reason of any person granted a Licence individually obtaining the power to secure (whether directly or indirectly) that any Relevant Service provided by a Licensee is provided in accordance with the wishes of that person; and

(ii)   has given to the Licensee written notice of his intention to do so and has given the Licensee not less than 28 days in which to make representations in relation to such revocation; or

(*e*)   if any Station for Wireless Telegraphy or item of Wireless Telegraphy Apparatus is comprised in the Applicable Systems and the Licensee fails to secure that there is in force in respect of the establishment and use of each such Station and the installation and use of each such item of Wireless Telegraphy Apparatus a licence granted under section 1 of the Wireless Telegraphy Act 1949, unless that Station or that Apparatus has been exempted from the need for such a licence by regulations made under that section.

3   The Secretary of State may at any time revoke this Licence in respect of any particular Licensee in the interests of national security or relations with the government of a country or territory outside the United Kingdom.

Service of notices

4   Any notice which is required to be given to a particular Licensee under paragraph 2 of this Schedule shall be given to the Licensee concerned by serving the documents by post to the address of the Licensee, provided however that, if it is not practicable to ascertain the name or address of the Licensee, the notice may be given by addressing it to a person by the description of 'the Licensee' of the Applicable Systems (describing them) and by delivering it to some person on premises where the Applicable Systems in respect of which the notice is given are situated or, if there is no person on those premises to whom it can be delivered, by affixing it or a copy of it to some conspicuous object on those premises.

5   In this Schedule:

(*a*)   'Appeal' includes further appeal and application for leave to appeal or further to appeal;

(*b*)   'Appeal Period' means:

(i)   where the Licensee appeals against neither conviction nor sentence, the period within which such an Appeal might have been brought; or

(ii)   where the Licensee appeals against conviction or sentence or both, the period ending on the date on which such an Appeal is finally disposed of:

(*c*)   'Group' means a parent undertaking and its subsidiary undertaking or undertakings within the meaning of section 258 of the Companies Act 1985 as substituted by section 21 of the Companies Act 1989; and 'Licensee's Group' means a Group in respect of which the Licensee is either a parent undertaking or a subsidiary undertaking;

(*d*)   'Relevant Service' means any telecommunication service which is provided by means of the Applicable Systems; and

(*e*)   'Station for Wireless Telegraphy' and 'Wireless Telegraphy Apparatus' have the same meaning as in the Wireless Telegraphy Act 1949.

SCHEDULE 3

AUTHORISATION TO CONNECT OTHER TELECOMMUNICATION SYSTEMS AND APPARATUS TO THE APPLICABLE SYSTEMS AND TO PROVIDE TELECOMMUNICATION SERVICES BY MEANS OF THE APPLICABLE SYSTEMS

1   Nothing in this Licence removes any need to obtain any other licence that may be required under any other enactment.

Connection authorisation

2   Subject to paragraph 1, this Licence authorises the connection to the Applicable Systems of:

(*a*)   any public telecommunication system;

(*b*)   any telecommunication system run under a Licence, which is situated on the same premises or in the same building as the Applicable Systems;

(c)   any telecommunication system run under a Licence which is specified by the Secretary of State for the purpose of this Licence and described in a list kept for the purpose by the Director and made available by him for inspection by the general public;

(d)   any telecommunication system run by the Crown;

(e)   any telecommunication system, the Licence for which authorises connection to the Applicable Systems;

(f)   any Offshore System, provided that:

(i)   the Licensee of the Applicable Systems to which that Offshore System is connected is the operator of an installation maintained in waters to which the Mineral Workings (Offshore Installations) Act 1971 applies; and

(ii)   no Messages conveyed by the Applicable Systems have been or are to be conveyed by means of the Offshore System to or from a telecommunication system in a country or territory outside the United Kingdom;

(g)   Apparatus of every description which is comprised in the Applicable Systems or comprised in a telecommunication system of a type described in paragraphs 2(a) to 2(f);

(h)   any Apparatus not comprised in the Applicable Systems which is for the time being Compliant Terminal Equipment or approved for connection to the Applicable Systems in accordance with section 22 of the Act; and

(i)   any hearing aid.

Service authorisation

3   Subject to paragraph 1, this Licence authorises the provision by means of the Applicable Systems of telecommunication services of any description, other than:

(a)   International Simple Voice Resale Services;

(b)   International Simple Data Resale Services, unless the Secretary of State has specified a description of such Services which may be provided by means of the Applicable Systems and such specification is described in a list kept for the purpose by the Director and made available by him for inspection by the general public;

(c)   conveyance of Messages for the delivery of one or more of the services specified in paragraphs (a) to (c) of Section 72(2) of the Broadcasting Act 1990 for simultaneous reception in two or more Dwelling-Houses; and

(d)   any telecommunication services involving the conveyance of Messages for more than 500 metres in lateral distance between points on a single set of premises, where any two points on the boundary of those premises are more than 5 kilometres in lateral distance from each other, unless the Secretary of State has specified that a particular Licensee may, on such conditions and in such circumstances as the Secretary of State may specify, provide such services and has notified that Licensee accordingly.

Definitions and interpretation

4   In this Schedule unless the context otherwise requires:

(a)   'Apparatus' means telecommunication apparatus within the extended definition in Schedule 2 to the Act;

(b)   'Applicable Terminal Equipment' means apparatus which is applicable terminal equipment within the meaning of regulation 4 of the Telecommunications Terminal Equipment Regulations 1992;

(c) 'Compliant Terminal Equipment' means Applicable Terminal Equipment which satisfies the requirements of regulation 8 of the Telecommunications Terminal Equipment Regulations 1992;

(d) 'Dwelling-House' has the same meaning as in section 202 of the Broadcasting Act 1990;

(e) 'International Private Leased Circuit' means a conmmunication facility which is:

(i)   comprised both in a public teleconununication system and in an equivalent telecommunication system in a country or territory other than the United Kingdom;

(ii)   for the conveyance of Messages between points, all of which are points of connection between telecommunication systems referred to in paragraph 4(e)(i) and other telecommunication systems;

(iii)   made available to a particular person or particular persons;

(iv)   such that all of the Messages transmitted at any of the points mentioned in paragraph 4(e)(ii) are received at every other such point; and

(v)   such that the points mentioned in paragraph 4(e)(ii) are fixed by the way in which the facility is installed and cannot otherwise be selected by persons or Apparatus sending Messages by means of that facility;

(f) 'International Simple Data Resale Services' means telecommunication services consisting in the conveyance of Messages which do not include two-way live speech, but include only such switching, processing, data storage or protocol conversion as is necessary for the conveyance of those Messages in real time, which have been or are to be conveyed by means of all of the following:

(i)   a Public Switched Network;

(ii)   an International Private Leased Circuit; and

(iii)   the equivalent of a Public Switched Network in another country or territory;

provided that conveyance of a Message by means of a Public Switched Network or, as the case may be, the equivalent of a Public Switched Network in another country or territory shall be disregarded where that Message is so conveyed from or to the telecommunication system by means of which that Message is initially sent or ultimately received exclusively for the purpose of carrying out such initial or final switching of that Message as could lawfully have been carried out by the person running that system or another on that person's behalf, under the Class Licence for the Running of Self Provided Telecommunication Systems granted by the Secretary of State under section 7 of the Telecommunications Act 1984 on 30 July 1992 and any successors to that Licence, on the premises where that Message was initially sent, or, as the case may be, ultimately received;

(g) 'International Simple Voice Resale Services' means telecommunication services consisting in the conveyance of Messages which include two-way live speech which have been or are to be conveyed by means of all of the following:

(i)   a Public Switched Network;

(ii)   an Internationial Private Leased Circuit; and

(iii)   the equivalent of a Public Switched Network in another country or territory;

provided that conveyance of a Message by means of a Public Switched Network or, as the case may be, the equivalent of a Public Switched Network in another country or territory shall be disregarded where that Message is so conveyed from or to the telecommunication system by means of which that Message is initially sent or ultimately received exclusively for the purpose of carrying out such initial or final switching of that Message as could lawfully have been carried out by the person running that system or another on that person's behalf, under the Class Licence for the Running of Self Provided Telecommunication Systems granted by the Secretary of State under section 7 of the Telecommunications Act 1984 on 30 July 1992 and any successors to that Licence, on the premises where that Message was initially sent, or, as the case may be, ultimately received;

(*h*) 'Message' means anything failing within paragraphs (a) to (d) of section 4(1) of the Act;

(*i*) 'Offshore System' means a telecommunication system which is on any installation which is maintained in waters to which the Mineral Workings (Offshore Installations) Act 1971 applies;

(*j*) 'Private Leased Circuit' means a communication facility which is:

(i)   provided by means of one or more public telecommunication systems;

(ii)   for the conveyance of Messages between points, all of which are points of connection between telecommunication systems referred to in paragraph 4(j)(i) and other telecommunication systems;

(iii)   made available to a particular person or particular persons;

(iv)   such that all of the Messages transmitted at any of the points mentioned in paragraph 40(j)(ii) are received at every other such point; and

(v)   such that the points mentioned in paragraph 40(j)(ii) are fixed by the way which the facility is installed and cannot otherwise be selected by persons or Apparatus sending Messages by means of that facility; and

(*k*)   'Public Switched Network' means a public telecommunication system by means of which two-way telecommunication services are provided whereby Messages are switched incidentally to their conveyance, and, for the avoidance of doubt, a Public Switched Network does not include Private Leased Circuits.

5   Expressions cognate with those referred to in this Schedule shall be construed accordingly.

ANNEX A

THE APPLICABLE SYSTEMS

1   The Applicable Systems are telecommunication systems of every description within the United Kingdom provided that each such system satisfies each of the following conditions:

(*a*)   all of the Apparatus comprised in that system:

(i)   is situated within a single set of premises; or

(ii)   if not so situated, consists of Apparatus situated in different sets of premises together with any Apparatus run exclusively for the purpose of enabling messages to be conveyed between those premises, where none of the sets of premises in question is more than 200 metres in lateral distance from any other; or

(iii)   is situated within a single building; or

(iv)   is run by the same Licensee and is situated on premises which the Secretary of State has specified for the time being for the purpose of this

Annex and are described in a list kept for the purpose by the Director and made available by him for inspection by the general public; and

(b) none of the Apparatus consists of Wireless Telegraphy Apparatus designed or adapted for the purpose of transmitting or receiving Messages to or from Apparatus which is designed or adapted to be capable of use whilst in motion.

2 For the purposes of this Annex, premises whose boundaries touch and which are owned or occupied by the same person shall be deemed to be a single set of premises.

3 For the purposes of this Annex:

(a) 'Apparatus' means telecommunication apparatus within the extended definition in Schedule 2 to the Act;

(b) 'Message' means anything falling within paragraphs (a) to (d) of section 4(1) of the Act; and

(c) 'Wireless Telegraphy Apparatus' has the same meaning as in the Wireless Telegraphy Act 1949.

ANNEX B
INFORMATION REQUIRED UNDER CONDITION 13 OF SCHEDULE 1

1 The information which is required under Condition 13 to be kept by the Licensee and made available is as follows:

(a) in all cases:

(i) the name of the Licensee;

(ii) the address of the Licensee's Major Office;

(iii) the public telecommunication systems to which the Applicable Systems are or are to be connected;

(b) where the Applicable Systems are or are to be connected to any International Private Leased Circuit:

(i) particulars of that International Private Leased Circuit; and

(ii) particulars of any other telecommunication system connected to that International Private Leased Circuit; and

(c) any information required in respect of relevant technical requirements laid down by the Director in accordance with Condition 3 of Schedule 1.

Note

The Licence no longer requires the keeping of detailed information about any Call Routing Apparatus and Serially Connected Equipment compised in the system. This follows on from the abolition of the designated maintenance regime.

CLASS LICENCE TO RUN TELECOMMUNICATION SYSTEMS FOR THE PROVISION OF SATELLITE TELECOMMUNICATION SERVICES GRANTED BY THE SECRETARY OF STATE FOR TRADE AND INDUSTRY UNDER SECTION 7 OF THE TELECOMMUNICATIONS ACT 1984

2 AUGUST 1991

TABLE OF CONTENTS

Part 1:   Conditions applying to all Applicable Systems
1   Requirements under the Wireless Telegraphy Act
2   Essential Interfaces
3   Approval of Apparatus
4   Compliance with European Community Requirements
Part 2:   Conditions applying to all Applicable Systems by means of which
telecommunication services are provided to others
5   Application of Conditions 6 to 10
6   Prohibition on Undue Preference and Undue Discrimination
7   Preparation of Accounts
8   Prohibition of Cross-Subsidies
9   Prohibition of Linked Sales
10   Privacy and Confidentiality
Part 3:   Requirement to Furnish Information
11   Requirement to Furnish Information to the Director
Part 4:   Exceptions and Limitations
12   Exceptions and Limitations on Conditions in Schedule 1
Schedule 2:   Revocation
Schedule 3;   Authorisation to connect other telecommuniccation systems
and apparatus to the applicable systems and to provide telecommunications
services by means of the applicable systems
Annex A: The applicable systems

THE LICENCE

1   The Secretary of State, in exercise of the powers conferred on him by
section 7 of the Telecommunications Act 1984 (hereinafter referred to as 'the
Act') having consulted the Director General of Telecommunications ('the
Director') hereby grants to all persons of the class described in paragraph 2
below (each such person being hereinafter referred to as 'the Licensee') a
Licence, for the period specified in paragraph 3, subject to the Conditions set
out in Schedule 1 and to revocation as provided for in Schedule 2, to run the
telecommunication systems specified in Annex A (each such system being
hereinafter referred to as 'the Applicable System') and authorises the Licensee to do all or any of the acts specified in Schedule 3.
2   The class of persons to whom this Licence is granted is all persons
except for the British Broadcasting Corporation and any persons in respect
of whom the Secretary of State or the Director has revoked this Licence in
accordance with Schedule 2 and whose names and particulars are for the time
being entered upon a list kept for the purpose by the Director and open for
inspection by the general public.
3   This Licence shall enter into force on 2 August 1991 and shall be of 25
years' duration unless previously revoked in accordance with Schedule 2.
4   In this Licence:
    'Apparatus' means telecommunications apparatus within the extended
    definition in Schedule 2 of the Act, and any apparatus which is connec-
    ted to a telecommunication system;
    'Appeal Period' means
        (a)   where the Licensee appeals against neither conviction nor
    sentence, the period within which such an Appeal might have been brought;

(*b*)   where the Licensee appeals against conviction or sentence or both, the period ending on the date on which such Appeal is finally disposed of;

'Appeal' includes further appeal and application for leave to appeal or further to appeal;

'Licence' means a licence granted or having effect as if granted under section 7 of the Act;

'Message' means anything falling within paragraphs (a) to (d) of section 4 (1) of the Act;

'Station for Wireless Telegraphy', 'Wireless Telegraphy Apparatus', and 'Wireless Telegraphy' have the same meaning as in the Wireless Telegraphy Act 1949.

5   The Interpretation Act 1978 shall apply for the purpose of interpreting this Licence as if it were an Act of Parliament.

6   Any word or expression used in this Licence shall unless the context otherwise requires have the same meaning as it has in the Act.

7   For the purpose of interpreting this Licence headings and titles shall be disregarded.

Rt Hon Peter Lilley MP
Secretary of State for Trade and Industry

2 August 1991

Note
The Licence authorises the provision of a wide range of satellite services and is available to all operators with the exception of the BBC. The DGT may prevent other operators — for example BT and Mercury — from using the licence if they could run their satellite systems under other licences which contain different conditions. There is no requirement to register or pay any fee in order to run under the Licence.

SCHEDULE 1
CONDITIONS INCLUDED UNDER SECTION 7 OF THE ACT

PART 1:   CONDITIONS APPLYING TO ALL APPLICABLE SYSTEMS

Condition 1   Requirements under the Wireless Telegraphy Act

1.1   The Licensee shall secure that there is in force in respect of the establishment and use of each Station for Wireless Telegraphy and the installation and use of each item of Wireless Telegraphy Apparatus comprised in the Applicable Systems a licence granted under section 1 of the Wireless Telegraphy Act 1949, unless that Station or that Apparatus has been exempted from the need for such a licence by regulations made under that section.

Note
Receive-only earth stations are covered by Wireless Telegraphy Act exemption orders and some kinds of mobile and portable equipment are also covered by similar exemptions. All other earth stations require a licence.

Condition 2   Essential Interfaces

2.1   Where the Licensee implements in its Applicable Systems an interface which the Director has specified as an 'Essential Interface', it shall secure that that interface conforms with the relevant European Telecommunications Standard or recommendation of the International Telecommunications Union or in the absence or inadequacy of either with such other standard, recommendation or document (including requirements or recommendations of the Director or any other person) as the Director may determine for the purpose of this Condition.

2.2   In paragraph 2.1 of this Condition 'Essential Interface' means in respect of a point of connection an interface on which in the opinion of the Director it is essential that interoperability between the Applicable Systems and the respective Operator's systems is available.

2.3   For the purposes of this Condition 'Operator' means any person who is authorised to run a telecommunication system under a Licence which authorises connection of that system to the Applicable Systems.

Note
The DGT reserves powers to specify interface standards for the purpose of ensuring interoperability between networks should future developments make this necessary.

Condition 3   Approval of Apparatus

3.1   Where the Applicable Systems are connected whether directly or indirectly to any public telecommunication system, all the telecommunication apparatus comprised in the Applicable Systems and all the apparatus connected to them shall unless the Director has consented otherwise and has not withdrawn that consent, be apparatus which is approved for the time being under section 22 of the Act or in such other manner as the Director may determine for the purposes of that public telecommunications system, and in respect of which any conditions specified in the relevant approval or determination are complied with.

Note
OFTEL issued on 2 August 1991 General Approval No: NS/G/123/100015 to cover fixed and mobile earth stations. Equipment standards for certain kinds of satellite earth stations are covered by ETSI (See Web site-http://www.etsi.fr).

Condition 4   Compliance with European Community Requirements

4.1   The Director may from time to time specify requirements relating to the specification, functioning or use of the Applicable Systems which the Secretary of State has notified to the Director are necessary to fulfil any European Community obligation of the United Kingdom, and the Licensee shall comply with any such requirement so specified.

4.2   Any requirement specified under paragraph 4.1 above shall be described in a list kept by the Director and made available by him for inspection by the general public.

Note
These obligations are listed at OFTEL.

PART 2: CONDITIONS APPLYING TO ALL APPLICABLE
SYSTEMS BY MEANS OF WHICH TELECOMMUNICATION
SERVICES ARE PROVIDED TO OTHERS

Condition 5   Application of Conditions 6 to 10

5.1   Condition 6 to 10 of this Schedule shall apply only to Licensees who provide telecommunication services to others by means of the Applicable Systems.
5.2   In Conditions 6 to 10 of this Schedule
'Relevant Service' means a service authorised in Schedule 3 to this Licence, and
'Relevant Services Business' means that part of the Licensee's activities which consists in the provision of Relevant services.

Condition 6   Prohibition on Undue Preference and Undue Discrimination

6.1   The Licensee shall not (whether in respect of the charges or other terms or conditions applied or otherwise) show undue preference to or exercise undue discrimination against particular persons or persons of any class or description in respect of:
(a)   the provision of any Relevant Service;
(b)   the connection to any of the Applicable Systems of any telecommunication apparatus or any other system which, in either case, is not and is not to be comprised in any of the Applicable Systems; or
(c)   the granting of permission to connect such systems or apparatus to, or to provide services by means of, any of the Applicable Systems.
6.2   The Licensee shall be deemed to have shown such undue preference or to have exercised such undue discrimination if it unfairly favours to a material extent a business carried on by it in relation to any of the matters mentioned in paragraph 6.1 so as to place at a significant competitive disadvantage persons competing with that business.
6.3   Nothing done in any manner by the Licensee shall be regarded as undue preference or undue discrimination if and to the extent that the Licensee is required to do that thing in that manner by or under any provision of this Licence.

Condition 7   Preparation of Accounts

7.1   The Licensee shall maintain accounting records in such a form that its Relevant Services Business is separately identifiable or separately attributable in the books of the Licensee, being records sufficient to show and explain the transactions of that part of the Licensee's business.

Condition 8   Prohibition of Cross-subsidies

8.1   The Licensee shall secure that its Relevant Services Business is not unfairly cross-subsidised from any other source.
8.2   The Licensee shall as soon as practicable and in any event not later than 12 months after beginning to provide any service under this Licence

record, except where the Director agrees otherwise, any material transfer at full cost between its Relevant Services Business and any other part of its undertaking or any other person.

8.3   In this Condition:

(*a*)   a transfer from one undertaking to another undertaking or a company takes place when any thing (including any service or money) produced or acquired by, normally used in, or otherwise at the disposal of, the first mentioned business is made available for the purposes of the other undertaking; and

(*b*)   'full cost' in the case of money transferred includes the market rate of interest for that money.

Condition 9   Prohibition of Linked Sales

9.1   The Licensee shall not make the provision to any person of any Relevant Service conditional upon the acquisition or use by any person of any other telecommunication service or telecommunication apparatus save where that Relevant Service cannot otherwise be provided.

9.2   Except with the agreement of the Director the Licensee shall not provide any combination of:

(*a*)   a Relevant Service or Relevant Services;

(*b*)   another telecommunication service or other telecommunication services;

(*c*)   an item or items of telecommunications apparatus;

by means of or in relation to the Applicable Systems in a manner or for charges or on terms or conditions more favourable than would have been available for doing any of those things separately and without the other thing or things.

9.3   Notwithstanding paragraph 9.2, the Licensee may, in providing by means of or in relation to the Applicable Systems, a combination of any of the items set out at (a) to (c) of that sub-paragraph, which are so related as to permit cost savings when they are provided together, offer quantity discounts or more favourable terms and conditions in respect of quantity for those services.

Condition 10   Privacy and Confidentiality

10.1   Subject to the other provisions of this Licence, and except where Messages are broadcast for general reception, the Licensee shall take all reasonable steps to safeguard the privacy and confidentiality of any Message conveyed by means of the Applicable Systems and of information acquired by it in relation to such conveyance.

PART 3:   REQUIREMENT TO FURNISH INFORMATION

Condition 11   Requirement to Furnish Information to the Director etc.

11.1   The Licensee shall furnish or procure and furnish to the Director, in such manner and at such times as the Director may reasonably require such documents, accounts, estimates, returns, or other information as he may reasonably require for the purpose of exercising the functions assigned or transferred to him by or under Parts II and III of the Act.

11.2   In making any such request the Director shall ensure that no undue burden is imposed on the Licensee in procuring and furnishing such information and that the Licensee is not required to procure or furnish information which would not normally be available unless the Director considers the information essential to enable him to exercise his functions, in particular to satisfy himself that the Licensee is complying with the terms of this licence.

11.3   The Licensee shall permit the Director and any person authorised by him in writing to inspect the Applicable Systems at any reasonable time for the purpose of verifying whether

(a)   the Licensee is running the Systems in accordance with this Licence; or

(b)   the connection or the proposed connection of any other system to the Applicable Systems causes or would cause any contravention of the Licence under which that other system is run.

11.4   If the Licensee is convicted of an offence under Section 5 (2) of the Act relating to the Applicable Systems, the Licensee shall, not later than fourteen days after the expiry of the Appeal Period, notify the Director that the Licensee has been so convicted, specifying the offence, the date of such conviction, the name and address of the Court concerned and the penalty imposed.

PART 4:   EXCEPTIONS AND LIMITATIONS

Condition 12   Exceptions and Limitations on Conditions in Schedule 1

12.1   Unless the context otherwise requires, the Licensee's obligations under these Conditions have effect subject to the following exceptions and limitations.

12.2   The Licensee is not obliged to do anything which is not practicable.

12.3   The Licensee shall not be held to have failed to comply with an obligation imposed upon it by or under these Conditions if and to the extent that the Licensee is prevented from complying with that obligation by any physical, topographical or other natural obstacle, by the malfunction or failure of any apparatus or equipment due to circumstances beyond the control of the Licensee, by the act of any national authority, or local authority or international organisation or as the result of fire, flood, explosion, accident, emergency, riot or war.

SCHEDULE 2
REVOCATION

1   The Secretary of State may revoke this Licence in its entirety at any time by giving not less than 30 days' notice published in such manner as the Secretary of State considers appropriate.

2   The Secretary of State or the Director may at any time revoke this Licence in respect of any particular Licensee or in respect of all or any of the Applicable Systems run by a particular Licensee:

(a)   where the Licensee has failed to comply with a final order (or a provisional order confirmed) under section 16 of the Act and the Secretary of State or the Director, as the case may be, has given the Licensee not less than 30 days' notice in writing that, if the Licensee fails to comply with the order within that period of 30 days, he intends to revoke the Licence in respect of that Licensee or in respect of any of the Applicable Systems run by that Licensee; no such notice of intention shall be given where the question of the validity of the order is the subject of any court proceedings, and where that question becomes so subject during the 30 day notice period, that period shall cease to run until the final disposal of those proceedings (including any Appeal);

(b)   if the Director receives notification under Condition 11.4 of Schedule 1 that the Licensee has been convicted of an offence under section 5(2) of the Act in relation to the Applicable Systems, or in default of the Licensee giving such notification, not later than three months after the Director first having had actual notice of the conviction, or the expiry of the Appeal Period, whichever is the later; or

(c)   by giving to that Licensee not less than 30 days' notice where the Secretary of State or the Director, as the case may be, considers that that Licensee is relying, has relied or is likely to rely on this Licence in order to run any telecommunication system so as to be relieved wholly or in part of any obligation, limitation or restriction imposed on the Licensee in respect of the provision of any telecommunication services run under a Licence granted to the Licensee individually.

3   The Secretary of State may at any time revoke this Licence in respect of any particular Licensee in the interests of national security or relations with the Government of a country or territory outside the United Kingdom.

4   Any notice which is required to be given to a particular Licensee under paragraph 2 of this Schedule shall be given to the Licensee concerned by serving the document by post to the address of the Licensee, provided however that if it is not practicable to ascertain the name or address of the Licensee the notice may be given by addressing it to a person by the description of 'the Licensee' of the System (describing it) and by delivering it to some person on premises where the System in respect of which the notice is given is situated or, if there is no person on those premises to whom it can be delivered, by affixing it or a copy of it to some conspicuous object on those premises.

Note

The Licence may be revoked under Schedule 2 in respect of a particular operator who uses the licence in order to avoid obligations imposed on them by any individual licence which they hold and which they should be using to operate the systems in question. For example, this provision can be used to prevent BT or Mercury from operating under the licence rather than under their individual licences which enable them to operate satellite systems.

SCHEDULE 3
AUTHORISATION TO CONNECT OTHER
TELECOMMUNICATION SYSTEMS AND APPARATUS TO THE
APPLICABLE SYSTEMS AND TO PROVIDE
TELECOMMUNICATION SERVICES BY MEANS OF
THE APPLICABLE SYSTEMS

1   Nothing in this Licence removes any need to obtain any other licence that may be required under any other enactment.

Connection Authorisation

2   Subject to the limitation in paragraph 1 above, this Licence authorises the connection to the Applicable Systems of:

(i)   any other Applicable System;

(ii)   any earth orbiting apparatus, provided that:

(aa)   the relevant requirements, if any, for consultation and compliance with specified operating parameters under the INTELSAT Agreement, INMARSAT Convention and EUTELSAT Convention have been and continue to be satisfied; and

(bb)   the relevant rules and standards, if any, issued under the INTELSAT Operating Agreement, INMARSAT Operating Agreement and the EUTELSAT Operating Agreement, have been and continue to be satisfied; and

(cc)   it is not earth orbiting apparatus to which the Secretary of State has notified the Licensee that the Licensee should not, or as the case may be should cease to, connect the Applicable System;

(iii)   any Private Leased Circuit, Offshore Private Circuit or International Private Leased Circuit;

(iv)   any telecommunication system run under the Licence entitled 'Class Licence for the running of Branch Telecommunication Systems' granted by the Secretary of State for Trade and Industry on 8 November 1989, or any successor thereto;

(v)   any telecommunication system run under the Licence entitled 'Class Licence for the Running of Self Provided Telecommunication Systems' granted by the Secretary of State for Trade and Industry on 2 August 1991, or any successor thereto;

(vi)   any telecommunication system run under a Licence which authorises the provision of Radiopaging Services;

(vii)   any telecommunication system run by the Crown;

(viii)   any telecommunication system in the United Kingdom the Licence for which authorises it to be connected to the Applicable Systems;

(ix)   any telecommunication system run under any Licence which was in force on the date on which this Licence was granted or subsequently comes into force and which is specified by the Secretary of State for the purpose of this Licence and described in a list kept for that purpose by the Director and made available by him for inspection by the general public;

(x)   telecommunications apparatus comprised in the Applicable Systems;

(xi)   telecommunication apparatus comprised in a telecommunication system mentioned in sub-paragraphs (i) to (ix) above; and

(xii)   any hearing aid.

Service Authorisation

3   Subject to the limitation in paragraph 1 above, this Licence authorises the provision by means of the Applicable Systems of any telecommunication service consisting in the transmission of Messages to or the reception of Messages from earth orbiting apparatus except for

(i)   the transmission and reception of Messages which have been or are to be conveyed by means of a Public Switched Telecommunication

System, except where the only connection to that Public Switched Telecommunication System is by means of earth orbiting apparatus and a telecommunication system in the United Kingdom, the Licence for which authorises that system to be connected to that Public Switched Telecommunication System, or where the Applicable System is a Mobile or Transportable System; and

(ii)   the reception of Messages comprised in Television Programme Services and Sound Broadcasting Services for subsequent delivery to two or more dwelling houses by means other than Wireless Telegraphy.

Interpretation

4   In this Schedule:
'EUTELSAT Convention' means the Convention establishing the European Telecommunications Satellite Organisation EUTELSAT including its Preamble and its Annexes, opened for signature by Governments at Paris, France on 15 July 1982 and any subsequent amendments made to it.
'EUTELSAT Operating Agreement' means the Operating Agreement relating to the European Telecommunications Satellite Organisation EUTELSAT, including its Preamble and Annexes, opened for signature at Paris, France on 15 July 1982 and any subsequent amendments made to it.
'INTELSAT Agreement' means the Agreement including its Annexes but excluding all titles of Articles, opened for signature by Governments at Washington DC, USA, on 20 August 1971 by which the International Telecommunications Satellite Organisation INTELSAT was established, and any subsequent amendments made to it.
'INTELSAT Operating Agreement' means the Agreement, including its Annex but excluding all titles of Articles, opened for signature at Washington DC, USA, on 20 August 1971, by Governments or telecommunications entities designated by Governments in accordance with the provisions of the INTELSAT Agreement, and any subsequent amendments made to it.
'INMARSAT Convention' means the Convention establishing the International Maritime Satellite Organisation INMARSAT including its Preamble and its Annex, opened for signature by governments at London, England on 3 September 1976 and any subsequent amendments made to it.
'INMARSAT Operating Agreement' means the Agreement, including its Annex, opened for signature at London, England on 3 September 1976 by entities designated by governments party to the INMARSAT Convention, and any subsequent amendments made to it.
'International Private Leased Circuit' means a communication facility which is
(i)   comprised both in a public telecommunication system and in a telecommunication system in a country or territory other than the United Kingdom;
(ii)   for the conveyance of Messages between points, all of which are points of connection between telecommunication systems referred to in sub-paragraph (i) above and other telecommunication systems;

(iii)   which is made available to a particular person or particular persons;

(iv)   which is such that all of the Messages transmitted at any of the points mentioned in sub-paragraph (ii) above are received at every other such point;

(v)   and which is such that the points mentioned in sub-paragraph (ii) above are fixed by the way in which the facility is installed and cannot otherwise be selected by persons or apparatus sending Messages by means of that facility.

'Mobile or Transportable System' means an Applicable System which is designed or adapted for use while in motion, or is portable and not intended for permanent use in any one location, and in either case is not connected directly or indirectly to any Public Switched Telecommunication System other than by means of earth orbiting apparatus.

'Offshore Private Circuit' means a communications facility which is

(i)   provided by means of both a telecommunication system comprised in a public telecommunication system and a telecommunication system which is on any installation which is maintained in waters to which the Mineral Workings (Offshore Installations) Act 1971 applies (an 'offshore system');

(ii)   for the conveyance of Messages between points, all of which are points of connection between telecommunication systems referred to in sub-paragraph (i) above and other telecommunication systems;

(iii)   which is made available to a particular person or particular persons;

(iv)   which is such that all of the Messages transmitted at any of the points mentioned in sub-paragraph (ii) above are received at every other such point; and

(v)   which is such that the points mentioned in sub-paragraph (ii) above are fixed by the way in which the facility is installed and cannot otherwise be selected by persons or apparatus sending Messages by means of that facility.

'Private Leased Circuit' means a communication facility which is:

(i)   provided by means of one or more public telecommunication systems;

(ii)   for the conveyance of Messages between points, all of which are points of connection between telecommunication systems referred to in sub-paragraph (i) above and other telecommunication systems;

(iii)   made available to a particular person or particular persons;

(iv)   such that all of the Messages transmitted at any of the points mentioned in (ii) above are received at every other such point; and

(v)   such that the points mentioned in (ii) above are fixed by the way in which the facility is installed and cannot otherwise be selected by persons or apparatus sending Messages by means of that facility.

'Public Switched Telecommunication System' means a telecommunication system providing a two-way switched telecommunication service which is run by a public telecommunications operator, or in the case of a country or territory outside the United Kingdom by the administration of that country or territory or by a person recognised by that administration for the purposes of the International Telecommunication

Convention and acting in that capacity, except where that system is a Private Leased Circuit, International Private Leased Circuit, or an Offshore Private Circuit.

'Radiopaging Services' means any telecommunication service provided by means of Wireless Telegraphy where every Message, apart from simple acknowledgement, can be transmitted only from a fixed Station for Wireless Telegraphy to apparatus designed or adapted for use while in motion.

'Television Programme Service' and 'Sound Broadcasting Services' have the same meaning as in the Broadcasting Act 1990.

Notes

1. The systems to which an earth station run under the Licence may be connected include: other systems on the same premises run under the Licence or under the Branch Systems General Licence; earth orbiting apparatus; private leased circuits (but not the public switched network), international private leased circuits and offshore private circuits; self-provided circuits run under the class licence for self-provided systems; terrestrial outside broadcast links; radio-paging systems; systems run by the Crown and any system which is run under a licence which permits that system to be connected to a system under this licence. The Secretary of State may also specify additional permitted connections after the licence has been issued.

2. Paragraph 2 (ii) of Schedule 3 lays down the conditions for use of satellite capacity: if satellite capacity is to be provided by INTELSAT, EUTELSAT or INMARSAT, their technical requirements must, where relevant, be complied with. Transponder capacity from these organisations may normally be obtained only through BT's Signatory Affairs office who will advise on the appropriate arrangements. This does not apply to capacity leased on a private satellite, but operators are required to ensure that the services they provide fall within the operating terms agreed for that satellite under INTELSAT, EUTELSAT or INMARSAT consultation procedures.

3. The Licence does not allow messages to be directly conveyed under any circumstances between an earth station and the PSN or to be indirectly sent via another terrestrial system such as a private leased circuit. If operators wish to use a satellite earth station for conveying such messages, they must apply to the DTI for an individual licence to do so.

4. Paragraph 3 (i) does permit messages to be sent from an earth station to the PSN by means of a satellite under certain circumstances. Subject to paragraph 7, signals which have been or are to be conveyed over the PSN may be received or transmitted by an earth station run under the licence provided that the connection to the PSN is by means of a satellite and an earth station run under a licence which authorises its connection to the PSN. Transmissions may, for example, be uplinked under the Licence for reception by BT or Mercury who may then pass them onto the PSN under their own PTO licences.

5. Messages from a fixed earth station which are intended to be received by a downlink overseas and then passed onto the PSN may not be transmitted under the Licence. Connections to the PSN via an overseas downlink are permitted under the Licence only if the earth station used in the UK is mobile or transportable within the definition used in the Licence (designed or adapted for use while in motion, or portable and not intended for permanent use in any one location, and in either case not connected directly or indirectly to the PSN other than indirectly by means of a satellite link).

6. Paragraph 3 (ii) also prevents a cable television system being run under the licence, and stops a downlink run under this licence being connected to a cable television system run under another licence. This does not, however, restrict the uplinking of programmes intended for reception on cable television systems.

ANNEX A

THE APPLICABLE SYSTEMS

1 The Applicable Systems are telecommunication systems within the United Kingdom provided that a System is an Applicable System only to the extent that the System is a Station for Wireless Telegraphy or Wireless Telegraphy Apparatus used to transmit Messages to or receive Messages from earth orbiting apparatus.

Note
The types of telecommunication systems covered by the Licence are satellite transmit and/or receive earth stations of any kind, whether fixed, mobile or transportable. Subject to the restrictions set out in the Licence it permits the provision of any kind of satellite service, whether one-way or two-way, point to point or point to multipoint, including voice, data, vision or any other kind of message, for reception within the UK or in any overseas country.

LICENCE GRANTED BY THE SECRETARY OF STATE FOR TRADE AND INDUSTRY TO NYNEX CABLECOMMS BURY AND ROCHDALE IN RESPECT OF THE CABLE FRANCHISE IN BURY AND ROCHDALE

TABLE OF CONTENTS

1   Lines.
2   Resiting of lines installed above the ground.
3   Cabinets, boxes, pillars, pedestals and other similar apparatus.
4   Guidelines on the installation of apparatus.
5   Conservation Areas.
6   Sites of Special Scientific Interest.
7   Listed Buildings and Ancient Monuments.
8   National Trust.
9   Maintainable Highways.
10   Placing of underground lines in ducts.
11   Maintenance and safety of apparatus.
12   Arrangements with electricity suppliers.
13   Replacement of Apparatus.
14   Needs of Disabled Persons.
15   Instructions for the installation of apparatus.
16   Records of apparatus.
17   Emergency works and urgent works.
18   Public or private events and construction sites.
19   Public inspection of Code related licence conditions.
20   Funds for meeting liabilities.
Annex A: The Applicable Cabled Systems.
Annex B: Map of the Licensed Area.

Notes
1. Although the whole contents of the Licence is set out, only extracts of the licence itself are reproduced in the text. This is because many conditions are similar in all licences, although not necessarily identical, and there is not space in this Handbook to reproduce all the selected licences in full. However, the conditions and other parts of the licence which are special or particular to this type of licence are reproduced.
2. This licence and other cable licences will be further amended in the light of recent changes to BT's licence particularly in relation to fair trading.

THE LICENCE

1   The Secretary of State, in exercise of the powers conferred on him by section 7 of the Telecommunications Act 1984 (hereinafter referred to as 'the Act') and after consultation with the Director hereby grants to NYNEX CableComms Bury and Rochdale (hereinafter referred to as 'the Licensee') a licence, for the period specified in paragraph 3, subject to the Conditions set out in Schedule 1 and to revocation as provided for in Schedule 2, to run the telecommunication systems specified in Annex A (hereinafter referred to as 'the Applicable Cabled Systems') and authorises the Licensee to do all or any of the acts specified in Schedule 3.

2   The Telecommunications Code contained in Schedule 2 to the Act shall apply to the Licensee in the Licensed Area, that is to say the area within the red line on the map attached at Annex B to this Licence, for all purposes except those not relating to the Applicable Cabled Systems and subject to the other exceptions and conditions set out in Schedule 4 for so long as this Licence is one to which section 8 of the Act applies.

3   This Licence enters into force on the date of signature and shall continue in force until the expiry of the period of 23 years beginning on the

date specified by the Secretary of State for the purpose of this Licence after consulting the Licensee and notified by him in writing to the Licensee.

Patrick McLoughlin MP
Parliamentary Under Secretary
of State for Trade and
Technology
14th December 1993

Note
This Licence has been chosen as a recent example of a typical broadband cable operator's licence.

SCHEDULE 1
CONDITIONS INCLUDED BY VIRTUE OF SECTION 7 OF THE ACT

PART 1:　DEFINITIONS, INTERPRETATIONS AND
TRANSITIONAL PROVISIONS RELATING TO THE CONDITIONS
IN SCHEDULE 1

(1)　In these Conditions unless the context otherwise requires:
(a)　'Applicable Terminal Equipment' means apparatus which is applicable terminal equipment within the meaning of regulation 4 of the Telecommunications Terminal Equipment Regulations 1992;
(b)　'Associate' of the Licensee means any member of the Licensee's Group or a Subsidiary of, or another body corporate controlled by, the Licensee;
(c)　'Bringing into Service' means the process of connecting by means requiring the use of a tool telecommunication apparatus (including apparatus comprised in a telecommunication system) or a telecommunication system to another telecommunication system, or the process of disconnecting by such means such apparatus or such system from another such system; and includes such testing or inspection of that apparatus or system and any other apparatus or system to which it is or is to be connected as is necessary for the purpose of ensuring that the apparatus or the system in which the apparatus is or is to be comprised, or the system, is authorised to be connected to any of the Applicable Cabled Systems; and expressions cognate with 'Bringing into Service' shall be construed accordingly;
(d)　'Call Box Services' and 'Public Call Box' have the meanings given to them in Condition 7;
(e)　'Compliant Terminal Equipment' means Applicable Terminal Equipment which satisfies the requirements of regulation 9 of the Telecommunications Terminal Equipment Regulations 1992;
(f)　'Connectable System' and 'Connection Service' have the meanings given to them in Condition 8;
(g)　'cost' includes a reasonable profit in all the circumstances of the case;
(h)　'to dial' includes any equivalent operation;
(i)　'Emergency' means an emergency of any kind, including any circumstance whatever resulting from major accidents, natural disasters and incidents involving toxic or radio-active materials;

(*j*) 'Emergency Organisations' has the meaning given to it in Condition 4;

(*k*) 'Fixed Wireless Telegraphy Station' means any 'Station for Wireless Telegraphy' or 'Wireless Telegraphy Apparatus' which is not used while in motion and which is not used to provide Mobile Radio Telecommunication Services;

(*l*) 'Group' means a group of companies consisting of a company and its Subsidiaries of which the Licensee is a member;

(*m*) 'Licence' means a licence granted or having effect as if granted under section 7 of the Act;

(*n*) 'Limited Maintenance Telecommunication System' and 'Limited Maintenance Telecommunication Apparatus' mean any telecommunication system or telecommunication apparatus as the case may be which is, or is to be, run under a Licence which requires Maintenance services to be provided in respect of it, if it is, or is to be, connected to any of the Applicable Cabled Systems, by either the Licensee or the person running any other public telecommunication system to which it is, or is to be, connected;

(*o*) 'Line' means any wire, cable, tube, pipe or other similar thing (including its casing or coating) which is designed or adapted for use in connection with the running of a telecommunication system together with any plug, socket or other connection apparatus;

(*p*) 'Local Authority' has the same meaning as in section 97 of the Act;

(*q*) 'Maintenance Services' means in relation to any apparatus which has been installed:

(i) Pre-Maintenance Inspection;

(ii) carrying out repairs;

(iii) verifying or ensuring that:

(aa) the apparatus performs in accordance with its specification or as may be required by the operator of the Connectable System in which such apparatus is incorporated;

(bb) the apparatus continues to comply with any condition contained in an approval of that apparatus under section 22 of the Act or in the designation of a standard under that section;

(cc) apparatus which is Compliant Terminal Equipment continues to comply with the requirements of Regulation 8 of the Telecommunications Terminal Equipment Regulations 1992;

(dd) any terms or conditions regarding the apparatus or its connection or use that may be stipulated by the Licensee and which must be observed if the Connectable System is or is to remain connected to the Applicable Cabled Systems are observed;

(iv) any activity involving the removal of the outer cover of the apparatus or alteration of the apparatus including alterations of any stored commands capable of affecting the compliance of the apparatus with the technical requirements and conditions mentioned in (iii) above; or

(v) any activity involving the use of any test apparatus or other equipment not forming a permanent part of the apparatus

but shall not include operations incidental to the installation, Bringing into Service or routine use of the apparatus to convey Messages;

(*r*) 'Message' means anything falling within paragraphs (a) to (d) of section 4(1) of the Act;

(*s*) 'Mobile Radio Telecommunication Services' means any telecommunication service provided by means of a telecommunication system for the conveyance of Messages through the agency of wireless telegraphy where every Message that is conveyed thereby has been, or is to be, conveyed by means of a telecommunication system which is designed or adapted to be capable of being used while in motion;

(*t*) 'Network Connecting Apparatus', 'Network Termination Point' and 'Network Termination and Testing Apparatus' have the meanings given to them in Annex A;

(*u*) 'Operator' has the meaning given to it in Condition 8;

(*v*) 'Pre-Maintenance Inspection' means any inspection reasonably necessary to ensure that apparatus has been properly installed in a manner rendering it fit to be maintained by the person making the inspection, but does not include any inspection for the purpose of Bringing into Service;

(*w*) 'Private Circuit' means a circuit which is:

(i) provided by means of a telecommunication system comprised in the Applicable Cabled Systems;

(ii) made available to a particular person or particular persons for the conveyance of messages between fixed points within that system; and

(iii) installed in such a way that persons sending Messages by means of that circuit are not able to select the destination within that system to which Messages are conveyed;

(*x*) 'Public Emergency Call Service' has the meaning given to it in Condition 4;

(*y*) 'Relevant Connectable System' has the meaning given to it in Condition 8;

(*z*) 'Relevant Service' means any service which is provided in whole or in part by means of any of the Applicable Cabled Systems and which could have been provided on 30 April 1987 under and in accordance with the Class Licence for the running of telecommunication systems providing value added and data services granted by the Secretary of State on 30 April 1987 in whole or in part by means of a telecommunication system the running of which was authorised by that Licence;

(*aa*) 'Relevant Terminal Apparatus' has the meaning given to it in Annex A;

(*bb*) 'Served Premises' has the meaning given to it in Annex A;

(*cc*) 'Specified Public Telecommunication System' has the meaning given to it in Condition 2;

(*dd*) 'Station for Wireless Telegraphy' and 'Wireless Telegraphy Apparatus' have the same meaning as in the wireless Telegraphy Acts 1949 to 1967;

(*ee*) 'Subsidiary' has the same meaning as in section 736 of the Companies Act 1985, as substituted by section 144(1) of the Companies Act 1989;

(*ff*) 'Supplemental Services Business' has the meaning given to it in Condition 18;

(*gg*) 'switched telecommunication service' has the meaning given to it in Condition 3;

(*hh*) 'Systems Business' has the meaning given to it in Condition 19;

(*ii*) 'Telephone' means an item of telecommunication apparatus capable when connected to the Licensee's Applicable Cabled Systems of transmitting and receiving uninterrupted simultaneous two way speech conveyed, or as the case may be to be conveyed, by means of those Applicable Cabled Systems; and

(jj) 'Wholly owned Subsidiary' means a body corporate all the issued shares in which are held by or on behalf of the Licensee.

(2) The Interpretation Act 1978 shall apply for the purpose of interpreting these Conditions as if they were an Act of Parliament.

(3) Any word or expression used in these Conditions shall unless the context otherwise requires have the same meaning as it has in the Act.

(4) For the avoidance of doubt it is hereby declared that for the purposes of these Conditions references to the supply of telecommunication apparatus do not include the making available of apparatus comprised or to be comprised in any of the Applicable Systems.

(5) For the purposes of interpreting these Conditions headings and titles to any Condition shall be disregarded.

(6) Any reference in any of these Conditions, however expressed, to the Director notifying the Licensee of any matter, consulting the Licensee about any matter, affording the Licensee an opportunity to make representations, taking representations made by the Licensee into account, or explaining, or giving reasons for, any matter to the Licensee, shall be without prejudice to any obligation of due process or similar obligation which the Director is or may be under by virtue of any rule or principle of law or otherwise.

PART 2

SPECIAL CONDITIONS REFERRED TO IN SCHEDULE 8 OF THE ACT

Condition 1 Installation of Applicable Cabled Systems and Provision of Telecommunication Services

1.1   The Licensee shall, except to the extent that the Director otherwise determines, provide to every person who requests the provision of such services at any place in an area where the Applicable Cabled Systems have been installed in accordance with paragraphs 1.2 or 1.3, telecommunication services (other than voice telephony services) consisting in the conveyance of Messages by means of the Applicable Cabled Systems, and the Licensee shall ensure that one or more Network Termination Points comprised in Network Termination and Testing Apparatus are installed, kept installed and run for those purposes on the premises occupied by every such person.

1.2   Subject to paragraph 1.3 the Licensee shall install and keep installed and run, or secure that there are installed and kept installed and run, the Applicable Cabled Systems such that there are by the end of the period ending on:

(a)   (i)   31 December 1994 not less than 10,000 premises;
      (ii)   31 December 1995 not less than 25,000 premises;
      (iii)   31 December 1996 not less than 45,000 premises
      (iv)   31 December 1997 not less than 75,000 premises; and
      (v)   31 December 1998 not less than 105,000 premises

such premises being premises at which telecommunication services could be provided by means of those Systems; and (*b*) 31 December 1999 not less than 143,000 premises at which telecommunication services could be provided by means of those Systems and the Licensee shall within 42 days of any of the dates mentioned in paragraph 1.2(a) or (b) take all reasonable steps to satisfy the Director that the requirements of those subparagraphs have been met.

1.3 Where at any time before 31 December 1998 the Licensee gives written notice to the Director that it is satisfied that it would be in the interests of the sound commercial development of the Applicable Cabled Systems if the dates or numbers of premises, or both, set out in paragraph 1.2(a) were modified as set out in the notice, the Director, if satisfied that the proposed modification or any variation thereof would enable the Licensee more easily to comply with the obligation imposed by paragraph 1.2(b), may by written notice to the Licensee determine that the Licensee shall install and keep installed and run, or secure that there are installed and kept installed and run, Applicable Cabled Systems in accordance with the terms of the Licensee's notice or in accordance with those terms as so varied, and the Licensee shall comply with any such determination.

1.4 For the avoidance of doubt, a determination under paragraph 1.3 shall not affect the obligation imposed by paragraph 1.2(b).

Condition 2   Connection of the Applicable Cabled Systems to Specified Public Telecommunication Systems

2.1 Subject to paragraph 2.3 if any person to whom the Licensee provides telecommunication services by means of the Applicable Cabled Systems requests the provision of a telecommunication service which requires the connection of the Applicable Cabled System to any public telecommunication system run by the operator of a Specified Public Telecommunication System, the Licensee shall take all reasonable steps to secure that such an agreement as is referred to in Condition 8 is made with the operator of such a system so that there are established and maintained such one or more points of connection between the Applicable Cabled Systems and that Specified Public Telecommunication System as are reasonably required and are of sufficient capacity and in sufficient number to enable Messages conveyed or to be conveyed by means of the Applicable Cabled Systems to be conveyed by means of that Specified Public Telecommunication System in such a way as conveniently to meet all reasonable demands for the conveyance of Messages between the Applicable Cabled Systems and any Specified Public Telecommunication System.

2.2 Subject to paragraph 2.3 the Licensee shall secure that the person running any Specified Public Telecommunication System which is connected to the Applicable Cabled Systems provides Connection Services in relation to any Message conveyed or to be conveyed by means of the Applicable Cabled Systems.

2.3 The obligations in paragraphs 2.1 and 2.2 shall not apply where in the opinion of the Licensee:

(*a*)   they would require an adjustment to, or modification of, any of the Applicable Cabled Systems whether by incorporation of apparatus or otherwise or the provision by the Licensee of services or information which in any particular case would not be reasonably required;

(*b*) it would not be reasonably practicable to require the Licensee to do the thing required, or to permit it to be done, having regard to the state of technical development of the Applicable Cabled Systems or any other matter which appears to the Director to be relevant;

(*c*) the provision of telecommunication services by the Licensee in accordance with paragraph 2.1 would unreasonably prejudice its ability to finance the cost of providing other telecommunication services by means of the Applicable Cabled Systems; or

(*d*) the demand or the prospective demand for the service requested is not sufficient, having regard to the revenue likely to be earned from the provision of that service, to meet the costs of establishing the points of connection referred to in paragraph 2.1

and the Director has not expressed a contrary opinion.

2.4   In this Condition:

'Specified Public Telecommunication System' means any public telecommunication system run by British Telecommunications plc or Mercury Communications Limited or any other public telecommunication system which is specified by the Secretary of State for the purpose of this Licence and described in a list kept for that purpose by the Director and made available by him for inspection by the general public.

Condition 8   Connection of Systems providing Connection Services

8.1   Without prejudice to Condition 2 and subject to the provisions of this Condition the Licensee shall, unless it is impracticable to do so, enter into an agreement with the Operator, that is to say any person who is authorised by a Licence to run a Relevant Connectable System, if the Operator requires it to do so:

(*a*) to connect, and keep connected, to any of the Applicable Cabled Systems, or to permit to be so connected and kept connected, that Relevant Connectable System and accordingly to establish and maintain such one or more points of connection as are reasonably required and are of sufficient capacity and in sufficient number to enable Messages conveyed or to be conveyed by means of the Operator's system to be conveyed by means of any of the Applicable Cabled Systems in such a way as conveniently to meet all reasonable demands for the conveyance of Messages between the Relevant Connectable System and any of the Applicable Cabled Systems; and

(*b*) without prejudice to paragraph 8.1(a) where the Operator is a Long Line Public Telecommunications Operator to establish and maintain such points of connection as will enable persons running telecommunication systems connected to the Operator's system and persons running telecommunication systems connected to any of the Applicable Cabled Systems to exercise freedom of choice as to the extent to which Messages are conveyed by means of the Applicable Cabled systems and in routing Messages so conveyed; and

(*c*) to provide such other telecommunication services (including the conveyance of Messages which have been, or are to be, transmitted or received at such points of connection), information and other services as the Director determines are reasonably required (but no more than reasonably required) to secure that points of connection are established and maintained and to enable the Operator effectively to provide the Connection Services which he provides or proposes to provide.

8.2   The Licensee shall not be obliged under paragraph 8.1 to enter into an agreement to do anything if:

(*a*)   in the opinion of the Licensee it would be liable to cause the death of or personal injury to, or damage to the property of, the Licensee or any person engaged in the Licensee's business, or materially to impair the quality of any telecommunication service provided by means of any of the Applicable Cabled Systems or any telecommunication system (other than the Operator's system) connected thereto and the Director has not expressed a contrary opinion; or

(*b*)   in the opinion of the Licensee:

(i)   it would require an adjustment to, or modification of, any of the Applicable Cabled Systems whether by incorporation of apparatus or otherwise or the provision by the Licensee of services or information which in any particular case would not be reasonably required; or

(ii)   it would not be reasonably practicable to require the Licensee to do that thing, or permit it to be done, at the time or in the manner required by the Operator, having regard to the state of technical development of the Applicable Cabled Systems or any other matter which appears to the Director to be relevant

and the Director has not expressed a contrary opinion.

8.3   The Licensee may require that an agreement to be entered into under paragraph 8.1 should be subject to terms and conditions, but only such terms and conditions as are permitted in relation to that agreement in accordance with paragraphs 8.4, 8.5 and 8.6.

8.4   Subject to paragraphs 8.5 and 8.6 terms and conditions are permitted if they are agreed between the Operator and the Licensee and relate to all or any of the following matters:

(*a*)   the charges to be paid by the Operator for anything done under an agreement of the kind described in paragraph 8.1 or as a result of such agreement;

(*b*)   the method adopted or to be adopted to make or maintain the connection;

(*c*)   the points of connection in the Applicable Cabled Systems at which the connection is or is to be made (including arrangements for determining the point at which Messages will be transferred from one system to another and arrangements for conveying and re-routing Messages in cases of Emergency or difficulty);

(*d*)   any restrictions on the telecommunication services to be provided by the Licensee or the Operator being restrictions needed to satisfy international obligations or recommendations applying to and accepted by Her Majesty's Government or to which the Director consents from time to time;

(*e*)   the time when and period for which the Licensee or the Operator is to be obliged to do anything or to permit anything to be done and any arrangements for reviewing the terms and conditions of the agreement;

(*f*)   the form and manner in which Messages are to be transmitted or received at the points of connection including arrangements for numbering and the use of appropriate call progress tones and announcements;

(*g*)   the means of securing that any Message will be received by means of the connection with a signal quality which is in accordance with any obligations and recommendations of the International Telecommunications Union which apply to Her Majesty's Government and are accepted by them or with any other standard to which the Director consents for the purpose from time to time;

(*h*) arrangements for charging customers and others in respect of Messages conveyed by virtue of the agreement;

(*i*) arrangements for Messages conveyed or to be conveyed outside the United Kingdom;

(*j*) provision by the Operator of a reasonable indemnity against any loss or damage sustained by the Licensee in consequence of the agreement in circumstances where the Licensee provides to the Operator an equivalent indemnity; and

(*k*) any other matter of which the Director is satisfied that account should be taken in the special circumstances of any particular case or which is agreed between the Licensee and the Operator.

8.5   If after a period which appears to the Director to be reasonable for the purpose the Licensee has failed to enter into an agreement as required by the Operator under paragraph 8.1, then the Director shall, on the application of the Operator or the Licensee, determine the permitted terms and conditions for the purpose of that agreement which have not been agreed between the Licensee and the Operator being terms and conditions relating to the matters mentioned in paragraph 8.4 which appear to the Director reasonably necessary (but no more than reasonably necessary) to secure:

(*a*) that the cost of anything done pursuant to or in connection with the agreement including fully allocated costs attributable to the services to be provided and taking into account relevant overheads and a reasonable rate of return on attributable assets is apportioned equitably between the Licensee and the Operator;

(*b*) that the Licensee is properly indemnified against any liabilities to third parties or damage to the Applicable Cabled Systems or loss arising from such damage which may result from the performance of the agreement;

(*c*) that the Licensee is reasonably able in all the circumstances (including its obligations and reasonably foreseeable obligations to permit other Operators to provide services by means of points of connection under this Condition) to finance the other services which it is required by this Licence to provide and to recover costs which are incurred or are necessarily incidental thereto;

(*d*) that the quality of any telecommunication services provided by means of the Applicable Cabled Systems and any systems (other than the Operator's system connected thereto is maintained;

(*e*) that the requirements of fair competition are satisfied;

(*f*) that proper account is taken of any other matter reasonably required for the protection of the interests of the Licensee to the extent that no interest of the Operator is unduly prejudiced, including the need to ensure:

(i)   that arrangements for connection accord with good engineering principles and practice;

(ii)   that the commercial development of the Applicable Cabled Systems is not unduly impeded;

(iii) that charging arrangements take account of the overall pattern of the Licensee's costs;

(iv)   that Messages which originate on one system and are conveyed by another should pass through a point of connection as near as reasonably practicable to the place from which they are initially sent or at which they are ultimately received;

(v)   that the Operator does not rely unduly upon services provided by the Licensee as a means of satisfying his own obligations under his Licence;

(vi)   that the Licensee's obligations to the Operator are determined having due regard to its obligations and reasonably foreseeable obligations to establish points of connection for others;

(vii)   that arrangements made under this Condition are so far as circumstances allow in as similar a form as practicable notwithstanding the variety of Operators entitled to such arrangements under this Condition;

(viii)   that commercial and confidential information of the Licensee is properly protected; and

(ix)   that the technical evolution and numbering arrangements of the Applicable Cabled Systems are not unreasonably constrained; and

(g)   that without prejudice to paragraph 8.5A the Licensee may be required to carry out any work which the agreement requires it to carry out within an appropriate period of time having regard to all the circumstances which would be reasonable for an efficient telecommunications operator who was not required to give the particular work priority over work for the Licensee's customers generally.

8.5A   Where in pursuance of such an application as is referred to in paragraph 8.5 the Director determines any charge (or the means of calculating any charge) payable in respect of the establishment of a connection between the Applicable Cabled Systems and the system of the Operator he shall do so in accordance with the following provisions:

(a)   Any costs incurred in the establishment of such a connection, including (without limitation) the provision of dedicated capacity at a point (a 'point of connection') at which the Applicable Cabled Systems and the Operator's system are connected, but not transmission capacity, shall be shared between the parties according to the proportions in which each of them will bill the customers originating calls which are to be conveyed over the point of connection. The proportions shall be derived from forecasts by each party of the capacity required to convey those calls for which the respective parties will bill customers originating them. These costs shall be assessed on the basis of:

(i)   the Licensee's or the Operator's respective fully allocated costs of the establishment of the connection including a reasonable contribution to relevant overheads; and

(ii)   the application to relevant capital employed of a reasonable rate of return on attributable assets.

(b)   Any determination of any charge (or the means of calculating the same) to be payable under paragraph 8.5A(a) above may include a provision that no such charge shall be payable where the party imposing the charge fails to provide the connection within six months (or such longer period as the Licensee and the Operator may agree) of the date of the request therefor, provided that this provision shall not apply in any particular case unless it is reasonable in all the circumstances for it to apply. It shall be deemed not to be reasonable if:

    (i)   it was not reasonably practicable for any reason for the first party to provide the connection in time;

    (ii)   the other party's request for the connection was unreasonable in quantum having regard to its current and future needs; or

    (iii)   in order to comply with the time period the Licensee would have had to give priority to making the connection beyond that given to its own customers generally.

    (c)   The period referred to in paragraph 8.5A(b) shall be extended by such period as equates to or, if there is no period that equates, as is reasonably commensurate with, delays attributable to any default or lack of co-operation by the Operator, or to force majeure of any kind.

    (d)   Where one party has in pursuance of a provision in the agreement required the other party to provide a connection and subsequently cancels the order, it shall reimburse the other party for all costs (assessed on the basis of that party's fully allocated costs, together with a reasonable rate of return on attributable assets) incurred by the other party in the provision of the connection up to the date of cancellation.

8.6   Where the Licensee is required to enter into an agreement to do anything under paragraph 8.1(b) the permitted terms and conditions may relate to all or any of the matters mentioned in paragraph 8.4 but in determining the terms and conditions, in the event of a failure to agree, under paragraph 8.5 the Director shall have regard to (in addition to the matters specified in paragraph 8.5) the need to ensure:

    (a)   that, insofar as any freedom of choice is conferred upon persons running telecommunication systems connected to the Operator's system as to the extent to which Messages are conveyed by means of the Applicable Cabled Systems and in routing messages so conveyed, a corresponding freedom of choice is conferred so far as reasonably practicable on persons running telecommunication systems connected to the Licensee's system;

    (b)   that the requirements of fair competition, including the need for those to whom telecommunication services are provided to have a reasonable means of learning by whom the Messages sent by them are conveyed, are satisfied but paragraph 8.5 shall have effect for this purpose with the omission of sub-paragraph (f)(iv).

8.7   The Licensee shall not be obliged to enter into any agreement under paragraph 8.1 if he refuses to do so, giving his reasons in writing to the Operator and to the Director, and the Director determines that those reasons are proper ones having regard to the matters mentioned in paragraphs 8.5 and 8.6.

8.8   Where:

    (a)   an agreement has been entered into under paragraph 8.1 but for any reason (whether breach of that agreement or otherwise) anything which the Licensee is required to do under the agreement is not being done;

    (b)   the Director considers that the thing ought to be done in order to ensure that a connection made pursuant to that agreement is maintained or that a connection is established pursuant to that agreement and that Messages are conveyed by means of the connection in accordance with the agreement; and

    (c)   the Director is satisfied that the Operator is not able satisfactorily to enforce the agreement so that that thing is done within such time as the Director considers necessary.

then, if the Director so directs, the Licensee shall do that thing subject to such conditions as the Director determines to be reasonable in the circumstances, having regard, in particular, to the permitted terms and conditions which apply and to any thing which he may reasonably require the Operator to do in order to mitigate the effects of the Licensee's failure to do the thing which he is required to do.

8.8A.1   This paragraph 8.8A applies where:

(a)   an Operator establishes a prima facie case that the Licensee is unreasonably not performing an obligation which he is required to perform under an agreement entered into under paragraph 8.1;

(b)   the Director considers that:

(i)   the obligation ought to be performed in order to achieve the purposes of paragraph 8.1;

(ii)   the Operator is not able satisfactorily to enforce the agreement so that the obligation is performed within such time as the Director considers necessary and the balance of convenience requires the Director to take action under this paragraph rather than leave it to the Courts; and

(iii)   the Operator has performed all its obligations which are relevant to the Licensee's obligation that is allegedly not being performed; and

(c)   paragraph 8.8 does not apply.

8.8A.2   Where this paragraph 8.8A applies the Director may require the Licensee to perform the obligation subject to such conditions as are reasonable in the circumstances having regard, in particular, to the permitted terms and conditions which apply and to anything which the Operator may reasonably be expected to do in order to mitigate the effects of the Licensee's failure to perform its obligation.

8.8A.3   Before making a requirement under paragraph 8.8A.2 the Director shall notify the Licensee of the prima facie case established by the Operator, his conclusions thereon, and on the matters referred to in paragraph 8.8A.1(b) and the direction he proposes to make. The Licensee shall be afforded adequate time in which to make representations.

8.8B.1   Notwithstanding, and without prejudice to, any of the foregoing provisions of this Condition, if the Director considers that there is likely to be a category comprising a sufficient number of Operators seeking determinations under paragraph 8.5 for whom standard terms and conditions would be appropriate, he may require the Licensee to publish standard provisions (including, without limitation, charges or the method for calculating them) which set out the terms on which the Licensee will enter into an agreement under paragraph 8.1 with Operators of that particular category.

8.8B.2   If on an application by an Operator in that category the Director is satisfied that the Operator has established a prima facie case that any such standard term or condition proposed by the Licensee is unreasonable and that the Licensee has acted unreasonably in relation to negotiations on that term or condition, the Director may, if he considers it necessary to do so, either determine that the Licensee shall modify that standard provision in such a way as to make the term reasonable in the agreement with the Operator, or modify that standard provision in such a way in the provisions published under paragraph 8.8B.1. In applying this paragraph 8.8B.2:

(a)   any such standard provision shall be confined to the subject matter of the term or condition proposed by the Licensee except that, where the

Director considers that a term or condition is essential in relation to subject matter not covered by any term or condition proposed by the Licensee, he may determine a term or condition to cover the subject matter;

(b) the Licensee shall not be deemed to have acted unreasonably merely by virtue of having proposed the term or condition in question; and

(c) no determination may be made in relation to any provision which would be subject to the Unfair Contract Terms Act 1977.

8.8B.3 Before making a determination under paragraph 8.8B.2 the Director shall notify to the Licensee and the Operator the grounds of the Operator's application and his conclusions thereon and the modification he proposes to make or require the Licensee to make, and shall afford the Licensee and the Operator adequate time, being not less than 28 days, in which to make representations.

8.8B.4 Where an Operator makes an application to the Director under paragraph 8.5, the Director may treat the application as an application under paragraph 8.8B.2 above and act accordingly.

8.8B.5 For the avoidance of doubt the provisions of paragraphs 8.5 and 8.5A, shall apply in respect of any determination made under this paragraph as they apply in relation to a determination made under paragraph 8.5.

8.9 In this Condition:

'Connectable System' means a telecommunication system which is authorised to be run under a Licence which authorises connection of that system to any of the Applicable Cabled Systems;

'Connection Service' means a telecommunication service consisting in the conveyance of any Message which has been, or is to be, conveyed by means of any of the Applicable Cabled Systems;

'Long Line Public Telecommunications Operator' means a public telecommunications operator who is authorised by a Licence to provide telecommunication services consisting in the conveyance of Messages by fixed links run by him over distances greater than 50 linear kilometres; and

'Relevant Connectable System' means a Connectable System which is authorised to be run under a Licence which authorises the provision by means of that System of Connection Services for reward to the public, or any class of the public, not being a system:

(i) authorised to be run under a Licence granted to all persons or persons of any class; and

(ii) for the connection of which, and for the provision of matters necessary for such connection, the Licensee offers standard terms and conditions which satisfy the requirements of Condition 11

and not being a system which the Director has determined ought not to be deemed to be a Relevant Connectable System for the purposes of this Condition.

8.10 This Condition operates without prejudice to Condition 20 but due account shall be taken for the purposes of this Condition of any charge imposed on the Operator for the purposes of that Condition.

8.11 An agreement made pursuant to this Condition shall not contain any restrictive provision unless, before the agreement is made, the Director has expressly consented to the inclusion of such a provision or has determined that that provision should be included under paragraph 8.5 or 8.6 and, for the purposes of this paragraph, a provision in an agreement is a restrictive provision if by virtue of the existence of such a provision (taken alone or with other provisions) the agreement is one to which the Restrictive Trade Practices Act 1976 would apply but for paragraph 1(1) of Schedule 3 to that Act.

8.12 Where the Director so directs the Crown shall be treated for the purposes of this Condition as a person authorised to run a Relevant Connectable System and where he does so he may also direct that the Crown is to be treated as a Long Line Public Telecommunications Operator for those purposes.

Condition 8A Equal access

8A.1 This Condition applies in respect of any Long Line Public Telecommunications Operator (the term 'Operator' referring in this Condition 8A to such an Operator) with whom the Licensee has entered into an agreement as required by Condition 8.1 and where the Director has made a direction under paragraph 8A.2.

8A.2 (a) At any time after the date on which the Licensee first provides 25 per cent of the available Exchange Lines either in any local call charge area of British Telecommunications plc or in the Licensed Area the Director may, subject to the provisions of paragraph 8A.3, make a direction that whenever an Operator so requests after a date specified in the direction the Licensee shall make Equal Access available in respect of that Operator, in an area or areas in relation to which the condition set out above is met, on the basis set out in this Condition 8A.

(b) The direction shall contain a functional specification of exchange software for the provision of Equal Access. The specification shall be that submitted to the Director by the Licensee (following receipt of a request from the Director) or, if the Director, having carried out such consultation as appears to him appropriate, considers that specification to be unsatisfactory, in a form determined by the Director. Before making such a determination the Director shall notify the Licensee as to why the Licensee's specification is unsatisfactory and give the Licensee the opportunity to make representations.

8A.3 The Director shall not make a direction under paragraph 8A.2 unless:

(a) he has carried out a cost-benefit analysis comparing the likely benefits to telecommunications customers to be gained from the introduction of Equal Access with all costs likely to be incurred, including opportunity costs, which analysis indicates that the gains outweigh the likely costs; and

(b) in his opinion sufficient arrangements in relation to the pricing of telecommunication services provided by the Licensee have been made in relation to the following matters to achieve fair competition:

(i) the extent to which the Licensee has been able to balance its charges to align them more appropriately with costs;

(ii) the extent to which regulatory controls, whether imposed by this Licence or otherwise and including voluntary commitments, affect the balance referred to in paragraph 8A.3(b)(i);

(iii) the amount and structure of charges payable to the Licensee by virtue of agreements with Operators entered into by the Licensee under Condition 8; and

(iv)   the extent to which charges are payable to the Licensee by virtue of Condition 20.

8A.4   When carrying out the cost-benefit analysis referred to in paragraph 8A.3(a), the Director shall consult the Licensee and such other persons as appear to him appropriate, affording them a reasonable period, being not less than 28 days, in which to make representations, and he shall take their representations into account when reaching his conclusions. On conclusion of the analysis he shall make it available to the Licensee and such other persons.

8A.5   (a)   In this Condition 'Equal Access' means a facility provided to an Operator whereby he can arrange with a customer of the Licensee that, following a request by that customer to the Licensee, the customer may choose over which public telecommunications system, being a system run by a Long Line Public Telecommunications Operator, to route National and International calls made by means of an Exchange Line provided to him by the Licensee. The choice shall be exercisable in either of the following ways, at the option of the customer:

(i)   by pre-selection, that is to say that the customer may, by registering a preference with the Licensee, name a particular such Operator for the conveyance of all such calls. The Licensee may offer to provide a facility to override the preference in the case of any particular call; or

(ii)   on a call-by-call basis, that is to say that the customer must, for each call, exercise his choice by dialling a short initial code designated for the particular such Operator (or the Licensee) chosen by the customer for the call in question. The respective initial codes for the Licensee and for all Operators shall be of equal length.

'National' and 'International' calls shall be defined by reference to the Licensee's charges and other terms and conditions published in accordance with Condition 11.

(b)   The Licensee shall not require the customer to acquire any special equipment or to pay any fee as a prerequisite to his being able to obtain the Equal Access facility. For the avoidance of doubt the Licensee may impose a charge if a customer who has registered a preference changes that preference in any way.

8A.6   Where Long Line Public Telecommunications Operator (within the meaning of that term in Condition 8) requires the Licensee to provide Equal Access, and specifies exchanges forming part of the Applicable Cabled Systems at which it is to be provided, and the Licensee has not, after a reasonable period, entered into an agreement with that Operator for the provision of Equal Access, the Director may, on the application of either the Licensee or the Operator, determine the terms and conditions of the agreement, being terms and conditions necessary for the provision of Equal Access, or such terms and conditions which the Licensee and the Operator have failed to agree.

8A.7   Before making a determination under paragraph 8A.6, the Director shall:

(a)   carry out in relation to the Operator concerned an analysis taking into account the results of the analysis referred to in paragraph 8A.3(a) comparing the benefits likely to be gained with all the costs incurred and likely to be incurred, including opportunity costs. The provisions of paragraph 8A.4 shall apply to the analysis. The purpose shall be to decide whether, in relation to that Operator's request for Equal Access, the costs will outweigh the benefits; and

(i) if the Director concludes that the costs will outweigh the benefits, his determination shall secure that no part of those costs shall be borne by the Licensee;

(ii) if the Director concludes that the benefits will outweigh the costs, his determination shall secure that the costs are apportioned as provided in paragraph 8A.10; and

(b) notify the Licensee and that Operator in respect of which terms and conditions he proposes to make a determination, and why, and shall afford the Licensee and that Operator adequate time, being not less than 28 days, in which to make representations.

8A.8 In making a determination under paragraph 8A.6, the Director shall;

(a) subject to paragraph 8A.10, secure that the principles set out in Condition 8.5(a) to (g), so far as applicable, are achieved; and

(b) secure that the Licensee's obligation in relation to the provision of Equal Access is limited to:

(i) the acceptance of registrations of such preference as is referred to in sub-paragraph 8A.5(a)(i);

(ii) the delivering of calls to the Operator's system in accordance with the choice of the Licensee's customers as described in paragraph 8A.5; and

(iii) the provision of facilities contained in the specification referred to in paragraph 8A.2(b).

8A.9 (a) Where the Director makes a determination under paragraph 8A.6 he shall secure that any development of the Applicable Cabled Systems made necessary thereby is consistent with the Licensee's then planned programme of network modernisation and development and in particular that the Licensee is not required to introduce Equal Access at any exchange if to do so would involve either:

(i) modernising the exchange in a case where, but for the proposed introduction of Equal Access, the exchange would not have been modernised at that time; or

(ii) a significant risk of impairment to the quality of telecommunication services provided by means of the Applicable Cabled Systems.

(b) Subject to paragraph 8A.9(a), where the Director makes a determination under paragraph 8A.6 the following shall apply in relation to the preparation of exchanges for Equal Access.

(i) The determination may require the Licensee to introduce Equal Access within a reasonable period. At a digital exchange to which the determination relates which does not require conversion for the introduction of Equal Access, a reasonable period for adapting the exchange to provide Equal Access shall be six months. In relation to such an exchange which does require conversion, or any other exchange of an exchange type which is capable of conversion to provide Equal Access, a reasonable period for conversion and adaptation shall, subject to paragraph 8A.9(a), be eighteen months. Different periods may be specified for different exchanges.

(ii) Where at the date of the determination an exchange to which it relates is not digital, and is of an exchange type which is not capable of conversion to provide Equal Access, the Licensee shall ensure (subject to paragraph 8A.9(a)) that, when modernisation to digital is planned, the specification therefor provides for Equal Access.

8A.10   Where in an analysis carried out under paragraph 8A.7(a), the Director concludes that the benefits will outweigh the costs, any determination under paragraph 8A.6 shall secure that the Licensee's costs of introducing Equal Access are apportioned according to the following provisions.

(*a*)   The following costs of introducing Equal Access, among any others which the Director may consider relevant, shall be included among those brought into account:

(i)   costs incurred by the Licensee which are not related to any particular locality consisting of initial development and set-up costs including, without limitation, the costs of hardware design and production, the costs of software development and the costs of planning and training;

(ii)   costs incurred by the Licensee in relation to a particular locality where an Operator has requested the introduction of Equal Access, consisting of initial development and set-up costs in relation to that locality including, without limitation, the costs of installation of hardware and software and the costs of distribution of necessary documentation and instructions and of training;

(iii)   the incremental costs of providing at any particular locality Equal Access to any further Operator after the first Operator at that locality;

(iv)   the costs per customer of registering preferences and of implementing arrangements for the initial code referred to in paragraph 8A.5(a)(ii); and

(v)   the costs per customer of changing registered preferences or removing, in relation to any particular Exchange Line, arrangements for the initial code.

(*b*)   Subject to paragraph 8A.10(c) and (d):

(i)   the costs referred to in paragraph 8A.10(a)(i) shall be apportioned between the Licensee and Operators who make requirements under paragraph 8A.6. The costs shall initially be apportioned between the Licensee and the first such Operator. Procedures will be established for subsequent Operators to make a proportionate contribution to the costs in such manner as the Director shall determine from time to time;

(ii)   the costs referred to in paragraph 8A.10(a)(ii) shall be apportioned between the Licensee and Operators who make requirements under paragraph 8A.6 in relation to the particular locality. The apportionment rules set out in paragraph 8A.10(b)(i) shall apply *mutatis mutandis*.

(iii)   where the addition of an Operator at a locality reduces the contribution to the costs of Equal Access at that locality of the Licensee and the other Operators, the procedures in paragraph 8A.10(b)(i) shall apply *mutatis mutandis* to the costs referred to in paragraph 8A.10(a)(iii). In any other case that Operator shall pay such costs;

(iv)   the costs referred to in paragraph 8A.10(a)(iv) and (v) above shall be met by the Long Line Public Telecommunications Operator, whether the Licensee or an Operator, to whom the customer chooses to route calls by registering a preference or, where the customer exercises choice on a call-by-call basis, apportioned equitably among the Long Line Public Telecommunications Operators (including, where appropriate, the Licensee) to whom the customer has the option of routing calls from time to time.

(*c*) The apportionment of the costs referred to in paragraph 8A.10(a)(i), (ii) and (iii) shall reflect equitably the benefit to the Operator and his customers, actual and potential, of the implementation of Equal Access in relation to that Operator.

(*d*) Before determining any apportionment of any costs referred to in paragraph 8A.10(a), the Director shall inform the Licensee and the Operator of his proposed determination, together with a full explanation of how it is calculated, and shall allow the Licensee and the Operator a reasonable period, being not less than 28 days, in which to make representations.

8A.11 In this Condition 8A, 'potential' customers include those customers of the Licensee who it is reasonable to expect will apply for the Equal Access facility, and 'Exchange Line' shall have the meaning given to it in Condition 6.

8A.12 The provisions of this Condition form part of Condition 8 and accordingly shall be treated for all purposes as contained in and laid down in Condition 8.

Condition 8B   Essential Interfaces

8B.1 This Condition is without prejudice to Condition 8.

8B.2 (*a*) The Director may, having first notified the Licensee of his proposal, affording the Licensee adequate time, being not less than 28 days in which to make representations, specify an Essential Interface.

(*b*) 'Essential Interface' means in respect of a point of connection, as defined in Condition 8.5A(a), an interface at which in the opinion of the Director it is essential that interoperability between the Applicable Cabled Systems and the respective Operator's systems is available.

8B.3 (*a*) Where in pursuance of paragraph 8B.2 the Director specifies an interface as an Essential Interface, and the Licensee thereafter makes that interface available to an Operator in relation to its Applicable Cabled Systems, it shall do so in such a manner as it considers appropriate, but shall ensure such availability in compliance with the Relevant Standard if the Operator so requires.

(*b*) 'Relevant Standard' means:

(i)   an appropriate European or other international standard, or

(ii)   in the absence of such a standard, any other standard specified by the Director after notifying the Licensee of his proposal and allowing the Licensee adequate time, being not less than 28 days, in which to make representations, provided that the Director shall not specify a standard if an appropriate European or other international standard is expected to be promulgated within a reasonable time, including, by way of example, if the European Telecommunications Standards Institute have published a work programme for the development of such a standard,

to the extent that such a standard is necessary to ensure interoperability.

(*c*) Where in pursuance of paragraph 8B.3(b)(ii) the Director specifies a standard as a Relevant Standard, he shall include in that Standard a technical specification. The Director shall use all reasonable endeavours to obtain the agreement of the Licensee and other relevant licensees to a technical specification applicable to the Standard, being a specification defined by reference to:

(i)   an appropriate European or other international specification, or

(ii)   in the absence of such a specification, a specification defined by reference to any other standard having currency within the European Community at the time.

Where after a reasonable time the Director has been unable to secure the agreement of the Licensee and other relevant licensees to a technical specification, the Director shall adopt for inclusion in the Relevant Standard an appropriate technical specification selected by him which has been promulgated by a recognised standards body, including, by way of example, the European Telecommunications Standards Institute, or the British Standards Institution, or other such body as is recognised by the Director as representative of all relevant telecommunications interests.

(d)   In any event the Director shall specify a Relevant Standard in pursuance of paragraph 8B.3(b) only if the owners of relevant intellectual property rights have agreed to grant any necessary licences in respect thereof to the Licensee on reasonable terms.

8B.4   For the avoidance of doubt this Condition shall not:

(a)   without prejudice to paragraph 8B.3, prevent the Licensee using such interfaces as it considers appropriate in relation to the Applicable Cabled Systems; or

(b)   where it makes available to an Operator an interface which the Director has specified as an Essential Interface, require the Licensee to comply with the Relevant Standard if the Operator does not require it to do so.

8B.5   When implementing an Essential Interface, the Licensee shall not be obliged to conform with the Relevant Standard:

(a)   if to do so would necessitate the Licensee:

(i)   acquiring apparatus, software or other goods or supplies of any kind, or implementing any operation, incompatible with, as the case may be, apparatus, software or such other goods or supplies already at the time in use, or the subject at the time of contracts for their procurement for use, in connection with any of the Applicable Cabled Systems, or, in the case of an operation, incompatible with any other operation being carried out at the time in connection therewith; or

(ii)   incurring any cost, or having to resolve technical difficulties, disproportionate to the benefits to be gained from the implementation of the Relevant Standard,

provided that the Licensee shall take reasonable steps to incorporate the Relevant Standard in its plans for network development, with a view to implementation of that Standard in connection with the Applicable Cabled Systems, but without the Licensee incurring any incremental expenditure disproportionate to the benefits to be gained from the implementation of the Relevant Standard which, but for the implementation of the Relevant Standard, would not have been incurred;

(b)   if the Relevant Standard is inappropriate for the particular application for any reason, including, without limitation:

(i)   that it does not afford the Licensee adequate protection for the security of the Applicable Cabled Systems;

(ii)   that its implementation would be liable to cause material impairment in the quality of any telecommunications service provided by means of any of the Applicable Cabled Systems;

(iii)   that it does not cater adequately for billing, metering or other customer administration systems; or

(iv)   that it is technically inadequate in the light of technical developments which have taken place since it was originally created;

(c)   if the Essential Interface concerned is of a genuinely innovative nature and accordingly the use in connection with it of the Relevant Standard would not be appropriate;

(d)   if compliance with the Relevant Standard would involve the infringement by the Licensee of any intellectual property right vested in any person; or

(e)   if the Director so agrees.

8B.6   Where paragraph 8B.5(b) or (c) applies the Licensee shall notify the Director thereof, with an explanation why.

8B.7   It is a precondition of any obligation on the Licensee under this Condition that equivalent obligations as are contained in this Condition are included in the respective licences of all Operators;

8B.8   In this Condition 'Operator' has the meaning given to it in Condition 8.1.

Condition 15   Provision of Voice Telephony Services

15.1   If:

(a)   the Licensee has become, in the opinion of the Director, a well-established operator in the provision of voice telephony services within part of the Licensed Area; and

(b)   the arrangements made by the Licensee are inadequate to secure the availability of voice telephony services to any person within part of the Licensed Area who may reasonably request them,

the Director may direct the Licensee to take such steps as the Director considers appropriate for the purpose of securing that voice telephony services are available within that part or all of the Licensed Area to any person who may reasonably request them and the Licensee shall comply with any such direction.

15.2   The Licensee shall satisfy the Director within 42 days of each of the dates in Condition 1.2 (a) and (b) that the Applicable Cabled Systems are capable of providing services for the purpose of sending and receiving voice telephony messages between the Applicable Cabled Systems and any other Specified Public Telecommunications System.

15.3   In order to satisfy the Director that the requirement referred to in paragraph 15.2 has been met it shall be sufficient for the Licensee to demonstrate that the capacity to supply voice telephony services exists throughout the Licensed Area by the Applicable Cabled Systems being installed so that there is sufficient space within the ducts to permit the insertion of any additional cables necessary to meet the requirement set out in paragraph 15.2 and accordingly this paragraph shall apply without prejudice to any obligation in Schedule 4 to this Licence relating to the provision of spare capacity in any ducts installed by the Licensee.

15.4   Nothing in this Condition shall be taken to require the Licensee to commence carrying on business in the supply of voice telephony services.

15.5   For the purposes of paragraph 15.1 a 'well-established operator' means that the Licensee has 25% or more of what is in the opinion of the

Director the relevant market (excluding cable television services), within the Licensed Area.

15.6 For the purposes of paragraph 15.3 'duct' means a structure or apparatus (with appropriate entry points) installed underground in such a way that Lines can be installed in it without having to break up the surface of the highway; and

'Line' has the meaning given to it by sub-paragraph (a) of the definition of 'telecommunication apparatus' in paragraph 1 of Schedule 2 to the Act.

Condition 15A Arrangements for International Simple Resale Services

15A.1 The Licensee shall not provide any International Simple Voice Resale Service by means of the Applicable Cabled Systems unless such services involve the conveyance of Messages conveyed by the Applicable Cabled Systems which have been or are to be conveyed also by the equivalent of a Public Switched Network in any country or territory:

(i) which the Secretary of State has designated for the purpose of International Simple Voice Resale Services and is included in a list kept for the purpose by the Director and made available by him for inspection to the general public;

(ii) in respect of which the Secretary of State has notified the Licensee that he has made such a designation; and

(iii) which is not a country or territory in respect of which the Secretary of State has revoked such designation having first given the Licensee not less than 3 months' notice of his intention to do so.

15A.2 The Licensee shall not provide International Simple Data Resale Services by means of the Applicable Cabled Systems unless the Secretary of State has specified a description of such Services which may be provided by means of the Applicable Cabled Systems and that specification appears in a list kept for the purpose by the Director and made available by him for inspection by the general public.

15A.3 Where it appears to the Secretary of State to be requisite or expedient to do so in the interests of maintaining or promoting effective competition in the conveyance of Messages to or from one or more countries or territories designated under paragraph 15A.1(i) he may, after consulting the Director, give the Licensee not less than 28 days' notice of his intention that the provisions of paragraphs 15A.5 and 15A.6 should apply in respect of such countries or territories as the Secretary of State has specified in that notice and has not by a further notice given before the expiry of the first notice cancelled that specification.

15A.4 Any notice given under paragraph 15A.3 shall appear in a list kept by the Director and made available by him for inspection by the general public.

15A.5 Subject to paragraph 15A.6, in respect of each country or territory specified in a notice as varied by a second notice (if any) given under paragraph 15A.3 the Licensee shall secure that in any period specified in the notice ('the first period'), the ratio ('the first ratio') between:

(a) the volume of Messages comprised in International Simple Voice Resale Services and International Simple Data Resale Services which are conveyed by means of the Applicable Cabled Systems and are delivered to the United Kingdom from that country or territory; and

(*b*)   the volume of Messages comprised in International Simple Voice Resale Services and International Simple Data Resale Services which are conveyed by means of the Applicable Cabled Systems and are sent from the United Kingdom to that country or territory

does not differ from the ratio ('the second ratio') for the previous specified period ('the second period') (the second ratio and the second period both being specified in the notice) between:

(*c*)   the total volume of all Messages delivered to the United Kingdom from that country or territory; and

(*d*)   the total volume of all Messages sent from the United Kingdom to that country or territory.

15A.6   Where the Secretary of State is unable for any reason to specify the second ratio and has informed the Licensee accordingly, the Licensee shall secure that in the first period the volume of Messages of the sort described in paragraph 15A.5(a) shall be equal to the volume of Messages of the sort described in paragraph 15A.5(b).

15A.7   In this condition:

(*a*)   'Public Switched Network' means a public telecommunication system by means of which two-way telecommunication services are provided whereby Messages are switched incidentally to their conveyance, and, for the avoidance of doubt, a Public Switched Network does not include Private Leased Circuits or International Private Leased Circuits.

(*b*)   'International Private Leased Circuit' means a communication facility which is:

(i)   comprised both in a public telecommunication system and in an equivalent telecommunication system in a country or territory other than the United Kingdom;

(ii)   for the conveyance of Messages between points, all of which are points of connection between telecommunication systems referred to in (i) and other telecommunication systems;

(iii)   made available to a particular person or particular persons;

(iv)   such that all of the Messages transmitted at any of the points mentioned in (ii) are received at every other such point; and

(v)   such that the points mentioned in (ii) are fixed by the way in which the facility is installed and cannot otherwise be selected by persons or apparatus sending Messages by means of that facility.

(*c*)   'International Simple Data Resale Services' means telecommunication services consisting in the conveyance of Messages which do not include two-way live speech, but include only such switching, processing, data storage or protocol conversion as is necessary for the conveyance of those Messages in real time, which have been or are to be conveyed by means of all of the following:

(*a*)   a Public Switched Network;

(*b*)   an International Private Leased Circuit; and

(*c*)   the equivalent of a Public Switched Network in another country or territory;

provided that there shall be disregarded:

(aa)   any service provided by means of a Public Switched Network consisting only in such conveyance and switching which when carried out by a customer of that Public Switched Network over a telecommunication system run by him could be carried out under the Class Licence for the Running of Self Provided Telecommunication Systems granted by the Secretary of State under section 7 of the Telecommunications Act 1984 on 30 July 1992; and

(bb)   any service provided by means of the Applicable Cabled Systems consisting only in such conveyance and switching which when carried out by a person other than a public telecommunications operator over a telecommunication system run by him could be carried out under the Class Licence to Run Branch Systems to Provide Telecommunication Services granted by the Secretary of State under section 7 of the Telecommunications Act 1984 on 15 July 1992.

(d)   'International Simple Voice Resale Services' means telecommunication services consisting in the conveyance of Messages which include two-way live speech which have been or are to be conveyed by means of all of the following:

(a)   a Public Switched Network;

(b)   an International Private Leased Circuit; and

(c)   the equivalent of a Public Switched Network in another country or territory;

provided that there shall be disregarded:

(aa)   any service provided by means of a Public Switched Network consisting only in such conveyance and switching which when carried out by a customer of that Public Switched Network over a telecommunication system run by him could be carried out under the Class Licence for the Running of Self Provided Telecommunication Systems granted by the Secretary of State under section 7 of the Telecommunications Act 1984 on 30 July 1992; and

(bb)   any service provided by means of the Applicable Cabled Systems consisting only in such conveyance and switching which when carried out by a person other than a public telecommunications operator over a telecommunication system run by him could be carried out under the Class Licence to Run Branch Systems to Provide Telecommunication Services granted by the Secretary of State under section 7 of the Telecommunications Act 1984 on 15 July 1992.

(e)   'Private Leased Circuit' means a communication facility which is:

(a)   provided by means of one or more public telecommunication systems;

(b)   for the conveyance of Messages between points, all of which are points of connection between telecommunication systems referred to in paragraph (a) and other telecommunication systems;

(c)   made available to a particular person or particular persons;

(d)   such that all of the Messages transmitted at any of the points mentioned in paragraph (b) are received at every other such point; and

(e)   such that the points mentioned in paragraph (b) are fixed by the way in which the facility is installed and cannot otherwise be selected by persons or telecommunication apparatus sending Messages by means of that facility.

SCHEDULE 4
OTHER EXCEPTIONS AND CONDITIONS RELATING TO THE APPLICATION OF THE TELECOMMUNICATIONS CODE

Definitions and Interpretation

1   In this Schedule unless the context otherwise requires:

(*a*) 'Capping Points' means the point at which any Service Line is temporarily terminated in the Footway or elsewhere in the maintainable highway;

(*b*) 'Carriageway' and 'Footway' have the meanings given to them by section 329 of the Highways Act 1980;

(*c*) 'Conservation Area' means any area designated as such under section 69 of the Planning (Listed Buildings and Conservation Areas) Act 1990;

(*d*) 'Controlled Land' means land (not forming part of a street) in which immediately before the commencement of Part III of the New Roads and Street Works Act 1991 there was apparatus placed by virtue of Schedule 1 to the Public Utilities Street Works Act 1950 (authorisation of works in certain land abutting the highway);

(*e*) 'Director' means the Director General of the Office of Telecommunications;

(*f*) 'Duct' means a structure or apparatus (with appropriate entry points) installed underground in such a way that Lines can be installed in it without having to break up the surface of the highway;

(*g*) 'Emergency Works' has the same meaning as in Part III of the New Roads and Street Works Act 1991;

(*h*) 'Highway Authority' means the highway authority as defined in section 1 of the Highways Act 1980;

(*i*) 'Line' has the meaning given to it by sub-paragraph (a) of the definition of 'telecommunication apparatus' in paragraph 1 of Schedule 2 to the Act;

(*j*) 'maintainable highway', 'street' and 'telecommunication apparatus' have the meanings given to them by paragraph 1 of Schedule 2 to the Act; and for the avoidance of doubt, 'apparatus' means 'telecommunication apparatus';

(*k*) 'Planning Authority' means the local planning authority for the area in question having planning functions under part III of the Town and Country Planning Act 1990;

(*l*) 'Relevant Undertaker' has the meaning given to it by paragraph 23(10) of Schedule 2 to the Act, and includes persons mentioned in paragraph 23(10)(b) in respect of services and apparatus for the supply of water, or disposal of sewage, and additionally includes any undertaking for the supply of heat;

(*m*) 'Service Line' means any Line placed or intended to be placed for the purpose of providing any telecommunication service to the occupier from time to time of any land, as distinct from a Line placed or intended to be placed for the general purposes of any telecommunication system;

(*n*) 'Service Line Distribution Point' means the point at which any Line placed or intended to be placed for the general purposes of any telecommunication system is connected to any Service Line; and (*o*) 'Statutory List of Buildings' means the statutory list of buildings of special architectural or historic interest compiled by the Secretary of State under Section 1 of the Planning (Listed Buildings and Conservation Areas) Act 1990.

(*p*) 'Street' means the whole or any part of any of the following, irrespective of whether it is a thoroughfare:

(i)   any highway, road, land, footway, alley or passage,

(ii)   any square or court, and

(iii) any land laid out as a way whether it is for the time being formed as a way or not

and where a street passes over a bridge or through a tunnel, references to a street include that bridge or tunnel;

(*q*) 'Street Authority' has the meaning given to it by section 49 of the New Roads and Street Works Act 1991;

(*r*) 'Street Works Register' means a register of the kind kept by a Street Authority under section 53 of the New Roads and Street Works Act 1991;

(*s*) 'Traffic Authority' has the same meaning as in the Road Traffic Regulation Act 1984.

(*t*) 'Urgent Works' has the meaning given in Regulation 2 of the Streetworks (Registers, Notices, Directions and Determinations) Regulations 1992.

2   The Interpretation Act 1978 shall apply for the purpose of interpreting this Schedule as if it was an Act of Parliament.

3   Any word or expression used in this Schedule shall unless the context otherwise requires have the same meaning as it has in the Act.

4   For the purposes of interpreting this Schedule headings and titles shall be disregarded.

5   For the avoidance of doubt, it is hereby declared that the conditions in this Schedule apply in addition to any obligations of the Licensee under the New Roads and Street Works Act 1991.

Condition 1   Lines

1.1   Except in the case of Emergency Works, any Line installed by the Licensee after the date on which this Licence enters into force shall be installed underground.

1.2   Notwithstanding paragraph 1.1, but subject to Condition 7, nothing in this condition shall prevent the installation on or above the ground in any area other than a Conservation Area of a Service Line which is:

(*a*) affixed to and lying on the exterior surface of a building;

(*b*) affixed to and lying on the exterior surface of any permanent structure on the land occupied by the person to whom the service is being provided;

(*c*) flown from the eaves of one building to another provided that the distance between buildings is not more than eight metres; or

(*d*) flown from an existing pole in a locality where overhead Service Lines are already flown from poles for the purpose of providing telecommunication services.

1.3   Notwithstanding paragraph 1.1, but subject to Condition 7, nothing in this condition shall prevent the installation of a Line in any area other than a Conservation Area which is affixed to and lying either on the exterior surface of a building or the surface of any structure and which terminates at a Service Line Distribution Point.

1.4 Notwithstanding paragraph 1.1, and without prejudice to paragraphs 1.2 and 1.3, but subject to Condition 7, nothing in this condition shall prevent the installation of a Line on or above the ground in any area provided that:

(a) the Licensee has given written notice of the proposed installation to the Planning Authority; and

(b) the Planning Authority does not within 28 days of the giving of the notice given written notice to the Licensee that the Line, and any pole to which it may be attached, would detrimentally affect the visual amenity of the locality and should not be installed in the position proposed.

1.5 Where telecommunication services are to be provide to a person occupying or proposing to occupy a new development the Licensee shall use every reasonable endeavour to enter into an agreement with those responsible for the development and any Relevant Undertaker providing or proposing to provide a service to persons occupying that development to secure that Lines are installed underground on a shared cost basis.

1.6 Lines installed over a maintainable highway shall be placed at a height of not less than 5.5 metres above the Highway (or in the case of a designated high load route not less than 6.7 metres), except where the Highway Authority has previously otherwise agreed in writing.

Condition 2   Resiting of Lines Installed above the Ground

2.1 The Licensee shall consider carefully a request by any person that any Line which is already installed above the ground be resited, either underground or in another position above the ground. If the Licensee is satisfied that the person making the request will pay the costs of resiting any such Line the Licensee shall, wherever it is reasonable and practicable, so resite the Line. In other cases, except where the request is frivolous, the Licensee shall be obliged within 28 days of receiving it, to give notice of its decision whether or not to accede to the request in writing to the person making the request giving, where it decides to refuse, reasons.

Condition 3   Cabinets, Boxes, Pillars, Pedestals and other Similar Apparatus

3.1 Subject to the following paragraphs of this condition and except in the case of Emergency Works, any telecommunication apparatus installed after the date on which this licence enters into force shall be installed underground.

3.2 Notwithstanding paragraph 3.1, but subject to Condition 7, nothing in this condition shall prevent the installation of cabinets, boxes, pillars, pedestals and other similar apparatus on or above the ground, in any area other than a Conservation Area, provided that:

(a) the dimensions of the apparatus above the surface of the ground, excluding any plinth, do not exceed 1.5 metres in height by 2.0 metres in width by 0.6 metres in depth;

(b)   the Licensee has given the Planning Authority written notice of its intention to install the apparatus in question describing the apparatus and identifying the place where it is proposing to install the apparatus; and

(c)   the apparatus is installed in accordance with the notice referred to in sub-paragraph (b) above or, where the Planning Authority gives written notice within the period of 28 days beginning with the giving of that notice that the apparatus should be installed in accordance with conditions, the apparatus is installed in accordance with such of those conditions as are reasonable in all the circumstances of the case taking into account both the desirability of protecting the visual amenity of the locality in which the apparatus is to be installed and the cost of installing the apparatus.

3.3   Notwithstanding paragraph 3.1, nothing in this condition shall prevent the installation of cabinets, boxes, pillars, pedestals and other similar apparatus, the dimensions of which above the surface of the ground exceed those at paragraph 3.2(a), with the prior written consent of the Planning Authority.

3.4   Notwithstanding paragraph 3.1, but subject to Condition 7, nothing in this condition shall prevent the installation of a Service Line Distribution Point which is affixed to and lying either on the exterior surface of a building or the surface of any structure provided that the Point is not in a Conservation Area.

Condition 4   Guidelines on the Positioning and Visual Appearance of Apparatus

4.1   Without prejudice to any other condition in this Schedule and any of the Licensee's statutory obligations, the Licensee shall, in conjunction with the Planning Authority (and in the case of (a) below in conjunction also with the Highway Authority), use every reasonable endeavour to establish guidelines to be followed by the Licensee in connection with the positioning and colour of:

(a)   cabinets, boxes, pillars, pedestals and other similar apparatus installed on or above the ground;

(b)   Lines or Service Line Distribution Points affixed to and lying on the exterior surface of a building;

(c)   apparatus installed on or above the ground in proximity to a building in the Statutory List of Buildings; and

(d)   poles and lines flown from or between those poles.

4.2   The Licensee shall take all reasonable steps to secure (in particular by giving instructions to its employees and agents) that the guidelines established under this condition are followed.

Condition 5   Conservation Areas

5.1   Subject to paragraph 5.2, without prejudice to Condition 1.4 and except in the case of Emergency Works, any telecommunication apparatus installed by the Licensee in any Conservation Area after the date on which this Licence enters into force shall be installed underground.

5.2   Notwithstanding paragraph 5.1, but subject to Condition 7, the Licensee may install telecommunication apparatus on or above the ground in

any Conservation Area provided that the Licensee has given the Planning
Authority written notice of its intention to install the telecommunication
apparatus in question describing the apparatus and identifying the place
where it is proposing to install the apparatus including such precise location
plans and drawings as the Planning Authority deems necessary. Where the
Planning Authority notifies the Licensee in writing within 28 working days of
the giving of the notice that the installation would detrimentally affect the
character or appearance of the Conservation Area and that the installation
should not take place, the Licensee may install the apparatus only if the
Planning Authority subsequently agrees in writing or if the Secretary of State,
after having consulted the Planning Authority, so directs in writing.

Condition 6   Sites of Special Scientific Interest

6.1   Subject to paragraph 6.2 and except in the case of Emergency Works,
before installing any apparatus in any Site of Special Scientific Interest the
Licensee shall give the Nature Conservancy Council for England (English
Nature) written notice of its intention to do so describing the proposed
works.
6.2   Where the Council notifies the Licensee in writing within 40 days of
the giving of the notice under paragraph 6.1 that the proposed works would
be likely to destroy or damage the flora, fauna or geological or physiographical
features by reason of which the land is of special interest and that the
installation should not take place, the Licensee may install the apparatus only
if the Council subsequently agrees in writing or if the Secretary of State, after
having consulted the Council, so directs in writing.
6.3   The Licensee shall also comply with any direction given to it in
writing by the Secretary of State relating to giving notice to and considering
representations made by any other authority exercising statutory functions in
relation to Sites of Special Scientific Interest or such other environmentally
sensitive areas as may be specified in the direction.
6.4   'Site of Special Scientific Interest' means an area notified as such
under section 28 of the Wildlife and Countryside Act 1981 or an area in
respect of which the Secretary of State has made an order under section 29
of that Act.

Condition 7   Listed Buildings and Ancient Monuments

7.1   In respect of the Statutory List of Buildings, except in the case of
Emergency Works, the Licensee shall give written notice to the Planning
Authority before installing Lines or other telecommunication apparatus
    (*a*)   on any listed building; or
    (*b*)   on or above the ground in proximity to any Grade I or Grade II*
listed building.
Where the Planning Authority notifies the Licensee in writing within 28
working days of the giving of the notice that the installation would detrimentally affect the character or appearance of the building, or its setting, and that
the installation should not take place, the Licensee may install the apparatus
only if the Planning Authority subsequently agrees in writing or if the

Secretary of State, after having consulted the Planning Authority, so directs in writing.

7.2   For the avoidance of doubt it is hereby declared that nothing in this Licence affects:

(a)   the statutory requirement that the consent of the Secretary of State shall be obtained before any work is carried out which will affect the site of an ancient monument scheduled under section 1 and 2 of the Ancient Monuments and Archaeological Areas Act 1979; or

(b)   the obligation imposed on the Licensee by virtue of section 7 of the Planning (Listed Buildings and Conservation Areas) Act 1990 to obtain listed building consent for any works which affect the character of a listed building, or involve the demolition of any part of such a building.

Condition 8   National Trust

8.1   Except in the case of Emergency Works, before installing any tele-communication apparatus for the purpose of providing a service to the occupier of any land which the National Trust has notified the Licensee in writing that it owns, or holds any interest in, the Licensee shall give the relevant regional office of that body written notice of its intention to do so, describing the proposed works; and shall consider any written representations made within 28 days of the giving of such notice to it by that body.

Condition 9   Maintainable Highways

9.1   Subject to paragraph 9.2, before the Licensee executes any works involving the breaking up of a maintainable highway in connection with the installation, inspection, maintenance, adjustment, repair or alteration of any telecommunication apparatus in that highway, he shall:

(a)   in the case of an overhead Line or an underground Service Line, consider any written representations made by the Highway Authority within 7 working days after the giving of any such notice (which shall be effected by facsimile backed by first class post) as is required to be given to the Highway Authority under section 55 of the New Roads and Street Works Act 1991;

(b)   in all other cases, consider any such written representations made within 29 days of the giving of any such notice; and

(c)   unless the Highway Authority consents otherwise, shall not commence those works until the expiry of 7 working days, or 29 days, as the case may be.

9.2   Paragraph 9.1 above shall not apply in the case of:

(a)   Urgent Works; or

(b)   Emergency Works; or

(c)   works involving the breaking up of a part of a maintainable highway other than a Carriageway in order to install a Service Line in that part of that maintainable highway, in circumstances where that Service Line is to be connected to a Capping Point or Service Line Distribution Point which has already been installed following the giving of any notice required to be given to the Highway Authority under section 55 of the New Roads and Street Works Act 1991.

Condition 10   Placing of Underground Lines in Ducts

10.1   All Lines installed underground after the date on which this Licence enters into force in a maintainable highway or Street shall, whenever practicable, be installed in Ducts.

Condition 11   Maintenance and the Safety of Apparatus

11.1   The Licensee shall, where necessary and in any event not less than once per year, inspect its telecommunication apparatus which is not inside a building and which is on or above the surface of the ground with a view to ensuring that it will not cause harm to other persons or property; and the Licensee shall notify the Director and the Highway Authority of its arrangements for inspecting such apparatus.

11.2   In addition to carrying out its own inspections of its apparatus on or above the surface of the ground, the Licensee shall investigate any report (other than a frivolous one) of any of its apparatus (wherever situated) being in a dangerous state and shall remove any danger without delay.

Condition 12   Arrangements with Public Electricity Suppliers

12.1   Before exercising any rights under the telecommunications code the Licensee shall use every reasonable endeavour to enter into an agreement with the Relevant Suppliers as to the engineering principles to be adopted and the allocation and apportionment of costs which arise:

(a)   when the Licensee installs and keeps installed apparatus in proximity to plant which is already installed which is the responsibility of a Relevant Supplier; and

(b)   when a Relevant Supplier gives notice to the Licensee that it proposes to install its plant in proximity to any of the Licensee's apparatus which is already installed.

12.2   The Licensee shall:

(a)   within three months of this Licence coming into force; and

(b)   after the expiry of the period of three months beginning on the date when this Licence comes into force, within three months of the commencement of any negotiations for the making of any such agreement as is mentioned in paragraph 12.1 above;

inform the Director of the steps taken to implement paragraph 12.1 above and of the terms of any agreement entered into by it with the Relevant Suppliers.

12.3   Where the Licensee has not offered to enter into such an agreement as is mentioned in paragraph 12.1 being an agreement which makes reasonable provision for securing that:

(a)   the Licensee will, when installing its apparatus in proximity to plant of the Relevant Suppliers which is already installed, protect its apparatus from electrical interference from that plant;

(b)   each Relevant Supplier will, when installing its plant in proximity to apparatus of the Licensee which is already installed, protect that apparatus of the Licensee from electrical interference from that plant:

the Licensee shall only install apparatus of such a kind and in such a position as will not be adversely affected by any plant of the Relevant Supplier which is already installed.

12.4   In this Condition, 'Relevant Supplier' means the National Grid Company and NORWEB plc.

Condition 13   Replacement Apparatus

13.1   For the avoidance of doubt, it is hereby declared that, where by under any condition in this Schedule prior notification is required to be given to any person before installing any apparatus, that notification is also required to be given where apparatus is installed by way of replacement for apparatus previously installed except:

(a)   in the case of Emergency Works or Urgent Works; or

(b)   where the apparatus is not substantially different from the apparatus it replaces, and is not installed in a position substantially different from the position of the apparatus it replaces.

Condition 14   The Needs of Disabled Persons

14.1   In executing works in a street or in installing apparatus in a street, the Licensee shall have regard to the needs of disabled persons (including in particular the blind and those with impaired sight) in accordance with section 65(1) of the New Roads and Street Works Act 1991.

Condition 15   Instructions for the Installation of Apparatus

15.1   Without prejudice to any of its statutory obligations the Licensee shall take all reasonable steps to secure (in particular by giving instructions to its employees and agents) that:

(a)   where apparatus is to be installed underground in a maintainable highway or a street, the normal practice wherever practicable and subject to consultation with the Highway Authority will be to place it in the verge or Footway (or the prospective verge or Footway in the case of a street) if any rather than the Carriageway;

(b)   provision is made for any new Ducts installed after the date on which this Licence comes into force to contain sufficient spare capacity to meet demand which is reasonably foreseeable by the Licensee for telecommunication services provided by it;

(c)   effective liaison is maintained with the Highway Authority with a view to ensuring that works entailing the breaking up of a maintainable highway are carried out in advance of scheduled resurfacing works or together with other schemes affecting the highway;

(d)   effective liaison is maintained with the Street Authority in order to ensure that all works are executed in accordance with the provisions of, and made under, sections 65 to 69 of the New Roads and Street Works Act 1991;

(e)   effective liaison is maintained with Relevant Undertakers with a view to avoiding the disruption of the services provided by those persons;

(f)   effective liaison is maintained with the Street Authority in order to ensure that, following the execution of works, the Licensee discharges its duties of reinstatement of the street under sections 70 to 74 of the New Roads and Street Works Act 1991;

(g) before constructing new Ducts, and with a view to reducing to a minimum the need for the construction of new Ducts, the possibility of using Ducts or other conduits which are already installed is investigated;

(h) the minimum practicable number of items of apparatus is installed, allowing for estimated growth in demand for telecommunication services;

(i) Lines and other items of telecommunication apparatus are placed so that they do not present safety hazards (in particular to disabled persons, including the blind and those with impaired sight);

(j) the visual amenity of properties in proximity to which apparatus is installed is protected as far as practicable;

(k) where apparatus is installed underground in a maintainable highway or a street the Street Authority and Relevant Undertakers are consulted about the appropriate depth of cover of the apparatus and its lateral position in the highway or street;

(l) so far as is practicable, where a Line or other telecommunication apparatus is attached to a building, the fitting used to attach that apparatus will not stain that building through corrosion; and

(m) effective liaison is maintained with the Street Authority in order to ensure that the Street Works Register contains such information in respect of works carried out as may be prescribed under section 53 of the New Roads and Street Works Act 1991;

15.2 The Licensee shall within three months of the date on which this Licence enters into force and thereafter from time to time as the Director may require furnish details to the Director of the instructions given in accordance with paragraph 15.1 above.

15.3 The requirement specified in paragraph 15.1(j) is without prejudice to the requirements of Condition 7.1.

Condition 16   Records of Apparatus

16.1 The Licensee shall keep records of the location of any of its apparatus installed in or under a maintainable highway or Street, or under any other land, after the date on which this Licence enters into force and shall take all reasonable steps to ensure that those records are accurate for the purpose of those intending to undertake works in the vicinity of that apparatus.

16.2 The Licensee shall ensure that records of the kind referred to in paragraph 16.1 can be made available in the form of route plans drawn on an Ordnance Survey Map background of a scale to be determined by the Licensee in consultation with the Highway Authority.

16.3 The Licensee shall provide by means of a telecommunication system free of charge, to any Highway Authority or other person who is intending to undertake works in the vicinity of any telecommunication apparatus it has installed of the kind described in paragraph 16.1 above, a service furnishing information about the location of that apparatus and shall, as soon as possible:

(a) respond to bona fide enquiries; and

(b) where it is reasonable and practicable confirm its advice in diagrammatic form and make trained staff available to indicate, on site, the location and nature of the apparatus so installed;

and shall also respond to any other reasonable request from a Highway Authority or Relevant Undertaker for information about the location of the Licensee's apparatus installed in or under a maintainable highway or Street.

16.4   The Licensee shall co-operate in any joint projects involving the Highway Authority or Relevant Undertakers which have as their purpose the recording and making available of information about the location of underground apparatus, unless the Director agrees that it would be inappropriate having regard to its existing practice in the area concerned for it to do so.

Condition 17   Emergency Works and Urgent Works

17.1   Without prejudice to the duties of the Licensee under sections 55, 57 and 93 of the New Roads and Street Works Act 1991 concerning the giving of notice in respect of Emergency Works or Urgent Works, the Licensee shall provide, in addition to the information contained in any such notice, a reasonable estimate of the date by which the Emergency Works or the Urgent Works are expected to be completed and a statement of the grounds for the need to execute those Emergency Works or Urgent Works, as the case may be.

Condition 18   Public or Private Events and Construction Sites Etc.

18.1   Where the Licensee is to provide telecommunication services for a limited period at the site of a public or private event or a construction site, it may install Lines on or above the ground and any associated poles, notwithstanding Conditions 1, 3, 5 and 7 provided that:

(a)   the Planning Authority is notified as soon as is practicable of the proposed installation and is given a reasonable estimate of the date by which the apparatus concerned will be removed;

(b)   the limited period does not exceed 28 days in the case of a public or private event or 12 months in the case of a construction site; and

(c)   the Lines and poles are removed within a reasonable period after the end of the event or after the work at the construction site is complete.

18.2   The Licensee may install and keep installed Lines and associated poles on or above the ground for a period exceeding 28 days or, as the case may be, 12 months with the consent of the Planning Authority.

Condition 19   Public Inspection of Code Related Licence Conditions

19.1   The Licensee shall place a copy of this Schedule and of every direction given to the Licensee under section 10(4) of the Act at a publicly accessible part of its premises at Magnetic House, Waterfront Quay, Salford Quays, Manchester, M5 2XW, or such other office as the Director may agree from time to time in such a manner and in such a place that it is readily available for inspection free of charge by the general public during such hours as the Secretary of State may prescribe by order under section 19(4) of the Act for the register of licences and orders to be open for public inspection, or, in the absence of any such order having been made by the Secretary of State, during normal office hours.

19.2   The Licensee shall send a copy of this Schedule to the Chief Executive's Department of each Local Authority that has responsibility for any area falling within the area of red line of the map attached at Annex B to this Licence.

Condition 20   Funds for Meeting Liabilities

20.1   Subject to paragraph 20.3 below, the Licensee shall make arrangements which are adequate to secure that sufficient funds are available to the Appropriate Authorities after the Relevant Event occurs for meeting the liabilities described in paragraph 20.2 below which have arisen on or before the date on which that Event occurred or may arise thereafter from the exercise of rights conferred upon the Licensee by paragraph 9 of the telecommunications code.

20.2   The liabilities referred to in paragraph 20.1 above are:

(a)   liabilities, including for the payment of indemnities in respect of costs or expenses incurred, arising under the New Roads and Street Works Act 1991 towards:

(i)   any Appropriate Authority, Traffic Authority or other responsible authority under that Act;

(ii)   any other person having the authority to execute works in, or having apparatus in, a Street;

(iii)   any concessionaire within the meaning of section 1 of that Act.

(b)   any other costs or expenses reasonably incurred by any Appropriate Authority or other responsible authority in making good any damage caused by the installation or removal of telecommunication apparatus, whether such damage occurs before or after the Relevant Event;

(c)   any other costs or expenses reasonably incurred by any Appropriate Authority or other responsible authority after the Relevant Event occurs in removing any telecommunications apparatus:

(i)   which is installed under, over, along or across a street;

(ii)   which is not, or is no longer, used for the purposes of any telecommunication system and in relation to which there is no reasonable likelihood that it will be so used; and

(iii)   the removal of which is desirable having regard to any harm it may cause to other persons or property, or to the visual amenity of properties in proximity to which the apparatus is installed.

20.3   The funds available under paragraph 20.1 above shall include, in relation to any Relevant Period:

(a)   an amount which is equal to:

(i)   10% of the Gross Book Value; or

(ii)   £100,000

whichever is the lesser, or such greater amount as the Director may direct; and

(b)   an amount which, having regard to:

(i)   any works undertaken by the Licensee before the beginning of the Relevant Period in question; and

(ii)   any works which the Licensee reasonably believes will be undertaken by it during the Relevant Period in question,

is sufficient to meet any liabilities of the kinds described in paragraph 20.2(a) above which may arise.

20.4   The Licensee shall:

(*a*) within three months of this Licence coming into force; and

(*b*) once a year thereafter,

inform the Director of the steps taken to implement this condition.

20.5 Where:

(*a*) the Licensee has failed to inform the Director in accordance with paragraph 20.4 above; or

(*b*) the Director is not satisfied that the arrangements made by the Licensee are adequate to secure that sufficient funds are available after the Relevant Event occurs for meeting the liabilities described in paragraph 20.1 above;

the Director may direct the Licensee to take such steps as the Director considers appropriate for the purpose of securing that such sufficient funds are available and the Licensee shall comply with any such direction.

20.6 In this condition:

'Appropriate Authority' means a public authority of a type described in subsection 49(6) of the New Roads and Street Works Act 1991;

'Cost Price' means the cost of any item of telecommunication apparatus, including the full cost of its installation, calculated before any charges for depreciation by the Licensee and modified to take account of any alteration in the CSO Price Index for Buildings and Works since it was installed;

'Gross Book Value', in relation to any Relevant Period, means the sum of the Cost Price of each piece of telecommunication apparatus installed by or on behalf of the Licensee under paragraph 9 of the telecommunications code before the beginning of that Period;

'Relevant Event' means:

(*a*) the revocation of this Licence;

(*b*) where the Licensee is not immediately granted another similar licence to run the Applicable Cabled Systems, the expiry of this Licence; or

(*c*) any of the events specified in paragraph 1(d) of Schedule 2 to this Licence; provided that paragraph 2 of that Schedule shall have effect for the purposes of the definition as it has for the purposes of paragraph 1 of that Schedule; and

'Relevant Period' means:

(*a*) any of the 23 consecutive periods of 12 months, the first of which begins on the date this Licence enters into force; or

(*b*) taking into account the date specified pursuant to paragraph 3 of the Licence, any residual period during which this Licence remains in force, following consecutively from the end of the 23 periods specified in (a) above.

ANNEX A
THE APPLICABLE CABLED SYSTEMS

1 The Applicable Cabled Systems are telecommunication systems of every description within the Licensed Area, provided that for a system to be an Applicable Cabled System it must satisfy each of the following conditions:

(*a*) all the telecommunication apparatus comprised in the system is located within the Licensed Area;

(*b*)   the system is one by means of which Messages are conveyed or are to be conveyed:

(i)   from one Network Termination Point to another such Point;

(ii)   from a Network Termination Point to another place which is neither a Network Termination Point nor a Call Office or from such a place to such a Point;

(iii)   between a place which is neither a Network Termination Point nor a Call Office and another such place where their conveyance is not by way of provision of a service to another person; or

(iv)   between a Call Office and any other place

but in any case falling within sub-paragraphs (i)–(iv) above, not beyond a Network Termination Point;

(*c*)   none of the apparatus comprised in the system is Relevant Terminal Apparatus installed on premises occupied by a person to whom there are provided telecommunication services by means of the system; and

(*d*)   the system is not a telecommunication system which conveys Messages by means of wireless telegraphy, except where every Station for Wireless Telegraphy and every item of Wireless Telegraphy Apparatus comprised within the system constitutes a permanent or temporary Fixed Wireless Telegraphy Station.

2   In this Annex:

(*a*)   'Applicable Terminal Equipment' means apparatus which is Compliant Terminal Equipment or which is applicable terminal equipment within the meaning of regulation 4 of the Telecommunications Terminal Equipment Regulations 1992;

(*b*)   'Approved Apparatus' means in relation to any system apparatus which is Compliant Terminal Equipment or is approved under section 22 of the Act for connection to that system;

(*c*)   'Call Office' means telecommunication apparatus not supplied by the Licensee to any particular person but made available for use by the public or a class of the public;

(*d*)   'Compliant Terminal Equipment' means Applicable Terminal Equipment which satisfies the requirements of regulation 9 of the Telecommunications Terminal Equipment Regulations 1992;

(*e*)   'Fixed Wireless Telegraphy Station' means any 'Station for Wireless Telegraphy' or 'Wireless Telegraphy Apparatus' which is not used while in motion and which is not used to provide Mobile Radio Telecommunication Services;

(*f*)   'Group' means a group of companies consisting of a company and its Subsidiaries of which the Licensee is a member;

(*g*)   'Licence' means a licence granted or having effect as if so granted under section 7 of the Act;

(*h*)   'Message' means anything falling within paragraphs (a) to (d) of section 4(1) of the Act;

(*i*)   'Mobile Radio Telecommunication Services' means any telecommunication service provided by means of a telecommunication system for the conveyance of Messages through the agency of wireless telegraphy where every Message that is conveyed thereby has been, or is to be, conveyed by means of a telecommunication system which is designed or adapted to be capable of being used while in motion;

(*j*) 'Network Connecting Apparatus' means telecommunication apparatus comprised in the System which is not Network Termination and Testing Apparatus and is connected to another telecommunication system;

(*k*) 'Network Termination Point' means any point:

(i) within an item of Network Connecting Apparatus at which energy of any of the forms specified in section 4(1) of the Act is conveyed directly to or from apparatus comprised in a telecommunication system other than the one in which that Network Connecting Apparatus is comprised; or

(ii) within an item of Network Termination and Testing Apparatus at which such energy is conveyed directly to any Relevant Terminal Apparatus;

(*l*) 'Network Termination and Testing Apparatus' means an item of telecommunication apparatus comprised in the System installed in a fixed position on Served Premises which enables:

(i) Approved Apparatus to be readily connected to, and disconnected from, the System; and

(ii) the conveyance of Messages between such Apparatus and the System; and

(iii) the due functioning of the System to be tested;

but the only other functions of which, if any, are:

(aa) to supply energy between such Apparatus and the System;

(bb) to protect the safety or security of operation of the System; or

(cc) to enable other operations exclusively related to the running of any Applicable Cabled System to be performed or the due functioning of any system to which the System is or is to be connected to be tested (separately or together with the System);

(*m*) 'Relevant Terminal Apparatus' means:

(i) 'Terminal Apparatus' that is to say any telecommunication apparatus installed on Served Premises by means of which Messages are initially transmitted or ultimately received except a Call Office; and

(ii) any other telecommunication apparatus directly connected to Terminal Apparatus (including apparatus which is Terminal Apparatus by virtue of this sub-paragraph) which would, if it were run with such Terminal Apparatus and any other apparatus by means of which it is so connected, constitute a system authorised to be run by the person running that Terminal Apparatus under a Licence;

(*n*) 'Served Premises' means a single set of premises in single occupation where apparatus has been installed for the purpose of the provision of telecommunication services by means of the System at those premises;

(*o*) 'Station for Wireless Telegraphy' and 'Wireless Telegraphy Apparatus' have the same meaning as in the Wireless Telegraphy Acts 1949 to 1967; and

(*p*) 'Subsidiary' has the same meaning as in section 736 of the Companies Act 1985, as substituted by section 144(1) of the Companies Act 1989.

3 In determining whether any telecommunication system is an Applicable Cabled System for the purposes of this Annex:

(i) any point at which any two systems run by the Licensee neither of which is a system authorised to be run and which is run under another Licence are connected shall be deemed not to be a Network Termination Point;

(ii)   in determining whether Messages are conveyed by way of provision of a service all members of the Licensee's Group (that is to say the Licensee and its Subsidiaries taken together) shall be treated as one person; and

(iii)   apparatus shall be deemed to remain installed in a fixed position notwithstanding that it has been moved without authority.

4   For the purposes of this Annex:

(a)   any approval issued under section 16(2) of the British Telecommunications Act 1981; or

(b)   any acknowledgement by the Secretary of State or a person appointed for the purposes of section 16(2) of that Act that any apparatus conforms to a standard approved under section 16(1) of that Act
which was effective on 5 August 1984 under which apparatus is approved for indirect connection to a system run by British Telecommunications by way of connection to any other system shall be treated as an approval under section 22 of the Act for connection to such other system.

5   The Interpretation Act 1978 shall apply for the purposes of interpreting this Annex as if it were an Act of Parliament.

6   Any word or expression used in this Annex shall unless the context otherwise requires have the same meaning as it has in the Act.

LICENCE GRANTED BY THE SECRETARY OF STATE FOR TRADE AND INDUSTRY TO ORANGE PERSONAL COMMUNICATIONS SERVICES LIMITED UNDER SECTION 7 OF THE TELECOMMUNICATIONS ACT 1984

27 JULY 1995

TABLE OF CONTENTS

Notes

1.   Although the whole contents of the Licence is set out, only extracts of the licence itself are reproduced in the text. This is because many conditions are similar in all licences, although not necessarily identical, and there is not space in this Handbook to reproduce all the selected licences in full. However, the conditions and other parts of the licence which are special or particular to this type of licence are reproduced.

2.   This licence and other mobile operator licences will be amended as a result of recent amendments to BT's licence particularly relating to fair trading.

THE LICENCE

1   The Secretary of State, in exercise of the powers conferred on him by section 7 of the Telecommunications Act 1984 (hereinafter referred to as 'the Act') and after consulting the Director hereby grants to Orange Personal Communications Services Limited (hereinafter referred to as 'the Licensee') a licence, for the period specified in paragraph 3, subject to the Conditions set out in Schedule 1 and to revocation as provided for in paragraph 3 and in Schedule 2, to run telecommunication systems of every description within the United Kingdom ('the Applicable Systems') and authorises the Licensee to do all or any of the acts specified in Schedule 3.

2   The Telecommunications Code contained in Schedule 2 to the Act shall apply to the Licensee for all purposes except those not relating to the Applicable Systems and subject to the other exceptions and conditions set out in Schedule 4 for so long as this Licence is one to which section 8 of the Act applies

Duration

3   This Licence shall enter into force on the date of signature and shall be of 25 years' duration in the first instance but, without prejudice to Schedule 2 to this Licence, shall be subject to revocation thereafter on ten years' notice in writing of such revocation and such notice shall accordingly not be given before the end of the fifteenth year after the granting of this Licence.

Interpretation

4   The Interpretation Act 1978 shall apply for the purpose of interpreting this Licence as if it were an Act of Parliament. In this Licence, except as

hereinafter provided or unless the context otherwise requires, words or expressions shall have the meaning assigned to them and otherwise any word or expression shall have the same meaning as it has in the Act. For the purposes of interpreting this Licence, headings and titles shall be disregarded.

5 In this Licence, 'Licence' means a licence granted or having effect as if granted under section 7 of the Act.

6 For the purposes of this Licence the 'Applicable Systems' means any or all of the telecommunication systems run by the Licensee under this Licence unless the context otherwise requires.

7 Where the Licence provides for any power of the Secretary of State or the Director to give any direction or consent or make any specification, designation or determination it implies, unless the contrary intention appears, a power, exercisable in the same manner and subject to the same conditions or limitations, to revoke, amend or give or make again any such direction, consent, specification, designation or determination.

8 Any notification which is required to be given under this Licence by the Secretary of State or the Director shall be satisfied by serving the document by post on the Licensee at the Licensee's registered office.

Parliamentary Under Secretary of State
for Science and Technology
27 July 1995

Note
This Licence has been chosen as a recent example of a typical cellular network operator's licence.

SCHEDULE 1

CONDITIONS INCLUDED UNDER SECTION 7 OF THE ACT

PART 1 DEFINITIONS, INTERPRETATION AND TRANSITIONAL PROVISIONS RELATING TO THE CONDITIONS IN SCHEDULE 1

1 In this Schedule, unless the context otherwise requires:

(a) 'Apparatus Production Business' means the production of telecommunication apparatus insofar as it is undertaken in the United Kingdom by the Licensee or any wholly owned Subsidiary taken together;

(b) 'Apparatus Supply Business' means any of the following activities of the Licensee or of any wholly owned Subsidiary insofar as they are undertaken in the United Kingdom taken together and do not form part of the activities of the Direct Business, that is to say:

(i) the supply of telecommunication apparatus; and

(ii) the installation, maintenance, adjustment, repair, alteration, moving, removal or replacement of telecommunication apparatus,
which in either case is to be connected to but not comprised in or to be comprised in the Applicable Systems;

(c) 'Applicable Terminal Equipment' means apparatus which is applicable terminal equipment within the meaning of regulation 4 of the Telecommunications Terminal Equipment Regulations 1992;

(*d*) 'Approved Apparatus' means in relation to any system apparatus approved under section 22 of the Act for connection to that system;

(*e*) 'Associated Person' means any member of the Licensee's Group or a person with a Participating Interest in a member of the Licensee's Group or in whom a member of the Licensee's Group has a Participating Interest;

(*f*) 'Auditor' means the Licensee's auditor for the time being appointed in accordance with the requirements of the Companies Act 1985;

(*g*) 'Authorised Mobile' means a telecommunication system designed or adapted to be capable of being used while in motion which is lawfully connected to any telecommunication system (whether or not within the United Kingdom) which has been specified by the Secretary of State for the purpose of Inter-System Roaming and described in a list kept for that purpose by the Director and made available by him for inspection by the general public;

(*h*) 'Bringing into Service' means the process of connecting by means of a tool telecommunication apparatus (including apparatus comprised in a telecommunication system) or a telecommunication system to another telecommunication system, or the process of disconnecting by such means such apparatus or such system from another such system; and includes such testing or inspection of that apparatus or system and any other apparatus to which it is or is to be connected as is necessary for the purpose of ensuring that the apparatus or the system is authorised to be connected to the Applicable Systems;

(*i*) 'Call Box' means any kiosk, booth, acoustic hood, shelter or similar structure at which apparatus is installed for the provision of voice telephony services to the public or a class of the public together with such apparatus;

(*j*) 'Call Box Services' means the installation, repair and maintenance of Call Boxes; the service of conveying by means of the Applicable Systems voice telephony messages to and from such Boxes, directory information services relating to switched voice telephony services available at such Boxes and Public Emergency Call Services so available;

(*k*) 'Call Office' means telecommunication apparatus not supplied by the Licensee to any particular person but made available for use by the public or a class of the public;

(*l*) 'Cell' means a geographical area served by a Station for Wireless Telegraphy which is dedicated to transmitting or receiving Messages;

(*m*) 'Cellular System' means a telecommunication system in which:

(i)   the area in which telecommunication services are provided is divided up into a number of Cells;

(ii)   Stations for Wireless Telegraphy comprised in the system are automatically controlled by the central processor;

(iii)   Messages are conveyed through the agency of Wireless Telegraphy between:

(A)   Stations for Wireless Telegraphy comprised in the system (the first systems); and

(B)   telecommunication apparatus or telecommunication systems which in either case are designed or adapted to be capable of being used while in motion (the second systems);

(iv)   the Wireless Telegraphy frequencies used for the purpose of such conveyance are assigned automatically;

(v)   there is a control procedure which allows the telecommunication service consisting in the conveyance of Messages between any of the first systems and any of the second systems to be continued to be provided between a different first system and that particular second system as the second system moves from Cell to Cell; and

(vi)   the strength of the emissions of the Stations for Wireless Telegraphy comprised in the system is automatically controlled so as to secure as far as is technically possible that each such Station for Wireless Telegraphy can effectively provide services only in the Cell in which it is located;

(*n*)   'Chatline Service' means a service which consists of or includes the enabling of more than two persons ('the Participants') simultaneously to conduct a telephone conversation with one another without either:

(i)   each of them having agreed with each other; or

(ii)   one or more of them having agreed with the person enabling such a telephone conversation to be conducted,

in advance of making the call enabling them to engage in the conversation the respective identities of the other intended Participants or the telephone numbers on which they can be called, provided that a service by which one or more additional persons who are known (by name or telephone number) to one or more of the parties conducting an established telephone conversation can be added to that conversation by means of being called by one or more such parties is not on that account a Chatline Service if it would not otherwise be regarded as such a service;

(*o*)   'Compatibility' means that between the parties concerned there is no reasonably foreseeable risk of:

(i)   duplication of any Number; or

(ii)   any other related effect,

such as would introduce ambiguity or errors or impose undue restrictions on any user or group of users;

(*p*)   'Compliant Terminal Equipment' means Applicable Terminal Equipment which satisfies the requirements of regulation 8 of the Telecommunications Terminal Equipment Regulations 1992;

(*q*)   'Condition' means a Condition in this Schedule;

(*r*)   'Connectable System' means a telecommunication system which is authorised to be run under a Licence which authorises connection of that system to the Applicable Systems;

(*s*)   'Connection Service' means a telecommunication service consisting in the conveyance of any Message which has been, or is to be, conveyed by means of the Applicable Systems;

(*t*)   'Controlled Service' means:

(i)   a Chatline Service; or

(ii)   a Live Conversation Message Service;

(*u*)   'cost' includes a reasonable profit;

(*v*)   'Designated Rural Area' means any part of the United Kingdom which has been specified by the Director, after consultation with the Secretary of State, and in respect of which that specification has not been revoked by the Director after consultation with the Licensee, and which is described in a list kept for that purpose by the Director and made available by him for inspection by the general public;

(*w*) 'Direct Business' means any of the following activities of the Licensee or of any wholly owned Subsidiary insofar as they are undertaken in the United Kingdom taken together, that is to say:

(i) the supply of any telecommunication apparatus which is or is to be connected to:

(A) the Applicable Systems; or

(B) any telecommunication system connected to the Applicable Systems,

but which is not and is not to be comprised in the Applicable Systems;

(ii) the provision of any telecommunication service consisting in the installation, maintenance, adjustment, repair, alteration, moving, removal or replacement of any such apparatus; or

(iii) the provision of any telecommunication service by means of the Applicable Systems,

to or for any person who is not:

(1) a Service Provider;

(2) the Crown, an Emergency Organisation, or a person specified for the time being under Condition 1.3(c) of Schedule 1;

(3) the operator of a Relevant Connectable System; or

(4) a person running a telecommunication system or providing telecommunication services outside the United Kingdom,

including any activity to promote or market those activities;

(*x*) 'Dwelling-House' has the same meaning as in section 202 of the Broadcasting Act 1990;

(*y*) 'Emergency' means an emergency of any kind, including any circumstance whatever resulting from major accidents, natural disasters and incidents involving toxic or radio-active materials;

(*z*) 'Emergency Organisations' means in respect of any locality:

(i) the relevant public police, fire, ambulance and coastguard services for that locality; and

(ii) any other similar organisation in respect of which any public telecommunications operator licensed to operate in the locality in question is providing a Public Emergency Call Service on the day on which this Licence enters into force;

(*aa*) 'Essential Interface' means in respect of a Point of Connection an interface at which in the opinion of the Director it is essential that interoperability between the Applicable Systems and the respective Operator's systems is available;

(*ab*) 'GSM System' means:

(i) a telecommunication system run outside the United Kingdom and conforming to European Telecommunications Standards adopted by the European Telecommunications Standards Institute for use with the pan-European digital cellular radio system generically known as GSM; or

(ii) a telecommunication system run outside the United Kingdom and conforming to a technical standard which replaces or derives from the European Telecommunications Standards mentioned in paragraph 1(ab)(i) and which is specified by the Secretary of State for the purpose of this Licence after consultation with the Director and described in a list kept for that purpose by the Director and made available by him for inspection by the general public;

(*ac*) 'Group' means a parent undertaking and its subsidiary undertaking or undertakings within the meaning of section 258 of the Companies Act 1985 as substituted by section 21 of the Companies Act 1989 and 'Licensee's Group' means a Group in respect of which the Licensee is either a parent undertaking or a subsidiary undertaking;

(*ad*) 'Industrial or Intellectual Property' includes without prejudice to its generality, patents, registered designs, know-how and copyright;

(*ae*) 'International Business' means the provision of telecommunication services consisting in the conveyance of Messages to countries or territories outside the United Kingdom (and including, without limitation, International Simple Data Resale Services and International Simple Voice Resale Services) carried on under a Licence, other than any of the services described in paragraphs 3(d)(i) and 3(e) of Schedule 3, and includes the running of such parts of the Applicable Systems as are used for the provision of those services, and the installation, maintenance, adjustment, repair, alteration, moving, removal or replacement of such Systems and any apparatus comprised therein;

(*af*) 'International Connection Service' means a telecommunication service consisting in the conveyance of any Message which has been conveyed or is to be conveyed by means of any telecommunication system outside the United Kingdom the connection of which to the system by means of which that service is provided is authorised by a Licence;

(*ag*) 'International Private Leased Circuit' means a communication facility which is:

(i)   comprised both in a public telecommunication system and in an equivalent telecommunication system in a country or territory other than the United Kingdom;

(ii)   for the conveyance of Messages between points, all of which are points of connection between telecommunication systems referred to in paragraph 1(ag)(i) and other telecommunication systems;

(iii)   made available to a particular person or particular persons;

(iv)   such that all of the Messages transmitted at any of the points mentioned in paragraph 1(ag)(ii) are received at every other such point; and

(v)   such that the points mentioned in paragraph 1(ag)(ii) are fixed by the way in which the facility is installed and cannot otherwise be selected by persons or apparatus sending Messages by means of that facility;

(*ah*) 'International Simple Data Resale Services' means telecommunication services consisting in the conveyance of Messages which do not include two-way live speech, but include only such switching, processing, data storage or protocol conversion as is necessary for the conveyance of those Messages in real time, which have been or are to be conveyed by means of all of the following:

(i)   a Public Switched Network;

(ii)   an International Private Leased Circuit; and

(iii)   the equivalent of a Public Switched Network in another country or territory;

provided that conveyance of a Message by means of a Public Switched Network or, as the case may be, the equivalent of a Public Switched Network in another country or territory shall be disregarded where that Message is so conveyed in circumstances specified for the time being by the Secretary of

State as not being material for the purposes of paragraph 3 of Schedule 3 to this Licence and included in a list kept for the purpose by the Director and made available by him for inspection by the general public;

(*ai*) 'International Simple Voice Resale Services' means telecommunication services consisting in the conveyance of Messages which include two-way live speech which have been or are to be conveyed by means of all of the following:

(i)   a Public Switched Network;

(ii)   an International Private Leased Circuit; and

(iii)   the equivalent of a Public Switched Network in another country or territory;

provided that conveyance of a Message by means of a Public Switched Network or, as the case may be, the equivalent of a Public Switched Network in another country or territory shall be disregarded where that Message is so conveyed in circumstances specified for the time being by the Secretary of State as not being material for the purposes of paragraph 3 of Schedule 3 to this Licence and included in a list kept for the purpose by the Director and made available by him for inspection by the general public;

(*aj*) 'Inter-System Roaming' means the ability of a telecommunication system to convey Messages upon demand between any Authorised Mobile and a Public Switched Network or between any Authorised Mobile and another Authorised Mobile;

(*ak*) 'Live Conversation Message Service' means a Message Service (other than a directory information service) which consists in the provision of live telephone conversation for any purpose, whether or not including the provision of information of any kind:

(i)   between the person providing the service (or a person acting on his behalf) and a person who obtains the service; or

(ii)   between a person who has independently called the service for the purpose of conducting a telephone conversation with one other such person, and such another person,

and, for the avoidance of doubt, it does not include a service provided by a human operator of the Licensee which is incidental to the conveyance of a voice telephony message;

(*al*) 'Long Line Public Telecommunications Operator' means a public telecommunications operator who is authorised by a Licence to provide telecommunication services consisting in the conveyance of Messages by fixed links run by him over distances greater than 50 linear kilometres;

(*am*) 'Major Office' means the Licensee's registered office and such other offices as the Director, having consulted the Licensee, may direct;

(*an*) 'Message' means anything falling within paragraphs (a) to (d) of section 4(1) of the Act;

(*ao*) 'Message Service' means a service which consists of, or includes, the sending of speech, music or other sounds or signals to any person who obtains access to that service by means of a Public Switched Network;

(*ap*) 'Minimum Figure' means £185 per annum or such other amount as the Director and the Licensee may agree for the time being in respect of any Call Box or any description of Call Boxes, after consultation with the advisory bodies established by the Secretary of State under section 54(1) of the Act;

(*aq*) 'Mobile Radio Telecommunication Service' means any telecommunication service consisting in the conveyance of Messages by means of a telecommunication system where every Message that is conveyed thereby has been, or is to be, conveyed through the agency of Wireless Telegraphy to or from a telecommunication system which is designed or adapted to be capable of being used while in motion;

(*ar*) 'Network Connecting Apparatus' means telecommunication apparatus comprised in the Applicable Systems which is not Network Termination and Testing Apparatus and is connected to another telecommunication system;

(*as*) 'Network Termination Point' means any point:

(i)   within an item of Network Connecting Apparatus at which energy of any of the forms specified in section 4(1) of the Act is conveyed directly to or from apparatus comprised in a telecommunication system other than one in which that Network Connecting Apparatus is comprised; or

(ii)   within an item of Network Termination and Testing Apparatus at which such energy is conveyed directly to any Relevant Terminal Apparatus;

(*at*) 'Network Termination and Testing Apparatus' means an item of telecommunication apparatus comprised in the Applicable Systems installed in a fixed position on Served Premises which enables:

(i)   Approved Apparatus to be readily connected to, and disconnected from, the Applicable Systems;

(ii)   the conveyance of Messages between such Apparatus and the Applicable Systems; and

(iii)   the due functioning of the Applicable Systems to be tested, but the only other functions of which, if any, are:

(1)   to supply energy between such Apparatus and the Applicable Systems;

(2)   to protect the safety or security of operation of the Applicable Systems; or

(3)   to enable other operations exclusively related to the running of the Applicable Systems to be performed or the due functioning of any system to which the Applicable Systems are or are to be connected to be tested (separately or together with the Applicable Systems);

(*au*) 'Number' means any identifier which would need to be used in conjunction with any public switched service for the purposes of establishing a connection with any Network Termination Point, user, telecommunication apparatus connected to any Public Switched Network or service element, but not including any identifier which is not accessible to the generality of users of a public switched service:

(*av*) 'Numbering Plan' means a plan describing the method adopted or to be adopted for allocating and re-allocating a Number to any Network Termination Point, user, telecommunication apparatus or service element;

(*aw*) 'Operator' means any person who is authorised by a Licence to run a Relevant Connectable System;

(*ax*) 'Parent Undertaking' has the same meaning as in section 258 of the Companies Act 1985 as substituted by section 21 of the Companies Act 1989;

(*ay*) 'Participating Interest' has the same meaning as in Part VII of the Companies Act 1985 as amended by section 22 of the Companies Act 1989;

(*az*) 'PCN System' means:

(i)   a telecommunication system run outside the United Kingdom and conforming to European Telecommunications Standards adopted by the European Telecommunications Standards Institute for use with the digital cellular radio system generically known as DCS 1800; or

(ii)   a telecommunication system run outside the United Kingdom and conforming to a technical standard which replaces or derives from the European Telecommunications Standards mentioned in paragraph 1(az)(i) and which is specified by the Secretary of State for the purpose of this Licence after consultation with the Director and described in a list kept for that purpose by the Director and made available by him for inspection by the general public;

(*ba*) 'Point of Connection' means a point at which the Applicable Systems and an Operator's system are connected;

(*bb*) 'Prepayment Apparatus' means telecommunication apparatus which has as its function, or one of its functions, the automatic enabling of Messages to be transmitted or received on the prior provision of consideration by means of the insertion in the apparatus of cash, or tokens, or cards, or by similar means;

(*bc*) 'Private Call Box' means a Call Box owned by or supplied to a person other than the Licensee or another public telecommunications operator at which Call Box Services are or may be provided;

(*bd*) 'Private Leased Circuit' means a communication facility which is:

(i)   provided by means of one or more public telecommunication systems;

(ii)   for the conveyance of Messages between points, all of which are points of connection between telecommunication systems referred to in paragraph 1(bd)(i) and other telecommunication systems;

(iii)   made available to a particular person or particular persons;

(iv)   such that all of the Messages transmitted at any of the points mentioned in paragraph 1(bd)(ii) are received at every other such point; and

(v)   such that the points mentioned in paragraph 1(bd)(ii) are fixed by the way in which the facility is installed and cannot otherwise be selected by persons or telecommunication apparatus sending Messages by means of that facility;

(*be*) 'Private Call Box' means a Call Box to which the public has access at all times which is neither a Private Call Box nor a Temporary Call Box and at which Call Box Services are or may be provided;

(*bf*) 'Public Emergency Call Service' means a telecommunication service by means of which any member of the public may, at any time and without incurring any charge, by means of any item of telecommunication apparatus which is lawfully connected to the Applicable Systems and which is capable of transmitting and receiving unrestricted two-way voice telephony services when so connected, communicate as swiftly as practicable with any of the Emergency Organisations for the purpose of notifying them of an Emergency;

(*bg*) 'Public Switched Network' means a public telecommunication system by means of which two-way telecommunication services are provided whereby Messages are switched incidentally to their conveyance, and, for the avoidance of doubt, a Public Switched Network does not include Private Leased Circuits or International Private Leased Circuits;

(*bh*) 'Relevant Apparatus' means any apparatus which is, or is to be, connected to the switched Applicable Systems;

(*bi*) 'Relevant Company' means:

(i) the Licensee; or

(ii) A Parent Undertaking in relation to the Licensee;

(*bj*) 'Relevant Connectable System' means a Connectable System which is authorised to be run under a Licence which authorises the provision by means of that system of Connection Services for reward to the general public, or any class of the general public, not being a system:

(i) authorised to be run under a Licence granted to all persons or persons of any class; and

(ii) for the connection of which, and for the provision of matters necessary for such connection, the Licensee offers standard terms and conditions which satisfy the requirements of Condition 8 of Schedule 1, and not being a system which the Director has determined ought not to be deemed a Relevant Connectable System for the purposes of this Licence;

(*bk*) 'Relevant Consumer Body' means any of the bodies referred to in Condition 20 of Schedule 1;

(*bl*) 'Relevant Intellectual Property Right' means any right, which is wholly or partly controlled by the Licensee or a member of the Licensee's Group, in Industrial or Intellectual Property or is subject to an agreement, an arrangement or concerted practice to which the Licensee or a member of the Licensee's Group is a party;

(*bm*) 'Relevant Local Authority' means the smallest unit of local authority for the area where the Public Call Box is located;

(*bn*) 'Relevant Person' means a person:

(i) who requests that a telecommunication service be provided by means of or in relation to the Applicable Systems, or for whom or on whose behalf such a telecommunication service is provided; or

(ii) who requests that telecommunication apparatus or a telecommunication system be supplied or to whom or on whose behalf such apparatus or system is supplied; or

(iii) who requests that any telecommunication system or telecommunication apparatus be connected to the Applicable Systems or for whom or on whose behalf such a system or such apparatus is so connected;

(*bo*) 'Relevant System' means a Connectable System which is, or is to be, connected to any of the switched Applicable Systems;

(*bp*) 'Relevant Terminal Apparatus' means:

(i) 'Terminal Apparatus' that is to say any telecommunication apparatus installed on Served Premises by means of which Messages are initially transmitted or ultimately received except a Call Office; and

(ii) any other telecommunication apparatus directly connected to Terminal Apparatus (including apparatus which is Terminal Apparatus by virtue of this paragraph) which would, if it were run with such Terminal Apparatus and any other apparatus by means of which it is so connected, constitute a system authorised to be run by the person running that Terminal Apparatus under a Licence;

(*bq*) 'Revenue', in relation to services provided at any Public Call Box, means the actual amounts received by the Licensee in respect thereof, together with a notional sum equal to 24 per cent (or such other percentage as the Director and the Licensee may agree for the time being) of the aggregate of such amounts representing revenue earned in respect of transfer charge, credit and similar facilities provided at that Call Box and of services provided and paid for elsewhere which involve conveyance of Messages to that Call Box;

(*br*) 'Served Premises' means a single set of premises in single occupation where apparatus has been installed for the purpose of the provision of telecommunication services by means of the Applicable Systems at those premises;

(*bs*) 'Service Provider' means any person who is in the business of providing Mobile Radio Telecommunication Services to another by means of a telecommunication system lawfully connected to the Applicable Systems or who is in the business of securing the provision of such services by such means;

(*bt*) 'Shares' has the meaning given to it in section 259(2) of the Companies Act 1985, as substituted by section 144(1) of the Companies Act 1989, and the term 'Shareholding' is to be construed accordingly;

(*bu*) 'Specified Numbering Scheme' means a scheme for the allocation and re-allocation of Numbers for the purposes of any of the switched Applicable Systems and the systems of other licensed operators which is specified by the Director for the purpose of this Licence and described in a list kept for that purpose by him and made available by him for public inspection;

(*bv*) 'Specified Personal Telecommunications Operator' means Mercury Personal Communications Limited or any other operator of a public telecommunications system specified by the Secretary of State for the purpose of this Licence and described in a list kept for that purpose by the Director and made available by him for inspection by the general public;

(*bw*) 'Subscriber' means a person (other than a public telecommunications operator, a Service Provider or a person who is in the business of providing any telecommunication service which is not a Mobile Radio Telecommunication Service to another by means of a telecommunication system lawfully connected to the Applicable Systems or who is in the business of securing the provision of such services by such means) to whom there are provided switched voice telephony services by means of the Applicable Systems;

(*bx*) 'Subsidiary' has the meaning given to it in section 736 of the Companies Act 1985 as substituted by section 144(1) of the Companies Act 1989;

(*by*) 'Supplemental Services Business' means the following activities of the Licensee taken together:

(i) the provision in the United Kingdom by the Licensee of Value Added Or Data Services;

(ii) the installation, maintenance, adjustment, repair, alteration, moving, removal or replacement of any apparatus used solely to provide a Value Added Or Data Service; and

(iii) the conveyance by means of the Applicable Systems, but only to the extent that they are used for this purpose, of Messages comprised in Value Added Or Data Services provided by the Licensee;

(*bz*) 'Systems Business' means the following activities of the Licensee and of any wholly owned Subsidiary to the extent that they are undertaken in the United Kingdom taken together:

(i)   the running of the Applicable Systems except where such running is part of the Supplemental Services Business;

(ii)   the installation, maintenance, adjustment, repair, alteration, moving, removal or replacement of any apparatus comprised or to be comprised in the Applicable Systems where those activities are not part of the Supplemental Services Business;

(iii)   without prejudice to the generality of paragraph 1(bz)(i) or 1(bz)(ii) the Bringing into Service of any item of telecommunication apparatus or telecommunication system connected or to be connected to the Applicable Systems whether comprised in those systems or not; and

(iv)   without prejudice to the generality of paragraph 1(bz)(i) the conveyance of Messages (not including switching) by means of the Applicable Systems and switching incidental to such conveyance where such conveyance is not part of the Supplemental Services Business;

(*ca*)   'Telephone' means an item of telecommunication apparatus capable when connected to the Licensee's public switched system, of transmitting and receiving uninterrupted simultaneous two-way speech conveyed, or, as the case may be, to be conveyed, by means of the Applicable Systems;

(*cb*)   'Temporary Call Box' means a Call Box run by the Licensee which is mobile or is installed for a limited period or is permanently installed but at which Call Box Services are provided to the public or a class of the public for limited periods of time;

(*cc*)   'United Kingdom' includes any area which the provisions of the Act apply by virtue of section 107;

(*cd*)   'Utility Services' means services consisting in the provision of gas, water or electricity;

(*ce*)   'Value Added Or Data Service' means any telecommunication service consisting in the conveyance by means of the Applicable Systems of Messages, other than:

(i)   the conveyance of television programmes or sound programmes or both comprised in services that require to be licensed under the Broadcasting Act 1990 for delivery or subsequent delivery to two or more Dwelling-Houses; and

(ii)   a telecommunication service which forms the whole or part of a service, provided by means of the Applicable Systems, the only substantial element of which is conveyance of telex Messages or live speech; and

(*cf*)   'Wireless Telegraphy' and 'Station for Wireless Telegraphy' have the same meaning as in the Wireless Telegraphy Act 1949.

2   Any reference in any Condition in this Schedule, however expressed, to the Director notifying the Licensee about any matter, affording the Licensee an opportunity to make representations, taking representations by the Licensee into account, or explaining, or giving reasons for, any matter to the Licensee, shall be without prejudice to any obligation of due process or similar obligation which the Director is or may be under by virtue of any rule or principle of law or otherwise.

3   Expressions cognate with those referred to in this Schedule shall be construed accordingly.

4   Nothing which the Licensee may do, or omit to do, after the date on which any provision of the Conditions in this Schedule enters into force shall be held to constitute a failure to comply with an obligation imposed by or

under those Conditions to the extent that the Licensee is obliged to do or to omit to do (as the case may be) that thing by the terms of any contract subsisting immediately before 9 July 1991.

PART 2 SPECIAL CONDITIONS REFERRED TO IN SECTION 8 OF THE ACT

Condition 1 Requirements to Provide Telecommunication Services

1.1   Save where paragraph 1.2 applies the Licensee shall install, keep installed and run the Applicable Systems in such a way as:

(*a*)   to provide, or offer to provide, to Service Providers and the persons described in paragraph 1.3 on and following the date this Licence comes into force a Mobile Radio Telecommunication Service; and

(*b*)   on and following 31 December 1999:

(i)   in an area where 90% of the United Kingdom population live to provide, or offer to provide, such telecommunication services to Service Providers and the persons mentioned in paragraph 1.3 by means of the Applicable Systems, save that in Designated Rural Areas this obligation may be met by procuring services by means of Inter-System Roaming; and

(ii)   to ensure that the reasonable demands for the provision of such telecommunication service and for services procured by Inter-System Roaming in that area are capable of being satisfied.

1.2   Where the Licensee has entered into an arrangement for the provision of Inter-System Roaming in Designated Rural Areas with any Specified Personal Telecommunications Operator prior to 31 December 1997, and any such arrangement is terminated after 31 December 1997 and prior to 31 December 1999 and not resumed, the Licensee shall ensure that the obligation set out in paragraph 1.1(b) is met on and following 31 December 2004.

1.3   For the purposes of paragraph 1.1, the persons mentioned are:

(*a*)   The Crown;

(*b*)   Emergency Organisations; and

(*c*)   any person who is engaged in the provision of Utility Services or in public administration and who is for the time being specified for the purposes of this Condition by the Director.

1.4   Subject to Condition 34, if:

(*a*)   the Licensee is, in the opinion of the Director, a well established operator in the provision of any telecommunication service of a particular description other than a Mobile Radio Telecommunication Service in the United Kingdom or within any part or locality thereof; and

(*b*)   the arrangements made by the Licensee are inadequate to secure the availability of such a service within the United Kingdom or within that part or locality thereof to any person who may reasonably request it,

the Director may direct the Licensee to install, keep installed and run the Applicable Systems in such a way as to secure that such services are available within that part of the United Kingdom to any person who may reasonably request them and the Licensee shall comply with any such direction.

1.5   Any specification made by the Director under paragraph 1.3 shall be described in a list kept for that purpose by the Director and made available by him for inspection by the general public.

1.6   Paragraph 1.1(b)(ii) shall not apply to the extent that the Director, after consultation with the Licensee, determines, taking into account in particular:

(*a*)   whether the current and prospective demand for such telecommunication services to be provided by means of any additional Applicable Systems that would need to be installed within that area and the revenues likely to be derived from providing such services would not be sufficient to enable the Licensee to recover the costs incurred in installing and running any such additions to the Applicable Systems; and

(*b*)   any other factor involved in the sound commercial development of the Applicable Systems.

1.7   In this Condition, 'well established operator' means that the Licensee has 25% or more of what is in the opinion of the Director the relevant market.

Note
This Condition should be contrasted with BT's 'Universal Service' obligation under Conditions 1 and 2 of BT's licence.

Condition 5   Requirement to Provide Connection Services

5.1   Without prejudice to Condition 2 and subject to the following provisions of this Condition the Licensee shall, unless it is impracticable to do so, enter into an agreement with an Operator if that Operator requires it to do so:

(*a*)   to connect, and keep connected, to the Applicable Systems, or to permit to be so connected and kept connected, any Relevant Connectable System run by the Operator and accordingly to establish and maintain such one or more Points of Connection as are reasonably required and are of sufficient capacity and in sufficient number to enable Messages conveyed or to be conveyed by means of the Operator's system to be conveyed by means of the Applicable Systems in such a way as conveniently to meet all reasonable demands for the conveyance of Messages between the Relevant Connectable System and the Applicable Systems;

(*b*)   without prejudice to paragraph 5.1(a), where the Operator is a Long Line Public Telecommunications Operator to establish and maintain such Points of Connection as will enable persons running telecommunication systems connected to the Operator's system and persons running telecommunication systems connected to the Applicable Systems to exercise freedom of choice as to the extent to which Messages are conveyed by means of the Applicable Systems and in routing Messages so conveyed; and

(*c*)   to provide such other telecommunication services (including the conveyance of Messages which have been, or are to be, transmitted or received at such Points of Connection), information and other services as the Director determines are reasonably required (but no more than reasonably required) to secure that Points of Connection are established and maintained and to enable the Operator effectively to provide the Connection Services which he provides or proposes to provide.

5.2   The Licensee shall not be obliged under paragraph 5.1 to enter into an agreement to do anything if:

(*a*)   in the opinion of the Licensee it would be liable to cause the death of or personal injury to, or damage to the property of, the Licensee or any person engaged in the Licensee's business, or materially to impair the quality of any telecommunication service provided by means of the Applicable Systems or any telecommunication system (other than the Operator's system) connected thereto and the Director has not expressed a contrary opinion; or

(b)   in the opinion of the Licensee:

(i)   it would require an adjustment to, or modification of, the Applicable Systems whether by incorporation of apparatus or otherwise or the provision by the Licensee of services or information which in any particular case would not be reasonably required; or

(ii)   it would not be reasonably practicable to require the Licensee to do that thing, or permit it to be done, at the time or in the manner required by the Operator, having regard to the state of technical development of the Applicable Systems or any other relevant matter,

and the Director has not expressed a contrary opinion.

5.3   The Licensee may require that an agreement to be entered into under paragraph 5.1 should be subject to terms and conditions, but only such terms and conditions as are permitted in relation to that agreement in accordance with paragraphs 5.4, 5.5 and 5.7.

5.4   Subject to paragraph 5.5 and 5.7, terms and conditions are permitted if they are agreed between the Operator and the Licensee and relate to all or any of the following matters:

(a)   the charges to be paid by the Operator for anything done under an agreement of the kind described in paragraph 5.1 or as a result of such agreement;

(b)   the method adopted or to be adopted to make or maintain the connection;

(c)   the Points of Connection in the Applicable Systems at which the connection is or is to be made (including arrangements for determining the point at which Messages will be transferred from one system to another and arrangements for conveying and rerouting Messages in cases of Emergency or difficulty);

(d)   any restrictions on the telecommunication services to be provided by the Licensee or the Operator being restrictions needed to satisfy international obligations or recommendations applying to and accepted by Her Majesty's Government or to which the Director consents from time to time;

(e)   the time when and period for which the Licensee or the Operator is to be obliged to do anything or to permit anything to be done and any arrangements for reviewing the terms and conditions of the agreement;

(f)   the form and manner in which Messages are to be transmitted or received at the Points of Connection including arrangements for numbering and the use of appropriate call progress tones and announcements;

(g)   the means of securing that any Message will be received by means of the connection with a signal quality which is in accordance with any obligations and recommendations of the International Telecommunication Union which apply to Her Majesty's Government and are accepted by it or with any other standard to which the Director consents for the purpose from time to time;

(h)   arrangements for charging customers and others in respect of Messages conveyed by virtue of the agreement;

(i)   arrangements for Messages conveyed or to be conveyed outside the United Kingdom;

(j) provision by the Operator of a reasonable indemnity against any loss or damage sustained by the Licensee in consequence of the agreement in circumstances where the Licensee provides to the Operator an equivalent indemnity; and

(k) any other matter of which the Director is satisfied that account should be taken in the special circumstances of any particular case or which is agreed between the Licensee and the Operator.

5.5 If after a period which appears to the Director to be reasonable for the purpose the Licensee has failed to enter into an agreement as required by the Operator under paragraph 5.1 then the Director shall, on the application of the Operator or the Licensee, determine the permitted terms and conditions for the purpose of that agreement which have not been agreed between the Licensee and the Operator being terms and conditions relating to the matters mentioned in paragraph 5.4 which appear to the Director reasonably (but no more than reasonably necessary) to secure:

(a) that the cost of anything done pursuant to or in connection with the agreement including fully allocated costs attributable to the services to be provided and taking into account relevant overheads and a reasonable rate of return on attributable assets is apportioned equitably between the Licensee and the Operator;

(b) that the Licensee is properly indemnified against any liabilities to third parties or damage to the Applicable Systems or loss arising from such damage which may result from the performance of the agreement;

(c) that the Licensee is reasonably able in all the circumstances (including its obligations and reasonably foreseeable obligations to permit other Operators to provide services by means of Points of Connection under this Condition) to finance the other services which it is required by this Licence to provide and to recover costs which are incurred for the provision of those other services or are necessarily incidental thereto;

(d) that the quality of any telecommunication services provided by means of the Applicable Systems and any systems (other than the Operator's system) connected thereto is maintained;

(e) that the requirements of fair competition are satisfied;

(f) that proper account is taken of any other matter reasonably required for the protection of the interests of the Licensee to the extent that no interest of the Operator is unduly prejudiced, including the need to ensure:

(i) that arrangements for connection accord with good engineering principles and practice;

(ii) that the commercial development of the Applicable Systems is not unduly impeded;

(iii) that charging arrangements take account of the overall pattern of the Licensee's costs;

(iv) that Messages which originate on one system and are conveyed by another should pass through a Point of Connection as near as reasonably practicable to the place from which they are initially sent or at which they are ultimately received;

(v) that the Operator does not rely unduly upon services provided by the Licensee as a means of satisfying his own obligations under his licence;

(vi) that the Licensee's obligations to the Operator are determined having due regard to its obligations and reasonably foreseeable obligations to establish Points of Connection for others;

(vii) that arrangements made under this Condition are so far as circumstances allow in as similar a form as practicable notwithstanding the variety of Operators entitled to such arrangements under this Condition;

(viii) that commercial and confidential information of the Licensee is properly protected; and

(ix) that the technical evolution and numbering arrangements of the Applicable Systems are not unreasonably constrained; and

(g) that without prejudice to paragraph 5.6 the Licensee may be required to carry out any work which the agreement requires it to carry out within an appropriate period of time having regard to all the circumstances which would be reasonable for an efficient telecommunications operator who was not required to give the particular work priority over work for the Licensee's customers generally.

5.6 Where in pursuance of such an application as is referred to in paragraph 5.5 the Director determines any charge (or the means of calculating any charge), payable in respect of the establishment of a connection between the Applicable Systems and the system of the Operator, he shall do so in accordance with the following provisions:

(a) any costs incurred in the establishment of such a connection, including (without limitation) the provision of dedicated capacity at a Point of Connection, but not transmission capacity, shall be shared between the parties according to the proportions in which each of them will bill the customers originating calls which are to be conveyed over the Point of Connection. These proportions shall be derived from forecasts by each party of the capacity required to convey those calls for which the respective parties will bill customers originating them. These costs shall be assessed on the basis of:

(i) the Licensee's or the Operator's respective fully allocated costs of the establishment of the connection including a reasonable contribution to relevant overheads; and

(ii) the application to relevant capital employed of a reasonable rate of return on attributable assets;

(b) any determination of any charge (or the means of calculating the same) to be payable under paragraph 5.6(a) may include a provision that no such charge shall be payable where the party imposing the charge fails to provide the connection within six months (or such longer period as the Licensee and the Operator may agree) of the date of the request therefor, provided that this provision shall not apply in any particular case unless it is reasonable in all the circumstances for it to apply. It shall be deemed not to be reasonable if:

(i) it was not reasonably practicable for any reason, for the first party to provide the connection in time;

(ii) the other party's request for the connection was unreasonable in quantum having regard to its current and future needs; or

(iii) in order to comply with the time period the Licensee would have had to give priority to making the connection beyond that given to its own customers generally;

(c) the period referred to in paragraph 5.6(b) shall be extended by such period as equates to or, if there is no period that equates, as is reasonably commensurate with, delays attributable to any default or lack of co-operation by the Operator, or to force majeure of any kind; and

(d) where one party has, in pursuance of a provision in the agreement, required the other party to provide a connection and subsequently cancels the order, it shall reimburse the other party for all costs (assessed on the basis of that party's fully allocated costs, together with a reasonable rate of return on attributable assets) incurred by the other party in the provision of the connection up to the date of cancellation.

5.7 Where the Licensee is required to enter into an agreement to do anything under paragraph 5.1(b) the permitted terms and conditions may relate to all or any of the matters mentioned in paragraph 5.4 but in determining the terms and conditions in the event of failure to agree under paragraph 5.5 the Director shall have regard to (in addition to the matters specified in paragraph 5.5) the need to ensure:

(a) that, insofar as any freedom of choice is conferred upon persons running telecommunication systems connected to the Operator's system as to the extent to which Messages are conveyed by means of the Applicable Systems and in routing messages so conveyed, a corresponding freedom of choice is conferred so far as reasonably practicable on persons running telecommunication systems connected to the Licensee's system; and

(b) that the requirements of fair competition, including the need for those to whom telecommunication services are provided to have a reasonable means of learning by whom the Messages sent by them are conveyed, are satisfied, but paragraph 5.5 shall have effect for this purpose with the omission of paragraph 5.5(f)(iv).

5.8 The Licensee shall not be obliged to enter into any agreement under paragraph 5.1 if he refuses to do so, giving his reasons in writing to the Operator and to the Director, and the Director determines that those reasons are proper ones having regard to the matters mentioned in paragraph 5.5.

5.9 Where:

(a) an agreement has been entered into under paragraph 5.1 but for any reason (whether breach of that agreement or otherwise) anything which the Licensee is required to do under the agreement is not being done, and

(b) the Director considers that the thing ought to be done in order to ensure that a connection made pursuant to that agreement is maintained or that a connection is established pursuant to that agreement, and that Messages are conveyed by means of the connection in accordance with the agreement; and

(c) the Director is satisfied that the Operator is not able satisfactorily to enforce the agreement so that thing is done within such time as the Director considers necessary,

then, if the Director so directs, the Licensee shall do that thing subject to such conditions as the Director determines to be reasonable in the circumstances, having regard, in particular, to the permitted terms and conditions which apply and to any thing which he may reasonably require the Operator to do in order to mitigate the effects of the Licensee's failure to do the thing which he is required to do.

5.10 Where:

(a) an Operator establishes a prima facie case that the Licensee is unreasonably not performing an obligation which he is required to perform under an agreement entered into under paragraph 5.1;

(*b*)   the Director considers that:

(i)   the obligation ought to be performed in order to achieve the purposes of paragraph 5.1;

(ii)   the Operator is not able satisfactorily to enforce the agreement so that the obligation is performed within such time as the Director considers necessary and the balance of convenience requires the Director to take action under this paragraph rather than leave it to the Courts; and

(iii)   the Operator has performed all its obligations which are relevant to the Licensee's obligation that is allegedly not being performed; and

(*c*)   paragraph 5.9 does not apply,

the Director may require the Licensee to perform the obligation subject to such conditions as are reasonable in the circumstances having regard, in particular, to the permitted terms and conditions which apply and to anything which the Operator may reasonably be expected to do in order to mitigate the effects of the Licensee's failure to perform its obligation.

5.11   Before making a requirement under paragraph 5.10 the Director shall notify the Licensee of the prima facie case established by the Operator, his conclusions thereon, and on the matters referred to in paragraph 5.10(b) and the direction he proposes to make, affording the Licensee adequate time in which to make representations.

5.12   Notwithstanding, and without prejudice to, any of the foregoing provisions of this Condition, if the Director considers that there is likely to be a category comprising a sufficient number of Operators seeking determinations under paragraph 5.5 for whom standard terms and conditions would be appropriate, he may require the Licensee to publish standard provisions (including, without limitation, charges and the method for calculating them) which set out the terms on which the Licensee will enter into an agreement under this Condition with Operators of that particular category.

5.13   If on an application by an Operator in the category mentioned in paragraph 5.12 the Director is satisfied that the Operator has established a prima facie case that any such standard term or condition proposed by the Licensee is unreasonable and that the Licensee has acted unreasonably in relation to negotiations on that term or condition, the Director may, if he considers it necessary to do so, either determine that the Licensee shall modify that standard provision in such a way as to make the term reasonable, in any agreement with the Operator, or modify that standard provision in such a way in the provisions published under paragraph 5.12.

5.14   In applying paragraph 5.13:

(*a*)   any such standard provision shall be confined to the subject matter of the term or condition proposed by the Licensee except that, where the Director considers that a term or condition is essential in relation to subject matter not covered by any term or condition proposed by the Licensee, he may determine a term or condition to cover the subject matter;

(*b*)   the Licensee shall not be deemed to have acted unreasonably merely by virtue of having proposed the term or condition in question; and

(*c*)   no determination may be made in relation to any provision which would be subject to the Unfair Contract Terms Act 1977.

5.15   Before making a determination under paragraph 5.13 the Director shall notify to the Licensee and the Operator the grounds of the Operator's application and his conclusions thereon and the modification he proposes to make or require the Licensee to make, and shall afford the Licensee and the Operator adequate time, being not less than 28 days, in which to make representations.

5.16   Where an Operator makes an application to the Director under paragraph 5.5 the Director may treat the application as an application under paragraph 5.13 and act accordingly.

5.17   For the avoidance of doubt the provisions of paragraphs 5.5 and 5.6 shall apply in respect of any determination made under paragraph 5.13 as they apply in relation to a determination made under paragraph 5.5.

5.18   An agreement made pursuant to this Condition shall not contain any restrictive provision unless, before the agreement is made, the Director has expressly consented to the inclusion of such a provision or has determined that the provision should be included under paragraph 5.5 and, for the purposes of this paragraph, a provision in an agreement is a restrictive provision if by virtue of the existence of such a provision (taken alone or with other provisions) the agreement is one to which the Restrictive Trade Practices Act 1976 would apply but for paragraph 1(1) of Schedule 3 to that Act.

5.19   Where the Director so directs the Crown shall be treated for the purposes of this Condition as a person authorised to run a Relevant Connectable System and where he does so he may also direct that the Crown is to be treated as a Long Line Public Telecommunications Operator for those purposes.

Condition 6   Connection of Other Systems and Apparatus

6.1   Subject to Conditions 13 and 14 and to the following provisions of this Condition, the Licensee shall at the written request of:

(*a*)   a Service Provider to whom the Licensee is obliged to provide Mobile Radio Telecommunication Services; or

(*b*)   in any case where the Licensee has agreed to provide Mobile Radio Telecommunication Services to a person who is not a Service Provider, that person,

connect or permit the connection of the Applicable Systems to any telecommunication system designed or adapted to be capable of being used while in motion which is composed of apparatus which is approved under section 22 of the Act for connection to the Applicable Systems or is Compliant Terminal Equipment and shall not discontinue a connection of any such system lawfully made.

6.2   Subject to Conditions 13 and 14 and to the following provisions of this Condition and at the written request of:

(*a*)   a person to whom the Licensee is obliged to provide telecommunication services other than Mobile Radio Telecommunication Services; or

(*b*)   in any case where the Licensee has agreed to provide telecommunication services other than Mobile Radio Telecommunication Services to a person who is not a Service Provider, that person,

the Licensee:

(aa)   shall connect or have connected, at a Network Termination Point within Network Termination and Testing Apparatus, the Applicable Systems to:

(i)   any item of telecommunication apparatus which is approved for the time being for connection to the Applicable Systems under section 22 of the Act or is Compliant Terminal Equipment; or

(ii)   any other telecommunication system to which this Condition applies which is or is to be run by the Crown or which is composed of apparatus which is approved for connection to that system or is Compliant Terminal Equipment, which is owned by or supplied to another person where such connection is or is to be made by means requiring the use of a tool; and

(bb)   shall permit any person to connect, or to keep connected, at a Network Termination Point within Network Termination and Testing Apparatus comprised in the Applicable Systems any such apparatus or other such system where such connection is or is to be made by means that do not require the use of a tool,

and shall not discontinue any such connection of any such apparatus or system lawfully made.

6.3   Apparatus shall not be regarded as approved for connection to any system for the purposes of paragraphs 6.1 or 6.2 unless that apparatus is Compliant Terminal Equipment or has been so approved for connection:

(a)   by the Secretary of State; or

(b)   by some other person by virtue of an authorisation given by the Secretary of State being an authorisation which required the person authorised, before approving any apparatus or designating any standard to which apparatus must conform if it is to be approved, to be satisfied that connection of the apparatus to the system would not be likely:

(i)   to cause the death of, or personal injury to, or damage to the property of the Licensee or any person engaged in the running of that system; or

(ii)   materially to impair the quality of any telecommunication service provided by means of that system or any system connected to it (other than the system being connected).

6.4   No apparatus or system is required under paragraph 6.1 or 6.2 to be, or to be permitted to be, connected or kept connected to the Applicable Systems if that system or any apparatus comprised in that system:

(a)   conformed to any relevant standard or standards for the time being designated under section 22(6) of the Act at the time when the connection to the Applicable System was made but has, since that time, ceased to do so yet does not conform to the current relevant standard or standards (if any) so designated; or

(b)   was at the time when the connection to the Applicable Systems was made, but has since ceased to be, Compliant Terminal Equipment; or

(c)   while continuing to conform to any relevant standard, is in the opinion of the Licensee liable to cause the death of, or personal injury to, or damage to the property of, the Licensee, or any person engaged in the running of the Applicable Systems or materially to impair the quality of any telecommunication service provided by means of the Applicable Systems, unless the Director otherwise directs.

6.5   For the purposes of this Condition apparatus shall not be regarded as constituting a system if it would not, but for its connection to the Applicable Systems, constitute such a system and this Condition applies to any apparatus or system which is not a Relevant Connectable System.

Condition 7   Provision by Others of Services by means of the Applicable Systems

7.1   Without prejudice to the provisions of Condition 5.1, the Licensee shall permit any person who is:

(a)   running a telecommunication system lawfully connected to the Applicable Systems; and

(b)   licensed to run a Connectable System under a Licence which authorises him to provide telecommunication services to others, including Connection Services,

to provide such services whilst that Connectable System is connected to the relevant Applicable System.

7.2   Subject to the provisions of Condition 34, the Licensee shall permit any person:

(a)   using telecommunication apparatus which has been lawfully connected to the Applicable Systems or which is connected to another telecommunication system which itself has been lawfully connected to the Applicable Systems; or

(b)   running a telecommunication system which is so connected.

to provide by means of the Applicable Systems any service other than the installation, maintenance, adjustment, repair, alteration, moving, removal or replacement of telecommunication apparatus comprised in the Applicable Systems.

7.3   Where the Director determines that the Licensee has 25% or more of what is in the Director's opinion the relevant market as respects the provision of any telecommunication service of a particular description other than a Mobile Radio Telecommunication Service in any part or locality of the United Kingdom paragraphs 7.4 to 7.9 of this Condition shall come into force in respect of such services in such part or locality of the United Kingdom specified in that determination and on such date as the Director shall specify.

7.4   The Licensee shall, following a request by any Service Provider to do so, provide to that Service Provider any description of telecommunication service specified in any determination made under paragraph 7.3 and which the Licensee at the time the request is made offers to its customers generally and which is specified in the request, on terms which would not prohibit the Service Provider from contracting with another person to provide that person with that description of service.

7.5   (a)   If on an application by a Service Provider the Director is satisfied that the Service Provider has established a prima facie case that any charge, term or condition proposed by the Licensee is unreasonable and that the Licensee has acted unreasonably in relation to negotiations on it, the Director may, if he considers it necessary to do so, determine that the Licensee shall modify that provision in such a way as to make it reasonable, in the agreement with the Service Provider.

In applying this paragraph:

(i)   no determination made shall affect any exclusion or restriction equivalent to one which is, at the relevant time, included in the Licensee's current usual terms and conditions upon which the Licensee provides the same description of service to the generality of the Licensee's customers in a way which would or might have the effect of rendering the position of the Licensee in relation to the provision of the service the subject of the determination worse than the position of the Licensee in relation to the provision of the same description of service to the generality of the Licensee's customers;

(ii) any such modified provision shall be confined to the subject matter of the term or condition proposed by the Licensee except that, where the Director considers that a term or condition is essential in relation to subject matter not covered by any term or condition proposed by the Licensee, he may determine a term or condition to cover that subject matter;

(iii) the Licensee shall not be deemed to have acted unreasonably merely by virtue of having proposed the term or condition in question; and

(iv) no determination may be made in relation to any provision which would be subject to the Unfair Contract Terms Act 1977.

(b) Before making a determination under paragraph 7.5(a) the Director shall notify to the Licensee and the Service Provider the grounds of the Service Provider's application and his conclusions thereon and the modification he proposes to make or require the Licensee to make, and shall afford the Licensee and the Service Provider adequate time, being not less than 28 days, in which to make representations.

7.6 (a) Subject to the terms of this paragraph, any charge determined under paragraph 7.5 by the Director shall be determined by reference to the Licensee's usual charge ('the usual charge') for the provision to its customers generally of the service of the description in question ('the Service').

(b) Any charge determined under paragraph 7.5 by the Director shall not be:

(i) less than the usual charge for the Service by an amount which exceeds any cost savings of the Licensee which are shown to be likely; or

(ii) less than the usual charge for the Service plus any additional costs of the Licensee which are shown to be likely.

(c) Where the cost to the Licensee of the provision of a service to a Service Provider exceeds the usual charge no charge determined under paragraph 7.5 shall be less than the usual charge.

(d) In this paragraph 'costs' means fully allocated costs and a reasonable rate of return on capital employed.

7.7 If at any time it appears to the Director that the Service Provider no longer satisfies the criteria within paragraph 7.9(a), the Director may, on giving not less than three months notice to both the Licensee and the Service Provider of his intention to do so, direct the Licensee to cease providing that description of telecommunication service to the Service Provider.

7.8 Where a direction given by the Director under paragraph 7.7 contains a statement that it appears to him that the need to protect the customers of the Service Provider or to protect any other person requires that the direction should be made without delay, the Director shall not be required to give the notice required to be given by paragraph 7.7 or any notice.

7.9 In this Condition 'Service Provider' means:

(a) any person proposing to carry on the business of reselling any description of telecommunication service proposed to be provided to that person by the Licensee and in respect of whom the Licensee has no reason to believe that such person will be unable to carry on that business effectively, economically and efficiently; or (*b*)   any person actually carrying on that business from time to time; or

(*c*)   where, on the application of any person proposing to carry on that business to whom the Licensee has refused to provide any telecommunication service, the Director is satisfied that such service has been refused and has determined that such service should be provided by the Licensee to such person, that person;

but does not in any case mentioned in paragraph 7.9(a), 7.9(b) or 7.9(c) include any person who carries on or would carry on that business by means which necessarily involve the running of a telecommunication system by that person or on that person's behalf.

PART 3   OTHER CONDITIONS INCLUDED UNDER SECTION 7 OF THE ACT

Condition 10   Maintenance of Effective Competition where the Licensee has an International Connection Authorisation in a Designated Country

10.1   This Condition shall apply where the Licensee or any Associated Person is the operator of any telecommunication system other than a GSM System or a PCN System in a country or territory outside the United Kingdom designated for the time being by the Secretary of State for the purposes of Schedule 3 and the Licensee or any Associated Person may lawfully connect that system to any telecommunication system or apparatus outside that country or territory, not being earth orbiting apparatus for the purpose of conveyance of Messages both initially transmitted and ultimately received within that country or territory.

10.2   Where it appears to the Director that as a result of any act or omission of the Licensee either by itself or with or through any Associated Person competition in the provision of any telecommunication service or any particular description of telecommunication services in the United Kingdom is being or is likely to be restricted, distorted or prevented he may make a determination to that effect.

10.3   Where the Director makes a determination under paragraph 10.2, the Licensee shall take such steps as the Director may direct for the purposes of remedying the situation. In particular (and without prejudice to the generality of the foregoing) any such direction may provide for the publication by the Licensee of charges and other terms and conditions, or prohibit undue discrimination or undue preference by the Licensee, in relation to the provision of any telecommunication service within the United Kingdom.

Condition 11   Essential Interfaces

11.1   This Condition operates without prejudice to the provisions of Condition 5.

11.2   The Director may, having first notified the Licensee of his proposal and given the Licensee not less than 28 days in which to make representations, specify an Essential Interface.

11.3   Where in pursuance of paragraph 11.2 the Director specifies an interface as an Essential Interface, and the Licensee thereafter makes that interface available to an Operator in relation to its Applicable Systems, it shall do so in such a manner as it considers appropriate, but shall ensure such availability in compliance with a Relevant Standard if the Operator so requires.

11.4 For the purposes of paragraph 11.3 'Relevant Standard' means:

(a) an appropriate European or other international standard; or

(b) in the absence of such a standard, any other standard specified by the Director after he has notified the Licensee of his proposal to make the specifications in question and allowed the Licensee not less than 28 days in which to make representations, provided that the Director shall not specify a standard if an appropriate European or other international standard is expected to be promulgated within a reasonable time, including, by way of example, if the European Telecommunications Standards Institute have published a work programme for the development of such a standard,

to the extent that such a standard is necessary to ensure interoperability.

11.5 Where in pursuance of paragraph 11.4(b) the Director specifies a standard as a Relevant Standard, he shall include in that Relevant Standard a technical specification, using all reasonable endeavours to obtain the agreement of the Licensee and other relevant licensees to a technical specification applicable to that Relevant Standard, being a specification defined if possible by reference to:

(a) an appropriate European or other international specification; or

(b) in the absence of such a specification, a specification defined by reference to any other standard having currency within the European Community at the time.

11.6 Where after a reasonable time the Director has been unable in accordance with paragraph 11.5 to secure the agreement of the Licensee and other relevant licensees to a technical specification, the Director shall adopt for inclusion in the Relevant Standard an appropriate technical specification which has been promulgated by a recognised standards body, including, by way of example, the European Telecommunications Standards Institute, or the British Standards Institution, or such other body as the Director considers to be representative of all relevant telecommunications interests.

11.7 The Director shall specify a Relevant Standard in pursuance of paragraph 11.4 only if the owners of relevant intellectual property rights have agreed to grant any necessary licences in respect thereof to the Licensee on reasonable terms.

11.8 For the avoidance of doubt this Condition shall not:

(a) without prejudice to paragraph 11.3, prevent the Licensee using such interfaces as it considers appropriate in relation to the Applicable Systems; or

(b) where it makes available to an Operator an interface which the Director has specified as an Essential Interface, require the Licensee to comply with the Relevant Standard if the Operator does not require it to do so.

11.9 When implementing an Essential Interface, the Licensee shall not be obliged to conform with a Relevant Standard:

(a) if to do so would necessitate the Licensee:

(i) acquiring apparatus, software or other goods or supplies of any kind, or implementing any operation, incompatible with, as the case may be, apparatus, software or such other goods or supplies already in use at the time, or the subject of contracts for their procurement for use, in connection with the Applicable Systems, or, in the case of an operation, incompatible with any other operation being carried out at the time in connection therewith; or

(ii)   incurring any cost, or having to resolve technical difficulties, disproportionate to the benefits to be gained from the implementation of the Relevant Standard,

provided that the Licensee shall take reasonable steps to incorporate the Relevant Standard in its plans for network development, with a view to implementation of that Standard in the Applicable Systems, but without the Licensee incurring any incremental expenditure which, but for the implementation of the Relevant Standard, would not have been incurred;

(b)   if the Relevant Standard is inappropriate for a particular application for any reason, including, without limitation:

(i)   that it does not afford the Licensee adequate protection for the security of the Applicable Systems;

(ii)   that its implementation would be liable to cause material impairment in the quality of any telecommunication service provided by means of the Applicable Systems;

(iii)   that it does not cater adequately for billing, metering or other customer administration systems; or

(iv)   that it is technically inadequate in the light of technical developments which have taken place since it was originally created;

(c)   if the Essential Interface concerned is of a genuinely innovative nature and accordingly the use in connection with it of the Relevant Standard would not be appropriate;

(d)   if compliance with the Relevant Standard would involve the infringement by the Licensee of any intellectual property right vested in any person; or

(e)   if the Director so agrees.

11.10   Where the Licensee considers that paragraph 11.9(b) or 11.9(c) applies, the Licensee shall notify the Director thereof in writing, providing an explanation why.

11.11   It is a precondition of any obligation on the Licensee under this Condition that an equivalent Condition to this Condition is included in the respective Licences of all Operators running telecommunications systems that are connected to any of the Applicable Systems.

Condition 13   Provision of Mobile Radio Telecommunication Services to Service Providers

13.1   Subject to the following provisions of this Condition, the Licensee shall at the written request of a Service Provider or a person intending to be a Service Provider provide Mobile Radio Telecommunication Services by means of the Applicable Systems to that Service Provider or that person if that Service Provider or that person is able to demonstrate to the reasonable satisfaction of the Licensee that:

(a)   during the most recent year for which published accounts of that Service Provider are available not less than 80% by value of the telecommunication services provided by the Licensee to that Service Provider by means of the Applicable Systems were resold to persons outside that Service Provider's Group; or

(b)   in the event that no such telecommunication services were provided to that person for resale during that financial year not less than 80% by value of the telecommunication services to be provided by the Licensee to that person by means of the Applicable Systems during the following financial year will be resold to persons outside that person's Group.

13.2   The Licensee shall not be obliged under paragraph 13.1 or under Condition 1.1 or 1.4 to provide services to a Service Provider if in the opinion of the Licensee there is reasonable cause to doubt the likelihood (for whatever reason) of that Service Provider:

(a)   providing services to others in a proper and efficient manner; or

(b)   financing the provisions of services,

and the Director has not given a written contrary direction.

Condition 39   Payment of Fees

39.1   The Licensee shall pay the following amounts to the Secretary of State at the times stated:

(a)   on the grant of this Licence the sum of £37,000;

(b)   on 1 April 1996 and annually thereafter a renewal fee of (at the option of the Director) either £20,000 (the second and subsequent renewal fees being adjusted to take account of any fall or increase in the value of money since that date) or such amount which shall represent a fair proportion, to be determined each year by the Director according to a method that has been disclosed to the Licensee, of the estimated costs to be incurred in that fiscal year by the Director in the regulation and enforcement of telecommunication licences and in the exercise of his other functions under the Act. The first renewal fee shall be increased by the proportion which the period from the date of granting of this Licence until the next following 1 April bears to the period of one year; and

(c)   where the Director so determines, on 1 January 1996 and annually thereafter a special fee which shall represent a fair proportion, to be determined each year by the Director according to a method that has been disclosed to the Licensee of the amount, if any, by which the aggregate of:

(i)   the costs estimated to have been already incurred in that fiscal year by the Director in the regulation and enforcement of telecommunication licences and in the exercise of his other functions under the Act;

(ii)   the costs estimated to have been already incurred in that fiscal year by the Monopolies and Mergers Commission following licence modification references under section 13 of the Act; and

(iii)   the estimated costs to be incurred in the remainder of that fiscal year:

(A)   by the Director in the regulation and enforcement of telecommunication licences and in the exercise of his other functions under the Act; and

(B)   by the Monopolies and Mergers Commission following licence modification references under section 13 of the Act,

exceeds the renewal fee for that year,

save always that the aggregate of the renewal fee and the special fee for any fiscal year shall not exceed 0.08% of the annual turnover of the Systems Business in the financial year before the last complete financial year of the Licensee before the renewal fee is payable, or £35,000 (adjusted in the manner described in paragraph 39.1(b)), whichever is the greater (the 'normal aggregate fee'), unless the Director determines that the costs incurred in any fiscal year by him and the Monopolies and Mergers Commission in respect of the Licensee's activities exceeds the normal aggregate fee, in which case the aggregate of the renewal fee and the special fee for the following year shall be such amount (not exceeding 0.4% of the annual turnover of the Systems Business in the financial year before the last complete financial year of the Licensee before the renewal fee is paid) as the Director determines is sufficient to take account of that excess as well as of the other costs to be incurred as mentioned in this paragraph.

SCHEDULE 3

AUTHORISATION TO CONNECT OTHER TELECOMMUNICATION SYSTEMS AND APPARATUS TO THE APPLICABLE SYSTEMS AND TO PROVIDE TELECOMMUNICATION SERVICES BY MEANS OF THE APPLICABLE SYSTEMS

1 Nothing in this Licence removes any need to obtain any other licence that may be required under any other enactment.

Connection Authorisation

2 Subject to paragraph 1, this Licence authorises the connection to the Applicable Systems of:
    (*a*)   any telecommunication system run under a Licence;
    (*b*)   any telecommunication system run by the Crown;
    (*c*)   any telecommunication system situated on a vessel or hovercraft outside the United Kingdom which, if that system were inside the United Kingdom, would be authorised to be run under a Licence;
    (*d*)   any GSM System, PCN System or any telecommunication system run exclusively for the purpose of connecting a GSM System or a PCN System to the Applicable Systems;
    (*e*)   any telecommunication apparatus comprised in a telecommunication system mentioned in paragraphs 2(a) to 2(d);
    (*f*)   any telecommunication apparatus not comprised in any of the Applicable Systems which is for the time being Compliant Terminal Equipment or approved for connection to any of the Applicable Systems in accordance with section 22 of the Act; and
    (*g*)   any hearing aid,
provided that until 1 July 1997 nothing in this paragraph shall be taken as permitting the connection to the Applicable Systems of any telecommunication system or telecommunication apparatus run by any member of the Licensee's Group and which is used to convey the Messages described in paragraph 3(a).

Service Authorisation

3   Subject to paragraph 1, this Licence authorises the provision by means of the Applicable Systems of any telecommunication service except:
   (*a*)   until 1 July 1997, conveyance of Messages otherwise than through the agency of Wireless Telegraphy:
      (i)   between, or any part of the distance between, a Base Transceiver Station and a Switching Point, except where the Base Transceiver Station is installed in the same building as the Switching Point or where apparatus comprised in either is situated not more than 200 metres in lateral distance from a building or premises in which a Base Transceiver Station or Switching Point is installed, and including such conveyance between a Base Transceiver Station and a Base Station Controller and between a Base Station Controller and a Switching Point; or
      (ii)   between one Switching Point and another such point; or
      (iii)   between a Switching Point and telecommunication apparatus or a telecommunication system not comprised in or being an Applicable System;
   (*b*)   conveyance of Messages for the delivery of one or more of the services specified in paragraphs (a) to (c) of section 72(2) of the Broadcasting Act 1990 for simultaneous reception in two or more Dwelling-Houses;
   (*c*)   services consisting in the conveyance of Messages that have been or are to be conveyed by means of a telecommunication system of the description specified in paragraph 2(d) to which the Applicable Systems are connected and which are conveyed:
      (i)   from a telecommunication system in the United Kingdom, other than the Applicable Systems or a Cellular System, which is connected neither to the Applicable Systems nor to a Cellular System, ultimately to a system outside the United Kingdom which is neither connected to nor comprised in a GSM System or a PCN System; or
      (ii)   from a telecommunication system outside the United Kingdom which is neither connected to nor comprised in a GSM System or a PCN System, ultimately to a telecommunication system in the United Kingdom, other than the Applicable Systems or a Cellular System, which is connected neither to the Applicable Systems nor to a Cellular System;
   (*d*)   International Simple Voice Resale Services, unless such services:
      (i)   consist in the conveyance of Messages which have been or are to be conveyed by means of a telecommunication system of the description specified in paragraph 2(d) to which the Applicable Systems are connected and which are conveyed:
         (A)   from a telecommunication system in the United Kingdom comprised in or connected to the Applicable Systems or a Cellular System ultimately to a telecommunication system outside the United Kingdom either comprised in or connected to a GSM System or a PCN System; or
         (B)   from a telecommunication system outside the United Kingdom either comprised in or connected to a GSM System or a PCN System ultimately to a telecommunication system in the United Kingdom comprised in or connected to the Applicable Systems or a Cellular System; or
      (ii)   involve the conveyance of Messages conveyed by means of the Applicable Systems which have been or are to be conveyed also by means of the equivalent of a Public Switched Network in any country or territory:

(A)   which the Secretary of State has for the time being designated for the purpose of this Licence and which is included in a list kept for the purpose by the Director and made available by him for inspection by the general public;

(B)   in respect of which the Secretary of State has notified the Licensee that he has made such a designation; and

(C)   which is not a country or territory in respect of which the Secretary of State has revoked such designation having given the Licensee not less than 3 months' notice of his intention to do so;

(e)   International Simple Data Resale Services, unless:

(i)   such services consist in the conveyance of Messages which have been or are to be conveyed by means of a telecommunication system of the description specified in paragraph 2(d) to which the Applicable Systems are connected and which are conveyed:

(A)   from a telecommunication system in the United Kingdom comprised in or connected to the Applicable Systems or a Cellular System ultimately to a telecommunication system outside the United Kingdom either comprised in or connected to a GSM System or a PCN System; or

(B)   from a telecommunication system outside the United Kingdom either comprised in or connected to a GSM System or a PCN System ultimately to a telecommunication system in the United Kingdom comprised in or connected to the Applicable Systems or a Cellular System; or

(ii)   the Secretary of State has specified a description of such services which may be provided by means of the Applicable Systems and such specification is described in a list kept for the purpose by the Director and made available by him for inspection by the general public; and

(f)   Telepoint Services other than the running of portable handsets within the services authorised by the Class Licence for the Running of Self Provided Telecommunication Systems granted by the Secretary of State under section 7 of the Telecommunications Act 1984 on 30 July 1992 or any replacement thereof.

Definitions and interpretation

4   In this Schedule, unless the context otherwise requires:

(a)   'Applicable Terminal Equipment' means apparatus which is applicable terminal equipment within the meaning of regulation 4 of the Telecommunications Terminal Equipment Regulations 1992;

(b)   'Base Station Controller' and 'Base Transceiver Station' shall have the meaning given to those terms in the European Telecommunications Standards adopted by the European Telecommunications Standards Institute for use with the pan-European digital radio system known generically as GSM or shall mean apparatus conforming to a different technical standard but serving the same or an equivalent purpose as apparatus so defined;

(c)   'Cell' means a geographical area served by a Station for Wireless Telegraphy which is dedicated to transmitting or receiving Messages;

(d)   'Cellular System' means a telecommunication system in which:

(i)   the area in which telecommunication services are provided is divided up into a number of Cells;

(ii)   Stations for Wireless Telegraphy comprised in the system are automatically controlled by a central processor;

(iii) Messages are conveyed through the agency of Wireless Telegraphy between:

(A) Stations for Wireless Telegraphy comprised in the system (the first systems); and

(B) telecommunication apparatus or telecommunication systems which in either case are designed or adapted to be capable of being used while in motion (the second systems);

(iv) the Wireless Telegraphy frequencies used for the purpose of such conveyance are assigned automatically;

(v) there is a control procedure which allows the telecommunication service consisting in the conveyance of Messages between any of the first systems and any of the second systems to be continued to be provided between a different first system and that particular second system as the second system moves from Cell to Cell; and

(vi) the strength of the emissions of the Station for Wireless Telegraphy comprised in the system is automatically controlled so as to secure as far as is technically possible that each such Station for Wireless Telegraphy can effectively provide services only in the Cell in which it is located;

(e) 'Compliant Terminal Equipment' means Applicable Terminal Equipment which satisfies the requirements of regulation 8 of the Telecommunications Terminal Equipment Regulations 1992;

(f) 'Dwelling-House' has the same meaning as in section 202 of the Broadcasting Act 1990;

(g) 'Group' means a parent undertaking and its subsidiary undertaking or undertakings within the meaning of section 258 of the Companies Act 1985 as substituted by section 21 of the Companies Act 1989 and 'Licensee's Group' means a Group in respect of which the Licensee is either a parent undertaking or a subsidiary undertaking;

(h) 'GSM System' means:

(i) a telecommunication system run outside the United Kingdom and conforming to European Telecommunications Standards adopted by the European Telecommunications Standards Institute for use with the pan-European digital cellular radio system generically known as GSM; or

(ii) a telecommunication system run outside the United Kingdom and conforming to a technical standard which replaces or derives from the European Telecommunications Standards mentioned in paragraph 4(h)(i) and which is specified by the Secretary of State for the purpose of this Licence after consultation with the Director and described in a list kept for that purpose by the Director and made available by him for inspection by the general public;

(i) 'International Private Leased Circuit' means a communication facility which is:

(i) comprised both in a public telecommunication system and in an equivalent telecommunication system in a country or territory other than the United Kingdom;

(ii) for the conveyance of Messages between points, all of which are points of connection between telecommunication systems referred to in paragraph 4(i)(i) and other telecommunication systems;

(iii) made available to a particular person or particular persons;

(iv) such that all of the Messages transmitted at any of the points mentioned in paragraph 4(i)(ii) are received at every other such point; and

(v)   such that the points mentioned in paragraph 4(i)(ii) are fixed by the way in which the facility is installed and cannot otherwise be selected by persons or apparatus sending Messages by means of that facility;

(j)   'International Simple Data Resale Services' means telecommunication services consisting in the conveyance of Messages which do not include two-way live speech, but include only such switching, processing, data storage or protocol conversion as is necessary for the conveyance of those Messages in real time, which have been or are to be conveyed by means of all of the following:

(i)   a Public Switched Network;

(ii)   an International Private Leased Circuit; and

(iii)   the equivalent of a Public Switched Network in another country or territory;

provided that conveyance of a Message by means of a Public Switched Network or, as the case may be, the equivalent of a Public Switched Network in another country or territory shall be disregarded where that Message is so conveyed in circumstances specified for the time being by the Secretary of State as not being material for the purposes of paragraph 3 included in a list kept for the purpose by the Director and made available by him for inspection by the general public;

(k)   'International Simple Voice Resale Services' means telecommunication services consisting in the conveyance of Messages which include two-way live speech which have been or are to be conveyed by means of all of the following:

(i)   a Public Switched Network;

(ii)   an International Private Leased Circuit; and

(iii)   the equivalent of a Public Switched Network in another country or territory;

provided that conveyance of a Message by means of a Public Switched Network or, as the case may be, the equivalent of a Public Switched Network in another country or territory shall be disregarded where that Message is so conveyed in circumstances specified for the time being by the Secretary of State as not being material for the purposes of paragraph 3 included in a list kept for the purpose by the Director and made available by him for inspection by the general public;

(l)   'Message' means anything falling within paragraphs (a) to (d) of section 4(1) of the Act;

(m)   'PCN System' means:

(i)   a telecommunication system run outside the United Kingdom and conforming to European Telecommunications Standards adopted by the European Telecommunications Standards Institute for use with the digital cellular radio system generically known as DCS 1800; or

(ii)   a telecommunication system run outside the United Kingdom and conforming to a technical standard which replaces or derives from the European Telecommunications Standards mentioned in paragraph 4(m)(i) and which is specified by the Secretary of State for the purpose of this Licence after consultation with the Director and described in a list kept for that purpose by the Director and made available by him for inspection by the general public;

(n)   'Private Leased Circuit' means a communication facility which is:

(i)   provided by means of one or more public telecommunication systems;

(ii)   for the conveyance of Messages between points, all of which are points of connection between telecommunication systems referred to in paragraph 4(n)(i) and other telecommunication systems;

(iii)   made available to a particular person or particular persons;

(iv)   such that all of the Messages transmitted at any of the points mentioned in paragraph 4(n)(ii) are received at every other such point; and

(v)   such that the points mentioned in paragraph 4(n)(ii) are fixed by the way in which the facility is installed and cannot otherwise be selected by persons or telecommunication apparatus sending Messages by means of that facility;

(o)   'Public Switched Network' means a public telecommunication system by means of which two-way telecommunication services are provided whereby Messages are switched incidentally to their conveyance, and, for the avoidance of doubt, a Public Switched Network does not include Private Leased Circuits or International Private Leased Circuits;

(p)   'Switching Point' means the point at which a Message which is conveyed by means of the Applicable Systems is first switched incidentally to such conveyance or the point at which such a Message is last switched incidentally to such conveyance and, for the avoidance of doubt, a Switching Point shall not include a Base Station Controller or a Base Transceiver Station;

(q)   'Telepoint Services' means services provided through the agency of Wireless Telegraphy operating at frequencies in the range 864 to 868 MHz;

(r)   'United Kingdom' includes any area to which the provisions of the Act apply by virtue of section 107; and

(s)   'Wireless Telegraphy' and 'Station for Wireless Telegraphy' have the same meaning as in the Wireless Telegraphy Act 1949.

5   Expressions cognate with those contained in this Schedule shall be construed accordingly.

LICENCE GRANTED BY THE SECRETARY OF STATE FOR TRADE AND INDUSTRY TO CABLE & WIRELESS PLC UNDER SECTION 7 OF THE TELECOMMUNICATIONS ACT 1984

11 SEPTEMBER 1995

TABLE OF CONTENTS

Note

As a result of the Government's announcement on 6 June 1996 that facilities-based services on all routes would be liberalised. ISR licence holders have been informed that amendments to their licences are likely to be required.

THE LICENCE

1   The Secretary of State, in exercise of the powers conferred on him by section 7 of the Telecommunications Act 1984 (hereinafter referred to as 'the Act') and after consulting the Director, hereby grants to Cable & Wireless plc (hereinafter referred to as 'the Licensee') a licence, subject to the Conditions set out in Schedule 1 and to revocation as provided for in Schedule 2, to run the telecommunication systems specified in Annex A ('the Applicable Systems') and authorises the Licensee to do all or any of the acts specified in Schedule 3.

Duration

2   This Licence shall enter into force on the date of signature and shall be of one year's duration in the first instance but, without prejudice to Schedule 2 to this Licence, shall be subject to revocation thereafter on one month's notice in writing of such revocation.

Interpretation

3   The Interpretation Act 1978 shall apply for the purposes of interpreting this Licence as if it were an Act of Parliament. In this Licence, except as hereinafter provided or unless the context otherwise requires, words or expressions shall have the meaning there assigned to them and otherwise any word or expression shall have the same meaning as it has in the Act. For the purposes of interpreting this Licence, headings and titles shall be disregarded.

4   In this Licence, 'Licence' means a licence granted or having effect as if granted under section 7 of the Act.

5   For the purposes of this Licence the 'Applicable Systems' means any or all of the telecommunication systems run by the Licensee under this Licence unless the context otherwise requires.

6   Where this Licence provides for any power of the Secretary of State or the Director to give any direction or consent or make any specification, designation, or determination, it implies, unless the contrary intention appears, a power, exercisable in the same manner and subject to the same conditions or limitations, to revoke, amend or give or make again any such direction, consent, specification, designation or determination.

7   Any notification which is required to be given under this Licence by the Secretary of State or the Director shall be satisfied by serving the document by post on the Licensee at the Licensee's registered office.

Christopher Holmes
Department of Trade and Industry

11 September 1995

SCHEDULE 1
CONDITIONS INCLUDED UNDER SECTION 7 OF THE ACT

PART 1:   DEFINITIONS AND INTERPRETATION RELATING TO THE CONDITIONS IN SCHEDULE 1

1   In this Schedule unless the context otherwise requires:

(a)   'Apparatus' means telecommunication apparatus within the extended definition in Schedule 2 to the Act;

(b)   'Associated Person' [similar to the definition in Orange's Licence reproduced above];

(c)   'Compatibility' [similar to the definition in Orange's Licence reproduced above];

(d)   'Conventions' means a set of principles and rules governing the use and management of Numbers and related matters published from time to time by the Director after consultation with interested parties who are members of the Telecommunications Numbering and Addressing Body and, if the Director deems it appropriate, end users;

(e)   'Essential Interface' means, in respect of a point of connection, an interface at which in the opinion of the Director, it is essential that interoperability between the Applicable Systems and the respective Operator's telecommunication systems is available;

(f)   'Group' [similar to the definition in Orange's Licence reproduced above];

(g)   'International Business' [similar to the definition in Orange's Licence reproduced above];

(h)   'International Private Leased Circuit' [similar to the definition in Orange's Licence reproduced above];

(i)   'International Simple Data Resale Services' [similar to the definition in Orange's Licence reproduced above];

(j)   'International Simple Voice Resale Services' [similar to the definition in Orange's Licence reproduced above];

(k)   'Message' [similar to the definition in Orange's Licence reproduced above];

(*l*) 'Metering System' means the totality of all equipment, data, procedures and activities which the Licensee employs to determine the extent of any telecommunication services provided by means of any of the Applicable Systems;

(*m*) 'Number' [similar to the definition in Orange's Licence reproduced above];

(*n*) 'Operator' [similar to the definition in Orange's Licence reproduced above];

(*o*) 'Parent Undertaking' [similar to the definition in Orange's Licence reproduced above];

(*p*) 'Participating Interest' [similar to the definition in Orange's Licence reproduced above];

(*q*) 'Private Leased Circuit' [similar to the definition in Orange's Licence reproduced above];

(*r*) 'Public Switched Network' [similar to the definition in Orange's Licence reproduced above];

(*s*) 'Relevant Company' [similar to the definition in Orange's Licence reproduced above];

(*t*) 'Relevant Service' means any telecommunication service which is provided by means of the Applicable Systems;

(*u*) 'Shares' [similar to the definition in Orange's Licence reproduced above];

(*v*) 'Specified Numbering Scheme' [similar to the definition in Orange's Licence reproduced above];

(*w*) 'Specified Person' means a person specified for the time being by the Director (and who has consented to be so specified) for the purpose of keeping and making available for inspection by the general public a list such as is referred to in Condition 3.2(b); and

(*x*) 'Telecommunications Numbering and Addressing Body' means a body approved by the Director as representative of the Licensee, other public telecommunications operators and other persons whom the Director considers it appropriate to include in consultations about the content of the Conventions and the Specified Numbering Scheme.

2   Any reference in any Condition in this Schedule, however expressed, to the Director notifying the Licensee about any matter, affording the Licensee an opportunity to make representations, taking representations by the Licensee into account, or explaining, or giving reasons for, any matter to the Licensee, shall be without prejudice to any obligation of due process or similar obligation which the Director is or may be under by virtue of any rule or principle of law or otherwise.

3   Expressions cognate with those referred to in this Schedule shall be construed accordingly.

PART 2:   CONDITIONS INCLUDED UNDER SECTION 7 OF THE ACT

Condition 1   Essential Interfaces

1.1   Where the Licensee implements in its Applicable Systems an interface which the Director has specified as an Essential Interface it shall secure that the interface conforms with the relevant European Telecommunications Standard or recommendation of the International Telecommunication Union or, in the absence or inadequacy of either, with such other standard, recommendation or document (including requirements or recommendations of the Director or any other person) as the Director may determine for the purpose of this Condition.

Condition 2   Use of Automatic Calling Equipment

2.1   This Condition applies if the Applicable Systems, or any telecommunication apparatus comprised in them, are capable:

(*a*)   of automatically initiating a sequence of calls to each of more than one destination in accordance with instructions stored in the Applicable Systems or telecommunication apparatus comprised in them; and

(*b*)   of transmitting, for reception by persons at some or all of the destinations so called, sounds other than:

(i)   live speech; or

(ii)   sounds for the purpose of the transmission or reception of facsimile messages.

2.2   The Licensee shall, except in so far as the Director consents otherwise:

(*a*)   secure that the Applicable Systems are used to initiate calls to transmit the Messages of the description referred to in paragraph 2.1 (b) only to telecommunication systems which are run by the Licensee or by persons who have consented in writing to receive such calls and which are identified by reference to Numbers which are used to make calls to those telecommunication systems; and

(*b*)   maintain, or secure that there is maintained, a record giving particulars of the persons and the Numbers referred to in paragraph 2.2(a), and shall make that record available for inspection on reasonable notice by the Director.

Condition 3   Restrictions on Advertising and Supply Activities

3.1   Where the Licensee sends and conveys Messages on its own behalf, or on behalf of any member of its Group, by means of the Applicable Systems for the purposes of the advertising, the offering for supply or provision or the supply or provision of goods, services or any other thing, and receives from any person who runs a telecommunication system by means of which that person receives such Messages a request to cease so sending them to a telecommunication system run by that person, then:

(*a*)   the Licensee and every member of the Licensee's Group shall cease sending such Messages to any telecommunication system run by that person and identified for the purpose to the Licensee by reference to a Number which is used to make calls to that telecommunication system; and

(*b*)   the Licensee or a member of the Licensee's Group shall maintain, or secure that there is maintained, a record giving particulars of the persons and the Numbers referred to in paragraph 3.1 (a) and shall make that record available for inspection on reasonable notice by the Director.

3.2   Where:

(a) in respect of a telecommunication system run by him or on his behalf, a person has notified a Specified Person that he does not wish to receive unsolicited calls (whether of a general or a particular kind) made for the purpose of the advertising or the offering for supply or provision or the supply or provision of goods, services or any other thing; and

(b) a Specified Person keeps a list of such notifications in a form specified by the Director and made available for inspection by the general public,

neither the Licensee nor any member of the Licensee's Group nor their agent, subcontractor or employee shall make such unsolicited calls by means of the Applicable Systems to the telecommunication systems so listed.

3.3   Paragraph 3.2 shall have effect only where the Director has determined for the time being:

(a) the description of unsolicited call to which that paragraph shall apply;

(b) the description or descriptions of persons who shall be entitled to notify a Specified Person under that paragraph in relation to any such description of unsolicited call

and such determinations are described in a list kept for the purpose by the Director and made available by him for inspection by the general public.

Condition 4   Privacy, Confidentiality and Metering Systems

4.1   Subject to the other provisions of this Licence, the Licensee shall take all reasonable steps to safeguard the privacy and confidentiality of:

(a) any Message conveyed for a consideration by means of the Applicable Systems; and

(b) any information acquired by the Licensee in relation to such conveyance.

4.2   The Licensee shall take all reasonable steps to ensure the accuracy and reliability of any Metering System used in connection with the Applicable Systems and shall, in relation to any Metering System, keep such records as the Director has specified and notified to the Licensee.

Condition 5   Numbering Arrangements

5.1   Subject to paragraph 5.7, the Licensee shall, from the date on which the Licensee first provides a Relevant Service, adopt a numbering plan, in respect of Relevant Services provided or to be provided, for the allocation of any Numbers which:

(a) are not allocated in accordance with a Specified Numbering Scheme;

(b) are used or are intended to be used:

(i)   by the Licensee; or

(ii) by any person running a telecommunication system, other than a public telecommunications system, under a Licence, who provides a telecommunication service of a description which the Licensee could provide under and in accordance with the provisions of this Licence; or

(iii) by any public telecommunications operator; and

(c) are necessary for access to each separately distinguishable element of each Relevant Service.

5.2   The numbering plan shall describe the method adopted or to be adopted for allocating and re-allocating Numbers of a kind described in paragraph 5.1 and that method shall allow for sufficient Numbers to be available in relation to all telecommunication services, having regard to the reasonably foreseeable growth in demand for such services.

5.3   The Licensee shall:

(a)   not later than three months after the date on which this Licence comes into force; or

(b)   on or before the date on which he first provides a Relevant Service or as soon as practicable thereafter

whichever is the later, furnish details of the numbering plan to the Director and on request to any other person having a legitimate interest.

5.4   The Licensee shall furnish to the Director details of any proposals which the Licensee may have from time to time to change the arrangements for allocating or re-allocating Numbers within, or to develop, add to or replace, the numbering plan adopted and furnished in accordance with paragraphs 5.1 to 5.3.

5.5   Where any arrangements for allocating or re-allocating Numbers within the numbering plan or any developments, additions or replacements furnished in accordance with paragraph 5.4:

(a)   are insufficient to provide Compatibility with the numbering arrangements applied or to be applied by any public telecommunications operator or other person running a telecommunication system under a Licence who provides a service of a description which the Licensee could provide under and in accordance with the provisions of this Licence; or

(b)   do not allow for sufficient Numbers to be available in relation to all telecommunication services, having regard to the reasonably foreseeable growth in demand for such services; or

(c)   are not consistent with any obligations and recommendations of the International Telecommunication Union which apply to Her Majesty's Government and are binding on or are accepted by it;

the Licensee shall adopt the numbering plan with such developments, additions or replacements as are best calculated to secure such Compatibility or availability or consistency.

5.6   The Licensee shall allocate and re-allocate Numbers in accordance with the numbering plan it has adopted.

5.7   Numbers which are of a class described in CCITT Recommendations E160, E164 or F69 (relating to public switched telephone and telex networks) and are assigned to the Licensee shall be allocated only in accordance with a Specified Numbering Scheme. In relation to such Numbers, the Licensee shall also comply with any Conventions which are published from time to time by the Director.

Condition 6   Payment of Fees

6.1   The Licensee shall pay to the Secretary of State a fee of £75 within 30 days of the granting of this Licence.

Condition 7   Arrangements for International Simple Resale Services

7.1   This Condition shall apply only:

(a) if it appears to the Secretary of State to be requisite or expedient for this Condition to apply in the interests of maintaining or promoting effective competition in the conveyance of Messages to or from one or more countries or territories designated under paragraph 3(a) of Schedule 3;

(b) if, having consulted the Director, the Secretary of State has given the Licensee 28 days' notice of his intention that this Condition should apply; and

(c) in respect of such countries or territories and for such period ('the first period') as the Secretary of State has specified in that notice and has not, by a further notice given before the expiry of the notice, varied or cancelled that specification.

7.2   Any notice given under paragraph 7.1(b) or 7.1(c) shall appear in a list kept by the Director and made available by him for inspection by the general public.

7.3   Subject to paragraph 7.4, in respect of each country or territory specified in a notice given under paragraph 7.1(b) as varied by a notice (if any) given under paragraph 7.1(c), the Licensee shall secure that in the first period the ratio ('the first ratio') between:

(a) the volume of Messages comprised in International Simple Data Resale Services and International Simple Voice Resale Services which are conveyed by means of the Applicable Systems and are delivered to the United Kingdom from that country or territory; and

(b) the volume of Messages comprised in International Simple Data Resale Services and International Simple Voice Resale Services which are conveyed by means of the Applicable Systems and are sent from the United Kingdom to that country or territory

does not differ from the ratio ('the second ratio') for the previous specified period ('the second period') (the second ratio and the second period both being specified in the notice) between:

(c) the total volume of all Messages delivered to the United Kingdom from that country or territory; and

(d) the total volume of all Messages sent from the United Kingdom to that country or territory.

7.4   Where the Secretary of State is unable for any reason to specify the second ratio, and has informed the Licensee accordingly, the Licensee shall secure that in the first period the volume of Messages of the sort described in paragraph 7.3(a) shall be equal to the volume of Messages of the sort described in paragraph 7.3(b).

Condition 8   Maintenance of Effective Competition where the Licensee has an International Connection Authorisation in a Designated Country

8.1   This Condition shall apply where the Licensee or any Associated Person is the operator of any telecommunication system in a country or territory outside the United Kingdom designated for the time being by the Secretary of State for the purposes of Schedule 3 and the Licensee or any Associated Person may lawfully connect that system to any telecommunication system or apparatus outside that country or territory, not being earth orbiting apparatus for the purpose of conveyance of Messages both initially transmitted and ultimately received within that country or territory.

8.2   Where it appears to the Director that as a result of any act or omission of the Licensee either by itself or with or through any Associated Person competition in the provision of any telecommunication service or any particular description of telecommunication services in the United Kingdom is being or is likely to be restricted, distorted or prevented he may make a determination to that effect.

8.3   Where the Director makes a determination under paragraph 8.2 the Licensee shall take such steps as the Director may direct for the purposes of remedying the situation. In particular (and without prejudice to the generality of the foregoing) any such direction may provide for the publication by the Licensee of charges and other terms and conditions, or prohibit undue discrimination or undue preference by the Licensee, in relation to the provision of any telecommunication service within the United Kingdom.

Condition 9   Requirement to Furnish Information to the Director

9.1   Without prejudice to Condition 10 and subject to paragraph 9.2, the Licensee shall furnish to the Director, in such manner and at such times as the Director may reasonably request, such documents, accounts, estimates, returns or other information and procure and furnish to him such reports as he may reasonably require for the purpose of exercising the functions assigned or transferred to him by or under Parts II and III of the Act.

9.2   In making any such request the Director shall ensure that no undue burden is imposed on the Licensee in procuring and furnishing such information and, in particular, that the Licensee is not required to procure or furnish a report which would not normally be available to it, unless the Director considers the particular report essential to enable him to exercise his functions.

9.3   If the Licensee is convicted of an offence under section 5(2) of the Act relating to the Applicable Systems, the Licensee shall, not later than fourteen days after the expiry of the Appeal Period, notify the Director of such conviction, specifying the offence, the date of such conviction, the name and address of the Court concerned and the penalty imposed.

9.4   Without prejudice to the generality of paragraph 9.1 and notwithstanding paragraph 9.2, the Licensee shall:

(a)   in such manner and at such times as he may reasonably request, furnish to the Director:

(i)   accounts which show separately the annual turnover of the Relevant Service business; and

(ii)   particulars of a sample of retail call revenues disaggregated by categories of call;

(b)   keep accurate records and copies of all agreements and arrangements with any Associated Person and deliver copies of the same to the Director promptly in response to any request of the Director in respect of any agreement or arrangement; and

(c)   keep accurate records of all services, money and things transferred or supplied by the Licensee to any Associated Person or by an Associated Person to the Licensee, such records to include full details of the type and quantity, and the prices, charges and methodology of charging such prices.

Condition 10 Requirement to Submit Accounts to the Director

10.1 The Licensee shall maintain such accounting records dealing separately with its International Business carried on in the United Kingdom as will enable it to show and explain, in response to any request from the Director under paragraph 10.4, all the transactions to which paragraph 10.2 refers.

10.2 This paragraph refers to all transactions between that International Business and:

(a) any other business carried on by the Licensee whether in the United Kingdom or elsewhere; or

(b) the business of any Associated Person whether in the United Kingdom or elsewhere.

10.3 The Licensee shall update the accounting records referred to in paragraph 10.1 no less frequently than monthly and those records shall include in particular the costs (including capital costs), revenue and a reasonable assessment of assets employed in and liabilities attributable to that International Business and, separately, the amount of any material item of revenue, cost, asset or liability which has been either:

(a) charged from or to any other business of the Licensee or Associated Person together with a description of the basis of the value on which the charge was made; or

(b) determined by apportionment or attribution from an activity common to the business and any other business of the Licensee or any Associated Person and, if not otherwise disclosed, the basis of the apportionment or attribution.

10.4 The Director may at any time request from the Licensee copies of any of the accounting records which the Licensee is obliged to maintain by this Condition, covering any period between:

(a) the date on which the Licensee first carried on its International Business in the United Kingdom or, if later, the date of this Licence; and

(b) the date on which such records were, or should have been, last updated in accordance with paragraph 10.3.

The Licensee shall provide any such records requested by the Director within 14 days of receiving such a request in writing.

10.5 Accounting records submitted to the Director shall, so far as reasonably practicable, be prepared in the formats and in accordance with the accounting principles and rules which apply to the annual accounts of the Licensee and shall state the accounting policies used and where the Licensee is a body corporate incorporated outside the United Kingdom the preparation and adoption of those accounts shall comply with the requirements of sections 226 and 231 to 234A of the Companies Act 1985 as if that body corporate were incorporated in the United Kingdom.

10.6 Where it appears to the Director that to do so would be beneficial to the promotion or maintenance of competition he may direct the Licensee to publish the accounting statements submitted to the Director in such way as he sees fit. In so directing the Licensee the Director shall have regard to the need for excluding, so far as that is practicable, any matter where publication of that matter might, in the opinion of the Director, seriously and prejudicially affect the interests of the Licensee or any Associated Person.

Condition 11   Notification of Changes in Shareholdings

11.1   The Licensee shall notify the Secretary of State if an undertaking becomes a Parent Undertaking in relation to the Licensee.

11.2   Subject to paragraph 11.3, the Licensee shall notify the Secretary of State of:

(a)   any change in the proportion of the Shares held in a Relevant Company by any person;

(b)   the acquisition of any Shares in a Relevant Company by a person not already holding such Shares, and the proportion of such Shares held by that person immediately after that acquisition.

11.3   The Licensee shall be obliged to notify the Secretary of State of any acquisition of Shares or change in the Shareholding of a Relevant Company by any person only if, by reason of that acquisition or change, the total number of Shares in that Relevant Company held by that person together with any Shares held by any nominee or trustee for that person immediately after that change or acquisition:

(a)   exceeds 15 per cent of the total number of Shares in that company (where it did not exceed 15 per cent prior to that change or acquisition); or

(b)   exceeds 30 per cent of the total number of Shares in that company (where it did not exceed 30 per cent prior to that change or acquisition); or

(c)   exceeds 50 per cent of the total number of Shares in that company (where it did not exceed 50 per cent prior to that change or acquisition),

provided that where a Relevant Company is a public company as defined in section 1 of the Companies Act 1985, the obligation shall be discharged by forwarding to the Secretary of State as soon as practicable all information in respect of that acquisition or that change as is entered on or received for entry on the register required to be maintained by that Relevant Company under section 211 of the Companies Act 1985.

11.4   In any case referred to in paragraph 11.1 or 11.2, notification shall be given by a date which is 30 days prior to the taking effect of such change or acquisition, as the case may be, or as soon as practicable after that date.

Condition 12   Licensee's Group

12.1   Without prejudice to the Licensee's obligations under these Conditions in respect, in particular, of anything done on its behalf, where:

(a)   the Director determines either:

(i)   that a member of the Licensee's Group has done something which would, if it had been done by the Licensee, be prohibited or not be authorised under these Conditions; or

(ii)   that a member of the Licensee's Group has done something which would, if it had been done by the Licensee, require the Licensee to take or refrain from taking a particular action under these Conditions and that neither the Licensee nor the member has met that further requirement; and

(b)   the Director is not satisfied that the Licensee has taken all reasonable steps to prevent any member acting in that way,

then the Director may direct the Licensee to take such steps as the Director deems appropriate for the purpose of remedying the matter, including refraining from carrying on with that member such commercial activities connected with telecommunications as the Director may determine.

12.2   Where these Conditions apply in respect of the Applicable Systems they do not apply in respect of any other telecommunication system, whether run by the Licensee or another.

12.3   Where any person becomes a member of the Licensee's Group then the Licensee shall not be subject to paragraph 12.1 before that is reasonably practicable but shall be so not later than one year after that person becomes such a member or such later date as the Director may determine.

12.4   This Condition shall not apply to any particular member of the Licensee's Group if and to the extent that the Director so determines.

Condition 13   Exceptions and Limitations on Obligations in Schedule 1

13.1   Unless the context otherwise requires, the Licensee's obligations under these Conditions have effect subject to the following exceptions and limitations.

13.2   The Licensee is not obliged to do anything which is not practicable.

13.3   The Licensee shall not be held to have failed to comply with an obligation imposed upon the Licensee by or under these Conditions if (and to the extent that) the Licensee is prevented from complying with that obligation by any physical, topographical or other natural obstacle, by the malfunction or failure of any Apparatus or equipment owing to circumstances beyond the control of the Licensee, by the regulatory act of any national authority, local authority or international organisation or as the result of fire, flood, explosion, accident, emergency, riot or war.

13.4   Paragraph 13.2 does not apply to Condition 8 or 10.

SCHEDULE 2

REVOCATION

1   This Licence may be revoked by the Secretary of State at any time by giving notice in writing after having given one month's notice in writing that he intends to revoke this Licence.

SCHEDULE 3
AUTHORISATION TO CONNECT OTHER TELECOMMUNICATION SYSTEMS AND APPARATUS TO THE APPLICABLE SYSTEMS AND TO PROVIDE TELECOMMUNICATION SERVICES BY MEANS OF THE APPLICABLE SYSTEMS

1   Nothing in this Licence removes any need to obtain any other licence that may be required under any other enactment.

Connection Authorisation

2   Subject to paragraph 1, this Licence authorises the connection to the Applicable Systems of:

(*a*)   any public telecommunication system;

(*b*)   any telecommunication system run by the Crown;

(*c*)   telecommunication apparatus of every description which is comprised in a telecommunication system mentioned in paragraphs 2(a) to 2(b); and

(*d*)   any hearing aid.

Service Authorisation

3   Subject to paragraph 1, this Licence authorises the provision by means of the Applicable Systems of any telecommunication services except:

(*a*)   International Simple Voice Resale Services, unless such services involve the conveyance of Messages conveyed by the Applicable Systems which have been or are to be conveyed also by the equivalent of a Public Switched Network in any country or territory:

(i)   which the Secretary of State has designated for the purpose of this Licence and is included in a list kept for the purpose by the Director and made available by him for inspection by the general public;

(ii)   in respect of which the Secretary of State has notified the Licensee that he has made such a designation; and

(iii)   which is not a country or territory in respect of which the Secretary of State has revoked such designation having given the Licensee not less than 3 months' notice of his intention to do so;

(*b*)   International Simple Data Resale Services, unless the Secretary of State has specified a description of such Services which may be provided by means of the Applicable Systems and such specification is described in a list kept for the purpose by the Director and made available by him for inspection by the general public;

(*c*)   conveyance of Messages for the delivery of one or more of the services specified in paragraphs (a) to (c) of Section 72(2) of the Broadcasting Act 1990 for simultaneous reception in two or more Dwelling-Houses; and

(*d*)   any Mobile Radio Tails Service.

Definitions and interpretation

4   In this Schedule unless the context otherwise requires:

(*a*)   'Dwelling-House' has the same meaning as in section 202 of the Broadcasting Act 1990;

(*b*)   'International Private Leased Circuit' means a communication facility which is:

(i)   comprised both in a public telecommunication system and in an equivalent telecommunication system in a country or territory other than the United Kingdom;

(ii)   for the conveyance of Messages between points, all of which are points of connection between telecommunication systems referred to in paragraph 4(b)(i) and other telecommunication systems;

(iii)   made available to a particular person or particular persons;

(iv)   such that all of the Messages transmitted at any of the points mentioned in paragraph 4(b)(ii) are received at every other such point; and

(v)   such that the points mentioned in paragraph 4(b)(ii) are fixed by the way in which the facility is installed and cannot otherwise be selected by persons or telecommunication apparatus sending Messages by means of that facility;

(c) 'International Simple Data Resale Services' means telecommunication services consisting in the conveyance of Messages which do not include two-way live speech, but include only such switching, processing, data storage or protocol conversion as is necessary for the conveyance of those Messages in real time, which have been or are to be conveyed by means of all of the following:

(i)   a Public Switched Network;

(ii) an International Private Leased Circuit; and

(iii) the equivalent of a Public Switched Network in another country or territory;

provided that conveyance of a Message by means of a Public Switched Network or, as the case may be, the equivalent of a Public Switched Network in another country or territory shall be disregarded where that Message is so conveyed in circumstances specified for the time being by the Secretary of State as not being material for the purposes of paragraph 3 and included in a list kept for the purpose by the Director and made available by him for inspection by the general public;

(d) 'International Simple Voice Resale Services' means telecommunication services consisting in conveyance of Messages which include two-way live speech which have been or are to be conveyed by means of all of the following:

(i)   a Public Switched Network;

(ii) an International Private Leased Circuit; and

(iii) the equivalent of a Public Switched Network in another country or territory;

provided that conveyance of a Message by means of a Public Switched Network or, as the case may be, the equivalent of a Public Switched Network in another country or territory shall be disregarded where that Message is so conveyed in circumstances specified for the time being by the Secretary of State as not being material for the purposes of paragraph 3 and included in a list kept for the purpose by the Director and made available by him for inspection by the general public;

(e) 'Message' means anything failing within paragraphs (a) to (d) of section 4(1) of the Act;

(f) 'Mobile Radio Tails Service' means a telecommunication service consisting in the conveyance of Messages through the agency of Wireless Telegraphy to or from the Applicable Systems directly from or to any apparatus designed or adapted to be capable of being used while in motion;

(g) 'Private Leased Circuit' means a communication facility which is:

(i)   provided by means of one or more public telecommunication systems;

(ii) for the conveyance of Messages between points, all of which are points of connection between telecommunication systems referred to in paragraph 4(g)(i) and other telecommunication systems;

(iii) made available to a particular person or particular persons;

(iv) such that all of the Messages transmitted at any of the points mentioned in paragraph 4(g)(ii) are received at every other such point; and

(v)   such that the points mentioned in paragraph 4(g)(ii) are fixed by the way in which the facility is installed and cannot otherwise be selected by persons or telecommunication apparatus sending Messages by means of that facility;

(*h*) 'Public Switched Network' means a public telecommunication system by means of which two-way telecommunication services are provided whereby Messages are switched incidentally to their conveyance, and, for the avoidance of doubt, a Public Switched Network does not include Private Leased Circuits or International Private Leased Circuits; and

(*i*) 'Wireless Telegraphy' has the same meaning as in the Wireless Telegraphy Act 1949.

5   Expressions cognate with those referred to in this Schedule shall be construed accordingly.

ANNEX A
THE APPLICABLE SYSTEMS

1   The Applicable Systems are telecommunication systems of every description within the United Kingdom provided that each such system satisfies each of the following conditions:

(*a*)   all of the Apparatus comprised in the systems:

(i)   is situated within a single set of premises; or

(ii)   if not so situated, consists of Apparatus situated in different sets of premises together with any Apparatus run exclusively for the purpose of enabling messages to be conveyed between those premises, where none of the sets of premises in question is more than 200 metres in lateral distance from any other; or

(iii)   is situated within a single building; or

(iv)   is run by the Licensee and is situated on premises which the Secretary of State has specified for the time being for the purpose of this Annex and are described in a list kept for the purpose by the Director and made available by him for inspection by the general public; and

(*b*)   none of the Apparatus consists of Wireless Telegraphy Apparatus designed or adapted for the purpose of transmitting or receiving Messages to or from Apparatus which is designed or adapted to be capable of use whilst in motion.

2   For the purposes of this Annex, premises whose boundaries touch and which are owned or occupied by the same person shall be deemed to be a single set of premises.

3   For the purposes of this Annex:

(*a*)   'Apparatus' means telecommunication apparatus within the extended definition in Schedule 2 to the Act;

(*b*)   'Message' means anything falling within paragraphs (a) to (d) of section 4(1) of the Act; and

(*c*)   'Wireless Telegraphy Apparatus' has the same meaning as in the Wireless Telegraphy Act 1949.

SPECIFICATION BY THE SECRETARY OF STATE FOR THE PURPOSES OF PARAGRAPH 4 OF SCHEDULE 3 TO THE LICENCE GRANTED TO CABLE & WIRELESS PLC ON 11 SEPTEMEBER 1995

1   The Secretary of State in accordance with paragraphs 1(i) and 1(j) of Schedule 1 and paragraphs 4(c) and 4(d) of Schedule 3 to the licence granted

to Cable & Wireless plc under section 7 of the Telecommunications Act 1984 on 11 September 1995 ('the Licence') hereby specifies that the circumstances in paragraph 2 below are not material for the purposes of paragraph 3 of Schedule 3 to the Licence.

2   The circumstances referred to in paragraph 1 above are those where a Message is so conveyed from or to the telecommunication system by means of which that Message is initially sent or received exclusively for the purpose of carrying out such initial or final switching of that Message as could lawfully have been carried out by the person running that system, or another on that person's behalf, under the Class Licence for the Running of Self Provided Telecommunication Systems granted by the Secretary of State under section 7 of the Telecommunications Act 1984 on 30 July 1992 on the premises where that Message was initially sent or, as the case may be, ultimately received.

3   In this specification words and phrases shall have the same meaning as in the Licence.

Christopher Holmes
For the Secretary of State

11 September 1995

Note
This licence is a recent example of a typical international simple resale licence.

SPECIFICATION BY THE SECRETARY OF STATE FOR THE PURPOSES OF THE LICENCE GRANTED TO CABLE & WIRELESS PLC ON 11 SEPTEMBER 1995

The Secretary of State under paragraph 3(b) of Schedule 3 to the Licence granted to Cable & Wireless plc on 11 September 1995 (the 'Licence') hereby specifies for the purposes of the Licence the following description of International Simple Data Resale Services which may be provided by means of the Applicable Systems:

International Simple Data Resale Services of all descriptions to and from the countries listed below:

Australia	Ireland
Austria	Italy
Belgium	Liechtenstein
Canada	Luxembourg
Denmark	Netherlands
Finland	New Zealand
France	Norway
Germany	Portugal
Gibraltar	Spain
Greece	Sweden
Iceland	United States of America

In this specification words and phrases shall have the same meaning as in the Licence.

Christopher Holmes
For the Secretary of State

11 September 1995

Note
This list of countries is revised from time to time.

DESIGNATION BY THE SECRETARY OF STATE FOR THE PURPOSES OF THE LICENCE GRANTED TO CABLE & WIRELESS PLC ON 11 SEPTEMBER 1995

The Secretary of State under paragraph 3(a) of Schedule 3 to the Licence granted to Cable & Wireless plc on 11 September 1995 (the 'Licence') hereby designates for the purposes of the Licence the following countries:

Australia	New Zealand
Canada	Sweden
Finland	United States of America

In this designation words and phrases shall have the same meaning as in the Licence.

Christopher Holmes
For the Secretary of State

11 September 1995

Note
This list of countries should have been revised following the lifting of the 'equivalency' rules by the Government on 1 July 1996.

LICENCE GRANTED BY THE SECRETARY OF STATE FOR TRADE AND INDUSTRY TO UNISOURCE HOLDING (UK) LTD UNDER SECTION 7 OF THE TELECOMMUNICATIONS ACT 1984
18 December 1996

TABLE OF CONTENTS

**LICENCE GRANTED BY THE SECRETARY OF STATE FOR
TRADE AND INDUSTRY TO UNISOURCE HOLDING (UK) LTD
UNDER SECTION 7 OF THE TELECOMMUNICATIONS ACT 1984**

THE LICENCE
1. The Secretary of State, in exercise of the powers conferred on him by
section 7 of the Telecommunications Act 1984 (hereinafter referred to as 'the
Act') and after consulting the Director hereby grants to Unisource Holding
(UK) Ltd hereinafter referred to as 'the Licensee') a licence, for the period
specified in paragraph 3, subject to the Conditions set out in the Schedule 1

and to revocation as provided for in paragraph 3 and in Schedule 2 to run telecommunication systems of every description within the United Kingdom ('the Applicable Systems') and authorises the Licensee to do all or any of the acts specified in Schedule 3.

2.   The Telecommunications Code contained in Schedule 2 to the Act shall apply to the Licensee for all purposes except those not relating to the Applicable Systems and subject to the other exceptions and conditions set out in Schedule 4 for so long as this licence is one to which section 8 of the Act applies.

Duration

3.   This Licence shall enter into force on the date of signature and shall be of six months' duration in the first instance but, without prejudice to Schedule 2 to this Licence, shall be subject to revocation thereafter on one month's notice in writing of such revocation.

Interpretation

4.   The Interpretation Act 1978 shall apply for the purpose of interpreting this Licence as if it were an Act of Parliament. In this Licence, except as hereinafter provided or unless the context otherwise requires, words or expressions shall have the meaning assigned to them and otherwise any word or expression shall have the same meaning as it has in the Act. For the purposes of interpreting this Licence. headings and titles shall be disregarded.

5.   In this Licence. 'Licence' means a licence granted or having effect as if granted under section 7 of the Act.

6.   For the purposes of this Licence the 'Applicable Systems' means any or all of the telecommunication systems run by the Licensee under this Licence unless the context otherwise requires.

7.   Where this Licence provides for any power of the Secretary of State or the Director to give any direction or consent or make any specification, designation or determination, it implies, unless the contrary intention appears, a power, exerciseable in the same manner and subject to the same conditions or limitations, to revoke, amend or give or make again any such direction, consent, specification. designation or determination.

8.   Any notification which is required to be given under this Licence by the Secretary of State or the Director shall be satisfied by serving the document by post on the Licensee at the Licensee's registered office.

Ian Taylor
Parliamentary Under Secretary of State
for Science and Technology
18 December 1996

Notes

1.   In March 1996 the Government published a consultation paper on liberalising the provisions of international services over a company's own facilities. The results of this and further consultation was to produce two template licenses one without and one with code powers. This IFL is an example of a licence with code powers, and was issued with 44 other IFL's in December 1996.

2.   There has been some debate as to whether the DTI will issue IFLs to companies which hold ISR authorisations, and if so the need for corporate separation.

3. Operating the international facilities completes the last major step to liberalising the UK telecommunications market, which has been achieved well ahead of the EU objective of full liberalisation by 1 January 1998.

4. These licences have only been issued for 6 months as the DTI is considering revoking the new licences issued to operaters with a domestic PTO licence and reissuing a new licence combining the two authorisations.

5. OFTEL is in the process of issuing guidelines for the operation of IFLs and on arrangements for accounting in respect of international conveyance services.

6. This licence has been reproduced in full because it is the latest of a new category of licence.

SCHEDULE 1

CONDITIONS INCLUDED UNDER SECTION 7 OF THE ACT

PART 1: DEFINITIONS AND INTERPRETATION RELATING TO THE CONDITIONS IN SCHEDULE 1

1   In this Schedule unless the context otherwise requires:

(a)   'Accounting Rate Service' means each telecommunications service to each country and territory for which a separate accounting rate has been agreed, not including Transit Services;

(b)   'Applicable Terminal Equipment' means apparatus which is applicable terminal equipment within the meaning of regulation 4 of the Telecommunications Terminal Equipment Regulations 1992;

(c)   'Approved Apparatus' means in relation to any system apparatus approved under section 22 of the Act for connection to that system;

(d)   'Associated Person' means any member of the Licensee's Group or a person with a Participating Interest in a member of the Licensee's Group or in whom a member of the Licensee's Group has a Participating Interest;

(e)   'Authorised Overseas System' means any telecommunication system outside the United Kingdom which is authorised to be connected to the Applicable Systems under Schedule 3;

(f)   'Compatibility' means that between the parties concerned there is no reasonably foreseeable risk of:

(i)   duplication of any Number; or

(ii)   any other related effect,

such as would introduce ambiguity or errors or impose undue restrictions on any user or group of users;

(g)   'Compliant Terminal Equipment' means Applicable Terminal Equipment which satisfies the requirements of regulation 8 of the Telecommunications Terminal Equipment Regulations 1992;

(h)   'Condition' means a Condition in this Schedule;

(i)   'Connectable System' means a telecommunication system which is authorised to be run under a Licence which authorises connection of that system to the Applicable Systems;

(j)   'Connection Service' means a telecommunication service consisting in the conveyance of any Message which has been, or is to be, conveyed by means of the Applicable Systems;

(k)   'Dwelling-House' has the same meaning as in section 202 of the Broadcasting Act 1990;

(l) 'Emergency' means an emergency of any kind, including any circumstance whatever resulting from major accidents, natural disasters and incidents involving toxic or radio-active materials;

(m) 'Emergency Organisations' means in respect of any locality:

(i) the relevant public police, fire, ambulance and coastguard services for that locality; and

(ii) any other similar organisation in respect of which any public telecommunications operator licensed to operate in the locality in question is providing a Public Emergency Call Service on the day on which this Licence enters into force;

(n) 'Essential Interface' means in respect of a Point of Connection an interface at which in the opinion of the Director it is essential that interoperability between the Applicable Systems and the respective Operator's systems is available;

(o) 'Group' means a parent undertaking and its subsidiary undertaking or undertakings within the meaning of section 258 of the Companies Act 1985 as substituted by section 21 of the Companies Act 1989; and 'Licensee's Group' means a Group in respect of which the Licensee is either a parent undertaking or a subsidiary undertaking;

(p) 'International Business' means the business of providing telecommunication services including, without limitation, any services comprised in a Relevant International Function, which consist in the conveyance of Messages to countries or territories outside the United Kingdom carried on under a Licence and include the running of such parts of the Applicable Systems as are used for the provision of those services, and the installation, maintenance, adjustment, repair, alteration, moving, removal or replacement of such Systems and any apparatus comprised therein;

(q) 'International Conveyance Service' means a telecommunication service consisting in the conveyance of any Message which has been or is to be conveyed by means of any telecommunication system outside the United Kingdom the connection of which to the system by means of which that service is provided is authorised by a Licence;

(r) 'International Private Leased Circuit' means a communication facility which is:

(i) comprised both in a public telecommunication system and in an equivalent telecommunication system in a country or territory other than the United Kingdom;

(ii) for the conveyance of Messages between points, all of which are points of connection between telecommunication systems referred to in paragraph 1(r)(i) and other telecommunication systems;

(iii) made available to a particular person or particular persons;

(iv) such that all of the Messages transmitted at any of the points mentioned in paragraph 1(r)(ii) are received at every other such point; and

(v) such that the points mentioned in paragraph 1(r)(ii) are fixed by the way in which the facility is installed and cannot otherwise be selected by persons or telecommunication apparatus sending Messages by means of that facility;

(s) 'International Simple Data Resale Services' means telecommunication services consisting in the conveyance of Messages which do not include two-way live speech, but include only such switching, processing, data storage or protocol conversion as is necessary for the conveyance of those Messages in real time, which have been or are to be conveyed by means of all of the following:

(i)   a Public Switched Network;

(ii)   an International Private Leased Circuit; and

(iii)   the equivalent of a Public Switched Network in another country or territory;

provided that conveyance of a Message by means of a Public Switched Network or, as the case may be, the equivalent of a Public Switched Network in another country or territory shall be disregarded where that Message is so conveyed in circumstances specified for the time being by the Secretary of State as not being material for the purposes of paragraph 3 of Schedule 3 to this Licence and included in a list kept for the purpose by the Director and made available by him for inspection by the general public;

(t)   'International Simple Voice Resale Services' means telecommunication services consisting in the conveyance of Messages which include two-way live speech which have been or are to be conveyed by means of all of the following:

(i)   a Public Switched Network;

(ii)   an International Private Leased Circuit; and

(iii)   the equivalent of a Public Switched Network in another country or territory;

provided that conveyance of a Message by means of a Public Switched Network or, as the case may be, the equivalent of a Public Switched Network in another country or territory shall be disregarded where that Message is so conveyed in circumstances specified for the time being by the Secretary of State as not being material for the purposes of paragraph 3 of Schedule 3 to this Licence and included in a list kept for the purpose by the Director and made available by him for inspection by the general public;

(u)   'Long Line Public Telecommunications Operator' means a public telecommunications operator who is authorised by a Licence to provide telecommunication services consisting in the conveyance of Messages by fixed links run by that operator over distances greater than 50 linear kilometres;

(v)   'Major Office" means the Licensee's registered office and such other offices as the Director, having consulted the Licensee, may direct;

(w)   'Message' means anything falling within paragraphs (a) to (d) of section 4(1) of the Act;

(x)   'Network Connecting Apparatus' means telecommunication apparatus comprised in the Applicable Systems which is not Network Termination and Testing Apparatus and is connected to another telecommunication system;

(y)   'Network Termination Point' means any point:

(i)   within an item of Network Connecting Apparatus at which energy of any of the forms specified in section 4(1) of the Act is conveyed directly to or from apparatus comprised in a telecommunication system other than one in which that Network Connecting Apparatus is comprised; or

(ii)   within an item of Network Termination and Testing Apparatus at which such energy is conveyed directly to any Relevant Terminal Apparatus;

(z)   'Network Termination and Testing Apparatus' means an item of telecommunication apparatus comprised in the Applicable Systems installed in a fixed position on Served Premises which enables:

(i)   Approved Apparatus to be readily connected to, and disconnected from, the Applicable Systems;
(ii)   the conveyance of Messages between such Apparatus and the
Applicable Systems; and
(iii) the due functioning of the Applicable Systems to be tested,
but the only other functions of which, if any, are:
(1)   to supply energy between such Apparatus and the Applicable
Systems;
(2)   to protect the safety or security of the operation of the
Applicable Systems; or
(3)   to enable other operations exclusively related to the running of
the Applicable Systems to be performed or the due functioning of any system
to which the Applicable Systems are or are to be connected to be tested
(separately or together with the Applicable Systems).
(aa)   'Number' means any identifier which would need to be used in
conjunction with any public switched service for the purposes of establishing
a connection with any Network Termination Point. user, telecommunication
apparatus connected to any Public Switched Network or service element, but
not including any identifier which is not accessible to the generality of users
of a public switched service;
(ab)   'Numbering Plan' means a plan describing the method adopted or
to be adopted for allocating and re-allocating a Number to any Network
Termination Point, user telecommunication apparatus or service element;
(ac)   'Operator' means any person who is authorised by a Licence to
run a Relevant Connectable System;
(ad)   'Parent Undertaking' has the same meaning as in section 258 of the
Companies Act 1985 as substituted by section 21 of the Companies Act 1989;
(ae)   'Participating Interest' has the same meaning as in section 260 of
the Companies Act 1985 as substituted by section 22 of the Companies Act
1989;
(af)   'Point of Connection' means a point at which the Applicable
Systems and an Operator's system are connected;
(ag)   'Private Leased Circuit' means a communication facility which is:
(i)   provided by means of one or more public telecommunication
systems;
(ii)   for the conveyance of Messages between points, all of which are
points of connection between telecommunication systems referred to in
paragraph 1(ag)(i) and other telecommunication systems;
(iii) made available to a particular person or particular persons;
(iv)   such that all of the Messages transmitted at any of the points
mentioned in paragraph 1(ag)(ii) are received at every other such point; and
(v)   such that the points mentioned in paragraph 1(ag)(ii) are fixed
by the way in which the facility is installed and cannot otherwise be selected
by persons or telecommunication apparatus sending Messages by means of
that facility;
(ah)   'Public Emergency Call Services' means a telecommunication
service by means of which any member of the public may, at any time and
without incurring any charge, by means of an item of telecommunication
apparatus which is lawfully connected to the Applicable Systems and which
is capable of transmitting and receiving unrestricted two way voice telephony

services when so connected, communicate as swiftly as practicable with any of the Emergency Organisations for the purpose of notifying them of an Emergency;

(ai) 'Public Switched Network' means a public telecommunication system by means of which two-way telecommunication services are provided whereby Messages are switched incidentally to their conveyance, and, for the avoidance of doubt, a Public Switched Network does not include Private Leased Circuits or International Private Leased Circuits;

(aj) 'Relevant Apparatus' means any apparatus which is, or is to be, connected to any of the switched Applicable Systems;

(ak) 'Relevant Company' means:

(i)   the Licensee; or

(ii) a Parent Undertaking in relation to the Licensee;

(al) 'Relevant Connectable System' means a Connectable System which is authorised to be run under a Licence which authorises the provision by means of that system of Connection Services for reward to the general public, or any class of the general public, not being a system:

(i)   authorised to be run under a Licence granted to all persons or persons of any class; and

(ii) for the connection of which, and for the provision of matters necessary for such connection, the Licensee offers terms and conditions which satisfy the requirements of Condition 7 of Schedule 1,

and not being a system which the Director has determined ought not to be deemed a Relevant Connectable System for the purposes of this Licence;

(am) 'Relevant International Function' means the business of providing any of the following telecommunication services by means of the Applicable Systems:

(i)   International Simple Voice Resale and/or International Simple Data Resale;

(ii) provision to others of International Private Leased Circuits;

(iii) provision of services under any agreement falling within the description contained in Condition 5.1 in Schedule 1;

(iv) provision of International Conveyance Services (but not including International Simple Voice Resale or International Simple Data Resale), charges for which are to be settled at accounting rates;

(v)   provision of International Conveyance Services (but not including International Simple Voice Resale or International Simple Data Resale), charges for which are not to be settled at accounting rates, and where the Messages conveyed in the provision of such service are conveyed over a circuit which is capable of conveying two-way live speech;

(vi) provision of International Conveyance Services (including International Simple Voice Resale or International Simple Date Resale), charges for which are not to be settled at accounting rates, and where the Messages conveyed in the provision of such service are conveyed over a circuit which is not capable of conveying two-way live speech;

(vii) the installation, maintenance, adjustment, repair, alteration, moving, removal or replacement of any apparatus comprised or to be comprised in the Applicable Systems; or

(viii) provision of any other services included in the Licensee's International Business but not included in any of (am) (i) to (vii) above.

(an)   'Relevant System' means a Connectable System which is, or is to be, connected to any of the switched Applicable Systems;

(ao)   'Relevant Terminal Apparatus' means:

(i)   Terminal Apparatus', that is to say any telecommunication apparatus installed on Served Premises by means of which Messages are initially transmitted or ultimately received; and

(ii)   any other telecommunication apparatus directly connected to Terminal Apparatus (including apparatus which is Terminal Apparatus by virtue of this sub-paragraph) which would, if it were run with such Terminal Apparatus and any other apparatus by means of which it is so connected, constitute a system authorised to be run by the person running that Terminal Apparatus under a Licence;

(ap)   'Served Premises' means a single set of premises in single occupation where apparatus has been installed for the purpose of the provision of telecommunication services by means of the Applicable Systems at those premises;

(aq)   'Shares' has the same meaning as in section 259(2) of the Companies Act 1985, as substituted by section 22 of the Companies Act 1989, and the term 'Shareholding' is to be construed accordingly;

(ar)   'Specified Numbering Scheme' means a scheme for the allocation and reallocation of Numbers which is specified by the Director for the purpose of this Licence and described in a list kept for that purpose by him and made available by him for inspection by the general public.

(as)   'Subscriber' means a person (other than a public telecommunications operator) to whom there are provided switched voice telephony services by means of the Applicable Systems;

(at)   'Subsidiary' has the meaning given to it in section 736 of the Companies Act 1985, as substituted by section 144(1) of the Companies Act 1989;

(au)   'Systems Business' means the following activities of the Licensee or of any wholly owned Subsidiary to the extent that they are undertaken in the United Kingdom taken together:

(i)   the running of the Applicable Systems; and

(ii)   the installation, maintenance, adjustment, repair, alteration, moving, removal or replacement of any apparatus comprised or to be comprised in the Applicable Systems;

(av)   'Transit Service' means any telecommunications service consisting in the conveyance of any Message which originates outside the United Kingdom and is not to be terminated within the United Kingdom and for which a separate accounting rate has been agreed;

(aw)   'Well Established International Operator' means an Operator having 25% or more of what is in the opinion of the Director the relevant market, unless the Director determines that the Operator is not a Well Established International Operator, or an Operator having less than 25% of what is in the opinion of the Director the relevant market which is determined by the Director to be a Well Established International Operator.

2.   Any reference in any Condition in this Schedule, however expressed, to the Director notifying the Licensee about any matter, affording the Licensee an opportunity to make representations, taking representations by the Licensee into account, or explaining, or giving reasons for, any matter to

the Licensee, shall be without prejudice to any obligation of due process or similar obligation which the Director is or may be under by virtue of any rule or principle of law or otherwise.

3.   Expressions cognate with those referred to in this Schedule shall be construed accordingly.

PART 2:   SPECIAL CONDITIONS REFERRED TO IN SECTION 8 OF THE ACT

Condition 1   Requirements to Provide Telecommunication Services

1.   The Licensee shall take all reasonable steps to provide by means of the Applicable Systems to any Operator who so requests International Conveyance Services to the extent necessary to satisfy all reasonable demands for such Services by such Operator.

Condition 2   Directory Information

2.1   This Condition shall only apply where the Applicable Systems are connected to a telecommunication system not run under a Licence issued to a particular person.

2.2   Subject to paragraph 2.5, where the Licensee provides switched voice telephony services by means of any of the Applicable Systems which is connected to an Authorised Overseas System by means of which such services are provided, then, if a directory information service is provided by means of that Authorised Overseas System in respect of that Authorised Overseas System, the Licensee shall provide to any person to whom it provides switched voice telephony services by means of that Applicable System information as to how that person may avail himself by means of that Applicable System and that Authorised Overseas System when connected together of the directory information service provided and shall take all reasonable steps to secure that that can be done.

2.3   Where the Licensee provides switched voice telephony services by means of any of the Applicable Systems which is connected to both:

(a)   an Authorised Overseas System by means of which such services are provided; and

(b)   a Connectable System in the United Kingdom by means of which such services are provided which is run under a Licence which does not authorise the connection of that system to a system outside the United Kingdom so as to convey Messages from the United Kingdom to a place outside the United Kingdom

it shall not unreasonably refuse to provide to the operator of that Connectable System access to such directory information services relating to the Authorised Overseas System as the Licensee makes available to those to whom it provides voice telephony services.

2.4   The directory information service provided by the Licensee under paragraph 2.2 shall include a service satisfactory to the Director whereby directory information is made available in a form which is appropriate to meet their needs to persons who are so blind or otherwise disabled as to be unable to use a telephone directory in a form in which it is generally available to persons to whom the Licensee provides services; and the service so provided to such persons shall from the date on which this Licence enters into force be provided free of charge or, if the Director is satisfied that that is not practicable, the Licensee shall provide, in accordance with arrangements agreed with the Director, appropriate reasonable compensation in respect of charges that are paid.

2.5   The obligation in paragraph 2.2 shall not apply:

(a)   when the directory information requested relates to a person who has requested the Licensee or the operator of the connected telecommunication system not to provide such information in relation to him; or

(b)   in respect of any person to whom switched voice telephony services are provided by means of the Applicable Systems if that person has notified the Licensee in writing that he is able to obtain from another public telecommunications operator who provides switched voice telephony services within the United Kingdom to that person information as to how to avail himself of such directory information service as may be provided in respect of any Authorised Overseas System which is connected to the Applicable Systems.

2.6   This Condition is without prejudice to Condition 5.

Condition 3   Public Emergency Call Service

3.1   This Condition shall only apply where the Applicable Systems are connected to a telecommunication system not run under a Licence issued to a particular person.

3.2   The Licensee shall ensure, except to the extent that the Director determines is not reasonably practicable, that both the numbers 999 and 112 are available as emergency call numbers so that any member of the public by dialling either the number 999 or the number 112 on telecommunication apparatus which is lawfully connected to the Applicable Systems at any place in the United Kingdom and which is capable of transmitting and receiving unrestricted two way voice telephony services when so connected is provided with a Public Emergency Call Service.

3.3   Where the Director has made a determination in accordance with paragraph 3.2 the Licensee shall take all reasonable steps to ensure that persons to whom there are provided by means of the Applicable Systems services which do not include a Public Emergency Call Service are notified in writing that the services so provided do not include a Public Emergency Call Service.

3.4   For the purposes of this Condition telecommunication apparatus shall be regarded as capable of transmitting and receiving unrestricted two way voice telephony services only if it is capable of both:

(a)   transmitting for conveyance by means of an Applicable System specific signals designated by the Licensee for the purpose of establishing communication with voice telephony apparatus controlled by the Emergency Organisations; and

(b)   transmitting and receiving uninterrupted simultaneous two way speech to be conveyed, or as the case may be conveyed, by means of that Applicable System.

3.5   In this Condition, the United Kingdom does not include any area to which the Act is extended under section 107.

Condition 4   Planning and Implementation of Special Arrangements for Emergencies

4.1   The Licensee shall, after consultation with such authorities responsible for Emergency Organisations and such departments of central and local government as the Director may from time to time determine and whose names are notified to the Licensee by him for the purpose, make plans or other arrangements for the provision or, as the case may be, the rapid restoration of such telecommunication services as are practicable and may reasonably be required in Emergencies.

4.2   The Licensee shall, on request by any such person as is designated for the purpose in the relevant plans or arrangements, implement those plans or arrangements insofar as it is reasonable and practicable to do so.

4.3   Nothing in this Condition precludes the Licensee from:

(a)   recovering the costs which it incurs in making or implementing any such plans or arrangements from those on behalf of or in consultation with whom the plans or arrangements are made; or

(b)   making implementation of any plans or arrangements conditional upon the person or persons for whom or on whose behalf that plan or arrangement is to be implemented indemnifying the Licensee for all costs incurred as a consequence of the implementation.

Condition 5   Requirement to Provide Connection Services and Connection of Apparatus

5.1   Subject to the following provisions of this Condition the Licensee shall, unless it is impracticable to do so, enter into an agreement or agree to amend such an agreement, within a reasonable period (which shall not, unless the Director otherwise consents, exceed 6 months), with an Operator if that Operator requires it to do so:

(a)   to connect, and keep connected, to any of the Applicable Systems, or to permit to be so connected and kept connected, any Relevant Connectable System run by the Operator and any item of telecommunication apparatus which is required for that purpose and which is located on the same premises as the Applicable Systems and which is approved for the time being under section 22 of the Act or is Compliant Terminal Equipment, and accordingly to establish and maintain such one or more Points of Connection as are reasonably required and are of sufficient capacity and in sufficient number to enable Messages conveyed or to be conveyed by means of the Operator's system to be conveyed by means of the Applicable Systems in such a way as conveniently to meet all reasonable demands for the conveyance of Messages between the Relevant Connectable System and the Applicable Systems;

(b)   without prejudice to paragraph 5.1(a), where the Operator is a Long Line Public Telecommunications Operator, to establish and maintain such Points of Connection as will enable persons running telecommunication systems connected to the Operator's system and persons running telecommunication systems connected to the Applicable Systems to exercise freedom of choice as to the extent to which Messages are conveyed by means of the Applicable Systems and in routing Messages so conveyed; and

(c)   to provide such other telecommunication services (including the conveyance of Messages which have been, or are to be, transmitted or received at such Points of Connection), information and other services as the Director determines are reasonably required (but no more than reasonably required) to secure that Points of Connection are established and maintained and to enable the Operator effectively to provide the Connection Services which he provides or proposes to provide.

5.2   The Licensee shall not be obliged under paragraph 5.1 to enter into an agreement to do anything or agree to amend such an agreement to do anything if:

(a)   in the opinion of the Licensee it would be liable to cause the death of or personal injury to, or damage to the property of, the Licensee or any person engaged in the Licensee's business, or materially to impair the quality of any telecommunication service provided by means of the Applicable Systems or any telecommunication system (other than the Operator's system) connected thereto and the Director has not expressed a contrary opinion: or

(b)   in the opinion of the Licensee:

(i)   it would require an adjustment to, or modification of, the Applicable Systems whether by incorporation of apparatus or otherwise or the provision by the Licensee of services or information which in any particular case would not be reasonably required; or

(ii)   it would not be reasonably practicable to require the Licensee to do that thing, or permit it to be done, at the time or in the manner required by the Operator, having regard to the state of technical development of the Applicable Systems or any other relevant matter,

and the Director has not expressed a contrary opinion.

5.3   The Licensee may require that an agreement under paragraph 5.1 should be subject to such terms and conditions as are, in the opinion of the Director, reasonable.

5.4   Apparatus shall not be regarded as approved for connection to any system for the purposes of paragraph 5.1 unless that apparatus is Compliant Terminal Equipment or has been so approved:

(a)   by the Secretary of State; or

(b)   by some other person by virtue of an authorisation given by the Secretary of State being an authorisation which required the person authorised, before approving any apparatus or designating any standard to which apparatus must conform if it is to be approved, to be satisfied that connection of the apparatus to the system would not be likely:

(i)   to cause the death of, or personal injury to, or damage to the property of the Licensee or any person engaged in the running of that system; or

(ii)   materially to impair the quality of any telecommunication service provided by means of that system or any system connected to it (other than the system being connected).

5.5   No apparatus or system is required under paragraph 5.1 to be, or to be permitted to be, connected or kept connected to the Applicable Systems if the apparatus, or any apparatus comprised in that system, as the case may be:

(a) conformed to the relevant standard or standards at the time when the connection to the Applicable Systems was made but no longer does so and does not conform to the relevant standard or standards (if any) for the time being designated under section 22(6) of the Act; or

(b)   was at the time when the connection to the Applicable Systems was made but has since ceased to be Complaint Terminal Equipment; or

(c)   while continuing to conform to the relevant standard is in the opinion of the Licensee liable to cause the death of, or personal injury to, or damage to the property of, the Licensee, or any person engaged in the running of the Applicable Systems or materially to impair the quality of any telecommunication service provided by means of the Applicable Systems and the Director has not directed otherwise.

5.6   An agreement made pursuant to this Condition shall not contain any restrictive provision unless, before the agreement is made, the Director has expressly consented to the inclusion of such a provision. For the purposes of this paragraph, a provision in an agreement is a restrictive provision if by virtue of the existence of such a provision (taken alone or with other provisions) the agreement is one to which the Restrictive Trade Practices Act 1976 would apply but for paragraph 1(1) of Schedule 3 to that Act.

5.7   Where the Director so directs the Crown shall be treated for the purposes of this Condition as a person authorised to run a Relevant Connectable System and where he does so he may also direct that the Crown is to be treated as a Long Line Public Telecommunications Operator for those purposes.

Note
This Condition will be reconsidered in the light of the revised Condition 13 of BT's licence — see note 16 to that condition on page 220.

Condition 6   Provision by Others of Services by Means of the Applicable System

6.1   The Licensee shall permit any person, who is licensed to run a Connectable System under a Licence which authorises it to provide telecommunication services to others, including Connection Services, to provide such services whilst that Connectable System is connected to the relevant Applicable System.

6.2   The Licensee shall permit any person:

(a)   using telecommunication apparatus which has been lawfully connected to the Applicable Systems or which is connected to another telecommunication system which itself has been lawfully connected to the Applicable Systems; or

(b)   running a telecommunication system which is so connected,
to provide by means of the Applicable Systems any service other than the installation, maintenance, adjustment, repair, alteration, moving, removal or replacement of telecommunication apparatus comprised in the Applicable Systems.

Condition 7   Publication of Charges, Terms and Conditions to be Applied

7.1   The Licensee shall, subject to paragraph 7.2, except insofar as the Director may otherwise consent in writing and except in respect of charges, terms and conditions in agreements made or modified to comply with Condition 5:

(a)   publish in the manner and at the times specified in paragraph 7.4 a notice specifying, or specifying the method that is to be adopted for determining, the charges and other terms and conditions on which it offers:

(i)   to provide each description of telecommunication services by means of the Applicable Systems; or

(ii)   to maintain, adjust, repair or replace any apparatus comprised in the Applicable Systems; or

(iii)   to connect to the Applicable Systems any other system which is not and is not to be comprised in the Applicable Systems; or

(iv)   to grant permission to connect such systems to, or to provide services by means of, the Applicable Systems;

where such things are done in accordance with an obligation imposed by or under this Licence.

(b)   Where the Licensee does any of the things described in paragraphs 7.1(a)(i) to 7.1(a)(iv) it shall do those things at the charges and on the other terms and conditions so published and not depart therefrom. Provided that this obligation will not be breached by variations to the charges, terms and conditions referred to in paragraph 7(1)(a) to the extent that the method which is adopted for determining those variations has been disclosed to the Director, except insofar as those charges, terms and conditions relate to a particular market in respect of which the Director has made a determination that the Licensee is a Well Established International Operator.

7.2   Where the Director has made a determination that the Licensee is a Well Established International Operator in a particular market the Licensee shall specify the precise amount of such charges in accordance with paragraph 7.1(a), insofar as they relate to the market in respect of which such a determination has been made.

7.3   The requirement to publish under paragraph 7.1 shall not apply in respect of any service which is materially different from any service already provided by the Licensee by means of the Applicable Systems until such time as it is provided and a copy of the notice shall be sent to the Director at that time.

7.4   Publication of the notice shall be effected by:

(a)   sending a copy thereof to the Director to arrive not more than 28 days after the date on which the Licensee first provides services under the Licence and thereafter not less than one day before any proposal to amend any charge, term or condition or the method of determining the same is to become effective: provided that where the Director has made a determination that the Licensee is a Well Established International Operator in a particular market, this sub-paragraph shall have effect as if the words '28 days' were substituted for the words 'one day' insofar as any such proposal relates to the provision of services in relation to the market in respect of which such a determination has been made;

(b)   placing as soon as practicable thereafter a copy thereof in a publicly accessible part of every Major Office of the Licensee in such a manner and in such a place that it is readily available for inspection free of charge by members of the general public during such hours as the Secretary of State may by order prescribe under section 19(4) of the Act that the register of Licences and final and provisional orders is to be open to public inspection, or in the absence of any such order having been made by the Secretary of State, during normal office hours; and

(c)   sending a copy thereof or such part or parts thereof as are appropriate to any person who may request such a copy.

7.5   The obligations imposed on the Licensee by this Condition are without prejudice to any determination which the Director may make under Condition 9 of this Licence.

Condition 8   Prohibition on Undue Preference and Undue Discrimination

8.1   The Licensee shall not (whether in respect of the charges or other terms or conditions applied or otherwise) show undue preference to, or exercise undue discrimination against, particular persons or persons of any class or description as respects:

(a)   the connection to the Applicable Systems of any other system which is not and is not to be comprised in the Applicable Systems in accordance with an obligation imposed by or under this Licence; or

(b)   the maintenance, adjustment, repair or replacement of any apparatus comprised in the Applicable Systems in accordance with an obligation imposed by or under this Licence; or

(c)   the provision by means of the Applicable Systems of any telecommunication service in accordance with an obligation imposed by or under this Licence; or

(d)   the granting of permission to connect such systems to, or to provide services by means of the Applicable Systems in accordance with an obligation imposed by or under this Licence.

8.2   The Licensee may be deemed to have shown such undue preference or to have exercised such undue discrimination if it unfairly favours to a material extent a business carried on by it in relation to the doing of any of the things mentioned in paragraph 8.1 so as to place at a significant competitive disadvantage persons competing with that business.

8.3   Any question relating to whether any act done or course of conduct pursued by the Licensee amounts to such undue preference or such undue discrimination shall be determined by the Director, but nothing done in any manner by the Licensee shall be regarded as undue preference or undue discrimination if and to the extent that the Licensee is required or permitted to do the thing in that manner by or under any provision of this Licence.

8.4   The obligations imposed on the Licensee by this Condition are without prejudice to any determination which the Director may make under Condition 9 of this Licence.

PART 3:   OTHER CONDITIONS INCLUDED UNDER SECTION 7 OF THE ACT

Condition 9   Maintenance of Effective Competition where the Licensee Operates a System or Provides Services Overseas

9.1   This Condition shall apply where the Licensee or any Associated Person is the operator of any telecommunication system or provides telecommunication services in a country or territory outside the United Kingdom

9.2   Where it appears to the Director that as a result of any act or omission of the Licensee either by itself or with or through any Associated Person competition in the provision of any telecommunication service or any particular description of telecommunication services in the United Kingdom is being or is likely to be restricted, distorted or prevented he may make a determination to that effect.

9.3   Where the Director makes a determination under paragraph 9.2 the Licensee shall take such steps as the Director may direct for the purpose of remedying the situation. In particular (and without prejudice to the generality of the foregoing) any such direction may require compliance by the Licensee with any other Condition, as appropriate, including in particular any Condition providing for publication of charges, terms and conditions or prohibiting undue discrimination and undue preference, in relation to the provision of any telecommunication service within the United Kingdom notwithstanding that any condition precedent to the application of that Condition is not otherwise satisfied.

Condition 10   Fair Trading

10.1   The Licensee shall not do any thing, whether by act or omission. which has or is intended to have or is likely to have the effect of preventing, restricting or distorting competition where such act or omission is done in the course of, as a result of or in connection with, providing telecommunication services, or any particular description of telecommunication service, or running a telecommunication system.
For the purpose of this Condition such an act or omission will take the form of:

(a)   any abuse by the Licensee, either alone or with other undertakings. of a dominant position within the United Kingdom or a substantial part of it. Such abuse may, in particular, consist in:

(i)   directly or indirectly imposing unfair purchase or selling prices or other unfair trading conditions;

(ii)   limiting production, markets or technical development to the prejudice of consumers;

(iii)   applying dissimilar conditions to equivalent transactions with other parties, thereby placing them at a competitive disadvantage; or

(iv)   making the conclusion of contracts subject to acceptance by the other parties of supplementary obligations which, by their nature or according to commercial usage, have no connection with the subject of such contracts; or

(b)   the making (including the implementation) of any agreement, the compliance with any decision of any association of undertakings or the carrying on of any concerted practice with any other undertaking which has the object or effect of preventing, restricting or distorting competition within the United Kingdom.

10.2   (a)   An act or omission of a kind described in paragraph 10.1 is not prohibited where:

(i)   it has or would have no appreciable effect on competition; or

(ii)   it has or would have no effect on competition between persons engaged in commercial activities connected with telecommunications and it would have no effect on users of telecommunication services.

(b)   An act or omission of a kind described in paragraph 10.1(b) is not prohibited by this Condition if the agreement decision or concerted practice contributes to improving the provision of any goods or services or to promoting technical or economic progress, while allowing consumers a fair share of the resulting benefit and does not:

(i) impose on the parties concerned restrictions which are not indispensable to attaining those objectives; and

(ii) afford such parties the possibility of eliminating competition in respect of a substantial part of the goods or services in question.

(c) This Condition shall not apply to any provision of an agreement insofar as it is a provision by virtue of which the Restrictive Trade Practices Act 1976 applies to that agreement.

(d) This Condition shall not apply to a merger situation qualifying for investigation under the Fair Trading Act 1973.

10.3 Whether any act or omission is prohibited by this Condition shall be determined:—

(a) with a view to securing that there is no inconsistency with the general principles having application to similar questions of directly applicable competition law, in particular those laid down by the Court of Justice of the European Communities on the scope of the competition rules contained in the EC Treaty and block exemptions adopted by the European Commission under Article 85(3); and

(b) having regard to—

(i) any decision taken, or notice issued, by the European Commission in applying the competition rules contained in the EC Treaty and any relevant pronouncement of the Director General of Fair Trading or report of the Monopolies and Mergers Commission; and

(ii) any guidelines on the application of this Condition issued from time to time by the Director.

10.4 (a) If it appears to the Director that an act or omission of the Licensee is or was prohibited by this Condition he may make an initial determination to that effect (an 'Initial Determination').

(b) Before making an Initial Determination the Director shall give a notice to the Licensee:

(i) stating that he is investigating a possible contravention of this Condition;

(ii) setting out the reasons why it appears to him that this Condition may be being, or may have been, breached, including any matters of fact or law which he thinks relevant;

(iii) requesting within a reasonable period laid down by the Director such further information as he may require from the Licensee in order to complete his Determination; and

(iv) where appropriate, setting out the steps he believes the Licensee would have to take in order to remedy the alleged breach.

10.5 (a) Within 28 days of the Director—

(i) making an Initial Determination;

(ii) making a provisional order; or

(iii) giving notice of his proposal to make a final order under section 17(1) of the Act

in respect of the contravention in question, the Licensee may notify the Director that it—

(iv) requires him to make a final determination (a 'Final Determination') of the matter;

(v)   requires that in making the Final Determination he take into account a report of a body of experts appointed by him to consider the matter ('the Advisory Body').

(b)   Before making a Final Determination the Director shall—

(i)   give a notice to the Licensee setting out the matters referred to in paragraph 10.4(b); and

(ii)   if the Licensee has given notice under sub-paragraph (a) (v) above, take into account the report of the Advisory Body on the matter.

(c)   The Director shall then determine whether he is satisfied that the act or omission in respect of which the Initial Determination was made is or was prohibited by this Condition.

10.6   (a)   Before making his Initial Determination or Final Determination the Director shall give the Licensee, and any other person whom he considers it appropriate to consult, such period within which to make representations (both orally and in writing) in response to the notice as he considers reasonable in all the circumstances.

(b)   The Director shall notify the Licensee and any other person whom he considers it appropriate to notify of every Initial Determination and Final Determination made by him and of his reasons for making it; and he shall, if so requested by the Licensee, publish any report of the Advisory Body on the matter, subject to such exclusions as he may consider it appropriate to make of matters of a kind mentioned in section 48(2) of the Act.

10.7   The Director shall publish a description of his office's procedures for the enforcement of this Condition including the steps taken to ensure that he has access to appropriate independent advice in enforcing this Condition.

10.8   This Condition shall not limit or affect in any way the Licensee's obligations arising under any other Condition of this Licence nor limit the Director's powers of enforcement under sections 16 to 18 of the Act.

10.9   (a)   On the coming into force of any Act or subordinate legislation which—

(i)   contains a prohibition enforceable by the Director, or gives to the Director the power to enforce an existing prohibition, of any behaviour prohibited under paragraph 10.1;

(ii)   gives to third parties in respect of a breach of that prohibition at least the rights they have under section 18 of the Act in respect of a breach of a provisional or final order; and

(iii)   permits the imposition on the Licensee of monetary penalties in respect of the breach of that prohibition this Condition shall cease to apply to the behaviour prohibited by or the prohibition enforceable by such Act or subordinate legislation.

(b)   If this Condition still has effect on 31st July 2001, it shall cease to have effect after that date.

10.10   (a)   This Condition shall come into force on 31st December 1996.

(b)   The prohibition in paragraph 10.1(b) shall not apply to acts or omissions done prior to the expiry of three months from the date of this Licence in pursuance of agreements entered into prior to the date of this Licence.

Note
This Condition follows the format of the new fair trading Condition 18A inserted in BT's licence.

Condition 11 Essential Interfaces

11.1 This Condition operates without prejudice to the provisions of Condition 5.

11.2 The Director may, having first notified the Licensee of his proposal and given the Licensee not less than 28 days in which to make representations, specify an Essential Interface.

11.3 Where in pursuance of paragraph 11.2 the Director specifies an interface as an Essential Interface, and the Licensee thereafter makes that interface available to an Operator in relation to its Applicable Systems, it shall do so in such a manner as it considers appropriate, but shall ensure such availability in compliance with a Relevant Standard if the Operator so requires.

11.4 For the purposes of paragraph 11.3 'Relevant Standard' means:

(a) an appropriate European or other international standard; or

(b) in the absence of such a standard, any other standard specified by the Director after he has notified the Licensee of his proposal to make the specifications in question and allowed the Licensee not less than 28 days in which to make representations, provided that the Director shall not specify a standard if an appropriate European or other international standard is expected to be promulgated within a reasonable time, including, by way of example, if the European Telecommunications Standards Institute have published a work programme for the development of such a standard,

to the extent that such a standard is necessary to ensure interoperability.

11.5 Where in pursuance of paragraph 11.4(b) the Director specifies a standard as a Relevant Standard, he shall include in that Relevant Standard a technical specification, using all reasonable endeavours to obtain the agreement of the Licensee and other relevant licensees to a technical specification applicable to that Relevant Standard, being a specification defined if possible by reference to:

(a) an appropriate European or other international specification; or

(b) in the absence of such a specification, a specification defined by reference to any other standard having currency within the European Community at the time.

11.6 Where after a reasonable time the Director has been unable in accordance with paragraph 11.5 to secure the agreement of the Licensee and other relevant licensees to a technical specification, the Director shall adopt for inclusion in the Relevant Standard an appropriate technical specification which has been promulgated by a recognised standards body, including, by way of example. the European Telecommunications Standards Institute, or the British Standards Institution. or other such body as the Director considers to be representative of all relevant telecommunications interests.

11.7 The Director shall specify a Relevant Standard in pursuance of paragraph 11.4 only if the owners of relevant intellectual property rights have agreed to grant any necessary licences in respect thereof to the Licensee on reasonable terms.

11.8 For the avoidance of doubt this Condition shall not:

(a) without prejudice to paragraph 11.3, prevent the Licensee using such interfaces as it considers appropriate in relation to the Applicable Systems; or

(b)   where it makes available to an Operator an interface which the Director has specified as an Essential Interface, require the Licensee to comply with the Relevant Standard if the Operator does not require it to do so.

11.9   When implementing an Essential Interface, the Licensee shall not be obliged to conform with the Relevant Standard:

(a)   if to do so would necessitate the Licensee:

(i)   acquiring apparatus, software or other goods or supplies of any kind, or implementing any operation, incompatible with, as the case may be, apparatus, software or such other goods or supplies already in use at the time, or the subject of contracts for their procurement for use, in connection with the Applicable Systems, or, in the case of an operation, incompatible with any other operation being carried out at the time in connection therewith; or

(ii)   incurring any cost, or having to resolve technical difficulties, disproportionate to the benefits to be gained from the implementation of the Relevant Standard,

provided that the Licensee shall take reasonable steps to incorporate the Relevant Standard in its plans for network development, with a view to implementation of that Standard in connection with the Applicable Systems, but without the Licensee incurring any incremental expenditure which, but for the implementation of the Relevant Standard, would not have been incurred;

(b)   if the Relevant Standard is inappropriate for the particular application for any reason, including, without limitation:

(i)   that it does not afford the Licensee adequate protection for the security of the Applicable Systems;

(ii)   that its implementation would be liable to cause material impairment in the quality of any telecommunication service provided by means of the Applicable Systems;

(iii)   that it does not cater adequately for billing, metering or other customer administration systems; or

(iv)   that it is technically inadequate in the light of technical developments which have taken place since it was originally created;

(c)   if the Essential Interface concerned is of a genuinely innovative nature and accordingly the use in connection with it of the Relevant Standard would not be appropriate;

(d)   if compliance with the Relevant Standard would involve the infringement by the Licensee of any intellectual property right vested in any person; or

(e)   if the Director so agrees.

11.10   Where paragraph 11.9(b) or 11.9(c) applies, the Licensee shall notify the Director thereof in writing, providing an explanation why.

11.11   It is a precondition of any obligation on the Licensee under this Condition that an equivalent Condition to this Condition is included in the respective Licences of all Operators running telecommunication systems that are connected to the Applicable Systems.

Condition 12   Customer Interface Standards

12.1   This Condition shall only apply where the Applicable Systems are connected to a telecommunication system not run under a licence issued to a particular person.

12.2 The Licensee shall ensure that on each occasion on which it introduces an interface provided or to be provided at a Network Termination Point on the Applicable Systems not previously so provided a notice is published specifying the technical characteristics of the interface introduced.

12.3 The technical characteristics to be included in such a notice shall include:

(a) physical, electrical and other relevant characteristics;

(b) network interworking and service management protocols; and

(c) reference to national and international standards and recommendations with which the interface complies,

in sufficient detail for compatible terminal apparatus to be produced, tested and approved.

12.4 Subject to paragraph 12.5, any notice under this Condition shall be published in a manner appropriate for bringing the matters to which the notice relates to the attention of persons likely to be affected by or to have an interest in them.

12.5 Where the Director following any representation or observation made to him reasonably concludes that a notice under paragraph 12.2 has not been published in an appropriate manner he may direct the Licensee to carry out such further publication as he considers reasonably necessary to meet the requirements of paragraph 12.4.

Condition 13   Metering and Billing Arrangements

13.1 This Condition shall only apply where the Applicable Systems are connected to a telecommunication system not run under a Licence issued to a particular person.

13.2 As regards any description of Meter in use on a date specified by the Director in connection with the Applicable Systems and which has been specified by the Director, the Licensee shall apply for Approval as soon as is practicable and in any case not later than such date as the Director may determine in relation to that description of Meter.

13.3 As regards any description of Meter specified by the Director and not in use in connection with the Applicable Systems on the date specified under paragraph 13.2, the Licensee shall, unless the Director consents otherwise, apply for Approval not later than such date as is further specified by the Director or not fewer than six months before the date on which the Licensee intends to bring that Meter into such use, whichever shall be the later.

13.4 The Licensee shall not after such date as the Director may determine in relation to any description of Meter so specified by him, keep in use or bring into use in connection with the Applicable systems, any Meter of a description so specified which is not Approved or for which the Licensee has not made an application for Approval.

13.5 Where Approval is not granted to or is withdrawn from a particular description of Meter the Licensee shall, as soon as is reasonably practicable, either;

(a) inform the Director of the action to be taken by the Licensee to remedy the absence of Approval in relation to that description of Meter and the anticipated date of such Approval; or

(b)   inform the Director that the Licensee intends to cease use of that description of Meter in connection with the Applicable Systems within a time reasonably practicable for the Licensee whereupon, on request of the Director, the Licensee shall provide the Director with a timetable for the withdrawal of that description of Meter.

13.6   The Licensee shall not render any bill in respect of any description of telecommunication Service provided by means of the Applicable Systems unless every amount (other than an indication of unit charge) stated in that bill is no higher than an amount which represents the true extent of any such Service actually provided by the Licensee to the customer in question. In this paragraph 'customer' does not include an Operator.

13.7   Without prejudice to the generality of paragraph 13.6 the Licensee shall at all times maintain in operation such a Billing Process as facilitates compliance by the Licensee with, and is calculated to prevent contravention by it of, that paragraph.

13.8   The Licensee shall not be regarded as being in contravention of its obligation under paragraph 13.6 except where the failure is in relation to the Billing Process and the Licensee has failed to take all reasonable steps to prevent a contravention of that obligation.

13.9   The Licensee shall keep such records as may be necessary or as may be determined by the Director to be necessary for the purpose of satisfying the Director that the Billing Process has the characteristics required by paragraph 13.7, provided that nothing in this paragraph shall require the Licensee to retain any records for more than 2 years from the date on which they came into being.

13.10   For the purpose of giving the Director an independent quality assurance from time to time that the Billing Process has the characteristics required by paragraph 13.7, the Licensee shall, where the Director has prima facie grounds to believe the Billing Process does not have those characteristics and has so notified the Licensee, extend its prompt co-operation to the Director and, in particular, on request by the Director shall;

(a)   furnish the Director in accordance with the Director's reasonable requirements any Information, document (including any facility enabling him to read data not held in readable form) or other thing;

(b)   carry out (or cause to be carried out by such person having such special expertise as the Director may specify and to whom the Director has raised no reasonable objection) in such manner as the Director may specify an examination of the whole or of any part of the Billing Process and as soon as practicable after the conclusion of such examination furnish to the Director a written report by the Licensee or that specified person, as the case may be, of the results of such examination;

(c)   on reasonable notice by him allow at all reasonable times the Director and, in the case of any member of his staff, on production of his special authority in that behalf, access to any relevant premises, plant or equipment of the Licensee;

(d)   on reasonable notice by him allow at all reasonable times the Director and, in the case of any member of his staff, on production of his special authority in that behalf, to examine or test the whole or any part of the Billing Process including any plant or equipment whether or not forming part of the Applicable Systems;

(e) for the purpose of paragraphs 13.10(c) and 13.10(d), allow the Director to be accompanied by any person as the Director may specify and to whom the Licensee has raised no reasonable objection whose assistance he might reasonably require for the purpose described at the beginning of this paragraph provided that the Director shall have given the Licensee notice (save in exceptional circumstances) of at least 5 working days of the identity of that person; and

(f) install and keep installed any equipment (whether or not supplied by the Director) for the purpose of verifying;

(i) the accuracy and reliability of any equipment or apparatus (including any Meter) of the Licensee;

(ii) in the case of any Meter which is or is required to be Approved and is in use in connection with the Applicable Systems, compliance with any conditions or other matters which may be required as regards such use of that Meter.

13.11 In this Condition:

(a) 'Approval' and 'Approved' mean approval and approved under section 24 of the Act,

(b) 'Billing Process' means Metering systems and Billing Systems taken together, where 'Billing System' means the totality of all apparatus, data, procedures and activities which the Licensee employs to determine the charges to be sought for Service usage recorded by a Metering System based on published or previously negotiated pricing structures and to present these charges on customers' bills and 'Metering System' means the totality of all apparatus, data, procedures and activities which the Licensee employs to determine the extent of any telecommunication Services provided by means of the Applicable Systems;

(c) 'Information' includes accounts, estimates and returns;

(d) 'Meter' means any system or apparatus constructed or adapted for use in ascertaining the extent of telecommunication Services provided by means of the Applicable Systems; and

(e) 'Service' includes any service provided by any person to whom the Licensee is bound to account for any part of the amount charged by the Licensee.

Condition 14   Numbering Arrangements

14.1 This Condition shall only apply where the Applicable Systems are connected to a telecommunication system not being run under a Licence issued to a particular person, or where the Licensee has been granted Numbers by the Director.

14.2 The Licensee shall from the day on which it first provides a switched telecommunication service or any other telecommunication service in connection with which the Licensee allocates to users Numbers adopt a Numbering Plan and shall furnish details thereof to the Director and on request to any other person having a reasonable interest.

14.3 The Numbering Plan shall describe the method adopted and to be adopted for allocating and re-allocating in respect of each Network Termination Point such Number or Numbers as may be necessary for each item of Relevant Apparatus or each Relevant System that is or is to be connected by means of that Network Termination Point to any of the switched Applicable Systems.

14.4   The Licensee shall install, maintain or adjust its switched Applicable Systems so that those Systems convey Messages to Network Termination Points in respect of which Numbers have been allocated in accordance with the Numbering Plan.

14.5   The Licensee shall from time to time consult:

(a)   the Director about the arrangements for the allocation and reallocation of Numbers within the Numbering Plan; and

(b)   in one body approved by the Director for the purpose and representative of telecommunications operators and other persons whom the Director considers appropriate about any developments of, additions to or replacements of, the Numbering Plan.

14.6   The Licensee shall from time to time prepare, taking into account the consultations mentioned in paragraph 14.5(b), and furnish to the Director proposals for developing, adding to or replacing the Numbering Plan and changing the switched Applicable Systems to the extent necessary to secure that:

(a)   sufficient Numbers are made available, having regard to the anticipated growth in demand for telecommunication services, for a Number or Numbers to be allocated without undue delay;

(b)   Numbers include as few digits as practicable and their allocation does not confer any undue advantage on the Licensee or undue disadvantage on persons running Relevant Systems;

(c)   the cost of changing any of the switched Applicable Systems or any Relevant Apparatus or Relevant System in order to accommodate the revised Numbering Plan is reasonable; and

(d)   inconvenience caused by the alteration of the Numbering Plan to the Licensee and to persons using Relevant Apparatus or Relevant Systems in respect of which Numbers have previously been allocated is minimised.

14.7   If the Director determines that the Numbering Plan with any developments, additions and replacements submitted in accordance with paragraph 14.6 is sufficient to provide compatibility with the numbering arrangements applied or to be applied by telecommunications operators and to meet the objectives specified in paragraph 14.6 the Licensee shall adopt the Numbering Plan but, if the Director determines that it is not compatible with numbering arrangements applied or to be applied by another public telecommunications operator or will not be sufficient to achieve the objectives specified in paragraph 14.6, then the Licensee shall adopt the Numbering Plan with such developments, additions or replacements as the Director may determine are best calculated to secure the objectives specified in paragraph 14.6.

14.8   Before making a determination under paragraph 14.7 the Director shall take account of:

(a)   the state of technical development of the Applicable Systems and the Licensee's plans for their commercial development;

(b)   the balance of advantage between:

(i)   making developments of, additions to or replacements of numbering arrangements applied or to be applied, or making changes to systems run, by others; and

(ii)   making any requirement of the Licensee;

(c)   the cost to the Licensee and to those to whom the Licensee provides telecommunication services arising from any determination;

(d)   any obligations and recommendations of the International Tele-communication Union which apply to Her Majesty's Government and are accepted by it and any other standard to which the Director consents for the purpose from time to time; and

(e)   the views of the Licensee and such other persons (including operators of telecommunication systems, those to whom telecommunication services are provided or telecommunication apparatus is supplied and pro-ducers of telecommunication apparatus) as appear to the Director to have an interest in the matter.

14.9   Where the Licensee has adopted a Numbering Plan in accordance with paragraph 14.7, or the Director has made a determination under that paragraph (by virtue of which the Licensee shall adopt the Numbering Plan), the Numbering Plan so adopted shall be the Licensee's Numbering Plan until the Licensee adopts a Numbering Plan pursuant to the following provisions of this Condition. The Numbering Plan referred to in the following provi-sions of this Condition is the Numbering Plan adopted pursuant to those provisions.

14.10   The Director may determine a Specified Numbering Scheme (the 'Scheme') in accordance with the National Numbering Conventions (the 'Conventions') published in accordance with paragraph 14.14 and he will allocate Numbers from this Scheme to the Licensee in accordance with the Conventions. The initial allocation of Numbers to the Licensee shall be of those Numbers to which the Numbering Plan referred to in paragraph 14.3 relates and of any other Numbers to which any other Numbering Plan in force immediately before such allocation relates, provided that, at such time of initial allocation, those Numbers are currently in use by the Licensee, and where not so in use, the Director shall have due regard to the Licensee's plans and future requirements for its use and allocation of additional Numbers. The Director shall, at the request from time to time of the Licensee, allocate to it:

(a)   such quantity of additional Numbers as it may require; and

(b)   in accordance with the Conventions, such specific Numbers as it may request and which the Director is satisfied are not required for other purposes.

14.11   The Licensee shall adopt a Numbering Plan for such Numbers as the Director may allocate to it from time to time in accordance with the Conventions. It shall within three months of being notified of such allocation furnish details of the Numbering Plan to the Director. and keep him informed of material changes to the Numbering Plan as they occur. The Licensee shall also furnish details of the Numbering Plan together with any material changes to that Numbering Plan on request to any other person having a reasonable interest. Except where the Director agrees otherwise, the Numbering Plan shall be consistent with the Conventions published in accordance with paragraph 14.14. If the Numbering Plan is not consistent with those Con-ventions, the Director may direct the Licensee to adopt and furnish him with a new Numbering Plan or to take such other reasonable remedial action which does not cause undue inconvenience to the Licensee's customers, as may be necessary to ensure consistency.

14.12   The Licensee shall install, maintain and adjust its switched Applicable Systems so that those Systems route Messages and otherwise operate in accordance with the Numbering Plan. The Licensee shall not use Numbers other than those allocated to it from the Scheme except:

(a)   with the written consent of the Director; or

(b)   where the use of those Numbers is the subject of an agreement to which Condition 5 applies.

14.13   (a)   The Licensee shall provide to the Director, on request, such information about its operations under its Numbering Plan as he may reasonably require to administer the Scheme and in particular on:

(i)   the percentages of Numbers in significant ranges which have already been allocated to end-users or which for other reasons are unavailable for further allocation;

(ii)   any allocation of blocks of Numbers to any person for purposes other than end use;

(iii)   Numbers whose use has been transferred at an end-user's request to another Operator, and

(iv)   the Licensee's current forecasts of all of the above matters.

(b)   The Licensee shall not be required to provide information about individual end-user customers.

(c)   In making any such request the Director shall ensure that no undue burden is imposed on the Licensee in procuring and furnishing such information and, in particular, that the Licensee is not required to procure or furnish information which would not normally be available to it, unless the Director is satisfied that such information is essential to the administration of the Scheme.

14.14   (a)   The Conventions referred to in this Condition will be a set of principles and rules published from time to time by the Director after consultation with interested parties who are members of the Telecommunications Numbering and Addressing Body and, if deemed appropriate, with end-users.

(b)   In consulting the said interested parties, the Director shall afford a reasonable period, not being less than 28 days, for them to make representations, and he shall take the said representations into account when publishing the Conventions. The Conventions shall govern the specification and application of the Scheme and the Numbering Plan of the Licensee and may also include such other matters relating to the use and management of Numbers as (but not limited to):

(i)   criteria and procedures relating to the application for, allocation of and withdrawal of Numbers;

(ii)   dialling plans;

(iii)   access codes;

(iv)   prefixes;

(v)   standard ways of recording Numbers for convenience or ease of use, such as the grouping of digits in Numbers of particular lengths: and

(vi)   methods of enabling end-users to understand the meaning implicit in Numbers or other dialled digits. and in particular the rate at which a call to a particular Number will be chargeable.

(c)   The Director may from time to time amend or withdraw a Convention already published, after consultation with interested parties who are members of the Telecommunications Numbering and Addressing Body. The Licensee shall not be required to comply with any such amendment or withdrawal unless the Licensee has been given a reasonable period of notice, such notice not being less than three months. Numbers allocated to the Licensee may only be withdrawn after similar consultation and notice, and the Director shall consult end-users affected by such withdrawal. Subject to overriding national interests, or where there is no alternative solution available, the power to withdraw Numbers shall not apply to any Numbers which the Director has approved from time to time as part of a specific service of the Licensee, which, as a result of investment by the Licensee, has a recognised identity and quality associated with that particular Number and which the Licensee is using and plans to continue to use.

14.15   In deciding on the details of and any subsequent changes to the Scheme and the Conventions, and when making or changing Number allocations within the Scheme or making determinations under this Condition, the Director shall ensure that the Scheme complies with the Conventions and shall have regard to:

(a)   the need for sufficient Numbers to be made available, having regard to the anticipated growth in demand for telecommunication services, together with the need for good husbandry of that supply at any time;

(b)   the need to ensure Compatibility with the Numbering Plans adopted or to be adopted by telecommunications operators;

(c)   the convenience and preferences of end-users;

(d)   the requirements of effective competition;

(e)   the practicability of implementing the Conventions in licensed systems by the date when the Conventions are intended to apply;

(f)   any costs or inconvenience imposed on the Licensee, other telecommunications operators, end-users and other interested parties (including those overseas);

(g)   any relevant international agreements, recommendations or standards;

(h)   the views of the Licensee and other interested parties; and

(i)   any other matters he regards as relevant.

14.16   The Licensee shall not, unless the Director consents otherwise, charge any person for a Number which is allocated to him (other than a coveted Number allocated to a person who is not a public telecommunications operator at the request of such a person), but nothing in this Condition shall preclude the Licensee from recovering from the operator of a Relevant System the reasonable costs associated with allocating Numbers to and routing calls to that System; save that in the case of any dispute or difference as to those costs the Director may determine them and the Licensee shall not be obliged so to allocate Numbers and route calls unless such operator agrees to bear the costs so determined.

14.17   For the purposes of this Condition, 'Telecommunications Numbering and Addressing Body' means a body approved by the Director as representative of the Licensee and other persons whom the Director considers it appropriate to include in consultations about the content of the Conventions and the Scheme.

14.18   For the avoidance of doubt, it is hereby declared that this Condition applies notwithstanding any arrangements for numbering arising by virtue of any agreement to which Condition 5 applies. But nothing in this paragraph shall affect the operation of any such agreements entered into before the coming into force of this Licence.

14.19   The Numbers to which this Condition applies are Numbers:

(a)   of a class described in CCITT Recommendation E.160, E.163, E.164, E.165, E.166 or F.69 or their functional successors; or

(b)   which are of a class described in CCITT Recommendation X.121 and which include any Data Network Identification Code which has been:

(i)   allocated before 14 November 1986 in accordance with a Numbering Plan furnished to the Director; or

(ii)   specified by the Director for the purposes of this Licence and described in a list kept for that purpose by the Director and made available by him for inspection to the general public.

Condition 15   Arrangements for Proportionate Return

15.1   This Condition shall apply in respect of the conveyance of Messages to or from each country and territory in the world other than as specified from time to time by the Secretary of State.

15.2   Except insofar as the Director may otherwise consent in writing, the Licensee shall ensure (using the most up-to-date information available) that over each quarterly period for each Accounting Rate Service the First Ratio shall be no greater than the Second Ratio.

15.3   Where it appears to the Director that in respect of any country or territory the obligation imposed by paragraph 15.2 is being breached, he may make a determination to that effect and the Licensee shall take such steps as the Director may direct for the purpose of remedying the situation. In particular, and without prejudice to the generality of the foregoing, any such direction may require the Licensee to cease to convey any Messages to that country or territory.

15.4   In this Condition:

'First Ratio'   means the volume of Messages comprised in each Accounting Rate Service which are conveyed by the Applicable Systems and are delivered to the United Kingdom divided by the volume of all Messages comprised in each Accounting Rate Service which are delivered to the United Kingdom; and

'Second Ratio'   means the volume of all Messages comprised in each Accounting Rate Service which are conveyed by the Applicable Systems and are sent from the United Kingdom divided by the volume of all Messages comprised in each Accounting Rate Service which are sent from the United Kingdom.

Condition 16   Arrangements for Accounting in Respect of International Conveyance Services

16.1   This Condition shall apply in respect of the conveyance of Messages to or from each country and territory in the world other than as specified from time to time by the Secretary of State.

16.2   The Licensee shall inform the Director of accounting rates and methods of settlement and division of the accounting rates agreed for all Accounting Rate Services, before those rates are put into operation.

16.3   As soon as practicably possible after making any correspondent arrangement with an overseas operator the Licensee shall inform the Director and all other holders of a Licence authorising the provision of International Conveyance Services in the United Kingdom and who are operating, or who have announced an intention to operate on that particular route, of the terms of that arrangement, in particular and without prejudice to the generality of the foregoing, including details of any changes to existing accounting rates or methods of settlement or division of the accounting rates.

16.4   Where it appears to the Director that any accounting rate or methods of settlement or division of the accounting rates agreed by the Licensee in respect of any Accounting Rate Service has or is likely to have an effect to the detriment of providers and users of International Conveyance Services in the United Kingdom, he may make a determination to that effect and the Licensee shall take such steps as the Director may direct for the purpose of remedying the situation. In particular, and without prejudice to the generality of the foregoing, any such direction may require the Licensee to cease to convey any Messages to that country or territory.

Condition 17   Prohibition of Exclusive Dealing in International Services

17.1   The Licensee shall not enter into any agreement or arrangement with any person running an Authorised Overseas System on terms or conditions which unfairly preclude or restrict the provision by another public telecommunications operator of International Conveyance Services.

17.2   The Licensee shall not unreasonably exclude any other public telecommunications operator who is authorised by a licence to connect his system to another telecommunication system situated outside the United Kingdom so as to convey Messages to that other system from a reasonable opportunity to participate in any international arrangements into which it proposes to enter after the date on which this Licence enters into force for the installation and operation of any submarine cable linking any of the Applicable Systems to any telecommunication system outside the United Kingdom.

Condition 18   Notification of Changes in Shareholdings

18.1   The Licensee shall notify the Secretary of State if an undertaking becomes a Parent Undertaking in relation to the Licensee.

18.2   Subject to paragraph 18.3, the Licensee shall notify the Secretary of State of:

(a)   any change in the proportion of the Shares held in a Relevant Company by any person;

(b)   the acquisition of any Shares in a Relevant Company by a person not already holding any such Shares, and the proportion of any such Shares held by that person immediately after that acquisition.

18.3   The Licensee shall be obliged to notify the Secretary of State of any acquisition of Shares or change in the Shareholding of a Relevant Company by any person only if, by reason of that acquisition or change, the total number of Shares in that Relevant Company held by that person otherwise than as trustee or nominee for another person together with any Shares held by any nominee or trustee for that person immediately after that change or acquisition:

(a) exceeds 15 per cent of the total number of Shares in that company (where it did not exceed 15 per cent prior to that change or acquisition);

(b) exceeds 30 per cent of the total number of Shares in that company (where it did not exceed 30 per cent prior to that change or acquisition); or

(c) exceeds 50 per cent of the total number of Shares in that company (where it did not exceed 50 per cent prior to that change or acquisition),

provided that where a Relevant Company is a public company as defined in section 1 of the Companies Act 1985, the obligation shall be discharged by forwarding to the Secretary of State as soon as practicable all information in respect of that acquisition or that change as is entered on or received for entry on the register required to be maintained by that Relevant Company under section 211 of the Companies Act 1985.

18.4   In any case referred to in paragraph 18.1 or 18.2, notification shall be given by a date which is 30 days prior to the taking effect of such change or acquisition, as the case may be, or as soon as practicable after that date.

Condition 19   Licensee's Group

19.1   Without prejudice to the Licensee's obligations under these Conditions in respect, in particular, of anything done on its behalf, where:

(a) the Director determines either:

(i)   that a member of the Licensee's Group has done something which would, if it had been done by the Licensee, be prohibited or not be authorised under these Conditions; or

(ii) that a member of the Licensee's Group has done something which would, if it had been done by the Licensee, require the Licensee to take or refrain from taking a particular action under these Conditions and that neither the Licensee nor the member has met that further requirement; and

(b) the Director is not satisfied that the Licensee has taken all reasonable steps to prevent any member acting in that way,

then the Director may direct the Licensee to take such steps as the Director deems appropriate for the purpose of remedying the matter, including refraining from carrying on with that member such commercial activities connected with telecommunications as the Director may determine.

19.2   Where these Conditions apply in respect of the Applicable Systems they do not apply in respect of any other telecommunication system, whether run by the Licensee or another.

19.3   Where any person becomes a member of the Licensee's Group then the Licensee shall not be subject to paragraph 19.1 before that is reasonably practicable but shall be so not later than one year after that person becomes such a member or such later date as the Director may determine.

19.4   This Condition shall not apply to any particular member of the Licensee's Group if and to the extent that the Director so determines.

Condition 20   Payment of Fees

20.1   The Licensee shall pay the following amounts to the Secretary of State at the times stated:

(a)   on the grant of this Licence the sum of £7,000;

(b)   on 1 April 1997 a renewal fee of (at the option of the Director) either £8,000 or such amount which shall represent a fair proportion, to be determined each year by the Director according to a method that has been disclosed to the Licensee, of the estimated costs to be incurred in that fiscal year by the Director in the regulation and enforcement of telecommunication licences and in the exercise of his other functions under the Act. The first renewal fee shall be reduced by the proportion which the period from the date of granting of this Licence until the next following 1 April 1997 bears to the period of one year; and

(c)   when the Director so determines, a special fee which shall represent a fair proportion, to be determined by the Director according to a method that has been disclosed to the Licensee of the amount, if any, by which the aggregate of:

(i)   the costs estimated to have been already incurred in that fiscal year by the Director in the regulation and enforcement of telecommunication licences and in the exercise of his other functions under the Act;

(ii)   the costs estimated to have been already incurred in that fiscal year by the Monopolies and Mergers Commission following licence modification references under section 13 of the Act; and

(iii)   the estimated costs to be incurred in the remainder of that fiscal year:

(A)   by the Director in the regulation and enforcement of telecommunication licences and in the exercise of his other functions under the Act; and

(B)   by the Monopolies and Mergers Commission following licence modification references under section 13 of the Act,

exceeds the renewal fee for that year,

save always that the aggregate of the renewal fee and the special fee for any fiscal year shall not exceed 0.08% of the annual turnover of the Systems Business in the financial year before the last complete financial year of the Licensee before the renewal fee is payable, or £35,000 (adjusted in the manner described in paragraph 20.1(b), whichever is the greater (the 'normal aggregate fee'), unless the Director determines that the costs incurred in any fiscal year by him and the Monopolies and Mergers Commission in respect of the Licensee's activities exceeds the normal aggregate fee, in which case the aggregate of the renewal fee and the special fee for the following year shall be such amount as the Director determines is sufficient to take account of that excess as well as of the other costs to be incurred as mentioned in this paragraph.

Condition 21   Requirement to Furnish Information to the Director

21.1   Without prejudice to Condition 22, the Licensee shall furnish to the Director, in such manner and at such times as the Director may reasonably request, such documents, accounts, estimates, returns or other information and procure and furnish to him such reports as he may reasonably require for the purpose of exercising the functions assigned or transferred to him by or under Parts II and III of the Act.

21.2   In making any such request the Director shall ensure that no undue burden is imposed on the Licensee in procuring and furnishing such information and, in particular, that the Licensee is not required to procure or furnish a report which would not normally be available to it unless the Director considers the particular report essential to enable him to exercise his functions.

Condition 22   Requirement to Submit Accounts to the Director

22.1   The Licensee shall maintain such accounting records dealing separately with its International Business carried on in the United Kingdom as will enable it to show separately and explain, in response to any request from the Director under paragraph 22.4, all the transactions to which paragraph 22.2 refers.

22.2   This paragraph refers to:

(a)   all transactions between each Relevant International Function run as part of the Licensee's International Business; and

(b)   all transactions between the Licensee's International Business and:

(i)   any other business carried on by the Licensee whether in the United Kingdom or elsewhere; or

(ii)   the business of any Associated Person whether in the United Kingdom or elsewhere.

22.3   The Licensee shall update the accounting records referred to in paragraph 22.1 no less frequently than monthly and those records shall include in particular the costs (including capital costs), revenue and a reasonable assessment of assets employed in and liabilities attributable to the International Business and, separately, the amount of any material item of revenue, cost, asset or liability which has been either:

(a)   charged from or to any other business of the Licensee or Associated Person together with a description of the basis of the value on which the charge was made; or

(b)   determined by apportionment or attribution from an activity common to the business and any other business of the Licensee or any Associated Person and, if not otherwise disclosed, the basis of the apportionment or attribution.

22.4   The Director may at any time request from the Licensee copies of any of the accounting records and detailed attribution policies and procedures which the Licensee is obliged to maintain by this Condition, covering any period between:

(a)   the date on which the Licensee first carried on any International Business in the United Kingdom or, if later, the date of this Licence; and

(b)   the date on which such records were, or should have been, last updated in accordance with paragraph 22.3.

The Licensee shall provide any such records requested by the Director within 28 days of receiving such a request in writing..

22.5   (i)   Accounting records submitted to the Director shall, so far as reasonably practicable, be prepared in the formats and in accordance with the accounting principles and rules which apply to the annual statutory accounts of the Licensee and shall state the attribution policies and procedures used and where the Licensee is a body corporate incorporated outside the United Kingdom the preparation and adoption of those accounts shall comply with the requirements of sections 226 and 23 to 234A of the Companies Act 1985 as if that body corporate were incorporated in the United Kingdom.

(ii) The Licensee shall procure in respect of each set of accounting records submitted to the Director an audit report which shall conform to UK auditing standards by the Auditor in which he shall state whether in his opinion the record complies with paragraph 22.1 and is fairly presented in accordance with the formats, accounting principles rules and requirements referred to in paragraph 22.5(i).

22.6 Where it appears to the Director that to do so would be beneficial to the promotion or maintenance of competition he may direct the Licensee to publish the accounting statements submitted to the Director in such way as he sees fit. In so directing the Licensee the Director shall have regard to the need for excluding, so far as that is practicable, any matter where publication of that matter might, in the opinion of the Director, seriously and prejudicially affect the interests of the Licensee or any Associated Person.

Condition 23 Exceptions and Limitations on Obligations in Schedule 1

23.1 Unless the context otherwise requires and subject to paragraph 23.9, the Licensee's obligations under these Conditions have effect subject to the following exceptions and limitations.

23.2 The Licensee is not obliged to do anything which is not practicable.

23.3 The Licensee shall not be held to have failed to comply with an obligation imposed upon it by or under these Conditions if and to the extent that the Licensee is prevented from complying with that obligation by any physical, topographical or other natural obstacle, by the malfunction or failure of any apparatus or equipment owing to circumstances beyond the control of the Licensee, by the act of any national authority, local authority or international organisation or as the result of fire, flood, explosion, accident, emergency, riot or war.

23.4 An obligation to provide any telecommunication service shall not apply:

(a) where there is no reasonable demand for it; or

(b) where provision of the service requested would expose any person engaged in its provision to undue risk to health or safety; or

(c) where the Licensee is unable to obtain (either because it has not been developed or for some other reason beyond the Licensee's control) anything necessary to provide a service of the quality or standard required by the person who requests the provision of the service and, in the event of dispute, the Director's decision as to whether anything is necessary shall be final; or

(d) where the person to whom the Licensee would otherwise be under an obligation to provide any service requests a service at a place in which the apparatus necessary to provide that service in that area has not been installed (or in which the installation of such apparatus has not been completed) or as the case may be such apparatus has not been adapted or modified to make it capable of providing that service or the trained manpower necessary to provide that service is not available in that area, provided that in every case where the Licensee declines to provide a service to which this paragraph relates it shall have published, or furnished to the Director, within 28 days (or such longer period as the Director considers reasonable) following receipt by it of the request that that service be provided, proposals for:

(i)   progressively installing, or completing the installation, adaptation or modification of, the apparatus; or

(ii)   the allocation of the trained manpower,

necessary for the provision of that service in that area and the Director has not determined that those proposals are unreasonable or are not being effectively carried out; or

(e)   where the person to whom the Licensee would otherwise be under an obligation to provide any service requests a service at a place in an area in which the demand or the prospective demand for the service is not sufficient, having regard to the revenue likely to be earned from the provision of the service in that area, to meet all the costs reasonably to be incurred by the Licensee in providing the service there, including:

(i)   the cost of apparatus necessary for the provision of the service there;

(ii)   the cost of installing, maintaining and operating such apparatus for the purpose of providing the service there; and

(iii) the cost of the trained manpower necessary to provide the service there; or

(f)   where in the opinion of the Director it is not reasonably practicable in all the circumstances for the Licensee to provide the service requested at the time or place demanded.

23.5 The Licensee shall not be obliged to connect or to keep connected to the Applicable Systems or to permit to be so connected or kept connected any telecommunication system or telecommunication apparatus or to provide telecommunication services or to permit the provision of any service if the person to or for whom that is or is to be done:

(a)   has not entered or will not enter into a contract for the purpose with the Licensee for reasons other than the unreasonable refusal of the Licensee to agree terms for the purpose but this paragraph does not apply in a case where the Director is satisfied that:

(i)   the Licensee has not published standard terms and conditions which it proposes to apply for the purpose in question, or the transaction is not fit to be governed by such terms and conditions; and

(ii)   the Licensee has unreasonably refused to agree terms and conditions for the purpose;

(b)   is, or in the Director's opinion has given reasonable cause to believe that he may become:

(i)   in breach of a contract with the Licensee for the provision of telecommunication services by the Licensee; or

(ii)   in default in regard to any debt or liability owed to the Licensee in respect of any such contract;

(c)   is using, or permitting the use of, apparatus so connected or kept connected for any illegal purpose or has done so in the past and is likely to do so again: or

(d)   has obtained, or attempted to obtain, any telecommunication service from the Licensee by corrupt, dishonest or illegal means at any time.

23.6 Nothing in these Conditions shall prevent the Licensee from withdrawing from, or declining to provide to, any person any telecommunication service which the Licensee has notified the Director that it is providing in a limited area, or to a limited class of customers, for the purpose of evaluating the technical feasibility of, or the commercial prospects for, that service.

23.7 Nothing in these Conditions shall require the Licensee to provide any telecommunication service, or to provide any telecommunication service of any particular class or description, if it provides instead a service, or a service of a class or description, which satisfies the purposes of that requirement at least to the same extent.

23.8 This Condition shall apply without prejudice to any limitation or qualification of the requirements imposed by or under any other Condition.

23.9 This Condition does not apply to Condition 5, 8 or 10 and:

(a) only paragraphs 23.1, 23.2, 23.3 and 23.8 apply to Conditions 7, 13.2, 13.3, 19, 20 and 21;

(b) only paragraphs 23.1, 23.5(a) and 23.8 apply to Condition 4.2;

(c) only paragraphs 23.1, 23.2, 23.3, 23.5 and 23.8 apply to Condition 14;

(d) only paragraphs 23.1, 23.2, 23.3, 23.4(b), 23.5(a) and 23.8 apply to Condition 3; and

(e) only paragraphs 23.1, 23.2, 23.3, 23.4, 23.6 and 23.8 apply to Condition 4.1;

but paragraph 23.2 does not apply to Condition 9 or Condition 22.

SCHEDULE 2: REVOCATION

1. Notwithstanding paragraph 3 of the Licence the Secretary of State may at any time revoke this Licence by at least 30 days' notice given to the Licensee in writing in any of the following circumstances:

(a) if the Licensee agrees in writing with the Secretary of State that this Licence should be revoked; or

(b) if either

(i) an undertaking has become a Parent Undertaking in relation to the Licensee; or

(ii) a change or acquisition of a description specified in paragraphs 18.2 and 183 of Condition 18 of Schedule 1 to this Licence has taken place; and either

(iii) the Licensee has duly notified the Secretary of State in accordance with those paragraphs; or

(iv) the Licensee has failed to notify the Secretary of State that such event, change or acquisition has taken place in accordance with an obligation under that Condition; and

(v) the Secretary of State has notified the Licensee in writing that he is minded to revoke this Licence on the grounds either that:

(A) the event, change or acquisition would in his opinion be against the interests of national security or relations with the government of a country or territory outside the United Kingdom; or

(B) the Licensee has committed a breach of Condition 18 of Schedule 1; and

(vi) the event, change or acquisition has not been reversed or remedied within 30 days of the receipt by the Licensee of such notification or

(c) if, following a change or acquisition of the type referred to in Condition 18 of Schedule 1 to this Licence, the Secretary of State considers, or the Director has notified the Secretary of State that the Director considers, that the Licensee is relying, has relied or is likely to rely on this Licence in circumstances in which an effect of such reliance is, was or may be that the Licensee or any member of the Licensee's Group is or was relieved wholly or in part of any obligation, limitation or restriction imposed by a Licence issued to the Licensee or any member of the Licensee's Group; or

(d)   where the Licensee has failed to comply with a final order (or a provisional order confirmed) under section 16 of the Act and the Secretary of State has given the Licensee not less than 30 days' notice in writing that, if the Licensee fails to comply with the order within that period of 30 days, he intends to revoke the Licence, provided that no such notice of intention shall be given where the question of the validity of the order is the subject of any court proceedings, and where that question becomes so subject during the 30 day notice period, that period shall cease to run until the final disposal of those proceedings (including any Appeal); or

(e)   if the Licensee:

(i)   is deemed to be unable to pay its debts (within the meaning of section 123 of the Insolvency Act 1986 as applied for the purposes of this Licence by paragraph 2(b)), convenes any meeting with its creditors generally with a view to the general readjustment or rescheduling of its indebtedness or makes a general assignment for the benefit of its creditors generally; or

(ii)   enters into administration, receivership or liquidation; or

(iii)   ceases to provide telecommunication services of the type authorised in paragraph 3 of Schedule 3 to this Licence; or

(f)   if the Licensee or any other person takes any action for the voluntary winding-up or dissolution of the Licensee; or

(g)   if the Licensee enters into any scheme of arrangement under the Insolvency Act 1986 (other than in any such case for the purpose of reconstruction or amalgamation upon terms and within such period as may previously have been approved in writing by the Secretary of State); or

(h)   if an administrator, receiver, trustee or similar officer of the Licensee, or of all or any material part of the revenues and assets of it, is appointed; or

(i)   if any order is made for the compulsory winding-up or dissolution of the Licensee; or

(j)   if any amount payable under Condition 20 of Schedule 1 is unpaid 30 days after it becomes due and remains unpaid for a period of 14 days after the Secretary of State notifies the Licensee that the payment is overdue.

2.   For the purposes of paragraph 1(e)(i), in applying section 123 of the Insolvency Act 1986:

(a)   if a written demand served on the Licensee is satisfied prior to the expiry of the notice of revocation the Secretary of State shall not revoke the Licence; and

(b)   the figure of '£750', or such other money sum as may be specified from time to time pursuant to sections 123(3) and 416 of the Insolvency Act 1986, shall be deemed to be replaced by '£250,000' or such higher figure as the Director may from time to time determine.

3.   In this Schedule:

(a)   'Group' means a parent undertaking and its subsidiary undertaking or undertakings within the meaning of section 258 of the Companies Act 1985 as substituted by section 21 of the Companies Act 1989; and 'Licensee's Group' means a Group in respect of which the Licensee is either a parent undertaking or a subsidiary undertaking; and

(b) 'Parent Undertaking' has the same meaning as in section 258 of the Companies Act 1985 as substituted by section 21 of the Companies Act 1989.

4. For the purposes of this Schedule 'Appeal' includes further appeal and application for leave to appeal or further to appeal.

SCHEDULE 3: AUTHORISATION TO CONNECT OTHER TELECOMMUNICATION SYSTEMS AND APPARATUS TO THE APPLICABLE SYSTEMS AND TO PROVIDE TELECOMMUNICATION SERVICES BY MEANS OF THE APPLICABLE SYSTEMS

1. Nothing in this Licence removes any need to obtain any other licence that may be required under any other enactment.

Connection Authorisation

2. Subject to paragraph 1, this Licence authorises the connection to the Applicable Systems of:

(a) any telecommunication system run under a Licence;

(b) any telecommunication system outside the United Kingdom except a telecommunication system which the Secretary of State has notified the licensee should not, or as the case may be should cease to, be connected to the Applicable Systems;

(c) any earth orbiting apparatus, provided that:

(i) the relevant requirements, if any, for consultation and compliance with specified operating parameters under the INTELSAT Agreement, INMARSAT Convention and EUTELSAT Convention have been and continue to be satisfied;

(ii) the relevant rules and standards, if any, issued under the INTELSAT Operating Agreement, INMARSAT Operating Agreement and EUTELSAT Operating Agreement have been and continue to be satisfied; and

(iii) it is not earth orbiting apparatus to which the Secretary of State has notified the Licensee that the Licensee should not, or as the case may be should cease to, connect the Applicable Systems;

(d) any telecommunication system run by the Crown;

(e) telecommunication apparatus of every description which is comprised in a telecommunication system mentioned in paragraphs 2(a) to 2(d);

(f) any telecommunication apparatus not comprised in the Applicable Systems which is for the time being Compliant Terminal Equipment or approved for connection to the Applicable Systems in accordance with section 22 of the Act: and

(g) any hearing aid.

Service Authorisation

3. Subject to paragraph 1, this Licence authorises the provision by means of the Applicable Systems of any telecommunication services except:

(a) International Simple Voice Resale Services;

(b)   International Simple Data Resale Services;

(c)   conveyance of Messages for the delivery of one or more of the services specified in paragraphs (a) to (c) of section 72(2) of the Broadcasting Act 1990 for simultaneous reception in two or more Dwelling-Houses;

(d)   conveyance of Messages which have originated in the United Kingdom and are subsequently to be terminated in the United Kingdom, unless:

(i)   such Messages are also to be conveyed over a telecommunications system outside the United Kingdom; or

(ii)   such Messages are conveyed in compliance with any obligations imposed under Condition 2, Condition 3 or Condition 4 in Schedule I of this Licence; and

(e)   any Mobile Radio Tails Service.

Definitions and interpretation
4.   In this Schedule unless the context otherwise requires:

(a)   'Applicable Terminal Equipment' means apparatus which is applicable terminal equipment within the meaning of regulation 4 of the Telecommunications Terminal Equipment Regulations 1992;

(b)   'Compliant Terminal Equipment' means Applicable Terminal Equipment which satisfies the requirements of regulation 8 of the Telecommunications Terminal Equipment Regulations 1992;

(c)   'Dwelling-House' has the same meaning as in section 202 of the Broadcasting Act 1990;

(d)   'EUTELSAT Convention' means the Convention establishing the European Telecommunications Satellite Organisation EUTELSAT including its Preamble and its Annexes, opened for signature by governments at Paris, France on 15 July 1982, and any subsequent amendments made to it;

(e)   'EUTELSAT Operating Agreement' means the Operating Agreement relating to the European Telecommunications Satellite Organisation EUTELSAT, including its Preamble and Annexes, opened for signature at Paris, France on 15 July 1982, and any subsequent amendments made to it;

(f)   'INMARSAT Convention' means the Convention establishing the International Mobile Satellite Organisation (formerly the International Maritime Satellite Organisation) INMARSAT including its Preamble and its Annex, opened for signature by governments at London, England on 3 September 1976, and any subsequent amendments made to it;

(g)   'INMARSAT Operating Agreement' means the Agreement, including its Annex, opened for signature at London, England on 3 September 1976 by entities designated by governments party to the INMARSAT Convention, and any subsequent amendments made to it;

(h)   'INTELSAT Agreement' means the Agreement including its Annexes but excluding all titles of Articles, opened for signature by governments at Washington DC, USA, on 20 August 1971 by which the International Telecommunications Satellite Organisation INTELSAT was established, and any subsequent amendments made to it;

(i)   'International Private Leased Circuit' means a communication facility which is:

(i)   comprised both in a public telecommunication system and in an equivalent telecommunication system in a country or territory other than the United Kingdom;

(ii)   for the conveyance of Messages between points, all of which are points of connection between telecommunication systems referred to in paragraph 4(i)(i) and other telecommunication systems;

(iii)   made available to a particular person or particular persons;

(iv)   such that all of the Messages transmitted at any of the points mentioned in paragraph 4(i)(ii) are received at every other such point; and

(v)   such that the points mentioned in paragraph 4(i)(ii) are fixed by the way in which the facility is installed and cannot otherwise be selected by persons or telecommunication apparatus sending Messages by means of that facility;

(j)   'International Simple Data Resale Services' means telecommunication services consisting in the conveyance of Messages which do not include two-way live speech. but include only such switching, processing, data storage or protocol conversion as is necessary for the conveyance of those Messages in real time, which have been or are to be conveyed by means of all of the following;

(i)   a Public Switched Network;

(ii)   an International Private Leased Circuit; and

(iii)   the equivalent of a Public Switched Network in another country or territory;

provided that conveyance of a Message by means of a Public Switched Network or, as the case may be, the equivalent of a Public Switched Network in another country or territory shall be disregarded where that Message is so conveyed in circumstances specified for the time being by the Secretary of State as not being material for the purposes of paragraph 3 and included in a list kept for the purpose by the Director and made available by him for inspection by the general public:

(k)   'International Simple Voice Resale Services' means telecommunication services consisting in the conveyance of Messages which include two-way live speech which have been or are to be conveyed by means of all of the following:

(i)   a Public Switched Network;

(ii)   an International Private Leased Circuit; and

(iii)   the equivalent of a Public Switched Network in another country or territory;

provided that conveyance of a Message by means of a Public Switched Network or, as the case may be, the equivalent of a Public Switched Network in another country or territory shall be disregarded where that Message is so conveyed in circumstances specified for the time being by the Secretary of State as not being material for the purposes of paragraph 3 and included in a list kept for the purpose by the Director and made available by him for inspection by the general public;

(l)   'Message' means anything falling within paragraphs (a) to (d) of section 4(1) of the Act;

(m)   'Mobile Radio Tails Service' means a telecommunication service consisting in the conveyance of Messages through the agency of Wireless Telegraphy to or from the Applicable Systems directly from or to any apparatus designed or adapted to be capable of being used while in motion;

(n)   'Private Leased Circuit' means a communication facility which is:

(i)   provided by means of one or more public telecommunications systems:

(ii)   for the conveyance of Messages between points, all of which are points of connection between telecommunication systems referred to in paragraph 4(n)(i) and other telecommunication systems;

(iii)   made available to a particular person or particular persons;

(iv)   such that all of the Messages transmitted at any of the points mentioned in paragraph 4(n)(ii) are received at every other such point; and

(v)   such that the points mentioned in paragraph 4(n)(ii) are fixed by the way in which the facility is installed and cannot otherwise be selected by persons or telecommunication apparatus sending Messages by means of that facility;

(o)   'Public Switched Network' means a public telecommunication system by means of which two-way telecommunication services are provided whereby Messages are switched incidentally to their conveyance, and, for the avoidance of doubt, a Public Switched Network does not include Private Leased Circuits or International Private Leased Circuits; and

(p)   'Wireless Telegraphy' has the same meaning as in the Wireless Telegraphy Act 1949.

5.   Expressions cognate with those referred to in this Schedule shall be construed accordingly.

SCHEDULE 4:   EXCEPTIONS AND CONDITIONS RELATING TO THE APPLICATION OF THE TELECOMMUNICATIONS CODE

Definitions and Interpretation

1.   In this Schedule, unless the context otherwise requires:

(a)   'Agricultural' has the meaning given to it by paragraph 1 of Schedule 2 to the Act;

(b)   'Appropriate Authority' means a public authority of a type described in subsection 49(6) or, in Scotland, subsection 108(6) of the New Roads and Street Works Act 1991 or. in Northern Ireland, Article 7(5) of the Street Works (Northern Ireland) Order 1995;

(c)   'The Broads' means the area in which the Broads Authority exercises power of development control;

(d)   'Condition' means a Condition in this Schedule;

(e)   'Cost Price' means the cost of any item of Telecommunication Apparatus, including the full cost of its installation, calculated before any charges for depreciation by the Licensee and modified to take account of any alteration in the CSO Price Index for Buildings and Works since it was installed;

(f)   'Duct' means a structure or apparatus (with appropriate entry points) installed underground in such a way that lines can be installed in it without having to break up the surface of the highway;

(g)   'Emergency' means an emergency of any kind, including any circumstance whatever resulting from major accidents, natural disasters and incidents involving toxic or radio-active materials;

(h)   'Emergency Organisations' means in respect of any locality:

(i)   the relevant public police, fire, ambulance and coastguard services for that locality; and

(ii)   any other similar organisation in respect of which any public telecommunications operator licensed to operate in the locality in question is providing a Public Emergency Call Service on the day on which this Licence enters into force;

(i) 'Emergency Works' has the meaning given to it by section 52 or, in Scotland, section 111 of the New Roads and Street Works Act 1991 or, in Northern Ireland, Article 6 of the Street Works (Northern Ireland) Order 1995;

(j) 'Gross Book Value'. in relation to any period referred to in paragraph 13.3. means the sum of the Cost Price of each piece of Telecommunication Apparatus installed by or on behalf of the Licensee under paragraph 9 of the Telecommunications Code before the beginning of that period;

(k) 'Highway Authority' means, in England and Wales, the highway authority as defined in section 1 of the Highways Act 1980 and, in Northern Ireland, the Department of the Environment for Northern Ireland;

(l) 'Line' has the same meaning as in paragraph (a) of the definition of 'Telecommunication Apparatus' in paragraph 1 of Schedule 2 to the Act;

(m) 'Maintainable Highway' has the meaning given to it by paragraph 1 of Schedule 2 to the Act as amended by paragraph 113(1) of Schedule 8 of the New Roads and Street Works Act 1991, or in the case of Northern Ireland, as amended by paragraph 9(a)(i) of Schedule 3 to the Street Works (Northern Ireland) Order 1995;

(n) 'Major Office' means the Licensee's registered office and such other offices as the Director, having consulted the Licensee, may direct;

(o) 'New Forest' means the area defined in the New Forest Act 1964;

(p) 'Planning Authority' means:

(i) in relation to England and Wales, the local planning authority for the area in question within the meaning of section 1 of the Town and Country Planning Act 1990;

(ii) in relation to Scotland, a planning authority within the meaning of section 172(1) of the Local Government (Scotland) Act 1973; and

(iii) in relation to Northern Ireland, the Department of the Environment for Northern Ireland;

(q) 'Public Emergency Call Services' means a telecommunication service by means of which any member of the public may, at any time and without incurring any charge, by means of any item of telecommunication apparatus which is lawfully connected to the Applicable Systems and which is capable of transmitting and receiving unrestricted two way voice telephony services when so connected, communicate as swiftly as practicable with any of the Emergency Organisations for the purpose of notifying them of an Emergency;

(r) 'Public Road' has the same meaning as in paragraph 1(1) of Schedule 2 to the Act, as amended by the Roads (Scotland) Act 1984 and the New Roads and Street Works Act 1991;

(s) 'Relevant Area' means:

(i) in relation to England and Wales, any area designated as a conservation area under sections 69 and 70 of the Planning (Listed Buildings and Conservation Areas) Act 1990;

(ii) in relation to Scotland, any area designated as a conservation area under section 262 of the Town and Country Planning (Scotland) Act 1972;

(iii) in relation to Northern Ireland, any area designated as a conservation area under Article 50 of the Planning (Northern Ireland) Order 1991; and

(iv) a park within the meaning of the Parks Regulation Acts 1872 to 1974;

(t) 'Relevant Event' means:

(i) the revocation of this Licence;

(ii) where the Licensee is not immediately granted another similar licence to run the Applicable Systems, the expiry of this Licence; or

(iii) any of the events specified in paragraph 1(e) of Schedule 2 to this Licence; provided that paragraph 2 of that Schedule shall have effect for the purposes of this definition as it has for the purposes of paragraph 1 of that Schedule;

(u) 'Relevant Owner' means any person who owns or operates electric lines for the transport of electricity;

(v) 'Relevant Supplier' means in relation to an area in which the Licensee has installed or proposes to install any apparatus the person who is authorised by a licence granted under paragraph (b) or (c) of section 6(1) of the Electricity Act 1989, or in the case of Northern Ireland, under Article 10(1) of the Electricity (Northern Ireland) Order 1992 to transmit or supply electricity;

(w) 'Relevant Undertaker' has the meaning given to it by paragraph 23(10) of Schedule 2 to the Act, and includes persons mentioned in paragraph 23(10)(b) in respect of services and apparatus for the supply of water, or disposal of sewage, and additionally includes any undertaking for the supply of heat;

(x) 'Road' has the meaning given to it in section 107(1) of the New Roads and Street Works Act 1991;

(y) 'Road Works Authority' has the meaning given to it in section 108(1) of the New Roads and Street Works Act 1991;

(z) 'Roads Authority' has the same meaning as in section 151 of the Roads (Scotland) Act 1984;

(aa) 'Service Line' means any line placed or intended to be placed for the purpose of providing any telecommunication service to the occupier from time to time of any land, as distinct from lines placed or intended to be placed for the general purposes of any telecommunication system;

(ab) 'Statutory List of Buildings' is the list of buildings of special architectural or historic interest compiled by the Secretary of State under section 1(1) of the Planning (Listed Buildings and Conservation Areas) Act 1990 or under section 52 of the Town and Country Planning (Scotland) Act 1972 or in the case of Northern Ireland, compiled by the Department of the Environment for Northern Ireland under Article 42 of the Planning (Northern Ireland) Order 1991;

(ac) 'Street' has the meaning given to it by paragraph 1 of Schedule 2 to the Act, as amended by paragraph 113(1) of Schedule 8 of the New Roads and Street Works Act 1991, or in the case of Northern Ireland, as amended by paragraph 9(a)(ii) of Schedule 3 to the Street Works (Northern Ireland) Order 1995;

(ad) 'Street Authority' has the meaning given to it by section 49 of the New Roads and Street Works Act 1991, or in Northern Ireland by Article 7 of the Street Works (Northern Ireland) Order 1995;

(ae) 'Telecommunication Apparatus' shall have the extended meaning given to it by paragraph 1(1) of Schedule 2 to the Act;

(af) 'Traffic Authority' has the same meaning as in the Road Traffic Regulation Act 1984, or in Northern Ireland means the Department of the Environment for Northern Ireland; and

(ag) 'Urgent Works' in relation to England, Wales and Northern Ireland, has the meaning given in regulation 2 of the Street Works (Registers, Notices, Directions and Designations) Regulations 1992 and, in relation to Scotland, has the meaning given in regulation 2 of the Road Works (Registers, Notices, Directions and Designations) (Scotland) Regulations 1992.

2.   Any word or expression used in this Schedule shall unless the context otherwise requires have the same meaning as it has in the Act.

3.   For the purposes of interpreting this Schedule headings and titles shall be disregarded.

4.   For the avoidance of doubt, it is hereby declared that the conditions in this Schedule apply in addition to any obligations of the Licensee in relation to England, Wales and Scotland under the New Roads and Street Works Act 1991 and the Public Utilities Street Works Act 1950, insofar as not superseded by the New Roads and Street Works Act 1991, and in relation to Northern Ireland under the Street Works (Northern Ireland) Order 1995.

5.   Expressions cognate with those referred to in this Schedule shall be construed accordingly.

Condition 1   Conservation Areas

1.1   Subject to paragraph 1.2 and except in the case of Emergency Works, any Line installed by the Licensee after the date on which this Licence enters into force in any Relevant Area shall be installed underground and no pole shall be installed in any such area after that date.

1.2   Notwithstanding paragraph 1.1, nothing in this Condition shall prevent the installation on or above the ground of:

(a)   a Line or pole required temporarily for the purpose of Emergency Works;

(b)   a Line flown between poles or pylons belonging to a Relevant Owner and used by that Relevant Owner for the transport of electricity at a nominal voltage of at least 6,000 volts;

(c)   an overhead Service Line flown from a pole installed:

(i)   before the area was designated a conservation area; or

(ii)   under paragraphs 1.2(f) or 1.2(g),

provided that the Line is of not noticeably larger diameter than that of the majority of the Licensee's overhead Service Lines in the same locality;

(d)   an overhead Service Line flown from a building in a locality where overhead Service Lines attached to poles or buildings are already installed in adjacent streets or on neighbouring land by the Licensee for the purpose of providing telecommunication services, provided that the Line is of a not noticeably larger diameter than that of the majority of such other overhead Service Lines;

(e)   any other Line replacing an existing Line provided that the replacement Line is of a not noticeably larger diameter than that of the Line it replaces;

(f)   a replacement pole in a position not substantially different from the pole it replaces;

(g)   subject to paragraph 1.3, a pole (other than one mentioned in paragraph 1.2(f)) in a street or on neighbouring land where overhead Service Lines attached to poles are already installed by the Licensee in that street or on that neighbouring land for the purpose of providing telecommunication services; or

(h)   a Service Line affixed to and lying on the surface of the exterior structure of a building provided that the Line is of a not noticeably larger diameter than the majority of Service Lines affixed to and lying on the surface of the exterior structures of buildings in the same locality.

1.3   Before installing a pole under paragraph 1.2(g) the Licensee shall give the Planning Authority written notice of its intention to do so describing the proposed works and shall consider any written representations made by the Planning Authority within 28 days of the giving of the notice.

Condition 2   Listed Buildings and Ancient Monuments

2.1   Except in the case of Emergency Works, the Licensee shall before installing Lines, poles or other Telecommunication Apparatus in proximity to a building shown as Grade 1 or, as the case may be, Category A in the Statutory List of Buildings give written notice to the Planning Authority. Where the installation would detrimentally affect the character or appearance of the building, or its setting, and the Planning Authority indicates within 28 days of the giving of the notice that the installation should not take place, the Licensee may install the Apparatus only if the Secretary of State (after having consulted the Planning Authority) so directs in writing, or with the agreement of the Planning Authority.

2.2   For the avoidance of doubt it is hereby declared that nothing in this Licence affects:

(a)   the statutory requirement that the consent of the Secretary of State or, in the case of Northern Ireland, the Department of the Environment (NI), shall be obtained before any work is carried out which will affect the site of an ancient monument scheduled under Sections 1 and 2 of the Ancient Monuments and Archaelogical Areas Act 1979 or Article 3 of the Historic Monuments and Archaeological Objects (NI) Order 1995; or

(b)   the obligation imposed on the Licensee by virtue of section 7 of the Planning (Listed Buildings and Conservation Areas) Act 1990 (or by section 53 of the Town and Country Planning (Scotland) Act 1972 or by Article 44 of the Planning (Northern Ireland) Order 1991) to obtain listed building consent for any works which affect the character of a listed building, or involve the demolition of any part of such a building.

Condition 3   Overhead Lines

3.1   Without prejudice to Condition 1.1 and subject to paragraph 3.4, the Licensee shall take steps to ensure that, wherever practicable, taking into account the need to provide telecommunication services at the lowest reasonable cost, new Lines (other than overhead Service Lines flown from poles) installed after the date on which this Licence enters into force are installed underground.

3.2   The Licensee shall consider carefully a request by any person that any of its existing Lines be resited underground. If the Licensee is satisfied that the person making the request will pay the costs of placing any such Line underground, the Licensee shall, wherever it is reasonable and practicable, so place the Line. In other cases, except where the request is frivolous, the Licensee shall be obliged within 28 days of receiving it, to give notice in writing of its decision whether or not to accede to the request to the person making the request giving, where it decides to refuse, reasons.

3.3   Where telecommunication services are to be provided to a person occupying or proposing to occupy a new development the Licensee shall consider in conjunction with those responsible for the development and any other statutory undertaker providing or proposing to provide a service to persons occupying that development whether Lines can be installed underground on a shared cost basis.

3.4   Nothing in this Condition or Condition 4 shall prevent the Licensee from installing new overhead Telecommunication Apparatus where that Apparatus is supported on poles or pylons belonging to a Relevant Owner and used by that Relevant Owner for the transport of electricity at a nominal voltage of at least 6,000 volts.

Condition 4   National Parks etc

4.1   Subject to paragraph 4.2 and to Condition 3.4, and except in the case of Emergency Works, before installing overhead Telecommunication Apparatus in any National Park, Area of Outstanding Natural Beauty, National Nature Reserve, National Scenic Area, the New Forest, or the Broads, and before installing any Apparatus or undertaking any works involving the breaking up of any land within any Limestone Pavement Area, Site of Special Scientific Interest, Area of Special Scientific Interest, Marine Nature Reserve or Natural Heritage Area, the Licensee shall give the Relevant Authority written notice of its intention to do so describing the proposed works.

4.2   Where:

(a)   the Licensee has given notice of proposed works in accordance with paragraph 4.1; and

(b)   the Relevant Authority has, within 28 days of the giving of the notice, made written representations to the Licensee about the proposed works,

the Licensee shall consider those representations and if it considers that, notwithstanding those representations, the proposed works which are the subject of that notice should be carried out in the form proposed in that notice or with modifications to take account of those representations it shall, before carrying out the proposed works, give written notice to the Relevant Authority of its intentions to carry out the proposed works and of the modifications, if any, of the proposed works and the reasons for its decision to do so.

4.3   The Licensee shall also comply with any direction given to it in writing by the Secretary of State or, in the case of Northern Ireland, the Department of the Environment (NI), relating to giving notice to and considering representations made by any other authority exercising statutory functions in relation to any of the areas specified in paragraph 4.1 or such other environmentally sensitive areas as may be specified in the direction.

4.4   The Licensee shall not be required to give notice pursuant to paragraph 4.1 where the Apparatus to be installed consists solely of, or where works are to be undertaken on Apparatus consisting solely of:

(a)   an overhead Service Line affixed to and lying on the surface of the exterior structure of a building or flown from a pole provided that the line is of a not noticeably larger diameter than that of the majority of such overhead Service Lines in the same locality; or

(b)   a replacement pole installed in a position not substantially different from the pole it replaces

but in carrying out any such installation or works as are referred to in this paragraph the Licensee shall have regard to the need to liaise effectively with the Relevant Authority.

4.5   In this Condition:

(a)   in relation to England, Wales and Scotland:

(i)   'National Park' and 'Area of Outstanding Natural Beauty' respectively mean any area designated and confirmed as such under section 5 or section 87 of the National Parks and Access to the Countryside Act 1949; and the Relevant Authority in relation thereto shall be the Planning Authority;

(ii)   'Site of Special Scientific Interest' means an area designated as such under section 28 of the Wildlife and Countryside Act 1981 or an area in respect of which the Secretary of State has made an order under section 29 of that Act. In both cases the Relevant Authority in respect of any such area shall be: in England, English Nature, established under the Environmental Protection Act 1990; in Scotland, Scottish Natural Heritage, established under the Natural Heritage (Scotland) Act 1991; and in Wales, the Countryside Council for Wales, established under the Environmental Protection Act 1990;

(iii)   'Limestone Pavement Area' means an area designated by the Secretary of State or relevant authority under section 34 of the Wildlife and Countryside Act 1981; and the Relevant Authority in England and Wales is the Planning Authority and in Scotland is the Planning Authority exercising district planning functions;

(iv)   'National Scenic Area' means any area in Scotland designated as such under the Town and Country (Planning) Scotland Act 1972; and the Relevant Authority in relation thereto is Scottish Natural Heritage, established under the Natural Heritage (Scotland) Act 1991;

(v)   'Marine Nature Reserve' means an area designated by the Secretary of State under section 36 of the Wildlife and Countryside Act 1981. The Relevant Authority in relation thereto shall be in England, English Nature, established under the Environmental Protection Act 1990; in Scotland, Scottish Natural Heritage, established under the Natural Heritage (Scotland) Act 1991; and in Wales, the Countryside Council for Wales, established under the Environmental Protection Act 1990; and

(vi)   'Natural Heritage Area' means any area in Scotland designated as such under the Natural Heritage (Scotland) Act 1991 and the Relevant Authority in relation thereto shall be Scottish Natural Heritage, established under that Act; and

(b)   in relation to Northern Ireland:

(i)   'National Park' means any area designated as such under Article 12(1) of the Nature Conservation and Amenity Lands (NI) Order 1985 (SI 1985/170 (NI 1)); and the Relevant Authority in relation thereto shall be the Department of the Environment for Northern Ireland; and

(ii) 'Area of Outstanding Natural Beauty' means any area established in accordance with Section 10 of the Amenity Lands Act (Northern Ireland) 1965 or designated under Article 14(1) of the Nature Conservation and Amenity Lands (NI) Order 1985 (SI 1985/170 (NI 1)); and the Relevant Authority in relation thereto shall be the Department of the Environment for Northern Ireland; and

(iii) 'Area of Special Scientific Interest' means an area designated under Article 24(1) of the Nature Conservation and Amenity Lands (NI) Order 1985 (S.I. 1985/170 (NI 1)) as amended by Article 10 of the Nature Conservation and Amenity Lands (Amendment) (NI) Order 1989, as amended by Article 10 of the Nature Conservation and Amenity Lands (Amendment) (NI) Order 1989 (SI 1989/492 (NI 3)); and the Relevant Authority in relation thereto means the Department of the Environment for Northern Ireland; and

(iv) 'National Nature Reserve' means any land declared to be a national nature reserve under Article 18(1) of the Nature Conservation and Amenity Lands (NI) Order 1985 (SI 1985/170 (NI 1)); and the Relevant Authority in relation thereto shall be the Department of the Environment for Northern Ireland.

Condition 5   National Trust and National Trust for Scotland

5.1   Except in the case of Emergency Works, before installing any Telecommunication Apparatus for the purpose of providing a service to the occupier of any land which the National Trust or the National Trust for Scotland has notified the Licensee that it owns, or holds any interest in, the Licensee shall give the relevant regional office of whichever of those bodies is concerned written notice of its intention to do so, describing the proposed works; and shall consider any written representations made within 28 days of the giving of such notice to it by either of those bodies.

Condition 6   Maintainable Highways and Public Roads

6.1   Except in the case of Emergency Works or Urgent Works, before executing any works involving the breaking up of a Maintainable Highway or, in Scotland, a Public Road in connection with the installation, inspection, maintenance, adjustment, repair or alteration of any Telecommunication Apparatus in that Highway or that Road the Licensee shall:

(a) in the case of an overhead Line or an underground Service Line, consider any written representations made by the Highway Authority or, in Scotland, the Road Works Authority within seven working days after the giving of any such notice as is required to be given, in England and Wales, to the Highway Authority under section 55 of the New Roads and Street Works Act 1991 or, in Scotland, to the Road Works Authority under section 114 of the New Roads and Street Works Act 1991 or, in Northern Ireland, to the Highway Authority under paragraphs 1(3) and 3(2)(a) of Schedule 3 to the Electricity Supply (NI) Order 1972 as amended by the Telecommunications (Street Works) (NI) Order 1984;

(b) in all other cases. consider any such written representations made within 29 days of the giving of any such notice; and

(c) unless the Highway Authority or, in Scotland, the Road Works Authority consents otherwise, shall not commence those works until the expiry of seven working days or 29 days as the case may be.

Condition 7 Placing of Underground Lines in Ducts

7.1 All lines installed underground after the date on which this Licence enters into force, in a part of a Maintainable Highway which is paved or in a Street which the Highway Authority has notified the Licensee is to be paved, shall, whenever practicable, be installed in Ducts.

7.2 In Scotland, all lines installed underground after the date on which this Licence enters into force, in a part of a Road which is paved or in a Road which the Road Works Authority has notified the Licensee is to be paved, shall, whenever practicable, be installed in Ducts.

Condition 8 Height of Overhead Lines

8.1 Lines installed over the carriageway of a Maintainable Highway or, in Scotland, a Public Road shall be placed at a height of not less than 5.5 metres above the carriageway (or in the case of a designated high load route not less than 6.7 metres), except where the Highway Authority or, in Scotland, the Roads Authority has previously otherwise agreed in writing.

Condition 9 Maintenance and the Safety of Apparatus

9.1 The Licensee shall from time to time inspect its Telecommunication Apparatus which is not inside a building and which is on or above the surface of the ground with a view to ensuring that it will not cause physical harm to other persons or property; and the Licensee shall notify the Director and the Highway Authority of its arrangements for inspecting such Apparatus.

9.2 In addition to carrying out inspections of its own Apparatus on or above the surface of the ground the Licensee shall take such steps as are appropriate in the circumstances to investigate any report (other than a frivolous one) of any of its Apparatus (wherever situated) being in a dangerous state and to remove any danger.

Condition 10 Arrangements with Electricity Suppliers

10.1 Before exercising any rights under the Telecommunications Code in the authorised area of any Relevant Supplier, the Licensee shall use its best endeavours to enter into an agreement with that Relevant Supplier as to the engineering principles to be adopted and the allocation and apportionment of costs which arise:

(a) when the Licensee installs and keeps installed apparatus in proximity to plant which is already installed and which is the responsibility of a Relevant Supplier; and

(b) when a Relevant Supplier gives notice to the Licensee that it proposes to install its plant in proximity to any of the Licensee's apparatus which is already installed.

10.2 The Licensee shall:

(a)   within three months of this Licence coming into force; and

(b)   after the expiry of the period of three months beginning on the date when this Licence comes into force, within three months of the commencement of any negotiations for the making of any such agreement as is mentioned in paragraph 10.1,

inform the Director of the steps taken to implement paragraph 10.1 and of the terms of any agreement entered into by it with the Relevant Supplier.

10.3   Where the Licensee has not offered to enter into such an agreement as is mentioned in paragraph 10.1 being an agreement which makes reasonable provision for securing that:

(a)   the Licensee will, when installing its apparatus in proximity to plant of the Relevant Supplier which is already installed, protect its apparatus from electrical interference from that plant; and

(b)   the Relevant Supplier will, when installing its plant in proximity to apparatus of the Licensee which is already installed, protect that apparatus of the Licensee from electrical interference from that plant,

the Licensee shall only install apparatus of such a kind and in such a position as will not be adversely affected by or of itself adversely affects any plant of the Relevant Supplier which is already installed.

10.4   In this Condition, the words 'authorised area' have the meaning ascribed to them in section 6(9) of the Electricity Act 1989 and, in Northern Ireland, Article 3 of the Electricity (NI) Order 1991.

Condition 11   Instructions for the Installation of Apparatus

11.1   Without prejudice to any of its statutory obligations the Licensee shall take all reasonable steps to secure (in particular by giving instructions to its employees and agents) that:

(a)   where apparatus is to be installed underground in a Street or, in Scotland, a Road, the normal practice will be to place it in the verge or footway (or the prospective verge or footway), if any, rather than the carriageway;

(b)   provision is made for any new Ducts installed after the date on which this Licence comes into effect to contain sufficient spare capacity to meet demand which is reasonably foreseeable by the Licensee for telecommunication services provided by it;

(c)   where apparatus is to be installed underground in a Street or, in Scotland, a Road the Street Authority or, in Scotland, the Road Works Authority and Relevant Undertakers are consulted about the appropriate depth of cover for the apparatus and its lateral position in that Street or Road, as the case may be;

(d)   effective liaison is maintained with Highway Authorities or, in Scotland, Road Authorities with a view to ensuring that works which entail breaking up the surface of a Maintainable Highway or, in Scotland, a Public Road are carried out in advance of scheduled resurfacing works or together with other schemes affecting the highway;

(e)   effective liaison is maintained with Relevant Undertakers with a view to avoiding the disruption of the services provided by those persons;

(f)   effective liaison is maintained with the Street Authority or, in Scotland, the Road Works Authority in order to ensure that

(i)   all works are executed in accordance with the provisions of and made under sections 65 to 69 or, in Scotland, sections 124 to 128 of the New Roads and Street Works Act 1991 or, in Northern Ireland, Schedule 3 to the Electricity Supply NI) Order 1972 as amended by the Telecommunications (Street Works) (NI) Order 1984; and

(ii)   following the execution of the works, the Licensee discharges its duties of reinstatement of the Street under sections 70 to 73 or, in Scotland, sections 129 to 132 of the New Roads and Street Works Act 1991 or, in Northern Ireland, paragraphs 1 to 5 of Schedule 3 to the Electricity Supply (NI) Order 1972 as amended by the Telecommunications (Street Works) (NI) Order 1984; and

(iii)   in England and Wales the Street Works Register or, in Scotland. the Road Works Register contains such information in respect of the works carried out as may be required under section 53 or, in Scotland, section 112 of the New Roads and Street Works Act 1991;

(g)   with a view to reducing to a minimum the need for the erection of new poles or the construction of new Ducts, before installing any such poles or Ducts steps will be taken to investigate the possibility of using poles, Ducts or other conduits which are already installed;

(h)   the minimum practicable number of poles and other items of apparatus is installed, allowing for estimated growth in demand for telecommunication services;

(i)   the visual amenity of properties (in particular buildings in the Statutory List of Buildings which have been notified by the Planning Authority to the Licensee as deserving special consideration) in proximity to which poles or other items of apparatus are installed is protected as far as practicable;

(j)   Telecommunication Apparatus is placed so that it does not present safety hazards;

(k)   underground Lines to be installed in Agricultural land are installed at such a depth that they will not interfere with the use of the land for Agricultural purposes, unless the occupier, any superior lessee and the freeholder agree otherwise; and

(l)   effective liaison is maintained with the Planning Authority in respect of the arrangements for the installation of Telecommunication Apparatus in Local Nature Reserves designated under section 21 of the National Parks and Access to the Countryside Act 1949.

11.2   The Licensee shall within three months of the date on which this Licence enters into force, and thereafter from time to time as the Director may require, furnish details to the Director of the instructions given in accordance with paragraph 11.1.

11.3   The requirement specified in paragraph 11.1(i) is without prejudice to Condition 2.1.

Condition 12   Records of Apparatus

12.1   The Licensee shall keep records of any of its apparatus installed underground after the date on which this Licence enters into force which can be made available in the form of route plans based on Ordnance Survey map backgrounds of one of the following scales (1:500, 1:625, 1:1.250, 1:2,500, 1:10,000) according to the density of development in the area concerned.

12.2   The Licensee shall provide by means of a telecommunication system free of charge, to any Highway Authority or, in Scotland, any Roads Authority or other person who is intending to undertake works in the vicinity of any Telecommunication Apparatus it has installed underground, a service furnishing information about the location of that Apparatus and shall whenever practicable:

(a)   respond to bona fide enquiries; and

(b)   where necessary confirm its advice in diagrammatic form and make trained staff available to give on-site advice about such Apparatus so installed, and shall also respond to any other reasonable request from a Highway Authority or, in Scotland, a Roads Authority, for information about the location of the Licensee's apparatus installed underground.

12.3   The Licensee shall co-operate in any joint projects involving the Highway Authority or, in Scotland, the Roads Authority or Relevant Undertakers which have as their purpose the recording and making available of information about underground apparatus, unless the Director agrees that it would be inappropriate having regard to its existing practice in the area concerned for it to do so.

Condition 13   Funds for Meeting Liabilities

13.1   Subject to paragraph 13.3 the Licensee shall make arrangements which are adequate to ensure that sufficient funds are available after the Relevant Event occurs for meeting the liabilities described in paragraph 13.2 which have arisen on or before the date on which that Event occurred or may arise thereafter from the exercise of rights conferred upon the Licensee by paragraph 9 of the Telecommunications Code.

13.2   The liabilities referred to in paragraph 13.1 are:

(a)   liabilities, including those for the payment of indemnities in respect of costs or expenses incurred, or arising under the New Roads and Street Works Act 1991 towards:

(i)   any Appropriate Authority, Traffic Authority or other responsible authority under that Act;

(ii)   any other person having authority to execute works in, or having apparatus in, a Street;

(iii)   any concessionaire within the meaning of section 1 of that Act;

(b)   any other costs or expenses reasonably incurred by any Appropriate Authority or other responsible authority in making good any damage caused by the installation or removal of Telecommunication Apparatus, whether such damage occurs before or after the Relevant Event;

(c)   any other costs or expenses reasonably incurred by any Appropriate Authority or other responsible authority after the Relevant Event occurs in removing any Telecommunication Apparatus:

(i)   which is installed under, over, along or across a Street;

(ii)   which is not, or is no longer, used for the purposes of any telecommunication system and in relation to which there is no reasonable likelihood that it will be so used; and

(iii)   the removal of which is desirable having regard to any harm it may cause to other persons or property, or to the visual amenity of properties in proximity to which the Apparatus is installed.

13.3   The funds available under paragraph 13.1 shall include, in relation
to the period extending from the date on which this Licence enters into force
until 31 March 1997 and, thereafter, in relation to every period of one year
beginning on 1 April:
-   (a)   an amount which is equal to:
    -   (i)   10 per cent of the Gross Book Value; or
    -   (ii)   £1,000,000,

whichever is the lesser, or such greater amount as the Director may direct; and
-   (b)   an amount which, having regard to any works begun by the
Licensee before the beginning of the period in question, is sufficient to meet
any liabilities of the kinds described in paragraph 13.2(a) which may arise.

13.4   The Licensee shall:
-   (a)   within three months of this Licence coming into force; and
-   (b)   once a year thereafter,

inform the Director of the steps taken to implement this Condition.

13.5   Where:
-   (a)   the Licensee has failed to inform the Director in accordance with
paragraph 13.4; or
-   (b)   the Director is not satisfied that the arrangements made by the
Licensee are adequate to secure that sufficient funds are available after the
Relevant Event occurs for meeting the liabilities described in paragraph 13.1

the Director may direct the Licensee to take such steps as the Director
considers appropriate for the purpose of securing that such sufficient funds
are available and the Licensee shall comply with any such direction.

Condition 14   Emergency Works and Urgent Works

14.1   Without prejudice to the duties of the Licensee under sections 55,
57 and 93 or, in Scotland, sections 116 and 152 of the New Roads and Street
Works Act 1991 or, in Northern Ireland, paragraphs 6 and 6A of Schedule 3
to the Electricity Supply (NI) Order 1972 as amended by the Telecommunications (Street Works) (NI) Order 1984 concerning the giving of notice in
respect of Emergency Works or Urgent Works, the Licensee shall provide, in
addition to the information contained in any such notice, a reasonable
estimate of the date by which the Emergency Works or the Urgent Works are
expected to be completed and a statement of the grounds for the need to
execute those Emergency Works or Urgent Works, as the case may be.

Condition 15   Public Events and Construction Sites

15.1   Where the Licensee is to provide telecommunication services for a
limited period at the site of a public event or a construction site, it may install
overhead Lines and associated poles to provide that service notwithstanding
Conditions 1, 2, 4 and 5, provided that the Lines or poles are removed within
a reasonable period after the end of the event or after the work at the
construction site is complete.

Condition 16   Emergency Organisations

16.1   Where the Licensee is to provide any telecommunication service for
a limited period to an Emergency Organisation in an Emergency it may,

notwithstanding Conditions 1, 2, 4, 5, 6 and 8, install overhead Lines and associated poles for the purposes of providing such services as are made necessary by the Emergency provided that any such line or pole is removed within a reasonable period after such services cease to be required.

SPECIFICATION BY THE SECRETARY OF STATE FOR THE PURPOSES OF PARAGRAPHS 1 (s) AND 1 (t) OF SCHEDULE 1 AND PARAGRAPHS 4 (j) AND 4 (k) OF SCHEDULE 3 TO THE LICENCE GRANTED TO UNISOURCE HOLDING (UK) LIMITED ON 18 DECEMBER 1996

1. The Secretary of State in accordance with paragraphs 1 (s) and 1 (t) of Schedule 1 and paragraphs 4 (j) and 4 (k) of Schedule 3 to the Licence granted to Unisource Holding (UK) Limited under section 7 of the Telecommunications Act 1984 on 18 December 1996 (the 'Licence') hereby specifies that the circumstances in paragraph 2 below are not material for the purposes of paragraph 3 of Schedule 3 to the Licence.

2. The circumstances referred to in paragraph 1 above are those where a Message is so conveyed from or to a telecommunication system by means of which that Message is initially sent or received exclusively for the purpose of carrying out such initial or final switching of that Message as could lawfully have been carried out by the person running that system, or another on that person's behalf, under the Class Licence for the Running of Self Provided Telecommunication Systems granted by the Secretary of State under section 7 of the Telecommunications Act 1984 on 9 September 1996 and any successors to that licence on the premises where that Message was initially sent or, as the case may be, ultimately received.

3. In this specification words and phrases shall have the same meaning as in the Licence.

Iain Osborne
For the Secretary of State
18 December 1996

SPECIFICATION BY THE SECRETARY OF STATE FOR THE PURPOSES OF CONDITIONS 15 AND 16 OF THE LICENCE GRANTED TO UNISOURCE HOLDING (UK) LIMITED ON 18 DECEMBER 1996

1. The Secretary of State in accordance with paragraph 15 1 of Condition 15 and paragraph 16.1 of Condition 16 of Schedule 1 to the Licence granted to Unisource Holding (UK) Limited under section 7 of the Telecommunications Act 1984 on 18 December 1996 (the 'Licence') hereby specifies that the provisions of Conditions 15 and 16 to Schedule 1 shall not apply in respect of the countries and territories listed below:

Australia	Finland
Austria	France
Belgium	Germany
Canada	Gibraltar
Denmark	Greece

Iceland	New Zealand
Ireland	Norway
Italy	Portugal
Liechtenstein	Spain
Luxembourg	Sweden
Netherlands	United States of America.

2.   In this specification words and phrases shall have the same meaning as in the Licence.

Iain Osborne
For the Secretary of State
18 December 1996

Note
This list may change from time to time.

INTERCONNECT AGREEMENT

STANDARD INTERCONNECT AGREEMENT BETWEEN # [OPERATOR] AND BRITISH TELECOMMUNICATIONS PLC

DATED # 199

INDEX

SPECIFICATIONS

Generic Electrical & Physical Interface Specification
Generic C7 Signalling Interface Specification
Generic Transmission Interface Specification
Generic SDH Interface Specification

ANNEXES

Annex A   Planning and Operations
Annex B   Billing and Payment
Annex C   Schedules
Annex D   Definitions

Notes
1. This is a standard template interconnect agreement which is required to be published by BT under Condition 13 of their licence.
2. The Specifications and Annexes have been excluded from the Handbook.
3. BT may be required to review this agreement as a result of modifications to its licence, for example, in relation to Network Charges from 1997.

THIS AGREEMENT is made the # day of # [month] 199
between
[Operator] registered in England No. # [number] having its registered office at # [address]
and
BRITISH TELECOMMUNICATIONS public limited company registered in England No. 1800000 having its registered office at 81 Newgate Street, London, EC1A 7AJ.
Whereas
    A   A licence was granted to the Operator on # [date] under section 7 of the Telecommunications Act 1984 to run the Operator System.
    B   A licence was granted to British Telecommunications on 22 June 1984 under section 7 of the Telecommunications Act 1984 to run its telecommunication system and pursuant to paragraph 20 of schedule 5 to such Act such licence has effect as if granted to BT to run the BT System.
    C   The Parties have agreed to connect the Operator System to the BT System and to the supply of services and facilities, on the terms and conditions of this Agreement.

IT IS AGREED as follows:

1.   Definitions and Interpretation

    1.1   In this Agreement, except if the context requires otherwise, words and expressions are as defined in Annex D.

1.2   The Interpretation Act 1978 shall apply for the purpose of interpreting this Agreement as if this Agreement were an Act of Parliament.

1.3   The following documents form part of this Agreement and, in the event of any inconsistencies between them, the order of precedence shall (unless expressly stated to the contrary) be as follows:

1. main body of this Agreement
2. Annex D
3. Annexes A and B
4. Specifications
5. Annex C
6. Carrier Price List

1.4   It is hereby expressly agreed that the Manuals, the Technical Master Plan and the Customer Service Plan are not legally binding.

2.   Commencement and Duration

2.1   This Agreement takes effect on the date hereof and shall continue until:

2.1.1   either Party ceases to hold a licence granted to it pursuant to section 7 of the Act to run a Telecommunication System; or

2.1.2   termination pursuant to this Agreement.

2.2   A Party may terminate this Agreement by giving at any time to the other not less than 24 months' written notice to terminate.

2.3   After a notice has been given pursuant to paragraph 2.2 a Party may request the other Party to carry on good faith negotiations with a view to entering into a new agreement.

2.4   Following a request pursuant to paragraph 2.3, if, on termination of this Agreement either Party would be obliged under its Licence to enter into a new interconnection agreement with the other Party then the Parties shall carry on good faith negotiations with a view to entering into a new agreement to take effect on termination of this Agreement.

3.   Interconnection and Standards

3.1   The Parties shall connect and keep connected the BT System and the Operator System at Points of Connection using Customer Sited Interconnect or In-span Interconnect in accordance with this Agreement (to such extent permitted by the Operator Licence).

3.2   If this Agreement does not contain a Schedule for the joint provision by the Parties of In-span Interconnect and BT notifies the Operator that BT requires Capacity between particular Switch Connections on a particular date, the Operator shall include such Capacity in its next Capacity Profile. The Operator shall place a Capacity Order in a timely manner for such Capacity by way of Customer Sited Interconnect between the same Switch Connections, being an order for not less than the Capacity required by BT. No such Capacity Order shall be cancelled nor any resulting Interconnect Link rearranged by the Operator without BT's written consent. The provisions relating to payment for duct for such Interconnect Links shall not apply and the Capacity by way of Customer Sited Interconnect provided pursuant to this paragraph shall, unless otherwise agreed, be used solely for Traffic Types for which BT has responsibility pursuant to Annex A.

3.3   Each Party shall comply with the Specifications in so far as they apply to the provision of services pursuant to this Agreement.

3.4   In the practical implementation of the Specifications relating to the interconnection of the BT System and the Operator System the Parties shall apply standards and operating guidelines which in the first instance have due regard to the following in the order of precedence specified below:

3.4.1   any legal requirements imposed upon each of them including requirements arising from Condition 13B of the BT Licence and the equivalent Condition of the Operator Licence; and

3.4.2   any relevant specification notified by the Director General in implementation of the recommendations of the NICC; and

3.4.3   any recommendations by ETSI; and

3.4.4   any recommendations by ITU-T; and

3.4.5   the GSM memorandum of understanding (where applicable).

4.   System Alteration

4.1   A Party wishing to make a System Alteration shall give to the other Party not less than 7 months' written notice prior to the date of the anticipated System Alteration. The notice shall specify the technical details of the System Alteration and the date of the anticipated System Alteration. Following such notification each Party shall supply to the other such information as the other may reasonably request including in the case of the Party giving the notice, to the extent reasonably practicable, the potential impact on the other Party's System.

4.2   The Party receiving the notice pursuant to paragraph 4.1 shall notify the other as soon as practicable, but in any event not more than one month after receipt of such notice, of any alterations required to that Party's System as a result of the proposed System Alteration and, if the provisions in paragraph 4.6 do not apply, a quotation for the cost of such alterations calculated on the basis of the minimum cost consistent with good engineering practice.

4.3   If the Party giving the notice pursuant to paragraph 4.1 agrees the alterations required to the other Party's System and agrees the quotation (if any), the Parties shall agree a plan within three months of receipt of the notice referred to in paragraph 4.2 to implement the System Alteration and the other Party shall carry out such alterations in accordance with the agreed plan.

4.4   If the provisions in paragraph 4.6 do not apply, and if the Party giving the notice pursuant to paragraph 4.1 does not agree the alterations required and/or the quotation (if any), that Party shall so notify the other Party, and the Parties agree to treat the matter as a Dispute. The Party giving the notice pursuant to paragraph 4.1 shall not implement the relevant System Alteration until the Dispute is resolved.

4.5   On completion of the relevant alteration the Party receiving the notice pursuant to paragraph 4.1 shall invoice the other Party for such alteration for an amount not exceeding the agreed quotation.

4.6   Each Party shall pay its own costs arising out of the System Alteration if:

4.6.1   the Parties agree in writing to change their respective Systems for their mutual benefit; or

4.6.2   the System Alteration is lawfully directed by the Director General who also lawfully directs each Party to pay its own costs; or

4.6.3   the System Alteration is unanimously agreed by NICC; or

4.6.4   the altering Party is BT and the System Alteration is a change to the signalling system, which change is consistent with an upgrade path agreed by NICC.

4.7   The Parties shall amend the Specifications prior to a System Alteration.

4.8   If a Party makes a System Alteration it shall ensure that Calls handed over from the other Party are not prevented to any greater extent or hindered in any manner different from the generality of Calls made by the altering Party's Customers.

5. Scope

5.1   The Parties shall convey Calls and provide the services and facilities pursuant to the Schedules.

5.2   For the avoidance of doubt and notwithstanding the interconnection of the BT System and the Operator System neither Party shall hand over to the other Party, nor have an obligation to convey Calls of any category, unless the other Party has agreed to convey Calls of that category and there is express provision to convey Calls of that category in a Schedule.

5.3   Neither Party shall be obliged to provide or be entitled to access Ancillary Services unless there is express provision for the particular Ancillary Service in a Schedule.

6. Quality of Service

6.1   BT shall use reasonable endeavours to meet the Target Performance, applicable at the time of provision of the relevant Standard Service, specified in the Quality Schedule.

7. Transfer Charge Calls

7.1   If having been allocated an entire NNG the Operator has the exclusive use of that NNG and requests BT not to offer Transfer Charge Calls to Operator Customers on such NNG then subject to the Operator:

7.1.1   taking reasonable steps to ensure that Operator Customers on such NNGs do not accept or agree to pay for Transfer Charge Calls; and

7.1.2   giving BT written notice that the Operator does not wish Transfer Charge Calls to be conveyed to the relevant NNG;

BT shall instruct BT Operators not to make available Transfer Charge Calls to Operator Customers on such NNG, request operators of Authorised Overseas Systems not to make available Transfer Charge Calls to Operator Customers on such NNG, and request Third Parties who run Telecommunication Systems that provide public switched telephony within the United Kingdom pursuant to licences granted under the Act, other than licences available to classes of persons, not to make available Transfer Charge Calls to Operator Customers on such NNG.

7.2   If the Operator has complied with the provisions of paragraph 7.1, the Operator shall be released from any obligation to pay for Transfer Charge

Calls conveyed to the relevant NNG 28 Working Days after the date of receipt of the notice pursuant to paragraph 7.1.2.

7.3   If BT releases the Operator from the obligation to pay for any Transfer Charge Call pursuant to paragraph 7.2, the Operator shall release BT from the obligation to pay the Operator for the conveyance of such Call unless the Call was connected by the BT Operator.

8.   New Services

8.1   Either Party may, at any time, request from the other Party an agreement to interconnect their respective Systems for the provision of any service or facility which the other Party provides under interconnection agreements to Third Party Operators which, in the case of a request to:

8.1.1   BT, is an agreement which BT is required to enter into under Condition 13 of the BT Licence; or

8.1.2   the Operator, is an agreement which the Operator is required to enter into under the equivalent Condition of the Operator Licence.

8.2   BT shall, following a request by the Operator, offer to enter into an agreement to interconnect the Parties' respective Systems for the provision of the service or facility to the Operator on BT's then current standard terms. Upon acceptance of such offer, this Agreement shall be amended by the addition of a Schedule containing the terms applicable to such service or facility or, if appropriate, the Parties shall agree and enter into a new interconnection agreement.

8.3   The Operator shall, following a request by BT, enter into good faith negotiations with BT to agree terms for interconnection of the Parties' respective Systems for the provision of the service or facility by the Operator to BT on fair and reasonable terms. Upon terms being agreed, this Agreement shall be amended to give effect to the agreed terms or, if appropriate, the Parties shall agree and enter into a new interconnection agreement.

8.4   If a Party requests from the other Party an agreement for interconnection for the provision of a service or facility which is not made available by such other Party to Third Party Operators and such agreement is one which, if BT is the other Party, BT is required to enter into under Condition 13 of the BT Licence or, if the Operator is the other Party, the Operator is required to enter into under the equivalent Condition of the Operator Licence, the Parties shall enter into good faith negotiations to enter into an agreement for interconnection for the provision of such service or facility in accordance with paragraphs 8.5–8.9 (inclusive) or otherwise as the Parties may agree.

8.5   The Party requesting the other Party under paragraph 8.4 (the 'Requesting Party') shall provide at the time of such request the other Party (the 'Requested Party') with a written statement of its requirements addressing the matters contained in the New Services Manual.

8.6   Not later than 5 Working Days after receipt by the Requested Party of the statement of requirements, the Requested Party shall acknowledge such receipt in writing.

8.7   Not later than 30 calendar days after the acknowledgement under paragraph 8.6, the Requested Party shall confirm whether or not the statement of requirements is sufficient for the purpose and, if not, the Requested

Party shall request and the Requesting Party shall provide such further clarification of the statement of requirements as the Requested Party may reasonably require. The Parties shall use their reasonable endeavours to ensure that the Requested Party shall be in a position to confirm the sufficiency of the statement of requirements (with clarification, if any) within such 30 calendar day period.

8.8 Subject to the Requested Party confirming the sufficiency of the Requesting Party's statement of requirements under paragraph 8.7, the Requested Party shall not later than:

8.8.1 60 calendar days after the acknowledgement under paragraph 8.6, confirm in writing to the Requesting Party whether it accepts an obligation to enter into an agreement to meet those requirements in accordance with the cost and other principles embodied in the Requested Party's Licence; and

8.8.2 if it does accept an obligation to do so, 75 calendar days after the acknowledgement under paragraph 8.6, endeavour to agree with the Requesting Party a plan which addresses:

8.8.2.1 the testing of the feasibility of the requirements and, if so feasible, the implementation of those requirements;

8.8.2.2 the terms and conditions, including price, applicable to the requirements; and

8.8.2.3 any other relevant matter.

8.9 If the Requested Party does not accept under paragraph 8.8.1 an obligation to meet the Requesting Party's requirements or the Requested Party does accept under paragraph 8.8.1 an obligation to meet the Requesting Party's requirements but the Parties fail to agree on any aspect of the plan within the timescale referred to in paragraph 8.8.2, then the Requesting Party without prejudice to its other rights and remedies may immediately request a determination from the Director General under the provisions of the Requested Party's Licence.

8.10 If the Requested Party does not accept under paragraph 8.8.1 an obligation to meet the Requesting Party's requirements, negotiations to agree terms for interconnection for the provision of the service or facility may nevertheless continue, whether by further clarification of the statement of requirements or otherwise and without prejudice to the Requesting Party's right to request a determination from the Director General as referred to in paragraph 8.9.

8.11 The provisions of this paragraph 8 are intended to establish a framework for the interconnection of the Parties' respective Systems for the provision of any service or facility not already agreed to be provided under this Agreement, but are not intended to prejudice the rights, liabilities and obligations of the Parties created by and under their Licences.

9. Forecasts and Capacity

9.1 The Parties shall supply to each other forecasts in accordance with Annex A and as may be required in a Schedule.

9.2 The Parties shall order and provide Capacity in accordance with Annex A and as may be required in a Schedule.

10.   Provision of Information

10.1   Each Party shall provide free of charge, one copy of the information specified in paragraph 10.3 of the main body and in paragraphs 3, 7 and 16 of Annex A, and such other information as is reasonably required from time to time by the other Party for interconnection of the Systems and the provision of services or facilities pursuant to this Agreement.

10.2   Each Party shall promptly supply to the other upon request details of services and facilities which it provides to its Customers to which paragraph 8 may apply.

10.3   Subject to a Party's obligations of confidentiality to a Third Party, a Party may request and the other Party shall provide information on protocols in use by that other Party which are required for interconnection, conveyance of Calls or the provision of services specified in this Agreement between the BT System and the Operator System if such other Party has relevant information and the provision of such information is necessary as a consequence of the absence of international standards.

10.4   Notwithstanding any provision of this Agreement a Party shall not be obliged to provide information which is subject to a confidentiality obligation to a Third Party unless such Third Party consents to such disclosure.

10.5   The Disclosing Party will use reasonable endeavours to ensure that information disclosed is correct to the best of its knowledge at the time of provision of such information.

10.6   If a Disclosing Party provides information to a Receiving Party, the Disclosing Party shall have obtained all appropriate Third Party consents.

10.7   Subject to paragraph 23, the Receiving Party shall indemnify the Disclosing Party and keep it indemnified against all liabilities, claims, demands, damages, costs and expenses arising as a consequence of any failure by the Receiving Party to comply with the conditions imposed and identified at the time when the information was provided.

10.8   Nothing in this Agreement shall require a Party to do anything in breach of any statutory or regulatory obligation of confidentiality, including without prejudice to the generality of the foregoing, any obligation pursuant to the Data Protection Act 1984, the BT Licence or the Operator Licence as appropriate or any code of practice on the confidentiality of customer information issued by the Director General.

11.   CLI

11.1   If a Party's System requests CLI from the other System the originating System shall generate and convey CLI to the System requesting it to the extent that the originating System has such a capability.

11.2   A Party whose System receives CLI following a request pursuant to paragraph 11.1 shall only use the CLI for the following purposes:

11.2.1   routing Calls; and

11.2.2   compilation of inter Party bills; and

11.2.3   agreed administrative use in accordance with accepted industry practice from time to time which includes, at the date of this Agreement, call trace, malicious call identification, compilation of statistics relating to call origin and PRS Fraud prevention and detection; and

11.2.4 display to Customers suject to compliance with the 'Code of Practice' as referred to in the definition of CLI in Annex D as such code may be amended or replaced from time to time.

11.3 A Party conveying Calls handed over from a Third Party System or an Authorised Overseas System shall convey, to the extent received, the CLI associated with those Calls.

11.4 Notwithstanding other provisions of this Agreement a Party may use CLI to pass telephone numbers to Emergency Organisations.

11.5 The cost of generating and conveying CLI is included in the relevant conveyance rates for Calls. Neither Party shall apply additional charges for CLI.

11.6 If a Party desires to charge separately for the generation or conveyance of CLI such Party may initiate a review of this paragraph 11 pursuant to paragraph 19.1.3 on 1 April 1997 and each 1 April thereafter.

11.7 If there is a change in applicable law or regulation materially affecting the operation of CLI, the Parties shall change the operation of CLI to the extent necessary to comply with the applicable law or regulation.

Note
OFTEL's Code of Practice for network operators in relation to Line Identification Display Services and other related services dated December 1996 is now required to be incorporated into interconnection agreements between public network operators.

12. BT Services

12.1 If, at the commencement of the Financial Year In Question, the Director General has not determined the Interim Charge for a Standard Service (other than a Competitive Standard Service), the Pre-Interim Charge for that Standard Service shall be the same as the Interim Charge (or the Actual Charge, if applicable, for the relevant period) for that Standard Service for the Financial Year immediately preceding the Financial Year In Question provided always that such Interim Charge has been determined for such immediately preceding Financial Year.

12.2 If, for the Financial Year In Question, the Director General has not determined, before 1 July of such year, the Interim Charge for a Standard Service (other than a Competitive Standard Service) referred to the Director General pursuant to Condition 16B.2 of the BT Licence, BT shall, as soon as reasonably practicable following publication in the Carrier Price List of the determined Interim Charge for the Financial Year In Question, adjust and recalculate the charges in respect of such Standard Service for the Financial Year In Question using the determined Interim Charge and calculate any sum overpaid or underpaid.

12.3 As soon as reasonably practicable following a determination by the Director General of a charge (or the means of calculating that charge) for a Standard Service, BT shall make any necessary alterations to the Carrier Price List so that it accords with the full list of Standard Services maintained by BT pursuant to Condition 16B.8 of the BT Licence and shall send a copy of the alterations to the Carrier Price List to the Operator as soon as reasonably practicable.

12.4 After the Director General has determined the Final Charge (or the means of calculating that charge) for a Standard Service, BT shall, as soon as reasonably practicable following publication in the Carrier Price List of the determined Final Charge for the Financial Year In Question, adjust and recalculate the charges in respect of such Standard Service for the Financial Year In Question in accordance with the provisions of Condition 13.5A.3B of the BT Licence and calculate the interest for any sums overpaid or underpaid in accordance with the Oftel Interest Rate. For the purposes of this paragraph 12.4 Pre-Interim Charges shall be treated as Interim Charges.

12.5   If the Director General determines that a Standard Service is a Competitive Standard Service, BT may, specify and vary from time to time, the charge for such Competitive Standard Service by publication in the Carrier Price List and such charge shall take effect on the Effective Date being a date not earlier than the date of such publication. If BT increases the price of a Competitive Standard Service the Effective Date shall in addition be not earlier than 28 calendar days after the date of such publication.

12.6   If a determination referred to in paragraphs 12.3, 12.4 or 12.5 is subject to a legal challenge, the Parties shall, without prejudice, treat the determination as valid until the conclusion of the legal proceedings, unless the court otherwise directs. If the court finds a determination to be unlawful then the Parties agree to revert to the charges payable immediately prior to such determination being made and BT shall make any necessary alterations to the Carrier Price List. As soon as reasonably practicable following a redetermination by the Director General (as a result of a legal challenge) of a charge (or the means of calculating that charge) for a Standard Service, BT shall make any necessary alterations to the Carrier Price List so that it accords with the full list of Standard Services maintained by BT pursuant to Condition 16B.8 of the BT Licence and shall send a copy of the alterations to the Carrier Price List to the Operator as soon as reasonably practicable. BT shall, as soon as reasonably practicable following publication in the Carrier Price List of the redetermined charge for the Financial Year In Question, adjust and recalculate the charges in respect of such Standard Service for the Financial Year In Question and calculate the interest for any sums overpaid or underpaid in accordance with the Oftel Interest Rate.

12.7   For a service which is not a Standard Service or is a Standard Service for which there is no determined charge, BT may specify and vary from time to time, the charge for such a service by publication in the Carrier Price List and such charge shall take effect on the Effective Date being a date not earlier than the date of such publication.

12.8   Subject to paragraphs 12.9 and 12.10, the charge payable during the course of the relevant Financial Year In Question for each Standard Service, other than a Competitive Standard Service, shall be that specified in the column headed Interim Charge in the Carrier Price List for the relevant Financial Year In Question.

12.9   Subject to paragraph 12.10, the charge payable during the course of the relevant Financial Year In Question for each Standard Service, other than a Competitive Standard Service or a Standard Service for which there is no determined charge, in respect of a period for which there is no charge specified in the column headed Interim Charge, shall be that specified in the column headed Pre-Interim Charge in the Carrier Price List for the relevant Financial Year In Question.

12.10   The charge payable for each Standard Service, other than a Competitive Standard Service, in respect of a period for which a charge is specified in the column headed Actual Charge, shall be the charge specified in the column headed Actual Charge in the Carrier Price List for the said period for the relevant Financial Year In Question.

12.11 An adjustment and recalculation which is to be carried out using the Final Charge shall be based on the charge specified in the column headed Final Charge in the Carrier Price List for the relevant Financial Year In Question.

12.12 The charge payable for each Competitive Standard Service and a service which is not a Standard Service, shall be the charge specified from time to time in the column headed BT Charge in the Carrier Price List.

12.13 If there is a difference between a charge for a Standard Service (other than a Competitive Standard Service) specified in the Carrier Price List and a charge determined by the Director General, the charge determined by the Director General shall prevail.

12.14 All references to an entry in the Carrier Price List for Standard Services are references to the Carrier Price List relating to the Financial Year In Question.

12.15 The date of publication in the Carrier Price List shall be the date that BT first makes available or sends the Carrier Price List containing the relevant entries to a person other than BT.

13. Operator Services

13.1 As soon as reasonably practicable following agreement of a charge (or the means of calculating that charge) for a service provided by the Operator to BT, BT shall make any necessary alterations to the Carrier Price List so that it accords with that agreement and shall send a copy of the alterations to the Carrier Price List to the Operator as soon as reasonably practicable.

13.2 If the Parties have agreed on a provisional basis an Interim Charge for a service provided by the Operator to BT, such provisionally agreed charge shall be reviewed on:

13.2.1 a date agreed by the Parties; or

13.2.2 a date that a determination by the Director General of an Interim Charge for an equivalent service for the relevant Financial Year In Question is published;

13.2.3 a date that a determination by the Director General of a Final Charge for an equivalent service for the relevant Financial Year In Question is published;

whichever is the earlier and any variation to the provisionally agreed charge shall take effect from the date of the original agreement.

13.3 In circumstances other than where Condition 13.5.(1)(i) of the BT Licence or the equivalent Condition of the Operator Licence applies, if the Parties are unable to reach agreement of a charge (or the means of calculating that charge) for a service provided by the Operator to BT under the Agreement, either Party may serve a review notice on the other Party under paragraph 19.1.

13.4 If the Director General has previously determined the charge for a service provided by the Operator to BT, and if, at the commencement of the Financial Year In Question, the Director General has not determined the

Interim Charge for that service, the Pre-Interim Charge for that service shall be the same as the Interim Charge for that service for the Financial Year immediately preceding the Financial Year In Question provided always that such Interim Charge has been determined for such immediately preceding Financial Year.

13.5　If the Director General has previously determined the charge for a service provided by the Operator to BT, and if, for the Financial Year In Question, the Director General has not determined, before 1 July of such year, the Interim Charge for that service, the Operator shall, as soon as reasonably practicable following publication in the Carrier Price List of the determined Interim Charge for the Financial Year In Question, adjust and recalculate the charges in respect of that service for the Financial Year In Question using the determined Interim Charge and calculate any sum overpaid or underpaid.

13.6　As soon as reasonably practicable following a determination by the Director General of a charge (or the means of calculating that charge) for a service provided by the Operator to BT, BT shall make any necessary alterations to the Carrier Price List so that it accords with the determination and shall send a copy of the alterations to the Carrier Price List to the Operator as soon as reasonably practicable.

13.7　If the Director General has determined an Interim Charge for a service provided by the Operator to BT, after the Director General has determined the Final Charge (or the means of calculating that charge) for that service, the Operator shall, as soon as reasonably practicable following publication in the Carrier Price List of the determined Final Charge for the Financial Year In Question, adjust and recalculate the charges in respect of that service for the Financial Year In Question in accordance with the provisions of Condition 13.5B.1A of the BT Licence and calculate the interest for any sums overpaid or underpaid calculated in accordance with the Oftel Interest Rate. For the purposes of this paragraph 13.7 Pre-Interim Charges shall be treated as Interim Charges.

13.8　If the Director General has determined an Interim Charge for a service provided by the Operator to BT then either Party may request the Director General to determine the Interim Charge for that service for the next Financial Year In Question.

13.9　If a determination referred to in paragraphs 13.3, 13.6, 13.7 or 13.8 is subject to a legal challenge, the Parties shall, without prejudice, treat the determination as valid until the conclusion of the legal proceedings unless the court otherwise directs. If the court finds a determination to be unlawful then the Parties agree to revert to the charges payable immediately prior to such determination being made and BT shall make any necessary alterations to the Canier Price List. As soon as reasonably practicable following a redetermination by the Director General (as a result of a legal challenge) of a charge (or the means of calculating that charge) for such service, BT shall make any necessary alterations to the Carrier Price List so that it accords with redetermination and shall send a copy of the alterations to the Carrier Price List to the Operator as soon as reasonably practicable. The Operator shall, as soon as reasonably practicable following publication in the Carrier Price List of the redetermined charge for the Financial Year In Question, adjust and recalculate the charges in respect of such service for the Financial Year In

Question and calculate the interest for any sums overpaid or underpaid in accordance with the Oftel Interest Rate.

13.10 Subject to paragraphs 13.11 and 13.12, the charge payable during the course of the relevant Financial Year In Question for each service provided by the Operator to BT, shall be that specified in the column headed Interim Charge in the Carrier Price List for the relevant Financial Year In Question.

13.11 The charge payable during the course of the relevant Financial Year In Question for each service provided by the Operator to BT for which there is no determined charge, in respect of a period for which there is no charge specified in the column headed Interim Charge, shall be that specified in the column headed Pre-Interim Charge in the Carrier Price List for the relevant Financial Year In Question.

13.12 An adjustment and recalculation which is to be carried out using the Final Charge shall be based on the charge specified in the column headed Final Charge in the Carrier Price List for the relevant Financial Year In Question.

13.13 If any charge (or the means of calculating that charge) for a service provided by the Operator to BT has retrospective effect then the Operator shall adjust and recalculate the charges in respect of such service for the Financial Year in Question using the new charge and calculate the interest for any sum overpaid or underpaid at the Oftel Interest Rate.

13.14 If there is a difference between a charge for a service provided by the Operator to BT specified in the Carrier Price List and a charge determined by the Director General, the charge determined by the Director General shall prevail.

13.15 All references to an entry in the Carrier Price List for services provided by the Operator are references to the Carrier Price List relating to the Financial Year In Question.

13.16 The date of publication in the Carrier Price List shall be the date that BT first makes available or sends the Carrier Price List containing the relevant entries to a person other than BT.

14. Charges and Payment

14.1 Each Party shall pay the charges calculated in accordance with, and within the time specified in, this Agreement.

14.2 No charges shall be payable under this Agreement by one Party to the other unless such charges are specifically referred to in this Agreement.

14.3 The charges in this Agreement are exclusive of VAT unless such charges are stated to be inclusive of VAT.

14.4 Invoices are due and payable in pounds sterling.

14.5 Each Party shall pay the other Party the relevant charges specified in this Agreement for all Calls conveyed between the Parties except that if a Party has a Third Party Interconnect, and the other Party has a Third Party Interconnect Agreement containing provisions such that charges for Calls conveyed via the Third Party Interconnect are paid directly to that other Party by that Third Party, then the first Party shall be released from payment for such Calls subject to such Calls being conveyed in agreed separate Traffic Routes.

14.6   If an Operator has a liability to pay BT Access Deficit Contributions for Calls handed over directly to BT that liability shall continue notwithstanding that the Operator conveys such Calls to BT via a Third Party.

14.7   If the Operator hands over a Call to a Third Party Operator system and such Call is subsequently handed over to the BT System and conveyed to a BT Network Termination Point the Operator shall pay BT (in relation to such a Call) the same contribution to BT's Access Deficit as the Operator would have been liable to pay BT if such a Call had been handed over directly from the Operator System to the BT System.

14.8   The Operator shall not pay any Access Deficit Contribution in respect of a Call made on or after 8 February 1996.

15. Billing

15.1   Each Party shall provide to the other invoices of all amounts due to it, calculated in accordance with the provisions of Annex B and the Carrier Price List.

16. System Protection and Safety

16.1   Each Party is responsible for the safe operation of its System and shall take all reasonable and necessary steps in its operation and implementation of this Agreement to ensure that its System does not:

16.1.1   endanger the safety or health of employees, contractors, agents or Customers of the other Party; or

16.1.2   damage, interfere with or cause any deterioration in the operation of the other Party's System.

17. Approved Attachments and Customer Equipment

17.1   Neither Party shall connect or knowingly permit the connection to its System of anything that is not approved by the relevant approvals authority for attachment to its System.

17.2   If a Customer ceases wholly or partly to be a Party's Customer at any one site and becomes a Customer of the other Party, the first Party shall not hinder the second Party from:

17.2.1   gaining access to equipment rooms owned or occupied by the Customer,

17.2.2   gaining access to ducting and wiring owned by the Customer, and/or

17.2.3   obtaining consents and wayleaves from any Third Party
as shall be required for such access.

18. Numbering

18.1   Each Party shall use numbers in accordance with the United Kingdom national numbering scheme and shall comply with the numbering provisions in Annex A.

19.   Review

19.1   A Party may seek to amend this Agreement by serving on the other a review notice if:

19.1.1   either Party's Licence is materially modified (whether by amendment or replacement); or

19.1.2   a material change occurs in the law or regulations (including codes of practice whether or not having the force of law) governing telecommunications in the United Kingdom; or

19.1.3   this Agreement makes express provision for a review or the Parties agree in writing that there should be a review; or

19.1.4   a material change (including enforcement action by any regulatory authority) occurs which affects or reasonably could be expected to affect the commercial or technical basis of this Agreement; or

19.1.5   this Agreement is assigned or transferred by the other Party except if prior written consent to the assignment or transfer is not required under paragraph 25.1; or

19.1.6   there is a general review pursuant to paragraph 19.4; or

19.1.7   there is to be a review of charges for which a Review Date is specified in a Schedule.

19.2   A review notice shall set out in reasonable detail the issues to be discussed between the Parties.

19.3   Save as provided in paragraphs 19.4 or 19.5, a Party shall serve a review notice not later than the expiration of a 1 year period commencing on the date set opposite each paragraph as follows:

Paragraph	Period commencing on the date:
19.1.1	of publication of the modifications to the Licence
19.1.2	of occurrence of material change
19.1.3	of entitlement or occurrence of the date of written agreement
19.1.4	of occurrence of the material change
19.1.5	of notification of assignment or transfer

19.4   A Party may initiate a general review of this Agreement by serving a review notice during the period of three months commencing on 1st April 1998 and 1st April every 2 years thereafter.

19.5   A Party may initiate a review of charges in a Schedule or the Carrier Pnce List if there is a Review Date specified, by serving a review notice during the period of three months commencing on the Review Date.

19.6   On service of a review notice, the Parties shall forthwith negotiate in good faith the matters to be resolved with a view to agreeing the relevant amendments to this Agreement.

19.7   A variation of charges payable by one Party to the other following a review notice pursuant to paragraph 19.1.7 shall take effect as of the Review Date. All other variations of charges resulting from a determination by the

Director General shall, except where agreed otherwise, take effect from the date of the relevant review notice.

19.8   For the avoidance of doubt, the Parties agree that notwithstanding service of a review notice this Agreement shall remain in full force and effect.

20.   Determination

20.1   If the Parties fail to reach agreement on the subject matter of a review notice within 3 months (or within 6 months for a review notice under paragraph 19.4) in each case from the date of service of such review notice, either Party may, not later than 3 months after the expiration of the relevant period, request in writing the Director General to determine:

20.1.1   the matters upon which the Parties have failed to agree;

20.1.2   whether this Agreement should be modified to take account of such matters; and, if so

20.1.3   the amendment or amendments to be made.

The Parties may, at any time, agree in writing a variation to the time periods specified above in relation to a particular review notice.

20.2   On receipt of a request for a determination the Director General may make a determination if he is satisfied that:

20.2.1   the requirements of the relevant paragraphs in paragraph 19.1 have been satisfied; and

20.2.2   the modifications sought to this Agreement are material.

20.3   A determination by the Director General shall be limited to:

20.3.1   the subject matter of the request for a determination; and

20.3.2   matters on which the Parties have failed to agree which the Director General would have power to determine under either Condition 13 of the BT Licence or under the equivalent Condition of the Operator Licence if there was no agreement between the Parties.

20.4   In making a determination, the Director General shall act pursuant to the criteria contained from time to time either in Condition 13 of the BT Licence or in the equivalent Condition of the Operator Licence. The Parties shall have the rights and remedies whether arising at law or otherwise in relation to such determination as would be available under either Condition 13 of the BT Licence or under the equivalent Condition of the Operator Licence.

20.5   The Parties shall enter into an agreement to modify or replace the Agreement in accordance with the Director General's determination unless the determination is subject to a legal challenge.

20.6   If the determination is subject to a legal challenge then the Parties shall subject to paragraphs 12.6 and 13.9 modify or replace the Agreement at the conclusion of the legal proceedings in accordance with the Director General's determination and the result of the legal proceedings.

20.7   For the avoidance of doubt, determination of a charge may include a determination of the basis for calculating that charge.

21.   Confidentiality

21.1   Subject to the following provisions of this paragraph 21, a Receiving Party shall keep in confidence Confidential Information and will not (and will use its reasonable endeavours to ensure that its directors, employees, and professional advisers will not) disclose such information to any Third Party.

21.2 A Receiving Party shall exercise no lesser degree of care of Confidential Information than would a reasonable person with knowledge of confidential nature of the information. A Receiving Party shall exercise no lesser security or degree of care than that Party applies to its own Confidential Information of an equivalent nature.

21.3 A Receiving Party shall restrict disclosure of Confidential Information relating to the other Party to those persons who have a reasonable need to know. Confidential Information shall be used solely for the purposes for which it was disclosed.

21.4 A Receiving Party may disclose Confidential Information to an Associated Company, subject to the Associated Company undertaking to comply with obligations equivalent to these contained in this paragraph 21.

21.5 A Receiving Party may disclose Confidential Information to a contractor or agent, suject to the contractor or agent undertaking to comply with obligations equivalent to those contained in this paragraph 21.

21.6 The following shall not constitute a breach of this paragraph 21:

21.6.1 a disclosure authorised in writing by the Disclosing Party to the extent of that authority; or

21.6.2 a disclosure to an Emergency Organisation; or

21.6.3 publication of all or part of this Agreement or details of it pursuant to the BT Licence or publication in the Carrier Price List or Quality Schedule except in so far as the Director General has consented to the exclusion of any matter pursuant to Condition 16A of the BT Licence; or

21.6.4 a disclosure which is properly made pursuant to the Operator Licence or the BT Licence or a relevant statutory or other regulatory obligation; or

21,6.5 a disclosure properly and reasonably made to the Director General under paragraph 20, to an arbitrator, expert or any person appointed by the Parties for the resolution of a Dispute; or

21.6.6 a disclosure to obtain or maintain any listing on any recognised stock exchange,

subject to in the case of any disclosure specified in paragraphs 21.6.4 to 21.6.6 the Receiving Party informing the Disclosing Party as soon as reasonably practical, after such disclosure.

21.7 Unless otherwise agreed in writing, a Receiving Party shall not use the other Party's Confidential Information to provide commercial advantage to its retail business.

22. Force Majeure

22.1 Neither Party shall be liable for any breach of this Agreement caused by act of God, insurrection or civil disorder, war or military operations, national or local emergency, acts or omissions of government, highway authority or other competent authority, compliance with any statutory obligation, industrial disputes of any kind (whether or not involving BT's or the Operator's employees), fire, lightning, explosion, flood, subsidence, weather of exceptional severity, acts or omissions of persons for whom neither Party is responsible or any other cause whether similar or dissimilar outside its reasonable control and any such event or circumstance is a force majeure.

22.2   The Party initially affected by a force majeure shall promptly notify the other of the estimated extent and duration of its inability to perform or delay in performing its obligations ('force majeure notification').

22.3   Upon cessation of the effects of the force majeure the Party initially affected by a force majeure shall promptly notify the other of such cessation.

22.4   If as a result of a force majeure, the performance by the Party initially affected of its obligations under this Agreement is affected, such Party shall, subject to the provisions of paragraph 22.6, perform those of its obligations not affected by a force majeure. In performing those of its obligations not affected by a force majeure, the Party initially affected by a force majeure shall deploy its resources such that (when taken together with other obligations to its Customers and Third Parties) there is no undue discrimination against the other Party.

22.5   To the extent that a Party is prevented as a result of a force majeure from providing all of the services or facilities to be provided under this Agreement, the other Party shall be released to the equivalent extent from its obligations to make payment for such services or facilities or complying with its obligations in relation thereto.

22.6   Following a force majeure notification and if the effects of such force majeure continue for:

22.6.1   a continuous period of not more than 6 months from the date of the force majeure notification (whether or not notice of cessation has been given pursuant to paragraph 22.3) any obligation outstanding shall be fulfilled by the Party initially affected by the force majeure as soon as reasonably possible after the effects of the force majeure have ended, save to the extent that such fulfilment is no longer possible or is not required by the other Party;

22.6.2   a continuous period of 6 months or more from the date of the force majeure notification (and notice of cessation has not been given pursuant to paragraph 22.3), the Party receiving the force majeure notification shall be entitled (but not obliged) to terminate this Agreement by giving not less than 30 days' written notice to the other Party, provided that such notice shall be deemed not to have been given if notice of cessation is received by the Party receiving the force majeure notification prior to the expiry of the 30 days' notice. If this Agreement is not terminated in accordance with the provisions of this paragraph 22.6.2, any obligations outstanding shall be fulfilled by the Party initially affected by the force majeure as soon as reasonably possible after the effects of the force majeure have ended, save to the extent that such fulfilment is no longer possible or is not required by the other Party.

23.   Limitation of Liability

23.1   Neither Party has an obligation of any kind to the other Party beyond the obligations to exercise the reasonable skill and care of a competent telecommunications operator in performing its obligations under this Agreement.

23.2   Subject to paragraph 23.4 if a Party is in breach of any of its obligations under this Agreement to the other Party (excluding obligations arising under this Agreement to pay moneys in the ordinary course of business), or otherwise (including liability for negligence or breach of statutory duty) such Party's liability to the other shall be limited to one million pounds sterling (Stg £1,000,000) for any one event or series of connected events and two million pounds sterling (Stg £2,000,000) for all events (connected or unconnected) in any period of 12 calendar months.

23.3 Neither Party excludes or restricts its liability for death or personal injury caused by its own negligence or liability arising under Part I of the Consumer Protection Act 1987.

23.4 Neither Party shall be liable to the other in contract, tort (including negligence or breach of statutory duty) or otherwise for loss (whether direct or indirect) of profits, business or anticipated savings, wasted expenditure or for any indirect or other consequential loss whatsoever arising in connection with the operation of this Agreement, howsoever caused.

23.5 Each provision of this paragraph 23 is a separate limitation applying and surviving even if one or more such provisions is inapplicable or held unreasonable in any circumstances.

23.6 The amounts specified in paragraph 23.2, as adjusted pursuant to this paragraph 23.6, shall be adjusted on each 1st April after the date of this Agreement by the percentage change in the retail price index (published in the General Index of Retail Prices (RPI) published by the Central Statistical Office (or any successor index)) for the month of September immediately preceding each 1st April compared with the RPI published in September in the previous year.

24. Intellectual Property Rights

24.1 Except as expressly provided otherwise in this Agreement, Intellectual Property Rights shall remain the property of the Party creating or owning the same and nothing in this Agreement shall be deemed to confer any assignment or licence of the Intellectual Property Rights of one Party to the other Party.

25. Assignment

25.1 Unless otherwise agreed in writing, and subject to paragraph 25.2, no rights, benefits or obligations under this Agreement may be assigned or transferred, in whole or in part, by a Party without the prior written consent of the other Party.

25.2 No consent is required under paragraph 25.1 for an assignment of rights, benefits or obligations under this Agreement (in whole or in part) to a successor to all or substantially all of the assigning Party's System or to an Associated Company provided that such successor or Associated Company shall have had a licence granted to it under section 7 of the Act to run the Telecommunication System of the assigning Party.

25.3 The assigning Party shall promptly give notice to the other Party of any assignment permitted to be made without the other Party's consent. No assignment shall be valid unless the assignee/successor agrees in writing to be bound by the provisions of this Agreement.

26. Disputes

26.1   If a Party ('the disputing Party') wishes to invoke the dispute procedure specified in this paragraph it shall as soon as reasonably practicable notify the other Party's liaison contact specified from time to time in the Customer Service Plan. The disputing Party shall include with such notice all relevant details including the nature and extent of the Dispute.

26.2   Following a notification under paragraph 26.1 the Parties shall consult in good faith to try to resolve the Dispute at level 1. If agreement is not reached at level 1 the Dispute may be escalated to level 2. If agreement is not reached at level 2 the Dispute may be escalated to level 3. If a Party escalates a Dispute it shall record for the benefit of the next level all relevant details including what is agreed and what is not agreed concerning the Dispute.

26.3   The name of each Party's liaison contact and representatives at each level of consultation shall be as specified from time to time in the Customer Service Plan. No change to a liaison contact or representative shall be effective until it has been notified to the other Party.

26.4   The above procedures are without prejudice to any other rights and remedies that may be available in respect of any breach of any provision of this Agreement.

26.5   Nothing herein shall prevent a Party from:

26.5.1   seeking (including obtaining or implementing) interlocutory or other immediate relief, or

26.5.2   referring the Dispute to the Director General in accordance with any right (if any) either Party may have to request a determination or other appropriate steps for its resolution.

27. Breach, Suspension and Termination

27.1   If a Party's System adversely affects the normal operation of the other Party's System or is a threat to any person's safety, the other Party may suspend, to the extent necessary, such of its obligations hereunder, and for such period as it may consider reasonable to ensure the normal operation of its System or reduce the threat to safety.

27.2   If a Party is in material breach of (including failure to pay a sum due under) this Agreement, the other Party may serve a written notice (the 'breach notice') on the Party in breach specifying the breach and requiring it to be remedied within:

27.2.1   30 calendar days from the date of receipt of such breach notice; or

27.2.2   in case of emergency, within such shorter period as the Party not in breach may reasonably specify.

27.3   If, the Party in breach fails to remedy the breach within such period as may be specified by the Party not in breach pursuant to paragraph 27.2 the Party not in breach may, until such breach is remedied, suspend performance of such of its obligations under this Agreement as is reasonable in the circumstances.

27.4   If the Party in breach fails to remedy the breach within the period stated in the breach notice the Party not in breach may terminate this Agreement on three months' written notice provided always that if the Party in breach remedies the breach within such three months' notice period, this Agreement shall not terminate as a result of such notice.

27.5 This Agreement may be terminated by either Party by written notice forthwith (or on the termination of such other period as such notice may specify) if the other Party:

27.5.1 is unable to pay its debts within the meaning of section 123 (1) (e) of the Insolvency Act 1986; or

27.5.2 has a receiver or administrative receiver appointed in relation to all or any of its assets; or

27.5.3 has an order made or a resolution passed for its winding up (other than for the purpose of amalgamation or reconstruction); or

27.5.4 has an administration order made in respect of its business; or

27.5.5 enters into a voluntary arrangement under section 1 of the Insolvency Act 1986; or

27.5.6 ceases to carry on business.

27.6 Upon termination or expiry of this Agreement each Party shall take such steps and provide such facilities as are necessary for recovery by the other Party of equipment (if any) supplied by that other Party. Each Party shall use reasonable endeavours to recover equipment made available by it.

27.7 If 30 calendar days after the termination or expiry of this Agreement, a Party fails to recover equipment in good condition (fair wear and tear excepted) because of the acts or omissions of the other Party (or a Third Party appearing to have control of a site where such equipment is situate) the first Party may demand reasonable compensation from the other Party which shall be paid by the other Party within 10 calendar days of the date of the demand.

27.8 Without prejudice to a Party's rights upon termination or expiry of this Agreement, a Party shall refund to the other a fair and equitable proportion of those periodic sums (if any) paid under the Agreement for a period extending beyond the date of such termination or expiration.

27.9 Termination or expiry of this Agreement shall not be deemed a waiver of a breach of any term or condition of this Agreement and shall be without prejudice to a Party's rights, liabilities or obligations that have accrued prior to such termination or expiry.

27.10 Notwithstanding the termination or expiry of this Agreement paragraphs 10.6, 17.2, 21, 23, 27.6 to 27.11 inclusive shall continue in full force and effect.

27.11 Each of the Parties' right to terminate or suspend performance of this Agreement pursuant to this paragraph 27 is without prejudice to any other rights or remedies available to either Party.

28. Notices

28.1 A notice shall be duly served if:

28.1.1 delivered by hand, at the time of actual delivery;

28.1.2 sent by facsimile, upon its receipt being confirmed;

28.1.3 sent by recorded delivery post, 4 calendar days after the day of posting.

28.2 Except if otherwise specifically provided all notices and other communications relating to this Agreement shall be in writing and shall be sent as follows:

If to the Operator:

#[Operator]

If to BT:

Contract Liaison Manager, #[Operator]
PP #
British Telecommunications plc
Tenter House
45 Moorfields
London
EC2Y 9TH

or to such other addresses as the Parties may notify from time to time
pursuant to this paragraph 28.

29. Entire Agreement

29.1   This Agreement supersedes all previous understandings, commitments, agreements or representations whatsoever, whether oral or written, in
relation to the subject matter of this Agreement.

30. Variations

30.1   Except as expressly provided in this Agreement, no variation of this
Agreement shall be effective unless agreed in writing by the Parties and signed
by a person nominated in writing on behalf of:
    30.1.1   BT, by the director, UK Carrier Services (or his successor); and
    30.1.2   the Operator, by a director or the company secretary (or
equivalent office holder) of the Operator.

31. Waiver

31.1   The waiver of any breach of, or failure to enforce, any term or
condition of this Agreement shall not be construed as a waiver or a waiver of
any other breach of the same or any other term or condition of this
Agreement. No waiver shall be valid unless it is in writing and signed on
behalf of the Party making the waiver.

32. Restrictive Trade Practices

32.1   Notwithstanding any other provision of this Agreement no provision
of this Agreement, by virtue of which this Agreement is subject to registration
(if such be the case) under the Restrictive Trade Practices Acts 1976 and
1977, shall take effect until the day after the date on which particulars of the
Agreement have been furnished to the Director General of Fair Trading
pursuant to the requirement of those Acts. In this paragraph the expression
'this Agreement' includes any agreement or arrangement of which this
Agreement forms part and which is registrable, or by virtue of which this
Agreement is registrable, under those Acts.

33. Independent Contractors and Agency

33.1 Each of the Parties is and shall remain at all times an independent contractor fully responsible for its own acts or defaults (including those of its employees or agents). Neither Party is authorised and neither of the Parties nor their employees, agents or representatives shall at any time attempt to act or act on behalf of the other Party to bind the other Party in any manner whatsoever to any obligations. Neither Party nor its employees, agents or representatives shall engage in any acts which may lead any person to believe that such Party is an employee, agent or representative of the other Party. Nothing in this Agreement shall be deemed to constitute a partnership between the Parties.

33.2 If either Party appoints an agent for the purposes of this Agreement, and notifies the other Party, then the other Party shall deal with the appointed agent for such purposes until the first Party notifies the other Party that the appointment has been terminated.

34. Severability

34.1 The invalidity or unenforceability of any provision of the Agreement shall not affect the validity or enforceability of the remaining provisions of this Agreement.

35. Governing Law

35.1 The interpretation, validity and performance of this Agreement shall be governed in all respects by the laws of England and Wales and the Parties submit to the exclusive jurisdiction of the English Courts.

IN WITNESS WHEREOF THIS AGREEMENT was entered into the day and year first before written.

SIGNED for and on behalf of
#[OPERATOR]
Signed:
Name: _____
Position: _____

SIGNED for and on behalf of
BRITISH TELECOMMUNICATIONS plc
Signed:
Name: _____
Position: _____

PART II
EUROPEAN

INTRODUCTION

The past decade has seen an extraordinary level of regulatory activity in the telecommunications sector within the European Union. Over 100 different directives, decisions, regulations, recommendations and resolutions, relating to every aspect of the industry, have been officially adopted since 1986.[1] From a UK perspective, such significant regulatory intervention has seldom touched the wider public consciousness, largely due to the developments that had already been put in place under the Telecommunications Act 1984. However, some Member States have experienced significant domestic political consequences following on from Commission initiatives in the area, such as public sector industrial action.

The basis for Commission involvement in the telecommunications market has been founded in two different aspects of European law. While Commission Directorate-General IV has been concerned with the application of competition law to the industry; Directorate-General XIII has pursued telecommunications reform in terms of the establishment of the 'Information Market'.

In the early 1980s, the Commission went to court on significant telecommunication provision issues. The cases were taken under Article 86 of the Treaty of Rome concerning 'abuse of dominant position'. The first case involved the refusal by British Telecommunications (BT) to allow private message-forwarding agencies in the UK from relaying telex messages received from and intended for relay to another country.[2] The first issue for the Court to decide was whether BT, as a public body, was subject to the competition rules of the Treaty of Rome. The Court found that despite its public sector status, BT was essentially a commercial enterprise. It noted that any regulatory powers that had been given to BT were strictly limited and, therefore, the particular scheme in question, as part of BT's commercial activities, should be subject to Article 86. The Court stated that Article 86 would apply whether the conditions of the contract were that of a private monopolist or regulations of a public telecommunications authority. It would also make no difference if the activity had state encouragement or was clearly alluded to in the legislation of a Member State.

A final issue in the BT case concerned the provision of 'value-added telecommunication services'. It appeared that the Court would not allow

---

1 See http://www.ispo.cec.be/infosoc/legreg/telecom.html/ for copies of the latest publications in the area. A special edition compilation of all telecommunications related texts, 'Official Documents Community Telecommunications Policy, XIII (96) 19', can be obtained from: European Commission, DG XIII/A/1, BU31 2/07, Rue de la Loi 200, B-1049 Brussels, Belgium.

2 Case 41/83 *Italy v Commission* [1985] CMLR 386. Commonly referred to as the '*British Telecom* case', it was the Italian Government which appealed the Commission's original decision against British Telecom, while the British Government took the side of the Commission.

national PTT's to restrict the existence of value-added services, or reserve them for themselves. The issue was clarified in the *Tele-Marketing* case,[3] where the Court held that a radio station was obliged under Article 86 to provide its transmission facilities to the lessee regardless of the fact that the facilities will be used to provide value-added services to a third party. The lessee acts within European law as long as he is willing to pay the corresponding charges, including time or volume sensitive tariffs.

These cases were significant landmarks in the industry and led to further investigations by the competition authorities into the activities of European PTTs. In 1988, the Commission used its powers under Article 90(3) of the Treaty to issue a directive on competition in the market for telecommunications terminal equipment. This was followed by a further directive on telecommunication services in 1990. It was the first time the Commission had issued a directive under Article 90 and was viewed by a number of Member States as an illegal exercise of its powers. Both directives were challenged in the European Court of Justice, but the Court upheld the Commission's right to adopt such legislation. The Handbook contains all six such Commission directives.

The Commission has continued to apply European competition law to the activities of telecommunication operators, primarily through numerous investigations into commercial agreements, joint ventures and merger activities. The Handbook contains the Commission's 1991 Guidelines on the application of the competition rules in the telecommunications market and its most recent draft Notice with regard to 'access agreements'.

Most recently, the establishment of global and regional alliances between national telecom operators has been the focus of attention of competition regulators, with the Commission trying to protect the interests of European consumers against the inevitable commercial pressures created by the developing global economy. The Handbook contains two key decisions in this regard: BT/MCI and Deutsche Telecom and France Telecom.

The other aspect of the movement for reform of the telecommunications market has been tied up with the establishment of the Single Market, and in particular the 'Information Market'.[4] With regard to legislative reform, the Commission outlined its initial position on the role of telecommunications in the creation of the Single Market in the 1987 Green Paper.[5] This paper set out three basic principles upon which the regulatory framework would be established:

    (a)   liberalisation of areas currently under a monopoly provider;

    (b)   opening access to telecommunication networks and services, through harmonisation and the development of minimum standards;

    (c)   full application of the competition rules.

Regulatory initiatives in pursuance of the first two components have originated within the Commission's Directorate-General XIII. The concept of

---

3 Case 311/84 *Tele-Marketing* v *Compagnie Luxembourgeoise de Télédiffusion* [1984] 2 CMLR 558.
4 See Communication, 'Working Plan for Creating a Community Information Market' COM(85) 658 final.
5 Commission, 'on the Development of the Common Market for Telecommunications Services and Equipment', COM(87) 290 final of 30 June, 1987. See also Commission, 'On the Way to a Competitive Community-Wide Telecommunications Market in the Year 1992', COM (88) 48 final of 9 Feb, 1988.

the 'Information Market' has since evolved into the 'Information Society'[6] and telecommunications has become a key aspect of the Trans-European Networks initiative established under the Treaty on European Union.[7]

This section of the Handbook contains the key pieces of legislation in the main areas of European telecommunications law: telecommunications equipment, services, open network provision, satellites and licensing. The final section covers a related area of activity, data protection, where legislation has been specifically addressed to the telecommunications industry.

On 17 November 1994, the Council of Ministers committed themselves to the target date of 1 January 1998 for full liberalisation of the voice telephony monopoly and telecommunications infrastructure in the majority of Members States. This date has become the focal point for subsequent legislative initiatives. Although considerable regulatory activity is continuing in the telecommunications market, the regulatory agenda has shifted from basic liberalisation towards more complex market issues, such as universal service, interconnection and licensing. Existing proposals in these areas are changing month-by-month as the legislative process continues. The draft directives reproduced in this section are the most recently published official positions and, therefore, can only provide a general background to the issues currently under debate.

The future regulatory agenda can be expected to be driven by the needs of the 'Information Society'. The most distinctive feature of this developing landscape is likely to be the issue of convergence which is already occurring between previously distinct areas of activity, such as broadcasting.

---

6 See generally the Bangemann Report, 'Europe and the Global Information Society', May 1994.
7 Title XII, Article 129b provides that: '. . . within the framework of a system of open and competitive markets, action by the Community shall aim at promoting the interconnection and interoperability of national networks as well as access to such networks'.

TERMINAL EQUIPMENT

COUNCIL DIRECTIVE (86/361/EEC) OF 24 JULY 1986 ON THE INITIAL STAGE OF THE MUTUAL RECOGNITION OF TYPE APPROVAL FOR TELECOMMUNICATIONS TERMINAL EQUIPMENT
OJ 217/21, 5 August 1986

THE COUNCIL OF THE EUROPEAN COMMUNITIES,

Having regard to the Treaty establishing the European Economic Community, and in particular Article 100 thereof,

Having regard to the proposal from the Commission,

Having regard to the opinion of the European Parliament,[1]

Having regard to the opinion of the Economic and Social Committee,[2]

Whereas the mutual recognition of type approval for telecommunications terminal equipment features in the Commission communication to the Council of 18 May 1984 on telecommunications, in the Council recommendations of 12 November 1984 concerning the implementation of harmonization in the field of telecommunications and the first phase of opening up access to public telecommunications contracts, and in the Council conclusions of 17 December 1984 concerning a Community telecommunications policy;

Whereas the market in telecommunications terminal equipment and use of the full potential of the new telecommunications services are of considerable importance for the economic development of the Community;

Whereas it is absolutely essential to establish or consolidate a specifically European industrial potential in the technologies concerned;

Whereas it is highly desirable to make rapid progress towards establishing a common market in this sector, in particular to order to offer the industry an improved base for its operations and to facilitate the adoption of a joint position with respect to third countries;

Whereas the mutual recognition of type approval for telecommunications terminal equipment constitutes a major step towards the creation of an open and unified market for such equipment;

Whereas, since situations differ and technical and administrative constraints exist in the Member States, progress towards this objective should be made in stages;

---

1 OJ No C 36, 17. 2. 1986, p. 55.
2 OJ No C 303, 25. 11. 1985, p. 2.

Whereas in particular the mutual recognition of conformity tests on mass-produced terminal equipment should constitute an initial stage of the mutual recognition of type approval for such equipment;

Whereas such an approach must be based on the definition of common technical specifications based on international standards and specifications of the harmonization of general technical requirements for testing, measuring and approval procedures in the areas of telecommunications and information technology;

Whereas a general standardization programme is being implemented in the field of information technology in compliance with the Standards Code of the General Agreement on Tariffs and Trade (GATT);

Whereas there is a need for a more comprehensive framework to be drawn up in preparation for a second stage which would create an open and unified market in telecommunications terminal equipment, bearing in mind that for telecommunications this has to include both the free movement of equipment and unimpeded connection to networks, in accordance with harmonized requirements;

Whereas Council Directive 73/23/EEC of 19 February 1973 on the harmonization of the laws of the Member States relating to electrical equipment designed for use within certain voltage limits[3] and Council Directive 83/189/EEC of 28 March 1983 laying down a procedure for the provision of information in the field of technical standards and regulations[4] are applicable, *inter alia*, to the fields of telecommunications and information technology;

Whereas the Memorandum of Understanding between the European Conference of Postal and Telecommunications Administrations (CEPT) and the Commission concerning standards and type approval for telecommunications equipment and the general guidelines agreed with the Joint European Standards Institution CEN-CENELEC henceforth make it possible to entrust specialized technical harmonization work to those bodies;

Whereas the mechanism introduced by certain CEPT administrations, including those of the Community Member States, under the agreement drawn up at Copenhagen on 15 November 1985, incorporates a formal adoption procedure and an undertaking to implement certain CEPT recommendations, which are then designated as 'NETS' (Normes européenes de télécommunications);

Whereas it is necessary to set up a Committee, with the task of assisting the Commission in implementing this Directive and in progressively implementing the mutual recognition of type approval for terminal equipment,

HAS ADOPTED THIS DIRECTIVE:

Article 1

The Member States shall implement the mutual recognition of the results of tests of conformity with common conformity specifications for mass-produced telecommunications terminal equipment in accordance with the detailed rules set out in this Directive.

---

3 OJ No L 77, 26. 3. 1973, p. 29.
4 OJ No L. 109, 26. 4. 1983, p. 8.

Article 2

For the purposes of this Directive:

1. 'telecommunications administrations' means the administrations or private operating agencies recognized in the Community and providing public telecommunications services;

2. 'terminal equipment' means equipment directly or indirectly connected to the termination of a public telecommunications network to send, process or receive information;

3. 'technical specification' means a specification contained in a document which lays down the characteristics required of a product such as levels of quality, performance, safety or dimensions, including the requirements applicable to the product as regards terminology, symbols, testing and test methods, packaging, marking and labelling.

4. 'international technical specification in telecommunications' means the technical specification of all or some characteristics of a product, recommended by such organizations as the Comité international télégraphique et téléphonique (CCITT) or the CEPT;

5. 'common technical specification' means a technical specification drawn up with a view to uniform application to all Member States in the Community;

6. 'standard' means a technical specification adopted by a recognized standards body for repeated or continuous application, compliance with which is not compulsory;

7. 'international standard' means a standard adopted by a recognized international standards body;

8. 'approved testing laboratory' means a laboratory the conformity of which with the accreditation system established by the CEPT in close cooperation with specialized organizations and any relevant national accreditation organizations has been verified, with particular reference to the relevant ISO guides, by the appropriate Member State or a body recognized as competent by that State and which is approved by that Member State or body recognized as competent for conducting conformity tests on terminal equipment;

9. 'certificate of conformity' means the document certifying that a product or service conforms to given standards or technical specifications;

10. 'type approval of terminal equipment' means the confirmation delivered by the competent authority of a Member State that a particular terminal equipment type is authorized or recognized as suitable to be connected to a particular public telecommunications network;

11. 'conformity specification' means a document giving a precise and full description of the technical characteristics of the relevant terminal equipment (such as safety, technical parameters, functions and procedures and service requirements) together with a precise definition of the tests and test methods enabling the conformity of the terminal equipment with the prescribed technical characteristics to be verified;

12. 'type approval specification' means a specification setting out the full and precise requirements that must be satisfied by terminal equipment to be granted type approval. It includes the conformity specification and also administrative requirements and, where appropriate, requirements concerning quality control operations to be carried out during the manufacture of the equipment;

13. 'common conformity specification' means a conformity specification used in all the Community Member States by the authority competent for testing the conformity of terminal equipment. It also includes, where appropriate, requirements made necessary in a given State by historical network peculiarities or established national provisions concerning the use of radio frequencies;

14. 'common type approval specification' means a type approval specification which is used in all the Community Member States by all the authorities empowered to grant type approval for terminal equipment. It includes the common conformity specification and also administrative requirements and, where appropriate, requirements concerning quality control operations to be carried out during the manufacture of the equipment;

15. 'NET (Norme européene de télécommunications) is an approved technical specification recommendation of the CEPT or part or parts thereof which the signatories of the Memorandum of Understanding, established at the meeting of Directors-General of CEPT Administrations, in Copenhagen on 15 November 1985, adopted in accordance with the procedures set down in that Memorandum;

16. 'mutual recognition of the results of conformity tests on terminal equipment' means a situation where when an approved laboratory or the competent authority in a Member State issues a certificate, accompanied by test data and identification details, stating that a terminal is in conformity with a common conformity specification or a part thereof, that certificate is recognized in the other Member States, so that if the terminal in question is the subject of an application for type approval in another Member State, it no longer has to be subjected to the tests for verifying conformity with that specification, or with the part of that specification concerning the tests carried out:

17. 'essential requirements' means those aspects of common conformity specifications of such importance as to necessitate compliance as a matter of legal obligation for the implementation of the mutual recognition of the results of conformity tests on terminal equipment as an integral part of the type approval procedure. These essential requirements are at present:

— user safety in so far as this requirement is not covered by Directive 73/23/EEC,

— safety of employees of public telecommunications network operators in so far as this requirement is not covered by Directive 73/23/EEC,

— protection of public telecommunications networks from harm,

— interworking of terminal equipment, in justified cases.

Article 3

The Council, acting in accordance with the rules of the Treaty on a proposal from the Commission, shall supplement as necessary the list of essential requirements and shall make them more specific where necessary for certain products.

Article 4

The Commission shall:

1. draw up each year, after consulting the Committee referred to in Article 5 and with due regard to the general programme of standardization in the information technology sector:

— a list of international standards and international technical specifications in telecommunications to be harmonized,

— a list of terminal equipment for which common conformity specifications should be drafted as a matter or priority, on the basis above all of the essential requirements,

— a timetable for this work;

2. request the CEPT to draw up the common conformity specifications in the form of NETs, within the specified field time limits; in so doing the latter shall, when appropriate, consult other specialized standardization organizations such as the European Committee for Standardization (CEN) and the European Committee for Electrotechnical Standardization (CENELEC).

Article 5

1. In carrying out the tasks referred to in Article 4, the Commission shall be assisted by a Committee, which shall be the Working Party of Senior Officials on Telecommunications. The members of the Committee may be assisted by experts or advisers according to the nature of the question under discussion. The Committee shall be chaired by a Commission representative:

2. Apart from the cases listed in this Directive, the Commission shall consult the Committee on:

(a) the broad objectives and the future needs of the telecommunications standardization

(b) problems raised by the approval of testing laboratories, and in particular the accreditation system referred to in Article 2(8) and any amendment to that system which may appear necessary;

(c) the effect of technological progress on specification work already under way and the possible need to give a new or revised mandate to the CEPT.

At the request of its Chairman or of a Member State, the Committee may consider any question relating to the implementation of this Directive.

3. The Committee shall adopt its own rules of procedure.

4. The Secretariat of the Committee shall be provided by the Commission.

Article 6

1. For the purposes of this Directive, a 'NET' shall be regarded as the equivalent of the common conformity specification.

Reference to NETs shall be published in the *Official Journal of the European Communities*.

2. Without prejudice to the cases referred to in Article 8, the competent authorities of the Member States shall not have any further tests carried out in respect of a particular type of terminal equipment where results of tests carried out in accordance with Article 7 have given rise to the issue of a certificate of conformity with the relevant common conformity specification, the references to which are published in the *Official Journal of the European Communities*. Such certificate of conformity shall be recognized for the purposes of type approval of the terminal equipment in question.

3. The common conformity specifications shall be used in all Member States by the competent authorities for any verification demanded for type approval purposes of the relevant terminal equipment.

The procedure for exception referred to in Article 7 (4) may also be applied by the competent authorities of the Member States in respect to the first paragraph.

Article 7

1. Member States shall inform the Commission of the authority or authorities competent in their territory to issue type approval for terminal equipment. The Commission shall publish a list of these authorities in the *Official Journal of the European Communities.*

2. Member States shall send the Commission a list of the laboratories which they have approved, or which have been approved by bodies recognized by them as competent, for the purpose of verifying the conformity of terminal equipment with the common conformity specifications. They shall regularly submit a report on the activities of these laboratories in the field covered by this Directive. Such lists and reports shall be transmitted to the Committee referred to in Article 5 for information.

3. For the purposes of Article 6, the certificate of conformity issues by the approved laboratory which has carried out the tests must be accompanied by the data obtained from the measurements performed during the conformity tests, all the information necessary for precise identification of the terminal equipment on which the tests were made and a precise indication of the common conformity specification, or part thereof, used for the tests.

4. Member States shall ensure that telecommunications administrations use common conformity specifications when purchasing terminal equipment covered by such specifications except in the following cases:

(a) where the equipment is to replace equipment connected to the network before the adoption of common conformity specification and is to the same technical specification as the equipment it replaces, or where, during any transition period between two systems, which is accepted as necessary and which is defined within the NET, a Member State needs to add a limited number of pieces of equipment complying with the specification of the first system. In both cases, the Commission shall be informed when such a waiver is invoked and kept informed of the number of pieces of equipment involved; this information shall be given too the Committee referred to in Article 5;

(b) where a careful consultation of the market — ie including the publication of a call for declarations of interest in the *Official Journal of the European Communities* — shows there is no offer at economically acceptable conditions for such terminal equipment complying with those common conformity specifications. In this case, on the basis of an unavoidable need, a Member State may, for a limited period of time, apply only a part of the characteristics set out in the common conformity specifications. The Member State shall inform the Commission immediately and also state what departures from the common conformity specification it intends to permit. The Commission shall consult the Committee referred to in Article 5 as a matter of urgency and may request the CEPT to revise the particular common conformity specification. In addition the Committee shall review the situation at least every six months during the period when this waiver is applied.

In the event that a request for revision is not made to the CEPT then his waiver shall cease when another Member State presents evidence to the

Committee that terminal equipment conforming to that common conformity specification has been connected to its public telecommunication networks on a normal commercial basis.

However, a Member State may have the waiver extended provided that the Commission, on the advice of the Committee referred to in Article 5, agrees that the technical and economic conditions are sufficiently different in the two Member States as to warrant such an extension.

5. The Member States shall consult within the Committee referred to in Article 5, so as to create conditions of fair competition for carrying out the same series of conformity tests in all the approved laboratories.

Article 8

1. A Member State may, after examining the common conformity specification and the test results, suspend recognition of a certificate of conformity issued for the purpose of type approval:

(a) if it discovers shortcomings regarding the application of the common conformity specification;

(b) if it discovers that the common conformity specification itself fails to meet the essential requirements which it is supposed to cover.

If it exercises this option, the Member State concerned shall immediately inform the Commission and the other Member States, stating the reasons for its decision.

2. Where the decision of the Member State concerned the electrical safety of users of terminal equipment, the procedures set out in Article 9 of Directive 73/23/EEC shall apply.

3. If the reasons given for the Member State's decision are as described in paragraph 1 (a), the Commission shall immediately consult the Member States concerned. If no agreement is reached without four weeks, the Commission shall seek the opinion of one of the approved laboratories notified in accordance with Article 7 which is based outside the territory of the Member States concerned. The Commission shall communicate the opinion of this laboratory to all the Member States, which may submit their comments to it within a period of one month.

After taking note of any such comments the Commission shall, if necessary formulate appropriate recommendations or opinions.

If in preparing its opinion a laboratory consulted unavoidably incurs expenditure, which may if necessary include additional tests, the Commission will defray that expenditure on production of documentary evidence. If, however, further to an opinion a decision to suspend recognition of a certificate of conformity is not maintained, the Member State which took it shall reimburse the Commission, in accordance with the procedures for the payment then negotiated with the Member State.

4. If the reasons invoked in support of the Member State's decision are as described in paragraph 1 (b), the Commission shall refer the matter to the Committee referred to in Article 5, which shall express its opinion as a matter of urgency. On the basis of that opinion the Commission shall decide whether or not to withdraw the common specification in question from the list published in the *Official Journal of the European Communities*. If it withdraws the specification, the Commission shall inform the CEPT and may entrust it with a further brief.

5. If a Member State considers that terminal equipment which has already been approved does not meet one or more of the essential requirements, it may revoke the type approval granted and shall in that case immediately apply the procedures set out in paragraphs 1 and 2.

Article 9

The Commission shall examine the detailed rules for the second stage of the establishment of a market in telecommunication terminal equipment without internal frontiers covering, in particular, the implementation of mutual recognition of type approval for terminal equipment. To this end it shall submit proposals to the Council within a period of two years following the implementation of this Directive.

Article 10

This Directive shall not prejudice the application of Directive 83/189/EEC.

Article 11

1. Member States shall introduce the measures necessary to comply with this Directive within a period of not more than one year following adoption thereof. It shall forthwith inform the Commission thereof.
2. Member states shall ensure that the Commission is informed of the main provisions of national law which they adopt in the field governed by this Directive.

Article 12

This Directive is addressed to the Member States.
Done at Brussels, 24 July 1986.

For the Council
The President
A. Clark

Note
In April 1988, CEPT established the European Telecommunications Standards Institute (ETSI), based in Nice, France (http://www.etsi.fr/).

COMMISSION DIRECTIVE (88/301/EEC) OF 16 MAY 1988 ON COMPETITION IN THE MARKETS IN TELECOMMUNICATIONS TERMINAL EQUIPMENT OJ L131/73, 27 May 1988

THE COMMISSION OF THE EUROPEAN COMMUNITIES
Having regard to the Treaty establishing the European Economic Community, and in particular Article 90 (3) thereof,
Whereas:
1. In all the Member States, telecommunications are, either wholly or partly, a State monopoly generally granted in the form of special or exclusive

rights to one or more bodies responsible for providing and operating the network infrastructure and related services. Those rights, however, often go beyond the provision of network utilization services and extend to the supply of user terminal equipment for connection to the network. The last decades have seen considerable technical developments in networks, and the pace of development has been especially striking in the area of terminal equipment.

2.   Several Member States have, in response to technical and economic developments, reviewed their grant of special or exclusive rights in the telecommunications sector. The proliferation of types of terminal equipment and the possibility of the multiple use of terminals means that users must be allowed a free choice between the various types of equipment available if they are to benefit fully from the technological advances made in the systems.

3.   Article 30 of the Treaty prohibits quantitative restrictions on imports from other Member States and all measures having equivalent effect. The grant of special or exclusive rights to import and market goods to one organization can, and often does, lead to restrictions on imports from other Member States.

4.   Article 37 of the Treaty states that 'Member States shall progressively adjust any State monopolies of a commercial character so as to ensure that when the transitional period has ended no discrimination regarding the conditions under which goods are procured and marketed exists between nationals of Member States.

The provisions of this Article shall apply to any body through which a Member State, in law or in fact, either directly or indirectly supervises, determines or appreciably influences imports or exports between Member States. These provisions shall likewise apply to monopolies delegated by the State to others. Paragraph 2 of Article 37 prohibits Member States from introducing any new measure contrary to the principles laid down in Article 37 (1).

5.   The special or exclusive rights relating to terminal equipment enjoyed by national telecommunications monopolies are exercised in such a way as, in practice, to disadvantage equipment from other Member States, notably by preventing users from freely choosing the equipment that best suits their needs in terms of price and quality, regardless of its origin. The exercise of these rights is therefore not compatible with Article 37 in all the Member States except Spain and Portugal, where the national monopolies are to be adjusted progressively before the end of the transitional period provided for by the Act of Accession.

6.   The provision of installation and maintenance services is a key factor in the purchasing or rental of terminal equipment. The retention of exclusive rights in this field would be tantamount to retention of the exclusive marketing rights. Such rights must therefore also be abolished if the abolition of exclusive importing and marketing rights is to have any practical effect.

7.   Article 59 of the Treaty provides that 'restrictions on freedom to provide services within the Community shall be progressively abolished during the transitional period in respect of nationals of Member States who are established in a State of the Community other than that of the person for whom the services are intended.' Maintenance of terminals is a service within the meaning of Article 60 of the Treaty. As the transitional period has ended, the service in question, which cannot from a commercial point of view be

dissociated from the marketing of the terminals must be provided freely and in particular when provided by qualified operators.

8. Article 90 (1) of the Treaty provides that 'in the case of public undertakings and undertakings to which Member States grant special or exclusive rights, Member States shall neither enact nor maintain in force any measure contrary to the rules contained in this Treaty, in particular to those rules provided for in Article 7 and Articles 85 to 94.'

9. The market in terminal equipment is still as a rule governed by a system which allows competition in the common market to be distorted: this situation continues to produce infringements of the competition rules laid down by the Treaty and to affect adversely the development of trade to such an extent as would be contrary to the interests of the Community. Stronger competition in the terminal equipment market requires the introduction of transparent technical specifications and type-approval procedures which meet the essential requirements mentioned in Council Directive 86/361/EEC[1] and allow the free movement of terminal equipment. In turn, such transparency necessarily entails the publication of technical specifications and type approval procedures. To ensure that the latter are applied transparently, objectively and without discrimination, the drawing-up and application of such rules should be entrusted to bodies independent of competitors in the market in question. It is essential that the specifications and type-approval procedures are published simultaneously and in an orderly fashion. Simultaneous publication will also ensure the behaviour contrary to the Treaty is avoided. Such simultaneous, orderly publication can be achieved only by means of a legal instrument that is binding on all the Member States. The most appropriate instrument to this end is a directive.

10. The Treaty entrusts the Commission with very clear tasks and gives it specific powers with regard to the monitoring of relations between the Member States and their public undertakings and enterprises to which they have delegated special or exclusive rights, in particular as regards the elimination of quantitative restrictions and measures having equivalent effect, discrimination between nationals of Member States, and competition. The only instrument, therefore, by which the Commission can efficiently carry out the tasks and powers assigned to it, is a Directive based on Article 90 (3).

11. Telecommunications bodies or enterprises are undertakings within the meaning of Article 90 (1) because they carry on an organized business activity involving the production of goods or services. They are either public undertakings or private enterprises to which the Member States have granted special or exclusive rights for the importation, marketing, connection, bringing into service of telecommunications terminal equipment and/or maintenance of such equipment. The grant and maintenance of special and exclusive rights for terminal equipment constitute measures within the meaning of that Article. The conditions for applying the exception of Article 90(2) are not fulfilled. Even if the provision of a telecommunications network for the use of the general public is a service of general economic interest entrusted by the State to the telecommunications bodies, the abolition of their special or exclusive rights to import and market terminal equipment would not obstruct, in law or in fact, the performance of that service. This is all the more

---

1 OJ No L, 217. 5. 8. 1986, p. 21.

true given that Member States are entitled to subject terminal equipment to type approval procedures to ensure that they conform to the essential requirements.

12.   Article 86 of the Treaty prohibits as incompatible with the common market any conduct by one or more undertakings that involves an abuse of a dominant position within the common market or a substantial part of it.

13.   The telecommunications bodies hold individually or jointly a monopoly on their national telecommunications network. The national networks are markets. Therefore, the bodies each individually or jointly hold a dominant position in a substantial part of the market in question within the meaning of Article 86.

The effect of the special or exclusive rights granted to such bodies by the State to import and market terminal equipment is to:

— restrict users to renting such equipment, when it would often be cheaper for them, at least in the long term to purchase this equipment. This effectively makes contracts for the use of networks subject to acceptance by the user of additional services which have no connection with the subject of the contracts.

— limit outlets and improve technical progress since the range of equipment offered by the telecommunications bodies is necessarily limited and will not be the best available to meet the requirements of a significant proportion of users.

Such conduct is expressly prohibited by Article 86 (d) and (b), and is likely significantly to affect trade between Member States.

At all events, such special or exclusive rights in regard to the terminal equipment market give rise to a situation which is contrary to the objective of Article 3 (f) of the Treaty, which provides for the institution of a system ensuring that competition in the common market is not distorted, and requires a future that competition must not be eliminated. Member States have an obligation under Article 5 of the Treaty to abstain from any measure which could jeopardize the attainment of the objectives of the Treaty, including Article 3 (f).

The exclusive rights to import and market terminal equipment must therefore be regarded as incompatible with Article 86 in conjunction with Article 3, and the grant or maintenance of such rights by a Member State is prohibited under Article 90 (1).

14.   To enable users to have access to the terminal equipment of their choice, it is necessary to know and make transparent the characteristics of the termination points of the network to which the terminal equipment is to be connected. Member States must therefore ensure that the characteristics are published and that users have access to termination points.

15.   To be able to market their products, manufacturers of terminal equipment must know what technical specifications they must satisfy. Member States should therefore formalize and publish the specifications and type approval rules, which they must notify to the Commission in draft form, in accordance with Council Directive 83/189/EEC.[2] The specifications may be extended to products imported from other Member States only insofar as they are necessary to ensure conformity with the essential requirements

---

specified in Article 2 (17) of Directive 86/361/EEC that can legitimately be required under Community law. Member States must, in any event, comply with Articles 30 and 36 of the Treaty, under which an importing Member State must allow terminal equipment legally manufactured and marketed in another Member State to be imported in another Member State to be imported on to its territory, and may only subject it to such type approval and possibly refuse approval for reasons concerning conformity with the above-mentioned essential requirements.

16. The immediate publication of these specifications and procedures cannot be considered in view of their complexity. On the other hand, effective competition is not possible without such publication, since potential competitors of the bodies or enterprises with special or exclusive rights are unaware of the precise specifications with which their terminal equipment must comply and of the terms of the type-approval procedures and hence their cost and duration. A deadline should therefore be set for the publication of specifications and the type-approval procedures. A period of two-and-a-half years will also enable the telecommunications bodies with special or exclusive rights to adjust to the new market conditions and will enable economic operators, especially small and medium-sized enterprises, to adapt to the new competitive environment.

17. Monitoring of type-approval specifications and rules cannot be entrusted to a competitor in the terminal equipment market in view of the obvious conflict of interest. Member States should therefore ensure that the responsibility for drawing up type-approval specifications and rules is assigned to a body independent of the operator of the network and of any other competitor in the market for terminals.

18. The holders of special or exclusive rights in the terminal equipment in question have been able to impose on their customers long-term contracts preventing the introduction of free competition from having a practical effect within a reasonable period. Users must therefore be given the right to obtain a revision of the duration of their contracts.

HAS ADOPTED THIS DIRECTIVE:

Article 1

For the purposes of this Directive:
— 'terminal equipment' means equipment directly or indirectly connected to the termination of a public telecommunications network to send, process or receive information. A connection is indirect if equipment is placed between the terminal and the termination of the network. In either case (direct or indirect), the connection may be made by wire, optical fibre or electromagnetically.

Terminal equipment also means receive-only satellite stations not reconnected to the public network of a Member State.
— 'undertaking' means a public or private body, to which a Member State grants special or exclusive rights for the importation, marketing, connection, bringing into service of telecommunications terminal equipment and/or maintenance of such equipment.

Article 2

Member States which have granted special or exclusive rights within the meaning of Article 1 to undertakings shall ensure that those rights are withdrawn.

They shall, not later than three months following the notification of this Directive, inform the Commission of the measures taken or draft legislation introduced to that end.

Article 3

Member States shall ensure that economic operators have the right to import, market, connect, bring into service and maintain terminal equipment. However, Member States may;

— in the absence of technical specifications, refuse to allow terminal equipment to be connected and brought into service where such equipment does not, according to a reasoned opinion of the body referred to in Article 6, satisfy the essential requirements laid down in Article 2 (17) of Directive 86/361/EEC.

— require economic operators to possess the technical qualifications needed to connect, bring into service and maintain terminal equipment on the basis of objective, non-discriminatory and publicly available criteria.

Article 4

Member States shall ensure that users have access to new public network termination points and that the physical characteristics of these points are published not later than 31 December 1988.

Access to public network termination points existing at 31 December 1988 shall be given within a reasonable period to any user who so requests.

Article 5

1. Member States shall, not later than the date mentioned in Article 2, communicate to the Commission a list of all technical specifications and type approval procedures which are used for terminal equipment, and shall provide the publication references.

Where they have not as yet been published in a Member State, the latter shall ensure that they are published not later than the dates referred to in Article 8.

2. Member States shall ensure that all other specifications and type approval procedures for terminal equipment are formalized and published. Member States shall communicate the technical specifications and Commission in accordance with Directive 83/189/EEC and according to the timetable set out in Article 8.

Article 6

Member States shall ensure that, from 1 July 1989, responsibility for drawing up the specifications referred to in Article 5, monitoring their application and granting type approval is entrusted to a body independent of public or private undertakings offering goods and/or services in the telecommunications sector.

Article 7

Member States shall take the necessary steps to ensure that undertakings within the meaning of Article 1 make it possible for their customers to terminate, with maximum notice of one year, leasing or maintenance contracts which concern terminal equipment subject to exclusive or special rights at the time of the conclusion of the contracts.

For terminal equipment requiring type-approval. Member States shall ensure that this possibility of termination is afforded by the undertakings in question no later than the dates provided for in Article 8. For terminal equipment not requiring type-approval. Member States shall introduce this possibility no later than the date provided for in Article 2.

Article 8

Member states shall inform the Commission of the draft technical specifications and type-approval procedures referred to in Article 5 (2):

— not later than 31 December 1988 in respect of equipment in category A of the list in Annex I.

— not later than 30 September 1989 in respect of equipment in category B in the list in Annex I.

— not later than 30 June 1990 in respect of other terminal equipment in category C of the list in Annex I.

Member States shall bring these specifications and type approval procedures into force after expiry of the procedure provided for by Directive 83/189/EEC.

Article 9

Member States shall provide the Commission at the end of each year with a report allowing it to monitor compliance with the provisions of Articles 2, 3, 4, 6 and 7.

An outline of the report is attached as Annex II.

Article 10

The provisions of this Directive shall be without prejudice to the provisions of the instruments of accession of Spain and Portugal, and in particular Articles 48 and 208 of the Act of Accession.

Article 11

This Directive is addressed to the Member States.

Done at Brussels, 16 May 1988.

For the Commission
Peter Sutherland
Member of the Commission

ANNEX I LIST OF TERMINAL EQUIPMENT
REFERRED TO IN ARTICLE 8

	Category
Additional telephone set; private automatic branch exchanges (PABXs)	A
Modems	A
Telex terminals	B
Data transmission terminals	B
Mobile telephones	B
Receive only satellite stations not reconnected to the public network of a Member State	B
First telephone set	C
Other terminal equipment	C

ANNEX II OUTLINE OF THE REPORT
PROVIDED FOR IN ARTICLE 9

Implementation of Article 2
 1.   Terminal equipment for which legislation is being or has been modified.
By category of terminal equipment:
— date of adoption of the measure or,
— date of introduction of the bill or,
— date of entry into force of the measure.
 2.   Terminal equipment still subject to special or exclusive rights:
— type of terminal equipment and rights concerned.

Implementation of Article 3
— terminal equipment, the connection and/or commissioning of which has been restricted,
— technical qualifications required, giving reference of their publication.

Implementation of Article 4
— references of publications in which the physical characteristics are specified,
— number of existing network termination points,
— number of network termination points now accessible.

Implementation of Article 6
— independent body or bodies appointed.

Implementation of Article 7
— measures put into force, and
— number of terminated contracts.

Notes
1. A considerable amount of case law has arisen under this Directive. In particular, see the case brought by the French Republic, with other Member State support: Judgment of the Court of 19 March 1991 in Case C-202/88: *French Republic* v *Commission of the European Communities* ([1991] ECR I-1223; [1992] 5 CMLR 552; OJ C 96/06, 12 April 1991). The Court held the following:

'(1)   Declares Article 2 of Commission Directive 88/301/EEC of 16 May 1988 on competition in the markets in telecommunications terminal equipment void in so far as it requires Member States which grant undertakings special rights regarding the importation, marketing, connection or bringing into service of terminal equipment and/or maintenance of such equipment to withdraw such rights and to inform the Commission of the measures taken or draft legislation introduced to that end;
  (2)   Declares void Article 7 of the Directive;
  (3)   Declares Article 9 of the Directive void in so far as it refers to the provisions of Article 2 which are concerned with special rights and to Article 7 of the Directive;
  (4)   Dismisses the remainder of the application; . . .'
See also generally: *Rouffeteau & Badia* [1994] Case C-314/93, ECR I-3257, [OJ 94/C233/13]; where the ECJ held:
  'Neither Article 30 of the EEC Treaty nor Directive 88/301/EEC precludes national rules which prohibit traders, with penalties for infringement, from importing terminal equipment which has not been approved for release for consumption, possessing it with a view to sale, selling, distributing or advertising it, even if the importer, holder or vender has clearly stated that such equipment is intended solely for re-export, where there is no certainty that it will actually be re-exported, and is therefore not suitable for connection to the public network.'
See also *RTT* v *GB-INN0*-BM [1991] Case C-18/88, ECR I-5941; where the ECJ held:
  'Articles 3(f), 90 and 86 of the EEC Treaty preclude a Member State from granting to the undertaking which operates the public telecommunications network the power to lay down standards for telephone equipment and to check that economic operators meet those standards when it is itself competing with those operators on the market for that equipment;'.
2.   With regard to **Article 3,** the 'essential requirements' referred to in Article 2(17) of Directive 86/361/EEC are user safety; safety of employees of public telecommunications network operators, protection of the public telecommunications network from harm and interworking of terminal equipment, in justified cases. These were extended in Directive 91/263 at Article 4.
3. Cases which specifically address **Article 6**: see *Procureur du Roi* v *Lagauche & Others, Evrard* [1993] Cases C-46/90 and C-93/91, ECR I-5267, [OJ 93/C316/3]; *Ministere Public* v *Decoster* [1993] Case C-69/91, ECR I-5335, [OJ 93/C332/7]; *Ministere Public* v *Taillandier-Neny* [1993] Case C-92/91, ECR I-5383, [OJ 93/C338/ 6]. Most recently, see *Thierry Tranchant and Tlphone Store SARL* [1995] Case C-91/94, ECR I-3911, [OJ 96/16/6]; where the ECJ held that Article 6:

'must be interpreted as precluding the application of national rules which prohibit economic agents from, and penalize them for, manufacturing, importing, stocking for sale . . . terminal equipment without furnishing proof, in the form of a type-approval or another document regarded as equivalent, that such equipment conforms to certain essential requirements . . . where there is no guarantee that a test laboratory responsible for technically monitoring the conformity of the equipment with the technical specifications is independent from economic agents offering goods and services in the telecommunications sector.'

COUNCIL DIRECTIVE (91/263/EEC) OF 29 APRIL 1991 ON THE APPROXIMATION OF THE LAWS OF THE MEMBER STATES CONCERNING TELECOMMUNICATIONS TERMINAL EQUIPMENT, INCLUDING THE MUTUAL RECOGNITION OF THEIR CONFORMITY
OJ L128/1, 23 May 1991

THE COUNCIL OF THE EUROPEAN COMMUNITIES,

Having regard to the Treaty establishing the European Economic Community, and in particular Article 100a thereof,

Having regard to the proposal from the Commission,[1]

In cooperation with the European Parliament,[2]

Having regard to the opinion of the Economic and Social Comittee,[3]

Whereas Directive 86/361/EEC[4] introduced the initial stage of the mutual recognition of type approval for telecommunications terminal equipment and in particular in its Article 9 envisaged a further stage for full mutual recognition of type approval for terminal equipment;

Whereas Decision 87/95/EEC[5] sets out the measures to be implemented for the promotion of standardization in Europe and the preparation and implementation of standards in the field of information technology and telecommunications;

Whereas the Commission has issued a Green Paper on the development of the common market for telecommunications services and equipment proposing to accelerate the introduction of the full mutual recognition of type approval as the measure vital for the development of a competitive Community-wide terminal market;

Whereas the Council, in its resolution of 30 June 1988 on the development of the common market for telecommunications services and equipment up to 1992,[6] considers as a major goal in the telecommunications policy the full mutual recognition of type approval for terminal equipment on the basis of the rapid development of common European conformity specifications;

Whereas the terminal equipment sector is a vital part of the telecommunications industry, which is one of the industrial mainstays of the economy in the Community;

Whereas harmonizing conditions for the placing on the market of telecommunications terminal equipment will create the conditions for an open and unified market;

Whereas real, comparable access to third country markets for European manufacturers should preferably the achieved through multilateral negotiations within GATT, although bilateral talks between the Community and third countries may also contribute to this process;

Whereas the Council resolution of 7 May 1985 provides for a new approach to technical harmonization and standards;[7]

Whereas the scope of the Directive must be based on a general definition of the term 'terminal equipment' so as to allow the technical development of products;

Whereas Community law in its present form provides — notwithstanding one of the fundamental rules of the Community, namely the free movement of goods — that obstacles to movement within the Community, resulting from disparities in national legislation relating to the marketing of products, must be accepted in so far as such requirements can be recognized as being

1 OJ No C 211, 17. 8. 1989, p. 12.
2 OJ No C 113, 7. 5. 1990; and OJ No C 19, 28. 1. 1991, p. 88.
3 OJ No C 329, 30. 12. 1989, p. 1
4 OJ No L 217, 5. 8. 1986, p. 21.
5 OJ No L 36, 7. 2. 1987, p. 31.
6 OJ No C 257, 4. 10. 1988, p. 1.
7 OJ No C 136, 4. 6. 1985, p. 1.

necessary to satisfy imperative requirements; whereas, therefore, the harmonization of laws in this case must be limited only to those requirements
necessary to satisfy the essential requirements relating to terminal equipment;
whereas these requirements must replace the relevant national requirements
because they are essential;

Whereas the essential requirements must be satisfied in order to safeguard
the general interest; whereas these requirements must be applied with
discernment to take account of the state of the art at the time of manufacture
and economic requirements;

Whereas Council Directive 73/23/EEC of 19 February 1973 on the
harmonization of the laws of the Member States relating to electrical
equipment designed for use within certain voltage limits[8] and Council
Directive 83/189/EEC of 28 March 1983 laying down a procedure for the
provision of information in the field of technical standards and regulations,[9]
as amended by Directive 88/182/EEC,[10] are applicable, *inter alia*, to the fields
of telecommunications and information technology;

Whereas Council Directive 89/336/EEC of 3 May 1989 on the approximation of the laws of Member States relating to electromagnetic compatibility[11] is applicable, *inter alia*, to the fields of telecommunications and
information technology; whereas it is, however, appropriate to delete the
provisions of Directive 89/336/EEC in so far as they refer to the definition of
telecommunications terminal equipment and to the conformity assessment
procedures to be applied for such equipment;

Whereas in respect of the essential requirements and in order to help
manufacturers to prove conformity to those requirements, it is desirable to
have standards harmonized at European level to safeguard the general interest
in the design and manufacture of terminal equipment and in order to allow
checks of conformity to those requirements; whereas these standards harmonized at European level are drawn up by private-law bodies and must
retain their nonbinding status; whereas for this purpose the Europen Committee for Standardization (CEN), the European Commttee for Electrotechnical Standardization (Cenelec) and the European Telecommunications
Standards Institute (ETSI), are the bodies recognized as competent to adopt
harmonized standards; whereas, within the meaning of this Directive, a
harmonized standard is a technical specification (European standard or
harmonization document) adopted by one of these bodies, on the basis of a
remit from the Commission in accordance with the provision of Directive
83/189/EEC, and in accordance with the general guidelines referred to above;

Whereas in respect of the essential requirements related to interworking
with public telecommunications networks, and in cases where it is justified,
through such networks, it is in general not possible to comply with such
requirements other than by the application of unique technical solutions;
whereas such solutions shall therefore be mandatory;

Whereas the proposals for common technical regulations are, as a general
rule, drawn up on the basis of harmonized standards, and, in order to ensure
an appropriate technical coordination on a broad European basis, of

8 OJ No L 77, 26. 3. 1973, p. 29.
9 OJ No L 109, 26. 4. 1983, p. 8.
10 OJ No L 81, 26. 3. 1988, p. 75.
11 OJ No 1, 139, 23. 5. 1989, p. 19.

additional consultations, in particular with the Telecommunications Regulations Application Committee (TRAC) set up by members of the European Conference of Postal and Telecommunications Administrations (CEPT) in a memorandum of understanding signed in 1991;

Whereas it is essential to ensure that notified bodies are of a high standard throughout the Community and meet minimum criteria of competence, impartiality and financial and other independence from clients;

Whereas it is appropriate to set up a committee bringing together parties directly concerned with the implementation of this Directive, in particular the national bodies designated for certifying conformity, to assist the Commission in executing the tasks entrusted to it by this Directive; whereas representatives from the telecommunication organizations, users, consumers, manufacturers, service providers and the trade unions should have the right to be consulted;

Whereas the Member States' responsibility for safety, health and the other aspects covered by the essential requirements on their territory must be recognized in a safeguard clause providing for adequate Community protection procedures;

Whereas the addressees of any decision taken under this Directive must be informed of the reasons for such a decision and the means of appeal open to them;

Whereas measures must be adopted with the aim of progressively establishing the internal market over a period expiring on 31 December 1992; whereas the internal market comprises an area without internal frontiers in which the free movement of goods, persons, services and capital is ensured,

HAS ADOPTED THIS DIRECTIVE:

CHAPTER 1   SCOPE, PLACING ON THE MARKET AND FREE CIRCULATION

Article 1

1.   This Directive shall apply to terminal equipment.
2.   For the purpose of this Directive:
— 'public telecommunications network' means the public telecommunications infrastructure which permits the conveyance of signals between defined network termination points by wire, by microwave, by optical means or by other electromagnetic means,
— 'terminal equipment' means equipment intended to be connected to the public telecommunications network, i.e.:
   (a)   to be connected directly to the termination of a public telecommunications network;
   or
   (b)   to interwork with a public telecommunications network being connected directly or indirectly to the termination of a public telecommunications network
in order to send, process or receive information.
The system of connection may be wire, radio, optical or other electromagnetic system,

— 'technical specification' means a specification contained in a document which lays down the characteristics required of a product such as levels of quality, performance, safety or dimensions, including the requirements applicable to the product as regards terminology, symbols, testing and test methods, packaging, marking and labelling,

— 'standard' means a technical specification adopted by a recognized standards body for repeated or continuous application, compliance with which is not compulsory.

3. The intended purpose of the equipment, shall be declared by the manufacturer or supplier of the equipment. However, terminal equipment within the meaning of paragraph 2 which makes use of a system of communication employing the radio frequency spectrum is presumed to be intended for connection to the public telecommunications network.

Article 2

1. Notwithstanding Article 1, equipment which is capable of being connected to the public telecommunications network, but is not intended for such a purpose, shall be accompanied by a manufacturer's or supplier's declaration, the model of which is to be found in Annex VIII and by the operating manual. At the time of placing the equipment on the market for the first time, a copy of such documentation shall be transmitted to the notified body referred to in Article 10 (1) in the Member State where this first placing on the market takes place. In addition, such equipment shall be subject to the provisions of Article 11 (4).

2. The manufacturer or supplier shall be prepared to justify once, at the request of any notified body referred to in Article 10 (1), the intended purpose of such equipment on the basis of its relevant technical characteristics, its functions and indications of the market segment it is intended for.

Article 3

1. Member States shall take all appropriate measures to ensure that terminal equipment may be placed on the market and put into service only if it complies with the requirements laid down in this Directive when it is properly installed and maintained and used for its intended purpose.

2. Member States shall also take all appropriate measures to ensure that equipment referred to in Article 2 may be placed and allowed to remain on the market only if it complies with the requirements laid down by this Directive for this equipment and may not be connected to the public telecommunications network within the meaning of Article 1 (2).

3. Member States shall also take all appropriate measures to ensure that terminal equipment or equipment referred to in Article 2 is disconnected from the public telecommunications network if it is not used for its intended purpose. Member States may moreover take all appropriate measures, according to their national laws, to prevent connection to the public telecommunications network of terminal equipment that is not used in conformity with its intended purpose.

Article 4

Terminal equipment shall satisfy the following essential requirements:

(a)   user safety, in so far as this requirement is not covered by Directive 73/23/EEC;

(b)   safety of employees of public telecommunications networks operators, in so far as this requirement is not covered by Directive 73/23/EEC;

(c)   electromagnetic compatibility requirements in so far as they are specific to terminal equipment;

(d)   protection of the public telecommunications network from harm;

(e)   effective use of the radio frequency spectrum, where appropriate;

(f)   interworking of terminal equipment with public telecommunications network equipment for the purpose of establishing, modifying, charging for, holding and clearing real or virtual connection;

(g)   interworking of terminal equipment via the public telecommunications network, in justified cases.

The cases where terminal equipment supports:

(i)   reserved service according to Community law;

or

(ii)   a service which the Council has decided that there should be Community-wide availability,

are considered as justified cases and the requirements concerning this interworking are determined in accordance with the procedure provided for in Article 14.

In addition, after consultation of representatives of the bodies referred to in Article 13 (3) and taking due account of the result of these consultations, the Commission may propose that this essential requirement is recognized as being justified for other terminal equipment in accordance with the procedure provided for in Article 14.

Article 5

Member States shall not impede the placing on the market and the free circulation and use on their territory of terminal equipment which complies with the provisions of this Directive.

Article 6

1.   Member States shall presume compliance with the essential requirements referred to in Article 4 (a) and (b) in respect of terminal equipment which is in conformity with the national standards implementing the relevant harmonized standards, the references of which have been published in the *Official Journal of the European Communities*. Member States shall publish the references of such national standards.

2.   The Commission shall, in accordance with the procedure laid down in Article 14, adopt:

— as a first step, the measure identifying the type of terminal equipment for which a common technical regulation is required, as well as the associated scope statement for that regulation, with a view to its transmission to the relevant standardization bodies,

— as a second step, once they have been prepared by the relevant standardization bodies, the corresponding harmonized standards, or parts thereof, implementing the essential requirements referred to in Article 4 (c)

to (g) which shall be transformed into common technical regulations, compliance with which shall be mandatory and the reference of which shall be published in the *Official Journal of the European Communities*.

Article 7

Where a Member State or the Commission considers that the harmonized standards referred to in Article 6 exceed or do not entirely meet the essential requirements referred to in Article 4, the Commission or the Member State concerned shall bring the matter before the Committee referred to in Article 13, hereinafter referred to as 'the Committee', giving the reasons therefor. The Committee shall deliver an opinion as soon as possible.

In the light of the Committee's opinion and after consultation of the standing Committee set up by Directive 83/189/EEC, the Commission shall inform the Member States whether or not it is necessary to withdraw reference to those standards and any related technical regulations from the *Official Journal of the European Communities* and shall take the necessary steps to correct the shortcomings noted in the standards.

Article 8

1. Where a Member State finds that terminal equipment bearing the markings under the provision laid down in Chapter III does not comply with the relevant essential requirements when properly used in accordance with the purpose intended by the manufacturer, it shall take all appropriate measures to withdraw such products from the market or to prohibit or restrict their being placed on the market.

The Member State concerned shall immediately inform the Commission of any such measure indicating the reasons for its decision, and in particular whether non-compliance is due to:

(a) incorrect application of the harmonized standards or common technical regulations referred to in Article 6;

(b) shortcomings in the harmonized standards or common technical regulations referred to in Article 6 themselves.

2. The Commission shall enter into consultation with the parties concerned as soon as possible. Where, after such consultation, the Commission finds that any measure as referred to in paragraph 1 is justified it shall immediately so inform the Member State that took the action and the other Member States. Where the decision referred to in paragraph 1 is attributed to shortcomings in the harmonized standards or common technical regulations, the Commission, after consulting the parties concerned, shall bring the matter before the Committee within two months if the Member State which has taken the measure intends to maintain them, and shall initiate the procedure referred to in Article 7.

3. Where terminal equipment which does not comply with the relevant essential requirements bears the CE mark the competent Member State shall take appropriate action against whomsoever has affixed the mark and shall inform the Commission and the other Member States thereof.

4. The Commission shall keep the Member State informed of the progress and outcome of this procedure

CHAPTER II   CONFORMITY ASSESSMENT

Article 9

1.   According to the choice of the manufacturer or his authorized representative established within the Community, terminal equipment shall be subject to either the EC type-examination, as described in Annex I, or to the EC delcaration of conformity, as described in Annex IV.

2.   An EC type-examination as described in Annex I shall be accompanied by a declaration issued according to the EC declaration of conformity to type procedure as described in Annex II or Annex III.

3.   The records and correspondence relating to the procedure referred to in this Article shall be in an official language of the Member State where the said procedure will be carried out, or in a language acceptable to the notified body involved

4.   Article 10 (4) of Directive 89/336/EEC is hereby deleted.

Article 10

1.   Member States shall notify to the Commission the bodies established in the Community and their identifying symbols, which they have designated for carrying out the certification, product checks, and associated surveillance tasks pertaining to the procedures referred to in Article 9. Member States shall apply the minimum criteria, set out in Annex V, for the designation of such bodies. Bodies that satisfy the criteria fixed by the relevant harmonized standards shall be presumed to satisfy the criteria set out in Annex V.

2.   Member States shall inform the Commission of test laboratories established in the Community which they have designated for carrying out tests pertaining to the procedures referred to in Article 9. Notified bodies shall apply the criteria fixed by the appropriate parts of the relevant harmonized standards for the designation of such laboratories.

3.   The Commission shall publish the list of notified bodies and the list of test laboratories together with the tasks for which they have been designated in the *Official Journal of the European Communities* and shall ensure that this list is kept up to date.

4.   A Member State has designated a notified body or a test laboratory under paragraph 1 or 2 shall annul the designation if the notified body or the test laboratory no longer meets the relevant cirteria for designation. It shall immediately inform the other Member States and the Commission accordingly and withdraw the notification. Where a Member State or the Commission considers that a notified body or a test laboratory designated by a Member State does not meet the relevant criteria the matter shall be brought before the Committee referred to in Article 13, which shall give its opinion within three months; in the light of the Committee's opinion the Commission shall inform the Member State concerned of any changes needed if that notified body or test laboratory is to retain its recognized status.

5.   In order to facilitate the determination of conformity of terminal equipment with technical regulations and standards, the notified bodies shall recognize documentation issued by third country relevant bodies, when agreements between the Community and the third country concerned have been concluded on the basis of a mutually satisfactory understanding.

6.   The notified bodies referred to in Article 10 (1), when issuing an EC type-examination certificate as referred to in Annex I, followed by the appropriate document referred to in Annex II or III, or a decision on quality assurance assessment as referred to in Annex IV, issue at the same time an administrative approval for the connection of the concerned terminal equipment to the public telecommunications network.

CHAPTER III   CE MARK OF CONFORMITY AND INSCRIPTIONS

Article 11

1.   The marking of terminal equipment complying with this Directive shall consist of the CE mark consisting of the symbol 'CE', followed by the identifying symbol of the notified body responsible and a symbol indicating that the equipment is intended and is suitable to be connected to the public telecommunications network. The CE mark and these two symbols are shown in Annex VI.
2.   The affixing of marks which are likely to be confused with the marks of conformity specified in Annex VI shall be prohibited.
3.   Terminal equipment shall be identified by the manufacturer by means of type, batch and/or serial numbers and by the name of the manufacturer and/or supplier responsible for placing it on the market.
4.   Equipment manufacturers or suppliers who place on the market equipment as referred to in Article 2 shall affix the symbol specified in Annex VII in such a way that it follows the CE mark and visually forms an integral part of the total marking.

Article 12

Where it is established that the marking referred to in Article 11 (1) has been affixed to terminal equipment which:
— does not conform to an approved type,
— conforms to an approved type which does not meet the essential requirements applicable to it,
or, where the manufacturer has failed to fulfil his obligations under the relevant EC declaration of conformity,
the notified body shall withdraw the EC type-examination certificate referred to in Annex I, the EC quality system approval decision referred to in Annex III or the EC quality system approval decision as referred to in Annex IV, notwithstanding any decisions taken under Article 8.

CHAPTER IV   COMMITTEE

Article 13
1.   The Commission shall be assisted by a Committee of an advisory nature composed of the representatives of the Member States and chaired by the representative of the Commission. The Committee shall be called the Approvals Committee for Terminal Equipment (ACTE).
2.   The representative of the Commission shall submit to the Committee a draft of the measure to be taken. The Committee shall deliver its opinion

on the draft, within a time limit which the chairman may lay down according to the urgency of the matter, if necessary by taking a vote.

The opinion shall be recorded in the minutes; in addition, each Member State shall have the right to ask to have its position recorded in the minutes.

The Commission shall take the utmost account of the opinion delivered by the Committee. It shall inform the Committee of the manner in which its opinion has been taken into account.

3. The Commission will periodically consult the representative of the telecommunications organizations, the consumers, the manufacturers, the service providers and trade unions and will inform the Committee on the outcome of such consultations, with a view to taking due account of the outcome.

Article 14

1. Notwithstanding Article 13 (1) and (2), the following procedure shall apply for matters covered by Articles 4 (g) and 6 (2).

2. The representative of the Commission shall submit to the Committee established in Article 13 a draft of the measures to be taken as referred to in Articles 4 (g) and 6 (2). The Committee shall deliver its opinion on the draft within a time limit which the chairman may lay down according to the urgency of the matter. The opinion shall be delivered by the majority laid down in Article 148 (2) of the Treaty in the case of decisions which the Council is required to adopt on a proposal from the Commission. The votes of the representatives of the Member States within the Committee shall be weighted in the manner set out in that Article. The chairman shall not vote.

3. The Commission shall adopt the measures envisaged if they are in accordance with the opinion of the Committee.

4. If the measures envisaged are not in accordance with the opinion of the Committee, or if no opinion is delivered, the Commission shall, without delay, submit to the Council a proposal relating to the measure to be taken. The Council shall act by qualified majority. If, within three months from the date of referral to it, the Council has not acted, the proposed measure shall be adopted by the Commission.

CHAPTER V   FINAL AND TRANSITIONAL PROVISIONS

Article 15

The Commission shall draw up every second year a report on the implementation of this Directive, including progress on drawing up the relevant harmonized standards and on transforming them into technical regulations, as well as any problems that have arisen in the course of implementation. The report will also outline the activities of the Committee, and assess progress in achieving an open competitive market for termimal equipment at Community level consistent with the essential requirements referred to in Article 4.

Article 16

1. Directive 86/361/EEC is hereby repealed, with effect from 6 November 1992. References made to the repealed Directive shall be construed as being made to this Directive.

2. Notwithstanding paragraph 1 and Article 10 (2), Member States may designate as test laboratories such bodies which have been notified under Directive 86/361/EEC, without applying the criteria of Article 10 (2) for a period of 18 months after the effective date of repeal of Directive 86/361/ EEC, it being understood that these laboratories will continue to observe the criteria for which they were notified.

3. Notwithstanding paragraph 1, any type approval granted by Member States in accordance with Directive 86/361/EEC may remain valid under the legislation of the Member States within the criteria of validity appropriate to the original approval.

4. Notwithstanding paragraph 1, measures adopted under Directive 86/ 361/EEC shall be submitted to the Committee under the procedure of Article 14 for possible transposition into common technical regulations.

Article 17

1. Member States shall take the measure necessary to comply with this Directive not later than 6 November 1992. They shall forthwith inform the Commission thereof.

When Member States adopt these measure, they shall contain a reference to this Directive or shall be accompanied by such reference on the occasion of their official publication. The methods of making such a reference shall be laid down by the Member States.

2. Member States shall inform the Commission of the main provisions of domestic law which they adopt in the field governed by this Directive.

Article 18

This Directive is addressed to the Member States.

Done at Luxembourg, 29 April 1991.

For the Council
The President
R. Goebbels

ANNEX I   EC TYPE-EXAMINATION

1. EC type-examination is that part of the procedure whereby a notified body ascertains and attests that a specimen, representative of the production envisaged, meets the provisions of the Directive that apply to it.

2. The application for the EC type-examination shall be lodged by the manufacturer or his authorized representative established within the Community with a notified body of his choice.

The application shall include:

— the name and address of the manufacturer and, if the application is lodged by the authorized representative, his name and address in addition,

— a written declaration that the same application has not been lodged with any other notified body,

— the technical documentation, as described in point 3.

The applicant shall place at the disposal of the notified body a specimen, representative of the production envisaged and hereinafter called 'type'.[12] The notified body may request further specimens if needed for carrying out the test programme.

3. The technical documentation shall enable the conformity of the product with the essential requirements of the Directive to be assessed. It shall, as far as relevant for such assessment, cover the design, manufacture and operation of the product.

For example, the documentation shall contain as far as is relevant for assessment:

— a general type-description sufficient to identify the product preferably by provision of photographs,

— design and manufacturing drawings and lists of components, sub-assemblies, circuits, etc.,

— descriptions and explanations necessary for the understanding of said drawings and lists and the operation of the product,

— a list of the standards referred to in Article 6, applied in full or in part, and descriptions of the solutions adopted to meet the essential requirements of the Directive when the standards referred to in Article 6 have not been applied,

— results of examinations carried out, etc.,

— test reports,

— proposed user information or handbook.

4. The notified body shall:

4.1. examine the technical documentation, verify that the type has been manufactured in conformity with it and identify the elements which have been designed in accordance with the relevant provisions of the standards referred to in Article 6 (1), as well as the components of those standards;

4.2. perform, or have performed, the appropriate examinations and necessary tests to check whether the solutions adopted by the manufacturer meet the essential requirements of the Directive which are specified in Article 4 (a) and (b);

4.3. perform, or have performed, the appropriate examinations and necessary tests to check that the type meets the relevant common technical regulations specified in Article 6 (2);

4.4. agree with the applicant on the location where the examinations and necessary tests are to be carried out.

5. Where the type meets the provisions of the Directive, the notified body shall issue an EC type-examination certificate to the applicant. The certificate shall contain the name and address of the manufacturer, conclusions of the examination, conditions for its validity and the necessary data for identification of the approved type.

A list of the relevant parts of the technical documentation shall be annexed to the certificate and a copy kept by the notified body.

6. The applicant shall inform the notified body that holds the technical documentation concerning the EC type-examination certificate of all modifications to the approved product which must receive additional approval

---

12 A type may cover several versions of the product provided that the differences between the versions do not affect the level of safety and the other requirements concerning the performance of the product.

where such changes may affect the conformity with the essential requirements or the prescribed conditions for use of the product. This additional approval is given in the form of an addition to the original EC type-examination certificate.

7. Each notified body shall communicate to the other notified bodies the relevant information concerning the EC type-examination certificates and additions issued and withdrawn.

8. The other notified bodies may request copies of the EC type-examination certificates and/or their additions. The Annexes to the certificate shall be kept at the disposal of the other notified bodies.

9. The manufacturer or his authorized representative shall keep with the technical documentation copies of EC type-examination certificates and their additions for a period ending at least 10 years after the last product has been manufactured.

Where neither the manufacturer nor his authorized representative is established within the Community, the obligation to keep the technical documentation available shall be the responsibility of the person who places the product on the Community market.

ANNEX II   CONFORMITY TO TYPE

1. Conformity to type is that part of the procedure whereby the manufacturer or his authorized representative established within the Community ensures and declares that the products concerned are in conformity with the type as described in the EC type-examination certificate and satisfy the requirements of the Directive that applies to them. The manufacturer shall affix the marks referred to in Article 11 (1) to each product and draw up a written declaration of conformity to type.

2. The manufacturer shall take all measures necessary to ensure that the manufacturing process assures compliance of the manufactured products with the type as described in the EC type-examination certificate and with the requirements of the Directive that apply to them.

3. The manufacturer or his authorized representative shall keep a copy of the declaration of conformity for a period ending at least 10 years after the last product has been manufactured.

Where neither the manufacturer nor his authorized representative is established within the Community, the obligation to keep the declaration of conforming to type available shall be the responsibility of the person who places the product on the Community market.

4. A notified body chosen by the manufacturer shall carry out, or have carried out, product checks at random intervals. An adequate sample of the final products, which may be taken on site by the notified body or on its behalf, shall be examined and appropriate tests shall be carried out to check the conformity of products with the relevant requirements of the Directive. In those cases where one or more of the products checked do not conform, the notified body shall take appropriate measures.

ANNEX III   PRODUCTION QUALITY ASSURANCE

1. Production quality assurance is the procedure whereby the manufacturer who satisfies the obligations of point 2 ensures and declares that the

products concerned are in conformity with the type as described in the EC type-examination certificate and satisfy the requirements of the Directive that apply to them. The manufacturer shall affix the marks referred to in Article 11 (1) to each product and draw up a written declaration of conformity to type.

2. The manufacturer shall operate an approved quality system for production, final product inspection and testing as specified in point 3 and shall be subject to monitoring as specified in point 4.

3. Quality system

3.1. The manufacturer shall lodge an application for assessment of his quality system with a notified body of his choice, for the products concerned.

The application shall inlcude:

— all relevant information for the product category envisaged,

— the documentation concerning the quality system,

— if applicable, the technical documentation of the approved type and a copy of the EC type-examination certificate.

3.2. The quality system shall ensure compliance of the products with the type as described in the EC type-examination certificate and with the requirements of the Directive that apply to them.

All the element, requirements and provisions adopted by the manufacturer shall be documented in a systematic and orderly manner in the form of written policies, procedures and instructions. The quality system documentation must permit a consistent interpretation of the quality programmes, plan, manuals and records.

It shall contain in particular an adequate description of:

— the quality objectives and the organizational structure, responsibilities and powers of the management with regard to product quality,

— the manufacturing, quality control and quality assurance techniques, processes and systematic actions that will be used,

— the examinations and tests will be carried out before, during and after manufacture, and the frequency with which they will be carried out,

— the quality records, such as inspection reports and test data, calibration data, qualification reports of the personnel concerned, etc.,

— the means to monitor the achievement of the required product quality and the effective operation of the quality system.

3.3. The notified body shall assess the quality system to determine whether it satisfies the requirements referred to in point 3.2. It shall presume conformity with these requirements in respect of quality systems that implement the relevant harmonized standard.[13]

The auditing team shall have at least one member with experience of evaluation in the product technology concerned. The evaluation procedure shall include an inspection visit to the manufacturer's premises.

The decision shall be notified to the manufacturer. The notification shall contain the conclusions of the examination and the reasoned assessment decision.

3.4. The manufacturer shall undertake to fulfil the obligations arising out of the quality system as approved and to uphold it so that it remains adequate and efficient.

---

13 This harmonized standard will be EN 29002, supplemented, if necessary, to take into account the specific nature of the procedure for which it is implemented.

The manufacturer or his authorized representative shall keep the notified body that has approved the quality system informed of any intended updating of the quality system.

The notified body shall evaluate the modifications proposed and decide whether the amended quality system will still satisfy the requirements referred to in point 3.2. or whether a re-assessment is required.

It shall notify its decision to the manufacturer. The notification shall contain the conclusions of the examination and the reasoned assessment decision.

4.   Surveillance under the responsibility of the notified body

4.1.   The purpose of surveillance is to make sure that the manufacturer duly fulfils the obligations arising out of the approved quality system.

4.2.   The manufacturer shall allow the notified body access for inspection purpose to the locations of manufacture, inspection and testing, and storage and shall provide it with all necessary information, in particular:

— the quality system documentation,

— the quality records, such as inspection reports and test data, calibration data, qualification reports of the personnel concerned, etc.

4.3.   The notified body shall carry out audits at reasonable intervals to make sure that the manufacturer maintains and applies the quality system and shall provide an audit report to the manufacturer.

4.4.   Additionally, the notified body may pay unexpected visits to the manufacturer. During such visits the notified body may carry out, or cause to be carried out, tests to verify that the quality system is functioning correctly, if necessary. The notified body shall provide the manufacturer with a visit report and, if a test has taken place, with a report.

5.   The manufacturer shall, for a period ending at least 10 years after the last product has been manufactured, keep at the disposal of the national authorities:

— the documentation referred to in the second indent of point 3.1.,

— the updating referred to in the second paragraph of point 3.4.,

— the decisions and reports from the notified body which are referred to in the final paragraph of points 3.4., 4.3. and 4.4.

6.   Each notified body referred to in Article 10 (1) shall make available to the other notified bodies referred to in that Article the relevant information concerning the quality system approvals issued and withdrawn.

ANNEX IV   FULL QUALITY ASSURANCE

1.   Full quality assurance is the procedure whereby the manufacturer who satisfies the obligations of point 2 ensures and declares that the products concerned satisfy the requirements of the Directive that apply to them. The manufacturer shall affix the marks referred to in Article 11 (1) to each product and draw up a written declaration of conformity.

2.   The manufacturer shall operate an approved quality system for design, manufacture and final product inspection and testing as specified in point 3 and shall be subject to surveillance as specified in point 4.

3.   Quality system

3.1.   The manufacturer shall lodge an application for assessment of his quality system with a notified body.

The application shall include:
— all relevant information for the products envisaged,
— the quality system's documentation.
3.2.   The quality system shall ensure compliance of the products with the requirements of the Directive that apply to them.

All the elements, requirements and provisions adopted by the manufacturer shall be documented in a systematic and orderly manner in the form of written policies, procedures and instructions. This quality system documentation shall ensure a common understanding of the quality policies and procedures such as a quality programmes, plans, manuals and records.

It shall contain in particular an adequate description of:
— the quality objectives and the organizational structure, responsibilities and powers of the management with regard to design and product quality,
— the technical specifications, including the harmonized standards and technical regulations as well as relevant test specifications that will be applied and, where the standards referred to in Article 6 (1) will not be applied in full, the means will be used to ensure that the essential requirements of the Directive that apply to the products will be met,
— the design control and design verification techniques, processes and systematic actions that will be used when designing the products pertaining to the product category covered,
— the corresponding manufacturing, quality control and quality assurance techniques, processes and systematic actions that will be used,
— the examinations and tests will be carried out before, during and after manufacture, and the frequency with which they will be carried out; as well as the results of the tests carried out before manufacture where appropriate,
— the means by which it is ensured that the test and examination facilities respect the appropriate requirements for the performance of the necessary test,
— the quality records, such as inspection reports and test data, calibration data, qualification reports of the personnel concerned, etc.,
— the means to monitor the achievement of the required design and product quality and the effective operation of the quality system.
3.3.   The notified body shall assess the quality system to determine whether it satisfies the requirements referred to in point 3.2. It shall presume compliance with these requirements in respect of quality systems that implement the relevant harmonized standard.[14]

The notified body shall assess in particular whether the quality control system ensures conformity of the products with the requirements of the Directive in the light of the relevant documentation supplied in respect of points 3.1. and 3.2. including, where relevant, test results supplied by the manufacturer.

The auditing team shall have at least one member experienced as an assessor in the product technology concerned. The evaluation procedure shall include an assessment visit to the manufacturer's premises.

The decision shall be notified to the manufacturer. The notification shall contain the conclusions of the examination and the reasoned assessment decision.

---

14 This harmonized standard shall be EN 29001, supplemented, if necessary, to take into account the specific nature of the products for which it is implemented.

3.4. The manufacturer shall undertake to fulfil the obligations arising out of the quality system as approved and to uphold it so that it remains adequate and efficient.

The manufacturer or his authorized representative shall keep the notified body that has approved the quality system informed of any intended updating of the quality system.

The notified body shall evaluate the modifications proposed and decide whether the amended quality system will still satisfy the requirements referred to in point 3.2. or whether a re-assessment is required.

It shall notify its decision to the manufacturer. The notification shall contain the conclusions of the examination and the reasoned assessment decision.

4. EC surveillance under the responsibility of the notified body

4.1. The purpose of surveillance is to make sure that the manufacturer duly fulfils the obligations arising out of the approved quality system.

4.2. The manufacturer shall allow the notified body access for inspection purposes to the locations of design, manufacture, inspection and testing, and storage and shall provide it with all necessary information, in particular:

— the quality system documentation,

— the quality records as foreseen by the design part of the quality system, such as results of analyses, calculations, tests, etc.

— the quality records as foreseen by the manufacturing part of the quality system, such as inspection reports and test data, calibration data, qualification reports of the personnel concerned, etc.

4.3. The notified body shall carry out audits at reasonable intervals to make sure that the manufacturer maintains and applies the quality system and shall provide an audit report to the manufacturer.

4.4. Additionally, the notified body may pay unexpected visits to the manufacturer. At the time of such visits, the notified body may carry out tests or have them carried out in order to check the proper functioning of the quality system where necessary; it shall provide the manufacturer with a visit report and, if a test has been carried out, with a test report.

5. The manufacturer shall, for a period ending at least 10 years after the last product has been manufactured, keep at the disposal of the national authorities:

— the documentation referred to in the second indent of point 3.1.,

— the updating referred to in the second paragraph of point 3.4.,

— the decisions and reports from the notified body which are referred to in the final paragraph of points 3.4., 4.3. and 4.4.

6. Each notified body referred to in Article 10 (1) shall make available to the other notified bodies referred to in that Article the relevant information concerning quality system approvals including references to the product(s) concerned, issued and withdrawn.

ANNEX V   MINIMUM CRITERIA TO BE TAKEN INTO ACCOUNT BY MEMBER STATES WHEN DESIGNATING NOTIFIED BODIES IN ACCORDANCE WITH ARTICLE 10 (1)

1. The notified body, its director and the staff responsible for carrying out the tasks for which the notified body has been designated shall not be a

designer, manufacturer, supplier or installer of terminal equipment, or a network operator or a service provider, nor the authorized representative of any of such parties. They shall not become directly involved in the design, construction, marketing or maintenance of terminal equipment, nor represent the parties engaged in these activities. This does not preclude the possibility of exchanges of technical information between the manufacturer and the notified body.

2.   The notified body and its staff must carry out the tasks for which the notified body has been designated with the highest degree of professional integrity and technical competence and must be free from all pressures and inducements, particularly financial, which might influence their judgment or the results of any inspection, especially from persons or groups of persons with an interest in such results.

3.   The notified body must have at its disposal the necessary staff and facilities to enable it to perform properly the administrative and technical work associated with the tasks for which it has been designated.

4.   The staff responsible for inspections must have:

— sound technical and professional training,

— satisfactory knowledge of the requirements of the tests or inspections that are carried out and adequate experience of such tests or inspections,

— the ability to draw up the certificates, records and reports required to authenticate the performance of the inspections.

5.   The impartiality of inspection staff must be guaranteed. Their remuneration must not depend on the number of tests or inspections carried out nor on the results of such inspections.

6.   The notified body must take out liability insurance unless its liability is assumed by the State in accordance with national law, or the Member State itself is directly responsible.

7.   The staff of the notified body is bound to observe professional secrecy with regard to all information gained in carrying out its tasks (except *vis-à-vis* the competent administrative authorities of the State in which its activities are carried out) under this Directive or any provision of national law giving effect thereto.

ANNEX VI   MARKING FOR TERMINAL EQUIPMENT REFERRED TO IN ARTICLE 11 (1)

   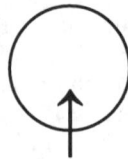   

Symbol of the notified body

ANNEX VII MARKING FOR EQUIPMENT REFERRED TO IN ARTICLE 11 (4)

ANNEX VIII MODEL OF A DECLARATION REFERRED TO IN ARTICLE 2 (1)

The manufacturer/supplier[15] ....

....

....

Declares that[16] ....

....

is not intended to be connected to a public telecommunications network.

The connection of such equipment to a public telecommunications network in the Community Member State will be in violation of the national law implementing Directive 91/263/EEC on the approximation of the laws of the Member States concerning telecommunication terminal equipment, including the mutual recognition of their conformity.

DATE, PLACE AND SIGNATURE

Notes
1.   Amended by Council Directive 93/68/EEC (OJ L220/1, 30 August 1993), Article 11, with respect to 'CE' marking.
2.   The Commission issued infringement proceedings against Member States, under Article 169 of the EEC Treaty, for failure to implement the Directive: e.g. Belgium (OJ 94/C275/162) and Ireland (OJ 94/C288/3).
3.   For the UK implementing regulations see: SI 1992/2423 (The Telecommunications Terminal Equipment Regulations 1992); SI 1994/3129 (The Telecommunications Terminal Equipment (Amendment and Extension) Regulations 1994) and SI 1995/144 (The Telecommunications Terminal Equipment (Amendment) Regulations 1995).
4.   See also subsequent legislation made under 91/263:
  Council Directive of 29 October 1993 supplementing Directive 91/263/EEC in respect of satellite earth station equipment (93/97/EEC; OJ L290/1, 24.11.93);
  Commission Decision of 21 December 1993 on a common technical regulation for the general attachment requirements for public pan-European cellular digital land-based mobile communications (94/11/EC; OJ L8/20, 12.1.94);

---

15 Name and address.
16 Equipment identification.

Commission Decision of 21 December 1993 on a common technical regulation for the telephony application requirements for public pan European cellular digital land-based mobile communications (94/12/EC; OJ L8/23, 12.1.94);

Commission Decision of 18 July 1994 on a common technical regulation for attachment requirements for terminal equipment interface for ONP 2048 kbit/s digital unstructured leased line (94/470/EC; OJ L194/87, 29.7.94);

Commission Decision of 18 July 1994 on a common technical regulation for general terminal attachment requirements for Digital European Cordless Telecommunications (DECT) (94/471/EC; OJ L194/89, 29.7.94);

Commission Decision of 18 July 1994 on a common technical regulation for telephony application requirements for Digital European Cordless Telecommunications (DECT) (94/472/EC; OJ L194/91, 29.7.94);

Commission Decision of 18 November 1994 on a common technical regulation for the pan-European integrated services digital network (ISDN) primary rate access (94/796/EC; OJ L329/1, 20.12.94);

Commission Decision of 18 November 1994 on a common technical regulation for the pan-European integrated services digital network (ISDN) basic access (94/797/EC; OJ L329/14, 20.12.94);

Commission Decision of 9 December 1994 on a common technical regulation for attachment requirements for terminal equipment interface for ONP 64 kbit/s digital unstructured leased line (94/821/EC; OJ L339/81, 29.12.94);

Commission Decision of 17 July 1995 on a common technical regulation for public land-based European radio message system (ERMES) receiver requirements (95/290/EC; OJ L182/21, 2.8.95);

Commission Decision of 28 November 1995 on a common technical regulation for attachment requirements for terminal equipment for Digital European Cordless Telecommunications (DECT), Public Access Profile (PAP) applications (95/525/EC; OJ L300/35, 13.12.95);

Commission Decision of 28 November 1995 on a common technical regulation for Integrated Services Digital Network (ISDN); Telephony 3,1 kHz teleservice, attachment requirements for handset terminals (95/526/EC; OJ L300/38, 13.12.95);

5.   See also related legislation: e.g. Council Directive of 28 April 1992 amending Directive 89/336/EEC on the approximation of the laws of the Member States relating to electromagnetic compatibility (92/31/EEC; OJ L126/11, 12.5.92).

TELECOMMUNICATION SERVICES

COMMISSION DIRECTIVE (90/388/EEC) OF 28 JUNE 1990
ON COMPETITION IN THE MARKETS FOR
TELECOMMUNICATIONS SERVICES
OJ L192/10, 24 July 1990

THE COMMISSION OF THE EUROPEAN COMMUNITIES,

Having regard to the Treaty establishing the European Economic Community, and in particular Article 90 (3) thereof,

Whereas:

(1) The improvement of telecommunications in the Community is an essential condition for the harmonious development of economic activities and a competitive market in the Community, from the point of view of both service providers and users. The Commission has therefore adopted a programme, set out in its Green Paper on the development of the common market for telecommunications services and equipment and in its communication on the implementation of the Green Paper by 1992, for progressively introducing competition into the telecommunications market. The programme does not concern mobile telephony and paging services, and mass communication services such as radio for television. The Council, in its resolution of 30 June 1988,[1] expressed broad support for the objectives of this programme, and in particular the progressive creation of an open Community market for telecommunications services. The last decades have seen considerable technological advances in the telecommunications sector. These allow an increasingly varied range of services to be provided, notably data transmission services, and also make it technically and economically possible for competition to take place between different service providers.

(2) In all the Member States the provision and operation of telecommunications networks and the provision of related services are generally vested in one or more telecommunications organizations holding exclusive or special rights. Such rights are characterized by the discretionary powers which the State exercises in various degrees with regard to access to the market for telecommunications services.

(3) The organizations entrusted with the provision and operation of the telecommunications network are undertakings within the meaning of Article 90 (1) of the Treaty because they carry on an organized business activity, namely the provision of telecommunications services. They are either public

---

1 OJ No C 257, 4. 10. 1988, p. 1.

undertakings or private enterprises to which the State has granted exclusive or special rights.

(4)   Several Member States, while ensuring the performance of public service tasks, have already revised the system of exclusive or special rights that used to exist in the telecommunications sector in their country. In all cases, the system of exclusive or special rights has been maintained in respect of the provision and operation of the network. In some Member States, it has been maintained for all telecommunications services, while in others such rights cover only certain services. All Member States have either themselves imposed or allowed their telecommunications administrations to impose restrictions on the free provision of telecommunications services.

(5)   The granting of special or exclusive rights to one or more undertakings to operate the network derives from the discretionary power of the State. The granting by a Member State of such rights inevitably restricts the provision of such services by other undertakings to or from other Member States.

(6)   In practice, restrictions on the provision of telecommunications services within the meaning of Article 59 to or from other Member States consist mainly in the prohibition on connecting leased lines by means of concentrators, multiplexers and other equipment to the switched telephone network, in imposing access charges for the connection that are out of proportion to the service provided, in prohibiting the routing of signals to or from third parties by means of leased lines or applying volume sensitive tariffs without economic justification or refusing to give service providers access to the network. The effect of the usage restrictions and the excessive charges in relation to net cost is to hinder the provision to or from other Member States of such telecommunications services as:

— services designed to improve telecommunications functions, e.g. conversion of the protocol, code, format or speed,

— information services providing access to data bases,

— remote data-processing services,

— message storing and forwarding services, e.g. electronic mail,

— transaction services, e.g. financial transactions, electronic commercial data transfer, teleshopping and telereservations,

— teleaction services, e.g. telemetry and remote monitoring.

(7)   Articles 55, 56 and 66 of the Treaty allow exceptions on non-economic grounds to the freedom to provide services. The restrictions permitted are those connected, even occasionally, with the exercise of official authority, and those connected with public policy, public security or public health. Since these are exceptions, they must be interpreted restrictively. None of the telecommunications services is connected with the exercise of official authority involving the right to use undue powers compared with the ordinary law, privileges of public power or a power of coercion over the public. The supply of telecommunication services cannot in itself threaten public policy and cannot affect public health.

(8)   The Court of Justice caselaw also recognizes restrictions on the freedom to provide services if they fulfil essential requirements in the general interest and are applied without discrimination and in proportion to the objective. Consumer protection does not make it necessary to restrict freedom to provide telecommunications services since this objective can also be

attained through free competition. Nor can the protection of intellectual property be invoked in this connection. The only essential requirements derogating from Article 59 which could justify restrictions on the use of the public network are the maintenance of the integrity of the network, security of network operations and in justified cases, interoperability and data protection. The restrictions imposed, however, must be adapted to the objectives pursued by these legitimate requirements. Member States will have to make such restrictions known to the public and notify them to the Commission to enable it to assess their proportionality.

(9)   In this context, the security of network operations means ensuring the availability of the public network in case of emergency. The technical integrity of the public network means ensuring its normal operation and the interconnection of public networks in the Community on the basis of common technical specifications. The concept of interoperability of services means complying with such technical specifications introduced to increase the provision of services and the choice available to users. Data protection means measures taken to warrant the confidentiality of communications and the protection of personal data.

(10)   Apart from the essential requirements which can be included as conditions in the licensing or declaration procedures, Member States can include conditions regarding public-service requirements which constitute objective, non-discriminatory and transparent trade regulations regarding the conditions of permanence, availability and quality of the service.

(11)   When a Member State has entrusted a telecommunications organization with the task of providing packet or circuit switched data services for the public in general and when this service may be obstructed because of competition by private providers, the Commission can allow the Member State to impose additional conditions for the provision of such a service, with respect also to geographical coverage. In assessing these measures, the Commission in the context of the achievement of the fundamental objectives of the Treaty referred to in Article 2 thereof, including that of strengthening the Community's economic and social cohesion as referred to in Article 130a, will also take into account the situation of those Member States in which the network for the provision of the packet or circuit switched services is not yet sufficiently developed and which could justify the deferment for these Member States until 1 January 1996 of the date for prohibition on the simple resale of leased line capacity.

(12)   Article 59 of the Treaty requires the abolition of any other restriction on the freedom of nationals of Member States who are established in a Community country to provide services to persons in other Member States. The maintenance or introduction of any exclusive or special right which does not correspond to the abovementioned criteria is therefore a breach of Article 90 in conjunction with Article 59.

(13)   Article 86 of the Treaty prohibits as incompatible with the common market any conduct by one or more undertakings that involves an abuse of a dominant position within the common market or a substantial part of it. Telecommunications organizations are also undertakings for the purposes of this Article because they carry out economic activities, in particular the service they provide by making telecommunications networks and services available to users. This provision of the network constitutes a separate

services market as it is not interchangeable with other services. On each national market the competitive environment in which the network and the telecommunications services are provided is homogeneous enough for the Commission to be able to evaluate the power held by the organizations providing the services on these territories. The territories of the Member States constitute distinct geographical markets. This is essentially due to the existing difference between the rules governing conditions of access and technical operation, relating to the provision of the network and of such services. Furthermore, each Member State market forms a substantial part of the common market.

(14)   In each national market the telecommunications organizations hold individually or collectively a dominant position for the creation and the exploitation of the network because they are the only ones with networks in each Member State covering the whole territory of those States and because their governments granted them the exclusive right to provide this network either alone or in conjunction with other organizations.

(15)   Where a State grants special or exclusive rights to provide telecommunications services to organizations which already have a dominant position in creating and operating the network, the effect of such rights is to strengthen the dominant position by extending it to services.

(16)   Moreover, the special or exclusive rights granted to telecommunications organizations by the State to provide certain telecommunications services mean such organizations:

(a)   prevent or restrict access to the market for these telecommunications services by their competitors, thus limiting consumer choice, which is liable to restrict technological progress to the detriment of consumers;

(b)   compel network users to use the services subject to exclusive rights, and thus make the conclusion of network utilization contracts dependent on acceptance of supplementary services having no connection with the subject of such contracts.

Each of these types of conduct represents a specific abuse of a dominant position which is likely to have an appreciable effect on trade between Member States, as all the services in question could in principle be supplied by providers from other Member States. The structure of competition within the common market is substantially changed by them. At all events, the special or exclusive rights for these services give rise to a situation which is contrary to the objective in Article 3 (f) of the Treaty, which provides for the institution of a system ensuring that competition in the common market is not distorted, and requires *a fortiori* that competition must not be eliminated. Member States have an obligation under Article 5 of the Treaty to abstain from any measure which could jeopardize the attainment of the objectives of the Treaty, including that of Article 3 (f).

(17)   The exclusive rights to telecommunications services granted to public undertakings or undertakings to which Member States have granted special or exclusive rights for the provision of the network are incompatible with Article 90 (1) in conjunction with Article 86.

(18)   Article 90 (2) of the Treaty allows derogation from the application of Articles 59 and 86 of the Treaty where such application would obstruct the performance, in law or in fact, of the particular task assigned to the telecommunications organizations. This task consists in the provision and

exploitation of a universal network, i.e. one having general geographical coverage, and being provided to any service provider or user upon request within a reasonable period of time. The financial resources for the development of the network still derive mainly from the operation of the telephone service. Consequently, the opening-up of voice telephony to competition could threaten the financial stability of the telecommunications organizations. The voice telephony service, whether provided from the present telephone network or forming part of the ISDN service, is currently also the most important means of notifying and calling up emergency services in charge of public safety.

(19)   The provision of leased lines forms an essential part of the telecommunications organizations' tasks. There is at present, in almost all Member States, a substantial difference between charges for use of the data transmission service on the switched network and for use of leased lines. Balancing those tariffs without delay could jeopardize this task. Equilibrium in such charges must be achieved gradually between now and 31 December 1992. In the meantime it must be possible to require private operators not to offer to the public a service consisting merely of the resale of leased line capacity, i.e. including only such processing, switching of data, storing, or protocol conversion as is necessary for transmission in real time. The Member States may therefore establish a declaration system through which private operators would undertake not to engage in simple resale.

However, no other requirement may be imposed on such operators to ensure compliance with this measure.

(20)   These restrictions do not affect the development of trade to such an extent as would be contrary to the interests of the Community. Under these circumstances, these restrictions are compatible with Article 90(2) of the Treaty. This may also be the case as regards the measures adopted by Member States to ensure that the activities of private service providers do not obstruct the public switched-data service.

(21)   The rules of the Treaty, including those on competition, apply to telex services; however, the use of this service is gradually declining throughout the Community owing to the emergence of competing means of telecommunication such as telefax. The abolition of current restrictions on the use of the switched telephone network and leased lines will allow telex messages to be retransmitted. In view of this particular trend, an individual approach is necessary. Consequently, this Directive should not apply to telex services.

(22)   The Commission will in any event reconsider in the course of 1992 the remaining special or exclusive rights on the provision of services taking account of technological development and the evolution towards a digital infrastructure.

(23)   Member States may draw up fair procedures for ensuring compliance with the essential requirements without prejudice to the harmonization of the latter at Community level within the framework of the Council Directives on open network provision (ONP). As regards data-switching, Member States must be able, as part of such procedures, to require compliance with trade regulations from the standpoint of conditions of permanence, availability and quality of the service, and to include measures to safeguard the task of general economic interest which they have entrusted to a telecommunications organization. The procedures must be based on specific

objective criteria and be applied without discrimination. The criteria should in particular be justified and proportional to the general interest objective, and be duly motivated and published. The Commission must be able to examine them in depth in the light of the rules on free competition and freedom to provide services. In any event, Member States that have not notified the Commission of their planned licensing criteria and procedures within a given time may no longer impose any restrictions on the freedom to provide data transmission services to the public.

(24) Member States should be given more time to draw up general rules on the conditions governing the provision of packet- or circuit-switched data services for the public.

(25) Telecommunications services should not be subject to any restriction, either as regards free access by users to the services, or as regards the processing of data which may be carried out before messages are transmitted through the network or after messages have been received, except where this is warranted by an essential requirement in proportion to the objective pursued.

(26) The digitization of the network and the technological improvement of the terminal equipment connected to it have brought about an increase in the number of functions previously carried out within the network and which can now be carried out by users themselves with increasingly sophisticated terminal equipment. It is necessary to ensure that suppliers of telecommunication services, and notably suppliers of telephone and packet or circuit-switched data transmission services enable operators to use these functions.

(27) Pending the establishing of Community standards with a view to an open network provision (ONP), the technical interfaces currently in use in the Member States should be made publicly available so that firms wishing to enter the markets for the services in question can take the necessary steps to adapt their services to the technical characteristics of the networks. If the Member States have not yet established such technical interfaces, they should do so as quickly as possible. All such draft measures should be communicated to the Commission in accordance with Council Directive 83/189/EEC,[2] as last amended by Directive 88/182/EEC.[3]

(28) Under national legislation, telecommunications organizations are generally given the function of regulating telecommunications services, particularly as regards licensing, control of type-approval and mandatory interface specifications, frequency allocation and monitoring of conditions of use. In some cases, the legislation lays down only general principles governing the operation of the licensed services and leaves it to the telecommunications organizations to determine the specific operating conditions.

(29) This dual regulatory and commercial function of the telecommunications organizations has a direct impact on firms offering telecommunications services in competition with the organizations in question. By this bundling of activities, the organizations determine or, at the very least, substantially influence the supply of services offered by their competitors. The delegation to an undertaking which has a dominant position for the provision and exploitation of the network, of the power to regulate access to the market

---

2 OJ No L 109, 26. 4. 1983, p. 8.
3 OJ No L 81, 26. 3. 1988, p. 75.

for telecommunication services constitutes a strengthening of that dominant position. Because of the conflict of interests, this is likely to restrict competitors' access to the markets in telecommunications services and to limit users' freedom of choice. Such arrangements may also limit the outlets for equipment for handling telecommunications messages and, consequently, technological progress in that field. This combination of activities therefore constitutes an abuse of the dominant position of telecommunications organizations within the meaning of Article 86. If it is the result of a State measure, the measure is also incompatible with Article 90(1) in conjunction with Article 86.

(30)   To enable the Commission to carry out effectively the monitoring task assigned to it by Article 90(3), it must have available certain essential information. That information must in particular give the Commission a clear view of the measures of Member States, so that it can ensure that access to the network and the various related services are provided by each telecommunications organization to all its customers on non-discriminatory tariff and other terms. Such information should cover:

— measures taken to withdraw exclusive rights pursuant to this Directive,
— the conditions on which licences to provide telecommunications services are granted.

The Commission must have such information to enable it to check, in particular, that all the users of the network and services, including telecommunications organizations where they are providers of services, are treated equally and fairly.

(31)   The holders of special or exclusive rights to provide telecommunications services that will in future be open to competition have been able in the past to impose long-term contracts on their customers. Such contracts would in practice limit the ability of any new competitors to offer their services to such customers and of such customers to benefit from such services. Users must therefore be given the right to terminate their contracts within a reasonable length of time.

(32)   Each Member State at present regulates the supply of telecommunications services according to its own concepts. Even the definition of certain services differs from one Member State to another. Such differences cause distortions of competition likely to make the provision of cross-frontier telecommunications services more difficult for economic operators. This is why the Council, in its resolution of 30 June 1988, considered that one of the objectives of a telecommunications policy was the creation of an open Community market for telecommunications services, in particular through the rapid definition, in the form of Council Directives, of technical conditions, conditions of use and principles governing charges for an open network provision (ONP). The Commission has presented a proposal to this end to the Council. Harmonization of the conditions of access is not however the most appropriate means of removing the barriers to trade resulting from infringements of the Treaty. The Commission has a duty to ensure that the provisions of the Treaty are applied effectively and comprehensively.

(33)   Article 90(3) assigns clearly-defined duties and powers to the Commission to monitor relations between Member States and their public undertakings and undertakings to which they have granted special or exclusive rights, particularly as regards the removal of obstacles to freedom to

provide services, discrimination between nationals of the Member States and competition. A comprehensive approach is necessary in order to end the infringements that persist in certain Member States and to give clear guidelines to those Member States that are reviewing their legislation so as to avoid further infringements. A Directive within the meaning of Article 90 (3) of the Treaty is therefore the most appropriate means of achieving that end,

HAS ADOPTED THIS DIRECTIVE:

Article 1

1.   For the purposes of this Directive:
— 'telecommunication organizations' means public or private bodies, and the subsidiaries they control, to which a Member State grants special or exclusive rights for the provision of a public telecommunications network and, when applicable, telecommunications services,
— 'special or exclusive rights' means the rights granted by a Member State or a public authority to one or more public or private bodies through any legal, regulatory or administrative instrument reserving them the right to provide a service or undertake an activity,
— 'public telecommunications network' means the public telecommunications infrastructure which permits the conveyance of signals between defined network termination points by wire, by microwave, by optical means or by other electromagnetic means,
— 'telecommunications services' means services whose provision consists wholly or partly in the transmission and routing of signals on the public telecommunications network by means of telecommunications processes, with the exception of radio-broadcasting and television,
— 'network termination point' means all physical connections and their technical access specifications which form part of the public telecommunications network and are necessary for access to and efficient communication through that public network,
— 'essential requirements' means the non-economic reasons in the general interest which may cause a Member State to restrict access to the public telecommunications network or public telecommunications services. These reasons are security of network operations, maintenance of network integrity, and, in justified cases, interoperability of services and data protection. Data protection may include protection of personal data, the confidentiality of information transmitted or stored as well as the protection of privacy,
— 'voice telephony' means the commercial provision for the public of the direct transport and switching of speech in real-time between public switched network termination points, enabling any user to use equipment connected to such a network termination point in order to communicate with another termination point,
— 'telex service' means the commercial provision for the public of direct transmission of telex messages in accordance with the relevant Comité consultatif international télégraphique et téléphonique (CCITT) recommendation between public switched network termination points, enabling any user to use equipment connected to such a network termination point in order to communicate with another termination point,

— 'packet- and circuit-switched data services' means the commercial provision for the public of direct transport of data between public switched network termination points, enabling any user to use equipment connected to such a network termination point in order to communicate with another termination point,

— 'simple resale of capacity' means the commercial provision on leased lines for the public of data transmission as a separate service, including only such switching, processing, data storage or protocol conversion as is necessary for transmission in real time to and from the public switched network.

2.   This Directive shall not apply to telex, mobile radiotelephony, paging and satellite services.

Article 2

Without prejudice to Article 1 (2), Member States shall withdraw all special or exclusive rights for the supply of telecommunications services other than voice telephony and shall take the measures necessary to ensure that any operator is entitled to supply such telecommunications services.

Member States which make the supply of such services subject to a licensing or declaration procedure aimed at compliance with the essential requirements shall ensure that the conditions for the grant of licences are objective, non-discriminatory and transparent, that reasons are given for any refusal, and that there is a procedure for appealing against any such refusal.

Without prejudice to Article 3, Member States shall inform the Commission no later than 31 December 1990 of the measures taken to comply with this Article and shall inform it of any existing regulations or of plans to introduce new licensing procedures or to change existing procedures.

Article 3

As regards packet- or circuit-switched data services, Member States may, until 31 December 1992, under the authorization procedures referred to in Article 2, prohibit economic operators from offering leased line capacity for simple resale to the public.

Member States shall, no later than 30 June 1992, notify to the Commission at the planning stage any licensing or declaration procedure for the provision of packet- or circuit-switched data services for the public which are aimed at compliance with:

— essential requirements, or

— trade regulations relating to conditions of permanence, availability and quality of the service, or

— measures to safeguard the task of general economic interest which they have entrusted to a telecommunications organization for the provision of switched data services, if the performance of that task is likely to be obstructed by the activities of private service providers.

The whole of these conditions shall form a set of public-service specifications and shall be objective, non-discriminatory and transparent.

Member States shall ensure, no later than 31 December 1992, that such licensing or declaration procedures for the provision of such services are published.

Before they are implemented, the Commission shall verify the compatibility of these projects with the Treaty.

Article 4

Member States which maintain special or exclusive rights for the provision and operation of public telecommunications networks shall take the necessary measures to make the conditions governing access to the networks objective and non-discriminatory and publish them.

In particular, they shall ensure that operators who so request can obtain leased lines within a reasonable period, that there are no restrictions on their use other than those justified in accordance with Article 2.

Member States shall inform the Commission no later than 31 December 1990 of the steps they have taken to comply with this Article.

Each time the charges for leased lines are increased, Member States shall provide information to the Commission on the factors justifying such increases.

Article 5

Without prejudice to the relevant international agreements, Member States shall ensure that the characteristics of the technical interfaces necessary for the use of public networks are published by 31 December 1990 at the latest.

Member States shall communicate to the Commission, in accordance with Directive 83/189/EEC, any draft measure drawn up for this purpose.

Article 6

Member States shall, as regards the provision of telecommunications services, and existing restrictions on the processing of signals before their transmission via the public network or after their reception, unless the necessity of these restrictions for compliance with public policy or essential requirements is demonstrated.

Without prejudice to harmonized Community rules adopted by the Council on the provision of an open network, Member States shall ensure as regards services providers including the telecommunications organizations that there is no discrimination either in the conditions of use or in the charges payable.

Member States shall inform the Commission of the measures taken or draft measures introduced in order to comply with this Article by 31 December 1990 at the latest.

Article 7

Member States shall ensure that from 1 July 1991 the grant of operating licences, the control of type approval and mandatory specifications, the allocation of frequencies and surveillance of usage conditions are carried out by a body independent of the telecommunications organizations.

They shall inform the Commission of the measures taken or draft measures introduced to that end no later than 31 December 1990.

Article 8

Member States shall ensure that as soon as the relevant special or exclusive rights have been withdrawn, telecommunications organizations make it possible for customers bound to them by a contract with more than one year to run for the supply of telecommunications services which was subject to such a right at the time it was concluded to terminate the contract at six months' notice.

Article 9

Member States shall communicate to the Commission the necessary information to allow it to draw up, for a period of three years, at the end of each year, an overall report on the application of this Directive. The Commission shall transmit this report to the Member States, the Council, the European Parliament and the Economic and Social Committee.

Article 10

In 1992, the Commission will carry out an overall assessment of the situation in the telecommunications sector in relation to the aims of this Directive.

In 1994, the Commission shall assess the effects of the measures referred to in Article 3 in order to see whether any amendments need to be made to the provisions of that Article, particularly in the light of technological evolution and the development of trade within the Community.

Article 11

This Directive is addressed to the Member States.

Done at Brussels, 28 June 1990.

For the Commission
Leon Brittan
Vice-President

Notes
1. 'See, in particular, the case brought by certain Member States against the directive: Judgment of the Court of 17 November 1992 in Cases C-271/90, C-281/90 and C-289/90: *Kingdom of Spain and others* v *Commission of the European Communities* ([1992] ECR I-5833; OJ C326/8, 11 December 1992). The Court held the following:
    (1)   Annuls Commission Directive 90/388/EEC of 28 June 1990 on competition in the markets for telecommunications services to the extent to which it purports to govern special rights;
    (2)   Annuls Article 8 of the directive
    (3)   For the rest, dismisses the application; . . .'
2. The Commission issued infringement proceedings against Member States, under Article 169 of the EEC Treaty, for failure to implement the Directive: e.g. action brought against Greece (Case C-281/94, OJ 94/C351/12).
3. See Commission Communication on the status and implementation of Directive 90/388/EC on competition in the markets for telecommunications services, COM(95) 113, 4 April 1995.

COMMISSION DIRECTIVE (95/51/EC) OF 18 OCTOBER 1995 AMENDING DIRECTIVE 90/388/EEC WITH REGARD TO THE ABOLITION OF THE RESTRICTIONS ON THE USE OF CABLE TELEVISION NETWORKS FOR THE PROVISION OF ALREADY LIBERALIZED TELECOMMUNICATIONS SERVICES
OJ L256/49, 26 October 1995

THE COMMISSION OF THE EUROPEAN COMMUNITIES,

Having regard to the Treaty establishing the European Community, and in particular Article 90 (3) thereof,

Whereas:

(1) Under Commission Directive 90/388/EEC of 28 June 1990 on competition in the markets for telecommunications services,[1] as amended by Directive 94/46/EC,[2] certain telecommunications services were opened to competition, and the Member States were requested to take the measures necessary to ensure that any operator was entitled to supply such services; as far as voice telephony services to the general public are concerned, the Council Resolution of 22 July 1993[3] acknowledges that this exception can be terminated by 1 January 1998, with a transitional period for some Member States; the telex service, mobile communications and radio and television broadcasting to the public were specifically excluded from the scope of the Directive; satellite communications were included in the scope of the Directive through Directive 94/46/EC.

During the public consultation organized by the Commission in 1992 on the situation in the telecommunications sector, following the Communication of the Commission of 21 October 1992, the effectiveness of the measures liberalizing the telecommunications sector and in particular the liberalization of data communications, value added services and the provision of data and voice services to corporate users and closed user groups, was questioned by many service providers and users of such services.

(2) The regulatory restrictions preventing the use of alternative infrastructure for the provision of liberalized services, and in particular the restrictions on the use of cable TV networks, are the main cause of this continuing bottleneck situation. Potential service providers must now rely on transmission capacity — 'leased lines' — provided by the telecommunications organizations, which are often also competitors in the area of liberalized services. To remedy this problem, the European Parliament, in its Resolution of 20 April 1993,[4] called upon the Commission to adopt as soon as possible the necessary measures to take full advantage of the potential of the existing infrastructure of cable networks for telecommunications services and to abolish without delay the existing restrictions in the Member States on the use of cable networks for non-reserved services.

(3) Following that resolution the Commission completed two studies on the use of cable TV networks and alternative infrastructures for the delivery of those telecommunications services which have already been opened to competition under Community law: 'The effects of liberalisation of satellite

---

1 OJ No L 192, 24. 7. 1990, p. 10.
2 OJ No L 268, 19. 10. 1994, p. 15.
3 OJ No C 213, 6. 8. 1993, p. 1.
4 OJ No C 150, 31. 5. 1993, p. 39.

infrastructure on the corporate and closed user group market', Analysis, 1994 and 'L'impact de l'autorisation de la fourniture de services de télécommunications libéralisés par les câblo-opérateurs' by Idate, 1994. The basic findings of those studies emphasize the potential role for, amongst other things, cable TV networks, in meeting the concerns raised about the relatively slow pace of innovation and delayed development of liberalized services in the European Community. Opening such networks would help to overcome the problems of high pricing levels and lack of suitable capacity, which are largely due to current exclusive provision of infrastructure in most Member States. The networks operated by authorized cable TV providers indeed offer opportunities for the supply of an increasing number of services, apart from TV broadcasts, if additional investment is forthcoming. The example of the US market shows that new services combining image and telecommunications emerge when certain regulatory barriers are removed.

(4)   Some Member States have therefore abolished previous restrictions on the provision of some data services and/or non-reserved telephone services on cable TV networks. One Member State permits voice telephony. Other Member States have, however, maintained severe restrictions on the provision of services other than the distribution of TV broadcasts on those networks.

(5)   The current restrictions imposed by Member States on the use of cable TV networks for the provision of services other than the distribution of TV broadcasts aim to prevent the provision of public voice telephony by means of networks other than the public switched telephone network, to protect the main source of revenue of the telecommunications organizations.

Exclusive rights to provide public voice telephony were granted to most of the telecommunications organizations of the Community, to guarantee them the financial resources necessary for the provision and exploitation of a universal network, that is to say, one having general geographical coverage and provided to any service provider or user upon request within a reasonable period of time.

(6)   Since those restrictions on the use of cable TV networks are brought about by State measures and seek, in each of the national markets where they exist, to favour telecommunications organizations, which the Member States own or to which they have granted special or exclusive rights, the restrictions must be assessed under Article 90 (1) of the EC Treaty. This Article requires Member States not to enact or maintain in force any measures regarding such undertakings which defeat the object of Treaty provisions, and in particular of the competition rules. It includes a prohibition on maintaining measures regarding telecommunications organizations which result in limiting the free provision of services within the Community or lead to abuses of a dominant position to the detriment of the users of a given service.

(7)   The granting of exclusive rights to the telecommunications organizations to provide transmission capacity for the provision of telecommunications services to the public and the consequent regulatory restrictions on the use of cable TV networks for purposes other than the distribution of radio and television broadcasting programmes, in particular, for new services such as interactive television and video on demand as well as multimedia-services in the Community, which otherwise cannot be provided, necessarily limits the freedom to provide such services to or from other Member States. Such

regulatory restrictions cannot be justified for public policy reasons or in terms of essential requirements, since the latter, and in particular the essential requirement of interworking networks wherever cable TV networks and telecommunications networks are interconnected, can be guaranteed by less restrictive measures, such as objective, non-discriminatory and transparent declaration or licensing conditions.

(8)   The measures granting exclusive rights to the telecommunications organizations for the provision of transmission capacity and the consequent regulatory restrictions on the use of cable TV infrastructure for the provision of other telecommunications services already open to competition are therefore a breach of Article 90, read in conjunction with Article 59 of the Treaty. The fact that the restrictions apply without distinction to all companies other than the relevant telecommunications organizations is not sufficient to remove the preferential treatment of the latter from the scope of Article 59 of the Treaty. Indeed it is not necessary for all the companies of a Member State to be favoured in relation to the foreign companies. It is sufficient that the preferential treatment should benefit certain national operators.

(9)   Article 86 of the Treaty prohibits as incompatible with the common market any conduct by one or more undertakings holding dominant positions that constitutes an abuse of a dominant position within the common market or a substantial part of it.

(10)   In each relevant national market the telecommunications organizations hold a dominant position for the provision of transmission capacity for telecommunications services because they are the only ones with a public telecommunications network covering the whole territory of those States. Another factor in this dominant position concerns the peculiar characteristics of the market and in particular its highly capital-intensive nature. Taking account of the amount of investment needed to duplicate a network, there is a high reliance on use of existing networks. This enhances the structural dominance of the relevant telecommunications organizations and constitutes a potential barrier to entry. Thirdly, as a result of their market share, the telecommunications organizations further benefit from detailed information on telecommunications flows which is not available to new entrants. It includes information on subscribers' usage patterns, necessary to target specific groups of users, and on price elasticities of demand in each market segment and region of the country. Finally, the fact that the relevant telecommunications organizations enjoy exclusive rights for the provision of voice telephony also contributes to their dominance in the neighbouring, but distinct, market for telecommunications capacity.

(11)   The mere creation of a dominant position within a given market through the grant of an exclusive right is not, as such, incompatible with Article 86. A Member State is, however, not allowed to maintain a legal monopoly where the relevant undertaking is compelled or induced to abuse its dominant position in a way that is liable to affect trade between Member States.

(12)   The prohibition of the use of other infrastructure, and in particular CATV networks, for the provision of telecommunications services has encouraged the telecommunications organizations to charge high prices in comparison with prices in other countries, whereas innovation in European corporate networking and competitive service provision as well as the imple-

mentation of applications proposed in the 'Report on Europe and the global information society', are critically dependent on the availability of infrastructure, in particular of leased circuits, at decreasing costs. Tariffs for such high-capacity infrastructure are on average ten times higher in the Community than equivalent capacity over equivalent distances in North America. In the absence of a justification, in the form of (for example) higher costs, these tariffs must be considered abusive within the meaning of point (a) of the second paragraph of Article 86.

Those high prices in the Community are a direct consequence of the restrictions imposed by Member States on the use of infrastructures other than those of the telecommunications organizations, and in particular of those of the cable TV operators, for the provision of telecommunications services. Such high prices cannot only be explained by the underlying costs, given the substantial differences in tariffs between Member States where similar cost structures could be expected.

(13)   Moreover, the State measures preventing the CATV operators from offering transmission capacity in competition with the telecommunications organizations for the provision of liberalized services restrict the overall supply of capacity in the market and eliminate incentives for telecommunications organizations to quickly increase the capacity of their networks, to reduce average costs and to lower tariffs. The resulting high tariffs charged by the telecommunications organizations for, and the shortage of, the basic infrastructure provided by these organizations over which liberalized services might be offered by third parties have delayed widespread development of high-speed corporate networks, remote accessing of databases by both business and residential users and the deployment of innovative services such as telebanking, distance learning, computer-aided marketing, etc. (See Communication to the European Parliament and the Council of 25 October 1994 'Green Paper on the liberalization of telecommunications infrastructure and cable television networks: Part One'). The networks of the telecommunications organizations currently fail to meet all potential market demand for transmission capacity for the provision of these telecommunications services, as emphasized by users and suppliers of such services ('Communication to the Council and the European Parliament on the consultation on the review of the situation in the telecommunications sector' of 28 april 1993, p. 5 point 2; the findings made during the review thus showed that the mere obligation to provide leased lines on demand was not sufficient to avoid restrictions on access to the markets in telecommunications services and limits on user's freedom of choice).

The current restrictions on the use of CATV networks for the provision of such services therefore create a situation in which the mere exercise by the telecommunications organization of their exclusive right to provide transmission capacity for public telecommunications services limits, within the meaning of point (b) of the second paragraph of Article 86 of the Treaty, the emergence of *inter alia* new applications such as pay per view, interactive television and video on demand as well as multimedia-services in the Community, combining both audio-visual and telecommunications, which often cannot adequately be provided on the networks of the telecommunications organizations.

On the other hand, given the restrictions on the number of services which they may offer, cable TV operators often postpone investments in their networks and in particular the introduction of optical-fibre which could be profitable if they were to be spread over a larger number of services provided. Consequently, restrictions on the use of cable TV networks to provide services other than broadcasting also have the effect of delaying the development of new telecommunications and multimedia services, and thus holding back technical progress in this area.

(14) Lastly, as was recalled by the Court of Justice of the European Communities in its Judgment of 19 March 1991 in Case C-202/88, *France* v *Commission*,[5] a system of undistorted competition, as laid down in the Treaty, can be guaranteed only if equality of opportunity is secured between the various economic operators. Reserving to one undertaking which markets telecommunications services the task of supplying the indispensable raw material — transmission capacity — to all companies offering telecommunications services proved, however, tantamount to conferring upon it the power to determine at will which service could be offered by its competitors, at which costs and in which time periods, and to monitor their clients and the traffic generated by its competitors, thereby putting that undertaking at an obvious advantage over its competitors.

(15) The exclusive rights granted to the telecommunications organization to provide transmission capacity for telecommunications services to the public and the resulting restrictions on the use of cable TV networks for the provision of liberalized services are therefore incompatible with Article 90 (1) in conjunction with Article 86 of the Treaty. Article 90 (2) of the Treaty provides for an exception to Article 86 in cases where the application of the latter would obstruct the performance, in law or in fact, of the particular tasks assigned to the telecommunications organizations. Pursuant to that provision, the Commission investigated the impact of liberalizing the use of the cable networks for the provision of telecommunications and multimedia services.

Pursuant to Directive 90/388/EEC, Member States may until a certain date continue to reserve the provision of voice telephony to their national telecommunications organization so as to guarantee sufficient revenues for the establishment of a universal telephone network. Voice telephony is defined in Article 1 of Directive 90/388/EEC as the commercial provision for the public of the direct transport and switching of speech in real time between public switched network termination points, enabling any user to use equipment connected to such a network termination point in order to communicate with another termination point. Where cable TV networks are transformed into switched networks providing voice telephony to any subscriber, such networks should likewise be considered to be public switched networks and their termination points as termination points of such networks. The relevant voice service would then become voice telephony, which according to Article 2 of Directive 90/388/EEC could further be prohibited on cable TV networks by the Member States.

It appears that such temporary prohibition of the provision of voice telephony on the cable TV network can be justified on the same grounds as for telecommunications networks. Conversely where switched voice services for closed user groups, and/or transparent transmission capacity in the form of leased lines, are provided on cable TV networks, those networks do not

---

5 [1991] ECR I-1271, paragraph 51.

represent public switched networks and Member States should not restrict the relevant services, even when they involve the use of one connection point with the public switched telephone network.

Besides the case of voice telephony, no other restrictions for the provision of liberalized services is justified under Article 90 (2), particularly if regard is had to the small contribution made to the turnover of the telecommunications organizations by those services, currently provided on their own networks, which could be diverted towards the cable TV networks. It is recalled that the measures liberalizing the provision of voice telephony should take into account the need to finance a universal service including any development in the concept, see point V.2 in the Communication from the Commission to the Council and the European Parliament of 3 May 1995.

(16)   Notwithstanding the abolition of the current restrictions on the use of cable TV networks, where the provision of services is concerned, the same licensing or declaration procedures could be laid down as for the provision of the same services on the public telecommunications networks.

(17)   In addition, the distribution of audiovisual programmes intended for the general public via those networks, and the content of such programmes, will continue to be subject to specific rules adopted by Member States in accordance with Community law and is not, therefore, subject to the provisions of this Directive.

(18)   Where Member States grant to the same undertaking the right to establish both cable TV and telecommunications networks, they put the undertaking in a situation whereby it has no incentive to attract users to the network best suited to the provision of the relevant service, as long as it has spare capacity on the other network. In that case, the undertaking has, on the contrary, an interest for overcharging for use of the cable infrastructure for the provision of non-reserved services, in order to increase the traffic on their telecommunications networks. The introduction of fair competition will often require specific measures that take into account the specific circumstances of the relevant markets. Given the disparities between Member States, the national authorities are best able to assess which measures are the most appropriate, and in particular to judge whether a separation of the activities is indispensable. In early stages of liberalization, detailed control of cross-subsidies and accounting transparency are essential. To allow the monitoring of any improper behaviour, Member States should therefore at least impose a clear separation of financial records between the two activities, though full structural separation is preferable.

(19)   In order to allow the monitoring of any improper cross-subsidies between the broadcasting tasks of cable TV operators which are provided under exclusive rights in a given franchise area and their business as providers of capacity for telecommunications services, Member States should guarantee transparency as regards the use of resources from one activity which could be used to extend the dominant position to the other market. Given the complexity of the financial records of network providers, it is extremely difficult to detect cross-subsidies within it between the reserved activities and the services provided under competitive conditions. It is thus necessary to require those cable TV operators to keep separate financial records, and in particular to identify separately costs and revenues associated with the provision of the services supplied under their exclusive rights and those

provided under competitive conditions once they achieve a significant turn-over in telecommunications activities in the licensed area. For the time being, a turnover of more than ECU 50 million should be considered a significant turnover. Where such a requirement would constitute an excessive burden on the relevant undertaking, Member States may grant deferments for limited periods, subject to prior notification to the Commission of the underlying justifications.

The operators concerned should use an appropriate cost accounting system which can be verified by accounting experts and which ensures the production of recorded figures.

The above separation of accounts should, for this purpose at least, apply the principles setout in Article 10 (2) of Council Directive 92/44/EEC of 5 June 1992 on the application of open network provision to leased lines,[6] as amended by Commission Decision 94/439/EC.[7] Hybrid services, made up of elements falling variously within the reserved and the competitive services, should distinguish between the costs of each element.

(20)   In the event that, in the meantime, no competing home-delivery system is authorized by the relevant Member State, the Commission will reconsider whether separation of accounts is sufficient to avoid improper practices and will assess whether such joint provision does not result in a limitation of the potential supply of transmission capacity at the expense of the services providers in the relevant area, or whether further measures are warranted.

(21)   Member States should refrain from introducing new measures with the purpose or effect of jeopardizing the aim of this Directive,

HAS ADOPTED THIS DIRECTIVE:

Article 1

Directive 90/388/EEC is hereby amended as follows:
   1.   Article 1(1) is amended as follows:
      (a)   the fifth indent is replaced by the following:
      '—"telecommunications services" means services whose provision consists wholly or partly in the transmission and/or routing of signals on a telecommunications network.'
      (b)   the following is added after the last indent:
      '—"cable TV network" means any mainly wire-based infrastructure approved by a Member State for the delivery or distribution of radio or television signals to the public.
   This Directive shall be without prejudice to the specific rules adopted by the Member States in accordance with Community law, governing the distribution of audiovisual programmes intended for the general public, and the content of such programmes.'
   2.   In Article 4, the following is inserted after the second paragraph:
   'Member States shall:

---

6 OJ No L 165, 19. 6. 1992, p. 27.
7 OJ No L 181, 15. 7. 1994, p. 40.

— abolish all restrictions on the supply of transmission capacity by cable TV networks and allow the use of cable networks for the provision of telecommunications services, other than voice telephony;

— ensure that interconnection of cable TV networks with the public telecommunications network is authorized for such purpose, in particular interconnection with leased lines, and that the restrictions on the direct interconnection of cable TV networks by cable TV operators are abolished.'

Article 2

When abolishing restrictions on the use of cable TV networks, Member States shall take the necessary measures to ensure accounting transparency and to prevent discriminatory behaviour, where an operator having an exclusive right to provide public telecommunications network infrastructure also provides cable TV network infrastructure; and in particular to ensure the separation of financial accounts as concerns the provision of each network and its activity as provider of telecommunication services.

Where an operator has an exclusive right to provide cable television network infrastructure in a given area Member States shall also ensure that the operator concerned keeps separate financial accounts regarding its activity as network capacity provider for telecommunications purposes as soon as it achieves a turnover of more than ECU 50 million in the market for telecommunications services other than the distribution of radio and broadcasting services in the relevant geographic area. Where such requirement would constitute an excessive burden on the relevant undertaking, Member States may grant deferments for limited periods, subject to prior notification to the Commission of the underlying justification.

Where a single operator provides both networks or both services as referred to in the first paragraph, the Commission shall, before 1 January 1998, carry out an overall assessment of the impact of such joint provision in relation to the aims of this Directive.

Article 3

Member States shall supply to the Commission, not later than nine months after this Directive has entered into force, such information as will allow the Commission to confirm that Articles 1 and 2 have been complied with.

Article 4

This Directive shall enter into force on 1 January 1996.

Article 5

This Directive is addressed to the Member States.

Done at Brussels, 18 October 1995.

For the Commission
Karel Van Miert
Member of the Commission

COMMISSION DIRECTIVE (96/2/EC) OF 16 JANUARY 1996 AMENDING DIRECTIVE 90/388/EEC WITH REGARD TO MOBILE AND PERSONAL COMMUNICATIONS
OJ L20/59, 21 January 1996

THE COMMISSION OF THE EUROPEAN COMMUNITIES,

Having regard to the Treaty establishing the European Community, and in particular Article 90 (3) thereof,

Whereas:

(1)   In its communication on the consultation on the Green Paper on mobile and personal communications of 23 November 1994, the Commission set out the major actions required for the future regulatory environment necessary to exploit the potential of this means of communication. It emphasized the need for the abolition, as soon as possible, of all remaining exclusive and special rights in the sector through full application of Community on competition rules and with the amendment of Commission Directive 90/388/EEC of 28 June 1990 competition in the markets for telecommunications services,[1] as last amended by Directive 95/51/EC,[2] where required. Moreover, the communication considered removing restrictions on the free choice of underlying facilities used by mobile network operators for the operation and development of their networks for those activities which are allowed by the licences or authorizations. Such a step was seen as essential in order to overcome current distortions of fair competition and, in particular, to allow such operators control over their cost base.

(2)   The Council Resolution of 29 June 1995 on the further development of mobile and personal communications in the European Union[3] gave general support to the actions required, as set out in the Commission's communication of 23 November 1994, and considered as one of the major goals the abolition of exclusive or special rights in this area.

(3)   The European Parliament, in its Resolution of 14 December 1995 concerning the draft Commission Directive amending Directive 90/388/EEC with regard to mobile and personal communications,[4] welcomed this Directive in both its principles and its objectives.

(4)   Several Member States have already opened up certain mobile communications services to competition and introduced licensing schemes for such services. Nevertheless, the number of licences granted is still restricted in many Member States on the basis of discretion or, in the case of operators competing with telecommunications organizations subject to technical restrictions such as a ban on using infrastructure other than those provided by the telecommunications organization. Many Member States, for example, have still not granted licences for DCS 1800 mobile telephony.

In addition, some Member States have maintained exclusive rights for the provision of certain mobile and personal communications services granted to the national telecommunications organization.

(5)   Directive 90/388/EEC provides for the abolition of special or exclusive rights granted by Member States in respect of the provision of telecommunications services. However, the Directive does not as yet apply to mobile services.

---

1 OJ No L 192, 24. 7. 1990, p. 10.
2 OJ No L 256, 26. 10. 1995, p. 49.
3 OJ No C 188, 22. 7. 1995, p. 3.
4 Resolution A4-0306/95.

(6) Where the number of undertakings authorized to provide mobile and personal communications services is limited by Member States through the existence of special rights and *a fortiori* exclusive rights, these constitute restrictions which would be incompatible with Article 90 in conjunction with Article 59 of the Treaty whenever such limitation is not justified under specific Treaty provisions or the essential requirements, since these rights prevent other undertakings from supplying the services concerned, to and from other Member States. In the case of mobile and personal communication networks and services, the applicable essential requirements encompass the effective use of the frequency spectrum and the avoidance of harmful interference between radio-based, space-based or terrestrial technical systems. Consequently, provided that the equipment used to offer the services also satisfies these essential requirements, the current special rights and *a fortiori* exclusive rights on the provision of mobile services are not justified and therefore should be treated in the same way as the other telecommunications services already covered by Directive 90/388/EEC. The scope of application of that Directive should accordingly be extended so as to include mobile and personal communications services.

(7) When opening the markets for mobile and personal communications to competition Member States should give preference to the use of Pan-European standards in the area, such as GSM, DCS 1800, DECT and ERMES, in order to allow development and transborder provision of mobile and personal communications services.

(8) Certain Member States have currently granted licences for digital mobile radio-based services making use of frequencies in the 1 700 to 1 900 Mhz band, according to the DCS 1800 standard. The Commission communication of 23 November 1994 established that DCS 1800 is to be seen as part of the GSM system family. The other Member States have not authorized such services even where frequencies are available in this band, thereby preventing the cross-border provision of such services. This is also incompatible with Article 90 in conjunction with Article 59. To remedy this situation, Member States which have not yet established a procedure for granting such licences should do so within a reasonable time-frame. In this context, due account should be taken of the requirement to promote investments by new entrants in these areas. Member States should be able to refrain from granting a licence to existing operators, for example to operators of GSM systems already present on their territory, if it can be shown that this would eliminate effective competition in particular by the extension of a dominant position. In particular, where a Member State grants or has already granted DCS 1800 licences, the granting of new or supplementary licences for existing GSM or DCS 1800 operators may take place only under conditions ensuring effective competition.

(9) Digital European cordless telecommunications (DECT) services are also an essential element for the development towards personal communications. DECT provides an alternative to the current local loop access to the public switched telephone network. On 3 June 1991, the Council, by Directive 91/287/EEC, designated coordinated frequency bands for the introduction of DECT into the Community[5] to be implemented not later

---

5 OJ No L 144, 8. 6. 1991, p. 45.

than 31 December 1991. Certain Member States are, however, preventing the use of these frequencies for such services by refusing to grant licences to companies which intend to start offering DECT services. Where telecommunications organizations were granted exclusive rights for the establishment of the public switched telephone network, the effect of such refusals is to strengthen their dominant position and also to delay the emergence of personal communications services and therefore restricts technical progress at the expense of the users contrary to Article 90 of the Treaty in conjunction with point (b) of Article 86. To remedy this situation Member States which have not yet established a procedure for granting such licences should also do so within a reasonable time-frame.

(10)   Even where licences were granted to competing mobile operators, Member States have in certain cases granted to one of them, in a discretionary manner, special legal advantages which were not granted to others. In such a situation, these advantages may be counterbalanced by special obligations and do not, necessarily, preclude the latter from entering and competing in the market. The compatibility of these advantages with the Treaty must therefore be assessed on a case-by-case basis taking into account their impact on the effective freedom of other entities to provide, in an efficient manner, the same telecommunications service and their possible justifications regarding the activity concerned.

(11)   The exclusive rights that currently exist in the mobile communications field were generally granted to organizations which already enjoyed a dominant position in creating the terrestrial networks, or to one of their subsidiaries. In such a situation, these rights have the effect of extending the dominant position enjoyed by those organizations and therefore strengthening that position, which, according to the case-law of the Court of Justice, constitutes an abuse of a dominant position contrary to Article 86 of the Treaty. The exclusive rights granted in the mobile and personal communications field are consequently incompatible with Article 90 read in conjunction with Article 86. These exclusive rights should consequently be abolished.

(12)   Moreover, as regards new mobile services, given the difficulty of ensuring that telecommunications organizations in those Member States with less developed networks which would qualify for a transitional time period for the abolition of the exclusive rights for the establishment and use of infrastructures required for a given mobile service, would not use this position to extend it to the market of the relevant mobile service, the Member States should, in order to prevent abuses of dominant positions contrary to the Treaty, abstain from granting such telecommunications organization, or any associated organization, a licence for this mobile service. Where telecommunications organization, do not or no longer enjoy exclusive rights for the establishment and the provision of the public network infrastructure, they should, however, not *a priori* be excluded from such licensing procedures.

(13)   Exclusive rights not only limit access to the market, but they also have the effect of restricting or preventing, to the disadvantage of users, the use of mobile and personal communications on offer, thereby holding back technical progress in this area. The telecommunications organizations have, in particular, maintained higher tariffs for mobile radiophony in comparison with fixed voice telephony which hinders competition at the expense of their main source of revenues.

Where investment decisions are taken by undertakings in areas where they enjoy exclusive rights, these undertakings are in a position whereby they can decide to give priority to fixed network technologies, whereas new entrants may exploit mobile and personal technology even to compete with fixed services, in particular as regards the local loop. Thus, the exclusive rights imply that there is a restriction on the development of mobile and personal communications and this is incompatible with Article 90, read in conjunction with Article 86.

(14) In order to establish the conditions under which mobile and personal communications systems are to be provided, Member States may introduce licensing or declaration procedures to ensure compliance with the applicable essential requirements and public service specifications in the form of trade regulations, subject to the proportionality principle. Public service specifications in the form of trade regulations relate to conditions of permanence, availability, and quality of the service. Such conditions may include the obligation to give service providers access to airtime on terms at least as favourable as those available to a service provision business owned by, or with ownership links to, a mobile network. This framework is without prejudice to the harmonization of the framework for licensing in the Community.

The number of licences may be limited only in the case of scarcity of the frequency resources. Conversely, licensing is not justified when a mere declaration procedure would suffice to attain the relevant objective.

As regards airtime resale and other mere provision of services by independent service providers or directly by mobile network operators on already authorized mobile sytems, none of the applicable essential requirements would justify the introduction or maintenance of licensing procedures, given that such services do not consist of the provision of telecommunications services or the operation of a mobile communications network, but of the retail of authorized services, the provision of which is likely to be subject to conditions ensuring compliance with essential requirements or public service specifications in the form of trade regulations.

They could therefore, besides the application of national fair trade rules concerning all similar retail activities, only be subject to a requirement of a declaration of their activities to the National Regulatory Authority of the Member States where they choose to operate. Mobile network operators could on the other hand refuse to allow service providers to distribute their services, in particular where these service providers did not adhere to a code of conduct for service providers in conformity with the competition rules of the Treaty, as far as such code exists.

(15) In the context of mobile and personal communications systems radiofrequencies are a crucial bottleneck resource. The allocation of radiofrequencies for mobile and personal communications system by Member States according to criteria other than those which are objective, transparent and non-discriminatory constitutes a restriction incompatible with Article 90 in conjunction with Article 59 of the Treaty to the extent that operators from other Member States are disadvantaged in these allocation procedures. The development of effective competition in the telecommunications sector may be an objective justification to refuse the allocation of frequencies to operators already dominant in the geographical market.

Member States should ensure that the procedure for allocation of radiofrequencies is based on objective criteria and without discriminatory effects.

In this context Member States should, with regard to future designation of frequencies for specific communications services, publish the frequency plans as well as the procedures to be followed by operators to obtain frequencies within the designated frequency bands. Current frequency allocation should be reviewed by the Member States at regular intervals. In cases where the number of licences was limited on the basis of spectrum scarcity, Member States should also review whether advances in technology would allow spectrum to be made available for additional licences. Possible fees for the use of frequencies should be proportional and levied according to the number of channels effectively granted.

(16) Most Member States currently oblige mobile operators to use the leased line capacity of telecommunications organizations for both internal network connections and for the routing of long distance portions of calls. As the charges for leased line rental represent a substantial proportion of the mobile operator's cost base, this requriement gives the supplying telecommunications organization, i.e. in many cases its direct competitor, a considerable influence on the commercial viability and cost structure of mobile operators. In addition, restrictions on the self-provision of infrastructure and the use of third party infrastructure is slowing down the development of mobile services, in particular because effective pan-European roaming for GSM relies on the widespread availability of addressed signalling systems, a technology which is not yet universally offered by telecommunications organizations throughout the Community.

Such restrictions on the provision and use of infrastructures constrain the provision of mobile and personal communications services by operators from other Member States and are thus incompatible with Article 90 in conjunction with Article 59 of the Treaty. To the extent that the competitive provision of mobile voice services is prevented because the telecommunications organization is unable to meet the mobile operator's demand for infrastructures or will only do so on the basis of tariffs which are not oriented towards the costs of the leased line capacity concerned, these restrictions inevitably favour the telecommunications organization's offering of fixed telephony services, for which most Member States still maintain exclusive rights. The restriction on the provision and use of infrastructure thus infringes Article 90, in conjunction with Article 86 of the Treaty. Accordingly, Member States must lift these restrictions and grant, if requested, the relevant mobile operators on a non-discriminatory basis access to the necessary scarce resources to set up their own infrastructure including radiofrequencies.

(17) Currently, the direct interconnection between mobile communications systems as well as between mobile communications systems and fixed telecommunications networks within a single Member State or between systems located in different Member States is restricted in mobile licences granted by many Member States without any technical justification. Furthermore, restrictions exist for the interconnection of such networks via networks other than the public telecommunications networks. In the Member States concerned, mobile operators are required to interconnect with other mobile operators via the telecommunications organization's fixed network. Such requirements result in additional costs and thus impede, in particular, the development of transborder provision of mobile communication services in the Community and therefore infringe Article 90, in conjunction with Article 59.

As in most Member States exclusive rights for the provision of voice telephony and public fixed network infrastructure are maintained, potential abuses of the relevant telecommunications organization's dominant position can be prevented only if Member States ensure that interconnection of public mobile communications systems is made possible at defined interfaces with the public telecommunications network of those telecommunications organizations and that the interconnection conditions are based on objective criteria, justified by the cost of providing the interconnection service, are transparent, non-discriminatory, published in advance and allow the necessary tariff flexibility, including the application of off-peak rates. In particular, transparency is required in respect of cost-accounting of operators providing both fixed networks and mobile telecommunications networks. Special and exclusive rights in respect of the establishment of cross-border infrastructure for voice telephony are not affected by this Directive.

In order to be able to ensure the full application of this Directive as regards interconnection, information on interconnection agreements must be available to the Commission on request.

The drawing up of such national procedures for licensing and interconnection, is without prejudice to the harmonization of the latter at Community level by European Parliament and Council Directives, in particular within the framework of Directives on open network provision (ONP).

(18) Article 90 (2) of the Treaty provides for an exception to the Treaty rules, and in particular to Article 86, in cases where the application of the latter would obstruct the performance, in law or in fact, of the particular tasks assigned to the telecommunications organizations. Pursuant to that provision, Directive 90/388/EEC allows exclusive rights to be maintained for a transitional period in respect of voice telephony.

Voice telephony is defined in Article 1 of Directive 90/388/EEC as the commercial provision for the public of the direct transport and switching of speech in real time between public switched network termination points, enabling any user to use equipment connected to such a network termination point in order to communicate with another termination point. The direct transport and switching of speech via mobile and personal communications networks is not implemented between two public switched termination points and is therefore not voice telephony within the meaning of Directive 90/388/ EEC.

On the basis of Article 90 (2) of the Treaty, public service specifications in the form of trade regulations applicable to all authorized operators of mobile telecommunications services provided to the public, are, however, justified to ensure the fulfilment of objectives of general economic interest, such as ensuring geographical coverage or the implementation of Community-wide standards.

(19) In its assessment of current restrictions imposed on mobile operators concerning the establishment and use of their own infrastructure and/or the use of third party infrastructures, the Commission will further consider the need for additional transition periods for Member States with less developed networks as called for in the Council's Resolution of 22 July 1993 on the review of the situation in the telecommunications sector and the need for further development in that market[6] in addition to the Council's Resolution

6 OJ No C 213, 6. 8. 1993, p. 2.

of 22 December 1994 on the principles and timetable for the liberalization of telecommunications infrastructures.[7] Although not covered by these resolutions there should be the possibility of requesting an additional transition period as regards the direct interconnection of mobile networks. The Member States which may request such an exception are Spain, Ireland, Greece and Portugal. However, only certain of these Member States do not allow GSM mobile operators to use own and/or third party infrastructures. A specific procedure should be provided in order to assess the possible justification for the maintenance of that regime for the provision of mobile and personal communications services for a transitional time period as set out in the said Council resolutions.

(20)   This Directive does not prevent measures being adopted in accordance with Community law and existing international obligations so as to ensure that nationals of Member States are afforded equivalent treatment in third countries,

HAS ADOPTED THIS DIRECTIVE:

Article 1

Directive 90/388/EEC is amended as follows:

1.   Article 1 (1) is amended as follows:
(a)   the following indents are inserted after the ninth indent:
'—"mobile and personal communications services" means services other than satellite services whose provision consists, wholly or partly, in the establishment of radiocommunications to a mobile user, and makes use wholly or partly of mobile and personal communications systems,
—"mobile and personal communications systems" means systems consisting of the establishment and operation of a mobile network infrastructure whether connected or not to public network termination points, to support the transmission and provision of radiocommunications services to mobile users,';
(b)   the thirteenth indent is replaced by the following:
'—"essential requirements" means the non-economic reasons in the public interest which may cause a Member State to impose conditions on the establishment and/or operation of telecommunications networks or the provision of telecommunications services. These reasons are the security of network operations, maintenance of network integrity, and where justified, interoperability of services, data protection, the protection of the environment and town and country planning objectives as well as the efficient use of the frequency spectrum and the avoidance of harmful interference between radio-based telecommunications systems and other space-based or terrestrial technical systems.
Data protection may include protection of personal data, the confidentiality of information transmitted or stored as well as the protection of privacy.'
2.   Article 1 (2) is replaced by the following:
'2.   This Directive shall not apply to telex.'

7 OJ No C 379, 31. 12. 1994, p. 4.

3.   The following Articles 3a to 3d are inserted:

'Article 3a

In addition to the requirements set out in the second paragraph of Article 2 Member States shall, in attaching conditions to licences or general authorizations for mobile and personal communications systems, ensure the following:

(i)   licensing conditions must not contain conditions other than those justified on the grounds of the essential requirements and, in the case of systems for use by the general public, public service requirements in the form of trade regulation within the meaning of Article 3;

(ii)   licensing conditions for mobile network operators must ensure transparent and non-discriminatory behaviour between fixed and mobile network operators in common ownership;

(iii)   licensing conditions should not include unjustified technical restrictions. Member States may not, in particular, prevent combination of licences or restrict the offer of different technologies making use of distinct frequencies, where multistandard equipment is available.

As far as frequencies are available, member States shall award licences according to open, non-discriminatory, and transparent procedures.

Member States may limit the number of licences for mobile and personal communications systems to be issued only on the basis of essential requirements and only where related to the lack of availability of frequency spectrum and justified under the principle of proportionality.

Licence award procedures may consider public service requirements in the form of trade regulation within the meaning of Article 3, provided the solution which least restricts competition is chosen. The relevant conditions related to trade regulations may be attached to the licences granted.

Member States which are granted an additional implementation period to abolish the restrictions with regard to infrastructure as provided for in Article 3c, shall not during that period grant any further mobile or personal communications licence to telecommunications organizations in such Member States do not or no longer enjoy exclusive or special rights, within the meaning of points (b) and (c) of the first paragraph of Article 2, for the establishment and the provision of the public network infrastructure, they shall not a priori be excluded from such licensing procedures.

Article 3b

The designation of radiofrequencies for specific communication services must be based on objective criteria. Procedures must be transparent and published in an appropriate manner.

Member States shall publish every year or make available on request, the allocation scheme of frequencies reserved for mobile and personal communications services, according to the scheme set out in the Annex, including the plans for future extension of such frequencies.

This designation must be reviewed by Member States at regular appropriate intervals.

Article 3c

Member States shall ensure that all restrictions on operators of mobile and personal communications systems with regard to the establishment of their own infrastructure, the use of infrastructures provided by third and the sharing of infrastructure, other facilities and sites, subject to limiting the use of such infrastructures to those activities provided for in their licence or authorization, are lifted.

Article 3d

Without prejudice to the future harmonization of national interconnection rules in the context of ONP, Member States shall ensure that direct interconnection between mobile communications systems, as well as between mobile communications systems and fixed telecommunications networks, is allowed. In order to achieve this, restrictions on interconnection shall be lifted.

Member States shall ensure that operators of mobile communications systems for the public have the right to interconnect their systems with the public telecommunications network. To this end, Member States shall guarantee access to the necessary number of points of interconnection to the public telecommunications network in the licences for mobile services. Member States shall ensure that the technical interfaces offered at such points of interconnection are the least restrictive interfaces available as regards the features of the mobile services.

Member States shall ensure that interconnection conditions with the public telecommunications network of the telecommunications organizations are set on the basis of objective criteria, are transparent and non-discriminatory, and compatible with the principle of proportionality. They shall ensure that, in case of appeal, full access to interconnection agreements is given to National Regulatory Authorities and that such information is made available to the Commission on request.'

4. In the first sentence of Article 4 the word 'fixed' is inserted before the words 'public telecommunications networks'.

Article 2

1. Without prejudice to Article 2 of Directive 90/388/EEC, and subject to the provision set out in paragraph 4 of this Article, Member States shall not refuse to allocate licences for operating mobile systems according to the DCS 1800 standard at the latest after adoption of a decision of the European Radiocommunications Committee on the allocation of DCS 1800 frequencies and in any case by 1 January 1998.

2. Member States shall, subject to the provision set out in paragraph 4, not refuse to allocate licences for public access/Telepoint applications, including systems operation on the basis of the DECT standard as from the entry into force of this Directive.

3.   Member States shall not restrict the combination of mobile technologies or systems, in particular where multistandard equipment is available. When extending existing licences to cover such combinations Member States shall ensure that such extension is justified in accordance with the provisions of paragraph 4.

4.   Member States shall adopt, where required, measures to ensure the implementation of this Article taking account of the requirement to ensure effective competition between operators competing in the relevant markets.

Article 3

Member States shall supply to the Commission, not later than nine months after this Directive has entered into force, such information as will allow the Commission to confirm that Article 1 as well as Article 2 (2) have been complied with.

Member States shall supply to the Commission, not later than 1 January 1998, such information as will allow the Commission to confirm that Article 2 (1) has been complied with.

Article 4

Member States with less developed networks may request at the latest three months from the entry into force of this Directive an additional implementation period of up to five years, in which to implement all or some of the conditions set out in Article 3c and in Article 3d (1) of Directive 90/388/EEC, to the extent justifiable by the need to achieve the necessary structural adjustments. Such a request must include a detailed description of the planned adjustments and a precise assessment of the timetable envisaged for their implementation. The information provided shall be made available to any interested party on demand.

The Commission will assess such requests and take a reasoned decision within a time period of three months on the principle, implications and maximum duration of the additional period to be granted.

Article 5

This Directive shall enter into force on the 20th day following its publication in the *Official Journal of the European Communities*.

Article 6

This Directive is addressed to the Member States.

Done at Brussels, 16 January 1996.

For the Commission
Karel Van Miert
Member of the Commission

COMMISSION DIRECTIVE (96/19/EC) OF 13 MARCH 1996 AMENDING DIRECTIVE 90/388/EEC WITH REGARD TO THE IMPLEMENTATION OF FULL COMPETITION IN TELECOMMUNICATIONS MARKETS
OJ L74/13, 22 March 1996

THE COMMISSION OF THE EUROPEAN COMMUNITIES

Having regard to the Treaty establishing the European Community, and in particular Article 90 (3) thereof,

Whereas:

(1) According to Commission Directive 90/388/EEC of 28 June 1990 on competition in the markets for telecommunications services,[1] as last amended by Directive 96/2/EC,[2] telecommunications services, with the exception of voice telephony to the general public and those services specifically excluded from the scope of that Directive, must be open to competition. These services were the telex service, mobile communications and radio and television broadcasting to the public. Satellite communications were included in the scope of the Directive through Commission Directive 94/46/EC.[3] Cable television networks were included in the scope of the Directive through Commission Directive 95/51/EC,[4] and mobile and personal communications were included in the scope of the Directive through Directive 96/2/EC. Under Directive 90/388/EEC, Member States must take the measures necessary to ensure that any operator is entitled to supply such services.

(2) Subsequent to the public consultation organized by the Commission in 1992 on the situation in the telecommunications sector (the 1992 Review), the Council, in its resolution of 22 July 1993,[5] unanimously called for the liberalization of all public voice telephony services by 1 January 1998, subject to additional transitional periods of up to five years to allow Member States with less developed networks, i.e. Spain, Ireland, Greece and Portugal, to achieve the necessary adjustments, in particular tariff adjustments. Moreover, very small networks should, according to the Council also be granted an adjustment period of up to two years where so justified. The Council subsequently unanimously recognized, in its resolution of 22 December 1994,[6] that the provision of telecommunications infrastructure should also be liberalized by 1 January 1998, subject to the same transitional periods as agreed for the liberalization of voice telephony. Furthermore, in its resolution of 18 September 1995,[7] the Council established basic guidelines for the future regulatory environment.

(3) Directive 90/388/EEC establishes that the granting of special or exclusive rights to telecommunications services to telecommunications organizations is in breach of Article 90 of the Treaty, in conjunction with Article 59 of the Treaty, since they limit the provision of cross-border services. As far as telecommunications services and networks are concerned such special rights were defined in that Directive.

---

1 OJ No L 192, 24. 7. 1990, p. 10.
2 OJ No L 20, 26. 1. 1996, p. 59.
3 OJ No L 268, 19. 10. 1994, p. 15.
4 OJ No L 256, 26. 10. 1995, p. 49.
5 OJ No C 213, 6. 8. 1993, p. 1.
6 OJ No C 379, 31. 12. 1994, p. 4.
7 OJ No C 258, 3. 10. 1995, p. 1.

According to Directive 90/388/EEC exclusive rights granted for the provision of telecommunications services are also incompatible with Article 90 (1) of the Treaty, in conjunction with Article 86 of the Treaty, where they are granted to telecommunications organizations which also enjoy exclusive or special rights for the establishment and the provision of telecommunications networks since their grant amounts to the reinforcement or the extension of a dominant position or necessarily leads to other abuses of such position.

(4) In 1990, the Commission, however, granted a temporary exception under Article 90 (2) in respect of exclusive and special rights for the provision of voice telephony, since the financial resources for the development of the network still derived mainly from the operation of the telephony service and the opening-up of that service could, at that time, threaten the financial stability of the telecommunications organizations and obstruct the performance of the task of general economic interest assigned to them, consisting in the provision and exploitation of a universal network, i.e. one having general geographic coverage, and that connection to it is being provided to any service provider or user upon request within a reasonable period of time.

Moreover, at the time of the adoption of Directive 90/388/EEC, all telecommunications organizations were also in the course of digitalizing their network to increase the range of services which could be provided to the final customers. Today, coverage and digitalization are already achieved in a number of Member States. Taking into account the progress in radio frequency applications and the on-going heavy investment programmes, optic fibre-coverage and network penetration are expected to improve significantly in the other Member States in the coming years.

In 1990, concerns were also expressed against immediate introduction of competition in voice telephony while price structures of the telecommunications organizations were substantially out of line with costs, because competing operators could target highly profitable services such as international telephony and gain market share merely on the basis of existing substantially distorted tariff structures. In the meantime efforts have been made to balance differences in pricing and cost structures in preparation for liberalization. The European Parliament and the Council have in the meantime recognized that there are less restrictive means than the granting of special or exclusive rights to ensure this task of general economic interest.

(5) For these reasons, and in accordance with the Council resolutions of 22 July 1993 and of 22 December 1994, the continuation of the exception granted with respect of voice telephony is no longer justified. The exception granted by Directive 90/388/EEC should be ended and the Directive, including the definitions used, amended accordingly. In order to allow telecommunications organizations to complete their preparation for competition and in particular to pursue the necessary rebalancing of tariffs, Member States may continue the current special and exclusive rights regarding the provision of voice telephony until 1 January 1998. Member States with less developed networks or with very small networks must be eligible for a temporary exception where this is warranted by the need to carry out structural adjustments and strictly only to the extent necessary for those adjustments. Such Member States should be granted, upon request, an additional transitional period respectively of up to five and of up to two years, provided it is necessary to complete the necessary structural adjustments. The

Member States which may request such an exception are Spain, Ireland, Greece and Portugal with regard to less developed networks and Luxembourg with regard to very small networks. The possibility of such transitional periods has also been called for in the Council resolutions of 22 July 1993 and of 22 December 1994.

(6)   The abolition of exclusive and special rights as regards the provision of voice telephony will in particular allow the current telecommunications organizations from one Member State to directly provide their service in other Member States as from 1 January 1998. These organizations currently possess the skills and the experience required to enter into the markets opened to competition. However, in almost all Member States, they will compete with the national telecommunications organizations which are granted the exclusive or special right to provide not only voice telephony but also to establish and provide the underlying infrastructure, including the acquisition of indefeasible rights of use in international circuits. The flexibility and the economies of scope which this allows will prevent this dominant position being challenged in the normal course of competition once the liberalization of voice telephony takes place. This will make it possible for the telecommunications organizations to maintain their dominant position on their home markets unless the new entrants in the voice telephony market were entitled to the same rights and obligations. In particular, if new entrants are not granted free choice as regards the underlying infrastructure to provide their services in competition with the dominant operator, this restriction would *de facto* prevent them from entering the market for voice telephony, including for the provision of cross-border services. The maintenance of special rights limiting the number of undertakings authorized to establish and provide infrastructure would therefore limit the freedom to provide services contrary to Article 59 of the Treaty. The fact that the restriction on establishing own infrastructure would apparently apply in the Member State concerned without distinction to all companies providing voice telephony other than the national telecommunications organizations would not be sufficient to remove the preferential treatment of the latter from the scope of Article 59 of the Treaty. Given the fact that it is likely that most new entrants will originate from other Member States such a measure would in practice affect foreign companies to a larger extent than national undertakings. On the other hand, while no justification for these restrictions appears to exist, less restrictive means such as licensing procedures would in any event be available to ensure general interests of a non-economic nature.

(7)   In addition, the abolition of exclusive and special rights on the provision of voice telephony would have little or no effect, if new entrants would be obliged to use the public telecommunications network of the incumbent telecommunications organizations, with whom they compete in the voice telephony market. Reserving to one undertaking which markets telecommunications services the task of supplying the indispensable raw material, i.e. the transmission capacity, to all its competitors would be tantamount to conferring upon it the power to determine at will where and when services can be offered by its competitors, at what cost, and to monitor their clients and the traffic generated by its competitors, placing that undertaking in a position where it would be induced to abuse its dominant position. Directive 90/388/EEC did not explicitly address the establishment and provision of telecommunications networks, as it granted a temporary excep-

tion under Article 90 (2) of the Treaty in respect of exclusive and special rights for the by far most important service in economic terms provided over telecommunications networks, i.e. voice telephony. However, the Directive provided for an overall review by the Commission of the situation in the whole telecommunications sector in 1992.

It is true that Council Directive 92/44/EEC of 5 June 1992 on the application of open network provision to leased lines, amended by Commission Decision 94/439/EC,[8] harmonizes the basic principles regarding the provision of leased lines, but it only harmonizes the conditions of access and use of leased lines. The aim of that Directive is not to remedy the conflict of interest of the telecommunications organizations as infrastructure and service providers. It does not impose a structural separation between the telecommunications organizations as providers of leased lines and as service providers. Complaints illustrate that even in Member States which have implemented that Directive, telecommunications organizations still use their control of the access conditions to the network at the expense of their competitors in the services market. Complaints show that telecommunications organizations still apply excessive tariffs and that they use information acquired as infrastructure providers regarding the services planned by their competitors, to target clients in the services market. Directive 92/44/EEC only provides for the principle of cost-orientation and does not prevent telecommunications organizations to use the information acquired as capacity provider as regards subscribers' usage patterns, necessary to target specific groups of users, and on price elasticities of demand in each service market segment and region of the country. The current regulatory framework does not resolve the conflict of interest mentioned above. The most appropriate remedy to this conflict of interest is therefore to allow service providers to use own or third party telecommunications infrastructure to provide their services to the final customers instead of the infrastructure of their main competitor. In its resolution of 22 December 1994 the Council also approved the principle that infrastructure provision should be liberalized.

Member States should therefore abolish the current exclusive rights on the provision and use of infrastructure which infringe Article 90 (1) of the Treaty, in combination with Articles 59 and 86 of the Treaty, and allow voice telephony providers to use own and/or any alternative infrastructure of their choice.

(8)   Directive 90/388/EEC states that the rules of the Treaty, including those on competition, apply to telex services. At the same time it establishes that the granting of special or exclusive rights for telecommunications services to telecommunications organizations is in breach of Article 90 (1) of the Treaty, in conjunction with Article 59 of the Treaty, since they limit the provision of cross-border services. However, it was considered in the Directive that an individual approach was appropriate, as a rapid decline of the service was expected. It the meantime it has become clear that the telex service will continue to coexist with new services like facsimile in the forseeable future, given that the telex network is still the only standardized network with worldwide coverage and providing legal proof in Court. It is therefore no longer justified to maintain the initial approach.

---

8 OJ No L 165, 19. 6. 1992, p. 27.

(9)   As regards the access of new competitors to the telecommunications markets, only mandatory requirements can justify restrictions to the fundamental freedoms provided for in the Treaty. These restrictions should be limited to what is necessary to achieve the objective of a non-economic nature pursued. Member States may therefore only introduce licensing or declaration procedures where it is indispensable to ensure compliance with the applicable essential requirements and, with regard to the provision of voice telephony and the underlying infrastructure, introduce requirements in the form of trade regulations where it is necessary in order to ensure, in accordance with Article 90 (2) of the Treaty, the performance in a competitive environment of the particular tasks of public service assigned to the relevant undertakings in the telecommunications field and/or to ensure a contribution to the financing of universal service. Other public service requirements can be included by Member States in certain categories of licences, in line with the principle of proportionality and in conformity with Articles 56 and 66 of the Treaty.

The provisions of Directive 90/388/EEC are therefore not to prejudice the applicability of provisions laid down by law, regulation or administrative action providing for the protection of public security and in particular the lawful interception of communications.

In the framework of the adoption of authorization requirements under Directive 90/388/EEC, it appeared that certain Member States were imposing obligations on new entrants which where not in proportion with the aims of general interest pursued. To avoid such measures being used to prevent the dominant position of the telecommunications organizations being challenged by competition once the liberalization of voice telephony takes place, thus making it possible for the telecommunications organizations to maintain their dominant position in the voice telephony and public telecommunications networks markets and thereby strengthening the dominant position of the incumbent operator, it is necessary that Member States should notify any licensing or declaration requirements to the Commission, before they are introduced, to enable the latter to assess their compatibility with the Treaty and in particular the proportionality of the obligations imposed.

(10)   According to the principle of proportionality, the number of licences may only be limited where this is unavoidable to ensure compliance with essential requirements concerning the use of scarce resources. As the Commission stated in its communication on the consultation on the Green Paper on the liberalization of telecommunications infrastructure and cable television networks, the sole reason in this respect should be the existence of physical limitations, imposed by the lack of necessary frequency spectrum.

As regards the provision of voice telephony, public fixed telecommunications networks and other telecommunications networks involving the use of radio frequencies, the essential requirements would justify the introduction or maintenance of an individual licensing procedure. In all other cases, a general authorization or a declaration procedure suffices to ensure compliance with the essential requirements. Licensing is not justified when a mere declaration procedure would suffice to attain the relevant objective.

As regards the provision of packet- or circuit-switched data services, Directive 90/388/EEC allowed the Member States under Article 90 (2) of the Treaty to adopt specific sets of public service specifications in the form of trade regulations with a view to preserving the relevant public service requirements. The Commission has in the course of 1994 assessed the effects of the measures adopted under this provision. The results of this review were made public in its Communication on the status and the implementation of Directive 90/388/EEC. On the basis of that review, which also took account of the experience in most Member States where the relevant public service objectives were achieved without the implementation of such schemes, there is no justification to continue this specific regime and the current schemes should be abolished accordingly. However, Member States may replace these schemes by a declaration or a general authorization procedure.

(11)   Newly authorized voice telephony providers will be able to compete effectively with the current telecommunications organizations only if they are granted adequate numbers to allocate to their customers. Moreover, where numbers are allocated by the current telecommunications organizations, the latter will be induced to reserve the best numbers for themselves and to give their competitors insufficient numbers or numbers which are commercially less attractive, for example, because of their length. By maintaining such power in the hands of their telecommunications organizations Member States would therefore induce the former to abuse their power on the market for voice telephony and infringe Article 90 of the Treaty, in conjunction with Article 86 of the Treaty.

Consequently, the establishment and administration of the national numbering plan should be entrusted to a body independent from the telecommunications organization, and a procedure for the allocation of numbers should, where required, be drafted, which is based on objective criteria, is transparent and without discriminatory effects. Where a subscriber changes service providers, telecommunications organizations should communicate, in the way and to the extent required by Article 86 of the Treaty, the information on his new number for a sufficient period of time to parties seeking to contact him under his old number. Subscribers changing service providers should also have the possibility of keeping their numbers in return for a reasonable contribution to the cost of transferring the numbers.

(12)   As Member States are obliged by this Directive to withdraw special and exclusive rights for the provision and operation of fixed public telecommunications networks, the obligation set out in Directive 90/388/EEC to take the necessary measures to ensure objective, non-discriminatory and published access conditions should be adapted accordingly.

(13)   Subject to reasonable compensation, the right of new providers of voice telephony to interconnect their service for call completion purposes with the existing public telecommunications network at the necessary interconnection points, including access to customer databases necessary for the provision of directory information, is of crucial importance in the initial period after the abolition of the special and exclusive rights regarding voice telephony and telecommunications infrastructure provision. Interconnection should in principle be a matter for negotiation between the parties, subject to the application of the competition rules addressed to undertakings. Given the imbalance in negotiating power of new entrants compared with the telecommunications organizations whose monopoly position results from their special and exclusive rights, it is likely that, as long as a harmonized regulatory framework has not been established by the European Parliament and the Council, interconnection would be delayed by disputes as to terms and

conditions to be applied. Such delays would jeopardize the market entry of new entrants and hence prevent the abolition of special and exclusive rights to become effective. The failure by Member States to adopt the necessary safeguards to prevent such a situation would lead to a continuation *de facto* of the current special and exclusive rights, which as set out above are considered to be incompatible with Article 90 (1) of the Treaty, in conjunction with Articles 59 and 86 of the Treaty.

In order to allow for effective market entry and to prevent the *de facto* continuation of special and exclusive rights contrary to Article 90 (1) of the Treaty, in conjunction with Articles 59 and 86 of the Treaty, Member States should ensure that, during the time period necessary for such entry by competitors, telecommunications organizations publish standard terms and conditions for interconnection to the voice telephony networks which they offer to the public, including interconnect price lists and access points, no later than six months before the actual date of liberalization of voice telephony and telecommunications transmission capacity. Such standard offers should be non-discriminatory and sufficiently unbundled to allow the new entrants to purchase only those elements of the interconnection offer they actually need. Furthermore, they may not discriminate on the basis of the origin of the calls and/or the networks.

(14) Moreover in order to allow the monitoring of interconnection obligations under competition law, the cost accounting system implemented with regard to the provision of voice telephony and public telecommunications networks should, during the time period necessary to allow for effective market entry, clearly identify the cost elements relevant for pricing interconnection offerings and, in particular for each element of the interconnection offered, identify the basis for that cost element, in order to ensure in particular that this pricing includes only elements which are relevant, namely the initial connection charge, conveyance charges, the share of the costs incurred in providing equal access and number-portability and of ensuring essential requirements and, where applicable, supplementary charges aimed to share the net cost of universal service, and provisionally, imbalances in voice telephony tariffs. Such cost accounting should also make it possible to identify when a telecommunications organization charges its major users less than providers of voice telephony networks.

The absence of a quick, cheap and effective procedure to solve interconnection disputes, and one which would prevent the telecommunications organizations causing delays or using their financial resources to increase the cost of available remedies under applicable national law or Community law, would make it possible for the telecommunications organizations to maintain their dominant position. Member States should therefore establish a specific recourse procedure for interconnection disputes.

(15) The obligation to publish standard charges and interconnection conditions is without prejudice to the requirement on undertakings in a dominant position, under Article 86 of the Treaty, to negotiate special or tailor-made agreements for a particular combination or use of unbundled public switched telephony network components and/or the granting of discounts for particular service providers or large users where these are justified and non-discriminatory. Any interconnection discounts should be justified on an objective basis and be transparent.

(16)   The requirement to publish standard interconnection conditions is also without prejudice to the obligation of dominant undertakings under Article 86 of the Treaty to allow interconnected operators on whose network a call originates to remain responsible for setting the tariff for the customer between the calling and the called party and for routing its clients' traffic up to the interconnection point of its choice.

(17)   A number of Member States are currently still maintaining exclusive rights with regard to the establishment and provision of telephone directory and enquiry services. These exclusive rights are generally granted either to organizations which are already enjoying a dominant position in providing voice telephony, or to one of their subsidiaries. In such a situation, these rights have the effect of extending the dominant position enjoyed by those organizations and therefore strengthening that position, which, according to the case-law of the Court of Justice of the European Communities, constitutes an abuse of a dominant position contrary to Article 86. The exclusive rights granted in the area of telephone directory services are consequently incompatible with Article 90 (1) of the Treaty, in conjunction with Article 86. These exclusive rights consequently have to be abolished.

(18)   Directory information constitutes an essential access tool for telephony services. In order to ensure the availability of directory information to subscribers to all voice telephony services, Member States may include obligations for the provision of directory information to the general public within individual licences and general authorizations.

Such an obligation should not, however, restrict the provision of such information by new technological means, nor the provision of specialized and/or regional and local directories contrary to Article 90 (1) of the Treaty, in conjunction with point (b) of the second paragraph of Article 86 of the Treaty.

(19)   In the case where universal service can be provided only at a loss or provided under costs falling outside normal commercial standards, different financing schemes can be envisaged to ensure universal service. The emergence of effective competition by the dates established for full liberalization would, however, be seriously delayed if Member States were to implement a financing scheme allocating too heavy a share of any burden to new entrants or were to determine the size of the burden beyond what is necessary to finance the universal service.

Financing schemes disproportionately burdening new entrants and accordingly preventing the dominant position of the telecommunications organizations being challenged by competition once the liberalization of voice telephony takes place, thus making it possible for the telecommunications organizations to entrench their dominant position, would be in breach of Article 90 of the Treaty, in conjunction with Article 86 of the Treaty. Whichever financing scheme they decide to implement, Member States should ensure that only providers of public telecommunications networks contribute to the provision and/or financing of universal service obligations harmonized in the framework of ONP and that the method of allocation amongst them is based on objective and non-discriminatory criteria and is in accordance with the principle of proportionality. This principle does not prevent Member States from exempting new entrants which have not yet achieved any significant market presence.

Moreover, the funding mechanisms adopted should seek only to ensure that market participants contribute to the financing of universal service, and not to other activities not directly linked to the provision of the universal service.

(20) As regards the cost structure of voice telephony, a distinction must be made between the initial connection, the monthly rental, local calls, regional calls and long distance calls. The tariff structure of voice telephony provided by the telecommunications organizations in certain Member States is currently still out of line with cost. Certain categories of calls are provided at a loss and are cross-subsidized out of the profits from other categories. Artificially low prices, however, impede competition since potential competitors have no incentive to enter into the relevant segment of the voice telephony market and are contrary to Article 86 of the Treaty, as long as they are not justified under Article 90(2) of the Treaty as regards specific identified end-users or groups of end-users. Member States should phase out as rapidly as possible all unjustified restrictions on tariff rebalancing by the telecommunications organizations and in particular those preventing the adaptation of rates which are not in line with costs and increase the burden of universal service provision. Where this is justified, the proportion of net costs insufficiently covered by the tariff structure may be reapportioned among all parties concerned in a non-discriminatory and transparent manner.

(21) As re-balancing could make certain telephone service less affordable in the short term for certain groups of users, Member States may adopt special provisions to soften the impact of re-balancing. In this way, the affordability of the telephone service during the transitional period would be guaranteed while telecommunications operators would still be able to continue their re-balancing process. This is in line with the statement of the Commission concerning the Council resolution on universal service,[9] which states that there should be reasonable and affordable prices throughout the territory for initial connection, subscription, periodic rental, access and the use of the service.

(22) Where Member States entrust the application of the financing scheme of universal service obligations to their telecommunications organization with the right to recoup a share of it from competitors, the former will be induced to charge a higher amount than justified, if Member States would not ensure that the amount charged to finance universal service is made separate and explicit with respect to interconnection (connection and conveyance) charges. In addition, the mechanism should be closely monitored and efficient procedures for timely appeal to an independent body to settle disputes as to the amount to be paid must be provided, without prejudice to other available remedies under national law or Community law.

The Commission should review the situation in Member States five years after the introduction of full competition, to ascertain whether this financing scheme does not lead to situations which are incompatible with Community law.

(23) Providers of public telecommunications networks require access to pathways across public and private property to place facilities needed to reach the end users. The telecommunications organizations in many Member

---

9 OJ No C 48, 16. 2. 1994, p. 8.

States enjoy legal privileges to install their network on public and private land, without charge or at charges set simply to recover incurred costs. If Member States do not grant similar possibilities to new licensed operators to enable them to roll out their network, this would delay them and in certain areas be tantamount to maintaining exclusive rights in favour of the telecommunications organization.

Moreover Article 90 of the Treaty, in conjunction with Article 59 of the Treaty, requires that Member States should not discriminate against new entrants, who generally will originate from other Member States, in comparison with their national telecommunications organizations and other national undertakings, which have been granted rights of way facilitating the roll out of their telecommunications networks.

Where essential requirements, in particular with regard to the protection of the environment or with regard to town and country planning objectives, would oppose the granting of similar rights of way to new entrants which do not already have their own infrastructure, Member States should at least ensure that the latter have, where it is technically feasible, access, on reasonable terms, to the existing ducts or poles, established under rights of way by the telecommunications organization, where these facilities are necessary to roll out their network. In the absence of such requirements the telecommunications organizations would be induced to limit access by their competitors to these essential facilities and thus abuse their dominant position. A failure to adopt such requirements would therefore be contrary to Article 90 (1) of the Treaty, in conjunction with Article 86 of the Treaty.

In addition, pursuant to Article 86, all public telecommunications network operators having essential resources for which competitors do not have economic alternatives are to provide open and non-discriminatory access to those resources.

(24) The abolition of special and exclusive rights in the telecommunications markets will allow undertakings enjoying special and exclusive rights in sectors other than telecommunications to enter the telecommunications markets. In order to allow for monitoring under the applicable rules of the Treaty of possible anti-competitive cross-subsidies between, on the one hand, areas for which providers of telecommunications services or telecommunications infrastructures enjoy special or exclusive rights and, on the other, their business as telecommunications providers, Member States should take the appropriate measures to achieve transparency as regards the use of resources from such protected activities to enter in the liberalized telecommunications market. Member States should at least require such undertakings once they achieve a significant turnover in the relevant telecommunications service and/or infrastructure provision market, to keep separate financial records, distinguishing between *inter alia*, costs and revenues associated with the provision of services under their special and exclusive rights and those provided under competitive conditions. For the time being, a turnover of more than ECU 50 million could be considered as a significant turnover.

(25) Most Member States also currently maintain exclusive rights for the provision of telecommunications infrastructure for the supply of telecommunications services other than voice telephony.

Under Directive 92/44/EEC, Member States must ensure that the telecommunications organizations make available certain types of leased lines to all providers of telecommunications services. However, the Directive provides only for such offer of a harmonized set of leased lines up to a certain bandwidth. Companies needing a higher bandwidth to provide services based on new high-speed technologies such as SDH (synchronous digital hierarchy) have complained that the telecommunications organizations concerned are unable to meet their demand whilst it could be met by the optic fibre networks of other potential providers of telecommunications infrastructure, in the absence of the current exclusive rights. Consequently, the maintenance of these rights delays the emergence of new advanced telecommunications services and therefore restricts technical progress at the expense of the users contrary to Article 90 (1) of the Treaty, in conjunction with point (b) of the second paragraph of Article 86 of the Treaty.

(26)   Given that the lifting of such rights will concern mainly services which are not yet provided and does not concern voice telephony, which is still the main source of revenue of those organizations, it will not destabilize the financial situation of the telecommunications organization. There is consequently no justification to maintain exclusive rights on the establishment and use of network infrastructure for services other than voice telephony. In particular, Member States should ensure that all restrictions on the provision of telecommunications services other than voice telephony over networks established by the provider of the telecommunications service, the use of infrastructures provided by third parties and the sharing of networks, other facilities and sites are lifted as from 1 July 1996.

In order to take account of the specific situation in Member States with less-developed networks and in Member States with very small networks, the Commission will grant, upon request, additional transitional periods.

(27)   Whilst Directive 95/51/EC lifted all restrictions with regard to the provision of liberalized telecommunications services over cable television networks, some Member States still maintain restrictions on the use of public telecommunications networks for the provision of cable television capacity. The Commission should assess the situation with regard to such restrictions in the light of the objectives of that Directive once the telecommunications markets approach full liberalization.

(28)   The abolition of all special and exclusive rights which restrict the provision of telecommunications services and underlying networks by undertakings established in the Community is without regard to the destination or the origin of the communications concerned.

However, Directive 90/388/EEC does not prevent measures regarding undertakings, which are not established in the Community, being adopted in accordance with Community law and existing international obligations so as to ensure that nationals of Member States are afforded comparable and effective treatment in third countries. Community undertakings should benefit from effective and comparable access to third country markets and enjoy a similar treatment in a third country as is offered by the Community framework to undertakings owned, or effectively controlled, by nationals of the third country concerned. World Trade Organization telecommunications negotiations should result in a balanced and multilateral agreement, ensuring effective and comparable access for Community operators in third countries.

(29)   The process of implementing full competition in telecommunications markets raises important issues in the social and employment fields.

These are referred to in the Commission's communication on the consultation on the Green Paper on the liberalization of telecommunications infrastructure and cable television networks of 3 May 1995.

Always remaining in line with a horizontal policy approach, efforts should now be undertaken to support the transition process to a fully liberalized telecommunications environment; responsibility for such measures rests mainly at Member State level, although Community structures, such as the European Social Fund, may also play a part. In line with existing initiatives, the Community should play a role in facilitating the adaptation and retraining of those whose traditional activities are likely to disappear during the process of industrial restructuring.

(30) The establishment of procedures at national level concerning licensing, interconnection, universal service, numbering and rights of way is without prejudice to the harmonization of the latter by appropriate European Parliament and Council legislative instruments, in particular in the framework of open network provision (ONP). The Commission should take whatever measures it considers appropriate to ensure the consistency of these instruments and Directive 90/388/EEC,

HAS ADOPTED THIS DIRECTIVE:

Article 1

Directive 90/388/EEC is amended as follows:
1.   Article 1 is amended as follows:
   (a)   Paragraph 1 is amended as follows:
      (i)   The fourth indent is replaced by the following:
      '—"public telecommunications network" means a telecommunications network used *inter alia* for the provision of public telecommunications services;
      '—"public telecommunications service" means a telecommunications service available to the public,'.
      (ii)   The 15th indent is replaced by the following:
      '—"essential requirements" means the non-economic reasons in the general interest which may cause a Member State to impose conditions on the establishment and/or operation of telecommunications networks or the provision of telecommunications services. These reasons are security of network operations, maintenance of network integrity, and, in justified cases, interoperability of services, data protection, the protection of the environment and town and country planning objectives as well as the effective use of the frequency spectrum and the avoidance of harmful interference between radio based telecommunications systems and other, space-based or terrestrial, technical systems.
      Data protection may include protection of personal data, the confidentiality of information transmitted or stored as well as the protection of privacy.'
      (iii)   The following indents are added:
      '—"telecommunications network" means the transmission equipment and, where applicable, switching equipment and other resources which permit the conveyance of signals betweeen defined termination points by wire, by radio, by optical or by other electromagnetic means;

'—"interconnection" means the physical and logical linking of the telecommunications facilities of organizations providing telecommunications networks and/or telecommunications services, in order to allow the users of one organization to communicate with the users of the same or another organization or to access services provided by third organizations.'

(b)   Paragraph 2 is deleted.

2.   Article 2 is replaced by the following:

'Article 2

1.   Member States shall withdraw all those measures which grant:

(a)   exclusive rights for the provision of telecommunications services, including the establishment and the provision of telecommunications networks required for the provision of such services; or

(b)   special rights which limit to two or more the number of undertakings authorized to provide such telecommunications services or to establish or provide such networks, otherwise than according to objective, proportional and non-discriminatory criteria; or

(c)   special rights which designate, otherwise than according to objective, proportional and non-discriminatory several competing undertakings to provide such telecommunications services or to establish or provide such networks.

2.   Member States shall take the measures necessary to ensure that any undertaking is entitled to provide the telecommunications services referred to in paragraph 1 or to establish or provide the networks referred to in paragraph 1.

Without prejudice to Article 3c and the third paragraph of Article 4, Member States may maintain special and exclusive rights until 1 January 1998 for voice telephony and for the establishment and provision of public telecommunications networks.

Member States shall, however, ensure that all remaining restrictions on the provision of telecommunications services other than voice telephony over networks established by the provider of the telecommunications services, over infrastructures provided by third parties and by means of sharing of networks, other facilities and sites are lifted and the relevant measures notified to the Commission no later than 1 July 1996.

As regards the dates set out in the second and third subparagraphs of this paragraph, in Article 3 and in Article 4a (2), Member States with less developed networks shall be granted upon request an additional implementation period of up to five years and Member States with very small networks shall be granted upon request an additional implementation period of up to two years, provided it is needed to achieve the necessary structural adjustments. Such a request must include a detailed description of the planned adjustments and a precise assessment of the timetable envisaged for their implementation. The information provided shall be made available to any interested party on demand having regard to the legitimate interest of undertakings in the protection of their business secrets.

3.   Member States which make the supply of telecommunications services or the establishment or provision of telecommunications networks

subject to a licensing, general authorization or declaration procedure aimed at compliance with the essential requirements shall ensure that the relevant conditions are objective, non-discriminatory, proportionate and transparent, that reasons are given for any refusal, and that there is a procedure for appealing against any refusal.

The provision of telecommunications services other than voice telephony, the establishment and provision of public telecommunications networks and other telecommunications networks involving the use of radio frequencies, may be subjected only to a general authorization or a declaration procedure.

4.   Member States shall communicate to the Commission the criteria on which licences, general authorizations and declaration procedures are based together with the conditions attached thereto.

Member States shall continue to inform the Commission of any plans to introduce new licensing, general authorization and declaration procedures or to change existing procedures.'

3.   Article 3 is replaced by the following:

'Article 3

As regards voice telephony and the provision of public telecommunications networks, Member States shall, no later than 1 January 1997, notify to the Commission, before implementation, any licensing or declaration procedure which is aimed at compliance with:
— essential requirements, or
— trade regulations relating to conditions of permanence, availability and quality of the service, or
— financial obligations with regard to universal service, according to the principles set out in Article 4c.

Conditions relating to availability can include requirements to ensure access to customer databases necessary for the provision of universal directory information.

The whole of these conditions shall form a set of public-service specifications and shall be objective, non-discriminatory, proportionate and transparent.

Member States may limit the number of licences to be issued only where related to the lack of availability spectrum and justified under the principle of proportionality.

Member States shall ensure, no later than 1 July 1997, that such licensing or declaration procedures for the provision of voice telephony and of public telecommunications networks are published. Before they are implemented, the Commission shall verify the compatibility of these drafts with the Treaty.

As regards packet- or circuit-switched data services, Member States shall abolish the adopted set of public-service specifications. They may replace these by the declaration procedures or general authorizations referred to in Article 2.'

4.   In Article 3b, the following paragraph is added:
'Member States shall ensure, before 1 July 1997, that adequate numbers are available for all telecommunications services. They shall ensure that

numbers are allocated in an objective, non-discriminatory, proportionate and transparent manner, in particular on the basis of individual application procedures.'

5.   In Article 4, the first paragraph is replaced by the following:

'As long as Member States maintain special or exclusive rights for the provision and operation of fixed public telecommunications networks they shall take the necessary measures to make the conditions governing access to the networks objective and non-discriminatory and shall publish them.'

6.   The following Articles 4a to 4d are inserted:

'Article 4a

1.   Without prejudice to future harmonization of the national interconnection regimes by the European Parliament and the Council in the framework of ONP, Member States shall ensure that the telecommunications organizations provide interconnection to their voice telephony service and their public switched telecommunications network to other undertakings authorized to provide such services or networks, on non-discriminatory, proportional and transparent terms, which are based on objective criteria.

2.   Member States shall ensure in particular that the telecommunications organizations publish, no later than 1 July 1997, the terms and conditions for interconnection to the basic functional components of their voice telephony service and their public switched telecommunications networks, including the interconnection points and the interfaces offered according to market needs.

3.   Furthermore, Member States shall not prevent that organizations providing telecommunications networks and/or services who so request can negotiate interconnection agreements with telecommunications organizations for access to the public switched telecommunications network regarding special network access and/or conditions meeting their specific needs.

If commercial negotiations do not lead to an agreement within a reasonable time period, Member States shall upon request from either party and within a reasonable time period, adopt a reasoned decision which establishes the necessary operational and financial conditions and requirements for such interconnection without prejudice to other remedies available under the applicable national law or under Community law.

4.   Member States shall ensure that the cost accounting system implemented by telecommunications organizations with regard to the provision of voice telephony and public telecommunications networks identifies the cost elements relevant for pricing interconnection offerings.

5.   The measures provided for in paragraphs 1 to 4 shall apply for a period of five years from the date of the effective abolition of special and exclusive rights for the provision of voice telephony granted to the telecommunications organization. The Commission shall, however, review this Article if the European Parliament and the Council adopt a directive harmonizing interconnection conditions before the end of this period.

Article 4b

Member States shall ensure that all exclusive rights with regard to the establishment and provision of directory services, including both the publication of directories and directory enquiry services, on their territory are lifted.

Article 4c

Without prejudice to the harmonization by the European Parliament and the Council in the framework of ONP, any national scheme which is necessary to share the net cost of the provision of universal service obligations entrusted to the telecommunications organizations, with other organizations whether it consists of a system of supplementary charges or a universal service fund, shall:

(a) apply only to undertakings providing public telecommunications networks;

(b) allocate the respective burden to each undertaking according to objective and non-discriminatory criteria and in accordance with the principle of proportionality.

Member States shall communicate any such scheme to the Commission so that it can verify the scheme's compatibility with the Treaty.

Member States shall allow their telecommunications organizations to rebalance tariffs taking account of specific market conditions and of the need to ensure the affordability of a universal service, and, in particular, Member States shall allow them to adapt current rates which are not in line with costs and which increase the burden of universal service provision, in order to achieve tariffs based on real costs. Where such rebalancing cannot be completed before 1 January 1998 the Member States concerned shall report to the Commission on the future phasing out of the remaining tariff imbalances. This shall include a detailed timetable for implementation.

In any case, within three months after the European Parliament and the Council adopt a Directive harmonizing interconnection conditions, the Commission will assess whether further initiatives are necessary to ensure the consistency of both Directives and take the appropriate measures.

In addition, the Commission shall, no later than 1 January 2003, review the situation in the Member States and assess in particular whether the financing schemes in place do not limit access to the relevant markets. In this case, the Commission will examine whether there are other methods and make any appropriate proposals.

Article 4d

Member States shall not discriminate between providers of public telecommunications networks with regards to the granting of rights of way for the provision of such networks.

Where the granting of additional rights of way to undertakings wishing to provide public telecommunications networks is not possible due to applicable essential requirements, Member States shall ensure access to existing facilities established under rights of way which may not be duplicated, at reasonable terms.'

7. In the first paragraph of Article 7, the words 'numbers, as well as the' are inserted before the word 'surveillance'.

8. Article 8 is replaced by the following:

'**Article 8**

Member States shall, in the authorization schemes for the provision of voice telephony and public telecommunications networks, at least ensure that where such authorization is granted to undertakings to which they also grant special or exclusive rights in areas other than telecommunications, such undertakings keep separate financial accounts as concerns activities as providers of voice telephony and/or networks and other activities, as soon as they achieve a turnover of more than ECU 50 million in the relevant telecommunications market.'

9. Article 9 is replaced by the following:

'**Article 9**

By 1 January 1998, the Commission will carry out an overall assessment of the situation with regard to remaining restrictions on the use of public telecommunications networks for the provision of cable television capacity.'

Article 2

Member States shall supply to the Commission, not later than nine months after this Directive has entered into force, such information as will allow the Commission to confirm that points 1 to 8 of Article 1 are complied with.

This Directive is without prejudice to existing obligations of the Member States to communicate, no later than 31 December 1990, 8 August 1995 and 15 November 1996 respectively, measures taken to comply with Directives 90/388/EEC, 94/46/EC and 96/2/EC.

Article 3

This Directive shall enter into force on the 20th day following its publication in the *Official Journal of the European Communities*.

Article 4

This Directive is addressed to the Member States.

Done at Brussels, 13 March 1996.

For the Commission
Karel Van Miert
Member of the Commission

Note
Under this Directive, the Commission has published a Communication on Assessment Criteria for National Schemes for the Costing and Financing of Universal Service in Telecommunications and Guidelines for the Member States on Operation of such Schemes, COM(96) 608 (27.11.1996).

OPEN NETWORK PROVISION

COUNCIL DIRECTIVE (90/387/EEC) OF 28 JUNE 1990 ON THE ESTABLISHMENT OF THE INTERNAL MARKET FOR TELECOMMUNICATIONS SERVICES THROUGH THE IMPLEMENTATION OF OPEN NETWORK PROVISION OJ L192/1, 24 July 1990

THE COUNCIL OF THE EUROPEAN COMMUNITIES,

Having regard to the Treaty establishing the European Economic Community, and in particular Article 100a thereof,

Having regard to the proposal from the Commission,[1]

In cooperation with the European Parliament,[2]

Having regard to the opinion of the Economic and Social Committee,[3]

Whereas Article 8a of the Treaty stipulates that the internal market shall comprise an area without internal frontiers in which the free movement of services is ensured, in accordance with the provisions of the Treaty;

Whereas the Commission submitted a Green Paper on the development of the common market for telecommunications services and equipment, dated 30 June 1987, and a communication on the implementation of that Green Paper up to 1992, dated 9 February 1988;

Whereas the Council adopted on 30 June 1988 a resolution on the development of the common market for telecommunications services and equipment up to 1992;[4]

Whereas the full establishment of a Community-wide market in telecommunications services will be promoted by the rapid introduction of harmonized principles and conditions for open network provision;

Whereas, since situations differ and technical and administrative constraints exist in the Member States, this objective should be realized in stages;

Whereas the conditions of open network provision must be consistent with certain principles and must not restrict access to networks and services except for reasons of general public interest, hereinafter referred to as 'essential requirements';

Whereas the definition and application of such principles and essential requirements must take full account of the fact that any restrictions of the right to provide services within and between Member States must be

---

1 OJ No C 39, 16. 2. 1989, p. 8.
2 OJ No C 158, 26. 6. 1989, p. 300, OJ No C 149, 18. 6. 1990.
3 OJ No C 159, 26. 6. 1989, p. 37.
4 OJ No C 257, 4. 10. 1988. p. 1.

objectively justified, must follow the principle of proportionality and must not be excessive in relation to the aim pursued;

Whereas the conditions of open network provision must not allow for any additional restrictions on the use of the public telecommunications network and/or public telecommunications services except those restrictions which may be derived from the exercise of special or exclusive rights granted by Member States and which are compatible with Community law;

Whereas tariff principles should be clearly laid down to ensure fair and transparent conditions for all users;

Whereas this entire Directive must be read in the light of Annex III which lays down a work programme for the first three years;

Whereas the establishment of harmonized conditions of open network provision must be a progressive process and must be prepared with the assistance of a committee composed of representatives of the Member States, which consults the representatives of the telecommunications organizations, the users, the consumers, the manufacturers and the service providers; whereas this process must also be open to all parties concerned and therefore sufficient time must be given for public comment;

Whereas the Community-wide definition of harmonized technical interfaces and access conditions must be based on the definition of common technical specifications based on international standards and specifications;

Whereas work to be undertaken in this area must take full account, *inter alia*, of the framework resulting from the provisions of Council Directive 83/189/EEC of 28 March 1983 laying down a procedure for the provision of information in the field of technical standards and regulations,[5] as last amended by Directive 88/182/EEC,[6] Council Directive 86/361/EEC of 24 July 1986 on the initial stage of the mutual recognition of type approval for telecommunications terminal equipment[7] and Council Decision 87/95/EEC of 22 December 1986 on standardization in the field of information technology and telecommunications;[8]

Whereas the formal adoption on 12 February 1988 of the statutes of the European Telecommunications Standards Institute (ETSI) and of the associated internal rules has created a new mechanism for producing European telecommunications standards;

Whereas the Council in its resolution of 27 April 1989 on standardization in the field of information technology and telecommunications[9] supported the work of ETSI and invited the Commission to contribute to the coherent development of ETSI and lend it its support;

Whereas the Community-wide definition and implementation of harmonized network termination points establishing the physical interface between the network infrastructure and users' and other service providers' equipment will be an essential element of the overall concept of open network provision;

Whereas Commission Directive 88/301/EEC of 16 May 1988 on competition in the markets in telecommunications terminal equipment[10] requires

---

5 OJ No L 109, 26. 4. 1983, p. 8.
6 OJ No L 81, 26. 3. 1988, p. 75.
7 OJ No L 217, 5. 8. 1986, p. 21.
8 OJ No L 36, 7. 2. 1987, p. 31.
9 OJ No C 117, 11. 5. 1989, p. 1.
10 OJ No L 131, 27. 5. 1988, p. 73.

Member States to ensure that users who so request are given access to network termination points within a reasonable time period;

Whereas one of the principal aims of the establishment of an internal market in telecommunications services must be the creation of conditions to promote the development of Europe-wide services;

Whereas, in its abovementioned resolution of 30 June 1988, the Council considered the taking fully into account of the external aspects of Community measures on telecommunications to be a major policy goal;

Whereas the Community attaches very great importance to the continued growth of cross-border telecommunications services, to the contribution that telecommunications services provided by companies, firms or natural persons established in a Member State may make to the growth of the Community market, and to the increased participation of Community service providers in third country markets; whereas it will therefore be necessary, as specific Directives are drawn up, to ensure that these objectives are taken into account with a view to reaching a situation where the progressive realization of the internal market for telecommunications services will, where appropriate, be accompanied by reciprocal market opening in other countries;

Whereas this result should be achieved preferably through multilateral negotiations in the framework of GATT, it being understood that bilateral discussions between the Community and third countries may also contribute to this process;

Whereas this Directive should not address the problems of mass media, meaning problems linked to broadcasting and distribution of television programmes via telecommunications means, in particular cable television networks, which need special consideration;

Whereas neither should this Directive address the question of communication via satellite for which, according to the abovementioned Council resolution of 30 June 1988, a common position should be worked out;

Whereas the Council, on the basis of a report which the Commission is to submit to the European Parliament and the Council, and in accordance with Article 100b of the Treaty, will review, during 1992, any remaining conditions for access to telecommunications services which have not been harmonized, the effects of these conditions on the workings of the internal market for telecommunications services, and the extent to which this market needs to be further opened up,

HAS ADOPTED THIS DIRECTIVE:

Article 1

1.   This Directive concerns the harmonization of conditions for open and efficient access to and use of public telecommunications networks and, where applicable, public telecommunications services.

2.   The conditions referred to in paragraph 1 are designed to facilitate the provision of services using public telecommunications networks and/or public telecommunications services, within and between Member States, and in particular the provision of services by companies, firms or natural persons established in a Member State other than that of the company, firm or natural person for whom the services are intended.

Article 2

For the purposes of this Directive:

1. 'telecommunications organizations' means public or private bodies, to which a Member State grants special or exclusive rights for the provision of a public telecommunications network and, where applicable, public telecommunications services.

For the requirements of this Directive, Member States shall notify the Commission of the bodies to which they have granted special or exclusive rights;

2. 'special or exclusive rights' means the rights granted by a Member State or a public authority to one or more public or private bodies through any legal, regulatory or administrative instrument reserving them the right to provide a service or undertake an activity;

3. 'public telecommunications network' means the public telecommunications infrastructure which permits the conveyance of signals between defined network termination points by wire, by microwave, by optical means or by other electromagnetic means;

4. — 'telecommunications services' means services whose provision consists wholly or partly in the transmission and routing of signals on a telecommunications network by means of telecommunications processes, with the exception of radio broadcasting and television;

— 'public telecommunications services' means telecommunications services whose supply Member States have specifically entrusted *inter alia* to one or more telecommunications organizations;

5. 'network termination point' means all physical connections and their technical access specifications which form part of the public telecommunications network and are necessary for access to and efficient communication through that public network;

6. 'essential requirements' means the non-economic reasons in the general interest which may cause a Member State to restrict access to the public telecommunications network or public telecommunications services. These reasons are security of network operations, maintenance of network integrity and, in justified cases, interoperability of services and data protection.

Data protection may include protection of personal data, the confidentiality of information transmitted or stored as well as the protection of privacy;

7. 'voice telephony' means the commercial provision for the public or direct transport of real-time speech via the public switches network or networks such that any user can use equipment connected to a network termination point to communicate with another user of equipment connected to another termination point;

8. 'telex service' means the commercial provision for the public of direct transport of telex messages in accordance with the relevant 'Comité consultatif international télégraphique et téléphonique' (CCITT) recommendation via the public switched network or networks, whereby any user can use equipment connected to a network termination point to communicate with another user using another termination point;

9. 'packet- and circuit-switched data services' means the commercial provision for the public of direct transport of data via the public switched

network or networks such that any equipment connected to a network termination point can communicate with equipment connected to another termination point;

10. 'open network provision conditions' means the conditions, harmonized according to the provisions of this Directive, which concern the open and efficient access to public telecommunications networks and, where applicable, public telecommunications services and the efficient use of those networks and services.

Without prejudice to their application on a case-by-case basis, the open network provision conditions may include harmonized conditions with regard to:

— technical interfaces, including the definition and implementation of network termination points, where required,

— usage conditions, including access to frequencies where required,

— tariff principles;

11. 'technical specifications', 'standards' and 'terminal equipment' are given the same meaning for those terms as in Article 2 of Directive 86/361/EEC.

Article 3

1. Open network provision conditions must comply with a number of basic principles set out hereafter, namely that:

— they must be based on objective criteria,

— they must be transparent and published in an appropriate manner,

— they must guarantee equality of access and must be non-discriminatory, in accordance with Community law.

2. Open network provision conditions must not restrict access to public telecommunications networks or public telecommunications services, except for reasons based on essential requirements, within the framework of Community law, namely:

— security of network operations,

— maintenance of network integrity,

— interoperability of services, in justified cases,

— protection of data, as appropriate.

In addition, the conditions generally applicable to the connection of terminal equipment to the network shall apply.

3. Open network provision conditions may not allow for any additional restrictions on the use of the public telecommunications networks and/or public telecommunications services except the restrictions which may be derived from the exercise of special or exclusive rights granted by Member States and which are compatible with Community law.

4. The Council, acting in accordance with Article 100a of the Treaty, may, if necessary, modify the points set out in paragraphs 1 and 2.

5. Without prejudice to the specific Directives provided for in Article 6 and in so far as the application of the essential requirements referred to in paragraph 2 of this Article may cause a Member State to limit access to one of its public telecommunications networks or services, the rules for uniform application of the essential requirements, in particular concerning the interoperability of services and the protection of data, shall be determined,

where appropriate, by the Commission, in accordance with the procedure laid down in Article 10.

Article 4

1. Open network provision conditions shall be defined in stages under the procedure set out hereafter.
2. Open network provision conditions shall concern the areas selected in accordance with the list in Annex I.
The Council, acting in accordance with Article 100a of the Treaty, may, if necessary, modify this list.
3. Using the list referred to in paragraph 2, the Commission shall draw up a work programme each year, under the procedure laid down in Article 9.
4. For the work programme referred to in paragraph 3, the Commission shall:
  (a) initiate detailed analysis, in consultation with the committee referred to in Article 9, and draw up reports on the results of this analysis;
  (b) invite, by publication of a notice to that effect in the *Official Journal of the European Communities*, public comment by all parties concerned on the reports on the detailed analysis provided for in subparagraph (a). The period for submitting such comment shall be not less than three months from the date of publication of the said notice;
  (c) request, where appropriate, the European Telecommunications Standards Institute (ETSI) to draw up European standards, taking account of international standardization as a basis for setting up, where required, within specified time limits, harmonized technical interfaces and/or service features. In so doing, ETSI shall coordinate, in particular, with the Joint European Standards Institution CEN/Cenelec;
  (d) draw up proposals for open network provision conditions in accordance with Article 3 and with the open network provision reference framework described in Annex II.
5. For 1990, 1991 and 1992 a work programme shall be drawn up in order to implement the guidelines in Annex III.

Article 5

1. Reference to European standards drawn up as a basis for harmonized technical interfaces and/or service features for open network provision according to Article 4 (4) (c) shall be published in the *Official Journal of the European Communities* as suitable for open network provision.
2. The standards mentioned under paragraph 1 shall carry with them the presumption:
  (a) that a service provider who complies with those standards fulfils the relevant essential requirements, and
  (b) that a telecommunications organization which complies with those standards fulfils the requirement of open and efficient access.
3. If the implementation of European standards within the meaning of Article 5 (2) appears inadequate to ensure the interoperability of transfrontier services in one or more Member States, reference to European standards may be made compulsory under the procedure laid down in Article 10, to the

extent strictly necessary to ensure such interoperability and to improve freedom of choice for users. The procedure provided for in this paragraph may in no way affect the implementation of Articles 85 and 86 of the Treaty.

4.   Where a Member State or the Commission considers that the harmonized standards mentioned under paragraph 1 do not correspond to the objective of open and efficient access, in particular the basic principles and the essential requirements referred to in Article 3, the Commission or the Member State concerned shall bring the matter before the committee referred to in Article 9, giving the reasons therefore. The committee shall deliver an opinion without delay.

5.   In the light of the committee's opinion and after consultation of the standing committee set up by Directive 83/189/EEC, the Commission shall inform the Member States whether or not it is necessary to withdraw references to those standards from the Official Journal of the European Communities.

Article 6

Following the completion of the procedures set out in Articles 4 and 5, and acting in accordance with Article 100a of the Treaty, the Council shall adopt specific Directives establishing open network provision conditions including a time schedule for implementing them.

Article 7

The Council, acting in accordance with Article 100a of the Treaty, taking Article 8c of the Treaty into consideration, shall, where required, adopt measures for harmonizing declaration and/or licensing procedures for the provision of services via public telecommunications networks, with a view to establishing conditions in which there would be mutual recognition of declaration and/or licensing procedures.

Article 8

During 1992 the Council, on the basis of a report which the Commission shall submit to the European Parliament and the Council, shall review progess on harmonization and any restrictions on access to telecommunications networks and services still remaining, the effects of those restrictions on the operation of the internal telecommunications market, and measures which could be taken to remove those restrictions, in conformity with Community law, taking account of technological development and in accordance with the procedure provided for under Article 100b of the Treaty.

Article 9

1.   The Commission shall be assisted by a committee of a advisory nature composed of the representatives of the Member States and chaired by the representative of the Commission.

The committee shall, in particular, consult the representatives of the telecommunications organizations, the users, the consumers, the manufacturers and the service providers. It shall lay down its rules of procedure.

2.   The representative of the Commission shall submit to the committee a draft of the measures to be taken. The committee shall deliver its opinion on the draft, within a time limit which the chairman may lay down according to the urgency of the matter, if necessary by taking a vote.

The opinion shall be recorded in the minutes; in addition, each Member State shall have the right to ask to have its position recorded in the minutes.

The Commission shall take the utmost account of the opinion delivered by the committee. It shall inform the committee of the manner in which its opinion has been taken into account.

Article 10

1.   Notwithstanding the provisions of Article 9, the following procedure shall apply in respect of the matters covered by Article 3 (5) and Article 5 (3).

2.   The representative of the Commission shall submit to the committee a draft of the measures to be taken. The committee shall deliver its opinion on the draft within a time limit which the chairman may lay down according to the urgency of the matter. The opinion shall be delivered by the majority laid down in Article 148 (2) of the Treaty in the case of decisions which the Council is required to adopt on a proposal from the Commission. The votes of the representatives of the Member States within the committee shall be weighted in the manner set out in that Article. The chairman shall not vote.

3.   The Commission shall adopt the measures envisaged if they are in accordance with the opinion of the committee.

4.   If the measures envisaged are not in accordance with the opinion of the committee, or if no opinion is delivered, the Commission shall, without delay, submit to the Council a proposal relating to the measures to be taken. The Council shall act by a qualified majority.

If on the expiry of a period of three months from the date of referral to the Council, the Council has not acted, the proposed measures shall be adopted by the Commission.

Article 11

1.   Member States shall bring into force the laws, regulations and administrative provisions necessary in order to comply with this Directive before 1 January 1991 at the latest. They shall forthwith inform the Commission thereof.

2.   Member States shall communicate to the Commission the texts of the provisions of national law which they adopt in the field governed by this Directive.

Article 12

This Directive is addressed to the Member States.

Done at Luxembourg, 28 June 1990.

For the Council
The President
M. Geoghegan-Quinn

ANNEX I   AREAS FOR WHICH OPEN NETWORK PROVISION CONDITIONS MAY BE DRAWN UP IN ACCORDANCE WITH ARTICLE 4

Areas shall be selected from the following list in accordance with the procedures laid down in Article 4:

1. leased lines;
2. packet- and circuit-switched data services;
3. Integrated Services Digital Network (ISDN);
4. voice telephony service;
5. telex service;
6. mobile services, as applicable;

subject to further study,

7. new types of access to the network, such as access, under certain conditions, to the circuits connecting subscriber premises to the public network exchange ('data over voice') and access to the network's new intelligent functions, according to progress on definition and technological development;

8. access to the broadband network, according to progress on definition and technological development.

ANNEX II   REFERENCE FRAMEWORK FOR DRAWING UP PROPOSALS ON OPEN NETWORK PROVISION CONDITIONS IN ACCORDANCE WITH ARTICLE 4 (4) (d)

Proposals on open network provision conditions as defined in Article 2 (10) should be drawn up in accordance with the following reference framework:

1. Common principles

In drawing up the conditions described in this Annex, due account will be taken of the relevant rules of the Treaty.

Open network provision conditions shall be drawn up in such a way as to facilitate the service providers' and users' freedom of action without unduly limiting the telecommunications organizations' responsibility for the functioning of the network and the best possible condition of communications channels.

Member States may, in accordance with Community law, take any measure enabling the telecommunications organizations to develop the new opportunities deriving from open network provision.

2. Harmonized technical interfaces and/or service features

In drawing up open network provision conditions the following scheme should be taken into account for the definition of technical interfaces at appropriate open network termination points:

— for existing services and networks, existing interfaces should be adopted;

— for entirely new services or the improvement of existing services, existing interfaces should also be adopted, as far as feasible. When existing interfaces are not suitable, enhancements and/or new interfaces will have to be specified;

— for networks that are still to be introduced, but for which the standard-ization programme has already commenced, open network provision require-ments falling within the terms of Article 3 should be taken into account when specifying new interfaces.

Open network provision proposals must, wherever possible, be in line with the ongoing work in the European Conference of Postal and Telecommuni-cations Administrations (CEPT), CCITT, ETSI and CEN-Cenelec.

Work undertaken in this area shall take full account of the framework resulting from the provisions of Council Directive 83/189/EEC of 28 March 1983 laying down a procedure for the provision of information in the field of technical standards and regulations,[11] as last amended by Directive 88/182/EEC,[12] Council Directive 86/361/EEC of 24 July 1986 on the initial stage of the mutual recognition of type approval for telecommunications terminal equipment[13] and Council Decision 87/95/EEC of 22 December 1986 on standardization in the field of information technology and telecommunica-tions.[14]

Additional features will be identified where required. They may be classi-fied as:

— inclusive if they are provided in association with a specific interface and included in the standard offering,

— optional if they can be requested as an option with regard to a specific open network provision offering.

Work shall include the drawing up of proposals for time schedules for the introduction of interfaces and service features, taking account of the state of development of telecommunications networks and services in the Commu-nity.

3. Harmonized supply and usage conditions

Supply and usage conditions shall identify conditions of access and of provision of services, as far as required.

They may include as applicable:

    (a)   supply conditions such as:

       — maximum provision time (delivery period),

       — quality of service, in particular the quality of transmission,

       — maintenance,

       — network malfunction reporting facilities;

    (b)   usage conditions such as:

       — conditions for resale of capacity,

       — conditions for shared use,

       — conditions for interconnection with public and private networks.

Usage conditions may include conditions regarding access to frequencies, as applicable, and measures concerning protection of personal data and confidentiality of communications, where required.

4. Harmonized tariff principles

Tariff principles must be consistent with the principles set out in Article 3 (1).

---

11 OJ No L 109, 26. 4. 1983, p. 8.
12 OJ No L 81, 26. 3. 1988, p. 75.
13 OJ No L 217, 5. 8. 1986, p. 21.
14 OJ No L 36, 7. 2. 1987, p. 31.

These principles imply, in particular, that:

— tariffs must be based on objective criteria and especially in the case of services and areas subject to special or exclusive rights must in principle be cost-oriented, on the understanding that the fixing of the actual tariff level will continue to be the province of national legislation and is not the subject of open network provision conditions. When these tariffs are determined, one of the aims should be the definition of efficient tariff principles throughout the Community while ensuring a general service for all,

— tariffs must be transparent and must be properly published,

— in order to leave users a choice between the individual service elements and where technology so permits, tariffs must be sufficiently unbundled in accordance with the competition rules of the Treaty. In particular, additional features introduced to provide certain specific extra services must, as a general rule, be charged independently of the inclusive features and transportation as such,

— tariffs must be non-discriminatory and guarantee equality of treatment.

Any charge for access to network resources or services must comply with the principles set out above and with the competition rules of the Treaty and must also take into account the principle of fair sharing in the global cost of the resources used and the need for a reasonable level of return on investment.

There may be different tariffs, in particular to take account of excess traffic during peak periods and lack of traffic during off-periods, provided that the tariff differentials are commercially justifiable and do not conflict with the above principles.

ANNEX III   GUIDELINES FOR IMPLEMENTATION OF THE FRAMEWORK DIRECTIVE UP TO 31 DECEMBER 1992

In an initial phase, and without prejudice to the procedures laid down in Article 4 (2) and (3), work to be undertaken in 1990, 1991 and 1992 concerning Articles 4, 5 and 6 will implement the following priorities:

1.   adoption of specific Directives pursuant to Article 6 covering leased lines and the voice telephony service;

2.   implementation by 1 January 1991 of harmonized technical interfaces and/or service features for packet-switched data services and ISDN (Integrated Services Digital Network); reference to such interfaces and features may be made compulsory before that date in accordance with the procedure set out in Article 5 (3);

3.   adoption by the Council by 1 July 1991, acting on a proposal from the Commission, of a recommendation on the supply of technical interfaces, conditions of usage and tariff principles applying to provision of packet-switched data services complying with open network principles; this recommendation would in particular call on Member States to ensure that at least one such service was provided on their territory;

4.   adoption by the Council by 1 January 1992, acting on a proposal from the Commission, of a similar recommendation on ISDN;

5.   examination in 1992, with a view to its adoption, on a proposal from the Commission, of a specific Directive on packet-switched data services. That proposal should take into account the initial results of the implementation of the recommendation referred to in point 3;

6. subsequent examination of a proposal for a Directive on ISDN. That proposal should also take into account the initial results of the implementation of the recommendation referred to in point 4.

Notes
1. See the Proposal for a European Parliament and Council Directive amending Council Directives 90/387/EEC and 92/44/EEC for the purpose of adaptation to a competitive environment in telecommunications, COM(95) 543 final - 95/0290(COD); OJ C62/3, 1 March 1996. See also the amended proposal (OJ C291/18, 4 October 1996) and the Common Position (OJ C315/41, 24 October 1996).
2. See also Council Recommendation of 5 June 1992 on the harmonised provision of a minimum set of packet-switched data services (PSDS) in accordance with open network provision (ONP) principles (92/382/EEC; OJ L200/1, 18 July 1992); and Council Recommendation of 5 June 1992 on the provision of harmonised integrated services digital network (ISDN) access arrangements and a minimum set of ISDN offerings in accordance with open network provision (ONP) principles (92/383/EEC; OJ L/200/10, 18 July 1992).
3. On **infrastructure liberalisation** see:
    Council Resolution of 22 July 1993 on the review of the situation in the telecommunications sector and the need for further development of that market, OJ C213/1, 6.8.93.
    Council Resolution of 22 December 1994 on the principle and timetable for the liberalisation of telecommunications infrastructures, OJ C379/4, 31.12.94.
4. On **ONP standards**, see: Telecommunications: open network provision (ONP) list of standards (fourth issue), OJ C266/2, 13.10.95.

COUNCIL DIRECTIVE (92/44/EEC) OF 5 JUNE 1992 ON THE APPLICATION OF OPEN NETWORK PROVISION TO LEASED LINES
OJ L165/27, 19 June 1992

THE COUNCIL OF THE EUROPEAN COMMUNITIES,
    Having regard to the Treaty establishing the European Economic Community, and in particular Article 100a thereof,
    Having regard to the proposal from the Commission,[1]
    In cooperation with the European Parliament,[2]
    Having regard to the opinion of the Economic and Social Committee,[3]
    (1) Whereas Council Directive 90/387/EEC of 28 June 1990 on the establishment of the internal market for telecommunications services through the implementation of open network provision,[4] provides that the Council shall adopt specific open network provision conditions for leased lines;
    (2) Whereas in this Directive the concept of leased lines covers the offer of transparent transmission capacity between network termination points as a separate service and does not include on-demand switching or offers which form part of a switched service offered to the public;
    (3) Whereas, in accordance with Commission Directive 90/388/EEC of 28 June 1990 on competition in the markets for telecommunications

1 OJ No C 58, 7. 3. 1991, p. 10.
2 OJ No C 305, 25. 11. 1991, p. 61 and Decision of 13 May 1992 (not yet published in the Official Journal).
3 OJ No C 269, 14. 10. 1991, p. 30.
4 OJ No L 192, 24. 7. 1990, p. 1.

services,[5] Member States which maintain special or exclusive rights for the provision and operation of public telecommunications networks shall take the necessary measures to make the conditions governing access to and use of the network objective and non-discriminatory and publish them; whereas it is necessary to harmonize which specifications should be published and under which form, in order to facilitate the provision of competitive services using leased lines, within Member States and between Member States, and in particular the provision of services by companies, firms or natural persons established in a Member State other than that of the company, firm or natural person for whom the services are intended;

(4)   Whereas, in application of the principle of non-discrimination, leased lines shall be offered and provided on request without discrimination to all users;

(5)   Whereas the principle of non-discrimination as laid down in the Treaty applies to, *inter alia*, availability of technical access, tariffs, quality of service, provision time (delivery period), fair distribution of capacity in case of scarcity, repair time, availability of network information and customer proprietary information, subject to relevant regulatory provisions on data protection;

(6)   Whereas a number of technical restrictions have been applied, in particular for the interconnection of leased lines among each other or for the interconnection of leased lines and public telecommunications networks; whereas such restrictions, which impede the use of leased lines for the provision of competitive services, are not justified, as they can be replaced by less restrictive regulatory measures;

(7)   Whereas, in accordance with Community law, access to and use of leased lines may only be restricted in application of essential requirements as defined in this Directive and to safeguard exclusive or special rights; whereas those restrictions must be objectively justified, must follow the principle of proportionality and must not be excessive in relation to the aim pursued; whereas it is necessary to specify the application of these essential requirements in respect of leased lines;

(8)   Whereas, in accordance with Directive 90/388/EEC which does not apply to telex, mobile radiotelephony, paging and satellite services, Member States shall withdraw all special or exclusive rights for the supply of telecommunications services other than voice telephony; whereas this is the commercial provision for the public of the direct transport and switching of speech in real-time between public switched network termination points, enabling any user to use equipment connected to such a network termination point in order to communicate with another termination point;

(9)   Whereas Member States may, until the dates provided in Directive 90/388/EEC prohibit, as regards packet- or circuit-switched data services, economic operators from offering leased line capacity for simple resale to the public; whereas there should be no other restriction on the use of leased lines, in particular in respect of the transmission of signals which are not originated by the user who subscribed to the leased line offering, the transmission of signals which are not finally destined for the user who subscribed to the leased line offering, or the transmission of signals which are neither originated by nor finally destined for the user who subscribed to the leased line offering;

---

5 OJ No L 192, 24. 7. 1990, p. 10.

(10)   Whereas, in accordance with Directive 90/387/EEC, the Community-wide definition of harmonized technical interfaces and access conditions must be based on the definition of common technical specifications based on international standards and specifications;

(11)   Whereas, in accordance with Directive 90/388/EEC, Member States which maintain special or exclusive rights for the provision and operation of public telecommunications networks shall ensure that those who so request can obtain leased lines within a reasonable period;

(12)   Whereas, in order to make leased lines available to a sufficient extent to users for their own use, for shared use or for the provision of services to third parties, it is necessary that Member States ensure that a harmonized set of leased lines with defined network termination points is made available in all Member States both for communications within a Member State and between Member States; whereas it is therefore necessary to determine which type of leased lines should be included in the harmonized set and within which time limit if they are not yet available; whereas given the dynamic technological development in this sector, it is necessary to establish a procedure for adjusting or enlarging such a set;

(13)   Whereas other leased lines, in addition to the harmonized minimum set, will also be provided subject to market demand and the state of public telecommunications network; whereas the other provisions of this Directive apply to these leased lines; whereas however it should be ensured that the provision of these other leased lines does not impede the provision of the minimum set of leased lines;

(14)   Whereas in conformity with the principle of separation of regulatory and operational functions and in application of the principle of subsidiarity, the national regulatory authority of each Member State will play an important role for the implementation of this Directive;

(15)   Whereas common ordering procedures, as well as one-stop ordering and one-stop billing are needed in order to encourage the use of leased lines throughout the Community; whereas any cooperation of the telecommunications organizations in that respect is subject to compliance with Community competition law; whereas, in particular, such procedures should respect the principle of cost orientation and should not result in any price fixing or market sharing;

(16)   Whereas the implementation of one-stop ordering and one-stop billing procedures by telecommunications organizations must not prevent offers by service providers other than telecommunications organizations;

(17)   Whereas, in accordance with Directive 90/387/EEC, tariffs for leased lines must be based on the following principles; they must be based on objective criteria and must follow the principle of cost-orientation, taking into account a reasonable time needed for rebalancing; they must be transparent and properly published; they must be sufficiently unbundled in accordance with the competition rules of the Treaty and they must be non-discriminatory and guarantee equality of treatment; whereas tariffs for leased lines provided by one or more telecommunications organization must be based on the same principles; whereas a favourable prejudice is given to a tariff based on a flat-rate periodic rental, except where other types of tariffs are justified by cost;

(18)   Whereas any charge for access to and use of leased lines must comply with the principles set out above and with the competition rules of

the Treaty and must also take into account the principle of fair sharing in the global cost of the resources used and the need for a reasonable level of return on investment which is required for the further development of the telecommunications infrastructure;

(19)   Whereas, in order to ensure the application of the tariff principles set out in the previous two recitals, telecommunications organizations shall use an appropriate transparent cost accounting system which can be verified by accounting experts ensuring the production of recorded figures; whereas such requirement can be fulfilled for example by the implementation of the principle of fully distributed costing;

(20)   Whereas to enable the Commission to monitor effectively the application of this Directive, it is necessary that Member States notify to the Commission which national regulatory authority will be responsible for its implementation and provide the relevant information requested by the Commission;

(21)   Whereas the Committee referred to in Articles 9 and 10 of Directive 90/387/EEC should play an important role for the application of this Directive;

(22)   Whereas disagreements between users and telecommunications organizations on the provision of leased lines will normally be solved between these parties involved; whereas it must be possible for parties to refer their case to a national regulatory authority and the Commission in cases where this is considered necessary; whereas this does not prejudice normal application of the procedures laid down in Articles 169 and 170 and the competition rules of the Treaty;

(23)   Whereas a specific procedure must be established in order to examine whether, in justified cases, the time limit set out in this Directive for the provision of a minimum set of leased lines and for the implementation of an appropriate cost accounting system may be extended;

(24)   Whereas this Directive does not apply to leased lines one network termination point of which is located outside the Community,

HAS ADOPTED THIS DIRECTIVE:

Article 1   Scope

This Directive concerns the harmonization of conditions for open and efficient access to and use of the leased lines provided to users on public telecommunications networks, and the availability throughout the Community of a minimum set of leased lines with harmonized technical characteristics.

Article 2   Definitions

1. The definitions given in Directive 90/387/EEC shall apply, where relevant, to this Directive.

2.   In addition, for the purposes of this Directive,

— *leased lines* means the telecommunications facilities provided in the context of the establishment, development and operation of the public telecommunications network, which provide for transparent transmission capacity between network termination points and which do not include on-demand switching (switching functions with the user can control as part of the leased line provision),

— *ONP Committee* means the Committee referred to in Articles 9 and 10 of Directive 90/387/EEC,

— *users* means end users and service providers, including telecommunications organizations where the latter are engaged in providing services which are or may be provided also by others,

— *national regulatory authority* means the body or bodies in each Member State, legally distinct and functionally independent of the telecommunications organizations, entrusted by that Member State inter alia with the regulatory functions addressed in this Directive,

— *simple resale of capacity* means the commercial provision on leased lines for the public of data transmission as a separate service, including only such switching, processing, data storage or protocol conversion as is necessary for transmission in real time to and from the public switched network,

— *common ordering procedure* means an ordering procedure for the procurement of intra-Community leased lines which ensures that there is commonality across the telecommunications organizations in the information that has to be suplied by the user and the telecommunications organizations, and in the format in which the information is presented,

— *one-stop-ordering* is a system whereby all transactions involving a user, required for the procurement of intra-Community leased lines, supplied by more than one telecommunications organization to a single user, can be completed at one location between the user and a single telecommunications organization,

— *one-stop-billing* is a system whereby the billing and payment transaction for intra-Community leased lines supplied by more than one telecommunications organization to a single user can be completed at one location between the user and a single telecommunications organization.

Article 3 Availability of information

1. Member States shall ensure that information in respect of leased lines, offerings on technical characteristics, tariffs, supply and usage conditions, licensing and declaration requirements, and the conditions for the attachment of terminal equipment is published in accordance with the presentation given in Annex I. Changes in existing offerings shall be published as soon as possible and, unless the national regulatory authority agrees otherwise, no later than two months before the implementation.

2. The information referred to in paragraph 1 shall be published in an appropriate manner so as to provide easy access for users to that information. Reference shall be made in the national Official Journal of the Member State concerned to the publication of this information.

Member States shall notify to the Commission before 1 January 1993, and thereafter in case of any change, the manner in which the information is made available. The Commission will regularly publish reference to such notifications.

3. Member States shall ensure that information concerning new types of leased line offerings will be published as soon as possible, and no later than two months before the implementation of the offering.

Article 4 Information on supply conditions

The supply conditions to be published pursuant to Article 3 shall include at least:

— information concerning the ordering procedure

— the typical delivery period, which is the period, counted from the date when the user has made a firm request for a leased line, in which 80% of all leased lines of the same type have been put through to the customers.

This period will be established on the basis of the actual delivery periods of leased lines during a recent time interval of reasonable duration. The calculation must not include cases where late delivery periods were requested by users. For new types of leased lines a target delivery period shall be published instead of the typical delivery period,

— the contractual period, which includes the period which is in general foreseen for the contract and the minimum contractual period which the user is obliged to accept,

— the typical repair time, which is the period, counted from the time when a failure message has been given to the responsible unit within the telecommunications organization up to the moment in which 80 % of all leased lines of the same type have been re-established and in appropriate cases notified back in operation to the users. For new types of leased lines a target repair time period shall be published instead of the typical repair time. Where different classes of quality of repair are offered for the same type of leased lines, the different typical repair times shall be published,

— any refund procedure.

Article 5 Conditions for the termination of offerings

Member States shall ensure that existing offerings continue for a reasonable period of time, and that termination of an offering can be done only after consultation with users affected. Without prejudice to other rights of appeal provided for by national laws, Member States shall ensure that users can bring the case before the national regulatory authority where the users do not agree with the termination date as envisaged by the telecommunications organization.

Article 6 Access conditions, usage conditions and essential requirements

1. Without prejudice to Articles 2 and 3 of Directive 90/388/EEC, Member States shall ensure that when access to and usage of leased lines is restricted, these restrictions are aimed only at ensuring compliance with the essential requirements, compatible with Community law, and are imposed by the national regulatory authorities through regulatory means.

No technical restrictions shall be introduced or maintained for the inter-communication of leased lines and public telecommunications networks.

2. Where access to and use of leased lines are restricted on the basis of essential requirements, Member States shall ensure that the relevant national provisions identify which of the essential requirements listed in paragraph 3 are the basis of such restrictions.

3. The essential requirements specified in Article 3(2) of Directive 90/ 387/EEC shall apply to leased lines in the following manner:

(a) *Security of network operations*

A telecommunication organization may take the following measures in order to safeguard the security of network operations during the period when an emergency situation prevails:

— the interruption of the service,
— the limitation of service features,
— the denial of access to the service.

An emergency situation in this context means an exceptional case of *force majeure*, such as extreme weather, flood, lightning or fire, industrial action or lockouts, war, military operations, or civil disorder.

In an emergency situation the telecommunications organization shall make every endeavour to ensure that service is maintained to all users. The Member States shall ensure that the telecommunications organization immediately notifies to the users and to the national regulatory authority the beginning and the end of the emergency as well as the nature and extent of temporary service restrictions;

(b) *Maintenance of network integrity*

The user has the right to be provided with a fully transparent service, in conformity with the specifications of the network termination point, which he can use in an unstructured manner as he wants, e.g. where no channel allocations are forbidden or prescribed. There shall be no restrictions on the use of leased lines on the ground of the maintenance of network integrity, as long as the access conditions related to terminal equipment are fulfilled;

(c) *Interoperability of services*

Without prejudice to the application of Article 3 (5) and Article 5 (3) of Directive 90/387/EEC, the use of a leased line shall not be restricted on the grounds of the interoperability of services, when the access conditions related to terminal equipment are fulfilled;

(d) *Protection of data*

In respect of data protection, Member States may restrict the use of leased lines only to the extent necessary to ensure compliance with relevant regulatory provisions on the protection of data including protection of personal data, the confidentiality of information transmitted or stored, as well as the protection of privacy compatible with Community law.

4. Access conditions related to terminal equipment

Access conditions related to terminal equipment are considered to be fulfilled when the terminal equipment complies with the approval conditions set out for its connection to the network termination point of the type of leased line concerned, in accordance with Directive 91/263/EEC.[6]

In the case where a user's terminal equipment does not comply or no longer complies with these conditions, the provision of the leased line may be interrupted until the terminal is disconnected from the network termination point.

Member States shall ensure that the telecommunications organization immediately informs the user about the interruption, giving the reasons for

---

6 Council Directive 91/263/EEC of 29 April 1991 on the approximation of the laws of the Member States concerning telecommunications terminal equipment, including the mutual recognition of their conformity (OJ No L 128, 23. 5. 1991, p. 1).

the interruption. As soon as the user has ensured that the non-complying terminal equipment is disconnected from the network termination point, the provision of the leased line shall be restored.

Article 7   Provision of a minimum set of leased lines in accordance with harmonized technical characteristics

1.   Member States shall ensure that the respective telecommunications organizations separately or jointly provide a minimum set of leased lines in accordance with Annex II, in order to guarantee a harmonized offering throughout the Community.
2.   Where leased lines which implement the standards listed in Annex II are not yet available, Member States shall take the necessary measures to ensure that these types of leased lines will be implemented by the date resulting from the application of Article 15.
3.   The modifications necessary to adapt Annex II to new technical developments and to changes in market demand, including the possible deletion of certain types of leased lines from the Annex, shall be adopted by the Commission under the procedure provided for in Article 10 of Directive 90/387/EEC, taking into account the state of development of national networks.
4.   The provision of other leased lines beyond the minimum set of leased lines which must be provided by Member States shall not impede the provision of this minimum set of leased lines.

Article 8   Control by the national regulatory authority

1.   Member States shall ensure that the national regulatory authority lays down the procedures whereby it decides, on a case-by-case basis and in the shortest time period, to allow or not telecommunications organizations to take measures such as the refusal to provide a leased line, the interruption of the provision of leased lines or the reduction of the availability of leased line features for reasons of alleged failure to comply with the usage conditions by users of leased lines. These procedures may also foresee the possibility for the national regulatory authority to authorize, a priori, specified measures in the case of defined infringements of usage conditions.

Member States shall ensure that these procedures provide for a transparent decision-making process in which due respect is given to the rights of the parties. The decision shall be taken after having given the opportunity to both parties to state their case. The decision shall be motivated and notified to the parties within one week of its adoption: it shall not be enforced before its notification.

This provision shall not prejudice the right of the parties concerned to apply to the courts.
2.   The national regulatory authority shall ensure that telecommunications organizations adhere to the principle of non-discrimination when they make use of the public telecommunications network for providing services which are or may be provided also by other service providers. When telecommunications organizations use leased lines for the provision of services not covered

by special and/or exclusive rights, the same type of leased lines must be provided to other users on request and under equal conditions.

3. Where, in response to a particular request, a telecommunications organization considers it unreasonable to provide a leased line under its published tariffs and supply conditions, it must seek the agreement of the national regulatory authority to vary those conditions in that case.

Article 9   Common ordering and billing procedures

1. Member States shall encourage the establishment, by 31 December 1992 at the latest, in conformity with the procedural and substantive rules of competition of the Treaty and in consultation with users, of:
— a common ordering procedure for leased lines throughout the Community,
— a one-stop-ordering procedure for leased lines, to be applied where requested by the user,
— a one-stop-billing procedure for leased lines, to be applied where requested by the user. The procedure shall foresee that all price elements resulting from the national leased lines and the respective parts of international leased lines provided by the telecommunications organizations involved are identified separately in the bill for the user.

2. Member States shall report to the Commission one year after this Directive is brought into effect on the results achieved with respect to the procedures provided for in paragraph 1. These results shall be examined by the ONP Committee.

Article 10   Tariffing principles and cost accounting

1. Member States shall ensure that tariffs for leased lines follow the basic principles of cost orientation and transparency in accordance with the following rules:
   (a)   tariffs for leased lines shall be independent of the type of application which the users of the leased lines implement;
   (b)   tariffs for leased lines shall normally contain the following elements:
— an initial connection charge,
— a periodic rental charge, i.e. a flat-rate element.
When other tariff elements are applied, these must be transparent and based on objective criteria;
   (c)   tariffs for leased lines apply to the facilities provided between network termination points at which the user has access to the leased lines.
For leased lines provided by more than one telecommunications organization, half-circuit tariffs, i.e. from one network termination point to a hypothetical mid-circuit point, can be applied.

2. Member States shall ensure that their telecommunications organizations formulate and put in practice, by 31 December 1993 at the latest, a cost accounting system suitable for the implementation of paragraph 1.

Without prejudice to the last subparagraph, the system referred to in the first subparagraph shall include the following elements:

(a)   the costs of leased lines shall in particular include the direct costs incurred by the telecommunications organizations for setting up, operating and maintaining leased lines, and for marketing and billing of leased lines;

(b)   common costs, that is costs which can neither be directly assigned to leased lines nor to other activities, are allocated as follows:

(i)   whenever possible, common cost categories shall be allocated based upon direct analysis of the origin of the costs themselves;

(ii)   when direct analysis is not possible, common cost categories shall be allocated based upon an indirect linkage to another cost category or group of cost categories for which a direct assignment or allocation is possible. The indirect linkage shall be based on comparable cost structures;

(iii)   when neither direct nor indirect measures of cost allocation can be found, the cost category shall be allocated based upon a general allocator computed by using the ratio of all expenses directly assigned or allocated to, on the one hand, services which are provided under special or exclusive rights and, on the other hand, to other services.

After 31 December 1993, other cost accounting systems may be applied only if they are suitable for the implementation of paragraph 1 and have as such been approved by the national regulatory authority for application by the telecommunications organization, subject to the Commission being informed prior to their application.

3.   The national regulatory authority shall keep available, with an adequate level of detail, information on the cost accounting systems applied by the telecommunications organizations pursuant to paragraph 2. It shall submit this information to the Commission on request.

Article 11   Notification and reporting

1.   Member States shall notify before 1 January 1993 to the Commission their national regulatory authority as defined in Article 2, fourth indent.

2.   The national regulatory authority shall make available statistical reports showing the performance in relation to the supply conditions, in particular with respect to delivery time and repair time, published in accordance with Article 3 at least for each calendar year. The reports shall be sent to the Commission no later than five months after the end of the annual reporting period.

The national regulatory authority shall keep available and submit to the Commission on request the data on cases where the access to or use of leased lines has been restricted, in particular because of alleged infringements of special or exclusive rights or the prohibition of simple resale of capacity, as well as details of the measures taken, including their motivation.

Article 12   Conciliation procedure

Without prejudice to:

(a)   any action that the Commission or any Member State might take pursuant to the Treaty, and in particular Articles 169 or 170 thereof;

(b)   the rights of the person invoking the procedure in paragraphs 1 to 5 of this Article of the telecommunications organizations concerned or any

other person under applicable national law, except in so far as they enter into an agreement for the resolution of issues between them;
the following conciliation procedure shall be available to the user:

1.   Any user complaining that he has been or may be injured by the infringement of the provisions of this Directive, particularly regarding intra-Community leased lines, shall have the right to appeal to the national regulatory authority or authorities.

2.   Where agreement cannot be reached at a national level, the aggrieved party may invoke the procedure provided for in paragraphs 3 and 4, by way of a written notification to the national regulatory authority and the Commission.

3.   Where the national regulatory authority or the Commission finds that there is a case for further examination, following a notification based on paragraph 2, it can refer it to the Chairman of the ONP Committee.

4.   In the case referred to in paragraph 3, the Chairman of the ONP Committee shall initiate the procedure described below if he is satisfied that all reasonable steps have been taken at a national level:

(a)   the Chairman of the ONP Committee shall convene as soon as possible a working group including at least two members of the ONP Committee and one representative of the national regulatory authorities concerned and the Chairman of the ONP Committee or another official of the Commission appointed by him. The working group shall normally meet within 10 days of the meeting being convened. The Chairman may decide, upon proposal of any of the members of the working group, to invite a maximum of two other persons as experts to advise it.

(b)   the working group shall give the party invoking this procedure, the national regulatory authorities of the Member States, and the telecommunications organizations involved the opportunity to present their opinions in oral or written form;

(c)   the working group shall endeavour to reach agreement between the parties involved. The Chairman shall inform the ONP Committee of the results of this procedure.

5.   The party invoking the procedure referred to in this Article shall bear its own costs of participating in this procedure.

Article 13   Deferment of certain obligations

1.   When a Member State is not able to or can foresee that it will not be able to fulfil the requirements of Article 7 (1) or (2) or Article 10 (1) or (2), it shall notify the Commission of the reasons.

2.   Deferment of the obligations under Article 7 (1) or (2) can be accepted only in cases where the Member State concerned can prove that the actual state of development of its public telecommunications network or the conditions of demand are such that the obligations under Article 7 would impose an excessive burden on the telecommunications organization in that Member State.

3.   Deferment of the obligations under Article 10(1) or (2) can be accepted only in cases where the Member State concerned can prove that the fulfilment of the requirements would impose an excessive burden on the telecommunications organization in that Member State.

4.   The Member State shall inform the Commission of the date by which the requirements can be met and of the measures envisaged in order to meet this deadline.

5.   When the Commission receives a notification in accordance with paragraph 1, it shall inform the Member State whether it deems that the particular situation of the Member State concerned justifies, on the basis of criteria set out in paragraphs 2 and 3, a deferment for this Member State of the application of Article 7 (1) or (2) of Article 10 (1) or (2) and until which date such deferment is justified.

6.   No deferment can be granted in application of paragraph 2 where the non-compliance with Article 7 results from activities of telecommunications organizations of the Member State concerned in competitive areas within the meaning of Community law.

Article 14

The Commission shall examine and report to the European Parliament and to the Council on the functioning of this Directive, on the first occasion not later than three years after this Directive is brought into effect. The report shall be based *inter alia* on the information provided by the Member States to the Commission and to the ONP Committee. Where necessary, further measures can be proposed in the report for the full implementation of the aims of the Directive.

Article 15

1.   Member States shall take the measures necessary to comply with this Directive before 5 June 1993. They shall forthwith inform the Commission thereof.

When Member States adopt these measures, they shall contain a reference to this Directive or shall be accompanied by such reference on the occasion of their official publication. The methods of making such a reference shall be laid down by the Member States.

2.   Member States shall inform the Commission of the main provisions of national law which they adopt in the field governed by this Directive.

Article 16

This Directive is addressed to the Member States.

Done at Luxembourg, 5 June 1992.

For the Council
The President
Joaquim Ferreira Do Amaral

ANNEX I   PRESENTATION OF THE INFORMATION TO BE PROVIDED IN RESPECT OF LEASED LINES IN ACCORDANCE WITH ARTICLE 3 (1)

The information referred to in Article 3 (1) of this Directive shall follow the presentation given below:

A.   Technical characteristics

The technical characteristics include the physical and electrical characteristics as well as the detailed technical and performance specifications which apply at the network termination point, without prejudice to Council Directive 83/189/EEC of 28 March 1983 laying down a procedure for the provision of information in the field of technical standards and regulations.[7] Clear reference shall be made to the standards implemented.

B.   Tariffs

The tariffs include the initial connection charges, the periodic rental charges, and other charges. Where tariffs are differentiated, e.g. for reasons of different levels of quality of service or the number of leased lines provided to a user (bulk provision), this must be indicated.

C.   Supply conditions

The supply conditions include at least the elements defined in Article 4 (1).

D.   Licensing requirements

The information on licensing requirements, licensing procedures and/or licensing conditions provides a complete overview of all factors which have an impact on the usage conditions set out for leased lines. It shall include the following information, where applicable:

1.   a clear description of the service categories for which the licensing procedures have to be followed and for which the licensing conditions have to be met by the user of the leased line or by his customers;

2.   information on the character of the licensing conditions, in particular whether such licence is of a general nature which does not require individual registration and/or authorization, or whether the licensing conditions require registration and/or authorization on an individual basis;

3.   a clear indication of the validity in time of the licence, including a review date, where applicable;

4.   the conditions resulting from the application of the essential requirements in conformity with Article 6;

5.   other obligations which the Member States may impose on the users of leased lines in accordance with Directive 90/388/EEC as regards packet- or circuit-switched data services, requiring the adherence to conditions of permanence, availability, or quality of service;

6.   a clear reference to conditions aiming at the enforcement of the prohibition to provide services for which exclusive and/or special rights have been maintained by the Member State concerned in conformity with Community law;

7.   a list referring to all documents containing licensing conditions which the Member State imposes on the users of leased lines when these are using leased lines for the provision of services to others.

E.   Conditions for the attachment of terminal equipment

The information on the attachment conditions includes a complete overview of the requirements which terminal equipment to be attached to the relevant leased line has to fulfil in accordance with Directive 91/263/EEC.

---

7 OJ No L 109, 26. 4. 1983, p. 8. Directive last amended by Commission Decision 90/230/EEC (OJ No L 128, 18. 5. 1990, p. 15).

ANNEX II   DEFINITION OF A MINIMUM SET OF LEASED LINES
WITH HARMONIZED TECHNICAL CHARACTERISTICS, IN
ACCORDANCE WITH ARTICLE 7, TO BE PROVIDED AS SOON
AS POSSIBLE AND NOT LATER THAN THE DATE ON WHICH
THIS DIRECTIVE IS BROUGHT INTO EFFECT

Leased line type	Technical characteristics[8]	
	Interface specifications	Performance specifications
Ordinary quality voice bandwidth	2 or 4 wire analogue	CCITT M. 1040
Special quality voice bandwidth	2 or 4 wire analogue	CCITT M. 1020/M. 1025
64 kbit/s digital	CCITT G. 703[9]	Relevant CCITT G. 800 series recommendations
2 048 kbit/s digital unstructured	CCITT G. 703	Relevant CCITT G. 800 series recommendations
2 048 kbit/s digital structured	CCITT G. 703 and G. 704 (excluding section 5)[10]	Relevant CCITT G. 800 series recommendations In-service monitoring[11]

For the types of leased lines listed above, the specifications referred to also
define the network termination points (NTPs), in accordance with the
definition given in Article 2 of Directive 90/387/EEC.

Notes
1. See further:
    Telecommunications: open network provision for leased lines - Publication of
information in respect of leased lines; OJ C277/9, 15.10.93.
    Commission Decision of 15 June 1994 on amendment of Annex II of Council
Directive 92/44/EEC (94/439/EC; OJ L181/40, 15.7.94).
    Telecommunications: Open network provision (ONP) for leased lines - Concili-
ation procedure; OJ C214/4, 4.8.94.
2. See also ECJ reference (Case C-302/94) in *R* v *Secretary of State for Trade and
Industry, ex parte British Telecommunications plc* [1994] (OJ C380/3, 31 December
1994) regarding the implementation of the Directive in SI. 1994 No.2251 (Leased
Lines). For the ECJ decision, see the law report in the *Financial Times*, 17 December
1996.

---

8 The CCITT recommendations referenced refer to the 1988 version. ETSI has been requested
to carry out further work on standards for leased lines.
9 The majority of applications are converging towards the G. 703 specification. For an interim
period, leased lines may be provided using other interfaces, based on X.21 or X.21 (a), instead
of G. 703.
10 With cyclic redundancy checking in accordance with CCITT G. 706.
11 In-service monitoring can facilitate improved maintenance by the telecommunications
organization.

3. The Commission issued infringement proceedings against Member States, under Article 169 of the EEC Treaty, for failure to implement the Directive: e.g. Spain (OJ 94/C304/13) and Luxembourg (OJ 94/C254/10).

DIRECTIVE (95/62/EC) OF THE EUROPEAN PARLIAMENT AND OF THE COUNCIL OF 13 DECEMBER 1995 ON THE APPLICATION OF OPEN NETWORK PROVISION (ONP) TO VOICE TELEPHONY
OJ L321/6, 30 December 1995

THE EUROPEAN PARLIAMENT AND THE COUNCIL OF THE EUROPEAN UNION,

Having regard to the Treaty establishing the European Community, and in particular Article 100a thereof,

Having regard to the proposal from the Commission,[1]

Having regard to the opinion of the Economic and Social Committee,[2]

Acting in accordance with the procedure laid down in Article 189b of the Treaty,[3]

(1) Whereas Council Directive 90/387/EEC of 28 June 1990 on the establishment of the internal market for telecommunications services through the implementation of open network provision[4] provides *inter alia* for the adoption of a specific Directive establishing open network provision conditions for the voice telephony service;

(2) Whereas in accordance with Directive 90/387/EEC, open network provision (ONP) applies to public telecommunications networks and, where applicable, public telecommunications services; whereas therefore the application of ONP to the voice telephony service must also include the application of ONP to the network over which the voice telephony service is provided;

(3) Whereas ONP conditions for access to and use of the fixed public telephone networks and services must apply to all the network technologies currently in use in Member States, including analogue telephone networks, digital networks and the integrated services digital network (ISDN);

(4) Whereas this Directive does not apply to mobile telephony services; whereas it does apply to the use of fixed public telephone networks by operators of public mobile telephony services, in particular with respect to the interconnection of mobile telephone networks with the fixed public telephone network in a single Member State, in order to achieve comprehensive Community-wide services; whereas this Directive does not apply to direct interconnection between operators of public mobile telephony services;

(5) Whereas this Directive does not apply to services or facilities provided at network termination points located outside the Community;

(6) Whereas Commission Directive 90/388/EEC of 28 June 1990 on competition in the markets for telecommunications services[5] requires Mem-

---

1 OJ No C 122, 18. 5. 1995, p. 4.
2 OJ No C 236, 11. 9. 1995, p. 38.
3 Opinion of the European Parliament of 16 May 1995 (OJ No C 151, 19. 6. 1995, p. 27), common position of the Council of 12 July 1995 (OJ No C 281, 25. 10. 1995, p. 19), Decision of the European Parliament of 26 October 1995 (OJ No C 308, 20. 11. 1995) and Council Decision of 27 November 1995.
4 OJ No L 192, 24. 7. 1990, p. 1.
5 OJ No L 192, 24. 7. 1990, p. 10. Directive as amended by Directive 94/46/EC (OJ No L 268, 19. 10. 1994, p. 15).

ber States to abolish exclusive rights for the supply of telecommunications services other than voice telephony; whereas Directive 90/388/EEC does not apply to telex, mobile radiotelephony and paging services;

(7)   Whereas some Member States have abolished exclusive rights for the provision of voice telephony and the public telecommunications network; whereas those Member States should ensure that all users can subscribe to harmonized telephony services in accordance with this Directive; whereas the provisions of this Directive should not hinder entry to markets for voice telephony or the provision of the public telecommunications network;

(8)   Whereas the voice telephony service has become important for social and economic reasons, and everyone in the Community should have the right to subscribe to this service; whereas in application of the principle of non-discrimination, voice telephony service must be offered and provided on request without discrimination to all users; whereas the principle of non-discrimination applies to, *inter alia*, availability of technical access, tariffs, quality of service, delivery period, fair distribution of capacity in the event of scarcity, repair time, availability of network information and customers' information, subject to relevant legislation concerning the protection of personal data and privacy;

(9)   Whereas in accordance with Directive 90/388/EEC, Member States which maintain exclusive rights for the provision and operation of public telecommunications networks must take the necessary measures to make the conditions governing access to and use of the network objective and non-discriminatory and to publish them; whereas it is necessary to harmonize which specifications should be published and in what form, in order to facilitate the provision of telecommunications services within and between Member States, and in particular the provision of services by companies, firms or natural persons established in a Member State other than that of the company, firm or natural person for which or for whom the services are intended;

(10)   Whereas in conformity with the principle of separation of regulatory and operational functions, national regulatory authorities have been created in the Member States; whereas in application of the principle of subsidiarity, the national regulatory authority of each Member State should play an important role in the implementation of this Directive, particularly in matters relating to the publication of targets and performance statistics, dates for the implementation of new facilities, adequate consultation with users/consumers and user/consumer organizations, the control of numbering plans, the super-vision of conditions of use, and the resolution of disputes and in ensuring that users are given fair treatment throughout the Community; whereas they should have the necessary means to carry out these tasks fully;

(11)   Whereas quality of service as perceived by users is an essential aspect of the service provided, and quality-of-service parameters and achieved performance levels should be published for the benefit of users; whereas harmonized quality-of-service parameters and common measurement methods are required in order to assess Community-wide convergence of quality of service; whereas different categories of user require different levels of quality of service, for which different tariffs may be appropriate;

(12)   Whereas users of the fixed public telephone network should have at least similar rights when dealing with telecommunications organizations as they have with the providers of other goods and services, and

telecommunications organizations should not have any undue legal protection when dealing with users of the fixed public telephone network;

(13)   Whereas agreement between the parties involved can constitute a contract; whereas, in order to avoid unfair contractual clauses, it is necessary that national regulatory authorities have the right to require modifications of conditions imposed by telecommunications organizations on users in their contracts; whereas Member States may decide whether their national regulatory authority shall check these contractual conditions either before their use by telecommunications organizations, or at any time at the user's request;

(14)   Whereas Council Directive 93/13/EEC of 5 April 1993 on unfair terms in consumer contracts[6] already provides general protection for consumers with regard to contractual terms; whereas nevertheless for the purpose of this Directive it is necessary to complete this general protection by adding more specific rules which should apply to all users;

(15)   Whereas in addition to the basic voice telephony service made available to users it is desirable to ensure that, subject to technical feasibility and economic viability, a harmonized minimum set of advanced voice telephony facilities is offered to users for communications both within and between Member States;

(16)   Whereas an agreement on a *modus vivendi* between the European Parliament, the Council and the Commission concerning the implementing measures for acts adopted in accordance with the procedure laid down in Article 189b of the EC Treaty was reached on 20 December 1994;

(17)   Whereas the provision of other voice telephony facilities, provided in response to market demand in addition to the harmonized minimum set of voice telephony facilities described herein, should not impede the provision of the basic voice telephony facilities and should not lead to unreasonable increases in the prices for basic voice telephony service;

(18)   Whereas harmonized conditions for the voice telephony service should allow Member States flexibility to determine the timescales for implementation, given the different situations with regard to technical development of the network and market demand;

(19)   Whereas the Commission has issued Guidelines on the application of Community competition rules in the telecommunications sector[7] in order *inter alia* to clarify the application of Community competition law when telecommunications organizations cooperate in order to implement Community-wide interconnectivity between public networks and services;

(20)   Whereas, in order to provide efficient and effective telecommunications services, and to offer new applications, telecommunications service providers and other users may, in accordance with the principles of Community law, request access to the fixed public telephone network at points other than the network termination points offered to the majority of telephone users; whereas such requests must be reasonable in terms of technical feasibility and economic viability; whereas procedures must be introduced to provide a balance between the requirements of users and the justified concerns of telecommunications organizations; whereas it is essential that in making full and efficient use of the fixed public telephone network via such special network access, the integrity of the public network is maintained;

6 OJ No L 95, 21. 4. 1993, p. 29.
7 OJ No C 233, 6. 9. 1991, p. 2.

(21)   Whereas in accordance with the definition in Directive 90/387/EEC, the network termination point may be located on the premises of a telecommunications organization; whereas installation of equipment owned by service providers on the premises of a telecommunications organization is not specifically called for in this Directive;

(22)   Whereas it is necessary for adequate safeguards to be implemented by national regulatory authorities in order to ensure that telecommunications organizations do not discriminate against service providers with whom they are in competition, including, in particular, safeguards to ensure fair access to network interfaces; whereas the tariffs which apply to telecommunications organizations when using the fixed public telephone network for the provision of telecommunications services should be the same as the tariffs which apply to other users;

(23)   Whereas users should benefit from economies of scope and scale which may result from new intelligent network architectures; whereas the development of the Community market in telecommunications services calls for the widest availability of facilities such as those defined in this Directive; whereas the principle of non-discrimination should be applied in a manner that does not hinder the development of advanced telecommunications services;

(24)   Whereas telecommunications organizations should be encouraged to establish the necessary cooperation mechanisms in order to ensure full Community-wide interconnectivity between public networks, in particular for the voice telephony service; whereas national regulatory authorities should facilitate such cooperation; whereas such interconnection should be subject to regulatory supervision in order to safeguard the interests of users throughout the Community and ensure compliance with Community law, where appropriate in compliance with the existing international regulatory framework within the scope of the International Telecommunications Union (ITU); whereas therefore national regulatory authorities should have the right of access to full information about network interconnection agreements where required; whereas the Commission may request from Member States details of special network access agreements and interconnection agreements in so far as Community law so provides;

(25)   Whereas interconnection of public telephone networks is essential for the provision of Community-wide voice telephony services; whereas it is the responsibility of national regulatory authorities to ensure that the conditions governing interconnection with the fixed public telephone networks, including interconnection by telecommunications organizations from other Member States and operators of public mobile telephony services, are objective and non-discriminatory in accordance with Directive 90/387/EEC;

(26)   Whereas where the fixed public telephone network in a Member State is operated by more than one telecommunications organization, appropriate supervision of interconnection arrangements by national regulatory authorities is necessary in order to guarantee Community-wide provision of the voice telephony service; whereas such interconnection arrangements should take due account of the principles laid down in this Directive;

(27)   Whereas the principle of non-discrimination in relation to interconnection primarily aims at preventing abuse of a dominant position by telecommunications organizations;

(28)   Whereas in accordance with Directive 90/387/EEC common, efficient tariff principles, based on objective criteria and cost orientation, should be applied throughout the Community; whereas a reasonable transition period may be necessary in order to implement these tariff principles fully; whereas tariffs must nevertheless be transparent and properly published, must be sufficiently unbundled in accordance with the competition rules of the Treaty, and must be non-discriminatory and guarantee equality of treatment; whereas application of the principle of cost orientation should take account of the objective of universal service and may take account of town and country planning policies aimed at ensuring cohesion within a Member State;

(29)   Whereas national regulatory authorities should have responsibility for supervising tariffs; whereas tariff structures should evolve in response to technological development and user demand; whereas the requirement for cost-oriented tariffs means that telecommunications organizations should implement within a reasonable time limit cost accounting systems by which costs can be allocated to services as accurately as possible on the basis of a transparent cost accounting system; whereas such requirements can be fulfilled for example by implementation of the principle of fully distributed costing;

(30)   Whereas, within the overall principle of cost orientation, some flexibility is needed, under supervision of the national regulatory authority, in order to allow discount schemes for certain uses, or socially desirable tariffs for particular groups of people, for particular types of call, or at particular times of day; whereas discount schemes must be compatible with the competition rules of the Treaty, and in particular with the general principle that the conclusion of contracts must not be subject to acceptance of unrelated supplementary obligations; whereas, in particular, discount schemes must not link the supply of services provided under special or exclusive rights with services provided competitively;

(31)   Whereas users must be able to check the correctness of their bills by being given the possibility of itemized bills with a degree of detail compatible with user needs and with relevant legislation on data protection and privacy;

(32)   Whereas directories of users who subscribe to the voice telephony service should be readily available, since they are an important element for use of the voice telephony service; whereas directory information should be made available on fair and non-discriminatory terms; whereas users should have the choice of being included or excluded from directories, in conformity with relevant legislation on data protection and privacy; whereas this Directive does not change the regulatory situation regarding the supply of directories;

(33)   Whereas public pay-telephones provide an important means of access to the voice telephony service, especially in emergencies, and it is desirable to ensure that they are available to meet the reasonable needs of users;

(34)   Whereas, recognizing that users would benefit from a single type of telephone payment card usable in all Member States, the Commission has given the European Committee for Standardization (CEN)/the European Committee for Electrotechnical Standardization (Cenelec) a mandate to develop suitable standards; whereas, in addition to these standards, commercial agreements are needed to ensure that pre-payment cards issued in one Member State can be used in other Member States;

(35)   Whereas, within each Member State, measures may be taken to assist groups of people with special needs; whereas this may include provisions relating to the voice telephony service, because it is recognized as an important service for disabled people;

(36)   Whereas the Commission has requested the European Telecommunications Standards Institute (ETSI) to study the technical feasibility and economic viability of a harmonized single line network interface suitable for access to and use of the fixed public telephone network in all Member States; whereas, to ensure harmonized access for ISDN terminal equipment, it is desirable to set requirements for the corresponding network termination point, including specifications for the socket;

(37)   Whereas national telephone numbers are a resource which should be controlled by national regulatory bodies; whereas numbering schemes should be developed in close consultation with telecommunications organizations and in harmony with a long-term Europe-wide numbering framework and the international numbering scheme; whereas number changes are expensive for both telecommunications organizations and users, and should be kept to a minimum compatible with national and international long-term requirements;

(38)   Whereas the Council resolution of 19 November 1992 on the promotion of Europe-wide cooperation on numbering of telecommunications services[8] regards as a major policy goal the strengthening of cooperation on the numbering arrangements for services with pan-European applications; whereas there is a need to create a European numbering area in order to facilitate the implementation and use of Europe-wide voice telephony services, including freephone/green numbers;

(39)   Whereas in accordance with Directive 90/388/EEC Member States which make the supply of telecommunications services subject to a licensing or declaration procedure must ensure that the conditions for the grant of licences are objective, non-discriminatory and transparent, that reasons are given for any refusal, and that there is a procedure for appealing against any such refusal; whereas conditions for using the fixed public telephone network must be compatible with Community law and in particular Directive 90/387/EEC; whereas in accordance with Council Directive 92/44/EEC of 5 June 1992 on the application of open network provision to leased lines,[9] any restrictions aimed at ensuring compliance with the essential requirements should be compatible with Community law and imposed by the national regulatory authorities through regulatory means; whereas no technical restrictions may be introduced or maintained for the interconnection of leased lines and public telephone networks;

(40)   Whereas in accordance with Directive 90/387/EEC the essential requirements on the basis of which restrictions on access to and use of public telecommunications networks or services are justified are limited to the security of network operations, maintenance of network integrity, interoperability of services in justified cases and protection of data as appropriate; whereas, in addition, the conditions generally applicable to the connection of terminal equipment apply; whereas national regulatory authorities may auth-

8 OJ No C 318, 4. 12. 1992, p. 2.
9 OJ No L 165, 19. 6. 1992, p. 27. Directive as amended by Commission Decision 94/439/EC (OJ No L 181, 15. 7. 1994, p. 40).

orize procedures whereby a telecommunications organization can act immediately in the event of a serious breach of conditions of access or use;

(41) Whereas the principle of transparency should apply to the standards upon which voice telephony services are based; whereas in accordance with Directive 90/387/EEC, the harmonization of technical interfaces and access conditions must be based on common technical specifications which take account of international standardization; whereas in accordance with Council Directive 83/189/EEC of 28 March 1983 laying down a procedure for the provision of information in the field of technical standards and regulations,[10] new national standards must not be developed in areas where harmonized European standards are under development;

(42) Whereas, to enable the Commission to monitor effectively the application of this Directive, it is necessary that Member States notify to the Commission which national regulatory authorities will be responsible for the functions created by this Directive and the provision of the relevant information called for in this Directive;

(43) Whereas, in addition to the rights of recourse granted under national or Community law, there is a need for a simple conciliation procedure for disputes at both national and Community level; whereas this procedure should be responsive, inexpensive and transparent and should involve all the parties concerned;

(44) Whereas telecommunications services are subject to consumer protection legislation, data protection legislation and legislation concerning dissemination of information or material which may be considered offensive by the general public, and therefore no specific additional measures are envisaged in this Directive;

(45) Whereas transparency would be improved by regular and systematic dialogue with telecommunications organizations, users, consumers, manufacturers and service providers as regards Community-wide issues raised by this Directive; whereas consultation with trade unions is already covered by Commission Decision 90/450/EEC[11] which set up, to assist the Commission, a Joint Committee on Telecommunications Services consisting of representatives of employers and employees;

(46) Whereas given the dynamic development of this sector, the application of open network provision to voice telephony must be a progressive and ongoing process, and the regulatory conditions must be flexible enough to meet the demands of a changing market and changing technology; whereas a responsive procedure for technical adjustment should therefore be established which takes full account of the views of Member States and involves the ONP Committee;

(47) Whereas a procedure will probably have to be introduced for ensuring Community-wide convergence by determining harmonized targets and target dates for voice telephony services and facilities; whereas such a convergence procedure should involve the ONP Committee; whereas in such a procedure full account must be taken of the state of network development and market demand in the Community;

(48) Whereas the goal of an advanced cost-effective Community-wide voice telephony service — an essential foundation of the internal market —

---

10 OJ No L 109, 26. 4. 1983, p. 8. Directive as last amended by Directive 94/10/EC of the European Parliament and of the Council (OJ No L 100, 19. 4. 1994, p. 30).
11 OJ No L 230, 24. 8. 1990, p. 25.

cannot be realized satisfactorily at Member State level, and hence is better achieved at Community level by the adoption of this Directive;

(49) Whereas Decision 91/396/EEC[12] requires the introduction in the Community of a single European emergency call number;[12] whereas Council Directive 91/263/EEC of 29 April 1991 on the approximation of the laws of the Member States concerning telecommunications terminal equipment, including the mutual recognition of their conformity,[13] defines the conditions for connection of terminal equipment to the fixed public telephone network;

(50) Whereas Europe is shifting towards an information-based economy; whereas open access to networks is a critical issue at world level; whereas the Council has agreed a timetable for the liberalization of all telecommunication services, networks and infrastructures; whereas a balanced policy of liberalization and harmonization, including accompanying measures for universal service, will continue to ensure that business, industry and the public can access modern, economic and efficient communications infrastructures over which a rich and diverse range of services will be offered;

(51) Whereas the Council resolution of 22 July 1993[14] calls on the Commission to introduce the necessary proposals for legislation by 1 January 1996 and to consider how to adjust open network provision to future developments,

HAVE ADOPTED THIS DIRECTIVE:

Article 1 Scope

1. This Directive concerns the harmonization of conditions for open and efficient access to and use of fixed public telephone networks and public telephony services, and the availability throughout the Community of a harmonized voice telephony service.

2. This Directive does not apply to mobile telephony services in so far as it concerns interconnection between the networks used for public mobile telephony services and the fixed public telephone networks.

Article 2 Definitions

1. The definitions given in Directive 90/387/EEC shall apply, where relevant, to this Directive.

2. For the purposes of this Directive:

— 'fixed public telephone network' means the public switched telecommunications network which is used, *inter alia*, for the provision of voice telephony service between network termination points at fixed locations,

— 'users' means end-users, including consumers (e.g. residential end-users), and service providers, including telecommunications organizations where the latter provide services which are or may be provided also by others,

— 'national regulatory authority' means the body or bodies in each Member State, legally distinct and functionally independent of the telecommunications

---

12 OJ No L 217, 6. 8. 1991, p. 31.
13 OJ No L 128, 23. 5. 1991, p. 1. Directive as last amended by Directive 93/97/EEC (OJ No L 290, 24. 11. 1993, p. 1).
14 OJ No C 213, 6. 8. 1993, p. 1.

organizations, entrusted by that Member State, *inter alia*, with the regulatory functions addressed in this Directive,

— 'ONP Committee' means the committee created by Article 9 (1) of Directive 90/387/EEC,

— 'public pay-telephone' means a telephone available to the general public, for the use of which the means of payment are coins, credit/debit cards and/or pre-payment cards.

Article 3 Provision of service, connection of terminal equipment and use of the network

Member States shall ensure that the respective telecommunications organizations separately or jointly provide a fixed public telephone network and a voice telephony service in accordance with the provisions of this Directive, in order to guarantee a harmonized offering throughout the Community.

In particular Member States shall ensure that users can:

(a) obtain on request a connection to the fixed public telephone network;

(b) connect and use approved terminal equipment situated on the users' premises, in accordance with national and Community law.

Member States shall ensure that no restrictions other than those referred to in Article 22 are placed on the use made of the connection provided.

Article 4 Publication of and access to information

1. National regulatory authorities shall ensure that adequate and up-to-date information on access to and use of the fixed public telephone network and voice telephony service is published according to the list of headings given in Annex I.

Changes in existing service offerings and information on new offerings shall be published as soon as possible. The national regulatory authority may lay down a suitable period of notice.

2. The information referred to in paragraph 1 shall be published in such a way as to provide easy access for users to that information. Reference shall be made in the national Official Journal of the Member State concerned to the publication of this information.

3. National regulatory authorities shall notify to the Commission no later than one year after the adoption of this Directive — and thereafter in the event of any change — the manner in which the information referred to in paragraph 1 is made available; the Commission shall regularly publish a corresponding reference to such notifications in the *Official Journal of the European Communities*.

Article 5 Targets for supply time and quality of service

1. National regulatory authorities shall ensure that targets are set and published for the supply-time and quality-of-service indicators listed in Annex II. Definitions, measurement methods and the performance of telecommunications organizations in relation to those targets shall be published annually. Definitions, measurement methods and targets shall be reviewed at least every three years by the national regulatory authority.

2. Publication shall be in the manner laid down in Article 4.

3. Where appropriate, the Commission shall, in consultation with the ONP Committee, acting in accordance with the procedure laid down in Article 30, request ETSI to draw up European standards for common definitions and measurement methods.

Article 6   Conditions for the termination of offerings

1. National regulatory authorities shall ensure that service offerings continue for a reasonable period of time and that termination of an offering, or a change that materially alters the use that can be made of it, can take place only after consultation with users affected and an appropriate public notice period set by the national regulatory authority.

2. Without prejudice to other rights of appeal provided for by national law, Member States shall ensure that users, acting where national law provides for this in conjunction with organizations representing user and/or consumer interests, can bring before the national regulatory authority cases where the users affected do not agree with the termination date envisaged by the telecommunications organization.

Article 7   User contracts

1. National regulatory authorities shall ensure that users have a contract which specifies the service to be provided by a telecommunications organization. National regulatory authorities shall as a general rule require compensation and/or refund arrangements to be provided if the contracted service quality levels are not met, and shall ensure that any exceptions to this rule are justified by the telecommunications organization or organizations concerned and made clear in the users' contract.

2. Telecommunications organizations shall respond to a request for connection to the fixed public telephone network without delay and shall give the user an estimated date for provision of service.

3. National regulatory authorities shall be able to require alteration of the conditions of contracts and the conditions of any compensation and/or refund schemes used by telecommunications organizations. Users' contracts with telecommunications organizations shall contain a summary of the method of initiating procedures for the settlement of disputes.

4. Member States shall ensure that users have the right to institute proceedings against a telecommunications organization.

Article 8   Variation of published conditions

Where in response to a particular request a telecommunications organization considers it unreasonable to provide a connection to the fixed public telephone network under its published tariffs and supply conditions, it must seek the agreement of the national regulatory authority to vary those conditions in that case.

Article 9 Provision of advance facilities

1. National regulatory authorities shall ensure the provision, subject to technical feasibility and economic viability, of the facilities listed in Annex III (1), in accordance with the technical standards identified in Article 24.

2. National regulatory authorities shall facilitate and encourage provision of the services and facilities listed in Annex III (2), in accordance with the technical standards identified in Article 24, through commercial arrangements between telecommunications organizations and where applicable other persons providing the service or facilities, in compliance with the competition rules of the Treaty and in response to user demand.

3. National regulatory authorities shall ensure that dates for the introduction of the facilities listed in Annex III (1) are set, taking into account the state of network development, market demand and progress with standardization, and are published in the manner laid down in Article 4. They shall similarly encourage the setting and publication of dates for the services and facilities listed in Annex III (2).

Article 10 Special network access

1. National regulatory authorities shall ensure that telecommunications organizations respond to reasonable requests from users other than:

(a) operators of public mobile telephony services;

(b) telecommunications organizations when providing a voice telephony service;

for access to the fixed public telephone network at network termination points other than the network termination points referred to in Annex 1.

Where in response to a particular request a telecommunications organization considers it unreasonable to provide the special network access requested, it must seek the agreement of the national regulatory authority to restrict or deny that access. Users affected must be given the opportunity to put their case to the national regulatory authority before a decision is taken.

Where a request for special network access is denied, the user making the request must be given a prompt and reasoned explanation as to why the request has been refused; however, this provision shall not apply to any action taken under national regimes for the enforcement of licensing conditions in conformity with Community law or to proceedings before a national court.

2. Technical and commercial arrangements for special network access shall be a matter for agreement between the parties involved, subject to intervention by the national regulatory authority as laid down in paragraphs 1, 3 and 4. The agreement may include reimbursement to the telecommunications organization of the costs incurred *inter alia* in providing the network access requested; these charges shall fully respect the principles of cost orientation set out in Annex II to Directive 90/387/EEC.

3. National regulatory authorities may intervene on their own initiative at any time, and shall do so if requested by either party, in order to set conditions that are non discriminatory, are fair and reasonable for both parties and offer the greatest benefit to all users.

4. National regulatory authorities shall also have the right, in the interest of all users, to ensure that the agreements include conditions that meet the

criteria set out in paragraph 3, are entered into and implemented in an efficient and timely manner and include conditions on conformity with relevant standards, compliance with essential requirements and/or the maintenance of end-to-end quality.

5.   Conditions set by national regulatory authorities in accordance with paragraph 4 shall be published in the manner laid down in Article 4.

6.   National regulatory authorities shall ensure that telecommunications organizations adhere to the principle of non-discrimination when they make use of the fixed public telephone network for providing services which are or may also be supplied by other service providers.

7.   The Commission shall, in consultation with the ONP Committee, acting in accordance with the procedure laid down in Article 30, request ETSI to draw up, where appropriate, standards for new types of network access. Reference to such standards shall be published in the *Official Journal of the European Communities* in accordance with Article 5 (1) of Directive 90/387/EEC.

8.   Details of agreements for special network access shall be made available to the national regulatory authority upon request.

Article 11   Interconnection

1.   National regulatory authorities shall ensure that reasonable requests for interconnection with the fixed public telephone network from the organizations listed below are met, in particular to ensure Community-wide provision of voice telephony services:

(a)   telecommunications organizations providing fixed public telephone networks in other Member States, whose names have been notified in accordance with Article 26 (3);

(b)   operators of public mobile telephony services in the same Member State.

No request for interconnection shall be refused by a telecommunications organization without the prior agreement of its national regulatory authority.

Interconnection with the fixed public telephone network of operators of public mobile telephony services in other Member States, whose names have been notified in accordance with Article 26 (3), may also be agreed between the parties involved. No request for such interconnection shall be refused by a telecommunications organization without the prior agreement of its national regulatory authority.

2.   Technical and commercial arrangements for interconnection shall be a matter for agreement between the parties involved, subject to intervention by the national regulatory authority as laid down in Article 10 (3) and (4).

3.   National regulatory authorities shall ensure that telecommunications organizations adhere to the principle of non-discrimination when they enter into interconnection agreements with others.

4.   If interconnection agreements include specific compensation provisions for the telecommunications organization in situations where different operating conditions, e.g. price controls or universal service obligations, are imposed upon the respective parties, such compensation provisions shall be cost-oriented, non-discriminatory and fully justified, and shall only be applied with the approval of the national regulatory authority acting in accordance with Community law.

5. Details of interconnection agreements shall be made available, upon request, to the national regulatory authorities concerned.

Article 12   Tariff principles and transparency

1. National regulatory authorities shall ensure that tariffs for use of the fixed public telephone network and the voice telephony service follow the basic principles of transparency and cost orientation set out in Annex II to Directive 90/387/EEC, and comply with the provisions of this Article.

2. Without prejudice to application of the principle of cost orientation, national regulatory authorities may impose on telecommunications organizations tariff constraints relating to the objectives of universal telephone-service accessibility, including town and country planning aspects.

3. Tariffs for access to and use of the fixed public telephone network shall be independent of the type of application which the users implement, except to the extent that they require different services or facilities.

4. Tariffs for facilities additional to the provision of connection to the fixed public telephone network and provision of voice telephony service shall, in accordance with Community law, be sufficiently unbundled, so that the user is not required to pay for facilities which are not necessary for the service requested.

5. Tariffs shall normally contain the following elements, each of which should be itemized separately for the user:
— an initial charge for connection to the fixed public telephone network and subscription to the voice telephony service,
— a periodic rental charge based on the type of service and facilities selected by the user,
— usage charges which may, *inter alia*, take account of peak and off-peak periods.
Where other tariff elements are applied, they must be transparent and based on objective criteria.

6. Tariffs shall be published in the manner laid down in Article 4.

7. Tariff changes shall be implemented only after an appropriate period of public notice set by the national regulatory authority.

Article 13   Cost accounting principles

1. Member States shall ensure that their telecommunications organizations notified in accordance with Article 26 (2) operate by 31 December 1996 at the latest a cost accounting system suitable for the implementation of Article 12 and that compliance with such a system is verified by a competent body which is independent of those organizations. A statement concerning compliance shall be published periodically.

2. National regulatory authorities shall ensure that a description of the cost accounting system showing the main categories under which costs are gathered and the rules used for the allocation of costs to the voice telephony service is made available on request. National regulatory authorities shall submit, on request, to the Commission information on the cost accounting systems applied by the telecommunications organizations.

3. Without prejudice to the last subparagraph of this paragraph, the system referred to in paragraph 1 shall include the following elements:

(a)   the costs of the voice telephony service shall in particular include the direct costs incurred by the telecommunications organizations in setting up, operating and maintaining the voice telephony service and in marketing and billing the service.

(b)   common costs, that is to say costs which can be directly assigned to neither the voice telephony service nor other activities, shall be allocated as follows:

(i)   whenever possible, common cost categories shall be allocated on the basis of direct analysis of the origin of the costs themselves;

(ii)   when direct analysis is not possible, common cost categories shall be allocated on the basis of an indirect linkage to another cost category or group of cost categories for which a direct assignment or allocation is possible; the indirect linkage shall be based on comparable cost structures;

(iii)   when neither direct nor indirect measures of cost allocation can be found, the cost category shall be allocated on the basis of a general allocator, computed by using the ratio of all expenses directly or indirectly assigned or allocated, on the one hand, to the voice telephony service and, on the other hand, to other services.

Other cost accounting systems may be applied if they are suitable for the implementation of Article 12 and have been approved as such by the national regulatory authority for application by the telecommunications organizations, subject to the Commission being informed prior to their application.

4.   Detailed accounting information shall be made available to the national regulatory authority on request and in confidence.

5.   Member States shall ensure that the financial accounts of those telecommunications organizations notified in accordance with Article 26 are drawn up, published and submitted for audit in accordance with the provisions of national legislation.

Article 14   Discounts, low-usage schemes and other specific tariff provisions

1.   National regulatory authorities may agree that bulk discount schemes can be offered to users and shall make those schemes subject to supervision by the national regulatory authority.

2.   National regulatory authorities may agree special tariffs for the provision of socially useful services such as emergency services, or for low-usage users or specific social groups.

3.   National regulatory authorities shall ensure that tariff structures allow for reduced-rate calls within the Community at off-peak times, including night-time and weekends if appropriate.

4.   National regulatory authorities shall ensure that, where special tariffs are introduced for voice telephony services provided in connection with specific projects of limited duration, they shall be subject to prior notification to the national regulatory authority.

Article 15   Itemized billing

National regulatory authorities shall ensure that targets are set and published for the provision of itemized billing as a facility available to users on request, taking into account the state of network development and market demand.

Subject to the following paragraph and the level of detail permitted under relevant legislation on the protection of personal data and privacy, itemized bills shall show the composition of the charges incurred.

Calls which are free of charge to the caller, including calls to helplines, shall not be identified in the caller's itemized bill.

Within this framework, different levels of detail may be offered to users at reasonable tariffs.

Article 16   Directory services

Subject to the requirements of relevant legislation on the protection of personal data and privacy, national regulatory authorities shall ensure that:

(a)   directories of subscribers to the voice telephony service are made available to users in either printed or electronic form, and are updated on a regular basis;

(b)   users have the right to have or not to have an entry in publicly available directories;

(c)   telecommunications organizations make available on request public directory information concerning the voice telephony service on published terms which are fair, reasonable and non-discriminatory.

Article 17   Provision of public pay-telephones

National regulatory authorities shall ensure that public pay-telephones are provided to meet the reasonable needs of users, in terms of both numbers and geographical coverage, and that it is possible to make emergency calls from such telephones. Calls to the single European emergency call number referred to in Decision 91/396/EEC shall be free of charge.

Article 18   Telephone pre-payment cards

1.   The Commission shall ensure that standards for a harmonized telephone pre-payment card suitable for use in pay-telephones in all Member States, and associated network interface standards, are drawn up by ETSI and/or CEN/Cenelec, in order to make it possible for pre-payment cards issued in one Member State to be used in other Member States. A reference to these standards and to associated standards shall be published in the *Official Journal of the European Communities*.

2.   National regulatory authorities shall encourage the progressive introduction of public pay-telephones conforming to these standards.

Article 19   Specific conditions for disabled users and people with special needs

National regulatory authorities may draw up specific conditions to aid disabled users and people with special needs in their use of the voice telephony service.

Article 20   Specifications for network access, including the socket

1.   Where appropriate, the Commission shall, in consultation with the ONP Committee, acting in accordance with the procedure laid down in

Article 30, request ETSI to draw up standards for new types of harmonized network access, in accordance with the reference framework set out in Annex II (2) to Directive 90/387/EEC. References to these standards shall be published in the *Official Journal of the European Communities*.

2.   Where voice telephony service is supplied to users over the ISDN network at the S/T reference point, national regulatory authorities shall ensure that, after the implementation of this Directive, the introduction of a new network termination point complies with the relevant physical interface specifications, in particular those for the socket, referenced in the list of standards published in the *Official Journal of the European Communities*.

Article 21   Numbering

1.   Member States shall ensure that national telephone numbering plans are controlled by national regulatory authorities, in order to ensure fair competition. In particular the procedures for allocating individual numbers and numbering ranges shall be transparent, equitable and timely and the allocation shall be carried out in an objective, transparent and non-discriminatory manner.

2.   National regulatory authorities shall ensure that the main elements of the national numbering plan and all subsequent additions or amendments to them are published, subject only to limitations imposed on the grounds of national security.

3.   National regulatory authorities shall encourage appropriate use of any European numbering schemes for the provision of the facilities identified in Annex III (2).

Article 22   Conditions of access and use and essential requirements

1.   Member States shall ensure that conditions which restrict access to and use of fixed public telephone networks or voice telephony services are based only on the grounds given in paragraphs 3, 4 and 5, and are subject to the agreement of the national regulatory authority.

2.   National regulatory authorities shall draw up procedures in order to decide, on a case-by-case basis and as soon as possible, whether or not to allow telecommunications organizations to take measures such as the refusal to provide access to the fixed public telephone network or the interruption or reduction in availability of voice telephony service, on the grounds of a user's alleged failure to comply with the conditions of use. These procedures may also provide for the possibility of the national regulatory authority authorizing *a priori* specified measures in the event of defined infringements of the conditions of use.

The national regulatory authority shall ensure that these procedures provide for a transparent decision-making process which respects the rights of the parties. The decision shall be taken after both parties have been given the opportunity to state their case. The decision shall be duly substantiated and notified to the parties within one week of its adoption.

A summary of these procedures shall be published in the manner laid down in Article 4.

This provision shall not prejudice the rights of the parties concerned to apply to the courts.

3.   Any restrictions placed upon users on the basis of special or exclusive rights for voice telephony shall be imposed through regulatory means and shall be published in accordance with Article 4.

4.   Conditions for connection of terminal equipment to the fixed public telephone network shall comply with Directive 91/263/EEC and shall be published in accordance with Article 4 of this Directive.

Without prejudice to the provisions of Directive 91/263/EEC, where a user's terminal equipment does not comply or no longer complies with its approval conditions, or where it malfunctions in a way which adversely affects the integrity of the network, or where there is a danger of physical injury to persons, national regulatory authorities shall ensure that the following procedure is followed:

— service provision may be interrupted by the telecommunications organization until the terminal is disconnected from the network termination point,

— the telecommunications organization shall immediately inform the user about the interruption, giving the reasons for it,

— as soon as the user has ensured that the terminal equipment is disconnected from the network termination point, service provision shall be restored.

5.   When access to or use of the fixed public telephone network is restricted on the basis of essential requirements, national regulatory authorities shall ensure that the relevant national provisions identify which of the essential requirements set out in (a) to (d) below are the basis of such restrictions.

Restrictions imposed on the basis of essential requirements shall be published in the manner laid down in Article 4.

Restrictions derived from essential requirements shall be imposed through regulatory means.

Without prejudice to Articles 3 (5) and 5 (3) of Directive 90/387/EEC, the essential requirements specified in Article 3 (2) of that Directive shall apply to the fixed public telephone network and voice telephony service in the following manner:

(a)   *Security of network operations*

There shall be no restrictions on access to and use of the fixed public telephone network on the grounds of security of network operations except in emergency situations, when a telecommunications organization may take the following measures in order to safeguard the security of network operations:

— interruption of service,

— limitation of service features,

— denial of access to the network and service for new users.

An emergency situation in this context means catastrophic network breakdown or an exceptional case of *force majeure*, such as extreme weather, flood, lightning or fire, industrial action or lockout, war, military operations or civil disorder. In an emergency situation the telecommunications organization shall make every endeavour to ensure that service is maintained to all users.

National regulatory authorities shall ensure that telecommunications organizations have procedures in place whereby users and the national regulatory authority are immediately informed of the beginning and the end of the emergency, as well as the nature and extent of temporary service restrictions.

(b) *Maintenance of network integrity*

National regulatory authorities shall ensure that restrictions on access to and use of the fixed public telephone network on the grounds of maintenance of network integrity, in order to protect *inter alia* network equipment, software or stored data, are kept to the minimum necessary to provide for normal operation of the network. Restrictions shall be based on published, objective criteria and shall be applied in a non-discriminatory manner.

(c) *Interoperability of services*

When terminal equipment has been approved and is operating in compliance with Directive 91/263/EEC, no further restrictions on use shall be imposed on the grounds of interoperability of services.

Where the national regulatory authority imposes conditions concerning interoperability of services in contracts relating to interconnection of public networks or special network access, those conditions shall be published in the manner laid down in Article 4.

(d) *Protection of data*

Member States may restrict access to and use of the fixed public telephone network on the grounds of protection of data only to the extent necessary to ensure compliance with relevant regulatory provisions on the protection of data, including protection of personal data, the confidentiality of information transmitted or stored, and the protection of privacy, in a manner compatible with Community law.

6. National regulatory authorities shall ensure that, where appropriate, users are informed in advance by appropriate means by the telecommunications organizations of periods when access to or use of the fixed public telephone network may be restricted or denied as a result of planned maintenance activity.

Article 23 Non-payment of bills

Member States shall authorize specified measures, which shall be published in the manner laid down in Article 4, to cover non-payment of bills and any consequent service interruption of disconnection. These measures shall ensure that any service interruption is confined to the service concerned, as far as is technically feasible, and that due warning is given to the user beforehand.

Article 24 Technical standards

1. National regulatory authorities shall encourage the provision of services according to the standards listed below:
— standards published in the *Official Journal of the European Communities*, in accordance with Article 5 (1) of Directive 90/387/EEC,
or, in the absence of such standards,
— European standards adopted by ETSI, or CEN/Cenelec,
or, in the absence of such standards,
— international standards or recommendations adopted by the International Telecommunications Union (ITU), the International Organization for Standardization (ISO) or the International Electrotechnical Commission (IEC),

or, in the absence of such standards,
— national standards or specifications,
without prejudice to reference to European standards, which reference may
be made compulsory under Article 5 (3) of Directive 90/387/EEC.

2. National regulatory authorities shall ensure that telecommunications
organizations inform users on request of standards or specifications, including
any European and/or international standards which are implemented through
national standards, in accordance with which the services and facilities in this
Directive are provided.

Article 25 Provisions for Community-wide convergence

1. On the basis of the reports provided by the national regulatory
authorities under Article 26 (5) and the information published under Article
4, the Commission shall review progress towards convergence of targets and
implementation of common services and facilities within the Community.

2. If implementation of the requirements of Articles 5, 9 or 15 appears
inadequate to ensure the provision of harmonized services and facilities to
users at a Community level, harmonized targets and target dates may be
determined in accordance with the procedure laid down in Article 31.

The procedure initiated by the Commission shall take full account of the
state of network development and market demand in all individual Member
States.

3. In particular with regard to those facilities requiring Community-wide
cooperation described in Article 9 (2), where commercial agreements between telecommunications organizations cannot be concluded, conditions
necessary to achieve the provision of harmonized facilities to users may be
recommended.

The recommendations shall take due account of the state of network
development, the various architectures and market demand in the Community.

Article 26 Notification and reporting

1. Member States shall notify the name of their national regulatory
authority to the Commission by 13 December 1996.

2. Member States shall notify to the Commission the names of the
telecommunications organizations to which this Directive applies, in particular
to ensure the provision of the network and service in accordance with Article 3.

Without prejudice to the future applicability of ONP measures, Member
States which have abolished exclusive rights for voice telephony may apply
this Directive to organizations defined on the basis of a significant market
share or on the basis of a dominant position in their authorized area of
operation, in such a way as to ensure that at every point in their territory at
least one organization is subject to the provisions of this Directive.

Member States may ensure that telecommunications organizations are
obliged to supply the information necessary to determine the application of
this Directive.

3. National regulatory authorities shall notify to the Commission the
names of the telecommunications organizations in their territory which are
authorized to interconnect their fixed networks directly with those of telecom-

munications organizations in other Member States in order to provide voice telephony service.

National regulatory authorities shall notify to the Commission the names of the operators of public mobile telephony services in their territory which are authorized to interconnect directly with the fixed networks of telecommunications organizations in other Member States in order to provide voice telephony service.

4.   The Commission shall publish the names referred to in paragraphs 2 and 3 in the *Official Journal of the European Communities*.

5.   National regulatory authorities shall, each for the matters for which it is responsible, make available to the Commission once each calendar year a report covering the progress made in achieving the targets agreed by them under Articles 5, 9 and 15.

The annual report shall be sent to the Commission within five months of the end of the year.

6.   National regulatory authorities shall keep available and submit to the Commission on request details of individual cases brought before them, other than those covered by Article 23, where access to the public telephone network or voice telephony service or use of the network or service has been restricted or denied, including the measures taken and their justification.

However, this provision shall not apply to any action taken under national regimes for the enforcement of licensing conditions in conformity with Community law, or to proceedings before a national court.

Article 27   Conciliation of national dispute resolution

Without prejudice to:

(a)   any action that the Commission or any Member State may take pursuant to the Treaty;

(b)   the rights of the person invoking the procedure in paragraphs 3 and 4, of the telecommunications organizations concerned or of any other person under applicable national law, except in so far as they enter into an agreement for the resolution of disputes between them;

(c)   the provisions of this Directive which allow the national regulatory authorities to set the terms of contracts between telecommunications organizations and users,

the following procedures shall be available to the user:

(1)   Member States shall ensure that any party, including users, service providers, consumers, or other telecommunications organizations having an unresolved dispute with a telecommunications organization concerning an alleged infringement of the provisions of this Directive, shall have a right of appeal to the national regulatory authority or another independent body. Easily accessible and in principle inexpensive procedures shall be created at national level to resolve such disputes in a fair, transparent and timely manner. These procedures shall also apply in cases where users are in dispute with a telecommunications organization about their telephone bills.

(2)   A user or a telecommunications organization may, where the dispute involves telecommunications organizations in more than one Member State, invoke the conciliation procedure provided for in paragraphs 3 and 4 by means of a written notification to the national regulatory authority and to the

Commission. Member States may also allow their national regulatory authority to invoke the conciliation procedure.

(3)   Where the national regulatory authority or the Commission finds that there is a case for further examination, following a notification based on paragraph 2, it can refer the matter to the Chairman of the ONP Committee.

(4)   In the circumstances referred to in paragraph 3, the Chairman of the ONP Committee shall initiate the procedure described below if he is satisfied that all reasonable steps have been taken at national level:

(a)   the Chairman of the ONP Committee shall convene as soon as possible a working group including at least two members of the ONP Committee and one representative of the national regulatory authorities concerned, and the Chairman of the ONP Committee or another official of the Commission appointed by him. The working group shall be chaired by the representative of the Commission and shall normally meet within ten days of having been convened. The Chairman of the working group may decide, upon proposal by any of the members of the working group, to invite a maximum of two other persons as experts to advise it;

(b)   the working group shall give the party invoking this procedure, the national regulatory authorities of the Member States involved and the telecommunications organizations involved the opportunity to present their opinions in oral or written form;

(c)   the working group shall endeavour to reach agreement between the parties involved within three months of the date of receipt of the notification referred to in paragraph 2. The Chairman of the ONP Committee shall inform that Committee of the results of the procedure so that it may express its views.

(5)   The party invoking the procedure shall bear its own costs of participating in this procedure.

Article 28   Deferment of certain obligations

1.   When a Member State is unable to or can foresee that it will be unable to fulfil the provisions of Articles 12 and 13, it shall notify the Commission of the reasons.

2.   Deferment of obligations under Articles 12 or 13 can be accepted only in cases where the Member States concerned can prove that fulfilment of the obligation would impose an excessive burden on the telecommunications organizations in that Member State.

3.   The Member State shall inform the Commission of the date by which the obligation can be fulfilled and of the measures envisaged in order to meet that deadline.

4.   When the Commission receives a notification in accordance with paragraph 1, it shall inform the Member State whether the particular situation of the Member State concerned justifies, on the basis of criteria set out in paragraph 2, a deferment for that Member State of the application of Article 12 or Article 13 and until which date such deferment is justified.

Article 29   Technical adjustment

Modifications necessary to adapt Annex I (2), Annexes II and III to technological developments or to changes in market demand shall be determined in accordance with the procedure laid down in Article 31.

Article 30 Advisory Committee procedure

1. The Commission shall be assisted by the Committee set up by Article 9 (1) of Directive 90/387/EEC.

The Committee shall, in particular, consult the representatives of the telecommunications organizations, users, consumers, manufacturers and service providers.

2. The representative of the Commission shall submit to the Committee a draft of the measures to be taken. The Committee shall deliver its opinion on the draft within a time limit which the Chairman may lay down according to the urgency of the matter, if necessary by taking a vote.

The opinion shall be recorded in the minutes; in addition, each Member State shall have the right to ask to have its position recorded in the minutes.

The Commission shall take the utmost account of the opinion delivered by the Committee. It shall inform the Committee of the manner in which its opinion has been taken into account.

Article 31 Regulatory Committee procedure

1. Notwithstanding the provisions of Article 30, the following procedure shall apply in respect of the matters covered by Articles 25 and 29.

2. The representative of the Commission shall submit to the Committee a draft of the measures to be taken. The Committee shall deliver its opinion on the draft within a time limit which the Chairman may lay down according to the urgency of the matter. The opinion shall be delivered by the majority laid down in Article 148 (2) of the EC Treaty in the case of decisions which the Council is required to adopt on a proposal from the Commission. The votes of the representatives of the Member States within the Committee shall be weighted in the manner set out in that Article. The Chairman shall not vote.

3. The Commission shall adopt the measures envisaged if they are in accordance with the opinion of the Committee.

4. If the measures envisaged are not in accordance with the opinion of the Committee, or if no opinion is delivered, the Commission shall, without delay, submit to the Council a proposal relating to the measures to be taken. The Council shall act by a qualified majority.

If, within a period of three months from the date of referral to the Council, the Council has not acted, the proposed measures shall be adopted by the Commission.

Article 32 Review

1. The European Parliament and the Council shall decide by 1 January 1998, on the basis of a proposal which the Commission will submit to them in good time, on the revision of this Directive to adapt it to the requirements of market liberalization.

2. The Commission shall examine and report to the European Parliament and to the Council on the functioning of this Directive, on the first occasion not later than 13 December 1998. The report shall be based *inter alia* on the information provided by the Member States to the Commission and to

the ONP Committee. Where necessary, further measures may be proposed in the report for full implementation of the aims of the Directive.

Article 33   Implementation

1.   Member States shall take the measures necessary to comply with this Directive before 13 December 1996. They shall forthwith inform the Commission thereof.

When Member States adopt these measures, they shall contain a reference to this Directive or shall be accompanied by such reference on the occasion of their official publication. The methods of making such reference shall be laid down by the Member States.

2.   Member States shall inform the Commission of the main provisions of national law which they adopt in the field governed by this Directive.

Article 34   Entry into force

This Directive shall enter into force on the twentieth day following that of its publication in the *Official Journal of the European Communities*.

Article 35

This Directive is addressed to the Member States.

Done at Brussels, 13 December 1995.

For the European Parliament
The President
K. Haensch

For the Council
The President
J. L. Dicenta Ballester

ANNEX I   HEADINGS FOR INFORMATION TO BE PUBLISHED IN ACCORDANCE WITH ARTICLE 4

1.   Name(s) and address(es) of telecommunications organization(s)
i.e. name(s) and head office address(es) of the telecommunications organization(s) providing fixed public telephone networks and/or voice telephony services.

2.   Telecommunications services offered
2.1.   *Types of connection to the public fixed telephone network*
Technical characteristics of interfaces at commonly provided network termination points are required, including where applicable reference to national and/or international standards or recommendations, in accordance with Article 24:

— for analogue and/or digitally presented networks:
   (a)   single line interface;
   (b)   multi-line interface;

    (c)   direct dialling-in (DDI) interface;

    (d)   other interfaces commonly provided,

— for ISDN:

    (a)   specification of basic and primary rate interfaces at the S/T reference points, including the signalling protocol;

    (b)   details of bearer services able to carry voice telephony services;

    (c)   other interfaces commonly provided,

— and any other interfaces commonly provided.

In addition to the above information to be published on a regular basis in the manner laid down in Article 4, telecommunications organizations must inform terminal equipment suppliers, without undue delay, of any particular network characteristics which affect the correct operation of approved terminal equipment.

    2.2.   *Telephone services offered*

Description of the basic voice telephony service offered, indicating what is included in the subscription charge and the periodic rental charge (e.g. operator services, directories, maintenance).

    Description of optional facilities and features of the voice telephony service which are tariffed separately from the basic offering, including where applicable reference to the relevant technical standards or specifications to which they conform, in accordance with Article 24.

    2.3.   *Tariffs*

covering access, usage, maintenance, and including details of any discount schemes

    2.4.   *Compensation/refund policy*

including specific details of any compensation/refund schemes offered

    2.5.   *Types of maintenance service offered*

    2.6.   *Ordering procedure*

including designated contact points within the telecommunications organization

    2.7.   *Standard contract conditions*

including any minimum contractual period.

    3.   Licensing requirements

This shall include a clear description of all licensing conditions which have an impact on users, including service providers, containing at least:

— information on the nature of the licensing conditions, in particular whether registration and/or authorization is required on an individual basis, or whether the licence is of a general nature which does not require individual registration and/or authorization,

— the duration of any relevant licences or authorizations,

— a list referring to all documents containing relevant licensing conditions which the Member State imposes.

    4.   Conditions for attachment of terminal equipment

This shall include a complete overview of requirements for terminal equipment as regulated by the national regulatory authority, in line with the provisions of Directive 91/263/EEC, including, where appropriate, conditions concerning customer premises wiring and location of the network termination point.

    5.   Restrictions on access and use

This shall include any restrictions on access and use imposed in accordance with the requirements of Article 22.

    6.   Performance and quality-of-service parameters

Definitions, measurement methods, targets and achieved performance figures, in accordance with the requirements of Article 5.

7.   Targets for the introduction of new services, features, facilities and tariffs
Targets shall be published in accordance with the requirements of Articles 9 and 15.

8.   Conditions for special network access
This shall include conditions for special network access set by national regulatory authorities in accordance with Article 10 (5).

9.   Availability of the description of the cost accounting system
The address from which the description of the cost accounting system may be requested in accordance with the requirements of Article 13.

10.   Main elements of the national numbering plan
In accordance with the requirements of Article 21.

11.   Terms for the use of directory information
In accordance with Article 16 (c).

12.   Conciliation and dispute resolution procedure
This shall include guidelines for users on the appeal mechanisms available for conciliation and resolving disputes with telecommunications organizations, according to the procedure described in Article 27. This shall also include a summary of the procedures for resolving disputes referred to in Article 22 (2).

13.   Procedure in the event of non-payment of bills
In accordance with the requirements of Article 23.

ANNEX II   SUPPLY-TIME AND QUALITY-OF-SERVICE INDICATORS IN ACCORDANCE WITH THE REQUIREMENTS OF ARTICLE 5

The following list specifies areas where quality-of-service indicators are required for telecommunications organizations notified in accordance with Article 26 (2):
— supply time for initial network connection,
— fault rate per connection,
— fault repair time,
— call failure rates,
— dial tone delay,
— call set up delay,
— transmission quality statistics,
— response times for operator services,
— the proportion of coin and card-operated public pay-telephones in working order,
— billing accuracy.

ANNEX III   PROVISION OF ADVANCED FACILITIES IN ACCORDANCE WITH ARTICLE 9

1.   List of facilities referred to in Article 9 (1):
    (a)   *DTMF (dual-tone multifrequency operation)*
i.e. the fixed public telephone network supports the use of DTMF telephones for signalling to the exchange, using tones as defined in ITU-T Recommendation Q.23, and supports the same tones for end-to-end signalling through the network, both within a Member State and between Member States.

(b) *Direct dialling-in (or facilities offering equivalent functionality)*
i.e. users on a private branch exchange (PBX) or similar private system can be called directly from the fixed public telephone network without intervention by the PBX attendant.

(c) *Call forwarding*
i.e. incoming calls sent to another destination in the same or another Member State (e.g. on no reply, on busy, or unconditionally).

This facility should be provided in accordance with relevant legislation on data protection and privacy.

(d) *Calling-line identification*
i.e. the calling party's number is presented to the called party prior to the call being established.

This facility should be provided in accordance with relevant legislation on data protection and privacy.

2.   List of services and facilities referred to in Article 9 (2):

(a) *Community-wide access to green/freephone services*
Such services, variously known as green numbers, freephone services, 0800 numbers etc. include dial-up services where the caller pays either nothing for the call or only part of the total cost of the call.

(b) *Community-wide kiosk billing*
Kiosk billing means a facility whereby charges for the use of a service accessed through a telecommunications organization's network are combined with the network call charges ('premium rate service').

(c) *Community-wide call transfer*
i.e. transfer of an established call to a third party in the same or another Member State.

(d) *Community-wide automatic reverse charging service facility for calls which are terminated and originated within the Community.*
i.e. prior to the call being connected, the called party, at the caller's request, agrees to accept the cost of the call.

(e) *Community-wide calling-line identification*
i.e. the calling party's number is presented to the called party prior to the call being established.

This facility should be provided in accordance with relevant legislation on data protection and privacy.

(f) *Access to operator services in other Member States*
i.e. users in one Member State can call the operator/assistance service in another Member State.

(g) *Access to directory enquiry services in other Member States*
i.e. users in one Member State can call the directory enquiry service in another Member State.

Notes
1.   The following text consists only of the amended proposal. The referenced Official Journal contains both the original and the amended proposal.
2.   On **Universal Service** see further:
Council Resolution of 7 February 1994 on universal service principles in the telecommunications sector, OJ C48/1, 16.2.94.
Commission Statement concerning Council Resolution on universal service in the telecommunications sector, OJ C48/8, 16.2.94.

Commission Communication on 'universal service for telecommunications in the perspective of a fully liberalised environment', COM(96)73, 14 March 1996.

PROPOSAL FOR A EUROPEAN PARLIAMENT AND COUNCIL DIRECTIVE ON THE APPLICATION OF OPEN NETWORK PROVISION (ONP) TO VOICE TELEPHONY AND ON UNIVERSAL SERVICE FOR TELECOMMUNICATIONS IN A COMPETITIVE ENVIRONMENT (REPLACING EUROPEAN PARLIAMENT AND COUNCIL DIRECTIVE 95/62/EC)

THE EUROPEAN PARLIAMENT AND THE COUNCIL OF THE EUROPEAN UNION,

Having regard to the Treaty establishing the European Community, and in particular Article 100a thereof,

Having regard to the proposal from the Commission,[1]

Having regard to the Opinion of the Economic and Social Committee,[2]

Acting in accordance with the procedure laid down in Article 189b of the Treaty,[3]

1. Whereas from 1 January 1998, with transition periods for certain Member States, the provision of telecommunications services and infrastructure in the Community will be liberalised; whereas the Council,[4] the European Parliament,[5] the Economic and Social Committee[6] and the Committee of the Regions[7] have all recognised that liberalisation goes hand in hand with parallel action to create a harmonised regulatory framework which secures the delivery of universal service; whereas the concept of universal service must evolve to keep pace with advances in technology, market developments and changes in user demand; whereas progress has been made in the Community towards defining the scope of universal service and laying down rules for its costing and financing;[8] whereas the Commission has undertaken to publish a report on the monitoring of the scope, level, quality and affordability of the universal telephone service in the Community before 1 January 1998, and at regular intervals thereafter;[9]

1

2

3

4 Council Resolution 94/C48 of 7 February 1994 on Universal Service principles in the telecommunications sector, OJ C48, 16.2.1994, p. 1, and Council Resolution 95/C258 of 18 September 1995 on the implementation of the future regulatory framework for telecommunications, OJ C258, 3.10.1995, p. 1.

5 European Parliament Resolution of 19 May 1995 on the Green Paper on the liberalisation of telecommunications infrastructure and cable television networks — Part II A4-0111/95; OJ C151, 19.6.1995

6 Opinion of the Economic and Social Committee of 13 September 1995 on the Green Paper on the liberalisation of telecommunications infrastructure and cable television networks — Part II, OJ C301, 13.11.1995

7 Opinion of the Committee of the Regions on the Commission Communication: Europe's way to the information society. An action plan (COM(94) 347 final). CdR 21/95 ESP/ET/AG/ym and CdR 21/95 Appendix D/BAN/JKB/NF/as.

8 Common Position (EC) No 34/96 adopted by the Council on 18 June 1996 with a view to adopting Directive 96/ . . . /EC of the European Parliament and the Council on interconnection in telecommunications with regard to ensuring universal service and interoperability through application of the principles of open network provision (ONP). OJ C220, 29.07.1996, p. 13

9 See Commission Communication on Universal service for telecommunications in the perspective of a fully liberalised environment, COM(96) 73, 13 March 1996.

2. Whereas Council Directive 90/387/EEC of 28 June 1990 on the establishment of the internal market for telecommunications services through the implementation of open network provision,[10] provides a general framework for the application of ONP principles in specific areas;

3. Whereas Article 32(1) of European Parliament and Council Directive 95/62/EC of 13 December 1995 on the application of open network provision (ONP) to voice telephony[11] calls for the European Parliament and the Council to decide by 1 January 1998, on the basis of a proposal submitted by the Commission, on the revision of the Directive to adapt it to the requirements of market liberalisation; whereas Directive 95/62/EC does not apply to mobile telephony services; whereas in moving to a competitive market, there are certain obligations that should apply to all organisations providing telephone services over fixed networks, and others that should be retained only for as long as certain organisations continue to enjoy significant market power and thus have the ability to influence market conditions independently of their competitors; whereas full account has been taken of the user and consumer requirements for affordability, cost control and user facilities as expressed in the public consultation on universal service for telecommunications;[12] whereas, since the modifications required to Directive 95/62/EC are substantial, it is convenient for the sake of clarity to reformulate the said Directive; whereas the present Directive does not affect the timescales for Member States' implementation of Directive 95/62/EC as set out in Annex IV;

4. Whereas the basic universal service requirement is to provide users on request with a connection to the fixed public telephone network at a fixed location, at an affordable price; whereas there should be no constraints on the technical means by which the connection is provided, allowing for wire or wireless technologies; whereas affordability is a matter to be determined at national level in the light of specific national conditions, including town and country planning aspects; whereas the affordability of telephone service is related to the information users receive about telephone usage expenses as well as the relative cost of telephone usage compared to other services;

Whereas tariff rebalancing is leading to a move away from uniformly low and non cost-oriented tariffs; whereas until competition is effectively established safeguards may be necessary to ensure that price increases in remote or rural areas are not used to compensate for losses in revenue resulting from price decreases elsewhere; whereas price caps and similar schemes may be used to ensure that the necessary re-balancing does not affect users adversely, and that the differences between prices in high cost areas and prices in low cost areas do not endanger the affordability of telephone services;

5. Whereas the importance of the telephone network and service is such that it should be available to anyone reasonably requesting it; whereas in accordance with the principle of subsidiarity, it for Member States to decide which organisations have the responsibility for providing the various elements of the universal service for telecommunications as defined in this Directive; whereas corresponding obligations could be included as conditions in authorisations to provide voice telephony services; whereas only the net cost of obligations covered in this Directive should be shared under a universal service financing scheme;

---

10 192, 28.06.1990, p. 1.
11 OJ L321, 30.12.1995, p. 6
12 See COM(96) 73, 13 March 1996

6.   Whereas provision of directory services is a competitive activity; whereas European Parliament and Council Directive 95/46/EC of 24 October 1995 on the protection of individuals with regard to the processing of personal data and on the free movement of such data regulates the processing of personal data;[13] whereas progress has been made in the Community on a proposal for a Directive on the protection of personal data and privacy in the telecommunications sector which will give subscribers the right to be omitted, or to have certain data omitted, from a printed or electronic directory at his or her request;[14] whereas users and consumers desire comprehensive directories and directory enquiry service covering all listed telephone subscribers and their numbers (including fixed, mobile and personal telephone numbers); whereas the situation whereby certain telephone directories and directory services are provided in a manner that is perceived to be free of charge to the user is not affected by this Directive;

7.   Whereas Council Decision of 29 July 1991 on the introduction of a single European emergency call number[15] called for Member States to ensure that no later than 31 December 1996 the number <112> is introduced in public telephone networks as the single European emergency call number; whereas it is important that users are able to call emergency telephone numbers, and in particular the single European emergency call number <112>, free of charge from any telephone, including public pay-telephones, without the use of coins or cards;

8.   Whereas quality and price are key factors in a competitive market, and national regulatory authorities should be able to monitor achieved quality of service and take appropriate corrective measures where necessary; whereas these powers are without prejudice to the application of competition law by national and Community authorities;

9.   Whereas conditions on the access to and use of fixed public telephone networks or publicly available telephone services may be imposed exceptionally by a Member States on the grounds of essential requirements; whereas national regulatory authorities may authorise procedures whereby an organisation can act immediately to restrict access, in particular in the case of fraud; whereas, except in cases of persistent late payment or non payment of bills, consumers should be protected from immediate disconnection from the network on the grounds of an unpaid bill, and in particular in the case of disputes over high bills for premium rate services, should continue to have access to essential telephone services pending resolution of the dispute;

10.   Whereas the facilities of tone dialling and itemised billing are normally available on modern telephone exchanges and can therefore be provided inexpensively once old exchanges are modernised or new exchanges installed; whereas tone dialling is increasingly being used for interaction with special services and facilities, including value added services, and lack of this facility can prevent users accessing certain services; whereas itemised billing and selective call barring are valuable means for users to control and monitor their usage of telephone networks; whereas progress has been made in the

---

13 OJ L281, 23.11.1995, p. 31.
14 Common Position (EC) No /96 adopted by the Council on [date] with a view to adopting Directive 96/ . . . /EC of the European Parliament and the Council concerning the processing of personal data and protection of privacy in the telecommunications sector, in particular in the Integrated Services Digital Network (ISDN) and in digital mobile networks
15 OJ L 217, 06.08.1991, p. 31.

Community on a proposal for a Directive on the protection of personal data and privacy in the telecommunications sector which will safeguard the privacy of users with regard to itemised billing; whereas harmonised technical interface standards have been drawn up by the European standardisation organisations for access to the Integrated Services Digital Network (ISDN) at what is known as the S/T reference point;

11.   Whereas certain prior obligations concerning tariffs and cost accounting systems will no longer be appropriate once competition is introduced, and others can be relaxed by the competent national regulatory authority as soon as competition achieves the desired objectives; whereas in all cases the non-discrimination requirements of the competition rules of the Treaty apply;

12.   Whereas issues related to the level of affordability, the quality of service and the future scope of the universal service should be the subject of consultation at national level and at the European level with all interested parties; whereas such consultation requires that adequate information about the level, quality and affordability of universal service is available; whereas disabled users should wherever possible receive a broadly similar level of services compared to other users in terms of their access to or use of telephone services;

13.   Whereas the Commission has to be able to monitor effectively the application of this Directive, and European users need to know where to find published information about telephone services in other Member States;

14.   Whereas in view of the forecast convergence of fixed and mobile telephone services, the applicability of the Directive with respect to mobile services should be re-examined when the Directive is reviewed; whereas the review date of 31 December 1999 will allow for a coordinated review of all the ONP Directives in the light of experience with the liberalisation of public telecommunications networks and voice telephony services;

15.   Whereas the essential goals of ensuring universal service for telecommunications for all European users and of harmonising conditions for access to and use of fixed public telephone networks and publicly available telephone services, cannot be realised satisfactorily at Member State level;

HAVE ADOPTED THIS DIRECTIVE:

CHAPTER 1.   SCOPE, AIM AND DEFINITIONS

Article 1   Scope and aim

1.   This Directive concerns the harmonisation of conditions for open and efficient access to and use of fixed public telephone networks and publicly available telephone services in an environment of open and competitive markets, in accordance with the principles of open network provision (ONP).

The aims are to ensure the availability throughout the Community of good quality telephone services, and to ensure that all users, including consumers, have access to a defined set of telephone services at affordable prices.

2.   This Directive replaces Directive 95/62/EC.

Article 2   Definitions

1.   The definitions given in Directive 90/387/EEC shall apply, where relevant, to this Directive.

2.   For the purposes of this Directive:

— 'users' means individuals, including consumers, or organisations using or requesting publicly available telecommunications services;

— 'consumer' means any natural person who uses a *fixed public telephone network* or publicly available telephone service for purposes which are outside his or her trade, business or profession;

— 'fixed public telephone network' means those elements of the public switched telecommunications network which are used, in all or in part, for the provision of voice telephony service between network termination points which are at fixed locations;

— 'public pay-telephone' means a telephone available to the general public, for the use of which the means of payment are coins, credit/debit cards and/or pre-payment cards;

— 'publicly available telephone service' means a service made available to telephone users over a connection to the fixed public telephone network, which includes the availability of the facilities specified in this Directive;

— 'universal service' means a defined minimum set of services of specified quality which is available to all users independent of their geographical location and, in the light of specific national conditions, at an affordable price;

— 'national regulatory authority' means the body or bodies in each Member State, entrusted by that Member State, *inter alia*, with the regulatory functions addressed in this Directive;

— 'ONP Committee' means the Committee created by Article 9(1) of Directive 90/387/EEC;

— 'organisation with significant market power' means an organisation providing fixed public telephone networks and/or publicly available telephone services in a Member State which has been designated by the national regulatory authority in that Member State as having significant market power and notified to the Commission.

An organisation shall be presumed to have significant market power when it has a share of 25% or more of the relevant voice telephony market in a Member State.

National regulatory authorities may determine that an organisation with a market share of less than 25% in the relevant voice telephony market has significant market power. They may also determine that an organisation with a market share of more than 25% in the relevant voice telephony market does not have significant market power. In either case, the determination shall take into account the organisation's ability to influence market conditions, its turnover relative to the size of the market, its control of the means of access to end-users, its access to financial resources, its experience providing products and services in the market.

CHAPTER II.   PROVISION OF A DEFINED SET OF TELECOMMUNICATIONS SERVICES

Article 3   Availability of telecommunications services

1.   Member States shall ensure throughout their territory the availability of the services set out in this Chapter

Where these services cannot be commercially provided on the basis of conditions laid down by the Member State, Member States may set up universal service schemes for the shared financing of these services, in conformity with Community law.

Article 4 Affordability

1.   Member States shall ensure, in the light of their national conditions, the affordability of the services specified in this Chapter.

Taking into account the progressive adjustment of tariffs towards costs, Member States shall in particular maintain the affordability of the specified services for users in rural or high cost areas, where necessary by taking measures to ensure that price increases in rural areas are not used to compensate losses in revenue resulting from price decreases elsewhere, and for vulnerable groups of users such as the elderly, those with disabilities, those who do not use the telephone very much.

To this end, Member States shall remove obligations which prevent or restrict the use of special or targetted tariff schemes for the provision of the services specified in this Directive and may, in accordance with Community law, implement price caps or other similar schemes for some or all of the specified services, for a appropriate period of time.

Member States shall publish the rules and criteria for ensuring affordability at the national level, taking into account the consultation called for in Article 24.

2.   Member States shall publish regular reports on the evolution of tariffs.

Article 5 Provision of network connections and access to telephone services

1.   Member States shall ensure that all reasonable requests for connection to the fixed public telephone network and access to publicly available telephone services, at a fixed location, are met.

The connection provided shall allow users to make and receive national and international calls, supporting speech, facsimile and/or data communications.

2.   Where, taking into account the revenues generated as a result of that connection, the network provider states that the user concerned can only be served at a loss or under cost conditions falling outside normal commercial standards, the net cost of serving that user may be shared with other organisations under a universal service financing scheme.

Article 6 Directory services

1.   Subject to the requirements of relevant legislation on the protection of personal data and privacy, such as Directive 95/46/EC, Member States shall ensure that:

(a)   subscribers have the right to have an entry in publicly available directories, and to verify and if necessary correct or request removal of that entry;

(b)   directories of all subscribers who consent to be listed, including fixed and personal numbers, are available to users in printed and where appropriate, electronic form, and updated on a regular basis;

(c)   directory enquiry services covering all listed subscribers numbers are available to all users, including users of public pay-telephones.

2.   In order to ensure provision of the services in paragraph 2, Member States shall ensure that all organisations who assign telephone numbers to subscribers make available on request the relevant information in an agreed format on terms which are fair, reasonable and non-discriminatory.

3.   Member States shall ensure that organisations providing the service in paragraph 2 follow the principle of non discrimination in their treatment and presentation of information provided to them.

4.   Where a Member State finds that no organisation is willing to make telephone directories publicly available, or to provide directory enquiry services to all telephone users including users of public pay telephones, the net cost of providing these services may be shared amongst all organisations providing publicly available voice telephony services under a universal service financing scheme, in accordance with Community law.

Article 7   Public pay-telephones

1.   Member States shall ensure that public pay telephones are provided to meet the reasonable needs of users, in terms of both numbers and geographical coverage.

2.   Member States shall ensure that it is possible to make emergency calls from public pay-telephones using the single European emergency call number '112' referred to in Decision 91/396/EEC, and other national emergency numbers, all free of charge.

3.   Where a Member State finds that certain public pay telephones can only be served at a loss or under cost conditions falling outside normal commercial standards, the net cost of providing those public pay telephones may be shared amongst all organisations providing public telecommunications networks and/or publicly available voice telephony services under a universal service financing scheme, in accordance with Community law.

Article 8   Specific measures for disabled users and users with special needs
Member States shall, where appropriate, take specific measures to ensure access to and affordability of telephone services for disabled users *and users with special needs.*

CHAPTER III.   GENERAL PROVISIONS CONCERNING FIXED PUBLIC TELEPHONE NETWORKS AND PUBLICLY AVAILABLE TELEPHONE SERVICES

Article 9   Connection of terminal equipment and use of the network

Member States shall ensure that all users provided with a connection to the fixed public telephone network can:
(a)   connect and use terminal equipment suitable for the connection provided, in accordance with national and Community law;
(b)   access operator assistance services, and directory enquiry services in accordance with Article 6;

(c)   access Emergency Services at no charge, using the dialling code '112' and any other dialling codes specified by national regulatory authorities for use at a national level.

All connections to the fixed public telephone network installed after 1st January 1998 should be of a quality that supports, in addition to speech, data communications at rates suitable for access to online information services, ie 14400 bit/s or more.

Article 10   Contracts

1.   National regulatory authorities shall ensure that organisations providing access to fixed public telephone networks provide a contract which specifies the service and service quality levels to be provided, and the compensation and/or refund arrangements for users that apply if the contracted service quality levels are not met. Contracts shall contain a summary of the method of initiating procedures for the settlement of disputes in accordance with Article 26.

2.   Without prejudice to other rights of appeal provided for by national law, Member States shall ensure that users, and where national law so provides, organisations representing user and/or consumer interests, can bring before the national regulatory authority cases where compensation and/or refund arrangements are deemed to be unsatisfactory for users.

National regulatory authorities shall be able to require the alteration of the conditions of contracts referred to in paragraph 1, and the conditions of any compensation and/or refund schemes used.

Article 11   Publication of and access to information

1.   Member States shall ensure that all organisations providing fixed public telephone networks or publicly available telephone services publish adequate and up-to-date information on access to and use of the fixed public telephone networks and/or publicly available telephone services. In particular, national regulatory authorities shall ensure that tariffs are presented clearly and accurately.

2.   National regulatory authorities shall ensure that organisations providing fixed public telephone networks provide them with details of technical interface specifications for network access, as identified in Annex II, part 1, to be made available in accordance with paragraph 4. Changes in existing network interface specifications and information on new network interface specifications shall be communicated to the national regulatory authority in advance of implementation. The national regulatory authority may lay down a suitable period of notice.

3.   Where and for as long as the provision of public telecommunications networks and publicly available voice telephony services are subject to special or exclusive rights in a Member State, national regulatory authorities shall ensure that adequate and up-to-date information on access to and use of the fixed public telephone networks and publicly available telephone services is published according to the list of headings given in Annex II, part 2 in the manner laid down in paragraph 4.

4.   National regulatory authorities shall ensure that the information is made available in an appropriate manner in order to provide easy access to

that information for interested parties. Reference shall be made in the national Official Gazette of the Member State concerned to the manner in which this information is published.

5. National regulatory authorities shall notify to the Commission no later than 1 July 1997 the manner in which the information referred to in paragraph 2 and 3 is made available. The Commission shall regularly publish a reference to such notifications in the Official Journal of the European Communities. Any changes shall be immediately notified.

Article 12   Quality of service

1. Member States shall take the necessary steps to ensure quality of the services identified in this Directive. In particular, they may set performance targets in the authorisations that apply to organisations providing fixed public telephone networks and/or publicly available telephone services.

In the case of organisations who retain special or exclusive rights for the provision of fixed public telecommunications networks and/or voice telephony services, Member States shall ensure that targets are set and published for the relevant parameters laid down in Annex III, in accordance with Article 11(4).

2. National regulatory authorities shall ensure that organisations who have been providing fixed public telephone networks and/or publicly available telephone services for more than 18 months start to keep up-to-date information concerning their performance based on the parameters, definitions and measurement methods laid down in Annex III. This information shall be provided to the national regulatory authority on request.

3. Where appropriate, and in particular as a result of consultation with interested parties in accordance with the provisions of Article 24, national regulatory authorities shall ensure publication of the performance data referred to in paragraph 1, and may set performance targets for organisations providing fixed public telephone networks and/or publicly available telephone services where these do not exist already, in accordance with Article 11(4).

Persistent failure of an organisation to meet performance targets may result in specific measures being taken in accordance with conditions set out in the relevant authorisation for that organisation.

4. National regulatory authorities shall have the right to call for independent audits of the performance data in order to ensure the accuracy and comparability of the data made available by the organisations referred to in paragraph 1.

Article 13   Conditions of access and use and essential requirements

1. National regulatory authorities shall have procedures in order to decide, on a case-by-case basis and in the shortest possible time period, whether or not to allow organisations providing fixed public telephone networks and/or publicly available telephone services to take measures such as the refusal to provide access to the fixed public telephone network or the interruption or reduction in availability of service, for reasons of a user's alleged failure to comply with the conditions of use. These procedures may also provide for the possibility of the national regulatory authority authorising

a priori specified measures in the event of defined infringements of the conditions of use, in particular fraudulent use.

The national regulatory authority shall ensure that these procedures provide for a transparent decision-making process in which due respect is given to the rights of the parties. The decision shall be taken after both parties have been given the opportunity to state their case. The decision shall be duly substantiated and notified to the parties within one week of its adoption.

A summary of these procedures shall be published in the manner laid down in Article 11(4).

This provision shall not prejudice the rights of the parties concerned to apply to the courts.

2.   Member States shall ensure that, when access to or use of fixed public telephone networks and/or publicly available telephone services is restricted on the basis of essential requirements, the relevant national provisions identify which of the essential requirements set out in (a) to (e) below are the basis of such restrictions.   .

These restrictions shall be imposed through regulatory means which can be challenged in court, and shall be published in the manner laid down in Article 11(4).

Without prejudice to action which may be taken in accordance with Articles 3(5) and 5(3) of Directive 90/387/EEC, the following essential requirements shall apply to the fixed public telephone network and publicly available telephone services in the following manner:

(a)   *Security of network operations*

Member States shall take all necessary steps to ensure that the availability of fixed public telephone networks and publicly available telephone services is maintained in the event of catastrophic network breakdown or in cases of *force majeure*, such as extreme weather, earthquakes, flood, lightning or fire.

In the event of the circumstances referred to in the first subparagraph, the bodies concerned shall make every endeavour to maintain the highest level of service to meet any priorities laid down by the competent authorities.

National regulatory authorities shall ensure that any restrictions on access to and use of the fixed public telephone network on the grounds of the security of networks are proportionate and non-discriminatory, and are based on objective criteria identified in advance.

(b)   *Maintenance of network integrity*

Member States shall take all necessary steps to ensure that the integrity of fixed public telephone networks is maintained. National regulatory authorities shall ensure that restrictions on access to and use of the fixed public telephone network on the grounds of maintenance of network integrity, in order to protect *inter alia* network equipment, software or stored data, are kept to the minimum necessary to provide for normal operation of the network. Such restrictions shall be non-discriminatory, and be based on objective criteria identified in advance.

(c)   *Interoperability of services*

When terminal equipment is operating in compliance with Directive 91/263/ EEC, no further restrictions on use shall be imposed on the grounds of interoperability of services.

(d)   *Protection of data*

Conditions on access to and use of fixed public telephone networks and/or publicly available telephone services based on the grounds of protection of data may be imposed only in accordance with relevant legislation on the protection or personal data and privacy, such as Directive 95/46/EC.

(e) *Effective use of the frequency spectrum*

Member States shall take all necessary steps to ensure the effective use of the frequency spectrum and the avoidance of harmful interference between radio-based systems that could restrict or limit access to or use of fixed public telephone networks and publicly available telephone services.

3. Where and for as long as Member States maintain special or exclusive rights for the provision of public telecommunications networks and voice telephony services, conditions imposed on users on the basis of such special or exclusive rights shall be imposed through regulatory means and with the agreement of the national regulatory authority.

CHAPTER IV.   SPECIFIC PROVISIONS CONCERNING PUBLIC TELEPHONE NETWORKS AND PUBLICLY AVAILABLE TELEPHONE SERVICES

Article 14   Itemised billing, tone dialling and selective call barring

1. Member States shall ensure that all organisations providing publicly available telephone services over fixed public telephone networks make available, as early as possible, the facilities of:

— tone dialling

— itemised billing and selective call barring as facilities available on request.

Tone dialling and selective call barring are specified in Annex I, part 1.

National regulatory authorities shall ensure that these facilities are offered to most telephone users before 31 December 1998, and are generally available before 31 December 2002.

2. Subject to the requirements of relevant legislation on the protection of personal data and privacy, such as Directive 95/46/EC, itemised bills shall show a sufficient level of detail to allow verification and control of the charges incurred in using the fixed public telephone network and/or publicly available telephone services.

A basic level of itemised billing shall be available at no extra charge to the user. Where appropriate, additional levels of detail may be offered to users at reasonable tariffs. National regulatory authorities may lay down the basic level of itemised bill.

Calls to helplines which are free of charge to the caller shall not be identified in the caller's itemised bill.

Article 15   Provision of additional facilities

1. National regulatory authorities shall ensure that organisations with significant market power in the provision of telephone services over fixed public telephone networks provide, subject to technical feasibility and economic viability, the facilities listed in Annex I, part 2.

2. National regulatory authorities shall facilitate and encourage provision of the services and facilities listed in Annex I, part 3, in compliance with the competition rules of the Treaty.

3.   National regulatory authorities shall ensure that dates for the introduction of the facilities listed in Annex I, part 2 are set, taking into account the state of network development, market demand and progress with standardisation, and are published in the manner laid down in Article 11(4).

Article 16   Special network access

1.   National regulatory authorities shall ensure that the organisations with significant market power in the provision of fixed public telephone networks deal with reasonable requests from organisations providing telecommunications services for access to the fixed public telephone network at network termination points other than the commonly provided network termination points referred to in Annex II, part 1.

2.   The organisation making such a request shall be granted the opportunity to put its case to the national regulatory authority before a final decision is taken to restrict or deny access in response to a particular request.

Where a request for special network access is denied, the organisation making the request should be given a prompt and justified explanation as to why the request has been refused.

3.   Technical and commercial arrangements for special network access shall be a matter for agreement between the parties involved, subject to intervention by the national regulatory authority as laid down in paragraphs 2, 4 and 5. The agreement may include reimbursement to the organisation of its costs incurred *inter alia* in providing the network access requested; these charges shall fully respect the principles of cost orientation set out in Annex II to Directive 90/387/EC.

4.   National regulatory authorities may intervene on their own initiative at any time, and shall do so if requested by either party, in order to set conditions that are non discriminatory, are fair and reasonable for both parties and offer the greatest benefit to all users.

5.   National regulatory authorities shall also have the right, in the interest of all users, to ensure that the agreements include conditions that meet the criteria set out in paragraph 4, are entered into and implemented in an efficient and timely manner and include conditions on conformity with relevant standards, compliance with essential requirements and/or the maintenance of end-to-end quality.

6.   Conditions set by national regulatory authorities in accordance with paragraph 5 shall be published in the manner laid down in Article 11(4).

7.   National regulatory authorities shall ensure that organisations with significant market power referred to in paragraph 1 adhere to the principle of non-discrimination when they make use of the fixed public telephone network, and in particular use any form of special network access, for providing publicly available telecommunications services.

8.   Where appropriate, the Commission shall, in consultation with the ONP Committee, acting in accordance with the procedure laid down in Article 29, request ETSI to draw up standards for new types of network access. Reference to such standards shall be published in the Official Journal of the European Communities in accordance with Article 5 of Directive 90/387/EEC.

9.   Details of agreements for special network access shall be made available to the national regulatory authority upon its request.

Article 17 Tariff principles

1. Without prejudice to the specific provisions of Article 4 in relation to affordability, national regulatory authorities shall ensure that organisations with significant market power for the provision of voice telephony services over fixed public telephone networks comply with the provisions of this Article.

2. Tariffs for use of the fixed public telephone network and publicly available telephone services shall follow the basic principles of cost orientation set out in Annex II to Directive 90/387/EC. In particular, the facilities referred to in Article 14 of this Directive shall be provided at affordable prices.

3. Tariffs for access to and use of the fixed public telephone network shall be independent of the type of application which the users implement, except to the extent that they require different services or facilities.

4. Tariffs for facilities additional to the provision of connection to the fixed public telephone network and publicly available telephone services shall, in accordance with Community law, be sufficiently unbundled, so that the user is not required to pay for facilities which are not necessary for the service requested.

5. Tariff changes shall be implemented only after an appropriate public notice period, set by the national regulatory authority, has been observed.

6. A Member State may authorise its national regulatory authority not to apply the requirements of paragraphs 2, 3, 4 or 5 in a specific geographical area where it is satisfied that there is effective competition in the relevant telephone services market.

Article 18 Cost accounting principles

1. Member States shall ensure that, where an organisation has an obligation for its tariffs to follow the principle of cost orientation in accordance with Article 17, the cost accounting systems operated by such organisations are suitable for the implementation of Article 17 and that compliance with such systems are verified by a competent body which is independent of those organisations. National regulatory authorities shall ensure that a statement concerning compliance is published annually.

2. National regulatory authorities shall ensure that a description of the cost accounting system referred to in paragraph 1, showing the main categories under which costs are gathered and the rules used for the allocation of costs to the voice telephone service, is made available to it on request. National regulatory authorities shall submit to the Commission on request information on the cost accounting systems applied by the organisations concerned.

3. Where and as long as the provision of public telecommunications networks and voice telephony services are subject to special or exclusive rights in a Member State, the system referred to in paragraph 1 shall, without prejudice to the last subparagraph of this paragraph, include the following elements:

(a) the costs of the voice telephony service shall in particular include the direct costs incurred by the telecommunications organisations in setting up, operating and maintaining the voice telephony service and in marketing and billing the service.

(b) common costs, that is costs which cannot be directly assigned to either the voice telephony service or other activities, shall be allocated as follows:

(i) whenever possible, common cost categories shall be allocated on the basis of direct analysis of the origin of the costs themselves;

(ii) when direct analysis is not possible, common cost categories shall be allocated on the basis of an indirect linkage to another cost category or group of cost categories for which a direct assignment or allocation is possible; the indirect linkage shall be based on comparable cost structures;

(iii) when neither direct nor indirect measures of cost allocation can be found, the cost category shall be allocated on the basis of a general allocator computed by using the ratio of all expenses directly or indirectly assigned or allocated, on the one hand, to the voice telephony service and, on the other hand, to other services.

Other cost accounting systems may be applied if they are suitable for the implementation of Article 17 and have been approved as such by the national regulatory authority for application by the telecommunications organisations, subject to the Commission being informed prior to their application.

4. Member States shall ensure that the financial accounts of all organisations providing fixed public telephone networks and/or publicly available telephone services are drawn up, submitted to audit and published in accordance with the provisions of national and Community legislation applying to commercial undertakings. Detailed accounting information shall be made available to the national regulatory authority on its request and in confidence.

Article 19 Discounts and other special tariff provisions

Member States shall ensure that, where an organisation has an obligation for its tariffs to follow the principle of cost orientation in accordance with Article 17, discount schemes for end users (including consumers) are fully transparent and published and applied in accordance with the principle of non-discrimination.

National regulatory authorities may require such discount schemes to be modified or withdrawn.

Article 20 Specifications for network access, including the socket

1. Standards suitable for access to fixed public telephone networks shall be published in the ONP List of Standards referred to in Article 5 of Directive 90/387/EC.

2. Where telephone services are supplied to users over the ISDN network at the S/T reference point, national regulatory authorities shall ensure that the ISDN network termination points comply with the relevant physical interface specifications, in particular those for the socket, referenced in the ONP List of Standards.

Article 21   Non-payment of bills

Member States shall authorise specified measures, which shall be proportion-ate, non-discriminatory and published in the manner laid down in Article 11(4), to cover non-payment of telephone bills for use of the fixed public telephone network. These measures shall ensure that due warning is given to the subscriber beforehand of any consequent service interruption or discon-nection.

Except in cases of persistent late or non payment, these measures shall ensure, as far as is technically feasible, that any service interruption is confined to the service concerned, and that complete disconnection takes place only after a stated period during which calls are permitted that do not incur a charge to that subscriber.

Article 22   Conditions for the termination of offerings

1.   The provisions of this article shall apply where and for as long as the provision of public telecommunications networks and publicly available voice telephony services are subject to special or exclusive rights in a Member State.

2.   National regulatory authorities shall ensure that service offerings of organisations with such special or exclusive rights continue for a reasonable period of time and that termination of an offering, or a change that materially alters the use that can be made of it, can be done only after consultation with users affected and an appropriate public notice period set by the national regulatory authority.

3.   Without prejudice to other rights of appeal provided for by national law, Member States shall ensure that users, and where national law so provides, organisations representing user and/or consumer interests, can bring before the national regulatory authority cases where the users affected do not agree with the termination date as envisaged by the organisation concerned.

Article 23   Variation of published conditions

1.   The provisions of this article shall apply where and for as long as the provision of public telecommunications networks and publicly available voice telephony services are subject to special or exclusive rights in a Member State.

2.   Where in response to a particular request an organisation with such special or exclusive rights considers it unreasonable to provide a connection to the fixed public telephone network under its published tariffs and supply conditions, it must seek the agreement of the national regulatory authority to vary those conditions in that case.

CHAPTER V   PROCEDURAL PROVISIONS

Article 24   Consultation

Member States shall ensure consultation, in accordance with national pro-cedures, with the representatives of organisations providing public telecom-munications networks, of users, consumers, manufacturers and service providers on issues related to the scope, affordability and quality of telephone services. Where appropriate, the Commission shall ensure additional consultation at the European level on these issues.

Article 25   Notification and reporting

1.   Member States shall notify to the Commission any changes in the information which had to be published under Directive 95/62/EC. The Commission shall publish this information in the Official Journal of the European Communities.

2.   Member States shall also notify to the Commission:
— organisations with significant market power for the purposes of this Directive
— details of situations where organisations providing fixed public telephone networks and/or publicly available telephone services no longer have to follow the principle of cost orientation of tariffs, in accordance with Article 17(6)
The Commission may request national regulatory authorities to provide their reasons for classifying or not classifying organisations in these two categories.

3.   Where a Member State maintains special or exclusive rights for the provision of public telecommunications networks and publicly available telephone services, national regulatory authorities shall keep available and submit to the Commission on request details of individual cases brought before them, other than those covered by Article 21, where access to or use of the fixed public telephone network or voice telephony service has been restricted or denied, including the measures taken and their justification.

Article 26   Conciliation and national dispute resolution

Without prejudice to:
   (a)   any action that the Commission or any Member State may take pursuant to the Treaty;
   (b)   the rights of the person invoking the procedure in paragraphs 3 and 4, of the organisations concerned or of any other person under applicable national law, except insofar as they enter into an agreement for the resolution of disputes between them;
   (c)   the provisions of Article 10(2) which allow the national regulatory authorities to alter the conditions of subscriber contracts,
the following procedures shall be available:
   (1)   Member States shall ensure that any party, including for example users, service providers, consumers, or other organisations having an unresolved dispute with an organisation providing fixed public telephone networks and/or publicly available telephone services concerning an alleged infringement of the provisions of this Directive, shall have a right of appeal to the national regulatory authority or another independent body. Easily accessible and in principle inexpensive procedures shall be available at a national level to resolve such disputes in a fair, transparent and timely manner. These procedures shall in particular apply in cases where users are in dispute with an organisation about their telephone bills, or the terms and conditions under which telephone service is provided.

(2)   A user or an organisation may, where the dispute involves organisations in more than one Member State, invoke the conciliation procedure provided for in paragraphs 3 and 4 by means of a written notification to the national regulatory authority and to the Commission. Member States may also allow their national regulatory authority to invoke the conciliation procedure.

(3)   Where the national regulatory authority or the Commission finds that there is a case for further examination, following a notification based on paragraph 2, it can refer the matter to the Chairman of the ONP Committee.

(4)   In the circumstances referred to in paragraph 3, the Chairman of the ONP Committee shall initiate the procedure described below if satisfied that all reasonable steps have been taken at national level:

(a)   the Chairman of the ONP Committee shall convene as soon as possible a working group including at least two members of the ONP Committee and one representative of the national regulatory authorities concerned, and the Chairman of the ONP Committee or another official of the Commission appointed by him. The working group shall be chaired by the representative of the Commission and shall normally meet within ten days of having been convened. The Chairman of the working group may decide, upon proposal by any of the members of the working group, to invite a maximum of two other persons as experts to advise it;

(b)   the working group shall give the party invoking this procedure, the national regulatory authorities of the Member States involved and the organisations involved the opportunity to present their opinions in oral or written form;

(c)   the working group shall endeavour to reach agreement between the parties involved within three months of the date of receipt of the notification referred to in paragraph 2. The Chairman of the ONP Committee shall inform that Committee of the results of the procedure so that it may express its views.

(5)   The party invoking the procedure shall bear its own costs of participating in this procedure.

Article 27   Deferment of certain obligations

1.   The dates laid down in any deferments granted in relation to Article 12 and 13 of Directive 95/62/EC shall remain unchanged.

Article 28   Technical adjustment

Modifications necessary to adapt Annexes I, II and III to this Directive to technological developments or to changes in market demand shall be determined in accordance with the procedure laid down in Article 30.

Article 29   Advisory Committee procedure

1.   The Commission shall be assisted by the ONP Committee.

The Committee shall, in particular, consult the representatives of the organisations providing fixed public telephone networks, publicly available telephone services, users, consumers and manufacturers.

2.   The representative of the Commission shall submit to the Committee a draft of the measures to be taken. The Committee shall deliver its opinion

on the draft within a time limit which the Chairman may lay down according to the urgency of the matter, if necessary by taking a vote.

The opinion shall be recorded in the minutes; in addition, each Member State shall have the right to ask to have its position recorded in the minutes.

The Commission shall take the utmost account of the opinion delivered by the Committee. It shall inform the Committee of the manner in which its opinion has been taken into account.

Article 30   Regulatory Committee procedure

1.   Notwithstanding the provisions of Article 29, the following procedure shall apply in respect of the matters covered by Article 28.

2.   The representative of the Commission shall submit to the Committee a draft of the measures to be taken. The Committee shall deliver its opinion on the draft within a time limit which the Chairman may lay down according to the urgency of the matter. The opinion shall be delivered by the majority laid down in Article 148(2) of the Treaty in the case of decisions which the Council is required to adopt on a proposal from the Commission. The votes of the representatives of the Member States within the Committee shall be weighted in the manner set out in that Article. The Chairman shall not vote.

3.   The Commission shall adopt the measures envisaged if they are in accordance with the opinion of the Committee.

4.   If the measures envisaged are not in accordance with the opinion of the Committee, or if no opinion is delivered, the Commission shall, without delay, submit to the Council a proposal relating to the measures to be taken. The Council shall act by a qualified majority.

If, on the expiry of a period of three months from the date of referral to the Council, the Council has not acted, the proposed measures shall be adopted by the Commission.

Article 31   Review

The Commission shall examine and report to the European Parliament and to the Council on the functioning of this Directive, on the first occasion not later than 31 December 1999, taking into account the Report on Universal service to be published by the Commission before 1 January 1998. The review shall be based *inter alia* on the information provided by the Member States to the Commission, and shall in particular examine:

— the scope of the Directive, and in particular whether some of its provisions should apply to mobile telephony

— the provisions in chapter II in the light of changes in market conditions, users demand and technological progress

— the maintenance of the obligations imposed under Articles 17, 18 and 19 in the light of the emergence of competition.

Where necessary, further periodic reviews may be proposed in the report.

Article 32   Transposition

1.   Member States shall take the measures necessary to comply with this Directive before 31 December 1997. They shall forthwith inform the Commission thereof.

When Member States adopt these measures, they shall contain a reference to this Directive or shall be accompanied by such reference on the occasion of their official publication. The methods of making such reference shall be laid down by the Member States.

2.   Member States shall inform the Commission of the main provisions of national law which they adopt in the field governed by this Directive.

Article 33   Repeal of Directive 95/62/EC

Directive 95/62/EC is hereby repealed with effect from 31 December 1997, without prejudice to Member States' obligations for implementation of that Directive according to the timescales laid down in Annex IV.

References made to the repealed Directive shall be construed as being made to this Directive.

Annex V provides a table showing the relationship between the Articles of Directive 95/62/EC and the Articles of this Directive.

Article 34   Entry into force

This Directive shall enter into force on the twentieth day following that of its publications in the Official Journal of the European Communities.

Article 35   Addressees

This Directive is addressed to the Member States.

Done at Brussels, [date]

For the European Parliament ....For the Council
   The President ....The President

ANNEX I   DESCRIPTION OF FACILITIES REFERRED TO IN ARTICLES 14 AND 15

Part 1   Facilities referred to in Article 14(1)
   (a)   *Tone dialling or DTMF (dual-tone multifrequency operation)*
i.e. the fixed public telephone network supports the use of DTMF telephones for signalling to the exchange, using tones as defined in ITU-T Recommendation Q.23, and supports the same tones for end-to-end signalling through the network, both within a Member State and between Member States.
   (b)   *Selective call barring for outgoing calls*
i.e. the facility whereby the subscriber can, on request to the telephone service provider, bar outgoing calls of defined types or to defined types of numbers.

Part 2   List of facilities referred to in Article 15(1)
   (a)   *Calling-line identification*
i.e. the calling party's number is presented to the called party prior to the call being established.

This facility should be provided in accordance with relevant legislation on protection of personal data and privacy, such as Directive 95/46/EC.

(b)   *Direct dialling-in (or facilities offering equivalent functionality)*
i.e. users on a private branch exchange (PBX) or similar private system can be called directly from the fixed public telephone network, without intervention of the PBX attendant.

(c)   *Call forwarding*
i.e. incoming calls sent to another destination in the same or another Member State (e.g. on no reply, on busy, or unconditionally).

This facility should be provided in accordance with relevant legislation on protection of personal data and privacy, such as Directive 95/46/EC.

Part 3   List of services and facilities referred to in Article 15(2)

(a)   *Community-wide access to green/freephone services*
These services, variously known as green numbers, freephone services, 0800 numbers etc. cover dial-up services where the caller pays nothing for the call to the number dialled.

(b)   *Shared cost services*
These services cover dial-up services where the caller pays only part of the cost of the call to the number dialled.

(c)   *Community-wide premium rate services/shared revenue services*
Premium rate service is a facility whereby charges for the use of a service accessed through a telecommunications network are combined with the network call charges.

(d)   *Community-wide calling-line identification*
i.e. the calling party's number is presented to the called party prior to the call being established.

This facility should be provided in accordance with relevant legislation on protection of personal data and privacy, such as Directive 95/46/EC.

(e)   *Access to operator services in other Member States*
i.e. users in one Member State can call the operator/assistance service in another Member State.

(f)   *Access to directory enquiry services in other Member States*
i.e. users in one Member State can call the directory enquiry service in another Member State.

This facility should be provided in accordance with relevant legislation on protection of personal data and privacy, such as Directive 95/46/EC.

ANNEX II   HEADINGS FOR INFORMATION TO BE PUBLISHED IN ACCORDANCE WITH ARTICLE 11

PART 1   INFORMATION TO BE SUPPLIED TO THE NATIONAL REGULATORY AUTHORITY IN ACCORDANCE WITH ARTICLE 11(2)

TECHNICAL CHARACTERISTICS OF NETWORK INTERFACES

Technical characteristics of interfaces at commonly provided network termination points are required, including where applicable reference to relevant national and/or international standards or recommendations:

— for analogue and/or digitally presented networks:
   (a)   single line interface;

    (b)   multiline interface;
    (c)   direct dialling-in (DDI) interface;
    (d)   other interfaces commonly provided;
— for ISDN: (where provided)
    (a)   specification of basic and primary rate interfaces at the S/T reference points, including the signalling protocol;
    (b)   details of bearer services able to carry voice telephony services;
    (c)   other interfaces commonly provided;
— and any other interfaces commonly provided.

In addition to the above information to be submitted to the National regulatory authority on a regular basis in the manner laid down in Article 11(2), all organisations providing fixed public telephone networks must inform their National regulatory authority, without undue delay, of any particular network characteristics which are found to affect the correct operation of terminal equipment. The national regulatory authority shall make this information available on request to terminal equipment suppliers.

PART 2   INFORMATION TO BE PUBLISHED IN ACCORDANCE WITH ARTICLE 11(3)

Note. The national regulatory authority has a responsibility to ensure that the information in this Annex is published, in accordance with Article 11(3). It is for the national regulatory authority to decide which information is to be published by the organisations providing telecommunications networks and/or publicly available telephone services, and which by the national regulatory authority itself.

1. Name(s) and address(es) of organisation(s)

i.e. names and head office addresses of organisations providing fixed public telephone networks and/or publicly available telephone services.

2 Telephone services offered

2.1   *Scope of the basic service*
Description of the basic telephone services offered, indicating what is included in the subscription charge and the periodic rental charge (e.g. operator services, directories, directory services, selective call barring, itemised billing, maintenance etc).
    Description of optional facilities and features of the telephone service which are tariffed separately from the basic offering, including where applicable reference to the relevant technical standards or specifications to which they conform.
2.2   *Tariffs*
covering access, all types of call charges, maintenance, and including details of discounts applied and special and targetted tariff schemes.
2.3   *Compensation/refund policy*
    including specific details of any compensation/refund schemes offered.
2.4.   *Types of maintenance service offered*
2.5.   *Standard contract conditions*
including any minimum contractual period, if relevant.

3. Conditions for attachment of terminal equipment

This shall include a complete overview of requirements for terminal equipment in line with the provisions of Directives 91/263/EEC or 93/97/EEC, including, where appropriate, conditions concerning customer premises wiring and location of the network termination point.

4. Restrictions on access and use

This shall include any restrictions on access and use imposed in accordance with the requirements of Article 13

ANNEX III   SUPPLY-TIME AND QUALITY-OF-SERVICE
INDICATORS, DEFINITIONS AND MEASUREMENT METHODS
IN ACCORDANCE WITH THE REQUIREMENTS OF ARTICLE 12

INDICATOR (NOTE 1)	DEFINITION	MEASUREMENT METHOD
supply time for initial connection	ETSI ETR 138	ETSI ETR 138
fault rate per access line	ETSI ETR 138	ETSI ETR 138
fault repair time	ETSI ETR 138	ETSI ETR 138
unsuccessful call ratio	ETSI ETR 138	ETSI ETR 138
call set up time	ETSI ETR 138	ETSI ETR 138
response times for operator services	ETSI ETR 138	ETSI ETR 138
response times for directory enquiry services	as for operator services	as for operator services
proportion of coin and card operated public pay-telephones in working order	ETSI ETR 138	ETSI ETR 138
billing accuracy	see note 2	see note 2

Note 1.
Indicators should allow for performance to be analysed at a regional level (i.e. no less than level 2 in the Nomenclature of Territorial Units for Statistics (NUTS) established by Eurostat.)

Note 2.
Billing accuracy. National definitions and measurement methods should be used until such time as a common definition and measurement method are agreed at the European level.

ANNEX IV TIMESCALE REFERRED TO IN ARTICLE 33

Date by which Member States must take the necessary measures
to comply with Directive 95/62/EC ....13 December 1996

ANNEX V COMPARATIVE TABLE

Article No. in Directive 95/62/EC	Title of Article	Article Number in this Directive
1	Scope and aim	1
2	Definitions	2
	Availability of telecommunications services	
	Affordability	4
3	Provision of service, connection of terminal equipment and use of the network	5, 9
4	Publication of and access to information	11
5	Quality of service	12
6	Conditions for the termination of offerings	22
7	User Contracts	10
8	Variation of published conditions	23
9	Provision of additional facilities	15
10	Special network access	16
11	Interconnection	—
12	Tariff principles	17
13	Cost accounting principles	18
14	Discounts and other special tariff provisions	19
15	Itemized billing and other facilities	14
16	Directory services	6
17	Public pay-telephones	7
18	Telephone pre-payment cards	—
19	Specific measures for disabled users	8
20	Specifications for network access, including the socket	20
21	Numbering	—
22	Conditions of access and use and essential requirements	13
23	Non-payment of bills	21

Article No. in Directive 95/62/EC	Title of Article	Article Number in this Directive
24	Technical standards	—
25	Provisions for Community wide convergence	—
	Consultation	24
26	Notification and reporting	25
27	Conciliation and national dispute resolution	26
28	Deferment	27
29	Technical adjustment	28
30	Advisory Committee procedure	29
31	Regulatory committee procedure	30
32	Review	31
33	Implementation	32
	Repeal of directive 95/62/EC	33
34	Entry into force	34
35	Addressees	35
Annex 1	Headings for information to be published	Annex II
Annex II	Supply-time and quality-of-service indicators	Annex III
Annex III	Description of facilities	Annex I

AMENDED PROPOSAL FOR A EUROPEAN PARLIAMENT AND COUNCIL DIRECTIVE (96/C 178/04) ON INTERCONNECTION IN TELECOMMUNICATIONS WITH REGARD TO ENSURING UNIVERSAL SERVICE AND INTEROPERABILITY THROUGH APPLICATION OF THE PRINCIPLES OF OPEN NETWORK PROVISION (ONP)[1]
OJ C178/3, 21 June 1996

COM(96) 121 final — 95/0207(COD)

(Submitted by the Commission pursuant to Article 189a (2) of the EC Treaty on 20 March 1996)

AMENDED TEXT

Recital 1

Whereas from 1 January 1998 (with, subject to certain conditions, the possibility of transition periods in some Member States) the provision of

---

1 OJ No C 313, 24.11.1995, p. 7.

telecommunication services and infrastructure in the Community will be liberalized; whereas in order to promote Community-wide telecommunications services there is need to ensure interconnection of networks between different national and Community operators; whereas Council Directive 90/387/EEC of 28 June 1990 on the establishment of the internal market for telecommunications services through the implementation of open network provision (ONP)[2] lays down harmonized principles for open and efficient access to and use a public telecommunications networks and where applicable services; whereas the Council resolution of 22 July 1993 on the review of the situation in the telecommunications sector and the need for further development in that market[3] recognizes that open network provision measures provide an appropriate framework for harmonizing interconnection conditions;

Recital 4

Whereas, following the removal of special and exclusive rights for telecommunications services and infrastructure in the Community, the provision of telecommunications networks or services may require some form of authorization by the relevant public authority, in accordance with the subsidiarity principle; whereas all organizations authorized to provide public telecommunications networks or public telecommunications services in all or part of the Community should be free to negotiate interconnection agreements on a commercial basis in accordance with Community law, subject to supervision and intervention by the relevant authorities; whereas it is necessary to ensure adequate interconnection within the Community of certain networks and services essential for the social and economic well-being of Community users, notably public telephone networks and services, and leased lines;

Recital 6

Whereas obligations for the provision of universal service contribute to the Community objective of socioeconomic cohesion and territorial equity; whereas the aim should be to introduce new technologies like the integrated services digital network (ISDN) as soon as possible and on as broad a basis as possible in the Member States; whereas the current level of deployment of ISDN in Member States means that it cannot be made available to all users everywhere and therefore it cannot at present be subject to a universal service obligation; whereas there may be more than one organization in a Member State with obligations of providing universal service; whereas the calculation of the net cost of universal service should take due account of costs and revenues, as well as economic externalities and the intangible benefits resulting from providing universal service but, in order not to hinder the on-going process of tariff rebalancing, should not include elements which are due to historic tariff imbalances, given that the fixed costs associated with the existing network are at present partly taken into account in the tariff shared by all users of that network; whereas costs of universal service obligations

---

2 OJ No L 192, 24.7.1990, p. 1.
3 OJ No C 213, 6.8.1993, p. 1.

should be calculated on the basis of transparent procedures; whereas financial contributions related to the sharing of the cost of universal service obligations should be unbundled from charges for interconnection;

Recital 7

Whereas it is important to lay down principles to guarantee transparency, access to information, non-discrimination and equality of access, in particular for organizations with significant market power; whereas the market power of an organization depends on a number of factors including its share of the relevant product or service market in the relevant geographical market, its turnover relative to the size of the market, its ability to influence market conditions, its control of the means of access to end-users, its international links, its access to financial resources, its experience providing products and services in the market; whereas, for the purpose of this Directive, an organization with a share of more than 25% of a particular telecommunications market in the geographical area in a Member State within which it is authorized to operate would be presumed to enjoy significant market power, unless the relevant regulatory authority determined that this was not the case; whereas, for an organization falling below this threshold market share, the relevant regulatory authority may nevertheless determine that the organization enjoyed significant market power;

Recital 8

Whereas pricing for interconnection is a key factor to determine the structure and the intensity of competition in the transformation process towards a liberalized market; whereas organizations with significant market power must be able to demonstrate that their interconnection charges are set on the basis of objective criteria and follow the principles of transparency and cost orientation, and are sufficiently unbundled in terms of network and service elements offered; whereas publication of a list of interconnection services, charges, terms and conditions enhances the necessary transparency and non-discrimination; whereas flexibility in the methods of charging for interconnection traffic should be possible, including capacity-based charging; whereas the level of charges should promote productivity and encourage efficient and sustainable market entry, and should not be below a limit calculated by the use of long-run incremental cost and cost allocation and attribution methods based on actual cost causation, nor above a limit set by the stand-alone cost of providing the interconnection in question;

Recital 9

Whereas where an organization enjoys significant market power, appropriate accounting separation between interconnection activities and other activities ensures transparency of internal cost-transfers; whereas, where an organization with special or exclusive rights in a non-telecommunications field also provides telecommunications services, accounting separation is an appropriate means to discourage unfair cross-subsidies;

Recital 11

Whereas, in accordance with Directive 90/387/EEC, the essential requirements on which restrictions on access to and usage of public telecommunications networks or services are justified are limited to security of network operations, maintenance of network integrity, interoperability of services in justified cases, and protection of data as appropriate; whereas the reasons for these restrictions must be made public;

Recital 12

Whereas facility-sharing can be of benefit for town planning, environmental, economic or other reasons, and should be encouraged by national regulatory authorities on the basis of voluntary agreements; whereas compulsory facility-sharing may be appropriate in some circumstances, but should be imposed on organizations only after full public consultation; whereas virtual collocation may in normal circumstances provide a satisfactory alternative to physical collocation of telecommunications equipment;

Recital 22

Whereas the essential goal of interconnection of networks and services throughout the Community and the provision of trans-European networks and services cannot be realized satisfactorily at Member State level, and is better achieved at Community level by this Directive; whereas it may appear desirable, when this Directive is reviewed, to envisage the possibility of establishing a European regulatory authority to ensure those tasks carried out by the Commission or the national regulatory authority according to this Directive, which would be more efficiently fulfilled through such a European regulatory authority;

Article 1(1)

1. This Directive establishes a regulatory framework for securing the interconnection and interoperability of telecommunications networks and services in the Community and ensuring universal service, in an environment of open and competitive markets.

Article 2(1)(h) (new)

(h) 'universal service' means a defined minimum service or set of services of specified quality which is accessible to all users everywhere and, in the light of specific national conditions, at an affordable price.

Article 3(1)

1. Member States shall take all necessary measures to remove any restrictions which prevent organizations authorized in Member States to provide telecommunications networks and telecommunications services from negotiating interconnection agreements between themselves in accordance

with Community law. The organizations concerned may be in the same Member State or in different Member States. Technical and commercial arrangements for interconnection shall be a matter for agreement between the parties involved, subject to the provisions of this Directive and the competition rules of the Treaty.

Article 3(3)

3.   Member States shall ensure that organizations which interconnect their facilities to public telecommunications networks and/or public telecommunications services respect at all times the confidentiality of information transmitted or stored, except when required by their national law for the protection of public order.

Article 5(5)

5.   Where a mechanism for sharing the net cost of universal service obligations as referred to in paragraph 4 is established, national regulatory authorities shall ensure that the principles for cost sharing, and details of the mechanism used, are open to public inspection in accordance with Article 14(2).

Article 6(1)

For interconnection to the public telecommunications networks and public telecommunications services identified in Annex I provided by organizations which have significant market power, Member States shall ensure that:

Article 6(d)

(d)   interconnection agreements and changes to them are communicated to the relevant national regulatory authorities and the Commission, and made available on request to interested parties, in accordance with Article 14(2), with the exception of those parts which deal with the commercial strategy of the parties. The national regulatory authority shall decide which parts deal with the commercial strategy of the parties. In every case, details of interconnection charges, terms and conditions and any contributions to universal service obligations shall be made available on request to interested parties.

Article 6(e) (new)

(e)   Information received from an organization seeking interconnection shall be used only for the purpose for which it was supplied. It shall not be passed on to other departments, subsidiaries or partners for whom such information could provide a competitive advantage.

Article 7(3)

3.   Charges for interconnection shall be based on the costs of providing the interconnection services requested, and shall normally contain the following elements, each of which should be itemized separately:

— a charge to cover reimbursement of the one-time costs incurred in providing the specific elements of the interconnection requested; (i.e. the initial and subsequent cost of any engineering work needed to provide the interconnection facilities requested);

— usage charges related to the utilization of the network elements and resources requested. These may include capacity-based charges and/or traffic related charges;

Annex IV indicates the types of costs that may be included in each of these tariff elements. Where other tariff elements are applied, these must be transparent and based on objective criteria, and approved by the national regulatory authority.

Charges for interconnection may include bulk discount schemes. In some cases, these may be available only to organizations identified in Annex II. Such schemes shall be based on objective criteria and applied in a non-discriminatory manner.

Article 7(5)

5.   National regulatory authorities shall ensure the publication, in accordance with Article 14(1), of terms and conditions for interconnection. This shall include a list of interconnection services and relevant tariffs broken down into components, according to market needs.

Article 7(5)(a) (new)

5.(a)   In order to provide a common basis for the derivation of interconnection charges, the Commission shall draw up, acting in accordance with the procedure in Article 15, guidelines on cost-accounting systems in relation to interconnection.

Article 7(8)

8.   Member States shall ensure that published interconnection charges, terms and conditions, and charges related to the sharing of the cost of universal service obligations are made available to the ONP Committee at the request of the Commission.

Article 7(9)(deleted)

Article 8(3)(a) (new)

3.(a)   the Commission shall, acting in accordance with the procedure laid down in Article 15, draw up guidelines on accounting separation in relation to interconnection.

Article 8(4)

4.   The financial accounts of organizations providing public telecommunications networks or public telecommunications services shall be drawn up, submitted to independent audit and published. The audit shall be carried out

in accordance with the relevant rules of national legislation, and its results shall be made public.

The first subparagraph shall also apply to the separate accounts established as required in paragraphs 1 and 2.

Article 8(6) (deleted)

Article 9(1)

1.   National regulatory authorities shall encourage and secure adequate interconnection in the interests of all users, exercising their responsibility in a way that provides maximum economic efficiency and gives the maximum benefit to end-users.

In particular, national regulatory authorities shall take into account:
— the need to ensure satisfactory end-to-end communications for users,
— the need to stimulate a competitive market,
— the need to ensure the fair and proper development of a seamless harmonious European telecommunication home market, thus coordinate their policies, guidelines and actions with their counterparts in other Member States and with the Commission,
— the need to promote the establishment and development of trans-European networks and services, and the interconnection and interoperability of national networks and services, as well as access to such networks and services.
— the principles of non-discrimination (including equal access) and proportionality,
— the need to maintain the universal service.

Article 9(5)

5.   In the event of an interconnection dispute between organizations operating under authorizations granted by the same Member State, the national regulatory authority of that Member State shall, on request of either party, take steps with a view to resolving the dispute.

In so doing, the national regulatory authority shall take into account, *inter alia*:
— the user interest,
— the need to maintain a universal service,
— regulatory obligations or constraints imposed on any of the parties,
— the desirability of stimulating innovative market offerings, and of providing users with a wide range of telecommunications services at a national and at a Community level,
— the availability of technically and commercially viable alternatives to the interconnection requested,
— the desirability of ensuring equal access arrangements,
— the need to maintain the integrity of the public telecommunications network and the interoperability of services,
— the nature of the request in relation to the resources available to meet the request,
— the relative market positions of the parties,
— the public interest (e.g. the protection of the environment).

Article 9(6)(a) (new)

6.(a)   National regulatory authorities shall provide help and assistance to their counterparts in other Member States whenever required in order to implement this Directive. The Commission may at any time request a national regulatory authority to intervene on specific issues. National regulatory authorities shall take due account of the Commission's request and inform the Commission in detail and without undue delay of the steps taken.

Article 10(e) (new)

(e)   Protection of the environment:
Member States may impose conditions in interconnection agreements in order to ensure the protection of the environment or comply with objectives of town-planning, and in particular to impose physical collocation of lines and ducts. The need to protect the environment does not constitute a valid reason for refusal to negotiate terms of interconnection.

Article 11(1)

Where an organization is granted a general right under national legislation to install facilities for telecommunications purposes on, over or under public or private land, or may take advantage of a procedure for the expropriation or use of property for telecommunications purposes, national regulatory authorities shall encourage the sharing of such facilities and property with other organizations providing public telecommunications networks and services.

Article 12(2)

In order to ensure full interoperability of European-wide networks and services, Member States shall ensure the coordination of their national positions in international organizations and forums where numbering decisions are taken, taking into account possible future developments in numbering at a European level.

Article 12(3)

3.   Member States shall ensure that national telecommunications numbering plans are controlled by the national regulatory authority, in order to guarantee independence from organizations providing public telecommunications networks or public telecommunications services and facilitate number portability. In order to ensure effective competition, national regulatory authorities shall ensure that the procedures for allocating individual numbers and/or numbering ranges are transparent, equitable and timely and the allocation is carried out in an objective, transparent and non-discriminatory manner. National regulatory authorities may lay down conditions for the use of certain prefixes or certain short codes, in particular where these are used for services of general public interest (e.g. freephone service, kiosk-billed services, directory services, emergency services), or to ensure equal access.

Article 12(5)

5. National regulatory authorities shall encourage the earliest possible introduction of the facility whereby end-users who so request can retain, against a reasonable contribution, their national number at a specific location independent of the organization providing service, and shall ensure that this facility is available at least in all major centres of population before 1 January 2003. If this facility is not yet in use, national regulatory authorities shall ensure that, once a user has changed supplier, a telephone call to his old number is rerouted to the user, or that during a reasonable period callers are given an indication of the new number.

Article 16(2)

2. Any party may refer the dispute to the national regulatory authorities concerned. The national regulatory authorities shall coordinate their efforts and shall inform the Commission in order to bring about a resolution of the dispute, in accordance with the principles set out in Article 9(1).

Article 16(5)

5. The position agreed in accordance with the procedure referred to in paragraph 4 shall form the basis of a solution to be implemented at a national level without delay. If an agreed position is not reached, or if an agreed position is not implemented within a reasonable time which shall not, except in justified cases, exceed two months, the appropriate solution shall be adopted by the Commission in accordance with the procedure laid down in Article 15. This solution does not prejudice the possibilities which exist in national legislation for one party to claim in the relevant courts for the granting of damages if it appears that the behaviour of another party has led to financial losses due to distortion of competition. However, issues which have been settled at EU level cannot be questioned under these claims.

Article 17(2)

2. National regulatory authorities shall notify to the Commission by 31 January 1997, and immediately thereafter in the event of any change, the names of those organizations which:
— have universal service obligations for the provision of the public tele-communications networks and services identified in Annex I, Part I,
— are subject to the provisions of this Directive concerning organizations with significant market power,
— are covered by Annex II.
The Commission may request national regulatory authorities to provide their reasons for classifying an organization as having significant market power or for not classifying an organization as such.

Article 19(1)

1. Member States with less-developed networks which are granted an additional period of up to five years in which to implement all or some of the

obligations under Directive 96/. . ./EC may request a corresponding deferment of some or all of the requirements of Articles 3(1) and 9(3), to the extent justified by any special or exclusive rights for telecommunications services and infrastructure allowed under Community law.

Article 19(2)

2.   Deferment from the obligations under Article 12(5) may be requested where the Member State concerned can prove that they would impose an excessive burden on certain organizations or classes of organization.

The Member State shall inform the Commission of the reasons for requesting a deferment, the date by which the requirements can be met, and the measures envisaged in order to meet this deadline. The Commission shall consider the request taking into account the particular situation in that Member State and the existing possibilities of otherwise meeting the requirements, and shall inform the Member State whether it deems that the particular situation in that Member State justifies a deferment and, if so, until which date such deferment is justified.

Article 21(2)

2.   The Commission shall examine and report to the European Parliament and to the Council on the functioning of this Directive, on the first occasion not later than 31 December 1999. For this purpose, the Commission may request information from the Member States. Where necessary, the report shall examine what provisions of this Directive should be adapted in the light of the developments in the market. Further measures can be proposed in the report for the full implementation of the aims of this Directive; in particular, the report shall examine the possibility of establishing a European regulatory authority to ensure those tasks carried out by the Commission or the national regulatory authorities according to this Directive, which would be more efficiently fulfilled through such a European regulatory authority.

ANNEX I   PART 1

The fixed public telephone service

The fixed public telephone service means the provision to end-users at fixed locations of a service for the originating and receiving of national and international calls, and includes access to emergency (112) services, the provision of operator assistance, directory information services, provision of public pay phones, provision of service under special terms and/or provision of special facilities for customers with disabilities.

ANNEX II(4)

4.   Organizations providing telecommunications services which are included in this category at their own request, under relevant national licensing or authorization schemes.

ANNEX VII   PART 2(n) (NEW)

(n)   provision of facility sharing,

ANNEX VII   PART 2(o) (NEW)

(o)   maintenance and quality of interconnection services

ANNEX VII   PART 2(p) (NEW)

(p)   protection of confidential information

ANNEX VII   PART 3(b)

(deleted)

ANNEX VII   PART 3(e)

(deleted)

SATELLITES

COMMISSION DIRECTIVE (94/46/EC) OF 13 OCTOBER 1994 AMENDING DIRECTIVE (88/301/EEC) IN PARTICULAR WITH REGARD TO SATELLITE COMMUNICATIONS
OJ L268/15, 19 October 1994

THE COMMISSION OF THE EUROPEAN COMMUNITIES,

Having regard to the Treaty establishing the European Community, and in particular Article 90 (3) thereof,

Whereas:

1. The Green Paper on a common approach in the field of satellite communications in the European Community, adopted by the Commission in November 1990, set out the major changes in the regulatory environment necessary to exploit the potential of this means of communications. This Satellite Green Paper called for, *inter alia*, full liberalization of the satellite services and equipment sectors, including the abolition of all exclusive or special nights in this area, subject to licensing procedures, as well as for the free (unrestricted) access to space segment capacity.

2. The Council Resolution of 19 December 1991 on the development of the common market for satellite communications services and equipment,[1] gave general support to the positions set out in the Commission's Satellite Green Paper, and considered as major goals: the harmonization and liberalization of the market for appropriate satellite earth stations, including where applicable the abolition of exclusive or special rights in this field, subject in particular to the conditions necessary for compliance with essential requirements.

3. The European Parliament, in its Resolution on the development of the common market for satellite communications services and equipment[2] calls upon the Commission to enact the necessary legislation in order to create the environment to enable existing constraints to be removed and new activities developed in the field of satellite communications, while stressing the need to harmonize and liberalize the markets in satellite equipment and services.

4. Several Member States have already opened up certain satellite communications services to competition and have introduced licensing schemes. Nevertheless, the granting of licences in some Member States still does not follow objective, proportional and non-discriminatory criteria or, in the case

---

1 OJ No C 8, 14. 1. 1992, p. 1.
2 OJ No C 42, 15. 2. 1993, p. 30.

of operators competing with the telecommunications organizations, is subject to technical restrictions such as a ban on connecting their equipment to be switched network operated by the telecommunications organization. Other Member States have maintained the exclusive rights granted to the national public undertakings.

5.   Commission Directive 88/301/EEC of 16 May 1988 on competition in the markets in telecommunications terminal equipment,[3] as amended by the Agreement on the European Economic Area, provides for the abolition of special or exclusive rights to import, market, connect, bring into service and maintain telecommunications terminal equipment. It does not cover all types of satellite earth station equipment.

6.   In its judgment in Case C-202/88, *France* v. *Commission*,[4] the Court of Justice of the European Communities upheld Commission Directive 88/301/ EEC. However, in so far as it relates to special rights, the Directive was declared void on the grounds that neither the provisions of the Directive nor the preamble thereto specify the type of rights which are actually involved and in what respect the existence of such rights is contrary to the various provisions of the Treaty. As far as importation, marketing, connection, bringing into service and maintenance of telecommunications equipment are concerned, special rights are in practice rights that are granted by a Member State to a limited number of undertakings, through any legislative, regulatory or administrative instrument which, within a given geographical area,

— limits to two or more the number of such undertaking, otherwise than according to objective, proportional and non-discriminatory criteria, or

— designates, otherwise than according to such criteria, several competing undertakings, or

— confers on any undertaking or undertakings, otherwise than according to such criteria, legal or regulatory advantages which substantially affect the ability of any other undertaking to engage in any of the abovementioned activities in the same geographical area under substantially equivalent conditions.

This definition is without prejudice to the application of Article 92 of the EC Treaty.

7.   The existence of exclusive rights has the effect of restricting the free movement of such equipment either as regards the importation and marketing of telecommunications equipment (including satellite equipment), because certain products are not marketed, or as regards the connection, bringing into service or maintenance because, taking into account the characteristics of the market and in particular the diversity and technical nature of the products, a monopoly has no incentive to provide these services in relation to products which it has not marketed or imported, nor to align its prices on costs, since there is no threat of competition from new entrants. Taking into account the fact that in most equipment markets there is typically a large range of telecommunication equipment, and the likely development of the markets in which there are as yet a limited number of manufacturers, any specialy right which directly or indirectly — for example by not providing for an open and non-discriminatory authorization procedure — limits the numb-

---

3 OJ No L 131, 27. 5. 1988, p. 73.
4 [1991] ECR I-1223.

er of the undertakings authorized to import, market, connect, bring into service and maintain such equipment, is liable to have the same kind of effect as the grant of exclusive rights.

Such exclusive or special rights constitute measures having equivalent effect to quantitative restrictions incompatible with Article 30 of the EC Treaty. None of the specific features of satellite earth stations or of the market for their sale or maintenance is such as to justify their being treated differently in law from other telecommunications terminal equipment. Thus it is necessary to abolish all existing exclusive rights in the importation, marketing, connection, bringing into service and maintenance of satellite earth station equipment, as well as those rights having comparable effects — that is to say, all special rights except those consisting in legal or regulatory advantages conferred on one or more undertakings and affecting only the ability of other undertakings to engage in any of the abovementioned activities in the same geographical area under substantially equivalent conditions.

8.   Satellite earth station equipment must satisfy the essential requirements harmonized by Council Directive 93/97/EEC[5] with special reference to the efficient use of frequencies. It will be possible to monitor the application of these essential requirements partly through the licences granted for the provision of the services concerned. Alignment on the essential requirements will be achieved mainly through the adoption of common technical rules and harmonization of the conditions attached to licences. Even where these conditions are not harmonized, Member States will nevertheless have to adapt their rules. In either case, Member States must in the meantime ensure that the application of such rules does not create barriers to trade.

9.   The abolition of special or exclusive rights relating to the connection of satellite earth station equipment makes it necessary to recognize the right to connect this equipment to the switched networks operated by the telecommunications organizations so that licensed operators can offer their services to the public.

10.   Commission Directive 90/388/EEC of 28 June 1990 on competition in the markets for telecommunications services,[6] as amended by the Agreement on the EEA, provides for the abolition of special or exclusive rights granted by Member States in respect of the provision of telecommunications services. However, the Directive excludes satellite services from its field of application.

11.   In Joined Cases C-271/90, C-281/90 and C-289/90, *Spain* v. *Commission*,[7] the Court of Justice of the European Communities upheld this Commission Directive on 17 November 1992. However, in so far as it relates to special rights, the Directive was declared void by the Court of Justice on the grounds that neither the provisions of the Directive nor the preamble thereto specify the type of rights which are actually involved and in what respect the existence of such rights is contrary to the various provisions of the Treaty. Consequently, these rights must be defined in this Directive. As far as telecommunications services are concerned, special rights are in practice rights that are granted by a Member State to a limited number of undertakings, through any legislative, regulatory or administrative instrument which, within a given geographical area,

---

5 OJ No L 290, 24. 11. 1993, p. 1.
6 OJ No L 192, 24. 7. 1990, p. 10.
7 [1992] ECRI-5833.

— limits to two or more, otherwise than according to objective, proportional and non-discriminatory criteria, the number of undertakings which are authorized to provide any such service, of

— designates, otherwise than according to such criteria, several competing undertakings as those which are authorized to provide any such service, or

— confers on any undertaking or undertakings, otherwise than according to such criteria, legal or regulatory advantages which substantially affect the ability of any other undertaking to provide the same telecommunications service in the same geographical area under substantially equivalent conditions.

This definition is without prejudice to the application of Article 92 of the EC Treaty.

In the field of telecommunications services, such special legal or regulatory advantages may consist, among other things, in a right to make compulsory purchases in the general interest, in derogations from law on town-and-country planning, or in the possibility of obtaining an authorization without having to go through the usual procedure.

12.   Where the number of undertakings authorized to provide satellite telecommunications services is limited by a Member State through special rights, and *a fortiori* exclusive rights, these constitute restrictions that could be incompatible with Article 59 of the Treaty, whenever such limitation is not justified by essential requirements, since these rights prevent other undertakings from supplying (or obtaining) the services concerned to (or from) other Member States. In the case of satellite network services, such essential requirements could be the effective use of the frequency spectrum and the avoidance of harmful interference between satellite telecommunications systems a other space-based or terrestrial technical systems. Consequently, provided that equipment used to offer the services satisfies the essential requirement applicable to satellite communications, separate legal treatment of the latter is not justified. On the other hand, special rights consisting only in special legal or regulatory advantages, do not, in principle, preclude other undertakings from entering the market. The compatibility of these rights with the EC Treaty must therefore be assessed on a case-by-case basis, regard being had to their impact on the effective freedom of other entities to provide the same telecommunications service and their possible justifications regarding the activity concerned.

13.   The exclusive rights that currently exist in the satellite communications field were generally granted to organizations that already enjoyed a dominant position in creating the terrestrial networks, or to one of their subsidiaries. Such rights have the effect of extending the dominant position enjoyed by those organizations and therefore strengthening that position. The exclusive rights granted in the satellite communications field are consequently incompatible with Article 90 of the EC Treaty, read in conjunction with Article 86.

14.   These exclusive rights limiting access to the market also have the effect of restricting or preventing, to the detriment of users, the use of satellite communications that could be offered, thereby holding back technical progress in this area. Because their investment decisions are likely to be based on exclusive rights, the undertakings concerned are often in a position to decide to give priority to terrestrial technologies, whereas new entrants might exploit

satellite technology. The telecommunications organizations have generally given preference to the development of optical-fibre terrestrial links, and satellite communications have been used chiefly as a technical solution of last resort in cases where the cost of the terrestrial alternatives has been prohibitive, or for the purpose of data broadcasting and/or television broadcasting, rather than being used as a fully complementary transmission technology in its own right. Thus the exclusive rights imply a restriction on the development of satellite communication, and this is incompatible with Article 90 of the Treaty, read in conjunction with Article 86.

15. However, where the provision of satellite services is concerned, licensing or declaration procedures are justified in order to ensure compliance with essential requirements, subject to the proportionality principle. Licensing is not justified when a mere declaration procedure would suffice to attain the relevant objective. For example, in the case of provision of a satellite service which involves only the use of a dependent VSAT earth station in a Member State, the latter should impose no more than a declaration procedure.

16. Article 90 (2) of the Treaty provides for an exception to Article 86 in cases where the application of the latter would obstruct the performance, in law or infact, of the particular tasks assigned to the telecommunications organizations. Pursuant to that provision, Directive 90/388/EEC allows exclusive rights to be maintained for a transitional period in respect of voice telephony.

'Voice telephony' is defined in Article 1 of Directive 90/388/EEC as the commercial provision for the public of the direct transport and switching of speech in real-time between public switched network termination points, enabling any user to use equipment connected to such a network termination point in order to communicate with another termination point. In the case of direct transport and switching of speech via satellite earth station networks, such commercial provision for the public in general can take place only when the satellite earth station network is connected to the public switched network.

As regards all services other than voice telephony, no special treatment under Article 90(2) is justified especially in view of the insignificant contribution of such services to the turnover of the telecommunications organizations.

17. The provision of satellite network services for the conveyance of radio and television programmes is a telecommunications service for the purpose of this Directive and thus subject to its provisions. Notwithstanding the abolition of certain special and exclusive rights in respect of receive-only satellite earth stations not connected to the public network of a Member State and the abolition of special and exclusive rights in respect of satellite services provided for public or private broadcasters, the content of satellite broadcasting services to the general public or private broadcasters, the content of satellite broadcasting services to the general public provided via frequency bands defined in the Radio Regulations for both Broadcasting Satellite Services (BSS) and Fixed-Satellite Services (FSS) will continue to be subject to specific rules adopted by Member States in accordance with Community law and is not, therefore, subject to the provisions of this Directive.

18. This Directive does not prevent measure being adopted in accordance with Community law and existing international obligations so as to ensure

that nationals of Member States are afforded equivalent treatment in third countries.

19.   The offering by satellite operators of space segment capacity of national, private or international satellite systems to licensed satellite earth station network operators, is still, in some Member States, subject to regulatory restrictions other than those compatible with frequency and site coordination arrangements required under the international commitments of Member States. These additional restrictions are contrary to Article 59, which implies that such satellite operators should have full freedom to provide their services in the whole Community, once they are licensed in one Member State.

20.   Tests to establish whether satellite earth stations of licensed operators other than national operators conform to specifications governing technical and operational access to intergovernmental satellite systems, are, in most of the Member States, carried out by the national Signatory of the nation upon whose territory the station is operating. These conformity assessments are therefore performed by service providers which are competitors.

This is not compatible with the Treaty provisions, notably Articles 3 (g) and 90, read in conjunction with Article 86. Member States therefore need to ensure that these conformity assessments can be carred out direct between the satellite earth station network operator concerned and the intergovernmental organization itself, under supervision of the regulatory authorities alone.

21.   Most of the available space segment capacity is offered by the international satellite organizations. The charges for using such capacity are still high in many Member States because the capacity can be acquired only from the signatory for the Member State in question. Such exclusivity, permitted by some Member States, leads to a partitioning of the Common Market to the detriment of customers requiring capacity. In its resolution of 19 December 1991, the Council consequently called on the Member States to improve access to the space segment of the intergovernmental organizations. As regards the establishment and use of separate systems, restrictive measure taken under international conventions signed by Member States could also have effects incompatible with Community law, by limiting supply at the expense of the consumer within meaning of Article 86 (b). Within the international satellite organizations, reviews of the provisions of the relevant constituent instruments are under way, *inter alia*, in respect of improved access and in respect of the establishment and use of separate systems. In order to enable the Commission to carry out the monitoring task assigned to it by the EC Treaty, instruments should be provided to help Member States to comply with the duty of cooperation enshrined in the first paragraph of Article 5, read in conjunction with Article 234 (2), of the Treaty.

22.   In assessing the measures of this Directive, the Commission, in the context of the achievement of the fundamental objectives of the Treaty referred to in Article 2 thereof, including that of strengthening the Community's economic and social cohesion as referred to in Article 130 (a), will also take into account the situation of those Member States in which the terrestrial network is not yet sufficiently developed and which could justify the deferment for these Member States, as regards satellite services and to the extent necessary, of the date of full application of the provisions of this Directive until 1 January 1996,

HAS ADOPTED THIS DIRECTIVE:

Article 1

Directive 88/301/EEC is hereby amended as follows:
  (a) The last sentence of the first indent is replaced by the following:
'Terminal equipment also means satellite earth station equipment'.
  (b) The following indents are added after the second indent:
  — special rights' means rights that are granted by a Member State to
a limited number of undertakings, through any legislative, regulatory or
administrative instrument, which, within a given geographical area,
  — limits to two or more the number of such undertakings, otherwise than according to objective, proportional and non-discriminatory
criteria, or
  — designates, otherwise than according to such criteria, several
competing undertakings, or
  — confers on any undertaking or undertakings, otherwise than
according to such criteria, any legal or regulatory advantages which
substantially affect the ability of any other undertaking to import,
market, connect, bring into service and/or maintain telecommunication
terminal equipment in the same geographical area under substantially
equivalent conditions;
  — 'satellite earth station equipment' means equipment which is capable of being used for the transmission only, or for the transmission and
reception ('transmit/receive'), or for the reception only ('receive-only') of
radiocommunication signals by means of satellites or other space-based
systems'
  2. The first paragraph of Article 2 is replaced by the following text.
'Member States which habe granted special or exclusive rights to
undertakings shall ensure that all exclusive rights are withdrawn, as well
as those special rights which
  (a) limit two or more the number of undertakings within the
meaning of Article 1, otherwise than according to objective, proportional
and non-discriminatory criteria, or
  (b) designate, otherwise than according to such criteria, several
competing undertakings within the meaning of Article 1.'
  3. The first indent of Article 3 is replaced by the following text:
  '— in the case of satellite earth station equipment, refuse to allow such
equipment to be connected to the public telecommunications network
and/or to be brought into service where it does not satisfy the relevant
common technical regulations adopted in pursuance of Council Directive 93/97/EEC[1] or, in the absence thereof, the essential requirements
laid down in Article 4 of that Directive. In the absence of common
technical rules of harmonized regulatory conditions, national rules shall
be proportionate to those essential requirements and shall be notified to
the Commission in pursuance of Directive 83/189/EEC where that
Directive so requires.
  — in the case of other terminal equipment, refuse to allow such
equipment to be connected to the public telecommunications network
where it does not satisfy the relevant common technical regulations

adopted in pursuance of Council Directive 91/263/EEC or, in the absence thereof, the essential requirements laid down in Article 4 of that Directive.

Notes to the amendment
1 OJ No L 290, 24.11.1993, p. 1.
2 OJ No L 128, 23.5.1991, p. 1.

Article 2

Directive 90/388/EEC is hereby amended as follows:

1. Article 1 is amended as follows:
    (a) Paragraph 1 is amended as follows:
        (i) the seconds indent is replaced by the following:
        '— exclusive rights' means the rights that are granted by a Member State to one undertaking through any legislative, regulatory or administrative instrument, reserving it the right to provide a telecommunication service or undertake an activity within a given geographical area.';
        (ii) The following is inserted as the third indent:
        '—"special rights" means the rights that are granted by a Member State to a limited number of undertakings through any legislative, regulatory or administrative instrument which, within a given geographical area,
        — limits to two or more the number of such undertakings authorized to provide a service or undertake an activity, otherwise than according to objective, proportional and non-discriminatory criteria, or
        — designates, otherwise than according to such criteria, several competing undertakings as being authorized to provide a service or undertake an activity, or
        — confers on any undertaking or undertakings, otherwise than according to such criteria, legal or regulatory advantages which substantially affect the ability of any other undertaking to provide the same telecommunications service or to undertake the same activity in the same geographical area under substantially equivalent conditions.'
        (iii) The fourth indent is replaced by the following:
        '— "telecommunications services" means services whose provision consists wholly or partly in the transmission and routing of signals on a public telecommunications network by means of telecommunications processes, with the exception of radio- and television-broadcasting to the public, and satellite services.'
        (iv) the following indents are inserted after the fourth indent:
        '— "satellite earth station network" means a configuration of two or more earth stations which interwork by means by means of a satellite;
        — "satellite network services" means the establishment and operation of satellite earth station networks; these services consist, as a minimum, in the establishment, by satellite earth stations, of radiocommunications to space segment ('uplinks'), and in the establishment of radiocommunications between space segment and satellite earth stations ('downlinks');
        — "satellite communications services" means service whose provision makes use, wholly or partly, of satellite network services;

— "satellite services" means the provision of satellite communications services and/or the provision of satellite networks services;'

(v) the second sentence of the sixth indent is replaced by the following text:

'Those reasons are security of network operations, maintenance of network integrity, and, in justified cases, interoperability of services, data protection and, in the case of satellite network services, the effective use of the frequency spectrum and the avoidance of harmful interference between satellite telecommunications systems and other space-based or terrestrial technical systems.'

(b) Paragraph 2 is replaced by the following:

'2. This Directive shall not apply to the telex service or to terrestrial mobile radiocommunications.'

2. Article 2 is amended as follows:

(a) The first paragraph is replaced by the following:

'Without prejudice to Article 1 (2), Member States shall withdraw all those measures which grant:

(a) exclusive rights for the supply of telecommunications services otherwise than voice telephony and

(b) special rights which limit to two or more the number of undertakings authorized to supply such telecommunication services, otherwise than according to objective, proportional and non-discriminatory criteria, or

(c) special rights which designate, otherwise than according to such criteria, several competing undertakings to provide such telecommunication services.

They shall take the measures necessary to ensure that any operator is entitled to supply any such telecommunications services, otherwise than voice telephony'.

(b) The following paragraphs are added:

'Member States shall communicate the criteria on which authorizations are granted, together with the conditions attached to such authorizations and to the declaration procedures for the operation of transmitting earth stations.

Member States shall continue to inform the Commission of any plans to introduce new licensing procedures or to change existing procedures'.

3. Article 6 is amended as follows:

(a) The following paragraphs are added after the second paragraph:

'Member States shall ensure that any fees imposed on providers of services as part of authorization procedures, shall be based on objective, transparent and non-discriminatory criteria.

Fees, the criteria upon which they are based, and any changes thereto, shall be published in an appropriate and sufficiently detailed manner, so as to provide easy access to that information.

Member States shall notify to the Commission no later than nine months after publication of this Directive, and thereafter whenever changes occur, the manner in which the information is made available. The Commission shall regularly publish references to such notifications.'

(b) The following paragraph is added:

'Member States shall ensure that any regulatory prohibition or restrictions on the offer of space-segment capacity to any authorized satellite earth station network operator are abolished, and shall authorize within their territory any space-segment supplier to verify that the satellite earth station network for use in connection with the space segment of the supplier in question is in conformity with the published conditions for access to his space segment capacity.'

Article 3

Member States which are party to the international conventions setting up the international organizations Intelsat, Inmarsat, Eutelsat and Intersputnik for the purposes of satellite operations shall communicate to the Commission, at its request, the information they possess on any measure that could prejudice compliance with the competition rules of the EC Treaty or affect the aims of this Directive or of the Council Directives on telecommunications.

Article 4

Member States shall supply to the Commission, not later than nine months after this Directive has entered into force, such information as will allow the Commission to confirm that Articles 1 and 2 have been complied with.

Article 5

This Directive shall enter into force on the twentieth day following that of its publication in the *Official Journal of the European Communities.*

Article 6

This Directive is addressed to the Member States.

Done at Brussels, 13 October 1994.

For the Commission
Karel Van Miert
Member of the Commission

Notes

1. On **satellite personal communications services** see:
    Council Resolution of 7 December 1993 on the introduction of satellite personal communications in the Community, OJ C339/1, 16.12.93.
    Council Resolution of 29 June 1995 on the further developments on mobile and personal communications in the European Union, OJ C188/3, 22.7.95.
    Proposal for a European Parliament and Council Decision on an action at a Union level in the field of satellite personal communications services in the European Union, COM(95)529, 8 November 1995.
See also the amended proposal: on a common framework for the harmonised development of satellite personal communications services in the European Union (OJ C350/14, 21.11.96).

2. On the **encryption of satellite signals** see:
    Commission Green Paper on legal protection of encrypted services in the internal market COM (96) 76, 6 March 1996.

COMPETITION

GUIDELINES ON THE APPLICATION OF EEC COMPETITION RULES IN THE TELECOMMUNICATIONS SECTOR
(91/C 233/02)
OJ C233/2, 6 September 1991

PREFACE

These guidelines aim at clarifying the application of Community competition rules to the market participants in the telecommunications sector. They must be viewed in the context of the special conditions of the telecommunications sector, and the overall Community telecommunications policy will be taken into account in their application. In particular, account will have to be taken of the actions the Commission will be in a position to propose for the telecommunications industry as a whole, actions deriving from the assessment of the state of play and issues at stake for this industry, as has already been the case for the European electronics and information technology industry in the communication of the Commission of 3 April 1991.[1]

A major political aim, as emphasized by the Commission, the Council, and the European Parliament, must be the development of efficient Europe-wide networks and services, at the lowest cost and of the highest quality, to provide the European user in the single market of 1992 with a basic infrastructure for efficient operation.

The Commission has made it clear in the past that in this context it is considered that liberalization and harmonization in the sector must go hand in hand.

Given the competition context in the telecommunications sector, the telecommunications operators should be allowed, and encouraged, to establish the necessary cooperation mechanisms, in order to create — or ensure — Community-wide full interconnectivity between public networks, and where required between services to enable European users to benefit from a wider range of better and cheaper telecommunications services.

This can and has to be done in compliance with, and respect of, EEC competition rules in order to avoid the diseconomies which otherwise could result. For the same reasons, operators and other firms that may be in a dominant market position should be made aware of the prohibition of abuse of such positions.

---

1 The European electronics and information technology industry: state of play, issues at stake and proposals for action, SEC(91) 565, 3 April 1991.

The guidelines should be read in the light of this objective. They set out to clarify, *inter alia*, which forms of cooperation amount to undesirable collusion, and in this sense they list what is *not* acceptable. They should therefore be seen as one aspect of an overall Community policy towards telecommunications, and notably of policies and actions to encourage and stimulate those forms of cooperation which promote the development and availability of advanced communications for Europe.

The full application of competition rules forms a major part of the Community's overall approach to telecommunications. These guidelines should help market participants to shape their strategies and arrangements for Europe-wide networks and services from the outset in a manner which allows them to be fully in line with these rules. In the event of significant changes in the conditions which prevailed when the guidelines were drawn up, the Commission may find it appropriate to adapt the guidelines to the evolution of the situation in the telecommunications sector.

I SUMMARY

1.   The Commission of the European Communities in its Green Paper on the development of the common market for telecommunications services and equipment (COM(87)290) dated 30 June 1987 proposed a number of Community positions. Amongst these, positions (H) and (I) are as follows:

'(H)   strict continuous review of operational (commercial) activities of telecommunications administrations according to Articles 85, 86 and 90 of the EEC Treaty. This applies in particular to practices of cross-subsidization of activities in the competitive services sector and of activities in manufacturing;

(J)   strict continuous review of all private providers in the newly opened sectors according to Articles 85 and 86, in order to avoid the abuse of dominant positions;'.

2.   These positions were restated in the Commission's document of 9 February 1988 'Implementing the Green Paper on the development of the common market for telecommunications services and equipment/state of discussions and proposals by the Commission' (COM(88)48). Among the areas where the development of concrete policy actions is now possible, the Commission indicated the following:

'Ensuring fair conditions of competition:

Ensuring an open competitive market makes continuous review of the telecommunications sector necessary.

The Commission intends to issue guidelines regarding the application of competition rules to the telecommunications sector and on the way that the review should be carried out.'

This is the objective of this communication.

The telecommunications sector in many cases requires cooperation agreements, *inter alia*, between telecommunications organizations (TOs) in order to ensure network and services interconnectivity, one-stop shopping and one-stop billing which are necessary to provide for Europe-wide services and to offer optimum service to users. These objectives can be achieved, *inter alia*, by TOs cooperating — for example, in those areas where exclusive or special rights for provision may continue in accordance with Community law, including competition law, as well as in areas where optimum service will require certain features of cooperation. On the other hand the overriding objective to develop the conditions for the market to provide European users with a greater variety of telecommunications services, of better quality and at lower cost requires the introduction and safeguarding of a strong competitive structure. Competition plays a central role for the Community, especially in view of the completion of the single market for 1992. This role has already been emphasized in the Green Paper.

The single market will represent a new dimension for telecoms operators and users. Competition will give them the opportunity to make full use of technological development and to accelerate it, and encouraging them to restructure and reach the necessary economies of scale to become competitive not only on the Community market, but worldwide.

With this in mind, these guidelines recall the main principles which the Commission, according to its mandate under the Treaty's competition rules, has applied and will apply in the sector without prejudging the outcome of any specific case which will have to be considered on the facts.

The objective is, *inter alia*, to contribute to more certainty of condititions for investment in the sector and the development of Europe-wide services.

The mechanisms for creating certainty for individual cases (apart from complaints and ex-officio investigations) are provided for by the notification and negative clearance procedures provided under Regulation No 17, which give a formal procedure for clearing cooperation agreements in this area whenever a formal clearance is requested. This is set out in further detail in this communication.

II INTRODUCTION

3.   The fundamental technological development worldwide in the telecommunications sector[2] has caused considerable changes in the competition conditions. The traditional monopolistic administrations cannot alone take up the challenge of the technological revolution. New economic forces have appeared on the telecoms scene which are capable of offering users the numerous enhanced services generated by the new technologies. This has given rise to and stimulated a wide deregulation process propagated in the Community with various degrees of intensity.

This move is progressively changing the face of the European market structure. New private suppliers have penetrated the market with more and more transnational value-added services and equipment. The telecommunications administrations, although keeping a central role as public services providers, have acquired a business-like way of thinking. They have started competing dynamically with private operators in services and equipment. Wide restructuring, through mergers and joint ventures, is taking place in order to compete more effectively on the deregulated market through economies of scale and rationalization. All these events have a multiplier effect on technological progress.

---

2 Telecommunications embraces any transmission, emission or reception of signs, signals, writing, images and sounds or intelligence of any nature by wire, radio, optical and other electromagnetic systems (Article 2 of WATTC Regulation of 9 December 1988).

4. In the light of this, the central role of competition for the Community appears clear, especially in view of the completion of the single market for 1992. This role has already been emphasized in the Green Paper.

5. In the application of competition rules the Commission endeavours to avoid the adopting of State measures or undertakings erecting or maintaining artificial barriers incompatible with the single market. But it also favours all forms of cooperation which foster innovation and economic progress, as contemplated by competition law. Pursuing effective competition in telecoms is not a matter of political choice. The choice of a free market and a competition-oriented economy was already envisaged in the EEC Treaty, and the competition rules of the Treaty are directly applicable within the Community. The abovementioned fundamental changes make necessary the full application of competition law.

6. There is a need for more certainty as to the application of competition rules. The telecommunication administrations together with keeping their duties of public interest, are now confronted with the application of these rules practically without transition from a long tradition of legal protection. Their scope and actual implications are often not easily perceivable. As the technology is fast-moving and huge investments are necessary, in order to benefit from the new possibilities on the market-place, all the operators, public or private, have to take quick decisions, taking into account the competition regulatory framework.

7. This need for more certainty regarding the application of competition rules is already met by assessments made in several individual cases. However, assessments of individual cases so far have enabled a response to only some of the numerous competition questions which arise in telecommunications. Future cases will further develop the Commission's practice in this sector.

Purpose of these guidelines

8. These guidelines are intended to advise public telecommunications operators, other telecommunications service and equipment suppliers and users, the legal profession and the interested members of the public about the general legal and economic principles which have been and are being followed by the Commission in the application of competition rules to undertakings in the telecommunications sector, based on experience gained in individual cases in compliance with the rulings of the Court of Justice of the European Communities.

9. The Commission will apply these principles also to future individual cases in a flexible way, and taking the particular context of each case into account. These guidelines do not cover all the general principles governing the application of competition rules, but only those which are of specific relevance to telecommunication issues. The general principles of competition rules not specifically connected with telecommunications but entirely applicable to these can be found, *inter alia*, in the regulatory acts, the Court judgments and the Commission decisions dealing with the individual cases, the Commission's yearly reports on competition policy, press releases and other public information originating from the Commission.

10. These guidelines do not create enforceable rights. Moreover, they do not prejudice the application of EEC competition rules by the Court of Justice of the European Communities and by national authorities (as these rules may be directly applied in each Member State, by the national authorities, administrative or judicial).

11. A change in the economic and legal situation will not automatically bring about a simultaneous amendment to the guidelines. The Commission, however, reserves the possibility to make such an amendment when it considers that these guidelines no longer satisfy their purpose, because of fundamental and/or repeated changes in legal precedents, methods of applying competition rules, and the regulatory, economic and technical context.

12. These guidelines essentially concern the direct application of competition rules to undertakings, i.e. Articles 85 and 86 of the EEC Treaty. They do not concern those applicable to the Member States, in particular Articles 5 and 90(1) and (3). Principles ruling the application of Article 90 in telecommunications are expressed in Commission Directives adopted under Article 90 (3) for the implementation of the Green Paper.[3]

Relationship between competition rules applicable to undertakings and those applicable to Member States

13. The Court of Justice of the European Communities[4] has ruled that while it is true that Articles 85 and 86 of the Treaty concern the conduct of undertakings and not the laws or regulations of the Member States, by virtue of Article 5 (2) of the EEC Treaty, Member States must not adopt or maintain in force any measure which could deprive those provisions of their effectiveness. The Court has stated that such would be the case, in particular, if a Member State were to require or favour prohibited cartels or reinforce the effects thereof or to encourage abuses by dominant undertakings.

If those measures are adopted or maintained in force *vis-à-vis* public undertakings or undertakings to which a Member State grants special or exclusive rights, Article 90 might also apply.

14. When the conduct of a public undertaking or an undertaking to which a Member State grants special or exclusive rights arises entirely as a result of the exercise of the undertaking's autonomous behaviour, it can only be caught by Articles 85 and 86.

When this behaviour is imposed by a mandatory State measure (regulative or administrative), leaving no discretionary choice to the undertakings concerned, Article 90 may apply to the State involved in association with Articles 85 and 86. In this case Articles 85 and 86 apply to the undertakings' behaviour taking into account the constraints to which the undertakings are submitted by the mandatory State measure.

Ultimately, when the behaviour arises from the free choice of the undertakings involved, but the State has taken a measure which encourages the

---

3 Commission Directive 88/301/EEC of 16 May 1988 on competition in the markets in telecommunications terminal equipment (OJ No L 131, 27. 5. 1988, p. 73).

Commission Directive 90/388/EEC of 28 June 1990 on competition in the markets for telecommunications services (OJ No L 192, 24. 7. 1990, p. 10).

4 Judgment of 10. 1. 1985 in Case 229/83, *Leclerc/gasoline* [1985] ECR 17; Judgment of 11. 7. 1985 in Case 299/83, *Leclerc/books* [1985] ECR 2517; Judgment of 30. 4. 1986 in Cases from 209 to 213/84, *Ministère public* v *Asjes* [1986] ECR 1425; Judgment of 1. 10. 1987 in Case 311/85, *Vereniging van Vlaamse Reisbureaus* v *Sociale Dienst van de Plaatselijke en Gewestelijke Overheidsdiensten* [1987] ECR 3801.

behaviour or strengthens its effects, Articles 85 and/or 86 apply to the undertakings' behaviour and Article 90 may apply to the State measure. This could be the case, *inter alia*, when the State has approved and/or legally endorsed the result of the undertakings' behaviour (for instance tariffs).

These guidelines and the Article 90 Directives complement each other to a certain extent in that they cover the principles governing the application of the competition rules: Articles 85 and 86 on the one hand, Article 90 on the other.

Application of competition rules and other Community law, including open network provision (ONP) rules

15. Articles 85 and 86 and Regulations implementing those Articles in application of Article 87 of the EEC Treaty constitute law in force and enforceable throughout the Community. Conflicts should not arise with other Community rules because Community law forms a coherent regulatory framework. Other Community rules, and in particular those specifically governing the telecommunications sector, cannot be considered as provisions implementing Articles 85 and 86 in this sector. However it is obvious that Community acts adopted in the telecommunications sector are to be interpreted in a way consistent with competition rules, so to ensure the best possible implementation of all aspects of the Community telecommunications policy.

16. This applies, *inter alia*, to the relationship between competition rules applicable to undertakings and the ONP rules. According to the Council Resolution of 30 June 1988 on the development of the common market for telecommunications services and equipment up to 1992,[5] ONP comprises the 'rapid definition, by Council Directives, of technical conditions, usage conditions, and tariff principles for open network provision, starting with harmonized conditions for the use of leased lines'. The details of the ONP procedures have been fixed by Directive 90/387/EEC[6] on the establishment of the internal market for telecommunications services through the implementation of open network provision, adopted by Council on 28 June 1990 under Article 100a of the EEC Treaty.

17. ONP has a fundamental role in providing European-wide access to Community-wide interconnected public networks. When ONP harmonization is implemented, a network user will be offered harmonized access conditions throughout the EEC, whichever country they address. Harmonized access will be ensured in compliance with the competition rules as mentioned above, as the ONP rules specifically provide.

ONP rules cannot be considered as competition rules which apply to States and/or to undertakings' behaviour. ONP and competition rules therefore constitute two different but coherent sets of rules. Hence, the competition rules have full application, even when all ONP rules have been adopted.

18. Competition rules are and will be applied in a coherent manner with Community trade rules in force. However, competition rules apply in a non-discriminatory manner to EEC undertakings and to non-EEC ones which have access to the EEC market.

---

5 OJ No C 257, 4. 10. 1988, p. 1.
6 OJ No L 192, 24. 7. 1990. p. 1.

III   COMMON PRINCIPLES OF APPLICATION OF ARTICLES 85 AND 86

Equal application of Articles 85 and 86

19.   Articles 85 and 86 apply directly and throughout the Community to all undertakings, whether public or private, on equal terms and to the same extent, apart from the exception provided in Article 90 (2).[7]
The Commission and national administrative and judicial authorities are competent to apply these rules under the conditions set out in Council Regulation No 17.[8]
20.   Therefore, Articles 85 and 86 apply both to private enterprises and public telecommunications operators embracing telecommunications administrations and recognized private operating agencies, hereinafter called 'telecommunications organizations' (TOs).
TOs are undertakings within the meaning of Articles 85 and 86 to the extent that they exert an economic activity, for the manufacturing and/or sale of telecommunications equipment and/or for the provision of telecommunications services, regardless of other facts such as, for example, whether their nature is economic or not and whether they are legally distinct entities or form part of the State organization.[9] Associations of TOs are associations of undertakings within the meaning of Article 85, even though TOs participate as undertakings in organizations in which governmental authorities are also represented.
Articles 85 and 86 apply also to undertakings located outside the EEC when restrictive agreements are implemented or intended to be implemented or abuses are committed by those undertakings within the common market to the extent that trade between Member States is affected.[10]

Competition restrictions justified under Article 90 (2) or by essential requirements

21.   The exception provided in Article 90 (2) may apply both to State measures and to practices by undertakings. The Services Directive 90/388/ EEC, in particular in Article 3, makes provision for a Member State to impose specified restrictions in the licences which it can grant for the provision of certain telecommunications services. These restrictions may be imposed under Article 90 (2) or in order to ensure the compliance with State essential requirements specified in the Directive.
22.   As far as Article 90 (2) is concerned, the benefit of the exception provided by this provision may still be invoked for a TO's behaviour when it

---

7 Article 90 (2) states: 'Undertakings entrusted with the operation of services of general economic interest or having the character of a revenue-producing monopoly shall be subject to the rules contained in this Treaty, in particular to the rules on competition, in so far as the application of such rules does not obstruct the performance, in law or in fact, of the particular tasks assigned to them. The development of trade must not be affected to such an extent as would be contrary to the interests of the Community'.
8 OJ No 13, 21. 2. 1962, p. 204/62 (Special Edition 1959–62, p. 87).
9 See Judgment of the Court 16. 6. 1987 in Case 118/85, *Commission v Italy — Transparency of Financial Relations between Member States and Public Undertakings* [1987] ECR 2599.
10 See Judgment of the Court of 27. 9. 1988 in Joined Cases 89, 104, 114, 116, 117, 125, 126, 127, 129/85, *Ålström others v Commission ('Woodpulp')*, [1988] ECR 5193.

brings about competition restrictions which its Member State did not impose in application of the Services Directive. However, the fact should be taken into account that in this case the State whose function is to protect the public and the general economic interest, did not deem it necessary to impose the said restrictions. This makes particularly hard the burden of proving that the Article 90 (2) exception still applies to an undertakings's behaviour involving these restrictions.

23. The Commission infers from the case law of the Court of Justice[11] that it has exclusive competence, under the control of the Court, to decide that the exception of Article 90 (2) applies. The national authorities including judicial authorities can assess that this exception does not apply, when they find that the competition rules clearly do not obstruct the performance of the task of general economic interest assigned to undertakings. When those authorities cannot make a clear assessment in this sense they should suspend their decision in order to enable the Commission to find that the conditions for the application of that provision are fulfilled.

24. As to measures aiming at the compliance with 'essential requirements' within the meaning of the Services Directive, under Article 1 of the latter,[12] they can only be taken by Member States and not by undertakings.

The relevant market

25. In order to assess the effects of an agreement on competition for the purposes of Article 85 and whether there is a dominant position on the market for the purposes of Article 86, it is necessary to define the relevant market(s), product or service market(s) and geographic market(s), within the domain of telecommunications. In a context of fast-moving technology the relevant market definition is dynamic and variable.

(a)   The product market

26. A product market comprises the totality of the products which, with respect to their characteristics, are particularly suitable for satisfying constant needs and are only to a limited extent interchangeable with other products in terms of price, usage and consumer preference. An examination limited to the objective characteristics only of the relevant products cannot be sufficient: the competitive conditions and the structure of supply and demand on the market must also be taken into consideration.[13]

The Commission can precisely define these markets only within the framework of individual cases.

27. For the guidelines' purpose it can only be indicated that distinct service markets could exist at least for terrestrial network provision, voice communication, data communication and satellites. With regard to the equipment market, the following areas could all be taken into account for the purposes of market definition: public switches, private switches, transmission

---

11 Case 10/71, *Mueller-Hein* [1971] ECR 723; Judgment of 11. 4. 1989 in Case 66/86, *Ahmed Saeed* [1989] ECR 803.
12 '. . . the non-economic reasons in the general interest which may cause a Member State to restrict access to the public telecommunications network or public telecommunications services.'
13 Case 322/81, *Michelin v Commission*, 9 November 1983 [1983] ECR 3529, Ground 37.

systems and more particularly, in the field of terminals, telephone sets, modems, telex terminals, data transmission terminals and mobile telephones. The above indications are without prejudice to the definition of further narrower distinct markets. As to other services — such as value-added ones — as well as terminal and network equipment, it cannot be specified here whether there is a market for each of them or for an aggregate of them, or for both, depending upon the interchangeability existing in different geographic markets. This is mainly determined by the supply and the requirements in those markets.

28.   Since the various national public networks compete for the installation of the telecommunication hubs of large users, market definition may accordingly vary. Indeed, large telecommunications users, whether or not they are service providers, locate their premises depending, *inter alia*, upon the features of the telecommunications services supplied by each TO. Therefore, they compare national public networks and other services provided by the TOs in terms of characteristics and prices.

29.   As to satellite provision, the question is whether or not it is substantially interchangeable with terrestrial network provision:

(a)   communication by satellite can be of various kinds: fixed service (point to point communication), multipoint (point to multipoint and multipoint to multipoint), one-way or two-way;

(b)   satellites' main characteristics are: coverage of a wide geographic area not limited by national borders, insensitivity of costs to distance, flexibility and ease of networks deployment, in particular in the very small aperture terminals (VSAT) systems;

(c)   satellites' uses can be broken down into the following categories: public switched voice and data transmission, business value-added services and broadcasting;

(d)   a satellite provision presents a broad interchangeability with the terrestrial transmission link for the basic voice and data transmission on long distance. Conversely, because of its characteristics it is not substantially interchangeable but rather complementary to terrestrial transmission links for several specific voice and data transmission uses. These uses are: services to peripheral or less-developed regions, links between non-contiguous countries, reconfiguration of capacity and provision of routing for traffic restoration. Moreover, satellites are not currently substantially interchangeable for direct broadcasting and multipoint private networks for value-added business services. Therefore, for all those uses satellites should constitute distinct product markets. Within satellites, there may be distinct markets.

30.   In mobile communications distinct services seem to exist such as cellular telephone, paging, telepoint, cordless voice and cordless data communication. Technical development permits providing each of these systems with more and more enhanced features. A consequence of this is that the differences between all these systems are progressively blurring and their interchangeability increasing. Therefore, it cannot be excluded that in future for certain uses several of those systems be embraced by a single product market. By the same token, it is likely that, for certain uses, mobile systems will be comprised in a single market with certain services offered on the public switched network.

(b)   The geographic market

31.   A geographic market is an area:
— where undertakings enter into competition with each other, and
— where the objective conditions of competition applying to the product or service in question are similar for all traders.[14]

32.   Without prejudice to the definition of the geographic market in individual cases, each national territory within the EEC seems still to be a distinct geographic market as regards those relevant services or products, where:
— the customer's needs cannot be satisfied by using a non-domestic service,
— there are different regulatory conditions of access to services, in particular special or exclusive rights which are apt to isolate national territories,
— as to equipment and network, there are no Community-common standards, whether mandatory or voluntary, whose absence could also isolate the national markets. The absence of voluntary Community-wide standards shows different national customers' requirements.

However, it is expected that the geographic market will progressively extend to the EEC territory at the pace of the progressive realization of a single EEC market.

33.   It has also to be ascertained whether each national market or a part thereof is a substantial part of the common market. This is the case where the services of the product involved represent a substantial percentage of volume within the EEC. This applies to all services and products involved.

34.   As to satellite uplinks, for cross-border communication by satellite the uplink could be provided from any of several countries. In this case, the geographic market is wider than the national territory and may cover the whole EEC.

As to space segment capacity, the extension of the geographic market will depend on the power of the satellite and its ability to compete with other satellites for transmission to a given area, in other words on its range. This can be assessed only case by case.

35.   As to services in general as well as terminal and network equipment, the Commission assesses the market power of the undertakings concerned and the result for EEC competition of the undertakings' conduct, taking into account their interrelated activities and interaction between the EEC and world markets. This is even more necessary to the extent that the EEC market is progressively being opened. This could have a considerable effect on the structure of the markets in the EEC, on the overall competitivity of the undertakings operating in those markets, and in the long run, on their capacity to remain independent operators.

IV   APPLICATION OF ARTICLE 85

36.   The Commission recalls that a major policy target of the Council Resolution of 30 June 1988 on the development of the common market for telecommunications services and equipment up to 1992 was that of:

---

14 Judgment of 14. 2. 1978 in Case 27/76, *United Brands* v *Commission* [1978] ECR 207, Ground 44. In the telecommunications sector: Judgment of 5. 10. 1988 in Case 247/86, *Alsatel-Novasam* [1988] ECR 5987

'. . . stimulating European cooperation at all levels, as far as compatible with Community competition rules, and particularly in the field of research and development, in order to secure a strong European presence on the telecommunications markets and to ensure the full participation of all Member States'.

In many cases Europe-wide services can be achieved by TOs' cooperation — for example, by ensuring interconnectivity and interoperability

(i) in those areas where exclusive or special rights for provision may continue in accordance with Community law and in particular with the Services Directive 90/388/EEC; and

(ii) in areas where optimum service will require certain features of cooperation, such as so-called 'one-stop shopping' arrangements, i.e. the possibility of acquiring Europe-wide services at a single sales point.

The Council is giving guidance, by Directives, Decisions, recommendations and resolutions on those areas where Europe-wide services are most urgently needed: such as by recommendation 86/659/EEC on the coordinated introduction of the integrated services digital network (ISDN) in the European Community[15] and by recommendation 87/371/EEC on the coordinated introduction of public pan-European cellular digital land-based mobile communications in the Community.[16]

The Commission welcomes and fully supports the necessity of cooperation particularly in order to promote the development of trans-European services and strengthen the competitivity of the EEC industry throughout the Community and in the world markets. However, this cooperation can only attain that objective if it complies with Community competition rules. Regulation No 17 provides well-defined clearing procedures for such cooperation agreements. The procedures foreseen by Regulation No 17 are:

(i) the application for negative clearance, by which the Commission certifies that the agreements are not caught by Article 85, because they do not restrict competition and/or do not affect trade between Member States; and

(ii) the notification of agreements caught by Article 85 in order to obtain an exemption under Article 85 (3). Although if a particular agreement is caught by Article 85, an exemption can be granted by the Commission under Article 85(3), this is only so when the agreement brings about economic benefits — assessed on the basis of the criteria in the said paragraph 3 — which outweigh its restrictions on competition. In any event competition may not be eliminated for a substantial part of the products in question. Notification is not an obligation; but if, for reasons of legal certainty, the parties decide to request an exemption pursuant to Article 4 of Regulation No 17 the agreements may not be exempted until they have been notified to the Commission.

37.   Cooperation agreements may be covered by one of the Commission block exemption Regulations or Notices.[17] In the first case the agreement is automatically exempted under Article 85 (3). In the latter case, in the Commission's view, the agreement does not appreciably restrict competition and trade between Member States and therefore does not justify a Commis-

---

15 OJ No L 382, 31. 12. 1986, p. 36.
16 OJ No L 196, 17. 7. 1987, p. 81.
17 Reported in 'Competition Law in the European Communities' Volume I (situation at 31. 12. 1989) published by the Commission.

sion action. In either case, the agreement does not need to be notified; but it may be notified in case of doubt. If the Commission receives a multitude of notifications of similar cooperation agreements in the telecommunications sector, it may consider whether a specific block exemption regulation for such agreements would be appropriate.

38.   The categories of agreements[18] which seem to be typical in telecommunications and may be caught by Article 85 are listed below. This list provides examples only and is, therefore, not exhaustive. The Commission is thereby indicating possible competition restrictions which could be caught by Article 85 and cases where there may be the possibility of an exemption.

39.   These agreements may affect trade between Member States for the following reasons:

(i)   services other than services reserved to TOs, equipment and spatial segment facilities are traded throughout the EEC; agreements on these services and equipment are therefore likely to affect trade. Although at present cross-frontier trade is limited, there is potentially no reason to suppose that suppliers of such facilities will in future confine themselves to their national market;

(ii)   as to reserved network services, one can consider that they also are traded throughout the Community. These services could be provided by an operator located in one Member State to customers located in other Member States, which decide to move their telecommunications hub into the first one because it is economically or qualitatively advantageous. Moreover, agreements on these matters are likely to affect EEC trade at least to the extent they influence the conditions under which the other services and equipment are supplied throughout the EEC.

40.   Finally, to the extent that the TOs hold dominant positions in facilities, services and equipment markets, their behaviour leading to — and including the conclusion of — the agreements in question could also give rise to a violation of Article 86, if agreements have or are likely to have as their effect hindering the maintenance of the degree of competition still existing in the market or the growth of that competition, or causing the TOs to reap trading benefits which they would not have reaped if there had been normal and sufficiently effective competition.

A.   *Horizontal agreements concerning the provision of terrestrial facilities and reserved services*

41.   Agreements concerning terrestrial facilities (public switched network or leased circuits) or services (e. g. voice telephony for the general public) can currently only be concluded between TOs because of this legal regime providing for exclusive or special rights. The fact that the Services Directive recognizes the possibility for a Member State to reserve this provision to certain operators does not exempt those operators from complying with the competition rules in providing these facilities or services. These agreements may restrict competition within a Member State only where such exclusive rights are granted to more than one provider.

---

18 For simplification's sake this term stands also for 'decisions by associations' and 'concerted practices' within the meaning of Article 85.

42.   These agreements may restrict the competition between TOs for retaining or attracting large telecommunications users for their telecommunications centres. Such 'hub competition' is substantially based upon favourable rates and other conditions, as well as the quality of the services. Member States are not allowed to prevent such competition since the Directive allows only the granting of exclusive and special rights by each Member State in its own territory.

43.   Finally, these agreements may restrict competition in non-reserved services from third party undertakings, which are supported by the facilities in question, for example if they impose discriminatory or inequitable trading conditions on certain users.

44.   (aa) *Price agreements*: all TOs' agreements on prices, discounting or collection charges for international services, are apt to restrict the hub competition to an appreciable extent. Coordination on or prohibition of discounting could cause particularly serious restrictions. In situations of public knowledge such as exists in respect of the tariff level, discounting could remain the only possibility of effective price competition.

45.   In several cases the Court of Justice and the Commission have considered price agreements among the most serious infringements of Article 85.[19]

While harmonization of tariff structures may be a major element for the provision of Community-wide services, this goal should be pursued as far as compatible with Community competition rules and should include definition of efficient pricing principles throughout the Community. Price competition is a crucial, if not the principal, element of customer choice and is apt to stimulate technical progress. Without prejudice to any application for individual exemption that may be made, the justification of any price agreement in terms of Article 85 (3) would be the subject of very rigorous examination by the Commission.

46.   Conversely, where the agreements concern only the setting up of common tariff structures or principles, the Commission may consider whether this would not constitute one of the economic benefits under Article 85 (3) which outweigh the competition restriction. Indeed, this could provide the necessary transparency on tariff calculations and facilitate users' decisions about traffic flow or the location of headquarters or premises. Such agreements could also contribute to achieving one of the Green Paper's economic objectives — more cost-orientated tariffs.

In this connection, following the intervention of the Commission, the CEPT has decided to abolish recommendation PGT/10 on the general principles for the lease of international telecommunications circuits and the establishment of private international networks. This recommendation recommended, *inter alia*, the imposition of a 30 % surcharge or an access charge where third-party traffic was carried on an international telecommunications leased circuit, or if such a circuit was interconnected to the public telecommunications network. It also recommended the application of uniform tariff coefficients in order to determine the relative price level of international

19 PVC, Commission Decision 89/190/EEC, OJ No L 74, 17. 3. 1989, p. 1; Case 123/85, *BNIC* v *Clair* [1985] ECR 391; Case 8/72, *Cementhandelaren* v *Commission* (1972) ECR 977; Polypropylene, Commission Decision 86/398/EEC (OJ No L 230/1, 18. 8. 1986, p. 1) on appeal Case179/86.

telecommunications leased circuits. Thanks to the CEPT's cooperation with the Commission leading to the abolition of the recommendation, competition between telecoms operators for the supply of international leased circuits is re-established, to the benefit of users, especially suppliers of non-reserved services. The Commission had found that the recommendation amounted to a price agreement between undertakings under Article 85 of the Treaty which substantially restricted competition within the European Community.[20]

47.   (ab)   *Agreements on other conditions for the provision of facilities*

These agreements may limit hub competition between the partners. More-over, they may limit the access of users to the network, and thus restrict third undertakings' competition as to non-reserved services. This applies especially to the use of leased circuits. The abolished CEPT recommendation PGT/10 on tariffs had also recommended restrictions on conditions of sale which the Commission objected to. These restrictions were mainly:

— making the use of leased circuits between the customer and third parties subject to the condition that the communication concern exclusively the activity for which the circuit has been granted,

— a ban on subleasing,

— authorization of private networks only for customers tied to each other by economic links and which carry out the same activity,

— prior consultation between the TOs for any approval of a private network and of any modification of the use of the network, and for any interconnection of private networks.

For the purpose of an exemption under Article 85(3), the granting of special conditions for a particular facility in order to promote its development could be taken into account among other elements. This could foster technologies which reduce the costs of services and contribute to increasing competitiveness of European industry structures. Naturally, the other Article 85 (3) requirements should also be met.

48.   (ac)   *Agreements on the choice of telecommunication routes*

These may have the following restrictive effects:

(i)   to the extent that they coordinate the TOs' choice of the routes to be set up in international services, they may limit competition between TOs as suppliers to users' communications hubs, in terms of investments and production, with a possible effect on tariffs. It should be determined whether this restriction of their business autonomy is sufficiently appreciable to be caught by Article 85. In any event, an argument for an exemption under Article 85 (3) could be more easily sustained if common routes designation were necessary to enable interconnections and, therefore, the use of a Europe-wide network;

(ii)   to the extent that they reserve the choice of routes already set up to the TOs, and this choice concerns one determined facility, they could limit the use of other facilities and thus services provision possibly to the detriment of technological progress. By contrast, the choice of routes does not seem restrictive in principle to the extent that it constitutes a technical requirement.

49.   (ad)   *Agreements on the imposition of technical and quality standards on the services provided on the public network*

Standardization brings substantial economic benefits which can be relevant under Article 85 (3). It facilitates *inter alia* the provision of pan-European

---

20 See Commission press release IP(90) 188 of 6 March 1990.

telecommunications services. As set out in the framework of the Community's approach to standardization, products and services complying with standards may be used Community-wide. In the context of this approach, European standards institutions have developed in this field (ETSI and CEN-Cenelec). National markets in the EC would be opened up and form a Community market. Service and equipment markets would be enlarged, hence favouring economies of scale. Cheaper products and services are thus available to users. Standardization may also offer an alternative to specifications controlled by undertakings dominant in the network architecture and in non-reserved services. Standardization agreements may, therefore, lessen the risk of abuses by these undertakings which could block the access to the markets for non-reserved services and for equipment. However, certain standardization agreements can have restrictive effects on competition: hindering innovation, freezing a particular stage of technical development, blocking the network access of some users/service providers. This restriction could be appreciable, for example when deciding to what extent intelligence will in future be located in the network or continue to be permitted in customers' equipment. The imposition of specifications other than those provided for by Community law could have restrictive effects on competition. Agreements having these effects are, therefore, caught by Article 85.

The balance between economic benefits and competition restrictions is complex. In principle, an exemption could be granted if an agreement brings more openness and facilitates access to the market, and these benefits outweigh the restrictions caused by it.

50.　Standards jointly developed and/or published in accordance with the ONP procedures carry with them the presumption that the cooperating TOs which comply with those standards fulfil the requirement of open and efficient access (see the ONP Directive mentioned in paragraph 16). This presumption can be rebutted, *inter alia*, if the agreement contains restrictions which are not foreseen by Community law and are not indispensable for the standardization sought.

51.　One important Article 85 (3) requirement is that users must also be allowed a fair share of the resulting benefit. This is more likely to happen when users are directly involved in the standardization process in order to contribute to deciding what products or services will meet their needs. Also, the involvement of manufacturers or service providers other than TOs seems a positive element for Article 85 (3) purposes. However, this involvement must be open and widely representative in order to avoid competition restrictions to the detriment of excluded manufacturers or service providers. Licensing other manufacturers may be deemed necessary, for the purpose of granting an exemption to these agreements under Article 85 (3).

52.　(ae)　*Agreements foreseeing special treatment for TOs' terminal equipment or other companies' equipment for the interconnection or interoperation of terminal equipment with reserved services and facilities*

53.　(af)　*Agreements on the exchange of information*

A general exchange of information could indeed be necessary for the good functioning of international telecommunications services, and for cooperation aimed at ensuring interconnectivity or one-stop shopping and billing. It should not be extended to competition-sensitive information, such as certain tariff information which constitutes business secrets, discounting, customers and commercial strategy, including that concerning new products. The exchange of this information would affect the autonomy of each TO's commercial policy and it is not necessary to attain the said objectives.

B. *Agreements concerning the provision of non-reserved services and terminal equipment*

54.   Unlike facilities markets, where only the TOs are the providers, in the services markets the actual or potential competitors are numerous and include, besides the TOs, international private companies, computer companies, publishers and others. Agreements on services and terminal equipment could therefore be concluded between TOs, between TOs and private companies, and between private companies.

55.   The liberalizing process has led mostly to strategic agreements between (i) TOs, and (ii) TOs and other companies. These agreements usually take the form of joint ventures.

56.   (ba)   *Agreements between TOs*

The scope of these agreements, in general, is the provision by each partner of a value-added service including the management of the service. Those agreements are mostly based on the 'one-stop shopping' principle, i.e. each partner offers to the customer the entire package of services which he needs. These managed services are called managed data network services (MDNS). An MDNS essentially consists of a broad package of services including facilities, value-added services and management. The agreements may also concern such basic services as satellite uplink.

57.   These agreements could restrict competition in the MDNS market and also in the markets for a service or a group of services included in the MDNS:

   (i)   between the participating TOs themselves; and

   (ii)   *vis-à-vis* other actual or potential third-party providers.

58.   (i)   *Restrictions of competition between TOs*

Cooperation between TOs could limit the number of potential individual MDNS offered by each participating TO.

The agreements may affect competition at least in certain aspects which are contemplated as specific examples of prohibited practices under Article 85 (1) (a) to (c), in the event that:

— they fix or recommend, or at least lead (through the exchange of price information) to coordination of prices charged by each participant to customers,

— they provide for joint specification of MDNS products, quotas, joint delivery, specification of customers' systems; all this would amount to controlling production, markets, technical development and investments,

— they contemplate joint purchase of MDNS hardware and/or software, which would amount to sharing markets or sources of supply.

59.   (ii)   *Restrictive effects on third party undertakings*

Third parties' market entry could be precluded or hampered if the participating TOs:

— refuse to provide facilities to third party suppliers of services,

— apply usage restrictions only to third parties and not to themselves (e.g. a private provider is precluded from placing multiple customers on a leased line facility to obtain lower unit costs),

— favour their MDNS offerings over those of private suppliers with respect to access, availability, quality and price of leased circuits, maintenance and other services,

— apply especially low rates to their MDNS offerings, cross-subsidizing them with higher rates for monopoly services.

Examples of this could be the restrictions imposed by the TOs on private network operators as to the qualifications of the users, the nature of the messages to be exchanged over the network or the use of international private leased circuits.

60.   Finally, as the participating TOs hold, individually or collectively, a dominant position for the creation and the exploitation of the network in each national market, any restrictive behaviour described in paragraph 59 could amount to an abuse of a dominant position under Article 86 (see V below).

61.   On the other hand, agreements between TOs may bring economic benefits which could be taken into account for the possible granting of an exemption under Article 85 (3). *Inter alia,* the possible benefits could be as follows:

— a European-wide service and 'one-stop shopping' could favour business in Europe. Large multinational undertakings are provided with a European communication service using only a single point of contact,

— the cooperation could lead to a certain amount of European-wide standardization even before further EEC legislation on this matter is adopted,

— the cooperation could bring a cost reduction and consequently cheaper offerings to the advantage of consumers,

— a general improvement of public infrastructure could arise from a joint service provision.

62.   Only by notification of the cases in question, in accordance with the appropriate procedures under Regulation No 17, will the Commission be able, where requested, to ascertain, on the merits, whether these benefits outweigh the competition restrictions. But in any event, restrictions on access for third parties seem likely to be considered as not indispensable and to lead to the elimination of competition for a substantial part of the products and services concerned within the meaning of Article 85 (3), thus excluding the possibility of an exemption. Moreover, if an MDNS agreement strengthens appreciably a dominant position which a participating TO holds in the market for a service included in the MDNS, this is also likely to lead to a rejection of the exemption.

63.   The Commission has outlined the conditions for exempting such forms of cooperation in a case concerning a proposed joint venture between 22 TOs for the provision of a Europe-wide MDNS, later abandoned for commercial reasons,[21] The Commission considered that the MDNS project presented the risks of restriction of competition between the operators themselves and private service suppliers but it accepted that the project also offered economic benefits to telecommunications users such as access to Europe-wide services through a single operator. Such cooperation could also have accelerated European standardization, reduced costs and increased the quality of the services. The Commission had informed the participants that approval of the project would have to be subject to guarantees designed to

---

21 Commission press release IP(89) 948 of 14. 12. 1989.

prevent undue restriction of competition in the telecommunications services markets, such as discrimination against private services suppliers and cross-subsidization. Such guarantees would be essential conditions for the granting of an exemption under the competition rules to cooperation agreements involving TOs. The requirement for an appropriate guarantee of non-discrimination and non-cross-subsidization will be specified in individual cases according to the examples of discrimination indicated in Section V below concerning the application of Article 86.

64.   (bb)   *Agreements between TOs and other service providers*

Cooperation between TOs and other operators is increasing in telecommunications services. It frequently takes the form of a joint venture. The Commission recognizes that it may have beneficial effects. However, this cooperation may also adversely affect competition and the opening up of services markets. Beneficial and harmful effects must therefore be carefully weighed.

65.   Such agreements may restrict competition for the provision of telecommunications services:

    (i)   between the partners; and

    (ii)   from third parties.

66.   (i)   Competition between the partners may be restricted when these are actual or potential competitors for the relevant telecommunications service. This is generally the case, even when only the other partners and not the TOs are already providing the service. Indeed, TOs may have the required financial capacity, technical and commercial skills to enter the market for non-reserved services and could reasonably bear the technical and financial risk of doing it. This is also generally the case as far as private operators are concerned, when they do not yet provide the service in the geographical market covered by the cooperation, but do provide this service elsewhere. They may therefore be potential competitors in this geographic market.

67.   (ii)   The cooperation may restrict competition from third parties because:

— there is an appreciable risk that the participant TO, i.e. the dominant network provider, will give more favourable network access to its cooperation partners than to other service providers in competition with the partners,

— potential competitors may refrain from entering the market because of this objective risk or, in any event, because of the presence on the market-place of a cooperation involving the monopolist for the network provision. This is especially the case when market entry barriers are high: the market structure allows only few suppliers and the size and the market power of the partners are considerable.

68.   On the other hand, the cooperation may bring economic benefits which outweigh its harmful effect and therefore justify the granting of an exemption under Article 85 (3). The economic benefits can consist, *inter alia*, of the rationalization of the production and distribution of telecommunication services, in improvements in existing services or development of new services, or transfer of technology which improves the efficiency and the competitiveness of the European industrial structures.

69.   In the absence of such economic benefits a complementarity between partners, i.e. between the provision of a reserved activity and that of a service

under competition, is not a benefit as such. Considering it as a benefit would be equal to justifying an involvement through restrictive agreements of TOs in any non-reserved service provision. This would be to hinder a competitive structure in this market.

In certain cases, the cooperation could consolidate or extend the dominant position of the TOs concerned to a non-reserved services market, in violation of Article 86.

70. The imposition or the proposal of cooperation with the service provider as a condition for the provision of the network may be deemed abusive (see paragraph 98 (vi)).

71. (bc) *Agreements between service providers other than TOs*

The Commission will apply the same principles indicated in (ba) and (bb) above also to agreements between private service providers, *inter alia*, agreements providing quotas, price fixing, market and/or customer allocation. In principle, they are unlikely to qualify for an exemption. The Commission will be particularly vigilant in order to avoid cooperation on services leading to a strengthening of dominant positions of the partners or restricting competition from third parties. There is a danger of this occurring for example when an undertaking is dominant with regard to the network architecture and its proprietary standard is adopted to support the service contemplated by the cooperation. This architecture enabling interconnection between computer systems of the partners could attract some partners to the dominant partner. The dominant position for the network architecture will be strengthened and Article 86 may apply.

72. In any exemption of agreements between TOs and other services and/or equipment providers, or between these providers, the Commission will require from the partners appropriate guarantees of non-cross-subsidization and non-discrimination. The risk of cross-subsidization and discrimination is higher when the TOs or the other partners provide both services and equipment, whether within or outside the Community.

C. *Agreements on research and development (R&D)*

73. As in other high technology based sectors, R&D in telecommunications is essential for keeping pace with technological progress and being competitive on the market-place to the benefit of users. R&D requires more and more important financial, technical and human resources which only few undertakings can generate individually. Cooperation is therefore crucial for attaining the above objectives.

74. The Commission has adopted a Regulation for the block exemption under Article 85(3) of R&D agreements in all sectors, including telecommunications.[22]

75. Agreements which are not covered by this Regulation (or the other Commission block exemption Regulations) could still obtain an individual exemption from the Commission if Article 85(3) requirements are met individually. However, not in all cases do the economic benefits of an R&D agreement outweigh its competition restrictions. In telecommunications, one major asset, enabling access to new markets, is the launch of new products

---

22 Regulation (EEC) No 418/85, OJ No L 53, 22. 2. 1985, p. 5.

or services. Competition is based not only on price, but also on technology. R&D agreements could constitute the means for powerful undertakings with high market shares to avoid or limit competition from more innovative rivals. The risk of excessive restrictions of competition increases when the cooperation is extended from R&D to manufacturing and even more to distribution.

76.   The importance which the Commission attaches to R&D and innovation is demonstrated by the fact that it has launched several programmes for this purpose. The joint companies' activities which may result from these programmes are not automatically cleared or exempted as such in all aspects from the application of the competition rules. However, most of those joint activities may be covered by the Commission's block exemption Regulations. If not, the joint activities in question may be exempted, where required, in accordance with the appropriate criteria and procedures.

77.   In the Commission's experience joint distribution linked to joint R&D which is not covered by the Regulation on R&D does not play the crucial role in the exploitation of the results of R&D. Nevertheless, in individual cases, provided that a competitive environment is maintained, the Commission is prepared to consider full-range cooperation even between large firms. This should lead to improving the structure of European industry and thus enable it to meet strong competition in the world market place.

V   APPLICATION OF ARTICLE 86

78.   Article 86 applies when:

    (i)   the undertaking concerned holds an individual or a joint dominant position;

    (ii)   it commits an abuse of that dominant position; and

    (iii)   the abuse may affect trade between Member States.

Dominant position

79.   In each national market the TOs hold individually or collectively a dominant position for the creation and the exploitation of the network, since they are protected by exclusive or special rights granted by the State. Moreover, the TOs hold a dominant position for some telecommunications services, in so far as they hold exclusive or special rights with respect to those services.[23]

80.   The TOs may also hold dominant positions on the markets for certain equipment or services, even though they no longer hold any exclusive rights on those markets. After the elimination of these rights, they may have kept very important market shares in this sector. When the market share in itself does not suffice to give the TOs a dominant position, it could do it in combination with the other factors such as the monopoly for the network or other related services and a powerful and wide distribution network. As to the equipment, for example terminal equipment, even if the TOs are not involved in the equipment manufacturing or in the services provision, they may hold a dominant position in the market as distributors.

---

23 Commission Decision 82/861/EEC in the 'British Telecommunications' case, point 26, OJ No L 360, 21. 12. 1982, p. 36, confirmed in the Judgment of 20. 3. 1985 in Case 41/83, *Italian Republic* v *Commission* [1985] ECR 873, generally known as 'British Telecom'.

81.   Also, firms other than TOs may hold individual or collective dominant positions in markets where there are no exclusive rights. This may be the case especially for certain non-reserved services because of either the market shares alone of those undertakings, or because of a combination of several factors. Among these factors, in addition to the market shares, two of particular importance are the technological advance and the holding of the information concerning access protocols or interfaces necessary to ensure interoperability of software and hardware. When this information is covered by intellectual property rights this is a further factor of dominance.

82.   Finally, the TOs hold, individually or collectively, dominant positions in the demand for some telecommunication equipment, works or software services. Being dominant for the network and other services provisions they may account for a purchaser's share high enough to give them dominance as to the demand, i.e. making suppliers dependent on them. Dependence could exist when the supplier cannot sell to other customers a substantial part of its production or change a production. In certain national markets, for example in large switching equipment, big purchasers such as the TOs face big suppliers. In this situation, it should be weighed up case by case whether the supplier or the customer position will prevail on the other to such an extent as to be considered dominant under Article 86.

With the liberalization of services and the expansion of new forces on the services markets, dominant positions of undertakings other than the TOs may arise for the purchasing of equipment.

Abuse

83.   Commission's activity may concern mainly the following broad areas of abuses:

A.   *TOs' abuses*: in particular, they may take advantage of their monopoly or at least dominant position to acquire a foothold or to extend their power in non-reserved neighbouring markets, to the detriment of competitors and customers.

B.   *Abuses by undertaking other than TOs*: these may take advantage of the fundamental information they hold, whether or not covered by intellectual property rights, with the object and/or effect of restricting competition.

C.   *Abuses of a dominant purchasing position*: for the time being this concerns mainly the TOs, especially to the extent that they hold a dominant position for reserved activities in the national market. However, it may also increasingly concern other undertakings which have entered the market.

A.   *TOs' Abuses*

84.   The Commission has recognized in the Green Paper the central role of the TOs, which justifies the maintenance of certain monopolies to enable them to perform their public task. This public task consists in the provision and exploitation of a universal network or, where appropriate, universal service, i.e. one having general coverage and available to all users (including service providers and the TOs themselves) upon request on reasonable and non-discriminatory conditions.

This fundamental obligation could justify the benefit of the exception provided in Article 90 (2) under certain circumstances, as laid down in the Services Directive.

85.   In most cases, however, the competition rules, far from obstructing the fulfilment of this obligation, contribute to ensuring it. In particular, Article 86 can apply to behaviour of dominant undertakings resulting in a refusal to supply, discrimination, restrictive tying clauses, unfair prices or other inequitable conditions.

If one of these types of behaviour occurs in the provision of one of the monopoly services, the fundamental obligation indicated above is not performed. This could be the case when a TO tries to take advantage of its monopoly for certain services (for instance: network provision) in order to limit the competition they have to face in respect of non-reserved services, which in turn are supported by those monopoly services.

It is not necessary for the purpose of the application of Article 86 that competition be restricted as to a service which is supported by the monopoly provision in question. It would suffice that the behaviour results in an appreciable restriction of competition in whatever way. This means that an abuse may occur when the company affected by the behaviour is not a service provider but an end user who could himself be disadvantaged in competition in the course of his own business.

86.   The Court of Justice has set out this fundamental principle of competition in telecommunications in one of its judgments.[24] An abuse within the meaning of Article 86 is committed where, without any objective necessity, an undertaking holding a dominant position on a particular market reserves to itself or to an undertaking belonging to the same group an ancillary activity which might be carried out by another undertaking as part of its activities on a neighbouring but separate market, with the possibility of eliminating all competition from such undertaking.

The Commission believes that this principle applies, not only when a dominant undertaking monopolizes other markets, but also when by anti-competitive means it extends its activity to other markets.

Hampering the provision of non-reserved services could limit production, markets and above all the technical progress which is a key factor of telecommunications. The Commission has already shown these adverse effects of usage restrictions on monopoly provision in its decision in the 'British Telecom' case.[25] In this Decision it was found that the restrictions imposed by British Telecom on telex and telephone networks usage, namely on the transmission of international messages on behalf of third parties:

(i)   limited the activity of economic operators to the detriment of technological progress;

(ii)   discriminated against these operators, thereby placing them at a competitive disadvantage *vis-à-vis* TOs not bound by these restrictions; and

(iii)   made the conclusion of the contracts for the supply of telex circuits subject to acceptance by the other parties of supplementary obligations which had no connection with such contracts. These were considered

---

24 Case 311/84, *Centre belge d'études de marché Télémarketing (CBEM) SA v Compagnie luxembourgeoise de télédiffusion SA and Information Publicité Benelux SA*, 3 October 1985 [1985] ECR 3261, Grounds 26 and 27.
25 See Note 23.

abuses of a dominant position identified respectively in Article 86 (b), (c) and (d).

This could be done:

(a)   as above, by refusing or restricting the usage of the service provided under monopoly so as to limit the provision of non-reserved services by third parties; or

(b)   by predatory behaviour, as a result of cross-subsidization.

87.   The separation of the TOs' regulatory power from their business activity is a crucial matter in the context of the application of Article 86. This separation is provided in the Article 90 Directives on terminals and on services mentioned in Note 2 above.

(a)   Usage restrictions

88.   Usage restrictions on provisions of reserved services are likely to correspond to the specific examples of abuses indicated in Article 86. In particular:

— they may limit the provision of telecommunications services in free competition, the investments and the technical progress, to the prejudice of telecommunications consumers (Article 86 (b)),

— to the extent that these usage restrictions are not applied to all users, including the TOs themselves as users, they may result in discrimination against certain users, placing them at a competitive disadvantage (Article 86 (c)),

— they may make the usage of the reserved services subject to the acceptance of obligations which have no connection with this usage (Article 86 (d)).

89.   The usage restrictions in question mainly concern public networks (public switched telephone network (PSTN) or public switched data networks (PSDN)) and especially leased circuits. They may also concern other provisions such as satellite uplink, and mobile communication networks. The most frequent types of behaviour are as follows:

(i)   *Prohibition imposed by TOs on third parties:*

(a)   *to connect private leased circuits by means of concentrator, multiplexer or other equipment to the public switched network; and/or*

(b)   *to use private leased circuits for providing services, to the extent that these services are not reserved, but under competition.*

90.   To the extent that the user is granted a licence by State regulatory authorities under national law in compliance with EEC law, these prohibitions limit the user's freedom of access to the leased circuits, the provision of which is a public service. Moreover, it discriminates between users, depending upon the usage (Article 86 (c)). This is one of the most serious restrictions and could substantially hinder the development of international telecommunications services (Article 86 (b)).

91.   When the usage restriction limits the provision of non-reserved service in competition with that provided by the TO itself the abuse is even more serious and the principles of the abovementioned 'Télémarketing' judgment (Note 23 *supra*) apply.

92.   In individual cases, the Commission will assess whether the service provided on the leased circuit is reserved or not, on the basis of the Community regulatory acts interpreted in the technical and economic context of each case. Even though a service could be considered reserved according to the law, the fact that a TO actually prohibits the usage of the leased circuit only to some users and not to others could constitute a discrimination under Article 86 (c).

93.   The Commission has taken action in respect of the Belgian Régie des télégraphes et téléphones after receiving a complaint concerning an alleged abuse of dominant position from a private supplier of value-added telecommunications services relating to the conditions under which telecommunications circuits were being leased. Following discussions with the Commission, the RTT authorized the private supplier concerned to use the leased telecommunications circuits subject to no restrictions other than that they should not be used for the simple transport of data.

Moreover, pending the possible adoption of new rules in Belgium, and without prejudice to any such rules, the RTT undertook that all its existing and potential clients for leased telecommunications circuits to which third parties may have access shall be governed by the same conditions as those which were agreed with the private sector supplier mentioned above.[26]

(ii)   *Refusal by TOs to provide reserved services (in particular the network and leased circuits) to third parties*

94.   Refusal to supply has been considered an abuse by the Commission and the Court of Justice.[27] This behaviour would make it impossible or at least appreciably difficult for third parties to provide non-reserved services. This, in turn, would lead to a limitation of services and of technical development (Article 86 (b)) and, if applied only to some users, result in discrimination (Article 86 (c)).

(iii)   *Imposition of extra charges or other special conditions for certain usages of reserved services*

95.   An example would be the imposition of access charges to leased circuits when they are connected to the public switched network or other special prices and charges for service provision to third parties. Such access charges may discriminate between users of the same service (leased circuits provision) depending upon the usage and result in imposing unfair trading conditions. This will limit the usage of leased circuits and finally non-reserved service provision. Conversely, it does not constitute an abuse provided that it is shown, in each specific case, that the access charges correspond to costs which are entailed directly for the TOs for the access in question. In this case, access charges can be imposed only on an equal basis to all users, including TOs themselves.

96.   Apart from these possible additional costs which should be covered by an extra charge, the interconnection of a leased circuit to the public

---

26 Commission Press release IP(90) 67 of 29. 1. 1990
27 Cases 6 and 7/73 *Commercial Solvents* v *Commission* [1974] ECR 223; *United Brands* v *Commission* (Note 14, above).

switched network is already remunerated by the price related to the use of this network. Certainly, a leased circuit can represent a subjective value for a user depending on the profitability of the enhanced service to be provided on that leased circuit. However, this cannot be a criterion on which a dominant undertaking, and above all a public service provider, can base the price of this public service.

97.   The Commission appreciates that the substantial difference between leased circuits and the public switched network causes a problem of obtaining the necessary revenues to cover the costs of the switched network. However, the remedy chosen must not be contrary to law, i.e. the EEC Treaty, as discriminatory pricing between customers would be.

(iv)   *Discriminatory price or quality of the service provided*

98.   This behaviour may relate, *inter alia*, to tariffs or to restrictions or delays in connection to the public switched network or leased circuits provision, in installation, maintenance and repair, in effecting interconnection of systems or in providing information concerning network planning, signalling protocols, technical standards and all other information necessary for an appropriate interconnection and interoperation with the reserved service and which may affect the interworking of competitive services or terminal equipment offerings.

(v)   *Tying the provision of the reserved service to the supply by the TOs or others of terminal equipment to be interconnected or interoperated, in particular through imposition, pressure, offer of special prices or other trading conditions for the reserved service linked to the equipment.*

(vi)   *Tying the provision of the reserved service to the agreement of the user to enter into cooperation with the reserved service provider himself as to the non-reserved service to be carried on the network*

(vii)   *Reserving to itself for the purpose of non-reserved service provision or to other service providers information obtained in the exercise of a reserved service in particular information concerning users of a reserved services providers more favourable conditions for the supply of this information*

This latter information could be important for the provision of services under competition to the extent that it permits the targeting of customers of those services and the definition of business strategy. The behaviour indicated above could result in a discrimination against undertakings to which the use of this information is denied in violation of Article 86 (c). The information in question can only be disclosed with the agreement of the users concerned and in accordance with relevant data protection legislation (see the proposal for a Council Directive concerning the protection of personal data and privacy in the context of public digital telecommunications networks, in particular the integrated services digital network (ISDN) and public digital mobile networks).[28]

---

28 Commission document COM(90) 314 of 13. 9. 1990.

(viii) *Imposition of unneeded reserved services by supplying reserved and/or non-reserved services when the former reserved services are reasonably separable from the others*

99. The practices under (v) (vi) (vii) and (viii) result in applying conditions which have no connection with the reserved service, contravening Article 86 (d).

100. Most of these practices were in fact identified in the Services Directive as restrictions on the provision of services within the meaning of Article 59 and Article 86 of the Treaty brought about by State measures. They are therefore covered by the broader concept of 'restrictions' which under Article 6 of the Directive have to be removed by Member States.

101. The Commission believes that the Directives on terminals and on services also clarify some principles of application of Articles 85 and 86 in the sector.

The Services Directive does not apply to important sectors such as mobile communications and satellites; however, competition rules apply fully to these sectors. Moreover, as to the services covered by the Directive it will depend very much on the degree of precision of the licences given by the regulatory body whether the TOs still have a discretionary margin for imposing conditions which should be scrutinized under competition rules. Not all the conditions can be regulated in licences: consequently, there could be room for discretionary action. The application of competition rules to companies will therefore depend very much on a case-by-case examination of the licences. Nothing more than a class licence can be required for terminals.

(b) Cross-subsidization

102. Cross-subsidization means that an undertaking allocates all or part of the costs of its activity in one product or geographic market to its activity in another product or geographic market. Under certain circumstances, cross-subsidization in telecommunications could distort competition, i.e. lead to beating other competitors with offers which are made possible not by efficiency and performance but by artificial means such as subsidies. Avoiding cross-subsidization leading to unfair competition is crucial for the development of service provision and equipment supply.

103. Cross-subsidization does not lead to predatory pricing and does not restrict competition when it is the costs of reserved activities which are subsidized by the revenue generated by other reserved activities since there is no competition possible as to these activities. This form of subsidization is even necessary, as it enables the TOs holders of exclusive rights to perform their obligation to provide a public service universally and on the same conditions to everybody. For instance, telephone provision in unprofitable rural areas is subsidized through revenues from telephone provision in profitable urban areas or long-distance calls. The same could be said of subsidizing the provision of reserved services through revenues generated by activities under competition. The application of the general principle of cost-orientation should be the ultimate goal, in order, *inter alia*, to ensure that prices are not inequitable as between users.

104. Subsidizing activities under competition, whether concerning services or equipment, by allocating their costs to monopoly activities, however,

is likely to distort competition in violation of Article 86. It could amount to an abuse by an undertaking holding a dominant position within the Community. Moreover, users of activities under monopoly have to bear unrelated costs for the provision of these activities. Cross-subsidization can also exist between monopoly provision and equipment manufacturing and sale. Cross-subsidization can be carried out through:

— funding the operation of the activities in question with capital remunerated substantially below the market rate;

— providing for those activities premises, equipment, experts and/or services with a remuneration substantially lower than the market price.

105. As to funding through monopoly revenues or making available monopoly material and intellectual means for the starting up of new activities under competition, this constitutes an investment whose costs should be allocated to the new activity. Offering the new product or service should normally include a reasonable remuneration of such investment in the long run. If it does not, the Commission will assess the case on the basis of the remuneration plans of the undertaking concerned and of the economic context.

106. Transparency in the TOs' accounting should enable the Commission to ascertain whether there is cross-subsidization in the cases in which this question arises. The ONP Directive provides in this respect for the definition of harmonized tariff principles which should lessen the number of these cases.

This transparency can be provided by an accounting system which ensures the fully proportionate distribution of all costs between reserved and non-reserved activities. Proper allocation of costs is more easily ensured in cases of structural separation, i.e. creating distinct entities for running each of these two categories of activities.

An appropriate accounting system approach should permit the identification and allocation of all costs between the activities which they support. In this system all products and services should bear proportionally all the relevant costs, including costs of research and development, facilities and overheads. It should enable the production of recorded figures which can be verified by accountants.

107. As indicated above (paragraph 59), in cases of cooperation agreements involving TOs a guarantee of no cross-subsidization is one of the conditions required by the Commission for exemption under Article 85 (3). In order to monitor properly compliance with that guarantee, the Commission now envisages requesting the parties to ensure an appropriate accounting system as described above, the accounts being regularly submitted to the Commission. Where the accounting method is chosen, the Commission will reserve the possibility of submitting the accounts to independent audit, especially if any doubt arises as to the capability of the system to ensure the necessary transparency or to detect any cross-subsidization. If the guarantee cannot be properly monitored, the Commission may withdraw the exemption.

108. In all other cases, the Commission does not envisage requiring such transparency of the TOs. However, if in a specific case there are substantial elements converging in indicating the existence of an abusive cross-subsidization and/or predatory pricing, the Commission could establish a presumption of such cross-subsidization and predatory pricing. An appropriate separate accounting system could be important in order to counter this presumption.

109. Cross-subsidization of a reserved activity by a non-reserved one does not in principle restrict competition. However, the application of the exception provided in Article 90 (2) to this non-reserved activity could not as a rule be justified by the fact that the financial viability of the TO in question rests on the non-reserved activity. Its financial viability and the performance of its task of general economic interest can only be ensured by the State where appropriate by the granting of an exclusive or special right and by imposing restrictions on activities competing with the reserved ones.

110. Also cross-subsidization by a public or private operator outside the EEC may be deemed abusive in terms of Article 86 if that operator holds a dominant position for equipment or non-reserved services within the EEC. The existence of this dominant position, which allows the holder to behave to an appreciable extent independently of its competitors and customers and ultimately of consumers, will be assessed in the light of all elements in the EEC and outside.

B. *Abuses by undertakings other than the TOs*

111. Further to the liberalization of services, undertakings other than the TOs may increasingly extend their power to acquire dominant positions in non-reserved markets. They may already hold such a position in some services markets which had not been reserved. When they take advantage of their dominant position to restrict competition and to extend their power, Article 86 may also apply to them. The abuses in which they might indulge are broadly similar to most of those previously described in relation to the TOs.

112. Infringements of Article 86 may be committed by the abusive exercise of industrial property rights in relation with standards, which are of crucial importance for telecommunications. Standards may be either the results of international standardization, or *de facto* standards and the property of undertakings.

113. Producers of equipment or suppliers of services are dependent on proprietary standards to ensure the interconnectivity of their computer resources. An undertaking which owns a dominant network architecture may abuse its dominant position by refusing to provide the necessary information for the interconnection of other architecture resources to its architecture products. Other possible abuses — similar to those indicated as to the TOs — are, *inter alia*, delays in providing the information, discrimination in the quality of the information, discriminatory pricing or other trading conditions, and making the information provision subject to the acceptance by the producer, supplier or user of unfair trading conditions.

114. On 1 August 1984, the Commission accepted a unilateral undertaking from IBM to provide other manufacturers with the technical interface information needed to permit competitive products to be used with IBM's then most powerful range of computers, the System/370. The Commission thereupon suspended the proceedings under Article 86 which it had initiated against IBM in December 1980. The IBM Undertaking[29] also contains a commitment relating to SNA formats and protocols.

---

29 Reproduced in full in EC Bulletin 10-1984 (point 3.4.1). As to its continued application, see Commission press release No IP(88) 814 of 15 December 1988.

115. The question how to reconcile copyrights on standards with the competition requirements is particularly difficult. In any event, copyright cannot be used unduly to restrict competition.

C. Abuses of dominant purchasing position

116. Article 86 also applies to behaviour of undertakings holding a dominant purchasing position. The examples of abuses indicated in that Article may therefore also concern that behaviour.

117. The Council Directive 90/531/EEC[30] based on Articles 57 (2), 66, 100a and 113 of the EEC Treaty on the procurement procedures of entities operating in *inter alia* the telecommunications sector regulates essentially:

(i)   procurement procedures in order to ensure on a reciprocal basis non-discrimination on the basis of nationality; and

(ii) for products or services for use in reserved markets, not in competitive markets. That Directive, which is addressed to States, does not exclude the application of Article 86 to the purchasing of products within the scope of the Directive. The Commission will decide case by case how to ensure that these different sets of rules are applied in a coherent manner.

118. Furthermore, both in reserved and competitive markets, practices other than those covered by the Directive may be established in violation of Article 86. One example is taking advantage of a dominant purchasing position for imposing excessively favourable prices or other trading conditions, in comparison with other purchasers and suppliers (Article 86 (a)). This could result in discrimination under Article 86 (c). Also obtaining, whether or not through imposition, an exclusive distributorship for the purchased product by the dominant purchaser may constitute an abusive extension of its economic power to other markets (see 'Télémarketing' Court judgment (Note 23 *supra*)).

119. Another abusive practice could be that of making the purchase subject to licensing by the supplier of standards for the product to be purchased or for other products, to the purchaser itself, or to other suppliers (Article 86 (d)).

120. Moreover, even in competitive markets, discriminatory procedures on the basis of nationality may exist, because national pressures and traditional links of a non-economic nature do not always disappear quickly after the liberalization of the markets. In this case, a systematic exclusion or considerably unfavourable treatment of a supplier, without economic necessity, could be examined under Article 86, especially (b) (limitation of outlets) and (c) (discrimination). In assessing the case, the Commission will substantially examine whether the same criteria for awarding the contract have been followed by the dominant undertaking for all suppliers. The Commission will normally take into account criteria similar to those indicated in Article 27 (1) of the Directive.[31] The purchases in question being outside the scope of the

---

30 OJ No L 297, 29. 10. 1990, p. 1.
31 (See Note 27) Article 27 (1) (a) and (b). The criteria on which the contracting entities shall base the award of the contracts shall be: (a) the most economically advantageous tender involving various criteria such as delivery date, period for completion, running costs, cost-effectiveness, quality, aesthetic and functional characteristics, technical merit, after-sales services and technical assistance, commitments with regard to spare parts, security of supplies and price; or (b) the lowest price only.

Directive, the Commission will not require that transparent purchasing procedures be pursued.

### D.	*Effect on trade between Member States*

121.	The same principle outlined regarding Article 85 applies here. Moreover, in certain circumstances, such as the case of the elimination of a competitor by an undertaking holding a dominant position, although trade between Member States is not directly affected, for the purposes of Article 86 it is sufficient to show that there will be repercussions on the competitive structure of the common market.

VI APPLICATION OF ARTICLES 85 AND 86 IN THE FIELD OF SATELLITES

122.	The development of this sector is addressed globally by the Commission in the 'Green Paper on a common approach in the field of satellite communications in the European Community' of 20 November 1990 (Doc. COM(90) 490 final). Due to the increasing importance of satellites and the particular uncertainty among undertakings as to the application of competition rules to individual cases in this sector, it is appropriate to address the sector in a distinct section in these guidelines.

123.	State regulations on satellites are not covered by the Commission Directives under Article 90 of the EEC Treaty respectively on terminals and services mentioned above except in the Directive on terminals which contemplates receive-only satellite stations not connected to a public network. The Commission's position on the regulatory framework compatible with the Treaty competition rules is stated in the Commission Green Paper on satellites mentioned above.

124.	In any event the Treaty competition rules fully apply to the satellites domain, *inter alia*, Articles 85 and 86 to undertakings. Below is indicated how the principles set out above, in particular in Sections IV and V, apply to satellites.

125.	Agreements between European TOs in particular within international conventions may play an important role in providing European satellites systems and a harmonious development of satellite services throughout the Community. These benefits are taken into consideration under competition rules, provided that the agreements do not contain restrictions which are not indispensable for the attainment of these objectives.

126.	Agreements between TOs concerning the operation of satellite systems in the broadest sense may be caught by Article 85. As to space segment capacity, the TOs are each other's competitors, whether actual or potential. In pooling together totally or partially their supplies of space segment capacity they may restrict competition between themselves. Moreover, they are likely to restrict competition *vis-à-vis* third parties to the extent that their agreements contain provisions with this object or effect: for instance provisions limiting their supplies in quality and/or quantity, or restricting their business autonomy by imposing directly or indirectly a coordination between these third parties and the parties to the agreements. It should be examined whether such agreements could qualify for an exemption under Article 85 (3) provided that they are notified. However, restrictions on third parties' ability to compete are likely to preclude such an exemption. It should also be examined whether such agreements strengthen any individual or collective dominant position of the parties, which also would exclude the granting of an exemption. This could be the case in particular if the agreement provides that the parties are exclusive distributors of the space segment capacity provided by the agreement.

127.   Such agreements between TOs could also restrict competition as to the uplink with respect to which TOs are competitors. In certain cases the customer for satellite communication has the choice between providers in several countries, and his choice will be substantially determined by the quality, price and other sales conditions of each provider. This choice will be even ampler since uplink is being progressively liberalized and to the extent that the application of EEC rules to State legislations will open up the uplink markets. Community-wide agreements providing directly or indirectly for coordination as to the parties' uplink provision are therefore caught by Article 85.

128.   Agreements between TOs and private operators on space segment capacity may be also caught by Article 85, as that provision applies, *inter alia*, to cooperation, and in particular joint venture agreements. These agreements could be exempted if they bring specific benefits such as technology transfer, improvement of the quality of the service or enabling better marketing, especially for a new capacity, outweighing the restrictions. In any event, imposing on customers the bundled uplink and space segment capacity provision is likely to exclude an exemption since it limits competition in uplink provision to the detriment of the customer's choice, and in the current market situation will almost certainly strengthen the TOs' dominant position in violation of Article 86. An exemption is unlikely to be granted also when the agreement has the effect of reducing substantially the supply in an oligopolistic market, and even more clearly when an effect of the agreement is to prevent the only potential competitor of a dominant provider in a given market from offering its services independently. This could amount to a violation of Article 86. Direct or indirect imposition of any kind of agreement by a TO, for instance by making the uplink subject to the conclusion of an agreement with a third party, would constitute an infringement of Article 86.

VII   RESTRUCTURING IN TELECOMMUNICATIONS

129.   Deregulation, the objective of a single market for 1992 and the fundamental changes in the telecommunications technology have caused wide strategic restructuring in Europe and throughout the world as well. They have mostly taken the form of mergers and joint ventures.

(a)   Mergers

130.   In assessing telecom mergers in the framework of Council Regulation (EEC) No 4064/89 on the control of concentrations between undertakings[32] the Commission will take into account, *inter alia*, the following elements.

---

32 OJ No L 395, 30. 12. 1989, p. 1; Corrigendum OJ No L 257, 21. 9. 1990, p. 13.

131. Restructuring moves are in general beneficial to the European telecommunications industry. They may enable the companies to rationalize and to reach the critical mass necessary to obtain the economies of scale needed to make the important investments in research and development. These are necessary to develop new technologies and to remain competitive in the world market.

However, in certain cases they may also lead to the anti-competitive creation or strengthening of dominant positions.

132. The economic benefits resulting from critical mass must be demonstrated. The concentration operation could result in a mere aggregation of market shares, unaccompanied by restructuring measures or plans. This operation may create or strengthen Community or national dominant positions in a way which impedes competition.

133. When concentration operations have this sole effect, they can hardly be justified by the objective of increasing the competitivity of Community industry in the world market. This objective, strongly pursued by the Commission, rather requires competition in EEC domestic markets in order that the EEC undertakings acquire the competitive structure and attitude needed to operate in the world market.

134. In assessing concentration cases in telecommunications, the Commission will be particularly vigilant to avoid the strengthening of dominant positions through integration. If dominant service providers are allowed to integrate into the equipment market by way of mergers, access to this market by other equipment suppliers may be seriously hindered. A dominant service provider is likely to give preferential treatment to its own equipment subsidiary.

Moreover, the possibility of disclosure by the service provider to its subsidiary of sensitive information obtained from competing equipment manufacturers can put the latter at a competitive disadvantage.

The Commission will examine case by case whether vertical integration has such effects or rather is likely to reinforce the competitive structure in the Community.

135. The Commission has enforced principles on restructuring in a case concerning the GEC and Siemens joint bid for Plessey.[33]

136. Article 85 (1) applies to the acquisition by an undertaking of a minority shareholding in a competitor where, *inter alia*, the arrangements involve the creation of a structure of cooperation between the investor and the other undertakings, which will influence these undertakings' competitive conduct.[34]

(b) Joint ventures

137. A joint venture can be of a cooperative or a concentrative nature. It is of a cooperative nature when it has as its object or effect the coordination of the competitive behaviour of undertakings which remain independent. The principles governing cooperative joint ventures are to be set out in

33 Commission Decision rejecting Plessey's complaint against the GEC-Siemens bid (Case IV/33.018 *GEC-Siemens/Plessey*), OJ No C 239, 25. 9. 1990, p. 2.
34 *British American Tobacco Company Ltd and RJ Reynolds Industries Inc.* v *Commission* (Joined Cases 142 and 156/84) of 17. 11. 1987 (1987) ECR 4487.

Commission guidelines to that effect. Concentrative joint ventures fall under Regulation (EEC) No 4064/89.[35]

138.   In some of the latest joint venture cases the Commission granted an exemption under Article 85 (3) on grounds which are particularly relevant to telecommunications. Precisely in a decision concerning telecommunications, the 'Optical Fibres' case,[36] the Commission considered that the joint venture enabled European companies to produce a high technology product, promoted technical progress, and facilitated technology transfer. Therefore, the joint venture permits European companies to withstand competition from non-Community producers, especially in the USA and Japan, in an area of fast-moving technology characterized by international markets. The Commission confirmed this approach in the 'Canon-Olivetti' case.[37]

VIII IMPACT OF THE INTERNATIONAL CONVENTIONS ON THE APPLICATION OF EEC COMPETITION RULES TO TELECOMMUNICATIONS

139.   International conventions (such as the Convention of International Telecommunication Union (ITU) or Conventions on Satellites) play a fundamental role in ensuring worldwide cooperation for the provision of international services. However, application of such international conventions on telecommunications by EEC Member States must not affect compliance with the EEC law, in particular with competition rules.

140.   Article 234 of the EEC Treaty regulates this matter.[38] The relevant obligations provided in the various conventions or related Acts do not pre-date the entry into force of the Treaty. As to the ITU and World Administrative Telegraph and Telephone Conference (WATTC), whenever a revision or a new adoption of the ITU Convention or of the WATTC Regulations occurs, the ITU or WATTC members recover their freedom of action. The Satellites Conventions were adopted much later.

Moreover, as to all conventions, the application of EEC rules does not seem to affect the fulfilment of obligations of Member States *vis-à-vis* third countries. Article 234 does not protect obligations between EEC Member States entered into in international treaties. The purpose of Article 234 is to protect the right of third countries only and it is not intended to crystallize the acquired international treaty rights of Member States to the detriment of the EEC Treaty's objectives or of the Community interest. Finally, even if Article 234 (1) did apply, the Member States concerned would nevertheless be obliged to take all appropriate steps to eliminate incompatibility between their obligations *vis-à-vis* third countries and the EEC rules. This applies in particular where Member States acting collectively have the statutory

---

35 OJ No C 203, 14. 8. 1990, p. 10.
36 Decision 86/405/EEC, OJ No L 236, 22. 8. 86, p. 30.
37 Decision 88/88/EEC, OJ No L 52, 26. 2. 1988, p. 51.
38 'The rights and obligations arising from agreements concluded before the entry into force of this Treaty between one or more Member States on the one hand and one or more third countries on the other, shall not be affected by the provisions of this Treaty. To the extent that such agreements are not compatible with this Treaty, the Member State or States concerned shall take all appropriate steps to eliminate the incompatibilities established. Member States shall, where necessary, assist each other to this end and shall, where appropriate, adopt a common attitude . . . .'

possibility to modify the international convention in question as required, e.g. in the case of the Eutelsat Convention.

141. As to the WATTC Regulations, the relevant provisions of the Regulations in force from 9 December 1988 are flexible enough to give the parties the choice whether or not to implement them or how to implement them.

In any event, EEC Member States, by signing the Regulations, have made a joint declaration that they will apply them in accordance with their obligations under the EEC Treaty.

142. As to the International Telegraph and Telephone Consultative Committee (CCITT) recommendations, competition rules apply to them.

143. Members of the CCITT are, pursuant to Article 11(2) of the International Telecommunications Convention, 'administrations' of the Members of the ITU and recognized private operating agencies ('RPOAs') which so request with the approval of the ITU members which have recognized them. Unlike the members of the ITU or the Administrative Conferences which are States, the members of the CCITT are telecommunications administrations and RPOAs. Telecommunications administrations are defined in Annex 2 to the International Telecommunications Conventions as 'tout service ou département gouvernemental responsable des mesures à prendre pour exécuter les obligations de la Convention Internationale des télécommunications et des règlements' [any government service or department responsible for the measures to be taken to fulfil the obligations laid down in the International Convention on Telecommunications and Regulations]. The CCITT meetings are in fact attended by TOs. Article 11 (2) of the International Telecommunications Convention clearly provides that telecommunications administrations and RPOAs are members of the CCITT by themselves. The fact that, because of the ongoing process of separation of the regulatory functions from the business activity, some national authorities participate in the CCITT is not in contradiction with the nature of undertakings of other members. Moreover, even if the CCITT membership became governmental as a result of the separation of regulatory and operational activities of the telecommunications administrations, Article 90 in association with Article 85 could still apply either against the State measures implementing the CCITT recommendations and the recommendations themselves on the basis of Article 90 (1), or if there is no such national implementing measure, directly against the telecommunications organizations which followed the recommendation.[39]

144. In the Commission's view, the CCITT recommendations are adopted, inter alia, by undertakings. Such CCITT recommendations, although they are not legally binding, are agreements between undertakings or decisions by an association of undertakings. In any event, according to the case law of the Commission and the European Court of Justice[40] a statutory body entrusted with certain public functions and including some members appointed by the government of a Member State may be an 'association of undertakings' if it represents the trading interests of other members and takes decisions or makes agreements in pursuance of those interests.

---

39 See Commission Decision 87/3/EEC ENI/Montedison, OJ No L 5, 7. 1. 1987, p. 13.
40 See Pabst Richarz/BNIA, OJ No L 231, 21. 8. 1976, p. 24, AROW/BNIC, OJ No L 379, 31. 12. 1982, p. 1, and Case 123/83 BNIC v Clair (1985) ECR 391.

The Commission draws attention to the fact that the application of certain provisions in the context of international conventions could result in infringements of the EEC competition rules:

— As to the WATTC Regulations, this is the case for the respective provisions for mutual agreement between TOs on the supply of international telecommunications services (Article 1 (5)), reserving the choice of telecommunications routes to the TOs (Article 3 (3) (3)), recommending practices equivalent to price agreements (Articles 6 (6) (1) (2)), and limiting the possibility of special arrangements to activities meeting needs within and/or between the territories of the Members concerned (Article 9) and only where existing arrangements cannot satisfactorily meet the relevant telecommunications needs (Opinion PL A).

— CCITT recommendations D1 and D2 as they stand at the date of the adoption of these guidelines could amount to a collective horizontal agreement on prices and other supply conditions of international leased lines to the extent that they lead to a coordination of sales policies between TOs and therefore limit competition between them. This was indicated by the Commission in a CCITT meeting on 23 May 1990. The Commission reserves the right to examine the compatibility of other recommendations with Article 85.

— The agreements between TOs concluded in the context of the Conventions on Satellites are likely to limit competition contrary to Article 85 and/or 86 on the grounds set out in paragraphs 126 to 128 above.

Notes

1. For some post-Guidelines decisions see: *Alcatel/Telettra* (OJ L122/48, 17.5.91); *Infonet* (OJ C7/3, 11.1.92); *Encompass Europe* (OJ C233/2, 11.9.92; [1992] 5 CMLR 557); *STET/Italtel/AT&T/AT&T-NSI* (OJ C333/3, 17.12.92); *Astra* (OJ L20/23, 28.1.93); *Intrax* (OJ C117/3, 28.4.93; [1993] 5 CMLR 190); *Nordic Satellite Distribution* (OJ L53/20, 2.3.93); *Arospatiale/Alcatel Espace* (OJ C47/6, 15.2.94); *GEN* (OJ C55/3, 23.2.94); *CMC/Talkline* (OJ C221/9, 9.8.94); *International Private Satellite Partners* (OJ L354/75, 31.12.94); *MSG Media Service* (OJ C379/35, 31.12.94).

2. With regard to paragraph 49, *Agreements on the imposition of technical and quality standards on the services provided on the public network*, see also the European Telecommunications Standards Institute (ETSI) 'Interim Intellectual Property Rights Policy', approved by the ETSI General Assembly, 23 November 1994 (http://www.etsi.fr/).

COMMISSION DECISION (94/579/EC) OF 27 JULY 1994 RELATING TO A PROCEEDING PURSUANT TO ARTICLE 85 OF THE EC TREATY AND ARTICLE 53 OF THE EEA AGREEMENT
OJ L223/36, 27 August 1994

Case IV/34.857 — BT-MCI)
(Only the English text is authentic)
(Text with EEA relevance)

THE COMMISSION OF THE EUROPEAN COMMUNITIES,

Having regard to the Treaty establishing the European Community,

Having regard to the Agreement on the European Economic Area,

Having regard to Council Regulation No 17 of 6 February 1962, First Regulation implementing Articles 85 and 86 of the Treaty,[1] as last amended

---

1 OJ No 13, 21.2.1962, p. 204/62.

by the Act of Accession of Spain and Portugal, and in particular Articles 2, 6, and 8 thereof,

Having regard to the application for negative clearance and the notification for exemption submitted, pursuant to Articles 2 and 4 of Regulation 17, as converted on 18 September 1993 from the original notification pursuant to Council Regulation (EEC) No 4064/89 of 21 December 1989 on the control of concentrations between undertakings,[2]

Having regard to the request made by the parties on 10 February 1994, to extend the application and notification to Article 53 of the Agreement on the European Economic Area,

Having regard to the summary of the application and notification published pursuant to Article 19(3) of Regulation 17 and to Article 3 of Protocol 21 of the EEA Agreement,[3]

After consultation with the Advisory Committee for Restrictive Practices and Dominant Positions,

Whereas:

1. THE FACTS

A. INTRODUCTION

(1) The present case was originally notified as a concentration pursuant to Regulation (EEC) No 4064/89. However, the Commission concluded that none of the transactions notified constituted a concentration. The parties were so informed by the decision of 13 September 1993. Consequently, and at the request of the parties, the notification was converted into a notification for negative clearance and/or exemption pursuant to Regulation 17.

Following the entering into force of the Agreement on the European Economic Area (EEA Agreement), the parties requested the Commission to extend the notification to cover also Article 53 of the EEA Agreement. Given that the notified agreements will have a relevant impact on the EFTA countries and that such impact is expected to be very similar to that the notified agreements will have on the Community, the Commission will also apply Article 53 of the EEA Agreement in the present case.

(2) The notified operation actually comprises two main transactions:

(i) British Telecommunications plc (BT) is to take a 20% stake in MCI Communications Corporation (MCI), worth US$ 4,3 billion. BT will acquire new equity and will become the largest single shareholder in MCI, with proportionate board representation and investor protection. As will be further detailed later, several provisions have been included in the relevant agreement to impede BT from controlling or influencing MCI;

(ii) the creation of a joint-venture company Newco, for the provision of enhanced and value-added global telecommunications services to multinational (or large regional) companies. The parties will contribute their existing non-correspondent international network facilities, including Syncordia, BT's existing outsourcing business to Newco.

2 OJ No L 395, 30.12.1989, p. 1 (corrected version OJ No L 257, 21.9.1990, p. 13).
3 OJ No C 93, 30.3.1994, p. 3.

In the framework of the operation, the parties will rationalize their respective holdings in other telecommunications operators (TOs) and groupings in the world. In this respect, MCI has already acquired most of BT's existing business in North America

B. THE PARTIES

(3)   BT, the former UK monopolist telecommunications operator, and now a publicly quoted company, supplies telephone exchange lines to homes and businesses; local, trunk and international (to and from the United Kingdom) telephone calls; other telecommunications services and telecommunications equipment for customers' premises.

Worldwide turnover for BT in 1993 was ECU 17952 million, a figure that shows a slight decrease in respect of 1992 (ECU 18080 million). Over 95% of BT's turnover was obtained in the EEA, mainly (over 94%) in the United Kingdom. Outside the United Kingdom, BT has an established presence in France, the Netherlands, Germany and Spain, where it has recently announced a joint-venture agreement with Banco de Santander to provide data transmission services in Spain, where it has recently announced a joint-venture agreement with Banco de Santander to provide data transmission services in Spain in competition with the local TO.

BT is the world's fourth largest telecommunications company in terms of traffic (minutes of telecom traffic).

(4)   MCI is a telecommunications common carrier in the United States of America providing a broad range of US and international voice and data communications services including long-distance telephone, record communications and electronic mail services to and from the US.

Worldwide turnover for MCI in 1992 was ECU 8137 million. MCI's turnover in the Community for the same year was said by MCI to be ECU 326,27 million.

MCI is the second largest long-distance operator in the United States of America after AT&T and the world's fifth largest in terms of traffic.

C. THE RELEVANT MARKET

1. Newco

(5)   The market Newco will address is the emerging market for value-added and enhanced services to large multinational corporations, extended enterprises and other intensive users of telecommunications services provided over international intelligent networks. This market will cover a wide range of existing global trans-border services. including virtual network services, high-speed data services and outsourced global telecommunications solutions specially designed for individual customer requirements. Initially, however Newco will focus its development efforts on the biggest [. . .][4] multinationals.

(6)   In this market, Newco is expected to offer a portfolio of global products included in six categories of service offerings. Those global products will originally be based on a blend of existing products of the parent companies.

---

4 Blanks between square brackets indicate business secrets deleted pursuant to Article 21(2) of Regulation No 17.

The six categories are the following:
— data services: low-speed packet, high-speed packet and frame relay services, pre-provisioned, managed and circuit switched bandwidth,
— value-added application services: value-added messaging and video conferencing services,
— traveller services: global calling card services,
— intelligent network services,
— other services: Integrated VSAT network services,
— global outsourcing that will allow the distributor to offer its customers the ability to transfer responsibility and ownership of their global networks to either the distributor or Newco. In this respect, Newco will be able to integrate within its own offerings third-party products already owned by customers that they want to keep.

Given the needs of big companies to link locations geographically dispersed over the world (that means also providing broad coverage of delivery capacity and in-country support), those products must be global in nature and respond to a very particular set of requirements.

For a product to be global, it must have a number of special characteristics that make it different from similar products. Those characteristics are:
— to provide ubiquitous service across multiple horders,
— to provide consistent service levels and flexible delivery schedules,
— to make time-zones, languages and currencies irrelevant,
— to overcome inadequacies of local infrastructures,
— to make customers assume service is local when it is actually being provided from the other side of the world.

(7)   The requirements of big companies that a provider of services must meet, and that refer to all products or services being provided are:
— a single point of contact accountable for assuring service levels,
— seamless, uniform, flexible features/functionality across geography,
— end-to-end provisioning, installation, fault management and service support,
— reliable service,
— customized billing, management information, reporting with language and currency flexibility,
— speed, ease of implementation,
— products that meet existing and evolving needs.

Generally speaking, those requirements have not been adequately satisfied under the still existing structure of the global telecommunications market based on national monopolies. A national TO does not provide real one-stop-shop, end-to-end or seamless services to customers' premises located outside the national borders. What a TO was doing up to now was to cooperate with other TOs to link their respective networks. Doing so meant that customers were billed separately and in different currencies by the TO of each country where they had facilities, that services and features available in each country were different (or at least that some features available at home were not available abroad), and that they had to face many other problems linked to the differences in culture or language.

(8)   This situation began to change because of two elements. The starting Up, first in the United States of America, then in the United Kingdom and now in the rest of the Community, of the gradual liberalization process of the

global telecommunications market, and, secondly the rapid convergence of telecommunications and information technology. Both elements enabled the introduction of new services and products which vastly improved quality and range. One result was that multinationals and other big companies began to construct their own private networks. However, those private networks were costly because they eliminated scale economies of service and personnel, and because telecommunications was not the core business of those companies. For those reasons, now that the continued evolution of the said two elements has substantially changed the overall situation, those companies may consider turning to telecommunication service providers such as Newco.

(9) In addition, as regulation eases and technology advances, the border between services still under monopoly and liberalized services fades away. This fact adds further uncertainty to the market.

(10) In this context, what BT and MCI intend to offer through Newco is what the existing technology allows them to offer within the current regulatory limits. New products within existing categories and new categories of products could be offered by Newco in the years to come, that could include public basic telecommunications services.

(11) However, this Decision relates only to Newco's range of products and business scope as notified. Any substantial change thereof in the years to come, and in particular the offering by Newco of public basic telecommunications services will then require a new notification.

Structure of the market

(12) It is particularly difficult to give a precise picture of the existing structure of this emerging market because its principal feature is that it is in constant evolution. What is certain is that there is a very significant growth potential in the segment to be addressed by Newco, due to the continuing emergence of new technologies, improvements in basic infrastructure, the increasing standardization of services across borders, the increasing sophistication of customers and their reliance on telecommunications as a transport vehicle for information. All this is in the framework of a rapidly changing telecommunications regulatory environment, which, in the Community, will mean full liberalization telephony in 1998 (2003 for some Member States).

2. BT's investment in MCI

(13) The acquisition by BT of new equity equivalent to a 20% stake in MCI is intended to serve a common interest expressed by the parties to go global to better serve (and keep) their existing customers and to better address new areas of the market.

(14) The telecommunications market is developing fast and there is a high degree of uncertainty about how it will look in a few years' time: the prospect of full liberalization is pushing TOs to take positions, in order to be in the best possible situation when full liberalization comes. Many alliances are being announced, and most of them include provisions to enter the value-added segment, as a first step (in the EEA, value-added and enhanced services have already been liberalized), in particular as regards the provision of advanced value-added services to big multinationals. In this respect, the

creation of Newco and the investment of BT in MCI are steps taken by the two parent companies to pre-position themselves for when full liberalization is in place, steps that are being followed by many TOs who are creating sets of products comparable to those of Newco.

3. Geographic scope

(15) The geographic market to be addressed by Newco, and to be considered in respect of the investment of BT in MCI, is global. Such conclusion is based on the two following arguments.

Although national borders are still in place as regards the provisions of most telecommunications services, strategic alliances like the present one are being created now in anticipation of a market situation where national boundaries will have substantially disappeared.

In addition, both the services that Newco is going to offer, as indicated in definition of the business scope of Newco (see recital 23), and the customers it intends to serve are by nature international; consequently Newco will not be involved in the provision of services within one country only.

4. Market shares of Newco

(16) Newco's addressable market has been estimated by the parent companies at ECU [. . .] billion in 1994 and is projected to achieve over [. . .] annual growth over its first five years to achieve ECU [. . .] billion in 1999. It is also estimated that the Community will account for [. . .] of the market in 1994/95 rising to [. . .] in 1998/99.

According to Newco's business plan its market share, considering all categories of services together, will be [. . .] in 1994 and grow to over [. . .] by 1999 (assuming no dramatic change in the categories of products offered).

5. Main competitors of Newco

(17) Many companies, on their own or in cooperation with other partners, have entered or are entering the market for international value-added services (the precise set of services being offered is never exactly the same). Among them, the most important are: AT&T Worldsource, AT&T Istel, GEIS, International Private Satellite Partners (limited to North America and Europe), Eunetcom, Unisource, Infonet, Sprint International, FNA (limited to financial services), and IBM (through IBM's connect programme). Some of those projects are the current expression of strategic alliances between TOs, the real scope of which is not well determined yet, but which are similar to the present one between BT and MCI in that they are actions intended to position their partners with a view to the full liberalization to come and are not limited to the provision of value-added services.

In addition, almost every TO in Europe and in North America is trying to offer to its existing customers, at a national or a limited international level, an improved set of value-added and enhanced services.

For many of them, the range of specific products they want to offer and the kind of customers they want to serve are not clear yet. However, a substantial number intends to address the needs of the same companies Newco sees as potential customers, so that it is anticipated that there is going to be substantial competition at least at that level.

It should also be noted that a substantial number of major companies whose needs Newco intends to address have installed or are in the process of installing their own internal networks built on circuits leased from TOs. Those networks will be close substitutes of the Newco's services, in so far as they are to be offered to third parties.

6. Position of buyers

(18) The customers that Newco intends to serve are multinational corporations, extended enterprises, and other intensive users of telecommunications and in particular the biggest [. . .] of them. Many of them have huge telecommunication needs. In addition many have developed experience in the management of their own internal networks. They will only switch to providers such as Newco, if so doing proves to be cost-effective. Finally, given their knowledge of the market they are in a position to request offers from different competitors. All those factors give them considerable bargaining power which will give rise to pressure on margins and an expected high level of competition between suppliers.

D. THE TRANSACTION: THE NOTIFIED AGREEMENTS

(19) The complexity of the operation concluded between BT and MCI is reflected by the substantial number of agreements notified to the Commission. Those agreements are summarized below:

1. Agreements regarding Newco

(i) *The joint-venture agreement* (JVA)
This is the principal document creating Newco. Under it, the parent companies indicate their intention to achieve joint success in the global telecommunications market and to offer a seamless set of global enhanced and value-added products to the customers of MCI and BT.

(ii) *The intellectual property agreement* (IPA) concluded by BT, MCI and Newco concerning the licensing to Newco of the parent companies' technical information and intellectual property rights needed by Newco to carry out the business, and the licensing of Newco's technical information to the parent companies.

(iii) *The BT/MCI services agreements* (SA), under which Newco and each parent company (acting as supplier) agree on the terms and conditions of supply of support services to be provided by each parent company to Newco, related to the establishment by Newco of the global platform and on the provision by Newco of the global products and services.

(iv) *The BT/MCI distribution agreements* (DA) under which Newco appoints each parent company (acting as distributor) as its exclusive distributor for global products in the Americas, in the case of MCI, and in the rest of the world, in the case of BT.

(v) *The agreement for the sale and purchase of the business of Syncordia (with a disclosure letter)* concluded between Newco and BT setting the terms and conditions of the sale of the assets and business included in Syncordia, which up to now was BT's outsourcing unit.

(vi) *The Infonet indemnity agreement* concluded between BT and MCI under which MCI undertakes to indemnify and hold BT harmless from and against any legal action by Infonet against MCI, arising from MCI's ownership in Infonet.

2. Agreements regarding BT's investment in MCI

(20)(i) *The investment agreement* (IA) under which BT has agreed to purchase 20% of the outstanding shares of common stock of MCI.

(ii) *The registration rights agreement* concluded between BT and MCI, required in order for each party to effect the transactions contemplated by the IA.

(iii) *The McCaw indemnity agreement* under which BT undertakes or indemnify MCI and hold it harmless in respect of any legal action by the cellular phone company McCaw against BT as owner of a number of shares in McCaw.

(iv) Finally, the transaction also includes three agreements relating to the sale by BT to MCI of most of its existing activities in the United States of America and Canada.

3. Contractual provisions

(21) Relevant provisions of the agreements from a competition point of view are further detailed below.

A. *Concerning Newco*

(i) Structure of Newco

(22) Newco is an international joint-venture company, and according to the parties, the central focus of their alliance. Following the incorporation of Newco, 75,1% of its share capital will be owned by BT and 24,9 % by MCI. Each party will have the right to appoint Newco board directors in accordance with its shareholding. Thus BT will be entitled to nominate six out of eight directors (the A directors) and MCI two out of eight (the B directors).

Most decisions of the board are to be adopted by simple majority of the directors present at any board meeting. However, a number of important decisions cannot be adopted without the prior consent of both shareholders. Most important of those decisions are changes in business direction, management appointments (including the appointment of the chief executive officer) and approval of the five-year business plan and annual operating plan and budget, so that MCI has joint control of the company (this was the conclusion of the Commission in its decision of 13 September 1993).

The day-to-day management and operations of Newco will be delegated to a chief executive officer who will be responsible to the board for all matters in the ordinary course of business.

Newco will be incorporated in the United Kingdom with day-to-day management vested in a US-based service company. It is expected to employ around [. . .] people. It is anticipated that over the five initial years, the parent companies will invest US$ [. . .] billion (ECU [. . .] billion) in Newco including the assets which will be transferred to it prior to closing. BT will invest US$ [. . .] million and MCI US$ [. . .] million.

(ii)   Purpose and activities of Newco

(23)   Newco has been created for the provision of enhanced and value-added telecommunications services and outsourcing to big companies. By enhanced and value-added telecommunication services the parties mean any international telecommunication service (collectively referred to as global products) which the regulatory framework permits to be offered between two or more countries by members of a single group and which the regulatory framework permits to be managed on an end-to-end basis.[5]

To achieve that goal, Newco's precise activities can be split into planning and management on the one hand, and support and marketing on the other hand.

1.   Provisions concerning planning and management

In respect of planning and management activities, Newco will be responsible for:

(a)   the planning and development of global products. As part of this function, Newco will review the current products of the parent companies and the regulatory constraints still existing at any given moment;

(b)   the establishment of a global platform (i.e. a software package) over which the global products will be provided. Newco will provide a 'best-of-breed' platform comprised of a combination of any or all of transmission, switching, signalling, network intelligence and service management services. The architecture, design and continuing development shall be at the discretion of Newco, although it shall ensure that those parts of the distributor domestic system used are compatible with the overall design. Such platform will be based initially on the existing systems of the parent companies. Thus interworking those systems will consume the most important part of Newco's time and efforts in its early years of operation;

(c)   the provision of telecommunications services management to customers, including the acquisition and management of assets and staff from customers (global outsourcing).[6]

In order to carry out the foregoing, Newco will have a budget for R&D activities. However, as Newco will not have its own in-house facilities, the R&D activities will actually be undertaken mainly by the parent companies, under contract with Newco. The former will keep the ownership of their laboratories and of the existing technology being licensed to Newco.

2.   Support and marketing

Newco will derive its revenue from selling its services to its parent companies who will be the exclusive distributors of the Newco products. In this respect,

---

5 The following services are excluded from the definition: (i) voice international simple resale (ii) international direct distance dialling provided on a correspondent basis (iii) the provision of international private leased circuits and (iv) any services which for regulatory reasons must be offered on a correspondent basis.

6 In this respect, Syncordia, BT's existing outsourcing unit, will continue to exist, either as a division or as a separate branch within Newco.

it will not have direct contact with customers except as regards the provision and sale of global outsourcing services. Newco will nevertheless have a number of responsibilities and obligations towards the distributors:

(a) it will decide, according to principles set out in the business plan, who is going to be the main or 'lead' distributor in each contract for global products;

(b) it will provide technical and commercial support to each distributor in sales and marketing activities including assisting in identifying potential customers, advising on the most suitable means of meeting the requirements of a customer, supporting account management and assisting in the preparation of proposals to customers;

(c) it will provide billing services to distributors;

(d) it will provide second-level customer service in support of the first-level support provided by the distributors;

(e) it will carry out global market analysis and an annual products development plan.

(iii)   Provisions concerning dealings with/by Newco

(24) Pursuant to Article 17(1) of the JVA, transactions between Newco and a shareholder are to be on terms and conditions substantially as favourable to Newco as if such transaction had been entered into with a third party on an arm's-length basis (cost plus a reasonable market rate of return) but no more than that.

Pursuant to Article 17(3) of the JVA, Newco is to purchase all products, services and facilities from the parent companies only if in each case the relevant parent company can provide the same on terms at least as favourable as regards price, quality and service to Newco as would be obtainable in an arm's-length transaction from a supplier not related to Newco or the parent companies.

(iv)   Non-compete provisions

Pursuant to Article 18(1)(a) of the JVA, and except in accordance with the DA, each shareholder and its ultimate parent company undertakes to Newco and the other shareholder and its ultimate parent company that it will not carry on or be engaged or interested in the provision of enhanced and value added telecommunication services anywhere in the world or international outsourcing services or appoint any person to be a director of a business which provides such services other than as director of Newco or its subsidiary undertakings. In addition, and except in accordance with the distribution agreement, they also undertake not to solicit the custom of any person for the purpose of offering to it enhanced and value-added telecommunication services or international outsourcing services.

However, neither BT nor MCI will be in breach of the non-compete provision as a consequence of any actions undertaken by either of them in compliance with the licence granted to BT by the Secretary of State, or any applicable regulatory certificate, licence or any obligation imposed upon MCI by any authority in the United States of America (Articles 18(3) and 18(4) of the JVA). It has to be noted, however, that in such a case, and provided that the parent company involved cannot find an alternative means of complying with the non-compete provision, it shall pay to Newco an amount equal to any profits made as a result of such action (Article 18(5) of the JVA).

Finally, Articles 18(9) and 18(10) of the JVA ensure that in the case of deregulation of the US/UK (and vice versa) route for the provision of international voice services, BT and MCI will receive from each other the necessary support to compete; however, if the two parent companies cannot agree on a method to effectively compete with third parties except by means of international voice resale, then Newco will be authorized to offer basic international voice services on that deregulated route. As indicated in recital 11 should this occur, a new notification will be required.

(v)   Licences granted to Newco and by Newco to the distributors

(26)   Pursuant to Article 3(3) of the ITA, each parent company grants to Newco irrevocable, perpetual, non-exclusive, non-transferable licences to use the technical information solely for the purposes of the business. However, it has to be noted that the term 'technical information' excludes confidential information (the sharing of which between and among the parties is substantially restricted by the terms of a Data Segregation Schedule of the JVA) and trade secrets of a commercial nature.

Newco has the right to grant the following sub-licences to its parent companies:

(a)   to BT solely for its territory (i.e. the world excluding the Americas) and to MCI solely for the Americas, to use the technical information licensed from the parent companies in the distribution of Newco's products (Article 3(4)(a)(i) of the IPA). In addition, each distributor has the right to grant similar sub-sublicences to customers and an outside party for the sole purpose of discharging, in whole or in part, the licensed distributor's obligations under the relevant distribution agreement (but in any event restricted to the territory of that distributor).

(b)   to the so-called non-owning parent company (i.e. the parent company that does not own a specific technical intellectual property right), to use the licensed technical information in respect of products other than global products provided by Newco to customers connected to/or served by such parent company but limited to that parent company's territory as distributor (Article 3(4)(c) of the IPA).

Newco itself cannot sublicence an outside party with two exceptions:

(a)   where the distribution agreement has become non-exclusive (Article 3(5)(a) of the IPA);

(b)   where Newco is providing directly to any customer global outsourcing directly to any customer.

Furthermore, Newco grants to each parent company, upon request, similar licences to use the technical intellectual property rights (Article 6 of the IPA) of Newco.

Finally, it has to be noted that the sublicences granted to BT or to MCI under their respective technical intellectual property rights will survive termination of the agreement as irrevocable, perpetual and worldwide licences unrestricted as to use and licensing (Article 13(1)(b) and 13(2)(b) of the IPA), subject only to the payment by each parent company to the other of a given royalty during four years. In addition, they also receive similar licences for Newco's own intellectual property rights.

(vi)   Ownership by Newco of new technology

(27)   Pursuant to Article 7(1) of the IPA, Newco may be the owner of the technical intellectual property rights in new developments. In such a case, and assuming that a given development was actually made by one parent company under contract by Newco, such parent company (Newco does not have its own R&D activities) will receive from Newco a non-exclusive, irrevocable, perpetual licence to use that development for any purpose (Article 7(2) of the IPA). Conversely, where the new development is owned by the parent company that effected it. that parent company will grant a similar licence to Newco (Article 7(3) of the IPA).

(vii)   Trade mark provisions

(28)   Pursuant to Article 12(3)(a) and (b) of the IPA each parent company grants the other (this time without any intervention by Newco) a non-exclusive licence to use and license the trade marks of the one in the territory of the other in connection with the sale, distribution, provision or performance of global products only.

(viii)   Provisions regarding the distribution of Newco products

(29)   Pursuant to Article 2(1) of each DA, Newco appoints the distributor as its exclusive distributor in the territory. Such appointment means that the distributor has the exclusive right to promote, sell and distribute services in the territory (Article 3(1) of the DA) and the corresponding obligation to promote the sale of the global products in the territory (Article 8(1)). In addition, the distributor agrees to obtain from Newco, with some exceptions, all requirements for global products (Article 5(1)). Finally, in consideration of the provision of the services, the distributor pays to Newco (i) a variable annual charge based on the forecast that each distributor is obliged to provide to Newco each year of the aggregate requirements of its own customers for the following 12 months,[7] and (ii) a usage charge. Also, in consideration of the licences granted by Newco to the distributor pursuant to the intellectual property agreement, the distributor shall pay Newco an annual charge that for the first financial year will amount to US$ 6,5 million (Article 16).

Newco undertakes not to sell global products directly or indirectly in the territory other than to the distributor (Article 4(1)). However, Newco can sell global outsourcing services directly to customers when it is desirable to do so for tax or other reasons and assuming that in such a case the distributor releases Newco from its undertaking in Article 4(1) (Article 4(2)). The

---

7 It has to be noted that if the actual requirements of the distributor are less than those stated in the forecast, no part of the charge will be refunded by Newco.

provision of the global products to the distributor includes the provision by Newco of all necessary use of remote networks on the most competitive terms available, where the products are to be provided at one or more sites of one customer located outside the territory (Article 6(5)), and the provision by Newco of reasonable technical and commercial support to the distributor in sales and marketing activities (Article 9).

B. *Concerning BT's investment in MCI*

(i) Restriction on transfer of shares by BT and limits to the ability of BT to increase its shareholding in MCI

(30) Pursuant to Article 5(1) of the IA, BT undertakes not to dispose of its shares in any manner whatsoever for four years from the closing date. After that date, BT can sell, but must give a right of first refusal to MCI (Article 5(3) of the IA).

Pursuant to Article 6(1) of the IA, BT is granted the right to acquire any new shares issued by MCI necessary to maintain the percentage it has in MCI at that time or to increase it assuming that such purchase does not breach any foreign ownership restrictions under US law applicable at the relevant time (Articles 6(2)(d) and 6(4) of the IA).

However, pursuant to under Article 7(1) of the IA, BT has agreed not to acquire, directly or indirectly, the ownership of any additional equity of MCI to exceed 20% thereof until the 10th anniversary of the closing date. Furthermore, during the same period, BT has expressly undertaken not to seek to control or influence the company (Article 7(3) of the IA)

Once the 10-year's 'standstill' period has expired, BT can increase its shareholding up to the level then fixed by the US Communications Act as regards foreign ownership. However, even if those restrictions were completely eliminated. BT would generally only be allowed to exceed a 35% stake in MCI by a tender offer or business combination that has been approved by a majority of the independent directors and by a majority of the shareholders (other than BT) (Article 7(4) of the IA).

(ii) BT's consent rights and board representation

(31) The MCI board is to be composed of 15 directors. BT's representation on the MCI board will remain in proportion to its shareholding. BT is currently entitled to three directors. Four directors can be executive officers of MCI There is a similar representation on most MCI board committees. At least eight members of the MCI board must be fully independent of MCI and BT (Articles 9(7) and 9(9) of the IA).

BT, as the sole holder of MCI class. A common stock, has been granted substantial consent rights with respect to certain corporate actions of MCI concerning equity issuances, acquisition of core and of non-core business, sales of assets and borrowing above certain specified limits.

(iii)   Loss of rights provisions

(32)   Pursuant to Article 9 (12) of the IA, in the event that either BT or MCI engages, directly or indirectly, in the core business[8] of the other (in the Americas in the case of BT and outside the Americas in the case of MCI) or transfers or provides sales and marketing in connection with any person or acquires an interest in any person who is engaged in the core business of the other, then the engaging party will lose certain rights.

In the case of BT, its shares in MCI will be converted into common stock and it will lose its voting and consent rights and its board representation in MCI.

In the case of MCI, BT will cease to be bound by various obligations concerning future share transfers, voting or the standstill provisions mentioned above.

In any event, the loss of rights provisions will not be automatically triggered; there are a number of exceptions (listed in Article 9(12)(b) and (d) which include without limitation correspondent relationships in the ordinary course of business and any activities in connection with the ownership of Newco) and a procedure to be followed (including arbitration in case of disagreement) before a loss of rights is deemed to exist.

E.   THIRD PARTY OBSERVATIONS

(33)   Following the publication of a notice pursuant to Article 19(3) of Regulation 17 and to Article 3 of Protocol 21 of the EEA Agreement, comments were received from two interested third parties. One of them requested its comments and identity to remain confidential. The other set of comments received focused on the ability of BT to distort competition in the provision of enhanced and value-added services throughout Europe, given its control of local access facilities in the United Kingdom and on the necessity for the Commission to impose undertakings on the parties with respect to non-discriminatory treatment of competitors and cross-subsidization of competitive services with revenues derived from non-competitive operations, to facilitate the development of effective competition in the telecommunications market.

The Commission studied carefully the comments received and concluded that concerns expressed by those third parties had already been raised by the Commission and discussed in detail with BT and MCI, who had provided adequate answers and safe-guards. Consequently, those comments have not caused the Commission to modify its substantive position indicated in the Article 19(3) notice and expressed below, as regards the notified agreements.

---

8 Defined as all telecommunications and other electronic information services and equipment for the provision of such services, as they exist on the date of this agreement or hereafter exist, including (but not limited to) all forms of telecommunication access and egress; and value-added consumer and business services generated through or as a result of underlying telecommunications services using all technology (voice, data and image) and physical transport, network intelligence, and software applications, and including (i) information processing (ii) systems integration and outsourcing, (iii) transaction processing and (iv) cable television.

II. LEGAL ASSESSMENT

A. APPLICATION OF ARTICLES 85(1) OF THE EC TREATY AND 53(1) OF THE EEA AGREEMENT TO THE CREATION OF NEWCO AND TO BT's INVESTMENT IN MCI

1. The creation of Newco

(a) *Competition between the parent companies and/or Newco*

(34) The parent companies must be considered potential competitors of Newco and of each other in respect of the global products to be offered by Newco and actual competitors in the overall telecommunications market.

The inherent evolving nature of the business scope of Newco will have an effect on the issue of potential/actual competition; it is therefore considered that when (and if) Newco begins to offer some basic services (recital 11), the parent companies will become actual competitors of Newco.

(35) The above mentioned conclusions are based on the following arguments:

(a.a) potential competition in international value-added and enhanced services

(36) Newco's offering will consist of a mixture of the parent companies' existing products and networks. Prior to the incorporation of Newco, the parent companies were competitors, at least to a limited extent, for obtaining contracts for similar sets of products and services. Thus, BT won a contract with Hewlett Packard North America for the development of a global communications strategy focused mainly on Europe and Asia Pacific. In addition, customers of MCI for value-added services in the United States of America with branches abroad could obtain basically the same features (with some limitations depending on the number of locations abroad) in respect of these value-added services when entering into contact with their facilities abroad as when doing the same in the United States of America. Although many of those services are provided on a correspondent basis — i.e. by means of connecting MCI to another TO's network — some of them — MCI mail, for instance — are provided on a non-correspondent basis.

(37) The parties have indicated that they have withdrawn from the market that Newco will address. However, Newco has in fact received a licence from the parent companies to use the technologies and the latter retain the ownership of their respective know-how and intellectual property rights and also keep intact their respective R&D capabilities.

Newco will not do any research and development on its own but will award contracts mainly to its parent companies to do so. It is therefore considered that the parent companies will certainly keep and increase their proficiency and know-how in respect of the technologies required to stay in (or to re-enter) the market.

In addition, although the ownership of any new development could be awarded to Newco, it is possible (depending on the specific arrangements made in each case) that the developing parent company obtains the ownership, and, in any event, the parent companies will receive licences from Newco for using any such developed technology for any non-global product.

(38)   The parties have declared that they intend to offer to their intranational customers (that will usually be the national facilities of Newco's international customers) a set of services that for the customers will have an identical look and feel to the services offered by Newco in the international arena. For so doing they will receive from the other parent company through Newco the appropriate licences. Neither BT nor MCI are prevented, within their own territories, from setting up local subsidiaries in any given country to serve the local needs of companies in those countries. As a result a customer could be contracting at the same time with BT (or MCI), outside Newco, for its local needs and with BT (or MCI) as exclusive distributor of Newco for the customer's international needs.

(39)   Furthermore, customers may be international, but have such a concentration of traffic in either the United Kingdom or the United States of America that the relevant parent company's offering could be in direct competition with that of Newco were the customer to decide to forego Newco's international spread in order to get a good deal on domestic telecommunications which formed the bulk of its needs.

(40)   Finally, the patent companies will maintain their commercial presence and reputation intact. They will also keep, in particular because they will be the exclusive distributors of Newco, and increase their knowledge of the market in terms, for instance, of customers' needs.

All the above elements make the probability of such a (re)entry more credible.

(a.b)   Actual or at least potential competition in the overall market for telecommunications services

(41)   BT and MCI are the fourth and fifth largest telecommunications companies in the world in terms of traffic. BT, as the former monopolist in the United Kingdom, still keeps a very substantial amount of market power in that Member State as reflected by BT's overall market share (around 90% of the UK market). MCI is the second largest long-distance carrier in the United States of America, although significantly behind AT&T.

Under a traditional approach based on the state of international telecommunications prior to liberalization, TOs were limited to activities on their respective domestic markets and thus did not compete. However, this view cannot be maintained any longer, at least as far as large users of telecommunications are concerned. The different networks compete on features and prices for the installation of the telecommunication hubs of those large users. The intensity of this competition is bound to increase in the coming years as long as the liberalization process continues.

(42)   Both MCI and BT develop direct activities outside their home markets by means of subsidiaries and/or their activities in international organizations.

MCI employs 150 people in Europe and has several subsidiaries in different Member States (Germany, Belgium, France, Italy and the United Kingdom). Those subsidiaries provide the liaison office with the local TO involved, and also provide maintenance and repair of customer-based equipment, and coordination of billing information with multinational customers. They also support the sale of several of MCI's services (i.e. MCI Call USA, Vnet) which are available to European users and in competition with international direct dial services offered by BT or by other TOs in their respective home markets. Apart from the subsidiaries already mentioned, MCI has a branch office in the United Kingdom, MCI Ltd, to hold the name only, and another in the Netherlands, MCI Global Ventures BV, intended to be the holding company of a project that did not materialize. In addition, in Greece, Ireland, Spain and the Netherlands, MCI conducts liaison activities and sales support for services through independent contractors.

MCI currently provides enhanced private line services between the United States of America and the United Kingdom pursuant to a telecommunications services licence in the United Kingdom. In addition, MCI also provides data-only services for one customers worldwide reservation system using VSAT licences issued in Germany and France to Overseas Telecommunications Inc., an MCI subsidiary.

Finally, MCI has a 8,5% participation in the Financial Network Association (FNA), an association formed for the purpose of helping the supply, on a correspondent basis, of specialized telecommunication services to the global financial community. In addition. MCI had a 25% stake in Infonet, but has divested itself thereof.

BT has substantial activities in some Member States, in particular, France, the Netherlands, Germany and Spain (where it has recently created, together with the Spanish Banco de Santander, a joint venture to offer data services in Spain). However, the bulk of BT's activities abroad prior to the transaction with MCI was in the United States of America. As a result of the operation, most of British Telecom North America (BTNA) activities will be sold to MCI, and Syncordia will be transferred to Newco. Nonetheless, BT will keep a residual staff presence in the United States of America and BT USA Holdings, the US holding company. Apart from these, BT will retain BT US Capital Corporation (which is used by BT for obtaining funds in the US market), BT US Paging Inc., BT US Ventures Inc. and BT US Cableships. Finally, BT has held a 25% shareholding in McCaw but this has now been sold to AT&T in exchange for 2% of the outstanding voting power of AT&T, worth in the region of US$ 2 billion, which does not give BT any influence over AT&T's commercial strategy and which BT has declared it expects to sell at the appropriate time.

(b) *Applicability of Article 85 of the EC Treaty and Article 53 of the EEA Agreement to the creation of Newco*

(43) Having concluded that BT and MCI are, and for the foreseeable future will continue to be, at least potential competitors in the two markets concerned, it is necessary to assess whether the creation by them of Newco falls under Article 85(1).

It has not been demonstrated conclusively that the creation of Newco is the only objective means for the parent companies to enter and stay in the market for international and enhanced value-added services, because both parent companies are companies that currently have substantial activities in similar fields, including the provision of services to customers abroad, sometimes on a non-correspondent basis, and that have the financial and technological capacities required to enter the relevant market on their own. In doing so, they will be facing substantially the same constraints, in terms, for instance, of regulation, that Newco will be facing, when trying to enter the relevant market. In addition, the creation of Newco means that each parent company is unlikely itself to develop a similar set of products for use in the relevant market on its own. For these reasons, the creation of Newco falls within the scope of Article 85(1) of the EC Treaty and Article 53(1) of the EEA Agreement.

In addition, under its present structure, Newco can be considered as a vehicle for the parent companies to pool their respective intellectual property rights and to cross-license each other and Newco on an exclusive basis as far as the services to be offered by Newco are concerned, given in particular the non-compete provision, but also given the intellectual property agreements, the geographical scope of the licences granted to Newco by the parent companies and by Newco to them, and the terms of the exclusive distribution agreements. The Commission has indicated, in respect of reciprocal licences between competitors on an exclusive basis, that the benefits of the block exemption regulations on patent and know-how licence agreements to such licences are conferred only if the parties are not subject to any territorial restriction within the Community, including restrictions that isolate the Community against imports from non-member countries and thereby adversely affect the conditions of competition within the Community.

For the above mentioned reasons it is concluded that Newco falls within the scope of Article 85(1) of the EC Treaty and of Article 53(1) of the EEA Agreement.

2. BT's investment in MCI

(44) As a general rule, both the Commission and the Court of Justice have taken the view in the past that Article 85(1) does not apply to agreements for the sale or purchase of shares[9] as such. However, it might do so, given the specific contractual and market contexts of each case, if the competitive behaviour of the parties is to be coordinated or influenced.

The Commission consequently assessed whether the presence of BT's nominees to the board of MCI could give rise to coordination of the competitive behaviour of the two companies, in particular given the access that BT will have to MCI's confidential information. In this respect, the IA has been drafted in such a way that BT does not have the possibility to seek to control or influence the company. This is particularly so in the case of the obligations found in Articles 7(1) (not to increase shareholding for 10 years) and 7(3) (not to seek to control or influence the company).

In addition both American corporate and antitrust laws would impede any misuse of (or even the access to) any piece of confidential information of MCI by BT.

For the reasons mentioned above, it is concluded that the investment by BT in MCI does not fall within the scope of Article 85(1) of the EC Treaty or Article 53(1) of the EEA Agreement.

---

9 See the Decision in *Philip Morris/Rembrandt/Rothmans* referred to the 14th Report on Competition, points 98 to 100 and Joined Cases 142/84 and 156/84, *BAT and Reynolds* v *Commission*, [1987] ECR 4487.

B. APPLICATION OF ARTICLE 85(1) OF THE EC TREATY AND ARTICLE 53(1) OF THE EEA AGREEMENT TO CONTRACTUAL PROVISIONS

(45) The following provisions restrict competition:

(a) the appointment of BT as exclusive distributor of Newco (Article 2(1) of BT's DA) within the EEA;

(b) the obligation on the parties to obtain from Newco all requirements for global products (Article 3(1) of each DA);

(c) the non-compete provision as regards the activities of Newco (Article 18(1) of the JVA);

(d) the 'loss of rights' provisions pursuant to Article 9(12)(c) of the IA, as regards the activities of MCI in the territory of the EEA.

(46) Of these restrictions, the non-compete provision and the obligation to buy all requirements for global products from Newco are ancillary to the creation and successful initial operation of Newco. In this respect, they are considered to be subsumed under the joint venture and, consequently, they will not be assessed pursuant to Article 85(1) of the EC Treaty and Article 53(1) of the EEA Agreement separately from the joint venture itself.

Newco is the way chosen by BT and MCI to enter the relevant market. In this respect, both restraints are different expressions of the same firm commitment made by the two parent companies towards each other and towards Newco, and required for Newco to successfully enter the market, considering the characteristics of the emerging market for global value-added and enhanced services (and those of the overall market for telecommunications), in terms of uncertainty and associated risks, substantial investments required, and level of competition from similar ventures. Those characteristics are reflected in the fact that Newco is expected to incur substantial losses at least during its early years of operation.

The non-compete clause is aimed at ensuring that BT and MCI will concentrate their efforts on Newco, as regards the services to be offered by the joint venture; thus parallel activities by them (for instance in cooperation with other TOs) do not frustrate Newco's success in entering the relevant market.

The obligation on BT and MCI, as the exclusive distributors of Newco, to buy all requirements for global products from Newco, is aimed at ensuring a steady stream of funds for Newco and at increasing the credibility and market reputation of Newco; if the parent companies were free to obtain global products from other sources, in particular in cases where Newco could adequately satisfy a particular requirement, that might severely affect the credibility of Newco and its financial position. It has also to be noted that Newco itself is not obliged to obtain from its parent companies all of its requirements for telecommunications and other products and services.

Ancillary provisions are usually accepted for a limited period of time. In the present case, however, in view of the particular circumstances of the market in which Newco will be operating, including the substantial investments involved and the associated risks, those provisions will be accepted as ancillary for the entire duration of the exemption granted by this Decision to the joint venture.

(47) The appointment of BT as exclusive distributor of Newco within the EEA falls under Article 85(1) of the Treaty and under Article 53(1) of the

EEA Agreement because it has as its object or produces as its effect the isolation of the EEA against imports of the relevant services, as offered by Newco, from outside the EEA. Such fact will adversely affect the conditions of competition within the EEA. In addition, it cannot be considered ancillary to the creation of the joint venture taking in particular into account that the agreements foresee the possibility of the distribution becoming non-exclusive (Article 3(5)(a) of the IPA).

As to the appointment of BT as exclusive distributor of Newco in the BT territory outside the EEA territory and the corresponding provision under MCI's distribution agreement concerning the Americas, these provisions do not produce any appreciable effect in the EEA. For that reason they do not fall under either Article 85(1) of the EC Treaty or Article 53(1) of the EEA Agreement.

(48)   In view of the current state of development of the overall market for telecommunications, the 'loss of rights' provision affecting BT (Article 9(12)(a) of the IA) and, in so far as the territory of the EEA is not concerned, the 'loss of rights' provision affecting MCI (Article 9(12)(c) of the IA), will not produce any appreciable effect in the EEA. For that reason these provisions do not fall under either Article 85(1) of the Treaty or Article 53(1) of the EEA Agreement.

On the contrary, in so far as the territory of the EEA is concerned, the 'loss of rights' provision pursuant to Article 9(12)(c), already has an appreciable effect in the EEA and cannot be considered ancillary either to the investment of BT in MCI or the incorporation of Newco. It has as its object or produces the effect of significantly impeding any entry by MCI into the territory of the EEA using its existing technologies, in segments of the telecommunications market, that are currently outside the business scope of Newco but within the widely defined 'core business' of BT. In this respect, this provision, although it is not a non-compete provision as such, because MCI is not actually prevented from competing on its own in BT's territory (the effect of the provision is to make MCI pay a high price in case it decides to compete with BT in fields different from those covered by Newco), will nevertheless produce a practical effect very close to a non-compete obligation.

As a result, MCI might for instance in practice feel dissuaded from setting up a local company in any country within BT's territory to provide non-international value-added services, even though only using its existing range of products and services (that is, without infringing any intellectual property right belonging to BT or to Newco), within that country.

Any agreement which presents undertakings in third countries from becoming suppliers or competitors within the Community falls within the scope of Article 85(1) of the Treaty (and under Article 53(1) of the EEA Agreement). The assessment of the case has not shown the existence of any reason that would justify departing from that established practice.

In addition, a non-compete provision that extends beyond the field of activity of a joint venture cannot be accepted as such.[10]

For those reasons, the 'loss of rights' provision for MCI pursuant to Article 9(12)(c) of the IA falls under Article 85(1) of the Treaty (and Article 53(1) of the EEA Agreement) in so for as the territory of the EEA is concerned.

---

10 See Article 3(3) of Commission Regulation (EEC) No 2349/84, Article 6(a) of Commission Regulation (EEC) No 418/85 and Article 3(5) of Commission Regulation (EEC) No 556/89.

C. EFFECT ON TRADE BETWEEN MEMBER STATES AND BETWEEN MEMBER STATES AND EFTA COUNTRIES

(49)   In point 39(i) of the Guidelines on the application of EEC competition rules in the telecommunications sector[11] issued by the Commission, it is stated that as in the entire Community non-reserved services, equipment and space segment infrastructure are traded, any agreement concerning them may affect trade between Member States. This is the situation in the present case as Newco will cover the provision of value-added services not only between the EEA and abroad, but also between any two EEA countries. Such effect on trade between Member States, and between Member States and the EFTA countries, is going to be substantial in view of the growing size of the market, and of the further expansion expected for the coming years.

As regards non-ancillary provisions, they also affect trade between Member States, and between Member States and the EFTA countries, because they tend to insulate the entire EEA by impeding the development of existing or new activities by MCI within it, not only in respect of the products and the geographic areas within the business scope of Newco (as a result of the exclusive distribution arrangements) but also in respect of products or geographic areas that are outside the business scope of Newco (as a result of the 'loss of rights' for MCI).

As the provision of services between any two EEA countries is included in the business scope of Newco, such effect on trade is substantial.

D. CONCLUSION IN RESPECT OF ARTICLE 85(1) OF THE EC TREATY AND OF ARTICLE 53(1) OF THE EEA AGREEMENT

(50)   In conclusion it is considered that the creation of Newco falls under Article 85(1) of the Treaty and Article 53(1) of the EEA Agreement, and that this is also the case of the non-ancillary provisions mentioned above. The restrictive effect on competition and on trade between Member States is considered to be substantial.

E. APPLICATION OF ARTICLE 85(3) OF THE EC TREATY AND ARTICLE 53(3) OF THE EEA AGREEMENT

(51)   The objectives of the parent companies in entering this set of transactions are somewhat different. BT wants to become a leading global provider of international value-added and enhanced telecommunications services in the world, but with a particular emphasis in Europe and in the United States of America. Collaboration with a major American player was particularly important for BT to achieve those goals, and in particular to enter the US market, where 40% of multinational companies are located.

MCI's main interest was to maintain its competitive position in the Americas, in particular against AT&T. In order to do so, as customers' demand for global services was increasing, MCI considered it necessary to add a global dimension to its services but without having to establish itself abroad; it therefore chose the joint venture alternative. MCI first entered into

---

11 OJ No C 233, 6.9.1991, p. 2.

Infonet, but finally opted for an alliance with another TO. In this respect, after negotiating with different TO's it turned to BT. As a result of the transactions it will obtain the financial means to finance the improvement of its infrastructure in the United States of America.

(52) The agreements notified, in so far as they fall under Article 85(1) of the EC Treaty and Article 53(1) of the EEA Agreement, satisfy the conditions for exemption laid down in Article 85(3) of the Treaty and Article 53(3) of the EEA Agreement.

(a) Improvements

(53) It is considered that Newco will improve telecommunications services and technical/economic progress in the Community in the following ways:
— The combination of BT and MCI technologies will allow Newco to offer new services, based on the existing services of the parent companies, more quickly, cheaply and of a more advanced nature than either BT or MCI would have been capable of providing alone under their existing technologies Such combination will nevertheless require a very costly and time consuming effort as demonstrated by the fact that the set of services that Newco will offer will not be fully operational within five years. In addition, as a related consequence, MCI technology, which is said to be one of the most credible and user friendly in the world, will be made available to European customers of Newco (within the limits imposed by the non-ancillary provisions to be discussed below).
— The strategy of Newco for entering the market is to add value to basic transmission capacity (international private leased lines) obtained from local TOs. However, Newco will not use the features of each national network involved but will instead add its own switching systems, call prosessing/routing, signalling and databases as well as software to provide the international services on a truly seamless basis. This is considered to be a real advantage over existing international services that are provided (this is the case of BT and MCI) by interconnecting national networks that are usually incompatible in terms of structure, software, hardware and management systems. The result of a combined network so creative, is as strong as its weakest link and so the number of services and the features thereof are those supported by the less performant national network involved.
— In addition, if successful, Newco could allow the Community's most important companies to achieve levels of telecommunications performance on all international level currently only available at some national/local levels, that could enable them to better withstand global competition from other corporations operating from parts of the world where technological advance in telecommunications is becoming common-place.
— Finally, Newco will allow cost savings resulting from its operation of a single network architecture reflecting economies of scale at a technological and operational level, and possibly from cheaper interconnections obtained from TOs given Newco's expected size. In this respect, Newco will no doubt generate competition between the providers of international basic transmission capacity in order to obtain the lowest costs for its business, and will try to direct traffic over alternative routes in order to achieve the lowest cost routing available.

(54) Both the exclusive distribution arrangements in respect of BT and the 'loss of rights' for MCI as regards the EEA, are aimed at ensuring that each parent company concentrates its marketing efforts' in terms of prospecting for customers, investments on regional and/or national networks and other facilities, within its respective territory, as required by a successful market entry by Newco. At the same time, Newco will benefit from the reputation and track-record of its parent companies, *vis-à-vis* its potential customers.

(b) Consumers

(55) The incorporation of Newco will mean that consumers in general will benefit more rapidly from a set of new advanced services than Newco's parent companies would have been capable of providing separately.

In addition, consumers, big companies in this case, will benefit directly through the provision of:

— a greater product portfolio of developed and new services allowing them to operate more effectively on a global scale and to better compete with their global as well as with their Community and EEA competitors, and

— lower pricing resulting from the cost savings to be made by Newco as a result of operational effiencies or pressure on local TOs.

Such advantages will improve the competitive position of those company users in their respective markets, in particular against competitors that have at their disposal more advanced telecommunications.

In this respect, the exclusive distribution arrangements for BT will ensure in respect of its customers that there is a single person to contact in case of any kind of difficulties related to the continuous provision of the services anywhere in the world. In addition, the 'loss of rights' for MCI, seen as a means of permitting confidence between the parent companies to grow (see recital 62) would guarantee the necessary stability of the underlying relationship between BT and MCI necessary for it to be successful. A successful entry by Newco will increase the level of competition in the relevant market, and hence the possibilities of choice available for customers. Such stability is also a very important element for customers when considering giving a potential supplier responsibility over a strategic element as to their telecommunications needs.

(c) Remaining competition

(56) The creation of Newco will not afford the parties the possibility of eliminating competition in respect of the categories of services to be offered by Newco. Such conclusion is also applicable to the non-ancillary restrictions identified above, and is based on the following arguments:

— At Newco's level there will be significant third-party competition coming first of all from AT&T's Worldsource and from Eunectom (or from any enhancement of Eunectom if plans for a closer cooperation between Deutsche Bundespost Telekom and France Télécom go ahead). There will also be competition from other existing alliances, such as Unisource or IPSP, or from alliances to be concluded between TOs that have not taken a position until now (like Sprint, and the 'Baby Bells' in the United States of America,

NTT in Japan and some significant European TOs like Telefónica, Belgacom, Mercury or STET). Finally, the parties also expect competition, at least for components of global value-added telecommunications services, coming from other players including computer and data processing companies (like IBM, DEC and EDS) and information service companies (like Geis and Compuserve).

— Multinational or other big companies are sophisticated purchasers with the ability to build their own private network solutions or to attract offers from competitors of Newco. This gives the multinationals considerable bargaining power reflected in intense pressure on margins, and competition between the suppliers for customers.

(57)   In this context, the Commission has examined in detail and discussed with the parties, the extent to which access to MCI and BT networks by third parties is possible. This is an important question that can become of particular relevance in the near future, as is also the issue of possible cross-subsidization of Newco by BT, an issue that the Commission has also examined in detail.

In this respect, existing regulation to which BT and/or MCI are subjected in their respective countries prevents such cross-subsidization and/or discrimination from taking place.

As regards MCI, under the requirements of the Communications Act of 1934, as enforced by the Federal Communication Commission (FCC), MCI's network arrangements and services are described in publicly available tariff schedules or contracts.

The Communications Act and the FCC's policies prohibit MCI from making any unjust or unreasonable discrimination in the provision of its services including access to these services by MCI's competitors and foreign correspondents. In addition the FCC has a complaint process, should any party feel aggrieved by MCI's actions or inactions (or by those of any other TO in the United States of America).

The situation is similar as regards BT because under the terms of the Public Telecommunications Operator Licence that BT received under the Telecommunication Act 1984, which is enforced by the Office of Telecommunications (Oftel), BT cannot show undue preference or discrimination in the provision of certain services towards other persons, nor unfairly favour any part of its own business against competitors. In addition, a prohibition on exclusive dealing in the provision of international telecommunications services prevents BT from making arrangements with overseas correspondents, including MCI, which would exclude them from dealing with other operators in the United Kingdom. Finally, condition 18 of BT's licence (together with condition 38, in so far as the confidentiality of customer information is concerned),[12] empowers Oftel to act against any unfair cross-subsidy by BT and imposes upon BT an obligation to keep records of any material transfer between any parts of its business.

Those regulatory constraints are reflected in the agreements, so that actions undertaken by MCI or BT in complying with their respective obligations are excluded from the non-compete provision in the JJVA (Articles 18(3) and

---

12 The use of such information is also restricted by the Data Segregation Schedule of the JVA, to which reference is made in recital 26.

18(4)) and from the 'loss of rights' provisions in the IA (Articles 9(12)(b)(iii) and 9(12)(c)(iii))

The abovementioned regulatory constraints, together with the additional explanations provided by the parties, have permitted the Commission to conclude that it is not necessary for it to take any further action as of now, including requesting the parties to make appropriate undertakings to the effect that they will neither discriminate nor cross-subsidize. However, should this conclusion prove to be wrong in the future, the Commission will immediately apply the competition rules of the EC Treaty (and if applicable those of EEA Agreement as required.

(d) Indispensability

(i) *Newco*

(58) The formation of Newco itself is indispensable for the parent companies to successfully enter the relevant market:

— Newco will allow the time required for the relevant services to be marketed to be substantially shortened. As many other companies (mainly alliances) are entering the relevant market, the time required for being in the market with a comprehensive set of services is a competitive factor of the utmost importance.

— In addition, Newco will allow each parent company to substantially reduce the costs and risks inherently associated with the complex organization required to offer such services at the scale and with the other features required by multinationals and other big international users.

— Finally, as indicated in recital 7, Newco is a means to quickly overcome the inadequacies associated with the provision of the services and features (one-stop-shop, end-to-end and seamless basis, etc.) required by multinationals and other big international users, under the existing framework of cooperative relationships established by TOs.

(ii) *Exclusive distribution*

(59) Under BT's distribution agreement, BT is appointed by Newco as the exclusive distributor for Newco's products in a wide territory, covering the entire world excluding the Americas.

Such exclusivity is reinforced by the licensing provisions in the IPA. Thus, pursuant to Article 3(4)(a)(i), Newco sublicenses BT solely for the 'territory' and MCI solely for the Americas to use the combined technology it has received from its parent companies in the distribution of Newco's products. In addition, each parent company (or distributor) receives directly from the other a non-exclusive licence to use and license the trademarks of the latter within its own territory. Thus, BT grants MCI such a licence for the trademarks of BT but limited to the Americas (Article 12(3)(a) and (b)) and vice versa.

The parties have provided the Commission with an array of arguments supporting the indispensability of the exclusive distribution arrangements for BT in the transaction. Both have particularly stressed the protection of the valuable intellectual property rights they have contributed to the joint venture against outsiders but, in particular, against each other. In this context, both parties have stressed that they have not found a more efficient manner of organizing the distribution of the products in a balanced way.

Taking those facts into consideration, together with the high level of competition that the parent companies will be facing (as distributors of Newco) and the substantial bargaining power of customers, the exclusive distribution arrangement for BT (including here those provisions in the IPA that reinforce it) can be accepted as being indispensable to the positive effects (in particular the distribution of the products in an efficient manner) resulting from the restrictive clauses, provided that at least a possibility for passive sales is available for EEA customers. By passive sales is understood, as regards MCI, the possibility offered to a EEA customer of addressing himself to MCI for the provision of Newco products in the EEA with the support of Newco (as regards, for instance, the availability of leased lines or the required customer service) but without the intervention of BT or with the intervention of BT only as support distributor.

(60) The Commission has therefore examined the extent to which such passive sales are possible for all kinds of customers. The parties have confirmed that passive sales[13] will be possible irrespective of the actual size and location of customers, and the Commission considers (and the parties have recognized) that passive sales by each distributor to customers in the exclusive territory of the other are indeed a genuine possibility.[14] Thus, any potential European customer, with activities in at least two Member States, but no presence in the United States of America, can contract with MCI (instead of BT, the exclusive distributor for the EEA) the provision of Newco services in the EEA only. MCI will conclude the sale in America (without infringing any licence granted to it by Newco or any trademark licence granted by BT) and will then ask Newco to procure all necessary use of remote networks (third-party networks) on the most competitive terms available. For so doing, Newco could, in some cases, engage BT's services (in particular as regards regulated services still provided by BT), but will always be obliged to obtain supplies on a competitive basis. In addition, MCI will be responsible for that customer.

In conclusion, the exclusivity is considered indispensable within the meaning of Article 85(3) of the EC Treaty (and pursuant to Article 53(3) of the EEA Agreement).

(iii) *MCI's 'loss of rights' pursuant to Article 9(12)(c) of the IA*

(61) As explained above, Article 9(12)(c) of the IA provides for MCI to lose certain rights in the event that MCI becomes engaged in the core business of BT in a territory defined as 'the rest of the world', which includes the entire EEA.

---

13 The latest available version of the business plan even makes a distinction between 'remote sales' (where a customer requests a bid from one distributor for services in the other distributor's territory) and 'passive sales' (where a customer requests bids from a distributor which is not responsible for that territory or customer). Both sales can be effected. The relevant distributor will independently prepare a bid without consulting the other, and Newco, to the extent that it will be involved will not disclose to one distributor the prices or conditions it has provided to the other or any confidential information regarding the customer.
14 In addition, differences in MCI and BT prices for Newco services will occur in so far as each will be related to local conditions and supply costs.

(62)   This provision has to be considered against the imbalance between the very high value for each parent company of its proprietary software licensed to Newco (and to each other within their respective territory) and the low level of protection to which the software is entitled under most intellectual property laws in force. Basically, the same software is going to be used by Newco to serve the needs of its international customers and by each parent company to serve the intra-national needs of their customers within their respective territories. In addition, it has to be taken into account that through Newco (and the licences that Newco will grant to its parent companies in respect of any new development) the technologies of both parties will be increasingly interlinked and, hence, will be increasingly difficult to separate.

For these reasons, the parties decided not to include a termination provision in the IPA in case of infringement, and instead to include the 'loss of rights' provisions in the IA. In this respect, the latter can be seen as analogous to the territorial licensor protection permitted under both the patent licensing block exemption regulation (Regulation (EEC) No 2349/84) and the know-how licensing block exemption regulation (Regulation (EEC) No 556/89).

From this point of view, the 'loss of rights' pursuant to Article 9(12)(c) of the IA are indispensable in particular as a means of permitting confidence between the parent companies to grow and, consequently, to permit the necessary transfer of technology so as to allow Newco to succeed.

(63)   However, as indicated above, such provision will also produce the effect of substantially preventing MCI from entering the EEA using only its own proprietary technology. The Commission sees no justification for accepting this restrictive effect for as long as the agreements are in force.

For that reason, and following discussions with the Commission, the parties have modified the agreements so that the 'loss of rights' provision pursuant to Article 9(12)(c) of the IA, in so far as the EEA is concerned, will apply only for a period of five years. Once the five-year period in respect of those rights has expired, MCI's 'loss of rights' will be terminated in relation to the EEA.

This five-year period is adequate taking into account that the existing business plan for Newco commits the parent companies for five years and that, in addition, five years is the time required for the set of services to be marketed by Newco to be fully operational.

In view of this modification, the Commission considers that Article 9(12)(c) of the IA now fulfils the conditions for the granting of an exemption pursuant to both Article 85(3) of the EC Treaty and Article 53(3) of the EEA Agreement.

(e)   Conclusion

(64)   It is concluded that all the four conditions for the granting of an individual exemption pursuant to Article 85(3) of the EC Treaty and pursuant to Article 53(3) of the EEA Agreement in respect of the creation of Newco and in respect of the indispensable restrictions indentified above are satisfied.

F. DURATION OF THE EXEMPTIONS

(65)   Pursuant to Article 8 of Regulation No 17, a decision in application of Article 85(3) of the EC Treaty (and pursuant to Protocol 21 of the EEA Agreement in so far as Article 53(3) of the EEA Agreement is concerned) shall be issued for a specified period. Pursuant to Article 6 of that Regulation, the date from which such a decision takes effect cannot be earlier than the date of notification. In that respect, in the present case the Decision, in so far as it grants exemption, should take effect:

— from the date the notification was complete, that is from 16 November 1993 to 15 November 2000 as regards the joint venture created between BT and MCI, and the appointment of BT as exclusive distributor of Newco in the EEA,

— as regards the 'loss of rights' for MCI pursuant to Article 9(12)(c) of the IA, until the end of the fifth year from the date of the adoption of this Decision,

HAS ADOPTED THIS DECISION:

Article 1

On the basis of the facts in its possession, the Commission has no grounds for action pursuant to Article 85(1) of the EC Treaty and Article 53(1) of the EEA Agreement in respect of the agreements as notified, relating to the acquisition by BT of a 20% stake in the share capital of MCI, to the appointment of MCI as exclusive distributor of Newco in the Americas pursuant to Article 2(1) of MCI's Distribution Agreement, to the appointment of BT as exclusive distributor of Newco in the rest of the world excluding the EEA territory, to MCI's 'loss of rights' pursuant to Article 9(12)(c) of the Investment Agreement in so far as the territory of the EEA is not concerned, and to BT's 'loss of rights' pursuant to Article 9(12)(a) of the Investment Agreement.

Article 2

On the basis of the facts in its possession, the Commission has no grounds for action pursuant to Article 85(1) of the EC Treaty and Article 53(1) of the EEA Agreement for the duration of the exemption granted to the joint venture in respect of the obligation on BT and on MCI to obtain from Newco all requirements for global products pursuant to Article 3(1) of each Distribution Agreement and in respect of the non-compete provision as regards the activities of Newco pursuant to Article 18(1) of the Joint-Venture Agreement.

Article 3

Pursuant to Article 85(3) of the EC Treaty and Article 53(3) of the EEA Agreement, the provisions of Article 85(1) of the EC Treaty and of Article 53(1) of the EEA Agreement are hereby declared inapplicable for the period from 16 Nobember 1993 to 15 November 2000 to the joint venture, Newco, created between BT and MCI, as notified to the Commission, and to the appointment of BT as the exclusive distributor of Newco within the territory of the EEA pursuant to Article 2(1) of BT's Distribution Agreement.

Article 4

Pursuant to Article 85(3) of the EC Treaty and Article 53(3) of the EEA Agreement, the provisions of Article 85(1) of the EC Treaty and of Article 53(1) of the EEA Agreement are hereby declared inapplicable for a period of five years from the date of the adoption of this Decision to Article 9(12)(c) of the Investment Agreement.

Article 5

This Decision is addressed to:

British Telecommunications plc,
81 Newgate Street,
UK-London EC1A 7AJ.

MCI Communications Corporation,
1801 Pennsylvania Avenue, NW,
Washington, DC 20006,
USA.

Done at Brussels, 27 July 1994.

For the Commission
Karel Van Miert
Member of the Commission

**COMMISSION DECISION (96/546/EC) OF 17 JULY 1996 RELATING TO A PROCEEDING UNDER ARTICLE 85 OF THE EC TREATY AND ARTICLE 53 OF THE EEA AGREEMENT
OJ L239/23, 19 September 1996**

(Case No IV/35.337 — Atlas)
(Only the English, French and German texts are authentic)
(Text with EEA relevance)

THE COMMISSION OF THE EUROPEAN COMMUNITIES,
Having regard to the Treaty establishing the European Community,
Having regard to the Agreement on the European Economic Area,
Having regard to to Council Regulation No 17 of 6 February 1962, First Regulation implementing Articles 85 and 86 of the Treaty,[1] as last amended by the Act of Accession of Austria, Finland and Sweden, and in particular Articles 2, 6 and 8 thereof,
Having regard to the application for negative clearance and the notification for exemption submitted, pursuant to Articles 2 and 4 of Regulation No 17, on 16 December 1994,

---

1 OJ No 13, 21.2.1962, p. 204/62.

Having regard to the summary of the application and notification published pursuant to Article 19(3) of Regulation No 17 and Article 3 of Protocol 21 of the EEA Agreement,[2]

After consultation with the Advisory Committee for Restrictive Practices and Dominant Positions,

Whereas:

I. THE FACTS

A. INTRODUCTION

(1) The Atlas venture was notified to the Commission on 16 December 1994. This transaction brings about a joint venture owned as to 50% by France Télécom (FT) and as to 50% by Deutsche Telekom AG (DT). The notification of Atlas replaces the notification on 3 June 1993[3] of a joint venture formed by FT and DT (at the time Deutsche Bundespost Telekom) under the name of Eunetcom to which this Decision extends. Atlas is also the instrument of DT and FT's participation in a second transaction, notified under the name of Phoenix, with Sprint Corporation (Sprint).[4] Phoenix, since renamed as GlobalOne, is the object of a separate Decision pursuant to Article 85(3) of the EC Treaty.[5]

(2) Atlas is structured at two levels. A holding company established in Brussels. Atlas SA, incorporated as a *société anonyme* under the laws of Belgium, has three operating subsidiaries, namely Atlas Télécommunications SA (Atlas France) in France, Telekom Internationale Telekommunikationsdienste GmbH (Atlas Germany) in Germany, and one for the rest of Europe. Atlas France and Atlas Germany will initially provide technical and sales support to FT and DT, being the French and German distributors of Atlas and GlobalOne products. After full and effective liberalization of the telecommunications infrastructure and services markets in France and Germany, scheduled to occur by 1 January 1998, DT's subsidiary for the provision of X.25 packet-switched data communications, T-Data Gesellschaft für Datenkommunikation GmbH (T-Data)[6], will be merged with Atlas Germany while FT's subsidiary for the provision of X.25 packet-switched data communications, Transpac France, will be merged with Atlas France.

B. THE PARTIES

(3) Deutsche Telekom AG (DT) and France Télécom (FT) are the public telecommunications organizations (TOs) in Germany and France. Both supply telephone exchange lines to homes and businesses; local, trunk and international communications to and from their respective home country.

2 OJ No C 337, 15.12.1995, p. 2.
3 OJ No C 175, 26.6.1993, p. 11.
4 OJ No C 184, 18.7.1995, p. 11.
5 See p. 57 of this Official Journal.
6 The parties have submitted that T-Data is the new name of DT's former Datex-P division for the provision of X.25 packet-switched data communications services, incorporated after publication of the Commission notice pursuant to Article 19(3) of Council Regulation No 17 and Article 3 of Protocol 21 of the European Economic Area Agreement in this case; OJ No C 337, 15.12.1995, p. 2 (hereinafter the 'Article 19(3) notice').

Worldwide turnover in 1994 was ECU 31,8 billion, a 4,3% increase over 1993, for DT and ECU 21,7 billion, a 1,8% increase over 1993, for the FT group.

C. THE RELEVANT MARKET

1. Product markets

(4) Atlas will address the markets for the provision of non-reserved telecommunications services to corporate users both Europe-wide and nationally. Atlas will target two separate produce markets for non-reserved services, namely:

(5) *The market for customized packages of corporate telecommunications services.*

This market comprises mostly customized combinations of a range of existing telecommunications services, mainly liberalized voice services including voice communication between members of a closed group of users (virtual private network (VPN) services), high-speed data services and outsourced telecommunications solutions specially designed for individual customer requirements. The market for customized packages of corporate telecommunications services, enhanced by features such as tailored capacity allocation, billing, a 24-hour technical service, etc., is currently changing and evolving rapidly. Customers demand such packages of sophisticated telecommunications and information services offered by one single provider. That provider is expected to take full responsibility for all services contained in the package from 'end to end'. Accordingly, DT and FT intend to offer such customers through Atlas whatever services existing technology allows them to offer from time to time within the applicable regulatory framework. In this regard, the parties have indicated that Atlas will eventually extend to international voice traffic and other basic services, regulations permitting.

These services are provided over high-speed, large-capacity leased lines linking sophisticated equipment on customer premises to the service provider's nodes. Alternatively, other means of transmission, such as satellite or mobile radio capacity, can be used to ensure the geographic coverage demanded from time to time. Such services employ advanced state-of-the-art protocols, data compression techniques, equipment and software. In this market, Atlas is expected to offer a portfolio of services including the following (the 'Atlas services'):

— data services: high- and low-speed packet-switched, Frame Relay, Internet Protocol (IP) services,

— value-added application services: value-added messaging, video-conferencing and electronic document interchange (EDI) services,

— voice VPN services,

— value-added leased lines offerings: pre-provisioned, managed and circuit-switched bandwidth,

— very small aperture satellite (VSAT) network services, and

— outsourcing: customers are invited to transfer responsibility and ownership of their networks to Atlas. If they agree, Atlas may integrate into its own offerings any third-party products already owned by customers who wish to keep such offerings, as the case may be.

Of the above, some services will remain with DT and FT and therefore not be Atlas services These services are: (i) those national receive-only VSAT services in France which provide a single channel per carrier ('receive-only SCPC'); (ii) national messaging and EDI services in Germany; (iii) data network services using Asynchronous Transfer Mode (ATM) technology in France, Germany and any third country; and (iv) national VPN services in France and Germany. The integration into Atlas of any such service and/or its underlying network as well as of any broadband transmission capacity operated by DT and/or FT necessitates separate notification to the Commission.

(6)   Due to the high cost of building and operating the networks needed to provide customized packages of corporate telecommunications services, such services can be commercially viable only if provided to multinational corporations, extended enterprises, and other intensive users of telecommunications and in particular the largest among those customers generating continuous high traffic volumes.[7] Many of those potential customers have complex and specific needs and have often acquired expertise in managing own internal networks. Whether each of the services listed above constitutes a separate product market can be left open for present purposes, since a separate analysis would not affect the Commission's conclusions.

(7)   However this Decision relates only to Atlas' range of products and its business scope as notified. Any substantial change of products or business scope, and in particular (i) the integration into Atlas of broadband transmission capacity (such as Asynchronous Transfer Mode (ATM) networks) in France and Germany and (ii) the offering by Atlas of public basic telecommunications services (such as voice telephony services[8]) will require a new notification.

(8)   *The market for packet-switched data communications services*
Atlas will also be active on a separate market for packet-switched data communications services. The Commission considers data communications services to be a distinct telecommunications product market, without prejudice to the existence of narrower markets.[9] One narrower market is that for packet-switched data communications services.[10] Packet switching is a means to improve network capacity utilization and consists of splitting data sequences into 'packets', feeding these and other packets into the network optimizing utilization of available capacity, switching the packets to the desired destination and rearranging the packets to obtain the original data sequences. One standard used for the provision of packet-switched data communications services is the X.25 protocol. Packet-switched data services using this protocol (the 'X.25 data services') are slower than packet-switched data communications services using protocols such as Frame Relay,

7 See Commission Decision 94/579/EC of 27 July 1994 in Case No IV/34.857 — *BT-MCI*; OJ No L 223, 27.8.1994, p. 36.
8 Defined in the seventh indent of Article 1 of Commission Directive 90/388/EEC of 28 June 1990 on competition in the markets for telecommunications services; OJ No L 192, 24.7.1990, p. 10, hereinafter 'Services Directive', as last amended by Directive 96/19/EC; OJ No L 74, 22.3.1996, p. 13.
9 Commission's Guidelines on the application of Community competition rules in the telecommunications sector, OJ No C 233, 6.9.1991, p. 2, at paragraph 27.
10 Defined as 'packet- and circuit-switched services' in the ninth indent of Article 1(1) of the Services Directive — see footnote 8.

Asynchronous Transfer Mode (ATM) or Internet Protocol (IP), given that X.25 data services rely on smaller packets and require switches which allow charging per packet.

(9)   Packet-switched data communications services can be divided into different customer segments within the same product market.

1.   On the one hand, some customers generate mostly erratic and geographically widespread demand for low-speed, low-volume applications. These features are due either to the specific type of use (such as banks operating cash machines nationwide, networks of points-of-sale in shops) or to the size of such customers, as with small and medium-sized enterprises (SMEs). Such services are billed by volume sent, according to published tariffs. All incumbent Member State TOs including DT and FT operate dense public networks with nationwide coverage providing X.25 data services to this customer segment (the 'public packet-switched data networks'). There is only one public packet-switched network in each Member State, built by the incumbent TO under a public service obligation before market liberalization.

2.   On the other hand, larger corporate customers and other extended users generate more substantial and regular traffic. Often the requirements of these users make it worthwhile for either third-party service providers or the potential customer itself to assume the high cost of creating customized leased lines circuits (for example, to set up VPNs) to meet individual service demand. This demand is therefore increasingly met either by packet-switched services using protocols other than X.25, notably Frame Relay and ATM (for VPN applications) and IP (for both public and VPN applications) or by switched services (PSTN or ISDN services). Packet-switched data communications services to such users are billed according to negotiated rates that take account of the individual demand features of a particular customer.

(10)   Virtually all companies active in each individual Member State of the European Community are potential if not actual customers for national packet-switched data communications services. Such services are also required by SMEs, albeit in smaller volumes and possibly less regularly than by larger users. Seldom will such volumes make it worthwhile for service providers to invest in leased lines with the specific purpose of reaching these SMEs, which are therefore in a weak negotiating position and hardly capable to date of switching from the current provider, typically the incumbent TO, to a competitor.

(11)   Packet-switched data communications may also be offered as one service in a customized package of corporate services. However, even as part of such an arrangement, packet-switched data communications services are based on mature internationally standardized technology and provided over standard terrestrial infrastructure. At the national level, choice from a wider range of packet-switched data communications offerings than merely X.25 data services is available to larger customers that are not served over the TO's public packet-switched data networks but over customized leased-line circuits. However, most existing customers for packet-switched data communications currently generate annual turnover of far below ECU 10000 each and are not therefore potential users of customized packages of corporate telecommunications services. Therefore, packet-switched data communications services offered by Atlas constitute a product market separate from the market

for customized packages of corporate telecommunications services equally targeted by Atlas.

2. Geographic markets

The markets for customized packages of corporate telecommunications services

(12) Given that cost and price differences are quite substantial, demand for customized packages of corporate telecommunications services exists in at least three distinct geographic markets, namely at a global, at a cross-border regional and at a national level. Atlas will provide such packages to large users Europe-wide and nationally. Through GlobalOne, customized packages of corporate telecommunications services offered by Atlas will also have global 'connectivity' — the technical option of extending a given service offering beyond Europe by linking a customer's premises worldwide over Phoenix 'Global Backbone Network'.[11] Given the considerable costs involved, customized packages of corporate telecommunications services are today mainly demanded by large multinational corporations, extended enterprises, as well as major national and other intensive users of telecommunications. The Commission has discussed the requirements of such users in its Decision 94/579/EC (BT-MCI).[12]

(13) Due to the cost structure of providing customized packages of corporate telecommunications services, notably the cost of leasing the required infrastructure, prices of such services are related to geographic coverage, as is the cost of additional features (for example, one-stop-billing, help-desk and technical assistance around the clock, customized billing). There is evidence that increasing availability of trans-European networks will ultimately blur the distinction between national and cross-border or ultimately Europe-wide provision of non-reserved telecommunications services. However, certain sophisticated national non-reserved services currently available from DT and FT in Germany and France respectively will not be Atlas services, including DT and FT's national data network services based on ATM or equivalent packet-switching technology (Datex-M and Transrel respectively) and the national services mentioned at recital 5. This demonstrates that a distinction between national and cross-border provision of customised packages of corporate telecommunications services remains valid to date.

The markets for packet-switched data communications services

(14) Price differences for these services may be less than for customized packages of corporate telecommunications services. However, a national, cross-border regional and global geographic level can be distinguished for packet-switched data communications services. In terms of traffic volumes, supply and demand of packet-switched data communications services are mostly national. For instance, in Germany DT's existing T-Data packet-switched data communications services division hardly ever provides such

---

11 See *Phoenix* Decision in Case No IV/35.617, at recital 27.
12 See footnote 7.

services across the border while FT's German subsidiary Info AG, in spite of appertaining to FT's seamless cross-border Transpac network, only provides one fifth of its packet-switched data communications services across the border. This assessment was confirmed by interested third parties further to the Commission's notice on the Atlas notifications.[13]

(15) At a global and Europe-wide level, X.25 data services and customized packages of corporate telecommunications services may be partly converging to the extent that large customers of the latter do not require separate provision of X.25 data services once such services are available as part of service combinations offered over advanced networks. Accordingly, large European telecommunications users demand services with global 'connectivity', meaning that they may be extended beyond Europe if so required. DT and FT have moved to meet this demand in entering the GlobalOne agreements with Sprint. Along with increased availability of advanced, cross-border network infrastructure, the market is generally expected to overcome distinctions along national borders in the medium term. However, separate national geographic markets subsist to date for packet-switched data communications services and for the provision of customized packages of corporate telecommunications services respectively.

D. MARKET SHARES OF ATLAS

The market for customized packages of corporate telecommunications services

(16) The parties estimate the European markets for non-reserved corporate telecommunications services (exclusive of data communications services) to be worth approximately ECU 505 million (1993 figures). Of this total, end-to-end services accounted for approximately ECU 15,1 million, VPN services for approximately ECU 220,6 million, VSAT services for approximately ECU 173,2 million and outsourcing services for approximately ECU 96,4 million. According to the notification DT and FT's aggregate market shares (1993 figures) in the European Community were 25% in the end-to-end services market, 27% in the VPN services market and 2,3% in the outsourcing services market. Market shares for VSAT services are difficult to calculate given that TOs mostly use VSAT terminals either as back-up facilities for other services or to extend the geographic scope of services despite terrestrial infrastructure shortcomings; however, DT and FT taken together operated 10907 VSAT terminals by June 1994, equivalent to 29% of the total installed base of interactive, data one-way or business television VSAT terminals in the European Economic Area.

As to the national market for customized packages of corporate telecommunications services in France and Germany respectively, DT and FT's aggregate market shares for individual non-reserved corporate telecommunications services are 93% in the French VPN market (where DT has no presence) against 0% in the German VPN market, and 60% in the French market for end-to-end services against 35% in the equivalent German market DT and FT's outsourcing joint venture, Eunetcom B.V., achieved 36% of

13 Notification of a joint venture (Case No IV/35.337 — *Atlas*), OJ No. C 377, 31.12.1994, p. 9 and the Article 19(3) notice (see footnote 6 and recitals *et seq.*).

total outsourcing turnover generated in France and 29% of total outsourcing turnover generated in Germany. As for VSAT services, DT has installed approximately 25% of all VSAT terminals in Germany; this Member State accounts for 18% of the total installed base of such terminals in the EEA.

In third-country national markets, including all EEA member countries, DT and FT's presence is to date negligible or non-existent.

The market for packet-switched data communications services

(17)   DT and FT estimate the European market for data communications services to be worth approximately ECU 2,8 billion (1993 figures).

According to the notification DT and FT's aggregate shares (1993 figures) of this market were 35%. Among national markers, Atlas will have a particularly strong position in France and Germany. DT and F's aggregate market share for all data communications services is 79% in Germany and 77% in France, of which approximately half relates to services provided by DT's X.25 data services subsidiary (now incorporated as T-Data) and FT's Transpac France subsidiary. Both subsidiaries will remain outside the scope of Atlas until the French and German telecommunications infrastructure and services markets are fully and effectively liberalized, as is scheduled for 1 January 1998 (see recital 24).

E.   MAIN COMPETITORS OF ATLAS

The markets for customized packages of corporate telecommunications services

(18)   Since the BT-MCI Decision several players, acting alone or jointly with partners, have entered or are entering the international markets providing non-reserved corporate telecommunications services. The most important of these players, albeit with disparate geographic scope and target customers, include: AT&T WorldPartners, Concert, IBM-Stet, International Private Satellite Partners,[14] Unisource[15] or Uniworld.[16] Some of these strategic alliances are merely projects while others are awaiting regulatory approval. However, all of the above share the aim of positioning the respective partners in anticipation of the full liberalization.

The market for packet-switched data communications services

(19)   The market for packet-switched data communications services features a substantially larger number of players than that for customized packages of corporate telecommunications services. Among the global players in this market are the alliances mentioned at recital 18 competing with providers such as EDS, FNA, Infonet, SITA or Swift and operating subsidiaries of large global companies such as AT&T Istel, Cable & Wireless

---

14 See Commission Decision 94/895/EC of 15 December 1994 (Case No IV/34 768 — *International Private Satellite Partners*); OJ No L 354, 31.12.1994, p. 75.

15 Notification of a joint venture (Case No IV/35.830 — *Unisource/Telefónica*); OJ No C 94, 30.3.1996, p. 5.

16 Notification of a joint venture (Case No IV/35.738 — *Uniworld*); OJ No C 276, 21.10.1995, p. 9.

Business Networks, DEC's Easynet, or GEIS. In addition, a large number of smaller players competes at a cross-border regional or national level in the EEA. For instance, FT's indirect German subsidiary Info AG, which provides most of its data communications services within Germany, is DT's second-largest competitor in the German national market for packet-switched data communications services. None of these smaller players can compare to large alliances in terms of reach, access to transmission capacity and financial backing.

F. THE TRANSACTION

(20)   The Atlas transaction notified to the Commission comprises a set of agreements whose main features are described below.

1.   Agreements as originally notified

(a)   The Atlas Joint Venture Agreement (JV Agreement) is the main agreement providing for the establishment of the Atlas joint venture.

(b)   The Intellectual and Industrial Property Transfer and Licence Agreements were concluded by FT and DT respectively, with Atlas SA; under these agreements FT and DT make available to Atlas SA the intellectual property rights (the IPRs) needed to operate the Atlas business.

(c)   The Framework Services Agreements are framework agreements setting forth the basic terms and conditions with respect to the supply by DT and FT of certain services to Atlas SA and the supply by Atlas SA of certain services to FT and DT.

(d)   The Distribution Agreements are two substantially similar distribution agreements between Atlas SA and FT and DT respectively, regarding the marketing and sale of Atlas products in France and Germany respectively.

(e)   The Agency Agreements under which each parent appoints Atlas SA as non-exclusive worldwide agent for the sale of DT and FT's international leased lines (half-circuits), with the territorial exception of Germany as regards DT's half-circuits.

2.   Contractual Provisions

(21)   In particular, the above agreements provide for the following:

1.   *Structure of Atlas venture*

Atlas SA is created as joint venture between FT and DT, each owning half the share capital. The management structure of Atlas SA is as follows:

(a)   Shareholders' meeting: Prior approval by the shareholders' meeting is necessary for matters such as the amendment of the articles of association, changes of capital, issuance of shares, mergers, sale of all or a substantial part of the assets, and liquidation.

(b)   The board of directors: Atlas SA's board of directors has eleven members, five apiece being elected by DT and FT and one by Sprint. Prior approval by the board of directors is required for a number of important decisions such as the approval of business plans and annual budgets and changes in the scope of Atlas, the conclusion of important contracts, etc. Decisions on changes in the Atlas business, management appointments, and the approval of the business plan, the annual operating plan, and the budget require that at least two directors nominated by each party vote with the majority.[17]

(c)   Chief executive officers (CEOs): It is envisaged that Atlas SA will have two CEOs, one nominated by FT from among its representatives in the board of directors, the other by DT from among its representatives in the board of directors. The CEOs shall be jointly responsible for day-to-day operations and the management of the business and affairs of Atlas. Approval of both co-CEOs is required for all important decisions including the hiring or dismissal of key employees.

The parties will contribute to Atlas their existing European assets outside France and Germany (as well as some assets in France and Germany) used for the provision of services coming within the scope of Atlas.

2.   *Purpose and activities of Atlas*

The Atlas venture is to provide seamless national and international non-reserved services to corporate customers (that is, to multinational companies (MNCs) and SMEs alike). The portfolio of Atlas services comprises data network services, international end-to-end services (managed links), voice VPN services, customer-defined networks, outsourcing and VSAT services. These services are fully liberalized in the European Community and are widely liberalized worldwide. Atlas will have the responsibility for the services portfolio mentioned above, outside France and Germany.

In France and Germany, Atlas will provide sales support to FT and DT's sales forces as regards all services mentioned in the Atlas portfolio, with the exception of public packet-switched data network services within France and Germany, which will be provided by FT's Transpac France subsidiary and DT's T-Data subsidiary respectively until the telecommunications infrastructure and services markets are fully and effectively liberalized in France and Germany, as scheduled for 1 January 1998.

Each acting as an exclusive distributor, DT will sell Atlas services in Germany, while FT will sell ATlas services in France. Atlas products will be sold in France and Germany under the common globally used Atlas/GlobalOne brands. Passive sales of Atlas services by DT in France, by FT in Germany and by any Atlas operating entity in both Member States will be allowed. Outside France and Germany, Atlas products will be sold by the Atlas operating entity for the rest of Europe.

Pursuant to the JV Agreement, a balancing payment was made by DT at closing to equalize the respective contribution values of the two parties, DT or FT will make a further balancing payment upon contribution of T-Data and Transpac to Atlas to offset any difference in the valuation of T-Data and Transpac respectively.

3.   *Provisions concerning dealings with/by Atlas*

---

17 The originally envisaged Strategic Board of Atlas SA, described in the Article 19(3) notice (footnote 6) at paragraph 20(b), was deleted from the final Atlas Agreements.

Mutual service provision between Atlas and FT/DT is the subject of two Framework Services Agreements pursuant to which dealings between FT/DT and Atlas must be transparent, non-discriminatory and at arm's length.

As for services generally offered by DT or FT, the prices and other terms which DT or FT generally apply from time to time to their customers are to apply equally for Atlas. As for services not generally offered by FT or DT, market prices and terms apply and are negotiated between the Parties in good faith and at arm's length. Consequently, Atlas will purchase such services from DT or FT at similar prices and on similar conditions to those that any third party generally offering such services under equivalent circumstances would allow. If information on relevant market prices is not available, the prices applicable for Atlas are to be determined on the basis of a calculation model that is used, within FT, to make offers to customers with special requests and, within DT, to calculate intra-group transfer prices. Prices resulting from such calculation will cover, for the relevant period, all costs as well as a reasonable profit margin.

4. *Anti-competition provisions*

Pursuant to Article XIII of the Atlas JV Agreement, FT and DT will not engage anywhere in the production of services that are substantially the same or compete directly with the Atlas services, and will not engage outside France and Germany in the marketing, sale or distribution of services that are substantially the same or compete directly with the Atlas services. Furthermore, FT will not market or distribute Atlas services in Germany and DT will not market and distribute Atlas services in France; passive sales are, however, permitted by FT outside France, by DT outside Germany and by Atlas in both France and Germany.

5. *Provisions relating to intellectual and industrial property*

The parents each concluded an Intellectual and Industrial Property Transfer and Licence Agreement with Atlas SA under which DT, FT, T-Data and Transpac France (the 'IPR holders') are to make available to Atlas SA the IPRs which are needed to operate the Atlas business in accordance with the following principles:

   (a) IPRs owned by, or licensed to, the IPR holders that are used exclusively for the Atlas business will be transferred to Atlas SA;

   (b) IPRs owned by, or licensed to, the IPR holders that are used predominantly for the Atlas business shall be transferred to Atlas SA, and a sub-licence will be granted to the Parties (Grant-Back Licence sub-licence); and

   (c) IPRs owned by, or licensed to, the IPR holders that are used predominantly for the IPR holders' business are (sub-)licensed to Atlas SA.

G. CHANGES MADE FURTHER TO THE COMMISSION'S INTERVENTION AND CONDITIONS ATTACHED TO THIS DECISION

(22) Certain feature of the Atlas transaction as notified appeared to be incompatible with Community competition rules. Consequently, the Com-

mission by letter of 23 May 1995 informed the Parties of its concerns. In the course of the notification procedure the Parties have amended the original Agreements and given undertakings to the Commission.

1. Contractual changes

(23)   Non-appointment of Atlas SA as an agent for international half-circuits.

Further to the Commission's letter of 23 May 1995, DT and FT abolished the Agency Agreements and amended the original Service Agreements to take account of the non-appointment of Atlas SA as a non-exclusive agent for DT and FT's half-circuits.

(24)   Non-integration of French and German public packet-switched data networks before full and effective liberalization of the telecommunications infrastructure and service markets.

Atlas SA will not acquire legal ownership or control within the meaning of Article 3 of Council Regulation (EEC) No 4064/89[18] of the French and German public packet-switched data networks, Transpac France and T-Data respectively, before the telecommunications infrastructure and services markets are fully and effectively liberalized in France and Germany, as is scheduled to occur by 1 January 1998. Meanwhile:

1.   FT has split Transpac SA into Transpac France and Transpac Europe;

2.   FT has yielded Transpac Europe to Atlas;

3.   FT will keep Transpac France as a wholly owned subsidiary;

4.   DT has incorporated DT's X.25 data services division as a separate company under German law and a wholly owned subsidiary of DT;

5.   DT and FT have fully contributed their outsourcing joint venture, Eunetcom B.V., to Atlas SA; and

6.   Atlas SA has created a subsidiary in France and Germany (Atlas France and Atlas Germany respectively) to provide the following services:

(i)   sales support regarding Atlas products to distributors in France and Germany; and

(ii)   services within the scope of Atlas other than packet-switched data network services including:

— VSAT services,

— international end-to-end services,

— voice VPN services,

— customer-defined solutions (excluding national X.25 data services in France and Germany), and

— outsourcing services,

and excluding the services described in the last paragraph of recital 5.

Once the telecommunications infrastructure and services markets are fully and effectively liberalized in France and Germany, Transpac France and T-Data will be contributed to Atlas in such a way that Atlas France and Atlas Germany will be merged with Transpac France and T-Data respectively. For the purposes of such contribution, Transpac France and T-Data shall be read as comprising only the public packet-switched data networks for the provision

---

18 OJ No L 395, 30.12.1989, p. 1 (corrected version in OJ No L 257, 21.9.1990, p. 13); as amended by the Act of Accession of Austria, Finland and Sweden.

of packet-switched data communications services based on the X.25, IP, SNA and Frame Relay protocols respectively.

(25) Technical cooperation

Ahead of full and effective liberalization of the telecommunications infrastructure and service markets in France and Germany, DT and FT will cooperate in the development of common technical network elements. This Decision is subject to the condition that DT and FT's cooperation in this field will, until the date set in Article 2, comprise the following areas only:

1. FT and DT will cooperate in the development of common products and common technical network elements (namely such products and elements as share the same features, whilst being separately built and owned); such cooperation will extend to the French and Geman public packet-switched data networks. Only the following functions will be managed by Atlas SA for Transpac France and T-Data respectively:

(a) product management and development, namely: (i) product definition (definition of *inter alia* speed, terms and availability of interconnection and other technical and commercial features), (ii) product marketing, (iii) product life cycle management, (iv) specification of product requirements, (v) technical specifications and developments of the products and (vi) technical development of the products (hardware and software), provided that product branding and pricing as well as product implementation in the network is managed by Transpac France and T-Data respectively;

(b) certain network planning functions, namely: (i) central network engineering and optimization of the common transmission network so as to avoid an unreasonable duplication of resources, (ii) engineering and optimization of the networks for the various service platforms so as to ensure seamless services and (iii) central planning regarding the implementation of new network nodes (such as timing); and

(c) information systems, namely: (i) definition of the information system architecture (for example, development of common technical features for future information systems), (ii) specification of information system requirements and applications, (iii) technical development of hardware and software for information systems and (iv) central implementation planning of hardware and software, provided that central information system functions (for example, billing information and statistics) will be operated by Transpac France and T-Data respectively.

The above areas of cooperation are on no account to be tantamount to a *de facto* integration of the French and German public packet-switched data networks, which will be controlled by two separate network management centres. The restriction of DT and FT's technical cooperation to the elements set out above is attached to this Decision as a condition within the meaning of Article 8(1) of Regulation No 17.

2. Atlas may subcontract certain operational functions to Transpac France and T-Data respectively.

(26) Non-integration of assets of FT's indirect German subsidiary.

The assets of FT's German corporate telecommunications services provider Info AG shall not be integrated into Atlas save as indicated in the following undertaking:

'To meet the requirement of the European Commission that competition is not eliminated on the German telecommunications services market, France Télécom (FT) undertakes that it will irrevocably make available for sale, as a going business, Transpac's German subsidiary Info AG, or execute alternative remedies if such sale should not occur.

Scope of the divestiture

FT will divest of all assets as well as contracts of Info AG. Multinational clients whose headquarters are outside Germany to whom Info AG to date provides advanced network services as part of the Transpac network may be transferred to Atlas, to the extent to which the Commission is satisfied that such services are separable from the German activities of Info AG ("Info AG's business") without significantly lessening the value of those activities.

The two parts of Info AG's business (i.e. Disaster Recovery Services (DRS) and Network Services (NWS)) will be sold separately if no purchaser can be found for Info AG's business as a whole. For the purposes of this undertaking, the sale of Info AG will be considered as the sale of both the DRS and the NWS parts of Info AG's business.

Obligations of France Télécom

1. With regard to Info AG's present operations in respect of customers whose headquarters are located outside Germany, FT will, before the sale of Transpac's shares in Info AG to the party purchasing such shares (the "purchaser"), try to bring about a service agreement between Info AG and Transpac. Pursuant to such agreement, Transpac will continue providing for Info AG such services as Transpac is currently providing to Info AG.

2. The services covered by the agreement referred to in the preceding paragraph shall be provided so as not to impair Info AG's remaining business as presently conducted. Conclusion of such agreement with the purchaser is not a condition and cannot be required by FT for the purposes of complying with this undertaking.

3. FT also agrees to provide the purchaser with any assistance (e.g. licences and know-how) relating to the provision of Info AG's services to the extent possible under existing contractual obligations, as the case may be. FT may charge the purchaser a market-based fee for any such licence and know-how. The market-based fee shall be that normally obtainable on the market at the time that any licence or know-how is provided.

4. FT recognizes the Commission's objectives to (i) maintain the viability, marketability and competitiveness of Info AG's current business and (ii) to provide sufficient management and other resources for this purpose. To achieve these objectives, FT undertakes the following:

(a) to ensure that (i) Info AG's business is legally kept separate from both Transpac and T-Data and maintained as a distinct and saleable business; (ii) the value of Info AG's assets and of its business in every respect is maintained, pursuant to good business practice, at their current level, unless a change in the assets is necessary, in which case FT shall not make any signficant change without prior consultation with and approval of the European Commission; and (iii) all agreements necessary to maintain Info AG's business are entered into or continued according to their terms, consistent with past practice and the ordinary course of business; this notably includes all agreements and arrangements related to leased line capacity and interconnection with T-Data and/or Deutsche Telekom;

(b)   to keep all administrative and management functions relating to Info AG which have been carried out at all levels within FT and/or Transpac to maintain the viability, marketability and competitiveness of Info AG until divestiture is completed or until the trustee advises FT that such functions are no longer necessary, whichever ocurs earlier;

(c)   as soon as is practical and in any event no later than by 10 July 1996, to appoint a trustee (the "trustee"), such as an investment bank, subject to approval by the Commission (such approval shall not be withheld without good cause), provided that, subject to approval by the Commission (such approval shall not be withheld without good cause), FT may (i) terminate the trustee agreement should FT decide at any time after the appointment that the trustee does not perform its duties properly, and (ii) replace the previously appointed trustee by another trustee also approved by the Commission;

(d)   to give such trustee an irrevocable mandate to sell Info AG, on best possible terms and conditions, to an available purchaser making an offer before [. . .];[19] and

(e)   to establish and facilitate the management structure agreed with the trustee in the framework of the divestiture negotiations.

5.   When the trustee is appointed to sell Info AG, FT shall comply with the requirements of the trustee to maintain the value of Info AG's assets, to the extent legally permissible, unless a change in the assets is necessary, in which case FT shall not make any significant change without prior consultation with and approval of the European Commission. FT shall in particular ensure that all services provided by FT or any of FT's subsidiaries to Info AG continue to be provided efficiently and satisfactorily and that no increase is made in the charge (if any) made to Info AG for any service. FT shall not, except with the consent of the trustee, employ or offer employment to any employee or officer of Info AG until after the sale of Info AG.

Obligations of the trustee

6.   Pursuant to the agreement between FT and the trustee appointed with the Commission's consent, the trustee shall:

(a)   advise FT and Transpac on the best management structure to ensure the continued viability, marketability and competitiveness of Info AG's business. The trustee shall notably give advice on how to undertake any restructing of Info AG in a way that guarantees Info AG's viability, marketability and competitiveness;

(b)   advise FT and Transpac with regard to the satisfactory operation and management of Info AG to ensure the continued viability,

---

19 Business secret.

marketability and competitiveness of Info AG's business as well as supervise, monitor and control the implementation of the advice by Info AG. For the purposes of and to the extent necessary for such monitoring, the trustee shall have complete access to Info AG's personnel and facilities as well as to documents, books and records of both FT and Transpac, including such personnel, facilities, books and records which, even if not directly related to Info AG, may have an impact on the conduct of Info AG's operations;

(c) act as FT's investment banker in conducting good faith negotiations with interested third parties with a view to selling Info AG within [. . .][20] of the first closing date of the Atlas transaction as defined therein, i.e. before [. . .][21] (the "target date"). In the event that the trustee at any time prior to the target date but at least two months before that date determines together with the Commission that it is not possible to identify an acceptable purchaser for Info AG exclusive of the customers whose headquarters are located outside of Germany, the trustee, FT and the Commission will discuss appropriate alternatives to the proposed divestiture of Info AG, notably an extended divestiture;

(d) provide a written report before a binding contract is signed and in any event every month on all developments in its negotiations with third parties interested in purchasing Info AG; such reports, with supporting documentation, shall be furnished to the Commission with copy to FT;

(e) provide the Commission, with copy to FT, with a written report every two months concerning the monitoring of the operations and management of Info AG;

(f) at any other time upon the Commission's request provide the Commission with a written or oral report on any aspect of the duties and activities of the trustee in relation to Info AG and its possible purchasers. FT shall receive a copy of such written reports and shall be informed of the content of oral reports; and

(g) cease to perform its duties as trustee for the purpose of this undertaking when the sale of Info AG or any alternative remedy within the meaning of paragraph 6(c) above becomes effective.

7. The trustee shall be remunerated by FT. The trustee's remuneration shall provide incentives for a prompt divestiture, so that the trustee uses it best efforts in arranging a prompt and value-maximizing sale of Info AG.

8. FT undertakes to give all reasonable assistance requested by the trustee to sell Info AG by the target date. FT shall be deemed to have complied with its divestiture undertaking if by such date it has entered into a binding letter of intent or a binding contract for the sale of Info AG to a purchaser agreed by the Commission, provided that such sale is completed within a reasonable time limit, after the signing of such binding letter of intent or binding contract, agreed by the Commission.

9. The Commission may, upon FT's request and good cause provided, extend the period granted to FT for divestiture of Info AG by an additional six months after the target date (the 'extended target date').

20 Business secret.
21 Business secret.

10. The reports referred to in subparagraphs (6)(d) and (f) above shall indicate whether a proposed purchaser would be able to ensure that Info AG remains a competitive participant in the German telecommunications market and whether negotiations with such proposed purchaser should continue. If within 10 working days of the receipt of such indications from the trustee the Commission does not formally disagree with the trustee's favourable assessment of a proposed purchaser, negotiations with such proposed purchaser may proceed. The Commission may disagree with the trustee's assessment of a proposed purchaser if the proposed purchaser were in the Commission's view unlikely to compete effectively with T-Data, Atlas Germany and GlobalOne respectively.

11. The [. . .]^{22} period up to the target date and the six-month period up to the extended target date, as the case may be, are suspended in cases where the sale of Info AG is suspended due to a notification to a competition authority until such authority adopts its final decision with regard to the sale of Info AG.

12. Any dispute between FT and the purchaser(s) of Info AG with respect to FT's undertaking to divest of the Info AG business will be subject to arbitration by an independent third party. During such arbitration, the [. . .]^{23} period up to the target date will be suspended.

13. If the sale of Info AG's business does not seem likely to occur by the date stated in paragraph (4)(d), FT shall, at least two months before that date, submit alternative remedies sufficiently satisfactory to safeguard actual competition in the German market. These alternative remedies must be executed by the date stated in paragraph (4)(d).'

The Commission makes this Decision conditional on FT's compliance with the terms of the above undertaking. Where they are separable from the product divisions of Info AG that are to be divested, multinational clients to whom Info AG now provides network services as part of the Transpac network and whose headquarters are located outside Germany may be transferred to Atlas.

(27) FT, DT, Atlas and GlobalOne have given separate undertakings not to compete, for one year after the closing date of the sale of Info AG, with the purchaser for the provision of telecommunications services to customers of Info AG whose headquarters are located within Germany (the 'transferred customers') at the specific locations which Info AG served, except where such transferred customers decline in good faith to deal with the purchaser of Info AG. The Commission makes this Decision conditional on compliance by FT, DT, Atlas and GlobalOne comply with the requirements of this undertaking.

2. Non-discrimination condition

(28) In order to provide the services described under recital 5, Atlas or any other service provider is dependent on access to the public switched telecommunications network (PSTN), the integrated services digital network (ISDN) and to other essential facilities, and also on reserved services.^{24} Until

---

22 Business secret.
23 Business secret.
24 Reserved services are services which are provided pursuant to special or exclusive rights granted by the EU Member States to their respective TOs.

there is full and effective liberalization of infrastructure and services in France and Germany, as is scheduled to occur by 1 January 1998, only FT and DT provide access to the PSTN and the ISDN as well as reserved services. However, even when all telecommunications facilities and services are non-reserved, FT and DT will at least for a number of years remain indispensable suppliers of building blocks for the relevant services in France and Germany. Given that FT and DT are shareholders of Atlas it is essential for the safeguarding of fair competition between Atlas and other existing or future telecommunications services providers to eliminate the risk that the former might be granted more favourable treatment regarding the following facilities-related telecommunications services provided by FT and DT to Atlas in France and Germany respectively, pursuant to the Framework Services Agreements: (i) leased lines services, in particular international leased lines (half-circuits) and domestic leased lines, including any discounts, as the case may be; and (ii) PSTN/ISDN services including both access to such networks (namely analogue access; basic ISDN access; ISDN access to the public packet-switched data networks; special access from the public packet-switched data networks to ISDN (X.75 interface); and national and international voice VPN and VPN interconnection services) and traffic over such networks. Likewise, Atlas is not to be granted more favourable treatment than third parties in connection with other reserved facilities and services and with such facilities and services which remain an essential facility after full and effective liberalization of telecommunications infrastructure and services in France and Germany. Thus:

1. Terms and conditions

The terms and conditions applied by DT and FT to Atlas for the abovementioned services covered by the Framework Services Agreements and for the provision of other reserved and/or essential services (for example, provision of leased lines, allocation of numbers, addresses and names) in connection with the services described under recital 5 shall be similar to the terms and conditions applied to other providers of similar services. This requirement covers *inter alia* availability, price, quality of service, functionality, usage conditions, timetable for installation of requested facilities, connection of apparatus, or repair and maintenance services.

2. Scope of services available

Atlas is not to be granted terms and conditions, or to be exempted from any usage restrictions regarding the abovementioned services covered by the Framework Services Agreements and other reserved and/or essential services, which would enable it to offer services which competing providers are prevented from offering.

3. Technical information

DT and FT is not to discriminate between Atlas and any other service provider competing with Atlas in connection with either a decision to substantially modify technical interfaces for the access to reserved and/or essential facilities or services or the disclosure of any other technical information relating to the operation of the PSTN/ISDN. Competitors will, in particular, have access to technical information to which they can adapt lest their quality of services be reduced, such as signalling software information for the provision of voice services.

4. Commercial information

DT and FT is not to discriminate between Atlas and other providers of services as described under recital 5 as regards the disclosure of certain commercial information (for example, systemized and organized customer information derived exclusively from the operation the PSTN/ISDN or the provision of reserved and/or essential services) if such information would confer a substantial competitive advantage and is not readily and equally available elsewhere by service providers competing with Atlas.

To ensure the absence of third-party discrimination, this Decision in application of Article 85(3) of the EC Treaty and Article 53(3) of the EEA Agreement is to be valid only on condition that DT, FT and Atlas comply with the following additional conditions.

3. Other conditions attached to this Decision

(29) DT and FT have also entered into certain additional commitments. Where these commitments are too general or insufficient, the Commission has specified and supplemented the behavioural constraints imposed on the parents. Compliance with the constraints described below will be a condition for the validity of this Decision within the meaning of Article 8(1) of Regulation No 17.

1. Access to DT and FT's public packet-switched data networks

DT and FT have given the following undertaking:
'Each of FT and DT will as of 1 January 1996 establish and thereafter maintain third-party access to their public switched data networks in France and Germany respectively. Non-discriminatory, open and transparent access will be granted to all data services providers that offer X.25 packet-switched data communications services. To ensure non-discriminatory access to their national public X.25 packet-switched data networks, FT and DT shall:
    (a) establish and maintain standardized X.75 interfaces to access their national public X.25 packet-switched data networks; this interconnection is suitable for the provision of end-to-end services based on X.25 specifications for end-user access speeds up to 64 kbps; and
    (b) offer such access on non-discriminatory terms, including price, availability of volume or other discounts and the quality of interconnection provided.
    FT and DT shall further ensure non-discriminatory access by making publicly available the standard terms and conditions for such X.75 interface standards, including, if any, volume and other discounts, as of 1 January 1996. FT and DT will make available for inspection by the

Commission any agreements relating to such X.75 interfaces, including all specifically agreed terms. Until such time as Transpac France and T-Data are integrated into Atlas, neither Transpac France nor T-Data shall disclose to Atlas any such specifically agreed terms that are identified and maintained as confidential by the party obtaining interconnection through such X.75 interfaces. Finally, the above obligations shall likewise apply to any generally used CCITT-standardized interconnection protocol that may modify, replace or co-exist as a standard related to the X.75 standard and is used by FT and DT.

Proprietary interfaces may be retained or established among Transpac France, T-Data and Atlas; such interfaces are defined by the particular type of technology, hardware and software that a network operator uses to provide advanced or customized services. Atlas will be allowed to access the Transpac France and T-Data public packet-switched data networks through these proprietary interfaces, also for the provision of packet-switched data communications services, provided access granted to Atlas through such interfaces is economically equivalent to third-party access to the Transpac France and T-Data networks.'

The Commission makes this Decision subject to the condition that Transpac France, T-Data and eventually Atlas grant third-party access to the French and German public packet-switched data networks on non-discriminatory transparent terms and conditions which must be economically equivalent to the terms and conditions of Atlas' access to such networks.

2. Access to DT and FT's other networks and facilities

This Decision is conditional on DT's and FT's granting to any third party that operates a telecommunications facility ('telecommunications operator') and applies for the interconnection of such facility or systems facilities with DT or FT's networks, such as PSTN, ISDN or ATM networks and related broadband capacity, as the case may be, such interconnection on non-discriminatory terms vis-à-vis Atlas. Such terms must enable the telecommunications operator to provide telecommunications services or provide its telecommunications facilities without limitation in any respect within the reasonable capabilities of the telecommunications operator concerned.

3. Cross-subsidization

DT and FT have undertaken not to engage in cross-subsidization in connection with the Atlas venture. To prevent Atlas from benefiting from cross-subsidies stemming from the operation of public telecommunications infrastructure and of reserved services by either DT or FT, all entities formed pursuant to the Atlas venture will be established as distinct entities separate from DT and FT.

Atlas SA, T-Data and Transpac France shall obtain their own debt financing on their own credit, provided that FT and DT:

(a)   may make capital contributions or commercially reasonable loans to such entities as are required to enable Atlas SA, T-Data and Transpac France to conduct their respective businesses;

(b)   may pledge their venture interests in such entities, in connection with non-recourse financing for such entities, and

(c)   may guarantee any indebtedness of such entities, provided that FT and DT may only make payments pursuant to any such guarantee following a default by such entities in respect of such indebtedness.

Compliance with the above undertaking is a condition for the validity of this Decision under Article 8(1) of Regulation No 17. The Commission extends the following conditions as to conduct to cover all entities created pursuant to the Atlas agreement, T-Data and Transpac France. Such entities are not to allocate directly or indirectly any part of their operating expenses, costs, depreciation, or other expenses of their business to any parts of FT or DT's business units (including without limitation the proportionate costs based on work actually performed that are attributable to shared employees or sales or marketing of Atlas products and services by DT or FT employees); however, nothing is to prevent Atlas SA, T-Data and Transpac France from billing DT or FT for products and services provided to DT or FT by such entities on the basis of the same price charged third parties (in the case of products or services sold to third parties in commercial quantities) or full cost reimbursement or other arm's length pricing method (in the case of products and services not sold to third parties in commercial quantities).

4.   Accounting

The Commission imposes a condition on T-Data, Transpac France (including all subsidiaries) and all entities created pursuant to the Atlas agreements which operate in the EEA to keep separate accounting records (including profit and loss account and balance sheet or statement of capital employed) using international accounting standards for each service they provide in any country.

These accounting records will notably identify all services provided to such entities by DT and FT and payments or transfers to or from DT and FT; moreover, no entity created pursuant to the Atlas Agreement, nor T-Data or Transpac France will receive any material subsidy (including forgiveness of debt) directly or indirectly from DT or FT, or any investment or payment from DT or FT that is not recorded in the books of such entities as an investment in debt or enquiry.

The Commission also imposes a condition on DT and FT (including all subsidiaries) to keep separate accounting records of all services provided to any entity created pursuant to the Atlas Agreements operating in the EEA. To that end, DT and FT are to implement within one year from the date of the exemption pursuant to Article 1 of this Decision an accounting system which identifies detailed cost accounting data for any such service.

The records mentioned in the previous two subparagraphs will detail the following:

(a)   the cost standard used;

(b)   the accounting conventions used for the treatment of costs;

(c)   the full allocation and attribution of expenses or costs, revenues, assets and liabilities shared between such entities and their parents; and

(d)   the attribution method chosen.

5. Bundling

The Commission imposes a condition on DT and FT to sell DT and FT services respectively under contracts separate from the contracts for the sale of Atlas services concluded as distributors of Atlas in Germany and France respectively. Each separate contract will set out the terms and conditions of each individual service sold thereunder and notably attribute any quantity or other discounts to a particular service, as the case may be.

4. Obligations attached to this Decision

(30) The Commission attaches the following obligations within the meaning of Article 8(1) of Regulation No 17 to this Decision, pursuant to Article 85(3) of the EC Treaty and Article 53(3) of the EEA Agreement. These obligations will remain in force for the duration of the exemption. In so far as related to existing obligations under national or Community law, the obligations described below are intended to ensure the Parties' firm commitment to comply with the applicable legal framework. Pursuant to Article 8(3)(b) of Regulation No 17, the Commission may revoke this Decision where the parties breach any such obligation.

1. Auditing

Atlas SA (which includes its consolidated subsidiaries), Transpac France and T-Data are to be audited every year; such audit will confirm from an accounting viewpoint that:

(a)   the transactions between these entities, on the one hand, and FT and DT, on the other hand, have been conducted at arm's length;

(b)   these entities have adhered to the accounting procedures chosen within the framework set out under recital 29(4); and

(c)   the calculation numbers are accurate.

The first auditing reports, covering the 12-month period starting on the date on which this Decision comes into force, will be submitted to the Commission within 15 months of that date. This obligation will remain in force for the duration of this Decision.

2.   Recording obligations

DT, FT and all entities created pursuant to the Atlas Agreements will each keep records and documents suitable to prove compliance with the terms of the above conditions ready for inspection by the Commission.

3.   Inspection of records

For the purpose of ascertaining and ensuring compliance by DT, FT or Atlas with the above conditions, DT, FT and all entities created pursuant to the Atlas Agreements will, on reasonable notice, during office hours, and without a need for the Commission to invoke the powers of inspection pursuant to Regulation No 17, give the Commission access to DT, FT or Atlas's business premises to inspect records and documents covered by the above recording obligations and to receive oral explanations relating to such documents.

4. Reporting obligations

T-Data, Transpac France, DT, FT and all entities created pursuant to the Atlas Agreements will provide the Commission, for the purpose of ascertaining whether DT, FT and Atlas comply with the above obligations, with:

   (a) any records and documents in the possession or control of DT, FT or an entity created pursuant to the Atlas agreements necessary for that determination; in particular, every six months, starting one year after the date of the exemption pursuant to Article 1 of this Decision with unaudited accounting data as specified in recital 29(4); and

   (b) oral or written complementary explanations.

H. THE REGULATORY SITUATION

(31) In letters sent to the Commission, the French and German Governments have undertaken to take the necessary steps to effectively allow the use of alternative infrastructure for the provision of liberalized telecommunications services by 1 July 1996 and to liberalize the voice telephony service and all telecommunications infrastructure fully and effectively by 1 January 1998. The availability of alternative telecommunications infrastructure in Germany and France renders competitors of Atlas independent of DT and FT's infrastructure for the purposes of creating trunk network infrastructure to provide liberalized services.

Early alternative infrastructure liberalization in France and Germany adds to a regulatory framework in the home countries of the Atlas partners that is designed to ensure a level playing field in the telecommunications markets.

1. France

1. *Separation of regulatory and operative functions*

Pursuant to French Law, the Minister of Telecommunications shall ensure that regulation of the telecommunications markets is undertaken separately of service provision in these markets. A specific national regulatory authority (NRA), the Direction Générale des Postes et Télécommunications (DGPT), is competent for licensing providers of telecommunications networks and services in France based on objective and transparent criteria. The DGPT shall survey FT's market behaviour and approve FT's tariffs for (i) reserved services and leased lines and (ii) such liberalized services that are not in fact provided by a third party active in the French market.

2. *Non-discriminatory access*

Further to the adoption of the Commission Services Directive and Council Directive 90/387/EEC ('ONP Framework Directive'), [25] Article L 32-1-4° of the French Law of 29 December 1990 grants all users equal access to the public networks on objective, transparent and non-discriminatory conditions.

---

25 Council Directive 90/387/EEC of 28 June 1990 on the establishment of the internal market for telecommunications services through the implementation of open network provision; OJ No L 192, 24.7.1990, p. 1.

FT is under an obligation to effectively grant such access and must publish information on the network (such as technical features, tariffs and usage conditions) and on leased line offerings. The DGPT may verify FT's compliance with these obligations and investigate complaints filed against FT for non-compliance with these obligations. The DGPT is, further, to ensure compliance with FT's obligation to share available transmission capacity for liberalized services with competitors and shall publish annual statistical reports on FT's compliance with these obligations.

3. *Prevention of cross-subsidies*

To allow the DGPT to supervise FT's market behaviour, FT is under the legal obligation to keep an analytical accounting system that relates costs to each individual FT service. Where an offering comprises the provision of both reserved and liberalized services, FT must separate each kind of service in the contract and in the invoice. In this connection, FT's data communications services are already provided by a separate legal entity.

2. Germany

1. *Separation of regulatory and operative functions*

Pursuant to the German 1989 Poststrukturgesetz, the 1994 Postneuordnungsgesetz and the 1994 Post- und Telekommunikation-Regulierungsgesetz, regulatory competencies are assigned to a Federal agency created under the Federal Ministry of Post and Telecommunications (BMPT) while telecommunications operations are undertaken by DT, a fully State-owned joint stock corporation. Regulatory obligations of DT are policed by independent bodies, so-called regulatory chambers.

2. *Non-discriminatory access*

Under the current and future German regulatory framework, DT is to provide third parties with both access to monopoly infrastructure and reserved or mandatory services on a non-discriminatory and transparent basis according to objective criteria. Upon application, DT will supply state-of-the-art leased lines over service-neutral access points without delay. With the only restriction of voice telephony service provision, leased lines may be freely interconnected and used for any service. Leased lines must meet market demand and DT must publish data concerning availability and quality of such lines.

3. *Prevention of cross-subsidies*

The BMPT (i) will approve both tariffs and other price-sensitive contractual terms for DT's reserved services and (ii) may object to DT's tariffs for mandatory services. The BMPT may also seize DT's profits stemming from tariffs in excess of the approved amount and take any measure necessary to reestablish an effectively competitive environment jeopardized by unlawful cross-subsidization. Moreover, DT's subsidiaries and affiliates are to use reserved services for the provision of competitive services under equivalent terms as DT's customers and must use such terms to account internal services transfer.

1. THIRD-PARTY OBSERVATIONS

(32)   Following the publication of a notice pursuant to Article 19(3) of Regulation No 17 and to Article 3 of Protocol 21 of the EEA Agreement,[26] 10 interested third parties submitted comments to the Commission. These comments approved of the structural changes made by DT and FT to the original project, whilst suggesting that a swift divestiture of FT's indirect German subsidiary Info AG was crucial. Third parties also contributed to the Commission's definition of the relevant markets emphasizing the indispensability of (i) an effective liberalization of alternative infrastructure in France and Germany, namely actual access to alternative sources of infrastructure in these countries, before Atlas is exempted from Articles 85(1) of the EC Treaty and 53(1) of the EEA Agreement and (ii) surveillance of technical cooperation between DT and FT lest it extend to sales, marketing and pricing.

(33)   As for proposed behavioural restraints to be imposed on DT and FT, third parties submitted that obligations and conditions should remain in place until there was effective competition in France and Germany. Finally, third-party observations also pointed to the relevance of appropriate accounting systems and interconnection terms, including technically equivalent interfaces for the joint-venture companies and third parties, to ensure that Atlas's competitors are not harmed by cross-subsidies or discriminatory practices.

(34)   The Commission carefully reviewed all comments received and concluded that most concerns expressed therein had already been raised by the Commission and discussed in detail with DT and FT, who had provided adequate answers and safeguards. Those comments have not therefore affected the Commission's substantive position outlined in the Article 19(3) notice as regards the notified agreements. However, in the interests of legal certainty the Commission has spelled out in more detail in this Decision the scope and duration of some conditions and obligations imposed on DT and FT.

(35)   Subsequent to third-party observations, the Commission also requested that FT, DT, Atlas and GlobalOne give the undertakings reproduced under recitals *et seq.* and decided to attach as an additional condition to this Decision that DT and FT sell own products unbundled from Atlas products (see recital 29(5)).

II.   LEGAL ASSESSMENT

A.   ARTICLE 85(1) OF THE EC TREATY AND ARTICLE 53(1) OF THE EEA AGREEMENT

1.   Structural cooperative joint venture

The Atlas joint venture is structural and cooperative in nature.

---

26 See footnote 2.

(36) Potential competition in markets for Europe-wide and national telecommunications services.

Atlas will intially combine and develop products largely based on DT and FT's existing products, in respect of which DT and FT will act as exclusive distributors within their respective domestic markets. Although certain services transferred to Atlas in third-country national markets and Europe-wide remain with DT and FT in their respective home markets (see recital 5), interconnection allows the extension of any such service from the national home market into another geographic market. FT for instance provides an international extension to its domestic and international VPN services offerings. For both offerings this extension may include Germany where DT's national VPN services remain outside the scope of Atlas. Moreover, DT and FT will keep a residual staff presence at all their current foreign locations and continue to provide international leased lines, which are the 'building blocks' of self-provided private networks.

In this connection, Atlas will undertake own R + D activities but also award important R + D contracts to DT and FT. The parents will therefore keep and increase their proficiency and know-how in respect of the technologies required to stay in (or to re-enter) the relevant markets while keeping control of the necessary infrastructure in the single largest Member State telecommunications markets. Moreover, although Atlas may own new developments (see recital 21(5)) it is on the whole more likely that such ownership will revert to the developing parent. In any event, Atlas will license back to the respective parent most technology developed from IPRs contributed by DT or FT.

The Commission concludes that DT and FT remain potential competitors for Atlas services and other services in neighbouring and upstream transmission capacity) markets.

(37) Structural joint venture

Atlas combines DT and FT's activities in a range of Europe-wide and third-country markets for liberalized telecommunications services and is set to develop and take over new services in these markets. This venture entails major changes in the structures of DT and FT as two undertakings with very limited presence outside their respective home countries. Through Atlas the parents pool a significant number of assets in connection with the provision and marketing of telecommunications services. Atlas will employ 2500 people across Europe.

2. Applicability of Article 85(1) of the EC Treaty and Article 53(1) of the EEA Agreement to the creation of Atlas

The agreements between DT and FT fall within Article 85(1) of the EC Treaty and Article 53(1) of the EEA Agreement as they restrict competition and affect trade between Member States. The Commission cannot therefore give negative clearance to the Agreements as the Parties requested in their application.

(38) The Atlas venture eliminates actual and potential competition between DT and FT both in Germany and France and Europe-wide. DT and FT were already competing in some segments of the market for Europe-wide if not global provision of customized packages of corporate

telecommunications services to corporate users described at recitals 12 *et seq.*: prior to the implementation of their Eunetcom joint venture DT and FT tendered individually for outsourcing contracts, offering similar corporate services. As any European TO, DT and FT also competed on features and prices for the location of telecommunication hubs of international users.[27] While currently targeting only large businesses, this competition was set to intensify along with further liberalization and ultimately extend to private households. With the exception of outsourcing services and in spite of substantial market shares in their respective home markets, the parents were actual competitors for Europe-wide services only in Germany (see below).

(39)   In creating Atlas, DT and FT each abandon their own developments and activities in the relevant markets for cross-border and ultimately Europe-wide telecommunications services. In the case of FT, such activities were substantial to the point that FT's existing Transpac network is the starting base for Atlas' envisaged European backbone network. As for national services, the large numbers of providers of liberalized services, including FT's Transpac, in all European countries targeted by Atlas shows that the parents have the financial and technological capabilities required to address national markets across Europe on their own.

(40)   The elimination of competition between the parents is substantial as the Atlas venture is created by two internationally active TOs and covers the joint development and provision of services throughout the European Economic Area. DT and FT's respective dominant positions in the two single largest Member State telecommunications markets is reinforced by a legal infrastructure monopoly until such markets are fully and effectively liberalized, as is scheduled to occur by 1 January 1998, and will continue to rely on a dominant position for terrestrial transmission capacity for years thereafter. Current prices for infrastructure access — leased lines tariffs or interconnection rates — together with DT and FT's strengthened joint market position impair competitors' ability to create a competitive network of similar scope and density to DT and FT's in these countries.[28]

3. Application of Article 85(1) of the EC Treaty and Article 53(1) of the EEA Agreement to contractual provisions

(41)   The following individual provisions are restrictive of competition:
1. the anti-competition provision as regards the activities of Atlas (Article XII JV Agreement as amended and Article VII of both Distribution Agreements):
2. the obligation on DT and FT acting as distributors to obtain from Atlas all the requirements for Europe-wide products (Article VII of both Distribution Agreements); and
3. the appointment of DT and FT as exclusive distributors of Atlas products in the respective parent's home market (Article IV of both Distribution Agreements).

---

27 *BT-MCI* Decision (footnote 7), at recital 41.
28 See Commission Decision 93/49/EEC of 23 December 1992 — *Ford/Volkswagen*, OJ No L 20, 28.1.1993, p. 14, at recitals 18 to 21; Decision 94/322/EC of 18 May 1994 — *Exxon/Shell*, OJ No L 144, 9.6.1994, p. 20, at recitals 42 *et seq.*; and Decision 94/896/EC of 16 December 1994 — *Asahi/Saint Gobain*, OJ No L 354, 31.12.1994, p. 87, at recitals 16 to 22.

(42)   The Commission considers the anti-competition provision and DT and FT's obligation to obtain all requirements for global products from Atlas to be ancillary to the creation and operation of Atlas. Therefore, these restrictions are not assessed under Article 85(1) of the EC Treaty and Article 35(1) of the EEA Agreement separately from the joint venture as such. DT and FT chose creating Atlas as a way to strengthen their presence in the relevant cross-border and ultimately Europe-wide markets and as a first step towards entering the global markets for customized packages of corporate telecommunications services. In this respect, both the anti-competition provision and the exclusive purchasing obligation are different expressions of DT and FT's same commitment to the other parent and to their joint venture. Atlas requires both restraints to successfully establish itself in the emerging market for customized packages of global corporate telecommunications services given the uncertainty and risk associated with such market entry, the level of investment required, and competition from similar ventures.

1.   Anti-competition obligation

Given DT and FT's substantial investment in Atlas, this clause ensures that DT and FT concentrate their efforts in the relevant markets on Atlas lest parallel activities, perhaps in cooperation with other TOs, jeopardize Atlas' successful establishment in the market.

2.   Exclusive purchasing obligation

This restraint on DT and FT as exclusive distributors of Atlas services aims at ensuring Atlas a steady stream of funds and at increasing its credibility and market reputation. Were the parents free to obtain such products from other suppliers, notably in cases where Atlas is in a position to meet a particular demand requirement, this would affect Atlas' credibility and financial position alike. Inversely, Atlas is not under an obligation to obtain all its requirements for telecommunications and other products and services from the parents.

The Commission usually accepts ancillary provisions for a limited period of time only. In this case, however, given the particular features of the market in which Atlas will operate, notably the substantial investment required and the risks associated to such investment, the Commission accepts both the anti-competition clause and DT and FT's obligation to obtain all provisions for Europe-wide services from Atlas as ancillary restraints for the entire duration of this exemption Decision.

(43)   Exclusive distribution

DT and FT's exclusive distributorship in their respective home countries is caught by Article 85(1) of the EC Treaty and Article 53(1) of the EEA Agreement because it has the object or effect of isolating Germany and France against imports of Atlas services from other EEA Member States. This may adversely affect the conditions of competition within the EEA. Unlike the other restrictive provisions, the Commission cannot consider DT and FT's exclusive distributorship to be ancillary to the creation of the joint venture, as non-exclusive forms of distribution are possible which would not impair the performance or marketing of Atlas services. Given that Germany and France taken together account for more than 40% of all telecommunications revenues in the European Community, the restriction is appreciable.

4. Effect on trade between Member States

(44) Pursuant to the Commission's telecommunications guidelines, agreements concerning non-reserved services, equipment and space segment infrastructure potentially affect trade between Member States.[29] The creation of Atlas has an effect on inter-Member State trade in that Atlas will provide non-reserved services between any two Member States and within any Member State. The exclusive distribution provision caught by Article 85(1) of the EC Treaty and Article 53(1) of the EEA Agreement protect the parents within their respective home market and contribute to dividing the single market along national borders. Therefore, this non-ancillary provision affects trade among Member States and between Member States and the EFTA countries. The Commission concludes that the loss of two powerful independent and potentially competing service providers in the relevant markets generally and in France and Germany in particular has a considerable impact on trade.

B. ARTICLES 85(3) OF THE EC TREATY AND ARTICLE 53(3) OF THE EEA AGREEMENT

(45) DT and FT pursue different aims in entering this set of transactions. DT was for a long time restricted to domestic investments and additionally burdened with a programme of infrastructure modernization in the former German Democratic Republic territories. DT has little presence elsewhere in Europe and aims at becoming an international telecommunications services provider worldwide, albeit seeing European markets as a priority. Cooperating with a major European player present in all of DT's target markets is particularly important for DT to achieve its objectives, notably a sufficiently broad European base to justify an extension of its business into the United States market, where 40% of multinational companies are located.

(46) FT's main interest is to maintain its competitive position as a cross-border provider of business telecommunications services in Europe while addressing increasing customer demand for global services. The increasing presence of BT and MCI's Concert venture in Europe convinced FT of the need for wide coverage in Europe before adding a global dimension to its services; given that the scope of business of Infonet, in which FT held a stake, was limited compared to the range of envisaged Atlas services, FT opted for an alliance with another TO. DT and FT's joint aim now is to become leading providers of non-reserved telecommunications services in Europe. This requires a substantial investment in creating seamless networks in Europe, where DT and FT face strong competition from Concert and possibly from Uniworld.[30]

(47) The notified agreements, to the extent caught by Article 85(1) of the EC Treaty and Article 53(1) of the EEA Agreement, satisfy the conditions for an exemption set out in Article 85(3) of the EC Treaty and Article 53(3) of the EEA Agreement, for the following reasons:

---

29 Footnote 9, at paragraph 39.
30 See notice published in OJ No C 276, 21.10.1995, p. 9.

1. Technical progress

(48)   DT and FT will in the framework of Atlas implement a seamless Europe-wide network by adding value to basic transmission capacity purchased from local TOs. To that end, Atlas will not preserve the features of each national network involved but will instead implement harmonized technical features, own switching systems, call processing/routing, signalling and databases as well as software applications, notably fully compatible interfaces. This approach has substantial advantages over most existing international services that are provided by interconnecting national networks which are usually incompatible in terms of structure, software, hardware and management systems. Consequently, the number and features of services available is determined by the least sophisticated national network involved. The creation of a seamless trans-European network will allow the technical performance already requested by large business customers across Europe, which competitors such as Concert are also aiming at through distribution agreements and ventures.

(49)   Under the conditions attached to this Decision, the harmonized joint DT and FT network will also improve the level of services provided by competitors of Atlas which may: (i) interconnect with the public packet-switched data networks operated by Transpac France and T-Data and eventually by Atlas in France and Germany over X.75 interfaces; (ii) access these public packet-switched data networks from other networks, notably the public switched telecommunications network (PSTN) and the integrated services digital network (ISDN); and (iii) interconnect with DT and FT's other networks, notably the PSTN. The latter is indispensable for the viability of competitive voice services offerings. Third parties shall be offered access to the public packet-switched data networks, the PSTN and the ISDN on terms technically and commercially non-discriminatory with regard to Atlas. Any service provider who wishes to make applications for interconnection to DT and FT will be able to rely on a substantive non-discrimination duty attached to this Decision as a separate condition.

(50)   The combination of FT and DT's technology will enable Atlas from the outset to offer new services, albeit initially based largely on parents' existing services. By joining their R + D in the framework of the joint venture DT and FT will enable Atlas to provide more advanced features than either parent would be capable of providing independently within the same time frame. Jointly, DT and FT will also be able to make the substantial investment required to create a large seamless state-of-the-art trans-European network. This is a major improvement over the current situation in Europe, where many modern networks exist, but can only be interconnected at the price of a loss of features. At present, the most relevant example of shortcoming of interconnection is data transmission over state-of-the-art networks. Most advanced features of packet-switched data communications services, for example reverse charging, closed user group definition or end-to-end management, are lost as soon as several data communications networks are interconnected unless the respective technical specifications and interfaces are harmonized. As the Commission acknowledged in its BT-MCI Decision, successful implementation of trans-European networks will allow Europe's major undertakings to chose from international telecommunications services

improved to levels of quality which are currently available only nationally or even locally. Availability of international state-of-the-art telecommunications services is critical to face increasingly global competition stemming from parts of the world where advanced telecommunications technology and services are already widely available.

2. Economic progress

(51)   DT and FT jointly intend to undertake the investment necessary to bring about a qualitative improvement of European telecommunications which Atlas will also make available to SMEs. As the Commission acknowledged in its BT-MCI Decision, this requires a costly and time consuming effort. DT and FT will implement investment plans amounting to a total of ECU 5 billion linked to the creation or enhancement of services. Further to the Commission's preliminary position on the proposed alliance as expressed on 23 May 1995 the parties have: (i) changed their agreements in respect of Atlas' rôle outside France and Germany; and (ii) entered into a global alliance with a United States operator. A sizeable presence across the EEA is one requirement for the provision of such non-reserved services as targeted by Atlas. DT and FT have submitted data showing their commitment to substantial investment in Europe. Moreover, DT and FT have changed the original balance between Atlas' own services and services outsourced to the parents in Atlas' favour. Another requirement if service offerings are to progress beyond what is already available in the European market is the global extension of services as needed by multinational companies, so-called global connectivity of services. Atlas meets this requirement as a parent of the Phoenix alliance.

(52)   Given the current cost of leased line infrastructure, Atlas' investment will initially be driven by the large multi-national companies (MNCs) with most complex requirements in countries other than France and Germany. However, as a result of operating a single high-speed network architecture Atlas will allow economies of scale at both the technological and operational level, i.e. reduce the cost per channel. Atlas is further likely to reduce infrastructure costs in respect of interconnection agreements with other TOs by generating larger traffic volumes which allow lowest-cost routing. The effects of economies of scale along with increased availability of infrastructure further to the implementation of recent Community legislation[31] will eventually allow service offerings with sophisticated technical features to develop and become widely available.

3. Benefits to consumers

(53)   Atlas will shorten the time required by the parents individually for marketing new telecommunications services in a rapidly changing technological and commercial market environment. Business customers will benefit, more rapidly than if DT and FT acted separately, from both the provision of a larger product portfolio of newly developed services and lower pricing.

---

31 Commission Directive 96/19/EC of 13.3.1996 amending Directive 90/388/EEC with regard to the implementation of full competition in the telecommunications markets; OJ No L 74, 22.3.1996, p. 13.

Increased choice of telecommunications services and related cost benefits will spill over to other segments of the telecommunications market and economic sectors. Atlas will also provide an alternative option for the supply of customized offerings which cover the complete range of liberalized business telecommunications services.

(54)   Through its global alliance with Spring, Phoenix, Atlas will also offer European customers an expanded geographic reach of its customized packages of corporate telecommunications services. The possibility for European customers to reach remote locations worldwide either ad hoc or permanently without a loss of quality or technical features and without changing supplier is a major advantage for such customers, for example European companies endeavouring to establish a worldwide presence in an increasingly global economy. Customers have the advantages of seamless cross-border services through Atlas in Europe and through Phoenix worldwide at their convenience. Only global alliances can offer global connectivity of services. While the scope of Atlas is not in itself global, DT and FT's investment plans through Atlas ensure that a substantial number of European business customers will have the option of global scope.

(55)   The exclusive distributorship in Germany and France combined with the agreements concerning IPR licensing and grant-back licensing will provide an incentive for DT and FT to share with the joint venture any technical progress made in markets related to the relevant markets. This is an additional benefit for large non-reserved telecommunications service users in DT and FT's home countries, i.e. two of the Member States with a substantial number of potential customers for Atlas services.

4. Indispensability

(56)   The creation of Atlas
Creating Atlas is indispensable for the parents to bring about the benefits within the meaning of Article 8(3) of the EC treaty and 53(3) of the EEA Agreement discussed above. Compared to individual market entry or other forms of cooperation with a lesser level of integration, the degree of cooperation between DT and FT in the framework of Atlas is necessary to provide the relevant services. Atlas will shorten the time DT and FT would have required to compete with other providers of cross-border and Europe-wide services and substantially reduce the costs and risks borne by each parent. In rapidly changing market FT is forced to update its Transpac network and DT to establish itself as a European player. Last, Atlas is a means to quickly overcome the inadequacies of most services and features currently available by creating a major trans-European network which offers what multinationals and other large international users need.

(57)   Exclusive distribution
Pursuant to the Distribution Agreements, each parent is the exclusive distributor for Atlas products in its own home market. The exclusive distribution provisions are indispensable in that:

    1.   exclusivity together with the grant-back licensing provisions in the Intellectual and Industrial Property and Licence Agreements in respect of technology Atlas receives from each parent protects DT and FT's technology against third parties and against the other parent respectively; and

2.   using one such network instead of several is technically easier and therefore allows more efficient distribution. Atlas as a provider of Europe-wide services relies on national distribution networks with broad geographic coverage. The alternative to using the TO's distribution networks is either distribution by several smaller distributors or the construction of an own nationwide network in the parents' home countries. Both would deprive European telecommunications markets of the benefits of a technical harmon-ization of Europe's two largest existing public packet-switched data networks.

(58)   Atlas will use Transpac-France and T-Data as national distribution networks in France and Germany. Thus, DT or FT will provide the national services required and use Atlas to provide all cross-border and third-country connections needed. In the light of this, other distribution arrangements would be less protective of the parents intellectual property rights and less adequate to the importance of services DT and FT will initially provide to Atlas. The Commission therefore concludes that the exclusive distribution arrangement is indispensable within the meaning of Article 85(3) of the EC Treaty and Article 53(3) of the EEA Agreement.

5.   Non-elimination of competition

(59)   The conditions imposed on DT and FT and the general regulatory framework in the European Community will improve the environment for competition in FT and DT's home countries. This applies notably to the conditions regarding: (i) interconnection to the public packet-switched data networks on terms non-discriminatory and economically equivalent to those available to Atlas in France and Germany; (ii) non-discriminatory intercon-nection to the PSTN and the ISDN in France and Germany; and (iii) the prohibition on DT and FT to take advantage of their market position in distributing Atlas' services and own services through joint contracts.

(60)   The condition described in recital 29(5) requiring DT and FT to sell Atlas products under separate contracts from the sale of own products will ensure that possible differences in calculation are verifiable and thus that non-discriminatory interconnection works in practice. The outsourcing and value-added ('managed') leased lines services provided by Atlas are open to competition and returns on these services are relatively low. Given the legal monopoly and eventually the dominant position for infrastructure provision enjoyed by DT and FT for the duration of this Decision, DT and FT could eliminate competition by using discounts on reserved services (such as leased lines) to attract their clients to use Atlas' non-reserved services.

The sale of packages of different services under one single contract is common commercial practice in the telecommunications sector known as 'bundling.' In liberalized telecommunications markets, dominant providers are usually prohibited both from tying sales of different services and from granting discounts on packages of services without specifying: (i) the terms and conditions of each individual 'unbundled' service; and (ii) the individual service(s) subject to a discount. Also, dominant providers are under an obligation to publish all tariffs and must prove that discounts on packages of services are justified by savings specifically due to the offering of a package of services. However, given: (i) the imbalance between DT and FT's ubiquitous monopoly networks on the one side and the small presence and reliance on interconnection of new market entrants on the other; and (ii) the lack of sufficient regulatory transparency requirements for the relevant services, allowing DT and FT to negotiate single contracts for both liberalized and reserved services would at this stage effectively impair market entry by competitors in Germany and France. DT and FT could *inter alia* grant quantity discounts or more favourable conditions in respect of combined packages of such services in a way which would make individual pricing and notably justification of any discounts non-transparent. The requirement to sell such services under separate contracts would in itself be insufficient unless terms and conditions are set out for each particular service sold.

(61)   Moreover, the conditions and obligations imposed on DT and FT to keep and supply detailed accounting information ensures that the entities created pursuant to the Atlas Agreement and Atlas' parents gather sufficient information to allow the Commission a verification of their competitive behaviour. Accounting-related requirements attached to this Decision will also make it possible for national courts to order discovery of evidence of breaches of the substantive conditions attached to this Decisions and of any alleged anti-competitive behaviour where third parties seek remedies against such behaviour before the national courts. The Commission concludes that Atlas will not afford the parents the possibility of eliminating competition in respect of the envisaged set of services. In reaching this conclusion the Commission has taken into account the following elements.

Markets for cross-border and ultimately Europe-wide services

(62)   Competitors in the marketplace
Atlas is one of several alliances between TOs and/or other undertakings in the relevant markets. Several alliances have obtained regulatory clearance and are already active in the market.[32] DT and FT will also face competition, at least for certain non-reserved services that will integrate Atlas' Europe-wide packages of corporate telecommunications services. Competitors range from computer and data processing companies, for example IBM, DEC and EDS, to information services companies such as GEIS and Compuserve. However, most of these competitors have small market shares and are dependent on a substantive change in current competitive conditions to develop their presence in the non-reserved corporate telecommunications services markets. As for the provision of cross-border and ultimately Europe-wide services from and into Germany and France, these conditions will change as soon as the two main elements of competition are available, namely: (i) alternatives to using DT and FT's infrastructure; and (ii) access to DT and FT's networks on transparent and non-discriminatory terms.

Both elements are of particular relevance to innovative offerings of non-reserved corporate telecommunications services which require state-of-the-art, high-speed lines and distribution networks whose use does not entail a loss of features. The mere presence of competing providers of cross-border and ultimately Europe-wide services has had little impact in that market yet.

---

32 In addition to BT-MCI's Concert (footnote 7), the Commission has granted regulatory approval in Case No IV/M.595 — *BT/VIAG*, OJ No C 15, 20.1.1996, p. 4; Case No IV/M.618 — *Cable & Wireless/VEBA*, OJ No 23, 5.9.1995, p. 3, and Case No IV/M.689 — *ADSB/Belgacom* (Decision of 29 February 1996; OJ No C 194, 5.7.1996, p. 4).

For both economic and geographic reasons, service provision into or across Germany and France is key to competition in the markets for Europe-wide non-reserved corporate telecommunications services. DT and FT will not eliminate competition if prevented from abusing their market positions and from preventing effective market entry. The Commission concludes that the following conditions are indispensable to that end.

(63) Availability of alternative infrastructure

Alternative infrastructure options and competitive pressure on leased-line rates will be possible in Germany and France when at least two infrastructure licences for the provision of liberalized telecommunications services are awarded, as is scheduled to occur by 1 July 1996. Given the existence of several infrastructure operators in both Member States and given the chance these operators have had to prepare for early infrastructure liberalization, the award of at least two alternative infrastructure licences in Germany and France should mean choice of infrastructure there. Only from that moment will other telecommunications services providers be in a position to compete with Atlas without depending on Atlas' parents for their leased-line requirements.

(64) Interconnection on non-discriminatory technical terms

Atlas as any of its competitors, must: (i) create an own leased-line network to provide cross-border services; and (ii) interconnect to the public packet-switched data networks, the PSTN or the ISDN in France and Germany for final distribution of the Atlas services to customers. The use of DT and FT's networks as distribution networks will also be possible for competitors from the date of the exemption by interconnecting to such networks over X.75 interfaces. As to voice and sophisticated data services, DT and FT respectively must make available upon request adequate technical information relevant for PSTN or ISDN interconnection. This enables third-party competitors to provide services from and into DT and FT's home countries offering essential advanced features such as reverse charging, closed user group definition or end-to-end management. DT and FT's packet-switched ATM networks are not integrated into the Atlas venture; as was stated at recital 7, such integration would require a new notification. Atlas must therefore interconnect to such networks if so required for certain high-speed data communications services. The condition imposed on DT and FT not to discriminate between Atlas and third-party competitors as regards technical information on DT and FT's networks, such as full data on DT and FT's implementation of the Signalling System 7 (SS7)[33] for voice services interconnection to the PSTN, will ensure that technical performance options for Atlas' non-reserved services involving interconnection with DT and FT's networks are similar for any competitor.[34]

(65) DT and FT are constrained under their respective national regulations not to discriminate against third parties and to comply with Open

---

33 Major digital protocol/signalling system for managing and transmitting control and routing information in networks.

34 The Commission has decided similarly in previous cases featuring similar market structures and problems, e.g. Decision 93/403/EEC of 11 June 1993 — EBU/Eurovision System, OJ No L 179, 22.7.1993, p. 23, at recital 82; Decision 94/594/EC of 27 July 1994 — ACI, OJ No L 224, 30.8.1994, p. 28, at recital 66; and Decision 94/663/EC of 21 September 1994 — Night Services, OJ No L 259, 7.10.1994, p. 20, at recitals 80 and 82.

Network Provision (ONP) obligations such as providing a minimum set of lines at cost oriented and transparent tariffs.[35] More importantly, the exemption of the Atlas transaction is conditional upon DT and FT *inter alia* granting transparent and non-discriminatory terms of interconnection and implementing an accounting system which discloses the fully allocated costs of each service in anticipation of the ONP Interconnection Directive.[36] While the existing legal framework already provides for transparency, the Commission considers the additional conditions imposed on DT and FT as to separation and auditing of accounts, exclusion of cross subsidies and economically equivalent rates for interconnection to the German and French public packet-switched data networks are indispensable to ensure that the use of DT and FT's PSTN, Transpac-France in France and/or T-Data in Germany as distribution networks will be possible for Atlas and its competitors under equivalent conditions.

(66)   No privileged information

Atlas will not have a competitive advantage over competitors as regards access to DT and FT's privileged commercial information. The parents have also deleted from the Atlas Agreements those clauses originally notified that appointed Atlas as DT and FT's agents for half-circuits. Given that such international leased lines are sought either by service providers competing with Atlas or by MNCs and other private network operators which are potential clients for Atlas' outsourcing services, the agency agreement would have given Atlas a competitive information advantage over competitors.

(67)   Consumer bargaining power

MNCs or other large companies have the choice between either building their own private network solutions across national borders or purchasing them from service providers such as Atlas; they are not likely to choose the latter option unless this is cost-effective. Given their knowledge of the market these customers are in a position to request offers from different competitors. This gives MNCs considerable bargaining power, reflected in competition between the suppliers. This may equally apply to SMEs when lower infrastructure prices allow small suppliers to reach the scale necessary to enter the market.

French and German markets for packet-switched data communications services

(68)   DT and FT have substantial market presence in their respective home countries, where they own the only existing nationwide, packet-switched data communications networks. Actual competition existed in Germany and will not be eliminated, thanks to the divestiture of FT's indirect German subsidiary Info AG. However, the restriction of potential competition between FT and DT in France and Germany has a substantial impact on the respective markets for packet-switched data communications services. More than 80% of customers for this service in France and Germany are SMEs, which would not have sufficient bargaining power to counterbalance

---

35 Articles 7 and 10 of Council Directive 92/44/EC of 5 June 1992 on the application of open network provision to leased lines, OJ No L 165, 19.6.1992, p. 27.
36 See Articles 6 and 7 of the modified proposal for a European Parliament and Council Directive on interconnection in telecommunications with regard to ensuring universal service and interoperability through application of the principles of open network provision (ONP), OJ No C 178, 21.6.1996, p. 3.

the strengthening of DT and FT's market position through the creation of a joint public packet-switched data network.

(69)   For the purposes of this assessment the Commission defines two different albeit partly overlapping customer segments in the market for packet-switched data communications services, namely: (i) customers demanding casual, low-speed, low-volume applications, which are provided over the public packet-switched data networks in each Member State and billed by volume sent according to published tariffs (recital 9(1)); and (ii) customers that generate more substantial and regular demand traffic, which service providers meet increasingly by packet-switched services using protocols such as Frame Relay, ATM and IP or by switched services and bill according to individual demand features (recital 9(2)).

The choice of alternative infrastructure is not in itself sufficient to provide competitive alternatives to X.25 data and Transpac France offer in Germany and France respectively to the first customer segment described above. These services require dense networks with wide geographic coverage, which DT and FT's competitors will continue to lack for some time. This conclusion is based on two considerations. First, all alternative infrastructure currently available in Germany and France taken together amounts to only one third of total infrastructure owned by DT and FT respectively. Secondly, the market for X.25 data services is characterized by low margins. Consequently, investment in alternative infrastructure with nationwide coverage as is required to serve the first customer segment described in the previous recital will not begin to narrow the gap with the incumbent TO's infrastructure until new infrastructure can carry any telecommunications service and thus provide a better return on investment. The legal and administrative framework necessary to provide such new infrastructure is scheduled to be in place in France and Germany by 1 January 1998.

(70)   Competitive alternatives

No adequate competitive alternative to Atlas would exist in Germany and France for customers in the first segment described at recital 9(1) if DT and FT were to integrate their respective nationwide, public packet-switched data networks before at least two competing nationwide carriers are licensed in each of these Member States to provide public telecommunications services. The integration of these public packet-switched data networks into Atlas would reinforce Transpac France and T-Data's existing dominant position in the French and German markets for national packet-switched data communications services (more than 70% market share respectively). With hardly any competitive alternative yet for national services, Atlas would at this stage lock in existing Transpac France and T-Data customers with restrictive effects in the cross-border and ultimately Europe-wide geographic market as the Single Market develops. Keeping the French and German public packet-switched data networks separate from Atlas and prohibiting FT and DT from selling own services and Atlas services in the same contract, customers have the possibility to: (i) compare Transpac France and T-Data's national X.25 data services to emerging competitive alternatives such as more advanced packet-switched data communications and switched services (see below), for which FT and DT face stronger competition; and (ii) choose between Atlas and its competitors for separate provision of cross-border and ultimately Europe-wide X.25 data services if their requirements exceed the national scope.

Generally, competitive alternatives must be effectively available to have an appreciable impact on market conditions. However, as regards the French and German telecommunications markets, the Commission envisages that competitive conditions will already change substantially once telecommunications services and networks are fully and effectively liberalized and first nationwide carrier licences granted, as is scheduled to occur by 1 January 1998, and development quickly thereafter. To reach this conclusion, the Commission has taken into consideration: (i) the decreasing relevance of public packet-switched data networks using the X.25 protocol for the provision of corporate packet-switched data communications services; (ii) the outstanding economic importance and attraction of the French and the German telecommunications markets to telecommunications operators; (iii) the existence of operational expandable alternative infrastructure there and (iv) the positioning of a number of strong competing alliances ahead of full and effective liberalization of telecommunications networks and services in France and Germany by 1 January 1998 (see recital 18).

Ahead of full and effective liberalization of the French and German telecommunications markets it is possible in Germany to provide nationwide X.25 data services using the ISDN 'D' channel. Several of T-Data's competitors use this alternative to direct interconnection with DT's public packet-switched data networks (see next recital) at a total investment cost of approximately ECU 1,1 million. The ISDN 'D' channel is accessible in France using Transpac France as a transit network and direct access will be possible by the end of 1996. The Commission considers that increasing availability of the ISDN might eventually offer a competitive alternative for the provision of X.25 data services in the German customer segment described at recital 9(1). As for France however, the Commission concludes from the density of Transpac France's public packet-switched data networks that using the ISDN is unlikely to prove a sufficiently competitive alternative.

(71) Economically equivalent interconnection terms

Any third party can obtain non-discriminatory interconnection with T-Data and Transpac-France (before these entities are integrated into Atlas) or Atlas Germany and Atlas France (after T-Data and Transpac France have been integrated into Atlas) in Germany and France over X.75 interfaces. Services provided over two or more networks interconnected through X.75 interfaces are an alternative to using own networks in the market for packet-switched data communications services. This alternative is competitive only for service provision to customers in the second segment described at recital 9(2), albeit demand for X.25 data services in this segment is decreasing quickly. In this segment, most value is added to services provided over customized networks, and service providers rely on interconnection merely to relay customer data communications to third parties unconnected to the customized network (call termination).

While Atlas may use proprietary interfaces to interconnect with T-Data and Transpac France, non-discriminatory third-party access to T-Data and Transpac France via X.75 interfaces is sufficient to prevent Atlas from eliminating competition in the market for packet-switched data communications services. For instance, to date T-Data interconnects to most third-party networks over interfaces which use the X.75 protocol and do not therefore support certain advanced features. DT and FT's tariffs for interconnection to their public packet-switched data communications networks must disclose the mark-up on the fully allocated costs of providing such interconnection. Third-party interconnection must be non-discriminatory compared to inter-connection conditions for Atlas, *inter alia* as regards availability of ancillary services, provisioning time, repair and maintenance levels or technical information required. In the light of the above, the Commission concludes that the elimination of potential competition between T-Data and Transpac France in Germany and France respectively will not allow the parents to foreclose their home markets for the provision of standardized packet-switched data communications services.

Markets for national services in countries other than France and Germany

(72) At the third-country national level, Atlas is set to develop into a significant competitor for incumbent TOs: Atlas aims at becoming the second player on the data communications services markets of all major European markets with the exception of the UK. In respect of these services, the parents' submitted market share target for Atlas in all major national markets other than France and Germany is 20%. Atlas is therefore set to offer an alternative to dominant incumbent TOs rather than to eliminate actual competition in third countries.

Markets outside the scope of the Atlas venture

(73) The liberalized services subject to cooperation within Atlas contribute less than 10% to DT and FT's respective turnover. Even some liberalized services such as national VPN services and all data communications involving the use of DT and FT's ATM networks are not Atlas services and therefore subject to competition between the parents, while Atlas may purchase these services and access these networks under equivalent non-discriminatory, transparent conditions and at the same inter-connection rates as third-party competitors. The condition attached to this Decision restricting the exchange of sensitive information between DT, FT and Atlas limit the potentially negative effects of the joint venture both on competition between the parents acting as Atlas distributors and on overall competition between the parents.

Exclusive distribution arrangements in France and Germany

(74) In allowing passive sales the Distribution Agreements provide an opening for customers with bargaining power to exploit margins for competition between the Atlas parent acting as exclusive distributor in its home country and the other parent that may offer the same Atlas service at a lower price. More importantly, the restrictive effects of the exclusive distribution agreements are likely to be increasingly balanced by the availability of alternative infrastructure and the non-discriminatory terms of interconnection with T-Data and Transpac-France's networks, which will induce competition for Atlas and for DT and FT acting as Atlas distributors.

6. Conclusion

(75) It is the Commission's conclusion that all conditions for an individual exemption pursuant to Article 85(3) of the EC Treaty and Article 53(3)

of the EEA Agreement are met in respect of the creation of Atlas and in respect of the individual restrictions discussed above.

C. DURATION OF THE EXEMPTION, CONDITIONS AND OBLIGATIONS

(76)   Pursuant to Article 8 of Regulation No 17 and to Protocol 21 of the EEA Agreement respectively, a decision in application of Article 85(3) of the EC Treaty and Article 53(3) of the EEA Agreement shall be issued for a specified period and conditions and obligations may be attached thereto. Pursuant to Article 6 of Regulation No 17, the date from which such a decision takes effect cannot be earlier than the date of notification. In that respect, in the present case the Decision, in so far as it grants exemption, shall take effect:

(a)   as regards the creation of Atlas and related agreements as described above, except for the integration of Transpac France and T-Data into a joint venture, for five years from the date on which the second new infrastructure licence comes into force in both Germany and France authorizing the licensee to operate infrastructure for the provision of liberalized services in competition with the respective parent and the respective first licensee; and

(b)   as regards the integration of Transpac France and T-Data into a joint venture company, from the date on which licences to new applicants for the provision of nationwide infrastructure and national and international voice telephony services which provide two alternatives to DT and FT in a substantial part of Germany and France respectively come into force in both Germany and France to the expiry of the five-year period specified in the preceding recital.

(77)   This exemption Decision shall be subject to the conditions described in recitals 25 to 30(1). This exemption Decision shall further impose on DT, FT and the entities created pursuant to the Atlas agreements the obligations described in recital 30. These conditions are indispensable to prevent an elimination of competition in the relevant markets by the largest TOs in the EEA. The Commission will, upon the parties request, review the need for any particular condition or obligation attached to this Decision if circumstances change substantially before the period of exemption expires.

The most crucial behavioural requirements to safeguard competition in the EEA are attached as conditions rather than obligations to this Decision, given the need to prevent an elimination of effective competition. Strict compliance with these requirements is so important that the Commission must ensure immediate consequences in the event of a breach. Given the legal consequences of such breach of a condition, national courts can adequately and swiftly contribute to a decentralized policing of compliance and thus ensure that the competition rules will be respected for the benefit of private individuals.[37] However, the principle of proportionality requires that far-reaching legal, financial and commercial consequences do not ensue from occasional or individual mistakes whose effects on the market are negligible. Therefore, violations of the prohibitions on cross-subsidization, discrimina-

---

37 See Commission notice on cooperation between national courts and the Commission in applying Articles 85 and 86 of the EEC Treaty, OJ No C 39, 13.2.1993, p. 6.

tion and bundling cannot be considered to breach a condition attached to this Decision unless such violations have a substantial impact on market conditions, for instance if practices are committed systematically or repeatedly.

The condition relating to non-discriminatory treatment of Atlas and its competitors (recital 28) will also allow DT and FT to compete against each other at the distribution level, albeit through passive sales. Such competition is possible because the same atlas service may be sold from either end of the requested circuits, namely from Germany or from France. To limit the potentially negative effects of the joint venture on overall competition between the parents, the Commission considers it appropriate to impose restrictions on the exchange of sensitive information between the parents and Atlas (recital 28(4)).

(78) This Decision is without prejudice to the applicability of Article 86 of the EC Treaty and Article 54 of the EEA Agreement,

HAS ADOPTED THIS DECISION:

Article 1

Pursuant to Article 85(3) of the EC Treaty and Article 53(3) of the EEA Agreement and subject to Articles 2 to 5 of this Decision, the provisions of Articles 85(1) of the EC Treaty and Article 53(1) of the EEA Agreement are hereby declared inapplicable, for a period of five years from the date on which two or more licences for the construction or ownership and control of alternative infrastructure for the provision of liberalized telecommunications services take effect in both Germany and France, to:

(a)   the creation of the Atlas joint venture by Deutsche Telekom AG ('DT') and France Télécom ('FT'), as notified to the Commission, including the ancillary obligations imposed on DT and on FT:

(i)   to obtain from Atlas all requirements for global products under Article VII of both Distribution Agreements; and

(ii)   not to compete with the joint venture for the provision of Atlas services under Article XIII of the Joint Venture Agreement and Article VII of both Distribution Agreements; and to

(b)   the appointment of DT as the exclusive distributor for Atlas in Germany and of FT as the exclusive distributor for Atlas in France under Article IV of both Distribution Agreements.

Article 2

Pursuant to Article 85(3) of the EC Treaty and Article 53(3) of the EEA Agreement and subject to Articles 3, 4 and 5 of this Decision, the provisions of Article 85(1) of the EC Treaty and Article 53(1) of the EEA Agreement are hereby declared inapplicable to the integration into Atlas of the German and French public packet-switched data networks, provided that only networks providing packet-switched data communications services using the X.25, Frame Relay, SNA or Internet protocols shall be integrated, from the date on which both Germany and France have:

(a)   removed all legal prohibitions on entities other than DT and FT and their subsidiaries to:

(i)   build, own or control both national and international telecommunications infrastructure and use such infrastructure to provide any telecommunications service, and

(ii)   provide a national and international voice telephony service; and

(b)   granted and made effective at least two licences to applicants other than DT and FT for

(i)   the construction or ownership, and control of telecommunications infrastructure and either separately or in combination,

(ii)   the provision of national and international voice telephony services, provided that such licences provide two suitable alternatives to DT and FT respectively to serve all or a substantial part of the territory of Germany and France,

until the expiry of the five-year period specified in Article 1.

Article 3

Until the date specified in Article 2 of this Decision, the exemption from Article 85(1) of the EC Treaty and Article 53(1) of the EEA Agreement set out in Article 1 of this Decision is subject to the condition that cooperation between DT and FT in developing common technical network elements comprise the following areas only:

(a)   the following product management and development tasks:

(i)   product definition,

(ii)   product marketing,

(iii) product life-cycle management,

(iv)   specification of product requirements,

(v)   technical specifications and development of the products, and

(vi)   technical development of the products;

(b)   the following network planning functions:

(i)   central network engineering and optimization of the common transmission network so as to avoid an unreasonable duplication of resources,

(ii)   engineering and optimization of the networks for the various service platforms so as to ensure seamless services, and

(iii) central planning regarding the implementation of new network nodes; and

(c)   the following aspects of information systems:

(i)   definition of the information system architecture,

(ii)   specification of information system requirements and applications,

(iii) technical development of hardware and software for information systems, and

(iv)   central implementation planning of hardware and software.

Until the date specified in Article 2, all other aspects and functions of each of the French and the German public packet-switched data networks shall be controlled by two separate network management centres.

Article 4

The exemption from the application of Article 85(1) of the EC Treaty and Article 53(1) of the EEA Agreement set out in Articles 1 and 2 of this Decision is subject to the following conditions:

(a) Divestiture of Info AG
  (1) FT shall:
    (i) sell Transpac's shares in Info AG before [. . .].[38] The Commission may extend the period granted to FT for divestiture of Info AG by an additional six months after that date; FT shall be deemed to have complied with this condition by [. . .][39] if it has entered into a binding letter of intent or a binding contract for the sale of Info AG to a purchaser agreed by the Commission, provided that such sale is completed within a reasonable time limit, after the signing of such binding letter of intent or binding contract, agreed by the Commission;
    (ii) appoint a trustee subject to approval by the Commission to advise on the management and to sell Info AG, provided that, subject to approval by the Commission, FT may
      — terminate the trustee agreement should FT decide at any time after the appointment that the trustee is not performing its duties properly, and
      — replace the previously appointed trustee by another trustee also approved by the Commission;
    (iii) give the trustee an irrevocable mandate to sell Info AG, on best possible terms and conditions, to any available purchaser making an offer before [. . .];[40]
    (iv) remunerate the trustee providing incentives for a prompt divestiture;
    (v) give all reasonable assistance requested by the trustee to sell Info AG by the target date;
    (vi) establish and facilitate the management structure agreed with the trustee in the framework of the divestiture negotiations;
    (vii) provide the purchaser of Info AG with any licences and know-how relating to the provision of Info AG's services to the extent possible under existing contractual obligations, if any. FT may charge the purchaser a market-based fee for any such licence and know-how;
    (viii) keep all administrative and management functions relating to Info AG which have been carried out at all levels within FT and/or Transpac, so as to maintain the viability, marketability and competitiveness of Info AG until divestiture is completed or until the trustee advises FT that such functions are no longer necessary, whichever occurs earlier.
  (2) FT shall at all times use its best efforts to maintain the value of Info AG and of its business in every respect and, when the trustee is appointed to sell Info AG, shall consider the advice of the trustee to maintain this value. FT shall in particular ensure that all services provided by FT or any of FT's subsidiaries to Info AG continue to be provided efficiently and satisfactorily and that no increase is made in the charge (if any) made to Info AG for any such service. FT shall not, except with the consent of the trustee, employ or offer employment to any employee or officer of Info AG until after the sale of Info AG.
  (3) The trustee appointed by FT shall:
    (i) advise FT and Transpac on the best management structure to ensure the continued viability, marketability and competitiveness of Info AG's business, also in the event of a restructuring of Info AG;

---

38 Business secret.
39 Business secret.
40 Business secret.

(ii)   advise FT and Transpac with regard to the satisfactory operation and management of Info AG, so as to ensure the continued viability, marketability and competitiveness of Info AG's business, and shall supervise, monitor and control the implementation of the advice by Info AG; for these purposes the trustee shall have complete access to Info AG's personnel and facilities as well as to documents, books and records of both FT and Transpac, including such personnel, facilities, books and records which, even if not directly related to Info AG, may have an impact on the conduct of Info AG's operations;

(iii)   act as FT's investment banker in conducting bona fide negotiations with interested third parties with a view to selling Info AG. In the event that the trustee at any time prior to the target date determines together with the Commission that it is not possible to identify an acceptable purchaser for the business of Info AG other than the customers whose headquarters are located outside Germany, the Trustee, FT and the Commission shall discuss appropriate alternatives to the proposed divestiture of Info AG, notably an extended divestiture;

(iv)   provide the Commission with a written report before a binding contract is signed and in any event every month on all developments in its negotiations with third parties interested in purchasing Info AG;

(v)   provide the Commission with a written report every two months concerning the monitoring of the operations and management of Info AG;

(vi)   at any other time upon the Commission's request, provide the Commission with a written or oral report on any aspect of the duties and activities of the trustee in relation to Info AG and its possible purchasers, indicating whether a proposed purchaser would be able to ensure that Info AG remains a competitive participant in the German telecommunications market and whether negotiations with such proposed purchaser should continue; and

(vii)   cease to perform its duties as trustee for the purpose of this condition when the sale of Info AG or any alternative remedy within the meaning of point (iii) becomes effective.

(4)   Multinational clients to whom Info AG has so far provided network services as part of the Transpac network and whose headquarters are located outside Germany may be transferred to Atlas on condition that the Commission is satisfied that these services can be separated from the German activities of Info AG without significantly lessening the value of those activities.

(5)   With immediate effect from the date of notification of this Decision and until one year after the date of signature of the agreements between Transpac and the purchaser of Info AG, neither DT, FT, Atlas nor GlobalOne shall compete with Info AG for the provision of telecommunications services to customers of Info AG whose headquarters are located within Germany except where such customers decline to deal with Info AG.

(6)   If the sale of Info AG's business does not seem likely to occur by the date stated in point (1)(i), FT shall, at least two months before that date, submit alternative remedies sufficiently satisfactory to safeguard actual competition in the German market. These alternative remedies must be executed by the date stated in point (1)(i).

(b)   Non-discrimination

(1)   DT and FT shall not grant to any entity created pursuant to the Atlas Agreements terms and conditions dissimilar to the terms and conditions applied to other providers of similar services, nor exempt such entity from any usage restrictions which would enable such entity to offer services which competing providers are prevented from offering with regard to the following facilities-related telecommunications services provided by FT and DT in France and Germany respectively:

(i)   leased lines services, in particular international leased lines (half-circuits) and domestic leased lines, including any discounts, as the case may be; and

(ii)   PSTN/ISDN services including both access to such networks (namely analogue access; basic ISDN access; ISDN access to the public packet-switched data networks; special access from the public packet-switched data networks to ISDN; and national and international voice VPN and VPN interconnection services) and traffic over such networks.

Atlas shall not be granted more favourable treatment than third parties in connection with reserved facilities and services and with such facilities and services which remain an essential facility after full and effective liberalization of telecommunications infrastructure and services in France and Germany.

(2)   DT and FT shall grant any entity created pursuant to the Atlas Agreement and any third party operating a telecommunications facility that apply for the interconnection of such facility with DT or FT's networks such interconnection on non-discriminatory terms that enable such entity or person to provide telecommunications services or provide its telecommunications facilities without limitation in any respect within the reasonable capabilities of the operator concerned.

(3)   DT and FT shall not in any way discriminate between any entity created pursuant to the Atlas Agreements and any other service provider competing with such entity in connection with:

(i)   either a decision substantially to modify technical interfaces for the access to reserved services and/or essential facilities or services, or the disclosure of any other technical information relating to the operation of the PSTN/ISDN; competitors shall in particular have access to such software and interface information as is indispensable for maintaining the technical features of voice services where such competitors interconnect to the German or French PSTN/ISDN; and

(ii)   the disclosure of any commercial information that would confer a substantial competitive advantage and is not readily and equally available elsewhere by service providers competing with such entity.

(4)   Breaches of the requirements set out in points 1, 2 and 3 shall not be considered to infringe this condition unless such breaches have a substantial impact on the market.

(c)   Interconnection to DT and FT's public packet-switched data networks

(1)   FT and DT shall immediately:

(i)   establish and maintain standardized X.75 interfaces to access their national public packet-switched data networks;

(ii)   offer such access on non-discriminatory terms, including price, availability of volume or other discounts and the quality of interconnectrion provided; and

(iii)   publish the standard terms and conditions for such X.75 inter-face standards, including, if any, volume discounts and other discounts and make any agreements relating to such X.75 interfaces, including all specifi-cally agreed terms, available for inspection by the Commission.

(2)   Transpac France and T-Data shall, until such time as Transpac France and T-Data are integrated into Atlas, not disclose to any entity created pursuant to the Atlas Agreement any such specifically agreed terms as are identified and maintained as confidential by the party obtaining interconnection through standardized X.75 interfaces to access the French or German national public packet-switched data networks.

(3)   The conditions set out in points (1) and (2) shall likewise apply to any generally used CCITT-standardized interconnection protocol that may modify, replace or co-exist as a standard related to the X.75 standard and is used by FT and DT.

(4)   Any entity created pursuant to the Atlas Agreements may access the French and German public packet-switched data networks through propri-etary interfaces, even for the provision of data communications services, provided that access granted to such entity through such interfaces is economically equivalent to third-party access to those networks.

(5)   Breaches of the requirements set out in points 1 to 4 shall not be considered to infringe this condition unless such breaches have a substantial impact on the market.

(d)   Interconnection to DT and FT's other networks and facilities

(1)   DT and FT shall grant to any third party that operates a telecom-munications facility ('telecommunications operator') and applies for the interconnection of such facility or systems facilities with DT or FT's net-works, such interconnection on non-discriminatory terms as compared to the terms applied to Atlas. Such terms shall enable the telecommunications operator to provide telecommunications services or provide its telecommuni-cations facilities without limitation in any respect within the reasonable capabilities of the telecommunications operator concerned.

(2)   Breaches of the requirements set out in point 1 shall not be considered to infringe this condition unless such breaches have a substantial impact on the market.

(e)   Cross-subsidization

(1)   All entities created pursuant to the Atlas Agreements shall be established as distinct entities separate from DT and FT.

(2)   Atlas SA, T-Data and Transpac France shall obtain their own debt financing on their own credit, provided that FT and DT:

(i)   may make capital contributions or commercially normal loans to Atlas SA, T-Data and Transpac France, to enable them to conduct their respective businesses;

(ii)   may pledge their venture interests in such entities, in connection with non-recourse financing for such entities; and

(iii)   may guarantee any indebtedness of such entities, provided that FT and DT may only make payments pursuant to any such guarantee following a default by such entities in respect of such indebtedness.

(3)   All entities created pursuant to the Atlas Agreement, T-Data and Transpac France shall not allocate directly or indirectly any part of their operating expenses, costs, depreciation, or other expenses of their business to

any parts of FT or DT's business units (including without limitation the proportionate costs based on work actually performed that are attributable to shared employees or sales or marketing of Atlas products and services by DT or FT employees). These undertakings may bill DT or FT for products and services applied to DT or FT by such undertakings at:

    (i)   the same price charged third parties in the case of products or services sold to third parties in commercial quantities; or

    (ii)   on the basis of the full cost reimbursement or other arm's length pricing method in the case of products and services not sold to third parties in commercial quantities.

(4)   Breaches of the requirements set out in points 1, 2 and 3 shall not be considered to infringe this condition unless such breaches have a substantial impact on the market.

(f)   Bundling

(1)   DT and FT shall sell their services under contracts separate from the contracts for the sale of Atlas services concluded as distributors of Atlas in Germany and France respectively. Each separate contract shall set out the terms and conditions of each individual service sold thereunder and notably attribute any quantity or other discounts to a particular service, as the case may be.

(2)   Breaches of the above requirements shall not be considered to infringe this condition unless such breaches have a substantial impact on the market.

(g)   Accounting

(1)   T-Data, Transpac France (including all their subsidiaries) as well as all entities created pursuant to the Atlas Agreements which are operating in the EEA shall keep separate accounting records using international accounting standards for each service they provide in any country. DT and FT (including all subsidiaries) shall keep separate accounting records using international accounting standards for each service they provide to any entity created pursuant to the Atlas Agreements, operating in the EEA.

(2)   DT and FT shall, within one year of the date defined in Article 1, implement an accounting system which generates sufficiently detailed records of the services covered by point (1). Those records shall detail the following:

    (i)   the cost standard used;

    (ii)   the accounting conventions used for the treatment of costs;

    (iii)   the allocation and attribution of expenses or costs, revenues, assets and liabilities shared between any entity created pursuant to the Atlas Agreements and DT and/or FT; and

    (iv)   the attribution method chosen.

(3)   The accounting records referred to in points (1) and (2) shall identify all services provided to any entity created pursuant to the Atlas Agreements by DT and FT or transfers to or from DT and FT.

(4)   No entity created pursuant to the Atlas Agreement, nor T-Data or Transpac France shall receive any material subsidy directly or indirectly from DT or FT, nor any investment or payment from DT or FT that is not recorded in the books of such entities as an investment in debt or equity.

Article 5

The exemption granted under this Decision is subject to the following obligations:

(a)   Auditing

(1)   Atlas SA and any consolidated subsidiary of Atlas SA, Transpac France and T-Data shall be audited by an independent external auditor every 12 months, provided that such audit shall certify from an accounting viewpoint that:

(i)   all transactions between those undertakings, on the one hand, and FT and DT, on the other hand, have been conducted at arm's length;

(ii)   the undertakings have adhered to the accounting procedures; and

(iii)   the calculation numbers are accurate.

(2)   The first auditing report and certificate complying with point (1), covering the 12-month period starting on the date on which this Decision takes effect, shall be submitted to the Commission within 15 months of that date.

(b)   Other obligations

DT, FT, T-Data, Transpac France and all entities created pursuant to the Atlas Agreements shall each, for the purpose of ascertaining and ensuring compliance by these undertakings with the conditions set out in Article 4:

(1)   keep all detailed records and documents necessary to prove complete compliance with the terms of the conditions set out in Article 4 ready for inspection by the Commission and to enable the Commission to verify the correctness of the audit certificate referred to in point (a)(2);

(2)   give the Commission access to their business premises to inspect records and documents covered by the obligations set out under heading (a) and to receive oral explanations relating to such documents on reasonable notice, during office hours, and without the need for the Commission to invoke the powers of inspection pursuant to Regulation No 17; and

(3)   provide the Commission with:

(i)   any records and documents in the possession or control of those undertakings necessary for that determination;

(ii)   unaudited accounting data as specified in points (1) and (2) every six months, starting one year after the commencement date of the exemption pursuant to Article 1; and

(iii)   further oral or written explanations.

Article 6

This Decision is addressed to:

Deutsche Telekom AG,
Friedrich-Ebert-Allee 140,
D-53105 BONN;

France Télécom,
Place d'Alleray,
F-75505 PARIS.

Done at Brussels, 17 July 1996.

For the Commission
Karel Van Miert
Member of the Commission

Note

See also Commission Decision of 17 July 1996: Case IV/35.617 — Phoenix/Global One; OJ L239/57, 19 September 1996.

DRAFT

**NOTICE ON THE APPLICATION OF THE COMPETITION RULES
TO ACCESS AGREEMENTS
IN THE TELECOMMUNICATIONS SECTOR**

Framework, Relevant Markets and Principles

PREFACE

In the telecommunications industry, access agreements are central in allowing market participants the benefits of liberalization.

The purpose of this Notice is threefold:

— To set out access principles stemming from EU competition law as shown in a large number of Commission decisions in order to create greater market certainty and more stable conditions for investment and commercial initiative in the telecoms and multimedia sectors;

— To define and clarify the relationship between competition law and sector specific legislation under the Article 100A framework (in particular this relates to the relationship between competition rules and Open Network Provision legislation);

— To explain how competition rules will be applied in a consistent way across the converging sectors involved in the provision of new multimedia services, and in particular to access issues and gateways in this context.

This draft Notice is now published for public consultation only. The final version of the Notice will be adopted only once the ONP interconnection directive has been finally approved by Parliament and Council. This will guarantee complete coherence between the ONP interconnection framework and the application of the competition rules as set out in this draft Notice, and the taking into account of the final version of the ONP interconnection directive, in order to create market certainty before the 1 January 1998 liberalisation deadline.

TABLE OF CONTENTS

INTRODUCTION

0.   The timetable for full liberalisation in the telecommunications sector has now been established, and Member States are to remove the last barriers to the provision of telecommunications services in a competitive environment to consumers by 1 January 1998.[1] As a result of this liberalisation a second set of related products or services will emerge as well as the need for access to facilities necessary to provide these services. In this sector, interconnection to the public switched telecommunications network is a typical example of such access. The Commission has stated that it will define the treatment of access agreements under the competition rules.[2] This Notice, therefore, addresses the issue of how competition rules and procedures apply to access agreements in the context of harmonised EU and national regulation in the telecommunications sector.

1.   The regulatory framework for the liberalisation of telecommunications consists of the liberalisation directives issued under Article 90 EC and the Open Network Provision (ONP) framework. The ONP framework provides harmonised rules for access and interconnection to the telecommunications networks and the voice telephony services. The legal framework provided by the liberalisation and harmonisation legislation is the background to any action taken by the Commission in its application of the competition rules. Both the liberalisation legislation[3] and the harmonisation legislation[4] are aimed at ensuring the attainment of the objectives of the Community as laid

---

1 According to Directive 96/19/EC and 96/2/EC, certain Member States may request a derogation from full liberalisation for certain limited periods. See: Commission Decision of 27 November 1996 concerning the additional implementation periods requested by Ireland for the implementation of Commission Directives 90/388/EEC and 96/2/EC as regards full competition in the telecommunications markets. This Notice is without prejudice to such derogations, and the Commission will take account of the existence of any such derogation when applying the competition rules to access agreements, as described in this Notice.
2 Communication by the Commission to the European Parliament and the Council on the Green Paper on the liberalisation of telecommunications infrastructure and cable television networks, COM (95) 158 final, 3 May 1995.

out in Article 3 EC, and specifically, the establishment of '*a system ensuring that competition in the internal market is not distorted*' and 'an internal market characterised by the abolition, as between Member States, of obstacles to the free movement of goods, persons, services and capital'.

2.   The Commission has published Guidelines on the application of EEC competition rules in the telecommunications sector, OJ C 233/2 (1991). The present Notice is intended to build on those Guidelines, which do not deal explicitly with access issues.

3.   In the telecommunications sector, liberalisation and harmonisation legislation permit and simplify the task of Community firms in embarking on new activities in new markets and consequently allow users to benefit from increased competition. These advantages must not be jeopardised by restrictive or abusive practices of undertakings: the Community's competition rules are therefore essential to ensure the completion of this development. New entrants must in the initial stages be ensured the right to have access to the networks of incumbent telecommunications operators (TOs). Several authorities, at the regional, national and Community levels, have a role in regulating this sector. If the competition process is to work well in the Internal Market, effective coordination between these institutions must be ensured.

4.   Part I of the Notice sets out the legal framework and details how the Commission intends to achieve its intention of avoiding unnecessary duplication of procedures while safeguarding the rights of undertakings and users under the competition rules. In this context, the Commission's efforts to encourage decentralised application of the competition rules by national courts and national authorities aim at achieving remedies at a national level, unless a significant Community interest is involved in a particular case. In the

---

3 Commission Directive 88/301/EEC, on competition in the markets in telecommunications terminal equipment, OJ L131/73 (1988);

   Commission Directive 90/388/EEC, on competition in the markets for telecommunications services, OJ L 192/10 (1990);

   Commission Directive 94/46/EEC, amending Directive 88/301/EEC and Directive 90/388/ EEC in particular with regard to satellite communications, OJ L 268/15 (1994);

   Commission Directive 95/51/EC, amending Directive 90/388/EEC with regard to the abolition of the restrictions on the use of cable television networks for the provision of already liberalised telecommunications services, OJ L 256/49 (1995);

   Commission Directive 96/2/EC, amending Directive 90/388/EEC with regard to mobile and personal communications, OJ L 20/59 (1996);

   Commission Directive 96/19/EC, amending Directive 90/388/EEC OJ L 74/113 (1996).

4 Interconnection agreements are the most significant form of access agreement in the telecommunications sector. A basic framework for interconnection agreements is set up by the rules on Open Network Provision (ONP), and the application of competition rules must be seen against this background:

   Council Directive 90/387/EEC, on the establishment of the internal market for telecommunications services through the implementation of open network provision, OJ16L16192/1 (1990)

   Council Directive 92/44/EEC, on the application of open network provision to leased lines, OJ L 165/27 (1992);

   EP and Council Directive 95/62/EEC, on the application of open network provision to voice telephony, OJ L 321/6 (1995);

   Common Position for a European Parliament and Council Directive on interconnection in telecommunications with regard to ensuring universal service and interoperability through application of the principles of open network provision (ONP), OJ C220/13, 29 July 1996.

   Proposal for a European Parliament and Council Directive amending Council Directives 90/387/EEC and 92/44 EEC for the purpose of adaptation to a competitive environment in telecommunications, Com(95) 543 final, 14.11.1995.

telecommunications sector, specific procedures in the ONP framework likewise aim at resolving access problems in the first place at a decentralised, national level, with a further possibility for conciliation at Community level. Part II defines the Commission's approach to market definition in this sector. Part III details the principles that the Commission will follow in the application of the competition rules: it aims to help telecommunications market participants shape their access agreements by explaining the competition law requirements.

5.   The Notice is based on the Commission's experience in several cases,[5] and certain studies into this area carried out on behalf of the Commission.[6]

6.   This Notice does not in any way restrict the rights conferred on individuals or undertakings by Community law, and is without prejudice to any interpretation of the Community competition rules that may be given by the Court of First Instance or the European Court of Justice.

PART I: FRAMEWORK

1.   Competition Rules and Sector Specific Regulation

7.   Access problems in the broadest sense of the word (e.g. provision of leased lines, interconnection to networks, access to data concerning subscribers to voice telephone services) can be dealt with at different levels and on the basis of a range of legislative provisions, of both national and Community origin. A service provider faced with an access problem such as a TO's unjustified refusal to supply (or on reasonable terms) a leased line needed by the applicant to provide services to its customers could therefore contemplate a number of routes to seek a remedy. Generally speaking, aggrieved parties will experience a number of benefits, at least in an initial stage, in seeking redress at a national level. At a national level, the applicant has two main choices, namely (1) specific national regulatory procedures now established in accordance with Community law and harmonised under Open Network Provision (see footnote 3) and (2) an action under national and/or Community law before a national court or national competition authority.[7]

5.In the telecommunications area, notably Commission decision of 18 October 1991, *Eirpage*, OJ L 306/22 (1991), and Commission decisions of 17 July 1996, *Atlas* and *Phoenix*, OJ L 239. (1996). There are also a number of pending cases involving access issues.

6 Competition aspects of interconnection agreements in the telecommunications sector, June 1995; Competition aspects of access by service providers to the resources of telecommunications operators, December 1995. See also Competition Aspects of Access Pricing, December 1995.

7 In the case of the ONP leased line directive, ONP foresees the first stage which allows the aggrieved user to appeal to the National Regulatory Authority. This can offer a number of advantages. In the telecommunications areas where experience has shown that companies are often hesitant to be seen as complainants against the TO on which they heavily depend not only with respect to the specific point of conflict but also a much broader and far-reaching sense, the procedures foreseen under ONP are an attractive option. ONP procedures furthermore can cover a broader range of access problems than could be approached on the basis of the competition rules. Finally, these procedures can offer users the advantage of proximity and familiarity with national administrative procedures; language is also a factor to be taken into account.

Under ONP procedures, if matters cannot be resolved at the national level, a second stage is organised at the European level (conciliation procedure). Pursuant to the ONP leased line directive, an agreement between the parties involved must then be reached within two months, with a possible extension of one month if the parties agree.

It should be noted that in the Proposed ONP interconnection directive, as opposed to the

Complaints made to the Commission under the competition rules in the place of or in addition to national courts, national competition authorities and/or to national regulatory authorities under ONP procedures will be dealt with according to the priority which they deserve in view of the urgency, novelty and transnational nature of the problem involved and taking into account the need to avoid duplicate proceeding (see below, points 13 et seq.).

8. The Commission recognises that National Regulatory Authorities[8] have different tasks, and operate in a different legal framework to the Commission. First, the NRAs operate under national law, albeit often implementing European law. Secondly, that law, based as it is on considerations of telecommunications policy has objectives different to, but consistent with, the objectives of Community competition policy. The Commission cooperates as far as possible with the National Regulatory Authorities, and invites the National Regulatory Authorities to cooperate as far as possible between themselves. Under Community law, national authorities, including regulatory authorities and competition authorities, have a duty not to approve a practice or agreement contrary to Community competition law.

9. Community competition rules are not sufficient to remedy the various problems in the telecommunications sector. NRAs therefore have a significantly wider ambit and a significant and far-reaching role in the regulation of the sector. It should also be noted that as a matter of Community law, the NRAs must be independent.[9]

10. It is also important to note that the ONP framework imposes certain obligations on national telecommunications operators that go beyond those that would normally be imposed by Article 86 EC. NRAs may require strict standards relating to transparency, obligations to supply and pricing practices. These obligations can be enforced by the National Regulatory Authorities, which also have jurisdiction to take steps to ensure effective competition.[10]

11. This Notice is written, for convenience, in most respects as if the law was conceived with only one telecommunications operator controlling the only nation-wide public switched telecommunications network in each Member State. This will not necessarily be the case: new telecommunications networks offering increasingly wide coverage will develop progressively. These alternative telecommunications networks may ultimately be large and extensive enough to be partly or even wholly substitutable for the existing national networks, and this should be kept in mind.

---

leased line directive, a conciliation procedure is foreseen for transfrontier cases only, that is interconnection disputes in which more than one National Regulatory Authority is involved. If the National Regulatory Authorities dealing with an interconnection problem do not reach a solution to the problem, then one of them may notify the Commission thereof and invoke the conciliation procedure (Article 17 of the Proposed directive).

8 National Regulatory Authority is a sector specific national telecommunications regulatory created by a Member State in the context of the services directive as amended, and the ONP framework.

9 Article 7 of the services directive (Commission Directive 90/388/EEC, referred to above in footnote 2), and Communication by the Commission to the European Parliament and the Council on the status and implementation of Directive 90/388/EEC on competition in the markets for telecommunications services, 4 April 1995, Com (95) 133 final at p.21 et seq. See also Case C-91/94, Thierry Tranchant and Telephones Stores SARL, Judgment of the Court of Justice, 9 November 1995, not yet reported.

10 Proposed ONP interconnection Directive cited in footnote 3, Article 9(3).

12.　Given the Commission's responsibility for the Community's competition policy, the Commission must serve the Community's general interest. The administrative resources at the Commission's disposal to perform its task are necessarily limited and cannot be used to deal with all the cases brought to its attention. The Commission is therefore obliged, in general, to take all organisational measures necessary for the performance of its task and, in particular, to establish priorities.[11]

13.　The Commission has therefore indicated that it intends, in using its decision-making powers, to concentrate on notifications, complaints and own-initiative proceedings having particular political, economic or legal significance for the Community.[12] Where these features are absent in a particular case, notifications will not normally be dealt with by means of a formal decision, but rather a comfort letter (subject to the consent of the parties), and complaints should, as a rule, be handled by national courts or other relevant authorities. In this context, it should be noted that the competition rules are directly effective[13] so that EC competition law is enforceable in the national courts. Even where other Community legislation has been respected, this does not remove the need to comply with the Community competition rules.[14]

14.　Other national authorities, in particular National Regulatory Authorities acting within the ONP framework, have jurisdiction over certain access agreements (which must be notified to them). However, notification of an agreement to an NRA does not make notification of an agreement to the Commission unnecessary. The National Regulation Authorities must ensure that actions taken by them are consistent with EC competition law,[15] this duty requires them to refrain from action that would undermine the effective protection of Community law rights under the competition rules.[16] Therefore, they may not approve arrangements which are contrary to the competition rules.[17] If the national authorities act so as to undermine those rights, the Member State may itself be liable in damages to those harmed by this action.[18] In addition, National Regulatory Authorities have jurisdiction under the ONP directives to take steps to ensure effective competition.[19]

15.　Access agreements in principle regulate the provision of certain services between independent undertakings and do not result in the creation

---

11 Case T-24/90, Automec v Commission, 1992 ECR II-2223, at paragraph 77; and BEMIM 1995 ECR II 147.

12 Notice on cooperation between national courts and the Commission in applying Articles 85 and 86 of the EEC Treaty, OJ C 39/6 (1993), at paragraph 14.
　Draft Notice on cooperation between national competition authorities and the Commission.

13 Case 127/73, BRT v SABAM, 1974 ECR 51.

14 Case 66/86, Ahmed Saeed, 1989 ECR 838.

15 They must not, for example, encourage or reinforce or approve the results of anti-competitive behaviour: Ahmed Saeed, above; Case 153/93, Federal Republic of Germany v Delta Schiffahrts, 1994 ECR-I 2517; Case 267/86, Van Eycke, 1988 ECR 4769.

16 Case 13/77, GB-Inno-BM/ATAB, 1977 ECR 2115, at paragraph 33: *'while it is true that Article 86 is directed at undertakings, nonetheless it is also true that the Treaty imposes a duty on Member States not to adopt or maintain in force any measure which could deprive the provision of its effectiveness.'*

17 For further duties of national authorities see Case 103/88, Fratelli Costanzo SpA, 1989 ECR 1839.
　See Ahmed Saeed, above. *'Articles 5 and 90 of the EEC Treaty must be interpreted as (i) prohibiting the national authorities from encouraging the conclusion of agreements on tariffs contrary to Article 85(1) or Article 86 of the Treaty, as the case may be; (ii) precluding the approval by those authorities of tariffs resulting from such agreements'*

of an autonomous entity which would be distinct from the parties to the agreements. Access agreements are thus generally outside the scope of the Merger Regulation.[20]

16. Under Regulation 17,[21] the Commission could be seised of an issue relating to access agreements by way of a notification of an access agreement by one or more of the parties involved,[22] by way of a complaint against a restrictive access agreement or against the behaviour of a dominant company in granting or refusing access,[23] by way of a Commission own-initiative procedure into such a grant or refusal, or by way of a sector inquiry.[24] In addition, a complainant may request that the Commission take interim measures in circumstances where there is an urgent risk of serious and irreparable harm to the complainant or to the public interest.[25] It should however, be noted in cases of great urgency that procedures before national courts can usually result more quickly in an order to end the infringements than procedures before the Commission.[26]

17. There are a number of areas where agreements will be subject to both the competition rules and national or European sector specific regulation, most notably Internal Market regulation. In the telecommunications sector, the ONP Directive aims at establishing a regulatory regime for access agreements. Given the detailed nature of ONP rules and the fact that they may go beyond the requirements of Article 86, undertakings operating in the telecommunications sector should be aware that compliance with the Community competition rules does not absolve them of their duty to abide by obligations imposed in the ONP context, and vice versa.

2. Commission Action in Relation to Access Agreements[27]

18. Access agreements taken as a whole are of great significance, and it is therefore appropriate for the Commission to spell out as clearly as possible the Community legal framework within which these agreements should be concluded. Access agreements having restrictive clauses will involve issues under Article 85. Agreements which involve dominant, or monopolist, undertakings involve Article 86 issues: concerns arising from the dominance of one or more of the parties will generally be of greater significance in the context of a particular agreement than those under Article 85.

---

18 Joined Cases C-6 and 9/90, Francovich, 1990-I ECR 5357; Joined Cases C-46/93, Brasserie de Pêcheur SA v Germany and Case C-48/93, R v Secretary of State for Transport ex parte Factortame Ltd and others, judgment of 5 March 1996, not yet reported.

19 For example, recital 18 of the leased line directive referred to in footnote 3 and Article 9(3) of the draft ONP interconnection directive.

20 Council Regulation No 4064/89 of 21 December 1989 on the control of concentrations between undertakings, OJ L 395/1 (1989).

21 Council Regulation No 17 of 6 February 1962, first Regulation implementing Articles 85 and 86 of the Treaty, OJ 13/204 (1962), as amended.

22 Articles 2 and 4(1) of Regulation 17.

23 Article 3 of Regulation 17.

24 Articles 3 and 12 of Regulation 17.

25 Case 792/79R, Camera Care v Commission, 1980 ECR 119.
   See also Case T-44/90, La Cinq v Commission, 1992 ECR II-1.

26 See point 16 of the Notice on cooperation between national courts and the Commission cited above in footnote 10.

27 Article 2 or 4(1) of Regulations 17.

19.   In applying the competition rules, the Commission will build on the ONP framework, and the National Regulatory Authorities acts within that framework. Where agreements fall within Article 85(1), they must be notified to the Commission if they are to benefit from an exemption under Article 85(3). Where agreements are notified, the Commission intends to deal with one or more notifications by way of formal decisions, following appropriate publicity in the Official Journal, and in accordance with the principles set out below. Once the legal principles have been clearly established, the Commission then proposes to deal by way of comfort letter with other notifications raising the same issues.

3.   Complaints[28]

20.   Natural or legal persons with a legitimate interest may, under certain circumstances, submit a complaint to the Commission, requesting that the Commission by decision require that an infringement of Article 85 or Article 86 EC be brought to an end. A complainant may additionally request that the Commission take interim measures where there is an urgent risk of serious and irreparable harm.[29] A prospective complainant has other equally or even more effective options, such as an action before a national court. In this context, it should be noted that procedures before the national courts can offer considerable advantages for individuals and companies, such as in particular[30]:

— national courts can deal with and award a claim for damages resulting from an infringement of the competition rules;
— national courts can usually adopt interim measures and order the termination of an infringement more quickly than the Commission is able to do;
— before national courts, it is possible to combine a claim under Community law with a claim under national law;
— legal costs can be awarded to the successful applicant before a national court.

Furthermore, the specific national regulatory principles as harmonised under ONP principles can offer recourse both at the national and if necessary at Community level.

3.1   Use of national and ONP procedures

21.   As referred to above[31] the Commission will take into account the Community interest of each case brought to its attention. In evaluating the Community interest, the Commission examines:

. . . the significance of the alleged infringement as regards the functioning of the common market, the probability of establishing the existence of the

---

28 Article 3(2) of Regulation 17.
29 Camera Care and La Cinq, referred to above.
30 Notice on cooperation between national courts and the Commission cited above in footnote 10, point 16.
31 At paragraph 14.

infringement and the scope of the investigation required in order to fulfil, under the best possible conditions, its task of ensuring that Articles 85 and 86 are complied with . . .'[32]

Another essential element in this evaluation is the extent to which a national judge is in a position to provide an effective remedy for an infringement of Article 85 or 86. This may prove difficult, for example, in cases involving extra-territorial elements.

22. Article 85(1) and Article 86 EC produce direct effects in relations between individuals which must be safeguarded by national courts.[33] As regards actions before the National Regulatory Authority, the ONP Directive provides that such an authority has power to intervene and order changes in relation to both the existence and content of access agreements. National Regulatory Authorities must take into account, 'the need to stimulate a competitive market' and may impose conditions on one or more parties, *inter alia*, 'to ensure effective competition'.[34]

23. The Commission may itself be seised of a dispute either pursuant to the competition rules, or pursuant to an ONP Conciliation Procedure. Multiple simultaneous proceedings might lead to unnecessary duplication of investigative efforts by the Commission and the national authorities. Where complaints are lodged with the Commission under Article 3 of Regulation 17 while there are related actions before a relevant national or European authority or court, the Directorate-General for Competition will generally not initially pursue any investigation as to the existence of an infringement under Article 85 or 86 of the EC Treaty. This is subject, however, to the following points.

3.2   Safeguarding complainant's rights

24.   Undertakings are entitled to effective protection of their Community law rights.[35] These rights would be undermined if national proceedings were allowed to lead to an excessive delay of the Commission's action, without a satisfactory resolution of the matter at a national level. In the telecommunications sector, innovation cycles are relatively short, and any substantial delay in resolving an access dispute would in practice be equivalent to a refusal of access, thus prejudging the proper determination of the case.

25.   The Commission therefore takes the view that an access dispute before a National Regulatory Authority should be resolved within a reasonable period of time, normally speaking not extending beyond six months of the matter first being drawn to the attention of that authority or after initiation of ONP procedures, including the conciliation procedures.[36] This resolution could take the form of either a final determination of the action or another form of relief which would safeguard the rights of the complainant. If the matter has not reached such a resolution then, *prima facie*, the rights of

---

32 See Automec, footnote above, paragraph 86.
33 *BRT* v *SABAM*, footnote above.
34 Articles 9(1) and 9(3) of the Proposed ONP interconnection Directive.
35 Case 14/83, Von Colson, 1984 ECR 1891.
36 Telecommunications: Open network provision (ONP) for leased lines; Conciliation procedure; 94/C 214/04, OJ C 214/4 (1994).

the parties are not being effectively protected, and the Commission would in principle, upon request by the complainant, begin its investigations into the case in accordance with its normal procedures, after consultation and in cooperation with the national authority in question.

3.3   Interim measures

26.   As regards any request for interim measures, the existence of national proceedings is relevant to the question of whether there is a risk of serious and irreparable harm. Such proceedings should, *prima facie*, remove the risk of such harm and it would therefore not be appropriate for the Commission to grant interim measures in the absence of evidence that the risk would nevertheless remain.

27.   The availability of and criteria for injunctive relief is an important factor which the Commission must take into account in reaching this *prima facie* conclusion. If injunctive relief were not available, or if such relief was not likely adequately to take into account the complainant's rights under Community law, the Commission would consider that the national proceedings did not remove the risk of harm, and would therefore commence its investigation of the case.

4.   Own-Initiative Investigation and Sector Inquiries

28.   If it appears necessary, the Commission will open an own-initiative investigation. It can also launch a sector inquiry, subject to consultation of the Advisory Committee of Member State competition authorities.

5.   Fines

29.   The Commission may impose fines of up to 10% of the annual worldwide turnover of undertakings which intentionally or negligently breach Article 85(1) or Article 86.[37] Where agreements have been notified pursuant to Regulation 17 for an exemption under Article 85(3), no fine may be levied by the Commission in respect of activities described in the notification[38] for the period following notification. However, the Commission may withdraw the immunity from fines by informing the undertakings concerned that, after preliminary examination, it is of the opinion that Article 85(1) of the Treaty applies and that application of Article 85(3) is not justified.[39]

30.   The ONP interconnection Directive has two particular provisions which should be taken into account with respect to the question of fines under the competition rules. First, it provides that interconnection agreements must be communicated to the relevant National Regulatory Authorities and made available to interested third parties, with the exception of those parts which deal with the commercial strategy of the parties.[40] Secondly, it provides that the National Regulatory Authority must have a number of powers which it can use to influence or amend the interconnection

---

37 Article 15(2) of Regulation 17.
38 Article 15(5) of Regulation 17.
39 Article 15(6) of Regulation 17.
40 Article 6(c) of the Proposed ONP interconnection Directive.

agreements.[41] These provisions ensure that appropriate publicity is given to the agreements, and provide the National Regulatory Authority with the opportunity to take steps, where appropriate, to ensure effective competition on the market.

31. Where an agreement has been notified to a National Regulatory Authority, but has not been notified to the Commission, the Commission does not consider it would be generally appropriate as a matter of policy to impose a fine in respect of the agreement, even if the agreement ultimately proves to contain conditions in breach of Article 85. A fine would, however, be appropriate in some cases, for example where:

the agreement proves to contain provisions in breach of Article 86; and/or

the breach of Article 85 is particularly serious.

The size of the fine will depend on the gravity and duration of the infringement.

32. Notification to the NRA is not a substitute for a notification to the Commission and does not limit the possibility for interested parties to submit a complaint to the Commission, or for the Commission to begin an own-initiative investigation into access agreements. Nor does such notification limit the rights of a party to seek damages before a national court for harm caused by anti-competitive agreements.[42]

PART II: RELEVANT MARKETS

33. In the course of investigating cases within the framework set out in Part I above, the Commission will base itself on the following approach to the definition of relevant markets in this sector.

34. Firms are subject to three main sources of competitive constraints; demand substitutability, supply substitutability and potential competition, with the first constituting the most immediate and effective disciplinary force on the suppliers of a given product or service. Demand substitutability is therefore the main tool used to define the relevant product market on which restrictions of competition for the purposes of Articles 85(1) and 86 can be identified.

35. Supply substitutability is generally not used to define relevant markets. In practice it cannot be clearly distinguished from potential competition. Supply side substitutability and potential competition are used for the purpose of determining whether the undertaking has a dominant position or whether the restriction of competition is significant within the meaning of Article 85, or whether there is elimination of competition.

36. In assessing relevant markets it is necessary to look at developments in the market in the short term.

1.   Relevant product market

37. Section 6 of Form A/B defines the relevant product market as follows:

A relevant product market comprises all those products and/or services which are regarded as interchangeable or substitutable by the consumer, by reason of the products' characteristics, their prices and their intended use.

---

41 Inter alia, at Article 9 of the Proposed ONP interconnection Directive.
42 See footnote above.

38.   The ending of the legal monopolies in the telecommunications sector, whereby third parties can provide services to end-users, will lead to the emergence of a second type of market, related to the market for provision of services, that of access to facilities which are currently necessary to provide these services. In this sector, interconnection to the public switched telecommunications network would be a typical example of such access. Without interconnection, it will not be commercially possible for third parties to provide, for example, comprehensive voice telephony services.

39.   It is clear, therefore, that in the telecommunications sector there are at least two types of relevant product markets to consider — that of a service to be provided to end users and that of access to those facilities necessary to provide that service to end users (information, physical network, etc.). In the context of any particular case, it will be necessary to define the relevant access and services markets, such as interconnection to the public telecommunications network, and provision of public voice telephony services, respectively.

40.   When appropriate, the Commission will use the test of a relevant market which is made by asking whether, if all the suppliers of the services in question raised their prices by 5–10%, their collective profits would rise. According to this test, if their profits would rise, the market considered is a separate relevant market.

41.   The Commission considers that the principles under competition law governing these markets remain the same regardless of the particular market in question. Given the pace of technological change in this sector, any attempt to define particular product markets in this Notice would run the risk of rapidly becoming inaccurate or irrelevant. The definition of particular product markets is best done in the light of a detailed examination of an individual case.

1.1.   Services market

42.   This can be broadly defined as the provision of any telecommunications service to a user. Different telecommunications services will be considered substitutable if they show a sufficient degree of interchangeability for the end-user, which would mean that effective competition can take place between the different providers of these services.

1.2   Access to facilities

43.   For a service provider to provide services to end-users it will often require access to one or more (upstream or downstream) facilities. For example, to deliver physically the service to end-users, it needs access to the termination points of the telecommunications network to which these end-users are connected. This access can be achieved at the physical level through dedicated or shared local infrastructure, either self provided or leased from a local infrastructure provider. It can also be achieved either through a service provider who already has these end-users as subscribers, or through an interconnection provider who has access directly or indirectly to the relevant termination points.

44.   In addition to physical access, a service provider may need access to other facilities to enable it to market its service to end users: for example, a service provider must be able to make end-users aware of its services. Where, as is often the case, for example, with directory information, the facility can

only be obtained from the telecommunications operator, similar concerns arise as with physical access issues.

45. In many cases, the Commission will be concerned with physical access issues, where what is necessary is interconnection to the network of the telecommunications operator.[43]

46. Some incumbent telecommunications operators may be tempted to resist providing access to third party service providers or other network operators, particularly in areas where the proposed service will be in competition with a service provided by the telecommunications operator itself. This resistance will often manifest itself as a reluctance to allow access or a willingness to allow it only under disadvantageous conditions. It is the role of the competition rules to ensure that these prospective access markets are allowed to develop, and that incumbent operators are not permitted to use their control over access to stifle developments on the services markets.

It should be stressed that in the telecommunications sector, liberalisation can be expected to lead to the development of new, alternative networks which will ultimately have an impact on access market definition involving the incumbent telecommunications operator.

2. Relevant geographic market

47. Relevant geographic markets are defined in Form A/B as follows:

The relevant geographic market comprises the area in which the undertakings concerned are involved in the supply and demand of products or services, in which the conditions of competition are sufficiently homogeneous and which can be distinguished from neighbouring areas because the conditions of competition are appreciably different in those areas.

48. As regards the provision of telecommunication services and access markets, the relevant geographic market will be the area in which the objective conditions of competition applying to service providers are similar. It will therefore be necessary to examine the possibility for these service providers to access an end-user in any part of this area, under equivalent and economically viable conditions. Regulatory conditions such as the terms of licences, and any exclusive or special rights owned by competing local access providers are particularly relevant.[44]

---

43 Interconnection is defined in Directive 96/19/EC as:

'. . . *the physical and logical linking of the telecommunications facilities of organisations providing telecommunications networks and/or telecommunications services, in order to allow the users of one organisation to communicate with the users of the same or another organisation or to access services provided by third organisations.*'

In the full liberalization Directive and ONP Directives, telecommunications services are defined as:

'*services, whose provision consists wholly or partly in the transmission and / or routing of signals on a telecommunications network.*'

It therefore includes the transmission of broadcasting signals and CATV networks.

A telecommunications network is itself defined as:

'. . . *the transmission equipment and, where applicable, switching equipment and other resources which permit the conveyance of signals between defined termination points by wire, by radio, by optical or by other electromagnetic means*'.

44 Eurotunnel, OJ L 354/66 (1994).

PART III: PRINCIPLES

49. The Commission will apply the following principles in cases before it.
50. The Commission has recognised that:

Articles 85 and 86 . . . constitute law in force and enforceable throughout the Community. Conflicts should not arise with other Community rules because Community law forms a coherent regulatory framework . . . it is obvious that Community acts adopted in the telecommunications sector are to be interpreted in a way consistent with competition rules, so as to ensure the best possible implementation of all aspects of the Community telecommunications policy . . . This applies, inter alia, to the relationship between competition rules applicable to undertakings and the ONP rules.[45]

51. Thus, competition rules continue to apply in circumstances where other Treaty provisions or secondary legislation are applicable. In the context of access agreements the Internal Market and competition provisions of Community law are both important and mutually reinforcing for the proper functioning of the sector. Therefore in making an assessment under the competition rules, the Commission will seek to build as far as possible on the principles established in the harmonisation legislation. It should also be borne in mind that a number of the competition law principles set out below are also covered by specific rules in the context of the ONP framework. Proper application of these rules should often avoid the need for the application of the competition rules.

52. As regards the telecommunications sector, attention should be paid to the cost of universal service obligations. Article 90(2) EC may justify exceptions to the principles of Articles 85 and 86 EC. The details of universal service obligations are a regulatory matter. The field of application of Article 90(2) has been specified in the Article 90 Directives in the telecommunications sector, and the Commission will apply the competition rules in this context.

53. Articles 85 and 86 EC apply in the normal manner to agreements or practices which have been approved or authorised by a national authority,[46] or where the national authority has required the inclusion of terms in an agreement at the request of one or more of the parties involved.

54. However, if a national regulatory authority were to require terms which were contrary to the competition rules, the undertakings involved would in practice not be fined, although the Member State itself would be in breach of Articles 3(g) and 5 EC[47] and therefore subject to challenge by the Commission under Article 169 EC. Additionally, if an undertaking having special or exclusive rights within the meaning of Article 90, or a state-owned undertaking, were required or authorised by a national regulator to engage in behaviour constituting an abuse of its dominant position, the Member State would also be in breach of Article 90(1) and the Commission could adopt a decision requiring termination of the infraction.[48]

---

45 Guidelines on the application of the competition rules in the telecommunications sector, see footnote above, at paragraphs 15 and 16.
46 Commission Decision, BNIC/AROW, 82/896/EEC, OJ L 379/19 (1982).
47 See footnote above.
48 Joined Cases C-48 and 66/90, Netherlands and others v Commission, 1992 ECR I-565.

55.   National Regulatory Authorities may require strict standards of transparency, obligations to supply and pricing practices on the market, particularly where this is necessary in the early stages of liberalisation. When appropriate, legislation such as the ONP framework will be used as an aid in the interpretation of the competition rules.[49] Given the duty resting on National Regulatory Authorities to ensure that effective competition is possible, application of the competition rules is likewise required for an appropriate interpretation of the ONP principles. It should also be noted that many of the issues set out below are also covered by rules under the Full Competition Directive and the existing and proposed ONP, licensing and data protection Directives: effective enforcement of this regulatory framework should prevent many of the competition issues set out below from arising.

1.   Dominance (Article 86)

56.   In order for an undertaking to provide services in the telecommunications services market, it will need to obtain access to various facilities. For the provision of telecommunications services, for example, interconnection to the public switched telecommunications network will usually be necessary. Access to this network will almost always be in the hands of a dominant telecommunications operator. As regards access agreements, dominance stemming from control on facilities will be the most relevant to the Commission's appraisal.

57.   Whether or not a company is dominant does not depend only on the legal rights granted to that company. The mere ending of legal monopolies does not put an end to dominance. Indeed, notwithstanding the liberalisation Directives, the development of effective competition from alternative network providers with adequate capacity and geographic reach will take time.

58.   In the telecommunications sector, the concept of 'essential facilities' will in many cases be of direct relevance in determining the duties of dominant telecommunications operators. The phrase essential facility is used to describe a facility or infrastructure which is essential for reaching customers and/or enabling competitors to carry on their business, and which cannot be replicated by any reasonable means.[50]

A company controlling the access to an essential facility enjoys a dominant position within the meaning of Article 86. Conversely, a company may enjoy a dominant position pursuant to Article 86 without controlling an essential facility.

The following facilities could at present be expected to constitute essential facilities in the telecommunications sector: for example, the public telecommunications networks for voice and/or data services, leased circuit and related network terminating equipment, basic data regarding subscribers

---

49 See Ahmed Saeed, above, where internal market legislation relating to pricing was used as an aid in determining what level of prices should be regarded as unfair for the purposes of Article 86.

50 See also the definition included in the 'Additional commitment on regulatory principles by the European Communities and their Member States 'used by the Group on basic telecommunications in the context of the World Trade Organisation (WTO) negotiations:

'Essential facilities mean facilities of a public telecommunications transport network and service that

(a)   are exclusively or predominantly provided by a single or limited number of suppliers; and

(b)   cannot feasibly be economically or technically substituted in order to provide a service.'

to the public voice telephony service, numbering schemes and other customer or technical information.

1.1. Services market

59.   One of the factors used to measure the market power of an undertaking are the sales attributable to that undertaking, expressed as a percentage of total sales in the market for substitutable services in the relevant geographic area. As regards the services market, the Commission will assess, *inter alia*, the turnover generated by the sale of substitutable services, excluding the sale or internal usage of interconnection services and the sale or internal usage of local infrastructure,[51] taking into consideration the competitive conditions and the structure of supply and demand on the market.

1.2 Access to facilities

60.   The concept of 'access' as referred to above in point 45 can relate to a range of situations, including the availability of leased lines enabling a service provider to build up its own network, and an interconnection problem in the strict sense, i.e. interconnecting two telecommunication networks, e.g. mobile and fixed. In relation to access, incumbent operators often occupy a monopoly position, and even in areas where liberalisation of the legal framework has begun, it is probable that the incumbent will remain dominant in the future. The incumbent operator, which controls the facilities, is often also the largest service provider, and they have in the past not needed to distinguish between the conveyance of telecommunications services and the provision of these services to end-users. Today, an operator who is also a service provider does not require its downstream operating arm to pay for access, and therefore it is not easy to calculate the revenue to be allocated to the facility. In a case where an operator is providing both access and services it is necessary to separate so far as possible the revenues for the two markets before using revenues as the basis for the calculation of the company's share of whichever market is involved. Article 8(2) of the proposed Interconnection Directive should be helpful in this context as it calls for separate accounting for 'activities related to interconnection — covering both interconnection services provided internally and interconnection services provided to others — and other activities'.

61.   The economic significance of obtaining access also depends on the coverage of the network with which interconnection is sought. Therefore, in addition to using turnover figures, the Commission will, where this is possible, also take into account the number of customers who have subscribed to services comparable with those which the service provider requesting access intends to provide. Accordingly, market power for a given undertaking will be measured partly by the number of subscribers who are connected to termination points of the telecommunications network of that undertaking expressed as a percentage of the total number of subscribers connected to termination points in the relevant geographic area.

Supply-side substitutability

62.   As stated above (see point 37), supply-side substitutability is also

---

51 Case 6/72 Continental Can, 1973 ECR 215.

relevant to the question of dominance. A market share of over 50%[52] is usually sufficient to demonstrate dominance although other factors will be examined. For example, the Commission will examine the existence of other network providers, if any, in the relevant geographic area to determine whether such alternative infrastructures are sufficiently dense to provide competition to the incumbent's network and the extent to which it would be possible for new access providers to enter the market.

Other relevant factors

63. In addition to market share data, and supply-side substitutability, in determining whether an operator is dominant the Commission will also examine whether the operator has privileged access to facilities which cannot be duplicated, either for legal reasons or because it would cost too much.

64. As competing access providers appear and challenge the dominance of the incumbent, the scope of the rights they receive from Member States' authorities, and notably their territorial reach, will play an important part in the determination of market power. The Commission will closely follow market evolution in relation to these issues and will take account of any altered market conditions in its assessment of access issues under the competition rules.

1.3 Joint dominance

65. The wording of Article 86 makes it clear that the Article applies when more than one company shares a dominant position. The circumstances in which a joint dominant position exists, and in which it is abused, have not yet been fully clarified by the case law of the Community Courts or the practice of the Commission, and the law is still developing.

66. The words of Article 86 ('abuse by one or more undertakings') describe something different from the prohibition on anti-competitive agreements or concerted practices in Article 85. To hold otherwise would be contrary to the usual principles of interpretation of the Treaty, and would render the words pointless and without practical effect. This does not, however, exclude the parallel application of Articles 85 and 86 to the same agreement or practice, which has been upheld by the Commission and the Court in a number of cases,[53] nor is there anything to prevent the Commission from taking action only under one of the provisions, when both apply.

67. Two companies, each dominant in a separate national market, are not the same as two jointly dominant companies. National public voice telephony telecommunications operators are not likely to become jointly dominant until after liberalisation in the Community. For two or more companies to be in a joint dominant position, they must together have substantially the same position *vis-à-vis* their customers and competitors as a single company has if

---

52 It should be noted in this context that under the ONP framework an organisation may be notified as having significant market power. The determination of whether an organisation does or does not have significant market power depends on a number of factors, but the starting presumption is that an organisation with a market share of more than 25% will normally be considered to have significant market power. The Commission will take account of whether an undertaking has been notified as having significant market power under the ONP rules in its appraisal under the competition rules.
53 Case 85/76 Hoffmann La Roche, 1979 ECR 461, Racal Decca, Commission Decision of 21 December 1988, OJ L 43/27 (1989).

it is in a dominant position. With specific reference to the telecommunications sector, joint dominance could be attained by two telecommunications infrastructure operators covering the same geographic market.

68.   In addition, for two or more companies to be jointly dominant it is necessary, but not sufficient, for there to be no effective competition between the companies on the relevant market. This lack of competition may in practice be due to the fact that the companies have links such as agreements for cooperation, interconnection or roaming agreements. The Commission does not, however, consider that either economic theory or Community law implies that such links are legally necessary for a joint dominant position to exist.[54] It is a sufficient economic link if there is the kind of interdependence which often comes about in oligopolistic situations. There does not seem to be any reason in law or in economic theory to require any other economic link between those companies. This having been said, in practice such links will often exist in the telecommunications sector where national telecommunication operators nearly inevitably have links of various kinds with one another.

69.   To take as an example access to the local loop, in some Member States this could well be controlled in the near future by two operators - the incumbent telecommunications operator and a cable operator. In order to provide particular services to consumers, access to the local loop of either the telecommunications operator or the cable television operator is necessary. Depending on the circumstances of the case and in particular on the relationship between them, neither operator may hold a dominant position: together, however, they may hold a joint monopoly of access to these facilities.

2.   Abuses of Dominance

2.1   Refusal to grant access to essential facilities and application of unfavourable terms

70.   A refusal to give access may be prohibited under Article 86 if the refusal is made by a company which is dominant because of its control of facilities, as incumbent telecommunications operators will usually be for the foreseeable future. A refusal may have:

the effect of hindering the maintenance of the degree of competition still existing in the market *or the growth of that competition.*[55]

A refusal will only be abusive if it affects competition. Service markets in the telecommunications sector will initially have few competitive players and refusals will therefore generally affect competition on those markets. In all cases of refusal, any justification will be closely examined to determine whether it is objective.

71.   Broadly there are three relevant scenarios:

(a)   a refusal to grant access for the purposes of a service where another operator has been given access by the access provider to operate on that services market;

---

54 Nestlé/Perrier.
55 Case 85/76 Hoffmann La Roche, 1979 ECR 461.

(b)   a refusal to grant access for the purposes of a service where no other operator has been given access by the access provider to operate on that services market;

(c)   a withdrawal of supply of access from an existing customer.

72.   As to the first of the above scenarios, it is clear that a refusal to supply a new customer in circumstances where a dominant facilities owner is already supplying one or more customers operating in the same downstream market would constitute discriminatory treatment which, if it would restrict competition on that downstream market, would be an abuse. Where network operators offer the same, or similar, retail services as the party requesting access, they may have both the incentive and the opportunity to restrict competition and abuse their dominant position in this way. There may, of course, be justifications for such refusal - for example, *vis-à-vis* applicants which represent a potential credit risk. In the absence of any objective justifications, a refusal would usually be an abuse of the dominant position on the access market.

73.   In general terms, the dominant company's duty is to provide access in such a way that the goods and services offered to downstream companies are available on terms no less favourable than those given to other parties, including its own corresponding downstream operations.

74.   As to the second of the above situations, the question arises as to whether the access provider should be obliged to contract with the service provider in order to allow the service provider to operate on a new service market. Where capacity constraints are not an issue and where the company refusing to provide access to its facility has not provided access to that facility, either to its downstream arm or to any other company operating on that services market, then it is not clear what other objective justification there could be.

75.   If there were no commercially feasible alternatives to the access being requested, then unless access is granted, the party requesting access would not be able to operate on the service market. Refusal in this case would therefore limit the development of new markets, or new products on those markets, contrary to Article 86(b). In the transport field,[56] the Commission ruled that a firm controlling an essential facility must give access in certain circumstances.[57] The same principles apply to the telecommunications sector.

---

56 Commission decision, Sea Containers v Stena Sealink, 94/19/EC, OJ L15/8 (1994); Commission decision, Re Access to Facilities of Port Rodby, 94/119/EC, OJ L55/52 (1994).

57 See also (among others):

Judgments of the Court -

Cases 6 and 7/73, Commercial Solvents v. Commission, 1974 ECR 223;

Case 311/84, Télémarketing, 1985 ECR 3261;

Case C-18/88 RTT v. GB-Inno, 1991 ECR I-5941;

Case C-260/89, Elliniki Radiophonia Teleorassi, 1991 ECR I-2925;

Cases T-69, T-70 and T-76/89, RTE, BBC and ITP v. Commission, 1991 ECR II-485, 535, 575;

Case C-271/90, Spain v Commission, 1992 ECR I-5833;

Cases C-241 and 242/91P, RTE and ITP Ltd v Commission (Magill), 1995 ECR I-743

Commission Decisions —

76/185/EEC — National Carbonizing Company, OJ L 35/6 (1976);

88/589/EEC — London European v. Sabena, OJ L 317/47 (1988);

92/213/EEC — British Midland v. Aer Lingus, OJ L 96/34 (1992);

B & I v. Sealink, (1992) 5 CMLR 255; EC Bulletin, No 6 — 1992, point 1.3.30.

76.   The principle obliging dominant companies to contract in certain circumstances will often be relevant in the telecommunications sector. Currently, there are monopolies or virtual monopolies in the provision of network infrastructure for most telecom services in the EU. Even where restrictions have already been, or will soon be, lifted, competition in downstream markets will continue to depend upon the pricing and conditions of access to upstream network services that will only gradually reflect competitive market forces. Given the pace of technological change in the telecommunications sector, it is possible to envisage situations where companies would seek to offer new products or services which are not in competition with products or services already offered by the dominant access operator, but for which this operator is reluctant to provide access.

77.   The Commission must ensure that the control over facilities enjoyed by incumbent operators is not used to hamper the development of a competitive telecommunications environment. A company which is dominant on a market for services and which commits an abuse contrary to Article 86 on that market may be required, in order to put an end to the abuse, to supply access to its facility to one or more competitors on that market. In particular, a company may abuse its dominant position if by its actions it prevents the emergence of a new product or service.

78.   The starting point for the Commission's analysis will be the identification of an existing or potential market for which access is being requested. In order to determine whether access should be ordered under the competition rules, account will be taken of a breach by the dominant company of its duty not to discriminate (see below) or of the following elements, taken cumulatively:

access to the facility in question is generally essential in order for companies to compete on that related market;[58]

The key issue here is therefore what is essential. It will not be sufficient that the position of the company requesting access would be more advantageous if access were granted - but refusal of access must lead to the proposed activities being made either impossible or seriously and unavoidably uneconomic.

Although, for example, alternative infrastructure may as from 1 July 1996 be used for liberalised services, it will be some time before this is in many cases a satisfactory alternative to the facilities of the incumbent operator. Such alternative infrastructure does not at present offer the same dense geographic coverage as that of the incumbent telecommunications operator's network.

(a)   there is sufficient capacity available to provide access.

(b)   the facility owner fails to satisfy demand on an existing service or product market, blocks the emergence of a potential new service or product, or impedes competition on an existing or potential service or product market;

(c)   the company seeking access is prepared to pay the reasonable and non-discriminatory price and will otherwise in all respects accept non-discriminatory access terms and conditions.

---

58 Community law protects competition and not competitors, and therefore it would be insufficient to demonstrate that one competitor needed access to a facility in order to compete in the downstream market. It would be necessary to demonstrate that access is necessary for all except exceptional competitors in order for access to be made compulsory.

(d)   there is no objective justification for refusing to provide access.

Relevant justifications in this context could include an overriding difficulty of providing access to the requesting company, or the need for a facility owner which has undertaken investment aimed at the introduction of a new product or service to have sufficient time and opportunity to use the facility in order to place that new product or service on the market. However, although any justification will have to be examined carefully on a case-by-case basis. It is particularly important in the telecommunications sector that the benefits to end-users which will arise from a competitive environment are not undermined by the actions of the former state monopolists in preventing competition from emerging and developing.

In determining whether an infringement of Article 86 has been committed, account will be taken both of the factual situation in that and other geographic areas, and, where relevant the relationship between the access requested and the technical configuration of the facility.

79.   The question of objective justification will require particularly close analysis in this area. In addition to determining whether difficulties cited in any particular case are serious enough to justify the refusal to grant access, the relevant authorities must also decide whether these difficulties are sufficient to outweigh the damage done to competition if access is refused or made more difficult and the downstream service markets are thus limited.

80.   Three important elements relating to access which could be manipulated by the access provider in order, in effect, to refuse to provide access are timing, technical configuration and price.

81.   Dominant telecommunications operators have a duty to deal with requests for access efficiently: undue and unexplained delays in responding to a request for access may constitute an abuse. In particular, however, the Commission will seek to compare the response to a request for access with:

the usual time frame and conditions applicable when the responding party grants access to its facilities to its own subsidiary or operating branch;

(a)   responses to requests for access to similar facilities in other Member States;

(b)   the explanations given for any delay in dealing with requests for access.

82.   Issues of technical configuration will similarly be closely examined in order to determine whether they are genuine. In principle, competition rules require that the party requesting access must be granted access at the most suitable point for the requesting party, provided that this point is technically feasible for the access provider. Questions of technical feasibility may be objective justifications for refusing to supply — for example, the traffic for which access is sought must satisfy the relevant technical standards for the infrastructure — or questions of capacity restraints, where questions of rationing may arise.[59]

83.   Excessive pricing for access, as well as being abusive in itself,[60] may also amount to an effective refusal to grant access.

---

59 As noted above at paragraph 80.
60 See paragraph 91 below.

84.   There are a number of elements of these tests which require careful assessment. Pricing questions in the telecommunications sector will be facilitated by the obligations on ONP Directives to have transparent cost-accounting systems.

85.   As to the third of the situations referred to in point 72 above, some previous Commission decisions and the case law of the Court have been concerned with the withdrawal of supply from downstream competitors (the third case, above). In *Commercial Solvents*, the Court held that:

> an undertaking which has a dominant position on the market in raw materials and which, with the object of reserving such raw material for manufacturing its own derivatives, refuses to supply a customer, which is itself a manufacturer of these derivatives, and therefore risks eliminating all competition on the part of this customer, is abusing its dominant position within the meaning of Article 86.[61]

86.   Although this case dealt with the withdrawal of a product, there is no difference in principle between this case and the withdrawal of access. The unilateral termination of access agreements raises substantially similar issues to those examined in relation to refusals. Withdrawal of access from an existing customer will usually be abusive. Again, objective reasons may be provided to justify the termination. Any such reasons must be proportionate to the effects on competition of the withdrawal.

2.2   Other forms of abuse

87.   Refusals to provide access are only one form of possible abuse in this area. Abuses may also arise in the context of access having been granted. An abuse may occur *inter alia* where the operator is behaving in a discriminatory manner or the operator's actions otherwise limit markets or technical development. The following are non-exhaustive examples of abuses which can take place.

Network configuration

88.   Network configuration by a dominant network operator which makes access objectively more difficult for service providers[62] could constitute an abuse unless it were objectively justifiable. One objective justification would be where the network configuration improves the efficiency of the network generally.

Tying

89.   This is of particular concern where it involves the tying of services for which the telecommunications operator is dominant with those for which it is exposed to competition.[63] Where the vertically integrated dominant

---

61 Case 6 and 7/73, Commercial Solvents, 1974 ECR 223.
62 ie to use the network to reach their own customers.
63 This is also dealt with under the ONP framework: see Art 7(4) of the Interconnection Directive, Art 12(4) of the voice telephony Directive and Annex II of the ONP Framework Directive.

network operator obliges the party requesting access to purchase one or more services[64] without adequate justifications, this may exclude rivals of the dominant access provider from offering these elements of the package independently. This requirement could thus constitute an abuse under Article 86.

Pricing

90. Pricing problems in connection with access for service providers to a dominant operator's (essential) facilities will often revolve around excessively high prices:[65] in the absence of another viable alternative to the facility to which access is being sought by service providers, the dominant or monopolistic operator may be inclined to charge excessive prices.

Problems of unfairly low prices could arise in the context of competition between different telecommunications infrastructure networks, where a dominant operator may tend to charge unfairly low prices for access in order to eliminate competition from other (emerging) infrastructure providers, in violation of Article 86(a). In general a price is abusive if it is below the dominant company's average variable costs or if it is below average total costs and part of an anti-competitive plan.[66]

If a case arises, the ONP rules concerning accounting requirements and transparency will help to ensure the effective application of Article 86 in this context.

91. Where the operator is dominant in the product or services market, the margin between the price charged to all competitors on the downstream market (including the dominant company's own downstream operations, if any) for access and the price which the network operator charges in the downstream market must be large enough to allow a reasonably efficient service provider in the downstream market to obtain a normal profit unless the dominant company can show that its downstream operation is exceptionally efficient.[67] If this is not the case, competitors on the downstream market are faced by a 'price squeeze' which could force them out of the market.

---

64 ie including those which are superfluous to the latter, or indeed those which may constitute services the access requester itself would like to provide for its customers.

65 The Commission Communication on Assessment Criteria for National Schemes for the Costing and Financing of Universal Service and Guidelines for the Operation of such Schemes will be relevant for the determination of the extent to which the universal service obligation can be used to justify the prices charged. See also the reference to the universal service obligation at paragraph 53 above.

66 See AKZO, case C-62/86, [1991] ECR-3359

However, the average variable cost rule cannot be applied in many situations in the telecommunications sector, since the variable costs of providing access to an already existing network are almost zero. Accordingly, the test which the Commission considers should be applied is whether whether a company charges a price for goods and services - other than in the context of a new product or service16-which, although above the average variable cost of providing the specific goods or services for which the price in question is paid is so low that the overall revenues for all the goods or services in question would be less than its average total costs of providing them if it sold the same proportion of its output at the same price on a continuing basis, even where no intent to exclude a competitor is proved.

67 Commission Decision, Brown Napier/British Sugar, 88/518/EEC, OJ L 284/41 (1988): the margin between industrial and retail prices was reduced to the point where the wholesale purchaser with packaging operations as efficient as those of the wholesale supplier could not profitably serve the retail market. See also National Carbonising, footnote above.

Discrimination

92. A dominant access provider may not discriminate between different access agreements where such discrimination would restrict competition. Any differentiation based on the use which is to be made of the access rather than differences between the transactions for the access provider itself, if the discrimination is sufficiently likely to restrict or distort actual or potential competition, would be contrary to Article 86. This discrimination could take the form of imposing different conditions, including the charging of different prices, or otherwise differentiating between access agreements, except where such discrimination would be objectively justified, for example on the basis of cost or technical considerations or the fact that the users are operating at different levels. Such discrimination could be likely to restrict competition in the downstream market on which the company requesting access was seeking to operate, in that it might limit the possibility for that operator to enter the market or expand its operations on that market.[68]

93. With regard to price discrimination, Article 86(c) prohibits discrimination by a dominant firm between customers of that firm,[69] including discriminating between customers on the basis of whether or not they agree to deal exclusively with that dominant firm.

94. Discrimination without objective justification as regards any aspects or condition of an access agreement may constitute an abuse. Discrimination may relate to elements such as pricing, delays, technical access, routing,[70] numbering, restrictions on network use exceeding essential requirements and use of customer network data. However, the existence of discrimination can only be determined on a case by case basis. Discrimination is contrary to Article 86 whether or not it results from or is apparent from the terms of a particular access agreement.

95. There is, in this context, a general duty on the network operator to treat independent customers in the same way as its own subsidiary or downstream service arm. The nature of the customer and its demands may play a significant role in determining whether transactions are comparable. Different prices for customers at different levels (e.g. wholesale and retail) do not necessarily constitute discrimination.

96. Discrimination issues may arise in respect of the technical configuration of the access, given its importance in the context of access.

The degree of technical sophistication of the access: restrictions on the type or 'level' in the network hierarchy of exchange involved in the access or the technical capabilities of this exchange are of direct competitive significance. These could be the facilities available to support a connection or the type of

---

68 However, when infrastructure capacity is under-utilised, charging a different price for access depending on the demand in the different downstream markets may be justified to the extent that such differentiation permits a better utilisation of the infrastructure and a better development of certain markets, and where such differentiation does not restrict or distort competition. In such a case, the Commission will analyse the global effects of such price differentiation on all of the downstream markets.

69 Case C-310/93 P, BPB Industries PLC and British Gypsum Ltd v Commission [1995] ECR I-865, 904, applying to discrimination by BPB among customers in the related market for dry plaster.

70 ie to a preferred list of correspondent network operators.

interface and signalling system used to determine the type of service available to the party requesting access (e.g. intelligent network facilities).

The number and/or location of connection points: the requirement to collect and distribute traffic for particular areas at the switch which directly serves that area rather than at a higher level of the network hierarchy may be important. The party requesting access incurs additional expense by either providing links at a greater distance from its own switching centre or being liable to pay higher conveyance charges.

Equal access: the possibility for customers of the party requesting access to obtain the services provided by the access provider using the same number of dialled digits as are used by the customers of the latter is a crucial feature of competitive telecommunications.

Objective justification

97.   These could include factors relating to the actual operation of the network owned by the access provider, or licensing restrictions consistent with, for example, the subject matter of intellectual property rights.

2.3   Abuses of joint dominance

98.   In the case of joint dominance (see above, points 65 *et seq*.) behaviour by one of several jointly dominant companies may be abusive even if others are not behaving in the same way.

99.   In addition to remedies under the competition rules, if no operator was willing to grant access, and if there was no technical or commercial justification for the refusal, one would expect that the National Regulatory Authority would resolve the problem by ordering one or more of the companies to offer access, under the terms of the ONP Directive or under national law.

3.   Access agreements (Article 85)

100.   Restrictions of competition stemming from access agreements may have two distinct effects: to restrict competition between the two parties to the access agreement, or to restrict competition from third parties, for example through exclusivity for one or both of the parties of the agreement. In addition, where one party is dominant, conditions of the access agreement may lead to a strengthening of that dominant position, or to an extension of that dominant position to a related market, or may constitute an unlawful exploitation of the dominant position through the imposition of unfair terms.

101.   Access agreements where access is in principle unlimited are not likely to be restrictive of competition within the meaning of Article 85(1). Exclusivity obligations in contracts providing access to one company are likely to restrict competition because they limit access to infrastructure for other companies. Since most networks have more capacity than any single user is likely to need, this will normally be the case in the telecommunications sector.

102.   Access agreements can have significant pro-competitive effects as they can improve access to the downstream market. Access agreements in the

context of interconnection are essential to interoperability of services and infrastructure, thus increasing competition in the downstream market for services, which is likely to involve higher added value than local infrastructure.

103.   There is, however, obvious potential for anti-competitive effects of certain access agreements or clauses therein. Access agreements may, for example:

(a)   serve as a means of coordinating prices;
(b)   or market sharing;
(c)   have exclusionary effects on third parties;[71]
(d)   lead to an exchange of commercially sensitive information between the parties.

104.   The risk of price coordination is particularly acute in the telecommunications sector since interconnection charges often amount to 50% or more of the total cost of the services provided, and where interconnection with a dominant operator will usually be necessary. In these circumstances, the scope for price competition is limited and the risk (and the seriousness) of price coordination correspondingly greater.

105.   Furthermore, interconnection agreements between network operators may under certain circumstances be an instrument of market sharing between the network operator providing access and the network operator seeking access, instead of the emergence of network competition between them.

106.   In a liberalised telecommunications environment, the above types of restrictions of competition will be monitored by the national authorities and the Commission under the competition rules. The right of parties who suffer from any type of anti-competitive behaviour to complain to the Commission is unaffected by national regulation.

Clauses falling within Article 85(1)

107.   The Commission has identified certain types of restriction which would potentially infringe Article 85(1) EC and therefore require individual exemption. These clauses will most commonly relate to the commercial framework of the access.

108.   In the telecommunications sector, interconnecting parties may wish to exchange customer and traffic information. This exchange is likely to influence the competitive behaviour of the undertakings concerned, and could easily be used by the parties for collusive practices, such as market sharing.[72] Safeguards will therefore be necessary to ensure that either confidential information is only disclosed to those parts of the companies involved in making the interconnection agreements, or to ensure that the information is not used for anti-competitive purposes.

---

71 Commission Decision, Night Services, OJ L 259/20 (1994); Commission Decision, Eurotunnel, OJ L 354/66 (1994).
72 Case T-34/92, Fiatagri UK Ltd and New Holland Ford Ltd v Commission
  Case T/35/92, John Deere Ltd v Commission
  Both on appeal to the ECJ
  Appealing against Commission decision, UK Agricultural Tractor Registration Exchange, OJ L 68/19 (1992).

109.   Exclusivity arrangements, for example where traffic would be conveyed exclusively through the telecommunications network of one or both
parties rather than to the network of other parties which whom access
agreements have been concluded will similarly require analysis under Article
85(3). If no justification is provided for such routing, such clauses will be
prohibited.
110.   Access agreements that have been concluded with an anti-competitive object are extremely unlikely to fulfil the criteria for an individual
exemption under Article 85(3).
111.   Furthermore, access agreements may have an impact on the competitive structure of the market. Local access charges will often account for a
considerable portion of the total cost of the services provided to end-users
by the party requesting access, thus leaving limited scope for price competition. Because of the need to safeguard this limited degree of competition, the
Commission will therefore pay particular attention to scrutinising access
agreements in the context of their likely effects on the relevant markets in
order to ensure that such agreements do not serve as a hidden and indirect
means for fixing or co-ordinating end-prices for end-users, which constitutes
one of the most serious infringements of Article 85 EC.[73]
112.   In addition, clauses involving collective discrimination leading to the
exclusion of third parties are similarly restrictive of competition. The most
important is discrimination with regard to price, quality or other commercially significant aspects of the access to the detriment of the party requesting
access, which will generally aim at unfairly favouring the operations of the
access provider.

4.   Effect on trade between Member States

113.   The application of both Article 85 and Article 86 requires an effect
on trade between Member States.
114.   In order for an agreement to have an effect on trade between
Member States, it must be possible for the Commission to:

foresee with a sufficient degree of probability on the basis of a set of
objective factors of law or of fact that the agreement in question may have
an influence, direct or indirect, actual or potential, on the pattern of trade
between Member States.[74]

It is not necessary for each of the restrictions of competition within the
agreement to be capable of affecting trade,[75] provided the agreement as a
whole does so.
115.   As regards access agreements in the telecommunications sector, the
Commission will consider not only the direct effect of restrictions of competition on inter-state trade in access markets, but also the effects on inter-state
trade in downstream telecommunications services. The Commission will also
consider the potential of these agreements to foreclose a given geographic

73 Case 8/72 *Vereniging van Cementhandelaaren* v *Commission* [1972] ECR 977;
   Case 123/85 *Bureau National Interprofessionnel du Cognac* v *Clair* [1985] ECR 391;
74 Case 56/65, STM, 1966 ECR 235 at 249.
75 Case 193/83, Windsurfing International Inc v Commission, 1986 ECR 611.

market which could prevent undertakings already established in other Member States from competing in this geographic market.

116.   Telecommunications access agreements will normally affect trade between Member States as services provided over a network are traded throughout the EU and access agreements may govern the ability of a service provider or an operator to provide any given service.[76] Even where markets are mainly national, as is generally the case at present given the stage of development of liberalisation, abuses of dominance will normally speaking affect market structure, leading to repercussions on trade between Member States.

117.   Cases in this area involving issues under Article 86 will relate either to abusive clauses in access agreements, or a refusal to conclude an access agreement on appropriate terms or at all. As such, the criteria listed above for determining whether an access agreement is capable of affecting trade between Member States would be equally relevant here.

Conclusions

118.   The Commission considers that competition rules and sector specific regulation form a coherent set of measures to ensure a liberalised and competitive market environment for telecommunications markets in the EU.

119.   In taking action in this sector, the Commission will aim to avoid unnecessary duplication of procedures, in particular competition procedures and national/EU regulatory procedures as set out under the ONP framework.

120.   Where competition rules are invoked the Commission will consider which markets are relevant and will apply Articles 85 and 86 in accordance with the principles set out above.

---

76 See Telecommunications Guidelines, footnote above.

LICENSING

PROPOSAL FOR A EUROPEAN PARLIAMENT AND COUNCIL DIRECTIVE (96/C 90/05) ON A COMMON FRAMEWORK FOR GENERAL AUTHORIZATIONS AND INDIVIDUAL LICENCES IN THE FIELD OF TELECOMMUNICATIONS SERVICES

COM(95) 545 final — 95/0282(COD)
(Submitted by the Commission on 30 January 1996)

THE EUROPEAN PARLIAMENT AND THE COUNCIL OF THE EUROPEAN UNION,
Having regard to the Treaty establishing the European Community, and in particular Articles 57 (2), 66 and 100a thereof,
Having regard to the proposal from the Commission,
Having regard to the proposal of the Economic and Social Committee,
Acting in accordance with the procedure in Article 189b of the Treaty,
1. Whereas the Council Resolution of 22 July 1993 on the review of the situation in the telecommunications sector and the need for further development in that market,[1] together with Council Resolution of 22 December 1994 on the principles and timetable for the liberalization of telecommunications infrastructures,[2] as well as European Parliament Resolutions of 20 April 1993,[3] 7 April 1995[4] and 19 May 1995[5] have supported the process of complete liberalization of telecommunications services and infrastructures by 1 January 1998, with possible transition periods for certain Member States;
2. Whereas the Communication on the consultation on the green paper on the liberalization of telecommunications infrastructure and cable television networks has confirmed the need for principles at Union level, in order to ensure that general authorization and individual licensing regimes are based on the principle of proportionality and are open, transparent and non-discriminatory; whereas Council Resolution of 18 September 1995 on the implementation of the future regulatory framework for telecommunications[6] recognizes as a key factor for this regulatory framework in the Union the establishment, in accordance with the principle of subsidiarity, of common

---

1 OJ No C 213, 6. 8. 1993, p. 1.
2 OJ No C 379, 31. 12. 1994, p. 4.
3 OJ No C 150, 31. 5. 1993, p. 39.
4 OJ No C 109, 1. 5. 1995, p. 310.
5 OJ No C 151, 19. 6. 1995, p. 479.
6 OJ No C 258, 3. 10. 1995, p. 1.

principles for general authorizations and individual licensing regimes in the Member States, based on categories of balanced rights and obligations; whereas these principles should cover all authorizations which are required for the provision of any telecommunications services and for the establishment and/or operation of any infrastructure for the provision of telecommunications services;

3. Whereas a common framework should be established for general authorizations and individual licences granted by Member States in the field of telecommunications services; whereas under Community law and in particular under Commission Directive 90/388/EEC of 28 June 1990 on competition in the markets for telecommunications services,[7] as last amended, market entry should only be restricted on the basis of objective, transparent, proportionate and non-discriminatory selection criteria relating to the availability of scarce resources as well as on the basis of the implementation by national regulatory authorities of objective, transparent and non-discriminatory award procedures; whereas that directive also sets out principles regarding *inter alia* fees and rights of way; whereas these rules should be complemented and elaborated upon by the present text to determine this common framework;

4. Whereas conditions attached to authorizations are necessary in order to attain public interest objectives to the benefit of telecommunications users, such as requirements relating to consumer protection; whereas according to Articles 52 and 59 of the Treaty, the regulatory regime in the field of telecommunications should be consistent with the principles of freedom of establishment and freedom to provide services and should take into account the need to facilitate the introduction of new services as well as the widespread application of technological improvements; whereas therefore general authorization and individual licensing regimes should provide for the lightest possible regulation compatible with the achievement of applicable requirements; whereas Member States should not be required to introduce or maintain authorization regimes, in particular where the provision of telecommunications services or the establishment and/or operation of telecommunications infrastructure is not, at the date of entry into force of this directive, subject to such an authorization regime;

5. Whereas the present directive therefore will make a significant contribution to the entry of new operators on markets, in the perspective of the development of the Information Society;

6. Whereas Member States may define and grant different categories of authorizations; whereas this should not restrict undertakings, in particular those established in another Member State, from determining their own commercial strategies and, in particular, the type of telecommunications services or infrastructures that they wish to provide, subject to compliance with relevant regulatory obligations;

7. Whereas in order to facilitate the Union-wide provision of telecommunications services, priority should be given to market access regimes not requiring authorizations or relying on general authorizations, to be complemented where necessary by individual licences setting conditions for those elements which cannot be suitably dealt with by general authorizations;

---

7 OJ No L 192, 24. 7. 1990, p. 10.

8. Whereas any conditions attached to authorizations should be objectively justified in relation to the service concerned, non-discriminatory, proportionate and transparent; whereas authorizations should not impose non-telecommunications related obligations on the beneficiaries of such authorizations; whereas authorizations may be the means for applying conditions required by Community law, in particular in the area of Open Network Provision;

9. Whereas the harmonization of conditions attached to authorizations should significantly facilitate the free provision of telecommunications services in the European Community;

10. Whereas any fees imposed on undertakings as part of authorizations procedures must be based on objective, transparent and non-discriminatory criteria;

11. Whereas the introduction of individual licensing regimes should be restricted to limited, pre-defined situations; whereas Member States should not *a priori* limit the number of individual licences for any category of telecommunications services, except to the extent required to ensure the efficient use of radio frequencies;

12. Whereas Member States may be allowed to impose specific conditions on undertakings providing public telecommunications networks and telecommunications because of their market power; whereas the market power of an undertaking depends on a number of factors including its share of the relevant product or service market in the relevant geographical market, its turnover relative to the size of the market, its ability to influence market conditions, its control of the means of access to end-users, its access to financial resources, its experience providing products and services in the market; whereas, for the purpose of this directive, an undertaking with a share of more than 25% of a particular telecommunications market in the geographical area in a Member State within which it is authorized to operate would be presumed to enjoy significant market power, unless its national regulatory authority determined, in accordance with the European Union competition rules, that this was not the case; whereas, for an undertaking falling below this threshold market share, the national regulatory authority may nevertheless, only for the purposes of applying the provisions of the directive on interconnection, determine that the undertaking enjoyed significant market power;

13. Whereas telecommunications services have a role to play in strengthening social and economic cohesion, *inter alia* by furthering the achievement of universal service, in particular in remote, peripheral, land-locked and rural areas and islands; whereas Member States may therefore impose universal service obligations by means of individual licences;

14. Whereas in order to facilitate the granting of individual licences to undertakings applying for such licences in more than one Member States, a one-stop shopping procedure should be established;

15. Whereas any authorization regimes should defer to the need to contribute to the establishment of trans-European telecommunications networks as envisaged in Title XII of the Treaty establishing the European Community; whereas to this end co-ordination of national authorization procedures may prove useful for undertakings intending to provide a telecommunications service or to establish and/or operate telecommunications infrastructure in more than one Member State;

16.   Whereas European Community undertakings should benefit from effective and comparable access to third countries markets and enjoy a similar treatment in a third country as is offered by the Community framework to undertakings owned directly or through majority ownership, or effectively controlled, by nationals from the third country concerned; whereas World Trade Organization telecommunications negotiations scheduled to be finished in April 1996 should result in a balanced and multilateral agreement ensuring effective and comparable access for Community operators in third countries;

17.   Whereas a committee to assist the Commission should be established;

18.   Whereas, without prejudice to other procedures available to ensure the application of Community law, it is appropriate to provide for a specific procedure in order to facilitate the implementation of the principles set out in this directive;

19.   Whereas the functioning of this directive should be reviewed in due time in the light of the development of the telecommunications sector and of trans-European networks, as well as in the light of experience gained from the harmonization and one-stop-shopping procedures set out in this directive;

20.   Whereas on the basis of the full implementation of a competitive framework, in particular directive 90/388/EEC and its subsequent amendments, in order to achieve the essential goal of ensuring the development of the internal market in the field of telecommunications and specifically the free provision of telecommunications services and infrastructure throughout the European Union, the adoption of the present directive will substantially contribute to this goal; whereas Member States should, in particular through their national regulatory authorities, implement this common framework;

HAVE ADOPTED THIS DIRECTIVE:

SECTION I   SCOPE, DEFINITIONS AND PRINCIPLES

Article 1   Scope and aim

This directive concerns the procedures associated with the granting of authorizations and the conditions attached to such authorizations, for the purpose of providing telecommunications services.

Article 2   Definitions

1.   For the purposes of this directive,

(a)   'Authorization' means any 'general authorization' or 'individual licence' as defined below:

— 'general authorization': any permission regardless of whether it is regulated through a 'class licence' or through general law and regardless of whether such regulation requires registration, allowing undertakings to provide telecommunications services and, where applicable, to establish and/or operate infrastructure for the provision of these services;

— 'Individual licence': an authorization which is granted by a national regulatory authority and which gives an undertaking operating under a general authorization specific rights, or which subjects that undertaking's operations to specific obligations, where the undertaking is not entitled to exercise the rights concerned until it has received the decision by the national regulatory authority;

(b) 'National regulatory authority (NRA)' means the body or bodies, legally distinct and functionally independent of the telecommunications organizations, charged by a Member State with the granting, the supervision and the enforcement of authorizations.

(c) 'One-stop shopping procedure' means an arrangement facilitating the obtaining of individual licences from more than one national regulatory authority in a co-ordinated procedure and at a single location.

(d) 'Essential requirements' means the non-economic reasons in the public interest which may cause a Member State to impose conditions on the establishment and/or operation of telecommunications networks or the provision of telecommunications services. These reasons are security of network operations, maintenance of network integrity, and, where justified, interoperability of services, data protection, the protection of the environment and town and country planning objectives as well as the effective use of the frequency spectrum and the avoidance of harmful interference between radio based telecommunications systems and other, space-based or terrestrial, technical systems. Data protection may include protection of personal data, the confidentiality of information transmitted or stored as well as the protection of privacy.

(e) 'Telecommunications services' means services whose provision consists wholly or partly in the transmission and/or routing of signals on telecommunications networks.

(f) 'Public telecommunications service' means a telecommunications service available to the public.

(g) 'Universal service' means a defined minimum service or set of services of specified quality which is accessible to all users everywhere and, in the light of specific national conditions, at an affordable price.

2. Other definitions given in directive 90/387/EEC[8] and directive on interconnection shall apply, where relevant, to this directive.

Article 3 Principles governing authorizations

1. Where Member States make the provision of a telecommunications service subject to an authorization, the grant of any such authorization and the conditions to be attached to such authorization shall comply with the principles set out in this Article.

2. Authorizations may only contain conditions which are listed in Annex I.

Moreover, such conditions shall be objectively justified in relation to the service concerned, non-discriminatory, proportionate and transparent.

3. Member States shall ensure that telecommunications services can be provided either without authorization, or on the basis of general authorizations, to be complemented where necessary with rights and obligations requiring an individual assessment of applications and giving rise to one or more individual licences. Member States may only require an individual

---

8 OJ No L 192, 24. 7. 1990, p. 1.

licence to the extent that the beneficiary is given access to scarce physical and other resources, or is subject to particular obligations or benefits from particular rights, in accordance with the provisions of Section III.

SECTION II GENERAL AUTHORIZATIONS

Article 4 Conditions attached to general authorizations

1.   Where Member States subject the provision of telecommunications services to general authorizations, the conditions which may be attached, where justified, to such authorizations are set out in Annex I, part 2 and 3. Such authorizations shall develop the least onerous regime possible consistent with ensuring compliance with the relevant essential requirements and other public interest requirements set out in Annex I, parts 2 and 3.

2.   Member States shall ensure that the conditions attached to general authorizations are published in an appropriate manner so as to provide easy access to that information for interested parties. Reference shall be made in the national Official Journal of the Member State concerned to the publication of this information.

3.   When modifying the conditions attached to a general authorization, Member States shall give appropriate notice of their intention to do so and enable interested parties to express their views on the intended modifications.

Article 5 Procedures for the granting of general authorizations

1.   Member States shall not prevent an undertaking which complies with the applicable conditions set out in a general authorization in accordance with Article 4 from providing the intended telecommunications service.

2.   Member States may require that, before providing the service, the undertaking benefiting from the general authorization shall notify the national regulatory authority of its intention to do so, and shall communicate the information relating to the service concerned which is necessary for the purpose of ensuring compliance with the applicable conditions set out in accordance with Article 4. The undertaking may be required to observe a waiting period not exceeding two weeks before it can start providing the services covered by the general authorization.

3.   Where the beneficiary of a general authorization does not comply with a condition set out in a general authorization in accordance with Article 4, the national regulatory authority may inform the undertaking concerned that it is not entitled to benefit from the general authorization. The national regulatory authority shall give the undertaking concerned a reasonable opportunity to state its views on the application of the conditions and to remedy any breaches. If the undertaking concerned does not remedy the breaches, the national regulatory authority shall confirm its decision and state the reasons for its decision, which shall be communicated within one week of its adoption to the undertaking concerned. Member States shall provide for a procedure for appealing against the withdrawal of the benefit of the general authorization to an institution independent from the national regulatory authority.

4.   Member States shall ensure that information concerning the procedures related to general authorizations is published in an appropriate

manner, so as to provide easy access to that information. Reference shall be made in the national Official Journal of the Member State concerned to the publication of this information.

Article 6   Fees for general authorizations

1.   Member States shall ensure that any fees imposed on undertakings as part of authorizations procedures only aim at covering the administrative costs incurred in the implementation of the applicable general authorization scheme.

2.   Fees, the criteria upon which they are based and any changes thereto, shall be published in an appropriate and sufficiently detailed manner, so as to provide easy access to that information.

SECTION III   INDIVIDUAL LICENCES

Article 7   Scope

1.   Member States may, in addition to conditions attached to general authorizations for the telecommunications services including those mentioned in Annex II, require individual licences imposing conditions as listed in Annex I, part 4, only for the following purposes:

(a)   to allow the licensee access to specific radio frequencies or numbers;

(b)   to give the licensee particular rights with regard to access to public or private land;

(c)   to grant the licensee rights to provide public telecommunications infrastructure between the European Union and third countries;

(d)   to impose obligations on the licensee relating to the mandatory provision of public telecommunications services;

(e)   to impose specific obligations, in conformity with European Union competition rules, where the licensee has significant market power in relation to the provision of public telecommunications networks and telecommunications services.

2.   Undertakings wishing to provide services which are not yet covered by a general authorization and which cannot be provided without authorization, or wishing to benefit from additional rights not granted by the applicable general authorization, may apply for an individual licence.

3.   In the situation addressed in Article 7 (2) Member States shall, as rapidly as possible, either enable the provision of the service concerned or the establishment and/or operation of infrastructure concerned without authorization, or adopt the relevant general authorizations in accordance with Section II.

Article 8   Conditions attached to individual licences

1.   The conditions which may be attached, where justified, to individual licences are set out in Annex I, part 4.

The conditions attached to an individual licence shall only relate to the situations justifying the grant of such a licence, as defined in Article 7.

However, where appropriate, Member States may incorporate the terms of the applicable general authorizations into the individual licence.

2. The rights given under and the conditions attached to any general authorizations must not be varied by the granting of an individual licence, except in objectively justified cases and in a proportionate manner.

3. Member States shall ensure that information concerning the conditions which will be attached to any individual licence are published in an appropriate manner, so as to provide easy access to that information. Reference shall be made in the national Official Journal of the Member State concerned to this publication.

Article 9 Procedures for the granting of individual licences

1. Where a Member State grants individual licences, it shall ensure that information concerning the procedures for applying for individual licences are published in an appropriate manner, so as to provide easy access to that information. Reference shall be made in the national Official Journal of the Member State concerned to this publication.

2. In the situation addressed in Article 7 (2), Member States shall grant an individual licence before having completed the procedure set out in paragraph (1).

3. Where a Member State intends to grant individual licences, it shall do so by:

— granting individual licences through open, non-discriminatory, transparent procedures and, to this end, subject all applicants to the same procedures, unless there is an objective reason for differentiation, and

— setting reasonable time limits, and inter alia it shall communicate to the applicant a decision on the application as soon as possible but not later than six weeks after it has received the application.

4. Without prejudice to Article 10, paragraph (1), any undertaking which fulfils the conditions decided and published by Member States in accordance with the relevant provisions of the present directive is entitled to receive an individual licence.

5. Where the beneficiary of an individual licence does not comply with a condition set out in the licence in accordance with the relevant provisions of the present directive, the national regulatory authority may withdraw or suspend the benefit of the individual licence. The national regulatory authority shall give the undertaking concerned a reasonable opportunity to state its views on the application of the conditions and to remedy any breaches. If the undertaking concerned does not remedy the breaches, the national regulatory authority shall confirm its decision and state the reasons for its decision, which shall be communicated within one week of its adoption to the undertaking concerned.

6. Member States refusing to grant, withdrawing or suspending an individual licence shall state the reasons therefor. Member States shall provide for an appropriate procedure for appealing against such refusals, withdrawals or suspensions to an institution independent from the national regulatory authority.

Article 10   Limitation in the number of individual licences

1.   Member States may limit *a priori* the number of individual licences for any category of telecommunications services, only to the extent required to ensure the efficient use of radio frequencies and in conformity with European Union competition rules.

2.   Where a Member State intends to limit the number of individual licences granted, it shall:
— give due weight to the need to facilitate the development of competition and to maximise benefits for users,
— enable interested parties to express their views on any limitation,
— publish its decision to limit the number of individual licences, stating the reasons therefor,
— review the limitation at reasonable intervals,
— invite applications for licences.

3.   Member States shall grant such individual licences on the basis of selection criteria which must be objective, detailed, transparent, proportionate and non-discriminatory. Any such selection must give due weight to the need to facilitate the development of competition and to maximise benefits for users.

Member States shall ensure that information concerning such criteria are published in an appropriate manner, so as to provide easy access to that information. Reference shall be made in the national Official Journal of the Member State concerned to this publication.

4.   Where a Member State finds, either at its own initiative or following a request by an undertaking, either at the time of entry into force of this directive or at a later time, that the number of individual licences can be increased, it shall publish this fact and invite applications for additional licences.

Article 11   Fees for individual licences

1.   Member States shall ensure that any fees imposed on undertakings as part of authorization procedures only aim at covering the administrative costs incurred in the implementation of the applicable individual licence. Fees, the criteria upon which they are based and any changes thereto, shall be published in an appropriate and sufficiently detailed manner, so as to provide easy access to that information.

In addition, in the case of scarce resources Member States may allow their national regulatory authorities to impose, in a non-discriminatory manner, a fee for the granting of an individual licence. This fee shall take into account the need for the optimal use of this resource as well as for the introduction and the development of innovative services and competition.

SECTION IV   PROVISION OF TELECOMMUNICATIONS SERVICES THROUGHOUT THE EUROPEAN UNION

Article 12   Principle

Member States shall, in the formulation and application of their authorization regimes, facilitate the provision of telecommunications services between Member States.

Article 13   Co-ordination of authorizations procedures

1.   An undertaking intending to provide a telecommunications service or to establish telecommunications infrastructure in more than one Member State may request the national regulatory authorities concerned to co-ordinate their authorizations procedures in order to deliver the necessary authorizations on substantially the same conditions.

2.   Where the undertaking concerned is unable to obtain the necessary authorizations in one or more of those Member States within the time periods set out in this directive, or where significant variations between the authoriz-ations conditions in these Member States appear, the procedure described in paragraphs 3 to 5 shall be available.

3.   The undertaking concerned may refer the matter to the Chairman of the European Union Telecommunications Committee.

4.   Where the Chairman of the European Union Telecommunications Committee finds that there is a case for further examination, he shall convene as soon as possible a working group including at least two members of the European Union Telecommunications Committee and one representative of the national regulatory authorities concerned. The working group shall define its position within three months.

5.   The position agreed according to this procedure shall form the basis of a solution to be implemented by the Member State concerned, without delay. If an agreed position fails to be reached, or if an agreed position is not implemented within a reasonable time which shall not, except in justified cases, exceed two months, measures to resolve the issue shall be taken in accordance with the procedure set out in Article 17.

Article 14   Harmonization

1.   Without prejudice to the possibility for Member States to authorize additional services, Member States shall ensure that the categories of tele-communications services listed in Annex II can be provided either without authorization, or on the basis of a general authorization.

2.   Wherever necessary, the conditions attached to general authorizations for the provision of the telecommunications services listed in Annex II, the procedures for the grant of general authorizations and individual licences and the determination of the level of fees shall be harmonized.

The harmonization of conditions and procedures shall aim to develop the least onerous regime possible consistent with ensuring compliance with the relevant essential requirements and other public interest requirements set out in Annex I, parts 2 and 3.

Harmonization shall furthermore aim to elaborate balanced sets of rights and obligations for the beneficiaries of authorizations.

3.   The Commission shall, in accordance with the procedure laid down in Article 17, assign mandates to CEPT/ECTRA, CEPT/ERC or other relevant harmonization bodies. These mandates shall define the tasks to be performed and the categories of general authorizations to be harmonized, and lay down a time schedule for the elaboration of harmonised conditions and procedures. A decision shall be adopted in accordance with the procedure laid down in

relation to Article 17, setting out that the relevant telecommunications services can be provided on the basis of a harmonized general authorization.

4. The provisions of paragraph (3) will lapse on 1st January 2001, unless the Commission will have proposed to maintain or to modify it in the report referred to in Article 22.

Article 15   One-stop shopping procedure for individual licences

1. The Commission shall undertake the necessary steps to provide for the operation of a one-stop shopping procedure for individual licences, including suitable arrangements for its technical administration, in accordance with the procedure laid down in Article 17. References to such arrangements will be published in the *Official Journal of the European Communities*.

2. Such one-stop shopping procedure shall conform to the following conditions:

(a) The one-stop shopping procedure is open to all service providers wishing to operate telecommunications services in the European Community.

(b) The submission of applications and/or declarations at a single location in the European Union is possible and one or more bodies are defined with which the applications and/or declarations can be filed. Applications may include, where required, requests for frequency co-ordination and site clearance and/or for allocation and registration of names, numbers or addresses.

(c) Within seven days of filing, the application(s) and/or declaration(s) shall be provided to the national regulatory authorities concerned by the body with which the application was filed.

(d) The national regulatory authorities concerned shall take a decision on the grant of the licence within six weeks after they have received the application; they shall inform the applicant as well as the body with which the relevant application was filed of that decision within one week.

(e) Where possible, national regulatory authorities shall endeavour to shorten the time period of six weeks indicated in paragraph d) for certain categories of services, in response to commercial needs.

(f) Article 9 shall apply to applications for individual licences made by means of the one-stop shopping procedure.

(g) The body with which the applications and/or declarations may be filed shall report annually to the Commission on the operation of the one-stop shopping procedure, including in particular information on refusals of applications and objections raised to declarations.

SECTION V   EUROPEAN UNION TELECOMMUNICATIONS COMMITTEE

Article 16   Composition of the EUTC

The Commission shall be assisted by a committee of an advisory nature composed of representatives of the national regulatory authorities of the Member States and chaired by a representative of the Commission. The Committee shall be called the European Union Telecommunications Committee (EUTC).

Article 17   Procedures for the EUTC

1.   The representative of the Commission shall submit to the Committee a draft of the measures to be taken. The Committee shall deliver its opinion on the draft, within a time limit which the chairman may lay down according to the urgency of the matter, if necessary by taking a vote.

The opinion shall be recorded in the minutes; in addition each Member State shall have the right to ask to have its position recorded in the minutes.

The Commission shall take the utmost account of the opinion delivered by the committee. It shall inform the committee of the manner in which its opinion has been taken into account.

2.   The Commission shall where necessary inform the Committee on the outcome of regular consultations with the representatives of telecommunications organizations, users, consumers, manufacturers, service providers and trade unions.

In addition, the Committee shall, taking account of the European Community's telecommunications policy, foster the exchange of information between the Member States and between the Member States and the Commission, on the situation and the development of regulatory activities regarding the authorization of telecommunications services.

SECTION VI   FINAL PROVISIONS

Article 18   Application to undertakings from third countries

1.   With a view to ensuring effective and comparable access to third countries markets to the benefit of Community undertakings, Member States shall inform the Commission of any general difficulty encountered, *de jure* or *de facto*, by Community undertakings in obtaining authorizations and in operating under authorizations in third countries, which have been brought to their attention. Member States and the Commission shall ensure that commercial confidentiality is respected.

2.   Whenever the Commission establishes that a third country is not providing Community undertakings with rights to authorizations which are comparable to those which the Community grants to undertakings from that third country, the Commission may submit proposals to the Council for the appropriate mandate for negotiation with a view to obtaining comparable rights for Community undertakings. The Council shall decide by qualified majority.

3.   In the circumstances set out in paragraph (2), the Commission may at any time propose that the Council exempt one or more Member States from obligations laid down by this directive in relation to undertakings from that third country. The Commission may make such a proposal on its own initiative or at the request of a Member State. The Council shall act by qualified majority as soon as possible.

4.   Measures taken pursuant to this Article shall be without prejudice to the European Community obligations under any international agreement governing the liberalization of telecommunications networks and services.

Article 19   Confidentiality

1.   The Commission and the national regulatory authorities shall not disclose any information covered by the obligation of professional secrecy.

2.   The provisions of paragraph (1) shall not prevent publication of information on licensing conditions which does not include information of a confidential nature.

Article 20   Notification

1.   In addition to the information already required under directive 90/388/ EEC, Member States shall supply the Commission with the following information:

— the names and addresses of the national authorities and bodies competent to issue national authorizations;

— all information on national authorization regimes, including conditions and procedures, in particular whether and for which services individual licences are required and criteria on the basis of which applications are assessed;

— general national regulation specifically relevant in the area of telecommunications services.

2.   Member States shall notify any changes in respect of the information supplied under paragraph (1), within two weeks of its entry into force.

3.   At the request of a Member State or on its own initiative the Commission shall examine any conditions, criteria and/or procedures set out in a national authorization, in particular with regard to the justification of the measures and their compliance with the principle of proportionality. The Commission shall, within one month of receipt of a request and following the procedure set out in Article 17, decide whether the Member State may continue to apply the measure. The Commission shall communicate its decision to the Council and to the Member States.

Article 21   Authorizations existing at the date of entry into force of the directive

Member States shall make all necessary efforts to bring authorizations in force at the date of entry into force of this directive into line with the provisions of this directive by 1 January 1999. Obligations which have not been brought into line by that date with the provisions of this directive shall be inoperative. Where justified, Member States may be granted by the Commission, upon request, a deferment of the provisions of this Article.

Article 22   Review procedures

1.   Any modifications necessary to adapt the content of the Annexes of this directive to new technological developments and appropriate practical procedures shall be determined in accordance with the procedure laid down in Article 17.

2.   Before 1 January 2000 the Commission will review whether a modification of the provisions of this directive is necessary, on the basis of a report

to be provided to Parliament and Council. This report shall include an assessment, on the basis of the experience gained, of the need for further evolution of the regulatory structures as regards authorizations, in particular in relation to harmonization and to trans-European services and networks.

3.   Before 1 January 1999 the Commission shall report on the possibilities of access by Community undertakings to telecommunications markets in third countries. If appropriate, the Commission may submit proposals as mentioned in Article 18.

Article 23   Deferment

Where Member States with less developed networks make use of the deferment they have been granted in conformity with Commission Directive 90/388/EEC with regard to the obligation to remove special or exclusive rights in relation to voice telephony and the provision of public telecommunications networks, in order to achieve the necessary structural adjustments, these Member States shall be granted upon request a similar deferment for the application, to the provision of voice telephony and public telecommunications networks, of the provisions of Articles 7 (1), 10 (1) and 21 of this directive.

Where Member States with very small networks make use of the deferment they have been granted in conformity with Commission Directive 90/388/EEC with regard to the obligation to remove special or exclusive rights in relation to voice telephony and the provision of public telecommunications networks, in order to achieve the necessary structural adjustments, these Member States shall be granted upon request a similar deferment for the application, to the provision of voice telephony and public telecommunications networks, of the provisions of Articles 7 (1), 10 (1) and 21 of this directive.

Article 24   Implementation of the directive

1.   Member States shall bring into force the laws, regulations and administrative provisions necessary to comply with this directive by July 1st, 1997. They shall notify these measures to the Commission. These measures shall contain a reference to this directive.

2.   Member States shall notify to the Commission a list of representatives to the European Union Telecommunications Committee not later than two months after the publication of this directive.

Article 25   Addressees

This directive is addressed to the Member States.

ANNEX I   CONDITIONS THAT MAY BE ATTACHED TO AUTHORIZATIONS

1.   Any conditions that are attached to authorizations must comply with Commission Directive 90/388/EEC[9] and its amendments, in particular the

---

9 Commission Directive 90/388/EEC regarding the implementation of full competition in telecommunications markets, OJ L 192/10, 24.7.90.

amending directive 94/46/EEC[10], the amending directive 95/.../EEC,[11] the amending directive 95/.../EEC[12] and the amending directive 95/.../EEC.[13]

2.   Conditions that may be attached to all authorizations, where justified and subject to the principle of proportionality

2.1.   Conditions aiming at ensuring compliance with relevant essential requirements.

2.2.   The provision of information reasonably required to verify compliance with applicable conditions.

3.   Specific conditions that may be attached to general authorizations for the provision of public telecommunications services, and of infrastructure used for the provision of such services, where justified and subject to the principle of proportionality

3.1.   Conditions related to the protection of users, as set out in the directive on the application of open network provision to voice telephony[14] and, subject to part 1 of this Annex, to the protection of consumers, in particular in relation to:

— prior approval by national regulatory authority of the standard consumer contract,

— provision of detailed and accurate billing,

— provision of a dispute settlement procedure,

— publication and adequate notice of change of access conditions, including tariffs, quality and availability of service.

3.2./Financial contribution to the provision of universal service, according to the directive on interconnection.[15]

3.3.   Communication of customer database information necessary for the provision of universal directory information.

3.4.   Provision of emergency services.

3.5.   Special arrangements for disabled people.

3.6.   Conditions relating to interconnection, according to the directive on interconnection[16] and to obligations of Community law.

3.7.   Conditions related to the achievement of public interest requirements recognised by the EC Treaty and, in particular, Articles 36 and 56 of that Treaty, specifically in relation to public morality and public security.

4.   Specific conditions that may be attached to individual licences, where justified and subject to the principle of proportionality

---

10 Commission Directive of 13 October 1994 amending Directive 88/301/EEC and Directive 90/388/EEC in particular with regard to satellite communications, OJ L 268/15, 19.10.94.

11 Commission Directive of 18 October 1995 amending Directive 90/388/EEC with regard to the abolition of the restrictions on the use of cable television networks for the provision of already liberalized telecommunications services, C(95) 2422 final.

12 Draft Commission Directive amending Commission Directive 90/388/EEC with regard to mobile and personal communications, OJ C 197/5, 1.8.95.

13 Draft Commission Directive amending Commission Directive 90/388/EEC regarding the implementation of full competition in telecommunications markets, OJ C 263/6, 10.10.95.

14 Commission proposal for a Directive on the application of the principles of open network provision to voice telephony, COM(94) 689 final (OJ No C 122, 18.5.1995, p. 4) and Council common position of 12 July 1995 on that proposal.

15 Commission proposal for a Directive on interconnection to public telecommunications networks and public telecommunications services in the context of open network provision (ONP), adopted by the Commission on 19 July 1995, not yet published.

16 Commission proposal for a Directive on interconnection to public telecommunications networks and public telecommunications services in the context of open network provision (ONP), adopted by the Commission on 19 July 1995, not yet published.

4.1.   Specific conditions linked to the allocation of numbering rights (compliance with national numbering schemes . . .).

4.2.   Specific conditions linked to the allocation of specific radio frequencies.

4.3.   Specific environmental and specific town and country planning requirements, linked to the use of scarce resources.

4.4.   Maximum duration, only in order to ensure the efficient use of radiofrequencies, and without prejudice to other provisions concerning the withdrawal or the suspension of licences.

4.5.   Provision of universal service obligations according to the directives on interconnection and on the application of the principles of open network provision to voice telephony.[17]

4.6.   Conditions applied to operators having a significant market position, as notified by Member States under the directive on interconnection,[18] aiming at ensuring interconnection or specific monitoring requirements.

4.7.   Provision of information on ownership in other companies, where the procedure set out in Article 18 (3) is in operation.

4.8.   Requirements related to quality, availability and permanence of the service or the network, including the financial, managerial and technical competence of the applicant and conditions setting a minimum period of operation.

4.9.   Defence related requirements.

This list of conditions shall be without prejudice to the specific rules adopted by Member States in accordance with Community law and concerning the content of audio-visual programmes intended for the general public.

ANNEX II   SERVICES TO BE COVERED BY GENERAL AUTHORIZATIONS

1.   Bearer data services, including fixed packet- or circuit-switched data services offered to the public

2.   Other fixed telecommunications services other than voice telephony for the public, telex and bearer data services, including:

— value-added data transmission services, such as telefax services, X.400 services (message handling systems), X.500 services (global electronic directory)

— value-added voice transmission services, such as storage and voice-mail services, E-mail services, audiotex and teletex services, video-conferencing, re-forwarding of messages via PSTN (private switching), video-phones, enquiries

— premium rate services, such as shared cost, shared revenue or freephone services, calling cards

---

17 Commission proposal for a Directive on interconnection to public telecommunications networks and public telecommunications services in the context of open network provision (ONP), adopted by the Commission on 19 July 1995, not yet published. Commission proposal for a Directive on the appliction of the principles of open network provision to voice telephony, COM(94) 689 final (OJ No 122, 18.5.1995, p. 4) and Council common position of 12 July 1995 on that proposal.

18 Commission proposal for a Directive on interconnection to public telecommunications networks and public telecommunications services in the context of open network provision (ONP), adopted by the Commission on 19 July 1995, not yet published.

— voice telephony provided to closed user groups
3. Satellite personal communication services (S-PCS)
4. Satellite network and communication services other than S-PCS, including very small aperture terminal, satellite news gathering and mobile satellite services
5. Mobile communications
6. Voice telephony for the public
7. Leased lines

The general authorizations covered by this list of services shall be without prejudice to the specific rules adopted by Member States in accordance with Community law and concerning the content of audiovisual programmes intended for the general public.

Notes
1. Including the amended proposal for a European Parliament and Council Directive on a common framework for general authorisations and individual licences in the field of telecommunications services (OJ C291/12, 4 October 1996).
2. See also an earlier proposal: Proposal for a European Parliament and Council Directive on a policy for the mutual recognition of licences and other national authorisations for the provision of satellite network services and/or satellite communication services, OJ C36/2, 4 February 1994.

AMENDED PROPOSAL FOR A EUROPEAN PARLIAMENT AND COUNCIL DIRECTIVE (96/C 291/06) ON A COMMON FRAMEWORK FOR GENERAL AUTHORIZATIONS AND INDIVIDUAL LICENCES IN THE FIELD OF TELECOMMUNICATIONS SERVICES

(Text with EEA relevance)
COM(96) 342 final — 95/0282 (COD)

(Submitted by the Commission pursuant to Article 189a(2) of the EC Treaty on 31 July 1996)

AMENDED TEXT

Recital 5

Whereas this Directive therefore will make a significant contribution to the entry of new operators into the market, as part of the development of the information society, bearing in mind that major obstacles still exist for new operators in the sectors that have already been open to competition, as well as in those Member States where national schemes of liberalization of telecommunications have been implemented, such as the differentiated tariff policy of the incumbent operator, insufficient transparency and high costs for interconnection, and the lack of an asymmetrical treatment;

Recital 12

Whereas Member States should be allowed to impose specific conditions on undertakings providing public telecommunications networks and telecommunications services because of their market power, the market power of an undertaking being defined by the provisions of the European Parliament and Council Directive on interconnection to public telecommunications networks and public telecommunications services in the context of Open Network Provision (ONP);

Recital 13

Whereas telecommunications services have a role to play in strengthening social and economic cohesion, *inter alia* by furthering the achievement of universal service, in particular in remote, peripheral, landlocked and rural areas and islands; whereas Member States should therefore be allowed to impose universal service obligations to provide the universal service by means of individual licences; whereas obligations to contribute to the financing of universal service are not a justification for imposing individual licences;

Recital 19

Whereas the functioning of this Directive should be reviewed in due course; in the light of the development of the telecommunications sector and of trans-European networks, as well as in the light of experience gained from the harmonization and one-stop-shopping procedures set out in this Directive; whereas it seems reasonable that, when this Directive is reviewed, the possibility of the creation of a European regulatory authority is considered;

Article 1

This Directive concerns the procedures associated with the granting of authorizations and the conditions attached to such authorizations, for the purpose of providing telecommunications services and for the establishment and/or operation of any infrastructure for the provision of telecommunications services.

Article 2(1)(e)

(e) 'Telecommunications services' means services whose provision consists wholly or partly in the transmission and/or routing of signals on telecommunications networks. This Directive does not apply to radio and television broadcasting;

Article 4(2)

Member States shall ensure that the conditions attached to general authorizations are published in an appropriate manner so as to provide easy access to that information for interested parties. Reference to the publication of this information shall be made in the national official gazette of the Member State concerned and in the *Official Journal of the European Communities*.

Article 5(4)

Member States shall ensure that information concerning the procedures relating to general authorizations is published in an appropriate manner, so as to provide easy access to that information. Reference to the publication of this information shall be made in the national official gazette of the Member State concerned and in the *Official Journal of the European Communities.*

Article 7(1)

Member States may, in addition to conditions attached to general authorizations, require individual licences imposing conditions as listed in Annex I, point 4, but only for the following purposes:

    (a)   to allow the licensee access to specific radio frequencies or numbers;

    (b)   to give the licensee particular rights with regard to access to public or private land,

    (c)   to grant the licensee rights to provide public telecommunications infrastructure between the Community and third countries;

    (d)   to impose obligations and requirements on the licensee relating to the mandatory provision of public telecommunications services as defined in Annex I, points 4.5 and 4.8;

    (e)   to impose specific obligations, in conformity with Community competition rules, where the licensee has significant market power as defined by the provisions of the European Parliament and Council Directive on interconnection to public telecommunications networks and public telecommunications services in the context of Open Network Provision in relation to the provision of public telecommunications networks and telecommunications services.

Article 7(2)

National regulatory authorities must within two weeks grant a temporary individual licence to undertakings wishing to provide services which are not yet covered by a general authorization and which cannot be provided without authorization, or wishing to enjoy additional rights not granted by the applicable general authorization, or prove that the service has to be subject to an individual licence procedure for the purposes of paragraph 1. Member States shall lay down an appropriate procedure for appealing against a negative decision to an institution independent of the national regulatory authority.

Article 7(3)

In the situations addressed in paragraph 2 Member States shall, within one month, either consent to the provision of the service concerned or the establishment and/or operation of infrastructure concerned without authorization, or grant the relevant general authorizations in accordance with Section II.

Article 9(3) second indent

    — It shall set reasonable time limits; *inter alia* it shall communicate to the applicant a decision on the application as soon as possible but not later than six weeks after it has received the application. Extension is possible in situations that are set out in advance, in particular to ensure transparency and coordination with other Member States.

Article 10(1)

Member States may *a priori* limit the number of individual licences for any category of telecommunications services, and for establishment and/or operation of telecommunications infrastructure, only to the extent required to ensure the efficient use of radio frequencies and in conformity with Community competition rules.

Article 10(2), introduction

Where a Member State is entitled by virtue of the preceding paragraph to limit the number of individual licences granted, it shall:

Article 10(4)

Member States shall periodically review whether any opportunities exist to increase the availability of frequencies. They shall inform the Commission every two years on the situation and any measures taken. Where a Member State finds, that the number of individual licences can be increased, it shall publish this fact and invite applications for additional licences.

Article 11(2)

In addition, where the resources mentioned in Article 7(1)(a) are scarce, Member States may allow their national regulatory authorities to impose, in a non-discriminatory manner, a fee for the granting of an individual licence. This fee shall reflect the need for the optimal use of this resource as well as for the introduction and the development of innovative services and competition.

Article 13, Title

Coordination of general authorization procedures and individual licence procedures

(Article 13 to be moved and placed after Article 15)

Article 13(1)

Pending harmonization on the basis of Article 14, the national regulatory authority concerned shall allow derogations to their general authorizations at the request of an undertaking intending to provide a telecommunications service or to establish a telecommunications infrastructure in more than one Member State in order to enable the undertaking to operate in the Member States concerned on substantially the same conditions.

The national regulatory authority concerned shall issue the necessary individual licences on substantially the same conditions on the request of an undertaking intending to provide a telecommunications service or to establish a telecommunications infrastructure in more than one Member State.

Article 14, Title

Harmonization of general authorizations and procedures

Article 14(2)

Wherever necessary, with a view to ensuring lighthanded regulation, the conditions attached to general authorizations for the provision of the telecommunications services listed in Annex II, the procedures for the grant of general authorizations and individual licences, and the setting of fees shall be harmonized.

Article 20(3)

At the request of a Member State or on its own initiative the Commission may examine at any time any conditions, criteria and/or procedures set out in a national authorization, in particular with regard to the justifiability of the measures and their compliance with the principle of proportionality. The Commission shall, within one month of receipt of a request and following the procedure set out in Article 17, decide whether the Member State may continue to apply the measure. The Commission shall communicate its decision to the Council and to the Member States.

Article 22(2)

Before 1 January 2000 the Commission will review whether an amendment of the provisions of this Directive is necessary, on the basis of a report to be supplied to the European Parliament and Council. The report shall include an assessment, on the basis of the experience gained, of the need for further development of the regulatory structures as regards authorizations, in particular in relation to harmonization and to trans-European services and networks, the institutional arrangements, as well as numbering plans and number portability.

Article 24

Member States shall bring into force the laws, regulations and administrative provisions necessary to comply with this Directive and publish the conditions and procedures attached to authorizations by 1 July 1997. They shall immediately inform the Commission thereof.

When Member States adopt these provisions, these shall contain a reference to this Directive or shall be accompanied by such reference at the time of their official publication. The procedure for such reference shall be adopted by Member States.

Deleted

Annex I, point 4.5a (new)

(4.5a)   Compliance with substantive obligations concerning coverage of low population areas in particular.

Annex I, point 4.6

Conditions applied to operators having a significant market position, as notified by Member States under the Directive on interconnection, aiming at ensuring interconnection or the control of significant market power.

Annex I, point 4.9 (new)

(4.9a)   Specific conditions related to the supply of leased lines in conformity with Directive 92/44/EEC as modified by Directive 96/. . ./EC amending Council Directives 90/387/EEC and 92/44/EEC for the purpose of adaptation to a competitive environment in telecommunications.

DATA PROTECTION

COMMON POSITION (EC) No 57/96 (96/C 315/06) ADOPTED BY THE COUNCIL ON 12 SEPTEMBER 1996 WITH A VIEW TO ADOPTING DIRECTIVE 96/. . ./EC OF THE EUROPEAN PARLIAMENT AND OF THE COUNCIL, OF . . ., CONCERNING THE PROCESSING OF PERSONAL DATA AND THE PROTECTION OF PRIVACY IN THE TELECOMMUNICATIONS SECTOR, IN PARTICULAR IN THE INTEGRATED SERVICES DIGITAL NETWORK (ISDN) AND IN THE PUBLIC DIGITAL MOBILE NETWORKS
OJ L281/31, 23 November 1995

THE EUROPEAN PARLIAMENT AND THE COUNCIL OF THE EUROPEAN UNION,

Having regard to the Treaty establishing the European Community, and in particular Article 100a thereof,

Having regard to the proposal from the Commission,[1]

Having regard to the opinion of the Economic and Social Committee,[2]

Acting in accordance with the procedure referred to in Article 189b of the Treaty,[3]

(1) Whereas Directive 95/46/EC of the European parliament and of the Council of 24 October 1995 on the protection of individual with regard to the processing of personal data and on the free movement of such data[4] requires Member States to ensure the rights and freedoms of natural persons with regard to the processing of personal data, and in particular their right to privacy, in order to ensure the free flow of personal data in the Community;

(2) Whereas currently in the Community new advanced digital technologies are introduced in public telecommunications networks, which give rise to specific requirements concerning the protection of personal data and privacy of the user; whereas the development of the information society is characterized by the introduction of new telecommunications services; whereas the successful cross-border development of these services, such as video-on-demand, interactive television, is partly dependent on the confidence of the users that their privacy will not be at risk;

---

1 OJ No C 200, 22.7.1994, p.4.
2 OJ No C 159, 17.6.1991, p. 38.
3 Opinion of the European Parliament of 11 March 1992 (OJ No C 94, 13.4.1992, p. 198), Council common position of 12 September 1996 (not yet published in the Official Journal) and Decision of the European Parliament of . . . (not yet published in the Official Journal).
4 OJ No L 281, 23.11.1995, p. 31.

(3) Whereas this is the case, in particular, with the introduction of the integrated services digital network (ISDN) and digital mobile networks;

(4) Whereas the Council, in its resolution of 30 June 1988 on the development of the common market for telecommunications services and equipment up to 1992,[5] called for steps to be taken to protect personal data, in order to create an appropriate environment for the future development of telecommunications in the Community; whereas the Council re-emphasized the importance of the protection of personal data and privacy in its resolution of 18 July 1989 on the strengthening of the coordination for the introduction of the integrated services digital network (ISDN) in the European Community up to 1992;[6]

(5) Whereas the European Parliament has underlined the importance of the protection of personal data and privacy in the telecommunications networks, in particular with regard to the introduction of the integrated services digital network (ISDN);

(6) Whereas, in the case of public telecommunications networks, specific legal, regulatory, and technical provisions must be made in order to protect fundamental rights and freedoms of natural persons and legitimate interests of legal persons, in particular with regard to the increasing risk connected with automated storage and processing of data relating to subscribers and users;

(7) Whereas legal, regulatory, and technical provisions adopted by the Member States concerning the protection of personal data, privacy and the legitimate interests of legal persons, in the telecommunications sector, must be harmonized in order to avoid obstacles to the internal market for telecommunications in conformity with the objective set out in Article 8a of the Treaty; whereas the harmonization pursuant to the principle of subsidiary is limited to requirements that are strictly necessary to guarantee that the promotion and development of new telecommunications services and networks between Member States will not be hindered;

(8) Whereas these new services include interactive television and video-on-demand;

(9) Whereas, in the telecommunications sector, in particular for all matters concerning protection of fundamental rights and freedoms, which are not specifically covered by the provisions of this Directive, including the obligations on the controller and the rights of individuals, Directive 95/46/EC applies; whereas Directive 95/46/EC applies to non-publicly available telecommunication services;

(10) Whereas this Directive, similarly to what is provided for by Article 3 of Directive 95/46/EC, does not address issues of protection of fundamental rights and freedoms related to activities which are not governed by Community law; whereas it is for Member States to take such measures as they consider necessary for the protection of public security, defence, State security (including the economic well-being of the State when the activities relate to State security matters) and the enforcement of criminal law; whereas this Directive shall not affect the ability of Member States to carry out lawful interception of telecommunications, for any of these purposes;

---

5 OJ No C 257, 4.10.1988, p. 1.
6 OJ No C 196, 1.8.1989, p. 4.

(11) Whereas subscribers of a publicly available telecommunications service may be natural or legal persons; whereas the provisions of this Directive are aimed to protect, by supplementing Directive 96/46/EC, the fundamental rights of natural persons and particularly their right to privacy, as well as the legitimate interests of legal persons; whereas these provisions may in no case entail an obligation for Member States to extend the application of Directive 95/46/EC to the protection of the legitimate interests of legal persons; whereas this protection is ensured within the framework of the applicable Community and national legislation;

(12) Whereas the application of certain requirements relating to presentation and restriction of calling and connected line identification and to automatic call forwarding to subscriber lines connected to analogue exchanges must not be made mandatory in specific cases where such application would prove to be technically impossible or would require a disproportionate economic effort; whereas it is important for interested parties to be informed of such cases and the Member States should therefore notify them to the Commission;

(13) Whereas service-providers must take appropriate measures to safeguard the security of their services, if necessary in conjunction with the provider of the network, and inform subscribers of any special risks of a breach of the security of the network; whereas security is appraised in the light of the provision of Article 17 of Directive 95/46/EC;

(14) Whereas measures must be taken to prevent the unauthorized access to communications in order to protect the confidentiality of communications by means of public telecommunications networks and publicly available telecommunications services; whereas national legislation in some Member States only prohibits intentional unauthorized access to communications;

(15) Whereas the data relating to subscribers processed to establish calls contain information on the private life of natural persons and concern the right to respect for their correspondence or concern the legitimate interests of legal persons; whereas such data may only be stored to the extent that is necessary for the provision of the service for the purpose of billing and for interconnection payments, and for a limited time; whereas any further processing which the provider of the publicly available telecommunications services may want to perform for the marketing of its own telecommunications services may only be allowed if the subscriber has agreed to this on the basis of accurate and full information given by the provider of the publicly available telecommunications services about the types of further processing he intends to perform;

(16) Whereas the introduction of itemized bills has improved the possibilities for the subscriber to verify the correctness of the fees charged by the service-provider; whereas, at the same time, it may jeopardize the privacy of the users of publicly available telecommunications services; whereas therefore, in order to preserve the privacy of the user, Member States must encourage the development of telecommunications service options such as alternative payment facilities which allow anonymous or strictly private access to publicly available telecommunications services, for example calling cards and facilities for payment by credit card; whereas, alternatively, Member States may, for the same purpose, require the deletion of a certain number of digits from the called numbers mentioned in itemized bills;

(17) Whereas it is necessary, as regards calling line identification, to protect the right of the calling party to withhold the presentation of the identification of the line from which the call is being made and the right of the called party to reject calls from unidentified lines; whereas it is justified to override the elimination of calling line identification presentation in specific cases; whereas certain subscribers, in particular helplines and similar organizations, have an interest in guaranteeing the anonymity of their callers; whereas it is necessary, as regards connected line identification, to protect the right and the legitimate interest of the called party to withhold the presentation of the identification of the line to which the calling party is actually connected, in particular in the case of forwarded calls; whereas the providers of publicly available telecommunications services must inform their subscribers of the existence of calling and connected line identification in the network and of all services which are offered on the basis of calling and connected line identification and about the privacy options which are available; whereas this will allow the subscribers to make an informed choice about the privacy facilities they may want to use; whereas the privacy options which are offered on a per-line basis do not necessarily have to be available as an automatic network service but may be obtainable through a simple request to the provider of the publicy available telecommunications service;

(18) Whereas safeguards must be provided for subscribers against the nuisance which may be caused by automatic call-forwarding by others; whereas, in such cases, it must be possible for subscribers to stop the forwarded calls being passed on to their terminals by simple request to the provider of the publicly available telecommunications service;

(19) Whereas directories are widely distributed and publicly available; whereas the right to privacy of natural persons and the legitimate interest of legal persons require that subscribers are able to determine the extent to which their personal data are published in a directory; whereas Member States may limit this possibility to subscribers who are natural persons;

(20) Whereas safeguards must be provided for subscribers against intrusion into their privacy by means of unsolicited calls and faxes; whereas Member States may limit such safeguards to subscribers who are natural persons;

(21) Whereas it is necessary to ensure that the introduction of technical features of telecommunications equipment for data-protection purposes is harmonized in order to be compatible with the implementation of the internal market;

(22) Whereas in particular, similarly to what is provided for by Article 13 of Directive 95/46/EC, Member States can restrict the scope of subscribers' obligations and rights in certain circumstances, for example by ensuring that the provider of a publicly available telecommunications service may override the elimination of the presentation of calling-line identification in conformity with national legislation for the purpose of prevention or detection of criminal offences or State security;

(23) Whereas where the rights of the users and subscribers are not respected, national legislation must provide for judicial remedy; whereas sanctions must be imposed on any person, whether governed by private or public law, who fails to comply with the national measures taken pursuant to this Directive;

(24) Whereas it is useful in the field of application of this Directive to draw on the experience of the working party on the protection of individuals with regard to the processing of personal data composed of representatives of the supervisory authorities of the Member States, set up by Article 29 of Directive 95/46/EC;

(25) Whereas, given the technological developments and the attendant evolution of the services on offer, it will be necessary technically to specify the categories of data listed in the Annex to this Directive for the application of Article 6 of this Directive with the assistance of the committee composed of representatives of the Member States set up in Article 31 of Directive 95/46/EC in order to ensure a coherent application of the requirements set out in this Directive regardless of changes in technology;

(26) Whereas, to facilitate compliance with the provisions of this Directive, certain specific arrangements are needed for processing of data already under way on the date that national implementing legislation pursuant to this Directive enters into force,

HAVE ADOPTED THIS DIRECTIVE:

Article 1 Object and scope

1. This Directive provides for the harmonization of the provisions of the Member States required to ensure an equivalent level of protection of fundamental rights and freedoms, and in particular the right to privacy, with respect to the processing of personal data in the telecommunications sector and to ensure the free movement of such data and of telecommunications equipment and services in the Community.

2. The provisions of this Directive particularize and complement Directive 95/46/EC for the purposes mentioned in paragraph 1. Moreover, they provide for protection of legitimate interests of subscribers who are legal persons.

3. This Directive shall not apply to the activities which fall outside the scope of Community law, such as those provided for by Titles V and VI of the Treaty on European Union, and in any case to activities concerning public security, defence, State security (including the economic well-being of the State when the activities relate to State security matters) and the activities of the State in areas of criminal law.

Article 2 Definitions

In addition to the definitions given in Directive 95/46/EC, for the purposes of this Directive:

(a) *Subscriber* shall mean any natural or legal person who or which is party to a contract with the provider of publicly available telecommunications services for the supply of such services;

(b) *User* shall mean any natural person using a publicly available telecommunications service, for private or business purposes, without necessarily having subscribed to this service;

(c) *Public telecommunications network* shall mean transmission systems and, where applicable, switching equipment and other resources which permit the conveyance of signals between defined termination points by wire, by radio, by optical or by other electromagnetic means, which are used, in all or in part, for the provision of publicly available telecommunications services;

(d) *Telecommunications service* shall mean services whose provision consists wholly or partly in the transmission and routing of signals on telecommunications networks, with the exception of radio- and television broadcasting.

Article 3 Services concerned

1. This Directive shall apply to the processing of personal data in connection with the provision of publicly available telecommunications services in public telecommunications networks in the Community, in particular via the integrated services digital network (ISDN) and public digital mobile networks.

2. Articles 8, 9 and 10 shall apply to subscriber lines connected to digital exchanges and, where technically possible and if it does not require a disproportionate economic effort, to subscriber lines connected to analogue exchanges.

3. Cases where it would be technically impossible or require a disproportionate investment to fulfil the requirements of Articles 8, 9 and 10 shall be notified to the Commission by the Member States.

Article 4 Security

1. The provider of a publicly available telecommunications service must take appropriate technical and organizational measures to safeguard security of its services, if necessary in conjunction with the provider of the public telecommunications network with respect to network security. Having regard to the state of the art and the cost of their implementation, these measures shall ensure a level of security appropriate to the risk presented.

2. In case of a particular risk of a breach of the security of the network, the provider of a publicly available telecommunications service must inform the subscribers concerning such risk and any possible remedies, including the costs involved.

Article 5 Confidentiality of the communications

Member States shall ensure via national regulations the confidentiality of communications by means of public telecommunications network and publicly available telecommunications services. In particular, they shall prohibit listening, tapping, storage or other kinds of interception or surveillance of communications, by other than users, without the consent of the users concerned, except when legally authorized.

Article 6 Traffic and billing data

1. Traffic data relating to subscribers and users processed to establish calls and stored by the provider of a public telecommunications network and/or publicly available telecommunications service must be erased or made anony-

mous upon termination of the call without prejudice to the provisions of paragraphs 2, 3 and 4.

2.   For the purpose of subscriber billing and interconnection payments, data indicated in the Annex may be processed. Such processing is permissible only up to the end of the period during which the bill may lawfully be challenged or payment may be pursued.

3.   For the purpose of marketing its own telecommunications services, the provider of a publicly available telecommunications service may process the data referred to in paragraph 2, if the subscriber has given his consent.

4.   Processing of traffic and billing data must be restricted to persons acting under the authority of providers of the public telecommunications networks and/or publicly available telecommunications services handling billing or traffic management, customer enquiries, fraud detection and marketing the providers's own telecommunications services and it must be restricted to what is necessary for the purposes of such activities.

5.   Paragraphs 1, 2, 3 and 4 shall apply without prejudice to the possibility for competent authorities to be informed of billing or traffic data in conformity with applicable legislation in view of settling disputes, in particular interconnection or billing disputes.

Article 7   Itemized billing

1.   Subscribers shall have the right to receive non-itemized bills.

2.   Member States shall apply national provisions in order to reconcile the rights of subscribers receiving itemized bills with the right to privacy of calling users and called subscribers, for example by ensuring that sufficient alternative modalities for communications or payments are available to such users and subscribers.

Article 8   Presentation and restriction of calling and connected line identification

1.   Where presentation of calling-line identification is offered, the calling user must have the possibility via a simple means, free of charge, to eliminate the presentation of the calling-line identification on a per-call basis. The calling subscriber must have this possibility on a per-line basis.

2.   Where presentation of calling-line identification is offered, the called subscriber must have the possibility via a simple means, free of charge for reasonable use of this function, to prevent the presentation of the calling-line identification of incoming calls.

3.   Where presentation of calling-line identification is offered and where the calling identification is presented prior to the call being established, the called subscriber must have the possibility via a simple means to reject incoming calls where the presentation of the calling-line identification has been eliminated by the calling user or subscriber.

4.   Where presentation of connected line identification is offered, the called subscriber must have the possibility via a simple means, free of charge, to eliminate the presentation of the connected line identification to the calling user.

5.   The provisions set out in paragraph 1 shall also apply with regard to calls to third countries originating in the Community; the provisions set out

in paragraphs 2, 3 and 4 shall also apply to incoming calls originating in third countries.

6.   Member States shall ensure that where presentation of calling and/or connected line identification is offered, the providers of publicly available telecommunications services inform the public thereof and of the possibilities set out in paragraphs 1, 2, 3 and 4.

Article 9   Exceptions

Member States shall ensure that the provider of a public telecommunications network and/or publicly available telecommunications service may override the elimination of presentation of the calling-line identification:

(a)   on a temporary basis, on application of a subscriber requesting the tracing of malicious or nuisance calls; in this case, in accordance with national law, the data containing the identification of the calling subscriber will be stored and be made available by the provider of a public telecommunications network and/or publicly available telecommunications service;

(b)   on a per-line basis for organizations dealing with emergency calls and recognized as such by a Member State, including law enforcement agencies, ambulance services and fire brigades, for the purpose of answering such calls.

Article 10   Automatic call forwarding

Member States shall ensure that any subscriber is provided, free of charge and via a simple means, with the possibility to stop automatic call-forwarding by a third party to the subscriber's terminal.

Article 11   Directories of subscribers

1.   Personal data contained in printed or electronic directories of subscribers available to the public or obtainable through directory enquiry services should be limited to what is necessary to identify a particular subscriber, unless the subscriber has given his unambiguous consent to the publication of additional personal data. The subscriber shall be entitled, free of charge, to be omitted from a printed or electronic directory at his or her request, to indicate that his or her personal data may not be used for the purpose of direct marketing, to have his or her address omitted in part and not to have a reference revealing his or her sex, where this is applicable linguistically.

2.   Member States may allow operators to require a payment from subscribers wishing to ensure that their particulars are not entered in a directory, provided that the sum involved is reasonable and does not act as a disincentive to the exercise of this right.

3.   Member States may limit the application of this Article to subscribers who are natural persons.

Article 12   Unsolicited calls

1.   The use of automated calling systems without human intervention (automatic calling machine) or facsimile machines (fax) for the purposes of

direct marketing may only be allowed in respect of subscribers who have given their prior consent.

2.   Member States shall take appropriate measures to ensure that, free of charge, unsolicited calls for purposes of direct marketing, by means other than those referred to in paragraph 1, are not allowed either without the consent of the subscribers concerned or in respect of subscribers who do not wish to receive these calls, the choice between these options to be determined by national legislation.

3.   Member States may limit the application of paragraphs 1 and 2 to subscribers who are natural persons.

Article 13   Technical features and standardization

1.   In implementing the provisions of this Directive, Member States shall ensure, subject to paragraphs 2 and 3, that no mandatory requirements for specific technical features are imposed on terminal or other telecommunications equipment which could impede the placing of equipment on the market and the free circulation of such equipment in and between Member States.

2.   Where provisions of this Directive can be implemented only by requiring specific technical features, Member States shall inform the Commission according to the procedures provided for by Directive 83/189/EEC[7] which lays down a procedure for the provision of information in the field of technical standards and regulations.

3.   Where required, the Commission will ensure the drawing-up of common European standards for the implementation of specific technical features, in accordance with Community legislation on the approximation of the laws of the Member States concerning telecommunications terminal equipment, including the mutual recognition of their conformity, and Council Decision 87/95/EEC of 22 December 1986 on standardization in the field of information technology and telecommunications.[8]

Article 14   Extension of the scope of application of certain provisions of Directive 95/46/EC

1.   Member States may adopt legislative measures to restrict the scope of the obligations and rights provided for in Articles 5, 6 and Article 8(1), (2), (3) and (4), when such restriction constitutes a necessary measure to safeguard national security, defence, public security, the prevention, investigation, detection and prosecution of criminal offences or of unauthorized use of the telecommunications system, as referred to in Article 13(1) of Directive 95/46/EC.

2.   The provisions of Chapter III on judicial remedies, liability and sanctions of Directive 95/46/EC shall apply with regard to national provisions adopted pursuant to this Directive and with regard to the individual rights derived from this Directive.

3.   The working party on the protection of individuals with regarding to the processing of personal data established according to Article 29 of

7 OJ No L 109, 26.4.1983, p. 8. Directive as last amended by Directive 94/10/EC (OJ No L 100, 19.4.1994, p. 30).
8 OJ No L 36, 7.2.1987, p. 31. Decision as last amended by the 1994 Act of Accession.

Directive 95/46/EC shall carry out the tasks laid down in Article 30 of the abovementioned Directive also with regard to the protection of fundamental rights and freedoms and of legitimate interests in the telecommunications sector, which is the subject of this Directive.

4. The Commission, assisted by the committee established by Article 31 of Directive 95/46/EC, shall technically specify the Annex according to the procedure mentioned in this Article. The aforesaid committee shall be convened specifically for the subjects covered by this Directive.

Article 15 Implementation of the Directive

1. Member States shall bring into force the laws, regulations and administrative provisions necessary for them to comply with this Directive by 24 October 1998 at the latest.

When Member States adopt these provisions, they shall contain a reference to this Directive or shall be accompanied by such a reference at the time of their official publication. The procedure for such reference shall be adopted by Member States.

2. By derogation from the last sentence of Article 6(3), consent is not required with respect to processing already under way on the date the national provisions adopted pursuant to this Directive enter into force. In those cases the subscribers shall be informed of this processing and if they do not express their dissent within a period to be determined by the Member State, they shall be deemed to have given their consent.

3. Article 11 shall not apply to editions of directories which have been published before the national provisions adopted pursuant to this Directive enter into force.

4. Member States shall communicate to the Commission the text of the provisions of national law which they adopt in the field governed by this Directive.

Article 16 Addresses

This Directive is addressed to the Member States.

Done at . . .

For the European Parliament
The President

For the Council
The President

ANNEX LIST OF DATA

For the purpose referred to in Article 6(2) the following data may be processed: Data containing the:
— number or identification of the subscriber station,
— address of the subscriber and the type of station,
— total number of units to be charged for the accounting period,
— called subscriber number,
— type, start time and duration of the calls made and/or the data volume transmitted,

— other information concerning payments such as advance payment, payments by instalments, disconnection and reminders.

STATEMENT OF THE COUNCIL'S REASONS

I. INTRODUCTION

On 27 July 1990 the Commission submitted a proposal for a Directive, based on Article 100a of the EC Treaty, concerning the protection of personal data and privacy in the context of digital telecommunications networks, in particular the integrated services digital network (ISDN) and public digital mobile networks.

The Economic and Social Committee delivered its opinion on 24 April 1991. The European Parliament delivered its opinion on 11 March 1992.

After re-examining its proposal in the light of those opinions, the Commission submitted an amended proposal to the European Parliament and the Council.

The Council adopted its common position in accordance with Article 189b of the Treaty on 12 September 1996.

II. AIM OF THE PROPOSAL

The proposal sets out to apply for the specific purposes of telecommunications networks the general data protection principles laid down by Directive 95/46/EC of the European Parliament and of the Council of 24 October 1995. It is accordingly designed, in a constantly changing field, to prevent Member States' legislation from developing along different lines in ways that might jeopardize the single market in telecommunications services and terminal equipment, while ensuring a high level of protection of the rights of individuals, in particular their right to privacy.

III. ASSESSMENT OF THE COMMON POSITION

1. General comments

The common position adopted by the Council provides confirmation of the approach followed by the Commission in its amended proposal and of the Commission's objectives, even though the Council has been prompted to make some changes to the detailed provisions of that proposal.

In making such amendments, the Council was generally concerned to:

— align the provisions of this Directive on those of the general Directive (particularly as regards the scope, Articles 1 and 14),

— ensure that they are consistent with the Community rules already adopted or in preparation in the telecommunications sector (e.g. the definitions in Article 2),

— clarify the scope of some provisions or make them more flexible.

2. Specific comments

(i) With regard to the European Parliament's amendments, the Council took the following line:

— *Amendment 96, first part (private networks and services)*
Article 3 of the common position stipulates that the Directive applies to publicly available telecommunications services provided in public telecommunications networks. However, that Article is to be construed as allowing a Member State to apply its provisions to non-public or non-publicly available networks and services, with the proviso that Directive 95/46/EC in any case applies to the processing of personal data in the context of such networks and services.

— *Amendment 97 (development of technologies)*
The Council went along with the Commission, which did not include in its amended proposal the new recital 21(a) proposed by the European Parliament.

— *Amendments 96 second part (value-added services), 98 (special or exclusive rights), 107 and 108 (service-providers other than telecommunications organizations)*
These amendments could not be accepted as they were no longer consistent with the legal situation brought about by the new Community rules governing the telecommunications sector.

— *Amendment 99*
The definition of a telecommunications service given in this amendment has been included in Article 2(d).

— *Amendment 100 (directories of subscribers)*
The content of this amendment has mainly been included in Article 11 of the common position.

However, under that provision, the principle that the right to be omitted from the directory is applicable free of charge may be departed from, subject to certain conditions. Article 11(2) stipulates that Member States may allow operators to require a payment from subscribers for exercising that right, provided that the sum involved is reasonable and does not act as a discentive to the exercise of the right.

It should be noted that this paragraph is to be construed as reflecting the provision agreed on the same subject matter by the Council of Europe in its recommendation No R(95)4 of 7 February 1995.

— *Amendment 101 (electronic profiles of subscribers)*
The Council took the same line as the Commission in not including Article 4 of the original proposal, to which the amendment related. However, it believes that the protection sought by the European Parliament is in any event ensured, in general terms by Directive 95/46/EC and in the specific case of traffic and billing data by Article 6 of the common position, in particular paragraph 3.

— *Amendment 102 (protection of the contents of information transmitted)*
The Council took the same line as the Commission in not including Article 5 of the original proposal, to which the amendment related (see the following point for traffic and billing data).

— *Amendments 103 and 104 (traffic and billing data)*
The points about which the European Parliament was concerned have been accommodated in the various paragraphs of Article 6 of the common position.

The provision put forward by the Commission in its amended proposal with regard to traffic data is included in Article 6(1). (The Council has also followed the Commission in not including the provision corresponding to Article 10(1) of the original proposal — the subject of amendment 103 — which is already taken into account in the general Directive).

The provisions on billing data (Article 9 of the original proposal, Article 5 of the amended proposal) have been included in Article 6(2), with an exhaustive list of data which may be processed for the purpose of subscriber billing now being given in an annex to the Directive, in the interests of ensuring a high level of protection.

Under Article 14(4) of the common position, that list, which is the same as the one proposed by the Commission and endorsed by the European Parliament, may only be technically specified by the Committee established by Article 31 of Directive 95/46/EC (see Article 14(4)). This provision is to be construed as in no way allowing the substance of the Annex and of Article 6 to be changed, for example by adding or deleting categories of data, and as merely permitting the list of data to be particularized on account of changes in technology. Substantial amendments calling into question data protection may therefore be introduced only under the procedure laid down in Article 100a of the Treaty.

All data other than those listed in that Annex to the common position, moreover, should be regarded as having to be processed in accordance with the principles in Directive 95/46/EC, especially Article 16 of it.

Article 6(4) of the common position contains provisions on restriction of access to traffic and billing data that accommodate the concern expressed by the European Parliament in amendment 103.

— *Amendment 105 (automatic call-forwarding)*
This amendment is to a large extent taken into account in Article 10 of the common position, which enjoins Member States to ensure that any subscriber is provided, free of charge and via a simple means, with the possibility to stop automatic call-forwarding by a third party to the subscriber's terminal.

— *Amendment 106 (teleshopping service)*
The provisions contained in Article 16 of the original proposal have been omitted from the common position, as the European Parliament wished.

(ii)   The other main changes made in the common position are as follows:
— *Article 3:*
the Directive applies to services provided via digital and analogue networks. However, the provisions of Article 8, 9 (presentation of line identification) and 10 (automatic call-forwarding) are applicable to subscriber lines connected to analogue exchanges only where technically possible and if this does not require a disproportionate economic effort (paragraphs 2 and 3).

— *Article 4 (security)*
This Article corresponds to Article 8 of the original proposal.

The Article is to be understood as follows:
— the provisions of paragraph 1 are designed to establish a level of processing security consistent with that advocated by Article 17 of Directive 95/46/EC,

— as regards the provisions of paragraph 2, where, in spite of the security measures taken, there is still a particular risk of a breach of the security of the network, the provider of a telecommunications service, where appropriate together with the provider of the public telecommunications network, is in addition required to inform individuals of that risk and of possible remedies.

— *Article 5 (confidentiality of communications)*

The provisions on confidentiality of communications (Article 12 of the Commission proposal) have been redrafted more concisely and placed at the start of the enacting terms, after the provisions on security, in order to highlight the importance to be attached to that principle.

— *Article 7 (itemized billing)*

The Council has opted for a wording which reconciles the right of subscribers to be able to check the correctness of their bills with the right to the protection of privacy; recital 16 also stipulates that Member States may, in order to protect users' privacy more effectively, opt to require the deletion of a number of digits from the called number mentioned in itemized bills.

— *Article 8 (presentation of calling and connected line identification)*

The provisions in the amended Commission proposal with regard to calling-line identification have been redrafted so as not to be dependent upon any particular technology or terminal equipment and provisions on the connected line identification service have also been added.

With specific reference to the possibility, under paragraph 3, of rejecting a call from a user who has eliminated the presentation of identification of his line, it should be noted that this provision does not prevent Member States from prohibiting government agencies, public utilities and emergency services from rejecting calls where the presentation of the calling-line identification has been eliminated by the calling user or subscriber.

— *Article 12 (unsolicited calls)*

The provisions of this Article have been redrafted so as to tally with Article 10 of the common provision for the Directive on distance selling.

— *Article 13 of the amended proposal (technical application and modification)*

This Article has been deleted and technical adaptation is now confined to the Annex, under the procedure laid down in Article 31 of Directive 95/46/EC (see the comments above on Parliament's amendments 103 and 104).

— *Article 14(3) (working party on the protection of individuals)*

The Council, supported by the Commission, considers that the working party, set up under Article 29 of Directive 95/46/EC, which also has a role to play in the implementation of this Directive, could for the purposes of the Directive usefully draw on the expertise of the national regulatory authorities for telecommunications by where appropriate inviting representatives of those authorities to its meeting as experts.

— *Article 15 (implementation of the Directive)*

For transposition of the Directive into national law in the Member States, the Council has opted for the same time limit as for the general Directive, with a deadline of 24 October 1998.

Notes

1. See European Parliament and Council Directive (95/46/EC) on the protection of individuals with regard to the processing of personal data and on the free movement of such data (OJ No. L 281/31, 23 November 95).

2. See also the Council of Europe Recommendation No.R (95) 4 of the Committee of Ministers to Member States 'on the protection of personal data in the area of telecommunication services, with particular reference to telephone services'.

PART III
INTERNATIONAL LAW

INTRODUCTION

'Telecommunications is becoming the world's biggest economic sector, growing faster than anything else, being the real engine for growth in almost all economies . . . telecommunications is the key to development in all sectors . . .'
Pekka Tarjanne, Secretary-General, ITU, Africa Telecom 94

Although the focus of this book is clearly in UK and European law, wider international developments should not be ignored. Such developments can be sub-divided into two general categories:

(a)   regulatory initiatives undertaken in other countries;
(b)   and the regulatory activities of supra-national organisations.

Under the former category, a broad distinction can be made between regulatory activities based around the *liberalisation* of the telecommunications market, which chronologically can be seen as commencing in the US with the break-up of AT&T in 1982; and a second trend which concerns the *privatisation* of traditionally state-owned operating entities, which can be seen as emanating from the UK's experience.

A further differing perspective can be identified between those other industrialised countries, e.g. the US and New Zealand, where some form of liberalisation in the telecommunications sector has occurred, or is taking place; and the perspective of developing countries. Developing countries increasingly see the telecommunications sector as a key infrastructure component contributing towards general economic growth. In terms of facilitating trade-in-services, links into international telecommunication networks are seen as being critical to the integration of such countries into the global economy.

Within all countries, the changing regulatory environment can be seen to reflect a number of different and overlapping policy objectives, from the raising of government revenue to infrastructure modernisation. In this section, United States legislation has been included as a case study. As a pioneer of telecommunications liberalisation, the Communications Act of 1934 and Telecommunications Act of 1996 provide benchmarks of regulatory initiatives in this area. The 1934 Act established the first independent, quasi-judicial regulatory authority for the sector, the Federal Communications Commission. While the 1996 Act addresses many of the regulatory themes that are currently facing national legislators, such as universal service, convergence and control of content.

International telecommunications is governed primarily under the auspices of the International Telecommunications Union (ITU), which is a part of the United Nations system.[1] The regulatory role of the ITU is limited to the technical *means* of telecommunications, such as communication protocols and interconnection standards;[2] although message content can be an issue in certain areas, such as message security and authentication. The ITU operates in accordance with the International Telecommunications Convention.[3]

Over recent years, the telecommunications market has fallen within the scope of international free trade negotiations. The 1994 General Agreement on Tariffs and Trade was extended to cover services and within that a special annex on telecommunications was agreed and is reproduced in this section. Further major negotiations on basic telecommunication issues have recently resulted in an agreement between 68 countries under the auspices of the World Trade Organisation.

---

1 The International Telecommunications Union can be found at: http://www.itu.ch/.
2 The European Court of Justice was required to consider the status of ITU Recommendations in *Italy* v *Commission, re: British Telecommunications* (OJ L360, 21.12.82; [1985] ECR 873), with respect to the activities of private message-forwarding agencies. The Court held that a PTO could not legitimise an abuse of a dominant position (illegal under Article 86 of the Treaty of Rome) through reliance on an ITU recommendation.
3 The most recent revision was adopted in Geneva 1992.

INTERNATIONAL

URUGUAY ROUND GENERAL AGREEMENT ON TRADE IN SERVICES (GATS), ANNEX ON TELECOMMUNICATIONS

ANNEX ON TELECOMMUNICATIONS

1. Objectives

1.1 Recognizing the specificities of the telecommunications services sector and, in particular, its dual role as a distinct sector of economic activity and as the underlying transport means for other economic activities, the Members have agreed to the following Annex with the objective of elaborating upon the provisions of the Agreement with respect to measures affecting access to and use of public telecommunications transport networks and services. Accordingly, this Annex provides notes and supplementary provisions to the Agreement.

2. Scope

2.1 This Annex shall apply to all measures of a Member that affect access to and use of public telecommunications transport networks and services.[15]

2.2 This Annex shall not apply to measures affecting the cable or broadcast distribution of radio or television programming.

2.3 Nothing in this Annex shall be construed:

2.3.1 to require a Member to authorize a service supplier of any other Member to establish, construct, acquire, lease, operate, or supply telecommunications transport networks or services, other than as provided for in its schedule; or

2.3.2 to require a Member (or to require a Member to oblige service suppliers under its jurisdiction) to establish, construct, acquire, lease, operate or supply telecommunications transport networks or services not offered to the public generally.

3. Definitions

For the purposes of this Annex:

3.1 Telecommunications means the transmission and reception of signals by any electromagnetic means.

3.2 Public telecommunications transport service means any telecommunications transport service required, explicitly or in effect, by a Member to be offered to the public generally. Such services may include, inter alia, telegraph, telephone, telex, and data transmission typically involving the real-time transmission of customer-supplied information between two or more points without any end-to-end change in the form or content of the customer's information.

3.3 Public telecommunications transport network means the public telecommunications infrastructure which permits telecommunications between and among defined network termination points.

3.4 Intra-corporate communications means telecommunications through which a company communicates within the company or with or among its subsidiaries, branches and, subject to a Member's domestic laws and regulations, affiliates. For these purposes, 'subsidiaries', 'branches' and, where applicable, 'affiliates' shall be as defined by each Party Member. 'Intra-corporate communications' in this Annex excludes commercial or non-commercial services that are supplied to companies that are not related subsidiaries, branches or affiliates, or that are offered to customers or potential customers.

3.5 Any reference to a paragraph or subparagraph of this Annex includes all subdivisions thereof.

4. Transparency

4.1 In the application of Article III of the Agreement, each Member shall ensure that relevant information on conditions affecting access to and use of public telecommunications transport networks and services is publicly available, including: tariffs and other terms and conditions of service; specifications of technical interfaces with such networks and services; information on bodies responsible for the preparation and adoption of standards affecting such access and use; conditions applying to attachment of terminal or other equipment; and notifications, registration or licensing requirements, if any.

5. Access to and use of Public Telecommunications Transport Networks and Services

5.1 Each Member shall ensure that any service supplier of any other Member is accorded access to and use of public telecommunications transport networks and services on reasonable and non-discriminatory terms and conditions, for the supply of a service included in its schedule. This obligation shall be applied, inter alia, through paragraphs 5.2 through 5.6 below.[16]

5.2 Each Member shall ensure that service suppliers of any other Member have access to and use of any public telecommunications transport network or service offered within or across the border of that Member, including private leased circuits, and to this end shall ensure, subject to paragraphs 5.5 and 5.6, that such suppliers are permitted:

5.2.1 to purchase or lease and attach terminal or other equipment which interfaces with the network and which is necessary to supply a supplier's services;

5.2.2 to interconnect private leased or owned circuits with public telecommunications transport networks and services or with circuits leased or owned by another service supplier; and

5.2.3   to use operating protocols of the service supplier's choice in the supply of any service, other than as necessary to ensure the availability of telecommunications transport networks and services to the public generally.

5.3   Each Member shall ensure that service suppliers of any other Member may use public telecommunications transport networks and services for the movement of information within and across borders, including for intra-corporate communications of such service suppliers, and for access to information contained in data bases or otherwise stored in machine-readable form in the territory of any Member. Any new or amended measures of a Member significantly affecting such use shall be notified and shall be subject to consultation, in accordance with relevant provisions of the Agreement.

5.4   Notwithstanding the preceding paragraph, a Member may take such measures as are necessary to ensure the security and confidentiality of messages, subject to the requirement that such measures are not applied in a manner which would constitute a means of arbitrary or unjustifiable discrimi-nation or a disguised restriction on trade in services.

5.5   Each Member shall ensure that no condition is imposed on access to and use of public telecommunications transport networks and services other than as necessary:

5.5.1   to safeguard the public service responsibilities of suppliers of public telecommunications transport networks and services, in particular their ability to make their networks or services available to the public generally;

5.5.2   to protect the technical integrity of public telecommunications transport networks or services; or

5.5.3   to ensure that service suppliers of any other Member do not supply services unless permitted pursuant to commitments in a Member's schedule.

5.6   Provided that they satisfy the criteria set out in paragraph 5.5, conditions for access to and use of public telecommunications transport networks and services may include:

5.6.1   restrictions on resale or shared use of such services;

5.6.2   a requirement to use specified technical interfaces, including interface protocols, for inter-connection with such networks and services;

5.6.3   requirements, where necessary, for the inter-operability of such services and to encourage the achievement of the goals set out in paragraph 7.1;

5.6.4   type approval of terminal or other equipment which interfaces with the network and technical requirements relating to the attachment of such equipment to such networks;

5.6.5   restrictions on inter-connection of private leased or owned cir-cuits with such networks or services or with circuits leased or owned by another service supplier; or

5.6.6   notification, registration and licensing.

5.7   Notwithstanding the preceding paragraphs of this section, a develop-ing Member may, consistent with its level of development, place reasonable conditions on access to and use of public telecommunications transport networks and services necessary to strengthen its domestic telecommunica-tions infrastructure and service capacity and to increase its participation in international trade in telecommunications services. Such conditions shall be specified in the Member's schedule.

6. Technical Co-operation

6.1 Members recognize that an efficient, advanced telecommunications infrastructure in countries, particularly developing countries, is essential to the expansion of their trade in services. To this end, Members endorse and encourage the participation, to the fullest extent practicable, of developed and developing countries and their suppliers of public telecommunications transport networks and services and other entities in the development programmes of international and regional organizations, including the International Telecommunication Union, the United Nations Development Programme, and the International Bank for Reconstruction and Development.

6.2 Members shall encourage and support telecommunications co-operation among developing countries at the international, regional and subregional levels.

6.3 In co-operation with relevant international organizations, Members shall make available, where practicable, to developing countries information with respect to telecommunications services and developments in telecommunications and information technology to assist in strengthening their domestic telecommunications services sector.

6.4 Members shall give special consideration to opportunities for the least developed countries to encourage foreign suppliers of telecommunications services to assist in the transfer of technology, training and other activities that support the development of their telecommunications infrastructure and expansion of their telecommunications services trade.

7. Relation to International Organizations and Agreements

7.1 Members recognize the importance of international standards for global compatibility and inter-operability of telecommunication networks and services and undertake to promote such standards through the work of relevant international bodies, including the International Telecommunication Union and the International Organization for Standardization.

7.2 Members recognize the role played by intergovernmental and nongovernmental organizations and agreements in ensuring the efficient operation of domestic and global telecommunications services, in particular the International Telecommunication Union. Members shall make appropriate arrangements, where relevant, for consultation with such organizations on matters arising from the implementation of this Annex.

Notes

1. The World Trade Organisation can be found at: http://www.wto.org/
2. Compliance with the Annex will be monitored by a telecommunications committee operating within the World Trade Organisation (WTO) structure. Members will also be able to make use of the dispute settlement procedure established under Annex 2 of the Marrakesh Agreement, which established the WTO.
3. The WTO currently has a Negotiating Group on Basic Telecommunications (NGBT) considering the policitally more contentious issues of basic service provision. The NGBT negotiations were originally scheduled to complete their work in April 1996. Failure to reach agreement meant that the process was extended to February 1997.

UNITED STATES

COMMUNICATIONS ACT OF 1934, 47 U.S.C. 151 (EXTRACTS)

AN ACT To provide for the regulation of interstate and foreign communication by wire or radio, and for other purposes.

Be it enacted by the Senate and House of Representatives of the United States of America in Congress assembled,

TITLE I   GENERAL PROVISIONS

Section 1   Purposes of Act, creation of Federal Communications Commission

[47 U.S.C. 151]   For the purpose of regulating interstate an foreign commerce in communication by wire and radio so as to make available, so far as possible, to all the people of the United States a rapid, efficient, Nation-wide, and world-wide wire and radio communication service with adequate facilities at reasonable charges, for the purpose of the national defense, for the purpose of promoting safety of life and property through the use of wire and radio communication,[1] and for the purpose of securing a more effective execution of this policy by centralizing authority heretofore granted by law to several agencies and by granting additional authority with respect to interstate and foreign commerce in wire and radio communication, there is hereby created a commission to be known as the 'Federal Communications Commission,' which shall be constituted as hereinafter provided, and which shall execute and enforce the provisions of this Act.[2]

---

1 The provision relating to the promotion of safety of life and property was added by 'An Act to amend the Communications Act of 1934, etc.' Public Law 97, 75th Congress, approved and effective May 20, 1937, 50 Stat. 189.

2 Section 202 of Public Law 97-259, 96 Stat. 1087, 1099, Sept. 13, 1982, provides:

(a)   The National Telecommunications and Information Administration shall conduct a comprehensive study of the long-range international telecommunications and information goals of the United States, the specific international telecommunications and information policies necessary to promote those goals and the strategies that will ensure that the United States achieves them. The Administration shall further conduct a review of the structures, procedures, and mechanisms which are utilized by the United States to develop international telecommunications and information policy.

(b)   In any study or review conducted pursuant to this section, the National Telecommunications and Information Administration shall not make public information regarding usage or traffic patterns which would damage United States commercial interests. Any such study or review shall be limited to international telecommunications policies or to domestic telecommunications issues which *directly* affect such policies.

TITLE II   COMMON CARRIERS

Sec. 201   Service and charges

[47 U.S.C. 201]   (a)   It shall be the duty of every common carrier engaged in interstate or foreign communication by wire or radio to furnish such communication service upon reasonable request therefor; and, in accordance with the orders of the Commission, in cases where the Commission, after opportunity for hearing, finds such action necessary or desirable in the public interest, to establish physical connections with other carriers, to establish through routes and charges applicable thereto and the divisions of such charges, and to establish and provide facilities and regulations for operating such through routes.

(b)   All charges, practices, classifications, and regulations for and in connection with such communication service, shall be just and reasonable, and any such charge, practice, classification, or regulation that is unjust or unreasonable is hereby declared to be unlawful: *Provided,* That communications by wire or radio subject to this Act may be classified into day, night, repeated, unrepeated, letter, commercial, press, Government[45B] and such other classes as the Commission may decide to be just and reasonable, and different charges may be made for the different classes of communications: *Provided further,* That nothing in this Act or in any other provision of law shall be construed to prevent a common carrier subject to this Act from entering into or operating under any contract with any common carrier not subject to this Act, for the exchange of their services, if the Commission is of the opinion that such contract is not contrary to the public interest: *Provided further,* That nothing in this Act or in any other provision of law shall prevent a common carrier subject to this Act from furnishing reports of positions of ships at sea to newspapers of general circulation, either at a nominal charge or without charge, provided the name of such common carrier is displayed along with such ship position reports. The Commissioner may prescribe such rules and regulations as may be necessary in the public interest to carry out the provisions of this Act.[46]

45B Section 5266 of the Revised Statutes, as amended (U.S.C. 1940 edition title 47, sec. 3), concerning telegrams between several departments of the Government, their priority and rates, was amended by Public No. 4, 78th Congress, 1st Session, approved March 6, 1943, 57 Stat. 12, and repealed effective July 26, 1947 by Public Law 193, 80th Congress, 1st Session, 61 Stat. 327 sec. 2, Public Law 193 provided as follows:

SEC. 2. Nothing in this Act shall limit the authority of the Federal Communications Commission under the provisions of the Communications Act of 1934, as amended, to prescribe charges, classifications, regulations and practices, including priorities, applicable to Government communications.

Public Law 48, 80th Congress, 1st Session, May 13, 1947, 61 Stat. 83, provides 'That nothing in the Communications Act of 1934, as amended, or any other provision of Law shall be construed to prohibit United States common carriers from rendering free communication services to official participants in the world telecommunication conferences to be held in the United States in 1947 subject to such rules and regulations as the Federal Communications Commission may prescribe.'

46 This proviso was added by an Act 'To amend the Act approved June 19, 1934, entitled the Communication Act of 1934' Public Law 561, 75th Congress, approved May 31, 1938, 52 Stat. 555.

Sec. 202   Discrimination and preferences

[47 U.S.C. 202]   (a)   It shall be unlawful for any common carrier to make any unjust or unreasonable discrimination in charges, practices, classifications, regulations, facilities, or services for or in connection with like communication service, directly or indirectly, by any means or device, or to make or give any undue or unreasonable preference or advantage to any particular person, class of persons, or locality, or to subject any particular person, class of persons, or locality to any undue or unreasonable prejudice or disadvantage.

(b)   Charges or services, whenever referred to in this Act, include charges for, or services in connection with, the use of common carrier lines of communication, whether derived from wire or radio facilities, in chain broadcasting or incidental to radio communication of any kind.[47]

(c)   Any carrier who knowingly violates the provisions of this section shall forfeit to the United States the sum of $500 for each such offense and $25 for each and every day of the continuance of such offense.

Sec. 203   Schedules of charges

[47 U.S.C. 203]   (a)   Every common carrier, except connecting carriers, shall, within such reasonable time as the Commission shall designate, file with the Commission and print and keep open for public inspection schedules showing all charges for itself and its connecting carriers for interstate and foreign wire or radio communication between the different points on its own system, and between points on its own system and points on the system of its connecting carriers or points on the system of any other carrier subject to this Act when a through route has been established, whether such charges are joint or separate, and showing the classifications, practices, and regulations affecting such charges. Such schedules shall contain such other information, and be printed in such form, and be posted and kept open for public inspection in such places, as the Commission may by regulation require, and each such schedule shall give notice of its effective date; and such common carrier shall furnish such schedules to each of its connecting carriers, and such connecting carriers shall keep such schedules open for inspection in such public places as the Commission may require.

Sec. 207   Recovery of damages

[47 U.S.C 207]   Any person claiming to be damaged by any common carrier subject to the provisions of this Act may either make complaint to the Commission as hereinafter provided for, or may bring suit for the recovery of the damages for which such common carrier may be liable under the provisions of this Act, in any district court of the United States of competent jurisdiction; but such person shall not have the right to pursue both such remedies.

---

47 Section 202(b) was amended to read as above by Public Law 86–751, approved September 13, 1950 74 Stat. 888. It formerly read as follows:

(b)   Charges or or services, whenever referred to in this Act, include charges for, or services in connection with, the use of of wires in chain broadcasting or incidental to radio communication of any kind.

Sec. 208   Complaints to the Commission

[47 U.S.C 208]   (a)   Any person, any body politic or municipal organiz-ation, or State commission, complaining of anything done or omitted to be done by any common carrier subject to this Act, in contravention of the provisions thereof, may apply to said Commission by petition which shall briefly state the facts, whereupon a statement of the complaint thus made shall be forwarded by the Commission to such common carrier, who shall be called upon to satisfy the complaint or to answer the same in writing within a reasonable time to be specified by the Commission. If such common carrier within the time specified shall make reparation for the injury alleged to have been caused, the common carrier shall be relieved of liability to the complain-ant only for the particular violation of law thus complained of. If such carrier or carriers shall not satisfy the complaint within the time specified or there shall appear to be any reasonable ground for investigating said complaint, it shall be the duty of the Commission to investigate the matters complained of in such manner and by such means as it shall deem proper. No complaint shall at any time be dismissed because of the absence of direct damage to the complainant.

. . .

(h)   Nothing in this section shall impair or diminish the powers of any State commission.

Sec. 214   Extension of lines

[47 U.S.C. 214]   (a)   No carrier shall undertake the construction of a new line or of an extension of any line, or shall acquire or operate any line, or extension thereof, or shall engage in transmission over or by means of such additional or extended line, unless and until there shall first have been obtained from the Commission a certificate that the present or future public convenience and necessity require or will require the construction, or oper-ation, or construction and operation, of such additional or extended line: *Provided,* That no such certificate shall be required under this section for the construction, acquisition, or operation of (1) a line within a single State unless such line constitutes part of an interstate line, (2) local, branch, or terminal lines not exceeding ten miles in length, or (3) any line acquired under section 221 or 222 of this Act: *Provided further,* That the Commission may, upon appropriate request being made, authorize temporary or emerg-ency service, or the supplementing of existing facilities, without regard to the provisions of this section. No carrier shall discontinue, reduce or impair service to a community, or part of a community, unless and until there shall first have been obtained from the Commission a certificate that neither the present nor future public convenience and necessity will be adversely affected thereby; except that the Commission may, upon appropriate request being made, authorize temporary or emergency discontinuance, reduction, or impairment of service, or partial discontinuance, reduction, or impairment of service, without regard to the provisions of this section. As used in this section the term 'line' means any channel of communication established by the use of appropriate equipment, other than a channel of communication estab-lished by the interconnection of two or more existing channels: *Provided, however,* That nothing in this section shall be construed to require a certificate or other authorization from the Commission for any installation, replacement, or other changes in plant, operation, or equipment, other than new construction, which will not impair the adequacy or quality of service provided.

(b)   Upon receipt of an application for any such certificate, the Commission shall cause notice thereof to be given to, and shall cause a copy of such application to be filed with, the Secretary of Defense,[52] the Secretary of State (with respect to such applications involving service to foreign points), and the Governor of each State in which such line is proposed to be constructed, extended, acquired, or operated, or in which such discontinuance, reduction, or impairment of service is proposed, with the right to those notified to be heard; and the Commission may require such published notice as it shall determine.

(c)   The Commission shall have power to issue such certificate as applied for, to refuse to issue it, or to issue it for a portion or portions of a line, or extension thereof, or discontinuance, reduction or impairment of service, described in the application, or for the partial exercise only of such right or privilege, and may attach to the issuance of the certificate such terms and conditions as in its judgment the public convenience and necessity may require. After issuance of such certificate, and not before, the carrier may, without securing approval other than such certificate, comply with the terms and conditions contained in or attached to the issuance of such certificate and proceed with the construction, extension, acquisition, operation, or discontinuance, reduction, or impairment of service covered thereby. Any construction, extension, acquisition, operation, discontinuance, reduction, or impairment of service contrary to the provisions of this section may be enjoined by any court of competent jurisdiction at the suit of the United States, the Commission, the State commission, any State affected, or any party in interest.

(d)   The Commission may, after full opportunity for hearing, in a proceeding upon complaint or upon its own initiative without complaint, authorize or require by order any carrier, party to such proceeding, to provide itself with adequate facilities for the expeditious and efficient performance of its service as a common carrier and to extend its line or to establish a public office; but no such authorization or order shall be made unless the Commission finds, as to such provision of facilities, as to such establishment of public offices, or as to such extension, that it is reasonably required in the interest of public convenience and necessity, or as to such extension or facilities that the expense involved therein will not impair the ability of the carrier to perform its duty to the public. Any carrier which refuses or neglects to comply with any order of the Commission made in pursuance of this paragraph shall forfeit to the United States $100 for each day during which such refusal or neglect continues.[53]

---

52 The words *'the Secretary of the Army, the Secretary of the Navy'* were changed to *'the Secretary of Defense,'* in Subsections 214(b) and 222(c)(1), and *'the Secretary of State'* in Subsection 214(b) by Public Law 93-506, approved November 30, 1974, 88 Stat. 1577. Previously, the Department of War was designated the Department of the Army and the title of the Secretary of War changed to Secretary of the Army by Public Law 80-253, approved July 26, 1947, 61 Stat. 501.
53 Paragraphs (a), (b), (c), and (d) of Section 214 were amended to read as above by Public

Sec. 218   Inquiries into management

[47 U.S.C. 218]   The Commission may inquire into the management of the business of all carriers subject to this Act, and shall keep itself informed as to the manner and method in which the same is conducted and as to technical developments and improvements in wire and radio communication and radio transmission of energy to the end that the benefits of new inventions and developments may be made available to the people of the United States. The Commission may obtain from such carriers and from persons directly or indirectly controlling or controlled by, or under direct or indirect common control with, such carriers full and complete information necessary to enable the Commission to perform the duties and carry out the objects for which it was created.

Sec. 219   Annual and other reports

[47 U S.C. 219]   (a)   The Commission is authorized to require annual reports[54] from all carriers subject to this Act, and from persons directly or indirectly controlling or controlled by, or under direct or indirect common

---

Law 4, 78th Congress, 1st Sess., approved March 6, 1943, 57 Stat. 11, 12. Formerly, they read as follows:

SEC. 214.   (a)   No carrier shall undertake the construction of a new line or of an extension of any line, or shall acquire or operate any line, or extension thereof, or shall engage in transmission over or by means of such additional or extended line, unless and until there shall first have been obtained from the Commission a certificate that the present or future public convenience and necessity require or will require the construction or operation, or construction and operation, of such additional or extended line: Provided, That no such certificate shall be required under this section for the construction, acquisition, operation, or extension of (1) a line within a single State unless said line constitutes part of an interstate line, (2) local branch, or terminal lines not exceeding ten miles in length, or (3) any lines acquired under section 221 of this Act: Provided further, That the Commission may upon appropriate request being made, authorize temporary or emergency service, or the supplementing of existing facilities, without regard to the provisions of this section.

(b)   Upon receipt of an application for any such certificate the Commission shall cause notice thereof to be given to and a copy filed with the Governor of each State in which such additional or extended line is proposed to be constructed or operated, with the right to be heard as provided with respect to the hearing of complaints; and the Commission may require such published notice as it shall determine.

(c)   The Commission shall have power to issue such certificate as preyed for, or to refuse it, or to issue it for a portion or portions of a line, or extension thereof, described in the application, or for the partial exercise only of such right or privilege, and may attach to the issuance of the certificate such terms and conditions as in its judgment the public convenience and necessity may require. After issuance of such certificate, and not before, the carrier may, without securing approval other than such certificate, comply with the terms and conditions contained in or attached to the issuance of such certificate and proceed with the construction, acquisition, operation, or extension covered thereby. Any construction, acquisition, operation, or extension contrary to the provisions of this section may be enjoined by any court of competent jurisdiction at the suit of the United States, the Commission, the State commission, any State affected, or any party in interest.

(d)   The Commission may, after full opportunity for hearing, in a proceeding upon complaint or upon its own initiative without complaint, authorize or require by order any carrier, party to such proceeding, to provide itself with adequate facilities for performing its service as a common carrier and to extend its line; but no such authorization or order shall be made unless the Commission finds, as to such extension, that it is reasonably required in the interest of public convenience and necessity, or as to such extension or facilities that the expense involved therein will not impair the ability of the carrier to perform its duty to the public. Any carrier which refuses or neglects to comply with any order of the Commission mode in pursuance of this paragraph shall forfeit to the United States $100 for each each day during which such refusal or neglect continues.

54 Subsection (a) was amended by Public Law 87-444, approved April 27, 1962, 76 Stat. 63, by deleting the words under oath from the first sentence.

control with, any such carrier, to prescribe the manner in which such reports shall be made, and to require from such persons specific answers to all questions upon which the Commission may need information. Except as otherwise required by the Commission,[55] such annual reports shall show in detail the amount of capital stock issued, the amount and privileges of each class of stock, the amounts paid therefor, and the manner of payment for the same; the dividends paid and the surplus fund, if any; the number of stockholders (and the names of the thirty largest holders of each class of stock and the amount held by each); the funded and floating debts and the interest paid thereon; the cost and value of the carrier's property, franchises, and equipment; the number of employees and the salaries paid each class; the names of all officers and directors, and the amount of salary, bonus, and all other compensation paid to each; the amounts expended for improvements each year, how expended, and the character of such improvements; the earnings and receipts from each branch of business and from all sources; the operating and other expenses; the balances of profit and loss; and a complete exhibit of the financial operations of the carrier each year, including an annual balance sheet. Such reports shall also contain such information in relation to charges or regulations concerning charges, or agreements, arrangements, or contracts affecting the same, as the Commission may require.

Notes
1. The Federal Communications Commission can be found at: http://www.fcc.gov/
2. See also the decision breaking up AT&T: *United States* v *American Telephone and Telegraph Co.* 552 F.Supp 131 (1982).

TELECOMMUNICATIONS ACT OF 1996, PUB. L. No. 104-104, 110 STAT. 56 (1996) (EXTRACTS)

SECTION 1   SHORT TITLE; REFERENCES

(a)   Short Title. — This Act may be cited as the 'Telecommunications Act of 1996'.

(b)   References. — Except as otherwise expressly provided, whenever in this Act an amendment or repeal is expressed in terms of an amendment to, or repeal of, a section or other provision, the reference shall be considered to be made to a section or other provision of the Communications Act of 1934 (47 U.S.C. 151 et seq.).

SEC. 2   TABLE OF CONTENTS

The table of contents for this Act is as follows:
Sec. 1.   Short title; references.
Sec. 2.   Table of contents.
Sec. 3.   Definitions.

---

55 Subsection (a) was amended by Public No. 914, 84th Congress, 2d Sess., Aug. 2, 1956, 70 Stat. 931, by addition of the words 'Except as otherwise required by the Commission.'

SEC. 3   DEFINITIONS

(a)   Additional Definitions. — Section 3 (47 U.S.C. 153) is amended—
   (1)   in subsection (r)—
     (A)   by inserting '(A)' after 'means'; and
     (B)   by inserting before the period at the end the following: ', or (B) comparable service provided through a system of switches, transmission equipment, or other facilities (or combination thereof) by which a subscriber can originate and terminate a telecommunications service'; and
   (2)   by adding at the end thereof the following:
     '(33)   Affiliate. — The term "affiliate" means a person that (directly or indirectly) owns or controls, is owned or controlled by, or is under common ownership or control with, another person. For purposes of this paragraph, the term "own" means to own an equity interest (or the equivalent thereof) of more than 10 percent.
     (34)   AT&T consent decree. — The term "AT&T Consent Decree" means the order entered August 24, 1982, in the antitrust action styled United States v. Western Electric, Civil Action No. 82 0192, in the United States District Court for the District of Columbia, and includes any judgment or order with respect to such action entered on or after August 24, 1982.
     (35)   Bell operating company. — The term "Bell operating company"—
     (A)   means any of the following companies: Bell Telephone Company of Nevada, Illinois Bell Telephone Company, Indiana Bell Telephone Company, Incorporated, Michigan Bell Telephone Company, New England Telephone and Telegraph Company, New Jersey Bell Telephone Company, New York Telephone Company, U S West Com-

munications Company, South Central Bell Telephone Company, Southern Bell Telephone and Telegraph Company, Southwestern Bell Telephone Company, The Bell Telephone Company of Pennsylvania, The Chesapeake and Potomac Telephone Company, The Chesapeake and Potomac Telephone Company of Maryland, The Chesapeake and Potomac Telephone Company of Virginia, The Chesapeake and Potomac Telephone Company of West Virginia, The Diamond State Telephone Company, The Ohio Bell Telephone Company, The Pacific Telephone and Telegraph Company, or Wisconsin Telephone Company; and

(B) includes any successor or assign of any such company that provides wireline telephone exchange service; but

(C) does not include an affiliate of any such company, other than an affiliate described in subparagraph (A) or (B).

(36) Cable service. — The term "cable service" has the meaning given such term in section 602.

(37) Cable system. — The term "cable system" has the meaning given such term in section 602.

(38) Customer premises equipment. — The term "customer premises equipment" means equipment employed on the premises of a person (other than a carrier) to originate, route, or terminate telecommunications.

(39) Dialing parity. — The term "dialing parity" means that a person that is not an affiliate of a local exchange carrier is able to provide telecommunications services in such a manner that customers have the ability to route automatically, without the use of any access code, their telecommunications to the telecommunications services provider of the customer's designation from among two or more telecommunications services providers (including such local exchange carrier).

(40) Exchange access. — The term "exchange access" means the offering of access to telephone exchange services or facilities for the purpose of the origination or termination of telephone toll services.

(41) Information service. — The term "information service" means the offering of a capability for generating, acquiring, storing, transforming, processing, retrieving, utilizing, or making available information via telecommunications, and includes electronic publishing, but does not include any use of any such capability for the management, control, or operation of a telecommunications system or the management of a telecommunications service.

(42) Interlata service. — The term "interLATA service" means telecommunications between a point located in a local access and transport area and a point located outside such area.

(43) Local access and transport area. — The term "local access and transport area" or "LATA" means a contiguous geographic area—

(A) established before the date of enactment of the Telecommunications Act of 1996 by a Bell operating company such that no exchange area includes points within more than one metropolitan statistical area, consolidated metropolitan statistical area, or State, except as expressly permitted under the AT&T Consent Decree; or

(B) established or modified by a Bell operating company after such date of enactment and approved by the Commission.

(44)   Local exchange carrier. — The term "local exchange carrier" means any person that is engaged in the provision of telephone exchange service or exchange access. Such term does not include a person insofar as such person is engaged in the provision of a commercial mobile service under section 332(c), except to the extent that the Commission finds that such service should be included in the definition of such term.

(45)   Network element. — The term "network element" means a facility or equipment used in the provision of a telecommunications service. Such term also includes features, functions, and capabilities that are provided by means of such facility or equipment, including subscriber numbers, databases, signaling systems, and information sufficient for billing and collection or used in the transmission, routing, or other provision of a telecommunications service.

(46)   Number portability. — The term "number portability" means the ability of users of telecommunications services to retain, at the same location, existing telecommunications numbers without impairment of quality, reliability, or convenience when switching from one telecommunications carrier to another.

(47)   Rural telephone company. — The term "rural telephone company" means a local exchange carrier operating entity to the extent that such entity—

(A)   provides common carrier service to any local exchange carrier study area that does not include either—

(i)   any incorporated place of 10,000 inhabitants or more, or any part thereof, based on the most recently available population statistics of the Bureau of the Census; or

(ii)   any territory, incorporated or unincorporated, included in an urbanized area, as defined by the Bureau of the Census as of August 10, 1993;

(B)   provides telephone exchange service, including exchange access, to fewer than 50,000 access lines;

(C)   provides telephone exchange service to any local exchange carrier study area with fewer than 100,000 access lines; or

(D)   has less than 15 percent of its access lines in communities of more than 50,000 on the date of enactment of the Telecommunications Act of 1996.

(48)   Telecommunications. — The term "telecommunications" means the transmission, between or among points specified by the user, of information of the user's choosing, without change in the form or content of the information as sent and received.

(49)   Telecommunications carrier. — The term "telecommunications carrier" means any provider of telecommunications services, except that such term does not include aggregators of telecommunications services (as defined in section 226). A telecommunications carrier shall be treated as a common carrier under this Act only to the extent that it is engaged in providing telecommunications services, except that the Commission shall determine whether the provision of fixed and mobile satellite service shall be treated as common carriage.

(50)   Telecommunications equipment. — The term "telecommunications equipment" means equipment, other than customer

premises equipment, used by a carrier to provide telecommunications services, and includes software integral to such equipment (including upgrades).

(51) Telecommunications service. — The term "telecommunications service" means the offering of telecommunications for a fee directly to the public, or to such classes of users as to be effectively available directly to the public, regardless of the facilities used.'.

(b) Common Terminology. — Except as otherwise provided in this Act, the terms used in this Act have the meanings provided in section 3 of the Communications Act of 1934 (47 U.S.C. 153), as amended by this section.

(c) Stylistic Consistency. — Section 3 (47 U.S.C. 153) is amended—

(1) in subsections (e) and (n), by redesignating clauses (1), (2) and (3), as clauses (A), (B), and (C), respectively;

(2) in subsection (w), by redesignating paragraphs (1) through (5) as subparagraphs (A) through (E), respectively;

(3) in subsections (y) and (z), by redesignating paragraphs (1) and (2) as subparagraphs (A) and (B), respectively;

(4) by redesignating subsections (a) through (ff) as paragraphs (1) through (32);

(5) by indenting such paragraphs 2 em spaces;

(6) by inserting after the designation of each such paragraph—

(A) a heading, in a form consistent with the form of the heading of this subsection, consisting of the term defined by such paragraph, or the first term so defined if such paragraph defines more than one term; and

(B) the words 'The term;'

(7) by changing the first letter of each defined term in such paragraphs from a capital to a lower case letter (except for 'United States', 'State', 'State commission', and 'Great Lakes Agreement'); and

(8) by reordering such paragraphs and the additional paragraphs added by subsection (a) in alphabetical order based on the headings of such paragraphs and renumbering such paragraphs as so reordered.

(d) Conforming Amendments. — The Act is amended—

(1) in section 225(a)(1), by striking 'section 3(h)' and inserting 'section 3';

(2) in section 332(d), by striking 'section 3(n)' each place it appears and inserting 'section 3'; and

(3) in sections 621(d)(3), 636(d), and 637(a)(2), by striking 'section 3(v)' and inserting 'section 3'.

TITLE I TELECOMMUNICATION SERVICES
Subtitle A Telecommunications Services

Sec. 101 Establishment of Part II of Title II

(a) Amendment. — Title II is amended by inserting after section 229 (47 U.S.C. 229) the following new part:
'PART II DEVELOPMENT OF COMPETITIVE MARKETS

Sec. 251 Interconnection

(a) General Duty of Telecommunications Carriers. — Each telecommunications carrier has the duty—

(1)   to interconnect directly or indirectly with the facilities and equipment of other telecommunications carriers; and

(2)   not to install network features, functions, or capabilities that do not comply with the guidelines and standards established pursuant to section 255 or 256.

(b)   Obligations of All Local Exchange Carriers. — Each local exchange carrier has the following duties:

(1)   Resale. — The duty not to prohibit, and not to impose unreasonable or discriminatory conditions or limitations on, the resale of its telecommunications services.

(2)   Number portability. — The duty to provide, to the extent technically feasible, number portability in accordance with requirements prescribed by the Commission.

(3)   Dialing parity. — The duty to provide dialing parity to competing providers of telephone exchange service and telephone toll service, and the duty to permit all such providers to have nondiscriminatory access to telephone numbers, operator services, directory assistance, and directory listing, with no unreasonable dialing delays.

(4)   Access to rights-of-way. — The duty to afford access to the poles, ducts, conduits, and rights-of-way of such carrier to competing providers of telecommunications services on rates, terms, and conditions that are consistent with section 224.

(5)   Reciprocal compensation. — The duty to establish reciprocal compensation arrangements for the transport and termination of telecommunications.

(c)   Additional Obligations of Incumbent Local Exchange Carriers. — In addition to the duties contained in subsection (b), each incumbent local exchange carrier has the following duties:

(1)   Duty to negotiate. — The duty to negotiate in good faith in accordance with section 252 the particular terms and conditions of agreements to fulfill the duties described in paragraphs (1) through (5) of subsection (b) and this subsection. The requesting telecommunications carrier also has the duty to negotiate in good faith the terms and conditions of such agreements.

(2)   Interconnection. — The duty to provide, for the facilities and equipment of any requesting telecommunications carrier, interconnection with the local exchange carrier's network—

(A)   for the transmission and routing of telephone exchange service and exchange access;

(B)   at any technically feasible point within the carrier's network;

(C)   that is at least equal in quality to that provided by the local exchange carrier to itself or to any subsidiary, affiliate, or any other party to which the carrier provides interconnection; and

(D)   on rates, terms, and conditions that are just, reasonable, and nondiscriminatory, in accordance with the terms and conditions of the agreement and the requirements of this section and section 252.

(3)   Unbundled access. — The duty to provide, to any requesting telecommunications carrier for the provision of a telecommunications service, nondiscriminatory access to network elements on an unbundled basis at any technically feasible point on rates, terms, and conditions that

are just, reasonable, and nondiscriminatory in accordance with the terms and conditions of the agreement and the requirements of this section and section 252. An incumbent local exchange carrier shall provide such unbundled network elements in a manner that allows requesting carriers to combine such elements in order to provide such telecommunications service.

(4) Resale. — The duty—

(A) to offer for resale at wholesale rates any telecommunications service that the carrier provides at retail to subscribers who are not telecommunications carriers; and

(B) not to prohibit, and not to impose unreasonable or discriminatory conditions or limitations on, the resale of such telecommunications service, except that a State commission may, consistent with regulations prescribed by the Commission under this section, prohibit a reseller that obtains at wholesale rates a telecommunications service that is available at retail only to a category of subscribers from offering such service to a different category of subscribers.

(5) Notice of changes. — The duty to provide reasonable public notice of changes in the information necessary for the transmission and routing of services using that local exchange carrier's facilities or networks, as well as of any other changes that would affect the interoperability of those facilities and networks.

(6) Collocation. — The duty to provide, on rates, terms, and conditions that are just, reasonable, and nondiscriminatory, for physical collocation of equipment necessary for interconnection or access to unbundled network elements at the premises of the local exchange carrier, except that the carrier may provide for virtual collocation if the local exchange carrier demonstrates to the State commission that physical collocation is not practical for technical reasons or because of space limitations.

(d) Implementation.—

(1) In general. — Within 6 months after the date of enactment of the Telecommunications Act of 1996, the Commission shall complete all actions necessary to establish regulations to implement the requirements of this section.

(2) Access standards. — In determining what network elements should be made available for purposes of subsection (c)(3), the Commission shall consider, at a minimum, whether—

(A) access to such network elements as are proprietary in nature is necessary; and

(B) the failure to provide access to such network elements would impair the ability of the telecommunications carrier seeking access to provide the services that it seeks to offer.

(3) Preservation of state access regulations. — In prescribing and enforcing regulations to implement the requirements of this section, the Commission shall not preclude the enforcement of any regulation, order, or policy of a State commission that—

(A) establishes access and interconnection obligations of local exchange carriers;

(B) is consistent with the requirements of this section; and

(C) does not substantially prevent implementation of the requirements of this section and the purposes of this part.

(e) Numbering Administration.—

(1) Commission authority and jurisdiction. — The Commission shall create or designate one or more impartial entities to administer telecommunications numbering and to make such numbers available on an equitable basis. The Commission shall have exclusive jurisdiction over those portions of the North American Numbering Plan that pertain to the United States. Nothing in this paragraph shall preclude the Commission from delegating to State commissions or other entities all or any portion of such jurisdiction.

(2) Costs. — The cost of establishing telecommunications numbering administration arrangements and number portability shall be borne by all telecommunications carriers on a competitively neutral basis as determined by the Commission.

(f) Exemptions, Suspensions, and Modifications.—

(1) Exemption for certain rural telephone companies.—

(A) Exemption. — Subsection (c) of this section shall not apply to a rural telephone company until (i) such company has received a bona fide request for interconnection, services, or network elements, and (ii) the State commission determines (under subparagraph (B)) that such request is not unduly economically burdensome, is technically feasible, and is consistent with section 254 (other than subsections (b)(7) and (c)(1)(D) thereof).

(B) State termination of exemption and implementation schedule. — The party making a bona fide request of a rural telephone company for interconnection, services, or network elements shall submit a notice of its request to the State commission. The State commission shall conduct an inquiry for the purpose of determining whether to terminate the exemption under subparagraph (A). Within 120 days after the State commission receives notice of the request, the State commission shall terminate the exemption if the request is not unduly economically burdensome, is technically feasible, and is consistent with section 254 (other than subsections (b)(7) and (c)(1)(D) thereof). Upon termination of the exemption, a State commission shall establish an implementation schedule for compliance with the request that is consistent in time and manner with Commission regulations.

(C) Limitation on exemption. — The exemption provided by this paragraph shall not apply with respect to a request under subsection (c) from a cable operator providing video programming, and seeking to provide any telecommunications service, in the area in which the rural telephone company provides video programming. The limitation contained in this subparagraph shall not apply to a rural telephone company that is providing video programming on the date of enactment of the Telecommunications Act of 1996.

(2) Suspensions and modifications for rural carriers. — A local exchange carrier with fewer than 2 percent of the Nation's subscriber lines installed in the aggregate nationwide may petition a State commission for a suspension or modification of the application of a requirement or requirements of subsection (b) or (c) to telephone exchange service

facilities specified in such petition. The State commission shall grant such petition to the extent that, and for such duration as, the State commission determines that such suspension or modification—

(A)   is necessary—

(i)   to avoid a significant adverse economic impact on users of telecommunications services generally;

(ii)   to avoid imposing a requirement that is unduly economically burdensome; or

(iii)   to avoid imposing a requirement that is technically infeasible; and

(B)   is consistent with the public interest, convenience, and necessity.

The State commission shall act upon any petition filed under this paragraph within 180 days after receiving such petition. Pending such action, the State commission may suspend enforcement of the requirement or requirements to which the petition applies with respect to the petitioning carrier or carriers.

(g)   Continued Enforcement of Exchange Access and Interconnection Requirements. — On and after the date of enactment of the Telecommunications Act of 1996, each local exchange carrier, to the extent that it provides wireline services, shall provide exchange access, information access, and exchange services for such access to interexchange carriers and information service providers in accordance with the same equal access and nondiscriminatory interconnection restrictions and obligations (including receipt of compensation) that apply to such carrier on the date immediately preceding the date of enactment of the Telecommunications Act of 1996 under any court order, consent decree, or regulation, order, or policy of the Commission, until such restrictions and obligations are explicitly superseded by regulations prescribed by the Commission after such date of enactment. During the period beginning on such date of enactment and until such restrictions and obligations are so superseded, such restrictions and obligations shall be enforceable in the same manner as regulations of the Commission.

(h)   Definition of Incumbent Local Exchange Carrier.—

(1)   Definition. — For purposes of this section, the term "incumbent local exchange carrier" means, with respect to an area, the local exchange carrier that—

(A)   on the date of enactment of the Telecommunications Act of 1996, provided telephone exchange service in such area; and

(B)(i)   on such date of enactment, was deemed to be a member of the exchange carrier association pursuant to section 69.601(b) of the Commission's regulations (47 C.F.R. 69.601(b)); or

(ii)   is a person or entity that, on or after such date of enactment, became a successor or assign of a member described in clause (i).

(2)   Treatment of comparable carriers as incumbents. — The Commission may, by rule, provide for the treatment of a local exchange carrier (or class or category thereof) as an incumbent local exchange carrier for purposes of this section if—

(A)   such carrier occupies a position in the market for telephone exchange service within an area that is comparable to the position occupied by a carrier described in paragraph (1);

(B)   such carrier has substantially replaced an incumbent local exchange carrier described in paragraph (1); and

(C)   such treatment is consistent with the public interest, convenience, and necessity and the purposes of this section.

(i)   Savings Provision. — Nothing in this section shall be construed to limit or otherwise affect the Commission's authority under section 201.

Sec. 252   Procedures for Negotiation, Arbitration, and Approval of Agreements

(a)   Agreements Arrived at Through Negotiation.—

(1)   Voluntary negotiations. — Upon receiving a request for interconnection, services, or network elements pursuant to section 251, an incumbent local exchange carrier may negotiate and enter into a binding agreement with the requesting telecommunications carrier or carriers without regard to the standards set forth in subsections (b) and (c) of section 251. The agreement shall include a detailed schedule of itemized charges for interconnection and each service or network element included in the agreement. The agreement, including any interconnection agreement negotiated before the date of enactment of the Telecommunications Act of 1996, shall be submitted to the State commission under subsection (e) of this section.

(2)   Mediation. — Any party negotiating an agreement under this section may, at any point in the negotiation, ask a State commission to participate in the negotiation and to mediate any differences arising in the course of the negotiation.

(b)   Agreements Arrived at Through Compulsory Arbitration.—

(1)   arbitration. — During the period from the 135th to the 160th day (inclusive) after the date on which an incumbent local exchange carrier receives a request for negotiation under this section, the carrier or any other party to the negotiation may petition a State commission to arbitrate any open issues.

(2)   Duty of petitioner.—

(A)   A party that petitions a State commission under paragraph (1) shall, at the same time as it submits the petition, provide the State commission all relevant documentation concerning—

(i)   the unresolved issues;

(ii)   the position of each of the parties with respect to those issues; and

(iii)   any other issue discussed and resolved by the parties.

(B)   A party petitioning a State commission under paragraph (1) shall provide a copy of the petition and any documentation to the other party or parties not later than the day on which the State commission receives the petition.

(3)   Opportunity to respond. — A non-petitioning party to a negotiation under this section may respond to the other party's petition

and provide such additional information as it wishes within 25 days after the State commission receives the petition.

(4) Action by state commission.—

(A) The State commission shall limit its consideration of any petition under paragraph (1) (and any response thereto) to the issues set forth in the petition and in the response, if any, filed under paragraph (3).

(B) The State commission may require the petitioning party and the responding party to provide such information as may be necessary for the State commission to reach a decision on the unresolved issues. If any party refuses or fails unreasonably to respond on a timely basis to any reasonable request from the State commission, then the State commission may proceed on the basis of the best information available to it from whatever source derived.

(C) The State commission shall resolve each issue set forth in the petition and the response, if any, by imposing appropriate conditions as required to implement subsection (c) upon the parties to the agreement, and shall conclude the resolution of any unresolved issues not later than 9 months after the date on which the local exchange carrier received the request under this section.

(5) Refusal to negotiate. — The refusal of any other party to the negotiation to participate further in the negotiations, to cooperate with the State commission in carrying out its function as an arbitrator, or to continue to negotiate in good faith in the presence, or with the assistance, of the State commission shall be considered a failure to negotiate in good faith.

(c) Standards for Arbitration. — In resolving by arbitration under subsection (b) any open issues and imposing conditions upon the parties to the agreement, a State commission shall—

(1) ensure that such resolution and conditions meet the requirements of section 251, including the regulations prescribed by the Commission pursuant to section 251;

(2) establish any rates for interconnection, services, or network elements according to subsection (d); and

(3) provide a schedule for implementation of the terms and conditions by the parties to the agreement.

(d) Pricing Standards.—

(1) Interconnection and network element charges. — Determinations by a State commission of the just and reasonable rate for the interconnection of facilities and equipment for purposes of subsection (c)(2) of section 251, and the just and reasonable rate for network elements for purposes of subsection (c)(3) of such section—

(A) shall be—

(i) based on the cost (determined without reference to a rate-of-return or other rate-based proceeding) of providing the interconnection network element (whichever is applicable), and

(ii) nondiscriminatory, and

(B) may include a reasonable profit.

(2) Charges for transport and termination of traffic.—

(A) In general. — For the purposes of compliance by an incumbent local exchange carrier with section 251(b)(5), a State commission shall not consider the terms and conditions for reciprocal compensation to be just and reasonable unless—

(i) such terms and conditions provide for the mutual and reciprocal recovery by each carrier of costs associated with the transport and termination on each carrier's network facilities of calls that originate on the network facilities of the other carrier; and

(ii) such terms and conditions determine such costs on the basis of a reasonable approximation of the additional costs of terminating such calls.

(B) Rules of construction. — This paragraph shall not be construed—

(i) to preclude arrangements that afford the mutual recovery of costs through the offsetting of reciprocal obligations, including arrangements that waive mutual recovery (such as bill-and-keep arrangements); or

(ii) to authorize the Commission or any State commission to engage in any rate regulation proceeding to establish with particularity the additional costs of transporting or terminating calls, or to require carriers to maintain records with respect to the additional costs of such calls.

(3) Wholesale prices for telecommunications services. — For the purposes of section 251(c)(4), a State commission shall determine wholesale rates on the basis of retail rates charged to subscribers for the telecommunications service requested, excluding the portion thereof attributable to any marketing, billing, collection, and other costs that will be avoided by the local exchange carrier.

(e) Approval by State Commission.—

(1) Approval required. — Any interconnection agreement adopted by negotiation or arbitration shall be submitted for approval to the State commission. A State commission to which an agreement is submitted shall approve or reject the agreement, with written findings as to any deficiencies.

(2) Grounds for rejection. — The State commission may only reject—

(A) an agreement (or any portion thereof) adopted by negotiation under subsection (a) if it finds that—

(i) the agreement (or portion thereof) discriminates against a telecommunications carrier not a party to the agreement; or

(ii) the implementation of such agreement or portion is not consistent with the public interest, convenience, and necessity; or

(B) an agreement (or any portion thereof) adopted by arbitration under subsection (b) if it finds that the agreement does not meet the requirements of section 251, including the regulations prescribed by the Commission pursuant to section 251, or the standards set forth in subsection (d) of this section.

(3) Preservation of authority. — Notwithstanding paragraph (2), but subject to section 253, nothing in this section shall prohibit a State commission from establishing or enforcing other requirements of State law in its review of an agreement, including requiring compliance with intrastate telecommunications service quality standards or requirements.

(4)   Schedule for decision. — If the State commission does not act to approve or reject the agreement within 90 days after submission by the parties of an agreement adopted by negotiation under subsection (a), or within 30 days after submission by the parties of an agreement adopted by arbitration under subsection (b), the agreement shall be deemed approved. No State court shall have jurisdiction to review the action of a State commission in approving or rejecting an agreement under this section.

(5)   Commission to act if state will not act. — If a State commission fails to act to carry out its responsibility under this section in any proceeding or other matter under this section, then the Commission shall issue an order preempting the State commission's jurisdiction of that proceeding or matter within 90 days after being notified (or taking notice) of such failure, and shall assume the responsibility of the State commission under this section with respect to the proceeding or matter and act for the State commission.

(6)   Review of state commission actions. — In a case in which a State fails to act as described in paragraph (5), the proceeding by the Commission under such paragraph and any judicial review of the Commission's actions shall be the exclusive remedies for a State commission's failure to act. In any case in which a State commission makes a determination under this section, any party aggrieved by such determination may bring an action in an appropriate Federal district court to determine whether the agreement or statement meets the requirements of section 251 and this section.

(f)   Statements of Generally Available Terms.—

(1)   In general. — A Bell operating company may prepare and file with a State commission a statement of the terms and conditions that such company generally offers within that State to comply with the requirements of section 251 and the regulations thereunder and the standards applicable under this section.

(2)   State commission review. — A State commission may not approve such statement unless such statement complies with subsection (d) of this section and section 251 and the regulations thereunder. Except as provided in section 253, nothing in this section shall prohibit a State commission from establishing or enforcing other requirements of State law in its review of such statement, including requiring compliance with intrastate telecommunications service quality standards or requirements.

(3)   Schedule for review. — The State commission to which a statement is submitted shall, not later than 60 days after the date of such submission—

(A)   complete the review of such statement under paragraph (2) (including any reconsideration thereof), unless the submitting carrier agrees to an extension of the period for such review; or

(B)   permit such statement to take effect.

(4)   Authority to continue review. — Paragraph (3) shall not preclude the State commission from continuing to review a statement that has been permitted to take effect under subparagraph (B) of such paragraph or from approving or disapproving such statement under paragraph (2).

(5) Duty to negotiate not affected. — The submission or approval of a statement under this subsection shall not relieve a Bell operating company of its duty to negotiate the terms and conditions of an agreement under section 251.

(g) Consolidation of State Proceedings. — Where not inconsistent with the requirements of this Act, a State commission may, to the extent practical, consolidate proceedings under sections 214(e), 251(f), 253, and this section in order to reduce administrative burdens on telecommunications carriers, other parties to the proceedings, and the State commission in carrying out its responsibilities under this Act.

(h) Filing Required. — A State commission shall make a copy of each agreement approved under subsection (e) and each statement approved under subsection (f) available for public inspection and copying within 10 days after the agreement or statement is approved. The State commission may charge a reasonable and nondiscriminatory fee to the parties to the agreement or to the party filing the statement to cover the costs of approving and filing such agreement or statement.

(i) Availability to Other Telecommunications Carriers. — A local exchange carrier shall make available any interconnection, service, or network element provided under an agreement approved under this section to which it is a party to any other requesting telecommunications carrier upon the same terms and conditions as those provided in the agreement.

(j) Definition of Incumbent Local Exchange Carrier. — For purposes of this section, the term "incumbent local exchange carrier" has the meaning provided in section 251(h).

Sec. 253 Removal of Barriers to Entry

(a) In General. — No State or local statute or regulation, or other State or local legal requirement, may prohibit or have the effect of prohibiting the ability of any entity to provide any interstate or intrastate telecommunications service.

(b) State Regulatory Authority. — Nothing in this section shall affect the ability of a State to impose, on a competitively neutral basis and consistent with section 254, requirements necessary to preserve and advance universal service, protect the public safety and welfare, ensure the continued quality of telecommunications services, and safeguard the rights of consumers.

(c) State and Local Government Authority. — Nothing in this section affects the authority of a State or local government to manage the public rights-of-way or to require fair and reasonable compensation from telecommunications providers, on a competitively neutral and nondiscriminatory basis, for use of public rights-of-way on a nondiscriminatory basis, if the compensation required is publicly disclosed by such government.

(d) Preemption. — If, after notice and an opportunity for public comment, the Commission determines that a State or local government has permitted or imposed any statute, regulation, or legal requirement that violates subsection (a) or (b), the Commission shall preempt the enforcement of such statute, regulation, or legal requirement to the extent necessary to correct such violation or inconsistency.

(e)   Commercial mobile service providers. — Nothing in this section shall affect the application of section 332(c)(3) to commercial mobile service providers.

(f)   Rural Markets. — It shall not be a violation of this section for a State to require a telecommunications carrier that seeks to provide telephone exchange service or exchange access in a service area served by a rural telephone company to meet the requirements in section 214(e)(1) for designation as an eligible telecommunications carrier for that area before being permitted to provide such service. This subsection shall not apply—

(1)   to a service area served by a rural telephone company that has obtained an exemption, suspension, or modification of section 251(c)(4) that effectively prevents a competitor from meeting the requirements of section 214(e)(1); and

(2)   to a provider of commercial mobile services.

Sec. 254   Universal Service

(a)   Procedures to Review Universal Service Requirements.—

(1)   Federal-state joint board on universal service. — Within one month after the date of enactment of the Telecommunications Act of 1996, the Commission shall institute and refer to a Federal-State Joint Board under section 410(c) a proceeding to recommend changes to any of its regulations in order to implement sections 214(e) and this section, including the definition of the services that are supported by Federal universal service support mechanisms and a specific timetable for completion of such recommendations. In addition to the members of the Joint Board required under section 410(c), one member of such Joint Board shall be a State-appointed utility consumer advocate nominatèd by a national organization of State utility consumer advocates. The Joint Board shall, after notice and opportunity for public comment, make its recommendations to the Commission 9 months after the date of enactment of the Telecommunications Act of 1996.

(2)   Commission action. — The Commission shall initiate a single proceeding to implement the recommendations from the Joint Board required by paragraph (1) and shall complete such proceeding within 15 months after the date of enactment of the Telecommunications Act of 1996. The rules established by such proceeding shall include a definition of the services that are supported by Federal universal service support mechanisms and a specific timetable for implementation. Thereafter, the Commission shall complete any proceeding to implement subsequent recommendations from any Joint Board on universal service within one year after receiving such recommendations.

(b)   Universal Service Principles. — The Joint Board and the Commission shall base policies for the preservation and advancement of universal service on the following principles:

(1)   Quality and rates. — Quality services should be available at just, reasonable, and affordable rates.

(2) Access to advanced services. — Access to advanced telecommunications and information services should be provided in all regions of the Nation.

(3) Access in rural and high cost areas. — Consumers in all regions of the Nation, including low-income consumers and those in rural, insular, and high cost areas, should have access to telecommunications and information services, including interexchange services and advanced telecommunications and information services, that are reasonably comparable to those services provided in urban areas and that are available at rates that are reasonably comparable to rates charged for similar services in urban areas.

(4) Equitable and nondiscriminatory contributions. — All providers of telecommunications services should make an equitable and nondiscriminatory contribution to the preservation and advancement of universal service.

(5) Specific and predictable support mechanisms. — There should be specific, predictable and sufficient Federal and State mechanisms to preserve and advance universal service.

(6) Access to advanced telecommunications services for schools, health care, and libraries. — Elementary and secondary schools and classrooms, health care providers, and libraries should have access to advanced telecommunications services as described in subsection (h).

(7) Additional principles. — Such other principles as the Joint Board and the Commission determine are necessary and appropriate for the protection of the public interest, convenience, and necessity and are consistent with this Act.

(c) Definition.—

(1) In general. — Universal service is an evolving level of telecommunications services that the Commission shall establish periodically under this section, taking into account advances in telecommunications and information technologies and services. The Joint Board in recommending, and the Commission in establishing, the definition of the services that are supported by Federal universal service support mechanisms shall consider the extent to which such telecommunications services—

(A) are essential to education, public health, or public safety;

(B) have, through the operation of market choices by customers, been subscribed to by a substantial majority of residential customers;

(C) are being deployed in public telecommunications networks by telecommunications carriers; and

(D) are consistent with the public interest, convenience, and necessity.

(2) Alterations and modifications. — The Joint Board may, from time to time, recommend to the Commission modifications in the definition of the services that are supported by Federal universal service support mechanisms.

(3) Special services. — In addition to the services included in the definition of universal service under paragraph (1), the Commission may designate additional services for such support mechanisms for schools, libraries, and health care providers for the purposes of subsection (h).

(d)   Telecommunications Carrier Contribution. — Every telecommunications carrier that provides interstate telecommunications services shall contribute, on an equitable and nondiscriminatory basis, to the specific, predictable, and sufficient mechanisms established by the Commission to preserve and advance universal service. The Commission may exempt a carrier or class of carriers from this requirement if the carrier's telecommunications activities are limited to such an extent that the level of such carrier's contribution to the preservation and advancement of universal service would be de minimis. Any other provider of interstate telecommunications may be required to contribute to the preservation and advancement of universal service if the public interest so requires.

(e)   Universal Service Support. — After the date on which Commission regulations implementing this section take effect, only an eligible telecommunications carrier designated under section 214(e) shall be eligible to receive specific Federal universal service support. A carrier that receives such support shall use that support only for the provision, maintenance, and upgrading of facilities and services for which the support is intended. Any such support should be explicit and sufficient to achieve the purposes of this section.

(f)   State Authority. — A State may adopt regulations not inconsistent with the Commission's rules to preserve and advance universal service. Every telecommunications carrier that provides intrastate telecommunications services shall contribute, on an equitable and nondiscriminatory basis, in a manner determined by the State to the preservation and advancement of universal service in that State. A State may adopt regulations to provide for additional definitions and standards to preserve and advance universal service within that State only to the extent that such regulations adopt additional specific, predictable, and sufficient mechanisms to support such definitions or standards that do not rely on or burden Federal universal service support mechanisms.

(g)   Interexchange and Interstate Services. — Within 6 months after the date of enactment of the Telecommunications Act of 1996, the Commission shall adopt rules to require that the rates charged by providers of interexchange telecommunications services to subscribers in rural and high cost areas shall be no higher than the rates charged by each such provider to its subscribers in urban areas. Such rules shall also require that a provider of interstate interexchange telecommunications services shall provide such services to its subscribers in each State at rates no higher than the rates charged to its subscribers in any other State.

(h)   Telecommunications Services for Certain Providers.—

(1)   In general.—

(A)   Health care providers for rural areas. — A telecommunications carrier shall, upon receiving a bona fide request, provide telecommunications services which are necessary for the provision of health care services in a State, including instruction relating to such services, to any public or nonprofit health care provider that serves persons who reside in rural areas in that State at rates that are reasonably comparable to rates charged for similar services in urban areas in that State. A telecommunications carrier providing service under this paragraph shall be entitled to have an amount equal to the difference, if any, between the rates for services provided to health care providers for rural areas in a State and the rates for similar services provided to other customers in comparable rural areas in that State treated as a service obligation as a part of its obligation to participate in the mechanisms to preserve and advance universal service.

(B) Educational providers and libraries. — All telecommunications carriers serving a geographic area shall, upon a bona fide request for any of its services that are within the definition of universal service under subsection (c)(3), provide such services to elementary schools, secondary schools, and libraries for educational purposes at rates less than the amounts charged for similar services to other parties. The discount shall be an amount that the Commission, with respect to interstate services, and the States, with respect to intrastate services, determine is appropriate and necessary to ensure affordable access to and use of such services by such entities. A telecommunications carrier providing service under this paragraph shall—

(i) have an amount equal to the amount of the discount treated as an offset to its obligation to contribute to the mechanisms to preserve and advance universal service, or

(ii) notwithstanding the provisions of subsection (e) of this section, receive reimbursement utilizing the support mechanisms to preserve and advance universal service.

(2) Advanced services. — The Commission shall establish competitively neutral rules—

(A) to enhance, to the extent technically feasible and economically reasonable, access to advanced telecommunications and information services for all public and nonprofit elementary and secondary school classrooms, health care providers, and libraries; and

(B) to define the circumstances under which a telecommunications carrier may be required to connect its network to such public institutional telecommunications users.

(3) Terms and conditions. — Telecommunications services and network capacity provided to a public institutional telecommunications user under this subsection may not be sold, resold, or otherwise transferred by such user in consideration for money or any other thing of value.

(4) Eligibility of users. — No entity listed in this subsection shall be entitled to preferential rates or treatment as required by this subsection, if such entity operates as a for-profit business, is a school described in paragraph (5)(A) with an endowment of more than $50,000,000, or is a library not eligible for participation in State-based plans for funds under title III of the Library Services and Construction Act (20 U.S.C. 335c et seq.).

(5) Definitions. — For purposes of this subsection:

(A) Elementary and secondary schools. — The term "elementary and secondary schools" means elementary schools and secondary schools, as defined in paragraphs (14) and (25), respectively, of section 14101 of the Elementary and Secondary Education Act of 1965 (20 U.S.C. 8801).

(B) Health care provider. — The term "health care provider" means—

(i)   post-secondary educational institutions offering health care instruction, teaching hospitals, and medical schools;

(ii)   community health centers or health centers providing health care to migrants;

(iii)   local health departments or agencies;

(iv)   community mental health centers;

(v)   not-for-profit hospitals;

(vi)   rural health clinics; and

(vii)   consortia of health care providers consisting of one or more entities described in clauses (i) through (vi).

(C)   Public institutional telecommunications user. — The term "public institutional telecommunications user" means an elementary or secondary school, a library, or a health care provider as those terms are defined in this paragraph.

(i)   Consumer Protection. — The Commission and the States should ensure that universal service is available at rates that are just, reasonable, and affordable.

(j)   Lifeline Assistance. — Nothing in this section shall affect the collection, distribution, or administration of the Lifeline Assistance Program provided for by the Commission under regulations set forth in section 69.117 of title 47, Code of Federal Regulations, and other related sections of such title.

(k)   Subsidy of Competitive Services Prohibited. — A telecommunications carrier may not use services that are not competitive to subsidize services that are subject to competition. The Commission, with respect to interstate services, and the States, with respect to intrastate services, shall establish any necessary cost allocation rules, accounting safeguards, and guidelines to ensure that services included in the definition of universal service bear no more than a reasonable share of the joint and common costs of facilities used to provide those services.

Sec. 255   Access by Persons with Disabilities

(a)   Definitions. — As used in this section—

(1)   Disability. — The term "disability" has the meaning given to it by section 3(2)(A) of the Americans with Disabilities Act of 1990 (42 U.S.C. 12102(2)(A)).

(2)   Readily achievable. — The term "readily achievable" has the meaning given to it by section 301(9) of that Act (42 U.S.C. 12181(9)).

(b)   Manufacturing. — A manufacturer of telecommunications equipment or customer premises equipment shall ensure that the equipment is designed, developed, and fabricated to be accessible to and usable by individuals with disabilities, if readily achievable.

(c)   Telecommunications Services. — A provider of telecommunications service shall ensure that the service is accessible to and usable by individuals with disabilities, if readily achievable.

(d)   Compatibility. — Whenever the requirements of subsections (b) and (c) are not readily achievable, such a manufacturer or provider shall ensure that the equipment or service is compatible with existing peripheral devices or specialized customer premises equipment commonly used by individuals with disabilities to achieve access, if readily achievable.

(e) Guidelines. — Within 18 months after the date of enactment of the Telecommunications Act of 1996, the Architectural and Transportation Barriers Compliance Board shall develop guidelines for accessibility of telecommunications equipment and customer premises equipment in conjunction with the Commission. The Board shall review and update the guidelines periodically.

(f) No Additional Private Rights Authorized. — Nothing in this section shall be construed to authorize any private right of action to enforce any requirement of this section or any regulation thereunder. The Commission shall have exclusive jurisdiction with respect to any complaint under this section.

Sec. 256 Coordination for Interconnectivity

(a) Purpose. — It is the purpose of this section—

(1) to promote nondiscriminatory accessibility by the broadest number of users and vendors of communications products and services to public telecommunications networks used to provide telecommunications service through—

(A) coordinated public telecommunications network planning and design by telecommunications carriers and other providers of telecommunications service; and

(B) public telecommunications network interconnectivity, and interconnectivity of devices with such networks used to provide telecommunications service; and

(2) to ensure the ability of users and information providers to seamlessly and transparently transmit and receive information between and across telecommunications networks.

(b) Commission Functions. — In carrying out the purposes of this section, the Commission—

(1) shall establish procedures for Commission oversight of coordinated network planning by telecommunications carriers and other providers of telecommunications service for the effective and efficient interconnection of public telecommunications networks used to provide telecommunications service; and

(2) may participate, in a manner consistent with its authority and practice prior to the date of enactment of this section, in the development by appropriate industry standards-setting organizations of public telecommunications network interconnectivity standards that promote access to—

(A) public telecommunications networks used to provide telecommunications service;

(B) network capabilities and services by individuals with disabilities; and

(C) information services by subscribers of rural telephone companies.

(c) Commission's Authority. — Nothing in this section shall be construed as expanding or limiting any authority that the Commission may have under law in effect before the date of enactment of the Telecommunications Act of 1996.

(d) Definition. — As used in this section, the term "public telecommunications network interconnectivity" means the ability of two or more public telecommunications networks used to provide telecommunications service to communicate and exchange information without degeneration, and to interact in concert with one another.

Sec. 257 Market Entry Barriers Proceeding

(a) Elimination of Barriers. — Within 15 months after the date of enactment of the Telecommunications Act of 1996, the Commission shall complete a proceeding for the purpose of identifying and eliminating, by regulations pursuant to its authority under this Act (other than this section), market entry barriers for entrepreneurs and other small businesses in the provision and ownership of telecommunications services and information services, or in the provision of parts or services to providers of telecommunications services and information services.

(b) National Policy. — In carrying out subsection (a), the Commission shall seek to promote the policies and purposes of this Act favoring diversity of media voices, vigorous economic competition, technological advancement, and promotion of the public interest, convenience, and necessity.

(c) Periodic Review. — Every 3 years following the completion of the proceeding required by subsection (a), the Commission shall review and report to Congress on—

(1) any regulations prescribed to eliminate barriers within its jurisdiction that are identified under subsection (a) and that can be prescribed consistent with the public interest, convenience, and necessity; and

(2) the statutory barriers identified under subsection (a) that the Commission recommends be eliminated, consistent with the public interest, convenience, and necessity.

Sec. 258 Illegal Changes in Subscriber Carrier Selections

(a) Prohibition. — No telecommunications carrier shall submit or execute a change in a subscriber's selection of a provider of telephone exchange service or telephone toll service except in accordance with such verification procedures as the Commission shall prescribe. Nothing in this section shall preclude any State commission from enforcing such procedures with respect to intrastate services.

(b) Liability for Charges. — Any telecommunications carrier that violates the verification procedures described in subsection (a) and that collects charges for telephone exchange service or telephone toll service from a subscriber shall be liable to the carrier previously selected by the subscriber in an amount equal to all charges paid by such subscriber after such violation, in accordance with such procedures as the Commission may prescribe. The remedies provided by this subsection are in addition to any other remedies available by law.

Sec. 259   Infrastructure Sharing

(a)   Regulations Required. — The Commission shall prescribe, within one year after the date of enactment of the Telecommunications Act of 1996, regulations that require incumbent local exchange carriers (as defined in section 251(h)) to make available to any qualifying carrier such public switched network infrastructure, technology, information, and telecommunications facilities and functions as may be requested by such qualifying carrier for the purpose of enabling such qualifying carrier to provide telecommunications services, or to provide access to information services, in the service area in which such qualifying carrier has requested and obtained designation as an eligible telecommunications carrier under section 214(e).

(b)   Terms and Conditions of Regulations. — The regulations prescribed by the Commission pursuant to this section shall—

(1)   not require a local exchange carrier to which this section applies to take any action that is economically unreasonable or that is contrary to the public interest;

(2)   permit, but shall not require, the joint ownership or operation of public switched network infrastructure and services by or among such local exchange carrier and a qualifying carrier;

(3)   ensure that such local exchange carrier will not be treated by the Commission or any State as a common carrier for hire or as offering common carrier services with respect to any infrastructure, technology, information, facilities, or functions made available to a qualifying carrier in accordance with regulations issued pursuant to this section;

(4)   ensure that such local exchange carrier makes such infrastructure, technology, information, facilities, or functions available to a qualifying carrier on just and reasonable terms and conditions that permit such qualifying carrier to fully benefit from the economies of scale and scope of such local exchange carrier, as determined in accordance with guidelines prescribed by the Commission in regulations issued pursuant to this section;

(5)   establish conditions that promote cooperation between local exchange carriers to which this section applies and qualifying carriers;

(6)   not require a local exchange carrier to which this section applies to engage in any infrastructure sharing agreement for any services or access which are to be provided or offered to consumers by the qualifying carrier in such local exchange carrier's telephone exchange area; and

(7)   require that such local exchange carrier file with the Commission or State for public inspection, any tariffs, contracts, or other arrangements showing the rates, terms, and conditions under which such carrier is making available public switched network infrastructure and functions under this section.

(c)   Information Concerning Deployment of New Services and Equipment. — A local exchange carrier to which this section applies that has entered into an infrastructure sharing agreement under this section shall provide to each party to such agreement timely information on the planned deployment of telecommunications services and equipment, including any software or upgrades of software integral to the use or operation of such telecommunications equipment.

(d) Definition. — For purposes of this section, the term "qualifying carrier" means a telecommunications carrier that—

(1) lacks economies of scale or scope, as determined in accordance with regulations prescribed by the Commission pursuant to this section; and

(2) offers telephone exchange service, exchange access, and any other service that is included in universal service, to all consumers without preference throughout the service area for which such carrier has been designated as an eligible telecommunications carrier under section 214(e).

Sec. 260 Provision of Telemessaging Service

(a) Nondiscrimination Safeguards. — Any local exchange carrier subject to the requirements of section 251(c) that provides telemessaging service—

(1) shall not subsidize its telemessaging service directly or indirectly from its telephone exchange service or its exchange access; and

(2) shall not prefer or discriminate in favor of its telemessaging service operations in its provision of telecommunications services.

(b) Expedited Consideration of Complaints. — The Commission shall establish procedures for the receipt and review of complaints concerning violations of subsection (a) or the regulations thereunder that result in material financial harm to a provider of telemessaging service. Such procedures shall ensure that the Commission will make a final determination with respect to any such complaint within 120 days after receipt of the complaint. If the complaint contains an appropriate showing that the alleged violation occurred, the Commission shall, within 60 days after receipt of the complaint, order the local exchange carrier and any affiliates to cease engaging in such violation pending such final determination.

(c) Definition. — As used in this section, the term "telemessaging service" means voice mail and voice storage and retrieval services, any live operator services used to record, transcribe, or relay messages (other than telecommunications relay services), and any ancillary services offered in combination with these services.

Sec. 261 Effect on Other Requirements

(a) Commission Regulations. — Nothing in this part shall be construed to prohibit the Commission from enforcing regulations prescribed prior to the date of enactment of the Telecommunications Act of 1996 in fulfilling the requirements of this part, to the extent that such regulations are not inconsistent with the provisions of this part.

(b) Existing State Regulations. — Nothing in this part shall be construed to prohibit any State commission from enforcing regulations prescribed prior to the date of enactment of the Telecommunications Act of 1996, or from prescribing regulations after such date of enactment, in fulfilling the requirements of this part, if such regulations are not inconsistent with the provisions of this part.

(c) Additional state requirements. — Nothing in this part precludes a State from imposing requirements on a telecommunications carrier for intrastate services that are necessary to further competition in the provision of telephone exchange service or exchange access, as long as the State's requirements are not inconsistent with this part or the Commission's regulations to implement this part.'.

(b) Designation of Part I. — Title II of the Act is further amended by inserting before the heading of section 201 the following new heading:

'PART I COMMON CARRIER REGULATION'.

(c) Stylistic Consistency. — The Act is amended so that—

(1) the designation and heading of each title of the Act shall be in the form and typeface of the designation and heading of this title of this Act; and

(2) the designation and heading of each part of each title of the Act shall be in the form and typeface of the designation and heading of part I of title II of the Act, as amended by subsection (a).

Sec. 102 Eligible Telecommunications Carriers

(a) In General. — Section 214 (47 U.S.C. 214) is amended by adding at the end thereof the following new subsection:

'(e) Provision of Universal Service.—

(1) Eligible telecommunications carriers. — A common carrier designated as an eligible telecommunications carrier under paragraph (2) or (3) shall be eligible to receive universal service support in accordance with section 254 and shall, throughout the service area for which the designation is received—

(A) offer the services that are supported by Federal universal service support mechanisms under section 254(c), either using its own facilities or a combination of its own facilities and resale of another carrier's services (including the services offered by another eligible telecommunications carrier); and

(B) advertise the availability of such services and the charges therefor using media of general distribution.

(2) Designation of eligible telecommunications carriers. — A State commission shall upon its own motion or upon request designate a common carrier that meets the requirements of paragraph (1) as an eligible telecommunications carrier for a service area designated by the State commission. Upon request and consistent with the public interest, convenience, and necessity, the State commission may, in the case of an area served by a rural telephone company, and shall, in the case of all other areas, designate more than one common carrier as an eligible telecommunications carrier for a service area designated by the State commission, so long as each additional requesting carrier meets the requirements of paragraph (1). Before designating an additional eligible telecommunications carrier for an area served by a rural telephone company, the State commission shall find that the designation is in the public interest.

(3) Designation of eligible telecommunications carriers for unserved areas. — If no common carrier will provide the services that are

supported by Federal universal service support mechanisms under section 254(c) to an unserved community or any portion thereof that requests such service, the Commission, with respect to interstate services, or a State commission, with respect to intrastate services, shall determine which common carrier or carriers are best able to provide such service to the requesting unserved community or portion thereof and shall order such carrier or carriers to provide such service for that unserved community or portion thereof. Any carrier or carriers ordered to provide such service under this paragraph shall meet the requirements of paragraph (1) and shall be designated as an eligible telecommunications carrier for that community or portion thereof.

(4) Relinquishment of universal service. — A State commission shall permit an eligible telecommunications carrier to relinquish its designation as such a carrier in any area served by more than one eligible telecommunications carrier. An eligible telecommunications carrier that seeks to relinquish its eligible telecommunications carrier designation for an area served by more than one eligible telecommunications carrier shall give advance notice to the State commission of such relinquishment. Prior to permitting a telecommunications carrier designated as an eligible telecommunications carrier to cease providing universal service in an area served by more than one eligible telecommunications carrier, the State commission shall require the remaining eligible telecommunications carrier or carriers to ensure that all customers served by the relinquishing carrier will continue to be served, and shall require sufficient notice to permit the purchase or construction of adequate facilities by any remaining eligible telecommunications carrier. The State commission shall establish a time, not to exceed one year after the State commission approves such relinquishment under this paragraph, within which such purchase or construction shall be completed.

(5) Service area defined. — The term "service area" means a geographic area established by a State commission for the purpose of determining universal service obligations and support mechanisms. In the case of an area served by a rural telephone company, "service area" means such company's "study area" unless and until the Commission and the States, after taking into account recommendations of a Federal-State Joint Board instituted under section 410(c), establish a different definition of service area for such company.'.

Sec. 103   Exempt Telecommunications Companies

The Public Utility Holding Company Act of 1935 (15 U.S.C. 79 and following) is amended by redesignating sections 34 and 35 as sections 35 and 36, respectively, and by inserting the following new section after section 33:

'Sec. 34   Exempt Telecommunications Companies

(a) Definitions. — For purposes of this section—

(1) Exempt Telecommunications Company. — The term "exempt telecommunications company" means any person determined by the Federal Communications Commission to be engaged directly or in-

directly, wherever located, through one or more affiliates (as defined in section 2(a)(11)(B)), and exclusively in the business of providing —

(A)   telecommunications services;

(B)   information services;

(C)   other services or products subject to the jurisdiction of the Federal Communications Commission; or

(D)   products or services that are related or incidental to the provision of a product or service described in subparagraph (A), (B), or (C).

No person shall be deemed to be an exempt telecommunications company under this section unless such person has applied to the Federal Communications Commission for a determination under this paragraph. A person applying in good faith for such a determination shall be deemed an exempt telecommunications company under this section, with all of the exemptions provided by this section, until the Federal Communications Commission makes such determination. The Federal Communications Commission shall make such determination within 60 days of its receipt of any such application filed after the enactment of this section and shall notify the Commission whenever a determination is made under this paragraph that any person is an exempt telecommunications company. Not later than 12 months after the date of enactment of this section, the Federal Communications Commission shall promulgate rules implementing the provisions of this paragraph which shall be applicable to applications filed under this paragraph after the effective date of such rules.

(2)   Other terms. — For purposes of this section, the terms "telecommunications services" and "information services" shall have the same meanings as provided in the Communications Act of 1934.

(b)   State Consent for Sale of Existing Rate-Based Facilities. — If a rate or charge for the sale of electric energy or natural gas (other than any portion of a rate or charge which represents recovery of the cost of a wholesale rate or charge) for, or in connection with, assets of a public utility company that is an associate company or affiliate of a registered holding company was in effect under the laws of any State as of December 19, 1995, the public utility company owning such assets may not sell such assets to an exempt telecommunications company that is an associate company or affiliate unless State commissions having jurisdiction over such public utility company approve such sale. Nothing in this subsection shall preempt the otherwise applicable authority of any State to approve or disapprove the sale of such assets. The approval of the Commission under this Act shall not be required for the sale of assets as provided in this subsection.

(c)   Ownership of ETCS by Exempt Holding Companies. — Notwithstanding any provision of this Act, a holding company that is exempt under section 3 of this Act shall be permitted, without condition or limitation under this Act, to acquire and maintain an interest in the business of one or more exempt telecommunications companies.

(d)   Ownership of ETCS by Registered Holding Companies. — Notwithstanding any provision of this Act, a registered holding company shall be permitted (without the need to apply for, or receive, approval from the Commission, and otherwise without condition under this Act) to acquire and hold the securities, or an interest in the business, of one or more exempt telecommunications companies.

(e) Financing and Other Relationships Between ETCS and Registered Holding Companies. — The relationship between an exempt telecommunications company and a registered holding company, its affiliates and associate companies, shall remain subject to the jurisdiction of the Commission under this Act: Provided, That—

(1) section 11 of this Act shall not prohibit the ownership of an interest in the business of one or more exempt telecommunications companies by a registered holding company (regardless of activities engaged in or where facilities owned or operated by such exempt telecommunications companies are located), and such ownership by a registered holding company shall be deemed consistent with the operation of an integrated public utility system;

(2) the ownership of an interest in the business of one or more exempt telecommunications companies by a registered holding company (regardless of activities engaged in or where facilities owned or operated by such exempt telecommunications companies are located) shall be considered as reasonably incidental, or economically necessary or appropriate, to the operations of an integrated public utility system;

(3) the Commission shall have no jurisdiction under this Act over, and there shall be no restriction or approval required under this Act with respect to (A) the issue or sale of a security by a registered holding company for purposes of financing the acquisition of an exempt telecommunications company, or (B) the guarantee of a security of an exempt telecommunications company by a registered holding company; and

(4) except for costs that should be fairly and equitably allocated among companies that are associate companies of a registered holding company, the Commission shall have no jurisdiction under this Act over the sales, service, and construction contracts between an exempt telecommunications company and a registered holding company, its affiliates and associate companies.

(f) Reporting Obligations Concerning Investments and Activities of Registered Public-Utility Holding Company Systems.—

(1) Obligations to report information. — Any registered holding company or subsidiary thereof that acquires or holds the securities, or an interest in the business, of an exempt telecommunications company shall file with the Commission such information as the Commission, by rule, may prescribe concerning—

(A) investments and activities by the registered holding company, or any subsidiary thereof, with respect to exempt telecommunications companies, and

(B) any activities of an exempt telecommunications company within the holding company system,

that are reasonably likely to have a material impact on the financial or operational condition of the holding company system.

(2) Authority to require additional information. — If, based on reports provided to the Commission pursuant to paragraph (1) of this subsection or other available information, the Commission reasonably

concludes that it has concerns regarding the financial or operational condition of any registered holding company or any subsidiary thereof (including an exempt telecommunications company), the Commission may require such registered holding company to make additional reports and provide additional information.

(3) Authority to limit disclosure of information. — Notwithstanding any other provision of law, the Commission shall not be compelled to disclose any information required to be reported under this subsection. Nothing in this subsection shall authorize the Commission to withhold the information from Congress, or prevent the Commission from complying with a request for information from any other Federal or State department or agency requesting the information for purposes within the scope of its jurisdiction. For purposes of section 552 of title 5, United States Code, this subsection shall be considered a statute described in subsection (b)(3)(B) of such section 552.

(g) Assumption of Liabilities. — Any public utility company that is an associate company, or an affiliate, of a registered holding company and that is subject to the jurisdiction of a State commission with respect to its retail electric or gas rates shall not issue any security for the purpose of financing the acquisition, ownership, or operation of an exempt telecommunications company. Any public utility company that is an associate company, or an affiliate, of a registered holding company and that is subject to the jurisdiction of a State commission with respect to its retail electric or gas rates shall not assume any obligation or liability as guarantor, endorser, surety, or otherwise by the public utility company in respect of any security of an exempt telecommunications company.

(h) Pledging or Mortgaging of Assets. — Any public utility company that is an associate company, or affiliate, of a registered holding company and that is subject to the jurisdiction of a State commission with respect to its retail electric or gas rates shall not pledge, mortgage, or otherwise use as collateral any assets of the public utility company or assets of any subsidiary company thereof for the benefit of an exempt telecommunications company.

(i) Protection Against Abusive Affiliate Transactions. — A public utility company may enter into a contract to purchase services or products described in subsection (a)(1) from an exempt telecommunications company that is an affiliate or associate company of the public utility company only if—

(1) every State commission having jurisdiction over the retail rates of such public utility company approves such contract; or

(2) such public utility company is not subject to State commission retail rate regulation and the purchased services or products—

(A) would not be resold to any affiliate or associate company; or

(B) would be resold to an affiliate or associate company and every State commission having jurisdiction over the retail rates of such affiliate or associate company makes the determination required by subparagraph (A).

The requirements of this subsection shall not apply in any case in which the State or the State commission concerned publishes a notice that the State or State commission waives its authority under this subsection.

(j) Nonpreemption of Rate Authority. — Nothing in this Act shall preclude the Federal Energy Regulatory Commission or a State commission from exercising its jurisdiction under otherwise applicable law to determine whether a public utility company may recover in rates the costs of products or services purchased from or sold to an associate company or affiliate that is an exempt telecommunications company, regardless of whether such costs are incurred through the direct or indirect purchase or sale of products or services from such associate company or affiliate.

(k) Reciprocal Arrangements Prohibited. — Reciprocal arrangements among companies that are not affiliates or associate companies of each other that are entered into in order to avoid the provisions of this section are prohibited.

(l) Books and Records. — (1) Upon written order of a State commission, a State commission may examine the books, accounts, memoranda, contracts, and records of—

(A) a public utility company subject to its regulatory authority under State law;

(B) any exempt telecommunications company selling products or services to such public utility company or to an associate company of such public utility company; and

(C) any associate company or affiliate of an exempt telecommunications company which sells products or services to a public utility company referred to in subparagraph (A),

wherever located, if such examination is required for the effective discharge of the State commission's regulatory responsibilities affecting the provision of electric or gas service in connection with the activities of such exempt telecommunications company.

(2) Where a State commission issues an order pursuant to paragraph (1), the State commission shall not publicly disclose trade secrets or sensitive commercial information.

(3) Any United States district court located in the State in which the State commission referred to in paragraph (1) is located shall have jurisdiction to enforce compliance with this subsection.

(4) Nothing in this section shall—

(A) preempt applicable State law concerning the provision of records and other information; or

(B) in any way limit rights to obtain records and other information under Federal law, contracts, or otherwise.

(m) Independent Audit Authority for State Commissions.—

(1) State may order audit. — Any State commission with jurisdiction over a public utility company that—

(A) is an associate company of a registered holding company; and

(B) transacts business, directly or indirectly, with a subsidiary company, an affiliate or an associate company that is an exempt telecommunications company,

may order an independent audit to be performed, no more frequently than on an annual basis, of all matters deemed relevant by the selected auditor that reasonably relate to retail rates: Provided, That such matters relate, directly or indirectly, to transactions or transfers between the public utility company subject to its jurisdiction and such exempt telecommunications company.

(2)   Selection of firm to conduct audit. — (A) If a State commission orders an audit in accordance with paragraph (1), the public utility company and the State commission shall jointly select, within 60 days, a firm to perform the audit. The firm selected to perform the audit shall possess demonstrated qualifications relating to—

(i)   competency, including adequate technical training and professional proficiency in each discipline necessary to carry out the audit; and

(ii)   independence and objectivity, including that the firm be free from personal or external impairments to independence, and should assume an independent position with the State commission and auditee, making certain that the audit is based upon an impartial consideration of all pertinent facts and responsible opinions.

(B)   The public utility company and the exempt telecommunications company shall cooperate fully with all reasonable requests necessary to perform the audit and the public utility company shall bear all costs of having the audit performed.

(3)   Availability of auditor's report. — The auditor's report shall be provided to the State commission not later than 6 months after the selection of the auditor, and provided to the public utility company not later than 60 days thereafter.

(n)   Applicability of Telecommunications Regulation. — Nothing in this section shall affect the authority of the Federal Communications Commission under the Communications Act of 1934, or the authority of State commissions under State laws concerning the provision of telecommunications services, to regulate the activities of an exempt telecommunications company.'.

Sec. 104   Nondiscrimination Principle

Section 1 (47 U.S.C. 151) is amended by inserting after 'to all the people of the United States' the following: ', without discrimination on the basis of race, color, religion, national origin, or sex,'.

Subtitle B   Special Provisions Concerning Bell Operating Companies

Sec. 151   Bell Operating Company Provisions

(a)   Establishment of Part III of Title II. — Title II is amended by adding at the end of part II (as added by section 101) the following new part:
'PART III   SPECIAL PROVISIONS CONCERNING BELL
OPERATING COMPANIES

Sec. 271   Bell Operating Company Entry into Interlata Services

(a)   General Limitation. — Neither a Bell operating company, nor any affiliate of a Bell operating company, may provide interLATA services except as provided in this section.

(b)   InterLATA Services to Which This Section Applies.—

(1)   In-region services. — A Bell operating company, or any affiliate of that Bell operating company, may provide interLATA services originating in any of its in-region States (as defined in subsection (i)) if the Commission approves the application of such company for such State under subsection (d)(3).

(2)   Out-of-region services. — A Bell operating company, or any affiliate of that Bell operating company, may provide interLATA services originating outside its in-region States after the date of enactment of the Telecommunications to subsection (j).

(3)   Incidental interLATA services. — A Bell operating company, or any affiliate of a Bell operating company, may provide incidental interLATA services (as defined in subsection (g)) originating in any State after the date of enactment of the Telecommunications Act of 1996.

(4)   Termination. — Nothing in this section prohibits a Bell operating company or any of its affiliates from providing termination for interLATA services, subject to subsection (j).

(c)   Requirements for Providing Certain In-Region InterLATA Services.—

(1)   Agreement or statement. — A Bell operating company meets the requirements of this paragraph if it meets the requirements of subparagraph (A) or subparagraph (B) of this paragraph for each State for which the authorization is sought.

(A)   Presence of a facilities-based competitor. — A Bell operating company meets the requirements of this subparagraph if it has entered into one or more binding agreements that have been approved under section 252 specifying the terms and conditions under which the Bell operating company is providing access and interconnection to its network facilities for the network facilities of one or more unaffiliated competing providers of telephone exchange service (as defined in section 3(47)(A), but excluding exchange access) to residential and business subscribers. For the purpose of this subparagraph, such telephone exchange service may be offered by such competing providers either exclusively over their own telephone exchange service facilities or predominantly over their own telephone exchange service facilities in combination with the resale of the telecommunications services of another carrier. For the purpose of this subparagraph, services provided pursuant to subpart K of part 22 of the Commission's regulations (47 C.F.R. 22.901 et seq.) shall not be considered to be telephone exchange services.

(B)   Failure to request access. — A Bell operating company meets the requirements of this subparagraph if, after 10 months after the date of enactment of the Telecommunications Act of 1996, no such provider has requested the access and interconnection described in subparagraph (A) before the date which is 3 months before the date the company makes its application under subsection (d)(1), and a statement of the terms and conditions that the company generally offers to provide such access and interconnection has been approved or permitted to take effect by the State commission under section 252(f). For purposes of this subparagraph, a Bell operating company shall be considered not to have received any request for access and interconnection if the State commission of such State certifies that the only provider or providers making such a request have (i) failed to negotiate in good faith as required by section 252, or (ii) violated the terms of an agreement approved under section 252 by the provider's failure to comply, within a reasonable period of time, with the implementation schedule contained in such agreement.

(2)   Specific interconnection requirements.—

(A)   Agreement required. — A Bell operating company meets the requirements of this paragraph if, within the State for which the authorization is sought—

(i)(I)   such company is providing access and interconnection pursuant to one or more agreements described in paragraph (1)(A), or

(II)   such company is generally offering access and interconnection pursuant to a statement described in paragraph (1)(B), and

(ii)   such access and interconnection meets the requirements of subparagraph (B) of this paragraph.

(B)   Competitive checklist. — Access or interconnection provided or generally offered by a Bell operating company to other telecommunications carriers meets the requirements of this subparagraph if such access and interconnection includes each of the following:

(i)   Interconnection in accordance with the requirements of sections 251(c)(2) and 252(d)(1).

(ii)   Nondiscriminatory access to network elements in accordance with the requirements of sections 251(c)(3) and 252(d)(1).

(iii)   Nondiscriminatory access to the poles, ducts, conduits, and rights-of-way owned or controlled by the Bell operating company at just and reasonable rates in accordance with the requirements of section 224.

(iv)   Local loop transmission from the central office to the customer's premises, unbundled from local switching or other services.

(v)   Local transport from the trunk side of a wireline local exchange carrier switch unbundled from switching or other services.

(vi)   Local switching unbundled from transport, local loop transmission, or other services.

(vii)   Nondiscriminatory access to—

(I)   911 and E911 services;

(II)   directory assistance services to allow the other carrier's customers to obtain telephone numbers; and

(III)   operator call completion services.

(viii)   White pages directory listings for customers of the other carrier's telephone exchange service.

(ix)   Until the date by which telecommunications numbering administration guidelines, plan, or rules are established, nondiscriminatory access to telephone numbers for assignment to the other carrier's telephone exchange service customers. After that date, compliance with such guidelines, plan, or rules.

(x)   Nondiscriminatory access to databases and associated signaling necessary for call routing and completion.

(xi)   Until the date by which the Commission issues regulations pursuant to section 251 to require number portability, interim telecommunications number portability through remote call forwarding, direct inward dialing trunks, or other comparable arrangements, with as little impairment of functioning, quality, reliability, and convenience as possible. After that date, full compliance with such regulations.

(xii) Nondiscriminatory access to such services or information as are necessary to allow the requesting carrier to implement local dialing parity in accordance with the requirements of section 251(b)(3).

(xiii) Reciprocal compensation arrangements in accordance with the requirements of section 252(d)(2).

(xiv) Telecommunications services are available for resale in accordance with the requirements of sections 251(c)(4) and 252(d)(3).

(d) Administrative Provisions.—

(1) Application to commission. — On and after the date of enactment of the Telecommunications Act of 1996, a Bell operating company or its affiliate may apply to the Commission for authorization to provide interLATA services originating in any in-region State. The application shall identify each State for which the sought.

(2) Consultation.—

(A) Consultation with the attorney general. — The Commission shall notify the Attorney General promptly of any application under paragraph (1). Before making any determination under this subsection, the Commission shall consult with the Attorney General, and if the Attorney General submits any comments in writing, such comments shall be included in the record of the Commission's decision. In consulting with and submitting comments to the Commission under this paragraph, the Attorney General shall provide to the Commission an evaluation of the application using any standard the Attorney General considers appropriate. The Commission shall give substantial weight to the Attorney General's evaluation, but such evaluation shall not have any preclusive effect on any Commission decision under paragraph (3).

(B) Consultation with state commissions. — Before making any determination under this subsection, the Commission shall consult with the State commission of any State that is the subject of the application in order to verify the compliance of the Bell operating company with the requirements of subsection (c).

(3) Determination. — Not later than 90 days after receiving an application under paragraph (1), the Commission shall issue a written determination approving or denying the authorization requested in the application for each State. The Commission shall not approve the authorization requested in an application submitted under paragraph (1) unless it finds that—

(A) the petitioning Bell operating company has met the requirements of subsection (c)(1) and—

(i) with respect to access and interconnection provided pursuant to subsection (c)(1)(A), has fully implemented the competitive checklist in subsection (c)(2)(B); or

(ii) with respect to access and interconnection generally offered pursuant to a statement under subsection (c)(1)(B), such statement offers all of the items included in the competitive checklist in subsection (c)(2)(B);

(B)   the requested authorization will be carried out in accordance with the requirements of section 272; and

(C)   the requested authorization is consistent with the public interest, convenience, and necessity.

The Commission shall state the basis for its approval or denial of the application.

(4)   Limitation on commission. — The Commission may not, by rule or otherwise, limit or extend the terms used in the competitive checklist set forth in subsection (c)(2)(B).

(5)   Publication. — Not later than 10 days after issuing a determination under paragraph (3), the Commission shall publish in the Federal Register a brief description of the determination.

(6)   Enforcement of conditions.—

(A)   Commission authority. — If at any time after the approval of an application under paragraph (3), the Commission determines that a Bell operating company has ceased to meet any of the conditions required for such approval, the Commission may, after notice and opportunity for a hearing—

(i)   issue an order to such company to correct the deficiency;

(ii)   impose a penalty on such company pursuant to title V; or

(iii)   suspend or revoke such approval.

(B)   Receipt and review of complaints. — The Commission shall establish procedures for the review of complaints concerning failures by Bell operating companies to meet conditions required for approval under paragraph (3). Unless the parties otherwise agree, the Commission shall act on such complaint within 90 days.

(e)   Limitations.—

(1)   Joint marketing of local and long distance services. — Until a Bell operating company is authorized pursuant to subsection (d) to provide interLATA services in an in-region State, or until 36 months have passed since the date of enactment of the Telecommunications Act of 1996, whichever is earlier, a telecommunications carrier that serves greater than 5 percent of the Nation's presubscribed access lines may not jointly market in such State telephone exchange service obtained from such company pursuant to section 251(c)(4) with interLATA services offered by that telecommunications carrier.

(2)   IntraLATA toll dialing parity.—

(A)   Provision required. — A Bell operating company granted authority to provide interLATA services under subsection (d) shall provide intraLATA toll dialing parity throughout that State coincident with its exercise of that authority.

(B)   Limitation. — Except for single-LATA States and States that have issued an order by December 19, 1995, requiring a Bell operating company to implement intraLATA toll dialing parity, a State may not require a Bell operating company to implement intraLATA toll dialing parity in that State before a Bell operating company has been granted authority under this section to provide interLATA services originating in that State or before 3 years after the date of enactment of the Telecommunications Act of 1996, whichever is earlier. Nothing in this subparagraph precludes a State from issuing an order requiring intraLATA toll dialing parity in that State prior to either such date so long as such order does not take effect until after the earlier of either such dates.

(f) Exception for Previously Authorized Activities. — Neither subsection (a) nor section 273 shall prohibit a Bell operating company or affiliate from engaging, at any time after the date of enactment of the Telecommunications Act of 1996, in any activity to the extent authorized by, and subject to the terms and conditions contained in, an order entered by the United States District Court for the District of Columbia pursuant to section VII or VIII(C) of the AT&T Consent Decree if such order was entered on or before such date of enactment, to the extent such order is not reversed or vacated on appeal. Nothing in this subsection shall be construed to limit, or to impose terms or conditions on, an activity in which a Bell operating company is otherwise authorized to engage under any other provision of this section.

(g) Definition of Incidental InterLATA Services. — For purposes of this section, the term "incidental interLATA services" means the interLATA provision by a Bell operating company or its affiliate—

(1)(A) of audio programming, video programming, or other programming services to subscribers to such services of such company or affiliate;

(B) of the capability for interaction by such subscribers to select or respond to such audio programming, video programming, or other programming services;

(C) to distributors of audio programming or video programming that such company or affiliate owns or controls, or is licensed by the copyright owner of such programming (or by an assignee of such owner) to distribute; or

(D) of alarm monitoring services;

(2) of two-way interactive video services or Internet services over dedicated facilities to or for elementary and secondary schools as defined in section 254(h)(5);

(3) of commercial mobile services in accordance with section 332(c) of this Act and with the regulations prescribed by the Commission pursuant to paragraph (8) of such section;

(4) of a service that permits a customer that is located in one LATA to retrieve stored information from, or file information for storage in, information storage facilities of such company that are located in another LATA;

(5) of signaling information used in connection with the provision of telephone exchange services or exchange access by a local exchange carrier; or

(6) of network control signaling information to, and receipt of such signaling information from, common carriers offering interLATA services at any location within the area in which such Bell operating company provides telephone exchange services or exchange access.

(h) Limitations. — The provisions of subsection (g) are intended to be narrowly construed. The interLATA services provided under subparagraph (A), (B), or (C) of subsection (g)(1) are limited to those interLATA transmissions incidental to the provision by a Bell operating company or its affiliate of video, audio, and other programming services that the company or its affiliate is engaged in providing to the public. The Commission shall ensure that the provision of services authorized under subsection (g) by a Bell operating company or its affiliate will not adversely affect telephone exchange service ratepayers or competition in any telecommunications market.

(i)   Additional Definitions. — As used in this section—

(1)   In-region state. — The term "in-region State" means a State in which a Bell operating company or any of its affiliates was authorized to provide wireline telephone exchange service pursuant to the reorganization plan approved under the AT&T Consent Decree, as in effect on the day before the date of enactment of the Telecommunications Act of 1996.

(2)   Audio programming services. — The term "audio programming services" means programming provided by, or generally considered to be comparable to programming provided by, a radio broadcast station.

(3)   Video programming services; other programming services. — The terms "video programming service" and "other programming services" have the same meanings as such terms have under section 602 of this Act.

(j)   Certain Service Applications Treated as In-Region Service Applications. — For purposes of this section, a Bell operating company application to provide line service, or their equivalents that—

(1)   terminate in an in-region State of that Bell operating company, and

(2)   allow the called party to determine the interLATA carrier, shall be considered an in-region service subject to the requirements of subsection (b)(1).

Sec. 272   Separate Affiliate; Safeguards

(a)   Separate Affiliate Required for Competitive Activities.—

(1)   In general. — A Bell operating company (including any affiliate) which is a local exchange carrier that is subject to the requirements of section 251(c) may not provide any service described in paragraph (2) unless it provides that service through one or more affiliates that—

(A)   are separate from any operating company entity that is subject to the requirements of section 251(c); and

(B)   meet the requirements of subsection (b).

(2)   Services for which a separate affiliate is required. — The services for which a separate affiliate is required by paragraph (1) are:

(A)   Manufacturing activities (as defined in section 273(h)).

(B)   Origination of interLATA telecommunications services, other than—

(i)   incidental interLATA services described in paragraphs (1), (2), (3), (5), and (6) of section 271(g);

(ii)   out-of-region services described in section 271(b)(2); or

(iii)   previously authorized activities described in section 271(f).

(C)   InterLATA information services, other than electronic publishing (as defined in section 274(h)) and alarm monitoring services (as defined in section 275(e)).

(b) Structural and Transactional Requirements. — The separate affiliate required by this section—

(1) shall operate independently from the Bell operating company;

(2) shall maintain books, records, and accounts in the manner prescribed by the Commission which shall be separate from the books, records, and accounts maintained by the Bell operating company of which it is an affiliate;

(3) shall have separate officers, directors, and employees from the Bell operating company of which it is an affiliate;

(4) may not obtain credit under any arrangement that would permit a creditor, upon default, to have recourse to the assets of the Bell operating company; and

(5) shall conduct all transactions with the Bell operating company of which it is an affiliate on an arm's length basis with any such transactions reduced to writing and available for public inspection.

(c) Nondiscrimination Safeguards. — In its dealings with its affiliate described in subsection (a), a Bell operating company—

(1) may not discriminate between that company or affiliate and any other entity in the provision or procurement of goods, services, facilities, and information, or in the establishment of standards; and

(2) shall account for all transactions with an affiliate described in subsection (a) in accordance with accounting principles designated or approved by the Commission.

(d) Biennial Audit.—

(1) General requirement. — A company required to operate a separate affiliate under this section shall obtain and pay for a joint Federal/State audit every 2 years conducted by an independent auditor to determine whether such company has complied with this section and the regulations promulgated under this section, and particularly whether such company has complied with the separate accounting requirements under subsection (b).

(2) Results submitted to commission; state commissions. — The auditor described in paragraph (1) shall submit the results of the audit to the Commission and to the State commission of each State in which the company audited provides service, which shall make such results available for public inspection. Any party may submit comments on the final audit report.

(3) Access to documents. — For purposes of conducting audits and reviews under this subsection—

(A) the independent auditor, the Commission, and the State commission shall have access to the financial accounts and records of each company and of its affiliates necessary to verify transactions conducted with that company that are relevant to the specific activities permitted under this section and that are necessary for the regulation of rates;

(B) the Commission and the State commission shall have access to the working papers and supporting materials of any auditor who performs an audit under this section; and

(C) the State commission shall implement appropriate procedures to ensure the protection of any proprietary information submitted to it under this section.

(e) Fulfillment of Certain Requests. — A Bell operating company and an affiliate that is subject to the requirements of section 251(c)—

(1) shall fulfill any requests from an unaffiliated entity for telephone exchange service and exchange access within a period no longer than the period in which it provides such telephone exchange service and exchange access to itself or to its affiliates;

(2) shall not provide any facilities, services, or information concerning its provision of exchange access to the affiliate described in subsection (a) unless such facilities, services, or information are made available to other providers of interLATA services in that market on the same terms and conditions;

(3) shall charge the affiliate described in subsection (a), or impute to itself (if using the access for its provision of its own services), an amount for access to its telephone exchange service and exchange access that is no less than the amount charged to any unaffiliated interexchange carriers for such service; and

(4) may provide any interLATA or intraLATA facilities or services to its interLATA affiliate if such services or facilities are made available to all carriers at the same rates and on the same terms and conditions, and so long as the costs are appropriately allocated.

(f) Sunset.—

(1) Manufacturing and long distance. — The provisions of this section (other than subsection (e)) shall cease to apply with respect to the manufacturing activities or the interLATA telecommunications services of a Bell operating company 3 years after the date such Bell operating company or any Bell operating company affiliate is authorized to provide interLATA telecommunications services under section 271(d), unless the Commission extends such 3-year period by rule or order.

(2) InterLATA information services. — The provisions of this section (other than subsection (e)) shall cease to apply with respect to the interLATA information services of a Bell operating company 4 years after the date of enactment of the Telecommunications Act of 1996, unless the Commission extends such 4-year period by rule or order.

(3) Preservation of existing authority. — Nothing in this subsection shall be construed to limit the authority of the Commission under any other section of this Act to prescribe safeguards consistent with the public interest, convenience, and necessity.

(g) Joint Marketing.—

(1) Affiliate sales of telephone exchange services. — A Bell operating company affiliate required by this section may not market or sell telephone exchange services provided by the Bell operating company unless that company permits other entities offering the same or similar service to market and sell its telephone exchange services.

(2) Bell operating company sales of affiliate services. — A Bell operating company may not market or sell interLATA service provided by an affiliate required by this section within any of its in-region States until such company is authorized to provide interLATA services in such State under section 271(d).

(3)   Rule of construction. — The joint marketing and sale of services permitted under this subsection shall not be considered to violate the nondiscrimination provisions of subsection (c).

(h)   Transition. — With respect to any activity in which a Bell operating company is engaged on the date of enactment of the Telecommunications Act of 1996, such company shall have one year from such date of enactment to comply with the requirements of this section.

Sec. 273   Manufacturing by Bell Operating Companies

(a)   Authorization. — A Bell operating company may manufacture and provide telecommunications equipment, and manufacture customer premises equipment, if the Commission authorizes that Bell operating company or any Bell operating company affiliate to provide interLATA services under section 271(d), subject to the requirements of this section and the regulations prescribed thereunder, except that neither a Bell operating company nor any of its affiliates may engage in such manufacturing in conjunction with a Bell operating company not so affiliated or any of its affiliates.

(b)   Collaboration; Research and Royalty Agreements.—

(1)   Collaboration. — Subsection (a) shall not prohibit a Bell operating company from engaging in close collaboration with any manufacturer of customer premises equipment or telecommunications equipment during the design and development of hardware, software, or combinations thereof related to such equipment.

(2)   Certain research arrangements; royalty agreements. — Subsection (a) shall not prohibit a Bell operating company from—

(A)   engaging in research activities related to manufacturing, and

(B)   entering into royalty agreements with manufacturers of telecommunications equipment.

(c)   Information Requirements.—

(1)   Information on protocols and technical requirements. — Each Bell operating company shall, in accordance with regulations prescribed by the Commission, maintain and file with the Commission full and complete information with respect to the protocols and technical requirements for connection with and use of its telephone exchange service facilities. Each such company shall report promptly to the Commission any material changes or planned changes to such protocols and requirements, and the schedule for implementation of such changes or planned changes.

(2)   Disclosure of information. — A Bell operating company shall not disclose any information required to be filed under paragraph (1) unless that information has been filed promptly, as required by regulation by the Commission.

(3)   Access by competitors to information. — The Commission may prescribe such additional regulations under this subsection as may be necessary to ensure that manufacturers have access to the information with respect to the protocols and technical requirements for connection with and use of telephone exchange service facilities that a Bell operating company makes available to any manufacturing affiliate or any unaffiliated manufacturer.

(4) Planning information. — Each Bell operating company shall provide, to interconnecting carriers providing telephone exchange service, timely information on the planned deployment of telecommunications equipment.

(d) Manufacturing Limitations for Standard-Setting Organizations.—

(1) Application to bell communications research or manufacturers. — Bell Communications Research, Inc., or any successor entity or affiliate—

(A) shall not be considered a Bell operating company or a successor or assign of a Bell operating company at such time as it is no longer an affiliate of any Bell operating company; and

(B) notwithstanding paragraph (3), shall not engage in manufacturing telecommunications equipment or customer premises equipment as long as it is an affiliate of more than one otherwise unaffiliated Bell operating company or successor or assign of any such company. Nothing in this subsection prohibits Bell Communications Research, Inc., or any successor entity, from engaging in any activity in which it is lawfully engaged on the date of enactment of the Telecommunications Act of 1996. Nothing provided in this subsection shall render Bell Communications Research, Inc., or any successor entity, a common carrier under title II of this Act. Nothing in this subsection restricts any manufacturer from engaging in any activity in which it is lawfully engaged on the date of enactment of the Telecommunications Act of 1996.

(2) Proprietary information. — Any entity which establishes standards for telecommunications equipment or customer premises equipment, or generic network requirements for such equipment, or certifies telecommunications equipment or customer premises equipment, shall be prohibited from releasing or otherwise using any proprietary information, designated as such by its owner, in its possession as a result of such activity, for any purpose other than purposes authorized in writing by the owner of such information, even after such entity ceases to be so engaged.

(3) Manufacturing safeguards. — (A) Except as prohibited in paragraph (1), and subject to paragraph (6), any entity which certifies telecommunications equipment or customer premises equipment manufactured by an unaffiliated entity shall only manufacture a particular class of telecommunications equipment or customer premises equipment for which it is undertaking or has undertaken, during the previous 18 months, certification activity for such class of equipment through a separate affiliate.

(B) Such separate affiliate shall—

(i) maintain books, records, and accounts separate from those of the entity that certifies such equipment, consistent with generally acceptable accounting principles;

(ii) not engage in any joint manufacturing activities with such entity; and

(iii) have segregated facilities and separate employees with such entity.

(C) Such entity that certifies such equipment shall—

(i) not discriminate in favor of its manufacturing affiliate in the establishment of standards, generic requirements, or product certification;

(ii) not disclose to the manufacturing affiliate any proprietary information that has been received at any time from an unaffiliated manufacturer, unless authorized in writing by the owner of the information; and

(iii) not permit any employee engaged in product certification for telecommunications equipment or customer premises equipment to engage jointly in sales or marketing of any such equipment with the affiliated manufacturer.

(4) Standard-setting entities. — Any entity that is not an accredited standards development organization and that establishes industry-wide standards for telecommunications equipment or customer premises equipment, or industry-wide generic network requirements for such equipment, or that certifies telecommunications equipment or customer premises equipment manufactured by an unaffiliated entity, shall—

(A) establish and publish any industry-wide standard for, industry-wide generic requirement for, or any substantial modification of an existing industry-wide standard or industry-wide generic requirement for, telecommunic equipment or customer premises equipment only in compliance with the following procedure:

(i) such entity shall issue a public notice of its consideration of a proposed industry-wide standard or industry-wide generic requirement;

(ii) such entity shall issue a public invitation to interested industry parties to fund and participate in such efforts on a reasonable and nondiscriminatory basis, administered in such a manner as not to unreasonably exclude any interested industry party;

(iii) such entity shall publish a text for comment by such parties as have agreed to participate in the process pursuant to clause (ii), provide such parties a full opportunity to submit comments, and respond to comments from such parties;

(iv) such entity shall publish a final text of the industry-wide standard or industry-wide generic requirement, including the comments in their entirety, of any funding party which requests to have its comments so published; and

(v) such entity shall attempt, prior to publishing a text for comment, to agree with the funding parties as a group on a mutually satisfactory dispute resolution process which such parties shall utilize as their sole recourse in the event of a dispute on technical issues as to which there is disagreement between any funding party and the entity conducting such activities, except that if no dispute resolution process is agreed to by all the parties, a funding party may utilize the dispute resolution procedures established pursuant to paragraph (5) of this subsection;

(B) engage in product certification for telecommunications equipment or customer premises equipment manufactured by unaffiliated entities only if—

(i)   such activity is performed pursuant to published criteria;

(ii)   such activity is performed pursuant to auditable criteria; and

(iii)   such activity is performed pursuant to available industry-accepted testing methods and standards, where applicable, unless otherwise agreed upon by the parties funding and performing such activity;

(C)   not undertake any actions to monopolize or attempt to monopolize the market for such services; and

(D)   not preferentially treat its own telecommunications equipment or customer premises equipment, or that of its affiliate, over that of any other entity in establishing and publishing industry-wide standards or industry-wide generic requirements for, and in certification of, telecommunications equipment and customer premises equipment.

(5)   Alternate dispute resolution. — Within 90 days after the date of enactment of the Telecommunications Act of 1996, the Commission shall prescribe a dispute resolution process to be utilized in the event that a dispute resolution process is not agreed upon by all the parties when establishing and publishing any industry-wide standard or industry-wide generic requirement for telecommunications equipment or customer premises equipment, pursuant to paragraph (4)(A)(v). The Commission shall not establish itself as a party to the dispute resolution process. Such dispute resolution process shall permit any funding party to resolve a dispute with the entity conducting the activity that significantly affects such funding party's interests, in an open, nondiscriminatory, and unbiased fashion, within 30 days after the filing of such dispute. Such disputes may be filed within 15 days after the date the funding party receives a response to its comments from the entity conducting the activity. The Commission shall establish penalties to be assessed for delays caused by referral of frivolous disputes to the dispute resolution process.

(6)   Sunset. — The requirements of paragraphs (3) and (4) shall terminate for the particular relevant activity when the Commission determines that there are alternative sources of industry-wide standards, industry-wide generic requirements, or product certification for a particular class of telecommunications equipment or customer premises equipment available in the United States. Alternative sources shall be deemed to exist when such sources provide commercially viable alternatives that are providing such services to customers. The Commission shall act on any application for such a determination within 90 days after receipt of such application, and shall receive public comment on such application.

(7)   Administration and enforcement authority. — For the purposes of administering this subsection and the regulations prescribed thereunder, the Commission shall have the same remedial authority as the Commission has in administering and enforcing the provisions of this title with respect to any common carrier subject to this Act.

(8)   Definitions. — For purposes of this subsection:

(A)   The term "affiliate" shall have the same meaning as in section 3 of this Act, except that, for purposes of paragraph (1)(B)—

(i)   an aggregate voting equity interest in Bell Communications Research, Inc., of at least 5 percent of its total voting equity, owned directly or indirectly by more than one otherwise unaffiliated Bell operating company, shall constitute an affiliate relationship; and

(ii)   a voting equity interest in Bell Communications Research, Inc., by any otherwise unaffiliated Bell operating company of less than 1 percent of Bell Communications Research's total voting equity shall not be considered to be an equity interest under this paragraph.

(B)   The term "generic requirement" means a description of acceptable product attributes for use by local exchange carriers in establishing product specifications for the purchase of telecommunications equipment, customer premises equipment, and software integral thereto.

(C)   The term "industry-wide" means activities funded by or performed on behalf of local exchange carriers for use in providing wireline telephone exchange service whose combined total of deployed access lines in the United States constitutes at least 30 percent of all access lines deployed by telecommunications carriers in the United States as of the date of enactment of the Telecommunications Act of 1996.

(D)   The term "certification" means any technical process whereby a party determines whether a product, for use by more than one local exchange carrier, conforms with the specified requirements pertaining to such product.

(E)   The term "accredited standards development organization" means an entity composed of industry members which has been accredited by an institution vested with the responsibility for standards accreditation by the industry.

(e)   Bell Operating Company Equipment Procurement and Sales.—

(1)   Nondiscrimination standards for manufacturing. — In the procurement or awarding of supply contracts for telecommunications equipment, a Bell operating company, or any entity acting on its behalf, for the duration of the requirement for a separate subsidiary including manufacturing under this Act—

(A)   shall consider such equipment, produced or supplied by unrelated persons; and

(B)   may not discriminate in favor of equipment produced or supplied by an affiliate or related person.

(2)   Procurement standards. — Each Bell operating company or any entity acting on its behalf shall make procurement decisions and award all supply contracts for equipment, services, and software on the basis of an objective assessment of price, qualify, delivery, and other commercial factors.

(3)   Network planning and design. — A Bell operating company shall, to the extent consistent with the antitrust laws, engage in joint network planning and design with local exchange carriers operating in the same area of interest. No participant in such planning shall be allowed to delay the introduction of new technology or the deployment of facilities to provide telecommunications services, and agreement with such other carriers shall not be required as a prerequisite for such introduction or deployment.

(4)   Sales restrictions. — Neither a Bell operating company engaged in manufacturing nor a manufacturing affiliate of such a company

shall restrict sales to any local exchange carrier of telecommunications equipment, including software integral to the operation of such equipment and related upgrades.

(5)   Protection of proprietary information. — A Bell operating company and any entity it owns or otherwise controls shall protect the proprietary information submitted for procurement decisions from release not specifically authorized by the owner of such information.

(f)   Administration and Enforcement Authority. — For the purposes of administering and enforcing the provisions of this section and the regulations prescribed thereunder, the Commission shall have the same authority, power, and functions with respect to any Bell operating company or any affiliate thereof as the Commission has in administering and enforcing the provisions of this title with respect to any common carrier subject to this Act.

(g)   Additional Rules and Regulations. — The Commission may prescribe such additional rules and regulations as the Commission determines are necessary to carry out the provisions of this section, and otherwise to prevent discrimination and cross-subsidization in a Bell operating company's dealings with its affiliate and with third parties.

(h)   Definition. — As used in this section, the term "manufacturing" has the same meaning as such term has under the AT&T Consent Decree.

Sec. 274   Electronic Publishing by Bell Operating Companies

(a)   Limitations. — No Bell operating company or any affiliate may engage in the provision of electronic publishing that is disseminated by means of such Bell operating company's or any of its affiliates' basic telephone service, except that nothing in this section shall prohibit a separated affiliate or electronic publishing joint venture operated in accordance with this section from engaging in the provision of electronic publishing.

(b)   Separated Affiliate or Electronic Publishing Joint Venture Requirements. — A separated affiliate or electronic publishing joint venture shall be operated independently from the Bell operating company. Such separated affiliate or joint venture and the Bell operating company with which it is affiliated shall—

(1)   maintain separate books, records, and accounts and prepare separate financial statements;

(2)   not incur debt in a manner that would permit a creditor of the separated affiliate or joint venture upon default to have recourse to the assets of the Bell operating company;

(3)   carry out transactions (A) in a manner consistent with such independence, (B) pursuant to written contracts or tariffs that are filed with the Commission and made publicly available, and (C) in a manner that is auditable in accordance with generally accepted auditing standards;

(4)   value any assets that are transferred directly or indirectly from the Bell operating company to a separated affiliate or joint venture, and record any transactions by which such assets are transferred, in accordance with such regulations as may be prescribed by the Commission or a State commission to prevent improper cross subsidies;

(5)   between a separated affiliate and a Bell operating company—

(A)   have no officers, directors, and employees in common after the effective date of this section; and

(B)   own no property in common;

(6)   not use for the marketing of any product or service of the separated affiliate or joint venture, the name, trademarks, or service marks of an existing Bell operating company except for names, trademarks, or service marks that are owned by the entity that owns or controls the Bell operating company;

(7)   not permit the Bell operating company—

(A)   to perform hiring or training of personnel on behalf of a separated affiliate;

(B)   to perform the purchasing, installation, or maintenance of equipment on behalf of a separated affiliate, except for telephone service that it provides under tariff or contract subject to the provisions of this section; or

(C)   to perform research and development on behalf of a separated affiliate;

(8)   each have performed annually a compliance review—

(A)   that is conducted by an independent entity for the purpose of determining compliance during the preceding calendar year with any provision of this section; and

(B)   the results of which are maintained by the separated affiliate or joint venture and the Bell operating company for a period of 5 years subject to review by any lawful authority; and

(9)   within 90 days of receiving a review described in paragraph (8), file a report of any exceptions and corrective action with the Commission and allow any person to inspect and copy such report subject to reasonable safeguards to protect any proprietary information contained in such report from being used for purposes other than to enforce or pursue remedies under this section.

(c)   Joint Marketing.—

(1)   In general. — Except as provided in paragraph (2)—

(A)   a Bell operating company shall not carry out any promotion, marketing, sales, or advertising for or in conjunction with a separated affiliate; and

(B)   a Bell operating company shall not carry out any promotion, marketing, sales, or advertising for or in conjunction with an affiliate that is related to the provision of electronic publishing.

(2)   Permissible joint activities.—

(A)   Joint telemarketing. — A Bell operating company may provide inbound telemarketing or referral services related to the provision of electronic publishing for a separated affiliate, electronic publishing joint venture, affiliate, or unaffiliated electronic publisher, provided that if such services are provided to a separated affiliate, electronic publishing joint venture, or affiliate, such services shall be made available to all electronic publishers on request, on nondiscriminatory terms.

(B)   Teaming arrangements. — A Bell operating company may engage in nondiscriminatory teaming or business arrangements to engage in electronic publishing with any separated affiliate or with any other electronic publisher if (i) the Bell operating company only provides facilities, services, and basic telephone service information as authorized by this section, and (ii) the Bell operating company does not own such teaming or business arrangement.

(C) Electronic publishing joint ventures. — A Bell operating company or affiliate may participate on a nonexclusive basis in electronic publishing joint ventures with entities that are not a Bell operating company, affiliate, or separated affiliate to provide electronic publishing services, if the Bell operating company or affiliate has not more than a 50 percent direct or indirect equity interest (or the equivalent thereof) or the right to more than 50 percent of the gross revenues under a revenue sharing or royalty agreement in any electronic publishing joint venture. Officers and employees of a Bell operating company or affiliate participating in an electronic publishing joint venture may not have more than 50 percent of the voting control over the electronic publishing joint venture. In the case of joint ventures with small, local electronic publishers, the Commission for good cause shown may authorize the Bell operating company or affiliate to have a larger equity interest, revenue share, or voting control but not to exceed 80 percent. A Bell operating company participating in an electronic publishing joint venture may provide promotion, marketing, sales, or advertising personnel and services to such joint venture.

(d) Bell Operating Company Requirement. — A Bell operating company under common ownership or control with a separated affiliate or electronic publishing joint venture shall provide network access and interconnections for basic telephone service to electronic publishers at just and reasonable rates that are tariffed (so long as rates for such services are subject to regulation) and that are not higher on a per-unit basis than those charged for such services to any other electronic publisher or any separated affiliate engaged in electronic publishing.

(e) Private Right of Action.—

(1) Damages. — Any person claiming that any act or practice of any Bell operating company, affiliate, or separated affiliate constitutes a violation of this section may file a complaint with the Commission or bring suit as provided in section 207 of this Act, and such Bell operating company, affiliate, or separated affiliate shall be liable as provided in section 206 of this Act; except that damages may not be awarded for a violation that is discovered by a compliance review as required by subsection (b)(7) of this section and corrected within 90 days.

(2) Cease and desist orders. — In addition to the provisions of paragraph (1), any person claiming that any act or practice of any Bell operating company, affiliate, or separated affiliate constitutes a violation of this section may make application to the Commission for an order to cease and desist such violation or may make application in any district court of the United States of competent jurisdiction for an order enjoining such acts or practices or for an order compelling compliance with such requirement.

(f) Separated Affiliate Reporting Requirement. — Any separated affiliate under this section shall file with the Commission annual reports in a form substantially equivalent to the Form 10 K required by regulations of the Securities and Exchange Commission.

(g)   Effective Dates.—

(1)   Transition. — Any electronic publishing service being offered to the public by a Bell operating company or affiliate on the date of enactment of the Telecommunications Act of 1996 shall have one year from such date of enactment to comply with the requirements of this section.

(2)   Sunset. — The provisions of this section shall not apply to conduct occurring after 4 years after the date of enactment of the Telecommunications Act of 1996.

(h)   Definition of Electronic Publishing.—

(1)   In general. — The term "electronic publishing" means the dissemination, provision, publication, or sale to an unaffiliated entity or person, of any one or more of the following: news (including sports); entertainment (other than interactive games); business, financial, legal, consumer, or credit materials; editorials, columns, or features; advertising; photos or images; archival or research material; legal notices or public records; scientific, educational, instructional, technical, professional, trade, or other literary materials; or other like or similar information.

(2)   Exceptions. — The term "electronic publishing" shall not include the following services:

(A)   Information access, as that term is defined by the AT&T Consent Decree.

(B)   The transmission of information as a common carrier.

(C)   The transmission of information as part of a gateway to an information service that does not involve the generation or alteration of the content of information, including data transmission, address translation, protocol conversion, billing management, introductory information content, and navigational systems that enable users to access electronic publishing services, which do not affect the presentation of such electronic publishing services to users.

(D)   Voice storage and retrieval services, including voice messaging and electronic mail services.

(E)   Data processing or transaction processing services that do not involve the generation or alteration of the content of information.

(F)   Electronic billing or advertising of a Bell operating company's regulated telecommunications services.

(G)   Language translation or data format conversion.

(H)   The provision of information necessary for the management, control, or operation of a telephone company telecommunications system.

(I)   The provision of directory assistance that provides names, addresses, and telephone numbers and does not include advertising.

(J)   Caller identification services.

(K)   Repair and provisioning databases and credit card and billing validation for telephone company operations.

(L)   911 E and other emergency assistance databases.

(M)   Any other network service of a type that is like or similar to these network services and that does not involve the generation or alteration of the content of information.

(N)   Any upgrades to these network services that do not involve the generation or alteration of the content of information.

(O)   Video programming or full motion video entertainment on demand.

(i)   Additional Definitions. — As used in this section—

(1)   The term "affiliate" means any entity that, directly or indirectly, owns or controls, is owned or controlled by, or is under common ownership or control with, a Bell operating company. Such term shall not include a separated affiliate.

(2)   The term "basic telephone service" means any wireline telephone exchange service, or wireline telephone exchange service facility, provided by a Bell operating company in a telephone exchange area, except that such term does not include—

(A)   a competitive wireline telephone exchange service provided in a telephone exchange area where another entity provides a wireline telephone exchange service that was provided on January 1, 1984, or

(B)   a commercial mobile service.

(3)   The term "basic telephone service information" means network and customer information of a Bell operating company and other information acquired by a Bell operating company as a result of its engaging in the provision of basic telephone service.

(4)   The term "control" has the meaning that it has in 17 C.F.R. 240.12b 2, the regulations promulgated by the Securities and Exchange Commission pursuant to the Securities Exchange Act of 1934 (15 U.S.C. 78a et seq.) or any successor provision to such section.

(5)   The term "electronic publishing joint venture" means a joint venture owned by a Bell operating company or affiliate that engages in the provision of electronic publishing which is disseminated by means of such Bell operating company's or any of its affiliates' basic telephone service.

(6)   The term "entity" means any organization, and includes corporations, partnerships, sole proprietorships, associations, and joint ventures.

(7)   The term "inbound telemarketing" means the marketing of property, goods, or services by telephone to a customer or potential customer who initiated the call.

(8)   The term "own" with respect to an entity means to have a direct or indirect equity interest (or the equivalent thereof) of more than 10 percent of an entity, or the right to more than 10 percent of the gross revenues of an entity under a revenue sharing or royalty agreement.

(9)   The term "separated affiliate" means a corporation under common ownership or control with a Bell operating company that does not own or control a Bell operating company and is not owned or controlled by a Bell operating company and that engages in the provision of electronic publishing which is disseminated by means of such Bell operating company's or any of its affiliates' basic telephone service.

(10)   The term "Bell operating company" has the meaning provided in section 3, except that such term includes any entity or corporation that is owned or controlled by such a company (as so defined) but does not include an electronic publishing joint venture owned by such an entity or corporation.

Sec. 275   Alarm Monitoring Services

(a)   Delayed Entry Into Alarm Monitoring.—

(1)   Prohibition. — No Bell operating company or affiliate thereof shall engage in the provision of alarm monitoring services before the date which is 5 years after the date of enactment of the Telecommunications Act of 1996.

(2)   Existing activities. — Paragraph (1) does not prohibit or limit the provision, directly or through an affiliate, of alarm monitoring services by a Bell operating company that was engaged in providing alarm monitoring services as of November 30, 1995, directly or through an affiliate. Such Bell operating company or affiliate may not acquire any equity interest in, or obtain financial control of, any unaffiliated alarm monitoring service entity after November 30, 1995, and until 5 years after the date of enactment of the Telecommunications Act of 1996, except that this sentence shall not prohibit an exchange of customers for the customers of an unaffiliated alarm monitoring service entity.

(b)   Nondiscrimination. — An incumbent local exchange carrier (as defined in section 251(h)) engaged in the provision of alarm monitoring services shall—

(1)   provide nonaffiliated entities, upon reasonable request, with the network services it provides to its own alarm monitoring operations, on nondiscriminatory terms and conditions; and

(2)   not subsidize its alarm monitoring services either directly or indirectly from telephone exchange service operations.

(c)   Expedited Consideration of Complaints. — The Commission shall establish procedures for the receipt and review of complaints concerning violations of subsection (b) or the regulations thereunder that result in material financial harm to a provider of alarm monitoring service. Such procedures shall ensure that the Commission will make a final determination with respect to any such complaint within 120 days after receipt of the complaint. If the complaint contains an appropriate showing that the alleged violation occurred, as determined by the Commission in accordance with such regulations, the Commission shall, within 60 days after receipt of the complaint, order the incumbent local exchange carrier (as defined in section 251(h)) and its affiliates to cease engaging in such violation pending such final determination.

(d)   Use of Data. — A local exchange carrier may not record or use in any fashion the occurrence or contents of calls received by providers of alarm monitoring services for the purposes of marketing such services on behalf of such local exchange carrier, or any other entity. Any regulations necessary to enforce this subsection shall be issued initially within 6 months after the date of enactment of the Telecommunications Act of 1996.

(e)   Definition of Alarm Monitoring service. — The term "alarm monitoring service" means a service that uses a device located at a residence, place of business, or other fixed premises—

(1)   to receive signals from other devices located at or about such premises regarding a possible threat at such premises to life, safety, or property, from burglary, fire, vandalism, bodily injury, or other emergency, and

(2) to transmit a signal regarding such threat by means of transmission facilities of a local exchange carrier or one of its affiliates to a remote monitoring center to alert a person at such center of the need to inform the customer or another person or police, fire, rescue, security, or public safety personnel of such threat,

but does not include a service that uses a medical monitoring device attached to an individual for the automatic surveillance of an ongoing medical condition.

Sec. 276 Provision of Payphone Service

(a) Nondiscrimination Safeguards. — After the effective date of the rules prescribed pursuant to subsection (b), any Bell operating company that provides payphone service—

(1) shall not subsidize its payphone service directly or indirectly from its telephone exchange service operations or its exchange access operations; and

(2) shall not prefer or discriminate in favor of its payphone service.

(b) Regulations.—

(1) Contents of regulations. — In order to promote competition among payphone service providers and promote the widespread deployment of payphone services to the benefit of the general public, within 9 months after the date of enactment of the Telecommunications Act of 1996, the Commission shall take all actions necessary (including any reconsideration) to prescribe regulations that—

(A) establish a per call compensation plan to ensure that all payphone service providers are fairly compensated for each and every completed intrastate and interstate call using their payphone, except that emergency calls and telecommunications relay service calls for hearing disabled individuals shall not be subject to such compensation;

(B) discontinue the intrastate and interstate carrier access charge payphone service elements and payments in effect on such date of enactment, and all intrastate and interstate payphone subsidies from basic exchange and exchange access revenues, in favor of a compensation plan as specified in subparagraph (A);

(C) prescribe a set of nonstructural safeguards for Bell operating company payphone service to implement the provisions of paragraphs (1) and (2) of subsection (a), which safeguards shall, at a minimum, include the nonstructural safeguards equal to those adopted in the Computer Inquiry-III (CC Docket No. 90 623) proceeding;

(D) provide for Bell operating company payphone service providers to have the same right that independent payphone providers have to negotiate with the location provider on the location provider's selecting and contracting with, and, subject to the terms of any agreement with the location provider, to select and contract with, the carriers that carry interLATA calls from their payphones, unless the Commission determines in the rulemaking pursuant to this section that it is not in the public interest; and

(E) provide for all payphone service providers to have the right to negotiate with the location provider on the location provider's selecting and contracting with, and, subject to the terms of any agreement with the location provider, to select and contract with, the carriers that carry intraLATA calls from their payphones.

(2) Public interest telephones. — In the rulemaking conducted pursuant to paragraph (1), the Commission shall determine whether public interest payphones, which are provided in the interest of public health, safety, and welfare, in locations where there would otherwise not be a payphone, should be maintained, and if so, ensure that such public interest payphones are supported fairly and equitably.

(3) Existing contracts. — Nothing in this section shall affect any existing contracts between location providers and payphone service providers or interLATA or intraLATA carriers that are in force and effect as of the date of enactment of the Telecommunications Act of 1996.

(c) State Preemption. — To the extent that any State requirements are inconsistent with the Commission's regulations, the Commission's regulations on such matters shall preempt such State requirements.

(d) Definition. — As used in this section, the term "payphone service" means the provision of public or semi-public pay telephones, the provision of inmate telephone service in correctional institutions, and any ancillary services.'.

(e) Review of Entry Decisions. — Section 402(b) (47 U.S.C. 402(b)) is amended—

(1) in paragraph (6), by striking '(3), and (4)' and inserting '(3), (4), and (9)'; and

(2) by adding at the end the following new paragraph:

'(9) By any applicant for authority to provide interLATA services under section 271 of this Act whose application is denied by the Commission.'.

TITLE IV   REGULATORY REFORM

Sec. 401   Regulatory Forbearance

Title I is amended by inserting after section 9 (47 U.S.C. 159) the following new section:

Sec. 10   Competition in Provision of Telecommunications Service

(a) Regulatory flexibility. — Notwithstanding section 332(c)(1)(A) of this Act, the Commission shall forbear from applying any regulation or any provision of this Act to a telecommunications carrier or telecommunications service, or class of telecommunications carriers or telecommunications services, in any or some of its or their geographic markets, if the Commission determines that—

(1) enforcement of such regulation or provision is not necessary to ensure that the charges, practices, classifications, or regulations by, for, or in connection with that telecommunications carrier or telecommunications service are just and reasonable and are not unjustly or unreasonably discriminatory;

(2) enforcement of such regulation or provision is not necessary for the protection of consumers; and

(3)   forbearance from applying such provision or regulation is consistent with the public interest.

(b)   Competitive Effect To Be Weighed. — In making the determination under subsection (a)(3), the Commission shall consider whether forbearance from enforcing the provision or regulation will promote competitive market conditions, including the extent to which such forbearance will enhance competition among providers of telecommunications services. If the Commission determines that such forbearance will promote competition among providers of telecommunications services, that determination may be the basis for a Commission finding that forbearance is in the public interest.

(c)   Petition for Forbearance. — Any telecommunications carrier, or class of telecommunications carriers, may submit a petition to the Commission requesting that the Commission exercise the authority granted under this section with respect to that carrier or those carriers, or any service offered by that carrier or carriers. Any such petition shall be deemed granted if the Commission does not deny the petition for failure to meet the requirements for forbearance under subsection (a) within one year after the Commission receives it, unless the one-year period is extended by the Commission. The Commission may extend the initial one-year period by an additional 90 days if the Commission finds that an extension is necessary to meet the requirements of subsection (a). The Commission may grant or deny a petition in whole or in part and shall explain its decision in writing.

(d)   Limitation. — Except as provided in section 251(f), the Commission may not forbear from applying the requirements of section 251(c) or 271 under subsection (a) of this section until it determines that those requirements have been fully implemented.

(e)   State Enforcement After Commission Forbearance. — A State commission may not continue to apply or enforce any provision of this Act that the Commission has determined to forbear from applying under subsection (a).'.

TITLE V   OBSCENITY AND VIOLENCE

Subtitle A   Obscene, Harassing, and Wrongful Utilization of Telecommunications Facilities

Sec. 501   Short Title

This title may be cited as the 'Communications Decency Act of 1996'.

Sec. 502   Obscene or Harassing use of Telecommunications Facilities Under the Communications Act of 1934

Section 223 (47 U.S.C. 223) is amended—
(1)   by striking subsection (a) and inserting in lieu thereof:
      '(a)   Whoever—
         (1)   in interstate or foreign communications—
            (A)   by means of a telecommunications device knowingly—

(i)   makes, creates, or solicits, and

(ii)   initiates the transmission of,

any comment, request, suggestion, proposal, image, or other communication which is obscene, lewd, lascivious, filthy, or indecent, with intent to annoy, abuse, threaten, or harass another person;

(B)   by means of a telecommunications device knowingly—

(i)   makes, creates, or solicits, and

(ii)   initiates the transmission of,

any comment, request, suggestion, proposal, image, or other communication which is obscene or indecent, knowing that the recipient of the communication is under 18 years of age, regardless of whether the maker of such communication placed the call or initiated the communication;

(C)   makes a telephone call or utilizes a telecommunications device, whether or not conversation or communication ensues, without disclosing his identity and with intent to annoy, abuse, threaten, or harass any person at the called number or who receives the communications;

(D)   makes or causes the telephone of another repeatedly or continuously to ring, with intent to harass any person at the called number; or

(E)   makes repeated telephone calls or repeatedly initiates communication with a telecommunications device, during which conversation or communication ensues, solely to harass any person at the called number or who receives the communication; or

(2)   knowingly permits any telecommunications facility under his control to be used for any activity prohibited by paragraph (1) with the intent that it be used for such activity,

shall be fined under title 18, United States Code, or imprisoned not more than two years, or both.'; and

(2)   by adding at the end the following new subsections:

(d)   Whoever—

(1)   in interstate or foreign communications knowingly—

(A)   uses an interactive computer service to send to a specific person or persons under 18 years of age, or

(B)   uses any interactive computer service to display in a manner available to a person under 18 years of age,

any comment, request, suggestion, proposal, image, or other communication that, in context, depicts or describes, in terms patently offensive as measured by contemporary community standards, sexual or excretory activities or organs, regardless of whether the user of such service placed the call or initiated the communication; or

(2)   knowingly permits any telecommunications facility under such person's control to be used for an activity prohibited by paragraph (1) with the intent that it be used for such activity,

shall be fined under title 18, United States Code, or imprisoned not more than two years, or both.

(e)   In addition to any other defenses available by law:

(1)   No person shall be held to have violated subsection (a) or (d) solely for providing access or connection to or from a facility, system, or network not under that person's control, including transmission, down-

loading, intermediate storage, access software, or other related capabilities that are incidental to providing such access or connection that does not include the creation of the content of the communication.

(2)   The defenses provided by paragraph (1) of this subsection shall not be applicable to a person who is a conspirator with an entity actively involved in the creation or knowing distribution of communications that violate this section, or who knowingly advertises the availability of such communications.

(3)   The defenses provided in paragraph (1) of this subsection shall not be applicable to a person who provides access or connection to a facility, system, or network engaged in the violation of this section that is owned or controlled by such person.

(4)   No employer shall be held liable under this section for the actions of an employee or agent unless the employee's or agent's conduct is within the scope of his or her employment or agency and the employer (A) having knowledge of such conduct, authorizes or ratifies such conduct, or (B) recklessly disregards such conduct.

(5)   It is a defense to a prosecution under subsection (a)(1)(B) or (d), or under subsection (a)(2) with respect to the use of a facility for an activity under subsection (a)(1)(B) that a person—

(A)   has taken, in good faith, reasonable, effective, and appropriate actions under the circumstances to restrict or prevent access by minors to a communication specified in such subsections, which may involve any appropriate measures to restrict minors from such communications, including any method which is feasible under available technology; or

(B)   has restricted access to such communication by requiring use of a verified credit card, debit account, adult access code, or adult personal identification number.

(6)   The Commission may describe measures which are reasonable, effective, and appropriate to restrict access to prohibited communications under subsection (d). Nothing in this section authorizes the Commission to enforce, or is intended to provide the Commission with the authority to approve, sanction, or permit, the use of such measures. The Commission shall have no enforcement authority over the failure to utilize such measures. The Commission shall not endorse specific products relating to such measures. The use of such measures shall be admitted as evidence of good faith efforts for purposes of paragraph (5) in any action arising under subsection (d). Nothing in this section shall be construed to treat interactive computer services as common carriers or telecommunications carriers.

(f)(1)   No cause of action may be brought in any court or administrative agency against any person on account of any activity that is not in violation of any law punishable by criminal or civil penalty, and that the person has taken in good faith to implement a defense authorized under this section or otherwise to restrict or prevent the transmission of, or access to, a communication specified in this section.

(2)   No State or local government may impose any liability for commercial activities or actions by commercial entities, nonprofit libraries, or institutions of higher education in connection with an activity or

action described in subsection (a)(2) or (d) that is inconsistent with the treatment of those activities or actions under this section: Provided, however, That nothing herein shall preclude any State or local government from enacting and enforcing complementary oversight, liability, and regulatory systems, procedures, and requirements, so long as such systems, procedures, and requirements govern only intrastate services and do not result in the imposition of inconsistent rights, duties or obligations on the provision of interstate services. Nothing in this subsection shall preclude any State or local government from governing conduct not covered by this section.

(g)   Nothing in subsection (a), (d), (e), or (f) or in the defenses to prosecution under (a) or (d) shall be construed to affect or limit the application or enforcement of any other Federal law.

(h)   For purposes of this section—

(1)   The use of the term "telecommunications device" in this section—

(A)   shall not impose new obligations on broadcasting station licensees and cable operators covered by obscenity and indecency provisions elsewhere in this Act; and

(B)   does not include an interactive computer service.

(2)   The term "interactive computer service" has the meaning provided in section 230(e)(2).

(3)   The term "access software" means software (including client or server software) or enabling tools that do not create or provide the content of the communication but that allow a user to do any one or more of the following:

(A)   filter, screen, allow, or disallow content;

(B)   pick, choose, analyze, or digest content; or

(C)   transmit, receive, display, forward, cache, search, subset, organize, reorganize, or translate content.

(4)   The term "institution of higher education" has the meaning provided in section 1201 of the Higher Education Act of 1965 (20 U.S.C. 1141).

(5)   The term "library" means a library eligible for participation in State-based plans for funds under title III of the Library Services and Construction Act (20 U.S.C. 355e et seq.).'.

Sec. 503   Obscene Programming on Cable Television

Section 639 (47 U.S.C. 559) is amended by striking 'not more than $10,000' and inserting 'under title 18, United States Code,'.

Sec. 504   Scrambling of Cable Channels for Nonsubscribers

Part IV of title VI (47 U.S.C. 551 et seq.) is amended by adding at the end the following:

'Sec. 640   Scrambling of Cable Channels for Nonsubscribers

(a)   Subscriber Request. — Upon request by a cable service subscriber, a cable operator shall, without charge, fully scramble or otherwise fully block the audio and video programming of each channel carrying such programming so that one not a subscriber does not receive it.

(b) Definition. — As used in this section, the term "scramble" means to rearrange the content of the signal of the programming so that the programming cannot be viewed or heard in an understandable manner.'.

Sec. 505   Scrambling of Sexually Explicit Adult Video Service rogramming

(a) Requirement. — Part IV of title VI (47 U.S.C. 551 et seq.), as amended by this Act, is further amended by adding at the end the following:

'Sec. 641   Scrambling of Sexually Explicit Adult Video Service Programming

(a) Requirement. — In providing sexually explicit adult programming or other programming that is indecent on any channel of its service primarily dedicated to sexually-oriented programming, a multichannel video programming distributor shall fully scramble or otherwise fully block the video and audio portion of such channel so that one not a subscriber to such channel or programming does not receive it.

(b) Implementation. — Until a multichannel video programming distributor complies with the requirement set forth in subsection (a), the distributor shall limit the access of children to the programming referred to in that subsection by not providing such programming during the hours of the day (as determined by the Commission) when a significant number of children are likely to view it.

(c) Definition. — As used in this section, the term "scramble" means to rearrange the content of the signal of the programming so that the programming cannot be viewed or heard in an understandable manner.'.

(b)   Effective Date. — The amendment made by subsection (a) shall take effect 30 days after the date of enactment of this Act.

Sec. 506   Cable Operator Refusal to Carry Certain Programs

(a)   Public, Educational, and Governmental Channels. — Section 611(e) (47 U.S.C. 531(e)) is amended by inserting before the period the following: ', except a cable operator may refuse to transmit any public access program or portion of a public access program which contains obscenity, indecency, or nudity'.

(b)   Cable Channels for Commercial Use. — Section 612(c)(2) (47 U.S.C. 532(c)(2)) is amended by striking 'an operator' and inserting 'a cable operator may refuse to transmit any leased access program or portion of a leased access program which contains obscenity, indecency, or nudity and'.

Sec. 507   Clarification of Current Laws Regarding Communication of Obscene Materials Through the Use of Computers

(a)   Importation or Transportation. — Section 1462 of title 18, United States Code, is amended—

(1) in the first undesignated paragraph, by inserting 'or interactive computer service (as defined in section 230(e)(2) of the Communications Act of 1934)' after 'carrier'; and

(2) in the second undesignated paragraph—

(A) by inserting 'or receives,' after 'takes';

(B) by inserting 'or interactive computer service (as defined in section 230(e)(2) of the Communications Act of 1934)' after 'common carrier'; and

(C) by inserting 'or importation' after 'carriage'.

(b) Transportation for Purposes of Sale or Distribution. — The first undesignated paragraph of section 1465 of title 18, United States Code, is amended—

(1) by striking 'transports in' and inserting 'transports or travels in, or uses a facility or means of,';

(2) by inserting 'or an interactive computer service (as defined in section 230(e)(2) of the Communications Act of 1934) in or affecting such commerce' after 'foreign commerce' the first place it appears;

(3) by striking ', or knowingly travels in' and all that follows through 'obscene material in interstate or foreign commerce,' and inserting 'of'.

(c) Interpretation. — The amendments made by this section are clarifying and shall not be interpreted to limit or repeal any prohibition contained in sections 1462 and 1465 of title 18, United States Code, before such amendment, under the rule established in United States v. Alpers, 338 U.S. 680 (1950).

Sec. 508 Coercion and Enticement of Minors

Section 2422 of title 18, United States Code, is amended—

(1) by inserting '(a)' before 'Whoever knowingly'; and

(2) by adding at the end the following:

'(b) Whoever, using any facility or means of interstate or foreign commerce, including the mail, or within the special maritime and territorial jurisdiction of the United States, knowingly persuades, induces, entices, or coerces any individual who has not attained the age of 18 years to engage in prostitution or any sexual act for which any person may be criminally prosecuted, or attempts to do so, shall be fined under this title or imprisoned not more than 10 years, or both.'.

Sec. 509 Online Family Empowerment

Title II of the Communications Act of 1934 (47 U.S.C. 201 et seq.) is amended by adding at the end the following new section:

'Sec. 230 Protection for Private Blocking and Screening of Offensive Material

(a) Findings. — The Congress finds the following:

(1) The rapidly developing array of Internet and other interactive computer services available to individual Americans represent an extraordinary advance in the availability of educational and informational resources to our citizens.

(2)   These services offer users a great degree of control over the information that they receive, as well as the potential for even greater control in the future as technology develops.

(3)   The Internet and other interactive computer services offer a forum for a true diversity of political discourse, unique opportunities for cultural development, and myriad avenues for intellectual activity.

(4)   The Internet and other interactive computer services have flourished, to the benefit of all Americans, with a minimum of government regulation.

(5)   Increasingly Americans are relying on interactive media for a variety of political, educational, cultural, and entertainment services.

(b)   Policy. — It is the policy of the United States—

(1)   to promote the continued development of the Internet and other interactive computer services and other interactive media;

(2)   to preserve the vibrant and competitive free market that presently exists for the Internet and other interactive computer services, unfettered by Federal or State regulation;

(3)   to encourage the development of technologies which maximize user control over what information is received by individuals, families, and schools who use the Internet and other interactive computer services;

(4)   to remove disincentives for the development and utilization of blocking and filtering technologies that empower parents to restrict their children's access to objectionable or inappropriate online material; and

(5)   to ensure vigorous enforcement of Federal criminal laws to deter and punish trafficking in obscenity, stalking, and harassment by means of computer.

(c)   Protection for "Good Samaritan" Blocking and Screening of Offensive Material.—

(1)   Treatment of publisher or speaker. — No provider or user of an interactive computer service shall be treated as the publisher or speaker of any information provided by another information content provider.

(2)   Civil liability. — No provider or user of an interactive computer service shall be held liable on account of—

(A)   any action voluntarily taken in good faith to restrict access to or availability of material that the provider or user considers to be obscene, lewd, lascivious, filthy, excessively violent, harassing, or otherwise objectionable, whether or not such material is constitutionally protected; or

(B)   any action taken to enable or make available to information content providers or others the technical means to restrict access to material described in paragraph (1).

(d)   Effect on Other Laws.—

(1)   No effect on criminal law. — Nothing in this section shall be construed to impair the enforcement of section 223 of this Act, chapter 71 (relating to obscenity) or 110 (relating to sexual exploitation of children) of title 18, United States Code, or any other Federal criminal statute.

(2)   No effect on intellectual property law. — Nothing in this section shall be construed to limit or expand any law pertaining to intellectual property.

(3)   State law. — Nothing in this section shall be construed to prevent any State from enforcing any State law that is consistent with this section. No cause of action may be brought and no liability may be imposed under any State or local law that is inconsistent with this section.

(4)   No effect on communications privacy law. — Nothing in this section shall be construed to limit the application of the Electronic Communications Privacy Act of 1986 or any of the amendments made by such Act, or any similar State law.

(e)   Definitions. — As used in this section:

(1)   Internet. — The term "Internet" means the international computer network of both Federal and non-Federal interoperable packet switched data networks.

(2)   Interactive computer service. — The term "interactive computer service" means any information service, system, or access software provider that provides or enables computer access by multiple users to a computer server, including specifically a service or system that provides access to the Internet and such systems operated or services offered by libraries or educational institutions.

(3)   Information content provider. — The term "information content provider" means any person or entity that is responsible, in whole or in part, for the creation or development of information provided through the Internet or any other interactive computer service.

(4)   Access software provider. — The term "access software provider" means a provider of software (including client or server software), or enabling tools that do any one or more of the following:

(A)   filter, screen, allow, or disallow content;

(B)   pick, choose, analyze, or digest content; or

(C)   transmit, receive, display, forward, cache, search, subset, organize, reorganize, or translate content.'.

Subtitle B   Violence

Sec. 551   Parental Choice in Television Programming

(a)   Findings. — The Congress makes the following findings:

(1)   Television influences children's perception of the values and behavior that are common and acceptable in society.

(2)   Television station operators, cable television system operators, and video programmers should follow practices in connection with video programming that take into consideration that television broadcast and cable programming has established a uniquely pervasive presence in the lives of American children.

(3)   The average American child is exposed to 25 hours of television each week and some children are exposed to as much as 11 hours of television a day.

(4)   Studies have shown that children exposed to violent video programming at a young age have a higher tendency for violent and aggressive behavior later in life than children not so exposed, and that children exposed to violent video programming are prone to assume that acts of violence are acceptable behavior.

(5) Children in the United States are, on average, exposed to an estimated 8,000 murders and 100,000 acts of violence on television by the time the child completes elementary school.

(6) Studies indicate that children are affected by the pervasiveness and casual treatment of sexual material on television, eroding the ability of parents to develop responsible attitudes and behavior in their children.

(7) Parents express grave concern over violent and sexual video programming and strongly support technology that would give them greater control to block video programming in the home that they consider harmful to their children.

(8) There is a compelling governmental interest in empowering parents to limit the negative influences of video programming that is harmful to children.

(9) Providing parents with timely information about the nature of upcoming video programming and with the technological tools that allow them easily to block violent, sexual, or other programming that they believe harmful to their children is a nonintrusive and narrowly tailored means of achieving that compelling governmental interest.

(b) Establishment of Television Rating Code.—

(1) Amendment. — Section 303 (47 U.S.C. 303) is amended by adding at the end the following:

'(w) Prescribe—

(1) on the basis of recommendations from an advisory committee established by the Commission in accordance with section 551(b)(2) of the Telecommunications Act of 1996, guidelines and recommended procedures for the identification and rating of video programming that contains sexual, violent, or other indecent material about which parents should be informed before it is displayed to children, provided that nothing in this paragraph shall be construed to authorize any rating of video programming on the basis of its political or religious content; and

(2) with respect to any video programming that has been rated, and in consultation with the television industry, rules requiring distributors of such video programming to transmit such rating to permit parents to block the display of video programming that they have determined is inappropriate for their children.'.

(2) Advisory committee requirements. — In establishing an advisory committee for purposes of the amendment made by paragraph (1) of this subsection, the Commission shall—

(A) ensure that such committee is composed of parents, television broadcasters, television programming producers, cable operators, appropriate public interest groups, and other interested individuals from the private sector and is fairly balanced in terms of political affiliation, the points of view represented, and the functions to be performed by the committee;

(B) provide to the committee such staff and resources as may be necessary to permit it to perform its functions efficiently and promptly; and

(C) require the committee to submit a final report of its recommendations within one year after the date of the appointment of the initial members.

(c) Requirement for Manufacture of Televisions That Block Programs. — Section 303 (47 U.S.C. 303), as amended by subsection (a), is further amended by adding at the end the following:

'(x)   Require, in the case of an apparatus designed to receive television signals that are shipped in interstate commerce or manufactured in the United States and that have a picture screen 13 inches or greater in size (measured diagonally), that such apparatus be equipped with a feature designed to enable viewers to block display of all programs with a common rating, except as otherwise permitted by regulations pursuant to section 330(c)(4).'.

(d)   Shipping of Televisions That Block Programs.—
(1)   Regulations. — Section 330 (47 U.S.C. 330) is amended—
(A)   by redesignating subsection (c) as subsection (d); and
(B)   by adding after subsection (b) the following new subsection (c):

'(c)(1)   Except as provided in paragraph (2), no person shall ship in interstate commerce or manufacture in the United States any apparatus described in section 303(x) of this Act except in accordance with rules prescribed by the Commission pursuant to the authority granted by that section.

(2)   This subsection shall not apply to carriers transporting apparatus referred to in paragraph (1) without trading in it.

(3)   The rules prescribed by the Commission under this subsection shall provide for the oversight by the Commission of the adoption of standards by industry for blocking technology. Such rules shall require that all such apparatus be able to receive the rating signals which have been transmitted by way of line 21 of the vertical blanking interval and which conform to the signal and blocking specifications established by industry under the supervision of the Commission.

(4)   As new video technology is developed, the Commission shall take such action as the Commission determines appropriate to ensure that blocking service continues to be available to consumers. If the Commission determines that an alternative blocking technology exists that—
(A)   enables parents to block programming based on identifying programs without ratings,
(B)   is available to consumers at a cost which is comparable to the cost of technology that allows parents to block programming based on common ratings, and
(C)   will allow parents to block a broad range of programs on a multichannel system as effectively and as easily as technology that allows parents to block programming based on common ratings,
the Commission shall amend the rules prescribed pursuant to section 303(x) to require that the apparatus described in such section be equipped with either the blocking technology described in such section or the alternative blocking technology described in this paragraph.'.

(2)   Conforming amendment. — Section 330(d), as redesignated by subsection (d)(1)(A), is amended by striking 'section 303(s), and section 303(u)' and inserting in lieu thereof 'and sections 303(s), 303(u), and 303(x)'.

(e)   Applicability and Effective Dates.—
(1)   Applicability of rating provision. — The amendment made by subsection (b) of this section shall take effect 1 year after the date of

enactment of this Act, but only if the Commission determines, in consultation with appropriate public interest groups and interested individuals from the private sector, that distributors of video programming have not, by such date—

(A) established voluntary rules for rating video programming that contains sexual, violent, or other indecent material about which parents should be informed before it is displayed to children, and such rules are acceptable to the Commission; and

(B) agreed voluntarily to broadcast signals that contain ratings of such programming.

(2) Effective date of manufacturing provision. — In prescribing regulations to implement the amendment made by subsection (c), the Federal Communications Commission shall, after consultation with the television manufacturing industry, specify the effective date for the applicability of the requirement to the apparatus covered by such amendment, which date shall not be less than two years after the date of enactment of this Act.

Sec. 552 Technology Fund

It is the policy of the United States to encourage broadcast television, cable, satellite, syndication, other video programming distributors, and relevant related industries (in consultation with appropriate public interest groups and interested individuals from the private sector) to—

(1) establish a technology fund to encourage television and electronics equipment manufacturers to facilitate the development of technology which would empower parents to block programming they deem inappropriate for their children and to encourage the availability thereof to low income parents;

(2) report to the viewing public on the status of the development of affordable, easy to use blocking technology; and

(3) establish and promote effective procedures, standards, systems, advisories, or other mechanisms for ensuring that users have easy and complete access to the information necessary to effectively utilize blocking technology and to encourage the availability thereof to low income parents.

Subtitle C   Judicial Review

Sec. 561   Expedited Review

(a) Three-Judge District Court Hearing. — Notwithstanding any other provision of law, any civil action challenging the constitutionality, on its face, of this title or any amendment made by this title, or any provision thereof, shall be heard by a district court of 3 judges convened pursuant to the provisions of section 2284 of title 28, United States Code.

(b) Appellate Review. — Notwithstanding any other provision of law, an interlocutory or final judgment, decree, or order of the court of 3 judges in an action under subsection (a) holding this title or an amendment made by this title, or any provision thereof, unconstitutional shall be reviewable as a matter of right by direct appeal to the Supreme Court. Any such appeal shall be filed not more than 20 days after entry of such judgment, decree, or order.

TITLE VII   MISCELLANEOUS PROVISIONS

Sec. 702   Privacy of Customer Information

Title II is amended by inserting after section 221 (47 U.S.C. 221) the following new section:

'Sec. 222   Privacy of Customer Information

(a)   IN GENERAL — Every telecommunications carrier has a duty to protect the confidentiality of proprietary information of, and relating to, other telecommunication carriers, equipment manufacturers, and customers, including telecommunication carriers reselling telecommunications services provided by a telecommunications carrier.

(b)   CONFIDENTIALITY OF CARRIER INFORMATION — A telecommunications carrier that receives or obtains proprietary information from another carrier for purposes of providing any telecommunications service shall use such information only for such purpose, and shall not use such information for its own marketing efforts.

(c)   CONFIDENTIALITY OF CUSTOMER PROPRIETARY NETWORK INFORMATION—

(1)   PRIVACY REQUIREMENTS FOR TELECOMMUNICATIONS CARRIERS—

Except as required by law or with the approval of the customer, a telecommunications carrier that receives or obtains customer proprietary network information by virtue of its provision of a telecommunications service shall only use, disclose, or permit access to individually identifiable customer proprietary network information in its provision of (A) the telecommunications service from which such information is derived, or (B) services necessary to, or used in, the provision of such telecommunications service, including the publishing of directories.

(2)   DISCLOSURE ON REQUEST BY CUSTOMERS — A telecommunications carrier shall disclose customer proprietary network information, upon affirmative written request by the customer, to any person designated by the customer.

(3)   AGGREGATE CUSTOMER INFORMATION — A telecommunications carrier that receives or obtains customer proprietary network information by virtue of its provision of a communications service may use, disclose, or permit access to aggregate customer information other than for the purposes described in paragraph (1). A local exchange carrier may use, disclose, or permit access to aggregate customer information other than for purposes described in paragraph (1) only if it provides such aggregate information to other carriers or persons on reasonable and nondiscriminatory terms and conditions upon reasonable request therefor.

(d)   EXCEPTIONS — Nothing in this section prohibits a telecommunications carrier from using, disclosing, or permitting access to customer proprietary network information obtained from its customers, either directly or indirectly through its agents—

(1)   to initiate, render, bill, and collect for telecommunications services;

(2)   to protect the rights or property of the carrier, or to protect users of those services and other carriers from fraudulent, abusive, or unlawful use of, or subscription to, such services; or

(3)   to provide any inbound telemarketing, referral, or administrative services to the customer for the duration of the call, if such call was initiated by the customer and the customer approves of the use of such information to provide such service.

(e)   SUBSCRIBER LIST INFORMATION — Notwithstanding subsections (b), (c), and (d), a telecommunications carrier that provides telephone exchange service shall provide subscriber list information gathered in its capacity as a provider of such service on a timely and unbundled basis, under nondiscriminatory and reasonable rates, terms, and conditions, to any person upon request for the purpose of publishing directories in any format.

(f)   DEFINITIONS — As used in this section:

(1)   CUSTOMER PROPRIETARY NETWORK INFORMATION — The term "customer proprietary network information" means—

(A)   information that relates to the quantity, technical configuration, type, destination, and amount of use of a telecommunications service subscribed to by any customer of a telecommunications carrier, and that is made available to the carrier by the customer solely by virtue of the carrier-customer relationship; and

(B)   information contained in the bills pertaining to telephone exchange service or telephone toll service received by a customer of a carrier; except that such term does not include subscriber list information.

(2)   AGGREGATE INFORMATION — The term "aggregate customer information" means collective data that relates to a group or category of services or customers, from which individual customer identities and characteristics have been removed.

(3)   SUBSCRIBER LIST INFORMATION — The term "subscriber list information" means any information—

(A)   identifying the listed names of subscribers of a carrier and such subscribers' telephone numbers, addresses, or primary advertising classifications (as such classifications are assigned at the time of the establishment of such service), or any combination of such listed names, numbers, addresses, or classifications; and

(B)   that the carrier or an affiliate has published, caused to be published, or accepted for publication in any directory format.'.

Sec. 706   Advanced Telecommunications Incentives

(a)   IN GENERAL — The Commission and each State commission with regulatory jurisdiction over telecommunications services shall encourage the deployment on a reasonable and timely basis of advanced telecommunications capability to all Americans (including, in particular, elementary and secondary schools and classrooms) by utilizing, in a manner consistent with the public interest, convenience, and necessity, price cap regulation, regulatory forbearance, measures that promote competition in the local telecommunications market, or other regulating methods that remove barriers to infrastructure investment.

(b)   INQUIRY — The Commission shall, within 30 months after the date of enactment of this Act, and regularly thereafter, initiate a notice of inquiry concerning the availability of advanced telecommunications capability to all Americans (including, in particular, elementary and secondary schools and classrooms) and shall complete the inquiry within 180 days after its initiation. In the inquiry, the Commission shall determine whether advanced telecommunications capability is being deployed to all Americans in a reasonable and timely fashion. If the Commission's determination is negative, it shall take immediate action to accelerate deployment of such capability by removing barriers to infrastructure investment and by promoting competition in the telecommunications market.

(c)   DEFINITIONS — For purposes of this subsection:

(1)   ADVANCED TELECOMMUNICATIONS CAPABILITY — The term 'advanced telecommunications capability' is defined, without regard to any transmission media or technology, as high-speed, switched, broadband telecommunications capability that enables users to originate and receive high-quality voice, data, graphics, and video telecommunications using any technology.

(2)   ELEMENTARY AND SECONDARY SCHOOLS — The term 'elementary and secondary schools' means elementary and secondary schools, as defined in paragraphs (14) and (25), respectively, of section 14101 of the Elementary and Secondary Education Act of 1965 (20 U.S.C. 8801).

Note
1.   Title V 'Obscenity and Violence' is also known as the Communications Decency Act (CDA), which was put forward by US Senator Exon. The CDA has subsequently been challenged in the courts. On June 12, 1996, a Philadelphia court granted the Citizens Internet Empowerment Coalition a preliminary injunction against the implementation of the CDA on the grounds that it would unconstitutionally restrict the right of free speech. On July 29, 1996, a New York court, in *Shea* v *Reno* ruled the CDA unconstitutional.

INDEX

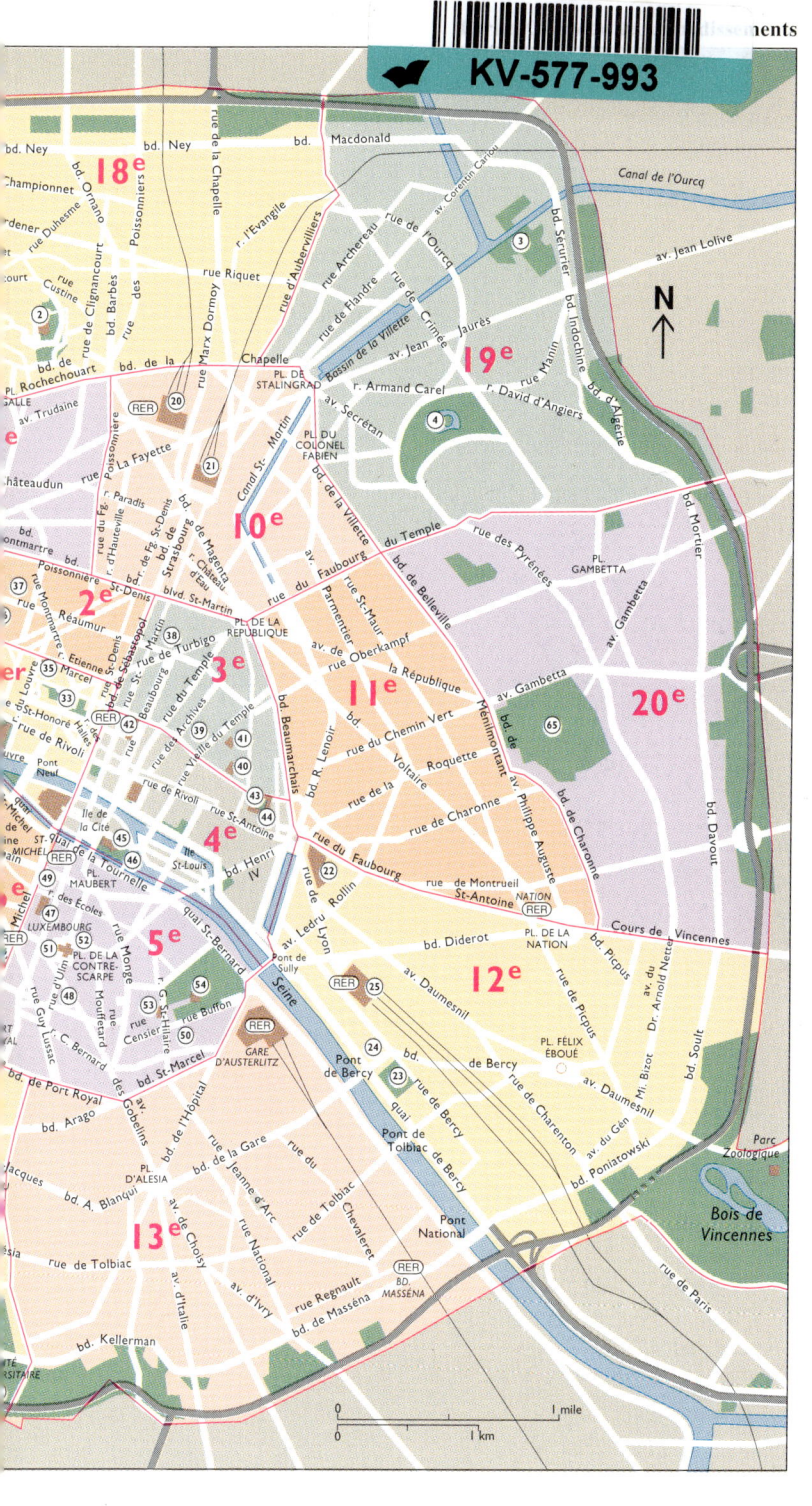

ments

18e

bd. Ney · bd. Ney · Macdonald · Canal de l'Ourcq

Championnet · bd. Ornano · Poissonniers

rdener Duhesme · rue Duhesme · r. l'Evangile · rue Archereau · rue de l'Ourcq · av. Corentin Cariou · av. Jean Lolive

court · rue Custine · rue de Clignancourt · rue Barbès · rue Marx Dormoy · rue d'Aubervilliers · rue de Flandre · rue de Crimée · bd. Sérurier · bd. Indochine · bd. d'Algérie

2 · rue Riquet · Bassin de la Villette · av. Jean Jaurès

Chapelle · **19e**

Pl. Rochechouart · bd. de la Chapelle · PL. DE STALINGRAD · r. Armand Carel · r. David d'Angiers

SALLE · av. Trudaine · RER · 20 · PL. DU COLONEL FABIEN · av. Secrétan · 4 · bd. Mortier

e · r. Poissonnière · r. La Fayette · 21 · Canal St. Martin · bd. de la Villette · rue du Temple · rue des Pyrénées · PL. GAMBETTA

hâteaudun · r. Paradis · r. du Fg. St-Denis · r. de Magenta · **10e**

bd. Montmartre · r. d'Hauteville · r. de Strasbourg · r. Château d'eau · rue St-Maur · bd. de Belleville · av. Gambetta

37 · Poissonnière · St-Denis · blvd. St-Martin · rue du Faubourg · rue St-Denis · Parmentier · rue de Oberkampf · **20e**

9 · rue Montorgueil · Réaumur · **2e** · 38 · PL. DE LA RÉPUBLIQUE · la République · av. Gambetta · 65

35 · r. Etienne Marcel · rue de Turbigo · **3e** · rue du Temple · bd. · rue du Chemin Vert · bd. de Charonne

er · 33 · r. St-Honoré · Halles · RER · 42 · rue Beaubourg · rue des Archives · 39 · 41 · rue Vieille du Temple · 40 · rue de la Roquette · Voltaire

Pont Neuf · rue de Rivoli · 43 · rue St-Antoine · 44 · rue de Charonne · bd. Davout

ne · St-Quai de la Tournelle · Ile de la Cité · 45 · Ile St-Louis · bd. Henri IV · **4e** · rue du Faubourg · rue de Montreuil · St-Antoine · NATION RER · Cours de Vincennes

ain · RER · 46 · MICHEL · 49 · r. des Ecoles · PL. MAUBERT · 22 · rue de Lyon · rue · Rollin · St-Antoine · bd. Picpus · av. du Dr. Arnold Netter

Michel · 47 · 52 · LUXEMBOURG · rue Monge · PL. DE LA CONTRE-SCARPE · bd. Diderot · PL. DE LA NATION · av. Daumesnil · Mt. Bizot · av. du Gén · bd. Soult

51 · **5e** · 48 · rue Mouffetard · 53 · r. Censier · 54 · r. Buffon · 25 · **12e** · PL. FÉLIX ÉBOUÉ · rue de Picpus · av. Daumesnil · bd. Poniatowski

PL. de Guy Lussac · C. Bernard · 50 · quai St-Bernard · RER · GARE D'AUSTERLITZ · Pont de Bercy · 24 · bd. · de Bercy · rue de Charenton · Parc Zoologique

bd. de Port Royal · des Gobelins · bd. St-Marcel · Pont de Sully · Seine · 23 · rue de Bercy · Pont de Tolbiac · quai · de Bercy

bd. Arago · PL. D'ALESIA · rue de l'Hôpital · rue du · Pont de Tolbiac

Jacques · bd. A. Blanqui · rue de la Gare · rue de Jeanne d'Arc · rue de Tolbiac · Pont National · Bois de Vincennes

esia · rue de Tolbiac · **13e** · av. de Choisy · rue National · rue Chevaleret · rue Regnault · rue de Masséna · RER · BD. MASSÉNA · rue de Paris

TÉ · ISITAIRE · bd. Kellerman · av. d'Italie · av. d'Ivry

N ↑

1 mile · 1 km

Paris: 1er and 2e

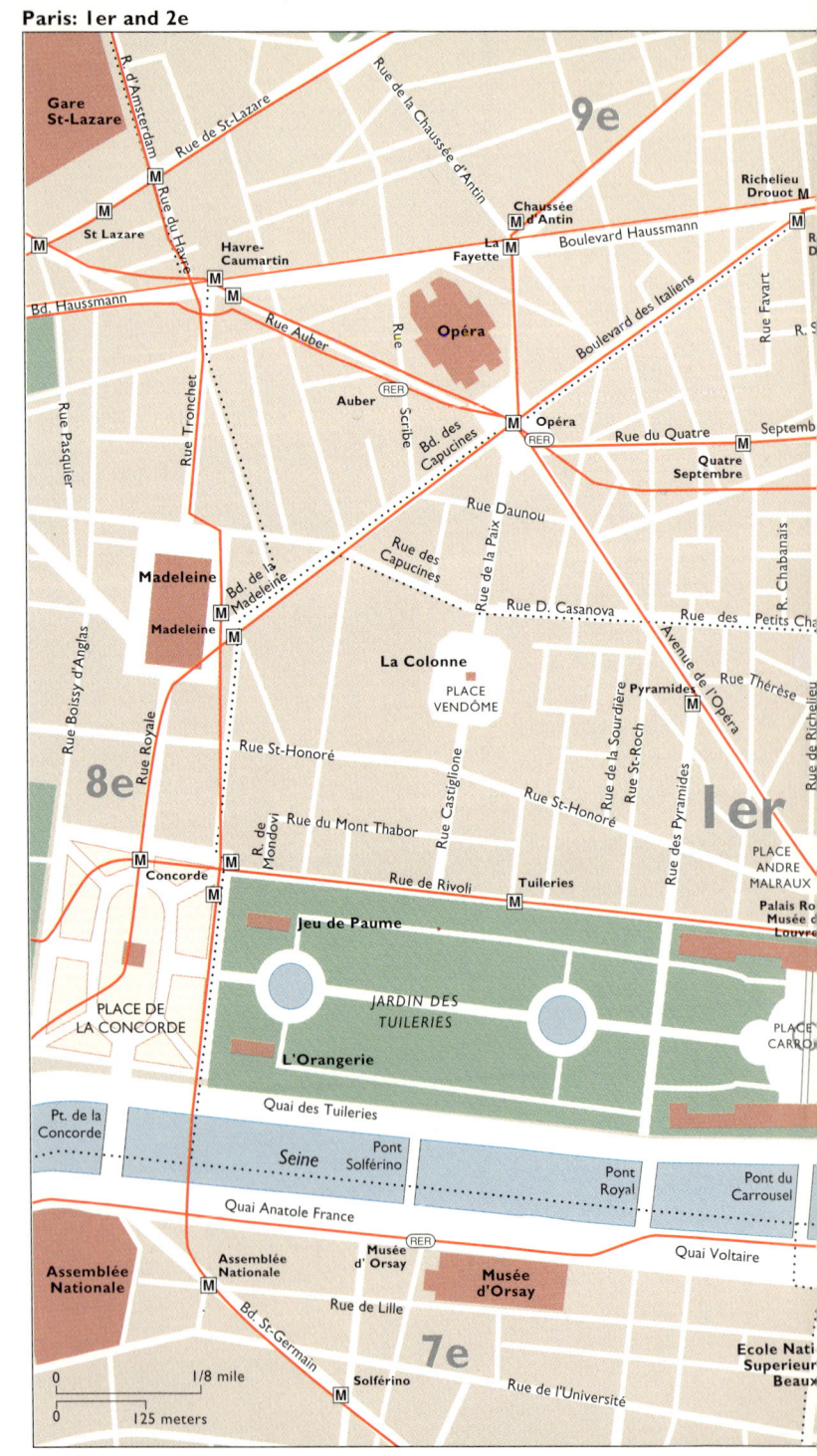

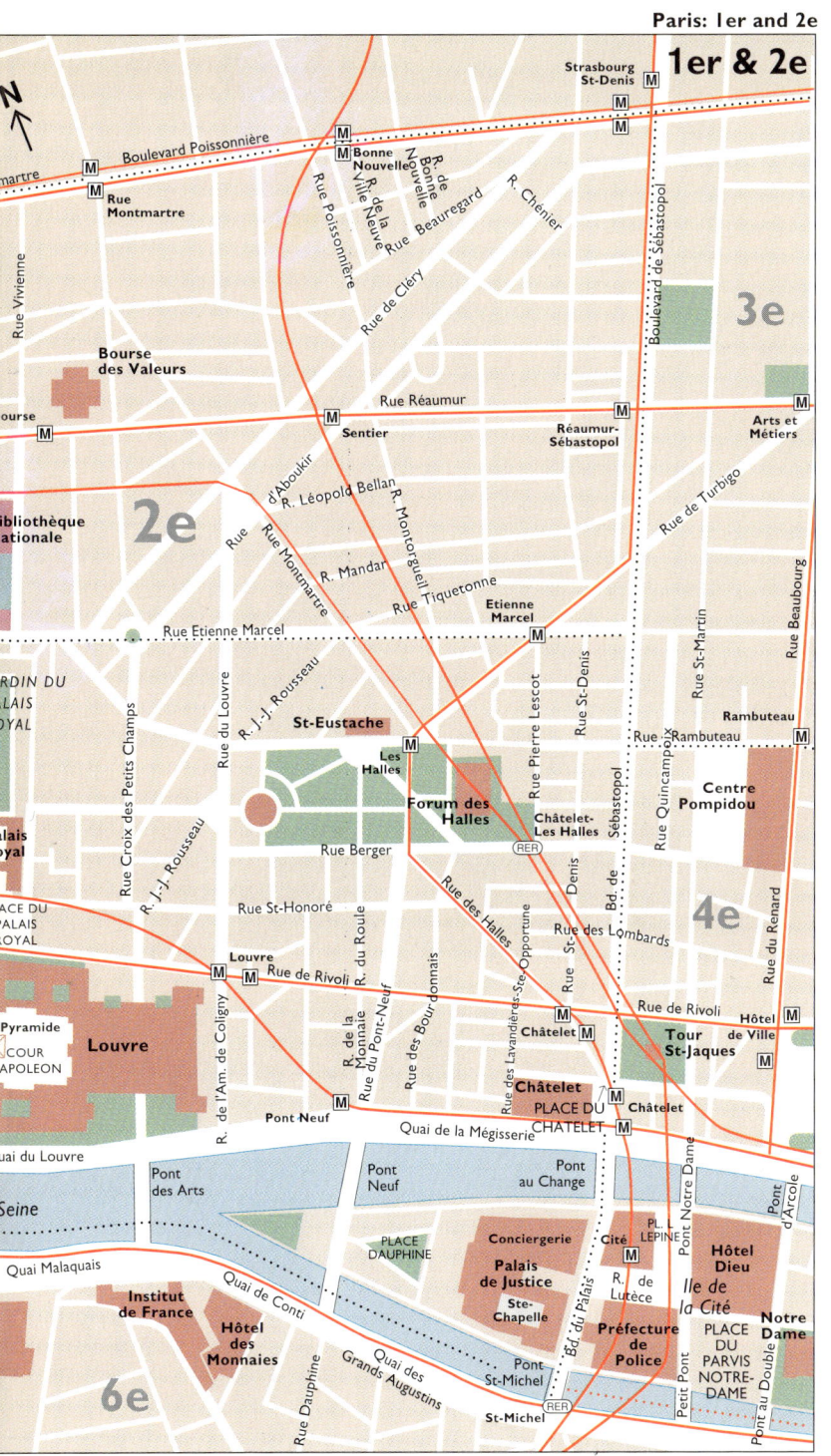

N

Strasbourg
St-Denis

Boulevard Poissonnière

Rue
Montmartre

Bonne
Nouvelle

R. de
Bonne
Nouvelle

R. de la
Ville Neuve

Rue Poissonnière

Rue Beauregard

R. Chénier

Boulevard de Sébastopol

3e

Rue de Cléry

Bourse
des Valeurs

Bourse

Rue Réaumur

Sentier

Réaumur-
Sébastopol

Arts et
Métiers

Bibliothèque
Nationale

2e

d'Aboukir

R. Léopold Bellan

Rue

Rue Montmartre

R. Mandar

R. Montorgueil

Rue Tiquetonne

Rue de Turbigo

Rue Beaubourg

Etienne
Marcel

Rue Etienne Marcel

JARDIN DU
PALAIS
ROYAL

Rue du Louvre

R. J.-J. Rousseau

St-Eustache

Les
Halles

Forum des
Halles

Rue Pierre Lescot

Rue St-Denis

Rue St-Martin

Rambuteau

Rue Rambuteau

Centre
Pompidou

Palais
Royal

Rue Croix des Petits Champs

R. J.-J. Rousseau

Rue Berger

Châtelet-
Les Halles

RER

Bd. de Sébastopol

Rue St. Denis

Rue Quincampoix

Rue du Renard

4e

PLACE DU
PALAIS
ROYAL

Rue St-Honoré

Louvre

Rue de Rivoli

R. du Roule

Rue des Halles

Rue des Lombards

Rue de Rivoli

Hôtel
de Ville

Pyramide
COUR
NAPOLEON

Louvre

R. de l'Am. de Coligny

R. de la
Monnaie

Rue du Pont-Neuf

Rue des Bourdonnais

Rue des Lavandières-Ste-Opportune

Châtelet

Tour
St-Jaques

Pont Neuf

PLACE DU
CHATELET

Châtelet

Châtelet

Quai du Louvre

Quai de la Mégisserie

Pont Notre Dame

Pont
d'Arcole

Seine

Pont
des Arts

Pont
Neuf

Pont
au Change

Cité

PL.
LEPINE

Hôtel
Dieu

Quai Malaquais

PLACE
DAUPHINE

Conciergerie

Palais
de Justice

Ste-
Chapelle

R. de
Lutèce

Ile de
la Cité

Notre
Dame

Institut
de France

Hôtel
des
Monnaies

Quai de Conti

Quai des Grands Augustins

Rue Dauphine

Bd. du Palais

Préfecture
de
Police

Pont
St-Michel

Petit Pont

PLACE
DU
PARVIS
NOTRE-
DAME

Pont au Double

6e

St-Michel

RER

Palais du Louvre

Pont Neuf

Châtelet

Quai du Louvre

1er

Pont du Carrousel

Pont des Arts

Pont au Change

Pont Neuf

Conciergerie

Cité

Hôtel Dieu

Quai Malaquais

Ste-Chapelle

Palais du

Île de la Cité

Rue de la Cité

Ecole Nationale Superieure des Beaux Arts

Quai de Conti

Institut de France

Hôtel des Monnaies

Quai des Grands Augustins

Pont St-Michel

R. Bonaparte

Rue des Sts-Pères

Rue Jacob

Rue de Seine

Rue Mazarine

Rue Dauphine

Pont St-Michel

St-Michel

St-Michel

Pl. St-Michel

Rue St-Jaques

R. de l'Abbaye

PLACE ST-GERMAIN-DES-PRÉS

St-Germain Des Prés

Rue St-André des Arts

Rue Danton

Bd. St-Germain

Musée du Cluny

Bd. St-Germain

7e

St-Germain des Prés

Mabillon

Odéon

Bd. St-Germain

R. du Four

Rue de l'Odéon

Rue Racine

Boulevard

Sorbonne

R. de Sèvres

R. du Vieux Colombier

R. du Saint Sulpice

Rue de Tournon

PLACE DE L'ODÉON

PLACE DE LA SORBONNE

St-Michel

R. du Cherche Midi

PLACE ST-SULPICE

St-Sulpice

Rue Soufflot

R. d'Assas

R. de Rennes

St-Sulpice

Palais du Luxembourg

Bd. Raspail

R. de Vaugirard

6e

Rennes

JARDIN DU LUXEMBOURG

Luxembourg

Rue Gay-Lussac

St Placide

Notre-Dame des Champs

Rue du Montparnasse

Rue Vavin

Rue Notre-Dame des Champs

Rue d'Assas

Rue St-Jaques

Montparnasse Bienvenüe

Vavin

Boulevard du Montparnasse

Avenue de

Boulevard St-Michel

Port Royal

R. du Depart

Boulevard Raspail

14e

Edgar Quinet

Boulevard Edgar Quinet

la Observatoire

Paris Métro

- The stations Liège and Rennes are closed after 8pm and on Sundays and holidays.
- Beyond the city limits, *Metro Urbain* tickets are not valid on the RER.

Paris: Métro

Paris: Overview and Arrondissements

1 Cimetière de Montmartre
2 Sacré Coeur Basilica
3 Parc La Villette
4 Parc des Buttes Chaumont
5 Jardins du Trocadero
6 Palais Chaillot
7 Cimetière de Passy
8 American Embassy
9 British Embassy
10 Petit Palais
11 Grand Palais
12 Arc de Triomphe
13 Madeleine
14 Gare St-Lazare
15 Parc Monceau
16 Palais de la Découverte
17 Opéra Garnier
18 Galeries Lafayette
19 Printemps
20 Gare du Nord
21 Gare de l'Est
22 Opéra Bastille
23 Palais Omnisports de Bercy
24 Ministère des Finances
25 Gare de Lyon
26 Parc de Montsouris
27 Cité Universitaire
28 Cimetière Montparnasse
29 Gare Montparnasse

30 Bureau des Objets Trouvés
    (Lost and Found)
31 Louvre
32 Palais Royale
33 Forum des Halles
34 Musée de l'Orangerie
35 Central Post Office
36 Bourse
37 Bibliothèque Nationale
38 Ecole des Arts et Métiers
39 Archives Nationales
40 Musée Carnavalet
41 Musée Picasso
42 Centre George Pompidou
43 place des Vosges
44 Musée Victor Hugo
45 Notre Dame
46 Mémorial de la Déportation
47 Université de Paris (Sorbonne)

48 Ecole Normal Supérieure
49 Musée de Cluny
50 Museum Nationale d'Histoire
    Naturelle
51 Panthéon
52 Eglise St-Etienne du Mont
53 La Mosquée
54 Jardin des Plantes
55 Jardins du Luxembourg
56 Eglise St-Sulpice
57 Théâtre Nationale de l'Odéon
58 Eiffel Tower
59 Champs de Mars

60 Ecole Militaire
61 UNESCO
62 Hôtel des Invalides
63 Assemblée Nationale
64 Musée d'Orsay
65 Cimetière de l'Est du Père Lachaise

4e

Hôtel
de Ville

R. St-Paul

R. de l'Ave Maria

Bastille M

Boulevard Henri IV

Pont Marie M
Quai des Célestins

Pont
Louis Philippe

Pont Marie

e du
tre Dame

Rue St-Louis

Rue des
Deux Ponts

en l'Ile
Ile St-Louis

Musée
Mickiewicz

M

Sully
Morland

Notre
Dame

Pont St-Louis

Pont de la
Tournelle

Pont de Sully

e Montebello

Musée de
l'Assistance
Publique

Quai de la
Rapeo

M

R. de Bièvre

Boulevard St-Germain

Institut
du Monde
Arabe

Musée de la
Sculpture en
Plein Air

Seine

CE
ERT

M

R. des Bernadins

R. de Pontoise

R. de Poissy

Rue du Cardinal Lemoine

Rue des Fosses
St-Bernard

Musée de
Minéralogie

Quai

St-Bernard

des Ecoles

R. Monge

Rue Cuvier

PLACE
VALHUBERT

RER

Cardinal
Lemoine M

Rue
Jussieu

M
Juissieu

JARDIN
DES PLANTES

Gare
d'Austerlitz

M

St-Etienne
du Mont

Arènes
de Lutèce

Rue Lime

Rue Cujas

Rue Rollin

Gare
d'Austerlitz

nthéon

Rue Lacepede

5e

Musée
d'Histoire
Naturelle

de l'Estrapade

Rue Geoffroy
Saint Hilaire

Place Monge

Rue Lhomond

Rue Mouffetard

PLACE
MONGE

Institut Musulman
et Mosque

Rue Buffon

Rue Erasme Brossolette

Rue Monge

Rue Poliveau

St-Marcel M

Bd. de l'Hôpital

Rue Claude Bernard

Censier
Daubenton

M

e Grâce

Rue Berthollet

Boulevard St- Marcel

Campo
Formio M

M Gobelins

Boulevard de Port Royal

13e

Avenue des Gobelins

5e & 6e

Paris: RER

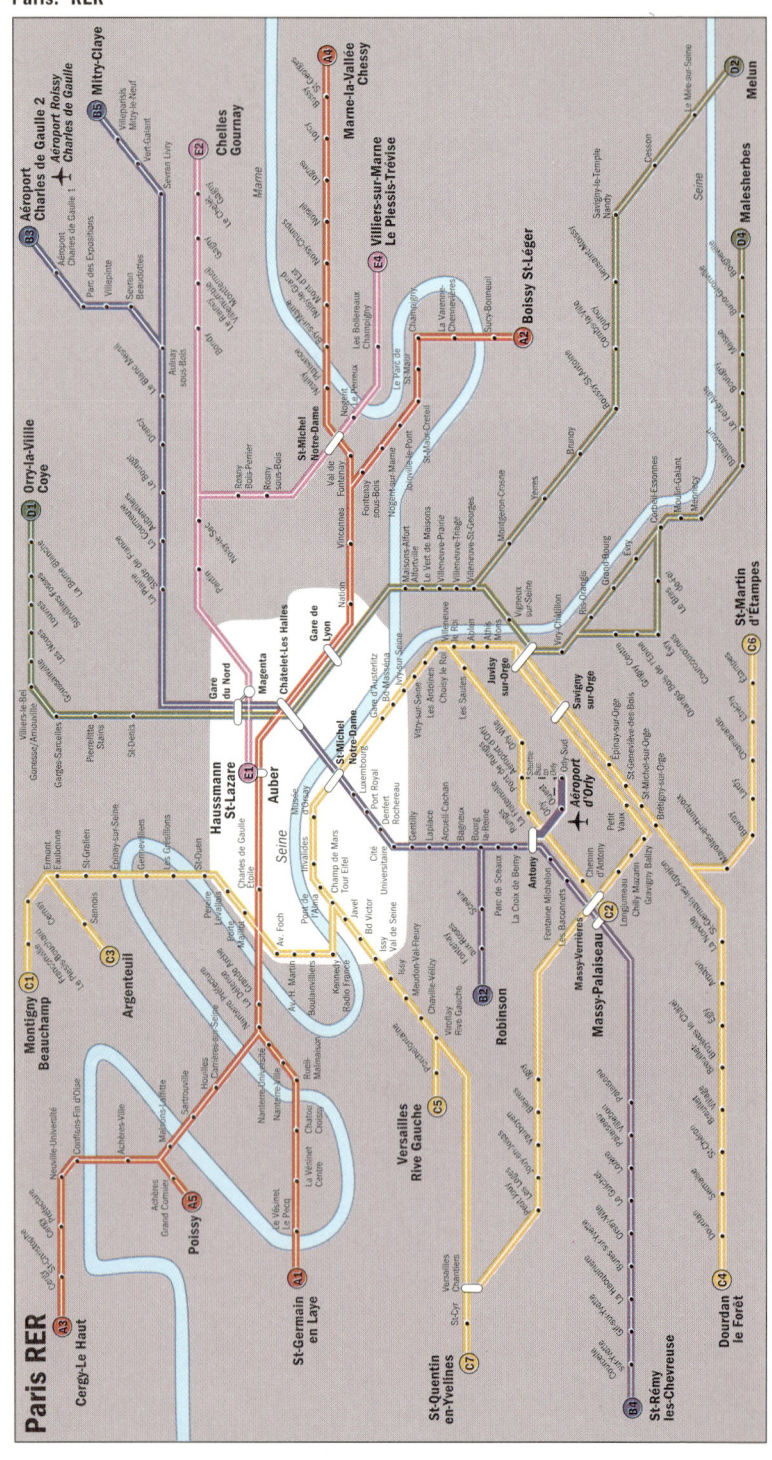

 Let's Go writers travel on your budget.

"Guides that penetrate the veneer of the holiday brochures and mine the grit of real life."

—The Economist

"The writers seem to have experienced every rooster-packed bus and lunar-surfaced mattress about which they write."

—The New York Times

"All the dirt, dirt cheap."

—People

Great for independent travelers.

"The guides are aimed not only at young budget travelers but at the independent traveler; a sort of streetwise cookbook for traveling alone."

—The New York Times

"Flush with candor and irreverence, chock full of budget travel advice."

—The Des Moines Register

"An indispensible resource, *Let's Go*'s practical information can be used by every traveler."

—The Chattanooga Free Press

Let's Go is completely revised each year.

"Only *Let's Go* has the zeal to annually update every title on its list."

—The Boston Globe

"Unbeatable: good sightseeing advice; up-to-date info on restaurants, hotels, and inns; a commitment to money-saving travel; and a wry style that brightens nearly every page."

—The Washington Post

All the important information you need.

"*Let's Go* authors provide a comedic element while still providing concise information and thorough coverage of the country. Anything you need to know about budget traveling is detailed in this book."

—The Chicago Sun-Times

"Value-packed, unbeatable, accurate, and comprehensive."

—Los Angeles Times

Let's Go Publications

Let's Go: Alaska & the Pacific Northwest 2000
Let's Go: Australia 2000
Let's Go: Austria & Switzerland 2000
Let's Go: Britain & Ireland 2000
Let's Go: California 2000
Let's Go: Central America 2000
Let's Go: China 2000 **New Title!**
Let's Go: Eastern Europe 2000
Let's Go: Europe 2000
Let's Go: France 2000
Let's Go: Germany 2000
Let's Go: Greece 2000
Let's Go: India & Nepal 2000
Let's Go: Ireland 2000
Let's Go: Israel 2000 **New Title!**
Let's Go: Italy 2000
Let's Go: Mexico 2000
Let's Go: Middle East 2000 **New Title!**
Let's Go: New York City 2000
Let's Go: New Zealand 2000
Let's Go: Paris 2000
Let's Go: Perú & Ecuador 2000 **New Title!**
Let's Go: Rome 2000
Let's Go: South Africa 2000
Let's Go: Southeast Asia 2000
Let's Go: Spain & Portugal 2000
Let's Go: Turkey 2000
Let's Go: USA 2000
Let's Go: Washington, D.C. 2000

Let's Go *Map Guides*

Amsterdam	New Orleans
Berlin	New York City
Boston	Paris
Chicago	Prague
Florence	Rome
London	San Francisco
Los Angeles	Seattle
Madrid	Washington, D.C.

Coming Soon: *Sydney* and *Hong Kong*

Let's Go 2000

FRANCE

Daryush Jonathan Dawid
Editor
Valerie de Charette de la Contrie
Associate Editor
Benjamin E. Lytal
Associate Editor

Researcher-Writers:
Tova Carlin   **Nicole López**
Brady Gunderson   **Ashika Singh**
Nenita Ponce de León Elphick
Daisy Stanton

Macmillan

Published in Great Britain 2000 by Macmillan, an imprint of Macmillan Publishers Ltd, 25 Eccleston Place, London, SW1W 9NF, Basingstoke and Oxford Associated companies throughout the world
www.macmillan.co.uk

Maps by David Lindroth copyright © 2000, 1999, 1998, 1997, 1996, 1995, 1994, 1993, 1992, 1991, 1990, 1989, 1988 by St. Martin's Press.

Published in the United States of America by St. Martin's Press.

ISBN: 0 333 77985 1
First edition
10 9 8 7 6 5 4 3 2 1

Let's Go: France is written by Let's Go Publications, 67 Mount Auburn Street, Cambridge, MA 02138, USA.

Let's Go® and the thumb logo are trademarks of Let's Go, Inc.
Printed in the USA on recycled paper with biodegradable soy ink.

HOW TO USE THIS BOOK

For 40 years, *Let's Go* has been enjoying France as we've aged and matured. For the year 2000, we've handpicked web addresses and the latest boutiques, yet we've still got all the tips you wouldn't know you needed until you landed in Paris. You'll find ski lift prices, English bookstores, trains that run from beaches to mountains, and all the gritty details you need to thrive and travel without a hitch.

How to use this book? Whether you're going to hole up in a Parisian bed and breakfast or spend a month combing the Côte d'Azur, first read through our **Essentials** section, 50 pages of hard information on everything from sleeping bags to visas. Of course we know the real reason you're going to France is not for sunshine or fine wine, but for culture. Therefore, turn to our **History and Culture** section to prep for all the museum and cathedral placards you'll come across. The heart of the book is divided into six **chapters,** beginning with Paris and then the Center, moving counterclockwise around the country after that. Each chapter includes a historical introduction along with climate information and suggested sights. These big chapters are earmarked by black tabs that can be seen without even opening the book, in case you get lazy. Each chapter is further subdivided into more particular regions, and after that into towns and cities, the basic building block of *Let's Go: France.* All but the smallest towns include an **Orientation and Practical Information** section that includes everything from train times to internet access. After that come **Accommodations, Food, Sights,** and **Entertainment;** listings in these sections are ranked according to quality and value. Entries with a ▩ are really super; we'd print these entries in red if we weren't saving the colored ink for the maps of Paris that sandwich the book at front and back. While reading, don't forget to look up strange French words in the **Appendix,** and if you ever tire of our detailed, easy-reading travel writing, or if there's actually an emergency, you can always check out the emergency, transit, and communication information listed on the inside back cover.

As you plan your trip, sift through towns you're interested in by looking at their introductions and sights sections. Or, if you don't mind taking our word for it, the new **Discover** section outlines tours that take you straight to the best of France—either sweeping through a single region or hitting the highlights of the whole country. If you're dazzled by the choice on offer, but still prefer to plan your own itinerary, the **Let's Go Picks** overleaf give our favorite destinations in the whole country. If you'd prefer to concentrate on a given region of France, the **Suggestions** at the beginning of each chapter give pointers on where to go, while within chapters, the smaller regions are each prefaced by a **Highlights of the Region** box, listing four or five places we think are tops in the neighborhood.

Besides being better than all the other guides, just as France is better than all other...well—*Let's Go: France 2000* includes over 35 new towns, reorganized regions with expanded introductions, and smashing new formats for sights. You hold in your hands all the information you need to hit the highlights or spend six months in Strasbourg. Basically, you can do what you want to. Now let's go do it.

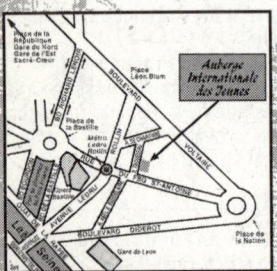

CONTENTS

MAPS

COLOR INSERTS

RESEARCHER-WRITERS

Tova Carlin   *Brittany and western Normandy*
Brokenhearted young men litter northwestern France, forlornly mourning that magical young American-Basque who passed so quickly through their towns. Tova enjoyed her job possibly more than any R-W in *Let's Go* history, even roping her family into helping with her work. Always the intrepid researcher, Tova braved dark, winding roads at all hours of the night, to bring you the beautifully crafted prose you read today.

Nenita Ponce de León Elphick   *Provence, Lyon and the Auvergne, and Burgundy*
While Lyon recovered from this *León*, Nenita found the cushy solution to traveling on the cheap: get wooed by natives with wheels. In beat-up buses, silver bullets, and black beemers she roared through southeastern and central France, letting her experienced eye and pithy pen slash and burn through years of grime. Generally hardheaded, it only takes a *cervoise* to soften her heart.

Brady Gunderson   *Côte d'Azur, Corsica, and the Alps*
Ah, what can be said about the mysterious Brady… although a family man, he speedo-ed around the south of France in the skimpiest of swimwear. Infiltrating nudist colonies, high-rolling casinos, and exclusive nightclubs, he disarmed doubters with his smooth talk and toothy grin, letting no human temptation interfere with his dedication to his work and his tan lines. Time had no meaning for this laid-back surfer dude, who emailed back cyber-copy with no margin for error.

Nicole López   *Périgord, Languedoc-Roussillon,*
Aquitaine, the Pays Basque, and Gascony
As feisty as a jalapeño pepper, stalwart Nikki careened around the Southwest at the whim of local bus schedules. Though hobbled by juicy blisters, bent double under her pack, and with laptop in one hand and camera in the other, Nikki was no *escargot*, finishing her itinerary in record time. Her sidesplitting marginalia aside, Nikki showed her respect for previous researchers in her copy. Akin to the Aztec rain god, every beach she touched upon was blessed with torrents from the sky.

Ashika Singh   *Champagne, Alsace, Lorraine, Franche-Comté,*
Flanders, the Pas de Calais, and eastern Normandy
Probably the only *Let's Go* researcher who called in on her own Hong Kong-registered cell phone, Ashika is the "abstract poetic representing from Queens." Now commuting back and forth between the South China Sea, Long Island Sound, and Massachusetts Bay, jet-set Ashika proved as adaptable as you'd expect, easily juggling numerous visits to wine cellars and Alsatian breweries while copy flowed from her fingers like vintage champagne.

Daisy Stanton   *Berry-Limousin, Poitou-Charentes, and the Loire Valley*
Having unravelled the mysteries of her Twingo, rocket-propelled Daisy left others far behind, gathering new info faster than an internet search engine. Daisy left no stone unturned, no path unbiked, no wine unsipped, and no château unexplored in her quest for truth. Overcoming her fear of French sanitation, she prodded and poked her way through France's finest kitchens—proof positive that even a vegetarian who hates cheese and chocolate can make it out of France alive.

Anna M. Schneider-Mayerson	*Paris Editor*
Silas Alben	*Paris*
Judith Batalion	*Paris*
Whitney Bryant	*Paris*

ACKNOWLEDGMENTS

These books don't just put themselves together, you know. They are assembled by machine.

TEAM FRANCE THANKS: "Punctuality" Paloff; "Iron" Anne Chisholm; Production for daily technological miracles; Reception for sorting through our deluge of fan mail; Matt and Melissa for their Byzantine iconography (and delicious cakes); Maps for all their highlighters; Christian for the Belle and Sebastian; Caleb for giving Sarah flowers every day; Sarah for keeping her flowers in the office; Brendan for his patience; Aarup for being nicer than anyone has a right to be; Olivia for the Belle and Sebastian; Julie for reminding us that there's life outside the Go; Anna for Paris; and Monique and Mamie Arnal, Lucie Fromental, Fabrice Gouriou, Nanay, Tatay, Lola Toughbird, Krzysztof Owerkowicz, and Tova's entire family for indispensable on-the-road assistance.

JONATHAN DAWID THANKS: Valerie for giving us credibility; Ben for the Belle and Sebastian; Gabor and Yoav for the days on the river; Amir for the messages; Gwendolen for all her sweetness; Doolin and Zippy for the company; NPR for broadcasting the BBC; Dolly for her smile; my family for suffering me all these years; and Mme Mimran, the best French teacher in the world.

VALERIE DE CHARETTE THANKS: Jonathan Darling, for calling me every day—what a thoughtful guy; my parents, for obvious emotional and fiscal reasons; fabulous Sarah Rotman, for her noisy house and all sorts of advice; Luscious Lytal; the pod, for listening to Newsies; and NYC and all my hoochie mamas there.

BEN LYTAL THANKS: His keyboard, the closest he came to guitar this year; Tim for gardening; Luke and Teri for catching the Crimson rebound; John for a spate of Tulsa; Jonathan for being so chill, for the rare ice cream, and for being the G in organization (Valerie being the Z); Valerie for so apt yet seemly an epithet; the pod also for ice cream and the more workaday indulgences; the connecting hallway for its necessary hip-swerves; the smaller pods, branching off, for their diverse atmospheres and thermostats; and everybody under this same Germany page.

Editor
Daryush Jonathan Dawid
Associate Editors
Valerie de Charette de la Contrie
Benjamin Lytal
Managing Editor
Benjamin Paloff

Publishing Director
Benjamin Wilkinson
Editor-in-Chief
Bentsion Harder
Production Manager
Christian Lorentzen
Cartography Manager
Daniel J. Luskin
Design Managers
Matthew Daniels, Melissa Rudolph
Editorial Managers
Brendan Gibbon, Benjamin Paloff,
Kaya Stone, Taya Weiss
Financial Manager
Kathy Lu
Personnel Manager
Adam Stein
Publicity & Marketing Managers
Sonesh Chainani,
Alexandra Leichtman
New Media Manager
Maryanthe Malliaris
Map Editors
Kurt Mueller, Jon Stein
Production Associates
Steven Aponte, John Fiore
Office Coordinators
Elena Schneider, Vanessa Bertozzi,
Monica Henderson

Director of Advertising Sales
Marta Szabo
Associate Sales Executives
Tamas Eisenberger, Li Ran

President
Noble M. Hansen III
General Managers
Blair Brown, Robert B. Rombauer
Assistant General Manager
Anne E. Chisholm

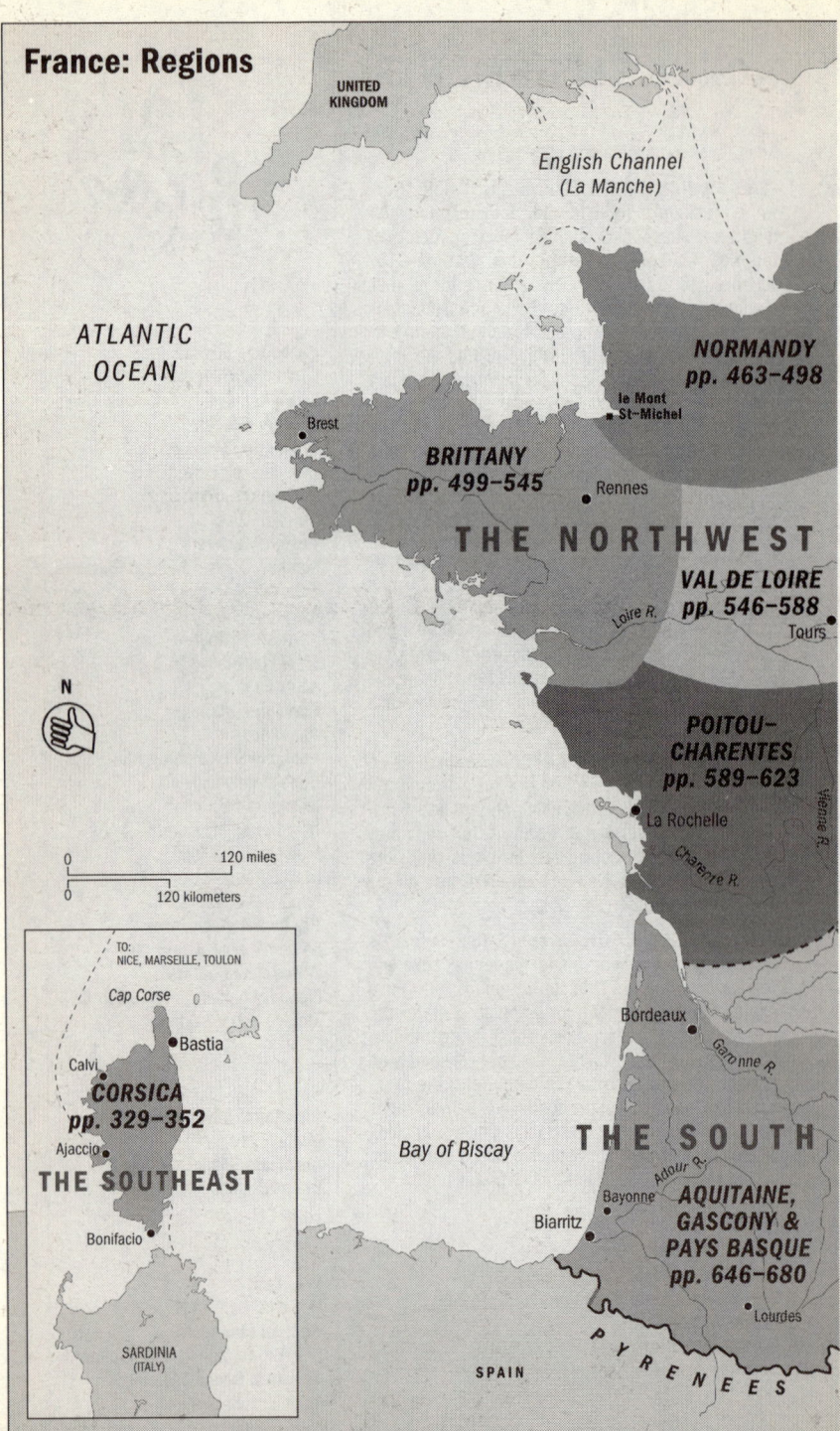

France: Regions

UNITED KINGDOM

English Channel
(La Manche)

ATLANTIC OCEAN

NORMANDY
pp. 463–498

le Mont St~Michel

BRITTANY
pp. 499–545

Brest

Rennes

THE NORTHWEST

VAL DE LOIRE
pp. 546–588

Loire R.

Tours

N

POITOU- CHARENTES
pp. 589–623

Vienne R.

La Rochelle

Charente R.

0   120 miles
0   120 kilometers

Bordeaux

Garonne R.

TO:
NICE, MARSEILLE, TOULON

Cap Corse

Bastia

Calvi

CORSICA
pp. 329–352

Ajaccio

THE SOUTHEAST

Bonifacio

SARDINIA (ITALY)

Bay of Biscay

THE SOUTH

Adour R.

Bayonne

Biarritz

AQUITAINE, GASCONY & PAYS BASQUE
pp. 646–680

Lourdes

P Y R E N E E S

SPAIN

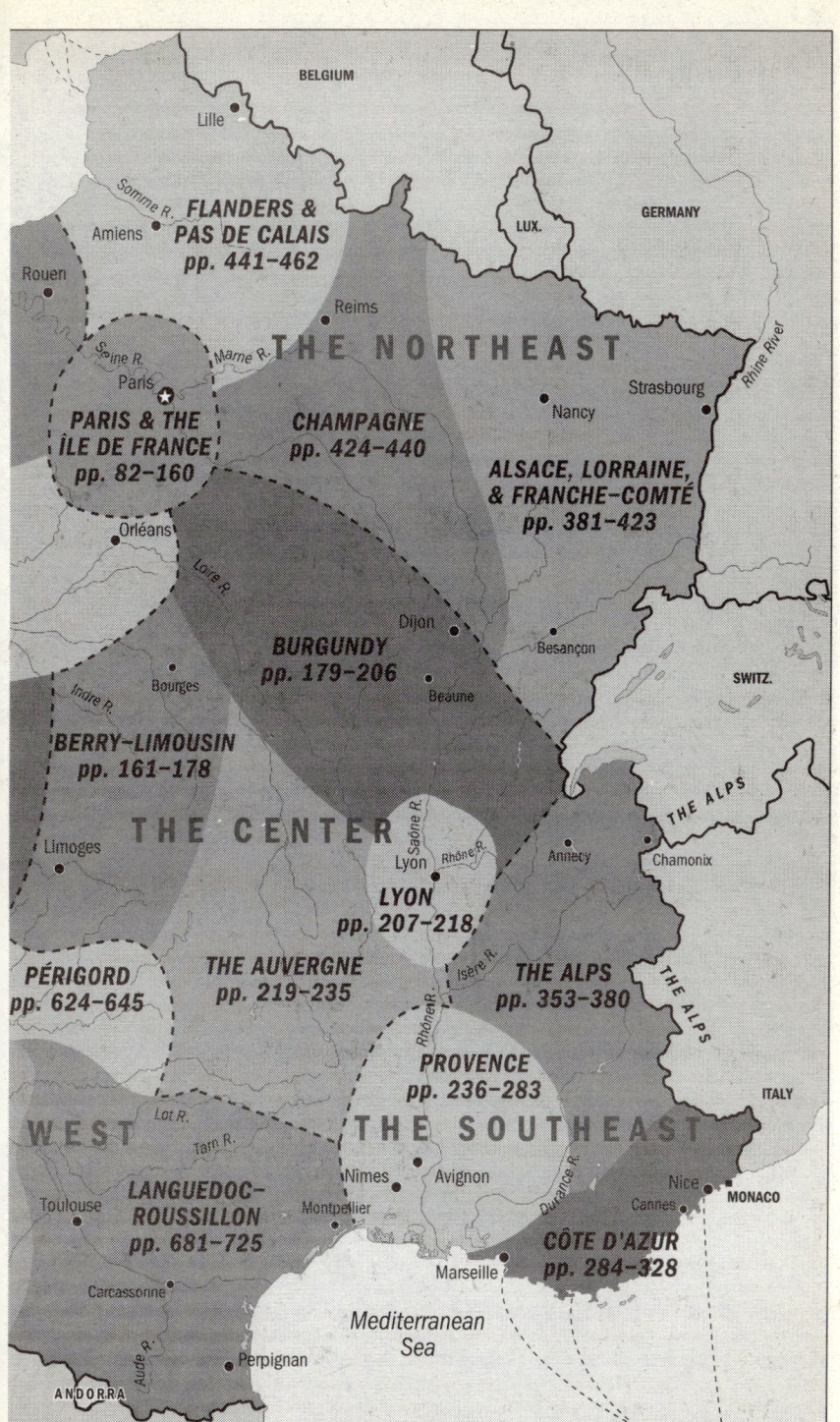

BELGIUM

Lille

Somme R.

**FLANDERS &
PAS DE CALAIS**
pp. 441–462

Amiens

LUX.

GERMANY

Rouen

Reims

THE NORTHEAST

Rhine River

Seine R.

Paris ★

Marne R.

Strasbourg

**PARIS & THE
ÎLE DE FRANCE**
pp. 82–160

CHAMPAGNE
pp. 424–440

Nancy

**ALSACE, LORRAINE,
& FRANCHE-COMTÉ**
pp. 381–423

Orléans

Loire R.

Dijon

Besançon

SWITZ.

BURGUNDY
pp. 179–206

Beaune

Indre R.

Bourges

BERRY–LIMOUSIN
pp. 161–178

THE ALPS

Limoges

THE CENTER

Saône R.

Lyon

Rhône R.

Annecy

Chamonix

LYON
pp. 207–218

PÉRIGORD
pp. 624–645

THE AUVERGNE
pp. 219–235

Isère R.

Rhône R.

THE ALPS
pp. 353–380

THE ALPS

PROVENCE
pp. 236–283

ITALY

Lot R.

WEST

Tarn R.

THE SOUTHEAST

Durance R.

Nîmes

Avignon

Nice

Cannes

MONACO

**LANGUEDOC–
ROUSSILLON**
pp. 681–725

Toulouse

Montpellier

CÔTE D'AZUR
pp. 284–328

Carcassonne

Marseille

Aude R.

Perpignan

*Mediterranean
Sea*

ANDORRA

Highways

GREAT BRITAIN

Exeter

Southampton

Portsmouth

English Channel
(La Manche)

ATLANTIC OCEAN

CHANNEL ISLANDS

Guernsey

Jersey

Étretat

N29

Cherbourg

Le Havre
Deauville

A13

Bayeux

Coutances

Caen

Granville

N175

N138

Paimpol

St-Malo

Avranches

Brest

N12

Morlaix

St Brieuc

Dinan

N12

Alençon

Quimper

Carhaix-Plouguer

N164

Rennes

N175

N12

A81

A11

N165

Lorient

Le Mans

Concarneau

Vannes

Angers

N138

Quiberon

St-Nazaire

A11

N147

Tours

Belle-Ile

Nantes

Saumur

N152

N137

N149

Poitiers

N147

Ile d'Yeu

Hills of Vendée

N137

Les Sables d'Olonne

Niort

A10

La Rochelle

Rochefort

N137

Saintes

N141

le Verdon-sur-Mer

Royan

Cognac

Angoulême

N150

A10

Périgueux

Bordeaux

N89

Bergerac

Arcachon

A63

N21

A62

N10

Agen

Mont-de-Marsan

Auch

Bay of Biscay

Bayonne

Biarritz

St-Jean-de-Luz

A63

Anglet

A63

A64

Pau

N21

Bilbao

San Sebastian

St-Jean-Pied-de-Port

Lourdes

Cauterets

SPAIN

P Y R E N E E S

A10	Highways Roads (Autoroutes)
N76	National Roads (Routes Nationales)
- - -	Ferry

0 ————— 120 miles

0 ————— 120 kilometers

N

TO:
NICE, MARSEILLE, TOULON

Cap Corse

Calvi

Bastia

CORSICA

Corte

Ajaccio

Aléria

Propriano

Sartène

Porto-Vecchio

Bonifacio

SARDINIA
(ITALY)

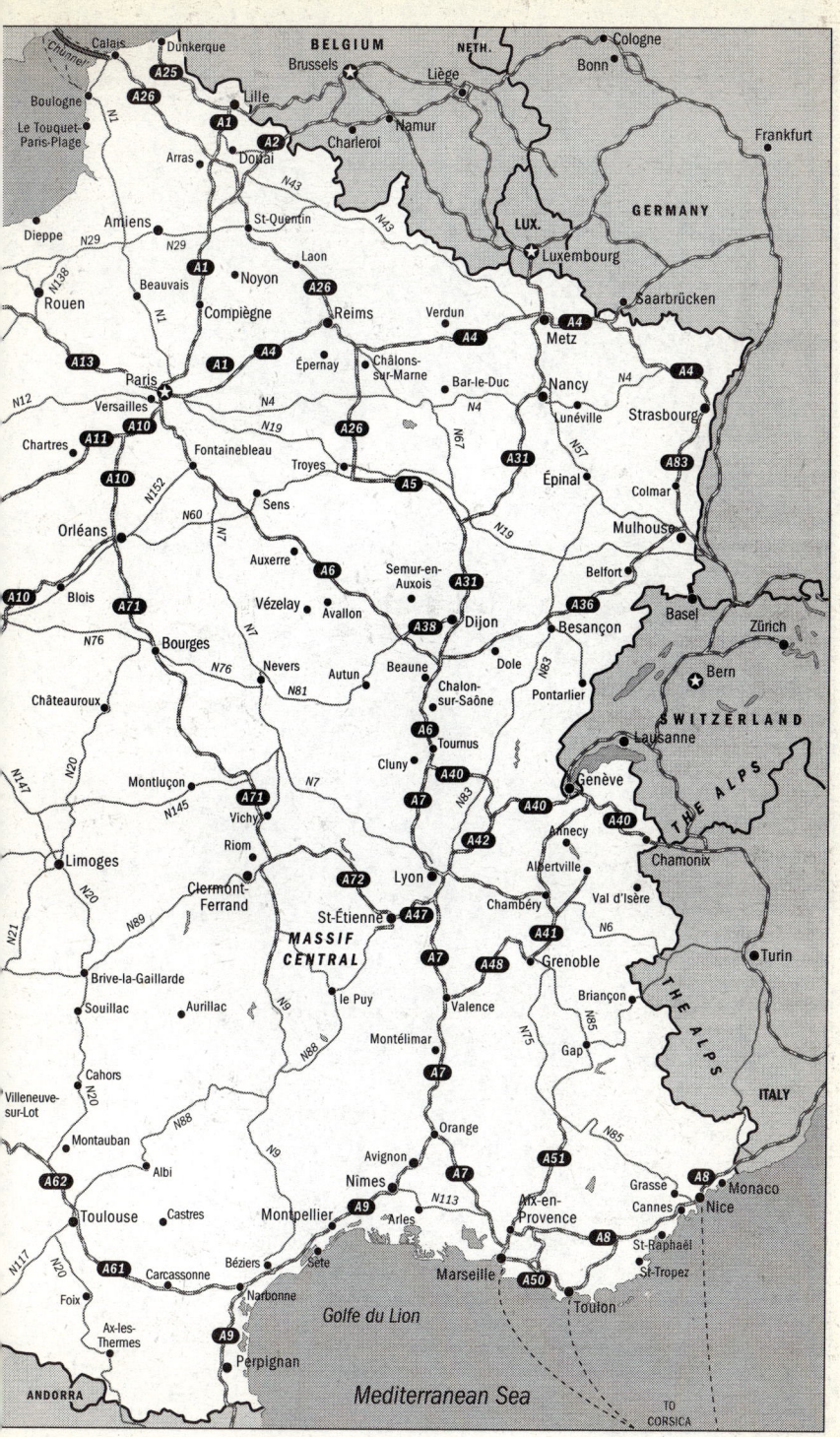

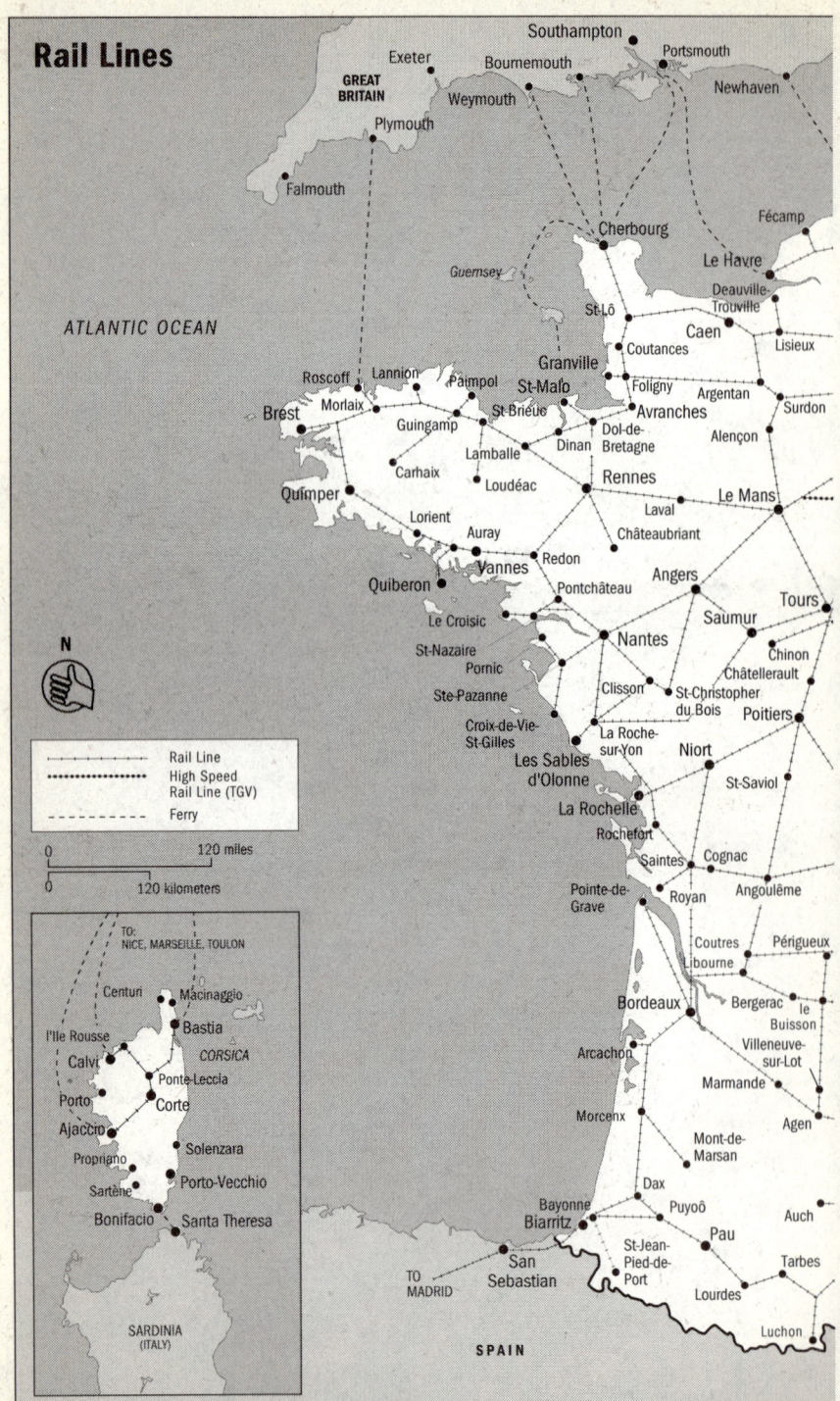

Rail Lines

GREAT BRITAIN

ATLANTIC OCEAN

Legend:
- Rail Line
- High Speed Rail Line (TGV)
- Ferry

0 — 120 miles
0 — 120 kilometers

N

Great Britain / Channel:
Southampton, Exeter, Bournemouth, Portsmouth, Weymouth, Newhaven, Plymouth, Falmouth, Guernsey, Fécamp

France (north/Normandy/Brittany):
Cherbourg, Le Havre, Deauville-Trouville, St-Lô, Caen, Lisieux, Coutances, Granville, St-Malo, Foligny, Argentan, Surdon, Roscoff, Lannion, Paimpol, Avranches, Morlaix, St-Brieuc, Dol-de-Bretagne, Alençon, Brest, Guingamp, Dinan, Lamballe, Rennes, Le Mans, Carhaix, Loudéac, Quimper, Laval, Auray, Redon, Châteaubriant, Lorient, Vannes, Angers, Tours, Quiberon, Pontchâteau, Saumur, Le Croisic, Nantes, Chinon, St-Nazaire, Châtellerault, Pornic, Clisson, St-Christopher du Bois, Poitiers, Ste-Pazanne, Croix-de-Vie-St-Gilles, La Roche-sur-Yon, Niort, Les Sables d'Olonne, St-Saviol, La Rochelle, Rochefort, Cognac, Saintes, Angoulême, Pointe-de-Grave, Royan, Périgueux, Coutres, Libourne, Bordeaux, Bergerac, le Buisson, Arcachon, Villeneuve-sur-Lot, Marmande, Morcenx, Agen, Mont-de-Marsan, Dax, Auch, Bayonne, Puyoô, Pau, Biarritz, St-Jean-Pied-de-Port, Tarbes, San Sebastian, Lourdes, Luchon

TO MADRID

SPAIN

Corsica inset:
TO: NICE, MARSEILLE, TOULON
Centuri, Macinaggio, l'Ile Rousse, Bastia, Calvi, CORSICA, Porto, Ponte-Leccia, Corte, Ajaccio, Solenzara, Propriano, Sartène, Porto-Vecchio, Bonifacio, Santa Theresa, SARDINIA (ITALY)

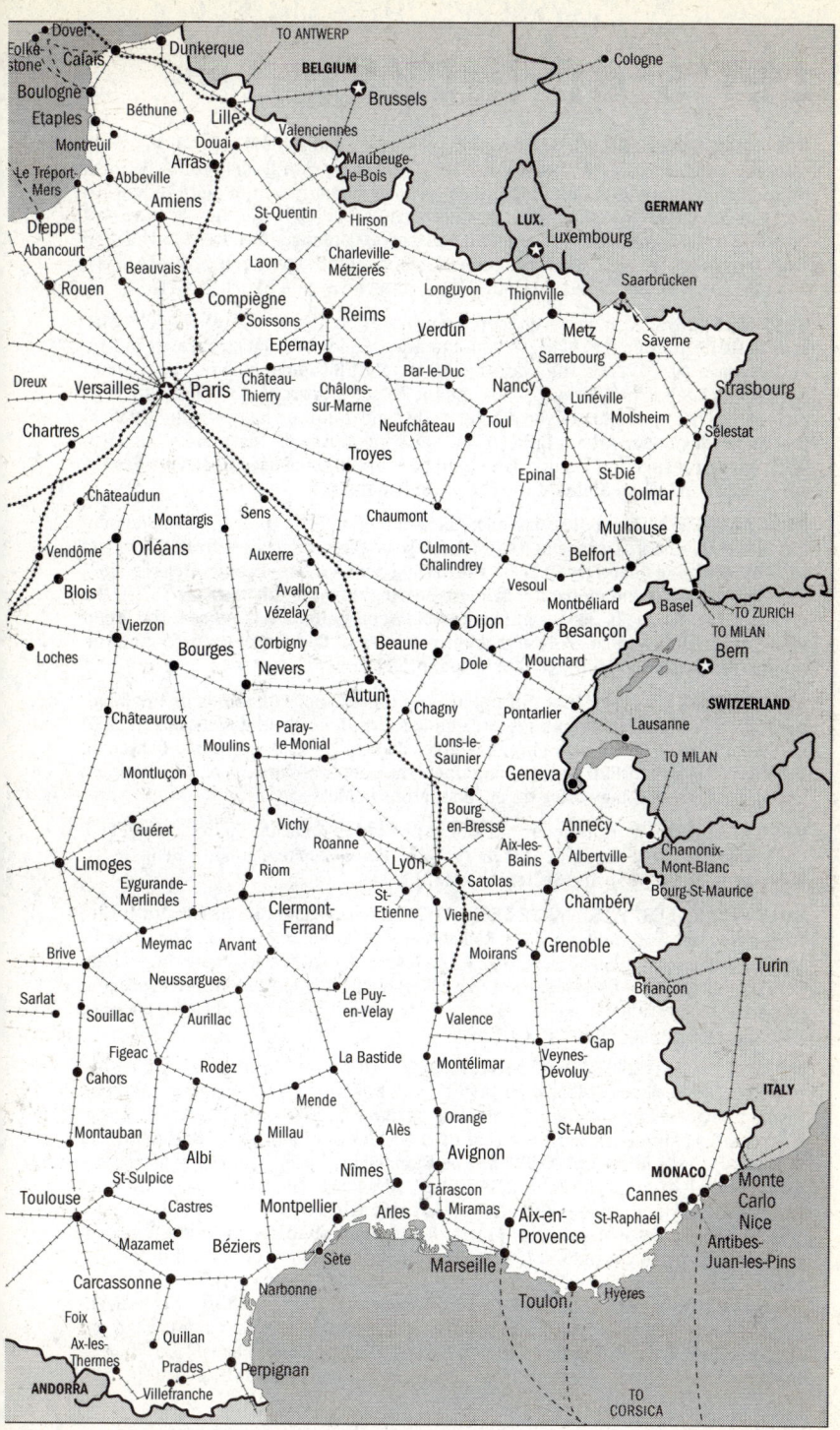

LET'S GO PICKS

BEST CITIES AND TOWNS: Lille, with Flemish beer and French style (p. 442); oh-too-pretty **Collioure,** the Matisse's muse (p. 704); **Nîmes,** with Roman ruins, Spanish bullfights, and fabulous French gardens (p. 274); nonstop action and the world's best cuisine in **Lyon** (p. 207); with its soaring cathedral and beautiful old town, it's no wonder the Germans kept annexing **Strasbourg; Cordes-sur-Ciel,** must have fallen from the clouds (p. 692); **Grenoble,** cultural capital of the sky-piercing Alps (p. 354); and of course, **Paris**—in the springtime, gay, or any way you like it (p. 84).

BEST MUSEUMS: You've never seen a museum as funky as the psychedelic **Maisons Satie** in Honfleur (p. 478), though the ultra-modern **Fondation Vasarely** in Aix-en-Provence (p. 247) and the graffitied **Musée d'Art Moderne** in Céret (p. 703) are hard on its heels. The **Louvre** (p. 136) and the **Musée d'Orsay** (p. 137), both in Paris, may be the heavyweights of the established scene, but they have worthy rivals in the **Musée des Beaux Arts** in Lille (p. 442) and the **Musée de Tessé** in Le Mans (p. 582). No self-respecting fashion fan could pass up on the **Musée Historique des Tissus** (p. 216), in Lyon, capital of the French silk industry.

BEST SCENERY: The endless **lavender fields** of the Lubéron (p. 260); the spectacularly-lit walls of **Carcassonne** at night (p. 693); the panoramic view from the *haute ville* of charming **Chauvigny** (p. 595); the darling cobbled streets of **Le Mans** (p. 582) and **Blois** (p. 555); the menacing glaciers bearing down on **Chamonix** (p. 370); the coves of **Cap Corse** (p. 348), sandwiched between mountains and sea; the steep white cliffs of **Étretat** (p. 474) and sheer red ones of **Cap Frehel** (p. 515); and the public transportation employees in **Nîmes** (p. 274).

BEST OUTDOOR ACTIVITIES: Hiking around the extinct volcanoes of the **Mont-Dore** (p. 225); climbing mountains and skiing down them around **Chamonix** (p. 370) and **Val d'Isère** (p. 376); canoeing in **Georges du Tarn** (p. 723) and **Grand Canyon du Verdon** (p. 317); the **GR20** trail running down the center of **Corsica** (p. 332); and just sitting outside drinking coffee on pl. Mandarous in **Millau** (p. 722).

BEST BEACHES: Work on your tan and your strut in **Arcachon** (p. 655), **Anglet** (p. 658), **Mimizan-Plage** (p. 657), **St-Malo** (p. 507), **Porto Vecchio** (p. 350), **Belle-Île** (p. 536), **Île de Ré** (p. 615), and **St-Tropez** (p. 322).

HOLY PICKS: BEST PILGRIMAGE DESTINATIONS. Rocamadour and its beautiful Cité Réligeuse built into a cliff (p. 640); **Conques** and its stolen relics of St. Foy (p. 724); **Lourdes** and its sacred grotto (p. 674); **Mont-St-Michel,** commissioned by the archangel himself (p. 496); **Chartres,** the fullest flower of early Gothic architecture and protector of the Sancta Camisia, Mary's birthing robe (p. 154); and **Le Puy-en-Velay,** with its sky-scraping churches (p. 228).

MORBID PICKS: BEST ROYAL NECROPOLISES. All but three kings of France are buried in the **Basilique St-Denis,** Paris (p. 134), while their sworn enemies, the Plantagenêt kings of England, lie at **Fontevraud l'Abbaye** (p. 577). Princess Grace (a.k.a. Grace Kelly) slumbers with the rest of the Grimaldi clan in the **Cathédrale de Monaco** (p. 304). **BEST CEMETERIES.** The **Catacombs,** Paris (p. 133), is an underground maze of bone-filled tunnels. Arles's **Alyscamps** (p. 266), was the Roman Empire's most famous cemetery. In Paris's **Père Lachaise** (p. 133) slumber Chopin, Wilde, Molière, Proust, and Jim Morrison—to name but five of its million residents. Rows of headstones stand in silent memory to those who died defending France and freedom in two World Wars at **Vimy** (p. 450), **Verdun** (p. 395), and by the **D-Day beaches** (p. 488). **BEST SOLO TOMBS.** Napoleon lies buried within nine concentric coffins at Les Invalides, Paris—this time they made sure he wouldn't get out (p. 131). **Richelieu** is entombed beneath his hat in the **Sorbonne chapel** (p. 128). **Nostradamus** checks his predictions from inside his coffin in **Salon de Provence** (p. 252).

DISCOVER FRANCE

Every year, 80 million visitors descend on France, making it by far the most popular tourist destination in the world. For a country which, though the largest in western Europe, is small by international standards, this is an impressive achievement. To the French, it is natural that the world should wish to pay homage to their beloved *patrie*. While reminders of the past abound everywhere in countless *châteaux*, Roman monuments, and medieval villages, France is also relentlessly modern. Most French people do their shopping in one of the 1100 hypermarkets and travel the country by TGV, the world's fastest train.

To the French, though, the future is not so obviously rosy. Canute-like, the government tries with diminishing success to stem the rising tide of American-style mass culture, and its insistence on French being an international language on a par with English and Spanish is increasingly untenable. The people themselves are preoccupied by the North-African immigrants who are taking their post-colonial revenge on France, undermining (in the eyes of the far right) the cultural integrity of the country by their refusal to assimilate French culture. While to outside observers their *banlieues* (suburbs) are the source of the most exciting and vibrant music, art, and cinema in France today, to the increasingly popular National Front they are an affront to the imaginary purity of the French people.

In reality, much of what is commonly considered "French" has been imposed on France's diverse regions by Kings and governments in Paris anxious to weld their diverse nation together. At the time of the revolution, in 1789, only half of the population spoke French, and at the extremities of the country you can still hear people speaking Basque, Breton, German, and Provençal. Every region has its own unique cultural traditions, which are too often ignored by the hordes of tourists who see no more of French culture than that which is already processed for mass consumption. You'll do far better, and get a far truer picture of France, if you take time out to visit smaller, less touristed towns, to enjoy the countryside, and to simply slow down, look around you, and take a breath of French air.

FACTS AND FIGURES

- **Official Name** République Française
- **Population** 59 million
- **Capital** Paris
- **Average Income** US$23,500
- **President** Jacques Chirac (1995-2002)
- **Major Religions** 76% Catholic, 5.5% Muslim, 2.5% Protestant
- **Area** 543,965km^2
- **Highest Peak** Mont Blanc (4807m)
- **Longest River** Loire (1024km)

WHEN TO GO

There is never a bad time to visit France, but you should plan your visit carefully depending on when you want to go. In July and August, everywhere is crowded and there seems to be more English and German spoken on the streets than French. This is the time that the beach resorts buzz, with the Mediterranean coast becoming one long party strip. Foreigners concentrate on the famous towns of the Côte d'Azur, while the French flock to resorts further west and to Corsica. In August, Paris heads south for the month and the city goes dead but for the click of camera shutters and the rumbling of tourist buses. Parisians and tourists crowd the city in the spring, while winters are cold and grey. All in all, early summer and autumn are the best times to visit the city. The north and west of France are prone to wet, though mild, winters and springs, while summers are warm but often unsettled. The center and east of the country have a more continental climate, with often harsh winters and long, dry summers; they are also generally the least crowded and most unspoiled regions—with some exceptions. December to February, the Alps provide some of the best skiing in the world, while the Pyrenees offer a less frenetic, if less climactically dependable, alternative. For a climate chart of major French cities, see the **Appendix** (p. 726).

THINGS TO DO

The vast majority of the millions who visit France every year are interested only in those sights and towns which fortune has propelled to worldwide fame. Though it would be a crime to totally neglect places such as Paris, the Loire châteaux, or the Côte d'Azur, France is so steeped in history and culture that there are hundreds of places equally deserving of attention, but happily so far "undiscovered." To help you decide what you want to see, we've given a brief summary of what sights, places, and towns we think are the best of their kind in France. In addition, each chapter includes a **Suggestions** paragraph for the area, while within each region the **Highlights of the Region** box has local recommendations.

CITIES

Though **Paris** (pp. 84-153) struts the world stage as one of its great cities, you'll find plenty to do in France's major regional centers. In **Marseille's** (p. 238) 2600-year history, this vibrant working city—the third largest in France—has never failed to make itself heard. **Lyon** (p. 220), France's second city, has long had a reputation for staid *bourgeoisie*. Don't be taken in by this—the undisputed culinary capital of France was also the center of the Resistance in World War II. **Nice** (p. 287) is a party town packed with museums, but be warned—there's no sand on its famous beach. Then again, with the rest of the Côte d'Azur but a pebble's throw away, who cares? Perhaps the new capital of Europe will be **Strasbourg** (p. 395). With a hybrid Franco-German culture, it's an obvious home for the European Parliament. The west of France isn't devoid of cities either. **Rennes** (p. 500) mixes a medieval *vieille ville*, major museums, and a frenetic youth culture, while **Toulouse** (p. 682) holds the Languedoc together with nightlife, monuments, and modern art.

CHÂTEAUX

French châteaux range from imposing feudal ruins to the well-preserved country homes of 19th-century industrialists. The greatest variety and concentration is to be found in the **Loire Valley** (pp. 546-589). Here the defensive hilltop fortresses of **Chinon** (p. 571) and **Saumur** (p. 573) contrast with the Renaissance grace of **Chenonceaux** (p. 568) and **Chambord** (p. 559). The Loire has no monopoly on châteaux, though. Near Paris you can find tributes to two great French monarch's even greater egos, **Versailles** (p. 156) and **Fontainebleau** (p. 157). In Provence, you'll be hard-pressed to decide whether the Palais des Papes in **Avignon** (p. 254) is a castle or a palace, while nearby the craggy ruins of **Les Baux** (p. 263) will take you back to the age of chivalry. Perhaps the most impressive château is the fortress of **Carcassonne** (p. 693), a medieval citadel which still stands guard over the Languedoc.

CATHEDRALS AND CHURCHES

France was one the Christian kingdom, and over the centuries has remained one of the most loyal to the Catholic church. This piety has resulted in the construction of thousands of abbeys, churches, and cathedrals throughout the country. Paris's **Nôtre Dame** (p. 116) is the most famous, but a more exquisite Gothic jewel is to be found a few hundred meters away in the **Sainte-Chapelle** (p. 117). The Gothic style first reached maturity at **Chartres** (p. 154), while other medieval masterpieces await at **Strasbourg** (p. 395) and **Reims** (p. 426). Skipping the centuries, a different sensibility animates Le Corbusier's masterpiece at **Ronchamp** (p. 419), while Henri Matisse's swansong is his chapel at **Vence** (p. 296).

THE OUTDOORS

Everyone's heard of the Alps, and some of the best hiking and skiing in the world can be found around the **Val d'Isère** (p. 377) and **Chamonix** (p. 370). But the Alps are just one of France's four major mountain ranges. Just north of them, you can get into the **Jura mountains** (p. 421) in Franche-Comté, while at the center of the country **Le Mont Dore** (p. 225), in the Massif Central, is a spectacular area. To the southwest, climb into Spain from the **Pyrénées occidentales** (p. 677). If snow-capped peaks aren't your thing, more lowland pleasures can be found in the flamingo-filled plains of the **Camargue** (p. 271), the hills of the **Lubéron** (p. 260), and the fantastic **Gorges du Tarn** (p. 723). For advanced hikers, it's possible to walk the length of rugged **Corsica's** unspoiled interior (pp. 329-353).

TOTAL HEDONISM

The Côte d'Azur attracts two types of people—the stars who make its glamor, and the masses who come looking for it. You'll party among the tanned youth of Europe in **Nice** (p. 287) and **Juan-les-Pins** (p. 309). Surfers should head straight for the big rollers of the Atlantic coast in **Anglet** (p. 658), while if sun and sand are your only desires, try **Porto Vecchio** (p. 350) in Corsica. If you're willing to brave the risk of rain, some of France's most beautiful beaches await in Brittany, at **Belle-Île** (p. 536) and **St-Malo** (p. 507).

SUGGESTED ITINERARIES

THE CREAM OF FRANCE (1 MONTH)

To see everything worth seeing in France in only a few weeks may seem impossible, but you can still try! You'll need at least 4-5 days to see the sights and shops of **Paris** (p. 84)—make sure to make time for a daytrip to **Versailles** (p. 156). Next, slip down to the Loire Valley. The château of **Amboise** (1 day; p. 561) was home to four French kings, while **Saumur** (1 day; p. 573) is famous for its castle, its riding school, and its sparkling wines. Then travel up to the island abbey of **Mont-St-Michel** (1 day; p. 496). A little further along the coast is popular **St-Malo** (1 day; p. 507), with ramparts, beaches, and fantastic seafood. Next, head down to **Nantes** (2 days; p. 541) for medieval sights and modern nightlife, before soaking up the sun in beach-blessed, historical **La Rochelle** (2 days; p. 610). For a change of pace, contemplate times past in medieval **Sarlat** (1 day; p. 641), and the 17,000-year-old cave paintings of **Les-Eyzies-de-Tayac** (1 day; p. 630). Test your taste buds in the vineyards of **Bordeaux** (2 days; p. 648) before zipping southwards to *basque* on the beach in **Biarritz** (2 days; p. 663). From there, follow the pilgrims to miraculous **Lourdes** (1 day; p. 674). Keep heading east to reach the stunning walls of **Carcassonne** (1 day; p. 693), guarding the town as they have done for centuries. No less formidable are the fortifications of the Palais-des-Papes in festive **Avignon** (1 day; p. 254). Students have been partying in elegant **Aix-en-Provence** (1 day; p. 247) for 600 years, but for non-stop action go to **Nice** (2 days; p. 287), undisputed capital of the Riviera. For a change of scenery, climb into the Alps to reach dynamic **Grenoble** (2 days; p. 354). You'll find highs of a different sort in **Beaune** (1 day; p. 186), home of Burgundy's most precious wines, while northeastwards, **Strasbourg** (2 days; p. 395) offers Alsatian wines and a hybrid Franco-German culture. Finally, finish off in style with a tasting at one of the many champagne *caves* in **Reims** (1 day; p. 426).

WEST COAST WONDERLAND (3 WEEKS) Kick off with a couple of days in **Rennes** (p. 500), the action-packed capital of Brittany, before exploring the rugged Atlantic scenery of the **Crozon Peninsula** (1 day; p. 528). Next, nip down the coast to **Quiberon** (p. 534), where you can catch a ferry to the idyllic beaches of **Belle-Île** (2 days; p. 536). Back on the mainland, **Nantes** (2 days; p. 541) is the next stop, packed with

Suggested Itineraries

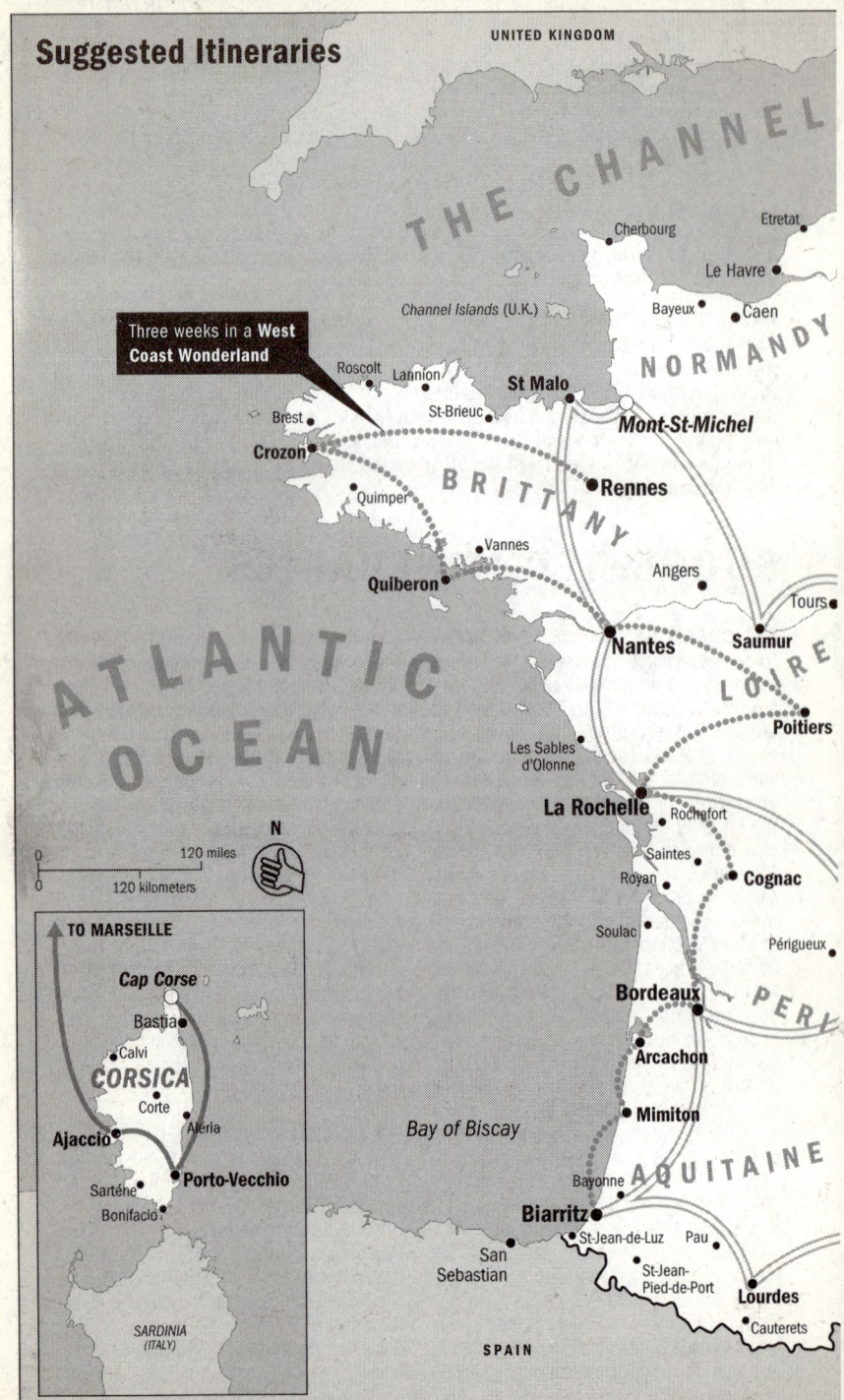

UNITED KINGDOM

THE CHANNEL

Cherbourg
Etretat
Le Havre
Bayeux
Caen

NORMANDY

Channel Islands (U.K.)

Three weeks in a **West Coast Wonderland**

Roscolt
Lannion
St-Brieuc
St Malo
Mont-St-Michel
Brest
Crozon
Quimper
Rennes

BRITTANY

Vannes
Angers
Quiberon
Nantes
Saumur

Tours

LOIRE

Poitiers

ATLANTIC OCEAN

Les Sables d'Olonne
La Rochelle
Rochefort
Saintes
Royan
Cognac
Soulac
Périgueux

0 ———— 120 miles
0 ———— 120 kilometers

N

Bordeaux

PERI

TO MARSEILLE

Cap Corse
Bastia
Calvi
CORSICA
Corte
Aleria
Ajaccio
Sarténe
Porto-Vecchio
Bonifacio

Arcachon

Mimiton

Bay of Biscay

AQUITAINE

Bayonne
Biarritz
St-Jean-de-Luz
San Sebastian
St-Jean-Pied-de-Port
Pau
Lourdes
Cauterets

SARDINIA (ITALY)

SPAIN

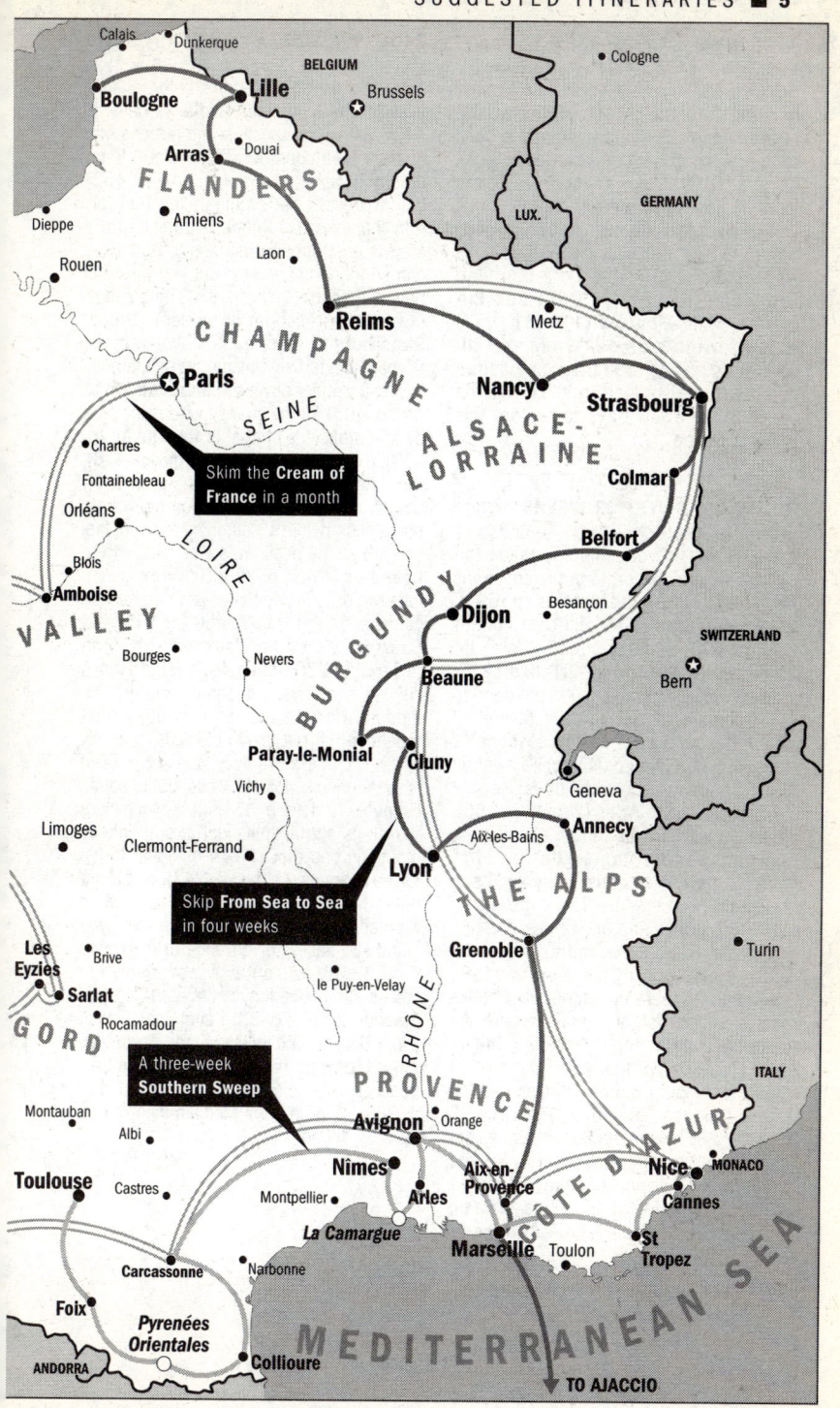

DISCOVER

ancient sights and youthful students. Take a brief trip inland to **Poitiers** (2 days; p. 590), where you'll find France hurtling into the 21st century at the **Futuroscope** theme-park. Then it's back to the beach in beautiful **La Rochelle** (2 days; p. 610). Make a stop to taste the local liquids in **Cognac** (1 day; p. 600) and rumbling **Bordeaux** (2 days; p. 648) before getting out your surfboards for a whirlwind sweep of the Côte d'Argent. **Arcachon** (2 days; p. 655) has the crowds, while **Mimizan** (1 day; p. 657) is lost in the Landes. When you hit **Anglet** (p. 658), you'll be in Basque country; base yourself in glitzy **Biarritz** (p. 663) for a few days to explore this unusual region.

SOUTHERN SWEEP (3 WEEKS) When you arrive, head straight for **Toulouse** (3 days; p. 682); from this capital of the southwest you can explore ancient towns like **Albi** (p. 688) and **Castres** (p. 692). Then head down to redoubtable **Foix** (1 day; p. 697) before climbing into the spectacular **Pyrénées Orientales** (2 days; p. 697). Spend a day in picture-perfect **Collioure** (p. 704) before taking refuge in the solid walls of **Carcassonne** (2 days; p. 693). Even older stones await in the Roman monuments of **Nîmes** (2 days; p. 274) and **Arles** (2 days; p. 266). While you're there, spend an afternoon in the otherworldly **Camargue** (p. 271) national park. More past glory awaits in **Avignon** (2 days; p. 254), home to numerous popes and anti-popes. The oldest city in France, **Marseille** (2 days; p. 238) is also one of the most modern; make sure to taste the inimitable *bouillabaisse*, king of fish dishes. From here, it's on to the glitter of the Côte d'Azur. **St-Tropez** (1 day; p. 322) may be the "jewel of the Riviera," but **Cannes** (2 days; p. 310) is the flashiest diamond and **Nice** (2 days; p. 287) wears the crown as its capital. If you've any money left, hit the world-famous casino of **Monte-Carlo** (1 day; p. 299) before nipping back east for a final night of hedonism in **Antibes** (1 day; p. 307).

FROM SEA TO SEA (4 WEEKS) Start off in **Boulogne** (1 day; p. 456), the most enticing of the Channel ports, before shifting inland to bustling, flemish **Lille** (2 days; p. 442). Pay your respects to the millions who died for their countries at the World War I memorials around Vimy (1 day; p. 450) before toasting the eventual French victory with champagne in **Reims** (2 days; p. 426). Moving east, more reminders to past wars can be found in Lorraine, but find peace in beautiful **Nancy** (1 day; p. 384) before moving onto the linchpin of modern Europe, **Strasbourg** (2 days; p. 395), home of the EU parliament. Don't blame intoxication following a wander down the **Route du Vin** (1 day; p. 403) for the strange visions induced by Le Corbusier's chapel in **Ronchamp** (p. 419), a daytrip from **Belfort** (1 day; p. 416). Older sights await in **Dijon** (2 days; p. 180), capital of Burgundy. Fill up on rich *boeuf bourgignon* before succumbing to sweet inebriation at the acclaimed vineyards of the **Côte d'Or** (1 day; p. 190). Travelling south, take two days to see the great Romanesque churches of **Paray-le-Monial** (p. 195) and **Cluny** (p. 198). France's second city, **Lyon** (3 days; p. 220), offers the best in French cuisine and a bevy of sights ancient and modern. Now it's time to work off all that weight you've put on—in the Alps, the only way is up. Ancient **Annecy** (2 days; p. 366) is surrounded by forests, while further south, **Grenoble** (2 days; p. 354) offers world-class museums and nightlife with a stupendous mountain backdrop. Power on south to hip **Aix-en-Provence** (1 day; p. 247), just a few miles from the southern sea at bustling **Marseille** (2 days; p. 238). From here you could slip east into Provence or west onto the Côte d'Azur, but why not follow the French and take a ferry or plane to Corsica? **Ajaccio** (2 days; p. 332) combines French sophistication with Italian charm, **Porto Vecchio** (1 day; p. 350) has perhaps the best beaches in Europe, and **Cap Corse** (1 day; p. 348) sticks into the Mediterranean like a *Let's Go* thumb.

HISTORY AND CULTURE

Straddling the European peninsula, France occupies a special place in Western consciousness. The largest country in Western Europe, it is also the most geographically diverse; bounded on the north by the North Sea and the English Channel, on the west by the Atlantic, and to the south by the Mediterranean, it shares land borders with eight countries. This unique position means that France has always played on the centre of the European stage, from the 17,000-year-old cave paintings at Lascaux, to the launch of the **euro** in 1999 (see p. 37).

AN HISTORICAL OVERVIEW

A BRUSH WITH PREHISTORY

In 1868, the skull of an advanced hominid was unearthed at **Cro-Magnon,** France. Dated to 27,000 years ago, Cro-Magnon man is proof that France's hospitable environment has attracted people since the dawn of time. Ten thousand years later, his artistic descendents were busy decorating their caves around the Dordogne valley, and by 4500 BC Neolithic peoples were carving out their place in history with giant stone monuments. These mysterious creations were held in awe by the celtic **Gauls,** who arrived from the east around 600 BC. Trade flourished between the Gauls and their new neighbors, the Phocean **Greeks,** who had founded a colony in the 7th century BC at Massilia (present day Marseille, p. 238). It took the local tribes 500 years to realize that the Greeks were getting the better end of the bargain, and to defend themselves the Massilians were forced to call for help from an expanding **Rome** in 125 BC. In less than three years, Rome had established control of southern France, though fierce northern Gauls resisted Roman incursions until Julius Cæsar's victory at **Alesia** in 52 BC. Gaul would remain an integral part of the Empire until its collapse, and Rome's legacy ranges from the well-preserved monuments of Provence (p. 237) to the French language itself.

THE FRANK ASCENDANCY

By the time Rome finally fell in AD 476, Gaul had suffered periodic Germanic invasions for centuries. While many tribes simply plundered and passed on, the **Franks** eventually dominated Gaul and bequeathed it their name. Under the Romans, the population had been Christianized, but the Franks remained pagan until the baptism of their king **Clovis,** first of the Merovingian dynasty, in 507. Clovis chose the minor town of Paris as his capital, and extended his rule over most of Gaul. Frankish inheritance laws, which divided territories equally among all the king's sons, did nothing to support his legacy and the kingdom rapidly fragmented. When the dashing **Charles Martel** (the Hammer) reunited the Frankish domains and defeated the previously unstoppable Moors at Poitiers in 732, the way was open for his diminutive son **Pépin le Bref** (the Short) to usurp the throne in 754. Pépin was the first monarch to be crowned by the pope, earning for France the moniker "eldest daughter of the Church." Despite his own achievements, Pépin was outshone by his son, the magnificent **Charlemagne,** who gave his name to the Carolingian dynasty. With hopes of reviving the Roman Empire, he added what is now Germany, Austria, and Switzerland to his domains, fulfilling his dream in 800 when the pope crowned him Holy Roman Emperor. The territorial squabbles following his death in 814 were only resolved in 843 with the Treaty of Verdun, which divided the empire amongst Charlemagne's grandsons. The western part, Francia (as France was then called), was given to **Charles le Chauve** (the Bald).

FEUD FOR THOUGHT The early Middle Ages saw the old Roman administration combine with Frankish tribal traditions to develop into the **feudal system.** A complex pyramid of authority, with serfs at the bottom and the king at the top, the organizing principle was one of **vassalage** and **suzerainty.** At each level, the vassal owed allegiance only to his suzerain, for whom he was bound to perform certain well-defined duties. In return, the suzerain kept order in his lands and dispensed justice. The independence enjoyed by local lords was necessary in an age of dangerous travel and unreliable communication, but it concentrated great power in their hands. Constantly at war amongst themselves, and often openly rebellious against the king, it was the dukes and counts who held the real power. This state of semi-permanent civil war throughout the Middle Ages was responsible for the profusion of castles in France, as each lord sought to protect his domains from greedy neighbors.

STORMING NORMANS AND POWER-HUNGRY PLANTAGENETS

In the 10th century a new wave of invaders took advantage of internal turmoil. Vikings, or **Normans,** no longer content with raiding the coasts, beached their longboats and forced the ailing Carolingians to grant them the duchy of Normandy. When the last Carolingian died in 987, the nobles elected **Hugh Capet** as king. Surrounded by powerful vassals, the king's power only extended over Paris and the tiny Île-de-France; he relied on the prestige of his position and their own insecurity to keep the nobles in check. But when the Duke of Normandy gained a kingdom and an epithet by conquering England in 1066, this balance was upset; the exploits of **William the Conqueror** are told in the famous Bayeux tapestry (p. 486). By passing the English succession into continental hands, the Norman conquest would pave the way for centuries of Anglo-French warfare. Things got serious for France in 1152 after Henry Plantagenêt, Duke of Anjou, married the well-endowed **Eleanor of Aquitaine.** Now master of more of France than **Louis VII** himself, he went on to inherit the English crown two years later as **Henry II.** However, when his chivalrous heir, **Richard the Lionheart,** departed for the Crusades, England was left in the inept hands of **John Lackland.** When John ignored a summons to the court of French king **Philippe-Auguste** (1180-1223), by feudal law he forfeited his French territories. With the English threat to his kingdom over, a series of astute marriages left Philippe one of the most powerful men in Europe by the end of his reign.

OF MONKS AND MEN

This endless warfare devastated peasant life, and many sought refuge inside the monasteries and convents which had sprung up all over Europe. In addition to offering sincerely believed promises of eternal salvation, the Church offered plebeians a rare opportunity for advancement outside the feudal hierarchy. While townspeople raised cathedrals to the honour of God, monasteries and convents swelled with the ranks of novitiates. Soon the power of the monasteries was as great as that of the aristocracy, and in the 11th century the abbot of **Cluny** (p. 198) was as influential as any monarch. As the Church grew in wealth, many turned away from its ostentation and luxury. A young Burgundian, **St. Bernard,** sought do away with corruption, influencing popes and kings from his abbey at **Clairvaux,** which he founded in 1115. Twenty years earlier, **Pope Innocent II** had proclaimed the first Crusade from Clermont (p. 220), hoping to wrest Jerusalem from the Saracens. Thousands, from kings to peasants, flocked to take the cross, swayed by the promise of guaranteed salvation (and not a little plunder). Though only the first of the eight Crusades launched between 1095 and 1271 had any military success, exposure to the advanced civilizations of the east and the revival of international trade played an important part in awakening Europe from the cultural lethargy of the early Middle Ages.

ONE HUNDRED YEARS OF INCERTITUDE

The French throne was thrown into question in 1328 on the death of **Charles IV,** last of the Capetians. Charles had only daughters, and since French law prohibited a woman from inheriting the throne, the nobles gave the throne to **Philippe de Valois.** But when he encroached upon English Aquitaine, Charles IV's nephew, **Edward III** of England, claimed the throne for himself, starting off the **Hundred Years' War.** The first twenty years went badly for the French, but they regained the upper hand under **Charles V** (1364-1380). The recovery was brief, though; his son, **Charles VI,** suffered bouts of insanity and was unable to rule effectively. After **Henry V** of England annihilated the French cavalry at Agincourt in 1415 and occupied Paris; the French were obliged to recognize Henry's son as heir to their throne, and on Charles's death the child-king Henry VI of England was crowned king of France. Salvation for the French came in 1429, when a 17-year old peasant girl claiming divine inspiration forced her way through to his court in Chinon (see p. 571). Leading the French army, **Joan of Arc** won a string of victories before her betrayal and capture by Burgundians, who were at that time allied to the English. They handed her over to the English authorities, who had her convicted of witchcraft and burnt her at the stake in Rouen in 1430 (see p. 466). But the tide of war had turned, and by 1453 only Calais was left in English hands.

THE THREE R'S: REBIRTH, REFORMATION, AND RELIGIOUS WAR

With the English confined to their island, the French kings spent the rest of the century consolidating their position, arm-twisting their way into Provence and Burgundy by the end of the 15th century. In 1515 **François I** set off to recapture his great-grandmother's heritage in swinging Italy; initial victory was followed ten years later by disaster at the battle of Pavia. Captured and imprisoned by his arch-rival, the Holy Roman Emperor **Charles V,** he also found himself conquered by the dazzling artistic forces of the **Renaissance** (French for "rebirth"), and after his release in 1526 he worked to bring France into the new age.

Meanwhile, in Germany, a monk called **Martin Luther** had kicked off the **Reformation** with his tirades against the obscurity and pomp of Catholic worship. Under the influence of Frenchman **Jean Calvin,** these ideas spread rapidly through French society. Though **Catherine de Medici,** regent for her son **Charles IX,** king of France, tried to reconcile Huguenots (French Protestants) with Catholics, the powerful **duc de Guise** would accept nothing less than papal supremacy. In 1562, civil war became inevitable after de Guise initiated the St. Bartholemew's Day Massacre. This saw the death of over 3000 Huguenots who had gathered in Paris to celebrate the wedding of **Henri III**'s sister Marguerite to their leader, Henri of Navarre. When the king's son died, leaving protestant Henri heir to the throne, de Guise planned to seize power for himself. Aware of the danger, the King retaliated by ordering the duke's murder in 1588, but even so was assassinated himself a year later. Ascending the throne as **Henri IV,** the new king said *"Paris vaut bien une messe"* ("Paris is well worth a mass"), referring to his recent conversion to Catholicism—a political necessity. But he did not abandon his Huguenot friends, and in 1598 the **Edict of Nantes** guaranteed their religious and political rights.

THE KINGDOM OF THE SUN

First of the Bourbon line, Henri IV succumbed to an assassin's dagger in 1610 and was succeeded by **Louis XIII.** Louis' capable and ruthless minister, **Cardinal Richelieu,** consolidated political power in the hands of the monarchy and created the centralized, bureaucratic administration so characteristic of France to this day. When Richelieu and Louis died within months of each other in 1642, they were succeeded by another king-and-cardinal combo, **Louis XIV** and **Cardinal Mazarin.** Since Louis was only five years old at the time, once again the cardinal took charge, but by 1661 the 24-year-old monarch had decided he was ready to rule alone. Not known for his modesty, Louis adopted the motif of the Sun King and took the motto *"l'état, c'est moi"* ("I am the state"). Following this, he brought a personal touch to national affairs, moving the government to his new 14,000-room palace of Versailles (p. 156), revoking the Edict of Nantes in 1685 at the behest of his mistress, and initiating the ruinous War of the Spanish Succession (1701-1713). As the nobles vegetated at court, most didn't even notice their complete loss of political power. When Louis finally died in 1715, he had outlasted even his grandsons, and was succeeded by the two-year old **Louis XV.** Coming to its senses, the aristocracy made a grab to reclaim power, as the national debt soared and a series of disastrous wars led to the loss of France's colonies in Canada and India.

A BOURBON ON THE ROCKS: REVOLUTION AND REGICIDE

When **Louis XVI** succeeded to the throne in 1774, the country was in a desperate financial state. While peasants blamed the soon-to-be-*ancien* regime for their mounting debts, the useless aristocrats detested the king for his attempts at reform. In 1789, to get out of this no-win situation, Louis XVI called a meeting of the Estates General, an assembly of delegates from the three classes of society: aristocrats, clergy, and everyone else. This anachronistic body had not met since 1614, and after weeks of wrangling over legalities, the bourgeois-dominated **Third Estate** broke away and declared itself to be the National Assembly. Inviting the other Estates to join it, it vowed not to disband until the country had a constitution. The king sent in troops to intimidate the Assembly, whereupon they received the immortal reply that "the assembled nation cannot receive orders." As rumors multiplied, the initiative passed to the Parisian mob, known as *sans-culottes* ("without breeches"—i.e. working class). When they stormed the **Bastille** (see p. 126) on July 14th, a destructive orgy exploded across the nation as peasants burnt the records of their debts and obligations. The Assembly responded in August with the abolishment of feudal privileges and the **Declaration of the Rights of Man.** When the petrified king, by now under virtual house arrest, tried to flee the country in 1791 he was arrested and imprisoned; meanwhile Austria and Prussia mobilized in order to stamp out this democratic disease. As the revolutionary armies miraculously defeated the invaders, the radical Jacobin faction took control of the Assembly, abolished the monarchy, and declared the **Republic.** In January 1793, the king was guillotined; the *ancien régime* was over.

DEATH AND TRANSFIGURATION: FROM GUILLOTINE TO EMPIRE

The revolution had taken on a radical turn. When the Church refused to be subjugated to the National Assembly, it was abolished and replaced by the oxymoronic **Cult of Reason.** Confusing rationalization with decimalization, a new calendar was introduced with 10-day weeks; though this did not catch on, the Revolutionary **metric** system of measurement is now the international standard. As counter-revolutionary paranoia set in, power lay with the "incorruptible" **Robespierre** and his McCarthyesque Committee of Public Safety. The least suspicion of royalist sympathy led straight to the gallows, and Dr. Guillotine himself did not escape the vengeance of his fearful invention. Fearful of his position, Robespierre ordered the execution of his revolutionary rivals, including the popular **Danton,** before his own denunciation and death in 1794. The **Terror** was over, and power was entrusted to a five-man Directory. Meanwhile, war continued. In a brilliant campaign, a young Corsican general swept through northern Italy and forced the Austrians to capitulate on his terms. Fearful of his rising popularity, the Directory jumped at **Napoleon Bonaparte**'s idea of invading Egypt to threaten the British colonies in India. Though successful on land, the destruction of his fleet at the Battle of the Nile left his disease-ridden army marooned in Cairo. Ever the pragmatist, Napoleon responded by abandoning it, and hurried back to France to salvage his political career. Riding a wave of public support, Napoleon deposed the despised Directory, declaring himself First Consul in 1799, Consul for Life in 1802, and ultimately **Emperor** in 1804. While not at war, Napoleon crafted a legal code which would be his most lasting achievement; elements of it remain incorporated into French law today. Though it remained largely faithful to revolutionary ideals, the **Code Napoléon** bears touches of his autocratic approach to life, re-establishing slavery and requiring wives to show total obedience to their husbands. Napoleon also made peace with the

Church and reformed the education system, but with his popularity contingent on military victory, war remained his specialty. After crushing the Austrians at Austerlitz, the Prussians at Jena and the Russians at Friedland, only Britain remained undefeated, safe in her island refuge following **Nelson**'s destruction of the French fleet at Trafalgar in 1807. Napoleon's unravelling came during the Russian campaign of 1812. The Russians withdrew before the advancing *Grande Armée*, ravaging their own land to deny the enemy food and shelter. After occupying a deserted Moscow, Napoleon was forced to withdraw at the onset of winter. The freezing cold decimated the French ranks, and of the 700,000 men he had led out to Russia, barely 200,000 returned. Napoleon's enemies sensed their time had come and attacked. Though Napoleon rose to the challenge with what many consider to be militarily the greatest of his campaigns, he had finally lost the support of his war-weary people. In return for abdicating in 1814, he was given the Mediterranean island of Elba, and the monarchy was reinstated under **Louis XVIII,** brother of his headless predecessor. The story had a final twist: Napoleon, leaving Elba and landing near Cannes on March 26, 1815, marched northwards to a rapturous reception as the king fled back to England. The adventure of the Hundred Days ended three months later on the field of Waterloo in Flanders, where the **Duke of Wellington** triumphed as much by luck as by skill. The ex-Emperor threw himself on the mercy of the English, who banished him to remote St. Helena in the south Atlantic, where he died in 1821, probably poisoned by royalist French agents. Popularly regarded as a hero in France, thousands still flock to pay their respects at his grandiose tomb at Les Invalides, Paris (p. 131).

REVOLUTION AND EMPIRE: PART TWO

Though initially forced to recognize the achievements of the Revolution, the reinstated monarchy soon returned to its despotic ways. When **Charles X** restricted the press and limited the electorate to the landed classes, the people had had enough. Remembering the fate of his brother, Charles abdicated quickly, following the **July Revolution** of 1830, and a constitutional monarchy was created under the "citizen king," **Louis-Philippe,** Duke of Orleans. While the middle classes prospered, the industrialization of France created a class of urban poor receptive to the new ideas of **socialism.** When the king and his bourgeois government refused to reform, the people were well practised: there followed the **February Revolution** of 1848 and the declaration of the **Second Republic** with universal male suffrage for the first time. Playing on the myth of his name, the emperor's nephew **Louis Napoleon** was elected president. Since the constitution barred him from seeking a second term despite his immense popularity, he seized power in a coup in 1851, followed a year later by a referendum which declared him **Emperor Napoleon III.** During his reign, France's prestige was restored; her factories hummed and **Baron Haussmann** rebuilt Paris, knocking down the medieval street plan so conducive to street fighting and replacing it with grand boulevards along which troops could rapidly be deployed. The confident French did not notice the storm clouds gathering across the Rhine, where **Bismarck** had almost completed the unification of Germany. Tricking the French into declaring war, the Iron Chancellor's troops swiftly overran the country; the emperor was captured and as German armies advanced the **Third Republic** was declared. Paris held out for four months, with the residents reduced to eating rats and communicating with the outside world by hot-air balloon, but its position was hopeless. When the government admitted defeat, the Parisian mob revolted and declared the **Commune;** it was crushed only after 4000 *communards* died in street battles, and in the name of order 25,000 more Parisians were summarily executed. The Third Republic was further undermined by the **Dreyfus affair,** as the humiliated army searched for a scapegoat. An army captain, the Jewish Dreyfus was convicted in 1894 on trumped-up charges of treason, and exiled. When the army refused to consider the case even after proof of Dreyfus' innocence was uncovered, France became polarized between the Dreyfusards, who argued for his release, and the reactionary right-wing Antidreyfusards, to whom Dreyfus was an unpatriotic traitor regardless of the evidence. After **Émile Zola** condemned the army, the government, and society for its anti-semitic prejudice in his dramatic diatribe *J'accuse*, the Dreyfusard momentum became unstoppable; Dreyfus was finally pardoned in 1904.

WAR AND PEACE... AND WAR AGAIN

The 1871 unification of Germany had fundamentally changed the balance of power in Europe. After centuries of conflict, the **Entente Cordiale** brought the British and the French into cooperation in 1904. Together with tsarist Russia the three nations of the **Triple Entente** faced the **Triple Alliance** of Germany, Italy, and the Austro-Hungarian Empire. When **World War I** erupted in 1914, German armies rapidly advanced into France in a seeming replay of the previous conflict, but a stalemate soon emerged as the opposing armies dug into trenches along the length of the country. The withdrawal of newly revolutionary Russia in 1917 was balanced by the entry of the USA, and victory for the West came in 1918. It is still possible to visit the fields where a generation laid down their lives; see **Memorials near Verdun,** p. 395, for details. Devastated by four years of fighting on her territory, and with 1.3 million men dead, France pushed for crippling reparations from Germany; the ensuing social breakdown would aid **Hitler**'s rise to power. During the **great depression** of the 1930s, France was politically paralyzed and incapable of dealing with the rising threat of Nazi Germany. **World War II** began with the German invasion of Poland in 1939. France declared war on Germany in response, and in May, 1940, the German response swept through Belgium, bypassing the Maginot Line, a string of fortresses along the German border which formed France's main defensive position. Allied defenses collapsed, and France capitulated in June. The country was partitioned, with the north under German occupation, and a puppet state in the south ruled from **Vichy** by WWI hero **Maréchal Pétain.** Though evidence indicates that many French people willingly collaborated with the Germans, today France prefers to commemorate the brave men and women of the **Resistance;** their headquarters in Lyon have now been made into a museum (p. 220). Those French forces that escaped the Germans were led by the French government-in-exile, under General **Charles de Gaulle.** It was at his insistence that French troops led the liberation of Paris on August 25th, 1944.

AFTER THE WAR: A NEW HOPE FOR EUROPE

The **Fourth Republic** was proclaimed in 1944, but its wartime leader de Gaulle quit in 1946, unable to adapt to the deadlock of democratic politics. Like the Third Republic, it lacked a strong executive to keep the country running when the legislature stalemated, and over the next 14 years France saw 25 governments. Despite these problems, the Fourth Republic presided over an economically resurgent France, and when the constitution was reformed in 1958, the **Fifth Republic,** under the renewed leadership of the still-revered de Gaulle, inherited a sound industrial base. Fiercely nationalist, de Gaulle's foreign policy was a success, delicately playing the USA against the USSR to France's advantage, but his domestic conservatism brought growing problems at home. In **May 1968,** what started as a student protest against the university system rapidly grew into a full-scale revolt as workers striked in support of social reform. The National Assembly was dissolved and things looked to be heading for revolution yet again, averted only when fresh elections returned the Gaullists to power. However, the aging General had lost his magic touch, and he resigned following a referendum defeat in 1969. During his reign, the structure of France's relations with the world had changed significantly. Defeat in Indochina (now Vietnam) in 1954, and Algerian independence in 1962 following eight years of civil war in between native Arabs and *Pieds Noirs* (French settlers), ended France's role as a colonial power. Meanwhile a new era of European cooperation began, designed to put an end to the disastrous cycle of war which had devastated the continent. What began as the European Coal and Steel Community in 1952, a pact of industrial cooperation between Belgium, France, Holland, Luxembourg and West Germany, became the **European Economic Community** (EEC) following the 1957 **Treaty of Rome.** With the Maastricht Treaty of

1992 the EEC evolved into the more closely knit **European Union** (EU), and in 1995 the **Schengen agreement** created a six-nation zone without border controls. 1999 saw the extension of this zone to the entire EU bar the U.K., Ireland, and Denmark, as well as the birth of the European single currency, the **euro.**

CULTURAL CONNECTIONS

Artistically active throughout the Middle Ages, since its unification in the 16th century, France has always been at the fore of Western intellectual development. As the inheritors of René Descartes, Victor Hugo, and Henri Matisse, the immense pride the French show in their cultural achievements is not without justification.

EARLY DAYS: FROM CAVEMEN TO THE DARK AGES

France was endowed with a rich artistic heritage long before the arrival of the "civilizing" influence of Greeks and Romans. Protected from 17,000 years of history deep within the caves of the Perigord region, the paintings of Lascaux (p. 631) and Les Eyzies-de-Tayac (p. 631) remained hidden until the 19th century, while five millennia of wind and rain have not diminished the majesty of the huge stones which still guard their secrets near Carnac in Brittany (p. 537). No such impressive monuments stand to the memory of the ancient Gauls, whose legacy was swept away by Roman conquerors. Rome's legacy is most visible in Provence, such as the theater at Orange (p. 280) and the arena and temple at Nîmes (p. 274). Nearby, the golden arches of the Pont du Gard aqueduct (p. 279) served up 44 million gallons of fresh water to Nîmes' thirsty citizens every day.

The fall of Rome ushered in the evocatively named **Dark Ages.** A troubled time of invasion and destruction, it was not until the ninth century that intellectual life could re-emerge from the monasteries where it had cowered for centuries. Though Charlemagne tried to emulate the Romans, during the intervening years artistic sensibilities had undergone a profound change. No longer merely imitating nature, art now served to teach the scriptures in an illiterate age.

THE MIDDLE AGES: THE ROMANESQUE PERIOD

Only religious buildings survive from the early Middle Ages, treated with reverence by the plundering armies which continually criss-crossed the land. Inspired by surviving Roman basilicas, the **Romanesque** style emerged at the end of the 10th century, using semicircular arches and vaults supported on massive columns to create an impression of simple grandeur, as can be seen at the Cathédrale St-Étienne in Nevers (p. 198). The 11th century saw new developments as the monastic cults established at Cluny (p. 198) and Clairvaux spread throughout Europe. The rectangular plan of the earlier churches was crossed with a transept and supplemented by private chapels, while pointed vaults allowed masons to build ever higher. Meanwhile, the doorways of churches acquired their own distinctive sculptural function. The Église St-Trôphime in Arles (p. 270) displays a typical tympanum above the door featuring Christ surrounded by the evangelists. Around this were carved such scenes as the Apocalypse or the Last Judgement. It is instructive to recall that medieval sculptures were originally brightly painted; only rarely has the coloring survived centuries of sun and rain. For the same reason medieval paintings appear dull and faded, and it is only in the pages of **manuscripts** that the brilliant colors and detailed drawings of the age have survived intact. Unfortunately, almost all are locked away safely in library vaults, with the largest collection being at the Bibliothèque Nationale in Paris (p. 120).

Choral music also flourished in monasteries, where monks, by adding more voices to the single melodic line of Gregorian chants, developed **polyphony** in the 10th and 11th centuries. This was brought to perfection in the 12th century under **Léonin** at Nôtre-Dame in Paris. Of the **secular music** of the time, we know little since musical notation was neither well developed nor commonly used outside the Church. Then, as now, songs were more popular than instrumental music, and while most tunes have long been lost, in many cases the words remain. In the flourishing courts of 11th century Provence, **troubadours** sang songs of love and chivalry in the southern *langue d'oc* tongue, while farther north, **trouvères** wrote in the *langue d'oil*, the predecessor of modern French. Regarding women as objects of veneration rather than disposable chattels, the troubadours instigated the sexual revolution that became embodied in the chivalric code, while the literary forms they developed influenced all future European lyric poetry. **Epic poetry** was represented by the *chansons de geste*, of which the most famous is the *Chanson de Roland* (circa 1100), the story of Charlemagne's nephew and his doomed struggle against the Moors. From such songs developed the 12th century *romance*, written in rhyming couplets; one early example, *le roman d'Alexandre*, gave its name to the **alexandrine,** the dominant meter for French verse until the 20th century. The satirical *Roman de Renart*, a 13th century *Animal Farm*, was so popular that its canine protagonist gave his name to the French word for fox, *renard*.

THE LATE MIDDLE AGES: THE GOTHIC EXPLOSION

In the 13th century, poetry devolved from song, as a growing merchant class demanded a more serious approach to writing. Though generally considered the last and greatest *trouvère*, **Rutebeuf** (1245-1285) wrote unaccompanied poems treating subjects such as corruption and personal belief. It was the marriage of secular words with sacred music, under Léonin's successor **Pérotin** (d. 1238), which gave birth to the popular motet. These multi-part choral works, in which each part sings a different text, rapidly lost their holy origins; while the original Latin text survived in the tenor, the upper voices sang unrelated secular French verse. Motets form the largest body of work by **Guillaume de Machaut** (1300-1377), the leading figure of the **Ars Nova** style. This was marked by the development of isorhythm, in which repeated rhythms in each part overlapped to create a remarkably modern sound—and in fact the technique was revived by 20th composers.

The increased complexity of music and literature mirrored the development of architecture as the Romanesque style gave way to the **Gothic** towards the end of the 12th century. In their quest for height, master builders developed the ribbed vault, small rectangular vaults supported by diagonal arches and strung together in series to create the main nave. St-Rémy-de-Reims (built 1162-1181; p. 430) and Nôtre-Dame-de-Paris (started 1163; p. 116) are examples of the early Gothic style, but it is with the cathedral of Chartres (built 1194-1220; p. 154) that the art reached maturity. The use of flying buttresses, exterior supports which leap from the side-aisles to support the nave, allowed ceilings to soar up to 48 meters into the air. With the walls freed of structural duties, they could be filled with windows, so that from within, the ceiling appears to float above on a sea of shimmering stained glass. Dominating the ends of the nave, the circular rose window became common in the 13th century, and the way in which the "petals" radiate out from the centre gave its name to the **Rayonnant** style. This emerged around 1230, when the ultimate height limit of stone vaulting was reached and attention turned from structure to decoration. Windows became still larger and the supporting stone was carved into delicate tracery; a delectable example is the Sainte-Chapelle in Paris (finished 1248; p. 117), with an almost continuous glass curtain on three sides of the chapel. Rayonnant further evolved into the highly ornamental **Gothic Flamboyant** style at the end of the 14th century. *"Flamboyant"* is French for "flaming," and refers to the shape of the sinuous traceries of the windows, such as at La Trinité in Vendôme (p. 586). By this time the sculpted portals of Romanesque churches had evolved into great porches, with layers of attendant saints and angels to welcome the faithful; at the same time sculpture became less stylized and more naturalistic, as can be seen in the church of the Madeleine in Troyes (p. 434). The relative peace and prosperity of the late Gothic period encouraged the development of civic architecture, and Gothic motifs may often be found in the houses of rich merchants. The Hôtel Jacques-Coeur in Bourges (p. 167) is a good example of a where a successful 15th-century entrepreneur might have lived.

14TH TO 16TH CENTURY: THE FLOWERING OF HUMANISM

When Pope Clement V decided to move from Rome to Avignon (p. 254) in 1309, Provence became the centre of Christendom. The **Palais des Papes** his successors constructed is a masterpiece of late Gothic architecture, aggressively defensive from the outside, yet sumptuously decorated within. Among those attracted to the Papal court was the poet **Petrarch,** and it was in Avignon on April 6, 1327, that he first saw the beautiful Laura of his sonnets. A few miles south lay the flourishing court of **Les Baux** (p. 263), long a magnet for troubadours; a Florentine exile called **Dante** would spend time there. The fantastical surroundings of the neighboring **Val d'Enfer** ("Valley of Hell") provided the perfect setting for his **Inferno.** These seeds of the Renaissance did not take root farther north for another century, as the continuing saga of the Hundred Years' War diverted French attention.

When François I inherited a strong, united country in 1515, the time had come for France's initiation into the new artistic universe. Exposed to the Renaissance during his Italian campaigns, the king invited the greatest living artists to work in France, including **Leonardo da Vinci** and **Il Rosso.** At his new palace of **Fontainebleau** (1527, p. 157), Italian designers and French craftsmen laid the foundations for the French Renaissance style. The **École de Fontainebleau** combined Italian and Flemish influence with a French sensibility in the works of father-and-son team Jean and François **Clouet.** Known for its subtle eroticism, the Fontainebleau school followed the Renaissance movement away from religious subjects, toward scenes of court life and classical mythology. French Renaissance architecture, though perfected at Fontainebleau, had been developing since the 16th century. Gunpowder had made nonsense of medieval siege tactics, and as war moved to the battlefield, once-fearsome châteaux could be transformed into stately pleasure domes. This transition is most visible in the Loire Valley, the favored haunt of the Valois monarchs; the château of **Amboise** (p. 561) is a case in point. Charles VIII first took to renovating the feudal building in 1492, and his Gothic wing contrasts sharply with that started in an Italian Renaissance style by Louis XII.

This cultural promiscuity resulted in a renaissance of French letters during the 16th century, as the end of Provençal independence hastened the demise of the *langue d'oc.* Brightest star of the Pleiades, poet Pierre de **Ronsard** (1524-1585; see p. 587) found inspiration in the literature of classical Greece and Rome. The publication of François **Rabelais'** novel *Pantagruel* (1532) delighted many with its unusual combination of bodily functions and progressive ideas on education, but did not impress the skeptical Michel de **Montaigne.** Deeply disturbed by the wars of religion, Montaigne created a new literary genre with his *Essays* (1580), a collection of musings on the frailty of truth. His *Journal de Voyage,* which describes his travels around Europe, prefigured *Let's Go*'s observant literary style by 380 years. Early 15th century music was dominated by the **Burgundian school,** under the influence of Guillaume **Dufay,** father of the musical mass.

THE 17TH CENTURY: THE SPLENDOR OF THE BAROQUE

The 17th century found France at the acme of cultural and political power as **Louis XIII** and **Louis XIV** recognized the power of art to project an image of unchallenged royal authority. With the court established in the Île de France, Paris became the screen on which they projected their grandeur. **Baroque** architecture was introduced from Italy by Louis XIII's mother, Marie de Medici, who commissioned the Palais de Luxembourg in Paris (1615; p. 128), but it reached its peak with the château of Vaux-le-Vicomte (1657, p. 158), which brought architect Louis **Le Vau,** artist Charles **Le Brun,** and landscaper Louis **Le Nôtre** together for the first time. Louis XIV was so impressed with their work that he commissioned them to build him a new palace at Versailles (p. 156). When Le Vau died, architectural responsibility for the palace passed to Jules **Hardouin-Mansart,** who had gained fame for his church at Les Invalides in Paris (1675; p. 131). Under the approval of his egocentric master, the size of the palace was trebled until it could house a quarter of the king's retinue of 20,000. Among the pampered nobility, martial prowess gave way to cultural refinement as the mark of distinction. This was embodied in the yin and yang concepts of the *honnête homme*, the cultivated and moderate gentleman who delighted in social discourse, and the *précieuse*, the lady of affectation and extravagance. Baroque sculpture also centred around Versailles, from **Giradon's** outdoor *Apollo Tended by the Nymphs* (1666), to Antoine **Coysevox's** busts reflected in the Hall of Mirrors. Baroque painting became a clear favorite after Simon **Vouet** returned from Rome in 1627, but he was soon obscured by the genius of Nicolas **Poussin.** Poussin, who spent the majority of his career in Rome, is crediting with developing the **Academic** style, espoused by the *Académie Royale* after its foundation in 1648. Under style dictator Le Brun, the Academy became the sole arbiter of taste in all matters artistic.

As science emerged from the shadows of religion, René **Descartes** placed his trust firmly in logic and set out to understand the world. The greatest of French philosophers, in his 1637 *Discourse on Method* Descartes proved his own existence with the irrefutable deduction "I think, therefore I am." A gifted mathematician, the father of analytical geometry also introduced the notation "x" for an unknown quantity. Opposing Descartes was the equally diverse genius of **Blaise Pascal**. After a youth misspent inventing the mechanical calculator and the science of probabilities, he became a devotee of Jansenism, an influential Catholic reform movement which sought salvation through inner peace and contemplation. Retiring from public life, Pascal expounded the virtues of solitude in his best-known work, the *Pensées* (1658). Another important Jansenist was the classically-oriented tragedian **Jean Racine,** whose *Phèdre* (1677) is considered by many to be the greatest play in the French literary canon. His comic counterpart, **Molière**, satirized the social pretensions of his age in comedies of manner, which combined classical structures with hilarious farce. Molière's actors formed the basis for the the **Comédie Française,** the world's oldest national theater company, which still produces the definitive versions of French classics at its theatre in Paris (p. 141). Molière himself died in 1673, ironically during a performance of his satire on hypochondria, *The Imaginary Invalid.* His manner of death was bested by that of his collaborator, composer Jean-Baptiste **Lully,** who died in 1687 from self-inflicted injuries sustained with his baton during some vigorous conducting. During his long career, this ambitious Italian rose from a humble violinist to the ranks of the aristocracy, and by 1674 he could veto any opera performance in France. He is credited with developing the French opera-ballet (often starring Louis XIV himself), with its distinctive overture and accompanied recitative.

THE 18TH CENTURY: AN ENLIGHTENED AGE

The tensions created in French society under Louis XIV would give rise to a period of intense philosophical activity in the years leading up to the Revolution. This **Enlightenment** was dominated by the intellectual and literary activity of three men; Charles-Louis de **Montesquieu, Voltaire,** and Jean-Jacques **Rousseau.** The oldest of the three, Montesquieu achieved recognition in 1721 for the *Persian Letters*, a compelling and damning picture of Parisian culture seen through the eyes of two visiting Persians. This was followed in 1748 by *The Spirit of Laws*, which revolutionized political theory by emphasizing the principles of government over its institutions. Meanwhile, Voltaire (the pen name of François Marie Arouet) illuminated the entire century with his insistence on liberty and tolerance. A period of exile across the Channel in 1726-1728 laid the basis for his seminal *Philosophical Letters* (1734), an exposition of the merits of the English constitution. Voltaire's reputation as a writer rests on his short stories, such as *Candide* (1758), a comic refutation of the optimistic philosophy that "all is for the best in this best of all possible worlds." In the same year he chose to move to Ferney, on the Franco-Swiss border; with enemies on both sides of the border, he found it expedient to be able to switch countries at a moments notice. Even more unwelcome were the ideas of Rousseau. While Voltaire and Montesquieu proposed progressive reforms, Rousseau thought that society needed to be entirely reshaped. In the *Social Contract* (1762), he opens with the statement that "man was born free, but he is everywhere in chains," and proceeds to develop his utopian vision. Asserting that only in solitude can true freedom be realized, he proposed the total subjugation of people to the state. Able to act upon the united "general will" of its people, the republic itself could act as a lone, free super-being.

Voltaire and Rousseau were both members of the *philosophes* ("philosophers"), a diverse group of thinkers bent upon social reform. They were led by Denis **Diderot,** who directed the landmark *Encyclopédie* in collaboration with the scientist Jean **d'Alembert.** This enormous undertaking aimed to encompass the entire body of human knowledge, with contributions from all the leading French intellectuals of the time. Somehow Diderot also found time to write novels, including *Rameau's Nephew,* in which he questions the meaning of virtue via the life of the good-for-nothing nephew of Jean-Philippe **Rameau.** The greatest French composer of his day, Rameau brought a new harmonic complexity to French music, as in the opera *Pygmalion* (1748). His elaborate Baroque style eventually brought him into conflict with a young Rousseau, himself no mean composer, on the charge that an emphasis on harmony stifled artistic freedom. Not a man of letters, Rameau came off the worst in this philosophically heated argument, and the melodic **Classical** style Rousseau favored soon triumphed in the concert hall.

In the fine arts, the early 18th century brought on the **Rococo** style. Reacting against the formal simplicity of Baroque ideals, its asymmetric curves and profusion of ornamentation were perhaps more successful in the **Louis XV style** of interior design than in architecture. Catering to the tastes of the nobility, Antoine **Watteau** and François **Boucher** painted playful pastoral landscapes and scenes from courtly life. Boucher's protégé Jean-Honoré **Fragonard** was famous for such crowd-pleasers as *The Swing,* in which the flying skirts of an oscillating woman afford a young man a refreshing glimpse. Such decadent art could not long escape the attentions of the interfering *philosophes,* and under the thundering criticism of Diderot and company, the playful Rococo style gave way to severe **Neoclassicism,** exemplified by Jacques-Germain **Soufflot's** grandiose **Église Ste-Geneviève** in Paris (1757). Deconsecrated during the Revolution, it was re-dedicated, as the **Panthéon,** to the *"great men of the fatherland,"* and now serves as the fitting final resting place of Voltaire and Rousseau (see p. 128).

THE REVOLUTION AND ITS AFTERMATH

After a century of philosophical fomentation, the Revolution seemed inevitable. Concerned more with the implementation of the *philosophes'* agenda rather than its further development, this time of social upheaval saw little in the way of new political thought. When the Rousseauist **Robespierre** came to power, he declared the necessity of forging a "single will" for the people. Meanwhile, the people rallied to the strains of **revolutionary music,** such as Rouget **de Lisle's** *War Song of the Army of the Rhine.* Composed in 1792 to rally French forces fighting the Prussians, it was taken up with gusto by volunteers from Marseille; dubbed the *Marseillaise,* it became the national anthem in 1795.

NOBLESSE OBLIGE In early July, 1789, the Marquis de Sade shouted to the crowds to storm the Bastille, where he had been incarcerated for his sexual perversions. Unfortunately for him, he was transferred to an insane asylum just days before the mob took his advice. In fact, he had already been sentenced to death and executed in 1772–though only in effigy, since he had fled the country. Taking refuge in his château at Lacoste, in the Lubéron (p. 260), de Sade and his wife preyed upon local men and women until he was finally imprisoned in 1777. He spent the next 13 years writing plays and novels, such as *120 Days of Sodom.* Released in 1790, he spoke on behalf of the revolution but was condemned to death again (for moderatism of all things!); he was saved this time by the fall of Robespierre. Finally, with Napoleon in charge, he was forced to play the submissive, and remained in captivity until his death in 1814. Though his wholesale abuse of the peasantry might seem to rank among the worst excesses of the *ancien régime,* others detect in his amorality the ultimate expression of the intellectual liberation of the Enlightenment.

Amid the turmoil, science rapidly advanced, despite the suppression of the Academy of Sciences in 1793. This retrograde step was opposed by Antoine-Laurent **Lavoisier,** the "father of modern chemistry," who demonstrated that oxygen (which he named) was indispensable for respiration. His political activism led him to the guillotine in 1794, and on his death the mathematician Joseph-Louis **Lagrange** remarked that "it required only a moment to sever that head, and perhaps a century will not be sufficient to produce another like it." Lagrange's magnum opus, *Analytical Mechanics* (1788), laid the foundations for modern physics. Pierre-Simon de **Laplace,** another friend of Lavoisier, set troubled minds to rest in 1787 when he demonstrated the stability of the solar system. But he had a far greater effect on world history as an examiner for the Artillery corps; impressed with a young Corsican cadet's mathematical skill, Laplace recommended Napoleon Bonaparte for a commission in the army.

Napoleon's reign saw an entrenchment of neo-classicism as he used the artistic language of ancient Rome to buttress the image of his reign. Jacques-Louis **David** created giant canvases on Classical themes, painting in a clear style which sacrificed atmosphere for detail and design. Perhaps his most famous work is the *Coronation* (1807), depicting the moment Napoleon crowned himself Emperor. In the decorative arts, the **Empire style** supplemented Roman models with a Pharaonic frenzy inspired by Napoleon's Egyptian exploits. The Neoclassical agenda was best fulfilled in the two architectural monuments dedicated to the Empire's glory. The Église de la Madeleine in Paris (p. 122), a giant imitation of a Greco-Roman temple, was commissioned in 1806 as a shrine to the Empire's *Grande Armée* (Great Army). However, this role was quickly taken over by the imposing Arc de Triomphe (p. 123), begun in the same year but not finished until 1836.

THE EARLY 19TH CENTURY: INCURABLE ROMANTICS

The 19th century saw an emotional reaction against Enlightenment rationality. Though anticipated in some ways by Rousseau, the expressive ideals of **Romanticism** first came to prominence in Britain and Germany rather than analytically-minded France. One of the first works of the Romantic era in France came with the publication of François-René de **Chateaubriand's** novel *Attala* (1801), inspired by the time he spent waiting out the excesses of the revolution with native Americans around Niagara falls. Goethe and the German Romantics were greatly admired by the stylish Mme de **Staël,** whose *Delphine* (1802) and *Corinne* (1807) reflect upon the injustices of being a talented woman in a chauvinist world. It was during this time that the novel became the pre-eminent literary medium, under such great writers as **Stendhal** and **Balzac,** but it was Victor **Hugo** who dominated the Romantic age. While his novels *The Hunchback of Notre-Dame* (1831) and *Les Misérables* (1862) have achieved near-mythical status, he was also a prolific playwright and poet. An early blow for feminism was struck by Aurore Dudevant. After leaving her husband and her childhood home of La Châtre (p. 173) in 1831, she took the pen-name Georges **Sand** and started a successful career as a novelist, condemning the social conventions which bound women into unhappy marriages in books such as *Valentine* (1832). Sand was as famous for her scandalous lifestyle as for her prose, with a string of high-profile relationships, including a 10-year dalliance with Frédéric **Chopin.**

Half French, half Polish, Chopin (1810-1849) started composing at the age of seven, and his complex work transcends the Romantic style to attain universality. Although French music remained under the influence of Beethoven in the early 19th century, by the 1830s Paris had again become the musical centre of Europe. Here Chopin mixed with the Hungarian Franz Liszt, the Austrian Felix Mendelssohn, and the French **Hector Berlioz.** Berlioz's unconventional compositional style gave birth to the modern orchestra by requiring a far greater range of musicians; his *Requiem* (1837) is scored for 166 musicians and a chorus of 290, as well as four brass sections placed around the concert hall. It was to handle such a complex orchestra that Berlioz developed the dictatorial conducting style that persists today. He also espoused the Romantic notion of **program music,** which uses careful instrumentation to narrate a story, as in the *Symphonie Fantastique* of 1830.

While the Romantic movement scarcely affected French architecture, its influence in the visual arts was immense. Even though Jean-Auguste-Dominique **Ingres** took up the neo-classical mantle of David after the latter's death in 1825, his interest in medieval and religious themes betrayed the Romantic taste for all things Gothic. His most celebrated work, the sensuous reclining nude of *La Grande Odalisque* (1814; now in the Louvre, p. 136), prefigures the oriental fascination of his younger contemporary Eugène **Delacroix.** A master of Romantic art, Delacroix's dramatic shading and masterly use of color contrasts sharply with Ingres' restrained, academic painting. The bold brushwork seen in *Liberty leading the people* (1830; also in the Louvre) would prepare the way for Impressionism later in the century.

THE MID-19TH CENTURY: POSITIVELY REALIST

While Neoclassicists and Romantics treated themes far removed from everyday life, in the 1830s a group of painters settled near Fontainebleau to paint nature as they saw it. Led by Théodore **Rousseau** and Jean-François **Millet,** the artists of the **École de Barbizon** celebrated the land and the humble life of those who worked it. In the 1850s, this grew into the **Realist** movement under Gustave **Courbet,** whose treatment of everyday subjects on a grand scale shocked the public. When his painting *The Artist's Studio* (now in the Louvre) was rejected by the Universal Exhibition of 1855, he responded by opening his own "Pavilion of Realism." The tempestuous seascapes he painted during stays in Étretat, Normandy (p. 474), would profoundly influence the young Edouard Manet (see below). Normandy also provided the setting for Gustave **Flaubert's** Realist novel *Madame Bovary* (1856), in which the author developed his characters' psychology though detailed descriptions of their experiences. Flaubert narrowly escaped being convicted of immorality in 1857, but six months later the same tribunal fined the poet Charles **Baudelaire** 50F. Baudelaire thus gained a reputation for obscenity, although his condemned work, *The Flowers of Evil*, is now recognized as the most influential piece of French poetry of the 19th century.

Baudelaire participated in the 1848 revolution, and his radical political views closely resembled those of the anarcho-socialist innovator Pierre-Joseph **Proudhon.** In 1840 he published the leaflet *What is Property?* His inflammatory reply was that "property is theft." At his trial in 1842, he was acquitted only because the jury could not understand his ideas. A pivotal figure in the history of socialism, Proudhon inspired the *syndicaliste* trade-union movement of the 1890s. A more optimistic philosophy was provided by the **Positivism** of Auguste **Comte.** Comte discerned three stages in human progress, beginning with the theological stage when man ascribed events he did not understand to supernatural beings. The second metaphysical stage rejected divine intervention and attributed phenomena to ill-defined abstract forces. Finally, with the development of science the positive stage allowed a rational explanation of nature. Science certainly demonstrated a great deal of progress at the time; Louis **Pasteur** (1822-1895) showed that disease and fermentation were both caused by micro-organisms; famous for his milk pasteurization process, he also solved the problem of transporting beer long distances without its spoiling.

In architecture alone, Neoclassicism reigned throughout the 19th century, advocated by the dominant École de Beaux Arts. Innovation came through the back door as the use of iron for buildings allowed vast spaces to be spanned; in the Bibliothèque Ste-Geneviève in Paris (1838; opposite the Panthéon), Henri **Labrouste** used an iron framework to fashion a light, airy reading room in an otherwise wholly classical building. The ultimate expression of 19th century classicism is to be found in Charles **Garnier's** Paris opera house (1862-1875, p. 120), a vast, ornate stone fantasy. The *Opéra* was part of Baron **Haussmann's** grand redesign of the capital in the 1860s. Sweeping away the medieval tangle of streets, he replaced them with tree-lined avenues bordered by majestic buildings; the wide open sidewalks he created permitted the establishment of outdoor cafés and encouraged that peculiarly Parisian form of entertainment, *flânerie*, the art of walking with no purpose but to see and be seen.

THE LATE 19TH CENTURY: SYMBOLIC IMPRESSIONS

As the Industrial Revolution spread its smoky arm across France, a rapidly evolving society called for an art better able to deal with its incessant change. In the 1860s, the young Edouard **Manet** began to move away from Realism as he found the handling of his subject more interesting than the fidelity of its reproduction. The small group of artists who clustered around him were united more by this emphasis on visual effect than any particular style or technique, and for this reason they became known as **Impressionists.** The sunny landscapes of Claude **Monet,** the rosy-cheeked faces of Auguste **Renoir,** and the working scenes of Camille **Pissarro** all combine prosaic, contemporary subjects with a sense of immediacy and freshness. The most revolutionary aspect of Impressionism was that the artists painted outside, directly from life, rather than working in the studio from sketches made earlier. But every movement inspires its reaction, and in the 1880s and 1890s the **Post-impressionists** concentrated their technical explorations in search of solidity and permanence. Georges **Seurat** developed **Pointillism,** the use of small dots of primary colors placed scientifically to build up a final image, and in *La Grande Jatte* (1885), millions of such points bathe his picture in a light unattainable by conventional means. In Aix-en-Provence (p. 247), Paul **Cézanne** created solidity and mass using geometric forms and a limited palette; his technique was so painstakingly slow that he had to use artificial fruit for his still lifes. Also drawn to Provence was the dutch painter Vincent **van Gogh,** who developed an expressive personal style of swirling brush strokes and intense colors. After a brief, tempestuous stay with van Gogh in Arles (p. 266), the ex-stockbroker Paul **Gauguin** settled in Tahiti. Here, influenced by folk art, he developed a style involving broad expanses of color to create a flat, spiritual effect.

The idealism of Gauguin's art caused him to be identified with the **Symbolist** movement in poetry. Like Impressionism, Symbolism reacted against stale conventions and used new techniques to capture instants of perception. Led by Stéphane **Mallarmé** and Paul **Verlaine,** the movement was instrumental in the creation of modern poetry as we understand it today, particularly through the work of the precocious Arthur **Rimbaud** (see greybox below). In 1880, a loose grouping of novelists proclaimed the birth of **Naturalism,** a development of Realism which

---

REBEL WITHOUT A CAUSE The life of **Arthur Rimbaud** makes most modern teen idols seem as adventurous as Trappist monks. During the Franco-Prussian war of 1870, the 16-year-old Rimbaud ran away from home to start a revolution, but was foiled when he was arrested at the train station for traveling without a ticket. Undeterred, he ran away again a year later to defend the Paris Commune, abandoning it only days before its bloody suppression. Politically disillusioned, Rimbaud put his trust in the pen rather than the bayonet, and set out to change the world through poetry. By abandoning traditional forms, trusting to his visions, and torturing himself to achieve new experiences, he attempted to "derange all the senses." The confident 17-year-old sent some verses to Paul Verlaine, who was so impressed that he invited Rimbaud to stay with him. Arriving in Paris in 1871, Rimbaud seduced the older man, who abandoned his wife and child; after two years they separated acrimoniously. In 1875, at the ripe old age of twenty-one, Rimbaud abandoned poetry and set off to explore the world. Traveling to Indonesia and Egypt, he finally settled down to a peaceful career running guns into Ethiopia. When cancer forced his return to France in 1891, he found himself famous: during his absence, Verlaine, believing him dead, had published the works of "the late Arthur Rimbaud." Rimbaud died in Marseille later that year, and today he is recognized as one of the greatest French poets.

attempted to use a scientific, analytic approach to dissect and reconstruct reality. Obscure enough in theory, in practise there was little to unite the works of writers like Émile **Zola** and Guy de **Maupassant.** Zola's life work was *Les Rougon-Macquart,* a 20-novel series which uses the life of the title family to examine every aspect of French life during the Second Empire.

For the moment, music remained aloof from the influence of Impressionism; the densely expressive sounds of the **Post-romantics** took their cue from Wagner's operatic exploits across the Rhine. Composers such as César **Franck** and Camille **Saint-Saëns** both wrote symphonic poems. A development of the program music of the romantic age, these single-movement orchestral works aimed to evoke a scene more than narrate a story; a well-loved example is Saint-Saëns *Carnival of the Animals* (1886). Saint-Saëns' pupil Gabriel **Fauré** shot to number one in the charts recently when his *Requiem* was chosen as the theme music for the 1998 World Cup.

Architecture finally reawoke as engineers began taking matters into their own hands. In 1876, Gustave **Eiffel,** together with architect Louis-Auguste **Boileau,** designed a new building for *Le Bon Marché,* the world's first department store, creating large skylit interior spaces in which to display merchandise. Nicknamed the "magician of iron," Eiffel is most famous for the tower that bears his name (p. 130), the star exhibit of the Universal Exhibition of 1889. Twice as tall as any other building in the world, it excited violent passions, and most Parisians of the time thought it unspeakably ugly, not to mention unstable. A century later, of course, it stands as the best-loved landmark in France. Truly a monumental figure, Eiffel also designed the internal structure of the Statue of Liberty.

THE DAWN OF THE 20TH CENTURY: LA BELLE ÉPOQUE

The decadence and social snobbery of the turn of the century was captured by Marcel **Proust** in the seven-volume *Remembrance of Things Past* (1913-1927). Revolutionary in technique, this autobiographical portrait of upper-class society during the *Belle Époque* inspires a fanaticism which puts Star Wars to shame. Illiers, the model for Proust's fictional town of Combray, renamed itself "Illiers-Combray" (p. 156) and there is even a cookbook to help devotees relive their experiences. Like most serious French authors of his time, Proust published in the influential *Nouvelle Revue Française.* Founded in 1909, this literary journal rose to prominence under the guidance of André **Gide,** who won the Nobel Prize in 1947 for morally provocative novels such as *The Counterfeiters* (1924). Throughout his career, the liberal Gide battled Catholic revivalist Paul **Claudel.** Claudel struggled unsuccessfully to persuade Gide that divine grace would overcome worldly desires, the basic theme behind plays such as *The Satin Slipper* (1924).

Today, Claudel is perhaps less well known than his sister Camille, student, muse, and lover of the great sculptor Auguste **Rodin.** Rodin finally achieved recognition at the age of 35, when critics found his nude *The Age of Bronze* (1877) to be so real that they accused him of casting it from life. However, his greatest influence on the future course of sculpture comes from his later movement away from realism. In the towering *Balzac* (1898), the coarse modelling of Rodin's broodily draped figure paves the way for abstraction. Too advanced for the public of its day, it remained under wraps until the 1930s,when it was erected at the intersection of bd. Raspail and bd. de Montparnasse in Paris. Music too broke free of historical constraints as Claude **Debussy** abandoned the excesses of his predecessors for a restrained new harmony. Though his style is called **Impressionist,** this owes more to Debussy's admiration for the visual movement than any application of its methods. His sole opera, *Pelléas et Mélisande* (1902), seamlessly integrates the singers and the orchestra through the careful use of the sonorities of the French language. Its quiet, tragic tone could not differ more from Maurice **Ravel's** boisterous *The Spanish Hour* (1911). Though he is often classified with Debussy, Ravel's music shows great versatility; Spanish rhythms betray his Basque origins, while a trip to North America opened his eyes to the possibilities of jazz. When a listener screamed "but he is mad!" at the premiere of his most famous work, the hypnotic *Boléro* (1928), the composer retorted, "aha! She has understood."

Each summer from 1909 to 1929, musicians and artists alike eagerly awaited the summer season of the *Ballets Russes*. Under the leadership of Sergei **Diaghilev,** this Russian dance company astounded audiences with the dancing of Vaslav **Nijinsky** and the music of Igor **Stravinsky**. Stravinsky's ballet *The Rite of Spring* caused a riot at its 1913 premiere, and its violently rhythmic dissonance sounded the clarion call for the modernist movement. No less shocking was the first night of *Parade* (1917), organized jointly by Diaghilev and the multi-talented Jean **Cocteau.** In this landmark ballet, composer Erik **Satie's** score used sirens and typewriters while Pablo **Picasso** provided the costumes and decoration. Poet and critic Guillaume **Apollinaire** coined the word "surreal" to describe the effect of the performance. A leading member of the avant garde, Apollinaire vocally supported innovation in all the arts; in his innovative *Calligrammes* (1918), he created visual poems (or "calligrams") by using words to draw out pictures on the page.

In 1907, Apollinaire was arrested on suspicion of having stolen the Mona Lisa from the Louvre after noticing the great interest taken in it by his close friend Picasso. The most prolific artist of the 20th century, the spanish artist developed a bewildering number of styles during his 80-year career, almost all of it spent in France. Arriving in Paris in 1900, it was not until 1907 that he shot to notoriety with *Les demoiselles d'Avignon*. This shocked both for its illicit subject (the title referred to a street in Barcelona's red light district) and for the angular treatment of the figures which presaged **Cubism.** Developed by Picasso and Georges **Braque,** this radical movement was really a continuation of Cézanne's geometric approach; by presenting the subject from many different angles at once, the artist tried to capture the whole three-dimensional object on a flat plane. The word "Cubism" was coined by Picasso's friend and great rival Henri **Matisse**. Struggling with pointillism, during a trip to Collioure in the Languedoc (p. 704) Matisse abandoned it and started squeezing paint from the tube directly onto the canvas. Shocked Parisian critics called the artists associated with the expressive new style *Fauves* (wild animals), and the name stuck. While **Fauvism** made only a brief splash on the canvas of time, Matisse's art remained a vibrant celebration of life; in mature works such as *The Dance* (1931-32; now in the Musée d'art moderne de la ville de Paris, p. 139) his mastery of line and color animate the composition to create a sense of movement and joy.

BETWEEN WORLD WARS: DADA AND SURREALISM

The first world war shattered Europe's complacency, and a generation of young artists turned their backs on a world descending into chaos. Appearing first in Zurich, this nihilistic anti-art movement became known under the nonsense name of **Dada.** Already in 1913 Marcel **Duchamp** had exhibited *Bicycle Wheel* (now lost), a bicycle wheel on a stool. This was the first of his "ready mades," and by exhibiting such commonplace, mass-produced objects Duchamp started off the whole "but is it art?" question. In France, Dada took a literary bent under the influence of Romanian born Tristan **Tzara,** whose poems of nonsensically scrambled words attacked the structure of language. Tzara's colleagues André **Breton** and Louis **Aragon** soon became dissatisfied with the anarchy of Dada, and set about developing a more organized protest. In 1924, Breton published the *Surrealist Manifesto*, in which he expounded its guiding principal: the artistic supremacy of the subconscious. Like Dadaism, Surrealism rejected all traditional notions of art, but it was fundamentally a constructive movement, plumbing the hidden creative depths of the mind. Though Breton was initially skeptical that Surrealist principals could be applied to art, the paintings of René **Magritte,** Joan **Miró,** and Salvador **Dalí** reached a far larger public than his own work. Rather than directly expressing the subconscious, the dreamlike fantasies of surrealist art aim to unsettle and liberate the unconscious creativity of the viewer.

The disconcerting influence of Surrealism bypassed the public of the 1920s, who were busy throwing themselves into the wild excesses of the post-war *années folles.* In the Great Depression which followed, the avant-garde reasserted itself on the public consciousness, and an audience weary of fifty years of shock tactics was grateful for the relative peace of a new neoclassicism. The young members of the Group of Six, led by Francis **Poulenc** and Darius **Milhaud,** attracted concert-goers with their lighthearted, melodic style. Milhaud developed **polytonality** by scoring music simultaneously in a number of keys; an early example is the jazzy *The Bull on the Roof* (1918). Meanwhile, the rising threat of Nazi Germany spurred a call to arms by writers, led by the indomitable André **Malraux.** Active in the Chinese and Spanish civil wars, the former supplied the subject for his master-piece, *The Human Condition* (1933). Another adventurer, Antoine de **Saint-Exupéry,** used his experiences as an early aviation pioneer to create classics such as *Earth of Men* (1939) and the well-loved *The Little Prince* (1943). Neoclassi-cism was more literally adhered to in theatre, where audiences thrilled to updated treatments of Greek myth such as Jean Cocteau's *Orpheus* (1926) and Jean **Girau-doux's** *The Trojan War Will Not Take Place* (1935).

In 1930 Cocteau had produced the surrealist film *Beauty and the Beast* (1940), which featured an early use of special effects to show the monster changing into a handsome man. Though cinema had been invented in 1895 by the Lumière broth-ers in Lyon, it remained a novelty until ex-magician Georges **Méliès** produced the science-fiction blockbuster, *Journey to the Moon* (1902). Fourteen minutes in length, and with 30 scenes, this was the first motion picture to realize the story-telling possibilities of the medium. Although the first world war allowed Holly-wood to wrest celluloid dominance from a shattered Europe, in the 1920s and 1930s French cinema was the most critically acclaimed in the world under such great directors as Jean **Renoir,** son of the Impressionist painter. *The Great Illu-sion*, which he directed in 1937, is a powerful anti-war statement; set in the pris-oner of war camps of World War I, it is a desperate plea for humanity released in the shadow of Nazi Germany.

DILEMMAS OF POST-WAR EXISTENCE

The swift French defeat in 1940, and slightly slower German retreat in 1944, spared Paris the devastating bombing which had destroyed so many cities. With France free again, the city of light could sparkle once more.

The period following the war was intellectually dominated by Jean-Paul **Sartre,** Grand High Master of **Existentialism.** This held that life, in itself, was meaningless; only by choosing and then committing yourself to a cause could existence take on a purpose. Sartre committed his own ideas to the stage, dominating French theatre in the 1940s and 1950s; in *No Exit* (1946), four people in a small room discover they are there for eternity; as they find out, *"l'enfer, c'est les autres"* ("hell is other people"). His companion, Simone **de Beauvoir,** concentrated on writing nov-els, but his best known for the seminal *The Second Sex* (1949), an essay attacking the myth of femininity. Though Albert **Camus** is often classed with Sartre, he could scarcely be more different. Born into poverty in Algeria, Camus edited the Resis-tance newspaper *Combat* while Sartre was working under censorship in occupied Paris. Camus' existentialism was marked by a sense of decency; commitment was not enough if it was unfair to others. He achieved fame with his debut novel *The Outsider* (1942), which tells the story of a dispassionate social misfit condemned to death for an unrepentant murder. Camus' play *Caligula* (1945) was an early example of **Anti-theatre,** whose adherents laid bare the strangeness of life and exposed the inadequacies of language. In Irish emigré Samuel **Beckett's** *Waiting for Godot* (1953), two men wait and wait, without knowing why or for whom. *Rhi-noceros* (1960), by Romanian immigrant Eugène **Ionesco,** portrays the protago-nist's perplexity as everyone else turns into horned african mammals. Meanwhile, the novel was in the hands of the equally inaccessible **Anti-novel,** which rejected the fictional pretense that people interact meaningfully with an indifferent universe. Instead, by presenting the world subjectively through their characters' words and thoughts, the authors limited the readers' involvement in their world. In Claude

Mauriac's *The Dinner Party* (1959), we follow a dinner-table conversation, with no pretense to plot or purpose.

Already famous for his monochromatic *Blue* paintings, in 1960 Yves **Klein** presented *The Monotone Symphony*. In this performance piece, three naked models painted the wall blue with their bodies while the artist conducted an orchestra on one note for 20 minutes. Somewhat less messy, though no less radical, is the music of composer Pierre **Boulez**. Boulez was an adept of the **Neo-serialist** school, which used the 12-tone system developed in the 1920s by Austrian Arnold Schoenberg. Always innovative, Boulez's output includes aleatory music, partial works which leave aspects of their completion to the performer. His greatest influence on modern music, however, has been as director of IRCAM, a centre for avant-garde music in Paris. Boulez's earlier work owes a debt to his teacher, the late Olivier **Messaien** (d. 1992). Messaien suffered from synesthesia, a sensory disorder which confuses sound and vision; different harmonies appeared to him in different colors, and this dual perception affected his composition. Messaien was also fascinated by birdsong, and both these influences are apparent in *Chronochromie* (1960). Another important composer who studied under Messaien was Iannis **Xenakis**. Xenakis's music uses computers to coordinate and even compose music according to advanced mathematical techniques. Xenakis was an engineer by training, and his first major composition, *Metastasis* (1954), was a translation into sound of the design of the Philips Pavilion in the 1958 Brussels Exposition. He was working on this as an assistant to the architect Charles-Edouard Janneret, known as **Le Corbusier.** A prominent member of the **International school,** Le Corbusier dominated his field from the 1930s until his death in 1965, and is famous for such buildings as the *Unité d'habitation* in Marseille (1947). Following his principles; the building itself is raised on stilts, while the absence of ornamentation brings out the essential qualities of its concrete construction.

With the exception of fashionable Existentialism, the public remained unimpressed by the stream of unintelligible innovation gushing from the fount of French intellectualism. They were far happier with the songs of crooner Charles **Aznavour** and the unregrettable Édith **Piaf.** Aznavour starred in François **Truffaut's** *Shoot the Pianist* (1960), one of the first films of the **New Wave.** While Truffaut was the driving force behind this group of young critics-turned-directors who rebelled against the over-polished, lush productions of "quality cinema," it was Jean-Luc **Godard** who made the movement his own. Godard's *Breathless* (1959), which Truffaut produced, was shot without a script, relying instead on improvisation from sketches Godard worked out between rehearsals. Three years earlier, a star was born when Jean **Vadim** sent the incomparable **Brigitte Bardot** shimmying naked across the stage in *And God Created Woman*.

FRANCE TODAY

RECENT HISTORY AND CURRENT AFFAIRS

Many feared that the Fifth Republic would collapse after de Gaulle, its founding father, resigned in 1969. It endured, of course, but its tone changed fundamentally. De Gaulle was succeeded by the *Gaulliste* Georges **Pompidou,** who combined a laissez-faire position towards business and with less assertive foreign policy. Following Pompidou's unexpected death in 1974, his conservative (but non-Gaullist) successor Valéry Giscard **d'Estaing** assumed the presidency. D'Estaing's term saw the construction of Richard Rogers' and Renzo Piano's **Centre Pompidou** (p. 119) as a tribute to his dead predecessor. This post-modern center for the arts, incorporating galleries and performance spaces, is (in)famous for its radical inside-out design. As it turned out, the *Centre Pompidou* was only the first of a new spate of monumental architecture in Paris.

When D'Estaing's term expired in 1981, the socialist François **Mitterrand** was elected president, a position he would hold until 1995. While Mitterrand began his term with widespread nationalization and expanded benefits, the international climate could not support this socialist economy. By 1986, the right had control of parliament, and Mitterrand had to appoint the ruthless conservative Jacques **Chirac** as Prime Minister. At the same time, the **far right** began to flourish under the leadership of Jean-Marie **Le Pen,** who formed the **Front National (FN)** upon an anti-immigration platform. The healthy French post-war economy had led to the development of a new working class from North Africa, and Le Pen was able to capitalize on a racism towards these immigrants that is often phrased—euphemistically—in terms of "cultural difference." Meanwhile, Mitterrand withdrew to control foreign affairs, allowing Chirac to assume a great deal of domestic power. Chirac privatized many industries, but a transport strike and widespread terrorism damaged the right, allowing Mitterrand to win a second term in 1988.

As France's great intellectuals gave way to a lesser generation in the late 80s (see **Current Thought,** below), the cultural spotlight shifted toward architecture. Mitterrand sought immortality in stone, steel, and concrete, commissioning a number of controversial buildings, including **I.M. Pei's** radical glass **pyramid** at the Louvre (p. 136), the perennially troubled **Opéra Bastille** (p. 126), and the massive **Grande Arche de la Défense** (p. 133). The people were more concerned with scandals involving Mitterrand's ministers than with these grandiose projects, however, and the left suffered crushing parliamentary defeats in the early 90s which forced him to again appoint a conservative prime minister. Mitterrand further lost prestige when the 1991 referendum on the **Maastricht Treaty,** which would transform the European Community into the more closely integrated European Union (EU), scraped through with a 51% approval rating despite massive government support.

In the mid-nineties, Mitterrand made two startling confessions. The first was that he had collaborated with the Vichy government before joining the Resistance in 1943. The second, and more shocking, revelation was that he was seriously ill with cancer, and had been so for many years. His death in January, 1996, came shortly after the presidency had finally been won by his arch-rival Jacques Chirac. The ascendancy of the right was short-lived; in 1997, elections returned a socialist parliament and Chirac was forced to accept his one-time presidential rival **Lionel Jospin** as Prime Minister. Though Chirac's term does not expire until 2002, the left appears firmly in control of France. Chirac's Gaullist **RPR** party is the dominant conservative party, with Jospin's **PS** party leading the socialist left. A recent split between Le Pen and his deputy has caused a fragmentation of the far right, with two different *Front National* parties competing for the extremist vote.

CURRENT THOUGHT: POSTMODERNISM

To many, **Postmodernism** is just another French fashion, unduly mimicked by provincial thinkers everywhere. To the French intelligentsia, however, Postmodernism is associated with America, the land of superficial mass culture. In *The Postmodern Condition: A Report on Knowledge*, Jean François **Lyotard** turned a routine report commissioned by the Canadian government into a manifesto of Postmodernism, arguing that modernist thought was too stable and thus was constraining. It was not long before a slew of French thinkers were hashing out the problems of contemporary life, discussing our information-age world in terms of paradoxes and word-games. Over recent decades, Postmodern discourse and its cousin, **Poststructuralism,** have continued to flourish, and the French tendency to turn intellectuals into celebrities has had many personalities to lionize or deride. To many, these intellectuals and their colleagues represent the most important thinking done in the post-war world.

CONTEMPORARY CINEMA

Political and sexual censorship of film was loosened in the 70s, a decade when cinema business decreased as television kept viewers at home. Nonetheless, the world impact of French cinema during the 60s propelled it into the international spotlight, and New Wave directors dominated though the 70s. Even so, the biggest-grossing film of the decade was a middle-brow comedy, Gérard **Oury's** *Les Adventures de Rabbi Jacob* (1973). Between Oury and the *auteurs*, a number of artful, sometimes intellectual and usually sensual films were embraced by an attentive international audience. In the past few decades the *Three Colors* trilogy, *Manon des Sources*, and *Au Revoir les Enfants* have moved movie-goers around the world. Actor Gérard **Depardieu** (*Cyrano de Bergerac*, *Jean de Florette*) is renowned for roles both serious and comic, but Jean **Reno** has had more luck making the transition into Hollywood following the success of Luc **Besson**'s *The Professional*. Yet contemporary French cinema is constantly battling Hollywood hegemony, and anxiety over its future was clearly evident in the GATT trade negations of 1993. The French government subsidizes the film industry as part of French culture, but American studios, which dominate the French market, call it "unfair." Very different from the *Belle de jour* fare beloved of "Foreign Film" rentals is the recent spate of **cinéma beur,** made by second-generation North Africans coming to terms with life in the HLMs (municipal housing) of suburban Paris. These inexpensive, grafitti-decor films, such as Mathieu **Kassovitz**'s *La Haine* (1995), confront the traumas of urban racism. Facing up to a history of colonialism, meanwhile, is a preoccupation in Claire **Denis**'s *Chocolat* (1988). The art cinema continues to prosper under Marcel **Hanoun** (*Bruit d'Amour et de Guerre*, 1997) and Jacques **Doillon** (*Ponette*, 1997*)*, while the French flock to hilarious low-budget comedies like Jean-Marie **Poiré**'s *Les Visiteurs* (1992). France retains a vibrant film culture, with 12 annual festivals in addition to the May festival at **Cannes.** Foreign films are normally dubbed into French; watch out for listings marked *version originale (v.o.)* to see an English language film graced by French subtitles.

THE MEDIA

France has relatively few daily **papers** for its size; instead, weekly **magazines** dominate print media. Conservatives should check the weekly *L'Express*, while for a more left-wing, intellectual magazine, try *Le Nouvel Observateur*. Among national dailies, the two most popular are *Le Figaro*, a quality right-wing paper, and *Le Parisien*, a more moderate and accessible daily. *Le Monde*, an evening paper, is internationally renowned for its comprehensive analysis. Local publications often list events that most tourists miss; *Let's Go* gives info about them in most towns. **TV guides** are the most popular publications in France, with *Télé 7 jours* leading the pack. French **radio** went commercial in 1984, though the success of large conglomerates means few stations remain independent. National stations include *Fun Radio* for teens; *Skyrock*, a noisy and provocative rock station; and *Nostalgie*, an adult-oriented station with quiz shows and emotional music. Public stations include *France-Inter*, a general interest station, and *France Info*, an all-news station.

As radio and vinyl records made recordings a viable platform for stardom in the early 50s, a few singer-songwriters rose to fame. Perhaps the best loved was Georges **Brassens,** who is commemorated in his home town of Sète (p. 714). Then, in the late 50s and the 60s, a unique French take on American rock emerged: the movement was termed, in a stroke of onomatopoetic brilliance, **yé-yé.** In the 70s bands came and went, but in the 80s a number of solid groups emerged, and in recent years, ethnic hybrids have had a huge influence on French pop music. Today, the bulk of **popular music** played on French radio will be familiar to anglophone travelers, despite a 1996 law requiring that francophone music make up 40% of radio stations' playlists—much of that quota gets filled between 1 and 6am. The problem facing French music is not so much one of quality as of distribution; it still has a strong following in France outside the mainstream, but most of the music industry is in the hands of multinational corporations.

SPORTS

In a dramatic prelude to the 1998 *Coupe Mondial* (World Cup), French organizers reserved two-thirds of all tickets for domestic spectators, provoking global outrage. This was surprising since playing international hosts comes naturally to the French; the **French Open** tennis tournament and the gruelling **Tour de France** bicycle race attract rapt international attention each year. At the domestic level, *le foot* (soccer) is by far the most popular spectator sport, and Mitterrand himself re-inaugurated the tradition of officially attending the French cup final. Although the sport has suffered several drug and bribery scandals in the 90s, its popularity continues to increase. Rugby is also very popular, especially in the southwest. Both sports also feature countless local clubs, all organized under government associations. In recent decades unorganized "street sports" like basketball and "california sports" like wind-surfing have given French sportsmanship a personalized flair. **Individual sports** of a more legitimate pedigree include tennis and skiing, both of which were democratized in the 70s and 80s as low prices put them in the reach of the man on the street. Finally, in a country of small towns and villages, cycling unites the nation in more ways than one.

A FRENCH FOOD PRIMER

Today French cuisine is recognized as one of the great culinary achievements of the world, but it has not always been so popular. Indeed, in some respects *la cuisine française* is not even French; it was only under the influence of the Italian Renaissance tastes of Catherine de Medici, Queen to Henri II, that it became the refined, delicately flavored fare we know today. Meals developed into 12-hour, multi-course feasts during the reign of Louis XIV, whose chefs held official titles. Although eating time has since been cut down considerably, *la gastronomie* remains an important part of French culture. Despite the infiltration of fast-food, elite restaurants look disdainfully upon Coca-Cola and expect patrons to respect the traditional course order at **le dîner** (dinner): *entrée* (appetizer), *plat* (main dish), *salade*, *fromages* (a board of selected cheeses), *dessert*, and a *café* (always black; white coffee is for breakfast). No meal is complete without wine, while some places will also suggest a pre-dinner *apéritif* such as *kir*, white wine with a blackcurrant liqueur, *pastis*, a licorice liqueur diluted with water, or *martini*. Finish off after coffee with a *digestif*, such as *cognac*, *armagnac*, or *calvados*.

Le déjeuner (lunch), while not as elaborate as dinner, is still very important, and the entire country seems to shut down between noon and 2pm. **Le petit déjeuner** (breakfast) is much more casual, usually a *café crème* (espresso with hot milk) or *chocolat chaud* (hot chocolate, often served in a bowl), with a *croissant* or a *tartine* (bread with butter and jam). It's normally cheaper and nicer to eat breakfast at a café than at a hotel (but watch out—many hotels have obligatory breakfast). **Picnicking** is the cheapest option for lunch, and your taste-buds won't suffer either. The unadventurous can find everything from smelly cheese to American cereals in the numerous **supermarket chains** that have infiltrated even traditional France. Major chains include Carrefour, Casino, Monoprix, Leclerc, and Prisunic. A better idea is to do it the old fashioned way; after buying bread from the *boulangerie* (bakery), stock up on *pâté*, *saucisson* (hard sausage), *jambon* (ham), or *quiches* from a *charcuterie*, or buy a delicious freshly roasted chicken from the *boucherie* (butcher's). Local produce is always fresh from the local *marché* (market), nor-

CHEESE, PLEASE! France produces over 400 kinds of cheese, and cheese is almost as much a staple of French meals as bread. Every restaurant offers a board of selected cheeses for the end of the meal. Usually this includes a **bleu,** carefully fermented and strewn with mold to create the blue color and surface of the moon texture. These come either from *Roquefort* (more crumbly and made with sheep's milk) or *Auvergne* (creamier). **Chèvre,** a mild goat's milk cheese is popular cold and even grilled as an appetizer. The notoriously smelly **Camembert** comes from Normandy. Legend has it that Marie Harel was given the recipe by a priest from Meaux (the home of **Brie**) in return for hiding him during the Revolution. Good Camembert should be aged until it is light brown on the outside and creamy and runny within. Above all, don't be scared off when you smell the cheese plate before your waiter has left the kitchen!

mally held at least once a week; *Let's Go* lists times and places for markets in each town. If you want someone else to do the work, *boulangeries* often sell a variety of fresh sandwiches with ham, cheese, pâté, and other cold cuts, and you'll always end sweetly with a pastry or cake from a *pâtisserie*.

Eating out in France is one of the finer pleasures in life, and you can almost always find good food without paying gastronomical prices. Aside from ubiquitous fast-food joints and pizzerias, you can choose between traditional French restaurants and something more exotic. Traditional restaurants usually serve a regional speciality, while ethnic restaurants generally represent France's two main immigrant communities, North Africans and Vietnamese. North African restaurants serve delicious *couscous*, hot semolina with a meat or vegetable sauce. Don't go to a Vietnamese restaurant without trying *Nem* (cold pastry rolls filled with vegetables and meat). Spicy food is often toned down for the delicate French palate. Most restaurants, traditional and ethnic alike, offer a range of *menus*, complete meals that cost less than ordering *à la carte*. A *menu* normally includes at least *entrée*, *plat*, and *dessert*. At lunchtime many places offer a cheaper, two-course *formule* for people in a hurry. There'll be no unhealthy snacking between meals at a restaurant because they only open at mealtimes; noon-2pm for lunch and 7-10pm for dinner, earlier in rural areas. For odd-hour cravings go to a *brasserie* for a limited range of standard fare; they remain open between lunch and dinner. But don't expect less from a *brasserie;* some are fancier than most restaurants. For a cheap treat, flip out at a *crêperie*. These serve *crêpes*, super-thin pancakes with sweet and savory fillings. In Brittany, where the *crêpes* originated, savory fillings are served on *galettes*, buckwheat versions of their sweet cousins. Many cafés also have a *crêpe* stand for take out; check to see that your pancake is freshly cooked rather than being reheated from a pile prepared earlier.

Cafés, those French institutions which gained legendary status as the favored hunting ground of writers and intellectuals from Hemingway to Sartre, do in fact figure prominently in the French daily routine. When choosing a café, remember that you pay for its location. Those on a major boulevard can be much more expensive than smaller establishments a few steps down a sidestreet. Prices in cafés are two-tiered, cheaper at the counter *(comptoir)* than in the seating area *(salle)*. Some even have a third price level for outdoor seating *(la terrasse)*. Coffee, beer, and (in the south) *pastis* are the staple café drinks, but there are other refreshing options. Try a *citron pressé*, a glass of freshly squeezed lemon juice with iced water and sugar on the side, or a *diabolo menthe*, soda with mint syrup. If you order *café*, you'll get espresso; for coffee with milk, ask for a *café crème*. *Bière à la pression*, or draught beer, is always lager, either *blonde* (pale) or *brune* (dark). Ask for a *bière*, and you'll get 660 ml, about a pint; for something smaller ask for a *demi* (330ml). A glass of *vin rouge* (red wine) is the cheapest wine in a café (starting at 4-6F), with *vin blanc* (white wine) costing about twice as much. Besides breakfast, cafés offer a range of snacks all day long, such as *croque-monsieur*, a hot cheese and ham sandwich, making them a great place in which to pore over your *Let's Go*.

Most French fare originated as **regional specialties,** and there are some dishes whose popularity has made them staples in restaurants all over the country. You could start off with *crudités* (plate of raw vegetables), *une assiette anglaise* (a plate of cold cuts), or *soupe à l'oignon* (beef-based onion soup with a rich cheese topping) at almost any traditional restaurant, and then follow it with *boeuf bourguignon* (beef a and red wine stew), *steak tartare* (uncooked ground beef mixed with a raw egg and herbs), *ratatouille* (a tomato, eggplant, and zucchini stew), or *coq au vin* (chicken simmered in red wine). Other dishes are still best closer to their origins, such as *bouillabaisse* (a giant fish stew) in Provence, *cassoulet* (stew with beans and sausages) in Languedoc, and fantastic *fruits de mer* in Brittany. Those searching for that textbook experience will find *escargots* (snails) in Poitou and *cuisses de grenouilles* (frogs' legs) in the Loire Valley. **Vegetarians** in France should be especially cautious; even an innocent sounding salad may have a slice of ham lurking under the lettuce. You'll probably have most luck at *crêperies*, ethnic restaurants and places catering to a younger crowd; if all else fails, you can always order an *omelette*.

WINE

Le vin pervades French culture, and no occasion is complete without a glass or four of wine. The range and variety of wines available is enormous, and terrifying for the uninitiated. Not only does the character and quality of a wine depend upon which of the 60 grape varieties it is made from, the climate and soil type also have a crucial effect. White wine *(vin blanc)* can be made from both white grapes *(blanc de blancs)*, or red *(blanc de noirs)*; in the latter case care must be taken to prevent the skins from coloring the wine. Red wine *(vin rouge)* and *rosé* is always made from red grapes; the skins remain in contact with the juice for a brief time for rosé; this period is much longer with red wines.

Wine-producing regions are distributed throughout the country. Centered on the Dordogne and Garonne rivers, the famous **Bordeaux** region produces mostly red and white Pomerol, Médoc and Graves, and sweet white Sauternes. Note that red Bordeaux is often called **claret** in English. **Burgundy** is especially famous for its reds, from the wines of *Chablis* and the *Côte d'Or* in the north, to the Beaujolais and Mâconnais in the south. **Alsatian** whites tend to be dry and fruity, and match well with spicy foods. Delicately-bouqueted whites predominate in the **Loire Valley;** major vineyards are found in *Anjou, Touraine* and *Sancerre.* In **Provence,** the *Côtes de Provence* around Marseille are recognized for their rosés, while around Avignon the *Côtes du Rhône* produce celebrated reds such as the famous *Châteauneuf du Pape,* and the sweet white *Muscat de Beaumes-de-Venise.* Although many areas produce sparkling wines *(vins mousseux)*, only those grown and produced in **Champagne** can legally bear its name.

Other grape-based intoxicators include **Cognac** and **Armagnac,** which come from Charente and Gascony respectively. Technically distinguished from brandy by strict government regulations, Cognac is a double distilled spirit and so has a higher alcohol content than the single-distilled but more flavorful Armagnac. Unlike other wines, Cognac and Armagnac are usually enjoyed as *digestifs.*

France passed the first comprehensive wine legislation in 1935, and since then a variety of regulations have ensured the quality and reputation of French wines. All wines are categorized according to place of origin, alcohol content, and wine-making practices. Categories include the elite *Appellation d'Origine Contrôlée* regulations *(AOC* or "controlled place of origin"), closely followed by *Vins Délimités de Qualité Supérieure (VDQS;* "restricted wines of superior quality") and the more modest but still fine *Vins de Pays* (country wines). Still, a budget traveler in France can be pleasantly surprised by even the least expensive *vins de tables* (table wines), which is what most French drink.

...AND WHICH WINE DOES MADAME DESIRE?

Embarrassed that the *garçon* (waiter) will scoff at your inexpert handling of wine? Stop biting your nails and read on to discover all that a wine connoisseur needs to know about tasting. First, when the *garçon* presents the wine, nod knowingly; show no fear. Briefly hold your glass to the light and against a white surface. Check that the liquid is clear and limpid. Then hold it to your nose and take a sniff. If it smells sulfurous, vinegary or moldy, tell the *garçon* "non". You are an expert; no one call pull the wool over your eyes. Now swirl the wine several times and smell it again. This scent should be much stronger. To really show off your expertise, sniff the middle of the wine as well by tipping the glass sideways and sticking your nose well over the side of it. The wine has now passed the initial tests and is ready for tasting. Sip the wine delicately, letting some air enter your mouth with the liquid (this brings the flavor out more). Try to taste the wine on each region of your tongue to distinguish between the bitter, sweet, acidic, and salty sensations. If the smell or taste is not as strong as you would like, ask the waiter to put your wine in a carafe so it can breath a little more.

ESSENTIALS

DOCUMENTS AND FORMALITIES

ENTRANCE REQUIREMENTS.
Passport (p. 31). Required for all non-EU citizens, plus UK and Irish citizens.
Visa (p. 34). For stays of under 90 days, required of citizens of South Africa. Over 90 days, required of Australian, Canadian, New Zealand, and US citizens.
Work Permit (p. 34). Required for Australian, Canadian, New Zealand, South African, and US citizens.

FRENCH CONSULAR SERVICES ABROAD

Always call ahead, since different services have varying opening hours; those listed are for visa concerns. Most consulates will also receive inquiries in the afternoon provided you call ahead and make an appointment.

AUSTRALIA. Sydney: Consulate General, Level 26 St. Martins Tower, 31 Market St., Sydney NSW 2000. Tel. 02 926 157 79; www.france.net.au/site/administration/consulats/sydney/index.htm. Open M-F 9am-1pm. **Melbourne:** Consulate General, 492 St. Kilda Rd., Melbourne VIC 3004. Tel. 03 982 009 21; www.france.net.au/site/administration/consulats/melbourne/index.htm. Open M-F 9am-12:30pm.

CANADA. Montréal: Consulate General, 1 pl. Ville Marie, 26th floor, Montréal QC H3B 4. Tel. 514 878 4385; www.consulfrancemontreal.org. Open M-F 8:30am-noon. **Toronto:** Visa Service, Consulate General, 130 Bloor Street West, Suite 401 Toronto, Ontario M5S 1N5. Tel. 416 925 8233; web.idirect.com/~fs1tto/index.htm. Open M-F 9:30am-1:30pm. **Vancouver:** Consulate General, 1100-1130 West Pender St., Vancouver BC V6E 4A4. Tel. 604 681 4345; www.consulfrancevancouver.org. Open M-F 9:30am-noon. Also in **Quebec City** and **Halifax.**

IRELAND. Dublin: French Embassy, Consulate Section, 36 Ailesbury Rd., Ballsbridge, Dublin 4. Tel. 01 260 16 66; www.ambafrance.ie. Open M-F 9am-noon.

NEW ZEALAND. Wellington: French Embassy and Consulate, 34-42 Manners St. P.O. box 11-343, Wellington. Tel. 04 802 7793; www.ambafrance.net.nz.

SOUTH AFRICA. Pretoria: French Embassy and Consulate, 807 George Ave. Arcadia, Pretoria 0083. Tel. 12 429 7030; www.france.co.za. Open M-F 8:30am-12:30pm and 2-5pm. **Johannesburg:** Consulate General, Carlton Center, 35th floor, Commissioner St., PO box 11278, Johannesburg 2000. Tel. 11 331 34 68. Open M-F 8:15am-1pm. **Cape Town:** Consulate, 2 Dean St., PO box 1702, 8001 Cape Town. Tel. 21 423 1575. Open M-F 9am-12:30pm.

UNITED KINGDOM. London: Consulate General, 21 Cromwell Rd., London SW7 2 EN. Tel. 020 7838 2000; www.ambafrance.org.uk/db.phtml?id=consulat. Open M-W 8:45am-3pm, Th-F 8:45am-noon. **Edinburgh:** Consulate General, 11 Randolph Crescent, Edinburgh EH3 7TT. Tel. 013 1225 7954. Open M-F 9am-5:30pm.

UNITED STATES. Washington D.C.: Consulate General, 4101 Reservoir Rd. NW, Washington D.C. 20007. Tel. 202 944 6000; www.france-consulat.org/dc/dc.html.

Open 8:45am-12:30pm. **Los Angeles:** Consulate General, 10990 Wilshire Blvd., 3rd Floor, Los Angeles CA 90024. Tel. 310 235 3200; www.etats-unis.com/consulat-la. Open M-F 9am-noon. **New York:** Consulate General, 934 Fifth Ave., New York NY 10021; visa office is separate; call for address. Tel. 212 606 3600; www.francecon-sulatny.org. Open M-F 9am-1pm. Also in **Atlanta, Chicago, Houston, New Orleans, San Francisco,** and **Miami.**

FOREIGN CONSULAR SERVICES IN FRANCE

Call before visiting any of these embassies; various services have different hours of availability. Visa services tend to be available only in the morning. If you find yourself in serious trouble, call your country's embassy or consulate; they should be able to provide legal advice, and may be able to advance you some money in a dire emergency. Don't expect them to get you out of every scrape, though: you must always abide by French law while in France, and if you are arrested the consulate can do little but point you towards a lawyer. Dual citizens of France cannot call on the consular services of their second nationality for assistance.

AUSTRALIA. Australian Embassy and Consulate, 4 rue Jean Rey, 75015 Paris. Tel. 01 40 59 33 00; www.austgov.fr. Open 9:25am-noon and 2-4:30pm.

CANADA. Canadian Embassy and Consulate, 35 Ave. Montaigne, 75008 Paris. Tel. 01 44 43 29 00. Hours: 9am-noon and 2-5pm. General Delegation of Quebec, 66 rue Pergolèse, 75016 Paris. Tel. 01 40 67 85 00. Open 9am-5:30pm.

IRELAND. Irish Embassy and Consulate, 4 rue Rude, 75116 Paris. Tel. 01 44 17 67 00. Open M-F 9:30am-noon.

NEW ZEALAND. New Zealand Embassy and Consulate, 7 rue Leonardo da Vinci, 75116 Paris. Tel. 01 45 00 24 11. Open M-F 9am-1pm and 2-5pm.

SOUTH AFRICA. South American Embassy, 59 Quai d'Orsay, 75007 Paris. Tel. 01 53 59 23 23. Open M-F 8:30am-5:15pm.

UNITED KINGDOM. British Embassy, Consulate Section, 18bis rue d'Anjou, 75008 Paris. Tel. 01 44 51 31 02; www.amb-grandebretagne.fr. Open M-F 9:30am-12:30pm and 2:30-5pm. Also in **Bordeaux, Lille,** and **Marseille.**

UNITED STATES. Consulate General, 2 rue St-Florentin, 75008 Paris. Tel. 01 43 12 22 22. Open M-F 9am-3pm. Also in **Strasbourg** and **Marseille**.

PASSPORTS

REQUIREMENTS

Citizens of Australia, Canada, Ireland, New Zealand, South Africa, the UK, and the US need valid passports to enter France and to re-enter their own country. To enter France, your passport must be valid for three months beyond your expected date of departure. Returning home with an expired passport is illegal, and may result in a fine.

PHOTOCOPIES. It is a good idea to photocopy the page of your passport that contains your photograph, passport number, and other identifying information, along with other important documents such as visas, travel insurance policies, airplane tickets, and traveler's check serial numbers. Carry one set of copies in a safe place apart from the originals and leave another set at home. Consulates also recommend that you carry an expired passport or an official copy of your birth certificate in a part of your baggage separate from other documents.

ESSENTIALS

LOST PASSPORTS

If you lose your passport in France, immediately notify the local police and the nearest embassy or consulate of your home government. To expedite its replacement, you will need to show identification and proof of citizenship. A replacement may take weeks to process, and it may be valid only for a limited time. Any visas stamped in your old passport will be irretrievably lost. In an emergency, ask for temporary traveling papers that will permit you to re-enter your home country. Your passport is a public document belonging to your nation's government. You may have to surrender it to a foreign government official, but if you don't get it back in a reasonable amount of time, inform the nearest mission of your home country.

NEW PASSPORTS

All applications for new passports or renewals should be filed well in advance of your planned departure date. Most passport offices offer expedited services for an extra charge. Citizens residing abroad who need a passport or renewal should contact their nearest embassy or consulate.

Australia: Apply in person at a post office or a passport office. Passport offices are located in Adelaide, Brisbane, Canberra, Darwin, Hobart, Melbourne, Newcastle, Perth, and Sydney. AUS$126 (for a 32-page passport) or AUS$188 (64-page), children AUS$63 (32-page) or AUS$94 (64-page). Valid for 10 years, child passports 5 years. For more info, call toll-free 13 12 32, or visit www.dfat.gov.au/passports.

Canada: Application forms are available at all passport offices, many travel agencies, and Northern Stores in northern communities. CDN$60 plus CDN$25 consular fee. Valid for 5 years. For more info, contact the Canadian Passport Office, Department of Foreign Affairs and International Trade, Ottawa, ON, K1A OG3 (tel. 613 994 3500; www.dfait-maeci.gc.ca/passport). Or call 800 567 6868 (24hr.); in Toronto, 416 973 3251; in Vancouver, 604 586 2500; in Montreal, 514 283 2152.

Ireland: Apply by mail to either the Department of Foreign Affairs, Passport Office, Setanta Centre, Molesworth St., Dublin 2 (tel. 01 671 16 33; fax 671 1092; www.irlgov.ie/iveagh), or the Passport Office, Irish Life Building, 1A South Mall, Cork (tel. 021 27 25 25). Obtain an application at a local Garda station or post office, or request one from a passport office. IR£45. Valid for 10 years. Those under 18 or over 65 can request a 3-year passport (IR£10).

New Zealand: Application forms are available from most travel agents. Standard processing time is 10 working days. NZ$80, children NZ$40. Valid for 10 years, child passports 5 years.

South Africa: South African passports are issued only in Pretoria. Tourist passports around SAR80, under 16 SAR60. Valid for 10 years, child passports 5 years. Processing takes 3 months or more. For more info, contact the nearest Department of Home Affairs Office (www.southafrica-newyork.net/passport.htm).

United Kingdom: Application forms are available at passport offices, main post offices, and many travel agents. Apply by mail or in person to one of the passport offices, located in London, Liverpool, Newport, Peterborough, Glasgow, or Belfast. UK£31, under 16 UK£11. Valid for 10 years, child passports 5 years. Allow 1 month, but the London office offers a five-day, walk-in rush service; arrive early. For more info, contact the UK Passport Agency (tel. 0870 521 04 10; www.open.gov.uk/ukpass/ukpass.htm).

United States: Apply at any courthouse or post office authorized to accept passport applications, or at a US Passport Agency, located in most major cities. US$60, under 18 US$40. Valid 10 years, child passports 5 years. Passports may be renewed by mail or in person for US$40. Processing takes 3-4 weeks. For more info, contact the 24hr. US Passport Information (tel. 202 647 0518; http://travel.state.gov/passport_services.html).

 YOU AND THE EU. Traveling between the fifteen member states of the **European Union** (EU) has never been easier, especially for EU citizens. Citizens of EU member states need only a valid state-issued identity card to travel within the EU, and have right of residence and employment throughout the Union, though some regulations do apply (see **Visas, Invitations, and Work permits,** p. 34). **Freedom of mobility** within the EU was established on May 1st 1999; henceforth, with the exception of the UK, Ireland, and Denmark, checks will be abolished at internal EU borders. Travelers should always carry a passport or EU-member issued identity card as police controls may still be carried out.

There are **no customs** at internal EU borders (travelers arriving in one EU country from another by air should take the **blue channel** when exiting the baggage claim), and travelers are free to transport whatever legal substances they like across the Union provided they can demonstrate that it is for their personal (i.e. non commercial) use. In practise this means quantities in excess of 800 cigarettes, 10L of spirits, 90L of wine (60L of sparkling wine), and 110L of beer—quite enough for most people! Correspondingly, on June 30th 1999, **duty-free was abolished** for travel between EU member states. Those arriving in the EU from outside will still have a duty-free allowance. January 1st 1999 saw the launch of the **Euro,** a common currency for 11 of the EU nations. While it exists only in electronic form as yet, in the future it will mean far fewer money-changing headaches for travelers in Europe (see **Money,** p. 36).

The fifteen member states of the EU are: Austria, Belgium, Denmark, Finland, France, Germany, Greece, Ireland, Italy, Luxembourg, the Netherlands, Portugal, Spain, Sweden, and the United Kingdom.

VISAS AND WORK PERMITS

French visas are valid for travel throughout the **common travel area** (the entire EU, except the UK and Ireland, plus Iceland and Norway), but if the primary object of your visit is a country other than France you should apply to their consulate for a visa. **EU citizens** do not require a visa to visit, reside in, or work in France; however there are some formalities to complete for stays of over 90 days (see below).

All visitors to France are required to register their presence with the police in the town in which they are staying; this is normally done automatically by hotels and hostels and when signing a lease with a landlord.

VISITS OF UNDER 90 DAYS. Citizens of South Africa need a **short-stay visa;** citizens of Australia, Canada, New Zealand, and the US do not need visas. In addition to the application form you require 2 passport-sized photos, proof of a hotel reservation or an organized tour, or, if you intend to stay with relatives or friends, a certificate of accommodation stamped by the police station or town hall (2 copies), a return ticket, and proof of medical insurance. A single/multiple entry visa for 30 days or under costs 165F; for 31-90 days the cost is 195F for single entry, 230F for multiple entry. Short-stay visas for South African nationals usually take 2 days to process. Visa fees are payable in local currency according to an exchange rate determined by the consulate.

VISITS OF OVER 90 DAYS. All non-EU citizens require a **long-stay visa** for stays of over 90 days. These need to be applied for well in advance and require no less than 8 copies of the application form and 8 passport photos, along with proof of residence in your home country, financial independence during your stay in France, medical insurance, and that you do not have a criminal record. Visas can take two months to process and cost 650F. Visa fees are payable in local currency according to an exchange rate determined by the consulate.

Within 60 days of their arrival, all foreigners (including EU citizens) who plan to stay over 90 days must apply for a **residence permit** *(carte de séjour);* apply at the local **préfecture, mairie,** or **commissariat;** in Paris go to the **préfecture de Police.** You must show sufficient resources to support yourself for the duration of your stay. **Unemployed EU citizens** are given 90 days from their entry to France to find employment; if they succeed they will be issued a residence permit valid for 10 years and automatically renewable after that; if they do not, but can show proof of financial independence, they will be issued with a permit valid for 5 years. All other foreign nationals cannot work without applying a work permit (see below). Residence permits are issued free of charge to EU citizens; otherwise they cost 220F. In addition, non-EU citizens must take a medical examination before being issued a card; these cost 360F for students and 1050F for others.

STUDY AND WORK PERMITS. EU citizens (see p. 33) do not need a visa to work and study in France. Others wishing to **study** in France must apply for a **student visa,** for which you will need proof of admission to a French university, financial independence, and medical insurance. Foreigners studying in France must apply for a residence permit within two months of their arrival. Non-EU citizens wishing to **work** in France must have a firm offer of employment before applying for a **work visa;** the employer should arrange for an official contract to be sent to you, which must be presented upon arrival in France. You must also apply for a residence permit within 8 days of arrival. For **au pairs, scientific researchers,** and **teaching assistants,** special rules apply; check with your local consulate. For more information, see **Alternatives to Tourism,** p. 76.

IDENTIFICATION

French law requires that all people carry official identification—either a passport or an EU government-issued identity card. The police have the right to demand to see identification at any time and you risk running a large fine if you do not comply. Minority travelers should be especially careful to carry proof that they are in France legally. In general, when traveling it is advisable to carry two or more forms of identification on your person, including at least one photo ID. A passport combined with a driver's license or birth certificate usually serves as adequate proof of your identity and citizenship. Many establishments, especially banks, require several IDs before cashing traveler's checks. Never carry all your IDs together. It is useful to carry extra passport-size photos to affix to the various IDs or railpasses you may acquire.

STUDENT, YOUTH, AND TEACHER IDENTIFICATION. The **International Student Identity Card (ISIC)** is the most widely accepted form of student identification. Flashing this card can procure you discounts for sights, theaters, museums, meals, buses, and other services. ISICs are preferable to institution-specific cards since they are widely recognized. For US cardholders traveling abroad, the ISIC also provides basic health insurance; see **Insurance,** p. 48. In addition, cardholders have access to a toll-free 24hr. ISIC helpline whose multilingual staff can provide assistance in medical, legal, and financial emergencies overseas (tel. 800 626 2427 in the US and Canada; elsewhere call collect UK (country code: 44) 20 8666 9025).

Many student travel agencies around the world issue ISICs, including STA Travel in Australia and New Zealand; Travel CUTS in Canada; USIT in Ireland and Northern Ireland; SASTS in South Africa; Campus Travel and STA Travel in the UK; and Council Travel, STA Travel, and on the web (www.counciltravel.com/idcards/index.htm) in the US. The card is valid from September of one year to December of the following year and costs AUS$15, CDN$15, US$20, or UK£6. Because of the proliferation of phony ISICs, many airlines and some other services require additional proof of student identity, such as a signed letter from the registrar attesting to your student status that is stamped with the school seal or your school ID card. The **International Teacher Identity Card (ITIC)** offers the same insurance coverage, and similar discounts. The fee is AUS$13, UK£5, or US$20.

Travelers who are under 25 years old but not students can receive many of the same benefits as the ISIC with an **International Youth Travel Card (IYTC,** formerly GO25). Most organizations that sell the ISIC also sell the IYTC. A brochure that lists discounts is free when you purchase the card. To apply, you will need either a passport, valid driver's license, or copy of a birth certificate, and a passport-sized photo with your name printed on the back. The fee is US$20.

For more information on these cards, contact the **International Student Travel Confederation (ISTC),** Herengracht 479, 1017 BS Amsterdam, Netherlands (tel. (country code: 31) 20 421 28 00; fax 020 421 28 10; email istcinfo@istc.org; www.istc.org).

CUSTOMS

ARRIVING IN FRANCE

Upon entering France from a non-EU country, you must declare items which exceed the legal allowance and pay duty on them as established by French law. (For allowances on travel between EU countries, see p. 33.) Keeping receipts for purchases made abroad will help establish values when you return. It is wise to make a list, including serial numbers, of any valuables that you carry with you from home; if you register this list with customs before your departure and have an official stamp it, you will avoid import duty charges and ensure an easy passage upon your return.

RECLAIMING VALUE-ADDED TAX

Most purchases in France include a 20.6% value-added tax **(TVA).** Non-EU residents (including EU citizens who reside outside the EU) can in principal reclaim the tax on purchases for export worth over 1200F made in one store. Only certain stores participate in this **vente en détaxe** refund process; ask before you buy. You must show a non-EU passport or proof of non-EU residence at the time of purchase, and

ESSENTIALS

ak the vendor for a tripartite form called a *bordereau de vente à l'exportation*; make sure that they fill it out, including your bank details. When leaving the country, present the receipt for the purchase together with the completed form to a French customs official. If you're at an airport, look for the window labeled *douane de détaxe*, and be sure to budget at least an hour for the intricacies of French bureaucracy. On a train, find an official (they won't find you) or get off at a station close to the border. Once home, you must send a copy back to the vendor within 6 months; eventually the refunds will work their way into your account. Some shops will exempt you from paying the tax at the time of purchase; you must still complete the above process. Note that food products, tobacco, medicine, unmounted precious stones, cars, and "cultural goods" do not qualify for a refund.

GOING HOME

Upon returning home, you must declare all articles acquired abroad exceed the allowance established by your country's customs service, and pay duty on them. There is normally a different, smaller allowance for goods and gifts purchased at **duty-free** shops abroad; if you exceed this you must declare and pay duty and possibly sales tax on them as well. "Duty-free" merely means that you need not pay a tax in the country of purchase. Note that from June 30th, 1999, Duty Free has been abolished for trips starting and ending within the EU. For more information on customs requirements, contact the following information centers:

Australia: Australian Customs National Information Line 13 003 632 63; www.customs.gov.au.

Canada: Canadian Customs, 2265 St. Laurent bd., Ottawa, ON K1G 4K3 (tel. 613 993 0534 or 24hr. automated service 800 461 9999; www.revcan.ca).

Ireland: The Collector of Customs and Excise, The Custom House, Dublin 1 (tel. 01 679 27 77; fax 01 671 20 21; email taxes@revenue.iol.ie; www.revenue.ie/customs.htm).

New Zealand: New Zealand Customhouse, 17-21 Whitmore St., Box 2218, Wellington (tel. 04 473 60 99; fax 04 473 73 70; www.customs.govt.nz).

South Africa: Commissioner for Customs and Excise, Private Bag X47, Pretoria 0001 (tel. 012 314 9911; fax 012 328 64 78).

United Kingdom: Her Majesty's Customs and Excise, Custom House, Nettleton Road, Heathrow Airport, Hounslow, Middlesex TW6 2LA (tel. 020 8910 3602/3566; fax 020 8910 3765; www.hmce.gov.uk).

United States: US Customs Service, Box 7407, Washington D.C. 20044 (tel. 202 927 6724; www.customs.ustreas.gov).

MONEY

If you stay in hostels and prepare your own food, expect to spend anywhere from 100-140F per person per day. **Accommodations** start at about 130F per night for a double room, while a basic sit-down meal with wine costs 65F. Personal checks from home will meet with blank refusal, and even traveler's checks are not widely accepted outside tourist-oriented businesses; moreover, many establishments will only accept franc- or euro-denominated traveler's checks. The bottom line is, carry enough cash to take you through the day, and take care.

CURRENCY AND EXCHANGE

The national currency of France is the **franc français** or French Franc (abbreviated to FF or F), though it has now been superseded by the **euro** (symbol €; see box above for more information). Each franc is divided into 100 **centimes**. The franc is available in brightly colored 50F, 100F, 200F and 500F notes, smart two-tone 10F and 20F coins, as well as silvery 5F, 2F, 1F and 0.50F coins and pale copper 5, 10 and 20 *centimes* pieces. There are a still a few old 20F notes around, too.

THE EURO. On January 1, 1999, 11 EU countries, including France, adopted the **euro** as their common currency. Euro notes and coins will not be issued until January 1st 2002, and until that time the euro will exist only in electronic transactions and traveler's checks. On June 1st 2002, the franc will be entirely withdrawn from circulation and the euro will become the only legal currency in France. *Let's Go* lists all prices in French francs, as these will still be most relevant in 2000. However, French businesses must by law quote prices both in Francs and euros.

Travelers who will be passing through more than one nation in the euro-zone should note that exchange rates between the 11 national currencies were irrevocably fixed on January 1st 1999. Henceforth, *bureaux de change* must interchange euro-zone currencies at the official rate and with **no commission,** though they may still charge a nominal **service fee** of up to 3%. Euro-denominated **traveler's checks** can be used commission-free throughout the euro-zone.

The **11 euro countries** are: Austria, Belgium, Finland, France, Germany, Ireland, Italy, Luxembourg, the Netherlands, Portugal, and Spain. Updated information on the euro can be found on the EU's website at www.europa.eu.int/.

ESSENTIALS

The currency chart below is based on published exchange rates from August 1999, except for the Euro rate which is fixed permanently at the value given. For a quick conversion, note that one euro is approximately equal to one US dollar.

EURO€1 = 6.55957F	1F = EURO€0.152449
US$1 = 6.23F	1F = US$0.16
CDN$1 = 4.16F	1F = CDN$0.24
UK£1 = 9.94F	1F = UK£0.10
IR£1 = 8.33F	1F = IR£0.12
AUS$1 = 3.97F	1F = AUS$0.25
NZ$1 = 3.29F	1F = NZ$0.30
SAR1=1.02F	1F = SAR0.982

As a general rule, it's cheaper to convert money in France. Bring enough foreign currency to last for the first 24-72 hours of a trip to avoid being penniless after banking hours or on a holiday. Travelers living in the US can get foreign currency from the comfort of their home; **Capital Foreign Exchange** (tel. 888 842 0880) or **International Currency Express** (tel. 888 278 6628) will deliver foreign currency (for over 120 countries) or traveler's checks overnight (US$15) or second-day (US$12) at competitive exchange rates.

Watch out for commission rates and check newspapers for the standard rate of exchange. Banks generally have the best rates. Look for a better deal elsewhere if the bank or *bureau de change* has more than a 5% margin between their buy and sell prices. Since you lose money with each transaction, convert in large sums (unless the currency is depreciating rapidly). If you use traveler's checks or bills, carry some in small denominations (US$50 or less), especially for times when you are forced to exchange money at disadvantageous rates.

TRAVELER'S CHECKS

Traveler's checks are one of the safest and least troublesome means of carrying funds, since they can be refunded if stolen. Several agencies and banks sell them, usually with a small percentage commission. A number of places in France only accept traveler's checks in francs or euros, so keep that in mind when buying checks. **American Express** and **Visa** are the most widely recognized. If you're ordering checks from a bank, do so well in advance, especially if requesting large sums. American Express offices often sell traveler's checks in major currencies over the counter.

ESSENTIALS

Money From Home In Minutes.

If you're stuck for cash on your travels, don't panic. Millions of people trust Western Union to transfer money in minutes to 165 countries and over 50,000 locations worldwide. Our record of safety and reliability is second to none. For more information, call Western Union: USA 1-800-325-6000, Canada 1-800-235-0000. Wherever you are, you're never far from home.

www.westernunion.com

WESTERN UNION | MONEY TRANSFER®

The fastest way to send money worldwide:

Each agency provides refunds if your checks are lost or stolen, and many provide additional services, such as toll-free refund hotlines in the countries you're visiting, emergency message services, and stolen credit card assistance.

In order to collect a **refund** for lost or stolen checks, keep your check receipts separate from your checks and store them in a safe place or with a traveling companion. Record check numbers when you cash them, leave a list of check numbers with someone at home, and ask for a list of refund centers when you buy your checks. Never countersign your checks until you are ready to cash them, and always bring your passport with you when you plan to use the checks.

American Express: Tel. 800 251 902 (Australia); 0800 441 068 (New Zealand); 0800 52 1313 (UK); or 800 221 7282 (Canada and US). Elsewhere, call US collect (country code: 1) 801 964 6665; www.aexp.com. Checks can be purchased for a small fee (1-4%) at American Express Travel Service Offices, banks, and American Automobile Association offices. AAA members can buy checks commission-free. AmEx offices cash their checks commission-free, but often at slightly worse rates than banks. Cheques for Two can be signed by either of two people traveling together. The booklet *Traveler's Companion* lists travel office addresses and stolen check hotlines for France.

Citicorp: Tel. 800 645 6556 (US and Canada); in France, Ireland, the UK, and South Africa, call UK 020 7508 7007; from elsewhere, call US collect 813 623 1709. Commission 1-2%. Guaranteed hand-delivery of traveler's checks when a refund location is not convenient.

Thomas Cook MasterCard: Tel. 800 223 7373 (US or Canada); 0800 622 101 (UK); elsewhere, call UK (country code: 44) 01733 318 950 collect. Commission 2% to buy; checks cashed commission-free. Offices are widespread in France.

Visa: Tel. 800 227 6811 (US); 0800 895 078 (UK); elsewhere, call UK (country code: 44) 1733 318 949 collect. Any of these can tell you the location of their nearest office.

CREDIT CARDS

Credit cards are accepted in most businesses in France, though normally only for purchases of over 100F. Major credit cards can be used to extract cash advances in francs from associated banks and cash machines throughout France. Credit card companies get the wholesale exchange rate, which is generally 5% better than the retail rate used by banks and other currency exchange establishments. The most commonly accepted cards, in both businesses and cash machines, are **Visa** (also known as Carte Bleue in France), and **Mastercard** (also called Eurocard). French-issued credit cards are fitted with a micro-chip (such cards are known as *cartes à puce*) rather than a magnetic strip (*cartes à piste magnétique*); in untouristed areas, cashiers may attempt (and fail) to scan the card with a microchip reader. In such circumstances you should ask for a more senior staff member who (hopefully) will know to swipe your card through the magnetic strip reader. If in doubt, explain: say **"Ceci n'est pas une carte à puce, mais une carte à piste magnétique."** (This card does not have a microchip, but a magnetic strip.) Self-service and cash machines should have no problem scanning magnetic cards. **American Express** cards also work in some cash machines, as well as at AmEx offices and major airports. All such machines require a **Personal Identification Number (PIN).** You must ask your credit card company for a PIN before you leave; without it, you will be unable to withdraw cash with your credit card outside your home country. If you already have a PIN, check with the company to make sure it will work in France. Credit cards often offer an array of other services, from insurance to emergency assistance. Check with your company to find out what is covered.

Visa (US tel. 800 336 8472) and **MasterCard** (US tel. 800 307 7309) often include some purchase protection; **gold cards** often come with comprehensive insurance packages. Call your card issuer for details. **American Express** (US tel. 800 843 2273) cardholder services include the option of cashing personal checks at AmEx offices, a 24-hour hotline with medical and legal assistance in emergencies (tel. 800 554 2639 in US and Canada; from abroad call US collect 202 554 2639), and the American Express Travel Service.

CASH CARD ALERT. To use a cash or credit card to withdraw money from a machine in France, you must have a four-digit **Personal Identification Number (PIN).** These are not usually automatically assigned to credit cards, so ask your card issuer to assign you one before you leave. There are no letters on the keypads of most French cash machines, so use the following chart to work out your PIN: 1=QZ; 2=ABC; 3=DEF; 4=GHI; 5=JKL; 6=MNO; 7=PRS; 8=TUV; and 9= WXY. If you mistakenly punch the wrong code into a French machine three times it will swallow your card for good. If you **lose your card** in France, call for help at the following numbers, all of which have English-speaking operators: **Mastercard** (tel. 08 00 90 13 87), **Visa** (tel. 08 00 90 20 33), and **American Express** (tel. 01 47 77 72 00).

CASH CARDS

24-hour **cash machines** (also called **ATMs**) are widespread in France; they can normally be found at post offices as well as banks. Depending on the system that your home bank uses, you can probably access your personal bank account whenever you need money. ATMs get the same wholesale exchange rate as credit cards. Despite these perks, do some research before relying too heavily on automation. There is normally a limit on the amount of money you can withdraw per day (usually about US$500), and computer networks sometimes fail. Your home bank may also charge a fee for using ATM facilities abroad. If your PIN is longer than four digits, ask your bank whether the first four digits will work.

The two major international money networks are **Cirrus** (US tel. 800 4 CIRRUS (424 7787)) and **PLUS** (US tel. 800 843 7587 for the "Voice Response Unit Locator").

GETTING MONEY FROM HOME

American Express: Cardholders can withdraw cash from their **checking** or **current accounts** without fees at any of AmEx's major offices and many of its representatives' offices, up to US$1000 every 21 days. AmEx also offers Express Cash at their ATMs in France. Express Cash withdrawals are automatically debited from the Cardmember's checking account or line of credit. AmEx Green card holders may withdraw up to US$1000 in a seven day period. For more info or to enroll in Express Cash, tel. 800 CASH NOW (227 4669) in the US; outside the US call collect (US country code: 1) 336 668 5041. The AmEx national number in France is 01 47 77 70 00.

Western Union: Travelers from the US, Canada, and the UK can wire money abroad through Western Union's international money transfer services. Tel. 800 325 6000 (US); 0800 833 833 (UK); 800 235 0000 (Canada). You can send money to any Western Union office; there are some located in French post offices. Rates for sending cash are generally US$10-11 cheaper than with a credit card, and the money is usually available at the place you're sending it to within an hour.

US State Department (US Citizens): In emergencies, US citizens can have money sent via the State Department. For US$15, they will forward money within hours to the nearest consular office, which will disburse it according to instructions. The office serves only Americans in the direst of straits abroad; non-American travelers should contact their embassies for information on wiring cash. Check with the State Department or the nearest US embassy or consulate for the quickest way to have the money sent. Contact the Overseas Citizens' Service, American Citizens Services, Consular Affairs, Room 4811, US Department of State, Washington, D.C. 20520 (tel. 202 647 5225; nights, Sundays, and holidays 202 647 4000; fax 202 647 3000; http://travel.state.gov).

TIPPING

By law, service must be included at all restaurants, bars, and cafés in France. It is not unheard of to leave extra *monnaie* (change) at a café or bar, maybe a franc or two per drink; exceptionally good service may be rewarded with a 5-10% tip. Otherwise, tipping is only expected for **taxis** and **hairdressers;** 10-15% is the norm. People (like hotel concierges) may also expect to be tipped for services beyond their call of duty; in such cases, never tip less than 10F.

SAFETY AND SECURITY

EMERGENCY AND CRISIS TELEPHONE NUMBERS	Police: 17 Ambulance: 15 Fire: 18 English language crisis line: 01 47 23 80 80 (3-11pm)

Personal safety in France is on a par with the rest of Western Europe, with a far lower rate of violent crime than the US. It's best not to be complacent, though, since tourists are often seen as (and often are) easy victims. Always take care in big cities. **Con artists** can work singly or in gangs, and the most efficient are often innocent-looking children. Be especially suspicious in unexpected situations; do not respond or make eye contact, walk quickly away, and keep a solid grip on your belongings. Contact the police if a hustler is insistent or aggressive. A common scam is for one person to distract the victim with a question about directions while their accomplice snatches his or her bag. In city crowds and especially on public transportation, **pickpockets** are amazingly deft at their craft. In **Paris,** be especially careful on public transportation at rush hour and on the way to and from the airport. Theft is also common on Metro line #1 and at department stores. Outside Paris, tourist-targeted crime is most prevalent on the **Côte d'Azur,** as well as in **Marseille** and **Montpellier.** If you are driving, keep your doors locked at all times and keep bags away from the windows; scooter-borne thieves often snatch wallets, purses, and bags from cars stopped at red lights. Pedestrians should also be careful as purse-snatching is common.

BLENDING IN

Tourists are particularly vulnerable to crime because they often carry large amounts of cash and are not as street savvy as locals. Try to blend in as much as possible; what may look perfectly innocuous in Miami will mark you out instantly in Marseille. The French are known for their conservative stylishness—it's unlikely you'll be able to compete with them. Go for restrained sneakers or closed shoes, solid colored pants or jeans, and plain T-shirts or button-down shirts, rather than teva sandals, baggy pants, and torn jeans. Shorts shouldn't be too short, nor should they feature strategically ripped butt areas. Skirts or dresses for girls are more appropriate and just as good in hot weather. Carrying a large bag with you everywhere is another giveaway, as well as being a burden—leave it behind!

Women and men should remember that they are expected to dress respectfully before entering churches. Women should wear long pants or a long skirt, and cover their shoulders; men should remove their hats and cover their upper bodies. Beach wear is totally unacceptable in churches.

The gawking camera-toter is a more obvious target than the low-profile observer. Familiarize yourself with your surroundings before setting out; if you must check a map on the street, duck into a café, shop, or at least a doorway. Also, carry yourself with confidence, as an obviously bewildered bodybuilder is more likely to be harassed than a stern and confident weakling. If you are traveling alone, be sure that someone at home knows your itinerary and **never admit that you're traveling alone.**

EXPLORING

Extra vigilance is always wise, but there is no need for panic when exploring a new city or region. Find out about unsafe areas from tourist offices, from the manager of your hotel or hostel, or from a local whom you trust. Whenever possible, *Let's Go* warns of unsafe neighborhoods and areas. When walking at night, stick to busy, well-lit streets and avoid dark alleyways. If you feel uncomfortable, leave as quickly and directly as you can, but don't allow fear of the unknown to turn you into a hermit. Careful, persistent exploration will build confidence and make your stay in an area that much more rewarding.

TERRORISM

While terrorist attacks are not unknown in France, tourists are rarely targeted. In the past, Algerian Islamicists have carried out bombings in Paris, but terrorism is most common in **Corsica** and the **Pays Basque,** where there are well-established separatists movements. The Basque Separatist Party (ETA) is not as active or as widely supported in France as it is in Spain, and it targets mainly local government offices. The National Front for the Liberation of Corsica (FLNC) also carries out political assassinations and car-bombings. Always be on the alert for unattended packages and parcels.

DRIVING

The French have a not-undeserved reputation for aggressive, dangerous driving. They take advantage of excellent roads to widely flout speed limits, and in a country where it's not uncommon to start the day with a stiff drink, drunk driving is a problem all day (and all night) long. Corsican roads are some of the most lethal in Europe; think twice about driving here, and don't be intimidated by drivers trying to overtake you on narrow, twisting coast roads. Always be on the look out for mopeds, especially in the south, which can speed out from narrow alleys, pedestrian zones, and sidewalks. Wearing a seatbelt is required by law of all passengers. In cities, and especially on the Côte d'Azur, be sure to park your vehicle in a well-lit, popular area. For information on road conditions, contact the **Association for**

Safe International Road Travel (ASIRT), 5413 West Cedar Lane 103C, Bethesda, MD 20814 (tel. 301 983 5252; fax 301 983 3663; email asirt@erols.com; www.asirt.org).

Sleeping in your car is one of the most dangerous (and often illegal) ways to get your rest; don't do it. If your car breaks down on an *autoroute*, wait for the police to assist you. *Let's Go* does not recommend **hitchhiking** under any circumstances, particularly for women—see **Getting Around,** p. 63 for more information.

FURTHER INFORMATION

The following government offices provide travel information and advisories by telephone or on their websites: **Australian Department of Foreign Affairs and Trade** (tel. 02 6261 1111; www.dfat.gov.au); **Canadian Department of Foreign Affairs and International Trade** (tel. 800 267 8376, from Ottawa tel. 613 944 4000; www.dfait-maeci.gc.ca), offering the free booklet, *Bon Voyage...But;* **United Kingdom Foreign and Commonwealth Office** (tel. 020 7238 4503; www.fco.gov.uk); **United States Department of State** (tel. 202 647 5225; http://travel.state.gov).

FINANCIAL SECURITY

PROTECTING YOUR VALUABLES

To prevent easy theft, don't keep all your valuables and documents in one place. **Photocopies** of important documents allow you to recover them in case they are lost or filched. Carry one copy separate from the documents and leave another copy at home or with a friend. Label every piece of luggage both inside and out. Don't put a wallet in your back pocket. Never count your money in public and carry as little as possible. If you carry a handbag, buy a sturdy one with a secure clasp, and carry it crosswise on the side, away from the street with the clasp against you. Secure packs with small combination padlocks. A **money belt** combines convenience and security, and is the best way to carry cash; you can buy one at most camping stores. A **neck pouch** is equally safe, although far less accessible; refrain from pulling it out in public. Keep some money separate from the rest to use in an emergency or in case of theft.

ACCOMMODATIONS AND TRANSPORTATION

Never leave your belongings unattended; crime occurs in even the most demure-looking hostel or hotel. If you feel unsafe, look for places with either a curfew or a night attendant. Lockers are available in many hostels and a few major train stations: *Let's Go* lists availability. You may need your own padlock for hostel lockers. Most hotels also provide lock boxes free or for a minimal fee.

Be particularly careful on **buses,** carry your backpack in front of you where you can see it, and don't trust anyone to "watch your bag for a second." Thieves thrive on **trains;** professionals wait for tourists to fall asleep and then carry off everything they can. Keep important documents and other valuables on your person and try to sleep on top bunks with your luggage stored above you (if not in bed with you). If you travel by **car,** try not to leave valuable possessions in it while you are away. Lock all bags—however innocuous-looking—out of sight in the trunk; otherwise you may well come back to find a window smashed and your belongings gone.

DRUGS

Possession of **illegal drugs** in France can end your vacation abruptly; convicted offenders can expect a jail sentence and fines. Never bring any illegal drugs across a border. It is vital that **prescription drugs,** particularly insulin, syringes, or narcotics, be accompanied by the prescriptions themselves and a statement from a doctor and left in original, labeled containers. In France, police may stop and search anyone on the street—no reason is required. It is not unknown for a pusher to increase profits by selling drugs to a tourist and then turning that person in to the authorities for a reward. If you are arrested, your home country's consulate can provide a list of attorneys and inform family and friends, but it cannot get you out of jail. Write the Bureau of Consular Affairs, Public Affairs #6831, Department of State, Washington, D.C. 20520 (tel. 202 647 1488) for more info.

HEALTH

Common sense is the simplest prescription for good health while you travel. Travelers complain most often about their feet and their gut, so take precautionary measures; drink lots of fluids to prevent dehydration and constipation, wear sturdy, broken-in shoes and clean socks, and use talcum powder to keep your feet dry. To minimize the effects of jet lag, "reset" your body's clock by adopting the time of your destination as soon as you board the plane.

BEFORE YOU GO

Preparation can help minimize the likelihood of contracting a disease and maximize the chances of receiving effective health care in the event of an emergency.

For minor health problems, bring a compact **first-aid kit**, including sticking plasters, pain killer, antiseptic, a thermometer, a Swiss army knife with tweezers, motion sickness remedy, medicine for diarrhea or stomach problems (Pepto Bismol tablets or liquid Immodium), and insect repellent. **Contact lens** wearers who use heat disinfection might consider switching to chemical cleansers.

In your **passport,** write the names of any people you wish to be contacted in case of a medical emergency, and also list any **allergies** or medical conditions you would want doctors to be aware of. Allergy sufferers might want to obtain a full supply of any necessary medication before the trip. Matching a prescription to a foreign equivalent is not always easy, safe, or possible. Carry up-to-date, legible prescriptions or a statement from your doctor stating the medication's trade name, manufacturer, chemical name, and dosage. While traveling, be sure to keep all medication with you in your carry-on luggage.

USEFUL ORGANIZATIONS

The US **Centers for Disease Control and Prevention (CDC)** (tel. 888 232 3299; www.cdc.gov) is an excellent source of information for travelers around the world and maintains an international fax information service. The CDC also publishes the booklet "Health Information for International Travelers" (US$20), an annual global rundown of disease, immunization, and general health advice, including risks in particular countries. Order by phone (tel. 202 512 1800) or send a check or money order to the Superintendent of Documents, US Government Printing Office, P.O. Box 371954, Pittsburgh, PA, 15250-7954.

The **United States State Department** (http://travel.state.gov) compiles Consular Information Sheets on health, entry requirements, and other issues for all countries of the world. For quick information on travel warnings, call the **Overseas Citizens' Services** (tel. 202 647 5225; after-hours 202 647 4000). To receive the same Consular Information Sheets by fax, dial 202 647 3000 directly from a fax machine and follow the recorded instructions. The State Department's regional passport agencies in the US, field offices of the US Chamber of Commerce, and US embassies and consulates abroad provide the same data; or send a self-addressed, stamped envelope to the Overseas Citizens' Services, Bureau of Consular Affairs, #4811, US Department of State, Washington, D.C. 20520.

MEDICAL ASSISTANCE ON THE ROAD

Medical care in France is as good (and as expensive) as anywhere in the world, and all but the smallest towns have a hospital, listed under the Practical Informations for towns covered by *Let's Go.* Every town has a **24-hour pharmacy** *(pharmacie de garde);* this burden rotates among the various pharmacies in town. The police will be able to tell you which one is open on any given night; on Sundays pharmacies must post a list on their door saying which is on duty.

EU citizens can get reciprocal health benefits, entitling them to immediate urgent care, by filling out an **E-111** form before departure; this is available at major post offices. EU citizens studying in France also qualify for long-term care. Other travelers should ensure they have adequate medical insurance before leaving; if your regular **insurance** policy does not cover travel abroad, you may wish to purchase additional coverage. With the exception of Medicare, most health insurance plans cover members' medical emergencies during trips abroad; check with your insurance carrier to be sure. For more information on, see **Insurance,** p. 48.

If you need a doctor **(un medecin),** call the local hospital for a list of nearby practitioners. If you are receiving reciprocal health care, make sure you call a **honoraires opposables** doctor, who will be linked to the state health care system. They may not charge more than 110F for a consultation at their surgery. Doctors described as **honoraires libres** are free to charge whatever they like, and their fees will not be reimbursed under reciprocal health care agreements. Note that the same medicines may go under different names in France from your home country; check with your doctor before you leave.

If you are concerned about being able to access medical support while traveling, contact one of these two services: **Global Emergency Medical Services (GEMS)** has products called *MedPass* that provide 24-hour international medical assistance and support coordinated through registered nurses who have online access to your medical information, your primary physician, and a worldwide network of screened, credentialed English-speaking doctors and hospitals. Subscribers also receive a personal medical record that contains vital information in case of emergencies, and GEMS will pay for medical evacuation if necessary. Prices start at about US$35 for a 30-day trip and run up to about $100 for annual services. For more information contact them at 2001 Westside Dr. #120, Alpharetta, GA 30004 (tel. 800 860 1111; fax 770 475 0058; www.globalems.com). The **International Association for Medical Assistance to Travelers (IAMAT)** has free membership and offers a directory of English-speaking doctors around the world who treat members for a set fee schedule, and detailed charts on immunization requirements, various tropical diseases, climate, and sanitation. Chapters include: **US,** 417 Center St., Lewiston, NY 14092 (tel. 716 754 4883, 8am-4pm; fax 519 836 3412; email iamat@sentex.net; www.sentex.net/~iamat); **Canada,** 40 Regal Road, Guelph, ON, N1K 1B5 (tel. 519 836 0102) or 1287 St. Clair Avenue West, Toronto, ON M6E 1B8 (tel. 416 652 0137; fax 519 836 3412); **New Zealand,** P.O. Box 5049, Christchurch 5 (fax 03 352 4630; email iamat@chch.planet.org.nz).

MEDICAL CONDITIONS

Those with medical conditions (e.g. diabetes, allergies to antibiotics, epilepsy, heart conditions) may want to obtain a stainless steel **Medic Alert** identification tag (US$35 the first year, $15 annually thereafter), which identifies the condition and gives a 24-hour collect-call information number. Contact the Medic Alert Foundation, 2323 Colorado Ave., Turlock, CA 95382 (tel. 800 825 3785; www.medicalert.org). Diabetics can contact the **American Diabetes Association,** 1660 Duke St., Alexandria, VA 22314 (tel. 800 232 3472), to receive copies of the article "Travel and Diabetes" and a diabetic ID card, which carries messages in 18 languages explaining the carrier's diabetic status.

If you are **HIV** positive, contact the Bureau of Consular Affairs, #4811, Department of State, Washington, D.C. 20520 (tel. 202 647 1488; auto-fax 202 647 3000; http://travel.state.gov).

OUTDOOR HAZARDS

France is a densely populated, medically advanced country, so travelers may be tempted to neglect safety concerns. However, those hiking or spending a lot of time outdoors should always take care. The heat in summer can lead to rapid dehydration, especially for those undertaking physical exertions, and sunburn is another hazard. If you go mountaineering or on long-distance hikes in the Alps, the

ESSENTIALS

Pyrenees, or Corsica, remember that storms can strike at any time of year; every year sees a number of deaths of climbers who were ill-prepared for their route. When hiking, plan your route carefully and tell the local authorities where you are going; see **Wilderness Safety,** p. 55, for more information.

Heat exhaustion and dehydration: Avoid heat exhaustion, whose symptoms include fatigue, headaches, and nausea, by eating salty foods and imbibing enough clear drinks to keep your urine clear. Stay off alcoholic and caffeinated drinks, which are dehydrating. Wear a hat, and a lightweight long-sleeved shirt in hot sun, and take time to acclimatize to a hot destination before seriously exerting yourself. Continuous heat stress can eventually lead to **heatstroke,** characterized by rising body temperature, severe headache, and cessation of sweating. Heatstroke is rare but serious, and victims must be cooled off with wet towels and taken to a doctor as soon as possible.

Sunburn: If you are planning on spending time near water, in the desert, or in the snow, you are at risk of getting burned, even through clouds. Wear good sunglasses, since long exposure to the bright sunshine can damage the retina. If you get sunburned, drink more fluids than usual and apply Calamine or an aloe-based lotion.

Hypothermia and frostbite: A rapid drop in body temperature is the clearest warning sign of overexposure to cold. Victims may also shiver, feel exhausted, have poor coordination or slurred speech, hallucinate, or suffer amnesia. Seek medical help, and *do not let hypothermia victims fall asleep*—it may prove fatal. To avoid hypothermia, keep dry, wear layers, and stay out of the wind. In wet weather, wool and synthetics such as pile retain heat. Most other fabrics, especially cotton, will make you colder. When the temperature is below freezing, watch for **frostbite.** If a region of skin turns white, waxy, and cold, do not rub the area. Drink warm beverages, get dry, and slowly warm the area with dry fabric or steady body contact, until a doctor can be found.

High altitude: Travelers to high altitudes must allow their bodies a couple of days to adjust to lower oxygen levels in the air before exerting themselves. At high altitude, alcohol is more potent, and the risk of sunburn is greater, even in cold weather.

PREVENTING DISEASE

TICK- AND INSECT-BORNE DISEASES

Many diseases are transmitted by insects and ticks. **Mosquitoes** are most active from dusk to dawn. Use insect repellents, wear long pants and long sleeves, and buy a mosquito net. Wear closed shoes and socks, and tuck long pants into socks. Soak or spray your gear with permethrin, which is licensed in the US for use on clothing. Calamine lotion or topical cortisones (like Cortaid) may stop insect bites from itching, as can a bath with a half-cup of baking soda or oatmeal. **Ticks**—responsible for Lyme and other diseases—can be particularly dangerous in rural and forested regions. Pause periodically while walking to brush off ticks using a fine-toothed comb on your neck and scalp. Do not try to remove ticks by burning them or coating them with nail polish remover or petroleum jelly.

Tick-borne encephalitis, a viral infection of the central nervous system, is transmitted during the summer by tick bites and by consumption of unpasteurized dairy products. The disease occurs most often in wooded areas. Symptoms range from headaches and flu to swelling of the brain (encephalitis). A vaccine is available in Europe, but the immunization schedule is impractical for most tourists, and the risk of contracting the disease is relatively low, especially if you take precautions against tick bites.

Lyme disease, also carried by ticks, is a bacterial infection marked by a circular bull's-eye rash of 5cm or more that appears around the bite. Other symptoms include fever, headache, tiredness, and aches and pains. Antibiotics are effective if administered early. Left untreated, lyme can cause problems in joints, the heart, and the nervous system. If you find a tick attached to your skin, grasp the tick's head parts with tweezers as close to your skin as possible and apply slow, steady traction. If you remove a tick within 24 hours, you greatly reduce your risk of infection.

FOOD- AND WATER-BORNE DISEASES

Prevention is the best cure: be sure that everything you eat is cooked properly and that the water you drink is clean. This is unlikely to be a problem in France, although most French people prefer to drink mineral water as a matter of taste and style; in rural areas you may wish to imitate them. Never drink water from rivers or ponds; in addition to harmful organisms it may contain high levels of chemical waste and agricultural run-off.

Traveler's diarrhea in France is usually nothing more than your body's temporary reaction to bacteria in unfamiliar food ingredients, and tends to last 3-7 days. If the nasties hit you, have quick-energy, non-sugary foods with protein and carbohydrates to keep your strength up. Over-the-counter remedies (such as Immodium) provide symptomatic relief, but they can complicate serious infections; only use them in conjunction with rehydration salts. These can be purchased, but are simple to make: mix one cup of clean water with half a teaspoon of sugar or honey and a pinch of salt. Soft drinks without caffeine and salted crackers are also good. Down several of these remedies a day, rest, and wait for the disease to run its course. If you develop a fever or symptoms persist longer than five days, consult a doctor. If children develop diarrhea, consult a doctor, since treatment is different.

Weil's disease (Leptospirosis) is a water-borne bacterial disease spread by contamination from animal urine. Do not expose cuts or burns to untreated fresh water, especially in agricultural areas. The incubation period is normally 5-15 days, though it can be as long as 30 days and short as 48hr.; early symptoms are fever, chills, muscular aches and pains, loss of appetite, and nausea when lying down. After five days, this may be followed by bruising, anemia, sore eyes, nose bleeds, and jaundice. The disease is often fatal if untreated; always tell your doctor if you suspect you are infected, or you may be misdiagnosed with flu.

INFECTIOUS DISEASES

Rabies is transmitted through the saliva of infected animals. It is fatal if untreated. Avoid contact with wild or stray animals. If you are bitten, wash the wound thoroughly and seek immediate medical care. Once you begin to show symptoms (thirst and muscle spasms), the disease is in its terminal stage. If possible, try to locate the animal that bit you to determine whether it does indeed have rabies. A rabies vaccine is available but is only semi-effective. Three shots must be administered over one year.

Hepatitis B is a viral infection of the liver transmitted through the transfer of bodily fluids, by sharing needles, or in unprotected sex. Its incubation period varies and can be much longer than a month. A person may not begin to show symptoms until many years after infection. Vaccination is recommended for health-care workers, sexually active travelers, and anyone planning to seek medical treatment abroad. Vaccination consists of a 3-shot series given over a period of time, and should begin 6 months before traveling.

Hepatitis C is like Hepatitis B, but the modes of transmission are different. Intravenous drug users, those with occupational exposure to blood, hemodialysis patients, or recipients of blood transfusions are at the highest risk, but the disease can also be spread through sexual contact and sharing of items like razors and toothbrushes.

AIDS, HIV, STDS

Acquired Immune Deficiency Syndrome (AIDS; SIDA in French) is a major problem in France; Paris has the largest HIV-positive community in Europe. There are as many heterosexuals infected as homosexuals in France, and among heterosexuals more women are infected than men. The easiest mode of HIV transmission is through direct blood-to-blood contact; *never* share intravenous drug, tattooing, or other needles. The most common mode of transmission is sexual intercourse; you can greatly reduce the risk by using latex condoms; these are widely available in France from pharmacies, supermarkets, and vending machines.

For more information on AIDS, call the **US Centers for Disease Control's** 24-hour hotline at 800 342 2437. In Europe, contact the **World Health Organization,** Attn: Global Program on AIDS, Avenue Appia 20, 1211 Geneva 27, Switzerland (tel. 022 791 21 11; fax 022 791 31 11), for statistical material on AIDS internationally. Council's brochure, *Travel Safe: AIDS and International Travel,* is available at all Council Travel offices and at their website (www.ciee.org/study/safety/travelsafe.htm).

Sexually transmitted diseases (STDs) such as gonorrhea, chlamydia, genital warts, syphilis, and herpes are easier to catch than HIV, and some can be just as deadly. **Hepatitis B** and **C** are also serious sexually transmitted diseases (see **Infectious Diseases,** above). Warning signs for STDs include: swelling, sores, bumps, or blisters on sex organs, rectum, or mouth; burning and pain during urination and bowel movements; itching around sex organs; swelling or redness in the throat, flu-like symptoms with fever, chills, and aches. If these symptoms develop, see a doctor immediately. When having sex, condoms may protect you from certain STDs, but oral or even tactile contact can lead to transmission.

NO PRÉSERVATIFS ADDED Having invented the French kiss, the speakers of the language of love have long had *savoir faire* in all things amorous—safety included. In the age of responsibility, French pharmacies provide 24-hour condom dispensers, which unabashedly adorn public streets. But for you health buffs, don't ask for foods *"sans préservatifs."* Funny looks will greet you as listeners wonder what condoms would be doing in a jar of jam, *Bonne Maman* no less.

WOMEN'S HEALTH

Women are vulnerable to **urinary tract** and **bladder infections,** common and severely uncomfortable bacterial diseases that cause a burning sensation and painful and sometimes frequent urination. To avoid these infections, drink plenty of vitamin-C-rich juice and clean water, and urinate frequently. Untreated, these infections can lead to kidney problems, sterility, and even death.

Women are also susceptible to **vaginal yeast infections,** a treatable but uncomfortable illness likely to flare up in hot and humid climates. Wearing loosely fitting trousers or a skirt and cotton underwear will help. Yeast infections can be treated with an over-the-counter remedy like Monostat or Gynelotrimin. Bring supplies from home if you are prone to infection, as they may be difficult to find on the road. Some travelers opt for a natural alternative such as plain yogurt and lemon juice douche if other remedies are unavailable.

Contraception is readily available in most pharmacies and supermarkets. To obtain **condoms** in France, visit a pharmacy and tell the clerk, *"Je voudrais une boîte de préservatifs"* (zhuh-voo-DRAY oon BWAHT duh PREY-zehr-va-TEEF). The French branch of the International Planned Parenthood Federation, the **Mouvement Français pour le Planning Familiale (MFPF;** tel. 01 42 60 93 20; 10 rue Vivienne, 750002 Paris), can provide more information.

Women who need an **abortion** while abroad should contact the **International Planned Parenthood Federation,** European Regional Office, Regent's College Inner Circle, Regent's Park, London NW1 4NS (tel. 020 7487 7900; fax 487 7950), for more information.

INSURANCE

Travel insurance generally covers four basic areas: medical/health problems, property loss, trip cancellation/interruption, and emergency evacuation. Be sure to check whether your regular insurance policies extend to travel-related accidents; even if they do, you may consider purchasing travel insurance if the cost of potential trip cancellation/interruption or emergency medical evacuation is greater than you can absorb.

US residents' **medical insurance** (especially university policies) often covers costs incurred abroad; check with your provider. **Medicare does not cover foreign travel.** Canadians are protected by their home province's health insurance plan for up to 90 days after leaving the country; check with the provincial Ministry of Health or Health Plan Headquarters for details. **Homeowners' insurance** (or your family's coverage) often covers theft during travel and loss of travel documents (passport, plane ticket, railpass, etc.) up to US$500.

ISIC and **ITIC** (see **Identification,** p. 34) provide basic insurance benefits, including US$100 per day of in-hospital sickness for a maximum of 60 days, US$3000 of accident-related medical reimbursement, and US$25,000 for emergency medical transport. This might sound like a lot, but in reality won't even cover a major operation. Cardholders have access to a toll-free 24-hour helpline whose multilingual staff can provide assistance in medical, legal, and financial emergencies overseas (tel. 800 626 2427 in the US and Canada; elsewhere call the US collect 713 267 2525.)

Prices for travel insurance purchased separately generally run about US$50 per week for full coverage, while trip cancellation/interruption may be purchased separately at a rate of about US$5.50 per US$100 of coverage. **Council** and **STA** (see p. 59 for complete listings) offer a range of budget policies around the world.

PACKING

Pack light: a good rule is to lay out only what you absolutely need, then take half the clothes and twice the money. The less you have, the less you have to lose (or store, or carry on your back). Don't forget the obvious things: no matter when you're traveling, it's always a good idea to bring a rain jacket, a warm jacket or wool sweater, and sturdy shoes and thick socks. You may also want to add one outfit beyond the jeans and t-shirt uniform, and maybe a nicer pair of shoes if you have the room. Remember that wool will keep you warm even when soaked through, whereas wet cotton is colder than wearing nothing at all. If you plan to be doing a lot of hiking, see **Outdoors,** p. 54.

Backpacks: If you plan to cover most of your itinerary by foot, a sturdy **frame backpack** is unbeatable. **Internal-frame** packs mold better to your back, keep a lower center of gravity, and can flex adequately on difficult hikes that require a lot of bending and maneuvering. **External-frame** packs are more comfortable over even terrain—like city streets—since they keep the weight higher and distribute it more evenly. Look for a pack with a strong, padded hip belt to transfer weight from your shoulders to your hips. Good packs cost US$150-500—this is one area where it's not worth economizing. Before you buy a pack, try it on and imagine carrying it, full, a few miles up a rocky incline. Better yet, insist on filling it with something heavy and walking around the store to get a sense of how it distributes weight before committing to buy it. Organizations that sell packs via mail-order are listed on p. 54.

Suitcases: Toting a suitcase is fine if you plan to live in one or two cities and explore from there, but a very bad idea if you're going to be moving around a lot. Make sure suitcases have wheels and consider how much they weigh even when empty. Hard-sided luggage is more durable but more weighty and cumbersome. Soft-sided luggage should have a PVC frame, a strong lining, and triple-stitched seams.

Sleepsacks: Some youth hostels require that you have your own sleepsack or rent one of theirs. If you plan to stay in hostels you can avoid linen charges by making the requisite sleepsack yourself: fold a full size sheet in half the long way, then sew it closed along the open long side and one of the short sides. Sleepsacks can also be bought at any Hostelling International outlet store.

Electricity: In France, electricity is 220 volts AC, enough to fry any 110V North American appliance. 220V Electrical appliances don't like 110V current, either. Visit a hardware store for an adapter (which changes the shape of the plug) and a converter (which changes the voltage). Don't make the mistake of using only an adapter (unless appliance instructions explicitly state otherwise).

Film: Expect to pay US$4-10 for a 24-exposure ISO200 35mm color film. If you're not a serious photographer, you might want to consider bringing a **disposable camera** or two rather than an expensive permanent one. Airport carry-on X-ray machines should not affect film speeds of 400 and under; always pack film in your carry-on luggage, since higher-intensity X-rays are used on checked luggage.

ACCOMMODATIONS

HOSTELS

A HOSTELER'S BILL OF RIGHTS. There are certain standard features that we do not include in our hostel listings. Unless we state otherwise, you can expect that every hostel has: no lockout, no curfew, a kitchen, free hot showers, secure luggage storage, and no key deposit.

Hostels generally offer dormitory accommodations in large single-sex rooms with 6-10 beds, though some have as many as 60, while at the other end of the scale, many offer private singles and doubles. They sometimes have kitchens and utensils for your use, bike rental, storage areas, and laundry facilities. There can be drawbacks: some hostels close during certain daytime "lock-out" hours, have a curfew, don't accept reservations, and/or impose a maximum stay. In France, a bed in a hostel will average around 60-90F.

If you plan on doing a lot of hostelling, it is definitely worth joining **Hostelling International (HI)** before you leave home; to do so, contact one of the national organizations listed below. Many hostels in France are HI affiliates; members get lower rates and can reserve in advance, often through the **International Booking Network** (tel. 02 9261 1111 from Australia, 800 663 5777 from Canada, 01629 581 418 from the U.K., 01 301 766 from Ireland, 09 379 4224 from New Zealand, 800 909 4776 from US; www.hiayh.org/ushostel/reserva/ibn3.htm) for a nominal fee. For information on HI-affiliated hostels in France, contact the **Fédération Unie des Auberges de Jeunesse (FUAJ),** 4 bd. Jules ferry, 75011 Paris (tel. 01 43 57 02 60; www.fuaj.org). Other comprehensive hostelling websites include www.hostels.com and www.eurotrip.com/accommodation. If you only decide to start hostelling when you arrive, you can stay at HI member hostels by getting a **guest card** when you arrive. For 19F per night, you will receive a **welcome stamp;** after six stamps, you automatically become a full HI member.

Australian Youth Hostels Association (AYHA), 422 Kent St., Sydney NSW 2000 (tel. 02 9261 1111; fax 02 9261 1969; email yha@yhansw.org.au; www.yha.org.au). One-year membership AUS$44, under 18 AUS$13.50.

Hostelling International-Canada (HI-C), 400-205 Catherine St., Ottawa, ON K2P 1C3 (tel. 800 663 5777 or 613 237 7884; fax 613 237 7868; email info@hostellingintl.ca; www.hostellingintl.ca). One-year membership CDN$25, under 18 CDN$12; 2-yr. CDN$35.

An Óige (Irish Youth Hostel Association), 61 Mountjoy St., Dublin 7 (tel. 01 830 4555; fax 01 830 5808; email anoige@iol.ie; www.irelandyha.org). One-year membership IR£10, under 18 IR£4, families IR£20.

Youth Hostels Association of New Zealand (YHANZ), P.O. Box 436, 173 Cashel St., Christchurch 1 (tel. 03 379 9970; fax 03 365 4476; email info@yha.org.nz; www.yha.org.nz). One-year membership NZ$24, ages 15-17 NZ$12, under 15 free.

Hostelling International South Africa, P.O. Box 4402, Cape Town 8000 (tel. 021 24 2511; fax 021 24 4119; email info@hisa.org.za; www.hisa.org.za). One-year membership SAR50, under 18 SAR25, lifetime SAR250.

Scottish Youth Hostels Association (SYHA), 7 Glebe Crescent, Stirling FK8 2JA (tel. 01786 891 400; fax 01786 891 333; email info@syha.org.uk; www.syha.org.uk). Membership UK£6, under 18 UK£2.50.

Youth Hostels Association of England and Wales (YHA), 8 St. Stephen's Hill, St. Albans, Hertfordshire AL1 2DY, England (tel. 01727 855 215 or 845 047; fax 01727 844 126; email yhacustomerservices@compuserve.com; www.yha.org.uk). One-year membership UK£11, under 18 UK£5.50, families UK£22.

Hostelling International Northern Ireland (HINI), 22-32 Donegall Rd., Belfast BT12 5JN, Northern Ireland (tel. 01232 324 733 or 315 435; fax 01232 439 699; email info@hini.org.uk; www.hini.org.uk). One-year membership UK£7, under 18 UK£3, families UK£14.

Hostelling International-American Youth Hostels (HI-AYH), 733 15th St. NW, Suite 840, Washington, D.C. 20005 (tel. 202 783 6161 ext. 136; fax 202 783 6171; email hiayh-serv@hiayh.org; www.hiayh.org). One-year membership US$25, over 54 US$15, under 18 free.

HOTELS

Two or more people traveling together will often save money staying in cheap hotels over hostels, and while you may lose the camaraderie of hosteling, you'll be recompensed with more privacy and the freedom to come and go when you like. The French government employs a ratings system which graces hotels with zero to four stars, awarded according to the facilities they provide. Most hotels listed by *Let's Go* are zero or one star, with a smattering of two stars, but are chosen and ranked according to qualities such as charm, friendliness, convenience, and value for money. Hotels in each town are listed in our order of preference; particularly outstanding ones are awarded the *Let's Go thumb* (🖐). Prices are generally per room, although *demi-pension* (half-board: includes room, breakfast, and/or dinner) and *pension* (room and all meals) are always quoted per person. Expect to pay at least 110F for a single room and 130F for a double. If you want a room with twin beds, make sure to ask for *une chambre avec deux lits* (oon chAMBR-avEK duh LEE; a room with two beds); otherwise you may find yourself in *une chambre avec un grand lit* (oon chAMBR-avEK inh grANH LEE; a room with a double bed). You may also have to pay a **taxe de séjour** (residency tax) of 5-10F per person per night, depending on the region. Breakfast in hotels normally runs 25-40F, which should include coffee or hot chocolate and bread and/or croissants; check whether it's obligatory, since you'll probably get a better deal at a local café. Rooms in cheap hotels normally have no en suite facilities, and often not even a sink; normally facilities are to be found on the hallway. Occasionally you will have to pay extra for a hot shower (10-25F), and some very cheap hotels have no washing facilities at all; *Let's Go* notes if this is the case. Otherwise, rooms can come with a variety of add-ons: *avec WC* or *avec cabinet* means with sink and toilet, *avec douche* means with shower, and *avec salle de bain* is with a full bathroom. Most bathrooms also have a *bidet*, a low toilet-like apparatus which is intended for cleaning genitalia; no matter how desperate you are, do not use a bidet as a toilet. All French hotels must display on the back of each room's door a list showing the prices of rooms, breakfast, and any residency tax. It is illegal for them to charge you more than is shown, though you can try to bargain for a lower rate if you are staying longer than a few days.

The hotels listed by *Let's Go* are generally small, family-run establishments close to sights of interest, but France also has a number of hotel chains that cater to the budget traveler. To be found on the outskirts of most major towns, and often accessible only by car, unrated chains such as *Hôtels Formule 1*, *Étap Hôtel*, and *Hôtels Première Classe* charge about 140F for rooms for one, two, or three people. All rooms have a sink and TV, with hall showers, toilets, and telephones. When the reception is closed, you can rent a room with your credit card.

If you plan to visit a popular tourist area, especially during a festival, it is advisable to write or fax ahead for reservations. Most hotel owners will require either a deposit or a credit card number as a guarantee of your reservation: if you don't show up or stay less time than you booked for, they have the right to charge you for their loss of earnings. When in doubt, reserve for just one night; you can usually extend your stay once you arrive.

ESSENTIALS

OTHER OPTIONS

GÎTES D'ÉTAPE AND MOUNTAIN REFUGES. Gîtes d'étape are rural accommodations for cyclists, hikers, and other ramblers. They are located in less populated areas, normally on popular trails, and provide lodgings in farmhouses, cottages, and even campgrounds. Though they vary widely in price and quality, you can expect *gîtes* to provide beds, a kitchen facility, and a resident caretaker. Facilities range from single rooms and hot showers to a bare bed and hole-in-the-ground toilets; as the scouts say, be prepared. During the high season, *gîtes* in resort towns fill up fast, so reserve in advance. Averaging 60F a night and spaced along hiking trails, *gîtes* allow you to pass through for a night or stay several days, and sometimes to take advantage of guided hikes led by caretakers. Don't confuse *gîtes d'étapes* with *gîtes ruraux*, country houses available for rent by the week, or *Gîtes de France*, an organization of small hotels.

Another type of French lodging used mostly by hikers and skiers on extended treks is a **refuge,** a rustic shelter generally guarded by a caretaker moonlighting as a chief, fix-it person, and sage. *Refuges* dot the wilderness and range in price from 45-80F. Expect to pay another 80F for a hot, home-cooked meal—while you're savoring it, remember that supplies often have to be carried up by hand or mule! *Refuges* are not always guarded year-round, but the doors generally remain open throughout the seasons to accommodate hikers and skiers on the road.

CHAMBRES D'HÔTES (BED AND BREAKFAST). Many French house-owners supplement their income by letting out rooms to weary travelers. These **Chambres d'Hôtes,** or Bed and Breakfasts, range from acceptable rooms in modern townhouses to palatial accommodation in Baroque châteaux, and are priced accordingly; most cost 200-300F per night, with a few slightly lower prices as well as many edging into the stratosphere. Often rooms in old farmhouses, those restricted to public transportation may find them hard to reach; but for drivers, hikers, and bikers, they can provide a perfect base in the French countryside. For a comprehensive listing of *chambres d'hôtes* in France, write to or call **Bed & Breakfast (France),** PO box 66, Bell St., Henley-on-Thames, Oxon. RG9 1XS, UK (UK tel. 01491 57 88 03; fax 01491 41 08 06). Catalogues cost UK£7.99, IR11, NZ$38, or CDN$34; for other countries, the charge is UK£15.99. You can also call the **Association Française BAB France** (France tel. 01 34 68 83 15; fax 01 34 72 29 31). **Fleurs de Soleil** lists *chambres d'hôtes* throughout France at www.fleurs-soleil.tm.fr/index.html.

UNIVERSITY HOUSING. In many French towns, universities open their residence halls to travelers when not in session, and some do so even in term-time. These accommodations are often close to student areas—good sources for information on things to do—and are usually very clean. Getting a room may take a couple of phone calls and require advanced planning, but rates tend to be low and you'll normally get a single or double room. Look in the accommodation listings for each town to see if university accommodation is available.

HOME EXCHANGE AND RENTALS. Home exchange offers the traveler various types of homes (houses, apartments, condominiums, villas, even castles in some cases), plus the opportunity to live like a native and to cut down dramatically on accommodation fees—usually only an administration fee is paid to the matching service. On the other hand, you have to give up your own castle to someone else while you're away. Once you join or contact one of the exchange services listed below, it is then up to you to decide with whom you would like to exchange homes. Most companies have pictures of member's homes and information about the owners. A great site listing many exchange companies can be found at www.aitec.edu.au/~bwechner/Documents/Travel/Lists/HomeExchange-Clubs.html. If you're unwilling to hand your house over to strangers, **home rentals**

can still work out much cheaper than hotels for larger groups. Both home exchanges and rentals are ideal for families with children or travelers with special dietary needs.

HomeExchange, P.O. Box 30085, Santa Barbara, CA 93130. Tel. 805 898 9660; email admin@HomeExchange.com; www.homeexchange.com.

Intervac International Home Exchange, 230 bd. Voltaire, 75011 Paris. Tel. 01 43 70 21 22; fax 01 43 70 73 35; www.intervac.com.

The Invented City: International Home Exchange, 41 Sutter St., Suite 1090, San Francisco, CA 94104 (tel. 800 788 2489 in the US or 415 252 1141 elsewhere; fax 415 252 1171; email invented@aol.com; www.invented-city.com). For US$75, you get your offer listed in 1 catalog and unlimited access to the club's database containing thousands of homes for exchange.

FURTHER READING. *Campus Lodging Guide* (18th Ed., B&J Publications, US$15); *The Complete Guide to Bed and Breakfasts, Inns and Guesthouses in the US, Canada, and Worldwide,* by Pamela Lanier (Ten Speed Press, US$17).

CAMPING AND THE OUTDOORS

With over three thousand years of settled history, true wilderness in France is limited to the most inhospitable mountain peaks, and almost nowhere is more than a few kilometers from some human activity. The French are very keen campers, but it is not camping as those from the New World know it. Forget setting up your tent in some forgotten spot and cooking freshly-fished trout on a wood fire. It's illegal to camp in most public spaces, including and especially national parks, and you wouldn't want to be caught lighting your own fire, either. Instead, look forward to organized *campings* (campsites), where you'll be but one tent amongst many. Camping in France is a social rather than a solitary pursuit, and it's a great way to meet people. Most campsites have toilets, showers, and electrical outlets, though you may have to pay extra for such luxuries (10-40F); you'll often need to pay a supplement for your car, too (20-50F). Otherwise, expect to pay 50-90F per site.

USEFUL PUBLICATIONS AND WEB RESOURCES

A variety of publishers offer hiking guidebooks to meet the educational needs of novices or experts. For information about camping, hiking, and biking, write or call the publishers listed below to receive a free catalogue. Consider buying an International Camping Carnet; similar to a hostel membership card, it's required at a few campgrounds and provides discounts at others. It is available in North America from the Family Campers and RVers Association and in the UK from The Caravan Club (see below).

Automobile Association. Orders and enquiries to TBS Frating Distribution Centre, Colchester, Essex, CO7 7DW, UK (tel. 01206 25 56 78; www.theaa.co.uk). Publishes *Camping and Caravanning: Europe* (UK£9). They also offer Big Road Atlases for France.

The Caravan Club, East Grinstead House, East Grinstead, West Sussex, RH19 1UA, UK (tel. 01342 32 69 44; www.caravanclub.co.uk). Members receive a 700-page directory and handbook, discounts and a monthly magazine (£27.50).

Family Campers and RVers/National Campers and Hikers Association, Inc., 4804 Transit Rd., Bldg. #2, Depew, NY 14043 (tel. or fax 716 668 6242). Membership fee (US$25) includes their publication *Camping Today.*

The Mountaineers Books, 1001 SW Klickitat Way, #201, Seattle, WA 98134 (tel. 800 553 4453 or 206 223 6303; email alans@mountaineers.org; www.mountaineers.org). Over 400 titles on hiking (the *100 Hikes* series), biking, mountaineering, natural history, and conservation.

The **Institut Géographique National (IGN)** publishes the acclaimed **Blue Series** of 1:8000 scale maps for hikers, as well as a full range of road maps. They are sold throughout France; for more information contact their map superstore in Paris, **Éspace IGN** (tel. 01 43 98 80 00; fax 01 43 98 85 11; email espace-ign@ign.fr), 107 rue La Boétie 75008 Paris, or use the clickable map on their website at www.ign.fr/GP/adresse/. You can buy IGN maps in **Australia** from **Hema maps,** 24 Allgas Street, Slacks Creek 4127, P.O Box 2660, Logan City D.C. 4114, Brisbane (tel. 07 329 003 22; fax 07 329 004 78), in **Canada** from **Ulysse,** 4176 St Denis, Montrea, Québec H2W 2M5 (tel. 514 843 9882; fax 514 843 9448; guidly@ulysse.ca; www.ulysse.ca/), in the **UK** from World Leisure Marketing, Unit 11, Newmarket Court, Newmarket Drive, Derby DE24 8NW (tel. 01332 57 37 37; fax 01332 57 33 99; office@wlmsales.co.uk; www.map-guides.com/), and in the **USA** from Map Link Inc., 30 S. La Patera Lane, Unit #5, Santa Barbara, CA 93117 (tel. 805 692 6777; fax 805 692 6787; email billhunt@maplinkinc.com).

CAMPING AND HIKING EQUIPMENT

Good camping equipment is both sturdy and light. Camping equipment is generally more expensive in France than in North America.

Sleeping Bag: Most good sleeping bags are rated by "season," or the lowest outdoor temperature at which they will keep you warm ("summer" means 30-40°F or 0-4°C at night and "four-season" or "winter" often means below 0°F or -18°C). Sleeping bags are made either of down (warmer and lighter, but expensive and miserable when wet) or synthetic material (heavier, more durable, and warmer when wet). Prices vary, but might range from US$80-210 for a summer synthetic to US$250-300 for a good down winter bag. **Sleeping bag pads,** including foam pads (US$10-20) and air mattresses (US$15-50) cushion your back and neck and insulate you from the ground. Bring a **"stuff sack"** or plastic bag to store your sleeping bag and keep it dry.

Tent: The best tents are free-standing, with their own frames and suspension systems; they set up quickly and only require staking in high winds. Low-profile dome tents are the best all-around. When pitched, their internal space is almost entirely usable, which means little unnecessary bulk. Tent sizes can be somewhat misleading: two people *can* fit in a two-person tent, but will find life more pleasant in a four-person. If you're traveling by car, go for the bigger tent, but if you're hiking, stick with a smaller tent that weighs no more than 5-6lbs (2-3kg). Good two-person tents start at US$90, four-person tents at US$300. Seal the seams of your tent with waterproofer, and make sure it has a rain fly. Other tent accessories include a **battery-operated lantern,** a **plastic ground-cloth,** and a **nylon tarp.**

Backpack: If you intend to do a lot of hiking, you should have a frame backpack. For a run-down on different types of pack, prices, and choosing a pack, see **packing,** p. 49. Any serious backpacking requires a pack of at least 4000 cubic inches (16 liters). Allow an additional 500 cubic inches (2 liters) for your sleeping bag in internal-frame packs. A **waterproof backpack cover** will prove invaluable. Otherwise, plan to store all of your belongings in plastic bags inside your backpack.

Boots: Be sure to wear hiking boots with good **ankle support** which are appropriate for the terrain you plan to hike. Your boots should fit snugly and comfortably over one or two wool socks and a thin liner sock. Breaking in boots properly before setting out requires wearing them for several weeks; doing so will spare you from painful and debilitating blisters.

Other Necessities: Raingear in two pieces, a top and pants, is far superior to a poncho. **Synthetics,** like polypropylene tops, socks, and long underwear, along with a pile jacket, will keep you warm even when wet. When camping in autumn, winter, or spring, bring along a **"space blanket,"** which helps you to retain your body heat and doubles as a groundcloth (US$5-15). Plastic **canteens** or water bottles keep water cooler than metal ones do and are virtually shatter- and leak-proof. Large, collapsible **water sacks** will significantly improve your lot in primitive campgrounds and weigh practically nothing when empty, though they are bulky and heavy when full. Bring **water-purification tablets** for when you can't boil water, unless you are willing to shell out money for a portable water-purification system. Since virtually everywhere in France forbids fires and the gathering of firewood, you'll need a **camp stove.** The classic Coleman stove starts at about US$40. You will need to purchase a **fuel bottle** and fill it with propane to operate it. A **first aid kit, swiss army knife, insect repellent, calamine lotion,** and **waterproof matches** or a **lighter** are other essential camping items.

The mail-order/online companies listed below offer lower prices than many retail stores, but a visit to a local camping or outdoors store will give you a good sense of items' look and weight.

Discount Camping, 880 Main North Rd., Pooraka, South Australia 5095, Australia (tel. 08 8262 3399; fax 08 8260 6240; www.discountcamping.com.au).

Mountain Designs, P.O. Box 1472, Fortitude Valley, Queensland 4006, Australia (tel. 07 3252 8894; fax 07 3252 4569; www.mountaindesign.com.au).

Eastern Mountain Sports (EMS), 327 Jaffrey Rd., Peterborough, NH 03458 (tel. 888 463 6367 or 603 924 7231; www.emsonline.com; email emsmail@emsonline.com) Call the above number for the branch nearest you.

Campmor, P.O. Box 700, Upper Saddle River, NJ 07458-0700 (US tel. 888 226 7667, outside US call 201 825 8300; email customer-service@campmor.com; www.campmor.com).

L.L. Bean, Freeport, ME 04033-0001 (US/Canada tel. 800 441 5713; UK tel. 0800 962 954; elsewhere, call US (country code:1) 207 552 6878; www.llbean.com). If your purchase doesn't meet your expectations, they'll replace or refund it.

YHA Adventure Shop, 14 Southampton St., London, WC2E 7HA, UK (tel. 020 7836 8541). The main branch of one of Britain's largest outdoor equipment suppliers.

WILDERNESS SAFETY

Stay warm, stay dry, stay hydrated. The vast majority of dangerous wilderness situations result from a breach of this simple dictum. On any hike, however brief, you should pack enough equipment to keep you alive should disaster befall. This includes **raingear, hat** and **mittens,** a **first-aid kit,** a **reflector,** a **whistle, high energy food,** and extra **water.** Dress in warm layers of **synthetic materials** designed for the outdoors, or **wool.** Pile fleece jackets and Gore-Tex raingear are excellent choices. **Never rely on cotton for warmth**. This "death cloth" will be absolutely useless should it get wet. Make sure to check all equipment for any defects before setting out, and see **Camping and Hiking Equipment,** above, for more information.

Check **weather forecasts** and pay attention to the skies when hiking. Weather patterns can change suddenly. Whenever possible, let someone know when and where you are going hiking, either a friend, your hostel, a park ranger, or a local hiking organization. Do not attempt a hike beyond your ability—you may be endangering your life. See **Health,** p. 44 for information about outdoor ailments as well as basic medical concerns and first-aid.

KEEPING IN TOUCH
MAIL

SENDING MAIL TO, AND RECEIVING MAIL IN, FRANCE

Airmail letters under 1 oz. between the US and France take 4 to 7 days and cost US$1.00. Letters from Canada cost CDN$0.95 for 20g. Allow at least 5 working days from Australia (postage AUS$1.00 for up to 20g) and 3 days from Britain (postage UK£0.30 for up to 20g). Envelopes should be marked *"par avion"* (airmail) to avoid having letters sent by sea.

Mail can be held for pick-up through **Poste Restante** (French for General Delivery) to almost any city or town with a post office. Address letters to: <u>DOE</u>, Jane; Poste Restante: Recette Principale; [5-digit postal code] TOWN; FRANCE; mark the envelope HOLD. *Let's Go* lists post offices and postal codes; we also note when the Poste Restante has a different postal code, or if it sent to a different branch to that listed. The mail will go to the central post office, unless you specify a branch office by address or postal code. As a rule, it's best to use the main post office in the area, and mail may be sent there regardless of what is written on the envelope. When picking up your mail, bring a passport. There is generally a small charge per item to pick up. If the clerks insist that there is nothing for you, have them check under your first name as well. Note that post offices will not accept courier service deliveries for Poste Restante.

If regular airmail is too slow, **Federal Express** (US tel. for international operator 800 247 4747; UK 0800 123 800; Australia 13 26 10; Ireland 1800 535 800; South Africa 011 923 8000; New Zealand 0800 733 339) can get a letter from New York to Paris in two days for a whopping US$25.50; rates among non-US locations are prohibitively expensive (overnight from London to Paris, for example, costs upwards of UK$36). Using a **US Global Priority Mail** flat-rate envelope, a letter from New York would arrive within four days and would cost US$5.

Surface mail is by far the cheapest and slowest way to send mail. It takes one to three months to cross the Atlantic and two to four to cross the Pacific—appropriate for sending large quantities of items you won't need to see for a while. When ordering books and materials from abroad, always include one or two **International Reply Coupons (IRCs)**—a way of providing the postage to cover delivery. IRCs should be available from your local post office and those abroad (US$1.05).

SENDING MAIL HOME FROM FRANCE

Aerogrammes, printed sheets that fold into envelopes and travel via airmail, are available at post offices. Mark it **par avion** (airmail) if it is not already. Most post offices will charge exorbitant fees or simply refuse to send aerogrammes with enclosures. Airmail from France to the USA averages 7 to 10 days; within Europe letters can arrive in as little as 3 days. To send a **letter** to anywhere in the EU (including within France) costs 3F for up to 20g, to South Africa 3.90F, to North America costs 4.40F, and to Australia and New Zealand 5.20F.

TELEPHONES

CALLING FRANCE FROM HOME

To call France direct from home, dial:

1. The **international access code** of your home country. These are listed in the **Appendix** (p. 726).

2. 33 (France's country code).

3. The French number **without the first zero**.

Thus if a French number was listed as 01 23 45 67 89, you would dial the international access code followed by 33 1 23 45 67 89.

CALLING HOME FROM FRANCE

A **calling card** is the most convenient way to call home from abroad, but it's not always cheaper. There are two basic types. In the first, the card is issued free or for a small charge, but calls are billed either to your home account or to the person you are calling. It's lucky that you won't see the bill until you get home, as calls with these cards can be ruinously expensive. On no account use them for calls inside France or to other countries than the issuing one, since you'll probably be charged for a call back to your home country and then out again to the person you're calling. Far cheaper are prepaid cards, in which you buy a card which contains a certain amount of calling credits. The former is more convenient and better if you don't expect to be using it much, but the latter is often cheaper for long calls.

BILLED CARDS. Calls are billed either collect or to your account. **MCI World-Phone** also provides access to MCI's Traveler's Assist, which gives legal and medical advice, exchange rate information, and translation services. Other phone companies provide similar services to travelers. **To obtain a calling card** from your national telecommunications service before you leave home, contact the appropriate company for your country. The second number given is the local access number to dial for an operator when in France.

Australia: Telstra **Australia Direct** (tel. 13 22 00; in France 0 800 99 00 61).

Canada: Bell Canada **Canada Direct** (tel. 800 565 4708; in France 0 800 99 00 16 or 0 800 99 02 16).

Ireland: Telecom Éireann **Ireland Direct** (tel. 0800 250 250; in France 0 800 99 03 53).

New Zealand: Telecom New Zealand (tel. 0800 000 000; in France 0 800 99 00 64).

South Africa: Telkom South Africa (tel. 09 03; in France 0 800 99 00 27).

UK: British Telecom **BT Direct** (tel. 0800 34 51 44; in France 0 800 99 02 44).

US: AT&T (tel. 888 288 4685; in France 0 800 99 00 11); **Sprint** (tel. 800 877 4646; in France 0 800 99 00 87); or **MCI** (tel. 800 444 4141; in France 0 800 99 00 19).

PREPAID CARDS. You can buy prepaid cards at home or in France which can be used anywhere in the world; the number of varieties available is bewildering but beware that the cheaper the calls offered, the more likely you are to have trouble getting through. Most major telecommunications companies issue them too; these are generally widely available in kiosks and travel stores. Common prepaid cards you can buy at home include Telstra **PhoneAway** (Australia), Telecom Éireann **Ireland Direct Prepaid,** AT&T **Global Prepaid Card** (USA), Telecom New Zealand **talkaway,** and Canada Direct **Hello!** You can also buy prepaid cards in France; the most popular is the **Carte Intercall Monde,** available in most *tabacs*. These are available in 50F and 100F denominations, and give up to 75% off standard French international call rates.

DIRECT DIAL. If you must use a pay phone, prepare yourself in advance with a fully charged **télécarte** (see **calling within France,** below), and be ready to watch the units drop. Calls are cheaper between 7pm and 8am Monday to Friday, noon-midnight Saturday and all Sunday. Expect to pay about 3F per minute to the UK, Ireland, and North America, and about 10F per minute to Australia and New Zealand. Use only public **France Télécom** payphones, as private ones often charge more. Although convenient, in-room hotel calls invariably include an arbitrary and sky-high surcharge (as much as US$10).

If you do dial direct, you must first insert a *télécarte*, then dial 00 (the international access code for France), the country code, and then the number of your home. **Country codes** include: Australia 61, Ireland 353, New Zealand 64, South Africa 27, UK 44, US and Canada 1. Note that when calling the UK from abroad you should drop the first zero of the area code.

CALLING COLLECT. The expensive alternative to dialing direct or using a calling card is using an international operator to place a **collect call** (also called reverse-charges; *faire un appel en PCV* in French). An English-speaking operator from your home nation can be reached by dialing the appropriate service provider listed above, and they will typically place a collect call even if you don't possess one of their phone cards.

CALLING WITHIN FRANCE

French public payphones only accept stylish microchip-toting phonecards called **Télécartes**; some payphones in Paris also take credit cards. *Télécartes* are available in 50 unit (41F) and 120 unit (98F) denominations; a unit lasts about a minute for a local call. A small digital screen on the phone will issue a series of simple commands; press the small button marked with a British flag to get instructions in

> ## I'LL TRADE YOU MY '52 MANTLE FOR YOUR '88 GERARD LONGUET
> If you're going to be in France for any length of time, you'll eventually give up the futile search for coin-operated telephones and invest in a *télécarte*. These cards, of course, only last so long, so where is the *télécarte* graveyard? The answer is simple but shocking: collectors' albums. The ads and artwork on the cards turn some designs into valuable commodities—so valuable that an entire *télécarte* collection business has developed around the credit-card sized *chef d'oeuvres*. Common and uncommon cards may be sold in stores for 5-10F each, while rare specimens reside under protective covering in acrylic cases. The condition of a card, of course, drastically affects its value, while the number of call-enabling *unités* is irrelevant. A 1987-88 carte by Gerard Longuet is one of the gems in the *télécarte* collector's crown. Only 40 exist, and an unblemished one will net you 34,000F. For the real prize, seek out the November 1988 card "Les Boxeurs," with artwork by Gilles Chagny. There are 100 out there, but only one is signed by the artist. Maybe it's down at your feet right now as you make your call—it's worth checking; if it *is* there, you've just stumbled across a cool 60,000F.

English. If none exists, proceed with caution, as French payphones are as unforgiving and infuriating as the bureaucracy they serve. *Décrochez* means pick up; you will then be asked to *patientez* (wait) before you can put your card in. Only when you are told *numérotez* or *composez* should you dial. *Racrochez* means "hang up," and this generally means you've done something wrong. If you want to make another call, don't hang up at the end of the first one; just press the green button. French phone boxes also normally display a complicated wall chart showing phone rates depending on the time of day, the day of the week, and the place you are calling. In very remote rural areas, as well as in most bars, hotels, and cafés, you will still find coin operated telephones; be warned that privately owned pay phones can be far more expensive.

EMAIL

Email is the fastest and cheapest way to send messages to friends around the world. Most large towns in France have a cybercafé; check the 'Practical Information' section of town listings to see if there is one. Rates and speed of connection vary widely; occasionally there are free terminals in technologically-oriented museums or exhibition spaces. **Cybercafé Guide** (www.cyberiacafe.net/cyberia/guide/ccafe.htm#working_france) can help you find cybercafés in France.

To send and receive email you will need an email account. Free, web-based email providers include **Hotmail** (www.hotmail.com), **RocketMail** (www.rocketmail.com), and **Yahoo! Mail** (www.yahoo.com).

Travelers who have the luxury of a laptop with them can use a **modem** to call your home internet service provider; beware that many hotel switchboards use the **PBX** system, which will fry most modems. Long-distance phone cards specifically intended for such calls can defray normally high phone charges. Check with your long-distance phone provider to see if they offer this option.

GETTING TO FRANCE

BY PLANE

When it comes to flights, a little effort can save you a bundle. If your plans are flexible enough to deal with the restrictions, courier fares are the cheapest. Tickets bought from consolidators and standby seating are also good deals, but last-minute specials, airfare wars, and charter flights often beat these fares. The key is to hunt around, to be flexible, and to persistently ask about discounts. Students, seniors, those under 26, and those who plan ahead should never pay full price.

DETAILS AND TIPS

Timing: Prices to France peak between June and September, while Easter and Christmas are also expensive periods in which to travel. Most cheap fares require a Saturday night stay. Flexibility is usually not an option for the budget traveler; traveling with an "open return" ticket can be pricier than fixing a return date when buying the ticket and paying later to change it. Most budget tickets, once bought, allow no date or route changes to be made; student tickets sometimes allow date changes for a price.

Route: Round-trip flights are the cheapest; "open-jaw" (arriving in and departing from different cities) and round-the-world, or RTW, flights are pricier but reasonable alternatives. Patching one-way flights together is the least economical way to travel. Flights between capital cities or regional hubs will offer the most competitive fares.

Checking in: Whenever flying internationally, pick up tickets for international flights well in advance of the departure date, and reconfirm by phone within 72 hours of departure. Most airlines require that passengers arrive at the airport at least two hours before departure. However, for scheduled flights departing from an EU country, you are entitled to full compensation if a flight is overbooked and you have a confirmed ticket (indicated by an 'OK' in the relevant box on the ticket), provided that you checked in on time. One carry-on item (max 5kg) and two pieces of checked baggage weighing up to 60kg total is the norm for non-courier intercontinental flights; for flights within Europe, the checked baggage allowance is normally 20-30kg, regardless of the number of pieces.

Fares: Round-trip fares to Paris from the US range from US$200-400 (during the off-season) to US$200-550 (during the summer); fares to other cities tend to be much higher. From Australia, count on paying between AUS$1600 and AUS$3000, depending on the season. From New Zealand, fares start at about NZ$5000 and climb to $9000. Flights from the UK to France are a comparative snip at UK£80-140 for London-Paris, while a return flight from Dublin to Paris can cost as little as IR£120 return. For flights between the UK or Ireland and France, see **Budget Airlines,** p. 60.

BUDGET AND STUDENT TRAVEL AGENCIES

A knowledgeable agent specializing in flights to Europe can make your life easy and help you save, too, but agents may not spend the time to find you the lowest possible fare—they get paid on commission. Students, teachers, and under-26ers holding **ISIC, ITIC, or IYTC cards** (see **Identification,** p. 34), respectively, qualify for discounts from student travel agencies.

Campus/Usit Youth and Student Travel. The head office is at 52 Grosvenor Gardens, London SW1W 0AG (tel. 0870 240 1010). Other offices include: 19-21 Aston Quay, O'Connell Bridge, Dublin 2 (tel. 01 677 8117; fax 01 679 8833); New York Student Center, 895 Amsterdam Ave., New York, NY, 10025 (tel. 212 663 5435; email usitny@aol.com). Additional offices in Cork, Galway, Limerick, Waterford, Coleraine, Derry, Belfast, and Greece.

Council Travel (www.counciltravel.com) has offices in most major US cities and universities, as well as many locations abroad. In US call 800 2 COUNCIL (226 8624) to locate your nearest branch. To locate an office in the **UK** contact 28A Poland St. (Oxford Circus), **London,** W1V 3DB (tel. 020 7287 3337). In **France,** call 01 44 41 89 89.

CTS Travel, 44 Goodge St., **London** W1 (tel. 020 7636 00 31; fax 020 7637 5328; email ctsinfo@ctstravel.com.uk).

STA Travel, 6560 Scottsdale Rd. #F100, Scottsdale, AZ 85253 (US tel. 800 777 0112 fax 602 922 0793; www.sta-travel.com). STA caters to students and youth with over 150 offices worldwide, mostly on or near university campuses. **US** offices include: **Los Angeles,** CA 90046 (tel. 323 93 8722); 10 Downing St., **New York,** NY 10014 (tel. 212 627 3111); 2401 Pennsylvania Ave., Ste. G, **Washington, D.C.** 20037 (tel. 202 887 0912). In the **UK,** 6 Wrights Ln., **London** W8 6TA (tel. 020 7938 47 11). In **New Zealand,** 10 High St., **Auckland** (tel. 09 309 04 58). In **Australia,** 222 Faraday St., **Melbourne** VIC 3053 (tel. 03 9349 2411).

Travel CUTS (Canadian Universities Travel Services Limited), 187 College St., Toronto, Ont. M5T 1P7 (tel. 416 979 2406; fax 416 979 8167; www.travelcuts.com). 40 offices in **Canada.** Also in the **UK,** 295-A Regent St., **London** W1R 7YA (tel. 020 7255 19 44).

Wasteels, Victoria Station, London, UK SW1V 1JT (tel. 020 7834 70 66; fax 020 7630 7628; www.wasteels.dk/uk). European chain with 203 locations, many in France.

ESSENTIALS

COMMERCIAL AIRLINES

The commercial airlines' lowest regular offer is the **APEX** (Advance Purchase Excursion) fare, which provides confirmed reservations and allows "open-jaw" tickets. Generally, reservations must be made 7-21 days in advance, with 7- to 14-day minimum and up to 90-day maximum-stay limits, and hefty cancellation and change penalties (fees rise in summer). Book peak-season APEX fares early, since by May you will have a hard time getting the departure date you want.

Although APEX fares are probably not the cheapest possible fares, they will give you a sense of price from which to measure other bargains. Specials advertised in newspapers may be cheaper but have more restrictions and fewer available seats. Popular carriers include:

Icelandair (US tel. 800 223 5500; www.centrum.is/icelandair) has last-minute offers and standby fares on some flights between North America and Europe. Reservations must be made within three days of departure.

Air France (tel. 0 802 802 802 in France; from abroad call (country code: 33) 8 36 64 08 02; www.airfrance.com) is France's national airline, connecting France to the world with 162 flights per week to the US alone.

United Airlines (US tel. 800 538 2929 for international reservations; www.ual.com). Mammoth US carrier offers last-minute special E-fares deals available only online.

TowerAir (tel. 800 348 6937; www.towerair.com) offers flights from the US to Paris.

BUYING TICKETS OVER THE INTERNET. There are many advantages to browsing for travel bargains on the Web. Many airlines sites offer special last-minute deals to internet customers, and you can spend as long as you like exploring options without driving your travel agent insane. Make sure that the site uses a secure server before handing over any credit card details. Useful sites include **STA online** (www.sta-travel-com), for student-rate flights and insurance, and **Travelocity** (www.travelocity.com), which offers a comprehensive range of travel services, including flights and car hire. At **Priceline** (www.priceline.com) you choose how much you want to pay, though you are obliged to buy the ticket if it finds one; be prepared for antisocial hours and odd routes.

BUDGET AIRLINES

UK and Irish residents can take advantage of the growing number of no-frills carriers operating in Europe. In return for giving up free in-flight food and drink, and a few inches of legroom, these offer flights to a number of regional destinations at prices that often beat rail. To keep costs down, they only accept direct booking by phone or internet; you won't find them quoted by any travel agent.

easyJet (UK tel. 0870 6 000 000; www.easyjet.co.uk) flies from London and Liverpool to Nice up to four times per day from UK£48 one-way (including tax).

Ryanair (Ireland tel. 01 609 7800; UK 0870 333 1250; www.ryanair.co.ie) flies from Dublin and Glasgow to Paris, and from London to Dinard, Biarritz, Carcassonne, and St-Étienne. Prices start at UK£29.99 one-way.

Virgin Express (UK tel. 020 7744 0004; Ireland tel. 061 70 44 70; France tel. 0800 528 528; www.virgin-express.com) connects London and Shannon to Nice via Brussels from UK£39 one-way.

OTHER CHEAP ALTERNATIVES

AIR COURIER FLIGHTS. Couriers help transport cargo on international flights by guaranteeing delivery of the baggage claim slips from the company to a representative overseas. Generally, couriers must travel light (carry-ons only) and deal with complex restrictions on their flight. Most flights are round-trip only with short fixed-length stays (usually one week) and a limit of a single ticket per issue. Most of these flights also operate only out of the biggest cities, like New York. Generally, you must be over 21 (in some cases 18), have a valid passport, and procure your own visa, if necessary. Groups such as the **Air Courier Association** (tel. 800 282 1202; www.aircourier.org) and the **International Association of Air Travel Couriers,** 220 South Dixie Hwy., P.O. Box 1349, Lake Worth, FL 33460 (tel. 561 582 8320; email iaatc@courier.org; www.courier.org) provide their members with lists of opportunities and courier brokers worldwide for an annual fee. For more information, consult *Air Courier Bargains* by Kelly Monaghan (The Intrepid Traveler, US$15) or the *Courier Air Travel Handbook* by Mark Field (Perpetual Press, US$10).

CHARTER FLIGHTS. Charters are flights a tour operator contracts with an airline to fly extra loads of passengers during peak season. Charters can sometimes be cheaper than flights on scheduled airlines, some operate nonstop, and restrictions on minimum advance-purchase and minimum stay are more lenient. However, charter flights fly less frequently than major airlines, make refunds particularly difficult, and are almost always fully booked. Schedules and itineraries may also change or be cancelled at the last moment (as late as 48 hours before the trip, and without a full refund), and check-in, boarding, and baggage claim are often much slower. As always, pay with a credit card if you can, and consider travel insurance against trip interruption.

  Discount clubs and **fare brokers** offer members savings on last-minute charter and tour deals. Study their contracts closely; you don't want to end up with an unwanted overnight layover. **Travelers Advantage,** Stamford, CT (tel. 800 548 1116; www.travelersadvantage.com; US$60 annual fee includes discounts, newsletters, and cheap flight directories), specializes in European travel and tour packages.

STANDBY FLIGHTS. To travel standby, you will need considerable flexibility in the dates and cities of your arrival and departure. Companies that specialize in standby flights don't sell tickets but rather the promise that you will get to, or near, your destination within a certain window of time (anywhere from 1-5 days). You may only receive a monetary refund if all available flights which depart within your date-range from the specified region are full, but future travel credit is always available. Do not be surprised if you are stranded for some time, especially during the tourist high season.

  Carefully read agreements with any company offering standby flights, as tricky fine print can leave you in the lurch. To check on a company's service record, call the Better Business Bureau of New York City (tel. 212 533 6200). It is difficult to receive refunds, and clients' vouchers will not be honored when an airline fails to receive payment in time.

  Airhitch, 2641 Broadway, 3rd Fl., **New York,** NY 10025 (tel. 800 326 2009 or 212 864 2000; fax 212 864 5489; www.airhitch.org) and **Los Angeles,** CA (tel. 310 726 5000). In Europe, the flagship office is in **Paris** (tel. 01 47 00 16 30). Flights to Europe from the Northeast (US$159 one-way), the West Coast ($239), the Northwest ($239), the Midwest ($209), and the Southeast ($189). Also travel within Europe ($79-$139).

TICKET CONSOLIDATORS. Ticket consolidators, or **"bucket shops,"** buy unsold tickets in bulk from commercial airlines and sell them at discounted rates. The best place to look is in the Sunday travel section of any major newspaper, where many bucket shops place tiny ads. Call quickly, as availability is typically extremely limited. Not all bucket shops are reliable establishments, so insist on a receipt that gives full details of restrictions, refunds, and tickets, and pay by credit card. For more information, check the website **Consolidators FAQ** (www.travel-library.com/air-travel/consolidators.html) or the book *Consolidators: Air Travel's Bargain Basement*, by Kelly Monaghan (Intrepid Traveler, US$8).

FURTHER RESOURCES: BY PLANE

WEBSITES. *Air Traveler's Handbook* (www.cs.cmu.edu/afs/cs.cmu.edu/user/mkant/Public/Travel/airfare.html); *TravelHUB* (www.travel-hub.com), a directory of travel agents that includes a database of fares from over 500 consolidators.

BOOKS. *The Worldwide Guide to Cheap Airfares*, by Michael McColl (Insider, US$15); *Discount Airfares: The Insider's Guide*, by George Hobart (Priceless, US$14); *The Official Airline Guide*, an expensive tome available in libraries, has flight schedules, fares, and reservation numbers.

BY BUS

For British travelers buses are the cheapest way of getting to France, with return fares starting around UK£50 including ferry/chunnel transport. On the downside, buses take far longer than trains and planes and are more susceptible to delays.

Europe's largest international coach operator is **Eurolines,** 4 Cardiff Rd., Luton, Beds. L41 1PP (tel. 08705 143 219); in London, 52 Grosvenor Gardens, London SW1V 1BS (tel. 020 7950 1661; fax 020 7950 1662; email welcome@euro-lines.uk.com; www.eurolines.co.uk). A **Eurolines Pass** offers unlimited 30-day (under 26 and over 60 UK£199, 26-60 UK £229) or 60-day (UK£249/£279) travel between 30 major cities. Return fares between London and Paris start at UK£49. Eurolines also offers **Euro Explorers,** seven travel loops throughout Europe with set fares and itineraries.

BY BOAT

Ferries across the English Channel *(La Manche)* link France to England and Ireland. The shortest route, between Dover and Calais, is also the most popular with departures every hour. Interestingly, in recent years the journey time has actually increased from an hour to an hour and a half, as ferry companies try to tempt passengers into spending more money on board; their giant "super-ferries" are little more than floating malls with a passenger business on the side. Catering to claustrophobes in a hurry, the fastest non-tunnel crossings are provided by Hoverspeed, with hovercraft and catamaran services. Many people in England (and everyone in Ireland) who holiday in the west of France choose to take longer crossings to Brittany and Normandy, and Le Havre has the fastest road connections to Paris. Take the longer crossings overnight and you can awake refreshed and ready to start your day in France. All the ferries cater both to car and foot passengers, and French ports all have excellent rail and autoroute connections to the national networks. The following details are based on **one-way** trips; for most operators have special fares for fixed-period returns.

P&O Stena Line: Tel. 0990 980 980 (UK); 08 02 01 00 20 (France); www.posl.com. **Dover-Calais:** every 45 minutes 7am-1am and hourly through the night. Foot passengers UK£24; car with 2 people UK£105-143; car and up to 8 passengers UK£108-148.

SeaFrance: Tel. 08705 711 711 (UK); www.seafrance.co.uk. **Dover-Calais:** 16 departures daily. Foot passengers UK£15; car and driver UK£80; UK£1 extra car passenger.

Hoverspeed: Reservations and bookings tel. 08705 240 241 (UK); 03 21 46 14 54 (France). High speed hovercraft and catamaran services. **Dover-Calais:** 35-50min., 12-

20 per day. Foot passengers UK£25-30; car and driver UK£104-140; car and 2 passengers UK£105-145. **Folkestone-Boulogne:** 55 minutes, 3-4 daily. Foot passengers UK£25, car and driver UK£94-130; car and 2 passengers UK£95-135. **Newhaven-Dieppe:** 2hr., 2-3 per day. Foot passengers UK£25, car and driver UK£114-153, car and 2 passengers UK£115-160.

P&O European ferries: Tel. 0870 2424 999 (UK); 01 44 51 00 51 (France); www.poef.com. **Portsmouth-Le Havre:** 2-3 per day Jan. 1-Dec. 23; special schedule Dec. 24-31. **Portsmouth-Cherbourg:** 5-7 per day Mar. 20-Dec. 23; 1 per day Jan. 1-Mar. 19; special schedule Dec. 24-31. Both 5½hr., 8hr. at night. Foot passenger UK£18-32, car and 2 people UK£78-142, extra person UK£7. The high-speed Superstar Express also operates between Portsmouth and Cherbourg (2¾hr.); call for details.

Brittany ferries: Tel. 0870 90 12 400 (UK); 08 03 82 88 28 (France); www.brittanyferries.co.uk. **Portsmouth-Caen:** 6hr., 1-3 per day, 140-290F, 410-1280F with car. **Portsmouth-St-Malo:** 8¾hr., 1-2 per day, none F during low season; foot passengers 150-320F, 50F extra for bikes in high season, 480-1460F with car. **Plymouth-Roscoff:** 6hr., 1 per week during low season, 1-3 per day otherwise; foot passengers 140-300F, 50F extras for bike in high season, 440-1340F with car. **Poole-Cherbourg:** 4¼hr., 1-2 per day, none on weekends during low season; foot passengers 140-290F, 50F extra for bike in high season, 410-1280F with car. **Cork-Roscoff:** 14hr.; foot passengers 340-650F, 100-150F extra for bike, 1040-2770F with car. 10% student discount on all standard fares. Special prices available for roundtrip tickets with a set return date.

Irish Ferries: Tel. 01 638 3333 (Ireland); 01 42 66 90 90 (France); www.irishferries.ie. Summer services **Rosslare-Cherbourg** and **Rosslare-Roscoff;** destination alternates every 2 days. Foot passengers IR£45-85, students and seniors IR£41-71; car and two passengers IR£129-309; additional passengers IR£5-32. Cabins from IR£26.

BY CHANNEL TUNNEL

Though still dogged by huge debts, the Channel Tunnel is increasing in popularity every year as people overcome their fear of traveling 27 miles under the sea. Undoubtedly the fastest and most convenient, yet least scenic route from England to France, the Chunnel offers two types of passenger service. **Eurostar** is the high-speed train which links London to Paris and Brussels, with stops at Ashford in England and Calais and Lille in France; **Le Shuttle** is a drive-on train service which ferries cars and coaches between Folkestone and Calais.

Eurostar: Reservations tel. 01233 61 75 75 (UK); 01 49 70 01 75 (France); www.eurostar.co.uk. Eurostar tickets can also be bought at most major travel agents. **London-Paris:** 3hr., 18-23 departures daily; roundtrip fares UK£249 standard, under 25 UK£79, over 60 UK£119, child (4-11) UK£55; restricted fares from UK£79. Fares slightly lower to **Lille** (2hr., 9-12 per day) and **Calais** (1½hr., 3-5 per day). 1 per day to **Disneyland Paris;** fares slightly higher. Slightly fewer departures from Ashford; fares are same as for London departures.

Le Shuttle: Tel. 0800 096 9992 (UK); 03 21 00 61 00 (France); www.eurotunnel.co.uk. 20min., 1-3 departures per hour. Services run throughout the night. Roundtrip prices for car and all passengers: day UK£110-150; economy (open) UK£219-299; minibreaks (5 day return) UK£139-195.

GETTING AROUND FRANCE

Most travelers take advantage of France's comprehensive rail system to get around, since its network of high-speed services and local trains connect all but the most minor towns. In some areas buses fill in gaps in service, but where the bus and train compete along the same route the bus is normally only marginally cheaper and somewhat slower—though over short distances buses can be faster than slow local trains. While France is also blessed with an extremely efficient and well-maintained network of roads, high *autoroute* tolls and expensive gasoline can make driving more expensive than trains for one or two people, even without including the price of renting a car. However, a car will offer greater freedom to explore the countryside, and you will no longer be at the whim of timetables designed primarily for local needs.

To buy a one-way ticket for a train, bus, or plane in France, ask for **un billet aller-simple;** for a roundtrip ticket, request **un billet aller-retour.** Roundtrip fares are often cheaper than two one-ways.

HOW TO USE TRANSPORTATION LISTINGS: CENTER-OUT.
Let's Go employs a center-out principle for transportation listings: from each town we give details only on how to get to towns of similar or greater importance. So if you're in a big city and we don't list a bus or train to nearby towns, don't despair— the information you're looking for will be in the transportation information for the towns themselves.

BY PLANE

Only real high-flyers get around France by plane. With most major cities linked by high-speed rail lines, flying really doesn't save any time once you've counted getting to out-of-the-way airports, checking in, taxiing around runways, waiting for luggage, and then getting from the arrival airport into the city. The one exception is getting to **Corsica** and back; frequent services from Nice, Marseille, and Paris to Ajaccio and Bastia offer serious competition to 10-hour ferry crossings. See **Corsica, Getting There,** p. 330, for details; expect to pay about US$100 round-trip from **Nice** to Corsica, or US$150 from **Paris.**

BY BOAT

FERRIES. Aside from the many coastal islands dotted around the French seaboard, the only time you're likely to want to take a ferry within France is to get to Corsica and back. While far, far slower than flying (expect a 7- to 12-hour trip), and barely any cheaper, ferries offer a relaxing break from endless sights, and make a great place to meet people. By traveling overnight, you won't waste any time, either. Expect to pay about 600F (US$100) roundtrip per person and 200-600F per car. There is also a high-speed hydrofoil service from Nice to Calvi and Bastia, which takes about 3 hours. For details see **Corsica: Getting There,** p. 330.

RIVERBOATS. France has over 8500km of navigable rivers and canals, and every year thousands take advantage of them for relaxing vacations spent meandering through the French countryside. It's possible to boat from the English channel right through to the Mediterranean, though this takes planning and experience. For details of regulations get the French Government Tourist Office to send you a copy of their pamphlet *Boating on the Waterways.* For a list of companies renting out boats and organizing waterborne vacations, contact the **Syndicat National des Louers de Bateaux de Plaisance** (tel. 01 44 37 04 00; fax 01 45 77 21 88), Port de la Bourdonnais, 75007 Paris, or check out the *Maison de la France* website on www.francetourism.com/activities/boatrent.htm.

BY TRAIN

SNCF HOTLINE | Tel. **08 36 35 35 35** for timetable info and reservations.

The French national railway company, **SNCF,** operates one of the most efficient transportation systems in the world; their **TGVs** *(Train à grande vitesse,* or high-speed train) are the fastest trains in the world. Many high speed and intercity services require a supplement to be paid in addition to the regular ticket price; railcard holders must generally pay these too. If you're not in a hurry, you can take the slower **Rapide** service; local trains are slowest of all and confusingly called **Express.** Trains, however, are not always safe; keep your valuables on your person. For long trips make sure you are on the correct carriage, as trains are sometimes split to two different destinations. Towns listed in parentheses on French train schedules require a change of train.

Even a ticket or railpass does not guarantee you a seat on a train; during busy periods it's advisable to buy a **reservation** for a small extra cost—these are required for TGV services. For overnight travel, a tight, open bunk called a **couchette** is an affordable luxury (80F). These are mixed, with up to six people in triple-stacked bunks per compartment, so be prepared to sleep in your day clothes. Both seat and couchette reservations can be made by a travel agent or in person at the train station. TGV reservations can be made up to a few minutes before departure; for other services reserve before noon for departures after 5pm, and before 8pm the previous day for departures before 5pm.

 COMPOSTEZ! Before you board a train, you must validate your ticket by having it *composté* (stamped with the date and time) by one of the orange machines found near platforms. Otherwise, you'll be treated as a fare-dodging criminal.

RAILPASSES

Ideally, a railpass would allow you to jump on any train in the specified zone, go wherever you want whenever you want, and change your plans at will for a set length of time. In practice, it's not so simple; you must still wait to pay for supplements, seat reservations, and couchette reservations. More importantly, railpasses don't always pay off. France has a bevy of different discount fares (see **Discount Rail Tickets,** p. 66), and you should be able to get away without paying full-price. For ballpark estimates, consult the SNCF website for prices of point-to-point tickets, add them up, and compare with railpass prices. Prices listed below are for second-class travel; first-class passes can be bought at considerably higher prices.

FRANCE-ONLY RAILPASSES

SNCF offers a number of railpasses valid only in France, which can be bought through agents such as **RailEurope** or **Eurail** (see below for details). All of them also feature savings on Eurostar services from Paris to London.

France Railpass: 3 days unlimited rail travel in any 30-days. US$175 for 1 adult, $140 each for 2 traveling together. Add up to 6 extra days for $30 each.

France Rail'n'drive pass: 3 days rail travel and 2 days Avis car hire (excl. insurance) for US$255 for 1 adult, US$187 each for 2 traveling together. Additional rail days $30 each, additional car days $50.

France Youthpass: For travelers under 26. 4 days of unlimited travel within a 2 month period for US$158; add up to 6 days for $26 each.

Euro-Domino passes are available to anyone who has been resident at least 6 months in Europe. These single-country passes are available for 29 European countries and Morocco; they include TGV and most other high-speed supplements, but reservations must still be purchased separately. You also get a 25% discount on rail travel from the country of residence to the destination country. Tickets should be bought in your country of residence at travel agents or major train stations. The prices given only refer to Euro-Domino passes for France bought in the UK; each country has its own rates.

Euro-Domino France pass: 3 days UK£105, 5 days £145, 10 days £220.

Euro-Domino France Youth pass: Must be under 26. 3 days UK£85, 5 days £115, 10 days £185.

ESSENTIALS

EUROPEAN PASSES FOR NON-EUROPEAN RESIDENTS

A **Eurailpass** remains the best option for non-European travelers who plan on hitting major cities in several countries. Eurailpasses are valid in Austria, Belgium, Denmark, Finland, France, Germany, Greece, Hungary, Italy, Luxembourg, Netherlands, Norway, Portugal, Republic of Ireland, Spain, Sweden, and Switzerland. These passes must be sold at uniform prices determined by the EU, so no particular travel agent is better than another as far as the pass itself is concerned. However, some agents tack on a $10 handling fee. First-class passes are also available.

Eurail Saverpass: Unlimited first-class travel for those traveling in a group of 2-5. 15 days US$470, 21 days $610, 1 month $1072, 2 months $1072, 3 months $1324.

Eurail Youthpass: Unlimited second-class travel for those aged 12-25. 15 days US$388, 21 days $499, 1 month $623, 2 months $882, 3 months $1089.

Youth Flexipasses: Second-class travel for those under 26. 10 days (US$458), 15 days (US$599); children 4-11 pay half price and children under 4 travel free.

With a **Europass** you can travel throughout France, Germany, Italy, Spain, and Switzerland on any of 5-15 days within a window of 2 months. Second-class youth tickets begin at US$233 and increase incrementally by about $29 for each extra day of travel. For a fee, you can add associate countries; call for details. Be sure to plan your itineraries in advance before buying a Europass; if you cut through a country you haven't purchased, you'll be fined. Europasses are not appropriate if you like to take lots of side trips—you'll waste rail days. If you're tempted to add lots of rail days and associate countries, consider the Eurailpass.

It's best to buy your Eurailpass/Europass before leaving; they are hard to find in Europe, and you will probably have to use a credit card to buy over the phone from a travel agent in a non-participating country (one on the North American east coast will be closest), who can send the pass to you by express mail. Contact Council Travel, Travel CUTS (see **Budget Travel Agencies,** p. 27), or almost any travel agent handling European travel. Eurailpasses are not refundable once validated; if your pass is completely unused and unvalidated and you have the original purchase documents, you can get an 85% refund from the place of purchase. You can get a replacement for a lost pass only if you have purchased insurance on it under the Pass Protection Plan (US$10). All Eurailpasses can be purchased from a travel agent or from **Rail Europe Group,** 500 Mamaroneck Ave., Harrison, NY 10528 (in the US tel. 888 382 7245; fax 800 432 1329; in Canada tel. 800 361 7245; fax 905 602 4198; www.raileurope.com), which also sells point-to-point tickets. They offer special rates for groups of ten or more traveling together.

EUROPEAN RAILPASSES FOR EUROPEAN RESIDENTS

European residents planning to cover more than one country should consider **InterRail Passes.** Tickets are also available from travel agents or main train stations throughout Europe; they should be purchased in your country of residence.

Under 26 InterRail Card: 14 days or 1 month of unlimited travel within 1, 2, 3, or all of the 7 zones into which InterRail divides Europe. If you buy a ticket which includes your country of residence, you must pay 50% of the fare for travel with your country. UK£159-259.

Over 26 InterRail Card: unlimited second-class travel in 20 countries (Austria, Bulgaria, Croatia, Czech Republic, Denmark, Finland, Germany, Greece, Hungary, Republic of Ireland, Luxembourg, Netherlands, Norway, Poland, Romania, Slovakia, Slovenia, Sweden, Turkey, and Yugoslavia) for 15 days or 1 month. UK£215-275.

DISCOUNT RAIL TICKETS

SNCF offers a wide range of discounted roundtrip tickets for travelers in France which go under the name **tarifs Découvertes**—you should rarely have to pay full price. Get a calendar from a train station detailing **période bleue** (blue period), **péri-**

ode blanche (white period), and période rouge (red period) times and days; blue gets the most discounts, while red gets none. The Découverte à deux, Découverte Séjour, and Découverte 12-25 all give a 25% discount on tickets on a limited number of seats on all TGV services and on any other journey starting during a blue period. They differ in eligibility requirements. The *Découverte à deux* is only available to two adults traveling together on both legs of a roundtrip journey, the *Découverte Séjour* applies to short roundtrip journeys (under 200km), and requires a stay over a Saturday night, and the *Découverte 12-25* is only available to travelers between the ages of 12 and 25. Travelers who plan ahead can take advantage of the special Découverte J30 and Découverte J8. These are available on all trains and include the cost of reservation and/or couchette, but must be booked in advance for a specific train and are not exchangeable.

Those under the age of 25 can also take advantage of the Carte 12-25. These are available for 270F at SNCF stations and is valid for a year from the date of purchase; you'll need proof of age and a passport-sized photo to buy one. With it you get 25-50% off all TGV trains, 50% off all other trips which started during a blue period, and 25% off those starting in a white period. You can also take advantage of a 25% reduction on Avis car rentals (for those over 21), 25% off Eurostar tickets, and (in case you lose your ticket home) a 25% discount on United flights between France and the USA. The SNCF often has special offers for youth travelers—check their website for details (see below).

For international rail journeys, travelers under 26 buy BIJ tickets (*Billets Internationals de Jeunesse*), which knock 20-40% off regular second-class fares. Tickets are good for 60 days after purchase and allow a number of stopovers along the normal direct route of the train journey. Issued for a specific international route between two points, they must be used in the direction and order of the designated route and must be bought in Europe. They are available from European travel agents, at Wasteels or Eurotrain offices (usually in or near train stations), or directly at the ticket counter in some stations. Contact Wasteels (see Budget and Student Travel Agencies, p. 59). Wasteels agents are widespread in France, and *Let's Go* lists them in town write-ups wherever possible.

FURTHER RESOURCES: BY TRAIN

WEBSITES. *SNCF* (www.sncf.fr); *SNCF 12-25* (http://12-25.sncf.fr.); *Wasteels* (www.voyages-wasteels.fr); *European Railway Server:* (http://mercurio.iet.unipi.it/home.html).

BOOKS. *On the Rails Around Europe*, by Melissa Shales (Passport Books, US$19). *Traveling Europe's Trains*, by Jay Brunhouse (Pelican Publishing, US$16). *Europe By Eurail 1999*, by Laverne Ferguson (Globe Pequot, US$16). *Eurail and Train Travel Guide to Europe* (Houghton Mifflin, US$15).

BY BUS

In France, long-distance buses are very much a secondary transportation choice, and service is fairly rare and infrequent compared to most other European countries. However, within a given region buses can be indispensable for reaching out-of-the-way towns and villages, and in some areas they rival trains for speed. Many bus services are operated by the SNCF itself; these accept railpasses. Other services are operated by regional companies; prices and punctuality are variable. *Let's Go* lists the local bus companies and relevant destinations for each town.

BY CAR

Unless you are three or more, you won't save money traveling long distance by car rather than train, thanks to *autoroute* tolls, high gasoline costs, and rental charges. On the upside, cars offer speed, freedom, access to the countryside, and an escape from the town-to-town mentality of trains. If you can't decide between train and car travel, you may benefit from a combination of the two; RailEurope and other railpass vendors offer rail-and-drive packages for both individual countries and all of Europe.

The French drive on the right-hand side of the road; speed limits on *autoroutes* are 130km/h (about 80 mph) and 100km/h (60mph) on smaller roads. However, they are widely flouted. One quirk of the French highway code is that cars entering a road from the right have priority, even on roundabouts and when joining major roads; thus be prepared for people to turn onto the road in front of you with little or no warning. If you see inverted triangle road signs with exclamation marks proclaiming *"vous n'avez pas la priorité"* or *"cédez le passage,"* this rule does not apply and you will be expected to give way before turning right; this is normally the case on major roundabouts. An invaluable internet resource for those planning to drive in France is **iTinéraire** (www.iti.fr); you tell it your starting and end points, and it will draw up a choice of routes according to speed and budget, along with estimates of driving time and toll and gas costs.

FINDING YOUR WHEELS

RENTALS. You can **rent** a car from an international firm (e.g. Avis, Budget, or Hertz) with European offices, from a European-based company with local representatives (e.g. Europcar), or from a tour operator (e.g. Auto Europe, Europe By Car, or Kemwel Holiday Autos) which will arrange a rental for you from a European company at its own rates. Multinationals offer greater flexibility, but tour operators often strike better deals. Expect to pay at least US$150 per week, plus 20.6% tax, for a small car; you'll probably have to purchase insurance as well (see below). Generally automatic gearboxes are unavailable on the cheaper cars and cost extra; most Europeans prefer the performance and economy of stick-shifts. Reserve well before leaving for France and pay in advance if at all possible. Always check if prices quoted include tax, unlimited mileage, and collision insurance; some credit card companies will cover this automatically. Ask about discounts and check the terms of insurance, particularly the size of the deductible. Non-Europeans should check with their national motoring organization (like AAA or CAA) for international coverage. Ask your airline about special fly-and-drive packages; you may get up to a week of free or discounted rental. The minimum age for renting in France is usually 21; those under 25 will often have to pay a surcharge. At most agencies, all that's needed to rent a car is a valid drivers' license and proof that you've had it for a year.

You can rent cars in Europe from the following rental agencies. **Auto Europe:** US tel. 888 223 5555; fax 800 235 6321; www.autoeurope.com. **Avis:** US and Canada tel. 800 331 1084; UK 0990 900 500; Australia 800 225 533; www.avis.com. **Budget:** US tel. 800 472 3325; Canada 800 527 0700; UK 0800 181 181; Australia, 013 2727; www.budgetrentacar.com. **Europe by Car:** US tel. 800 223 1516 or 212 581 3040; www.europebycar.com. **Europcar:** US tel. 800 227 3876; Canada 800 227 7368; France 01 45 00 08 06; www.europcar.com. **Hertz:** US tel. 800 654 3001; Canada 800 263 0600; UK 0990 996 699; Australia 13 30 39; www.hertz.com.

LEASING. An option only for non-EU residents, **leasing** can be cheaper than renting for periods longer than 17 days; it is often the only option for those aged 18-21. The cheapest leases are agreements to buy the car and then sell it back to the manufacturer at a prearranged price. As far as you're concerned it's a lease and doesn't entail enormous financial transactions. While the base price of a lease may not seem very different from a regular car rental, recall they include comprehensive insurance, unlimited mileage, and are tax-free—you just pay what's quoted, plus gas. Expect to pay at least US$1200 for 60 days. Contact **Auto Europe, Europe by Car,** or **Kemwel Holiday Autos** (see above). There's a fair deal of paperwork to be done in advance—you should arrange the lease at least 30 days before your departure.

BUYING. If you're brave and know what you're doing, buying a used vehicle in France and reselling it before you leave can provide the cheapest wheels for long trips. Check with consulates for import-export laws concerning used vehicles, registration, and safety and emission standards. Camper-vans and motor homes give the advantages of a car without the hassle and expense of finding lodgings. Most of these vehicles are diesel-powered and deliver roughly 24-30 miles per gallon.

PERMITS AND CAR INSURANCE

INTERNATIONAL DRIVING PERMIT (IDP). Those in possession of a valid EU-issued driving license are entitled to drive in France with no further ado. While others may be legally able to drive in France on the strength of their national licenses for a few months, not all the police know it; it's safest to get an International Driving Permit (IDP), which is essentially a translation of your regular license into 10 languages, including French. The IDP, valid for one year, must be issued in your own country before you depart. You must be 18 years old to receive the IDP. The IDP is an addition, not a replacement, for your home license, and is not valid without it. An application for an IDP usually needs to include one or two photos, a current local license, an additional form of identification, and a fee.

> **Australia:** Contact the Royal Automobile Club (RAC) or the National Royal Motorist Association (NRMA) if in NSW or the ACT (tel. 08 9421 4298; www.rac.com.au/travel). AUS$15.

> **Canada:** Contact any Canadian Automobile Association (CAA) branch office in Canada, or write to CAA, 1145 Hunt Club Rd., Suite 200, K1V 0Y3 Canada. (tel. 613 247 0117; fax 247 0118; www.caa.ca/CAAInternet/travelservices/internationaldocumentation/idptravel.htm). CDN$10.

> **New Zealand:** Contact your local Automobile Association (AA) or their main office at Auckland Central, 99 Albert St. (tel. 09 377 4660; fax 09 302 2037; www.nzaa.co.nz.). IDP NZ$8.

> **South Africa:** Contact your local Automobile Association of South Africa office or the head office at P.O. Box 596, 2000 Johannesburg (tel. 711 799 1000; fax 711 99 1010). SAR28.50.

> **US:** Visit any American Automobile Association (AAA) office or write to AAA Florida, Travel Related Services, 1000 AAA Drive (mail stop 100), Heathrow, FL 32746 (tel. 407 444 7000; fax 407 444 7380). You do not have to be a member of AAA to purchase an IDP. US$10.

CAR INSURANCE. EU residents driving their own cars do not need any extra insurance coverage in France. For those renting, paying with a gold credit card usually covers standard insurance; if your home car insurance covers you for liability, make sure you get a **green card**, or **International Insurance Certificate** to prove it. If you have a collision abroad, the accident will show up on your domestic records if you report it to your insurance company. Otherwise, be prepared to shell out US$5-10 per day for insurance on a rental car. Leasing should include insurance and the green card in the price. Some travel agents offer the card; it may also be available at border crossings.

BY MOPED AND MOTORCYCLE

Motorbikes don't use much gas and are a good compromise between the high cost of car travel and the limited range of bicycles. However, they're uncomfortable for long distances, dangerous in the rain, and unpredictable on rough roads and gravel. Always wear a helmet, and never ride with a backpack. If you've never been on a moped before, a twisting Alpine road is not the place to start. Expect to pay about US$20-35 per day; try auto repair shops, and remember to bargain. Motorcycles are more expensive and require a license, but are better for long distances. **Bosenberg Motorcycle Excursions**, Mainzer Str. 54, 55545 Bad Kreuznach, Germany (tel. 671 673 12; www.bosenberg.com), arranges tours in the Alps, Austria, France, Italy, and Switzerland; they also rent motorcycles April to October.

Before renting, ask if the quoted price includes tax and insurance, or you may be hit with an unexpected additional fee. Avoid handing your passport over as a deposit; if you have an accident or mechanical failure you may not get it back until you cover all repairs. Pay ahead of time instead.

For **further information,** consult *Europe by Motorcycle*, by Gregory Frazier (Arrowstar Publishing, US$20).

BY BICYCLE

Today, biking is one of the key elements of the budget European vacation. With the proliferation of mountain bikes, you can do some serious natural sight-seeing.

If you are nervous about striking out on your own, **Blue Marble Travel** (tel. 519 624 2494 in Canada; 800 258 8689 or 973 326 9533 in US; 01 42 36 02 34 in France; www.bluemarble.org) offers bike tours designed for adults aged 20 to 50. Pedal with or without your 10 to 15 companions through the Alps, Austria, France, Germany, Italy, Portugal, Scandinavia, and Spain. Full-time graduate and professional students may get discounts, and "stand-by" rates may be obtained in Europe through the Paris office. **CBT Tours,** 415 W. Fullerton, #1003, Chicago, IL 60614 (tel. 800 736 BIKE (2453) or 773 404 1710; www.cbttours.com), offers full-package one- to seven-week biking, mountain biking, and hiking tours (around US$115 per day). Tours run June to September, with departures every 7-10 days. In 2000, CBT will visit Belgium, the Czech Republic, France, Germany, Holland, Hungary, Ireland, Italy, Luxembourg, Switzerland, and the UK.

Many airlines will count your bike as your second piece of luggage, and a few charge extra. The additional fee runs about US$60-110 each way. Bikes must be packed in a cardboard box with the pedals and front wheel detached; airlines sell bike boxes at the airport (US$10). Most ferries let you take your bike for free or for a nominal fee. You can always ship your bike on trains, though the cost varies.

Riding a bike with a frame pack strapped on it or your back is about as safe as pedaling blindfolded over a sheet of ice; panniers are essential. The first thing to buy, however, is a suitable **bike helmet** (US$25-50). **U-shaped locks** are expensive (starting at US$30), but by far the most secure. For mail order equipment, **Bike Nashbar,** 4111 Simon Rd., Youngstown, OH 44512 (tel. 800 627 4227; www.nashbar.com), beats all competitors' offers and ships anywhere in the US or Canada.

Renting a bike beats bringing your own if your touring will be confined to one or two regions. *Let's Go* lists bike rental shops for most cities and towns. Some youth hostels rent bicycles for low prices.

For **further information, Mountaineers Books,** 1001 S.W. Klickitat Way #201, Seattle, WA 98134 (tel. 800 553 4453 or 206 223 6303; www.mountaineers.org), offers tour books for France, and Europe By Bike, by Karen and Terry Whitehill (US$15).

BY FOOT

France's grandest scenery can often be seen only by foot. *Let's Go* describes many daytrips and short hikes for those who want to hoof it, but tourist offices, locals, hostel owners, and fellow travelers are the best source of tips. France is crisscrossed by over 30,000km of footpaths known as **sentiers de grandes randonées** or just **GR,** signposted and dotted with campsites and *refuges.* The **Fédération française de randonée pédestre (FFRP),** 14 rue Riquet, 75019 Paris (tel. 01 44 89 93 93; fax: 01 40 35 85 67; www.ffrp.asso.fr) publishes the *Topoguide* series of guides for each GR route in French, with maps and details of accommodations on the way.

The route of the GR65, which runs from Le Puy-en-Velay in the Massif Central to St-Jean-Pied-de-Port on the way to Santiago de Compostella in Spain, was trodden for centuries before hiking became a fashionable form of relaxation. Many thousands of people still undertake **pilgrimages** on foot; Le Puy and Santiago are the oldest and best-known destinations, and trails lead to them from all over Europe. Pilgrims can stay along the way at monasteries and special pilgrim hostels; to stay there you will need a letter from your local priest confirming that you are a bona-fide pilgrim. For more information on monastic stays, contact **La Procure,** 3 rue de Mézières, 75006 Paris (tel. 01 45 48 20 25).

BY THUMB

No one should hitch *("faire l'autostop")* without careful consideration of the risks involved. Not everyone can be an airplane pilot, but any bozo can drive a car. Hitching means entrusting your life to a random person who happens to stop beside you on the road, risking theft, assault, sexual harassment, and unsafe driving. In spite of this, some travelers report favorable hitching experiences, such as allowing you to meet local people and to get where you're going where public transportation is poor. Be warned that many consider France the hardest country in Europe in which to get a lift. If you're a woman traveling alone, don't hitch. It's just too dangerous. A man and a woman are a safer combination, two men will have a hard time getting lifts, and three will go nowhere.

 BEWARE YOUNG HITCHHIKER. *Let's Go* strongly urges you to consider seriously the risks before you choose to hitch. We do not recommend hitching as a safe means of transportation, and none of the information presented here is intended to do so.

Where you stand is vital. Experienced hitchers pick a spot outside built-up areas, where drivers can stop and return to the road safely, and have time to look over potential passengers as they approach. Hitching (or even standing) on *autoroutes* is illegal; one may only thumb at rest stops or at highway entrance ramps.

Finally, success will depend on what you look like. Successful hitchers travel light and stack their belongings in a compact but visible cluster. Most Europeans signal with an open hand, rather than a thumb; many write their destination on a sign in large, bold letters and draw a smiley-face under it. Drivers prefer hitchers who are neat and wholesome. No one stops for anyone wearing sunglasses.

Safety issues are always imperative, even for those who are not hitching alone. Safety-minded hitchers avoid getting in the back of a two-door car and never let go of their backpacks. They will not get into a car that they can't get out of again in a hurry. If they ever feel threatened, they insist on being let off, regardless of where they are. Acting as if they are going to open the car door or vomit on the upholstery will usually get a driver to stop. Hitchhiking at night can be particularly dangerous; experienced hitchers stand in well-lit places and expect drivers to be leery of nocturnal thumbers (or open-handers).

Most Western European countries offer a ride service (listed in the **Practical Information** for major cities), a cross between hitchhiking and the ride boards common at many universities, which pairs drivers with riders; the fee varies according to destination. **Eurostop International** (**Allostop** in France) is one of the largest in Europe. Riders and drivers can enter their names on the Internet through the **Taxistop** website (www.taxistop.be). Not all of these organizations screen drivers and riders; ask in advance.

SPECIFIC CONCERNS

WOMEN TRAVELERS

NATIONAL RAPE HOTLINE	SOS Viol: 0 800 05 95 95 offers counseling and assistance in French. Open M-F 10am-7pm.

Women exploring on their own face additional safety concerns, but it's easy to be adventurous without taking undue risks. If you are concerned, consider staying in hostels which offer single rooms that lock from the inside. Communal showers in some hostels are safer than others; check before settling in. Stick to central accommodations and avoid solitary late-night walks or travel.

Women traveling alone or in small groups are inevitably going to encounter some unwanted attention, especially in the south of France. French men often regard solo women travelers as soft targets; the best response to their advances is the one French women have developed: a withering, icy stare. Speaking to *dragueurs* (as the French call them), even to say "NO!", is only inviting a reply, but if you feel threatened don't hesitate to call out to others or to draw attention to yourself. A loud *"laissez-moi tranquille!"* (leh-SEH mwa tranhk-EEL; "leave me alone!") or *"au secours!"* (oh-S'KOOR; "help!") will embarrass them and hopefully send them on their way. Harassment can be minimized by making yourself as inconspicuous as possible; see **Blending In**, p. 42, for tips, though in some cities you may be harassed no matter how you're dressed. Wearing a conspicuous **wedding ring** may dissuade unwanted overtures. Even a mention of a husband waiting back at the hotel may be enough in some places to discount your potentially vulnerable, unattached appearance.

Hitching is never safe for lone women, or even for two women traveling together. If traveling long-distance by train, choose coach-style carriages over compartments; if this is impossible, choose a compartment occupied by other women or couples. Always look as if you know where you're going and consider approaching older women or couples for directions if you're lost or feel uncomfortable.

Don't hesitate to seek out a police officer or a passerby if you are being harassed. *Let's Go* lists crisis numbers in the Practical Information listings of most cities. **In an emergency, dial 17 for police assistance.** Carry a **whistle** or an airhorn on your keychain, and don't hesitate to use it in an emergency. A **model mugging** self-defense course will not only prepare you for a potential attack, but will also raise your level of awareness of your surroundings and your confidence. Women also face some specific health concerns when traveling (see **Women's Health,** p. 48).

TRAVELING ALONE

There are many benefits to traveling alone, among them greater independence and challenge. As a lone traveler, you have greater opportunity to interact with the residents of the region you're visiting. Without distraction, you can write a great travel log in the grand tradition of Marco Polo, Mark Twain, or John Steinbeck.

On the other hand, any solo traveler is a more vulnerable target of harassment and street theft. Lone travelers need to be well-organized and look confident at all times. Try not to stand out as a tourist, and be especially careful in deserted or very crowded areas. If questioned, never admit that you are traveling alone. Maintain regular contact with someone at home who knows your itinerary.

A number of organizations supply information for solo travelers, and others find travel companions for others. A few are listed here. For further information, consult *Traveling Solo*, by Eleanor Berman (Globe Pequot, US$17).

Connecting: Solo Traveler Network, P.O. Box 29088, 1996 W. Broadway, Vancouver, BC V6J 5C2, Canada (tel. 604 737 7791; email info@cstn.org; www.cstn.org). Bi-monthly newsletter features going solo tips, single-friendly tips and travel companion ads. Annual directory lists holiday suppliers that avoid single supplement charges. Advice and lodging exchanges facilitated between members. Membership US$25-35.

Travel Companion Exchange, P.O. Box 833, Amityville, NY 11701 (tel. 516 454 0880 or 800 392 1256; www.travelalone.com). Publishes the pamphlet *Foiling Pickpockets & Bag Snatchers* (US$4) and *Travel Companions*, a bi-monthly newsletter for single travelers seeking a travel partner (subscription US$48).

OLDER TRAVELERS

Almost all museums and sights in France offer discounts for senior citizens, and many cities also offer special rates for public transportation. France is very popular with older travelers, and major sights are well equipped to deal with their special needs. However, budget accommodations are not so accommodating; for example, they rarely have elevators (and often have extremely steep stairs). Make sure to call ahead to check facilities if you have any special concerns.

Agencies for senior group travel are growing in enrollment and popularity. These are but a few:

Elderhostel, 75 Federal St., Boston, MA 02110-1941 (tel. 617 426 7788 or 877 426 8056; email registration@elderhostel.org; www.elderhostel.org). Programs at colleges, universities, and other learning centers in Europe on varied subjects lasting 1-4 weeks. Must be 55 or over (spouse can be of any age).

The Mature Traveler, P.O. Box 50400, Reno, NV 89513 (tel. 775 786 7419 or 800 460 6676). Has soft-adventure tours for seniors. Subscription $30.

Walking the World, P.O. Box 1186, Fort Collins, CO 80522 (tel. 970 498 0500; fax 970 498 9100; email walktworld@aol.com; www.walkingtheworld.com), sends trips to France.

FURTHER READING. *No Problem! Worldwise Tips for Mature Adventurers*, by Janice Kenyon (Orca Book Publishers, US$16); *A Senior's Guide to Healthy Travel*, by Donald L. Sullivan (Career Press, US$15); *Unbelievably Good Deals and Great Adventures That You Absolutely Can't Get Unless You're Over 50*, by Joan Rattner Heilman (Contemporary Books, US$13).

BISEXUAL, GAY, AND LESBIAN TRAVELERS

France has been changing its ways alongside the rest of the modern world; gay communities, with help lines, bars, and meeting places have sprung up in all its major cities. But, in general, the French countryside and even most smaller towns have not lost their traditional stereotypes. To avoid possibly offending or uncomfortable situations, use discretion when interacting with your significant other in public. Listed below are contact organizations, mail-order bookstores and publishers which offer materials addressing some specific concerns.

Gay's the Word, 66 Marchmont St., London WC1N 1AB (tel. 020 7278 7654; email gays.theword@virgin.net; www.gaystheword.co.uk). The largest gay and lesbian bookshop in the UK Mail-order service available. No catalogue of listings, but they will provide a list of titles on a given subject.

Giovanni's Room, 345 S. 12th St., Philadelphia, PA 19107 (tel. 215 923 2960; fax 923 0813; email giophilp@netaxs.com). An feminist, lesbian, and gay bookstore with mail-order service which carries the publications listed here.

International Gay and Lesbian Travel Association, 4331 N. Federal Hwy., Suite 304, Fort Lauderdale, FL 33308 (tel. 954 776 2626 or 800 448 8550; fax 954 776 3303; email IGLTA@aol.com; www.iglta.com). An organization of over 1350 companies serving gay and lesbian travelers worldwide. Call for lists of travel agents, accommodations, and events.

International Lesbian and Gay Association (ILGA), 81 rue Marché-au-Charbon, B-1000 Brussels, Belgium (tel./fax 032 2 502 24 71; email ilga@ilga.org; www.ilga.org). Not a travel service. Provides political information, such as homosexuality laws of individual countries.

FURTHER READING. *Spartacus International Gay Guide*, by Bruno Gmunder (Verlag, US$33); *Damron's Accommodations* and *The Women's Traveller* (Damron Travel Guides, US$14-19); *Ferrari Gay Paris, Ferrari Guides' Gay Travel A to Z, Ferrari Guides' Men's Travel in Your Pocket, Ferrari Guides' Women's Travel in Your Pocket,* and *Ferrari Guides' Inn Places* (Ferrari Guides, US$14-18); *The Gay Vacation Guide: The Best Trips and How to Plan Them,* by Mark Chesnut (Citadel Press, US$15).

TRAVELERS WITH DISABILITIES

Many museums and sights are fully accessible to wheelchairs and some provide guided tours in sign language. Unfortunately, budget hotels and restaurants are generally ill-equipped to handle the needs of handicapped visitors. Handicapped-accessible bathrooms are virtually non-existent among hotels in the one- to two-star range. The brochure **Paris-Île-de-France for Everyone** (available in French and English for 60F at most Paris tourism offices) lists accessible sites, hotels, and restaurants, as well as indispensable practical tips. Travelers are encouraged to ask restaurants, hotels, railways, and airlines if they are wheelchair accessible.

Rail is probably the most convenient form of travel for disabled travelers in France. SNCF offers wheelchair compartments on all TGV services, while availability on other services is indicated by a wheelchair icon on train timetables. Ask for the *Guide du voyageur a mobilité réduite* at train stations for more details. Guide dog owners from Britain and Ireland will have trouble getting their pooches past quarantine on the return trip; others should inquire as to the specific quarantine policies of their own country, as well as regulations for entering France. In Paris and other major cities, public transport has seats which are earmarked for disabled or infirm passengers; though it may not always be easy to persuade the person occupying it to move. Taxis are obliged to take wheelchair-bound passengers and to help you in and out of your vehicle; they must also take guide-dogs. Hertz, Avis, and National car rental agencies have hand-controlled vehicles at some locations, but they must be reserved at least 48 hours in advance.

The following organizations provide information or publications that might be of assistance:

Association des paralysées de France (APF), 17 bd. Auguste-Blanqui, 75013 Paris (tel. 01 40 78 69 00), has information on wheelchair-accessible accommodations in France.

Comité nationale française de liaison pour la réadaptation des handicapées (CNRH), 236bis rue de Tolbiac, 75013 Paris (tel. 01 52 80 66 66), is an information service which produces numerous guides for disabled travelers.

Moss Rehab Hospital Travel Information Service (tel. 215 456 9600; www.mossresourcenet.org). A telephone and internet information resource center on international travel accessibility and other travel-related concerns for those with disabilities.

Society for the Advancement of Travel for the Handicapped (SATH), 347 Fifth Ave., #610, New York, NY 10016 (tel. 212 447 1928; fax 212 725 8253; email sathtravel@aol.com; www.sath.org). Advocacy group publishing a quarterly color travel magazine *OPEN WORLD* (free for members or US$13 for nonmembers). Also publishes a wide range of information sheets on disability travel facilitation and accessible destinations. Annual membership US$45, students and seniors US$30.

The following organizations arrange tours or trips for disabled travelers:

Access Travel, 16 Haysewater Ave., Astley, Lancs. M29 7BL, UK (tel. 01942 888 844), is a specialized tour operator which arranges vacations in France for disabled travelers.

Directions Unlimited, 720 N. Bedford Rd., Bedford Hills, NY 10507 (tel. 800 533 5343; in NY 914 241 1700; fax 914 241 0243; email cruisesusa@aol.com). Specializes in arranging individual and group vacations, tours, and cruises for the physically disabled.

FURTHER READING. *Access in Paris,* by Gordon Couch (Quiller Press, US$12); *Resource Directory for the Disabled,* by Richard Neil Shrout (Facts on File, US$45); *Wheelchair Through Europe,* by Annie Mackin. (Graphic Language Press, US$13); *Global Access* (www.geocities.com/Paris/1502/disability-inks.html) has links for disabled travelers in France.

MINORITY TRAVELERS

Like many European countries, France has experienced a wave of reverse-coloni-zation in the past few decades. By far the biggest group of immigrants are North Africans, who number over a million, followed by West Africans and Vietnamese. This influx has led to a surge in support for the far-right National Front party, and many French people are sympathetic to its cry of *"la France pour les français"* (France for the French). Travelers who could be taken for North Africans may encounter verbal abuse, especially in the South, and are also more likely to be arbitrarily stopped and questioned by French police. However, French prejudice is more cultural than color-oriented; the most common complaint is that immigrants do not adopt French culture and customs. Minority travelers from abroad are likely to be treated simply as foreigners; James Baldwin and Charles Mingus fled the USA for Paris in the 1950s to escape racism.

TRAVELERS WITH CHILDREN

Family vacations often require that you slow your pace, and always require that you plan ahead. If you're thinking of staying at a B&B, call ahead and make sure it's child-friendly. If you rent a car, make sure the rental company provides a car seat for younger children. Be sure that your child carries some sort of ID in case of an emergency or he or she gets lost, and arrange a reunion spot in case of separa-tion when sight-seeing.

French restaurants welcome children. At least, they welcome French children who are used to eating regularly in restaurants and eat what they're served; par-ents of fussy eaters should make sure there's something acceptable before choos-ing a restaurant. Often cheaper restaurants have a children's menu, typically featuring a hamburger and fries; while elegant establishments will not turn up there noses at young customers, they will not go out of their way to accommodate them, either. Virtually all museums and tourist attractions also have a children's rate. Children under two generally fly for 10% of the adult airfare on international flights (this does not necessarily include a seat). International fares are usually discounted 25% for children from two to 11.

FURTHER READING. *Backpacking with Babies and Small Children,* by Goldie Silverman (Wilderness Press, US$10); *Take Your Kids to Europe,* by Cyn-thia W. Harriman (Globe Pequot, US$17); *How to take Great Trips with Your Kids,* by Sanford and Jane Portnoy (Harvard Common Press, US$10); *Have Kid, Will Travel: 101 Survival Strategies for Vacationing With Babies and Young Children,* by Claire and Lucille Tristram (Andrews and McMeel, US$9); *Adven-turing with Children: An Inspirational Guide to World Travel and the Out-doors,* by Nan Jeffrey (Avalon House Publishing, US$15); *Trouble Free Travel with Children,* by Vicki Lansky (Book Peddlers, US$9).

ESSENTIALS

DIETARY CONCERNS

France may be the country of gastronomy, but sometimes it seems so caught up in its own eating traditions that those with special dietary requirements can feel left behind. **Vegetarians** will find eating out difficult (see **A French Food Primer,** p. 27), and **vegans** almost impossible—to the French, the idea of someone who eats neither meat nor cheese verges on the incomprehensible. Both are most likely to find something palatable at ethnic restaurants; though the French are very fond of salads, be especially careful to make sure the *patron* understands that you want neither ham nor fish nor chicken livers nor cheese with your greens.

For more information about vegetarian travel, contact the **North American Vegetarian Society**, P.O. Box 72, Dolgeville, NY 13329 (tel. 518 568 7970; email navs@telenet.com; www.cyberveg.org/navs/) for a copy of *Transformative Adventures*, a guide to vacations and retreats (US$15).

Kosher food certainly exists in France, which has one of Western Europe's largest Jewish populations, but tracking it down may prove difficult. It can be hard to find a kosher restaurant or deli in rural regions. Travelers who keep kosher should contact synagogues in larger cities for information on kosher restaurants; your own synagogue or college Hillel should have access to lists of Jewish institutions across the nation. If you are strict in your observance, you may have to prepare your own food on the road.

FURTHER READING. *The Vegetarian Traveler: Where to Stay if You're Vegetarian,* by Jed Civic (Larson Pub, US$16); *Europe on 10 Salads a Day*, by Greg and Mary Jane Edwards (Mustang Publishing, US$10); *The Jewish Travel Guide*, by Betsy Sheldon (Hunter, US$17).

ALTERNATIVES TO TOURISM

STUDY

Every year, thousands of people from all over the world descend on France to study, whether for a few weeks of French language immersion or to enroll in an advanced degree program. In response to this demand, hundreds of institutions offer courses to cater to every taste. You don't even need to speak French to get a degree; in 1999, in a bid to bolster the long-term standing of France (and earn a little foreign currency on the side), the French government announced a program to offer certain degree courses in English to overseas students.

All non-EU citizens need a study visa if they intend to spend more than three months studying in France, while everyone will need a residency permit. As long as you have been accepted into a course and can show proof of financial independence, you should have no trouble getting a study visa. For details, see **Visas and Work Permits,** p. 34.

FRENCH UNIVERSITIES

French **universities** (except for the *Grandes Écoles;* see below) must admit anyone holding a *baccalaureat* (French school-leaving certificate) or a recognized equivalent to their first year of courses. (US students must have a high school diploma and two years of college to be admitted.) Non-native French speakers must also pass a written and oral language test. At the end of the first year, exams separate the wheat from the chaff. The cream of the academic crop go to the elite **Grandes Écoles,** which have notoriously difficult entrance examinations which require a year of preparatory schooling in themselves.

French universities are far, far cheaper than their American equivalents, including programs offered by US universities in France; however, it can be hard to receive academic credit at home for work completed on a non-approved program. Expect to pay at least 2500F per month in living expenses. EU citizens studying in France can take advantage of the **SOCRATES** program, which offers grants to support inter-European educational exchanges. Most UK and Irish universities will have details of the grants available and the application procedure. EU law dictates that educational qualifications be recognized across the Union (with the exception of some professional subjects such as medicine). The universities and organizations listed below can supply further information and help organize an academic program in France.

Agence EduFrance, 173 bd. Saint-Germain, 75006 Paris (Tel. 01 53 63 35 00; www.edufrance.fr), is a one-stop resource for foreigners thinking about studying for a degree in France. Information on courses, costs, grant opportunities, and student life in France. Website available in English, with a downloadable questionnaire that will prepare a tailor-made list of contacts.

The British Council, 11 Portland Place, London W1N 4EJ (tel. 020 7930 8466; fax 020 7389 3199; www.britishcouncil.org), has information on educational exchanges between the UK and France, and also administers the SOCRATES educational exchange program in Britain.

Université Paris-Sorbonne, 1 rue Victor Cousin, 75230 Paris cedex 05 (tel. 01 40 46 22 11; fax 01 40 46 25 88; www.paris4sorbonne.fr), the grand-daddy of French universities, was founded in 1253 and is still going strong. Inscription into degree courses cost about 2500F per year. Also offers programs for US students lasting 3-9 months.

American University of Paris, 31 Avenue Bosquet, 75007 Paris (tel. 01 40 62 06 00; www.aup.fr), offers US-accredited degrees and summer programs taught in English at its Paris campus. Tuition and living expenses total about US$28,000 per year.

Central College Abroad, Office of International Education, 812 University, Pella, IA 50219 (tel. 800 831 3629 or 515 628 5284; fax 515 628 5316; email Study-Abroad@Central.edu; http://studyabroad.com/central/). Offers semester- and year-long study abroad programs in France. US$25 application fee. Scholarships available. Applicants must be at least 18, have completed their freshman year of college, and have a minimum 2.5 GPA.

LANGUAGE SCHOOLS

Language schools are offered in the summer by many French universities, while independent organizations run language classes throughout the year. The American University in Paris also runs a summer program (see above for contact details). For more information on language courses in France, contact your national **Institut Français,** official representatives of French Culture attached to French embassies around the world (contact your nearest French embassy or consulate for details). The Canadian chapter has created a fantastic **clickable map** of language schools in France at www.ambafrance.org:80/COURS/index_eng.html. Other well-known schools include:

Alliance Française, École Internationale de Langue et de Civilisation Françaises, 101 bd. Raspail, 75270 Paris Cedex 06 (tel. 01 45 44 38 28; fax 01 45 44 89 42; info@alliancefrancaise.fr; www.alliancefrancaise.fr). Instruction at all levels, with specialized courses in legal and business French. From 1400F per month for evening classes (1¾hr. per day) to 3200F per month for an intensive course (4hr. per day).

Cours de Civilisation Française de la Sorbonne, 47 rue des Écoles, 75005 Paris (tel. 01 40 46 22 11; fax 01 40 46 32 29; www.fle.fr/sorbonne/). Offers instruction at all levels in the French language, together with a comprehensive lecture program of French cultural studies taught by professors of the Sorbonne. Must be at least 18 and have completed high school. Semester- and year-long courses during the academic year, and 4-, 6-, 8-, and 11-week summer programs.

Eurocentres, 101 N. Union St. #300, Alexandria, VA 22314 (tel. 800 648 4809, 703 684 1494 for consumer representative; fax 703 684 1495; www.eurocentres.com) or Eurocentres, Head Office, Seestrasse 247, CH-8038 Zurich, Switzerland (tel. (country code: 41) 1 485 5040; fax 1 481 6124). Language programs and homestays for about US$1132 a month. 2 weeks to full academic year programs for beginners to advanced.

FURTHER READING

Academic Year Abroad and *Vacation Study Abroad* (Institute of International Education Books, US$40-45); *Peterson's Study Abroad Guide* (Peterson's, US$30).

WORK

Anyone hoping to come to France and slip easily into a job will face a tough reality on their arrival. French unemployment stubbornly remains above 10%, and unqualified foreigners are unlikely to meet with much sympathy from French employers.

OPTIONS FOR WORK

Non-EU citizens will find it well-nigh impossible to get a work permit without a firm offer of a job; networking among your fellow country-men will prove your best bet for (illegal) employment. Agricultural work is another option; the autumn *vendages* (grape harvest) provides plentiful opportunities for backbreaking work in return for a small allowance and a lot of cheap wine. Full-time students at a US universities can apply to work permit programs run by **Council on International Educational Exchange (Council)** and its member organizations. For a US$225 application fee, Council can procure 3- to 6-month work permits and a handbook to help you find work and housing. Among other options for legal, gainful employment are **Au pair** positions, which offer lodging, board, and a small stipend to young women in return for childcare and household chores. You are unlikely to land a job **teaching English** in France unless you have a **TEFL** (Teaching of English as a Foreign Language) certificate or equivalent and a couple of years experience. If you are an experienced English teacher, though, you can try for an official position as a **Teaching Assistant** in a French school; contact your national French embassy for details. For more information on visas, see **Study and Work Permits**, p. 34.

EU citizens can work in France without a visa or work permit, though they will still need a **residency permit** (see p. 34). Those without an offer of employment have a grace period of three months in which to seek work; during this time they are eligible for social security benefits. To receive benefits, you must arrange it in advance with your local social security office before leaving for France; beware that French bureaucracy often takes most of the three months just to process the paperwork. If you do not succeed in finding work in that time, you must return home unless you can prove your financial independence. By law, all EU citizens must be given equality of opportunity when applying to jobs not directly related to national security, so theoretically if you speak French you have as much chance of finding a job as an equivalently qualified French person. Theoretically. If your parents were born in an EU country, you may be able to claim dual citizenship or at least the right to a work permit.

AU PAIR

L'Accueil Familial des Jeunes Étrangers, 23 rue du Cherche-Midi, 6ème Paris (tel. 01 42 22 50 34; fax 01 45 44 60 48). Arranges summer and 6-10 month au pair jobs (placement fee 680F for EU citizens, 800F otherwise). Will help switch families if you are unhappy.

Accord Cultural Exchange, 750 La Playa, San Francisco, CA 94121 (tel. 415 386 6203; fax 415 386 0240; email leftbank@hotmail.com; www.cognitext.com/accord), offers Au pair jobs to people aged 18-29 in France. Au pairs work 5-6 hours a day, 30 hours a week, plus 2 evenings of babysitting. Program fees US$750 for the summer, US$1200 for the academic year. US$40 application fee.

Childcare International, Ltd., Trafalgar House, Grenville Place, London NW7 3SA (tel. 020 8906 3116; fax 020 8906 3461; office@childint.demon.co.uk; www.childint.demon.co.uk) offers *au pair* positions in France. Provides information on qualifications required and local language schools. The organization prefers a long placement but does arrange summer work. UK£80 application fee.

TEACHING ENGLISH

International Schools Services, Educational Staffing Program, P.O. Box 5910, Princeton, NJ 08543 (tel. 609 452 0990; fax 609 452 2690; edustaffing@iss.edu; www.iss.edu). Recruits teachers and administrators for American and English schools in France. All instruction in English. Applicants must have a bachelor's degree and two years of relevant experience. Nonrefundable US$100 application fee. Publishes *The ISS Directory of Overseas Schools* (US$35).

Office of Overseas Schools, A/OS Room 245, SA-29 Dept. of State, Washington, D.C. 20522 2902 (tel. 703 875 7800; fax 703 875 7979; overseas.school@state.gov; http://state.gov/www/about_state/schools/). Keeps a list of schools abroad and agencies that arrange placement for Americans to teach abroad.

HERITAGE WORK

REMPART, 1 rue des Guillemites, 4ème Paris (tel. 01 42 71 96 55; fax 01 42 71 73 00). Offers summer and year-long programs geared toward protecting the French heritage. Restores churches, monuments, and the environment. Anyone 15 or over is eligible. 40-50F per day, plus a 220F insurance fee.

Club du Vieux Manoir, 10 rue de la Cossonnerie, 75001 Paris (tel. 01 45 08 80 40 or 03 44 72 33 18). Offers year-long and summer programs, as short as 15 days, restoring castles and churches throughout France. Anyone 15 or over is eligible. 80F per day, plus 90F application fee.

FINDING WORK ONCE YOU'RE THERE

Check help-wanted columns in French newspapers, especially *Le Monde, Le Figaro*, and the English-language *International Herald Tribune*, as well as *France-USA Contacts*, a free weekly circular filled with classifieds, which can be picked up in Yankee hangouts. Many of these jobs are "unofficial" and therefore illegal (one risks deportation), but many people find them convenient because they often don't ask for presentation of a work permit. However, the best tips on jobs for foreigners come from other travelers. Be aware of your rights as an employee, and always get written confirmation of your agreements. Youth hostels frequently provide room and board to travelers willing to help run the place.

In Paris, start your job search at the **American Church,** 65 Quai d'Orsay, Paris 75007 (tel. 01 40 62 05 00) which posts a bulletin board (view M-Sa 9am-10pm) full of job and housing opportunities targeting Americans abroad. Those with ambition and an up-to-date resume, in both French and English, should stop by the **American Chamber of Commerce in France,** 21 av. George V, 1st floor, 8ème (tel. 01 40 73 89 90; fax 01 47 20 18 62; open M-F 9am-5pm), an association of American businesses in France. Your resume will be kept on file for two months and placed at the disposal of French and American companies. Chamber of Commerce membership directories can be browsed in the Paris office. Filled with practical info on working as an American abroad, it is useful to have it sent to you before your arrival in France. (Library open Tu and Th 10am-12:30pm. Admission 50F.) The **Agence Nationale Pour l'Emploi (ANPE),** 4 impasse d'Antin, 8ème (tel. 01 43 59 62 63; fax 01 49 53 91 46; www.enpe.fr), has specific info on employment. (Open M-W and F 9am-5pm, Th 9am-noon.) Remember to bring your work permit and, if you have one, your *carte de séjour*. The **Centre d'Information et de Documentation Jeunesse (CIDJ),** 101 quai Branly, 15ème (tel. 01 44 49 12 00; fax 01 40 65 02 61), an invaluable state-run youth center provides info on education, resumés, employment, and careers. English spoken. Jobs are posted at 9am on the bulletin boards outside. (Open M-F 9am-6pm, Sa 9:30am-1pm.)

FURTHER READING

Overseas Summer Jobs 1999, Work Your Way Around the World, and *Directory of Jobs and Careers Abroad* (Peterson's, US$17-18 each); *International Jobs: Where they Are, How to Get Them,* by Eric Koocher (Perseus Books, US$16); *How to Get a Job in Europe,* by Robert Sanborn (Surrey Books, US$22).

VOLUNTEER

Volunteer jobs are readily available almost everywhere. You may receive room and board in exchange for your labor. You can sometimes avoid the application fees charged by the organizations that arrange placement by contacting the individual work camps directly; check with the organizations.

Service Civil International Voluntary Service (SCI-VS), 814 NE 40th St., Seattle, WA 98105 (tel./fax 206 545 6585; email sciivsusa@igc.apc.org), arranges placement in work camps in Europe for those aged 18 and over. (Registration US$50-250, depending on location.)

For **further information,** consult *The International Directory of Voluntary Work*, by Victoria Pybus (Vacation Work Publications, US$16), or *The Alternative Travel Directory*, by Clayton Hubbs (Transitions Abroad, US$20).

OTHER RESOURCES

USEFUL PUBLICATIONS

The following is a very small selection of thousands of books published about France. Many of them may only be available on order or from a specialist travelers' bookstore: check local listings to see if there is one near you.

French or Foe? Getting the Most Out of Visiting, Living and Working in France, Polly Platt. Distribooks Intl, 1998 (US$16.95). A popular guide to getting by in France

Cultural Misunderstandings: The French-American Experience, Raymonde Carroll, transl. Carol Volk. University of Chicago Press, 1990 (US$11.95). For Americans baffled by the French outlook on life.

Wicked French, Howard Tomb. Workman, 1989 (US$4.95). A hilarious guide to everything you really didn't need to know how to say in French.

A Traveller's Wine Guide to France, Christopher Fielden. Traveller's Wine Guides, 1997. (US$17.95). Exactly what it says it is, by a well-known oenophile.

Michelin Green Guides. Michelin. Around US$20. The authoritative guide to France, this series covers the country in 24 regional books with unbeatable information on towns and sights. You'll still need your trusty *Let's Go* for all your practical information, accommodations, and food needs. Some regions are only available in French.

Traveller's Literary Companion: France, Ed. John Edmonson. Passport Books, 1997 (US$17.95). For those rare times when *Let's Go* doesn't reach that literary high, these 120 extracts from great French writers provide another perspective on France.

THE WORLD WIDE WEB

The Web is catching on in France in a big way, making it an ever more useful resource for travelers as businesses realize the advantages of cyberspace. Websites relevant to specific concerns and businesses mentioned above are given in the relevant sections.

Maison de la France (www.maison-de-la-france.com:8000/) is the main government tourist site. Up-to-date information on tourism in France, including a calendar of festivals and major events, regional info with links to local servers, and a host of tips on everything from accommodation to smoking laws. English version available.

France Diplomatie (www.france.diplomatie.fr/) is the French Department of Foreign Affairs site, with information on visas and other official matters as well as comprehensive presentations on French history, culture, geography, politics, and current affairs. Most information is available in English.

Secretariat for Tourism (www.tourisme.gouv.fr) has a number of governmental documents and press releases relating to the state of tourism in France, plus links to all the national, regional and departmental tourist authorities. In French.

Tourism in France (www.tourisme.fr) has information on all types of tourism in France, an extensive directory of links to local resources and features on "unwonted stays to discover France." In French and mildly amusing English.

Nomade (www.nomade.fr) and **French Excite** (www.excite.fr) are a popular French search engines—though they're not very useful if you can't read French.

TF1 (www.TF1.com) is the home page of France's most popular TV station, and with news, popular culture, and weather and traffic reports in French.

Météo-France (www.meteo.fr) has 2-day weather forecasts and maps for France.

Let's Go (www.letsgo.com) is where you can find our newsletter, information about our books, up-to-the-minute links, and more.

FURTHER READING. *How to Plan Your Dream Vacation Using the Web*, by Elizabeth Dempsey (Coriolis Group, US$25); *Nettravel: How Travelers Use the Internet*, by Michael Shapiro (O'Reilly & Associates, US$25); *Travel Planning Online for Dummies*, by Noah Vadnai. (IDG Books, US$25).

ESSENTIALS

PARIS AND THE ÎLE DE FRANCE

To the French, their country is divided into two parts: Paris and *province*—everywhere else. To the men and women of the provinces, the excesses of the capital are greeted with a shrug and a wry *"Eh bien, ça c'est Paris,"* while to the denizens of the capital, the inhabitant rest of the country—whether they be from a Pyreneean village or Lyon—are *paysans*, mythical guardians of French traditions. Meanwhile, the Île de France, the historic heart of the country, has long been little more than an extension of Paris's *banlieues*, swallowing up châteaux and parks in its suburban sprawl.

HISTORY

Paris owes its name to its first inhabitants, the Gaulish Parisii tribe who settled in the Île de la Cité in the 3rd century BC. In an early display of Parisian pride, the inhabitants chose to burn down their city rather than surrender it to Julius Cæsar in 52BC. Though the Romans established Lutetia on its site, the town was just another provincial city until Clovis captured it for the Franks and made it his capital at the end of the 5th century. The area bounded by the Seine, the Marne, the Beuvronne, the Oise, and the Nonette rivers thus became known as Francia, and, as Francia became France, its water-bound heartland took the name Île de France. Though the Carolingians retained Paris as their nominal capital, it was only when the Count of Paris, Hugh Capet, became king in 987 that the city definitively became the urban hub of the kingdom—not that there was much else left of the kingdom outside the Île de France anyway. Nevertheless, the city prospered, and merchants' guilds became increasingly powerful. The river-merchants' crest of ships was adopted as the city's coat-of-arms, and when Philippe-Auguste left for the Crusades in 1190, he entrusted the city to the guilds. Thirty years later, the king formally recognized the three distinct quarters of medieval Paris: the university on the left bank, the merchants on the right, and the *cité* on the island.

Philippe-Auguste was also responsible for extending the fractured royal domain from the Île de France to encompass the rest of the country. But while France was more or less unified, trouble was brewing in the capital. The merchants viewed with a greedy eye the success of the free Flemish towns to the north, and coveted independence. In 1356, their leader Étienne Marcel had the royal administrators murdered and allied himself with the English invaders. While French control was soon reinstated, in 1415 an Anglo-Burgundian alliance occupied the city with little resistance, and Paris accepted the English Henry VI as its king. Only in 1437 did Charles VII make his triumphal entry into the city, and, perhaps unsure of its loyalty, he and his heirs chose to reside in the Loire valley. During the Wars of Religion in the 16th century, Paris came down firmly on the Catholic side after the St. Bartholomew's Day Massacre in 1572. The city rose against the religiously moderate Henri III in 1588 and refused entry to the Protestant Henri IV in 1590. In 1594, Henri gave in—as he said, "Paris is worth a Mass"—converted to Catholicism, and took up residence in the Louvre. Under his son Louis XIII, Paris sparkled. Squares and gardens were laid out, Richelieu built the Palais Royal, the aristocracy moved into mansions in the Marais, and two previously uninhabited Seine islands were joined together to make the Île St-Louis.

Paris remained at the center of French cultural life even when Louis XIV moved the court to Versailles in the 17th century. The Sun King continued to expand the Louvre, which had been rebuilt under François I, and laid out the Champs-Élysées, while the centralization of government under his reign increased the power and wealth of the city. However, the discontent of Parisians boiled over in 1789 as the Revolution unfolded in the capital and then spread to the provinces. The dread Guillotine was set up in place de la Concorde, its blade falling on Louis XVI in 1793. Despite all the construction, Paris remained very much a medieval city; conditions were so bad that a cholera epidemic in 1832 killed almost 20,000 people, while the maze of streets allowed mobs to assemble and disperse with impunity. In 1852, Napoleon III ordered Baron Haussmann to remodel the city, and over the next 18 years medieval buildings were razed, grand avenues laid out, and modern Paris was created. Revitalized, Paris held out for three months when the Second Empire collapsed before the Prussian advance in 1870. After the peace was signed, the new Third Republic did not prove to the city's liking, and disenchantment boiled over into the left-wing Communard revolt of 1871, ruthlessly crushed by the city authorities.

In the 19th century, the industrialized city was captured by Impressionists, from Toulouse Lautrec's scenes of Parisian nightlife to Monet's smoke-filled *Gare St-Lazare*. The international pre-eminence of Paris was evident at the Universal Exhibition in 1889, crowned by the new Eiffel Tower. Paris remained the intellectual capital of the world until WWII, attracting artists from Sisley to Brancusi and writers from Wilde to Hemingway, but France's defeat in 1939 forced many into exile or hiding. While the city suffered little structural damage from the war, a new generation of thinkers could not disguise that fact that Paris had lost its cultural crown to an upstart across the Atlantic. Nevertheless, the city continues to hold its head high as it enters the new millennium. The Grande Arche, a 20th-century reply to the Arc de Triomphe, towers over high-tech La Défense; the Louvre has been revitalized by I.M. Pei's pyramid; and Paris demonstrated that its proud spirit is still alive after France's 1998 World Cup victory at the new Stade-de-France.

GEOGRAPHY AND CLIMATE

Though only two million people live in Paris proper, over 10 million inhabit the Île de France, making it the most densely populated region in the country. Geographically, the Paris Basin occupies a depression (which would account for all the dour faces), with a climate typical of central France: cold but not severe winters and hot, dusty summers. The population flees in August, leaving a ghost city inhabited only by tourists and pigeons, while autumn brings unsettled weather and rapidly shortening days. As for Paris in the springtime, what more need be said?

SUGGESTIONS

Paris is first and foremost an international city, and only second capital of France. Wandering down the grand **Champs-Élysées** (p. 123), the studenty **Latin Quarter** (p. 127), the ex-aristocratic **Marais** (p. 120), and medieval **Montmartre** (p. 124) will give you a good feel for the city. No-one can visit Paris without seeing the **Louvre** (p. 136), the **Eiffel Tower** (p. 130), and **Notre-Dame** (p. 116), but don't neglect Paris's past in the **Musée de Cluny** (p. 138), the other side of iron-age construction in the **Grand Palais** (p. 139), or Gothic architecture's finest jewel, **La Sainte-Chapelle** (p. 117). Of the châteaux near Paris, **Versailles** (p. 156) and **Fontainebleau** (p. 157) are the best known, but **Vaux-le-Vicomte** (p. 158) is just as exquisite, and far less crowded. Literary pilgrims should make their way to **Illiers-Combray** (p. 156), site of Marcel Proust's *Swann's Way* and near the great cathedral of **Chartres** (p. 154). The French formal garden is at its best in the **Jardins de Luxembourg** (p. 128), while the **Bois de Boulogne** (p. 135) sprawls languidly to the west. For a different outdoor experience, head to **Père Lachaise** cemetery (p. 133), burial place of Oscar Wilde, Proust, Chopin, and Jim Morrison.

PARIS

Paris, it might be thought, needs no introduction. It is, after all, the City of Lights and the city of love; it has appeared in a thousand films and on a million postcards. Everyone recognizes the Eiffel Tower, everyone aspires to wear clothes by Paris-based designers, and everyone knows that Parisians are unspeakably rude to foreigners. With such a wealth of clichés blanketing every aspect of the city, it's no wonder that so many visitors leave without having seen anything but what they expected to see; that for them Paris is the Louvre, Notre-Dame, the Champs-Élysées, and nothing more. It's sometimes hard to remember that behind the façade of *grands avenues* and grander museums there lies a living, pulsating city, a city that left behind years ago the tourists who continue to sip over-priced coffee in the old haunts of long-dead philosophers and flock to restaurants that Parisians abandoned before WWII. To be sure, there's no shame to marvelling at the Mona Lisa, living it up at the Moulin Rouge, or finding love under the Pont Neuf—but don't feel bound to limit yourself. Give some effort to discovering Paris and you will be rewarded many times over. Drop your preconceptions, loosen your purse-strings, and lose yourself in its visual tapestry. For more detailed coverage of Paris and its surroundings, consult *Let's Go: Paris 2000*.

▓ ORIENTATION

The **Île de la Cité** and neighboring **Île St-Louis** sit at the geographical center of the city, while the **Seine**, flowing east to west, splits Paris into two large expanses: the **Rive Gauche** (Left Bank) to its south and the **Rive Droite** (Right Bank) to its north. Administratively, Paris is divided into 20 **arrondissements** that spiral clockwise around the Louvre.

RIVE GAUCHE. The **Latin Quarter**, encompassing the 5ème and parts of the 6ème *arrondissements*, has been home to students for centuries. The boundary between the two, **bd. St-Michel** (abbreviated to *le boul'Mich* by students) overflows with cafés, cinemas, boutiques, and bookstores. Crossing bd. St-Michel and running east-west, **bd. St-Germain** welcomes literary pilgrims to the former drinking haunts of Hemingway, Sartre, and Camus. To the west, the sparkling gold dome of the **Invalides** and the stern Neoclassical **École Militaire**, which faces the Eiffel tower across the **Champ-de-Mars**, recall the military past of the 7ème and northern 15ème, now a civil servant haven filled with traveling businesspeople. To the south of the Latin Quarter, **Montparnasse**, in the 14ème and eastern 15ème, lolls in the shadows of its tower, central Paris's only real skyscraper. The glamorous **bd. du Montparnasse** belies the more residential districts around it—once home to many a penniless artist, including Modigliani and Chagall. Farther south in the 14ème, the area around the **Denfert-Rochereau** RER station is far off the tourist map, while right on the *arrondissement's* southern boundary, the **cité universitaire** complex is home to many of the capitals' students. The eastern *rive gauche*, comprising the 13ème, is home to much of Paris's East Asian community and is currently Paris's newest up-and-coming hotspot, centered on the **pl. d'Italie.**

RIVE DROITE (RIGHT BANK). Paris's royal past is conspicuous in the area around the **Louvre** and **rue de Rivoli,** occupying the sight- and tourist-packed 1er and the more business oriented 2ème. Home to *ancien régime* magnates in the 17th and Jewish immigrants in the late 19th century, the **Marais** (3ème and 4ème) escaped Haussmann's destruction of ancient Paris. Palatial mansions have become exquisite museums, and the tiny twisting streets have been adopted by fashionable boutiques and galleries. From **pl. de la Concorde,** the western end of the 1er, **av. des Champs-Élysées** bisects the swish 8ème as it sweeps up towards the Arc de Triomphe at **Charles de Gaulle-Étoile.** South of the Étoile, money old and new makes its home in the exclusive 16ème, bordered to the east by the **Bois de Boulogne** park and to the west by the Seine and the **Trocadéro,** facing the Eiffel Tower across the river. Moving back to central Paris, just north of the 1er, the 9ème is defined by the sumptuous **Opéra.** It's also home to most of Paris's major department stores. To the east of the 9ème, the 10ème holds little allure but the promise of cheap lodgings and escape via the **Gare du Nord** and the **Gare de l'Est.** The 10ème and 3ème meet at **pl. de la République.** The *place* marks the start of the happening 11ème, which climaxes to the south at **Bastille.** South of Bastille, the 12ème clusters around the **Gare de Lyon,** petering out at the **Parc de Vincennes,** while east of Bastille the party atmosphere gives way to the quiet 20ème, whose only real attraction is **Père Lachaise** cemetery, burial place of Apollinaire and Victor Hugo. Circling counter-clockwise, the 19ème has little to offer, while the 18ème is home to **Montmartre,** capped by the **Sacré-Cœur.** To the east the 17ème starts in the sordidness of **Pigalle** but mutates into swishness as it approaches the Étoile and the 16ème. Continuing along the *grande axe* defined by the Champs-Élysées through the suburb of **Neuilly** is Paris's newest quarter, **La Défense,** which erects its space-age skyscrapers just across the loop of the Seine as it curves up on the other side of the Bois de Boulogne.

⌐ TRANSPORTATION

GETTING IN AND OUT OF PARIS

PLANES

Paris has two major airports. Most international flights arrive at **Roissy-Charles de Gaulle** airport to the north of the city, while domestic, budget, and charter flights often land at **Orly,** to the south.

AÉROPORT ROISSY-CHARLES DE GAULLE

The airport has two terminals; as a general rule, the newer **Terminal 2** *(aérogare 2)* serves Air France and its affiliates, while the ageing **Terminal 1** *(aérogare 1)* serves other airlines. There are many ways of getting to Roissy from Paris; the RER is cheap and reliable, but shuttle buses are more convenient. For 24hr. airport info in English, call 01 48 62 22 80.

RER: The RER line B3 links central Paris to Roissy, stopping at Luxembourg, St-Michel, Châtelet-les-Halles, and the Gare du Nord in central Paris. From Roissy, a free bus shuttles to the RER station from Terminal 1 gate 28, Terminal 2A gate 5, Terminal 2B gate 6, and Terminal 2D gate 6. Going to Roissy, make sure the RER train number starts with an "E." Try to get an express train, which is significantly faster; signs on the platform indicate at which stations the train stops (45min., every 20min. 5am-12:30am, 48F).

Shuttle Buses: Roissybus (tel. 01 48 04 18 24) runs from the AmEx office, rue Scribe (M: Opéra), to Terminal 2A gate 10 (also serves terminal 2C), Terminal 2D gate 12 (also serves Terminal 2B), and Terminal 1 gate 30, arrivals level (45min., every 15min. 5:45am-11pm, 45F). **Air France Buses** (tel. 01 41 56 89 00) has two lines; both stop at Terminals 2A-2F and outside exit 34 at Terminal 1. **Line #2** leaves from the Arc de Triomphe (M: Charles de Gaulle-Étoile) at 1 av. Carnot, with a stop at Porte de Maillot/ Palais des Congrès (M: Porte de Maillot) on bd. Gouvion St-Cyr (35min.; every 20min. 5:50am-11pm; one-way 60F, round-trip 105F). **Line #4** leaves from rue du Commandant Mouchette in front of the Hôtel Méridien, near Gare Montparnasse (M: Montparnasse-Bienvenue), with a stop at Gare de Lyon (M: Gare de Lyon), at 20 bd. Diderot (every 30 min. 7am-9pm; one-way 70F, round-trip 120F). Buy tickets on the bus.

Door-to-door shuttles: Airport Shuttle (tel. 01 45 38 55 72). 120F for one person, 89F each for 2 or more. **Paris Shuttle** (tel. 01 43 90 91 91). 85F per person for 2 or more. **Paris Airports Service** (tel. 01 49 62 78 78). 145F for one person, 180F for two.

Paris: Central Accommodations

1er & 2ème

A Hôtel Louvre-Richelieu
B Hôtel Montpensier
C Centre International (BVJ)/Paris Louvre
D Hôtel Saint-Honoré
E Henri IV
F Hôtel des Boulevards
G Hôtel La Marmotte
H Hôtel Tiquetonne

5ème & 6ème

I Hôtel d'Esmeralda
J Centre International (BVJ): Paris Quarter Latin
K Hôtel le Central
L Hôtel des Médicis
M Hôtel Gay Lussac
N Young & Happy Hostel
O Hôtel des Alliés
P Hôtel de Neslé
Q Dhely's Hotel
R Foyer International des Etudiantes
S Hôtel de Chevreuse

11ème, 12ème, & 14ème

T Hôtel Moderne
U Hôtel Rhétia
V Mistral Hôtel
W Centre International du Séjour de Paris: "Ravel"
X Hôtel du Parc
Y Ouest Hôtel
Z Hôtel de Blois

For Accommodations in 3ème, 4ème, 7ème, 8ème, 9ème, and 10ème, and more in 11ème, please see the maps of 3ème and 4ème, 7ème, 8ème, and 9ème.

3ème

rue de Fbg. St-Denis
bd. de Strasbourg
rue du Château d'Eau
STRASBOURG ST-DENIS
bd. St-Martin
rue St-Martin
ARTS ET MÉTIERS
rue de Turbigo
rue Beaubourg
RAMBUTEAU
rue du Temple
rue des Archives
rue Vieille du Temple
rue de Bretagne
Musée Picasso
Musée Carnavalet
rue de Rivoli
Hôtel de Ville
ST-PAUL
PL. DES VOSGES
rue St-Antoine
4ème
SULLY MORLAND
bd. Henri IV
Ile St-Louis
rue de Fourcy
rue Quetampi
ST-SÉBASTIEN FROISSART
bd. Beaumarchais
RICHARD LENOIR
CHEMIN VERT
rue Lenoir
rue du Chemin Vert
ST-AMBROSE
BRÉGUET SABIN
BASTILLE
rue du Faubourg St-Antoine
rue de la Roquette
PL. LÉON BLUM
VOLTAIRE
11ème
bd. Voltaire
rue de Charonne
CHARONNE
rue de Reuilly
Opéra Bastille
LEDRU-ROLLIN
FAIDHERBE CHALIGNY
rue de Montreuil
REUILLY DIDEROT
5ème
quai St-Bernard
Seine
QUAI DE LA RAPÉE
JUSSIEU
Jardin des Plantes
SEE 3ÈME & 4ÈME MAP
av. Ledru-Rollin
av. Daumesnil
12ème
rue de Lyon
rue Chaligny
bd. Diderot
GARE DE LYON
Gare de Lyon
Pont de Sully
GARE D'AUSTERLITZ
RER
Gare d'Austerlitz
RER
La Mosquée
rue Buffon
rue Censier
rue G. St-Hilaire
rue de l'Hôpital
bd. St-Marcel
ST-MARCEL
13ème
Pont de Bercy
QUAI DE LA GARE
bd. de Bercy
rue de Bercy

N
TO W (2km)

0 300 yards
0 300 meters

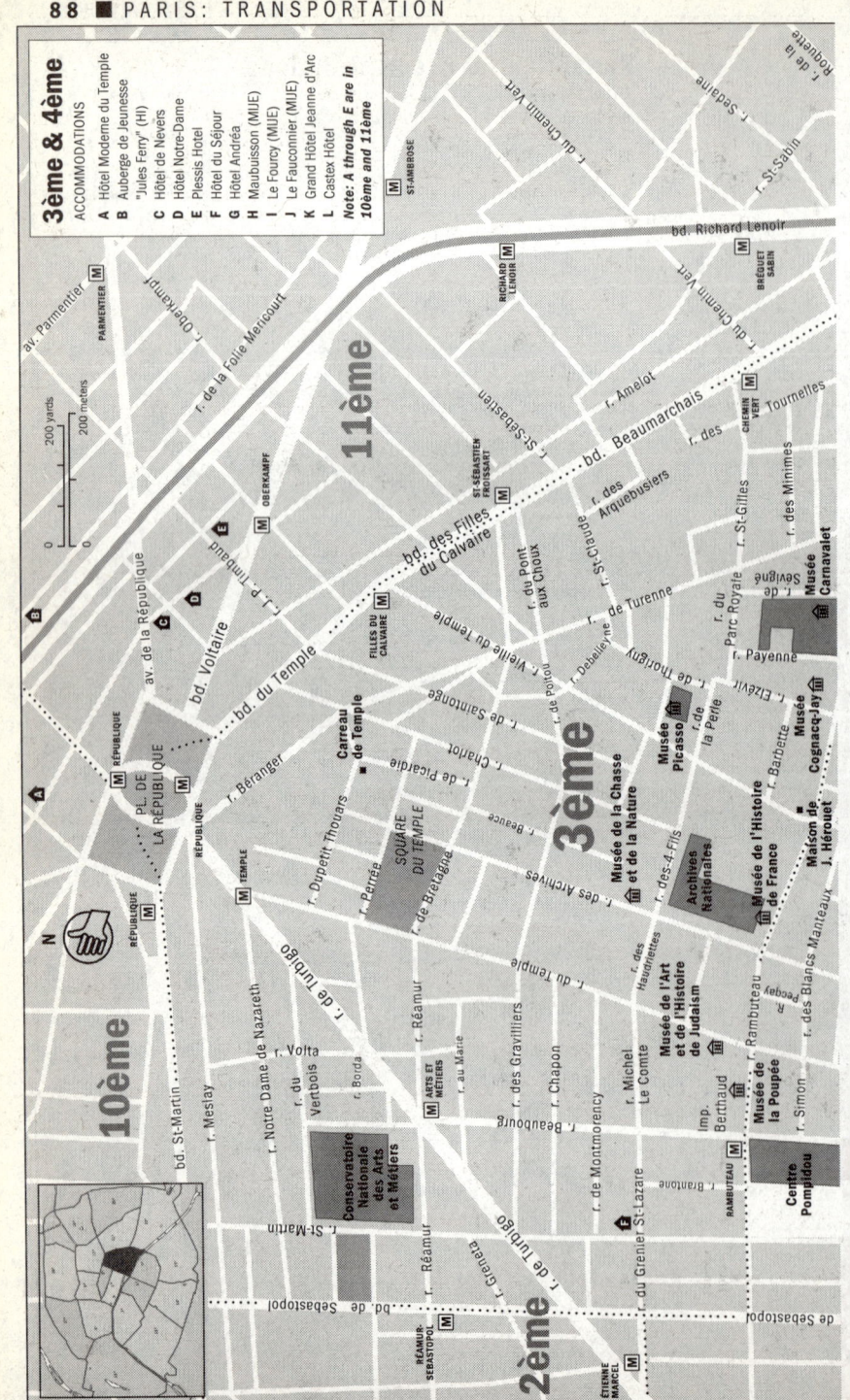

3ème & 4ème

ACCOMMODATIONS

A Hôtel Moderne du Temple
B Auberge de Jeunesse "Jules Ferry" (HI)
C Hôtel de Nevers
D Hôtel Notre-Dame
E Plessis Hotel
F Hôtel du Séjour
G Hôtel Andréa
H Maubuisson (MIJE)
I Le Fourcy (MIJE)
J Le Fauconnier (MIJE)
K Grand Hôtel Jeanne d'Arc
L Castex Hôtel

Note: A through E are in 10ème and 11ème

0   200 yards
0   200 meters

10ème

11ème

3ème

2ème

Conservatoire Nationale des Arts et Métiers

Carreau de Temple

SQUARE DU TEMPLE

Musée de la Chasse et de la Nature

Musée Picasso

Musée Cognacq-Jay

Musée de l'Histoire de France

Archives Nationales

Maison de J. Hérouet

Musée Carnavalet

Musée de l'Art et de l'Histoire du Judaïsm

Musée de la Poupée

Centre Pompidou

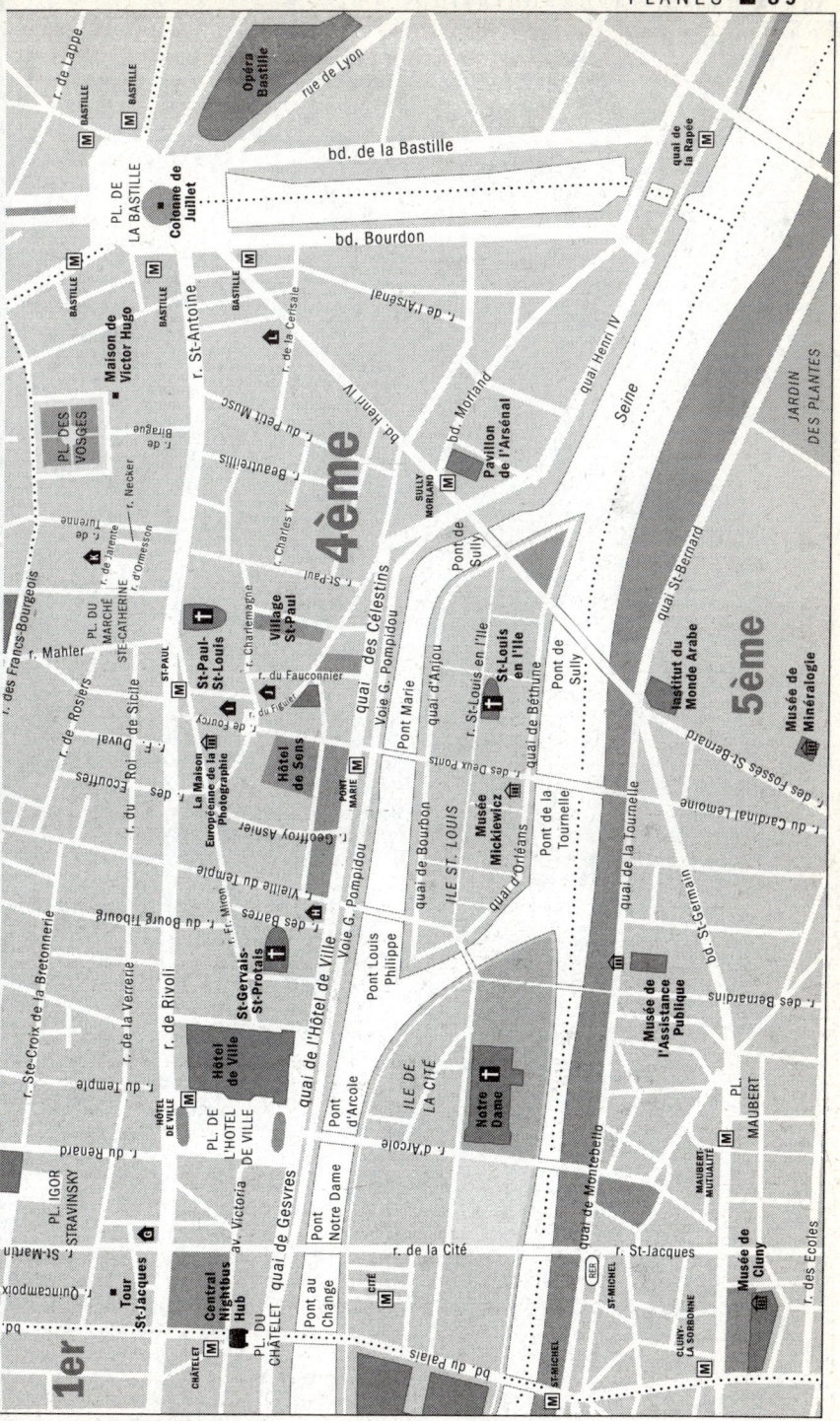

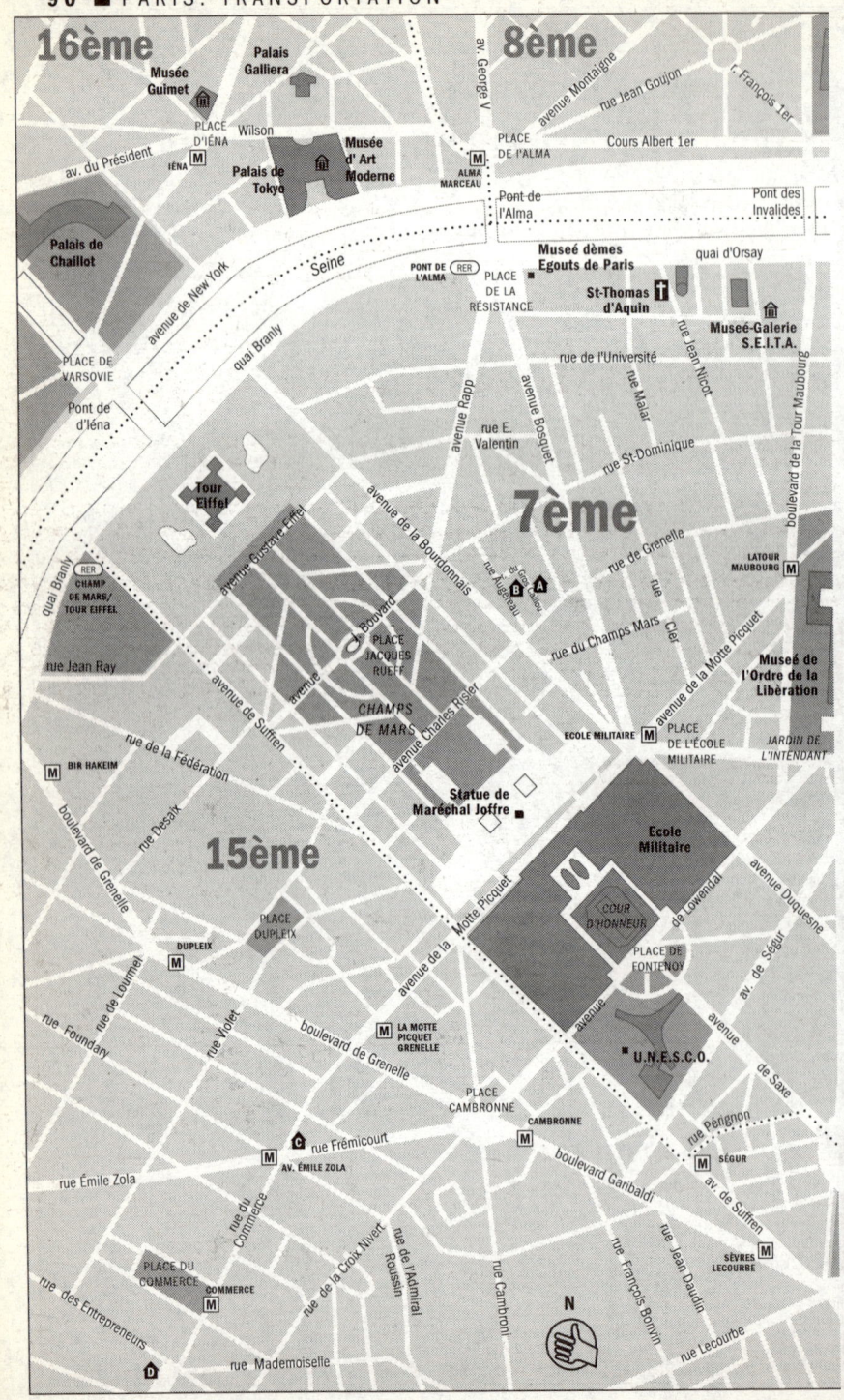

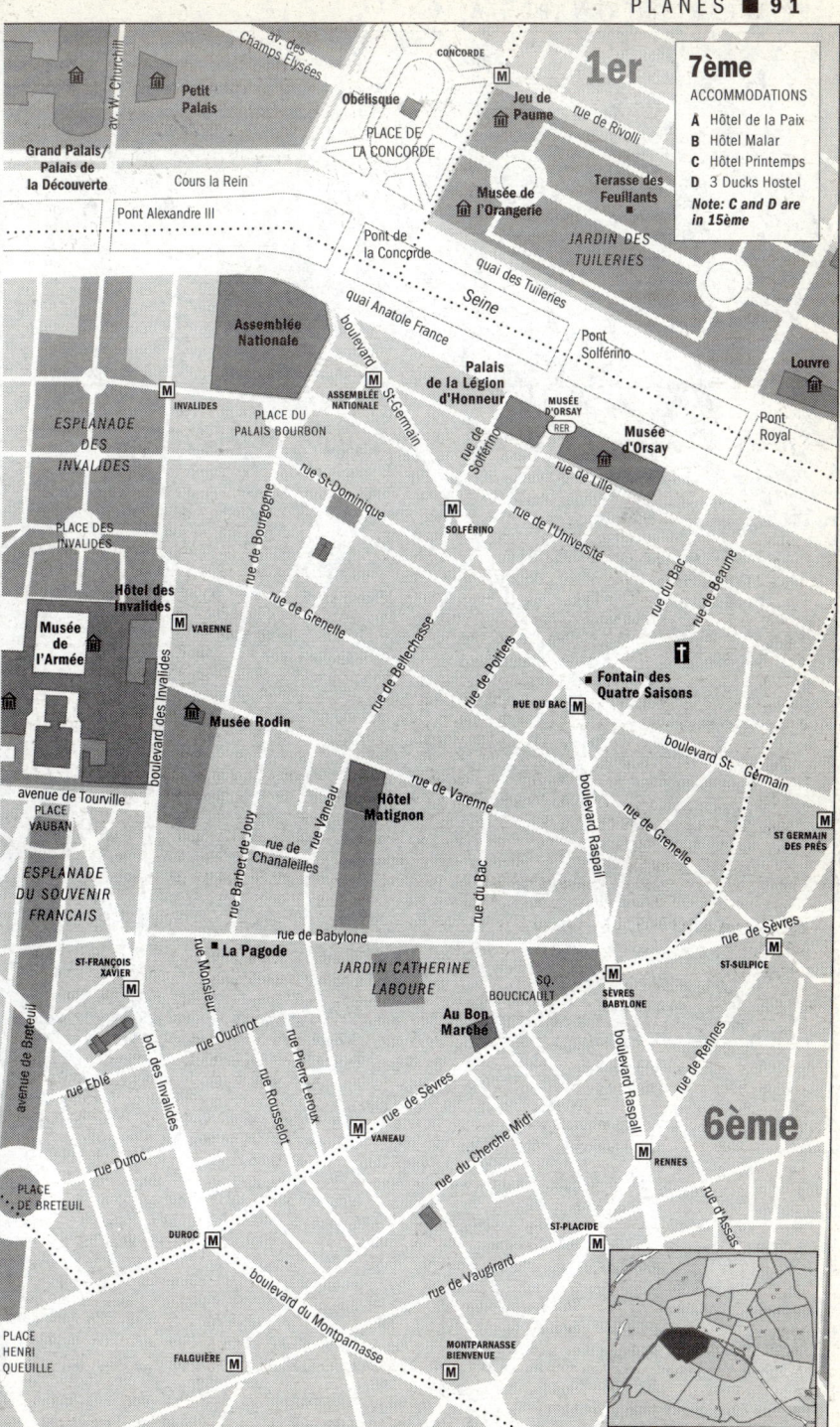

av. des Champs Élysées

CONCORDE

1er

7ème
ACCOMMODATIONS
A Hôtel de la Paix
B Hôtel Malar
C Hôtel Printemps
D 3 Ducks Hostel
Note: C and D are in 15ème

av. W. Churchill

Petit Palais

Grand Palais/ Palais de la Découverte

Cours la Rein

Pont Alexandre III

Obélisque

PLACE DE LA CONCORDE

Jeu de Paume

rue de Rivoli

Musée de l'Orangerie

Terasse des Feuillants

JARDIN DES TUILERIES

Pont de la Concorde

quai des Tuileries

Seine

quai Anatole France

Pont Solférino

Louvre

Assemblée Nationale

boulevard St-Germain

ASSEMBLÉE NATIONALE

Palais de la Légion d'Honneur

MUSÉE D'ORSAY

RER

Musée d'Orsay

Pont Royal

INVALIDES

PLACE DU PALAIS BOURBON

rue de Solférino

rue de Lille

ESPLANADE DES INVALIDES

rue St-Dominique

rue de l'Université

rue du Bac

rue de Beaune

SOLFÉRINO

PLACE DES INVALIDES

rue de Bourgogne

rue de Grenelle

Hôtel des Invalides

VARENNE

rue de Bellechasse

rue de Poitiers

Fontain des Quatre Saisons

Musée de l'Armée

boulevard des Invalides

Musée Rodin

RUE DU BAC

boulevard St- Germain

avenue de Tourville

PLACE VAUBAN

rue de Varenne

rue de Grenelle

boulevard Raspail

ST GERMAIN DES PRÉS

ESPLANADE DU SOUVENIR FRANCAIS

rue Barber de Jouy

rue Vaneau

Hôtel Matignon

rue de Babylone

rue de Chanaleilles

rue du Bac

ST-FRANÇOIS XAVIER

La Pagode

rue Monsieur

JARDIN CATHERINE LABOURE

SQ. BOUCICAULT

SÈVRES BABYLONE

ST-SULPICE

rue de Sèvres

avenue de Breteuil

rue Eblé

bd. des Invalides

rue Oudinot

rue Pierre Leroux

rue Rousselot

Au Bon Marché

rue de Sèvres

boulevard Raspail

rue de Rennes

6ème

PLACE DE BRETEUIL

rue Duroc

VANEAU

rue du Cherche Midi

RENNES

rue d'Assas

DUROC

ST-PLACIDE

PLACE HENRI QUEUILLE

FALGUIÈRE

boulevard du Montparnasse

rue de Vaugirard

MONTPARNASSE BIENVENUE

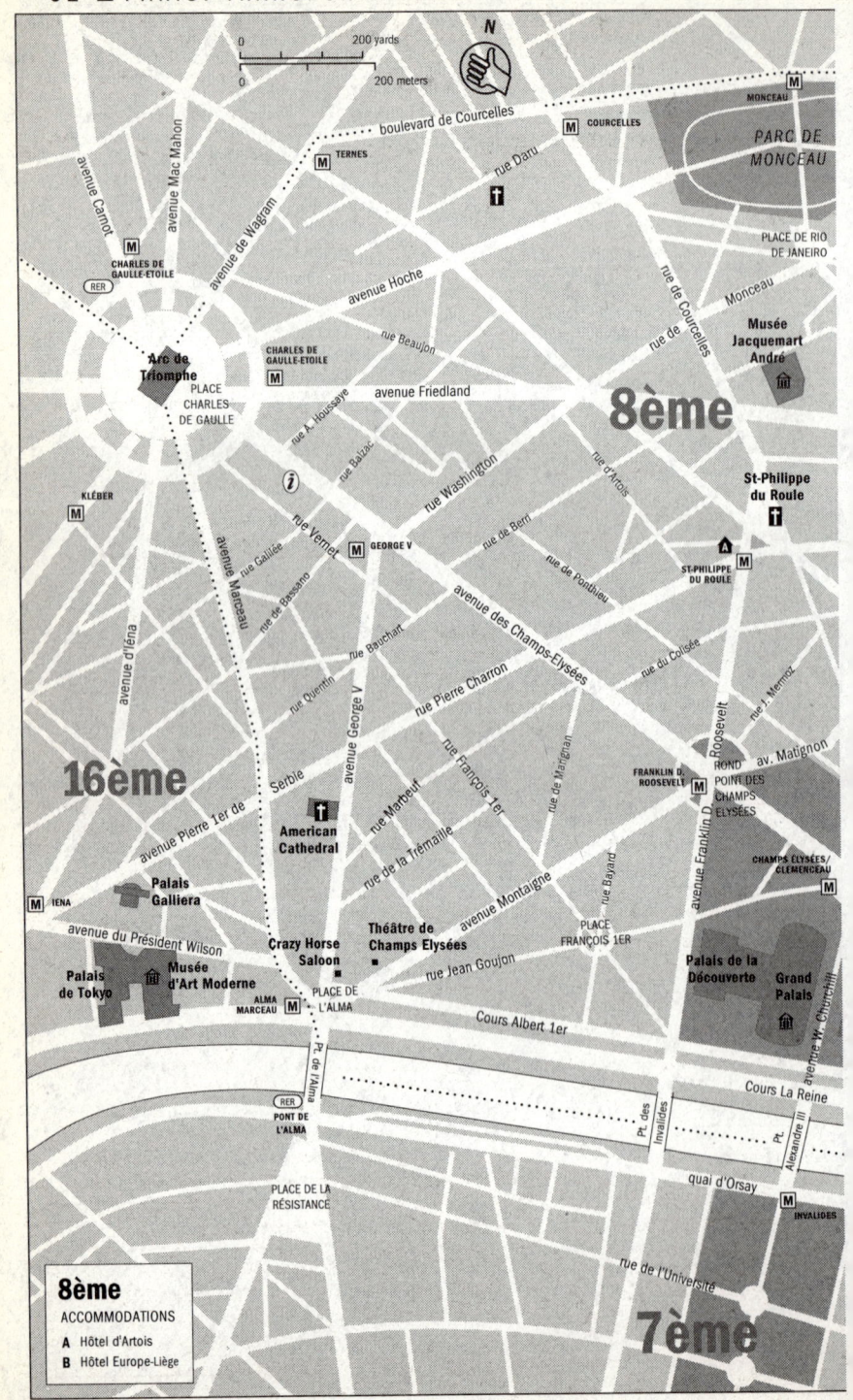

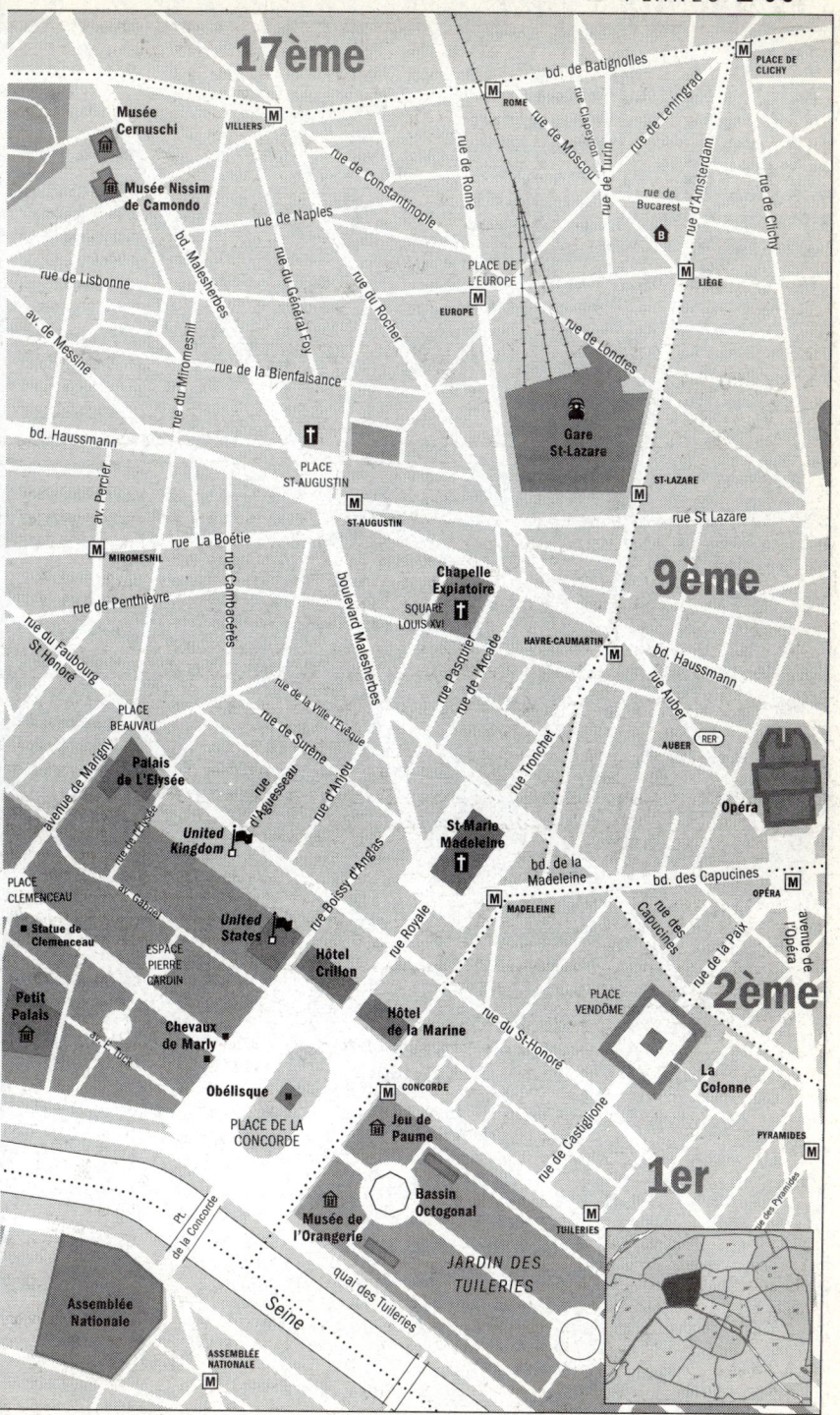

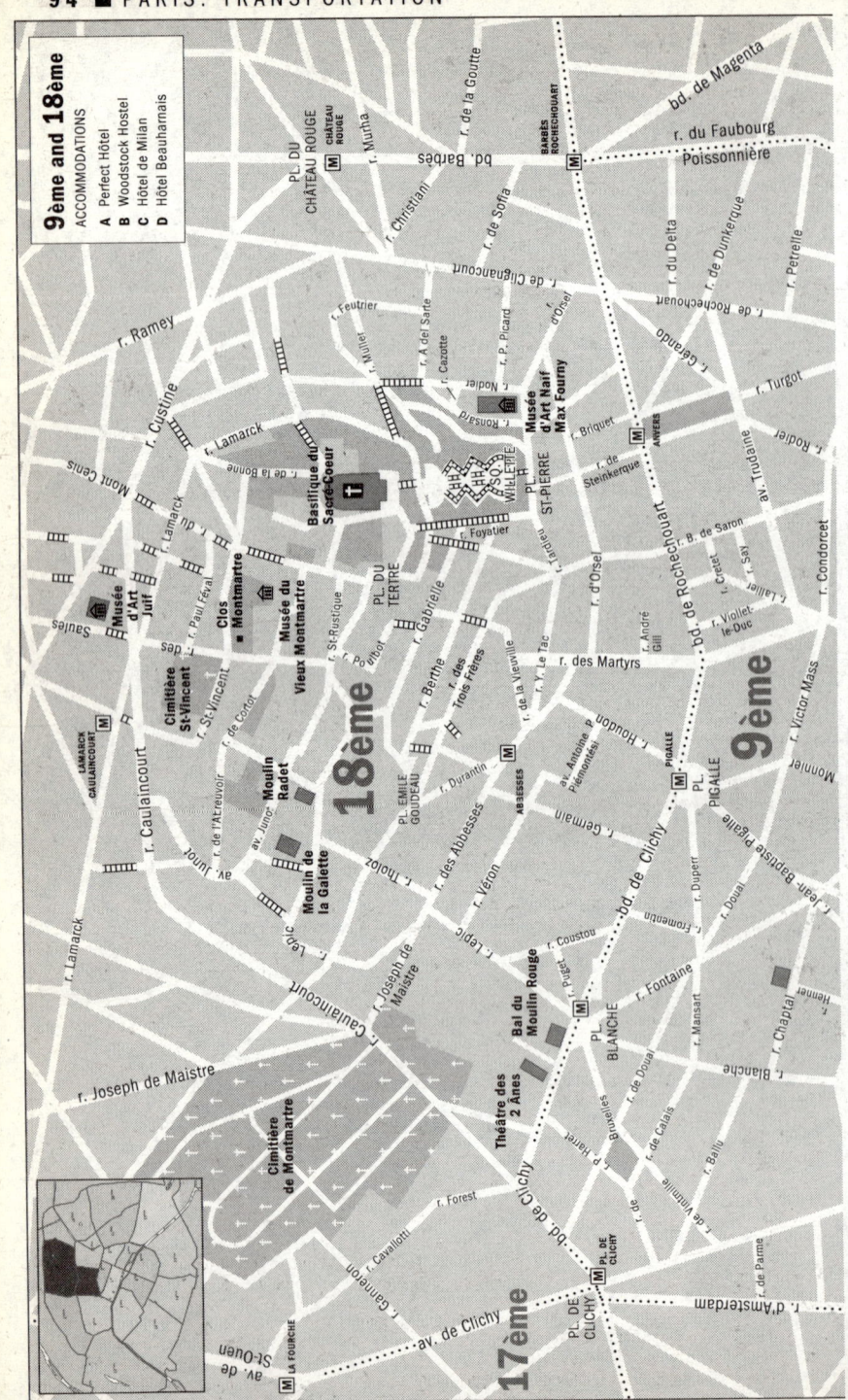

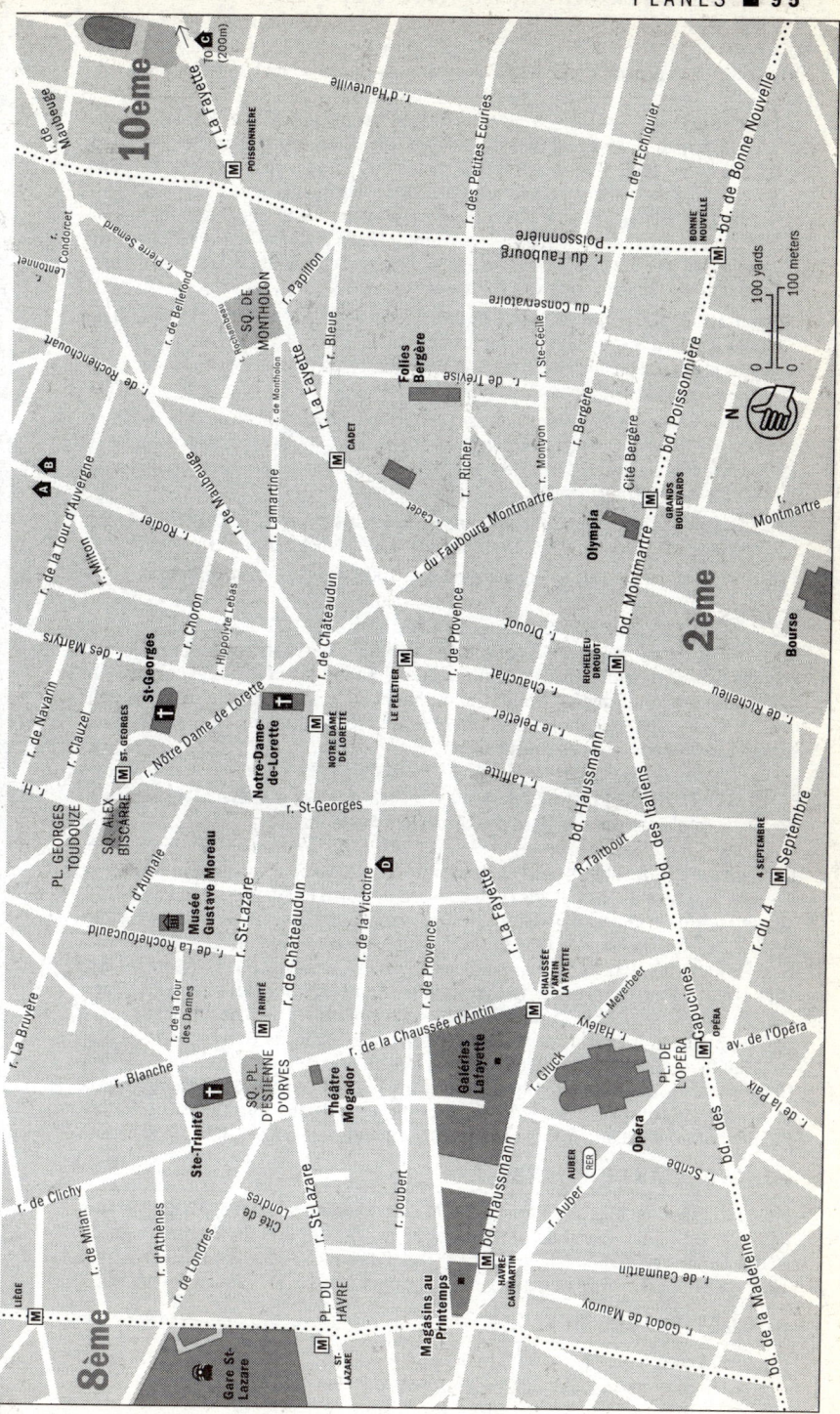

ORLY

Orly is closer to central Paris than Roissy, but harder to reach by metro/RER.

RER/Metro: Line C2 heads from Pont de Rungis/Aéroport d'Orly to central Paris, stopping at Invalides, Musée d'Orsay, St-Michel, and Gare d'Austerlitz (25min., every 15min. 6am-11pm, 35F). The **Orly-Rail** shuttle bus links the RER station to Orly Sud gate H and gate I platform 1, and Orly Ouest arrival level gate F (every 15min 5:40am-11:15pm). **Jetbus** goes from Orly Sud gate H platform 2 and Orly Ouest arrival level gate C to M: Villejuif-Louis Aragon, line 7 (every 12min. 5:45am-11:30pm, 22F). **Orly-bus** goes to RER: Denfert-Rochereau, line B from Orly Sud gate H platform 4 and Ouest level 0 gate J (30min., every 13-20min. 6am-11pm, 30F).

Orlyval: Tel. 01 43 46 14 14. Take RER B to Antony-Orly (make sure the station is lit up on the indicator board), and transfer to the VAL train. You need to buy an Orlyval ticket from a metro station or an RATP office in Orly (Ouest gate W level 1, Sud gate K) before starting your journey (30min.; VAL runs M-Sa 6am-10:30pm, Su 7am-10:57pm; 57F).

Air France Buses: To Gare Montparnasse, 36 rue du Commandant Mouchotte (M: Montparnasse-Bienvenüe), and the Invalides Air France office, pl. des Invalides, stopping at Orly Sud gate J and Orly Ouest gate E arrivals level (30min.; every 12min. 6am-11pm; 45F one-way, 75F round-trip).

Door-to-door Shuttles: Airport Shuttle and **Paris Shuttle** prices as for Charles de Gaulle. **Paris Airports Service** (tel. 01 49 62 78 78). 115F for one person, 135F for two.

Taxis: At least 45min. and 120F during the day, 160F at night and on weekends.

TRAINS

Each of Paris's six major train stations has two divisions: **banlieue** (suburban) and **grandes lignes** (long distance). Within a given station, each division has its own ticket counters, information booths, and timetables; make sure you're at the right one. There is a free telephone with direct access to the stations on the right-hand side of the Champs-Élysées tourist office.

 STATION SAFETY. Each terminal shelters its share of thieves. Take particular care in the **Gare du Nord** and the **Gare d'Austerlitz** at night.

Each *grande ligne* station serves destinations in a particular region of France or Europe. The **Gare du Nord** heads (you guessed it) north to Flanders, the Pas de Calais, and northern and north-eastern Europe, including Eurostar services to Britain. Head east from the **Gare de l'Est** to Champagne, Alsace, and Lorraine, and eastern Europe including Luxembourg, southern Germany, and Austria. The **Gare de Lyon** (this is getting too easy) heads to Lyon and the south, serving Burgundy, Provence, the Alps, the Côte d'Azur, parts of Switzerland, and Italy. The **Gare d'Austerlitz** goes to... trick! not to Austerlitz at all, but southwest to Spain, as well as Berry-Limousin, Aquitaine, Gascony, the Pays Basque, Languedoc, and occasionally to Poitou-Charentes. More TGVs to Poitou-Charentes leave from the **Gare Montparnasse** (hint: it's in Montparnasse), which also serves Brittany and the Loire Valley. Finally, for no linguistic reason, trains to Normandy leave from the **Gare St-Lazare**.

LONG DISTANCE BUSES

Most international buses to Paris arrive at **Gare Routière Internationale du Paris-Galliéni** (M: Galliéni), just outside Paris at 28 av. du Général de Gaulle, Bagnolet 93170. **Eurolines,** 55 rue St-Jacques, 5ème (tel. 08 36 69 52 52; www.eurolines.fr; M: Maubert-Mutualité) sells tickets to many European and a few French destinations.

BUDGET TRAVEL OFFICES

Council Travel, 1 pl. Odéon, 6ème (tel. 01 44 41 89 80; fax 01 40 51 89 12; CouncilTravelFrance@ciee.org). M: Odéon. Travel service for the under 26. Flights, train tickets,

BIJ/Eurotrain, guidebooks, and ISICs (60F). Replaces lost Council Travel tickets. English spoken. Open M-F 9:30am-6:30pm and Sa 10am-5pm.

Office de Tourisme Universitaire (OTU), 2 rue Malus, 5ème (tel. 01 44 41 74 74). M: Place Monge. Reduced train, plane, and BIJ tickets for students under 26 and ISICs (60F). Bring a government-issued ID. English spoken. Open M-F 10am-6:30pm. Also at 119 rue St-Martin, 4ème (tel. 01 40 29 12 12), M: Rambuteau. Open Sa 10am-5pm.

GETTING AROUND PARIS

Paris, when you exclude the sprawling suburbs, is small for its fame—much smaller than London or New York—and is best seen by foot. It takes only two hours to walk across the city from *porte* to *porte.* To explore, arm yourself with a pocket map, such as **Streetwise Paris** (US$5.95), or the comprehensive Michelin series **Paris: Atlas par arrondissements**. Of course, those hours walking add up and you're bound to need some faster way of traversing the city. Luckily, Parisian public transportation is swift, well maintained, and relatively cheap.

PUBLIC TRANSPORTATION

Public transportation in Paris is run by the **RATP** (Régie Autonome des Transports Parisiens; www.ratp.fr). Every metro station gives out free RATP network maps as well as displaying a map of the neighborhood. RATP information is available from: **La Maison de la RATP** (M: Gare de Lyon); **Bureau de Tourisme RATP,** pl. de la Madeleine, 8ème (tel. 01 40 06 71 44; M: Madeleine; open M-Sa 8:30am-6:45pm, Su 6:30am-1pm); and the English-language **RATP helpline** (tel. 08 36 68 77 14; 2.33F per minute; open daily 6am-9pm).

The transportation system is divided into five **zones**; central Paris *(section urbaine)* is Zone 1. All metros and all services in Zone 1 (metro, bus, and RER) use the same flat-rate ticket, available at metro stations; outside Zone 1 prices rise. **Tickets** for Zone 1 cost 8F each; a *carnet* of 10 costs 52F.

 USEFUL TIPS: PUBLIC TRANSPORTATION.
Always carry an extra ticket: ticket windows often close long before the last train departs—sometimes as early as 10pm.
At night, stay away from the most **dangerous stations:** Barbès-Rochechouart, Pigalle, Anvers, Châtelet-Les-Halles, Gare du Nord, and Gare de l'Est.

Metro: Inaugurated in 1898, the *métropolitain* is one of the world's oldest subway systems. Stations are marked with an "M" or with Art-Nouveau *"métropolitain"* lettering designed by Hector Guimard. There are 14 lines, numbered 1-14; within the system, lines are referred to by their final destinations. Tickets are valid for transfers to other metro lines and the RER if made within a station, but it is not always possible to reverse direction on the same line without exiting the station. Connections are indicated by orange *Correspondance* signs, exits by blue *Sortie* signs. You must keep your ticket until you have left the system. Service 5:30am-12:15am.

RER: The *Réseau Express Régional* is a rapid-transit system that connects the center of Paris to the outlying suburbs; within the city they travel at speed and make few stops. There are five lines, A-E. Each line is divided into branches (which split off in the suburbs), indicated by letters: e.g. B3 goes to Roissy-Charles de Gaulle. Express trains do not stop at some suburban stations; platform indicators show which stops will be made. Cars are divided into first and second class; standard tickets are for second-class travel.

Bus: Often neglected by tourists, Paris's bus system provides an efficient way to get from one sight to another *and* see some of Paris on the way. You'll need a bus map to unravel the mysteries of the system; the free *Autobus Paris-Plan du Réseau* is available at the tourist office and all metro information booths. The routes of each line are also posted at each stop. Push the red buttons on board to request a stop. Punch your ticket in the machine by the driver as you enter, or buy one from the driver. Tickets are not valid for bus-bus or metro-bus transfers. If you have a pass, show it to the driver when you enter. Service 6:30am-8:30pm; service marked **Autobus du Soir** run until 1am.

Noctambus: Limited all-night bus service. Buses depart the central "Châtelet" stop 1:30-5:30am, hourly M-Th, every 30min. F-Sa; the return trips run 1am-6am. Noctambus stops are marked with a bug-eyed moon. 3 tickets required for one bus, 4 tickets allows one transfer; all passes are valid. Ask at a major metro station or the Gare de l'Est RATP info booth for more information.

Balabus: A special tourist bus from Gare de Lyon to Bastille, St-Michel, Louvre, Musée d'Orsay, Concorde, Champs-Élysées, Charles-de-Gaulle-Étoile, Porte Maillot, Pont de Neuilly, and Grande Arche de La Défense (1¼hr.). Stops marked Balabus (Bb). Requires 1-3 tickets, depending on distance. Runs on Su and national holidays Apr. 2-Sept. 24 every 20min., 1:30-8:30pm from Gare de Lyon, 12:30-8pm from La Défense.

RATP PASSES

Whether you're staying in Paris for a few days or a few months, if you'll be using RATP services a lot you'll probably save money with one of their many passes.

Carte Orange: Coupons available in *hebdomadaire* (weekly, 80F) and *mensuel* (monthly, 271F). Valid for all RATP and SNCF *banlieue* services in Zone 1; adding zones costs extra. Weekly cards start Monday; monthly cards start the first of the month. You must have a passport-size photograph for the *carte* issued with your first coupon; you must write the number of your ID on the coupon to validate it.

Mobilis: Valid for one day on all RATP services in Zone 1 and 2. 32F.

Paris Visite: Unlimited travel on RATP services in Zone 1 plus discounts on many sights, tours, and bike rentals. 70F for 2 days; longer periods available (but not worth it).

TAXIS

Rates vary according to time of day and area, but they're never cheap. Count on paying a base rate of 13F plus: 4F per km for **Tarif A** (journeys within central Paris 7am-7pm); 5.83F per km for **Tarif B** (M-Sa 7pm-7am, all day Su, 7am-7pm from the airports and immediate suburbs); or 7.16F per km for **Tarif C** (to and from the airports 7pm to 7am). All taxis have lights on their roofs indicating the rate being charged. Additional charges (6F) are added for luggage over 5kg, a fourth adult, or for taxis leaving from train stations and taxi stops. Calling a cab is more expensive than hailing one from designated taxi stands. Radio-cab providers include: **Alpha Taxis,** tel. 01 45 85 85 85; **Taxis Radio Étoile,** tel. 01 41 27 27 27; **Taxis G7,** tel. 01 47 39 47 39; **Taxis Bleus,** tel. 01 49 36 10 10; and **Taxis 7000,** tel. 01 42 70 00 42.

TWO-WHEELERS

If you've never ridden a bike in heavy traffic, don't use central Paris as a testing ground. Bicycles can be transported on all RER lines, but not on the metro. If renting, ask for a helmet and inquire about insurance. **Bike rental** companies include: **Paris à vélo, c'est sympa!,** 37 bd. Bourdon, 4ème (tel. 01 48 87 60 01; M: Bastille; 60F per half-day, 80F per day, 150F per 24hr.; 2500F or credit card deposit); **La Maison du Vélo,** 11 rue Fénelon, 10ème (tel. 01 42 81 24 72; M: Poissonière; 90F per day; 2000F deposit; open Tu-Sa 10am-7pm); and **Paris-Vélo,** 2 rue de Fer-à-Moulin, 5ème (tel. 01 43 37 59 22; M: Censier Daubenton; 90F per day; 2000F deposit; open M-Sa 10am-12:30pm and 2pm-7pm). **Active Bike,** 20 rue Acacias, 17ème (tel. 01 40 55 02 02; M: Charles de Gaulle-Étoile), rents **scooters.** (From 200F per day, 950F per week; 6000F deposit.) Many of the above establishments also run **bike tours** of the city; call for details.

⏏ USEFUL SERVICES

TOURIST OFFICES

Tourist offices are packed in the summer; expect waits of up to one hour. All offices stock brochures, maps, and pamphlets and offer a **same-day accommodations service,** charging 8F to book a hostel, 20F for a one-star hotel, 25F for a two-star, and 40F for a three-star. The **main office,** 127 av. des Champs-Élysées, 8ème (tel. 08 36 68 31 12, 2.23F per minute; www.paris-touristoffice.com; M: Charles-de-Gaulle-Étoile) has **currency exchange** with decent rates. (Open daily 9am-8pm.) Other **major branches** include: **Gare de Lyon,** 12ème (tel. 01 43 43 33 24; M: Gare de Lyon; open M-Sa 8am-8pm); **Tour Eiffel,** Champs de Mars, 7ème (tel. 01 45 51 22 15; M: Champs de Mars; open May-Sept. daily 11am-5pm). At the **airports,** branches are found at: **Orly Sud,** near gate H (tel. 01 49 75 00 90) and **Orly Ouest,** near gate F (tel. 01 49 75 01 39; both open daily 6am-11:30pm); and **Roissy-Charles de Gaulle,** near gate 36 arrival level (tel. 01 48 62 27 29; open daily 7am-10pm).

USEFUL PUBLICATIONS AND LISTINGS

The weeklies *Pariscope* (3F) and *Officiel des Spectacles* (2F) are the most comprehensive listings of movies, plays, exhibits, festivals, clubs, and bars. *Pariscope* also includes an English-language section called *Time Out Paris*. The tourist office's free monthly *Where: Paris* highlights exhibitions, concerts, walking tours, and events. *Free Voice,* a monthly English-language newspaper published by the American Church, and the bi-weekly *France-USA Contacts (FUSAC)* list jobs, housing, and information for English speakers, are both available free from English-language bookstores, restaurants, and travel agencies throughout Paris. For a run-down of the latest on music, fashion, and street-culture trends, pick up the monthly *Technik Art* (18F). Gay and lesbian readers should consult *Têtu* (30F) for the latest in politics, fashion, and events.

CURRENCY EXCHANGE

Many, but not all, banks will exchange money from 9am-noon and 2-4:30pm. Beware of bureaux de change at airports, train stations, and in touristy areas; banks are normally a better bet. **Banque de France** normally has good rates, but their exchange desks are open only in the morning. **American Express,** 11, rue Scribe, 9ème (tel. 01 47 77 79 33; fax 01 47 77 74 57; M: Opéra or Auber), across from the back of the Opéra, offers tolerable exchange rates with no commission. (Open M-F 9am-6:30pm, Sa 10am-5:30pm, exchange counters only Su 10am-5pm.)

YOUTH SERVICES

Council on International Educational Exchange (CIEE), 1 pl. de l'Odéon, 6ème (tel. 01 44 41 74 99; fax 01 43 26 97 45; infofrance@ciee.org). M: Odéon. Answers questions about work and study abroad and offers mail service, phone service, and computers for use in the office. The library has useful info on jobs, travel, and housing, but is only available to students registered as Council participants. Information meetings Fridays at 12:30am. Register in Paris (1800F) or contact your CIEE office at home before you leave. Open M-F 9am-6pm; library open M-F 3am-6:30pm.

American Church in Paris, 65 quai d'Orsay, 7ème (tel. 01 40 62 05 00). M: Invalides or Alma-Marceau. A community center and a church. Bulletin boards list jobs, rides, apartments, and personals. Open M-Sa 9am-10pm, Su 9am-7pm. Free concerts Sept.-June Su 6pm. Flea market 1st Sa of every month (2-5pm).

HEALTH AND CRISES

Hospitals: Hospitals in Paris are numerous and efficient. Unless your French is exceptionally good, you'll have the best luck at one of the anglophone hospitals. **Hôpital Franco-Britannique de Paris,** 3 rue Barbès, Levallois-Perret (tel. 01 46 39 22 22). M: Anatole-France. State-run hospital; has some English-speakers, but don't count on it. On the other hand, it charges state prices and EU travelers should receive reciprocal treatment, **Hôpital Américain de Paris,** 63 bd. Victor Hugo, Neuilly (tel. 01 46 41 25 25). M: Port Maillot, then bus #82 to the end of the line. Private hospital. American (or at least English-speaking) doctors, American prices. You can change US dollars at the in-hospital *bureau de change* or use their ATM. Probably the only place in France you will be able to get a proper US insurance claim form and have it filled out.

24hr. Pharmacies: Every arrondissement should have a **pharmacie de garde** which will open in case of emergencies. The locations change, but the name of the nearest one is posted on each pharmacy's door.

Birth control: Mouvement Français pour le Planning Familial (MFPF), 10 rue Vivienne, 2ème (tel. 01 42 60 93 20). M: Bourse. Counseling and medical evaluations in French on family planning concerns. Appointment required to see generalist (115F) or gynæcologist (255F). Morning-after pill on demand (10F donation). Fridays, the clinic is held at 94 Blvd. Massana, 13ème (M: Porte Ivry), in the Tour Mantoue, door code 38145 (tel. 01 45 84 28 25). Open M-F 9:30am-5:30pm (hours vary in summer; call ahead).

AIDS: AIDES, 247 rue de Belleville, 20ème (tel. 01 44 52 00 00). M: Télégraphe. Free 24hr. hotline in French and English (tel. 0 800 84 08 00). Office open M-Sa 9am-6pm and Su 2-6pm. The **Free Anglo-American Counseling Treatment and Support (FACTS)** hotline (tel. 01 44 93 16 69) at the American Church (See **Youth Services,** above) also provides HIV/AIDS support in English M, W, and F 6-10pm.

Drug Problems: Hôpital Marmottan, 17-19 rue d'Armaillé, 17ème (tel. 01 45 74 00 04). M: Charles de Gaulle-Étoile or Argentine. Not an emergency service, but a general hospital that specializes in drug problems. For consultation or treatment, open M, W-Th noon-7pm, F 10am-7pm, and Sa noon-6pm; Aug. M-F only.

Emotional Health: Services and aid are provided by a number of organizations. **SOS Crisis Help Line: Friendship** (tel. 01 47 23 80 80). Support and information for the depressed and lonely in English. Open daily 3-11pm. For personalized crisis-control and counseling (for anything from pregnancy to homesickness), the American Church (see **Youth Services,** above) offers the **International Counseling Service** (ICS; tel. 01 45 50 26 49), which provides access to psychologists, psychiatrists, social workers, and a clerical counselor. First consultation free; payment thereafter is negotiable. Open M-F 9:30am-6pm, Sa 9:30am-1pm. Office staffed irregularly July-Aug. but will respond if you leave a message on its answering machine. Call for an appointment.

COMMUNICATIONS

Main Post Office: 52 rue du Louvre, 1er (tel. 01 40 28 20 40) M: Louvre. All Poste Restante sent to Paris is held here. Open daily 7am-6:20am!

Postal codes: Paris postal codes are all of the form 750XX, where XX is the two-digit number of the *arrondissement;* thus the main post office's postal code is 75001.

Internet: WebBar, 32 rue de Picardie, 3ème (tel. 01 42 72 66 55), M: République; **Cyber Cube,** 5 rue Mignon, 6ème (tel. 01 53 10 30 50), M: St-Michel or Odéon; also at rue Daval, 11ème (tel. 01 49 29 67 67), M: Bastille; and **Luxembourg Micro,** 83 bd. St-Michel, 5ème (tel. 01 46 33 27 98), RER: Luxembourg.

▟ ACCOMMODATIONS

While rooms are more expensive in Paris than in the rest of France, compared to other big cities around the world they're still a bargain. You should count on paying around 120F for dorm accommodations, and at least 200F per night for a double in an outer *arrondissement,* though advance planning can bring costs down.

Paris's **hostels** are generally restriction free—no sleepsheets, curfews, and the like—but they do have maximum stays. There are six HI hostels or affiliates in Paris; most dorm-like accommodations are either in private hostels or *foyers.* Check for availability by calling ahead or arrive very early in the morning. For two or more travelers staying together, **hotels** can often undercut hostels.

High season in Paris falls around Easter and May to October, peaking in July and August. Paris has a **taxe de séjour** of 1-5F per person per day within the city. Most hostels and *foyers* include the tax in their listed prices, but many hotels do not. Ask about this and other expenses, such as direct telephone service, before making a reservation, and check the locks in the room where you are staying.

ACCOMMODATIONS SERVICES

It's best to make reservations in advance, but don't panic if you arrive in Paris without one. **Tourist offices** (see p. 98) can help you find a room, although the lines may be long and the selections not necessarily the cheapest. Below are some organizations that can help with finding and booking rooms.

Centre Régional des Oeuvres Universitaires (CROUS), 39 av. Georges Bernanos, 5ème (tel. 01 40 51 36 00; lodging tel. 01 40 51 37 17 or 01 40 51 36 99). RER: Port-Royal. Info on student housing in Paris (2 nights-1 year) and on university restaurants throughout the city. Open M-F 9am-5pm; accommodations office open M-F 1-5pm.

La Centrale de Réservations (FUAJ-HI), 4 bd. Jules Ferry, 11ème (tel. 01 43 57 02 60; fax 01 40 21 79 92). M: République. Follow the rue du Fbg du Temple away from pl. de la République and cross the park-like entity that divides bd. Jules Ferry. La Centrale is half a block up on your left. One of the best ways to secure a bed in a hostel (115F per night per person). Same-day reservations in one of their affiliated youth hostels or budget hotels. The earlier you show up the better. Books beds for groups throughout France and Europe, arranges excursions, and procures plane and bus tickets. Open 24hr.

OTU-Voyage, 119 rue St-Martin, 4ème (tel. 01 40 29 12 12; see **Budget Travel Offices,** p. 96). Across the pedestrian mall from the Pompidou. Even in the busiest months, OTU-Voyage guarantees same-day "decent and low-cost lodging" for a 10F fee. You must pay the full price of the room when making your reservation, even before seeing it. Employees speak English. Also at 2 rue Malus, 5ème (tel. 01 44 41 74 74). M: Place Monge. Open M-F 10am-6:30pm, St-Martin branch open Sa 10am-5pm.

ACCOMMODATIONS BY PRICE

The establishments below have been ranked by price per person for hostels and *foyers*, and by the price of the cheapest double rooms for hotels. Note that the price of other rooms, including other doubles, may vary significantly. Full listings of the each establishment are given under **Accommodations by Location** (p. 102).

HOSTELS

Woodstock Hostel. 97F. *Opéra.*

Young and Happy (Y&H) Hostel. 117F, off season 97F. *Latin Quarter.*

Three Ducks Hostel. 117F, off-season 97F. *La Motte Piquet.*

Centre International de Paris (BVJ): Louvre. 120F. *Louvre-Rivoli.*

Centre International de Paris (BVJ): Quartier Latin. 120F. *Latin Quarter.*

Foyer International des Étudiantes. 120F. *Latin Quarter.*

Hôtel des Jeunes (MIJE). 140F. *Marais.*

Auberge de Jeunesse "Jules Ferry" (HI). 120F. *République.*

Centre International du Séjour de Paris: CISP "Rave." 143F. *Nation.*

HOTELS

UNDER 200F

Hôtel Printemps. *Champ de Mars.*

Hôtel Moderne. *Bastille.*

Ouest Hôtel. *Montparnasse.*

Hôtel Moderne du Temple. *République.*

Henri IV. *Île de la Cité.*

Hôtel La Marmotte. *Louvre-Rivoli.*

Hôtel des Médicis. *Latin Quarter.*

Hôtel de Milan. *Gare du Nord.*

Hôtel de Nevers. *République.*

Hôtel Notre-Dame. *République.*

200-300F

Hôtel Rhétia. *Bastille.*

Hôtel des Boulevards. *Louvre-Rivoli.*

Mistral Hôtel. *Bastille.*

Plessis Hôtel. *République.*

Hôtel Louvre-Richelieu. *Louvre-Rivoli.*

Hôtel le Central. *Latin Quarter.*

Hôtel des Alliés. *Latin Quarter.*

Hôtel de Blois. *Denfert-Rochereau.*

Hôtel Tiquetonne. *Louvre-Rivoli.*

Hôtel Picard. *Marais.*

Hôtel du Séjour. *Marais.*

Hôtel Andrea. *Marais.*

Hôtel du Parc. *Montparnasse.*

Perfect Hôtel. *Opéra.*

☙ **Dhely's Hôtel.** *Latin Quarter.*

Hôtel d'Artois. *Champs-Élysées.*

Hôtel de Chevreuse. *Latin Quarter.*

Castex Hôtel. *Marais.*

Hôtel Gay-Lussac. *Latin Quarter.*

☙ **Hôtel Beauharnais.** *Opéra.*

Hôtel de la Paix. *Champ de Mars.*

☙ **Hôtel Malar.** *Champ de Mars.*

Hôtel de Neslé. *Latin Quarter.*

300-400F

☙ **Grand Hôtel Jeanne d'Arc.** *Marais.*

☙ **Hôtel Montpensier.** *Louvre-Rivoli.*

Hôtel St-Honoré. *Louvre-Rivoli.*

OVER 400F

☙ **Hôtel d'Esmerelda.** *Latin Quarter.*

☙ **Hôtel Europe-Liège.** *Champs-Élysées.*

PARIS & ÎLE DE FRANCE

ACCOMMODATIONS BY LOCATION

ÎLE DE LA CITÉ AND LOUVRE-RIVOLI (1ER & 2ÈME)

In the shadow of the Louvre, Cartier and the Banque de France set the mood. Don't let the financiers and ladies-who-lunch scare you away: a few budget options remain. Those who stay near Châtelet-Les-Halles will revel in the central location but should use a safer metro station at night. Try not to stray too far into the northeastern quarter past rue d'Aboukir, especially near seedy rue St-Denis.

☙ **Centre International de Paris (BVJ): Louvre,** 20 rue J.-J. Rousseau, 1er (tel. 01 53 00 90 90; fax 01 53 00 90 91). M: Louvre or Palais-Royal. From M: Louvre take rue du Louvre away from the river then turn left on rue St-Honoré and right on rue J.-J. Rousseau. Courtyard hung with brass lanterns and strewn with chairs. 200 places in bright 2- to 10-bed dorms. 120F. Breakfast included. 2-course meals 40F, 4-course 60F. Reception 24hr. Weekend reservations up to 1 week in advance. Reserve by phone; rooms held only 10min. after expected check-in; call if you'll be late.

☙ **Hôtel Montpensier,** 12 rue de Richelieu, 1er (tel. 01 42 96 28 50; fax 01 42 86 02 70). M: Palais-Royal. Walk around the left side of the Palais-Royal to rue de Richelieu. Good taste distinguishes it from most hotels in this area and price range. Brightly lit lounge with stained-glass ceiling. Small elevator. Singles and doubles 310F, with toilet, shower, and TV 420F, with toilet, bath, and TV 510F. Shower 25F. Breakfast 37F. Extra bed 80F. Reserve 2 weeks ahead. V, MC, AmEx.

Henri IV, 25 pl. Dauphine, 1er (tel. 01 43 54 44 53). M: Cité. Walk toward the Conciergerie and turn right on bd. du Palais, left on quai de l'Horloge, and left at the front of the Conciergerie onto pl. Dauphine. In a 400-year-old building on the Île de la Cité, this hotel combines a great location with a great price. Simple, attractive furnishings. Singles 125-160F; doubles 170-205F, with shower 250F; triples 240-265F; quads 290F. Showers 15F. Reserve 1 month in advance.

Hôtel Saint-Honoré, 85 rue St-Honoré, 1er (tel. 01 42 36 20 38 or 01 42 21 46 96; fax 01 42 21 44 08). M: Louvre, Châtelet, or Les Halles. From M: Louvre, cross rue de Rivoli on rue du Louvre and turn right on rue St-Honoré. Comfortable renovated rooms in dashing black and mauve. Friendly, anglophone staff. All rooms have bathroom, most have TVs. Singles 290F; doubles 320-350F, with bath 380F; triples and quads 480F. Breakfast 29F. Fridge access. Reserve and confirm 1 night before. V, MC, AmEx.

Hôtel Louvre-Richelieu, 51 rue de Richelieu, 1er (tel. 01 42 97 46 20; fax 01 47 03 94 13). M: Palais-Royal. See directions for Hôtel Montpensier, above. Plastic flowers and faux Monet prints decorate these smallish rooms with radios, phones, and a view of the bustling thoroughfare—except in the otherwise charming skylit attic doubles. English spoken. Reserve 3 weeks ahead in summer. Singles 190-210F, with shower or bath and toilet 280-345F; doubles 230F, with shower or bath and toilet 420F; triples with shower and toilet 490F. Extra bed 50F. Showers 10F. Breakfast 35F. V, MC.

Hôtel des Boulevards, 10 rue de la Ville Neuve, 2ème (tel. 01 42 36 02 29; fax 01 42 36 15 39). M: Bonne Nouvelle. From metro, turn south onto rue de la Ville Neuve. Quiet, aqua rooms with TVs and phones. Bag storage in the basement. Singles and doubles 210-230F, with shower 235-285F; double with bath 320F. Extra person 60F. 10% *Let's Go* discount. Reserve 2 weeks ahead. V, MC, AmEx.

Hôtel Tiquetonne, 6 rue Tiquetonne, 2ème (tel. 01 42 36 94 58; fax 01 42 36 02 94). M: Étienne Marcel. Walk against traffic on rue de Turbigo; turn left on rue Tiquetonne. Near Marché Montorgueil and St-Denis' sex shops, is this study in false finishes, from fake-marble corridors to "I-can't-believe-it's-not-wood" doors. Singles with shower 143-213F; doubles with shower and toilet 246F. Shower 30F. Breakfast 25F. Closed Aug. and 1 week at Christmas. V, MC.

Hôtel La Marmotte, 6 rue Léopold Bellan, 2ème (tel. 01 40 26 26 51). M: Sentier. Take rue Petits Carreaux and turn right at rue Léopold Bellan. Reception in ground-floor bar of a modern building. Quiet, spacious rooms with TVs, phones, marmots, and safe-boxes. Singles and doubles 180-220F, with shower 270-300F; twins 320F. Shower 15F. Breakfast 25F. Reserve 2-3 weeks ahead. V, MC, AmEx.

THE MARAIS (3ÈME & 4ÈME)

Once home to Paris's noblest families, the Marais' 17th-century mansions now house a number of budget accommodations. The plethora of bars in the neighborhood make going out easy and worry-free. Even if you venture past the *arrondissement*, Paris's night buses converge in the 4ème at M: Châtelet. Many hotels are on quiet streets, so it's a great place to stay even if you're not nocturnal.

🏅 **Hôtel des Jeunes (MIJE;** tel. 01 42 74 23 45; fax 10 40 27 81 64; www.mije.com/; MIJE@wanadoo.fr) books beds in **Le Fourcy, Le Fauconnier,** and **Maubuisson** (see below), 3 small hostels in old Marais residences. The most picturesque and best-located youth accommodations around. No smoking. English spoken. Ages 18-30 only. 7-day max. stay. 4- to 9-bed dorms 140F; singles 220F; doubles 340F; triples 450F. Breakfast and sheets included. Free lockers (2F deposit). Lockout noon-3pm. Curfew 1am. Quiet after 10pm. Open M-F 11:30am-1:30pm and 6:30-8:30pm. Reception 7am-1am. Reserve at least 1 month in advance and arrive before noon.

Le Fourcy, 6 rue de Fourcy, 4ème. M: St-Paul or Pont Marie. From St-Paul, walk against the traffic down rue François-Miron and turn left on rue de Fourcy. Hostel surrounds a large social courtyard ideal for meeting travelers and open-air picnicking. **Internet access** 1F per min. Restaurant with 52F 3-course *menu.*Elevator.

Le Fauconnier, 11 rue du Fauconnier, 4ème. M: St-Paul or Pont Marie. From St-Paul take rue du Prevôt, turn left on rue Charlemagne, and right on rue du Fauconnier. Ivy-covered building steps away from the Seine and Île St-Louis. 4-bed dorms, some doubles and singles.

Maubuisson, 12 rue des Barres, 4ème. M: Hôtel-de-Ville or Pont Marie. From Pont Marie, walk against traffic on rue de l'Hôtel de Ville and turn right on rue des Barres. Half-timbered former convent that looks out onto a silent street by the St-Gervais monastery. Smaller 2- to 7-bed rooms with nice views. Elevator.

🏅 **Hôtel du Séjour,** 36 rue du Grenier St-Lazare, 3ème (tel./fax 01 48 87 40 36). M: Étienne Marcel or Rambuteau. From Étienne Marcel follow the traffic on rue Étienne Marcel, which becomes rue du Grenier St-Lazare. One block from Les Halles and the Centre Pompidou, this hotel is mid-renovation; ask for a new room. Most of the 20 rooms bright with large windows. Singles 180F; doubles 260F, with shower and toilet 320F. Extra bed 150F. Showers 20F. Reception 7am-10:30pm.

🏅 **Grand Hôtel Jeanne d'Arc,** 3 rue de Jarente, 4ème (tel. 01 48 87 62 11; fax 01 48 87 37 31; www.hoteljeannedarc.com). M: St-Paul or Bastille. From St-Paul walk against traffic on rue de Rivoli, turn left on rue de Sévigné then right on rue de Jarente. On a quiet side-street, the stylish rooms all have showers, toilets, and TVs. 2 ground-floor rooms wheelchair accessible. Elevator. Singles 300-400F; doubles 305-500F; triples 540F; quads 600F. Extra bed 75F. Breakfast 35F. Reserve 2 months in advance. V, MC.

Hôtel Picard, 26 rue de Picardie, 3ème (tel. 01 48 87 53 82; fax 01 48 87 02 56). M: Temple. Walk against traffic down rue du Temple, turn on rue Dupetit Thouars and right at the end of the street. Simple pastel rooms. Elevator. Singles 210F, with TV and bathroom 260F; doubles 250-270F, with TV and bathroom 330F; triples 520F. Showers 20F. Breakfast 30F. 10% *Let's Go* discount. Reserve 1 week ahead. V, MC.

Castex Hôtel, 5 rue Castex, 4ème (tel. 01 42 72 31 52; fax 01 42 72 57 91). M: Bastille or Sully-Morland. Exit Bastille on bd. Henri IV and take 3rd right on rue Castex. Spotless rooms look onto street or courtyard. All rooms have phone and sink. TV room. Singles 240-290F; doubles 320-360F; triples 460F. Extra bed 70F. Breakfast 30F. Check-in 1pm. Reserve by fax and credit card 1 month in advance. V, MC, AmEx.

Hôtel Andréa, 3 rue St-Bon, 4ème (tel. 01 42 78 43 93; fax 01 44 61 28 36). M: Hôtel-de-Ville. Follow traffic on rue de Rivoli and turn right on rue St-Bon. On a quiet street 2 blocks from Châtelet. Comfortable rooms with phones; top floor rooms have balconies. Singles 250F, with bathroom and TV 325F; doubles 260F, with bathroom and TV 360F; triples 435F; quads 500F. Showers 20F. Breakfast 30F. Reserve 3 weeks ahead. V, MC.

THE LATIN QUARTER (5ÈME & 6ÈME)

The 5ème has many of the best budget lodgings in the city. Hotel and hostel owners here often bend over backwards to help clueless Anglo tourists. Most hotels could easily fill up at twice their summer rates; the key to getting a room is to **reserve well in advance**—from one week in the winter to two months in the summer.

Centre International de Paris (BVJ): Quartier Latin, 44 rue des Bernardins, 5ème (tel. 01 43 29 34 80; fax 01 53 00 90 91). M: Maubert-Mutualité. Walk with traffic on bd. St-Germain and turn right on rue des Bernardins. Ultra-modern hostel with shiny cafeteria. Friendly, boisterous crowd congregates in the huge common area. Kitchen, TV, message service. Showers in rooms. Lockers 10F. 138 beds. 2- to 10-bed dorms 120F; singles 150F. Breakfast included. Check-in 2:30pm. Check-out 9am. Reception 24hr. Reserve well in advance and confirm, or arrive at 9am to check for available rooms.

Young and Happy (Y&H) Hostel, 80 rue Mouffetard, 5ème (tel. 01 45 35 09 53; fax 01 47 07 22 24). M: Monge. Cross rue Gracieuse and take rue Ortolan to rue Mouffetard. A lively hostel in the heart of the student quarter, serving cheap beer with a smile. Clean rooms—basic but cheerful. Commission-free **currency exchange.** Dorms 117F, 97F off-season; doubles 137F/117F. Sheets 15F. Towels 5F. Breakfast included. Lockout 11am-5pm. Curfew 2am. Reserve with 1 night deposit or show up at 8am. V, MC.

Foyer International des Étudiantes, 93 bd. St-Michel, 6ème (tel. 01 43 54 49 63). RER: Luxembourg. Across from Jardins du Luxembourg. Spacious rooms with elegant wood paneling, some with balconies. Library, TV lounge, kitchenettes, laundry. Women only Oct.-June. 2-bed dorms 120F; singles 170F. Breakfast included. Check-out 10am. Call ahead or arrive at 10am to check for no-shows. Reserve in writing 2 months ahead off-season, by January for summer; 300F deposit if confirmed.

Hôtel d'Esmeralda, 4 rue St-Julien-le-Pauvre, 5ème (tel. 01 43 54 19 20; fax 01 40 51 00 68). M: St-Michel. Walk along the Seine on quai St-Michel toward Nôtre-Dame and turn right at parc Viviani. Rooms have an old feel, with solid, rustic chairs and desks. Some reveal views of the park, the Seine, and Nôtre-Dame. Singles 160F, with shower and toilet 320F; doubles 420-490F; triples 550F; quads 600F. Breakfast 40F.

Hôtel de Neslé, 7 rue du Neslé, 6ème (tel. 01 43 54 62 41; fax 01 43 54 31 88). M: Odéon. Walk up rue Mazarine, turn right onto rue Dauphine and left on rue du Neslé. Fantastical and sparkling, the Neslé stands out in a sea of nondescript budget hotels. The recently renovated rooms feature theme accoutrements with murals depicting the history of Paris. For a treat, book the double with a Turkish steam bath (500F). Singles 175F; doubles 350-500F. No reservations; arrive 10am and hope for the best.

Dhely's Hôtel, 22 rue de l'Hirondelle, 6ème (tel. 01 43 26 58 25; fax 01 43 26 51 06). M: St-Michel. Steps from pl. St-Michel and the Seine, the Dhely's wood paneling, flower boxes, modern facilities, and quiet location make for a pleasant stay. TV and phone in all rooms. Singles 200F; doubles 290F, with shower 380F; triples 370F, with shower 490F. Extra bed 100F. Showers 25F. Breakfast 35F. Advance payment required for all nights. Reserve in advance with deposit. V, MC, AmEx.

Hôtel le Central, 6 rue Descartes, 5ème (tel. 01 46 33 57 93). M: Maubert-Mutualité. From metro, walk up rue de la Montaigne Ste-Geneviève. Great location near rue Mouffetard and the Panthéon. Crooked stairs lead to bright, newly-painted rooms with discount furnishings. Rooms on pl. Contrescarpe somewhat noisy. All rooms have shower. Singles 160-213F; doubles and triples 236-266F.

Hôtel des Alliés, 20 rue Berthollet, 5ème (tel. 01 43 31 47 52; fax 01 45 35 13 92). M: Censier-Daubenton. From metro, walk down rue Monge toward bd. Port-Royal, turn right on rue Claude Bernard and left on rue Berthollet. Rooms large with quality furnishings. Singles 180F; doubles and triples 235-320F. Showers 15F. Breakfast 28F. V, MC.

Hôtel Gay Lussac, 29 rue Gay-Lussac, 5ème (tel. 01 43 54 23 96; fax 01 40 51 79 49). M: Luxembourg. From metro walk down rue Gay-Lussac to rue St-Jacques. Stately old rooms, some with fireplaces. A bit worn, but with good beds. Elevator. Breakfast included. Singles 185F; doubles 320-350F; triples 450-480F; quads 570F.

Hôtel des Médicis, 214 rue St-Jacques, 5ème (tel. 01 43 54 14 66). M: Luxembourg. From metro turn right on rue Gay-Lussac and left on rue St-Jacques. Rickety old place that shuns right angles; perhaps that's why Jim Morrison slummed here (room #4) for three weeks in 1971. Some guests have ensconced themselves in the musty rooms for more than five years. Singles and doubles 180-190F. Reception 9am-11pm. No reservations in summer; arrive early in the morning and hope for a vacancy.

Hôtel de Chevreuse, 3 rue de Chevreuse, 6ème (tel. 01 43 20 93 16; fax 01 43 21 43 72). M: Vavin. Walk up bd. du Montparnasse away from the Tour and turn left on rue de Chevreuse. Clean, quiet rooms with TV. Singles 235F; doubles 295F, with shower, toilet, and TV 355F, with bath, toilet, and TV 395F; triples with bath, toilet, and TV 535F. Breakfast 35F. Reserve 1 week ahead and confirm by fax. V, MC.

CHAMP DE MARS-INVALIDES (7ÈME AND 15ÈME)

With no hostels and few budget options, this quiet area attracts mainly business travelers, older couples, and families. Most reasonably priced hotels are near École Militaire; expect telephones and TVs, breakfast in bed, bathtubs, and a short walk to the tallest thing in Paris.

Hôtel Malar, 29 rue Malar, 7ème (tel. 01 45 51 38 46; fax 01 45 55 20 19). M: Latou-Maubourg. From metro, follow traffic on bd. de la Tour Maubourg, turn left on rue St-Dominique, and right on rue Malar. Family resort feel in a classy neighborhood. All rooms have TVs, phones, showers, and hairdryers. Singles 295-370F; doubles 350-500F. Extra bed 100F. Breakfast 35F. Reserve one month ahead. V, MC, AmEx.

Hôtel de la Paix, 19 rue du Gros-Caillou, 7ème (tel. 01 45 51 86 17; fax 01 45 55 93 28). M: École Militaire. Cheap with amusing white-and-tan 70s decor. Small, but pleasant and clean. Singles 180F, with shower 255F; doubles with shower 320F, with shower and toilet 350F-395F. Breakfast 32F. Reserve one week ahead.

Hôtel Printemps, 31 rue du Commerce, 15ème (tel. 01 45 79 83 36; fax 01 45 79 84 88). M: La Motte-Picquet-Grenelle. In the middle of a busy, bourgeois neighborhood surrounded by shops and restaurants, this hotel is clean and cheap. Singles and doubles 150F, with shower 190F; twins with shower and toilet 230F. Showers 15F. Breakfast 20F. Reserve 3-4 weeks ahead. V, MC.

CHAMPS-ÉLYSÉES (8ÈME)

The 8ème is more for jet-setters than budget travelers. While you might spot a movie star dining at Fouquet's or hopping into a car outside Christian Dior, you'll be hard-pressed to find comfortable, affordable lodging nearby.

Hôtel Europe-Liège, 8 rue de Moscou, 8ème (tel. 01 42 94 01 51; fax 01 43 87 42 18). M: Liège. From metro, walk down rue d'Amsterdam and turn left on rue de Moscou. Very pleasant, quiet hotel with newly painted rooms. All rooms have TV, hairdryer, phone, and shower or bath. 2 handicap-accessible rooms on the ground floor. Singles 370F; doubles 480F. Breakfast 35F. V, MC, AmEx.

Hôtel d'Artois, 94 rue La Boëtie, 8ème (tel. 01 43 59 84 12 or 01 42 25 76 65; fax 01 43 59 50 70). M: St-Philippe de Roule. From the metro, turn left onto rue La Boëtie. A stone's throw from the Champs. A bit worn, but with spacious bathrooms and large bedrooms. Singles 255F, with shower 365F, with bathroom 405F; doubles 290F, with shower 440F; triples with bathroom 580F. Showers 22F. Breakfast 28F. V, MC.

OPÉRA (9ÈME)

The 9ème's central location makes it an ideal base. The hotels to the south are generally safe and clean, but many along the northern edge serve clients paying by the hour. Avoid the areas around Pigalle and Barbès-Rochechouart. Just a few streets south of bd. de Clichy and rue Pigalle, the neighborhood shifts from a red-light district to a quiet and diverse residential quarter.

🖼 **Woodstock Hostel,** 48 rue Rodier, 9ème (tel. 01 48 78 87 76; fax 01 48 78 01 63). M: Anvers or Gare du Nord or bus #85 (probably the best way). From Anvers, walk against traffic on pl. Anvers, turn right on av. Trudaine and then left on rue de Rodier. From Gare du Nord turn right on rue Dunkerque (with the station at your back); at pl. de Roubaix, veer left on rue de Maubeuge, veer right on rue Condorcet, and turn left on rue Rodier. (15min.). Near Sacré-Cœur; clean with quiet, affordable rooms. Courtyard nicer than most cafés. Communal kitchen, safe box, and fax. Apr.-Oct. 4-bed dorms 97F; doubles 107F per person; Sept.-May dorms 87F; doubles 97F. Call ahead. V, MC.

🖼 **Hôtel Beauharnais,** 51 rue de la Victoire, 9ème (tel. 01 48 74 71 13). M: Le Peletier. Follow traffic on rue de la Victoire and look for flower boxes—there's no sign and the lobby looks like a sitting room. The witty, gregarious Mme Bey dispenses helpful advice in English to young travelers. Cozy rooms with showers are dressed in antiques and mirrors. *Let's Go* rates for stays of 2-3 days: Doubles 320F; triples 490F. Breakfast 30F.

Perfect Hôtel, 39 rue Rodier, 9ème (tel. 01 42 81 18 86; fax 01 42 85 01 38). Opposite the Woodstock Hostel. While not quite living up to its name, this hotel offers workable rooms with phones and great views from the upper floors. Elevator. Singles and doubles 180-205F; triples with bath 265F. V, MC, AmEx.

RÉPUBLIQUE (10ÈME & 11ÈME)

At the junction of the 10ème, 11ème, and 3ème *arrondissements*, the bustling pl. de la République swarms with young people in search of a good time. Hotels in the area tend to be cheap with vacancies year-round, though hostels are packed.

🖼 **Auberge de Jeunesse "Jules Ferry" (HI),** 8 bd. Jules Ferry, 11ème (tel. 01 43 57 55 60). M: République. Walk east on rue du Fbg du Temple and turn right on the far side of bd. Jules Ferry. In front of the park and next to pl. de la République, with a crowded party atmosphere. **Internet access** 1F per min. Laundry. 100 bunks in 4- to 6-bed dorms 120F; doubles 250F. Breakfast included. Sheets 5F. Lockers 10F. Flexible 4-night max. Reception 24hr. Lockout 10am-2pm. No reservations; arrive by 8am. V, MC.

Plessis Hôtel, 25 rue du Grand Prieuré, 11ème (tel. 01 47 00 13 38; fax 01 43 57 97 87). M: Oberkampf. From the metro, walk north on rue du Grand Prieuré. Clean, bright rooms, some with balconies. TV, drinks machines, and leather chairs in the lounge. Singles 195F, with shower, toilet, and TV 280F, with bath, toilet, and TV 295F; doubles 215F, with shower, toilet, and TV 325F, with bath, toilet, and TV 350F. "American" breakfast 38F. 10% discount after 3rd night. Elevator. Open Sept.-July. V, MC, AmEx.

Hôtel Nôtre-Dame, 51 rue de Malte, 11ème (tel. 01 47 00 78 76; fax 01 43 55 32 31; hotelnotredame@wanadoo.fr). M: République. Descend av. de la République and turn right on rue de Malte. Tidy, renovated rooms with tasteful, bright decor. Cheerful lounge. Elevator. Singles 200-370F; doubles 190F, with shower 280F, with shower or bath and toilet 330F; twins 380F. Breakfast 35F. Showers 20F. Reserve 1 month ahead. V, MC.

Hôtel Moderne du Temple, 3 rue d'Aix, 10ème (tel. 01 42 08 09 04; fax 01 42 41 72 17). M: Goncourt. Walk with the traffic on rue du fbg du Temple and turn right onto the quiet rue d'Aix. Czech-owned hotel has tastefully decorated rooms, some overlooking a courtyard. Singles 120-140F, with shower 170F, with shower and toilet 220F; doubles

160F, with shower 190F, with shower and toilet 240F; triples 180F, with shower 280F, with shower and toilet 320F. Breakfast 23F. AmEx.

Hôtel de Nevers, 53 rue de Malte, 11ème (tel. 01 47 00 56 18; fax 01 43 57 77 39). M: Oberkampf or République. From metro, walk down av. de la République and turn right on rue de Malte. Spotless, spacious rooms. Higher rooms escape street noise. Fridge access. Singles and doubles 180F, with shower 235F, with shower and toilet 260-275F; triples with shower and toilet 335F; quads with shower and toilet 410F. Extra bed 50F. Breakfast 25F. Showers 20F. 24hr. reception. Reserve 2 weeks ahead. V, MC.

BASTILLE (11ÈME & 12ÈME)

The area around Bastille is short on sights but long on nightlife. Inexpensive hotels cluster around the Opéra Bastille, providing easy access to clubs, bars, and cafés. In the 12ème's southeast corner, hotels are far enough from central Paris to be both cheap and comfortable.

Hotel Moderne, 121 rue de Chemin-Vert, 11ème (tel. 01 47 00 54 05; fax 01 47 00 08 31). M: Père Lachaise. A few blocks from the metro along rue de Chemin-Vert, on the right. Modern, bright, and clean. Prices likely to rise with new look. Singles 120F, with shower 200F, with shower and toilet 250F; doubles 140F, with shower 245F, with shower and toilet 250F. Reserve ahead. V, MC.

Hôtel Rhétia, 3 rue du Général Blaise, 11ème (tel. 01 47 00 47 18; fax 01 48 06 01 73). M: Voltaire. From metro, take av. Parmentier, turn right on rue Rochebrune and left on rue du Général Blaise. In a calm, quiet neighborhood, some rooms overlook a park, others a courtyard. Clean rooms with lacquered furniture. Singles 180F, with shower 220F; doubles 200F, with shower 240F; triples 240F, with shower 290F. Breakfast 15F. Showers 10F. Reception daily 7:30am-10pm.

Mistral Hôtel, 3 rue Chaligny, 12ème (tel. 01 46 28 10 20; fax 01 46 28 69 66). M: Reuilly-Diderot. Walk west on bd. Diderot and turn left onto rue Chaligny. Each spectacularly clean room is unique, with furniture from chandeliers to wicker headboards. All rooms have TV and phone. Parking. Singles 205F, with shower 250F; doubles 210F, with shower 260F; twins with shower 290F; triples with shower and toilet 340F; quads with shower and toilet 400F. Breakfast 35F. Showers 15F. Reserve 2 weeks in advance and confirm in writing or by fax with deposit. V, MC, AmEx.

MONTPARNASSE (14ÈME & 15ÈME)

The area around Montparnasse combines an almost central location with cheaper-than-chi-chi prices. It may not afford Paris's most outstanding views, but its busy, safe streets and interesting history make it an agreeable place to stay.

Ouest Hôtel, 27 rue de Gergovie, 14ème (tel. 01 45 42 64 99; fax 01 45 42 46 65). M: Pernety. Walk against traffic on rue Raymond Losserand and turn right on rue de Gergovie. Super-cheap with friendly staff, but beware of the occasional bug-infested pillow. Singles 120F; singles with larger bed and doubles 160F, with shower 220F; twins 200F, with shower 230F. Shower 20F (sometimes long waits). Breakfast 20F. V, MC.

Hôtel du Parc, 6 rue Jolivet, 14ème (tel. 01 43 20 95 54; fax 01 42 79 82 62; www.hotelduparc.com). M: Edgar-Quinet. Facing the tower, turn left on rue de la Gaîté, right on rue du Maine, then right on rue Jolivet. Creatively colored rooms with TVs and phones open onto the courtyard or a park. 32 rooms. Singles and doubles 260F; triples with shower 450F. Shower 20F. Breakfast 30F. V, MC, AmEx.

OTHER NEIGHBORHOODS

Towards the city limits, the primarily residential neighborhoods cease to have well-recognized nicknames. But just because these areas are devoid of famous sights, you shouldn't neglect them as bases in which to stay. The lack of tourists means that prices have stayed lower and welcomes friendlier, while Paris is still small enough that you're never *that* far from the action.

☑ **Three Ducks Hostel,** 6 pl. Étienne Pernet, 15ème (tel. 01 48 42 04 05; fax 01 48 42 99 99). M: Félix Faure. Walk against traffic on the left side of the church; hostel will be on your left. Aimed at young Anglo fun-seekers, the Three Ducks wants you to rock with them at the in-house bar until the 2am curfew. Kitchen. Lockers. 2- to 8-bed dorm rooms. Laundry nearby. Mar.-Oct. 117F; Nov.-Feb. 97F. Breakfast included. Sheets 15F. Towels 5F. Reserve with credit card deposit several days ahead in peak season. V, MC.

Centre International du Séjour de Paris: "Ravel," 6 av. Maurice Ravel, 12ème (tel. 01 44 75 60 00; fax 01 43 44 45 30). M: Porte de Vincennes. Walk east on cours de Vincennes then right on bd. Soult, left on rue Jules Lemaître, and right on av. Maurice Ravel (15min.). Large rooms with shower (most with 4 or fewer beds), art exhibits, auditorium, and access to outdoor pool next door (25F). Cafeteria open daily 7:30-9:30am, noon-1:30pm, and 7-8:30pm; restaurant open noon-1:30pm and 7:30-9:30pm. **Internet** 10F per 10min. Dorms 143F; singles with shower, toilet, and phone 191F; doubles with shower, toilet, and phone 322F. Breakfast included. Reception daily 7:30am-1:30am. Curfew 1:30am. Reserve a few days ahead by phone. V, MC.

☑ **Hôtel de Blois,** 5 rue des Plantes, 14ème (tel. 01 45 40 99 48; fax 01 45 40 45 62). M: Mouton-Duvernet. From metro, turn left on rue Mouton Duvernet then left on rue des Plantes. One of the better deals in Paris. Ornate ceilings and velvet chairs. TVs, phones, and big, clean bathrooms. Singles 230F; doubles 240-280F, with shower 270F, with bath 320-360F; triples 360F. Breakfast 27F. Reserve 10 days ahead. V, MC, AmEx.

Hôtel de Milan, 17 rue de St-Quentin, 10ème (tel. 01 40 37 88 50; fax 01 46 07 89 48). M: Gare du Nord. Follow rue de St-Quentin from Gare du Nord; hotel is on the right-hand corner of the 3rd block. Antique wooden elevator ascends the center of a spiral staircase. The well-kept rooms are slightly more expensive than other 10ème hotels, but the location right next to the Gare du Nord is very convenient for the Eurostar. Singles 160-280F; doubles 186-266F; triples 429F. Showers 18F. Breakfast 20F. V, MC.

🗂 FOOD AND DRINK

While *lyonnais* may beg to differ, to Parisians theirs is the gourmet capital of the world. Famous restaurants such as Maxims and La Tour d'Argent present well-dressed diners with superlative food and a bill longer than the maître d's face, but affordable dining is possible. This being Paris, *la cuisine française* is significantly more expensive than in the provinces—count on paying at least 70-80F for a 3-course *menu* at even the cheapest restaurants. But no other French city can match Paris for variety; Chinese, Vietnamese, and North and sub-Saharan African restaurants make up the majority of ethnic eateries, but you'll find food from every corner of the world, from Tibet to Argentina. Occupying the twilight zone between traditional French cuisine and extra-European *nourriture* is a new wave of offbeat, innovative restaurants mixing flavors from around the world.

Supermarchés (supermarkets) are found in every neighborhood. **Monoprix** and **Prisunics** litter the city (48, to be exact) and are usually open during the week until 9pm, although the Champs-Élysées Prisunic is open until midnight.

UNIVERSITY RESTAURANTS

For students strapped for cash, university restaurants provide cheap, if not always very appetizing, meals. Students can purchase meal tickets at each restaurant location while food is being served (14.50F for students enrolled in a French university; 23.50F for others with ISIC). The following university restaurants are most convenient, but the list is not nearly exhaustive. They open on a rotating schedule during the summer and on weekends—visit **CROUS (Centre Regional des Oeuvres Universitaires et Scolaires),** 39 av. Georges Bernanos, 5ème. (Tel. 01 40 51 37 10. M: Port-Royal. Open M-F 9am-5pm.) Most of the following offer a cafeteria-style choice of sandwiches, *plats*, and drinks: **Bullier,** 39 av. Georges Bernanos, 5ème (M: Port-Royal; open 8am-4:30pm); **Cuvier-Jussieu,** 8bis rue Cuvier, 5ème (M: Cuvier-Jussieu; open 9am-4:15pm); **Censier,** 31 rue Geoffroy St-Hilaire, 5ème (M: Censier-Daubenton; open 11am-3pm); **Châtelet,** 10 rue Jean Calvin, 5ème (M: Censier-

Daubenton; open 8-11am); **Assas**, 92 rue d'Assas, 6ème (M: Port-Royal or Nôtre-Dame-des-Champs; open 7:45am-6:15pm); **Mabillon**, 3 rue Mabillon, 6ème (M: Mabillon; open 11:30am-3:30pm and 6:30-8:30pm); **Grand Palais**, cours la Reine, 8ème (M: Champs-Élysées Clemenceau; open 11:30am-2pm and 6:15-7:45pm); **Cit-eaux**, 45 bd. Diderot, 12ème (M: Gare de Lyon; open 11:30am-2:30pm); **C.H.U. Pitié-Salpetrière**, 105 bd. de l'Hôpital, 13ème (M: St-Marcel; open 8am-4:30pm); **Dareau**, 13-17 rue Dareau, 14ème (M: St-Jacques; open 11:30am-2pm); **C.H.U. Necker**, 156 rue de Vaugirard, 15ème (M: Pasteur; open 9am-4pm); and **Dauphine**, av. de Pologne, 16ème (M: Porte Dauphine; open 8am-6pm).

FOOD AND DRINK BY GENRE

For complete listings of restaurants, cafés, markets, and the like, see **Food by Location**, below. Prices below are indicated by funky euro signs (€). For restaurants, one € means most *plats* cost under 50F, two €s 50-80F, and three €s 80-120F. For cafés and *salons de thé*, one € means an espresso will set you back under 15F; two €s 15-25F; and three €s over 25F. For snacks and sweets, it's more intuitive.

CAFÉS
🔲 **Café de l'Industrie.** *Bastille.* €
Pause Café. *Bastille.* €
Café de la Mosquée. *Latin Quarter.* €
Café du Marché. *Champ de Mars.* €-€€
Le Procope. *Latin Quarter.* €-€€€
🔲 **Le Fumoir.** *Louvre-Rivoli.* €€

FAMOUS CAFÉS
Le Sélect. *Montparnasse.* €-€€€
La Coupole. *Montparnasse.* €-€€€
Aux Deux Magots. *Latin Quarter.* €€
Café de Flore. *Latin Quarter.* €€€
Fouquet's. *Champs-Élysées.* €€€
Café de la Paix. *Opéra.* €€€

FOREIGN
Le Dogon (Malian). *République.* €
Le Singe d'Eau (Tibetan). *Champs-Élysées.* €
🔲 **Au Jardin des Pâtés** (Italian). *Latin Quarter.* €-€€
Un Saumon à Paris (Polish). *Bastille.* €€
🔲 **Paris-Dakar** (Senegalese). *Gare du Nord.* €€
🔲 **Chez Omar** (North African). *Marais.* €€
Sans Frontières (Greek). *Latin Quarter.* €€
Haynes Bar (American). *Opéra.* €€-€€€

MARKETS
Mouffetard. *Latin Quarter.* Tu, Th, Sa.
Port Royale. *Latin Quarter.* Tu-Su.
Bastille. *Bastille.* Th, Su.
Berthier. *Montmartre/Pigalle.* W, Sa.
Marché Popincourt. *République.* Tu, F.

OFFBEAT
🔲 **Café du Commerce.** *Pl. d'Italie.* €
Le Merle Moqueur. *Pl. d'Italie.* €
🔲 **Le Samson.** *Pl. d'Italie.* €-€€
🔲 **Papou Lounge.** *Louvre-Rivoli.* €€
Chez Ginette. *Montmartre.* €€-€€€
L'Ébauchoir. *Bastille.* €€€

SALONS DE THÉ
Le Soleil Gourmand. *Montmartre.* €€
Le Loir dans la Théière. *Marais.* €€
Le Marais Plus. *Marais.* €€€
Angelina's. *Louvre-Rivoli.* €€€
Ladurée. *Champs-Élysées.* €€€

SANDWICHES AND SNACKS
🔲 **L'As du Falafel.** *Marais.* €
Finkelsztajn's. *Marais.* €
Deli's Café. *Opéra.* €
🔲 **Antoine's.** *Champs-Élysées.* €€
🔲 **Così.** *Latin Quarter.* €€

SPECIALTY FOOD
Tang Frères (Chinese). *Pl. d'Italie.* €-€€
Fauchon (fancy). *Champs-Élysées.* €€€
Alléosse (cheese). *Champs-Élysées.* €€€
Poilâne (bread). *Latin Quarter.* €€€

SWEETS
🔲 **Berthillon Glaces.** *Île St-Louis.* €
La Maison du Chocolat. *Opéra.* €€

TRADITIONAL
Le Dénicheur. *Louvre-Rivoli.* €.
Crêperie le Josselin. *Montparnasse.* €
🔲 **Aux Artistes.** *Montparnasse.* €-€€
Les Listines. *Montparnasse.* €€

Au Petit Fer à Cheval. *Marais.* €–€€

🦐 La Varangue. *Champ de Mars.* €–€€

Phinéas. *Montparnasse.* €€

Au Pied de Fouet. *Invalides.* €€

Le Bistrot du Peintre. *Bastille.* €€

La Table de Margot. *Champs-Élysées.* €€

Les Fous de l'Isle. *Île St-Louis.* €€–€€€

VEGETARIAN

Le Kitch. *République.* €

La Victoire Suprême du Coeur. *Louvre.* €€

WINE BARS

Le Clown Bar. *République.* €€

Jacques Mélac. *Bastille.* €€

FOOD AND DRINK BY LOCATION

ÎLE ST-LOUIS AND LOUVRE-RIVOLI (1ER & 2ÈME)

The arcades on rue de Rivoli are filled with the chic and expensive, but tea or *chocolat chaud* at a *salon de thé* are affordable treats. Traditional restaurants cluster around the Palais-Royal, while Les Halles features cheaper, louder eateries. Near Les Halles, rue St-Denis' restaurants coexist with sex shops; during daylight hours, consider these eateries welcome bargains, but steer clear of them after dark. Rue Montorgueil is lined with bakeries, fruit stands, and specialty stores, while side streets like rue Marie Stuart and rue Mandar hide some worthwhile dining options. On Île St-Louis, **Berthillon,** 31 rue St-Louis-en-l'Île, 4ème (tel. 01 43 54 31 61; M: Cité or Pont Marie), is famous for its ice cream, with dozens of flavors ranging from chocolate to passion fruit and gingerbread. (Cones from 9F. Open Sept.-July 14. Takeout W-Su 10am-8pm; eat-in W-F 1-8pm, Sa-Su 2-8pm.)

🦐 **Papou Lounge,** 74 rue J.-J. Rousseau (tel. 01 44 76 00 03). M: Les Halles. Walk toward the Église St-Eustache, then turn right onto rue Coquillère and right onto rue J.-J. Rousseau. With house music, tiled floors, and voodoo dolls, Papou is a cross between a Tahitian lounge and a French café. The purple (!) *boudin* is wickedly good. Hamburgers 48-55F, beer 16-20F. Daily special 55F. Open daily 10am-2am. V, MC.

🦐 **Le Fumoir,** 6 rue de l'Amiral Colligny (tel. 01 42 92 05 05). M: Louvre. In this café across from the Louvre, decidedly untouristy types drink in deep green leather sofas or sup on the best brunch in Paris (120F). Smoked-salmon sandwiches 37F, coffee 15F. Open Su-Th 11am-midnight, F-Sa 11am-2am. V, MC, AmEx.

Les Fous de l'Isle, 33 rue des Deux-Ponts (tel. 01 43 25 76 67). M: Pont Marie. A café-bistro for the neighborhood crowd that displays the work of local artists and has mellow concerts every other Tuesday, except in summer. *Entrées* 30-65F, salads 50-65F. *Plats,* like *croustillant de saumon* and *noix de St-Jacques aux fruits de la passion,* 60-98F. Open Tu-F noon-11pm, Sa 6-11pm, Su noon-7pm. V, MC.

Angelina's, 226 rue de Rivoli (tel. 01 42 60 82 00; M: Concorde), was Audrey Hepburn's favorite *salon de thé.* Belle Époque paintings, gold-leaf interiors, and an atmosphere of propriety dampen all sounds but the clink of teacups. The *chocolat africain* (hot chocolate, 36F) and *Mont Blanc* (meringue with chestnut cream, 36F) are house specialties. Open M-F 9am-7pm, Sa-Su 9:30am-7:30pm. V, MC, AmEx.

La Victoire Suprême du Coeur, 41 rue des Bourdonnais (tel. 01 40 41 93 95). M: Châtelet. Follow traffic on rue des Halles then turn left on rue des Bourdonnais. Run by the devotees of the guru Sri Chinmoy, who have both body and soul in mind when creating dishes like *gratinée aux champignons.* All-day 3-course *formule* 89F, *plats* 47-67F. Open M-F noon-2:30pm and 6:30-10pm, Sa noon-10pm.

Le Dénicheur, 4 rue Tiquetonne (tel. 01 42 21 31 01). M: Étienne Marcel. Walk against traffic on rue de Turbigo and turn left on rue Tiquetonne. Lawn gnomes for sale, excellent food, and an affable crowd. Are upside-down Christmas trees sacrilegious? Only a *dénicheur* (antique hunter) knows. 2-course *menu* 50-55F; 3-courses 70F. Omelettes, sandwiches, and quiches 35F. Open daily noon-3:30pm and 7:30pm-2am.

THE MARAIS (3ÈME & 4ÈME)

The restaurants of the Marais, sometimes tucked away in courtyards and alleys, offer varied ethnic and French cuisine. Dinner can be pricey, but lunchtime *menus* are good deals. Rue des Rosiers is the promised land of Ashkenazi and Sephardi bakeries, delis, and restaurants, not all of which are kosher.

◢ **Chez Omar,** 47 rue de Bretagne (tel. 01 42 72 36 26). M: Arts et Métiers. Walk along rue Réamur, away from rue Saint Martin. Rue Réamur turns into rue de Bretagne. Adrenaline and heaps of couscous are the backdrop in this Art Déco-ish, mirrored restaurant. Couscous from 60F. Open M 7:30-11:30pm, Tu-Su noon-3pm and 7:30-11:30pm.

◢ **L'As du Falafel,** 34 rue des Rosiers (tel. 01 48 87 63 60). M: St-Paul. Follow the traffic a few steps down rue de Rivoli, turn right on rue Pavée, and left on rue des Rosiers. Lenny Kravitz credited this cheerfully decorated kosher place with "the best falafel in the world, particularly the special eggplant falafel with hot sauce." Falafel special 25F, lamb *shawerma* 32F. Open Su-Th 11:30am-11:30pm. V, MC.

Le Marais Plus, 20 rue des Francs-Bourgeois (tel. 01 48 87 01 40). The relaxed *salon de thé* of this wacky toy store and funky gift and book shop has tables which function as display counters, exhibiting toys, baby clothing, and cutlery. Teas 25F, cappucino 25F, salads 60F, *tartes salées* 50F. Open daily noon-6:30pm.

Au Petit Fer à Cheval, 30 rue Vieille-du-Temple (tel. 01 42 72 47 47), off rue de Rivoli. M: Hôtel-de-Ville or St-Paul. An oasis of *chèvre*, kir, and *gauloises*. The local crowd knows a good thing when they find it. Invisible from the front, a few tables huddle behind the bar. Life-changing *chèvre chaud* salad with prosciutto and toast 50F, sandwiches 20-35F, desserts 25-34F. Open M-F 9am-2am, Sa-Su 11am-2am.

Finkelsztajn's, 27 rue des Rosiers (tel. 01 42 72 78 91). M: St-Paul. Finkels has served homemade Eastern European Jewish delicacies since 1946. Bagels, *piroghi*, strudel, and latkes 14-32F; gargantuan sandwiches to go 32-45F. Open Sept.-July W-Th 10am-2pm and 3-7pm, F-Su 10am-7pm.

Le Loir Dans la Théière, 3 rue des Rosiers (tel. 01 42 72 90 61). M: St-Paul. Named after the character in *Alice in Wonderland,* this bohemian salon serves curiouser and curiouser caramel and jasmine tea (20F), coffees (12-30F), cakes and tarts (38-48F), and Sunday brunch (120F). Open daily noon-6:30pm. V, MC.

THE LATIN QUARTER (5ÈME & 6ÈME)

With the student population demanding inexpensive but proper meals at all hours, the 5ème is geared toward the budget *gourmand*—but beware the many tourist traps in the side streets around pl. St-Michel. Instead, head for rue Mouffetard and the streets off pl. de la Contrescarpe. Cheap Japanese restaurants congregate on rue M. le Prince, between Odéon and bd. St-Michel. Rue de Buci harbors bargain Greek restaurants, while rue Grégoire de Tours has the highest density of cheap restaurants (think greasy spoons). More options can be found along the streets near the Odéon metro stop. **Poilâne,** 8 rue Cherche-Midi (tel. 01 45 48 42 59; M: Sèvres-Babylone), has a tiny shop that services the huge bakery responsible for Paris's most famous bread. (Quarter-loaf 11F. Open M-Sa 7:15am-8:15pm.) There are also three **markets;** the most convenient is the small daily market on rue de Buci (M: Odéon). The colorful **Marché Port Royal** (M: Censier-Daubenton) is crowded with fresh produce, meat, fish, and cheese, as well as cheap shoes and houseware. To get there, turn right out of the metro and head toward bd. du Port-Royal (Tu, Th, and Sa 8am-1:30pm). The **Marché Mouffetard** (M: Monge) has the same selection, plus a few bakeries of high repute (Tu-Su 8am-1:30pm).

◢ **Au Jardin des Pâtes,** 4 rue Lacépède (tel. 01 43 31 50 71). M: Jussieu. From the metro, walk up rue Linné and turn right on rue Lacépède. Organic pastas with a variety of vegetables and sauces. Plenty for vegetarians. *Entrées* 19-31F, *plats* 39-77F. Reservations recommended. Open Tu-Su noon-2:30pm and 7-11pm. V, MC.

▨ **Così,** 54 rue de Seine (tel. 01 46 33 35 36). M: Mabillon. Enormous, tasty, and inexpensive sandwiches. The opera piped into the pleasant eating area makes it even better. Tomato, mozzarella, and *roquette* (38F); desserts (20F). Open daily noon-midnight.

Sans Frontières, 19 rue du Regard (tel. 01 45 48 87 67). M: St-Placide. Greek restaurant looking more like a pricey *brasserie*. Delightfully cheap, tasty, large, portions. 3-course lunch *menu* 65F, dinner 95F and 120F, all including a starter *meze* plate that is a meal in itself (hummus, tzatziki, eggplant—the works). Very kind staff keeps the techno hits coming. Open daily noon-2:30pm and 7-11pm. V, MC.

Café de la Mosquée, 39 rue Geoffrey St-Hilaire (tel. 01 43 31 38 20). M: Censier Daubenton. In the main Paris mosque, this cool café, with decorative tiles and tropical trees, offers mint tea (10F) and *Mahgrebin* pastries (10F). Indulge yourself in the Turkish steam bath (men Tu and Su; women M, Tu, Th, Sa). Café open daily 10am-midnight.

Aux Deux Magots, 6 pl. St-Germain-des-Prés (tel. 01 45 48 55 25). M: St-Germain-des-Prés. Sartre's second-choice café and de Beauvoir's first, its high ceilings and gilt mirrors have been home to literati since 1885. Named after two Chinese porcelain figures. *Café* 23F, pastries 12-24F. Open daily 7am-1:30am. V, AmEx.

Café de Flore, 172 bd. St-Germain (tel. 01 45 48 55 26). M: St-Germain-des-Prés. Sartre's favorite haunt also saw Apollinaire, Picasso, Breton, Thurber, and Prévert before the war; it's traded on its reputation ever since. Enjoy your drink on the terrace, Brigitte Bardot's favorite spot. *Café* 34F, *salade Flore* 68F. Open daily 7am-2am. V, MC.

Le Procope, 13 rue de l'Ancienne Comédie (tel. 01 40 46 79 00). M: Odéon. Founded in 1686 and the oldest café in Paris. Voltaire drank 40 coffees per day here while writing *Candide*. His table remains "a festimony of permanence" (sic). *Café* 14F, beer 21-28F, *menu* 299F(!). Open daily 11am-2am.

CHAMP DE MARS-INVALIDES (7ÈME)

This wealthy area does not boast many budget options. Moderately priced restaurants aimed at lawyers and government officials are more the norm. Some grocers and *boulangeries* have small tables for inexpensive eat-in.

▨ **La Varangue,** 27 rue Augereau (tel. 01 45 05 51 22). M: École-Militaire. Turn right on rue de Grenelle from av. de la Bourdonnais, then left onto rue Augereau. Intimate atmosphere and fresh food. 2-course lunch (55F) and dinner *menus* (77 and 98F) include wine or cider. *Grandes salades* 45F. Open M-F noon-2:30pm and 7-10pm. Dinner reservations recommended. V, MC, AmEx.

Au Pied de Fouet, 45 rue de Babylone (tel. 01 47 05 12 27). M: Vaneau. A small but well-known bistro, once frequented by Cocteau. Excellent place to try French home-cooking such as *confit de canard* (duck casserole, 60F). *Entrées* 13-20F, *plats* 45-65F, dessert 15F. Open M-F noon-2:30pm and 7-9pm, Sa noon-2:30pm.

Café du Marché, 38 rue Cler (tel. 01 47 05 51 27). M: École-Militaire. This is the main location on delightful rue Cler for whiling away the afternoon hours amid bustling bakeries and markets. Good range of croissants, *brioches*, and a reasonable cup of coffee (12-22F). Open M-Sa 7am-midnight, Su 8am-4pm. V, MC.

CHAMPS-ÉLYSÉES (8ÈME)

While the Champs-Élysées itself is increasingly taken over by international fast-food and home-grown, mid-price chains which cater to the throngs of strolling tourists and film-going Parisians, the area around it is as *chic* as it gets. If you're not interested in participating in such exuberant wastefulness, there are some affordable restaurants to be found, especially on side streets around rue La Boëtie. For an affordable taste of extravagance, nip into **Ladurée,** 16 rue Royale (tel. 01 42 60 21 79; M: Concorde), or 75 av. des Champs-Élysées (tel. 01 40 75 08 75; M: FDR) The adjunct store sells chocolates galore, while the *chocolat chaud* is nearly as rich as the women sipping tea in the salon. (Open daily 8:30am-7pm.) You'd do best just to window shop at **Fauchon,** 26 pl. de la Madeleine (tel. 01 47 42 60 11; M: Madeleine), a cross between a billionaire's supermarket and a museum. Tuxedoed attendants float about the store helping clients find their favorite pâté and galettes. (Open M-Sa 9:40am-7pm. V, MC, AmEx.) At the famous cheese emporium **Alléosse**, 13 rue Poncelet, 17ème (tel. 01 46 22 50 45; M: Ternes), you'll faint at the prices if not the smell. (Open Tu-Sa 9am-1pm and 4-7pm, Su 9am-1pm. V, MC.)

🗲 **Antoine's: Les Sandwichs des 5 Continents,** 31 rue de Ponthieu (tel. 01 42 89 44 20). M: FDR Walk toward the Étoile, turn right on av. F.D. Roosevelt, and left on rue de Ponthieu. 35F deal (*panini,* yogurt, and a drink) on bread that's probably worth 35F alone. Open M-Sa 8am-7pm.

La Table de Margot, 40 rue Ponthieu (tel. 01 53 96 06 88). M: FDR. Follow directions to Antoine's, above. French staples done well, with flattering lighting. *Plats* 67-69F, salads 56-58F. 2-course *menu* includes kir (89F). Open daily 11:30am-3pm and 7-10:30pm. V, MC, AmEx.

Le Singe d'Eau, 28 rue de Moscou (tel. 01 43 87 72 73). M: Europe. Proper Tibetan cuisine in a very colorful dining room. *Entrées* 18-40F, *plats* 45-55F. Lunch *menu* 65F. Plenty for vegetarians. Open Sept.-July M-Sa noon-3pm and 7-11pm. V, MC, AmEx.

Fouquet's, 99 av. des Champs-Élysées (tel. 01 47 2370 60). M: George V. Filled with French stars of song and screen, but it's also filled with American tourists—and the two groups rarely mix. Classic decor and snobbery so "French" that it seems like a caricature of itself. *Café* and a chance to be seen 25F. Open daily 8am-1am; unaffordable food served noon-3pm and 7pm-midnight. V, MC, AmEx.

OPÉRA-GARE DU NORD/GARE DE L'EST (9ÈME & 10ÈME)

Except for a few gems, meals close to the Opéra cater to the after-theater crowd and can be quite expensive. For truly cheap deals, head farther north. Many immigrants have found a home here, providing visitors with affordable North and West African, Latin American, and Middle Eastern delicacies. Catering to locals rather than tourists, these restaurants offer some of Paris's more colorful culinary creations. Passage Brady overflows with cheap Indian *restaus* and rue Lafayette with Japanese delights.

🗲 **Paris-Dakar,** 95 rue du fbg St-Martin (tel. 01 42 08 16 64). M: Gare de l'Est. Senegalese cuisine served with West African charm. Lunch *menu* (59F), dinner *menu* (129F), and African *menu* (179F) feature *tiébou dieune* (fish with rice and veg) and the house drink *bissap,* made from sorrel and fresh mint. Open Tu-Th and Sa-Su noon-3pm and 7pm-2am, F 7pm-2am. V, MC.

🗲 **Haynes Bar,** 3 rue Clauzel (tel. 01 48 78 40 63). M: St-Georges. Head uphill on rue Notre-Dame-de-Lorette and turn right on rue H. Monnier, then right on rue Clauzel till the end of the block. Former hangout of Louis Armstrong, James Baldwin, and Richard Wright. Fried chicken and fresh-baked corn bread 70F, BBQ spare ribs 80F. New Orleans jazz piano Friday nights. Closed Aug. Open Tu-Sa 7pm-midnight. V, MC, AmEx.

Deli's Café, 6 rue du Fbg Montmartre (tel. 01 48 24 24 04). M: Rue Montmartre. A small, affordable café with great sandwiches like chicken curry on spinach or tomato bread (16-21F), *panini* (18-23F), and *brioches* (25F). Open daily 7am-2am.

Café de la Paix, 12 bd. des Capucines (tel. 01 40 07 32 32). M: Opéra. On the left as you face the Opéra. This institution has drawn a classy crowd since it opened in 1862. *Café* 26F, ice cream 40-59F, *menus* 300F (gulp). Open daily 10am-1:30am.

La Maison du Chocolat, 8 bd. de la Madeleine (tel. 01 47 42 86 52). M: Madeleine. From milk to dark, and, for those tired of the usual consumption of solids, a mysterious distilled chocolate essence drink. Solid bar 28-39F. Open M-Sa 9:30am-7pm. V, MC. Also at 52 rue François 1er, 8ème (tel. 01 47 23 38 25).

RÉPUBLIQUE (10ÈME & 11ÈME)

Though not quite as youth-cool as nearby Bastille, the area around pl. de la République buzzes with a grittier style all its own. *Brasseries* and fast-food line the *place* itself along with the pre-requisite Tex-Mex joints. More budget restaurants cluster around the hip Oberkampf area (M: Oberkampf or Filles du Calvaire). Well-priced perishables are on offer at the **Marché Popincourt**, bd. Richard Lenoir. (M: Oberkampf. Tu and F 8am-1:30pm.)

Le Dogon, 30 rue René Boulanger (tel. 01 42 41 95 85). M: République. Follow bd. St-Martin from the metro; rue René Boulanger is on your right. Named after the owner's hometown in Mali, this West African restaurant is steps away from pl. de la République. White walls, batiks, and animal pelts serve as the backdrop for curries, couscous, and affordable lunch *menus* (55F). Popular bar in the evening. Open M-F noon-3pm and 7pm-1am, Sa-Su 7pm-1am. V, MC.

Le Kitch, 10 rue Oberkampf (tel. 01 40 21 94 19). M: Oberkampf or Filles du Calvaire. Despite the dollar-store decor, this restaurant-bar catches a hip crowd with affordable, tasty, primarily vegetarian dishes. Gazpacho 29F, vegetarian lasagna 52F. Open M-F 11am-3pm and 8pm-2am, Sa-Su 8pm-2am.

Le Clown Bar, 114 rue Amelot, (tel. 01 43 55 87 35). M: Filles du Calvaire. Across from the Cirque d'Hiver, and frequented by real live circus folk, this very cool wine-bar is very popular. By the glass starts at 15F. Open M-Sa noon-3:30pm and 7pm-1am. V, MC.

BASTILLE (11ᵉᵐᵉ & 12ᵉᵐᵉ)

Since the Bastille hit the spotlight as the place to be in the early 90s, it's become a victim of Tex-Mex, burger, and pizza chains. Head away from the *place* toward rue Charonne, rue Keller, and rue de Lappe, where a diverse selection of reasonable spots plays to a hip crowd. If you're around in the morning, spare an hour for **Marché Bastille**, on bd. Richard-Lenoir from pl. de la Bastille north to rue St-Sabin, which spreads god's bounty across the 11ᵉᵐᵉ from M: Richard Lenoir to M: Bastille. (Open Th and Su 7am-1:30pm.)

Café de l'Industrie, 16 rue St-Sabin (tel. 01 47 00 13 53). M: Breguet-Sabin. A huge and happy-ning café with neo-colonial touches and black-and-white prints that swells with a trendy but not pouty crowd. *Café* 10F, salads 45-58F; prices increase 4F after 10pm. Open Su-F 10am-2am, food served noon-12:30pm.

Pause Café, 41 rue de Charonne (tel. 01 48 06 80 33). M: Ledru-Rollin. Walk along av. Ledru Rollin and turn left onto rue de Charonne. Once a people-drooling, name-dropping, terrace-posing joint, Pause is now a downbeat, friendly, colorful café. Salads 40-50F, beer 15F. Open M-Sa 7:45am-2am, Su 8:30am-8:30pm. V, MC.

Un Saumon à Paris, 32 rue de Charonne (tel. 01 49 29 07 15). M: Ledru-Rollin. follow directions to Pause Café. In a school of its own, this smoked fish and caviar bar masterminds salmon and trout in more ways than you ever imagined (48-70F). 15 different vodkas. Lunch *menu* 69F. Open M-Sa 10:30am-3:30pm and 6pm-1am, Su 6pm-1am.

Le Bistrot du Peintre, 116 av. Ledru-Rollin (tel. 01 47 00 34 39). M: Ledru-Rollin. The dark wood, curvaceous mirrors, and floral tiles of this original Art Nouveau bistro are a treat. Omelettes 32-35F, *plats* 48-82F. Open M-Sa 7am-2am, Su 10am-8pm. V, MC.

L'Ébauchoir, 45 rue de Cîteaux (tel. 01 43 42 49 31). M: Faidherbe-Chaligny. Walk down rue du Fbg St-Antoine and turn left on rue de Cîteaux. Great balance of funky and French. Try the *foie de veau au miel et au coriandre* (veal liver with honey and coriander, 80F). *Entrées* 30-60F, *plats* 75-100F, desserts 25-40F. Open M-Th noon-2:30pm and 8-10:30pm, F-Sa noon-2:30pm and 8-11pm.

Jacques Mélac, 42 rue Léon Frot (tel. 01 43 70 59 27). M: Charonne. In September, children harvest and tread the grapes hanging from the bar's storefront—call ahead for the date and don't miss the party. Don't worry—the Mélac wines sold here come from his vineyard. 18F per glass. Open Sept.-July M 9am-5pm, Tu-F 9am-midnight. V, MC.

PLACE D'ITALIE (13ᵉᵐᵉ)

The up-and-coming 13ᵉᵐᵉ is a budget gourmand's dream. Southwest of pl. d'Italie, rue de la Butte aux Cailles' restaurants and bars fill with the young and high-spirited. Scores of Vietnamese, Thai, Cambodian, Laotian, and Chinese restaurants cluster in Paris's "Chinatown," south of pl. d'Italie on av. de Choisy, while a large North African community offers Moroccan, Tunisian, and Algerian specialties in the restaurants near the St-Marcel metro to the north. You can stock up on a range of Asian foods at ⬛ **Tang Frères,** 44 and 48 av. d'Ivry (tel. 01 45 70 80 00; M: Porte d'Ivry), which also has a restaurant, a café, and a gourmet shop. (No. 44 open M-Sa 10am-8:30pm; no. 48 open Tu-F 9am-7:30pm and Sa-Su 8:30am-7:30pm.)

⬛ **Café du Commerce,** 39 rue des Cinq Diamants (tel. 01 53 62 91 04). M: Pl. d'Italie. Take bd. Auguste Blanqui and turn left onto rue des Cinq Diamants; on the corner of rue Jonas. Funky fruit-i-ful place. Dinner *menus* (65-120F) include *éventail d'avocat aux framboises* (avocado fan with strawberries) and *entrecôte sauce roquefort.* Lunch *menu* 47-50F. Open daily 11:30am-3pm and 7pm-2am. Reserve Sa-Su. V, MC, AmEx.

⬛ **Le Samson,** 9 rue Jean-Marie Jégo (tel. 01 45 89 09 23). M: Pl. d'Italie. Take rue Bibelot and turn right on rue de la Butte aux Cailles and then right on rue Jean-Marie Jégo. Artsy, mellow, and jam-packed. Homemade sausages flambéed in whiskey 40F. Lunch *menu* 68F, dinner 78F. Open M-F noon-3pm and 8pm-midnight, Sa 8pm-midnight.

Le Merle Moqueur, 11 rue de la Butte aux Cailles (tel. 01 45 65 12 43). M: Corvisart. Take rue Bobillot south until rue de la Butte aux Cailles branches right. Bamboo walls, African music, and a shabby-cool ambiance. Cheap beer (14F) and food (nothing over 50F). No frills and few tourists. Most customers head for the terrace but the back room is cooler. Happy hour 5-8pm. Open daily 3pm-2am. V, MC.

MONTPARNASSE(14$^{\grave{e}me}$ & 15$^{\grave{e}me}$)

The 14$^{\grave{e}me}$ is bordered at the top by the busy bd. du Montparnasse, which is lined with restaurants ranging from Tex-Mex chains to famed cafés. Rue de Montparnasse, which intersects with the boulevard, teems with charming and reasonably priced *crêperies.* Cheap, easy bistros and *brasseries* trip over each other on rue du Commmerce. Restaurants off the main avenues rely on reputation, so they deserve the extra time it takes to get there.

⬛ **Aux Artistes,** 63 rue Falguière (tel. 01 43 22 05 39). M: Pasteur. Follow Pasteur away from the rails for two blocks and go right. Modigliani's old hangout, and still one of the *arrondissement's* coolest spots. Red walls, neo-Impressionist *oeuvres,* and a Hawaii license plate on the wall? Here, it all makes sense. Lunch *menu* 56F, dinner 78F. Open M-F noon-12:30am, Sa noon-2pm. V, MC.

Phinéas, 99 rue de l'Ouest (tel. 01 45 41 33 50). M: Pernety. Follow the traffic on rue Pernety and turn left on rue de l'Ouest. Specializing in *tartes,* this delightful restaurant doubles as a comic book shrine with elaborate candelabras and a suspended glimmering gold crown. *Plats* (some vegetarian) 58-80F. Open Tu-Sa 9am-noon for take-out and noon-11:30pm for sit-down meals. V, MC, AmEx.

Crêperie de Josselin, 67 rue du Montparnasse (tel. 01 43 20 93 50). M: Edgar Quinet. On a street full of *crêperies,* this small restaurant stands out. Wood-paneled dining room with lace coverings, colorful wall mosaics, and a collection of ceramics. *Crêpes* 22-70F. Open Tu-F noon-2pm and 6-11:45pm, Sa-Su noon-midnight

Restaurant Les Listines, 24 rue Falguière (tel. 01 45 38 57 40). M: Falguière. Pretty interior and delicately prepared seafood and meat dishes. *Menu* 79F. Open M-F noon-2:30pm and 7-10pm, Sa noon-2:30pm. V, MC, AmEx.

Le Sélect, 99 bd. du Montparnasse (tel. 01 45 48 38 24). M: Vavin. Opposite La Coupole. Trotsky, Satie, Breton, Cocteau, and Picasso all frequented this swank bistro/café. Coffee 6.50F at the counter, hot chocolate 35F. Open daily 7am-3am. V, MC.

La Coupole, 102 bd. du Montparnasse (tel. 01 43 20 14 20). M: Vavin. The Art Deco interior has hosted Lenin, Stravinsky, Hemingway, and Einstein. You can probably afford coffee (11F) or a *croque monsieur* (28F). Splash out after 10:30pm on the 132F *menu "Faim de Nuit,"* which offers oysters, steak tartare, and lemon tart. Open M-Th 7:30am-2am, F 9:30pm-4am, Sa 3-7pm and 9:30pm-4am. Dancing Sa-Su. V, MC.

MONTMARTRE (17ÈME & 18ÈME)

During the siege of Paris in 1814, Cossacks occupied Montmartre; being always in a hurry, they called the restaurants which satisfied their appetites *bistros* (Russian for "quick"). Today, charming *bistrots* and cafés lie between rue des Abbesses and rue Lepic. At the outdoor **marché Berthier,** on bd. de Reims between rue de Courcelles and rue du Marquis d'Arlandes (M: Porte de Champerret), vendors try to hard-sell the already underpriced meat, vegetables, and Middle-Eastern specialties (W and Sa 8am-1pm).

Chez Ginette, 101 rue Caulaincourt (tel. 01 46 06 01 49). Above M: Lamarck-Caulaincourt. A slice of Montmartre livened up by music at night. Inventive cooking, such as monkfish with prawn sauce (98F) or eggplant stuffed with goat cheese (50F). *Plats* 78-98F, salads 38-55F. Open Sept.-July M-Sa noon-2:30pm and 7:30pm-2am. V, MC.

Le Soleil Gourmand, 10 rue Ravignan (tel. 01 42 51 00 50). M: Abbesses. Facing the *église*, go right and take the rightmost of the three streets that diverge there. Artsy ambiance: cast-iron chairs, tiled tables, and scribbles on the walls. Perfect when you've OD'd on *coq au vin*, this *salon de thé* offers lighter fare, including oriental seafood salad (65F) and house-baked cakes (30-44F). Open daily 12:30-2:30pm and 8:30-11pm.

👁 SIGHTS

For all its grandeur, Paris is a small city. In just a few hours you can walk from Bastille in the east to the Eiffel Tower in the west, passing many of the city's principal monuments. You don't have a true sense of Paris until you know how close Nôtre-Dame is to the Centre Pompidou, or the *quartier latin* of students to the Louvre of kings. If you're not in a walking mood, **Parisbus** (tel. 01 42 30 55 50) runs bus tours in English covering all the major sights. (2hr.; 125F, students 100F, children 60F.) Another great way to see the city is by boat along the Seine, especially at night when the buildings are illuminated. **Bateaux-Mouches** (tel. 01 42 25 96 10; info line 01 40 76 99 99; M: Alma-Marceau) runs 1½-hour tours in English. (Every 30min. 10am-11:30pm from pier by Pont d'Alma. 40F, ages 4-14 20F.)

The sights below have been arranged in easily walkable geographical clusters that do not always correspond to the irregular *arrondissements*. **Museums** are described in a separate section of their own; see p. 136.

THE SEINE ISLANDS

ÎLE DE LA CITÉ

If any place could be called the heart of Paris, it is this slip in the river. It was here that the Parisii first settled in the 3rd century BC, and here that Clovis made his capital 900 years later. All distances from Paris are measured from *kilomètre zéro*, a sundial on the ground in front of Notre-Dame.

NÔTRE-DAME. Though Nôtre-Dame is by no means the most architecturally distinguished cathedral in France, its position as the spiritual heart of the nation is unchallenged. It was here that Joan of Arc was tried and condemned in 1429, and here that Napoleon was crowned Emperor in 1804. Begun in 1163, the cathedral's construction spanned 200 years, and incorporates the full gamut of Gothic techniques. After suffering the ravages of the Revolution—the façade was plastered over and statues defaced—popular affection for the cathedral was revived by Victor Hugo's *The Hunchback of Notre-Dame* (1831), and its restoration was undertaken by Viollet-le-Duc. The transept's largely original 13th-century rose windows form the highlight of the interior; the north window depicts the Virgin surrounded by Old Testament kings, the south the Evangelists, and the central window Christ and the Apostles. The **trésor,** south of the choir, contains an assortment of robes, sacramental cutlery, and other gilded artifacts. For a spectacular view of the *cité* and the city, climb the massive twin **towers.** In the south tower there's a 13-ton bell that even Quasimodo couldn't move. The **crypte archéologique** is an excavation site beneath the square in front of the cathedral; you can walk through Paris's history from Roman times to the 19th century. *(M: Cité. Tel. 01 42 34 56 10. Cathedral: Open M-F 8am-6:45pm, Sa-Su 8am-7:45pm. Tours in English W and Th noon, Sa 2:30pm; in French M-F noon, Sa 2:30pm. Towers: Open Apr.-Sept. 10am-6pm, Oct.-Mar. 10am-5pm. Trésor: Open M-Sa 9:30am-6pm; 15F, students and ages 12-17 10F, 6-12 5F. Crypt: Tel. 01 43 29 83 51. Open daily Apr.-Sept. 10am-6pm; Oct.-Mar. 10am-5pm; 35F, students 23F, under 12 free.)*

PALAIS DE JUSTICE. Justice has been dispensed here since Roman times. The present building incorporates Louis IX's 13th-century chambers and **Ste-Chapelle** and Philippe le Bel's **Conciergerie** palace, more famous as a Revolutionary prison. After Étienne Marcel slew Charles V's counselors before his eyes in 1538, the palace has not been kind to Royalty; Charles moved to the Louvre, as did all his successors save Louis XVI, Charles X, and Louis-Philippe—the same three who lost their thrones in revolutions. Today the complex still houses Paris's law courts. All trials are open to the public, but don't expect a *France vs. Dreyfus* every day. *(M: Cité. Tel. 01 44 32 51 51. Courtrooms open M-F 9am-noon and 1:30-5pm. Free.)*

STE-CHAPELLE. When St. Louis (Louis IX) bought the Crown of Thorns from the Venetians for 135,000 *livres* in 1239, he decided he needed a new chapel in which to house it. The result is one of the most exquisite examples of Flamboyant Gothic architecture in the world. Built on two floors, the muted lower chapel hardly prepares one for the incredible upstairs; sheer stained glass lines three sides of the chapel as the ceiling recedes into irrelevance. Read from bottom to top, left to right, the windows narrate the Bible from alpha to omega. *(M: Cité. Inside the Palais de Justice complex. Tel. 01 53 73 78 50. Open daily Apr.-Sept. 9:30am-6:30pm; Oct.-Mar. 10am-5pm. 35F, with Conciergerie 50F, seniors and ages 12-25 23F, under 12 free.)*

CONCIERGERIE. Around the corner of the Palais de Justice from the entrance to the Ste-Chapelle is this dark but fascinating monument to the Revolution. At the far-right corner, a stepped parapet marks the oldest tower, the **Tour Bonbec,** which once housed the prison's torture chambers. The modern entrance lies between the **Tour d'Argent,** stronghold of the royal treasury, and the **Tour de César,** which housed the Revolutionary tribunal. Follow the "rue de Paris," the corridor leading from the entrance, named for "Monsieur de Paris," the executioner's nickname. These same stones were trod by Marie-Antoinette on her way to the gallows. Farther down the hall is the cell where Robespierre awaited his death. *(1 quai de l'Horloge. M: Cité. Tel. 01 53 73 78 50. Open daily Apr.-Sept. 9:30am-6:30pm; Oct.-Mar. 10am-5pm. Tours in French at 11am and 3pm. 35F, students 23F.)*

MÉMORIAL DE LA DÉPORTATION. A simple but moving memorial erected for the French victims of Nazi concentration camps; 200,000 flickering lights represent the dead, and an eternal flame burns close to the tomb of an unknown deportee. Quotations are engraved into the walls, the most striking of which is the injunction *"Pardonne. N'oublie Pas"* ("Forgive. Do not forget"). *(Pl. de l'Île de France, behind the cathedral. M: Cité. Open daily Apr.-Sept. 10am-noon, 2-7pm; Oct.-Mar. 10am-noon, 2-5pm. Free.)*

PONT NEUF. The oldest bridge in Paris acquired its name when it was completed in 1604. Before the construction of the Champs-Élysées, the bridge was Paris's most popular thoroughfare, attracting peddlers, performers, thieves, and street physicians. The bridge is interesting for being the first not to be lined with houses.

ÎLE ST-LOUIS

Originally two small islands—the Île aux Vâches and the Île de Nôtre-Dame—this most elegant of Parisian addresses was originally considered fit only for cows. It became residential in the 17th century after the entrepreneur Christophe Marie joined the islands together and sold the land for development. Baudelaire and Cézanne number among its past residents; the *hôtels particuliers* now house an elite that includes Guy de Rothschild, the Aga Khan, and Pompidou's widow. The island's most beautiful mansions line the **quai d'Anjou,** between **Pont Marie** and **Pont**

de Sully. No. 29 once housed Ford Madox Ford's *Transatlantic Review,* the expatriate rag to which Hemingway frequently contributed. No. 9 was the address of Honoré Daumier, Realist painter and caricaturist, from 1846 to 1863. Loop around the end of the *quai* to get to the island's main thoroughfare, **rue St-Louis-en-l'Île,** home to art galleries, pricey restaurants, and the famous **Berthillon glacerie** (see **Sweets,** p. 109). Follow rue Budé to the **Musée Adam Mickiewicz,** 6 quai d'Orléans, the former home of the Polish poet. Exhibits on his circle of expat Polish artists, include Chopin's death mask. (Tours Th at 2, 3:30, and 5pm. 30F, students 15F, children free.) Another famous Pole, Marie Curie, lived on the other side of rue des Deux Ponts at 36 quai de Béthune. Behind the humdrum façade of the 17th-century **Église St-Louis-en-l'Île,** 3 rue Poulletier (tel. 01 46 34 11 60), is a blazing Rococo interior decorated with gold leaf, marble, and statuettes, and lit by more windows than seemed to exist on the outside. Designed by Le Vau, the church has legendary acoustics and hosts concerts throughout the year and every night in July and August. (Open Tu-Su 9am-noon and 3-7pm.)

RIVE DROITE (RIGHT BANK)
LOUVRE-RIVOLI (1ER)

In the shadow of the Louvre (see **Museums,** p. 136), the Sun King's well-tended gardens are now filled with sunbathers, cafés, and carnival rides. The Louvre's restoration, which began with the construction of the famous Pyramid in the early 90s, is now complete, freeing the once traffic-choked palace forecourt and reconnecting it to the Tuileries. There is a **color map** of the area in the front of this book.

JARDIN DES TUILERIES. Sweeping down from the **Louvre** to the **place de la Concorde,** the Jardin des Tuileries celebrates the victory of geometry over nature. Named after the long-gone Palais des Tuileries, which formerly made up the west wing of the Louvre, the gardens were first laid out in the Italian style by a homesick Catherine de Médici in 1564; in 1649, Le Nôtre imposed his preference for straight lines and sculpted trees. Framed by Napoleon's Arc du Carrousel and the Concorde's Obelisk, the garden is home to sculptures, cafés, and *pétanque* courts. In summer, the terrace becomes an amusement park with a huge ferris wheel. Towards pl. de la Concorde are the **Galerie National du Jeu de Paume,** now a contemporary art gallery, and the **Musée de l'Orangerie,** the crowded repository of Monet's Water Lilies. *(See p. 140. M: Tuileries. Tel. 01 40 20 90 43. Open daily Apr.-Sept. 7am-9pm; Oct.-Mar. 7:30am-7:30pm.)*

PLACE VENDÔME. Designed by Hardouin-Mansart for Louis XIV in 1687, the stately *place* remained nothing but a pretty façade for 15 years—the first lot was not sold until 1702, and the last house was built in 1720. In the center of the square is a large column topped by Napoleon dressed as Cæsar. The ever-modest Emperor commissioned it in 1805, modeled after Trajan's column in Rome, and surrounded with reliefs of military exploits. During the Commune, a group led by Gustave Courbet toppled the column, planning to replace it with a monument to the "Federation of Nations and the Universal Republic;" instead, Courbet was forced to pay for a replica of the old column.

PALAIS-ROYAL. Constructed in 1632 for Cardinal Richelieu, it became a Palais Royal when His Eminence gave it to Louis XIII. In 1784, the duc de Chartres rented out the elegant buildings to create a low-class mall whose arcades were a favorite

---

PUTTIN' ON THE... Founded by César Ritz at the turn of the century, the unaffordably opulent Ritz Hotel (no. 15 pl. Vendôme) stands as a monument to money. Most famous recently as the place where Princess Diana had her last meal, it also has happier stories to tell. Riding into Paris with the US Army in 1944, Ernest Hemingway gathered some troops and went to liberate the Ritz. Greeted by his old chum, the assistant manager, he proceeded to order 73 dry martinis.

for lewd encounters. On July 12, 1789, 26-year-old Camille Desmoulins leaped onto a café table and urged his fellow citizens to arm themselves. The crowd filed out and was soon skirmishing with cavalry in the Tuileries. Today, the galleries still contain shops and cafés with splendid views of the palace fountain, flower beds, and gardens. In the central courtyard stand the controversial striped columns installed by artist Daniel Buren in 1986. The southwest corner of the Palais houses the 18th-century **Comédie Française,** home to France's oldest dramatic troupe. For performance info, see p. 141. At the corner of rue Molière and rue Richelieu, Visconti's **Fontaine de Molière** is steps from where Molière died at no. 40.

OTHER SIGHTS. At the back of the Louvre, the **Pont Neuf** (see p. 117) leads to the Île de la Cité. Nearby is the Gothic **Église St-Germain l'Auxerrois.** On August 24, 1572, the church's bell gave the signal for the St. Bartholomew's Day Massacre. Within the church are buried a number of artists and architects, including Le Vau, Souflot, Boucher, and Chardin. Behind the church, the roof of **Samaritaine** department store has one of the best free views of Paris in the city (see p. 149).

LES HALLES-BEAUBOURG (1ER & WESTERN 4ÈME)

The area northwest of the Louvre is a testament to 70s urban planning. Les Halles housed Paris's main food market from the 12th century until 1969, when the market moved to the suburbs. The space under the market is now home to Paris's biggest metro-RER station and a subterranean shopping mall, the **Forum des Halles**— don't hang around underground at night. Above ground, a few remnants of the 19th-century iron-and-glass pavilions have been incorporated into a garden. Going right from the Forum des Halles main exit takes you to the **Fontaine des Innocents.** Built in 1548, the fountain is the last remnant of the Église and Cimetière des Sts-Innocents, destroyed in 1780 due to the stench of rotting corpses; today, punks and goths do their best to recreate the death æsthetic. Continuing west across the busy **bd. de Sébastopol** brings you to **Beaubourg,** another 70s creation. Now home to France's most popular tourist attraction, the **Centre Pompidou,** sometimes it seems like this former slums' old residents never moved out.

ÉGLISE DE ST-EUSTACHE. Towering over Les Halles, the church saw the baptisms of Richelieu and Molière as well as Louis XIV's first communion. Construction of began in 1532 in the Gothic style and dragged on for over a century; in 1754, the Renaissance façade was replaced with an incongruous Neoclassical pediment. In summer, concerts are played on the famous organ. Outside the church is Henri de Miller's 1986 sculpture *The Listener.* (M: Les Halles. Tel. 01 42 36 31 05. Open June-Aug. M-F 10am-8pm, Sa 9am-12:30pm and 2:30-8pm; Sept.-May M-F 9am-7pm. Concerts 80-150F.)

CENTRE POMPIDOU. Certain to elicit an opinion, the Centre was the brainchild of President Georges Pompidou. Finished in 1977, the building was designed inside-out by Richard Rogers and Renzo Piano. The prominent service tubes are color coded: yellow for electricity, green for water, and blue for ventilation. Even its designers did not anticipate its enormous popularity; the wear and tear caused by crowds far in excess of its capacity have necessitated a massive restoration project. When it reopens on December 31, 1999, people will again be able to visit the **Musée Nationale de l'Art Moderne** (see p. 137). The cobblestone square in front of the Pompidou gathers a mixture of caricaturists, musicians, and causeless rebels by day and rougher types by night. To the left of the Centre as you face it twirl the surreal aquatic sculptures of the **Fontaine Stravinsky.** Beneath the fountain is **IRCAM,** the contemporary music center directed by Pierre Boulez; its entrance is by the fountain's northwest corner. (M: Rambuteau.)

OTHER SIGHTS. Stretching north from the Halles gardens, the marble-cobbled **rue Montorgueil** has been home to gourmet food shops since the 13th century. To the left of rue Montorgueil stand the well-preserved remnants of the 15th-century **Tour de Jean Sans Peur,** on rue Étienne Marcel. Not as brave as all that, after ordering the successful assassination of the king's brother in 1408 Jean built himself this tower in which he could sleep *sans peur* of retribution.

PARIS & ÎLE DE FRANCE

OPÉRA (2ÈME & SOUTHWESTERN 9ÈME)

From Palais Royal, in the 1er, the av. de l'Opéra sweeps up to the palatial **Opéra Garnier,** cutting through the narrow, commercial 2ème. From wheeling and dealing at the **Bourse des Valeurs** to 19th-century shopping in the glass-covered *passages*, this *arrondissement* has long been Paris's financial heart. Avoid the seedy district to the east around rue St-Denis. Next to the Opéra is the quintessentially 19th-century **Café de la Paix** (see p. 113). Heading towards la Madeleine along bd. des Capucines takes you past the **Olympia** music hall, where Édith Piaf achieved fame. Taking bd. des Capucines the other way leads you past the **Opéra Comique;** at the road's end, bear right along bd. Montmartre to reach the waxworks of the **Musée Grévin** (see p. 140). West of the Opéra, the department stores **Au Printemps** and **Galeries Lafayette** stand on bd. Haussmann (see p. 149). For an overview of the area, refer to the **color map** at the front of this book.

OPÉRA GARNIER. Emerging from M: Opéra, your eyes will quickly be drawn to the grandiose Opéra, or at least to the enormous scaffolding covering its front. Charles Garnier's building epitomizes both the Second Empire's ostentation and its rootlessness. The interior, with its grand staircase, golden foyer, and five-tiered auditorium, was designed as a stage for socialites as much as arias. Opened in 1875, the Opéra is decorated with Gobelins tapestries and a six-ton chandelier that fell on the audience in 1896. In 1964, Chagall was commissioned to paint the ceiling. Since the opening of the Opéra Bastille in 1989, the Garnier has been used mainly for ballets. For information on performances, see **Music** (p. 142). The Opéra also houses a library and museum on the history of opera and dance. *(Tel. 01 44 73 13 99. Open daily July-Aug. 10am-6pm, Sept.-June 10am-5pm. Last entry 30min. before closing. Museum open daily 10am-noon and 2-5pm. Daily English tours noon in summer 60F, students, ages 10-16, and over 60 45F; under 10 25F. Tours often overbooked; for info, call 01 40 01 22 63. Admission including museum 30F, ages 10-16, over 60, and students 20F.)*

BIBLIOTHÈQUE NATIONALE. Since 1642, every book published in France has been required to enter the national archives. The main body of 10 million volumes has been relocated to the mammoth new **Bibliothèque de France** in the 13ème (see p. 134). Today, the **Galerie Mazarin** and **Galerie Mansart** host temporary exhibitions of books, prints, and lithographs. Opposite the main entrance, Visconti's 1839 fountain personifies the four great rivers of France as heroic women. *(58 rue de Richelieu. Main tel. 01 47 03 81 26; info tel. 01 53 79 59 59; galleries tel. 01 47 03 81 10. Mansart open Tu-Su 10am-7pm. 35F, students 24F.)*

LES PASSAGES. In the early 19th century, speculators built numerous glass-housed *galeries* or *passages* through which pedestrians could pass safe from the cold, rain, and mud of the streets—and do a little shopping on the side. Fewer than 20 of the originally over 100 *passages* survive. Today, they continue to house boutiques. **Galerie Colbert** is notable for its bronze sculptures and rotunda, while **Galerie Vivienne** is a showcase of pastel luxury and faux-marble columns; at the end the Bibliothèque National keeps an exhibition space. *(Both on rue des Petits Champs, next to Bibliothèque National. Call 01 47 03 85 71 for exhibit info. Exhibitions open M-Sa noon-8pm.)*

LA BOURSE. Founded in 1724, Paris's stock exchange opened well after those of Lyon, Toulouse, and Rouen. Construction of the present building began in 1808, proceeded slowly, and halted between 1814 and 1821 for lack of funds. The wings were added from 1902-1907. Today's traders' pit is quiet as *actions* change hands electronically—the entire process has been computerized since 1986. *(Rue Nôtre-Dame des Victoires. M: Bourse. Tel. 01 40 41 62 20. Hourly 45min. English tours M-F 1:15-4pm. English audioguides available during French tour with 50F deposit. 30F, students 15F.)*

THE UPPER MARAIS (3ÈME & NORTHERN 4ÈME)

Named for its swampy location, the Marais was drained in the 13th century to provide building space for the expanding city. With the construction of **pl. des Vosges** in the early 17th century, aristocrats moved into elegant *hôtels* with enclosed gardens. The Marais lost its charm under Louis XV as the royal scene shifted eastwards, and the area fell into disrepair, escaping Haussmanization in the 19th century and becoming a center for Jewish immigration in the early 20th. Since the 60s, the Marais has returned to the spotlight and trendy boutiques, cafés, and museums have moved in.

RUE DES FRANCS BOURGEOIS AND RUE VIEILLE DU TEMPLE. Slicing eastwards from Beaubourg to pl. des Vosges, **rue des Francs Bourgeois** divides the 3ème and 4ème *arrondissements*. Starting from the west, the 18th-century **Hôtel de Soubise** is home to the **Archives Nationales** and the **Musée de l'Histoire de France,** which preserves a number of historical documents, including the Declaration of the Rights of Man and Napoleon's will. Louis XVI's diary entry for July 14, 1789 reads simply *"rien."* (*60 rue des Francs Bourgeois. M: Rambuteau. Tel. 01 40 27 64 19 or 01 40 27 64 20. Open M and W-F noon-5:45pm, Sa-Su 1:45-5:45pm. 15F; students, seniors, and Su 10F, under 18 free.*) Continuing down the street, at the corner of rue des Francs Bourgeois and rue Vieille du Temple is the Flamboyant Gothic **Hôtel Hérouët**, built in 1528. Turn left and follow **rue Vieille du Temple,** lined with stately residences, to the **Hôtel de Rohan** (no. 87). Built between 1705 and 1708 for Armand-Gaston de Rohan, Bishop of Strasbourg and alleged love-child of Louis XIV, today it holds temporary exhibitions. (*Tel. 01 40 27 60 00. Open M-F 9am-6pm. Free.*) From Hôtel de Rohan, turn right into rue de la Perle and immediately left into rue de Thorigny to reach the **Hôtel Salé,** which now houses the **Musée Picasso** (see **Museums,** p. 139). Balzac, who once boarded here, based the Maison Vauquer in *le Père Goriot* on the place. Return to rue des Franc Bourgeois and turn left. At rue Pavée is the 16th-century **Hôtel de Lamoignon,** one of the finest *hôtels particuliers* in the Marais. Facing Lamoignon across rue des Francs Bourgeois, with its entrance on rue de Sévigné, is the 16th-century **Hôtel Carnavalet,** Mme de Sévigné's former house and now home to the **Musée Carnavalet** (see p. 140). Continue down rue des Francs Bourgeois to get to **pl. des Vosges.**

PLACE DES VOSGES. Perfectly symmetrical 17th-century terraces surround a park, itself centered around a splendid fountain. Before Henri IV ordered its construction, several kings had built mansions on the site, including the Palais de Tournelles, destroyed after Henri II died there in a jousting tournament in 1563. Originally named pl. Royale, during the Revolution it was renamed pl. des Vosges after the first *departement* in France to pay its taxes. Famous past residents include **Théophile Gautier** and **Alphonse Daudet** at no. 8, and **Victor Hugo** at no. 6, now a museum of his life and work. (*Open Tu-Su 10am-5:40pm. 22F, students 15F, under 18 free.*) Leave pl. des Vosges through the corner door at the right of the south face, which leads into the garden of the **Hôtel de Sully.** (*M: Chemin Vert or St-Paul.*)

THE LOWER MARAIS (4ÈME)

THE JEWISH MARAIS. The heart of Paris's Jewish community since the 13th century, the Marais witnessed an influx of Eastern European Jews in the 19th. Although its population was decimated during WWII, the community was rejuvenated by Jews fleeing Algeria in the '60s. Today, **rue des Rosiers** is at the center of a vibrant mix of Ashkenazi and Sephardi cultures. The Art Nouveau synagogue at 10 rue Pavée was designed by Hector Guimard in 1913. Between rue de Rivoli and the quai des Célestins is the **Mémorial du Martyr Juif Inconnu.** Upstairs, the **Centre de Documentation Juive Contemporaine** has exhibits on the treatment of Jews in France during the Occupation as well as frequent temporary exhibits. (*17 rue Geoffroy de l'Asnier. M: St-Paul. Tel. 01 42 77 44 72. Memorial: Open Su-Th 10am-1pm and 2-6pm, F 10am-1pm and 2-5pm. Centre: Open M-Th 2-6pm. Each 15F.*)

HÔTEL DE VILLE. The first major building on this site served as the meeting hall of the river-merchants' guild; François I had the medieval structure replaced with a Renaissance one in 1533. This survived until 1871, when *communards* burnt it to the ground. The current edifice is a faithful copy on the exterior; when Manet, Monet, Renoir, and Cézanne offered their services to repaint the interior, they were all turned down in favor of ponderous didactic artists. The Information

PARIS & ÎLE DE FRANCE

Office holds exhibits on Paris in the lobby. In front of the building, **pl. de l'Hôtel de Ville** was originally called pl. de la Grève. Poised on a marshy embankment (grève) of the Seine, the medieval square served as a meeting ground for angry workers, giving France the useful phrase être en grève (to be on strike). The square also saw Henri IV's assassin being torn apart by wild horses in 1610. (29 rue de Rivoli. M: Hôtel-de-Ville. Tel. 01 42 76 43 43. Open M-Sa 9am-6:30pm. Tours offered 1st M of each month at 10:30am; call 01 42 76 50 49 to reserve a place.)

OTHER SIGHTS. West of the Hôtel de Ville, the lonely, Flamboyant Gothic **Tour St-Jacques** is all that remains of the 16th-century Église St-Jacques-la-Boucherie. A statue of Pascal at its base commemorates his experiments on the weight of air, performed here in 1648. (39-41 rue de Rivoli. M: Châtelet.) Built in 1474, the **Hôtel de Sens** is a rare example of a well-preserved medieval house, with watch turrets and a square defensive tower against street violence. The hôtel was the residence of the Reine Margot, Henri IV's divorced first wife, famous for her romantic escapades and literary salon. The hôtel now houses the **Bibliothèque Forney,** a fine arts library that hosts some temporary exhibits. (1 rue du Figuier. M: Pont Marie.) In the **Hôtel Henault de Cantobre** (built 1706), **La Maison Européenne de la Photographie** hosts temporary exhibits of international photographers. The interesting permanent display Les Plus Beaux Plans du Monde presents photography and film from the late '50s to the present. (5-7 rue de Fourcy. M: St-Paul. Tel. 01 44 78 75 00; www.mep-fr.org. Open W-Su 11am-8pm. 30F, students 15F.)

CONCORDE (8ÈME)

PLACE DE LA CONCORDE. Paris's largest and most infamous square forms the eastern terminus of the Champs-Élysées. Constructed between 1757 and 1777 as a monument to Louis XV, this vast area soon became pl. de la Révolution, the site of the guillotine that severed 1,343 necks. On January 21, 1793, Louis XVI was beheaded near where the Brest statue now stands. After the Terror, the square was optimistically renamed pl. de la Concorde (place of Harmony). Much favored by film crews for its views of Paris's monuments, the square featured in the dream sequence in An American in Paris. At the center of the place spikes the 2300-year-old **Obélisque de Luxor,** offered to Charles X by the Viceroy of Egypt in 1829. It took seven more years to get it to its current spot. At night the obelisk and fountains are illuminated. Flanking the Champs stand the equine forms of the **Cheveaux de Marly.** Also known as Africans Mastering the Numidian Horses, the original 18th-century sculptures are now in the Louvre to protect them from pollution; replicas graciously hold their places on the place, along with eight large statues representing France's major cities. Juliette Drouet, Victor Hugo's mistress, allegedly posed for the town of Strasbourg, with Hugo posing as the horse. (M: Concorde.)

ÉGLISE DE LA MADELEINE. Since 1764, various architects had begun churches on the site, but when work finally got under way in 1806 it was to build a temple to Napoleon's Grande Armée. Louis XVIII decided that it should be a church after all, but construction dragged on until 1842. The structure is unique among Parisian churches, distinguished by its four ceiling domes that light the interior in lieu of windows, 52 exterior Corinthian columns, and a curious altarpiece. An immense sculpture of the ascension of Mary Magdalene, the church's dedicatee, adorns the altar. Marcel Proust spent most of his childhood nearby at 9 bd. Malesherbes, which might explain his penchant for madeleine coffee cakes. (Pl. de la Madeleine. M: Madeleine. Tel. 01 44 51 69 00. Open daily 7:30am-7:15pm. Regular organ and chamber concerts; tickets available at Virgin and FNAC.)

OTHER SIGHTS. Directly north of pl. de la Concorde stand Jacques-Ange Gabriel's 18th-century **Hôtel de Crillon** (left) and the **Hôtel de la Marine** (right). Chateaubriand lived in the Hôtel de Crillon from 1805-1807. Today, it is one of the most elegant hotels in Paris. (Single 2600-3200F, suite with shower 29,800F. V, MC, AmEx.) The world-renowned **Maxim's,** 3 rue Royale, won't even allow you a peek into what was once Richelieu's home. Instead, nibble some chocolate macarons from **Fauchon,** 24-30 pl. de la Madeleine (see p. 112).

THE ARCH-DECEIVER In 1805, Napoleon told his troops, newly victorious at Austerlitz, that they would "go home beneath triumphal arches." The first stone of said arch was placed the following year, but events conspired to necessitate a little *trompe l'œil*. In 1810, Napoleon was set to marry Marie-Louise, the daughter of the Austrian emperor. The only hitch was the still incomplete arch, through which he desired to process on the way to his wedding at the Louvre. Always one to have his way, the emperor had his architect Chalgrin build a full-scale mock-up for the couple to parade through on their way to the altar.

THE CHAMPS-ÉLYSÉES (8ÈME)

Crowding around the great sweep of the Champs-Élysées from the Arc de Triomphe to pl. de la Concorde, expansive mansions, expensive shops and restaurants, and grandiose monuments make the 8ème the most glamorous *arrondissement* of all. Crazily upscale salons and boutiques of *haute couture* line fashionable streets such as the rue du Faubourg St-Honoré while embassies crowd around the President's home, the Palais de l'Élysée.

THE ÉTOILE AND THE ARC DE TRIOMPHE. The 8ème really took off in the early 19th century with the construction of bds. Haussmann, Malesherbes, Victor Hugo, Foch, Kléber, and others that shoot out from the Arc de Triomphe in a radiating formation known as **l'Étoile** (the star). In 1907 the Étoile became the world's first traffic circle, and is today one of its most dangerous. To reach the **Arc de Triomphe** safely, use the underpasses on the even-numbered sides of both the Champs-Élysées and avenue de la Grande Armée. The arch was commissioned by Napoleon in 1805 to commemorate his victories; after Waterloo, Louis XVIII continued the work to commemorate his defeat. When it was finally finished in 1836, there was no consensus on what symbolic figure should cap the monument—its original theme of "Napoleon the Grand" was somewhat outdated—so it retains its simple flat-toped form. The most famous of the Arc's allegorical sculpture groups is Rude's *Departure of the Volunteers of 1792*, commonly known as *La Marseillaise*, to the right facing the arch from the Champs-Élysées. The **Tomb of the Unknown Soldier** has been under the Arc since November 11, 1920; the eternal flame is rekindled every evening at 6:30pm, when veterans lay wreaths decorated with blue, white, and red. Inside the Arc, climb 205 steps to the *entresol* between the Arc's two legs and then 29 more to tackle the lines at the elevator. The museum explains in French the Arc's architecture and history. Just 46 steps beyond, the observation deck provides a view of the Champs-Élysées, the tree-lined av. Foch, and the Axe Historique from the Arc de Triomphe du Carrousel and the Louvre Pyramid at one end to the Grande Arche de la Défense at the other. *(M/RER: Charles-de-Gaulle-Étoile. Tel. 01 55 37 73 77. Open daily Apr.-Sept. 9:30am-10:30pm; Oct.-Mar. 10am-6pm. Buy tickets in the underpasses. 40F, ages 12-25 25F.)*

AVENUE DES CHAMPS-ÉLYSÉES. The Champs-Élysées is the most famous of the 12 boulevards radiating from the Étoile. Allegedly the most beautiful avenue in the world, the Elysian Fields can disappoint on first sight, today being largely a tourist runway packed with mini-malls, burger bars, and famous cafés that hold on by reputation alone. Glimmers of its former glamour can be seen in the area around the **Rond-Point,** and the gardens leading up to the **pl. de la Concorde.** Le Nôtre planted trees here in 1667 to extend the Tuileries vista. During the 19th century, the Champs developed into a fashionable residential district. Mansions sprang up along its sides, then apartments and smart boutiques, making this strip of pavement the place to see and be seen in Paris. Balls, café-concerts, restaurants, and circuses drew enormous crowds. Today, you can watch others cling desperately to the Champs' glorious past at **Fouquet's,** a famous and outrageously expensive café-restaurant that hosts the French answer to the Oscars, the annual César awards.

AV. MONTAIGNE AND FBG ST-HONORÉ. About half-way down the Champs, six more avenues radiate out from the **Rond-Point des Champs-Élysées,** leading to all that is the most chic and most expensive in the known world. **Avenue Montaigne** runs southwest and shelters the houses of *haute couture*, including **Christian Dior** (no. 30) and **Chanel** (no. 42), along with some (sniff) Italian names. The other side of the rond-point heads out towards **rue du Fbg St-Honoré,** where you can gawk at **Cartier** (no. 23), **Hermès** (no. 24), and **Yves St-Laurent** (no. 38).

PALAIS DE L'ÉLYSÉE. Past the rond-point, av. de Marigny leads to the Palais de l'Élysée. Built in 1718, the *palais* was later home to the Marquis de Marigny, brother of Madame de Pompadour; since 1870, it has served as the official residence of the French president. If you want to get inside, call up Jacques and ask to be invited to the next state banquet. *(M: Champs-Élysées-Clemenceau.)*

GRAND PALAIS AND THE PETIT PALAIS. Facing av. de Marigny on the Champs are the Grand and Petit *palais*. Built for the 1900 World's Fair, both espouse the iron-and-glass construction of *fin-de-siècle* expo architecture and today host diverse cultural exhibitions. Most beautiful at night, the glass dome of the Grand Palais glows greenly from within, and its statues are backlit. Between the two *palais*, av. Churchill leads to the graceful **pont Alexandre III,** which leaps over to the Esplanade des Invalides in a single bound. *(See p. 139. M: Champs-Élysées-Clemenceau.)*

OTHER SIGHTS. Built by the Perret brothers in 1912 with bas-reliefs by Bourdelle, the **Théâtre des Champs-Élysées** staged the controversial premiere of Stravinsky's *Rite of Spring*. The three large halls still host performances. *(15 av. Montaigne.)* Around the corner from the theater, the **Crazy Horse Saloon,** long famous for its cabaret, still entertains fans of the *Art du Nu* ("Art of the Nude"). *(M: Alma-Marceau.)*

MONTMARTRE AND PIGALLE (18ÈME)

At the southern boundary of the 18ème, you'll find many of the cabarets and nightclubs that were the definitive hangouts of the Belle Époque, including the infamous **Bal du Moulin Rouge** (M: Blanche), immortalized by the paintings of Toulouse-Lautrec and the music of Offenbach. Today, the area between **pl. Blanche** and **pl. Pigalle** (M: Pigalle) is world renowned for seediness. Although Pigalle is undergoing a slow gentrification, tourists (especially women) should be wary of walking alone here at night. To the north of Pigalle rises **Montmartre,** 19th-century bohemian haunt and 20th-century tourist magnet. It's still worth a climb for the fantastic views of Paris and the neo-Byzantine **Basilique du Sacré-Cœur.** The hill is the nearest thing to a mountain for hundreds of kilometers and takes some huffing and puffing to get up. From M: Anvers, the walk up rue Steinkerque to the ornate switchbacked stairway is short and pretty but sometimes overcrowded with tourists and associated commerce. The longer climb from M: Abbesses, the safest at night, leads one past more worthwhile cafés and shops: follow rue de la Vieuville to rue Drevet, turning right on rue Gabrielle and left up the stairs to rue du Cardinal Dubois. For a less difficult ascent, use the glass-covered **funicular** from the base of rue Tardieu (from M: Anvers, walk up rue Steinkerque and take a left on rue Tardieu). Operated by the RATP, it will whisk you up 100m in 45 seconds. (Open 6am-12:45am. RATP tickets, 8F, and passes accepted.)

LA BUTTE MONTMARTRE. A rural area outside the city limits until the 20th century, the *butte* (hill) attracted artists to its low rents and fine vistas. Toulouse-Lautrec, in particular, is known for his posters for, and paintings of, disreputable local nightspots. A generation later, just before WWI smashed its spotlights and destroyed its crops, the hill welcomed Picasso, Modigliani, and Apollinaire into its artistic circle. Today, **pl. du Tertre** teems with tourist cafés, restaurants, and portrait artists. Around the corner, the **Musée Salvador Dalí,** 11 rue Poulbot, displays some lesser-known lithographs and sculptures by the mustachioed painter. *(Open daily Nov.-Mar. 10am-6pm, Oct.-Apr. 10am-9pm. 40F, students 25F.)* Still going strong at 22 rue des Saules, is the **Lapin Agile** cabaret. Frequented by Verlaine, Renoir, Modigliani, and Max Jacob, the establishment was known as the "Cabaret des Assassins" until André Gill decorated its façade with a rabbit. The cabaret immediately gained renown as the "Lapin à Gill," (Gill's rabbit), which rapidly transmuted into its current name. Overlooking the vineyard at 12 rue Cortot, the **Musée du Vieux Montmartre** presents a history of the neighborhood and has one of the few zinc bars to have escaped metal rationing during WWI. *(Open Tu-Su 11am-6pm. 25F, students and seniors 20F.)*

BASILIQUE DU SACRÉ-CŒUR. Following France's disastrous defeat in the Franco-Prussian war, public pressure persuaded the government to commission this basilica in 1873 to "expiate the sins" of the nation. After a massive fund-raising effort—largely contributed by adepts of the cult of the Sacred Heart, centered in Paray-le-Monial, Burgundy (p. 195)—the basilica was completed in 1914 and consecrated in 1919. Both its neo-Byzantine style and its white color sets it apart from the smoky grunge of most Parisian buildings. The church's bleached look is a quirk of its stone, which secretes white lime when wet. The narrow climb up the dome offers the highest vantage point in Paris and a view that stretches as far as 50km on clear days. *(35 rue du Chevalier de la Barre. Tel. 01 42 51 17 02. Open daily 7am-11pm. Dome and crypt open daily 9am-6pm. 15F each, students 8F.)*

ABBESSES. These days, restaurants, cafés, and *boulangeries* crowd this corner of Montmartre around rue des Abbesses and rue Lepic. Walking down rue Lepic will carry you past the **Moulin Radet,** one of the last remaining windmills on Montmartre. Farther down is the site of the **Moulin de la Galette,** depicted by Renoir during one of the frequent dances held there, and one of Van Gogh's former homes at 54 rue Lepic. Parallel to rue Lepic, rue Caulaincourt leads downhill to the landscaped, secluded **Cimetière Montmartre,** where Stendhal, Degas, Foucault, Berlioz, and François Truffaut are buried. In 1871, this cemetery became the site of huge mass graves after the siege of the Commune. *(20 av. Rachel. M: Pl. de Clichy or Blanche. Tel. 01 43 87 64 24. Open daily 8am-5:30pm.)*

RÉPUBLIQUE AND BASTILLE (10$^{\grave{E}ME}$, 11$^{\grave{E}ME}$, & 12$^{\grave{E}ME}$)

Three *arrondissements* collide at **pl. de la République.** Brasseries and cafés offer lunch by day; prostitutes and swindlers carouse by night. Nearby, to the northeast, the tree-lined Canal St-Martin makes a refreshing break from the city. A 10-minute walk south of pl. de la République takes you to **pl. de la Bastille,** famous for hosting the Revolutionary kick-off on July 14, 1789. Cutting-edge a few years ago, today Bastille is crowded with once-too-cool bars and cafés. It still has some hip areas, but overall it's laid back, cheap, and crowded.

PLACE DE LA RÉPUBLIQUE. The stretch from **porte St-Martin** to pl. de la République along rue René Boulanger and bd. St-Martin served as a lively theater district in the 19th century and has recently begun to retrieve some of its former sparkle. A shining example is the **Théâtre de la Renaissance,** with its sculpted façade of griffins and arabesques by Carrier-Belleuse. Newly refurbished, it has breathed new life into the neighborhood. **Pl. de la République** is the meeting point of the 3$^{\grave{e}me}$, 10$^{\grave{e}me}$, and 11$^{\grave{e}me}$ *arrondissements*. At its center, Morice's sculpture of *la République* glorifies France's many revolutionary struggles. Ironically, it was created by Haussmann to divide and conquer the rather-revolutionary arrondissements that border it. Buzzing by day, the *place* intimidates at night. *(M: République.)*

CANAL ST-MARTIN. The most pleasant area of the 10$^{\grave{e}me}$ is the tree-lined Canal St-Martin. 4.5km long, the canal was dug in 1825 as a shortcut for river traffic on the Seine. It was also a natural defense against the upstart eastern arrondissements. East of the canal, follow rue Bichat to the **Hôpital St-Louis.** Built in 1607 by Henri IV as a sanctuary/prison for victims of the plague, its distance from any water-source suggests that it was intended more to protect the city from contamination than to help the unfortunates inside.

PLACE DE LA BASTILLE. The 4ème, 11ème, and 12ème *arrondissements* touch noses at the site of the famous (but no longer extant) royal fortress and prison. Originally commissioned by Charles V to safeguard the eastern entrance to Paris, the Bastille became a state prison under Louis XIII. Notable prisoners included Mirabeau, Voltaire, and the Marquis de Sade. By 1789, the prison had almost fallen out of use; the Revolutionaries liberated all of five men incarcerated for insanity, but they were really after its supply of gunpowder. Demolition of the prison began the day after its capture and concluded in October 1792. Some of its stones were incorporated into the **Pont de la Concorde.** *(M: Bastille.)* Some residues of the Bastille's recent spurt of chicness can be found along the curvy **rue de la Roquette,** a 17th-century byway that was home to Verlaine (no. 17), and is now lined with cafés, bars, boutiques, and an avant-garde church. *(M: Bastille or Voltaire.)* **Jean-Paul Gaultier's gallery** is at 30 rue Faubourg-St-Antoine. *(M: Bastille or Ledru-Rollin.)*

AVENUE DAUMESMIL. South of the Opéra Bastille, the arches of an old railway viaduct along av. Daumesmil now house the **Viaduc des Arts,** providing work space and showrooms for potters, painters, weavers, glass blowers, and furniture manufacturers. On top of the viaduct runs the **Promenade Plantée,** Paris's longest and skinniest park, accessible only by train, elevator, or stairs. *(M: Bastille.)*

OPÉRA BASTILLE. Presiding over the **pl. de la Bastille** and designed by Carlos Ott, a Canadian mall architect, the Opéra opened in 1989 to protests over its design (nets still surround parts of the building to catch falling tiles). Many complain that the acoustics of the hall are defective. Worse yet, "the people" for whom the opera was supposedly designed often can't afford to go there. The Opéra has not struck a completely sour note, though, and has helped renew local interest in the arts. *(130 rue de Lyon. M: Bastille. Tel. 01 40 01 19 70; www.opera-de-paris.fr. Tours daily 1pm. 50F; students, under 16, and over 60 30F. For opera info, see p. 143.)*

TROCADÉRO (16ÈME)

In the lavish, residential 16ème, *hôtels particuliers* retire graciously from wide, quiet streets. Businesses, storefronts, and tackiness are at a minimum. Embassies and museums are plentiful, metro stops few and far between, and inexpensive restaurants non-existent. The steps of the Trocadéro provide a spectacular view of the Eiffel Tower.

PLACE D'IÉNA. The pl. d'Iéna positions you for a sweep of the most popular sights, including Henri Bouchard's impressive façade for the **Église St-Pierre de Chaillot** (1937), between rue de Chaillot and av. Pierre I de Serbie, and the **Musée Guimet,** containing a spectacular collection of Asian art but closed for renovations until spring 2000. *(Open M-Sa 9:30am-12:30pm and 3-7pm, Su 9:30am-12:30pm.)* A short walk east down av. du Président Wilson brings you to the **Palais de Tokyo,** home of the **Musée d'Art Moderne de la Ville de Paris** (see p. 139). Built for the 1937 World Expo, the palace took its name from the adjacent quai de Tokyo, which was renamed quai de New York after WWII. Across pl. de Tokyo, the gardens of the **Palais Galliera** draw children and sculpture enthusiasts to the allegorical figures representing painting, architecture, and sculpture. The Palais houses the **Musée de la Mode et du Costume,** which rotates its exhibits amongst its 30,000 outfits and 70,000 accessories. To enter the museum, follow either of the streets next to the garden to av. Pierre I de Serbie. *(10 av. Pierre I de Serbie. M: Iéna. Tel. 01 47 20 85 23. Open Tu-Su 10am-6pm. 45F, students and seniors 35F.)* Farther along av. Wilson, **pl. de l'Alma** carries a replica of the torch of Bartholdi's Statue of Liberty, France's most famous gift to the United States, and a memorial to Diana, Princess of Wales.

PALAIS DU CHAILLOT AND JARDINS DU TROCADÉRO. The pl. du Trocadéro is dominated by the **Palais de Chaillot,** a cultural temple housing three museums, a theater, and a cinema (see below). Today's building is but the latest of many monuments on the site, which owes its name to the duc d'Angoulême's fortress-like memorial to his victory over the Spanish at Trocadéro in the 1820s. Built for the

1937 World Exposition, Jacques Carlu's design features two curved wings cradling a gorgeous Art Deco courtyard and terrace overlooking spectacular cannon-fountains. Surveyed by the 7.5m tall bronze Henri Bouchard *Apollo*, the terrace attracts tourists, vendors, skateboarders, and skaters, and offers brilliant views of the Eiffel Tower and Champs de Mars, particularly at night. Below the palace, the **Jardins du Trocadéro** extend to the Seine. After a day of sight-seeing, children of all ages might enjoy the carousel (10F) in pl. de Varsovie in front of the Eiffel Tower.

INSIDE THE PALAIS DE CHAILLOT. The **Musée de l'Homme** is an anthropological museum illustrating world cultures. *(Tel. 01 44 05 72 00 or 01 44 05 72 72. Open W-M 9:45am-5:15pm. 30F, under 27 and seniors 20F. Films Sept.-July W and Sa, 3 and 4pm.)* The **Musée de la Marine** has model ships of incredible detail, and a couple of real boats, including the golden dinghy built for Napoleon in 1810. *(Tel. 01 53 65 69 69. Open W-M 10am-6pm. 38F, under 25 and seniors 25F.)* The remarkable **Musée National des Monuments Français** is unfortunately closed until 2001; when it reopens you will again be able to gaze in wonder at plaster replicas of all of France's major architectural monuments. The **Cinémathèque Française** is part of the **Musée du Cinéma,** and shows 2-3 classics or soon-to-be classics per day. *(Tel. 01 47 04 24 24 for show info. Foreign films usually in v.o. Buy tickets 15-20min. early. Open W-Su 5-9:45pm. 28F, students 17F.)*

PASSY. A few blocks south of Trocadéro on rue Franklin, Passy is best known as the setting for *Last Tango in Paris*, as well as for its expensive shopping. Running along the northern walls and shaded by a chestnut bower, the small **Cimetière de Passy** contains the tombs of Debussy, Fauré, and Manet. Ask the concierge at the entrance for directions to the grave sites. *(2 rue de Commandant Schloesing. M: Trocadéro. Open M-F 8am-6pm, Sa 8:30am-6pm, Su 9am-6pm; Nov. 6-Mar. 15 closes at 5:30pm.)* While completing the last volumes of *La Comédie Humaine*, Balzac lived at what is now the **Maison de Balzac.** Here the novelist sought refuge from bill collectors, writing for 17 hours a day. There are several rooms of portraits, memorabilia, manuscripts, and temporary exhibits. *(47 rue Raynouard. M: Passy. Tel. 01 55 74 41 80. Open Tu-Su 10am-5:40pm. 22F, students 15F, over 60 free.)* The large, white, round building at the end of rue Raynouard is the **Maison de Radio France,** which holds frequent concerts (see **Music,** p. 142). Just past it, rue de Boulainvilliers will take you down to the miniature **Statue of Liberty,** near pont de Grenelle. Donated by a group of American expats in 1885, it was moved here for the 1889 World Exposition.

RIVE GAUCHE (LEFT BANK)

LATIN QUARTER (5ÈME & EASTERN 6ÈME)

Even as wave after wave of tourists break on the Rive Gauche, the Latin Quarter maintains its reputation as the nerve center of young Paris, preserved by the annual influx of Parisian students. The twin axes of the *quartier* are the **bd. St-Michel,** running south from the Seine, and the **bd. St-Germain,** running roughly east-west. A **color map** of the area can be found in the front of this book.

BDS. ST-MICHEL AND ST-GERMAIN. The boulevard starts by the river at bustling **pl. St-Michel,** which nurtured both the Paris Commune in 1871 and the student uprising of 1968. The 1860 fountain incorporates a WWII memorial commemorating the students who fell here during the Liberation of Paris in August 1944. **Bd. St-Michel** stretches from the left of the fountain up towards **bd. St-Germain.** One block beyond the intersection of the two boulevards, the Gothic **Hôtel de Cluny,** 6 pl. Paul Painlevé, was once home to the abbots of the powerful Burgundian monastery of that name (see p. 193). Built upon the remains of the Gallo-Roman baths, today the building houses the **Musée de Cluny's** collection of medieval art, tapestries, and illuminated manuscripts (see p. 138). From the museum, cross bd. St-Michel and head down rue des Écoles de Médecine, next to the Gibert-Joseph bookstore, to reach **pl. Mondor** and M: Odéon. On the other side of bd. St-Germain is the pedestrian **Cour de Commerce St-André,** the site of Marat's house and now home to the beautiful Art Nouveau

Relais Odéon bistro. To the south, rue de l'Odéon leads to pl. de l'Odéon and the **Théâtre Odéon,** Paris's oldest theater and one-time home of the Comédie-Française. Completed in 1782, it saw the 1784 premiere of Beaumarchais' *The Marriage of Figaro*. Its present Neoclassical incarnation dates from an 1818 renovation overseen by David. On May 17, 1968, student protesters seized the building and destroyed much of its interior. From the back of the theater, rue de Vaugirard leads left to bd. St-Michel and **pl. de la Sorbonne**, while the **Palais** and **Jardin de Luxembourg** sit across the street.

SORBONNE AND COLLÈGE DE FRANCE. Place de la Sorbonne faces the Baroque **Sorbonne Chapel,** wherein Cardinal Richelieu lies entombed beneath his hat, which is suspended by threads from the ceiling. Legend has it that when Richelieu is freed from purgatory, the threads will snap and the hat will fall. The 1642 chapel is the oldest surviving building of the Sorbonne, which was founded in 1253 by Robert de Sorbon as a theological college; the rest of the edifice is 19th-century. Today, the Sorbonne is officially known as Paris IV, one of the University of Paris's 13 campuses, and specializes in the humanities. *(45-7 rue des Écoles. M: Cluny-La Sorbonne or RER: St-Michel. Open M-F 9am-5pm.)* Frustrated by the Sorbonne's inflexible curriculum, in 1530 François I founded a new college to teach the humanist ideas of the Renaissance. The **Collège de France** is still independent and its outstanding courses are free and open to all. Past professors have included Henri Bergson and Paul Valéry. *(Courses run Sept.-May. For info, call 01 43 29 12 11 or 01 44 27 12 11.)*

PALAIS AND JARDIN DE LUXEMBOURG. The **Palais du Luxembourg** was built in 1615 by Louis XIII's mother Marie de Médici. Homesick for Tuscany, she tried to recreate its architecture and gardens in central Paris. Her builders finished the Italianate palace in a mere five years, and Marie moved in 1625 only to be kicked out by Richelieu in 1630. In 1852 the palace first served its current function as the meeting place for the Senate. The **Musée du Luxembourg,** next to the palace on rue de Vaugirard, shows free exhibitions of contemporary art. *(Tel. 01 42 34 25 95. Open M-Sa 11am-6:30pm.)* You can't get into the Palace, but who cares when you've got the **Jardin de Luxembourg.** Parisians flock to these formal gardens to sunbathe, write, stroll, and gaze at the rose gardens and central pool. Children can sail toy boats in the fountain, ride ponies, and see the *grand guignol* puppet show (see p. 142) while their grandparents pitch *boules*. In spring, gardeners bring out the giant pots of palm and orange trees from their greenhouses. Don't miss Osip Zadkine's cubist sculpture in the southwest corner. *(M: Odéon; RER: Luxembourg. Garden open daily Apr.-Oct. 7:30am-9:30pm; Nov.-Mar. 8:15am-5pm. French tours 1st W of month Apr.-Oct. 9:30am, departing from pl. André Honorat behind the observatory.)*

THE PANTHÉON. Built on the **Montagne Ste-Geneviève,** the dome of the Panthéon towers over the Latin Quarter. After surviving a grave illness in 1744, Louis XV commissioned Jacques-Germain Soufflot to build a new church to honor St. Genevieve, Paris's patron saint. During the Revolution the church was deconsecrated, renamed, and dedicated to France's national heroes. In the crypt you will find Voltaire, Rousseau, Hugo, Zola, and Marie Curie. In 1851 Foucault demonstrated his famous pendulum here; a replica still swings under the dome, its continually changing plane of oscillation proof of the earth's rotation. Not all of France's luminaries are buried in the Panthéon. Pascal and Racine lie next door in the Flamboyant Gothic **Église St-Étienne-du-Mont.** *(Pl. du Panthéon. RER: Luxembourg. Tel. 01 44 32 18 01. Panthéon open daily 10am-6:30pm. 35F, students 23F.)*

PLACE DE LA CONTRESCARPE. A block behind the Panthéon, at the southern end of rue Descartes, **pl. de la Contrescarpe** is the geographical center of the 5ᵉᵐᵉ. Running south of the *place*, **rue Mouffetard** plays host to the liveliest street market in Paris. Hemingway lived near here at 74 rue du Cardinal Lemoine; John Dos Passos and Samuel Beckett were also local residents. At the intersection of rue de Navarre and rue des Arènes, the Roman **Arènes de Lutèce** were built to accommodate 15,000 spectators. The ruins were unearthed and reconstructed in 1910.

JARDIN DES PLANTES. In the eastern corner of the 5ème, the **Jardin des Plantes** offers 45,000 square meters of flowers and greenery. Opened in 1640 by Louis XIII's doctor, the gardens originally grew medicinal plants. In the 18th century, Thomas Jefferson spent much time here admiring the flora and fauna. Today, the gardens include the **Musée d'Histoire Naturelle** (see p. 140), two botanical theme parks, the **Jardin Alpin** and **Serres Tropicales,** and the small **Ménagerie** zoo. During the siege of Paris in 1870, residents were reduced to eating its inhabitants. *(M: Jussieu. Tel. 01 40 79 30 00. Jardin Alpin: open M-F 8-11am and 1:30-5pm. Tropicales: open W-M Apr.-Oct. 1-6pm; Nov.-Mar. 1-5pm; 15F, students 10F. Ménagerie: tel. 01 40 79 37 94; open Apr.-Sept. 9am-6pm; Oct.-Mar. 9am-5pm; 30F, students and ages 4-16 20F.)*

INSTITUT DU MONDE ARABE (IMA). Housed in one of the city's most striking buildings, the ship-like architecture represents the boats on which Muslim immigrants sailed to France. The south façade is made up of thousands of portals that open and close to admit the shifting sun. Inside are permanent and rotating exhibitions on Arab cultures as well as a library, research facilities, lectures, films, and a gorgeous rooftop terrace where you don't have to eat in the expensive restaurant to see the views of the Seine, Montmartre, and the Île de la Cité. *(23 quai St-Bernard. M: Jussieu. Tel. 01 40 51 38 38. Open Tu-Su 10am-6pm. 25F, ages 12-18 20F, under 12 free.)*

ST-GERMAIN-DES-PRÉS (6ÈME)

Until recently known as *le village de St-Germain-des-Prés*, the area around **bd. St-Germain** between St-Sulpice and the Seine is pocketed with cafés, restaurants, cinemas, and expensive boutiques. The fame of the area rests above all on a literary reputation garnered this century for being the haunt of Apollinaire, Hemingway, Camus, Sartre, and de Beauvoir among others.

Today the "village" trades on its past glory, announcing every spot where the gods of letters sat, slept, or spat, and hundreds follow their used grinds every day to the **Café de Flore** and **Aux Deux Magots,** next to each other on bd. St-Germain by the Église St-Germain-des-Prés (see p. 112). But the real intellectual heart of the neighborhood lies towards the Seine, in the **École de Beaux-Arts** and the **Institut de France.** On the way, you'll come upon some of the most tangled streets in central Paris; Haussmann retired before he could figure out a way to extend rue de Rennes across the Seine to meet up with rue de Louvre. Today the maze of streets around rue de Seine, rue Mazarine, rue Bonaparte, and rue Dauphine is home to gallery after gallery, all providing glimpses of contemporary art that has yet to make it to the public consciousness. A **color map** of the area may be found at the front of this book.

ÉGLISE ST-SULPICE. Designed by Servadoni in 1733, the massive Neoclassical church remains unfinished. Inside are Delacroix frescoes in the first chapel on the right, a *Virgin and Child* by Jean-Baptiste Pigalle in one of the rear chapels, and an enormous Chalgrin organ. An inlaid copper band runs along the transept floor, connecting a plaque in the south to an obelisk in the north. Holes in the windows are placed so that during the winter solstice a ray of light strikes a marked point on the obelisk at exactly mid-day, while a beam falls on the copper plaque at midsummer and behind the communion table on the spring and autumn equinoxes. *(M: St-Sulpice. Tel. 01 46 33 21 78. Open daily 7:30am-7:30pm. French tours daily 3pm.)*

ÉGLISE DE ST-GERMAIN-DES-PRÉS. A church has stood on this site since the 6th century—the first was consecrated by St. Germain himself. The present-day Romanesque building dates from the 11th century and was previously the abbey church of an important Benedictine community. The revolution put an end to the abbey, while the church was used as a munitions dump—until 15 tons of gunpowder exploded in 1794 and devastated the interior and treasures, including much of its renowned monastic library. Even 19th-century restorers couldn't destroy the peace and calm of the interior, whose blue vault is studded with regular gilt constellations. Poster displays in side-chapels detail the history of the abbey and church. In the second chapel on the right, a stone marks the interred heart of 17th-

PARIS & ÎLE DE FRANCE

RULES OF THE GAME The Institut de France incorporates the older and highly prestigious **Académie Française,** which, since its founding in 1635, has assumed the task of serving as guardian of the French language. Having already registered its disapproval of *le weekend, le walkman, le snack bar,* and other "Franglais" nonsense, the Academy recently triumphed with the passage of a constitutional amendment affirming French as the country's official language. It is so difficult to become elected to this arcane society—limited to 40 members—that Molière, Balzac, and Proust never made it. In 1981 novelist Marguerite Yourcenar became the first woman to join its hallowed ranks; in 1998 the academy decided to allow the use of feminine forms of normally masculine nouns, such as *avocate* (*avocat,* lawyer), reflecting the role of women in professions from which they were once *barred*.

century philosopher René Descartes. The church hosts frequent concerts; see p. 142 for details. *(3 pl. St-Germain-des-Prés. M: St-Germain-des-Prés. Tel. 01 43 25 41 71. Open daily 8am-7:45pm. Info office open Tu-Sa 10:30am-noon and 2:30-7pm.)*

ÉCOLE NATIONALE SUPÉRIEURE DES BEAUX ARTS. France's most famous art school was founded by Napoleon in 1811 and soon became the stronghold of the French Academic style. The current building was finished in 1838 and is a mishmash of styles and monuments to Old Masters. The public is not permitted in the building or courtyard, but look young and studenty and you'll have little trouble sneaking in. Otherwise get a look at the next Delacroix at the changing public shows in the Exhibition Hall at 13 quai Malaquais. *(14 rue Bonaparte, at quai Malaquais. M: St-Germain-des-Prés. Tel. 01 47 03 50 00; www.ensba.fr. For application information call 01 47 03 50 65.)*

INSTITUT DE FRANCE. Cardinal Mazarin provided for the foundation of a college in his will, and the building, with its famous black- and gold-topped dome, was designed by Le Vau. It has served as a school (1688-1793), a prison (1793-1805), and since 1806 as a mixture of the two, housing the humorless Académie Française. Founded in 1795, the *institut* was intended to be a storehouse for the nation's knowledge and a meeting place for France's greatest scholars. Waltz into the courtyard and turn right to see Coysevox's enormous sculpture topping Mazarin's tomb. *(Pl. de l'Institut. M: Pont-Neuf. 1 block east of the ENSB-A on quai Malaquai.)*

OTHER SIGHTS. Once the mint for all French coins, **Hôtel des Monnaies,** next to the *institut*, proudly displays its austere 17th-century façade. The **Pont des Arts,** across from the *institut*, is celebrated by poets and artists for its delicate ironwork, its beautiful views of the Seine, and its spiritual locus at the heart of France's most prestigious Academy of Arts and Letters. Built as a toll bridge in 1803, on the day it opened, 65,000 Parisians paid to walk across it; today it is less crowded, absolutely free, and still lovely.

INVALIDES-CHAMP DE MARS (7ÈME)

The 7ème is utterly dominated by Eiffel's magisterial "300m flagpole," as the engineer himself described it. In its shadow, the **Champ de Mars,** where Napoleon III reviewed his troops before riding off to ignominious defeat in 1870, rolls southward towards the Neoclassical façade of the **École Militaire,** where Napoleon I learned his trade rather more successfully. For a good view of the **Eiffel tower,** cross the river to the Palais de Chaillot and the Jardins du Trocadéro (see p. 126). Since the 18th century, the district around the **Esplanade des Invalides** has stood its ground as the city's most elegant residential district. Home to the National Assembly, Napoleon's tomb, and the *musées* **d'Orsay** and **Rodin** (see p. 137), this section of the Left Bank is a medley of France's social, artistic, and military achievements.

THE EIFFEL TOWER. Designed to be the tallest structure in the world, the Eiffel Tower was conceived as a monument to engineering and industry. Even before construction began in 1887, Parisians were expressing their doubts, and as they saw it rise from the ground their horror only increased. After the building's completion, Maupassant ate lunch every day at its restaurant—the only place in Paris, he claimed, from which he couldn't see the offensive thing. Nevertheless, as the showpiece of the 1889 Universal Exposition, it trembled to the popular acclaim of 4 million feet, and the *avant-garde* crowd flocked to defend it, including Apollinaire, Dufy, and Picasso. Due to be dismantled in 1909, the invention of radio settled the tower's fate; such an ideal broadcasting mast could not be given up.

Despite all the hype, the tower is a wonder to behold, supremely graceful despite its 9,100,000 kilograms of iron. Gustave had special elevators made to climb the curves up to the second floor, but for the fit it's cheaper (and more fun) to ascend by foot. The third and final floor is only accessible by elevator. The Cinemax, a relaxing stop midway through the climb on the first floor, shows films about the tower. The top floor offers the obvious reward of an unparalleled view of the city, and captioned aerial photographs help you locate landmarks. *(M: Bir Hakeim. Tel. 01 44 11 23 45; www.eiffel-tower.com. Open daily June-Aug. 9am-midnight; Sept.-May 9:30am-11pm. Last lift at 10:30pm. Elevator to 1st floor 21F, under 12 12F; 2nd floor 43F/22F; 3rd floor 60F/31F. Stairs to 1st and 2nd floors 15F.)*

CHAMP DE MARS. The Field of Mars long ago eschewed its military role as a drill ground and is now a flower-embroidered carpet stretching from the École Militaire to the Eiffel Tower. You'll find many groups of backpackers sprawled on the grass with bottles of wine in their hands—though they're liable to get kicked out by the *gardiens* at 3am. After the 1900 Exhibition, the municipal council considered parceling off the Champ de Mars for development, but concluded that Paris needed all the open space it could get. Today, contemporary sculpture is often exhibited in the gardens.

ÉCOLE MILITAIRE. Louis XV created the École Militaire at the urging of his mistress, Mme de Pompadour, who hoped to make educated officers of "poor gentlemen." In 1784, the 15-year-old Napoleon Bonaparte enrolled; within a few weeks he had presented administrators with a comprehensive plan for the school's reorganization. The building still belongs to the army today and is closed to visitors.

UNESCO. The École Militaire's utter antithesis, UNESCO (United Nations Educational, Scientific, and Cultural Organization), occupies the Y-shaped building across the road. The U.S. still refuses to rejoin the organization it resigned from in 1984. Among the building's decorations are a painting by Picasso, a meditation area, and an angel from the façade of a Nagasaki church destroyed in WWII. There are often small, free exhibits of art, science, or culture. *(7 pl. de Fontenoy. M: Ségur. Tel. 01 45 68 10 00; www.unesco.org. Bookstore open M-F 9am-1pm and 2-6pm.)*

INVALIDES. The Hôtel des Invalides was founded in 1670 by Louis XIV to provide for sick soldiers. Enter the building from either pl. des Invalides to the north or pl. Vauban and av. de Tourville to the south. The building's trademark gold-domed chapel was added in 1706 by Jules Hardouin-Mansart to spice the dour building up a bit, and now houses **Napoleon's tomb.** Finished in 1861, the Emperor's tomb actually consists of six concentric coffins, made of materials ranging from mahogany to lead—perhaps to make sure he doesn't escape again, like he did from Elba. The same ticket will allow you to peruse the trophies in the **Musée de l'Armée,** which celebrates French military history, and the **Musée de l'Ordre de la Libération,** entered from bd. de Latour-Maubourg, which tells the story of those who fought for the liberation of France. *(Esplanades des Invalides. M: Invalides. Tel. 01 44 42 37 72; www.invalides.org. Museums open daily Apr.-Sept. 10am-6pm; Oct.-Mar. 10am-5pm. 38F, students under 26 and ages 12-17 28F.)* Housed in a gallery of the *hôtel's* Cour d'Honneur, the **Musée d'Histoire Contemporaine** mounts two yearly exhibitions, probing recent history, propaganda, and popular culture. *(Tel. 01 44 42 54 91 or 01 44 42 38 39. Call for information regarding temporary exhibits and hours. 30F, students and ages 12-17 20F, under 12 free.)* The tree-lined **Esplanade des Invalides** runs from the *hôtel* to the **Pont Alexandre III,** which arches across the Seine to the Grands and Petits Palais (p. 139).

ASSEMBLÉE NATIONALE. Its original inhabitants would scarcely recognize the **Palais Bourbon** now. Built in 1722 for the daughter of Louis XIV, today the palace houses the French parliament. Free French tours, with English pamphlets, take you round the chambers, including the **Salon Delacroix** and the **library** (both spectacularly painted by Delacroix), and the Assembly chamber, or **Salle de Séances,** where the Président du Conseil presides. Members of the political right and left sit to the right and left of the president's seat, according to the tradition started in 1789. *(33 quai d'Orsay. M: Assemblée Nationale. Tel. 01 40 63 63 08. Open Oct.-June while the Assembly is in session. Tours Sa 10am and 2 and 3pm.)*

MONTPARNASSE (14ÈME, 15ÈME, & SOUTHERN 6ÈME)

Like Montmartre and the *quartier latin*, Montparnasse was a haven for 20th-century artists and writers. Generations of newly arrived immigrants have also called Montparnasse home; the first to arrive were Bretons, who left Brittany in the 19th century after failed harvests. Arriving en masse at the **Gare de Montparnasse,** they settled in the neighborhood around the station, now known as Petite Bretagne and packed with excellent Breton *crêperies. (M: Montparnasse-Bienvenüe.)*

BOULEVARD DU MONTPARNASSE. In the early 20th century, Montparnasse became a center for avant-garde artists including Modigliani, Utrillo, and Chagall, while political exiles like Lenin and Trotsky talked strategy over cognac in the cafés along the boulevard. After WWI, Montparnasse attracted American expats. Man Ray transformed an apartment into a photo lab, Calder worked on his first sculptures, Hemingway did some serious writing (and drinking), and Henry Miller produced the steamy *Tropic of Cancer* with the amorous help of Anaïs Nin. To see where Lenin and Sartre sat and racked (and Hemingway sat and soaked) their brains, check out the cafés **La Coupole,** 102-104 bd. Montparnasse, and **Le Sélect** at no. 99, to which Jake Barnes and Brett Ashley taxied in Hemingway's *The Sun Also Rises* (see p. 115). But even artists cannot live on coffee alone, as Gertrude Stein well understood; her open door, at 27 rue de Fleurus (off bd. Raspail), welcomed broke characters by the name of Picasso, Matisse, and Hemingway.

TOUR MAINE-MONTPARNASSE. Fifty-nine stories tall and completed in 1973, the tower looks out of place amid Montparnasse's 19th-century architecture. Shortly after it was erected, the city forbade further skyscraping, designating La Défense (p. 133) the sole home for future *gratte-ciels.* For an open-air view of Paris, ride the elevator to the 56th floor and climb three flights to the rooftop terrace. *(33 av. du Maine. M: Montparnasse-Bienvenüe. Tel. 01 45 38 52 56. Open May-Sept. daily 9:30am-11:30pm; Oct.-Apr. M-F 9:30am-10:30pm. 46F, students 35F, seniors 38F, under 14 30F.)*

CIMETIÈRE MONTPARNASSE. In the shadow of the modern Tour Montparnasse, the serene cemetery brings repose to both accused Jewish traitor Alfred Dreyfus and actual anti-Semitic traitor Maréchal Pétain, only feet from each other. Fate has also brought composer Camille Saint-Saëns together with 70s popster Serge Gainsbourg. Other famous corpses interred here include writers Maupassant, Sartre, de Beauvoir, Beckett, and Baudelaire, as well as artists Man Ray, Brancusi, and Bartholdi. With a free *Index des Célébrités* (available to the left of the entrance), you can pay your respects. *(3 bd. Edgar Quinet. M: Edgar Quinet. Tel. 01 44 10 86 50. Open mid-Mar. to Oct. M-F 8am-6pm, Sa 8:30am-6pm; Su 9am-6pm; Nov.-Mar. M-F 8am-5:30pm, Sa 8:30am-5:30pm, Su 9am-5:30pm.)*

INSTITUT PASTEUR. Founded by Louis Pasteur in 1887, the institute is now a center for biochemical research. It was here that Pasteur developed pasteurization, his technique for purifying milk products and beer. It was also here in 1983 that Dr. Luc Montaigner (in conjunction with Robert Gallo) first isolated HIV. The institute's small museum houses Pasteur's projects, lab, awards, and living quarters. Don't miss his tomb, an ornate marble and tile construction dedicated to the four virtues of faith, hope, charity, and science. *(25 rue du Dr. Roux. M: Pasteur. Tel. 01 45 68 82 82 or 01 45 68 82 83. Open Sept.-July M-F 2-5:30pm. 15F, students 8F.)*

PERIPHERAL SIGHTS

Many fascinating sights are scattered through Paris's outer *arrondissements*. While each will require a trip by itself, Paris is small enough that it probably won't take more than 30 minutes to get to any of them from the center of town. Moreover, with the central arrondissements losing artistic momentum due to high prices and numbing gentrification, the periphery has established itself as the seat of French intellectual and cultural life.

PÈRE LACHAISE CEMETERY. The antithesis of the church cemetery, Père Lachaise is like a 19th-century garden party for the dead. Many of the tombs strive to remind visitors of the dead's worldly accomplishments: the tomb of Géricault wears a reproduction of his *Raft of the Medusa*; on Chopin's Calliope sits lyre in hand. Oscar Wilde's grave bears a life-sized streaking Egyptian figure, whose penis was broken off by a scandalized warden soon after the monument was installed. The most visited grave is that of Jim Morrison. His graffiti-covered bust has been removed from the tomb; the sandbox in front of the stone is now the sanctioned site for the creative expression of those pensive mourners. Other famous residents include Balzac, Colette, David, Delacroix, Haussmann, Proust, Molière, and La Fontaine. Though the land for the cemetery was only purchased in 1803, Napoleon had these last two transferred there to persuade reluctant Parisians to bury their dead in the new plot. Since then, over a million have been buried in Père Lachaise, but far fewer are there at any one time; the cemetery is full and so the government makes room by digging up any grave that has not been visited in a certain number of years. To avoid this fate, some hire an official "mourner."

Perhaps the most moving site is the **Mur des Fédérés.** In May 1871, a group of communards murdered the Archbishop of Paris, who had been taken hostage at the beginning of the Commune. They dragged his mutilated corpse to their strong-hold in Père Lachaise and tossed it in a ditch. Four days later, the victorious Republican militia found the body. In retaliation, they lined up 147 communards against the eastern wall of the cemetery, shot them, and buried them on the spot. Ever since, the wall where they died has been a rallying point for the French Left. Free maps are supposedly available at guard booths by main entrances, but they're usually out; it may be worth the 10F or so to buy a detailed map from a nearby *tabac* before entering. *(16 rue du Repos. M: Père-Lachaise. Tel. 01 43 70 70 33; www.cemetery.org/lachaise/lachaise.intro.html. Open Mar.-Oct. M-F 8am-6pm, Sa 8:30am-6pm, Su and holidays 9am-6pm; Nov.-Feb. M-F 8am-5:30pm, Sa 8:30am-5:30pm, Su and holidays 9am-5:30pm. 2hr. English tour June-Sept. Sa 3pm; in French Sa 2:30pm, occasionally Tu 2:30pm and Su 3pm. 37F, students 26F; meet at bd. de Ménilmontant entrance.)*

THE CATACOMBS. At the intersection of six avenues, a miniature version of Bartholdi's **Lion of Belfort** (see **Belfort,** p. 416), commemorating Colonel Denfert-Rochereau's heroic (and successful) defense of that town in 1870-71, dominates **pl. Denfert-Rochereau.** Most visitors observe Leo from their place in the line to visit the **Catacombs,** a series of tunnels 20m below ground and 1.7km in length. They were originally excavated to provide building stone. By the 1770s, much of the Left Bank was in danger of caving in and digging stopped. The former quarry was then used as a mass grave to relieve the stench emanating from Paris's overcrowded cemeteries. The entrance warns "Stop! Beyond Here Is the Empire of Death." During WWII, the caves were full of life as the Resistance set up among the departed. The catacombs are like an underground city, with street names on walls lined with femurs and craniums. Beware the low ceilings and bring a sweater (and a flashlight if you have one). Not recommended for the faint of heart or leg; there are 85 steep steps to climb on the way out. *(Pl. Denfert-Rochereau. M: Denfert-Rochereau. Tel. 01 43 22 47 63. Open Tu-F 2-4pm, Sa-Su 9-11am and 2-4pm. 45min. tour 33F, ages 7-25 22F.)*

LA DÉFENSE AND THE GRANDE ARCHE. La Défense gained its name in the 19th century, when a monument was erected commemorating the defense of Paris in 1870-71. Since the government decided to create a commercial park here in 1958, the *quartier* has grown into a high-tech wonderland of modern architecture,

PARIS & ÎLE DE FRANCE

which also includes the giant **Les Quatre Temps** shopping center, one of the largest in Europe. The district is arranged along a wide plaza, and roller skaters practice stunts among sculptures by Miró, Calder, and César. La Défense's natural position on the "Axe Historique," the line connecting the Louvre, pl. de la Concorde, and the Arc de Triomphe, was crying out for a Big Idea to cap it off. President Mitterrand organized an architectural competition; 424 submissions were whittled down to four final designs which were presented anonymously to the president. He chose Danish architect Otto von Spreckelsen's **Grande Arche** for its "purity and strength." Spreckelsen backed out of the project before its completion, disheartened by red tape and by his own design, which he deemed a "monument without a soul." British engineer Peter Rice finished the work and designed the canvas tent "clouds" suspended to soften the arch's austere angles. The Arche was inaugurated on the French Republic's bicentennial, July 14, 1989. Ride the Willy Wonka-style outdoor glass elevators for a great view. *(M/RER: Grande Arche de la Défense. Note that La Défense is in RATP zone 3; standard tickets can be used on the metro, but the faster RER requires a specific ticket. Arch open daily 10am-7pm; last admission 6pm. 43F; under 18, students, and seniors 33F.)*

BASILIQUE ST-DENIS. In a neighborhood today more famous for its ethnic tensions and World Cup stadium, the Basilique St-Denis stands as an odd, archaic symbol of the long-dead French monarchy. In AD 475, a small church was built on the site, a former Gallo-Roman cemetery, to mark the grave of St. Denis. A larger basilica was built by Pepin le Bref, Charlemagne's father, the first monarch to be buried in what was to become the French royal necropolis. All but three of his successors lie entombed here, and their funerary monuments range from medieval simplicity to Renaissance extravagance. Dogs at the feet of the queens mark their fidelity; the kings have lions as symbols of their virility and courage.

Architecturally, the cathedral is remarkable for being the first example of Gothic architecture in the world; dissatisfied with the pokey windows of Romanesque edifices, in 1136 Abbot Suger began rebuilding the basilica in a new style that would open it to the "light of the divine." During the Revolution, most of the tombs were desecrated, and much of the basilica's stained glass shattered. Some of the original 12th-century windows can be seen in the center of the ambulatory. Look closely and you can discern something other than biblical tales—Suger ensured his immortality by having his likeness (a small monk prostrate before the Virgin) added to the design. *(1 rue de la Légion d'Honneur. Metro/RER: St-Denis. Walk towards the square and turn left at the tourist office. Tel. 01 48 09 83 54. Open Apr.-Sept. M-Sa 10am-6:30pm, Su noon-6:30pm; Oct.-Mar. M-Sa 10am-4:30pm, Su noon-4:30pm. French tours daily 11:15am and 3pm. Audioguides 25F, 2 people 35F. Nave, aisles, and chapels free; transept, ambulatory, and crypt 32F, seniors and students 12-25 21F, under 12 free.)*

MANUFACTURE DES GOBELINS. The Manufacture des Gobelins, a tapestry workshop over 300 years old, is all that is left of the 13ème's industrial past. In the mid-17th century, the Gobelins produced some of the priceless tapestries now displayed in the **Musée de Cluny** (p. 138). Extensive and interesting tours explain the intricacies of the weaving process. *(42 av. des Gobelins. M: Gobelins. Tel. 01 44 61 21 69. French tours with English handout 1½hr.; Tu-Th 2 and 2:45pm; 45F, ages 7-24 25F, under 7 free.)*

BIBLIOTHÈQUE DE FRANCE. Opened in 1996, the Bibliothèque de France was the last and most expensive of Mitterrand's *grand projets*. Replacing the old Bibliothèque Nationale in the 2ème (p. 120), the new library is open to the public and houses 10 million volumes. Designed by Dominique Perrault, the four L-shaped towers are designed to look like open books from above. *(M: Quai de la Gare or Bibliothèque François Mitterrand. Readers card 20F per day, 200F per year.)*

PARKS

While central Paris is graced with numerous parks, two enormous swathes of greenery stretch to the east and west of the capital. A refreshing oasis for those tired of the grime and grind of the capital, Parisians and tourists alike flock to

SMELLING TOO GOOD? The Pré Catelan is a neatly mani-cured meadow named for a troubadour who died in these woods. Arnault Catelan, riding from Provence to Paris in order to deliver gifts to Philippe le Bel, hired some men to protect him on his journey. Instead, they murdered him—and were not impressed to discover that Arnault's precious cargo was a collection of perfumes. The marauders were soon captured, being easily identified by their sweet smell. (*M: Porte Maillot then bus #244 to Bagatelle-Pré-Catelan. Tel. 01 40 19 95 33. Open daily 8:30am-7:30pm.*)

these open spaces on summer weekends. Both the **Bois de Boulogne** and the **Bois de Vincennes** have a similar history; originally royal hunting reserves, they were given to the city by Napoleon III. The Emperor had been much impressed with Hyde Park during his exile in London, and he told Haussmann to create something in the English style. The result was a naturalistic landscape of green meadows, hillocks, and clumps of trees quite unlike the dusty formal gardens which had dominated French horticulture since their introduction by Le Nôtre in the 17th century.

BOIS DE BOULOGNE. The Bois de Boulogne, neighboring Paris's wealthiest sub-urbs, rapidly became a fashionable spot; in the late 19th century, the upper classes would go for carriage rides and spend their weekends socializing in the park. Reminders of this period can be seen in the activities that take place in the *bois* today, which houses the **Hippodromes de Longchamp** and **d'Auteil** horsetracks and the **Roland Garros** tennis club, home of the French Open. More recently, the park's reputation has taken a beating; until a couple of years ago, the *bois* by night was a bazaar of sex and drugs, where transvestite prostitutes would stand along the roads and violent crime was quite common. Now, all lawn-crashers have been nudged out, and police are especially attentive to the *bois*, closing the roads at night and stepping up patrols. Even so, boulevards around its periphery continue to be lined with prostitutes at night—it's not a good place for a midnight stroll.

Attractions in the park include: the **Jardins d'Acclimatation** (M: Sablons; 12F), with a small zoo and numerous children's activities, plus a bowling alley and out-door jazz concerts; the **Musée en Herbe** (M: Porte Maillot; 16F), a modern art museum for children ages 4-11; and the **Jardin des Serres d'Auteuil** tropical green-house (M: Porte d'Auteuil or Michel-Ange Molitor; 3F). Free and prettier is the neighboring **Jardin des Poètes,** in which poems are attached to each flower bed. Inside the **Pré Catelan** (see greybox), the **Jardin de Shakespeare** (5F, students 3F, under 10 2F) features plants mentioned by the bard, grouped by play. At the cen-ter, the open-air **Théâtre de Verdure du Jardin Shakespeare** gives popular summer performances of Shakespeare's and others' plays in French. **Parc de la Bagatelle** (10F, ages 6-10 5F), an Anglo-Chinese garden, is famous for its stunning June rose exhibition (35F, seniors 25F; call 01 40 67 97 00 for dates) and for its water lilies, which the gardener added in tribute to Monet. You can **rent bikes** from the boat-house at the northern end of **Lac Inférieur** and in front of the entrance to the Jardin d'Acclimatation. (70F per half-day, 130F per day. Deposit 1000-1500F.) Organized rides 3-5pm, 100F. Call 06 07 35 40 17 for reservations.) More relaxing exercise can be had with a **boat** on Lac Inférieur, on the park's eastern edge. (M: Porte Dau-phine. 45F per hr., 400F deposit; with insurance 52F per hr., 200F deposit.)

BOIS DE VINCENNES. Annexed to a much poorer section of Paris than the Bois de Boulogne, the Bois de Vincennes was never as fashionable or as formal as its western sibling; in the 19th century, men would even strip to their shirtsleeves in exceptionally hot weather! The park's best known attractions are the **Parc Zoologique de Paris,** France's premier zoo, and the **Château de Vincennes,** so-called "Versailles of the Middle Ages" and residence of French kings from Charles V to Henri IV. (Zoo: 53 av. de St-Maurice. M: Porte Dorée. Tel. 01 44 75 20 10. Open May-Sept. M-Sa 9am-6pm, Su 9am-6:30pm; Oct.-Apr. M-Sa 9am-5pm, Su 9am-5:30pm. 40F; ages 4-16, students under 27, and those over 60 30F. Château: M: Château de Vincennes. Open daily May-Sept. 10am-noon and 1:15-6pm; Oct.-Apr.

10am-noon and 1:15-5pm. Guided tours: long tour 32F, students 21F; short tour 25F, students 15F; under 12 free.) Another gem is the **Parc Floral de Paris** (M: Château de Vincennes; 10F, ages 6-18 5F), which has a library, a butterfly garden, miniature golf, and assorted games for kids. Picnic areas, restaurants, and open-air concerts make it a metropolis of summer entertainment. You can also **rent boats** on **Lac Daumesnil.** (Mar.-Nov. daily 10:30am-5:30pm. 1-2 people 54F per hr., 3-4 people 60F. 50F deposit plus recommended tip.) The **Ferme de Paris,** with barnyard animals and agricultural fields, encourages kids and adults with some hands-on learning. (Tel. 01 43 28 47 63. Open Sa-Su and holidays in summer 1:30-7pm; rest of year 1:30-5:15pm.)

🏛 MUSEUMS

The **Carte Musées et Monuments** offers admission to 65 museums in the Paris area, plus the chance to skip long ticket lines (often over 30min. in summer) The card is sold at major museums and most metro stations. For more information, call **Association InterMusées,** 25 rue du Renard, 4ème (tel. 01 44 78 45 81; fax 44 78 12 23; www.intermusees.com). 80F per day, 3 days 160F, 5 days 240F. Multi-day passes valid for consecutive days only.

MUSÉE DU LOUVRE

The former residence of the French monarchy has been continually reconstructed, restored, and re-assigned ever since Philippe-Auguste built the original structure in 1190. Its function then was to defend Paris; the kings lived on the Île de la Cité, in what is now the Palais de Justice (see p. 117). Charles V was the first king to move to the Louvre, in the 14th century, but his successors preferred to live in more comfortable *hôtels* in Paris or châteaux elsewhere in the country. In 1527, François I returned to the Louvre and commissioned Pierre Lescot to build a new palace in the Renaissance style. All that remains of the old Louvre are its foundations, which are on display in the museum basement. The palace was further expanded by Louis XIV, at which point it consisted of the **cour Carrée,** the enclosed courtyard now at the rear of the building, the **Galerie de Bord de l'Eau** by the river, and the Tuileries palace, which once stood at the head of the Tuileries gardens but was pulled down in the 19th century. After Louis XIV abandoned Paris for Versailles in the late 17th century, the Louvre was let out to tenants. During the Revolution, Louis XVI was placed under house arrest in the Tuileries, which also served as home to all French rulers from Napoleon I to Napoleon III. Most of the palace you see today was built by the two Napoleons, including the wing along the rue de Rivoli and the **Cour Napoleon,** the open court at the front of the building. The palace was made into a museum in 1793, and Napoleon's conquests significantly expanded its collection. However, by the late 1970s it was clear that the Louvre was in need of updating; the **Grand Louvre** project, began in 1981, completely renovated both the palace exterior and the galleries; the last government ministries moved out, the Impressionist collection was transferred to the Musée d'Orsay in 1986, and the Cour Napoleon was converted from a parking lot to the centerpiece of the palace, capped by I.M. Pei's original glass pyramids.

Renaissance works include Leonardo da Vinci's *Mona Lisa (la Jaconde)* and canvases by Raphael and Titian, while French paintings number David's *Oath of the Horatii,* Ingres' sensual *Odalisque,* Géricault's gruesome *Raft of the Medusa,* and Delacroix's patriotic *Liberty Leading the People* among their better-known pieces. Sculptures include Michelangelo's *Slaves,* as well as an incredible collection of antiquities; be sure to see the *Venus de Milo* and the *Winged Victory of Samothrace.* The underground complex beneath the Pyramid also houses **temporary exhibitions** (30F).Visitors can either enter through the pyramid or directly from the metro into the new Carrousel du Louvre mall—follow the signs; if you have a *Carte Musée et Monuments* (see p. 136), you can enter directly from the Richelieu entrance, in the passage connecting the Cour Napoléon to the rue de Rivoli. Otherwise, you can buy full-price tickets from machines underneath the pyramid; reduced-rate tickets must be bought from ticket offices. The Louvre is less crowded on weekday afternoons and on Monday and Wednesday evenings, when it stays open until 9:45pm. The museum is enormous; you'll only be able to cover a fraction of it in any one visit. Pick up an updated **map** at the information desk blew the pyramid, or take an English tour. *(M: Palais-Royal/Musée du Louvre. Tel. 01 40 20 50 50; www.louvre.fr. Open M and W 9am-9:45pm, Th-Su 9am-6pm. English tours M and W-Sa 17F; call 01 40 20 53 17 for exact times. Admission: W-Sa 9am-3pm 45F, 3pm-close and all day Su 26F, under 18 and first Su of the month free. Combined ticket to museum and temporary exhibits 60F before 3pm, 40F after 3pm and on Su.)*

CENTRE POMPIDOU

Closed for renovation until December 31, 1999. Often called the Centre Beaubourg, the Centre National d'Art et de Culture Georges Pompidou has inspired architectural controversy ever since its inauguration in 1977. Named after French president Georges Pompidou, it fulfills his desire that Paris have a multidisciplinary cultural center. The Centre attracts more visitors per year than any other museum or monument in France—eight million compared to the Louvre's three. When it reopens, visitors will be able to explore the fantastic **Musée Nationale d'Art Moderne;** the Picasso and Matisse collections are particularly outstanding. The Centre is also home to the **Bibliothèque Publique d'Information** library and the **IRCAM** contemporary music center. See p. 119 for more information on the building. *(Rue Beaubourg, 4ème. M: Rambuteau. Tel. 01 44 78 12 33 or 01 44 78 14 63.)*

MUSÉE D'ORSAY

While the Musée d'Orsay has established itself as *the* Impressionist museum, those who come only to see the soft strokes of Monet, Degas, Manet, Pissarro, and co. will miss the breadth and excitement of its full collection. Paintings, sculpture, decorative arts, architecture, photography, and cinema from 1848-1914 are presented in this former Beaux Arts railway station.

The order in which to visit the museum is (counter intuitively) the ground floor, the top floor, and then the mezzanine. This is clearly indicated both by signs and maps. The central atrium is dedicated to **sculpture** and highlights the likes of Jean-Baptiste Carpeaux. Galleries around the atrium display 19th-century works of the **Neoclassical, Romantic, Barbizon,** and **Realist** schools; important canvases include Manet's *Olympia,* Ingres' *La Source,* Delacroix's *La Chasse aux Lions,* and Courbet's *Un Enterrement à Ornans.* The top floor is dedicated to the **Impressionists,** with important works by virtually all of the school of light's movers and shakers; famous works include Monet's *Gare St-Lazare* and Manet's *Déjeuner sur l'Herbe.* The **Post Impressionist** collection includes van Gogh's *Portrait of the Artist* (1889) and still lifes and landscapes by Cézanne. The small mezzanine, meanwhile, is dedicated to **Rodin,** and is dominated by his huge *Porte de l'Enfer.*

The museum is least crowded on Sunday mornings and Thursday evenings; avoid Tuesdays, when the Louvre is closed. In addition to the permanent collection, seven **temporary exhibition** spaces, called *dossiers,* are dispersed throughout the building. Call or pick up a free copy of *Nouvelles du Musée d'Orsay* to find out which temporary exhibitions are currently installed. The museum also hosts conferences, special tours, and concerts. Call 01 40 49 49 66 for more information. *(62 rue de Lille, 7ème. M: Solférino or RER: Musée d'Orsay. Tel. 01 40 49 48 48; recorded info 01 45 49 11 11; www.musee-orsay.fr. Open June 20-Sept. 20 Tu-W and F-Su 9am-5:45pm, Th 9am-9:30pm; Sept. 21-June 19 Tu-W and F-Su 10am-5:45pm, Th 10am-9:45pm. Last admission 30min. before closing. 40F, ages 18-25 and Su 30F, under 18 free. 90min. English tours leave regularly Tu-Sa from the group reception, 36F.)*

MUSÉE RODIN

Located in the elegant 18th-century Hôtel Biron, in which the artist lived and worked at the end of his life, the Musée Rodin highlights the work of one of France's greatest sculptors, Auguste Rodin (1840-1917). The museum houses many of Rodin's better known sculptures in plaster, bronze, and marble, such as

The Hand of God (1902) and *The Kiss* (1888-98), along with nearly 500 lesser-known works. *The Cathedral* shows two hands twisted around each other, palms facing and fingertips touching; look twice and you'll notice that both of the hands are right hands—one a man's and one a woman's. Rodin's training in drawing is evident everywhere; as he said, "my sculpture is but drawing in three dimensions." One room on the first floor is dedicated to a rotating display of drawings and studies. In addition, the museum has several arresting works by **Camille Claudel,** Rodin's muse, collaborator, and lover. The sculpture-scattered gardens are worth a visit by themselves and make a perfect picnic spot. *(77 rue de Varenne, 7ème. M: Varenne. Tel. 01 44 18 61 10; www.musee-rodin.fr. Open Apr.-Sept. Tu-Su 9:30am-5:45pm; Oct.-Mar. Tu-Su 9:30am-4:45pm. 28F; students, seniors, under 18, and Su 18F. Gardens only 5F.)*

MUSÉE DE CLUNY

The Hôtel de Cluny houses the **Musée National du Moyen Âge,** one of the world's finest collections of medieval art, jewelry, sculpture, and tapestries. The *hôtel* itself is a Flamboyant Gothic manor built on top of 1st-century Roman ruins. One of three ancient *thermæ* (public baths) in Roman Lutetia, the baths were purchased in 1330 by the Abbot of Cluny, who built his residence upon them. In 1843 the state converted the *hôtel* into a medieval museum. Today, the collection includes art from Paris's most important medieval churches; panels of brilliant stained glass in ruby reds and royal blues from the Ste-Chapelle line the ground floor, while the *galerie des rois* contains sculptures from Nôtre-Dame. The museum's collection of 15th- and 16th-century tapestries includes the famous series **La Dame et la Licorne** (The Lady and the Unicorn); its first five panels represent the five senses, while the sixth depicts a lady holding a necklace from a jewelry box. Some say that the lady is removing her necklace, locking it away, and rejecting the material, sensual world of the first five tapestries. The museum sponsors chamber music concerts in its Roman and medieval spaces. *(6 pl. Paul Painlevé, 5ème. M: Cluny-Sorbonne. Tel. 01 43 25 62 00. Open W-M 9:15am-5:45pm. Museum 30F; students, ages 18-25, over 60, and Su 20F; under 18 free. English tours W 12:30pm; 36F, under 18 25F. Concerts: tel. 01 53 73 78 00; F 12:30pm, Sa 5pm, and summer evenings; 60F, students and seniors 50F, under 18 20F.)*

LA VILLETTE

In the northeast corner of Paris, La Villette is a highly successful urban renewal project in the northeastern corner of Paris, with a park, museum complex, and performance spaces spread over its 55 hectares. A former meat-packing district, the area used to contain slaughterhouses that provided Paris with most of its pork and beef. Refrigeration technology made city *abattoirs* uneconomical, and the government closed down the meat industry in 1974. Work began on La Villette in 1979, and in 1985 the complex was inaugurated by President Mitterrand. La Villette has an extensive program of millennium activities planned for 2000.

CITÉ DES SCIENCES ET DE L'INDUSTRIE. Dedicated to bringing science to the young layperson, the star attraction of this science and technology museum complex is the **Explora** science museum. The architecture alone is worth a visit, but the exhibits, ranging from astronomy and mathematics to computer science and sound, are fabulous; kids will love them. The museum also features a **planetarium,** a **3D cinema,** a modest aquarium, and the **Cité des Enfants** with programs for kids ages 3-12. On the ground floor, **Technocité** (for ages 12 and older) challenges visitors to program their own computer games, design a bicycle, and experiment with industrial art. The enormous **Géode** features Omnimax movies on volcanos, glaciers, and other natural phenomena. To the right of the Géode, the 400-tonne, 50m-long **Argonaute** submarine (built in 1950) details the history of submersibles from Jules Verne to present-day nuclear-powered subs. Between the Canal St-Denis and the Cité, **Cinaxe** features inventive movies filmed in first-person perspective from vehicles like Formula One cars, low-flying planes, and Mars land-rovers, while hydraulic pumps simulate every curve and bump. *(Cité: M: Porte de la Villette. Tel. 01 40 05 80 00; www.cite-sciences.fr. Open M-Sa 10am-6pm, Su 10am-7pm. One-day Cité-Pass includes*

Explora, planetarium, 3-D cinema, and Argonaute; 50F. Argonaute: Open Tu-F 10:30am-5:30pm, Sa-Su 11am-6:30pm; separate admission 25F. Technocité and Cité des Enfants 25F each. Children's programs: 1½hr.; offered Tu and Th-F 9:30and 11:30am, and 1:30 and 3:30pm; W and Sa-Su 10:30am and 12:30, 2:30, and 4:30pm. Géode: Tel. 01 40 05 12 12; 57F. Cinaxe: Tel. 10 40 05 12 12. Open Tu-Su 11am-6pm. 34F, 29F with another cité sight ticket.)

CITÉ DE LA MUSIQUE. At the opposite end of La Villette from the Cité des Sciences, the City of Music was designed by Franck Hammoutène and completed in 1990. The stunning complex of buildings is full of curves and glass ceilings. The highlight is the **Musée de la Musique,** a collection of paintings, sculptures, and 900 instruments. Visitors don a pair of headphones that tune into musical excerpts and explanations of each instrument. *(M: Porte de Pantin. Tel. 01 44 84 44 84; info tel. 01 44 84 45 45; www.cite-musique.fr. Open Tu-Th noon-6pm, F-Sa noon-7:30pm, Su 10am-6pm. 35F, reduced 25F, children 6-18 10F, under 6 free. 10F more for temporary exhibits. Tours Sa 2:30pm, thematic tours F 7pm, kids tour Su 11am. 60F, reduced 45F, children 6-18 20F.)*

PARC DE LA VILLETTE. Cut through by the Canal de l'Ourcq and the Canal St-Denis, the Parc de la Villette separates the Cité des Sciences from the Cité de la Musique. Rejecting the notion of the park as natural oasis, Bernard Tschumi designed a 20th-century urban park, which feels like a step into the future; thematic gardens include the Garden of Childhood Fears.

GRAND AND PETIT PALAIS

These two ornate cathedrals of iron and glass, quite unlike any other building in Paris, were designed for the Universal Exposition of 1900. Most of the **Grand Palais** is taken up by the **Palais de la Découverte** (see below), but it also houses enormous temporary exhibitions. *(3 av. du Général Eisenhower, 8ème. M: Champs-Élysées-Clemenceau. Tel. 01 44 13 17 30 or 01 44 13 17 17. Open Th-M 10am-8pm, W 10am-10pm. Last entry 45min. before closing. Some exhibitions require reservations. Admission varies: typically 50F, students and M 35F, under 13 free.)*

PALAIS DE LA DÉCOUVERTE. Kids tear around the interactive science exhibits, pressing buttons that start comets on celestial trajectories, spinning on seats to investigate angular motion, and glaring at all kinds of camouflaged creepy-crawlies. The **Planetarium** (tel. 01 40 74 81 73) has four shows per day. *(Tel. 01 40 74 80 00 or 01 40 74 81 82. Open Tu-Sa 9:30am-6pm, Su 10am-7pm. 30F; students, seniors, and under 18 20F. 80F family ticket includes 2 adults and 2 children over 5, additional children 15F.)*

PETIT PALAIS. Also called the **Palais des Beaux-Arts de la Ville de Paris,** the palais houses 17th- to 20th-century northern European painting and sculpture, including Monet's *Sunset at Lavacourt* as well as works by Rubens, Rembrandt, Carpeaux, Cézanne, and Renoir. The Palais also houses a collection of medieval French crafts. *(Tel. 01 42 65 12 73. Open Tu-Su 10am-5:40pm. Last entry 5pm. Exhibitions 30F, students 25F, seniors and under 18 free. Permanent collection and exhibitions 55F/45F/free.)*

OTHER MAJOR COLLECTIONS

MUSÉE PICASSO. When Picasso died in 1973, his family paid inheritance tax in artwork. Although much of the booty is minor, the collection works admirably as a whole, housed in the 17th-century Hôtel Salé (see p. 121). Each room covers one period of Picasso's life, detailing the progression of both his technique and his personal life. *(5 rue de Thorigny, 3ème. M: Chemin-Vert. Tel. 01 42 71 63 15 or 01 42 71 70 84. Open Apr.-Sept. W-M 9:30am-6pm; Oct.-Mar. 9:30am-5:30pm; last admission 45min. before closing. 30F, ages 18-25 and Su 20F, under 18 free. French tours Sa-Su 36F, ages 7-18 25F.)*

MUSÉE D'ART MODERNE DE LA VILLE DE PARIS. Housed in magnificent galleries of the Palais de Tokyo (see p. 126), this museum contains one of the world's foremost collections of 20th-century art. Two pieces stand out: Matisse's *The Dance* and Raoul Dufy's high-voltage epic, *La Fée Électricité.* *(11 av. du Président Wilson, 16ème. M: Iéna. Tel. 01 53 67 40 00. Open Tu-F 10am-5:30pm, Sa-Su 10am-6:45pm. 30-45F, students and seniors 20-35F.)*

MUSÉE CARNAVALET. Housed in Mme de Sévigné's 16th-century *hôtel* (see p. 121), this museum traces Paris's history from its origins to the present. The philosopher's chamber guards Voltaire's and Rousseau's writing supplies. *(23 rue de Sévigné, 3ème. M: Chemin-Vert. Tel. 01 42 72 21 13. Open Tu-Su 10am-5:40pm. 30F, students 20F, seniors and under 18 free.)*

FONDATION CARTIER POUR L'ART CONTEMPORAIN. The glass façade deceives from afar—this is not a building, but a mammoth transparent bubble surrounding a garden, an "outdoor" theater, and diverse exhibitions. *Soirées Nomades* (Sept.-June Th 8:30pm) offer films, lectures, and performances linked to the current exhibition. *(261 bd. Raspail, 14ème. M: Raspail or Denfert-Rochereau. Tel. 01 42 18 56 51; www.fondation.cartier.fr. Open Tu-Su noon-8pm. 30F, students and seniors 20F, under 10 free.)*

MUSÉE GRÉVIN. This wax museum's ornate halls feature *personnages* from Marie-Antoinette to the King of Pop. The smaller branch in the Forum des Halles, 1er (tel. 01 40 26 28 50; M: Châtelet-Les-Halles), presents figures from the Belle Époque. *(10 bd. Montmartre, 9ème. M: Rue Montmartre. Tel. 01 42 46 13 26. Open daily Apr.-Aug. 10am-7pm; Sept.-Mar. 1-7pm. 58F, ages 6-14 38F.)*

MUSÉE D'HISTOIRE NATURELLE. Three science museums in one, scattered through the garden. The star is the four-floor **Grand Galerie d'Évolution,** a taxonomist's dream, which tells the story of evolution creatively. Next door, the **Musée de Minéralogie** displays gemstones along with an exhibit on volcanos. At the other end of the garden, the **Gallery of Comparative Anatomy and Paleontology** houses skeletons and fossils, including a 7m iguanodon. *(Jardin des Plantes, 5ème. M: Gare d'Austerlitz. Tel. 01 40 79 39 39. All museums open M and W-F 10am-5pm, Sa-Su 10am-6pm. Grand Galerie also open until 10pm Th; 40F, students 30F. Others museums 30F, students 20F.)*

MUSÉE DE L'ORANGERIE. Closed for renovations until spring 2001. Opened in 1927, the museum is home to works by Renoir, Cézanne, Rousseau, Matisse, and Picasso, but is most famous for Monet's *Water Lilies.* These 8 murals were the artist's gift to France on the day of the Armistice, *"comme un bouquet des fleurs."* *(In the southwest corner of the Jardin des Tuileries, 1er. M: Concorde.)*

GALERIE NATIONALE DU JEU DE PAUME. Huge windows bathe this spectacular exhibition space in afternoon sunlight. Connoisseurs and tourists alike come to appreciate the changing contemporary art exhibitions. *(Northwest corner of the Jardins des Tuileries, 1er. M: Concorde. Tel. 01 47 03 12 50. Open Tu noon-9:30pm, W-F noon-7pm, Sa-Su 10am-7pm. 38F, students under 26, seniors, and ages 13-18 28F, under 13 free.)*

MUSÉE MARMOTTAN MONET. Formerly the Musée Marmottan, the name-change highlights the 100+ Monets on view in the basement alongside works by Renoir, Pissarro, et al. The upstairs displays Napoleonic furniture, Renaissance tapestries, medieval illuminations, and Morisot paintings. *(2 rue Louis-Boilly 16ème. M: La Muette. Follow Chaussée de la Muette, which becomes av. Ranelagh, through Jardin du Ranelagh. Tel. 01 44 96 50 33. Open Tu-Su 10am-5pm. 40F, students and seniors 25F, under 8 free.)*

MUSÉE ZADKINE. Installed in the house, studio, and gardens where he worked, the museum highlights the extraordinary work of the relatively little-known Russian sculptor Ossip Zadkine (1890-1967), whose work spans from the extremes of Cubism to neo-Classicism. *(100bis rue d'Assas, 6ème. Just south of Jardin du Luxembourg. M: Vavin or Port-Royal. Tel. 01 43 26 91 90. Open Tu-Su 10am-5:30pm. 27F, students 19F.)*

ENTERTAINMENT

Crawling with swank lounges, hopping dance clubs, and smoky jazz bars, and bursting with theater, dance, music, film, and cultural programs, Paris has something to satisfy every taste. The bibles of Paris entertainment are the weekly **Pariscope** (3F) and the **Officiel des Spectacles** (2F), on sale at any kiosk or *tabac* and with every conceivable listing. Pariscope includes an English-language pull-out section. When going out, keep in mind that the neighborhoods around some popular night-spots, such as Pigalle, Gare St-Lazare, and Beaubourg, are not always safe. Also keep an eye on the time in order to avoid expensive late-night taxis; hop on the metro before 12:30am.

THEATER

Parisian theater offers something for every taste and budget, from classically staged spectacles in the Comédie Française to avant-garde productions in shoebox spaces. Many theaters close on Mondays and in July and August.

TICKET AGENCIES

Kiosque-Théâtre, 15 pl. de la Madeleine, 8ème. M: Madeleine. To the left of the church. Also in the 15ème in front of the Gare Montparnasse. M: Montparnasse-Bienvenüe. The best discount box office, selling discount tickets the day of the show. 16F per seat commission. Open Tu-Sa 12:30-7:45pm, Su 12:30-3:45pm. No credit cards.

Kiosque Info Jeune, 25 bd. Bourdon, 4ème (tel. 01 42 76 22 60). M: Bastille. Half price theater tickets and free passes to concerts, plays, and exhibits for those under 26. Open M-F 10am-7pm. Also at 101 quai Branly, 5ème (tel. 01 43 06 15 28). M: Bir Hakeim. Open M-F 9:30-6pm.

Alpha FNAC: Spectacles, 136 rue de Rennes, 6ème (tel. 01 49 54 30 00). M: Montparnasse-Bienvenüe. Also at Forum des Halles, 1-7 rue Pierre Lescot, 1er (tel. 01 40 41 40 00; M: Châtelet-Les-Halles); 26 av. des Ternes, 17ème (tel. 01 44 09 18 00; M: Ternes); and 71 bd. St-Germain, 5ème (automated tel. 01 44 41 31 50; M: Cluny). Easy pickup, but no discounts. Open M-Sa 10am-7:30pm. V, MC, AmEx.

SERIOUS THEATER

With the advantages of giant auditoriums, great acoustics, veteran acting troupes, and centuries of prestige, Paris's major stages put on popular and polished productions of dramatic classics. Unless you're banking on last-minute rush tickets, make reservations 14 days in advance. **La Comédie Française,** 2 rue de Richelieu, 1er (tel. 01 44 58 15 15; www.comedie-francaise.fr; M: Palais-Royal), was founded by Molière's actors, and is the granddaddy of all French theaters. They don't only play comedy—*comédien* is a general French word for actor. (Tickets 70-190F, remainders 60-70F for those under 27. Limited number of 30F tickets go on sale 45min. before curtain; arrive 1hr. before and don't expect a good view.) Plays, music, and dance concerts take place at the **Théâtre National de Chaillot,** pl. du Trocadéro, 16ème (tel. 01 53 65 30 00; M: Trocadéro), in the Palais de Chaillot. (Tickets 160F, under 25 and seniors 120F, same-day student standby 80F. Box office open M-Sa 11am-7pm, Su 11am-5pm. V, MC.) Founded in 1988, the **Théâtre Nationale de la Colline,** 15 rue Malte-Brun, 20ème (tel. 01 44 62 52 00; reservations 01 44 62 52 52; M: Gambetta), features French and foreign contemporary plays. (160F, over 60 130F, reductions for students and under 30; Tu shows 110F. Box office open M-Sa 11am-7pm, Su 2-5pm; phone reservations until 9pm on show days.)

CAFÉ-THÉÂTRES

Visit one of Paris's *café-théâtres* for an evening of word play and social satire in mostly black-box theater settings. Expect low-budget, high-energy skits filled with political puns and double-entendres. Knowledge of French is helpful if not essential. Well-loved *café-théâtres* include: **Café de la Gare,** 41 rue du Temple, 4ème (tel. 01 42 78 52 51; reservations 01 40 09 64 06; M: Hôtel-de-Ville), in the Centre de Danse du Marais, with a line-up ranging from solo comics to Addams Family Goth seances (100F, 25 and under 80F; shows W-Sa 8 and 10pm, Su 6:30pm; box office open daily 3-7pm and 30min. before curtain; V, MC); and **Point Virgule,** 7 rue Ste-Croix-de-la-Bretonnerie, 4ème (tel. 01 42 78 67 03; M: Hôtel-de-Ville), which is as immediate and interactive as theater can be, with crowds of 130 sitting shoulder-to-shoulder on benches; the frequent slapstick is ideal for non-French speakers (80F, students 65F; 2 shows 130F, 3 150F; 3 shows daily at 8, 9:15, and 10:15pm; open daily 5pm-midnight; reservations suggested).

GUIGNOLS

Grand guignol is traditional French marionette theater featuring the *guignol*, its classic stock character (like *Punch and Judy* without the domestic violence). Although the puppets speak French, you'll have no trouble understanding the slapstick, child-geared humor. Nearly all parks have *guignols;* check *Pariscope* for more information. The best-known is the **Marionettes du Luxembourg,** Jardin du Luxembourg, 6ème (tel. 01 43 26 46 47; M: Odéon or Vavin; RER: Luxembourg), where they've played the same classics since 1933: *Little Red Riding Hood*, *The Three Little Pigs*, etc. Very Grimm. (45min. shows generally M, W, and F-Sa. Call for schedules. Arrive 30min. early for good seats. 25F.)

CINEMA

With a tradition that goes back to the very birth of cinema, Paris is a *cinophile's* silver-screened heaven. Invented by *lyonnais* brothers Auguste and Louis Lumière, cinema had its world debut at the **Grand Café,** 14 bd. des Capucines, in 1895. At the time, Louis belittled his innovation as "an invention without a future." Today, you'll find scores of cinemas throughout the city. The center of movie action is on the Champs-Élysées, where Hollywood blockbusters and French hits can be seen in hi-tech luxury—and heard in *v.o.* (original language) rather than the otherwise ubiquitous dubbed *v.f.* Cinemas in the Latin Quarter also often run *v.o.* screenings. Always check the listings for those two magic letters or you may find your favorite actor has acquired a new voice and a perfect French accent. Cinemas offer student, senior, and family discounts. On Monday and Wednesday, prices drop about 10F for everyone. Reserve or arrive early for weekend showings.

Musée du Louvre, 1er (tel. 01 40 20 51 86 for info; 01 40 20 52 99 for schedules and reservations). M: Musée du Louvre. Art films, films on art, and silent movies with live musical accompaniment. 25-70F, students 15-50F. Open Sept.-June.

Les Trois Luxembourg, 67 rue M. le Prince, 6ème (tel. 01 46 33 97 77). M: Odéon. High-quality independent, classic, and foreign films, all in *v.o.* 40F, students 30F.

Action Christine, 4 rue Christine, 6ème (tel. 01 43 29 11 30). M: Odéon. International films from the 40s and 50s in *v.o.* 40F, 6-7pm shows 25F; M and students 30F.

L'Arlequin, 76 rue de Rennes, 6ème (tel. 01 45 44 28 80). M: St-Sulpice. A revival cinema with occasional visits from directors and first-run preview showings. Some films in *v.o.* Buy tickets in advance. 46F, W and students M-F 36F; Su matinée 30F. V, MC.

MUSIC

Paris's squares, churches, and concert halls feature performers from the world over. Acclaimed dance companies visit Paris frequently; watch for posters and read *Pariscope*. Connoisseurs will find the thick *Programme des Festivals* (free at *mairies* and tourist offices) an indispensable guide to seasonal music and, to a lesser extent, dance series and celebrations in and around Paris. The monthly *Paris Selection*, free at tourist offices, also keeps track of concerts in churches and museums, many of which are free or reasonably priced. Cheap seats are often available, but you gets what you pays for—expect poor views and poor acoustics. Try to see a floorplan and ask about unobstructed views before buying.

CLASSICAL MUSIC, OPERA, AND DANCE

Free concerts are often held in churches and parks, especially during summer festivals. Check *Pariscope* and *l'Officiel des Spectacles*, and the Alpha FNAC offices for concert notices. Concerts take place W-Su in the **Jardin du Luxembourg** bandstand, 6ème (tel. 01 42 34 20 23); show up early or prepare to stand. The **Maison de Radio France**, 116 av. du Président Kennedy, 16ème (tel. 01 42 30 15 16; M: Passy or RER: Av. du Pt. Kennedy/Maison de Radio France), hosts a wide range of concerts, some free, at France's public radio HQ.

Many churches hold pricey concerts that feature fantastic acoustics and atmosphere. Check the schedules at **Église St-Germain-des-Prés,** 3 pl. St-Germain-des-Prés, 6ème (tel. 01 44 62 70 90; M: St-Germain-des-Prés); **Église St-Eustache,** 2 rue du Jour, 1er (tel. 01 42 36 31 05; M: Les Halles); **Église de la Trinité,** pl. Estienne d'Orves, 9ème (tel. 01 48 74 12 77; M: Trinité); **Église St-Louis-en-l'Île,** 19bis rue St-Louis-en-l'Île, 4ème (tel. 01 46 34 11 60; M: Pont Marie); and **Église St-Julien-le-Pauvre,** 23 quai de Mortebello, 5ème (tel. 01 43 54 52 16). Arrive 30 to 45 minutes ahead for good seats. The **Ste-Chapelle** also hosts fabulous concerts a few times per week in summer. Contact the box office at 4 bd. du Palais, 1er (tel. 01 53 73 78 50; M: Cité).

GENERAL VENUES

Théâtre des Champs-Élysées, 15 av. Montaigne, 8ème (tel. 01 49 52 50 50; reservations 01 49 52 50 50). M: Alma Marceau. Top dance companies, classical and world music, and opera. Season Sept.-June. Box office open M-Sa 1-7pm; phone M-F 10am-noon and 2-6pm. 40-750F.

Théâtre Musical de Paris, pl. du Châtelet, 1er (tel. 01 40 28 28 40). M: Châtelet. Superb 2300-seat theater hosting orchestras, opera, and dance. Season Oct.-June; Generally 60-775F; remainders 50F 15min. before curtain, operas 100F. V, MC, AmEx.

Théâtre de la Ville, 2 pl. du Châtelet, 4ème (tel. 01 42 74 22 77). M: Châtelet. Innovative theater and dance, as well as classical and world music. Box office open M 11am-7pm, Tu-Sa 11am-8pm; phone lines open M-Sa 11am-7pm. Second venue in Montmartre: **Les Abbesses,** 31 rue des Abbesses, 18ème. Box office open Tu-Sa 5-8pm; phone times same. 95-190F, students 70-80F. V, MC, AmEx.

CONCERT HALLS

Cité de la Musique, at La Villette, 19ème (tel. 01 44 84 44 84; www.cite-musique.fr). M: Porte-de-Pantin. Everything from lute concerts to gospel in its enormous *salle des concerts* and smaller *amphithéâtre.* There are free concerts throughout the year in both spaces; call for information. Generally 65-200F; *carnet* of 4 tickets 160F.

IRCAM (Institut de Recherche et Coordination Acoustique/Musique), 1 pl. Igor Stravinsky, 4ème (tel. 01 44 78 48 43; http://mediatheque.ircam.fr). M: Rambuteau. Under the direction of Pierre Boulez since the 60s, this center for musical innovation often holds contemporary music concerts, sometimes accompanied by film or theater.

Musée du Louvre, 1er (tel. 01 40 20 51 86 for info; 01 40 20 52 99 for schedule; 01 40 20 84 00 for reservations; www.louvre.fr). M: Palais-Royal. Classical music in a classy auditorium. 100-135F, students 50F 30min. before concerts. Open Sept.-June.

Orchestre de Paris, 252 rue du Fbg St-Honoré, 8ème (tel. 01 45 61 65 60; www.orchestredeparis.com). M: Ternes. Semyon Bychkov conducts the orchestra for the Oct.-June season. 2-4 concerts per week, W-Sa. Box office open M-Sa 11am-6pm and until 8pm before concerts. 60-320F, students 50F 30min. before concerts. V, MC.

OPERA

Opéra de la Bastille, pl. de la Bastille, 11ème (tel. 08 36 69 78 68, 2.23F per min.; fax 01 44 73 13 74; www.opera-de-paris.fr). M: Bastille. Opened amidst controversy in 1989, this huge theater features elaborate opera and ballet, often with a modern spin. Phone lines open M-Sa 9am-7pm, box office M-Sa 11am-6:30pm. 60-670F; over 65 and students under 25 15min. before curtain 120F (operas), 70F (ballets) and 50F (concerts).

Opéra Comique, 14 rue Favart, 2ème (tel. 01 42 44 45 46; fax 01 49 26 05 93). M: Richelieu-Drouot. Lighter opera, from Rossini to Offenbach. Box office open M-Sa 11am-7pm. 35-550F, students 50F 15min. before curtain.

Opéra Garnier, pl. de l'Opéra, 9ème (tel. 08 36 69 78 68, 2.23F per min.; fax 01 44 73 13 74; www.opera-de-paris.fr). M: Opéra. Under renovation but still open, the historic Garnier is home to the Ballet de l'Opéra de Paris. Box office open M-Sa 11am-6pm. Ballets 30-420F; operas up to 670F. Remainders from 1hr. before curtain.

PARIS & ÎLE DE FRANCE

JAZZ

Jazz began to trickle into Paris with US servicemen during WWI, and by the 40s Paris had emerged as a jazz hot spot. Black musicians flocked to France in the 50s and 60s to escape oppression at home, and Paris welcomed them with open arms. Since then, French jazz musicians, including pianist and native Parisian Michel Petrucciani, have themselves become fixtures of the international scene. Herbie Hancock, McCoy Tyner, Benny Baily, Duffy Jackson, and Kenny Garrett frequent the Paris circuit. Nearly every type of jazz is represented, from New Orleans to cool jazz and acid jazz to hip hop and fusion.

Frequent summer festivals sponsor free or nearly free jazz concerts; see **Festivals**, p. 152, for details. French mags *Jazz Hot* (45F) and *Jazz Magazine* (35F) are great sources, as is the bimonthly *LYLO* (*Les Yeux, Les Oreilles;* free). *Pariscope* and *l'Officiel* also have jazz listings.

Au Duc des Lombards, 42 rue des Lombards, 1ᵉʳ (tel. 01 42 33 22 88). M: Châtelet. The best French jazz, with occasional US soloists and hot items in world music. Great acoustics, dark smoky atmosphere, and a hip crowd. Cover 80-100F, music students 50-80F. Beer 28-48F. Music 8:30 or 10pm to 3 or 4am. Open daily 7:30pm-4am. V.

Le Baiser Salé, 58 rue des Lombards, 1ᵉʳ (tel. 01 42 33 37 71). M: Châtelet. Lower-key than Lombards. Cuban, African, and Antillean music with modern jazz and funk upstairs. Music 10pm-3am (typically 3 sets). Cover 40-80F. Jam sessions M (no cover, 1 drink min.). Beer 26F, cocktails 46F. Bar open daily 4pm-dawn.

Le Petit Opportun, 15 rue des Lavandières-Ste-Opportune, 1ᵉʳ (tel. 01 42 36 01 36). M: Châtelet. Show up early for a spot in the front room. Younger crowd and some of the best modern jazz around, including many US performers. Nice pub upstairs. Cover 50-80F. Drinks 30-60F. Open Sept.-July Tu-Sa 9pm-5am; music begins 10:30pm.

L'Eustache, 37 rue Berger, 1ᵉʳ (tel. 01 40 26 23 20). M: Châtelet-Les Halles. Fun, relaxed bar near Les Halles featuring good, free jazz on weekends Sept.-June. Open daily 11am-4am; music starts 10:30pm. V, MC, AmEx.

Caveau de la Huchette, 5 rue de la Huchette, 5ᵉᵐᵉ (tel. 01 43 26 65 05). M: St-Michel. Dance the jitterbug, be-bop, swing, and jive in caves which served as tribunal, prison, and execution site for Danton and Robespierre. Be-bop dance lessons M-F before club opens (tel. 01 42 71 09 09). Crowded on weekends. Cover Su-Th 60F, F-Sa 75F; students 55F. Drinks 26-35F. Open daily 9:30pm-2:30am, F till 3:30am, Sa till 4am.

New Morning, 7-9 rue des Petites-Écuries, 10ᵉᵐᵉ (tel. 01 45 23 51 41). M: Château d'Eau. 400-seat former printing plant is everything a jazz club should be. All the greats have played here, and the club still attracts big names like Wynton Marsalis and Betty Carter. Open Sept.-July from 8pm; concerts usually at 9pm. Tickets, 110-140F, available at box office, FNAC, or Virgin Megastore. Drinks 35-65F. V, MC.

⊠ NIGHTLIFE

Parisian nightlife is a tough nut to crack. Exclusivity is a major part of its charm, but there are alternatives to the mega-trendy and mega-expensive out there. If you'd rather just drink and watch the world go by, bars and the cafés which blend into bars at sundown won't disappoint, with an establishment for every predilection. For gay and lesbian nightlife, Paris is tops, with many scenes to explore.

BARS

In the Latin Quarter, bars cater to students, while the Bastille and Marais teem with Paris's young and hip, gay and straight. Near Les Halles you'll find a slightly older set, while the outer *arrondissements* cater to locals. Like cafés, prices at the bar are cheaper than table service and rise after 10pm.

LOUVRE-RIVOLI-LES HALLES

Le Bar, 5 rue de la Ferronerie, 1er (tel. 01 40 41 00 10). M: Châtelet. Dark and filled with mirrors and throbbing techno, with a tiny underground disco. If you're looking for a break from the muscle-boys, Le Bar offers a crowd with all shapes, sizes, and ages. Happy hour 6-9pm. Beer 16F until 10:30pm, 18F after. Open daily 5pm-3am.

Jip's, 41 rue St-Denis, 1er (tel. 01 42 33 00 11). M: Châtelet-Les Halles. Overflows with Cuban music and murals, and strong rum-based cocktails. Carved wood interior, neon exterior. Cocktails 35-45F, beer 15-25F. Open M-Sa 10am-2am, Su 4pm-2am. V, MC.

MARAIS

🥇 **Le Détour,** 5 rue Elizéver, 3ème (tel. 01 40 29 44 04). M: St-Paul. Swank lounge beats with soul, jazz, and deep house. Cocktails 50-60F, beer 18F. Open daily 7pm-1:30am.

🥇 **Chez Richard,** 37 rue Vieille-du-Temple, 4ème (tel. 01 42 74 31 65). M: Hôtel-de-Ville. In a courtyard, this super-sexy bar and lounge screams drama. The secret: it's actually a fun, friendly place. Beer 22-40F, cocktails 50-60F. Open daily 5pm-2am. V, MC.

Au Petit Fer à Cheval, 30 rue Vieille-du-Temple, 4ème (tel. 01 42 72 47 47). M: Hôtel-de-Ville. A Marais institution with a horseshoe bar, sidewalk terrace, and small restaurant in the back. Paradise on earth. Beer 14-18F. Open M-F 9am-2am, Sa-Su 11am-2am.

LATIN QUARTER

🥇 **Le Bar Dix,** 10 rue de l'Odéon, 6ème (tel. 01 43 54 87 68). M: Odéon. A student hangout where you may be forced to eavesdrop on existentialist discussions. But after enough 15F sangria, being condemned to freedom seems OK. Open daily 5:30pm-2am.

Le Piano Vâche, 8 rue Laplace, 5ème (tel. 01 46 33 75 03). M: Cardinal Lemoine or Maubert-Mutualité. Poster-plastered bar hidden in the winding streets off pl. Contrescarpe. The bar of choice for French students. Beer 20-30F, cocktails 40F. Open July-Aug. M-F 6pm-2am, Sa-Su 9pm-2am; Sept.-June M-F noon-2am, Sa-Su 9pm-2am.

RÉPUBLIQUE-BASTILLE

Café Charbon, 109 rue Oberkampf, 11ème (tel. 01 43 57 55 13). M: Parmentier or Ménilmontant. *Fin-de-siècle* dance hall with mirrors, dark-wood bar, vintage booths, and chandeliers. Expect large crowds. Beer 15-20F. Open daily 9am-2am. V, MC.

China Club, 50 rue de Charenton, 12ème (tel. 01 43 43 82 02). M: Ledru-Rollin or Bastille. Hong Kong gentlemen's club with a speakeasy-style cellar and lacquered *fumoir chinois* look. High-class prices, but a Chinatown (gin fizz with mint) is hard to resist. Cocktails (70-90F) and jazz. Open M-Th 7pm-2am, F-Sa 7pm-3am. V, MC, AmEx.

PIGALLE

L'Endroit, 67 pl. du Dr. Félix Lobligeois, 17ème (tel. 01 42 29 50 00). M: Rome. The purveyor of cool in work-a-day Batignolles, it's the most happening place around, day or night. On a homey square facing the church, beer (22-30F), wine (20-25F), and liquor (45F) are just the start. Open daily noon-2am. V, MC.

Le Fourmi, 74 rue des Martyrs, 18ème (tel. 01 42 64 70 35). M: Pigalle. Popular stop-off before clubbing at Divan du Monde, this bar has character. More spacious than other bars and more energetic as well. Crowd is young and scrappy. Beer 25-35F, wine 25-40F, cocktails 30-60F. Open M-Sa 8:30am-2am, Su 10:30am-2am. V, MC.

PLACE D'ITALIE

Les Oiseaux de Passage, 7 passage Barrault, 13ème (tel. 01 45 89 72 42). M: Corvisart. Young, hip, and laid-back. Art openings, live music, multiple board games, and theme evenings, including silent discussion night. Very laid-back. Beer and *kir* 12F; most food under 55F. Open Tu-Su 10am-2am.

La Folie en Tête, 33 rue de la Butte aux Cailles, 13ème (tel. 01 45 80 65 99). M: Corvisart. Magazines, writing workshops, and musical instruments. Crowded concerts on Saturday nights. Beer 10F, coffee 7F, selection of 10F cocktails before 8pm, all prices increase 2F after 10pm. Open M-Sa 5pm-2am.

CLUBS AND LIVE MUSIC

Clubbing is less about hip DJs and cutting-edge beats than about dressing up, getting in, and being seen. Although admission can be selective, once inside clubs are soft-core and usually friendly. Drinks are expensive and people drink little. Many clubs accept reservations, which means that on busy nights there will be no available seating. To get into selective clubs, dress *very* well, arrive early, be confident but not aggressive about getting in, and come in a couple if you can. Clubs are usually busiest between 2 and 4am, and have very different feels on different evenings—check what music/scene is scheduled before heading out. Live music bar/clubs are a more relaxing, less exclusive way to spend your evening enjoyably.

FOR DANCERS

Rex Club, 5 bd. Poissonnière, 2ème (tel. 01 42 36 10 96). M: Bonne-Nouvelle. Non-selective club with a most selective DJ line-up. Young break-dancers and veteran clubbers fill this casual, subterranean venue for cutting-edge techno, break beats, and hip hop fusion from international DJs on one of the best music systems in Paris. Large dance floor. Open Tu-Sa 11:30pm-6am. Drinks 60-80F. Cover 70F. V, MC.

Batofar, facing 11 Quai François-Mauriac, 13ème (tel. 01 56 29 10 00). M: Quai de la Gare. On a *bateaux mouche* whose innards have been transformed into cavernous bar areas and a sizeable dance floor. Jungle, dub, drum'n'bass, eccentric electronic and Su live "blue note groove" jazz. Open summer daily 10pm-3am. Tapas 20F. Cover 40-60F.

What's Up Bar, 15 rue Daval, 11ème (tel. 01 48 05 88 33). M: Bastille. A rare Paris miracle: often free and always funky. In a concrete bunker, this bar/club has DJ competitions and its own magazine; it's also a good place to chill and chat. M drum'n'bass, W Electronic, F Garage, Sa Freestyle. Open M-F 10pm-2:30am, Sa-Su 10pm-5am. No cover M-Th, F-Sa 50F. Drinks from 25F. V, MC.

Niels, 27 av. des Ternes, 17ème (tel. 01 47 66 45 00). M: Ternes. Equal parts swank and soul, Niels is all-around fun. Music is mainstream but the dance floor is packed. Open daily 11:30pm-dawn. Drinks 95F. Cover Th-Sa 100F with drink.

Folies Pigalle, 11 pl. Pigalle, 9ème (tel. 01 48 78 25 56). M: Pigalle. This club is the largest and most popular in the once-sleazy Pigalle *quartier.* A former strip joint, the Folies Pigalle is popular among gay and straight clubbers, with some special girls-only events. Mostly house and techno. Very crowded at 4am. Open Tu-Sa 11pm-7am, Su 3-8pm. Cover 100F. Drinks 50F. V, MC, AmEx.

Divan du Monde, 75 rue des Martyrs, 18ème (tel. 01 44 92 77 66). M: Pigalle. Not quite global, but this grungy den does try with Brazilian music, live bands, English DJs, and funk evenings. Youngish crowd varies; frequent week-long festivals. Su is gay tea dance. Open daily 7:30pm-dawn. Cover 40-100F. Drinks from 20F. V, MC.

FOR POSERS

Les Bains, 7 rue du Bourg l'Abbé, 3ème (tel. 01 48 87 01 80). M: Réaumur-Sébastopol. Ultraselective, super-crowded, and very expensive. A former public bath visited by Marcel Proust; more recently Mike Tyson, Madonna, and Jack Nicholson stopped in to bathe in their own glory. Lots of models on the floor. House and garage grunge. Cover and 1st drink 120F, subsequent drinks 100F. Open daily midnight-6am. V, MC, AmEx.

Le Queen, 102 av. des Champs-Élysées, 8ème (tel. 01 53 89 08 90). The fiercest funk in town, where drag queens, superstars, models, moguls, and Herculean go-go boys get down to the mainstream rhythms of a 10,000 gigawatt sound system. At once one of the cheapest and one of the most fashionable clubs, and thus the toughest to get in to—especially for women. M disco (50F cover plus 50F drink), W "Respect" (no cover for the hottest spot in town), Th house (no cover), F-Sa house (80F entry, plus 50F drink), Su 80s (no cover). Open daily midnight-dawn.

Bus Palladium, 6 rue Fontaine, 9ème (tel. 01 53 21 07 33). M: Pigalle. The classiest of the mainstream clubs, Le Bus fills with a young and trendy crowd who rock the party that rocks the ex-rock'n'roll club, still sporting vintage posters and faded gilded décor. Cover 100F. Open Tu-Sa 11pm-dawn.

LIVE MUSIC

L'Arapaho, 30 av. d'Italie, Centre Commercial Italie 2, 13ème (tel. 01 45 89 65 05). M: Pl. d'Italie. It's the gray door on the right, just past Au Printemps. Since 1983, this place has built up a reputation for hosting some of the best hard-core, rap, pop, and metal bands to come through Paris. A stop on most indie bands' itineraries, past acts include Pavement, Sebadoh, Shellac, Bim Skala Bim, and Soul Asylum. Tickets 60-130F. Beer 20F, cocktails 50F. Open F (Asian Folly) and Sa (Cuban) 11pm-dawn. Cover 80F.

La Cigale, 120 bd. Rochechouart, 18ème (tel. 01 49 25 89 99). M: Pigalle. One of the two large rock clubs in Pigalle, seating 2000 for international indie, punk, and hard-core bands. Concerts 100-180F. The converted theater also brings in modern dance shows. Music starts at 8:30pm, box office open M-Sa noon-curtain. V, MC.

Élysée Montmartre, 72 bd. Rochechouart, 18ème (tel. 01 44 92 45 42). M: Anvers. The biggest-name rock, reggae, and rap venue in a neighborhood fixture. Featuring well-known British and American groups in addition to home-grown talent, and a large dance floor for disco and salsa nights. Drinks 30-50F, shows 80-150F. V, MC, AmEx.

Le Cithéa, 114 rue Oberkampf, 11ème (tel. 01 40 21 70 95). M: Parmentier. More of a bar with live music than a flash-dancing club. In the hip Oberkampf *quartier* and full of young, artsy folk, Le Cithéa features a wide variety of jazz, hip hop, and free jack fusion bands, as well as occasional DJs spinning drum'n'bass. Drinks 25-60F. Open daily 9:30pm-5:30am. Cover F-Sa 50F with 1 or 2 drinks. V, MC.

Le Bataclan, 50 bd. Voltaire, 11ème (tel. 01 47 00 39 12). M: Oberkampf. A concert space and café-bar that hosts indie rock bands like Guided By Voices and Beck. Funky sliding toward trendy. Tickets start at 100F and vary with show. Th (free) is low-key. F (80F) is gay night, and Sa (80F) is house. Open Sept.-July Th-Sa 11pm-dawn.

GAY AND LESBIAN ENTERTAINMENT

The center of lesbian and gay life is the Marais, while most gay establishments cluster around rue du Temple, rue Ste-Croix de la Bretonnerie, rue des Archives, and rue Vieille du Temple, in the 4ème. For the most comprehensive listing of gay and lesbian restaurants, clubs, hotels, organizations, and services, consult Gai Pied's *Guide Gai* (79F at kiosks), *Illico* (free at gay bars and restaurants), or *Le Guide Paris* (28F at gay shops). *Pariscope* has an English-language section called *A Week of Gay Outings*. **Les Mots à la Bouche,** Paris's largest gay and lesbian bookstore, serves as an unofficial information center for queer life and can also tell you what's hot and where to go (see **Books,** p. 150).

FOR MEN

▨ **Banana Café,** 13-15 rue de la Ferronerie, 1er (tel. 01 42 33 35 31). M: Châtelet. The most popular gay bar in the area. Two floors include a popular piano bar. Legendary theme nights. Beer 20F after 10pm. Half-price drink during "Crazy Time," 4:30-7pm. Open daily 4:30pm-dawn. V, MC, AmEx.

Le Duplex, 25 rue Michel Le Comte, 3ème (tel. 01 42 72 80 86). M: Rambuteau. This gay *bar d'art* has a funky mezzanine yet feels small and intimate. Not exclusively male, but few women hang out here. Open daily 8pm-2am.

Open Café, 17 rue des Archives, 4ème (tel. 01 42 72 26 18). M: Hôtel-de-Ville. Recently redone, the Open Café is the most popular of the Marais gay bars. Grit your teeth, grip your handbag, and bitch your way onto the terrace. Beer 18F, cocktails 35F. Su brunch (70-105F). Open daily 10am-2am.V, MC, AmEx.

Cox, 15 rue des Archives, 4ème (tel. 01 42 72 72 71). M: Hôtel-de-Ville. As the name suggests, this is a buns-to-the-wall bar with bulging and beautiful boys. So crowded the spillover blocks the traffic. Very cruisy; this isn't the place for a quiet cocktail. Happy hour (with beer half-off) M-Sa 6-8pm, Su 6-9pm. Beer 16-29F. Open daily 2pm-2am.

FOR WOMEN

🗨 **Le Champmeslé,** 4 rue Chabanais, 2ème (tel. 01 42 96 85 20). M: Pyramides or Quatre Septembre. Paris's most famous lesbian bar. Mixed at the front, women-only at the back. Cabaret Th, 10pm. Drinks 30-45F. Open M-W 5pm-2am, Th-Sa 5pm-5am. V, MC.

Les Scandaleuses, 8 rue des Écouffes, 4ème (tel. 01 48 87 39 26). M: St-Paul. Vibrant, ultra-hip lesbian bar set to techno beats. Open daily 6pm-2am.

Pulp!, 25 bd. Poissonnière, 2ème (tel. 01 40 26 01 93). M: Rue Montmartre. The legendary L'Entr'acte is now the swanky, glamorous Pulp! House, techno, and Latin are the mainstays. Drinks 30-60F. M-Th men admitted in the company of a woman; weekends women-only. Open W-Sa midnight-5am. F and Sa 50F cover. V, MC, AmEx.

JUST PLAIN QUIRKY

🗨 **La Main Jaune,** pl. de la Porte-de-Champerret, 17ème (tel. 01 47 63 26 47). M: Porte de Champerret. A roller-and-regular-dancing disco popular with the high school crowd. Open W and Sa-Su 2:30-7pm, F-Sa and holidays 10pm-dawn. 50F W and Sa-Su (including 1 drink; skate rental 10F); F-Sa non-skating disco with Portuguese music.

Le Piano Zinc, 49 rue des Blancs Manteaux, 4ème (tel. 01 42 74 32 42). M: Rambuteau. A mature crowd gathers to enjoy the hysterical cabaret performances of the gifted bar staff. Campy homage is paid to Liza, Eartha, Madonna, Bette, and Édith Piaf. All are welcome to perform (though attendance at 10pm rehearsals is recommended). Happy hour 6-8pm. Beer 10-14F, cocktails 37-44F. Open Tu-Su 6pm-2am. V, MC, AmEx.

L'Entrepôt, 7-9 rue Francis de Pressensé, 14ème (tel. 01 45 40 78 38; film schedule 08 36 68 05 87; restaurant reservations 01 45 40 60 70). M: Pernety. Alternative cinema coupled with a plush, trendy bar featuring live music and a garden patio. *Ciné-Philo*, a screening and discussion café, held Su 2:30pm and occasional other days (42F, students 32F). Open daily 11am-1:30am.

🛍 SHOPPING

Paris is an endless parade of all that is extravagant, form-fitting, and flattering, and stylish clothes and accessories are spread democratically through a variety of price ranges. In the more exclusive boutiques, assistants have perfected the art of disapproval—ignore them and waltz on in. After all, *they* can't afford to shop there, either. Budget shoppers should keep a keen eye out for big *soldes* signs— that's French for **sales,** and they can be outstanding, especially during **January** and **July** when most stores offer discounts of 30-50%. Non-EU residents who have made purchases worth over 1200F in one store should ask about getting a refund on the 20.6% value-added tax (see **Reclaiming Value-added Tax,** p. 35).

SHOPPING BY LOCATION

As in any big city, each area of Paris has its specialty when it comes to wooing consumers. The biggest names and biggest prices are found on the famous **rue du Fbg St-Honoré,** conveniently close to the presidential Élysée palace. Between the unaffordable swank of the rue de Rivoli and the tourist clutter around the Pompidou center, the 1er and 2ème lunge for the youth market. Here you'll find everything from classic black at Agnès B. on **rue du Jour,** to technicolor clubwear on **rue Étienne Marcel** and **rue Tiquetonne** (M: Étienne Marcel). Les Halles RER station exits into the **Forum Les Halles,** a subterranean mall providing the full urban warrior æsthetic. The alleys of the **Marais,** in the 3ème and 4ème (M: St-Paul or Hôtel-de-Ville), trade a streetwise edge for a consistent line up of affordable, trendy boutiques, mid-priced clothing chains, independent designer shops, and vintage stores that line **rue Vieille-du-Temple, rue de Sévigne, rue Roi de Sicile,** and **rue des Rosiers.** The best selection of affordable-chic men's wear in Paris can be found here, especially along **rue Ste-Croix-de-la-Bretonnerie.** Most stores are open late weekdays and hopping on Sundays. Farther east in the 11ème, **rue de la Roquette** (M: Bastille) is the shopping hub of **Bastille,** with numerous trendy clothing and accessories shops. **Rue de Keller** and its surrounding streets are lined with record shops.

Crossing the river into the Latin Quarter, **bd. St-Michel** in the 5ème caters to students, with vast bookstores, stationary shops, and mid-priced clothing chains. Heading into the 6ème and eventually the 7ème, **bd. St-Germain** (M: Odéon and Sèvres-Babylone) goes rapidly upscale; it may still be Rive Gauche, but it's distinctly Yves St-Laurent. Don't just settle for window shopping; rue du Four hosts fun and more affordable designers. South, in the 14ème, the discount outlet stores on **rue d'Alésia**, between rue Didot and Place Victor Basch (M: Plaisance or Alésia), are crowded on weekends but offer some real steals.

DEPARTMENT STORES

It's strange that a country where one must go to a thousand speciality shops to assemble one complete meal should be the birthplace of the *grand magasin*, those meccas of one-stop shopping. The old stores are as noteworthy for their Belle Époque architecture and Art Nouveau details as for their acres of accessories. You can see where it all started **Au Bon Marché,** 22-38 rue de Sèvres, 7ème (tel. 01 44 39 80 00; M: Sèvres-Babylone), the world's first department store, complete with a central hall designed by Gustave "Tour" Eiffel. (Open M-Sa 9:30am-7pm. V, MC.) **Samaritaine,** 67 rue de Rivoli, 1er (tel. 01 40 41 20 20; M: Pont-Neuf, Châtelet-Les-Halles, or Louvre), occupies four large buildings connected by tunnels and bridges. It may not be as chic as its rivals, but it's a lot more affordable. The rooftop observation deck provides one of the best views of the city. (Open M-W and F-Sa 9:30am-7pm, Th 9:30am-10pm. V, MC, AmEx.) The two real heavyweights slug it out on bd. Haussmann in the 9ème, where **Au Printemps,** at #64 (tel. 01 42 82 50 00), faces off with **Galeries Lafayette** at #40 (tel. 01 42 82 34 56). Neither have much in the budget category, but many hotels give out 10% discount cards for tourists. While some consider that Printemps has the better selection, Galeries Lafayette takes the prize for looks, with a giant perfume gallery crowned by a stained-glass dome. (Printemps: Open M-W and F-Sa 9:30am-7pm, Th 9:30am-10pm. V, MC. Lafayette: Open M-W and F-Sa 9:30am-7pm, Th 9:30-8pm. V, MC, AmEx.)

CLOTHES

OUTLET STORES

Stock is French for outlet store, where big names go for less—generally seconds or last season's remainders. Widen your portfolio and invest! Many are on rue d'Alésia in the 14ème (M: Alésia), including **Cacharel Stock** (#114; tel. 01 45 42 53 04; open M-Sa 10am-7pm; V, MC, AmEx), **Stock Daniel Hechter** (#92; tel. 01 47 07 88 44; open M-Sa 10am-7:30pm; V, MC), and a small **Stock Kookaï** (#111; open M 1-7pm and Tu-Sa 10am-7pm). A much larger **Stock Kookaï** bustles at 82 rue Réamur, 2ème. (Tel. 01 45 08 93 69. Open M-Sa 10:30am-7:30pm.)

BOUTIQUES

Once upon a time, famous designers such as Christian Dior and Chanel provided only custom-tailored *haute couture* to the rich and famous, but ever since St-Laurent produced the first *prêt-à-porter* (ready to wear) collection in the 1960s, designers have been falling over themselves to appeal to the masses. However, big-name labels still mean big price tags. Although the last few years have witnessed a Gap invasion in Paris, if you want affordable French style that your neighbors won't be wearing at home, try these mid-priced *magasins*.

- 🖎 **MKDM,** 24 rue de Sévigne, 4ème (tel. 01 42 77 00 74). M: St-Paul. 20% 'Independent Japanese designers', 30% 'chic-casual' and unisex, and 50% 'Paris-Tokyo tendencies.' Innovation doesn't come cheap: creations range 180-700F. Open daily 2-8pm.
- 🖎 **Le Shop,** 3 rue d'Argout, 2ème (tel. 01 40 28 95 94). M: Étienne-Marcel. Two levels, 1200 square meters, and 24 corners of club wear. Open M 1-7pm, Tu-Sa 11am-7pm.
- **A.P.C.,** 3-4 rue de Fleurus, 6ème (tel. 01 42 22 12 77; www.apc.fr). M: St-Placide. A resource for wardrobe staples, A.P.C. is hip without being outrageous. Open M-Sa 10:30am-7pm. V, MC, AmEx.

Agnès B., 2, 3, 6, 10, and 19 rue du Jour, 1er (tel. 01 45 08 56 56 or 01 42 33 04 13). M: Étienne Marcel. Upscale but affordable, these pieces are the kind of well-made clothes that are classic but stylishly French. Open M-Sa 10am-7pm. V, MC.

Mosquitos, 25 rue du Four, 6ème (tel. 01 43 25 25 16). M: Mabillon. Funky and chunky shoes in all colors and for all occasions. Open M-Sa 11am-7pm.

Kookaï, 12 rue Gustave-Gourbet, 16ème (tel. 01 47 55 18 00). M: Victor Hugo. The flagship store of the global chain, with sexed-up runway knock-offs and a hip young staff. Open M-Sa 10:30am-7:30pm. V, MC, AmEx.

Boy'z Bazaar, 5 rue Ste-Croix-de-la-Bretonnerie, 4ème (tel. 01 42 71 94 00). M: St-Paul. A large selection of all that's trendy-casual in men's wear from Énergie to Paul Smith. Open daily noon-midnight.

Loft Design By Paris, 12 rue du Faubourg-St-Honoré, 8ème (tel. 01 42 65 59 65). M: Concorde or Madeleine. Mostly for men; well-tailored shirts, casual sweaters. Branch at 12 rue de Sévigné, 4ème. M: St-Paul. Open M-Sa 10am-7pm. V, MC, AmEx.

MAGASINS DE TROC AND VINTAGE CLOTHES

Snazzy *magasins de troc* resell clothes bought and returned at more expensive stores. Their stock often includes lots of basics as well as some pretty wild finds—while prices aren't always low, savings are often massive. Paris's vintage clothing scene is marginal. A number of stylish vintage clothes shops can be found in the Marais, on rue de Mouffetard (5ème), around Les Halles (1er and 2ème), and around av. de Clichy and rue des Dames (17ème). If you don't find what you're looking for here, you may have better luck at one of Paris's flea markets (see below).

Mouton à Cinq Pattes: 8-10 and 18 rue St-Placide, 6ème (tel. 01 45 48 86 26; M: Sèvres-Babylone); 19 rue Grégoire de Tours, 6ème (tel. 01 43 29 73 56; M: Odéon); 15 rue Vieille de Temple, 4ème (tel. 01 42 71 86 30; M: St-Paul); and 130 av. Victor Hugo (tel. 01 47 55 42 25; M: Victor Hugo). A huge selection of designer clothing. Little costs less than 200F, but if you're willing to dig through the rainbow piles, you might find a pot of gold. Open M-F 10:30am-7:30pm, Sa 10:30am-8pm. V, MC, AmEx.

La Clef des Marques, 20 pl. du Marché St-Honoré, 1er (tel. 01 47 03 90 40). M: Pyramides. Two stories of designer merchandise, including lingerie, swimwear, basic cotton tops, and shoes. You may stumble upon Prada pumps or Gaultier Jean's for less than your hotel room. Open M-Sa 12:30am-7pm. V, MC.

Guerrisol, 19-29-31 and 33 av. de Clichy, 17ème (tel. 01 42 94 13 21; M: La Fourche); 9, 21, and 21bis bd. Barbès, 18ème (tel. 01 42 52 19 73: M: Barbès-Rochechouart); 45 bd. de la Chapelle, 10ème (tel. 01 45 26 80 85; M: La Chapelle); 116-118 rue Jean-Pierre Timbaud, 11ème (tel. 01 43 38 69 05; M: Courconnes); and 22 bd. Poissonière, 9ème (tel. 01 47 70 35 02; M: Bonne Nouvelle). Racks upon racks of vintage clothes. Silk shirts and leather coats; jeans 40-60F. Most branches open M-Sa 9:30am-7pm.

Tandem, 20 rue Houdron, 18ème (tel. 01 44 92 97 60). M: Abbesses. 60s and 70s polyester and glitter squeezed next to 40s and 50s retro-wear. Big menswear selection. Dresses and trousers 120-200F. Open Tu-Sa 11am-2:30pm and 3:30-8pm.

BOOKS

Book buying is such an avid Parisian habit that it long ago spilled from the shops onto the streets; endless stalls of *bouquinistes* line the Seine, promising rare first editions as often as unwanted paperbacks. The Latin Quarter has the highest density of bookstores, with second-hand shops offering musty wares on the side streets while students pile into the superstores of bd. St-Michel. The biggest of all is **Gibert Jeune,** 5 pl. St-Michel, 5ème (tel. 01 43 25 70 07; M: St-Michel), with six satellite branches clustered around the *place* selling everything from stationary to foreign books. (Open M-Sa 9:30am-7:30pm. V, MC, AmEx.) Jeune's main rival is the towering **Gibert Joseph,** 26-34 bd. St-Michel, 6ème (tel. 01 44 41 88 88; M: Odéon or Cluny-Sorbonne), a gigantic *librairie* and music store rolled into one with new and used books mixed together. (Open M-Sa 9:30am-7:30pm. V, MC.) **FNAC** has branches across Paris: the largest is at **Forum des Halles,** 1er (M: Les Halles.)

Today, numerous English-language bookstores cater to homesick expats, but the first was **Galignani**, 224 rue de Rivoli, 1er (tel. 01 42 60 76 07; M: Tuileries). Founded in 1804, it's all you'd expect from its age and location. (Open M-Sa 10am-7pm. V, MC.) **Shakespeare and Co.,** 37 rue de la Bûcherie, 5ème (M: St-Michel), seeks to recreate the atmosphere of the eponymous establishment where Sylvia Beach first published James Joyce's *Ulysses* in 1922. Profits support writers who live and work upstairs—former residents include Allen Ginsberg. The Sunday evening tea party is a good way to introduce yourself to the literary crowd. (Open daily noon-midnight.) The focus of Paris's English literary life is the **The Village Voice,** 6 rue Princesse, 6ème (tel. 01 46 33 36 47; M: Mabillon), with 3-4 readings, lectures, and discussions every month. It also stocks American and British newspapers and magazines. (Open M 2-8pm, Tu-Sa 11am-8pm. V, MC, AmEx.) Save yourself a Eurostar fare by nipping into Paris's very own **W.H. Smith,** 248 rue de Rivoli, 1er (tel. 01 44 77 88 99; M: Concorde), with the latest publications and a large selection of magazines. (Open M-Sa 9am-7:30pm, Su 1-7:30pm. V, MC, AmEx.)

Les Mots à la Bouche, 6 rue Ste-Croix-de-la-Bretonnerie, 4ème (tel. 01 42 78 88 30; M: St-Paul or Hôtel-de-Ville), has an extensive collection of gay and lesbian literature and is a must-visit for those in search of an inside line on gay and lesbian nightlife and political and cultural events. (Open M-Th 11am-11pm, F-Sa 11am-midnight, Su 2-8pm. V, MC.) **Presence Africaine,** 25bis rue des Écoles, 5ème (tel. 01 43 54 15 88; M: Maubert-Mutualité), is the store of the famous company which first published Césaire and Fanon, and is a resource for travelers seeking businesses that cater to black clientele. (Open M-Sa 9:30am-7pm. V, MC.)

MARKETS

Paris's many flea markets *(marchés aux puces)* are great options for vintage clothing, jewelry, and memorabilia. Feel free to haggle, but beware of "bargains" and watch your wallet—pickpockets are out in droves. The **Puces de St-Ouen,** just north of the 18ème (M: Porte de Clignancourt), began in the Middle Ages, when merchants resold the cast-off, flea-ridden clothing of aristocrats to peasant-folk on the edge of the city. Today, it's a highly structured, regular market alongside a wild, anything-goes street bazaar. From antique armoires and fine silverware to LPs and vintage 60s hippie gear, you'll find everything you need (and don't need) in the many acres of criss-crossing pedestrian alleys. (Market Sa-M 7am-7:30pm.) The **Puces de Vanves,** along rue Marc Sanguier between av. de la Porte de Vanves and av. Georges La Fenestre, 14ème (M: Porte de Vanves), carries an assortment of antique cameras, jewelry, furniture, lace, tableware, 19th-century books, and 20th-century comics (Sa-Su 8am-1pm). The **Puces de Montreuil,** extending from pl. de la Porte de Montreuil along av. du Professeur A. Lemierre and av. Galliéni, 20ème, is cheap in every sense. You'll find auto parts, tools, and stereos, but the market's heart is in its piles of used clothes and eccentric hats (most 5-50F). (Market Sa-M 7:30am-7:30pm.)

At the opposite end of the spectrum is the **Marché aux Fleurs,** on pl. Louis-Lépine just across from the M: Cité staircase, on the Île de la Cité. This permanent flower market fills the plaza near the Palais de Justice with color and fragrance and makes for a romantic walk down the Seine. (Open M-Sa 9am-7pm.) On Sunday a pet market appears instead (9am-6pm).

SPECTATOR SPORTS

Parisians follow sports with fierce interest. The **Palais Omnisports Paris Bercy,** 8 bd. de Bercy, 12ème (tel. 01 44 68 44 68; M: Bercy), hosts everything from beach volleyball to figure skating, horse jumping, and surfing beneath its sod-covered roof.

> **CITY-OF-LIGHT EXPRESS** If you've witnessed the Friday night "Roller Rally" that leaves pl. d'Italie at 9:45pm and winds throughout the city with 5000 skaters in tow, you know what mayhem is. Fear not—they're accompanied by a swift-footed fleet of about thirty policemen on skates. (*Rent* at FranScoop, 47 rue Servan, 11*ème*. Tel. 01 47 00 68 43. M: St-Maur. 45-90F per day, 120F per weekend, 240F per week. Open M-Sa 9:30am-1pm and 2-7:30pm.)

CYCLING. The **Tour de France** has its triumphal last stage in Paris. Call the sports journal *l'Équipe* (tel. 01 41 33 15 00), one of the tour's sponsors, for information about the itinerary and join the droves of spectators cheering their favorites to victory along the Champs-Élysées. Show up early and be prepared for a mob scene. The **Grand Prix Cycliste de Paris** is an annual time trial competition held in June in the Bois de Vincennes, 12*ème* (tel. 01 43 68 01 27).

FOOTBALL (LE FOOT). You'd have to have been in a coma not to have missed France defeating Brazil to win the 1998 World Cup at the new **Stade de France,** in St-Denis; but Parisians have been avid followers of the world's favorite sport since long before then. **Paris St-Germain** is the capital's best-known team, splitting its time between away games and matches at **Parc des Princes** stadium. Tickets (50-300F) can be purchased at the stadium box office, 24 rue du Commandant-Guibaud, 16*ème*. (Tel. 01 49 87 29 29. M: Porte d'Auteuil. Open M-F 9am-8pm, Sa 10am-5pm. V, MC.)

HORSING AROUND. An afternoon at a French track is a family outing, though the level of classiness climbs for championship races. **Hippodrome de Vincennes,** 2 rte. de la Ferme, Bois de Vincennes, 12*ème* (tel. 01 49 77 17 17; M: Château de Vincennes), has been home to harness racing since 1906. Big meets include the Prix d'Amérique (late Jan.), Prix de France (early Feb.), and Prix du Président de la République (late June). (All races 15-30F.) The **Hippodrome d'Auteuil,** Bois de Boulogne, 16*ème* (tel. 01 44 10 20 30; M: Porte d'Auteuil), has hosted steeplechases since 1873. For big races, shuttles run from the metro and RER stations. (Open Sept.-Nov. and Feb.-June. M-F 25F, Su 40F, major events 50F. No reservations.)

TENNIS. The *terre battue* (red clay) of the **Stade Roland Garros,** 2 av. Gordon Bennett, 16*ème* (M: Porte d'Auteuil), has ended more than one champion's quest for a Grand Slam. For two weeks during May and June, **Les Internationaux de France de Tennis,** a.k.a. the **French Open,** welcomes top players to Paris. Write to the Fédération Française de Tennis (tel. 01 47 43 48 00), at Roland Garros, in February for information on tickets. Call in March for prices; seats generally range 45-295F.

■ FESTIVALS

MUSIC

Festival de St-Denis, early June to early July (tel. 01 48 13 06 07). M: St-Denis-Basilique. 4-week concert series featuring classical and contemporary works. Held in the magnificent Basilique St-Denis and the Légion d'Honneur. Tickets 50-275F.

La Villette Jazz Festival, late June to early July (tel. 01 40 03 75 75 or 01 44 84 44 84; www.la-villette.com). M: Porte de Pantin. At Parc de la Villette. Past performers have included Herbie Hancock, Ravi Coltrane, and B.B. King. Some concerts free; call for info and prices. *Forfait-soirée* for one night 170F; students, under 26, and seniors 145F.

Festival Musique en l'Île, mid-July to Aug. (tel. 01 44 62 70 90). Chamber and classical music in some of Paris's most exquisite churches, including the Ste-Chapelle, Église St-Louis, and Église St-Germain-des-Près. Tickets 100-150F.

Paris, Quartier d'Été, mid-July to mid-Aug. (tel. 01 44 94 98 00; www.quartierdete.com). Dance, music of the world, a giant parade, promenade concerts, and jazz. Many events are held in the Jardin des Tuileries, Jardin du Luxembourg, and Parc de la Villette. From international ballet companies and top-10 rock bands to local performers.

Festival d'Automne, mid-Sept. to late Dec. (tel. 01 53 45 17 17; www.festival-automne. com). Notoriously highbrow and *avant-garde* drama, ballet, and music arranged around a different theme each year. Many events held at the Théâtre du Châtelet, Théâtre de la Ville, and Cité de la Musique. Ticket prices vary by venue.

Festival FNAC-Inrockuptibles, early Nov. The music megastore and France's primary music mag host indie and "alternative" concerts with artists like Beck, Fiona Apple, and others in varying venues. Consult *Pariscope* or *Les Inrockuptibles* for details.

FILM

Fête du Cinéma, around June 28. Purchase 1 full-price ticket at any cinema (choose a cheap one!) and receive a passport admitting you to all the films shown during the 3-day festival for 10F each. Expect long lines and get there at least 30min. early for popular movies. Look for posters in the metro or ask at cinemas for the specific dates.

Festival du Cinéma en Plein Air, mid-July to late Aug. (tel. 01 40 03 76 92; www.la-villette.com). M: Porte de la Villette or Porte de Pantin, at the Parc de la Villette, 19ème. Fabulous outdoor film festival. Movies usually focus on one theme, but exceptions are made for cult classics and blockbusters. Chairs 40F or bring a blanket. Tu-Su 10pm.

NATIONAL HOLIDAYS

Bastille Day (Fête Nationale), July 14. Festivities begin the night before, with traditional street dances at the tip of Île St-Louis. Free *bals pompiers* (firemen's balls) take place inside every Parisian fire station the night of the 13th, with DJs, bands, and cheap alcohol. There's dancing at pl. de la Bastille, but it's also full of kids throwing fireworks into the crowd. July 14 starts with the army parading down the Champs-Élysées at 10:30am and ends with fireworks at 10:30pm. For the parade and fireworks, metro stations along the Champs and at Trocadéro are closed.

New Year. Young punks and tourists throng the Champs-Élysées to set off fireworks, while restaurants host pricey evenings of *foie gras* and champagne galore. On New Year's day there is a parade with floats and dolled up dames from pl. Pigalle to pl. Jules-Joffrin.

MISCELLANEOUS

Course des Serveuses et Garçons de Café, 1 day in mid-June (tel. 01 42 96 60 75). Over 500 tuxedoed waiters and waitresses sprint through an 8km course carrying a full bottle and glass on a tray. Starts and finishes at the Hôtel de Ville (M: Hôtel de Ville).

Journées du Patrimoine, 3rd weekend of Sept. (tel. 01 44 61 21 00). National palaces, ministries, and monuments open to the public. The Hôtel de Ville should be on your list, as well as Jacques Chirac's bathroom in the Palais de l'Élysée. Free.

Fête des Vendanges à Montmartre, first weekend in Oct. Rue des Saules, 18ème (tel. 01 42 52 42 00). M: Lamarck-Caulaincourt. A celebration of the grape harvest from Montmartre's own vineyards. Folksongs, wine tasting, and costumed picking and stomping of grapes. Much wine is consumed.

Gay Pride (Fierté), June. Parties, special events, film festivals, demonstrations, exhibitions, concerts, and a huge parade through the Marais. For dates and events, call the **Centre Gai et Lesbien** (tel. 01 43 57 21 47) or check Marais bars for posters.

ÎLE DE FRANCE

With 10 million inhabitants, the region surrounding Paris is both the most densely populated in France and the nation's economic powerhouse. Though today it is little more than a giant suburb of the capital, historically the Île de France was the heartland of the country. Bounded by the Seine, the Marne, the Beuvronne, the Oise, and the Nonette rivers, the Île was the first area to be known as Francia (after its Frankish overlords), and for much of the Middle Ages was the only part of France to remain loyal to the king. The nucleus of the kingdom, it lost none of its importance when France was reunified under Philippe-Auguste in the 12th century, and its forests and châteaux provided diversion from city life for the monarchs and their courtiers. As time wore on and the kings grew more and more suspicious of the rebellious-minded inhabitants of their capital, nearby towns took on more importance. François I built a fantastic "hunting lodge" at Fontainebleau in the early 16th century, making it the artistic capital of France, and 150 years later Louis XIV abandoned Paris entirely for Versailles, a triumph of egomania over nature—untold numbers of workers died draining the swamps on which it was built. Though the Revolution brought the capital back to Paris, both Napoleons and the restored monarchy stayed frequently in the Île's palaces. It was at Fontainebleau, in 1814, that Napoleon I took a tearful farewell to his empire before leaving for Elba, while Napoleon III's wife, the Empress Eugénie, liked to amuse herself playing Marie-Antoinette at Versaille's Petit Trianon. During the siege of Paris in 1870-1871, King Wilhelm of Prussia made Versailles his home, and it was in the Hall of Mirrors that Bismarck had him crowned Kaiser of Germany. Forty-eight years later, a humbled Germany was forced to sign its surrender in the same room at the end of the World War I.

▐ GETTING AROUND

As befits a region which provides many of Paris's workers, public transportation is frequent, rapid, and almost exclusively connects each town to the capital and nowhere else. Towns and sights nearer to Paris are often accessible by the RER commuter express trains, although regular metro tickets won't work—you might be able to get on the trains with them, but you won't be able to get out without paying a hefty fine. Instead, make sure to clearly state your destination when buying tickets, which can be done at any metro station. Other towns are accessible by SNCF *banlieue* (suburban), and occasionally *grandes lignes* (long-distance) trains; make sure you know which you need.

CHARTRES

Clustered around its magnificent Cathédrale Notre-Dame, Chartres is still a medieval village at heart. The town's oldest streets are named for the trades once practiced there (rue de la Poissonerie was home to the fishmonger), while handsome stone bridges and iron-trimmed walkways cross the Eure River. Chartres's tangle of streets can be maddening; get a free map from the tourist office.

Without its **cathedral** (tel. 02 37 21 75 02 or 02 37 28 15 58), Chartres would be just another dormitory town near Paris. Though the towers and the base of the west façade are Romanesque, the cathedral's fame rests on its exquisite Gothic architecture. It was here that the style, born at St-Denis (see p. 134), reached maturity. A fire in 1194 occasioned the rebuilding of the cathedral, and thanks to the generosity of nobles and monks it took only 25 years to complete. The rapidity of construction resulted in a unity of style unique in medieval churches. Most of the **stained glass** dates from the 13th century and was preserved through both World Wars by heroic town authorities, who dismantled over 2000 square meters and stored the windows pane by pane out of harm's way. The famous **Blue Virgin window,** the **Tree of Jesse window,** and the **Passion and Resurrection of Christ windows** are among the surviving 12th-century stained glass. The center window of the Incarnation shows the story of Christ from the Annunciation to the ride into Jerusalem. Bring binoculars if you can, or rent them for 10F per hour plus ID or 300F deposit. (Cathedral open M-Sa 7:30am-7:15pm, Su and holidays 8:30am-7:15pm.)

No visit to Chartres would be complete without seeing the **Sancta Camisia,** the cloth supposedly worn by Mary when she gave birth to Christ and donated to Chartres in 875 by Charles le Chauve. It is kept in the cathedral's **treasury** along with other significant garments and objects from the building's history. (Open Apr.-Oct. Tu-Sa 10am-noon and 2-6pm, Su and holidays 2-6pm; Nov.-Mar. Tu-Sa 10am-11:40pm and 2:30-4:30pm, Su and holidays 2-5pm.) The adventurous can

Île-de-France

N

climb the **Tour Jehan-de-Beauce** for a view of the cathedral roof, the flying buttresses, and the city below. (Open May-Aug. M-Sa 9am-6pm, Su 2-6pm; Sept.-Mar.
M-Sa 9:30-11:30am and 2-5pm, Su 2-5pm. 25F, ages 12-25 15F.) Parts of Chartres's
crypt, such as a well down which Vikings tossed the bodies of their victims during
raids, date back to the 9th century. You can enter the subterranean crypt only as
part of a French tour that leaves from **La Crypte,** 18 Cloître Nôtre-Dame (tel. 02 37
21 56 33), the store opposite the cathedral's south entrance. (30min. tours Apr.-
Oct. M-Sa noon and 2:45pm; Nov.-Mar. 11am and 4:15pm. 11F, students 8F.) The
only English **tours** of the cathedral are given by Brit Malcolm Miller. (1¼hr., departing at the rear of the nave, Apr.-Jan. M-Sa noon and 2:45pm. 30F, students 20F.)

   If Chartres takes your fancy, bed down at **Le Boeuf Couronné,** 15 pl. Châtelet (tel.
02 37 18 06 06; fax 02 37 21 72 13), with small, airy rooms with TV and phone. From
the SNCF station, walk up av. Jehan de Beauce; the hotel is on the right-hand side
of the *place.* (Singles 158F, with shower and toilet 230F, with bath and toilet 247F;
doubles 167F, with shower and toilet 288F, with bath and toilet 310F; triples 340F.
Breakfast 30F. Showers 20F. V, MC, AmEx.) For a snack, try the wonderful *boulangerie* **Au Bon Croissant de Chartres,** 1 rue de Bois Merrain (tel. 02 37 21 36 28), at
the corner of rue de la Tonnellerie. (Sandwiches 10F, *tartes* 11F.)

   The **tourist office** (tel. 02 37 21 50 00; fax 02 37 21 51 91) is in front of the cathedral's main entrance at pl. de la Cathédrale. (Open Apr.-Sept. M-Sa 9am-7pm, Su
9:30am-5:30pm; Oct.-Mar. M-Sa 10am-6pm, Su 10am-1pm and 2:30-4:30pm.) Chartres is accessible by frequent trains from Paris's **Gare Montparnasse** (1hr.; hourly in
summer, less frequent in winter; round-trip 162F). To reach the cathedral from the
train station, walk straight along rue Jehan de Beauce to pl. de Châtelet and turn
left into the place, right onto rue Ste-Même, and left onto rue Jean Moulin.

NEAR CHARTRES: ILLIERS-COMBRAY

"Longtemps je me suis couché de bonne heure..." Thus opens **Marcel Proust's** seven-volume *Remembrance of Things Past*, considered by many to be the greatest novel of the century, and by adepts to be the greatest contribution to human civilization since our ancestors descended from the trees. The author often vacationed at his aunt's house in the sleepy village of Combray, and it served as the model for the fictional town of Illiers which dominates the first volume of the series, *Swann's way*. Already much frequented by book-carrying pilgrims, in 1971 the town celebrated Proust's 100th birthday by changing its name to Illiers-Combray. Uncut lawns, medieval ruins, half-timbered façades, and sloping roofs mark the town as an unhurried trace of the French past. Visitors should proceed from the train station down av. Georges Clemenceau and turn right onto rue de Chartres. Pick up a map of the town (10F) at the *papeterie* across from the **Église St-Jacques**—with *Swann's Way*, the *Guermantes' Way*, and other fondly remembered promenades clearly marked, the map is a pilgrim's necessity. The **Maison de Tante Léonie**, 4 rue Dr Proust, was the home of Proust's aunt who "had gradually declined to leave, first Combray, then her bedroom, and finally her bed." It was here that Proust dunked his aunt's memory-inducing *madeleines* in tea. Visits are by tour only. (Tel. 02 37 24 30 97. Open Jan. 15-Dec. 15. Tours Tu-Su 2:30 and 4pm, Sa-Su extra tour 11:30am in English; call to confirm. 30F, students 20F.) **Trains** to Illiers-Combray leave from **Chartres** irregularly; pick up a schedule before you begin your trip, and don't get left behind. (M-Sa first train 7:40am, last train back 6:40pm; Su first train 10:40am, last train back 9pm. Round-trip 54F.)

VERSAILLES

*To get to Versailles, take the **RER C5** from M/RER: Invalides in **Paris**; don't forget to buy a specific ticket, as regular metro tickets are not valid for the trip. Make sure the train name starts with "V," e.g. Vick or Vora. (30-40min., 28F).*

Today an appendage of the Parisian urban sprawl, in the early 17th century Versailles did not exist. Where today there stretch gardens, palaces, and a thriving suburban community was once just a marshy wasteland teeming with wildlife. It was the abundance of game which attracted Louis XIII to the spot; in 1624 he constructed a small hunting lodge on the remains of a feudal castle that occupied a small hill, the only dry spot in the region. When Louis XIV decided to move his capital out of Paris, he chose this spot so full of happy childhood memories and instructed his design team of Le Nôtre, Le Vau, and Le Brun to create the most magnificent palace the world had ever seen. Since the hill was too small to allow for the proposed new building, tons of earth were carried in to enlarge it, while 22,000 workmen toiled to drain the marshes and lay out the gardens; the Eure river was diverted to provide water for the fountains and ponds. Construction, begun in 1668, was not completed until 1708 (following Le Vau's death, the design had been taken over by Jules Hardouin-Mansart), and by its end Louis XIII's old hunting lodge had been enveloped by a palace capable of lodging the court's 3000 hangers-on. No one knows how much it cost—Louis XIV burnt the accounts—but its ostentation was doubtlessly a contributing factor to the Revolution. On October 5, 1789, 15,000 Parisians and National Guardsmen marched out to the palace and brought the royal family back to Paris.

Under Louis XIV, life in the **château** followed a complex daily routine centered on the king, starting with his dressing, a public spectacle attended by the courtiers who vied for his favor. Only a few rooms are open to the public, including the **grands appartements,** where the king held audience, the **Salon d'Apothon,** Louis XIV's throne room, and the **Hall of Mirrors.** The king and queen's **personal apartments** can only be seen by guided visits. (Château open Tu-Su May-Sept. 9am-6:30pm; Oct.-Apr. 9am-5:30pm. For general admission, go to Entrance A: 45F; ages 18-25, over 60, and after 3:30pm 35F. For 1hr. audio guides, go to Entrance C: 25F. For guided tours, go to Entrance D: 1hr. 25F, ages 7-17 17F; 1½hr. 37F, ages 7-17 26F; 2hr. 50F, ages 7-17 34F.)

The château, as magnificent as it is, is upstaged by the **gardens.** Filled with statues and fountains, their overall plan is due to Le Nôtre. In the center of the terrace lies the **Parterre d'Eau.** The south gate of the grove leads to the **Bassin de Bacchus,** one of four seasonal fountains. The **Parterre du Nord,** full of flowers, lawns, and trees, overlooks some of the garden's most spectacular fountains. The **Allée d'Eau** provides the best view of the **Bassin des Nymphes de Diane.** The path slopes toward the **Bassin du Dragon,** where a dying beast spurts water 25m into the air. Ninety-nine jets of water surround a menacing sea-god in the **Bassin de Neptune,** the gardens' largest fountain. On Sunday afternoons from mid-spring to mid-autumn, the fountains come to life with musical accompaniment for **Grandes Eaux Musicales.** A diminished version called the **Grande Perspective** runs 11am to noon. (Gardens open daily sunrise-sunset. Free except during Grands Eaux, mid-Apr. to mid-Oct. Sa-Su 3:30-5:30pm; 28F, under 10 free.)

The gardens hide two smaller palaces: the **Grand Trianon** and the **Petit Trianon,** built to provide respite from the pressure of château life. The Grand Trianon was built by Louis XIV, while Louis XV entertained Mme de Pompadour at the Petit Trianon. If you don't fancy walking to the Trianons (25min.), a *petit train* runs from the palace (32F, ages 3-12 20F). (Both open May-Sept. Tu-Sa 10am-6:30pm; Oct.-Apr. Tu-F 10am-12:30pm and 2-5:30pm, Sa-Su 10am-5:30pm. Grand Trianon 25F, reduced 15F. Petit Trianon 15F, reduced 10F. Combined ticket 30F, reduced 20F.)

FONTAINEBLEAU

*Hourly **trains** run to Fontainebleau from the banlieue section of Paris's **Gare de Lyon** (45min., 94F round-trip). The château is a 30-minute walk or 10-minute bus ride away. From the station, **Car Vert A** (tel. 01 64 22 23 88) runs buses (9.50F) after each train arrival from Paris; take the bus (direction "Château-Lilas") to "Château." You can also **cycle** to the château; rent a bike at the station from **MBK.** (Tel. 01 64 22 36 14. 60-120F per day. Helmets 10F. Open daily 9am-7pm. V, MC.) Opposite the château, the **tourist office,** 4 rue Royal (tel. 01 60 74 99 99; fax. 01 60 74 80 22), organizes village tours, helps find rooms, and has maps of Fontainebleau and Barbizon. (Open M-Sa 9:30am-6:30pm, Su 10am-4pm.)*

Kings of France had long enjoyed hunting in the Forêt de Fontainebleau before François I decided to build himself a not-so-modest hunting lodge there in 1528. A big fan of the Renaissance, François imported a drove of Italian artists to work on his new château, including Il Primatice and Michelangelo's pupil Il Rosso. Together with an army of French craftsmen, they created the first truly Renaissance château in France, and the palace gave rise to the first school of Renaissance French painting, the School of Fontainebleau. The château also saw many events of historical significance, including Louis XIII's birth, Louis XIV's revocation of the Edict of Nantes, and Napoleon's farewell to his empire in 1814.

The **Grands Appartements** provide a lesson in the history of French architecture and decoration. Printed guides (20-30F) will make your visit to the château, gardens, and Grands Appartements more meaningful. The **King's Cabinet** was the site of *le débotter*, the king's post-hunt boot removal. Since the 17th century, every queen and empress of France has slept in the gold and green **Queen's Bed Chamber;** the gilded wood bed was built for Marie-Antoinette. The N on the red and gold velvet throne of the **Throne Room** is a testament to Napoleon's humility, while his **Bed Chamber,** sandwiched between two mirrors, is a monument to either narcissism or eroticism. The château houses a number of Napoleon-oriented museums, including the **Musée Napoléon,** with a collection of the Emperor's toothbrush, shoes, field tent, his son's toys, and state gifts from European monarchs. The **Musée Chinois de l'Impératrice Eugénie** houses the Empress's collection of Chinese decorative art, porcelain, jade, and crystal. The **Petits Appartements,** private rooms of Napoleon and the Empress Josephine, are accessible only by guided tours. (Château: tel. 01 60 71 50 70; open July-Aug. W-M 9:30am-6pm, May-June and Sept.-Oct. W-M 9:30am-5pm, Nov.-Apr. W-M 9:30am-12:30pm and 2-5pm; 35F, students, seniors, and Su 23F, under 18 free; includes Musée Chinois. Musée Napoleon: 16F, under 26 and over 60 12F, under 18 free. Petits Appartements: tours M and holidays 10am, 11am, 2pm, and 3pm; 16F, under 26 and over 60 12F, under 18 free.)

Unlike Versailles's extensive formal gardens, Fontainebleau's modest **Jardin Anglais** and **Jardin de Diane** feature quiet grottoes guarded by statues of the Greek huntress and the **Étang des Carpes,** a carp-filled pond that you can explore by rowboat. (Boats available June-Aug. daily 10am-12:30pm and 2-7pm; Sept. Sa-Su 2-6pm. 50F per 30min., 80F per hr.) The **Forêt de Fontainebleau** is a thickly wooded, 20,000 hectare preserve with hiking trails, bike paths, and sandstone rock-climbing.

VAUX-LE-VICOMTE

*Vaux is 50km from Paris; getting here is exquisite torture. There is no bus service from the **RER** in **Melun** (45min., round-trip 90F), 7km away, and the 1½-hour walk is along a busy highway. The best option is to come by **car.** Take Autoroute A4 or A6 from Paris and exit at Val-Maubué or Melun, respectively. Head toward Meaux on N36 and follow the signs. The **tourist office,** 2 av. Galliéni (tel. 01 64 37 11 31), by the Melun station, helps with accommodations and provides free maps. Open Tu-Sa 10am-noon and 2-6pm.)*

It was Nicolas Fouquet, Louis XIV's minister of finance, who first assembled the famous triumvirate of Le Vau, Le Brun, and Le Nôtre to build Vaux-le-Vicomte (tel. 01 64 14 41 90; www.vaux-le-vicomte.com) in 1656. Upon its completion in 1661, Nick threw an extravagant 6000-guest party in honor of Louis XIV, premiering poetry by La Fontaine and a comedy by Molière. Louis wasn't just impressed by the château—he was infuriated at being outclassed by his minister. Fouquet was arrested, and the château's designers put to work on a new project: Versailles.

Vaux-le-Vicomte's designers integrated painting and sculpture, architecture and decor, incorporating a number of *trompe l'œil* tricks. The first to be aware of is that the moat is completely invisible from the road. In many ways, the château is a forerunner of Versailles; in the **Minister's Bedchamber,** an opulent red and gold bed stands under an allegorically decorated ceiling depicting Apollo bearing the lights of the world, while **Mme Fouquet's Closet** once had walls lined with mirrors. Le Brun's **Room of the Muses** is one of his finest decorative schemes. The ornate **King's Bedchamber** boasts an orgy of cherubs and lions fluttering around the centerpiece, Le Brun's *Time Bearing Truth Heavenward.* On Saturday evenings in summer, the château is candle-lit for night-time visits.

Vaux-le-Vicomte also presented Le Nôtre with his first opportunity to create an entire garden. Three villages, a small château, and 70 acres of trees were destroyed and a river rerouted to create the first true French formal garden, with sculpted shrubberies strategically placed to create classical harmony and optical illusions. The **Pool of the Crown,** named for the gold crown at its center, is the most ornate of the garden ponds, while the **Water Mirror** was designed to reflect the château perfectly. A climb to the **Farnese Hercules,** a 19th-century addition to the gardens, rewards with a nice vista. (Château and gardens open daily Mar. 11-Nov. 11 10am-6pm. Château and gardens 62F; students, seniors, and ages 6-16 49F. Gardens alone 30F; students, seniors, and ages 6-16 27F. Evening visits: May-Sept. Sa 8pm-midnight; 80F, students, seniors, and ages 6-16 70F.)

CHANTILLY

*Trains leave for Chantilly-Gouvieux from **Paris's** Gare du Nord (Grandes Lignes) (35min., approximately every hr. 5am-midnight, round-trip 82F). Free and frequent **shuttles** to the château leave from the bus station to the left as you exit the train station. Otherwise, the château is a pleasant half-hour walk from the station. The **tourist office,** 60 av. du Maréchal Joffre, offers brochures, maps, and a shuttle-bus schedule. To get there from the station, go straight ahead up rue des Ôtages; the office is on the right. (Tel. 03 44 57 08 58. Open daily May-Sept. 9am-6pm; Oct.-Apr. M-Sa 9am-12:30pm and 2-6pm.) To continue to the château, leave the office, turn left on av. Maréchal Joffre, and then right on rue de Connetable (2km).*

The small, picturesque **Château de Chantilly** is devoid of whipped cream, but instead offers gardens, lakes, and canals. The present-day château was built in the 1870s by the duc d'Aumale, Louis-Philippe's fifth son, but the main attraction is the **garden** laid out by Le Nôtre for Louis XIV's cousin, Le Grand Condé, in the 17th century. Directly in front of the château, the gardens' central expanse is designed in the French formal style, with neat rows of carefully pruned trees and calm statues overlooking geometric pools. To the right, hidden within a forest, the rambling English garden attempts untamed nature. Windows carved into the foliage allow you to see fountains in the formal garden as you stroll. The gardens also hide a play village **Hameau,** the inspiration for Marie-Antoinette's hamlet at Versailles. Elsewhere, a statue of Cupid reigns over the "Island of Love." If you want to see the château and grounds all at once, levitate for 10 minutes in the world's largest **hot air balloon** (attached to the ground by a cable), which rises 150m, providing a view as far as the Eiffel Tower in clear weather. Inside, the château's **Musée Condé** houses the duke's private collection of pre-modern paintings, the second largest in France. Among the 700 canvases are works by Raphael, Titian, Corot, Delacroix, and Ingres. Per the duc d'Aumale's will, the paintings and furniture are arranged as they were over a century ago. The rest of the castle can only be visited by frequent guided tours in French; highlights include a **Gutenberg Bible** and a facsimile of the château's most famous possession, the **Très Riches Heures du Duc de Berry,** a 15th-century manuscript illustrating medieval life in France by season. (Tel. 03 44 62 62 62. Open Mar.-Oct. W-M 10am-6pm; Nov.-Feb. M and W-F 10:30am-12:45pm and 2-5pm, Sa-Su 10:30am-5pm. Castle and park 39F, students 34F, children 12F. Castle, park, and boat tour 69F, students 64F, children 32F. Park only 17F, students 17F, children 10F. Balloon 49F, students 43F, children 28F.)

The approach to the castle passes the **Grandes Écuries,** which once housed 240 horses and hundreds of hunting dogs. The stables were originally founded by Louis-Henri Bourbon, who hoped to live in them when he was reincarnated as a horse. They now house the **Musée Vivant du Cheval,** a run-down museum dealing with all things equine. During the first weekend of every month and Christmas, holiday-themed equestrian shows, such as "Horse and Gospel" are a highlight. Two of France's premier horse races are held here in June. In mid-September, **Polo at the Hippodrome** is free to the public. (Château tel. 03 44 57 13 13. Open Apr.-Oct. M and W-F 10:30am-6:30pm, Sa-Su 10:30am-7pm; May-Aug. also open Tu 10:30am-5:30pm. Call for schedule of horse shows. Museum and shows 50F, students and seniors 45F.)

DISNEYLAND PARIS

*To get to Disneyland, take the **RER A4** from Paris to **Marne-la-Vallée;** make sure the stop is lit up on the departure board or the train will terminate earlier (45min., every 30min. until 12:22am, round-trip 76F). The extravagant or railpass-holders can take the **TGV** directly from Roissy-Charles de Gaulle airport (15min.). Otherwise, **Disneyland Paris Buses** make the rounds between the terminals of both Orly and Roissy/Charles de Gaulle airports and the bus station near the Marne-la-Vallée RER (40min.; every 45-60min. 8:30am-7:45pm, 8:30am-10pm at CDG on weekends; round-trip 85F). At weekends, it can take 2hr. in line to by a **ticket** (passeport) at the park; instead purchase them at the Paris tourist office on the Champs-Élysées, or at RER A stations. (Park open daily July 11-Aug. 9am-11pm; Apr.-May and Sept.-June hours vary. Apr.-Sept. and Dec. 23-Jan. 7 220F, ages 3-11 170F; off-season 175F, ages 3-11 145F. 2- and 3-day passeports also available.)*

It's a small, small world, and Disney is bent on making it even smaller. When Euro-Disney opened in 1992, Mickey was met by the jeers of French intellectuals and the popular press, who called the Disney theme park a "cultural Chernobyl." At first it seemed their hopes that the park would fail were justified, but since being renamed Disneyland Paris, it's taken off. To help visitors minimize their exposure to France, there's even a direct Eurostar service from London.

Inside, there are all the standard Disneyland attractions, annotated in a multitude of languages. The park entrance gives onto **Main Street USA,** a sanitized turn-of-the-century depiction of small town America. Not quite what Charles Perrault had in mind when he penned his fairy tale at the Château d'Ussé in the Loire Valley (see p. 570), the pink **Sleeping Beauty's Castle** stands over a plasticized cave containing a high-tech, smoke-breathing dragon. Behind the château lies the pre-school oriented **Fantasyland. Adventureland** awaits the intrepid with a mix of themes from so-called adventurous regions: the Middle East, West Africa, and the Caribbean. One of the better rides in the park is **Indiana Jones and the Temple of Doom,** featuring the first 360° loop on a Disney ride. Light-years away on the other side of the park, **Discoveryland** flaunts the park's latest technological wizardry. The newest ride is the frightening **Space Mountain** roller-coaster, which travels at speeds of 70km per hour through three loops in pitch blackness, while a synchronized eight-speaker sound track immerses you in the illusion that you're being shot all the way to the moon. Disney also puts on a variety of special daily events, including the **Disney Character Parade** and the evening **Main Street Electrical Parade,** both with many elaborate floats and performers. **Eating** in the park is expensive; though it's prohibited to bring your own food into the park (and they do search bags at the entrance), most French people smuggle in a picnic and eat it surreptitiously. If you are forced to sup in the Magic Kingdom, take solace in the fact that this is the only Disney-run attraction in the world where you can buy a beer.

THE CENTER

Central France is often overlooked by tourists speeding south from Paris towards the attractions of the coasts. Thanks to the benign neglect engendered by its smokestack reputation, most of the region has escaped the deleterious effects of mass tourism; still continuing in its traditional lifestyle, it is here that cliché meets reality. With medieval abbeys, *grands vins*, outstanding cuisine, and magnificent châteaux, this is France in all its preconceived glory. But there are other sides to central France: you can revel in unspoiled countryside, from the vineyards of the Beaujolais to the extinct volcanoes of the Massif Cen-

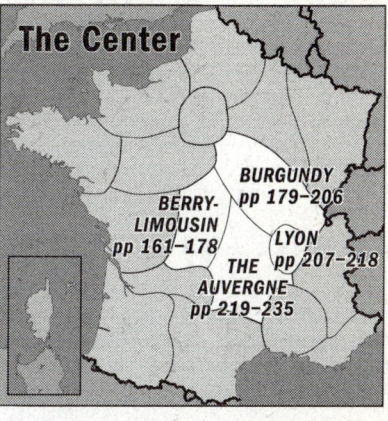

The Center

BURGUNDY pp 179–206

BERRY-LIMOUSIN pp 161–178

LYON pp 207–218

THE AUVERGNE pp 219–235

tral. While technophile France hurtles into the millennium in Lyon, a hundred miles away pilgrims still pay homage to the Virgin in the medieval town of Le Puy-en-Velay.

HISTORY: THE HEARTLAND OF A NATION

From heroic resistance against foreign invaders to deadly civil strife, the geographical center of the nation underlines its position as the historic heartland of France. The first evidence of the crucial role it was to play came as early as 53 BC, when Gaulish chieftain Vercingetorix delivered a stunning victory over Julius Cæsar at Gergovia in the Auvergne. This was followed a few months later by an even more stunning defeat at Alesia, in Burgundy, as the overconfident Gauls attacked a reinforced and vengeful Cæsar. Vercingetorix was paraded in chains through Rome and later strangled, Gaulish resistance collapsed, and the way was open for Roman domination of Western Europe.

In the 5th century a Germanic tribe from the Baltic, the Burgundians, took advantage of an enfeebled Roman Empire to move in and found a kingdom around the fertile plains of the Rhône valley. They themselves fell in 534 to the Franks, fresh from conquering the Auvergne in 507 under the recently-baptized Clovis (see p. 7). After Charlemagne's death in 814, war engulfed the Frankish empire until the treaty of Verdun (see p. 7) in 843, when the region was given to the new kingdom of West Francia—the prototype France. With the abbeys of Cluny, Cîteaux, and Clairvaux, Burgundy became the center of medieval Christianity, while in the Auvergne, Pope Urban III proclaimed the First Crusade from Clermont in 1095.

During the Middle Ages the kings of France struggled to impose their authority on the region. The Auvergne was brought under royal control by 1213, but Burgundy remained a threat, allying itself with the English in the Hundred Years' War. With half of France in hostile hands, his enemies mocked the dauphin Charles VII as "King of Bourges." In 1440, Duke Philip the Good switched sides to the French, bringing Flanders, Belgium, and Luxembourg under his control. Charles the Bold continued his father's territorial expansion, but upon his death in 1477 King Louis XI finally annexed Burgundy. The duke had the last laugh—his grandson was Charles V, Holy Roman Emperor and the nemesis of French king François I.

In the 15th century, Lyon became the financial center of Europe. Home to France's first printing press, Lyon's importance increased further with the establishment of the silk industry in the 16th century, and contented locals saw no reason to support the Revolution in 1789. In revenge, the Committee of Public Safety declared *"Lyon n'est plus"* ("Lyon is no longer") and guillotined thousands.

A new crisis arose in 1863. The deadly root disease phylloxera devastated the Beaujolais vineyards, reaching Burgundy in 1878. Since the native vines were help-less against the disease, the only solution was to plant American vines and graft cuttings of local stock onto the foreign stalks. In return, Lyon gave America the cinema, invented by the Lumière brothers in 1895.

When the Germans took control of Paris in 1940, the quiet spa town of Vichy achieved infamy as the seat of Pétain's collaborationist government. Vichy France would last until 1944, despite the valiant efforts of the Resistance, whose leader-ship took refuge in the twisting medieval tunnels of Lyon. In the 1970s and 1980s, the French government built an impressive network of *autoroutes* and high-speed rail links to allow travelers to more efficiently bypass this fascinating region.

CLIMATE AND GEOGRAPHY

The dominant geographical feature is the **Massif Central,** an enormous granite pla-teau extending from the Rhône Valley eastwards across the **Auvergne** and **Limousin.** Dotted with extinct volcanoes, hot springs and crater lakes serve as a reminder of its fiery past. Winter brings skiers to the highlands, while in summer hikers take advantage of the altitude to escape the heat of the plains. Between the Massif and the Parisian basin lie the fertile plains and gentle hills of **Berry.** North and east of Berry, the central plateaux of **Burgundy** suddenly drop into the plains of the Saône Valley, creating perfect grape-growing conditions on the east-facing slopes of the Côte d'Or. Clear weather in the winter brings cold weather to the highlands of the Morvan, while summers are warm and dry. Autumn is the most attractive season, pleasant and luminous—perfect for the grape harvest.

SUGGESTIONS

To many people, Burgundy means one thing: **wine.** The **Côte d'Or** (p. 190) produces more famous wines than seems possible for its tiny size; nestled between Bur-gundy and the Lyonnais, the **Beaujolais** (p. 218) harbors more affordable offerings. Those in search of a **religious experience** are spoilt for choice. Benedictine **Cluny** (p. 198) was the center of a monastic empire in the Middle Ages. Pity the **pilgrims** who must decide between worshipping the Sacred Heart at the magnificent basilica of **Paray-le-Monial** (p. 195), or the Virgin Mary at medieval **Le-Puy-en-Velay** (p. 228) in the Auvergne. You can take the waters while pondering the vagaries of history at **Vichy** (p. 232), or paraglide off the **Puy-de-Dôme** (p. 224) near Clermont-Ferrand. Anchor-ing the whole of southern France, **Lyon** (p. 220) is France's second-largest city, with all the history, fine art, and refined cuisine that that entails.

BERRY-LIMOUSIN

All too often passed over for beaches and bigger cities, Berry-Limousin offers peaceful countryside, tiny villages, and striking cities. Its land-locked position and lack of world-famous attractions have made it very much the poorer sister of its neighbors when it comes to attracting tourist dollars—so much the better for the intrepid few who do venture here! During the 50-year period of Angevin domi-nance (12th century), the region was absorbed into the empire of the Anglo-French king-dukes until Philippe-Auguste wrested it from John Lackland in 1200. In the 14th century, Limousin gave three popes to Avignon, the last of whom, Gre-gory XI, was responsible for the return of the papacy to Rome. During the same period, Berry was in the hands of Jean de Berry, third son of King Jean le Bon. Though his greed and treachery resulted in Berry being besieged by the Royal Army in 1412, the duke is most famous for commissioning the exquisite book of medieval miniatures, *Les Très Riches Heures du Duc de Berry.* On Jean's death,

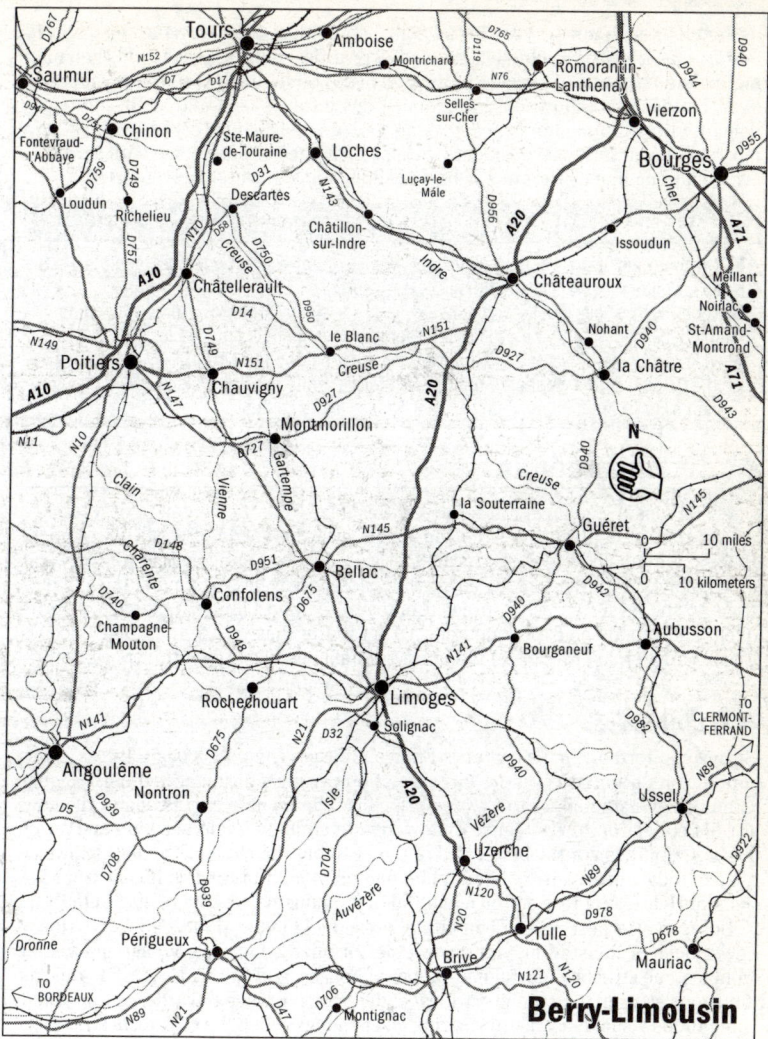

Berry-Limousin

Berry passed to the dauphin Charles VII—and just in time, for the English were in possession of Paris. Bourges found itself the capital of France, and benefited from the lavish attention of the kings' financier, Jacques Cœur, who built the lavish string of château now forming the Routes Jacques Cœur. In later years, Berry-Limousin proved its worth as a breeding ground for artistic and literary talent, giving the world Georges Sand, Auguste Renoir, and Jean Giraudoux.

Nourished by the waters of the Cher, Indre, Creuse, and Vienne rivers, the countryside is rippled by hills, forests, and yawning valleys. The land does not lend itself to agriculture but is perfectly suited to the Limousin cattle. The wrap-around *limousine* capes worn by the local herdsmen somehow gave their name to the first fabric-covered, enclosed luxury motor-cars.

While Berry produces wines of the highest quality—those of Sancerre, Menetou-Salon, Châteaumeillant, and Valençay are particularly well-known—local specialties such as *soupe au pain* (bread soup) sound less than enticing. Instead, try *poulet en barbouille*, chicken roasted over a fire, cut in pieces, and then simmered in a creamy sauce made of its own blood mixed with cream, egg yolk, and liver. Limousin is renowned throughout France for its beef and lamb, often garnished with walnuts, honey, *chèvre*, and local mushrooms (*cêpes*, truffles, and morrels). Local fruit-based liqueurs are also highly regarded; try one with a *clafoutis*, a pudding-like dessert of a light, eggy dough baked with black cherries.

HIGHLIGHTS OF BERRY-LIMOUSIN

■ **Oradour-sur-Glane**, a farming village whose inhabitants were massacred by SS troops, remains eerily unchanged since 1944 (p. 178).
■ Those with a slim pocketbook should head for sightly **Bourges**. Three museums, a stunning cathedral, and a maze of medieval streets can all be relished for free (p. 164).
■ Visit the home of George Sand in **Nohant**, near charming **La Châtre** (p. 173).
■ The 100km *Grand Sentier* of the **Val du Creuse** winds through a lush river valley past Roman ruins, 12th-century churches, and grassy lakeside beaches (p. 172).

GETTING AROUND

Berry-Limousin's greatest attraction—that it's far from the beaten tourist track—means that transportation is not designed with the needs of travelers in mind. Even if a limousine is out of your budget, you may want to consider renting a car or bike to explore the region, since while most towns have train and bus connections to the larger cities (Bourges, Châteauroux, and Limoges), service is infrequent and scheduled for commuters. To get to the châteaux of the Route Jacques Cœur or the smaller towns of the interior, you'll need your own transportation.

BOURGES

Sitting comfortably in the center of France, Bourges (pop. 76,000 *bourgeois*) owes much of its popularity to the largesse of a corrupt politician. In 1433, Jacques Cœur, financial minister to Charles VII, chose the humble city as one of the sites for his collection of châteaux. Endowed with some marvelous sights and a rich history, Bourges got the better end of the deal, but the city nonetheless shows its thanks today; nearly every laundromat and pizza joint in town is named after Mr. Jack of Hearts, not to mention a handful of monuments erected in his honor.

Bourges also possesses a beautifully preserved medieval *vieille ville;* within a few blocks of the station, you can wander through a fairy-tale village of twisting cobblestone streets, colorful half-timbered houses, and Gothic turrets. If you ever find your way out, one of the grandest cathedrals in France rewards visitors with a sumptuous visual feast. During spring and summer, when the city hosts two major music festivals, the bars of the old city overflow with live music.

ORIENTATION AND PRACTICAL INFORMATION

While its narrow streets delight camera-toters, they are frustrating to anyone with a specific destination. Head straight (well, crooked) from the station for the tourist office and its invaluable map.

Trains: Pl. Général Leclerc. To: **Nevers** (1hr., 7 per day, 50F); **Tours** (1½hr., 15 per day, 123F); **Clermont-Ferrand** (2hr., 4 per day, 123F); and **Paris** (2½hr., 4 per day, 153F). Many trains require a change at Vierzon. Info office open M-Sa 9am-6:30pm. Ticket office open daily 6am-9:15pm.

Buses: Rue Pré Doulet (tel. 02 48 24 36 42). Office closed July-Aug.; Sept.-June open M-Tu and Th-F 8-9:30am and 4-6pm, W and Sa 8am-noon. Services operated by **Cariane Centre**, 12 av. Jean Jaurès (tel. 02 48 70 45 89), **Socetra**, 88 rte. d'Orlenans (tel. 02

The Center

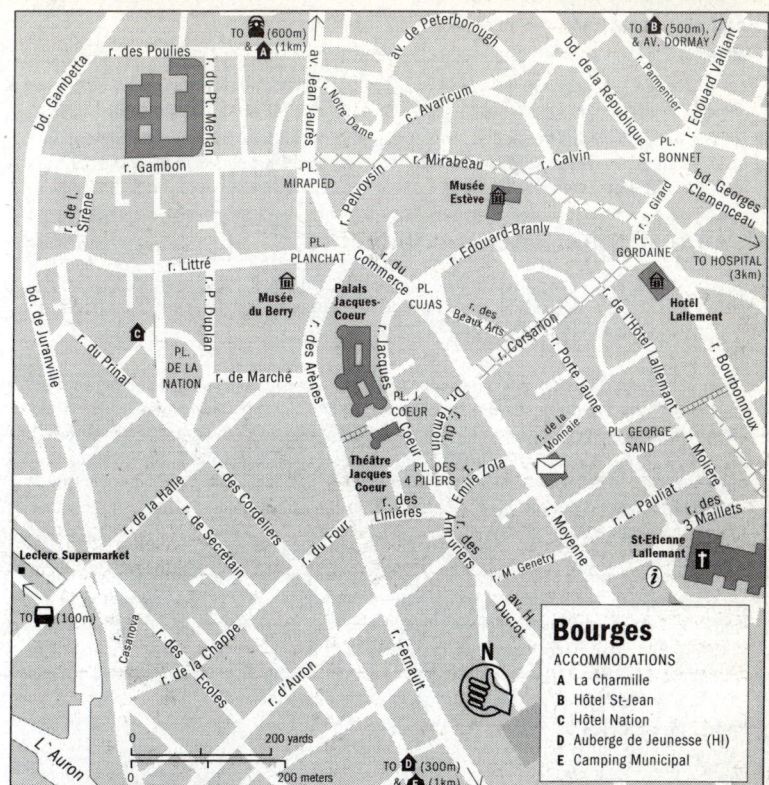

Bourges
ACCOMMODATIONS
A La Charmille
B Hôtel St-Jean
C Hôtel Nation
D Auberge de Jeunesse (HI)
E Camping Municipal

THE CENTER

48 23 90 10), and **TDM,** 169 chemin de Villeneuve (tel. 02 48 21 05 21). To: **Châteauroux** (1¾hr., 2 per day, 28F) and **Vierzon** (1¼hr., 3 per day, 20F). Schedules posted at the station.

Local Transportation: CTB (tel. 02 48 50 82 82). Schedules at station. Tickets 7F, *carnet* of 10 52F.

Taxis: Radio-Taxis de Bourges (tel. 02 48 24 50 00). 24hr.

Bike Rental: Narcy, 31 av. Marx-Dormoy (tel. 02 48 70 15 84). 40F per half-day, 60F per day. Credit card deposit. Open Tu-Sa 9am-noon and 2-7pm.

Tourist Office: 21 rue Victor Hugo (tel. 02 48 23 02 60; fax 02 48 23 02 69), facing rue Moyenne near the cathedral. To get there from the train station, follow av. H. Laudier and its continuation, av. Jean Jaurès, into the *vieille ville.* From there, bear left onto rue du Commerce, then right two blocks later onto rue Moyenne, which leads to the office (15min.). Or catch bus #1 (direction "Val d'Auron," 6F) to "Victor Hugo." Excellent free maps and info. **Walking tours** (1½hr., in French) July-Sept. daily at 3pm. (30F, students 20F.) **Night tours** July-Aug. F-Sa 8:30pm. (40F, students 30F.) Open July-Sept. M-Sa 9am-7:30pm, Su 10am-7:30pm; Oct.-June M-Sa 9am-6pm, Su 10am-12:30pm.

Money: Banque de France, 1bis av. Eugène Brisson (tel. 0800 10 15 20), behind the cathedral, has good rates of **currency exchange.** Exchange desk open M-F 9-11:30am.

Youth Center: BIJ, Halle/St-Bonnet, bd. de la République (tel. 02 48 24 77 19), offers information on local discounts, budget travel, and lodging. Open July-Aug. M-F 10am-noon and 2-5pm; Sept.-June 8:30am-noon and 1-5:30pm, W until 7pm.

Laundromat: Lavomatiques, 117 rue Édouard Valliant and 15 bd. Juranville. Open daily 7am-8pm.

Hospital: 145 rue François Mitterrand (tel. 02 48 48 48 48).

Police: 163 av. de St-Amand (tel. 02 48 55 85 00).

Post Office: 29 rue Moyenne (tel. 02 48 68 82 82). **Currency exchange.** Poste Restante code: 18012 Bourges Cedex. Open M-F 8am-7pm, Sa 8am-noon. **Postal code:** 18000.

Internet Access: Mediathèque, bd. Lamarck (tel. 02 48 23 22 50). To avoid waiting for the 3 computers, get a ticket and return in a few hours. Open July-Aug. Tu-Sa 12:30-6:30pm, Sa 9am-noon; Sept.-June M-F same hours plus Th until 8pm, Sa 10am-5pm.

█ ACCOMMODATIONS AND CAMPING

While the youth hostel is convenient and reliable, Bourges' cheaper hotels are outside the *centre ville*; moreover, unoccupied beds may be hard to find during major festivals and in the height of summer.

Auberge de Jeunesse (HI), 22 rue Henri Sellier (tel. 02 48 24 58 09), 10min. from the center of town. From the station, take av. H. Laudier onto av. Jean Jaurès to pl. Planchat. Head straight along rue des Arènes, which becomes rue Fernault. At the busy intersection, cross over to rue René Ménard, which curves around a pink wall to the right. Turn left at the brown fence (rue Henri Sellier), and follow the street about another block; the hostel is on the right, set back from the street behind a brown and white building (25min.). Alternatively, take bus #1 (direction "Val d'Auron") to "Conde." From the bus stop, cross the parking lot to your right, keeping your eye out for a paved footpath to the left that traverses the park patch in front of you. Take the path down, and continue straight ahead down rue Vieil Castel. The hostel is across the street at the bottom, 30m down a driveway slightly to your right. Bar, snack bar, laundry, slightly grimy kitchen, but clean 3- to 8-bunk rooms, some with private showers. 49F. Sheets 18F. Breakfast 19F. Reception M-F 8am-noon and 2-11pm, Sa-Su 8am-noon and 5-10pm. Ask for door code to avoid 11pm curfew and noon-2pm lockout.

Centre International de Séjour, "La Charmille," 17 rue Félix-Chédin (tel. 02 48 23 07 40; fax 02 48 69 01 21). Cross the footbridge over the tracks at the station and head up rue Félix-Chédin (5min.). This lively center—half hostel, half *foyer*—is the skateboard mecca of Europe, with bowls, ramps, and half-pipes to prove it. In summer, many of the world's best skaters offer classes. All rooms have showers. TV room. Laundry. Singles 99F, 73F for three or more. Breakfast. Meals 53F. V, MC.

La Nation, 24 pl. de la Nation (tel. 02 48 24 11 96), is the closest budget hotel to the *centre ville*, in a quiet, spacious square. Singles 105F, with shower 135F; doubles 120F; twins 155F. Breakfast 25F. Closed July 6-Aug. 4.

Hôtel St-Jean, 23 av. Marx-Dormoy (tel. 02 48 24 13 48; fax 02 48 24 79 98), offers well-furnished rooms with phone and TV. Singles 125F, with shower and toilet 135-150F, with bath 190F; doubles 145F, with shower and toilet 170-190F, with bath 210-160F. Shower 20F. Breakfast 21-28F. V, MC.

Camping Municipal, 26 bd. de l'Industrie (tel. 02 48 20 16 85). Follow directions to the *auberge* but continue on rue Henri Sellier and turn right on bd. de l'Industrie. 18F per person, 18F per tent and car, 26F per caravan. Open Mar. 15-Nov. 15.

█ FOOD

On **pl. Gordaine** and **rue des Beaux-Arts,** outdoor tables fill with convivial locals in spring and summer. If you want a touch more elegance, a few restaurants along rue Bourbonnoux allow you to sup on regional specialties in a more intimate setting. Look for specialties such as *poulet en barbouille* (chicken roasted in aromatic red wine) and *oeufs en meurette* (eggs in red wine). The largest **market** takes place on pl. de la Nation (Sa morning), another livens up pl. des Marronniers (Th until 1pm), and there is a smaller **covered market** at pl. St-Bonnet (Tu-Sa 7:30am-1pm and 3-7:30pm, Su 7:30am-1pm). Cheap sandwich shops lie on **rue Moyenne** and **rue Mirabeau,** while the huge **Leclerc supermarket,** rue Prado off bd.

Juraville, can provide the fixings for your own culinary experiments. (Open M-F 9:15am-7:20pm, Sa 8:30am-7:20pm.)

🅂 **Cake-Thé,** 74 promenade des Remparts (tel. 02 48 24 94 60). In an enchanting lavender-lined hidden passage, this beautiful little *salon de thé* pampers with soothing music, flowers and lace, and fresh brews. Bite into a cake or pastry (18-25F) for a slice of heaven while you take in the lovingly decorated interior. Teas 12-20F, coffee 18F. Open Tu-Sa 3-7pm; closed Aug. V, MC.

D'Antan Sancerrois, 50 rue Bourbonnoux (tel. 02 48 65 96 26). Excellent dining in a pleasant spot. Delicious grilled salmon in lemon thyme sauce (68F) will vie for your favor with the *jambon de Sancerre fumé aux sarments de vigne* (48F). *Oeufs en meurette* 36F. Deservedly popular, so arrive early or very late on weekends. Open Tu 7-10:30pm, W-Su noon-2pm and 7-10:30pm. V, MC, AmEx.

Le Phénicien, 13 rue Jean Girard off pl. Gordaine (tel. 02 48 65 01 37). This Middle Eastern house of nosh embodies the *Let's Go* creed, offering the penniless pita permutations for a pittance. Lunch *menu* with 4 appetizers and *plat* 42F, with dessert and *café* 53F. Open M-Sa 11am-11pm.

👁 SIGHTS

SIGHTS. One of France's most magnificent cathedrals, the 13th-century **Cathédrale St-Étienne** preserves a fantastic Gothic façade on its west side. Amongst its five portals is a Last Judgment scene, in which six rows of disciples swim minnow-like head to tail around the sitting Jesus; angelic smiles of souls bound for the eternal Jerusalem contrast with the grimaces of demons stewing the damned. The cathedral's design is unconventional, with no transepts opening up the nave in the center; running along these straight walls is a stunning set of 13th-century stained glass. Prominent organists play summer concerts; if you're lucky, you'll walk in on a practice session. (Tourist office has concert schedule; tickets 75F, students 50F. Cathedral open daily July-Aug. 8am-9pm, June and Sept. 8:30am-7:30pm; Oct.-May 8:30am-6:30pm. Crypt and towers open daily 9am-6pm, unguided visits 2-7pm only. 32F, students 21F; 30F *billet jumelé* includes Palais Jacques Cœur.)

Not exactly a testimony to the conniving financier's own egotistical motto *"A vaillants Cœurs, rien d'impossible"* ("To bold Hearts, nothing is impossible"), the **Palais Jacques-Cœur,** rue Jacques-Cœur (tel. 02 48 24 06 87), impresses nonetheless. This example of a successful 15th-century businessman's townhouse was restored just two years ago, the cleaned-up eastern façade glowing once again for the first time in 500 years. The palace is unfurnished, but exquisite carved mantelpieces, crooked ceilings built in the shape of ship galleys, and a dramatically decorated chapel still remain, along with a barrage of hearts and scallops (the symbol of St. James) to remind you who owned it all. In 45 minutes you'll see more of the palace than Jacques ever did; he was imprisoned in 1451, years before its completion. (French tours leave hourly July-Aug. 9:15am-6:10pm; Apr.-June and Sept. 9:15am-noon and 2-5:10pm; Oct.-Mar. 9:15am-noon and 2-4:10pm. Extensive English follow-along text available. 32F, ages 18-24 21F.)

Bourges also offers three free museums. The **Musée du Berry,** rue des Arènes (tel. 02 48 57 81 15), gathers locally-excavated prehistoric, Gallo-Roman, and medieval artifacts in a 16th-century *hôtel.* (Open W-Sa 10am-noon and 2-6pm, Su 10am-noon.) A 15th-century merchant built the **Hôtel Lallemant,** 6 rue Bourbonnoux (tel. 02 48 57 81 17), which houses furniture, tapestries, and decorative works from the 16th to 18th centuries. (Open Tu-Sa 10am-noon and 2-6pm, Su 10am-noon.) The **Musée Estève,** 13 rue Édouard Branly (tel. 02 48 24 75 38), displays paintings by the turn-of-the-century French artist. Estève's early realism gave way to a cubist bent; look for *le Sculpteur,* an amorphous composition which stretches the imagination to its limits. (Open W-Sa 10am-noon and 2-6pm, Su 10am-noon.)

If the free museums, a stunning cathedral, a 15th-century palace, and a dizzying rainbow of half-timbered houses isn't enough for you, make sure you discover

Bourges' more peaceful natural refuges. The **Archbishop's Garden,** behind the cathedral, is the perfect spot for a shady picnic, while the **Jardin des Près-Fichaux,** off bd. de la République, adds a beautiful river to the scene. The wonderful **promenade des Remparts** hides between rue Bourbonnoux and rue Molière, offering a quiet stroll past Roman ramparts and flower-filled back gardens.

🎵 🎆 ENTERTAINMENT AND FESTIVALS

ENTERTAINMENT. Bars and cafés pepper the *vieille ville,* and if you're there in spring or summer, you may be in for a late night. **La Comédie,** 10 pl. Mirepied (tel. 02 48 65 95 85), on the corner of rue du Commerce and av. Jean Jaurès, is a sleek underground club crowded with gay men during the week. (Open W-M 10pm-4am. 60F including first drink.) On rue d'Auron, close to rue Labbé, the late-night crowd gathers at **Pub Dublin** for pool and meters of beer (from 70F).

FESTIVALS. Over 200,000 ears perk up in April for the **Festival Printemps de Bourges.** Most tickets cost 50-180F, but some informal folk, jazz, classical, and rock concerts are free. (Contact the Association Printemps de Bourges, rue Henri Sellier. Tel. 02 48 70 61 11.) The city gets *avant-garde* in early June for the **Festival International des Groupes de Musique Experimentale de Bourges** (tel. 02 48 20 41 87). From June 21 until September 15, there is free culture every night during **Un Été à Bourges,** a conflagration of classical and rock concerts and theater (tickets 50-90F, some events free).

ROUTE JACQUES CŒUR

Jacques may have left his *cœur* in Bourges, but his ego spilled far into the surrounding countryside. The Route Jacques Cœur is the name given to a string of 17 châteaux (plus one 12th-century abbey thrown in for good measure), many once owned by Jacques, that stretches from La Buissière in the north to Culan in the south. Less ostentatious than those of the Loire, these castles see much less tourism than their northwestern neighbors. The tourist offices in Bourges (p. 164) and St-Amand-Montrond (see below) have free maps of the Route in English, and can provide information on transport and bus excursions. Make sure to get a stamp at each château—see four and the fifth is free. The châteaux are less than 90km from Bourges, but you'll need a car or bike to reach them; if you decide to stay the night, be sure to make arrangements in advance, or you could be in for a hefty bill. Bourges' **Comité Départmental de Tourisme du Cher,** 5 rue Sérancourt (tel. 02 48 67 00 18), can also help with arrangements.

SOUTH OF BOURGES

ST-AMAND-MONTROND

Eighty-five kilometers south of Bourges, St-Amand-Montrond (pop. 12,000) is a good base for exploring the southern part of the Route, encircled by a veritable jungle of forests, châteaux, and churches waiting to be explored. The **tourist office,** pl. de la République (tel. 02 48 96 16 86; fax 02 48 96 46 64), offers maps indicating sights and forest excursions. (Open M-Sa 9am-noon and 2-7pm.) **Établissements Aubrun,** 26 rue Henri Barbusse (tel. 02 48 96 16 38), **rents bikes.** (70F per day. 1000F deposit. Open Tu-Sa 9am-noon and 2:30-7pm. V, MC.) If you want to stay the night, contact **Hôtel l'Écu,** 9 rue de lÉcu (tel./fax 02 48 96 27 49; rooms 160-180F; closed Su) or **Hôtel le Point du Cher,** 2 av. de la Gare (tel. 02 48 96 00 51), in nearby Orval (rooms 150-240F; closed Su-M). To get to St-Amand, take the **train** from **Bourges** (45-75min.; M-Sa 8 per day, 3 on Su).

CHÂTEAU DE MEILLANT

A beautiful 8km bike ride from St-Amand through the **Grand Bois de Meillant** finds its terminus at the foot of the imposing **Château de Meillant** (tel. 02 48 63 32 05 or 02

48 63 30 58), a heavily spired 15th- to 16th-century structure with intricate façades and a beautifully furnished interior. Built on the remains of a feudal fortress, it was bought by the Amboise family in the 15th century, who imported Italian architects, sculptors, and decorators to create their numerous châteaux around the country. The château's exterior, while mainly Flamboyant Gothic, betrays early Renaissance influences; this curious mixture of styles is especially visible in the **Tour du Lion,** the upper part of which was designed by none other than Leonardo da Vinci. Head over to the east wing to see a surprisingly good exhibit of miniature scenes depicting daily life from the Middle Ages to the present. Don't forget to make time to enjoy the beautiful shady park which surrounds the château. To get to Meillant from **St-Amand,** take rue Nationale north out to the D10. *(Open daily Feb.-Dec. 14 for guided visits 9-11:45am and 2-6:45pm. Last visit leaves 30min. before closing; visits in autumn end at dusk. Château 45F, 25F students, ages 7-15 20F. Gardens only 30F, ages 7-15 20F.)*

ABBAYE DE NOIRLAC

A mere 4km west of St-Amand-Montrond, the **Abbaye de Noirlac** (tel. 02 48 62 01 01) sits peacefully surrounded by a nest of grass and trees. Originally built in 1150, it was renovated in the 13th and 14th centuries in the austere Cistercian style. The abbey is now beautifully restored, with eight buildings open to the public. Most of the monks' **chapter house** dates from the original 12th-century construction, but the upper floor holds a surprise; the main dormitory was broken up into separate rooms in the 17th century, each redone with wood panelling and classical decor. The light **Église Abbatial** has two 13th- to 14th-century arcades flanking the south cloister, while signature Cistercian arches and carved ornamentation line many of the remaining structures. Within the complex, the **Centre de l'Enluminure et de l'Image Médiévale** holds a collection of medieval art. In summer, **L'Été de Noirlac** fills the space with jazz and classical music; call for scheduling information. From St-Amand, take rue Henri Barbusse out to the D925 west (direction "Bourges") and follow the signs to the abbey. *(Open daily July-Aug. 9:45am-noon and 1:45-6:30pm; Apr.-May and Sept. 9:45am-noon and 1:45-6:30pm; Feb.-Mar. 9:45am-noon and 1:45-5pm; Oct.-Jan. same hours but closed Tu. Ticket office shuts 1hr. before closing. French tours offered every hr. from 10am; July-Aug. no tours noon-1:45pm. 35F, students 25F, under 16 20F.)*

NORTH OF BOURGES

LA VERRERIE

The 15th-century La Verrerie (tel. 02 48 58 06 91), 45km north of Bourges, is one of the most popular châteaux on the Route. Like many of its cousins on the Loire, it has a long history of British control, but this time for more peaceful reasons. Charles VII gave the picturesque site to the Stuarts of Scotland in the 15th century; it remained in their hands for two centuries, during which period the château was rebuilt in a Renaissance style. Though Louis XIV took the château back in 1670, only three years later control passed again to the other side of the channel when the Sun King gave it to the Duchess of Portsmouth, mistress of Charles II of England, himself a Stuart. Sitting picturesquely by a lake in the Ivoy forest, inside the château you can see Renaissance furnishings, 18th-century Beauvais tapestries, and a doll collection. There's also the fascinating library of Melchior de Vogüé, an archeologist who worked in Syria and Palestine in the late 19th century. *(Open Apr.-Nov. 10am-noon and 2-6pm.)*

MENETOU-SALON AND MAUPAS

For something a bit closer to home, the bike ride to Maupas and Menetou-Salon makes a perfect daytrip. **Menetou-Salon** (tel. 02 48 64 80 54) is closer, just 20km north of Bourges. Jacques bought the estate in 1448, but his bout with Charles and the architecturally devastating Revolution left the castle in ruins until the 19th century, when the Prince of Arenburg decided to finish its construction. Though the current prince resides in New York City and only visits his château/hunting camp four times a year, personal touches make Menetou a treat. Most impressive is his collection of cars, ranging from the Range Rover that roved from Alaska to Tierra del Fuego, to a snazzy Hispano-Suiza paraded by the Prince whenever he returns. From Bourges, take D940 north to D11 and follow the signs to Menetou-Salon. (*Open Easter-Sept. W-M 10am-noon and 2-6pm; last tour 5:15pm. No cameras. 50F, students 20F, under 15 free.*)

To continue to Maupas, head back into the town of Menetou-Salon and follow the signs to Parassy and Moroques. This 13th-century castle still preserves two original towers, but most of the building was transformed and updated in the 15th, 17th, and 18th centuries. In the 19th century it belonged to the Comte de Chambord, the last legitimate Bourbon pretender to the French throne. Today, the château's reputation rests on its collection of 887 porcelain plates which are displayed around the *escalier d'honneur*. (*Open daily July-Sept. 15 10am-noon and 2-7pm, Sept. 15-30 2-7pm, Oct. 1-15 2-6pm; Oct. 15-Nov. 15 Su only 2-6pm.*)

CHÂTEAUROUX

Named for the Château Raoul that lies peacefully to the west, Châteauroux (pop. 49,000) is a busy urban hub suitable for excursions into the *pays du Berry*. The town is quiet at night and offers little sightseeing, but its extensive *jardin publique* on the river Indre is a pleasant refuge from daytime traffic.

◪ **ORIENTATION AND PRACTICAL INFORMATION. SNCF trains** and **buses** leave pl. de la Gare, off rue Bourdillon, for **Bourges** via Vierzon (2hr., 13 per day, 76F), **Orléans** (1¼hr., 6 per day, 105F), **Tours** (2hr., 6 per day, 90F), **Paris** (2hr., 8 per day, 65F), and **Poitiers** (2½hr., 3 per day, 170F). Right next door, the *gare routière* (tel. 02 54 22 13 22) sends **buses** to **Bourges** (2hr., 5 per day, 28F), **Poitiers** (3hr., 2 per day, 96F), **Tours** (2¼hr., 3 per day, 90F), and **Blois** (2½hr., 3 per day, 75F). The **tourist office**, right across the street in pl. de la Gare (tel. 02 54 34 10 74; fax 02 54 27 57 97), gives out maps and will help you find a room for free. If you'll be in town for a weekend, ask for the events guide, as outdoor movies are often screened in the park by the campsite. (Open July-Aug. M-Sa 9am-7pm and Su 10am-3:30pm; rest of year M-Sa 9am-noon and 2-7pm.) The **post office**, 2bis rue du Palais de Justice (tel. 02 54 53 54 00), **exchanges currency.** (Open M-F 8am-6:30pm, Sa 8am-noon.)

◤ **ACCOMMODATIONS AND CAMPING.** Luckily for Berry cruisers, Châteauroux spills over with conveniently located hotels. If you want to crash close to the *gare*, look across the street to the left as you exit the station; above the green veranda of **Le Rallye**, 9 rue Bourdillon (tel. 02 54 34 37 41), await seven large, sea-green rooms. (155F. No breakfast. Closed Su.) Two blocks west, **La Boule d'Or**, 18 rue Bourdillon (tel. 02 54 60 24 24; fax 02 54 27 98 10), has 19 singles and doubles. (125-160F. Breakfast 30-35F. Closed F-Sa Mar.-May. V, MC.) For even cheaper rooms, **Hôtel Brogard**, 5 rue des Halles (tel. 02 54 34 53 45), two blocks north of pl. de la République, offers big, rickety rooms. (Singles 95-135F; doubles 105-155F. Breakfast 26F.) Four-star **Camping Municipal Le Rochat-Belle-Isle**, 17 av. du Parc des Loisirs (tel. 02 54 34 26 56; fax 02 54 60 85 26), rests by the river Indre 15 minutes north of the *centre ville;* a swimming pool and activities center sit 100m away. (Sites 15.90F, adults 13F, under 7 6F, cars 11F. Electricity 7-18F. Open May-Sept.)

◨ **FOOD.** There is a **permanent market** on **pl. des Halles** (Tu-Sa 7am-1pm and 2:30-7pm). There are **outdoor markets** at pl. Voltaire (Sa 7am-5pm) and pl. de la République (Sa 7am-1pm), and a **marché fermier** on pl. Monestier (F 3-6pm). A **Petit Casino supermarket**, 8 Cours St-Luc, near the Église St-Andre, is particularly well-stocked. It also has a **cafeteria** with surprisingly good *à la carte* options (20-50F), which is just as well if you're in town on a weekend night, since everything else shuts down. (Supermarket open M-Sa 9am-7:30pm. Cafeteria open daily 11:30am-9:15pm. V, MC.) During the week, a few spots show signs of life after 8pm. **Il Giardino d'Italia**, 61 rue Ledru Rollin (tel. 02 54 07 60 94), owned by bona-fide Italians, does the pizza-pasta-salad thing for 40-60F, and has outdoor tables in the back. (Open M-Sa noon-2pm and 7:30-10pm. V, MC.) Serving an older crowd, **L'Entrecôte,** 123 rue Grande (tel. 02 54 34 68 69), off pl. Monestier, grills and roasts French cuisine in 49F *plats du jour* and 69F *formules*. (Open M-Sa noon-2pm and 7-10pm. V, MC.)

📷 **SIGHTS.** The tourist office prints up a walking tour of the city (in French, Spanish, and Italian) that takes you past all the major sights in town. The 15th-century **Château Raoul** is not open to the public, but it makes for pretty viewing from the river. A prison until 1742, the château was later the birthplace of Napoleonic general Henri Bertrand and the property of George Sand's grandparents. *M. le Général's* former home is now the **Musée Hôtel Bertrand,** 2 rue Descente des Cordeliers (tel. 02 54 61 12 13). As well as featuring the general and his emperor, the museum holds diverse collection of artwork, including 2nd- to 3rd-century Gallo-Roman pieces, medieval sculptures, 15th- to 18th-century Flemish, Dutch, French, and Italian paintings, and temporary exhibitions of modern art. (Open June-Aug. Tu-F 10am-noon and 2-6pm, Sa-Su 10am-noon and 2-7pm. 20F.) The **Couvent des Cordeliers,** rue Alain Fournier (tel. 02 54 08 34 54), rotates temporary expositions and holds summer concerts in its beautifully renovated 13th-century abbey. (Same hours and admission as Musée Hôtel Bertrand.)

📷 **ENTERTAINMENT.** Groups congregate for drinks in Pizza-pub **Le Bureau,** 54 rue Ledru Rollin (tel. 02 54 08 97 97), and the **Brasserie de Paris,** pl. de la République (tel. 02 54 34 04 28). (Both open 10am-1am.) **Le Complèxe** bar and discothèque, 14 rue Diderot (tel. 02 54 32 02 79), lures a few locals in for its Thursday Salsa Latino night and Sunday House night specials (30F; open daily 10pm-4am), but, in general, nightlife consists of carloads of teenagers driving recklessly down the same streets looking for the party that's in some other town.

VALENÇAY

Midway between the châteaux of the Loire to the west and the castles of the Route Jacques Cœur to the east, the majestic château of Valençay has Renaissance and Neo-Classical architecture to match any of them. Dominating the quiet town and ripe vineyards that surround it, the luxurious château was built in 1540 upon the site of an earlier 12th-century fortress; its rich owner Jacques d'Étampes intended it to compete with the likes of Chambord and Chenonceau.

The château today preserves the traditions and history of its 19th-century owner, the cunning Charles-Maurice Talleyrand-Périgord. Even though Talleyrand began his career under Louis XVI, he survived the Revolution and was made Minister of Foreign Affairs by Napoleon. It was the Emperor who bought the château for Talleyrand, desiring that he entertain important guests here as extra insurance for the empire's popularity. After Napoleon deposed King Ferdinand VII of Spain in 1808, he sent the Spanish royal family to Talleyrand at Valençay. Here the princes and 50-plus ladies-in-waiting remained until 1814, when Ferdinand was reinstated as monarch. The wily Talleyrand survived both Napoleon's demise and the 1830 July Revolution, remaining in office until 1834. The exquisite interior contains a host of remarkable items, including the table used for the Congress of Vienna and a sumptuous dining room in which some of the most celebrated culinary creations in all of Europe slipped down the throats of Talleyrand's guests four nights a week.

Admission to the château comes with a free audio guide in English, and includes visits to the underground kitchens and wine cellars, the vast animal park, and the **Musée de l'Automobile,** a collection of early 20th-century vehicles which lies just off the park. In summer, costumed actors perform duels and short spectacles. *(Château tel. 02 54 00 10 66. Open daily July-Aug. 9:30am-7:30pm; Apr.-June and Sept.-Oct. 9:30am-6pm; Mar. M-F 2-5pm, Sa-Su 10am-5pm; Nov.-Feb. Sa-Su 2-5pm. Musée de l'Automobile will be moving to the center of town in Oct. 2000. June-Sept. admission 54F, students and ages 7-17 44F; Oct.-May 48F, students and 7-17 36F.)*

The **tourist office** is on av. de la Résistance (tel. 02 54 00 04 42). **Trains** run from rue de la Gare to **Salbris,** whence you can breeze on to **Orléans** (2hr., M-Sa 7 per day, 2 on Su, 97F) and **Paris** (3hr., M-Sa 7 per day, 2 on Su, 159F). **Buses** go to **Châteauroux** (1hr., M-Sa 2 per day, 1 on Su Sept.-July, 32F) and **Blois** (1½hr., 2 per day, 1 on Su Sept.-July, 46F). To get to the château from the bus stop at pl. de la Halle, continue straight down rue de l'Auditoire and take your second right into pl. Talleyrand. The château entrance is on your left.

VAL DE CREUSE

C'est peut-être la plus belle rivière du monde que la Creuse au mois d'avril.

Laura, George Sand

Between the small medieval town of St-Marcel and the wee provincial village of Crozant lies the *Sentier de Pays du Val de Creuse,* a 100km hiking and biking loop which hugs the insouciant wigglings of the river Creuse. Forging through lush, fertile valley, the trail affords marvelous views of the river and the surrounding countryside, while little hamlets along the way offer restauration and historical sights of mild interest. Perfect for day hike or a week-long escapade, the valley offers a peaceful natural beauty which has inspired in the past such artists as George Sand and Claude Monet.

The Val de Creuse is a welcome refuge of peace and natural beauty, but be forewarned: like any isolated spot, public transportation is infrequent and often inconvenient. The most convenient base is **Argenton,** at the north end of the valley; frequent **trains** and **SNCF buses** make it an easy trip from Châteauroux (15min.; 11 per day, 3 on Su; 39F). Other trains go to **Limoges** via St-Sebastien (1hr., 3 per day, 1 on Su, 82F) and **Poitiers** (2¼hr., 3 per day, 1 on Su, 79F). **L'Aile Bleue buses** (tel. 0800 77 86 21) offers two *services à la demande* buses per day from **Châteauroux** (#8, 28.50F). Two more travel on through the valley, making frequent stops *en route* to **Éguzon** (#7, 29.10F). Call two hours ahead to make reservations; schedules are available at tourist offices. The Argenton **tourist office,** pl. de la République (tel. 02 54 24 05 30; fax 02 54 24 28 13), sells **laminated maps** marking 8, 14, and 30km loops around Argenton (3F) as well as one of the entire *Sentier* (10F). You can **rent bikes** at **Bois Cycles,** 7 rue Grande. (Tel. 02 54 24 36 33. 50-70F per day.)

The valley is flecked with two- and three-star **campsites** and a few **gîtes d'étapes.** A good place to scout out is the **Moulin de Châteaubrun,** a turnoff from the D-45 in Cuzion (tel. 02 54 47 46 40), which has a *gîte d'étape* (55-65F per night), camping (40F per night), and bike, canoe, and kayak rental. (All 45F per half-day, 80F per day. Call ahead Sept.-June.) Further south, the **Base de Plein Air** *gîte d'étape* is near the Chambon beach, and offers canoe rental too. (Tel. 02 54 47 46 13. 56F per person. Canoes 60F per hour.) The local tourist offices can give you camping and *gîte* listings, and, if you don't feel like roughing it, guide you towards the valley's cheaper hotels. Éguzon and Argenton are good bets for campsites and hotels.

ST-MARCEL TO GARGILESSE

The *Sentier* begins just outside **St-Marcel,** a pretty village with cobblestone medieval streets and a set of 2nd-century **Roman ruins,** which include a temple, a sacred fountain, and an amphitheater. Objects excavated from the site are on show at the **Argentomagus museum,** rue Les Mercants. (Tel. 02 54 24 47 31. Open July-Aug. Tu 2-6pm, W-M 9am-noon and 2-6pm; rest of year W-M only. 20F, students and children 10F.) The trail then snakes along the river in lively **Argenton-sur-Creuse** (pop. 5200), whose charming main square leads off to a 12-century bridge. Wandering away from the river to **Le Pêchereau,** endowed with a modest château, the *Sentier* approaches the Creuse again after passing **Le Menoux.** At **Le Pin,** a panoramic view from the road looks down over the Creuse's first *boucle,* or C-shaped curl, while the conforming valley walls rise up in the shape of an amphitheater from below. Across the river (swim if you dare!) in

Ceaulmont lie a small medieval church and the *Moulin de Chenet* windmill. About 1.5km southeast of Le Pin is the picturesque **Gargilesse**, George Sand's "village of refuge" which she discovered with Chopin; today the **Villa Algira** (tel. 02 54 47 84 14) displays some of the writer's belongings. (Open Apr.-Oct. 9:30am-12:30pm and 2-7pm.) Also worth seeing is the 12th-century **Romanesque church,** which has fantastic carved capitals and 13th-century paintings on the walls of its crypt. Gargilesse's small **tourist office,** Le Pigeonnier (tel. 02 54 47 85 06 or 02 54 47 83 11), is open July and August only.

GARGILESSE TO CROZANT

From Gargilesse to Crozant, the river widens and twists ever more persistently, creating more *boucles* and scenic panoramas. From **Cuzion,** the two crumbling towers of Châteaubrun's former 12th-century fortress stand out against the greens and browns of the valley. About 500m south, the **Pont des Piles** passes a striking rock-climbing cliff face on its way to the west bank of the Creuse, where the hiking trail continues to the **Lac de Chambon.** Here a dam widens the river considerably, and popular grassy beaches line either bank. Watersports and beach activity are available on the **plage du Chambon,** while a free motorboat shuttles passengers and bikes over to the east bank's **plage Fougères** and quieter **plage Bonnu** to the north. Two kilometers northwest of Chambon lies the valley's southern transportation hub, **Éguzon-Chantome,** with a small museum of local history, the sole remaining tower of a 15th-century chateau, and a helpful **tourist office** at 2 rue Jules Ferry (tel. 02 54 47 43 69; fax 02 54 47 35 60). A pretty panoramic view awaits 5km south at **Pillemongin,** while at southernmost **Crozant,** the craggy ruins of a 6th- to 12th-century fortress dismantled by Richelieu sit hugged by the confluence of Creuse and Sedelle rivers. (Open daily 10am-noon and 2-6pm; until 7pm July-Aug.) After Crozant the *sentier* crosses to the opposite bank and works its way back up the Creuse on the other side.

LA CHÂTRE

Serving as an exceptionally pretty base from which to visit the plentiful nearby sights, **La Châtre** (pop. 5234) lies 36km southeast of Châteauroux. Its pleasant *centre ville,* lively Saturday market, and annual Chopin Festival at the end of July, earn it top marks as a place to stop in for a day or two of fun and relaxation.

The tourist office's info guide maps out a little pedestrian tour of La Châtre; the walk takes visitors past 15th-century houses, the 12th- to 14th-century **Église St-Germain,** and the **Musée George Sand et de la Vallée Noire,** 71 rue Venose (tel. 02 54 48 36 79), housed in a square 15th-century keep. The museum has plenty of Sand's souvenirs and drawings to pick over, as well as local art and a large ornithological collection. (Open daily July-Aug. 9am-7pm; Sept.-June 9am-noon and 2-5pm; Apr.-Sept. until 7pm. Closed Jan.) Temporary exhibitions are held in the Hôtel de Villaines next to the tourist office, while the second-to-last week in July ushers in the **Rencontres International Frédéric Chopin,** with seminars and nightly recitals in both La Châtre and nearby Nohant (tickets 30-220F).

If you call at least two days in advance, you can stay at the 52-bed **Auberge de Jeunesse (HI),** rue Moulin Borgnon (tel. 02 54 06 00 55; fax 02 54 48 48 10). A 20-minute walk from the tourist office, the hostel sits behind a park right by the river Indre. (55F. Sheets 20F. 10F extra for non-members. Reception daily 8am-9pm.) A very pretty trot down the Parcours de Sante across the river leads to the three-star **Camping le Val Vert.** (Tel 02 54 48 32 42; fax 02 54 48 32 87. 50F for car and 2 adults. Extra person 15F. Electricity 15F.) **Hôtel Le Paradis Breton,** 4 rue Alphonse Fleury (tel. 02 54 48 02 87; fax 02 54 48 44 43), has six rooms above a well-priced restaurant. (115-135F. Closed W Sept.-May.) Other pleasant **restaurants** in the *centre ville* are easily spotted, while a **market** fills up the pl. du Marché (Sa 8am-7pm).

To get to the **tourist office,** pl. George Sand (tel. 02 54 48 22 64; fax 02 54 06 09 15), from the *gare,* exit the parking lot and head straight out on av. Aristide Briand. About four blocks past pl. Jules Neraud, turn left on av. George Sand; the tourist

THE ORIGINAL BOY GEORGE While most girls called Amandine-Aurore-Lucile might like to give themselves a snappier title, a boy's name would not normally make it to the top of the list—especially in the 19th century. But George Sand (1804-1876) was never one to worry about convention. Prolific novelist, proto-feminist, and passionate lover, she achieved a fame and notoriety in her lifetime that could scarcely be expected from a provincial *mademoiselle* from Nohant. After leaving her home and husband for the excitement of the capital in 1831, she embarked on a series of amorous adventures—her conquests include Alfred de Musset, Prosper Mérimée (the author of *Carmen)*, and, most famously, Frédéric Chopin. Sand adopted male clothing as part of her protest against the social strictures of the day, which she attacked in her novels. She returned to Nohant in 1839 with a consumptive Chopin in tow; while he composed some of his best-loved works, she celebrated the beauty of her homeland with novels such as *La Mare au Diable* and *La Petite Fadette*.

office is ahead of you on your right, set back from the street in a pretty grassy area. Here you can get maps, info, and help with accommodations, all for free. (Open July-Aug. M-Sa 9am-12:30pm and 2:30-7pm, Su 10:15am-12:15pm and 4-7pm; Apr.-June and Sept. same hours M-Sa only; Oct.-Mar. M-Sa 9am-12:30pm and 2-6:30pm.)

Trains roll in from **Châteauroux** (46min., 5 per day, 36F), **Limoges** (2¼hr., 4 per day, 120F), and **Bourges** (3½hr., 1 per day, 82F). The station and *gare routière* are both a 25-minute walk from town, but there's another bus stop in rue du Champ de Foire, about three blocks west of the tourist office. The town's sole bus services goes to **Châteauroux** (1hr.; 7 per day, 4 on Su; 43F). The **SNCF Info Boutique,** 142 rue Nationale (tel. 02 54 48 00 06), in the center of town, can sell you tickets. (Open Tu-Sa 8:45am-noon and 2-6pm.)

NEAR LA CHÂTRE: NOHANT

The first stop on the *Route George Sand*, tiny **Nohant,** 8km out of La Châtre, houses the writer's childhood home, a pretty 17th-century house purchased by her grandmother in 1793 (tel. 02 54 31 06 04). It was here that Sand penned her first novel, *Indiana,* and here that so many great literary and artistic figures came to dine, among them Balzac, Delacroix, Flaubert, and Liszt. A guided tour in French leads you through the "modest dwelling." The presence of Frédéric Chopin, who stayed 10 years here with Sand, is not overlooked; the puppet theater downstairs which he built with Sand's son Maurice is still in perfect condition, as is the study upstairs where the composer wrote over fifteen of his piano works. (Open daily July-Aug. 9am-7:30pm; Apr.-June and Sept.-Oct. 15 9am-12:15pm and 2-6:30pm; Oct. 16-Mar. 10am-12:15pm and 2-4:30pm. Last tour 30min. before closing, 23F.)

To get to Nohant, take the **bus** (direction "Châteauroux," 10min., 3 per day, 6F) from **La Châtre.** When you get off, take the crosswalk across the highway and follow the road ahead of you into the main square. A fun time to visit is the last weekend in July, when **La Fête au Village** puts a little more sparkle into the tiny town square, with outdoor dining, music, and market vendors selling traditional wares and regional food specialties. If you'd like to explore the area, the Nohant **tourist office,** pl. de l'Église (tel. 02 54 31 07 37), hands out maps and **rents bikes.** (Office open daily 9:30am-7pm. Bikes 45F per half-day, 75F per day. 800F deposit.)

LIMOGES

Although Limoges (pop. 150,000) is acclaimed for its centuries-old traditions of porcelain- and enamel-making, its attractions extend far beyond its numerous ceramic-oriented museums. Once you've had your fill of *émaux d'art* and *faïenceries,* spend some time exploring the beautiful old town, the exquisite Gothic cathedral, and the relaxing gardens.

Worldwide Calling Made Easy

The MCI WorldCom Card, designed specifically to keep you in touch with the people that matter the most to you.

www.wcom.com/worldphone

Please cut out and save this reference guide for convenient U.S. and worldwide calling with the MCI WorldCom Card.

And, it's simple to call home or to other countires.

1. Dial the WorldPhone toll-free access number of the country you're calling from (listed inside).

2. Follow the easy voice instructions or hold for a WorldPhone operator. Enter or give the operator your MCI WorldCom Card number or call collect.

3. Enter or give the WorldPhone operator your home number.

4. Share your adventures with your family!

COUNTRY		WORLDPHONE TOLL-FREE ACCESS #
St. Lucia ÷		1-800-888-8000
Sweden (CC) ◆		020-795-922
Switzerland (CC) ◆		0800-89-0222
Taiwan (CC) ◆		0080-13-4567
Thailand ★		001-999-1-2001
Turkey (CC) ◆		00-8001-1177
United Kingdom	(CC) To call using BT ■	0800-89-0222
	To call using CWC ■	0500-89-0222
United States (CC)		1-800-888-8000
U.S. Virgin Islands (CC)		1-800-888-8000
Vatican City (CC)		172-1022
Venezuela (CC) ÷ ◆		800-1114-0
Vietnam ●		1201-1022

(CC)	Country-to-country calling available to/from most international locations.
÷	Limited availability.
▼	Wait for second dial tone.
▲	When calling from public phones, use phones marked LADATEL.
■	International communications carrier.
◆	Not available from public pay phones.
★	Public phones may require deposit of coin or phone card for dial tone.
●	Local service fee in U.S. currency required to complete call.
▶	Regulation does not permit Intra-Japan calls.
✧	Available from most major cities

MCI WorldCom Worldphone Access Numbers

The MCI WorldCom Card.

The easy way to call when traveling worldwide.

The MCI WorldCom Card gives you...

- Access to the US and other countries worldwide.
- Customer Service 24 hours a day
- Operators who speak your language
- Great MCI WorldCom rates and no sign-up fees

For more information or to apply for a Card call:

1-800-955-0925

Outside the U.S., call MCI WorldCom collect (reverse charge) at:

1-712-943-6839

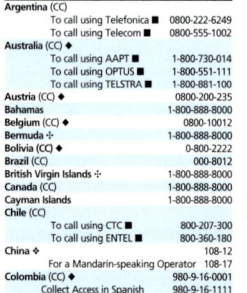

COUNTRY	WORLDPHONE TOLL-FREE ACCESS #
Argentina (CC)	
To call using Telefonica ■	0800-222-6249
To call using Telecom ■	0800-555-1002
Australia (CC) ♦	
To call using AAPT ■	1-800-730-014
To call using OPTUS ■	1-800-551-111
To call using TELSTRA ■	1-800-881-100
Austria (CC) ♦	0800-200-235
Bahamas	1-800-888-8000
Belgium (CC) ♦	0800-10012
Bermuda ÷	1-800-888-8000
Bolivia (CC) ♦	0-800-2222
Brazil (CC)	000-8012
British Virgin Islands ÷	1-800-888-8000
Canada (CC)	1-800-888-8000
Cayman Islands	1-800-888-8000
Chile (CC)	
To call using CTC ■	800-207-300
To call using ENTEL ■	800-360-180
China ✧	108-12
For a Mandarin-speaking Operator	108-17
Colombia (CC) ♦	980-9-16-0001
Collect Access in Spanish	980-9-16-1111
Costa Rica ♦	0800-012-2222
Czech Republic (CC) ♦	00-42-000112
Denmark (CC) ♦	8001-0022
Dominican Republic	
Collect Access	1-800-888-8000
Collect Access in Spanish	1121
Ecuador (CC) ÷	999-170
El Salvador	800-1767

COUNTRY	WORLDPHONE TOLL-FREE ACCESS #
Finland (CC) ♦	08001-102-80
France (CC) ♦	0800-99-0019
French Guiana (CC)	0-800-99-0019
Guatemala (CC) ♦	99-99-189
Germany (CC)	0-800-888-8000
Greece (CC) ♦	00-800-1211
Guam (CC)	1-800-888-8000
Haiti ÷	193
Collect Access in French/Creole	190
Honduras ÷	8000-122
Hong Kong (CC)	800-96-1121
Hungary (CC) ♦	00▼800-01411
India (CC) ✧	000-127
Collect Access	000-126
Ireland (CC)	1-800-55-1001
Israel (CC)	
BEZEQ International	1-800-940-2727
BARAK	1-800-930-2727
Italy (CC) ♦	172-1022
Jamaica ÷	Collect Access 1-800-888-8000
(From Special Hotels only)	873
(From public phones)	#2
Japan (CC) ♦	To call using KDD ■ 00539-121▶
To call using IDC ■	0066-55-121
To call using JT ■	0044-11-121
Korea (CC)	To call using KT ■ 00729-14
To call using DACOM ■	00309-12
To call using ONSE	00369-14
Phone Booths÷	Press red button, 03, then ✶
Military Bases	550-2255
Lebanon	Collect Access 600-MCI (600-624)

COUNTRY	WORLDPHONE TOLL-FREE ACCESS #
Luxembourg (CC)	0800-0112
Malaysia (CC) ♦	1-800-80-0012
To call using Time Telekom ■	1-800-18-0012
Mexico (CC)	Avantel 01-800-021-8000
Telmex ▲	001-800-674-7000
Collect Access in Spanish	01-800-021-1000
Monaco (CC) ♦	800-90-019
Netherlands (CC) ♦	0800-022-9122
New Zealand (CC)	000-912
Nicaragua (CC)	Collect Access in Spanish 166
(Outside of Managua, dial 02 first)	
Norway (CC) ♦	800-19912
Panama	108
Military Bases	2810-108
Philippines (CC) ♦	To call using PLDT ■ 105-14
To call using PHILCOM	1026-14
To call using Bayantel	1237-14
To call using ETPI	1066-14
Poland (CC) ÷	00-800-111-21-22
Portugal (CC) ÷	800-800-123
Puerto Rico (CC)	1-800-888-8000
Romania (CC) ♦	01-800-1800
Russia (CC) ♦ ÷	
To call using ROSTELCOM ■	747-3322
(For Russian speaking operator)	747-3320
To call using SOVINTEL ■	960-2222
Saudi Arabia (CC) ÷	1-800-11
Singapore	8000-112-112
Slovak Republic (CC)	00421-00112
South Africa (CC)	0800-99-0011
Spain (CC)	900-99-0014

▐ ORIENTATION AND PRACTICAL INFORMATION

To get to the tourist office from the train station, keep left by the train tracks down **av. du Général de Gaulle,** and follow the path which cuts diagonally across **pl. Jourdan** to **bd. de Fleurus.** The tourist office is at the end of bd. de Fleurus on the left.

Trains: Gare des Bénédictins, pl. Jourdans (tel. 05 55 11 11 80), off av. de Gaulle. Following a 1998 fire the dome of this 'symbol of Limoges' has been restored, returning the gare to its 1920s Art Deco splendor. To: **Brive** (1hr., 5 per day, 78F); **Poitiers** (2hr., 3 per day, 101F); **Bordeaux** (3hr., 7 per day, 148F); **Toulouse** (3½hr., 8 per day, 188F); **Paris** (3-4hr., 12 per day, 227F); and **Lyon** (5-7hr., 6 per day, 232F).

Buses: Bus station, pl. des Charentes (tel. 05 55 77 29 00). The entire timetable for the Limousin region **bus system** is available here and at the tourist office. Open M-F 7:45am-noon and 1:45-5pm, Sat. 8:30am-noon.

Taxis: Taxis Limoges (tel. 05 55 37 81 81.)

Tourist Office: Bd. de Fleurus (tel. 05 55 34 46 87; fax 05 55 34 19 12; e-mail ot.limoges.haute-vienne@en-france.com), near pl. Wilson. English-speaking staff has maps, lists of *chambres d'hôtes,* and mountains of brochures. **Currency exchange** with 4% commission. 2hr. theme **tours** of the city July-Aug. Open June 22-Sept. 20 M-Sa 9am-7pm, Su 10am-2pm; rest of year M-Sa 9am-noon and 2-6:30pm.

Tours: Limoges Tour Autocars, 3 rue Jean-Jaurès (tel. 05 55 34 38 22).

Budget Travel: Centre Régional Information Jeunesse, 27 bd. de la Corderie (tel. 05 55 45 18 70). Open in summer M 1:30-5:30pm, Tu-F 9am-12:30pm and 1:30-5:30pm, Sa 9am-noon; in winter M 2-6pm, Tu-F 9am-6pm.

Money: Banque de France, 8 bd. Carnot (tel. 05 55 11 53 00), works commission-free counters and offers good rates. Exchange desk open M-F 8:45am-noon.

Laundromat: Laverie, 49 rue de François Chenieux. Open daily 6am-10pm.

Police: 2 rue des Vénitiens (tel. 05 55 33 80 00).

Hospital: Tel. 05 55 33 33 33.

Post Office: Rue de la Préfecture near pl. Stalingrad. **Currency exchange.** Open M-F 8am-7pm, Sa 8am-noon. **Postal code:** 87000.

Internet Access: Free access in 14-computer multimedia room at the brand new **Bibliothèque Francophone Multimedia de Limoges,** 2 rue Louis Longequeue (tel. 05 55 45 96 00), just beyond the Hôtel de Ville. Open Tu and Th-F 1-7pm, W 10am-7pm, Sa 10am-6pm; other sections of the library also open M 2-6pm.

▐▗ ACCOMMODATIONS, CAMPING, AND FOOD

ACCOMMODATIONS. The **Auberge de Jeunesse,** 20 rue Encombe Vineuse (tel. 05 55 77 63 97), offers rooms with sinks and desks, as well as a kitchenette, a clean, well-lit bathroom on each floor, and a TV room on the ground floor. From the *gare,* walk around the right side of the station, take rue Théodore Bac to pl. Carnot, turn left onto av. Adrien Tarrade, and take the first left onto rue Encombe Vineuse (15min.). (Singles 85F, doubles 130F. Breakfast included. Reception daily 9am-noon, also: Su 2pm-2am, M-W 2pm-1am, Th-Sa all night.)

Hotel de Paris, 5 cours Vergniaud (tel. 05 55 77 56 96), has big beds in dark rooms. Huge 19th-century mirrors hang from the stair landings, and most rooms look out over the Champs de Juillet beyond a parking lot. (Singles 130-250F, doubles 170-280F. Breakfast 25F. V, MC.) **Mon Logis,** 16 rue du Gal-du-Bessol (tel. 05 55 77 51 40), has 14 pretty, light rooms for excellent prices as well as a series of hand-drawn pictures of Limoges from ancient times to the present running up the staircase. (Singles with shower 127F, with shower, toilet, and TV 195F; doubles 155F-190F. Breakfast 27-29F.) **Camping de la Vallée de l'Aurence** (tel. 05 55 38 49 43). 5km north of Limoges, this is the closest campground to town. Rest comfortably—you're pitching your tent on three-star grounds. (Take bus #20 M-Sa. Camping 15F per person, 15F per car.)

THE ANCIENT ART OF EMAIL If you're looking for internet access in Limoges, don't take things at face value. All those signs on stores and museums proclaiming "Email" actually refer to *émail* (pronounced "M-I"), or enamel. First discovered in the second millennium BC, the basic process consists of applying a thin layer of powdered soft glass to a metal base and firing it at high temperatures so that the metal becomes covered in a thin protective layer of glass. By adding metal oxides, almost any color can be achieved, while mixing in gold or silver foil adds lustre. Limoges is particularly famous for its *émaux d'art* because local mineral deposits provide uncommonly rich hues of enamel for artists to work with. Every summer, the Exposition de l'Hôtel de Ville displays thousands of enamels in the beautiful town hall.

FOOD. The central Les Halles **indoor market** faces pl. de la Motte (Su-F 7am-1pm, Sa 8am-1pm); a larger market brightens pl. Carnot Saturday mornings. There's also a Monoprix **supermarket** at 11 pl. de la République (open M-Sa 8:30am-8pm; V, MC), and two **STOC** counterparts in the Centre St-Martial on bd. Garibaldi (M-F 10am-2pm, Sa 9am-8pm) and off ave. Adrien Tarrade by the youth hostel (M-Sa 8:30am-7:30pm, Su 9am-noon). Restaurants in the old quarter provide a more chic (and expensive) dining experience than the restaurant-bars of the far less beautiful pl. de la République. For a younger, more relaxed crowd in a nice setting, try your luck at pl. Denis Dussoubs.

La Parenthèse (tel. 05 55 33 18 25) is bracketed in the cour de Temple, a Renaissance courtyard in the center of town, and offers light lunches. The *tartes salées* (38F) and colorful salads (42-50F) are proper preludes to the marvelous house pastries (21F). (Open M noon-2:30pm, Tu-F 11:45am-6pm, Sa noon-7pm.) **Le Glacier**, 12 pl. Denis Dussoubs (tel. 05 55 77 23 81), is a well-priced bar and restaurant popular with a slightly younger crowd. Despite its lively tropical-trees and Mexican-hats decor, it serves up full plates of regional salads, seafood, specialty *crêpes* (savory 40-45F, sweet 14-33F), meats (38-75F), omelettes, and sandwiches. For the kid in you, there's an entire menu of extra-terrestrial ice cream concoctions (37-85F), and you can eat out on the *place*. (Open daily 7am-2am; dining hours M-Sa 11am-2:30pm and 6-11:30pm, Su 6-11:30pm. V, MC.)

◉ SIGHTS

Limoges offers enough sights and variety to overwhelm most tourists. Plunge straight into the beautiful ancient quarter, which offers agreeable sight-seeing, lively window shopping, and wonderful dining along cobbled streets and open *places*. Most museums have brochures in English.

CATHÉDRALE ST-ÉTIENNE. Rebuilt on the remains of its Romanesque predecessor between the late 13th and mid-16th century, this is one of the few great Gothic edifices south of the Loire. The builders added a three-bay choir and ambulatory with pillars composed of bundles of narrow columns to emphasize slimness and verticality. The crypt and bell tower porch are the 11th-century original. *(Near the tourist office on pl. St-Étienne. Open to visitors M-Sa 9:30am-6:30pm, Su 2:30-6:30pm. Free tours in French M-Sa 11am.)*

MUSÉE NATIONAL ADRIEN-DUBOUCHÉ. Houses the largest porcelain collection in Europe, spanning centuries of craftsmanship. Over 11,000 items of porcelain, ceramics, glass, stoneware, and tin-glazed earthenware are on display. *(8bis pl. Winston Churchill. Tel. 05 55 33 08 50. Open W-M July-Aug. 10am-5:45pm; Sept.-June 10am-12:30pm and 2-5:45pm. Admission 25F, ages 18-25 and Su 15F, under 18 free.)*

CRYPTE ST-MARTIAL. The crypt is all that remains of the medieval Benedictine Abbey of St. Martial, which was demolished after the French Revolution. The saint, who evangelized Augustoritum (the Roman name for Limoges) in the late 3rd century, was also its first bishop. The abbey, once famed for its library, was run by monks of the Cluniac order. Now wholly underground, the ruins of the abbatial city, the surrounding Roman necropolis from the 1st century, and the tombs of St. Valérie and St. Martial may be visited by guided tour in French. *(Beneath pl. de la République. Open July-Sept. 9:30am-noon and 2:30-7pm; off-season ask at tourist office for a tour. Free.)*

ÉVÊCHÉ BOTANICAL GARDENS. These gardens are a gorgeous and relaxing place to spend time. Follow up by walking along the tree-lined promenade which runs between the 12th- and 13-century Pont St-Martial and the Pont St-Étienne on the far side of the Vienne river. The path meanders beside flowering gardens and an outdoor climbing wall. Locals fish and bring their young children to play by these two beautiful bridges, the former of which rests on 1st-century Roman foundations. Brasseries await snack-mongers at the bridges' ends. *(In front of the cathedral. Tel. 05 55 45 62 67. Guided visits by appointment.)*

VILLAGE DE LA BOUCHERIE. A sight unique to Limoges, the village is a district of narrow streets and medieval houses in the *centre ville* where the town's butchers have lived since the 10th century. For a slice of their life, visit the **Maison Traditionelle de la Boucherie,** just beyond the Chapelle St-Aurelien on your right. Friendly guides lead tours of a butcher's house. *(Open July-Sept. 10am-1pm and 3-7pm; Oct.-June ask tourist office for an appointment. Free.)*

OTHER SITES. Down from pl. de la Motte, the **Église St-Michel des Lions,** built between the 14th and 16th centuries, bears an exquisite carved stone chapel which hosts altars to Limoges natives St. Martial, St. Valérie, and St. Loup. Equally noteworthy is its 13th-15th century predecessor **St-Pierre-du-Queyroix,** whose Limousin-Romanesque bell tower was the model for both the Église St-Michel and the Cathedral. Each summer, Limoges's grandiose **Hôtel de Ville** dishes out an exhibit with such offbeat items as a porcelain watermill powering a porcelain chime, as well as ho-hum plates and statues. *(Pl. Louis Betoulle. Tel. 05 55 77 29 18. Open June-Sept. daily 9am-7pm. Free.)* The **Musée Municipal de l'Evêché** and the **Musée de l'Email** fill the 18th-century bishop's palace with their very impressive collections of Egyptian art, Merovingian capitals, masonry, sarcophagi, local Roman artifacts, and, of course, the inescapable enamels and porcelain. There are also four rather misty paintings by Auguste Renoir, who was born in Limoges in 1841. *(Next to the Cathedral. Tel. 05 55 34 44 09 or 05 55 45 61 75. Open June W-M 10-11:45am and 2-6pm; July-Sept. daily 10-11:45am and 2-6pm; Oct.-May W-M 10-11:45am and 2-5pm. Free.)*

🎵 🎍 ENTERTAINMENT AND FESTIVALS

ENTERTAINMENT. The nightlife in Limoges is nothing to get revved up about, but a smattering of small **bars and clubs** line the rue St-Michel in the center of town (generally no cover, but purchase of a drink required). People will find their own niche when they hit the street, but the **Blue Banana** is habitually packed. Young people congregate at the **Crazy Cub Café,** a small bar and lounge with a dance floor, and around the bar at the **Cheyenne Café.**

For those with earlier bedtimes, the **Grand theater,** 48 rue Jean Jaurès (tel. 05 55 33 08 00), presents 60 ballet, orchestral, opera, and choral productions from September to June, while the **Théâtre de l'Union,** 20 rue des Coopérateurs (tel. 05 55 79 90 00), has a season from September to May. The five **Centres Culturels Municipaux** put on a vast array of concerts, theater productions, cinema, and variety shows to meet every taste Monday through Friday at the Centre Culturel Jean Gagnant, 7 av. Jean Gagnant (tel. 05 55 34 45 49), and the Centre Culturel Jean Moulin, 76 rue des Sagnes (tel. 05 55 35 04 10).

FESTIVALS. The **Limousine Jazz Festival** livens up the city in November (tel. 05 55 10 90 28), while in January and February 2000 Limoges will host **Danse-Émoi** (tel. 05 55 34 45 49), a biennial festival of modern dance. The **Foire de la Saint-Loup,** a centuries-old fair which occurs around May 22, brings more than 400 merchants and thousands of people to peruse traditional wares and goodies in the *centre ville*. **Fête la Saint-Jean** on Pont St-Étienne takes place at the end of June and includes diving, fireworks, water shows, dancing, and traditional music performances. At the same time of year, look out for the 13th annual **International Meeting of Athleticism,** a mini-Olympics which draws over 200 track and field athletes from around the world to Limoges' Beaublanc sports arena. The popular *Festival des Arts de la rue*, **Urb Aka** (tel. 05 55 75 83 18), lasts from June 28 to July 1. Mid-October brings the mother of all Limousin meals with **La Frairie des petits ventres** (Festival of Small Stomachs), a street banquet where residents consume meat of every kind in mass quantities. Additionally, every seven years the butchers parade into the Chapelle St-Aurelien and retrieve the relics of St-Aurelien, their patron saint; they then proceed through the streets and eat more meat. The next feast is in 2002—start packing your sausages now.

ORADOUR-SUR-GLANE

On June 10, 1944, Nazi SS troops massacred all the inhabitants of the farming village **Oradour-sur-Glane** without warning or provocation before setting the whole town ablaze. Perhaps France's most vivid testimony to WWII, the town remains in ruins; train wires dangle from slanting poles, and 50-year-old cars rust next to crumbling walls. You can walk freely along the main thoroughfare and peer into the remnants of each home. Signs indicate the name and profession of each person who lived there. Mystery still enshrouds the reason for the Nazis' decision, although one theory maintains that they mistook this town for Oradour-sur-Vayres, an important center of the Resistance. The Nazis entered at two in the afternoon; by three-thirty the women and children had been corralled into the church and the men into six barns. At four, a shot was fired to start the massacre. Those in the church were burned alive; the men were tortured, shot, and set ablaze. By seven o'clock, 642 people, including 205 children, had been slaughtered. Six men, a schoolboy, and a woman who had jumped out the church window were the sole survivors. The event was overseen by Heinz Barth, an SS officer who was promoted to lieutenant colonel shortly after the attack. Barth is currently serving a life sentence for his war crimes. Plaques with heartbreaking messages and pictures mark two glass tombs containing the bones and ashes of the dead. A small museum between the cemetery and town displays bicycles, toys, and watches that were all stopped by the heat of the fire at the same moment. (Town open 24hr. Memorial open 9am-12:30pm and 2-5:30pm. Guide answers questions next to the church 9am-12:30pm and 2-5:30pm. Free English self-guided walking tour.) After some hesitation, a new Oradour (pop. 2000) was built next to the martyred village. To get there, catch a **bus** from Limoges (40min.; M-F 4 per day, 3 on Sa; 18F).

ST-LÉONARD-DE-NOBLAT

One of many small villages near Limoges worth visiting thanks to its history and picturesque beauty, St-Léonard-de-Noblat (pop. 5000) looks down upon the Briance and Vienne rivers from a hilltop perch. Named for the patron saint of prisoners, this *petite ville* was for centuries an important stop along the pilgrim route to Santiago de Compostela. The **Église de St-Léonard,** pl. Gay-Lussac, was begun in 1050 and subsequently developed during the next two centuries. The church, which houses St. Léonard's tomb, has at its far end a wide seven-chapel ambulatory, as well as the finest Limousin Romanesque bell tower in the region. (Open daily 9am-5pm.) You can also visit the **house of Joseph-Louis Gay-Lussac,** the great 19th-century physicist, which is now a small museum. (Rue Roger Salengro. Open July-Aug. 10am-noon and 2-6pm; rest of the year call tourist office for hours.) A small **HistoRail** museum, 18 rue de Beaufort (tel. 05 55 56 11 12), should be visited by railway fanatics. (Open July-Aug. daily 2:30-6pm, closed M Apr.-June and Sept.-Oct., Nov.-Mar. only for pre-arranged group visits). If you pass by St-Léonard in September, look out for the **Limousin Beef Fair;** at **la Quintaine** in November, riders imitate the destruction of a wooden fortress, reenacting how St-Léonard is said to have freed prisoners. For some peace and quiet, take a wander around the cemetery, off rue 19 de 1962, to catch a glimpse of the beautiful surrounding hills and countryside. Call the Limoges tourist office for details about bus tours to St-Léonard and other surrounding villages, or make your own day trip by **bus** (45min., 3-4 daily) or **train** (30min.; 4 per day M-Sa, 1 Su), both of which leave from the Gare des Bénédictins in **Limoges.** Get off in the *centre ville* and walk straight ahead to the tourist office, pl. du Champ de Mars (tel. 05 55 56 25 06), for a map. (Open July and Aug. M-Sa 9:30am-6:30pm, Su 10am-1pm; rest of year T-Sa 9:30am-noon and 2:30-5pm.)

BURGUNDY (BOURGOGNE)

Encompassing the Côte d'Or, the Plateau de Langres, and the wild, forested Morvan, Burgundy is best known for its Romanesque architecture and the 40 million bottles of wine it produces annually. Battleground of Gallic border wars in the 1st century BC, the region was a major player in the Roman conquest; Autun was founded as a Roman capital. In the 5th century, the Burgundians, one of many Germanic tribes to pour across the Roman Empire's borders during its final years, settled on the plains of the Saône and modestly named the region after themselves.

What the Loire is to châteaux, Burgundy is to churches. During the Middle Ages, the duchy was at the heart of the religious fever sweeping Europe. Magnificent cathedrals were constructed to welcome the pilgrims who flocked to their holy relics, while abbeys burgeoned in size and wealth. Most powerful of all was Cluny, whose abbot housed over 10,000 monks in the 12th century and was second only to the Pope in power and influence. While the Wars of Religion and the Revolution ended the pre-eminence of religious institutions in Burgundian life, the 19th century saw a revival, with new pilgrimages beginning to Paray-le-Monial and Nevers.

From the mid-14th century to the end of the 15th, the dukes of Burgundy were more powerful than the kings of France. This famous lineage began with Philippe le Hardi (the Strong), whose marriage to Marguerite de Flandres brought artists from the north to their capital at Dijon. The state reached its maximum size and power under Le Hardi's grandson, Philippe le Bon (the Good), who expanded his territories to include most of Holland, Belgium, Luxembourg, Flanders, Artois, Picardie, and the region bound by the Loire and the Jura. When good Philippe's son, Charles le Téméraire (the Bold), was found frozen to death and half-eaten by wolves, a delighted Louis XI took the opportunity to annex Burgundy to France.

With just a few French phrases, you can taste your way to connoisseurship of the finest wines. Burgundy's wine can be *fruité* (fruity), *moelleux* (mellow), *vif* (lively), or *velouté* (velvety). Châteaux feature whites such as the dry Pouilly-sur-Loire from Nièvre and Chablis from L'Yonne, and full-bodied reds including Vougeot, Gevrey-Chambertin, Nuits-St-George, and Corton from the Côte d'Or and Givry from Saône-et-Loire. Delectable cuisine goes hand in hand with stellar wine. Try *gougères* (puffed pastry filled with cabbage or cheese), a few *hélix pomatia* (escargots) in butter and garlic, or the esteemed *bœuf bourguignon*. The *jambon persillé* (a gelatin mold of ham and parsley) may be an acquired taste, but the traditional *coq au vin* (chicken in wine sauce) is fantastic from the start. Dijon mustard is divine—it's made with white wine instead of vinegar. Regional cheeses include soft St-Florentin and rich Chaource. Desserts include *pain d'épices* (gingerbread) and pastries filled with cherries and black currants.

HIGHLIGHTS OF BURGUNDY

■ Even if **Beaune** were not at the heart of the famous Côte d'Or vineyards, it would be worth visiting for the magnificent altarpiece in the **Hôtel-Dieu** (p. 186).

■ Walk around the ramparts in beautiful **Semur-en-Auxois** (p. 205).

■ Near the once-great abbey of **Cluny,** the 17th-century **Château de Cormatin** has beautifully preserved rooms, lush formal gardens, and a maze (p. 194).

■ The Second Crusade was declared by St. Bernard from the magnificent Romanesque basilica of **Vézelay,** which holds the relics of Mary Magdelene.

⌐ GETTING AROUND

With Dijon as its main transportation hub, Burgundy is crisscrossed by **train** lines. Towns which lack train stations are served by **SNCF** or **TRANSCO** buses (tel. 03 80 42 11 00 in Dijon). Be aware that Burgundy is primarily an agricultural region and timetables favor early morning departures and early evening returns. Hikers and cyclists will find the gently sloping lands well suited to their ventures, though harsh weather will dissuade them in winter. Parts of the Morvan and some small towns and isolated châteaux can only be reached by bike, car, thumb, or foot.

DIJON

Dijon (pop. 160,000) is renowned for its snobbery in France and for its mustard everywhere else. Beyond these two local products, the capital of Burgundy is a city endowed with a rich cultural patrimony, from fine medieval architecture to some of the world's greatest wines. While Dijon is clearly speeding along into the 21st century as both an industrial and administrative center, the *vieille ville* seems comfortably frozen in a non-specific past, with its plethora of *maisons en bois* and *hôtels particuliers*. In the late Middle Ages, the Dukes of Burgundy cast a disdainful eye on the weak sovereign in Paris, wielding power and prestige the monarchy could not hope to match. Nowadays, with its student population and mustard factories, the city is decidedly more democratic, but something of its ancient ways lingers in the *vieille ville*, as elite and refined as ever.

ⓩ ORIENTATION AND PRACTICAL INFORMATION

Despite its size, Dijon is easy to explore. Its main east-west axis, the pedestrian **rue de la Liberté,** runs roughly from **pl. Darcy** and the tourist office to **pl. St-Michel.** From the train station, follow av. Maréchal Foch straight to pl. Darcy (5min.). The *vieille ville* and most of Dijon's sights are on the small streets radiating north and south from rue de la Liberté. The **pl. de la République,** northeast of pl. Darcy, is the central roundabout for roads leading out of the city.

Trains: Cours de la Gare, at the end of av. Maréchal Foch. To: **Paris** (1¾hr., 12 per day, 222F); **Lyon** (1½hr., 9 per day, 132F); **Nice** (7-8hr., 9 per day, 373F); and **Clermont-Ferrand** (4hr., 1 per day, 184F). 24hr. ticket counters. Reservations and info office M-F 9am-7pm, Sa 9am-6pm. **SOS Voyageurs** (tel. 03 80 43 16 34) M-F 8:30am-7pm and Sa 8:30am-5pm. **Baggage storage** open M-F 8am-8pm and Sa-Su 9am-7pm, 15F.

Buses: TRANSCO, av. Maréchal Foch (tel. 03 80 42 11 00), connected to train station, to the left as you exit. Ticket and info office open M-F 7:30am-6:30pm, Sa 7:30am-12:30pm. At other times, go to the *chef du Gare's* office near the bus terminal or buy tickets on the bus. Service to the **Côte d'Or, Beaune, Chalon-sur-Saône,** and **Autun.**

Local Transportation: STRD (tel. 03 80 30 60 90), a groovy concrete booth on pl. Grangier. Office open M-Sa 6:30am-7:15pm. Map at the tourist office. Tickets 5.20F, available on bus. 12-trip pass 43.50F, 1-day pass 16F, 1-week pass 45.50F. 5-trip night pass 23F. Buses run 6am-8pm, with limited evening service until 12:15am.

Taxis: Taxi Dijon (tel. 03 80 41 41 12). 24hr.

Car and Bike Rental: Avis, 5 av. Maréchal Foch (tel. 03 80 43 60 76). **Cars** from 520F for 24hr., 250km, and insurance included; 1820F per week, 1750km, and insurance included. Open M-F 8am-noon and 2-7pm. **Travel Car,** 2 av. Poincaré (tel. 03 80 72 31 00; fax 03 80 73 38 40), off pl. Bouhey. **Bikes** 100F per day, 430F per week. 2000F deposit. Also rents cars, minivans, and a wide array of scooters and motorcycles. Open M-F 9am-noon and 2-7pm, Sa 9am-noon and 3-6pm. V, MC, AmEx.

Tourist Office: Pl. Darcy (tel. 03 80 49 11 44). Sells 2F map with museums and organizes daily **city tours** July-Aug., some in English (35F, students 25F). Accommodations service 15F plus 10% deposit on the first night. **Currency exchange.** Open daily July-Aug. 9am-8pm; Sept.-June 9am-7pm. **Branch** at 34 rue des Forges. Go just to climb up

THE CENTER

GERMANY

SWITZERLAND

Burgundy

the Renaissance staircase. Open May-Oct. 15 M-Sa 9am-1pm and 2-6pm; Oct. 16-Apr. M-F 9am-1pm and 2-6pm. **Accueil** office in the Palais des Ducs. Open M-F 8am-12:30pm and 1:30-6:30pm and Sa-Su 9am-12:30pm and 1:30-6:30pm.

English Bookstore: Librairie de l'Université, 17 rue de la Liberté (tel. 03 80 44 95 44). Paperbacks on 2nd floor. Open M 1-7pm, Tu-Sa 9:30am-7pm.

Youth Information: Centre d'Information Jeunesse de Bourgogne (CIJB), 18 rue Audra (tel. 03 80 44 18 44). Info on lodgings, French classes, grape-picking jobs, sports, and travel. Sells HI cards. Open M-F 9am–1pm and 2-6pm; 2-5pm in summer.

Budget Travel: Wasteels, 16 av. Foch (tel. 03 80 43 65 34). Open M-Th 9am-noon and 2-6pm, F 9am-noon and 2-7pm, Sa 9am-noon.

Laundromat: 36 rue Guillaume Tell. Open daily 6am-9pm.

Police: 2 pl. Suquet (tel. 03 80 44 55 00).

Medical Assistance: Centre Hospitalier Regional de Dijon, 3 rue fbg Raines (tel. 03 80 29 30 31). **SOS Médecins** (tel. 03 80 73 55 55) has doctors on call.

Post Office: Pl. Grangier (tel. 03 80 50 62 19), near pl. Darcy. Poste Restante code: 21031. **Currency exchange. Internet access.** Open M-F 8am-7pm, Sa 8am-noon. **Postal code:** 21000.

Internet Access: Station Internet, in the bus station. Open M-F noon-8pm, Sa noon-5pm. 40F per hr.

▶ ACCOMMODATIONS AND CAMPING

In summer, reasonably priced hotels fill quickly. Reserve or use the tourist office's accommodations service. The foyers are a 45-minute walk from the station. **CROUS,** 3 rue du Docteur Maret, may be able to arrange university housing for about 70F per night. (Tel. 03 80 40 40 23. Open M-F 9am-noon and 1:30-5pm.)

Foyer International d'Étudiants, 6 rue Maréchal Leclerc (tel. 03 80 71 70 00; fax 03 80 71 60 48). Take bus #4 from pl. Darcy (direction "St-Apollinaire") to "Parc des Sports." From av. Paul Doumer, turn right onto rue du Stade, then take the first left. You'll hear English, Japanese, German, and Spanish emanating from this neutral crossroads. TV rooms, tennis court, laundry, kitchen, and a lawn for sunbathing (the international sport). Cafeteria open on weekdays. Huge singles with big desks 90F. 24hr. reception.

Auberge de Jeunesse (HI), Centre de Rencontres Internationales, 1 av. Champollion (tel. 03 80 72 95 20; fax 03 80 70 00 61), 4km from the station. Take bus #5 (or night bus A) from "Bar Bleu" on pl. Grangier to "Épirey;" the stop is in front of the concrete megahostel. The complex offers a bar/disco, language courses in summer, game rooms, and laundry facilities. Dorms 52F. Clean but unattractive singles with shower 130F; doubles and triples with shower and toilet 144F. Breakfast 20F. Lunch or dinner 35-55F. Pool 6F. Lockers 10-20F. 24hr. reception. No keys before midday, no lockout. Reservations advised June-Sept.

Hôtel Montchapet, 26-28 rue Jacques Cellerier (tel. 03 80 53 95 00; fax 03 80 58 26 87). In a quiet neighborhood 10min. from the station, north of av. Première Armée Française off pl. Darcy. Fairy-tale proprietors let thoroughly homey rooms. Lots of students. Singles 150F, with toilet 190F, with shower 215F; doubles with toilet 230F, with shower 235F; triples 330F; quads 370F. Extra bed 40F. Shower 20F. Breakfast 32F. Reception 6am-midnight, check-out noon, will hold baggage. V, MC, AmEx.

Hôtel Monge, 20 rue Monge (tel. 03 80 30 30 15; fax 03 80 30 63 87). Set back from the street near the Église St-Jean, with a courtyard. Cozy rooms and friendly proprietors. Singles 125F, with shower 170F; doubles 135F, with shower 180F; 1 twin and 1 double with shower and toilet 280F. Some doubles with shower 210-240F. Extra person 10F. Shower 15F. TV in room 10F. Breakfast 28F. Reception 8am-10pm. V, MC, AmEx.

Hôtel du Sauvage, 64 rue Monge (tel. 03 80 41 31 21; fax 03 80 42 06 07), off rue de la Liberté. Located in a former 15th-century post office. Half-timbered façade opens into a cobblestone courtyard strewn with flowers and tapestries line the breakfast room.

THE CENTER

N

TO F (1.8km)

bd. de la Marne   bd. de Verdun   r. Davout   r. de Metz

bd. G. Clémenceau

r. de Mulhouse   r. Dietsch   bd. Thiers   r. du Lycée de   r. Diderot   Chambure   Paul Cabet   r. Jean Baptiste

PL. DU 30 OCTOBRE ET DE LA LÉGION D'HONNEUR

TO E (2.6km)

PL. DE LA RÉPUBLIQUE

r. du Nord   r. d'Assas   Verrerie   r. Comte Rousseau   Chaudronnerie   r. Jeannin   Sauvmèse   St-Michel

PL. DE STE-CHAPELLE   PL. ST-MICHEL

bd. de la Trémouille   bd. de la Préfecture   Notre-Dame   r. des Forges   Palais des Ducs   Musée des Beaux Arts   PL. DU THÉÂTRE   Musée Magnin   r. Buffon   r. Berbier   bd. Carnot   r. d'Auxonne

r. Devosge   PL. ST-BERNARD   r. Bannelier   r. Musette   Branch Office   PL. DE LA LIBÉRATION   PL. FR. RUDE   r. Amiral Roussin   r. Chabot Charny   r. P. Potel   r. Pasteur   PL. WILSON   r. Feutel

r. Courtépée   r. d'Ahuy   r. Colonel Marchand   r. Montigny   r. des Godrans   r. du Château   GRANGIER   PL. GRANGIER   Centre Commercial Dauphine   r. du Bourg   r. Mercier   r. Piron   PL. JEAN MACÉ   r. V. Dumay   PL. DES CORDELIERS   r. de la Synagogue   r. Turgot   r. du Chaignot   r. du Transvaal

r. des Roses   r. des Fleurs   r. de Brosses   PL. GUILLAUME DARCY   r. de la Poste   r. de la Liberté   Musée Archéologique   Cathédrale St-Bénigne   r. Michelet   r. Bossuet   PL. BOSSUET   r. Danton   r. Cazotte   PL. ÉMILE ZOLA   r. Berbisey   Ste-Anne   r. Colson   r. de Sem.

B   r. Cellerier   r. Montmartre   PL. de l'Égalité   AUGUSTE DUBOIS   r. Audra   PL. Square d'Arcy   av. 1ère Armée   Porte Guillaume   Dr. Maret   r. St-Philibert   PORTE St-BÉNIGNE   r. Condorcet   L. Monge   D   C   r. de Tivoli   PL. SUQUET   r. de la Manutention   r. de l'Hôpital

r. des Fleurs   r. de l'Égalité   r. Spuller   av. Victor Hugo   r. du Rosoir   r. Millotet   bd. de Sévigné   r. Mariotte   Rempart Miséricorde

r. Guillaume Tell   r. Docteur Remy   av. du M. Foch   r. de l'Arquebuse

r. Charles Briffaut   r. des Perrières   av. Albert 1er   Jardin de l'Arquebuse

r. Lamartine   r. de Marmuzots   r. A.Coubert   r. Nodot   r. de Faubourg Raines   av. de Louche

r. Th. de Béze   r. de Bellevue   r. des Perrières

r. Moreau   bd. de l'Ouest

300 yards
300 meters

TO A (1.2km)

Dijon

ACCOMMODATIONS

A Camping Municipal du Lac
B Hôtel Montchapet
C Hôtel Sauvage
D Hôtel Monge
E Foyer International d'Etudiants
F Auberge de Jeunesse (CRISD)

Courtyard restaurant grills meat and vegetables over a wood fire (*plats* 39-140F, lunch *menu* 65F). Singles with shower and toilet 20-300F; doubles 240-320F. Huge 5-person loft 520F. Parking garage 25F. Breakfast 33F. Reception 7am-11pm. Reserve 1-2 weeks in advance during the summer. V, MC.

Campsites: Camping Municipal du Lac, 3 bd. Kir (tel. 03 80 43 54 72). Exit the back of the station and turn left on av. Albert 1er. After 1km, turn left on bd. Kir, then follow the signs. Or take bus #12 from pl. Darcy (direction "Fontaine d'Ouche") to "Hôpital des Chartreux." A nearby park runs along the shady canal. Bring toilet paper. 16.50F per person, children under 10 8.50F, 12.50F per tent, 8.50F per car. Electricity 16F. Office open daily 8:30am-8pm. Open Apr.-Oct. 15.

▣ FOOD

Dijon's reputation for *haute cuisine* is well-deserved—and the restaurant prices reflect it. Still, *charcuteries* provide an economical way to sample *dijonnais* specialities such as the transplendent *tarte bourguignonne* (creamy meat and mushroom pie), *quiche aux champignons*, and *jambon persillé* (ham with parsley). *Dijonnais* chefs are delightfully liberal with local vinegars, wines, and, of course, mustards. Drunk all over France as an *apéritif*, *Kir*, a blend of *cassis* and white wine, is named after its inventor, a former Mayor of Dijon.

Rue Berbisey and **rue Monge** host a wide variety of reasonable restaurants. University cafeterias stay open all summer; contact **CROUS** (see **Accommodations**; cafeteria info tel. 03 80 40 40 40) for details. **R.U. Maret,** 3 rue Docteur-Maret (tel. 03 80 40 40 34), has an all-you-can-eat dinner for 14F. (Student ID required. Open M-F 11:30am-1:30pm and 6:30-8pm, Sa-Su 11:40am-1:15pm and 6:40-7:45pm.) There's a supermarket in the basement of the **Galeries Lafayette,** 41 rue de la Liberté (open M-Sa 9am-7:15pm), and on the first floor of **Prisunic** at 11 rue Piron, off pl. Jean Macé (open M-Sa 8:30am-8pm). There is a colorful **market** in the pedestrian area from **pl. F. Rude** to **rue Bannolier.** (Tu and Sa 6am-1pm.)

L'Entresol, 27-29 rue Musette (tel. 03 80 30 15 10), off pl. Grangier. Upstairs from the health-food *marché* La Vie Saine, this haven for hungry vegans and vegetarians has a direct line to organic ingredients. *Menus* 63F and 72F. Drinks include soy milk, fruit cocktails, and creamy café au (soy) lait. Open M-Sa 11:45am-2:30pm. V, MC, AmEx.

Le Germinal, 44 rue Monge (tel. 03 80 30 69 61). Bares a wide spread of frogs' legs, *paella*, and traditional Burgundian favorites on a street not lacking in fine food. The lunchtime *menu* is a steal at 60F. Dinner *menus* start at 98F. Open Tu-Su noon-2:30pm and 7-10:30pm, until 11pm F-Sa. V, MC, AmEx.

Le Rapido, 102 rue Berbisey (tel. 03 80 30 95 55). Young, hip café perfect for sidewalk chilling and spectating. The generous *entrées* (from 30F), *plats* (49-59F), and hepcat bar-hopping *dijonnais* will compete for your attention. The fresh salads are a meal in themselves (30F).

👁 SIGHTS

PALAIS DES DUCS DE BOURGOGNE (MUSÉE DE BEAUX-ARTS). In their heyday (1364-1477), the Dukes of Burgundy were fearless (Jean sans Peur), good (Philippe le Bon), and bold (Philippe le Hardi and Charles le Téméraire). At the center of the *vieille ville*, the 52m **Tour Philippe le Bon** is the most conspicuous vestige of ducal power, while the palace and its semi-circular arcade were designed in the late 17th century by the royal architect, Jules Hardouin-Mansart. Most of the buildings currently house administrative offices, but the elegant **Musée des Beaux-Arts,** pl. de la Ste-Chapelle (tel. 03 80 74 52 70), occupies the palace's east wing, and includes in its courtyard the 15th-century kitchens and a grand staircase leading to the Chapter House. The highlights of the museum are the Salle du Maître, Campin's exquisite "Nativity," (c.1420) depicting the vision of St. Brigit of Sweden, and the famous Salle des Gardes, dominated by the huge sarcophagi of Philippe le Hardi, Jean sans Peur, and Jean's wife Margaret. Tiny, delicately detailed figures of mourners keep vigil at the base of each tomb. *(Pl. de la Libération. Open W-M 10am-6pm. 22F, 28F for special exhibitions, free to students and on Su.)*

ÉGLISE NOTRE-DAME. The 13th-century church bears eloquent witness to some of Dijon's darkest moments. The defaced tympanum, which depicted the lives of the Virgin and Christ, remains a sad relic of the Revolution, but the 11th-century cult statue of the Black Virgin has happier stories to tell. She is credited with the liberation of the city on two desperate occasions: first in 1513 when the Swiss besieged Dijon, and second from the German occupation in 1944. Both liberations occurred on 11 September; two sumptuous tapestries depicting the miracles were commissioned for the Virgin in gratitude. The **Horloge à Jacquemart,** ticking above the church's tower, is worth a crick in the neck. Hauled off as plunder by Philippe le Hardi after his 1382 victory over the Flemish, the lonely male statue that sounded the hour (dubbed "Jacquemart" by the *dijonnais*) was given a spouse 200 years later. The couple later "bore" a son to strike the half-hour, and finally, in 1881, were blessed with a daughter to daintily announce the quarter-hour. Lower your gaze to drink in the magnificent façade, which displays three rows of leering gargoyles. The current monsters are 19th-century replicas, made after the original 13th-century creations were found to be too effective—the creature symbolizing Avarice fell from its perch, killing a money-lender. After leaving the church, touch the rubbed-down *chouette* (owl) on the left side of the exterior to ensure extra good luck. *(Pl. Notre Dame. Tel. 03 80 74 35 76.)*

ÉGLISE ST-MICHEL. Begun at the end of the Gothic era in the 15th century, the church's style transmuted from Flamboyant to Renaissance during its construction. Like Notre-Dame, the church suffered severe damage during the Revolution but was lovingly restored by Abbé Deschamps, who put his heart into the job—it's buried in one of the chapels. The Renaissance façade has been revamped and now sparkles above the oldest buildings in the old city. *(Pl. St-Michel. Tel. 03 80 63 17 84.)*

MUSÉE MAGNIN. The elegant 17th-century Hôtel Lantin now houses this extensive collection of 16th- to19th-century paintings. Though most of the art is obscure, the ensemble is well-worth a visit. With period furnishings, rich wallpapers, and works clustered in intimate groups, you'll feel as if you've been invited to the home of an ardent art collector for a private showing. *(4 rue des Bons Enfants. Tel. 03 80 67 11 10. Open Tu-Su 10am-noon and 2-6pm. 16F, students 12F; Su everyone 12F.)*

CATHÉDRALE ST-BÉNIGNE. This Burgundian-Gothic cathedral commemorates a 2nd-century missionary whose remains were unearthed nearby in the 6th century. Its brightly-tiled roof makes it one of Dijon's most prominent landmarks. Don't miss the 18th-century organ designed by Charles Joseph Riepp and the unusual (and somewhat spooky) circular crypt, originally the rotunda of an early 11th-century Romanesque church. *(Pl. St-Bénigne. Tel. 03 80 30 14 90. Crypt 7F.)*

MUSÉE ARCHÉOLOGIQUE. Next door to the cathedral, the Musée Archéologique unearths the history of the Côte d'Or. Housed in the former cloisters of St-Bénigne's abbey, it includes Gallo-Roman sculpture, medieval statuary, and neolithic finds. *(5 rue Docteur Maret. Tel. 03 80 30 88 54. Open Jan.-May and Oct.-Dec. W-M 9am-noon and 2-6pm; June-Sept. 9:30am-6:30pm. 14F, students 7F; free on Su.)*

OTHER SIGHTS. The **Jardin de l'Arquebuse** provides a welcome retreat from Dijon's churches and monuments. There are 3500 species in the meticulously laid out botanical garden, and the weeping willows and reflecting pools of the arboretum make it a pleasant spot to stroll. *(1 av. Albert 1er. Tel. 03 80 76 72 84. Open daily July-Sept. 7:30am-8pm; Oct.-Feb. 7:30am-5:30pm; Mar.-June 7:30am-7pm.)*

No trip to Dijon could be complete without a stop at **Grey Poupon,** 32 rue de la Liberté, *moutarde au vin* makers since 1777. Take home the famous mustard (from 12F), a handmade faïence jar (from 135F), or a silk mustard tie (220F).

♪ ❋ ENTERTAINMENT AND FESTIVALS

NIGHTLIFE. Rue Berbisey is lined with bars and cafés. At **Cappuccino,** 132 rue Berbisey (tel. 03 80 41 06 35), the staff and chic clientele mingle to rock and hip hop on the pastel terrace. (Open M-F 3pm-1am, Sa 3pm-2am.) **L'Univers',** 47 rue Berbisey (tel. 03 80 30 98 29), attracts a worldly bunch that spills onto the sidewalk. (Open M-Sa 11am-2am, Su 5pm-2am.) The cavo downstairs embraces the gay crowd. (Open 9pm-2am.) At **Atmosphère,** 7 rue Audra (tel. 03 80 30 52 03 or 03 80 30 66 03), *dijonnais* youth hang in the combo bar, pool hall, nightclub, and discothèque. Weekend crowds can be large, especially during the academic year. (Beer 20F, cocktails 35F. Open daily 2pm-3am.) Not to be missed is **Le Brighton,** 33 rue Auguste Comte, near Notre-Dame (tel. 03 80 73 59 32), a pseudo-English pub that caters to the yuppie crowd. (Half-pints 25-40F. Open daily noon-3am.) But your best bet is the friendly and always full **La Comédie,** 3 pl. du Théâtre (tel. 03 80 67 11 62), with beer for 12.50F and fine *kir.*

CULTURE. Opera and classical music are performed from mid-October to late April at the Théâtre de Dijon, pl. du Théâtre (tel. 03 80 68 46 40), a beautiful 18th-century opéra house. (Tickets 130-1540F, students 60F 1hr. before curtain.) Check out the shows (both classic and contemporary) at **Nouveau Théâtre de Bourgogne,** located at Théâtre du Parvis St-Jean, rue Danton (tel. 03 80 30 12 12), in a former Gothic church. The theater bar draws an artsy crowd. (Open noon-7pm.)

FESTIVALS. Dijon's **Estivade** (tel. 03 80 30 31 00) brings cheap dance, music, and theater to the streets and venues from late June to late July. Pick up a programme at the tourist office. (Tickets 0-50F.) The city devotes a week in late summer to the **Fêtes de la Vigne** and the **Folkloriades Internationales** (tel. 03 80 30 37 95), a well-attended grape celebration, accompanied by over 20 foreign dance and music troupes. (Tickets 30-70F.)

BEAUNE

The puns are easy enough to make: *le vin de Beaune, c'est du bon vin.* But the throngs of dapper 40-somethings and red-faced septuagenarians who come to this viticultural hotspot often don't speak enough French to get them. The only snippets of the local tongue you may hear are the names of vineyards, pronounced with enthusiasm by foreign wine connoisseurs. While Beaune is hardly French—yen, dollars, and deutchmarks drip from hallowed wine-presses—the bunches of visitors unite with locals in their deep love of the liquid which Louis Pasteur called "the healthiest and most hygienic drink." Nestled along the Côte d'Or 40km south of Dijon, the town serves as a base for shippers and wineries. Beneath Beaune's streets, a labyrinth of *caves* (cellars) protects the bottles from the tipsy throngs above. Not that wine-tasting in Beaune is a Bacchanalian affair—the dimly lit, centuries-old *caves* evoke a religious reverence. Meandering along the maze of Beaune's short cobblestone streets with the recent memory of a (free!) fine *cru* on the palate, you'll struggle to stumble away from this town.

⊟ ORIENTATION AND PRACTICAL INFORMATION

Almost everything there is to see lies within the circular ramparts that enclose Beaune's *vieille ville.* To get to the center of town from the train station, head straight on av. du 8 Septembre, which becomes rue du Château. Turn left onto rempart St-Jean, following it up and down the stairs as it crosses rue d'Alsace and mutates into rempart Madeleine. The fourth right is **rue de l'Hôtel-Dieu,** which leads to the Hôtel-Dieu and the **tourist office** (15min.). The streets of the *centre ville* run in concentric rings around **Basilique Notre-Dame.**

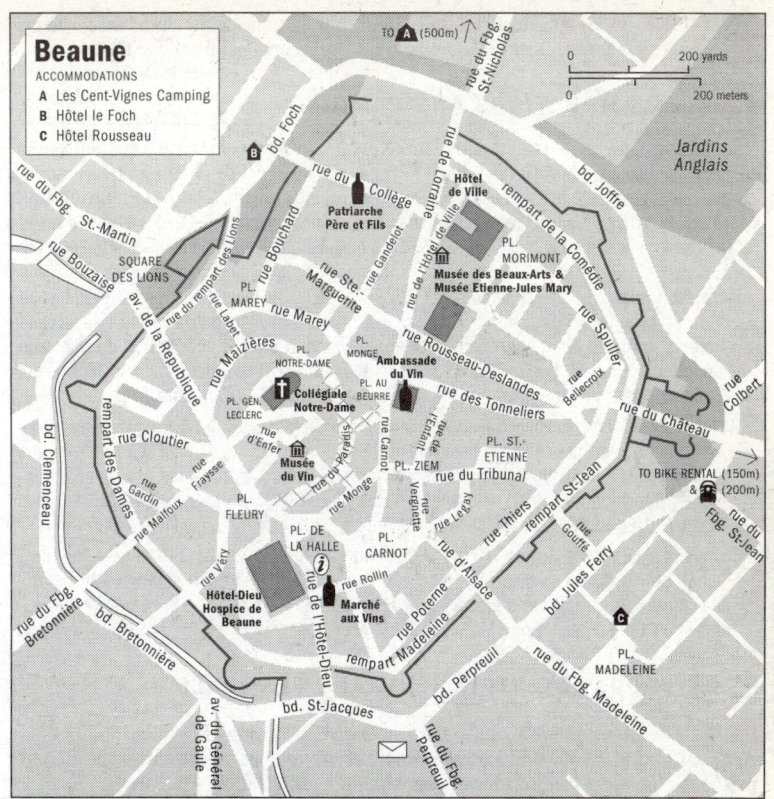

Beaune
ACCOMMODATIONS
A Les Cent-Vignes Camping
B Hôtel le Foch
C Hôtel Rousseau

THE CENTER

Trains: Av. du 8 Septembre (tel. 08 80 22 13 13). To: **Dijon** (25min., 21 per day, 38F); **Chalon-sur-Saône** (25min., 13 per day, 31F); **Lyon** (1½hr., 6 per day, 113F); and **Paris** (2hr., 2 per day, 286F). Ticket window open daily 6:15am-8:30pm.

Buses: TRANSCO (tel. 03 80 42 11 00 in Dijon). To: **Chalon-sur-Saône** (1hr., 2 per day); **Dijon** (1hr., 10 per day, 39.20F); **Autun** (80min., 1 per day). Stops along the **Côte d'Or.** Schedule available at the tourist office. Buses depart from several locations.

Car Rental: ADA, 26 av. du 8 Septembre (tel. 03 80 22 72 90; fax 03 80 22 72 92), across from the train station. From 209F for 24hr., 1599F per week with 1000km included. Open M-Sa. V, MC.

Bike Rental: Bourgogne Randonnées, 3 av. du 8 Septembre (tel. 03 80 22 06 03), near the station. Helpful English-speaking owner is full of advice. 20F per hr., 90F per day, 170F for 2 days, 400F per week. Passport deposit. Open daily 9am-noon and 1:30-7pm, Su 10am-noon and 2-6pm. V, MC.

Tourist Office: Rue de l'Hôtel-Dieu (tel. 03 80 26 21 30; fax 03 80 26 21 39). Free maps. Hotel reservations with 10% down payment, lists of *caves,* and daily *vieille ville* tours in English (July-Sept.; 40F per person, 65F per couple). 85F *passeporte* to sites and *dégustations.* **Currency exchange** on M when banks are closed. Open M-Sa 9am-8pm, Su 9am-6pm; June 15-Sept. 15 also Su 9am-7pm.

Laundromat: Blanc-matic, next to the supermarket off pl. Madeleine and at 26 fbg. Nicholas. Open daily 7:30am-7pm.

Police: 5 av. du Général de Gaulle (tel. 03 80 25 09 25).

Hospital: Centre Hospitalier, av. Guigone de Salins (tel. 03 80 24 44 44). **Ambulance** (tel. 03 80 24 64 00).

Post Office: Bd. St-Jacques (tel. 03 80 26 29 50), in a building with red steel girders. **Currency exchange.** Open M-F 8am-7pm, Sa 8am-noon. **Postal code:** 21200.

ACCOMMODATIONS AND CAMPING

The visitors swarm between April and November—especially on weekends—so it's best to make reservations at least a week in advance. For cheaper accommodations, base yourself in Dijon, a 25-minute train ride away. The hotels around pl. Madeleine tend to be less expensive than those in the *centre ville*. A **Villages** hotel is 2km out on rue Burgalat. (Tel. 03 80 24 14 50. Singles and doubles 155F.)

Hôtel Rousseau, 11 pl. Madeleine (tel. 03 80 22 13 59). From the station, head left on rue des Lyonnais until it turns into rue Celer, then turn right onto rue fbg. Madeleine. Hotel is in the far right-hand corner. Beautiful wooden beds in rooms that open onto a secluded courtyard. Singles from 135F; doubles from 180F, with shower 300F. Shower 20F. Breakfast included. Ask for the code to avoid the 11:30pm curfew.

Hôtel le Foch, 24 bd. Foch (tel. 03 80 24 05 65; fax 03 80 24 75 59). Take av. de la République from the tourist office and turn right on bd. Foch. Simple, carpeted rooms with TVs. One suite with a sitting room and futon couch costs the same as a double. Singles in nearby annex 100F; singles and doubles 160F, with shower 200-230F; quad 250F. Extra bed 40F. Breakfast 28F. Reception 7am-9pm. Free parking. V, MC.

Campsites: Les Cent-Vignes, 10 rue Dubois (tel. 03 80 22 03 91), 500m from the town center off rue du fbg. St-Nicolas. Head north on rue Lorraine from pl. Monge. Arrive early in summer. Restaurant and grocery store. Package 41F. Electricity 19F. Laundry. Reception daily 8am-10pm. Open Mar. 15-Oct. V, MC.

FOOD, ENTERTAINMENT, AND FESTIVALS

FOOD. Food here is not exactly *Beaune marché*—prices are high. The restaurants around **pl. Madeleine** and **pl. Carnot** serve the least exorbitant *menus*, but prices for the local *vin* may leave you whining in frustration. The streets just east of **pl. Monge** hawk sandwiches and cheap North African food. There are two **Casino supermarkets,** at 28 rue du fbg. Madeleine (open M-Sa 8:30am-7:30pm) and at 14 rue Monge (open M-Sa 7:30am-12:30pm and 3-7pm, Su 8am-12:30pm). A large **market** on pl. Carnot livens up Saturday mornings. If you're willing to dispense with formality, you can eat a full, good meal for under 60F at the locally popular cafeteria **Sun 7,** Stoc Centre Commercial, av. Charles de Gaulle. (Open daily 11am-9:30 pm.)

If you insist on service, you'll get the most fat for your franc at **Les Marinières,** 6 bd Jules-Ferry (tel. 03 80 22 14 42). Choose from 26 varieties of *moules frites*, from white wine and garlic to curry (55-80F). (Open Su and Tu-Th noon-2pm and 7-10pm, F-Sa until 10:30pm. V, MC.) An old favorite, **Les Tontons,** 22 rue du fbg. Madeleine (tel. 03 80 24 19 64), has been remodeled and now caters to more discerning palates. Try the *escargots*, or one of the delicious 95F and 159F *menus*. (Open M-Sa noon-2pm and 7-10:30pm. V, MC.) M. Neaux, the *chef de cuisine* wants you to try everything at **Relais de la Madeleine,** 44 Place Madeleine (tel. 03 80 22 07 47). You won't go wrong with *spécialités de la maison* like duck pâté, *boeuf bourgignon*, and peppered trout. Don't be dissuaded by the low-tech menu—this food is *haute cuisine. Menus* run 70F, 92F, and 145F. (Closed W during Oct.-Apr. V, MC.)

ENTERTAINMENT AND FESTIVALS. On July weekends, Beaune holds its annual **International Baroque Music Festival** with concerts in the courtyard of Hôtel-Dieu and the Basilique Notre-Dame (tickets at the tourist office 70-350F, students 50-300F). At night, it's always the best of times at **Pickwick's,** 2 rue Notre-Dame (tel. 03 80 24 72 59), near the cathedral, with a non-smoking wine bar in the *cave* downstairs. (Open M-Sa 11am-3pm and 5pm-1am; until 2am weekends and summer.)

🕐 SIGHTS AND SIPS

Though the 15th-century hospital might have cured any outward ills, it is wine that has always kept the city, if not its inhabitants, in good health. This tradition continues today, with visitors milling about the central squares and boulevards before descending into one of Beaune's many *caves*. Ask questions about the individual wine-making processes at each cave. For a crash course on wine tasting, see **...And Which Wine Does Madame Desire?** (p. 29); the guides in each *cave* will also be happy to instruct.

PATRIARCHE PÈRE ET FILS. The largest *cave* in Beaune is reached by a staircase descending from the altar of an 18th-century chapel. An audioguide tour will explain the mysteries of wine as you wonder at 10 million bottles maturing in 5km of corridors. *(5-7 rue du Collège. Tel. 03 80 24 53 7825 08 20. Open daily 9:30-11:30am and 2-5:30pm; try to arrive at least 1hr. before closing. 50F; all proceeds go to charity.)*

MARCHÉ AU VINS. A steady stream of tourists funnel to this 15th-century church from the nearby tourist office and Hôtel de Ville. From here you can descend into a candle-lit *cave* and follow a trail of 18 wine kegs. They save the best till last—*les grands crus* come near the end—and there's a one-hour limit on drinking. *(Rue Nicolas-Rolin. Tel. 03 80 25 08 20. Open daily 9:30am-noon and 2-6pm. 50F)*

MUSÉE DU VIN. If you can still walk, stagger to this museum housed inside the Hôtel des ducs de Bourgogne. Within the 15th- to 16th-century ducal mansion you can see the wine cellar, antique presses, and vats for free. The painstakingly detailed museum takes you past bar graphs, pie and temperature charts, and topographical maps with precise information about some of the greatest harvests. Other exhibits trace the evolution of the shapes of wine bottles, wine glasses, and carafes from ancient Rome to today. *(Rue d'Enfer, off pl. Général Leclerc. Tel. 03 80 22 08 19. Open daily 9:30am-6pm; closed Tu Dec.-Mar. Ticket booth closes at 5:30pm. 25F, students 15F. Includes admission to Musée de Beaux-Arts and Musée Étienne-Jules Marey, below.)*

HÔTEL-DIEU. In 1443, Nicolas Rolin, chancellor to the Duke of Burgundy, built this hospital to hasten the city's recovery from the ravages of war, poverty, and famine. The building continued to treat patients until 1971, and is now the town's biggest non-potable tourist attraction. The hospital managed to give its patients royal treatment through Rolin's bequest of 143 acres of the area's finest vineyards. Each year in November the most recent vintages are whipped out for the famous charity auction, which takes place on a Sunday afternoon. The courtyard is an excellent vantage point from which to admire the magnificent tiled roofs which make the Hôtel-Dieu the architectural icon of the region. Inside, La Salle des Pôvres (the Room of the Poor) is anything but, with rows of red-curtained beds. The Hôtel's great treasure, however, is the polytyptich Last Judgment by Roger van der Weyden, whose exquisite detail can be appreciated with the help of a giant automated magnifying glass. *(Open daily Mar. 22-Nov. 16 9am-6:30pm; Nov. 17-Mar. 21 9-11:30am and 2-5:30pm. 32F, students 25F. Guided tour 10F extra.)*

OTHER SIGHTS. The **Musée des Beaux-Arts** has a small collection of Gallo-Roman sculpture and a cache of paintings by 15th- and 16th-century Dutch and Flemish artists and 18th- to 19th-century French artists. The same building holds the **Musée Étienne-Jules Marey.** *(Rue de l'Hôtel de Ville. Both museums tel. 03 80 24 56 98 and open daily Apr.-Nov. 2-6pm. For admission, see Musée du Vin, above.)* No visit to Beaune is complete without a peep at the Burgundian-Romanesque **Collégiale Notre-Dame** and the set of late 15th-century tapestries behind its altar which depict the life of the Virgin. *(Open daily 8:30am-7pm.)*

THE CÔTE D'OR

The nectar fastidiously stored in Beaune's dark cellars began its life basking on the sunny acres of the Golden Slopes to the north and south. The Côte d'Or—a 60km strip of land from Dijon to the village of Santenay 20km south of Beaune—has nurtured grapes since around 500 BC. Traces of limestone in the soil, the right amount of rainfall, and the ideal inclination of the land for exposure and drainage make it the perfect place to cultivate grapes, placing it among the most valuable real estate in the world. This acknowledged heart of Burgundy produces less wine than the Médoc region of Bordeaux alone, and the price of a bottle reflects its scarcity.

The Côte d'Or is divided into two regions. The **Côte de Nuits**, stretching south from Dijon through **Nuits-St-Georges** to the village of **Corgoloin**, produces red wines made from the *Pinot Noir* grape. Running from Corgoloin south to **Santenay**, the **Côte de Beaune** produces its great white wines from *Chardonnay* grapes. The aptly-named **Route des grands crus** ("great wine route") winds through the region, passing through the famous vineyards and wine-producing villages. Without a car and plentiful funds, the villages are hard to get to, hard to stay in, and offer few services and attractions other than the *vignerons* peddling their high-priced wares. You can taste for free, but remember that most wine-makers will expect you to buy something.

The vineyards near Beaune are the only superior ones along the Côte d'Or easily accessible by public transportation; otherwise hire a **bike** or pull on your walking boots. It's cheapest to base yourself in **Dijon** and bike south along the Route des Grand Crus, returning with your bike on the train. Unfortunately, **trains** stop only in **Beaune** and **Nuits-St-Georges**. The reasonable distances between villages make it a pleasant few days **hike**. TRANSCO buses (tel. 03 80 42 11 00) head from **Dijon** throughout the Côte, with major stops at **Nuits-St-George** (30min., 7-8 per day, 24.50F) and **Beaune** (1hr., 7-8 per day, 39.20F). If you're in a hurry and have cash to spare, you can try one of **Bacchus Wine Tours'** guided minibus tours in English from Beaune (180-195F for 2hr. with *dégustation*; info at the tourist office), or **rent a car** in Beaune or Dijon (around 400F per day including tax, insurance, and gas).

Lodging on the Côte is expensive; some reasonable options are given below, but your best bet is to reserve a room days in advance at one of the many *chambres d'hôtes* dotting the villages. The tourist office in Beaune will supply you with a copy of *Chambres et Table d'hôtes*, a comprehensive list of bed and breakfasts along the Côte d'Or and throughout France.

GEVREY-CHAMBERTIN

Perhaps the finest vineyards in all of France may be found 10km south of Dijon around Gevrey-Chambertin. Nine of the Côte's 29 *grands crus* are grown here, all with "Chambertin" in their name. Perched atop of the vineyards, the **Château de Gevrey-Chambertin** offers a guided tour. The gracious proprietor takes you through her 10th-century château, built to protect the wine and the villagers (in that order). Louis XIV's doctor, who knew his wine perhaps better than his medicine, prescribed Chambertin for his corpulent patient. You'll see a millennium of history, including a 10th-century guard tower. The tour ends with a taste of her prized vintages, which sell for upwards of 90F a bottle. *(Open Apr.-Oct. daily 10am-noon and 2-6pm; Nov.-Mar. M-Sa 10am-noon and 2-5pm, Su 11am-noon and 2-5pm. 30min. tour 20F.)*

The Gevrey-Chambertin **tourist office** (tel. 03 80 34 38 40) is small. (Open M-Sa 10am-12:30pm and 2-6pm.) Bunk down near the restaurants *chez* the **Marchands**, 1 pl. du Monument aux Morts (tel. 03 80 34 33 60; fax 03 80 34 12 77; singles 150F, doubles 200-250F), or get some shut-eye closer to the château at the foot of the vineyards at **Clos-Saint-Jacques** (tel. 03 80 51 82 06; singles 150F, doubles 200F).

CHÂTEAU DE CLOS DE VOUGEOT

From Gevrey-Chambertin, the D122 turns back southward, passing just to the east of minor châteaux in Morey-St-Denis and Chambolle-Musigny before arriving at the **Château du Clos de Vougeot** (tel. 03 80 62 86 09), a few kilometers north of Nuit-

St-Georges. Built in 1098, it was renovated to its present state in the 15th century by Louis XI, who regarded it as one of his greatest conquests. Today, this magnificent castle stands sentinel in a 125-acre vineyard which its owners lease to several different *vignerons*. And it is these owners who give the château its spark: the **Confrérie des Chevaliers du Tastevin** (Brotherhood of the Knights of the Tastevin), was founded in 1934 to promote the sale of Burgundian *crus* during a slump in sales brought on by Prohibition and the Depression. The 12,000 members hold frequent parties at the château as part of their strict duty to spread the gospel of Burgundian wine: *"Jamais en vain, toujours en vin"* ("Never in vain, always in wine"). The *confrères* may have their fun here, but there's no wine tasting or buying at the château for the plebs. *(Open Apr.-Sept. Su-F 9am-6:30pm, Sa 9am-5pm; Oct.-Mar. Su-F 9-11:30am and 2-5:30pm, Sa 9-11:30am and 2-5pm; closes at nightfall during the winter. 1hr. guided visits depart every 30min. 20F, students and children 15F, under 8 free.)*

CHÂTEAU DE ROCHEPOT

Fifteen kilometers southwest of Beaune, the **Château de Rochepot** springs straight out of a fairy tale, flaunting its pointed turrets, slate roof, and wooden drawbridge. "To enter, knock three times," declares the ancient sign. Most of what you see today is a 19th-century restoration of the 15th-century original. The ornate well leads to secret underground tunnels which served as escape routes during attacks. The 45-minute tour includes a peek at the Guard Room, the ingenious kitchens, the dining room, the old chapel, and the "Chinese" room, a gift of the last empress of China. *(Tel. 03 80 21 71 37. Open July-Aug. W-M 10am-noon and 2-6pm; Sept. 10-11:30am and 2-5pm; Oct. 10-11:30am and 2-4:30pm; Apr.-June 10-11:30am and 2-5:30pm. 30F.)*

In la Rochepot, Serge and Solange Robin's *chambre d'hôtes* are on rte. de Nolay. *(Tel. 03 80 21 71 6. Singles 200F; doubles 220F.)* From here, the bike route again climbs steeply along the vaulted cliffs of St-Romain, where French rock-climbers belay each other up onto the highway from the vertical faces below. The road then descends through Pommard and back into Beaune.

MÂCON

Balanced between Burgundy and the Beaujolais, Mâcon (pop. 38,500) is considered the crossroads between the north and the south. Its location on the Saône helped make it an important Roman colony, Matisco, and later a frontier city between French lands and the Holy Roman Empire. Mâcon's main claim to fame is as the birthplace of Alphonse Prat de Lamartine (1790-1869), Romantic poet, politician, and ladies' man *par excellence*. For those with a car or bike (there's no rental in town), Mâcon also makes an ideal base from which to explore the Beaujolais vineyards (p. 218), as well as for daytrips to Cluny and Paray-le-Monial.

🛂 ORIENTATION AND PRACTICAL INFORMATION. Trains and **SNCF buses** leave from rue Bigonnet for **Dijon** (1¼hr., 6 per day, 94F), **Lyon** (1hr., 13 per day, 61F), and **Paris** (4½hr., 3 per day). (Info desk open M-F 9am-noon and 1:20-6:30pm, Sa 9am-12:45pm and 1:45-5:40pm.) TGVs stop at **Mâcon-Loche**, 6km away. SNCF buses shuttle occasionally between the two *gares* (7 per day); a *taxi* costs around 110F (tel. 06 85 10 73 79; 24hr.).

The *centre-ville* is a fairly compact area framed by rue Gambetta, rue Victor Hugo, cours Moreau, and the Saône. To reach the **tourist office**, 1 pl. St-Pierre (tel. 03 85 21 07 07; fax 03 85 40 96 00), from the *gare*, go straight down rue Gambetta and take the second left onto rue Carnot. The office's accommodations service charges 15F plus 10% down payment. (Open June-Sept. M-Sa 10am-7pm, Su 2-6pm, Oct.-May M-Sa 10am-6pm.) There's a **Laverie 7/7** at 22 rue Gambetta. (Open daily 7am-10pm.) The **police** are at 36 rue Lyon (tel. 03 85 32 63 63). The **post office**, 3 rue Victor Hugo (tel. 03 85 21 05 50), has **currency exchange**. (Open M-F 8:30am-7pm, Sa 8:30am-noon. **Postal code: 71019.**) **Internet access** is at **Le Victor Hugo Cafe**, 37 rue Victor Hugo. (Tel. 03 85 39 26 16. 1F per min. Open M-Sa 8am-1am, Su 3pm-1am.)

ACCOMMODATIONS. Budget accommodations come easy in Mâcon, though reservations are recommended in July and August. **Le Relais Fleuri,** 28 rue des Minimes (tel./fax 03 85 38 36 02), is centrally located on the street across from the tourist office, to the right of the Église St-Pierre. The homey atmosphere is complemented by the friendly proprietor. (Doubles 150F, with shower and toilet 180F; triples 180F; quads 200F. Breakfast 28F. Closed Su afternoon. Call ahead.) **Hôtel Escatel,** 4 rue de la Liberté (tel. 03 85 29 02 50, fax 03 85 34 19 97), feels like a college dorm. From the gare turn left onto rue V. Hugo and follow it past pl. de la Barre as it flows into rue de l'Héritan. The hotel is to the right across from the intersection of rue de l'Héritan and rue de Flace (15min.). It has a restaurant, bar, and pool. (Singles 129-145F; doubles 185F. Rooms with double bed, shower, toilet, and TV 170F for 1 person; 200F for 2, with bath instead of shower 235F. Extra bed 50F. Breakfast 38F. V, MC, AmEx.)

FOOD. Situated between mainstream Burgundy and the Beaujolais, Mâcon has the best of both wine worlds while also producing its own admirable Chardonnays, *Pouilly Fuissé* and *Mâcon Clessé.* They go nicely with *quenelles* (fishballs) and *coq au vin,* two regional specialties which grace almost every menu. A small **market** is held daily on pl. aux Herbes; a larger one is held on esplanade Lamartine (Sa 7am-1pm). Staples can be found at **Marché Plus,** 18 rue Lacretelle off rue V. Hugo. (Open M-Sa 7am-7pm and Su 9am-1pm.)

It's not difficult to find reasonable restaurants in Mâcon, but avoid the impersonal eateries on the *quais* next to the noisy highway. For a night on the town, start off with an *apéritif* at **La Maison de Bois,** 13 pl. aux Herbes (tel. 03 85 38 03 51), a friendly bar in a Renaissance house with grotesque carvings. (Open Tu-Sa 8-1 or 2am, Su-M noon-1am). **Chez Gilou,** 19 rue Dufour (tel. 03 85 40 95 47), off rue Carnot, has a fun Caribbean shack ambience and serves mussels *en masse.* The 55F lunch *menu* includes 250g of mussels with fries, dessert, and coffee, while more muscular *menus* cost 68F and 82F. (Open Tu-Sa noon-2pm and 7-10pm; July-Aug. also Su noon-2pm.) **L'Amuse Gueule,** 18 rue St-Vincent (tel. 03 85 38 16 24), near Vieux St-Vincent, is a homey place with a country-kitchen touch, tucked away from the main road. The *plat du jour* is 39F, with starter and dessert 45-60F. (Salads and pizzas 35-50F. Non-smoking. Open daily noon-2pm and 7-10pm.)

SIGHTS. The tourist office sells a **global pass** (40F), only worth it if you plan on seeing everything. The office also offers a guided tour of the city in French with a *dégustation* at a Mâconnais *cave* (1½hr.; July-Aug. F-Sa 1 per day; 25F).

From the tourist office, walk right a couple of steps to the **Résidence Soufflot,** 249 Carnot, a former hospital. The building was designed in 1752 by Soufflot, architect of Paris's Panthéon. It preserves a multi-level Italianate chapel, which allowed the sick to participate in mass without having to descend to the ground floor, and a *tonneau tournant* (revolving cupboard), which allowed mothers to orphan unwanted children anonymously. (Hours vary; inquire at tourist office.)

Rue Carnot and rue Dombey have a number of late medieval houses, the most famous being the **Maison de Bois,** now housing a bar (see **Food,** above) on the corner of rue Dombey and pl. aux Herbes. Built between 1490 and 1510, the façade has a marvelous array of carvings, with naughty monkeys and other animals, and the house is one of only four of its kind left in France. At rue du Pont, turn right and walk across the **Pont St-Laurent** for a good view of the city. During the Wars of Religion, Huguenot prisoners were tossed from the 11th-century bridge. Back in town stands the sad ruin of **Vieux St-Vincent,** rue de Strasbourg (tel. 03 85 39 90 38). All that's left is the 12th-century narthex with a defaced tympanum and two octagonal 11th- to 13th-century towers. (Narthex open June-Sept. Tu-Sa 10am-6pm, Su 10am-noon; Oct.-May M, W-Sa 10am-5:30pm, Su noon-5:30pm. South tower open June-Sept. M and W-Sa 10am-noon and 2-6pm, Su 2-6pm; Oct.-May call ahead. 15F, under 16 and students free.)

Two blocks behind Vieux St-Vincent is the **Musée des Ursulines,** 5 rue des Ursulines (tel. 03 85 39 90 38),which has displays on local prehistoric, Gallo-Roman, Merovingian, and later medieval archæology. The first floor is devoted to the ethnology and traditions of the Mâconnais, while the second holds a collection of paintings and furniture from the 16th to 20th centuries, including works by Le Brun and Corot. (Open Tu-Sa 10am-noon and 2-6pm, Su 2-6pm. 15F.) Eighteenth-century aficionados should not miss the **Hôtel-Dieu,** another Soufflot creation, at 344 rue des Épinoches (tel. 03 85 39 90 38) behind sq. de la Paix. The dome is impressively high, but the real highlight is the 1775 **apothecary.** Large porcelain pots announcing such delectable contents as eye of crayfish are displayed on mag-nificently-worked ash and oak shelves. (Open June-Sept. W-Su 2-7pm.) Another delight is the elegant Regency-style **Hôtel Senèce,** 41 rue Sigorgue. Built by the chancellor of Burgundy, it became the center for the Academy of Arts, Sciences and Letters in the early 19th century, presided over by Lamartine. Now it holds the **Musée Lamartine** (tel. 03 85 39 90 38), where devotees will find documents and per-sonal objects illustrating the operatic life of the poet-turned-politician. (Open M and W-Sa 10am-noon and 2-6pm. 15F.)

ENTERTAINMENT AND FESTIVALS. Cafés on the *quais* are full all day long and well into the evening. Just behind quai Jean Jaurès are lively concert-bars, including **La Bodega,** 41 rue Franche, which specializes in karaoke. (Open Th-Sa 5pm-2am.) The big summer event is the four-week **L'Été Frappé,** a festival that features a variety of free shows at indoor and outdoor venues around Mâcon. Films, jazz, classical music, comedians, and dancing are all packed into the pro-gramme, which usually unrolls between mid-July and mid-August. For goings-on in the region, ask the tourist office for the free annual *Guide Sortir.*

CLUNY

Cluny's population (5000) has not grown since it controlled 10,000 monks, 1200 monasteries, and more than a few kings at the height of its power at the end of the 11th century. Its once enormous abbey, which produced almost a dozen popes, faded into obscurity following the Wars of Religion and the Revolution. Lying between rolling green hills in the Grosne valley, Cluny now exports mustard jars and top-notch engineers from ENSAM *(École Nationale Supérieure d'Arts et Métiers)*, but it is the town's rich medieval heritage which keeps it on the map.

PRACTICAL INFORMATION. Cluny has no train station, but **SNCF buses** run to **Mâcon** (40min., 5 per day, 25F), **Châlon-sur-Saône** (80min., 3 per day, 46F), and **Paray-le-Monial** (2½hr., 1 per day, 56F). **Bike rental** (tel. 03 85 59 08 34 or 03 85 59 03 97) is available at the **campground.** (45F per day. 500F deposit. Open May-Oct. M and F 9am-noon and 2-6pm, Tu and Th 1-6pm, W and Sa 9am-noon and 2-7pm.) For a **taxi,** call 03 85 59 04 87. To get from the bus stop to the **tourist office,** 6 rue Mer-cière (tel. 03 85 59 05 34; fax 03 85 59 06 95), in the Tour des Fromages, walk against the traffic on rue Porte de Paris, turn right at pl. du Commerce; and con-tinue for five minutes. Here you'll find a helpful map, the free *Practical Guide to Cluny*, a schedule for **city tours** (25F, reduced rate 15F), and **currency exchange** on weekends. (Open daily July-Aug. 10am-7pm; Sept.-June 10am-12:30pm and 2:30-7pm.) The **police** are at rue Porte de Paris (tel. 03 85 59 06 32). The **post office** is off Chemin du Prado (tel. 03 85 59 07 98), near pont de la Levée. (Open M-F 8am-noon and 2-6pm, Sa 8am-noon. **Postal code:** 71250.)

ACCOMMODATIONS, CAMPING, AND FOOD. Budget lodgings fill quickly in summer; reserve early or daytrip from Mâcon. The best deal for groups is **Cluny Séjour,** rue Porte de Paris (tel. 03 85 59 08 83; fax 03 85 59 26 27), behind the bus stop. (Singles 115F; doubles 154F; triples 231F; quads 308F. Breakfast included. Reception opens 5pm.) Or try **Hôtel du Commerce,** 8 pl. du Commerce. (Tel. 03 85 59 03 09. Singles from 110F; doubles 140-155F, with shower 200F. Extra bed 40F. Breakfast 28F. Closed daily noon-3pm unless you call ahead. V, MC.) There is **camping** at **St-Vital,** rue de Griottons (tel. 03 85 59 08 34; fax 03 85 59 16 34), over the pont de la Levée and across a field. (18F, children under 7 9F; 9.50F per tent or car. Electricity 15F. Open May 15-Sept. Reservations recommended.)

Locals speak well of **Les Marronniers,** 20 av. Général de Gaulle (tel. 03 85 59 07 95), for regional specialties (including frogs legs) on their three- (47F) and four-course (61F) *menus.* (Open Tu-Sa noon-2pm and 7-9:30pm, Su noon-2pm. V, MC). There is a **Casino supermarket** at 29 rue Lamartine. (Open M-Sa 8am-12:30pm and Su 8am-noon.) The **local market** is held every Saturday morning near the abbey.

SIGHTS AND FESTIVALS. Begin your tour with a great view from atop the 120 steps of the **Tour des Fromages.** (6F, students 4F.) Then follow rue Mercière one block and turn right onto rue de la République. This area, particularly at rue d'Avril provides a peek at the well-preserved **Maisons Romanes** (medieval houses). The path leads straight through the **Porte d'Honneur,** which frames the abbey spires. The **Musée d'Art et d'Archéologie** (tel. 03 85 59 23 97), on the left, houses a reconstruction of the abbey and some religious art which escaped destruction. (Open July-Aug. 9am-7pm., Sept.-June 10am-noon and 2-6pm. 32F, under 25 21F; includes abbey tour in French, 8 per day July-Aug.) The Romanesque **abbey church,** dedicated to St. Peter and St. Paul, is the third church on the site and goes under the imaginative name of **Cluny III.** The order of the Cluniacs was founded in the 10th century in an effort to reform monastic life, but it quickly mushroomed. Forgetting its founding creed, it became immeasurably wealthy, attracting some of the brightest minds of the 11th and 12th centuries. At the height of its power Cluny controlled a vast network of daughter abbeys and by virtue of its unique charter escaped the control of every ruler except the pope. Cluny III was the largest church in the world until the construction of St. Peter's in Rome, and the abbot's power and wealth rivaled that of the popes. During the Wars of Religion and particularly the Revolution and its aftermath, the abbey was looted, sold, and used as a quarry. A mental reconstruction of its scale requires some effort, but its wealth can still be easily glimpsed in the ornamentation of the Gothic **Pope Gelasius** façade. What remains is now home to the **École Nationale Supérieure d'Arts et Métiers,** with a central cloister surrounded by students' rooms. Times have changed; cells that used to house one monk are now shared among four engineers!

Medieval nostalgia rules the town for a weekend in early July during **les Médiévales de Cluny.** Locals and tourists dress up in 13th-century robes to watch and participate in a series of jousting tournaments, falconry shows, and archery competitions. On Saturday there is a banquet in the abbey with troubadours and other period entertainment. (Reserve at tourist office. 30F per day, banquet extra.)

NEAR CLUNY: VAL LAMARTINIEN

The sights and roadsides of the area around Cluny are splashed with signs bearing verses by the Romantic poet Alphonse de Lamartine (1790-1869), who made his home in the **Château de St-Point** (tel. 03 85 50 50 30), 12km south of Cluny. This 12th-century château was restored by Lamartine in a neo-Gothic style and surrounded by an English-style park. Many of his possessions are still on display. (Open M-Tu and Th-Sa 10am-noon and 2-6pm, Su 2-6pm. Tours every 30min. 28F, ages 12-16 18F.) **La route Lamartine** tours some of the other châteaux around Cluny. The imposing **Château de Pierreclos** (tel. 03 85 35 73 73) belonged to four separate noble families, each with distinct decorative tastes. Take a brief spin through the interior, complete with France's largest and longest spiral staircase, and then head for the *caves* and a *dégustation* of local wines. (Open daily July-Aug. 9:30am-6pm; Sept.-June 9:30am-noon and 2-6pm. Guided tours. 35F, students 27F.)

Twelve kilometers to the north of Cluny is the 17th-century **Château de Cormatin** (tel. 03 85 50 16 55), with a moat, formal gardens, an aviary, and a maze. The château was probably designed by the royal architect for the governor of Châlon between 1605 and 1616; the monumental open well staircase in the north wing was the height of sophisticated engineering. The governor's heir paid homage to Maria de Médici through sumptuous interior decoration which copied the royal widow's preferred Italian style. The rooms, though unrestored, are well preserved. The château also bears traces of more eccentric owners, including Nina de Pierreclos, self-styled "siren" of this "enchanted island," who threw wild parties until the family lost the castle to her creditors. The château is easily **bikeable** from Cluny, or take an **SNCF bus** from **Cluny** (25min., 7 per day, 16F) or **Mâcon** (65min., 7 per day, 36F). (Open daily May-Sept. 10am-noon and 2-6:30pm; Easter-Apr. and Oct. 1-Nov. 11 10am-noon and 2-5:30pm. Tours in French with written translation every 30min. 38F, students 28F, children 22F.)

PARAY-LE-MONIAL

Paray-le-Monial owes its fame to a 25-year-old nun. It was here, in 1673, that Christ began to appear before Sister Marguerite-Marie Alacoque, revealing his heart and saying, "Here is the heart, which so loved mankind." The adoration of the Sacred Heart didn't catch on until the late 19th century, when pilgrimages were organized to the town. The growing cult provoked a visit by Pope Pius IX, who elevated the town's simple cathedral to the status of a basilica, while Sister M-M was canonized in 1920. Since then Paray has become a pilgrimage site second only to Lourdes in France, and it was money raised by the cult that paid for the Sacré-Cœur in Paris.

🔁 **PRACTICAL INFORMATION. Trains** (tel. 03 85 81 13 25) are infrequent; the last leaves early in the afternoon, so check times or risk getting stuck. They go to **Lyon** (3 per day, 95F), **Dijon** (1 per day, 97F), **Moulins** (4 per day, 58F), and indirectly to **Paris** (5 per day, 246F). You can ride **SNCF buses** to **Cluny** (2½hr., 1 per day, 56F), where you can change for **Mâcon** (72F), and to local hubs **Roannes** (5 per day, 45F) and **Le Creusot,** with a TGV terminal (5 per day, 52F). For a **taxi,** call 03 85 88 85 01. To get to the **tourist office** (tel. 03 85 81 10 92), exit left out of the station and turn right on av. de la Gare. Cross the canal bridge and veer right onto av. de Gaulle. At the end of the street, turn left on rue des Deux Ponts, continue straight until you cross the bridge over the Bourbince, with a view of the Basilica, and then turn right on av. Jean Paul II. When the road forks, you'll be in front of the office, next to the Basilica (15min.). (Open daily July-Aug. 9am-7pm; May-June and Sept.-Oct. M-Sa 9am-noon and 1:30-6:30pm, Su 10am-12:30pm and 2:30-6:30pm; Nov.-Apr. M-Sa 9am-noon and 1:30-6pm.) The **post office** is on rue du Marché. (Open M-F 9am-noon and 1:30-6pm, Sa 8am-noon. **Postal code:** 71600.)

🏕 **ACCOMMODATIONS AND CAMPING.** Paray draws pilgrims year-round, and rooms are difficult to find during religious sessions (mostly in the summer); reserving two months in advance is strongly recommended. Comfortable, cheap rooms can be found in the Christian Foyers near the basilica. The **Foyer du Sacré-Cœur,** 14 rue de la Visitation (tel. 03 85 81 11 01; fax 03 85 81 26 83; foyersc@club-internet.fr), is a charming, quiet place in the center of town. Rooms are tastefully decorated, some with crucifixes hovering protectively over the bed. Pilgrims predominate, but pagans and tourists are welcome. (Singles from 100F; doubles with 2 beds from 190-200F. Breakfast 22F, lunch 65F, dinner 60F. Reception 8am-12:30pm, 1:30-6:30pm and 8-9:30pm.) The **Hôtel du Nord,** 1 av. de la Gare (tel. 03 85 81 05 12), has simple rooms and a comfortable sitting room with TV. (Singles 150F; with shower 170F; doubles with bath, toilet, and TV 240F. Breakfast 30F. Showers 15F. Reception 6:30am-11pm. V, MC.) In town is **Hôtel du Champ de Foire,** rue Desrichard (tel. 03 85 81 01 68; fax 03 85 88 86 30), with clean, simple rooms and friendly proprietor. (Singles 140F; doubles 180-190F; triples 220F; quads 260F. Breakfast 25F. V, MC). **Camping de Mambré** is on route du Gué-Léger (tel. 03 85 88 89 20). From the end of av. de la Gare, turn left and follow it for 25 minutes. This bustling campsite has a pool and laundry. (Bungalows July-Aug. 260-320F, Sept.-June 180-200F. Tent 40F/34F, 20F/14F per person. Reception 8am-11pm. Open Apr.-Oct.)

🍴 **FOOD. Markets** are held on bd. du Collège (F until 1pm). A string of cheap eateries unravels on rue Victor Hugo off pl. Guignault, but a prettier place for lunch is in one of the cheap *brasseries* on the south side of the Bourbince, with views of the Basilica. There's an **Éco Service** grocery store on the corner of rue Victor Hugo and rue du Marché. (Open M-Sa 8am-12:30pm and 2:30-8pm, Su 8:30am-noon.) **La Tarterie,** 9 rue Victor Hugo (tel. 03 85 81 21 66), is the place to go if you like tarts. Solo tarts cost 20F, while the 45F *menu* offers salad plus tarts *salé* and *sucré*. (Open 10am-7pm daily Apr.-Oct., M-Sa Nov.-Mar. V, MC, AmEx.)

🏛 **SIGHTS.** The spire of the **Basilique du Sacré-Cœur** is visible throughout the town. Although Paray didn't emerge as a religious center until the first pilgrimage was organized in 1873, the basilica dates from the 11th century. It was built by order of St. Hugh, Abbot of Cluny, and in many ways is a miniature (not to mention extant) replica of the nearby abbey. This production of the Cluny architectural workshop is brought to you by the number three, symbolizing the Trinity, with a tripartite elevation and division on the façade, three major towers, and three radiating chapels. Unlike at Cluny, the design eschews sculptural decoration for clean lines, harmonious design, and soaring verticality. Some of the sculpture has geometric patterns which may have been inspired by Hugh's travels in Moorish Spain. In the semi-domed apse there is a massive 14th-century fresco of Christ in Majesty.

Rue de la Visitation leads from the Basilica to the other religious sights. The **Parc des Chapelains,** behind the church, is a peaceful spot for reflection in the outdoor chapel, whose nave is formed by plane trees. The **Acceuil Pèlerinage de Paray** (Pilgrimage Center; tel. 03 85 81 62 22) next door welcomes the curious with a multilingual video and info on religious sessions. (Open 9:30-noon and 2-6pm.) Continue along rue de la Visitation to the **Monastère de la Visitation,** sometimes referred to as *la Chapelle des Apparitions,* where Jesus is said to have revealed himself to Marguerite-Marie and where the relics of Marguerite-Marie can now be found. At the end of rue de la Visitation, turn left to get back to the *centre ville.* On **pl. Guignault,** the sand-colored façade of the early 16th-century **Maison Jayet** (now the **Hôtel de Ville**) is adorned with portraits of French royalty. The **Tour St-Nicholas,** also 16th-century, stands guard over pl. Guignault. Once the belfry of the long-gone St-Nicholas church, it is now another pretty façade adorned by a beautiful staircase. Occasional art exhibits are held inside.

AUTUN

Around 15 BC, Emperor Augustus founded Augustodunum—later shortened to Autun—to create a "sister and rival of Rome." Invading barbarians later performed a similar abbreviation to the town's glory; the only remaining proof of Autun's former status is an impressive collection of ruins. Things started to look up when the relics of St. Lazarus were brought to town in the 10th century, but the town's comeback really began in the 12th. Stirred by civic jealousy of nearby Vézelay's success, the town erected the Cathédrale St-Lazare (1120-1146) and made a successful push for the lucrative medieval pilgrimage business. Despite the ravages of eight none-too-kind centuries, the cathedral still boasts some of the finest Romanesque sculpture in the world. Though a recent lack of pilgrims has pushed Autun (pop. 20,000) off the beaten path, its serpentine streets, cathedral, and Roman ruins make it a compelling stop for anyone in Burgundy.

🚆 **ORIENTATION AND PRACTICAL INFORMATION. Trains** run from pl. de la Gare on av. de la République to **Lyon** (3½hr., 2 per day, 144F) and **Paris** via **Dijon** (5hr., 4 per day, 234F); most trains require a change at Chalon-sur-Saône or Étang. **SNCF buses** also leave the station for **Chalon-sur-Saône** (2hr., 4 per day, 72F) and **Dijon** (2hr., 4 per day, 94F). (Station office open M-F 7:05am-7:30pm, Sa 9:05am-12:30pm and 2:30-6:30pm, Su 12:05-7:30pm.) **TRANSCO buses** (tel. 03 80 42 11 00) go to **Dijon** daily at 5pm (2½hr., 79F). For a **taxi,** tel. 03 85 52 05 06.

THE CENTER

The main street, **av. Charles de Gaulle,** connects the station to the central **pl. du Champ de Mars.** To get to the *vieille ville* from the pl. de Champs de Mars, follow the signs leading to cathedral from rue aux Cordeliers. The **tourist office,** av. Charles de Gaulle (tel. 03 85 86 30 00; fax 03 85 86 10 17), is off pl. Champ de Mars. (Open July-Aug. daily 9am-7pm; Apr.-June and Sept. M-Sa 9am-noon and 2-7pm; Oct.-Mar. M-Sa 9am-noon and 2-6pm.) There's an **annex** at 5 pl. du Terreau (tel. 03 85 86 80 38), next to the cathedral. (Open July-Aug. daily 9am-7pm, June and Sept. M-Sa 9am-7pm.) The **hospital** is at 9 bd. Fr. Latouche (tel. 03 85 86 65 66). The **police** (tel. 03 85 52 14 22) are at 29 av. Charles de Gaulle. You can **exchange currency** at the **post office** on rue Pernette. (Tel. 03 85 52 20 93. Open M-F 8:30am-6:30pm, Sa 8:30am-noon. **Postal code:** 71400.)

▐ ACCOMMODATIONS AND CAMPING. Hotels near the *centre ville* tend to be pricey, but cheaper alternatives can be found across from the train station. Make reservations a couple of weeks in advance during the summer. **Hôtel de France,** 18 av. de la République (tel. 03 85 52 14 00), has many rooms with TV and phone. (Doubles 130-230F. Breakfast 27F. Reception daily 8am-11pm. Closed Su until 5:30pm.) **Hôtel Clarine,** 22 av. de la République (tel. 03 85 52 30 03; fax 03 85 86 39 09), offers huge, modern bathrooms, comfy beds, TVs, and telephones. (Doubles 275F; triples 300F. Breakfast 35F. AmEx.) Stake your claim at **Camping Municipal de la Porte d'Arroux** (tel. 03 85 52 10 82), an easy 20-minute walk from town. From the train station, turn left on av. de la République, left on rue de Paris, and go under the Porte d'Arroux. Cross the bridge and veer right on rte. de Saulien; the campground is on your left. There is a restaurant and a grocery store. (Stores open 8am-9:30pm. 14F per person, 13F per tent, 8.50F per car. Electricity 15F. July-Aug. 15F fee for campground security. Open Apr.-Oct.)

▐ FOOD. Regional fare awaits at the **Auberge de la Bourgogne,** 39-40 pl. du Champ de Mars (tel. 03 85 52 20 96). Choose zee leetle *escargots* (70F for 12) or *grenouilles* (frog's legs, 75F); *menus* start at 70F. (Open Tu-Su noon-2pm and 7-10pm. V, MC, AmEx.) Romanesque—or at least Italian—restaurants line the cobbled streets of the *haute ville*. Everything in **La Trattoria,** 2 rue des Bancs (tel. 03 85 86 10 73), is the color of a very ripe plum tomato and just as tasty. Choose from a dozen pizzas (42-50F) or pastas (45-60F). (Open Tu-Sa noon-2pm and 7:15-10pm, Su noon-2pm. V, MC.) Next door, **Le Petit Banc,** 4 rue des Bancs (tel. 03 85 52 64 32), has cheap sandwiches (22-30F) and *crêpes* (15-30F). (Open daily 10am-3:30pm and 6pm-midnight, except Th in winter.) If you're looking for authentic Roman ambience, Autun's ruins are prime picnicking territory. Prepare your feast at **Intermarché,** pl. du Champs de Mars. (Open M-Th 8:30am-12:45pm and 2:30-7:30pm, F-Sa 8:30am-7:30pm.) Champs de Mars is also the *place* for **markets** (W and F).

▣ SIGHTS. At the top of the *haute ville*, the **Cathédrale St-Lazare** rises above the Morvan countryside. In the course of 900 years of clerical quarrels, one group objected to the marvelous **tympanum** above the church doors and covered it in plaster, unwittingly protecting the masterpiece from the ravages of the Revolution. Today, Jesus still presides over the Last Judgment while Satan tinkers with the weighing of the souls. The artist's name, Gislebertus, is visible below Jesus'

THE WICKED SAMARITAN As you enter Autun's Cathédrale St-Lazare, look for the second and third capitols to the right. These tell the tale of Simon Magus, a Samaritan sorcerer who could reputedly change his shape, fly, and take his head off at will. When Jesus upstaged him on the miracle front, Simon lost his head and bribed the Apostles to sell him the Holy Ghost. The arrogant magician was soon brought down to earth—literally. His rise and fall are illustrated in the carvings; one shows Simon flying to demonstrate his power, while on the other he crashes to the ground as a result of the Apostles' prayers.

THE CENTER

feet. In the dimly lit nave, intricately carved capitals illustrate biblical scenes. To see some of the carvings at eye-level, climb up to the *salle capitulaire* above the sacristy. Beware the basilisk, an imaginary animal whose gaze reputedly turns humans into stone. (Open daily 8am-7pm.) The **Musée Rolin,** 3 rue des Bancs (tel. 03 85 52 09 76), next to the cathedral, houses a diverse historical collection in the 15th-century mansion of Burgundian chancellor Nicolas Rolin. It includes beautiful mosaics, a Roman helmet of bronze and gold shaped like a leafy human face, Gislebertus's poignant sculpture of Eve at the Fall, the noseless man of Nazareth, and paintings by Le Nain and Natoire. (Open Apr.-Sept. W-M 9:30am-noon and 1:30-6pm; Oct. W-Sa 10am-noon and 2-5pm, Su 10am-noon and 2:30-5pm; Nov.-Mar. W-Sa 10am-noon and 2-4pm, Su 2:30-5pm. 20F, students 10F.)

There isn't a huge amount left from the Roman period, considering that the city was once the largest in Gaul, but enough remains to more than merit a visit. The cushy way is to sit back and take a narrated tour on **le Petit Train,** which leaves from pl. du Champs de Mars and from the tourist office annex near the cathedral. (45min.; July-Aug. 7 French tours per day; 30F, children 20F.) If you plan do the ruins solo, be sure to arm yourself with a free map from the tourist office. Standing behind the train station, across the river Arroux, is the huge brick **Temple de Janus.** Once 24m high and 16m wide, this 1st-century temple was dedicated to an unknown Roman deity—not the double-headed Janus common in mythology. To reach the two walls that still exist, walk along rue de Paris until you pass under one of the city's two remaining Roman gates, the **Porte d'Arroux.** With two large arches for vehicles and two smaller ones for pedestrians, this gate led to the Via Agrippa, the main trade road between Lyon and Boulogne. Cross the river and take the footpath leading to the left. After passing the temple, the path returns to town via rue du fbg. St-Andoche. The other gate, the **Porte St-André,** is at the intersection of rue de la Croix Blanche and rue de Gaillon. The small Protestant church nearby is a former Roman guard house.

In the **Théâtre Romaine,** accessible by av. du Dragons off pl. de Charmasse, picnickers relax where once there sat 12,000 enthralled spectators. Occasionally the amphitheater whimpers back to life when 600 locals bring Cæsar, chariot races, and games to life in the show **Augustodunum,** during the first three weekends of August. (80F. Tickets sold at tourist office.) From the rear of the amphitheater, you can see a 30m pile of bricks of the **Pierre de Couhard.** The purpose of this heap remained unknown until excavations unearthed a 1900-year-old plaque that cursed anyone who dared to disturb the eternal slumber of the man buried inside. *Let's Go* does not recommend incurring dormant wrath. To reach it, follow a path that starts above the cathedral from rue du fbg. St-Blaise and climb into the hills.

The ramparts, towers, and spire are best seen from the hills above town; to get there, take the path from near the cathedral to the Pierre de Couhard.

NEVERS

Canals, forests, fields, and the Loire and Nièvre rivers all converge on Nevers (pop. 50,000). A primary subject of Marguerite Duras's screenplay *Hiroshima Mon Amour,* Nevers is also the final resting place of Bernadette Soubirous, a.k.a. St. Bernadette of Lourdes. She came to Nevers in July 1866, to enter the Couvent St-Gildard, and she's still there, preserved in the convent's chapel. Beyond the bustle of a modern industrial city, Nevers is a land of carefully tended parks, modest squares, exquisite medieval and Renaissance architecture, and a long tradition of decorative arts: glass, enamel, and most of all, porcelain. If at first you aren't impressed by this shy city, remember Duras's admonition: "Saying that Nevers is a tiny town is an error of both the heart and the spirit."

⌖ PRACTICAL INFORMATION. Trains pass through Nevers to: **Moulins** (35min., 8 per day, 53F), **Bourges** (55min., 5 per day, 59F), **Clermont-Ferrand** (1½hr., 6 per day, 117F), **Paris** (2½hr., 7 per day, 161F), and **Dijon** (2¾hr., 5 per day, 142F). (Counters open daily 5:45am-9:10pm.) To the left of the station as you exit is the bus station (tel. 03 86 57 16 39), with limited **bus service.** For a **taxi,** call 03 86 59 58 00. **Rent bikes** at **Belair,** 31bis rue de la Préfecture. (Tel. 03 86 61 24 45. 100F per day, 450F per week. 2000F deposit. Open M-Sa 8:30am-12:30pm and 1:30-7pm.) From the station, head four blocks up av. Général de Gaulle to Nevers's main road, pl. Carnot. The **tourist office** (tel. 03 86 68 46 00; fax 03 86 68 45 98) is in the Palais Ducal, across the square from av. de Gaulle on rue Sabatier. The office offers free maps and French **walking tours** on the city, porcelain, and St. Bernadette. (Tours July-Aug. M-Sa; 30F, students 20F. Office open June to mid-Sept. M-Sa 9am-7pm, Su 10am-7pm; mid-Sept. to May M-Sa 9am-noon and 2-6pm, Su 10am-noon and 2-7pm.) There's **currency exchange** at **Crédit Municipal,** pl. Carnot. The **Centre Hospitalier** is at 1 av. Colbert (tel. 03 86 68 30 30), the **police** at 6bis av. Marceau (tel. 03 86 60 53 00). The **post office,** 25bis av. Pierre Bérégovoy (tel. 03 86 21 50 21), has **currency exchange.** (Open M-F 8am-6:30pm, Sa 8am-noon. Poste Restante code: 58000. **Postal code:** 58019.) **Internet access** is online across the street at **France Télécom.** (Open M 10am-noon and 1:30-6pm, Tu-F 8:30am-noon and 1:30-6pm, Sa 9am-noon and 2:30-6pm.)

⌐ ACCOMMODATIONS AND CAMPING. The tourist office has a list of hotels and restaurants in the area. Rooms near the station and *centre ville* start around 115-130F. The friendly **Foyer Clairjoie,** 2 rue Cloître St-Cyr (tel. 03 86 59 86 00), right by the cathedral, caters mostly to long-term residents but also welcomes tourists. (150F. Breakfast included.) Several blocks to the left of the train station and opposite the convent, **Hôtel Beauséjour,** 5bis rue St-Gildard (tel. 03 86 61 20 84; fax 03 86 59 15 37), has clean, pleasant rooms with phones and TVs. (Singles 140F; doubles with shower and TV 180-190F, with TV and full bathroom 200-230F. Extra bed 50F. Shower 20F. Breakfast 28F. Reception 7am-10pm. V, MC.) The classy two-star **Hôtel Villa du Parc,** 16ter rue de Lourdes (tel. 03 86 61 09 48; fax 03 86 57 85 17), is across the park from pl. Carnot. Spanking new doubles look onto the park or the hotel garden. (Doubles with shower 175F, with bath 230F. Cable TV and telephones in every room. Extra bed 50F. Breakfast 28F. Parking 30F. Reception 7am-10:30pm. V, MC, AmEx.) The scenic **Camping Municipal** (tel. 03 86 37 56 52), surveys the *vieille ville* from across the Loire. From the cathedral, follow rue de la Cathédrale to the river, cross the bridge, and turn left. (15F per person, 15F per tent, 10F per car. Reception 7am-10pm. Open May-late Sept.)

⌐ FOOD. Nevers' *vieille ville* is studded with pricey *brasseries,* but there are inexpensive spots in all directions from pl. Carnot. **Rue du 14 Juillet,** between pl. Carnot and the cathedral, has many inexpensive restaurants. **Le Goemon,** 9 rue de 14 Juillet (tel. 03 86 59 00 96), has every kind of *crêpe* and *galette* (56F lunch *menu,* dinner *crêpes* 18-39F) in homey, rustic surroundings. (Open Tu-Sa until 11pm.) **Le Lusitania,** 64 rue de la Préfecture (tel. 03 86 59 00 96), serves Portuguese dishes to hungry troopers for 53-74F with *menus* at 60 and 85F. (Open M noon-2:30pm, Tu-Sa noon-2:30pm and 7-10:30pm. V, MC.) Young folks frequent **Restaurant La Tour,** 2 pl. du Palais (tel. 03 86 59 86 07), a public cafeteria connected to the *foyer.* There's not much choice, but you'll get a full meal for 50F. (Open M-F 11:30am-2pm and 7-8:30pm.) **Stoc supermarket,** 12 av. Général de Gaulle, is half a block from pl. Carnot. (Open M-F 9am-7:30pm, Sa 8:30am-7:30pm, Su 9am-noon.) The *boulangerie* **Quicroc** next door has a *petit dejeuner* for 9.50F and sandwiches and salads for 16-20F. **Marché Carnot** hosts a covered **market,** with entrances on rue Général de Gaulle and rue St-Didier. (Open M-Th 7am-12:30pm, F-Sa 7am-7pm.)

⌐ SIGHTS. Traces of the **Cathédrale St-Cyr et Ste-Juliette** (tel. 03 89 59 06 74) go back to the 6th century, but the bulk dated from the 10th to the 16th centuries before a devastating bombing raid in 1944 occasioned most of its reconstruction. St-Cyr's charm is in its unusual double-heeled arrangement—to the west is an enormous Romanesque apse with a fresco of Christ Pantokrator and the crypt, while to the east is the 14th-century Gothic response. The eclectic impulse carries on in the modern stained glass, which was created by five distinct artists between 1977 and 1983. (Open June-Sept. Tu-Sa 10am-noon and 2-7pm.) Opposite the cathedral, fairy-tale turrets cap the 15th-century **Palais Ducal** (tel. 03 86 68 46 00). Exhibits include an aquarium of local fish and an automated duke that gives history lessons. (Enter from tourist office, same hours as tourist office. Free.) On pl. Charte, to the east of the cathedral, the simplicity of the 11th-century **Église St-Étienne** obscures the fact that poor Duke William of Nevers spent so much on its construction that he couldn't afford to join his friends on the First Crusade. Two blocks away is the **Porte de Paris,** a triumphal arch commemorating the Battle of Fontenoy among Charlemagne's grandsons in 841. The **Couvent St-Gildard,** on the corner of rue Jeanne d'Arc and rue St-Gildard (tel. 03 86 57 79 99), houses the Congregation of the Sisters of Nevers and the body of St. Bernadette (d. 1879). A small museum gives a thorough overview of Bernadette's life and displays many artifacts, including her clothes, books of piety, and copies of letters describing her visions. The incorruptible saint reposes peacefully in a glass case in the chapel. (Open Apr.-Sept. 7am-7:30pm; Oct.-Mar. 7am-noon and 2-7pm. Free.)

A walk among the gardens lining the **Promenade des Remparts,** from the Loire to av. Général de Gaulle, follows the crumbled remains of 12th-century Nevers. Along the Promenade is the **Musée Municipal Frédéric Blandin** (tel. 03 86 23 92 89). Installed in the 13th-century Abbaye Notre-Dame, it houses a collection of the ceramics for which Nevers is famous. (Open Oct.-Apr. M and W-Sa 1:30-5:30pm, Su 10am-noon and 2-5:30pm; May-Sept. W-M 10am-6:30pm. 15F, reduced 8F, under 18 and students free.) Just outside the gardens is the **Porte du Croux,** an imposing example of 14th-century military architecture, which now houses an archæology museum. Before leaving Nevers, cross over the **Pont de Loire** for a last view.

LA CHARITÉ-SUR-LOIRE

Twenty-three kilometers north of Nevers, the red roofs, church spire, and ramparts of La Charité-sur-Loire make the tiny town on the banks of the upper Loire a pleasant excursion from Nevers. Founded in the 8th century and appropriated by Cluniac monks, La Charité grew in power and wealth until it was known as "the eldest daughter" of Cluny, with 400 dependent monasteries throughout Europe. But while La Charité was able to withstand Joan of Arc's siege in 1429, the abbey was no more immune than its neighbors to the destruction wrought upon religious buildings during the centuries that followed. The crumbling **Église Notre Dame** is La Charité's *raison d'être.* The tourist office has a detailed binder in English to guide you through the massive structure. A three-tiered transept and modern, blood-red *vitraux* line the interior. At the far end of the apse, a depiction of La Charité is depicted in the glass. You can peep into the galleried cloister from the north transept, while the opposite end has a Tympanium of the Transfiguration, whose execution in 1132 was undoubtedly linked to the festival, which had been freshly introduced in the Cluniac liturgy. Behind the church lies the only surviving portion of the original **Église St-Laurent,** discovered in 1975. Though it may not look like much, the site proved to be the find of the century for La Charité. From the ruins, you can get a good look at the apse, a 12th-century chapel, and the **Bell Tower of Bertrange.** Just downstairs from the cloister and cellars, the tiny **Musée Municipal,** 33 rue des Chapelains (tel. 03 86 70 34 83), shows prized artifacts from the excavation that now reside in the Hôtel Adam alongside rooms devoted to regional handicrafts, decorative arts, and a collection of dramatic sculptures and statues by Rodin's student Alfredo Pina (1887-1966). (Open Dec.-Mar. Sa 10am-noon, Su 2-6pm; Apr.-June and Sept.-Nov. W-Su 10am-noon and 2-6pm; July-Aug. W-M 10am-noon and 2-7pm. Free.)

From the museum, you can walk up along the grassy Roman ramparts to get a great view of the town and the Loire. For another look, cross the Pont de Pierre to the **Faubourg,** where you can picnic in the church's reflection. The **Forêt des Bertranges,** just 6km from town, has over 10,000 hectares of woods, trails, and fountains. To get there, go east on RN151 towards Auxerre. Turn off onto the D179 to follow signs for Raveau and the Forêt. From Raveau, take the D138 to the Petites Maisons; the sign for the Fontaine de la Vache will take you to a nearby spring.

Pl. de Gaulle is the site of the **Casino supermarket** (open M-Sa 8:45am-12:15pm and 3-7pm, Su 8:45am-12:15pm) and the morning **market** (Sa). **Camping municipal,** quai de la Saulaie (tel. 03 86 70 00 83), is 10 minutes from the tourist office. Cross rue des Chapelains and take rue du Pont over the Pont de Pierre. At the quai d'Aval turn right and follow it to the three-star campsite. (Package for 1 person 33F, for 2 people 56F, 20F for extra person. Electricity 12-15F. Open mid-Apr.-Sept.)

To get to the helpful **tourist office**, 5 pl. Ste-Croix (tel. 03 86 70 15 06), turn left on av. de la Gare and follow it downtown, always curving slightly to the right (10min.). The office is in the courtyard of the **Église Notre-Dame** and gives free maps and lists of accommodations. In the summer they organize tours in French of the church and surrounding city. (Tours July-Aug. M-Sa 3 per day; May-June and Sept. M-F 1 per day. Open daily July-Aug. 9am-7pm; Sept.-June 9am-noon and 2-6pm.) For a taxi, call **Taxi Regis** (tel. 03 86 69 67 12). The **post office,** 4 rue Charles Chevallier (tel. 03 86 69 42 82), has **currency exchange.** (Open M-F 8am-noon and 2-6pm, Sa 8am-noon.) Frequent **trains** connect La Charité to Nevers (25min., 11 per day, 30F).

AUXERRE

Auxerre (pronounced "oh-zehr") began its days as Autessiodrum, a Roman hub along the via Agrippa. Converted early, Auxerre's monastic community blossomed in the 5th century under the learned bishop Germain (378-448) and his successors, and throughout the Middle Ages, the town commanded respect as a pilgrimage site and center of religious learning. Though the ravages of wars and Revolution humbled the town's stature, the economy, however, found a saving grace in its Chablis wine, which was supplied *en masse* to the insatiable Parisian market. Today, Auxerre (pop. 41,000) is an administrative center, resting on its laurels amid the lush Yonne countryside.

7 ORIENTATION AND PRACTICAL INFORMATION. The **Gare Auxerre-St-Gervais,** rue Paul Doumer, east of the Yonne, sends **trains** to **Avallon** (1hr., M-Sa 6 per day, Su 3 per day, 50F), **Paris** (3hr., M-Sa 9 per day, Su 6 per day, 121F), **Dijon** (2½hr., 5-6 per day, 123F), and **Lyon** (3-5hr., 6 per day, 216F). **Les Rapides de Bourgogne buses,** 3 rue des Fontenottes (tel. 03 86 46 90 90), leave from the bus station (tel. 03 86 46 90 66), on rue des Migraines. From the tourist office, walk north on quai de la République, which becomes quai de la Matine. Turn left on bd. de la Chainette; rue des Migraines is directly across the roundabout. **Le Bus** (tel. 03 86 94 95 00) has service around town (M-Sa 7am-7:30pm). Line #1 circles the *centre ville,* passing the train and the bus stations every 30 minutes. (Schedules at tourist office. Ticket 6.50F.) For a **taxi,** call 03 86 46 78 78 or 03 86 46 77 88.

To reach the **tourist office,** 1-2 quai de la République (tel. 03 86 52 06 19; fax 03 86 51 23 27), from the station veer left and cross onto rue Jules Ferry. Turn right onto av. Gambetta, and cross the river on pont Bert. The office is on the right, three blocks down quai de la République (12min.). The staff offers an accommodations service (15F), **currency exchange** when banks are closed, and **rents bikes** (40F per half-day, 70F per day; 1500F and ID deposit). They also run biking and walking tours in French from mid-July to mid-September. (30F-40F, students 20F-30F). Ask for a free copy of *L'Yonne* for current goings-on. (Open mid-June-mid-Sept. M-Sa 9am-1pm and 2-7pm, Su 9:30am-1pm and 3-6:30pm; mid-Sept.-mid-June M-Sa 9am-12:30pm and 2-6:30pm, Su 10am-1pm.) **Hôpital Général** is at 2 bd. de Verdun (tel. 03 86 48 48 48), and the **police** are at 32 bd. Vaulabelle (tel. 03 86 40 85 00). The **post office,** pl. Charles-Surugue (tel. 03 86 72 68 60), has **currency exchange.** (Open M-F 8am-7pm, Sa 8am-12:15pm. **Postal code:** 89000.) **Internet connections** available at **Media 2,** 17 bd. Vauban (tel. 03 86 51 04 35), and **L'Étang Café,** chemin des Mesanges (tel. 03 86 72 96 60).

THE CENTER

★ ACCOMMODATIONS AND CAMPING. The **Foyer des Jeunes Travailleuses (HI)**, 16 bd. Vaulabelle (tel. 03 86 52 45 38), has simple singles. Follow the signs from the train station to the *centre ville*, cross the pont Bert, and turn left on quai de la République; the first right is rue Vaulabelle. The *foyer* is in an apartment building to the left; the building is back from the street, just past a gas station. (77F. Breakfast included. Meals 34F in the Maison de Worms—a German city, not *nematoda*. Reception daily 2-8pm.)

Hôtel la Renommée, 27 rue d'Égleny (tel. 03 86 52 03 53; fax 03 86 51 47 83), on the northern fringe of the *vieille ville*, has spacious rooms, some of which overlook a chatty courtyard, others a busy street. There's a lingering scent of cigarettes. The wildly popular restaurant downstairs has *menus* from 58F. (Singles 95F, with TV 115F, with shower 150F; doubles 110F, with shower and TV 165F. Breakfast 25F. Private parking. Reception daily 7am-midnight. Closed Su and last 3 weeks in Aug. V, MC.) **Hôtel l'Écu,** 5 rue Joubert (tel. 03 86 52 09 96), has small rooms in a 400-year-old house, but the price is right and the location's even better. (Singles 90F; doubles from 100-110F; doubles and triples with shower from 125F. Toilet outside rooms. Shower 10F. Reception M-Sa 8am-10pm.)

You can sleep under the stars (three, to be exact) at the **campsite** at 8 rte. de Vaux (tel. 03 86 52 11 15), south of town on D163. (13F per site, 15F per person, 13F per car. Electricity 12F. Reception daily Apr. 7am-8pm; May and Sept. 7am-9pm; June-Aug. 7am-10pm. Open Apr.-Sept.)

★ FOOD. Auxerre is a budget gourmand's dream, when the restaurants are open. **Le Mouflon d'Or,** 46 rue du Pont (tel. 03 86 52 72 12), has hefty helpings of couscous from 50F, salads 25F-35F, and *menus* for 65 and 95F. (Open Tu-Su noon-2pm and 6:30-10pm. V, MC.) The friendly **La Crêperie Rimbambelle**, rue Fecauderie, devotes its popular salad greenery to salads (35-45F), *omelettes* (20-28F), and *crêpes* (12-40F). (Open M-Th 11:45am-2pm and 7-10pm, F-Sa until 11pm. V, MC.) **Monoprix supermarket,** 10 pl. Charles Surugue, also has a cheap cafeteria, with *plats* 25-40F. (Supermarket open M-Sa 8:30am-8:30pm; cafeteria open 11:30am-2pm; *salon de thé* open 2:30-6pm.) **Markets** are held on pl. de l'Arquebuse (Tu morning, F until 6pm) and on pl. Degas, on the outskirts (Su morning).

★ SIGHTS. From the Pont Paul-Bert is a lovely view of the city and its distinct churches. The **Quartier de la Marine,** near the tourist office and around pl. St-Nicolas, is lined with the old wooden houses formerly occupied by Auxerrois rivermen. From the Yonne, wander up to the **Cathédrale St-Étienne,** started around 1215, whose wounded façade still displays statuettes decapitated by Huguenots when they occupied the city in 1567—only seven years after the cathedral was finally completed. The iconoclasts also smashed much of the stained glass, but didn't get as far as the 13th-century *vitraux* in the ambulatory, which depict Old Testament stories and saints' lives. The Gothic structure sits on top of an 11th-century Romanesque **crypt,** which preserves an ochre fresco of *Christ on Horseback*. The **treasury** on the south wall guards enamels, relics, illuminated manuscripts, and St-Germain's 5th-century tunic—in need of a good pressing by now. (Cathedral open M-Sa 9am-noon and 2-6pm, Su 2-6pm. Crypt and treasury 10F each.)

The Gothic **Abbaye St-Germain,** 2 pl. St-Germain, attracted pilgrims to the tomb of the saint and former bishop of Auxerre, as well as medieval scholars seeking the wisdom of its ecclesiastic college. Founded in the 5th century, the abbey quickly became a prestigious center of learning. Part Carolingian, the underground chapel preserves the oldest frescoes in France, depicting the life of St. Stephen and the Adoration of the Magi. Only monks were allowed in this privileged space; pilgrims had to be content to hand bits of cloth down into the tomb of St. Germain from the upper church. Next to the abbey church are the conventual buildings, now used for archæological displays of prehistoric, Gallo-Roman, and medieval material culture. (Open June-Sept. W-M 10am-6:30pm; Oct.-May 10am-noon and 2-6pm. Crypt tours every 30min.; 30F including Musée Leblanc, students under 26 free.)

Towards pl. de l'Hôtel de Ville, the **Tour de l'Horloge,** a two-faced 15th-century clock tower in gold and terra-cotta, serves as a gateway to the *vieille ville*. The **Musée Leblanc-Duvernoy,** 9bis rue d'Égleny (tel. 03 86 52 44 63), between rue Gaillard and rue de l'Égalité, contains elegant 18th-century Beauvais tapestries, as well as painting and pottery. (Open W-M 2-6pm. Separate admission 12F, free for students under 26.) Duck into the Neoclassical 17th-century **Chapelle des Visitandines,** (tel. 03 86 52 78 96), which shelters 72 expressive polychrome wooden sculptures. (Open W 9am-noon and 2-7pm, F-Sa 2-7pm. Free.)

AVALLON

The *vieille ville* of Avallon (pop. 10,000) peeks over medieval walls high on a granite mountain. The town's ramparts, designed by the prolific military architect Sébastien "The Fortifier" Vauban, provide a great vista of the entire Yonne region. No longer a military target, the town makes a sensible base from which to attack the nearby forest of the Morvan as well as a reasonable day-trip from Auxerre.

🛈 **PRACTICAL INFORMATION.** Avallon is hard to get to and from. **SNCF trains** and **buses** (tel. 03 86 34 01 01 for both) are rare and slow, running to **Auxerre** (1hr., M-Sa 5-6 per day, Su 3 per day, 50F), **Autun** (1¾hr., 2-3 per day, 71F), **Dijon** (2-3hr., 3 per day, 100F), and **Paris** (2½-3hr., 5 per day, 149F). (Station open M-Th 5:30am-9pm, F 5:30am-10pm, Sa 5:30am-8pm, Su 8:30am-10pm.) **TRANSCO buses** (tel. 03 80 42 11 00) roll from the train station to **Dijon** (2½hr., M-Sa 3 per day, Su 1 per day, 90F) with a stop in Semur-en-Auxois (45min., 40.20F); the tourist office has schedules. For a 24hr. **taxi** call 03 86 34 04 52. **Bikes** are available from **Touvelo,** 26 rue de Paris. (Tel. 03 86 34 28 11. 100F per day. No deposit. Open Tu-Sa 8am-noon and 2-7pm.) The **tourist office,** 4 rue Bocquillot (tel. 03 86 34 14 19), is next to the Église St-Lazare, a 15-minute walk from the station. Head straight on av. du Président Doumer and turn right onto rue Carnot. At the large intersection, turn left onto rue de Paris which passes a large parking lot, becomes the pedestrian Grande Rue A. Briand, passes through the Tour de l'Horloge, and lands you at the office. The staff offers a free map in English and free accommodations service. (Open daily July-Aug. 9:30am-7:30pm; Sept.-June 9:30am-12:30pm and 2:30-6:30pm; Nov.-Mar. same as Sept.-June but closed Su.) The **Centre Hospitalier** is at 1 rue de l'Hôpital (tel. 03 86 34 66 00). The **police** are at 2 av. Victor Hugo (tel. 03 86 34 17 17). The **post office** is at 9 rue des Odebert. (Tel. 03 86 34 91 08. Open M-F 8am-noon and 1:30-6pm, Sa 8am-noon. **Postal code:** 89200.)

🛏🍴 **ACCOMMODATIONS AND FOOD.** The **Foyer des Jeunes Travailleurs,** 10 av. de Victor Hugo (tel. 03 86 34 01 88; fax 03 86 34 10 95), is 20 minutes from the station and 15 from the *vieille ville*. From the station, walk straight ahead on av. du Président Doumer, turn right onto rue Carnot, which becomes rte. de Paris after the intersection, then go left onto av. de Pepinster at the next major intersection. Stay on Pepinster when it becomes av. du Morvan, and finally go left onto av. Victor Hugo. There, you'll find 70s-style singles in the modern high-rise. (80F per night. Breakfast 16F. Meals 46F. 24hr. reception.) Across from the *gare* stands **Hôtel du Parc** (tel. 03 86 34 17 00), in a 17th-century *hôtel* with a nice terrace bar. The friendly *patron* lets pleasant, well-maintained rooms. If you take a room without a shower, be warned—there are no hall showers. (Singles and doubles 115-130F, with shower 149-210F. Extra bed 55-75F. Breakfast 23F. No hall showers. Reception 7am-9:30pm. Closed late Dec.-mid-Jan. V, MC.) **Camping Municipal de Sous-Roche** (tel. 03 86 34 10 39) lies 2km away; walk straight from the train station onto av. du President Doumier, right onto rue Carnot, then straight through the big intersection. Head straight along rte. de Lourmes, then veer left on rue de Sous Roche. Climb to the riverside campground. (18F per person, 13F per site, 13F per tent or car. 18F for electricity. Reception 7am-10pm. Open Mar. 15-Oct. 15.) At the top of town, **La Tour,** 84 Grande Rue A. Briand (tel. 03 86 34 24 84), cooks up Italian food in a warm, if literally tumbledown, atmosphere—the whole street is braced. Big salads go for 28-35F, pizzas 34-50F, and pastas 43-45F. (Open daily 11:30am-2:30pm and 6:45-11pm. V, MC, AmEx.) The **Casino supermarket,** rue de Paris, is a block or two past the intersection with rue Carnot toward town. (Open Tu-Sa 8:15am-12:30pm and 3-7pm, Su 8:45am-noon.) More comestibles are available at the self-described **Mammouth,** rue de Général Leclerc; turn right after rue Carnot. (Open M-Sa 9am-8:30pm, F 9am-9pm.) Morning **markets** are held on pl. Vauban (Sa) and in the parking lot by the post office (Th).

🔲 **SIGHTS.** A walk along the narrow paths of the western and southern ramparts reveals an excellent view of the dense forests, verdant pastures, and crumbling châteaux of the Vallée du Cousin. The tourist office can give you a free detailed map of an 8km walk that covers the area's highlights and will also point out biking circuits. The charmingly amateur **Musée du Costume,** 6 rue Belgrand (tel. 03 86 34 19 95), off Grande Rue A. Briand, fills eight rooms of the prince of Condé's 17th-century house with bustles and *bijoux* (jewelry) each summer as mannequins don period dress for the annual exhibition. (Open daily Easter-Oct. 10:30am-12:30pm and 1:30-5:30pm. Tours in French. 25F, students 15F.) Two prominent remnants of days gone by stand side-by-side at the southern end of the *vieille ville.* Currently under reconstruction, the 15th-century slate **Tour de l'Horloge,** straddles Grande Rue A. Briand and keeps the *Avallonais* on schedule. Down the street, the **Église Collégiale St-Lazare** gained its present name in AD 1000 when Henry Le Grand, Duke of Burgundy, donated a part of St. Lazare's skull to the church. The main Romanesque portal is ornamented with a series of recessed arches, with carvings depicting cherubim, the Zodiac, and the Elders of the Apocalypse carrying musical instruments. Note the varied spiraling colonnettes on either side of the doors. The crypt below the church dates from the 4th century. (Open in summer daily 8:45am-7pm; rest of year 8:45am-6pm.) Behind the tourist office, the **Musée de l'Avallonais** (tel. 03 86 34 03 19) contains an interesting but poorly presented collection of artifacts, statues, and jewelry from Gallo-Roman times to the Middle Ages, as well as contemporary religious art. (Open June-Oct. W-M 2-6pm. 20F, students 15F.)

VÉZELAY

High up a hillside 15km from Avallon, the village of Vézelay (pop. 580) smiles on the valley below, watching over the surrounding fertile pastures and dense forests. The houses, covered with red tile roofs and wild roses, seem lost in time. Considered one of the most beautiful villages in France, Vézelay lives up to its promise—but its reputation does not rest on natural beauty alone. The town has been a major pilgrimage destination since the 11th century, thanks to the relics of St. Mary Magdelene held within the **Basilique Ste-Madeleine** (tel. 03 86 33 35 98), and it was here that St. Bernard of Clairvaux made his impassioned plea to launch the Second Crusade in 1146. The basilica he spoke in—and the one that still stands today—was reconstructed after a fire in 1120 destroyed the Carolingian original. The simple, cream-colored stone bears little ornamentation, which gives the airy interior a clean, dignified feel, while the tympanum above the narthex's main portal portrays a magnificent Christ in Glory, framed by the zodiac and converts to Christianity (including pygmies and dog-men!). St. Louis paid homage to the relics four times between 1240 and 1270, but their authenticity was thrown into doubt when another set was discovered at St-Maximin in Provence, near where Mary had reputedly landed in AD 40 (see p. 272), and the basilica declined in importance in the 13th century. The relics remain officially sanctified by the Church, though, and many still come to commune with them in the crypt. To appreciate the extraordinary carvings and the history of the basilica, take an informative tour given by a guild of volunteers. (Open daily 8am-7:30pm. Tours in English July-Aug. daily 10am-noon and 2-5:30pm, by appointment the rest of the year. 30F suggested donation.) In summer, a small **museum** above the chapter room displays 11th- and 12th-century stonework removed from the church and chronicles the 19th-century restoration. (Open late June-mid-Sept. W-M 10am-noon and 2-7pm. 10F.)

As in most towns where tourists outnumber residents ten to one, good cheap dining is well nigh impossible to find, so why not create your own feast at **Casino supermarket,** near the bottom of rue St-Étienne? (Open July-Aug. M-Sa 8am-8pm, Su 9am-8pm; Oct.-June M-Tu 8am-12:30pm and 3:30-8pm, W and Su 8am-12:30pm.) The **Hôtel de la Terasse** (tel. 03 86 33 25 50), in front of the basilica at pl. de la Madeleine, has salads for 28-42F and two- and three-course lunch *formules* for 45F and 58F respectively. The hotel also has large, attractive rooms in a great location. (Singles and doubles approx. 200F; triples or quads 230-350F. Breakfast 30F. Reception daily 8am-8pm, closed Tu and W morning Sept.-June.) Fifteen minutes from the bus stop, the rural **Auberge de Jeunesse (HI),** rte. de l'Etang (tel. 03 86 33 24 18), offers prosaic six-bed rooms. Follow the signs to the *gendarmerie;* the hostel is 400m past it on your left. (46F, non-members 56F. Reception 9-10am and 5-8pm. Lockout 10am-5:30pm. Open Feb.-Dec. Reservations recommended.) More in keeping with the spirit of the past is the **Maison Saint Bernard** (tel. 03 86 33 26 73), which offers a contemplative atmosphere to pilgrims and others for 80F. (Closed for restorations 1999; should open 2000, but call ahead.) There's a **campsite** behind the hostel. (18F per person, 5F per tent, 5 per car. Electricity 10F.)

Vézelay's tiny **tourist office,** rue St-Pierre (tel. 03 86 33 23 69; fax 03 86 33 34 00), just down the street from the church, offers free maps and a *guide pratique,* which has accommodations listings. During weekends in July-mid-Sept. they run tours in French (25F). (Open daily June 15-Oct. 10am-1pm and 2-6pm; Nov.-June 14 F-W 10am-1pm and 2-6pm.) The closest bank is in Avallon, but the **post office,** rue St-Étienne (tel. 03 86 33 26 35), has an ATM. (Open M-F 9am-noon and 2-5pm, Sa 8:45-11:45am. **Postal code:** 89450.)

There's no train station in Vézelay; **trains** run from **Paris** via **Auxerre** to **Sermicelles** (50min., 4 per day, 40F); from here you can wait for the weekly shuttle bus, or call **Taxi Vezelay** (tel. 03 86 32 31 88; 24hr.). An **SNCF bus** leaves Avallon for Vézelay in the morning and returns late afternoon (22min., 22F). Faced with such options, you might prefer to bike from (15km) Avallon or take a taxi (around 120F).

SEMUR-EN-AUXOIS

Although legend attributes Semur-en-Auxois' founding to Hercules, the earliest written record of the town (pop. 5100) dates from 606. In that year, monks of the Abbaye de Flavigny signed their charter in a village they called *Sene Muros*—the "old walls." Known as the "Athens of Burgundy," the *vieille ville'*s towers and ramparts crown an unspoiled provincial town of cobblestones and archways that overlook a bend in the Armençon river. Venture under the Sauvigny Gate (built in 1417) and the arch that bears the city's motto in old French: *Les Semurois se plaisent fort en l'acointance des Estrangers* (The people of Semur take great pleasure in welcoming strangers).

◪ PRACTICAL INFORMATION. Trains only run to **Montbard,** 18km away; a bus completes the journey to Semur (see below). You'd be better off catching one direct; **TRANSCO** (tel. 03 80 42 11 00) runs **buses** to **Montbard** (25min., M-Sa 3 per day, Su 2 per day, 14.70F), **Avallon** (¾hr., M-Sa 4 per day, Su 1 per day, 40.20F), and **Dijon** (1½hr., M-Sa 3 per day, Su 1 per day, 58.80F). For **Taxi Pommier,** call 03 80 97 09 71. The **tourist office,** pl. Gaveau (tel. 03 80 97 05 96), where rue de la Liberté meets the gates of the *vieille ville,* has bus schedules, free maps, and a list of hotels. The staff runs guided tours in English during the summer (20-25F, students 15F). (Open mid-June to mid-Sept. M-Sa 9am-9pm, Su 10am-noon and 3-6pm; rest of year M-Sa 8:30am-noon and 2-6:30pm.) The tourist office is also home to an **SNCF information and reservation office.** (Open Tu-F 9am-noon and 2-6pm, Sa 9am-noon and 2-5pm.) Most businesses in Semur are closed on Monday. The **police** (tel. 03 80 97 11 17) and the **hospital** (tel. 03 80 89 64 64) are on av. Pasteur. The **post office,** pl. de l'Ancienne Comédie (tel. 03 80 97 00 86), has **currency exchange.** (Open M-F 8:30am-noon and 1:30-5:30pm, Sa 8am-noon. **Postal code:** 21140.)

⬛ ACCOMMODATIONS AND CAMPING. The **Foyer des Jeunes Travailleurs,** 1 rue du Champ de Foire (tel. 03 80 97 10 22; fax 03 80 97 36 97), off rue de la Liberté and about 300m away from the tourist office, has comfortable if institutional singles, a TV room, phone, and cafeteria. Usually full in winter but worth a shot in the summer. (100F per night. Breakfast 10F, meals 48F. Reception M-F 9am-8pm, Sa-Su 11am-2pm and 6-8pm; call ahead if arriving at a different time.) The **Hôtel des Gourmets,** 4 rue Varenne (tel. 03 80 97 09 41; fax 03 80 97 17 95), offers large rooms in the heart of the *vieille ville.* (Singles and doubles 130-180F, with shower 210F; triples and quads 180F; sextuple 300F. Extra bed 25F. Breakfast 35F. Closed M evening and Tu, as well as Dec. and 1st week of June. Reception M 11am-2pm, W-F 11am-2pm and 5-9pm, Sa 11am-2pm and 6-8pm, Su 6-8pm. V, MC, AmEx.) **Camping Municipal du Lac de Pont** (tel. 03 80 97 01 26) offers a spot in the sun 3km south of Semur on a scenic lake with a beach. Rent a tennis court (20F per hour) or a **bike** (25F per hr., 50F per half-day, 75F per day). There's a laundry and a scenic mini-mart, too. (20F per person, 10F per site, 8F per car. Electricity 13F. Reception 9am-noon and 4-8pm. Open May-Sept. 15.)

⬛ FOOD. **Le Sagittaire,** 15 rue de la Liberté (tel. 03 80 97 23 91), hits the bull's-eye with inexpensive, tasty dishes. Pizzas cost 30-49F, huge salads 32-48F, a three-course weekday lunch *menu* 55F, and the dinner *menu* 90F. (Open M-Sa noon-2pm and 7-10:30pm.) You're welcome **Chez Madame Fanfan,** 15 rue Buffon (tel. 03 80 97 28 97), where you can try excellent local specialties served on a terrace. *Menus* cost 78F and 98F. (Open daily noon-2:30pm and 5-10:30pm. V, MC.) For groceries, stop at the small **Casino supermarket,** 32 pl. Notre Dame (open Tu-Sa 8:30am-12:30pm and 2:30-7:30pm), or head a few blocks down rue de la Liberté to **Intermarché,** av. du Général Maziller (open M-Th 9am-12:15pm and 2:30-7:15pm, F 9am-7:45pm, Sa 9am-7:15pm). **Markets** take place on Fridays at the Centre Commercial Champlon, and on pl. Notre Dame on Sunday mornings in summer.

⬛ SIGHTS. The tourist office offers free brochures with self-guided itineraries, scheduled walking tours, and a 45-minute *petit train* during the summer (25F, children 15F). Make sure to walk around the ramparts and then down by the river Armençon, where pretty orchards and enormous flowers line the banks. The *vieille ville* is illuminated nightly 10pm to midnight, mid-June to September.

In the medieval town, down rue Buffon, leering gargoyles menace the *place* from the 15th-century façade of the **Collégiale Notre-Dame.** The 13th-century tympanum on the **porte des Bleds** faces rue Notre-Dame, while on the skinny left pillar, two sculpted snails slime their way to St. Thomas's feet—no doubt seeking divine intervention from their likely fate in a tasty butter and garlic sauce. The church offers up a full three-course meal; after the snail *entrée*, gluttons can meditate in the Chapels of the Butchers and then the Bakers, donated by their respective guilds in the 15th century. (Open 9am-noon and 2-6pm; closes 5pm in winter. English pamphlet.) The mighty **Tour de l'Orle d'Or,** along the castle walls, has a collection on the medieval history of Semur. (Open daily in July-Aug. 10am-6pm. 10F, children 5F.)

The *beaux-arts* wing of the **Musée Municipal,** rue Jean-Jacques Collenot (tel. 03 80 97 24 25), off pl. de l'Ancienne Comédie, houses statues and carvings from the Middle Ages and painting and sculpture from the 17th to the 19th centuries—including three Corot canvases and plaster models by Augustin Dumont. The zoology section includes a 19th-century *fragonard* hidden in the corner—a dead infant injected with chemicals to preserve the cardiovascular system for study. Those without a cast-iron stomach should stick to the stuffed owls and ferrets. (Open W-M 2-6pm. 20F, students 10F.)

LYON

France's second-largest city is second in little else. With industrial and culinary *savoir faire*, Lyon (pop. 1.5 million) has established itself as a cultural and economic alternative to Paris. Despite its reputation for bourgeois snobbery, Lyon is friendlier and more relaxed than Paris, with a few centuries' more history.

Situated at the convergence of the Rhône and Saône rivers, Lyon has benefited from its position since Julius Cæsar used Lugdunum ("the hill of ravens") as a military base. Augustus ordered roads connecting this provincial capital of Gaul to Italy and the Atlantic, permanently establishing Lyon's status as a major crossroads and cultural capital. During the Renaissance, the city's tax-free *foires* encouraged foreign merchants and bankers to set up shop here, and after the invention of moveable type in the 15th century, Lyon assumed the role of Europe's press. Silkworms imported from China in the 16th century also contributed to Lyon's rise to economic power, helping to make it a focal point of the French Renaissance. The ornate façades and elegant courtyards of 16th-century townhouses lining the crooked streets of Vieux Lyon attest to this period of wealth.

Lyon's puppet and political satirist, the Guignol, is emblematic of its free-thinking history. Lyon's citizens refused the post-Revolution Terrorists' demands in the 1790s, prompting the massacre of thousands by Robespierre's lackeys, while local silk workers unsuccessfully rioted for better pay in 1831. The city also served as the headquarters of the Resistance in WWII. Today Lyon is the stomping ground of world-renowned chefs Paul Bocuse, Georges Blanc, and Jean-Paul Lacombe, who all learned to boil an egg here. There's no doubt you can eat *really* well at one of the spin-off restaurants. Other juices flow creatively in excellent art collections. This modern city has all the comforts for the urban sophisticate, with skyscrapers and cafés, nifty transport systems and flowering parks, and concert halls and *discothèques*. King of the culinary jungle and recently declared UNESCO World Heritage site, this is not a city to be taken lyon down.

HIGHLIGHTS OF LYON

■ Explore the mysterious **traboules,** a medieval network of subterranean passages used by Resistance fighters in WW2 (p. 214).
■ Save up for the best meal of your life at one of Paul Bocuse's quasi-budget spin-offs, **Le Nord** and **Le Sud** (p. 213).
■ Fashion fans mustn't miss the incredible **Musée Historique des Tissus,** which has displays on costume through the ages (p. 216).
■ Bartholi's fountain froths in Lyon's hip neighborhood of **Les Terreaux** (p. 215).

✤ ORIENTATION

Lyon is divided into nine *arrondissements*; the 1er, 2ème, and 4ème lie on the **presqu'île,** a narrow strip of land jutting southward toward the confluence of the Saône and Rhône rivers. Starting from the south, the 2ème *arrondissement* (the *centre ville*) includes the Perrache train station and **pl. Bellecour,** a retail area with most of the city's hotels and fast-food joints. The 1er is home to the nocturnal *terreaux* neighborhood, with its sidewalk cafés and student-packed bars. Further north, the *presqu'île* widens and climbs into the 4ème and the Croix-Rousse, a residential neighborhood that once dominated Lyon's silk industry.

To the west of the Saône is the oldest part of the city: Vieux Lyon, with its narrow streets and legion of traditional restaurants, and the **Fourvière** hill, with a Roman theater, basilica, and fabulous views of the city. East of the Rhône (3ème and 6-8ème) lies most of the city's population, the **Part-Dieu** train station, and its modern commercial complex. Orient yourself by Fourvière and its **Tour Metallique,** a mini-Eiffel Tower, to the west, and to the east by the **Tour du Crédit Lyonnais,** a reddish-brown crayon towering over Part-Dieu.

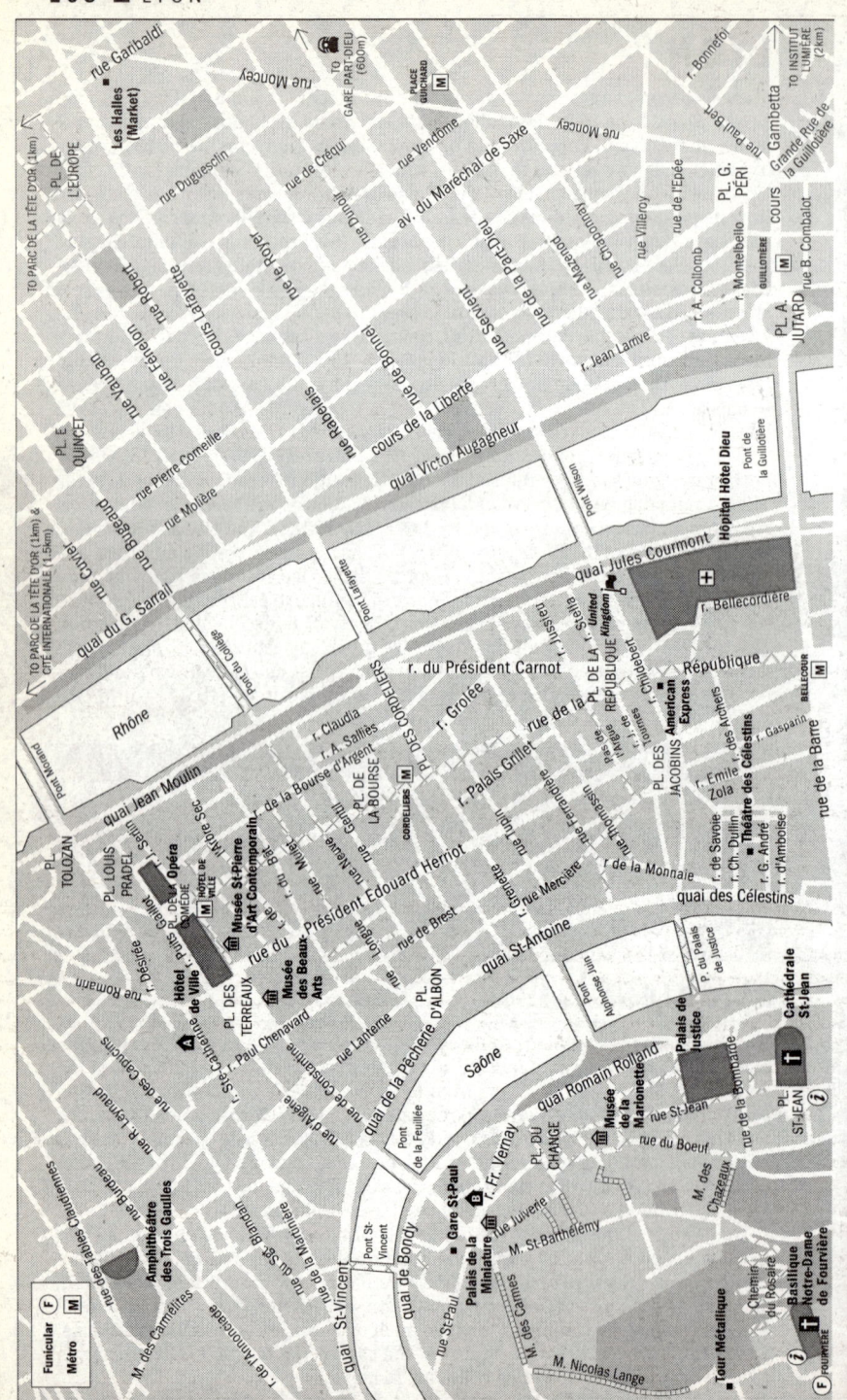

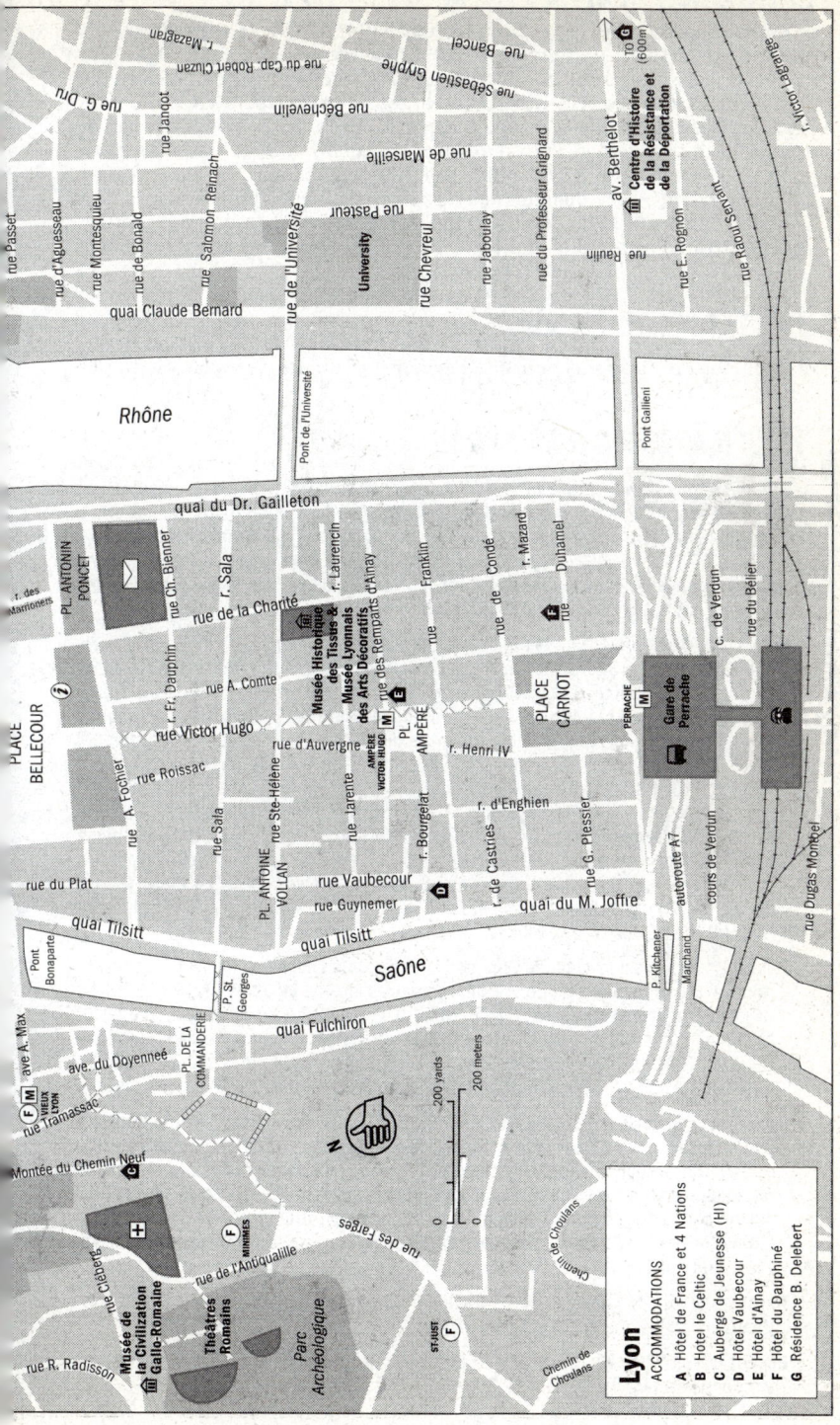

Lyon

ACCOMMODATIONS

A Hôtel de France et 4 Nations
B Hôtel le Celtic
C Auberge de Jeunesse (HI)
D Hôtel Vaubecour
E Hôtel d'Ainay
F Hôtel du Dauphiné
G Residence B. Delebert

Most trains terminating in Lyon stop at both the **Gare de Perrache** and the **Gare de la Part-Dieu;** those just passing through stop at Part-Dieu alone. Perrache is more central and considered safer at night, but both are connected to Lyon's efficient **metro,** which is the fastest way to the **tourist pavilion.** (Take line A from Perrache, B then A from Part-Dieu, to "Bellecour.") To walk from Perrache, head straight onto rue Victor Hugo and follow it until it ends at expansive pl. Bellecour; the tourist office is on the right (15min.). From Part-Dieu, exit the station by the fountains and turn right. Walk right for three blocks and turn left onto cours Lafayette. Cross the Rhône on pont Lafayette and continue as the street changes to pl. des Cordeliers. Turn left on rue de la République and follow it to pl. Bellecour (30min.).

Lyon is a reasonably safe city. For solo women, harassment is more irksome than dangerous; when ignored, *lyonnais* men usually go away. Don't respond to their *"Bonsoir,"* however, unless you want to get to know them better. Watch out for pickpockets inside Perrache, at pl. des Terreaux, and in pl. Bellecour's crowds.

◰ TRANSPORTATION

THE CENTER

Flights: Aéroport Lyon-Satolas (tel. 04 72 22 72 21). Flights within France and around Europe, North Africa, and the Middle East. The TGV, which stops at the airport, is cheaper and more convenient than the 50 daily flights to Paris. **Satobuses** (tel. 04 72 68 72 17; 50min., 48.50F) shuttle to **Perrache, Part-Dieu,** and subway stops **Jean Mace, Grange-Blanche,** and **Mermoz Pinel** (every 20min. until 9pm daily). **Air France,** 10 quai Jules Courmont, 2ème (tel. 08 02 80 28 02).

Trains: To: **Grenoble** (1¼hr., 15 per day, 96F); **Dijon** (2hr., 15 per day, 132F); **Paris** (2hr., 20 per day, 312-388F); **Geneva** (2hr., 8 per day, 118F); **Marseille** (3hr., 13 per day, 205F); **Nice** (6hr., 15 per day, 299F); and **Strasbourg** (6hr., 9 per day, 256F). Trains passing through Lyon stop only at **Gare de la Part-Dieu,** bd. Marius Vivier-Merle (M: Part-Dieu), in the business district on the east bank of the Rhône. SNCF info desk open M-F 9am-7pm, Sa 9am-6:30pm. Those terminating in Lyon make a further stop at **Gare de Perrache,** pl. Carnot (M: Perrache). SNCF info and reservation desk open M-Sa 8am-7:30pm. Station open 5am-midnight. At Perrache, **SOS Voyageurs** (tel. 04 78 37 03 31) provides wheelchairs, baby-changing facilities, and sick beds. Staff will meet you at the platform and help you find a connection if you call ahead. Open M-F 8am-8pm. On weekends, **Le Mail** (tel. 04 78 42 24 28) offers similar services, and even beds for the desperate (45F). Open Sa-Su 3:30-7:30pm.

Buses: On the lowest level of the Gare de Perrache. **Cars Faure** (tel. 04 78 96 11 44) to **Annecy** and **Grenoble.** Other domestic companies include **Philibert** (tel. 04 78 98 56 00) and **Transport Verney** (tel. 04 78 70 21 01), but it's generally cheaper and faster to take the train within France. **International bus terminal** across the hall. **Eurolines** (tel. 04 72 41 09 09) travels throughout Europe. Ask about student prices. Station open July-Aug. M-Sa 7:30am-6:30pm; Sept.-June M-Sa 6:30am-5pm.

Local Transportation: TCL (tel. 04 78 71 80 80) has info offices at both stations and major at metro stops. *Plan de Poche* (pocket map) available from tourist office or any TCL branch. Tickets 8F; *carnet* of 10 68F, students 58F. Valid 1hr. in 1 direction, connections included. *Ticket Liberté* day pass (24F) sold at tourist and TCL offices but not stations. **Metro** runs 5am-midnight. **Buses** run 5am-9pm (a few until midnight). **Funiculars,** between pl. St-Jean and the top of Fourvière and St-Just, run until 10pm.

Taxis: Taxi Radio de Lyon (tel. 04 72 10 86 86). 24hr. To airport from Perrache and Part-Dieu 200F during the day, 7pm-7am 280F.

Budget Travel: Wasteels (tel. 04 78 37 80 17), in Perrache's Galerie Machande. BIJ tickets. Long lines. Open M-F 9am-12:30pm and 2-6:15pm, Sa 9am-noon. V, MC.

ⓩ PRACTICAL INFORMATION

Tourist Office: In the Pavilion, at pl. Bellecour, 2ème (tel. 04 72 77 69 69; fax 04 78 42 04 32). M: Bellecour. Incredibly efficient. Brochures and info on rooms and restaurants. Hotel reservation office. **Map** with museum listings (4F). Wide range of excellent **city tours** in French and English all year long (50-60F, students 25-35F). Culture vultures can buy a *Lyon City Card* (90F), with admission to 7 museums and a day's public transportation. **SNCF desk** for tickets and info. Office open M-Sa 10am-7pm, Su 10am-6pm. **Annex** near the cathedral, av. Adolphe Max, 5ème, on pl. St-Jean. Open mid-June to mid-Sept. M-F 9am-7pm, Sa 9am-6pm; rest of year M-F 9am-1pm and 2-6pm, Sa 9am-5pm. For info on entertainment and cinema, try the weekly *Lyon Poche* (7F), or seasonal *Lyon Libertin* (10F) and *Guides de l'été de Lyon: Restaurant Nuits* (10F), all available in *tabacs*. For longer stays get the scarce but free gold mine, *Le Petit Pomme*.

Consulates: Canada, 21 rue Bourgelat, 2ème (tel. 04 72 77 64 07), 1 block west of the Ampere metro stop. Open M-F 9am-noon. **Ireland,** 58 rue Victor Lagrange, 7ème (tel. 06 85 23 12 03). Open M-F 9am-noon. **UK,** 24 rue Childebert, 2ème (tel. 04 72 77 81 70). M: Bellecour. Open M-F 9am-12:30pm and 2-5:30pm.

Money: Currency exchange in the tourist office, or for terrible rates after-hours at **Thomas Cook** in both stations. Part-Dieu (tel. 04 72 33 48 55): open M-Sa 8am-8pm, Su 9am-7:15pm. Perrache (tel. 04 78 38 38 84): open M-Sa 8am-7:30pm, Su 9:30am-noon and 1:30-6:45pm. No currency exchange at **American Express,** 6 rue Childebert, 2ème (tel. 04 72 77 74 50). Open M-Sa 9:30am-1pm and 2-6:30pm.

English Bookstore: Eton, 1 rue du Plat, 2ème (tel. 04 78 92 92 36), 1 street west of pl. Bellecour toward the Saône. Good selection, decent prices. Flash *Let's Go* for a 5% discount. Open M 2-7pm, Tu-Sa 10am-12:30pm and 1:30-7pm.

Youth Centers: CROUS, 59 rue de la Madeleine, 7ème (tel. 04 72 80 13 00; toll free 0 800 03 25 58). Info on university housing and cafeterias. Open M-F 10am-4pm. **Bureau d'Informations de Jeunesse (BIJ),** 9 quai des Célestins (tel. 04 72 77 00 66), lists jobs and sports events. Open M noon-6pm and Tu-F 10am-6pm.

Women's Center: Centre d'Information Féminine, 18 pl. Tolozan, 1er (tel. 04 78 39 32 25). Open M-F 9am-1pm and 1:30-5pm.

Laundromat: Lavadou, 19 rue Ste-Hélène, around pl. Ampère. Open 7:30am-8:30pm. **Lav 123,** 123 rue Jean Jaurès. Open 7am-8pm.

Police: 47 rue de la Charité (tel. 04 78 42 26 56).

Crisis Lines: SOS Amitié (tel. 04 78 29 88 88). **SOS Racisme** (tel. 04 78 39 24 44; M-F 6:30-8:30pm). **AIDS** info service, 2 rue Montebello, 3ème (tel. 04 78 62 39 88).

Hospitals: All hospitals should have English-speaking doctors on call. **Hôpital Edouard Herriot,** 5 pl. Arsonval (tel. 04 72 11 73 11). M: Grange Blanche. Best equipped for serious emergencies, but far from the center of town. More central is **Hôpital Hôtel-Dieu,** 1 pl. de l'Hôpital, 2ème (tel. 04 72 41 30 00), near quai du Rhône. **SOS Médecins,** 10 pl. Dumas de Loire (24hr. tel. 04 78 83 51 51), arranges home visits.

Post Office: Pl. Antonin Poncet, 2ème (tel. 04 72 40 65 22), next to pl. Bellecour. **Currency exchange, internet access,** and Poste Restante (code: 69002). Open M-F 8am-7pm, Sa 8am-noon. M-Sa 8am-midnight, Su 8am-2pm. **Postal codes:** 69000-69009; last digit indicates *arrondissement*.

Internet Access: Station-Internet, 4 rue du President Carnot, 2ème. 50F per hr. Open M-Sa 10am-7pm. Surf with style at **Connectix Café,** 19 quai St-Antoine, 2ème (tel. 04 72 77 98 85). 75F per hr. Open Su-Th 10am-8pm, F-Sa 10am-1am.

⌐ ACCOMMODATIONS

France's second financial center, Lyon fills its central hotels on weekday nights with businessmen who are gone by the weekend. Unlike most places in

France, it's easier and cheaper to find a place in summer. Budget hotels cluster east of pl. Carnot near Perrache. Prices rise as you approach pl. Bellecour, but there are some inexpensive options north of pl. des Terreaux. Vieux Lyon tends to break budgets. Students may be able to find housing through CROUS (see **Youth Centers,** above).

HOSTELS AND CAMPING

Auberge de Jeunesse (HI), 41-45 Montée du Chemin Neuf (tel. 04 78 15 05 50; fax 04 78 15 05 51; www.iyhf.org) in *Vieux Lyon.* M: Vieux Lyon. From pl. Bellecour, walk west toward the old city and cross the Saône at pont Bonaparte. Turn right through pl. St-Jean and then left onto rue de la Bombarde. Follow the hairpin turn left onto Montée du Chemin Neuf and prepare for a good climb. The hostel is 8min. up on the left (15min. from Bellecour, 25min. from Perrache). Features a view worthy of a luxury hotel. Bar, laundry, **internet access,** kitchen, 4- to 8- bunk rooms. 71F. Breakfast included. Sheets 17F. **Members only.** 24hr. reception. Reservations recommended.

Résidence Benjamin Delessert, 145 av. Jean Jaurès, 7ème (tel. 04 78 61 41 41; fax 04 78 61 40 24). M: Jean Macé. From Perrache, take bus #11 or 39 to "Jean Macé," walk under the tracks, and look left after 3 blocks. From Part-Dieu, take metro to "Jean Macé." TV room. Laundry. **Internet access** (60F for 100min.). Singles 90F, with shower 95F. 24hr. reception. Reserve in advance. Often full during academic year.

Camping Dardilly (tel. 04 78 35 64 55), 10km from Lyon in a dull suburb. From the Hôtel de Ville, take bus #19 (direction "Écully-Dardilly") to "Parc d'Affaires." Pool, TV, and restaurant. 60F per tent and car. Open all year. Reception daily mid-June to mid-Sept. 8am-noon and 4-9pm; mid-Sept. to mid-June 8am-11pm. V, MC.

PERRACHE AND BELLECOUR HOTELS

Hôtel d'Ainay, 14 rue des Remparts d'Ainay, 2ème (tel. 04 78 42 43 42; fax 04 72 77 51 90). M: Ampère-Victor Hugo. Near the station, on top of pl. Ampère. The sparkling hallways and rooms may be devoid of germs, but character has also been scrubbed away by the disinfectant. Cheap, sunny, comfortable rooms and happy anglophone staff. Singles from 139F, with shower from 208F; doubles 175F, with shower 235F. Breakfast 25F. Shower 15F. Reception 7am-11pm. V, MC.

Hôtel du Dauphiné, 3 rue Duhamel, 2ème (tel. 04 78 37 24 19; fax 04 78 92 81 52), near Perrache. Clean and comfortable rooms, all with showers. The pricier rooms are huge, and rooms over 205F have TV. Singles from 135F; doubles from 205F; triples from 280F; quads 300F. Breakfast 27F. 24hr. reception. V, MC.

Hôtel des Marronniers, 5 rue des Marronniers, 2ème (tel. 04 78 37 04 82), on pl. Belle-cour across from the post office. High ceilings but low lighting in a lively central loca-tion. Singles 150F, with shower 180F; doubles 190F, with shower 220F; triples with toilet 300F; quads with toilet 350F. Breakfast 25F. 24hr. reception.

VIEUX LYON AND TERREAUX HOTELS

Le Celtic, 10 rue Francois Vernay, 5ème (tel. 04 78 28 01 12; fax 04 78 28 01 34), in Vieux Lyon. M: Terreaux. The one affordable hotel in Vieux Lyon, near the Palais de la Miniature. Turn-of-the-century institutional feel. Singles 135F, with shower 165F; dou-bles 160F, with shower 200F; triples with shower and toilet 300F. Breakfast 35F. Shower 30F. 24hr. reception.

Hôtel de France et 4 Nations, 9 rue Ste-Catherine, 1er (tel. 04 78 28 11 01; fax 04 78 28 05 34), in Terreaux. On top of much of Lyon's nightlife and right behind pl. des Ter-reaux. Good sized, generally clean rooms, some on a quieter inner courtyard. Singles 170F, with cable TV and shower 190-210F, with TV, shower, and toilet 260F; doubles with TV and shower 200-290F; triples with TV and shower 290-370F. Breakfast 30F. 24hr. reception. V, MC, AmEx.

⬛ FOOD

The galaxy of Michelin stars adorning Lyon's restaurants confirms what the *lyonnais* know and proudly declare—this is the gastronomic capital of Western civilization. A typical delicacy consists of a flagrantly unacceptable cow part prepared in a subtle, creamy sauce. Since organs such as brain, stomach, and intestines are in high demand nowhere else, you might think their inevitable surplus would send prices plummeting. But attach the description *Specialité Lyonnaise*, and suddenly 200F seems reasonable. For dessert, finish off with *tarte tatin*, an apple tart baked upside-down and then turned over. *Lyonnais* food is as bizarre as it is elegant and as creative as it is delicious. Luckily, the tradition is a part of the city's fabric; you can sample fine food even in inexpensive restaurants.

THE PRIDE OF LYON

The pinnacle of the Lyon food scene is *chez* **Paul Bocuse,** 50 rue Plages Collonges au Mont d'Or (tel. 04 72 42 90 90), 9km out of town, where meals cost approximately the equivalent of Andorra's GNP. You need not sell your body organs to eager *lyonnais* chefs to enjoy Bocusian cuisine, however. The master has two places in Lyon charting the geography of scrumptious yet affordable food. At **Le Nord,** 18 rue Neuve, 2ème (tel. 04 72 10 69 69), traditional *lyonnais* food graces the 115F *menu*. (Open daily noon-2:30pm and 7pm-midnight. V, MC, AmEx.) Bocuse's kitchens serve up more Mediterranean fare at the appropriately named (and beautifully situated) **Le Sud,** 11 pl. Antonin Poncet, 2ème (tel. 04 72 77 80 00), which also has a 115F *menu*, but offers more affordable pizzas and pastas from around 70F, (Open noon-2pm and 7pm-midnight. V, MC, AmEx.) Whether you want to eat North or South, you'll need to reserve two to three days ahead.

Locals are proud of their *cocons* (chocolates wrapped in marzipan) at Lyon's grandest *pâtisserie*, **Bernachon,** 42 cours F. Roosevelt, 6ème (tel. 04 78 24 37 98). The showcases sparkle with pastries and ambrosial *palets d'or*, recognized as the best chocolates in France—and not only because they're made with gold dust.

OTHER FLEURS-DE-LYON

If *haute cuisine* doesn't suit your wallet, and university canteens don't suit your palate, try one of Lyon's many **bouchons,** descendants of the inns where travelers would stop to dine and have their horses *bouchonné* (rubbed down). These cozy restaurants serving local cuisine cluster in the Terreaux district and along rue Mercière in the 2ème. Most places in Vieux Lyon are sure to feed you very well; try the *bouchons* along rue St-Jean, where *menus* start around 75F. If the preponderance of innards in *lyonnais* cuisine doesn't entice you, or if its cavalier attitude towards price appalls you, consider the cheaper ethnic restaurants that congregate on the wide streets off **rue de la République** (2ème).

🍴 **Chez Mounier,** 3 rue des Marronniers, 2ème (tel. 04 78 37 79 26). This tiny place satisfies the discriminating local clientele with generous traditional specialties. 4-course *menus* for 59F, 83F, and 93F. Open Tu-Sa noon-2pm and 7-10:30pm, Su noon-2pm.

🍴 **Comptoir du Bœuf,** 3 pl. Neuve St. Jean, 5ème (tel. 04 78 92 82 35). *Lyonnais* cuisine with a lighter and more imaginative twist than most *bouchons*. Specialties include lentil and herring pâtés, lamb sautéed in ginger chutney, and the obligatory *andouillettes*. *Menus* 89-119F. Open daily noon-2pm and 7pm-midnight. V, MC.

L'Acteur, 5 Charles Dullin, 2ème (tel. 04 78 92 88 53). More innovative French than traditional *lyonnais*, but delicious all the same. The offerings change often but recently included rabbit pâté and smoked salmon salad. Lunch *menu* 75F; dinner from 82F. Open M-Sa noon-2pm and 7-11pm. V, MC.

Chabert et Fils, 11 rue des Marronniers, 2ème (tel. 04 78 37 01 94). One of the better known *bouchons* in Lyon. *Museau de bœuf* (snout of cattle) and *andouillettes* make it to the 99F menu. Lunch *menus* 61-71F. Open daily noon-2pm and 7-11pm. V, MC.

Chez Carlo, 22 rue du Palais Grillet, 2ème (tel. 04 78 42 05 79), near Garioud. Locals say this has the best pasta and pizza in town (40-55F). Extensive dessert list (30F). Open Tu-Sa noon-2pm and 7-11pm, Su noon-2pm. V, MC.

Le Patisson, 17 rue Port de Temple, 2ème (tel. 04 72 41 81 71). Small, simple vegetarian joint off quai des Célestins. 3-course *menus* 65F and 70F. *Plat du jour* 50F. Open M-Th 11:30am-2pm and 7pm-9:30am, F 11:30am-2pm. Non-smoking. V, MC, AmEx.

L'Étoile de l'Orient, 31 rue des Remparts d'Ainay, 2ème (tel. 04 72 41 07 87). M: Ampère-Victor Hugo. Regulars pack this star for food and decor straight out of "Casablanca." Taboulé salads 25-40F, 120F *menu.* Open Th-Tu noon-2pm and 7-11pm.

UNIVERSITY RESTAURANTS AND SUPERMARKETS

You won't find any culinary masterpieces in Lyon's many **university restaurants,** but they're sure to please your wallet. Operated by CROUS (see **Youth Centers,** p. 211), they include: **Résidence André Allix,** 2 rue des Sœurs Bauvier, 5ème (tel. 04 78 25 47 13); **Résidence Jean Mermoz,** 29 rue Prof. J. Nicolas, 8ème (tel. 04 78 74 41 64); **Résidence la Madeleine,** 4 rue Sauveur, 7ème (tel. 04 78 72 80 62); **Cafétéria Université Lyon 2,** 16 quai C. Bernard, 7ème (tel. 04 72 73 07 02); **Résidence Jussieu,** 3 av. A. Einstein, Villeurbanne (tel. 04 78 93 34 21); and **Puvis de Chavanne,** 29 rue Marguerite, Villeurbanne (tel. 04 78 89 62 02). The last two are open in summer.

Prisunic supermarket is on rue de la République at pl. des Cordeliers, 2ème. (Open M-Sa 8:30am-8:30pm.) If you're craving a more gourmet experience, buy your groceries at **Maréchal Centre,** rue de la Platière at rue Lanterne, 1er. (Open M-F 8:30am-12:30pm and 3-8:30pm, Sa 8:30am-8:30pm.)

◉ SIGHTS

VIEUX LYON

Stacked up against the Saône at the bottom of the Fourvière hill, the narrow streets of Vieux Lyon wind between lively cafés, tree-lined squares, and magnificent medieval and Renaissance houses. The colorful *hôtels particuliers*, with delicate carvings, shaded courtyards, and ornate turrets, arose from the great wealth Lyon gained as the center of Europe's silk and publishing industries from the 15th to 19th centuries. The regal homes around rue St-Jean, rue du Bœuf, and rue Juiverie have housed Lyon's elite for 400 years—and still do.

TRABOULES. The most distinguishing feature of Vieux Lyon townhouses is the *traboules*, long tunnels leading from the street through a maze of courtyards, often with vaulted ceilings and statuary niches. Although their original purpose is still debated, later traboules were constructed to transport silk safely from looms to storage rooms. During WWII, the passageways proved to be invaluable information gathering and escape routes for the local Resistance. If the door is open, peek in (many are open to the public at specific hours), get a list of addresses from the tourist office, or take one of their tours. *(June-Sept. 1 per week. 50F, students 25F.)*

CATHÉDRALE ST-JEAN. The southern end of Vieux Lyon is dominated by the Cathédrale St-Jean, whose soaring columns and delicately mullioned stained glass windows look too fragile to have withstood eight centuries of rampages. Paris might have been worth a mass, but Lyon got the wedding cake; it was here that Henri IV met and married Maria de Médici in 1600. Every hour between noon and 4pm, automatons pop out of the 14th-century astronomical clock in a charming re-enactment of the Annunciation—the Holy Spirit literally falls through the roof. The clock can also calculate Church feast days until 2019. *(Cathedral open M-F 8am-noon and 2-7:30pm, Sa-Su 2-5pm.)*

MUSEUMS. Down rue St-Jean, turn left at the pl. du Change for the **Hôtel de Gadagne** and its relatively minor museums. The **Musée de la Marionette** displays puppets from around the world, including models of **Guignol,** the famed local cynic, and his inebriated friend, Gnaffron. *(Pl. du Petit College, 5ème. M: Vieux Lyon. Tel. 04 78 42 03 61.*

Open W-M 10:45am-6pm. 25F, students 13F.) The **Palais de la Miniature** devotes itself to microscopic art and extraordinarily complex origami. The world's smallest bear is perched atop a pearl and visible with a magnifying glass. *(2 rue Juiverie. Tel. 04 72 00 24 77. Open 10am-noon and 2-7pm. 25F, students 20F.)*

FOURVIÈRE AND ROMAN LYON

From the corner of rue du Bœuf and rue de la Bombarde in Vieux Lyon, climb the stairs heading straight up to reach the **Fourvière Hill,** the nucleus of **Roman Lyon.** From the top of the stairs, continue up via the rose-lined **Chemin de la Rosaire,** a series of switchbacks that leads through a garden to the **Esplanade Fourvière,** where a model of the cityscape points out local landmarks. Most prefer to take the **funicular** from the head of av. Max in Vieux Lyon, off pl. St-Jean, to the top of the hill. The **Tour de l'Observatoire** offers a more acute angle on the city. On a clear day, scan for Mont Blanc, about 200km east. *(Chemin de la Roseraie: Open daily 6:30am-9:30pm. Tower: Open June-Sept. daily 10am-noon and 2-6pm; Oct.-May Sa-Su only. 10F, students 5F.)*

BASILIQUE NOTRE-DAME DE FOURVIÈRE. Lyon's archbishop vowed to build a church if the city was spared attack during the Franco-Prussian War. His bargain was met, and the bishop followed through. The basilica's merengue-like exterior is delectable from a distance. Multicolored mosaics, gilded pillars and statues, and elaborate carvings adorn every square inch of the interior. *(Behind the Esplanade.)*

MUSÉE GALLO-ROMAIN. The museum holds a huge collection of mosaics, jugs, helmets, swords, statues, jewelry, and a well-preserved bronze tablet inscribed with a speech by Lyon's native son, the Emperor Claudius. *(17 rue Cléberg, 5ème. Tel. 04 72 38 81 90. Open W-Su 9:30am-noon and 2-6pm. 20F, students 10F.)*

PARC ARCHÉOLOGIQUE. Just next door to the Musée Gallo-Romain, the Parc holds the well-preserved 2000-year-old **Théâtre Romain** and the smaller **Odéon,** discovered when modern developers dug into the hill to build apartment buildings. Both still function as venues for shows during the *Nuits de Fourvière* (see **Festivals**). *(Park open Apr. 15-Sept. 15 7am-9pm, Sept. 16-Apr. 14 7am-7pm. Free.)*

LE PRESQU'ÎLE AND LES TERREAUX

Monumental squares, statues, and fountains are the trademarks of the **Presqu'ile,** the lively area between the Rhône and the Saône. Its heart is **pl. Bellecour,** a barren expanse of Martian-red gravel fringed with shops and flower stalls that utterly dwarfs Limit's equestrian statue of Louis XIV. North along pedestrian **rue de la République,** the movie theaters, FNAC, and rushing crowds establish the street as the urban aorta of Lyon. It runs through **pl. de la République** and terminates at **pl. Louis Pradel** in the 1er, at the tip of the Terreaux district. Once a marshy wasteland, the area was filled with soil centuries ago, creating dry terraces *(terreaux)* and establishing the neighborhood as the place to be for chic Lyonnais. Sidewalk cafés (full after 11pm), bars, and clubs keep this area hopping into the night. At **pl. des Terreaux,** Bartholi's fountain of frenzied horses teems with kids splashing in the cool water. Across the square, at **pl. Louis Pradel,** is the spectacular 17th-century facade of the **Hôtel de Ville,** framed by an illuminated cement field of miniature geysers. The **Opéra,** pl. Louis Pradel, is the building that looks like an airplane hangar perched atop a 19th-century attempt at classical architecture.

MUSÉE DES BEAUX-ARTS. Second only to the Louvre in France, the museum's strengths include a distinguished collection of French paintings, works by Spanish and Dutch masters, a wing devoted to the Italian Renaissance, and a lovely sculpture garden. Even the more esoteric works mingled with all-star pre-, post-, and just-plain-Impressionist collections are delightful. Look for the Rodin miniatures and Monet's famous image of Charing Cross. *(Pl. des Terreaux. tel. 04 72 10 17 40. Open W-Su 10:30am-noon and 1:05-6pm, M 1-6pm. 25F, students 13F.)*

LA CROIX-ROUSSE AND THE SILK INDUSTRY

Lyon is proud of its historical dominance of European silk manufacture. Born in the 15th century, Lyon's silk industry operated 28,000 looms by the 18th century, mainly in the Croix-Rousse district on a hill in the 1er. The 1801 invention of the power-loom by *lyonnais* Joseph Jacquard intensified the sweatshop conditions endured by the *canuts* (silk workers). Unrest came to a head in the 1834 riot, in which hundreds were killed. Mass silk manufacturing is based elsewhere today, and Lyon's few remaining silk workers perform delicate handiwork, reconstructing and replicating rare patterns for museum and château displays.

LA MAISON DES CANUTS. Come here to discover the impressive weaving techniques of the canuts. The Maison's shop sells silk made by its own canuts. A scarf costs 130F and up, but you can take home a silkworm cocoon for a few francs. *(10-12 rue d'Ivry, 4ème. Tel. 04 78 28 62 04. Open M-F 8:30am-noon and 2-6:30pm, Sa 9am-noon and 2-6pm. 20F, 15F students.)*

MUSÉE HISTORIQUE DES TISSUS. It's not in the Croix-Rousse *quartier*, but textile and fashion fans will have a field-day here. This world-class collection includes wonderfully-preserved examples of 18th-century men's wear, scraps of luxurious Byzantine textiles, sumptuous vestments, embroidered wall-hangings, and rotating exhibits. Included with admission is the neighboring **Musée des Arts Décoratifs,** housed in an 18th-century *hôtel.* Wander through reconstructed rooms brimming with period porcelain, furniture, and all sorts of luxurious *bibelots. (34 rue de la Charité, 2ème. Tel. 04 78 38 42 00. Arts Déco.: Open Tu-Su 10am-noon and 2-3:30pm. Tissus: Open Tu-Su 10am-5:30pm. Maps in English. Tour in French Su 3pm. 30F, students 15F.)*

EAST OF THE RHÔNE AND MODERN LYON

Lyon's newest train station and monstrous space-age mall form the core of the ultra-modern **Part-Dieu district.** Many see the whole place as an eyesore and consider Part-Dieu's greatest virtue to be its shops—perhaps the only ones in France open between noon and 2pm. Locals call the commercial **Tour du Crédit Lyonnais,** on the other side of the mall, *le Crayon* for its unwitting resemblance to a giant pencil standing on end. Next to it, the shell-shaped **Auditorium Maurice Ravel** hosts major cultural events.

CENTRE D'HISTOIRE, DE LA RÉSISTANCE ET DE LA DÉPORTATION. The center is housed in a building in which Nazis tortured detainees during the Occupation. Here you'll find assembled documents, photos, and films of the Resistance, whose national headquarters were based in Lyon. *(14 av. Bertholet, 7ème. Take bus #11, 26, 32, or 39. Tel. 04 72 73 33 54. Open W-Su 9am-5:30pm. 25F, students 15F.)*

INSTITUT LUMIÈRE. Film buffs will dig this *institut*, a museum that examines the lives of the *lyonnais* brothers who in 1895 invented the first film projector. During the summer, free films are screened every Tuesday outside the institute. *(25 rue du Premier-Film, 8ème. M: Monplaisir/Lumière. Tel. 04 78 78 18 95. Open Tu-Su 2-7pm. 25F, students 20F.)*

MUSÉE D'ART CONTEMPORAIN. In the futuristic **Cité International de Lyon,** a super-modern complex with offices, shops, theaters, and Interpol's world headquarters, you'll find this extensive, wholly entertaining collection of modern art. *(Quai Charles de Gaulle, 6ème. M: Masséna or bus #4. Tel. 04 72 69 17 18. Open W-Su noon-7pm. 25F, students 13F.)*

PARC DE LA TÊTE D'OR. The massive park owes its name to a legend that a golden head of Jesus lies buried somewhere within its grounds. The park sprawls over 259 acres, and you can rent paddle boats to explore its artificial lake and artificial island. Very real lions, elephants, and a thousand other animals fill the zoo; giant greenhouses encase the botanical garden, and the rose gardens are stunning in summer. *(Tel. 04 78 89 02 03. Park open daily Apr.-Sept. 6am-11pm; Oct.-Mar. 6am-9pm.)*

🔊 ENTERTAINMENT

NIGHTLIFE

Nightlife in Lyon is fast and furious. Students congregate in a series of bars on **rue Ste-Catherine** (1ème) until 1am before heading to the clubs. Pound 10F tequilas like everyone else at **L'Abreuvoir,** 18 rue Ste-Catherine. (Open Su-Th 6pm-1am, F-Sa until 2am.) **Le Chantier,** 20 rue Ste-Catherine, is a bit classier, but you still have to slip down a spiral slide to reach the dance floor downstairs. (Open M-Sa 7:30pm-3am, sometimes later. Live music for a nominal cover W-Sa.) The British-style pubs across the street are bigger and offer occasional live music. **Le Voxx,** 1 rue d'Algérie, is the latest in a series of *quai* hotspots radiating off of pl. des Terreaux.

Lyon is crawling with nightclubs. There's a whole row of semi-exclusive joints off the Saône, on quais Romain Rolland, de Bondy, and Pierre Scize in Vieux Lyon (5ème), but the city's best and most accessible late-night spots are a strip of riverboat dance clubs by the east bank of the Rhône. **Le Fish,** across from 21 quai Augagneur (tel. 04 72 84 98 98), has theme nights with salsa, jungle, house, and disco in a swank floater. (Open Th 7pm-4:30am, F-Sa 10pm-6am. 60-80F includes 1st drink; free before 10pm.) Next door, **La Marquise** (tel. 04 72 61 92 92) spends less on the boat but more on drawing big-name DJs for jungle and house. (Open W-Sa 10:30pm till dawn. Usually free, occasional 30-40F cover.) More alternative night-life can be found in *Lyon Libertin* and *Guides de l'été de Lyon: Restaurant/Nuits*, both 10F at *tabacs*.

GAY AND LESBIAN NIGHTLIFE

The tourist office's city guide lists spots catering to Lyon's active gay community. The most popular gay spots cluster in the 1er. The weekend club circuit normally starts around midnight at **L'United Café,** impasse de la Pêcherie (tel. 04 78 29 93 18), which plays a mix of American and Latino dance hits interspersed by Latino and slow songs. Thursdays is theme night—from coal mines to 2001—and there are lip-shaped urinals to boot. (Open daily until 3am.) Unless you prefer United's French selection, **Le Village Club,** 6 rue Violi (tel. 04 72 07 72 62), is the best place to be on Sunday nights, and the second spot on the weekend circuit. The contemporary music attracts a mid-20s to mid-30s crowd. (Open F-Sa 11pm-5am, Su-W closes at 3am.) **La Divine Comédie,** 30 montée St-Sebastien (tel. 04 78 30 15 12), is up and around the corner from Le Village—just follow the crowd at 5am. The last stop on the weekend circuit features a makeout room downstairs, an expensive bar, and an 80s-style neon lit dancefloor. Lesbians schmooze at **Le Verre à Soi,** 25 rue des Capucins, 1er (tel. 04 78 28 92 44), with half-price drinks 11am-8pm (open M-F 11am-3am, Sa 5pm-3am), and party on down at **L'Échiquier,** 38 rue de l'Arbre-Sec (tel. 04 78 29 18 19), when they're not having fun at one of the above clubs.

LIVE PERFORMANCE AND CINEMA

Lyon's major theater is the **Théâtre des Célestins,** 4 rue Charles Dullin, 2ème. (Tel. 04 78 42 17 67. Tickets 65-250F; discounts for under 26 and over 65.) The **Opéra,** pl. de la Comédie, 1er (tel. 04 72 00 45 45), has pricey tickets (70-380F), but 50F tickets for under 26 and over 65 go on sale 15 minutes before the show. The acclaimed **Orchestre National de Lyon** plays a full season (Oct.-May; tel. 04 78 95 95 95). The **Théâtre National Populaire** is at 8 pl. Lazare-Goujon, in the suburb of Villeurbanne (tel. 04 78 03 30 40). The **Maison de la Danse** (tel. 04 72 78 18 00) keeps pace with the dance scene in Lyon. The birthplace of cinema, Lyon is a superb place to see quality film. The **Cinéma Opéra,** 6 rue J. Serlin (tel. 04 78 28 80 08), and **Le Cinéma,** 18 imp. St-Polycarpe (tel. 04 78 39 09 72), specialize in black-and-white oldies, all in *v.o.* (34-40F). You'll find avant-garde films and classics (44F) at **CNP Terreaux Cinéma,** 40 rue Président Edouard Herriot, 1er (tel. 04 78 27 26 25).

THE CENTER

✺ FESTIVALS

In the summer, Lyon bursts with festivals and special events nearly every week. The **Fête de la Musique,** June 21, and **Bastille Day,** here as elsewhere, engender major partying. **Les Vivats** is a three-day festival in late June with free concerts, plays, and films. July 1 starts the two-week **Festival du Jazz à Vienne,** welcoming jazz masters to Vienne, a medieval town a little south of Lyon, accessible by bus or train. For festival info, call 04 74 85 00 05 or Vienne's tourist office at 11 cours Brillier (tel. 04 74 85 12 62). **Les Nuits de Fourvière** (tel. 04 78 95 95 95), is a two-month summer festival held in the ancient Théâtre Romain and Odéon. 1999 acts included Blondie and *(bien sûr)* Johnny Hallyday, interspersed with classical concerts and plays. (Tickets and info at the FNAC shop on rue de la République.)

From the beginning of September to mid-October, Lyon hits its cultural peak with two annually alternating festivals. In odd-numbered years the **Festival de Musique du Vieux Lyon,** 5 pl. du Petit Collège, 5ème (tel. 04 78 42 39 04), brings artists from around the world to perform in the churches of Lyon's old town. (Mid-Nov. to mid-Dec. Tickets 90-230F.) Even-numbered years (like 2000!) erupt with the **Biénniale de la Danse Lyon,** Maison de Lyon, pl. Bellecour, 2ème (tel. 04 72 41 00 00), which draws modern dance performers from around the world. The celebration combines a major modern art exhibit with workshops on music and cinema. (Tickets 40-240F.) Every December 8, Lyon places candles in its windows and ascends with tapers to the basilica for the **Fête de Lumières.** The celebration (which becomes a city-wide block party) honors the Virgin Mary on the Feast of the Immaculate Conception for protecting Lyon from the Black Plague.

NEAR LYON: THE BEAUJOLAIS

The very mention of Beaujolais provokes the thirst for the cool, fruity wine that is one of the main exports from this region. Both the wine and the land owe their name to the Beaujeu clan, who controlled the territory from the 9th to the early 15th century. The Beaujolais lies roughly between the Loire and Saône, with Lyon at its foot and Mâcon at its head, and is home to an important textile and lumber industry, especially in the more mountainous regions to the west. Still, it's the charm of the vine that seduces most, and the tourist offices dotting the countryside are only too happy to furnish suggested bike or car routes that wind through seemingly endless vineyards, sleepy villages, and medieval chateaux, with a couple of *dégustations* thrown in for good measure.

The most beautiful areas in the Beaujolais are difficult to access by public transportation; trains run between Mâcon and Lyon, but mostly stop in uninteresting industrial towns such as Villefranche. The best option is to rent a car in Lyon or Macon or penetrate it by bike. Guided **bus tours** in English are also available from Lyon through the tourist office and **Philibert** (tel. 04 78 98 56 98), who offer an afternoon visit into the Beaujolais countryside winding up in Le Hameau (see below) for 195F. There are also twice-weekly bus tours in French (with *dégustation*) which leave in the morning from the Villefranche tourist office, 29 rue de Thizy. (Tel. 04 74 68 05 18. Half-day tour 50F; full-day 100F. Office open July-Aug. M-Sa 9am-noon and 2:30-7pm, Su 9am-noon; Sept.-June M-Sa 9am-noon and 1:30-6pm.)

A possible day-trip from Lyon or Mâcon is to **Le Hameau du Vin** (tel. 03 85 35 22 22), in Romaneche-Thorins, right at the train station. Through the use of wax dummies, automated figures, a 3-D film starring Paul Bocuse, and a number of viticulture artifacts, this multi-media museum is a fun intro to the world of the Beaujolais. The two-hour tour caps off with a *dégustation.* (Open daily 9am-6pm.)

THE AUVERGNE

France's visitors crowd Paris to the north and descend to Provence and the Riviera in the south. Wine lovers linger in Bordeaux or Beaune, and outdoor enthusiasts scale and ski the Alps or Pyrénées. Few, however, penetrate the country's interior. The lucky adventurer who does will find rugged beauty and lively cities—as elsewhere in France—but without mobs of tourists to increase prices or trample scenery. The Auvergne is a bizarre and breathtaking landscape. Giant lava needles, extinct volcanic craters, and verdant pine forests rise out of the Massif Central. The hills no longer spew forth molten lava but release icy, crystalline springs. The mineral waters of Vichy, Le Mont Dore, and Volvic attract both *curistes* and bottling entrepreneurs. The cathedrals and churches of the Auvergne are hewn from jet-black volcanic stone. During the Middle Ages popes, troubadours, and Bourbon kings added color to the intricate social tapestry, and Pope

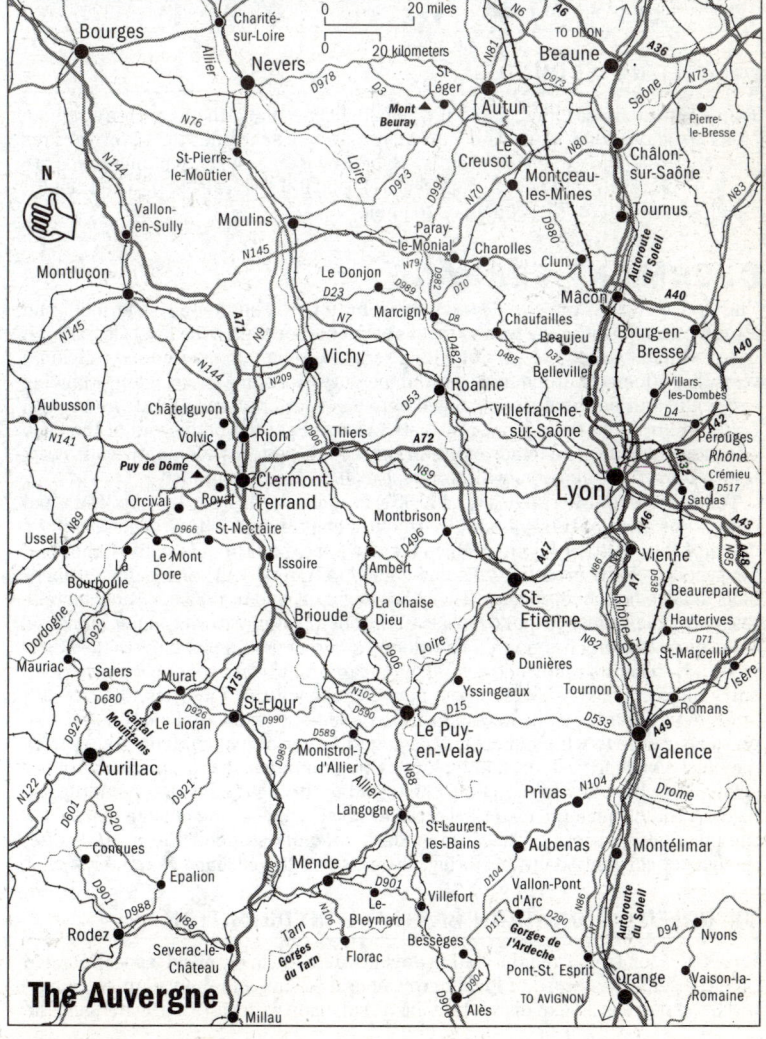

The Auvergne

Urban II chose Clermont-Ferrand as the launching pad for the First Crusade in 1095. During World War II the region achieved eternal infamy as Vichy, with its empty hotels designed for spa-goers, became headquarters for the collaborationist French government headed by Maréchal Philippe Pétain.

The farm kitchens of the Auvergne simmer with rich food—pork, cabbage, veal, turnips, and potatoes. Try *potée* (pork stew) or *tripoux* (sheep's feet stuffed with sheep's stomach). The sauces are often strong and laced with earthy red wines. Tarts and jams are filled with apricots from local orchards. The acclaimed *cantal* cheese is called *"fourme,"* a term from which the French have derived *"fromage."*

HIGHLIGHTS OF THE AUVERGNE

■ **Vichy**'s Belle Époque architecture and *curiste* culture will content your aesthetic and physical karma (p. 232).
■ Perched atop Le **Puy-en-Velay**'s stark volcanic rocks is the religious complex **Cité Episcopal**. The striking **Cathédrale Notre-Dame** is at its center (p. 231).
■ The jagged peaks of **Le Mont Dore** accommodate every level of hiking (p. 225).

THE CENTER

▐ GETTING AROUND

Trains run to major cities, and a few small villages along the way; more remote areas are served only by private bus companies with schedules timed for workers and local students rather than tourists. The Auvergne's steep, winding roads are made for the *Tour de France*, not a leisurely pedal. The locals tend to be friendly, which bodes well for those inclined to hitch.

CLERMONT-FERRAND

Clermont-Ferrand was two distinct cities during the Middle Ages: Clermont and Montferrand. It was in the former that Urban II first preached the First Crusade, an event which sparked the first of a long series of religious (and not so religious) wars that affected Europe until the 15th century. Back in France, a long-standing economic and political rivalry raged between Clermont and Montferrand until Louis XIII ordered their merger in 1630; Clermont got the better end of the deal. The city built walls to exclude Montferrand, and the latter, a 40-minute walk away, is now often forgotten; many locals simply call their city Clermont.

Today, Clermont-Ferrand (pop. 140,000) is slowly burnishing its smudged reputation. For most of this century, Clermont meant Michelin tires. Mme Daubrée, niece of the Scottish scientist Macintosh (whose experiments with rubber and benzene led to the invention of a damn good rainproof coat), made some rubber balls to keep her children busy. The balls caught on, and in 1886 her Michelin relatives used the rubber to make bicycle tires, kicking off the town's major industry.

Recently, the city has poured its resources into upgrading its universities; Clermont now boasts a renowned school of fine arts, a business school, a police academy, and a chemistry lab. Home to many smoke-spitting factories, the city still tends to be regarded by its neighbors as a soot-covered industrial landfill. But suppress your urge to whip out a sand-blaster; the color of the buildings comes from the black volcanic rock used in their construction rather than as the result of lingering pollution. If you happen to be treading through, consider spending the night. A roll through the historical areas of town is a welcome change of pace for the imaginative tourist. The porous, dark volcanic stone of the *vieille ville*, though not conventionally endearing, gives the streets a striking character.

▐ ORIENTATION AND PRACTICAL INFORMATION

Buses #2, 4, or 14 go from the station downtown to the lively **pl. de Jaude**. Bounded on either end by statues of local hero Général Desaix and the valiant Vercingetorix, the *place* is an expansive, tree-lined esplanade with cafés, a theater, and the modern **Centre Jaude,** a vast shopping center. If you'd rather make the 25-minute walk, go left from the station onto av. de l'Union Soviétique, left again onto bd. Fleury, and take a quick right onto av. Carnot. The street bends to the left and turns into rue Maréchal Joffre for two blocks, then curves back right, turning into rue Maréchal Juin and then bd. Desaix before it dumps you onto pl. de Jaude. Get a map at the tourist office in the train station before you go.

Trains: Av. de l'Union Soviétique. To: **Le Puy** (2½hr., 2 per day, 107F); **Lyon** (3hr., 11 indirect per day, 136F); and **Paris** (3½hr., 9 per day, 235F). Info office open M-Sa 8am-7:30pm; ticket window open daily 5:30am-10:30pm. **Baggage check** 20F. Open M-F 7am-7:30pm. In the station, **SOS Voyageurs** (tel. 04 73 30 12 79) helps travelers. Open M-F 8am-2:30pm and 4-7:30pm.

Buses: 69 bd. F. Mitterrand (tel. 04 73 93 13 61). Near the Jardin Lecoq. Buses throughout the Auvergne, including **Le Puy** (3¼hr., 1 per day Sept.-June, 69F). Office open M-Sa 8:30am-6:30pm. **Luggage storage** 4.50F per day.

Local Transportation: 15-17 bd. Robert Schumann (tel. 04 73 28 56 56). Buses blanket the city. Ticket 7F, day pass 25F. Service 5:30am-9pm.

Taxis: Taxi Radio Clermontois (tel. 04 73 19 53 53). 24hr.

Tourist Office: Pl. de la Victoire (tel. 04 73 98 65 00; fax 04 73 90 04 11). From the *gare,* follow directions for pl. Jaude but look out for rue St-Genès on your right during the rue Maréchal Joffre span. The office is right before the cathedral (20min.). Excellent map and bus schedules. **SNCF** tickets and info. Additional office specializes in the region. **Walking tours** depart pl. de la Victoire (M, W, and F 3pm; 30F, students 15F). Open June-Sept. M-Sa 8:30am-7pm, Su 9am-noon and 2-6pm; Oct.-May M-F 8:45am-6:30pm, Sa 9am-noon and 2-6pm, Su 9am-1pm. **Annex** at the *gare* (tel. 04 73 91 87 89). Open July-Aug. M-F 10am-5pm, Sa-Su. 10am-1pm and 2-7pm; June and Sept. M-Sa 9:15-11:30am and 12:15-5pm; Oct.-May M-F 9:15-11:30am, Sa 12:15-5pm.

Budget Travel: Wasteels, 69 bd. Trudaine (tel. 04 73 91 07 00). BIJ tickets and long lines. Open M-W 9am-noon and 2-6pm, Th-F 9am-noon and 1:30-4pm, Sa 9am-noon.

English Books: Librairie les Volcans, bd. Gergovia, across from the *gare routière*. Open Tu-Sa 9am-noon and 2-7pm.

Youth Centers: Espace Info Jeunes, 5 av. St-Genès (tel. 04 73 92 30 50). Open M-F 10am-6pm, Sa 10am-1pm and 2-6pm.

Laundromat: Laverie, 6 pl. Hippolye Renoux. Open daily 7am-8pm.

Police: 2 rue Pélissier (tel. 04 73 98 42 42).

Crisis Line: SOS Amitié (tel. 04 73 37 37 37), 24hr. friendship line.

Hospital: Hôpital Gabriel-Montpied, rue Montalembert (04 73 62 57 00). **SOS Médecins,** 28 av. Léon Blum (tel. 04 73 92 12 12).

24-Hour Pharmacy: Pharmacie Ducher, 1 pl. Delille (tel. 04 73 91 31 77).

Post Office: 1 rue Louis Renon (tel. 04 73 30 63 00). **Currency exchange.** Open M-F 8am-7pm, Sa 8am-noon. **Postal code:** 63000. **Branch** at pl. Galliard (tel. 04 73 31 70 00). Same hours and services. **Postal code:** 63100.

Internet Access: Internet Café, 31 rue Ballainvieliers (tel. 04 73 92 42 80). 1F per min., 45F per hr. Open M and Sa 11am-11pm, Tu-F 8am-11pm. **France Telecom,** 67 bd. F. Mitterand. 30F per 30min., students 10F. Open M-F 9am-6:30pm.

■ ACCOMMODATIONS AND CAMPING

There are a couple of inexpensive hotels clustered conveniently near the train station. Finding a cheap room in the center of town can be more challenging. Use the tourist office's *Guide Practique* to find other foyer accommodations.

Foyer des Jeunes Travailleurs (Corum Saint Jean), 17 rue Gauthier de Biauzat (tel. 04 73 31 57 00; fax 04 73 31 59 99), off pl. Gaillard. From the station, take bus #2 or 4 to "Gaillard." Modern complex holds well-furnished rooms (some with private bathrooms), a bar, basketball courts, and laundry facilities. Great location near the *vieille ville*. Singles, doubles, or triples 90-110F per person. Breakfast included. Meals 44F. Reception daily 9am-7pm. Often full; call ahead.

Auberge de Jeunesse "Cheval Blanc" (HI), 55 av. de l'Union Soviétique (tel. 04 73 92 26 39; fax 04 73 92 99 96). Across and to the right of the station. International clientele dig the cream stucco and red-tile façade. Squat toilets only. Kitchen. 1- to 8-bunk rooms 67F. Breakfast included. Dinner 50F. Sheets 17F. Reception daily 7-9:30am and 5-11pm. Lockout 9:30am-5pm. Curfew 11pm. Open Apr.-Oct. **Members only.**

Hôtel Zurich, 65 av. de l'Union Soviétique (tel. 04 73 91 97 98), right of the train station past the youth hostel. Homey, good-sized rooms. Grandmotherly patron. Singles and doubles without shower 120-140F, with shower 150-160F; twins with bath 180-220F. Discount for longer stays. Reception at variable hours. Best to call ahead.

Campsites: Le Chancet, av. Jean-Baptiste Marrou (tel. 04 73 61 30 73). From the station, take bus #4 (direction "Ceyrat") to "Préguille." Three-star site has volleyball, game room, and laundry. Resort-like July-Aug., with organized activities and biking and hiking excursions. 16.50F per person, 20F per tent, 8F per car. Electricity 22F. Open year-round. Reception 8am-8pm in summer.

FOOD

The area around **rue St-Dominique,** off av. des États-Unis, has dozens of ethnic eateries, while the narrow streets behind the cathedral, especially **rue des Chaussetiers,** specialize in local cuisine. There is the usual thrifty selection at the **Casino cafeteria** on av. Marx Dormoy. (Open M-Th 11am-9:30pm, F-Sa 11am-10pm.) There's a **supermarket** in **Galeries Lafayette,** on the east side of pl. de Jaude. (Open M-Sa 8:30am-7pm.) For local fruits, veggies, and cheese, head to the **Marché couvert/Espace St-Pierre,** off pl. Gaillard, a huge covered market with hundreds of *auvergnat* specialties. (M-Sa 7am-7:30pm.)

Au Bon Pinard/Mme Griffet, 7 rue des Petits Gras (tel. 04 73 36 40 95). Mme Griffet's two children wait and tend bar before heading back to their day jobs, while the cook is content stuffing her regular crowd of businessmen and workmen full of delicious *auvergnat* treats. The 63F lunch menu changes every day. Renowned throughout the city for quantity and quality. Open Tu-Sa noon-2pm.

Maiko, 65 rue du Port (tel. 04 73 90 79 15). An origami version of the Puy de Dôme greets customers in this charming Japanese restaurant. Tempura 45F. Lunch *menu* with miso soup, salad, and grilled fish and rice 55F. Dinner *menus* start at 70F. Open Tu-F noon-2pm and 7:30-10:30pm, Su-M noon-2pm. V, MC (200F min.).

Le Relais Pascal, 15 rue Pascal (tel. 04 73 92 21 04). Dozens of regional dishes and a selection of over 100 wines. 85F menu includes *assiette auvergnate* (local meats), *tripaux* (tripe) or steak, cheese, and dessert. 55F lunch *menu* changes.

1513, 3 rue des Chaussetiers (tel. 04 73 92 37 46). Travel back in time and dine in the garden or the candlelit cavern, both dating from 1513. Imaginative *crêpes à la carte* 20-59F. 55F lunch menu. *Plat du jour* or *steak frites* with salad and glass of wine 50F. Open 11:30am-1:30am. V, MC, AmEx (100F min.).

SIGHTS

The tourist office **Pass découverte** (52F) gives entry to the city's five major museums.

During his conquest of Gaul, Julius Cæsar suffered one major setback. In 52 BC, in modern-day Clermont-Ferrand, the chief of the local Arvernians and commander of the combined Gaulish forces, Vercingetorix, successfully beat off the Roman legions. A few months later, Cæsar got his revenge and carted Vercingetorix off in chains to Rome. The Roman ruins on nearby **Puy de Dôme** (see p. 224) and the relics housed in the city's museums are significant and well-preserved, revealing a history far deeper than the petty rivalry that later marked the town.

CLERMONT

The *vieille ville* of Clermont, called the *Ville Noire* (Black City), is one of the most fascinating old town districts in France. The buildings are made of black volcanic stone, which contrasts with the bright red roofs, to make the streets of Vieux Clermont wonderful for strolling.

CATHÉDRALE NOTRE-DAME DE L'ASSOMPTION. First built in 450, the church was completely reconstructed in the Gothic style between 1248 and 1295 and now commands attention from miles away. The strength of the lava-based material allowed the architects to elongate the graceful spires to a height of 100m; you can ascend the tower for a panoramic view. Up close, the three rose windows and the 13th-century *vitraux* in the chapels behind the altar gleam majestically through the dark. *(Pl. de la Victoire. Open M-F 8am-6pm, Sa 9:30am-7pm. Tower 10F. Free French tour of the windows mid-June to mid-Sept. Tu, Th, and Sa 3pm, W 10am.)*

BASILIQUE DE NOTRE-DAME-DU-PORT. Less magnificent but more intriguing than the cathedral is this 11th- to 12th-century church built in the local Auvergnat Romanesque style. The basilica has a particularly beautiful choir, surrounded by an ambulatory and radiating chapels. It was probably here that Urban II first preached the First Crusade. On the Sunday after May 14th, pilgrims stream in to see the icon of the Black Virgin; the ex-voto plaques in the crypt attest to recent miracles. *(Pl. Notre-Dame-du-Port. Open daily 8am-7pm.)*

FONTAINE D'AMBOISE. Near the basilica, the black fountain is framed by a view of the surrounding countryside. This fountain was erected in 1515 and is a lovely *melange* of late Gothic and Renaissance forms, all carved from volcanic stone. *(Pl. de la Poterne.)* The free tourist office brochure *Circuit des fontaines* details a walking tour past Clermont-Ferrand's many other interesting fountains.

THE MUSÉE BARGOIN. Undoubtedly the most interesting museum in Clermont, the Musée Bargoin is devoted to prehistoric and Gallo-Roman archæology. It displays artifacts recovered from the Temple of Mercury on the Puy de Dôme, as well as Pompeiian wall paintings, 2000-year-old hair braids, mummified infants, and bizarre wooden votive offerings. The **Musée du Tapis d'Art,** in the same building and on the same ticket, lays out a beautiful collection of Persian rugs. *(45 rue Ballainvilliers. Tel. 04 73 91 37 31. Both open Tu-Su 10am-6pm. 23F, students 13F.)*

MUSÉE LECOQ. In here, you'll find a natural history collection with its share of glassy-eyed stuffed animals. Just outside is the peaceful *Jardin Lecoq*, where you can while away the time in its winding shady paths, rose garden, and artificial lake. *(15 rue Bardoux. Tel. 04 73 91 93 78. Open Oct.-Apr. Tu-Sa 10am-noon and 2-5pm, Su 2-5pm; May-Sept. until 6pm. 23F, students 13F, free first Su of each month.*

MUSÉE DE RANQUET. Walk, don't rush, to the Musée de Ranquet, which hosts temporary exhibits and has a collection of regional artifacts, including two *pascalines*, counting machines perfected by native genius Blaise Pascal. *(34 rue des Gras. Tel. 04 73 37 38 63. Open Tu-Su 10am-6pm. 13F.)*

MONTFERRAND

Most of Montferrand's best sites are inconspicuous *hôtels particuliers*—private mansions which date from the Middle Ages and the Renaissance. The best way to visit the town, which rises above an unattractive commercial district 40 minutes away up av. de la République, is by a **walking tour** given by the tourist office. (Tours depart Tu, Th, and Sa from pl. Louis Deteix at 3pm; 30F, students 15F.) Take buses #17 (direction "Blanzat" or "Cébazat") or 10M (direction "Aulnat") from the *gare*. Like Clermont, Montferrand is dominated by a (less magnificent) volcanic stone church. **Notre-Dame-de-Prospérité** stands on the site of the long-demolished château of the *auvergnat* counts. For a more secular sight, take a look at the full moon on

the 15th-century carvings on the **Maison de l'Apothécaire**, corner of rue de Cordeliers and rue de la Rodade. Having served as everything from nunnery to police
headquarters, the 18th-century convent on rue du Seminaire now acts as the
region's **Musée des Beaux-Arts** (tel. 04 73 16 11 30). This old dog has learned its new
trick well. The modern structure in traditional stone leads you through 14 centuries, encompassing relics, sculpted capitals, and a wide range of impressive works
from the last 500 years. (Beaux-Arts open Tu-Su 10am-6pm. 23F, students 13F, free the first
Su of each month.)

NIGHTLIFE AND FESTIVALS

Clermont's students complain that the city's nightlife is sluggish, but they struggle
valiantly to start it up at a few popular nightspots. Check *Le Guide l'Étudiant
Clermont-Ferrand* (available at the tourist office) for complete listings. All types
play pool and drink cheap beer in one of the many bars across the street from the
gare. **Place de Jaude** plays host to the largest concentration of dance clubs.

Le Palais de la Bière, 3 rue de la Michodière (tel. 04 73 37 15 51), on the corner of pl.
Galliard and av. des États-Unis, is for real brew-hounds, lacking romantic ambience but
providing exotic beers and *brasserie* fare to boot. Open M-F noon-2pm and 7pm-1am, F
until 2am, Sa-Su 8pm-2am.

Club l'Arlequin, 2 rue d'Étoile (tel. 04 73 37 33 88), off av. des États-Unis, strives to be
an exclusive club in an inclusive city. Drinks 30-50F. No shorts or sneakers. 50F cover
includes first drink. Open F-Su midnight-4am.

Blue Sport Café (tel. 04 73 36 08 92), down the street from the club, will take you if
Arlequin gives you and your hiking gear the boot.

Sonic Rendez Vous, 3 bd. Desaix (tel. 04 73 93 12 52), blasts techno until 2am. 60F
cover.

FESTIVALS. During the first week in February, filmmakers from all over Europe
gather for Clermont-Ferrand's annual **Festival International du Court Métrage** (International Festival of Short Films), considered the "Cannes du Court." For info, contact Sauve Qui Peut le Court Métrage, 26 rue des Jacobins, 63000 Clermont-
Ferrand (tel. 04 73 91 65 73; fax 04 73 92 11 93).

PUY DE DÔME

Clermont-Ferrand's greatest attraction is its proximity to an extinct volcanic hin-
terland filled with crystal-clear lakes and pristine mountains. The **Parc Naturel
Régional des Volcans d'Auvergne** (tel. 04 73 62 21 45 or 04 73 65 64 00), west of Clermont-Ferrand, rewards hikers, bikers, and skiers with unspoiled terrain in
France's largest national park. A booklet available at the Clermont-Ferrand tourist
office marks and catalogues hiking paths. The protected area includes three main
sections: the **Monts Dore**, the **Monts du Cantal**, and the **Monts Dômes**—the last of
which is the best place for exploring the mountains.

From the top of the massive, flat-topped **Puy de Dôme** (1465m), you can see
across the teacup-shaped **Chaîne des Puys,** a ridge of extinct volcanos which runs
north-south from Clermont-Ferrand. If you scale the Dôme in late autumn, you
may behold the wondrous *mer de nuages* (sea of clouds); a blanket of clouds
obscures the plains below, and only isolated peaks protrude into the clear blue
sky. In 1648, Clermont native Blaise Pascal conducted experiments on air pressure
from the peak. Still earlier, Roman Gauls recognized the mystique of the spot and
lugged tons of marble all the way from Rome and the Pyrenees to erect a giant
temple to Mercury. Today only the foundation remains, and a 50m television tower
nearby diminishes some of its charm. Still, even on hazy days, the mountain
remains impressive for the beauty of its terrain and for the crazed paragliders
whisking by its steep sides. (Puy-de-Dôme open Mar.-Nov. daily, Nov.-Dec. Sa-Su,
and over Christmas holiday, weather permitting.) At the peak, the **Centre d'Accueil**

de **Puy de Dôme** (tel. 04 73 62 21 46) has informative displays and leads free tours of the summit. (Tours every 45min. Open May-Sept. 7am-10pm; Apr. and Oct. 8am-8pm; Nov.-Mar. 8am-6pm.) The **Comité Départemental de Tourisme du Puy de Dôme,** pl. de la Bourse in Clermont-Ferrand (tel. 04 73 42 21 23), has reams of pamphlets on the area and sells its colorful Puy-de-Dôme guide (50F) with historical and cultural info on the area's towns. (Open M-Th 8:30am-12:15pm and 1:45-5:30pm, F 8:30am-12:15pm and 1:45-5pm.) Also in Clermont, **Chamina Sylva,** 24 av. Édouard Michelin (tel. 04 73 90 94 82 or 04 73 92 81 44), sells maps and suggests hiking and climbing excursions. (Open M-F 9am-1pm and 2-6pm.)

Although Puy-de-Dôme is only 12km from Clermont-Ferrand, reaching it takes planning. The Clermont tourist office's **Espace Massif Central** desk has mountains of info on how to get there. **Voyage Maisonneuve,** 24 rue Clemenceau (tel. 04 73 93 16 72), organizes infrequent **bus excursions** to the summit and other parts of the Auvergne (5hr.; offered July-Sept., see tourist office for exact dates; 73F). Your best bet, though, is to hike or drive. Hitching is also possible, although *Let's Go* does not recommend hitching as a safe form of transport. Hikers take the regular bus line to Royat (#14); from there it's about a three-hour hike along the PR Chamina to the summit. Hitchers head out of town on av. du Puy de Dôme and follow the signs for about 8km to the base of the mountain. It's illegal to walk up the road that the cars take, and the rule is well enforced. Either stand at the toll for an easy hitch or follow the D941 another couple of kilometers west to the Col de Ceyssat, where you can grab the *sentier des muletiers,* a Roman footpath that leads to the top in about an hour. Buy a good map (such as the IGN Chaîne des Puys), and get a good weather forecast for the day, as conditions change rapidly—hailstorms on the summit are not uncommon, even in June. Bring warm clothes and rain gear. From 10am-6pm in July and August, and Sundays and holidays in May, June, and September, drivers must leave their cars at the base and take a bus (13F one-way, 21F round-trip; free parking at base and summit); otherwise, the toll is 22F.

LE MONT DORE

Like most ski resorts, Le Mont Dore (pop. 2000) lies at the highest point of an isolated valley, right at the foot of the biggest mountain in the area. The mountain chain is little more than a sleepy string of volcanoes in the heart of the Massif Central, but the odd rock phenomena, craggy peaks and ridges, varying shades of green, and deep craters convey a primordial scene: elephants, rhinoceri, and tigers once roamed bamboo forests in the region, and their fossils remain encrusted in volcanic rock. In the 18th century, a spa community sprung up around Le Mont Dore. Pine trees and lush meadows now cover the slopes, populated with *curistes* who seek relief from asthma and rheumatism in the warm waters that seep up through cracks in the lava. In the winter, skiers flock to Puy de Sancy (1886m), the highest peak in the Auvergne, on the southern tip of town. When the snow melts, the slopes give way to trails and hikers have their chance at this bizarre and beautiful region.

▐ **PRACTICAL INFORMATION. Trains** run from pl. de la Gare (tel. 04 73 65 00 02) to **Clermont-Ferrand** (1½hr., 4 per day, 66F). (Info desk open daily 6am-12:30pm and 2-6pm.) **Taxis** are run by **Claude Taxi** (tel. 04 73 65 01 05) and **Taxi Sepchat** (tel. 04 73 65 09 38). **Rent bikes** and **skis** at **Bessac Sports,** rue de Maréchal Juin. (Tel. 04 73 65 02 25. Bikes 60-130F per half-day, 90-200F per day. Passport or 600F deposit. Skis 45-135F per day. Open M-F summer 9am-noon and 2-7pm; winter 8:30am-7pm. V, MC.) From the train station, head up av. Michel Bertrand and follow the signs to the **tourist office,** av. de la Libération (tel. 04 73 65 20 21; fax 04 73 65 05 71), on the other side of the Dordogne, which distributes a practical guide to the city and organizes hikes and bike circuits in the summer. (Circuits 55F half-day, 90F full day. Open July-Aug. M-Sa 9am-12:30pm and 2-6:30pm, Su 10am-noon and 4-6:30pm; May-June and Sept. closes at 6pm on Su; Oct.-Apr. closed Su.) **Maisonneuve** (tel. 04 73 65 20 21) runs **excursions** to the region's lakes, volcanoes, châteaux, and farms (5hr., most leave 2pm, 82-132F); you can book them at the tourist office. The **police station** (tel. 04 73 65 01 70) is on av. M. Bertrand. The **post office,** pl. Charles de Gaulle (tel. 04 73 65 02 04), **exchanges currency.** (Open M-F 8:30am-noon and 1:30-5pm, Sa 8:30am-noon. **Postal code:** 63240.)

⌐ ACCOMMODATIONS AND CAMPING. The **Auberge de Jeunesse "Le Grand Volcan" (HI),** rte. du Sancy (tel. 04 73 65 03 53; fax 04 73 65 26 39), is 3km from town. From the station, climb av. Guyot-Dessaigne, which becomes av. des Belges. Continue on D983 (which changes names several times) into the countryside. When you see ski lifts, the hostel will be on your right. The train station has info on local buses which pass the hostel. The slope-side chalet at the foot of Puy de Sancy has one- to six-bed rooms, a TV room, a bar, a mini-game room, semi-outdoor kitchen facilities, and laundry. Avoid the cramped loft singles. Hikers visit to avoid rain, and faithful regulars come every year. (51F. Breakfast 19F. Meals 50F.)

A stone's throw from the *gare,* **Hôtel Terminus,** av. Guyot Dessaigne (tel. 04 73 65 00 23), is a great deal, with calm, bright, pristine rooms. (Singles and doubles from 125F, with bath 175F. Breakfast 38F.) **Hôtel Helvetia,** 5 rue de la Saigne (tel. 04 73 65 01 67), is cozy and clean and keeps a family restaurant downstairs with *pension* and *demi-pension* also available. From the station, follow av. Bertrand past pl. Charles de Gaulle and onto rue Meynadier. Keep going straight as it turns into av. Foch and then rue de la Saigne; the hotel will be on the left past rue du Maréchal Juin (20min.). (Singles and doubles with phone, some with lofts, 130F, with shower 160-180F. Extra bed 30F. Breakfast 25F.)

There are four **campsites** in and around town. The most convenient is **Des Crouzets,** av. des Crouzets (tel. 04 73 65 21 60), across from the station in a pleasant hollow along the Dordogne. You can set up first and pay later. (14.50F per person, 13.50F per site, car included. Electricity 10.50-31F depending on voltage. Office open daily 9am-noon and 3-6pm, Sa-Su 9-10:15am and 4:30-5:45pm. Open mid-Dec. to Oct.) One kilometer behind the station is **L'Esquiladou,** rte. des Cascades. (Tel. 04 73 65 23 74. 17.50F per person, 14.50F per tent. Electricity 10.50F. Reception daily July-Aug. 8am-noon and 3-8pm; Sept.-June 9am-noon and 3-6pm.)

⌐ FOOD. It's difficult to find a restaurant in Le Mont Dore that isn't hitched to a hotel. Such *pensions* serve everyone but usually give discounts to their guests. Most *menus* in town begin at 65F, and a good meal is 70-90F. For an affordable and friendly coffee, *crêpe* (12-35F), or light dinner, stop at the Belle Époque-ish ■ **Au Petit Paris,** 8 rue Jean Moulin. (Tel. 04 73 65 01 77. Open daily 8am-11pm.) Everything's fine at **À Tout Va Bien,** rue Marie-Thérèse (tel. 04 73 65 05 14), on the corner of av. Général Leclerc, covered with Asterix paraphernalia. In addition to a 60F *menu* of regional dishes, their *fondue gauloise* (73F) and *fondue auvergnate* (93F) allow you to stone-cook your own meat. (Open daily noon-2pm and 7-9pm.) The cheapest and most scenic meals are mountaintop picnics. **Éco Service supermarket** is on rue du Cap-Chazzotte. (Open M-Sa 7am-12:30pm and 3-7:30pm, Su 8am-12:30pm. V, MC.) There's a modest **covered market** on pl. de la République (daily 8am-noon and 2-7pm) which loses its inhibitions on Fridays and goes topless (8am-4pm).

⌐⌐ SIGHTS AND ENTERTAINMENT. There's not a whole lot to do in the town, but you can introduce yourself to the *curiste* tradition at the **Établissement Thermal,** pl. du Panthéon (tel. 04 73 65 05 10). Five of the springs used today were first channeled by the Romans, who found that the sources did wonders for their horses' sinuses. Around 1810, the present-day center was built as a "hospital." The curious can visit the *thermes* only via tours given in French. Visitors are invited to sample the miraculous juice from the glass-enclosed pool as it burps sulfuric and ferric gases. The visit ends with a dose of the thermes's celebrated *douche nasale gazeuse.* A tiny blast of carbonated gas and helium evacuates those sinuses like no sneeze ever could. (Tours daily 2:30-5:30pm. 15F.) Down the hill on av. Michel

Bertrand, the **Musée Joseph Forêt** (tel. 04 73 65 00 91) honors the celebrated art editor, a Mont Dore native who left much of his collection to the town in 1985. For his grand finale, Forêt recruited seven painters and seven writers to collaborate in the publication of the largest book in the world. Le Livre de l'Apocalypse, weighing a quarter-ton, includes works by Dalí and Cocteau. A facsimile—the original was sold in bits to pay for itself—sits in the back. (Call for hours. 15F, students 10F.)

⚐ HIKES AND BIKES. Trails through these volcanic mountains cover dense forests, crystal-clear waterfalls and cascades, and bizarre, moon-like rock outcroppings. Scaling the peaks is relatively easy—the summit of Puy de Sancy, 1775m, is a half-day hike—but as always, if you plan on taking an extended hike, go over your route with the tourist office. Leave an itinerary with the police at the base of Puy de Sancy for any multi-day route (tel. 04 73 65 04 06). All hikers should equip themselves with maps and weather reports—mist in the valley can be hail or snow in the peaks. The tourist office sells the pocket-sized *Massif du Sancy* (45F), with hiking and bike circuits; it is complemented by a detailed map (35F) with topographical information and routes. You may want to invest in their *Massif du Sancy et Artense* guide (94F), which elaborates 38 hikes originating from all areas of Le Sancy. An IGN map (either Massif du Sancy or the larger Chaîne des Puys) is a must for any serious trek (58F).

To get the views without all that exertion, you can avail yourself of the **téléphérique** (cable car; tel. 04 73 65 02 73), which whisks people up from the base station by the hostel to the Puy de Sancy. (Every 15-20min. July-Aug. 9am-6pm; Sept.-June 9am-noon and 1:30-6pm. 30F one-way, 36F round-trip.) A **funicular** runs from near the tourist office up to the Salon des Capucins (1245m).

If you have a car or a bike, don't miss the chance to visit one of the many volcanic lakes like **Lac Servière** (20km northeast of Le Mont Dore), which fill in the craters of the Mont Dore region and are suitable for windsurfing, sailing, fishing, and swimming. **Lac d'Aydat**, farther to the northeast, offers pedal-boats and other amusements. **Lac Chambon**, 20km east of Le Mont Dore via D996E, offers the same and is near Murol, where actors pretend it's the 13th century and fill a château with *repartee* in Old French. (Tel. 04 73 88 67 11. Call for seasonal hours. 40F.)

For an **easy hike,** try the **Grande Cascade.** From the **Thermes,** follow rue des Desportes a few meters to the right and climb the stairs on your left to join the Chemin de Melki Rose, which then leads into the Route de Bresse and the Chemin de la Grande Cascade. After crossing a road, the trail continues though birch woods and then winds up a narrow, pine-covered gorge. From there it's a quick climb on the metal stairway to the top of the waterfall, into the sweeping pastures above sharply defined cliffs (3.5km round trip, 1½hr.). Ambitious types continue up to join the GR4 (see **advanced hikes,** below). Another easy option is the **Salon du Capucin.** From the tourist office, take av. Jules Ferry and follow the signs. Lots of meandering half-paved roads lead up 200m to the Salon. From there it's an hour to the **Pic du Capucin.** (See below. 4.5km round-trip to Salon, 1½hr.)

A great **intermediate hike** begins at the base of the **Puy de Sancy,** near the hostel. Ascend the mountain via the **Val de Courre,** clearly labeled with yellow markers, 200m to the right of the cable car. You'll pass the source of the Dordogne along the way. At **Puy Redon,** yellow blazes join the **GR30,** and the trail climbs to the summit of **Puy de Sancy.** Summer snow patches are not uncommon at the summit, and on clear days the Alps are visible to the east. On the south side of the peak, wildflowers and other rare vegetation carpet the immense **Vallée de la Fontaine Salée.** Ask at the tourist office for trails that descend into this huge basin. Smart hikers who don't want to follow the **GR4** all the way back into town (see below) retrace their steps along the Val de Cour instead of suffering through the marked ski trails of the **GR4e.** (8km round-trip, 3-4hr.) Another half-day hike starts just off the D996, a few hundred meters west of **le Marais.** Follow the yellow-marked PR as it curves right and ascends through a thick wood. At the juncture of the GR30 you can turn left and follow a 2km detour to climb the **Puy Gros.** Otherwise, continue right for several kilometers, passing by another yellow-marked PR, and on to the Lac de

Guerey. From there, it's just a few paces to a picnic above the valley framed by the massive rocks of Tuilière and Sanadoire. To descend, retrace your steps to the PR juncture and head back down to the Marais. (5-6hr. round-trip.)

The most ambitious **advanced full-day hike** follows a series of trails that makes a complete loop around the town and hits all of the major natural attractions along the way. It's 15-20km long, but can easily be broken down into one- to two-hour excursions. Start from the tourist office and follow av. Jules Ferry and the signs to the **Salon du Capucin,** a towering mass of rocks overlooking town; you can also take the funicular (see above). Another vertical 200m takes you to the **Pic du Capucin,** where the minor PR trail hooks up with the GR30, marked with parallel red and white lines. If you see crossing red and white stripes, you've left the trail—turn around. The GR30 follows a narrow ridge and passes rugged coves and craters of the once-furious peaks, as well as vast pastures full of sheep, horses, and cows. It then skirts the summit of **Puy Redon,** hovering over the spectacular **Val de Courre,** and ascends another 100m to the summit of **Puy de Sancy,** the highest peak in the Massif Central. From there, follow the GR4 as it loops back north and descends a series of ski trails before climbing back into the trees. The weary should take the GR4e, which descends straight to the base of the ski mountain. After 2km of level hiking, the trail passes by the **Grande Cascade** before beginning a gradual descent into town, finishing up by the station.

LE PUY-EN-VELAY

In stark, surreal contrast to the gentle green hills around them, jutting crags of volcanic rock pierce the sky at Le Puy (pop. 21,000). Fifteen centuries ago, traveling bishops decided that these rocky towers were the perfect spots to worship the Virgin Mary. They recruited rich pilgrims, and the moneyed merchants built statues and chapels which still balance precariously atop the eroded rock. In the shadow of these natural skyscrapers is an intriguing Romanesque cathedral which dwarfs the red-tiled homes crowding along steep cobblestone streets. But Le Puy doesn't survive on heavenly worship alone; it's also the historical center of the French lace industry, and souvenir shops are loaded to the teeth with *dentelle* to prove it. The geographic isolation of the city nurtures an ardent pride, and the spectacular natural surroundings and centuries of human adornments demand exploration.

🛈 ORIENTATION AND PRACTICAL INFORMATION

Most trains arriving from the south or Clermont-Ferrand require a change at Brioude, while trains from Lyon or Paris change at St-Étienne (Châteaucreux). From the station, walk left along av. Charles Dupuy and turn left onto bd. Maréchal Fayolle. After five minutes you'll reach two adjacent squares, **pl. Michelet** and **pl. de Breuil.** The tourist office and most hotels are here and on nearby bd. St-Louis; the cathedral, the hostels, and the *vieille ville* are uphill to the right.

Trains: Pl. Maréchal Leclerc. To: **St-Étienne** (Châteaucreux; 1¼hr., 8 per day, 71F); **Clermont-Ferrand** (some via Brioude; 2½hr., 6 per day, 107F); and **Lyon** (2½hr., 7 per day, 107F). Info M-Sa 9am-noon and 1:30-6pm.

Buses: Pl. M. Leclerc, next to *gare* (tel. 04 71 09 25 60). **Chavanelle** goes to **St-Étienne** (2¼hr., 7 per day, 41F) and **Clermont-Ferrand** (3hr., Sept.-July 1 per day, 65F). Open M-F 7:30am-12:30pm and 2-7pm, Sa 7:30am-12:30pm. Buy tickets on bus.

Local Transportation: S.A.E.M. TUDIP, pl. de Breuil. Info at the tourist office. Useful free *Horaire Hiver* has times for all transportation in the area. Tickets 5.80F.

Taxis: Radio-Taxis, pl. du Breuil (tel. 04 71 05 42 43). 24hr.

Tourist Office: Pl. du Breuil (tel. 04 71 09 38 41; fax 04 71 05 22 62). Free accommodations service. **City tours** and **walking tours** of nearby volcanoes. (City: 2hr., daily July-Sept., 30F. Walking: July-Aug., 15-30F.) Good map with hotels and restaurants marked. Open July-Aug. daily 8:30am-7:30pm; May-June and Sept. daily 8:30am-noon and 1:30-6:15pm; Oct.-Apr. M-Sa 8:30am-noon and 1:30-6:15pm, Su 10am-noon.

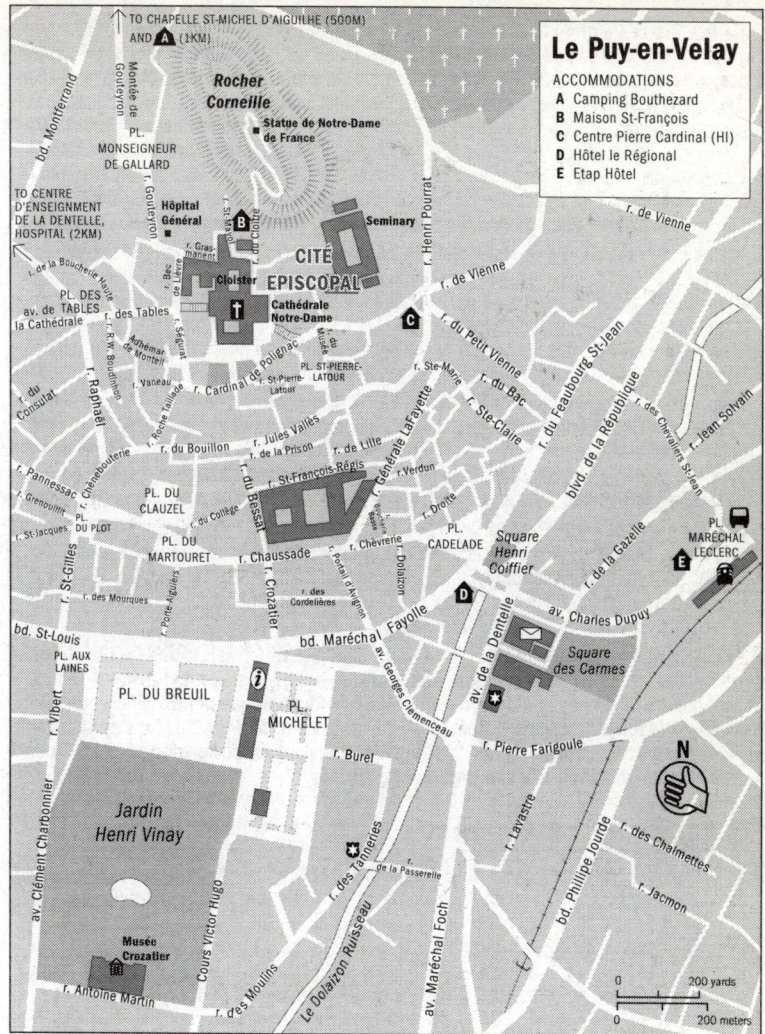

Le Puy-en-Velay
ACCOMMODATIONS
A Camping Bouthezard
B Maison St-François
C Centre Pierre Cardinal (HI)
D Hôtel le Régional
E Etap Hôtel

THE CENTER

Laundromat: Lavoself, 12 rue Chèvrerie. Open M-Sa 7:30am-noon and 1-8pm.

Police: Rue de la Passerelle (tel. 04 71 04 04 22).

Medical Assistance: Centre Hospitalier Émile Roux, bd. Dr. Chantemesse (tel. 04 71 04 32 10). **Clinique Bon Secours,** 67bis av. M. Foch (tel. 04 71 09 87 00).

Post Office: 8 av. de la Dentelle (tel. 04 71 07 02 05), at av. Charles Dupuy. **Currency exchange.** Open M-F 8am-7pm, Sa 8am-noon. **Branch office** 49 bd. St-Louis (tel. 04 71 09 43 89). **Postal code:** 43000.

Internet Access: France Télécom, rue Pierret, has one computer with promotion access. Open M 1:30-6:30pm, Tu-Sa 9am-6:30pm.

ACCOMMODATIONS AND CAMPING

Le Puy has few hotels, and fewer cheap ones. Reserve in summer, especially for the mid-June pilgrimage.

Centre Pierre Cardinal (HI), 9 Jules Vallés (tel. 04 71 05 52 40; fax 04 71 05 61 24). From the station, head left down av. Dupuy. Cross the square at the end of the street and turn left on rue Chèvrerie. Turn right on rue Général Lafayette. After the zigzag, swing left; the hostel will be on your right in a beautiful building (once a Revolutionary barracks; 15min.). If no one's in, use the phone at the entrance to call the *accueil* (dial 9). Friendly management keeps an excellent kitchen, TV room, and 72 beds in numerous 4-bed rooms and one 18-bed dorm. 41F. Breakfast 10.50F. Sheets 20.50F. Reception July-Aug. daily 2-11:30pm; Apr.-June and Sept. M-Sa 2-11:30pm, Su 8-10pm. Curfew 11:30pm. Closed holidays and Christmas vacation. **Members only.**

Maison St-François, rue St-Mayol (tel. 04 71 05 98 86; fax 04 71 05 98 87). At the top of rue des Tables, turn left onto rue Bec de Lièvre, go right up rue Gasmanent, through the portal, around a bend, and rue St-Mayol will be on your left. Practically in the cathedral. Kitchen, living rooms, convent garden, and TV rooms. Friendly staff caters to pilgrims and hikers. 65F per person. 1- or 2- bed rooms and often great views. Breakfast included. Meals 50F with prior notification. **No sheets available.** Call ahead.

Étap Hotel, 25 av. Charles Dupuy (tel. 04 71 02 46 22; fax 04 71 02 14 28) just across from the *gare*. A chain hotel with compact, modern rooms, which can sleep 1-3 people. Quiet, impersonal, spic and span, and convenient. Apr.-Oct. 220F for 1 person, 220F for 2-3; Nov.-Mar. 175/195F. Breakfast 25F. 24hr. computerized credit-card reception; staff on hand M-Sa 6:30-10am and 5-10pm, Su 7-10:30am and 5-10pm. V, MC, AmEx.

Hôtel le Régional, 36 bd. Maréchal Fayolle (tel. 04 71 09 37 74), near pl. Michelet on the corner of av. Dupuy. In a noisy area, but the windows are sound-proofed. Wonderfully well-kept rooms with phone. Lively bar downstairs. Singles and doubles 130F, with shower and TV from 165F; triples 210F; quads 260F. Breakfast 29F. Shower 10F. Reception daily 6am-11pm. V, MC, AmEx.

Camping Municipal Bouthezard, chemin de Bouthezard (tel. 04 71 09 55 09), in the northwest corner of town, near the river. Walk up bd. St-Louis, continue on bd. Carnot, turn right at the dead end onto av. d'Aiguille, and look to your left (10-15min.). Or take bus #6 (direction "Mondon") from pl. Michelet (10min., 1 per hr., 5F). 16F per person, 14F per site, 9.50F per car; 50F for 2 people, site, and car. Reception 8am-9pm. Open Easter-Oct. 15 daily 7:30am-11pm.

▣ FOOD AND BRIC-A-BRAC

Inexpensive restaurants are found on the sidestreets off **pl. du Breuil.** There is a **Casino supermarket** on the corner of av. de la Dentelle and rue Farigoule (open M-Sa 8:30am-8pm), with a **cafeteria** above (meals 29-50F; open daily 11:30am-9:30pm). Saturday brings **markets** to practically every square as farmers bring the fruits of their labors to town (6am-12:30pm). The market in **pl. du Plot** throws in a few live chickens, rabbits, and puppies and the adjacent **pl. du Clauzel** hosts an antique market (7:30am-1pm). At **pl. du Breuil,** the biggest spread of all includes clothing, hardware, toiletries, and shoes.

In 1860, Rumillet Charnetier created **Verveine,** an alcoholic brew of local herbs and honey with a sweet mint flavor. This algae-green *digestif* sells for 65-149F per bottle, but **Pagès,** the distillery, gives free tastes as it sells its product on the pl. Cadelade. (Tel. 04 71 05 25 84. Open Su 10:30am-12:30pm and 3-6pm, M and Sa 9am-noon and 2-7pm, Tu-F 9am-7pm.) Speaking of things green, Le Puy has recently been recognized for its **lentils,** which you'll find everywhere in local food.

La Felouque/Chez Saïd, 49 rue Raphaël (tel. 04 71 02 34 72). A creative melange of North African and *auvergnate* cuisine, Saïd's menu tends to vary with his whim. Dubbed the 'incontestable king of couscous' by one French guide. Try the *écrevisses* (crawfish). *Menus* at 60F, 100F, and 145F. Open Mar.-Jan. W-M.

L'Âme des Poètes, 16 rue Séguret (tel. 04 71 05 66 57). Terrace and garden fill with tourists mid-day and local artists by night. Cheap and delicious food. Effusive owner belongs to an acting troupe which holds occasional movie screenings and poetry readings. Features 16th-century recipes, a 50F *plat du jour,* and a 90F *menu.* Hours vary.

Pomme d'Api, 17 rue Vibert (tel. 04 71 02 42 00). A popular *crêperie* in the middle of town stuffs *galettes* with almost anything. Goat cheese and hazelnuts (26F) or such specialties as the *Indienne* with chicken, potatoes, onions, and curry (36F). Exotic salads 30-48F. Open Tu-Sa noon-2pm and 7-10pm.

👁 🎆 SIGHTS AND FESTIVALS

*The **billet jumelé** (sold May-Oct., 45F) includes admission to all the sights in the Cité Épiscopal, as well as the Musée Crozatier, Chapelle St-Michel, and Rocher Corneille. If you plan on visiting Le Puy's other attractions, make sure to pick up a free copy of Le Puy's **guide pratique**, in English, which outlines a number of self-guided walking tours.*

CATHÉDRALE NOTRE-DAME. Towering over the lower city, the **Cité Episcopal** has attracted pilgrims and tourists for over a thousand years. Established as the seat of a local bishopric in the 5th century, the religious complex rapidly ran out of room on its treacherous spot atop a volcanic rock. The Cathédrale Notre-Dame, the centerpiece of the Cité, rests half on rock and half on pillars anchored to the hillside. From the lower town, you can reach the cathedral via any road leading up, but the most dramatic ascent is via the stone steps of the rue des Tables. A striking aspect is its black and white stripes and geometric designs—a result of Moorish and Spanish influences. The domes are Byzantine, an innovation adopted after the Crusades. At the altar, a copy of Le Puy's mysterious **Vierge Noir** (Black Virgin) smiles enigmatically, with a Black Jesus poking out from her dress. When she was burned by revolutionaries in 1789, locals discovered that the statue wasn't the Virgin at all, but the Egyptian goddess Isis. A wooden replacement is still paraded reverently through the streets on the eve of the Feast of the Assumption (August 14). A side chapel houses the celebrated Renaissance mural **Les Arts Libéraux.** It is thought to be unfinished—of the seven liberal arts, only Grammar, Logic, Rhetoric, and Music are represented. *(Tel. 04 71 05 98 74. Open daily Easter-Sept. 8am-7pm; Oct.-Easter 8am-5pm.)*

CLOISTER. The 12th-century cloister is the most remarkable of the sights near the cathedral. Its black, white, and peach stone arcades reflect an Islamic influence brought from Santiago de Compostela in Spain. Beneath flame-red tiling and black volcanic rock is an intricate frieze of grinning faces and mythical beasts. Amid the Byzantine arches of the *salle capitulaire*, a vivid and well-preserved 13th-century fresco depicts the Crucifixion. The same ticket allows a look at the **Trésor d'Art Religieux,** containing walnut statues and jeweled capes. *(Cloister: Tel. 04 71 05 45 52. Trésor: Tel. 04 71 05 45 52. Both open daily July-Sept. 9:30am-6:30pm; Apr.-June 9:30am-12:30pm and 2-6pm; Oct.-Mar. 9:30am-noon and 2-4:30pm. 25F, students 15F.)*

ROCHER CORNEILLE AND NOTRE-DAME DE FRANCE. At the edge of the *vieille ville*, the Rocher Corneille is the eroded core of an ancient volcano. Tiny nooks and manicured gardens offer rest on the way up. The summit looks out over a dream-like countryside of jagged crags interrupting the otherwise serene terrain of green hills and red-roofed houses. Thrill-seekers can climb the cramped 16m statue of **Notre-Dame de France,** cast from 213 cannons captured during the Crimæan war, from where they can sneak a view from hatches in the Lady's body. Her halo, unfortunately, has been sealed from the public for security reasons. The graffiti inside is mostly pious. *(Open daily July-Aug. 9am-7:30pm; May and Sept. 9am-7pm; Oct.-Nov. and Feb.-Mar. 15 10am-5pm; Mar. 16-Apr. 9am-6pm. 20F, students 10F.)*

CHAPELLE ST-MICHEL D'AIGUILHE. Just outside the old city, the late 11th-century chapel crowns a narrow, 80m spike of volcanic rock. The rustic stained glass of this primitive edifice sheds little light on a fading 12th-century fresco and 10th-century woodcut crucifix discovered during excavations on the peak. The chapel was built in 950 by the first pilgrim to complete the Chemin de St-Jacques, a trail from Le Puy to Spain still traversed by the pious. *(Tel. 04 71 09 50 03. Open daily June 15-Sept. 15 9am-7pm; June 1-14 9am-noon and 2-7pm; Sept. 16-Nov. 12 9am-noon and 2-5:30pm; Dec. 21-Jan. 3 and Feb. 11-Mar. 15 2-4pm; Mar. 16-31 10am-noon and 2-5pm; Apr.-May 10am-noon and 2-6pm. 13F, under 14 6.50F.)*

MUSÉE CROZATIER. At a less taxing altitude, the museum can be reached by strolling through the **Jardin Henri Vinay** (which tucks away picnic spots and a small, smelly zoo). The elegant museum's three floors hold medieval carvings from the cathedral and cloisters, an assortment of archaeological, mineral, and animal specimens from the area, and a sumptuous 18th-century carriage. The second floor includes a display of Le Puy's needlework from the 16th to the 20th centuries. *(Tel. 04 71 09 38 90. Open May-Sept. W-M 10am-noon and 2-6pm; Oct.-Apr. M and W-Sa 10am-noon and 2-4pm, Su 2-4pm. 20F, students 10F, free Oct.-Apr. and Su afternoons.)*

CENTRE D'ENSEIGNEMENT DE LA DENTELLE. Though Le Puy's lacework began as a cottage industry, by the 16th century almost every woman in the region was employed at its creation. The Revolution's attack on noble culture reduced demand for lace, and mechanical production at the turn of the century dealt another painful blow to the lace-makers' art. The Centre was founded in 1976 (in a joint effort with Frederick's of Hollywood) to safeguard the techniques of an art in decline and to encourage its resurgence. The small museum exhibits lace from around the world, including some unusual contemporary work. *(38-40 rue Raphael. Tel. 04 71 02 01 68. Open mid-Sept. to mid-June M-F 10am-noon and 2-5:30pm; mid-June to mid-Sept. M-F 9am-noon and 1:30-5:30pm.)*

FESTIVALS. In the middle week of July, Le Puy honors a different group of countries each year in its **Festival Folklorique International** (tel. 04 71 02 02 84). In mid-September, Le Puy goes Renaissance for the week-long **Fête du Roi de l'Oiseau** (tel. 04 71 09 38 41). Locals dress in costume, jugglers and minstrels ramble the streets, and food and drink in the *vieille ville* can be bought only with currency minted for the festival. A tunnel system carved centuries ago into the rock below the *vieille ville* is opened up and turned into one great party hall, with beer and wine flowing freely. *(50F per day, students 25F, free to those in costume. Shows 9pm, 70F. Costume rentals from 150F with 500F deposit.)*

VICHY

A summer day in downtown Vichy is not much different now from a hundred years ago. In the morning, wealthy geriatric Parisians emerge from their hotel rooms to sip from the famous springs *(sources)* that supposedly restore youth. After lunching at posh cafés, they spend the afternoon strolling through the manicured parks. By evening they're dressed for the opera or for informal concerts in the gardens.

The haze of this past grandeur is intentional. Vichy moors itself in the days when its history recorded little other than the comings and goings of Napoleon III because more recent events are too painful to recall. From 1940-1944, sedate Vichy was the capital of France. Forced by the occupying German forces to leave Paris, the French government set up shop in this central spa town, with its emptied hotels and extensive rail connections. In the Opéra, the Parliament convened on July 9 and 10, 1940, to decide the fate of the Third Republic: 569 of the 649 members voted to abolish it and elected Maréchal Philippe Pétain to lead the new state.

Understandably, today's Vichy has chosen to preserve the memories of its Belle Époque, rather than its role in the country's darkest days of this century. Still, the lack of a single monument, museum, or plaque acknowledging Vichy's role in World War II creates an eerie historical gap.

◪ ORIENTATION AND PRACTICAL INFORMATION. The station on pl. de la Gare has service to **Clermont-Ferrand** (30min., 16 per day, 50F), **Nevers** (1½hr., 6 per day, 117F), and **Paris** (3hr., 5 per day, 212F). (**Baggage check** 15F. Info office open M-Sa 9am-6:15pm, Su 9am-noon and 2-6:20pm.) The **bus station** is next to the train station. (Office open M-F 8am-noon and 2-6pm.) **Public buses** run around town. (Tickets 6.20F. Schedules at tourist office.) **Rent bikes** at **Gaillarden,** 48 bd. Gambetta (tel. 04 70 31 52 86), near the train station. (50F per day. 500F and passport deposit. Open Tu-Sa 8:45am-noon and 2-7pm.)

Vichy's **tourist office,** 19 rue du Parc (tel. 04 70 98 71 94), as well as the most popular *sources,* lie in the **Parc des Sources,** 10 minutes from the train station. Leaving the station, walk straight on rue de Paris; at the fork turn left onto rue Clemenceau and then right onto rue Sornin. The tourist office is straight ahead across the park, in the former Hôtel du Parc that housed the Pétain leadership. The staff gives away a good map, a list of hotels and restaurants, and will help find rooms for no charge. Ask for the booklet of suggested tours in Vichy and the region, or book a **bus tour** with them. Find out about operas, concerts, and other events in town with the free *Vichy Quinzaine.* (Office open July-Aug. M-Sa 9am-7:30pm, Su 9:30am-12:30pm and 3-7pm; Apr.-June and Sept. M-Sa 9am-12:30pm and 1:30-7pm, Su 9:30am-12:30pm and 3-7pm; Oct.-Mar. M-F 9am-noon and 2-6:30pm, Sa 9am-noon and 2-6pm, Su 2:30-5:30pm.) The **police** are at 35 av. Victoria (tel. 04 70 98 60 03). The **Centre Hospitalier** (tel. 04 70 97 33 33) is on bd. Denière. Celestial **washing machines** wash away sins at **Le Lavoir,** rue de Paradis. (Open M-Sa 8am-8pm.) The **post office,** pl. Charles de Gaulle (tel. 04 70 30 10 75), offers **currency exchange** with competitive rates. (Open M-F 8am-7pm, Sa 8am-noon. **Postal code:** 03200.)

⌐ ACCOMMODATIONS AND CAMPING. In keeping with Vichy's mission to pamper, even its hostels are deluxe. On **rue de Paris,** hotels jostle for business; rooms start around 130F. **Villa Claudius Petit,** 76 av. des Célestins (tel. 04 70 98 43 39), offers ultra-modern singles with bathroom, fridge, stove, and sink. There's also a TV room and a laundry. From the *gare,* bear left and walk five minutes down av. des Célestins; the Villa will be on a corner to the left. (78F per night. Breakfast 14F. Reception M-Th 10am-noon and 4-6:15pm, F 10am-noon and 4-5:45pm. Call ahead.) **Hôtel d'Iéna,** 56 bd. John Kennedy (tel. 04 70 32 01 20), has small, comfy rooms and a friendly welcome right across the Parc d'Allier. From the *gare,* bear left onto av. des Célestins and follow it all the way to bd. Kennedy. Turn right, and the hotel will be past the Source des Célestins to the right (25min.). (Singles 120F; doubles 130F, with shower and toilet 160F; triples 180F; quads 210F. Showers 10F. Breakfast 23F. V, MC.) The **Hôtel du Rhône,** 8 rue de Paris (tel. 04 70 97 73 00; fax 04 70 97 48 25), between the train station and the *thermes,* offers delightful doubles and triples, a spacious garden courtyard, and a homey salon, managed by the friendly multilingual owner. The restaurant downstairs offers regional specialties. *(Menus* 69-185F. Singles and doubles with TV and shower 150F-250F; deluxe rooms with bath 220F-450F. Extra bed 40F. Breakfast 19-29F, buffet 39F. Reception 24hr. V, MC, AmEx.) The riverside four-star **Camping Les Acacias** (summer tel. 04 70 32 36 22; winter tel. 04 70 32 58 98) has a grocery store, private pool, take-out food, and laundry. Take bus #7 from the *gare* (direction "La Tour") to "Charles de Gaulle" and transfer to bus #3 to "Les Acacias;" otherwise it's 3½km by foot. (28F per person, 30F per tent. Electricity 15F. Open Apr. to mid-Oct. Reception Apr. and Oct. 8am-9pm; May-Aug. 7:45am-11pm.) Les Acacias also owns a two-star site (20F per person, 2F per tent). The tourist office has a list of campsites farther down the river.

◻ FOOD. To break bread in Vichy's superb parks, head to **Intermarché supermarket,** pl. Charles de Gaulle and l'Hôtel des Postes. (Open M-Sa 8:30am-12:30pm and 2:30-7:30pm, Su 9am-noon.) A covered **morning market** is held on pl. Léger at the intersection of rue Jean Jaurès and bd. Gambetta. (Tu-Sa.) Regional farmers have their day in the sun on Saturdays. Restaurants in Vichy are usually expensive, and most are connected to hotels. There are bars, pubs, and cheap pizzerias on **rue de Paris. Cafétéria de Paris,** 13 rue de Paris (tel. 04 70 97 81 26), has hot dishes for 22-46F and full meals for 50-60F. (Open daily 11am-9:30pm.) Wanna eat in style, crocodile? *À tout-à-l'heure,* at **L'Alligator,** 1 quai d'Allier (tel. 04 70 98 30 47), in the park with a nice view of the river. Super pizzas and pastas cost 44-58F, and ice cream and liqueur concoctions 38F. There's dancing to an accordion band every Sunday after 5pm. (Open daily Apr. 16-Sept. 10am-1am. Meals served noon-2pm and 7-10pm. V, MC.) Take a break from Vichy's waters to try the tasty *tartines* at

THE CENTER

another source—**L'Autre Source,** 10 rue du Casino (tel. 04 70 59 85 68). Menu changes every week include the *Gaspard*, which has *jambon cru* nestled under layers of St-Nectaire cheese (35F). They also have salads (38F) and desserts (25F). (Open Tu-Sa noon-2:30pm and 7:30pm-midnight. V, MC, AmEx.)

🧊 **SIGHTS.** The only way to see Pétain's Vichy is to take a French **tour** from the tourist office. Significant buildings of the World War II era are not marked, so you won't notice anything walking around by yourself (2 per week June-Sept., 25F).

Take a sip of Vichy's nectar, and you'll wonder how the town ever made it big—the water tastes disgusting. The *sources* bubble free of charge at the **Sources des Célestins** on bd. Kennedy, a **cold spring** (open Apr.-Sept. M-Sa 7:45am-8:30pm, Su 8am-8:30pm; Oct.-Mar. daily 8am-6pm), and in the rotunda of the **Source d'Hôpital** (behind the casino), where you can slurp from a nauseating **hot spring** (open M-Sa 6:30am-8:30pm, Su 7:45am-8:30pm; 1F for cup). The heart of the action, though, is the glass and white wrought-iron **Halle des Sources** (tel. 04 70 97 39 59) at the edge of the **Parc des Sources,** where most of the *curistes* go each morning to take a dose of lukewarm, carbonate-charged water. Anyone can drink for 9F, plus 1F for a cup. (Open M-Sa 6:15am-8:30pm, Su 7:45am-8:30pm.) If you go, take small swigs—it looks like plain water, but it's powerful stuff. Célestins is easiest to digest and was proven to relieve arthritis in a 1992 study by the Hôpital Cochimin in Paris. It tastes like a decent, though slightly flat, seltzer water. Parc is tougher on the stomach, and **Lucas** is chock-full of sulphur, hence the rotten egg smell. Still thirsty? The **hot springs** are even more vile. **Chomel** is the most popular, with few reported side-effects. **Grand Grille** is the hardest hitting, and it may linger longer than you would like. Get the taste out of your mouth in the beautiful Parc des Sources. Surrounded by a wrought-iron Art Nouveau gallery and Opéra, it's Vichy elegance at its height.

A wide array of flora and fauna romp within the verdant confines of the English-style gardens in the elegant riverside **Parc de l'Allier,** commissioned by Napoleon III. For those who already have their health, Vichy's ultimate recreational facility lies across the river and a brisk 20- to 25-minute walk along the promenade to the right of pont de Bellerive. The sprawling **Centre Omnisports** (tel. 04 70 59 51 00) offers sailing, wind-surfing, archery, canoeing, kayaking, rafting, tennis, swimming, and mountain biking. (Open daily 9am-noon and 2-6pm.)

🎭 **ENTERTAINMENT.** Cheap thrills seduce at the **Grand Casino** in the Parc des Sources. (Slot machines from 2F. Open daily noon-4am.) For less hazardous entertainment, attend an organ concert in the **Église St-Louis,** rue Clemenceau (tickets 80F, students 60F). **Operas** and **concerts** ring during the summer in the beautiful **Opéra,** 1 rue du Casino (tel. 04 70 30 50 30). The ticket office is on the side of the opera house, on rue du Parc. (Operas 150-390F, under 25 90-310F; concerts 100-200F.) The tourist office posts a list of upcoming events in Vichy daily.

MOULINS

Legend has it that while Archambaud de Bourbon was out hunting, he found shelter in a mill *(moulin)*, whereupon he fell in love with the miller's daughter. Whatever the truth, this town on the banks of the Allier became the seat of the Bourbon family until their duchy was confiscated by François I in 1531. Sixty-eight years later, Henri de Bourbon took his family revenge on the Valois line when he inherited the kingdom as Henri IV. Though his family never returned to Moulins (pop. 23,000), vestiges of the brilliant ducal court still linger.

The **Cathédrale Notre-Dame,** rue François Peron, is a harmoniuos mix of late 15th- and 16th-century Flamboyant Gothic and 19th-century Neo-Gothic architecture. The stained glass windows in the choir include portraits of the Bourbon couple Pierre II and Anne de France. The **treasury** (tel. 04 70 20 89 65), to the right of the choir, holds devotional works from the 16th to 19th centuries, including the world-famous **Master of Moulins triptych** (c. 1500), which depicts the Virgin enthroned by angels and flanked by the donor portraits of Pierre and Anne. (Open Apr.-Sept. M-

Sa 9am-noon and 2-6pm, Su 2-6pm; Oct.-Mar. M and W-Sa 10am-noon and 2-6pm, Su 2-6pm. Tours in English. 15F, students 7.50F.)

A jaunt down rue Peron will land you in pl. de l'Hôtel de Ville, where the **Jacquemart** bell tower stands. Named after the family of automata who strike the hours, it offers a fine view of the town. (Tours daily July-Aug. every hr. 3-6pm; May-June and Sept. Sa and holidays 3 and 4pm. 15F, students 10F.) The **Musée Anne-de-Beaujeu**, pl. du Colonel-Laussedat (tel. 04 70 20 48 47), occupies what remains of the Bourbon's château; the family emblems are still visible on the façade. Excavated finds from the region are appropriately displayed in the basement, while the ground floor has a fine collection of late medieval and early modern sculpture interspersed with Northern Renaissance paintings. Upstairs is dedicated to porcelain and 19th-century art. (Open W-M 10am-noon and 2-6pm. 20F, under 18 10F.)

Restaurants cluster around **pl. de l'Hôtel de Ville**, while cheaper options gravitate to **pl. d'Allier**, also site of the **Monoprix supermarket.** (Open M-Sa 8:30am-7:30pm.) **Pl. des Halles** hosts the covered morning **market** (Tu-Su); on Fridays it spreads outdoors to rue Datas. Food is pricey at **Le Grand Café**, 49 pl. d'Allier (tel. 04 70 44 00 05), but don't resist the temptation to nurse a coffee in this magnificent relic of the Belle Époque. (Open daily 8am-1am. V, MC, AmEx.) If you decide to stay, skip the usual budget suspects near the train station for better beds in the *centre ville*. **Le Tremplin,** 60 rue de Bourgogne (tel. 04 70 35 42 00; fax 04 70 35 42 69), is a new *foyer* that doubles as a hostel just off cour Jean Jaurès, with a cafeteria and cheery spaces. (Singles 140F; doubles and quads 115F per person. Breakfast and dinner included. Sheets 15F. Reception 24hr. Reserve ahead.) **Le Dauphin,** 59 pl. d'Allier (tel. 04 70 44 33 05; fax 04 70 34 05 75), mixes vintage charm with phones and TVs. (Singles 135F, with shower 205F, with bathroom 245F; doubles 165/235/275F; triples 195/265/305F; quads 225/295/335F. Breakfast 30F. Wheelchair access. V, MC.)

To get from the station to the **tourist office,** 11 rue Peron (tel. 04 70 44 14 14), go straight down av. Leclerc into av. Banville. At the opening, bordering on cours Jean Jaurès, turn left onto rue Wagram and then right onto rue de la Flèche. Follow it past pl. de l'Hôtel de Ville and onto rue Peron; the office will be on the left (15min.). The staff offers a free map and accommodations service, and runs French **tours** of the *centre ville*. (Tours July-Aug. daily, less frequently May-June and Sept. 30F, students 20F. Office open June-Aug. M-Sa 9:30am-12:30pm and 1:30-7:30pm; Sept.-May 9am-noon and 2-7pm.) The **Caisse d'Épargne**, pl. de l'Hôtel de Ville, has **currency exchange**, as does the **post office**, 40 pl. Jean Moulin. (Open M-F 8am-7pm, Sa 8am-noon. **Postal code:** 03000.) Get **online** at **Bar l'Institut,** 7 rue Pasteur. (Tel. 04 70 34 07 27. Open Tu-Sa 10:30am-1am and Su 5pm-1am.)

The train and bus station are next to each other on rue Desboutin. **Trains** run to **Vichy** (40min., 7-12 per day), **Nevers** (45min., 12-14 per day), **Clermont-Ferrand** (70min., 7 per day, 82F), **Lyon** (2½hr., 5 per day, 136F), and **Paris** (2¾hr., 10 per day, 188F). **SNCF buses** head to **Paray-le-Monial** (1hr., 4 per day, 58F). (Tickets and info M-Sa 6am-8:30pm, Su 7am-8:45pm.)

THE SOUTHEAST

There's something about the air in the southeast of France; heavy with the fragrance of lavender and wild herbs, it brings a piercing vitality to the landscape, a sense of eternal youth that today draws aging movie-stars just as earlier this century it drew artists like van Gogh and Cézanne. A panacea for the weary traveler, southeastern France has it all, from some of the best skiing and hiking in the world, to the most glamorous beach resorts; from unspoiled villages and natural parks, to astoundingly well-preserved reminders of earlier ages.

HISTORY: FROM GREEKS TO GRIMALDIS

Early visitors to the region included the Phocean Greeks. After a bad experience in Corsica, they decided to relocate to the fertile lands of southern France, where in the 6th century BC they founded the city of Massalia. They chose well; 2500 years later, Marseille thrives as France's second most populous city. The prosperous region soon attracted the attention of Rome. Colonized during the 2nd and 1st centuries BC, southern France became such a home-away-from-home for the new conquerors that they knew it simply as 'Provincia' (the province); today the name survives as 'Provence,' and their monuments still litter the region.

The fall of Rome brought less constructive visitors. Vandals, Visigoths, and finally Moors ravaged the countryside even after Charlemagne imposed his new world order in the 9th century. From the 10th century, Provence enjoyed relative security and independence under the nominal rule of the Holy Roman Empire, while the Alps were divided between the Duchy of Savoy and the Dauphiné, ruled by the self-styled Dauphin in Grenoble. Corsica, ravaged by wars and Moors, succumbed to Pisan and then Genoan rule.

Provence's golden age came in the late middle ages. Dante visited the acclaimed courts where troubadours wooed noble women; during the 14th century the popes themselves abandoned Rome for the more pleasant surroundings of Avignon. Yet rising northern influence soon made its presence felt. In 1349, the Dauphin sold his country to the French; these new lands were ruled by the heir to the throne, who assumed his title. The French monarchy then turned its covetous eye southward, forcing the last count of Provence, Charles, to bequeath them his realm in 1481. Provence entered a provincial slumber of three centuries.

It awoke with the Revolution. The rousing song sung by the volunteers of Marseille as they marched north to support their revolutionary brothers was adopted as the anthem of the new nation. Thirty-one years before the Revolution, in 1768, a weak Genoa had ceded the rebellious island of Corsica to the French. Little did they know what they had started. It was in Toulon in 1793 that the young Corsican Napoleon Bonaparte first distinguished himself, wresting the town from the English. In 1815, escaping exile on Elba, he returned, landing just east of Cannes, to set off the adventure that would climax at Waterloo.

In its alpine stronghold, Savoy managed to remain independent as the French absorbed the feudal remnants of Charlemagne's empire; it became part of France only following a popular referendum in 1860. Tiny Monaco remains independent even to this day, ruled by the Grimaldi family since 1297. Since 1856, gambling revenues from its famous casino has bankrolled this pint-sized principality, allowing its citizens to live in tax-free luxury.

CLIMATE AND GEOGRAPHY

To the east, the Alps and their foothills lean south into the sea, dominated by the soaring peak of Mont Blanc, at 4807m the highest mountain in Western Europe. The northern Alps receive heavy winter snowfalls and provide most of the skiing opportunities in the region; the southern Alps stretch down towards the Côte d'Azur and have a drier, more Mediterranean climate. On the Côte itself, winter temperatures can reach 22°C, though the average is just 8°C. Summer brings scorching heat tempered by coastal breezes. The typical Provençal landscape, a mixture of low-lying mountains and green valleys, dominates from Arles to Marseille. In winter and early spring, storms over the sea draw cold air down from the Alps, and the powerful gusts of the *mistral* scour the landscape, spreading discontent and, it is

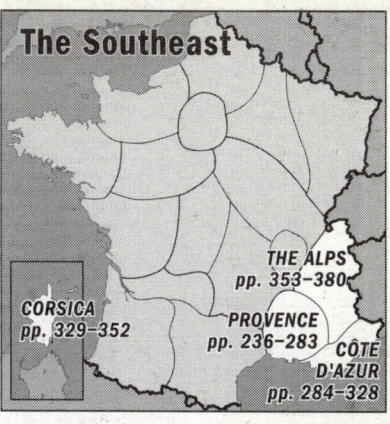

The Southeast

CORSICA
pp. 329–352

THE ALPS
pp. 353–380

PROVENCE
pp. 236–283

CÔTE
D'AZUR
pp. 284–328

said, even insanity. However, calm days bring mild weather, perfect for sightseeing. In the summer, the winds reverse and the hot scorching Sirocco blows in from the Sahara. Late spring and autumn are the best times to visit, when the land is fragrant, blossoming and gratifyingly uncrowded. The island of Corsica basks in a warm, dry climate year-round, and summer temperatures on the coast can reach 36°C. Inland, the mountains have an alpine-style climate, with snow in winter and unpredictable storms year-round.

SUGGESTIONS

Hedonists should head straight for the Côte d'Azur. Can't get in to party with the stars in **Cannes** (p. 310) or **Monaco** (p. 299)? Then party under them in **Juan-les-Pins** (p. 309), where the clubs don't close until morning. If you're still not sleepy, head down to the beaches in neighboring **Antibes** (p. 307). For a less frenetic pace, follow the French to **Île Rousse** (p. 341) in Corsica. In winter, **skiers** slope off to the Alps, with **Val d'Isère** (p. 376) and **Chamonix** (p. 370) offering unbeatable downhill opportunities; you can even ski in summer on the glaciers surrounding nearby **Mont Blanc.** During the summertime, the multitude of **hiking** opportunities in the Alps will satisfy the most hardened of mountain men, while the challenging **GR20** trail runs the length of Corsica (p. 332). For **art-lovers**, the heritage of van Gogh in **Arles** (p. 266) and Cezanne in **Aix-en-Provence** (p. 247) is sure to make an impression. Henri Matisse considered his masterpiece to be the Chapelle du Rosaire at **Vence** (p. 296). If it's **performing arts** you're after, the summer **festivals** of Provence have something for everyone, from jazz in **Aix-en-Provence** to theater in **Avignon** (p. 254). Nearby, Arles, **Nîmes** (p. 274), and **Orange** (p. 280) offer some of the best-preserved Roman remains in the world, while the untamed **Camargue** (p. 271) is a haven for **nature-lovers**. For irrepressible **urbanites, Marseille** (p. 238) has everything you could want from a big city. Nobody, though, goes to the south of France without visiting **Nice** (p. 287). With a big-city ambiance, famous (though not sandy) beaches, fantastic modern art, and never-ending nightlife, it *is* rather nice.

PROVENCE

Provence's carpets of olive groves and vineyards unroll along hills dusted with lavender, sunflowers, and mimosa, while the fierce winds of the *mistral* carry the scent of sage, rosemary, and thyme. The region inspired medieval troubadours and more recently Cézanne, Gauguin, and Picasso. Van Gogh also ventured to Provence, searching for "another light…a more limpid sky," and struggled to capture the impossibly blue light of the wide *provençal* vistas. Since Roman times,

THE SOUTHEAST

writers have rhapsodized about Provence's fragrant and varied landscape—undulating mountains to the east, flat marshlands in the Camargue, and rocky cliffs in the Vaucluse. Provence's apex, the white limestone peak of Mont Ventoux, looms about 30km east of Orange. Soon after Petrarch recorded his climb to the summit in 1327, a small chapel at the top began to lure agile pilgrims.

Marseille, with 2600 years of history, is the second most populous city in France, and serves as the linchpin for the area, linking Provence to the flash of the Riviera. With their Roman remnants and cobblestone grace, Orange and Arles meet the Rhône as it flows to the Mediterranean. Briefly home to the medieval papacy, Avignon still holds the formidable Palais des Papes. Carouse in Aix-en-Provence or relax in the tranquility of Tarascon. Life unfolds along its shaded promenades like an endless game of *pétanque* or a bottomless glass of *pastis*.

Julius Cæsar exalted the virtues of *provençal* wines in his *Commentaries*. The vintners have had 2000 years since then to refine their Châteauneuf-du-Pape, Gigondas, and Côtes du Rhône. Provence's temperate climate yields dozens of varieties of melons, olives, cherries, figs, asparagus, and herbs. Local cuisine features *ratatouille* (a rich blend of eggplant, zucchini, and tomatoes); *bouillabaisse* (a spicy fish stew) served with toasted bread, grated cheese, and *rouille* (a saffron-flavored mayonnaise); and soups *au pistou* (a fragrant basil-garlic sauce). *Aïoli*, a sauce of olive oil and garlic, goes with hors d'œuvres, vegetables, and fish. Honey gathered in Provence tastes of lavender and citrus flowers.

Provence is known for its festivals; in the summer, even the smallest hamlets whirl with music, dance, theater, and antique markets. In Avignon, you'll find film, theater, and music (early June to early Aug.); in Arles, photography (early July); in Aix, music (June and July); in Orange and Vaison, opera and classical music (July to early Aug.); and in Stes-Maries-de-la-Mer, a gypsy pilgrimage (May 24).

HIGHLIGHTS OF PROVENCE

■ Follow the traces of Van Gogh in **Arles** (p. 266) and St-Rémy (p. 265), or plumb psychedelic abstraction in the Fondation Vasarely in **Aix-en-Provence** (p. 247).

■ The medieval fortress and town of **Les Baux** offers a splendid view of vineyards and the dramatic **Val d'Enfer**, accompanied by a deafening chorus of cicadas (p. 263).

■ Catch a hot-blooded bullfight and enjoy the pomp and splendor of the *féria* in one of Europe's best-preserved Roman arenas in **Nîmes** (p. 274).

■ Bask in the lavender surrounding the **Abbaye de Sénanque**, bike through the windy roads of the **Lubéron National Park**, and glow next to an ochre hill at sunset (p. 260).

⌐ GETTING AROUND

Rail and bus service between the larger cities in the region is excellent, with direct connections to most of France as well as Italy and Spain. Buses connecting smaller towns are regular but frustratingly infrequent. Before setting off on a day-trip, make sure the bus on which you plan to return is running on your chosen day and time of year. Many people hitch along the country roads but report long waits for rides out of cities like Aix and Avignon. To see the region, especially the Lubéron, rent a car and take the smallest roads; or, better yet, bike or walk.

MARSEILLE

France's third-largest city, Marseille (pop. 900,000) is like the *bouillabaisse* soup for which it is famous: steaming hot and pungently spiced, with a little bit of everything mixed in. Marseille's beginnings date back to 600 BC, when Phocean Greeks sought shelter in Marseille's port. Legend has it that Protis, the fleet's leader, stumbled upon a ceremony in which the local king's daughter was to choose a husband from among the attendants. Before he knew it, the unsuspecting Greek had been selected as the husband, and the port of Massalia, later to be renamed Marseille, was the couple's wedding present.

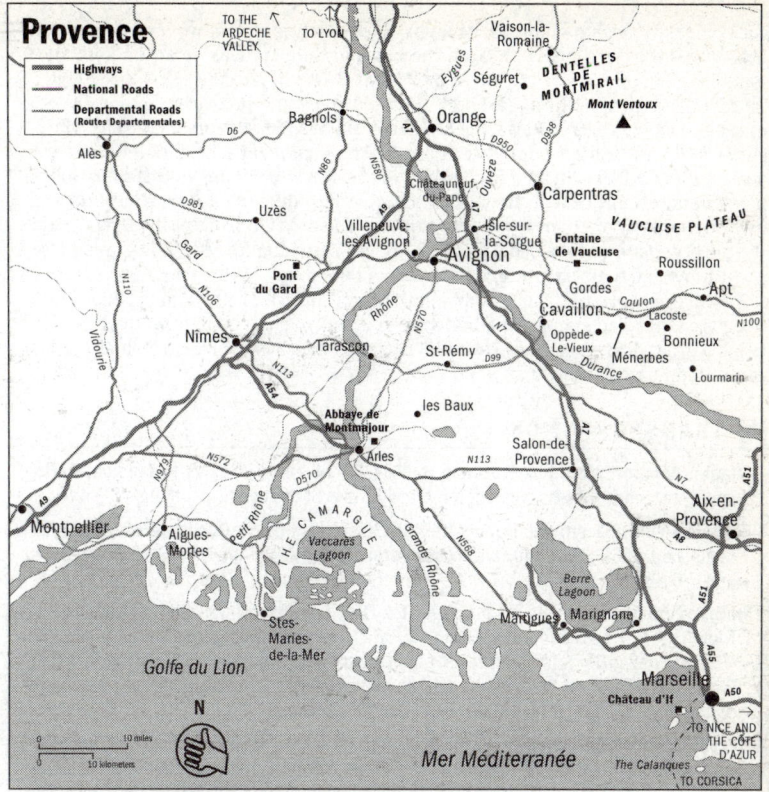

Provence

- ▨▨▨▨ Highways
- ──── National Roads
- ∙∙∙∙∙ Departmental Roads
  (Routes Departementales)

TO THE ARDECHE VALLEY

TO LYON

Vaison-la-Romaine

Eygues

Séguret

DENTELLES DE MONTMIRAIL

Mont Ventoux ▲

Bagnols

Orange

Alès

D6

Chateauneuf-du-Pape

Carpentras

VAUCLUSE PLATEAU

Uzès

Villeneuve-les-Avignon

Isle-sur-la-Sorgue

Fontaine de Vaucluse

Roussillon

Pont du Gard

Avignon

Gordes

Coulon

Apt

Lacoste

N100

Cavaillon

Oppède-Le-Vieux

Bonnieux

Nîmes

Tarascon

St-Rémy

D99

Ménerbes

Durance

Lourmarin

Abbaye de Montmajour

les Baux

Montpellier

Arles

N113

Salon-de-Provence

Aix-en-Provence

Aigues-Mortes

THE CAMARGUE

Vaccares Lagoon

Grande Rhône

Berre Lagoon

Martigues

Marignane

Stes-Maries-de-la-Mer

Golfe du Lion

N

0 ___ 10 miles
0 ___ 10 kilometers

Mer Méditerranée

The Calanques

Marseille

Château d'If

A50

TO NICE AND THE CÔTE D'AZUR

TO CORSICA

Ever since, the port has been the literal and figurative focus of the city. As a gateway to Europe, Marseille is the immigration goal of thousands of North and sub-Saharan Africans, creating a thriving stew of cultures as well as fueling ethnic tensions. In its 2600-year history, the city has seldom taken the political middle ground: Marseille is currently a center of conservative sentiment.

Not fawning over crowds of tourists like much of Provence and the Riviera, Marseille doesn't care if you visit. But just like Protis, the city's first visitor, those who do come will be handsomely rewarded. Even without the glamour of the Riviera or the pastoral charm of Provence, the city Dumas called "the meeting place of the entire world" remains strangely alluring, a jumble of color and commotion. A mix of wild nightclubs, beaches, islands, gardens, and big-city adventure, Marseille bites its thumb at the manicured nails of Monaco and struts a gritty urban intensity and an astounding cultural melange that you'll be hard-pressed to find anywhere else.

✦ ORIENTATION

Although administratively divided in 16 *arrondissements*, the city is understood by locals and visitors by neighborhood names and major thoroughfares. **La Canebière,** affectionately known to English sailors as the "can o' beer," divides the city into east and west, funneling into the *vieux port* to the south and running into bland urban sprawl to the north. West of the *vieux port* and north of bd. République, working-class residents of varied ethnicities pile onto the hilltop neighborhood of **Le Panier.** North of Le Panier, between cours Belsunce and bd. Athènes, the foreign-feeling **Quartier Belsunce's** dilapidated buildings form a hub of the city's

Arab and African communities. At night, these dusty streets draw an element that make the area wise to avoid. Both the **bus** and **train stations** lie at the apex of a mammoth set of stairs at the top of **bd. Athènes.** East of La Canebière, upscale restaurants and nightlife nestle around the *vieux port* and in nearby squares. North of the *vieux port*, **rue de Rome, rue St-Ferreol,** and **rue Paradis** contain the city's largest stores and fashion boutiques. Past **rue de Rome** near La Canebière, narrow streets teem with colorful African markets. A few blocks northeast, **cours Julien** has a counterculture feel. Head shops, book and music stores, restaurants and nightlife make it pleasant to wander around. The areas in front of the **Opéra** (near the port) and around **rue Curiol** (near rue Sénac) are often the meeting grounds for prostitutes and their clients; exercise particular caution here after dark.

Public transportation tames Marseille's urban sprawl. The two metro lines (M in text) are clean and simple. The bus system is thorough, if complex—the bus map helps a great deal. Buses are essential to get to beaches, which stretch along the coast, southeast of the *vieux port*.

▉ TRANSPORTATION

Flights: Aéroport Marseille-Provence (tel. 04 42 14 14 14). Flights to **Corsica, Paris,** and **Lyon.** Shuttle buses connect airport with Gare St-Charles (3 per hour, 45F).

Ferries: SNCM, 61 bd. des Dames (tel. 08 36 67 95 00). To **Corsica** (260-294F, students 160-176F), **Sardinia,** and **North Africa.** Open M-F 8am-6pm, Sa 8:30am-noon and 2-5:30pm.

Trains: Gare St-Charles, pl. Victor Hugo (tel. 04 91 08 50 50). M: Gare St-Charles. To: **Nice** (2¾hr., 1 per hour, 148F); **Lyon** (3½hr., 16 per day, 205F); and **Paris** (4¾hr., 12 TGVs per day, 406F). Info and reservations open M-Sa 9am-8pm. **SOS Voyageurs** (tel. 04 91 62 12 80), in the station, aids tourists. Cheery staff finds lodgings. Open summer M-Sa 9am-7pm; winter M-Sa 9am-noon and 1-7pm.

Buses: Gare des Autocars, pl. Victor Hugo (tel. 04 91 08 16 40), half a block from the train station. M: Gare St-Charles. Open M-Sa 7am-6:30pm, Su 9am-noon and 2-6:30pm. **Cartreize** (tel. 04 91 08 16 40) is an organization of local operators. Buy tickets on the bus (except to Nice), with exact change. To: **Aix-en-Provence** (5 per hour, 25F); **Avignon** (2hr., 5 per day, 89F); **Cannes** (2¼-3hr., 4 per day, 122F); **Nice** (2¾hr., 4 per day, 136F); and **Arles** (2-3hr., 7 per day, 85F).

Local Transportation: RTM, 6-8 rue des Fabres (tel. 04 91 91 92 10). Open M-F 8:30am-5:30pm, Sa 9am-5:30pm. Tickets sold at bus and metro stations, or use exact change (9F). Day pass 25F sold at tourist office. Long-term visitors should consider the 50-100F *Carte Liberté,* multiple tickets sold at a reduced rate. Metro lines #1 and 2 both stop at the train station. Line #1 (blue) goes to the *vieux port* (direction "Timone"). Metro runs 5am-9pm. The tourist office distributes the free *RTM Plan-Guide du Réseau.*

Taxis: Tel. 04 91 09 28 79 or tel. 04 91 02 20 20). 24hr. 80-130F to hostels.

▉ PRACTICAL INFORMATION

Consulates: UK, 24 av. du Prado (tel. 04 91 15 72 10). Open M-F 9am-noon and 2-5pm. **US,** 12 bd. Paul Peytral (tel. 04 91 54 92 00). Open by appointment M-F 8:30am-12:30pm and 1:30-5:30pm.

Tourist Office: 4 La Canebière (tel. 04 91 13 89 00; fax 04 91 13 89 20). Info on visiting nearby islands, annual festivals, and taxi tours of the city. Free maps and accommodations service. Bus and metro day pass 25F. Open daily July-Aug. 9am-8pm; Oct.-June M-Sa 9am-7pm, Su and holidays 10am-5pm. **Annex** (tel. 04 91 50 59 18) at train station. Open daily July-Aug. 10am-6pm; Sept.-June M-F 10am-1pm and 1:30-6pm. *Tak-Tik,* a weekly newspaper listing art exhibits, music, dance, theater, art, and film, is free at the tourist office and the FNAC in the Centre Bourse, a shopping mall 3 blocks from the *vieux port* on La Canebière.

Marseille
ACCOMMODATIONS

A Hôtel Béarn
B Hôtel Moderne (30, rue Breteuil) & Hôtel du Palais
C Hôtel Le Provencal
D Auberge de Jeunesse Bonnevine (HI)
E Hôtel Moderne
F Auberge de Jeunesse de Bois-Luzy

THE SOUTHEAST

Mediterranean Sea

Vieux Port

Jardin du Pharo

500 yards
500 meters

N

bd. de la Blancarde
av. Maréchal
TO (4m)
CINQ AVENUES LONGCHAMP
Palais Longchamp/ Musée des Beaux-Arts
bd. de la Libération
bd. du Longchamp
r. Monte Cristo
r. du Camas
r. du Chave
r. St-Pierre
TIMONE
bd. Eugène Pierre
bd. National
r. des Abeilles
bd. de la Volte
bd. Chave
bd. Chave
r. St. Pierre
r. Château
NOTRE DAME DU MONT-COURS JULIEN
r. de la Loubière Payan
r. de Lodi
bd. Baille
BAILLE
CANEBIÈRE REFORMES
PL JEAN JAURÈS
r. St. Savournin
CRS. F. Roosevelt
SQ. L. Gambetta STALINGRAD
allées
Gare St-Charles
PL. DES MARSEILLAISES
r. de la Volte
La Canebière
bd. Dugommier
NOAILLES
bd. Garibaldi
cours Lieutaud
cours Lieutaud
rue de Rome
av. Toulon
av. J. Cantini
cours Lieutaud
PL. CASTELLANE
CASTELLANE
av. du Prado
Dr. Escat
ST-CHARLES
PL. VICTOR HUGO
r. Longue des Capucins
r. de Rome
PL. DE ROME
cours Belsunce
d'Aubagne
Musée Cantini
ESTRANGIN PRÉFECTURE
r. Paradis
r. de Rome
r. St. Ferréol
r. Grignan
r. Breteuil
r. du Dragon
PL. JULES GUESDE
JULES GUESDE
r. d'Aix
St-barbe
Barbusse
H
PL. SADI-CARNOT
COLBERT
pavillon PL. DU GAL DE GAULLE
quai des Belges
cours J. Ballard
r. Sylabelle
r. Fontia
bd. Vauban
JOLIETTE
r. de la Joliette
bd. des Dames
r. de la République
PL. DE LA CORDERIE
crs. Pierre Puget
bd. Notre Dame
Basilique de Notre Dame de la Garde
r. de l'Evêché
r. R. Schumann
av. R. Schumann
r. Mazenod
r. du Panier
SQ PROTIS
r. Caisserie
r. de la Loge
quai du Port
VIEUX PORT– HÔTEL DE VILLE
quai de Rive Neuve
Sainte
bd. de la Corderie
bd. André Aune
bd. Tellene
ch. du Rouças Blanc
Cathédrale Nouvelle Major
quai de la Tourette
Tunnel
Abbaye St-Victor
bd. Notre Dame
quai de la Joliette
Bassin de la Grande Joliette
quai Jean Charcot
bd. Charles Livon
av. Pasteur
r. des Catalans
PL. DU 4 SEPTEMBRE
r. du Coteau
r. Chateaubriand
r. d'Endoume
corniche Prés. J.-F. Kennedy

Money: Comptoir Marseillais de Bourse, 22 La Canebière (tel. 04 91 54 93 94). Excellent rates and no commission. Open M-Sa 9am-7pm. **La Bourse,** 3 pl. Général de Gaulle (tel. 04 91 13 09 00). Good rates and no commission. Open M-F 8:30am-6:30pm, Sa 9am-5pm. **American Express,** 39 La Canebière (tel. 04 91 13 71 21). **Currency exchange.** Open M-F 8:30am-6pm, Sa 9am-noon and 2-5pm.

English Books: Librairie Fueri-Lamy, 21 rue Paradis (tel. 04 91 33 57 03). Slim paperback selection. Open M 1:30-7pm, Tu-Sa 9:30am-12:30pm and 1:45-7pm. V, MC.

Youth Information: Centre d'Information Jeunesse, 96 La Canebière (tel. 04 91 24 33 50). Info on sports, short-term employment, and activities, including climbing in the *calanques*. Pamphlets for people with disabilities. Open M-F 10am-6pm. **CROUS,** 42 rue du 141ème R.I.A. (tel. 04 91 62 83 60), has info on housing, work, and travel for students. Open daily 9am-noon and 2-4:30pm.

Laundromat: Point Laverie, 56 bd. de la Libération. Open daily 7am-9pm. Also at 8 rue de l'Académie.

Police: 2 rue du Commissaire Becker (tel. 04 91 16 29 50). Also in the train station on Esplanade St-Charles (same tel.; ask for *poste* 7097).

Crisis Lines: SOS Femmes Violées (tel. 04 91 56 04 10) is a 24hr. rape crisis hotline.

Hospital: Hôpital Timone, bd. Jean Moulin (tel. 04 91 38 60 00). Take metro line #1 to "Castéllane," then take bus #91. Ask the driver to drop you off at the hospital. **SOS Médecins** (tel. 04 91 52 91 52) has doctors on call.

Post Office: 1 pl. Hôtel des Postes (tel. 04 91 15 47 20). Follow La Canebière towards the sea and turn right onto rue Reine Elisabeth as it becomes pl. Hôtel des Postes. Poste Restante and **currency exchange** at this branch only. Open M-F 8am-7pm, Sa 8am-noon. **Branch office** at 11 rue Honnorat (tel. 04 91 62 80 80), near the station. **Postal code:** 13001.

Internet Access: Le Rezo, 68 cours Julien (tel. 04 91 42 70 02). Open M-Sa 10am-7pm. 40F per hr.

ACCOMMODATIONS AND CAMPING

Inexpensive hotels abound in Marseille, but walking home is sometimes potentially costly. Resist the cheap accommodations in the Belsunce quarter; the area may be dangerous after dark, and some hotels are fronts for brothels. Other hotels here could improve on cleanliness but have trustworthy owners, good locations, and ensure safety. Hotels listed here prioritize safety and location. Both hostels are far from the town center, with efficient, if time-consuming, bus service. They usually have space, even in summer, but call a day ahead.

Auberge de Jeunesse de Bois-Luzy (HI), allée des Primevères (tel./fax 04 91 49 06 18). By day, take bus #6 from cours J. Thierry at the top of La Canebière (away from the *port*) to "Marius Richard" and follow signs to the hostel, or bus #8 from "La Canebière" to "Bois-Luzy;" the hostel will be visible at the top of the hill. Night bus T also leaves "La Canebière" for "Marius Richard" at 9:10, 9:50, 10:40, 11:30pm, and 12:40am. The former home of a count and countess, the hostel has plain 3- to 6-bed dorms and a few doubles. 45F, 65F with breakfast. Camping 26F. Dinner 49F. Luggage storage 5F per day. Laundry. Reception daily 7:30-10am and 5-10:30pm. Lockout 10:30am-5pm. Strict curfew May-Oct. 11pm, Nov.-Apr. 10:30pm.

Auberge de Jeunesse Bonneveine (HI), impasse Bonfils (tel. 04 91 73 21 81; fax 04 91 73 97 23), off av. J. Vidal. From the station, take metro line #2 to "Rond-Point du Prado," and transfer (keeping your ticket) onto bus #44 to pl. Bonnefon. At the bus stop, walk left, turn left at J. Vidal. After #47, turn onto impasse Bonfils; the hostel is on the left. Swimming and sunbathing are just 200m away. Low-slung cement-block building with bar, restaurant, internet access, pool table, video games, drink and snack machines, travel agency, and 150 beds. Dorms 60-70F; doubles 80-90F. Breakfast included. Dinner 49F. Sheets 17F. Lockers 10F per day. Laundry. Reception daily 6am-1am. **Members only.** No lockout. Flexible 1am curfew. Closed Jan. V, MC.

■ **Hôtel du Palais,** 26 rue Breteuil (tel. 04 91 37 78 86). Competent, kind owner runs a tight ship and rents large, well-maintained rooms at great value for a 2-star hotel. Air-conditioning. Singles and doubles 185F; triples 280F. Breakfast 20F. V, MC.

Hôtel Béarn, 63 rue Sylvabelle (tel. 04 91 37 75 83; fax 04 91 81 54 98), between rue Paradis and rue Breteuil. Large rooms. Singles and doubles with shower 138F, with bath, toilet, and TV 188F; triples with shower, toilet, and TV 250F. Breakfast (with home-made jam) 20-25F. V, MC, AmEx.

Hôtel Le Provencal, 32 rue Paradis (tel. 04 91 33 11 15; fax 04 91 33 47 08). Modest rooms, but the low-key owner makes you feel more than welcome. Singles 120F; doubles 140F, with shower and TV 170F; triples with shower and TV 220F. V, MC.

Hôtel Moderne, 30 rue Breteuil (tel. 04 91 53 29 93). Dim but clean rooms, not far from the *vieux port.* Singles 110F, with shower 160F, with shower, toilet and TV 190F; doubles 170F, with shower 185F, with shower, toilet, and TV 190F. Breakfast 25F.

Hôtel Moderne, 11 bd. de la Libération (tel. 04 91 62 28 66). Decidedly the less *moderne* of the two. 10 rooms, each with a kitsch all its own, are bargains. One of the safer options in the decidedly dodgy train-station area. Singles 70-90F, with shower and TV 130F; doubles 120F, with shower and TV 150F; triples with shower 190-210F. Breakfast 20F. Shower 15F. V, MC.

■ FOOD

Marseille's dining scene is every bit as diverse as the people who hang their hat here. Once the staple of penniless fisherman, the city's trademark *bouillabaisse* has acquired prices to match its recently acquired *haute cuisine* status. North African restaurants are a budget traveler's dream, with excellent filling plates for under 40F. The restaurant density soars around the *vieux port*, concentrating on **pl. Thiars** and **Honoré d'Estienne d'Orvies**, where one can dine *en plein air* on fresh seafood for as little as 60F. For a more artsy crowd and cheaper fare, head up to **cours Julien** and take your pick from the bold and eclectic restaurants that line the pedestrian mall, most of which are in a budget price range. *Marseillais* stock up at the daily **fish market** on quai des Belges (9am-noon). There is a **vegetable market** on cours Julien (M-Sa 8am-1pm) and an **open-air market** on rue cours Pierre Puget, beginning at rue Breteuil (M-Sa, starts at 8am). Before you head for the hostels, stock up on the second floor of **BAZE supermarket,** on La Canebière, across from the AmEx office. (Open M-Sa 8:30am-8pm.)

■ **Ce Soleil Donne,** 70 Cours Julien (tel. 04 96 12 12 22). Popular spot with French-inflected cross-cultural dishes like kangaroo and bananas (59F) and curried salmon with papaya cream (59F). Equally exotic decor. Extensive patio gets crowded on weekends. Occasional live Cuban music. Open daily for lunch and dinner. V, MC.

L'Ecailler, 10 rue Fortia (tel. 04 91 54 79 39), off quai de Rive Neuve. True *marseillaise* cuisine can be eaten outside in summer or winter at this upscale restaurant. 3-course *menu* 65F. In summer and on weekends, call a day early to avoid a 20-30min. wait. Open daily 11:45am-2:30pm and 7-11:30pm. V, MC, AmEx.

Le Kahena, 2 rue de la République. Upscale North African cuisine in a muted pastel interior. Portions are filling, and the already tasty couscous (55-80F) gets extra kick from potent sauces. Closed Su lunch and dinner and M lunch. V, MC.

Country Life, 14 rue Venture (tel. 04 91 54 16 44; fax 04 91 33 90 29), off rue Paradis. The ground floor is a health food store; upstairs, a huge skylight and a forest of foliage provide a spacious atmosphere for enjoying the all-you-can-eat 58F vegan *menu* (students 35F). Open M-F 11:30am-2:30pm.

Brasserie Le 27, 27 quai de Rive Neuve (tel. 04 91 54 33 33). Marine *chic* is the feel at this friendly waterfront restaurant with reasonable prices for the *vieux port.* Fresh regional cuisine has a seafood focus, but pastas and pizzas (40-60F) are a cheaper bet. Open daily lunch and dinner, and as a café in between meals. V, MC.

L'Île de Gorée de Dakar, 30 rue du Musée (tel. 04 91 33 74 76). One of a handful of sub-saharan African restaurants in the area that serve up hearty portions of national staples in trinket-filled dining areas. Senegalese *Poulet-yaffa* (35F), *Riz-poisson* (35F).

Café le Parisien, 1 pl. Sadi Carnot (tel. 04 91 92 58 89). A mixed bag of moneyed hipsters, Marseille socialites, and card- and dice-playing old men sup at the city's most famous café. The stunning *trompe l'œil* interior recalls 1901, when the café first opened its doors. Decadent lunches are pricey, but coffee in all its incarnations costs much the same as elsewhere. Once a week, Le Parisien hosts guest presentations or exhibits running the artistic gamut and are open to the public.

👁 🌊 SIGHTS AND BEACHES

Spread out around the city and often poorly presented, Marseille's paucity of worthwhile museums and galleries are testament to the city's contentment at letting Paris play high-brow cultural capital, while it maintains a mind-boggling cultural diversity in its streets. Walking through Marseille's different neighborhoods will prove far more rewarding than a sight-oriented itinerary.

BASILIQUE DE NOTRE DAME DE LA GARDE. The 19th-century church glitters 160m above Marseille. Even in the summer haze of the Marseille skyline, the basilica's gilded Madonna shines over the Mediterranean Sea below. To see things from the Virgin's point of view—including the harbor islands, the Château d'If, and the surrounding mountains—take bus #60, or follow rue Breteuil from the *vieux port*, turn right on bd. Vauban, and turn right again on rue Fort du Sanctuaire. *(Tel. 04 91 13 40 80. Open in summer 7am-8pm; off-season 7am-7pm. Free.)*

ABBAYE ST-VICTOR. This imposing sanctuary evokes the ascetic beginnings of Christianity. The eerie 5th-century catacombs and basilica contain an extensive array of both pagan and Christian relics, including the remains of two 3rd-century martyrs. The abbey hosts sacred music concerts all year. *(Perched on rue Sainte at the end of quai de Rive Neuve, follow the signs from the quai. Tel. 04 96 11 22 60. Open daily 8:30am-6:30pm. 10F to go down to the crypts.)*

PALAIS LONGCHAMP. This elaborate 19th-century building was built as the ceremonious completion point of a massive aqueduct that brought water to the city. The highlight of the palace is the exterior. Two *long* stone staircases framing a set of complicated fountains and cascading waterfalls lead to two museums. On the left is the **Musée des Beaux-Arts.** The collections is strong in *provençal* painting, but the display is old and not viewer-friendly. It includes paintings of Marseille's early history, 16th- to 19th-century French canvases, and 17th- to 19th-century sculpture. Works by Courbet and Rubens, as well as a case of 36 satirical miniature busts by Daumier, round out the collection. Behind the Palais are the shady paths, playground, and pony rides of the former **Jardin Zoologique.** *(M: Cinq Avenues-Longchamp. Palais is at the eastern end of bd. Longchamp. Beaux-Arts: Tel. 04 91 14 59 30. Open Tu-Su June-Sept. 11am-6pm; Oct.-May 10am-5pm. 10F, students 5F.)*

LE JARDIN DES VESTIGES. The remains of the original port of Marseille rest in peace in this quiet garden behind the Centre Bourse, with limestone stacked like giant Legos. The grassy harbor makes a great picnic stop. Your ticket to the garden also admits you to the mildly interesting **Musée d'Histoire de Marseille.** *(Gardens open M-Sa noon-7pm. Museum tel. 04 91 90 42 22. 10F, students 5F.)*

HARBOR ISLANDS. The **Château d'If** looms ominously on the **Île d'If,** a small harbor island. The château's dungeon, immortalized in Dumas's *The Count of Monte Cristo,* imprisoned a number of Huguenots who never made it out alive. Nearby, the bald, barren, and windswept **Île Frioul** quarantined suspected plague victims for two centuries, starting in the 1600s. It was only marginally successful—an outbreak in 1720 killed half the city's 80,000 citizens. The ancient hospital is now a public monument and holds occasional raves. *(Boats depart from quai des Belges at M: quai des Belges, for both islands. Call the Groupement des Armateurs Côtiers, tel. 04 91 55 50*

09, for information. 20min., round-trip 45F for each island, 70F for both. Château tel. 04 91 59 02 30. Open daily Apr.-Sept. 9am-7pm; Oct.-Mar. 9am-1pm and 2-5:30pm. 26F, students 17F.)

OTHER SIGHTS. The memorable **Musée Cantini** features art from Fauvism to the present in permanent and temporary exhibits which form an excellent chronicle of area artistic feats of the last century. *(19 rue Grignan. Tel. 04 91 54 77 75. Open Tu-Su June-Sept. 11am-6pm; Oct.-May 10am-5pm. 10F, with temporary exhibits 15F, students half-price, over 65 or under 10 free.)* At the **Musée de la Mode,** praise or pan eccentric clothing and accessories from ever-changing but always wacky contemporary fashion exhibits. *(Espace Mode Méditerranée, 11 La Canebière. Tel. 04 91 56 59 57. Open Tu-Su noon-7pm. 15F, students 7.50F, over 65 free.)* The **MAC, Galeries Contemporaines des Musées de Marseille,** features art from the 1960s to today, including works by Pistoletto, César, and Wegman. *(69 av. d'Haifa. Tel. 04 91 25 01 07. Open Tu-Su 11am-6pm. 15F, students 7.50F.)* **Maison de l'Artisinat et des Metiers d'Art** has peculiar temporary exhibits that focus on different themes of Marseille past and present. The exhibitions do well at making specific subject matter accessible to everyone. *(21 cours Estienne d'Orves. Open Tu-Sa 1-6pm. Free.)*

BEACHES. Bus #83 (direction "Rond Pont du Prado") from the *vieux port* is your ticket to Marseille's public beaches. Catch it on the waterfront side of the street and get off just after it rounds the statue of David (20-30min.). Both **plage du Prado** and **plage de la Corniche** offer wide beaches, clear water, plenty of grass for impromptu soccer matches, and scenic views of the greyish-white cliffs surrounding Marseille, although the sand is not ideal. **Supermarché Casino,** across from the statue, will serve your every need. *Every* need. (Open M-Sa 8:30am-8:30pm.)

🎵 🎇 ENTERTAINMENT AND FESTIVALS

Don't let Marseille's seedy reputation scare you from its boisterous nightlife. Exercise cosmopolitan caution, and pick up a free magazine to keep up with club openings, theme nights, and concerts. People-watching and nightlife center around **cours Julien,** northeast of the harbor, and **pl. Thiers,** near the *vieux port*. Don't venture alone in the *vieux port* after dark, and after 10pm *everyone* should avoid the North African quarter, cours Belsunce, and bd. d'Athènes.

Theater buffs can check out the program at the **Théâtre National de Marseille,** 30 quai de Rive Neuve (tel. 04 91 54 70 54; tickets 80-135F; box office open Tu-Sa 11am-6pm), and **Théâtre Gymnase,** 4 rue du Théâtre Français (tel. 04 91 24 35 24; tickets 110-160F; box office open Sept.-July M-F 9:30am-6pm, Sa 9:30am-noon and 2-6pm). Unwind with the latest French and American **films** at **Le César,** 4 pl. Castallene (tel. 04 91 37 12 80; 40F, students and seniors 35F) and **Cinéma Breteuil,** 120 bd. Notre Dame (tel. 04 91 37 71 36; 38F, students and seniors 30F).

LIVE PERFORMANCE

L'Espace Julien, 39 cours Julien (tel. 04 91 24 34 10), hosts a variety of concerts, from African music to pop, in a quirky space full of wild 3-D decorations (9pm, 50-140F).

Chocolat Théâtre, 59 cours Julien (tel. 04 91 42 19 29), stages comic pieces and stand-up at 9pm (70-110F). Check out their restaurant and café for cool drinks on hot nights. Restaurant open noon-2am; café 9am-2am.

La Poste à Galene, 103 rue Ferrari (tel. 04 91 47 57 99), lures cutting-edge musicians of national and international fame into its nocturnal lair. Cover 30-80F.

BARS AND CLUBS

🗞 **Bar du Marche,** 15 pl. Notre-Dame du Mont (tel. 04 91 92 58 89). For no apparent reason, this outdoor café/bar is *the* night-time meeting spot for Marseille's youth and twenty-somethings. The hardest part is finding a seat. Beer from 18F.

L'Enigme, 22 rue Beauvau (tel. 04 91 33 79 20), parallel to rue Paradis and pl. de Gaulle, is the only gay place on a street rife with lively bars.

El Ache de Cuba, 9 pl. Paul Cézanne (tel. 04 91 42 99 79). A slice of Havana, with timbales and trumpets blaring out of speakers and on to the sidewalk of this friendly café. Ask about weekly latin-dance sessions. Ordering something requires you to become a member first (10F), but it's a ticket into the community. Everyone welcome.

Metal Café, 20 rue Fortia (tel. 04 91 54 03 03), off quai de Rive Neuve. Dress to impress to get into this small but wildly popular night spot. No cover but 1 drink required. Open 11pm-morning.

■ **Trolleybus,** 24 quai de Rive Neuve (tel. 04 91 54 30 45), is a mega-club with a room each for techno, rock, and acid jazz, as well as a gallery of contemporary art. Sa 60F cover. Open Th-Sa 11pm-7am.

New Can-Can, 3 rue Sénac (tel. 04 91 48 59 76). Dancing queens love this perpetual weekend party for the city's gay and lesbian community. Cover 60F Th and Su, 70F F, 80F Sa. Opens at 11pm; show at 2am.

FESTIVALS

Expect the **International Documentary Film Festival** in June and festivities surrounding the **Lesbian and Gay Pride March** in the middle of the same month. The **Festival de Marseille Méditerranée** and **Festival des Îles** keep Marseille bubbling with music, dance, and theater in July. December brings the **Festival de Musique,** a week-long jubilee of jazz, classical, and pop music at l'Abbaye de St-Victoire. Call the tourist office or the Culture Office (tel. 04 91 33 33 79) for info on all festivals.

LES CALANQUES

The **Calanques** are inlets of azure water surrounded by walls of jagged rock. Stretching from Marseille to Toulon, their precipices and seas shelter a fragile and rare balance of terrestrial and marine plants and wildlife. Bleached white houses skirt the hills, looking down on the swarms of scuba divers, mountain climbers, cliff divers, and those in search of a full body tan.

During July and August, the **Société des Excursionistes Marseillais,** 16 rue de la Rotonde (tel. 04 91 84 75 52), conducts free walking tours of the Calanques. To get to the area, they have boat trips leaving Marseille daily from the *vieux port*, across from the tourist office. (2 per week, round-trip 100F.) A far cheaper option is to take bus #21 to "Luminy" (9F); this leaves you near **Morgiou** and **Sormiou.** The first of the inlets, **Callelongue** also lies at the farthest reaches of Marseille bus lines. Take #19 from the *vieux port* to "Samena," then catch #20 and follow the coastal roads until its terminus. Service is sporadic, but you can kill time exploring trails in the nearby hills. Sometimes line #20 ends prematurely at **Goudes** (the town before Callelongue), which offers trails leading to secluded inlets.

CASSIS

Twenty-three kilometers from Marseille, the charming resort town of **Cassis** clings to a hillside overlooking the deep greens and blues of the Mediterranean. Immaculate white villas clump around the slopes above, while the town itself—a network of winding staircases, slender alleyways, and thick gardens—rests beside a devilishly bright port. Unfortunately, this is no undiscovered paradise. Swimmers should follow the signs to the **Calanque de Port-Pin,** about 45 minutes east of town. From there, it's a half-hour hike to the popular **En Vau** *calanque* and beach.

Cassis makes a terrific daytrip from Marseille, since hotel prices in the town itself can be steep. Eco-warriors can rejoice in the **Auberge de Jeunesse de la Fontasse (HI),** 20km from Marseille off D559 (tel. 04 42 01 02 72), near En Vau. For those on foot, the hostel is a spite-inducing 4km climb from the Cassis tourist office (1hr.), but the gorgeous panorama and friendly communal atmosphere may make it worth the effort. Flop on one of 66 beds in 6- to 10-person dormitories, powered by solar energy and irrigated with filtered rain water (from taps). There are no showers, but you can sponge-bathe at the sinks. Light chores are required of all guests. To get there, start from Cassis's port and follow signs for the Calanques. When the road ends at two paths, take the (very steep) right path and then watch closely for harmonious-with-nature signs printed on rocks. (46F. Kitchen open 5-10pm. **Members only.** Flexible reception daily 8-10am and 5-11pm.) To find **Camping Les Cigales** (tel. 04 42 01 07 34), take av. Agostina to av. Colbert, then turn right onto av. de la Marne (15-20min.). (60F for 1 person with tent, 90F for 2 people with tent. Cars and campers allowed. Open Mar. 15-Nov. 15.) Stock up at **Casino,** down the hill and on the left from the bus stop. (Open M-Sa 8:30am-12:30pm and 3:30-7:30pm.) Cheap eats and sangria can be had at **Le Petit Cassis,** 19 rue Michel Blanc. (Tel. 04 42 01 17 32. Open daily noon-2pm and 7-10:30pm.)

Since the train station is 3km outside town, it's simplest to take a **bus** from **Marseille** (30min.-1hr., 12-21 per day, 22F). One block down the hill from the bus stop, turn right into the Jardin Public. The **tourist office** is on your left as you leave the park; grab a map—they're especially helpful when navigating the hike to the hostel. (Tel. 04 42 01 71 17; fax 04 42 01 28 31. Open July-Aug. daily 9am-7:30pm; Sept.-June M-Sa 9am-6pm, Su 9am-12:30pm.) The tourist office's **beach-side annex** is open daily during the summer 10am-1pm and 3:30-10:30pm.

AIX-EN-PROVENCE

Aix (pronounced "X," pop. 150,000) is one of those rare cities which panders to tourists without being spoiled by them. The city of Paul Cézanne, Victor Vasarely, and Émile Zola, Aix's fame today rests on its festivals and flowing fountains. Though labyrinthine streets and local friendliness give Aix a small town feel, its large student population means that even outside the festival season there is always fun going on. The most exciting time to arrive is from the end of June through early August, when Aix bursts into revelry as dance, opera, jazz, and classical music take over the city. Concerts in Aix range from formal evening-wear occasions to impromptu street performances as violinists, xylophone players, and dancers vie for attention (and francs) along the crooked line of the rues G. de Saporta, M. Foch, and R. Bédarrides.

⊡ ORIENTATION AND PRACTICAL INFORMATION

The **cours Mirabeau** sweeps through the center of town, linking **La Rotonde** (a.k.a. **pl. du Général de Gaulle**) to the west with **place Forbin** to the east. Fountain-dodging traffic along the *cours* separates cafés on one side from banks on the other. The mostly pedestrian *vieille ville* snuggles inside the *périphérique*—a ring of boulevards including bd. Carnot and Cours Sextius. The tourist office and the central terminus for city buses are on **pl. du Général de Gaulle.** To reach them from the train station, go straight onto av. Victor Hugo and bear left at the fork, staying on av. Victor Hugo (5min.) until it feeds into **La Rotonde.** The tourist office is on the left. From the *gare routière*, facing the small terminal, go left across the parking lot and up the stairs on the right. The tourist office will be on your right.

Trains: At the end of av. Victor Hugo, off rue Gustave Desplace. To: **Marseille** (35min., every hr. until 9:53pm, 37F); **Avignon** (1hr., 6 per day, 112F); **Cannes** (2½hr., 8 per day, 150F); **Nice** (3½hr., 8 per day, 165F). Ticket window open daily 5:50am-9:45pm.

Buses: Rue Lapierre (tel. 04 42 27 82 54), behind the post office. A plethora of companies compete for the lucrative commuter route to **Marseilles,** with buses almost every 30min. **SATAP** (tel. 04 07 76 67 94) serves **Avignon** (2hr., 4 per day, 80F). **Phocéens Cars** (tel. 04 93 85 66 61) goes to **Cannes** (1¾hr., 5 per day, 120F) and **Nice** (2¼hr., 5 per day, 132F). **Ceyte** (tel. 04 90 93 74 90) runs to **Arles** (1¾hr., 5 per day, 70F). Ask for under-26 student discounts (ISIC required). Info desk open daily 6:45am-6pm.

Taxis: Tel. 04 42 27 71 11. 24hr. About 50F from *gare* to hostel.

Bike Rental: Cycles Zammit, 27 rue Mignet (tel. 04 42 23 15 53), located between pl. des Prêcheurs and pl. Bellegarde. Mountain bikes and regular bikes 80F per day, 200F Sa-Tu, 400F per week, and 25F for each additional day. Passport deposit. Open Tu-Sa 9am-noon and 3-7:30pm. V, MC, AmEx.

THE SOUTHEAST

Tourist Office: 2 pl. du Général de Gaulle (tel. 04 42 16 11 61; fax 04 42 16 11 62). Busy office provides hotel reservations and frequent tours of the city by foot and *petit train* as well as bus tours of the surrounding countryside. Some tours in English; call office for schedules. Sells city museum pass for 40F. Free monthly event guide, *Le Mois à Aix,* and the free French and English *Aix La Vivante: A Practical Guide,* with walking tours, museums, and more. Open daily July-Aug. 8:30am-10pm; May-June and Sept. 8:30am-9pm; Oct.-Apr. 8:30am-7pm.

International Music Festival Information: Call the Palais de l'Ancien Archevêché (tel. 04 42 17 34 34; www.aix-en-provence.com/festartlyrique). Festival lasts 2 months, with concerts in June and concerts and operas in July. Reserve early to guarantee a seat, though some may still be available the day of the performance (tel. 0800 84 08 00). Open mid-Apr. M-Sa 10am-7pm; from June 1 daily 10am-8pm. V, MC, AmEx.

Budget Travel: Council Travel, 12 rue Victor Leydet (tel. 04 42 38 58 82; fax 04 42 38 94 00), off pl. des Augustins. Flights at student prices, but even student status won't get you past the lines. Open M-F 9:30am-6:30pm, Sa 9:30am-12:30pm. V, MC, AmEx.

Money: Change Nazareth, 7 rue Nazareth (tel. 04 42 38 28 28), off cours Mirabeau, behind Monoprix. Good rates even with 3% commission. Open July-Aug. M-Sa 9am-7pm; Sept.-June M-Sa 9am-6:30pm. **American Express, L'Agence,** 15 cours Mirabeau (tel. 04 42 26 84 77; fax 04 42 26 79 03). Open July-Aug. M-Sa 9am-9pm, Su 10am-1pm and 4-7pm; Sept.-June M-Sa 9am-7pm.

English Bookstore: Paradox Bookstore, 15 rue du 4 Septembre (tel. 04 42 26 47 99). Used books and a board listing jobs. Open M-Sa 9am-12:30pm and 2-6:30pm.

Laundromat: Lavomatique, 61 Rue Bougelon. Open daily.

Help Lines: SOS Amitié (tel. 04 42 38 20 20), for instant friendship. **SIDA Info Service** (tel. 08 00 36 66 36) addresses AIDS-related issues. **SOS Viol** (tel. 04 91 56 04 10) is a sexual assault hotline. **SOS Médecins** (tel. 04 42 26 24 00) has medical advice (24hr.). **Service des Étrangers** (tel. 04 42 96 89 48) helps out strangers like yourself.

Police: 10 av. de l'Europe (tel. 04 42 93 97 00).

Internet Access: Hublot Cyber Café, 17 rue Paul Bert (tel. 04 42 21 37 31). 30F for 30min. or 50F per hr.; 5 computers available.

Post Office: 2 rue Lapierre (tel. 04 42 16 01 50), just off La Rotonde. Open M-F 8:30am-6:45pm, Sa 8:30am-noon. **Currency exchange. Annex,** 1 pl. de l'Hôtel de Ville (tel. 04 42 63 04 66), has same services. Open Sept.-July M-Tu and Th-F 8am-6:30pm, W 8:30am-6:30pm, Sa 8am-noon; Aug. M-Tu and Th-F 8am-noon and 2-6:30pm, W 8:30am-noon and 2-6:30pm, Sa 8am-noon. **Postal code:** 13100.

▶ ACCOMMODATIONS AND CAMPING

There are few inexpensive hotels near the center, and during the festival they may be booked in advance. Reserve early or hope for cancellations.

Auberge de Jeunesse (HI), 3 av. Marcel Pagnol (tel. 04 42 20 15 99; fax 04 42 59 36 12), quartier du Jas de Bouffan. Take bus #4 (A on weekends) from La Rotonde in front of the casino (every 15-30min. until 8pm, 7F) to "Vasarely." To walk, follow av. de Belges from La Rotonde and turn right on av. de l'Europe. At the first roundabout after the highway overpass, bear left and climb the hill. The hostel is on the left in a secluded wooded area before the Fondation Vasarely (35min.). Green-friendly rooms with push-button showers and energy-saving lighting in a roomy, modern hostel. TV room, bar, tennis, and volleyball. 69F for a spot in an 8-bed room, breakfast included. Dinner 50F. Linen 11F. No sleeping bags. No reception noon-5pm. Lockout 9am-4pm. Midnight curfew. No kitchen facilities. Laundry 35F. Reservations recommended June-Sept.

Hôtel Paul, 10 av. Pasteur (tel. 04 42 23 23 89; fax 04 42 63 17 80), past the Cathédrale St-Sauveur. Spacious, simple, immaculate rooms in a bright, modern hotel. Small and accessible garden in back; street-side rooms have sound-proofed glass. Proprietor speaks English. Reserve well ahead if you want one of the two 111-114F singles

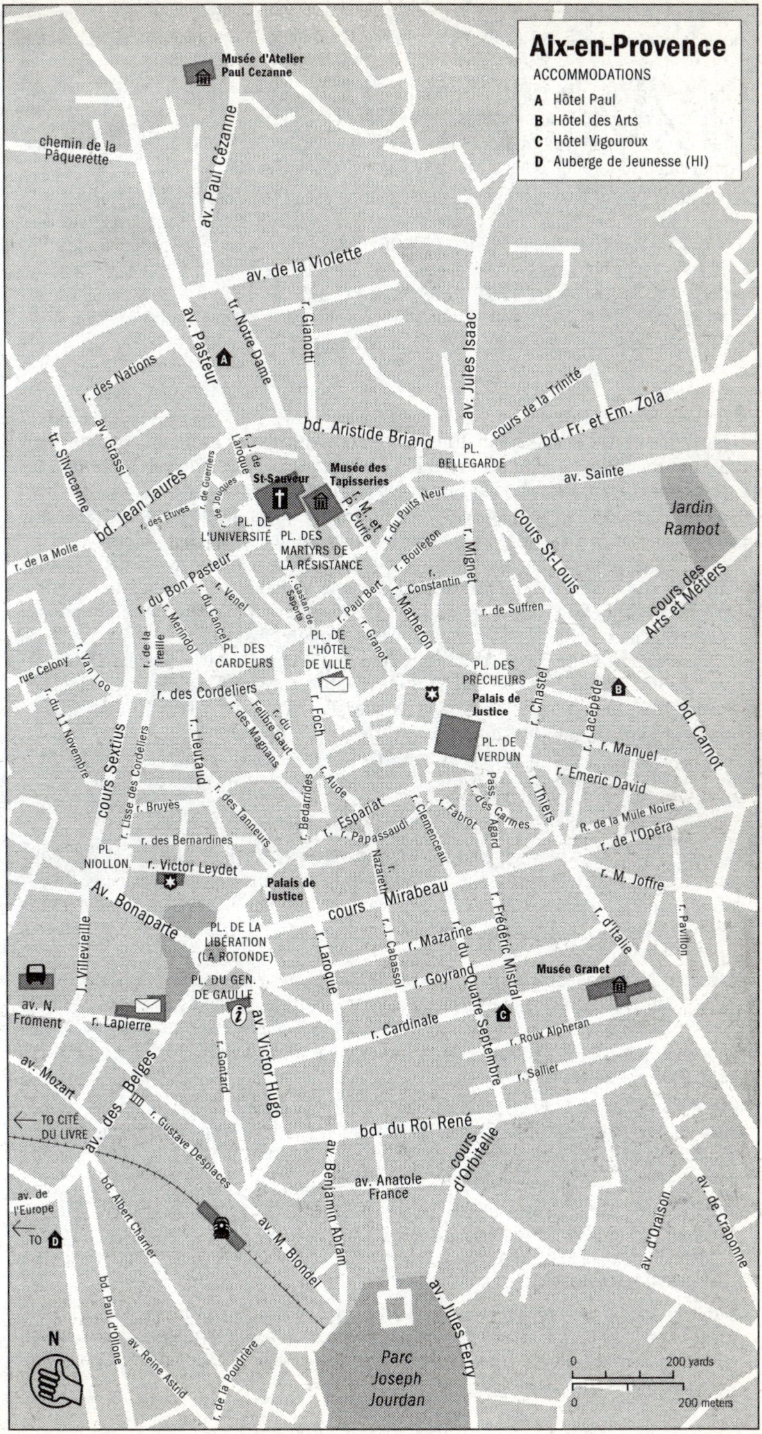

THE SOUTHEAST

with sink, but be warned—there is no shower available. Singles and doubles with shower and toilet 193-256F; triples 309F; 1 quad (2 adults and 2 kids only) 412F. Breakfast 28F. V, MC.

Hôtel des Arts, 69 bd. Carnot (tel. 04 42 38 11 70), where it meets rue Portalis. The identical, compact modern rooms all have shower, toilet, and phone. One large, comfy bed per room. Singles and doubles 180-205F, depending on whether you face the noisy boulevard or the quieter rue de la Fonderie. Breakfast 25F. V, MC.

Campsites: Two of the local campgrounds that lie out of town are accessible by bus #3 from La Rotonde at the "Trois Sautets" and "Val St-André" stops, respectively. **Arc-en-Ciel,** pont des Trois Sautets (tel. 04 42 26 14 28), rte. de Nice, 2km from the *centre ville*. Pool and hot showers. 34F per person, 35F for place, parking included. **Chantecler,** av. St-André (tel. 04 42 26 12 98; fax 04 42 27 33 53), by rte. de Nice, 3km from the *centre ville*. Swimming pool, hot showers, phones, restaurant, and bar. July-Aug. 30F per person, 35F per place. Both open year-round.

FOOD

Restaurants in Aix serve specialties seasoned with garlic aïoli sauce and local olives, but its culinary reputation stands on its *confiseries*. The city's *bonbon* is the *calisson d'Aix*, a small iced marzipan-and-melon treat created in 1473. Other specialties include soft nougat and hard praline candies. Peruse the *pâtisseries* on rue d'Italie or rue Espariat to feed your sweet dreams.

The **rue d'Italie** has a few *boulangeries, charcuteries,* and fruit stands. For the freshest produce, shop at the **markets** on pl. de la Madeleine (Tu, Th, and Sa 7am-1pm) and pl. Richelme (daily, same times). Supermarket aficionados can choose from two **Casinos,** at 1 av. de Lattre de Tassigny (open M-Sa 8:30am-8:30pm; V, MC) and 3 cours d'Orbitelle (open M-Sa 8am-1pm and 4-8pm; V, MC). **Monoprix** is at 25 cours Mirabeau. (Open M-Sa 8:30am-8pm. V, MC, AmEx.) The cheapest meal in town has to be the university **Cafétéria Les Gazelles.** Take av. Victor Hugo from La Rotonde, go left on bd. du Roi René, and right on cours d'Orbitelle, which turns into av. J. Ferry. Pass Parc Jourdan and it's up the incline to the left. (*Plat* 15F. Open M-F 11:45am-1:30pm and 6:45-8pm, Sa-Su 11:45am-1pm and 6:45-8pm.)

The Aixois like nothing better than to watch each other preen, and the cafés that line the **cours Mirabeau** encourage a polite voyeurism. Though eating on the cours Mirabeau is generally more expensive than the streets north of it in the **pl. des Cardeurs** and **pl. Ramus,** an espresso at the fancy **Café des Deux Garçons** (tel. 04 42 26 00 51), the former watering hole of Cézanne, costs a mere 9F (12F after 10pm), good for hours of choice people-watching.

Hacienda, 7 rue Mérindol (tel. 04 42 27 00 35), on pl. des Fontêtes off pl. des Cardeurs, serves delicious French platters despite its Spanish name. At lunch, enjoy two courses for 53F, three for 62F, wine included. At dinner the 3-course *menu* rises to 70F. Tasty tabouleh, roast beef, and lemon tart make a great meal. Salads 36-48F. Open M-Th noon-2pm, F-Sa noon-10pm.

Autour d'une Tarte, 13 rue Gaston de Saporta (tel. 04 42 96 52 12), off pl. de l'Hôtel de Ville. This tiny place offers quiches galore (20-40F, 12-18F take-out). *Menus* include a quiche, salad, and dessert *tarte* 50-65F. At lunch, quiche and salad 29-35F. The pear tarts are delicious. Open M-Sa 9am-7:30pm. V, MC.

L'Abre à Pain, 12 rue Constantin (tel. 04 42 96 99 95), for a *sympa* vegetarian meal in a colorful restaurant on a quiet, out-of-the way street. Salads (35-60F), lunch *menu* (78F), and dinner (110F and 150F). A splash of fish dishes too. Open Tu-Sa noon-2pm and 7:30-11:30pm. V, MC.

La Rose à Aix, 44 rue Espariat (tel. 04 42 26 38 16). A fun, friendly place to round off a meal or cool off from the sun. 56 kinds of gelati all made in the back to the hum of trance techno. The Snickers mix will have you rolling in the aisles. 13-40F. Open daily from late morning to at least midnight.

👁 SIGHTS

All museums but the Fondation Vasarely are included on the 40-60F pass, available at the tourist office or at any of the museums.

THE CHEMIN DE CÉZANNE. A self-guided walking tour, this trails the life and times of Paul Cézanne, Aix's most famous son. The English-language brochure (free at the tourist office) and sidewalk bronze markers will bring you to the artist's birthplace, his haunts, and his studio. Walking takes about two hours and leads through some of the more colorful parts of Aix. In his studio, **Atelier Paul Cézanne,** his beret still hangs inconspicuously in the corner of a large room filled with the props he used for his still-life's. Take bus #21 north of Aix. *(9 av. Paul Cézanne. Tel. 04 42 21 06 53. Open daily Apr.-Sept. 10am-noon and 2:30-6pm; Oct.-Mar. 10am-noon and 2-5pm. 25F; students, children, and seniors 10F; free for EU citizens under 25.)*

FONDATION VASARELY. This funky black-and-white museum is an absolute must-see for modern art fans. It was designed in the 1970s by the Hungarian-born artist Victor Vasarely, famed for his eye-boggling use of geometry. Some of his most monumental and original work is permanently exhibited in eight large hexagonal spaces. *(Av. Marcel-Pagnol, Jas-de-Bouffan, next to the youth hostel. Open M-F in summer 10am-1pm and 2-7pm, Sa-Su 10am-7pm; in winter 9:30am-1pm and 2-6pm. 35F, students 20F.)*

PAVILLON DE VENDÔME. This 17th-century building houses paintings and furniture from the turn of the 18th century in winter, while in summer the paintings are replaced by photography exhibitions. The glorious gardens offer soothing smells of boxwood and roses, a fountain, and shrubs cut into swirling, green merengues. It's so quiet you can hear the goldfish swimming amidst the water lilies. *(32 rue Célony. Tel. 04 42 21 05 78. Museum open W-M in summer 10am-noon and 2-6pm; in winter 9am-noon and 2-5pm. 10F. Gardens free and open the same hours as the Pavilion.)*

CITÉ DES LIVRES. Once one of France's largest match factories, this enormous building has been renovated into a free, widely used cultural center. The **Bibliothèque Méjanes** contains a library, contemporary art gallery, and café. Guarded by giant, rusty replicas of Camus's *L'Étranger* and Antoine de St-Exupéry's *Le Petit Prince*, this bright library stocks current *Newsweek*s and a collection of British and American literature. The **Discothèque** features a wide selection of music from around the world on CD for loan (with 95F membership). Relaxing music and lots of natural light will make you want to get a book and lounge in here. *(8-10 rue des Allumettes, behind the gare routière. Tel. 04 42 25 98 88. Both open Tu and Th-F noon-6pm; W and Sa 10am-6pm.)* You can ask the English-speaking staff at the *bibliothèque* to show you the way to the **Videothèque d'Art Lyrique,** where you can sit in air-conditioned splendor amidst old opera sets and view operas and concerts of past *Festivals d'Aix* for free. *(Tel. 04 42 37 70 89. Open Tu-F 1-6pm, Sa 10am-noon and 1-6pm.)*

CATHÉDRALE ST-SAVEUR. This dramatic mélange combines a 12th-century Romanesque nave and cloister with heavily-decorated Baroque chapels. The main attraction is the 16th-century carved panels of the main portal, which remain in mint condition. The interior hides the **Triptych du Buisson Ardent,** depicting Aix's Good King René and his queen oddly juxtaposed with the Virgin and Child and the burning bush of Moses. The work is usually only on show Tu 3-5pm, but you should ask the affable guard to open the cloister. *(Rue Gaston de Saporta, on pl. des Martyrs de la Résistance. Tel. 04 42 23 98 90. Open W-M 8am-noon and 2-6pm.)*

OTHER SIGHTS. The **Musée Granet** contains several lesser-known Cézannes and a smattering of works by David, Ingres and, Delacroix, as well as an archaeological section. Unfortunately, the museum is undergoing extensive renovations until 2005, so only a part of the full collection is visible. *(Pl. St-Jean-Marie-de-Malte. Tel. 04 42 38 14 70. Open daily 10-11:50am and 2-5:50pm, closed Tu. 10F, free under 25.)* A fine collection of 17th- and 18th-century tapestries hangs in the **Musée des Tapisseries,** the highlight of which is the series depicting the story of Don Quixote. The museum also includes contemporary art exhibits, oddly juxtaposed with the *ancien régime* decor. *(On the second floor of the Palais Archiepiscol, 28 pl. des Martyrs de la Résistance. Tel. 04 42 23 09 91. Open W-M 10am-noon and 2-6pm. 10F, under 25 free.)*

♪ ✿ ENTERTAINMENT AND FESTIVALS

NIGHTLIFE. Aix's students insist on revelry year-round; most clubs open at 11:30pm and don't get going until 2am, though pubs and bars have earlier hours. Cafés and bars, some lit by candles, line the **Forum des Cardeurs,** behind the Hôtel de Ville. **Le Scat,** 11 rue Verrerie (tel. 04 42 23 00 23), has both a pub and a terrific club with live music. (Open M-Sa 11pm until whenever. Concerts 80F.) **Bistro Aixois,** 37 Cours Sextius (tel. 04 42 27 50 10), off la Rotonde, packs students and bands in cramped quarters. (Open daily 6:30pm-3 or 4am. V, MC.) Techno and dance music surge at **Le Mistral,** 3 rue F. Mistral (tel. 04 42 38 16 49); don't show up here in shorts, jeans, or sandals. (Open Tu-Sa 11:30pm-5am. Women often free, cover 100F.) French music thumps at **Le Richelme,** 24 rue de la Verrerie. (Tel. 04 42 23 49 29. Open Tu-Sa 11:30pm-dawn. 80F cover includes 1 drink.) Students and professionals share the stages of **Théâtre 108,** 37 bd. A. Briand (tel. 04 42 21 06 70). **Ciné Mazarin,** 6 rue Laroque (tel. 04 42 26 99 85), off Cours Mirabeau, projects three foreign films at a time, some in English (35-45F).

FESTIVALS. The festival season kicks off in the beginning of June with **Cinestival,** a week-long film festival. If you pick up the free "billet scoop" from the tourist office, it's 20F per film. Aix's **International Music Festival** (tel. 04 42 17 34 34 or 04 42 21 14 40; www.aix-en-provence.com/festartlyrique/) is held from June to July. The program features operas in Le Grand Saint-Jean in Puyricard (125-350F), the Hôtel Maynier d'Oppède, 23 rue Gaston de Saporta (125-350F), and opera and orchestral concerts in the Théâtre de l'Archevêché (100-1200F). A 100F pass can also be purchased in April to sit in on master classes and morning and afternoon rehearsals. For two weeks at the end of July and the beginning of August, Aix holds a **Dance Festival** (tel. for info 04 42 96 05 01; for reservations 04 42 23 41 24) of ballet, modern, and jazz (90-150F, students 60-120F). Tickets can be bought at 1 pl. John Rewald or at the tourist office. At the end of June and beginning of July, the city puts on a two-week **Jazz Festival,** with concerts around town which also include salsa and big band music (80-150F). The **Comité Officiel des Fêtes** (tel. 04 42 63 06 75), on cours Gambetta at the corner of bd. du Roi René, can fill you in on all the festivals, while **Aix en Musique,** 3 place John Rewald (tel. 04 42 21 69 69), sponsors concerts year-round. Check the free *Le Mois* at the tourist office for listings.

SALON-DE-PROVENCE

Conveniently located between Aix-en-Provence and Arles, Salon-de-Provence (pop. 45,000) is a good base to penetrate the heart of the Rhône Valley. The surrounding countryside is bespeckled with olive trees, whose oil flows straight into the shops of Salon, where it gleams in bottles alongside the region's typical perfumed soaps and cheery blue and yellow textiles. Salon's most famous inhabitant by far was the physician with a predilection for prediction, Nostradamus (1503-1566), whose house and tomb can be visited. His study of the stars inspired *Centuries*, a cryptic book of predictions that is still freely interpreted by the supermarket tabloid industry. Of lesser international repute, but possibly more import, was the citizen Adam de Craponne (1527-1576), whose canal still irrigates the semi-arid lands and made possible the region's agricultural wealth.

◪ ORIENTATION AND PRACTICAL INFORMATION. Trains run to **Avignon** (65min.; M-Sa 7 per day, Su 5 per day; 49F) and **Marseilles** (1½ hr., 2 per day, 56F) from the *gare* on av. Émile Zola. (Ticket office open M-Th and Sa 5:45am-1pm and 1:15-8:15pm, F 5:45am-1pm and 1:15-9:15pm, Su 7:30am-9:15pm.) From the **bus station** on pl. Morgan (tel. 04 90 56 50 98), **Cartreize** coaches make the trip to **Arles** (70min., M-Sa 7 per day, 44.50F), **Aix** (45min., M-Sa 15 per day from 6:50am-6:30pm, 33F), and **Marseilles** (1¼hr., M-Sa 10 per day, 51F). Most of Salon's attractions are located within the small *centre ville*. From both the bus and the train station, walk down bd. Maréchal Foch, turn left onto cours Pelletan, and follow it as it flows into cours Carnot, cours Victor Hugo, and finally cours Gimon (12min. from *gare*, 5 min. from bus station). The **tourist office,** 56 cours Gimon (tel. 04 90 56 27 60 and 04 90 44 89 33; fax 04 90 56 77 09; www.salon-de-provence.org) gives out a free map and a list of restaurants, hotels, and museums. *Les Couleurs de l'Été* is a free brochure on the summer festivals in Salon. (Open June 15-Sept. 15 M-Sa 9am-noon and 2-7pm, Su 10am-noon; Sept. 16-June 14 M-Sa 9am-noon and 2-6:30pm.) Your best bet for **changing money** is **Crédit Commercial de France,** 93 bd. Maréchal Foch. (Tel. 04 90 56 89 56. Open M-F 8:15-11:55am and 1:20-4:30pm.) Aches and pains can be soothed across from the Bourg Neuf at **Pharmacie Roux,** on cours Gimon. (Open M-F 8:30am-12:15pm and 2-7:30pm, Sa 8:30am-12:15pm and 2-7pm.) More serious ailments can be treated at the **Centre Hospitalier de Salon,** 207 avenue Julien (tel. 04 90 44 91 44). Social ills are battled by the **Police** from avenue du Pays Catalan (tel. 04 90 17 04 00). Snail mail crawls out of the **post office** on rue Massanet (tel. 04 90 56 88 10). Here you'll find **currency exchange.** (Open M 9am-6:45pm, Tu-F 8:30am-6:45pm, Sa 8:30am-noon. **Postal code:** 13300.) Email beams up from behind the moss fountain at **Cybercafé Colissée-Oriental,** 1 pl. Crousillat. (Tel. 04 90 56 00 10. Open daily 6am-2am. 30F per half-hr., 50F per hr.)

▐ **ACCOMMODATIONS AND CAMPING.** If you're weary of the crowds of Arles and Aix, why not take temporary refuge in Salon? A tourist desert by area standards, hotels are reasonably priced and don't fill up as quickly as in more popular neighbors. Still, it's advisable to make reservations in July. Tucked away in a quiet street near the *centre ville*, the one-star **Hôtel Regina,** 245 rue des frères Kennedy (tel. 04 90 56 28 92; fax 04 90 56 77 43), has friendly owners, a rustic breakfast room, and a sweet dog. (Singles 130F, doubles 150F, quads with 2 double beds 240F. All rooms have shower and toilet. TV 20F. Breakfast 25F. Garage 22F. V, MC.) Conveniently located next to the *gare*, the one-star **Hôtel de Provence,** 450 bd. Maréchal Foch (tel. 04 90 56 27 04; fax 04 90 56 99 76), has an eclectic but homey mix of rooms. The quad is the old living room, with a painted ceiling and an antique fireplace. (Doubles with toilet 130F, with shower 160-170F, with both 220-260F; quad 310F. Breakfast 30F. No credit cards.) You're unlikely to find a crystal ball in any of the tents at **Camping Nostradamus,** rte. d'Eyguiere (tel. 04 90 56 08 36; fax 04 90 56 65 05). This 3-star site with pool and restaurant, on the road to Arles, is the closest to Salon. (75F per night for person and pitch. Open Mar.-Oct.)

▐ **FOOD.** Salon and the surrounding region are famous for their olive trees. Olives, olive oil, and fresh produce can be bought at one of the **markets.** (Tu 8am-12:15pm on av. de Wertheim, W 7:30am-12:30pm at pl. Morgan, F 7:30am-12:15pm on av. du Dauphiné, Sa 8am-12:15pm at les Bressons, and Su 8am-12:30pm at pl. du Général de Gaulle.) Market-less Mondays may force you into the **Petit Casino,** rue des frères Kennedy. (Open 7:30am-12:20pm and 3:30-7:30pm.) Unlike the hotels, most of the typical *provençale* restaurants within the old city are distinctly pricey, running around 100F for a menu. A good deal can be found in the busy **Le Sagittaire,** 32 cours Carnot (tel. 04 90 56 29 74). Savor their *terrine du lapin* (rabbit pâté) and *entrecôte grillé* in plush Edwardian-style booths for 70F with dessert.

▐ **SIGHTS.** In the middle of Salon's *centre ville* towers the fortified **Château de l'Emperi** (tel. 04 90 56 22 36), residence of the archbishop of Arles during the Middle Ages. Enter the Renaissance-style courtyard to visit the museum, which houses a vast and well-designed military collection, including the bed Napoleon slept in on St. Helena and a wisp of his hair. (Open July-Aug., M and W-F 10am-noon and 2-6:30pm, Tu and Sa-Su 2-6:30pm; Sept.-June M and W-F 10am-noon and 2-6pm, Tu and Sa-Su 2-6pm. 15F.) For something a little lighter, try out Salon's two wax museums. The **Musée Grevin de la Provence,** pl. des Centuries (tel. 04 90 56 36 30), is a fun way to brush up on *provençale* history and culture. The audio-tour can lead you, in seven languages, from the apocryphal arrival of a very sexy Mary Magdalene to those latter-day heros of Provence, Paul Cézanne and novelist Marcel Pagnol. (Open M-F 9am-noon and 2-6pm, Sa-Su 2-6pm. 20F.) If you're still not waxed out, mosey over to its counterpart, the **Maison de Nostradamus,** 13 rue Nostradamus (tel. 04 90 56 64 31). Housed in the former residence of the famous astrologer, this wax museum focuses on the *zeitgeist* of the late fifteenth and sixteenth centuries. Basking in the bizarreness of the flickering Zodiac room, you too may feel the urge to write obscure verse. (Open M-F 9am-noon and 2-6pm, Sa-Su afternoon only. 20F.) Groupies can find Nostradmus's **tomb** in the **Église St-Laurent** at the end of rue du Maréchal Joffre. Salon's other attraction is the **Musée de Salon de Provence et de La Crau** (tel. 04 60 56 28 37), which presents *provençale* craftwork and the natural history of the region. (Open M and W-F 10am-noon and 2-6pm, Tu and Sa-Su 2-6pm; July-Aug. 10am-noon and 2-6:30pm. 15F.) As you pass through the **Porte du Bourg Neuf,** don't miss the **Black Madonna and Child,** venerated by pregnant women in the late Middle Ages.

■ **FESTIVALS.** In mid-July the city shakes up with the **International Jazz Festival,** followed by the new **Gospel Festival** at the end of the month. Festivals abound in August with the **Festival de Musique de Chambre a l'Emperi** in the first week, the **Fiesta du Jazz dans la rue** in the second week, and the **Festival of the Olive** at the end of the month. Contact the tourist office (tel. 04 90 56 27 60) for further information.

AVIGNON

No wallflower, the city of Avignon (pop. 100,000) has danced with cultural and artistic brilliance since it snatched the papacy away from Rome some 700 years ago. Political dissent in Italy led French native Clement V to shift the Holy See to Avignon in 1309. During this "Second Babylonian Captivity of the Church," as it was dubbed by the stunned Romans, seven popes erected and expanded Avignon's Palais des Papes, a sprawling Gothic fortress, making the city a "Rome away from Rome." In 1377, Gregory XI returned the papacy to Rome, but his reform-minded Italian successor so infuriated the cardinals that they elected an alternate pope, who again set up court in Avignon, beginning the Great Schism. In 1403 the last "anti-pope" abandoned the luxurious ecclesiastical buildings, but the town remained Papal territory until the Revolution.

Stendhal may have described Avignon as "the city of pretty women," but it is chiefly known for its famous Festival d'Avignon, a celebration of theater *extraordinaire.* From early July until early August, this friendly town is animated by performers who roam the streets eager to steal both your heart and the show. Hotel and restaurant prices soar, accommodations become scarce, and authorities crack down on festival-induced vagrancy. Although Avignon calms down when the bards and players depart, a combination of sights, festivals, street performers, and plenty of young people continue to make Avignon an excellent base from which to explore the Alpilles (p. 263) and the Lubéron (p. 260).

ORIENTATION AND PRACTICAL INFORMATION

Avignon's 14th-century ramparts enclose a labyrinth of alleyways, cramped streets, and squares. To reach the tourist office from the train station, walk straight through porte de la République onto cours Jean Jaurès. The tourist office is about 200m up, on the right. Cours Jean Jaurès becomes rue de la République and leads directly to the pl. de l'Horloge, Avignon's central square. At night, lone travelers should avoid the area around rue Thiers and rue Philonarde. In addition, Avignon harbors many car thieves and pickpockets, especially during the festival.

Trains: Porte de la République (tel. 04 90 27 81 70). To: **Arles** (30min., 10 per day, 35F); **Nimes** (30min., 28 per day, 46F); **Montpellier** (1hr., 35 per day, 78F); **Marseille** (70min., 11 per day, 91F); **Lyon** (2hr., 17 per day, 149F); **Paris** (3½hr., 21 per day, 342-426F); **Nice** (3½hr., 11 per day, 203F); **Toulouse** (3½hr., 6 per day, 203F); and **Dijon** (4hr., 11 per day, 238F). Info desk open M-Sa 9am-6:15pm.

Buses: Bd. St-Roch, right of the *gare*. Info desk (tel. 04 90 82 07 35) open M-F 8am-noon and 1:30-6pm, Sa 9am-noon. **Cartreize** (tel. 06 07 76 67 94) to **Marseille** (2½hr., 4 per day, 91F). **Ceyte** (tel. 04 90 93 74 90) to **Arles** (45min., at least 4 per day, 40F). **Cevennes Cars** to **Nîmes** (1hr., at least 6 per day, 42F).

Bus tours: Autocars Lieutaud (tel. 04 90 85 57 07) offers excursions to **Vaison-la-Romaine,** the **Camargue,** and **Les Baux.** Apr.-Oct. 100-150F.

Local Transportation: TCRA, porte de la République (tel. 04 90 82 68 19) or pl. Pie (tel. 04 90 85 44 93). Tickets 6.50F, *carnet* of 10 or weekly pass 50F. Office open M-F 8:15am-noon and 1:45-6:30pm, Sa 8:45am-noon.

Taxis: Radio Taxi, pl. Pie (tel. 04 90 82 20 20). 24hr.

Bike Rental: Aymard Cycles Peugeot, 80 rue Guillaume Puy (tel. 04 90 86 32 49). 60F per day, 240F per week, 1000F deposit. Open T-Sa 8am-noon and 2-7pm. **Holiday Bikes,** 41 cours Jean Jaurès (tel. 04 90 27 92 61), next to the tourist office. 60-120F per day, 255-520F per week. 1000-3000F deposit. Open Apr.-Oct. M-Sa 9am-6:30pm and Su 9am-5pm. Rest of the year will deliver. V, MC, AmEx.

Tourist Office: 41 cours Jean Jaurès (tel. 04 90 82 65 11; fax 04 90 82 95 03; www.avignon-tourisme.com). Pick up the helpful *guide pratique* and the bimonthly *Rendez-Vous,* which lists all cultural events. Open Apr.-Sept. M-F 9am-1pm and 2-6pm, Sa-Su 9am-1pm and 2-5pm; Oct.-Mar. closed Su; during festival M-F 10am-7pm and Sa-Su 10am-5pm. **Annex** at pont St-Bénezet. Open Apr.-Sept. daily 9am-6:30pm; Oct. and Mar. 9am-1pm and 2-5pm; Nov.-Feb. Tu-Su 9am-1pm and 2-5pm. **Bureau du Festival,** 8bis rue de Mons (tel. 04 90 27 66 50), has festival info. Reservations start mid-June.

City tour: Les Trains Touristiques (tel. 04 90 82 64 44), in front of the Palais. 35min. city tours and shorter garden tours of the Rocher des Doms. (Daily Mar.-Oct. 10am-7pm. City tours every 35min., 35F. Gardens every 15min., 10F. 20% off with Pass.)

English Bookstore: Shakespeare Bookshop and Tearoom, 155 rue Carreterie (tel. 04 90 27 38 50), down rue Carnot towards the ramparts and the squash club. Sink into a paperback (from 20F) and an English cream tea (tea, 3 scones, jam and cream, 25F) in this haven for homesick anglophones. Open Tu-Sa 9:30am-12:30pm and 2-6:30pm.

Cultural Centers: Centre Franco-Américain de Provence, 10 montée de la Tour, in Ville-neuve (tel. 04 90 25 93 23; across Pont Daladier, or take bus #10). All nationalities welcome. Cultural exchanges, *au pair* stays, language courses, and the French-American Film Workshop. Open M-Sa 9am-noon and 2-6pm by appointment only. **Espace Info-Jeunes,** 102 rue Carreterie (tel. 04 90 14 04 05; fax 04 90 27 02 90). Help with housing, info on jobs, study, and work abroad. Open M-F 9am-noon and 2-5:30pm.

Laundromat: Laverie La Fontaine, on pl. des Corps Saints. Open daily 7am-8pm.

Police: Bd. St-Roch (tel. 04 90 16 81 00), left of the train station.

Hospital: Hôpital de la Durance, 305 rue Raoul Follereau (tel. 04 90 80 33 33).

Post Office: Cours Président Kennedy (tel. 04 90 27 54 00). **Currency exchange.** For Poste Restante specify Poste Restante-Avignon. Open M-F 8am-7pm, Sa 8am-noon. **Branch office** on pl. Pie (tel. 04 90 14 70 70). Open M-F 8:30am-12:30pm and 1:30-6:30pm, Sa 8am-12:30pm. **Postal code:** main office 84000.

Internet Access: Cyberdrome, 68 rue Guillaume Puy (tel. 04 90 16 05 15). Ultra-cool café with 15 stations and games. 50F per hr. Open M-Sa 7am-1am, Su 2pm-1am.

◤ ACCOMMODATIONS AND CAMPING

Outside festival season, Avignon's hotels and *foyers* usually have room, but unreserved beds vanish once the theater troops come to town. The tourist office has a list of organizations that set up inexpensive accommodations during the Festival, or you might consider staying in Tarascon, Arles, Orange, or Nîmes and commuting by train (23F, 35F, 29F, and 46F respectively). Note that all hotels and campsites sell reduced admission tickets to the *Palais*.

Foyer YMCA/UCJG, 7bis chemin de la Justice (tel. 04 90 25 46 20; fax 04 90 25 30 64; email ymca@avignon.packwan.net), in Villeneuve. From the *gare* turn left and follow the city wall; cross the second bridge (pont Daladier). After another 200m take a left onto chemin de la Justice; it will be up the hill on your left parallel to a *boulangerie* (30min.). From the post office, take bus #10 (direction "Les Angles-Grand Angles") to "Général Leclerc" or #11 (direction "Villeneuve-Grand Terme") to "Pont d'Avignon." Spiffy blue rooms with terraces and fab views of the Palais. Pool. Rooms 56-150F, rates drop after the 3rd night. Breakfast 25F. Reception daily 8:30am-8pm.

Foyer Bagatelle, Île de la Barthelasse (tel. 04 90 86 30 39; fax 04 90 85 78 45). Follow directions for YMCA to pont Daladier. Cross it; Bagatelle is to the right (15min.). Or take bus #10 or 11 (same directions as YMCA) to "la Barthelasse." Nice terrace with a view of the city. Simple rooms with 6-8 beds, plus some doubles. Supermarket, cafeteria, TV room, and bike rental (70F per day with 700F deposit). 62F per night; doubles 135F. Breakfast about 20F. **Camping** facilities available 17.80-23.80F per night, 10-13F per tent. Electricity 16-18F. V, MC.

Hôtel Mignon, 12 rue Joseph Vernet (tel. 04 90 82 17 30; fax 04 90 85 78 46). On a chic street near great shopping, this cutie lives up to its name with rooms bedecked in to-dream-for beds, phones, and TV with programming in five languages. All rooms with shower. Singles 150-185F; doubles with toilet 220F, with two beds 250-300F. Breakfast 25F. Parking nearby. V, MC.

Hôtel Splendid, 17 rue Perdiguier (tel. 04 90 86 14 46; fax 04 90 85 38 55), to the right off cours Jean Jaurès, near the tourist office. On a quiet street in a busy area. TV room.

A few rooms are small but all are clean with comfy beds. All rooms with shower. Singles 120-200F; doubles 170-270F. Extra bed 20F. Breakfast 25F. V, MC.

Hôtel du Parc, 18 rue Agricol Perdiguier (tel. 04 90 82 71 55; fax 04 90 85 64 86), right off cours Jean Jaurès, near tourist office. Sweet-smelling rooms with a rustic ambiance on a sleepy street near the park. Singles 150-165F, with shower 190F, with shower and toilet 205F; doubles 165F, with shower 215F, with shower and toilet 230F; triples with shower and toilet 285F. Shower 5F. V, MC.

Innova Hôtel, 100 rue Joseph Vernet (tel. 04 90 82 54 10; fax 04 90 82 52 39). Simple, relatively safe, clean, quiet, and 3min. from everything. Singles 140F; doubles 160F, with shower and TV 180F, with shower, toilet and TV 260F. Breakfast 25F. Bike storage available. V, MC, AmEx.

Campsite: St-Bénezet, 300 Île de la Barthelasse, 10min. past Foyer Bagatelle (tel. 04 90 82 63 50; fax 04 90 85 22 12). Hot showers, laundry (wash 20F per 7kg, dry 5F), restaurant, supermarket, and tennis and volleyball courts. Grassy, shady tent sites. 18-26.50F per adults, 9-11F per child, 16-19F per tent. Reception daily mid-Mar. to Oct. 8:30am-10pm. V, MC.

🔆 FOOD

Crooked **rue des Teinturiers** hosts a smattering of vivacious restaurants. The cafés of **pl. de l'Horloge** are best suited for after-dinner drinks, when clowns, street musicians, and mimes milk crowds for smiles and centimes. **Parc de Rocher des Doms,** overlooking the Rhône, provides scenic picnic spots and has an outdoor café near the pond. Provisions await in **Les Halles,** the large indoor **market** on pl. Pie (open Tu-Su 7am-1pm), at the less expensive **open-air market** outside the city walls near porte St-Michel (Sa-Su 7am-noon), and at the **Codec supermarkets** on rue de la République (open M-Sa 8:30am-8pm).

Terre de Saveur, 1 rue St-Michel (tel. 04 90 86 68 72), near the fountain on pl. des Corps Saints. Homey *provençal* restaurant makes hearty dishes with organic vegetables. *Menus* 72F and 90F. *Plats* 38-45F. Country-style rye bread offers a change from *baguettes.* Open M-Sa 11:30am-2:30pm, during festival also 7-9:30pm.

Woolloomoolloo, 16bis rue des Teinturiers, right past the water wheel (tel. 04 90 85 28 44). Bamboo-floored terrace, candle-filled interior, and comfy pillows in a restaurant that hosts culinary and cultural theme nights and tarot card readings. Vegetarian options aplenty. Main courses run around 78F. Open daily 11:30am-2pm.

Le Cloître, 9 pl. Deschataignes (tel. 04 90 85 34 63), at the intersection of rue de la Peyrolerie at the back of Cloître St-Pierre. Friendly staff and outdoor terrace. Salad and *galette* 60F. Open M 7pm-midnight, Tu-Sa noon-2pm and 7pm-midnight. V, MC.

Gambrinus, 62 rue Carreterie (tel. 04 90 86 12 32), 200m down the street from porte St-Lazare and the Squash Club. Specializes in *moules;* huge portions with fries (45F) awash in beer-sign light. *Moules marinières* (45F) and *à la crème* (55F) taste better than *à la bière* (50F), but you be the judge. If you prefer beer in a glass, drafts are 14F. Billiards 10F. Open daily 7am-1:30am. Closed Aug. 10-25 and Jan. 1-15. V, MC.

👁 SIGHTS

Avignon has instituted a **Pass** *system for visiting multiple sights. At the first monument or museum you pay full admission (regardless of age or status), but afterwards only the reduced price. The pass is good for all the sites listed except Maison Jean Vilar, and lasts 15 days.*

PALAIS DES PAPES. Facing the Rhône across a large open square, the majestic papal palace dominates the town from its austere battlements. Begun in 1335 by the third *avignonnais* pope Benoît XII and finished less than twenty years later by his successor Clément VI, it is the most stunning fortified Gothic palace extant. Although Revolutionary looting deprived the interior of its lavish furnishings, the giant rooms and their frescoed walls still more than impress. An audio-tour in

English is included with admission. Finish off with a climb to the tower for a superb view. Each year from May to September, the Palais houses an exhibition in the most beautiful rooms. In recent years, artists have included Picasso and Rodin; call for details on the 2000 exhibition. *(Tel. 04 90 27 50 00; www.palais-des-papes.com. Open daily May-June and Oct. 9am-7pm; July 9am-9pm; Aug.-Sept. 9am-8pm; Nov.-Mar. 9:30am-5:45pm. Last ticket 1hr. before closing. Palace and Exhibition separately each 45F, Pass 36F; together 55F, Pass 46F.)*

PONT ST-BÉNÉZET. This 12th-century bridge is known to all French children as the "Pont d'Avignon" immortalized in the French nursery rhyme. Legend has it that in 1177 Bénézet, a local shepherd boy, was commanded to build the bridge by angels; a series of miracles persuaded doubting townspeople to believe him and the bridge was finished by 1190. Despite the divinely-chosen location, the bridge has suffered a number of destructive setbacks thanks to warfare and the unruly Rhône, and today stretches only partway across the river. Housed on one of its four surviving arches is the **St-Nicolas Chapel,** dedicated to the patron saint of mariners. You can enjoy the bridge from the river banks; it costs 17F (pass 13F) to dance on it. *(Open daily May-Sept. 9am-7pm; Oct.-Mar. 9:30am-5:30pm.)* Further down the river, **Pont Daladier** makes it all the way across the river to the campgrounds and offers free views of the broken bridge and the Palais.

MAISON JEAN VILAR. Dedicated to the founder of the Festival, Avignon's affinity for the world of theater shines through just off pl. de l'Horloge. Has info about the history of theater festivals and *les arts du spectacle* in general. Video and audio recordings of performances, workshops, and lectures are open to the public, as is an elaborate exhibition of international costumes. *(8 rue de Mons. Tel. 04 90 86 59 64. Open Sept.-July Tu-F 9am-noon and 1:30-5:30pm, Sa 10am-5pm. Admission 26F.)*

OTHER SIGHTS. Avignon continued to prosper after the papacy finally left. Visit the elegant 18th-century *hôtel particulier* of the **Musée Calvet,** where you can ogle paintings by Manet, Raphaël, and Gericault, and a hall's worth of memorable marble sculptures. *(65 rue Joseph Vernet. Tel. 04 90 86 33 84. Open W-M 10am-1pm and 2-6pm. Admission 30F, Pass 15F.)* A 19th century *hôtel* houses the decorative arts collection of the **Musée Louis Vouland.** *(17 rue Victor Hugo. Tel. 04 90 86 03 79. Open June-Sept. Tu-Sa 10am-noon and 2-6pm; Oct.-May Tu-Sa 2-6pm. Admission 20F, Pass 10F.)* Other wonders can be glimpsed in the **Musée Lapidaire,** which displays Gallo-Roman statuary and stone carvings in a Baroque chapel. *(27 rue de la République. Tel. 04 90 85 75 38. Open W-M 10am-1pm and 2-6pm. Admission 10F, Pass 5F.)* Once home to cardinals, the **Musée du Petit Palais** (tel. 04 90 86 44 58), at the end of pl. du Palais, has a fine Italian primitive, Gothic, and Renaissance art collection. Botticelli's famous *La Vierge et l'Enfant* hides hauntingly in a corner. *(Open July-Aug. W-M 10:30am-6pm; Sept.-June 9:30am-noon and 2-6pm. Admission 30F, Pass 15F. Oct.-Mar. free on Su.)* Next to the Palais sits the 12th-century **Cathédrale Notre-Dame-des-Doms,** which contains the flamboyant Gothic tomb of Pope John XXII. *(Open daily 10am-7pm.)* On the hill above the cathedral, **Le Rocher des Doms,** a beautifully sculpted park, exposes vistas of Mont Ventoux, the fortifications of Villeneuve-les-Avignon, and the famous bridge.

♫ ❋ ENTERTAINMENT AND FESTIVALS

ENTERTAINMENT. Regular performances of opera, drama, and classical music take place in the **Opéra d'Avignon,** pl. de l'Horloge (tel. 04 90 82 23 44). Rue des Teinturiers is lined with theaters that have performances from the early afternoon through the wee hours of the morning, including the **Théâtre du Chien qui Fume** at no. 75 (tel. 04 90 85 25 87). The **Théâtre du Balcon,** 38 rue Guillaume Puy (tel. 04 90 85 00 80), and the **Théâtre du Chene Noir,** 8bis rue Ste-Catherine (tel. 04 90 82 40 57), are two other busy theaters. The **Utopia Cinéma** (tel. 04 90 82 65 36), on 4 rue Escalier Ste-Anne behind the Palais des Papes, screens a wide variety of flicks in their original versions (admission 32F, 10 showings 250F). The **Maison Jean Vilar,** 8 rue de Mons (tel. 04 90 86 59 64), a theater library (see **Sights**), shows free videos.

THE SOUTHEAST

Lively bars color **pl. des Corps Saints.** Cheap suds and a major sound system draw boisterous Australians and backpackers to the **Koala Bar,** 2 pl. des Corps Saints. (Tel. 04 90 86 80 87. Beer 10F, drinks 20F. Happy Hour W and F-Sa 9-10pm.) The *discothèque* **Le Yucatan** (tel. 04 90 27 00 84) heats up summer nights in the *gare routière.* (Open F-M 11pm until you drop.) **Le Blues,** 25 rue Carnot (tel. 04 90 85 79 71), is a piano bar that mellows the crowd with great music and 30F beers. (Open daily 10pm-5am.)

FESTIVALS. Rabelais called Avignon *"la ville sonnante"* ("the ringing city") for its clanging church bells. Modern Avignon peals from early July through early August with the riotous **Festival d'Avignon,** when Gregorian chanters rub shoulders with all-night *Odyssey* readers and African dancers (admission varies by activity; some are free). The official festival, also known as the **IN,** is the most prestigious theatrical gathering in Europe and offers at least 18 different venues. (Call 04 90 14 14 26 for tickets and information. Festival tickets free-200F per event. Reservations accepted from mid-June. Tickets also on sale at venue 45 minutes before the show; students get about a 50% discount.) The cheaper and more experimental **Festival OFF** presents over 400 plays, some in English, from mid-July to early August. (OFFice on pl. du Palais. Tel. 01 48 05 26 49.) You don't need to buy a ticket to get in on the act—fun, free theater overflows into the streets during the day and particularly at night during the Festival. The Centre Franco-Américain de Provence (tel. 04 90 25 93 23) sponsors the **French-American Film Workshop** (tel. 04 90 25 93 23) in late June and early July at the Cinéma Vox. The festival showcases feature-length and short films directed by young French and American aspirants, with an occasional attention-grabbing name (admission 40F, pass for a day 300F).

VILLENEUVE-LÈS-AVIGNON

On a hill overlooking Avignon sits quiet, complacent Villeneuve-lès-Avignon ("new town by Avignon"). Founded by the French in the late 13th-century as a border town to intimidate their *provençal* neighbors, it later became the home of choice for many of the dignitaries attending the papal court, earning it the nickname "City of Cardinals." Built up around an abbey, a monastery, and a fortress, this small town is only a short walk across the river, but the change of atmosphere makes its calmer streets feel miles away. The **tourist office,** 1 pl. Charles David (tel. 04 90 25 61 33; fax 04 90 25 91 55), will help you find out what's what. (Open July-Aug. daily 8:45am-12:30pm and 2:30-6:30pm; Sept.-June M-Sa 8:45am-12:30pm and 2-6pm.) **La Chartreuse du Val de Bénédiction,** rue de la République (tel. 04 90 15 24 24), was built by Pope Innocent VI in the 14th century and is one of the largest Cartusian monasteries in France. Though it makes a grueling walk, it's a feasible bike ride. (Open daily Apr.-Sept. 9am-6:30pm; Oct.-Mar. 9:30am-5:30pm. Admission 32F, Pass 21F.) Crowning Villeneuve's hill, Mont Andaon, is the Gothic **Fort Saint-André** (tel. 04 90 25 45 35). Built by the French king Philip the Fair in the 14th century, its fortified walls and double towers were meant to remind the Pope in Avignon that he did not hold a monopoly on power. (Open daily Apr.-Sept. 10am-12:30pm and 2-6pm; Oct.-Mar. 10am-noon and 2-5pm. Admission 25F, Pass 15F.) Inside the fortress, the 11th-century Benedictine **Abbaye Saint-André** was the first major construction in the area. Although the original buildings were largely destroyed during the Revolution, the 17th-century ramparts remain, sheltering gardens with panoramic views of the Rhône. (Same hours as fort. Admission 20F, Pass 15F.) Down the hill is the **Musée Municipal Pierre de Luxembourg,** rue de la République (tel. 04 90 27 49 66), which features both 14th- and 15th-century religious works and 17th- and 18th-century *provençal* paintings. The most prominent monument visible from Avignon is the Gothic **Tour Philippe Le Bel** (tel. 04 90 27 49 68), at the intersection of av. Gabriel Péri and Montée de la Tour. Once a dungeon, its only current method of punishment is the climb to the top for a panoramic view of Avignon and the Rhône Valley. (Museum and tower open Tu-Su; June-Sept. 10am-12:30pm and 3-7pm; Oct.-May 10am-noon and 2-5:30pm. Admission 20F, Pass 12F.) Take the scenic and less exhaustive route on the **Bateau Bus,** allées de l'Oulle (tel. 04 90 85 62 25), which cruises past Pont St-Bénézet and docks at Villeneuve. (6 trips per day 10am-6:45pm. Round-trip 40F, children 20F, 20% reduction with Pass.)

THE SOUTHEAST

THE LUBÉRON AND THE VAUCLUSE

"No nature is more beautiful."

-Petrarch

Just when you thought that nothing could possibly be more picturesque than Arles or Avignon, you find a region of such stunning beauty that it leaves you gasping for breath. The Vaucluse, and the neighboring national park of the Lubéron, is where all those picture-perfect postcards of Provence come from. Tiny medieval villages perched on rocky escarpments, fields of lavender as far as the eye can see, and ochre hills that seem to burn in the sunset are a backdrop to the omnipresent *vieux papies* drinking *pastis* and playing *pétanque* in the small village squares. For centuries, this mini-eden has been a home and inspiration to writers, from Petrarch to the Marquis de Sade to Samuel Beckett. So when the *foule* of the festivals in Avignon gets too oppressive, head east.

■ **GETTING AROUND.** The complexities of traveling in the area explain why so few people, with the exception of rich Parisians in Porsches, ever get here. By far the best way to appreciate the dramatic changes in landscape is at a leisurely pace, combining the occasional bus with walking or biking between towns (around 2-10km). Locals often choose to hitch, since rides are easy to come by. **Voyages Arnaud** (tel. 04 90 38 15 58) runs buses from **Avignon** to **Isle-sur-la-Sorgue** (40min., M-Sa 10 per day, Su 5, 17F) and on to **Fontaine de Vaucluse** (55min., 3 per day, 26F). More buses (tel. 04 90 82 07 35 or 04 90 82 07 35) scoot between **Avignon** and **Apt**, stopping at **Isle-sur-la-Sorgue** and **Bonnieux** (80min., 4-5 daily). Less regular buses run between **Bonnieux** and **Cavaillon**, stopping at **Lacoste, Ménerbes,** and **Oppède-le-Vieux** (1hr.; 1 per day in summer, 2 per day during school year). A good chunk of the Lubéron could easily be covered in two days by **car**, by far the easiest way to go. Pick one up in Avignon, which is chock-full of rental companies catering to people looking for more than the Palais des Papes. The N100 highway blows right through the middle of the Lubéron park and branches off to the smaller towns, but the most picturesque route is the twisting, sometimes tortuously lean roads from one small town to the next. Expect to pay 10-15F for parking in most villages.

However you travel, good walking shoes are a must since most of the villages are hilly and not always well paved. Bring enough **cash** to tide you over, since many restaurants and some hotels do not take credit cards, and banks are scarce.

L'ISLE-SUR-LA-SORGUE

Made popular by Peter Mayle's sardonic *provençal* portrait in *Hôtel Pastis*, **l'Isle-sur-la-Sorgue** (pop. 17,000) is the first step away from the bustle of Avignon and into the true Vaucluse countryside. You can pick up a hiking map of the Vaucluse in the **tourist office** (tel. 04 90 38 04 78; fax 04 90 38 35 43), in the church on pl. de l'Église. (Open Tu-Sa 9:30am-12:30pm and 2:30-6pm.) The town's main attraction is its **open-air market,** which provides food and mirth, especially on weekends when locals haggle with the hundreds of antique dealers who flood the downtown area. (Th and Su 7:30am-1pm.)

FONTAINE DE VAUCLUSE

Though Fontaine de Vaucluse (pop. 500) is famous for its chilly spring water, its grandeur and romantic history will warm your heart. It certainly worked for the father of the sonnet. After glimpsing "Laura," the lovely young wife of an early Marquis de Sade, in an Avignon church on April 6, 1327, Petrarch spent the next two decades here composing sonnets to her. His famous work, *De Vita Solitaria*, recounts the time he spent here; the 20m **Colonne,** built in 1804 in the center of town, commemorates his life and work. Continue up chemin de la Fontaine to get to **La Source,** a turquoise lagoon with near-freezing waters that even Jacques Cousteau couldn't fathom—300m down, he still didn't get to the bottom of the waters or the mystery of their source. Once owned by the de Sades, the ruined **Château de**

QUIT HOGGING THE TRUFFLES! If you see a group of diners in a French restaurant with their napkins over their heads, don't be alarmed. They're merely savoring the delicate aroma of the most sought-out mushroom in the world—the *truffe noir*, or black truffle. Not to be confused with the belgian chocolate blobs that bear a minimal visual resemblance to them, the real, honest-to-goodness truffle is to be found growing in the roots of oak and hazelnut trees. Picked fresh, a truffle is worth its weight in gold to the gastronomically obsessed. Why so *cher?* The truffle lurks hidden underground and defies systematic cultivation. Fortunately, nature has provided the French with the truffle-hunter *par excellence*. Pigs, which are attracted to the sexy odor emitted by the truffle, can snuffle out these delicacies in no time, and a good truffle-hunter is worth far more than his bacon. The biggest problem is making off with the treasured *truffe* with a greedy pig in hot pursuit.

Saumane reveals a stunning vista; return to the Colonne, cross the river, and take the stairs to a path leading to the castle. (10min. Sturdy shoes a must. Free.)

Fontaine also offers a number of small, locally-oriented museums down by the riverside. Just over the bridge and through a vaulted passageway is the small **Musée Petrarque** (tel. 04 90 20 37 20), which displays a collection of books and prints on the picturesque spot where Petrarch probably lived. (Open mid-Apr. to mid-Oct. W-M 10am-noon and 2-6pm. Admission 20F, students 10F.) On the other side of the river is a reconstruction of a **paper mill** and the **Musée du Santon** (tel. 04 90 20 20 83), which has an extensive collection of the little clay figurines so typical of Provence. (Mill open M-Sa 9am-12:20pm and 2-6:50pm, Su 10am-12:20pm and 2-6:50pm. Free. Musée du Santon open daily 10am-12:30pm and 2-6pm. 20F, students 10F.) Speleologists will get their thrills in the underground tours by the **Musée Norbert Casteret**. (Tel. 04 90 20 34 13. Open daily Apr.-Aug. 10am-noon and 2-6pm, tours every 30min.; Sept.-Nov. and Feb.-Mar 11am-1pm and 3-5pm, tours 1 per hour. 30F; under 12 20F.) Across the street is the sobering and reflective **Musée d'histoire 1939-1945** (tel. 04 90 20 24 00), with multi-disciplinary exhibitions dedicated to local life and the Resistance under the Occupation. (Open July-Aug. 10am-noon and 2-7pm; Apr. 1-June 30 and Sept. 15-Oct. 15 W-M 10am-noon and 2-6pm. 20F, students 10F, under 12 free.)

There is a **post office** with a rare **ATM** up the street from the Colonne, away from the river. (Open M-F 9am-noon and 2-7pm, Sa 8:30-11:30am.) Across from it you'll find a **mini-market**. (Open summer M-Sa 7:15am-8:30pm and Su 8:30am-7pm.) The rural **Auberge de Jeunesse (HI)**, chemin de la Vignasse (tel. 04 90 20 31 65), is 1km from town. Follow signs from the Colonne, or ask the bus driver to let you off closer to the *auberge*. Wake to a chorus of roosters in this idyllic stone country house. (48F, camping 27F. Sheets 16F. Breakfast 19F. Laundry 20F. Kitchen access. **Members only.** Reception daily 8-10am and 5-11pm. Curfew 11:30pm. Open Feb. 15-Nov. 15.) The hostel can also offer suggestions for **hiking** in the Lubéron, especially on the nearby national hiking trails, **GR6** and **GR91**.

OPPÈDE-LE-VIEUX

Clinging to the mountainside below a ruined château and above terraced rows of lavender, this medieval village was slowly deserted in the 16th century, and it was definitively abandoned in the early 20th century for the *hameau* in the plain. All that is left in this sun-baked village are a couple of artists' studios and a tiny square, where you can grab a bite to eat at **L'Echougette** (70F *menu*, salads 23-40F, *poulet aux olives* 50F). Obligatory parking is at the foot of the village (10F). Signs will direct you to the square and after that wander up to the 11th- to 13th-century **Église Notre-Dame d'Alidon** and to the château. The view of the valley from this vantage point is superb. **Buses** drop you off in the new town on the plain, from where it's a 10- to 15-minute hike up the hill to the old village.

MÉNERBES

This is the town made famous in Peter Mayle's *A Year in Provence*. Apparently, the popular author had to leave after he kept finding fans in his swimming pool—rumor has it that he's on his way back to the region, though. Despite this fame, the village is less touristy than other areas in the Lubéron. Another magnificent view of the valleys and neighboring stone quarries awaits from the church at the top of the village. Just outside town in the direction of Cavaillon is the **Musée du Tire-Bou-chon** (tel. 04 90 72 41 58), a collection of over 1000 corks in every shape and size from the 17th century on, appropriately topped off with a *dégustation*. (Open Apr.-Sept. M-F 9am-noon and 2-7pm, Sa-Su 10am-noon and 3-7pm; Oct.-Mar. M-F 9am-noon and 2-6pm, Sa 9am-noon.) The town is even big enough to have a **post office.** (Open M-F 9am-noon and 2-5pm, Sa 8:30-11:30am. **Postal code:** 84560.)

LACOSTE

Sleepy Lacoste seems to have shaken off the demons of its past—the pictur-esquely ruined château perched above the village was home to the **Marquis de Sade** from 1774-1778, and he abducted local peasants to satisfy his sexual needs until he was finally arrested and imprisoned. The raciest thing left in the village is a group of American art students, who rush around capturing the beauty of the site. Lacoste is home to one of the few affordable accommodations in the Lubéron, the **Café de Sade.** (Tel. 04 90 75 82 29; fax 04 90 75 95 68. Dormitories 70F; doubles 230-260F, with shower 290F. Breakfast 30F. Sheets 20F. *Menus* on the terraced restau-rant from 119F. Open Tu-Su, closed Jan.) The same street offers **bike rental** (tel. 04 90 75 90 05.) A somewhat brusque restaurant, but with a fabulous view from its ivy-covered terrace, is **Restaurant Loofoc** (tel. 04 90 75 89 76). A delightful place for lunch, their *formule rapide* costs 70F, and salads start at 45F. (Open daily for lunch and dinner, except Sa lunch. Closed Jan.-Feb.) There is also a **post office.** (Open M-F 9am-noon and 2-5pm, Sa 8:30am-12:30pm.) Nearby, a **market** is held on Tuesdays.

BONNIEUX

Yet another charming hillside town, but this time livelier and better-preserved than Lacoste or Oppède-le-Vieux. Bright flowers burst out of the balconies and windows of the stone houses. The panorama from the top of the town is worth the climb. *Baguette*-lovers mustn't miss the **Musée de la Boulangerie,** 12 rue de la République (tel. 04 90 75 88 34), which traces the history of French bread-making in a 17th-century bakery. (Open Apr.-Sept. W-M 10am-noon and 3-6:30pm. 20F, stu-dents 10F.) The **tourist office** (tel. 04 90 75 91 90) is located in the center of town. (Open Apr.-Oct. Tu-Sa 10:30am-12:30pm and 2:30-6:30pm.) Stave off hunger pangs at the **épicerie,** pl. Gambetta off rue Victor Hugo. (Open 8:30am-12:30pm and 3:30-6:30pm.) For **taxis,** call 04 90 75 85 98. You can camp at **Le Vallon** (tel. 04 90 75 91 90), 1km from town towards Ménerbes. (13F, children 7.50F. Electricity 15.50F. Tent 10.50F. Car 8.50F. Open mid-Mar.-mid-Nov.)

LOURMARIN

Situated on a plain at the entrance to the Lubéron range, this village is the final resting place of Albert Camus. Lourmarin also offers a glorious Renaissance châ-teau (tel. 04 90 68 15 23), where concerts and art exhibits are put up annually. Claiming to be the first Renaissance château in Provence, it was restored in the early 20th century and filled with 16th- to 18th-century furnishings. There are six obligatory guided tours every day in French with English documentation. (Open 10am-noon and 2:30-5:30pm.) The road from Bonnieux to Lourmarin is a beautiful but tricky drive down twisting roads and through dramatic rock formations. Just before town is the **Hostellerie du Paradou** (tel. 04 90 68 04 50; fax 04 90 08 54 94). Pricey but worth a splurge, it offers extensive gardens, a lovely terraced restau-rant, comfortable rooms, and friendly owners. Demi-pension (breakfast and din-ner) is obligatory but delicious. (Singles 440-480F, doubles 550-590F. MC, V.)

THE SOUTHEAST

ROUSSILLON

The most famous of the ochre villages, this is an un-missable stop even in this un-missable region. Playwright Samuel Beckett twiddled his thumbs here during the war, and the town was the inspiration behind Laurence Wylie's "Village in the Vaucluse." The site itself can been seen long before entering the village as the reddish-orange walls contrast wildly with the lush, green countryside. Take a peek at the village before checking out the **Sentier des Ochres,** where you can walk through a vast, dusty ochre deposit. White shoes and clothing are a bad idea. (Open daily 10am-6pm. 10F.) The **tourist office** in the center of town is open M-Sa 10am-noon and 2-6:30pm, with **currency exchange** 10-11:30am and 2-6pm.

GORDES

Perhaps the most picturesque of the hillside towns, Gordes is famous for its restored *bories*, drystone huts with pointed roofs often seen in the middle of provençal poppy fields. Their origins are pre-Roman, but they were built and used up until the mid-19th century. The **château** in the middle of town was originally a 12th-century fortress but was renovated in the 16th century. It houses a collection of 200 modern paintings in the **Musée Pol Mara.** (Open W-Sa and M 10am-noon and 2-6pm, Su 2-6pm.) The **tourist office** (tel. 04 90 72 02 75) is also in the château. (Open daily summer 9am-12:30pm and 2-6:30pm; winter 10am-noon and 2-6pm.) There's even an **ATM** in the *place* in front of it. **Sénanque Abbey** (tel. 04 90 72 05 72), an active Cistercian community famous for the fields of lavender which surround it, is 4km away from Gordes. The site was occupied by monks from 1148 until the Revolution and then re-populated and restored in the mid-19th century. You can buy the honey, lavender products, and *sénacole*, a liqueur produced by the monks in the abbey, which is also accessible to visitors. (Open Mar.-Oct. daily 10am-noon and 2-6pm, except Su mornings; Nov.-Feb. M-F 2-5pm, Sa-Su 2-6pm. Closed on church holidays. 25F, under 18 10F.)

THE ALPILLES

Caught between the thespian orations in Avignon and the clattering of camera shutters in Arles, the quiet hills of the Alpilles and their outlying towns await the attention they once commanded from prominent artists and authors. Vincent van Gogh spent the last year of his life painting the rugged beauty of the mini-mountain range from the asylum he had chosen in St-Rémy, while Tarascon's sleepy charm remains as authentic as when Alphonse Daudet immortalized it in *Tartarin de Tarascon*. From their eagle's perch in Les Baux, a mighty warrior family ruled over much of Provence during the Middle Ages, and troubadours flocked to the court in their now-ruined castle. The only poetry to the ears of many locals now is the sound of money ringing in the cash registers. While affordable accommodations can be found, the towns are very easily visited as daytrips from Arles and Avignon.

LES BAUX-DE-PROVENCE

"There is nothing terrible and savage belonging to feudal history of which an example may not be found in the annals of Les Baux."

John Addington Symonds

Les Baux-de-Provence (un-touristed pop. 458) is a magnificent site of feudal ruins, a demolished castle, and gracefully restored Renaissance homes, perched 245m up on a rocky escarpment. The powerful Baux lords traced their origins back to King Balthazar, one of the three Magi, and invoked him in their bloodthirsty war cry "Spare no-one, Balthazar!" Their regional court drew some of the finest troubadours (and a few spectacular debaucheries) until the Baux line died out in the late 14th century. It is thought that Dante came here while staying in nearby Arles, and that the tortured landscape of the *Val d'Enfer* (Valley of Hell) nearby provided the inspiration for his vision of hell in the *Inferno*. Under Anne de Montmorency and the Manville family, Les Baux regained its splendor in the 16th century, but was finally doomed when Louis XIII had its defences destroyed in 1632. Now the tiny *centre ville* has surrendered to souvenir shops, expensive ice cream stands, and cafés, all supported by over a million tourists annually. The unique and spectacular part of the town, the ruins of the **Château des Baux** (tel. 04 90 54 55 56), are carved out of the rocky mountain peak and cover an area five times that of the village below. It is a truly epic experience—those who arrive early will have the eerie treat of having the windy mountaintop, the valley, and the distant Mediterranean all to themselves. While in the château, don't miss the **Musée de l'Olivier.** Housed in a Romanesque chapel, Chopin accompanies a slide-show collection of van Gogh's and Cézanne's depictions of olive trees. (Open daily July-Aug. 9am-8:45pm; Sept.-Feb. 9am-6pm; Mar.-June 9am-5:30pm. 36F, students 28F, ages 7-17 22F.)

The **Fondation Louis Jou,** rue Frédéric Mistral (tel. 04 90 54 34 17), commemorates Les Baux's favorite son with major works by the local print-maker as well as engravings by Dürer and Goya. (Open only under group reservation. Admission 20F, students 10F.) An interesting and intimate portrait of an artist can be found at the **Musée Yves Brayer** (tel. 04 90 54 36 99), at the intersection of rue de l'Église and rue de la Calade. (Open daily Apr.-Sept. 10am-12:30pm and 2-6:30pm; Oct.-Dec. and mid-Feb.-Mar. 10am-12:30pm and 2-5pm. 25F, ages 15-19 15F, under 15 free.)

Les Baux gave its name to bauxite, the mineral from which aluminum is extracted and which was first discovered here in 1822. Just down the road from the old and new towns, an old bauxite mine has been converted into the **Cathédrale d'Images** (tel. 04 90 54 38 65). From the bus stop, continue down the hill, turn right at the crossroads, and follow the sign (10min.). Into this man-made cave, tens (if not hundreds) of projectors splash images from above, below, and all around. As you navigate the cavernous canvas, accompanying music will cool your soul, while the rocks cool your body (dress warmly!). Created by Albert Plécy in 1977, the *cathédrale* presents other caves with changing modern art exhibits. Shows change seasonally, so call to ask what's playing. (Open daily Mar.-Sept. 10am-7pm; Oct.-Feb.10am-6pm. 43F, students 38F, children 27F.)

Mas de la Fontaine (tel. 04 90 54 34 13) offers seven lovely rooms in a traditional *maison provençale*. At the foot of the village, it exudes quiet with its garden and pool. (Doubles 245-305F; triples 387F. Extra bed 62F. Breakfast 35F. Cash only. Open late Mar.-late Oct.) Most backpackers bring picnics to the Cité Morte; it's best to stock up before you come, but you can buy supplies at the small *épicerie* in the parking lot. Panini stands and *crêperies* abound. The **tourist office** in the Hôtel de Ville (tel. 04 90 54 34 39), about halfway up the hill between the parking lot and the Cité Morte, gives out a free map. (Open daily May-Oct. 9am-7pm.; Nov.-Dec. and Feb.-Mar. 9am-6pm; Dec.-Jan. 9am-5pm.) The **post office** (tel. 04 90 54 34 00) **exchanges currency** at decent rates. (Open M-F 10am-noon and 2-5pm, Sa 9-11am.) **Buses** to Les Baux run regularly from **Arles** (30min., M-Sa 4 per day, 28.50F). Contact **CTM,** 21 chemin du Temple, Arles (tel. 04 90 93 74 90).

TARASCON

The small city of Tarascon (pop. 12,000) is intimately linked to *provençal* folklore. First there was the *Tarasque*, an ur-creature from the black lagoon (actually the Rhône) who terrorized children and livestock by night. Legend has it that St. Martha finally domesticated the beast with the sign of the cross. For four days over the last weekend of June, a replica of the monster is paraded through the town accompanied by concerts, bullfights, horse shows, and folkloric events. Less happily for the locals, Tarascon inspired Alphonse Daudet's biting attack on provincial *provençals* in his novel *Tartarin*. Don't let the stereotype deter you, though. Tarascon's proximity to Arles (17km), Avignon (23km), and Nîmes (25km) makes it an easy daytrip or a good fallback if festivals clog the bigger cities' lodgings.

◪ **PRACTICAL INFORMATION.** You can get to Tarascon by **train** from **Arles** (10min., at least 6 per day, 17F) or **Avignon** (10min., at least 10 per day, 23F). **Cevennes Cars** (tel. 04 66 29 27 29) sends buses from in front of the *gare* to **Avignon**

(30min., M-Sa 4-5 per day, Su 2 per day, 24F) and **St-Rémy** (25min., 3 per day, 18F). **Station Total,** bd. Jules Ferry (tel. 04 90 91 13 90), **rents bikes.** (70F per day, 300F per week. Credit card or 1000F deposit.) From the *gare*, walk across the courtyard and turn left on cours Aristide Briand; walk two minutes, and rue des Halles will be on your right. The **tourist office,** 59 rue des Halles (tel. 04 90 91 03 52), is eager to help. Ask for the free *guide touristique.* (Open Apr.-Dec. M-Sa 9am-12:30pm and 2-6pm; Apr.-Oct. Su 10am-noon also; Jan.-Mar. closed Sa.) The banks along cours Aristide Briand **exchange currency.** If your clothes are standing up by themselves, hit the **Washmatic** on cours Aristide Briand. (17F for 7kg wash, 5F to dry. Open M-F 8am-noon and 2:30-7pm, Sa 8am-noon.) The **post office** (tel. 04 90 91 52 00) is to the left of the train station. (Open M-F 8:30am-5:30pm, Sa 9am-12:30pm. **Postal code:** 13150.)

▐ ACCOMMODATIONS. The **Auberge de Jeunesse (HI),** 31 bd. Gambetta (tel. 04 90 91 04 08), is roomy and has comfortable beds in 8- to 12-bed dorms, kitchen facilities, a secure bike area, and free parking. From the *gare*, turn right and follow the tracks until you reach bd. Victor Hugo. Cross the street and follow the path between the tracks and wall for 20m, turning left on the next major road. The hostel is another five minutes further, on your left near a phone booth. Reservations are accepted through email (tarascon@fuaj.org), but this gem of a hostel is rarely full. (48F per night. 19F breakfast obligatory first morning. Kitchen facilities available. Reception Mar. 2-Dec. 14 7:30-10am and 5:30-11pm. Lockout 10am-5:30pm.) **Hôtel du Viaduc,** 9 rue du Viaduc (tel. 04 90 91 16 67), has clean, cozy rooms. Popular with cyclists, it offers a locked bike area and free parking. (Singles 100F, with shower and toilet 130F; doubles 100-150F. Shower 10F. All-you-can-eat breakfast 25F.) **Camp** at **Tartarin,** bd. du Roy René (tel. 04 90 91 01 46), next to the castle, has a bar, snack stand, free showers, and lots of shade. (20F per person, 18F per place, 10F per car. Electricity 16F. Open Mar.-Oct.)

🏛 SIGHTS. The imposing 15th-century **Château de Tarascon** (tel. 04 90 91 01 93), on the wedge of the Rhône river, was a luxurious fortress built on the remains of a Romanesque castle by Louis II of Anjou and finished under King René. Having seen so few years of warfare, and having been maintained as a prison for centuries, the castle is in fantastic condition. Surrounded by a swampy moat, it boasts a lovely *provençal* garden, graffiti from the Middle Ages, an apothecary, an ornate courtyard, a set of stunning tapestries, and frequent art exhibitions. The climb to the roof is well worth it; from here, there is a picture-perfect view of its rival, the ruined Château de Beaucaire, across the river. (Open daily Apr.-Sept. 9am-7pm; Oct.-Mar. 9am-noon and 2-5pm. Admission 32F, ages 12-25 21F, under 12 free.) The **Collegiale Royale Sainte-Marthe** (tel. 04 90 91 09 50), with an austere Romanesque portal and elegant Gothic nave, is just across the street. St. Martha's remains allegedly lie in the crypt which can be peered at through thick iron bars. (Open 8am-noon and 2-6pm. Free.)

ST-RÉMY

Like Arles, its neighbor to the south, St-Rémy has a healthy smattering of Roman remnants and traces of Van Gogh. When the asylum let him out on good behavior, Vincent often ambled southward to the ruins of ancient Glanum.

The sights of St-Rémy center on two areas. The *centre ville* hosts the **Centre d'Art Présence van Gogh** within the Hôtel Estrine, 8 rue Estrine (tel. 04 90 92 34 72). Although lacking authentic *tableaux*, the museum excites with an ever-changing exhibit on different segments of Vincent's work, a graceful and compelling audio-visual presentation on his time here, and a rotating exhibit featuring modern artists. (Open Apr.-Dec. Tu-Su 10:30am-12:30pm and 2:30-6:30pm. Admission 20F, students 15F.) Also in the *centre ville*, the 15th-century **l'Hôtel de Stade,** rue de Parage (tel. 04 90 92 64 04; fax 04 90 92 64 02), houses all the best finds from nearby Glanum, including amazingly preserved glass work. (Open July-Aug. daily 10am-noon and 2-6pm; Apr.-Sept. Tu-Su same hours; Oct.-Dec. and Feb.-Mar. Tu-Su closes 5pm. 15F, 36F for both museum and Glanum.) **Glanum** lies nearly 1km south of the *centre ville*, past the tourist office on av. Vincent Van Gogh (15 min.). The capital of the Glaniques, a Celto-Ligurian tribe at the end of the 3rd century, the ruins provide a fascinating insight into the hybrid Gallo-Roman culture which emerged in Provence. Dedicated to Cybele, the Mother Goddess, the town prospered as a stop on the main ancient road *(Via Domitia)* linking Spain to Italy. (Open daily Apr.-Sept. 9am-7pm; Oct.-Mar. 9am-noon and 2-5pm. 32F, students 21F.) Standing in solitary splendor across the street are the well-preserved **Antiques,** a commemorative arch and mausoleum built during Augustus's reign. Also nearby, you can check out or into the monastery and invalids' home of **Saint-Paul de Mausole,** chemin des Carrières. It was here that van Gogh interned himself for the last year of his life. (Open Tu-Su 9:15am-6:15pm. 15F, students 10F.)

Whit Sunday (June 11, 2000) brings a veritable stampede of farm animals—mostly sheep—through the *centre ville* during the **Fête de la Traushumance,** a celebration of provençal migration traditions. The **Carreto Rondado,** a procession representing the local produce of St-Rémy, and the big **Féria Provençale,** where bulls are teased but not killed, take place around August 15th. See the *Patrimonie* handbook of St-Rémy for tons of cultural info.

Restaurants are pricey, but you can still partake of a filling lunch or dessert *crêpe* (22-42F) at **Crêperie Lou Planet,** 7 pl. Favier (tel. 04 90 92 19 81), near the statue of Nostradamus, a native of St-Rémy. (Open Tu-Su 11am-2pm and 6-11pm.) Just across the road is a **Coccinelle Marché.** (Open M-Sa 8am-12:30pm and 3:30-7:30pm, Su 8:30am-noon.) To take in the same vistas Vincent did, get the pamphlet which includes *"sur les pas de Vincent van Gogh"* from the **tourist office,** pl. Jean Jaurès (tel. 04 90 92 05 22; fax 04 90 92 38 52). From the bus stop, walk up av. Durand Maillane; the tourist office will be on the left next to the police station. Ask about guided tours in English (35F). (Open June-Sept. M-Sa 9am-noon and 2-7pm, Su 9am-noon; Oct.-Mar. M-Sa 9am-noon and 2-6pm.)

Buses (tel. 04 90 14 59 00) make the trek from **Tarascon** (25min., 3 per day, 16.50F) and **Avignon** (45min., M-Sa at least 7 per day, 32F).

ARLES

Just south of the Rhône's split into the Grand and Petit branches, times gone by collide in splendor within present-day Arles (pop. 35,000). The ghosts of the past live on in Arles, where their footsteps have left enduring impressions. Listening intently, one can hear the strokes of a paint-laden brush hitting blank canvas, the final, gurgling gasps of a beast giving up hope and spirit in the Roman arena, or the meditative chants of monks echoing through the *cloître*. Van Gogh spent two years (and left an ear) here capturing stunning vistas on his *tableaux*, while the passions of the bullfights lured Picasso and induced his benevolent donation of drawings to the city. Today, the international photography festival attracts both amateurs and professionals and transforms the city's halls, museums, nooks, and crannies into an inexhaustible exhibit. With the hills of the Alpilles (p. 263) and the wildlife and beaches of the Camargue (p. 271) close by, daytrips are a delight for those who can tear themselves away from Arles.

■ ORIENTATION AND PRACTICAL INFORMATION

Arles snuggles up to the Rhône on its northwestern side with the *gare* in the north, the tourist office in the south, and the heart of the *vieille ville* in between.

Trains: Av. P. Talabot. To: **Avignon** (30min., M-Sa 13 per day, 35F); **Nîmes** (30min., M-Sa 6 per day, 41F); **Marseille** (1hr., M-Sa 8 per day, 71F); and **Montpellier** (1hr., M-Sa 5 per day, 74F).

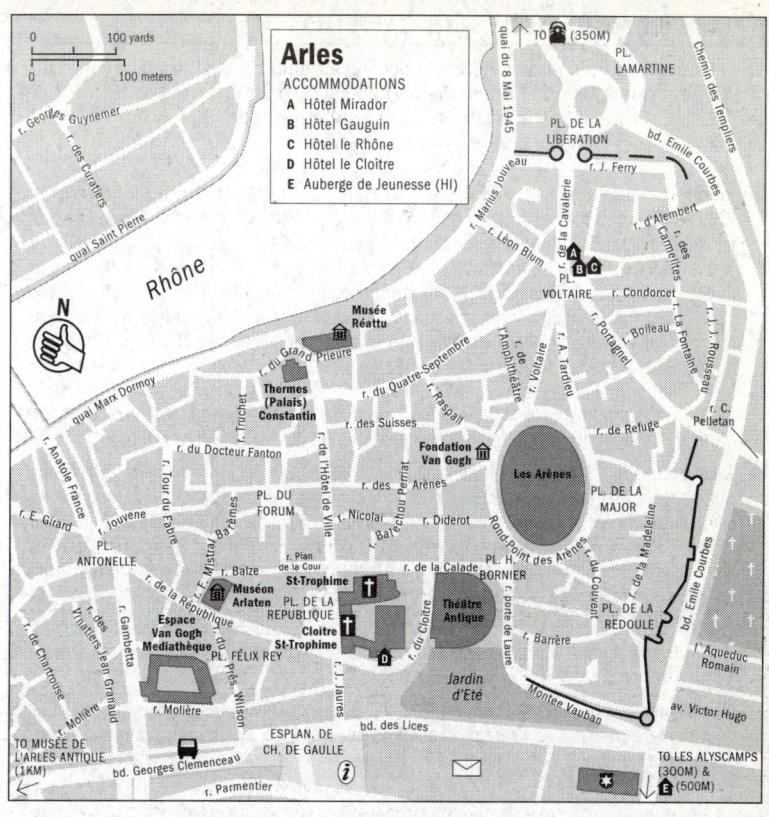

Arles
ACCOMMODATIONS
A Hôtel Mirador
B Hôtel Gauguin
C Hôtel le Rhône
D Hôtel le Cloître
E Auberge de Jeunesse (HI)

THE SOUTHEAST

Buses: Av. P. Talabot (tel. 04 90 49 38 01). Desk open M-F 6:45am-7:30pm, Sa 6:45am-noon. **Les Cars de Camargue,** 4 rue Jean-Mathieu-Artaud (tel. 04 90 96 36 25), run to **Nîmes** (50min., M-Sa 5 per day, 34F). **Cars Ceyte et Fils** and **CTM,** 21 chemin du Temple (tel. 04 90 93 74 90), go to **Avignon** (45min., M-Sa 4 per day, 40F).

Taxis: A.A.A. Arles Taxis (tel. 04 90 93 31 16); **Arles Taxis Radio** (tel. 04 90 96 90 03).

Tourist Office: Esplanade Charles de Gaulle (tel. 04 90 18 41 20; fax 04 90 18 41 29). Turn left outside the station and walk to pl. Lamartine; after the Monoprix turn left down bd. Émile Courbes. After 10min., cross the street and turn right onto bd. des Lices. The office is 2 minutes down on the left. Accommodations service 5F plus down payment. Open Apr.-Sept. daily 9am-7pm; Oct.-Mar. M-Sa 9am-6pm, Su 10am-noon. **Branch** in the *gare* (tel. 04 90 49 36 90) open July-Aug. daily 9am-7pm.

Money: Arène Change, 22bis rond-point des Arènes, takes no commission. Open W-M 9:30am-12:45pm and 2:30-6:45pm.

Laundromat: Lincoln Laverie, 6 rue de la Cavalerie. Open daily 7am-9pm.

Police: Bd. des Lices (tel. 04 90 18 45 00). **PAVIP,** 33 rue de la République (tel. 04 90 96 01 19), for victims of theft and aggression.

Hospital: Centre Hospitalier J. Imbert, quartier Fourchon (tel. 04 90 49 29 29).

Post Office: 5 bd. des Lices (tel. 04 90 18 41 00). **Currency exchange.** Open M-F 8:30am-7pm, Sa 8:30am-noon. **Postal code:** 13200.

■ ACCOMMODATIONS AND CAMPING

Arles teems with inexpensive hotels, especially around rue de l'Hôtel de Ville and pl. Voltaire. Note that hotel prices do not include the municipal residency tax (5F per person per night). Reservations are crucial during the photography festival and should often be made a month or two in advance.

Auberge de Jeunesse (HI), av. Maréchal Foch (tel. 04 90 96 18 25; fax 04 90 96 31 26), 10min. from the town center and 20min. from the station. Take the purple line bus #5 from bd. Émile Courbes, opposite Monoprix, to "Bigot" (last bus 7pm; 5.20F). If you're walking from the *gare,* follow the directions to the tourist office, but instead of turning on bd. des Lices, cross it and continue down av. des Alyscamps; follow the signs. Near the municipal pool and cinema. Modern with a quiet garden, but malodorous toilets. Personal lockers. Horrible rate of **currency exchange.** 100 beds in 8-bed dorms. 80F, breakfast included. Dinner 48F on nights when there are groups eating. Bar open until midnight. Reception daily 7-10am and 5pm-midnight. Lockout 10am-5pm. Curfew 11:30pm normally, 1-2am during the festivals. **Bike rental** 70F per day (500F deposit). Reserve by letter, fax, or through the internet. Call ahead Apr.-June.

 Hôtel Le Cloître, 16 rue du Cloître (tel. 04 90 96 29 50; fax 04 90 96 02 88). Pricey but worth it, this two-star hotel has a great location in the old town. The friendly young owners have a variety of comfortable rooms built on 12th-century vaults that were once part of the Cloître St-Trôphime; rear rooms look right down into the cloister. Doubles with shower 250F, with shower and toilet 270F; triples with shower and toilet 360F. Breakfast 34F. Parking 30F. TV 20F. English spoken. V, MC, AmEx.

Hôtel Gauguin, 5 pl. Voltaire (tel. 04 90 96 14 35; fax 04 90 18 98 87). This great value, two-star hotel has sweet-smelling rooms with telephones. Doubles with shower 160-180F; twins with shower and toilet 220F; triples 260F. Breakfast 25F. V, MC.

Hôtel Mirador, 3 rue Voltaire (tel. 04 90 96 28 05; fax 04 90 96 59 89). Impeccable, with modern rooms with TVs and phones. Pleasant lobby, lounge, and breakfast area. Singles and doubles with shower 190F, shower and toilet 240F, bath and toilet 260F. Extra bed 60F. Breakfast 28F. Parking 40F. V, MC, AmEx.

Hôtel le Rhône, 11 pl. Voltaire (tel. 04 90 96 43 70; fax 04 90 93 87 03). A cozy hotel with eager owners and an adorable breakfast room. Smallish rooms with modern bathrooms. Pl. Voltaire can be lively at night; ask for a room facing a quiet side street. Doubles 130-190F, with shower 170F, with shower and toilet 210F; twins with 1 big and 1 small bed 170-200F, with shower 210F, with shower and toilet 240F. V, MC, AmEx.

Campsites: The closest is **Camping-City,** 67 route de Crau (tel. 04 90 93 08 86), a 2-star site with pool, snack bar, and laundry. Take bus from bd. des Lices to "Graveaux" (direction "Pont de Crau"; 5.20F). 23F per person; site 23F; car 16F. Open Apr.-Sept.

◖ FOOD

The *arlésiens* have discovered that they can charge more for their delicious *provençal* food, but bargains still exist. Local specialties are seasoned with thyme, rosemary, and garlic, all of which grow in the region. Other regional produce fills the open-air markets on **bd. Émile Courbes** (W 7am-1pm) and **bd. des Lices** (Sa 7am-1pm). For the other days of the week there are two supermarkets in town. **Monoprix** is on pl. Lamartine, close to the train station and the city gates. (Open M-Th and Sa 8:30am-7:30pm, F 8:30am-8pm.) **Casino,** 26 rue Président Wilson, is off bd. des Lices towards the center of town. (Open Tu-Sa 7:30am-12:30pm and 3:30-7:30pm, Su 7:30am-12:30pm.) The *cafés* on **pl. Voltaire** are strung with colored lights and animated by rock and jazz music on Wednesday nights in summer. On summer evenings, the **pl. du Forum** bustles as much as it ever did in Roman days, with a multitude of *cafés* competing for business; if you don't feel like eating, order a *pastis* and watch the world go by.

La Désirade, 2 rue de Chiavary (tel. 04 90 49 60 03). Softly lit, but very friendly interior with a small terrace outside. The chef will lovingly produce a *salade camarguaise* and *daube de taureau* (beef stew) for the reasonable price of 68F (dessert included). His *pâté en croute à la confiture d'oignons* is also to die for. Open Th-Tu noon-2pm and 7-10pm or midnight depending on the season.

La Mûle Blanche, 9 rue du President Wilson (tel. 04 90 93 98 54). The perfect place to relax after a long day in the sun, with a shady terrace and vaulted medieval interior. Delicious, enormous salads 55-60F and a generous 89F lunch *menu* (110F for dinner). Piano and jazz music Friday nights in the winter. Open M-Sa noon-1am in the summer, winter same T-Sa, closed M night.

Blue Note, 14 rue du 4 Septembre (tel. 04 90 49 67 24). A happy mix of French and American culture, the Blue Note hops every Tuesday and Friday night with live salsa, rock, and blues bands. This may be the only place in France that serves Roquefort cheeseburgers (55F). Happy hour with half-price drinks 7-8:30pm. Open M-F noon-3pm and 7pm-late.

Vitamine, 16 rue du Docteur Fanton (tel. 04 90 93 77 36). Heaven-sent for vegetarians. Pasta (35-50F) and 38 different salads (20-50F). Try the *nougat glacé* for 30F. Open M-F noon-3pm and 7-10pm or midnight, depending on the season.

◧ SIGHTS

A 60F (40F for students) pass will cover the sites and museums listed with an asterisk; separate admission to each costs 15F (9F for students), unless otherwise indicated. Most museums are open Jan. daily 10am-noon and 2-4:30pm; Feb. 10am-noon and 2-5pm; Mar. 9am-12:30pm and 2-5:30pm; Apr.-June 15 9am-12:30pm and 2-7pm; June 16-Sept. 15 9am-7pm; Sept. 16-30 9am-12:30pm and 2-7pm; Oct. 10am-12:30pm and 2-5:30pm; Nov. 10am-12:30pm and 2-5pm; Dec. 10am-noon and 2-4:30pm. Exceptions are noted.

The cultural and historical wealth of Arles astounds. Be sure to get an English copy of *Arles et Vincent* (5F from the tourist office), which explains the four sets of ground markers that crisscross the city. A less strenuous way to get a glimpse of the historical city is by the **Petit Train** (tel. 06 12 66 17 09), a 35-minute guided tour. (Leaves from the Arena entrance daily in summer 10am-noon and 2-5pm. 30F.)

LES ARÈNES*. Though the *arènes* dominate Arles on postcards photographed from the air, it always comes as a surprise to emerge from the narrow medieval network of streets and be confronted with the largest surviving Roman amphitheater in France. Built in the 1st century AD, all the 25,000 spectators it seated could get in and out in five minutes thanks to the clever design. The high wall that separates the seating from the combat area protected enthralled spectators from combats between wild beasts. The sporadic *corridas* (Spanish-style bullfights) staged from Easter through September are as bloody as anything the Romans watched, but the *arlésiens* prefer their native *cocardes*. In the 8th century the arena was converted into a fortified village of its own, and two towers built during that era still remain, offering great views of Arles and the Rhône. The highest tower bears witness to a thousand years of vandalism—including names scratched in by WWII American GIs. *(Tel. 04 90 96 03 70. Bullfights from 90F, children 40F.)*

THÉÂTRE ANTIQUE*. Squeezed between the amphitheater and the gardens, the evocatively ruined theater serves as a reminder of the refined side of Roman culture. Capitols lie around the flower-filled backstage, and only two columns remain of the stage wall, but enough remains for modern productions to take advantage of the magnificent acoustics. *(Rue de la Calade. Tel 04 90 49 36 25; reservations 04 90 49 36 74.)* Just behind the theater, the shady **Jardin d'Été** is a great place to picnic and eavesdrop on concerts. *(Open daily May-Sept. 7am-8:30pm; Oct.-Apr. 7am-5:30pm.)*

CORRIDA OR COCARDE? In the Camargue and the South of France, there are two major types of bullfight: the Spanish **corrida,** and the *camarguais* **cocarde.** The *corridas* are the gory spectacles of bullfighting lore. The bull in a *corrida* is usually imported from Spain for the pleasure of spectators paying up to 500F to watch him fall to the matador's sword. The *cocardes,* on the other hand, hurt only the bull's ego and use free-range bulls raised in the swampy Camargue. Twenty to thirty *rasateurs,* usually dressed in white, hold a brightly colored mitt in one hand and a glove with a razor attached on the other; the bull has multi-colored pom-poms strung between his horns. The *rasateur* uses the mitted hand to distract the bull while attempting to swipe the pom-poms from the bull's head with the other.

MUSÉE D'ARLES ANTIQUE*. With its innovative use of light and space, this ultra-modern museum is 90s architecture at its best. Roman tools, statues, mosaics, sarcophagi, and other artifacts collected from the area sit alongside exceptionally detailed models of Roman engineering feats, including the ingenious pontoon bridge. *(Av. de la 1ère D.F.L. Tel. 04 90 18 88 88. 10min. from the centre ville. With your back to the tourist office, turn left, walk along bd. G. Clemenceau to its end, and follow the signs from there. Open W-M Apr.-Sept. 9am-7pm; Oct.-Mar. 10am-6pm. 35F, students 25F, children 5F.)*

LES ALYSCAMPS*. In its day one of the most famous burial grounds of the ancient world, this cemetery was later consecrated for Christian use by St-Trôphime. Holding the tombs of 80 generations of *arlésiens,* it even merited a mention in Dante's *Inferno.* The most elaborate sarcophagi have been destroyed or removed, but nothing could mar the tranquility and awe inspired by these ancient avenues. *(10min. from the centre ville. From the tourist office, head down bd. des Lices to its intersection with bd. Émile Courbes. Turn right onto av. des Alyscamps, cross the tracks, and follow the canal. Tel. 04 90 49 36 87. Closes 15min. earlier than schedule above.)*

CLOÎTRE ST-TRÔPHIME*. Famous for the elaborate carvings on its capitols, the medieval cloister provides a welcome oasis of calm and shade. The best sculpture is seen on the 12th-century Romanesque north side; the Gothic south and west sides date from the 14th century. You can also clamber over the roof and contemplate the cloister from above. Adjoining the cloister is the **Église St-Trôphime.** Built between the 11th and 15th centuries, the church has won a place in art-history books for its elaborate Romanesque façade. *(Pl. de la République. Tel. 04 90 49 33 53. Cloisters 20F, students 14F. Church free)*

FONDATION VAN GOGH. You'll find no van Gogh's here—only tributes to him by other artists. Though it houses some big names like Lichtenstein and Jasper Johns, some of the most moving elegies are found in the works of relatively unknown artists. A painting by Doutreleau captures what it would be like to pass Van Gogh on the street. Look out for temporary exhibits. *(26 rond-point des Arènes. Tel. 04 90 49 94 04. Open daily in summer 10am-7pm; call for winter hours. 30F, students and children 20F.)*

MUSEON ARLATEN*. Arles' more recent history can be discovered at this superb folk museum founded by author Frédéric Mistral, who dedicated his career to reviving traditional local customs; the name is *provençal* for "Museum of Arles." Mistral used the money he received from his 1904 Nobel Prize to buy the striking 16th-century building is built around the ruins of a small Roman forum. *(29 rue de la République. Tel. 04 90 96 08 23; fax 04 90 93 80 55. Open June-Aug. daily 9:30am-1pm and 2-6:30pm; Apr.-May and Sept. Tu-Su 9:30am-noon and 2-6pm; Oct.-Mar. Tu-Su 9:30am-noon and 2-5pm. 20F, students 15F.)*

MUSÉE RÉATTU*. Once a stronghold of the knights of St. John, this spacious museum now houses a collection of contemporary art, watercolors, oils of the Camargue by Henri Rousseau, and two rooms of canvases by the Neoclassical artist Réattu. The museum takes most pride in the 57 drawings with which Picasso honored the town in 1971. *(Rue du Grand Prieuré. Tel. 04 90 49 37 58. Open daily Apr.-Sept. 9am-noon and 2-7pm; Oct.-Mar. 10am-noon and 2-4:30pm. 20F, students 14F.)*

OTHER SIGHTS. Entered through the former Jesuit chapel on rue Balze, the **Cryp-toportiques du Forum*** provide an unforgettable experience. Dating from the 1st century BC, these gloomy underground galleries provided the foundations for the Roman forum. Hold your breath and walk into the darkness. The ruins of the **Thermes de Constantin*,** rue D. Maïsto, barely evoke what was once the largest Roman bath complex in Provence. For those spending more time in the city, the **Espace Van Gogh,** pl. Félix Rey (tel. 04 90 49 39 39), houses a book and video library, a small theater showing free films, art exhibitions, and the original walls of the hospital where Van Gogh lopped off his ear. *(Open Tu 12:30-7:30pm, W and Sa 10am-12:30pm and 2-5pm, F 12:30-6pm.)*

▓ FESTIVALS

The major cultural event of the year in Arles is the **Rencontres Internationales de la Photographie,** held in the second week of July. Undiscovered photographers from all over the world court agents by roaming around town with portfolios under their arms. More established photographers present their work in 15 locations (including parked train cars and a salt warehouse), conduct nightly slide shows (70F), participate in debates, and offer pricey workshops. When the festival crowd departs, the remarkable exhibits are still left behind. (10-30F per exhibit, under 25 free; global ticket 120F.) For more information, visit the tourist office or contact Rencontres, 10 rond-point des Arènes (tel. 04 90 96 76 06).

Of more interest to the casual tourist are Arles' many colorful *provençal* festivals. On May 1, the ancient *Confrèrie des Gardiens* ("brotherhood of herders" of the Camargue's wild horses) parades through town and gathers in the arena for the **Fête des Gardiens.** On the last weekend in June and the first in July, bonfires blaze in the streets and locals wear traditional costume to the beautiful **Fêtes d'Arles.** Half-way through the festival, bareback riders race through the bd. des Lices on white *camarguais* horses for the **course de Satin,** while at its end, the city crowns the *Reine d'Arles* (Queen of Arles), a young woman chosen to represent the region's language, customs, and history. Traditional ceremonies, dance performances, and fireworks occur in the arena at midnight (free). The next day brings the **Cocarde d'or,** when the new Queen crowns the winning *rasateur;* afterwards the bulls are run through the streets between the horses of the *gardiens.*

ABBAYE DE MONTMAJEUR

Just 7km from Arles is **Montmajeur Abbey,** a good place to wander around for an hour to picnic or just as a quick stop on the way to or from Les Baux. From a distance, the Benedictine abbey can be seen towering over the countryside. The complex consists of a motley group of buildings ranging from 948 to the 18th century. Isolated by marshlands, now drained, the monastery never had more than 60 monks. Nevertheless, time and money produced some notable architecture. Of particular interest is the **chapelle St-Pierre** (10th-11th century), which includes the confessional of St-Trôphime, and the 13th-century cloister, with vegetal and biblical scenes carved on its capitals. The 26m fortified tower was built in the late 14th century to protect the abbey from raids. *(8 buses per day from Arles M-Sa, 12.50F. Abbey open daily Apr.-Sept. 9am-7pm, rest of year W-M 10am-noon and 2-5pm. 35F, students 23F.)*

THE CAMARGUE

In stark visual contrast to the *provençal* hills to the north, this vast delta, with tall grasses and a bounty of wildlife, is an untamed wonder. Pink flamingos, black bulls, and the famous white Camargue horses roam freely across the flat expanse of wild marshland, protected by the confines of the national park. The human inhabitants include *gardiens*, rugged herders whose 2000-year tradition makes them the world's first cowboys, and the gypsies who have made the area one of their nomadic homes for 500 years. The Camargue is anchored to the north by Arles and to the south by Stes-Maries-de-la-Mer and Aigues-Mortes.

THE SOUTHEAST

Aspiring botanists and zoologists intrigued by the Camargue should stop along D570 at the **Centre d'Information de Ginès** (tel. 04 90 97 86 32), which distributes information on the region's unusual flora and fauna. (Open daily Apr.-Sept. 9am-6pm; Oct.-Mar. Sa-Th 9:30am-5pm.) Next door, the **Parc Ornithologique de Pont de Gau** (tel. 04 90 97 82 62), on the bus line between Stes-Maries and Arles, provides paths through the marsh and offers views of birds and grazing bulls. (Park open daily Apr.-Sept. 9am-sunset, Oct.-Mar. 10am-sunset. 35F, children 18F.)

The best way to see the Camargue is from **horseback,** and the region is dotted with stables offering tours throughout the park on *camarguais* horses. Most rides are oriented towards novices, so don't be afraid if you've never saddled up before. Other options include **Jeep Safaris** and **boat trips;** most leave from Stes-Maries, but some are offered in Arles and Aigues-Mortes as well. Although most of the trails are open only to horseback riders, **bicycle touring** is a great way to see much of the area. Keep in mind that bike trails may be sandy and difficult to ride on. Trail maps indicating length, level of difficulty, and danger spots are available from the tourist office. Bring an ample supply of fresh water—it gets hotter than Hades. A two-hour pedal will reveal some of the area, but you'll need a whole day if you plan to stop along the miles of wide, deserted white-sand **beaches** that line the bike trail.

STES-MARIES-DE-LA-MER

According to legend, in AD 40, a ship carrying Mary Magdalene, Mary Salomé (mother of the Apostles John and James), Mary Jacobé (Jesus's aunt), and their servant Sarah, washed ashore here. The unwitting arrivals came from Judea, where they had been put to sea to die a certain death. Today, Stes-Maries-de-la-Mer thrives on the force of this story, catering to tourists with overpriced snack trailers and honky-tonk stores willing to cast anything *provençal* in plastic. The village remains alluring, however, in its proximity to 30km of sandy beaches and to the Camargue national park.

7 ORIENTATION AND PRACTICAL INFORMATION. The town is wedged between untouched conservation land to the north, the sea to the south, and marsh to the east. **Buses** leave from **Arles** (1hr., 7 per day, 36.50F). Contact **Les Cars de Camargue,** 4 rue Jean-Mathieu, Arles (tel. 04 90 96 36 25) for info. The bus stop in Stes-Maries-de-la-Mer lies just north of pl. Mireille. Once here, **rent bikes** at **Le Vélociste,** pl. des Remparts. (Tel. 04 90 97 83 26. 80F per day, passport deposit. Open daily July-Aug. 8am-9pm and Sept.-June 9am-8pm). To get to the **tourist office,** 5 av. Van Gogh (tel. 04 90 97 82 55), walk towards the ocean down rue de la République from the bus station or down rue Victor Hugo from the church. Ask them for the free *Camargue Naturellement*, which gives a list of all the different kinds of bike, hiking, boating, and horse tours in the area. (Open daily July-Aug. 9am-8pm; Apr.-June and Sept. 9am-7pm; Oct.-Feb. 9am-5pm.) **Crédit Agricole** (tel. 04 90 97 95 09), next to the tourist office, **exchanges currency** for a 25F commission. (Open M-F 9am-12:30pm and 1:40-4:30pm, Sa 9am-12:15pm.) The police are on av. Van Gogh (tel. 04 90 97 89 50). The **post office** is on 6 av. Gambetta. (Open M-F 9am-noon and 1:30-3:30pm, Sa 8:30-10:50am. **Postal code:** 13460.)

┏ ACCOMMODATIONS AND CAMPING. Although sleeping on beaches is illegal, rows of cocooned tourists cover the sand at night. Hotels fill quickly in summer, and rooms under 100F are scarce. You can always base yourself in Arles and make the town a daytrip. North of the town, in the heart of the Camargue, lies the **Auberge de Jeunesse (HI),** hameau de Pioch Badet (tel. 04 90 97 51 72). Take the bus that runs between Stes-Maries and Arles to "Pioch Badet" (7 per day; 10 min., 11F50 from Stes-Maries; 40min., 28F from Arles). The quiet, camp-style hostel fills early in summer, so take the first bus. (Obligatory demi-pension 130F, full pension 175F, picnic 40F. Sheets 18F. Bikes 60F per day, passport deposit. Horse tours 60-285F. Reception Feb.-Nov. daily. 7:30-10:30am and 5-11pm. Call ahead if you plan to arrive later.) You'll find comfort close to the throng at **Hôtel Méditerranée,** 4 bd.

THE CAMARGUE ■ 273

Frédéric Mistral (tel. 04 90 97 82 09; fax 04 90 97 76 31), off rue Victor Hugo. A very pretty hotel exploding with flowers; reservations recommended in summer. (Doubles 180-230F, with shower and TV 230F, with bathroom and TV 250-280F. Shower 15F. Breakfast 28F. Open Feb. 15-Nov. 11 and over Christmas. V, MC.) Of course, stars like these beg to be slept under (though be forewarned that the mosquitoes can swarm thick); **camp** at **La Brise** (tel. 04 90 97 84 67), five minutes east of the *centre ville* with a pool, laundry, and tennis. (55F for 1 person and a car.)

🗹 **FOOD.** Rice is the Camargue's main crop; you will find it in gelatinous cakes sold at *pâtisseries*, at local restaurants, and on the shelves of **supermarkets** such as the **Petit Casino** on av. Victor Hugo. (Tel. 04 90 97 90 60; open daily in summer 8am-8pm; in winter 8am-noon and 4-8pm.) A **market** fills pl. des Gitanes on Monday and Friday mornings from 7am till noon. Restaurants cluster away from the waterfront around **av. Victor Hugo,** especially on **pl. Esprit Pioch,** where they serve French seafood dishes, the ubiquitous paella, *pavé de taureau*, and refreshing sangria. Most *menus* start around 65-70F, but some lunch ones can be found for 55F. **Le Provençal,** 1 pl. E. Pioch (tel. 04 90 97 94 23) is a shaking, Spanish-style pizzeria. (Pizzas 50-75F, *menu* 68F. Open summer daily, winter F-W.) A couple of doors down is the friendly **La Bouvine** (tel. 04 90 97 87 09), which makes a tasty *salade camarguaise* (42F) and *pavé de taureau* (57F). (2-course *menu* 63F. Open daily noon-2:30pm and 7-9:30pm or until 11pm in the summer.)

🖸 **SIGHTS.** The only major sight in town is the 12th-century **church** that protrudes high above the menagerie of snack bars. The lofty, fortified tower on top guards a view of the sunset over Stes-Maries, the sea, and the Camargue while the dark Romanesque interior offers a cool respite from the shadeless town. Go down to the crypt where the relics of the saints are visible year-round, except during pilgrimages when they glisten from the altar. The saints' power supposedly has cured the blind, healed the lame, and halted the *mistral* winds of 1833. The cult statue of St. Sarah also stands in the crypt surrounded by memorials of miracles rendered. (Church open daily 8am-noon and 2-7pm. Free. Roof and tower open daily in summer 10am-8pm; in winter 10am-12:30pm and 2-8:30pm. 10F.)

🎇 **FESTIVALS.** In keeping with the spirit of the legend, the Egyptian servant of the Marys, Sarah, has become the patron saint of gypsies. The relics of Sarah were exhumed by King René in 1448, initiating a tradition of pilgrimages by gypsy peoples. The **Pèlerinage des Gitans** unites gypsies from all over Europe annually (May 24-25). In traditional costumes, a procession from the church to the sea bears statues of the saints to re-enact their landing. The pilgrimage provides an unequaled opportunity to enjoy the art of flamenco. A festival on the weekend following October 22 honors the Marys, with ceremonies similar to Sarah's but without the gypsy gathering. During July and August, bullfights and horse shows occur regularly at the modern arenas (tickets 60-400F). In the second week of July, the **Féria du Cheval** brings horses from around the world for shows, competitions, and rodeos at the Stes-Maries and Mejanes arenas. (Call the Comité des Fêtes at 04 90 97 85 86 for details. Tickets 90-400F.)

🜨 **EXCURSIONS.** Stes-Maries is undoubtedly the capital of the Camargue, and the great majority of organized visits to the region leave from here. The exception are **horseback tours,** which are run by the many stables which line the road from Arles to Stes-Maries. Contact the **Association Camarguaise de Tourisme Équestre** (tel. 04 90 97 86 32) or pick up their list of members from the tourist office. Organized rides are geared mostly toward equestrian novices and follow somewhat limited routes; rates are the same from one establishment to another. (80F per hr., 200-230F for 3hr., 350F per day; meal usually included.) For **jeep safaris,** contact **Le Gitan,** 13 av. de la Plage. (Tel. 04 66 70 09 65 or 04 90 97 89 33. 2hr. for 200F and 4hr. for 230F in jeeps holding 7-8 people.) For viewing the coast from sea level, **Camargue** (tel. 04 90 97 84 72) sends **boats** from Port Gardien deep into the Petit Rhône for up-close bird and bull-watching. (1½hr., 3-4 per day. 60F, children 30F.)

THE SOUTHEAST

AIGUES-MORTES

Louis IX built Aigues-Mortes ("still waters") with the express purpose of using it as a springboard from which to reconquer the Holy Land; he launched the Seventh and Eighth Crusades from here in 1248 and 1270. The town is remarkable as a surviving testament to medieval planning, its grid still enclosed by thirteenth-century walls. Outside town, the Salins du Midi continue to provide chefs with the gourmet salt they have produced since the 8th century. The remarkable **Tour de Constance** (tel. 04 66 53 61 55) remains equipped with the latest in medieval defense stratagems and provides a view of the surrounding countryside and the sea of orange roofs of the *vieille ville.* A display of mannequins on the second floor includes one unfortunate Protestant woman looking longingly out the window of her dim room; the tableau is based on a painting by Jeanne Lombard. (Open daily June-Aug. 9:30am-8pm; Sept. and May 9:30am-7pm; Feb.-Apr. and Oct. 10am-6pm; Nov.-Jan. 10am-5pm. 32F, under 26 21F.) Down rue Jean Jaurès, on the corner of pl. St-Louis, stands the 13th-century **Notre Dame des Sablons.** The bizarre and beautiful modern stained-glass windows, designed by Bernard d'Honneur and Claude Viallat, illuminate the spartan interior. (Open daily 8:30am-noon and 2-7pm.)

L'Aventure (tel. 06 03 91 44 63) runs **boat tours** into the Camargue. (Daily; 35F for 1hr., 50F for 2hr.) If time is short or the sun too hot, let the images of the Camargue drift by without the mosquito bites in the **3-D Cinéma** across the canal. (Open Feb. 15-Nov. 15. Shows hourly 3-10pm July-Aug., 3-7pm Sept.-June. 37F, children 12 and under 22F.) For one weekend in late August, the **Fête de St-Louis** relives the past with historical pageants, jousting, and a medieval market. In the second week of October, *rasateurs* participate in the **Fête Votive**'s *camarguais* bullfights.

Lively, reasonable restaurants fill the central square, while fast food and small **markets** can be found on **rue Jean Jaurès.** The brightly colored **Casa Tora Luna** (tel. 04 66 53 68 75) has a 60F lunch *menu.* (Tapas served 9am-11:30pm; lunch noon-3pm, low season noon-2:30pm; dinner 7-11pm. Closed Tu low season.) Get holy behind St-Louis at **Les Capuchins** (tel. 04 66 53 12 12), which has a classy 79F shellfish *menu.* (Open daily for lunch and dinner in summer; erratic hours in winter.) If you fancy staying the night, **Hôtel Carrière,** 18 rue Pasteur (tel. 04 66 53 73 07; fax 04 66 53 84 75), half a block from pl. St-Louis, is an inexpensive option. Call at least 15 days in advance for reservations during the *fête.* (Singles with shower and toilet 200F; doubles 230F; triples 290F. Breakfast 30F. V, MC, AmEx.) The **Hôtel Tour de Constance,** 1 bd. Diderot (04 66 53 83 50), is just outside the walls near the canal, with basic, pastel-colored rooms. (Doubles 190F, with shower and TV 210F, with shower, toilet, and TV 230F; triples 260F, with shower, toilet and TV 280F; quads 330F. Breakfast 30F. Parking 30F. V, MC, AmEx.)

The town has barely grown since the Middle Ages, and most of it still lies within the original fortified *enceinte,* whose grid system makes it a cinch to navigate. The **tourist office,** pte. de la Gardette (tel. 04 66 53 73 00; fax 04 66 53 65 94), is on the inside of the main gate to the left. (Open July-Sept. M-F 9am-8pm, Sa-Su 10am-8pm; Oct.-June M-F 9am-6pm, Sa-Su 10am-noon and 2-6pm.) The **Petit Train** (tel. 04 66 53 85 20), outside the main gate, conducts tours around the city and also to the salt factories. (Written commentary in English. Daily Apr.-Sept. City tour: every 30min., 22F, children 4-12 15F. Salt factory tour: 6 per day, 35F, children 20F.) **SNCF** trains and buses run to **Nîmes.** (1hr., 4 per day, 39F; *Gare* open M-F 6:40am-7:30pm, Sa-Su 8am-7:30pm.) **STDG** runs buses to **Nîmes** (1hr., 5 per day, 37F) and **Montpellier** (65 min., M-Sa 4 per day, 35F).

NÎMES

Though technically outside Provence, Nîmes (pop. 132,000) has the best of all that is typically *provençale.* This beautiful site was colonized by legionnaires who accompanied Octavian (later the Emperor Augustus) on his campaign in Egypt. His victory over Anthony and the serpentine Cleopatra is commemorated in the city's omnipresent symbol, the crocodile shackled to a palm tree. The impressive

Roman arena remains the centerpiece for the *férias*, which pack the city for bull runs, *corridas*, flamenco dancing, and other forms of hot-blooded fanfare. Cafés and bodegas teem all night long as sangria flows to the strains of guitar music and the inevitable castanet. If you can leave, don't forget a special souvenir. The jeans you're sporting were made possible with *Nîmois serge*, a durable textile imported by Levi-Strauss for Californian gold-diggers. This indigo-colored cloth still indicates its origin in its name: de-nim.

ORIENTATION AND PRACTICAL INFORMATION

Nîmes's restaurants, shops, and museums cluster in the *vieille ville* between bd. Victor Hugo and bd. Admiral Courbet. From the *gare*, follow av. Feuchères, veer left around the small park, and scoot clockwise around the arena. Go straight on bd. Victor Hugo for 5 blocks until you reach the Maison Carré, a Roman temple in the middle of pl. Comédie, whose *façade* faces rue Auguste and the tourist office.

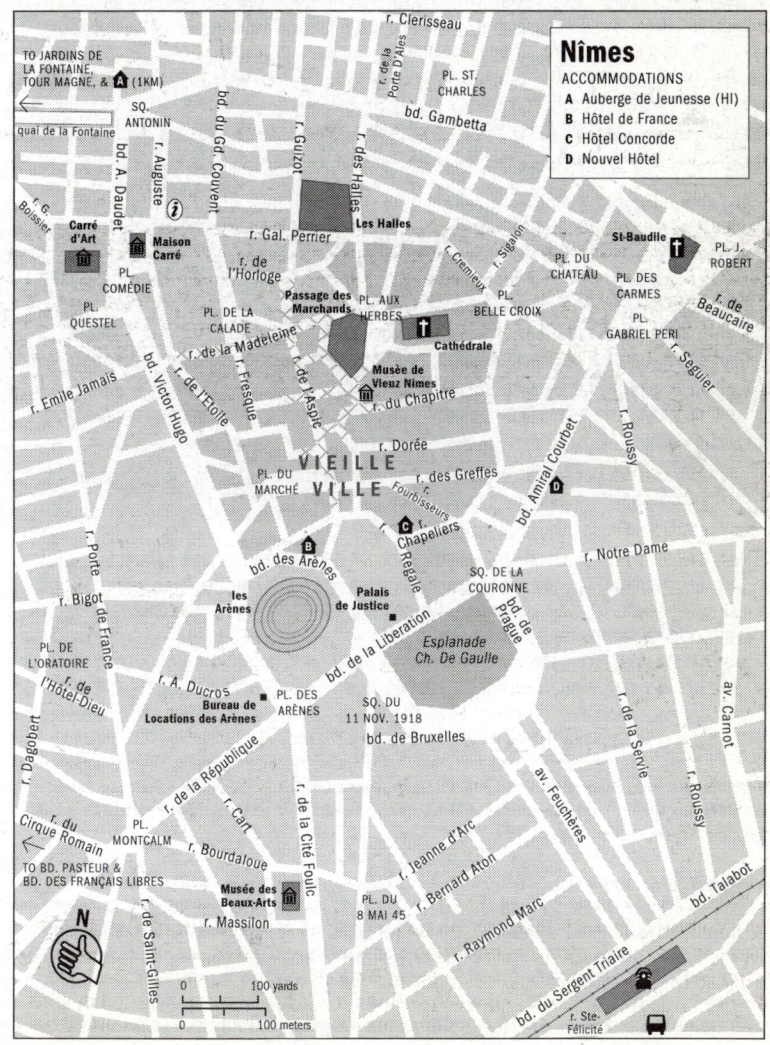

Nîmes

ACCOMMODATIONS

A Auberge de Jeunesse (HI)
B Hôtel de France
C Hôtel Concorde
D Nouvel Hôtel

Trains: Bd. Talabot. To: **Arles** (30min., 10 per day, 41F); **Montpellier** (30min., 1 or 2 per hr., 46F); **Marseille** (1¼hr., 10 per day, 95F); **Orange** (1½hr., 14 per day, 64F); **Toulouse** (3hr., 12 per day, 181F); **Paris** (4½hr., 7 per day, 350-400F); **Bordeaux** (5½hr., 6 per day, 290F). Info office open M-Sa 8am-6:30pm; ticket office open until 10pm.

Buses: At the *gare routière*, rue Ste-Félicité (tel. 04 66 29 52 00), behind train station. Info office open M-F 8am-noon and 2-6:30pm. **Société des Transports Départementaux du Gard (STDG)** (tel. 04 66 29 27 29). To: **Avignon** (1¼hr., M-F 8 per day, Sa 6 per day, Su 2 per day, 42F); **Arles** (M-F 5 per day, Sa 3 per day; 35F); and **Montpellier** (M-Sa 2 per day; 55F).

Local Transportation: T.C.N. (tel. 04 66 38 15 40). Tickets good for 1hr. Buses stop running at 7:30pm. Ticket 6F, *carnet* of 5 24.50F.

Taxis: TRAN office (tel. 04 66 29 40 11) in train station. 24hr. service.

Bike Rental: Piaggio SA, 22 bd. Talabot (tel. 04 66 21 91 03). 85F per day, 500F per week. 1500F and ID deposit. Open M-F 8am-noon and 2-7pm, Sa 8am-noon.

Tourist Office: 6 rue Auguste (tel. 04 66 67 29 11; fax 04 66 21 81 04). Free accommodations service. Info on bus and train excursions to Pont du Gard, the Camargue, and nearby towns. Free detailed map and festival info. **Currency exchange** at 1% commission. Open July-Aug. M-F 8am-8pm, Sa-Su 9am-7pm; Sept.-June M-F 8am-7pm, Sa 9am-7pm, Su 10am-6pm. **Branch office** (tel. 04 66 84 18 13) in the train station. Open July-Sept. M-Sa 9:30am-12:30pm and 2-6pm, Su 9:30am-12:30pm and 1:30-3:30pm; Oct.-June M-F 9:30am-12:30pm and 2-6pm. The free *Nimescope* lists events.

City tours: Le petit train (tel. 04 66 67 07 32). Every 45min. from Esplanade in front of Palais de Justice. mid-July to mid-Aug. 9:30am-9:30pm; Apr. to mid-July and mid-Aug. to Oct. 9:30-11:30am and 2:30-5:30pm. 30F, 25F reduced.

Budget Travel: Nouvelles Frontières, 1 bd. de Prague (tel. 04 66 67 38 94; fax 04 66 67 38 62). Open M-Sa 9am-7pm.

Money: Banque de France, 2 sq. du 11 Novembre (tel. 04 66 76 82 00), offers **currency exchange** with no commission. Exchange desk open M-F 8:30am-12:15pm.

English Books: 8 rue Dorée (tel. 04 66 21 17 04), in the *vieille ville,* is a little anglophone oasis. Some novels (popular and classics). Open M-Sa 9am-noon and 2-6pm.

Laundromat: Lavomatique, 5 rue des Halles. Open daily 7am-8pm.

Hospital: Gaston Doumergue, 5 rue Hoche, and **Hôpital Caremeau,** rue Professeur Robert Debré, share a helpful switchboard (tel. 04 66 68 68 68).

Police: 16 av. Feuchères (tel. 04 66 62 82 82).

Post Office: 1 bd. de Bruxelles (tel. 04 66 76 67 03), across from the park at the end of av. Feuchères. **Currency exchange** at no commission. Poste Restante code: 30006. Open M-F 8am-7pm, Sa 8am-noon. **Branch office:** 19 bd. Gambetta (tel. 04 66 76 67 90). **Postal codes:** 30000 and 30900.

Internet Access: Cybersnack Le Vauban, 34 rue Clérisseau (tel. 04 66 76 09 71). 50F per hr., 30F per 30min. Open daily 10am-10pm.

ACCOMMODATIONS AND CAMPING

The *vieille ville* is dotted with hotels offering reasonably priced rooms. It's best to reserve a couple of weeks ahead during the festival in early June and during the biggest summer concerts.

Auberge de Jeunesse (HI), chemin de l'Auberge de la Jeunesse (tel. 04 66 23 25 04; fax 04 66 23 84 27), off chemin de la Cigale, 3.5km from the station. **Closed for renovations Aug. 31 1999-Mar. 2000.** Take bus #2 (direction "Alès" or "Villeverte") to "Stade, Route d'Alès"; follow the signs up the hill. After buses stop running, the hostel minibus (if available, call hostel to arrange) will pick you up at the station for free, and take you back in the morning for 8F. To walk, pass the Maison Carrée (see **Orientation**) on bd. Victor Hugo and continue straight on bd. A. Daudet. Go left at sq. Antonin onto quai de la Fontaine. Pass the Jardins de la Fontaine park and continue straight on av. Roosevelt. Go right onto rte. d'Alès and bear left onto chemin de la Cigale. Follow the signs (45min.). Relaxed hostel in a park with very hospitable staff. Renovations will include 4- to 6-bed dorms, family rooms, laundry, and new kitchen. Bar until 1am. Ping-pong. Playground. 48F. Dinner 53F. Sheets 17F. Breakfast 19F. Camping 28F. Price rise likely after it reopens. **Members only.** Reservations advised. 24hr. reception (night guard). **Bikes** 50F per day. May-Oct. bike/kayak combo to Pont du Gard 130F. V, MC.

Nouvel Hôtel, 6 bd. Admiral Courbet (tel. 04 66 67 62 48). Spotless, very comfortable rooms with TV and in the heart of town. Singles and doubles 147F, with shower 185F; triples with shower 228F. Shower 20F. Breakfast 28F. V, MC, AmEx.

Hôtel de France, 4 bd. des Arènes (tel. 04 66 67 23 05; fax 04 66 67 76 93). Facing the arena. Singles 110F; doubles with shower and toilet 150F; triples and quads with shower and toilet 180F. Breakfast 25F. Reserve ahead. V, MC.

Hôtel Concorde, 3 rue des Chapeliers (tel. 04 66 67 91 03), off rue Regale. Warm, friendly proprietors run this hotel smack-dab in the *vieille ville*. Singles 110F, with shower 140-160F; doubles 120F, with shower, toilet, and TV 195F; one triple with shower and toilet 220F. Breakfast in bed 25F. Showers 20F—not strictly enforced. Reserve ahead. V, MC.

Campsite: Domaine de La Bastide (tel. 04 66 38 09 21), on rte. de Générac, 5km south of station. Take bus D (direction "La Bastide," last bus 7:30pm) to the terminus. By car, leave Nîmes heading to Montpellier, then get on rte. de Générac. Three-star site with grocery store, laundry, electricity, and recreational facilities. 41F per person, 68F for 2 people. Caravan with electricity 61F per person, 84F for 2 people. Open year-round.

FOOD

Nîmoise cooking is often seasoned with *herbes de Provence* (a mixture of local herbs) and *aïoli* (a thick sauce made with garlic and olive oil). Waiters will advise you to try *la brandade de morue*, dry cod crushed with olive oil and served as a turnover, pastry, or soufflé. On the sweet side, *caladons*, honey cookies sprinkled with almonds, are Nîmes' indigenous delight. The plethora of restaurants along **rue Fresques, bd. Admiral Courbet,** and around **pl. d'Assas, pl. aux Herbes,** and **pl. du Marché,** with its single palm tree and crocodile fountain, will keep you from going hungry. To get off the trampled path, cross bd. Victor Hugo and choose a Vietnamese restaurant or bistro along **imp. Porte-de-France** or **rue Bigot.** The terraced herb gardens and ponds on the back slopes of the **Jardins de la Fontaine** make for unforgettable picnicking. Hostelers can stock up at the **open-air market** on bd. Jean-Jaurès (F 7am-1pm) or the large **Marché U,** 19 rue d'Alès (tel. 04 66 64 14 29), just down the hill from the hostel (open M-Sa 8am-12:45pm and 3:30-8pm). For a crusty taste of history, **La Maison Villaret,** 13 rue de la Madeleine (tel. 04 66 67 41 79), has been baking bread in wood-burning ovens since 1775. (Open M-Sa 7am-7:30pm.)

The Pelican, 54 rte. de Beaucaire (tel. 04 66 29 63 28). Get cajun in this unbelievable reproduction of New Orleans. Cajun salad, spare ribs, and juice 58F. *Menus* 55-65F. Cream cider 21F. Desserts 20F. Open Tu-Su 6:30pm-1am.

Crêperie Les 4 Saisons, 3 rue des Greffes (tel. 04 66 67 21 70). Serves a 59F *menu* that includes wine. Specialty *crêpes* (34F) such as the *savoureuse* (mozzarella and smoked salmon) and the *délicieuse* (mushrooms and spinach) merit their names. Open M-Sa noon-2pm and 7-10:30pm. V, MC, AmEx.

Mogador Café, 2 pl. du Marché (tel. 04 66 21 87 90). While contemplating the broken columns of the crocodile fountain, enjoy *tartes* and *crêpes* (12-34F) in the bustling *place.* Open July-Sept. daily 8am-10pm; Oct.-Dec. and Apr.-June daily 8am-7pm; Jan.-Mar. M-Sa 8am-7pm. V, MC.

THE SOUTHEAST

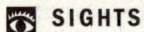 **SIGHTS**

*A three-day **pass** (60F, students 30F) to all sights is on sale at the tourist office and at the sights themselves.*

LES ARÈNES. This magnificent Roman amphitheater, the pride and joy of the city, is the best preserved in France. Built in the AD 50 for gory animal and gladiatorial combats and high-tech naval battles, the elliptical arena could hold approximately 23,000 people. During the Middle Ages the thick walls were used for a Visigothic fortress, a village, and a *prêt-à-porter* quarry. The arena is open for visits, but the best way to experience this ancient wonder is by attending one of the bullfights or concerts held there. *(Tel. 04 66 76 72 77. Open daily in summer 9am-6:30pm; in winter 9am-noon and 2-5pm. Admission 28F, students 20F.)*

MAISON CARRÉE AND CARRÉ D'ART. Despite its name, the **Maison Carrée** ("Square House") is actually a long rectangular temple, possibly dedicated to Jupiter, Juno, or Minerva during the 1st-century BC. By turns stable and meeting house, by the 18th century this Greco-Roman temple—one of the best preserved in the world—was admired so much it almost became a garden ornament at Versailles. Proportionally pleasing and exquisitely sculpted on the outside, the inner sanctum houses a motley crew of antiques. *(Open daily in summer 9am-noon and 2:30-7pm; in winter 9am-12:30pm and 2-6pm. Free.)* The Maison Carrée is gracefully reflected in Norman Foster's ultra-modern **Carré d'Art** across the square. Nîmes' cultural center houses the **Musée d'Art Contemporain,** which features an eclectic permanent collection and good temporary exhibits. *(Tel. 04 66 76 35 70. Library and museum open Tu-Su 10am-6pm. Library free; museum admission 28F, students 20F.)*

JARDINS DE LA FONTAINE. Wander up the quai de la Fontaine to while away the afternoon here amid the evocatively ruined **Temple of Diana,** numerous marble sculptures, and lush flora. This formal garden, built by an 18th-century military engineer after the 17th-century designs of Le Nôtre, uses water from the Nemausus spring in its fabulous fountains and reflecting pools. *(Off pl. Foch to the left along the canals from the Maison. Garden open June 15-Sept. 15 daily 7am-11pm; Sept. 16-Oct. and Apr.-June 14 8am-9pm; Nov.-Mar. 8am-7pm. Free.)* Climb the staircases up the park to reach the **Tour Magne.** Built in the Iron Age, it was renovated by Augustus in 15 BC for use in the city's ramparts. One of the few remnants of that fortification, the frayed tower now gazes over the entire city and the surrounding countryside. *(Tel. 04 66 67 65 56. Open daily July-Aug. 9am-6:30pm; Sept.-June 9am-5pm. 15F, students 12F.)*

MUSÉE DE BEAUX ARTS AND MUSÉE DE VIEUX NÎMES. The **Musée des Beaux-Arts,** housed in a Neoclassical building accented with marble pillars and Roman mosaic floors, contains paintings of the French, Italian, Flemish, and Dutch schools from the 15th to 19th centuries as well as temporary exhibits. The **Musée du Vieux Nîmes** resides in a 17th-century palace and boasts a remarkable collection of regional arts, furniture, and looms, including a meticulously detailed 18th-century billiard table. *(Beaux-Arts: Rue de la cité Foule. Tel. 04 66 67 38 21. Vieux Nimes: Pl. aux Herbes, next to cathedral. Tel. 04 66 36 00 64. Both open Tu-Su 11am-6pm. 28F, students 20F.)*

ENTERTAINMENT AND FESTIVALS

ENTERTAINMENT. During the *férias* (see below), many of the bars open late-night. Otherwise, **O'Flaherty's,** 21 bd. Admiral Courbet (tel. 04 66 67 22 63), has 22-34F pints of beer and live music on Thursday nights in the winter. Dishes like the *boeuf à la Guinness* (72F) will take you back to Dublin. (Open Su-Th 11am-2am, F-Sa 11am-3am.) **The Pelican** (see **Food,** above) has free weekly blues, country, and jazz concerts, while the area around **impasse Porte-de-France** is home to lots of hopping bars. **Lulu Club,** impasse de la Curaterie (tel. 04 66 36 28 70), is a gay dance club that occasionally features an act filled with flamboyant feather boas and chiffon. (30F cover includes 1 drink. Open T-Sa 11pm and on.) **Cinéma Le Sémaphore,**

25 rue Porte de France (tel. 04 66 67 88 04), plays foreign films in their original languages. (32F, 24F for noon shows. Closed July 9-Aug. 6.)

Concerts, movies, plays, and operas take place at the *arènes* throughout the year (60-300F). Summer acts have included Ray Charles and the Red Hot Chili Peppers. For info and reservations, contact the **Bureau de Location des Arènes,** 1 rue Alexandre Ducros. (Tel. 04 66 67 28 02. Open M-F 9am-noon and 2-6pm.)

FESTIVALS. In the spirit of the Roman gladiators, Nîmes sponsors three important *férias*: the **Féria de Primaveria** in February, the **Féria des Vendages** in mid-September, and the most boisterous, the **Féria de Pentecôte** (around June 11, 2000). For five days, the streets resound with the clattering of hooves as bulls are herded to the *arènes* for life and death combat. Meanwhile, nights are spend dancing, singing, and boozing. For the weak at heart and animal lovers, the **courses camarguaises,** in early September, offer more humane entertainment: fighters strip decorations from the bulls' horns and forehead. (Tickets 70-350F. Cheap seats are usually available the day of the event.) South American culture runs rampant in mid-July during the three-day **Horas Latinas** festival (tel. 04 66 67 29 11) which features extravagant music and dance shows. On summer evenings, **Les marchés du soir** sees local painters, artists, and musicians flock to the city center to entertain crowds. (Th 7-10pm July-Aug.)

PONT DU GARD

Built around 19 BC by Augustus's minion Agrippa to provide water to the growing city of Nîmes, the Pont du Gard is one of the biggest and best-preserved sections of a former Roman aqueduct. The original covered canal carried water 50km from the Eure springs near Uzès to Nîmes with only a 17m total fall in altitude, requiring uncannily skillful engineering and masonry. The Pont itself consists of 52 arches on three levels, spanning 275m over the Gard river. From the 5th to the 7th centuries, its stone was looted for building material. Subsequent restorations have returned the Pont du Gard to its original appearance, and a flow of tourists has replaced the 44 million gallons of water it once provided daily. On warm days many choose to sunbathe and swim in the cool river.

The best way to see the Pont du Gard is to start from **Collias,** 4km toward Uzès. Here **Kayak Vert** (tel. 04 66 22 84 83) rents two-person **canoes** (50F per hr., 145F per day), solo **kayaks** (35F per hr., 90F per day), and **bikes** (80F per half-day, 110F per day, passport deposit). You can also paddle 11km downstream from Collias to the Pont du Gard and then take a dip in the river before being shuttled back to Collias. (Kayak 105F, 70F for HI members. Canoe 180F.) If you're afraid to go into the water, the **Société des Transports Départementaux du Gard (STDG)** (tel. 04 66 29 27 29) runs daily buses from the *gare routière* in **Nîmes** to the Pont du Gard (30min., M-Sa 5 per day, Su 2 per day, 31F). Buses also leave for the Pont du Gard from **Avignon** (45min., 7 per day, 33F). The bus will drop you off and pick you up at the hotel L'Auberge Blanche in what seems to be the middle of nowhere. Follow signs to the parking lot (10min.). **Camping le Barralet,** rue des Aires in Collias (tel. 04 66 22 84 52), offers a pool in addition to river bathing. An *épicerie* is 200m away. (1 person 36-42F; 2 people with car 78F; 3 people 95F. 10% discount Apr.-June and Sept. Laundry 20F per wash; no dryers. Open Mar.-Sept. V, MC, AmEx.)

UZÈS

26km north of Nîmes, in lush, rolling countryside, lies the small city of Uzès. The **Duché** palace, pl. du Marché (tel. 04 66 22 18 96), which dominates the *vieille ville*, was built in the 11th-century and continuously renovated until the 18th. The result is an intriguing blend of period styles still enjoyed by the Uzès, descendants of the first duke and duchess of France, who still use this immaculate fortress as a home. The spirit evident in their family motto *"Ferro non auro"* ("By iron not gold") was embodied by the late Duchesse Anne, the first French woman to get her driver's license (and a fine for speeding). The interior features the furniture of Louis XIII and Louis XIV and a 15th-century chapel.

THE SOUTHEAST

Admission includes a tour in French with written English translation. (Open July-Sept. 15 10am-1pm and 2-6pm; Sept. 16-June 10am-noon and 2-6pm. Last visit 15min. before closing. 50F, students 35F.) The **Cathédrale St-Théodoric,** pl. de l'Evêché, was burned, rebuilt, and restored many times during its turbulent history and is now a mishmash of Renaissance, Baroque, and neo-medieval styles. The cathedral's remarkable 17th-century, 2772-pipe organ sports delicately carved shutters trimmed with gold. (Open daily 9am-6:30pm. Free organ concerts in Oct. and spring.) Next to the cathedral stands the 12th-century **Fenestrelle Tower,** the belltower of a Romanesque cathedral destroyed in the 16th-century. Across the street, to the cathedral's left, a stone balcony provides a magnificent view of the surrounding countryside.

Bulls stampede through the streets and cascades of *pastis* flow freely during the **Fête Votive** in the second week of August. Truffle buffs hit cloud nine the third Sunday of January during **la Journée de la Truffe,** when fresh truffles are trafficked en masse and truffling tips disclosed to the faithful. (Call 04 66 22 58 36 for information.) The second half of July 2000 will see the 30th anniversary of the **Nuits Musicales d'Uzès,** an international music festival. Tickets (70-220F per performance) are available at the **tourist office,** pl. Albert 1er (tel. 04 66 22 68 88; fax 04 66 22 95 19), where you can also pick up a free booklet on Uzès that includes a tourist-friendly map. (Open June-Sept. M-F 9am-6pm, Sa 10am-noon and 2-5pm, Su 10am-5pm; Oct.-May M-F 9am-noon and 1:30-6pm, Sa 10am-noon.)

Most accommodations are expensive, but a pool and sturdy bare-mattressed bunks in rooms for 2 to 14 people can be found at **Le Prieuré du Christ Roi,** rte. de Anduze (tel. 04 66 22 68 67). It's often full with groups, so call ahead. (80F. Sheets 20F. Dinner 60F.) To get there from the bus station, walk directly across the rotary road to Anduze. The *prieuré* is just past the Peugeot garage on the right (10min.). There is a cluster of middle-range restaurants around the fountain on the pl. aux Herbes. A cozier lunch option is **La Sorbetière,** pl. Albert 1er. (Tel. 04 66 22 34 32. 22-35F salads and 36-39F pizzas. Open daily noon-2pm.) Wednesday and Saturday mornings see a **market** on pl. aux Herbes and the surrounding boulevards.

STDG (tel. 04 66 29 27 29) runs buses to Uzès' tourist office from **Nîmes** (45min., M-Sa 8 per day, Su 2 per day, 31F) and **Avignon** (1hr., 3 per day, 47F). Three midday buses from **Uzès** to the **Pont du Gard** (20min., 20F) make the combination a good daytrip if timed correctly.

ORANGE

Despite its colorful name, this northern *provençal* town hasn't hosted a single citrus grove in its two millennia; "Orange" is a perversion of the name of the Roman city of "Arausio." Orange's juice comes from its renowned vineyards, producing the Côtes du Rhône vintage. *Caves* scattered throughout the region produce reds and rosés and offer *dégustations* to those willing to buy. The ancient Roman homes, arena, baths, and city walls from 36 BC have disappeared, but the immense theater and elaborate triumphal arch are astonishingly well-preserved among the 12th-century houses that dot the city. Many feel, however, that Orange (pop. 28,000) has soured with the 1995 success of the far-right Front National (see p. 24), which controls the city council.

☐ ORIENTATION AND PRACTICAL INFORMATION

Orange centers around **pl. Clemenceau, République,** and **aux Herbes.** To reach the main tourist office from the train station at the eastern edge of town, follow the signs to the *centre ville,* walking away from the station along **av. Frédéric Mistral,** and keep left as it becomes rue de la République; continue through pl. République, go around the building at the far end on its right side, and go straight on the smaller rue St-Martin, which becomes av. Charles de Gaulle. The tourist office will be across cours Aristide Briand and to your right (15min.).

Trains: Av. Frédéric Mistral. To: **Avignon** (20min., 21 per day, 29F); **Marseille** (1¼hr., 3 per day, 108F); **Lyon** (2½hr., 8 per day, 135F); and **Paris** (3½hr., 1 per day, 344F). Info desk open daily 5:20am-8:20pm.

Buses: Cours Pourtoules (tel. 04 90 34 15 59). Office open 8-11:50am and 2-4:50pm. To **Avignon** (55min.; M-Sa about every hr., Su 5 per day; 28.50F).

Taxi: Taxi Monge (tel. 04 90 51 00 00). 24hr.

Bike Rental: M.T.S. 84, 571 bd. Daladier (tel./fax 04 90 34 94 92). 120F per day, 100F after 2 days. Passport deposit. Open M 3-7pm, Tu-Sa 9am-noon and 3-7pm.

Tourist Office: 5 cours Aristide Briand (tel. 04 90 34 70 88; fax 04 90 34 99 62), near the *autoroute.* Spirited staff will help you in English and make last-minute reservations. **Currency exchange;** no commission but so-so rates. Open Apr.-Sept. M-Sa 9am-7pm, Su 10am-6pm; Oct.-Mar. M-F 9am-5pm. **Branch office** opposite Théâtre Antique on pl. des Frères Mounet. Open Apr.-Sept. M-Sa 10am-1pm and 2-7pm, Su 10am-6pm.

Laundromat: Lavomatique, 5 rue St-Florent, off bd. Daladier. Open daily 8am-8pm.

Hospital: Louis Giorgi, chemin de l'Abrian (tel. 04 90 11 22 22), on av. H. Fabré.

Police: 445 av. Charles de Gaulle (tel. 04 90 11 33 30).

Post Office: 679 bd. E. Daladier on cours Pourtoules (tel. 04 90 11 11 00). **Currency exchange.** Open M and W-F 8am-7pm, Tu 8am-noon and 1:15-7pm, Sa 8am-noon. **Postal code:** 84100.

Internet Access: Cyber Station, 2 cours Aristide Briand (tel. 04 90 34 27 27). 45F per hr. Open M and W-Th 9:30am-11pm, Tu 9:30am-7pm, F 9:30am-1am, Sa 11am-1am.

ACCOMMODATIONS AND CAMPING

Decent, cheap rooms should not be hard to find in Orange. During weekends in late July and early August, however, it's smart to book ahead.

Hôtel St-Florent, 4 rue du Mazeau (tel. 04 90 34 18 53; fax 04 90 51 17 25), near pl. aux Herbes. Friendly family paints frescoes on the walls of their lovely small hotel. California beach scene in breakfast room is their pride and joy. Phones included. Singles and doubles 160-300F, rooms 250F and up have toilet, shower, and TV; quads 400F. Extra bed 50F. Breakfast 30F. V, MC.

Arcotel, 8 pl. aux Herbes (tel. 04 90 34 09 23; fax 04 90 51 61 12). Friendly owners in a pleasant hotel overlooking a quiet plaza. A stone's throw from the Roman theater. Singles 110F; doubles 150-170F, with bathroom 200-220F; triples with bathroom 250-260F; quads with bathroom 300F. Breakfast 25-45F. TV 20F. V, MC.

Hôtel Clarine, 4 rue Caristie (tel. 04 90 34 10 07; fax 04 90 34 89 76). Very modern, well-kept chain hotel in a central location, with new furnishings, shower, toilet, and TVs. Rooms typically go for 300-450F, but if it isn't full and you mention *Let's Go,* the English-speaking staff might give you a room for 200F, even in summer. Breakfast 40F. Safe parking 30F. V, MC.

Campsites: Le Jonquier, rue A. Carrel (tel. 04 90 34 49 48; fax 04 90 51 16 97). From the tourist office, walk toward the *autoroute* and turn right after the big school onto av. du 18 Juin 1940. Take a left onto rue H. Nogueres, and after 5min. go right on rue Alexis Carrel; the site will be up on your left. 3-star site with pool, hot showers, and mini-mart. Mini-golf, horseback riding, and tennis extra. 64F for 2 people and tent, car included. Electricity extra. Reception daily 8am-8:30pm. Open Apr.-Sept. V, MC, AmEx.

FOOD

During the nights of the *Chorégies* (see **Entertainment,** below), the cafés on pl. aux Herbes and pl. de la République raise prices and keep concert-goers up until 3am. Many restaurants serve *pan bagna*, the traditional salad-filled sandwich of the south. For convenient grocery shopping, head to the **Petite Casino,** 16 rue de la République. (Open M-Sa 7:30am-12:30pm and 3:30-7:30pm.) Every Thursday the town erupts with an **open-air market** centered on pl. République and Clemenceau and cours Aristide Briand, with everything from produce to handmade jewelry (7am-1pm). Specialty food shops congregate on rue St-Martin between pl. République and cours A. Briand, with popular bakeries, a *pâtisserie*, and a fruit stand.

Le Phare Ouest, 9 pl. aux Herbes (tel. 04 90 11 04 44), is a colorful little *crêperie* with anything but little *crêpes.* Friendly Breton owner makes a mean *blini sucre* (pancake) for 32-42F. 36F lunch *menu* includes *galette, crêpe,* and wine or cider. Open in summer daily 11:30am-11:30pm; winter Tu-Sa 11:30am-2:30pm and 7-11:30pm. V, MC.

La Sangria, 3 pl. de la République (tel. 04 90 34 31 96), presents a delicious array of *provençal* specialties and basic favorites on a terrace in the lively *place. Moules* 52F, sangria 18F, 3-course *menu* 50F for lunch, 65F for dinner. Open M-Sa noon-2pm and 7-10pm; closed Tu night in the off-season. V, MC.

Le Yaca, 24 pl. Silvain (tel. 04 90 34 70 03), in a cozy little corner near the Roman theater, serves *provençal* plates (around 65F) and *menus* for 65F and 90F. Wheelchair accessible. Open Th-M noon-2pm and 7-10pm, Tu noon-2pm.

👁 🎵 SIGHTS AND ENTERTAINMENT

SIGHTS. Built around the 1st century, Orange's striking **Théâtre Antique** (tel. 04 90 51 17 60) is the best-preserved Roman theater in Europe, and one of only three in the world to have maintained its stage wall (103m wide by 37m tall). After the fall of Rome, this house of pagan entertainment fell into disrepair and peasants set up house in and around its walls. In the mid-19th century, engineers rediscovered its fantastic acoustics and used the remaining front three rows as a template for rebuilding the seating area, which can now accommodate 9000 (the theater reopened in 1869). A 3.5m headless statue, discovered in the orchestra pit and reconstructed in 1931 to resemble the city's founder, Augustus, presides over the scene from above the portal. The theater originally held 10,000 spectators and adjoined a gymnasium complete with running tracks, combat platform, sauna, and temple. Free, interesting history lessons disguised as one-hour tours in French are offered three times a day in July and August; call the tourist office for schedules. Across the street is the **Musée Municipal** (tel. 04 90 51 18 24), which includes many of the antique objects found in the excavations around Orange, as well as rooms dedicated to the more recent history of the Orange family and to the fabrication of *provençal* cloth. (Theatre and museum open daily Apr.-Sept. 9am-6:30pm; Oct.-Mar. 9am-noon and 1:30-5pm. Combined admission 30F, students 25F.)

Above the theater, the **Colline St-Eutrope** features a panoramic view and free, though acoustically poor, concert standing room amidst the ruins of the Princes of Orange's castle. Orange's other major monument, the **Arc de Triomphe,** stands on the ancient via Agrippa, which once connected Arles to Lyon. Built during Augustus' time, it was dedicated to Tiberius in AD 25 and now stands in the middle of a highway roundabout. Eight Corinthian columns adorn this three-arched monument, whose facades depict Roman victories on land and sea over the Gauls. During the Middle Ages, it was filled in and used to create a defense tower, the Tour de l'Arc. It stands today as an elaborate testament to the Romans' healthy self-confidence. **Le Petit Train** (tel. 04 90 34 71 89) visits these sites in the summer and leaves from the tourist office in front of the antique theater. (25F, children 10F.)

ENTERTAINMENT. In July, the theater returns to its original function with the **Chorégies,** a series of grand opera and choral productions. Info is available from the Maison des Chorégies, 18 pl. Sylvain (tel. 04 90 34 24 24), next to the theater. (Open Feb.-May M-F 9am-noon and 2-5pm; June M-Sa 9am-noon and 2-6pm; July daily 9am-7pm. Tickets run 40-890F. Under 18 and students under 28 can buy tickets for as little as 20F, and get up to 50% off on all other seats.) In August, more laid-back rock concerts, films, and variety shows take the stage (tickets free-800F). For info, call the Service Culturel (tel. 04 90 51 57 57).

FRENCH KISSIN'

Wondering how to get a little closer? Don't be shy! The *bise* (a small peck on the cheek) is *de rigueur* when meeting and greeting friends and family—even new acquaintances—in a social setting. Though males shake hands between themselves, in mixed or all-women settings everyone is expected to extend a cheek. Protocol varies by region, from two (one on each side, mind your nose during the switch) to four, which is most common in the south, to just one, a trend gaining popularity among Parisian teenagers. When in doubt of the magic number, pull back when they do. While lip-to-cheek contact is expected (a loud "mwaah" while kissing the air will not suffice), a *bise* should be no more than a crisp, methodical peck—not surprisingly, however, such an intimate opportunity isn't always thrown away lightly. Beware of (or indulge in) the soft, lingering *bise*; such tongue-on-cheek business bespeaks an interest beyond mere *amitié*.

VAISON-LA-ROMAINE

A drive through seemingly endless vineyards and past cozy hamlets tucked into the mountainside will bring you to Vaison-la-Romaine (pop. 6,000). This once-wealthy Roman town still charms, even if it requires a touch of imagination to conjure up the lavish villas and luxurious baths amidst the sprawling rubble. This *urbs opulentissima* had modest origins as a Ligurian settlement, before privileged Romans moved in to build their dream houses in the second half of the 1st century AD. Raymond of Toulouse built a defensive fortress on the neighboring hill in the 12th century, and the medieval town followed suite. Nowadays the Ouvèze river conveniently divides the cobblestoned, ivy-covered *haute ville* from the Roman excavations and the modern town. It is this relatively new quarter that is overrun every Tuesday by vendors' carts piled with *provençal* crafts, locally grown honey, lavender, olives, cheese, and, of course, wine. For wine connoisseurs, the tourist office will be happy to furnish a list of *caves* that offer *dégustations* of the local Ventoux or Gigondas reds.

▮ PRACTICAL INFORMATION. Vaison by **bus** to **Orange** (50min., M-Sa 2-3 per day, 25.50F) and **Avignon** (1½hr., M-Sa 2 per day, 38.50F). Call **Voyages Lieutard** for details (tel. 04 90 36 09 90). To reach the classy **tourist office,** pl. du Chanoine Sautel (tel. 04 90 36 02 11; fax 04 90 28 76 04), from the bus station, cross the parking lot of the gas station and turn right on av. Victor Hugo to pl. Monfort. Continue past the *place* for a block and turn right onto the Grande Rue. Walk two blocks to the tourist office on the right (10min.). They also offer **currency exchange** with commission. (Open July-Aug. daily 9am-12:30pm and 2-7pm; Sept.-June M-Sa 9am-noon and 2-6pm, Su 9am-noon.) Turn your nose up at the frustrating bus system and **rent a bike** at **Peugeot Motos Cycles,** 33 av. Jules Ferry. (Tel. 04 90 36 03 29. 50-80F per day. Passport deposit. Open M-Sa 9am-noon and 2-7pm.) Pick up *Livrets Cyclos Parcours* (35F) for route ideas. The **post office** is at pl. du 11 Novembre (tel. 04 90 36 06 40) and has no-commission **currency exchange.** (Open M-F 8:30am-noon and 2-5pm, Sa 8:30am-noon. **Postal code:** 84110.)

▮▮ ACCOMMODATIONS AND FOOD. Most hotels are pricey. **Hôtel du Théâtre Romain** (tel. 04 90 28 71 98; fax 04 90 28 86 96), on pl. de l'Abbé-Jautel near the tourist office, is the closest to cheap. Clean, sometimes stuffy rooms all have telephones and TVs. (Singles or doubles 155F, with shower 230F, with toilet 260F. Extra bed 70F. Breakfast 35F. V, MC.) The best source of inexpensive food is the Tuesday **market** in the town center (8am-1pm). During the rest of the week, squeeze melons at the **Super U supermarket,** on the intersection of av. Choralies and av. Victor Hugo. (Tel. 04 90 10 06 00. Open M-Sa 8:30am-8pm.) Most restaurants in Vaison have *menus* starting at 65F. **Chez Rina,** 19 Grande Rue (tel. 04 90 28 86 84), serves cheap, plentiful portions. (Pastas 35-55F, salads 17-45F, *menus* 58-110F. Open daily July-Sept. noon-11pm, Oct.-June noon-3pm and 6:30-11pm.)

☎ **SIGHTS.** Vaison-la-Romaine's tourist industry is refreshingly organized for your convenience, not theirs. A **"passport"** for 40F (under 25 years old 22F, 12-18 years 14F), good for the duration of your stay, allows access to all the sites and includes tours in French or English (ask at tourist office for times). To either side of the tourist office lie the **Quartier de Puymin** and the **Quartier de la Villasse,** where ruins of Roman houses, baths, and mosaics stretch over hills carpeted with roses, pines, and cypress trees. Although not much is left of the ancients' extravagance, the excellent city guides will conjure up the Roman *mode de vie*. The Puymin excavation includes a reconstruction of the **Roman theater** which regularly hosts events in the summer and offers a beautiful view of the surrounding vineyards. (Puymin daily open July-Aug. 9:30am-7pm, June and Sept. 9:30am-6pm. Villasse open daily July-Aug. 9:30am-noon and 2:30-7pm, June and Sept. 9:30am-noon and 2:30-6pm. Both ruins open Mar.-May and Oct. daily 10am-12:30pm and 2-6pm, Nov.-Feb. W-M 10am-noon and 2-4:30pm.) The best-preserved sculptures, mosaics, and ceramics from the excavations are housed in the small **Musée Theo Desplans.** (Open daily July-Aug. 9:30am-7pm; June and Sept. 9:30am-6pm; Mar.-May and Oct. 10am-12:30pm and 2:30-6pm; Nov.-Feb. W-M 10-11:30am and 2-4pm.)

Also included in the passport is the 12th-century **cloister** near the Quartier de la Villasse. With its columns and stylized capitals perfectly intact, the gallery has become a display case for remnants from the 6th-century Merovingian church. Connected to the cloister, the 11th- to 13th-century **Cathédrale de Notre-Dame** sits on a foundation of recycled Roman columns. (Both open daily July-Aug. 9:30am-noon and 2-6:30pm, June and Sept. 9:30am-noon and 2-5:30pm, Mar.-May and Oct. 10am-12:30pm and 2-5:30pm, Nov.-Feb. 10am-noon and 2-4pm. Cloister alone 8F.)

Across the well-preserved **Pont Romain** and up the hill is the medieval **Haute Ville,** where lush and flowery gardens spill over walks and wooden gates. The 12th-century **fortress,** built under Count Raymond V of Toulouse, still fends off invaders. Although the stronghold is locked up for safety reasons, the climb will give you a great view of the town below, the wine-covered Ouvèze valley, and **Mont Ventoux's** fabled peak (1912m). The tourist office in nearby **Malaucène** (tel. 04 90 65 22 59) organizes **night hikes** for the intrepid up to the Mont on Fridays in July.

🎭 **FESTIVALS.** Vaison doesn't always slumber in its golden past. From early July to early August, the city puts on an impressive **festival d'été,** which brings ballet, opera, drama, and classical music to the Roman theater almost nightly. (Reservations and information after mid-May tel. 04 90 36 02 11. Tickets 120-220F.) Other events of interest in Vaison include **Chorijazz,** a vocal jazz festival at the beginning of August (tickets 40-100F), and **Les Journées Gourmandes,** a celebration of the food of Provence in the second week of November.

THE CÔTE D'AZUR

A sunny place for shady people.

Somerset Maugham

Sparkling between Marseille and the Italian border, sun-drenched beaches and warm Mediterranean waters form the backdrop for this fabled playground of the beautiful and wealthy. Today, the area is a destination for low-budget backpackers and millionaires alike. Many French condemn the coast as a mere shadow of its former self, but the Côte remains an uncommon garden of delights bathed in vibrant colors. Pastel villas rim the sterling blue hues of the sea, while olive trees shelter roses and mimosas. By day, beaches invite swimming and sunning *au naturel;* by night, clubs and casinos cater to more expensive whims.

The Riviera's resort culture developed in the 18th and 19th centuries, when the English and Russian aristocracy came to its unspoiled fishing villages to cure winter ailments in the sun and sea. Soon Nice was drawing a steady crowd of the idle rich, whose favorite seaside sports included carriage-riding and seeing-and-dou-

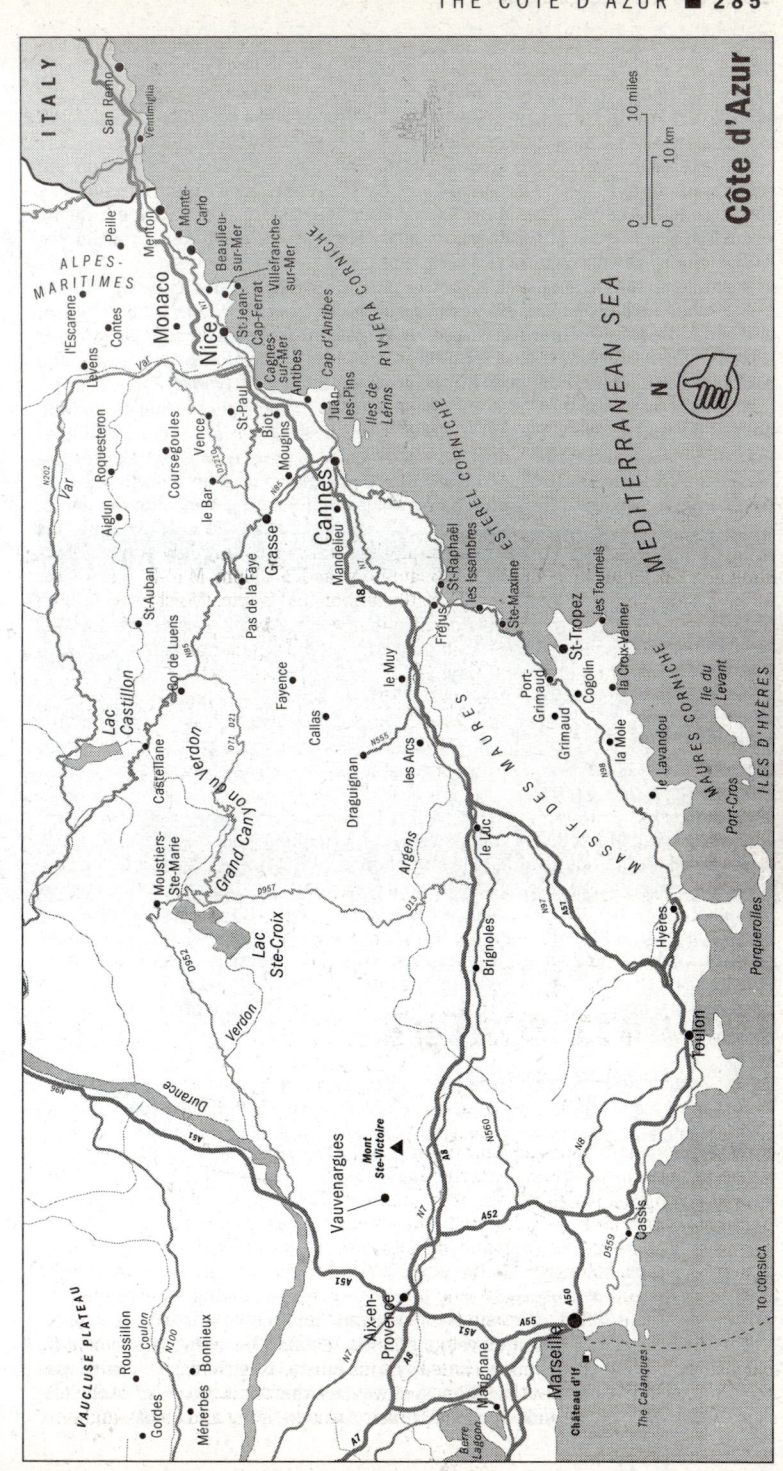

Côte d'Azur

bling. In the 1920s, Coco Chanel popularized the *provençal* farmer's healthy tan among her society customers; parasols went down, hemlines went up, and a religion of sun worship was born. The Côte began to see proletarian vacationers only after World War II, when new highways and railroads and a government-mandated increase in paid vacation time made the area accessible to the commoner.

Some of the past century's greatest artists came to the Côte for restoration and inspiration, from F. Scott Fitzgerald and Cole Porter at Cap d'Antibes, to Picasso, Renoir, and Matisse in Nice. Many towns along the eastern stretch of the Côte lay claim to a chapel, room, or wall decorated by Matisse or Chagall. Other regular visitors included Queen Victoria and Tsar Nicolas III.

Nightlife on the Riviera is wild. There's raucous revelry in Nice's *Carnaval* (late Feb.), while high-society magazines live on fodder from the Cannes Film Festival and the Monte-Carlo Grand Prix, both in May. Jazz festivals enrich the summer nights in most towns, and Monaco's Fireworks Festival explodes in August. Take a break from it all on the islands off the coast of Cannes or Hyères.

The food is simple and fresh all along the Côte. Regional specialities include *bouillabaisse* (a hearty fish and seafood stew), *soupe au pistou* (a brew of pine nuts, fresh basil, and garlic), *aïoli* (a creamy garlic dip to accompany fresh vegetables), and fresh seafood. The rough, full reds of the nearby Côte du Rhône and clean, lavender rosés of the Côte de Provence will infuse any meal with radiance.

HIGHLIGHTS OF CÔTE D'AZUR

■ **Nice's** palm-lined promenades, outstanding museums, high-class boutiques, and labyrinthine old town make it a must-see stop on any *tour de France* (p. 287).

■ High-rollers still strut in **St-Tropez,** easily the most chic spot on the Côte (p. 322).

■ The tranquility of the Riviera is concentrated in **Antibes,** home to the cliffside **Musée Picasso,** the shanty that housed the artist in 1946 (p. 307).

■ The best **beaches** snuggle between major towns. Try **Cap d'Ail,** between Monaco and Menton (p. 299), or **St-Raphaël,** between Cannes and St-Tropez (p. 319).

▐ GETTING AROUND

The coast from Marseille to Italy is served by frequent, inexpensive trains and buses. Most attractions lie along the stretch from St-Raphaël to Menton. Trains for the Côte leave Paris's Gare de Lyon hourly in summer; the trip on the TGV to Marseille takes five hours, to Nice seven to eight hours. Hitchhiking, never a safe pursuit, is said to be difficult along the coastal highway but less trying on inland country roads. You might want to base yourself in a sedate, less expensive town and make daytrips to the purse-emptying cities and inviting beaches. The Riviera is best visited in early June and in September, when crowds and prices are low and hotel vacancies and temperature high.

 A cautionary note: every woman who has traveled on the Riviera has a story to tell about men in the big beach towns. Unsolicited pick-up techniques range from subtle invitations to more naked displays of interest. Most can be brushed off with a biting *"laissez-moi tranquille!"* ("leave me alone") or stony indifference, but don't be shy about enlisting the help of passers-by or the police to fend off Mediterranean Don Juans.

◐ BEACHES

In summer, the optimal swimming time is from 7pm to 9pm, just before sunset. Bring a beach mat (20F at supermarkets); even the sand beaches are a bit rocky. Since almost all the towns on the *Côte* lie along one local rail line, just hop off and on to see what you can find. The largest cities have the worst beaches: Marseille's is artificial, Nice's are rocky, Cannes' private, and St-Tropez's remote. Alcoves between towns, like Cap Martin (between Monaco and Menton), Cap d'Ail (between Monaco and Nice), and St-Raphaël (between Cannes and St-Tropez), are calmer. Nearly all beaches are topless, while those who like to bare it all will find a wealth of secluded shores. At Héliopolis on the Île du Levant, and in the *calanques* between Èze-sur-Mer and Cap d'Ail, *naturistes* will find plenty of company. Don't neglect less-frequented islands: Porquerolles, the Île du Levant, and the Îles de Lérins off Cannes all have fine rock ledges and secluded coves.

Although crashing on the beach is illegal and dangerous, many travelers sleep where they sun. A number of beaches provide showers, toilets, and towels for a small fee (10-15F). Those who try to spend the night on the beaches at Nice, Cannes, and Juan-les-Pins may run afoul of more than the law. You could find yourself bedding down next to groups of "respectable"-looking youths whose summer salary is earned in tourists' jewelry, mopeds, and cash.

NICE

Cosmopolitan and chic, sun-drenched and spicy, Nice sparkles as the unofficial capital of the Riviera. A rite of passage for young travelers, the city holds an energetic nightlife tuned to the tastes of the anglophones who constantly flood it. Top-notch museums, vibrant art, and a bustling shore make Nice an urban destination, with excellent local and regional transportation, decent cheap lodgings, and a populace accustomed to tourists. You may also encounter the down-side of big-city life—at night, personal safety can be a concern.

During the famous annual *Carnaval*, native *niçois* and thousands of temporary inhabitants ring in Lent with wild floral revelry, grotesque costumes, and raucous merriment. Even if you can't make it for Carnival, you'll find plenty of merrymaking year round in the streets of Vieux Nice. Tucked into the southeastern pocket of the city, the old town's labyrinthine pedestrian streets teem with markets in the mornings. At night, peddlers give way to the boisterous bars, clubs, and restaurants that smaller Riviera towns lack. Be prepared to make friends, to hear more English than French, and to have more fun than you'll remember.

✴ ORIENTATION

The train station, Nice-Ville, is in the center of town next to the tourist office on av. Thiers. The area around the station is somewhat seedy but packed with cheap restaurants and budget hotels. To the left as you stumble out of the station, you'll hit **av. Jean Médecin,** which runs toward the water to **pl. Masséna** (10min.). Heading right from the train station, you'll run into **bd. Gambetta,** the other main street running directly to the water. Sweeping along the coast, the **promenade des Anglais** (which becomes quai des États-Unis east of av. Jean Médecin) is a people-watching paradise, as are the cafés, boutiques, and overpriced restaurants of the pedestrian zone west of pl. Masséna. To the southeast pulsates **Vieux Nice.** Farther to the east, on the opposite side of Le Château, lies **Port Lympia,** a warren of alleyways, boulevards, brasseries, and *tabacs.*

Unfortunately, Nice's big-city appeal is coupled with big-city crime. At night, women may want to avoid walking alone, and everyone should exercise caution around the train station, Vieux Nice, and on the Promenade des Anglais.

▪ TRANSPORTATION

Flights: Aéroport Nice-Côte d'Azur (tel. 04 93 21 30 30). Airport open daily 6:15am-10:30pm. **Air France,** 10 av. Félix-Faure (tel. 04 93 80 66 11 for info, 04 93 18 89 89 for reservations), serves **Paris** (800-1200F, 450-880F under 25) and **Corsica** (500-800F, 300-500F under 25). Open M-Sa 9am-6pm. **easyJet** flies to **London;** see **Budget Airlines,** p. 60. To get to the airport, take Sunbus #23 (direction "St-Laurent," every 20min. 6am-9pm, 10F) from the station. Be sure to ask for the Sunbus stop. The more expensive airport bus (21F; tel. 04 93 56 35 40) runs from pl. Masséna every 20min.

Trains: Gare SNCF Nice-Ville, av. Thiers (tel. 04 92 14 81 62). To: **Cannes** (40min., every 15-45min., last train midnight, from 32F); **Marseille** (2¾hr., every 30-90min., 148F); **Monaco** (25min., every 10-30min., last train 12:30am, 20F); **Paris** (7hr., change in Marseille, June-Sept. about 7, rest of year 4, 420-522F). Open daily 8am-8pm. **Luggage storage** daily 7am-10pm (30F per day per piece). **Gare du Sud,** 4bis rue Alfred Binet (tel. 04 93 82 10 17), 800m from Nice-Ville. Smaller trains, the *chemins de fer de la Provence,* run through the southern Alps to **Digne** (3¼hr.; 5 per day, 3 on Su; 110F). Info office open M-Sa 8am-6:30pm, Su 8:30-11:15am and 2-6pm.

Buses: 5 bd. Jean Jaurès (tel. 04 93 85 61 81). Ticket counters and booth open M-Sa 6:30am-8pm. Buy most tickets on the bus. To: **Monaco** (30min.; 4 per hr. M-Sa, 3 Su; last bus 7:30pm; 20F); **Cannes** (1¼hr.; 3 per hr. M-Sa, 2 per hour Su; 30F).

Local Transportation: Sunbus, 10 av. Félix Faure (tel. 04 93 16 52 10), near pl. Leclerc and pl. Masséna. Long treks to museums, the beach, and hostels make the 24F day pass, 72F 10-ticket carnet, 88F 5-day pass, or 115F 7-day pass well worth it. Buy passes at the agency (open M-F 7am-7pm, Sa 7am-6pm), the kiosk at sq. Leclerc (open M-F 6:30am-9:30pm), or on board. Individual tickets 8F. Bus #12 links the station, pl. Masséna, and the beach every 12min. Ask at the tourist office for the **"Plan Sunbus"** bus map and the **"Guide Infobus,"** which lists schedules and routes.

Ferries: SNCM, quai du Commerce (tel. 04 93 13 66 66; fax 04 93 13 66 81), at the port. Take bus #1 or 2 (direction "Port") from pl. Masséna. Service to Corsica: see **Corsica: Getting there,** p. 330, for more info. 270-310F one-way, ages 12-25 240-280F, children 135-155F; bikes 91F; cars 200-1200F. Open M-F 8am-7pm, Sa 8am-noon.

Taxis: Central Taxi Riviera (tel. 04 93 13 78 78). Get a price range before boarding, and make sure the meter is turned on. Airport 150-200F. Often 50F minimum at night.

Bike and Car Rental: Cycles Arnaud, 4 pl. Grimaldi (tel. 04 93 87 88 55), near pedestrian zone. Bikes 100F per day, 2000F or credit card deposit. Reductions for longer rentals. Open M-Sa 9am-noon and 2-7pm. **JML Location,** 34 av. Auber, opposite the station (tel. 04 93 16 07 00; fax 04 93 16 07 48). Bikes 60-80F per day, 300-390F per week. Scooters 130-310F per day, 800-1850F per week; 2000-5000F credit card deposit. Cars 259F per day with 200km free, 0.70F each additional km. Minimum age 21. Open M-F 8am-1pm and 2-6:30pm, Sa 8am-1pm.

🔢 PRACTICAL INFORMATION

Tourist Office: Av. Thiers (tel. 04 93 87 07 07; fax 04 93 16 85 16; www.nice-coteazur.org), beside the train station. Limited reservation service from 8am; stake out a place in line early. Ask for the English *Nice: A Practical Guide,* a bus map and schedule, the English *Museums of Nice,* and a detailed map (essential in Vieux Nice). To find out what's happening, pick up the free monthly *Le Mois à Nice* and the free weekly *Scènes d'Azur,* with cultural and live music listings. *Semaine des Spectacles* (8F at *tabacs*), published every Wednesday, lists entertainment for the entire Côte. Open daily June 15-Sept. 15 7:30am-8pm; Sept. 16-June 14 8am-7pm. **Branches:** 5 prom. des Anglais (tel. 04 92 14 48 00; fax 04 92 14 48 03; open June 15-Sept. 15 daily 8am-8pm, Sept. 16-June 14 M-Sa 9am-6pm); Nice Ferber, prom. des Anglais, near the airport (tel. 04 93 83 32 64; fax 04 93 72 08 27; same hours as prom. des Anglais office); and airport terminal 1 (tel. 04 93 21 44 11; fax 04 93 21 44 50; open daily 8am-10pm).

Budget Travel Offices: USIT, 15 rue de France (tel. 04 93 87 34 96; fax. 04 93 87 10 91), near pl. Masséna. Open M-F 9:30am-6pm, Sat 10am-1pm.

Consulates: Canada, 64 av. Jean Médecin (tel. 04 93 92 93 22). **USA,** 31 rue Maréchal Joffre (tel. 04 93 88 89 55; fax 04 93 87 07 38). Open M-F 9-11:30am and 1:30-4:30pm. **UK,** 11 rue Paradis (tel. 04 93 82 32 04). Open T-Th 10am-noon.

Money: Cambio, 17 av. Thiers (tel. 04 93 88 56 80), opposite the train station. No commission. Open daily 7am-midnight. **Change,** 10 av. Félix Faure (tel. 04 93 80 36 67), AmEx traveler's checks, no commission. Open M-Sa 9:30am-1:30pm and 2:30-5:30pm. **American Express:** 11 promenade des Anglais (tel. 04 93 16 53 53; fax 04 93 16 53 42), at the corner of rue des Congrès. Open daily 9am-9pm.

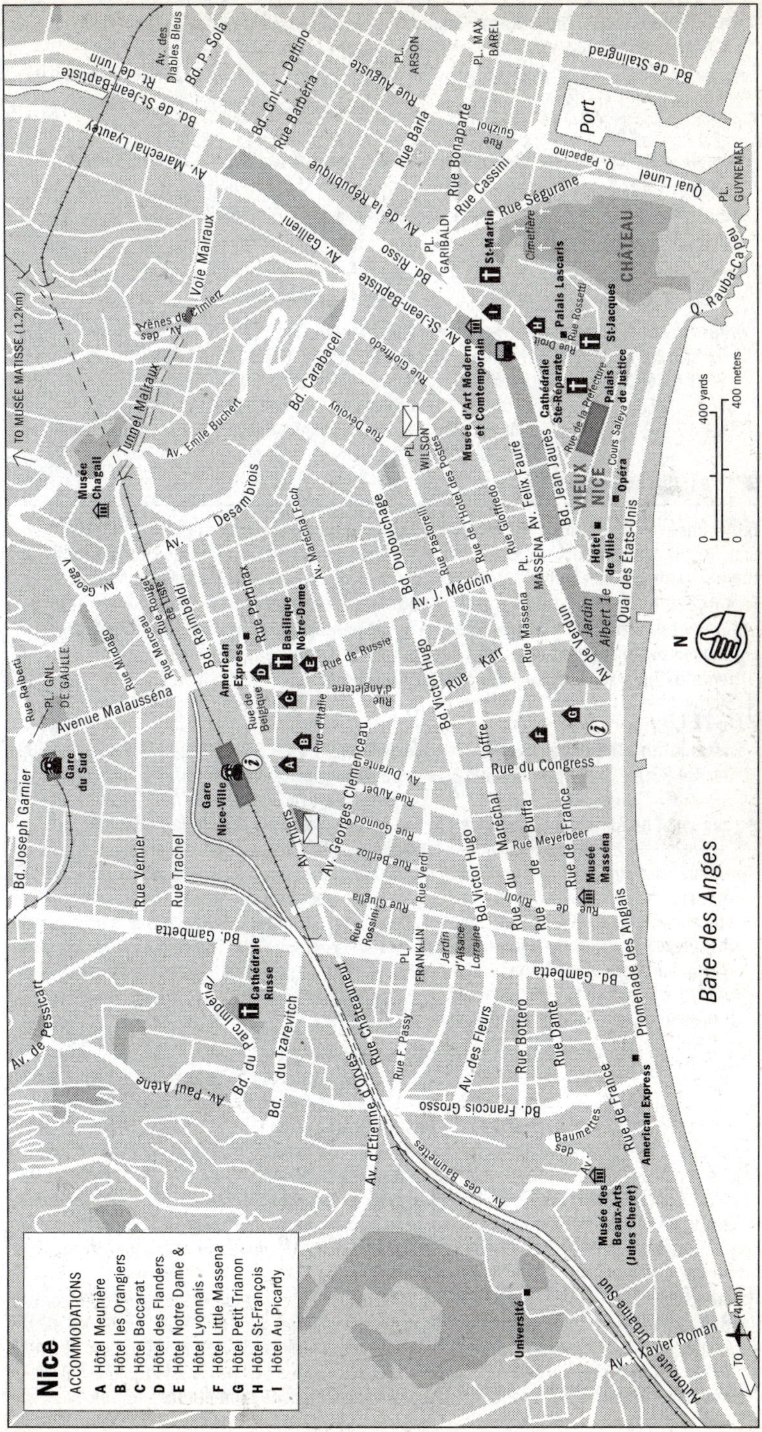
Nice
ACCOMMODATIONS
A Hôtel Meunière
B Hôtel les Orangiers
C Hôtel Baccarat
D Hôtel des Flanders
E Hôtel Notre Dame & Hôtel Lyonnais
F Hôtel Little Massena
G Hôtel Petit Trianon
H Hôtel St-François
I Hôtel Au Picardy
Baie des Anges
Promenade des Anglais
Quai des États-Unis
Quai Lunel
Q. Rauba-Capeu
Q. Papacino
Port
Bd. de Stalingrad
CHÂTEAU
Cimetière
VIEUX NICE
Cours Saleya
Palais de Justice
Cathédrale Ste-Réparate
Palais Lascaris
St-Jacques
St-Martin
Opéra
Hotel de Ville
Musée d'Art Moderne et Contemporain
Musée Chagall
Musée Masséna
Musée des Beaux-Arts (Jules Cheret)
Cathédrale Russe
Basilique Notre-Dame
American Express
Gare Nice-Ville
Gare du Sud
Université
Jardin Albert 1er
Jardin d'Alsace-Lorraine
PL. MASSENA
PL. GARIBALDI
PL. WILSON
PL. FRANKLIN
PL. GNL. DE GAULLE
PL. ARSON
PL. MAX BAREL
PL. GUYNEMER
Av. Jean Médecin
Av. Félix Faure
Bd. Jean Jaurès
Av. de Verdun
Av. de la République
Av. St-Jean-Baptiste
Bd. Risso
Av. Gallieni
Bd. Carabacel
Av. Desambrois
Bd. Dubouchage
Bd. Victor Hugo
Rue de France
Rue Masséna
Rue Pastorelli
Rue de l'Hôtel des Postes
Rue Gioffredo
Rue Defly
Av. Maréchal Foch
Rue Pertinax
Rue de Russie
Rue d'Angleterre
Rue d'Italie
Rue de Belgique
Rue Alphonse Karr
Rue Maréchal Joffre
Rue du Congrès
Rue Meyerbeer
Rue de Rivoli
Rue du Buffa
Rue Dante
Rue Bottero
Av. des Fleurs
Rue F. Passy
Rue Rossini
Rue Verdi
Rue Gounod
Rue Berlioz
Rue Auber
Av. Durante
Rue Gustave Deloye
Av. Thiers
Av. Georges Clemenceau
Bd. Gambetta
Rue Trachel
Rue Vernier
Bd. Joseph Garnier
Avenue Malausséna
Bd. Raimbaldi
Rue Marceau
Rue Rouget de Lisle
Rue Midi
Rue Raiberti
Av. George V
Av. Emile Buchert
Tunnel Malraux
Voie Malraux
Arènes de Cimiez
Av. des Arènes
TO MUSÉE MATISSE (1.2km)
Av. Maréchal Lyautey
Bd. de St-Jean-Baptiste
Rt. de Turin
Bd. P. Sola
Av. des Diables Bleus
Bd. Gnl. L. Delfino
Rue Barbéris
Rue Auguste
Rue Barla
Rue Bonaparte
Rue Cassini
Rue Ségurane
Rue Guizol
Rue Rossetti
Rue Droite
Rue de la Préfecture
Av. de Pessicart
Av. Paul Arène
Bd. du Parc Impérial
Bd. du Tzarevitch
Av. d'Etienne d'Orves
Rue Châteauneuf
Bd. François Grosso
Av. des Baumettes
Autoroute Urbaine Sud
Av. Xavier Roman
TO (4km)
400 yards
400 meters
N

English Bookstore: The Cat's Whiskers, 26 rue Lamartine (tel. 04 93 80 02 66). Great selection. Open M-Sa 9:30am-12:15pm and 2-6:45pm (3-6:45pm in summer).

Youth Center: Centre d'Information Jeunesse, 19 rue Gioffredo (tel. 04 93 80 93 93; fax 04 93 80 30 33), close to outer edge of prom. du Paillion. Board with student summer jobs. Open M-F 10am-7pm.

Laundromat: Laverie Automatique, rue de Suisse (tel. 04 93 88 78 52), between rue Paganini and rue d'Angleterre. Close to hotels around the station. Open daily 7am-9pm.

Police: Tel. 04 93 17 22 22. At opposite end of bd. M. Foch from bd. Jean Médecin.

Hospital: St-Roch, 5 rue Pierre Devoluy (tel. 04 92 03 33 75).

Post Office: 23 av. Thiers (tel. 04 93 82 65 22), near the station. Open M-Tu, Th-F 8am-7pm, W 8:30am-7pm, Sa 8am-noon. **Postal code:** 06000.

Internet Access: Organic Cafe, 16 rue Paganini (tel 04 93 16 97 82). Mention *Let's Go* for special rates: 10F for 15min, 35F for 1hr. Open M-Sa 10am-10pm, Su 2pm-8pm. **Web Nice,** 25bis promenade des Anglais (tel. 04 93 88 72 75). Open Tu-Sa 10am-8pm. 30F for 30min, 50F for 1hr. **Cyber Café La Douche,** 34 cours Saleya (tel. 04 93 62 40 20), a dark, black-lit bar/club. 25F for 30min., 45F 1hr. Open 4pm-2:30am.

⌐ ACCOMMODATIONS

Nice's hostels are out of the way and often full; call three to five days in advance. For hotels, you need to choose between the cluster of budget options around the train station, or the pricier, less modern hotels close to the action in Vieux Nice. Reserve at least one to two weeks ahead in the summer or you may be joining the legions of visitors who camp outside the train station, which moonlights as one of the largest and most dangerous bedrooms in France. In the morning, the tourist office may be able to help with accommodations.

HOSTELS

Relais International de la Jeunesse "Clairvallon," 26 av. Scudéri (tel. 04 93 81 27 63; fax 04 93 53 35 88), in Cimiez, 4km out of town. Take bus #15 to "Scudéri" (direction "Rimiez," 20min., every 10min.) from the train station or pl. Masséna. Get off the bus, turn right heading uphill and take the first left. To walk from the station, turn left and left again on av. Jean Médecin, then right before the overpass on bd. Raimbaldi. Go 6 blocks and turn right on av. Comboul, then left on bd. Carabacel. Follow it up the hill as it turns into bd. de Cimiez. Turn right before the hospital onto av. de Flirey, keep trudging uphill until you reach av. Scudéri, then turn left and follow the signs. It's you and 160 new friends in the luxurious villa of a deceased marquis. Too bad for him, but you get tennis, basketball courts, and a lovely TV, and a dining room, all in a pretty residential part of Nice. 4- to 10-bunk rooms. Bed and breakfast 72F. 3-course dinner 50F. Check-in 5pm. Lockout 9:30am-5pm. Curfew 11pm.

Auberge de Jeunesse (HI), route Forestière du Mont-Álban (tel. 04 93 89 23 64; fax 04 92 04 03 10), 4km away from it all. From the bus station, take bus #14 (direction "Mont Baron") to "l'Auberge" (M-F every 15min., Sa-Su every 30min.; last bus 7:30pm). From the train station, take #17 and tell the driver you need to switch to the #14. Otherwise it's a 50min. walk. From the train station, turn left and then right on av. Jean Médecin. Follow it through pl. Masséna and turn left on bd. Jaurès. Pass the Musée d'Art Contemporain and turn right on rue Barla, following the signs up the hill. The hostel draws a cool, friendly crowd, so you can start a *fête* of your own. 56 beds in 8- to 10-bed dorms. Kitchen. 68F. Breakfast included. Lockout 10am-5pm. 12:30am curfew.

NEAR THE TRAIN STATION

▧ Hôtel Les Orangiers, 10bis av. Durante (tel. 04 93 87 51 41; fax 04 93 82 57 82). Large, bright 6-bed dorms and rooms with sky-themed walls, most with showers and fridges. A few rooms with balconies are a real treat. Singles are small. Helpful English-speaking owner offers free beach mat loan and luggage storage. He may be able to direct you elsewhere if he's full. Dorms 85F; singles 100F; doubles 210F; triples 285F; quads 360F. Prices 10F lower in off-season. Breakfast 20F. Closed Nov. V, MC.

Hôtel Baccarat, 39 rue d'Angleterre (tel. 04 93 88 35 73; fax 04 93 16 14 25). Large, well-kept rooms, some renovated with tasteful lighting, pastel trimmings, and new beds. Friendly, no-nonsense staff create a homey ambience with concern for security. Some "romantic" suites. All rooms and dorms have bathroom. 3- to 5-person dorms 84-90F; singles 174F; doubles 217F. Prices drop 10-20F off-season. Breakfast 15F. V, MC.

Hôtel des Flanders, 6 rue de Belgique (tel. 04 93 88 78 94; fax 04 93 88 74 90). Large rooms with phones, big bathrooms, and worn carpets. Friendly owners will negotiate for long stays. Pretty TV parlor. 5-bed dorm for students 90F; singles 200F; doubles 220-250F; triples 340F; quads 360-400F. Extra bed 60F. Breakfast 25F. V, MC.

Hôtel Notre Dame, 22 rue de Russie (tel. 04 93 88 70 44; fax 04 93 82 20 38), at the corner of rue d'Italie 1 block west of av. Jean Médecin. Elegant, quiet rooms with phones and pleasing decor. If full, they'll shuttle you to another of their nearby hotels. Singles 200F; doubles 240F; triples 300F; quad apartments 350F. Extra person 85F. Breakfast 20F. Shower 10F. V, MC, AmEx.

Hôtel Belle Meunière, 21 av. Durante (tel. 04 93 88 66 15), near the train station, on a street facing the train station. Hostelers hang out in the hallways and gardens and jest with the owner. 4- to 5-bed co-ed dorms 76-101F; doubles 160-275F; triples 243-330F. Breakfast included. Luggage storage 10F.

Hôtel Lyonnais, 20 rue de Russie (tel. 04 93 88 70 74; fax 04 93 16 25 56). Pleasant rooms, some with street-side balconies, some facing a quieter courtyard. Singles 145-200F; doubles 160-260F; triples 240-290F; quads 300-390F, depending on facilities. 10% off-season Let's Go discount. Breakfast 22F. Shower 15F. V, MC, AmEx.

VIEUX NICE

Hôtel Little Masséna, 22 rue Masséna (tel./fax 04 93 87 72 34; fax 04 93 87 72 34). Intimate family-run hotel in a boisterous and touristy part of town. Standard rooms have TV and kitchenette. Singles and doubles 150F, 200F with shower, 250F with shower and toilet. Extra person 30F. Prices 10-30F cheaper in off-season. V, MC.

Hôtel Au Picardy, 10 bd. Jean-Jaurès (tel. 04 93 85 75 51), across from the bus station. The abundance of orange and brown is painful but proximity to Vieux Nice more than compensates. Older rooms can be noisy if on the street. Singles 170F, 190F with shower; doubles 200F. V, MC.

Hôtel Petit Trianon, 11 rue Paradis (tel. 04 93 87 50 46). Long-time owners offer humble rooms with elegant chandeliers. Close to beach, pl. Masséna and Vieux Nice. Singles 100F; doubles 200F; triples 300F. Showers 10F. Breakfast 25F.

Hôtel St-François, 3 rue St-François (tel. 04 93 85 88 69; fax 04 93 85 10 67). From the bus station entrance, cross the street and enter p. St-François. Turn right on rue St-François. It's on your right surrounded by *boucheries*. Great location a short stumble from the city's best nightlife. Dim, plain, but super-cheap rooms are stuffy in summer. Singles 95-135F; doubles 158F; triples 215-240F. Showers 15F.

◖ FOOD

A smorgasbord of international gastronomic delights complement seafood and *la cuisine niçoise,* flavored by local herbs and olives, and North African spices. Inexpensive local specialties are easy to find at *pâtisseries* and *boulangeries.* Sample *pan bagnat,* a round, crusty bread with tuna, sardines, and vegetables (20-28F), *pissaladière,* a pizza topped with onions, anchovies and olives (10-15F), and *socca,* a thin, soft, olive oil-flavored chickpea bread (10F). *Salade niçoise* is made with tuna, potatoes, tomatoes, and a spicy mustard dressing.

Cafés and food stands along the beach are expensive, so shop for lunch before you hit the waves. The fruit, fish, and flower **market** at cours Saleya is the best place to pick up fresh local olives, cheeses, and melons. (Tu-Su dawn-1pm.) You'll find everything else at **Prisunic supermarket,** 42 av. Jean Médecin (tel. 04 93 62 38

90; open M-Sa 8:30am-8:30pm), or **Casino supermarket** rue Deudor, behind the Nice Étoile on av. Jean Médecin (open M-Sa 8:30am-8pm), and behind Espace Magnan, on av. Gloria. For generous pizza portions, hit **av. Masséna** in the pedestrian zone. **Restaurant Université,** 3 av. Robert Schumann (tel. 04 93 97 10 20), serves students filling meals for about 36F. (Open Sept.-June daily 11:30am-1:30pm and 6-8pm.)

🦪 **Nissa Socca,** 5 rue Ste-Réparate (tel. 04 93 80 18 35). Practically a town landmark, the restaurant is famous for filling 35F *niçois* dishes in a homey aura. *Plat du jour* 49F and brick-oven-baked pizza 42-47F, all nestled in the narrow streets of Vieux Nice. Open M-Sa noon-2pm and 7-11pm.

🦪 **Acchiardo,** 38 rue Droite (tel. 04 93 85 51 16). Serves wonderful, simple *niçois* dishes that are immensely popular with a loyal local clientele. Surprisingly reasonable with pastas from 36F. Open M-F noon-1:30pm and 7-9:30pm.

Lou Pilha Leva, 10 rue du Collet (tel. 04 93 80 29 33), in Vieux Nice. Always bustling, this is where to get a lot of *niçois* food for little money. After ordering from the counter, settle down at one of the dark wood benches and feast on 15F pizzas, 10F *socca,* or 12F *pissaladière.* 40F *moules* (mussels) are hard to resist. Open daily 8am-11pm.

Indyana, 10 rue Chauvain (tel. 04 93 80 67 69). Trendy dinner spot for Nice's young and hip. Lighting scheme places an orange glow over the whole room. Always crowded, never cheap, but salads and pizzas are as well priced as anywhere. V, MC.

La Merenda, 4 rue de la Terrasse, no phone. Unlike other Vieux Nice restaurants, Le Merenda doesn't cater to tourists, and outsiders may feel out of place. The brave can savor the creations of a culinary master who abandoned chefdom in a four-star hotel to open this totem to *niçois* cuisine. Deliciously good value for the area (40-75F).

Voyageurs aux Nissart, 19 rue Alsace-Lorraine (tel. 04 93 82 19 60). Between Durante and Paganini. A good bet if you're stuck eating around the train station. Best deal is the four course 65F dinner, but less expensive options are available. V, MC, AmEx.

L'Authentic, 18 rue Biscarra (tel. 04 93 62 48 88). Inviting bistro ambience in a low-key neighborhood close to many budget hotels. Sampling plates from 56F are cheapest, but 68F and 87F *menus* are rewarding for those willing to spend more. V, MC.

👁 SIGHTS

Upon arriving in Nice, many head straight for the beaches and don't retreat from sun and water until the day is done, but the city houses a wealth of art and historical artifacts in its many museums. If nothing else, be sure to visit the Chagall museum and the Matisse museum, two stellar galleries devoted to the work of the one-time residents. The city itself is a museum with an oddball mix of architecture, a variety of ethnic influences, and a seemingly eternal bustle.

PROMENADE DES ANGLAIS. Stretching the length of Nice's waterfront and rocky beach, the promenade is a sight unto itself. Named after the affluent English community in Nice who had it built, the palm-lined boulevard was intended as a coastal response to other European cities' grand walking thoroughfares. Today the promenade is filled with luxury hotels like the stately **Negresco,** toward the west end of the promenade, where the staff still don top hats and uniforms that recall centuries past. Just east of the Negresco, the **Musée Masséna,** 35 prom. des Anglais, contains baubles and paintings from around the world, but is temporarily closed for renovation. **Private beaches** crowd the water between bd. Gambetta and the Opéra, but lots of public spaces compensate, especially west of bd. Gambetta. Whatever dreams you've had of Nice's beaches, the hard reality is a stretch of rocks somewhat smoothed by the sea—bring a beach mat. East of av. Jean Jaurès the promenade becomes **quai des États-Unis,** which abuts Vieux Nice and hosts the **Musée-Galerie Aléxis et Gustav-Adolf Mossa.** Here you'll find landscapes and symbolist works by *niçois* father and son team of the same name. *(59 quai des États-Unis. Tel. 04 93 62 37 11. Open Tu-Sa 10am-noon and 2-6pm, Su 2-6pm. 15F, students 9F.)*

LE CHÂTEAU. At the eastern end of the promenade, Le Château is a flowery, green hillside park crowned with the remains of an 11th-century cathedral and an artificial waterfall. Despite its name, there's no château—it was demolished in a battle during the 8th century. Jog blithely up more than 400 steps for a spectacular view of the rooftops of Nice and the sparkling blue Baie des Anges. Or ascend via elevator, by the Tour Bellanda. *(Park open 7am-8pm. Elevator runs 9am-7:30pm. 7F.)*

VIEUX NICE. Sprawling southeast from bd. Jean Jaurès, this *quartier* is the center of nightlife and a mix of tourist-trap cafés, shops, and *niçois* residences. The labyrinthine streets contain a number of buildings of historical significance. In the northeast corner of the quartier is the **Église St-Martin**, pl. St-Augustine, the city's oldest church. Its principal claim to fame is that the Italian revolutionary Garibaldi was baptized here. *(Open daily, 9am-noon and 2-6pm.)* Just south, **place St-François** holds a lively fish market on weekday mornings, though more æsthetically pleasing is the concurrent flower market on **cours Saleya,** next to the promenade. In an attempt to cash in on its appeal, knick-knack stands fill the cours throughout the day. By night its many cafés become prime spots for people-watching.

MUSÉE NATIONAL MARC CHAGALL. Radiating a universal holiness, the mesmerizing collection beautifully showcases Chagall's huge, color-saturated canvases, which fuse folklore and religion in his highly personal style. The centerpiece is the *Song of Songs*, a series of 17 paintings based on the Old Testament. A photo gallery offers a cursory visual biography of the man and his work. The stained glass windows in the small auditorium and the mosaic outside were created by Chagall specifically for the museum. In the wonderful garden, the otherwise expensive cafe serves reasonably priced coffee. *(Av. du Dr. Ménard. 15min. walk north of the station. Or take bus #15, direction "Rimiez" and "Les Sources," to "Musée Chagall." Tel. 04 93 53 87 20. July-Sept. open W-M 10am-5:40pm, 38F, students and seniors 28F. Oct.-June. open W-M 10am-4:50pm, 30F, students and seniors 20F.)*

MUSÉE MATISSE. If the Musée Chagall provides a religious experience, the Musée Matisse is truly a transcendental one. Henri Matisse lived and worked in Nice from 1917 until his death in 1954. Although he was best know for his paintings, the museum emphasizes his artistry in other media. The collection, which changes periodically, includes initial sketches, a model for his Chapelle du Rosaire in Vence, and books illustrated by the artist. *(164 av. des Arènes de Cimiez. Take bus #15, 17, or 20 to "Arènes". Tel. 04 93 81 08 08. Open W-M Apr.-Sept. 10am-6pm; Oct.-Mar. 10am-5pm. 25F, students 15F. Call for info on lectures, free with admission.)*

MUSÉE DES BEAUX-ARTS. Housed in the former villa of Ukrainian Princess Kotschoubey, the collection of 19th- and early 20th-century French artists highlights the work of Fragonard, Monet, Sisley, Bonnard, and Degas. It also features sculptures by Rodin and Carpeaux. Some rooms are more engaging than others. *(33 av. Baumettes. From the train station, take bus #38 to "Chéret" or #12 to "Grosseo". Tel. 04 92 15 28 28. Open Tu-Su 10am-noon and 2-6pm. Admission 25F, students 15F.)*

MUSÉE D'ART MODERNE ET D'ART CONTEMPORAIN. The museum is part of a large concrete, glass, steel, and marble complex that parallels its content: bold, new, and strangely elegant. It features over 400 European and American avant-garde pieces from 1960 to the present, emphasizing French New Realists and American Pop Art with works by Lichtenstein, Warhol, and Klein. *(Promenade des Arts, at the intersection of av. St-Jean Baptiste and Traverse Garibaldi. Take bus #5, direction "St-Charles", from the station to "Garibaldi". The museum is right behind the bus station. Tel. 04 93 62 61 62. Open Su-M and W-Th 11am-6pm, F 11am-10pm.)* Across from the museum sits another epic piece of modern architecture, the conspicuous gold **Acropolis.** This befountained eyesore is hard to miss. Though both exterior and interior resemble a sci-fi film set, its actual function is more prosaic; the complex is a conference center, office space, and shopping center.

MUSÉE ET SITE ARCHÉOLOGIQUE DE CIMIEZ. Built next to the site of ancient Nice's Gallo-Roman baths, the museum digs deep into the region's past. It contains relics found in the area from the Bronze to the Middle Ages, including excavated coins, jewelry, and sarcophagi. Visitors can walk around the well-preserved baths next door. *(160 av. des Arènes de Cimiez, next to Musée Matisse. Tel. 04 93 81 59 57. Open Apr.-Sept. T-Su 10am-noon and 2-6pm, Oct.-Mar. 10am-1pm and 2-5pm. 25F, students 15F.)*

CATHÉDRALE ORTHODOXE RUSSE ST-NICOLAS. Also known as the **Église Russe,** this awe-inspiring cathedral is a welcome departure from the region's all-pervasive Gothic and Romanesque ecclesiastical architecture. Built in 1912 under the patronage of Tsar Nicholas II and a princess mourning for her lost love, this gorgeous church is a reminder of the days when the Côte d'Azur was a getaway for Russian nobility. Its design borrows from the 17th-century Yaroslav style typified by the Kremlin. *(17 bd. du Tsarévitch, 5min. west of the train station. Tel. 04 93 96 88 02. Open June-Aug. 9am-noon and 2:30-6pm, Sept.-May 9:30am-noon and 2:30-5pm. 12F.)*

MONASTÈRE CIMIEZ. This monastery housed Nice's Franciscan brethren from the 13th to the 18th century and is now a museum. Religious artwork basks under an intricately painted ceiling, and the monks' living quarters are furnished as if the inhabitants had just stepped out to pray. The museum, the cloister, the lovely and peaceful gardens, and the crowded cemetery in which Matisse is buried are free and open to the public. *(Pl. du Monastère. Take bus #15, direction "Rimiez" and "Les Sources", or 17, direction "Cimiez", to "Monastère" from the station, or follow the signs and walk from the Musée Matisse. Tel. 04 93 81 55 41. Museum open M-Sa 10am-noon and 3-6pm; church open daily 8:30am-12:30pm and 2:30-6:30pm. Free.)*

JARDIN ALBERT IER AND ESPACE MASSÉNA. The most central of the city's parks, this fragrant, shaded garden is a quiet refuge with benches, fountains, and an ornate 18th-century fountain. It also contains the **Théâtre de Verdun,** a small amphitheater that hosts a variety of summer events, including jazz and outdoor theater. Espace Masséna is a picnic-perfect, creative public space with a large fountain and plenty of shady benches. *(Between av. Verdun and bd. Jaurès, off prom. des Anglais and quai des États-Unis. Theater box office open daily 10:30am-noon and 3:30-6:30pm.)*

🎵 🌴 ENTERTAINMENT AND FESTIVALS

BARS. Nice guys do finish last—here, the party crowd swings long after the folks in St-Tropez and Antibes have called it a night. The bars and nightclubs around rue Masséna and Vieux Nice frolic with constant dance, jazz, and rock, and the sheer number of night-time establishments in Vieux Nice ensures that everyone will find something to suit their style. For info on events pick up *l'Exés*, a free brochure available at the tourist office and some bars. To enjoy Nice's nightlife without spending a *centîme*, head down to the promenade des Anglais, where street performers, musicians, and hundreds of people wander the beach and boardwalk into the night. The bar and pub scene is steamy in the summer, especially in Vieux Nice; lone female travelers or even those in small groups should be extremely careful when walking at night. Everyone should be careful later at night around the promenade, where local men have a reputation for hassling people. Women should think twice about being there alone.

De Klomp, 6 rue Mascoinat (tel. 04 93 92 42 85). A Dutch pub with a kitschy brothel theme. The scantily clad mannequins are just for show, but you can really have one of their 40 whiskys (from 35F) or 18 beers on tap (pint 40F). A variety of live music from salsa to jazz every night. Open M-Sa 5pm-2:30am

The Hole in the Wall, 3 rue de l'Abbaye (tel. 04 93 80 40 16), is short on space but big on character. People pack into this tiny (you guessed it) hole in the wall for engaging acoustic acts who banter with the audience. Open daily 8pm-1am.

Le Bar Des Deux Frères, 1 rue du Moulin (tel. 04 93 80 77 61). Behind the façade of an old restaurant, this hip yet friendly local favorite is guaranteed to show everyone a good time. On summer weekends, the front room can spontaneously become a dance floor. Open daily 9pm-2 or 3am, winter closed Su or M.

Le Tapas, 2 bis rue de l'Abbaye (tel. 04 93 62 27 46). The bar resembles a revolutionary secret meeting spot, but the only plotting you will have to do is how to get home after braving the *bar o mètre* (100F), a meter-long wooden box of shots. Sissies can take 50cm for 60F or 25cm for 40F. Tequila and Vodka 10F. Live music M-Th.

Bar des Oiseaux, (tel. 04 93 80 27 33), at the intersection of rue de l'Abbaye and rue de St-Vincent. The classy, exotic bar caters to an artsy crowd. Theater at 9pm 2-3 times per week, jazz and folk other nights. Cover 20-50F. Open 11am-3pm and 7pm-2am.

La Trappa, corner of rue de la Prefecture and rue J. Gilly (tel. 04 93 80 33 69). Swanky Latin bar-cum-lounge which tends to draw a 25+ crowd into its colorful den. Tapas (20-60F) and margaritas (45-65F). Open till 2am.

Wayne's, 15 rue de la Préfecture (tel. 04 93 13 46 99), is the place to be for young anglophones on the prowl, with live music every night in the summer and karaoke on Sundays. A reverent hush descends Sunday nights, as locals and homesick Americans watch undubbed episodes of *The Simpsons*. Open daily 2:30pm-12:30am.

NIGHTCLUBS. Nice's nightclubs can quickly drain your funds. Going on Thursdays, Sundays, before midnight or being female are all good ways to bring down the cover. Cover usually includes first *conso* (drink).

Le Duke, 11 rue Alexandre Mari (tel. 04 93 80 40 50), near the Palais de Justice, is Nice's most exclusive club, luring a moneyed, well-dressed crowd into its chic ambience. Cover generally upwards of 100F. Before 1am, women get a free drink. Any night, women may be able to skirt the cover. Open W-Sa.

Le Studio, 29 rue Alphonse Karr (tel. 04 93 62 81 31). Popular with locals and sometimes hosts hip-hop or R&B shows. 90F, free F before 1am. Open Th-Su 11pm-6am.

Butterfly, 2 quai des États-Unis (tel. 04 93 92 27 31), has a prime seaside location and a thumping dance floor. 50F. Doors open 11pm. Closed Tu.

Blue Boy, 9 rue Jean-Baptiste Spinetta (tel. 04 93 44 68 24), in west Nice, is the city's most popular gay club.

CULTURE. The **Théâtre du Cours,** 2 rue Poissonnerie in Vieux Nice, stages traditional dramatic performances. (Th-Sa at 9pm and Su at 7pm. 75F.) The more experimental **Central Dramatique National,** prom. des Arts (tel. 04 93 80 52 60), at the corner of av. St-Jean Baptiste and traverse Garibaldi, offers a show almost every weekend for 50-160F. The grand **Théâtre de Nice,** on the promenade des Arts (tel. 04 93 80 52 60), hosts concerts and theater performances (50-200F), while the **Nice Opéra,** 4 rue St-François de Paule (tel. 04 93 85 67 31), has an annual performance series of visiting symphony orchestras and soloists (75-250F). The **FNAC** in the Nice Étoile shopping center at 24 av. Jean Médecin, sells tickets for virtually every musical or theatrical event in town.

FESTIVALS. In mid-July, the **Nice Jazz Festival** attracts world-famous jazz and non-jazz musicians from around the world. 1999's line-up included Van Morrison and James Brown. (Parc et Arènes de Cimiez. Tel. 04 93 21 68 12, fax 04 93 18 07 92. Tickets 50-250F.) During **Carnaval,** in late February, Nice gives Rio a run for its money with two weeks of parades, outlandish costumes, fireworks, and parties.

VENCE AND ST-PAUL

Just inland from the bustling metropolis of Nice, the small towns of St-Paul and Vence hide artistic treasures in a quiet environment untouched by the bustle on the coast. Both make an easy daytrip from Nice, but when you step off the bus onto their flower-laden hillsides, you may just want to drop your pack and stay.

THE SOUTHEAST

SAP Buses (tel. 04 93 58 37 60) sends bus #400 to Vence and St-Paul from **Nice** (19 per day, 55min., 20F). To get to St-Paul from **Cannes,** take the train to Cagnes-sur-Mer and change to the bus #400 (9.50F). The trip from Vence to St-Paul costs 7.50F. The last #400 leaves St-Paul for Nice and Cagnes at 6:50pm from the stop just outside the town entrance. The **tourist office** (tel. 04 93 32 86 95; fax 04 93 32 60 27), near the entrance of the village, dispenses free maps and info on galleries and exhibitions. (Open June-Sept. daily 10am-7pm; Oct.-Apr. 10am-noon and 2-6pm.)

VENCE

The former Roman market town of Vence (pop. 15,000) snoozes in the green hills above Nice. Less touristy and cramped than its neighbor St-Paul, this medieval village provides a refreshing break from the glitz and bustle of nearby Nice. The **cathedral** in its center is unremarkable save for a paintbox-bright mosaic of *Moses in the Bulrushes* by Marc Chagall. Vence is better known for the masterpiece of another artistic maestro: Henri Matisse, who completely designed and oversaw the construction of Vence's architectural centerpiece, the **Chapelle du Rosaire** (tel. 04 93 58 03 26). From the bus stop, facing the tourist office, turn left and walk up av. de la Résistance. Take a right on av. Élise and a left on av. des Poilus; at the roundabout go right onto av. de Matisse, cross the bridge, and follow the signs (1.5km). The stark white interior is softened by pale green, blue, and yellow rays of light filtered through the large stained-glass windows. On one of the walls sits Matisse's interpretation of the Christ story, expressed in bold black brush strokes. (Open Tu and Th 10-11:30am and 2:30-5:30pm; additional summer hours on W, F, and Sa. Call Chapelle or tourist office to confirm. 5F donation requested.)

A few kilometers from Vence is the **Galerie Beaubourg** (tel. 04 93 24 52 00; fax 04 93 24 52 19), skirted by surreal gardens where bizarre three-meter angels stick out of the ground and metallic girls eternally swing on metallic swing sets, in the 19th-century **Château Notre-Dame des Fleurs.** Modern works by the likes of César, Klein, and Warhol grace the walls. (Open Tu-Sa 11am-7pm. 30F, students 15F.)

Spending the night in Vence provides a more relaxing pace than in nearby coastal towns, and reasonable accommodations make the idea even more appealing. **La Closerie des Genets,** 4 impasse Maurel, (tel. 04 93 58 33 25; fax 04 93 58 97 01) just off av. Maurel at the southern end of the *vieille ville,* offers by far the nicest budget rooms in a small, carefully-maintained hotel. (Singles 180-280F; doubles 250-350F. V, MC.) **La Victoire,** pl. du Grand-Jardin (tel. 04 93 58 61 30; fax. 04 93 58 74 68) offers less by way of rooms, but has a location in the thick of things. (Singles 150-210F; doubles 180-210F. V, MC.) **Hotel des Alpes,** 2 ave G. Leclerc (tel. 04 93 58 13 30), with older, humbler rooms, is worth trying if the other two are full. (Singles and doubles 180-230F.) The **tourist office,** pl. du Grand Jardin (tel. 04 93 58 06 38; fax 04 93 58 91 81), near the bus stop, shells out free maps and more. (Open July-Sept. M-F 9am-1pm and 2-7pm, Sa 9am-1pm and 3-7pm, Su 10am-noon; Oct.-June M-Sa 9am-12:30pm and 2-6:30pm.)

ST-PAUL

The impossibly narrow pedestrian streets of St-Paul retain their medieval flavor as they wind through the impeccable town. An art lover's paradise, St-Paul abounds with attractive, pricey boutiques filled with local paintings, pottery, and handicrafts. Restaurants in this artists' colony are expensive and the only grocery option is a mini-mart near the town's entrance, so pack a picnic in Nice.

The pride of St-Paul is the **Fondation Maeght** (tel. 04 93 32 81 63; fax 04 93 32 53 22), 1km from the town center. Get off at the "St-Paul" bus stop and follow the signs first down then up the steep, winding chemin des Gardettes. Designed by Joseph Sert, the Fondation is part museum and part park, with shrubs and fountains mixed in among works by Miró, Calder, Arp, and Léger. Maeght, an art dealer, was inconsolable after the death of his eldest son. Encouraged by his friends Braque and Miró, he commissioned a small, somber chapel with stained glass by Braque and Ubac. The works lean towards abstraction and morbidity, and will appeal most to lovers of modern art. The Fondation's excellent **library** is open to the public—call for hours. (Open July-Sept. daily 10am-7pm; Oct.-June daily 10am-12:30pm and 2:30-6pm. 45F, students 35F. Photography permit 10F.) Throughout July and August, the entire city becomes a stage as St-Paul puts on operas, concerts and plays in its streets and squares. Call the tourist office for details. (Tickets 80-120F, students and children 60F.)

THE CORNICHES

Rocky shores, pebble beaches, and luxurious villas glow along the coast between hectic Nice and high-rolling Monaco. More relaxing than their glam-fab neighbors, these tiny towns are like freshwater pearls—similar in brilliance, yet gratifyingly unique. Interesting museums, architectural finds, and breathtaking countryside are among the many gifts the coast has to offer. The train offers an exceptional glimpse of the coast up close, while buses manoeuvering along the high roads of the *corniches* provide a bird's-eye view of the steep cliffs and crashing sea below. Take one method of transport out and the other back—you won't be disappointed.

⌐ TRANSPORTATION. Trains and buses between Nice and Monaco serve most of the Corniche towns frequently. With a departure about every hour, **trains** from **Nice** to **Monaco** stop at **Villefranche-sur-Mer** (7min., 8F), **Beaulieu-sur-Mer** (10min., 9F), **Èze-sur-Mer** (16min., 11F), and **Cap d'Ail** (20min., 13F).

Numerous numbered **RCA buses** (tel. 04 93 85 64 44 or 04 93 55 24 00) run between Nice and Monaco, making different stops along the way. **#111** leaves Nice, stopping in **Villefranche-sur-Mer** (8 per day M-Sa). Three buses continue on to **St-Jean-Cap-Ferrat. #117** runs between Nice and **Villefranche-sur-Mer** 11 times daily. **#112** runs 7 times per day (3 on Su) between Nice and Monte-Carlo, stopping in **Èze-le-Village.** Both **RCA #100** (every 15-30min. M-Sa 6:45am-7:45pm, Su every 20-40min.) and the cheaper **Autocars Broch** (tel. 04 93 31 10 52 or 04 93 07 63 28; daily every hour) run between Nice and **Villefranche-sur-Mer** (10min., RCA 8.50F/Broch 7.50F), **Beaulieu-sur-Mer** (20min., 12F/10.50F), **Èze-le-Village** (25min., 13.50F/12F), **Cap d'Ail** (30min., 16.50F/14.50), **Monaco-Ville** (40min., 20F/17F), and **Monte-Carlo** (45 min., 20F/17.50F). Autocars Broch tickets include free same-day return.

VILLEFRANCHE-SUR-MER

The narrow streets and pastel houses of Villefranche-sur-Mer, are twice as nice as Nice. Villefranche has enchanted *artistes* from Aldous Huxley and Katherine Mansfield to Tina Turner and Bono. Though there are notable sights here, everything plays second fiddle to the song of sun, surf, and sand.

As you stroll from the station along quai Ponchardier, a sign to the *vieille ville* points the way to **rue Obscure,** the oldest street in Villefranche. Built in the 13th century, this spooky, dungeonesque lane has since been layered with so many homes and shops that the only light comes from lonely iron chandeliers hanging from its "ceiling." On quai Courbet stands the pink and yellow 14th-century **Chapelle St-Pierre** (tel. 04 93 76 90 70), decorated from floor to ceiling by Jean Cocteau—former resident, film-maker, and jack-of-all-arts—with boldly executed scenes from the life of St. Peter and the Camargue gypsies, all dedicated to the fishermen of the area. (Hours fluctuate—call ahead. Open June 21-Sept. 21 Tu-Su 10am-noon and 4-8:30pm; Sept. 22-Dec. 20 9:30am-noon and 2-6pm; Dec. 21-Mar. 19 9:30am-noon and 2-5pm; Mar. 20-June 20 9:30am-noon and 3-7pm. 12F.)

The rather dull 16th-century **Citadelle** houses three small museums, the most interesting of which is the **Musée Volti** (tel. 04 93 76 33 27). Here you'll find creatively displayed works by native Antoniucci Volti, who experimented with bronze, clay, copper, and canvas to create lounging, curvaceous female forms. The cubism of Henri Goetz and Christine Boumeester taunts the viewer with vivid color and abstract yet familiar images in the **Musée Goetz-Boumeester** (tel. 04 93 76 33 44). Ask yourself: is this a horse or a hairbrush? (Open July-Aug. M and W-Sa 10am-noon and 3-7pm, Su 3-7pm; June and Sept. W-Sa and M 9am-noon and 3-6pm, Su 3-6pm; Oct.-May W-Sa 10am-noon and 2-5pm, Su 2-5pm. Free.)

If you want to stay, try the basic but well-maintained **La Régence,** 2 av. Maréchal Foch, across from the tourist office. (Tel. 04 93 01 70 91. Singles 183F, doubles 246-266F, triples 309F.) You'll feel at home at **Le Home,** av. de Grande-Bretagne, (tel. 04 93 76 79 88), where large, beautiful rooms run 230-280F. To reach the **tourist office** (tel. 04 93 01 73 68; fax 04 93 76 63 65) from the train station, exit on quai 1 and head inland on av. G. Clemenceau. Continue straight when it becomes av. Sadi Carnot. The office is at the end of the street in the Jardin François. The staff gives out maps and suggests excursions to regional villages. (Open July-Aug. daily 9am-8pm; mid-Sept. to June M-Sa 9am-noon and 2-6pm.)

BEAULIEU-SUR-MER

Although its rocky beaches (known as "little Africa" and "bay of Ants") don't size up with those in neighboring towns, Beaulieu-sur-Mer lives up to its name as a pretty place by the sea. Archæologist Theodore Reinach built his dream villa **Kérylos** (tel. 04 93 01 01 44) in imitation of an ancient Greek dwelling, and lived his version of an Athenian's life amid frescoes, mosaics, alabaster, and marble embellishments until his death in 1928. This "sea swallow" perched on the Beaulieu cliffs rewards its visitors with a gratifying Mediterranean vista. (Open daily July-Aug. 10am-7pm; Sept. 10am-6pm; late Feb. and early Nov. 10:30am-12:30pm and 2-6pm; mid-Dec. to mid-Feb. 2-6pm. 40F, students 25F.) The **tourist office** (tel. 04 93 01 02 21; fax 04 93 01 44 04), is at pl. de la Gare next to the station. (Open July-Sept. M-Sa 9am-12:15pm and 2-7pm; Oct.-June M-Sa 9am-12:15pm and 2-6pm.)

ST-JEAN-CAP-FERRAT

If the Riviera ever needed a trump card, St-Jean-Cap-Ferrat would be it. While the harbor and town itself are quite lovely, the **plage Paloma** and **plage Passable** beaches and Baroness Rothschild's mansion give St-Jean-Cap-Ferrat a set of aces. A 25-minute walk between Beaulieu and St-Jean-Cap-Ferrat, along a seaside path full of lavish villas, secluded rocky beaches, and once-beautiful docks and moorings, makes getting there the best part.

The **Fondation Ephrussi de Rothschild** (tel. 04 93 01 33 99; fax 04 93 01 31 10) is just off av. D. Semeria, in between the tourist office and the Nice-Monaco road. An æsthete's paradise, the stunning villa houses the furniture and art collections of the Baroness de Rothschild. Monet canvases, Gobelins tapestries, Chinese vases, and a stunning tea room all stand within spectacular grounds. Each of the seven gardens reflects a different part of the world, from Spain to Japan and, *bien sûr,* France. You can also reach the villa directly from Beaulieu. Follow the sea path toward St-Jean, turning right after the three-pronged tree and before the white villa that separates the path from the Mediterranean; from the top of this walled shore access, turn left and follow the road up, turning right at the sign to the Fondation. (Open July-Aug. daily 10am-6pm; Sept.-Oct. and Feb. 14-June daily 10am-6pm; Nov.-Feb.14 M-F 2-6pm, Sa-Su 10am-6pm. 46F, students 35F.)

St-Jean's alluring **beaches** have earned the area the nickname *"presqu'île des rêves"* ("peninsula of dreams"). Attracting mainly locals, who descend from their stately villas to bask in the sun, beaches here have a fun neighborhood feel. Try the misnamed **plage Passable,** just down the hill from the tourist office, at the base of chemin de Passable. On the other side of the peninsula, **plage Paloma** is past the port on av. Jean Mermoz. The tiny **tourist office,** 59 av. Denis Séméria (tel. 04 93 76 08 90; fax 04 93 76 16 67) is half-way along the winding street that runs from the Nice-Monaco road to the port. It has free maps of the region and **St-Jean-Cap-Ferrat à Petits Pas,** free walking tour maps of the peninsula's 11km of trails that will help you find your own idyllic beach. (Open July-Aug. M-Sa 8:30am-12:30pm and 1-5:30pm, Su 1-5:30pm; Sept.-June M-Sa 8:30am-noon and 1-5:30pm, Su 1-5:30pm.)

ÈZE

Three-tiered Èze perches precariously on the corniches, a medieval gem on the modern Côte d'Azur. The most colorful of the towns from Nice to Monaco, it is also the most difficult to navigate. **Èze Bord-de-Mer,** also called **Èze-sur-Mer,** houses the train station and a stretch of pebble beach popular with windsurfers, kayakers, and sailors. The middle tier sits 429m above sea level—straight up—and holds the heart of the town, **Èze-le-Village.** This medieval town bears the marks of visitors over the centuries, from the Moors to the Piedmontese to the King of Sweden, who built a castle here in 1920. **Le Col d'Èze,** a more residential area, keeps watch above.

In the imposing medieval city, the **Porte des Maures** remembers its glory days, when it served as a gate to admit a surprise attack by the Moors. Also in the old city is the newly-renovated Baroque **Église Paroissial,** shimmering with old-fashioned Catholic gilt and decorated with a unique combination of Christian and Egyptian symbols. (Open daily 9am-noon and 2-6pm.) Èze-le-Village offers more than narrow streets and pretty views, though—the **Fragonard Parfumerie** (tel. 04 92 42 34 34), based in Grasse, has its second-largest factory here and offers warehouse prices, free 15-minute tours explaining the process of making perfume, and ample opportunities for spritzing and whiffing. (Open daily 8:15am-6:45pm.) The more intimate **Parfumerie Galimard** (tel. 04 93 41 10 70) also lures in customers with free tours of their museum. (Open Mar. 15-Oct. daily 9am-12:30pm and 2-6pm.)

The best views go to those who venture 40 minutes up or down the **Sentier Friedrich Nietzsche,** a windy trail where its namesake found inspiration to compose the third part of *Thus Spake Zarathustra*. The trail begins in Èze Bord-du-Mer, 100m east of the train station and tourist office, and ends near the base of the medieval city, by the Fragonard parfumerie.

From June 15 to October 15, a **Navette mini-bus** connects Èze's three tiers (20F) stopping in **Èze Bord-du-Mer** in front of the tourist office and in **Èze-le-Village** where the main road meets the path to the medieval city.

CAP D'AIL

Filled with lavish, imposing villas, Cap d'Ail (pop. 5000) isn't a place to visit for provincial flavor. Instead, 3km of cliff-framed, foamy seashore, a beachside villa hostel, and numerous airy footpaths make Cap d'Ail a singular place to bask in the sun, especially in your birthday bathing suit. At **Les Pissarelles,** hundreds of *naturistes* make sure there's always a full moon over the Cap. To join them, or to seek the sun on the more modest **plage Mala,** turn left from the train station and make another left into a stone tunnel with 15 steps down to the rocky inlets and the winding path of the **sentier bord de Mer.** The path will lead you first to Mala and eventually to the nudist beach. A more treacherous path curves along the cliffs in front of the village; look for steps with a blue railing on the left after the hostel.

The **Relais International de la Jeunesse** on bd. de la Mer (tel. 04 93 78 18 58) has an amazing location for the price and draws a friendly, fun-loving crowd. Share prime beachfront property with mansions and their accompanying Rolls Royces, as waves lull you to sleep. Men and women are housed separately—no exceptions. (70F. Breakfast included. Dinner 50F. Free luggage storage. 3-night max. stay when busy. Lockout 9:30am-5pm. Curfew midnight.) Hostelers who miss the curfew sometimes take their chances illegally bedding down on Plage Mala, as few of Cap d'Ail's finest *gendarmes* want to walk down the 152 steps just to oust sleeping backpackers. *Let's Go* recommends you find a legal bed.

Free maps and lists of walking or biking daytrips are available from the **tourist office,** 104 av. de 3 Septembre (tel. 04 93 78 02 33; fax 04 92 10 74 36). Walk uphill, keeping left until you leave the residential area. Turn right at the village, continuing on av. de la Gare. Turn right on rue du 4 Septembre, and the office will be on your right (20min.). (Open M-F 9am-noon and 2-6:30pm, Sa 9am-noon and 1-6pm.)

MONACO AND MONTE-CARLO

The world's playground for the rich and famous, Monaco's golden glory may not be immediately evident to the newly initiated. Nestled into cliffs, and comprising just two priceless square kilometers of the Côte d'Azur, Monaco (native pop. 5000, 25,000 with hangers-on) compensates for its steep topography with a web of escalators and elevators to ensure that no one breaks a sweat after having waltzed down the yacht's gangplank into the awaiting sports car or private jet. Since *Monégasques* pay no income tax, one may wonder how Prince Rainier funded the prickly Jardin Exotique, ritzy aquarium, and all those hard-working street cleaners. Well, as the Italians say, gambling is a tax on fools—and one the Grimaldi princes have levied since 1856. Monaco makes a superb daytrip from Nice, and is just one stop from the lovely hostel in Cap d'Ail, but don't look to get any exotic new stamps on your passport. There are no border guards, and the electricity, tap water, military, and money are all French. You can, however, send off postcards emblazoned with the principality's very own stamps.

▨ ORIENTATION AND PRACTICAL INFORMATION

Monaco is 18km east of Nice and 12km west of the French-Italian border. Small enough to be considered a town, the principality consists of four *quartiers:* Monaco-Ville, Monte-Carlo, La Condamine, and Fontvieille. When you exit the train station, turn right onto **av. du Port,** then left onto **bd. Albert Ier** overlooking the harbor. Above you on the right sits **Monaco-Ville** with its *vieille ville,* the Prince's palace, and the museum/mall complex **Fontvieille.** To the left of the port rises fabled **Monte-Carlo** and its grand casino. **La Condamine** is where you're standing; it includes the port and the area inland which connects Monaco-Ville and Monte Carlo. Just above Monte Carlo, and across the imperceptible border with France, is the less ritzy **Beausoleil.** With so much to see condensed in so little space, Monaco should be a walker's dream. But steep streets and winding, car-oriented roads make it difficult to navigate the area by foot. Consider public transportation to move between the *quartiers.*

Trains: Av. Prince Pierre. Direct connections to: **Nice** (25min., every 30min., 19F); **Antibes** (45min., every 30min., 38F); **Cannes** (70min., every 30min., 46F); and **Menton** (10min., every 30min., 12F). Station open 5:30am-11pm. Information desk open M-F 8:05-11:55am and 2-5:35pm. **Lockers** 15-32F per night.

Buses: Buses to **Nice** (19F) and **Menton** (12F) leave from pl. du Casino. For info on buses, call 04 93 85 61 81 in Nice or ask the tourist office. Call **Autocars Broch** in Nice (tel. 04 93 31 10 52) for cheaper round-trip day fares (17F to Nice and back).

Public Transportation: Six routes (tel. 93 50 62 41) connect the entire hilly town every 11min., M-Sa 7am-9pm (Su and holidays every 20min. 7:30am-8:45pm). Bus #4 links the train station to the Casino in Monte-Carlo. Tickets 8.50F each, 19F for a *carnet* of 4, 30F for a *carnet* of 8. Buy them on board.

Taxis: Tel. 93 50 56 28 or 93 15 01 01. Around 50F from pl. de Casino to the hostel, 80-100F to the Relais de Jeunesse in Cap d'Ail.

Bike Rental: Auto-Moto Garage, 7 rue de Millo (tel. 93 50 10 80). 85F per day, 500F per week. Credit card deposit. Open M-F 8am-noon and 2-7pm, Sa 8am-noon.

Tourist Office: 2a bd. des Moulins (tel. 92 16 61 16; fax 92 16 60 00), near the casino. Helpful, English-speaking staff makes free **room reservations** and gives out maps of the city, the handy English brochure *Tourist Attractions,* and a guide to shopping in Monaco (all free). **Annexes** are set up in the train station and in the port June 15-Sept. 30. Main office open M-Sa 9am-7pm, Su 10am-noon.

Money: Compagnie Monégasque de Change, parking des Pêcheurs (tel. 93 25 02 50), next to the Musée de l'Océanographie, has reasonable rates and no commission. Open M-Sa 9:30am-5:30pm. Closed Nov.-Dec. 25. Also in the **train station,** open M-Sa 10am-6:30pm. **American Express,** 35 bd. Princesse Charlotte (tel. 93 25 74 45; fax 93 25 74 45). Open M-F 9am-noon and 2-6pm, Sa 9am-noon.

English Bookstore: Scruples, 9 rue Princesse Caroline (tel. 93 50 43 52). Impressive selection includes *Let's Go: France.* Open M-W and F-Sa 9:30am-noon and 2:30-7pm, Th 9:30am-7pm. V, MC, AmEx.

Police: 3 rue Louis Notari (tel. 93 15 30 15).

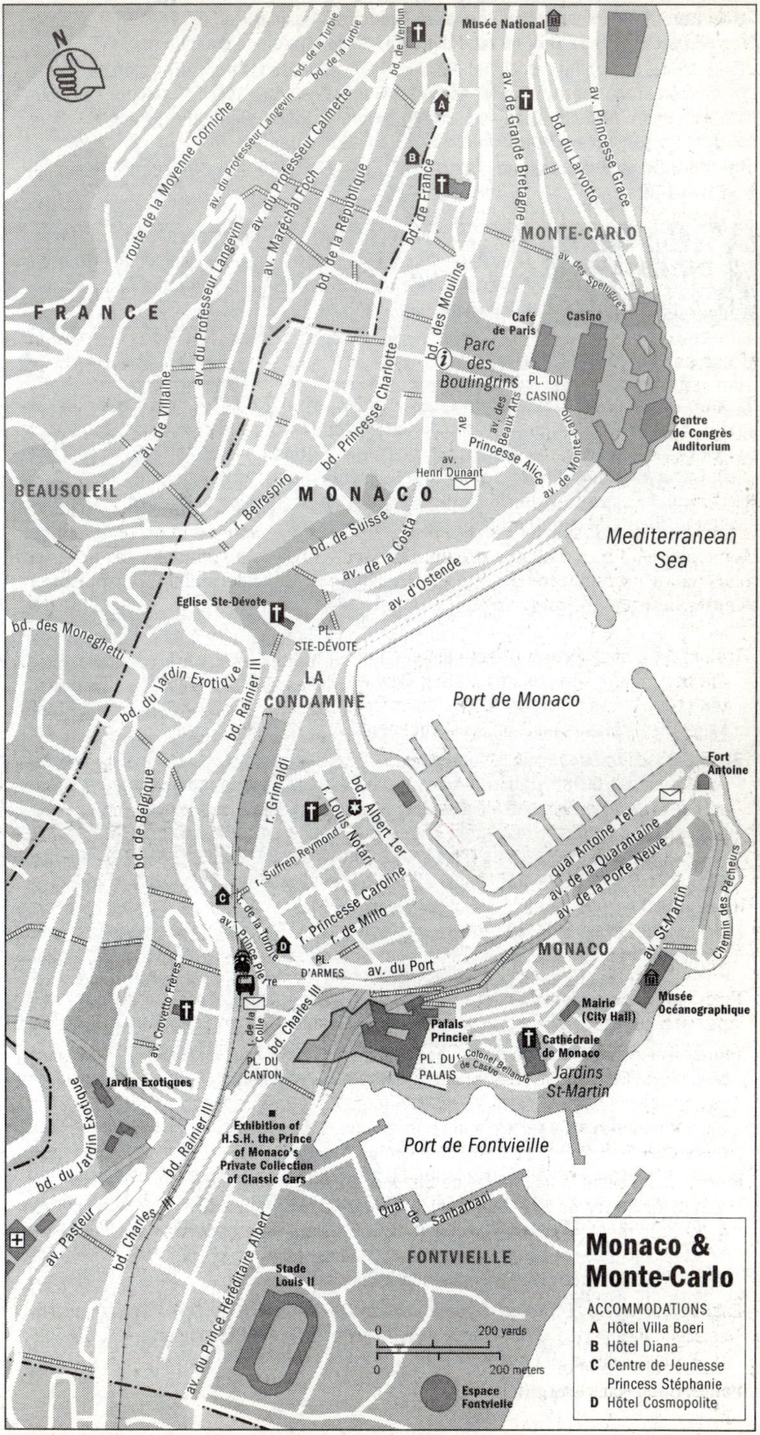

N

Musée National 🏛

av. de Verdun

av. de Grande Bretagne

av. du Lavotto

av. Princesse Grace

A

route de la Moyenne Corniche

bd. de la Turbie

bd. de la Turbie

av. du Professeur Langevin

av. du Professeur Calmette

av. du Maréchal Foch

bd. de la République

bd. de France

B

MONTE-CARLO

av. des Spélugues

av. du Professeur Langevin

FRANCE

bd. des Moulins

ℹ

Café de Paris

Casino

Parc des Boulingrins

PL. DU CASINO

av. des Beaux Arts

av. de Villaine

bd. Princesse Charlotte

Centre de Congrès Auditorium

av. de Monte-Carlo

Princesse Alice

r. Bellespiro

MONACO

av. Henri Dunant ✉

BEAUSOLEIL

bd. de Suisse

Mediterranean Sea

av. de la Costa

av. d'Ostende

bd. des Moneghetti

Eglise Ste-Dévote 🏛

bd. du Jardin Exotique

PL. STE-DÉVOTE

bd. Rainier III

LA CONDAMINE

Port de Monaco

Fort Antoine

bd. de Belgique

r. Grimaldi

r. Suffren Reymond

bd. Albert 1er

r. Louis Notari

🏛

✉

quai Antoine 1er

av. de la Quarantaine

av. de la Porte Neuve

r. Princesse Caroline

r. de Milto

C

av. de la Turbie

D

PL. D'ARMES

av. du Port

MONACO

av. St-Martin

Chemin des Pêcheurs

bd. du Pont Pierre

r. Crovetto Frères

🏛

bd. Charles III

PL. DU CANTON

PL. DU PALAIS

Colonel Bellando de Castro

Palais Princier

Mairie (City Hall)

🏛 Musée Océanographique

🏛 Cathédrale de Monaco

Jardins St-Martin

Jardin Exotiques

bd. du Jardin Exotique

bd. Rainier III

Exhibition of H.S.H. the Prince of Monaco's Private Collection of Classic Cars

Port de Fontvieille

av. Pasteur

✚

bd. Charles III

Quai de Sanbarbani

FONTVIEILLE

av. du Prince Héréditaire Albert

Stade Louis II

Espace Fontvieille

0   200 yards
0   200 meters

Monaco & Monte-Carlo

ACCOMMODATIONS
A Hôtel Villa Boeri
B Hôtel Diana
C Centre de Jeunesse
   Princess Stéphanie
D Hôtel Cosmopolite

THE SOUTHEAST

Hospital: Centre Hospitalier Princesse Grace, av. Pasteur (tel. 97 98 99 00 or emergency tel. 97 98 97 69), off bd. Rainier III, which runs along the train tracks.

Post Office: Pl. Beaumarchais (tel. 93 50 69 87). Monaco issues its own stamps; French stamps can not be used in Monaco. For Poste Restante, specify Palais de la Scala, Monte-Carlo. **Branch office** across from the train station. Both offices open M-F 8am-7pm, Sa 8am-noon. **Postal code: MC 98000 Monaco.**

Internet: Stars N' Bars on quai Antoine 1er (tel. 97 97 95 95). 40F per hr. Open daily 11am-1:30am.

PHONING TO AND FROM MONACO	Monaco's country code is 377. To telephone Monaco from France, dial 00377, then the 8-digit Monaco number. To call France from Monaco, dial 0033, and drop the first zero of the French number.

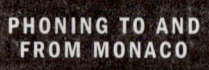

ACCOMMODATIONS

Monaco is glittering and glamorous, but unless your Rolls is parked outside the Casino, you probably can't afford to stay within a stone's throw of the Palace. A couple of bargains can be found near the train station or across the border in **Beausoleil. Cap d'Ail,** one train stop or a gorgeous walk along the beach away, is an ideal alternative to spending all that money you won at the slot machines. For those staying in Nice, the trip to Monaco is quick, cheap, and easy.

Centre de Jeunesse Princesse Stéphanie, 24 av. Prince Pierre (tel. 93 50 83 20; fax 04 93 25 29 82). From the train station, turn left up the hill and follow the signs 100m to the hostel, a pink building, which will be straight ahead of you. Hostel is extremely well-run with comprehensive binders holding as much information as a tourist office. Cooking, eating, smoking, and alcohol forbidden in dorms. 80F, cash only. Breakfast included. Sheets free with ID deposit. Lockers in rooms (30F key deposit). Laundry 30F. Must be aged 16-26 (students 16-31). 7-day max. stay. Reception July-Aug. 31 7am-1am, Sept. 16-June 7am-midnight. Check-out 9:30am. Curfew strictly enforced.

Hôtel Cosmopolite, 4 rue de la Turbie (tel. 93 30 16 95; fax 93 30 23 05), very near the train station. Exit the station, cross rue Prince Pierre and look for a small stairway between Bar de la Gare and Monasouca Shop. Stairs take you to rue de la Turbie. Plain, clean, functional rooms decorated in mustard or mint green. All rooms have sink and bidet, none have toilets, some have showers or balconies. Singles 200-310F; doubles 228-336F; triples 338-440F; quads 380-563F. Breakfast 35F. Free luggage storage.

Hôtel Villa Boeri, 29 bd. du Général Leclerc (tel. 04 93 78 38 10; fax 04 93 41 90 95), in Beausoleil, France. Clean rooms with big wooden beds and garden bouquet bedspreads. Mirrored halls reminiscent of casino or bowling alley. All rooms with toilet, shower, satellite TV, and telephone. Singles 195-270F; doubles 230-340F; triples 315-465F; quads 465-545F. Prices rise 10-25% July-Aug. Breakfast 35F. V, MC, AmEx.

Hôtel Diana, 17 bd. du Général Leclerc (tel. 04 93 78 47 58; fax 04 93 41 88 94) in Beausoleil, France. Simple accommodations with a 70s flair. Singles 180-290F; doubles 180-360F; triples 360-385F. Breakfast 38F. V, MC, AmEx.

FOOD AND DRINKS

With many of Monaco's restaurants aimed at billionaires, budget travelers will find few affordable eating options. Picnics are a good bet and there is no shortage of ideal spots to lay out a meal *en pleine air*. Stop by the fruit and flower **market** on pl. d'Armes (open daily 6am-1pm) at the end of av. Prince Pierre or the huge **Carrefour** (tel. 92 05 57 00) in Fontvieille's shopping plaza. From the station, turn right and then right again onto rue de la Colle until you reach pl. du Canton; cross the street, and head down the escalator. (Open M-Sa 8:30am-10pm.) A **Casino** supermarket sits on bd. Albert 1er. (Open M-Sa 8:30am-8pm.) For those who don't hit up the casino after dinner, a number of restaurants transform into bars and become the bulk of Monaco nightlife.

L'Escale, 17 bd. Albert 1er (tel. 93 39 13 44), on the waterfront near the Olympic pool. One of many waterfront restaurants vying for attention, L'Escale's fare is tastier and not as hard on the wallet. Pizzas and pastas from 45F, seafood risotto 55F.

Stars 'N' Bars, Quai Antoine 1er (tel. 97 97 95 95), in La Condamine. Join hordes of Anglophones to talk about the old country over pricey burgers and pizzas (55-90F). It may look like just another tourist trap, but the outdoor patio, indoor bar, and weekend disco (until 4am) are all extremely lively; locals join in the frivolity.

Bombay Frigo, 3 av. Princess Grace (tel. 93 25 57 00), on the waterfront, west of the Jardin Japonais. Do as the *monégasque* do and splurge. A trendy *mélange* of Mediterranean and Indian influences in cuisine and decor. May be out of dinner range—the risotto (60F) is the cheapest *plat* by a long shot—but a beer (22F) won't break the bank. Top DJs from Monaco radio spin on weekends. Being well-dressed is a prerequisite, being beautiful is preferred.

◉ SIGHTS

MONTE-CARLO CASINO. The wealth, mystery, and intrigue of Monte-Carlo revolve around the famed casino where Mata Hari once shot a Russian spy and Richard Burton wooed Liz Taylor. Surrounded by gardens overlooking the coast, the 1878 building was designed by Charles Garnier and resembles his Paris opera house. The interior, shining with 19th-century extravagance—red velvet curtains, gilded ceilings, and gold and crystal chandeliers—is worth visiting even if you're not a gambler. The car show outside represents the chic-est, sleekest, and priciest on wheels—that is, if you don't have your wings parked in Monaco's private airport. The slot machines open at 2pm, while blackjack, craps, and roulette (25F minimum) open at 3pm. The Monte-Carlo casino also houses the sumptuous **Atrium du Casino** theater (tel. 92 16 22 99), one-time venue for Diaghilev's Ballets-Russes. You can visit only by attending a ballet or opera performance; tickets cost 150-600F (students 75F, advance or standby). If you need to start your gambling fix before noon, head next door to the **Café de Paris** (opens 10am). Peeking at the *salons privés*, where such French games as *chemin de fer* and *trente et quarante* begin at 3pm, will cost you 50-100F. All casinos have **dress codes** (no shorts, sneakers, sandals, or jeans) and require you to be at least **21 years old.** Bring a passport as proof of age.

MUSÉE OCÉANOGRAPHIQUE. The tremendous museum brings you the deep seas of every corner of the earth. The loving attentions of former directors—sea-czar Jacques Cousteau and energetic marine biologist-cum-prince Albert I—have made the aquarium a virtual temple to Poseidon and his thousands of species of fish and creepy-crawlies. The amazing collection features rare feathered fish, whale skeletons, and strange sea creatures. It is built out of 100,000 tons of white stone on the edge of a cliff. *(Av. St-Martin. Tel. 93 15 36 00. Open daily July-Aug. 9am-8pm; Apr.-June and Sept. 9am-7pm; Oct. and Mar. 9:30am-7pm; Nov.-Feb. 10am-6pm. Admission 60F, students and ages 6-18 30F.)*

PALAIS PRINCIER. Even if you've lost your shirt at the casino, you can still admire the royal robes here. Perched on a cliff high above Monte-Carlo, the palace is the sometime home of Prince Rainier and his tabloid-darling family. The Grimaldis have ruled this small but fiercely independent principality since 1297, when things got too hot in Genoa for François Grimaldi. He escaped with a few men-at-arms dressed as monks to capture unsuspecting Monaco. Hence the Grimaldi coat of arms you'll see at the palace: a pair of armed monks. Things have cooled down since the sordid succession dramas of the 16th century, which ended with a splash when disgruntled *monagésques* tossed Prince Honoré I into the sea. Ever-vigilant for renegade monks, Monaco performs the **changing of the guard** outside the palace daily at 11:55am and 5pm. This ritual, given the size of the principality, may seem less than urgent. In their summer uniforms, complete with dainty white gun holders (they change to black after Labor Day, in accordance with the laws of fashion), the soldiers look as functional as the palace cannon, strategically positioned to bombard the shopping district. When the flag is down, the prince is away and the doors open to tourists. Take a tour of the small but lavishly decorated palace with stunning frescoes and marble inlay. Also on display are the hall of mirrors, Princess Grace's official state portrait, Prince Rainier's throne, and—of special interest to American patriots—the chamber where England's King George III died. (*Tel. 93 25 18 31. Open June-Sept. 9:30am-6pm; Oct. 10am-5pm. 30F, students 20F before 5pm.*)

CATHÉDRALE DE MONACO. The Grimaldis are buried within this white neo-Romanesque-Byzantine church, whose ceiling is decorated with saints and palms. Prince Rainier and Grace Kelly were wed here in 1956. The victim of a tragic 1982 car accident, Princess Grace lies in a tomb behind the altar marked simply with her latinized name, "Patritia Gracia." Her younger daughter, Princess Stéphanie, chose a local judge's chambers for her marriage to her former bodyguard two years ago but stopped by the cathedral on her wedding day to place flowers on her mother's grave. A full choir sings mass every Sunday from September to June at 10:30am and on Saturdays at 6pm. (*4 rue du Colonel Bellando de Castro, next door to the Palais. Tel. 93 30 88 13. Open daily 9am-12:30pm and 1:30-4:30pm. Free.*)

JARDIN EXOTIQUE. The Jardin sticks out in a principality famed for its gardens by virtue of its cactus collection. The garden has exquisite coastal views and dungeon-like grottoes with stalagmites and stalactites. (*Bd. du Jardin Exotique. Tel. 93 30 33 65. Open May 15-Sept. 15 daily 9am-7pm; Sept. 16-May 14 9am-6pm or nightfall. 37F, students 18F.*)

CAR COLLECTION. The mouthful **Exhibition of H.S.H. the Prince of Monaco's Private Collection of Classic Cars** is the best of an assemblage of small museums on the Terasses de Fontvielle. All 105 of the sexiest cars ever made are part of Prince Rainier's personal collection. It includes the toy race cars of the fun-loving Prince Albert and the 1956 Rolls Royce Silver Cloud that carried Prince Rainier and his movie-star bride on their wedding day. The museum also displays the car that won the first Grand Prix de Monaco in 1929. Explanatory placards sit on sculptures made with engine parts designed by the Prince himself. (*Terraces de Fontvieille. Tel. 92 05 28 56. Open daily Dec.-Oct. 10am-6pm. 30F, students 15F.*)

OTHER SIGHTS. Napoleonophiles and war enthusiasts will appreciate the **Collections des Souvenirs Napoléonais et des Archives Historiques du Palais,** just to the left of the palace entrance. The small museum houses Napoleon paraphernalia on the bottom floor, and a haphazard collection intended to explain the history of Monaco through coins, documents, and paintings on the top. (*Next to the Palais Princier entrance. Tel. 04 93 25 18 31. Open Jun.-Sept. daily 9:30am-6:30pm; Oct. daily 10am-5pm; Dec.-May Tu-Su 10:30am-12:30pm and 2-5pm. 20F, students 10F.*) For all the money spent on public works, the only real beach in Monaco, **Lavotto,** on av. Princesse Grace, is rather unspectacular. It is large, though, and if it's simply surf and sun you seek, you'll find it here. If you've come to Monaco for enlightenment, head west to the **Jardin Japonais,** designed by Japanese architect Yasua Beppu. The newest addition to Monaco's fabulous foliage, its garden, cherry trees, and tea house will bring you to a zen state, even in the Riviera sun. (*Open daily 9am-sunset. Free.*)

✸ FESTIVALS

For details about Monaco's events, festivals, and **the Grand Prix,** call the tourist office or the **Comité des Fêtes** (tel. 92 10 12 10). In the last week of July and the first week of August, the sky lights up for the internationally competitive **Fireworks Festival.** From January 20-27th, 2000, Monaco hosts the **Festival International du Cirque,** featuring the world's top circuses and culminating on the final evening when a gala showcases the best acts. The last week of May and the first week of June attracts floral enthusiasts to the **Flower Festival.** June 1-4 sees the 2000 edition of the **Festival St-Devote**—a ship burned in front of the *église* of the same name.

MENTON

Often called the "Secret Riviera," Menton (pop. 30,000; pronounced "MON-ton") holds an often-overlooked allure. Finally annexed to France in 1860, Menton and its former owner, Monaco, have flip-flopped between French and Sardinian control since 1346, leaving vestiges of Italian flavor in both the cuisine and the local accents. This *mélange* has attracted an even more eclectic group of visitors, from Le Corbusier to Coco Chanel. As the warmest winter spot on the coast, the town is a hit with the senior set and can occasionally appear like one big convalescent home, but the alluring *vieille ville*, a gorgeous church, and an extensive beach ensure that Menton will impress.

⚑ ORIENTATION AND PRACTICAL INFORMATION.

Trains leave pl. de la Gare every half hour for **Monaco** (10min., 12F), **Nice** (35min., 26F), and **Cannes** (80min., 50F). They also run to **Ventimiglia** (15min., 14F), the first stop in Italy, where you can connect to **Genoa** (4hr., 7 per day, 52F). (Open 8:30am-noon and 3-7pm. **Luggage storage** 20F per day.) **Buses** depart from promenade Maréchal Leclerc. (Tel. 04 93 28 43 27. Open M-F 8am-noon and 2-6pm, Sa 8am-noon.) **Autocars Broch** (tel. 04 93 31 10 52) sends 'em on the hour, 7am-8pm, to **Nice** (25F) and **Monaco** (11F); prices are the same for one-way or day-return ticket. **Rapides Côte d'Azur** (tel. 04 93 85 64 44) sends three buses an hour to **Nice** (26F). **Taxis** at the station (tel. 04 92 10 47 02 or 04 92 10 47 00) charge about 40F to go to the hostel. To get to the **tourist office** from the station, walk to the left of the restaurant Le Terminus onto av. de la Gare. After two blocks, turn right onto av. Boyer; the office is on the left at no. 8 (tel. 04 93 57 57 00; fax 04 93 57 51 00). The English-speaking staff hands out free maps. (Open July-Aug. M-Sa 9am-7pm, Su 9am-1pm; Sept.-June M-Sa 8:30am-12:30pm and 1:30-6pm.) To see everything in town take a tour with **Service du Patrimoine**, 5 rue Ciapetta. (Tel. 04 92 10 33 66; fax 04 93 28 46 85. 2hr. tour in French 30F. Call for times.) **Crédit Lyonnais**, 2 av. Boyer (tel. 04 93 28 60 60), has a competitive 24hr. **currency exchange machine**. The **post office** offers **currency exchange** across from the tourist office at cours George V. (Tel. 04 93 28 64 84. Open M-W and F 8am-6:30pm, Th 8am-6pm, Sa 8am-noon. **Postal code:** 06500.)

Like so many other towns on the Riviera, Menton is divided into the *vieille ville*, the new town, and the beach. **Av. du Verdun** or **av. Boyer** (depending on the side of the street) is the main thoroughfare for the new town. The *vieille ville* revolves around crowded pedestrian **rue St-Michel**. **Rue Longue** and the serpentine streets past **pl. St-Michel** are immensely rewarding to get lost in, bearing a strong sense of neighborhood and some good local food stores. Beaches line the waterfront through much of the town. **Plage des Sablettes** below the Église St-Michel is the largest and has the most youthful character.

⚑ ACCOMMODATIONS AND CAMPING.

Menton's year-round warmth makes winter its high season, when it may be better visited as a daytrip. Many of the cheaper options cluster around the train station. Your best bet, however, is by far the most inconvenient. To get to the **Auberge de Jeunesse (HI)**, plateau St-Michel (tel. 04 93 35 93 14; fax 04 93 35 93 07), head dead straight from the station, follow ave. de la Gare, and cross under the train tracks at the bridge. Take the first right onto allée de Namur up the hill, the second left onto Escaliers des Orangers, and brace yourself for the 300 steps, always following the signs for "Camping St-Michel." The hostel is at the end of the campsite. If your boots weren't made for walking, take bus #6 from the *gare routière*, which makes four trips per day (8F), or call the hostel minibus (20F per person for 1-2 people, 10F per person for 3 or more). The friendly, English-speaking staff runs a tight ship, and is eager to share traveling tales. (66F. Breakfast and great view included. Sleepsack 14F. Dinner 49F. Laundry 35F. Reception daily 7am-noon and 5pm-midnight. Open Feb.-Nov.)

Behind and below the train station is **Hôtel Beauregard**, 10 rue Albert 1er (tel. 04 93 28 63 63; fax 04 93 28 63 79). Take the steps behind Le Chou Chou *bar-tabac* and turn right onto rue Albert 1er. Squeaky-clean rooms with a beach motif, TV, and phone are an excellent value. (Singles and doubles 170F, with toilet 190F, with shower and toilet 210F; triples with the works 270F. Extra bed 55F. Breakfast 29F.) More central is the **Hôtel des Arcades,** 41 av. Felix Faure (tel. 04 93 35 70 62; fax 04 93 35 35 97). From the train station, head straight down av. de la Gare, cross the boulevard, then right on av. Boyer and left on av. Felix Faure. Rooms are standard but hotel is well situated for ambling through the *vieille ville.* All rooms have WC, TV, and telephone. (Singles 180-260F, doubles 220-260F, depending on time of year. WC, shower, and TV are 40F extra. V, MC, AmEx.) Campers can find shelter in Parc St-Michel at **Camping Municipal du Plateau St-Michel,** 50 steps shy of the hostel on route des Ciappes de Castellar (tel. 04 93 35 81 23). Enjoy free hot showers and a panoramic view of the bay. (17F per person, 17F per site. Reception M-F 8:30am-noon and 3-7pm, Sa-Su 8:30am-noon and 5:30-7pm.)

📷 **FOOD.** Meet your fresh food needs at the **Marché Carëi,** on av. Sospel at the end of av. Boyer (open daily 7am-12:30pm) or at the **Shopi supermarket,** 35 rue Félix Faure (open M-Sa 8:30am-7pm). Otherwise, wander the **plage des Sablettes,** next to the *vieille ville,* with its assortment of stuccoed restaurants and cafés. The pedestrian rue St-Michel in the *vieille ville* overflows with shops and restaurants (expect 60-70F *menus*). Look for *boulangeries* on rue Partouneux, or join the legions of ice-cream lickers in pl. aux Herbes. Surprisingly, two of Menton's more delectable dining options are found in hotels. **Le Terminus,** pl. de la Gare (tel. 04 92 10 49 80), offers excellent dinners of local specialties, often with a seafood focus. Your best budget bet is the 50F *menu.* (Open daily. V, MC, AmEx.) **Hôtel des Arcades** (see Accommodations, above) dishes out substantial portions of regional cuisine from its 55F *menu.* (Open daily. V, MC, AmEx.)

🏛 **SIGHTS.** Menton's prize attraction is the **Musée Jean Cocteau,** quai Napoléon II (tel. 04 93 57 72 30), on promenade du Soleil. Although best known for his brilliant work in film and drama, Cocteau was also skilled in the plastic arts. This 17th-century stronghold houses sketches, photographs of Cocteau, Picasso, and Poulenc, playfully designed cuff-links, a vase shaped like a woman's face, and a pebbly mosaic of a lizard basking in the sun. (Open W-M 10am-noon and 2-6pm. Admission 20F, students 15F, 18 and under free; free to all first Su of each month.) Another place of pilgrimage for Cocteau fans is the **Salle des Marriages** in the Hôtel de Ville. The only state-recognized locale where residents can get hitched, Cocteau decorated this wonderfully odd, windowless room as Greek temple, and then added personal touches like leopard rugs and red leather. (Open M-F 8:30am-12:30pm and 1:30-5pm. 10F.) Rising above the municipal market is the bell-tower of the **Église St-Michel.** Although the building has been repeatedly tinkered with since the first stones were laid in 1629, the church's Baroque architecture remains remarkably cohesive. Originally constructed in the 17th century, with the bell-tower built in 1704 and much of the current façade built during the 19th-century. The 12 side-chapels which connect the entrance to the choir were decorated by local artists through the ages. (Open Su-F 10am-noon and 3-6pm.) **Place St-Michel,** in front of the church, is also home to the humble **Chapelle des Penitents Blancs**—closed to the public, but with an admirable façade—and a glorious view of the Plage des Sablettes below and the Italian coastline beyond.

The **Monastère Annonciade,** site of the original Menton, sits calmly on a mountain overlooking the town. Get there via the **Chemin de Rosaire** (just west of the gare routiere, before the *gendarmerie*), a path built by a *monégasque* princess to thank God she hadn't caught the plague. It is lined with chapels that lead to the monastery. The half-hour walk up the hill may seem tough on your legs, but think of the pilgrims who did it on their knees. The amount of graffiti and the desecration of several of the small chapels is disturbing, but the small monastery that awaits up on top is eerie and beautiful, complete with its own set of proudly displayed femurs and other bony relics.

ANTIBES

Tripartite Antibes (pop. 70,000) is like Nice but better. The beaches are sandy, the museums are close to the city, and the city itself is clean and pleasant. The immense port and **Vieux Antibes** comprise the center of town, home to strolling tourists, a covered market, a handful of museums, and a panoply of restaurants. **Cap d'Antibes**, F. Scott Fitzgerald's old stomping ground, is a luxurious peninsula of reclusive villas hiding within pine groves, while come summer **Juan-les-Pins** (see below) is synonymous with debaucherous nightlife. While Antibes' beautiful beaches and its Picasso museum have been drawing crowds for years, the theater and music festivals and a seaside youth hostel have made it an increasingly popular destination on the budget itinerary. Beat the rush, save a spot on the sand, and unload your pack in town for a few days of music, sun, and relaxation.

Ⅶ PRACTICAL INFORMATION. Av. Robert Soleau connects the train station with **pl. de Gaulle**, center of the new town and home to the tourist office. From here, a short walk along rue de la République runs past the bus station into Vieux Antibes. Continuing straight down tree-lined bd. Albert 1er and turning right at the water brings you to a long stretch of beach and the beginning of **Cap d'Antibes** (15min.), although the hostel and the tip of the peninsula are 30 minutes further.

Trains leave av. Robert Soleau for **Cannes** (10min., every 30min., 14F), **Nice** (18min., every 30min., 22F), and **Marseille** (2½hr., 15 per day, 136F). (Station open 9am-noon and 2-6:40pm.) To get to the **bus station**, pl. Guynemer (tel. 04 93 34 37 60), from the tourist office, cross pl. de Gaulle and turn left onto bd. Wilson. Service to **Cannes** (25min., every 20min., 7:10am-9:40pm, 13F) and **Nice** (1¼hr., every 20min., 6:30am-8:05pm, 25F). (Open M-F 8am-noon and 2-6pm, Sa 9am-noon and 2-6pm.) You can **rent cars** and **bikes** from **French Riviera Location**, 43 bd. Wilson. (Tel. 04 93 67 65 67. Bikes from 75F per day, 1000F deposit. Scooters from 130F per day, deposit 5000F. Cars from 240F per day. Open June-Sept. daily 9am-noon and 2-7pm; Oct.-May M-Sa 9am-noon and 2-7pm. V.)

The **tourist office**, 11 pl. de Gaulle (tel. 04 92 90 53 00; fax 04 92 90 53 01), has free maps and info on accommodations, camping, and festivals. The staff can help with some night reservations. (Open July-Aug. daily 8:45am-7:30pm; Sept.-June M-F 9am-noon and 2-6pm, Sa 9am-noon and 2-6pm.) There is a **branch** at the train station. (Open July-Aug. M-F 8:30am-6:30pm, Sa 8:30am-12:30pm.) **Exchange currency** at **Numismatique Change**, 17 bd. Albert 1er. (Tel. 04 93 34 12 76. Open M-Sa 9am-noon and 2-7pm.) Wash off the grime at the **laundromat**, 42 bd. Wilson. (Open daily 7am-8:30pm.) There is a **hospital** (tel. 04 92 91 77 77) on rue de la Fontaine. The **post office** is on pl. des Martyrs de la Résistance (Tel. 04 92 90 61 00. Open M-Tu and Th-F 8am-7pm, W 8:30am-7pm, Sa 8am-noon. **Postal code:** 06600.)

Ⅰ ACCOMMODATIONS AND CAMPING. Antibes lacks the extensive budget accommodations of Nice and Cannes, but a few options are scattered around the area. Be conscious that the location of your hotel may define your Antibes experience, as the *vieille ville*, Cap d'Antibes, and Juan-les-Pins are all a 20 to 40-minute walk from each other. Reservations are essential during the summer.

It's a 40-minute walk along the shore from Antibes or Juan-les-Pins to the **Relais International de la Jeunesse**, at the intersection of bd. de la Garoupe and av. l'Antiquité (tel. 04 93 61 34 40). From Juan-les-Pins, walk south on bd. Edouard Baudoin, which becomes bd. du M. Juin, and cross the peninsula on chemin des Ondes. Turn right on bd. Francis Meillard, then left on bd. de la Garoupe, following signs for Juan-les-Pins Bord de Mer. Or take bus #2A from the bus station in Juan-les-Pins (every 30min.-1hr., last bus 7:15pm). The hostel offers high ceilings inside, room to pitch your tent outside, and a central picnicking area. (75F. Camping 40F per person. Breakfast included. Sheets 10F. Fridge available. Reception daily 8-10am and 6-11pm. Lockout 10am-5:30pm. No curfew.)

Hôtel Jabotte, 13 av. Max Maurey at the base of Cap D'Antibes (tel. 04 93 61 45 89; fax 04 93 61 07 04), is two minutes from the sea. Its central courtyard provides a homey respite from sun and sand. The very friendly and helpful managers preside over all-white rooms with phones, some with TVs. Follow bd. Albert 1er from pl. de Gaulle to its end, turn right on Maréchal Leclerc, and follow the beach for 10min.; av. Max Maurey is a right turn off the beach. Or take the free bus *gratuit*, which leaves every hour and stops at the beach. (Singles and doubles 180-270F, with shower and toilet 220-370F; triples 350-520F; quad/quint apartment 450-720F. Breakfast 30F. V, MC, AmEx.) **Nouvel Hotel,** 1 av. du 24 Août (tel. 04 93 34 44 07), across the street from the bus station, has large, nondescript rooms, above a restaurant. (Singles 150F, doubles 200-300F; triples 260-350. V, MC.) At **Stella's Bed and Bedfast,** 5 av. Paul Arène (tel. 04 93 34 12 14), Stella lets new beds in her beautiful home, with ultra-clean five-bed dorms and large, homey doubles, catering mostly to the port clientele. From the station, cross the street and take av. de la Libération towards the port. Av. Paul Arène is the third right after the roundabout. (Dorms 125F; doubles 350F.)

✪ FOOD. *Vieille* Antibes is loaded with restaurants, although many feel overtly touristy. The local **market**, on cours Masséna near the Picasso museum, is considered one of the best on the Côte d'Azur, with plenty to sample even if you're not going to buy. (Open daily 6:30am-12:30pm.) Supermarket options include **Inter-marché,** across pl. de Gaulle from the tourist office. (Open M-Sa 8am-7:30pm, Su 8:30am-12:30pm.) **La Famiglia,** 34 av. Thiers (tel. 04 93 34 60 82), is a popular family-run Italian restaurant where the only thing larger than the owner's welcome are the hearty pizzas and pastas. (Dishes 40-66F. Open Th-Tu noon-3pm and 7-11pm.) Try **Silverado,** 18 rue du Marc (tel. 04 93 34 99 34), for a long, satisfying dinner of regional cuisine. The 85F *menu* or cheaper salad and *à la carte* options will not disappoint. (Closed M. V, MC.) **Adieu Berthe,** 26 rue Vauban (tel. 04 93 34 78 84), provides a cozy, candle-lit ambience, and serves a dazzling array of *crêpes* starting at 30F. (Open Su-M and W-F 7pm-1am, Sa 7pm-3am.)

✪ SIGHTS. Antibes hides a handful of galleries and several superior museums within its *vieille ville*, which stretches between bd. Maréchal Foch and rue port d'Antibes. Once home to Pablo Picasso, Graham Greene, and Max Ernst, Antibes takes great pride in its resident *artistes*. **Musée Picasso,** pl. Mariejol (tel. 04 92 90 54 20), in the Château Grimaldi, housed Picasso for a productive six months in 1946. His work is executed in a variety of mediums, reflecting both war-time rationing and an inexhaustible, versatile genius. Ceramics, canvases, and sketches range from the gleeful to the disturbing. The small museum also features works by de Staël, Hartung, and Mathieu. (Open June-Sept. Tu-Su 10am-6pm; Oct.-May 10am-noon and 2-6pm. 30F, students 18F.) **Musée Peynet,** pl. Nationale (tel. 04 92 90 54 30), is known as the "Museum of Love." Its collection displays over 300 drawings made by local artist Raymond Peynet. Funny, colorful, and touching, Peynet's characters have brought literature to life for children and adults alike. The only other collection of Peynet's work is in Japan. (Open daily 10am-noon and 2-6pm. 25F, students 15F.) The **Musée Archéologique** (tel. 04 92 90 54 35) is on the waterfront in the Bastion St-André-sur-les-Remparts. The museum displays archaeological finds from the area and features exhibits on the history of Antipolis, the ancient Greek city on the same site. (Open Tu-Su 10am-noon and 2-6pm. 10F, students 5F.) The attractive **Musée Naval et Napoléonien,** av. Kennedy in Cap d'Antibes (tel. 04 93 61 45 32), contains Bonaparte paraphernalia and related objects like Canova's bust of the Emperor. (Open M-F 9:30am-noon and 2:15-6pm, Sa 9:30am-noon. 20F, students 10F.) Next door, the luxurious **Hôtel du Cap** is worth a walk through the lobby and grounds, although spending the night will cost a pretty *centime*. As the largest private marina on the Mediterranean, **Port Vauban** is at any given time host to some spectacular vessels. The 16th-century **Fort Carré** stands guard over the waters of the port. While plans to convert the Fort to a museum are in the works, the 20F admission is hardly worth your while at present. (Open May-Sept. 15 Tu-Su 10am-noon and 1:30-7pm; Sept. 16-Oct. Tu-Su 10am-12:30pm and

1:30-4:30pm; Nov.-Apr. W and Sa-Su 10am-12:30pm and 1:30-4pm. Last entrance 1hr. before closing.) The quai which extends beyond Fort Carré was constructed in the 1970's when a Saudi Arabian prince discovered that the existing port wasn't large enough for his boat. He personally financed the extension.

🎭 🎪 ENTERTAINMENT AND FESTIVALS. At night, your best bet for action is a trip to Juan-les-Pins; if you prefer to nurse a beer, stay put in Antibes. Bd. d'Aguillon, near the port, is lined with bars that get going early (6pm) for happy hours favored by the port crowd. Bawdily decorated **La Gaffe,** 6 bd. d'Aguillon (tel. 04 93 34 04 06; open 11:30am-2:30am), and the Irish **The Hop Store,** 39 bd. d'Aguillon (tel. 04 93 34 15 33), are two favorites. Just off bd. d'Aguillon, **Le Blue Lady,** rue Lacan (tel. 04 93 34 41 00), has a local atmosphere. (Beer from 15F. Open 7:30am-11pm.) In July, Antibes is taken over by festivals, making the town even more vibrant and rooms even harder to find.

During the last week of July, Antibes holds the annual **Été Musicale** in front of the château. Tickets (60-300F) for jazz and classical concerts and operas are available at the Antibes and Juan-les-Pins tourist offices. Some years, Antibes also offers a **Festival de Théâtre,** which coincides with the Été Musical. The **Festival d'Art Lyrique** (tel. 04 92 90 54 60 or 04 92 90 53 00), during the first two weeks of July, brings world-class soloists to the *vieux port.* (50-150F.)

JUAN-LES-PINS

Juan-les-Pins crams as much fun into the summer nights as possible. Although officially joined as one city, known as Antibes-Juan-les-Pins, Antibes and Juan-les-Pins are 3km apart and have separate train stations, post offices, and tourist offices. They also jive to a different tempo—Juan-les-Pins is younger and more hedonistic; the streets are packed with people seeking sun, sea, and sex (not necessarily in that order). In the summer, boutiques stay open until midnight, cafés until 2am, and nightclubs close when dancers head back to the beach. The cafés are cheaper and almost as lively as the clubs; even the most miserly traveler can join in the nightly bash.

🛈 PRACTICAL INFORMATION. The **train station** is on av. l'Esterel, where it joins av. du Maréchal Joffre. Trains leave about every 20 minutes for **Antibes** (5min., every 30min. until 12:25am, 7F), **Nice** (30min.) and **Cannes** (10min., 11F). To **walk from Antibes,** follow bd. Wilson from pl. du Général de Gaulle for 1.5km and turn left onto av. Dautheville. The English-speaking staff at the **tourist office,** 51 bd. Guillaumont (tel. 04 92 90 53 05), distributes maps, makes hotel reservations, and provides info and reservations for Juan-les-Pins' numerous music festivals. From the station, walk straight on av. du Maréchal Joffre and turn right onto av. Guy de Maupassant; the office is a two-minute walk on the right, at the intersection of av. Admiral Courbet and av. Gillaumont. (Open June M-F 9am-12:30pm and 2-6:30pm, Sa 9am-noon and 2-6pm; July-Aug. M-Sa 8:30am-7:30pm, Su 10am-1pm; Sept.-May M-F 9am-noon and 2-6pm.) There's also a **branch office** in the station. (Open July-Aug. M-Sa 9am-noon and 2-6pm.)

🏠🍴 ACCOMMODATIONS AND FOOD. Juan-les-Pins has little in the way of budget lodgings, but **Hôtel Trianon,** 14 av. de l'Estérel (tel. 04 93 61 18 11), has reasonable rooms and prices. To get there, take a right coming out of the train station. (Singles 200F; doubles 200-300F; triples 350F. Breakfast 30F. V, MC, AmEx.) **Hôtel Parisiana,** 16 av. de L'Estérel (tel. 04 93 61 27 03; fax 04 93 67 97 21), has more inviting rooms with TVs, plus 30F discounts for four-night stays and tickets to private beaches. (Singles 177-210F; doubles 245-295F; triples 285-388F. Extra bed 52-72F. Breakfast 25F. V, MC, AmEx.) Although it's illegal and not recommended by *Let's Go,* many serious carousers seem to fancy the beach's soft sand as a mattress. Before hitting the clubs and cafés, dinner at **La Bamba,** av. Dautheville (tel. 04 93 61 32 64), is favored by locals and tourists for better renditions of the same meals served everywhere else in town. (Open daily noon-3pm and 7pm-midnight. V, MC, AmEx.) Or assemble your own feast at the **Casino supermarket** on av. Amiral Courbet (tel. 04 93 61 00 56), near the tourist office and close to the beach. (Open M-Sa 8am-12:30pm and 4-8pm, Su 8am-1pm.)

ENTERTAINMENT AND FESTIVALS. Juan-les-Pins's nightlife emanates from the Casino area, and cruising the strip can be entertainment in itself. *Discothèques* all open around 11pm and close around 5am, with cover charges around 100F including one drink. Look for posters around town advertising special events, such as the *mega-mousse* party, where club-goers dance in a sea of foamy bubbles. **Le Village,** 1 bd. de la Pinède (tel. 04 92 93 90 00), is notorious throughout the Riviera for its lively dance floor. The psychedelic **Whisky à Gogo,** bd. de la Pinède (tel. 04 93 61 26 40), lets you dance the night away amid water-filled columns and ample lounge space (beer 50F). **Vertigo,** at the intersection of av. Maupassant and bd. Wilson, is a newcomer to the *discotheque* scene, but is quickly gaining a reputation. The dress code at all clubs is simple: look good. Apart from Whiskey à Gogo, in the off-season most *discothèques* only open on the weekends. Fortunately, the bar scene rivals discos in merrymaking. Crowds pile onto the patio of hip **Che Cafe,** 1 bd. de la Pinède (tel. 04 92 93 90 80). Serving a slightly older crowd, **Pam Pam Rhumerie,** 137 bd. Wilson (tel. 04 93 61 11 05), has a decisively tropical feel, with nightly dance shows and drinks with names like *Waikiki, Bora-Bora,* and *Macumba* (from 68F). If you have any money left after clubbing, you can lose it at the **Eden Casino,** bd. Baudoin. (Tel. 04 92 93 71 71. Open daily 10am-5am. Min. age 18. No shorts or sneakers. Free, if you're lucky.) In mid-July, Juan-Les-Pins becomes saturated with visitors for the **Festival International de Jazz (Jazz à Juan),** one of the Riviera's biggest summer events with an outstanding musical program that last year included Dave Brubeck, Ben Harper, and Ray Charles. (Tickets 110-200F, available at tourist offices in Juan-les-Pins and Antibes.)

CANNES

Cannes (pop. 78,000) scintillates with flashy cars, flashy people, and the sandy beach that you—and thousands of other bathing beauties—have been combing for on the stony Riviera. Here millionaires work-out their wallets in swanky cafés, plush hotels, cozy *couturiers*, and palm-lined boardwalk.

Cannes was just another sleepy Riviera fishing village until 1836, when a cholera outbreak forced Lord Brougham, an English aristocrat, to winter there *en route* to Nice. Brougham's aristocratic friends came over to keep him company, and the rest is revelry. Today, Cannes remains a favorite stop for the international jet-set. Less reclusive than St-Tropez, Cannes allows even the unshaven budget traveler to tan like the stars without spending a franc. You may be shockingly underdressed, but Yves Saint-Laurent will avert his gaze.

ORIENTATION AND PRACTICAL INFORMATION

Nouveau Cannes, between the station and the sea with rue d'Antibes running through its center, is the city's shopping hub. Heading right from the station on rue Jean-Jaurès leads to the pedestrian district and *vieux* Cannes, known as **le Suquet,** where cheap eats await on **rue Meynadier, rue St-Antoine,** and upscale restaurants line the steps of **rue du Suquet.** Eager star-gazers and those seeking the **tourist office** should follow rue des Serbes (across from the station) to **bd. de la Croisette,** Cannes's long and lavish coastal promenade. The tourist office is on the right in the huge Palais des Festivals.

Most of Cannes' daytime activity (and spending) pulses between **rue Félix-Faure** and the **waterfront.** Cafés, shops, *grandes dames*, and poodles line this quarter of town. Stroll down lovely rue Meynadier, one of Cannes' few pedestrian streets, or down the boardwalk along bd. de la Croisette and the **beach.** Sandy public beaches are sandwiched between parasol-studded private ones, all of which are dotted with multi-million-dollar yachts.

Cannes

ACCOMMODATIONS

A Hôtel National
B Auberge de Jeunesse
  –Le Chalit
C Hôtel du Nord
D Hôtel Cybelle
E Hôtel Bourgogne
F Hôtel Mimont
G Auberge de Jeunesse (HI)

THE SOUTHEAST

Baie de Cannes

Vieux Port

Plages de la Croisette

av. Windsor
PT. DES GABRES
bd. du Général Vautrin
r. Dr. Zamenhof
r. Latour-Maubourg
r. Rouaze
r. Pasteur
r. du Canada
Carlton Casino
r. Elnesy
r. F. Amouretti
bd. de la Croisette
r. Molière
r. Victor Cousin
r. d'Antibes
r. du Cdt. André
r. Macé
r. des États-Unis
r. des Serbes
r. des Belges
Main Tourist Office
Croisette Casino
r. N. Dame
r. Bivouac Napoléon
PL. DE GAULLE
Gare Maritime
quai St-Pierre
SQ. J. HIBERT
Musée de la Castre
r. Louie Perisol
r. du Pré
r. Georges Clémenceau
bd. Jean Hibert
r. Hibert
r. J. Dollus
r. des Suisses
av. des Anc. Combattants d'AFN
bd. Guynemer
r. L. Pasteur
av. de Grasse
r. Guy de Maupassant
r. Louis Blanc
r. Dr. Cazagnaire
La Pantiero
r. Félix Faure
r. Mandelieu
r. Tunis
r. Maréchal Joffre
PL. DU 18 JUIN
r. Jean de Riouffe
r. Buttura
r. d'Antibes
r. du Mal. Foch
av. du 24 Août
PL. DE LA GARE
r. Hoche
r. Jean Jaurès
H. Vagliano
Voie Ferrée
PL. GAMBETTA
bd. de Lorraine
r. du Colliwipbol
r. de Constantine
bd. d'Alsace
r. Louis Nouveau
bd. Montfleury
av. d'Isola Bella
PL. DU CDT. MARIA
av. de Valauris
r. Merle
bd. de la République
r. de Mimont
av. St-Nicolas
av. du Mal Galliéni
r. de Suffren
av. la Chaude
r. 11 Novembre
bd. Carnot
PL. VAUBAN
PL. G. PHILIPE
Lattre de Tassigny
r. Borniol
av. de Grasse
Voie Ferrée
r. Louis Blanc
r. de Grasse
r. Volta

N
300 yards
300 meters

Trains: 1 rue Jean-Jaurès. Connections approximately every 30min., 6am-midnight, to: **St-Raphaël** (25min., 34F); **Antibes** (15min., 14F); **Nice** (35min., 32F); **Monaco** (50min., 46F); and other coastal stops. Hourly trains to **Marseille** (2hr., 6:30am-11:05pm, 129F). TGV to **Paris** via Marseille 463F. Info desk open daily 8:30am-5:40pm. Ticket sales 6am-midnight.

Buses: Bus Azur (tel. 04 93 39 18 71). Info and departure from pl. de l'Hôtel de Ville. Open M-Sa 7am-7pm. Many buses make a prior and final stop by the train station (tel. 04 93 39 11 39 or 04 93 39 31 37). To: **Nice airport** (45min., every hr. 6am-7pm, 70F) and **Nice** (1½hr., every 20min., 32F).

Local Transportation: Bus tickets 7.50F; *carnet* of 10 50F. Weekly pass 54F.

Taxis: Allô Taxis Cannes (tel. 04 92 99 27 27).

Bike and Scooter Rental: Holiday Bikes, 16 rue du 14 Juillet (tel. 04 93 94 61 00). Bikes 60-80F, mopeds 120F, scooters from 150F. Deposits from 1000F. Helmet included. Open M-Sa 8:30am-7pm, Su 9am-noon and 5-7pm. V, MC, AmEx.

Tourist Office, 1 bd. de la Croisette (tel. 04 93 39 24 53; fax 04 92 99 84 23; semof-lou@palais-festivals-Calais.fr). Loads of info and free lodging service. Open July-Aug. daily 9am-7pm; Sept.-June M-Sa 9am-6:30pm. Longer hours during festivals. The **branch office,** 1 rue Jean-Jaurès (tel. 04 93 99 19 77), at the station, has less extensive services. Open July-Sept. M-Sa 8:30am-noon and 3-7pm; Oct.-June M-F 9am-12:30pm and 2-6:30pm.

Money: Office Provençal, 17 rue Maréchal-Foch (tel. 04 93 39 34 37), across from the train station, **exchanges currency.** Open daily 8am-8pm. **American Express,** 8 rue des Belges (tel. 04 93 38 15 87; fax 04 92 98 01 01), off bd. de la Croisette. Open M-F 9am-noon and 2-6pm, Sa 9am-noon.

English Bookstore: Cannes English Bookshop, 11 rue Bivouac Napoléon (tel. 04 93 99 40 08). Open M-Sa 10am-1pm and 2-7pm. V, MC, AmEx.

Youth Center: Cannes Information Jeunesse, 5 quai St-Pierre (tel. 04 93 06 31 31). Info on housing, jobs, and more. Open 8:30am-noon and 2-4:45pm.

Laundromat: Laverie, av. Latour-Maubourg. Open daily 7am-10pm.

Police: 2 quai St-Pierre (tel. 04 93 47 56 02).

Hospitals: Pierre Nouveau, 13 av. des Broussailles (tel. 04 93 69 70 00). **Sunny Bank Anglo-American Hospital,** 133 av. du Petit Juas (tel. 04 93 06 31 06).

Post Office: 22 rue Bivouac Napoléon (tel. 04 93 06 26 50), off allée de Liberté near Palais des Festivals. Open M-Tu and Th-F 8am-7pm, W 8:30am-7pm, Sa 8am-noon. **Branch office** at 37 rue Mimont (tel. 04 93 06 27 00). Open M-F 8:30am-noon and 1:30-5pm, Sa 8am-noon. For Poste Restante, designate "Cannes-Mimont" for the branch office. **Postal code:** 06400.

Internet Access: Asher M.C.S., 44 bd. Carnot (tel. 04 92 99 03 01). 10F per ¼hr. Open M-Th 9am-7pm and F-Su 9am-noon.

ACCOMMODATIONS AND CAMPING

Though eating and drinking in Cannes may force you to streeeetch your budget, you can get a good night's sleep at reasonable prices. For the film festival, expect a huge boost in rates, and book as much as a year ahead. Plan well in advance for high season. Prices drop dramatically when the crowds and stars leave.

Auberge de Jeunesse—Le Chalit, 27 av. Maréchal Galliéni (tel./fax 04 93 99 22 11 or tel. 06 15 28 07 09; ANNIKGEF@club_internet.fr). Take the stairs leading to a passage under the train station; signs will point you to the hostel (5min.). In the evening, travelers may want to avoid the dark tunnel—instead, as you exit the station, turn right on bd. Carnot and follow it straight until av. 11 November. Take a right on 11 Nov. and a left onto av. Galliéni. Cozy, movie poster-lined quarters and friendly hosts who give out coupons for local discounts. 4- to 8-bed dorms 90F. Sheets 17F. Reception daily 8:30am-12:30pm. Lockout 12:30-5pm. 24hr. access with door code.

Auberge de Jeunesse de Cannes (HI), 35 av. de Vallauris (tel./fax 04 93 99 26 79). Take the stairs that lead to a passageway under the station; follow the signs to the right to the hostel (10min.), past the unfortunately named Pizza Dick on your left. At the pl. du Cdt. Maria, veer left. New hostel with friendly owner, a short hike from the town center. Big comfy beds in 6-bed co-ed dorms. Kitchens, laundry, common room. 70-80F. Reception daily 8am-1pm and 3-11:30pm. Midnight curfew.

Hôtel Mimont, 39 rue de Mimont (tel. 04 93 39 51 64; fax 04 93 99 65 35), behind the train station next to bd. de la République. Large, clean rooms in a neighborhoody area. All with showers and TV. Singles 160F; with toilet 190F; doubles 200F; with toilet 220F; triples with toilet 285F. Extra person 65F. Breakfast 30F. Reception 7:30am-11pm, after that use your key. V, MC, AmEx.

Hôtel du Nord, 6 rue Jean-Jaurès (tel. 04 93 38 48 79; fax 04 92 99 28 20), across from the station. Welcoming rooms despite orange bedspreads and paisley halls. All have toilet; pricier rooms include shower and TV. Singles 180-260F; doubles 200-300F; triples 300-360F; quads 350-430F. Breakfast 20-30F. Open Jan.-Oct. V, MC, AmEx.

Hotel Cybelle, 14 rue du 24 Août (tel. 04 93 38 31 33; fax 04 93 38 43 47). Owners run a tight ship and offer bright rooms in between the train station and the beach. Singles 120-140F; doubles 200-250F. V, MC, AmEx.

Hôtel de Bourgogne, 11 rue du 24 Août (tel. 04 93 38 36 73; fax 04 92 99 28 41), on a small street off rue Jean-Jaurès. Spotless, muted rooms, some with TV. Singles 140-250F; doubles 180-280F; triples with shower 270-350F. Breakfast 25F. V, MC, AmEx.

Hôtel National, 8 rue Maréchal Joffre (tel. 04 93 39 91 92; fax 04 92 98 44 06). Standard rooms are well-situated, near rue Meynadier and the *vieille ville*. Singles 150-200F; doubles 220-260F; triples 350F. Breakfast 30F. V, MC.

Campsites: Le Grand Saule, 24 bd. Jean Moulin (tel. 04 93 90 55 10; fax 04 93 47 24 55), in nearby Ranguin. Take bus #9 from pl. de l'Hôtel de Ville toward Grasse (8F). 3-star site with pool. 70F per person, 124F for 2 people and tent, car 16F. Open Apr.-Oct. V, MC. **Caravaning Bellevue,** 67 av. M. Chevalier (tel. 04 93 47 28 97; fax 04 93 48 66 25). Take the #2 bus to "Poésie." 211 spaces. 61F per person with tent; 2 people and tent 82F; car 12F. 2-day max. stay at peak times. Open Apr.-Sept.

FOOD

Looking forward to delectable *and* affordable food? Sorry, no Cannes-do. Walking around at night, you'll pass many a table of smiling diners feasting on delectable dishes you probably can't afford. Be prepared to spend dearly, or settle for second-tier options. A morning **market** offers fresh food on the *place* between rue Mimont and av. de la République. (Daily 7am-noon.) Other supplies await at **Champion supermarket,** 6 rue Meynadier, in the pedestrian zone. (Open in summer M-Sa 8:45am-8pm; off-season M-Sa 8:45am-7:30pm.) Picnic options beckon at **Le Pain d'Olivier,** 18 rue Meynadier (tel. 04 93 39 37 74), a wonderful *boulangerie-pâtisserie* where you'll want one of everything. Complete the picnic at the *charcuterie* next door. The cool shade and breezes of palm-tree-filled **Jardin de la Croisette** render it the perfect picnic spot. Reasonably tasty and reasonably priced restaurants are located in the pedestrian zone, centered on **rue Meynadier.**

Mi Figue, Mi Raison, 27 rue du Suquet (tel. 04 93 39 51 25), towards the top of the stairs. The exception to prove the rule. Dishes explore the crossroads of *provençal* and North African cuisine. 65F couscous and 85F *aïoli provençal* are good value for the pricey Suquet. Closed W outside July-Aug. V, MC.

Le Domino, 7 rue du Pré (tel. 04 92 98 65 88). Small, informal restaurant near the top of busy Suquet, serving high quality *crêpes* (18-36F), salads (28-50F), and *plats du jour* (50F). Open M-Sa noon-3pm and 7:30-11pm.

Le Lion d'Or, 45 bd. de la République (tel. 04 93 38 56 57), serves excellent *cuisine provençale*, with super service and an unbeatable 3-course, 67F *menu*, that make up for the lackluster setting. Try the hearty *soupe de poissons*. Open Su-F noon-2pm and 7pm-midnight. V, MC.

THE SOUTHEAST

Le Caveau des Années "30," 45 rue Félix Faure (tel. 04 93 39 06 33). The affordable end of swank, the food is still overpriced, but forking over 60-70F for pasta allows you to admire the Frank Lloyd Wright-style dining room at this outlandish Cannes institution. Open nightly. V, MC.

■ SIGHTS AND SHOPS

SIGHTS. Castre Cathédrale and its courtyard stand on the hill where *vieux* Cannes was built. The tranquil shade of pines and the striking view of Cannes and the Îles de Lérins provide a soothing alternative to the speeding luxury land yachts and the stuffy heat below. Housed in the church, the **Musée de la Castre** (tel. 04 93 38 55 26) exhibits weapons, masks, and instruments from Ghana, Congo, and Nigeria. Within the cathedral, *provençal* paintings are displayed in the Chapelle Ste-Anne. (Open July-Sept. W-M 10am-noon and 3-7pm; Oct.-Mar. 10am-noon and 2-5pm; Apr.-June 10am-noon and 2-6pm. 10F, students free.)

SHOPPING. Blessed with streets and streets of designer boutiques, Cannes has the best window shopping on the Riviera. **Rue d'Antibes,** running parallel to the sea, and **bd. de la Croisette,** passing right along the shore, sport familiar runway names—Christian Dior, Hermès, and Gianni Versace.

■ ENTERTAINMENT AND FESTIVALS

ENTERTAINMENT. If you know how to hold 'em and when to fold 'em, Cannes offers three casinos. The most accessible, **Le Casino Croisette,** 1 jetée Albert Edouard (tel. 04 93 38 12 11), next to the Palais des Festivals, mainly has slot machines, but also offers blackjack and roulette. (Gambling daily 5pm-4am, open for slots at 10am. No shorts. Ages 18+.) To enter one of Cannes's elite clubs, get decked out in your finest and sport an attitude. In summer, the focus shifts to **Palm Beach** at the eastern edge of Cannes. If club covers leave you in a cold sweat, enjoy the cheaper and less formal entertainment at pubs and cafés near the waterfront.

Morrison's, 10 rue Teisseire (tel. 04 92 98 16 17). This Irish pub rivals any Dublin counterpart, especially Wednesdays, when the crowd goes crazy for live and rowdy Irish folk music. Thursdays see live blues and rock. Beer from 18F. Music starts at 10pm.

Jane's, 38 rue des Serbes (tel. 04 93 43 93 69), in the Hôtel Gray d'Albion remains Cannes' favorite *discothèque*. Fridays are theme nights. Cover includes first drink. Th and before midnight 50F, Su women free before 1am, otherwise 100F. Open Th-Su.

Whisky à Go Go, 115 av. de Lérins (tel. 04 93 43 25 72), revs it up nightly by Palm Beach. Also look for the nearby **Mocambo** which sets up shop here July-Aug. Both are immensely popular during the summer.

Al Modo Bar, corner of rue Dr. Monod and rue Bateguier (tel. 04 93 68 22 24). It doesn't get any more modo than this hip staple for Cannes' younger jet set, with the requisite beautiful people, unfriendly bouncers, and top-notch DJs.

Le Loft, rue du Dr. Monod (tel. 04 93 39 40 39). No cover, no attitude, just a lively dance floor upstairs and an easy-going patio with a busy happy hour. Open nightly.

César Palace, 48 bd. de la République (tel. 04 93 68 23 23). A good bet for hostelers who don't want to stray too far from their abode. Sporadic theme nights.

Zanzibar, 85 rue Féliz Faure (tel. 04 93 39 30 75). Intimate patio and candle-lit cavern cater to an older gay clientele.

FESTIVALS. In May, the world of cinema comes to town for the **Festival International du Film.** Executives sign multi-million-dollar deals on cocktail napkins while silver screen heart-throbs stand by waiting to be taken seriously. None of the festival's 350 screenings is open to the public, but the sidewalk circus is free. On July 4 and 14, Cannes hosts its annual **Fête Americaine** and **Fête Nationale**—fireworks burst overhead, and spirits run high as the whole city takes to the streets.

THE MAN IN THE IRON MASK Mythologized in Alexandre Dumas's novel, *Dix Ans plus tard ou le Vicomte de Bragelonne (The Man in the Iron Mask)*, the truth about this mystery man remains unsolved. The only concrete information about the shadowy figure is that he was in the prison Pignerol before 1681 and died in the Bastille on Nov. 19, 1703. The name "Marchioly" and "aged about 45" were the only inscriptions on his tombstone. The theory proposed by Voltaire and adopted by Dumas is that he was the twin of Louis XIV, imprisoned and forced by his brother to wear the mask to prevent a challenge to the throne. Others claimed that he was the king's bastard elder brother or else his illegitimate son, imprisoned to prevent a war for the succession. A less romantic, if more credible, theory maintains that the masked prisoner was Eustache Dauger, arrested in July 1669, for reasons unknown. In prison, Dauger became the valet for former finance minister Nicolas Fouquet. Upon Fouquet's death, Dauger's identity was hidden for fear that he might divulge state secrets. And the iron mask was actually a veil of black velvet.

ÎLES DE LÉRINS

Both Îles de Lérins provide a welcome respite from fast-paced Cannes. The smaller island, **St-Honorat,** harbors pine forests and an active monastery, the **Abbaye de Lérins.** In the 10th century, St. Honorat settled on this secluded island in an attempt to escape the visitors that continually accosted him in his coastal grotto. Today, the order of monks he founded still works the land. In high season and on weekends, tourists invade the island's gravel paths and the monastery's gift shop, which sells homemade honey and wine. When less crowded, the islet is an isolated paradise, scattered with ancient chapels and serenaded by a host of chattering birds. On the southeast corner of the island, the original monastery stands broken and deserted, full of rooms to be explored. (Open daily June-Sept. 9:40am-4:40pm, Oct.-May 10:40am-3:30pm. Free.)

Four times the size of its neighbor, **Ste-Marguerite** hosts only twice as many visitors and manages to preserve lusher forests. The island was once home to St. Honorat's equally holy sister, St. Marguerite. The massive, star-shaped **Forte Ste-Marguerite,** where the Man in the Iron Mask (see greybox) was imprisoned, has become a national monument Within the walls is **La Musée de la Mer** (tel. 04 93 43 18 17), but the collection of marine paraphernalia is less interesting than the fort itself. (Both open W-M June-Sept. 10:30am-noon and 2-6:30pm; Oct.-Dec. and Feb.-May 10:30am-noon and 2-4:30pm. 10F, students free.)

Compagnie Esterel Chanteclair (tel. 04 93 39 11 82; fax 04 92 98 80 32) sends **boats** from **Cannes'** *gare maritime*, in the old port near the Palais des Festivals. A brochure from Le Chalit Hostel gets you a 10F reduction on prices. (Every 30min. July-Aug., 7:30am-6pm, otherwise 6 per day. St-Honorat 30min., round-trip 50F; Ste-Marguerite 15min., round-trip 45F. Circuit of both islands 70F.)

MOUGINS AND MOUANS-SARTOUX

Mougins and Mouans-Sartoux were recently villages but have now become affluent suburbs of Cannes, well worth a stop on your itinerary if you can spare the time. **Mougins'** narrow stone streets harbor lots of boutiques, and pricey shaded cafés ring the outside of the village—but you are paying for the view. The **Musée de la photographie,** rue Maréchal Foch (tel. 04 93 75 85 67; fax 04 93 90 15 15), displays photos of a trendy, striped-shirted Picasso at work and play. The museum lends a key to the **clock tower,** from which you have a 360° view of the countryside, including nearby St-Paul and Vence. (Open July-Aug. daily 2-11pm; Sept.-Oct. and Dec.-June W-M 1-6pm. 5F.) The **tourist office,** 15 av. Jean-Charles Mallet (tel. 04 93 75 87 67; fax 04 92 92 04 03), provides plenty of info on the area, including the enormous **Forest la Valmasque.** (Open daily July-Aug. 10am-8pm; Sept.-June 10am-5:30pm.) Eight kilometers away, you can reach Mougins by the #600 bus from **Cannes'** train station (direction "Val du Mougins," 17min., every 30min., 9F). From there, walk 25m back down the road and take a left, following signs to Mougins (25min.).

A couple stops past Mougins on the road to Grasse, the same bus stops at **Mouans-Sartoux** (11F). Here the town's wealth seems less *passé* than Cannes, with trendy restaurants and boutiques housed in the picturesque old village, and interesting contemporary art exhibits housed in the stately château.

VALLAURIS

Vallauris, a few kilometers inland and east of Cannes, has long been the pottery capital of France. Picasso was entranced by the town's ceramics and worked here shortly after World War II. The **Musée National de Picasso,** pl. de la Libération (tel. 04 93 64 16 05), holds the master's *War and Peace.* (Open W-M July-Aug. 10am-12:30pm and 2-6:30pm; Sept.-June 10am-noon and 2-6pm. 17F, students 10.50F.) The galleries **M. Musarra, Siffre di Sculpteur,** and **Les 3 Flammes** on rue Clemenceau all show Picasso originals. To reach Vallauris, take a bus from the station or pl. de l'Hôtel de Ville in **Cannes** (40min., every hr. 8am-7:30pm, 12F), or from the *gare routière* in **Antibes** (5 per day, 14F) to "Picasso." From the stop, follow av. Clemenceau to the **tourist office,** sq. du 8 Mai 1945 (tel. 04 93 63 82 58; fax 04 93 63 13 66), for info on Vallauris's biannual exhibition of international ceramics and modern art. (Open daily in summer 9am-7pm; in winter 9am-noon and 2-6pm.)

GRASSE

When you're burnt crispy by the sun and tired of wearing your darkest t-shirt every day just because it shows the least dirt, head for the hills to drift in the floral-scented air of Grasse. The fragrant oxygen in the perfume-manufacturing capital of the world can overpower you, but at France's three largest, oldest, and most distinguished *parfumeries,* smelling good is a science as much as a sales pitch. For those who prefer the odor of physical activity, Grasse is near the GR4 trail and serves as an excellent springboard for exploration of local prehistoric caves and the Grand Canyon du Verdon. Staying put in town is equally enticing, as Grasse boasts one of the most appealing *vieilles villes* on the Côte d'Azur. Either way, Grasse is a treat for the senses.

⚫ ORIENTATION AND PRACTICAL INFORMATION. Grasse's proximity to Cannes makes it a pleasant afternoon excursion. Although the town spreads into the valley below, most tourist destinations are concentrated on the south-facing hillside. Museums cluster around **pl. du Cours,** a large plateau where old men while away the day sitting on benches and playing *petanque.* The **bus station,** pl. de la Buanderie (tel. 04 93 36 37 37), has service daily to **Cannes** (35min., every 30min., 23F) and **Nice** (1¼hr., every 30min., every hour on weekends, 37F). Call **SOMA** (tel. 04 93 36 49 61) or **RCA** (tel. 04 93 55 24 00) for times. No trains stop at Grasse, but the **SNCF info office,** across the *place,* can attend to your rail needs. (Open M-Sa 8:30am-5:30pm.) The **tourist office** (tel. 04 93 36 66 66; fax 04 93 36 86 36) is found near the Casino on cours Honoré Cresp in the Palais des Congrés. (Open mid-June to July M-Sa 9am-7pm; Aug. to mid-June 9am-12:30pm and 1:30-6pm.) There is also an **annex** near the bus station on pl. de la Foux. (Tel. 04 93 36 21 07. Open July-mid-Sept. 9am-12:30pm and 1:30-6pm.) Both make reservations, and give advice on walks and hikes. Cash in at **Change du Casino,** cours H. Cresp (tel. 04 93 36 48 48), near the casino. (Open Tu-Sa 9:30am-noon and 2-7pm.) The **post office** (tel. 04 93 36 24 19) is in the parking garage under the bus station. (Open M and W-F 8am-6:30pm, Tu 9am-6:30pm, Sa 8am-noon. **Postal code**: 06130.)

⚫🛏 ACCOMMODATIONS AND FOOD. If the narrow, walled *traversées* (stairways cut into the hill) and the welcoming aroma of the *parfumeries* induce you to spend the night, Grasse provides several low-cost, spartan rooms with luxurious vistas of the valley below. Perched above town, **Hôtel Ste-Thérèse,** 39 bd. Y.E. Baudoin (tel. 04 93 36 10 29; fax 04 93 36 11 73), has rooms managed by kind nuns surrounding an internal chapel. To reach this sanctum, climb bd. du Jeu de Balloon behind the tourist office annex and turn left onto bd. Baudoin (15min.). (Singles 160-220F; doubles 220-270F. Extra bed 30F. Breakfast 28F.) **Pension Les Palmiers,** 17 bd. Y.E Baudoin (tel./fax 04 93 36 07 24), on the way to Hôtel Ste-Thérèse, has an inviting home-like setting. (Singles 130-190F; doubles 170-235F. Breakfast 30F. V, MC.) **Oasis,** at the bus station (tel. 04 93 36 02 72; fax 04 93 36 11 73), is less inviting, with poorer views, but more central. The characterless rooms are reasonably well-maintained. (Singles 170F, doubles 240F. Breakfast 30F. V, MC.)

Grasse hoards a wealth of specialty food stores in the *vieille ville*. Much of the culinary action centers around the cobblestone **pl. aux Aires.** Also in the vicinity is a **Monoprix supermarket,** rue Paul Goby. (Open M-Sa 8:45am-7:30pm.) **Markets** bustle on pl. aux Herbes (Th-Tu 7am-noon), and on pl. aux Aires. For a prepared meal, **Le Gazan,** rue Gazan (tel. 04 93 36 22 88), has a fish and seafood focus, but you can't miss with anything from the 85F *menu*. (Open M-Sa noon-3pm and 7-10pm. V, MC.) **La Galerie Gourmande,** 3 rue des Fabreries (tel. 04 93 36 80 69), just off rue Amiral de Grasse below pl. aux Aires, serves lovingly prepared *provençale* specialties in a cozy alley setting. (89F *menu*. Open Tu-Sa 7-10:30pm. V, MC.)

■ **SIGHTS AND SMELLS.** A walk through the serpentine alleys of Grasse's *vieille ville* is immensely rewarding, but take a map or risk walking in circles for hours. The tourist office map includes an annotated 1½hr. walking tour. One of the neighborhood's many highlights, the Romanesque **Cathédrale Notre-Dame-du-Puy** has works by Rubens, Fragonard, and others gracing its walls. Grasse's three largest *parfumeries* provide variations on the theme of olfactory titillation: **Fragonard's** original 1873 factory, 20 bd. Fragonard (tel. 04 93 36 44 65; open daily in summer 9am-6:30pm, winter M-Sa 9am-12:30pm and 2-6pm; free 15min. English tours every 10min.); **Molinard,** 60 bd. Victor Hugo (tel. 04 93 36 01 62; free English tours M-Sa 9am-7pm, Su 9am-noon and 2-6pm); and **Galimard,** 73 rte. de Cannes (tel. 04 93 09 20 00; open in summer daily 9am-6:30pm, winter 9am-12:30pm and 2-6pm; Free tours daily). The **Musée International de la Parfumerie,** 8 pl. du Cours (tel. 04 93 36 80 20), instructs and fascinates: the second floor displays a 3000-year-old mummy's perfumed hand and foot preserved due to the perfuming process. Amid fourth-floor greenery, sniff the base elements of your favorite perfumes—it takes a tonne of flowers to make a liter of fragrance. (Open June-Sept. daily 10am-7pm; Oct.-May W-Su 10am-noon and 2-5pm. 25F, students 12.50F.)

The **Musée d'Art et d'Histoire de Provence,** 2 rue Mirabeau (tel. 04 93 36 01 61), provides a brilliant ethnography of the region through decorated rooms depicting different aspects and eras of the *provençal* lifestyle. (Open June-Sept. daily 10am-7pm; Oct.-May W-Su 10am-noon and 2-5pm. 20F, students 10F.) In the 18th-century artist's brightly painted villa, the **Musée Jean-Honoré Fragonard,** 23 bd. Fragonard (tel. 04 93 36 01 61), features originals and reproductions of local painters' work. A visit ensures you will leave Grasse having seen enough Fragonard and Granet paintings to last you a while. (Open June-Sept. daily 10am-7pm; Oct.-May W-Su 10am-noon and 2-5pm. 20F, students 10F.)

❀ **FESTIVALS.** Grasse hosts several festivals throughout the year. In early May **Exporose** (tel. 04 93 40 53 00) attracts rose growers from around the world for the largest exhibition of its kind (50F). The town spices up again in late June for **Jazz Rallye** (tel. 04 93 36 66 66), when musicians play the town's pubs.

GRAND CANYON DU VERDON

The plunging cliffs of the Grand Canyon du Verdon are—geological determinism aside—quite different from the scenery, pace, and lifestyle of the coast. They provide a memorable, if slow, way to move between the Riviera and the Alps. **Castellane,** 17km east of the canyon, is the largest town in the area, providing, numerous outdoor organizations for exploring the canyon. From September to June, don't count on public transport to the canyon.

CASTELLANE

Though the canyon is most easily reached from Castellane, the town is otherwise out of the way. **Autocars Sumian** (tel. 04 42 54 72 82) runs to **Aix-en-Provence** (3hr.; July-Aug. 3 per week, rest of year 1 per week; 95F) and **Marseille** (3½hr., same frequency, 116F). **VFD** (tel. 04 76 47 77 77) runs to **Grasse** (70min., 1 per day, 68F) and **Nice** (2hr., 1 per day, 97F). From Castellane, **Girieud Voyages** (tel. 04 92 83 40 27) sends buses into the **Canyon** (July-Aug. M-Sa 2 per day). The **tourist office** (tel. 04 92 83 61 14; fax 04 92 83 76 89) gives out hotel listings and maps of the canyon. Especially detailed canyon maps are worth the 12F. (Open July-Aug. 9am-12:30pm and 1:30-7pm; Sept.-June M-Sa 9:15am-noon and 2-6pm.) The **police** (tel. 04 92 83 60 08) are at the end of town on the road to the Canyon. For the **hospital**, call 04 92 83 62 64. The **post office** is on pl. Église (tel. 04 92 83 63 69). (Open M-F 9am-noon and 2-5pm, Sa 9am-noon. **Postal code:** 04120.)

Castellane has no shortage of accommodations, but in summer rooms fill quickly. With nature everywhere, camping is popular but often difficult to access. The closest hostel is the **Auberge de Jeunesse (HI)**, 20km from Castéllane in pleasant La-Palaud-sur-Verdon (tel./fax 04 92 77 38 72). There's no public transportation; from Castellane, take D952 towards the canyon, which runs to La-Palaud-sur-Verdon. Then continue on D23 and follow signs for the hostel. The friendly manager can tell you about his favorite hiking trails. The mostly eight-bed rooms are clean and comfortable, with gorgeous views and kitchen access. (68F. Breakfast included. Sheets 16F. Camping 28F. Reception open Mar.-Oct. 8am-noon and 5-9pm. Lockout 10am-5pm.) Near the heart of the canyon you'll find **Chalet C.A.F. Refuge de la Maline** (tel. 04 92 77 38 05), the last canyon bus stop. By car, follow directions to the youth hostel above but continue on D23 and follow the signs for the chalet. Large dorms cater to groups but are open to individuals. (74F. Breakfast 24F. Dinner 72F. Picnic lunch 40F. Kitchen. Open Mar. 26 -Nov. 11.)

If the hike to the hostel leaves you weak in the knees, dorm-style options are available in *gîtes d'étape* closer to town; the tourist office has a complete list. The cheapest beds are at the **Gîtes d'Étape L'Oustau** (tel. 04 92 83 77 27; fax 04 92 83 78 02), with immaculate beds in four- to six-bed dorms. Private rooms with bathrooms are also available. To get there take the alley next to Bar de l'Étape on the main road next to pl. M. Sauvaire and follow the road, right along the river. It's three minutes ahead on your left. (Dorms 75F, 95F with breakfast; doubles 220F per room; triples 320F.) **Hôtel du Roc**, pl. Église (tel. 04 92 83 62 85), has large, cheerful rooms with shower and toilet. (Singles and doubles 215-260F; triples 300F. V, MC.) **Auberge bon Accueil** (tel. 04 92 84 12 86) has cheaper options with dark, cozy, cabin-like rooms. (Singles 100-130F; doubles 150-280F; triples 180-320F; quads 360F.) **Camping Frédéric Mistral** (tel. 04 92 83 62 27) is a two-minute walk down the main road to the canyon. (Tent 15F, each person 22F, electricity 19F, free hot showers and water.) There's a **Casino supermarket** on pl. de l'Église. (Open M-Sa 9am-noon and 2-6pm, Su 9am-noon.) **La Main à la Pâte** serves up superlative pizzas and pastas (40-55F) in a cheery yellow room with a patio (closed W).

THE CANYON

Although the tree-speckled, chalky rock canyon is appealing unto itself, it is the Verdon river and its final destination, the immense Lac de Ste-Croix, that form the lifeblood of the area. Hiking trails, guided trips down the river, and swimming spots in the river and lake are all spectacular ways to take in sun, swimming, and the unusual landscape. The canyon's most beaten track is **Sentier Martel**, a.k.a. the **GR4** trail. The six- to eight- hour hike (one way) traces the river from **La Maline** east to **Point Sublime** as the gorge widens and narrows, passing through tunnels, vistas, and caves rumored to have been hiding places for fugitives long ago. Flashlights are useful for the tunnels. Taking the *sentier* east to west means steep grades with rewarding views. Red and white markers lead the way in either direction. One of the more popular ways to explore the Verdon is with one of a number of **outdoor rafting** companies which coordinate trips through the canyon. **Aboard Rafting**, 8 pl.

de l'Église, (tel. 04 92 83 76 11) offers all types of trips and has an English-speaking staff; **Acti-Raft,** Route des Gorges du Verdon (tel. 04 92 83 76 64; fax 04 92 83 76 74), **Aqua Viva Est,** 11 rue Nationale (tel./fax 04 92 83 75 74), and **Aqua Verdon,** 9 rue Nationale (tel. 04 92 83 72 75), all run comparable outfits. **Rafting** is the most conventional way of descending the river (1½hr. trip 190F; full day 490F). **Canyoning** involves climbing up and rapelling (abseiling) down parts of the canyon and then jumping, sliding, swimming, and floating down the river. (1½hr. 200F, full day 390F.) **Aqua-Rando** is canyoning without the rapelling and rock climbing. **Hydrospeeding** involves doing the river on kickboard-like contraptions and flippers (290F). A couple of organizations also run **kayaking** trips (1½hr. 200F). Cavaliers can trot their way through the canyon on **horseback** with **Les Pionniers** in La Palaud-sur-Verdon. (Tel./fax 04 92 77 38 30. 160F for 2hr., 380F full day.)

All that flowing water culminates in **Lac de Ste-Croix,** a mellow lake, with an even mellower atmosphere at the mouth of the gorge. The GR4 trail past La Palaud-Sur-Verdon will eventually take you there by foot. By car, taking D952 past La Palaud to Moustiers and then following signs to Ste-Croix-de-Verdon or taking D957 before Moustiers to Les Salles-sur-Verdon both provide good access to the lake.

ST-RAPHAËL AND FRÉJUS

With neither the charm of the Riviera's smaller towns nor the liveliness of its more cosmopolitan centers, the twin cities of St-Raphaël and Fréjus are of dubious appeal; yet each summer tourists throng to the large stretch of beach running the length of both towns. The towns are not connected in any walkable way, and each has its advantages. St-Raphaël is less attractive but provides an affordable way to visit St-Tropez, while the Fréjus youth hostel is one of the Riviera's best.

ST-RAPHAËL

St-Raphaël offers more by way of tourist amenities and nightlife, but as a town remains an unappealing assemblage of boutiques, knick-knack stores, and hotels which seem all too eager for your money.

■ **ORIENTATION AND PRACTICAL INFORMATION.** Separated from Cannes to the east by the Massif de l'Esterel, 40km of red volcanic rock and dry vegetation, St-Raphaël is a major stop on the coastal train line. Hotels and restaurants rest in between the train station and the waterfront, a few blocks straight out of the rue Waldeck Rousseau exit.

Trains run from pl. de la Gare approximately every 30 minutes to **Cannes** (25min., 34F) and **Nice** (1hr., 56F), and every hour to **Toulon** (1hr., 60F) and **Marseille** (1¾hr.). (Station open daily 5:30am-11:30pm. Info office open M-Sa 8am-7:30pm.) Store **luggage** at Lucky Bikes, 20 rue Waldeck Rousseau (tel. 04 94 95 86 35), across the street from the *gare;* the sign reads "Location Vélo." (Open daily 8am-9pm. 20F per day.) **Buses** leave from behind the station. **Forum Cars** speeds off to **Fréjus** (26min., every hr., 6.50F) and to **Cannes** (70min., 8 per day, 33F). **Sodetrav** (tel. 04 94 95 24 82) goes to **Toulon** (1½hr., 42F) and **St-Tropez** (1½hr., 15 per day, 49F); and **Phocéens** runs to **Nice** (1¼hr., 3 per day, 130F). **Taxis** (tel. 04 94 95 04 25) sit outside the train station. **Les Bateaux de St-Raphaël** (tel. 04 94 95 17 46; fax 04 94 83 88 55), at the *vieux port,* float to **St-Tropez** (50min.; July-Aug. 5 per day, otherwise 2 per day; 60F one-way, 100F round-trip). If you are staying at the hostel in Fréjus, ask about ticket reductions.

The **tourist office** is opposite the train station on rue Waldeck Rousseau (tel. 04 94 19 52 52; fax 04 94 83 85 40). Get the scoop on transportation and room availability as well as free maps. (Open July-Aug. daily 8:30am-7pm; Sept.-June M-Sa 9am-12:30pm and 2-6:30pm.) Commission-free **currency exchange** is on offer at **Cambio Wechsel,** Centre Commercial de la Gare. (Tel. 04 94 95 67 91. Open daily 8:30am-12:30pm and 2:30-6:30pm.) The **police** are on rue Admiral Baux (tel. 04 94 95 24 24), off the *vieux port.* The **post office** is on av. Victor Hugo (tel. 04 94 19 52 00), behind the train station. (Open M-F 8:30am-6:30pm, Sa 8:30am-noon. **Postal code:** 83700.)

Surf the web near the beach at **Blue Jibe-Le Cyber Café**, upstairs at the beachfront **Glacier Le Poussin Bleu**, 41 bd. de la Libération. (Tel. 04 94 19 84 58. Open M-Sa 1pm-midnight, Su 1pm-1am. 35F per ½hr., 60F per hr.)

┌ ACCOMMODATIONS AND CAMPING. St-Raphaël's intense package tourism makes hotels less service-oriented to the independent traveler, but accommodations are more plentiful than in Fréjus, and cheaper than in St-Tropez, an easy daytrip away. Be sure to book ahead in July and August. The fun **hostel** is a short ride away in **Fréjus** (see below). The two-star **Le Touring**, 1 quai Albert 1er (tel. 04 94 95 01 72; fax 04 94 95 86 09), has reasonably welcoming rooms despite many hazy shades of brown. From the station, exit right and Albert 1er will be your third left. All rooms have toilet, shower, TV, and phone, some have views of the ocean. (Singles and doubles with one bed 150-260F; twins and triples 290-350F. Breakfast 30F. Open Dec. 16-Nov. 14. V, MC.) Also two-star, **Hôtel des Pyramides** (tel. 04 94 95 05 95), has green and white pharaoh-approved rooms near the beach all with telephone, TV, and bathroom. (Singles 150F; doubles 220-340F; triples 335F; quads 370F. Breakfast 30F. Open Mar. 15-Nov. 15. V, MC.) The best value in town is **La Bonne Auberge**, 54 rue de la Garonne (tel. 04 94 95 69 72). Some simple rooms are somewhat dingy, others are bright and airy. (Singles 120-140F; doubles 140-170F, with shower and toilet 200F; triples 210F. Breakfast 35F. Open Feb.-Nov. V, MC.) Pitch your pavilion at **Royal Camping** (tel./fax 04 94 82 00 20), on Camp-Long along the bus route to Cannes. Perks include hot showers, a supermarket, and a restaurant. (90-125F for 2 people. Open mid-Mar. to Oct.)

⊡ FOOD. *Gourmet* magazine will not be visiting St-Raphaël any time soon. In a town full of hotel restaurants where meals are packaged with your room, interesting dining spots are hard to come by. Affordable restaurants center around the **vieux port**, bd. de la Libération. The **Monoprix supermarket** is on bd. de Félix Martin (tel. 04 94 19 82 82), off av. Alphonse Karr near the St-Raphaël train station. (Open daily Sept.-June 8:30am-7:30pm; July-Aug. 8:30am-8:30pm.) A **morning market** colors pl. Victor Hugo, down the hill from the bus station. (Tu-Su 7am-12:30pm.)

Le Bishop, 84 rue Jean Aicard (tel. 04 94 95 04 63), serves sanctified platters of paella and delicious pasta (40-55F), but is otherwise pricey. (Open daily noon-2pm and 7-11pm.) **La Taverne Del Matto**, 32 rue Boëtman (tel. 04 94 95 15 16), serves 65-105F *menus*, 38-50F pizzas, and 15-48F salads on a sunny sidewalk near the church. (Open M-F noon-2:30pm and 7-10:30pm, Sa-Su 7-10:30pm. V, MC, AmEx.)

⊿ BEACHES. Beachcombers will find kilometers of sand running all along the coast from St-Raphaël west through Fréjus—whose beach is actually closer to St-Raphaël's town center than Fréjus's—and east through Boulouris, which is more isolated and consequently less crowded. There are plenty of public beaches, but numerous snack stands mar the area's natural beauty.

▒ FESTIVALS. The first weekend in July is the **Competition Internationale de Jazz New Orleans** in St-Raphaël. Hundreds of musicians face off in the streets and around the port—and it's free. (Call tourist office for info.)

FRÉJUS

Since Julius Cæsar set up shop here with a trading post along the Aurelian Way in 49 BC, Fréjus has borne witness to a significant historical past. When the Roman Empire declined and fell, Fréjus flourished as a medieval town, which remains today in the form of the *vieille ville*. Reminders of the past figure large here: a Roman amphitheater, a sanctuary with medieval and Renaissance architecture, a Cocteau chapel, and a World War I monument are sure to quench any history buff's thirst for the past. More contemporary additions, like the oppressive sprawl of apartment complexes that stretch from the *vieille ville* to the beach, will be of little interest to anyone.

🖅 PRACTICAL INFORMATION. Trains leave rue Martin Bidoure (tel. 04 94 82 16 92) for **St-Raphaël** (5min.; M-F 10 per day, Sa-Su 5; 8F), **Nice** (1hr.; M-F 10 per day, Sa-Su 5; 56F), **Cannes** (30min.; M-F 10 per day, Sa-Su 5; 35F), **Toulon** (1hr., 6 per day, 72F), and **Marseille** (2hr, 6 per day, 112F). (Ticket office open M-F 7am-2:15pm and 2:30-6:30pm, Sa 9:15am-1pm and 2:30-6:30 pm.) **Local buses** (6.50F) connect the *vieille ville* with the beach, outlying sights, and **St-Raphaël**. The **bus station,** pl. Paul Vernet, is next to the tourist office but the *gare SNCF* is a stop for a number of local routes. For **taxis,** call 04 94 51 51 12.

With Fréjus beach physically and spiritually closer to St-Raphaël (at least a 20-minute walk from Fréjus *centre ville*), visitors should stick to the *vieille ville* and its surrounding sights. Fréjus is connected to St-Raphaël by regular buses until around 7pm. To get to the **tourist office,** av. Verdon (tel. 04 94 51 83 83; fax 04 94 51 00 26), from St-Raphaël, take bus #6 to "pl. Paul Vernet." (Open July-Aug. M-F 9am-5:30pm, Sa-Su 10am-noon and 2-5:30pm; Sept.-June M-F 9am-5:30pm. Frequent changes make calling ahead an act of wisdom.) The **Hôpital Inter-communal** (tel. 04 94 40 21 21) is on the corner of av. André Léotard and av. de St-Lambert. The **police** lock'em up at av. Einaudi (tel. 04 94 51 90 00). The **post office,** av. Aristide Briand (tel. 04 94 17 60 80), is just down the hill from the tourist office. (Open M-F 8:30am-6:30pm, Sa 8:30am-noon. **Postal code:** 83600.)

🛏 ACCOMMODATIONS AND CAMPING. One of the best hostels on the Côte is the **Auberge de Jeunesse de St-Raphaël-Fréjus (HI),** chemin du Counillier (tel. 04 94 52 93 93; fax 04 94 53 25 86). From the **Fréjus** tourist office take av. du 15ème Corps d'Armée, and then turn left on chemin de Counillier after the next roundabout (20min.). From **St-Raphael,** a shuttle bus (6.50F) leaves *quai* #7 of the bus station for the hostel at 6pm; return buses leave the hostel at 8:30am, 6pm, and 7pm. Local buses run every hour 7:30-11:30am and 2-8pm; get off at "Les Chênes" and walk up av. Jean Calliès to chemin du Counillier. The hostel is at the top of the unpaved road. Kind managers make this hostel fit for royalty. 4- to 8-person single-sex dorms have a restful view of the inland valley. Rooms for 4-6 people in a brand-new *châtelet* have more modern facilities. Ask about reductions on bike rentals, tickets for boats to St-Tropez, and excursions. (66F, *châtelet* 82F. Breakfast included. Sheets 17F. **Camping** 32F per person with tent. Hearty dinner 49F. Lock-out 10am-6pm. Curfew 11pm.)

La Riviera, 90 rue Grisolle (tel. 04 95 51 31 46), a couple of blocks below pl. de la Liberté, has small rooms with a kind of dated charm. (Singles and doubles 150-200F.) Next to the tourist office, **Bellevue,** pl. Paul-Vernet (tel 04 94 51 39 04; fax 04 94 51 35 20), has standard, well-sized rooms. (Singles and doubles 250-350F.)

🍴 FOOD. Budget restaurants cluster around **pl. de la Liberté.** The **Marché Provençal** decorates Fréjus's **rue de Fleury** and **pl. Formige.** (W and Sa mornings.) If you're coming from the hostel, ask the morning bus driver to drop you off directly. There's a **Super Rallye supermarket,** 168 av. André Léotard (tel. 04 94 51 47 30), at the bottom of the hill near the hostel. (Open M-Sa 8:30am-8pm, Su 8:30am-12:30pm.) **La Riviéra** (see **Accommodations,** above) serves a delicious meat-heavy 85F *menu,* in a spiffy rustic, dining room. (Open daily lunch and dinner. V, MC.)

🏛 SIGHTS. The city's **Roman amphitheater,** rue Henri Vadon (tel. 04 94 17 19 19), was constructed to entertain rowdy soldiers looking for a home away from Rome. Built in the 1st and 2nd centuries, the amphitheater is free of the elaborate embellishments of the those in Nîmes or Arles, which were designed to appeal to more discerning patrician eyes. Recently renovated, the former wrestling ground for gladiators and lions is now the site of bullfights and rock concerts. To get there from the tourist office, take rue Jean Jaurès to pl. de la Liberté, then turn right on rue de Gaulle. Continue straight until the roundabout where the amphitheater is. (Open daily Apr.-Sept. 9:30-11:45am and 2-6:15pm; Oct.-Mar. 9-11:45am and 2-4:15pm.) Other remnants of **Forum Julii,** Fréjus's Roman city, include the **Roman the-**

ater, whose original wall remains intact, although much of the rest of the structure has been replaced to accommodate concerts and plays today. To get there, take rue Bret from the roundabout at the tourist office for 250m. (Open daily Apr.-Sept. 9:30-11:45am and 2-6:15pm; Oct.-Mar. 9-11:45am and 2-4:15pm.) Pillars and a few arches are all that remain of the **aqueduct,** past the theater along av. du 15ème corps d'Armée, but a little visualization lends a sense of its epic length.

Groupe Épiscopal de Fréjus (Cathédrale Close), on pl. Formige (tel. 04 94 51 26 30), in the middle of the *vieille ville*, is a remarkable sanctuary whose present configuration is the result of over 15 centuries of construction and reconstruction. Viewable from a side entrance on pl. Formige, the octagonal **baptistry** dates back to the 5th century, making it one of France's oldest buildings. At the two corners next to the iron grille stand doors used during the baptism, one to enter before the ceremony, and one leading to the cathedral, where the newly-baptized would attend their first mass. Through the front entrance, the spectacular 12th- to 14th-century **cloisters** feature marble columns and wooden-beamed ceilings with hundreds of miniature beasts and figures depicting the Apocalypse. The Gothic **cathedral,** originally built during the 12th and 13th centuries, maintains its architectural integrity, despite added adornments and constant updating. (Cathedral open daily 9am-noon and 4-6pm. Office open Oct.-Mar. W-M 9am-noon and 2-5pm; Apr.-Sept. daily 9am-7pm. Tours 25F, students 15F.)

Pagode Hong-Hiên, 13 rue H. Giraud (tel. 04 94 53 25 29), 10 minutes up av. Jean Calliès from the hostel. The pagoda was built in 1919 to honor Vietnamese soldiers based at Fréjus who died defending France in World War I. The Tibetan-style Buddhist temple still functions as a spiritual center. (Open daily 9am-noon and 3-6:30pm.) **Villa Aurélienne,** av. du Général d'Aimée Calliès (tel. 04 94 53 11 30), is on the hill next to the hostel. The elegant 19th-century villa houses a museum and cultural center. The 20-hectare park hosts photography exhibitions, a 3-day flower festival in early Apr. known as the **Fête des Plantes,** and a 4-day contemporary art exhibit, the **Art Tendence Sud.** (Open summer Tu-Su 2-7pm; off-season Tu-Sa 2-6pm.) The **Cocteau Chapel,** av. Nicola (tel. 04 94 40 76 30), is a short distance out of town on the RN7 to Cannes. Die hard fans of film director, artist, and *"prince des poètes"* Jean Cocteau can visit the circular chapel, which Cocteau designed and built, although it was left unfinished when he died in 1963. Bus #3 from "Les Chênes" in Fréjus comes every other hour. (Officially open Apr.-Sept. W-M 2-6pm; Oct.-Mar. 2-5pm. Call to confirm.)

ST-TROPEZ

Nowhere is the glitz and glamour of the Riviera more apparent today than in St-Tropez. Where other landmark towns cling nostalgically to past glory, Saint Trop d'Aise's (Saint Too-Much-Luxury) religious devotion to the holy trinity of sun, sand, and big boats remains in full bloom. Originally a small fishing hamlet, St-Tropez first caught the public eye when Paul Signac brought a wave of post-Impressionists here in 1892, and the city soon became a haven for a slew of other artists, including Matisse and Braque. This obsession with new forms eventually gave way to an obsession with *nue* forms after Brigitte Bardot bared all on St-Tropez's beaches in the 60s. The inhabitants quickly switched from fishing for fish to fishing for compliments, and yachts began crowding out trawlers. Although its fishing hamlet days are long gone, the port, narrow streets, and vivid landscape have not relinquished the ambience that attracted the palates of artists more than a century ago. With sobering prices and inconvenient transportation, St-Tropez works hard to keep the riff-raff out, but remains the real highlight of the Côte d'Azur.

◪ **ORIENTATION AND PRACTICAL INFORMATION.** Reaching this self-proclaimed "jewel of the Riviera" requires some effort, as it lies well off the rail line. Once here, leaving the town for beaches and villages on the St-Tropez peninsula is an additional hassle, and you won't have much luck hitching around St-Tropez—

you'd soil the Porsche's upholstery. The town itself is condensed and walker-friendly, with constant activity between the port and pl. des Lices.

The fastest, nicest, and with the Fréjus hostel voucher, cheapest, way to get here is by **boat**. **Les Bateaux de St-Raphaël** (tel. 04 94 95 17 46 or 04 94 82 71 45), at the *vieux port*, sail in from **St-Raphaël** (50min.; July-Aug. 5 per day, rest of year 2 per day; 60F one way, 100F round-trip, 80F with hostel reduction) and **Cannes** (tel. 04 93 39 11 82; July-Aug. only; 1 per day Tu, Th, and Sa; 100F). Otherwise, **Sodetrav buses** (tel. 04 94 97 88 51 or 04 94 95 24 82) leave from av. Général Leclerc, across from the ferry dock and public parking, for **St-Raphaël** (1½-2¼hr., 15 per day, 48F) and **Toulon** (2¼hr., 8 per day, 80F). Once in town, get around with the help of **bikes** and **scooters** from Louis Mas, 3-5 rue Quarenta. (Tel. 04 94 97 00 60. Bikes 50-80F per day; deposit 1000-2000F. Mopeds 210F per day; deposit 2500-5000F. Open Easter-Oct. 15 M-Sa 9am-7:30pm, Su 9am-1pm and 5-7:30pm.)

The **tourist office** is on quai Jean Jaurès (tel. 04 94 97 45 21; fax 04 94 97 82 66). Arriving by bus or ferry, walk into town along the waterfront until you hit a series of cafés. It's on the corner just before cafe Senequier. The extremely competent English-speaking staff can help with (almost) anything. The guide *Manifestations* has updates on local events, gallery openings, and exhibits. (Open daily 9:30am-1:30pm and 3:30-11pm.) You can **exchange currency** at **Master Change,** 18 rue Allard. (Tel. 04 94 97 80 17. Open May-Sept. daily 10am-8pm.) The **police** are on rue François Sibilli (tel. 04 94 97 00 58), near the church. The **hospital** is on av. Foch, off pl. des Lices (tel. 04 94 79 47 30). There is a **post office** on pl. A. Celli at the *nouveau port*. (Tel. 04 94 54 86 65. Open M-F 9am-5:30pm, Sa 9am-noon.)

⌂ ACCOMMODATIONS AND CAMPING. Not even a fairy godmother could find you a budget hotels in St-Tropez, and by mid-June just about every option is booked solid. Staying in St-Raphaël or Hyères is easier on the wallet, but forces you to limit your time here. The closest **hostel** is in Fréjus. **Camping** is the cheapest option but still requires reservations, and no sites are within walking distance of town. The tourist office will tell you which have space, but don't trust to your luck.

Your best option is the central **La Méditerranée,** 21 bd. Louis Blanc (tel. 04 94 97 00 44; fax 04 94 97 47 83). From the ferry dock or *gare routière*, walk inland to av. Général Leclerc and turn left. After a four minute walk, bd. Louis Blanc and the hotel will be on your right. Small rooms are bright and cheery. (Singles and doubles 250-450F; triples and quads 200-500F. Breakfast 35-40F. Open Mar. 21-Nov. 16. V, MC.) Otherwise the only affordable alternative is **Hôtel Les Chimères,** port du Pilon (tel. 04 94 97 02 90; fax 04 94 97 63 57). From the ferry dock or bus station, walk inland to av. Général Leclerc and turn right. The hotel is a three minute walk ahead on the left, across from the gas station. Rooms vary widely in appeal but all are reasonably clean and attractive. Roadside rooms are noisier but cheaper. (Singles and doubles 150-250F Oct.-May; 330-360F June-Sept.; closed mid-Nov. to mid Dec. V, MC.) **Campers** can try the 4-star **La Croix du Sud** (tel. 04 94 79 80 84; fax 04 94 79 89 21), rte. des Plages, in **Ramatuelle** (85F for 1-2 people; 120F for 3; open Easter-Sept.), or **Kon Tiki** (tel. 04 94 79 80 17; 113F per car, tent, and 2 people). Both are behind Pampelonne beach. Camping on the beach is actively prohibited.

◻ FOOD. Like everything else in St-Tropez, eating is a glamorous but costly affair. The *vieux port* and the narrow streets behind the waterfront are the hubs of St-Tropez's restaurant and café culture. If you prefer to create your own ambience, head to the fabulous **grand marché** on **pl. des Lices** (daily 5am-2pm), or the morning **market** on **pl. aux Herbes,** behind the tourist office. An all-day option is **Prisunic supermarket,** 7 av. du Général Leclerc. (Tel. 04 94 97 07 94. Open M-Sa 8am-10pm, summer also Su 8:30am-1pm and 3-10pm.) **Lou Regalé,** 12 rue du Colonel Guichard (tel. 04 94 97 16 18), next to the Église Paroissiale, serves pasta, roast chicken, and *keufte riz pilaf* (a Greek specialty) in its 50F *menu*. (Open daily noon-2:30pm and 7-11pm.) Around the corner, **Chez Bruno,** 2 rue de l'Église (tel. 04 94 97 05 18), has pizzas (45-65F) as their specialty in an intimate countrified dining room. (Open daily from 12:50pm for lunch, 7:15pm for dinner.)

☎ SIGHTS. La Musée de l'Annonciade, pl. Grammont (tel. 04 94 97 04 01), hosts an impressive collection of Fauvist and neo-Impressionist paintings. Many of the painters featured here paid their artistic dues in St. Tropez. A number of the paintings depict recognizable locales in the area. (Open W-M June-Sept. 10am-noon and 3-7pm; Oct.-May 10am-noon and 2-6pm; closed Nov., Jan. 1, and May 1. 30F, students 15F.) **The Citadel,** perched above the picturesque port, appropriately contains the **Musée Naval** (tel. 04 94 97 59 43). The reasonably interesting collection hosts a statue of the street-namesake Pierre-André, a national hero, as well as displays on St-Tropez's military history through WWII. Perhaps the best part of the museum is the view of the sea and its troop of screaming peacocks. (Open daily summer 10am-7pm, winter 10am-5pm, closed Nov. 25F, students 15F.)

☑ BEACHES. Excellent beaches only add to St-Tropez's appeal, until you discover how difficult it is to reach them. **Sodetrav** buses (see **Orientation and Practical Information,** above) takes you there on the "St-Tropez-Ramatuelle" line (M-Sa 3 per day, 9F), stopping at **plage Tahiti,** which has the most wealth, **plage des Salins,** which has the most public space, and **plage de Pampelonne,** which has the most sand (all 10min.). Further along the peninsula, great swimming and good rock climbing await at **plage de L'Escalet,** 15km away. Contact the tourist office about public transportation there. Picnic spots await along the water only 10 minutes from the *vieux port.* Follow chemin des Graniers, which curves around the citadel and the water, to the small, uncrowded **plage des Graniers.** At the beachside **Les Graniers** (tel. 04 94 97 38 50) restaurant and bar, barefoot waiters serve tables planted in the sand. If you choose to arrive by boat, drop anchor and wait for the restaurant's motorboat to whisk you ashore. Of course, this decadence will cost you; stick to the 14F espresso. (Open daily 9am-sunset. V, MC.) A small path continues past the beach and snakes between the shore and villas. Choose a cove and bask *au naturel*—in St-Tropez, tan-lines mean you just got here.

♫ ENTERTAINMENT. During the summer, **Le Pigeonnier,** 13 rue de la Ponche (tel. 04 94 97 84 26), and **La Plage,** 11 rue de la Ponche (tel. 04 94 97 33 14), move to the beat of perfected tans and wealth to spend. Backpackers are few and far between, but for a 100F cover and a smooth outfit, you can join in. **Le Papagayo** (tel. 04 94 97 07 56), on the port bustles year-round with a trendy clientele on two floors. For a more sedentary evening, **Café de Paris** (tel. 04 94 97 00 56), centrally located on the port, offers equal people watching opportunities and the same expensive drinks. Stick to beer and wine (from 30F), or go for broke. Gold, plush velvet, and *belle époque* mirrors and chandeliers fill the inside, but the lively patio is just as enticing. Further along the port, **Kelly's Irish Pub** attracts a sizeable Anglophone community and is casual by St-Tropez standards.

✹ FESTIVALS. St-Tropez maintains its image of the good life with a string of golf tournaments and yacht regattas. Every May 16-18, St-Tropez celebrates the Saint's arrival with **Les Bravades,** three intense days of costumed parades. The spectacle is comically repeated in summer, with two months of strangely dressed foreigners parading the streets and firing cameras. June 27th brings **St. Peter's Day** and a torch-lit procession honoring the patron saint of fishermen.

THE ST-TROPEZ PENINSULA

Less ritzy, but no less endearing, the inland villages of the St-Tropez peninsula make excellent daytrips and prove rewarding places to spend a night for those who seek a slower pace. Although quieter than the coastal Riviera, these hilltop villages, with picture-perfect settings, more temperate weather, and memorable vistas, are becoming highly desirable places to live. Architecture is meticulously maintained and commerce is conspicuously upscale. The villages are also losing their status as "secret gems" as tour groups want a piece of the charm. Bound by their hilly topography and provincial flavor, each town has an appeal of its own.

GRIMAUD

Grimaud is, in a word, adorable. With remarkable stone houses lining narrow, meandering, fountain-filled streets, one gets the sense that to adjust anything is to blemish a masterpiece. Place Neuve and the narrow streets above are home to boutiques, antique shops, and some expensive restaurants. Above pl. Neuve, signs point to the simply adorned Romanesque **Église St-Michel.** (Open daily 9am-6pm.) Above the church, what remains of the château is but a remnant of the original fortification, although the views from atop are just as scenic as those the Knights Templar enjoyed. Below pl. Neuve, on the main road, the **Musée d'Art et Traditions Populaires** is worth a peek for its collection of exactly what its name suggests. Paraphernalia from agricultural and domestic life in the region during past centuries provide a thorough sense of the region. (Open Apr.-Oct. M-Sa 3-6:30pm. Free.)

Sodetrav (tel. 04 94 97 88 51 or 04 94 12 55 12) sends two **buses,** Monday to Saturday, from **St-Tropez** (40min., 19F). Buses tend to leave Grimaud around 8am and 1pm and St-Tropez around noon and 5pm, but schedules change often. Visiting Grimaud will inevitably be a day trip, since there are no budget hotels and the closest campsite is a couple of kilometers away. Restaurants are generally overpriced, so opt for treats from **Le Pâtissier du Château** (tel. 04 94 43 21 16), tucked away at the bottom of pl. Neuve. A few doors down from the museum, the **tourist office** is at 1 bd. des Aliziers. (Tel. 04 94 43 26 98. Open M-Sa July-Aug. 9am-12:30pm and 3-7pm; Sept.-June 9am-12:30pm and 2:30-6:30pm.)

RAMATUELLE

With exquisite panoramas surveying vineyards, orchards, and the sea, Ramatuelle milks its hilltop status for maximum effect. Next to pl. de l'Ormeau, the Romanesque **Église Notre Dame** is an intimate church with lavish decoration. The medieval village above the church consists of concentric circles of stone houses, stores, and a local theater. If you're coming by bus, consider spending the night or you'll only have a couple of hours in the morning to enjoy the town. **Le Saint Gilles,** 31 rue G. Clemenceau, (tel. 04 94 79 20 46) at the end of the main commercial street, has large comfortable rooms, above the friendly village bar. (Singles and doubles with shower 200F.) Many farmers open up their land to **campers;** the **tourist office,** pl. de l'Ormeau (tel. 04 94 79 26 04), keeps a constantly updated lists of which campsites are open. (Open Sept.-June M-F 8:30am-12:30pm and 2:30-6:30pm, Sa 9am-12:30pm and 3-6:30pm; July-Aug. M-Sa 9am-1pm and 3-6:30pm, and Su 10am-1pm and 3-7pm.) A great reason to hang around after dark is a strip of memorable restaurants just below the rotary that serve up incredible food. Splurge at **La Farigoulette** (tel. 04 94 79 20 49), at the bottom of the block in a stunning country house where the *provençal* cuisine lives up to the restaurant's appearance. Main dishes start around 80F. A few doors uphill and across the street, **L'Estable** (tel. 04 94 79 10 76) and its stone dining room are a cheaper bet with pizzas and pastas as well as regional specialties like fisherman's soup (55F) and *lapin* (rabbit; 75F). Unfortunately, coming and going offers little flexibility. **Sodetrav buses** (tel. 04 94 54 62 36) provides the only public transportation (25min., 1 per day Tu-W and F-Sa, 16.50F), leaving St. Tropez around 8:45am and Ramatuelle around 11:15am (3:30pm on F).

TOULON

Visions of the French Riviera seldom include racial tensions, extreme-right wing politics, or a faltering naval economy, but Toulon's troubled history stands in stark contrast to the charmed life of neighboring towns. Toulon's first call to fame was promising enough when, during the Roman era, the purple dye produced from pointed conches found on its coasts became essential to the production of the imperial toga. Toulon also served as raw material for the decoration of a later Emperor; in his first military action, Napoleon Bonaparte executed a daring and successful assault on the English-occupied port in 1793. More recently, Toulon's status as the second-largest port on the south coast has made it the first landfall

THE SOUTHEAST

for many North African immigrants, leading to a rise in ethnic tensions. In the mid-90s the city responded by being the first French city to elect the extreme right-wing *Front National* party.

The city is working hard to make itself a place worth visiting. The recent relocation of university buildings from the *banlieux* (suburbs) into the city center has brought a vital infusion of idealistic, youthful vigor. As it sorts out its waning economic problems and ethnic tensions, Toulon (pop. 185,000) can hardly be considered a must on any Riviera itinerary, but beneath its grimy facade is a rare urban grit too often forgotten on the sandy beaches of the Côte d'Azur.

ORIENTATION AND PRACTICAL INFORMATION

Toulon's main street, whose name changes from **av. du Maréchal Leclerc** to **bd. de Strasbourg** as it passes through **pl. de la République,** is the northern border of the tangle of narrow streets and shady, befountained *places* known as *vieux Toulon*. At night, action is centered on pl. Victor Hugo. Take care after dark on the streets between rue Jean Jaurès and the port, and stick to well-lit main thoroughfares.

Trains: Bd. Toesca and av. Vauban. Trains leave every half-hour to: **Marseille** (40min., 56F); **St-Raphaël** (1hr., 60F); **Nice** (2hr., 118F); and **Cannes** (80min., 94F). Open daily 6am-10pm. Info office open M-Sa 8am-7pm. Ticket office open daily 5am-11pm.

Ferries: SNCM, 21 and 49 av. de l'Infanterie de Marine (tel. 04 94 16 66 66), at the far eastern end of port. To **Corsica** (7-9hr.; 1-2 per day; roundtrip 370-400F, students 320-370F). **SITCAT** boats (tel. 04 94 46 35 46) on quai Stalingrad run to **La Seyne** and **St-Maudrier** on the other side of the bay (10F).

Buses: Tel. 04 94 93 11 39, across from the *bagages/consigne* office in the train station. Office open daily 6:15am-7pm. **Sodetrav** (tel. 04 94 92 26 41) runs to **St-Tropez** (2½hr., 7 per day, 80F), with a stops at **Hyères** (35min., 1 per hr., 34F). **Francelignes** (tel. 04 91 61 83 27) runs to **Aix-en-Provence** (1¼hr., 3 per day, 84F).

Public Transportation: RMITT (tel. 04 94 03 87 03). Buses gather in front of the train station at the traffic circle to Toulon, suburbs, and beaches. Tickets 11F.

Taxis: Tel. 04 94 93 51 51 or 04 94 93 51 84, near the train station. 24hr.

Bike or Moped Rental: Sun Bikes Location, 748 bd. de la Marine (tel. 04 94 57 39 11; fax 04 94 38 34 75), near the Toulon airport. Bikes 70-80F. Deposit 800-1000F. Motorcycles, waterskis, and jet skis available. Open daily 9am-7pm. V, MC.

Tourist Office: Pl. Raimu (tel. 04 94 18 53 00; fax 04 94 18 53 09). Free maps. Hotel reservations 10F. Open M-Sa 9am-6pm. The office has free copies of *Le Petit Bavard,* an entertainment guide written annually by Toulon's students.

Money: Bureau de change, in the train station. No commission. Open daily July-Aug. 9am-noon and 2-7pm. Also at **15 quai Stalingrad** (tel. 04 94 92 60 40), by the port. Open daily July-Aug. 9am-9pm; Sept.-June 9am-7pm.

Laundromat: Laverie, 25 rue Baudin and 16 rue Peirisc. Open daily 7am-9pm.

Hospital: Ste-Anne, 3 bd. Ste-Anne (tel. 04 94 09 90 00), off av. Victoire de 8 Mai 1945, just behind the station. **SOS Medecins** tel. 04 94 31 33 33.

Police: Rue Commandant Morandin (tel. 04 94 09 80 00).

Post Office: Rue Prosper Ferrero (tel. 04 94 18 51 00), at the western end of the pedestrian zone, off rue Jean Jaurès. For Poste Restante, specify "rue Prosper Ferrero." Open M-F 8am-7pm, Sa 8am-noon. **Postal code:** 83000.

ACCOMMODATIONS

Finding a room in Toulon is easier than elsewhere on the Riviera, but it is still wise to book ahead in the summer.

Foyer de la Jeunesse, 12 pl. d'Armes (tel. 04 94 22 62 00; fax 04 94 22 02 10). This new university dorm pampers backpackers aged 16-25. Spacious singles and doubles equipped with bathroom, phone, and the occasional balcony. Ping-pong, TV lounge, and cheap student cafeteria. 100F per person. Sheets 30F. July-Sept. is prime time.

Hôtel Molière, 12 rue Moliere (tel. 04 94 92 78 35; fax 04 94 62 85 82), next to the opera on pl. Victor Hugo. Ideally situated with cheerful management. Each room has its own character. Showers in all but one room. TV lounge. Singles 95-125F; doubles 110-180F; triples 210F. Breakfast 25F. V, MC, AmEx.

Hôtel Little Palace, 6 rue Berthelot (tel. 04 94 92 26 62; fax. 04 94 62 16 74). On pl. Puget in the pedestrian zone. Owner rents out small rooms, most with view of pl. des Trois Dauphins. Singles and doubles 90-150F, with shower 120-180F. V, MC, AmEx.

Hôtel Le Jaurès, 11 rue Jean Jaurès (tel. 04 94 92 83 04). Quiet, simple rooms with TV, shower, and toilet. Singles and doubles 150-170F; triples 200F. Breakfast 20F. V, MC.

⬛ FOOD

Inexpensive restaurants serving French, North African, and Asian cuisine dot Toulon's pedestrian zone. For seafood, try the *vieux port*, but expect to pay waterfront prices. For those who prefer park benches and picnic tables, **Cours Lafayette** is a cornucopia of breads, pastries, and *plats à emporter* (take-out). In the morning, a huge **market** stretching along the cours from the sea to bd. de Strasbourg booms with vendors' voices and the smells of apricots and olives. At 1pm, vegetables and fruits are swept away, revealing storefronts selling fresh breads, roasted chickens, and Vietnamese take-out. To the left of the *cours*, the Mayol shopping center houses the **Carrefour supermarket.** (Open M-Sa 8:30am-9pm.)

La Feuille de Chou, 15 rue de la Glacière (tel. 04 94 62 09 26). Unforgettable lunch spot with innovative variations on salads and bistro fare (55-65F) amidst pale green decor and wonderful patio. Open M-F 8am-6pm, Sa 8am-9pm.

Café Louis Blanc, on pl. Louis Blanc (tel. 04 94 46 06 41). Popular local seafood joint. Pick your own shellfish at their in-house market. The 58F *menu* includes a huge bowl of mussels (3 different styles), french fries, and a beer. Closed M and July-Aug.

Al Dente, 30 rue Gimeli (tel. 04 94 93 02 50). Decorated to the teeth with black lacquer. Eight varieties of fresh homemade pasta. Weekday lunch *menu* 55F. Open daily noon-2pm and 7-11pm. Closed Aug. V, MC.

Carthage, pl. du Murier (tel. 04 94 42 05 42), next to the Mayol Shopping Center. Hearty portions of couscous and *tajines* (50-60F) in a bazaar-like setting. Finish off by sampling their huge selection of North African pastry desserts (8F). V, MC.

👁 🎵 SIGHTS AND ENTERTAINMENT

SIGHTS. If you can visit only one of the many maritime museums on the Côte d'Azur, make it the **Musée Naval,** pl. Ingenieur Général Monsenergue (tel. 04 94 02 02 01). On display are meticulously crafted models of the strange ships that have sailed into Toulon's ports and mastheads from Toulon's ancient fleet. (Open daily 10am-noon and 2:30-7pm. 24F, students 12F.) The **Musée de Toulon,** 113 bd. Maréchal Leclerc, has small but generally worthwhile temporary exhibits housed in the 19th-century *bibliothèque.* (Open daily 1-7pm. Free.) The **Cathédrale Ste-Marie,** pl. de la cathédrale (tel. 04 94 92 28 91), off rue Émile Zola, was originally built in a Romanesque style, but reconstruction during the 17th century incorporated Neoclassical influences. (Open daily 8:30am-12:30pm and 2:30-5pm.)

During the day, Toulon's expansive and pedestrian-friendly *vieille ville* is a great place to get lost among merchants, tea-rooms, and Tunisian bakeries. In **cours Lafayette,** after the vegetable market is closed, vendors hawking Persian rugs, tapestries, and fake jewelry flood the kilometer-long strip, while book and music stores lend the area a college feel. **Mont Faron** offers a trance-inducing view of Toulon's reflections in the Mediterranean. To ascend the mount, take the *téléphérique* (cable car) from bd. Amiral Vence (tel. 04 94 92 68 25), several blocks behind the station. (Open June 16-Aug. 9:30am-7pm; rest of year 9:30am-noon and 2-6:30pm. 38F round-trip.) Atop the mount a few trails allow low-key hiking with panoramic vistas, including *Les Sentiers des Douaniers*, which traces the paths of officers who protected the port from smugglers and pirates.

Beaches are not Toulon's strong point and are a bit of a trek from the center of town. **Plage du Mourillan** is popular with locals and is seldom overcrowded. To get there, walk to the *vieux port* and follow av. de la République and av. de Lattre de Tassigny east (20min.). Buses make the trip. Much better sun-basking opportunities lie just over the bay from Toulon harbor and over the isthmus of La Seyne-sur-Mer. **Les Sablettes** are carpeted with the most finely ground sand on the Côte d'Azur. Yellow **SITCAT** boats leave from quai Stalingrad in Toulon harbor for Les Sablettes every two hours (8F).

ENTERTAINMENT. Toulon's sometimes reputation as a dangerous and generally undesirable city doesn't help its nightlife. Yet it possesses a sizable student population, and one can occasionally detect traces of cosmopolitanism and counter-culture. In particular, Toulon is nationally recognized for a thriving punk scene. *Le Petit Bavard* (see **Tourist Office,** above) is an indispensable guide for nightlife. Stay clear of bars near the port, especially on rue Chevalier Paul, which cater to navy libidos—they're overpriced anyway. **Le B des Cochons,** 503 av. de la République (tel. 04 94 03 04 75), a simultaneous shrine to pigs and Che Guevara, draws an eclectic crowd to its colorful restaurant/bar. **Café Lecture,** 18 rue d'Antrechaus (tel. 04 94 62 44 52), is a community-oriented café that regularly invites speakers and holds discussions and concerts for local and national artists, writers, and musicians. On other nights, settle down with your java (1-25F) and a book from the library. (Open M-Sa 8am-9pm.) **Boy's Paradise,** 1 bd. Pierre Toesca (tel. 04 94 09 35 90), near the train station, attracts a colorful and party-ready gay crowd.

ÎLES D'HYÈRES

Named after the color of the islands at dusk, the Îles d'Hyères ("Golden Isles") boast an exotic landscape and few signs of civilization. On sunny days, their rugged coasts are great for swimming and sunning, while interesting hikes await on the islands' trails. An off-season visit can be an isolated, almost eerie experience.

The largest island, **Porquerolles** (pop. 300), has the most colorful history. It was home to a religious order until François I, in a stroke of genius, declared it an asylum for criminals who had agreed to defend the mainland against pirates. Of course, the convicts promptly transformed the island into a base for their own piratical ambitions. A century later, Louis XIV, fixer of all things, finally put a stop to their raiding. Today, mainlanders and tourists seeking respite from the hectic Riviera come here to find peace in rugged cliffs and small, hidden coves. Pick your favorite inlet and swim all day without seeing a soul. The **Île du Levant** was also originally settled by monks, but its former inhabitants would be shocked if they could see it today, covered with naked people. Its **Héliopolis** is perhaps Europe's most famous nudist colony. Except for the western tip where ferries land, the entire island goes *au naturel*, but be careful where you and your birthday suit wander. The western part of the island, closed to the public, is an active military base. Day trippers are welcome, but visitors eager for one big peep-show are not. Upon disembarking from the ferry, orient yourself with the map posted on a board listing accommodations and trails on the island. Walking straight uphill from the port, you'll eventually reach what passes for a town square, with restaurants, hotels, and a piano bar. Hotels tend to be expensive, but **camping** at **Colombero** (tel. 04 94 05 90 29), straight uphill from the ferry, is a good bet, and it goes without saying that you don't need to pack much. (38F per person.) The smallest of the islands, **Port-Cros** revolves around a few buildings on the port, including a couple of restaurants and food stands. Beyond these, Port-Cros is a walker's paradise, with plenty of spots to drop down to the water and relax in your own scenic cove.

Ferries to the island run from the town of **Hyères,** to the east of Toulon. Get there by **train** from **Toulon** (9 per day, 48F) or **Marseille** (6 per day, 86F), or by **bus: Sodetrav** (tel. 04 94 12 55 00) runs to **Toulon** (every 20min., 37F) and **St-Tropez** (8 per day, 77F), while **Phoceens-Cars** (tel. 04 93 85 66 61) go to **Cannes** (2 per day, 130F) and **Nice** (2 per day, 140F). To get to the ferry ports, catch **Sodetrav local bus** #67 to **Port La Gavine** (12F) or **La Tour Fondue** (16F). **TVM Ferries** run to **Porquerelles** from **Tour Fondue.** (Tel. 04 94 58 21 81. 20min. July-Aug. 21 per day, off-season 6 per day; round-trip 80F.) Ferries also run to the islands of **Port-Cros** (1hr.) and **Île du Levant** (1½hr.), from **Port Le Gavine.** (Tel. 04 94 57 44 07. July-Aug. 5 per day, off-season 3 per day; round-trip each 115F.) From May to September, boats connect **Port-Cros** with **Île du Levant** (130F for both). If you're attracted to Hyères, stop by the **tourist office,** in the pale yellow Rotonde Jean Saluse on av. du Belgique, for more information on the town. (Tel. 04 94 65 18 55. Open daily July-Aug. 8am-7pm; Apr.-June and Sept.-Oct. M-F 8:30am-6pm, Sa 9am-noon and 2-6pm; Nov.-Mar. M-F 8:30am-5:30pm, Sa 10am-noon and 2-5pm.)

CORSICA (LA CORSE)

A story told to Corsican children goes something like this: On the sixth day of Creation, God made Corsica. He mixed the turquoise waters of the Mediterranean, the snow-capped splendor of the Alps, and the golden sunshine of the Riviera, and with them created the island the Greeks called *Kallysté* (the most beautiful).

With a total population of less than 250,000, Corsica offers refuge in its wilderness and tiny villages, and Corsicans will go out of their way to enhance your tryst with their island. The snootiness that mainland French often have a reputation for is nowhere to be seen on Corsica; then again, you'd be happy and friendly all day if you could call this island home. Corsica is relatively safe for women traveling alone, but they may encounter the same unwanted compliments and invitations that plague all of the Mediterranean.

Though dominated for centuries by Genoan and French masters, Corsicans deny being anything but Corsican. Corsica's only real brush with independence came after a series of uprisings in 1729 initiated the Corsican War of Independence, also known as the Forty Years' War. In 1755, the revered Pasquale Paoli proclaimed the island autonomous, created a university, and drafted the island's (and indeed the world's) first modern constitution. The retreating Genoese ceded their protectorate to the French, who humiliated Paoli's army on May 8, 1769. Among the Corsican officers who quickly swore allegiance to France was a certain Carlo Buonaparte. On August 15, 1769, his son Napoleone was born in Ajaccio. Napoleon (as he rechristened himself in France) was no believer in Corsican independence, though, and was execrated by Paoli for refusing to support his second bid for independence in 1783. In the past, the French government has prohibited Corsicans from using their language (a Romance language most closely related to medieval Tuscan) or even implementing Corsican place names; Corsicans fought back by refusing to pay taxes. Today, the Front de Libération National de la Corse (FLNC) continues to try bombing its way to independence. Most Corsicans deplore this extremism and question the wisdom of total independence from France, which directly provides 70% of Corsica's GNP. These politics will have little effect on tourists, who are warmly received throughout the island.

Between June 15 and August 31, tourist services improve and prices soar. The summer climaxes in a double-barreled blast on August 15, when all of France celebrates the **Fête de l'Assomption,** and Corsicans observe **Napoleon's birthday** on the same day. Tourists depart by September, when the weather is at its best and the waters their warmest. Winter visitors can either stay in sleepy coastal towns or head inland to the snow-capped mountains for skiing.

THE SOUTHEAST

Corsican cuisine is hearty, fresh, and pungent; what it lacks in refinement, it makes up for in earthiness. Herbs from the *maquis* (an impenetrable tangle of lavender, laurel, myrtle, rosemary, and thyme growing on Corsica's hillsides) impart a distinct flavor to local specialties, including honey made from its flowers. Along the coast, seafood is excellent; try *calamar* (squid), *langouste* (spiny lobster), *gambas* (prawns), or *moules* (mussels). Other delicacies include *pâté de merle* (blackbird pâté), *saucisson* (pork sausage), and *sanglier* (wild boar). Cheeses include *brocciu*, a white goat cheese, and *niolo*, a sharp goat cheese. Honeys, nougats, cakes, jams, and spices are flavored with the ubiquitous *maquis*. The fragrant, flavorful Corsican wines are as inexpensive as their cousins on the mainland and are often made using inventive ingredients like chestnuts.

Corsican tourist offices have free guides to all of Corsica's accommodations, published by **Agence du Tourisme de la Corse,** 17 bd. du Roi Jérôme, Ajaccio (tel. 04 95 21 56 56; fax 04 95 51 14 40). There are few budget hotels, and they fill by early morning in summer. Campsites lie close to most cities; a ban on unofficial camping is strictly enforced. Inland, *gîtes* provide little more than a roof over your head; they rarely take reservations, but you can usually pitch a tent outside.

HIGHLIGHTS OF CORSICA

■ The vast expanses of fine white sand around **Porto Vecchio** win the cut-throat competition for the island's best beaches (p. 350).
■ The scenic **train ride** from **Calvi** to **Île Rousse** trundles past church ruins and unadulterated views of the turquoise Mediterranean (p. 341).
■ The **GR20, Da Mare a Mare,** and **Da Mare a Monti** will test hikers through diverse, dazzling landscapes (see **By Foot,** p. 332).
■ **Cap Corse** juts into the Mediterranean, lined with tiny fishing villages that are connected by streets wide enough for only one Yugo (p. 348).

 GETTING THERE

BY PLANE. Air France and its subsidiary **Air Inter** fly to **Bastia, Ajaccio, Calvi,** and **Porto Vecchio** from **Paris** (2200F, students 1200-1900F), **Nice** (1037F, students 737F), **Marseille** (1155F, students 815F), and **Lyon** (2400F, students 1700F). There's also a direct link from **Lille** to **Bastia** (3600F, students 1500F). Call Air France in Marseille (tel. 04 91 39 36 36) or Paris (tel. 01 45 46 90 00). Air Inter's offices are at the airports in Ajaccio (tel. 04 95 29 45 45) and Bastia. In Ajaccio, the Air France/Air Inter office is at 3 bd. du Roi Jérôme (tel. 0 802 802 802). As with all airfares, you can get significant reductions if you hunt around; ask a budget travel agency in France.

BY BOAT. Ferry travel between the mainland and Corsica can be a rough trip and not much cheaper than a plane. High speed ferries run between Nice and Corsica. Overnight ferries from Toulon and Marseille take upwards of 10 hours. The **Société National Maritime Corse Méditerranée (SNCM)** sends ferries from **Marseille** (305-360F, under 25 265-305F), **Nice** (260-305F, under 25 235-260F) and **Toulon** (305-360F, under 25 265-305F) to **Bastia, Calvi, Île Rousse, Ajaccio, Porto Vecchio,** and **Propriano.** It costs 160-1210F to take a car, depending on the day and the car. In summer, up to eight boats float daily between Corsica and the mainland, dropping to two out of season. Schedules fluctuate, so call to confirm and arrive in good time.

MARE (tel. 04 95 73 00 96) and **Mobylines** (tel. 04 95 73 00 29) run from **Santa Teresa,** Sardinia, to **Bonifacio** (3-14 per day depending on the season, 65F per person and 120-200F per car one way). **Corsica Ferries** crosses from **Livorno** and **Savona** in Italy to **Bastia** (140-200F), with offices in **Bastia,** 5 bd. Chanoine-Leschi (tel. 04 95 32 95 95; fax 04 95 32 14 71); **Nice,** 3 quai Papacino (tel. 04 93 55 54 04); and **Paris,** 25 rue de l'Arbre sec (tel. 01 47 03 96 30). Call the Bastia office for reservations.

THE SOUTHEAST

Corsica

Ligurian Sea

MARSEILLE–
TOULON
NICE

Tollaré
TOULON
MARSEILLE
NICE
SAN REMO

Rogliano

Pino
D 180
Cap Corse

Sisco
D 80

Nonza
D 32

Golfe de
St-Florent

LA SPEZIA GENOVA
LIVORNO

Désert des
Agriates
Patrimonio
St-Florent
D 80
Bastia

Algajola
Ile-Rousse
N 197
▲ Mt. Asto
N 193

Calvi
N 197

Forêt de
Tartagine
Asco
Vescovato

D 81

Forêt de
Bonifato
▲ Mt. Padro

Stagno
Moriani
Plage

Galéria
Girolata
Col de
la Croix
▲ Mt. Cinto
Calacuccia
N 193
Corte
Cervione

Golfe de
Porto
Porto
D 124
Forêt de
Valdo-Niello
Venaco
▲ Mt.
San Petrone

Piana
Forêt d'
Aitone
Gorges de la Restonica
D 84
▲ Mt.
Rotondo
N 200

D 23

Sagone
▲ Mt. d'Oro
Forêt de
Vizzavona
Ghisoni
Aléria
Côte Orientale

Cargèse
Sari-d'Orcino
D 344
N 198

Tiuccia
N 193
▲ Mt. Renoso
Ghisonaccia

Golfe de
Sagone
Bastélica
D 757

Ajaccio
Iles
Sanguinaires
D 11
N 196
Zicavo

MARSEILLE-TOULON
Porticcio
D 55
D 83
▲ Mt.
L'Incudine
Col de
Bavella
Solenzara

MARSEILLE
TOULON
D 302
D 420
Forêt de
Bavella
D 268

PORTO TORRES
Olmeto
D 157
Zonza

Golfe de Valinco
D 69
D 368
Pinarello
MARSEILLE
PORTO SANTO STEFANO

Propriano
Forêt de l'Ospedale
Porto-Vecchio

Sartène
D 48
Golfe de
Porto-Vecchio

N 196
N 198

Golfe de
Sta-Manza
Tyrrhenian Sea

- - - - Ferry Route

0   20 miles
0   20 kilometers

Bonifacio
Iles
Lavezzi

Mediterranean
Sea

Santa Teresa

SARDINIA

N

Wine Regions

VIN DE CORSE-
COTEAUX DU CAP CORSE
PATRIMONIO
Patrimonio

Ile Roussé
Calvi
VIN DE CORSE-
CALVI

Corte

Porto
Aléria

VIN DE CORSE
AJACCIO

Ajaccio
Sartène
VIN DE CORSE-
PORTO VECCHIO

VIN DE CORSE-
SARTENE
Figari
Porto Vecchio

VIN DE CORSE-
FIGARI

⌐ GETTING AROUND

ON WHEELS. Rumor has it that Machiavelli and the Marquis de Sade collaborated on the design for Corsica's transportation system. **Train** service in Corsica is slow and limited to the half of the island north of Ajaccio—nor does it accept rail passes. Not for the faint of stomach, the antiquated trains are heinous to travel on in windy mountainous areas. Still, at least trains tend to be on time, which is more than can be said for **buses.** Bus companies are neither cheaper nor more frequent than trains, but offer a more comprehensive service. Call **Eurocorse Voyages** (tel. 04 95 21 06 30) for further info. Patient travelers report some success at hitching; they often carry a sign displaying both their destination and their willingness to pay for gas: *"Je vous offre l'essence."* Ten liters of gas (about 60F) usually covers 100km on flat roads, but buses are safer and about as cheap.

Corsica allegedly has the most lethal roads in Europe, but if you're foolhardy enough to rent a **car,** expect to pay at least 350-530F per day or 1450-1806F per week. The unlimited mileage deals are best; otherwise you'll be coughing up 2-4F per km. Gas stations are scarce; the police will sometimes help if you run out. **Bicycle** rental can be pricey (about 90-120F per day with 1500F deposit). Puttering **mopeds** *(mobilettes)* or scooters run about 130-200F per day, with a 3000F deposit. Narrow mountain roads and high winds make cycling difficult and risky; drivers should be careful and honk before rounding mountain curves.

BY FOOT. Hiking may be the best way to explore the island's mountainous interior. The longest marked route, the **GR20,** is a difficult 160km, 13- to 15-day trail that takes hikers across the island from Calenzana (southeast of Calvi) to Conca (northeast of Porto-Vecchio). Do *not* tackle this trail alone, and be prepared for cold, snowy weather, even in early summer. Two other popular routes are the **Mare e Monti,** a seven-day trail from Calenzana to Cargèse, and the easier **Da Mare a Mare,** which crosses the southern part of the island between Porto-Vecchio and Propriano (4-6 days). The **Parc Naturel Régional de la Corse,** 2 rue Major-Lambroschini, Ajaccio (tel. 04 95 51 79 10; fax 04 95 21 88 17), publishes maps, an invaluable guide to *gîtes d'étapes,* and an assortment of other brochures. **Editions Didier et Richard,** 9 Grande Rue, 38000 Grenoble, makes the best trail maps for the GR20. January through May, additional trails are available for cross-country skiing. For further information, contact the Parc Naturel Régional. For skiing information, contact the **Station de Ski Renoso** in Ghisoni (tel. 04 95 57 01 45).

AJACCIO (AIACCIU)

As the Frenchest town in Corsica, Ajaccio (pop. 60,000) often eschews Corsican nationalism in favor of the *français* side of life. It swings like nowhere else on the island, and with all the swank, you might think you're a few hundred kilometers north, on the Riviera—perhaps the Côte d'Azur's little sister has a Napoleon complex. If Ajaccio seems like a year-long celebration of Napoleon, wait until his birthday (August 15), when the city really goes out to conquer Europe. This love affair is odd, considering that Napoleon himself hopped the island for good as soon as he sniffed success. Although beaches here don't match those elsewhere on the island, Ajaccio provides a balance between beach resort relaxation and bustling urbanity.

⁊ ORIENTATION AND PRACTICAL INFORMATION

Cours Napoléon, which runs from pl. de Gaulle past the train station, is the city's main thoroughfare. The pedestrian **rue C. Fesch** starts at pl. Maréchal Foch and runs roughly parallel to cours Napoléon. Both are thick with cafés and boutiques. **Pl. Foch, pl. de Gaulle,** and the **citadel** (still an active military base) enclose the *vieille ville.*

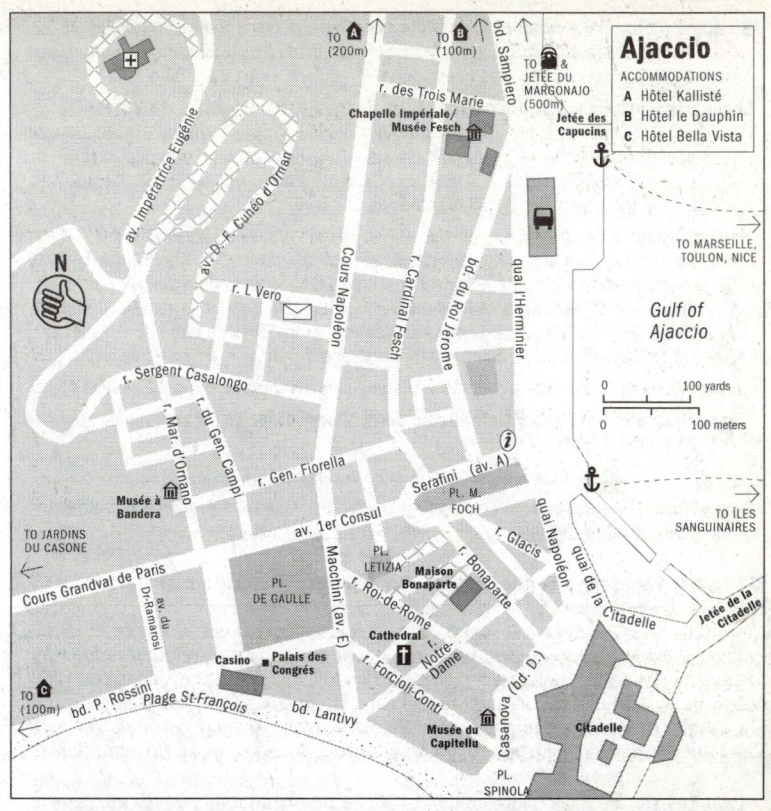

Ajaccio

ACCOMMODATIONS
A Hôtel Kallisté
B Hôtel le Dauphin
C Hôtel Bella Vista

Flights: Aéroport Campo dell'Oro (tel. 04 95 51 55 45), is 5km away. To: **Nice, Marseille,** and **Paris.** For info call **Air France/Air Inter,** 3 bd. du Roi Jerôme (tel. 08 02 80 28 02 for both). A bus (tel. 04 95 51 43 23) shuttles hourly between the airport and the bus station (20F).

Ferries: Gare Maritime (tel. 04 95 29 66 63). Open M-F 8-11:45am and 2-4pm, Sa 8-11:45am, and around ferry departure and arrival times. **SNCM,** quai l'Herminier (tel. 04 95 29 66 99), across from the bus station, sends ferries to **Nice** (4hr. by day, 10hr. overnight; 1-2 per day), **Marseille** (8½hr., 6 per week), and **Toulon** (7hr., 1 per week). 280-320F, students 250-280F.

Trains: Rue Jean-Jérôme Levie (tel. 04 95 23 11 03). Bear right from *gare maritime* away from the *vieille ville* and citadel on quai l'Herminier. Station is on the left, past pl. Abbatucci. Open daily 6am-8pm. To: **Corte** (2hr., 5 per day, 67F); **Calvi** via Ponte Leccia (5hr., 2 per day, 138F); and **Bastia** (4hr., 4 per day, 118F). **Luggage storage** 15F.

Buses: Quai l'Herminier (tel. 04 95 21 28 01), part of the *gare maritime.* Services and companies change seasonally; info kiosk will help you find up-to-date info. Open summer daily 6:30am-8pm; rest of year M-Sa 6:30am-8pm, Su 4-8pm. **Eurocorse Voyages** (tel. 04 95 21 06 30) goes via **Porto-Vecchio** (3hr., 4 per day, 110F) to **Bonifacio** (3½hr., 110F) and via **Corte** (1½hr., 2 per day, 60F) to **Bastia** (3hr., 105F). **Autocars SAIB** (tel. 04 95 22 41 99) go via **Porto** (2¾hr., 2 per day, 65F) to **Calvi** (6hr., 130F).

Taxis: Accord Ajaccio Taxis, pl. de Gaulle (tel. 04 95 21 00 87). To airport 100-110F.

Car Rental: Budget (tel. 04 95 21 17 18). 390F per day, 1660F per week, unlimited mileage. **Ada Rent-a-Car** (tel. 04 95 23 56 57). 356F per day, 1500F per week, unlimited mileage. **Europcar,** 16 cours Grandval (tel. 03 95 21 05 49). Open M-F 8am-noon and 2-6pm, Sa 8am-noon. Also at the airport (tel. 04 95 23 57 01).

Bike and Motorbike Rental: Ajaccio Moto Location, 61 cours Napoleon (tel. 04 95 23 56 36) and at the airport (tel. 04 95 23 56 36). Bikes from 80F per day. Motorbikes from 130F per day. 2000F credit card deposit required. Open daily 8am-7pm.

Local Transportation: TCA, Diamant 111, pl. de Gaulle (tel. 04 95 51 43 23; fax 04 95 50 15 06). Buses run every 20min. 7am-7pm. Tickets 7.50F, *carnet* of 10 58F, longer trips cost extra. Take bus #1 from pl. de Gaulle to the train station and airport (20F) or down cours Napoléon. Bus #5 from av. Dr. Ramaroni stops at Marinella and the beaches on the way to the **Îles Sanguinaires** (11.50F).

Tourist Office: 3 bd. du roi Jerome (tel. 04 95 51 53 03; fax 04 95 51 53 01). Free maps and slick quadrilingual guide *Ajaccio: Practical Information.* Open June 16-Aug. 31 M-Sa 8am-8:30pm, Su 9am-1pm; Sept.-June 15 M-Sa 8am-6pm and Su 9am-1pm. Get **hiking info** at **Parc Naturel Régional,** 2 rue Sergeant Cazalonga (tel. 04 95 51 79 10; fax 04 95 21 88 17), next to the *préfecture.* Maps of trails and info on shelters. Open M-Th 9am-noon and 2-6pm, F 9am-noon and 2-5pm.

Money: Currency exchange at airport and along cours Napoléon and rue C. Fesch.

Hospital: Centre Hospitalier Notre-Dame de la Miséricorde, 27 av. Impératrice Eugénie (tel. 04 95 29 90 90).

Police: In the Hôtel de Ville, on pl. Maréchal Foch (tel. 04 95 29 21 47).

Post Office: 13 cours Napoléon (tel. 04 95 51 84 75). Open M-F 8am-6:30pm, Sa 8am-noon. **Postal code:** 20000.

ACCOMMODATIONS AND CAMPING

Ajaccio has many hotels, but brace yourself for prices that exceed those in Paris. Call ahead from June to August, when rates soar and vacancies plummet. One way to save a bit is to ask hotels for the absolute cheapest room they have, and then follow up by asking if there's anything cheaper than that. Some hotels have a couple of older rooms they generally don't offer or list, but you may get one if you ask. The tourist office can help you find a hotel or recommend short-term apartments.

Hôtel Kallisté, 51 cours Napoléon (tel. 04 95 51 34 45; fax 04 95 21 79 00). Serene and peaceful despite being on Ajaccio's busiest street, with tasteful modern rooms and bits of rock peeping out of the wall. All rooms have TV, toilet, and shower. Singles 200-300F; doubles 250-340F; triples 360-450F; quads 400-560F. Breakfast 35F. Separate night reception desk upstairs. Studios with kitchen available for longer term rent. V, MC.

Hôtel Bella Vista, bd. Lantivy (tel. 04 95 21 07 97; fax 04 95 21 81 88). Older hotel with caring owners and reasonable-quality rooms with showers and toilet. Singles 190-240F; doubles 210-270F; triples 260-330F; quads 380F. Breakfast 25F. V, MC, AmEx.

Hôtel le Dauphin, 11 bd. Sampiero (tel. 04 95 21 12 94 or 04 95 51 29 96; fax 04 95 21 88 69), halfway between the train station and *gare maritime.* All rooms, many newly renovated, come with TV, telephone, toilet, and shower. Lively bar and restaurant downstairs (dinner *menu* 60F). Free garage for bikes. Singles 230-250F; doubles 260-290F; triples 320-390F. Extra bed 50F. Prices include 30F breakfast; haggle if you don't want it. Ask about cheaper rooms (from 130F) in their building next door. V, MC.

Campsites: Barbicaja (tel. 04 95 52 01 17), 4km away, is closest to town. Take bus #5 from av. Dr. Ramaroni just past pl. de Gaulle to "Barbicaja" (last bus at 7pm). 38F per person, 12F per tent, 12F per car. **U Prunelli** (tel. 04 95 25 19 23), near the bridge of Pisciatello, next to Porticcio, is accessible by bus (tel. 04 95 25 40 37; 10F). 35F per person, 12F per tent, 14F per car.

FOOD

The **morning market,** on bd. du roi Jérôme and pl. César Campinchi behind the tourist office, offers up all manner of scrumptious comestibles. A smaller market operates near the train station at pl. Abatuzzi on cours Napoléon. (Open Tu-Su 6am-

12:30pm.) Try the **rue St-Charles** for a selection of restaurants serving local dishes. Pizzerias (pizzas 35-50F) and *boulangeries* congregate on **rue Cardinal Fesch** and the pedestrian streets off pl. Foch towards the citadel. At **Monoprix supermarket,** 31, cours Napoléon (tel. 04 95 51 76 50), cheap foods leap into customers' baskets. (Open M-Sa 8:30am-7:15pm.) **Caramelys,** 15 rue roi de Rome (tel. 04 95 51 10 66), with 210 *sortes de bonbons*, dishes out enough sugar to kill you, but at least you'll die happy. (Open M 3-7:15pm, Tu-Sa 9am-noon and 3-7:15pm.)

🖾 **Da Mamma** (tel. 04 95 21 39 44), off cours Napoleon, by the post office on Passage Guinguetta. Serves up the mother of Corsican cuisine and more on a shaded patio. Discerning locals flock to this hole-in-the-wall. Mouth-watering *menus* 65F, 95F. Mention *Let's Go* for a free *apéritif*. (Open daily noon-2pm and 7:30-10:30pm. V, MC.)

La Calata, rue Danielle Casanova (tel. 04 95 21 26 77), on the *quai* near the citadel. Dine on the terrace by candlelight under a glorious web of vines or inside in a cozy booth. Large portions of meat and seafood paella 90F. Pizzas 45-48F, pasta 30-50F. Open daily noon-2pm and 6:30-11:30pm. V, MC, AmEx.

Cafétéria La Serre, 91 cours Napoléon (tel. 04 95 22 41 55), past the train station as you head to the airport. Beautiful indoor greenery; the primarily concrete outdoor garden is less appealing. Self-service salads 12-40F. Desserts 12-20F. Open daily in summer 11:30am-3pm and 6:30-10pm, in winter 11:30am-3pm and 6:30-9:30pm.

👁 🅰 SIGHTS AND EXCURSIONS

SIGHTS. If you're a Napoleonophile, you'll find Ajaccio's sights better than another 100 days. Otherwise, Ajaccio is the center of Corsica's museum life. Visiting a few will enlighten you to the island's culture and history, but you can't go far without encountering an imperial edification.

Grab the Corsican bull by the horns and start at the **Musée National de la Maison Bonaparte,** rue St-Charles (tel. 04 95 21 43 89), between rue Bonaparte and rue Roi-de-Rome. Modestly tucked away in the *vieille ville*, the slightly dingy house contains everything from Napoleon's baby pictures to his death mask. Security guards may let curious visitors into "off-limit" rooms. Ironically, the house briefly sheltered Hudson Lowe, Napoleon's jailer on St-Helena. (Open M 2-6 pm, Tu-Su 10am-noon and 2-6pm. 22F, ages 18-25 15F, under 18 free.)

Napoleon's uncle Fesch piled up a stash of money as a merchant during the Revolution. When he renounced his worldly goods for the Church, the new cardinal used the booty to amass a significant collection of 15th- and 16th-century Italian art; to house the art, he donated his residence to the city in 1839 and made it a museum where Corsican youth could improve their cultural education. Now the **Musée Flesch,** 50-52 rue Cardinal Fesch (tel. 04 95 21 48 17; fax 04 95 21 80 94), inside you'll find an exhausting collection including works by Raphael, Botticelli, and Titian. Interspersed modern exhibits provide a peculiar counterpoint. Within the complex is the **Chapelle Impériale,** the final resting place of most of the Bonaparte family—though Napoleon himself is buried in a modest Parisian tomb. (Open June 15-Aug. 30 Tu-Th 10am-5:30pm, F 10am-6:30pm and 9:30pm-midnight, Sa-Su 10am-4:30pm; Sept. 1-June 15 Tu-Sa 9:15am-12:15pm and 2:15-5:15pm. Museum 25F, students 15F; with chapel 39F, students 20F.)

The **Musée à Bandera,** 1 av. Général Levie (tel. 04 95 51 07 34), traces Corsican history from 3000 BC to World War II and has (of course) one room dedicated to Napoleon. Mannequins in period-era garb lean good-naturedly in the corners. (Open July-Aug. M-Sa 9am-7pm, Sept.-June 10am-noon and 2-6pm. 20F, students 10F.) If you've had enough of the Bonaparte craze, seek respite in the **Musée du Capitellu,** 18 bd. Danielle Casanova (tel. 04 95 21 50 57), opposite the citadel, which instead presents the history of Ajaccio in paintings, sculptures, and artifacts from the island's Genoan days to the present. (Open Apr.-Oct. M-Sa 10am-noon and 2-6pm, Su 10am-noon; also July-Aug. nightly 9-11pm. 25F, students 10F.)

EXCURSIONS. The **Îles Sanguinaires** bare their black cliffs to the sea, southwest of Ajaccio at the mouth of the gulf. **Promenades en Mer** (tel. 04 95 51 31 31) runs excursions to the islands daily April through October (120F). Visible from these boats, the Genoese **Tour de la Parata** can be reached by bus #5 from av. Dr. Ramaroni (1 per hour 7am-7pm, 12F). The bus stops at numerous beaches along the way. The closest beach to the town center is **plage St-François**, beyond the citadel.

NIGHTLIFE AND FESTIVALS

NIGHTLIFE. Unlike many other Corsican cities, fair Ajaccio can serve up a wild night on the town. To know the happenings on a given night, check out the posters that adorn street lampposts. **Le Sun Club** (tel. 04 95 50 06 17) is on residence Plein Soleil. **La Cinquième Avenue,** rte. des Sanguinares (tel. 04 95 52 09 77), requires a car or motorbike, but is Ajaccio's definitive nightclub. Locals flock to the slightly more distant **Le Blue Moon** (tel. 04 95 25 07 70), in Porticcio. (Open nightly in summer, off-season weekends only.) The best bet, if you want to stay put in town, is **La Place,** on quai de la Citadelle. Clubs tend to have no cover, but expect an obligatory one-drink minimum (40-50F). These clubs and the lively late-night cafés along quai de la Citadelle are usually safe for women.

FESTIVALS. Ajaccio often hosts a summer theater or classical music festival. Call the tourist office for more details. August 15 brings the three-day **Fêtes Napolé3** (tel. 04 95 21 50 90), when the city celebrates the birth of its municipal obsession. Napoleonic plays, a parade, and special ceremonies culminate in a *pyrosymphonie* (firework display) in the bay. But Ajaccio natives' real mania is apparent in the July and August **Shopping Festival,** when stores stay open until midnight on Friday nights, and everyone stays out late.

PORTO

If there had been an eighth day of creation, God would surely have conjured up Porto for the avid outdoor enthusiast. Captured within the city's surrounding area, the splendid natural spectacles that make Corsica unique are all here. Grandiose mountains shrouded in mist descend abruptly to meet the azure waters of the protected Gulf. While the town itself has been somewhat cheapened by tourism, it does provide the weary adventurer with mellow views of the setting sun, compromised only by the area's dizzying narrow mountain ledges. Don't miss the gorgeous exploration opportunities: the awe-inspiring red cliffs of Les Calanches, the balmy and fragrant eucalyptus forest, and the fishing hamlet of Girolata, accessible by boat and footpath only.

The town's tawdry cluster of tourist shops should be left as soon as possible. Run to the Citadel, built in 1540, and to the melancholy beauty of the sepulchres and cliffs that line the road up to the sweet, peaceful village of Ota. The surrounding forests' eucalyptus fragrance snuffs the marina's cheap perfume.

ORIENTATION AND PRACTICAL INFORMATION. Autocars SAIB (tel. 04 95 22 41 99 in Ajaccio; 04 95 26 13 70 in Porto) run at breakneck speeds along twisting roads to **Ajaccio** (2¼hr., M-Sa 2 per day, 75F) and **Calvi** (3hr., M-Sa 1 per day, 100F). **Autocars Mordiconi** (tel. 04 95 48 00 04 in Corte) go to **Corte** (July-Aug. M-Sa, 100F). **Taxis Ceccaldi Félix** (tel. 04 95 26 12 92) will take you to other villages for a hefty price. **Rent wheels** from **Porto Location** (tel. 04 95 26 10 13), opposite the supermarket in Haute Porto,. (**Bikes** 90F per day, 400F per week; passport deposit. **Mopeds** 400F per day, 1500F per week; 4000F deposit. **Cars** 420F per day, 2200F per week. Open May-Sept. daily 8am-8pm. V, MC.)

Porto is split into an upper town, **Haut Porto,** also called **Quartier Vaita,** and the coastal area, **Porto Marina,** where some 15 hotels and restaurants scramble for space. The main road has no name, but it's the only one leading straight to the port. The **tourist office** (tel. 04 95 26 10 55; fax 04 95 26 14 25), a green glass building in front of the marina off the main road, provides information on day hikes, water sports, boat trips, beaches, and accommodations. (Open June-Sept. M-F 9am-noon and 3:30-6:30pm; Oct.-May M-F 9am-noon and 2-4:30pm.) For info on longer hikes, try the **Parc Naturel Régional de la Corse** (tel. 04 95 26 15 14), 10m from the tourist office. (Open July-Aug. M-F 8:30am-12:30pm and 2-6pm.) **Changing money** here is a bad idea; if you have to, try **Porto Change,** near the port (open daily 9am-12:30pm and 3-7:30pm), or next to the pharmacy (open daily 8:30am-8pm). The **post office** (tel. 04 95 26 10 26) is midway between the marina and Haute Porto. (Open July-Aug. M-F 9am-12:30pm and 1:30-3:30pm, Sa 9am-noon; Sept.-June M-F 9am-12:30pm and 2-4pm, Sa 9-11am. **Postal code:** 20150.)

Ⲭ ACCOMMODATIONS AND CAMPING. For a small town, Porto teems with hotels; make sure yours doesn't require you to buy meals with your room *(demi-pension)* in the high season. Prices drop dramatically from September to May.

The family atmosphere of **l'Hôtel du Golfe** (tel. 04 95 26 13 33), directly across from the tourist office, will welcome you in from the sun. All rooms have shower and toilet. (Singles 210F; doubles 260F; quads 350F. Breakfast 25F. V, MC.) **Hôtel Colombo** (tel. 04 95 26 10 44) has no-frills rooms but a seaside location. (Singles and doubles 250-310F. V, MC.) The cheapest way to stay in Porto is to stake a tent at one of the three manicured **campgrounds** in Porto proper. The largest, **Camping Sole e Vista** (tel. 04 95 26 15 71), accessible either on your right as you enter Porto before the supermarkets, or 800m up the road to Ota, has showers and a rockin' bar. (29F per adult, 10F per tent, 10F per car.) **Camping Municipal** (tel. 04 95 26 17 76; fax 04 95 26 14 12) is as cozy as camping in your own backyard. (30F per person, 11F per tent, 10F per car. Electricity 17F. Reception open daily 9am-noon and 1-8pm.) **Camping Les Oliviers** (tel. 04 95 26 14 49; fax 04 95 26 12 49), on the road to Calvi, has great facilities. (28-36F per person according to season, 14F per tent, 14F per car. Electricity 20F. Reception open daily 8am-8pm.)

Cheaper accommodations are available in the pleasant village of **Ota,** 5km inland and upwards, and a starting point for many hikes. At the fork before the pharmacy, veer left and follow the signs. **Chez Marie** (tel. 04 95 26 11 37) offers spartan dorms and rock-bottom prices in three- to six-bed rooms. (66F per night, *demi-pension* 160F.)

⌁ FOOD. In tourist-saturated Porto, if a building isn't a hotel, it's probably a restaurant. *Loup* (sea bass) is usually freshly caught. **La Marine** (tel. 04 95 26 10 19) offers reasonable fare close to the marina, with 35-50F pizzas and 58-95F *menus.* (Open 10am-midnight.) Two **supermarkets** sit next to the bus stop on the D81: **Super Banco** (tel. 04 95 26 10 92; open daily 8am-noon and 3-7pm) and **Supermarché Timy** (open M-Sa 8am-noon and 3-7pm, Su 8:30am-noon; V, MC). Practice taking the plunge with the modeled male **scuba** instructors of the beachside **Generation Bleue.** (Tel./fax 04 95 26 24 88. 200F.)

◉ Ⲕ SIGHTS AND NEARBY HIKES AND TOWNS. Porto's best view stretches beneath Corsica's first **Genoese tower,** built in 1540 by the Italian governor when he annexed the town. From this height, even the strip of hotels seem regal as you gaze at the austere cliffs majestically dropping to the sea. The crowd thins out after 4pm. Cross the stream via footbridge and frolic on the long, wide beach or sun yourself on the rocks that stretch away from the old tower.

Hikes start from the Chalet des Roches Bleues, 8km from Porto on D81. Take the bus towards Ajaccio and ask the driver to let you off there. The Dog's Head rock, on the sea-hugging side of D81 about 700m from the chalet towards Porto, marks an easy trailhead to the boulder known as the Château Fort. Start near the Virgin Mary chapel 400m uphill from the chalet towards Piana for a rewarding vista of the port. Two other steep trails begin closer to the chalet; the one on its Porto side near the bridge is an exquisite semi-torture.

ENTERTAINMENT. After watching the sun set, head for one of Porto's numer-ous beachside bars, or dance the night away in one of its four *discothèques*. **La Bergerie** (tel. 04 95 26 13 15) thumps out all types of music on two levels of lounges and dance floors. Enter for free but dish out 45F for drinks. (Open 10:30pm until you decide to leave.)

GIROLATA

20km north and a 4km hike from the trail leading northwest of Osani, rests the fishing hamlet of Girolata and its fewer than 20 inhabitants. The hamlet's nearby **plage de Tuara** is a little piece of paradise. Spend the night at the *gîte d'étape* **Le Cor-moran Voyageur.** (60F per night. Breakfast 30F. Open Mar.-Oct.) The only other way to get here is aboard a boat. **Stradimare Promenade en Mer** (tel. 04 95 26 15 16) sends boats over (2 per day, 170F). They also go to the **Réserve Naturelle de Scandola,** por-tions of which are completely closed to human traffic in order to grant France's last pair of *balbuzards* (sea or fishing eagles) some romantic time to themselves. East of Porto along the D124, the road ascends as you pass Ota on your way to a wealth of challenging hikes through the **Gorges de la Spelunca.** Descending into the depths of the gorges is a great way to escape the sun for a moment, check out nearby natural caves, and experience an utterly different landscape, just inland from the coast.

LES CALANCHES

The most astounding scenery on the entire island may be south of Porto, where the geological formations of the Calanche are, as Guy de Maupassant wrote, a "menagerie of nightmares petrified by the whim of some extravagant god." The inhabited center-piece of this area is Piana. As picturesque a village as anywhere on the island, Piana is unfortunately becoming one big tourist trap. Visit soon while it still maintains any semblance of its original appeal. To experience the beauty a little longer and stock up on post cards, get a room at **Les Calanches,** on the waterfront (tel. 04 95 27 80 83; fax 04 95 27 82 08). (Singles 200-230F; doubles 250-290F. All rooms have shower and toilet. V, MC.)

CALVI

One of Corsica's smaller ferry ports, Calvi (pop. 5000) boasts the charm of a centu-ries-old city that has also fared well in modern times. The bare mountain rock faces sandy beaches, warm aquamarine waters, misty mountains, and nearly 2400 hours of sunshine per year (as opposed to Paris's 1700). This city could well be paradise—but surely no benevolent god would charge these prices! Despite the rates, in summer this small resort attracts tourists *en masse*, ballooning into a ver-itable United Nations of 25,000 Samsonite-wielding sun-seekers. While the endless beach can be hard to leave, the incredible citadel is just as much a reason to visit.

ORIENTATION AND PRACTICAL INFORMATION. The **Aéroport de Calvi Ste-Catherine** is 7km southeast of town; the taxi ride in costs 60-75F. **Air France/Air Inter** (tel. 04 95 65 88 68; flight info 08 36 68 34 24) fly to **Paris, Nice, Marseille, Lyon,** and **Lille** (see **Getting There,** p. 330). For info and tickets for **SNCM ferries,** call **Agence TRAMAR** (tel. 04 95 65 01 38), on quai Landry in the Port de Plaisance. (Open M-F 8:30am-noon and 2-5:30pm, Sa 8:30am-noon.) **Corsica Ferries,** Port du Commerce (tel. 04 95 65 43 21), sail to **Nice.** (Open M-F 9am-noon and 3-7pm.) The **train station,** pl. de la Gare (tel. 04 95 65 00 61), is at the end of Corso di la Repubblica near Port de Plaisance. Trains run to **Bastia** (3hr., 2 per day, 93F), **Corte** (2½hr., 2 per day, 78F), and **Île Rousse** (45min., 2 per day, 17F). **Tramways de la Balagne** provide regu-lar service to the further reaches of Calvi's beaches on the way to **Île Rousse** (45min.; 7 per day in season, 4 in the off-season; 30F). (Station open daily 6am-7pm. **Luggage storage** 16F per day.) **Autocar SAIB buses** (tel. 04 95 26 13 70 in Porto) go to **Porto** (3hr., M-Sa 1 per day, 100F), and **Les Beaux Voyages** (tel. 04 95 65 15 02), on av. Wilson, run to **Bastia** (2¼hr., daily, 80F). Buses stop at pl. Porteuse d'Eau

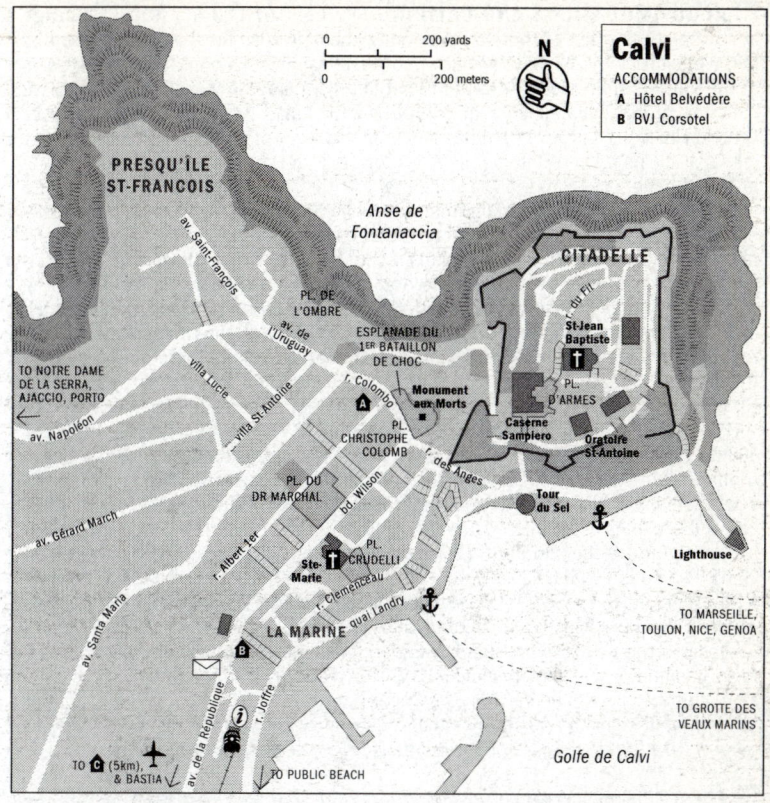

Agence; buy tickets on board. (Open M-Sa 9am-noon and 2-6pm.) **Car rental** is offered by **Hertz,** 2 rue Maréchal Joffre (tel. 04 95 65 06 64 in Calvi; 04 95 65 02 96 at the airport; 395F per day, 1425F per week) and **Europcar,** av. de la République (tel. 04 95 65 10 35 in Calvi; 04 95 65 10 19 at airport; from 415F per day, 749F per week). **Calvi Moto Location,** R.N. 197 (tel. 04 95 65 16 78), rents **bikes** and **scooters**. (Bikes 100F per day, 500F per week. Scooters 260F per day. 2000F deposit. Open May-Oct. 8:30am-7pm.) For **taxis,** call 04 95 65 03 10 (24hr.).

The city is manageable in size and easy to walk, threaded by one north-south street that starts at the citadel and changing name from **bd. Wilson,** to **av. de la République,** and again to **av. Christophe Colombe.** To reach the **tourist office,** Port de Plaisance (tel. 04 95 65 16 67; fax 04 95 65 14 09), exit from the back of the train station, facing the beach, turn left, and follow the signs. The chic staff is as well versed in Calvi's history as its nightlife, though their English is limited. They won't make reservations, but they do keep abreast of vacancies. (Open daily July-Aug. M-Sa 9am-7pm, Su 9am-1pm and 2:30-7pm; Sept.-June M-Sa 9am-noon and 2-6pm.) If you must **exchange currency** here, use one of the banks on bd. Wilson. **Change Wilson,** bd. Wilson (tel. 04 95 65 37 44), between the Institut de Beauté and Barbara Boutique, changes American Express traveler's cheques at mediocre rates, no commission. (Open daily 7am-7pm; 8pm-8am, same service offered by restaurant/ bar **Café du Port,** at Caltata Landry.) The **police** are on rte. d'Ajaccio (tel. 04 95 65 09 94). The **post office,** bd. Wilson (tel. 04 95 65 90 90), is across from the *gare* and tucked away into the hill, left of the Agence les Beaux Voyages. (Open M-F 8:30am-5:30pm, Sa 8:30am-noon. **Postal code:** 20260.)

█ ACCOMMODATIONS AND CAMPING. Prices for Calvi's hotels change according to the flux of tourists. Reserving ahead is wise for the summer months and a must for July. Weekly rentals are often cheaper; ask about *tarifs dégressifs* at the tourist office. Don't be afraid to bargain with hotel owners in the off season.

In a beautiful, isolated site 5km from town, the **Relais International de la Jeunesse U Carabellu** (tel. 04 95 65 14 16) has large, appealing rooms, some with spectacular views of the bay. There's no public transport; exit the station, turn left along av. de la République, pass Super U, turn right at rte. de Pietra-Maggiore and follow the signs 5km up the mountain. Continue past Bella Vista camping until the road forks at a stop sign; veer right and continue. It's a beautiful but lonely hike—women may not want to go alone. There's no campsite, but the staff will let those who ask pitch a tent for free. Families get their own room; otherwise single-sex dorms hold three to five beds. (75F. Breakfast included. Sheets 20F. Open May-Sept.) **BVJ Corsotel,** av. de la République (tel. 04 95 65 14 15; fax 04 95 65 33 72), has airy dorms holding two to eight beds with matching blankets, shower, and sink; doubles are reserved for couples. The noisy street-side rooms may have the best view in town. (120F. Breakfast included. Check out 10am. 24hr. reception. Open late Mar.-Oct.)

Hôtel Sole Mare, rte. de St-François (tel. 04 95 65 09 50; fax 04 95 65 36 64), is 300m from the *centre ville* on a residential street after the citadel and the St-Christophe Hôtel. The eager-to-please staff let functional rooms with shower and toilet. You'll remember the fabulous view and the super pool. (Singles 160-180F; doubles 200-400F; triples 300-450F; quads 350-500F. Breakfast 35F. Open Apr.-Oct.) In a prime location at the corner of bd. Wilson, **Hôtel Belvédère,** av. de l'Uruguay (tel. 04 95 65 01 25; fax 04 95 65 33 20), has bright Art Deco halls and small, fresh rooms with toilet, shower, and TVs. Reservations are a must. (Doubles 240-480F; triples 350-550F; quads 400-600F, depending on season. Breakfast 30F. Open Apr.-Oct.)

Close to the beach, with super friendly staff, an on-site bar, and bands every night in summer make **International,** R.N. 197 (tel. 04 95 65 01 75 or 04 95 65 36 11), a hot spot for the young'uns. It's past Super U and Hotel L'Onda, immediately after the mini golf sign—a trek that women might not want to do at night. (20-27F per person, 10-13F per child, 12-15F per tent, 8-10F per car. Open Apr.-Oct.)

█ FOOD. Pickings are slim for cheap food in Calvi; your best bet is to buy the elements for a Corsican feast yourself. Try the **Super U Supermarché,** av. Christophe Colombe. (Open M-F 8:30am-12:30pm and 3-7pm, Sa 8:30am-7pm.) The narrow rue Clemenceau has the highest concentration of food shops in Calvi and hosts a daily covered market (7am-1pm). Pizzerias line rue de la République. The stylish restaurants along the Port de Plaisance may offer tasty food and a great view, but at **La Main à la Pâte** (tel. 04 95 65 27 80), at the end of rue Clemenceau, near the citadel, you'll get local atmosphere and better prices. (Pasta 50-65F. Open daily lunch and dinner. V, MC.) Of the *vieux port* restaurants, **Café de la Transat** (tel. 04 95 65 00 20) is reasonably priced for noshing while you nurse your drink. (V, MC.)

█ SIGHTS. The inscription at the gates of the **citadel,** *"civitas Calvi semper fidelis"* (the city of Calvi is always faithful), recalls Calvi's loyalty to Genoa during the 16th century. Just beyond the entrance, an information center sells a *Guide of the Fort* (in English, 7F) that includes a map. Like several other Mediterranean towns, Calvi claims to be the birthplace of Christopher Columbus; a small plaque marks the house where he may have been born. Calvi's other famous house tells a more likely story: Napoleon and his family sojourned here in 1793 when fleeing from political opponents in Ajaccio. A particularly beautiful time to visit the citadel is at the end of the day, when watching the sunset at the far end of the citadel is a bit of a tradition. The 16th-century **Cathédrale St-Jean-Baptiste** has been stuffed with as many relics as would fit in one house of worship; wind your way to the top of the citadel to take a peek. The Baroque cathedral holds ecclesiastical works of art, as does the museum in the **Oratoire St-Antoine,** built in 1510. (Cathedral: Open daily 9am-noon and 2-7pm. Free. Oratory: Obligatory tour; call the tourist office.)

45F per person, groups 15F per person.) The other major place of worship is **Chapelle de Notre Dame de la Serra,** with a breathtaking view of Calvi and beyond. (Open 9am-noon and 2-7pm. Free.)

BEACHES. Gorgeous sand and water as far as the eye can see are hard to tire of. For much of the coast around Calvi, shallow water allows you to walk many meters into the water. With strong winds, windsurfing is particularly good here and has become a popular activity. If the 6km stretch of expansive **public beach** gets too windy, the rocks surrounding the citadel offer a secluded shelter to bask in the sun. The **Tramways de la Balagne** (see trains) can take you to more remote coves further out of town.

ENTERTAINMENT. The bars on the **port de Plaisance** glitter brightly in the summer. Signs posted all over town advertise party nights in different spots along the northern coast. Special occasion or not, locals come from far and wide to **La Camargue** (tel. 04 95 65 08 70), a *discothèque* 25 minutes along the road to Île Rousse. Things start to get good after midnight; call for the schedule of shuttle buses running from Calvi. For a mellower atmosphere and older crowd, the **Tao** piano bar and French/Asian restaurant (tel. 04 95 65 00 73), in the citadel, is a source of local pride. A spectacular vista outshines live music of varying genres.

FESTIVALS. Calvi hosts several festivals, including the **Festival du Jazz** (tel. 04 95 65 16 67) in the last week of June, when over 200 musicians give impromptu performances. Calvi becomes Calvary at Easter, with a dramatic re-creation of the crucifixion, **La Passion du Christ** (tel. 04 95 65 23 57), complete with self-flagellating penitents. Mid-September, the **Rencontres Polyphoniques** (tel. 04 95 65 23 57) celebrates traditional Corsican singing; in October, the **Festival du Vent** (tel. 04 95 65 16 67) glorifies everything that involves the wind, from wind quintets to windsurfing.

ÎLE ROUSSE

Stretching east from Calvi to Île Rousse, Corsica's luscious northern coast is lined with a largely unblemished coast, freckled with some not too exciting resort areas. In 1758 Pasquale Paoli, disgruntled leader of independent Corsica, built the town of Île Rousse (Isula) to compete with Genoese-dominated Calvi. Here you'll find a quieter, less yacht-club-dominated opportunity to bask in opalescent water and powdery sand, though the scenic train ride could justify the trip in itself.

To learn about what's under all that azure water, walk ten minutes along the beach toward Bastia to the **Musée Océanographique de l'Île Rousse** (tel. 04 95 60 27 81). You can learn about the fish you'll be eating that night, and can touch lots of soft and slimy aquatic life. There's also a 1½-hour video, in alternating English, German, and French, that was filmed in the wreck of a crashed plane. (Call for schedule. 44F, children 34F.)

Picnicking on the beach is allowed as long as you clean up after yourself. The **covered market** off pl. Paoli is filled with local fruits, the tentacled and finned catch of the day, and 10 different types of honey. (Open daily 7am-1pm.) The local **Super U,** av. Paul Doumer (tel. 04 95 60 02 46), off av. Piccioni, carries on where the market leaves off. (Open M-Sa 8:45am-12:30pm and 3:30-7:30pm.) Inexpensive pizza and pasta await in the snack bars along pl. Paoli, but you'll be rewarded if you move beyond their glitz to **Restaurant des Voyageurs,** rue Graziani (tel. 04 95 60 00 39). Their Corsican *bruschetta* (35-42F) is worth the trip from Calvi. (Open daily 9am-10pm or midnight, depending on the crowd.) Pretty much the only budget hotel in town is **Hôtel le Grillon,** 10 av. Paul Doumer, past pl. Paoli on the road to Bastia (tel. 04 95 60 00 49; fax 04 95 60 43 69), which has tranquil, sunny rooms with shower, toilet, firm mattresses, and balconies. (Singles 190-290F; doubles 200-310F; triples 240-350F, depending on season. Breakfast 30F. Open Mar.-Oct. V, MC, AmEx.) You'll have more luck **camping;** campsites appear fairly regularly all along the Balagne coast, so just hop off the train when you see one you like. In Île

THE SOUTHEAST

BUZZ OFF! Things looked grim for the inhabitants of Calenzana on January 14, 1732. An army of German mercenaries, hired by the Genoans to reconquer the rebellious island, was advancing from Calvi; the Corsicans had less than 20 rifles between them. But the Germans hadn't counted on the canny Corsican's secret weapon. Gathering together the hives from which they collected their precious honey, the Corsicans rained bees on the invaders from under the shelter of their homes. The Germans, in panic, dropped their weapons and ran for cover. News of this victory spread through the island, and, faced with renewed insurrections, the Genoans sued for peace.

Rousse, **Les Oliviers** (tel. 04 95 60 19 92 or 04 95 60 25 64) is 800m from the town center on the road to Bastia. (29F per person, 16F per tent, 10F per car. Open Apr.-Oct.) Another place to try is **Camping Bodri** (tel. 04 95 60 19 70), 1.5km on the trains line toward Calvi. (22F per person, 20F per tent, 12F per car.)

The **Tramways de la Balagne** trains hug the coast on the way to **Calvi** (45min.; July-Aug. 7 per day, Sept.-June 4 per day). The line is divided into three sections; each costs 9F, a *carnet* of six tickets 45F. Several beaches and campsites lie along the route—just ask the ticket collector in your carriage to let you off when you see one that looks particularly enticing. **SNCM** sends **ferries** to **Nice** (3-10hr.; 2-7 per week; 270-310F, students 244-270F). Call **Agence TRAMAR** on av. J. Calizi (tel. 04 95 60 08 56; fax 04 95 65 09 75) for more info. (Open M-F 9am-noon and 1:45-5:30pm, Sa 8:45am-noon.) Departing from either the ferry port or train depot, the walk past the station rte. du Port east into the square and pillared marketplace is quick and easy. The **tourist office** (tel. 04 95 60 04 35; fax 04 95 60 24 74) is at the opposite side of the square. The friendly staff speaks English and distributes detailed maps. (Open July-Aug. M-Sa 9am-noon and 4-6pm, Su 10am-noon; Sept.-June M-F 9am-noon and 2-6pm, Sa 9am-noon.)

NEAR ÎLE ROUSSE: LA BALAGNE

The **Balagne** is dotted with olive trees and pristine mountain villages, many of which are accessible by foot. **Lumio** is 15 minutes by train from Calvi or 30 minutes from Île Rousse. Here, on the mountain that the Romans called *Ortus Solis* (where the sun rises), the modern village lies meters away from its ancient counterpart Occi, mysteriously abandoned one morning in 1852. Not far off is the **Site archéologique du Monte Ortu,** where neolithic artifacts have recently been discovered. Further inland, and on the famous **GR20** trail, lies **Calenzana,** known as "the garden of the Balagne," with a 17th-century Baroque church named for St. Blaise that overlooks the peaceful **Cimetière des Allemands.** Every May 21, local Catholics make a pilgrimage to the **Sanctuaire de Ste-Restitude,** 1.5km out of town, named for the regional patron saint.

Sant' Antonino, with its stone roofs, is to the east toward Île Rousse. The highest village in the Balagne, it was built on a peak by the Moors in the 9th century, and its narrow streets remain accessible only by foot. Home to the renowned music school **Bartimore,** the village plays host to many musical concerts throughout the year, and local craftsmen make traditional Corsican instruments (call 04 95 61 77 31 for concert info). **Autocars Mariani,** bd. Wilson in Calvi (tel. 04 95 65 00 47 or 04 95 65 04 72), can take you to these sleepy old villages in a comfy tour bus. (Tours from 75F. Open M-Sa 9am-noon and 2-7pm.) The Calvi and Île Rousse tourist offices have info on routes for hikers and bikers. To learn about local handicrafts featured in each village, ask for the free booklet *Strada di l'Artigiani.*

CORTE (CORTI)

Precariously perched on the edge of a cliff face, Corte's citadel represents a physical manifestation of Corsica's turbulent history of independence movements—at any second it could come crashing down. Known to natives as "the heart of Corsica," Corte is enfolded amidst huge sheer cliffs and snow-capped peaks, appearing from a distance like a fairy tale illustration. The town gave birth to Pasquale Paoli's national constitution in 1731 and to this day boasts the most pro-independence graffiti on the island. Corsica's intellectual center, Corte houses the island's only university, and students (2600 of its 6000 residents) keep prices fairly low. Unexpected fountains and wild roses lend grace to this mountain refuge. History, splendor, and welcoming people await those with a strong heart and strong legs.

⏾ ORIENTATION AND PRACTICAL INFORMATION. The **train station** (tel. 04 95 46 00 97) is at the rotary where av. Jean Nicoli and the N193 meet. Trains run to **Bastia** (1¾hr., 4 per day, 58F), **Calvi** via Ponte-Leccia (2½hr., 2 per day, 78F), and **Ajaccio** (2½hr., 4 per day, 66F). (**Luggage storage** 14F. Open Apr.-Sept. daily 7:45am-6:30pm; Oct.-Mar. 7:45am-noon and 2-6:30pm.) **Eurocorse Voyages** (tel. 04 95 31 03 79) runs buses to **Bastia** (1¼hr., 3 per week, 55F) and **Ajaccio** (45min., M-Sa 2 per day, 65F). Call to find stops, as there's no office in Corte. **Autocars Mordiconi** (tel. 04 95 48 00 04) go to **Porto** (2½hr., July-Sept. M-Sa 1 per day, 100F). Call for their off-season schedule. **Taxis Salviani** (tel. 04 95 46 04 88) wait at the station. You can rent four wheels from **Europcar,** 28 cours Paoli. (Tel. 04 95 46 02 79. 575F per day, 1806F per week. 2F per km above 200km. Open M-F 8:30am-noon and 2-6pm.)

To reach the *centre ville* from the train station, turn right on D14 (alias av. Jean Nicoli), cross two bridges, and follow the road until it ends at **cours Paoli.** To reach the **citadel,** turn left onto cours Paoli until you reach **pl. Paoli,** the pizzeria *place* to be. Struggle up the steep **rue Scoliscia** until you faint at the citadel's gates and the **tourist office,** a.k.a. the **Commission Municipale du Tourisme** (tel. 04 95 46 26 70; fax 04 95 46 34 05). The office has helpful info on activities around Corte, a useful bus schedule, and the free bilingual *Corte: Heart of the Island.* (Open July-Aug. M-F 9am-1pm and 2-7pm, Sa 10am-1pm and 3-7pm; Sept.-June M-F 9am-noon and 2-6pm.) The **Parc Naturel Régional** office (tel. 04 95 46 27 44), at the Citadel, has **hiking** info and advice for excursions. (Open July-Sept. 9am-1pm and 4-7pm.) You can get the low-down on local **youth happenings** at the **Bureau Information Jeunesse de Corte,** rampe Ste-Croix. (Tel. 04 95 61 03 26. Open M-Th 8:30am-noon and 2-6pm, F 8:30am-noon and 2-5pm.) **Hôpital de Corte** is on allée du 9 Septembre (tel. 04 95 45 05 00), while the **police** (tel. 04 95 46 00 17) are southeast from town on N200. The **post office** is at 3 av. du Baron Mariani (tel. 04 95 46 08 20). (Open M-F 8am-noon and 2-5pm, Sa 8am-noon. **Postal code:** 20250.)

⏾ ACCOMMODATIONS AND CAMPING. Students take off in the summer, leaving plenty of affordable university housing behind; contact **CROUS,** 7 av. Jean Nicoli (tel. 04 95 45 21 00; fax 04 95 61 01 57). Students with an ID can stay in housing in the summer for 60F per night, 593F per month. (Office open M-F 9am-noon and 2-3:30pm.) Corte also has champion camping facilities. Always call ahead.

The fabulous owners of the **Gîte d'Étape: U Tavignanu,** Chemin de Balari (tel. 04 95 46 16 85; fax 04 95 61 49), will win your heart with a lovely converted farmhouse and gorgeous campsites. Turn left out of the station and bear right when the road forks, first following allée du 9 Septembre and then the signs at the base of the Citadel (20min.). Settle into the bar, or revel in the babbling brook and five poodles. (80F with breakfast; *demi-pension* 160F. Camping 20F per person, 10F per tent.)

Near the public pool and tennis courts, the **Hôtel-Residence Porette (H-R),** 6 allée du 9 Septembre (tel. 04 95 61 01 21), has functional rooms. Bear left from the station to the stadium and follow it around for 100m. There's also a sauna (29F), weight room, and a pseudo-swank restaurant. The staff has information on hiking in the area and offers guided tours in the National Forest as well as discounts on car rentals and train tickets. (Singles 135-180F; doubles 145-279F; triples 289-349F; quads 299F. Breakfast 29F. Open daily in summer 7am-10:30pm; off-season 7am-2pm and 4-10:30pm.) **Hôtel de la Poste,** 2 pl. du Padoue (tel. 04 95 46 01 37), is off cours Paoli and near (surprise) the post office. The 12 lovely rooms have bright bedspreads and showers, and the hallways smell deliciously of fresh bread in the morning. (Singles and doubles 170-230F; triples 200-250F. Breakfast 25F. V, MC.)

The closest **campsite** to town is **Camping Restonica** (tel. 04 95 46 11 59; fax 04 95 46 11 24 40). Follow the directions from the station to H-R Porette and continue until a sign points downhill (1¼km). The site is on a cozy stream-side setting. (29F per person, 14F per tent, 13F per car. Electricity 20F.) **U Sognu** (tel. 04 95 46 09 07) is on rte. de la Restonica. From pl. Paoli, turn right on av. Xavier Luciani and then right again. From the train station, follow the directions to the *gîte* above, until a blue and white sign indicates an earlier turn-off. A five-minute walk brings you to the campground's clean facilities and neat rows of pretty trees. (29F per adult, 13F per child, 16F per tent, 15F per car. Snack bar. Gates close 10pm. Open Mar.-Oct.)

FOOD AND ENTERTAINMENT. The university presence brings a plethora of cheap eats and smiles to the faces of budget travelers. **Pl. Paoli** seems to have a bylaw ensuring that every third building sells pizza. Above pl. Paoli, restaurants in the *vieille ville* around the Église de l'Annonciation deal a good dose of local atmosphere. Despite all the students, Corte lacks any real nightlife, save for a few cafés on cours Napoléon. There are two supermarkets in Corte: **Eurospar,** av. Xavier Luciani (tel. 04 95 46 08 59; open daily 7:30am-12:30pm and 3-8pm), and the huge **Casino,** next to the H-R on allée du 9 Septembre (open M-F 8:30am-12:30pm and 3-7:30pm, Sa 8:30am-7:30pm). **Exotic Fast Food,** pl. Paoli, is a godsend. Ignore the descriptor and go for the large *panini* sandwiches served on delicious bread (18-25F). To attract the university crowd, the establishment has named its sandwiches after great European scientific figures—Pasteur, Freud, and the Curies. (Open 9am-midnight.) **U Passa Tempu,** Rampe Ste-Croix off cours Paoli (tel. 04 95 46 21 20), serves provincial Corsican cuisine in a huge wooden dining room. Local specialties include *sanglier* (wild boar; 58F), and Corsican soup (39F). Nobody hikes up to the Belvedere and **Osteria Diu Castello** (tel. 04 95 46 32 50) for the food, but you'll come back for the atmosphere. Dine *en pleine air* surrounded by trees and lush greenery, near the very top of Corte. (Open only in summer.)

SIGHTS AND EXCURSIONS. The *vieille ville* of Corte, with its steep, inaccessible topography and stone **citadel** peering over the Tavignano and Restonica valleys, has always been a bastion of fierce Corsican patriotism. At the top of the *vieille ville*, the focus of the **Citadel** is the brand new **La Musée de la Corse** (tel. 04 95 45 25 45). Easily giving the best one-stop orientation of Corsica past and present, the museum moves beyond its interesting and well-presented displays to contemplate issues like the role of tourism in shaping Corsica's character and economy. The museum also provides entrance to the higher fortifications of the citadel, which is worth visiting for its temporary exhibitions. (Museum open June 16-Aug. 31 daily 10am-8pm; Sept. 1-June 15, M-Sa 10am-noon and 2-5:45pm. Citadel closes 1hr. earlier than museum. Citadel 20F; museum and citadel 35F, students 25F.) Trudging uphill from pl. Paoli and turning left at the Église de l'Annonciation will bring you to the **Belvedere** (view point) on the oldest portion of the 15th-century city walls, a 360° panorama with plenty of photo-ops.

Leaving town, countless trails through the areas mountains and valleys are nothing short of spectacular. Choose from **hiking** (tel. 04 95 21 56 54 for maps and trail info; tel. 04 95 51 79 10 for weather conditions), **biking** (if you can procure one—there are no rentals in town), and **horse riding** (tel. 04 95 46 24 55; 90F per hour, 200F per half-day, 400F per day).

GORGES DE LA RESTONICA

Southwest of Corte, the tiny D623 stretches 16km through the Gorges de la Restonica. One of Corsica's loveliest and least-populated areas, you can visit many parts of it in less than a day. Biking here is best left to Tour de France veterans, but swimming is possible, if chilly, in the surrounding lakes and rivers. Breathtaking views from the pristine peaks will make you feel like you've conquered the world. Follow the D623 in the direction of the river to the trail, marked in orange, that leads to the **Lac de Melo** (1hr.). This snow-fed beauty lies at 1711m, near the foot of

MOMMY DEAREST As you wander through the citadel amid wildflowers, imagine desperate Genoese soldiers defending the thick stone ramparts against a Corsican attempt to reclaim the city. In 1749, the coarse band of attackers followed Jean-Pierre Gaffori, a local physician who later became leader of the free Corsican nation, up the mountainside to besiege the city. As the Corsicans reached the top, the Genoese soldiers played their trump card: they held Gaffori's young son by the ankle from the citadel's eagle's-nest lookout. The bewildered Corsicans stopped dead, not daring to fire their cannons and risk hurting their leader's child. Suddenly, a woman leapt in front of the Corsican patriots, crying "Fire! Fire!" She was Faustine Gaffori, wife of their General and mother of the dangling child. "Don't think of my son!" she shouted, "Think of the homeland!" Reinvigorated, the Corsicans continued their assault and conquered the citadel, where they found the boy safe and sound.

Mont Rotondo (2622m), and is ringed by peaks including Corsica's highest—**Mont Cinto** (2700m). You can continue to **Lac de Capitellu** (1930m) and join the red-and-white-marked **GR20**, the challenging trail (best attempted mid-June-Oct.) that winds its way across the entire breadth of Corsica. In winter, cross-country ski trails replace many of the summer hiking paths. Be prepared for cold, even snowy weather as late as June. For info and itinerary help, see the **Parc Naturel Régional** office in Corte (see **Tourist Information**, p. 343). The pamphlet *Vallée de la Restonica* is helpful for planning daytrips. Topographic maps, essential for all longer hikes, are available from local bookstores.

BASTIA

Corsica's second largest city, Bastia (pop. 45,000) is somehow neither cosmopolitan nor over-touristed. Rather, the city seems content with processing half the island's tourist traffic through its port and airport. Although the American bombardment of '43 destroyed 80% of Bastia, forcing residents to rebuild *en masse*, the city's port, busy pl. St-Nicholas, Église St-Jean Baptiste, and the *glacier* on av. Émile Sari have outlived the concrete. Those who savor urban grit will be satiated with the area between the old port and the citadel, filled with crumbling apartment buildings. The city also maintains a reasonably deserved reputation for organized crime, but for the casual visitor Bastia should pose no particular safety concerns.

⬛ ORIENTATION AND PRACTICAL INFORMATION. Flights arrive at **Bastia-Poretta** (tel. 04 95 54 54 54), 23km away. An airport bus scheduled to coincide with flights leaves from pl. de la Gare, by the *préfecture* (30min., 38F; tel. 04 95 31 06 65). **Air Inter** and **Air France,** both at 6 av. Emile Sari (tel. 04 95 31 79 79), fly to **Marseille, Nice,** and **Paris.** (Office open M-F 8:30am-noon and 2-5pm.) **Ferries** leave from quai de Fangs, next to pl. St-Nicolas; turn left from av. Maréchal Sebastiani just past pl. St-Nicolas. **SNCM** (tel. 04 95 54 66 66) sails to **Nice, Marseille,** and **Toulon.** (Office open M-F 8-11:45am and 2-5:30pm.) **Corsica Ferries,** 5bis rue Chanoine Leschi (tel. 04 95 32 95 95), float to **Sardinia** and mainland **Italy.** For details on air and ferry connections to mainland France, see **Corsica: Getting there** (p. 330).

Trains leave pl. de la Gare (tel. 04 95 32 80 61), off av. Maréchal Sebastiani, for **Corte** (2hr., 5 per day, 58F), **Calvi** (3hr., 2 per day, 96F), and **Ajaccio** (4hr., 5per day, 122F). The station offers **luggage storage** (20F per bag per day). **Eurocorse** (tel. 04 95 21 06 30) runs **buses** to **Ajaccio** (3hr., 2 per day, 114F). Other destinations are provided by **Rapides Bleus,** 1 av. Maréchal Sebastiani. (Tel. 04 95 31 03 79. Open M-F 8am-noon and 2:30-6pm, Sa 8am-noon and 2:30-6:00pm.) **Rent cars** from **ADA Location,** 35 rue César Campinchi (tel. 04 95 31 09 02; fax 04 95 31 17 43), or at the airport (tel. 04 95 54 55 44). (300F per day, 1790F per week, unlimited mileage. Open M-Sa 8am-noon and 2-7pm.) A **taxi** to the airport will cost around 200F on weekdays. (Tel. 04 95 34 07 00 or 04 95 32 70 70. 24hr.)

Paved, rectangular **pl. St-Nicolas** is a friendly place to find your bearings as well as the tourist office. The main thoroughfares are **bd. Charles de Gaulle,** which runs along the *place,* and the parallel **bd. Paoli** and **rue César Campinchi.** The **tourist office,** pl. St-Nicholas (tel. 04 95 55 96 96; fax 04 95 55 96 00), offers a free accommodations service. (Open June-Aug. M-Sa 8am-8pm, Sept.-May M-Sa 8am-6pm.) For **currency exchange,** try **Banque de France,** 2 cours Pierangeli. (Tel. 04 95 32 82 00. Exchange desks open M-F 8:15am-12:10pm.) Young people can find info on jobs and travel at the **Centre Information Jeunesse,** 3 bd. Auguste Gaudin. (Tel. 04 95 32 12 13. Open M 2-6pm, Tu-Th 8am-noon and 2-6pm, F 8am-noon and 2-5pm.) The **Centre Hospitalier Général (CHG)** is on rue Impériale (tel. 04 95 55 11 11), and the **police** are on Cartier Montésoro (tel. 04 95 54 50 22). The **post office** (tel. 04 95 32 80 70) is on av. Maréchal Sebastiani. (Open M-Tu and Th-F 8am-7pm, W 8am-12:30pm and 1:30-7pm, Sa 8am-noon. **Postal code:** 20200.)

⌐ ACCOMMODATIONS AND CAMPING. Bastia's hotels are more affordable than those in Corsica's more popular resort towns. Off-season discounts and vacancies are also common, but it's prudent to call ahead. At **Hôtel Central,** 3 rue Miot (tel. 04 95 31 71 12; fax 04 95 31 82 40), the kind motherly owner will make you feel welcome if the rest of the staff doesn't. True to its name, the centrally-located hotel has beautifully tiled hallways and lovely rooms, some with TV and ceiling fans, most with shower, toilet, and charming balconies. If they're full, the owner is happy to direct you to other hotels. (Singles 200-280F; doubles 250-380F; triples 330-440F; quads 460F. Extra person 60F. Breakfast 30F. V, MC, AmEx.) The miniature **Hôtel Athena,** 2 rue Miot (tel. 04 95 34 88 40; fax 04 95 31 26 41), religiously follows a mint-green color scheme. The quirky owner insists that it's *"un hôtel avec charme,"* and she's right. (Singles 160F, with shower 200F, with shower and toilet 260F; doubles 190F, with shower 220F, with shower and toilet 280F; triples 230F, with shower 260F, with shower and toilet 360F; quads 260-400F.) **Campsites,** as always, are some way out of town. Beachside **Les Orangiers** is 4km north in Miomo. (Tel. 04 95 33 24 09 or 04 95 33 23 65. 24F per person, 12F per tent. Open May-Sept.) **Camping San Damiano** (tel. 04 95 33 68 02), on rte. de la Lagune de Pinette, is 5km south of Bastia. (32F per person, 12F per tent, 22F per car. Open Apr.-Oct.)

⌐ FOOD. Inexpensive cafés crowd **pl. St-Nicholas.** Eating in the **citadel** is a real treat, with some great restaurants and a very residential feel. Early birds hit the **market** on pl. de l'Hôtel de Ville (Tu-Su 6am-1pm). **SPAR supermarket** is at 14 rue César Campinchini. (Open M-Sa 7:30am-1pm and 6-9pm, Su 7:30am-1pm.) Bastia's sweetest, cheapest thrill is unquestionably the *banane* gelato (5F) in a small unnamed **glacier** at 1 Av. Émile Sari. (Tel. 04 95 31 64 95. Open daily 10am-8pm; in summer 10am until late.)

La Sampiero, in the citadelle (tel. 04 95 32 27 43), provides thoroughly Mediterranean cuisine and an atmosphere you won't forget. Main dishes begin at 65F. (Open from 9:30am daily. V, MC.) **Chez Mémé** (tel. 04 95 31 44 12), at the north end of quai des Martyrs de la Libération, has an unbeatable five-course Corsican *menu* for 80F. (Open daily 9am-1pm and 6pm-1:30am. V, MC, AmEx.)

◫◪ SIGHTS AND BEACHES. The 18th-century **Église St-Jean Baptiste,** pl. de l'Hôtel de Ville, is a stunning centerpiece for the photogenic port. Its immense proportions, gilded domes, and sky-high *trompe l'œil* nearly nullifies the graffiti outside that reads *"Jesus est mort."* Between the citadel and pl. St-Nicholas you'll find the Baroque **Oratoire de St-Roch** and the more lavishly adorned **Oratoire de L'Imaculée Conception,** both built during in the early 17th century as displays of Genoese power. Hugging an incline next to the citadel, the **Jardins Ramieu** are less a garden than a grove. (Open July-Aug. 8am-8pm; Sept.-June 8am-5pm.)

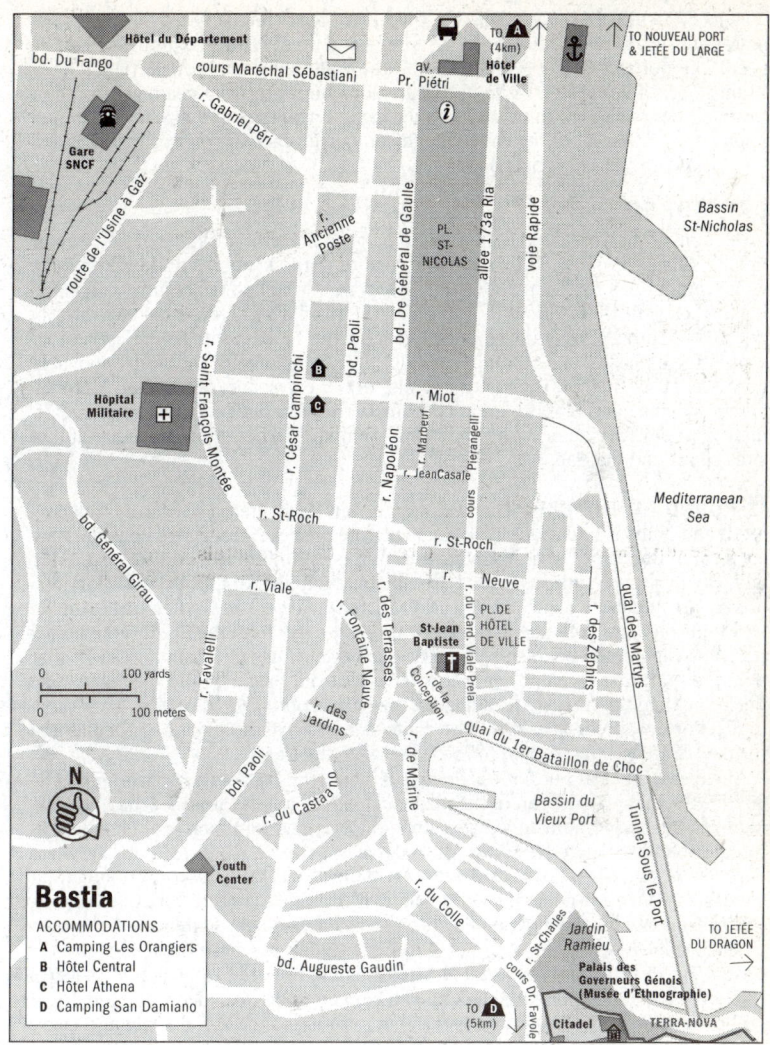

The **Citadel**, also called Terra Nova, was the spot from which the Genoese projected their power over the island. The beautiful 15th-century **Palais des Gouv-
erneurs Génois** overlooking the port, houses the **Musée d'Ethnographie** (tel. 04 95 31
94 95), which in turn houses geological specimens, archæological artifacts, and
exhibits on Corsican life. The citadel also holds the cells of condemned patriotic
fighters Climb the steps in the far left corner of the museum courtyard until you
reach the shady garden above, then follow the steps to the clock tower for an unri-
valed view of the coast. (Open M-F 9am-noon and 2-6pm. 15F.) Nearby is the 16th-
century **Oratoire Sainte-Croix,** which was redecorated in the 18th century with a lavish application of gilt work and an intricate mosaic at its entrance.

  Beach time in Bastia is reserved for hard-core sun-worshipers. If sharing a pebble beach with hordes of schoolchildren isn't your style, make the trek to the beautiful beaches of **L'Arinella** at **Montesoro.** Follow the road that leaves Bastia just
beyond the citadel for 1km.

◻ **ENTERTAINMENT. Café Wha,** on the *vieux port* (tel. 04 95 34 25 79), caters margaritas (30F) and a hip vibe to the young and thirsty souls eager to see and be seen. The portrait of George Michael on the wall is the final touch. (Open daily 11am-1am.) **Le Velvet** (tel. 04 95 31 01 00), along the waterfront road, just south of town, allows you to continue way into the night, if you've got wheels or don't mind a long, long walk. Features dance and disco music, catering primarily to a 25- to 30-year-old crowd. (No cover!)

CAP CORSE

Stretching north from Bastia, the Cap Corse peninsula is a necklace of tiny former fishing villages connected by a narrow road of perilous curves and breathtaking views; mountains rise 1km above the sleepy, rocky shores. Gracefully withstanding the heavy flow of visitors they deserve, the 18 villages on the cape have largely resisted the lures of over-development, making the 140km route from Bastia to St-Florentine exquisite in its natural splendor. Life is less hectic and more enjoyable here; the air is fresher, the water is bluer, and the greenery is greener. Unfortunately, staying overnight is hard to coordinate with few budget hotels, most requiring you to pay for dinner with your room. Camping is a better option; a handful of sites sit around the Cap.

◻ **ROUNDING THE CAP.** The best way to view its sheltered coves and tree-covered mountains is undoubtedly by some private means of transport; consider **renting a car** in Bastia or Calvi. A driving tour of the entire Cap will take at least half a day. Be alert and cautious; roads are narrow, winding, and poor, and Corsican drivers are apparently suicidal. It's best to drive on a weekend, when traffic on the D80 thins out, and you might consider starting the trip from the St-Florentine area (the west side of the peninsula), where your vehicle hugs the mountainside rather than the sparkling cerulean sea below. To start from Bastia on the west side, take bd. Paoli, then bd. Auguste Gaudin past the citadel onto D81 (direction "St-Florentine"). For the daredevil east-to-west route, simply drive through pl. St-Nicolas and turn left at the second rotary, following signs to the Cap.

Cheaper than a car but far less flexible is a **bus tour. Transports Michele** (tel. 04 95 35 61 08 in Ersa), at the top of the peninsula, offers full-day tours of the Cap leaving from **Bastia,** stopping at villages along the way and for lunch (not included) at the glorious blue slate beach at Albo (departs 1 rue de Nouveau Port, July-late Sept. M-Sa 9am, 84F). From **Calvi, Autocars Mariani** (tel. 04 95 65 05 32) runs similar excursions once a week, leaving at 7am and returning about 7:30pm, usually on Fridays but call for the updated day of the week. (June-Sept., 148F).

The cheapest way to see Cap Corse is to take **public bus** #4 from pl. St-Nicolas in **Bastia.** They'll only take you as far as **Sisco** (30min., 15F), but you'll get to **Erbalunga** (25min., 11F) and experience the Cap at a bargain price. Ask nicely and the driver will drop you off wherever you feel the urge to explore. (M-F 6:30am and every 30min. 8am-noon and 1:30-7pm, Sa 6:30am and every hr. 8am-noon and 2-7pm, Su every hr. 8am-noon and 2-7pm. 15F.)

◻ **NOT-TO-BE-MISSED SIGHTS.** The only danger with Cap Corse is that once you visit **Erbalunga,** you may never leave. The steep path to the ever-peaceful **Monastère des Benedictines du St-Sacrement** offers a lush view of the town and the Mediterranean. Built in 1862, it now houses eight nuns and one priest. A girls' school operated here from 1899 to 1963; the buildings have now been turned into a reception center. From the bus stop, walk two minutes and take a left on the little road after La Petite Auberge. When you reach the arch with the cross on top, follow the signs to the *église.* The divine shade of the monastery's walls is ample compensation for the hike. The entrance is the far door on the right.

Erbalunga is home to **La Petite Auberge** (tel. 04 95 33 20 78), where M and Mme. Morganti offer the freshest fish around (80-100F), pizza (45-55F), and pasta (45-60F). (Open daily 7am-3pm and 5:30pm until the restaurant empties. V, MC,

AmEx.) On the weekends, **Pizz'anto** (tel. 04 95 33 92 70) offers a small selection of pizzas (35-45F), salads (35F), and desserts (5-20F) served 10 feet from the azure waters of the Mediterranean. Walk three minutes from the bus stop toward Sisco to find this secluded getaway. The town also has a small supermarket across the street from the post office.

The famous sanctuary in **Lavasine,** just south of Erbalunga, draws pilgrims every September 8. The curved, pebble beach of **Miomo,** about 10 minutes from Bastia, draws people in search of more secular pleasures. Unfortunately, the only sand on the Cap is at **Pietra Carbona,** well out of the path of the public bus. If you do have a car, be sure not to miss **Rogliano.** Its precarious perch on the mountain defies gravity, and its ruins of a Genoese castle, Château de San Colombano, and a large 16th-century church, San Agnello, seem to defy time. If these stately edifices appear out-of-scale for the small village, note that Rogliano's population has dwindled to 800 since the glory days when it stood 4000 strong. Rogliano's beachside sister town, **Macinaggio,** is where Corsican leader Paolo Paoli returned to his beloved island in 1790, after 20 years in exile. 40km from Bastia, it's one of the few port towns where you can find supplies and services—including gas, a supermarket, and a **tourist office** (tel. 04 95 35 40 34), right on the port. **Camping** is a good bet here at the beachside **U Stazzu.** (Tel. 04 95 35 43 76. 27F per person, 16F per tent.)

In the miniature port of **Centuri,** on the other side of the peninsula, boats bring in their daily haul of lobsters, mussels, and fish. You can mingle with these soon to be sumptuous dinners while swimming out to a small nearby island, accessible on calm days. Although there's no beach, the rocky shore is certainly scenic.

For updates on Cap-related tourism, contact the **Communauté du Commune du Cap Corse,** Maison du Cap Corse, 20200 Ville di Pietra Bugno (tel. 04 95 31 02 32).

ALÉRIA

Present-day Aléria pales in comparison to its past incarnations, but the window it provides into the Roman era is precisely the reason to pay a visit. Beyond historical and archæological offerings, Aléria is a tiny laid-back resort town, where the beaches are even mellower than the little town center.

🛈 ORIENTATION AND PRACTICAL INFORMATION. With essentially one main road, tiny Aléria is hard to get lost in. In the middle of town, the main road intersects with a road to Cateraggio and the beach (3km east). **Buses** stop and pickup in front of the post office running daily to **Bastia** (60F), **Porto Vecchio** (68F), and **Bonifacio** (80F). Further down the road, the **tourist office** (tel. 04 95 57 01 51) is open June 16-Aug. M-F 9am-7pm, Sa 9am-noon and 3-7pm, Su 9am-noon, and Sept.-June 15 M-F 9am-noon and 3-5pm. Banking needs can be taken care of at the **Crédit Agricole** (tel. 04 95 57 20 00). The **post office** (tel. 04 95 57 00 00) is open Monday to Friday 8am-noon and 2-5pm. **(Postal code: 20270.)**

🛏🍴 ACCOMMODATIONS AND FOOD. The few hotels in Aléria generally have vacancies, but it's wise to call ahead in July and August. Camping is separated from the town and a chore to get to without a car, but is ideally located once you get there. **L'Empereur,** on the main road (tel. 04 95 57 02 13), has large, modern rooms surrounding a cute courtyard. All rooms with toilet and shower. Singles 260F; doubles 280F. V, MC. **Les Orangers** (tel. 04 95 57 00 31) has average rooms but kind management. Rooms have toilet and shower. (Singles 230F; doubles 250F. V, MC.) **Camping Marina d'Aleria** (tel. 04 95 57 01 42) is the closest **campsite** to town, 3km east in an attractive forested-beachside setting. (39F per person, 10F per tent, 12F per car. Electricity 18F.)

Throughout town, restaurants are virtually all the same, offering seafood at the more expensive end and pizza and pastas for the money-conscious diner. For slightly pricier and tastier fare head to **L'Atrachjata** (tel. 04 95 57 08 03) where fish dishes are some of the best around. (Open daily lunch and dinner. V, MC.)

THE SOUTHEAST

☎ **SIGHTS.** The **Musée Jérôme Carcopino** (tel. 04 95 57 00 92) contains an amazing collection of relics from the Roman city, providing insight into the Roman way of life. Highlights of the museum include meticulously designed oil lamps bearing Christian markings and a series of paintings dating back to the 5th century. Just past the museum stands the **Roman city** itself, lending a sense of where it all took place. Visitors enter into the middle of the forum; to the left a temple rises above the forum to distinguish worship from secular affairs, and to the right, past Augustus's arch, are the extensive baths, which were the first portion of the city to be excavated. Beyond the bath, minimal excavation leaves parts of the city a mystery, but a network of shops and bedrooms are slowly revealing themselves to the patient archæologists who labor here. At the eastern edge of the city, portions of a **Greek acropolis** have also been discovered. (Museum open May 16-Sept. 31 daily 8am-noon and 2-7pm; Oct. 1-May 15 M-F 8am-noon and 2-5pm; Roman city same hours but closes 30min. before museum. 10F for both.) When all this contemplation of things past becomes exhausting, relish the present and head for the sandy beach at **plage de Padulone**, 3km east of town.

PORTO VECCHIO

Conceived in 1539 as the final piece in Genoa's coastal fortification system, Porto Vecchio is today a stronghold of beaches. During July and August, visitors wile away days sunbathing and nights strolling through the trendy citadel, and you should too—if you can afford it. Steep prices and the inaccessibility of the beaches to pedestrians are considerable deterrents to the budget traveler, but Porto Vecchio remains one of Corsica's most appealing coastal towns.

🖪 **ORIENTATION AND PRACTICAL INFORMATION. Intersud Voyages,** at the port (tel. 04 95 70 06 03), can provide **ferry** info. **SNCM** (tel. 08 36 67 95 00) sails to **Marseille** (14½hr.; 3 per week; 265-295F, students 244-265F). **Eurocorse buses** (tel. 04 95 70 13 83 for Bonifacio info; 04 95 21 06 30 for Ajaccio info) stop in front of Trinitours on rue Pasteur, running to **Bonifacio** (30min., M-Sa 5 per day, 40F) and **Ajaccio** (3¼hr.; July-Aug. M-Sa, Sept.-June M-F 1 per day; 110F). **Autocars Rapides-Bleus** (tel. 04 95 31 03 79) stop outside the citadel walls in front of Corsicatours, rue Jean Jaurès, on their way to **Bastia** (3hr., M-Sa 2 per day, 115F).

The **citadel** is centered on pl. de la République and the Église St-Jean-Baptiste, and bisected by cours Napoléon. At the west of the citadel, rue Général Leclerc leads to the port and Bonifacio, while to the east rue Pasteur goes to the port. Downhill from the Église St-Jean-Baptiste, **porte Gênoise** provides the best pedestrian access between the citadel and the port below. The **tourist office** (tel. 04 95 70 09 68; fax 04 95 70 03 72) is just around the corner from pl. de la République. From rue Napoléon, walk through pl. de la République and turn right. The office can provide very helpful hiking information. (Open June-Sept. M-Sa 9am-8pm, Su 9am-1pm; Oct.-May M-F 9am-noon and 2-6pm.) **Self Laverie Picciocchi** (tel. 04 95 70 22 10) is in the Galerie Commerciale Géant. The **hospital** (tel. 04 95 73 80 00) is just north of town on rte. de Bastia. **Internet access** is available next to the tourist office, at **Tabac Terrazzoni**, 6 rue Serra (tel. 04 95 70 01 39), a grocery store with one computer. (Open daily 8am-12:30pm and 2:30pm-midnight.) The **post office** (tel. 04 95 70 95 00) is on rue Général Leclerc, north of rue Scaramoni. (Open M-F 9am-noon and 2-5pm, Sa 9am-noon. **Postal code:** 20137.)

🛏🍴 **ACCOMMODATIONS AND FOOD.** Price is the tie that binds sleeping options in Porto Vecchio. Call ahead and pray there are vacancies at the following recommendations or you'll be forking over a pretty *centime* for your bed. **Le Modern,** 10 cours Napoleon (tel. 04 95 70 06 36), has simple blue rooms with a Mediterranean flair. Before getting a room without a shower, know that there's only one common shower for the whole hotel. (Doubles 200-550F depending on facilities and season. Closed mid-Oct.-early Apr. V, MC.) **Hôtel Panorama,** 12 rue Jean-Nicoli (tel. 04 95 70 07 96; fax 04 95 46 78), is just outside the citadel walls on the way to Bonifacio. (Doubles 240F, with shower 280F, with shower and toilet 330F. Breakfast 40F. Open April-Sept. V, MC.)

The citadel is well-armed with restaurants, all catering to tourists, and most quite expensive. Sticking to Italian cuisine generally translates into more affordable meals. All around the citadel, huge summer crowds make dining a fun, if hectic, affair, while restaurants around the port tend to be either very expensive or depressing. ▧ **Filippi,** pl. de la Mairie (tel. 04 95 70 12 04) is at the back of pl. de la République next to the Église St-Jean-Baptiste. Here you'll find gourmet Italian cuisine in a chic silver and brick dining room. Quality pizzas and pastas cost 54F and up. (Open daily noon-2pm and 6pm-midnight. V, MC, AmEx.) **Chez Mimi,** 5 rue de Général Abbaluci (tel. 04 95 70 28 54), by the Église St-Jean-Baptiste, offers an 80F *menu Corse* and some vegetarian choices. Opt to eat on the street, for there's not much atmosphere within. (Open daily noon-2:30 and 7pm-about midnight. V, MC.)

◪ **BEACHES.** Porto Vecchio's daytime itinerary is simple and easy to follow: hit the sand. On an island full of memorable beaches, those on the Golfe de Porto Vecchio are something to write home about. Reaching them, however, is no easy task. From July to September, **Trinitours** (tel. 04 94 95 70 13 83) go to **Palombaggia** and **San Cipriano** (1 per day, 20F one way), but the schedule rarely works for spending the day at the beach. Updated schedules are posted on the tourist office wall.

Palombaggia manages to fill up during the summer; luckily it's about a mile long, and crowds thin out the further you walk from the parking lot. Heading south from Porto Vecchio, the first turnoff for Palombaggia is actually the longer way, winding around the peninsula past a few small beaches and a large nudist colony where a full body tan can be obtained on half a mile of sand. Further south, **Santa Giulia** is no stranger to crowds either, but just snatches first prize in the beach beauty contest. Slightly removed from the spotlight, beaches north of Porto Vecchio also provide stunning spectacles of sand and ocean. **Punta di Benedettu** is the first beach you get to, but it's generally worth continuing on. **San Cipriano** is fairly laid back, attracting anchored sailboats into its calm cove. Another 2km north, **Pinarellu** looks out onto the Île de Pinarellu and the remains of a medieval castle.

▤ **ENTERTAINMENT.** Cafes and *glaciers* on pl. de la République are the main evening hangouts; bars in the port and old town cater to older, staider crowds. The two discos between Porto Vecchio and Bonifacio are famous throughout Corsica, and for good reason. **Via Notte** (tel. 04 95 72 02 12) is an elaborate outdoor club with a number of cabana bars around swimming pools. **Amnesia,** 9km from Bonifacio, is renowned throughout the island for staying crowded until early morning with internationals, mainland French, and locals. (Covers for both 80-100F.)

BONIFACIO (BONIFAZIU)

Easily the most unique inhabited landscape on the island, Bonifacio enjoys a spectacular vantage point atop white chalky cliffs that drop straight into the sea. The town Paul Valéry called "the picturesque capital of Corsica" appears both beautiful and bizarre, equally at home on a postcard and in a science fiction novel. Situated at the southern tip of the island, Bonifacio is closer to Sardinia than to the next closest Corsican town; accordingly, the town has a strong Italian influence evident in names and food. It is the 16th-century Genoans, however, who left the most prominent mark on the town, in the architecture of the *haute ville* and citadel. Bonifacio can be tough to reach and will surely be expensive, but it's worth the extra effort to pay a visit.

🔃 ORIENTATION AND PRACTICAL INFORMATION. Eurocorse Voyages (tel. 04 95 21 06 30 in Ajaccio; 04 95 70 13 83 in Porto Vecchio) sends **buses** to **Ajaccio** (3½hr.; July-Aug. 3 per day, Sept.-June 2 per day; 110F) with stops at **Sartène** (1½hr., 110F) and **Propriano** (1½hr., 110F), as well as to **Porto Vecchio** (30min., 5 per day M-Sa, 40F), where connections can be made to **Bastia**. There's no office, but buses stop and pick up at the port parking lot. **Ferries** to Sardinia leave from the *gare maritime*, at the far end of the port. **Moby Lines** (tel. 04 85 73 00 29; fax 0495 73 05 50) and **MARE** (tel. 04 95 73 00 96; fax 04 95 73 13 37) share the 26.5km route to **Santa Teresa** (July-Aug. 14 per day, off-season 3 per day; 65F one-way, cars 120-200F). For a **taxi**, call **Borne d'Appels** (tel. 04 95 73 19 08) or **Di Meglio Louis** (tel. 04 95 73 02 86). You can **rent motorbikes** from **Corse Moto Services**, quai Nord, on the port. (Tel. 04 95 73 15 16. From 150F per day, 2000F deposit. V, MC.)

Bonifacio is divided into the **port** and the **haute ville,** with a steep climb in between. Upon entering town, the port will be on your right. An almost immediate left turn onto D58 heads to beaches on the nearby peninsula. The most direct route to the *haute ville* and the **tourist office** (tel. 04 95 73 11 88; fax 04 95 73 14 97), at the corner of av. de Gaulle and rue F. Scamaroni, is by walking along the café-lined port and then up the stairs before the *gare maritime*. (Office open July-Sept. daily 9am-8pm; Oct.-June M-F 8:30am-noon and 2-7pm.) **Currency exchange** at poor rates is found throughout the *ville haute* and the port. The **police** (tel. 04 95 73 00 17) are on the port, and the **hospital** (tel. 04 95 73 95 73) is on D58, toward the beaches. The **post office** is on rue du S. Vari, uphill from pl. Napoléon. (Tel. 04 95 73 73 73. Open M-F 9am-noon and 2-5pm, Sa 9am-noon.)

📌 ACCOMMODATIONS AND CAMPING. Throughout the summer, finding rooms is virtually impossible, and if you do the price may scare you away. Camping is easily the cheapest option, while neighboring Porto Vecchio has a couple of cheaper hotels, making day trips a good bet. Basic rooms in an older building can be found at **Hôtel des Étrangers**, av. Sylvère Bohn (tel. 04 95 73 01 09; fax 04 95 73 16 97), the first building in town on the only road into Bonifacio. (High season doubles 300-450F, rest of year 180-300F.) **Le Royal,** 8 rue Fred Scamaroni (tel. 04 95 73 00 51; fax 04 95 73 04 68), has small modern rooms in calming blue and white hues, and is centrally located a block uphill from the tourist office. (July-Aug. singles and doubles 300-500F, rest of year 250-300F.) **Campo di Liccia** (tel. 04 95 73 03 09; fax 04 95 73 03 09) is the cheapest of a cluster of campsites on the road to Porto Vecchio. (4.5km from the beach. 30F per person, 19F per car, 12F per tent. Electricity 16F. Open May 15- Sept. 30.) **L'Araguina,** av. Sylvère-Bohn (tel. 04 95 73 00 41; fax 04 95 73 01 62), at the beginning of town after Hôtel des Étrangers but before the port, makes up for an unceremonious and crowded camping arrangement by being within easy walking distance to everything in town and not far from a beach. (33F per person, 11F per tent. Electricity 17F. Open Mar. 15-Oct. 31.)

🔆 SIGHTS. Walking around and exploring the **ville haute** is the best way to experience Bonifacio—anything you have to pay to enter generally isn't worth it. A good place to start your tour is to head up the montée Rastello steps from the port by the *gare maritime*. At av. de Gaulle, a lookout provides excellent views of the harsh cliffs extending east from Bonifacio. Continue up montée St-Roch to the lookout at the **Porte des Gênes,** which during Genoan days was the only access to the *ville haute*. Just inside the door, the **Bastion de L'Étendard** contains the only remains of the original fortification. Be content to know it's there; it's not worth paying 20F to see it, and comparable views are free from other spots in the *ville haute*. Continue along rue des Deux Empéreurs and take the third left to the **Église Sainte-Mairie-Majeure.** The oldest building in Bonifacio, the church houses one of its most important objects—a morsel of the **true cross,** stripped from a shipwreck. The remnant was used to ward off storms by Bonifacians who would kneel on the cliffs and hold it to the sea while they prayed.

Expensive **boat tours** (120-140F) provide the best access to the coastal cliff-scape; boats go past hidden coves, through limestone caves, and by those peculiar rocks jutting out of the sea. **Thalassa-Le Corsaire** (tel. 06 86 34 00 49) is one of the many companies lined up conspicuously on the port—bargaining is not unheard of. While you're at the port, check out the small **aquarium,** where you'll see that some crabs can fly and some lobsters are blue. (Open daily 10am-7pm. 24F.)

■📖 **BEACHES AND NIGHTLIFE.** Bonifacio's beaches are hard to get to but hard to leave once you're there. The only beach actually in town is accessible from a path next to camping l'Araguina or a path at the north end of the port. The paths meet up and take you to **plage de la Catena,** and then **plage de l'Arinella,** two small beaches wedged between cliffs. The peninsula east of Bonifacio is filled with beaches, but you'll need your own wheels. At the port, take D58 towards the water; virtually every road stemming from it leads to a beach. **Cala Longa's** isolated locale 8km away makes it particularly desirable. If you stay on D58, you will end up at **plage Maora** (6km), a large beach with facilities in a natural harbor that keeps the water calm. The turnoff for camping Rondinara, 10km north, would appear to lead to a secret cove, but **plage de la Rondinara** is one of Corsica's most famous beaches. Dunes separate the beach from the sea for a dazzling effect.

The *ville haute* gets tucked in after dinner, but port cafés are lively in the summer, generally drawing an older crowd. The young and restless head to two of the islands best **clubs** in between Bonifacio and Porto Vecchio (see **Porto Vecchio: Entertainment,** p. 351). **Amnesia** runs a free shuttle from the port, and usually advertises its schedule on a billboard there.

THE ALPS (LES ALPES)

Natural architecture is the Alps' real attraction. The curves of the Chartreuse Valley rise to rugged crags in the Vercors range and ultimately crescendo into Europe's highest peak, Mont Blanc. Winter skiers enjoy some of the most challenging slopes in the world; summer hikers take over the same mountains for their endless vistas and clean air. With two high seasons a year, you'll have to choose between the dependable crowds, dependable prices, and dependable weather of summer and winter, and the quieter but less predictable months between them.

The Alps are split between two historical provinces, Savoie and Dauphiné. The Dauphiné includes the Chartreuse Valley, the Vercors regional park, the Ecrins national park in the east, and the Belledonne and Oisans mountains. The region first became independent in the 11th century, under Guiges I. His great-grandson Guiges IV, evidently tiring of his family's favorite name, took the title "dauphin" (dolphin); worn out by that burst of originality, the family adopted *dauphin* as its favorite name. In the 14th century, when the last independent dauphin sold his lands to France, the French monarchs adopted the practice of ceding the province to the heir to the throne, who thus came to be known as dauphin. In the 15th century, Louis XI established a permanent *parlement* (court) in Grenoble; it has since been the region's cultural and intellectual capital. Savoie, which includes the peaks of Haute Savoie, the Olympic resorts in the expansive Tarentaise valley, and the awesome Vanoise park, bears the name of the oldest royal house in Europe. Around 1034, the region became the possession of Humbert aux Blanches Mains, founder of the House of Savoie. Humbert settled at Chambéry and began extracting tolls from neighbors who wanted to march through. By the 14th century, his kingdom included Nice, the Jura, Piedmont, and Geneva. In 1860, Victor Emmanuel II ceded Savoy to France in return for the prize of being the first King of Italy.

Once you get to the Alps, head in the most logical direction—up. After the spring thaw, flowery meadows, icy lakes, and staggering views reward experienced and amateur hikers alike. Trails are clearly marked, but serious climbers should invest in a *Topo-Guide* (hiking map). Talk with local hiking info offices for advice on trail and weather conditions and itineraries. Skiing arrangements should be made a couple of months in advance. Chamonix, and Val d'Isère serve as excellent bases. The cheapest months are January, March, and April; most resorts close in October and November, between hiking and skiing seasons. **FUAJ**, the French Youth Hostel Federation (see p. 50), offers week-long skiing and sports packages.

Food here takes a Swiss twist. Regional specialties include *fondue savoyarde* (bread dipped in a blend of cheeses, white wine, and kirsch), *raclette* (strong cheese melted and served with boiled potatoes and onions), and *gratin dauphinois* (sliced potatoes baked in a creamy cheese sauce). Alpine cheeses are mild and creamy: try *tomme*, the oldest of Savoie cheeses, *St-Marcellin* (half goat's milk), *beaufort*, and *reblochon*. Regional wines include the whites of Apremont, Marignan, and Chignin, and the rich reds produced in Montmélian and St-Jean-de-la-Porte. If there's room left for dessert, try *roseaux d'Annecy* (liqueur-filled chocolates), *St-Genux* (a *brioche* topped with pink praline), or *gâteau de Savoie* (a light sponge cake). *Eaux de vie*, strong liqueurs distilled from fruits, are popular here, especially when made from local *framboises* (raspberries).

HIGHLIGHTS OF THE ALPS

■ Hikers and skiers ascend and descend the slopes above **Val d'Isère,** home of Olympic legend Jean-Claude Killy (p. 376).

■ The **Téléphérique** in Chamonix, host of the first Olympic Games, pulls cable cars up 3842m for a vista of Mont Blanc, Europe's highest peak (p. 374).

■ The *centre ville* of **Annecy** is a model of civic charm, with public parks, a Lover's Bridge, and a 12th-century château nearby (p. 366).

■ **Grenoble's** cosmopolitan charms will keep you out of the hills for a while (p. 354).

GETTING AROUND

TGV **trains** will whisk you from Paris to Grenoble and Annecy; from there it's either slow trains, special slow mountain trains, or more often, torturously slow **buses.** Always allow much longer than you think it should take to go anywhere. The farther into the mountains you want to get, the harder it is to get there, both in terms of travel time and frequency. Service is at least twice as frequent, especially on buses, during the skiing season (Dec.-Apr.). **Biking** through the Alps is, needless to say, an option only for the most serious cyclist. **Hiking** can range from simple strolls through mountain meadows to some of the most difficult climbing in the world. *Always* check with local hiking bureaus before starting *any* hike; even in summer you can encounter snowstorms and avalanches.

GRENOBLE

When 40,000 students descend on Grenoble (pop. 160,000) every September, it becomes one of the most dynamic cities in the country. Lodged in a narrow valley between four mountain ranges, it's easy to see why so many students prefer it. The city hosts the eccentric cafés, dusty bookshops, shaggy radicals, and serious politics you'll find in any university town, but it also boasts snow-capped peaks and sapphire-blue lakes cherished by hikers, skiers, bikers, aesthetes, and set designers alike. Stendhal, the city's most famous bookworm, grumbled that "at the end of every street, there is a mountain."

The immigrant influx to France in the 60s gave Grenoble a sizable North and West African population which combines with the droves of students to give the city a cosmopolitan pulse. Despite the commercialization of much of the Alps, Grenoble remains a convenient and economical base for jaunts to nearby mountains as well as an intriguing city in its own right. Its pedestrian *vieille ville* dates from medieval days and entertains trendy shops, dozens of colorful festivals, and all those young'uns. Whether you're here to huff up the hills or puff cigarettes in cafés, Grenoble will impress.

The Alps

⁊ ORIENTATION AND PRACTICAL INFORMATION

To get to the tourist office and the center of town from the station, turn right onto pl. de la Gare and take the third left onto av. Alsace Lorraine, following the tram tracks. Continue along the tracks on rue Félix Poulat and rue Blanchard; the tourist complex will be on your left, just before the tracks fork (10min.).

Flights: Aéroport de Grenoble St-Geoirs, St-Étienne de St-Geoirs (tel. 04 76 65 48 48). Buses leave 1¼hr. before each flight from the bus station (30F). Domestic flights only. **Air France,** pl. Victor Hugo (tel. 08 02 80 28 02). Open M-F 8:30-11:15am and 1:30-6pm, Sa 8:45am-12:15pm.

Trains: Gare Europole, pl. de la Gare. To: **Chambéry** (30min., 15 per day, 55F); **Lyon** (1½hr., 16 per day, 96F); **Annecy** (2hr., 9 per day, 89F); **Marseille** (3½hr., 14 per day, 222F); **Paris** (4hr., 11 per day, 362F); and **Nice** (6½hr., 8 per day, 316F). Office open daily 8:30am-7:45pm.

Buses: Gare routière, left of train station. **VFD** (tel. 04 76 47 77 77) has buses to: **Geneva** (2¾hr., 1 per day, 150F); **Chamonix** (3hr., 1 per day, 159F); and **Nice** (9hr., 1 per day, 307F). Office open 8:30am-noon and 1:30-5:30pm.

Public Transportation: Transports Agglomeration Grenobloise (TAG). Desk in the tourist office open Su-F 8:30am-6:30pm, Sa 9am-6pm. Ticket 7.50F, *carnet* of 10 49F. Two tram lines run roughly every 10min. 5am-midnight; buses run 6am-9pm.

Taxis: Tel. 04 76 54 42 54. 24hr. A ride to the far-out airport costs (gulp) 325F.

Car Rental: Auto, 24 rue Emile Gueymard (tel. 04 76 50 96 96), near the train station. One day from 335F, 250km included. Weekend 541F, 600km included.

Tourist Office: 14 rue de la République (tel. 04 76 42 41 41; fax 04 76 51 28 69). Tram line A (direction "Grande Place") runs to "Maison du Tourisme." The complex is the center of a visitor's universe, complete with a **bank, SNCF** counter, and **post office.** Good map, hotel info, train and bus schedules, and reservation service. Pick up a free copy of *Grenoble Magazine,* an English annual with feature articles and info on museums and points of interest; *Échappée Belle* also lists museums and sights. The *Guide DAHU* (20F) is a French publication written annually by local students which lists *restos,* bars, discos, and sights, and can be purchased at *tabacs* throughout the city. Guided tours of the old city July-Aug. Office open M-Sa 9am-6pm and 1:30-6pm, Su 10am-1pm.

Hiking Information: CIMES (Centre Informations Montagnes et Sentiers) (tel. 04 76 42 45 90; fax 04 76 15 23 91), above the tourist office. Runs hiking trips and sells detailed guides of hiking, mountaineering, and cross-country skiing trails. Free informative brochures. Open M-F 9am-noon and 2-6pm, Sa 10am-noon and 2-6pm. **Club Alpin Français,** 32 av. Félix-Viallet (tel. 04 76 87 03 73), has advice on mountain activities and a map library. Organizes hiking, climbing, and parachuting trips. Open M 2-7pm, Tu-W 10am-7pm, Th-F 10am-8pm, Sa 9am-noon. **Weather:** tel. 08 36 78 02 38.

Ski and Climbing Equipment Rental: Borel Sport, 42 rue Alsace-Lorraine (tel. 04 76 46 47 46). Rents climbing equipment. Shoes 25F per day. Skis 65-110F per day. 1000F or credit card deposit. Open M-Sa 9am-noon and 2-7pm; May-Nov. closed M. V, MC.

Budget Travel: Jeunes Sans Frontière-Wasteels, 50 av. Alsace-Lorraine (tel. 04 76 47 34 54), and 20 av. Félix-Viallet (tel. 04 76 46 36 39). BIJ and cheap packages. Both offices open M-F 9am-noon and 2-6:30pm, Sa 9am-noon and 2-5:30pm. V, MC.

English Bookstore: Just Books, 1 rue de la Paix (tel. 04 76 44 78 81). Pricey paperbacks, big used books section. Open Sept.-July Tu-Sa 9am-noon and 2-7pm.

Youth Center: Centre Régional d'Information Jeunesse, 8 rue Voltaire (tel. 04 76 54 70 38), near the tourist office. Info on housing, jobs, study, and events. BIJ tickets. Open M and F 1-6pm, Tu-Th 10am-6pm, Sa 2-6pm.

Laundromat: Lavomatique, 14 rue Thiers. Open daily 7am-7pm.

Police: 36 bd. Maréchal Leclerc (tel. 04 76 60 40 40). Take bus #31 to "Hôtel de Police" (direction "Malpertuis").

Hospital: Centre Hospitalier Régional de Grenoble, La Tronche (tel. 04 76 76 75 75).

THE SOUTHEAST

Grenoble

ACCOMMODATIONS

A Camping Les 3 Pucelles
B Auberge de Jeunesse (HI)
C Hôtel Victoria
D Hôtel de l'Europe
E Hôtel de la Poste
F Foyer de l'Etudiante

Tram Stops
Tramway B
Tramway A

N

0   200 yards
0   200 meters

l'Isère

Cimitière St-Roch

PARC PAUL MISTRAL

Hôtel de Ville

rue Bizanet
rue Masséna
parc A. Michalon
av. du Maréchal Randon
rue du Sonnant
av. St-Roch
rue Am. on de Chissé
parc de l'Île Verte
rue Joseph
Chanron
rue Hébé
av. de Jeanne d'Arc
av. de Verdun
pont du Sablon
chemin de Halage
bd. des Adieu
rue Malakoff
bd. Maréchal Leclerc
rue de l'Alma
rue des Eug. Faure
rue Clémond
rue D. Villars
Jardin des Plantes
boulevard Jean Pain
rue Fourier
rue Haxo

Musée de Grenoble
Pl. du Vieux Temple
rue Très Cloîtres
NOTRE DAME
rue Barnard
de la Paix
PL. STE-CLAIRE
rue Raoul Blanchard
PL. DE VERDUN
Préfecture
rue Fantin Latour
rue de la Liberté

l'Isère
quai Xavier Jouvin
pont de la Citadelle
Pl. de Lavalette
rue St-Laurent
quai St-Laurent
pont St-Laurent
Pl. St-Laurent
rue Chinoise
Pl. St-André
rue Brocherie
Palais de Justice
Musée Stendhal
rue des Clercs
Grande Rue
rue Rousseau
rue de la République
rue Vicat
rue St-Jacques
rue de la Poste
rue de Bonne
rue Beyle Stendhal
rue de Strasbourg
PL. DE METZ
rue Casimir Perier
bd. Mal. Lyautey
rue Hoche

Musée Dauphinois
Montée de Chalemont
Téléphérique to La Bastille
quai Stéphane-Jay
quai Perrière
rue Maurice Gignoux
Jardin de Ville
Pl. GRENETTE
rue Montorge
rue de Bonne
rue de Sault
boulevard Agutte Sembat
rue Lesdiguières
rue Rahoult

PARC GUY PAPE
Jardin des Dauphins
Fort de la Bastille
TÉLÉPHÉRIQUE TERMINAL (150m)
quai Crêqui
pont M. Gontard
rue Hector Berlioz
rue de Belgrade
Pl. de Belgrade
rue Desprez
rue Mallet
rue Félix Poulat
PL. VICTOR HUGO
cours La Fontaine
boulevard Gambetta
rue Lakanal

ESPLANADE BRIAND
quai de France
PL. HUBERT DUBEDOUT
quai de la Porte de France
rue de Paranka
boulevard Edouard Rey
rue Docteur Mazet
boulevard Gambetta
rue Thiers
rue Génissieu
rue Bergers
rue Condorcet

TO LYON
autoroute A48
quai Claude Bernard
rue Casimir Brenier
rue Émile Gueymard
quai de la Graille
rue Jean Macé
avenue Félix Viallet
rue Berges
cours Jean Jaurès
rue Lorraine
rue Jay
rue Rochleau
rue Denfert Rochereau
cours Berriat
rue Joseph Rey
av. de la Vizelle
rue Sémard
rue Chorier

PL. DE LA GARE
PL. ST-BRUNO
TO B (4km)
TO A (3.5km)
av. Alsace
rue Crêqu

Post Office: 11 rue Beyle-Stendhal (tel. 04 76 43 51 39). Open M-F 8am-7pm, Sa 8am-noon. **Branch office** at 12 rue de la République. Open M 8am-6pm, Tu-F 8am-6:30pm, Sa 8am-noon. Both have **currency exchange. Postal code:** 38000.

Internet Access: Cybernet Café, 3 rue Bayard (tel. 04 76 51 73 18). 50F per hr. Bar Happy Hour 6-8:30pm, internet Happy Hour (buy 1 get 1 free) noon-2pm and 10pm-1am. Kicks it late night as a bar. Open M-Sa noon-1am.

ACCOMMODATIONS AND CAMPING

Plenty of budget hotels are scattered throughout the pedestrian zone. Most do good business year-round, so it's wise to call ahead. You'll normally have more luck with vacancies in hotels outside the pedestrian zone. For rentals, see the tourist office's board *Locations Meubles.*

Auberge de Jeunesse (HI), 10 av. du Grésivaudan (tel. 04 76 09 33 52; fax 04 76 09 38 99), about 4km from Grenoble in Echirolles. From the station, follow tram tracks down av. Alsace-Lorraine to cours Jean Jaurès; turn right and the bus stop is 25m to your right. Take bus #8 (direction "Pont Rouge") to "La Quinzaine." The hostel is one block behind the Casino supermarket. If walking, follow cours Jean Jaurès and turn right just before Casino (1 long hr.). Modern building with garden, bar, game room, kitchen, laundry, and TV. Four- to 6-bed rooms. 68F per person. Breakfast included. Sheets 17F. Open M-Sa 7:30am-11pm, Su 7:30-10am and 5:30-11pm. V, MC, AmEx.

Le Foyer de l'Étudiante, 4 rue Ste-Ursule (tel. 04 76 42 00 84; fax 04 76 44 36 85), near pl. Notre-Dame, on a ,,,quiet street near the center. From the tourist office, follow pl. Ste-Claire to pl. Notre-Dame and take rue du Vieux Temple on the far right. Dorm rooms, some with lofts. Backpackers and summer students mix for a friendly atmosphere. Kitchen, TV, piano, and laundry facilities. Dorms 50F; singles 80F; doubles 70F per person. Shower and sheets for dorm room 15F. 24hr. reception. Accepts men and women mid-June to mid-Sept.; mid-Sept. to mid-June women only for month-long stays.

Hôtel de L'Europe, 22 pl. Grenette (tel./fax 04 76 46 16 94). A dark, well-run 2-star giant with a wide range of price levels and a swell location in the old city. Sauna and small gym. Singles from 140F, with shower 190F; doubles from 160F, with shower 220F; triples 340F; quads 360F. Breakfast 30F. 24hr. reception.

Hôtel de la Poste, 25 rue de la Poste (tel. 04 76 46 67 25), in the bosom of the pedestrian zone. Friendly managers, petunias, and a yapping little dog welcome you to aging but spacious rooms, all with new beds. Singles 130F; doubles 160-220F, with shower 200F; triples 190F; quads 220F. English breakfast 30F, continental breakfast 25F. 24hr. reception. V, MC.

Hôtel Victoria, 17 rue Thiers (tel. 04 76 46 06 36). Kind managers, elegant lobby, and large, immaculate rooms, some with TV. Singles with shower 178F; doubles with shower 198-223F; triples with shower and toilet 268F; quads with shower and toilet 298F. Breakfast 28F. Reception 7am-11:30pm. V, MC.

Camping Les 3 Pucelles, in Seyssins (tel. 04 76 96 45 73), just on the southwest corner of Grenoble. Take tram A to "Fontaine," then take bus #51 to "Mas des Îles" (direction "Les Nalettes"). Not terribly scenic but the closest campsite to town and the only one open all year. 60 sites. 30F per person and tent. Call ahead in the summer.

FOOD

Grenoble boasts many affordable restaurants with a refreshing variety of specialties, and some offer discounts or inexpensive student *menus*. With so many students, cafeteria cuisine is almost a local specialty. **University Restaurants** open during the school year; **CROUS** (tel. 04 76 57 44 00) sells meal tickets (13F). Call to find out what's open and when. **Prisunic,** across from the tourist office (open M-Sa 8:30am-7:30pm), or **Casino,** near the youth hostel (open M-Sa 8:30am-8:30pm), will supply your *al fresco* feasts. **Markets** are held on pl. St-André, pl. St-Bruno, pl. Ste-Claire, and pl. aux Herbes (all Tu-Su).

Regional restaurants cater to locals around **pl. de Gordes,** between pl. St-André and the Jardin de Ville. There's a smattering of Chinese and Vietnamese restaurants between pl. Notre Dame and the river, and they virtually own **rue Condorcet.** *Pâtisseries* and North African joints congregate around **rue Chenoise** and **rue St-Laurent,** between the pedestrian area and the river (*menus* 50-55F). Cafés and restaurants cluster around **pl. Notre-Dame** and **pl. St-André,** both in the heart of the *vieille ville.* Crusts are tossed in dozens of lively, cheap pizzerias across the river on quai Perrière, below the *téléphérique;* locals recommend **Chez Rofolo** and **Pompeii.**

La Galerie Rome, rue du Vieux Temple (tel. 04 76 42 82 01). A true gourmande, the owner presides over flawless French cuisine including Grenoble's trademark dish, the artery clogging *gratin dauphinois.* He takes his art as seriously as his food—the restaurant is also a vibrant gallery showing off his artist friends from around the globe. *La Nocturne* (60F), a mixed plate of local fare, is a cheap way to enjoy this beautiful restaurant built around a Roman era stone wall. Open Tu-Su lunch and dinner. V, MC, AmEx.

Le Tonneau de Diogène, 6 pl. Notre-Dame (tel. 04 76 42 38 40). Simple food served at outdoor tables, though there are no bathtub diners. Salads (15-36F) and a variety of omelettes (18-25F); a 40F *menu* includes *steak-frites,* salad, and cheese. After 10pm, it's both a restaurant and a lively bar. Open daily 9am-1am. The stairs in the back of the bar lead to **Le Sphinx** (tel. 04 76 44 55 08), Grenoble's unparalleled philosophy library/bookstore. (Open Tu-F 9:30am-midnight, Sa 9am-7pm.)

Le Couscous, 19 rue de la Poste (tel. 04 76 47 92 93). How can you have time for a better name when you're busy making couscous this good? Huge plates of the North African staple, served every way you like it (35-80F). Open Tu-Su.

Le Valgo, 2 rue St-Hughes (tel. 04 76 51 38 85), at pl. Notre-Dame. Friendly service, a cozy interior, and excellent food make this a favorite for *Hautes-Alpes* specialties. Serves hearty meat pies (*oreilles d'Anes*), turnovers (*tourtes*), and *ravioles* (40-70F). *Menus* start at 65F. Open Tu-W lunch, Th-Sa lunch and dinner. V, MC.

Moitié Toi Moitié Moi, 7 rue Très-Cloîtres (tel. 04 76 15 22 99), dishes up food from Cameroon in portions you could split with a friend. Meat dishes (45F, students 35F) come with soup, *gingembre* (home-made gingerbeer), African sweet *frites* or rice, and a *digestif.* Open for lunch and dinner. Closed Su.

SIGHTS

Grenoble supports enough fine museums for a city twice its size, but don't miss just walking around Grenoble. Students and recent immigrants now occupy most of the 18th-century houses on the river bank, Grenoble's most attractive neighborhood Straddling the river, the Victorian **Pont St-Laurent,** an early suspension bridge, has taken the place of a former Gallo-Roman bridge.

MUSÉE DAUPHINOIS. Towards the bottom of the Bastille hill on the north bank of the Isère, this former 17th-century convent is a far cry from the standard docile regional museum—this one boasts constantly updated futuristic exhibits under funky lighting, complete with multimedia extravagance. The latest, *"La Grande Histoire du Ski"* (The Great History of Skiing), recounts the sport from its early days to the present high-tech pursuit. (*30 rue Maurice Gignoux. Tel. 04 76 85 19 00. Open May-Oct. W-M 10am-7pm; Nov.-Apr.10am-6pm. 20F, students 10F, W free after 2pm.*)

TÉLÉPHÉRIQUE GRENOBLE-BASTILLE. The bubble gondolas that pop out of the city every 10 minutes for the **Bastille,** a 16th-century fort hovering ominously 800 feet above the town, have become an icon of Grenoble. From the top of the cable car station, the **Mont-Jalla** path leads for another hour on to the peak of Mont Jalla, but the views don't improve too much. From the top, you can look north toward the Lyon valley and its two converging rivers; the real peaks lie to the south, over the ridge of snow-capped mountains on the other side of Grenoble.

Back at the cable station restaurant and souvenir shop, descend via the **Parc Guy Pape,** which criss-crosses through the other ends of the fortress and deposits you at Place Aristide Briande, just across the river from the train station. *(Parc: Open June-Aug. daily 9am-7:30pm; Sept.-Oct. and Apr.-May 9am-7pm; Nov.-Feb. 9am-4pm; Mar. 9am-5:30pm. Téléphérique: Quai Stéphane-Jay. Tel. 04 76 44 33 65. Open July-Aug. M 11am-12:30am, Tu-Su 9am-12:30am; Sept. 1-14 and June 15-30 M 11am-midnight, Tu-Su 9am-midnight; Sept. 15-Oct. and Apr.-June 14 M 11am-7:30pm, Tu-Sa 9am-midnight, Su 9am-7:30pm; Nov.-Mar. M 11am-6:30pm, Tu-Su 10am-6:30pm. 23F students 18F; roundtrip 34/27F.)*

PALAIS DE JUSTICE. Overlooking the manicured **Jardin de Ville,** the elaborate Renaissance palace is noted for a set of intricate ceilings. Organized palace visits depart from pl. St-André at 10am on the first Saturday of each month (30F)—you have to sneak a look the rest of the time.

MUSUEMS. The Musée de Grenoble is housed in a half-pipe shaped building across the river. Half of the museum displays Italian Renaissance and French art while the other half houses contemporary works. *(5 pl. de Lavalette. Tel. 04 76 63 44 44. Open Th-M 11am-7pm, W 11am-10pm. 25F, students 15F.)* In a former warehouse built by Gustave Eiffel, **MAGASIN (Centre National d'Art Contemporain)** is today an exhibition center for great displays of contemporary art. *(155 cours Berriat. Tel. 04 76 21 95 84. Open Tu-Su noon-7pm. 15F, students 10F.)* Next to the Jardin de Ville, the old Hôtel de Ville is now home to the **Musée Stendhal,** which investigates Grenoble's most reluctant 19th-century citizen through a somewhat dry retrospective of his personal and professional life. *(1 rue Hector Berlioz. Tel. 04 76 54 44 14. Open T-Su 2-6pm. Free.)* Below Église St-Laurent and its mesmorizing *vitraux* stained glass, the **Musée Archéologique Saint Laurent** contains the remaining vestiges of Grenoble from the Roman era. Relics are in surprisingly good shape. *(Pl. St-Laurent. Open daily 9am-noon and 2-6pm. 20F, 10F students, free W 2-6pm.)*

♫ ❋ ENTERTAINMENT AND FESTIVALS

ENTERTAINMENT. Hot nightspots in Grenoble come and go quickly, but they're relatively easy to find; the *Guide DAHU* will generally point to the area between pl. St-André and pl. Notre Dame. On warm nights, students flood the outdoor terraces of the area's many cafés. Bars are less expensive than clubs, where covers cost 50-100F and drinks nearly as much. The **Maison de la Culture,** 4 rue Paul Claudel (tel. 04 76 25 05 45), tram stop "Maison de la Culture," so hip it calls itself Le CARGO, imports international performers to its world-class theater and dance spaces. For jazz, head to **La Soupe aux Choux,** 7 rte. de Lyon (tel. 04 76 87 05 67).

Le **Couche-Tard,** 1 rue du Palais (tel. 04 76 44 18 79), is a small bar with graffiti-covered walls that goes crazy after 11pm. (Open M-Sa 6pm-2am. Happy Hour M and W 8-10pm.) It's easy to wile away an evening at the student-hip café/bar **La Bibliothèque,** pl. St-Claire. The crowded yet still friendly **Le Saxo,** 5 pl. Agier (tel. 04 76 51 06 01), takes up an entire square by itself. (Open daily 7pm-2am.) If its dancing you're after, get your ISIC and head down to **Le Club des Étudiantes,** 50 rue St-Laurent (tel. 04 76 42 00 68).

FESTIVALS. Grenoble's annual offerings include February **ice car racing,** a mid-August outdoor **Feast of the Assumption,** and the spectacular July 14th fireworks over its very own (and still extant) Bastille. The **Festival du Court Métrage** (short films) takes place in early July and features flicks both indoors and outside in pl. St-André. Contact the **Cinémathèque,** 4 rue Hector Berlioz (tel. 04 76 54 43 51). The **European Theatre Festival,** with shows ranging from free-100F, hams it up in July; call the Bureau du Festival at 04 76 44 60 92 for further info. (Open 10am-11pm.) The festival scene is mapped out in the tourist office's free *Festivals, Spectacles, and Manifestations. Le Petit Bulletin,* free in cinemas and some cafés and restaurants, has schedules of Grenoble's movies, from the trashy to the vogue.

⚠ THE OUTDOORS

While four mountainous regions surround Grenoble, they aren't the only source of daytrips in the area. Dauphiné is proud of its *"Huit Merveilles"* (Eight Wonders), which include elaborate natural caves. The tourist office carries information on excursions to towns such as **Pont-en-Royans** and other natural beauties. That said, Grenoble, a short bus ride from Olympic slopes, has a lot to do with **skiing.** Rent equipment in Grenoble to avoid high prices at the resorts. The biggest ski areas lie in **Oisans** to the east. The **Alpe d'Huez** (rising above one of the most challenging legs of the Tour de France) boasts an enormous 2250m vertical drop and sunny south-facing slopes. The 220km of trails cover all difficulty levels, but lift tickets are a bit pricey. (189F per day, 1000F per week. Tourist office tel. 04 76 11 44 44; fax 04 76 80 69 54; ski area tel. 04 76 80 30 30.) **Les Deux Alpes** has the biggest skiable glacier in Europe and limited summer skiing—it also offers the added bonus of a slope-side youth hostel, and is most popular with advanced skiers. Its lift system includes two gondolas to whisk you up the 2000m vertical. Lift tickets are 188F per day and 940F per week. (Tourist office tel. 04 76 79 22 00; fax 04 76 79 01 38. Ski area tel. 04 76 79 75 00. Youth hostel tel. 04 76 79 22 80; fax 04 76 79 26 15.)

The **Belledonne** region, northeast of Grenoble, lacks the towering heights of the Oisans but compensates with lower prices. **Chamrousse** is its biggest and most popular ski area. It offers a lively atmosphere (with a youth hostel), but the skiing pales in comparison to the Oisans. Nonetheless, if conditions are right, there's plenty of good skiing at great value, especially for beginners. Lift tickets are 125F per day, 700F per week. (Tourist office tel. 04 76 89 92 65; fax 04 76 89 98 06. Youth hostel tel. 04 76 89 91 31; fax 04 76 89 96 66.) Only half an hour from Grenoble, the resort also makes an ideal daytrip in the summer (49F bus ride). Chamrousse maintains four **mountain bike** routes of varying difficulty and has a 230km network of **hiking** trails. In January, the town hosts a renowned humor film festival.

The neighborly slopes and tiny prices of the **Vercors**, south of Grenoble, are popular among locals. In traditional villages with small ski resorts, such as **Gresse-en-Vercors** (tourist office tel. 04 76 72 38 31), vertical drops hover at 1000m, and the drive from Grenoble can take 25 minutes (46F bus ride). Rock-bottom prices (tickets about 60F per day, 300F per week) make the area a stress-free option for beginners or anyone looking to escape the hassles of major resorts. Teeming with ibex and country villages, the Vercors and its regional park have plenty of great **hikes.** Contact **CIMES** (see p. 356) for maps and details.

HAUTERIVES

The village of Hauterives is an unlikely place for a palace, but sometimes the most extraordinary things happen to the most ordinary places and people. On an April day in 1879, the local postman tripped over an oddly shaped rock as he was making his 32km of daily rounds. Absentmindedly, he shoved it in his pocket and drifted off into a daydream. Well, one pebble led to another, and soon Ferdinand Cheval was taking a wheelbarrow into the fields every evening to collect piles of odd little rocks. The neighbors may have thought him a bit eccentric, but that was only the beginning. Over the next 32 years, he shaped his stones into a fantasy palace just outside the village. Rock by rock, it grew into an unbelievably detailed world of grimacing giants, frozen palms, and swirling staircases. When the postman finally laid down his trowel, the "Palais Idéal" (Ideal Palace) was almost 80m long and over two stories high. The palace, an indescribable mix of Middle Eastern architecture and hallucinatory images, has become a national monument. In the spirit of its free-form construction, you can climb all over the castle and explore for yourself the caves and crevices, mottoes and mysteries sculpted by two hands and the postman's unshakable faith. It is without a doubt the funkiest thing in all of Gaul. (Tel. 04 75 68 81 19. Open Apr. 15-Sept. 15 daily 9am-7pm; Sept. 16-Nov. and Feb.-Apr. 14 9:30am-5:30pm; Dec.-Jan. 10am-4:30pm. 24F, under 16 17F.)

Driving from Grenoble, take A48 north; at Voreppe, switch to A49 toward Romans. At Romans, take D538 north to Hauterives (about 1hr.; from Lyon, head south on A7 and change to D538 at Vienne). During school vacations, **La Régie Drôme** (tel. 04 75 02 30 42) sends a morning **bus** from **Romans** to Hauterives and an early evening bus back (40min., 25F; call for schedules). You can take the **train** from Grenoble to **Romans** (1hr., 10 per day, 61F). **Hauterives's tourist office** can give you schedules. (Pl. de Janauer. Tel. 04 75 68 86 82. Open Apr.-Oct. daily 9:30am-noon and 1:30-6pm; Nov.-Mar. M-Sa 10am-noon and 1:30-5pm.)

CHARTREUSE

North of Grenoble rise the electric green slopes of the **Chartreuse** mountain range, which boasts its own handful of ski areas. However, the most interesting thing here is not the snow but the liqueur. In 1605, the monks of the Monastère de la Grande Chartreuse tried to manufacture the elixir of long life; they came up with the celebrated yellow-green Chartreuse (around 70F in town). Only three monks know the 130-ingredient recipe. You can't visit the monastery (the monks live in silence and seclusion), but there's a great view of it from St-Pierre-de-Chartreuse, about 1km from the main road. The **Musée de la Correrie** (tel. 04 76 88 60 45), in St-Pierre-de-Chartreuse, details the monks' daily routine with spooky hooded models. (Museum open May-Sept. 9:30am-noon and 2-6:30pm; Apr. and Oct. 10am-noon and 2-6pm. 15F.) The **St-Pierre tourist office** (tel. 04 76 88 62 08) has more information. From Grenoble, **buses** run to St-Pierre (1-2 per day, 35F). Check the return schedule before you go or risk getting stuck in St-Pierre until morning.

CHAMBÉRY

In 1232, the savvy counts of Savoie settled in a magnificent château in this crucial gateway town. Because all traffic through the Alps passed beneath their windows, the dukes' control of Chambéry brought them enormous influence and wealth. Today the château is run by the no-less-fearsome French bureaucracy, and its towers dominate the covered arcades and wide boulevards of the pedestrian *vieille ville*. The city serves as a gateway to the high Alps, but it is a destination itself. The *vieille ville* is almost painfully cute, and Chambéry's museums are surprisingly top-notch. Perfect if you want to be outdoors by day but in town at night, Chambéry (pop. 57,000) is also a good place from which to explore the Lac du Bourget.

■ ORIENTATION AND PRACTICAL INFORMATION

The *centre ville* lies south of the train station, with the château and the *vieille ville* in the southwest corner. To reach the tourist office from the station, walk left on rue Sommeiller for one long block and cross pl. du Centenaire to bd. de la Colonne (5min.).

Trains: Pl. de la Gare. To: **Grenoble** (30min., 15 per day, 55F); **Annecy** (1hr., 13 per day, 48F); **Lyon** (1½hr., 10 per day, 83F); **Geneva** (2hr., 7 per day, 80F); and **Paris** (4hr., 18 indirect per day, 340F). Info office open M-F 8:30am-12:20pm and 1:30-6:50pm, Sa 8:30am-5:50pm.

Buses: Several companies run from the bus station, pl. de la Gare (tel. 04 79 69 11 88; office open M-F 8am-noon and 1:45-6pm), across from the station. A good, if slow, option for visiting Alpine villages. To: **Annecy** (1hr., 8 per day, 48F) and **Grenoble** (1hr., 6 per day, 50F).

Public Transportation: STAC, bd. de la Colonne (tel. 04 79 69 61 12 or 04 79 69 61 12). Runs 7:30am-7pm. Kiosk at bd. de la Colonne, at bus stop "Éléphants." Open M-F 7:15am-7:15pm, Sa 7:20am-12:20pm and 2:20-5:40pm. Ticket 6.50F; *carnet* of 10 37.20F, students 27F.

Bike Rental: Magique Cycles, 56 av. de Turin (tel. 04 79 70 13 54). 50F per day. Open Tu-Sa 8:30am-noon and 2-7pm.

Taxi: Allo Taxi (tel. 04 79 69 11 12). 24hr.

Tourist Office: 24 bd. de la Colonne (tel. 04 79 33 42 47; fax 04 79 85 71 39). Wheelchair access from 19 av. des Ducs de Savoie. English-speaking, brochure-wielding staff. Open June 15-Sept. 15 M-Sa 9am-12:30pm and 1:30-6:30pm, Su 10am-12:30pm; Sept. 16-June 14 M-Sa 9am-noon and 1:30-6pm. In the same building, the **Association Départementale de Tourisme de la Savoie** (tel. 04 79 85 12 45) dispenses information on hotels, campgrounds, and ski resorts (same hours).

Hiking Information: Club Alpin Français, 70 rue Croix d'Or (tel. 04 79 33 05 52). Advice on hiking and skiing. Open Tu-F 5:30-7:30pm, Sa 10am-noon.

Youth Information Center: Centre d'Information et de Documentation Jeunesse (CIDJ), 4 pl. de la Gare (tel. 04 79 62 66 87). Info on sports, hostels, and *foyers*. Bulletin board posts rides, jobs, babysitting, and housing information. BIJ/Transalpino tickets. Open M-F 9:30am-12:30pm and 1:30-6pm, Sa 10am-noon.

Laundromat: 1 rue Doppet. Open daily 7:30am-8pm.

Hospital: Centre Hospitalier, pl. François-Chiron (tel. 04 79 96 50 50).

Police: 585 av. de la Boisse (tel. 04 79 62 84 00).

Post Office: Sq. Paul Vidal (tel. 04 79 96 69 15). **Currency exchange** with commission. Open M-F 8am-7pm, Sa 8am-noon. **Postal code:** 73000.

ACCOMMODATIONS, CAMPING, AND FOOD

ACCOMMODATIONS. The nearest hostel is in Aix-les-Bains, 10 minutes away by train, but Chambéry provides a much more enjoyable place to stay. There are several budget hotels in the center of town, but most are older and above bars. **Art Hôtel,** 154 rue Sommeiller (tel. 04 79 62 37 26; fax 04 79 62 49 98), is an upscale hotel with a minimalist black and white theme and phones and TVs in its stylish rooms—but these luxuries are reflected in its prices. (Singles and doubles 245-280F. Breakfast 35F. V, MC.) **Hôtel le Mauriennais,** 2 rue Ste-Barbe (tel. 04 79 69 42 78; fax 04 79 69 46 86), near the château, offers great value and airy rooms in an older hotel. (Singles 90-110F; doubles 120F; triples 160F; quads 180F. Breakfast 25F. Reception 10am-10pm.) **Hôtel du Château,** 37 rue Jean-Pierre Veyrat (tel. 04 79 69 48 78), is near the château, of course, with large, simple rooms in a great part of town. Locals drink all day long in the bar downstairs. (Singles 90-130F; doubles 130-180F; triples and quads 180F. Breakfast 23F. Reception 7am-9pm.) **Hôtel des Voyageurs,** 3 rue Doppet (tel. 04 79 33 57 00), has basic rooms in a central location. (Singles 130F, with shower 150F; doubles 160F, with shower 190F; quads 240F, with shower 280F. Breakfast 25F. Reception 7:30am-9:30pm.) **Camping Le Nivolet,** 3km away in Bassens (tel. 04 79 85 47 79), has basic facilities in a not-so-scenic suburban location. Take bus "C" (direction "St-Alban") from Éléphants; note that on weekends and holidays there are only two buses. (15F per person, 7F per car, 15F per tent. Reception May-Sept. 9am-noon and 2-8pm.) Better camping lies a few miles north on Lac Bourget in Aix-Les Bains.

FOOD. Budget meals are easy to find in the *vieille ville*, and the restaurants near the château are particularly delicious. The town's market is held in **Les Halles,** pl. de Genève (Sa mornings). **Prisunic supermarket** lies on the corner of rue de Boigne and pl. du 8 Mai (open M-Sa 8:15am-7pm), but a better bet is to stock up on food at the specialty stores in the *vieille ville*. When you've got what you think you need, head over to **Au Fidèle Berger,** 15 rue de Boigne, a *chocolatier* that has been turning out sweet bliss since 1838. Locals crowd into **La Poterne,** 3 pl. Maché (tel. 04 79 96 23 70), a popular restaurant at the entrance to the château, for regional dishes renowned throughout Savoie. *Menus* start at 57F for lunch and 92F for dinner. (Open M noon-2pm, Tu-Sa noon-2pm and 7-10:30pm. V, MC.) **La Table de Marie,** 193 rue Croix d'Or (tel. 04 79 85 99 76), has local cuisine and local color (well, as much as you can have in the *vieille ville*), with 51-69F *menus* and 79-90F *fondues*.

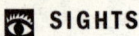 **SIGHTS**

CHÂTEAU DES DUCS DE SAVOIE. For three centuries, Savoie's power emanated from the 13th-century château. At the height of their power, the dukes commanded a realm that stretched from Neufchâtel to Nice and from Turin to Lyon. The château's last prominent master was Victor Emmanuel II, the first king of unified Italy. Enter through the intimidating 15th-century Porte de l'Église St-Dominique. The Ste-Chapelle presents a two-faced exterior, the result of an 18th-century fire and its subsequent rebuilding and repainting (in the 19th century) in a *trompe l'oeil* style. Invasions by French kings eventually convinced the dukes to transfer the capital, and Jesus' alleged burial cloth (kept in the chapel in the 16th century), to Turin, Italy, where the shroud has remained ever since. In the absence of the famous relic, Ste-Chapelle's largest attraction is its set of 70 bells, the largest and loveliest in all of Europe. *(Concerts every Sa 11am-noon and 6-6:30pm. 1hr. tours July-Aug. M-Sa 10:30am and 2:30-5:30pm; Sept. and May-June M-Sa 2:30pm; Oct.-Apr. Sa-Su 2:30 and 4pm. Entrance includes tour of* vieille ville. *25F; Nov.-Mar. 35F.)*

LA MUSÉE DES CHARMETTES. The best site in the town actually lies two kilometers to the south. The *musée* is the house in which Jean-Jacques Rousseau put his political theorizing on hold from 1736-1742 to live in semi-debauchery with the older and wiser Mme de Warens. The episode was the source of his famous *Confessions*. The museum displays Rousseau memorabilia, while the vine-covered garden looks out onto Chambéry and the mountains. Getting there is half the fun—though not nearly so much fun as Rousseau had. From pl. de la République, follow rue de la République, which becomes rue Jean-Jacques Rousseau and eventually chemin des Charmettes. From there, it's a 15-minute walk along a bubbling brook and mountain meadows. It's also all uphill; the museum appears just after you run out of breath. In summer, actors in period dress put on a show loosely based on Rousseau's stay at the cottage. *(Tel. 04 79 33 39 44. Shows July at 9pm, Aug. at 8:30pm; 2hr.; 100F. Musée open Apr.-Sept. W-M 10am-noon and 2-6pm; Oct.-Mar. W-M 10am-noon and 2-4:30pm. 20F, students 10F.)*

LE MUSÉE SAVOISIEN. This gorgeous museum displays a brilliant ethnography of the Savoie region through the ages with crafts, maps, ecclesiastical paraphernalia, and the like. The museum moves chronologically from prehistoric pottery to the present, with château life and the pivotal role of the Savoie during WWII as particular highlights. *(Sq. de Lannoy de Bissy. Leave the tourist office by the back door, turn left on bd. de la Colonne and walk past the Fontaine des Éléphants. Open W-M 10am-noon and 2-6pm. 20F, students 10F.)*

MUSÉE DES BEAUX-ARTS. Home to an extensive collection of Italian and other European paintings of the 17th-19th centuries. Masterworks by Titian and Tintoretto hang by French works by Watteau and Fragonard and a small Dutch collection, including a Rubens. Some of the most engaging paintings are religious works by lesser-known painters. *(Tel. 04 79 33 75 03. North of the aquatic stampede in pl. du Palais de Justice. Museum open W-M 10am-noon and 2-6pm. 20F, students 10F.)*

LA FONTAINE DES ÉLÉPHANTS. The best-known monument in Chambéry was erected in 1838 to honor the Comte de Boigne. After leading military exploits in India, the Comte returned with the spoils to his beloved Chambéry and spent most of it on public works for the city. True to the Comte's own history, the *fontaine* fuses East and West with elephants standing in the traditional form of the Savoie cross, spouting showers of water under the weight of de Boigne himself. Locals call them *"les quatre sans culs"*—the "buttless four".

THE VIEILLE VILLE. There are several Italian-influenced *hôtels particuliers* on rue Croix-d'Or, pl. St-Léger, as well as the arcades of rue de Boigne. The medieval rue Basse du Château looks as though it belongs in an Italian city; it even features a modest "bridge of sighs." The tourist office has a list of the most interesting *hôtels*, while from June to September they lead a 1½-hour tour of the *vieille ville*; evening tours include a *dégustation* in a 16th-century *cave*. *(Daily 4 and 9pm. 30F.)*

LAC DU BOURGET AND AIX-LES-BAINS

Aix-les-Bains (pop. 25,000) would be just another overpriced *station thermale* stuffed with ageing *curistes* undergoing smelly treatments at the sulfurous springs, were it not for the lake which laps at its feet. The Lac du Bourget, France's largest natural lake, provides the fountain of youth missing from the *thermes* in town, and its beaches are dominated by windsurfers and sunbathers.

There's only one thing to do in the town itself; follow the crowds of invalids to the **Thermes Nationaux** (tel. 04 79 35 38 50), across from the tourist office. You can plunge into the thermal *piscine* (29F per 30min.; open 6am-noon) or take a tour of the modern baths followed by a descent to see the remains of the Roman ones (20F; Tu-Sa 3pm, buy tickets by 2:30pm). Outside, visit the grottoes and the sinus-clearing sulphur springs. The **Musée Faure**, bd. des Côtes (tel. 04 76 61 06 57), atop a hill overlooking the town, diverts sodden spirits with works by Sisley, Pissarro, Rodin, and Degas. (Open M and W-F 9:30am-noon and 1:30-6pm, Sa-Su 9:30am-noon and 2-6pm. 20F, students 10F, under 15 free.)

Far more pleasant than the waters of the *thermes* are those of the lake. Take bus #2 (direction "Plage d'Aix") from Grand Port and get off when you see a site you like. When you've finished marveling at the mountains reflected in the water, jump in at the **plage Municipale** or the **plage de Mémars**, at opposite ends of the developed rocky coast (both free). The **Centre Nautique**, pl. Daniel-Rops (tel. 04 79 61 48 80), offers a heated pool on its private beach. (28F, under 18 20F. Open daily 9am-7pm.) In Grand Port, **Nautis-Aix** rents **sailboats** and **motorboats**. (Tel. 04 79 88 24 34. 180-450F per hr. Open daily 9am-7pm.)

For food, **Prisunic supermarket** is at 17 rue de Genève (open M-Sa 8:30am-12:30pm and 2-7:30pm), and morning **markets** are held on pl. Clemenceau (W and Sa). **Grand Port** is dotted with eateries offering lake views and servings of the lake's scaly ex-residents, called *fritures* or *fletans*. Try them at **Skiff Pub**, Grand Port. (*Menus* 85F and 110F. Tel. 04 79 63 41 00. Open daily 7:30am-1:30am. V, MC.)

The **Auberge de Jeunesse (HI),** promenade de Sierroz (tel. 04 79 88 32 88; fax 04 79 61 14 05), is near the lake. Take bus #2 from the station (direction "Plage d'Aix;" 7.50F) to "Camping," and walk three minutes along the stream away from the lake. The modern hostel often attracts groups to its spotless three to six bed dorms with skylights. (53F. Sheets 19F. Breakfast 19F. Dinner 50F. Laundry. Reception daily 7-10am and 6-10pm. Lockout 10am-6pm, 10am-2pm in summer. Ask for a key if you'll be out past 10pm.) The **Hôtel Broisin,** 10 ruelle du Kevet (tel. 04 79 35 06 15; fax 04 79 88 10 10), is in a quiet courtyard on an alley off rue des Bains. The comfortable rooms have TV and phone. (Singles 130F; doubles 150F, with shower 190F; twins 200F. Breakfast 25F. Reception 6:30am-8pm. Reserve ahead.) **Camping Municipal Sierroz** (tel. 04 79 61 21 43) is across from the lake next to the hostel, with a grocery store and volleyball. (18F per person, 39F tent, 18F car. Electricity 10F. Reception daily 8am-6:30pm. Reserve required July-Aug. Open Mar. 15-Nov. 15. V, MC.)

Aix's center is just east of the train station; the lake is a 25-minute walk in the opposite direction. To get to the **tourist office** pl. Maurice Mollard (tel. 04 79 35 05 92; fax 04 79 88 88 01), cross bd. Wilson, head down av. de Gaulle, cross pl. Moulin, and walk along the edge of the park for one block. (Open Apr.-Sept. M-Sa 9am-6:30pm, Su 9:30am-12:30pm; Oct.-Apr. M-Sa 9am-noon and 2-6pm.) There's a lakeside **annex** at Grand Port, pl. Herriot. (Tel. 04 79 34 15 80. Open June-Sept. daily 10am-noon and 2-6pm.) **Extreme Sports**, 60 bd. Franklin Roosevelt (tel. 04 79 69 11 88), at the edge of town on the way to Annecy, **rents bikes** from 100F per day. The **post office,** av. Victoria (tel. 04 79 35 15 10), has **currency exchange**. (Open M-F 8am-7pm, Sa 8am-noon. **Postal code:** 73100.)

Trains from pl. de la Gare go to **Annecy** (30min., 13 per day, 38F), **Grenoble** (1hr., 12 per day, 65F), **Lyon** (1½hr., 15 per day, 90F), and **Paris** (3½hr., 14 per day, 358F). (Office open M-Sa 8:30am-noon and 2-6:30pm.) **Buses** (tel. 04 79 69 11 88) leave the station for **Annecy** (6 per day, 29.50F) and **Chambéry** (8 per day, 15.70F).

ABBAYE D'HAUTECOMBE

Gregorian chants emanate from mass at the Benedictine Abbaye d'Hautecombe (tel. 04 79 54 26 12), restored in the 19th century and housing the tombs of the princes of Savoie. (Open M and W-Sa 10-11:30am and 2-5pm, Su 10:30am-noon and 2-5pm. Free.) The abbey makes an ideal daytrip by bicycle. From Grand Port, follow av. du Grand Port away from the lake and turn left onto rue St-Innocent (D991). Follow the Tour du Lac signs north to Groisin, where you'll see signs for the abbey (3hr. round-trip). For the less adventurous, the **boat** from Grand Port gives views of the abbey rising dramatically from the water (2½hr.; 3 per day, 1-2 per day Sept.-June; 56F). A trip to Sunday mass leaves at 8:30am (tel. 04 79 88 92 09 for info). Other excursions cover the history and ecology of the lake (56-90F).

ANNECY

You may forget Annecy is a real town when you walk through the *centre ville*. With narrow cobblestone streets, winding canals, a turreted castle, and over-stuffed flower boxes—all bordering the purest lake in Europe—Annecy appears more like a fiberglass fairy-tale fabrication than a modern city with a metropolitan population of 120,000. This capital of Haute Savoie consistently claimed the title in the National Flower City contest until its continued success forced it to withdraw permanently from the competition. Annecy has ceded its floral crown, but visitors still can't resist the magic of the lake and mountains.

◪ ORIENTATION AND PRACTICAL INFORMATION

Most activity centers around the lake, southeast of the train station. The canal runs east to west through the old town, leaving the elevated château on one side and the main shopping area, closer to the *centre ville*, on the other. To reach the tourist office from the train station, take the underground passage from the station to rue Vaugelas, turn left, and follow rue Vaugelas for four blocks. The tourist office is straight ahead in the large, modern Bonlieu shopping mall.

Trains: Pl. de la Gare. To: **Chambéry** (1hr., 13 per day, 48F); **Lyon** (2hr., 9 per day, 113F); **Grenoble** (2hr., 9 per day, 89F); **Chamonix** (2¼hr., 7 per day, 106F); **Paris** (4hr., 10 per day, 375F); and **Nice** (8hr., 2 per day, 352F). Office open M-Sa 8:40am-7:15pm, Su 9:10am-7:15pm.

Buses: Adjacent to the train station. **Voyages Frossard** (tel. 04 50 45 73 90) runs to **Geneva** (1hr., 6 per day, 52F) and **Lyon** (3hr., 2 per day, 92F).

Public Transportation: SIBRA (tel. 04 50 10 04 04). Tickets 7.50F, *carnet* of 8 40.50F. Schedule at booth in Bonlieu, near the tourist office. Open M-Sa 9am-7pm. Extensive service, but only minibuses run on Su (including #91 to the hostel).

Bike and Ski Rental: Annecy Sports Passion, 3 av. de Parmelan (tel. 04 50 51 46 28). Bike 70F per half-day, 100F per day, 140F per weekend. Skis 90F per day, boots 30F. Passport or credit card deposit. Open Tu-Sa 8:30am-noon and 2-7pm. V, MC.

Taxis: Stand at the train station call 24hr. (tel. 04 50 45 05 67).

Tourist Office: 1 rue Jean Jaurès (tel. 04 50 45 00 33 or 04 50 45 56 66; fax 04 50 51 87 20), at pl. de la Libération. Detailed maps, info on hiking, hotels, campgrounds, rural lodgings, excursions, and climbing. Ask for the helpful *Guide Pratique d'Annecy* or, for hikes, the *Sentiers Forestiers* (20F) or the free *Randonnées Pedestres*. 2hr. tours (32F) in summer M-Sa 10am and 3pm. Topo guides 57F. Open daily July-Aug. 9am-6:30pm; Sept.-June M-Sa 9am-noon and 1:45-6:30pm, Su 3-6pm.

Money: The **24hr. change machine** outside the tourist office has good rates.

Laundromat: Lav'Presse, 13 rue Revon. Open Su-F 8am-7pm, Sa 8am-5pm.

Hospital: 1 av. des Trésun (tel. 04 50 88 33 33).

The journey *is* the reward....
-Tao saying

Council *Travel*

Stop by one of our 65 offices listed on www.counciltravel.com
Or call: 1-800-2COUNCIL

save on airfares • lodging • attractions • theaters

ISIC International Student Identity Card

your compass for **travel discounts** & **benefits** around the world.

International *Student* Identity Card
Carte d'étudiant internationale / Carné internacional de estudiante
STUDENT
Studies at / Étudiant à / Est. de Enseñanza
Colorado State U.
Name / Nom / Nombre
McKormick, Kendra
Born / Né(e) le / Nacido/a el
16/06/80
Validity / Validité / Validez
09/1999 – 12/2000
ISIC

Call **1-800-2-Council** or visit **www.counciltravel.com**
for your nearest **ISIC** issuing office.

phone calls • trains • car rentals • museums & more

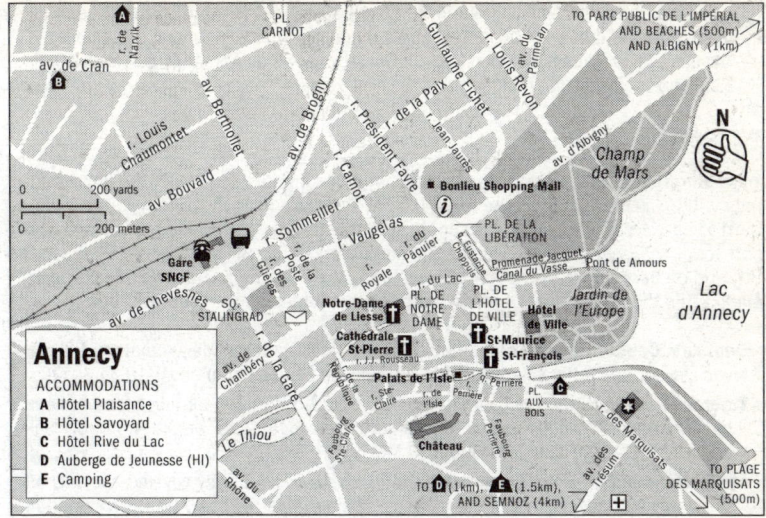

Annecy

ACCOMMODATIONS

A Hôtel Plaisance
B Hôtel Savoyard
C Hôtel Rive du Lac
D Auberge de Jeunesse (HI)
E Camping

Police: 17 rue des Marquisats (tel. 04 50 52 32 00).

Post Office: 4 rue des Glières (tel. 04 50 33 67 00), off rue de la Poste, down the street from the train station. **Currency exchange.** Poste Restante code 74011. Open M-F 9am-noon and 2-5pm, Sa 9am-noon. **Postal code:** 74000.

▐ ACCOMMODATIONS AND CAMPING

Annecy's prices confirm its popularity. Most budget hotels are in the neighbor-hood behind the station. Hotels around the lake and *vieille ville* are much poorer in value, but Annecy is so pretty that it makes sense to pick a room by location. Reservations are recommended, especially in high season.

Auberge de Jeunesse "La Grande Jeanne" (HI), rte. de Semnoz (tel. 04 50 45 33 19; fax 04 50 52 77 52). Minibus #91 (direction "Semnoz") leaves the station and drops you off at the hostel, but only runs in summer (7F, last bus 6pm). At other times, take bus #1 (direction "Marquisats") from the station to "Hôtel de Police." Follow D41 and signs pointing to Semnoz. After a 10min. uphill hike, the hostel will be on your right. Gorgeous new chalet in the woods near trails. Small rooms with 3-5 beds and shower. Bar, game room, kitchen, laundry, and TV room. 74F. Breakfast included. Sheets 17F. Reception daily 7am-midnight. No lockout or curfew. Reserve in summer.

Hôtel Savoyard, 41 av. de Cran (tel. 04 50 57 08 08), in a residential area behind the station. Pretty chalet with courtyard. From the train station, exit left, walk around the station to av. Berthollet, and turn left again on av. de Cran. Enthusiastic managers define hospitality and are particularly backpacker-friendly. Great, large, rustic singles and doubles 100-120F, with bathroom 180F. Breakfast 20F. Discounts in low season.

Hôtel Plaisance, 17 rue de Narvik (tel. 04 50 57 30 42). Pleasant building hung with vines and rosebushes. Bright, large rooms. TV room. Charming owner caters to young, foreign clientele. Singles 130F; doubles 140-235F; triples 235F; quads 285F. Shower 13F. Breakfast 25F. V, MC.

Hôtel Rive du Lac, 6 rue des Marquisats (tel. 04 50 51 32 85; fax 04 50 45 77 40). Simple rooms and some traffic noise, but the location by the lake and canals is ideal. Singles and doubles from 138F; triples 186F; quads 207F. Breakfast 24F. Shower 5F. Restaurant downstairs serves a 70F *menu*. V, MC.

Campsites: 8 rte. de Semnoz (tel. 04 50 45 48 30; fax 04 50 45 55 56). Close to the youth hostel and busy. (60F for tent and 1-2 people. TV room, laundry, ping-pong. 17F per car. 20F for electricity. Open Dec. 15-Oct. 15. Reception Apr.-Aug. daily 8am-10pm. Ring buzzer off-season. V, MC.)

FOOD

Whether you choose a restaurant on the canal or a lakeside picnic, the surroundings will be as enjoyable as the food. It's hard to eat poorly in Annecy, but it's also hard to eat *really* well, so pick a scenic spot to eat. Fill your picnic basket with the soft local *reblochon* cheese at the morning **markets** on pl. Ste-Claire (Tu, F, and Su) and on **bd. Taine** (Sa). Grocery stores line av. de Parmelan, and a **Prisunic supermarket** fills the better part of pl. de Notre-Dame. (Open M-Sa 8:30am-7:30pm.)

Quoi de n'Oeuf, 19 fbg Ste-Claire (tel. 04 50 45 75 42). Eggheads jump at the 50F all-you-can-eat *tartiflette,* salad, and dessert. Open M-Sa noon-2pm and 7-10pm. V, MC.

Taverne le Freti, 12 rue Ste-Claire (tel. 04 50 51 29 52). A find for those fond of flambéed *fromage. Raclette* 61-67F; *fondue savoyarde* (64F); other varieties 56-98F. Salads 20-39F. Open Tu-Su 7-11:30pm. V, MC.

Le Phénix Imperial, 8 rue Poquier (tel. 04 50 45 48 57), in a tiny covered alleyway off rue Vaugelas, specializes in Vietnamese cuisine. Most dishes 20-50F. Vegetarian dishes 20-25F. Open M-Sa noon-2pm and 6:30-10:30pm. V, MC.

SIGHTS

VIEILLE VILLE. A stroll through the *vieille ville* may cost you several rolls of film and a hundred sighs. The **Palais de l'Isle** (tel. 04 50 33 83 62) is a 12th-century fortress which was originally the home of the de l'Isle family. The tiny, turreted building forming a skinny island in the middle of the canal was converted into a prison in the 1400s and is now a museum devoted to Annecy's history—it's far more impressive from the outside. The passages of **quai Perrière, rue de l'Isle,** and **rue Ste-Claire** to the south of the fortress are Annecy at its most charming.

GARDENS. Cross the street from the tourist office to walk through the **Champ de Mars,** a long grass field dotted with *boules* players, sunbathers, and picnickers stretching out to the lake. At the mouth of the Canal du Vassé, which runs along the Champ de Mars, is the **Pont des Amours** (Bridge of Love) and one of few that merits its cheesy name. The **Jardin de l'Europe,** a web of paths surrounding manicured hedges, fountains, and statues, lies on the other side of the bridge and sticks out like a thumb into the water.

THE LAKE. After a stroll through the bustling streets, you may opt for a swim in the cold, crystalline lake. **Plage des Marquisats,** south of the city down rue des Marquisats, is free but crowded. The **Club de Voile Française** rents **kayaks** from the Plage des Marquisats (35F per hr.). Or escape on a pedal boat from **Bateaux Dupraz** on quai Napoleon; some boats have a slide to aid your descent into the water. *(Tel. 04 50 51 52 15. 35-52F per 30min., 60-88F per hr.; tours of the lake 52-55F. V, MC.)* It costs 18F to swim at the glamorous **Parc Public de l'Impérial,** an aquatic wonderland with waterslides, sailing, tennis, swim lessons, and a casino. *(20min. up av. d'Albigny. Tel. 04 50 23 11 82. Open May-Sept. daily 10am-7:30pm.)*

CHÂTEAU. The 12th-century château towers over Annecy, a short but steep climb from the *vieille ville.* Once a stronghold of the counts of Geneva, the castle and its imposing parapets now house unexciting archaeological and artistic exhibits. The 15th-century wooden statuary is worth a look. Temporary shows are often well-mounted, and the **Observatoire Régional des Lacs Alpins,** in the rear of the castle, has displays on lake ecosystems as well as a cool aquarium. If the exhibits don't impress you, the view will. *(Tel. 04 50 33 87 30. Open June-Aug. daily 10am-6pm; Sept.-May W-M 10am-noon and 2-6pm. Château 30F, students 10F. Grounds free.)*

⚠ EXCURSIONS

Although it may be hard to tear yourself away from the city's cosmetic charms, a hike or bike ride through its Alpine forests will prove that Annecy is also a natural beauty. A dozen breathtaking hikes begin on the **Semnoz,** a limestone mountain south of the city. The **Office National des Forêts** distributes a color map, *Sentiers Forestiers*, with several routes (20F at the tourist office or hostel). One of the best begins at the Basilique, right near the youth hostel. If you're staying in town, take bus #91 (summer only) to "Tillier." Then, from the Basilique, continue along the road until you reach a small parking lot. From there, follow the signs for la Forêt du Crêt du Maure. A two-hour hike with beautiful views of the lake, the city, and the mountains follows the Ste-Catherine and GR96 trails in a meandering circle around the Semnoz forest. Long-haulers may consider a bigger portion of the GR96, which circles the lake on a trail marked with yellow and red lines. There's an exquisite, 16km scenic *piste cyclable* (bike route) that hugs the lake shore from Sevrier to Doussard. After that, you can complete the entire loop (32km) on the main road, but be careful for increased traffic. The **Bureau des Guides,** 17 fbg Ste-Claire (tel. 04 50 45 60 61), covers all mountaineering activities, including hikes, rock-climbing, ice-climbing, and canyoning excursions. (Open daily 5:30-6:30pm. Hikes 80F per half-day, 120F per day. Sign up night before.) For info on sports in the area, call **Annecy Sport Information,** 7 fbg Ste-Claire (tel. 04 50 33 88 31; M-F 3-7pm). The *Guide Pratique* has info on outdoor recreation.

♫ 🌴 ENTERTAINMENT AND FESTIVALS

ENTERTAINMENT. After a hard day shooting the rapids or conquering the slopes, relax at the bars lining the canal in the *vieille ville*. Students stream into **Le River's Café,** 2 rue de la Gare (tel. 04 50 45 48 11), which overflows with cheap drinks, billiards, and funky painted patio furniture. **Redz,** 14 rue Perrière (tel. 04 50 45 17 13), caters to an older and more moneyed crowd, but really packs 'em in after 11pm. **Café Curtis,** 35 rue Ste-Claire (tel. 04 50 51 74 75), maintains an easy-going atmosphere in its crowded blond-wood bar with 10F wine and 13F Kronenbourg. Performing arts and cinema go up at the **Théâtre d'Annecy** (tel. 04 50 33 44 11) in the Bonlieu Mall across from the tourist office (about 95F, students 40F).

FESTIVALS. *Fête* fetishists can pick up schedules at the Comité des Fêtes kiosk across from the tourist office. A small **jazz festival** heats up the middle two weekends of July (60-100F). The grandpappy of them all is the **Fête du Lac,** the first Saturday in August, with fireworks and water shows (35-270F). Each year the floats on the lake take on wacky themes such as "Monsters and Legends," "Adventures in the Far West," and "Beyond the Planet Earth."

AROUND LAC D'ANNECY

Ten kilometers west of Annecy, waterfalls roar over the cliffs of the glacier-carved **Gorges du Fier.** (Call 04 50 46 23 07 for info. Open daily June 15-Sept. 10 9am-6pm; Mar. 15-June 14 and Sept. 11-Oct. 15 9am-noon and 2-5pm. 24F.) The **Château de Montrottier** (tel. 04 50 46 23 02) is five minutes from the entrance to the gorges. The castle contains centuries-old Asian costumes, armor, and pottery. (Open June-Aug. daily 9am-noon and 2-6pm; Mar. 15-May 31 and Sept. 1- Oct. 15 closed Tu. Tour 25F, students 20F.) To get there, take the bus to Lovagny (10min., 3-4 per day at odd hours, 12F) and walk the 800m to the gorges. Alternatively, you can take a bus tour that includes admission to the gorges and the château. (Contact **Voyages Crolard,** tel. 04 50 45 09 18. 105F.)

The smaller villages on the Lac d'Annecy make for excellent daytrips. All are within 20km of Annecy and accessible by bus (call **Voyages Crolard;** 8-9 per day in high seasons, 15-75F). Driving, take D909 along the east shore, which intersects with N508 at Doussard on the southern point of the lake, to return to Annecy along the west lake shore. **Talloires,** 13km from Annecy, makes a good starting point for the one-hour hike to the waterfalls at **La Cascade d'Angon** and to the beautiful gardens of the **Ermitage de St-Germain** (also 1hr.). To reach the waterfalls, follow the Closettaz path out of the village and follow the signs. The trail passes under the raging 100m-high torrent and then climbs the rocks up to the top for a better vantage point. Ask the tourist office in Annecy or Talloires (tel. 04 50 60 70 64) about boat rides from Annecy to Talloires. **Doussard,** south of the lake and surrounded by nature preserves, is known as "the source of the lake" because its rivers fill Lac d'Annecy (tourist office tel. 04 50 44 60 24; fax 04 50 44 45 96). Nearby **St-Jorioz** has great views of the mountains (tourist office tel. 04 50 68 61 82; fax 04 50 68 96 11).

The nearest **skiing resort** is **La Clusaz**, 32km away, with 130km of *pistes* and 56 lifts. Contact the **tourist office** in La Clusaz (tel. 04 50 32 65 00; fax 04 50 32 65 01) at Boîte Postale 7, 74220 La Clusaz, for info. There is a **youth hostel** (tel. 04 50 02 41 73; fax 04 50 02 65 85) outside La Clusaz on rte. du Col de la Croix Fry.

CHAMONIX

In other Alpine towns, the peaks provide harmless backdrops; in Chamonix (pop. 20,000), daggers of mammoth glaciers seem to reach down and menace the village. Mont Blanc, Europe's highest peak (4807m), reigns just to the east. Squeezed in between the mountainous walls of Le Brévent (2525m) and L'Aiguille du Midi (3842m), Chamonix has exploited its surroundings since 19th-century gentlemen-climbers scaled the peaks in crew-neck sweaters. The town hosted the first Winter Olympics in 1924, and many of its streets bear the names of climbers.

Two countries lie within skiing distance of Chamonix, filling its hostel and ski dorms with climbers and skiers who swap tall tales in many languages. Chamonix's slopes are among the toughest in the world, and its mountains are supremely challenging to scale. Some 62 lifts and *téléphériques* (cable cars) defeat gravity to take you to hiking trails that wag their way up the mountain to icy lakes, creeping glaciers, and treacherous, snow-covered ridges. Inexpensive dorms provide eye-popping views and excellent opportunities to retreat to the land of perpetual snow and soaring heights. In any season, the valley has enough to keep the outdoor enthusiast euphoric for a week. Depending on the season, hiking, cycling, and skiing options are hard to match. But be careful—an astonishing number of people die on Chamonix's mountains every year.

🛈 ORIENTATION AND PRACTICAL INFORMATION

The center of town is the intersection of **av. Michel Croz, rue du Docteur Paccard,** and **rue Joseph Vallot,** each named for a past conqueror of Mont Blanc's summit. From the station, follow av. Michel Croz through town, turn left onto rue du Dr. Paccard, and take the first right to the pl. de l'Église and the tourist office (5min.).

TRANSPORTATION AND SERVICES

Trains: Av. de la Gare (tel. 04 50 53 00 44). Chamonix is served by a special train running from St-Gervais to Martigny; all other destinations require a change of train. To: **Annecy** (2½hr., 6 per day, 106F); **Geneva** (2½hr., 4 per day, 108F); **Grenoble** (4hr., 5 per day, 172F); **Lyon** (5hr., 4 per day, 184F); and **Paris** (8hr., 1 per day, 373F). Info office open daily 9am-noon and 2-6:30pm.

Buses: Société Alpes Transports, at the train station (tel. 04 50 53 01 15). To: **Courmayeur, Italy** (40min., 8 per day, 53F); **Geneva** (2hr., 2 per day, 148F to town, 188F to airport); **Annecy** (2¾hr., 2 per day, 98F); and **Grenoble** (3½hr., 1 per day, 156F).

Local Transportation: Chamonix Bus, pl. de l'Église (tel. 04 50 53 05 55). The area is divided into sections; you pay by the number of sections you go through. Tickets 7.50F per section; *carnet* of 6 38F, of 10 59F. Buses do a good job of connecting with ski slopes and hiking trails.

Taxis: Tel. 04 50 53 13 94. 24hr.

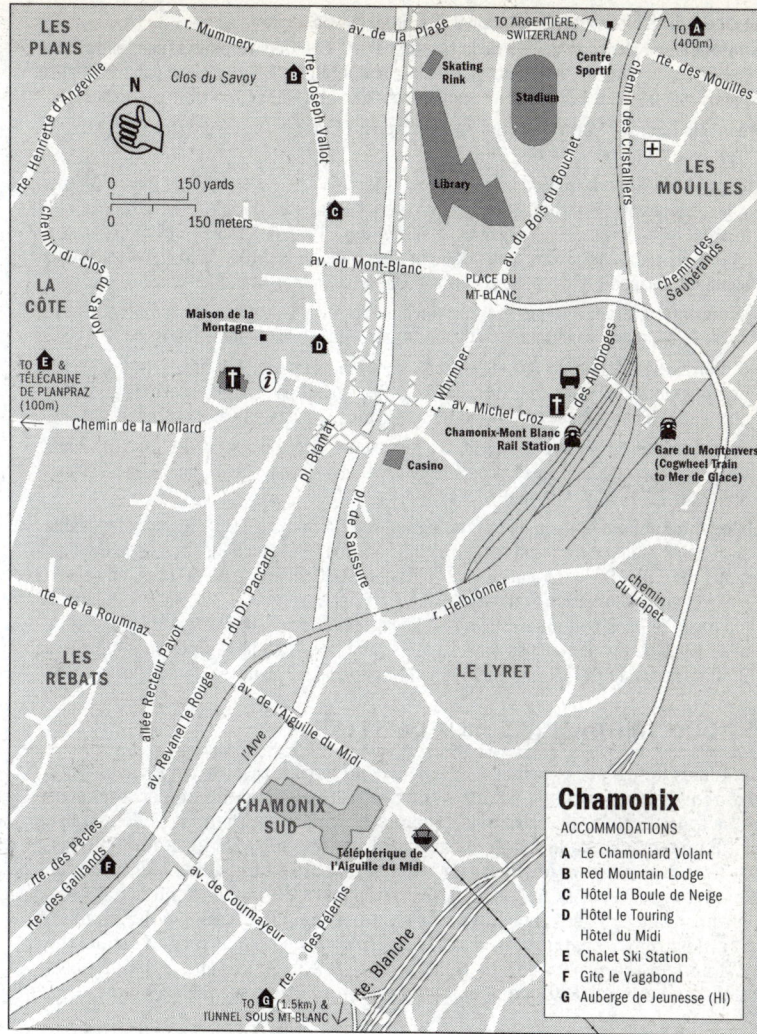

Chamonix

ACCOMMODATIONS

A Le Chamoniard Volant
B Red Mountain Lodge
C Hôtel la Boule de Neige
D Hôtel le Touring
   Hôtel du Midi
E Chalet Ski Station
F Gîte le Vagabond
G Auberge de Jeunesse (HI)

Tourist Office: 85 pl. du Triangle de l'Amitié (tel. 04 50 53 00 24; fax 04 50 53 58 90). Lists of hotels and dorms and a map of campgrounds. Reservations service (30F deposit for stays over 2 nights). Hiking map *Carte des Sentiers d'Été* (25F) and free *Chamonix Magazine*. Details on area cable cars. User-friendly computer gives numbers and weather conditions in English. **Currency exchange** with good rates. Open daily high season 8:30am-7:30pm; low season 8:30am-12:30pm and 2-7pm.

English Books: Librairie V.O., 20 av. Ravanel le Rouge (tel. 04 50 53 24 41). Paperback best-sellers and classics. Open daily 9am-11pm.

Laundromat: Lav'matic, 40 impasse Primevère. Open daily 8am-8pm.

Hospital: Centre Hospitalier, 509 rte. des Pélerins (tel. 04 50 53 84 00).

Police: 48 rue Hôtel de Ville (tel. 04 50 55 99 58).

Post Office: Pl. Jacques-Balmat (tel. 04 50 53 15 90), by the Arve bridge. **Currency exchange.** Open M-F 8:30am-noon and 2-6pm, Sa 8:30am-noon. **Postal code:** 74400.

SKIING, BIKING, AND HIKING RESOURCES

Weather Conditions: At Maison de la Montagne and Club Alpin Français (see below), the tourist office, and in the window of Pharmacie Mont Blanc where av. Croz and rue Vallot meet. Call 08 36 68 02 74 for a French recording of weather and road conditions.

Mountain Rescue: PGHM Secours en Montagne, 69 rte. de la Mollard (tel. 04 50 53 16 89). Emergency service open 24hr.

Bike and Ski Rental: Dozens of places rent skis; don't pay over 80F per day, 350F per week. **Chamonix Mountain Bike,** 132 rue des Moulins (tel. 04 50 53 54 76). Bike with helmet, lock, and maps 30F per hr., 95F per day, 450F M-Sa. Skis 39-100F per day, 200-500F per week. Snowboards 95F per day, with boots 140F; 595F per week, boots included. Passport or credit card deposit. Open daily 9am-7pm. V, MC.

Cycling Information: Pick up the free, invaluable map/guide *Itinéraires Autorisés aux Vélos Tout Terrain,* at the tourist office or at mountain biking rental shops.

Ski Information: École du Ski, downstairs from Maison de la Montagne. Next door, the **Compagnie des Guides** (tel. 04 50 53 00 88) organizes skiing and climbing lessons and leads guided summer hikes and winter ski trips. Register the evening before 5-7pm.

Hiking Equipment: Sanglard Sports, 31 rue Michel Croz (tel. 04 50 53 24 70). Boots 45F per day, 270F per week. Open July-Aug. 9am-7:30pm; Sept.-June 9am-12:30pm and 2:30-7:30pm. V, MC, AmEx.

Hiking Information: Maison de la Montagne, (tel. 04 50 53 22 08). The knowledgeable staff helps plan your adventures, gives info on weather conditions, and sells detailed maps (54-69F). Open daily in summer 8:45am-12:30pm and 2:30-6:15pm; off-season closed Sa-Su. **Club Alpin Français,** 136 av. Michel-Croz (tel. 04 50 53 16 03). Info on mountain *refuges* and road conditions. Register with guides 6-7:30pm the day before hikes. Bulletin board matches drivers, riders, and hiking partners. Open July-Aug. M-Sa 9:30am-noon and 3-7:30pm; Sept.-June M-Tu and Th-F 3-7pm, Sa 9am-noon.

■ ACCOMMODATIONS AND CAMPING

Chamonix's hotels are expensive. The *gîtes* and dormitories, when you can get a spot, are very basic, but still a budget traveler's dream. During summer weekends call the tourist office for availability: there are many more than *Let's Go* can list, they fill up fast, and it's possible to wander from one full *gîte* to another all day. Most *gîtes* are on mountainsides or in valleys, and are better suited to hiking than Chamonix nightlife. Both hotels and *gîtes* are packed during the winter (reserve 6 weeks in advance), ease up in autumn and spring, and fill up again in the summer. The hardest time to get a room is early February, when a car race overruns the city. Mountain *refuges* tend to be remote, have few facilities, and are sometimes unattended. For information on nearby mountain *refuges,* see **Hiking,** below.

Auberge de Jeunesse (HI), 127 montée Jacques Balmat (tel. 04 50 53 14 52; fax 04 50 55 92 34), in Les Pèlerins, at the foot of the Glacier de Bossons. Take the bus from pl. de l'Église (direction "Les Houches") to "Pèlerins École" (7F), and follow the signs uphill to the hostel. By train, get off at "Les Pèlerins" and follow the signs. You can also walk down rte. des Pèlerins (30min.). The glacier looks close enough to touch from your window. Vibrant, international crowd. **Bike rental** 30F per day. All-inclusive winter ski packages 2500-3500F per week. Dorms 76F; singles 98F; doubles 85F per person. Breakfast included. Meals 50F; vegetarian meals on request. Sheets 19F. Reception daily 8am-noon, 4-7:30pm, and 8:30-10pm; drop bags off any time. V, MC.

Red Mountain Lodge, 435 rue Joseph-Vallot (tel. 04 50 53 94 97). Cozy, superbly renovated chalet in the middle of town has a friendly international atmosphere, great communal space, and some of the best views around. Spring-autumn, the friendly Ozzie owner can provide info on hikes and outdoor activities, and will even coordinate them for a fee. If full, he can send you to his newly-opened other hotel, where jacuzzi access is available to customers of both hotels (40F). Barbecues twice a week (around 60F).

In winter the chalet is contracted out for groups only. Beautiful dorms 100F per person; doubles and triples 120F, with shower 160F. Includes sheets and breakfast.

Le Chamoniard Volant, 45 rte. de la Frasse (tel. 04 50 53 14 09; fax 04 50 53 23 25), 15min. from town center. From the station, turn right, go under the bridge, and turn right across the tracks, left on chemin des Cristalliers, and right on rte. de la Frasse. Climbers and hikers pack this popular *gîte*. Kitchen facilities. *Fondue* or *tartiflette* dinner 80F; 4-course *menu* 70F. 70 beds in 4- to 8-bed dorms 67F, 62F with *Let's Go*. Breakfast 28F. Sheets 20F first night, free thereafter. Reception daily 10am-10pm.

Chalet Ski Station, 6 rte. des Moussoux (tel. 04 50 53 20 25), near *télécabine* de Planpraz. Straight up the hill from the tourist office (follow signs to Les Moussoux). Space for cooking if you have a camp stove. 4- to 9-bunk dorms 65F. Shower 5F. Sheets 30F. Reception daily Dec. 20-May 10 and June 25-Sept. 20 9am-11pm. Check-out 11am. Reduced rates (20%) on the Brévent *téléphérique* in summer.

Gîte le Vagabond, 365 av. Ravanel-le-Rouge (tel. 04 50 53 15 43; fax 04 50 53 68 21). A sparkling-new *gîte* near the center of town. Kitchen and laundry facilities. Hip bar and restaurant downstairs. Dorms 70F with 100F key deposit. Sheets 6F. Showers 5F. Breakfast 25F. Veggie or meat dinner 40F. Reception noon-2pm and 4pm-1am.

Hôtel le Touring, 95 rue Joseph-Vallot (tel. 04 50 53 59 18). Large, older rooms with charming alpine decor, all with showers. Singles 165-210F depending on season; doubles 220-390F. Extra bed 60F. Breakfast 34-42F. Reception 8am-10pm. V, MC.

Hôtel du Midi (tel. 04 50 53 05 62; fax 04 50 53 67 25). Around the corner from le Touring and under the same management. Gorgeous courtyard, smaller rooms, and views. Singles 165-215F; doubles 200-280F; triples and quads 253-360F. Breakfast 32F. Reception 8am-10pm. V, MC.

Hôtel la Boule de Neige, 362 rue Joseph-Vallot (tel. 04 50 53 04 48; fax 04 50 55 91 09). Simple but inviting chalet-style rooms, some with Mont Blanc view. Singles 160-220F; doubles 205-245F; triples 285-345F; quads 355-425F. Breakfast 30F. V, MC.

Campsites: Several sites lie near the foot of the Aiguille du Midi cable car. It is illegal to pitch tents in the Bois du Bouchet. **L'Île des Barrats,** rte. des Pèlerins (tel. 04 50 53 51 44), has one of the nicest views but gets crowded. From the cable car, turn left, pass the busy intersection, continue 5min., and look right. 27F per person, 22F per tent, 12F per car. Electricity 16F. Reception daily July-Aug. 8am-noon and 2-8pm; May-June and Sept. 9am-noon and 4-7pm. Closed in winter. **Les Rosières,** 121 clos des Rosières (tel. 04 50 53 10 42), off rte. de Praz, is the closest site on the other side of Chamonix and often has space. Follow rue Vallot for 2km or take a bus to "Les Nants." 24F per person, 11F per tent, 11F per car. Open Dec. 15-Oct. 15. Reception daily 8am-9pm

🍴 FOOD

The Chamonix tourist machine produces better restaurants than most towns with such a high percentage of visitors. Many bars in town serve good meals. Regional fare like *fondue* and *raclette*, share menu space with international ski staples. It's hard to go too wrong—but it's also hard to eat cheap. The **Super U,** 117 rue Joseph Vallot, is the cheapest place for groceries. (Open M-Sa 8:15am-7:30pm, Su 8:15am-12:15pm.) Morning **markets** are held on pl. du Mont Blanc (Sa) and Chamonix Sud (Tu), near the foot of the Aiguille du Midi *téléphérique*. The **Jekyll** (see **Entertainment,** below) is a popular bar that also serves food.

Le Panier des 4 Saisons, 24 rue Paccard in the Galerie Blanc Neige (tel. 04 50 53 98 77). *The* place to go in Chamonix, if you want to splurge. 98F *menu* will get you 3 very gratifying courses of fresh local cuisine. Open Th-Tu. V, MC.

Wild Wallabies, rue de la Tour (tel. 04 50 53 01 31). Bring your bathing suit—the pool is free to patrons. Specialties include calamari (35F), barbecue (65F), an enormous 99F *menu,* and Aussie brews. Open daily 11am-2am.

La Cantina, 37 impasse des Rhododendrons (tel. 04 50 53 64 20), is a rowdy Mexican restaurant with 55-75F *plats*. Its small basement bar features live music and has a good vibe when it fills up. Open daily lunch and dinner.

🎵 🎭 ENTERTAINMENT AND FESTIVALS

Chamonix's three discos are popular in the winter when people shake what's left of their ski-weary bodies after bars close down—but during the summer they can be painfully empty, as hikers swap tales over beers. On bar-filled **rue des Moulins,** you won't have to crawl far between drinks.

The Jekyll, 71 rte. des Pélerins (tel. 04 50 55 99 70). Straight out of Dublin, the place is run (and overrun) by friendly foreigners. A Chamonix landmark, the bar also serves huge portions of food—down your Guinness (33F) with a burger (64F), scampi (59F), or fantastic salads (30-50F). Open daily 4pm-2am, earlier in bad weather.

Les Choucas, 224 rue Paccard. Alpine swank in a revamped chalet named after a local little black bird. Mixes bar atmosphere with night-club energy. Open nightly.

Le Garage, 200 av. de l'Aiguille (tel. 04 50 53 64 49), is generally considered the best of the Chamonix discos. Things get rolling after 1am. No cover, but one drink required (from 30F). Open nightly in winter 10pm-4am; rest of year Th-Sa.

Dick's Tea Bar, rue du Moulins (tel. 04 50 53 19 10), is the flagship of a bar saturated street. It's like a UN meeting where all the ambassadors can dance. Closed in summer.

Arbate, 80 chemin du Sapi (tel. 04 50 53 44 43), draws in a vast array of live music acts into its large 2-floor bar. 8-9pm means happy hour. Cover only for well-known bands.

Every July and August, the **Semaines Musicales du Mont-Blanc** bring chamber music and jazz to Chamonix (tickets 80-120F at tourist office).

🏔 OUTDOOR PURSUITS

Whether you've come to climb up these mountains or to ski down them, you're in for a challenge, and general precautions are in order. Steep grades, potential avalanches, and unique terrain means that this is not the place to do things you haven't done before. **La Mer de Glace** (tel. 04 50 53 12 54) is accessible by special trains running from a small station next to the main *gare*, and is a must for those who have never been on a glacier. (56F, round-trip 73F. May-Sept. daily 8:30am-5:30pm.) From the Mer, a cable-car runs down to an **ice cave** that is carved afresh every year—the glacier slides 30m per year so look for last year's cave further down the wall of ice. The adventurous prefer the two-hour hike (in summer only; see **Intermediate Hikes,** below, for directions). Consider taking the train up and then hiking back. It's downhill, and just as you run out of breath, the **Luge d'Été,** a concrete chute, whisks you to the bottom. You can also ride the luge without the hike. (Tel. 04 50 53 08 97. Open July-Aug. daily 10am-7:30pm; Sept. and June daily 2:30-5:30pm; Oct.-Nov. Sa-Su 1:30-5:30pm. 21F.)

TÉLÉPHÉRIQUES. Whether you're hiking in summer or skiing in winter, chances are you'll need to take a *téléphérique* (cable car) part of the way. Even if you're not the outdoors type, don't miss a chance to ride one for a spectacular and unmissable view. A board on pl. de l'Église lists the lifts currently open.

The **Aiguille du Midi** (tel. 04 50 53 30 80; 24hr. reservations 04 50 53 40 00) runs all year. Those with acrophobia (fear of heights) or argentophobia (fear of shelling out big bucks) might avoid the pricey and often frightening ride, which ascends above towering forests and rocky, snow-covered cliffs to the needlepoint peak at the top. Among the brave and well-to-do, however, few are disappointed by the ride. Go early, as clouds and crowds usually gather by mid-morning. It's not worth getting off at the first stop, **Plan de l'Aiguille** (64F, round-trip 82F), less than halfway to the second stop, **l'Aiguille du Midi** ("Needle of the South"). At the Aiguille, the panorama is magnificent but the experience of being 3842m high is equally worthwhile. Bring warm clothes and take it easy up top. Don't bother paying the additional 13F to go right to the top of the summit for a marginally better view (1½hr., round-trip 180F). Instead, if you've gone that far, you might as well pay an extra 96F for the round-trip to **Helbronner.** Four-person gondolas take you into the heart of the glacial beast and let you rest in **Italy** for great views of three countries, the **Matterhorn** and **Mont Blanc,** as well as the opportunity for a picnic on the glacier. The *téléphérique* descends the other side of the mountain into Italy at **La Palud,** near the resort town of **Courmayeur.** Bring a passport and cash—the Italian side doesn't accept credit cards for the cable car. Check that the entire *téléphérique* route is in operation before setting out for this trip. (*Téléphérique* open daily July-Aug. 6am-5pm; Apr.-June and Sept. 9am-3pm.)

There are several other *téléphériques* open year-round. **Le Brévent** (2525m) leaves from the corner of rte. Henriette and La Mollard up the street from the tourist office, and offers more stunning views of Mont Blanc and Chamonix from the opposite side of the valley. (One-way 55F, round-trip 80F. Open July-Aug. 8am-6pm; Sept.-June 9am-5pm.) **L'Index** (2385m) accesses some of the most popular hiking trails on the same side of the valley as Le Brevent and leaves from Les Praz, east of the city on rue Joseph-Vallon. The gondolas stop at **La Flégère** (43F, round-trip 55F) before finally getting to L'Index (67F, round trip 79F). (Open July-Aug. 8am-5pm; June and Sept. 8am-12:30pm and 1:30-4:45pm.)

SKIING. If you're in town a few days, buy daily lift tickets at individual areas—one area is more than enough per day. If you plan to ski for four or more days, con-

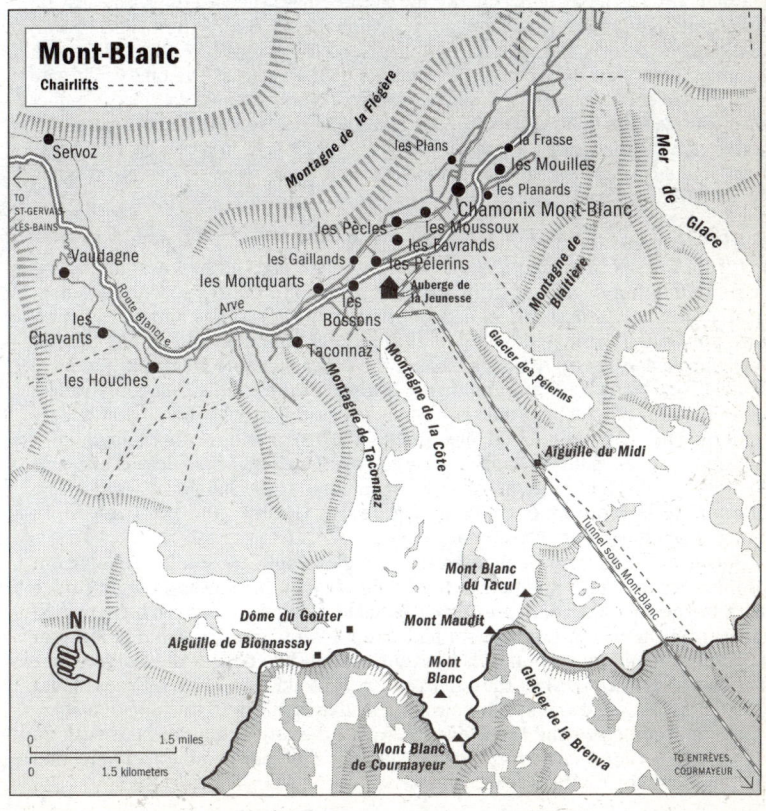

THE SOUTHEAST

sider a **Skipass Mont Blanc** (about 1000F per week), available at the tourist office, which is valid on all lifts in the valley and also good at **Courmayeur-Val Veny** in Italy.

Situated in a valley, Chamonix is surrounded by skiable mountains. On the southern side, **Le Tour-Col. de Balme** (tel. 04 50 54 00 58), above the village of **Le Tour,** cuddles up to the Swiss border and provides excellent views on sundrenched slopes, making it a delightful spot for intermediate skiers. (1-day lift pass 120F.) Just west, **Grands Montets** (3275m) is the grande dame of Chamonix's ski spots and the reason many a skier comes here. It's virtually all advanced terrain, and most skiers should test their mettle elsewhere before ascending. Almost directly above Chamonix, the **Vallée Blanche** requires no lift ticket, just a healthy dose of courage and insanity. The ungroomed, unmarked 20km trail with no ski patrol descends down a glacier from the summit of the Aiguille du Midi *téléphérique* down to Chamonix (144F for *téléphérique;* reserve in high season). Check the conditions before you go, and bring means to call for aid. Going with a guide who understands the terrain is highly recommended; going alone is simply stupid. Reserve a spot on the *téléphérique* in high season (tel. 08 36 68 00 67).

At the far west end of the valley, the village of **Les Houches** offers good slopes at the beginner-intermediate end. On the northern side of the valley, **Le Brevent** (2525m; tel. 04 50 53 13 18), a famous proving ground for experts, has also expanded skiing for beginners and intermediates. (1-day lift pass 230F.) Le Brevent also has lift connections with **La Flégère** (2595m), where endless open slopes are best suited to intermediate and advanced skiers. For either you can start your day at the La Flégère, Le Brévent, or Plan Praz *téléphériques.*

Chamonix has many opportunities for **glacier skiing.** The vast expanses provide breathtaking views, but glaciers are not snow fields. Stay within sight of trail markers, or you may end up at the bottom of a *crevasse.* If you ski off-*piste*, check your route with the **ski patrol** or the **Office de Haut Montagne.** The only really safe way to glacier ski, especially if you're new to Chamonix, is with a guide. Contact the **Compagnie des Guides** (see p. 372; about 350F per person). Beginners can get on a glacier at the **Glacier du Mont Blanc** (tel. 04 50 53 12 39). It's not that big (400m vertical), but it is near the huge **Glacier des Bossons,** and has night skiing. (Night skiing W-Th. 50F, 1-day pass 80F.)

HIKING. Chamonix has hundreds of kilometers of hikes through terrain ranging from forests to glaciers. A web of trails, each marked by lines painted on trees indicating degree of difficulty, wraps around the town. The 25F map, available at the tourist office, lists all the mountain *refuges* and gives departure points and estimated length of all the trails. Climbers should buy the **IGN topographic map** (see p. 54), available at the **Office de Haute Montagne** and local bookstores. Many trails start out in the further reaches of the Chamonix valley, but a handful of excellent ones are easily accessible from town. If you're very experienced, you can ascend **Mont Blanc** (4807m), a two- or three-day hike— but don't try this solo. Even in August you can be caught in a vicious blizzard; in 1996 the top had more snow in summer than at the height of winter. The Maison de la Montagne, the Compagnie des Guides, and the Club Alpin Français all have crucial information.

Because of Chamonix's almost vertical valley walls, most hikes leading out of the town are steep and take several hours to gain the **balcony,** the first ridge with the best views. There are some **easy hikes** along the southern balcony that start from the top of the Brevent and Index *téléphériques*. From **le Planpraz** (1999m, the middle station of le Brevent), follow the GRP trail west over the **Col de Brevent** (2368m) to the top of le Brevent ski-lift (1¾hr.). From **l'Index** (2385m), follow the signs and the rolling trail as it skirts to the side of a steep ridge and comes to the **Lac Blanc** (1¼hr.), a beautiful glacial lake with an expensive *refuge* nearby (tel. 04 50 53 49 14). (270F per person, including dinner and breakfast.) Make reservations.

For an **intermediate-level** hike, follow the signs from Montenvers *gare* and the trail as it ascends diagonally across the valley some 900m vertically to the foot of the **Mer de Glace** glacier and the **refuge Montenvers** (tel. 04 50 53 00 33; one-way 2½hr.). Mountaineers use this *refuge* as a base for serious ice climbing. (78F, with breakfast and dinner 203F. Open May-Sept.) From rte. Blanche at the foot of the Aiguille *téléphérique*, a series of steep trails (all 3½hr. one-way) ascend 1300m vertical to the **refuge Plan de l'Aiguille** (tel. 04 50 53 55 60), just below the first cable-car stop. (60F, with breakfast and dinner 165F. Open mid-June-mid-Sept.) From **Les Praz**, a steep switch-backing trail (3hr. one-way) runs to the right of the cable-car and ascends 800m vertical to the middle station, the tree-line, and the *refuge* **Chalet de la Flégère**. (July-Aug., including dinner and breakfast 180F. June and Sept., night only, 63F.) From there it's another 1¾ hours and 500m over the **Montagne de la Flégère** to **Lac Blanc**.

VAL D'ISÈRE

Val d'Isère (pop. 3000; 1850m) is named for the river that flows through the town, but it makes its livelihood from the peaks above. The Val's sole purpose is to worship the mountains, the snow, and native son Jean-Claude Killy, who won gold in *all* the men's downhill events in the 1968 Grenoble Winter Olympics. But that's not the only reason he's a hero here; Killy is the dynamo who brought Olympic events to Val d'Isère in 1992, just after he helped turn its main street into a tourist-laden strip of expensive hotels, restaurants, and ski boutiques that looks like one big wooden development. He must have made a Killyng—only the minuscule *vieille ville* remains as a memory of the original hamlet. The Espace Killy, an immense network of trails and lifts connecting Val d'Isère to Tignes on the other side of the mountain, covers well over 10,000 hectares (21,700 acres). With an average annual snowfall of 10m, Val d'Isère is not modest about its powdered slopes. In summer, snow and prices melt, bikers and climbers fill the hotels that stay open, and skiers retreat to the Glaciers du Pissaillas, where slushy white stuff persists until mid-August. A particularly good or bad time to come, depending on whether you want to share it with huge crowds, is Dec. 8-12, when the **Criterium de la Premiere Neige**, the first international competition of the season, comes to Val.

🚻 ORIENTATION AND PRACTICAL INFORMATION

Val d'Isère has no train station—getting here takes time and money. The nearest station is in **Bourg-St-Maurice**, 30km to the north; a bus leaves for Val d'Isère (three per day, 66F). If you're going to the hostel, get off at **Les Boisses**, 7km short of Val d'Isère (57F). In summer, the last bus leaves around 6pm; service is more frequent in winter. There are no street names in the town, but the tourist office map includes every building in town in a funky 3D design.

Trains: Pl. de la Gare in **Bourg St-Maurice**. To: **Annecy** (3-4 per day, 138F); **Lyon** (3-4 per day, 164F); and **Grenoble** (3-4 per day, 128F).

Buses: Autocars Martin (tel. 04 79 06 00 42 for reservations), 100m down the street from tourist office. Open July-Aug. M-Sa. 9-11am and 2-8pm; Oct.-June daily 9-11am and 2-8pm. **Main office** at pl. de la Gare in Bourg St-Maurice (tel. 04 79 07 04 49). Open daily 8am-noon and 2-6pm. In winter, buses go to **Geneva airport** (4hr.; M-F 3 per day, Sa-Su 5 per day; 268F). Buses to and from **Les Boisses** and the **hostel** (10min., 18F). **SNCF** info and reservation desk (tel. 04 79 06 03 55) are in the same building. Open Tu-Sa 9:30am-noon and 2:30-6pm.

Public Transportation: Val d'Isère runs free shuttles *(navettes)* about town. The "Rouge STVI" runs between La Daille and Le Fornet, while the "Manchet" runs only in summer from the tourist office up to le Manchet Sports complex. Both are very useful for shaving time off of the treks to the *refuges*. The last shuttles are generally around 7:30pm.

Bike and Ski Rental: Jean Sports (tel. 04 79 06 04 44), 100m up from the tourist office. Bikes 90F per half-day, 110F per day. Skis 30-50F per day in summer; 110-170F in winter. Boots 20F per day. Passport deposit. Open daily in summer 8:30am-7:30pm; in winter 8:30am-8pm; closed May-June and Sept.-Oct.

Taxis: Tel. 04 79 06 19 92. 24hr.

Hitchhiking: Infrequent buses, no trains, and sympathetic locals make hitching a popular mode of transport. Those going from the hostel to Val d'Isère cross the dam and wait by the highway. No one hitches after dark. Even you.

Tourist Office: Tel. 04 79 06 06 60; fax 04 79 06 04 56. Send mail to Boîte Postale 228. Free maps, brochures, and accommodations service. Open June 30-Sept. 5 and Dec. to mid-May 8:30am-7:30pm; Sept. 4-Nov. 31 and mid-May to June 2 9am-noon and 2-7pm. **Annex** at the entrance to town, a small shack on the right as you make your way up from La Daille (tel. 04 79 06 19 67). Ask for the summer or winter guide. Open daily June-Aug. 7 10am-noon and 3-7pm; Dec.-Apr. Sa-Su 9am-noon and 2-7pm.

Laundromat: La Grande Lessive, 200m below the tourist office, left at the roundabout. Open daily Nov.-Apr. 7:30am-10pm and May-Oct. 9am-8pm.

Weather, Ski, and Road Info: Call tourist office or listen to **Radio Val** (96.1FM; tel. 04 79 06 18 66). **Weather forecast,** call 08 36 68 02 73. **Ski info,** call 04 79 06 25 55; **Ski Lifts,** call 04 79 06 00 35; **Ski Patrol,** call 04 79 06 02 10.

Hospital: In Bourg St-Maurice (tel. 04 79 41 79 79).

Police: Tel. 04 79 06 03 41.

Post Office: Across from the tourist office (tel. 04 79 06 06 99). **Currency exchange.** Open in ski season M-F 8:30am-6:30pm, Sa 8:30am-noon; rest of year M-F 9am-noon and 2-6:30pm, Sa 9am-noon. **Postal code:** 73150.

■ ACCOMMODATIONS AND CAMPING

World class slopes only feet away make finding a room very tough in winter, while finding rooms in summer is generally hassle-free. During the off-season, many hotels close, so it can be hard to find a place to stay. The cheapest beds are at the two *refuges*, **Le Prarion** and **Le Fond Des Fours,** each at least a two hour hike from downtown (see **Intermediate Hikes,** below, for directions and prices). In the winter, their hospitality and location pack these places with off-*piste* skiers who attach *peaux de phoques* (seal skins) for uphill traction on the way to the *refuges*.

Auberge de Jeunesse "les Clarines" (HI) (tel. 04 79 06 35 07; fax 04 79 41 03 36; reservations tel. 04 79 41 01 93), in the village of **Les Boisses** at the junction of the routes to Val d'Isère (7km south) and Tignes (5km west). From Val d'Isère, a pleasant, well-marked trail begins at La Daille, the foot of the valley. Follow the river down to the lake and bear left along the shore until you ford a cascading creek. Turn right, cross the bridge, and take the small, unmarked path ascending to the right until it meets the road. To the right is Les Boisses and the hostel (1½hr.). Or take the "Tignes/Val Claret" bus to "Les Boisses" from Bourg-St-Maurice (57F) or Val d'Isère (18F). A free shuttle runs between Tignes and Les Boisses 2-3 times per day, more in winter. Spotless rooms, some with bath and shower, as well as a TV room, a bar, and info on outdoor activities. The hostel also runs **packages** of **skiing, hiking, biking,** and **water sports** (1870-4380F per week), as well as **paragliding** excursions and **horse riding, biking,** and **rock-climbing** trips. Trips are led by experts, and prices are the lowest around. 120F dorms include breakfast and dinner—a steal in the Val. Reception 5-10pm, drop off bags any time. Ask for the code if you're going to be out past 10pm. Reserve in Sept. for Dec. or Feb. and six weeks ahead for Jan., Mar., or Apr.

Moris Pub (tel. 04 79 06 22 11). Friendly, English pub rents bright rooms upstairs for what in Val d'Isère are considered astonishingly cheap prices. 150F per person includes breakfast. Reception in pub open daily 11am-1am. Open in summer. V, MC.

Le Relais du Ski (tel. 04 79 06 02 06; fax 04 79 41 10 64), past the tourist office on the left. The once-expensive hotel has been cut in two; the cheaper half lacks views and in-room showers. Hearty restaurant (*plat du jour* 48F, *menu* 105F). Singles 210-270F; doubles from 150F per person; triples 140F per person; quads 125F per person. Breakfast 45F. V, MC.

Hôtel Sakura/Les Crêtes Blanches (tel. 04 79 06 04 08), below the tourist office on a side street. Friendly couple rents spacious, wood-paneled rooms with balcony and TV. Also shelters a huge salon/breakfast room with snooker, a terrace, and glorious views. Prices vary according to season; rooms are cheapest in July, with singles from 180F and doubles from 250F. 2-person apartments from 1600F per week, negotiable for several nights. Breakfast included. Open July-Aug. for short stays; Oct.-June 1-week min. stay.

Campsites: Camping les Richardes (tel. 04 79 06 26 60), 500m up from tourist office. Plain campground in a beautiful setting with few trailers, yet close enough to amenities in town. Crowded in Aug. 12F per person, 8F per tent, 8F per car. Electricity 12F. Showers 6F. Reception 9am-noon and 5-8pm. Open June 15-Sept.

🖐🎵 FOOD AND ENTERTAINMENT

Perhaps someday Jean-Claude Killy will bring affordable dining to Val d'Isère just as Prometheus descended with fire to primitive man. Until then, the supermarkets will have to suffice. Pack for the slopes at **Marché U**, 100m below the tourist office. (Open daily 8:30am-1pm and 3:30-7:30pm.) During ski season, restaurants buzz with boasts of ski adventures; the rest of the year, many restaurants and virtually all nightlife close up. During the winter, **Café Face** (tel. 04 79 06 29 80), on the way to Le Bananas (see below), warms up the night with hip music and atmosphere.

La Perdrix Blanche (tel. 04 79 06 12 05). On the main road 100m below the tourist office. Immensely popular. Pizzas from 46F, including a vegetarian special (51F). Pasta (48F) and *crêpes* (15-45F) are other favorites. Wooden chalet walls are lined with pots, pans, paintings and posters. V, MC.

Le Bananas (tel. 04 79 06 04 23). Turn off the main road at Maison Chevallot, 100m below the tourist office. It's the last building on the right. Kooky little chalet serving even kookier dishes that riff off of Tex-Mex cuisine. *Ratatouille* tacos (60F) and banana salad (60F). Happy hour is from 7-8pm, but you can play backgammon or just hang out at the bar all night. V, MC.

The Bar-Restaurant L'Olympique (tel. 04 79 06 04 88), 200m up and across the street from the tourist office. Has a hearty 90F *menu* and *fondue savoyarde* with green salad (80F) in a relaxed atmosphere.

🏔 OUTDOOR ACTIVITIES

Skiing is king in Val d'Isère, with over 100 lifts giving access to 300km of trails; in summer, many hiking paths cross vast expanses of gravelly *pistes* (slopes). *Let's Go* has listed hikes which keep as clear of ski slopes and lifts as possible. The hostel (see above) runs outdoor adventure packages in winter and summer and arranges a variety of excursions. There's really no reason to come to Val d'Isère if you're not the outdoors type, but for a relaxing trip to the summit, take a *téléphérique* (cable car), which will whisk you up the peaks as spectacular vistas unfold before you. *Téléphériques* run to **Solaise** (ascents 9am-4pm; last descent 4:55pm) and **Bellevarde,** site of the 1992 Olympic downhill (ascents 9:30am-4:30pm; last descent 4:40pm). Both cost 55F, round-trip 70F and you can bring a bike or parasail on board for free.

SKIING. In Val d'Isère, you can ski for a week without repeating a run. Lift tickets cost 156F per half-day, 224F per day, and are cheaper over longer periods. They're valid on the entire **Espace Killy**, including **Val d'Isère** and **Tignes**. Excellent high-altitude beginner runs descend from the **Marmottes** and **Borsat Express** in the valley between Val d'Isère and Tignes. There's challenge in the expanses of off-*piste* skiing in the **Gorges de Malpasset** or the **Pisaillas glacier.** Check weather conditions and let the ski patrol know your itinerary. Never ski off-*piste* alone. Pisaillas is skiable July to mid-August; the snow softens after 11am. (110F per half-day, 140F per day; after 11am 98F per half-day, 110F per day. Lifts open at 7:30am.)

HIKING. Before hiking around Val d'Isère, be sure to check the weather report and to bring warm clothing. Snowstorms and winter weather are possible even in the summer. Some intermediate trails, when snow-covered, are passable only for those with the proper equipment and experience. Even though the trails around the Val are well-marked with blazes and signs, hikers should buy both the detailed *Val d'Isère—Balades et Sentiers* and a **hiking map** (25F for the guide, 45F for the map) in English at the tourist office. They include over 40 routes spanning 100km. **Mountain Guides** (tel. 04 79 06 06 60) has **ice climbing** (420F morning session) and **rock climbing** (180F afternoon session) schools and whole-day **canyoning** trips (420F). They also lead nature expeditions for all levels. Their desk in the tourist office opens at 6pm and closes with the office.

Until the construction of modern ski areas in the 60s, **Le Fornet** (1950m) was the highest year-round inhabited village in the French alps. It can be reached via an **easy** 4km, 1½-hour hike. Follow the main road up from the tourist office. After the church at the Tapia chalet, make a right on the small pedestrian paved road and continue straight on rue des Célibataires. Cross the village and follow the signs for the Combe du Laisisant. To return, descend the stairway to the main road, cross it, and look for the sign for the *Sentier des Charrières.* There's also a free shuttle bus if you're tired or lazy.

The most classic **intermediate** hikes in Val d'Isère also lead to the two closest *refuges.* To reach the **Refuge de Fornet** from le Fornet (one-way 3km, 1¾hr., 300m vertical), cross the bridge and, from the trail signs, take the trail that heads left out of town. After you cross the **pont St-Charles,** the marked trail switchbacks several times out of the far end of the parking lot before beginning a steep straight ascent up the **Gorges du Malpasset.** The trail then gains a plateau and continues gently to the *refuge.* There is plenty of wildlife, especially the ubiquitous furry marmots. (*Refuge* tel. 04 79 06 06 02. Staffed Nov.1-May 15 and June 15-Sept. 15. At other times, there is wood, gas, utensils, covers, and a tin box for your money. 68F per person. Hot showers 12F, animal-skin sleeping sacks 10F. Breakfast 32F, *à la carte* lunch 28-39F, meals 80F. Reserve 48hr. ahead at the tourist office and get a map.) From Prariond, you can climb another two hours and 600m vertical to the **Col de la Galise** (2987m), which affords one of the most stunning panoramas in the region. Coming out of the *refuge,* take the trail to the right. At the **Roche des Coses** (2750m), you can branch right for a 45-minute excursion into Italy and similarly stupendous vistas. Take care, since this trail is usually snow-covered year-round.

For the **Refuge des Fours,** take the free shuttle to **le Manchet** (see public transportation), and continue up the road to the trailhead near a cluster of old stone farmhouses. Take the trail on your right marked *"refuge des fours."* From there it's a steady climb to the hut in a high valley across from the Méan Martin glacier and alpine lakes. (One-way hike from le Manchet: 1¾hr., 560m vertical. *Refuge* tel. 04 79 06 16 90; same prices and staffing months as Refuge de Fournet.)

An **advanced full-day trek** heads from le Fornet to the **Lac de la Sassiere;** descend slightly and head away from town on the *Sentier des Charrières* before branching off to the right. The **Balleta** trail then climbs steeply for 800m (!!) to the small **Lac de la Balleta** (2½hr.) where it reaches a *col* and descends gradually to the larger **Lac de la Sassière.** This man-made lake is crammed with trout and surrounded by *chamois,* deer, and marmots. To return, retrace your steps for several hundred meters until the sign for **Picheru,** a steeper and more difficult path than the Bailleta route. Picheru passes over several very exposed knife-edge ridges before crossing just to the right of **Le Dome** and descending gradually into town. (Round-trip to Lac de la Sassiere: 12.2km, 7hr., 940m vertical.) Another advanced trek heads from the campground; grab the **GR5** (marked with red and white) and hold on tight for a harrowing ascent to the **Col de l'Iseran** (2770m). About half-way up, you'll cross the RD902 and wonder why you didn't just hitch. From the top there's a different glacier in every direction. (One-way to Col: 6km, 3hr., 914m vertical.)

THE NORTHEAST

Commonly ignored by travelers except as a rest stop between France and the rest of Europe, the "frontier regions" of the northeast represent the final frontier in French tourism. Sprawling clockwise from the Chunnel terminus to a mountainous border with Switzerland, the regions of Flanders, Champagne, Alsace, Lorraine, and Franche-Comté have been remembered as battlefields since the Middle Ages, and for many travelers the northeast will be of interest for reasons primarily historical. Yet the fields of Champagne, the wine towns surrounding Strasbourg, and the splendid hiking trails in the Jura

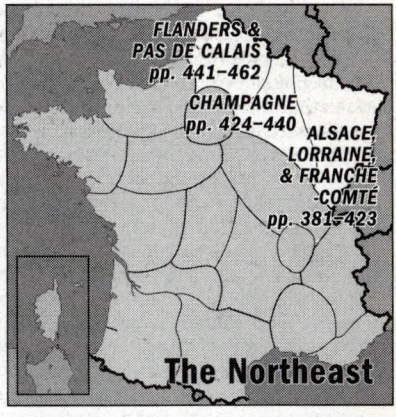

FLANDERS &
PAS DE CALAIS
pp. 441–462

CHAMPAGNE
pp. 424–440

ALSACE,
LORRAINE,
& FRANCHE-
COMTÉ
pp. 381–423

The Northeast

mountains suggest another motive for visiting the area. Furthermore, the bloody history of these regions has done more than leave behind solemn monuments—it has left behind a culturally independent region as unique as any other in France.

HISTORY: INVITATIONS TO INVASION

Though Alsace had been won for the Roman Empire by Cæsar himself, by the 3rd century AD barbarian incursions across the Rhine had become all too commonplace, and Germanic tribes had overrun the region by the Empire's fall in the 5th century. To the north, Frankish settlers soon outnumbered the original inhabitants, replacing the Gallo-Roman proto-French with a Germanic tongue that would evolve into modern-day Flemish. The entire region was incorporated into Charlemagne's empire in the 9th century, but his death brought lasting divisions. The treaty of Verdun in 843 split Flanders between the nascent French Kingdom and the Holy Roman Empire to the east; Alsace and Lorraine, initially contested, were firmly in the control of the Emperor by the end of the century. Whoever had nominal control over the region, the realities of feudal politics put power firmly in local hands. Champagne was born in the 10th century as the union of Troyes and Meaux, and grew in power until the Counts of Champagne had encircled the holdings of the impotent French king in the 12th century. The threat to the Kingdom was removed in 1284 when the heiress of Champagne, Joan de Navarre, married the future King Philip IV; with the accession of their son Louis X to the throne, Champagne became irreversibly united to France.

Effectively independent from their overlords in France and Germany, the Counts of Flanders created an efficient post-feudal state. Relative freedom and the rule of law soon led to a business boom that made Flemish merchants the wealthiest in Europe. When Count Baldwin unexpectedly found himself Emperor of Byzantium in 1205, French King Philippe-Auguste took the opportunity to become embroiled Flemish politics. A century of war followed, culminating in a Flemish victory in 1302 and French recognition of Flemish independence. Farther south, Count Raynald III of Cisjuran Burgundy had managed the same trick with his German overlords in 1127; the idea of an independent count was so novel that his territory was re-christened the Free County, or Franche-Comté.

The 14th century was dominated by the rise of Burgundy to the southeast; Duke Philip the Bold inherited both Franche-Comté and Flanders in 1384, while Burgundian armies advanced into Lorraine. When Duke Charles the Bold's widow married the Emperor Maximilian I in 1477, Franche-Comté and Flanders were added to Hapsburg holdings in Germany and Spain. This alarmed French monarchs, who found themselves encircled by a powerful rival. Over the next two centuries, Franche-Comté served as a battlefield until the French conquered it definitively in 1674. The same period saw French armies taking advantage of turmoil in Germany to occupy Lorraine, while an Alsatian appeal for French protection against their religiously intolerant neighbors led their incorporation into France by the end of the 17th century. A century later, expansion during the Revolutionary era brought Flanders back into the French orbit, though the northern half of the province was incorporated into the Netherlands (and later Belgium) after the fall of Napoleon. Though by the mid-19th century France's northeastern boundary looked much as it does today, the region's turbulent history was by no means over. Napoleon III's defeat and capture by Bismarck's Prussians at Sedan in 1870 sealed the fate of Alsace-Lorraine as a German province for the next 45 years, while Colonel Denfer-Rochereau's heroic defence of Belfort kept Franche-Comté in French hands. French resentment over Alsace-Lorraine helped feed the fires that led to WWI, when millions died on the battlefields of the Somme and Verdun. 1918 brought Alsace and Lorraine back into French hands, but the heavy border fortifications of the Maginot Line along the Rhine stood silent in 1939 as Hitler's troops poured through Belgium and drove the allied armies into the sea at Dunkerque. Happily, since 1945 peace has returned, and the region, with its close links to Belgium, Germany, and England across the channel, has become a symbol of renewed European unity.

CLIMATE AND GEOGRAPHY

As befits that part of France closest to England, Flanders and the channel coast is cool and rainy throughout the year, though the sea tempers winter frosts. The beaches of the north, bisected by the waters of the Somme, give way to the fields of Champagne. Here a more continental climate holds sway, with long dry summers ideal for vines and cold, harsh winters. East of Champagne, the rolling plains of Lorraine slope down into Alsace where the Rhine marks a natural border with Germany. Most Alsatian towns lie a few miles to the west of the Rhine, on the smaller, parallel river Ill. Lying low in the Rhine and Moselle valleys, this area shares the hot summers but escapes the freezing winters of its higher western neighbor. In southern Alsace the Vosges mountains meet the Jura range at Belfort, marking the beginning of France-Comté. The Jura mountains are craggy in the east but gentle in the west, with the two halves being separated by a high, wooded plateau. Skiing is possible in the winter in the south-eastern Jura, while in the summer the cooler mountains provide ideal hiking conditions. Most of Franche-Comté's population resides north of the mountains, on the banks of the Doubs.

SUGGESTIONS

If you're traveling to or from Britain, **Boulogne** (p. 456) is the most pleasant port of arrival. Before zipping south, stop in **Arras** (p. 448), for historical delights and Flemish highlights, or in **Amiens** (p. 459) to see a Notre-Dame twice the size of that in Paris. Those suffering from millenial hangovers will find the source of all their troubles in the champagne tunnels of **Reims** (p. 426) and **Épernay** (p. 431). More colorful alcoholic tourism thrives along the **Route du Vin** (p. 403), running between semi-germanic **Strasbourg** (p. 395) and the more clichéd **Colmar** (p. 406). For a sobering experience, visit the war memorials at **Verdun** (p. 393). The **Jura mountains** (p. 421) have some of the best cross-country skiing and hiking in Europe.

ALSACE, LORRAINE, AND FRANCHE-COMTÉ

The northeastern frontier of France has had a tumultuous and varied history, defined by its place as first prize in the ceaseless border wars between France and Germany. Alsace and Lorraine have been political pawns since the 3rd century, when barbarian tribes first swept westward through these regions into Roman Europe. Ravaged after the Franco-Prussian War of 1870-1871, and ceded to Germany, Alsace-Lorraine suffered far worse devastation during France's drive for *revanche* in WWI and Germany's response in WWII. Snuggling up to the Jura mountains in the south is Franche-Comté, long a pawn of its powerful neighbors. Though the inhabitants had violently opposed France's final 1674 conquest of their land, 193 years later their valiant defense against the invading Prussians earned them the right to stay French in 1871.

With such a politically varied history, the whole region maintains a fascinating blend of local *patois* (dialect), cuisine, and architecture. While many associate Alsace with Lorraine, natives disagree. In Alsace's Vosges, wooded hills slope down to sunlit valleys and deep blue lakes, where hiking, camping, and cross-country skiing flourish. On the eastern foothills lie the striped, shiny vineyards of the Route de Vin, and Alsace's well-preserved towns offer geranium-draped, half-timbered Bavarian houses flanking tiny crooked streets and canals. In contrast, Lorraine unfolds to the west among wheat fields and gently undulating plains. The serenely elegant *lorrainais* cities feature broad, tree-lined boulevards and stately Baroque architecture, a far cry from the fairy-tale cottages and narrow cobbled streets of Alsace. Often overlooked by visitors to northeastern France, Franche-Comté is beginning to burst into the spotlight. Known for their lush, seemingly endless forests, the verdant, peaceful Jura mountains are a haven of serenity from the tourist-oriented kitsch to the north, and their green summits make excellent destinations for summer hikes. Blanketed in snow in the winter, the Jura is home to some of France's finest cross-country skiing, including the **Grand Traversée de Jura,** a 400km network of trails that spans the entire region.

The region's Germanic influences are most apparent in its cuisine, which pairs *baguettes* and fine wine with sauerkraut and heavy German meats. Among traditional Alsatian dishes are *tarte à l'oignon, choucroute garnie* (sauerkraut cooked in white wine sauce and topped with sausages and ham) and *coq au Riesling* (chicken in a white wine sauce). Alsace's much-touristed wine route boasts the dry Riesling, one of the world's finest whites, which presides over even the sharper, fragrant Gewurztztraminer. The Jura has a wine route of its own; vineyards stretching from Arbois to Lons-le-Saunier produce respectable *appellations* with a decidedly fruity flair, including the famous *vin jaune*. The regional cheese is the sharp *comté*. In Lorraine, what the culinary specialities lack in delicacy they make up in heartiness: bacon, butter, and cream are key ingredients in artery-hardening dishes such as *quiche lorraine*. Desserts include *madeleines* (lemony tea cakes) from Commercy and *macarons* from Nancy.

HIGHLIGHTS OF ALSACE, LORRAINE, AND FRANCHE COMTÉ

■ The birthplace of *La Marseillaise* and Gutenberg's printing press, **Strasbourg** is home to the European Parliament as well as a stunning cathedral (p. 395).

■ The vineyards of the **Route du Vin** align themselves along a narrow mountain corridor running 170km from Strasbourg to Mulhouse (p. 403).

■ Hike or ski the **Jura mountains**, renowned for their cross-country trails (p. 421).

■ The **WWI battlefields** around Verdun are marked by military cemeteries and somber crypts (p. 395).

■ **Nancy** pulsates around its splendidly gilded pl. Stanislas (p. 411).

▣ GETTING AROUND

Metz, Nancy, Besançon, and Strasbourg are major train hubs with frequent service to the rest of France, Germany, Belgium and Switzerland. Between smaller towns, notably Verdun and the Route du Vin, buses are more practical and less expensive. Within Lorraine and especially Alsace, biking is a good option, although too hilly for the casual rider. Keep in mind that the Vosges, the small mountain range dividing the two, will seem a lot larger when you're huffing and puffing your way up. For hikers, hundreds of kilometers of trails dotted with *fermes auberges* (overnight farm refuges) are marked on maps and guides available from tourist offices. Renting a car or bike, or taking a tour bus, are practical ways to see the battlefields at Verdun and many of the villages on the Route du Vin. Hitchers take advantage of the heavy industrial traffic, especially in Lorraine.

NANCY

After the Duke of Lorraine gave up his holdings for the more lucrative title of Holy Roman Emperor in 1737, Louis XV offered the vacant duchy refuge to his father-in-law Stanislas Lesczynski, the dethroned King of Poland. Nancy (pop. 100,000) owes its gilded beauty to the good Duke Stanislas, whose passion for town planning transformed the city into a model of 18th century classicism, with broad plazas, wrought-iron grillwork, and cascading fountains. The town is more than just a pretty face, however; Nancy still reigns as the cultural and intellectual heart of Lorraine, boasting resident symphony, ballet and opera companies, and several fascinating museums. The city's 30,000 students fuel a passion for jazz, manifested both in the live bands at bars and restaurants and the many festivals.

▣ ORIENTATION AND PRACTICAL INFORMATION

The heart of the city is **pl. Stanislas.** As you exit the station to the left, take a right at the Hôtel Altéa on rue Raymond Poincaré (not to be confused with the parallel rue Henri Poincaré), which turns into rue Stanislas and opens onto pl. Stanislas and the tourist office. Be careful around the train station at night.

Flights: Aéroport de Metz-Nancy Lorraine (tel. 03 87 56 70 00). To **Paris, Lyon, Toulouse, Marseille,** and **Nice.** Shuttles run to the train station (1hr., 5 per day, 40F).

Trains: pl. Thiers (tel. 03 83 22 10 00). To: **Metz** (40min., 31 per day, 51F); **Strasbourg** (1hr., 11 per day, 109F); and **Paris** (3hr., 15 per day, 206F). Ticket office open M-F 5:30am-7:30pm, Sa 5:30am-6:30pm, Su 6am-8:30pm.

Buses: Rapides de Lorraine, 89 rue St-Georges (tel. 03 83 32 80 00). Departs pl. Colonel Driant across the street. Day return to **Paris** 170F. Open M-F 8am-noon and 2-6pm.

Local Transportation: Agence Bus, 3 rue Dr. Schmitt (tel. 03 83 35 54 54). Free route maps at tourist office. Most buses stop at Point Central on rue St-Georges. Buy tickets on board, at the train station or from automatic distributors. Tickets 7.50F, *carnet* of 10 51F. Buses run 5:30am-8pm; some lines run until midnight.

Taxis: Taxi Nancy, 2 bd. Joffre (tel. 03 83 37 65 37). *Centre ville* to hostel around 70F at night.

Bike Rental: Michenon, 91 rue des 4 Églises (tel. 03 83 17 59 59).

Tourist Office: pl. Stanislas (tel. 03 83 35 22 41; fax 03 83 35 90 10), to the right as you enter the *place* from rue Stanislas. Free fold-out map. Ask for a copy of *Le Fil d'Ariane,* a free, comprehensive guide written and researched each year by a squad of students. **Currency exchange** when banks are closed. Reservation service 15F. Open M-Sa 9am-7pm, Su 10am-5pm; Oct.-May closed Su afternoon.

City tour: Tourist office leads 1½hr. tours. July-Aug. Sa 4pm and Su 10:30am; Sept.-Nov. and Mar.-June Sa 4pm. 35F. Call ahead for English tour, or rent headphones (35F, 300F deposit).

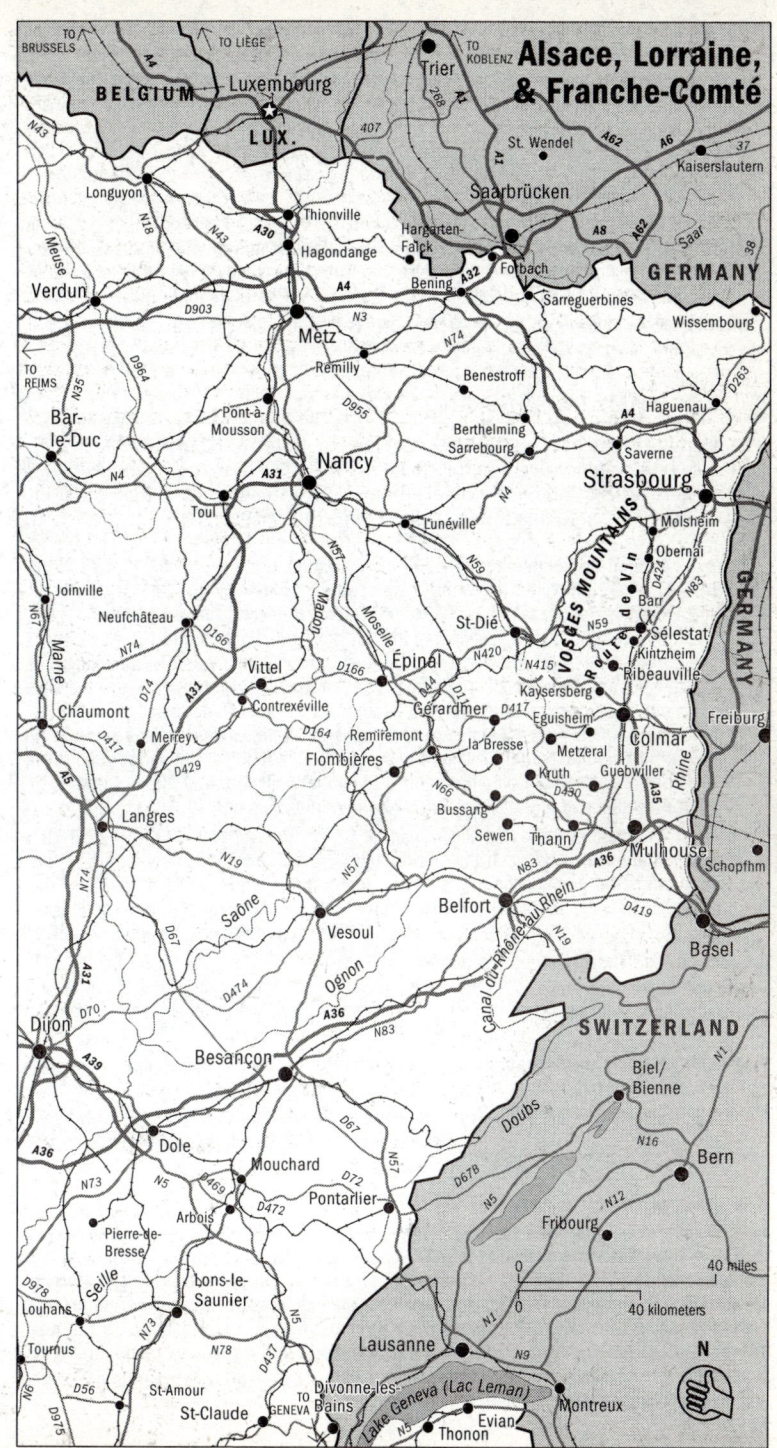

Alsace, Lorraine, & Franche-Comté

TO BRUSSELS
TO LIÈGE
TO KOBLENZ

BELGIUM
Luxembourg
LUX.
Trier
St. Wendel
Kaiserslautern
Saarbrücken
GERMANY
Longuyon
Thionville
Hargarten-Falck
Hagondange
Bening
Folbach
Sarreguebines
Verdun
Metz
Remilly
Benestroff
Wissembourg
TO REIMS
Bar-le-Duc
Pont-à-Mousson
Berthelming
Sarrebourg
Haguenau
Saverne
Nancy
Strasbourg
Toul
Lunéville
Molsheim
Obernai
Joinville
Neufchâteau
St-Dié
Barr
Sélestat
Kintzheim
Ribeauvillé
Vittel
Épinal
Kaysersberg
Contrexéville
Gérardmer
Eguisheim
Colmar
Chaumont
Remiremont
la Bresse
Metzeral
Freiburg
Merrey
Flombières
Kruth
Guebwiller
Bussang
Langres
Sewen
Thann
Mulhouse
Schopfhm
Vesoul
Belfort
Basel
Dijon
Besançon
SWITZERLAND
Biel/Bienne
Dole
Doubs
Bern
Mouchard
Pontarlier
Fribourg
Arbois
Pierre-de-Bresse
Lons-le-Saunier
Louhans
Tournus
Lausanne
St-Amour
St-Claude
Divonne-les-Bains
TO GENEVA
Montreux
Evian
Thonon
Lake Geneva (Lac Leman)

VOSGES MOUNTAINS
Route de Vin
Rhine
Rhein
Saône
Ognon
Canal du Rhône au Rhein
Selle

0   40 miles
0   40 kilometers

N

THE NORTHEAST

Budget Travel: Wasteels, 1bis pl. Thiers (tel. 03 83 35 42 29). Specializes in student passes and discount rates. Open M-F 9am-6:30pm, Sa 9am-5pm.

Laundromat: Self Lav-o-matic, 107 rue Gabriel Mouilleron. Open daily 8am-8pm. **Le bateau lavoir,** 125 rue St-Dizier (tel. 03 83 35 47 47). Open daily 7:45am-9:30pm.

English Books: Le Hall du Livre, 38 rue St-Dizier (tel. 03 83 35 53 01). Large pool of magazines, classics, and best-sellers. Open M-Sa 9am-8pm, Su 11am-7pm.

Police: Commissariat Central, 38 bd. Lobau (tel. 03 83 17 27 37).

Hospital: CHU Nancy, 29 av. de Lattre de Tassigny (tel. 03 83 85 85 85).

Post Office: 8 rue Pierre-Fourier (tel. 03 83 39 27 10), behind the Hôtel de Ville and pl. Stanislas. Branch on bd. des Aiguillettes, in Villers-lès-Nancy. Poste Restante code: Nancy-RP 54039. Open M-F 8am-7pm, Sa 8am-noon. **Postal code:** 54000.

Internet Access: Voyager, on rue St-Jean across from the cinema. 25F for 15min., 35F for 30min. Open M-Sa 9am-midnight, Su 2-11pm.

◤ ACCOMMODATIONS AND CAMPING

The hostel is lovely but far. **CROUS,** 75 rue de Laxou (tel. 03 83 91 88 00), can help students find summer accommodations in University dorms. (Open M-F 8am-6pm.) There are several budget hotels around rue Jeanne d'Arc, behind the train station, which are at least a 15min. walk from pl. Stanislas.

Centre d'Accueil de Remicourt (HI), 149 rue de Vandoeuvre (tel. 03 83 27 73 67; fax 03 83 41 41 35), in Villers-lès-Nancy, 4km southwest of town in the Château de Remicourt. From the station, take bus #26 to "St-Fiacre" (direction "Villiers Clairlieu," 2 per hr., last bus at 8pm). Just downhill from the bus stop, turn right onto rue de Vandoeuvre and walk uphill. Look for the signs. Bus #4 runs more frequently and until midnight; at Garenne take a bus to "Basch" (direction "Vandoeuvre/CHU Brabois"). Follow the sign for "Faculté des Sciences"; the hostel, a beautiful château in Nancy's suburban hills, is on the right (10min. walk). Simple rooms with hilltop views. Limited facilities include TV room and a beautiful garden. 3- and 4-bed dorms 80F; doubles with shower and toilet 95F. Breakfast included. Co-ed bathrooms. Reception daily 9am-10:30pm. Check-in 5-10:30pm; call ahead and plead if arriving earlier. **Members only.** V, MC.

Hôtel de l'Académie, 7 rue des Michottes (tel. 03 83 35 52 31; fax 03 83 32 55 78). Phenomenal location between the station and pl. Stanislas. The 29 spare, tidy rooms with showers are grouped around a small, bright atrium with a trickling fountain. The wrought-iron balustrade of the staircase shares historical ties with pl. Stanislas. Singles 130-150F; doubles 150-180F. Extra bed 30F. Breakfast 20F. 24hr. reception. V, MC.

Hôtel Le Jean Jaurès, 14 bd. Jean-Jaurès (tel. 03 83 27 74 14; fax 03 83 90 20 94). Beautiful, colorful, somewhat dim rooms, all with bathroom. Some overlook a little garden, others (with sound-proof glass) a busy street. Separate non-smokers' breakfast room. Singles 175-210F; doubles 230-260F. Breakfast 25F. V, MC, AmEx.

Campsites: Camping de Brabrois, av. Paul Muller (tel. 03 83 27 18 28), near the Centre d'Accueil. Take bus #23 or 46 to "Camping" (direction "Villiers Clairlieu"). Overlooks the town. Access to woodland trails. Telephones, showers, and grocery store. (Grocery open 8am-1pm and 8-9pm.) 16F per person, 7F per tent, 7F per car. Electricity 18F. Reception Apr.-Oct. 15 7am-10pm.

◤ FOOD

Nancy's signature *bergamote* is a bitter hard candy flavored by the orangey spice used in Earl Grey tea. Off rue St-Dizier, pl. Henri Mengin plays host to the **Marché Central** (Tu-Sa 6am-6pm). A **Prisunic supermarket** sits behind the post office on rue St-Georges. (Open M-Sa 8:30am-8pm.) Restaurants densely pack the **rue des Maréchaux,** spilling over onto the nearby **pl. Lafayette** and up along **Grande Rue** to **pl. St-Epvre.** For afternoon snacks, there are waffle and *crêpe* stands behind pl. Stanislas on the **Terrace de la Pépinière.**

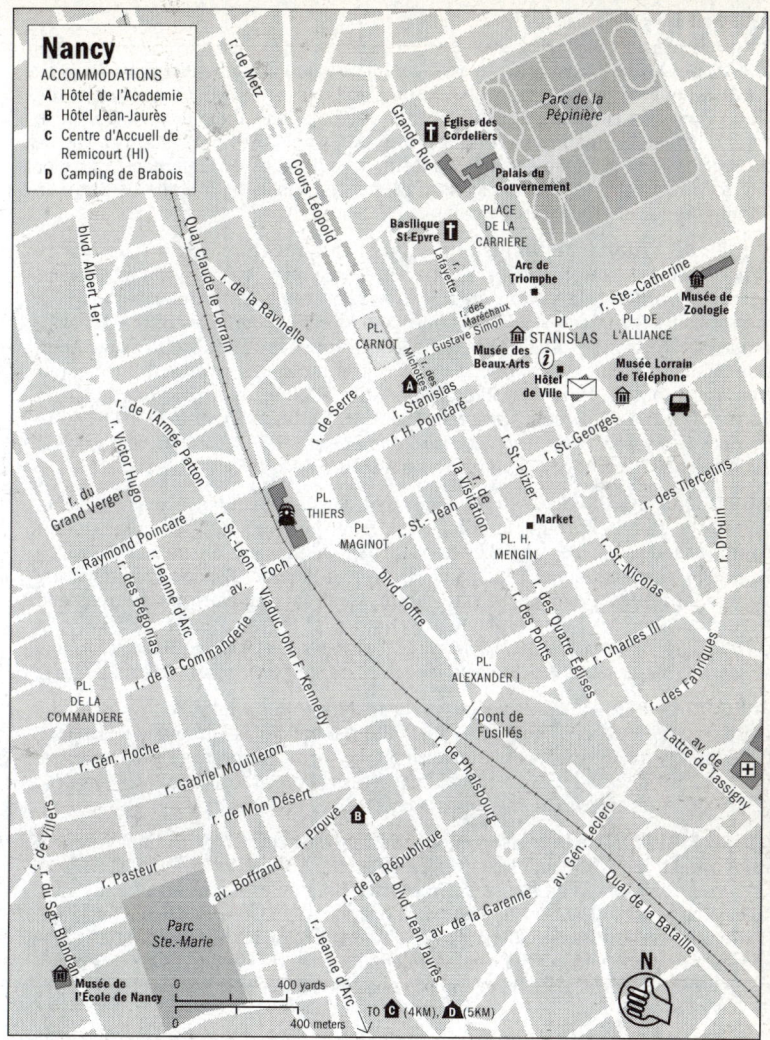

Nancy

ACCOMMODATIONS
A Hôtel de l'Academie
B Hôtel Jean-Jaurès
C Centre d'Accueil de Remicourt (HI)
D Camping de Brabois

🍴 **Aux Délices du Palais,** 69 Grande Rue. (Tel. 03 83 30 44 19). Swivel on zebra-striped bar stools while digging into a large sandwich (22-27F). Come early at lunchtime or you'll be crowded out by locals. Open Tu-F noon-3:30pm and 7-9:30pm, Sa noon-6pm.

Mère Grand, 1 pl. Lafayette (tel. 03 83 35 66 47), offers hearty regional fare beside a tinkling fountain. Try the lethal *eau de vie* made locally from *mirabelle* plums. Four-course *menu* 55F, *plats* 40-80F. (Open W-M noon-2pm and 7-11pm. V, MC, AmEx.)

La Gavotte, 47 Grande Rue (tel. 03 83 37 65 64). Satisfy the Breton in you at this *crêperie* adorably decorated with art and pottery straight from Brittany. The *galettes* include specialities such as *les Balanec* (with mushrooms, smoked duck, and goose-liver). (Open M-Sa noon-2pm and 7:30-11pm, Su evening. V, MC over 150F only.)

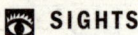 **SIGHTS**

PLACE STANISLAS. Designed by 18th-century architect Emmanuel Héré, Nancy's magnificent central *place* wraps its Baroque gilt iron arms around a statue of the Good Duke. On summer nights, light from the balconies illuminates and shades each curlicue, reflecting them in the fountain pools. From pl. Stanislas, pass through the five-arch **Arc de Triomphe** to the tree-lined **pl. de la Carrière,** a former site for jousts and tourneys, reconstructed by Stanislas with a mix of Baroque architecture and wrought-iron ornaments.

MUSÉE DE L'ÉCOLE DE NANCY. Illustrates the development of the Nancy School, Nancy's contribution to the turn-of-the-century Art Nouveau movement. Set in a converted villa, visitors are free to wander from room to room, all of which are furnished with the exaggerated lines and sweeping curlicues of the Art Nouveau style. Features works by Emile Gallé, creator of the Paris Métro signs. Additional Art Nouveau elements can be found on buildings scattered throughout Nancy; the tourist office distributes a guide with walking tours. *(36-38 rue du Sergent Blandan. Take bus #5, direction "Vandoeuvre Cheminots," to "Nancy Thermal." Tel. 03 83 40 14 86. Open June 1-July 27 W-M 10am-7pm, Jan. 2-Apr. 23 and July 27-Dec. 31 M 2-6pm and W-Su 10:30am-6pm. 35F, students 25F. Guided tours W-M at 4:30pm, 15F.)*

MUSÉE DES BEAUX-ARTS. Newly-renovated, this excellent museum is housed in one of the stately Baroque buildings that front pl. Stanislas. The collection of paintings and sculptures stretches from 1380 to the present, and includes gems by Rubens, Delacroix, Monet, Modigliani, Dufy, and Picasso. Especially noteworthy are the fantastical creations of 20th-century sculptors Lipchitz and Laurens and the collection of Art Nouveau Daum glasswork. *(3 pl. Stanislas. Tel. 03 83 85 30 72; fax 03 83 85 30 76. Open W-M 10:30am-6pm. 30F; students and children 15F; combined with Musée de l'École de Nancy 40F. Students free W and first Su of each month 10:30am-1:30pm.)*

PARC DE LA PÉPINIÈRE. Peacocks preen in the free zoo while people pose in the outdoor café. Portals of pink roses lead into the deliciously aromatic **Roseraie,** a collection of gaudy specimens from around the world. *(Just north of pl. de la Carrière. Open June-Aug. 6:30am-11:30pm; May 1-30 and Sept. 1-14 closes at 10pm; Mar-Apr. and Sept. 15-Nov. 30 closes at 9pm; Dec.-Feb. closes at 8pm.)*

OTHER SIGHTS. The late-19th-century **Basilique St-Epvre** has brilliant *vitraux* from around the world and free evening concerts. *(Just off Grande Rue at pl. St-Epvre. Open daily 2:30-6pm.)* The **Musée du Téléphone,** on a quiet street off pl. Stanislas, traces the history of man's quest to reach out and touch someone, from telegraph stations to the cordless wonders of today. The collection is varied and smartly presented, complete with stiffly-posed mannequins to set the scene. *(11 rue Maurice Barrès. Tel. 03 83 34 85 89. Open W-F 10am-noon and 2-6pm. 15F, students 10F.)*

THE NORTHEAST

♫ **ENTERTAINMENT**

In summer, nightly concerts from Beethoven to The Boss float from the Roseraie at **parc de la Pépinière.** In mid-October, **Jazz-Pulsations** beats from dusk to dawn in the park. **Pl. Stanislas** lights up on summer evenings with a free historical *son et lumière.* (July-Aug. daily 10-10:20pm.) The respected **Opéra de Nancy et de Lorraine** resides in an imposing building on the *place.* The 2000 season includes *Carmen* in January and *Béatrice et Bénédict,* Berlioz's operatic interpretation of *Much Ado About Nothing,* in February. (Tel. 03 83 85 30 60 M-F 1-7pm; stop in Tu-F 1-7pm; or email opera@mairie-nancy.fr. Tickets 40-315F, ask about student discounts.)

For more frivolous fun, soak up the evening beauty of the illuminated pl. Stanislas at its ritzy cafés, or grab a cheaper drink at one of their poorer relatives on rue Stanislas. To get you groovin', the tunnels of **Le Blue Note III,** 3 rue des Michottes (tel. 03 83 30 31 18), echo with live jazz. (Open M-Th 6pm-4am, F 6pm-5am, Sa 8pm-5am, Su 8pm-4am. 30F cover F-Sa.) Nancy's boys gather at **Le Batchi Bar,** 3 pl. St-Epvre (tel. 03 83 35 45 38), a lively gay watering hole near the Basilica. (Open M-F

11:30am-2am, F-Su 6pm-2am.) At **Le Hoops,** 4 rue Piroux (tel. 03 83 32 20 20) near the train station, the DJs spin techno and more till the wee hours of the morning. For mellower nights, the **Be Happy Bar,** 23 rue de Gustave Simon (tel. 03 83 35 56 41), is relaxing and warm. (Open M-Sa 4pm-2am.)

METZ

Settled by the Romans, Metz (the t is silent) was converted to Christianity in the 2nd century by St. Clement. According to legend, the town agreed to follow the pilgrim's religion if he would slay *le Graouilly,* a fire-breathing fiend with a penchant for gobbling up unwitting citizens. Clement, confident of his divine purpose, simply tossed his coat at the menacing beast, blinding it before closing in for the kill. After a century of unofficial occupation during the 16th and 17th centuries, the city was recognized as French by the 1648 Treaty of Westphalia but fell to the Germans following the 1871 Treaty of Frankfurt. In 1918, Maréchal Pétain wrenched Metz from the Kaiser's hands, only to relinquish it 22 years later as head of the Vichy government. Modern Metz (pop. 200,000) reflects its history of mixed Franco-German parentage. The city maintains classic fountains, sculptured gardens, verdant canals, and golden cobblestone streets without mobs of tourists. Though proud of its vibrant past, Metz is ready to blast into the 21st century; the glass and steel Technopole, to the southeast of the town center, is the first technological park in Europe specializing in software and communications.

■ ORIENTATION AND PRACTICAL INFORMATION

The honey-colored *vieille ville* is largely pedestrian (but heed the buses). The cathedral dominates the skyline of the **pl. d'Armes;** the tourist office is just across the way in the Hôtel de Ville. To get there from the station, turn right and then left onto rue des Augustins. At pl. St-Simplice, turn left onto the pedestrian rue de la Tête d'Or, then right onto rue Fabet. You can also take bus #11 from pl. Charles de Gaulle (direction "St-Eloy") directly to pl. d'Armes. Metz is a big city; use cosmopolitan caution.

Trains: pl. du Général de Gaulle. To: **Nancy** (40min., 31 per day, 51F); **Luxembourg** (45min., 15 per day, 84F); **Strasbourg** (1½hr., 13 per day, 115F); **Paris** (3hr., 10 per day, 209F); **Lyon** (5hr., 6 per day, 281F); and **Nice** (10-12hr., 3 per day, 493F). Info office open M-F 8:30am-7:30pm, Sa 8:30am-6pm.

Buses: Les Rapides de Lorraine, 2 rue de Nonnetiers (tel. 03 87 75 26 62, for schedules 03 87 36 23 43), across the tracks from the train station and to the left. To: **Verdun** (1hr., 7 per day, 69F); **Nancy** (2hr., 7 per day, 56F); and tiny regional towns. Ticket window open M-F 8am-noon and 2-6pm; Sa 8am-noon.

Local Transportation: TCRM, 1 av. Robert Schumann (tel. 03 87 76 31 11), runs every 10min. 6am-9pm. Ticket 5.30F, 2 trips 10F, *carnet* of 6 25.30F. Late-night bus 10F (10pm-midnight). Buses pass pl. de la République, pl. d'Armes, and the train station.

Taxis: (tel. 03 87 56 91 92) at the train station.

Bike Rental: Majchzak, 29 bd. Maginot (tel. 03 87 74 13 14). 80F per day, 3000F deposit. Open M 2-7pm, Tu-Sa 9am-noon and 2-7pm.

Tourist Office: pl. d'Armes (tel. 03 87 55 53 76 or 03 87 55 53 78; fax 03 87 36 59 43; email metz@tourisme.norsys.fr), facing the cathedral. Warm and competent staff makes hotel reservations and distributes maps (in French and English) of the *centre ville,* bus system, and walking tours. **Currency exchange.** Office open July-Aug. M-Sa 9am-9pm, Su 10am-1pm and 2-5pm; Sept.-June M-Sa 9am-7pm.

City Tours: Organized by the tourist office. M-Sa 3pm, 45F, call ahead for English. Tours of illuminated monuments every Sa night July-Aug. (50F).

Budget Travel: Agence Wasteels, 3 rue d'Austrasie (tel. 03 87 66 65 33). Student rates and passes. Open M-Th 9am-noon and 2-6pm, F 9am-noon and 2-7pm, Sa 9am-noon.

Youth Center: Centre Regional d'Information Jeunesse, 1 rue de Coëtlosquet (tel. 03 87 69 04 50). Open M-F 10am-noon and 1:30-6pm. Tons of info.

Laundromat: Lavomatique, 22 rue du Pont-des-Morts (tel. 03 87 31 38 81).

Police: 6 rue Belle Isle (tel. 03 87 37 91 11).

Hospital: Hôpital Notre-Dame-de-Bon-Secours, 1 pl. Phillipe de Vignuelles (tel. 03 87 55 31 31).

Post Office: 1 pl. du Général de Gaulle (tel. 03 87 56 73 00). Poste Restante code: 57037. **Currency exchange. Branch office** next to the theatre on pl. de la Comédie (tel. 03 87 30 38 58). Both open M-F 8am-7pm and Sa 8am-noon. **Postal code:** 57000.

Internet Access: Net Café, 1-3 rue Paul Bezanson (tel. 03 87 76 30 64), in the cour St-Étienne near the cathedral. Student rate 30F for 30min. Open M-Sa 1-6pm.

▌ ACCOMMODATIONS AND CAMPING

Hotels in the heart of the pedestrian district are expensive and hard to come by. Turn left from the train station onto **rue Lafayette** for several large, impersonal, 150F-range hotels.

Auberge de Jeunesse (HI), 1 allée de Metz Plage (tel. 03 87 30 44 02; fax 03 87 33 19 80), by the river. Walking is possible but tricky and long (30min.). From the station, take bus #3 (direction "Metz-Nord") or #11 (direction "St-Eloy;" last bus 8:50pm) to "Pontiffroy." Free bike and boat loans, laundry service (30F), and kitchen. 1- to 4-bed dorms 49F. Breakfast 19F, meals from 28F. Sheets 17F. No curfew or lockout. Reception 7:30-10am and 5-10pm. **Members only.** Flash *Let's Go* for a 10% discount.

Association Carrefour/Auberge de Jeunesse (HI), 6 rue Marchant (tel. 03 87 75 07 26; fax 03 87 36 71 44). From the station, turn right onto rue Vauban, which becomes av. Jean XXIII, and follow it around through as it becomes bd. Maginot and bd. Paixhans. Rue Marchant will be on your left after 20min. Or take minibus from the station to "Ste-Ségolène" (every 15min., 7:30am-7:15pm, 5.30F), and take a left up the hill. Central, residential atmosphere. Laundry. Co-ed bathrooms. 3-, 4-, and 8-bed dorms 71F. Singles and doubles 82F per person. Breakfast included. Meals 37.70F. Paper sheets 19.50F, real ones (more than 2 nights) 26F. 24hr. reception. **Members only.** V, MC.

Hôtel Métropole, 5 pl. du Général de Gaulle (tel. 03 87 66 26 22; fax 03 87 66 29 91). Pleasant by-the-station behemoth with spacious, elegant rooms. Singles 125-140F; singles and doubles with shower 160-290F. Nice breakfast 28F. 24hr. reception. Wheelchair accessible. V, MC, AmEx.

Hôtel Bristol, 7 rue Lafayette (tel. 03 87 66 74 22; fax 03 87 50 67 89), a small, serviceable place behind the train station. Aquamarine hallways lead to rather depressing wood-panelled rooms with a drab olive color scheme. The larger rooms—some with minibar—are cheerier. All have shower, toilet, and phone. Singles 165-270F; doubles 170-270F. Breakfast 29F. 24hr. reception. V, MC.

Campsite: Metz-Plage, allée de Metz-Plage (tel. 03 87 32 05 58), by the Moselle and the hostel. Enter from rue de la Piscine, behind the hospital on rue Belle Isle. Privacy can be elusive. Showers, grocery store, TV room, and fishing. Wheelchair accessible. 15F per person, 15F per tent, 10F per car, 35-40F per trailer incl. electricity. Reception daily 7am-8:30pm. 24hr. pedestrian access, 7am-10pm for cars. 28-day max. stay.

▌ ▐ FOOD AND ENTERTAINMENT

FOOD. *Boulangeries,* sandwich shops, and other cheap eateries cluster near the Auberge de Jeunesse on **rue du Pont des Morts,** in the **pedestrian district,** and toward the station on **rue Coisin.** The Centre St-Jacques (a mall off pl. St-Jacques) contains a number of specialty stores and cheap eateries, as well as an **ATAC supermarket.**

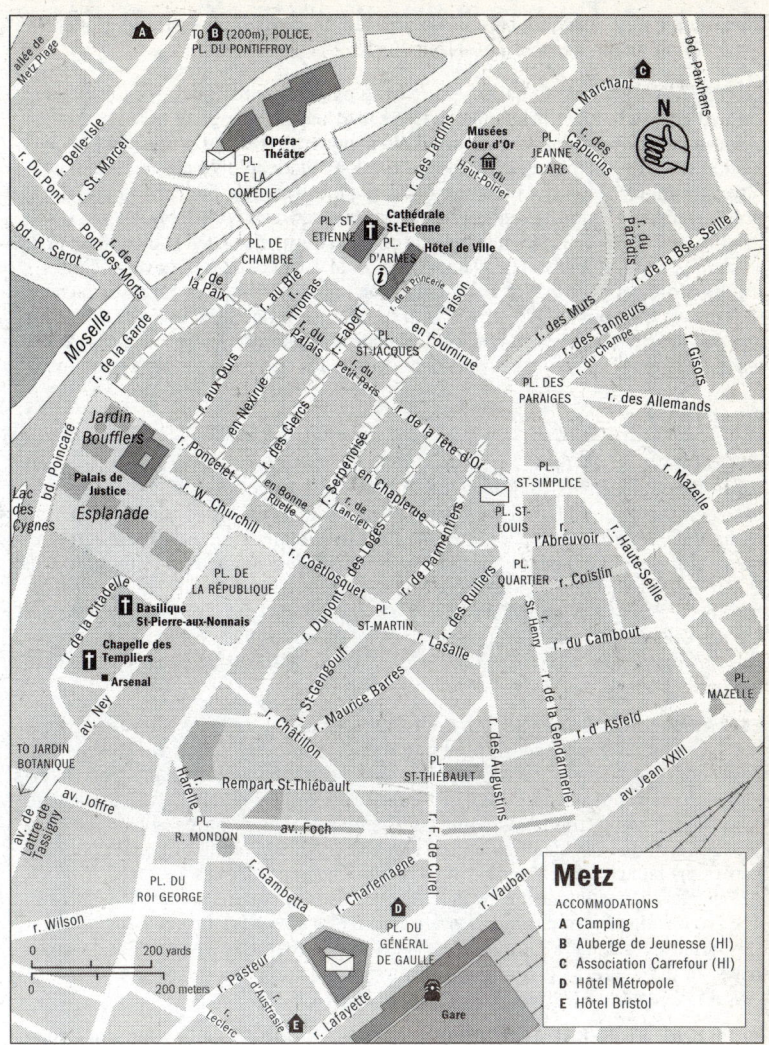

Metz
ACCOMMODATIONS
A Camping
B Auberge de Jeunesse (HI)
C Association Carrefour (HI)
D Hôtel Métropole
E Hôtel Bristol

(Open M-Sa 8:30am-7:30pm.) The biggest **markets** (Th and Sa 7am-2pm) are next to the Cathedral (mid-Apr. to Sept.) or on pl. St-Jacques (Oct. to mid-Apr.).

Traditional *lorraine* cuisine may be found more cheaply and readily in Nancy, but 20F kebab shops sprout like mushrooms on every street corner. The ▨ **Crêperie St-Malo,** 14 rue des Clercs (tel. 03 87 74 56 85), serves hundreds of stuffed *galettes* (13-55F) and *crêpes* (from 9F) on the tiny terrace or in the crammed dining room. (Open M-Sa 11:45am-11pm. V, MC.) Best for people-watching, **Le Beverly,** 2 pl. St-Jacques (tel. 03 87 37 35 33), offers great big salads (30-50F), quiches, and pastas. Eat in the swanky interior or on the immense terrace that sprawls across pl. St-Jacques. (Open 7am-2am. V, MC.) Popular and busy at meal-times, **Paul Le Boulanger,** rue du Petit Paris (tel. 03 87 75 38 53), is a wheat-themed *salon de thé* with omelettes (30F) and fruity *tartines*. 45F daily lunch *menus* are a farm-fresh deal. (Open M-Sa 7am-7pm, Su 8:30am-12:30pm and 2:30-6pm.) Cheery blue and yellow decor and sumptuous pizza and pasta dishes are the hallmark of **Le Moulin**

Bleu, rue Fabert. Sorry, no blue windmills, but there are dinner *menus* from 68F. (Open Tu-Su noon-2pm and 7:30-11pm. V, MC.)

ENTERTAINMENT. After dark, be sure to stop by the cathedral to see the glowing stained-glass windows. In summer, a free **son et lumière,** complete with Vegas-style colored lights, fountains, and assorted tunes by Wagner, *Les Beatles,* and Elvis is held at dusk on the pond at the foot of the Esplanade. (July-Sept. F-Su and holidays.) Students pack the bars and cafés at **pl. St-Jacques,** the central gathering point at night. Grind the night away at zebra-crazy **Le Club Tiffany,** 24 rue Coët-losquet (tel. 03 87 75 23 32), just outside pl. de la République. On Ladies Night (W), women get in free before 12:30am. (Open W-M 10am-5am. 60F cover includes 1 drink.) More zebras await at **Les 2 Zebras,** an impossibly hip bar on pl. St-Jacques that draws the young, chic crowd with funky tunes pounding in a sleek interior and packed see-and-be-seen terrace. **Le Tunnel,** 27 pl. Quarteau (tel. 03 87 36 62 99), leads to a huge TV screen; the outside terrace leads to a pleasant conversation.

◼ SIGHTS

CATHÉDRALE ST-ÉTIENNE. In France, only the naves of St-Pierre in Beauvais and Notre Dame in Amiens soar higher than this mustard-colored cathedral. Erected between the 13th and 16th centuries, Metz authorities joined the two existing cathedrals together (the pillars of the older sections are simpler in design than those of the new) in an attempt to build a church large enough to impress Rome. The most spectacular of the *vitraux* are the modern ones; several in the western transept are by Chagall. Before you enter from the pl. des Armes, note the twin statues of "Church" and "Synagogue," located on opposite sides of the outer archway. *(Pl. d'Armes. Tel. 03 87 75 54 61. Tours in French available May-Sept. daily 10am, 2pm, and 6pm. 15-25F.)*

ESPLANADE AND GARDENS. At the other end of the rue des Clercs from pl. d'Armes lies the Esplanade, a broad, formal garden overlooking the Moselle Valley. Metz's patchwork of gardens and promenades offers a refreshing green alternative to the yellow urban core. The tourist office publishes a map with trails up to 10km long. Down the steps from the Esplanade, shady paths wind their way through wooded parkland along the Lac aux Cygnes. Paddle or pedal your way across the lac with a boat rented at **La Flotille.** *(1 quai des Régates. Tel. 03 87 36 86 71. 57F for 30min.)* In summertime, watch the brightly lit fountains dance to music from J.S. Bach to Louis Armstrong. *(June 18-Sept. 5 F-Su at nightfall. Free.)* Swans preen at the **Jardin Botanique,** a Latinophile's heaven of packed flower beds and tagged trees. In the center, a greenhouse nurtures ferns and palm trees. *(Open May-Sept. daily 9-11:30am and 2-6:45pm; Oct.-Apr. 9:30-11:30am and 2-4:45pm.)*

BASILIQUE ST-PIERRE-AUX-NONNAIS. Nestled in the green beyond the Esplanade lies this tiny ancient church. Built by the Romans in the 4th century as part of a large set of baths, and perhaps the oldest church in France, it has been rebuilt four times—see if you can figure out where. Today, St-Pierre and the Chapelle des Templiers serve a secular function as an annex for exhibitions by **Arsenal,** the local cultural center which presents several concerts per month. Exhibitions are also held periodically. *(Basilica: Open daily 2-6:30pm, closed winter weekends. Arsenal: Tel. 03 87 39 92 00 for info. Exhibits open Apr.-Sept. Tu-Su 1-6:30pm. Student concert tickets 50F.)*

MUSÉE D'ART ET D'HISTOIRE. Includes an extensive archæological section which traces in detail Metz's rise from Roman settlement through Germanic capital to a prosperous city-state. Lose yourself (literally) in the dimly lit, labyrinthine passageways. The top two floors are dedicated to a **Musée des Beaux-Arts,** which presents *oeuvres* from the 15th to 20th century, and a **military history museum** with a focus on Napoleonic times. *(2 rue du Haut-Poirier, in the Cour d'Or. Tel. 03 87 75 10 18. Open daily 10am-noon and 2-6pm. 30F, students 15F. Audioguide in 5 languages 15F.)*

PL. DE LA COMÉDIE. Built on a former swamp, the *place* served a less-than-comedic function during the Revolution, when the guillotine was its main attraction. Its centerpiece is the 1751 theater, where opera, ballet, dance, and drama (classical and modern) continue to flourish at the **Opéra-Théâtre.** *(Tel. 03 87 55 51 71. For tickets, call the Bureau de Location at 03 87 75 40 50. Open M-F 1:30-6pm.)*

VERDUN

Verdun and its war memorials testify to the horror of the battles fought in the area between France and Germany during WWI. Each side lost almost 400,000 soldiers in the Battle of Verdun in 1916. Through its system of troop rotations, roughly three-quarters of the French Army experienced what some have called the worst battle in history, while 80 percent of the city was destroyed in the battle meant to end the "War to End All Wars." Eerie reminders of the destruction surround the city; the 15,000 marble crosses in the National Cemetery, the Trench of Bayonets, where most of France's 137th Regiment perished, and Verdun's chosen symbol, a dove with clasped wings.

Despite the long shadow cast by wartime devastation, Verdun (pop. 30,000) has painstakingly rebuilt itself into an attractive town that is popular with French and with foreigner travelers alike. Much of Verdun is modern and commercial, built to blend with the remnants of the original town.

■ **ORIENTATION AND PRACTICAL INFORMATION.** Verdun is split in two by the Meuse, with the train station, the cathedral, and the hostel on one side, and the tourist office and war memorials on the other. **Trains** from Verdun's station (built by Gustav Eiffel), on pl. Maurice Genovoix, run infrequently to **Metz** (1½hr., 4 per day, 73F). (Ticket booth open M 4:45am-6:50pm, Tu-F 5:45am-6:50pm, Sa 9:45am-noon and 2-7pm, Su 12:30-7:30pm.) You'll have more luck at the bus station (tel. 03 29 86 02 71) on pl. Vauban, at the other end of av. Garibaldi; **buses** go to **Metz** (2hr., 7per day, 69F) and **Nancy** (2½hr., 8 per day, 91F). (Open M-Sa 6am-8pm.) **Grand Garage de la Meuse,** 6 av. Colonel Driant (tel. 03 29 86 44 05), **rents cars.** (Open M-F 8am-noon and 1:45-6pm, Sa 8am-noon.) **Rent bikes** near the train station at **Flavenot Damien,** 1 Rond-Point des Etats-Unis (tel. 03 29 86 12 43). (100F per day. Passport deposit. Open M 9am-noon, Tu-Sa 9am-noon and 2-7pm.)

To get to the **tourist office,** pl. de la Nation (tel. 03 29 86 14 18; fax 03 29 84 22 42), from the train station, walk straight ahead on av. Garibaldi (the street to the extreme left) until you reach the bus station. Then turn left onto rue Frères Boulhaut and continue until you reach the Port Chaussée. Turn left again and cross the bridge onto pl. de la Nation; the tourist office will be on your right. The staff offers a free brochure map of the *centre ville*, a larger fold-out map for 3F, and info on the memorials as well as **currency exchange.** They also lead a daily 4-hour **tour** of major battlefields and monuments around the city. (Tours in French and English depart May-Sept. 15 daily at 2pm, 145F; call before noon to reserve a seat. Office open July-Aug. M-Sa 8am-8pm, Su 9am-5pm; Dec.-Feb. M-Sa 9am-noon and 2-5pm, Su 10am-1pm; Mar.-Apr. and Oct.-Nov. M-Sa 9am-noon and 2-6pm, Su 10am-1pm, but Su 9am-5pm in Apr.; May-June and Sept. 8:30am-6:30pm, Su 9am-5pm.) Launder **Laundry** late at the *laverie* on av. de la Victoire. (Open 6:30am-11pm). The **police** are at pl. du Gouvernement. The **hospital** is at 2 rue d'Anthouard (tel. 03 29 83 84 85). The **post office** is on av. de la Victoire (tel. 03 29 83 45 58), across the river from the tourist office. (Open M-F 8am-7pm, Sa 8am-noon. Poste Restante code: 55107 Verdun, B.P. 729. **Postal code:** 55100.)

■ **ACCOMMODATIONS AND CAMPING.** The **Auberge de Jeunesse** at the "Centre Mondial de la Paix," pl. Monseigneur Ginisty (tel. 03 29 86 28 28; fax 03 29 86 28 82), next to the cathedral, may not save the world, but it does provide lodgings and a hilltop view of Verdun. From the train station, cross to the island with the Match in front of the station and turn a bit right onto rue Louis Maury. When you reach the square, continue up on rue de la Belle Vierge. The hostel is at the end of the cathedral. Use the stairs in the corner of the parking lot in front of the cathedral to get down from the hill into the *centre ville*. Hallways decorated with modern stained glass give way to large quads, most with toilet, shower, and dim lighting. There's a stove available, but no phones. (49F. Singles 133F. Breakfast 19F. Sheets 17F. Reception M-F 8am-noon and 5-11pm, Sa-Su 8-10am and 5-11pm. No curfew or lockout. Cash only.) In the heart of the *vieille ville*, **Le Montaulbain**, 4 rue de la Vieille Prison (tel. 03 29 86 00 47; fax 03 29 84 75 70), offers fairly large, well-decorated rooms with TV and phone. (Singles 150-170F, doubles 170-200F. Breakfast 25F. Reception 7:30am-10pm. V, MC.) Around the corner from the train station, **Le Franc Comtois**, 9 av. Garibaldi (tel. 03 29 86 05 46), lets small, clean rooms with cream coverlets on squishy beds. (Singles 110-150F, doubles 140-220F. Breakfast 25F. Reception 7am-midnight. V, MC.) A crowded, three-star **camping** site lies 1km from town at **Les Breuils,** allée des Breuils (tel. 03 29 86 15 31; fax 03 29 86 75 76), past the Citadelle Souterraine on av. du Cinquième R.A.P. Take a right onto av. Général Boichut and then the first left. You'll find a bar, a grocery store, showers, and a pool. (21F per person, 15F per car or tent. Open Apr.-Oct. 15 7:30am-10pm.)

■ **FOOD.** Verdun's contribution to sweets is the *dragée*, almonds coated with sugar and honey. Verdun's main **covered market** is on rue de Rû. (F 8am-2pm.) Stock up at **Match supermarket,** in front of the train station on Rond-Point des États-Unis. (Open M-F 9am-12:15pm and 2:15-7:30pm, Sa 9am-7:30pm.) Restaurants and cafés co-exist in the pedestrian area along **rue Chaussée** and **rue Royeurs,** and by the canal along the **quai de Londres.** Pile your face at **Pile au Face,** 54 rue des Royeurs (tel. 03 29 84 20 70), where they serve paper-thin *crêpes* (12-40F) on the terrace or in the adorable dining room. (Open Tu-Su 10am-11pm. V, MC.) For hearty regional dishes, tuck your chair into **La Table d'Alsace,** 31 rue Royeurs (tel. 03 29 86 58 36), with a generous 60F *menu*. (Open daily 11:45am-2:30pm and 6:45-10pm.) For a light or vegetarian meal visit **F. Stadelmann,** 16 rue Chaussée (tel. 03 29 86 04 10), a *pâtisserie* and *salon de thé* that serves large salads (40-49F), *quiche* (15F), and tasty strawberry tarts (14F). (Open daily 7am-7:30pm.)

■ **SIGHTS.** Built in 1350, **Porte Chaussée,** on the quai de Londres (tel. 03 29 86 23 41), served as a prison and guard tower before providing passage into the city for troops during the Great War. Peer into the pitch-black dungeons 10am to 11:45am daily. At the other end of the rue Frères Boulhaut, Rodin's bronze **Victory** guards the Port St-Paul. Marking the edge of the *haute ville*, the traditionally-styled **Monument à la Victoire** rises above a flight of 72 granite steps. Atop the monument, a determined statue of a soldier aims bronzed cannons towards the German front.

The **Musée de la Princerie** (tel. 03 29 86 10 62), an elegant Renaissance building with galleries built around a cloister, hides behind the monument at the top of the hill. Devoted to archæology, medieval art and architecture, and old *faïence* pottery, the museum holds several treasures like an intriguing 12th-century ivory comb engraved with scenes of the Resurrection and an apparition of Mary Magdalene. The tower's lengthy spiral staircase leads absolutely nowhere. (Open Apr.-Oct. W-M 9:30am-noon and 2-6pm. 10F.) A few blocks away, the beautiful **Cathédrale Notre-Dame** crowns Verdun's *haute ville*. Although partially destroyed by shelling, its reconstructed Romanesque interior still displays a fine collection of stained glass. (Open daily 9am-noon and 2-6pm.) **Parc Municipal Japiot,** across from the tourist office, rolls out the green carpet along the shady banks of the Meuse. (Open Apr.-Sept. 8:30am-8pm; Oct. and Mar. 9am-6pm; Nov.-Feb. 9am-5pm.)

The massive cement and stone **Citadelle Souterraine** (down rue de Rû) sheltered 10,000 soldiers on their way to the front. The 4km of underground galleries were equipped with everything to support an army. Today, a small, very chilly section of the tunnels can be seen on a tour in roller coaster-like cars. Prepare to see WWI as if played out by holograms. (30min. tours in French or dubiously dubbed English every 5min. Open daily July-Aug. 9am-7pm; May-June 9am-6pm; Sept. and Apr.

9am-noon and 2-5:30pm; Oct.-Dec. 19 and Feb. 15-Mar. 10am-noon and 2-5pm, Dec. 20-Feb. 14 2-4pm. 35F.) Verdun also hosts a **son et lumière festival.** (June-July. Call 03 29 84 50 00 for info.)

MEMORIALS NEAR VERDUN

Many sites to the east of Verdun commemorate the 10-month Battle of 1916. As most are 5-8km away, they are difficult to reach without a car. The four-hour tourist office tour (see **Verdun,** above) visits all of the memorials mentioned below in rapid but thorough check-mark succession. The more contemplative may want to find their own transportation.

After Alsace and parts of Lorraine were annexed by Germany in 1870, Verdun found itself 40km from the German border and strongly protected by 38 new French forts. These fortifications were the linchpin of France's northeastern defenses, and so were expressly targeted by German General von Falkenhayn in planning the 1916 offensive. The first to fall was also the strongest; the immense **Fort de Douaumont,** covering 3 hectares and 3km of passageways, was left with only 57 soldiers after most of its arms and troops were transferred to weaker areas in Champagne and Artois. As a result, it was easily captured by a German brigade in February 1916, and held for eight months. The Fort now holds the bones of hundreds of German soldiers killed in an artillery explosion on May 8, 1916. (Open daily July-Aug. 10am-7pm; June 10am-6:30pm; Apr.-May and Sept. 10am-6pm; Oct. 10:30am-1pm and 2-5:30pm; Feb.-Mar. and Nov.-Dec. 10:30am-1pm and 2-5pm; Jan. 2-31 11am-4pm. 15F.)

Fort de Vaux, the smallest of the fortifications, surrendered to the Germans in June 1916 after seven days of siege and hand-to-hand combat. The French made numerous appeals for reinforcements to the Verdun garrison, but none came; inside the fort stands a statue of a carrier pigeon named Valiant, who bore the last message out of the fort. (Open daily May-Sept. 9am-6:30pm; Oct.-Dec. 19 9:30am-noon and 1-5pm; Feb.-Mar. 9:30am-noon and 1-4:30pm; Apr. 9am-6pm. 15F.)

On the site of the town of Fleury, a tiny village that was demolished during the Battle and never rebuilt, now stands the grim **Musée de Fleury.** The museum was built in 1967 through the efforts of Verdun veterans, as a memorial to their compatriots who died during the battle. Don't miss the evocative 20-minute film that conveys a sense of life in the trenches. (Open daily Mar.15–Sept. 12 9am-6pm; Sept. 13-Dec. and Feb. 8-Mar. 14 9am-noon and 2-6pm. 20F, under 16 10F.)

The central and most striking monument on the battlefields is the austere **Ossuaire de Douaumont,** a vast crypt crowned by a 46m granite tower that resembles a cross melded to an artillery shell. A brief philosophical film is shown, chronicling the events of the battle. Inside the Ossuary, vaults hold the remains of some 130,000 unknown French and German soldiers. Fifteen thousand more, whose remains were identifiable, lie buried in the military cemetery that stretches out before the Ossuary. Christian graves are marked by rows of white crosses, while Muslims lie beneath gravestones pointing towards Mecca and a wall commemorates the dead Jewish soldiers. (Open daily May-Sept. 5 9am-6:30pm, Apr. 4-Apr. 30 9am-6pm; Mar.-Apr. 3 and Oct. 9am-noon and 2-5:30pm; Sept. 6-Sept. 30 9am-noon and 2-6pm; Nov. 9am-noon and 2-5pm. Ossuary admission free; 20min. film 16F, children 10F; tower 6F, children 4F; film and tower 19F, children 12F.) Nearby, the **Tranchée des Baionettes** marks the trench where a detachment of France's 137th infantry regiment was buried alive while sheltering from heavy enemy fire. After the battle ended, the only visible sign of the men were the points of their bayonettes protruding from the ground.

STRASBOURG

"Willkommen, bienvenue, welcome." A few kilometers from the Franco-German border, cosmopolitan Strasbourg (pop. 260,000) seems to belong to both cultures. German is heard on the streets almost as often as French, and as many *winstubs* line the squares as *pâtisseries.* When France annexed Strasbourg 30 years after

the rest of Alsace in 1681, the townspeople demanded a charter as a free city. Since then, despite the bilingual street signs and prominent displays of civic culture, the city has cast its lot with the République; the *Marseillaise* was even composed here. The vibrantly beautiful city also serves as an administrative center of the European Union, hosting the European Parliament, the Council of Europe, and the European Commission for the Rights of Man. Its independence and energy is perpetuated by the large student population. Founded in 1566, and counting Goethe among its alumni, the Université de Strasbourg enrolls over 35,000 French students. At night, they drop their books and pack the clubs and squares.

▣ ORIENTATION AND PRACTICAL INFORMATION

The *vieille ville* is an eye-shaped island in the center of the city, bounded on the north by a large canal and on the south by the river Ill. From the station, go straight down rue du Maire-Kuss, cross pont Kuss, and make a quick right and then left onto Grande Rue, which becomes rue Gutenberg. Turn right at pl. Gutenberg and head towards the Cathedral down rue Mercière. Turning right after crossing the bridge from the station leads to **La Petite France,** a neighborhood of old Alsatian houses, narrow canals, and restaurants.

Airport: Strasbourg-Entzheim (tel. 03 88 64 67 67), 15km from Strasbourg. **Air France,** 15 rue des Francs-Bourgeois (tel. 03 88 55 26 05), and other carriers send frequent flights to **Paris** (students from 585F round-trip), **Lyon,** and **London.** Shuttle buses (tel. 03 88 77 70 70) run from "Baggarsee" (12min., every 15min. 5:30am-11pm, 25F).

Trains: pl. de la Gare (tel. 03 88 22 50 50; reservations tel. 03 88 32 07 51). To: **Paris** (4hr., 16 per day, 235F); **Luxembourg** (2½hr., 6 per day, 167F); **Frankfurt** (3hr., 12 per day, 237F); and **Zurich** (3hr., 12 per day, 265F). Ticket office open M 5am-8:50pm, Tu-Sa 5:30am-8:50pm, Su 6am-8:50pm.

Local Transportation: Compagnie des Transports Strasbourgeois (CTS), pl. Kléber. (tel. 03 88 77 70 70). Open M-F 7:30am-6:30pm, Sa 9am-12:30pm and 1:30-5pm. Also at the Gare Centrale. Open M-F 7:15am-6:30pm. Extensive bus service. A single north-south **tram** line rumbles every 5-8min. 7am-7pm, less frequently 4:30-7am and 7pm–midnight. Tickets 7F. 31F *Carnet* of 5 and 20F day pass available from *tabacs.*

Taxis: Taxi 13, pl. de la République (tel. 03 88 36 13 13). 24hr. Also offers city tours (180F for 1-4 people) and service to the Route du Vin.

Car Rental: Europ'Car, 13 pl. de la Gare (tel. 03 88 15 55 66). Open M-F 8am-noon and 2-7pm, Sa 8am-noon and 2-5pm. **Garage Sengler,** rue Jean Giradow (tel. 03 88 30 00 75) in Hautepierre, will rent you a car (149F per day plus 1F per km) even if you're under 21, as long as you've had a license for a year.

Bike Rental: Vélocation at 4 locations: 4 rue du Maire Kuss (tel 03 88 52 01 01), near the *gare;* 10 rue des bouchers (tel 03 88 52 01 01), in the town centre; in pl. du Château (tel. 03 88 21 06 38); and at Ponts Couverts (tel. 03 88 22 59 19) in la Petite France. Bikes 20F per half-day, 30F per day. Tandems 40F per day. 300F and passport deposit. *Gare* location open M-F 6am-8pm, Sa 8am-7pm, Su 9am-7pm. Others open Tu-F 9am-noon and 1:30-7pm, Sa-Su 9am-7pm. Ponts Couverts also rents bikes equipped with an audio guide tour of the city. 65F per bike with guide.

Tourist Office: 17 pl. de la Cathédrale (tel. 03 88 52 28 28), next to the cathedral. **Branches** at pl. de la Gare (tel. 03 88 32 51 49) and pont de l'Europe (tel. 03 88 61 39 23). The best map deal is the free one with the list of important sights, festival info, and hotel list. Other maps 3-24F. Hotel reservations 10F. Pick up the free *Shows and Events* guide, *Strasbourg Actualités* (with parliament sessions, market days, concerts, and bands), or *Strassbuch,* a free guide researched by students. Open June-Sept. M-Sa 8:30am-7pm, Su 9am-6pm; Oct.-May daily 9am-6pm. **Departmental Tourist Office,** 9 rue du Dôme (tel. 03 88 15 45 80), has info on the Route du Vin. Open M 10am-noon and 2-6pm, Tu-F 9:30am-noon and 2-6pm, Sa 10am-1pm and 2-6pm.

Strasbourg

ACCOMMODATIONS

A   CIARUS
B   Hôtel de Bruxelles
C   Hôtel le Grillon
D   Hôtel Kléber
E   Auberge de Jeunesse
    R. Cassin (HI)
F   Hôtel Michelet
G   Hostel Parc du Rhin

THE NORTHEAST

City Tours: The tourist office organizes tours of the *vieille ville* and the cathedral, available in English for groups of 5 or more. 38F, students 19F. Tours offered July 1-14 daily 2:30pm; July 15-Aug. Tu-Su 1:30pm and Sa 2:30pm; May-June and Sept.-Oct. Tu and F 2:30pm; Dec. Tu, F, and Sa 2:30pm. 1½hr. theme tours every Sa 2:30pm and Tu-Sa 8:30pm mid-July to Aug.

Budget Travel: Havas Voyages, 23 rue de la Haute-Montée (tel. 03 88 32 99 77). Open M-F 9am-12:30pm and 1:30-6:30pm, Sa 9am-12:30pm and 1:30-5pm.

Consulates: Canada, rue du Ried (tel. 03 88 96 65 02), in La Wantzenau. Open M-F 9am-noon. **US,** 15 av. d'Alsace (tel. 03 88 35 31 04, cultural services 03 88 35 38 20), next to pont John F. Kennedy. Open M-F 9am-noon and 2-5pm.

Money: 24hr. automatic currency exchange at **Crédit Commerciale de France,** pl. Gutendberg at rue des Serruriers. **American Express** at 19 rue du Francs-Bourgeois (tel. 03 88 21 96 59). Open M-F 9am-noon and 1:30-6pm, Sa 9am-6pm.

English Books: Librairie Internationale Kléber, 1 rue des Francs-Bourgeois (tel. 03 88 15 78 88). Best-sellers and some classics. Open Tu-Sa 9:15am-7pm.

Youth Center: CROUS, 1 quai du Maire-Dietrich (tel. 03 88 21 28 00; fax 03 88 36 77 79). Meal vouchers to University restaurants sold to students M-F 10am-noon. 23F per meal. **Centre d'Information Jeunesse (CIJA),** 7 rue des Écrivains (tel. 03 88 37 33 33), has info about jobs and lodgings. Open M-F 10am-noon and 1-6pm. Check out **Planète Jeune** next door. Open M-Sa 10am-7pm.

Laundromat: 15 rue des Veaux. Wash 8kg for 24F; dry 5min. for 2F. Open daily 7am-9pm. Bring your own soap. Also at 2 rue Deserte, near the *gare.*

Police: 11 rue de la Nuée-Bleue (tel. 03 88 32 99 08).

Hospital: Hospices Civils de Strasbourg, 1 pl. de l'Hôpital (tel. 03 88 11 67 68). South across the canal from the *vieille ville.*

Post Office: 5 av. de la Marseillaise (tel. 03 88 52 31 00). **Branches** at cathedral and 1 pl. de la Gare. All have **currency exchange.** Poste Restante (code: 67074) at main office. Main office open M-F 8am-7pm, Sa 8am-noon. **Postal code:** 67000.

Internet Access: Le Midi-Minuit, 5 pl. du Corbeau (tel. 03 88 36 09 92). Internet café and *salon de thé.* 30F per 30min. Open M-W 7am-7pm, Th-Sa 7am-10pm, Su 8am-7pm. Also at **Centre International d'Accueil** (see **Accommodations**).

⌐ ACCOMMODATIONS AND CAMPING

Strasbourg plays host to everyone. It's best to make reservations early. A cluster of relatively inexpensive hotels ring the train station.

Centre International d'Accueil de Strasbourg (CIARUS), 7 rue Finkmatt (tel. 03 88 15 27 88; fax 03 88 15 27 89; email ciarus@media-net.fr). From the station, take rue du Maire-Kuss to the canal, turn left, and follow quais St-Jean, Kléber, and Finkmatt. Take a left onto rue Finkmatt at the Palais de Justice; the hostel is on the left (15min.). Or take bus #10 (direction "Brant Université") or #20 (direction "Place de Bordeaux") to "Place de Pierre." Large, spotless facilities and international atmosphere. TV room, ping-pong, cafeteria, and internet access. Private bathrooms. 6- to 8-bed rooms 92F; 3- to 4-bed rooms 103F; 2-bed rooms 124F; singles 206F. Discounts after 2nd night. Breakfast 20F. Towels 7-15F. Check-in 3:30pm, call ahead if arriving earlier. Check-out 9am. Curfew 1am. Wheelchair access. Reserve in advance year-round. V, MC, AmEx.

Auberge de Jeunesse René Cassin (HI), 9 rue de l'Auberge de Jeunesse (tel. 03 88 30 26 46; fax 03 88 30 35 16), 2km from station. To get to bus stop "Ste-Marguerite" from the station, go up rue du Maire-Kuss, take a right just before canal onto quai St-Jean (turns into quai Altoffer) and follow until second bridge; the bus stop is up rue Ste-Marguerite, to the right. Take bus #3 (direction "Holtzheim-Entzheim Ouest") or #23 (direction "Illkirch") to "Auberge de Jeunesse" (15min.; every 30min., last bus 11:30pm, Su every hr.; 7F). To walk, turn right from the station onto bd. de Metz and follow it as it becomes bd. Nancy and bd. de Lyon. Turn right onto rue de Molsheim and go through the underpass. Be careful in this area at night. Follow rte. de Schirmeck 1km to rue de l'Auberge de Jeunesse, on the right (30min.). The setting is beautiful, by the canal and park, but rooms are slightly worn. TV room, kitchen, and cafeteria. 3- to 6-bed dorms 73F per person; doubles 100F; singles 149F. Sheets for dorms 18F. Camping 42F. Non-members 19F supplement. Breakfast included. Reception 7am-12:30pm, 1:30-7:30pm, and 8:30-11pm. Curfew 1am. Open Feb.-Dec. Wheelchair access.

Auberge de Jeunesse, Centre International de Rencontres du Parc du Rhin, rue des Cavaliers on the Rhine (tel. 03 88 45 54 20; fax 03 88 45 54 21). 7km from station, but less than 1km from Germany. Take tram to "Homme de Fer," then bus #2 to "Pont du Rhin" (30min.). Or take bus #21 (direction "Kehl") to "Parc du Rhin" from "Gutenberg" or "Porte de l'Hôpital" tramstop. Turn right opposite the tourist office entrance onto rue des Cavaliers. Private showers and toilets. Volleyball and basketball courts. Karaoke bar. July-Aug. and Nov.-Feb.: 3-4 bed rooms 98F per person; doubles 138F; singles 184F. Sept.-Oct. and Mar.-May: 86/118/115F. Fills with school groups in summer. Breakfast included. **Members only.** Reception 7am-11:30pm. Curfew 1am. V, MC.

Hôtel le Grillon, 2 rue Thiergarten (tel. 03 88 32 71 88; fax 03 88 32 22 01), 1 block from the station towards the *centre ville*. The beautiful, clean rooms are reminiscent of an alpine ski lodge. Rooms are cheaper on the top floor. Singles 170-230F; doubles 220-270F. Extra bed 70F. Reception 6am-2am. Breakfast 30F.

Hôtel Michelet, 48 rue du Vieux Marché aux Poissons (tel. 03 88 32 47 38). The cathedral is right around the corner from these dim, tidy rooms with phone but no TV. Riveting location with decent prices. Singles 145-210F; doubles 170-255F. Breakfast 25F. Reception 7am-8pm, otherwise call ahead. V, MC.

Hôtel de Bruxelles, 13 rue Kuhn (tel. 03 88 32 45 31; fax 03 88 32 06 22). Situated just up the street from the *gare*, the hotel is across the canal from the *vieille ville*. Slightly shabby hallways lead to large, beautiful rooms with antique-looking wood furnishings. Close to the *gare*. Singles and doubles 155-280F. Extra bed 40F. Shower 20F. Breakfast 28F. 24hr. reception. V, MC.

Hôtel Kléber, 29 pl. Kléber (tel. 03 88 32 09 53; fax 03 88 32 50 41). Right around the corner from the main tram and bus stop at "Homme de fer," the location is great but space is tight. All rooms have shower and TV. 24hr. reception—call ahead at night. Singles 185-346F; doubles 215-400F; triples 393-455F. Breakfast 31-40F. V, MC, AmEx.

Campsite: Terrain Municipal Montagne Verte, 2 rue Robert Ferrer (tel. 03 88 30 25 46). Perks include showers, tennis courts, and a bar. 26F per site, 20F per person, 10F per child, electricity 15-21F. Tent and car included. Car curfew 10pm. Reception in summer 7am-11pm, off-season 8am-noon and 2-8pm.

◖ FOOD

Streets around the cathedral are filled with restaurants—especially **pl. de la Cathédrale, rue Mercière,** and **rue du Vieil Hôpital.** A little further away, off pl. Gutenberg, pretty cafés line **rue du Vieux Seigle** and **rue du Vieux Marché-aux-Grains.** All sorts swarm the cafés and restaurants of tiny **pl. Marché Gayot,** hidden off of rue des Frères. In **La Petite France,** especially along rue des Dentelles and petite rue des Dentelles, you'll find small *winstubs* (VIN-shtoob)—informal places traditionally affiliated with individual wineries, with timber exteriors and checkered tablecloths. *Strasbourgeois* restaurants are known for *choucroute garnie,* sauerkraut served with meats. Several **markets** come to town every week. Those most accessible from the *centre ville* are pl. du Marché-aux-Poissons (Sa 7am-1pm), pl. de la Gare (M and Th 10am-6pm), and pl. Kléber (W and F 7am-6pm). Several supermarkets are also scattered around the *vieille ville,* including **ATAC,** 47 rue des Grandes Arcades (tel. 03 88 32 51 53), off pl. Kléber. (Open M-Sa 8:30am-8pm.)

◣ Poêles de Carottes, rue de la Krutenau (tel. 03 88 35 74 74). Perhaps the only unabashedly vegetarian restaurant this side of Paris, the tiny dining room is carrot orange and salad green, and the menu is a little photo album of eclectic vegetable postcards. The *gratins* and "pizzas" (dough stuffed with veggies) are great. Lunch *menu* 50F; dinner 98F. Open M-Sa noon-2:30pm and 7-10:30pm. V, MC.

La Korrygane, 12 pl. du Marché Gayot (tel. 03 88 37 07 34). This *crêperie's* versions are delightful. A lovely cobblestone terrace overlooks the flame breathers on summer nights. *Crêpes, galettes,* and salads 18-54F. Open daily 11am-midnight. V, MC.

Au Pont St-Martin, 13-15 rue des Moulins (tel. 03 88 32 45 13). Peer down at canal locks over huge servings of seafood, salads, and sauerkraut from this triple-decker *winstub* in La Petite France. Acoustic music rotates between floors M-Sa 8pm. Midweek lunch *menu* 60F. Vegetarian options. Open daily in summer noon-11pm; winter noon-2:30pm and 6:30-11pm. V, MC, AmEx.

👁 SIGHTS

CATHÉDRALE DE STRASBOURG. From the middle of the city, the majestic, rosy Cathédral de Strasbourg thrusts 142m into the sky. What Victor Hugo called the "prodigy of the gigantic and the delicate" is outstanding in form, color, and height. Inside the southern transept, the massive wooden **Horloge Astronomique** demonstrates the wizardry of 16th-century clockmakers. At 12:30pm, the apostles troop out of the face while a cock crows to greet St. Peter. Get there at least half an hour early in July and August. In front of the clock, the cathedral's central **Pilier des Anges,** decorated by a 13th-century master from Chartres, depicts the Last Judgment. Goethe scaled the 330 steps of the tower regularly to cure his fear of heights. *(Tel. 03 88 24 43 34. Cathedral open M-Sa 7-11:45am and 12:45-7pm, Su 12:45-6pm. Guided tours July-Aug. M-F 10:30am and 2:30 and 3:30pm; Sa 10:30am and 2:30pm; Su 2:30pm and 3:30pm. 15F. Horloge tickets, 5F, go on sale at 11:30am at the south entrance. Commentary in French, English, and German at noon. Tower open 9am-6:30pm. 20F, children 10F.)*

MUSÉE D'ART MODERNE ET CONTEMPORAIN. Opened in 1998, this is an excellent museum with a collection that ranges from late 19th-century impressionists and realists to the cutting edge artists of today and tomorrow. Works by Monet, Gauguin, Picasso, Dufy, and Ernst are featured, as well as an entire room devoted to the work of *strasbourgeois* artists Hans Jean Arp and his wife. *(1 pl. Hans Jean Arp. Tel. 03 88 23 31 31. 30F, students 20F, audio guide 20F.)*

PALAIS ROHAN. This magnificent 18th-century building houses a trio of small museums. The **Musée des Arts Décoratifs** grants visitors a surprising degree of freedom to explore restored chambers. Upstairs, the **Musée des Beaux-Arts** stocks a solid collection from the 14th to the 19th century, including works by Giotto, Botticelli, Raphael, Rubens, El Greco, Van Dyck, and Goya. The **Musée Archéologique** presents the history of Alsace from 600,000 BC to AD 800. *(2 pl. du Château. Tel. 03 88 52 50 00. Open M and W-Sa 10am-noon and 1:30-6pm, Su 10am-5pm. Museums 20F each, 40F for all 3, students 20F.)*

MAISON DE L'OEUVRE NOTRE-DAME. This 14th- to 16th-century mansion traces the evolution of Rhenish art from the 11th to the 17th century. Of particular note are the statues from the cathedral as well as 12th- to 14th-century stained glass. Behind the house, a recreated medieval garden, complete with trickling fountain and rows of herbs, smiles in sunny serenity. *(3 pl. du Château. Tel. 03 88 52 50 00. Open Tu-Sa 10am-noon and 1:30-6pm, Su 10am-5pm. Admission 20F, students 10F.)*

LA PETITE FRANCE. The old tanners' district, reposes in the southwest corner of the *centre ville.* Its slender Alsatian houses, with steep roofs and carved wooden facades, overlook narrow canals. Enjoy the burble of the water over the locks and the strolling accordion music at one of the numerous cafés lining the banks of the canal. Swans glide beneath the shadow of the Ponts Couverts, the remains of the 14th-century fortifications linking several small islands.

L'ORANGERIE. Strasbourg's largest and most spectacular park was designed by Le Nôtre in 1692, after he cut his teeth on Versailles. Waterways with ponds and waterfalls can be explored by rowboat. You can peer into the moon-and-stars well or rebel against the kids-only sign and scale the marvelous rope-climbing contraption. There are free concerts summer evenings at the Pavillon Joséphine. *(Concerts Th-Tu 8:30pm. Boats 30F for 30min. Take bus #23, 30, or 72 to "l'Orangerie.")*

PALAIS DE L'EUROPE, seat of the Council of Europe and the European Parliament, lies at the northwest edge of the Orangerie. During sessions (one week per month), you may register at the desk to sit in the visitors' gallery, where headsets translate debates into several languages. *(Av. de l'Europe. Tel. 03 87 17 20 07. Bring your passport. 1hr. guided tours by advance request only.)*

BREWERIES. The **Kronenbourg** brewery provides a taste of Alsace's German side, offering a free tour, a look at different stages of brewing, a film, and a tasting session. *(68 rte. d'Oberhausbergen. Tel. 03 88 27 41 59; fax 03 88 27 42 06. Take the tram to "Ducs d'Alsace." Visits by appointment only, M-F 9-10am and 2-3pm, as well as 11am and 4pm during the summer. Available in English.)* **Heineken** also offers free tours of its brewery in English, French, and German. *(4-10 rue St-Charles, Schiltgheim. Tel. 03 88 19 59 53. By appointment only; call to schedule, M-Sa.)*

🎵 🌸 ENTERTAINMENT, NIGHTLIFE, AND FESTIVALS

ENTERTAINMENT. Laze away summer afternoons and evenings on **pl. de la Cathédrale,** where musicians, flame-eaters, and acrobats perform. In summer, organ concerts reverberate through the cathedral accompanied by dancing *lumières*. (May 14-Aug. 28 F-Sa 9pm, July-Aug. also W. 34F, students 17F.) On summer nights, pl. du Château shows **Nuits de Strass,** a funny, free projection show with a time machine and laser circuit of space-time. **Water-jousting** competitions take place summer evenings on the Ill River outside the Palais des Rohan (July-Aug. Tu and Th 8:30pm). If your yearning for **aquabatics** has not been sated, fountains dance to lights and music while a tightrope walker traverses the two towers of Vauban's Ponts Converts. (July-Aug. daily 10:30pm.) **Strasbourg Fluvial** (tel. 03 88 32 75 25) sends boats out on 1¼hr. tours, including at night.

From October through June, the **Orchestre Philharmonique de Strasbourg** (tel. 03 88 15 09 09 for tickets, 03 88 15 09 00 for info) performs at the Palais de la Musique et des Congrès, behind pl. de Bordeaux. The **Théâtre National de Strasbourg,** 1 rue André Malraux (tel. 03 88 24 88 00), stages productions from September to May. (Tickets 70-120F, students 50-85F.) The **Opéra du Rhin** features opera and ballet in its 19th-century hall. (19 pl. Broglie. Tel. 03 88 75 48 01. Tickets 70-330F, students half-price.) **Forum Européen du Cinéma d'Art et d'Essai,** 32 rue du Vieux-Marché-aux-Vins (tel. 03 88 75 06 95), unreels quality film each November and December.

NIGHTLIFE. Nightlife in Strasbourg picks up from September to June, when the students are in town. Bars and pubs lie in the cathedral's shadow on **pl. du Marché Gayot,** especially along the rue des Frères. **L'Alchimiste,** 3 rue des Soeurs (tel. 03 88 37 02 83), is a tiny, conspiratorial café-bar with glowing pumpkins and mystical music. (Open M-Sa 6pm-4am, Su 8pm-4am.) A favorite with aspiring beatniks is **Le Gayot,** 18 rue des Frères (tel. 03 88 36 31 88), an intimate candlelit café with crowded terrace. Students play jazz piano nightly. (Open 10:30am-2am. Live music Sept.-June W-Sa. V, MC.) ■ **Les 3 Brasseurs,** 22 rue des Veaux (tel. 03 88 36 12 13), is a micro-brewery that serves a glass of each of the four home brews for 28F. During happy hour (5-7pm daily), two drinks go for the price of one and *tartes flambées* are 15F. The ambiance is warm and friendly, and the menu is a veritable newspaper packed with info on the history of beer-making in Alsace and other fun stuff. (Open daily 11am-1am).

Slightly seedier but no less fun is the area between **pl. d'Austerlitz** and **pl. de Zurich,** across the canal from the *vieille ville*. Numerous bars and cafés cluster there, particularly around the tiny **pl. des Orphelins.** The owners of Le Gayot recently opened **Le Funambule,** 3 rue Klein (tel. 03 88 36 90 20), a chic bar that caters to a more fast-paced crowd. Hip music pounds throughout the gleaming interior.

(Open Tu-Sa until 4am.) The bohemian, zebra-striped ground floor of **Café des Anges,** 5 rue Ste-Catherine (tel. 03 88 37 12 67), pulsates to salsa. (Ground floor open Tu-Sa 9pm-3am. Basement open W-Sa 10pm-4am. No cover.)

FESTIVALS. June brings the **Festival International de Musique,** a month-long extravaganza joining some of Europe's best classical musicians. In the past it has featured Jessye Norman and the London Philharmonic. The **Festival de Jazz** spans the first two weeks of July and traditionally draws giants of the jazz world to Strasbourg (tickets 160-230F, students 130-150F). For info on both festivals, contact **Wolf Musique,** 24 rue de la Mésange (tel. 03 88 32 43 10). **Musica** (tel. 03 88 23 47 23), a contemporary music festival from mid-September to early October, includes concerts, operas, and films. For more serious carousing, Schiltigheim hosts **La Fête de la Bière** in the first week of August, with beer, food, and fun for all.

SAVERNE

The 3rd-century Roman travel guide *Itinerarium Antonin* recommended Saverne as a "good place to rest." This 21st-century guidebook agrees. With its sleepy canals, picture-book square, and sculpted Vosges scenery, Saverne (pop. 10,000) remains a soothing place to stay. Germanic influence remains strong in the town, with half-timbered houses and cascading flower boxes. Saverne's position on a narrow pass through the Vosges mountains has made it a town long contested by kings and armies, from 12th-century crusaders to WWII Germans. Today, it makes a pleasant base for exploring the surrounding castles, towns, and forests.

◪ ORIENTATION AND PRACTICAL INFORMATION. Trains (tel. 03 88 91 33 66) leave from pl. de la Gare for: **Strasbourg** (25min., 24 per day, 42F), **Nancy** (1hr., 8 per day, 81F), and **Metz** (1hr., 5 per day, 86F). (Ticket office open M-F 6:30am-7:30pm, Sa 8:30am-6pm, Su 10am-8:30pm.) To get to the **tourist office,** 37 Grande Rue (tel. 03 88 91 80 47; tourisme.saverne@wanadoo.fr), from the train station, cross the square and turn right onto rue de la Gare. Cross the Zorn river and take a left onto Saverne's main street, **Grande Rue;** continue past the château on pl. de Gaulle and the office will be on your left. The irrepressibly friendly staff dispense various maps, a hefty town guidebook (in French, 15F), information on local sights, and hiking information along with a variety of trail maps. (Open May-Oct. M-Sa 9am-12:30pm and 2-7pm, Su 10am-12:30pm and 2-5pm; Nov.-Apr. M-Sa 9am-12:30pm and 2-7pm.) **Rent bikes** at **Cycles OHL,** 10 rue St-Nicolas (tel. 03 88 91 17 13). **Hôpital Ste-Catherine** is at 19 côte de Saverne (tel. 03 88 71 67 67). The **police** reside at 29 rue St-Nicolas (tel. 03 88 91 19 12). The **post office** is at 2 pl. de la Gare. (Tel. 03 88 71 56 40. Open M-F 8am-noon and 1:30-6:30pm, Sa 8am-noon. **Postal code:** 67700.)

▨ ACCOMMODATIONS AND FOOD. Why stay in a pricey Saverne hotel when you can stay in a castle? The ▨ **Auberge de Jeunesse** (tel. 03 88 91 14 84) occupies the fourth floor of the Château des Rohan, right in the center of town. Recently renovated rooms have great views. (Kitchen, TV. 4-bed dorms 46F per person; Singles and doubles with breakfast 85F per person. Breakfast 19F. Lockout 10am-5pm. Reception 8-10am and 5-11pm; ask for a key if you plan to be out late.) **Camping de Saverne,** rue du Père Libermann (tel. 03 88 91 35 65), is a rose-flowered three-star campground near tennis courts and trails to the Vosges. (14F per person, 13F per tent, 13F with car. Electricity 11F. 4F daily *taxe séjour* and insurance. Open Apr.-Sept. 7am-10pm.)

Saverne was called "Tres Tabernae" (Three Taverns) in Roman times, thanks to its reputation for welcoming travelers with hearty food in a cozy environment. ▨ **S'zawermer Stuebel,** 4 rue des Frères (tel. 03 88 71 29 95), proves itself the inheritor of this fine tradition, serving up delectably filling pasta (34-38F) and pizzas (30-45F) in an intimate converted wine cellar with vaulted ceilings. 48F and 69F 3-course *menus* are an unbeatable delicious deal. (Open daily 11:30am-2:30pm and 6:30-10pm. V, MC.) **Muller Oberling,** 66-68 Grande Rue (tel. 03 88 91 13 30), is a *salon de thé* offering quiche, *tarte à l'oignon*, and gourmet pizza for 20-35F. (Open Tu-F 7am-7pm, Sa 7am-6pm, Su 8am-noon and 1:30-6pm. V, MC.) Regional cuisine (40-70F) and cheap ethnic food options line **rue des Cles** on the far side of the hill. There is a giant **Match supermarket** at 8 rue Ste-Marie (tel. 03 88 91 23 63), a 10min. walk from the town center. (Open M-Th 8:30am-7:30pm, F 8:30am-8pm, Sa 8am-6pm.) Look out for the **market,** pl. de Gaulle, on Thursday mornings.

SIGHTS AND HIKING. "Oh! What a lovely garden!" exclaimed Louis XIV upon visiting Saverne, and he would no doubt say the same again if he had occasion to wander in the **Roseraie,** a botanical garden that sprawls out to the left of Grande Rue, along the Zorn. Over 8500 blooms shimmy their pretty heads here, bolstering Saverne's claim to be "The City of Roses." Several varieties have been named in honor of young blossoms of the past, among them Ingrid Bergman and Catherine Deneuve. (Open June-Sept. daily 9am-7pm. 15F, students 10F.)

The majestic **Château des Rohan,** home to the bishop-princes of Strasbourg from the 15th century to the Revolution, spreads its elegant Neo-Classical arms along the pl. de Gaulle in the center of town. The château now hosts the **Musée du Château des Rohan** (tel. 03 88 91 06 28), in reality a trio of museums that can help you while away your day. The Gallo-Roman remains and small art and history collection are fairly unremarkable, but the chic **Musée de Louise Weiss** compensates with panache. Dedicated to the local feminist, journalist, and Resistance fighter, the museum slickly recreates her life and times with audio-visual displays and assorted memorabilia. (Open Mar.-June 14 and Sept. 16-Nov. 30 W-M 2-5pm; June 15-Sept. 15 W-M 10am-noon and 2-6pm; Dec.-Feb. Su 2-5pm. 16F, students 10F.)

HIKES. Saverne's greatest asset is its endless, clearly-marked web of forested **hiking** and **biking trails** weaving through the farmlands. **Club Vosgien** maintains phenomenal trails and also runs hikes in the area; ask the tourist office for information. Bikers can pick up the free brochure *Cyclo Tourisme*, with a map and suggested routes, from the tourist office. Even if you're not up for a long hike, try the 45min. jaunt through shaded woods to the lovely 12th-century castle **Le Haut Barr;** pick up a map at the tourist office and follow rue du Haut Barr (D17) southwest. The castle saw its heyday in the 16th century as the home of Jean de Manderscheid, a gregarious scamp who formed a drinking club for local noblemen; membership required drinking six pints of wine non-stop out of a bull's horn. Nearby is the **Tour du Télégraphe Chappe** (tel. 03 88 52 98 99), the first telegraph tower along the Paris-Strasbourg line. (Open May Sa-Su noon-6pm; June-Aug. Tu-Su noon-6pm. 5F, children 3F.)

THE ROUTE DU VIN

The vineyards of Alsace flourish along a 170km corridor known as the Route du Vin that stretches along the foothills of the Vosges from Strasbourg to Mulhouse. The Romans were the first to ferment Alsatian grapes, but the locals, knowing a good thing when they tasted it, enthusiastically continued the tradition. Today over 150 million bottles are sold yearly. Hordes of tourists are drawn to the medieval villages along the route, with their picture-book half-timbered houses and numerous *caves* offering free *dégustations*. Unique among French *appellations*, Alsatian wines are named for the grape varieties from which they are made rather than the area they are grown in. Particularly renowned are fine whites such as the robust Riesling and the pungent Gewurtraminer, but the Pinot Noir reds and smoky rosés also deserve a mention.

The *Route* includes nearly a hundred towns, making for a lot of ground to cover. Accommodations tend to be expensive, so consider staying in **Colmar** (p. 406) or **Sélestat** (p. 409), larger towns which anchor the Route. **Buses** run frequently from Colmar to towns on the southern part of the Route, but many of the smaller towns are not well served by public transportation. **Car rental** is practical, if expensive, from Strasbourg and Colmar. **Biking** is a viable alternative, especially from Colmar, but the gentle yet persistent hills may challenge novices. The trails and turn-offs are very well marked. **Trains** connect **Sélestat, Molsheim, Barr, Colmar,** and **Mulhouse.** The best source of info on regional *caves* is the **Centre d'Information du Vin d'Alsace,** 12 av. de la Foire aux Vins (tel. 03 89 20 16 20; fax 03 89 20 16 30), at the Maison du Vin d'Alsace in Colmar. The departmental tourist offices in Strasbourg (p. 395) dispenses regional advice, including the excellent *Alsace Wine Route* brochure. From April to October, **Astra** (tel. 03 88 21 52 40) runs bus tours from Strasbourg to the Château de Haut Koenigsbourg, Ribeauvillé, and Riquewihr (Sa 9am, 160F). Call the Strasbourg tourist office (p. 396) for info and bookings.

KAYSERSBERG

Not just another storybook village along Alsace's meandering Route de Vin, **Kaysersberg** (pop. 2,755) is a little town with a lot of history. Its name, from the Latin "Cæsaris Mons" (Cæsar's Mountain), signifies the importance of this town during Roman times, when it commanded one of the most important passes between Gaul and the Rhine Valley. Perhaps it was this martial history which drove native son Albert Schweitzer to the Nobel Peace prize. His home has since been converted into the pastel green **Centre Culturel Albert Schweitzer,** 126 rue Général de Gaulle, which contains copious memorabilia retracing the life and works of the good doctor. (Open May 2-Oct. 31 daily 9am-noon and 2-6pm. 10F, students 5F.) Also noteworthy is the 12th- to 15th-century **church,** with a magnificent wooden triptych altarpiece carved by Jean Bongartz of Colmar in 1518. Between the church and the museum are the remains of the 15th- to 16th-century **fortified bridge.** Clamber up for a view of the ruined castle on the hill above the town.

Kaysersberg has no train station, but **buses** run frequently to **Colmar** (20min, 12F). The **tourist office,** 39 rue Général de Gaulle (tel 03 89 78 22 78; email ot.kaysersberg@rmcnet.fr), is sequestered in the Hôtel de Ville; cross the bridge behind the bus stop and walk straight up the road to a little square with a fountain to reach it. (Open M-F 8:30am-noon and 1-5:30pm, Sa 9am-noon.)

MOLSHEIM

A medieval university center, **Molsheim** is a large, accessible wine town that is quite heavily touristed. Car designer Ettore Bugatti established a factory here, and the 16th-century **Charterhouse Priory,** 4 Cours des Chartreux (tel. 03 88 38 25 10), houses Bugatti memorabilia as well as the **Musée de Molsheim,** a mélange of art, history, and archæology. The best-preserved Renaissance building in town, the **Metzig,** 1 pl. de l'Hôtel de Ville, retains its 16th-century tower, clock, and moondial. (Open Th-Tu noon-2:30pm and 6:30-10:30pm.) The town is connected by frequent **trains** to **Strasbourg** (20min., 21F) and **Sélestat** (35min, 33F). The **tourist office** is at 19 pl. de l'Hôtel de Ville (tel. 03 88 38 11 61; fax 03 88 49 80 40). It organizes visits to the vineyards and *caves,* a free *dégustation* (July-Aug. 2 per week), and horse-drawn carriage tours. (Open June-Sept. M-F 8am-noon and 2-6pm, Sa 9am-noon and 2-6pm, Su 10am-noon and 2-5pm; Oct.-May M-F 8am-noon and 2-6pm, Sa 10am-noon and 2-4pm.) The annual **Molsheim Wine Fair** takes place on May 1.

BARR

On the slopes of Mont Ste-Odile, **Barr** rests peacefully beneath vineyards which arch dramatically up the foothills of the Vosges. The old town's winding streets cut into the hillside, lined with tightly packed, half-timbered houses. From the *gare,* follow rue de la Gare to the right, past the roundabout, and into town as it becomes rue de l'Hôpital. Take a left on Grande Rue and a right on rue Taufflier (which flows into rue des Bouchers) to reach the **tourist office.** (Tel. 03 88 08 66 65. Open Sept.-June M-F 8am-noon and 2-6pm, Sa 9am-noon and 2-4pm; July-Aug. M-F 9am-12:30pm and 1:30-7pm, Su 10am-noon and 2-6pm.) From the pl. de l'Hôtel de Ville, a right on rue du Dr. Sultzer leads to several *caves.* To the left stands the massive, unornamented **Église Protestante,** the starting point for the *sentier viticole* (vineyard trail) leading through the hills. Walkable alone or in a guided tour organized by the tourist office, the path winds 2km through fields of glistening grapes as signs illustrate various stages in the development of the grape. The second week of July sees the **Foire aux Vins,** and the **Fête des Vendanges** (Grape Harvest Festival) takes place the first Sunday in October. **Trains** to Barr run from **Strasbourg** (45min., 33F) and **Sélestat** (25min., 18F).

RIQUEWIHR

Certainly the most visited village along the Route, the 16th-century walled hamlet of **Riquewihr** anchors a number of Alsace's best-known wine-shipping firms—but you may want to ship yourself somewhere less zoo-like in the summer months. Christmas time sees a celebratory market with mulled wine. The beautiful **Tour des Voleurs** (Thieves' Tower) contains a grisly, stocked torture chamber. (Open July-Aug. daily 9:15am-noon and 1:30-6:30pm. 10F.) The 13th-century **Tour du Dolder,** rue du Général de Gaulle, served as a sentinel post. (Open July-Aug. daily 9:15am-noon and 1:30-6:30pm; Apr.-June and Sept.-Oct. Sa-Su 9:15am-noon and 1:30-6:30pm. 10F.) Summer nights bring free *son et lumière* shows. (Mid-June to mid-Sept. F 10pm; July-Aug. Tu and F 10pm.) The **Wine Festival** takes place on the second to last weekend in July, and the first Sunday of September comes alive with song during the **Minstrel's Festival.** The **tourist office,** 2 rue de la 1ère Armée (tel. 03 89 49 08 40), leads free walking tours. (July-Aug. daily 5:30pm. Office open July-Aug. M-F 9:30am-12:30pm, Sa-Su 10am-12:30pm and 1:30-6pm; Mar.-June and Sept.-Nov. M-Sa 10am-12:30pm and 1:30-6pm.) You can pitch a tent at **Camping Intercommunal** (tel. 03 89 47 90 08), 1.5km from the town center. (20F per person, 25F per site. Reception 8:30-11:30am and 2-7pm. Open Apr.-Oct.)

SÉLESTAT

Halfway between Colmar and Strasbourg, Sélestat (pop. 17,200) is often overlooked by tourists on their way between the two larger cities. As a result, it has avoided acquiring the looniness of some of the Route du Vin's more frequented towns. Part of the Holy Roman Empire from AD 1217 and a center of humanism in the 15th century, Sélestat has painstakingly preserved its rich cultural heritage, including the ultimate in Rhineland bragging rights—the first recorded Christmas tree. *Vieux Sélestat* tucks away cranky old wells, brooding churches, nearly a dozen pocket-sized squares, and shady, tree-lined boulevards.

◪ **ORIENTATION AND PRACTICAL INFORMATION.** From pl. de la Gare, **trains** run to **Strasbourg** (30min., 41F) and **Colmar** (20min., 24F). The **tourist office,** 10 bd. Général Leclerc (tel. 03 88 58 87 20; fax 03 88 92 88 63; www.ville-selestat.fr), in the Commanderie St-Jean, is north of the *centre ville,* a 10-minute hike from the *gare.* Go straight on av. de la Gare, through pl. Général de Gaulle, to av. de la Liberté. Turn left onto bd. du Maréchal Foch, which veers right and becomes bd. Général Leclerc after pl. Schaal. The office is a few blocks down on your right. The efficient staff can **change currency** and rent you a bike. (Open May-Sept M-F 9am-12:30pm and 1:30-7pm, Sa 9am-noon and 2-5pm, Su 9am-3pm. Bikes 35F for 2 hours, 50F per half-day, 80F per full day.) The **hospital** is at 23 av. Pasteur (tel. 03 88 57 55 55), behind the *gare.* The **police** are at bd. du Général Leclerc (tel. 03 88 58 84 22). The **post office** is on rue de la Poste. (Tel. 03 88 58 80 10. Open M-F 8am-noon and 1:30-6pm, Sa 8am-noon. **Postal code:** 67600.)

◪◪ **ACCOMMODATIONS, CAMPING, AND FOOD.** The **Hôtel de l'Ill,** 13 rue des Bateliers (tel. 03 88 92 91 09), off bd. des Thiers, is a lovely white stucco building with pastel blue shutters. All rooms have newly-installed showers; simple but cheerful. (Singles 150F; doubles 180F-240F; triples 350F. Breakfast 28F. Reception daily 7am-10pm. V, MC, AmEx.) **Camping Les Cigognes** (tel. 03 88 92 03 98) is outside the ramparts on the south edge of the *vieille ville.* Public tennis courts and parks are nearby. (15.30F per person, 15.30F per site. Electricity 10.20F. Reception 7:30am-noon and 2-10pm.)

Boulangeries, *épiceries*, and other sources of edible treats are scattered throughout the *vieille ville*, especially on **rue des Chevaliers** and **rue de l'Hôpital**. Every Tuesday morning, an **open air market** fills the town center with cabbage and other necessities. For a casual setting, stop at **Halte Pizzas,** 14 rue d'Iéna (tel. 03 88 82 91 91). They have a huge selection of pizzas from 29F, to eat in or take out. (Open M-W 11am-2pm and 5-10pm, F-Sa 11am-2pm and 5-11:30pm, Su 5-10:30pm.) In a quiet square around the corner from the churches, **Au Bon Pichet,** 10 pl. du Marché-aux-Choux (tel. 03 88 82 96 65), prepares Alsatian favorites: large salads with *foie gras*, duck, or smoked salmon (48F), or meat dishes (60-85F). (Open Tu-Sa 11am-2:30pm and 7-11pm, Su-M 11am-2:30pm. V, MC, AmEx.)

☎ 🎭 **SIGHTS AND FESTIVALS.** According to local legend, Sélestat was founded by the gigantic Sletto. His massive thigh bone (a mere mammoth tusk, disbelievers claim) is only one of the treasures in the building that also houses Sélestat's extraordinary **Bibliothèque Humaniste,** 1 rue de la Bibliothèque (tel. 03 88 92 03 24). Founded in 1452, this contains a fascinating collection of ancient documents, reflecting Sélestat's status as a center of humanist learning in the 15th century. Included among the volumes are Charlemagne's 9th-century regulations and the 16th-century *Cosmographiae Introductio*, the first book to mention "America" by name. (Open M, W-F 9am-noon and 2-6pm, Sa 9am-noon; July-Aug. also Sa-Su 2-7pm. Admission 20F.) Surrounded by ivy-covered homes, the 12th-century **Église Ste-Foy** rises above the *vieille ville* and the pl. Marché-aux-Poissons. Constructed by Benedictine monks, Ste-Foy is one of the most beautiful Romanesque churches in the region. Resentful of the monastery's power, the townspeople responded with the 13th- to 15th-century **Église St-Georges** across the square. The essentially Gothic church's 14th- and 15th-century frescoes contrast with Max Ingrand's 1960s vibrant stained-glass windows. Religious and political disorder made the 16th and 17th centuries a dark period in Sélestat's history. The crumbling 13th-century **Tour des Sorcières,** in front of pl. Maréchal de Lattre de Tassigny, held over 100 "witches" imprisoned by the Catholic church between 1629 and 1642.

In odd-numbered years, the town hosts a contemporary art exhibition cleverly named **Sélest'Art** (mid-Sept. to mid-Oct.). Sélestat's major festival is its **Corso Fleuri,** or flower festival, the second Sunday in August, with elaborate, colorful floats made of fresh local flowers. The celebration is capped by an impressive fireworks display in the evening. (Adults 40F. Email corso@ville-selestat.fr for more info.)

NEAR SÉLESTAT: CHÂTEAU DE HAUT KOENIGSBOURG

Towering 757m over the town of Kintzheim, just to the east of Sélestat, this château housed the Hapsburgs in the 15th century during Alsace's sojourn as part of their Empire. The castle was demolished by the Swedes during the Thirty Years War and left in ruins until Emperor Wilhelm II of Hohenzollern reconstructed it at the beginning of the 20th century. (Tel. 03 88 82 50 60; fax 03 88 82 50 61. Open daily Mar.-Apr. and Oct. 9am-noon and 1-5:30pm, May-June and Sept. 9am-6pm, July-Aug. 9am-6:30pm, Jan.-Feb. and Nov.-Dec. 9:30am-noon and 1-4:30pm. Free, or guided tour.)

COLMAR

Surrounded by vineyards and the craggy Vosges ranges, Colmar (pop. 65,000) derives its name from the *colombes* (doves) Charlemagne kept at his estate on the Lauch river. Most of the sights lie within the cobblestone streets of the pedestrian zone and the scenic 15th- and 16th-century alleyways. In the city's former Dominican monastery and church are two superb works of Renaissance art—Grünewald's *Isenheim Altarpiece* and Schongauer's *Virgin in the Rose Bower*—which justify a visit in themselves. Anchoring the south of the Route du Vin, the streets teem with tourists in summer, but the crooked lanes and pretty pastel houses manage to retain a measure of bucolic charm.

TRUE LOVE Koenigsbourg has figured in tales of love as well as war; legend speaks of the Rathsamhausen and Tierstein families, who struggled against each other for control of the castle at the end of the 15th century. The Rathsamhausens appealed to Maximin of Ribeaupierre for help. To end the feud Maximin had to pick a side, and he decided to throw his daughter Isabella into the deal as well, to cement the alliance. Miffed that she hadn't been consulted, Isabella de Ribeaupierre disguised herself as a minstrel in order to sneak into the castle and catch a glimpse of Wilhelm de Tierstein, one of the prospective bridegrooms. Unbeknownst to her, however, Wilhelm had switched places with his valet Pépin and donned minstrel's garb as well, hoping to thereby uncover Isabella's true feelings towards him. A comedy of errors worthy of Shakespeare ensued, which is reenacted during the Château's *Soirées Médiévales*. (Apr. 30-Oct. 16 F and Sa 8:15pm. 230F including 4-course dinner.)

◪ ORIENTATION AND PRACTICAL INFORMATION. Trains go to **Mulhouse** (30min., 41F); **Strasbourg** (30min., 57F); **Paris** (5hr., 10 per day, 239F); and **Lyon** (5hr., 7 per day, 260F). (Office open M-F 6:30am-8pm, Sa 8:30am-6:30pm, Su 8:30am-7:30pm. Info office open M-F 9am-7pm, Sa 9am-6pm.) **Buses** are to the right as you exit the station, on pl. de la Gare. Numerous companies run to small towns on the *Route*. Ease tired feet by using **Allo Trace local transportation,** rue Unterlinden (tel. 03 89 20 80 80), next door to the tourist office. (Open M-F 8:30am-12:15pm and 1-6:15pm, Sa 8:30am-12:15pm. Tickets 5.60F, *carnet* of 10 41.50F. Buses run 6am-8pm, night *Somnabus* M-Sa 8pm-midnight.) 24hr. **taxis** (tel. 03 89 41 40 19 or 03 89 80 71 71) can be hailed at pl. de la Gare. **Bike rentals** are available at **La Cyclothèque,** 31 rte. d'Ingersheim. (Tel. 03 89 79 14 18. 50F per half-day, M-F 70F per full day, Sa-Su 150F. Open M 2-6:30pm, W-Sa 8am-noon and 2-6:30pm.) To get from the station to the **tourist office,** 4 rue des Unterlinden (tel. 03 89 20 68 92; email accueil@ot-colmar.fr), take the first left onto av. de la République. Follow it as it becomes rue Kléber and curves right through pl. du 18 Novembre into the main pl. Unterlinden; the tourist office is straight ahead. The staff offers cash only **currency exchange** and makes hotel reservations with a night's deposit. Ask for *Actualités Colmar*, a free events booklet with local bus schedules. From April till October, they also run **city tours** for 25F (students 15F); consult the schedule at the office. (Open July-Aug. M-Sa 9am-7pm, Su 9:30am-2pm; Apr.-June and Sept.-Nov. M-Sa 9am-6pm, Su 10am-2pm; Nov.-Mar. M-Sa 9am-noon and 2-6pm, Su 10am-2pm.) The **police** are at 6 rue du Chasseur (tel. 03 89 24 75 00). **Hôpital Pasteur** is at 39 av. de la Liberté (tel. 03 89 80 40 00). The **post office,** 36-38 av. de la République (tel. 03 89 41 19 19), across from the Champ-de-Mars, has **currency exchange.** (Open M-F 8am-6:30pm, Sa 8am-noon. **Postal code:** 68000.)

⚑ ACCOMMODATIONS AND CAMPING. There's precious little in budget range. The smattering of one- and two-star hotels in the center of town are perfectly located but overpriced. To reach the **Auberge de Jeunesse (HI),** 2 rue Pasteur (tel. 03 89 80 57 39), take bus #4 (direction "Logelbach") to "Pont Rouge." To walk, take the underground passage in the train station and exit to the right onto rue du Tir; follow it as it merges with av. Général de Gaulle. Turn left onto rue du Florimont halfway across the bridge over the railroad tracks, then take a right on rue du Pont Rouge; continue through the intersection on the rte. d'Ingersheim to rue Pasteur (20min.). (68F per person in 7-bunk dorms; 92F in singles or doubles. Breakfast included. **Members only.** Lockout 9am-5pm. Sheets 20F. Midnight curfew. Reception 7-10am and 5pm-midnight. Cash only. Closed Dec. 15-Jan. 15.)

Hôtel Kempf, 1 av. de la République (tel. 03 89 41 21 72), offers large, simple rooms with lovely bedspreads in a perfect location. (Singles and doubles 180-280F, triples 350F. Breakfast 30F. Reception 8am-1am. V, MC.) **La Chaumière,** 74 av. de la République (tel. 03 89 41 08 99), is situated around the corner from the train station and a brisk 5min. walk down the street from the center of town. Some of the serviceable, red-carpeted rooms are set around a balcony overlooking an inner courtyard, and there is a small but pretty *brasserie* downstairs. (Singles and doubles 150-180F, with shower 240F; triples 270F. Breakfast 28F. Reception daily 7am-midnight; July-Aug. closed Su 1-5pm. V, MC.) Sitting by the river, **Camping de l'Ill,** rte. Horbourg-Wihr (tel. 03 89 41 15 94), is about 3km from town. Take bus #1 (direction "Horbourg-Wihr") to "Plage d'Ill." Immaculate bathrooms, store, and restaurant. (Site 20F, tent 10F, adult 17F. Reception M-F 7am-9pm, Sa-Su 8am-9pm. Open Feb.-Nov., May-Sept. for tents. Fills quickly in summer.)

🍴 **FOOD.** There is a **Monoprix supermarket** at pl. Unterlinden. (Open M-F 8:30am-8:25pm, Sa 8am-7:55pm.) **Markets** are set up in pl. St-Joseph (Sa morning) and pl. de l'Ancienne Douane (Th morning), a popular café spot.

Tropic'ice, pl. des Dominicains (tel. 03 89 41 31 36), combines Caribbean beach house decor with over 100 permutations of *galettes, crêpes,* and *coupes glacées.* The packed terrace faces the massive Église des Dominicains. (Open daily 11:30am-midnight.) **Bier-u-Winstub,** 23-25 Grande Rue (tel. 03 89 23 66 26), offers *tartes flambées* and other hearty Alsatian fare, as well as a great selection of local beers and wines. The red-and-white checkered table-clothes and the intimacy of the people-watching terrace give it a cosy feel. (Open daily 10am-1am, hot food served 11:30am-11:30pm.) The big, brassy **Brasserie des Dominicains,** pl. des Martyrs (tel. 03 89 23 68 21), is tucked away behind the church. Popular eatery by day and piano bar by night, the *brasserie* serves up regional favorites (40-85F) amid burnished wood paneling. (Open daily 7:30am-1:30am. Food 11am-midnight.)

Being on the southern end of the Route du Vin, Colmar boasts a number of *viticulteurs.* A friendly welcome, a great selection of local wines (26F and up), and a 400-year legacy await at **Robert Karcher et Fils,** 11 rue de l'Ours (tel. 03 89 41 14 42; fax 03 89 24 45 05), in the *vieille ville.* (Open daily 8am-noon and 2-7pm. V, MC.)

🔎 **SIGHTS.** The city's restored Alsatian houses glisten in freshly-painted pastel hues. For the best specimens, visit the **quartier des Tanneurs** then follow rue des Tanneurs over a small canal to the area called **la petite Venise.** Carved wooden doors face the canals, and geraniums repose in window boxes above cobblestone streets. Renaissance **Maison des Têtes,** rue des Têtes, owes its name to the grinning masks that festoon its facade. Housed in a 13th-century Dominican cloister, the **Musée Unterlinden,** 1 rue d'Unterlinden (tel. 03 89 20 15 50), contains a spectacular and eclectic collection that includes Romanesque sculpture, medieval and Renaissance art, and an armory. Especially notable is Mathias Grunewald and Nikolaus Haguenauer's *Isenheim Altarpiece* (1500-1516), an ambitious polytych depicting scenes of the Crucifixion with an unsettling sense of desolation. (Open Apr.-Oct. daily 9am-6pm; Nov.-Mar. W-M 10am-5pm. 35F, students 25F.) The **Église des Dominicains,** pl. des Dominicains (tel. 03 89 24 46 57), is now little more than a showroom for Martin Schongauer's exquisite *Virgin in the Rose Bower* (1473), but it makes a splendid showroom indeed. Fourteenth-century stained glass illuminates the artwork with a golden glow. The German-captioned painted panels on the wall date from the German occupation of Alsace after the 1870 Franco-Prussian war. (Open daily 10am-12:45pm and 3-5:45pm. 8F, students 6F.) The **Collégiale St-Martin,** pl. de la Cathédrale, was built between 1234 and 1365 upon the ruins of an 11th-century church. The 14th-century stained glass was taken from the monastery that houses the museum. (Open daily 8am-7pm except during mass.) Frédéric Auguste Bartholdi (1834-1904) is best known for sculpting a 47m statue of his mother entitled *Liberty Enlightening the World*—though Americans insist on calling it the *Statue of Liberty*. His home has become the wonderful **Musée Bartholdi,** 30 rue des Marchands (tel. 03 89 41 90 60), housing his personal art collection, his drawings, and models of his monuments. (Open Mar.-Dec. W-M 10am-noon and 2-6pm. 20F, students 15F.)

⬛ ▓ ENTERTAINMENT AND FESTIVALS. The 10-day **Foire aux Vins d'Alsace** in early August is the region's largest wine fair. Concerts given by popular French and European musicians are held in the evenings at 9pm. (Tel. 03 09 50 50 50; www.colmar.expo.fr. Admission 10F until 5pm. Concerts 35-170F.) In the first two weeks of July, the **Festival International de Colmar** features two dozen concerts with world-class musicians. (Tickets 90-295F, students 45-110F). **Église St-Pierre** stages concerts mid-August to early September. (Th 8:45pm. 45F, under 21 25F.) The Collégiale St-Martin's organists pipe on Tuesdays at 8:45pm at the **Heures Musicales** during the last week of July and early August. (50F, students 40F.) In late September, the **Journée de la Choucroute et de la Bière** (Sauerkraut and Beer Day!), means feasting, dancing, and meals devoted to sauerkraut.

MULHOUSE

If the Route du Vin forms the heart of Alsace and Strasbourg is its mind, then prosperous Mulhouse (pop 110,000) provides the muscle. Granted a charter as a free city in the 13th century by the Holy Roman Emperor, Mulhouse chugged along happily for centuries as a tiny republic binding itself loosely with chunks of Switzerland and various other Alsatian towns. In 1798, city leaders took stock of their limited potential, decided that prosperity lay within the expanding French republic, and invited French soldiers into the territory. Having accumulated wealth and a sharp business sense through long involvement in the textile trade, Mulhouse is a modern city with a thriving commercial center, a welcome respite from the gingerbread kitsch of its northern neighbors in the Haut-Rhin. Its industrial heritage has endowed the town with a host of first-rate museums and an infectious energy that permeates the busy streets.

🛈 PRACTICAL INFORMATION

Trains run from bd. Général Leclerc to **Basel,** Switzerland (30min., 6 per day, 83F); **Belfort** (30min., 24 per day, 46F); **Strasbourg** (1hr., 22 per day, 81F); and **Paris** (4½hr., 9 per day, 260F). **Tram** (tel. 03 89 66 77 77) runs buses from **Porte Jeune,** north of the pedestrian district. (Most services 7am-7pm, evening routes 8:30-11:30pm. Tickets 7F, *carnet* of 10 50F, day pass 18F; all available at tourist office.) The **tourist office,** 9 av. Foch (tel. 03 89 35 48 48), lies two blocks straight ahead from the right-most edge of the *gare,* across from a park. Hotel reservations and maps of walking tours await. (Open July-Aug. M-Sa 9am-7pm, Su 10am-1pm; Sept.-June M-Sa 9am-7pm.) **Rent bikes** at **Cycles Beha,** pl. de la Concord (tel. 03 89 45 13 46). The **police** are at 12 rue Cochern (tel. 03 89 59 07 70). The **hospital** emergency room is located behind the *gare* at 20 rue du Dr. Läennec (tel. 03 89 64 64 64). The nearby central **post office,** 3 pl. de Gaulle, **exchanges money.** (Office open M-F 7:30am-7pm, Sa 8am-noon. Poste Restante code: 68074. **Postal code:** 68100.) Access the **internet** at **La Filature,** 20 allée Nathan Katz (tel. 03 84 36 28 28).

🏠🏕🍴 ACCOMMODATIONS, CAMPING, AND FOOD

ACCOMMODATIONS. Mulhouse's hotels cater to suits. Dirt-cheap rooms in town are elusive, but a galaxy of comfortable two-star establishments compete for clients. Rates drop on weekends.
The **Auberge de Jeunesse (HI),** 37 rue d'Ilberg (tel. 03 89 42 63 28), prepares cheerful spots in four to eight bed rooms with co-ed bathrooms. Take bus #2 (direction "Loteaux"; #S1 after 8:30pm) to "Salle des Sports." (48F per person. Breakfast 19F. Linen 17F. Bike rental 35F per half-day, 50F per day. **Members only.** Reception 8am-noon and 4-11pm, until midnight in summer, closed Su noon-5pm.) ▣ **Hôtel St-Bernard,** 3 rue des Fleurs (tel. 03 89 45 82 32; fax 03 89 45 26 32), conveniently located near the center of town, amazes with gorgeous Belle Époque decor and bright, immaculate rooms. Some have elaborate

murals painted on the ceiling, and all have showers, phones, and TVs with 32 channels. Also included is access to the small library, internet, bicycles, and, of course, a shaggy St. Bernard doggie, all for free. (Singles and doubles 170-280F. Breakfast 35F. Reception 7am-9:30pm. V, MC, AmEx.) ⬛ **Hôtel de Bâle,** 19-21 Passage Central (tel. 03 89 46 19 87), second in a row of three hotels on a bustling side street, provides modern, pastel-colored accommodations and a delightful first-floor breakfast room. (Singles from 160F, with shower 175-225F; doubles with shower 195F, with bath and toilet 195-310F. Extra bed 55F. Breakfast 37F. Room rates often 15-30F lower on weekends. V, MC.) **Camping de l'Ill,** rue Pierre de Couberlin (tel. 03 89 06 20 66), has a grocery store and sports facilities. (18.50F per person, site 18.50F. Open Apr.-Sept.)

FOOD. Mulhouse *menus* go for Swiss prices, but a community of students fosters inexpensive options on **rue de l' Arsenal. La Couscoussière,** 33 rue de l'Arsenal (tel. 03 89 56 65 07), has hearty pots of the signature dish (50-75F), as well as a 42F *plat du jour* and a summer selection of 30F salads. (Open Tu-Sa noon-2:30pm and 7-11:30pm, Su-M noon-2:30pm). *Crêpes* (13-43F) and *galettes* (32-45F) are served in a homey atmosphere at **Crampous Mad,** 14 impasse des Tondeurs. (Tel. 03 89 45 79 43. Open M-F 11:30am-10pm, Sa 11:30am-11pm.) For do-it-yourself types, **Monoprix** looms at the corner of rue du Sauvage and rue des Maréchaux. (Open M-F 8:15am-8pm, Sa 8:15am-7pm.) A few doors down, **Le Globe** *épicerie* awaits with delicacies bound to satisfy your inner *gourmand*.

👁 SIGHTS

Mulhouse's historical district centers upon the festive **pl. de la Réunion,** named for the dates in 1798 and 1918 when French troops "reunited" the city with distant Paris. Further afield, the city's industrial past has spawned a set of worthy museums focused on technology, from textile-making to trains. On a sunny day, you might like to hang out with rare animals amidst the 20,000 flowers of the **Parc Zoologique et Botanique.** *(Tel. 03 39 31 85 10. Take bus #12, direction "Moenschsberg" to "Zoo." Open May-Aug. 9am-7pm; Apr. and Sept. 9am-6pm; Mar. and Oct.-Nov. 9am-5pm; Dec.-Feb. 10am-4pm. Admission Mar.-Oct. 45F, Nov.-Feb. 20F; students 20F.)*

TEMPLE DE ST-ÉTIENNE. One of France's few Protestant Gothic cathedrals, the *temple* casts a long shadow across the cafés and the carousel on pl. de la Réunion. Inside, visitors are free to climb up to the galleries to inspect the 14th-century stained glass. The lower level displays temporary exhibits of modern art, and if the whole experience seems distinctly secular, it's because the burghers bought the church, lock, stock, and barrel, from the Catholics in 1890. *(Tel. 03 89 66 30 19. Open May-Sept. M and W-F 10am-noon and 2-6pm, Sa 10am-noon and 2-5pm, Su 2-6pm.)*

MUSÉE FRANÇAIS DU CHEMIN DE FER. A stunning collection of slick, gleaming engines and railway cars stand permanently *en retard* in this hanger-like museum. Peer into the perfectly restored compartments of legends such as the Orient Express for a trip back in railway history. Every hour on the half-hour a massive 1949 steam engine, the last of its kind, chugs into action; the timid can plunk 2F into a machine in the lobby to start a much smaller network rolling through miniature Alsatian villages and farms. A walkway dedicated to the history of wooden railway ties leads to the **Musée du Sapeur Pompier.** *Sapeurs-Pompiers*, France's heroic fireman-cum-medics, consider themselves part of a pedigree tradition; in addition to the fire trucks, the museum displays medals, regimental banners, portraits, and silly plumed hats. *(2 rue Alfred de Glehn. Tel. 03 89 42 25 67. Take bus #17, direction "Musées," from Porte Jeune Place or #18, direction "Technopole," from the train station. From MGEN, head left and then turn left onto the industrial road. Open daily Apr.1-Sept. 30 9am-6pm; Oct. 1-Mar. 31 9am-5pm. Admission 45F, students 20F, children 10F; includes entry to Musée du Sapeur Pompier. Guided tours are available in English, French, Italian, and German upon reservation, for 24F. Free parking.)*

ÉLECTROPOLIS. This zippy new museum indoctrinates kids into the wonderful world of energy through hands-on exhibits, films, and historical collections. The 170-ton *Grande Machine* whirls and clicks in the heart of the building. *(Next to the railway museum. Open July-Aug. daily 10am-6pm; Sept.-June Tu-Su 10am-6pm. Admission 48F, students 23F, combined with railroad museum 68F.)*

MUSÉE NATIONAL DE L'AUTOMOBILE. This temple to gas-guzzlers presents the staggering car collection of the brothers Schlumpf. 500 mint-condition autos, from a 1878 Jacques à vapeur to spunky 1950s coupes and the bubble-like electric cars of the future, repose grandly in a converted 19th-century woolen mill. *(192 av. de Colmar. Tel. 03 89 33 23 23. Take bus #1, 4, 11, 13, or 17 north to "Musée Auto." Open W-M 10am-6pm. Admission 57F, students 27F, with railway museum 81F.)*

MUSÉE DE L'IMPRESSION SUR ÉTOFFES. Around the corner from the train station, this makes a good first or last stop. The museum chronicles Mulhouse's 250-year love affair with textiles; miles of gorgeous swatches from around the world grace the walls forming a collection of nearly 50,000 pieces. Also featured are displays demonstrating the craft of textile-printing and the evolution of fashionable prints. *(14 rue J. J. Henner. Tel. 03 89 46 83 00. Open daily 10am-6pm. Admission 36F, students 18F, children 15F. Wheelchair access.)*

BESANÇON

Surrounded by the Doubs river on three sides and by a steep bluff on the fourth, Besançon (pop. 120,000) has intrigued military strategists from Julius Cæsar in the 1st century BC to Vauban 1800 years later. Today the brooding citadel has been transformed into a favorite picnic spot and tourist's playground, and few scars from its military past remain to sully Besançon's cheerful face. As home to a major university and an international language center, Besançon maintains a harmonious balance between rural and urban, forest and pavement. The population is young and on the move, strolling along the river or through the hills during the day, crowding into cafés, bars, and sweaty discos by night, and escaping to nearby Alpine ski slopes when the routine becomes too much. With the prosperity afforded by its status as France's watch-making capital, Besançon is a large city, but the friendliness of the locals gives it a small-village feel.

ⓘ ORIENTATION AND PRACTICAL INFORMATION

Everything of interest in Besançon lies within a thumb-shaped turn of the Doubs. To reach the tourist office, head down the hill from the station and cross the road onto av. Maréchal Foch, which curves downhill and to the left. Pass pont Denfert-Rochereau and continue straight (as av. Foch becomes av. de l'Helvétie) to pl. de la Première Armée Française. The office is in the park to your right, and the *vieille ville* is across the pont de la République (10min.).

Trains: av. de la Paix. To: **Belfort** (1hr., 10 per day, 77F); **Dijon** (1hr., 9 per day, 73F); **Paris** via Dole and Dijon (2hr., 7 per day, 263-309F); **Lyon** (2½hr., 10 per day, 163F); **Strasbourg** (3hr., 10 per day, 180F). Info office open M-Sa 8:30am-6:15pm.

Buses: Monts Jura, 9 rue Proudhon (tel. 03 81 21 22 00). To **Pontarlier** (55min., 6 per day, 51F). Office open M-F 8am-6:30pm, Sa 8am-1pm and 2:30-5:30pm.

Local Transportation: CTB, pl. du 8 Septembre (tel. 03 81 48 12 12). Open M-Sa 10am-12:45pm and 1:15-7pm. Tickets 6F, *carnet* of 10 51F. Valid 1hr. All-day ticket 20F. Buy on bus.

Taxis: (tel. 03 81 88 80 80). 24hr. service. Minimum charge 22F.

Bike Rental: Véloland, 4 rue des Chalets (tel. 03 81 53 51 54; fax 03 81 53 32 65). Mountain bikes 80F per day, 60F per half-day, discounts for over 2 days. Includes helmet and lock. ID deposit. Open M 10am-7pm, Tu-F 9am-7:30pm, Sa 9am-7pm.

THE NORTHEAST

Tourist services: Tourist Office, 2 pl. de la 1ère Armée Française (tel. 03 81 80 92 55; fax 03 81 80 58 30; www.besancon.com). Lists of hotels and restaurants, info on excursions and festivals. Ask for a free copy of the student guide *La Besace.* Free accommodations service. Guided tours for individuals (in French; 37F, students 27F) and groups (in French, English, or German). Provides **currency exchange** when banks are closed. Open June 15-Sept 15 M 10am-7pm, Tu-Sa 9am-7pm, Su 10am-noon and 3-5pm. April 1-June 14 and Sept. 15-30 same hours, but closed Su. Closed Oct.-Mar. **Besançon Informations,** 2 rue Megevand (tel. 03 81 83 08 24). Info on sports, wheel-chair facilities, health care, lodging, and festivals. Open July-Aug. M-F 8am-noon and 1:30-5:30pm; Sept.-June M-F 8am-noon and 1:30-6pm, Sa 9am-noon. Pick up the pamphlet *Culture Info.*

Laundromat: Blanc-Matic, 54 rue Bersot, near the bus station, and 57 rue des Cras, near the Foyer Mixte. 23F per 7kg to wash, 5F per 10min. to dry. Open 7am-8pm.

Youth Center: Centre Information Jeunesse (CIJ), 27 rue de la République (tel. 03 81 21 16 16). Info on internships, jobs, cultural events, and apartments. Train, bus and plane tickets, ride board. Hosteling cards and ISICs sold. Open M 1:30-6pm, Tu-F 10am-noon and 1:30-6pm, Sa 1:30-6pm. Closed Sa July-Aug. V, MC.

Hiking Information: Club Alpin Français, 14 rue Luc Breton (tel. 03 81 81 02 77), in the *vieille ville.* Sponsors organized hikes and outdoor activities. Information about mountain biking, climbing, and skiing in the area. Guidebooks and maps can be read in the library or photocopied. Open Tu-F 5-7pm.

Police: av. de la Gare d'Eau (tel. 03 81 21 11 22).

Hospital: Centre Hospitalier Universitaire, pl. St-Jacques (tel. 03 81 66 81 66).

Post Office: 23 rue Proudhon (tel. 03 81 65 55 82), off rue de la République. Currency exchange. Open M-F 8am-7pm, Sa 8am-noon. **Postal code:** 25019. **Main office** at 4 rue Demangel (tel. 03 81 53 81 12), in the new town. Poste Restante code: 25031 Besançon-Cedex. **Postal code:** 25000.

Internet Access: Rom Collection, 22 rue du Lycée (tel. 03 81 81 65 00). Open M, W-F 10am-12:30pm and 2-7:30pm, Tu and Sa 10am-12:30pm and 2-10pm. 1F per minute, 50F per hour.

▶ ACCOMMODATIONS AND CAMPING

Except during festivals and special events, hotels in Besançon are generally affordable and rarely full. For just a few francs more, you can stay in the *vielle ville* and avoid the arduous trek up the hill to the hostels.

Foyer Mixte de Jeunes Travailleurs (HI), 48 rue des Cras (tel. 03 81 40 32 00; fax 03 81 40 32 01). Turn left from the station on av. de la Paix, which turns into rue de Belfort. After 10min., turn left on rue Marie-Louise, which turns into rue des Cras. Hostel is uphill on the right (15min.). Ask locals for "Foyer Les Oiseaux," but don't worry, it's not really for the birds. Or take bus #7 from pl. Flore (off rue de Belfort on av. Carnot) to "Oiseaux" (direction "Orchamps," 3 per hr.). Large, bright rooms with private bath-rooms, and a TV room and game room. Quiet at night. Singles 90F, 80F the 2nd night; doubles 90F per person, 80F the 2nd night. Showers, sheets, and breakfast included. Lunch or dinner 40F. Reception 9am-8pm. Often full. No reservations.

Centre International de Séjour, 19 rue Martin-du-Gard (tel. 03 81 50 07 54; fax 03 81 53 11 79). Take bus #8 from the "Foch" stop near the station (direction "Campus") to "Intermarché." To get to "Foch" from the station, follow av. de la Paix as it curves down-hill to the left. Take the first right onto av. Foch; the stop is on the left. Restaurant, TV room, and foosball. Singles 99F, with shower and toilet 154F; doubles with 2 beds 64F per person, with shower and toilet 92F; triples or quads 53F per person. Breakfast 25F. Meals 58F, *plat du jour* 35F. Reception 7am-1am. Check-in 3pm, check-out 9am.

Hôtel du Nord, 8 rue Moncey (tel. 03 81 81 34 56; fax 03 81 81 85 96), on a quiet side street in the heart of the old town. Clean, full-sized rooms with shower and toilet. Singles 175F; doubles 195F. Larger singles or doubles with TVs 280F-320F. Call ahead

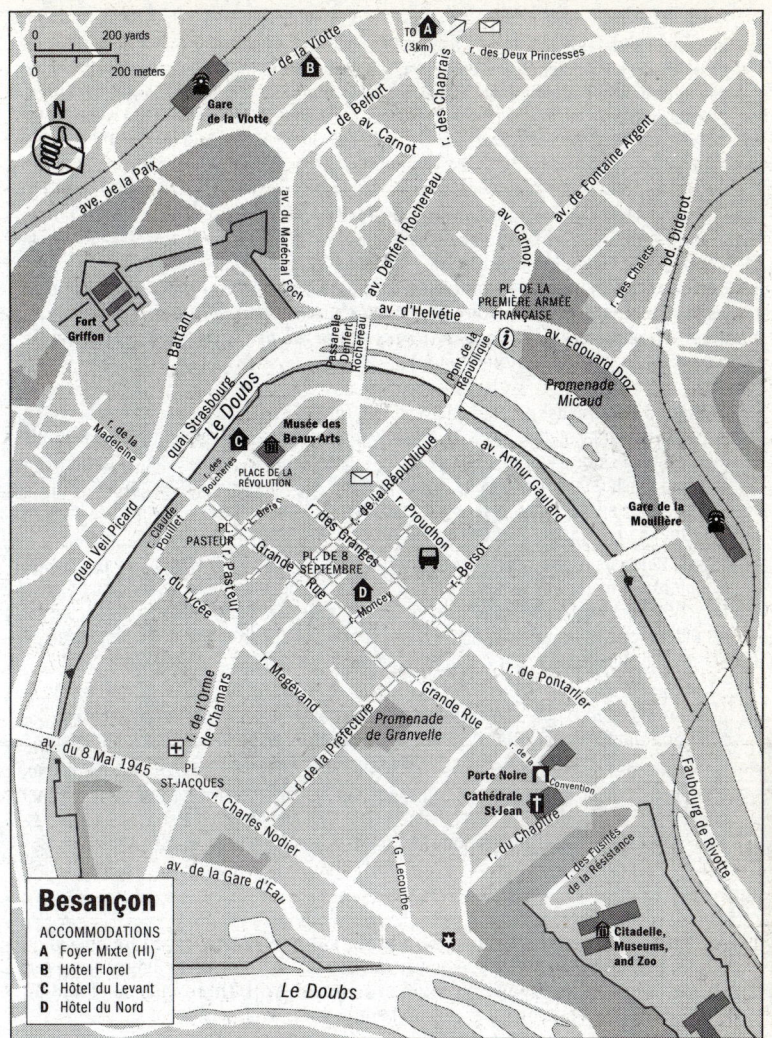

Besançon

ACCOMMODATIONS
A Foyer Mixte (HI)
B Hôtel Florel
C Hôtel du Levant
D Hôtel du Nord

THE NORTHEAST

to reserve large rooms at small room prices during low season and weekends. Breakfast 33F. Extra bed 30F. Reception 7am-8pm. Check-in and check-out at noon. V, MC.

Hôtel du Levant, 9 rue des Boucheries (tel. 03 81 81 07 88), on pl. de la Révolution. Somewhat cramped, but well located. If you take a room without a shower, you won't be washing. Singles 96-115F, with shower 140F; doubles 140F, with shower 160-190F. Breakfast 22F. Restaurant downstairs, with terrace, has *menus* from 57F and *plats* from 32F. Reception 7am-12:30am. V, MC.

Hôtel Florel, 6 rue de la Viotte (tel. 03 81 80 41 08; fax 03 81 50 44 40), the last in a row of functional hotels to the left of the station. Utilitarian but spacious rooms with TV and phone. Singles and doubles with toilet 170F, with shower 180-205F, with bath 195-225F. Shower 20F. Breakfast 27F. 24hr. reception. Check-in and check-out at noon. V, MC.

Campsites: Camping de la Plage, rte. de Belfort in Chalezeule (tel. 03 81 88 04 26), northeast of the city. Take bus #1 (direction "Palente") to the end (5min.). Shuttle bus during summer months, otherwise its a 35min. walk down rte. de Belfort. A 4-star municipal campground with free access to pool. Near a highway but manages to retain a certain bucolic charm. 20F per person, 29F per car or tent. 20% discount with French or international camping card. Breakfast 25F, *plats* 25-40F. Reception 8:30-10pm. Open Apr.-Oct. 5.

⬛ FOOD

A diverse group of restaurants along **rue Claude-Pouillet** caters to Besançon's cosmopolitan students, while **rue des Boucheries** is aimed more at tourists. Pl. de la Révolution stages an **outdoor market** (Tu and F 6am-12:30pm, Sa 6am-7pm). Buy groceries at **Monoprix,** 12 Grande Rue. (Open M-Sa 8:30am-8pm.) Sharp *comté* cheese is abundant in Besançon. Wash it down with *vin jaune*, one of the more famous Arbois wines. Many *charcuteries* along **rue des Granges** sell *jambon de Haut Doubs*, a regional smoked ham.

⬛ **La Boîte à Sandwiches,** 21 rue du Lycée (tel. 03 81 81 63 23), off rue Pasteur near a popular student nightlife area. Over 50 wittily-named sandwiches (11-30F). Exotic ingredients include heart of palm, grapefruit, and bananas; ask the waiter to translate to avoid disastrous combinations. Every possible salad concoction, warm or cold (15-35F). Rapid service; eat in or take out, and enjoy a glass of local wine while you're waiting. Open M-F 11:30am-2:30pm and 6:30pm-midnight, Sa noon-2:30pm.

Au Petit Polonais, 81 rue des Granges (tel. 03 81 81 23 67). This dignified restaurant, the oldest in town, was established in 1870 by a Polish immigrant. Generous *menus* from 60F offer local specialties such as fondue and salads heaped with *comté* cheese. An older crowd is drawn in at dinner-time, seeking refuge from the noisy *brasseries* on nearby rue Bersot. Open M-F 11:30am-2pm and 7-10pm, Sa 11:30am-2pm.

Au Gourmand, 5 rue Megevand (tel. 03 81 81 80 45 62). Tucked away on a quiet street near rue Pasteur. Hearty rice and pasta dishes garnished with provincial cheeses (35-50F) and warm salads served with potatoes (30-40F). Open M-F for lunch and dinner.

Restaurant au Feu Vert, 11 rue des Boucheries (tel. 03 81 82 17 20), a small restaurant on pl. de la Révolution that provides an informal, inexpensive way to enjoy regional specialties. *Menus* from 49-119F, *plats* 25-78F. The Algerian chef also steams up couscous specials (55-80F). Lunch from 11:30am, dinner from 6pm. V, MC, AmEx.

⬛ SIGHTS

Besançon's *vielle ville* is graced with remarkably well-preserved Renaissance buildings, providing plenty of eye-candy for *flâneurs*. The true delights, however, await high above the city within Vauban's citadel, with three museums and an array of other pleasant surprises within its imposing walls.

THE CITADEL. *At the end of rue des Fusilles de la Resistance. Tel 03 81 65 07 50. Open daily Nov.-Mar. 10am-5pm; July-Aug. 9am-7pm; Apr.-June and Sept.-Oct. 9am-6pm. Admission 40F, students 30F, includes entrance to museums and all other facilities. Audio guide 10F.*
A gruelling trek uphill from the town, but well worth every stitch in your side. Entrance to the first level is free, and it includes a deer park, beautifully sculpted lawns perfect for picnicking, and a wondrous panorama of the city below. The real treats, however, lie within the inner fortress. To the right of the gates, the **Salle de Vauban** offers a comprehensive trip back to the times of the Sun King and his favorite military architect, including a detailed presentation explaining the conquest of Franche-Comté and the construction of the citadel.

Still within the citadel, the vivid and harrowing **Musée de la Résistance et de la Deportation** warns the visitor, that "not to bear witness would be to betray their memory." Besançon's citadel bore sad witness indeed to the events of WWII; 100 members of the Résistance were shot here when the Germans occupied the town. The museum uses letters, artifacts, and photographs to chronicle the Nazi rise to power and the German occupation of France. Ask a guard to open the exhibition room on the third floor, which contains a collection of sculptures and drawings by two local men who were deported to Nazi concentration camps. *(Tel. 03 81 65 07 55. No children under 10. Open daily 10am-5pm in winter and 9am-6pm in summer.)*

Three sights to delight children include the **Musée d'Histoire Naturelle,** with its displays of mammals, birds, and fish that fell victim to the taxidermist's tools. The small **Aquarium** next door houses species of fish indigenous to the region. A re-created kitchen in the **Insectarium** shows you all the little nasties that hide in your home; you'll never leave leftovers out overnight again. A **zoological park** sprawls out along the back wall of the citadel, where tigers lounge in the sun and monkeys bicker over fruit while children chase squawking chickens at the **petit ferme**. On the other side of the zoo, raccoons and other nighttime creepy-crawlies await to scare kiddies in the pitch-black **Noctarium**.

On your way out, stop by the **Musée Comtois** which features folk art and crafts from Franche-Comté. Head left or right from the museum's base to climb to one of the twin watchtowers that survey the surrounding region. Either provides an excellent starting point for a stroll along the ramparts with a view of the Doubs, slowly winding its way through the town below.

CATHÉDRALE ST-JEAN. Perched on the hill beneath the citadel, its interior mixes architectural styles from the 12th- to 18th-century. Look for the beautiful Rose de St-Jean, a circular altar of white marble dating from the 11th-century. Set atop the church, the **Horloge Astronomique** is more than the sum of its 30,000 parts. Assembled in the 19th-century, the clock runs 70 dials that give 122 different indices. Every hour, Jesus leaps from his tomb as Hope blesses Faith and Charity. You must pay for the guided tour to visit the clock. Descending the hill back into town necessitates passage through the **Porte Noire** (Black Gate) in front of the cathedral. This stern Roman triumphal arch was probably constructed during the reign of Marcus Aurelius in the 2nd-century. *(Cathedral tel. 03 81 83 34 62. Open W-M 9am-7pm. Free. Horloge tel. 03 81 81 12 76. Apr.-Sept. tours W-M at 9:50, 10:50, and 11:50am, 2:50, 3:50, 4:50, and 5:50pm; Oct.-May tours Th-M. Admission 15F, 9F children.)*

MUSÉE DES BEAUX-ARTS. The museum houses Egyptian mummies, amulets, and statuettes. The exceptional painting and sculpture collection includes more than 6000 works by Tintoretto, David, Ingres, Géricault, Van Dyck, Rubens, Titian, Constable, Courbet, Matisse, Picasso, Renoir, and other masters. *(pl. de la Révolution. Tel. 03 81 82 39 92. Open W-M 9:30am-6pm. 21F, free for students and on Su and holidays.)*

BOAT TRIPS. Les Vedettes Bisontines runs daily *bâteau-mouche* cruises on the Doubs and the citadel canals from pont de la République, near the tourist office. *(Tel. 03 81 68 13 25. Apr.-Oct. 1¼hr.; 3 per day; 52F, children 37F, students 30F.)* Or cross the bridge to **Les Bâteaux Mouches's** "Le Pont Battant"; they operate cruises with commentary from July to September. *(Tel. 03 81 68 05 34. 4 per day; 49F, children 39F. Days and tours vary for both; call ahead.)*

♪ 🌿 ENTERTAINMENT AND FESTIVALS

ENTERTAINMENT. The students of Besançon pack bars and discos until early morning everyday of the week. Be forewarned, homebodies: silent nights are scarce. Small, cavernous bars where the student nightlife is friendly and welcoming proliferate throughout the town, particularly on **rue Pasteur**. Rue Bersot sports a string of buzzing *brasseries*, including **The Cactus Club,** where everyone who's anyone stops by to see and be seen.

The king of Besançon's dance clubs is **Le Queen** (tel. 03 81 61 17 49), about 1km from the tourist office at 8 av. de Chardonnet. The street is not well-lit; best go in a group. A large dance floor with London Underground decor is surrounded by plush couches, two bars, and many drunken *bisontin* students. (50F cover, 30F on W and Th includes 1 drink. Open W-Th 10:30pm-4am, F-Sa 10:30pm-5am.) **Sypssi,** pl. Granvelle (tel. 03 81 83 51 32), has three dance floors complete with disco balls,

416 ■ ALSACE, LORRAINE, AND FRANCHE-COMTÉ

plush red carpet, and floor lights. The club attracts an older crowd than Le Queen and plays all disco on weekends. (50F cover includes 1 drink. Open Tu-Su 10:30pm-4am.) On rue Pasteur, **Le Globe** (tel. 03 81 82 18 45) attracts an eclectic mix of students and aging hipsters for drinking and the occasional local band downstairs in the *cavo*. (Open 7:30am-1am.)

FESTIVALS. The tourist office publishes several comprehensive lists of events. In July and August, the city sponsors **Festiv'été,** with theater, music, dance, expositions, and a film festival. (Many events are free. Call the tourist office for info.) **Jazz en Franche-Comté** brings a flurry of concerts in June and July, uniting jazz musicians from all across France. (Tickets range from 80-130F with reductions for students, and some events are free. Call 03 81 83 39 09 for info.)

The **Festival International de Musique** erupts during the middle two weeks of September with classical concerts every night. Orchestras from across Europe participate, performing well-worn favorites as well as more obscure gems. (Tickets 80-300F depending on the locale; 20% discount for students. Tel 03 81 25 05 85; fax 03 81 81 52 15.) For more information on all three festivals, check out Besançon's website at www.besancon.com.

The hostel (ASEP-FJT les Oiseaux) also sponsors an array of events each month. Pick up a schedule at the tourist office.

BELFORT

Occupying a valley between the mountains of the Vosges to the north and the Jura to the south, Belfort has been a favorite target of invading armies for centuries. Practice makes perfect, and this doughty town (pop 52,000) has built up quite a reputation for withstanding sieges. While neighboring Alsace-Lorraine was snatched by the Germans during the Franco-Prussian War of 1870, 16,000 French troops withstood a 103-day siege by 44,000 Germans. To commemorate this extraordinary feat, Frédéric "Statue of Liberty" Bartholdi was commissioned to construct a monument to the town's bravery. His magnificent Lion reposes under Vauban's citadel to this day, ready to pounce on any further potential marauders.

Not content to rest on its laurels, the old town has since spawned a thriving industrial city specializing in high-technology—TGV trains are manufactured here. Numerous face-lifts have transformed the former garrison town, adding pretty half-timbered houses and shady plazas, but Belfort's most enduring attraction remains the ochre sprawl of the old fortifications crowned by the citadel. Silent witness to countless battles, its austere lines and towering battlements form a poignant contrast to the cheerful bustle of the town below.

7 ORIENTATION AND PRACTICAL INFORMATION. Trains run from Belfort to to **Mulhouse** (30min., very frequently, 25F); **Besançon** (1hr., 10 per day, 77F); **Strasbourg** (1½hr., 10 per day, 72F); and **Paris** (4hr., 6 per day, 285-315F). Once in town, **CTRB,** pl. Corbis (tel. 03 84 21 08 08), offers extensive and frequent service around town. (Office open M-F 9am-12:15pm and 1:45-6:15pm.) **Taxis Radio Belfortains** await your call at 44 rue André Parant (tel. 03 84 22 13 44), while **bikes** are at **Velocité,** av. Jean Moulin. (Tel. 03 84 28 32 52. 95F per day.) To get from the station to the **tourist office,** 2bis rue Clemenceau (tel. 03 84 55 90 90; fax 03 84 55 90 99), head left down av. Wilson and then bear right on fbg de France. When the river comes into sight; turn left on fbg des Ancêtres and follow it to rue Clemenceau; the office is to the right across rue Clemenceau, set back from the road. Here, a young staff can outfit you with free maps, hotel and restaurant listings, and info on excursions to the countryside. Ask for *Le Petit Geni,* a comprehensive guide to Belfort that includes discounts at local stores and restaurants. (Open June 15-Sept. 15 M-Sa 9am-7pm; July 1-Aug. 31 M-Su 10am-12:30pm and 2-7pm.) There is an automatic **currency exchange** machine at **Caisse d'Epargne,** pl. de la Résistance (tel. 03 84 57 77 77). Get all sudsy at **Laverie Actuel Plus,** 60 fbg de Montbeliard. (Tel. 03 84 22 68 40. Open daily 7am-9pm.) The **police** are at 1 rue du

Monnier (tel. 03 84 58 50 00), and medical care can be found at the **Centre Hospitalier**, 14 rue du Mulhouse (tel. 03 84 57 40 00). The **post office** is at 19 fbg des ancêtres. (Tel. 03 84 57 67 56. Open M-F 8am-7pm, Sa 8am-noon. **Postal code:** 90000.) **Get online** at **Hi-Fi Territory,** Centre Commercial des 4 As rue de l'As de Carreau. (Tel. 03 84 90 13 56. 35F per hour.)

◤ ACCOMMODATIONS AND CAMPING. Belfort has a nice smattering of one- and two-star hotels that are rarely full in summer, but truly budget prices are few and far between. Luckily, **Résidence Madrid,** 6 rue Madrid, (tel. 03 84 21 39 16), is well-located near the station and the *centre ville*. Bright and friendly, this hostel welcomes youths over 16 all year round. To reach it from the *gare*, follow rue Parisot from behind the station as it turns into av. Général Leclerc; rue Madrid will be on your left after about 7 minutes. (70F per person. Breakfast 14F. Reception open 8:30am-12:30pm and 2-7:30pm.)

The owners of ▨ **Hôtel Au Relais d'Alsace,** 5 av. de la Laurencie (tel. 03 84 22 15 55; fax 03 84 28 70 48), might just be the sweetest people on the planet. The rooms, all with shower and TV, are imaginatively decorated in bright colors, and those on the top floor have a stunning view of the Citadel. *Let's Go* readers get a free glass of freshly squeezed orange juice! (Singles 150F, doubles 210F. Limited rooms for 3-4 people available. Breakfast 28F. 24hr. reception. V, MC.) The best location in town belongs to **Hôtel St-Christophe,** pl. d'Armes (tel. 03 84 55 88 88; fax 03 84 54 08 77). Across from the cathedral in the heart of the *vieille ville*, this beautiful old hotel is the place to stay in style. The main hotel offers larger, more comfortable rooms, but the annex across the square is a better deal. All rooms are equipped with shower, TV, and toilet. (Singles 285F; doubles 330F. Annex singles 230F; doubles 280F. Breakfast buffet 38F. Reception open 7am-11pm. V, MC.)

The three-star **Camping international de l'Étang des Forges,** 4 rue du Général Bethouart (tel. 03 84 22 54 92; fax 03 84 22 76 55), enjoys a splendid location on the Étang des Forges, a sparkling lake 10 minutes from the center of town. Nature trails and a water sports center await. (70F per night for one person with tent, car or caravan. Reception open 8am-10pm.)

◖ FOOD. Fauborg de France, the main shopping street that cuts across the new town from the river to the train station, is rife with cafés, bakeries, and anything else your rumbling tummy might desire. Cafés and restaurants cluster thickly in the old town, especially near **place des Armes.** The best for people-watching is indubitably **Cafe Bruxelles,** which also offers a *plat du jour* for 43F. Don't leave town without sampling the *belflore*, a delectable local pastry consisting of raspberries covered with an almond meringue. If all else fails, a **Casino** supermarket (tel 03 84 21 02 13) awaits by the hostel at 2 rue de Madrid for your picnicking pleasure.

Aux Crêpes d'Antan, 13 rue du Quai (tel. 03 84 22 82 54), presents a staggering selection of *crêpes* and *galettes* (15-50F) just around the corner from the cathedral. Omlettes and local specialities are also available, and the sunny blue and yellow color scheme brightens even the dullest day. (Open daily noon-3pm and 7pm-midnight.) On the other side of the Savoreuse, the ▨ **Canadian Trapper,** 12bis fbg des ancêtres (tel. 03 84 21 88 44), puts a hearty new world twist on traditionally French dishes amid rustic, hunting lodge decor. The menu consists mainly of meat and salmon, but vegetarian options are available. *Menu du jour* 60F. (Open M-Sa noon-2pm and 7pm-midnight, Su noon-2pm only.)

◈ SIGHTS. Belfort's **citadel** has not yet been converted into a playground for tourists like that of Besançon, and a circuit of the grounds affords an instructive lesson in military history as well as incomparable panoramas of the countryside. Originally the site of a medieval fortress, the citadel and fortifications were expanded and reinforced by Vauban when the French laid claim to Belfort after the Thirty Years War. Successive generals throughout the 18th and 19th centuries ordered further expansions and modifications, resulting in the immense sprawl that still exists today. Orange arrows direct you along a tour of the fort that leads up meandering passageways, over walls, and through a cool, dank tunnel. The citadel lies above the *vielle ville* and can be reached by ascending the winding road from the pl. des Bourgeois. (Free guided tours are also available from June 1-Sept. 19 10am-noon and 2-6pm. Call 03 84 54 25 51 for details.)

A passageway on one of the lower levels leads to the viewing platform of the **Belfort Lion,** Bartholdi's regal creation which commemorates the town's intractability in 1870. Carved entirely of red sandstone, the reclining beast is 22m long and 11m high. (Platform open daily 8-11:45am and 2-6:45pm. Admission 4F.) The château at the heart of the fortifications houses the **Musée d'art et d'histore.** The museum's diverse collection encompasses the art and history of the region, featuring neolithic, Gallo-Roman, and Merovingian artifacts; uniforms, guns, and other military relics, as well as paintings and sculptures by the likes of Dore, Lefèvre, and Rodin. (Open Oct. 1-Apr. 30 W-M 10am-noon and 2-5pm; May 1-Sept. 30 daily 10am-7pm. 12F adults, 9F students.) The **terrace** above the museum is the best place for a view of the land below; diagrams at the north, south, and eastern sides point out pertinent landmarks. Heading back into town, remnants of the octagonal fortifications that once surrounded the *vieille ville* are still intact, including several guard towers. Some, such as **Tour 46 (Tower 64),** now host free, temporary exhibitions. (Open M-Sa 8:30am-noon and 2-6pm.) On the other side of town, the **Porte de Brisach** is a perfectly-preserved gateway constructed by Vauban in 1687. At the heart of the old town, the **Cathédral St-Christophe** presides over pl. des Armes. As ruddy as the citadel above, the graceful Classical facade conceals several notable treasures, including a gilded wrought iron grill around the choir and marvelously solemn transept paintings by Belfort painter G. Dauphin.

🎵 🎭 **ENTERTAINMENT AND FESTIVALS.** Belfort has sprouted a profusion of bars, but dance clubs lurk only in the outlying suburbs. The **Piano Bar,** 23 fbg de France (tel. 03 84 28 93 35), entertains with live music from rock to jazz, with karaoke on Thursday nights. (Open M-F 8pm-1am, Sa until 2 am.) Numerous **concerts** are held around town in July and August, at the citadel on Wednesday nights and at the cathedral on Thursdays. Call the tourist office for details.

Every July, some 80,000 enthusiastic music fans from all over Europe descend upon Belfort for **Les Eurockéennes,** France's largest open-air rock festival. The 1999 repertoire, extending over 4 days, included Metallica, The Black Crowes, and the irascible Marilyn Manson along with 39 other acts. (Tel. 08 36 68 90 88; www.eurockeenes.fr. 4-day tickets 630F, 3-day 450F, 1-day 190-250F in advance; roughly 20% mark-up on-site.) At the end of May, musicians from around the world hit town to participate in the **Festival International de Musique Universitaire,** a three-day extravaganza that offers over 200 free concerts, from classical to folk to rock to jazz. (Tel. 03 84 54 24 43; www.fimu.com; email: infos@fimu.com.) The last week of November brings **Entrevues,** a film festival that features fresh, young directors as well as retrospectives. (Tel. 03 84 54 25 53; festival-entrevues.com.)

🏔 **EXCURSIONS.** With the Jura on one side and the Vosges on the other, Belfort is an ideal base for exploring the surrounding countryside. The tourist office has numerous pamphlets detailing rambles, hikes, and other outdoor pursuits that can be enjoyed in and around the town. **Bessoncourt,** 4km to the east, is an important departure point for *petites randonnées* (short rambles) as well as the daunting **E5** trail that stretches from the Adriatic to the Atlantic. To the north, the towering summit of the **Ballon d'Alsace** (1247m) is a meeting point for three major long distance trails, the GR5, GR7, and GR59. The **Lac de Malsaucy,** just to the west of Belfort, is a dream for the nature lover and sports enthusiast alike, boasting an environmental protection center as well as water sports and recreation. **Hot-air ballooning** is a popular regional pastime; ask the tourist office for details.

RONCHAMP

Hidden in the hills to the west of Belfort, the tiny town of Ronchamp (pop. 3,000) would no doubt be living out its life in quiet provincial anonymity if it were not home to one of the most awe-inspiring and unusual pieces of modern architecture in France. The chapel **Notre-Dame-du-Haut** sprouts from between the trees like an overgrown mushroom 472m above the town on Bourlemont Hill, a site where French soldiers were felled by German attack in 1944. Created by master architect Le Corbusier in 1954 (see p. 24), the chapel is more sculpture than building, its sleek, geometric lines sweeping upwards towards the heavens in a gesture that conveys both mute supplication and inestimable grandeur. The strangely evocative interior is as spare as the stark, white-washed facade suggests. Narrow stained-glass windows cut randomly into the walls dapple the pews with soft, tinted light, and the sole other decoration is a statuette of Virgin Mary reposing in a niche behind the altar. To reach the chapel, turn onto rue de la Chapelle from rue le Corbusier and lug yourself up the steep, winding road for 1.5km. The hike can be gruelling and is the only way up, other than bike or car, but not to worry; one look at this serene masterpiece will melt all your earthly pains away. A walk around the grounds of the chapel guarantees exceptional vistas of the valley below. *(Tel. 03 84 20 65 13. Open daily Apr.-Oct. 9am-7pm, Nov.-Mar. 9am-4pm. Admission 10F, children 3F).*

If you have some extra time on your hands when you get back to town, the **Maison de la Mine,** 33 pl. de la Mairie (tel. 03 84 20 70 50), houses an interesting collection of tools, letters, and artwork detailing Ronchamp's two centuries as a center of coal-mining. The remains of an old mine shaft can still be seen halfway up the hill to the chapel. *(Museum open W-M, Apr.-May and Sept.-Nov. 1 2-6pm, June-Aug. 10am-noon and 2-7pm. 15F adults, 8F children.)*

To reach Ronchamp, hop on an SNCF **bus** or **train** in **Belfort;** both leave from the *gare SNCF* (20min.; M-F 7 per day, Sa 3 per day, Su 2 per day; 25F). The **tourist office** (tel. 03 84 63 50 82) is off rue le Corbusier, behind the church. (Open M 2-5:30pm, T-F 9am-noon and 2-5:30pm, Sa 9am-noon.) For a meal, **La Pomme d'Or,** 34 rue le Corbusier (tel. 03 84 20 62 12), will help replenish any calories sweated off during the trek to the chapel with their delicious *galettes* (58F) and other specialities drenched in the local *comté* cheese. If you miss the last train home, you can also spend the night here. (Singles 175F, doubles 230F.)

DOLE

As you munch on your cereal in the morning, give thanks to this quiet corner of Franche-Comté: Louis Pasteur, the world's most celebrated scientist-milkman, was born here in 1882. Although pasteurization is nothing to sneeze at, germ-free living is not all that Dole (pop. 30,000) has to offer. Its winding, flower-edged canals have been enjoyed by other illustrious people; Stendhal noted the "picturesque view" over the canals from the central cours St-Marius, and transcribed his memories of it into *The Red and the Black* as the "Cours de la Fidélité." Dole's tranquil atmosphere might leave some travelers itching to move on, but others will welcome the change of pace in this quiet corner of Franche-Comté.

◪ **ORIENTATION AND PRACTICAL INFORMATION. Trains** leave the pl. de la Gare (tel. 03 84 79 72 09) for **Dijon** (30min., 25 per day, 44F); **Besançon** (30min., 20 per day, 43F); **Strasbourg** (3½hr., 10 per day, 180F); and **Paris** (6 per day, 2hr., 236-286F). You can get around town on the local **Dolebus** (tickets 5F, *carnet* of 10 40F), or pay 7F per kilometer on a **taxi** (tel. 03 84 82 13 20), but the town is quite walkable. Those desperate for wheels can hire **bikes** from **Griffon,** 2 av. Léon Jouhaux. (Tel. 03 84 72 40 47. 80F per day, 250F per week, 2000F deposit. Open M-Sa 8am-noon and 1:45-7pm.) To get to the **tourist office,** 6 pl. Grévy (tel. 03 84 72 11 22), turn left on av. Aristide Briand as you exit the *gare* and follow it until it ends at the Place Boyvin. Turning left on rue de la Gouvernment will lead you directly into pl.

Grévy; the tourist office lies straight ahead. Here friendly staff can provide you with a free map and list of hotels, as well as brochures on the nearby Jura mountains. 25F will but you a city tour, 20F if you wave your ISIC. (Open M 2:30-5:30pm, Tu-F 8:45am-noon and 2-5:45pm, Sa 9am-noon.) In the same building, **Jura Vert** (tel. 03 84 82 33 01) offers guided expeditions in the Jura. The **police** survey their surroundings from 1 rue du 21 Janvier (tel. 03 84 79 63 10), while ambulances park at the **Centre Hospitalier Louis Pasteur,** av. L. Jouhaux (tel. 03 84 79 80 80). The **post office,** 5 av. Aristide Briand (tel. 03 84 79 42 41), has **currency exchange.** (Open M-F 8am-6:30pm, Sat. 8am-noon. **Postal code:** 39100.)

▌ ACCOMMODATIONS AND CAMPING. Comfortable student *foyers* welcome budget travelers throughout the year, and Dole's reasonably priced hotels usually have space. To get to the **Auberge de Jeunesse le St-Jean (HI),** pl. Jean XXIII (tel. 03 84 82 36 74; fax 03 84 79 17 69), turn right out of the station and then left onto rue Jantet. Follow it to the end and make a right on bd. Wilson, then turn left onto av. Pompidou at the second big intersection. Take the next right onto rue Général Lachiche, and walk straight into the hostel's gravel parking lot where the street makes a sharp left (15min.). Spacious and clean rooms, but call ahead to reserve a spot. (Singles and doubles 66F per person. Breakfast 20F. Lunch or dinner 40F. Laundry. Reception M-F 8:30-11:30am and 4-8pm, Sa-Su 12-2pm and 6-8pm.) No room at the Auberge? No worries; head down to the **Foyer L'Accueil Dolois,** 8 rue Charles Sauria (tel. 03 84 82 15 21; fax 03 84 82 25 81). From the station, head left, then straight ahead on av. Aristide Briand until the road ends. Cross the parking lot and turn right onto rue Raguet-Lépine; the *foyer* is at the end of the street. Housed in a beautiful former religious school in the center of town, this *foyer* caters mostly to local youth looking for spotless, bright singles. You can meet them in the bar, the TV room, the library, or over a game of ping pong. (84F per person; 150F per couple. Under 30s only. Breakfast included. Kitchen and laundry. Reception 9am-midnight. No lockout. Often full during the academic year.)

If only a hotel will do, the **Hôtel Moderne,** 40 av. Aristide Briand (tel. 03 84 72 27 04), is conveniently located above a bar across from the *gare.* Two can crowd into its functional singles. (Singles 80F, with bath 130F; larger rooms with bath 180F. Reception 7am-midnight. V, MC, AmEx.) Those carrying their housing with them can set up in an idyllic spot on an island at **Camping du Pasquier** (tel. 03 84 72 02 61). From the tourist office, follow the signs from pl. Grévy. (1 person and tent 45F; 2 people and tent 53F; 2 people, car, and tent 63F. Open Mar.15-Oct.15 daily 7am-10pm., Oct. 16- Mar. 14 8am-noon and 3-10pm. Call ahead.)

◉ FOOD. The **rue de Besançon** offers *charcuteries*, *épiceries*, and a **Casino supermarket.** (Open M-Sa 7:30am-12:30pm and 3-7:15pm, Su 8:15am-midnight; closed W afternoon.) A larger selection and lower prices can be found at **Intermarché** on the corner of av. L. Johaux and av. Georges Pompidou. (Open M-Th 8:30am-12:15pm and 2:30-7pm, F 8:30am-12:15pm and 2:30-7:15pm, Sa 8:30am-7pm.) Near the Basilica, the **Marché de la Ville** will warm your heart and appease your grumbling stomach. (Tu, Th, Sa 8am-noon.) Once you've collected various foodstuffs, Dole's meandering canals make a lovely site for a picnic.

If you're feeling doleful in Dole, you can spice up your life at **Taj Mahal,** 73 rue Pasteur (tel. 03 84 72 01 57), a genuine slice of India in the midst of rural France. Enormous 45F lunch *menu* includes tandoori, curries, rice, and dessert, but the best deal in the house is the 20F vegetarian *legumes korma.* (Open daily 11:45am-2:30pm and 6:30-11pm. V, MC, AmEx.) More locally-oriented cuisine can be found overlooking the canal at **La Demi-Lune,** 39 rue Pasteur (tel. 03 84 72 82 82). The terrace provides the perfect setting to enjoy *galettes* (12-75F) along with local specialties—*jurasienne* items feature the ever-present *comté* cheese. (Open daily noon–2pm, and 7:30pm-12am.)

⊚ SIGHTS. The **Maison Natale de Louis Pasteur,** 43 rue Pasteur (tel. 03 84 72 20 61; fax 03 84 72 14 63) is the cream of Dole's sights. The house has been converted into a museum honoring the man, his work, and his family. Pasteur was not only a model child, a biological genius, and an outspoken humanitarian, but also a gifted artist. You can wander through the impressive variety of exhibits at your own pace; an English translation of the French explanations is available on request. (Open April 1-Oct. 31 M-Sa 10am-12pm and 2-6pm, Sun 2-6pm. Admission 20F, students 10F, under 12 free.) A passageway to the right of the house leads to the **Canal des Tanneurs,** where Pasteur's father cured hides. A stroll along the banks of the canal reveals willow-lined estuaries and picture-perfect stone bridges, Dole's most endearing attractions.

The *dolois* play endless games of *boules* in the **cours St-Marius,** across from pl. Jules Grévy. Even non-players should stroll down the *cours* for the best view in town. The 16th-century **Basilique Notre-Dame** presides over pl. Nationale Charles de Gaulle, its 74m bell tower an easily discernible landmark. The church is the largest in the region, and a magnificent organ set in a tribune of polychrome marble looms in the back. Free concert events are listed at the tourist office. The **Musée des Beaux-Arts,** two blocks away on 85 rue des Arènes (tel. 03 84 72 27 72), contains works by Vouet, Le Brun, Courbet, and others, as well as an archaeological section with Celtic, Gallo-Roman, and Merovingian displays. (Open Tu-Su 10am-noon and 2-6pm; free.)

THE JURA MOUNTAINS

As France's forgotten mountain range, the Jura is often overlooked by foreigners who flock to the Alps further south. Much older than its neighbor, the Jura has grown rounder and smoother with age, and is covered with dense pine forests, sunny meadows, and countless trails for hiking, mountain biking, and skiing. It's easiest to use Pontarlier (see below) as a base for heading out into the mountains.

LONS-LE-SAUNIER

If you're beginning to feel patriotic about France, head to Lons-le-Saunier, which bore Rouget de Lisle, author of *la Marseillaise*, in 1760. Lons (pop. 20,000) is peppered with monuments to Rouget's glory, but was a place of repute long before his time: the town was the site of a neolithic settlement and has been heralded since Roman times for the healing quality of its thermal springs. Even if you're unwilling or unable to front the cash for a treatment at the luxurious spa, Lons makes a convenient base for exploring the natural splendor of the nearby Jura mountains.

⁊ ORIENTATION AND PRACTICAL INFORMATION. Trains roll frequently to **Dole** (67F) and **Besançon** (72F). **SNCF** also runs **buses** from the *gare* to **Dole.** (Tel. 08 36 35 35 35 for bus and train info.) Local buses run from Lons to the outlying villages; inquire at the tourist office for a schedule. Taxis (tel. 03 84 24 11 16) stand to attention outside the station. You can rent **bikes** at **Dominique Maillard,** 17 rue Perrin (tel. 03 84 24 24 07). To get to the **tourist office,** pl. due 11 Novembre, (tel. 03 84 65 01, fax 03 84 43 22 59), cross the *place* in front of the station and head up rue Aristide Briand until it forks. Take the left fork (av. Thurel) to rue Rouget de Lisle and then take another left; the tourist office lies in a corner of the old theatre to your right, behind the cafe. This font of regional information has free maps, hotel and restaurant listings, and guides to excursions in the Jura. The office runs **tours** of the town and the surrounding countryside. (Town tour 20F. Countryside tours 17-150F. Office open M-F 8am-noon and 2-6pm, Sa 8am-noon and 2-5pm.) There is a **laundromat** at 26 rue des Cordeliers (tel. 06 80 92 08 37). The **Commissariat de Police** sits at 6 av. du 44ème R.I. (tel. 03 84 35 17 10), and the **Centre Hospitalier** at 55 rue docteur Jean Michel (tel. 03 84 35 60 00). The **post office** is on av. Aristide Briand. (Tel. 03 84 85 83 12. Open M-F 8am-7pm, Sa 8am-noon. Post Restante code: 39021. **Postal code:** 39000.)

ACCOMMODATIONS AND FOOD. There are no hostels in town, but there are a couple of cheap hotels near the pl. de la Liberté. The **Hôtel Terminus,** 37 av. Aristide Briand (tel. 03 84 24 41 83), located conveniently just across from the train station, features spacious but pricey rooms. (Singles 210F-270F with shower, 280-370F with bath. Larger rooms for 2-4 people from 350F. Breakfast 40F. Reception 7:15am-10pm. V, MC, Amex.)

Scouring the *vieille ville* for vittles uncovers a number of delights. Next to the tourist office, drinkers leisurely sip their *kirs* at the **Grand Café de Strasbourg,** next door to the tourist office. The gleaming interior recalls the early 1900s, when productions at the old theater around the corner were in full swing. *Charcuteries, pâtisseries,* and *boulangeries* live side by side on the **rue de Commerce.** If something still lacks from your picnic hamper, stock up at the **Casino supermarket** next door. (Tel. 03 84 24 48 64. Open M-Sa 7:30am-12:30pm, 3pm-7:30pm, Su 8am-12:15pm.) *Jurassienne* feasts await at **Le Roesti,** 7-9 rue Tamisier, (tel. 03 84 47 26 46), a charming restaurant on a quiet side street off the Place de la Liberté. Local specialities such as fondues made of tangy *comté* cheese are served up amid decor reminiscent of a farmhouse kitchen. The lunchtime *formules,* from 45F, are the best deal. (Open M-Sa 12-2pm and 7-10pm.) Pancake cravings can be satisfied at **Le Clovis,** 30 rue Lecourbe (tel 03 84 47 20 58), a *brasserie* by day and a *crêperie* by night, which also offers regional specialities. (Open M-W 8:30am-2:30pm, Th-Sa 8:30am-2:30pm, evenings daily from 7pm. V, MC.)

SIGHTS. All roads in Lons lead to the **place de la Liberté,** site of the old **Théâtre.** Following a devastating fire, the theatre's rococo facade was reconstructed in 1901, and now every hour a clock keeps time by chiming out a refrain from *la Marseillaise.* Fire also played a part in the making of the pretty **rue du Commerce,** off the *place,* whose houses were rebuilt in stone after the great conflagration of 1637. If you have some time to spare, pop into no. 24, the birthplace of Rouget de Lisle. Now the **Musée Rouget de Lisle** (tel. 03 84 24 65 01), it houses a smattering of personal and *Marseillaise*-related memorabilia, including a recreation of his birth chamber and various editions of the famous song. (Open M-F 10am-noon and 2-6pm, Sa-Su 2-5pm, free.) Following the rue du Commerce to its end and bearing left leads to the **Musée des beaux arts,** pl. Philibert de Chalon (tel. 03 84 47 64 30). This provincial museum boasts a splendid collection of Perraud statuary, a couple nice Courbets, and precious little else. To get to the more interesting **Musée d'archéologie,** 25 rue Richebourg (tel. 03 84 47 12 13), veer right when the rue du Commerce forks and follow it as it becomes rue Trouillot, then turn right onto rue Richebourg. Many of the exhibits, including a dugout canoe, were excavated in or near the town itself. (Both museums open M and W-F 10am-noon and 2-6pm, weekends 2-5pm. 10F adults, 5F children, free on Wednesdays.) Between the two museums lies the **Puits Salé,** the remains of the old saltwater baths that first drew the Romans to Lons. The spring is now connected via an underground canal to the **Thermes Ledonia** (tel. 03 84 24 20 34), a luxurious spa offering cures for ailments from rheumatism to cellulite—a full-scale cure can run to thousands of francs, though a dip in the pool is marginally more affordable. Following rue Richebourg back towards the center of town leads to the **place de la Chevalerie,** which features an imposing statue of Rouget de Lisle sculpted by Bartholdi. The sculptor went on to recreate Rouget's stirring pose, one arm aloft, when working on a little lady now known as the Statue of Liberty.

EXCURSIONS. Just 10km from Lons slumbers the little town of **Baume-les-Messieurs,** a gem of great historical interest. The magnificent *abbaye* (tel. 03 84 44 61 41) was founded in the 6th century by St. Columban. Originally called *Baume-les-moines* (Baume-the-monks), by the 16th century the abbey attracted so many nobles *(messieurs)* that the name changed accordingly. There is also an extensive network of caves near the town, featuring underground lakes and vaults up to 80m high, which can be visited by guided tours in the summer. (Tel. 03 84 44 61 58 for information. Caves open Apr. 1-Sept. 30, daily 9am-6pm.) If you're seeking nature in all her splendor, the tourist office will happily smother you with suggestions on how best to explore the cascading waterfalls, crystal lakes, and green hills and forests of the Jura. Several hiking trails run near Lons, as well as paths for biking and horseback riding. Certain tour operators guide trips through the Jura for groups; contact **Juragence,** 19 rue Jean Moulin (tel 03 84 47 27 27) for details.

PONTARLIER

Eight hundred and forty meters in the sky sits the quiet town of Pontarlier, a good base from which to reach even greater heights in the Haut-Jura mountains. Only 12km from Switzerland, Pontarlier's proximity to its Alpine neighbor is evident in the châlet-style homes that climb up the steep mountainside. The *vieille ville,* permeated by chocolate aromas from the nearby Nestlé factory, is a tiny provincial village startled by the unsightly urban sprawl that has grown up around it in the past 30 years. Pontarlier itself offers little to the visitor, but who cares when some of France's most spectacular mountain scenery awaits just beyond the city limits?

▐ PRACTICAL INFORMATION. The **train station** (tel. 03 81 46 56 99) is on the Germanic-sounding pl. de Villingen-Schwenningen. Trains go to **Dole** (1hr., 4 per day, 75F); **Dijon** (1½hr.; 6 per day M-F, 7 Sa-Su; 100-110F); and **Paris** (3hr., 5 per day, 328F). Station open 5am-9:25pm. Pontarlier is easily reached from **Besançon** by **Monts Jura buses.** (Tel. 03 81 39 19 54. 55min., 6 per day, 51F. Office open M-F 9am-noon and 3-6:40pm.) To reach the **tourist office,** 14bis rue de la Gare (tel. 03 81 46 48 33; fax 03 81 46 83 32), from the train station, cross through the rotary and head left one block on rue de la Gare. From the bus station, the office is visible to the left down rue Michaud. The staff has info on hiking, skiing, and other outdoor sports. Ask for the free regional guide, *Le Doubs: C'est Pratique.* A full-color topographical map of the region's hiking and biking trails is 58F, but smaller maps that cover the area piece by piece cost 12F, and are adequate for less ambitious jaunts. The office also provides a *Guide Pratique* that lists every service you could possibly need, along with a variety of cheap mountain lodgings. (Open M-F 9am-noon and 2-7pm.) Rent a bike at **Cycles Pernet,** 23 rue de la République (tel. 03 81 46 48 00) for 60F per half-day, 80F per day. (Passport deposit. Open Tu-Sa 9am-noon and 2-7pm. V, MC, AmEx.) The **hospital** is at 2 fbg St-Étienne (tel. 03 81 38 54 54). **Police** are at 10 rue Michaud (tel. 03 81 38 51 10). The **post office** is across the street at 17 rue de la Gare (tel. 03 81 38 49 44). (Open M-F 8am-6:30pm, Sa 8am-noon. **Postal code:** 25300.)

▐▐ ACCOMMODATIONS, CAMPING, AND FOOD. Expect to add a 5F *taxe de séjour* per person per night in Pontarlier. **L'Auberge de Pontarlier (HI)** (tel. 03 81 39 06 57; fax 03 81 39 24 34) is quiet, clean, comfortable, and centrally located. From the tourist office, go left on rue Marpaud. The hostel is on your left after 100m at 2 rue Jouffroy. (49F. Sheets 17F. Breakfast 19F. Reception 8am-noon and 5:30-10pm. Reservations advised.) **Hôtel de France,** 8 rue de la Gare (tel. 03 81 39 05 20; fax 03 81 46 24 43), offers cozy beds and spacious rooms with TVs. The spiffy bar downstairs, replete with dartboard and neon lights, is always hopping. (Singles 105F, with shower 135F; doubles 150F, with shower 160F; triples 200F, with shower 250F; quad with shower 300F. Hall shower free. 24hr. reception.) The most scenic option is the **campground** on rue du Tolombief (tel. 03 81 46 23 33; fax 03 81 46 83 34). Turn right onto Rocade Georges Pompidou from the train station, cross the river, and bear left onto rue de l'Industrie. Take the first right onto av. de Neuchâtel and follow the signs (15 min.). Has a bar, game room, TV, and ping-pong (35-79F per night). They also rent *châlets.* (220F per day for 2, additional person 20F, 6-person capacity; weekly 2200F; monthly 7500F. Off-season prices lower.) The tourist office makes arrangements for the vacationing owner on Wednesdays and Thursdays.

Pontarlier earns much of its living by trafficking cheese and chocolate, and local cuisine is smothered with both. **Les Rives du Doubs,** 2 rue de la République (tel. 03 81 46 20 27), has a pleasant riverside terrace where you can watch the Doubs slither by as you enjoy traditional specialities such as the *fondue comtois* (49F) and *tartiflette au Mont d'Or* (55F). It's a *salon de thé* in the afternoons. (Open M and W-Sa noon-1:30pm and 6:45-9:45pm, Su and Tu noon-1:45pm. V, MC.) **Pizzeria Gambetta,** 15 rue Gambetta (tel. 03 81 46 67 17), has a wood oven that pumps out over 20 varieties of pizza (38-54F) with toppings ranging from the more traditional to eggs, tuna, and potatoes. Design your own for 54F. They also serve regional grilled meat dishes (*plat du jour* 41F) and ice cream, and the friendly staff will make any of their dishes for the road. Stock up for a picnic at the **Casino** on rue de la République. (Open M-F 8am-12:30pm and 2:30-7pm, Sa 8:30am-7pm.)

☝ SKIING, HIKING, BIKING, AND RIDING. The Jura mountains are best known for **cross-country skiing,** and are covered with 60km of long distance trails right around the city. Eight trails on two slopes, *Le Larmont* and *Le Malmaison*, cover every difficulty level. A daily pass costs around 30F, ages 10-16 20F. **Le Larmont** (tel. 03 81 46 55 20) is the alpine ski area nearest to Pontarlier. For ski conditions, call **Allo-Neige,** Massif de Jura (tel. 03 81 53 55 88). The Jura are much colder than the Alps; dress in layers to avoid a loss of feeling in crucial outer digits. **Sport et Neige,** 4 rue de la République, Pontarlier, (tel. 03 81 39 04 69), rents equipment for 45F per day, 245F per week, children 40-210F. (Open 9am-noon and 2-6pm. V, MC.) The prices for lift tickets, food, lodging, and equipment rental are far cheaper than those in the Alps, though the snow is less predictable. **Metabief Mont d'Or** (tel. 03 81 49 13 81) has day and night skiing and is accessible by bus from Pontarlier. (Lift tickets 100F per day. 30 min. shuttle ride 10F.)

In the summer, skiing gives way to **fishing, hiking,** and **mountain biking.** There are two **mountain bike** departure points in Portarlier, to the north and south of town. If you like to **hike,** the **GR5,** an international 262km trail, runs through Pontarlier. The **GR6** leads to a narrow valley dominated by the dramatic *Château de Joux*, standing over the ancient Franco-Swiss border. (Château open July-Aug. 9am-6pm; Sept. 10-11:30am and 2-4:30pm; Oct.-Jan. tours at 10 and 11:15am, and 2 and 3:30pm; Feb.-June 10-11:30am and 2-4:30pm.) The tourist office's map (12F) marks the trails and six departure points around town, including one near the train station at pl. St-Claude. **Le Poney Club,** 37 rue du Cret, Pontarlier (tel. 03 81 46 71 67), adjacent to the campground, rents affectionate horses for all skill levels (60F per hour, 300F per day). For organized rides, call at least eight days in advance.

CHAMPAGNE

Brothers, brothers, come quickly! I am drinking stars!

—Dom Pérignon

John Maynard Keynes once remarked that his major regret in life was not having consumed enough champagne. A trip through the rolling vineyards and fertile plains of Champagne will allow you to escape Keynes' mistake, as well as drink in the fascinating monuments to the rich history of the region, from the awe-inspiring grandeur of the Reims Cathedral, to the ancient Roman ramparts of Langres, to the half-timbered houses and crooked streets of Troyes.

According to European law, the word "champagne" may only be applied to wines made from regional grapes and produced according to the rigorous, time-honored method, which involves the blending of three varieties of grape, two stages of fermentation, and frequent realignment of bottles by *remueurs* (highly trained bottle turners) to facilitate removal of sediment. So fiercely guarded is their name that when Yves Saint-Laurent brought out a new perfume called "Champagne," the powerful *maisons* sued to force him to change it—and won. You can see the *méthode champénoise* in action at the region's numerous wine

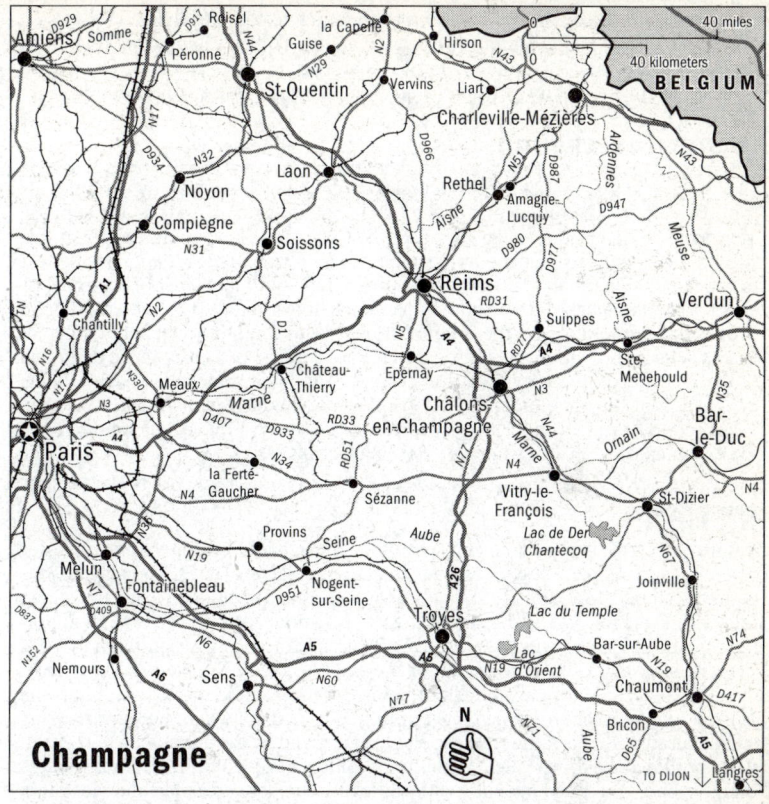

Champagne

cellars *(caves)*, at their best in the glitzy towns of Reims and Épernay. To sample the efforts of this rigorous process, partake in the tasting that caps most *cave* tours, or order a *coupe de champagne* in any café or bar. Even regional gastronomical specialities tend to center around a champagne base; try *volaille au champagne* (poultry) or *civet d'oie* (goose stew).

Champagne, however, played a pivotal role in French history long before Dom Pérignon made the region a household name. In 496, Reims witnessed the conversion of the Frankish King Clovis to Christianity, an act that forged a close (and often troubled) bond between crown and cross that lasted 14 centuries. Nearly every king from Henri I to Charles X returned to Reims's cathedral for their coronation, preserving the city's importance in French tradition. During the Middle Ages, Champagne was among the first provinces to rejoin the expanding French Kingdom, and cities like Troyes and Chaumont flourished as centers of trade and learning. Northern Champagne's fortunes changed rapidly in the 18th and 19th

HIGHLIGHTS OF CHAMPAGNE

■ Effervesce your way through the moldy **champagne *caves*** in **Épernay** (p. 431).
■ The **Cathédrale de Notre-Dame** in **Reims,** with stained glass by Chagall, presides where Clovis was baptized in the 5th century (p. 426).
■ **Troyes** boasts a disproportionate array of churches, from the gothic splendor of the **Cathédrale St-Pierre and St-Paul** to the ancient **Église Ste-Madeleine** (p. 434)
■ The **ramparts** of **Langres** contain a gate dating from the 1st century AD and provide stunning views over the Marne Valley (p. 440).

THE NORTHEAST

centuries with the explosion of the vine, and ancient Reims became reborn as a bourgeois city of shady parks and broad avenues. Today, Champagne remains a region of contrasts. The golden vineyards and *beaux arts* flavor of Reims and Épernay seem a world away from the quiet citadels and forests of the south.

⌐ GETTING AROUND

Champagne is a great place for excursions into the countryside by car, bike, or foot. Drivers should follow any of the lovely *routes de champagne* through the Montagne de Reims, the Val de Marne, or the Côtes des Blancs. Tourist offices distribute road maps; ask for the free pamphlet *The Champagne Road*. Wander off to the small villages and lakes that dot the region south and west of Épernay, or check out Champagne's two national parks, ideal for hiking. The tourist office in Troyes has information on the Forêt d'Orient to the southeast, while the office in Reims sells a booklet of trails through the Parc Naturel de la Montagne de Reims (15F). The Forêt de Verzy, a curious forest of twisted, umbrella-shaped dwarf beeches *(tortillards)*, and the vast Forêt de Germaine are also worth visiting. Trains connect Reims and the larger towns to the rest of France, but you will have to rely on capricious buses to reach the smaller villages.

REIMS

Reims (pop. 185,000; pronounced "rrrranhce") has had a presence in the lives of French leaders since Clovis was baptized here in AD 507 (p. 7). The magnificent cathedral stands today on the site of his baptism, and has enjoyed a centuries-long link with French kings as the site of their coronation; Joan of Arc won an important symbolic victory when she brought Charles VII to be crowned there in 1429. The city also claims the dubious honor of being the site of Napoleon's last victory, causing General Marmont to declare Reims "the last smile of Fortune." Fortune frowned on another would-be conqueror on May 7, 1945, when the German army surrendered in Reims' little red schoolhouse. Scarred by the great wars of the 20th century, Reims has since been rebuilt to its 19th-century glory. Enormous squares blend broad, tree-lined avenues with the wide, sun-soaked fields and vineyards that surround the city. Packed with bars, cafés, and shops, the central plazas are as lively and effervescent as the champagne that is the city's lifeblood.

ℹ ORIENTATION AND PRACTICAL INFORMATION

The **cathedral** is the center of town, with sights, restaurants, and hotels fanning out to the west. The best way to find it is to head for the towers. From the train station, follow the right-hand curve of the traffic circle in front of the station to **pl. Drouet d'Erlon**, a wide, café-riddled pedestrian street. Turn left after Église St-Jacques onto rue de Vesle, passing through the shopping district, then turn right after the theater onto **rue du Trésor**. The tourist office is before the cathedral, on the left.

Trains: Bd. Joffre (tel. 03 26 78 60 60). To: **Épernay** (20min., 15 per day, 33F); **Laon** (1hr., 7 per day, 49F); and **Paris** (1½hr., 9 per day, 116F). Info desk open M-F 8:30am-7pm, Sa 9am-6pm. Ticket counters open daily 5:45am-8:30pm.

Local Transportation: Transport Urbains de Reims (TUR) buses stop in front of the train station. Information office at 6 rue Chanzy (tel. 03 26 04 38 00). Open M-F 7am-8pm and Sa 7am-7pm. 5F per ticket, 34F per *carnet* of 10.

Bike Rental: Cycl'o Vert, located in distant Verzy (tel. 03 26 97 97 77). Half-day 70F, full day 110F, 2 days 170F. Open F-Su 9am-6pm.

Taxis: Tel. 03 26 47 05 05 or 03 26 02 15 02. 24hr.

Tourist Office: 2 rue Guillaume de Machault (tel. 03 26 77 45 25; fax 03 26 77 45 27; VisitReims@netvia.com), in a pint-sized ruin beside the cathedral. The always-busy office dispenses a free map with sights and caves, provides free accommodations ser-

Reims

ACCOMMODATIONS
A Auberge de Jeunesse (HI)
B Hôtel Jeanne d'Arc
C Ardenn' Hôtel
D Au Bon Accueil
E Central Hôtel

vice, and **exchanges currency.** Audioguides in 6 languages are available (50F), as well as guided tours of the town on foot, by carriage, or by tourist train (tel. 03 26 02 95 23). Local events are listed in the weekly *Les Rendez-vous Rémois.* Office open July-Aug. M-Sa 9am-8pm, Su 9:30am-7pm; April 24 (Easter)-June and Sept. M-Sa 9am-7:30pm, Su 9:30am-6:30pm; Oct.-Easter M-Sa 9am-6:30pm, Su 9:30am-5:30pm.

Budget Travel: Wasteels, 26 rue Libergier (tel. 03 26 85 79 79). ISIC cards, cheap flights, and BIJ tickets. Open M-F 9am-noon and 2-7pm, Sa 9am-noon and 2-6pm.

English Bookstore: Bookshop, 21 rue des Élus (tel. 03 26 84 99 81). Extensive selection of English books and some videos. Open M 2-7pm, Tu-Sa 10am-noon and 2-7pm.

Youth Center: Centre Régionale d'Information Jeunesse, 41 rue Talleyrand (tel. 03 26 79 84 79; fax 03 26 79 84 72). Oodles of information: jobs, local events, etc. Open summer M-F 1-6pm; winter M-F noon-7pm, Sa 3-6pm.

Laundry: Laverie de Vesle, 129 rue de Vesle. Open daily 7am-2am.

Hospital: Rue Cognac Jay (tel. 03 26 78 76 02).

Police: 40 bd. Louis Roederer (tel. 03 26 40 02 48).

Post Office: Rue Olivier-Métra (tel. 03 26 50 58 22), at pl. de Boulingrin, near the Porte Mars. Open M-F 8am-7pm, Sa 8am-noon. **Branch office,** 1 rue Cérès (tel. 03 26 77 64 80), on pl. Royale closer to the *centre ville.* Open M-F 8:30am-6pm, Sa 8:30am-noon. Poste Restante pick-up fee 35F per item; specify "51084 Reims-Cérès" for branch. Another branch on rue de Veste close to hostel. **Postal code:** 51100.

Internet Access: L'Arobace, 21 av. de Laon (tel. 03 26 88 55 51), in the Porte Mars area. 1F per min. Open M-Sa in summer 10:30am-midnight; in winter 7am-midnight. **Centre Culturel Saint-Exupéry** (tel. 03 26 77 41 41), next to the hostel. 10F per hr. access, with a 50F Sept.-June membership.

▌ ACCOMMODATIONS AND CAMPING

Inexpensive hotels cluster west of pl. Drouet d'Erlon, in the area above the cathedral, and near the *mairie.* Reims is popular; call ahead.

Centre International de Séjour/Auberge de Jeunesse (HI), chaussée Bocquaine (tel. 03 26 40 52 60; fax 03 26 47 35 70), next to La Comédie-Espace André Malraux. Cross the park in front of the station, following the right-hand side of the traffic circle. Turn right onto bd. Général Leclerc, follow it to the canal and cross the first bridge (pont de Vesle, on your left). Take the first left onto Chaussée Bocquaine (10-15min.). Fabulous facilities in airy building, with mini-balconies on each floor. Singles 85F; doubles and triples 69F per person. Breakfast 15F. Kitchen 8am-11pm. Laundry. Reception 7am-midnight, night porter midnight-7am. Non-members pay one-time 10F fee. V, MC.

Au Bon Accueil, 31 rue Thillois (tel. 03 26 88 55 74; fax 03 26 05 12 38). Great value for the money; just off the central pl. d'Erlon. Sloping floors lead to large, sunny rooms. Singles 80-140F, doubles 120-170F. Shower 10F. Breakfast 25F. Pets 15F. 24hr. reception. V, MC.

Ardenn' Hôtel, 6 rue Caqué (tel. 03 26 47 42 38; fax 03 26 09 48 56). Not far from pl. d'Erlon and the *gare,* the pleasant, newly renovated rooms match the pleasant, new owners. All rooms have sink, shower, toilet, and TV. 24hr. reception. Singles 170-180F; doubles 220-240F. Breakfast 35F. V, MC, AmEx.

Central Hotel, 16 rue des Telliers (tel. 03 26 47 30 08; fax 03 26 86 87 76). Pastel orange manages to be fetching. Well-decorated, largish rooms on a private street close to everything. All rooms have sink and shower. Singles 149-179F; doubles 169-199F; triples 219-239F. Breakfast 25F. Reception 7am-11pm. V, MC, AmEx.

Hôtel Jeanne d'Arc, 26 rue Jeanne d'Arc (tel. 03 26 40 29 62). Clean, cheap, and close. Unfortunately, there's no magic here: the hallways are dark and dusty, and the beds sag. Singles 95-135F; doubles 115-155F, some with shower. Showers only on the first floor. No breakfast. 24hr. reception, no visitors after 7pm. Checkout 11:30am. V, MC.

⚑ FOOD

Pl. Drouet d'Erlon is the foolproof spot to find food and people, day or night; *boulangeries* and sandwich shops squish side by side with cheap cafés and classier restaurants. A **Monoprix supermarket** occupies a 19th-century building on the corner of rue de Vesle and rue de Talleyrand. (Open M-Sa 8:30am-9pm.) The smaller **Marché Plus supermarket** on rue de Vesle is open Sundays. (daily 9am-1pm.) The main **open-air market** is on pl. du Boulingrin near Porte Mars. (W and Sa 6am-1pm.)

🍴 **Boeuf ou Salade?** 41 pl. d'Erlon (tel. 03 26 40 44 22). Underneath the silly sign and the (answer:) cow mascot is a terrace covered in (counter-answer:) greenery. The variety of vegetarian *salade-repas* (45-49F) is huge and appealing. Open daily 11am-midnight.

Taj Mahal Indian Restaurant, 151 rue de Vesle (tel. 03 26 40 03 50). This intimate Indian restaurant offers grills and curries (45-68F), weekday lunch *menu* (55F), and a plethora of veggie options. The marvelous, brilliant orange cocktail *maison* (25F) is a must. Open daily 11am-2:30pm and 7:30-11pm. V, MC.

Le Petit Basque, 13 rue de Colonel Fabien (tel. 03 26 09 96 26), around the corner from the hostel. A taste of the southwest in the northeast! The glorious fresh paella (65F) is delicious, and the red-and-white checkered tablecloths as irrepressibly cheery as the owner. *Plat du jour* 38F; *menu* 55F. Open Tu-Su 11:30am-3pm and 7-11pm. V, MC.

🍴 **La Coupole,** 73 pl. Drouet d'Erlon (tel 03 26 47 86 28), is one of the classiest *brasseries* on the pl. Erlon. Relax in the posh interior or on the sprawling canopied terrace, while enjoying fresh seafood dishes, their speciality. Open daily 11am-midnight. V, MC.

👁 SIGHTS

The most popular sights are around the *centre ville* and are easily accessible by foot. Other than the cathedral, the champagne *caves* are indubitably the biggest draw in town. Four hundred kilometers of *crayères* (Roman chalk quarries) wind under Reims, along with more recently-dug tunnels, sheltering the treasured bottles of the great Champagne firms. Many houses give tours by appointment only; the tourist office has information on hours and prices. It's not always cheaper to buy champagne at the houses; ask the advice of wine shops near the cathedral and look for sales on local brands—or check the prices at Monoprix (see **Food**, above). Good bottles start at 60F, half the cost outside France.

CATHÉDRALE DE NOTRE-DAME. Cathedrals on this site presided over the baptism of Clovis in the 5th century and the coronation of Charles VII at the end of the Hundred Years' War a millennium later. The present edifice, the third to occupy the site, is built with blocks of golden limestone quarried from caves now used to age champagne. Most of the stained-glass windows are in the eastern portion of the cathedral; visit in the morning for the best view. The most spectacular are a sea-blue set by Marc Chagall integrating elements from Genesis to the baptism of Clovis. For tours in English, consult the tourist office. *(Tel. 03 26 47 55 34 or tourist office. Open daily 7:30am-7:30pm. Tours July-Aug. M-Sa 10:30am, Su 11am, and daily 2:30pm and 4:30pm; tours depart less frequently late Mar.-mid June and Oct. 35F, ages 12-25 15F.)*

CHAMPAGNE CAVES. Of the many tours offered, by far the most elegant is that offered by **Pommery.** Mme Pommery became one of France's foremost vintners when she took over her late husband's business; since then she has brought art into the workplace, lining the *cave* walls with exquisite carvings by Gustave Navlet. *(5 pl. du Général Gouraud. Tel. 03 26 61 62 56; fax 03 26 61 62 96. 40F, students 20F, children free. Tours by appointment only daily Apr.-Oct. 10am-5:30pm; Nov.-Mar. M-F 10am-4:30pm.)* For a more earthy attitude to the fermenting business, **Mumm's** the word. Here visitors are entertained by cheeky red-uniformed guides and an inspiring film. *(34 rue du Champ de Mars. Tel. 03 26 49 59 70. Follow the billboard signs from pl. de la République. 20F. Tours daily Mar.-Oct. 9-11am and 2-5pm; Nov.-Feb. M-F 9-11am and 2-5pm, Sa-*

Su 2-5pm.) If *caves* are your thing, you'll be overjoyed at the gloom in **Taittinger's** spooky tunnels. *(9 pl. St-Nicaise. Tel. 03 26 85 45 35. 25F. Open Mar.-Nov. M-F 9:30am-noon and 2-4:30pm, Sa-Su 9-11am and 2-5pm; Dec.-Feb. closed weekends.)*

PALAIS DU TAU. The former archbishop's residence acquired its name from the original floor plan, which resembled a "T." Magnificent 16th-century tapestries line the walls. The dazzling collection includes reliquaries dating back as early as Charlemagne, and an entire room of robes and sacramental objects from the 1825 crowning of Charles X. *(Pl. du Cardinal Luçon, enter from inside the cathedral. Tel. 03 26 47 81 79. Open July-Aug. daily 9:30am-6:30pm; Sept. 1-Nov. 14 and Mar. 16-June 30 9:30am-12:30pm and 2-6pm; Nov. 15-Mar. 15 M-F 10am-noon and 2-5pm, Sa-Su 10am-noon and 2-6pm. 32F, students 21F.)*

BASILIQUE ST-RÉMI. The basilica reposes on a bed of purple wildflowers at the other end of town from the cathedral, near the Pommery and Taittinger *caves.* A Romanesque church with Gothic tinges, it was built around the tomb of St. Rémi himself, the bishop who baptized Clovis. *(Pl. St-Rémi. Open M-W, F, and Su 8am-7pm or dusk, whichever comes first; Th and Sa 9am-7pm or dusk).* Next door, the **Abbaye St-Rémi,** adjacent to the basilica, shelters an extensive collection of religious art, military uniforms, and artifacts from the Merovingian and Carolingian eras. *(53 rue Simon. Tel. 03 26 85 23 36. Open M-F 2-6:30pm, Sa-Su 2-7pm. 10F.)*

SALLE DE REDDITION. The simple schoolroom where the Germans signed the surrender to the Allies on May 7, 1945, is on the other side of the railroad tracks. The small **Musée de la Reddition** leads up to the room itself with a short film and several galleries of photos and timelines, more evocative than factual. The actual room has been glassed off and preserved with quiet audio echoes of Eisenhower and de Gaulle. *(12 rue Franklin Roosevelt. Tel. 03 26 47 84 19. Open Apr.-Nov. W-M 10am-noon and 2-6pm. 10F.)*

PORTE MARS. This crumbling triumphal Roman arch, once the largest in the Roman Empire, was one of four erected in honor of Augustus two centuries after his death. The 3rd-century ruins anachronistically frame the modern pl. de la République, up the road from the *gare.*

♪ ❧ ENTERTAINMENT AND FESTIVALS

ENTERTAINMENT. Comédie de Reims, chaussée Bocquaine (tel. 03 26 48 49 00; fax 03 26 88 76 95), presents a wide variety of plays (around 120F, students 75F). **Cinéma Gaumont,** 72 pl. Drouet d'Erlon (tel. 03 26 47 54 54), and **Opéra Cinémas,** 3 rue Théodore Dubois (tel. 03 26 47 29 36), show mainstream and independent flicks (tickets 30-50F). Opéra Cinémas generally has a couple of films running in *version original,* but they're not always English-language.

At night the biggest concentration of people is at **pl. Drouet d'Erlon,** where cafés and bars stay open until 3am on weekends. The crowd at **Jour et Nuit,** 81 pl. d'Erlon (tel. 03 26 40 19 46), is a little younger and the beer is cheaper than at the more dignified **Au Bureau** across the way. (Both open until 3am.) Boldly step out of the pedestrian district to the enormous **L'Échiquier,** 110 av. Jean Jaurès (tel. 03 26 89 12 38), which promises three different scenes under one roof. (Open Th-Sa 10pm-5am.) **Le Curtayn Club,** 7 bd. Général Leclerc (tel. 03 26 40 09 02), is a little closer to town, but generally draws older crowds to its garish interior. (Open nightly 10pm-4am.) The best entertainment is to be found walking by the illuminated cathedral.

FESTIVALS. Throughout July and August, Reims hosts the fantastic **Flâneries Musicales d'Été,** with more than a hundred free concerts in 60 days. For more fun, head to the cathedral every Friday and Saturday night in July and August for **Cathédrale de Lumière,** a one-hour spectacle illuminating the cathedral and nearby buildings and culminating in a light show on the cathedral façade. (1hr.; 11pm in July, 10pm in Aug. 40F adults, 20F kids; buy tickets at Palais du Tau 2-6pm.)

ÉPERNAY

Situated at the juncture of three wealthy grape-growing regions, Épernay (pop. 30,000) is a ritzy town. The world's most distinguished champagne producers—Moët & Chandon, Perrier-Jouet, Mercier, and De Castellane, among others—have put their labels on the palatial mansions along av. de Champagne and buried their 700 million bottles of treasure in miles of subterranean tunnels. Unlike the more metropolitan Reims, Épernay strips away all the distractions of the city and devotes itself heart and soul to the production of champagne. Perhaps as a result, streets not dedicated to the sparkling nectar have a rather abandoned air; if you're looking for a pretty little provincial town, you've come to the wrong place. If, however, you're burning for bubbly, Épernay caters to connoisseurs and amateurs alike; tour a *cave*, raise a glass, and taste the stars.

▶ ORIENTATION AND PRACTICAL INFORMATION. Trains leave cour de la Gare for **Reims** (20min., 15 per day, 33F); **Paris** (1¼hr., 14 per day, 109F); and **Strasbourg** (4½hr., 3 per day, 215F). (Ticket counters open Su-F 6am-8pm, Sa 7am-7pm. Info office open M-Sa 9am-noon and 2-6pm.) **STDM buses** (tel. 03 26 65 17 07) offer service to **Paris, Reims,** and many small towns in Champagne. **Local buses** are operated infrequently by **Sparnabus,** 30 pl. des Arcades. (Tel. 03 26 55 55 50. Tickets 6.50F, *carnet* of 10 42F. Open M-F 9am-noon and 1:45-6pm, Sa 9am-noon.)

To get to the **tourist office,** 7 av. de Champagne (tel. 03 26 53 33 00; fax 03 26 51 95 22), from the station, walk straight ahead through pl. Mendès France (you'll pass a fountain) and one block up rue Gambetta to the central **pl. de la République;** turn left onto av. de Champagne and you're there (5min.). The welcoming staff can outfit you with free maps, a list of hotels, and info on Épernay's *caves,* plus suggestions for 3 different *routes champenoises.* They also publish a free monthly guide, *On Sort?,* which lists local events and festivities. (Open April 24-Oct. 15 M-Sa 9:30am-12:30pm and 1:30-7pm, Su 11am-4pm; rest of year M-Sa 9:30am-12:30pm and 1:30-5:30pm.) **Exchange currency** at **Banque de France,** pl. de la République. (Tel. 03 26 55 59 00. Open M-F 8:45am-noon and 1:45-4pm.) You can do **laundry** at the turbocharged **Salon Lavoir GTI,** 18 av. Jean Jaurès. (Tel. 03 26 54 96 15. Open daily 7am-8pm.) Wounds are patched at **Hôpital Auban-Moët,** 137 rue de l'Hôpital (tel. 03 26 58 70 70), while the **police** watch for drunk drivers from 7 rue Jean-Moët (tel. 03 26 54 11 17), one block from pl. de la République down rue Fleuricourt. The **post office,** pl. Hugues Plomb (tel. 03 26 53 31 60), offers mediocre rates of **currency exchange.** (Open M-F 8am-7pm, Sa 8am-noon. **Postal code:** 51200.) Send messages over the **Internet** faster than a speeding *bouchon* from **l'Icone Café,** 25 rue de l'Hôpital Auban Moët. (Tel. 03 26 55 73 93. 25F first 30min., 20F next 30min. Open M-Sa 9:15am-midnight, Su 3pm-midnight.)

▶ ACCOMMODATIONS AND CAMPING. Épernay caters to the champagne set—budget hotels are rare. The closest hostel is in Verzy (20km), on rue du Bassin. (Tel. 03 26 97 90 10. 59F B&B. See **Reims,** p. 426, for Verzy bike rental.) For hostel-style accommodations without the ambience, the **Foyer des Jeunes Travailleurs,** 2 rue Pupin (tel. 03 26 51 62 51; fax 03 26 54 15 60), offers large, four-bed rooms with desks and sinks, laundry facilities, and a cafeteria (M-F lunch and dinner, Sa lunch only). From the station, cross the grassy square, turn left onto rue de Reims, and make an immediate right onto rue Pupin. (85F with breakfast. Kitchen Sa and Su nights only. Meal 47F; main dish only 37F. Reception M-F 9am-8pm, Sa 10am-2pm. During meals, enter at 8 rue de Reims.) The homey **Hôtel St-Pierre,** 14 av. Paul-Chandon (tel. 03 26 54 40 80; fax 03 26 57 88 68), is a block away from pl. d'Europe, with darkly floral hallways, large beautiful rooms, and a welcoming *salon.* (No hall showers. Singles 118-186F; doubles 130-202F. Breakfast 28F. Reception 7am-11pm. V, MC.) There is a **campground** about 4km from the station (direction "Reims") at allée de Cumières. (Tel. 03 26 55 32 14. 16F per person, 19F per tent and car. Electricity 17F. Open Apr.-mid-Sept. daily 7am-10pm.)

⌐ **FOOD.** The pedestrian district around pl. des Arcades and pl. Hugues Plomb is rich in food shops. More than a *marché*, there's a **Marché Plus** at 13 pl. Hugues Plomb. (Tel. 03 26 51 89 89. Open M-Sa 7am-9pm, Su 9am-1pm.) Halle St-Thibault hosts a **market.** (W and Sa 8am-noon.) The cafeteria at the **Foyer** (see **Accommodations and Camping,** above) is open 11:30am-1:30pm.

Intimate and elegant, **La Cave à Champagne,** 16 rue Gambetta (tel. 03 26 55 50 70), serves a 79F dinner *menu* with a wide selection of appetizers, main dishes, desserts, and (surprise) champagne. (Open daily noon-2:30pm and 7-10:30pm. V, MC.) **Le Darjeeling,** 32 pl. des Arcades (tel. 03 26 51 56 80), in the pedestrian district, has a smart terrace (10% price hike) frequented by ritzy tourists, and serves *salade-repas* (52-67F) in the afternoons. A *chocolaterie* lies inside. (Open M-Th 8:30am-7:30pm, F-Sa 8:30am-11pm. V, MC.)

■ **SIGHTS.** The **av. de Champagne** lives up to its name with palatial *maisons de champagne* pouring out the bubbly to hordes of visitors every day. The tours below are all offered in French or English for walk-ins. All include a *petite dégustation*, but sorry kids—over 16s only. *Caves* are cold (usually around 10°C)—bring a sweater. They may all be in the same business, but each firm's tour gives a different twist to the tale.

The grandpappy of them all is **Moët & Chandon,** 20 av. de Champagne (tel. 03 26 51 20 20), who've been "turning nature into art" since 1743. The tour is lively and engaging, and the caves don't look like a tourist set-up, though the 7-minute film is rather tame. (Open daily Mar. 15-Nov. 19 9:30am-11:30am and 2-4:30pm; Nov. 19-Mar. 14 closed weekends. 1hr. tour with tasting 40F, 25F under 16.) Slightly less popular but just as swanky, **Mercier,** 70 av. de Champagne (tel. 03 26 51 22 22; fax 03 26 51 22 23), lies a 10-minute walk away, in the middle of a vineyard. The self-proclaimed most popular champagne in France, Mercier certainly knows how to market. The slick film is little more than a lushly scored advert, but the 30-minute tour, in roller-coaster-like cars, fascinates. (Open Mar.-Nov. M-Sa 9:30-11:30am and 2-4:30pm, Su until 5pm; Dec.-Feb. closed Tu-W. 30F, ages 12-16 15F, under 12 free.) Across the street, **De Castellane,** 57 rue de Verdun (tel. 03 26 51 19 11), supplies the famed Parisian restaurant Maxim's. Ascending the tower affords a magnificent panorama of the valley below, and the museum sports a unique collection of champagne-related paraphernalia from old posters to tools. (Open daily 10am-noon and 2-6pm. Full tour 30F, tower and museum only 20F.) **Demoiselle Vranken,** 42 rue de Champagne (tel. 03 26 59 50 50), is a relatively new arrival. The tours are usually smaller and more intimate, and include a happy marriage of flashing slide shows and melodramatic music. (Open M-F 9am-noon and 2-6pm, Sa 9:30am-noon and 2-4:30pm. 20F.)

▢ **ENTERTAINMENT.** In keeping with Épernay's preoccupation with dark, moldy *caves*, the city's watering holes are flooded until the wee hours. At night, **Le Tap-Too,** 5 rue des Près Dimanche (tel. 03 26 51 56 10; *not* the café on pl. de la République), houses four clubs in one, each dance floor spinning a different genre of tunes. (Open daily 10pm-4am. Su-F 60F; Sa 40F before 11pm, 80F after. Includes first drink.) The trendy **Le Progrès,** 5 pl. de la République (tel. 03 76 58 22 72), is the place to sip champagne and watch the world go by. (Open daily 6am-midnight.) From the end of June to the beginning of August, free classical and jazz **concerts** are held at the Chateau Perrier on av. de Champagne. (Tu and Th at 7pm.)

▟ **HIKES.** At the heart of the *Route Touristique du Champagne*, Épernay is also an excellent base for exploring the surrounding countryside. The **Champagne route** is a set of hikes through vineyards, châteaux, and mountains. The tourist office provides brochures in French or English that map out treks and provide regional practical information.

CHÂLONS-EN-CHAMPAGNE

Having hidden out for years under the alias Châlons-sur-Marne, Châlons-en-Champagne (pop. 60,000) recently reverted to its original name; otherwise, not much has changed here for centuries. A hotbed of activity during Roman times, Châlons won prestige in 451 AD when Gallo-Roman armies overcame the hordes of Attila the Hun. Since the Middle Ages, however, the town has settled into bourgeois complacency, befitting its status as the administrative capital of Champagne. Once an important religious center, Châlons' main attractions remain its churches, particularly the Cathédrale-St-Étienne and Notre-Dame-en-Vaux. Half-timbered cottages and flower-lined waterways provide occasional photo-moments in a town that is too busy to worry about being attractive. Châlons' location in the center of Champagne, makes it a worthwhile stop for those traversing northeastern France.

▮ ORIENTATION AND PRACTICAL INFORMATION. The Marne flows through Châlons, conveniently dividing the *gare* and the industrial sector from the *centre ville*. **Trains** run from av. de la Gare to **Reims** (30min., 8 per day, 42F) and **Paris** (90min., 7-10 per day, 120F). **STDM buses,** 86 rue de Fagnières (tel. 03 26 65 17 07), provide service to surrounding smaller towns, while within Châlons **SITAC,** pl. Monseigneur Tissier (tel. 03 26 69 59 00), will supply **local transportation** needs. **Taxis** (tel. 03 26 65 95 95) lie in wait 24 hours at the station. To reach the **tourist office,** 3 quai des Arts (tel. 03 26 65 17 89; fax 03 26 65 35 65), from the station, take a left at the roundabout onto av. Jean Jaurès and follow it across the river as it turns into rue de la Marne; the office is set back from the road on the left in a pretty half-timbered mansion (10-15min). Taking a right a bit farther along onto the pedestrian rue de Lombards leads to the central **place de la République.** The friendly and knowledgeable staff can provide you with a map and info on local *caves.* They also run **city tours,** which visit a different local curiosity every day. (Office open June-Aug. M-Sa 9am-12:30pm and 1:30-6:30pm, Su 10:30am-12:30pm and 2:30-5:30pm. Rest of the year M-Sa 9am-noon and 1:30-6:30pm. Tours offered July-Sept. M-Sa 3pm. 25F, children 15F.) The **police** keep watch from pl. aux Cheviots (tel. 02 26 66 27 27), and the **hospital** treats the sick at 57 rue Commandant Derrien (tel. 03 26 69 60 60). The **post office** (tel. 03 26 68 77 11), rue de la Marne, **exchanges currency.** (Open M-F 8am-7pm, Sa 8am-noon. Poste Restante: specify 51001 Châlons-Cathédrale. **Postal code:** 51000.)

▮ ACCOMMODATIONS. The lively and attractive central **pl. de la République** is by far the most pleasant place to stay, but the hotels lining the square are overpriced. The hostel is on the outskirts of town and rather grim; those determined to visit Châlons on a tight budget would probably be best off making a daytrip from Reims. To get to the **Auberge de Jeunesse (HI),** 6 rue Kellermann (tel. 03 26 68 13 56), take bus #4 or 5 from the *gare* to pl. Mgr. Tissier, then switch to #3 (direction "Vallée St-Pierre") to "Doulcet;" the hostel sits in the enclosure behind the bus stop. To walk, follow av. Jean Jaurès from the station across town, bearing with its name changes as it crosses pl. Foch, the Hôtel de Ville, and pl. Mgr. Tissier, to become Grande Étape and finally rue Chevalier. The hostel will be on your right, across from the grassy sq. St-Loup, after about 30 minutes. The cool young staff oversee two single-sex, cramped, 20-bunk barracks, with separate bathrooms. (40F. Breakfast 22F. 24hr. reception in summer; otherwise 7:30-10am and 5:30-10pm.) Pricey, but with the best location in town, is ▮ **Hôtel du Pot d'Etain,** 18 pl. de la République (tel. 03 26 68 09 09; fax. 03 26 68 58 18). The whitewashed rooms are small but they sparkle, and the owner, a baker, serves up freshly-made croissants for breakfast. (Singles 270F; doubles 350F. Breakfast 37F. Reception open 7am-midnight. V, MC.) A great compromise between price and comfort is ▮ **Hôtel de la Cité,** 12 rue de la Charrière, (tel. 03 26 64 31 20; fax 03 26 70 96 22). A charming hotel near the Auberge de Jeunesse, it makes up for its distance from the action with great value. The large, sunny rooms are gorgeous, with brocaded armchairs and antique cabinets. Eat breakfast on the garden terrace and pretend you're in "House and Garden." (Singles and doubles 130-230F. Breakfast 30F. Reception 7:30am-10:30pm. V, MC.)

FOOD. Cheap eats abound at the cafés lining **pl. de la République,** while *boulangeries*, *épiceries*, and the like are strung along **rue de la Marne**. For a treat, loosen your belt and head for ■ **Les Ardennes,** 34 pl. de la République (tel. 03 26 68 21 42). Even discriminating gastronomes couldn't fault the 78F 2-course *menu*. (Open Tu-Su noon-2pm and 7:30-9pm. V, MC.) **La Bourse** (tel. 03 26 65 18 04), next door, is the most popular brasserie on the *place*, and its easy to see why; the burnished wood and brass interior is reminiscent of famous Parisian cafés, and the packed terrace is ideal for surveying the nonstop bustle of the square. (Open daily until 11pm.) Heading away from the pl. de la République towards the cathedral, **La Landolina,** 5 rue des Cordeliers (tel. 03 26 70 55 94), grills pizzas (from 31F) to perfection in its wood oven. Salads, pasta, and traditional meat dishes are also available, all to be consumed in the pretty peach dining room. (Open Tu-Sa noon-1:30pm and 7:30-9:30pm, M lunch only. V, MC.)

SIGHTS AND ENTERTAINMENT. Châlons-en-Champagne houses a famous collection of well-preserved medieval churches. The most compelling is the graceful **Notre-Dame-en-Vaux,** an artful mélange of Romanesque and Gothic styles built between 1157 and 1217. (Open daily 10am-noon and 1:30-7pm, except during Mass.) The church sits serenely alongside the Mau canal in one of the prettier areas of town, sandwiched between the fountain-spewing pl. Mgr. Tissier and the Hôtel de Ville on pl. Foch. Behind the church, the tiny **Cloître de Notre-Dame-en-Vaux,** rue Nicolas-Durand (tel 03 26 64 03 87), displays statuary unearthed from the ancient church cloister, much of it dating from the 12th century. A fragment of the old cloister wall, which takes up one side of the display room, features an unusual polychrome pietà sculpted in 1512. (Open W-M Apr. 1-Sept. 30 10am-noon and 2-6pm; Oct. 1-Mar. 31 10am-noon and 2-5pm. 25F, students and children 15F.) On the other side of town, the **Cathédrale St-Étienne** contains some remarkable stained glass that spans the 13th to 20th centuries. All that remains of the original Romanesque edifice, completed in 1147, is the crypt and northern tower. (Open W-M 2:30-6:30pm.) Châlons wears its prettiest clothes at its magnificently sculpted gardens along the Marne River. **Le Petit Jard,** a country garden in the style of Napoleon III, is famous for its fantastical floral clock, while the nearby **Grand Jard** is criss-crossed by vast tree-lined esplanades. Cross the bridge over the canal to reach **le Jardin anglais,** a cunning replica of a typical English garden.

FESTIVALS. Châlons bursts into song with the **F'Estival des Musiques d'Ici et d'Ailleurs,** a musical extravaganza featuring 36 free concerts held throughout July and August in the pl. de la République. The festival draws artists from the US to Ireland to Africa; concerts usually start at 9pm. Contact **Musiques sur la Ville** (tel. 03 26 68 47 27; www.chez.com/musville) for info. The huge **Foire-Exhibition,** from the end of August to the beginning of September, draws 120,000 visitors yearly to town. Displays range from automobiles to local handicrafts to wines.

TROYES

Troyes blossomed as a center of art and learning in the High Middle Ages under the Counts of Champagne, when Chrétien de Troyes penned the tale of *Parsifal*, Rachi guided the perplexed through the Talmud, and a local shoemaker's son made it to the top spot in Rome as Pope Urban IV. The Renaissance revitalized the arts, as the famous School of Troyes churned out masterworks of sculpture, painting, and stained glass; many can still be seen in the town's churches. The knitwear industry took off in the 18th century, fattening local wallets and paving the way for the garment business that sustains the town today.

Modern Troyes (pop. 60,000) bears little resemblance to its grape-crazy northern neighbors. It has no *caves*, and the old town's nickname—"*bouchon de champagne*" (champagne cork)—stems from its outline, not the success of its wine. *Parisiennes* may be drawn to Troyes by the ring of factory outlets on the outskirts, but the town's real charm lies in its ancient center. Troyes has preserved whole tracts of 16th-century houses and spiced them up with teeming cafés and strong collections of modern art. Although the weathered oak beams and gray stone may feel cold, they breathe an ancient air.

ⓘ ORIENTATION AND PRACTICAL INFORMATION

Troyes' train station is just three blocks from the *vieille ville*. The main tourist office is on your right one block from the station; another outpost lurks near the town center.

Trains: Av. Maréchal Joffre (train info. and reservations tel. 08 36 35 35 35). To: **Paris** (1½hr., 12 per day, 115F); **Mulhouse** (3hr., 4 per day, 191F). Info office open M-F 8:30-11:45am and 2-7pm, Sa 9-11:45am, 2-6:30pm. Station house open M-Sa 4:45am-9pm, Su 6am-10:15pm.

Buses: Go left as you exit the *gare*. **SDTM TransChampagne** (tel. 03 26 65 17 07), goes to **Reims** (2hr., 4 per day, 109F). **Les Rapides de Bourgogne** (tel. 03 86 46 90 90) hop to **Auxerre** (2½hr., 1 per day, 85F) and **Reims** (2hr., M-F 3 per day, Sa 2 per day; 105F).

Local Transportation: Bus L'Autoville (tel. 03 25 70 49 00), office in front of market. Extensive and frequent service. Ticket 7F, 3 for 17F.

Taxis: Taxis Troyens (tel. 03 25 78 30 30), in the circle outside the station. 24hr.

Car Rental: Europcar, 2 rue Voltaire (tel. 03 25 73 27 66). Cars start at 326F per day. 100km free, 1.21F/km after that. Open M-F 8:30am-noon and 2-7pm, Sa 2:30-6pm.

Tourist Office: Two outposts, one near the *gare* on 16 bd. Carnot (tel. 03 25 82 62 70; www.ot-troyes.fr) and the other near the heart of the *vieille ville* on rue Mignard (tel. 03 25 73 36 88). Free detailed city map. Room reservation service 15F. Bus schedules and calendar of local events. From July to early Sept. guided tours of the city leave daily; in English by appointment only, 35F. The rue Mignard bureau offers an audio guide. Both open M-Sa 9:30am-8:30pm, Su 10am-noon and 2-5pm.

Cultural Center: Maison du Boulanger, 16 rue Champeaux (tel. 03 25 43 55 00). Info on festivals, exhibitions, and concerts. Open M-F 9am-noon and 2-5pm, Sa 10am-noon and 2-5 pm.

Budget Travel: Havas Voyages, 30 bd. Victor Hugo. Open M 9:30am-noon and 2-6:30pm, Tu-F 8:30am-noon and 2-6:30pm, Sa 9am-noon and 2-6:30pm.

Money: Société Générale, 11 pl. Maréchal Foch (tel. 03 25 43 57 00) has **currency exchange.** Open M-F 8:30am-12:20pm and 1:30-5:30pm.

Laundromat: Laverie Automatique, 11 rue Clemenceau. Wash 24F, dry 2F for 5min. Open daily 7:30am-8pm.

Police: Tel. 03 25 43 51 00.

Hospital: 101 av. Anatole France (tel. 03 25 49 49 49).

Post Office: 2 pl. Général Patton (tel. 03 25 73 22 72). One block to the right as you exit the train station. Poste Restante code: "10013 Troyes-Voltaire". Open M-F 8am-6:30pm, Sa 8am-noon. **Postal code:** 10000.

▶ ACCOMMODATIONS, CAMPING, AND FOOD

ACCOMMODATIONS AND CAMPING. The **Hôtel Ambassy Club,** 49 rue Raymond Poincaré (tel. 03 25 93 12 03), is situated several blocks away from the center of town; with your back to the town hall follow rue de la République as it becomes rue Raymond Poincaré. Somewhat dingy hallways lead to surprisingly airy and bright rooms decorated with a floral theme. Toilets are on every floor; showers are only on the first. The hip *brasserie* downstairs serves snacks and drinks all day. (Singles and doubles 120F; triples 150F. Breakfast 30F. Reception 7am-3am. V, MC, AmEx.) ◪ **Les Comtes de Champagne,** 56 rue de la Monnaie (tel. 03 25 73 11 70; fax 03 25 73 06 02), is nestled in a half-timbered mansion just footsteps away from the heart of town and minutes from the train station. The family-run inn breathes an air of quiet elegance that wouldn't jive well with noisy party-hounds, but those seeking privacy and relaxation will appreciate the large, tranquil rooms. (Singles 150F, with shower from 180F; doubles from 170F, with shower from 200F; triples 270-300F; quads 290-320F; some large rooms can take 5 or 6. Extra bed 30F. Breakfast 29F. Parking at hotel garage 30F. Reception 7am-11pm. V, MC, Diners.) The **Camping Municipal** (tel. 03 25 81 02 64) is on N60, 2km from town. Take bus #1 (direction "Pont St-Marie") to this three-star site with showers, toilets, TV, and laundry. (25F per person, 30F per tent or car. Open Apr.-Oct. 15.)

FOOD. The **quartier St-Jean** has many inviting restaurants; cafes, *brasseries*, and inexpensive *crêperies* line the pedestrian rue Champeaux as it makes its way to pl. Alexander Israël. On the other side of the *vieille ville*, reasonably priced international eateries can be found on **rue de la Cité** near the cathedral. **Les Halles,** a covered market behind the main bus station (turn left down the rue de la République from the town hall), offers a fresh selection of produce from the Aube region. (Open M-Th 8am-12:45pm and 3:30-7pm, F-Sa 7am-7pm, Su 9am-12:30pm.) Try the creamy *fromage de Troyes* or the *andouillette de Troyes*, a tasty tripe sausage. For sanitized, pre-packaged fare, there is always the **Prisunic supermarket,** 78 rue Émile Zola. (Open M-Sa 8:30am-8pm.) 🎗 **Au Crieurs du Vin,** 4-6 Place Jean Jaurès (tel. 03 25 40 01 01), a bistro, bar, and *cave*, offers an elegant alternative to the noisy *brasseries* a few blocks away on rue Champeaux. The decor may be an eclectic mix of rustic and art nouveau, but the food is traditional and satisfying (*plats* 58F). Ask the friendly and knowledgeable staff for a *petit dégustation* of local wines.

👁 🎭 SIGHTS AND EXCURSIONS

"What do they do in Troyes?... They ring bells!" was a popular saying of old, as medieval and Renaissance churches are the prime attractions of the *vieille ville*. Troyes also offers an unusual array of museums; a 60F pass (students 10F) will allow you to visit all but the Maison de l'Outil. Free maps available at the tourist office lay out the major sights in a convenient walking tour format.

MUSÉE DE L'ART MODERNE. Truly the jewel in Troyes' crown, the museum boasts a collection of over 2,000 works of French art from the period 1850-1950, including sculptures, drawings, and paintings by Rodin, Degas, Courbet, Seurat, and Picasso. Not to be missed are the impressive examples of fauvism by artists such as Derain and Marinot. *(Pl. St-Pierre; head down rue Georges Clemenceau from the town hall. Tel. 03 25 76 26 80. Open W-M 11am-6pm. Tours on first and third Sunday of the month from 11-4pm. 30F, students and children 5F; free W.)*

CATHÉDRALE ST-PIERRE ET ST-PAUL. A 13th- to 17th-century Gothic masterpiece, the church features Flamboyant detailing on the facade, 1500 square meters of stained glass windows, and one of the longest naves in France. Tapestries hang about the altar, and the treasury houses the jewels of the counts of Champagne as well as manuscripts, statues, and relics dating from the 9th century to the present. *(Pl. St-Pierre; directions as above. Open daily 10am-noon and 2-4pm.)*

ÉGLISE STE-MADELEINE. To reach this 12th-century church, the oldest in Troyes, duck off rue Champeaux onto **Ruelle des Chats,** a covered alleyway so named because the houses are packed together tightly enough for cats to stroll from roof to roof. Inside the church is the particularly impressive stone *jubé*, a structure erected to separate the nave from the chancel. One of only seven in France, it was crafted by Jehan Gailde, a confident master mason of the 16th century, who lies buried at its foot under the epigraph "He happily waits for Judgement Day with no fear of being crushed." *(Open daily 10am-noon and 2-6pm.)*

BASILIQUE ST-URBAIN. Presiding over pl. Vernier, St-Urbain's buttresses extend outwards like the legs of a satiated spider. Illuminated by 13th-century stained-glass windows, the Basilica was founded in 1261 when Jacques Pantaléon became Pope Urbain IV. The structure lies on the site of his father's cobbler shop. *(Walk down rue Clemenceau from Town Hall. Tel. 03 25 73 37 13. Open daily 10am-noon and 2-6 pm.)*

MUSÉE DES BEAUX-ARTS. Housed in the old Abbaye St-Loup, this museum displays an array of archæological finds, medieval sculptures, and a large collection of 15th- to 19th-century paintings. A glass door upstairs affords a peek into one of France's oldest libraries; many of the 85,000 volumes inside are 1300 years old. *(21 rue Chrétien-de-Troyes, near the cathedral. Tel. 03 25 42 33 33. Open July-Aug. W-M 10-noon and 2-7pm, Sept.-June W-M 10am-noon and 2-6pm. 30F, students and children 5F; free W.)*

OTHER SIGHTS. The **Maison de l'Outil et de la Pensée Ouvrière,** filled with wooden carvings, is located in a restored 16th-century half-timbered *hôtel* that was once the central workshop of the town's knitwear industry. The building now houses a collection of over 7000 tools of 17th- and 18th-century craftsmen, offering a fascinating window into a bygone world. *(7 rue de la Trinité, off rue Emile Zola. Tel. 03 25 73 28 26. Open M-F 9am-1pm and 2-6:30pm, Sa-Su 10am-1pm and 2-6pm. 40F, students 30F.)* Housed in the 19th-century Hôtel Dieu, the **Pharmacie Musée** is stacked to the rafters with painted wood boxes, faïence, and majolica. *(Quai des Comtes de Champagne. Follow rue Clemenceau from the Hôtel de Ville until it crosses the canal; the museum is on the right. Tel. 03 25 80 98 97. Open July-Aug. W-M 10am-6pm, Sept.-June W and Sa-Su 2-6 pm.)*

EXCURSIONS. Troyes is a short distance from over 12,500 acres of freshwater lakes. The lakes of the **Forêt d'Orient** offer watersports, hikes, and biking for nature enthusiasts. The sunny waters of **Lake Orient** welcome sunbathers, swimmers, and windsurfers. Wilder **Lake Temple** is reserved for fishing and bird watching, and **Lake Amance** roars with speedboats (some tugging waterskiers) from **Port Dierville.** The **Comité Départemental du Tourisme de l'Aube,** 34 quai Dampierre (tel. 03 25 42 50 91; fax 03 25 42 50 88), provides free brochures and info on hotels and restaurants in the area. The tourist office has bus schedules for the Troyes-Grands Lacs routes.

♫ ENTERTAINMENT

Movie theaters, arcades, and pool halls rub elbows with chic boutiques on rue Emile Zola. On warm evenings, *Troyens* swarm the cafés and taverns of **rue Champeaux** and **rue Mole** near pl. Alexandre Israël. Overlooking the *place,* **Le Taverne de Maître Kanter,** 4 rue Champeaux (tel. 03 25 73 25 60) affords music lovers front row seats and plentiful drinks to enjoy the summer concerts held in front of the town hall. (Open daily 11:30am-midnight.) Hang with a gregarious pub crowd at **Bar Montabert,** 24 rue Paillot de Montabert (tel. 03 25 73 58 04), for a tankard of beer amid convivial surroundings, or duck into one of the many nooks and crannies among the plentiful timbering for a private *tête à tête.* (Open daily 6pm-3am.)

For fun more in the family vein, Troyes offers a host of festivals and special events throughout the summer. **Le Chemin des Bâtisseurs de Cathédrales** is a free sound and light spectacle held on summer evenings in the churches of St-Nicholas and St-Nizier. Summer also marks the coming of Troyes' **"Ville en Musique,"** a series of concerts held every Friday and Saturday night in churches or the open air. (Tel. 03 25 43 55 00 for more information.)

CHAUMONT

Trains approach Chaumont over a magnificent 19th-century viaduct, giving the visitor ample opportunity to appreciate the beauty of the town's location. Balanced on a plateau between the Marne and Suize Valleys, Chaumont (pop. 27,000) maintains an equilibrium between old and new. Its heyday as the seat of the Counts of Champagne from 1228 to 1239 has long passed, but the narrow, winding streets of the *vieille ville* retain much of their medieval charm. The ancient mansions with their idiosyncratic towers recall an older age, but beneath the surface is a town as comfortable with the present as the past, with a young, modern population and a state-of-the-art graphic design center. A visit to Chaumont also provides the perfect opportunity to explore the natural beauty of the surrounding countryside.

⚐ ORIENTATION AND PRACTICAL INFORMATION. To get from the *gare* to the *vieille ville*, walk straight ahead to the roundabout and turn right down rue Verdun. The heart of the old town comprises only a handful of streets branching off from pl. de la Concorde, site of the Hôtel de Ville, but hidden delights lurk on the outskirts as well. **Trains** (pl. du Général de Gaulle) chug to **Paris** (8-10 per day, 165F), **Reims** (4 per day, 130F) and **Troyes** (11 per day, 72F). **CTE buses** (tel. 03 80 42 11 00) swing by **Langres.** Zip around town on *Le Bus*, the **local bus service** (7 rue Jules Trefousse, tel. 03 25 01 88 42), or rent your own transport at **Avis,** pl. Aristide Briand. (Tel. 03 25 32 00 79. Open M-Sa 8:30am-noon and 2-6:30pm.) Across from the station, the **tourist office,** pl. de la Gare (tel. 03 25 03 80 80), gives out a free map and an audio guide in English (25F) and also **exchanges currency.** (Open M-F July-Aug. M-F 9am-7pm, Sept.-June M-Sa 9:30am-12:30pm; Su all year and holidays 10am-noon and 2-5pm.) 35F will buy you an hour in cyberspace at the **Net'Cafe,** 27 av. Debernadi (tel. 03 25 02 92 76) near pl. Aristide Briand. The **police** patrol from 1 et 3 av. Carnot (tel. 03 25 03 70 30). The **Centre Hospitalier** can be found at 2 rue Jeanne d'Arc (tel. 03 25 30 70 30). The **post office,** 39 rue Victoire de la Marne (tel. 03 25 30 66 81), sits up the road from the town hall. **Postal code:** 52000.

⚐ ACCOMMODATIONS AND CAMPING. In Le Cavalier, a district south of the *centre ville*, there is a **Foyer des Jeunes Travailleurs (HI)** at 1 rue Carcassonne (tel. 03 25 03 22 77). Follow rue Lévy Alphandéry behind the train station for about 1km, then turn right on rue du Cavalier; the *foyer* lies at the end of the road (15min.). The tired or lazy can take bus #2 from the station to "Suize." The hostel offers serviceable rooms with access to a kitchen, laundry, sports equipment, satellite TV, video games, ping-pong, and plenty of kids to play with. The cafeteria serves a 45.80F meal. (Singles 74F, 108F for non-members; doubles 63F, 92F non-members. Sheets 17F. Breakfast included. Reception daily 3-9pm; call before 6pm to reserve a room. Cash only. Cafeteria open M-F 11:45am-1pm and 7-8pm.)

Those seeking ritzier accommodations can tumble off their train and into a bed at the three-star **Hôtel Terminus Reine,** pl. Général de Gaulle (tel. 03 25 03 66 66, fax 03 25 02 28 95), opposite the *gare*. The tasteful, if garishly colored, rooms all have TV and telephone. The pricey hotel restaurant may well be the best in town, but the budget-conscious can find cheaper fare at the pizzeria in the basement. (Singles and doubles 190F, with shower 290F, with bath 390F. Extra bed 40F. Breakfast 40F.) The best bargain in town is the ⚐ **Hôtel-Brasserie St-Jean,** 2 place Aristide Briand (tel. 03 25 03 00 79; fax 03 25 03 08 81), 10 minutes up av. Victoire de la Marne from the town hall. Across from the sq. du Boulingrin park, the kindly manager presides over spanking-clean pastel-colored rooms. (Singles 130F, 170F with bathroom; doubles with bathroom 210F; triples and quads with bathroom 270F.)

Rough it at **Camping Municipal,** rue des Tanneries (tel. 03 25 32 11 98; fax 03 25 02 59 50). The campground is a 10 minute walk from the train station; follow rue de la Tour Charton from the roundabout in front of the station to square Bad Nauheim, then turn left onto rue des Tanneries. (9F per adult and per tent, 5F per child, 6F per car. Electricity 13F. Open May 1-Sept. 30.)

⚐ FOOD. When mealtime rolls around, Chaumont does not disappoint. *Boucheries*, *pâtisseries*, and other eateries line the streets of the *vieille ville*, particularly **rue Verdun** and **rue Victoire de la Marne,** along with the standard assortment of cafés and *brasseries*. The best place for people-watching is indubitably **pl. de la Concorde,** situated just across from the town hall. **Les Halles,** off rue Georges Clemenceau, displays the bounty of nearby farms on Wednesdays and Saturdays. For a *crêperie* with a twist, the poetically named ⚐ **Bleu Comme Orange,**

11 rue St-Louis (tel. 03 25 01 26 87), off rue Victoire de la Marne, is well worth a visit. The chef serves up mouth-watering *crêpes* and *galettes* stuffed with regional specialties such as *andouillettes* (tripe sausages). Arrive early to assure yourself a seat; at midday this tiny restaurant is packed with locals partaking of the express lunch, an unbeatable deal offering a *galette*, *crêpe*, cider, and coffee for 50F. **La Toscana**, 21 rue de Verdun (tel. 03 25 32 41 36), presents standard French pizzeria fare amid pleasant floral decor. (Open M-Sa for lunch and dinner.)

🕿 **SIGHTS.** Chaumont retains a number of monuments to its former medieval glory. The **Donjon** is all that remains of the castle of the Counts of Champagne. Built between the 11th and 12th centuries on a bluff overlooking the Suize Valley, the squat tower has served as a defensive outpost, barracks, and jail. The serene vistas of the undulating hills are unforgettable, and free if you skip the climb to the top and take it in from the garden at the base. (Tower open M, W-F 2:30-6:30pm, weekend 2:30-7pm. Admission 5F.) Follow the steps down from the garden to the **Musée d'art et d'histoire,** which offers a veritable hodge-podge of local goodies, from gallo-roman archæological finds to a room detailing the rise and fall of Chaumont's glovemaking industry. Both the Donjon and the museum are located at the end of rue du Palais, just behind the Palais du Justice. Walk up rue du Palais away from the medieval keep and turn left on the Desprez to reach the **Basilique St-Jean-Baptiste**, an impressive 12th- to 16th-century church. Particularly remarkable is the interior artwork, which includes Renaissance paintings, an exquisite Tree of Jesse, and numerous wooden carvings by celebrated *chaumontais* sculptor J.B. Bouchardon. Around the corner from the Basilica, on rue des Frères Mistarlet, sits the **Musée de la Creche,** which features an extensive collection of Neapolitan nativity scenes. (Both museums open M-W 2-6pm. Admission 5F, free for students.)

🎵 **ENTERTAINMENT.** Entertain yourself with a drink at one of Chaumont's numerous bars, most of which cluster around the roads branching off the **Place de la Concorde.** For a smarter evening, mingle with the *chic* at **Les Foyes,** 9 rue Clemenceau (tel. 03 25 02 01 13), a bar and *brasserie* just behind the town hall. The crowd is friendly, the kitchen dishes out delectable local specialities, and the gleaming chrome and marble *art nouveau* interior are *très* elegant. (Open daily 11am-11pm.) Mediaphiles will find their ultimate playground at **Les Silos** (tel. 03 25 03 86 86), a former agricultural co-op that now houses a graphic design studio, *mediathèque*, and exhibition space. Visitors can partake of the extensive facilities, including books, newspapers, CD-ROMs, CDs, and videos, for free. (Open Tu and Th-F 2-7pm, W and Sa 10am-6pm. Su 2-6pm, exhibition space only.)

LANGRES

Tiny Langres (pop. 10,000) rises high on a plateau where Champagne, Burgundy, and Franche-Comté meet amidst fields of wheat. Long ago deemed a crucial strategic site by Gauls and Romans, Langres assured itself lasting esteem with the birth of Enlightenment philosopher Denis Diderot in 1713; and a statue of the eminent Encyclopedist smirks at passersby from the Place Diderot in the center of town. After only a few minutes within its 2000-year-old walls, it is easy to see why Langres has been named one of the 50 prettiest towns in France; the well-preserved houses of the *vieille ville* exude Renaissance charm, and spectacular views are never more than a few steps away.

🛈 **ORIENTATION AND PRACTICAL INFORMATION.** Langres sits 3km away—and 0.5km up—from its *gare*. **Trains** roll west to **Paris** (3hr., 3 per day, 180F) and **Troyes** (1¼hr., 3 per day, 97F), and north to **Reims** (2½hr., 4 per day, 188F). **Local buses** (5.75F) run frequently between the station and the town center, so there's no need to make the sweaty hike. The impatient can call a taxi (tel. 03 25 87 41 31), while the brave can **rent bikes** from **Diderot Cycles et Loisirs**, 67 rue Diderot. (Tel. 03

25 87 06 98. Open Tu-Sa 8:30am-noon and 2-7pm.) The **tourist office** (tel. 03 25 87 67 67) stands across from the bus stop in the *centre ville*. The helpful staff provides a 2F regional guide and reserves rooms for 5F. (Office open July-Aug. M-Sa 9am-12:30pm and 1:30-7pm, Su 10:30am-12:30pm and 2-6pm; May-June and Sept. M-Sa 9:30am-12:30pm and 2-6:30pm.) Numerous **tours** are also organized by the tourist office. (Daily July-Aug. at 3pm; May-June and Sept. Su only. 2hr., 35F, students 20F, under 12 free. Audio guide 20F.) Alternatively, rumble along the ramparts for an hour on the *petit train touristique* (July-Aug. 5 departures daily from 2-6pm; May-June and Sept. 3 departures W and Sa-Su afternoons. Tickets 28F for adults, 20F for children.) Sleuth out the **police** at the Hôtel de Ville (tel. 03 25 87 00 40). Medical care awaits at the **Centre Hospitalier**, 10 rue de la Charité (tel. 03 25 87 88 88). On Mondays the only **currency exchange** options are the tourist office and the **post office,** rue Général Leclerc. (Tel. 03 25 84 33 30. Open M-F 8am-noon and 1:30-6pm, Sa 8am-noon. **Postal code:** 52200.

ℱ ACCOMMODATIONS AND CAMPING. Set right outside the Porte des Moulins by the tourist office, the **Foyer des Jeunes Travailleurs (HI)**, pl. Bel Air (tel. 03 25 87 09 69), offers pleasant, modern dorm rooms with outstanding views, kitchen access, and an adjoining cafeteria. (Singles 70F; doubles 100F. Discount after 4 nights. Breakfast 16.50F. Sheets 16F. Cash only. Reception M-F 9am-12:30pm and 2-7pm, Sa 10:30am-noon. Cafeteria open 9am-noon and 7-9:30pm; *plats* 25-30F.) If the hostel is full, try the **Auberge Jeanne d'Arc**, 26 rue Gambetta (tel. 03 25 87 03 18), on pl. Jenson across from the Église St-Martin. Tiny stairways lead to countrified bedrooms decorated in a blue and white theme. All rooms have a bathroom and telephone. (Singles 130-170F, doubles 170-220F, quad 230F. Breakfast 30F. Reception 7am-10pm. V.) **Camping Navarre** (tel. 03 25 88 14 93) occupies a prime hilltop space on the edge of the old town, with fabulous views over the ramparts. (11F, 7F under 7, 23F per place and car. Electricity 18F. Reception 8-10am, 4-8pm. Gates closed 10pm-6:30am.)

⎙ FOOD. Langres' proud contribution to French cuisine is its eponymous cheese, a mild, soft variety whose round orange casing recalls the celebrated ramparts. Pick up a wheel at the **market** at pl. Bel Air on Friday morning. Restaurants, like everything else in town, gravitate towards **rue Diderot. Le Moulin de la Galette,** 19 rue Jean Roussat (tel. 03 25 84 76 67), whips up sumptuous *crêpes* which can be enjoyed on the terrace as you watch the languid world of Langres pass by. (Open Tu-Su noon-2pm and 7-10pm.) Standard **supermarket** fare can be found in the town center at **Coccinelle**, pl. Jenson. (Open M-Sa 9am-12:15pm and 2-7pm; July-Aug. also Su 9am-noon.) Look for cheaper generic goods just outside at **Aldi**, rue des Chavannes. (Open M-F 9am-12:15pm and 2-7pm, Sa 9am-7pm.)

◉ SIGHTS. A stroll along the beautiful ramparts of Langres offers a panorama of the surrounding countryside, with azure lakes, red-roofed farmhouses, and gentle hills frosted dark green with trees. A complete circuit can begin nearly anywhere, but you may as well start with the first century AD **Porte Gallo-Romane,** the oldest of the seven gates which pierce the fortifications. Farther on clockwise stands the **Tour du Petit Sault,** which claims an unobstructed vantage point over the Marne Valley and the wooded Montagne Langroise. Continuing on, you can see the remains of the **Old Cog Railway,** the first mechanical contraption devised by the Langrois to link their town to the valley below. The view from **pl. de la Crémaillère** overlooks farmland and the glittering **réservoir de la Liez,** a nearby lake offering swimming, boating, and camping. A few steps ahead lies the **Table d'Orientation,** a 19th-century panel which identifies visible landmarks and the direction to Moscow and Constantinople. Several meters farther, the zippy glass **Panoramics,** a 20th-century answer to the cog railway, whisks visitors and locals down to the parking lot and the road below. The most famous of the towers is the squat **Tour de Navarre,** on the southwest corner of town. Opened in 1521 by François I, its 7m thick walls and spiral ramp for moving artillery recall its effectiveness as a defensive outpost. (Tower open May-June and Sept. weekends from 2:30-5:30pm; July-Aug. daily 10am-12:30pm and 2:30-7pm. Adults 10F, children and students 8F.) If a daytime promenade along the ramparts fails to sufficiently conjure up the past, visitors can join the **Ronde des Hallebardiers** in the evening. This costumed recreation of the night watchmen's patrol transports you back to more turbulent times. (Every Friday and Saturday in August; begins at Cathedral cloister at 9:15 pm.)

The best view in town is not from the ramparts but from the south tower of the **Cathédrale Mammès,** which dominates the center of town. Built between 1150 and 1196, the cathedral is an impressive combination of the Burgundian-Romanesque and Gothic styles. St-Mammès, a 3rd-century wonder-child, spread the gospel until he was stoned to death by local officials. (Cathedral open daily 8am-7pm. Free. Tower and treasury open July-Aug. W-M 2:30-6pm. Admission to both 10F, students 8F.) Down the road sits Langres' modern **Musée d'art et d'histoire,** pl. du Centaire (tel. 03 25 87 08 05). Displays include Egyptian artifacts and an extensive Roman collection featuring a geometric mosaic salvaged from a villa. (Open W-M 10am-noon and 2-6pm, may close in winter. Admission 20.50F, students 10.50F.) Around the corner, the **Maison Renaissance,** 20 rue Cardinal Morlot, is a beautifully preserved mansion dating from the mid-16th century. Pass through the corridor to the garden to admire the remarkable facade, featuring Ionic and Corinthian pillars topped by an elaborate frieze. (Corridor open daily 9am-6pm; free.)

FLANDERS AND THE PAS DE CALAIS

Even after five decades of peace, the memory of two World Wars is never far from the inhabitants of northern France. The world's battlefronts have moved across the region four times in this century alone. Nearly every town bears scars from merciless bombing in World War II, and German-built concrete observation towers still peer over the dunes. Regiments of tombstones stand as reminders of the terrible toll exacted at Arras, Cambrai, and the Somme.

Flanders, on the Belgian border, the coastal Pas de Calais, and Picardy farther inland remain the final frontier of tourist-free France. Although thousands traveling to and from Britain pass through Calais, Boulogne, and Dunkerque every day, surprisingly few take the time to explore the ancient towns between the ports and Paris. This is perhaps fortunate, as it has left the countryside unspoiled by commercial traffic and the natives welcoming to travelers. Chalk cliffs loom over the beaches along the rugged coast, and cultivation gives way to cows and sheep grazing near collapsed bunkers and coils of rusty barbed wire. Once part of an independent state, the wooden windmills and gabled houses still reflect its Flemish architectural influence. In Picardy, tranquil seas of wheat extend in all directions, while the eruption of red poppies from every yard and roadside signals the coming of summer. Many towns have earned an unfair reputation as soot-heaps to be avoided if at all possible. As you flee the ferry ports, don't overlook the hidden treasures: the cathedrals of Amiens and Laon, the intriguing Flemish culture of Arras, the world-class art collections of Lille, and the historic rural charm of small towns like Montreuil-sur-Mer, whose imposing ramparts smile upon an undulating green valley. In the 19th century, the looms and coal mines of the North transformed the region into the industrial heartland of France.

Sample the local specialties: *moules* (mussels swathed in an astounding variety of sauces) and beer along the coast and in Flanders; and in Picardy, *pâté de canard* (duck pâté), *flamiche aux poireaux* (a creamy quiche-like tart with leeks), and *ficelle Picarde* (a cheese, ham, and mushroom crêpe).

THE NORTHEAST

HIGHLIGHTS OF FLANDERS AND THE PAS DE CALAIS

■ **Lille** is an all-around wonder town, with a beautiful *vieille ville* and fantastic museums (p. 442).
■ Walk around the ramparts of **Montreuil-sur-Mer,** where the hostel is part of the old royal citadel (p. 458).
■ The **Vimy Memorial** marks the sacrifice of over 60,000 Canadian soldiers in World War I (p. 450).
■ The Gothic **Cathédrale de Notre-Dame** in Amiens (p. 461) is twice the size of that other Notre-Dame in Paris.

GETTING AROUND

A logical base for a visit to the North is **Lille,** the capital of the region and a major transportation hub. Getting to smaller towns often involves changing trains in **Amiens.** Ferries usually dock in **Calais,** where no one wants to linger; **Boulogne** is a far more pleasant port of arrival. The **Channel Tunnel** connects France to Britain at Calais and provides a viable alternative to ferries (for more Chunnel info, see **Getting There: By Channel Tunnel,** p. 63). The countryside is flat enough to allow bicycling, but towns are far apart. Consult local tourist offices for maps and routes.

LILLE

Founded in the 11th century as a transit station for boats passing down the Deûle, Lille (pop. 175,000) is no longer an island, but remains an international hub just across from Brussels. In 1363, the town was presented to Burgundy as dowry when Margaret of Flanders married Philip the Bold. Charles de Gaulle's hometown still retains much of its Flemish flavor, evident in its architecture and in the inhabitants' consumption of mussels and beer. Lille feels virtually tourist-free and is much more inviting than the region's gaudy ports. Whether shopping and strolling on the festive rue Béthune or downing a beer in the intimate *vieille ville,* here you can enjoy big city amenities with li'lle of the big city hassle.

ORIENTATION AND PRACTICAL INFORMATION

Lille is easy to get around and has a metro, but be sure to get a map before tackling *vieille Lille,* a maze of narrow streets running from the tourist office north to the cathedral. The newer part of town, with wide boulevards and 19th-century buildings, culminates in the **Wazemmes market.** Lille has a large shopping district off **pl. du Théâtre.** Cheaper goods lie in the area around the tourist office, around **rue de Béthune.** The areas around the train station and the Marché de Wazemmes may be unsafe at night. A word of caution: the route from M: Gare Lille Flandre to rue Rousseau runs through several seedy streets and is dark and narrow; women should not walk here alone.

Flights: Aéroport de Lille-Lesquin (tel. 03 20 49 68 68). **Cariane Nord** (tel. 03 20 66 26 63) shuttles leave from rue le Corbusier at Gare Lille Flandres (6 per day 9:30am-6:15pm, 30F).

Trains: Lille has two stations. One is **Gare Lille Flandres,** pl. de la Gare. To: **Arras** (40min., 30 per day, 54F); **Paris** (1hr., 20 per day, 199F); and **Brussels** (1½hr., 19 per day, 100F). **Currency exchange.** Information desk open M-Sa 9am-7pm. The other, **Gare Lille Europe,** rue le Corbusier (tel. 03 20 87 30 00), M: Gare Lille Europe, services **Eurostar** (to **London** and **Brussels**) and all TGVs to the South of France. To **Paris** (1hr., 6 per day, 199F). **SOS Voyageurs** (tel. 03 20 31 62 12), on *voie* 9 in Gare Lille Flandres, helps travelers in difficulty. Open summer M-F 9am-6pm, Sa 9am-noon and 3-6pm; in winter M-F 8:30am-7pm, Sa 8:30-11am and 2-5pm.

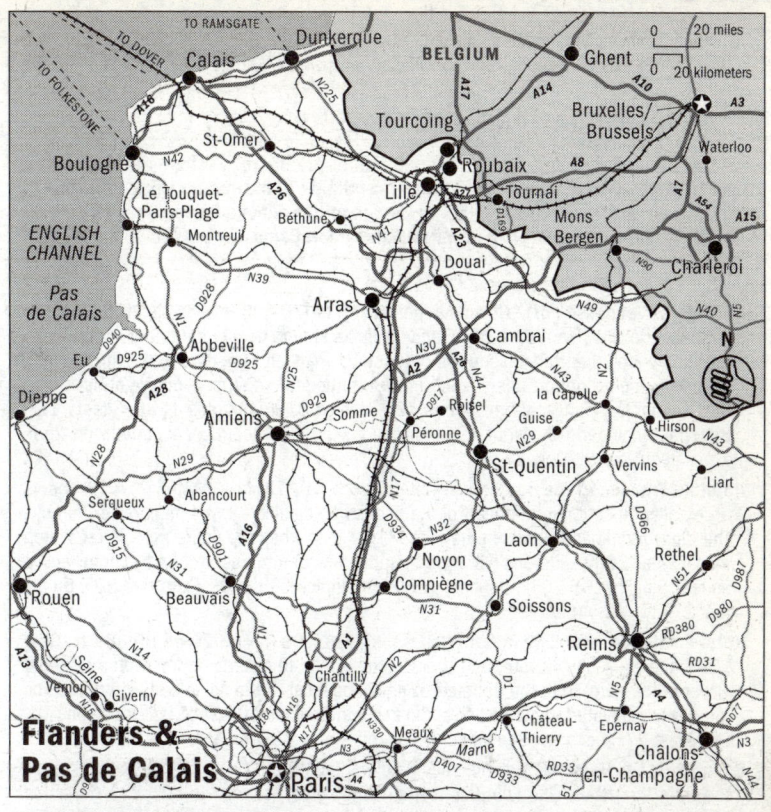

Flanders &
Pas de Calais

Local Transportation: Transpole central bus terminal next to the train station. **Metro (M)** and **trams** serve the town and periphery M-Sa 5:12am-12:12am, Su 6:24am-6:26pm. Tickets 7.50F. Info at the tourist office or the office below Gare Flandres (tel. 03 20 40 40 40). Office open M-F 7am-7pm, Sa 9am-5pm.

Taxis: Taxi Union (tel. 03 20 06 06 06).

Bike Rental: Peugeot Cycles, 64 rue Léon Gambetta (tel. 03 20 54 83 39). 100F per day. Deposit 1120F. Open M 2-7pm, Tu-Sa 9am-noon and 2-7pm.

Tourist Office: Pl. Rihour (tel. 03 20 21 94 21; fax 03 20 21 94 20). M: Rihour. From Gare Lille Flandres, head straight down rue Faidherbe 2 blocks and turn left through pl. du Théâtre and pl. de Gaulle. Beyond pl. de Gaulle, there's a huge monument; behind it is the castle housing the tourist office. Free maps, including an essential mass transit guide. Free accommodations service. Ask about the various guided tours. **Currency exchange.** Open M 1-6pm, Tu-Sa 9:30am-6:30pm, Su 10am-noon and 2-5pm.

Budget Travel: Wasteels, 25 pl. des Reignaux (tel. 03 20 06 24 24). Open M-Th 9am-noon and 2-6pm, F 9am-1pm and 2-6pm, Sa 9am-noon.

English Bookstore: Le Furet du Nord, pl. de la République (tel. 03 20 78 43 43), has an extensive selection on the 8th floor.

Police: 10 rue Ovigneur (tel. 03 20 57 41 22).

Hospital: 2 av. Oscar Lambret (tel. 03 20 44 59 62). M: CHR-Oscar Lambret.

Post Office: 8 pl. de la République (tel. 03 20 12 74 72). M: République. Limited **currency exchange** (U.S., U.K.). Poste Restante code: 59035 Lille Cedex. Open M-F 8am-7pm, Sa 8am-noon. **Branch** on bd. Carnot, near pl. du Théâtre. Open M-F 8am-6:30pm and Sa 8am-noon. **Postal code:** 59000.

Internet Access: NetPlayer Games, 25 bd. Carnot (tel. 03 20 31 20 29), 35F first 30min, 30F each additional 30min. Official hours M-Sa 10am-1am.

▶ ACCOMMODATIONS AND CAMPING

Lille has recently opened a new HI hostel in an old hospital, close to the heart of town. University-run singles (41F) may be available in the summer from **CROUS,** 74 rue de Cambrai (tel. 03 20 88 66 00), in the distant **Résidence Hélène Boucher** (tel. 03 20 43 43 77; M: Cité Scientific) and **Résidence Henri Camus** (tel. 03 20 43 44 61; M: 4 Cantons).

Auberge de Jeunesse (HI), 12 rue Malpart (tel. 03 20 57 08 94; fax 03 20 63 98 93), M: Mairie de Lille. From Gare Lille Flandres, circle around the station to the left and take rue du Molinel, then the second left onto rue de Paris and the third right onto rue Malpart. A welcome option despite the lingering hospital smell and dim lighting. Co-ed bathrooms. No lounge. 6-bed dorms 73F; singles 113F; doubles 123F. Sheets 18F. Breakfast included. Checkout 10:30am, curfew 2am. Reception 7am-noon and 2pm-1am. Open Jan. 31-Dec. 17.

Hôtel de France, 10 rue de Béthune (tel. 03 20 57 14 78; fax 03 20 57 14 78), offers an excellent location in the heart of the pedestrian district, but not much else—for now. The dingy rooms and antique plumbing will be gone when the entire hotel is renovated for the year 2000; add-ons will include spiffy new bathrooms, a laundry room, and a sauna! Singles 135-205F; doubles 155-265F; triples 285-370F. Extra bed 30F. Breakfast 27F. V, MC, AmEx.

Hôtel Faidherbe, 42 pl. de la Gare (tel. 03 20 06 27 93; fax 03 20 55 95 38). M: Gare Lille Flandres. A tiny elevator and spackled halls lead to cheerful rooms with a splendid view of...the *gare*. Still, the double-glazing keeps most of the noise out, and the rooms are newly renovated, most with TVs. Singles and doubles 160-240F. Extra person 50F. Breakfast 27F. *Let's Go* readers get a 10% discount. 24hr. reception. V, MC.

Campsites: Les Ramiers, 1 chemin des Ramiers (tel. 03 20 23 13 42), in Bondues. Take the tram from Gare Lille Flandres to Tourcoing center; change to bus #23 (direction "Bondues Église") to "Bondues centre," then follow rue César Loridan 1km. 14F per site, 10F per person, 5F per car. Showers, electricity, volleyball. Open mid-Apr.-Nov.

▶ FOOD

Decently priced restaurants and cafés pepper the fashionable pedestrian area around rue de Béthune, a neighborhood also filled with *pâtisseries*, *boulangeries*, pizzerias, and ice-cream stands. Lille is known for *maroilles* cheese, *genièvre* (juniper berry liqueur) and, this being Flanders, mussels—though the sea is nowhere in sight. Dusty **rue Léon Gambetta** is a paradise for picnic-seekers, culminating in the enormous **Marché de Wazemmes,** pl. de la Nouvelle Aventure. Here you'll find **markets** both indoors (M-Th 7am-1pm, and F-Sa 7am-8pm, Su 7am-3pm) and outdoors (Su, Tu, and Th 7am-2pm). **EuraLille,** the big, black shopping center next to the train station, has an enormous **Carrefour supermarket** with everything from Tintin towels to *camembert.* (Open M-Sa 9am-10pm.) **Match,** on the intersection of rue Masséna and rue Solférino (open M-Sa 9am-9pm), and **Monoprix,** on rue du Molinel near Gare Lille Flandres (open M-Sa 8:30am-8pm), are further testaments to the glories of air-conditioned grocery shopping.

Aux Moules, 34 rue de Béthune (tel. 03 20 57 12 46; fax 03 20 12 90 92). This popular restaurant accumulates the city's largest pile of mussel shells by the day's end. Do your part with the *plat du jour* (45-65F) or speed through the lunchtime *formule TGV-midi* (69F). Open daily noon-midnight. V, MC, AmEx.

Les 3 Brasseurs, 22 pl. de la Gare (tel. 03 20 06 46 25). Another branch of the microbrewery micro-chain. Try all four home-brews for 28F. There is also a selection of *menus*

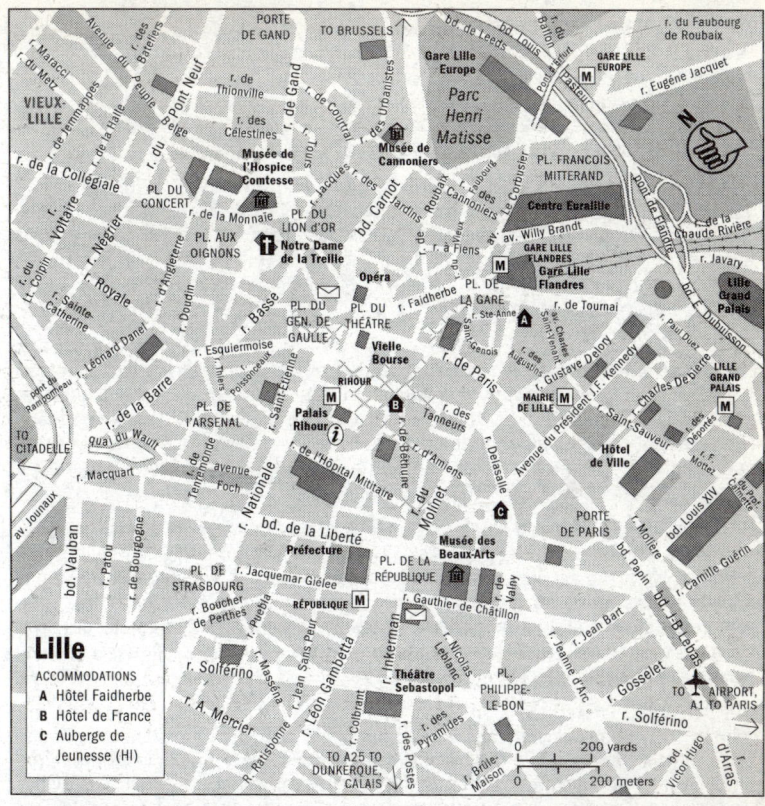

(67-69F) and a wide variety of *tartes flambées*, a nod to the restaurants' Alsatian origins. Open daily 11am-midnight.

■ **Le Maharajah,** 4 rue du Sec Arembault (tel. 03 20 57 67 77), in the pedestrian district. Dim, serene Indian restaurant specializing in tantalizing vegetarian plates (51-55F). An extensive selection of meats are served as well; meditate over your meal while listening to the soft sitar music. Open M-Sa noon-2pm and 7-10:30pm. V, MC.

■ SIGHTS

Lille's main draws are threefold: a number of high-quality museums, several fascinating old churches, and a variety of architectural marvels that invite you to just sit back and stare.

MUSÉE DES BEAUX-ARTS. Housed in a pretty 19th-century mansion, and surrounded by lovely gardens, the museum holds one of the most respected collections in France, including an encyclopædic display of 15th-20th century French and Flemish masters. Other highlights include ceramics from the 17th-18th centuries and a particularly renowned collection of Dutch paintings. *(Pl. de la République. M: République. Tel. 03 20 06 78 00; for tours tel. 03 20 06 78 17. Open M 2-6pm, W-Th and Sa-Su 10am-6pm, F 10am-7pm. 30F, students 20F.)*

MUSÉE D'ART MODERNE. In the suburb of Villeneuve d'Ascq, this houses an impressive collection of Cubist and Postmodernists art, including works by Braque, Picasso, Léger, Miró, and Modigliani. *(1 allée du Musée. Take bus #10 or 41 to "Parc Urbain-Musée." Tel. 03 20 19 68 68. Open W-M 10am-6pm; guided visits Sa 3pm and Su 4pm 15F. 25F, students 15F.)*

MUSÉE DE L'HOSPICE COMTESSE. Founded in 1237, the museum was used as a hospital from the 1400s to 1797. Now it displays antique furniture and art, but is most noted for the 17th-century tile work on its walls. The back building houses an exhibit on musical instruments with violins of all sizes and a clarinet in the shape of a snake. (*32 rue de la Monnaie, near Cathédrale Notre-Dame de la Treille. Tel. 03 20 49 50 90. Open W-M 10am-12:30pm and 2-6pm. 15F, children and students 5F.*)

CHARLES DE GAULLE'S BIRTHPLACE. *Vive la France! Vive la République!* Hard-core *Gaullistes* should jump at this chance to browse through a vast collection of photographs and newspaper clippings. Also featured are the General's car and the robe in which the leader of the Free French and two-time French president was baptized. (*9 rue Princesse, on the northern edge of the vieille ville. Tel. 03 20 31 96 03. Keep following rue de la Monnaie up away from town center. Open W-Su 10am-noon and 2-5pm. 15F, children 7F.*)

ÉGLISE ST-MAURICE. Ensconced in the heart of the pedestrian district and just steps from the *gare*, this church was begun in the 14th century but not finished until the 19th. A shrine to St. Maurice has stood on this spot at least since 1066. The forest of pillars inside, holding up the five naves, are characteristic of the "hallerkerque" (Flemish for "market church"), a type of church common in Flanders. (*Rue de Paris. M: Rihour. Open M-Sa 9am-6pm, Su 2-6pm, except during mass.*)

VIEILLE BOURSE. The old stock exchange is of particular architectural interest, epitomizing the Flemish Renaissance. The garland-like mouldings encircling the building give it the appearance of an elaborate, oversized wedding cake. Its four sides border a courtyard that once served as France's only stock exchange, and now house flower and book markets. (*Pl. du Général de Gaulle between rue des Sept Acaches and rue Manneliers.*) Nearby stands another masterpiece: the **Chamber of Commerce and Industry** and its tower on pl. du Théâtre.

THE CITADEL. This fortress on the city's north side was resculpted in the 17th century to Vauban's specifications. The impressive fortifications illustrate Louis XIV's military architect at the height of his considerable powers. To tour this active army base, sign up at the tourist office. (*In French, May-Aug. Su 3-5pm, 45F.*) Otherwise, settle for a view from the **Jardin Vauban** across the street.

🎵 🎆 ENTERTAINMENT AND FESTIVALS

ENTERTAINMENT. Party-hunters head to two distinct areas. Around les Halles Centrales, pubs line **rue Solférino** and **rue Masséna.** For billiards, VH-1 pop-ups, and 10F beer, head to **Gino Billiard.** (Tel. 03 20 54 45 55. Open noon-2am.) The crowd spills over next door at **Father Moustache.** On the other side of town, **L'Angle-Saxo,** 36 rue d'Angleterre (tel. 03 20 51 88 89), is a jazz bar with a lounge and fiery 45F drinks. (Open 9pm-2am.) **L'Illustration,** 18 rue Royale (tel. 03 20 12 00 90), serves up martinis (35F) by candlelight to a stylish crowd. (M-Sa noon-2am, Su 7pm-2am.)

FESTIVALS. Lille has a plethora of parties planned to ring in the millennium. **New Year's Eve** is set to kick off with the inauguration of the new belfry, followed by a street party that will last until dawn and a fireworks display on the evening of January 1. For more sedate entertainment, the last week in April plays host to the **Marché aux Fleurs,** carpeting the center of town with flowers. In mid-June Lille will welcome the **Train des Écrivains,** 90 writers from 45 European countries who are riding the rails from Bilbao to Berlin to meet and talk with readers.

DOUAI

Douai is an energetic, modern town with a lovely 18th-century face. As the seat of the Flemish parliament from 1713 to the French Revolution, Douai (metropolitan pop. 200,000) acquired streets filled with elegant mansions and government buildings that miraculously bear few scars of the onslaught suffered during both World Wars. The town's grace and beauty made it a muse for French authors from Balzac to Hugo. Today Douai remains attractive despite its industrial surrounds in the heart of mining country. A few remarkable monuments and a prominent place on the train line between Paris and the North make the town a worthwhile stop.

🔽 ORIENTATION AND PRACTICAL INFORMATION. Douai is divided by the River Scarpe; the liveliest shopping streets and the tourist office lie on one side, with the museum on the other. Trains speed to **Arras** (15min., 15-19 a day, 33F), **Lille** (30min., 6 per day, 46F), and **Paris** (1hr., 12 per day, 106F). Turn left from the *gare* and then right at the Porte de Valenciennes to reach **place d'Armes,** the center of town and home to the **tourist office,** 70 pl. d'Armes (tel. 03 27 88 26 79; fax 03 27 99 38 78). The staff can give you a map marking major sights, a list of hotels and restaurants, and a guided tour of the Hôtel de Ville (11F). (Open July-Aug. daily 9am-noon and 2-7pm; Sept-June closed Su.) **Local transport** is provided by **TUB.** (Tel. 03 27 95 77 77. Tickets 6.10F, *carnet* of 10 51F.) For **taxis,** tel. 03 27 88 85 31. Medical care is disbursed at the **Centre Hospitalier,** rte. de Cambrai (tel. 03 27 99 61 61). The **post office** is hidden on pl. Général de Gaulle (tel. 03 27 93 55 20), behind pl. d'Armes. (**Postal code:** 59500.)

🔽🔽 ACCOMMODATIONS AND FOOD. True budgeteers may want to daytrip in from the hostels in Arras or Lille. **Le Djurdjura,** 370 pl. du Bartlet (tel. 03 27 88 74 65), is just down the road from the pl. d'Armes. The restaurant downstairs serves up North African specialities from noon-3pm and 7:30-11pm, but the most exotic thing about the *chambres* is that there's no separation between the bathroom and the room. (Singles 190F, doubles 210F, triples 230F. Reception open 8am-midnight. V, MC.) **Le Carnot,** 47 pl. Carnot (tel. 03 27 87 39 41), overlooks the lively but slightly run-down pl. Carnot. Prices in town don't get lower than this, and rooms don't get any more basic, either. Still, the decor is pleasant and the cosy café downstairs is always buzzing. (Singles 110F, doubles with shower 150F. Breakfast 22F. Reception open M-Sa 7:30am-11pm.)

Cheap cafés line the **pl. d'Armes** and **pl. Carnot;** *boulangeries* and the like can be found on **rue de Bellain,** which links the two. **La Crêperie,** 1 pl. du Général de Gaulle (tel. 03 27 88 92 08), flips *crêpes* and *galettes* (from 12F) before your eyes, to be devoured on the packed terrace or in the wood-panelled dining room. Huge salads (42-45F) are also available. (Open daily from 11am, closed Su afternoons.) For a pizza, visit **La Fata Morgana,** 68 rue des Ferronniers (tel. 03 27 88 60 95), off rue de Bellain. Pizzas fresh from the wood-fired oven and pastas (31-69F) await. (Open daily noon-2pm and 7:30-10pm; June-Aug. closed Su.)

🔽🔽 SIGHTS AND FESTIVALS. The star attraction is the fantastic, Flamboyant Gothic **Hôtel de Ville,** just up the road from the pl. d'Armes. Popularized by Victor Hugo, who passed through Douai in 1837, its belfry rises to a height of 64m and is crowned with a delightfully gaudy assortment of tourelles and spires. Started in the 14th century, today it holds 62 bells, the largest collection in Europe. Every quarter hour the bells play a few notes of a tune, and there are concerts every Monday in July and August at 8:45pm. (Guided tours offered daily July-Aug. 10am-5pm; Sept.-June M-Sa 2-5pm, Su 10am-5pm.) Following rue Gambetta to the right of the Hôtel de Ville leads to the **Église St-Pierre.** From the outside, this gives the curious impression of being two churches melded together, its 16th-century Gothic façade joined with a red-brick addition built in 1903. On the other side of the river, the **Musée de la Chartreuse,** 130 rue de la Chartreuse (tel. 03 27 71 38 80), inhabits an ancient monastery. The collections of painting and sculpture includes 16th-century Flemish altarpieces, an exceptional array of 17th-century northern masters, and bronzes by Rodin. Skip the archæology museum around the corner. (Open M and W-Sa 10am-noon and 2-5pm, Su 10am-noon and 3-6pm. 12F, students 6F.)

Douai is at its most festive during the **Fête des Géants,** a tradition that began in 1479 with a procession through the streets to celebrate a Flemish victory over France. The first giant, constructed by basket makers, joined the procession in 1530, and the next year a wife was made to accompany him. Today Gayant (the Picardy form of the word *géant*) and his wife Marie Cagenon parade through the streets for three days along with their giant children. (Su-Tu before Bastille Day; call tourist office for info.)

ARRAS

Although historians say that the name "Arras" derives from the hanging tapestries produced here in the 16th century, locals maintain that the name honors a band of rats that stalked the unfortunate city in the Middle Ages. Every year on Whit Sunday, the Fête des Rats pays homage to the rodents. In 1758, Arras (pop. 80,000) gave birth to the biggest rat of the Revolution—Robespierre, architect of the Terror that took thousands to the guillotine. Rows of gabled townhouses, Flemish arcades, and the lilting melody of the belfry bells linger as a reminder of Arras's vibrant past. Used as a base for the British and Commonwealth soldiers who manned nearby trenches in World War I, Arras today welcomes their children, grandchildren, and great-grandchildren who come to retrace their footsteps.

🛈 **ORIENTATION AND PRACTICAL INFORMATION. Trains** leave pl. Maréchal Foch for **Lille** (45min., 25 per day, 54F), **Paris** (50min., 12 per day, 168F), **Amiens** (1hr., 10 per day, 69F), **Dunkerque** (1¼-1½hr., 19 per day, 87-102F), and **Lyon** (3hr., 2 per day, 420F). (Info desk open M-F 8am-7pm, Sa 8am-6pm. Ticket counters open M-F 6am-8:30pm, Sa-Su 8:30am-7:30pm.) To get to the **bus station** (tel. 03 21 51 34 64) from the train station, turn left onto rue du Dr. Brassart. After crossing the bridge, turn right; it will be on your left, via the red pedestrian overpass. (Open summer M-F 8am-noon and 4-8:30pm, Sa 10am-1pm; winter M-F 7am-7pm, Sa 7am-1pm.) **Local transportation** is operated by **STCRA.** (Tel. 03 21 58 08 58. Tickets 6.20F.) **Arras Taxi** (tel. 03 21 23 69 69) awaits travelers at the station 24 hours.

To get to the **tourist office,** pl. des Héros (tel. 03 21 51 26 95; fax 03 21 71 07 34), from the station, walk straight across pl. Foch, past the fountain, and onto rue Gambetta. Turn right onto rue Ronville (opposite the post office) to reach the cobbled **Petit'Place,** one of Arras's two main squares. Continue past the Église St-Jean-Baptiste and turn left onto rue de la Housse by the church. The office is across pl. des Héros, inside the Hôtel de Ville. The town's other main square, **Grand'Place,** is on the other side of pl. des Héros. In the office, the bilingual staff offers reservations service and a free map. (Office open Oct. 5-Apr. 25 M-Sa 9am-noon and 2-6pm, Su 10am-12:30pm and 3-6:30pm; Apr. 26-Oct. 3 M-Sa 9am-6:30pm, Su 10am-1pm and 4:30-6:30pm.) **Crédit Agricole,** 9 Grand'Place (tel. 03 21 50 41 80), **exchanges currency.** (Open Tu-F 9am-12:30pm and 2-6pm, Sa 9:15am-12:45pm and 2-4pm.) **Laundry** spins at **Superlav,** pl. Ipswich, next to the Église St-Jean-Baptiste. (Open daily 7am-8pm.) The **police station** is at 18 bd. de la Liberté (tel. 03 21 24 50 17), and there is a **hospital** at 57 av. Winston Churchill (tel. 03 21 24 40 00). The **post office,** 13 rue Gambetta (tel. 03 21 22 94 94), has **currency exchange.** (Open M-F 8am-6:30pm, Sa 8am-noon. **Postal code:** 62000.)

🛏 **ACCOMMODATIONS AND CAMPING.** Arras has precious few budget hotels. During high season, it's wise to reserve in advance at the central **Auberge de Jeunesse (HI),** 59 Grand' Place (tel. 03 21 22 70 02; fax 03 21 07 46 15), which occupies one of the Flemish townhouses on Grand'Place. Despite the spartan quarters (stripped-down rooms with 2-7 beds and no locks), this is quite a friendly place—and the price and location are unbelievable. (48F. Sheets 17F. Breakfast 19F. Strict lockout 10am-5pm. Curfew 11pm. Reception 7:30-noon and 5-11pm. Open Feb.-Nov. **Members only.**) No room at the hostel? Try the ostel; to be specific ⌂ **Ostel des Trois Luppars,** 47 Grand'Place (tel. 03 21 07 41 41; fax 03 21 24 24 80). Here, tidy, adorable rooms with wood-beamed ceilings and modern decor welcome guests in a 15th-century building. Steam for free in the sauna! Phones, showers, toilet, and TV in every room. (Singles from 190F; doubles 260-270F; triples and quads 350F. Breakfast 30F. Reception 5:30am-1am. V, MC, AmEx.) Everything will be OK at the **OK Pub et Hôtel,** 8 pl. de la Vacquerie (tel. 03 21 21 30 60; fax 03 21 21 30 61), behind the Hôtel de Ville. Not as classy as the Ostel, but drawing a younger crowd, here you'll find serviceable, though occasionally tiny, rooms with TV and telephone. Downstairs is a *brasserie* with a large games room and a garden terrace. (Singles 140F; doubles from 180F. Breakfast 33F. V, MC, AmEx.) To carry on **camping,** head to 138 rue du Temple (tel. 03 21 71 55 06), at av. Fernand Lobbedez. From the station, turn left onto rue du Dr. Brassart, then left on av. du Maréchal Leclerc. Cross the bridge; rue du Temple is the sixth street on the left (10min.). (15F per person, 8F per site, 8F per car. Electricity 15.30F. Reception 7am-10pm. Open Apr.-Sept.)

◘ **FOOD.** Inexpensive cafés skirt **pl. des Héros** and the pedestrian area; more elegant restaurants adorn the **Grand'Place.** Fence with a delicious meal at ▨ **La Rapière,** 44 Grand'Place (tel. 03 21 55 09 92; fax 03 21 22 24 29), which serves up high quality food at eminently reasonable prices in its posh dining room. Try the 88F 3-course *menu;* the chicken cooked in beer is a delectable local speciality. (Open daily 9am-3:30pm and 6:30-11pm. V, MC, AmEx.) The **Restaurant aux Grandes Arcades,** 8-12 Grand'Place (tel. 03 21 23 30 89; fax 03 21 71 50 94), serves cheap *brasserie* fare as well as gourmet 120-160F menus, on a huge floral terrace with a Grand'Place view. (Open 7am-10pm. V, MC, AmEx.) *Les Best Ribs in Town*—and probably the only ribs in town—cost 60F at **Le Saint-Germain,** 14 Grand'Place (tel. 03 21 51 45 45; fax 03 21 71 35 58), where France and America shake greasy hands. *Crème brûlée* costs 29F, but gumballs are free. (Open daily noon-12:30am. V, MC, AmEx.) The pedestrian shopping area between the post office and the Hôtel de Ville bustles with *boulangeries* and other specialty shops, plus a huge **Monoprix supermarket** on rue Gambetta across from the post office. (Open M-Sa 8:30am-8pm.) The pl. des Héros erupts into vibrant color during Arras's boisterous open-air **market.** (W and Sa 8am-1pm.)

◙ **SIGHTS.** Arras's two great squares are both framed by rows of nearly identical houses. **Grand'Place's** Flemish homogeneity is ruffled by the lone Gothic housefront (the Ostel des Trois Luppars), which dates from 1430. Although barbed wire divided the square down the middle during World War I when the French and Germans occupied opposite sides, it shows few battle scars. A block away, boutiques, bars, and cafés line the smaller, sootier, livelier **pl. des Héros.**

The current **Hôtel de Ville** is a faithful copy of the 15th-century original that reigned over pl. des Héros from the 15th century until its destruction in 1914. You can peep into the municipal chamber, the reception room, and the marriage chamber. A short elevator ride and vertiginous stairs lead you to the all-seeing, 75m-tall **belfry.** (14F, students 8F.) Underneath the town hall, the underground tunnels of **Les Boves** are an eerie subterranean maze first bored into the soft chalk as early as the 10th century. The tunnels last saw use as a clearing hospital for the British in WWI. The tourist office leads tours daily. (20F. Call 03 21 51 26 95 for info.)

A few blocks behind the Hôtel de Ville lies the well-named **Abbaye St-Vaast.** Founded in 667 AD on the hill where St. Vaast used to pray, the current gigantic structure dates from the 18th century. The abbey's 19th-century **church** combines a neo-classical style with a traditional Gothic floor plan. The plain white walls and massive columns shelter a stunning pipe organ. (Open daily 2:15-6:30pm; closed 6pm in winter.) Also in the abbey, the sophisticated **Musée des Beaux-Arts,** 22 rue Paul Doumer (tel. 03 21 71 26 43), displays a collection of medieval sculpture and tapestry, including fascinating funeral monuments. Look for the gruesome skeletal sculpture of Guillaume le Franchois with worm-infested entrails, and galleries of 17th-century French paintings. (Open Apr.-Sept. M,W, and F 10am-noon and 2-6pm, Th 10am-5pm, Sa 10am-noon and 2-6pm, Su 10am-noon and 3-6pm; Oct.-Mar. closes at 5 M and W-F. Closed Tu. 20F, students 10F.)

🖪 **ENTERTAINMENT. Pl. des Héros, Grand'Place,** and the surrounding pedestrian roads are where the evening action is; the area is peppered with fairly indistinguishable bars and cafés sure to wet your whistle. **Le Couleur Café,** 35 pl. des Héros (tel. 03 21 71 08 70), is crowded with the college set into the wee hours. Arras is at its most cosmopolitan at the **Noroit,** 6-9 rue des Capuchins (tel. 03 21 71 30 12), which plays international art-house films, and hosts concerts and plays several times a month.

WORLD WAR 1 MEMORIALS AND BATTLEFIELDS

The green countryside around Arras, which saw heavy fighting during WWI, is dotted with more than 20 war cemeteries and countless unmarked graves. Many cemeteries are accompanied by memorials, but they're tricky to reach without a car. For a comprehensive list, consult the Arras tourist office (tel. 03 21 51 26 95).

THE VIMY MEMORIAL. The Vimy Memorial (tel. 03 21 58 19 34 or 03 21 48 98 97), 12km northeast of Arras along N17, honors the more than 66,000 Canadian soldiers killed during WWI. The memorial itself is a vast limestone monument, consisting of two towering pylons rising from a rectangular base. Sculpted figures surround the edifice; the most poignant is that of a cowled and sorrowing woman carved from a single 30-ton limestone block, which represents Canada mourning her dead. The surrounding park, whose soil was shipped from Canada, is dedicated to the crucial victory at Vimy Ridge of April 1917: the re-capture of Hill 145. The land is morbidly beautiful here; tiny hills and large craters, carved out by shells and underground mines, are now covered in grass and grazed by sheep. Follow the path from the monument back towards the entrance and bear left to explore trenches, both Canadian and German, at times no more than 10m apart. Stay on marked paths, since the land is peppered with undetonated mines. The kiosk near the trenches is the starting point for an underground tour of the crumbling tunnels dug by British and Canadian soldiers to facilitate access to the front. The registration room, the commander's desk, and the little relief maple leaf chiseled in the chalk by an anonymous soldier remain as evocative reminders of the soldiers' daily plight. *(Memorial open daily sunrise to sunset. Free tunnel tours Apr.-Nov. 15 10am-6pm in English and French every 30min. Interpretive center open daily 10am-6pm.)*

The Vimy memorial is located 2-3km from the town of **Vimy.** The easiest, but most expensive, option is to catch a taxi in **Arras** (around 100F); if you get a group together, it won't be much more expensive than public transportation. Otherwise, seven **trains** go daily from **Arras** to Vimy (6:30am-6:30pm, 12F), but only three of them are between 10am and 6pm (only 1 train Su). From the train station, walk to the top of the road and take a right at the T-intersection; you'll find signs on your left which point to a trail that travels through the forest to the memorial. You can also catch one of seven daily **buses** from **Arras** to Vimy (20min., 12F).

NOTRE-DAME-DE-LORETTE. North of Neuville on D937 is the French cemetery, basilica, and museum of **Notre-Dame-de-Lorette** (tel. 03 21 29 30 62). The bodies of 22,970 unknown and 19,000 listed soldiers from the 1914-1915 Battle of Lorette rest here, arranged in eight ossuaries around the central Tour-Lanterne. Maréchal Pétain laid the first stone of the tower in 1921. The museum's first floor displays letters and photos sent by families. **Buses** run from Arras (direction "Lens") to "Souchez/Notre-Dame-de-Lorette" (4 per day, 14F). Notre-Dame-de-Lorette is 250m from the bus station via shortcuts to the left. Avoid the highway; ask locals for the path if you're confused. *(Basilica open daily June-Aug. 8am-7pm; Sept. 8am-6pm; Oct.-Nov. and Mar. 8am-5pm; Dec.-Feb. 9am-4:30pm; Apr.-May 8am-6pm. Museum open daily 9am-8pm. 20F, students 10F.)*

NEUVILLE-ST-VAAST. Farther west along D49, the cemetery at **Neuville-St-Vaast** holds the graves of over 44,000 German soldiers marked by grim black crosses representing 4 soldiers apiece. The Jewish graves, marked by plain headstones, stand out in stark contrast. There is also a large French cemetery and a small British one nearby. The **Musée La Targette,** across from the Monument au Flambeau, displays over 2500 painstakingly collected documents, uniforms, and objects used by soldiers. The exhibits are the property of an individual collector, whose grandfather was a Verdun veteran. Neuville-St-Vaast is accessible by bus from Arras (4 per day, 14F). *(Tel. 03 21 59 17 76. Open daily 9am-8pm. 20F, students 10F.)*

LAON

Viewed from afar, the great cathedral of Laon soars out of the surrounding farmland as on a cloud. Enclosed within ramparts, Laon's ancient *haute ville* looks down with haughty disdain on the sprawling modern *basse ville* below. Residence in the fortified acropolis was once reserved for kings: Laon (pop. 26,000) was the capital of France during the mighty Carolingian Empire of the 9th and 10th centuries. The town gave birth both to Charlemagne's mother and the great folk hero Roland, the Emperor's nephew. The town today has few royal visitors, but the winding cobbled streets of the *haute ville* retain a venerable dignity and charm befitting this former seat of kings.

⚐ ORIENTATION AND PRACTICAL INFORMATION. Laon's *haute ville* is built around one main street, whose name changes from rue du Cloître next to the cathedral and rue de Bourg next to the Hôtel de Ville. **Trains** leave pl. de la Gare (tel. 03 23 79 10 79) for **Reims** (1hr., 8 per day, 49F), **Paris** (1¼hr., 13 per day, 105F), and **Amiens** (1½hr., 7 per day, 86F). (Ticket office open M-F 5:15am-8:30pm, Sa 6am-8:30pm, Su 6:15am-9pm.) The **POMA** car (tel. 03 23 79 07 59) takes a roller-coaster ride every two minutes from the station to the *haute ville* and tourist office and allows a first breathtaking peek at the *ville basse* from above. (July-Aug. M-Sa 7am-8pm, Su 2-6pm; Sept.-June M-Sa only. Tickets 6.40F, round-trip 8.50F, *carnet* of 10 54F.) From the POMA station, cross the parking lot and turn left across pl. Général Leclerc onto rue Sérurier. The **tourist office,** pl. du Parvis (tel. 03 23 20 28 62; fax 03 23 20 68 11), occupies the **Hôtel-Dieu,** a squat 12th-century stone structure that served as France's first hospital. The staff organizes tours of the cathedral (daily 3pm) and the medieval city (Su 10:30am). (Tours 35F, students 20F. Office open July-Aug. M-Sa 9am-1pm and 2-7pm, Su 10am-1pm and 2-7pm; Mar.-June and Sept.-Oct. M-Sa 9am-12:30pm and 2-6:30pm, Su 11am-1pm and 2-5pm; Nov.-Feb. M-Sa 9am-12:30pm and 2-6pm, Su 11am-1pm and 2-5pm.) **Police** keep the peace from 2 bd. de Gras Boncourt (tel. 03 23 78 23 82), and there is a **hospital** at rue Marcellin-Berthelot (tel. 03 23 24 33 33). There is a **post office** (tel. 03 23 21 55 74) next to the station on pl. de la Gare, with **currency exchange.** (Open M-F 8am-7pm, Sa 8am-noon. **Postal code:** 02000.)

⚐ ACCOMMODATIONS AND CAMPING. Les Chevaliers, 3-5 rue Sérurier (tel. 03 23 27 17 50; fax 03 23 23 40 71), has enormous bathrooms and handsome rooms just a block from the cathedral. Breakfast is included, and the cozy *salon de thé* downstairs has a garden terrace. (Singles 150-275F; doubles 180-320F; triples 390F; quads 400F. Extra bed 50F. Reception 6:30am-9pm. V, MC.) The likeable proprietor of **Hôtel Welcome,** 2 av. Carnot (tel. 03 23 23 06 11), in the *ville basse*, lets pleasant rooms with a pink theme and attractive old wooden wardrobes. The three rooms facing the courtyard are more peaceful during the day. (Singles and doubles 130-150F; triples 160F; quads 180F. Reception M-Sa 7:15am-10pm, Su 7:15am-noon. Breakfast 25F. V, MC.) **Camping Municipale,** allée de la Chênaie (tel. 03 23 20 25 56), is a summer option. (14.50F per person, 9F per site, 9F per car. Electricity 16F. Reception 7am-11pm. Open Apr.-Oct.)

⚐ FOOD. Rue Chatelaine, which leads left from pl. Général Leclerc towards the cathedral, is the place to head for *boulangeries* and cheap sandwich shops. **L'Aziza,** 11 rue de la Herse (tel. 03 23 20 44 44), one block from the cathedral, offers

Moroccan couscous dishes (40-90F), fresh mint tea, and a beautiful deep-blue bong. (Open Tu-Sa 10am-2:30pm and 7pm-midnight. V, MC.) Right in front of the cathedral, **Le Parvis,** 3 pl. du Parvis (tel. 03 23 20 27 27), has a great view from the terrace, hosts jazz *soirées*, and lures travelers with a 60F 3-course *menu*. (Open daily 8am-11pm.) The ever-reliable **Monoprix supermarket** lies on rue de Bourg. (Open M-F 8:30am-7pm, Sa 9am-noon and 2-7pm.)

🔂 **SIGHTS.** A maze of narrow, twisting alleys and medieval walls surrounds Laon's airy **Cathédrale de Notre-Dame** (tel. 03 23 25 14 18), one of the earliest and finest examples of Gothic architecture in France. Construction began in 1155 and was completed 80 years later. Only five of the seven original towers survived the Revolution; the oxen carved on them refer to the two that miraculously appeared to bring building materials to the workers on the top of the hill. (Open daily 8am-7pm. Tours July-Aug. Su-F 3pm and 4:30pm, Sa 5pm; Sept.-Nov. and Apr.-June Sa-Su and holidays 3pm. 35F, students 20F.)

The **ramparts** encircling the *haute ville* are excellent for an post-prandial stroll, offering a pretty panorama of the *ville basse* and the surrounding countryside. The lovely, cool **Église St-Martin,** neglected sister of the cathedral, is open weekend afternoons. Two blocks from Notre-Dame on rue Georges Ermant, within a budding grove, sit the tiny **Musée de Laon** (tel. 03 23 20 19 87) and the 13th-century **Chapelle des Templiers.** Note the carved 14th-century "skeleton" of Guillaume de Harcigny, physician to Charles VI, and the two statues of prophets that once supported the cathedral façade. The museum contains a notable collection of Greek and Egyptian antiquities, as well as paintings from medieval times to the 19th century. (Both open Apr.-Sept. W-M 10am-noon and 2-6pm; Oct.-Mar. W-M 10am-noon and 2-5pm. Museum 16F, students 10F. Chapel free.)

🎎 **FESTIVALS.** September 17 to October 8, 2000, will see Laon's acclaimed **Festival de Musique Française** (tel. 03 23 20 87 50). Noted musicians from across the country will be performing a wide-ranging mix of classical and modern pieces. For more music, the town hosts **free concerts** during the summer at various monuments. (mid-July to Aug., Su 5pm.) May 6 and 7 will take you back to Laon's glorious medieval heyday at **Les Euromédievales,** with jousts, falconry, music, street performers, and a taste of medieval food and drink. The last week of March brings the avant-garde to town with the **Festival International du Cinéma Jeune Public,** an international film festival aimed at young audiences.

🔂 **EXCURSIONS.** To the south of Laon, the **Chemin des Dames** winds across the Aisne region, a scenic and historic route of great importance since Roman times. Following a ridge that rises to heights of over 200m, the route forms a natural barrier with a strategic value first noted by Cæsar when he conquered Northern Gaul in 57 BC. Its name dates from the 18th century, when the road was frequently used by Victoire and Adelaïde, daughters of Louis XV; the *dames* would take it from Paris to visit their governess at the Château de la Bove. The Chemin has since been traveled by those with rather less peaceful intentions; it was the site of Napoleon's last victory before Waterloo, and of crucial strategic import during WWI when it was held by the Germans from 1914-1918. Today the route is peppered with monuments to this turbulent history, including the **Caverne des Dragons,** (tel. 03 23 25 14 18), a former quarry used by the Germans as a barracks in WWI and later converted into a museum of remembrance. (Open Feb.-early Dec. daily 10am-6pm; open until 7pm July-Aug. 30F, children 15F.) A trip along the Chemin des Dames is feasible really only with your own transportation; for information on group visits contact the Comité Departmental du Tourisme (tel. 03 23 27 76 78; cdt@aisne.com; www.aisne.com). The Laon tourist office has additional information on the Chemin and can provide you with directions.

THE CHANNEL PORTS

They're big, they're bad, they're ugly. Such is the conventional wisdom regarding the sprawling ports that constitute the first contact between France and many travelers from Britain and beyond. Towns on the strip of land fronting the English Channel have been wrangled over from the Hundred Years' War until WWII, but today's visitor is often left wondering what made them such hot commodities; with their rather soggy weather, schlocky boutiques, and cafés promising genuine steak and kidney pie, the ports seem at times to combine the worst of both worlds. No wonder, perhaps, that many visitors only get off the ferry long enough to stock up on cheap wine, beer, and cigarettes, before heading back to Blighty. Scratch the surface, however, and these towns reveal a charm and a character uniquely their own, from Boulogne's ancient walled *haute ville*, to Rodin's renowned *Burghers of Calais* and Dunkerque's lively beach area, Malo-les-Bains. You might not go out of your way to get here, but if you're passing through, take some time out to explore what they've got to offer—you'll be surprised.

🚢 BOATS TO BRITAIN. All three towns offer frequent service to the UK, though Calais is by far the busiest. **Eurostar** trains zip under the tunnel from London and Ashford, stopping outside Calais on their way to Lille, Brussels, and Paris; **Le Shuttle** carries cars between Ashford and Calais. **Ferries** from Calais cross to Dover, while Boulogne services Folkestone and Dunkerque Ramsgate. For details of operators, schedules, and fares, see **Getting There: By Boat** (p. 62) and **Getting There: By Channel Tunnel** (p. 63).

DUNKERQUE

Dunkerque entered the history books in June 1940, when battleships, yachts, rowboats, and anything else British that could float gathered here to evacuate the last defenders of France. After a short stay in this workaday port (the third busiest in France), you too may find yourself scouring the horizon for a means of escape. The last French city to be liberated, over 80% of Dunkerque was razed before the Allies landed; it was resurrected in the concrete-slab style characteristic of postwar architecture and hardly compares to the gems further inland. What fun there is can be found in the lively beach resort of Malo-les-Bains, a short bus-ride away and home to the busy hostel.

🗺 ORIENTATION AND PRACTICAL INFORMATION. Bd. Alexandre III connects pl. de la Gare and the *centre ville*, which is focused on two main squares, **pl. Jean Bart** and **pl. Général de Gaulle**. Along the beach, **digue de Mer** turns into **digue des Alliés** on the west side, which is closer to the *centre ville*.

Trains leave pl. de la Gare for **Calais** (45min., 6 per day, 45F), **Lille** (1¼hr., 16 per day, 72F), **Arras** (1½hr., 15 per day, 88F), and **Paris** (1½hr., 210-280F). (Ticket counters open M-Sa 5:30am-7:45pm, Su 6:45am-9:35pm.) **BCD buses** leave the *gare* for **Calais** (35min., M-F 8 per day, 3 Sa, 40F) and **Boulogne** (1hr., M-F 5 per day, 2 Sa, 60F). **DK'BUS,** 12 pl. de la Gare (tel. 03 28 59 00 78), provides **local transportation.** Routes #3 and 3A connect the station and *centre ville* with the hostel and Malo-les-Bains (every 10-20min. 6:30am-9pm). **Taxibus** does the same Friday and Saturday nights (10:30pm-12:30am). (Tickets 8F, students and children 4F, *carnet* of 10 50F.) **Taxis** (tel. 03 28 66 73 00; 24hr.), wait at the *gare*, pl. de la République, and pl. Jean Bart. **Rent bikes** at **Loca Plage,** 4 digue des Alliés. (Tel. 03 28 63 66 06. 50F per half-day, 80F per day. Open summer 9:30am-noon and 2-6pm, rest of year 2-6pm.)

To reach the **tourist office,** rue Amiral Ronarch (tel. 03 28 26 27 28; fax 03 28 63 38 34; dunkerque@tourisme.norsys.fr), from the station, cross pl. de la Gare to rue du Chemin de Fer and follow the main road, bd. Alexandre III, which becomes rue Clemenceau when it veers left at pl. Jean Bart. The office is in a belfry on the left. Here you'll find free maps and **currency exchange.** (Open daily 9am-6:30pm.) For the **police,** call 03 28 26 26 72. **Hôpital de Dunkerque** is at 130 av. Louis Herbeaux (tel. 03 28 28 59 00). The **post office,** 20 rue du Président Poincaré (tel. 03 28 65 91 65), next to pl. de Gaulle, has **currency exchange** with good rates. (Open M-F 8:30am-6:30pm, Sa 8:30am-noon. **Postal codes:** Dunkerque 59140; Malo-les Bains 59240.) **Cyberkids** can get a free fix at the **Bibliothèque Universitaire du Littorcel,** quai de la Citadelle. (Tel. 03 28 23 74 74. Open Sept.-July M-Sa 9am-6pm.)

ACCOMMODATIONS AND CAMPING. The busy **Auberge de Jeunesse (HI),** pl. Paul Asseman (tel. 03 28 63 36 34; fax 03 28 63 24 54), sits on the beachfront. From the station, take bus #3 or 3A to "Piscine." Turn left and walk past the pool and rink; the hostel will be on your right. Walking, follow bd. Alexander III across town through its various name-changes. At pl. de la Victoire, turn left onto av. des Bains, cross the bridge, and turn left onto allée Fenelon; pl. Asseman is on the right (30min.). The single-sex, 8-bed barracks are cramped but clean. (48F. Sheets 19F. Breakfast 21F. Meals 43.50F. Co-ed bathrooms. Reception M-F 8:30am-12:30pm and 2-11pm, Sa-Su 6-11pm. Curfew Sept.-June 11pm. **Members only** in summer.)

Also on the beach, in a prime location, is ⚑ **Hôtel Eole,** 77-79 digue de Mer (tel. 03 28 69 13 64; fax 03 28 69 52 57). Take bus #3 or 3A to pl. Turenne and walk past the church towards the beach, then turn right on digue de Mer; otherwise it's a 30- to 45-minute hike from the *gare*. All the rooms have a TV, telephone, shower, and toilet. Being the only hotel facing the sea, rooms with a view are more expensive. (Singles 150-250F; doubles 180-300F. Breakfast 30F. Arrive early or call. V, MC, AmEx.) If you're stuck in town, try **Hôtel le Lion d'Or,** 2 rue de Chemin de Fer (tel. 03 28 66 08 24), just up the road from the *gare*. Rooms are decently pretty, decently clean, and decently sized. (Singles and doubles from 120F. No reception Sa-Su afternoons. V, MC, AmEx.) You can camp near the sand at **Dunkerque Camping Municipal,** bd. de l'Europe (tel. 03 28 69 26 68). Take bus #3 or 3a to "Malo CES Camping" or follow av. des Bains east for 4km. (23-26F per person, 15F per tent, 14F per car. Reception 9am-noon and 2-8pm. Open Apr.-Nov.)

FOOD. The cheapest pizzerias and *crêperies* flourish between #30 and 60 digue de Mer, in Malo, but you get what you pay for. Various indistinguishable cafés offering lunchtime *formules* line bd. Alexander III around pl. Jean Bart. Sample a local speciality with *potje vlesch,* a *dunkerquois* dish made with rabbit, chicken, and lamb in aspic, served cold. For vegetarians, it's easy being green at **La Chlorophylle,** 47 digue de Mer (tel. 03 28 63 12 31), where enormous salads (from 49F), omelettes, and meaty *plats* are attractively presented. (*Plat du jour* 43F, daily catch 49F. Open Jan. 10-Dec. 10 Tu-F 10am-10:30pm, Sa-Su 10am-11pm. V, MC.) A **Monoprix** supermarket is at pl. République. (Open M-Sa 8:30am-8pm.) There is also a **market** at pl. Général de Gaulle (W and Sa 9am-4:30pm), with a smaller suburban version at pl. Turenne (Tu summer 7am-2pm; winter 7am-1pm).

SIGHTS. Although not beautiful, the beach area of **Malo-les-Bains** is a hotbed of activity on sunny summer days. Cafés and bars line the **digue des Alliés** and the **digue de Mer.** Jet skis and windsurfing equipment can be rented on the beach.

Opposite the tourist office on rue Clemenceau, the 15th-century **Église St-Éloi** shelters Flemish paintings within Gothic walls. The church is the final resting place of Jean Bart (1650-1702), the famous *dunkerquois* pirate knighted by Louis XIV after he saved France from famine. The church's 500-year-old **belfry,** across the street, houses 48 bells, including the enormous seven-tonne "Jean Bart" bell. In the summer, the tourist office opens the belfry's viewing deck for surveying the city.

The **Musée des Beaux-Arts** (tel. 03 28 66 21 57), near the theater on pl. du Général de Gaulle, houses a collection of 16th- to 18th-century paintings by French and Flemish artists and a few delightfully playful 19th-century works. (Open W-M 10am-noon and 2-6pm. 20F, students 10F, Su free.) To learn more about this port's historic sea trade, visit the **Musée Portuaire,** 9 quai de la Citadelle (tel. 03 28 63 33 39), housed in a 19th-century tobacco factory, one of the few buildings not destroyed during World War II. (Open W-M July-Aug. 10am-6pm; Sept.-June 10am-12:45pm and 1:30-6pm. 25F, children 20F; half-price with Musée des Beaux Arts.)

◪ ENTERTAINMENT. In summer, the party's on the beachfront all night long; everyone packs the bars along **digue de Mer** and **digue des Alliés.** Like clockwork, twenty-something regulars fill the **Milk Bar,** 46 digue de Mer (tel. 03 28 59 12 52). For a faster pace, **NASA,** 67 digue de Mer (tel. 03 28 69 07 75), launches reggae from 10pm until dawn. On Sundays, dance your way through teatime at the *thé dansant,* starting at 4pm.

CALAIS

More lively and congenial than Dunkerque, Calais (pop. 80,000) has come a long way since the Middle Ages, when it served as a staging post for British invasions of France. Today, the town is firmly in French hands, but the Brits are still coming, and in even greater numbers since the opening of the Channel Tunnel next door. If you're here for any length of time (most aren't), duck over to the faux Flamboyant Gothic Hôtel de Ville, where Rodin's *Burghers of Calais* awaits, or watch the white ships glide by from one of the town's wide beaches.

◪ ORIENTATION AND PRACTICAL INFORMATION. Free **buses** connect the hoverport, ferry terminal, and train station every 30 minutes. Avoid the area around the ferry terminals and harbor at night. **Eurostar** stops outside town at the new **Gare Calais-Fréthun,** but most **SNCF trains** stop in town at the **Gare Calais-Ville,** bd. Jacquard. Service is offered to **Boulogne** (30min., 19 per day, 44F), **Dunkerque** (45min., 3 per day, 45F), **Lille** (1¼hr., 12 per day, 84F), and **Paris** (1-3hr., 10 per day, 198-265F). (Ticket office open M-Sa 5am-8pm, Su 7am-9pm.) **BCD buses** stop in front of the *gare* on the way to **Dunkerque** (45min., M-F 6 per day, Sa 3 per day, 40F) and **Boulogne** (30min.; 8 per day, Sa 3 per day; 38F). **STCE,** 22 rue Caillette (tel. 03 21 00 75 75), operates **local buses.** Line #3 from Gare Calais-Ville is your ticket to the beach, the hostel, and campgrounds (direction "Blériot/Plage"; M-Sa 7am-8pm, Su 10:30am-8pm; 5.10F). For **Taxis Radio Calais,** call 03 21 97 13 14 (24hr.).

The **tourist office,** 12 bd. Clemenceau (tel. 03 21 96 62 40; fax 03 21 96 01 92), is one block from the *gare;* cross the street, turn left, cross the bridge, and it's on your right. The staff offers a free reservations service, **currency exchange,** and a basic map; a better map costs 20F. (Open M-Sa 9am-7pm, Su 10am-1pm.) With people arriving from the UK throughout the day, **currency exchange** is no problem; exchange at the ferry or hovercraft terminals (both 24hr.), the post office, or most banks. Wash your armor at **Lavorama,** 34 rue de Thermes. (Open daily 7am-9pm.) The **police** are on pl. de Lorraine (tel. 03 21 19 13 17). The **Hôpital du Calais** is at 11 quai du Commerce (tel. 03 21 46 33 33). The **post office** is on pl. d'Alsace. (Tel. 03 21 85 52 85. Open M-F 8:30am-6pm, Sa 8:30-noon.) A **branch office** is located on pl. du Reims. (Open M-F 8:30am-6pm, Sa 8:30am-11:30am. **Postal code:** 62100.)

◪ ACCOMMODATIONS AND CAMPING. The few budget hotels fill up quickly in summer, so owners recommend calling 10-14 days ahead. The tourist office provides a list of hotels with prices. The modern ◪ **Centre Européen de Séjour/Auberge de Jeunesse (HI),** av. Maréchal Delattre de Tassigny (tel. 03 21 34 70 20; fax 03 21 96 87 80), is one block from the beach. From the station, turn left and follow the main road through its name changes, past pl. d'Armes; cross the bridge and take a left at the roundabout onto bd. de Gaulle. Walk past the high-rise and go right on tiny rue Alice Marie; the white hostel is the third building on your left. Or take bus #3 to stop "Pluviose." From the ferry, take a shuttle bus to pl. d'Armes; your first right down the bus route is the main road (rue Royale). The 84 blue doubles share a bathrooms in pairs. There's also a pool table, a bar, and a cafeteria (open M-F 7-9am, noon-1pm, and 5-8pm; Sa 7-9am and noon-1pm), and you can **rent bikes** for 40F per day. (80F per night. Breakfast included. Sheets 14F. Non-members 10F supplement and 1 night max. stay. 24hr. reception. Checkout 11am.)

Hôtel Bristol, 15-13 rue du Duc de Guise (tel./fax 03 21 34 53 24), off the main road, has neat, undistinguished rooms; double-glazing keeps out the noise. (Singles 130-200F; doubles 150-220F. Breakfast 25F. 24hr. reception. V, MC.) The garrulous owner also runs the adorable ☒ **Hôtel Tudor,** 6 rue Marie Tudor (tel. 03 21 96 08 15), around the corner, which has more comfortable rooms, some with kitchenettes. (Singles 180F; doubles 220F; 3-5 people 250-350F.) The **Camping Municipal,** av. Raymond Poincaré (tel. 03 21 97 89 79), off the main road (rue de Mer), packs them in like sardines on a great location near the beach. (17F per person plus 12.40F per car/tent. Reception M-Sa 8am-noon and 2-5pm, Su 8am-noon.)

⎙ **FOOD.** Calais caters to that rare breed looking for boring food at middling prices. Morning **markets** are held on pl. Crèvecœur (Th and Sa) and pl. d'Armes (W and Sa). Otherwise, look for a *boulangerie* on **bd. Gambetta, bd. Jacquard,** and **rue des Thermes. Match supermarket,** pl. d'Armes (open M-Sa 8:30am-7:30pm, Su 10am-7pm), and **Prisunic supermarket,** 17 bd. Jacquard (open M-Sa 8:30am-7:30pm, Su 9am-7pm), provide packaged treats. Restaurants line **rue Royale** and **bd. Jacquard.** Try **Le Napoli Pizzeria** (tel. 03 21 34 49 39), on rue Jean de Vienne not far from the tourist office. The 46F *menu* includes two courses and coffee. The hostel and campsite cafeterias are inexpensive.

☒ **SIGHTS.** Rodin's evocative sculpture, **The Burghers of Calais,** stands in front of the **Hôtel de Ville** at the juncture of bd. Jacquard and rue Royale, and depicts a story from the Hundred Years' War. When Calais was first captured in 1347, six of the town's leading citizens surrendered the keys to the city and offered their lives to England's King Edward III in exchange for those of the starving townspeople. Edward's French wife Philippa pleaded for mercy, and at the last minute they were spared. The best part of Calais is its **beach;** follow rue Royale through its name changes to rue de Mer until the road ends. Walk west along the shore, away from the unattractive harbor.

Directly across from the town hall, in Parc St-Pierre, a camouflaged German bunker now houses the **War Museum** (tel. 03 21 34 21 57), providing a display of battlefield models and old newspapers. (Open daily 10am-6pm; closed Dec.-Jan. 20F, children 15F.) **Le Musée des Beaux-Arts et de la Dentelle,** 25 rue Richelieu (tel. 03 21 46 48 40), near the tourist office, houses an exhibition detailing Calais' love affair with lace, as well as a room dedicated to Rodin and other 19th-century sculptors, Flemish and Dutch paintings, and modern pieces by Picasso, Dubuffet, and Alechinsky. (Open M and W-F 10am-noon and 2-5:30pm, Sa 10am-noon and 2-6:30pm, Su 2-6:30pm. 15F, students 10F, free W.)

BOULOGNE-SUR-MER

Legend has it that in AD 636, a boat carrying a statue of the Virgin Mary, patron saint of fishermen, washed up on the beach of Boulogne. The spot became a great pilgrimage site, and the population has since swelled to 50,000. By far and away the most attractive Channel port, Boulogne has achieved a happy marriage of modern bustle to age-old charm; in the summer the *quais* throb with commerce while the walled *haute ville* looks on from above. The busy port cuts into the heart of town and unloads quantities of Britons seeking a continental getaway.

▮ **ORIENTATION AND PRACTICAL INFORMATION.** The river Liane splits Boulogne into two parts: on the west bank is the ferry terminal, and on the east bank is everything else. Leaving the station, check the large map at the front doors. To reach central **pl. Frédéric Sauvage** from Gare Boulogne-Ville, turn right on bd. Voltaire then follow bd. Danou to the left to pl. Angleterre; the tourist office is just ahead on the left. **Pont Marquet,** next to the tourist office, leads to the **ferry port.** The streets between **pl. Frédéric Sauvage** and **pl. Dalton** form the busy *centre ville.*

Trains leave **Gare Boulogne-Ville,** bd. Voltaire for **Paris** (2-2¾hr., 8 per day, 161F-280F), **Lille** (2½hr., 12 per day, 102-135F), and **Calais** (30min., 19 per day, 44F). (Info office open M-Sa 8:15am-6:45pm.) **BCD** buses leave pl. Dalton for **Calais** (30min., 4 per day, 38F) and **Dunkerque** (80min., 4 per day, 60F). **TCRB** (tel. 03 21 83 51 51) sends **local bus** #7 from the train station to pl. de Sauvage; change to line #4 or 5 to reach the *haute ville* (tickets 6F). **Radio Taxis Boulogne** (tel. 03 21 91 25 00) sit around at the station.

At the **tourist office**, quai de la Poste, Forum Jean Noël, off pl. Frédéric Sauvage (tel. 03 21 31 68 38; fax 03 21 33 81 09; boulogne@tourisme.norsys.fr), the staff has bus info and makes hotel reservations; ask them for the fold-out town map. They also run **tours** of the *vieille ville* (daily 3:30pm, 20-32F). (Open M-Sa 8:45am-6pm, Su 9:30am-1pm and 2:30-5:30pm; July-Aug. M-Sa 9am-7pm, Su 10am-12:30pm and 2-5:30pm.) **Banks** lie between the tourist office and the *vieille ville*. **Crédit Agricole,** 26 rue Nationale, has a 24-hour **currency exchange** machine. There's a **Laundromat** on rue Lampe, down the road from the tourist office. (Open daily 7am-2am.) The **police** are at 9 rue Perrochel (tel. 03 21 99 48 48), while **Hôpital Duchenne** is on allée Jacques Monad (tel. 03 21 99 33 33). The **post office** is on pl. Frédéric Sauvage. (Tel. 03 21 99 09 09. Open M-F 8am-7pm, Sa 8am-12:30pm. **Postal code:** 62200.)

⚑ ACCOMMODATIONS. Many hotel rooms in the 110-160F range are clustered near the ferry terminal. The tourist office publishes a list of hotels and prices. The excellent 🏠 **Auberge de Jeunesse (HI),** 56 rue Rouget de Lisle (tel. 03 21 99 15 30; fax 03 21 80 45 62), is across from the train station. The non-smoking rooms, each with bathroom, hold three to four beds. There's even **internet access** (30F per 30min.). (72F, non-members 91F. Breakfast including. Sheets 17F. Wheelchair accessible. Check-out noon, check-in 5pm. Curfew 1am. Reception 8:30am-1am. V, MC.)

The central **Hôtel de Londres,** 22 pl. de France (tel. 03 21 31 35 63; fax 03 21 83 50 07), is behind the post office, with a prime view of a bus loading zone. The pleasant rooms all have TVs and the bathrooms are modern. The restaurant downstairs serves *menus* from 65F (open daily 8am-2am). (Singles and doubles 150-309F. Extra bed 25F. Breakfast 32F. V, MC, AmEx.) **Hôtel le Mirador,** 2-4 rue de la Lampe (tel. 03 21 31 38 08; fax 03 21 83 21 79), is on pl. d'Angleterre. The dim staircase leads to newly-renovated rooms, all with telephone and bathroom. (Single 195F; doubles 245F. Extra bed 45F. V, MC.)

🍴 FOOD. Restaurants, cafés, bakeries, and other food shops abound in the *centre ville*. An excellent **market** is held on pl. Dalton. (W and Sa 7:30am-12:30pm.) The **STOC supermarket,** 54 rue Daunou, is in the Centre Commercial de la Liane mall, just up the road from the hostel. (Open M-Sa 8:30am-8pm.) Next to it is the **Casino Cafétéria,** where steak and veg goes for 40F. (Open daily 11:30am-7:30pm.)

Charming restaurants cluster on **rue de Lille** in the *vieille ville*. Adequate, cheap food can be found on the waterfront along **bd. Gambetta.** The *café-brasserie* **Le Thiers,** 80 rue Thiers (tel. 03 21 31 67 32), greets guests with "roaring 20s" murals and hats. (Open M-Sa 7:30am-8pm.) At **Joly-Desenclos,** 44 rue de Lille (tel. 03 24 15 15 02), quiches cost 27F, salads 12F, omelettes 25F, and *crêpes* from 10F. (Open W-M 7am-8pm.) Bars and cafés also line **pl. Dalton.**

🏛 SIGHTS. Boulogne's *vieille ville* stands atop the hill where the Romans settled to survey their domain. The 13th-century walls surround a labyrinth of crooked streets. Walk along the ramparts for exhilarating views of the harbor, town, and countryside before descending into the cobbled maze below.

The massive **Château-Musée,** rue de Bernet (tel. 03 21 10 02 20 or 03 21 80 56 78 for a tour in French or English), dominates the east corner of the ramparts. Built from 1227-1231 for Philippe Hurepel, son of King Philippe-Auguste, it now houses an impressive collection which includes African masks, regional paintings and porcelain, and, last but not least, Napoleon's second-oldest hat. (Open M and W-Sa 10am-12:30pm and 2-5pm, Su 10am-12:30pm and 2:30-5:30pm. 20F, children 13F; tours 32F/20F.) Inside the walls of the old city, on pl. Goddefroy de Bouillon, the 13th-century **belfry** of the **Hôtel de Ville** sends acrophobes into a swoon with its dizzying view of the port and claustrophobes into a panic with its narrow and treacherous staircase. (Open M-Sa 9am-noon and 2-6pm. Free.)

Just down rue de Lille is the 19th-century **Basilique de Notre-Dame,** which sits above the labyrinthine crypts of a 12th-century edifice. One of the 14 chambers contains the remnants of a 3rd-century Roman temple; another exhibits relics and religious objects. (Open M-Sa 9am-noon and 2-6pm. Crypt 10F.)

When the residents of Boulogne aren't catching fish or eating them, they're admiring them at **Le Grand Nausicaā**, bd. Ste-Beuve (tel. 03 21 30 98 98; www.nausicaa-sea-centres.com). Sea lions frolic around the transparent tunnel as a cartoon manta ray guides you in English. With schools of children facing off with schools of fish, Nausicaā can get crowded; try to come late in the day. (Open July-Aug. daily 9:30am-8pm; Sept.-May 9:30am-6:30pm. 65F, ages 3-12 45F.)

Next to Nausicaā is the beach, where you can rent boards for **windsurfing** (60F per hr., 600F per week), **catamarans** (300F per 2hr., 700F per week), and windsurfer-on-wheels **chars à voile** (80F per hr.; tel. 03 21 83 25 48).

■ **ENTERTAINMENT.** In the evening, check out the neon-blinking bars at **pl. Dalton,** in particular **Au Bureau,** a local favorite that also serves a *plat du jour* (48-50F) till 11pm. Bars squish side by side on tiny **rue Doyen,** just off the *place;* drink a glass in memory of John-John and his dad at the **Pub "J.F. Kennedy,"** 20 rue du Doyen (tel. 03 21 83 97 05), which offers mounds of mussels (42F) and beer (15F). (Open 9am-1am. Food available noon-11pm.)

■ **FESTIVALS.** Boulogne and other towns along the coast rock during July with the **Festival de la Côte d'Opale,** a month-long festival that features rock and pop musicians from around the world playing venues up and down the coast (for info call 03 21 30 40 33). The last weekend in August sees the reenactment of the legend surrounding the town's founding with the **Grande Procession à Notre Dame de Boulogne;** a statue of the Virgin Mary arrives in a boat and is escorted with great pomp and circumstance from pl. Dalton to the cathedral.

MONTREUIL-SUR-MER

Montreuil and its surroundings provide an idyllic location for tranquil walks, hikes, and picnics. Its red-tiled houses and crumbling castle make a pleasant break from the hustle of the port towns. The "on-the-sea" suffix to the town's title belies the fact that not a drop of salt water has been seen here since the 13th century. Fortunately for Montreuil, the fickle sea's retreat left a rich countryside fed by the Canche river. Victor Hugo chose Montreuil as the meeting place of Jean Valjean, Fannette, and Inspector Javert at the beginning of *Les Misérables*, a testament to a thousand years of struggle and graceful endurance.

■ **ORIENTATION AND PRACTICAL INFORMATION.** The **train station** (tel. 03 21 06 05 09) lies just outside the walls of the citadel in the *ville basse.* Trains dash to **Boulogne** (30min., 7 per day, 38F), **Calais** (1hr., 4 per day, 69F), **Arras** (1½hr., 6 per day, 72F), **Lille** (2hr., 7 per day, 92F), and **Paris** via Étaples (3hr., 4 per day, 150F). (Ticket office open M-F 5am-8pm, Sa 6am-8pm, Su 7:30am-8pm.)

To reach the **tourist office,** 21 rue Carnot (tel. 03 21 06 04 27; fax 03 21 06 57 85), beside the citadel, climb the stairs across from the *gare* and turn right on av. du 11 Novembre. Pass through the gate into the city. At the sign for the hostel (Auberge de Jeunesse), turn right onto quiet rue des Bouhers. then turn left onto the footpath at the shrine of Notre Dame; the office is straight ahead. The staff distributes a map and brochures. (Open June-Aug. M-Sa 9:30am-12:30pm and 2-6:30pm, Su 10am-12:30pm and 2:30-5pm; rest of year open M-Sa 10am-12:30pm and 2-6:30pm.)

Because of its tiny size and narrow, cobblestone streets, Montreuil is best tackled on foot. To get into the countryside, rent **bicycles** from **Oxygène,** 11 pl. de Gaulle. (Tel. 03 21 86 14 25. 25F per hour, 50F per half day, 80F per day. Open Tu-Sa 9:30am-12:30pm and 2-7:30pm, Su-M 2-7:30pm.) **BNP,** pl. Darnétal, will **exchange currency.** (Open Tu-F 8:45am-noon and 1:35-5:45pm, Sa 8:45am-noon and 1:35-4pm.) The closest **hospital** (tel. 03 21 89 45 45) is in nearby Rang du Fliers. The **post office** (tel. 03 21 06 70 00) is on pl. Gambetta. (Open M-F 9am-noon and 2:30-5:30pm, Sa 8:30-11:30am. **Postal code:** 62170.)

ACCOMMODATIONS AND CAMPING. The **Auberge de Jeunesse "La Hulotte" (HI)** (tel. 03 21 06 10 83), is inside the citadel on rue Carnot, across the bridge to the right from the tourist office. It offers rustic, summer camp-style accommodations, kitchen access, and free reign of the medieval citadel after hours.(40F. Curfew 10pm. Open Feb.-Sept.) **Hôtel le Vauban,** 32 pl. de Gaulle (tel. 03 21 06 04 95; fax 03 21 06 04 00), provides attractive yellow and blue rooms in a candy-pink building on the central *place.* (Singles 170-240F; doubles 200-270F. Breakfast 35F. Reception 8am-7pm. V, MC.) ■ M. and Mme Renard, at 4 av. du 11 novembre (tel. 03 21 86 85 72), offer large, old-fashioned **chambres d'hôtes,** at the top of the stairs from the *gare.* Don't drop your cheese. (Singles 180F; doubles 220F. Breakfast and cute black dog included.) There's a beautiful **campground** in the *ville basse,* 744 rte. d'Étaples (tel. 03 21 06 07 28). It is situated by the banks of the river, near a pool, restaurant, and tennis courts. (35F for one person, 9F additional person.)

FOOD. Restaurants are centered around **pl. de Gaulle,** which is also the place to find *boulangeries.* Bathed in flowers, **Le Bistrot,** pl. de Gaulle (tel. 03 21 86 20 20), offers 59F *menus* and a 42F *plat du jour.* (2F terrace supplement. Open daily 9am-10pm.) Across the square, **La Paloma,** 50 pl. de Gaulle (tel. 03 21 86 36 75), bills itself as a pizzeria but whips up gigantic 38F omelettes and great 20F ice cream sundaes. (Open daily 9:30am-10pm. V, MC.) For cheap-cheap, nearby **Aux Chevaux d'Or,** 23 pl. de Gaulle (tel. 03 21 06 17 40), hawks sandwiches and salads for 15F. (Open summer daily 9am-midnight, winter Th-Tu 9am-9pm.) Picnic fare for the ramparts can be found at **Supermarket Shopi,** pl. de Gaulle. (Open Tu-F 8:45am-12:30pm and 2:30-7:15pm, Sa 9am-7:15pm, Su 9am-12:15pm.)

SIGHTS. Walking atop Montreuil's 3km-long **ramparts** is like the glorious minute after take-off. Green rivers slip through fields peppered with wildflowers, grazing cows, and sooty red rooftops. Stop along the way to visit the **citadel,** built in the 16th century on the site of the old royal castle, and which now houses the hostel. (Open W-M 10am-noon and 2-6pm. 15F, children 6F.)

Picture-perfect tumbledown cottages line the **rue du Clape en Bas** and the **Cavée St-Firmin;** the latter has been featured in several films, including the first celluloid version of *Les Misérables.* The liveliest streets are **rue d'Herambault** and those surrounding **pl. de Gaulle.** The **Chapel de l'Hôtel Dieu** and the **St-Saulve Abbey,** impressively carved Gothic churches on pl. Gambetta, have withstood the spasms of a 1467 earthquake and the iconoclastic riots of the Revolution. **Bassin de la Canche,** 4 rue Moulin des Orphelins (tel. 03 21 06 20 16), across the canal from the *gare,* rents canoes and kayaks for the Canche river. (Open 10am-noon and 2-5pm.)

FESTIVALS. At the end of July, the townsfolk stage a *son et lumière* based on *Les Misérables*—in the novel, Jean Valjean is mayor of the town when Inspector Javert brings about his downfall. August 15 brings the **Day of the Street Painters,** an exuberant celebration of theater, opera, and dance. 2001 will see the return of **Les Malins Plaisirs** (tel. 03 21 98 12 26), a two-week theatre festival in mid-August which stages productions by French playwrights from Molière to Anouilh.

AMIENS

Amiens' glory reached its pinnacle in 1533, when the spire was finally placed atop its cathedral, one of Europe's finest examples of Gothic architecture. The otherwise unremarkable town has two other star attractions: the Quartier St-Leu, a twisting maze of streets and canals, and the tranquil *hortillonages,* former marshlands cultivated since the Romans set up a winter camp here in 12 BC. Although it isn't necessary to go 20,000 leagues out of your way to get here, Jules Verne's home city merits a stop on your itinerary.

⎘ ORIENTATION AND PRACTICAL INFORMATION. Trains leave the **Gare du Nord,** pl. Alphonse Fiquet, for **Paris** (1hr., 15 per day, 98F), **Lille** (1½hr., 7 per day, 95F), **Rouen** (1½hr., 6 per day, 91F), **Boulogne** (1½hr., 15 per day, 90F), and **Calais** (2hr., 12 per day, 114F). (Ticket office open daily 7am-8:30pm. Info office open M-Sa 8:45am-6:20pm.) **Buses** leave from under the shopping center to the right of the station for **Beauvais** (1¼hr., 13 per day, 68F). **SEMTA,** left as you exit the station on 10 pl. Alphonse Figuet (tel. 03 22 71 40 00), provides **local transportation.** All buses stop at the train station; buy tickets on the bus or at the office. (Office open M-F 7am-7pm, Sa 8am-5:30pm. Buses run 6am-9pm.) For a **taxi,** call 03 22 91 30 03 (24hr.) You can **rent bikes** at **Amiens Cycles,** 4 rte. de Paris. (Tel. 03 22 95 03 39. 100F per day M-F, 150F Sa-Su. 1000F or passport deposit. Open Tu-Sa 9am-7pm.)

To get to the **tourist office,** 6bis rue Dusevel (tel. 03 22 71 60 50; fax 03 22 71 60 51), turn right from the station parking lot, pass the mall, and turn left onto rue Gloriette. Continue through several name changes and pl. St-Michel; after the cathedral, turn left onto rue Dusevel; the office is on the left. The staff has an excellent free map of the *centre ville,* a reservations service (20F), and organizes walking tours (30F, child 20F). A map of the whole city costs 23.50F. (Open Easter-Oct. 31 M-Sa 9am-6:30pm, Su 2-6:30pm; Nov. 1-Easter closes 5 pm Su.) Not a cybercafé, **Net Express,** 10 rue André (tel. 03 22 72 33 33), launders near the cathedral. (Open daily 7am-9pm.) To get to **Hôpital Nord,** pl. Victor Pauchet (tel. 03 22 66 80 00), take bus #10 (direction "Collège César Frank"); #11 makes the return trip. The **police** are at 1 rue Maré-Lanselles (tel. 03 22 71 53 00). The **post office** is at 7 rue des Vergeaux. (Open M-F 8am-7pm, Sa 8am-noon. Poste Restante code: 80050. **Postal code:** 80000.) There is a **branch** next to the station on the right.

⎘ ACCOMMODATIONS. There are several reasonable hotels (130-150F) in the *centre ville.* Cheaper hotels (110-120F) can be found on pl. Maréchal Foch, but it's far from the action. The tourist office publishes a list of hotels with price ranges.

Snuggled into a quiet street behind the cathedral, **La Résidence,** 6 rue Porion (tel. 03 22 92 46 16), could be *la résidence* of your grandmother, with antique furnishings and four-poster beds. Treat yourself to a little luxury. (Singles from 250F; doubles from 320F; triples 340F. Breakfast 36F. Reception closed Su 2-5pm.) A boisterous large family runs (and lives in) the **Hôtel Puvis de Chavannes,** 6 rue Puvis de Chavannes (tel. 03 22 91 82 96; fax 03 22 92 74 02). The pretty rooms have sinks in an adorably tiled "bathroom corner" and luxurious comforters. (Singles and doubles 140-200F. Breakfast 27F. Shower 10F. Pets 10F. V, MC.) The same family owns the **Hôtel Victor Hugo,** 2 rue l'Oratoire (tel. 03 22 91 57 91; fax 03 22 92 74 02). A chic white stairway leads to large green and white rooms, all with TVs and all slightly worn. The breakfast room is lovely. (Singles and doubles 135-230F; with two beds 210-250F. Breakfast 27F. Shower 10F. Pets 10F. V, MC.)

⎘ FOOD. Picardy's regional specialties, *pâté de canard* (duck pâté), *tuiles amiénoises* (chocolate macaroons), and *ficelles picarde* (thin crêpes stuffed with mushrooms, ham, and cream), are consumed with gusto in Amiens' restaurants and cafés. Most *confiseries* carry *macarons d'Amiens* (almond macaroons), a city treat since the 16th century.

There's food and much more in the shops around the **Hôtel de Ville,** including **Shopi supermarket,** 20 pl. Hôtel de Ville. (Open M 10am-12:30pm and 2-7:30pm, Tu-Th 9am-12:30pm and 2-7:30pm, F-Sa 9am-1pm and 2-7:30pm.) **Match supermarket** is in the mall to the right of the station. (Open M-Sa 9am-8pm.) Amiens' main **market** is held on pl. Pasmentier (Sa), selling vegetables grown in Les Hortillonages (see **Sights**). Smaller markets are held on pl. Beffroi (W and Sa).

⎘ Le T'chiot Zinc, 18 rue de Noyon (tel. 03 22 91 43 79), offers delicious and obscenely large Cambodian and *picard* dishes for around 50F, and turns into a busy hang-out spot at night. (Open M 6:30-10:30pm, Tu-Sa noon-2:30pm and 6:30-10:30pm. V, MC, AmEx.) **La Mangeoire,** 3 rue des Sergents (tel. 03 22 91 11 28), serves succulent *crêpes* (12-48F) and *cidre* in clay *bolées* (13F). (Open Tu-Sa 11:30am-3pm and 5-10pm. V, MC, AmEx.)

THE NORTHEAST

⏣ SIGHTS. When Wallon de Sarton returned in 1206 from the Fourth Crusade with the head of John the Baptist, the burghers of Amiens decided to build a cathedral worthy of housing the sacred object. The resulting **Cathédrale de Notre-Dame** soars above with a 42m nave; the impressive cathedral is twice the size of its namesake in Paris. The astounding west façade, currently being cleaned, displays 4000 figures acting out episodes from the Old and New Testaments. Inside, look behind the choir for the small Weeping Angel, which became famous when the WWI Allied soldiers mailed thousands of postcards of it home to celebrate their victory in taking the town from the Germans. The treasury, which holds a collection of holy valuables from across the centuries, is closed, but the relic of John the Baptist's *tête* is on display in the left arm of the transept. (Open Easter-Sept. 8:30am-6:45pm; Oct. and Mar. closes at 6pm; Nov.-Feb. 8:30am-noon and 2-5pm. Guided tours July-Aug. W-M 1:45-6pm; contact tourist office for details.)

Just north of the Somme River, the **Quartier St-Leu** is the oldest and most attractive part of Amiens. Built along a system of waterways and canals, its narrow, cobbled streets and flower-strewn squares allow it to vaunt itself as France's "Venice of the North." Nearby are the **hortillonages,** market gardens spread over the inlets created when the Romans built canals through the marshland. Paths wander among the canals, which still supply Amiens with fruit, vegetables, and flowers. **Embarcaderie d'Amont** (tel. 03 22 92 16 40) offers barge tours of the waterways.

The **Picardy Museum,** 48 rue de la République (tel. 03 22 97 14 00), houses a distinguished collection of French paintings, an impressive variety of sculpture from the Middle Ages to the 19th century, and an exhibit on Roman Amiens in a graceful Second Empire building. (Open Tu-Su 10am-12:30pm and 2-6pm. 20F, under 17 and students 10F.) Its sister, the **Musée de l'Hôtel de Berny,** 36 rue Victor Hugo (same tel.) is a 17th-century mansion housing original furniture, tapestries, and an exhibit on locks. (Open in summer Su 10am-12:30pm and 2-6pm; will open outside those hours for groups upon request. 10F, under 18 free.)

Jules Verne (1828-1905) spent most of his life in Amiens and wrote his prophetic novels here; his former house now bears the impressive title of **Centre de documentation Jules Verne,** at 2 rue Dubois, near the Cirque on the southern edge of town. Today it is a small but appropriately quirky museum, with holographic models of the Nautilus and a dummy of Verne himself. (Open Tu-F 9am-noon and 2-6pm, Sa 9am-noon. 15F, children under 6 5F.) Verne himself lies 0.00046 leagues under the earth in the **Cimitière de Madeleine,** a 20-minute walk from the center of town.

🎵 ENTERTAINMENT. At night, the gas-lit, cobbled **pl. du Don** and the **rue Belu,** in the Quartier St-Leu, teem with energetic French students. The **Riverside Café,** 3 pl. du Don (tel. 03 22 92 50 30), draws the biggest crowd. Modeled on a 50s American bar, the place rocks inside, while tables invite cozy discussion outside. (Beer 13-52F. Open daily 4pm-2am, closed Su in winter.) More hotspots pepper **rue des Francs Mûriers,** left of the pl. du Don with your back to the cathedral; groove it up with Jules' ghost at **Le Némo,** 9 rue des Francs Mûriers (tel. 03 22 97 96 71), which spins house and more. (Open W-Sa from 10:30pm-4am.)

BEAUVAIS

A crossroads since Roman times, Beauvais endured 1500 years of war and misery which culminated in a 1472 siege by the Burgundian army. As the town's defenses were crumbling, Jeanne Laîné, the feisty daughter of a local artisan, seized the Burgundian banner from the hands of a soldier who had scaled the ramparts and knocked him off the walls. Her action revived the sagging morale of the local troops and enabled them to hold off the besiegers until reinforcements arrived. Jeanne's heroics earned her the nickname La Hachette (the hatchet) and a yearly celebration in her honor. In 1664, as part of his effort to restore France's exhausted treasury, Louis XIV's finance minister Colbert establish the *Manufacture Nationale de la Tapisserie* (National Tapestry Factory) in Beauvais; the city's tapestries and carpets soon became world-renowned. While the carpet trade has since dwindled, the 13th-century Gothic cathedral remains magnificent.

⑦ ORIENTATION AND PRACTICAL INFORMATION. The station, pl. de la Gare, has service to **Paris** (1hr., 9 per day, 71F) and **Amiens** via Crieil (2hr., 8 per day, 89F). (Open M-Sa 4:50am-9:05pm, Su 6:40am-9:50pm.) **Buses** leave from 47 rue Corréus (tel. 03 44 48 08 47). To get to the **tourist office**, 1 rue Beauregard (tel. 03 44 15 30 30; fax 03 44 15 30 31), from the station, walk straight ahead for just over a block and turn left onto rue de la Madeleine. At pl. Jeanne Hachette, turn right, and then left at the fountain; the office will be on the corner on the left. Here you can avail yourself of a free map of the *centre ville*, several brochures, and **currency exchange.** (Open M 10am-1pm and 2-6pm, Tu-Sa 9:30am-7pm, Su 10am-5pm.) Renovate your dirty clothes at **Renov'vit**, 8 rue Phillippe de Dreux. The **Hôtel de Police** is on rue de la Banque (tel. 03 44 48 09 84). The **hospital** is on av. Léon Blum (tel. 03 44 11 21 21). The central **post office**, 1 rue Gambetta (tel. 03 44 06 24 80), offers **currency exchange.** (Open M-F 8am-7pm, Sa 8am-noon. **Postal code:** 60000.) **Email** is wired at **Cyber Square**, 2 rue de la Tapisserie. (Tel. 03 44 79 80 90. 30F per 30min. Open Tu-Th and F noon-6:30pm, Sa 2-6:30pm.)

⑦⑦ ACCOMMODATIONS AND FOOD. The tourist office has a brochure with hotels and prices. Beauvais lacks hostel or dorm accommodations, but **Hôtel du Commerce**, 11-13 rue Chambiges (tel. 03 44 15 34 34), offers simple, spacious rooms one block from the cathedral. (Doubles 120F, with shower 145F. Breakfast 20F.) More elegant accommodations are found at the **Hôtel du Cygne**, 24 rue Carnot (tel. 03 44 48 68 40), in the pedestrian district. (Doubles 200-250F. Breakfast 35F. Extra bed 50F. V, MC.) **Camping Municipal** is at 2 rue Aldebert Bellier. (Tel. 03 44 02 00 22. 12.50F per person, 8F per car, 8F per site. Open May-Sept.)

Markets are held on pl. des Halles (W and Sa). **La Nouvelle Galerie supermarket** is on pl. Jeanne Hachette. (Open M 9am-12:30pm, Tu-Sa 9am-7pm.) The **pedestrian zone, rue Carnot,** and **rue des Jacobins** are brimming with restaurants. For a more period, picturesque setting, venture out to the late-night eateries on pedestrian **Rue du 27 Juin.**

⑤ SIGHTS. The **Cathédrale Saint-Pierre**, erected between 1225 and 1573, is the acme of the Flamboyant Gothic style. Money ran out for the nave, but the choir, at 48.5m, is the tallest in the world. To bear the enormous strains, the apse is ringed by a crown of graceful supporting towers nearly as tall as the church itself. Inside, the light-drenched cathedral features a few surviving panels of stained glass dating from the 13th to 16th centuries. Also popular is the religiously-themed **astronomical clock**, designed in 1865. This oak and gilt behemoth's 52 displays allow you to track religious holidays and phases of the moon. A 25-minute audio-visual tour of the clock's functions lets visitors witness the 68 biblical characters leap into action. Behold as Jesus, perched on a golden throne, raises his arms in judgment over virgins and sinners who parade below. (Shows in English and French at 10:40am and 2:40, 3:40, and 4:40pm, except Su mornings and religious holidays. 22F, students 15F. Cathedral open daily May-Oct. 9am-12:15pm and 2-6:15pm; Nov.-Apr. 9am-12:15pm and 2-5:30pm. Free.)

Visitors expecting yet another faded Renaissance scene will be pleasantly surprised by the **Galerie Nationale de la Tapisserie**, 22 rue St-Pierre, next to the cathedral. Constructed in 1976 against ruined 3rd-century Roman walls, the museum showcases works produced in the years after Napoleon restored the weavers to the state payroll in 1804. Thrill to the lush hues of the many butterflies, flowers, and imperial emblems that line the walls. (Open Apr.-Sept. W-M 9:30-11:30am and 2-6pm; Oct.-Mar. W-M 10-11:30am and 2:30-4:30pm. 15F, under 25 5F.)

THE NORTHWEST

Northwestern France spikes into the sea, dividing the Atlantic from the English Channel and pointing two fingers suggestively across the water. The home of Loire châteaux, D-day beaches, and a fictional village of indomitable Gauls, the Northwest is hardly an unknown region of France. Beyond the must-see sights besieged by holiday makers there lies a wealth of small towns, rugged coastline, and idyllic islands that have yet to succumb to the lures of mass tourism.

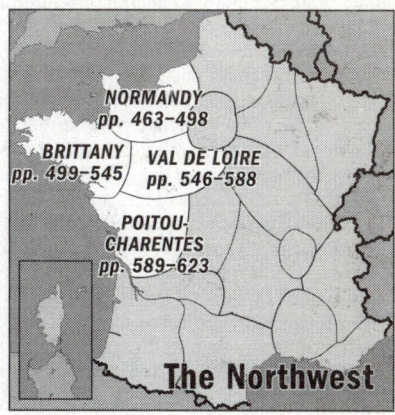

NORMANDY pp. 463–498

BRITTANY pp. 499–545

VAL DE LOIRE pp. 546–588

POITOU-CHARENTES pp. 589–623

The Northwest

HISTORY: THE ENGLISH BATTLEFIELD

Since the beginning of history, the fate of northwestern France has been caught up with that of its neighbor across the Channel. There can be little doubt that the culture which left vast arrangements of standing stones near Carnac 7000 years ago was also linked to Stonehenge, and it is well known that the Gauls kept close ties with their Celtic cousins across the sea. Whether or not a small village held out against Cæsar's armies in 56 BC with the help of a cunning moustached warrior, a menhir delivery man, and generous helpings of magic potion, it is true that the people of Armor (Gaulish for "seaside") were never fully part of Gallo-Roman culture. When Anglo-Saxon invasions sent British Celts scurrying across the channel from the 5th to the 7th century, they naturally chose to settle with their brethren in the region that came to be called Brittany, or Little Britain.

The rest of the Northwest had succumbed to Clovis's Franks in the 6th century, but Brittany stubbornly held out against the Germanic tide, grudgingly submitting to Charlemagne only in 799. Frankish domination lasted all of 46 years before the great folk hero Nominoë roused Brittany to rebellion and 700 years of independence. Soon both Bretons and Franks were faced with a new threat: adventurers from Scandinavia, who had long raided the coasts, began to settle along the channel, founding the town of Dieppe and moving into Rouen. While the Bretons repelled them at great cost, Louis the Simple had no choice but to grant them official title to the land they already occupied; thus the Duchy of Normandy came into being, named after the Frankish word for Viking, *norman*.

Norman power grew by leaps and bounds. In 1066 William the Conqueror added England to the list of Norman conquests; by the time his great-grandson ascended the English throne as Henry II, the Anglo-Norman lands stretched from Scotland to the Pyrenees. Henry's son, Richard the Lionheart, is famous for being a dashing and chivalrous warrior; yet his boundless appetite for war left his empire weak. Within a few years of his death in 1199, French king Phillipe Auguste had recovered all the territory lost over the previous 300 years.

The English returned with a vengeance in 1346 at the start of the Hundred Years' War. Normandy was invaded and subdued, while the French monarchy retreated from Paris to the Loire. In 1429, Joan of Arc burst into the dauphin's council chamber at Chinon and declared her divine mission to "boot the English out of France." Though Joan was captured in 1430 and burned a year later at the stake in English-occupied Rouen, Normandy was reconquered in 1450 and the war ended in 1453.

With France strong and confident, Brittany's independent days were numbered. Anne de Bretagne did her best, marrying successive French kings while somehow keeping her duchy separate, but her daughter Claude irrevocably ceded Brittany to her husband François I in 1532. François and his successors resided in the Loire Valley, building opulent châteaux and hunting while the Wars of Religion raged around them. The government returned to Paris with the accession of Henri IV in 1598, but religious strife still dogged the region, culminating in the siege of the Huguenot stronghold of La Rochelle by Louis XIII (and a certain Captain of the Musketeers named d'Artagnan). After a 15-month blockade, the town surrendered; three quarters of the population had already died of hunger.

The peasant farmers who dominated the Northwest in the 18th century had little time for the new ideas of the Enlightenment, and their lukewarm reaction to the Revolution turned to outright hostility following the execution of Louis XVI and the suppression of the church. Brittany and the Vendée became Royalist strongholds. For three years the Catholic and Royal Armies, under the command of François-Athanase Charette de la Contrie, fought for the *ancien régime* before being crushed by Général Hoche in 1796; 30,000 Vendéens died in one battle alone.

After further Royalist revolts in 1799, 1815, and 1830, the region settled down to a period of prosperity. Railways brought the burgeoning middle-classes to the coast to enjoy the sea air and swim in full-length bathing suits. But the region's bloody history could not long lie low, and the Conqueror's descendants returned to Normandy in 1944 at the start of their crusade to liberate Europe from the Nazi yoke. Today, the Northwest is again peaceful and prosperous, welcoming further waves of invaders from across the Channel every summer.

CLIMATE AND GEOGRAPHY

Pounded by waves, Brittany, Normandy, and Poitou-Charentes are dominated by the sea. In the north, forbidding cliffs line the Channel coasts, interspersed with myriad coves, estuaries, and beaches. To the west, the land gives way only grudgingly to the ocean, breaking up into a string of small islands. In contrast to the striking coastal landscape, the interior of the country undulates gently, from the forests of Brittany to the broad valleys of the Loire and the Seine.

The Atlantic climate tempers the weather, with mild winters blending into pleasant summers, though occasional storms blowing in from the ocean can bring raging seas and howling winds. Tides on the Channel coast are among the highest in Europe, and treacherous to the unwary; those at Mont-St-Michel famously speed in faster than a galloping horse. Low tide reveals vast expanses of sand and rock pools strewn with mussels and shellfish. Further inland, Poitou and the Loire Valley benefit from mild winters while enjoying warm, generally dry summers. In late summer, sunflowers blossom, and giant golden hay-bales dot the landscape.

SUGGESTIONS

The Northwest has a plethora of must-see sights. **Normandy** offers the **Bayeux tapestry** (p. 486), **Mont-St-Michel** (p. 496), and the **D-Day beaches** (p. 488), while **Brittany** has craggy **Belle-Île** (p. 536) and bustling, student-oriented **Rennes** (p. 500). Further south, **Cognac's distilleries** tempt the traveler (p. 600), as do **La Rochelle's** picturesque town and pristine beaches (p. 610). The **Loire valley** has numerous **châteaux** for every taste, from the austerely defensive ruins of **Chinon** (p. 571) to the Renaissance fantasies of **Chenonceau** (p. 568) and **Chambord** (p. 559). If you'd rather get away from the crowds, nip up to the Loire's equally attractive but less popular sister, the **Loir** (p. 586), to the windswept **Île d'Ouessant,** the westernmost point in France (p. 526), or to the calm canals of the **Marais Poitevin** (p. 618). If it's adrenaline you're after, brave the waves and winds on **Cap Fréhel,** or catch a competition at the acclaimed motor-racing circuit of **Le Mans** (p. 582).

NORMANDY (NORMANDIE)

In 911, Rollo, the leader of a band of Vikings who had settled around Rouen, accepted the title of Duke of Normandy from the hands of King Louis the Simple, whose name reflected his honesty rather than any wide-eyed innocence. After being baptized, Rollo assumed the name of Robert and set about making the town a worthy capital for his new duchy. Over the next few centuries, Norman power grew beyond even Robert's wildest dreams. The most famous Norman achievement, of course, was the successful 1066 invasion of the island just across the Channel, celebrated by the magnificent tapestry that still hangs in Bayeux. Scarcely less remarkable was the way in which bands of roaming Norman Knights seized control of southern Italy and Sicily, came within a plague-ridden flea's breath of conquering the Byzantine Empire, and even won for themselves the title King of Jerusalem following the First Crusade. Invaded and occupied by an English King Edward III in search of his Norman roots in 1346, by 1450 their war-torn nation was definitively incorporated into France. The English did not attempt another invasion until June 6, 1944, when they returned with American and Canadian allies to wrest Normandy from German occupation.

In the intervening centuries, Normandy exchanged its warlike reputation for a quiet agricultural role. Far removed from the border wars which raged between France and its neighbors, the towns and villages remained virtually unchanged from the Middle Ages. Tragically, much of this architectural heritage was lost during the heavy fighting following the D-Day landings. Gustave Flaubert, Normandy's most famous author, set his tale of provincial woe, *Madame Bovary*, in

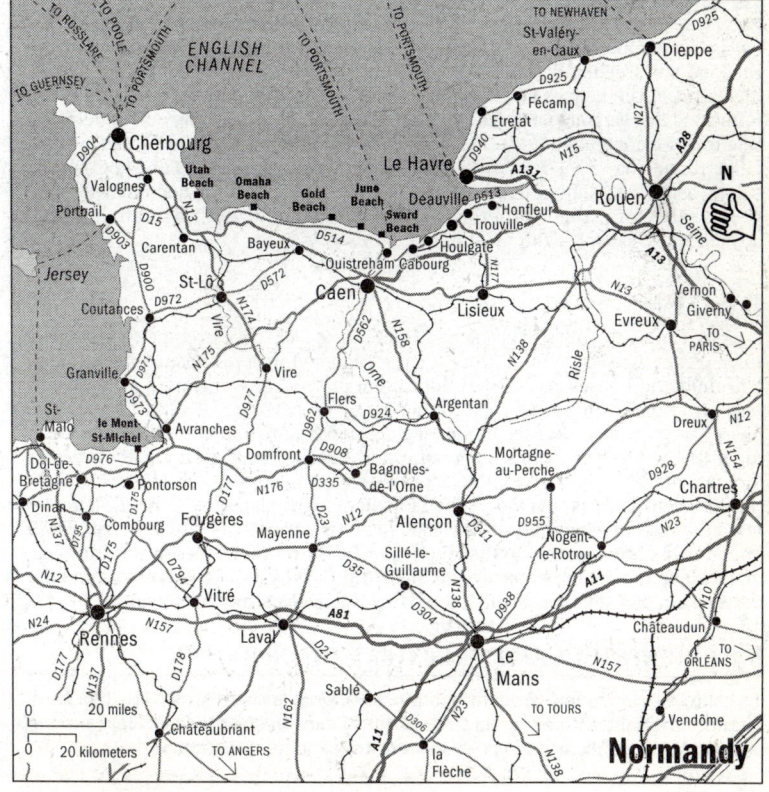

THE NORTHWEST

his homeland. Later in the 19th century, a landscape painter from Honfleur, Eugène Boudin, persuaded a young Claude Monet to take up serious painting. Monet and his friends became regular visitors to the stormy coast and calm Seine estuary in the 1860s. In the 1930s, Jean-Paul Sartre served as a teaching assistant in Le Havre, which he renamed Bouville (Mudtown) in his first novel, *Nausea*.

Normandy's cuisine is based on apples and the produce of the famous Norman cows, which supply all France with milk and butter. The creamy, pungent *camembert* cheese is best when soft in the middle, and smellable from a mile away. Flaubert once wrote of his embattled countrymen, "All of us Normans have a drop of cider in our veins. It's a bitter, fermented drink which sometimes bursts the gut." The province's traditional *cidre* comes both dry *(brut)* and sweet *(doux)*. *Calvados*, an apple brandy aged 12 to 15 years, ranks with the finest cognacs, while *poire* is to pears as cider is to apples. A local *apéritif* is *pommeau*, which sits halfway between cider and *calvados*.

HIGHLIGHTS OF NORMANDY

■ **Rouen's** imposing **Cathédrale de Notre-Dame** reflects the range and evolution of Gothic design (p. 466).
■ The lush **Seine Valley** includes the 11th-century **Abbaye de Jumiège,** consecrated in front of William the Conqueror in 1067 (p. 470).
■ The **D-Day beaches,** near Bayeux and Caen, recall the tragedy of WWII (p. 488).
■ The abbey of **Mont-St-Michel** rises from the sea above shifting sands (p. 496).
■ You've never seen a museum as funky as the **Maisons Satie** in **Honfleur** (p. 478).

▸ GETTING AROUND

Le Havre, Dieppe, Caen, and Cherbourg welcome travelers arriving by water from England and Ireland. Within Normandy, only major towns are connected by rail; buses fill in the gaps. The major bus operator in *Basse Normandie* (west of Rouen) is **Bus Verts du Calvados** (in Caen tel. 02 31 44 77 44). They offer the **Carte Liberté,** allowing unlimited travel on their lines and on the Caen city bus system. (100F for one day, 150F for three, and 250F per week.) Even if you don't opt for the *Carte*, ask about youth reductions. Since many spots lie off the main roads, a bike or car helps for extended touring. Cyclists should note that roads are hilly and coastal winds blow roughly west to east.

ROUEN

Despite Emma Bovary's experiences, Rouen (pop. 400,000) is no petty provincial town. From the 10th to the 12th century, it bloomed with Gothic architecture and half-timbered houses, as befitted the capital of the Norman empire. Joan of Arc was held prisoner here and tried for heresy by French clergy in 1431. The clerics passed down a life sentence, but under English pressure this was changed to burning at the stake. The saint's name adorns the main thoroughfare and droves of monuments, as well as every hotel, souvenir shop, and *tabac* for miles around. In the 19th century, Victor Hugo dubbed Flaubert's birthplace and Corneille's hometown the "city of a hundred spires," mainly in deference to its imposing cathedral, and Monet's attempts to capture the play of light on the cathedral's façade has made it a fixture in museums around the world. Though Rouen was not spared the devastation of WWII, the reconstructed city is a lively, attractive town.

◪ ORIENTATION AND PRACTICAL INFORMATION

To get to the *centre ville* from the station, follow **rue Jeanne d'Arc** several blocks. A left onto the cobblestone rue du Gros Horloge leads to **pl. de la Cathédrale** and the tourist office; a right leads to **pl. du Vieux-Marché** and its restaurants.

Rouen

ACCOMMODATIONS

A Hôtel du Palais
B Hôtel des Arcades
C Hôtel Normandya

Hôpital Charles Nicolle

r. des Sapins
PL. ST-HILAIRE
r. St-Hilaire
r. du Mont
rampe St-Hilaire
bd. de Verdun
r. Dieutre
av. Georges Metzler
r. des Frères Nicolle
Francis Yard
r. L. Bouilhet
r. Hyacinthe Langois
r. Jouvenet
PL. DU BOULINGRIN
BOULINGRIN Ⓜ
av. Porte des Champs
r. Poussin
bd. de l'Yser
rampe Beauvoisine
r. St-Vivien
Germont
Édouard Adam ✚
r. Joyeuse
r. Orbe
r. des Faulx
r. d'Amiens
bd. Gambetta
av. A. Briand
r. Schumann
Carel
r. Armand
PL. ST-MARC
r. Victor Hugo
r. Als. Lorraine
quai de Paris
Musée des Antiquités 🏛
rte. de Neufchâtel
BEAUVOISINE Ⓜ PL. BEAUVOISINE
bd. de l'Yser
r. de l'Avalasse
rte. d'Ernemont
r. Louis Ricard
PL. DU G. DE GAULLE
St-Ouen ✝
de la République
St-Maclou ✝
Champs des Oiseaux
Tour Jeanne d'Arc
r. du Cordier
r. Beauvoisine
Musée le Secq de Tournelles 🏛
PL. B. TISSOT
GARE-RUE VERTE Ⓜ
r. Verte
r. du Donjon
Musée de la Céramique 🏛
Musée des BeauxArts 🏛
r. Ganterie
des Carmes
Cathédrale de Notre-Dame ✝
quai P. Corneille
Pont Corneille
rue Jeanne d'Arc
r. Bouquet
St-Lô
aux Juifs
ⓘ PL. DE LA CATHÉDRALE
PL. LELIEUR
G. Leclerc
du Grand pont
quai P. Corneille
Pont Boieldieu
r. St-Maur
r. Guy de Maupassant
rampe Bouvreuil
bd. de la Marne
r. Jean Lecanuet
r. des Bons Enfants
PL. DU MARCHÉ
Musée Jeanne d'Arc 🏛
Palais de Justice
Gros Horloge ■ Gros Horloge
aux Ours
Théâtre des Arts
q. de la Bourse
Pont Pierre
r. St-Gervais
PL. CAUCHOISE
r. Cauchoise
r. de Crosne
r. de Fontenelle
Pierre Corneille Museum 🏛
THÉÂTRE DES ARTS Ⓜ
Métrobus
Pont Jeanne d'Arc
quai Jean Moulin
r. Taboure
r. Chasselièvre
r. des Forgettes
PL. CAUCHOISE
r. du G. Giraud
r. des Charrettes
Gare Routière
av. Cartier
JOFFRE-MUTUALITÉ Ⓜ
quai Cavalier de la Salle
bd. d'Orléans
r. Coulon
r. Stanislas Girardin
r. du Renard
PL. DE LA MADELEINE 🏛
r. de Lecat
r. A. France
HENRI IV
la Seine
bd. Jean de Béthencourt
bd. de Banneville
r. Tanger
r. du Pré de la Bataille
Musée Flaubert et d'Histoire de la Médecine ✚
av. Pasteur
r. Duguay Trouin
quai Gaston-Boulet
Pont 6-le Conquérant
PL. DU M. DE LATTRE
r. Brisout de Banneville
bd. des Belges
r. le Nostre
r. de Buffon
bd. de Boisguilbert
bd. du Mont Riboudet

300 yards
300 meters

N

Trains: Rue Jeanne d'Arc. To: **Dieppe** (45min., 7-9 per day, 55F); **Le Havre** (1hr., 12 per day, 71F); **Paris** (1½hr., every hr., 103F); **Caen** via Serquigny (2hr., 5 per day, 114F); and **Lille** (3hr., 2 per day, 159F). Information office open M-Sa 7:15am-7pm.

Buses: SATAR and **CNA**, at the corner of rue St-Éloi and rue des Charrettes (tel. 02 35 52 92 00). To **Dieppe** (2hr., 1-2 per day, 63F) and **Le Havre** (3hr., 2-3 per day, 80F), as well as various small towns along the **Seine Valley**. Office open M-F 8am-12:30pm and 1:45-6:45pm, Sa 8:30am-12:30pm. Station open daily 6am-7:30pm.

Local Transportation: Métrobus, rue Jeanne d'Arc, in front of the Théâtre des Arts (tel. 02 35 52 52 52). Subway and bus run M-Sa 7am-7pm. 1hr. ticket 8F, *carnet* of 10 61F. Day pass 20F, 2-days 30F. Info office at train station open M-Sa 6:30am-7pm.

Taxis: 67 rue Jean Lecanuet (tel. 02 35 88 50 50). 24hr. stands at the train and bus stations, as well as the Palais de Justice on rue Jeanne d'Arc.

Bike Rental: Rouen Cycles, 45 rue St-Éloi (tel. 02 35 71 34 30). 120F per day. Passport deposit. Open Tu-Sa 9am-12:30pm and 2-7:30pm. V, MC.

Tourist Office: 25 pl. de la Cathédrale (tel. 02 32 08 32 40; fax 02 32 08 32 44). Free map. **Exchanges currency** commission-free. Open Apr.-Sept. M-Sa 9am-7pm, Su 9:30am-12:30pm and 2:30-6pm; Oct.-Mar. M-Sa 9am-6:30pm, Su 10am-1pm.

Budget Travel: Wasteels, 111bis rue Jeanne d'Arc (tel. 08 03 88 70 87; fax 02 35 07 48 75). Open M-F 9am-noon and 2-7pm, Sa 9am-noon and 2-6pm. **Forum Voyages,** 72 rue Jeanne d'Arc (tel. 02 35 98 32 59; fax 02 35 70 24 43). Open M-F 9:30am-7pm, Sa 10am-12:30pm and 2-6pm.

English Bookstore: ABC Bookshop, 11 rue des Faulx, behind Église St-Ouen (tel. 02 35 71 08 67). Windows display ads for *au pairs* and tutors for hire. Open Tu-Sa 10am-6pm; closes 3pm in July. Usually closed around Aug. 1-15.

Youth Center: Centre Rouen Information Jeunesse (CRIJ), 84 rue Beauvoisine (tel. 02 35 98 38 75), helps find work and has info on activities. Also makes hostel reservations. Open M-F 10:30am-6:30pm, closes earlier June-Aug.

Laundromat: 73 rue Beauvoisine (tel. 02 35 70 80 10). Open daily 8am-8:30pm. Another on rue Cauchoise near pl. de Vieux Marché. Open daily 7am-9pm.

Hospital: Hôpital Charles Nicolle, 1 rue de Germont (tel. 02 32 88 89 90).

Police: 9 rue Brisout de Barneville (tel. 02 32 81 25 00).

Post Office: 45bis rue Jeanne d'Arc (tel. 02 35 15 66 66). **Currency exchange. Branch** at 122 rue Jeanne d'Arc. Both open M-F 8am-7pm, Sa 8am-noon. **Postal code:** 76000.

Internet Access: Place Net, 37 rue de la République (tel. 02 32 76 02 22), near the Église St-Maclou. 37F for 1 hr. Open M 1-9pm, Tu-Sa 11am-9pm.

▶ ACCOMMODATIONS AND CAMPING

Cheap lodgings lie on the side streets between the train station and Hôtel de Ville.

Hôtel Normandya, 32 rue du Cordier (tel. 02 35 71 46 15), near the train station off rue du Donjon. Owned by an exuberantly friendly, *Let's Go*-loving couple who could be your grandparents. Most rooms are well-lit, nicely decorated, and have excellent views of the city. In others the only natural light is supplied by a skylight (in other words, no views). Tiny toilets. Singles and doubles 110-150F. Shower 10F. Reception open 8am-8pm.

Hôtel des Arcades, 52 rue de Carmes (tel. 02 35 70 10 30; fax 02 35 70 08 91), features comfy rooms with curtained bathroom corner and a jolly owner. Singles and doubles 150F, with shower and TV 205F, with toilet 245F. Breakfast 32F. Reception open 7am-8am daily. V, MC, Amex.

Hôtel du Palais, 12 rue Tambour (tel. 02 35 71 41 40), off rue du Gros Horloge. Clean, large rooms can be noisy during the day but quiet down by evening. Singles 120F; doubles 140F, with shower 170-180F, with toilet and shower 200-220F. Extra bed 40F. Breakfast 25F. V, MC, AmEx.

Campsite: Camping Municipal de Déville, rue Jules Ferry in Déville-les-Rouen (tel. 02 35 74 07 59), 4km from Rouen. Take bus #2 from station to "Mairie." Attractive sites with squeaky-clean bathrooms and hot showers. 24F per person, 8F per tent or car, 15F per caravan. Open May-Sept. for tents; year-round for caravans.

🎭🎵 FOOD AND ENTERTAINMENT

FOOD. Outdoor cafés and *brasseries* crowd around **pl. du Vieux-Marché.** A **market** is held on the *place* itself (Tu-Su 7am-12:30pm). There are also plenty of eateries near the **Gros Horloge. Monoprix supermarket** is at 73-83 rue du Gros Horloge (open M-Sa 8:30am-9pm), and **Marché U** is on pl. du Vieux-Marché (open M-Su 9am-12:45pm and 2:30-7:45pm; V, MC).

🗽 **Natural Gourmand'grain,** 3 rue du Petit Salut (tel. 02 35 98 15 74), off pl. de la Cathédrale. Delicious organic vegetarian food in a small, informal setting. 69F *menu* offers plate of grains and vegetables, drink (try carrot-orange juice), dessert, and coffee; 45F *formule* has the plate and dessert. Also a small health-food store and a *salon du thé* after 3pm. Open Tu-Sa noon-2pm and 7-9pm. Store open noon-6pm. V, MC.

Les Flandres, 5 rue des Bons-Enfants (tel. 02 35 98 45 16). Traditional French food in an informal, vinyl-covered setting. The lunchtime *formule* is a great deal at 55F; 72F *menus* are also available, and the *plat du jour* is 41F. Open M-F noon-2pm and 7:30-9pm, Sa noon-2pm. V, MC, with 100F min.

Al Dente, 24 rue Cauchoise (tel. 02 35 70 24 45), off pl. du Vieux-Marché. Munch on pizzas (52F) and pastas (49F) surrounded by irrepressibly cheery blue and yellow decor and equally cheery Italian waiters. The 59F lunch *menu* includes a drink, pizza or pasta, and dessert. Open Tu-Su 11am-2:30pm and 6-10:30pm. V, MC.

Le Queen Mary, 1 rue du Cercle (tel. 02 35 71 52 09), off pl. du Vieux-Marché. A dozen different delicious mounds of *moules* with fries (44-75F). Super salads 38-45F. Open July-Aug. daily 11:30am-2pm and 7:30-11pm; Sept.-May closed M. V, MC.

ENTERTAINMENT. Rouen's yuppies flock to **Au Bureau,** pl. du Vieux-Marché, when they leave the office, while a younger crowd, heads to **Le Scottish,** 21 rue Verte (tel. 02 35 71 46 22), with weekend jazz concerts on the terrace. (Cocktails 48-52F, beer 18-65F. Open M-Sa 12:30pm-2am.) **The Underground Pub,** 26 rue des Champs Maillets (tel. 02 35 98 44 84), offers billiards and darts. (Beer 15-20F. Open M-Sa 5pm-2am. V, MC.) One of few gay bars in town is **Le Kox,** 138 rue Beauvoisine. (Tel. 02 35 07 71 97. Open daily 6pm-2am. V, MC.)

👁 SIGHTS

Sights in Rouen fall into three basic categories: museums, churches, and museums and churches related to Joan of Arc. The real show-stoppers are the cathedral, the fine arts museum, and Flaubert's former house. *Désolé*, Joan.

CATHÉDRALE DE NOTRE-DAME. The cathedral is among the most important in France, and incorporates nearly every intermediate style of Gothic architecture. Many of the *vitraux* destroyed during WWII have been replaced with frosted glass, giving the cathedral the atmosphere of a very holy bathroom, but the church is becoming gradually brighter and more beautiful as a result of continuing renovations. Don't miss the stained glass in the **Chapelle St-Jean de la Nef** depicting the beheading of St. John the Baptist. To the left of Notre-Dame stands the 12th-century **Tour St-Romanus.** To the right lies the 17th-century **Tour de Beurre,** which was financed through dispensations granted to those who wanted to eat butter during Lent. The cathedral, whose central spire is the tallest in France (151m), is illuminated nightly in summer. *(Pl. de la Cathédrale. Open M-Sa 8am-8pm, Su 8am-6pm. Guided tours daily in summer 10am-5pm.)*

THE NORTHWEST

MUSÉE DES BEAUX-ARTS. Set amidst the lush greenery of sq. Verdel, this excellent museum is attractive inside and out. It holds works by European masters from the 16th through 20th centuries—Monet, Sisley, Renoir, Modigliani, and Marcel Duchamp—as well as works by Rouen natives Jacques-Émile Blanche and Géricault. *(Sq. Verdrel, down rue Jeanne d'Arc from the train station. Wheelchair access is at 26bis rue Jean-Lecanuet, to the right of the main entrance. Tel. 02 35 71 28 40. Open W-M 10am-6pm. 20F; ages 18-25 and groups 13F; handicapped, under 18, and art history students free.)*

MUSÉE FLAUBERT ET D'HISTOIRE DE LA MÉDECINE. Gustave Flaubert grew up on these premises, which have since been converted into a fascinating museum. The building houses a few of Flaubert's possessions, as well as a collection of gruesome medical instruments (including a battlefield amputation kit and gallstone crushers) used by Flaubert's father, a physician. *(51 rue de Lecat, next door to the Hôtel-Dieu hospital. Tel. 02 35 15 59 95. Follow rue de Crosne from pl. de Vieux Marché. Open Tu 10am-6pm, W-Sa 10am-noon and 2-6pm. Free English brochure. Guided visits Sa 2:30pm. 12F; ages 18-25 8F; senior citizens, under 18, and students free.)*

ÉGLISE ST-MACLOU. Built in just 80 years, St-Maclou displays extraordinary Gothic uniformity. The organ, with elaborately carved friezes of saints and musicians, is its most stunning feature. Beyond the church, a poorly marked passageway at 186 rue de Martainville leads to the **Aitre St-Maclou**. This cloister served as the church's slaughterhouse and cemetery during the Middle Ages—including the years of the deadly plagues. Evidence of this legacy can be found in the grisly 15th-century frieze that decorates the beams of the inner courtyard. The *Rouennais* entombed a live cat inside the walls to exorcise spirits; a glass panel to the right of the entrance lets visitors see the unlucky feline. *(Pl. Barthélémy, behind the cathedral. Open M-Sa 10am-noon and 2-5:30pm, Su 3-5:30pm. Aitre: Open daily 8am-8pm. Free.)*

ÉGLISE STE-JEANNE D'ARC. A massive structure designed in 1979 to resemble an overturned Viking long-boat, its unconventional shape disguises the fact that the interior "church in the round" is actually quite tiny. The wall of luminous stained glass was recovered from the Église St-Vincent, destroyed during WWII. A 6.5m cross outside marks the spot where Joan met a fiery martyrdom on May 30, 1431. *(Pl. de Vieux Marché. Open M-F 10am-12:30pm and 2-6pm, Sa-Su 2-6pm.)*

TOUR JEANNE D'ARC. This is the last remaining tower of the château that confined Joan before she was burned to death on May 30, 1431, in the pl. du Vieux-Marché. Except for true fans of Joan, there isn't that much to see. *(To the left of the station on rue du Donjon. Due to renovations, the entrance is on rue Bouvreuil. Open W-Sa and M 10am-12:30pm and 2-6pm, Su 2-6pm only.)*

OTHER SIGHTS. The **Musée des Antiquités** houses a fine collection of Gallo-Roman to Renaissance objects, from crosses and croziers to tapestries and cathedral columns. *(198 rue Beauvoisine, in Cloître Ste-Marie. Tel. 02 35 98 55 10. Open M and W-Sa 10am-12:30pm and 1:30-5:30pm, Su 2-6pm. 20F, seniors 10F, students free.)* You can visit the great dramatist **Pierre Corneille's** former home at 4 rue de la Pie, off pl. du Vieux-Marché. *(Tel. 02 35 71 63 92. Open Th-M 10am-noon and 2-6pm, W 2-6pm. 5F, under 18 free.)* Built into a bridge across rue du Gros Horloge, the **Gros Horloge** (Big Clock) is charmingly inaccurate. When the belfry is eventually repaired, visitors will be able to ascend for a view of the 14th-century clockwork and the rooftops of Rouen. Next to the war-marked Palais de Justice stands the 11th-century **Monument Juif** (Jewish Monument). Uncovered during the 1980s, the structure may have been a synagogue, a Talmudic school, or a private house; regardless, it is one of the few remaining traces of the Jewish presence in medieval Europe. You must call the tourist office two days in advance to take a guided tour in French.

THE SEINE VALLEY

Following the Seine River on its lackadaisical course towards the sea reveals a number of natural and historic treasures strung out along its gently undulating valley. A diverse string of sights awaits along the looping waterway; castles, abbeys, and national parks are spread among rolling farmland and craggy cliffs. There are various routes that can be taken alongside the looping river, including an historic route, an Impressionist route, and a route that hits major castles and mansions, but perhaps the most fascinating is the *Route des Abbayes*, which connects some of the most venerable abbeys in France. The first you'll encounter out of Rouen is the still-functioning **Abbaye St-Martin de Boscherville,** but the star of the bunch is the **Abbaye de Jumièges** (tel. 02 35 37 24 02), founded by St. Philibert in 654. Now a splendid ruin, the abbey is set in lush grounds that incorporate a 17th-century French garden. Of central importance to local history and legend since Merovingian times, the abbey was turned into a stone quarry after being sold during the Revolution, but was bought by the State and restored to an outline of its former grandeur in 1947. (Open daily Apr. 15-Sept. 15 9:30am-7pm and Sept. 16-Apr. 14 9:30am-1pm and 2:30-5:30pm. Guided tours available in French every hour. 35F, children and students 23F.) The **Parc Naturel Regional de Brotonne** sprawls across the Seine midway to Le Havre, an ideal haven for nature-lovers that offers extensive biking, horse-riding, and hiking trails; inquire at the Rouen tourist office for details. The town of Caudebec-en-Caux, easily accessible by bus from Rouen or Le Havre, provides an excellent base to explore the park. A bit further on towards the sea, the town of Villequiers, the site of the tragic drowning of Victor Hugo's daughter Léopoldine and her husband Charles Vacquerie, now houses the **Musée Victor Hugo,** rue Ernest Binet (tel. 02 35 56 78 31). The museum holds memorabilia from the Hugo and Vacquerie families, as well as drawings and first editions by Hugo himself. Cap off your tour of the valley with a gander at the enormous **Pont de Normandie,** the stark, futuristic bridge that joins the northern and southern banks of the Seine just above Le Havre.

It's easiest to get around the valley by car, but **CNA buses** (tel. 02 35 52 92 00) hit most of the major sites. Line #30A runs from Rouen's bus station to several of the abbeys, including Jumièges (45min., 4 per day, 32F). Change buses at Caudebec-en-Caux to reach the Musée Victor Hugo at Villequiers. **Biking** is feasible as well, though distances are far. The Rouen tourist office can provide you with information on excursions and a map detailing all the major sights along the valley.

GIVERNY

Drawn by the verdant hills, haystacks, and lily pads on the Epte river, Impressionist Claude Monet and his eight children settled in Giverny in 1883. By 1887, John Singer Sargent, Paul Cézanne, and Mary Cassatt had placed their easels beside Monet's and the village became an artists' colony. (For more on Impressionism, see **Cultural Connections,** p. 20.) When he was not painting water lilies, Monet devoted much time to his garden, explaining "My garden is my most beautiful masterpiece".

Today, the **Fondation Claude Monet,** 84 rue Claude Monet (tel. 02 32 51 28 21), maintains Monet's house and gardens. From April to July, Giverny overflows with roses, hollyhocks, poppies, and honeysuckle, and the pond beneath the little bridge blooms with water lilies—but the crowds don't leave much room for contemplation. Get there early, preferably in spring when the gardens have just been reopened after months of meticulous grooming. Monet's thatched house is home to his collection of 18th- and 19th-century Japanese prints. Like his studio and the blue- and white-tiled kitchen, each room is bathed in light and flooded by garden scents. The second-floor windows offer lovely views of the Japanese garden. (Open Apr.-Oct. Tu-Su 10am-6pm. 35F, students and ages 12-18 25F, ages 7-12 20F. Gardens only 25F.) Near the foundation, the **Musée d'Art Américain,** 99 rue Claude Monet (tel. 02 32 51 94 65), houses a small number of works by James Whistler, John Singer Sargent, and Mary Cassatt. (Open Apr.-Oct. Tu-Su 10am-6pm. 35F, students, seniors, teachers, and ages 12-18 20F, under 12 15F.)

The nearest **train station** to Giverny is in **Vernon,** 6km away; from here, trains head to **Rouen** (40min., 9-10 per day) and **Paris** (40-60min., 10-16 per day). To get to Giverny, you can **rent a bike** from the Vernon station (tel. 02 32 51 01 72; 55F per day; 1000F or credit card deposit) or take a **bus** (tel. 02 32 71 06 39; 10min.; M-Sa 6 per day each way, Su and holidays 4 per day each way; 12F, round-trip 20F). **Taxis** in front of the train station are another option (one-way 65F weekdays, 80F weekends). The beautiful **hike** along a pedestrian and cyclist path is long and lacks shade; get a free trail map at the Vernon tourist office.

DIEPPE

The first boats to come to this town were those of the Vikings, who creatively named the harbor "Dieppe," from the Norse word meaning "deep." Since the 19th century, Dieppe's pebble-strewn beach has been a favorite spot for British and Parisian vacationers. On August 19, 1942, the beaches were home to less leisurely activity as thousands of Allied (mostly Canadian) troops fought in vain to wrest the port from Nazi control. The *dieppois* have been expressing their gratitude ever since with plaques, monuments, and even a rue de 19 août 1942. Though the town (pop. 36,000) is now a tourist haven, Dieppe's fisherman still support the city's economy with boatloads of *fruits de mer*. The bounteous seafood, imposing château, and gorgeous beach certainly merit a weekend away from Normandy's larger cities.

■ **ORIENTATION AND PRACTICAL INFORMATION.** Two ferry services shuttle between Dieppe and **Newhaven** from the *gare maritime* across the canal at the outer point. For **Stena ferries,** call 08 02 01 00 20 for info and foot passenger reservations, or 02 35 06 39 04 for cars. (2¼-4¼hr.; June-Sept. 4 per day, Oct.-May 1 per day; 110-250F, bikes free. Office open M-Sa 8am-8pm.) For **Hoverspeed,** call 08 00 90 17 77 (2hr.; 2-3 per day; 90-159F on foot, 390-890F with car). Ferry ticket holders can take advantage of a free shuttle between the ferry terminal and the **train station,** bd. Clemenceau (tel. 02 35 06 69 33). Trains go to **Rouen** (45min., 7-9 per day, 55F); all other major destinations require a change at Rouen. (Ticket office open M-F 5:45am-6:30pm, Sa 6:15am-7:35pm, Su 7:15am-8:50pm. Information office open M-Sa 9am-12:30pm and 1:30-6:30pm.) **CNA buses** (tel. 02 35 84 21 97), next to the train station, go to **Fécamp** (1½hr., M-Sa 4 per day, Su 2 per day, 73F) and **Rouen** (2hr., 4 per day, 68F). Buy your tickets on board. (Information office open M-Sa 8am-12:15pm and 2-6:15pm.) **Stradbus,** 1 pl. Ventabren (tel. 02 35 84 49 49), runs buses throughout Dieppe. (Tickets 6.50F, *carnet* of 10 40F.) For a **taxi,** call 02 35 84 20 05. (24hr.) **MJC,** 8 rue du 19 Août 1942 (tel. 02 35 84 16 92), **rents bikes** (55F per half-day, 90F per day), **kayaks,** and **windsurfing equipment** (both 45F per half-day, 65F per day). In summer, MJC relocates to the beach.

A courtesy bus runs from the ferry terminal to the **tourist office,** pont Jehan Ango (tel. 02 32 84 16 92; fax 02 32 14 40 61). Otherwise, follow the fishy smell to the waterfront in the *centre ville.* The friendly, multilingual staff book rooms (20F) and provides maps and info about the town. (Open daily July-Aug. 9am-1pm and 2-8pm; May-June and Sept. M-Sa 9am-1pm and 2-7pm, Su 10am-1pm and 3-6pm; Oct.-Apr. M-Sa 9am-noon and 2-6pm.) Check out the biweekly *Les Informations Dieppoises,* which lists local happenings and hotspots. (Published Tu and F, 6F at *tabacs.*) There's a **Laundromat** at 48 rue de l'Écosse. (Open daily 7:15am-10pm.) The **police** are on bd. Clemenceau, next to the station (tel. 02 32 14 49 00), and the **hospital** is on av. Pasteur (tel. 02 35 06 76 76). The **post office,** 2 bd. Maréchal Joffre (tel. 02 35 06 99 20), has **currency exchange.** (Open M-F 8-11am and 2-6pm, Sa 8am-noon. **Postal code:** 76200.) **La Cybercabine de Dieppe,** 48 rue de l'Épée (tel. 02 35 84 64 36), has **internet access.** (0.85F per min. Open Tu-Sa noon-7pm, Su 2-6pm.)

■ **ACCOMMODATIONS AND CAMPING.** Inexpensive hotels are scattered throughout the town, although truly cheap rates are hard to come by, especially in summer. Two-star establishments line the beach and are a reasonable alternative should cheaper stays be unavailable. Reserve well in advance for August.

The **Auberge de Jeunesse (HI),** 48 rue Louis Fromager (tel. 02 35 84 85 73), has clean, spacious, modern single-sex rooms with bunk beds, in a somewhat odd arrangement. To get there, take bus #2 (direction "Val Druel") from the Chambre

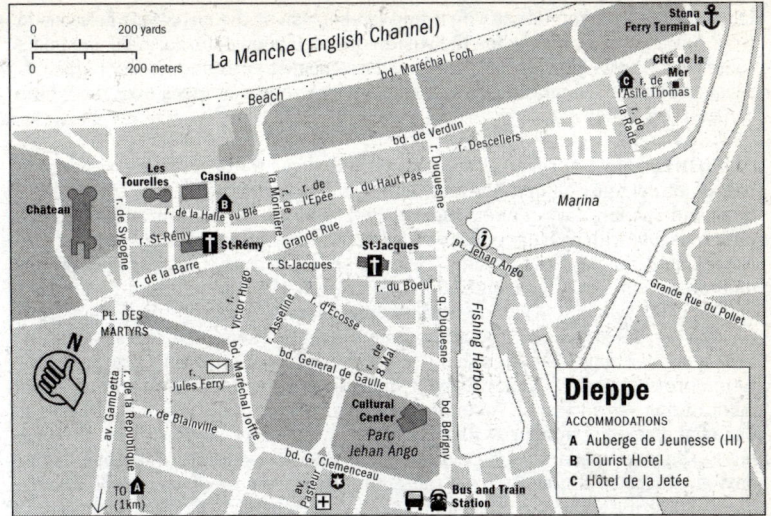

Dieppe

ACCOMMODATIONS
A Auberge de Jeunesse (HI)
B Tourist Hotel
C Hôtel de la Jetée

de Commerce, 200m down quai Duquesne from the station, to "Château Michel." Walk back down the hill a bit and take the first left. Or, if walking, turn left outside the station onto bd. Clemenceau, which later becomes rue de Blainville. At the end of the street, turn right on rue de la République and make a sharp left on rue Gambetta. Climb the hill and keep on truckin'. Turn right at the roundabout onto D925, and left again 200m up the hill (rue Louis Fromager). The hostel is on your right (30min.). (67F. Sheets 17F. Reception 8-10am and 5-10pm.)

Tourist Hôtel, 16 rue de la Halle au Blé (tel. 02 35 06 10 10; fax 02 35 84 15 87), is just behind the beach. From quai Dusquesne, turn left onto rue du Haut Pas, which becomes rue de l'Epée and eventually rue de la Halle au Blé. The polished rooms have large bathrooms. (Singles and doubles with toilet 165F, with shower 135-195F, with both 245F. Breakfast 30F.) Also near the beach, **Hôtel de la Jetée,** 5 rue de l'Asile Thomas (tel. 02 35 84 89 98), has worn but comfortable rooms. Take quai Dusquesne to Quai Henri IV; turn left onto rue de la Rade and then right onto rue d'Asile Thomas. (Singles and doubles 150-210F; triple with shower 300F; 4- to 6-person room 310F. Extra bed 35F. Breakfast 26-32F.)

Camping Vitamin (tel. 02 35 82 11 11) lies on the coast a few kilometers from downtown Dieppe on chemin des Vertus. Take bus #2 (direction "Val Druel") or bus #10 (direction "St-Aubin-sur-Scie") from the station to "Vasarely." Here you'll find a bar, a café, a pool—bliss. (22.50F per person, 25.50F per small tent, 40F per large tent. Reception until 7:30pm.)

ⓘ FOOD. Inexpensive *brasseries*, *boulangeries*, and *crêperies* are found on Grande Rue, quai Henri IV, and around the Église St-Jacques. The *centre ville's* side streets hold small restaurants that proudly serve up the local fish specialties: *sole dieppoise*, *harengs marinés* (marinated herring), *soupe de poisson* (fish soup), and *marmite dieppoise* (a fish and shellfish chowder). Head to ▧ **Les Tourelles,** 43 rue Commandant Fayolles (tel. 02 35 84 15 88), for a delicious and inexpensive meal. Three-course *menus* start at 59F; seafood dishes cost 45-62F. (Open Tu-Su noon-2:30pm and 6:45-10:30pm.) An upscale option is the tasteful **Comptoir Deep,** 8 pl. Camille St-Saëns (tel. 02 35 06 09 11). The 80F *menu* includes local specialties and a few more creative options. (Open Tu-Su noon-2:15pm; July-Aug. also 7-10:30pm.) The seaside picnicker should try **Shopi supermarkets,** with two locations, on rue Gambetta near the hostel (open M-Sa 8:30am-12:30pm and 3-7:30pm, Su 9:30am-noon) and on rue de la Barre (open daily 9am-7:30pm). If canned tuna gets you down, you'll find livelier fish at the **marché de poissons** in front of the tourist office when the weather is good enough for local fishing boats to go out. (Starts 8am, M-Sa.) There's also a **market** surrounding the Église St-Jacques (Tu and Th mornings), and another large one that takes over the whole *centre ville* all day Saturday.

🔊 **SIGHTS.** Most of Dieppe's summer visitors come to roast on the long pebbly beach, bordered by cliffs to the west and by the port to the east. Atop these cliffs rises an imposing 15th-century **château** (tel. 02 35 84 19 76), now an impressive civic museum with an ivory collection, 18th- to 20th-century paintings, and temporary exhibits ranging from a study of *les sirènes* to Georges Braques prints. (Open daily June-Sept. 10am-noon and 2-6pm; Oct.-May W-M 10am-noon and 2-5pm. 15F, children and groups 10F.) In town, **Église St-Jacques** offers a cool stone refuge from the sun (or, since this *is* Normandy, from the rain). The structure was begun in 1182 but was ravaged so often that it wasn't completed until 1543. Ongoing restoration projects seek to repair damage done more recently by German bombardment during World War II. A somber reminder of this is the chillingly beautiful **Canadian Cemetery** in nearby **Hautot-sur-Mer,** where each identified gravestone bears a poem or inscription in English. Visit in the early morning or late evening to have the place to yourself. To get there, turn right from the hostel, walk 20 minutes, and turn right at the cross and sign. Or take bus #2, which leaves every 20 minutes from the tourist office. In the eastern part of town, atop the cliffs, the **Chapelle de Notre-Dame-de-Bon-Secours** commands a stunning view of the harbor. It's a long way, but you'll get terrific pictures of the city and cliffs. Take bus #1 (direction "4 Poteaux") or 8 (direction "Puys"). The **GR21** hiking trail stretches along the cliff tops for miles, providing excellent views of the sea. Dieppe's newest attraction is the **Cité de la Mer,** 37 rue de l'Asile Thomas (tel. 02 35 06 93 20). This sea museum contains aquariums as well as exhibits detailing fishing technology and demonstrating how a maritime economy has influenced the development of the city. (Open daily May-Aug. 10am-7pm; Sept.-Apr. 10am-noon and 2-6pm; closed Dec. 24-Jan 1. 28F, ages 4-16 16F.)

📺 **ENTERTAINMENT.** For a boisterous night, **Le Brunswick,** rue St-Rémy, bowls over a young crowd with loud music, a friendly atmosphere, and occasional free concerts. **Djin's Club** (tel. 02 35 82 33 60) strobes it up at the **Casino,** 3 bd. de Verdun. (Admission Tu-F 50F, Sa 80F, free for women F before midnight. Cover includes first drink.) Other bars cluster on Grande Rue and rue du Haut Pas.

🎆 **FESTIVALS.** In July and August, Dieppe's Centre Jean Renoir, 1 quai Bérigny (tel. 02 35 82 04 43), hosts **L'Été au Cinéma,** a film festival with screenings ranging from Renoir himself to Tim Burton. In late August and early September, look for the **Festival de Musique Ancienne de Dieppe** (tickets 100F per concert, students 70F). In even-numbered years (look who planned for Y2K!), Dieppe soars for the first two weeks in September with the **International Kite Festival.** Write to Dieppe Capitale du Cerf-Volant, Les Tourelles, bd. de Verdun, 76200, Dieppe (tel. 02 32 90 04 95; fax 02 32 90 07 72). Dieppe also hosts its **Herring and Scallop Fair** during the first weekend after November 11th, with tastings and street performers on the quai.

THE HIGH NORMANDY COAST

ÉTRETAT

Heading southwest along the coast from Fécamp leads you to the small resort town of Étretat (pop. 1600), a glorious spot to stop whether it be for an extended vacation or a quick day trip. A favorite destination for British and French holidaymakers, Étretat occupies perhaps the most spectacular spot on the channel coast, its pebble beach sandwiched between soaring chalk cliffs. The blue of the sea, the white of the cliffs, and the tempestuous cloudscape will win your heart. The arching western cliff, known as the **Falaise d'Aval,** was likened by Guy de Maupassant to an elephant dipping its trunk into the sea. Ascend the stairs on the west end of the promenade (to the left facing the sea) to ramble along the cliff top for spectacular views up and down the coast. The eastern cliff, **Falaise d'Amont,** is similarly compelling. Perched atop it is the tiny **Chapelle Notre Dame de la Garde,** constructed by the Jesuits in 1854. Behind the church sits the **Musée Nungesser et Coli** and a monument dedicated to the first aviators to attempt crossing the Atlantic; their plane was lost off the coast of Étretat in 1927. (Open daily June 15-Sept. 15 10am-noon and 2-6pm.) The town itself is fairly small, consisting of a handful of adorably crooked streets that wend their way between the main avenue, Georges V, and the beach. Smuggled among them is the house formerly inhabited by crime novelist extraordinaire Maurice Leblanc. **Le Clos Lupin,** 15 rue de Maupassant (tel. 02 35 27 08 23), is now home to a *son et lumière* spectacle that allows the visitor a peek into the life and times of Leblanc's creation, gentleman burglar Arsène Lupin.

For a break from the usual French fare, try the unrealistically good Vietnamese and Chinese fare on offer at the gracious **Hoa Binh,** 44bis rue Alphonse Karr, by the beach. (Open Tu-Sa 12:15-2:30pm and 7:15-10:30pm. V, MC.) There are a plethora of hotels in town, but none are truly budget, and the closer to the beachfront, the higher the rates. Reservations are crucial in summertime. **Hôtel l'Angleterre,** 35 av. Georges V (tel. 02 35 27 01 65; fax 02 35 28 78 44), may not be cheap, but is still a wonderful value for the money, with gorgeous, sunny rooms decorated in a tasteful tropical theme. It's just steps from the beach, and there's a shower, toilet, and TV in every room. (Singles and doubles 260F; triples and quads 350F; lower prices Sept.-Easter. Reception daily 8am-8pm. V, MC.) Campers can bed down at the town **campsite** (tel. 02 35 27 07 67), straight down rue Guy de Maupassant from the tourist office. It may be dirt cheap, but it's about the only place in town to be far from the beach. (13F per person, children 6.50F; 13.50F per car. Reception 9am-noon and 3-7pm. Lockout 10:30pm-7am.)

The **tourist office** (tel. 02 35 27 05 21; fax 02 35 28 87 20), just behind the bus stop, can outfit you with a free map, a **bike** (50F for 2hr.), and a guided tour. (Open June-Aug. daily 10am-7pm, shorter hours in winter.) **Les Autocars Gris** (tel. 02 35 27 04 35) run from **Le Havre** (1hr., 10-12 per day, 39F) and **Fécamp** (35min., 12 per day, 29F) to the center of town.

FÉCAMP

Tucked among craggy cliffs, Fécamp (pop. 20,000) is one of the jewels of the High Normandy coast, well worth a daytrip from Dieppe or Rouen. While the city bustles today as France's major cod-fishing port, Fécamp first found fame as a pilgrimage site in the 6th century, when some drops of Christ's blood *(précieux-sang)* allegedly washed ashore in a fig-tree trunk. Pilgrims still come in numbers to adore the holy plasma, which is held in the **Église Abbatiale de la Trinité,** rue des Forts. Legend has it that as the bishops were arguing over the dedication of the church, an angel appeared and commanded that it should be placed under the patronage of the Holy Trinity; the heavyweight messenger left a footprint to mark his passage. Though the original 10th-century church burnt down, you can still see the footprint to the right of the altar in today's 12th- to 13th-century edifice. The nave, at 127m, is as long as Notre-Dame's in Paris, and the tower stands 70m tall. At the eastern end of the nave, near the chapel to the Virgin, sits a gold box containing the relic of the *précieux-sang.*

Other than on pilgrimage days (Tuesday and Thursday after Trinity Sunday in late May or early June), most visitors to Fécamp are after a different precious liquid entirely. From the 16th-18th century, Fécamp's Benedictine monks mixed a mysterious concoction of 27 regional plants and Asian spices as a healing agent. Local wine merchant Alexandre Le Grand rediscovered the recipe, lost during the Revolution, and built a *palais* in 1888 to distill the spirit, christened in homage to the monks who invented it. Today the **Palais Bénédictine,** 110 rue Alexandre Le Grand (tel. 02 35 10 26 10), remains the towns greatest draw; admire the collection of medieval and Renaissance artifacts while sipping a taste of the potent liqueur. (Open daily May 13-Sept. 5 9:30am-6pm; Sept. 6-Nov. 15 and Mar. 13-May 12 10am-noon and 2-5:30pm; Nov. 16-Mar. 12 10-11:15am and 2-5pm. 29F.) Entry to the Palais is half-price if you combine it with a ticket to Fécamp's two lesser museums, the **Musée des Terre-Neuvas et de la Pêche,** 27 bd. Albert 1er (tel. 02 35 28 31 99), dedicated to the adventures of the local cod fishermen, and **Le Musée Centre-des-Arts,** near the abbey at 21 rue Alexandre Legros (tel. 02 35 28 31 99), which displays regional art and objects such as furniture, carvings, and armor. (Both open July-Aug. daily 10am-noon and 2-5:30pm; Sept.-June closed Tu. 20F, 10F students.)

If you plan on spending the night in town, try the **Hôtel Martin,** 18 pl. St-Étienne (tel 02 35 28 23 82; fax 02 35 28 61 21), which has clean, cheery rooms and a delightful restaurant downstairs. (Singles and doubles 150-200F. Reception open 7:30am-11pm, closed Su evening and M. V, MC, AmEx.) For food, there's a **Marché-Plus supermarket** at 83 quai Berigny. (Open M-Sa 7am-9pm, Su 9am-1pm. V, MC.)

The *centre ville* is behind the Église St-Étienne, across the street from the station and up the stairs. To reach the **tourist office,** 113 rue Alexandre Le Grand (tel. 02 35 28 51 01; fax 02 35 27 07 77), follow rue St-Étienne to the right as it becomes rue de Mer. Turn left at the Palais Bénédictine; the office is across from its entrance. The staff dispenses maps and books rooms for 10F. (Open July-Aug. M-F 10am-6pm, Sa-Su 10am-noon and 2-6pm; Sept.-June M-F 9am-12:15pm and 1:45-6pm, closed Su from Nov.-Easter.)

Fécamp is accessible by **train** from **Le Havre** (45min., 5 per day, 43F), **Rouen** (75min., 7 per day, 68F), and **Paris** (2½hr., 7 per day, 146F), and by **CNA bus** (tel. 02 35 84 21 97) from **Dieppe** (2hr., 4 per day, 68F).

LE HAVRE

Everybody comes to Le Havre (pop. 197,000), but no one stays. Founded in 1517 by François I, the town can boast of being the largest transatlantic port in France and little else. Le Havre's answer to WWII's devastation was to call in architect Auguste Perret, who created an eulogy to reinforced concrete, compounding the unsightliness of the already utilitarian harbor. Important as a first port of call for many British and American travelers, the town is at best a stopover on the way to more congenial climes; get in, get out, and no one gets hurt.

▮ ORIENTATION AND PRACTICAL INFORMATION. P&O European Ferries, av. Lucien Corbeaux (tel. 02 35 19 78 50), depart from Terminal de la Citadelle (tel. 08 03 01 30 13) for **Portsmouth.** See **Getting There: By Boat,** p. 62, for details of service. (Ticket and info office open daily 7am-6pm. Terminal closes at 11pm.) **Trains** leave from cours de la République (tel. 02 35 98 50 50) for **Fécamp** via **Étretat** (45min., 5 per day, 43F), **Paris** (1hr., 7-9 per day, 150F), and **Rouen** (1hr., 9-12 per day, 71F). (Info office open M-Sa 9am-6:30.) The **bus station** (tel. 02 35 26 67 23) is by the train station on bd. de Strasbourg. **CNA** run to **Rouen** (3hr., M-Sa 8 per day, Su 2 per day, 85F); **Bus Verts** (tel. 08 01 21 42 14) to **Caen** (1½hr., 6 per day, 124F) and **Honfleur** (30min., 6 per day, 45F); and **Autocars Gris** (tel. 02 35 28 19 88) to **Fécamp** via **Étretat** (100min., 8 per day, 50F). **Bus Océane,** 115 rue Jules Lecesne (tel. 02 35 19 75 75), run about town. (Tickets 8F, *carnet* of 10 50F. *Ticket ville* day pass 20F.) **Radio-Taxis** (tel. 02 35 25 81 81 or 02 35 25 81 00) wait at the train station (24hr.).

To reach the **tourist office,** 186 bd. Clemenceau (tel. 02 32 74 04 04; fax 02 35 42 38 39), from the station, follow bd. de Strasbourg across town as it changes to av. Foch, to bd. Clemenceau; the tourist office is on your left. From the ferry terminal, walk left down quai de Southampton and then right up bd. Clemenceau. **Beware** of walking anywhere alone at night, especially around the train station and harbor. The businesslike staff can outfit you with a list of hotels and restaurants and a free map. (Open Oct.-Apr. M-Sa 9am-6:30pm, Su 10am-1pm; May-Sept. M-Sa 9am-7pm, Su 10am-12:30pm and 2:30-6:30pm.) The **hospital** is at 29 av. Pierre Mendès-France, Montivilliers (tel. 02 32 73 32 32), and the

police are on rue de la Victoire (tel. 02 32 74 37 00). The **post office** is on rue Jules Siegfried. (Tel. 02 32 92 59 00. Open M-F 8am-7pm, Sa 8am-noon. **Postal code:** 76600.) **Cybermetro,** on cours de la République across from train station, has **internet access.** (30F for 30min., 45F per hr.; student discounts. Open daily 8am-midnight.)

■ ■ **ACCOMMODATIONS AND FOOD.** Cheap one-star hotels, offering mostly singles, line the seedy cours de la République across from the train station. Pricier and marginally prettier two-star establishments line bd. de Strasbourg. **Hôtel Jeanne d'Arc,** 91 rue Émile Zola (tel. 02 35 21 67 27; fax 02 35 41 26 83), offers delightful, homey rooms, all with TVs and phones. (Singles 140-150F; doubles 160-165F; triples 230F. Breakfast 20F. V, MC.) **Hôtel Le Monaco,** 16 rue de Paris (tel. 02 35 42 21 01), near the ferry terminal, has spacious rooms with classy, country house decor. There's a good *brasserie* downstairs. (Singles 140-210F; doubles 165-260F; triples 240-300F; quads 350F. Breakfast 30F. Shower 25F. Reception 6:30am-11pm. V, MC.) For the lowest prices, head to cramped but clean **Hôtel Le Commerce,** 12 rue Dupleix (tel. 02 35 42 64 60), behind the AmEx Office on quai Georges V. (Singles and doubles 100-138F. Shower 15F. Breakfast 27F.)

Le Havre offers no shortage of cheap eateries, but don't set your sights too high. Restaurants crowd rue Victor Hugo near the Hôtel de Ville, while the streets between rue de Paris and quai Lamblardie frame a plethora of neighborhood restaurants frequented by locals. At **Le P'tit Comptoir,** av. Faidherbe by the port, workers, execs, and tourists rub elbows over the 67F and 95F *menus.* (Open daily noon-2pm and 7-9:30pm. V, MC.) For a quick, cheap meal, hit the **YMCA cafeteria** at 138 bd. de Strasbourg, which offers a 37F *formule.* Stock up for the ferry voyage at **Nouvelles Galeries supermarket,** quai George V (open M-Sa 8:30am-7pm; V, MC), or at **Monoprix,** 38-40 av. René Coty (open M-Sa 8:30am-8:30pm; V, MC).

■ ■ **SIGHTS AND ENTERTAINMENT.** The skyscraper visible from practically everywhere in town is actually a church; the **Église St-Joseph** is yet another verse in Perret's paean to the wonders of concrete. The quiet shade of the weeping willows in the **Jardin Sarraute,** off av. Foch, provide a refreshing counterpoint to the town's unremitting griminess, as do the sparkling fountains on **pl. de l'Hôtel de Ville.** If you are stuck in town overnight, treat yourself to an evening of the performing arts at the **Maison de la Culture du Havre,** the bizarre white structure on pl. Gambetta that looks like the unholy union of a nuclear power plant and overturned toilet bowl. Nicknamed "Le Volcan," the controversial building houses a state-of-the-art theater which hosts renowned orchestras and plays, as well as a cinema that screens new releases and classics. (Open Tu-Sa 1:30-7pm. Closed July 20-Aug. 30. Call 02 35 19 10 10 for info.) The recently renovated **Musée des Beaux Arts André Malraux,** where bd. Kennedy meets bd. Clemenceau (tel. 02 35 19 62 62), features an interesting collection of pre-Impressionist works. (Open W-M.)

THE CÔTE FLEURIE

In contrast to Normandy's working port cities, the smaller villages along the coast of Lower Normandy, known as the Côte Fleurie, are decidedly playful. Doubling as resort towns and thalassotherapy centers where the wealthy come to be slathered in mud or massaged with healing oils, these coastal towns have served as weekend destinations for Paris's elite since the mid-19th century. Today they cater to a more international crowd, which means the tourist office won't turn up its nose at your French. Of course, such hospitality has its price. You'll find precious few budget hotels, although the beach is *compris,* and some get away with sleeping on it. *Let's Go* does not recommend sleeping on the beach. Hostels or hotels in Caen serve as good budget bases; Bus Verts provides regular connections between coastal towns and to Caen and Bayeux. Consider their *Carte Liberté* bus passes if you'll be doing a lot of touring (see p. 466).

THE NORTHWEST

HONFLEUR

Honfleur's history is inextricably intertwined with the sea. The town's name is from the old Norman expression Hon Flaw ("important harbor") and is testimony to its maritime heritage. The town was a defensive bastion against English invaders during the Hundred Years' War, the port from which Champlain sailed on his trip to found Québec, and the birthplace of composer Erik Satie. It managed to escape unscathed from World War II and looks with pride to the marvelously intact 15th- and 16th-century buildings that line the streets of the *centre ville*. The artistic facet of Honfleur's *patrimoine* is seen in the streets filled with painters and the art galleries scattered all over town. Painters today say that during one day in Honfleur, one experiences all the colors of the seasons—the morning is spring, the mid-afternoon summer, the evening fall, and the night winter.

🛈 PRACTICAL INFORMATION. The bus station (tel. 02 31 89 28 41) is located at the end of quai Lepaulmier near the Bassin de l'Est. **Bus Verts** connect Honfleur to **Le Havre** (30min., 6 per day, 37F) and **Caen** (1½hr., 15 per day, 85F). To get to the **tourist office,** 33 pl. Arthur Boudin (tel. 02 31 89 23 30; fax 02 31 89 31 82), follow quai Lepaulmier to the right from the bus station and turn right on rue de la Ville. The office is at the end of the street. (Open Oct.-Easter M-Sa 9:30am-noon and 2-6pm; Easter-June and Sept. M-Sa 9:30am-12:30pm and 2-6:30pm, Su 10am-1pm; July-Aug. M-Sa 9:30am-7pm, Su 10am-1pm.) Free spirits can **rent bikes** at **Station Fina,** cours Jean de Vienne (tel. 02 31 89 91 73).

🛏 ACCOMMODATIONS. Budgeteers should make Honfleur a daytrip—hotels here have more stars than most constellations. **Les Cascades,** 17 pl. Theirs (tel. 02 31 89 41 77; fax 02 31 89 48 09), however, offers comparatively inexpensive rooms in an ideal location right next to the port. The marble staircase leads to comfortable rooms with minimal but agreeable decor and phones. (Doubles 170-200F, with shower and toilet 210-240F, with TV 250-280F, with TV and bath 270-300F. Lower prices represent off-season. Breakfast 35F. Open Feb.-Nov. V, MC.) The seaside **Le Phare Campsite** (tel. 02 31 89 10 26) rests at a quiet location 300m from the *centre ville* at the end of rue Haute. It gets crowded in summer, so arrive early to get a spot in the shade. (28F per person, 35F per tent and car. Shower 8F. Reception 9am-noon and 2-7pm. Automobile curfew 10pm-7am. Open Apr.-Sept.)

🍴 FOOD. Though it's decor leaves something to be desired, **Le Goéland,** 21 rue de la Ville, in a central location near the *vieux bassin*, serves *galettes* and a tasty 82F *menu* including such specialties as *truite aux amandes*. Like its pricier neighbors, it also has a pleasant terrace on the cobblestones. (Open Feb.-Dec. Tu-Su noon-10pm.) For a sweet splurge, the homemade ice cream at **Aimé Stéphan,** 60 quai Ste-Catherine (tel. 02 31 89 55 25), is worth the steep prices; generous portions in flavors like ginger and saffron bring cool and interesting relief from the heat of the sunny port. For groceries, drop by the **Champion supermarket,** pl. Sorel. The regular **market** takes place on place Ste-Catherine, in front of the *église* (Sa morning), while pl. St-Léonard sees an organic **Marché Bio** (W morning).

MILKIN' IT FOR ALL ITS WORTH

The houses on quai Ste-Catherine, lining the Vieux Bassin, stand on ground once belonging to Mademoiselle de Montpensier, a cousin of Louis XIV. In 1630, the last of the city ramparts were torn down to allow economic development. Mlle Montpensier, a shrewd businesswoman looking to make the largest profit possible, divided her property into the smallest lots possible before selling them, accounting for the extreme narrowness of the building fronts. In looking at the buildings one can see that, after the 3rd floor, the style of the windows changes; she made an extra profit by the fact that her property was on a hill—the change in architecture corresponds to the "ground" floor of another house whose front door opens up onto the back.

⚙ SIGHTS. Honfleur is for the curious; while the port and roads hold delights for the casual stroller, a close eye to tucked-away streets and corners will reveal any number of delights. Part of the ramparts that once surrounded the fishing village, the **Porte de Caen** at the end of quai Ste-Catherine is the only remaining door (of two) through which the king would ride into the fortified town. A block away from the Bassin's waters is the 15th-century **Église Ste-Catherine**, pl. Ste-Catherine. The largest all-wood church in France, the choice of material came upon the burning of the first church in 1450 and the desire of religious (and cheapskate) local sailors to have a church erected as soon as possible, at minimum cost. The ceiling looks much like two overturned hulls. (Open daily 9am-noon and 2-6pm.)

Worth the trip to Honfleur by itself is the new **Maison de Satie**, 67 bd. Charles V (tel. 02 31 89 11 11), an extraordinary and original museum commemorating the town's famous composer, musician, artist, and author, Erik Satie. Breathtaking, fanciful, and a little psychedelic, a self-guided tour through a maze of rooms is like taking a stroll through the mind of an artist; each room is a surprise. Accompanied by excerpts from Satie's works (provided by bilingual digital-quality headsets), each scene uses a different set of objects and images relating directly to themes present in his music and his life. Expect starry ceilings, indoor rainshowers, and floating images filled with color. (30F, students and seniors 20F. Open July-Aug. W-M 10am-7pm; Sept.-June W-M 10:30am-6pm.)

Paintings of Honfleur by Eugène Boudin and his circle became popular in the 19th century. Many critics consider their works to be precursors of Impressionism; visitors can decide for themselves at the **Musée Eugène Boudin,** pl. Erik Satie (tel. 02 31 89 54 00), off rue de l'Homme de Bois. Along with the vast collection of paintings on the upper level, the lower level contains an informative, interesting display on Norman ethnography. (Open in summer W-M 10am-noon and 2-5pm; off-season W-M 2-5pm, Sa 10am-noon and 2-5pm. 30F, students 25F.) For the full maritime treatment, check out the **Musée de la Marine,** quai St-Étienne (tel. 02 31 89 14 12), on the Vieux Bassin in the former Église St-Étienne. The tiny but packed museum tells the tale of Honfleur's affair with the sea. (Open Apr.-Sept. Tu-Su 10am-noon and 2-6pm; Oct.-Dec. and Feb. 15-Mar. M-F 2-6pm, Sa-Su 10am-noon and 2-6pm. 15F, students 10F.)

To eat your lunch or *casse-croute*, head to the shady **public gardens** on the bd. Charles V, just beside the port. Carefully planted flower beds, swingsets, a wading pool, and a waterfall should provide some cool entertainment during the hottest hours of the day. (Open June 15-Aug. 9:30am-9:30pm; Sept. 1-14 8am-8pm; Sept. 15-30 7:30am-7:30pm; Oct.-Nov. 14 7:30am-6pm; Nov. 15-Mar. 14 7:30am-5pm; Mar. 15-June 14 7:30am-8pm.) A spectacular photo opportunity of the looming Pont de Normandie awaits at the peak of **Mont-Joli.** Fill your water bottle and follow rue du Puits from pl. Ste-Catherine to a steep asphalt ramp sloping up to the right.

DEAUVILLE AND TROUVILLE

Deauville and Trouville are traditionally treated as a pair, but lead quite different lives on opposite banks of the river Touques. Since its founding in 1861 by Napoleon's cousin, le Duc de Morny, **Deauville** has consistently drawn the Parisian upper crust to its sandy shores, counting among its devotees Colette, Josephine Baker, and Maurice Chevalier. Its evolution as a resort town manifests itself today in its flagrant and self-proclaimed prestige; don't even think about walking into a boutique in flip-flops. Besides, if a fight ever broke out inside over the last taupe Hermès handbag, you might get your eyes gouged out by the gargantuan diamonds which grace pinkies and thumbs all over town. Better to stick to the comparatively inexpensive and somewhat more welcoming **Trouville,** where hotels are cheaper and there is no dress code for shopping.

⚑ DISORIENTATION AND PRACTICAL CONFUSION. Like siamese twins, Trouville and Deauville share the same train and bus stations. **Trains** (tel. 02 31 88 28 80) go to **Paris, Caen,** and **Rouen. Bus Verts** (tel. 0801 214 214) do an excellent job of joining Deauville-Trouville with **Honfleur** (20min., 22F), **Le Havre** via Honfleur (1hr., 59F), **Caen** (70min., 53F), and **Houlgate** and **Cabourg** (20min., 22F). **Agence Fournier**, pl. du Maréchal Foch in Trouville (tel. 02 31 88 16 73), runs **shuttles** between Deauville and Trouville. (9.50F per ticket, 15-trip pass 100F.) For **taxis** call 02 31 88 35 33 or 0800 51 41 41.

To get to **Trouville** from the *gare*, exit and turn right across the bridge, which will land you on the main bd. Fernand Moureaux; turn right and the tourist office is a 1-minute walk to the right in the direction of the *centre ville*. The **Trouville tourist office** is at 32 quai Ferdinand Moureaux (tel. 02 31 14 60 70; fax 02 31 14 60 71). The very helpful staff distributes *Le Guide: Trouville*, a complete vacationing guide; also available are a short history of Trouville, walking tours in the area, and a town map. Free guided walking tours in English are available upon request. The office also runs a free club for 14- to 18-year-olds on the beach, including watersports, tennis, volleyball, and a pool. (Open Nov.-Mar. 9:30am-noon and 2-6pm; Apr.-June and Sept.-Oct. 9:30am-noon and 2-6:30pm; July-Aug. 9:30am-7pm.)

To get to **Deauville** from the *gare*, turn left as you exit; at the first major round-about take the second right (rue Desiré le Hoc) and follow it two blocks to pl. Morny. Continue another block and the tourist office will be on a street corner in front of you (10min.). The **Deauville tourist office,** pl. de la Mairie (tel. 02 31 14 40 00; fax 02 31 88 78 88), can supply you with information about the prestigious film and music festivals that take place in Deauville throughout the year, as well as info concerning the hippodrome and equestriamania for which the resort town is famous. They'll also tell you all about the prestige of their town during their 2½-hour guided tours. (Open Sept. 15-Apr. 30 M-Sa 9am-12:30pm and 2-6:30pm; May-June M-Sa 9:30am-6:30pm; July-Sept. 15 9am-7pm; Su year-round 10am-1pm and 2-5pm; July-Aug. 10am-6pm.)

📠 **ACCOMMODATIONS AND CAMPING.** You'll have to stay in Trouville if you want to sleep without pawning your pack. **Hôtel La Reynita,** 29 rue Carnot (tel 02 31 88 15 13), welcomes guests to its spacious rooms and huge bathrooms. All rooms have minibar, TV, and phone; some even have internet jacks. The hotel will be renovated for 2000. (Doubles 265F; triples 370-450F. Breakfast 35F. V, MC.) The brisk owner at **Le Florian** lets clean, somewhat worn rooms in a slightly dingy building at 30 rue de la Plage (tel. 02 31 88 17 40; fax 02 31 39 61 41). All rooms have phones and TVs, while some get a sea view. The proximity to the beach compensates for occasionally peeling wallpaper. (Singles 200-220F; doubles 300-400F; triples 360-480F. Extra bed 80F. Breakfast 27F, subject to change.) **Camping Hamel,** 55 rue des Sœurs de l'Hôpital (tel. 02 31 88 15 56), is five minutes from the station. At the bridge turn right, and in front of you will be rue Biesta. Follow it until it turns into rue des Sœurs de l'Hôpital; the campsite will be on your left, in a large enclosed field in a residential neighborhood. It's not deluxe, but it's convenient for the *centre ville*. (12F per adult, 6F per tent. Electricity 10F.) **Camping Le Chant des Oiseaux,** 11 rte. d'Honfleur (tel 02 31 88 06 42; fax 02 31 98 16 09), is 2km from town on cliffs overlooking the sea; take the Bus Verts (direction "Honfleur") to "Camping." It has beach access, a restaurant, games room, and minigolf. (28F per tent, 25F per adult. Shower 2F.)

🍴 **FOOD.** Because many of the restaurants face the west and receive the rays of the setting sun, in the evenings beachcombers and locals flock to *trouvillais* terraces to eat and sun themselves. The tiny and delightful **Tivoli Bistro,** 27 rue Charles Mozin, is like eating in the kitchen of a family friend. Christine and Gérard welcome families and friends alike with a 3-course 78F *menu* in a small wooden dining hall. (Open daily noon-2:30pm and 7-10:45pm; closed W evening and Th off-season.) A number of seafood restaurants with reasonable *menus* line the pedestrian street rue des Bains; among them try the **Restaurant-Crêperie des Bains,** 8 rue des Bains (tel. 02 31 88 76 15), which offers *menus* for 68F, 115F, and 145F, as well as salads and *crêpes à la carte* in a somewhat gaudy interior—try the terrace for a little fresh air. (Open noon-3pm and 6-11pm, Sa-Su noon-midnight. Closed Tu and W in the off-season.) There is a **Monoprix Supermarket** on bd. F. Moureaux. (M-Sa 9am-7:30pm.) A **market** fills pl. Maréchal Foch in Trouville (W and Sa morning).

🏛 🎵 **SIGHTS AND ENTERTAINMENT.** The original and best attraction at both Trouville and Deauville is, of course, the beach. The boardwalk promenades are the respective prides of each town, especially in Trouville where a stroll along the wooden planks affords a view of the spectacular houses that inspired Flaubert.

A short walk outside town is **Villa Montebello,** 64 rue du Général Leclerc (in Trouville tel. 02 31 88 16 26), a magnificent Second Empire residence built in 1865 after the style of Louis XIII. It holds a series of rotating and permanent exhibits featuring artists' depictions and representations of the town. (Open Apr. 3-Sept. 26 2-6pm daily except Tu.) The somewhat eclectic **Aquarium-Vivarium de Trouville** (tel. 02 31 88 46 04; fax 02 31 81 20 70), along the boardwalk, offers fun out of the sun for reptile lovers; somewhat akin to the house of an eccentric collector, the glass aquariums hold finches, tarantulas, and geckos amidst a collection of local and tropical fish. (Open July-Aug. 10am-7:30pm; Sept.-Oct. 10am-noon and 2-7pm; Nov.-Easter 2-6:30pm; Easter-June 10am-noon and 2-7pm. 35F, 30F for students.)

Trouville's casino, **Louisiane Follies,** pl. du Maréchal Foch on the beachfront (tel. 02 31 87 75 00), has an adjoining nightclub and cinéma, and offers a somewhat more laid-back atmosphere than the **Casino de Deauville** (tel. 02 31 14 31 14). **Café Trouville,** a series of café-side concerts held in July and August (4-5 per week), can be enjoyed on the terrace of the café *du jour* or out on the sidewalk for free (see tourist office for details). The third weekend in June sees both the **Festival Folklorique** in Trouville, with music and dance groups from all over the world performing in the street, as well as the town's **Carnaval.** The wine bar **La Maison,** 66 rue des Bain (tel. 02 31 81 43 10), in Trouville, offers a sophisticated and laid-back setting. Grass mats and wrought-iron furniture give a dreamy, Spanish flavor to the warmly-lit interior; the terrace provides a great people-watching spot on the central rue des Bains. (Open June-Sept. daily 11am-1am; closed W Oct.-May.)

Deauville, famous for activities surrounding its four-legged equine demi-god, also hosts a number of festivals, including **Swing'In Deauville,** in the third week of June, and the **American Film Festival** in April, as well as a series of culturally-diverse concerts and festivals ranging from classical music to modern dance. Contact the Deauville tourist office for festival details.

HOULGATE

Quieter and more affordable than its neighbors to the east, Houlgate's 1.5km of sandy beach is strewn with seashells. Farther east, the sea swells crash into the **Vache Noir** (Black Cow) cliffs, so named because the fossil deposits of ancient crustaceans lend a dark hue to the cliffs' exposed limestone.

Room prices rise in July and August; ask for a list of *chambres d'hôtes* at the tourist office. If you like feeling the vibrations from the tent beside you, try the extra cozy **Camping de la Plage,** at the end of rue Henri Dobert (tel./fax 02 31 28 73 07). It's literally on the beach, just as you will be literally on top of your neighbor in high season. (20F per person, 23F per car, 15F per tent. Electricity 17F. Shower 5F. Gates closed 10pm-7:30am. Open Apr.-Sept.) **La Fromentine,** 36 rue du Général Leclerc (tel. 02 31 24 53 25), serves tasty *crêpes* (5-46F), *galettes*, and pizzas (42-59F) for as cheap as they'll come in this town. (Open daily noon-2:30pm and 7-10pm. V, MC.) At the laid-back **Le Globe Bar,** 44 rue des Bains (tel. 02 31 28 74 50), you can find both *moules* and pizza for around 40F. (V, MC.) A **8 à huit supermarket** slaves at 39 rue des Bains, near the beach. (Open daily 7am-9pm.)

A tide table is available at Houlgate's **tourist office** (tel. 02 31 24 34 79; fax 02 31 24 42 27), to the right of the town hall on bd. des Belges, diagonally across from the Bus Verts stop. (Open July-Aug. M-Sa 9am-7pm; in winter Su only 9am-12:30pm and 2-6:30pm.) The **post office,** at the corner of bd. des Belges and bd. de St-Philbert, **exchanges currency.** (Open M-F 8:30am-12:30pm and 2-5pm, Sa 8:30am-noon.) **Bus Verts** run to Houlgate from Caen (37F) through Cabourg (from Cabourg, 10F).

CABOURG

A little to the west of Houlgate, Cabourg's beachfront attracts hordes of preening Parisians. Marcel Proust (see p. 21) spent many summers looking for himself and penning his *Remembrance of Things Past* at Cabourg's **Grand Hôtel.**

For those seeking time to write their own masterpieces, tranquil **Hôtel Rally,** 5 av. Général Leclerc (tel. 02 31 91 27 35; fax 02 31 91 51 11), offers small, cheery, and comfortable pastel rooms 10m from the "Pasteur" bus stop. There's a phone and TV in all rooms. (Doubles and triples with shower 200F, with shower and toilet 230F. Breakfast 27F.) The *brasserie* downstairs has *moules marinières* for 35F. The pretty and spacious rooms of **L'Oie qui Fume,** 18 av. de la Brèche-Buhot (tel. 02 31 91 27 79; fax 02 31 91 40 02), 300m from the beach at the opposite end of av. Georges Clemenceau from the tourist office, come with quiet gardens but no cigar-toting geese. All rooms have phone, TV, and radio. (Singles and doubles 280F, with shower 295F, with bath and shower 300F. Extra bed 40F. Breakfast 35F. V, MC.) To camp in Cabourg, take the bus to "Oasis" and follow chemin Cailloué to **Camping de la Pommeraie** (tel. 02 31 91 54 58), with extensive grounds a little close for comfort to the main road. (25F, tent 32F. Open Apr.-Sept.)

For the hungry, a short walk from the beach leads you away from the wind and higher prices. The popular and often very crowded **Le Champagne,** pl. du Marché (tel. 02 31 91 02 29), offers a satisfying meal after a day in the sun with 3-course *menus* at 78F and 4-course *menus* from 95F. (Open daily mid-June-Aug. noon-2pm and 7-9pm; Sept.-mid-June Tu-Sa only. V, MC.) Many pizzerias and *crêperies* flank the hopping **av. de la Mer.** The folks at the **Brasserie, Bar, et Restaurant du Marché,** pl. du Marché (tel. 02 31 91 02 29), get their food straight from the market in front of the establishment. *Menus* of local specialties run 60-120F. (Open Tu-Su noon-2:30pm and 6:30-9:30pm.) The aforementioned **market** takes place on weekdays in summer, and Wednesday mornings the rest of the year. There is a **Champion supermarket** between the campsites and the *centre ville* where rte. de Caen (D513) becomes av. Guillaume le Conquérant. (Open M-Sa 9am-7:45pm, Su 9am-noon.)

The **tourist office,** Jardins du Casino (tel. 02 31 91 01 09; fax 02 31 24 14 49), lies immediately in front of the posh hotel at the edge of its formal gardens. (Open daily July-Aug. 9am-7pm; Sept.-June M-F 9:30am-12:30pm and 2-6:30pm, Sa 9:30am-7:30pm, Su 10am-12:30pm and 2:30-6pm.) Across the Dives River, the Dives-Cabourg **train station** (tel. 02 31 91 00 74) serves **Paris** (2hr.; mid-June-Sept. 2 per day, rest of year Sa-Su only; 158F). **Bus Verts** (0 801 214 214) run from any of five in-town stops ("pl. du 8 Mai" is closest to the beach and tourist office) to **Caen** (34F), **Houlgate, Honfleur,** and **Le Havre.** Rent **bikes** at **Cycles Cabourg,** pl. du Marché (tel. 02 31 91 10 10), near the center of town. (25F per hour, 80F per day.)

CAEN

The Battle of Normandy left 40,000 of Caen's then 60,000 citizens homeless. Not one of the city's medieval monuments was left untouched by Allied bombing—indeed, only a quarter of Caen's buildings were still standing in 1944. Fortunately, the Caennais exhibited tasteful discretion in rebuilding their home, and today the city exhibits none of the post-apocalyptic stagnation or architectural ghoulishness so common in other cities blasted in the War. A chic student population, international travelers, and the young but already legendary Musée de la Paix have made this city (pop. 115,000) a major rail, ferry, historical, and party center. Less scholarly than stylish, the students lingering in cafés and bookstores keep the city pumping at night during the year. Summer vacationers elbow them out to cultivate well-defined tan lines at nearby beaches or to explore the city's famous Romanesque edifices. For maximum nightlife, try to arrive before mid-July, when most of the students head to the beaches after finishing their exams.

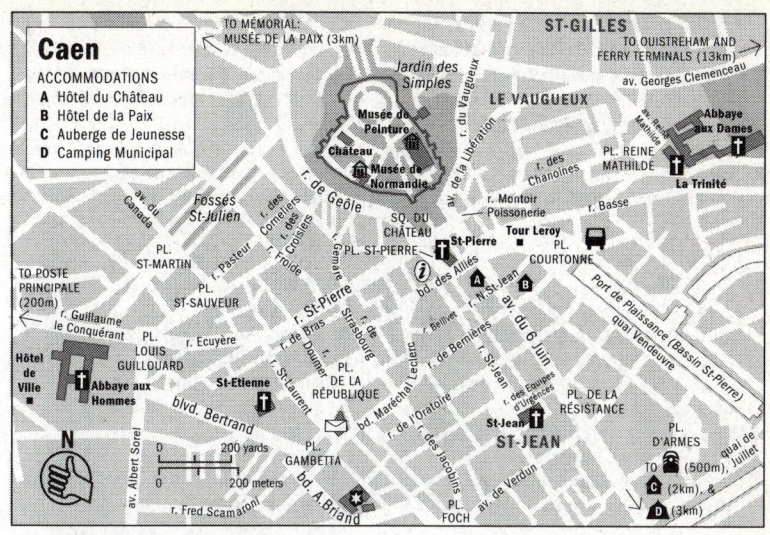

Caen

ACCOMMODATIONS
A Hôtel du Château
B Hôtel de la Paix
C Auberge de Jeunesse
D Camping Municipal

TO MÉMORIAL:
MUSÉE DE LA PAIX (3km)

ST-GILLES

Jardin des Simples

TO OUISTREHAM AND
FERRY TERMINALS (13km)

av. Georges Clemenceau

LE VAUGUEUX

Musée de Peinture

Château

Musée de Normandie

r. de Geôle

r. des Chanoines

PL. REINE MATHILDE

Abbaye aux Dames

La Trinité

Fossés St-Julien

r. Montoir
Poissonerie

r. Basse

SQ. DU CHÂTEAU

PL. ST-MARTIN

PL. ST-SAUVEUR

PL. ST-PIERRE

St-Pierre

Tour Leroy

PL. COURTONNE

Port de Plaisance (Bassin St-Pierre)

quai Vendeuvre

av. du Canada

r. Pasteur

r. St-Pierre

r. de Bras

r. Ecuyère

r. de Strasbourg

r. St-Laurent

PL. LOUIS GUILLOUARD

St-Etienne

PL. DE LA RÉPUBLIQUE

r. de Bernières

r. St-Jean

av. du 6 Juin

PL. DE LA RÉSISTANCE

TO POSTE PRINCIPALE (200m)

r. Guillaume le Conquérant

Hôtel de Ville

Abbaye aux Hommes

blvd. Bertrand

bd. Maréchal Leclerc

r. de l'Oratoire

r. des Jacobins

St-Jean

ST-JEAN

PL. D'ARMES

quai du Juillet

av. Albert Sorel

PL. GAMBETTA

bd. A. Briand

av. de Verdun

PL. FOCH

TO (500m)
C (2km), &
D (3km)

200 yards

200 meters

r. Fred Scamaroni

ℹ ORIENTATION AND PRACTICAL INFORMATION

Caen's train station and youth hostel are on the south side of the Orne River, far enough from the *centre ville* that you may want to take the bus (6.20F). The life-saving **Bus Verts Carte Liberté** grants liberal access to Caen's convenient and luxurious city buses (see p. 466). All of the buses leaving from the front of the train station stop in the vicinity of the Église St-Pierre and the *centre ville*. You can get a map at the CTAC kiosk before heading into the city. From the station, av. du 6 Juin and rue St-Jean parallel each other northwest to the *centre ville*. The liveliest commercial districts are located between **rue St-Pierre** and **rue de l'Oratoir**.

Trains: Pl. de la Gare. To: **Cherbourg** (1½hr., 7-10 per day, 5 on Su, 98F); **Rouen** (2hr., 4 per day, 113F); **Paris** (2½hr., 5-7 per day, 152F); **Rennes** (3hr., 2 per day, 163F); and **Tours** (3½hr., 6 per day, 168F). Info open M-Sa 8am-7pm, Su 9:15am-6:30pm.

Buses: To the left of the train station (tel. 02 31 44 77 44). Additional kiosks in pl. Courtonne and the Hippodrome. **Bus Verts** blanket the region. To: **Bayeux** (1hr., 3 per day, 37F) and **Le Havre** (2-3hr., 14 per day, 106F). Office open M-F 7:30am-7pm, Sa 8:15am-7pm, Su 9am-6pm.

Local Transportation: CTAC (tel. 02 31 15 55 55). Info booth outside station. Tickets 6.20F, *carnet* of 10 50F; 1-day pass 16F. Booth open M-F 7am-7:30pm, Sa 9am-1:45pm and 2:15-5:20pm.

Ferries: Brittany Ferries go to **Portsmouth** from Ouistreham, 13km north of Caen. See **Getting There: By Boat** p. 62. Bus Verts links Ouistreham to Caen's *centre ville* and *gare* (30min.).

Taxis: Abbeilles Taxis Caen, 19 pl. de la Gare (tel. 02 31 52 17 89). 24hr.

Tourist Office: Pl. St-Pierre (tel. 02 31 27 14 14; fax 02 31 27 14 18), by the Église St-Pierre. Accommodations service (10F). Numerous biking itineraries and "cider routes." Vague map 2F, detailed map 24F. Tours of the city in French by day or night (July-Aug. 2 per day, 30F). **Currency exchange** with decent rates. Open July-Aug. M-Sa 9:30am-7pm, Su 9:30am-1pm and 2-5pm; Sept.-June M-Sa 10am-1pm and 2-6pm, Su 10am-1pm. *Le Mois à Caen* lists concerts and miscellaneous happenings (also at *tabacs*).

Money: Currency exchange at **Crédit Agricole,** on the corner of rue St-Jean and bd. Maréchal Leclerc (1 block from the tourist office).

English Books: Stephen King lurks in a corner of **FNAC,** Centre Paul Doumer on rue Doumer. Open M 2-7pm, Tu-F 10am-7pm, Sa 9:30am-7pm.

Youth Center: Centre Information Jeunesse, 16 rue Neuve-St-Jean (tel. 02 31 85 73 60), off av. du 6 Juin next to the Hôtel de la Paix. Sells BIJ tickets. Brochures on events, jobs, and lodging. Open M 1-6pm, Tu-F 10am-6pm.

Laundromat: 15 rue des Équipes d'Urgence, near the Église St-Jean. Open M-Sa 7am-8pm, Su 8am-noon.

Hospital: Centre Hospitalier Universitaire, av. Côte de Nacre (tel. 02 31 27 27 27).

Police: Esplanade Jean-Marie Louvel (tel. 02 31 30 45 50).

Post Office: Pl. Gambetta (tel. 02 31 39 35 78). From pl. St-Pierre, take rue St-Pierre and turn left on rue St-Laurent. **Currency exchange.** For Poste Restante designate "Gambetta". Open M-F 8am-7pm, Sa 8am-noon. **Postal code:** 14000.

Internet Access: In the library at **Memorial: Un Musée Pour la Paix,** you can check email but not send any. Take bus #17 from the *centre ville* or the *gare.* 20F per 30min. Open daily 10am-1pm and 2-6pm. Ask tourist office for new locations.

▐ ACCOMMODATIONS AND CAMPING

There are many hotels in Caen's *centre ville*, but few go for under 150F. Student accommodations are also plentiful, but they fill up quickly; reserve in advance.

Auberge de Jeunesse (HI), Foyer Robert Reme, 68bis rue Eustache-Restout (tel. 02 31 52 19 96; fax 02 31 84 29 49). From the station, turn right and then take the second right onto rue de Vaucelles. Walk up a block and look for the bus stop on your left. Take bus #5 or 17 (direction "Fleury" or "Grace de Dieu") to "Lycée Fresnel." On foot, take a right out of the station and cross the street. Follow it until the road curves to the left and up the hill. Walk uphill until you reach bd. Leroy, at the first major intersection, and then turn right and continue about 10min. Turn left onto rue Eustasche Restout (look for sign to "Lycée Fresnel") and continue 15min. through a residential area. The road turns right after a large school; the hostel will be on your right. Clean 4-person, single-sex rooms with showers and kitchen facilities inside each room in a building that doubles as a *foyer* for young workers. Happening place with super-friendly staff; the single woman traveler may be made to feel a little bit uncomfortable by loitering residents, though the hostel is guarded 24hr. Ping-pong, TV, and billiards. 58 beds. 62F. Breakfast 10F. Sheets 15F. Reception 5-10pm.

Hôtel de la Paix, 14 rue Neuve-St-Jean (tel. 02 31 86 18 99; fax 02 31 38 20 74), off av. du 6 Juin. Extra friendly owner welcomes guests in a convivial atmosphere. Beautiful lobby and small cozy breakfast room. Clean, simple rooms, all with phone and TV. Singles with toilet, shower, or both 140-175F; doubles 20F more; triples with shower 240F, with shower and toilet 260F. Breakfast 28F. V, MC.

Hôtel du Château, 5 av. du 6 Juin (tel. 02 31 86 15 37; fax 02 31 86 58 08). 24 attractively-decorated rooms with TV; one handicapped accessible. Rooms under the eaves with skylights are sunny and pretty. Doubles and triples with toilet and TV 150-170F, add shower 190-240F. Breakfast 30F. V, MC.

Campsites: Terrain Municipal, rte. de Louvigny (tel. 02 31 73 60 92). Take bus #13 (direction "Louvigny") to "Camping." Near the river in the suburbs. 20F per person, 14F per tent, 11F per car. Reception 8am-9pm. Open May-Sept.

▐ FOOD

Crêperies, brasseries, and ethnic restaurants line the aged streets of the **Quartier Vaugueux** near the château and gather between the Église St-Pierre and the Église St-Jean. **Markets** take place Friday mornings in pl. St-Sauveur and Sunday morning in front of the Église St-Pierre. Culinary daredevils should seek out *tripes à la mode de Caen*—bovine stomachs cooked in an earthenware pot with vegetables, herbs, and calvados. There's a **Monoprix supermarket** at 45 bd. du Maréchal Leclerc. (Open M-Sa 8am-8:30pm.)

Le Filao, 2 av. de la Libération (tel. 02 31 94 14 19 90). Amidst beautiful batik table-cloths and highly decorated walls, friendly waiters serve African specialties to the constant tune of Senegalese and other music. Huge portions of spicy flavors are served in gargantuan hollowed-out wooden bowls. Poulet Yassa (a chicken dish), grilled fish, and meat dishes are 60F. *Menus* at 85F and 120F, lunch *menu* 55F. Open daily noon-2pm and 6-11pm, closed Su evening and M afternoon.

Couscous Le Kouba, 12 rue du Vaugueux (tel. 02 31 93 68 47). Le Kouba offers 59F and 86F menus to diners who come to sit on the outdoor terrace An extensive wine list accompanies a selection of meats and couscous (60-75F). 4-course *menu* (65F) features curries and salads. Vegetarian couscous is not on the menu but is available for 40F. Open Tu-Su 11:45am-2:30pm and 7-11:30pm, closed Su afternoon. V, MC.

Aux 4 Épices. In a beautifully decorated setting, the often-full restaurant serves such delicacies as plantains and apricot *beignets*. *Plats* 48-79F, wonderful tropical salads 35-47F. Open Tu-Sa 11:30am-2:30pm and 7-11pm, Su dinner only.

👁 🎵 SIGHTS AND ENTERTAINMENT

SIGHTS. Commemorating an era of turbulence, the powerful **Mémorial de Caen** (tel. 02 31 06 06 44) presides over manicured lawns in the northwest corner of the city. A must for any visit to Caen, it incorporates a unique array of WW II footage, high-tech audio-visual aids, and displays on pre-war Europe and the Battle of Normandy to relate a remarkably even-handed version of the events leading up to and during WWII. The short, haunting testimonial to the victims of the Holocaust is particularly moving. Similarly striking are the films about the D-Day landings and the Battle of Britain. A futuristic tunnel details the accomplishments of Nobel Peace Prize laureates, while the Canadian and American memorial gardens outside offer a touching tribute to the dead. From the *centre ville*, take bus #17 to "Mémorial." (Open daily July-Aug. 9am-8pm; Feb. 15-June and Sept.-Oct. 9am-7pm; Jan. 20-Feb. 14 and Nov.-Jan. 4 9am-6pm. 72F, students 63F, veterans free.)

Caen got its start as the seat of William the Conqueror's duchy from 1035 to 1087; the city's legacy of first-class Romanesque architecture is due chiefly to William himself, who married his distant cousin Matilda despite the pope's interdiction. As penance, the duke and his wife built several ecclesiastical structures, most notably Caen's twin abbeys. In 1066, William began the **Abbaye-aux-Hommes** (tel. 02 31 30 42 81), off rue Guillaume le Conquérant, to hold his tomb (and his place in heaven). Rebuilt in the 18th century, the abbey has served as a high school and now functions as Caen's Hôtel de Ville. (Guided tours in French daily 9:30 and 11am, and 2:30 and 4pm. 10F, students 5F, under 18 free.) The adjacent **Abbatiale St-Étienne,** which sheltered citizens during the Battle of Caen in 1944, features a cavernous 11th-century façade and nave and a brilliant rose window. (Open 8:15am-noon and 2-7:30pm.) The smaller, more intimate **Église de la Trinité** of the **Abbaye-aux-Dames,** off rue des Chanoines (Matilda's resting place and the penance for her marriage), has two 16th-century towers and a thoroughly-renovated Romanesque interior with sparkling *vitraux*. To visit the crypt, enter through the low doorway in the south transept. (Open daily 8am-6pm. Free guided tours in French daily at 10:30am, and 2:30 and 4pm.)

Across from the tourist office sprawl the ruins of William's **château.** (Open daily May-Sept. 6am-1am; Oct.-Apr. 6am-7:30pm.) The château's walls hide the somewhat strangely laid-out **Musée des Beaux-Arts** (tel. 02 31 85 28 63), which contains a fine selection of 16th- and 17th-century Flemish painting with works by Rubens and van Dyck, and Impressionist paintings of Normandy by Monet, Courbet, and Boudin, as well as a small and rather eclectic collection of 20th-century works. (Open W-M 9:30am-6pm. 25F, students 15F, free W.) The small **Jardin des Simples** holds a collection of plants used for murderous or medicinal purposes in the Middle Ages. (Open May-Sept. daily 6am-9:30pm; Oct.-Apr. 6am-7:30pm.)

Just beyond is the **Musée de Normandie** (tel. 02 31 86 06 24), which houses a truly impressive exhibit of artifacts from the beginning of Norman history to the

THE NORTHWEST

present. (Open daily except Tu and holidays 9:30am-12:30pm and 2-6pm. 10F, students 5F.) For a break from the bustle of Caen's *centre ville*, take a walk around the castle walls on rue de Geôle, turning left on rue Bosnières, to reach the sheltered, romantic **Jardin des Plantes** on pl. Blot. (Open June-Aug. daily 8am-sunset; Sept.-May 8am-5:30pm.)

ENTERTAINMENT. Caen's streets pulsate by night, especially around **rue de Bras, rue des Croisiers,** and **rue St-Pierre.** Locals head to the gaudy, kitschy **Joy's Club,** 10 rue Strasbourg (tel. 02 31 85 40 40), to flail to techno. (Open daily 10pm-5am. 60F cover includes first drink.) The same owner runs the popular karaoke bar **Bus Stop Café,** 7 rue de Bras. (Tel. 02 31 85 72 72. Beer costs 15-30F. Open M-Sa 3pm-3:45am, Su 3-8pm.) The wood interior and billiards draw locals to the more laid-back **Le Dakota,** 54 rue de Bernières (tel. 02 31 50 05 25); beer starts at 15F. (Open M-Sa 4pm-4am, Su 8:30pm-2am.) Anglophiles and *caennais* mingle at **The Glue Pot,** 18 quai Vendenure (tel. 02 31 86 29 15), an old-style pub with plush red carpeting, 8 beers on tap, 20 types of whisky, and hardly any elbow room by midnight. (Beer from 15F. Open M-Sa 4pm-4am, Su 8pm-2am.) **Le Zinc,** 12 rue du Vaugueux (tel. 02 31 93 20 30), which fills quickly with a mixed gay and straight crowd, pulsates amid the restaurants of the street Vaugueux with loud techno music and a well-dressed crowd. (Open Tu-Th 6:30pm-2am, F-Sa 6pm-4am.)

BAYEUX

Though Bayeux (pop. 15,000) will forever be famous for its tapestry—which is in fact not a tapestry at all, but a 70m long embroidery—numerous inviting surprises can be found in and around town. The streets and *vieille ville* merit a stroll, and the cathedral is quite spectacular. Founded 20 centuries ago as a Gallo-Roman settlement, Bayeux's cultural heritage has been remarkably well preserved in both its museums and its architecture. Proximity to the D-Day beaches and cemeteries and easy train access to Caen make Bayeux an easy day trip in itself or a great base from which to explore the war memorials.

◪ ORIENTATION AND PRACTICAL INFORMATION. Trains leave the station on pl. de la Gare (tel. 02 31 92 80 50) for **Caen** (20min., 12 per day, 33F), **Cherbourg** (50min., 4 per day, 78F), and **Paris** (2½hr., 5 per day, 164F). (Ticket counters open M-F 6am-9pm, Sa-Su 7am-9pm.) **Bus Verts,** also at pl. de la Gare (tel. 02 31 92 02 92), head west to small towns and east to **Le Havre** and **Caen** (1hr., 4 per day, 38F). Buy tickets from the driver or at the office. (Open M-F 9:15am-12:15pm and 1:45-6pm.) For a **taxi,** call 02 31 92 92 40 (24hr.).

To get from the station to the **tourist office,** pont St-Jean (tel. 02 31 51 28 28; fax 02 31 51 28 29; www.bayeux-tourism.com), turn left onto the highway (bd. Sadi-Carnot), then bear right at the roundabout, still on bd. Sadi-Carnot, following the signs to the *centre ville.* Once there, continue up rue Larcher until it hits rue St-Martin, Bayeux's commercial avenue. The office will be on your right, at the edge of the pedestrian zone. The staff offers **currency exchange** (Su and M only), **internet access** (50F per hr.), and books **rooms.** (Open M-Sa 9am-noon and 2-6pm, Su 9:30am-noon and 2:30-6pm; Sept. 15-June closed Su.) There's a **laundromat** at 10 rue Maréchal Foch. (Open daily 8am-8pm.) The **police station** is on pl. de la Liberté (tel. 02 31 92 94 00), and the **hospital** is on rue de Nesmond (tel. 02 31 51 51 51), next to the tapestry center. The **post office,** rue Larcher (tel. 02 31 51 24 90), has **currency exchange,** and **internet access.** (Open M-F 8am-6:30pm, Sa 8am-noon. Internet 50F per hour. **Postal code:** 14400.)

⌐ ACCOMMODATIONS AND CAMPING. Inexpensive lodging does exist in Bayeux, but demand often outstrips supply, especially in summer; arrive early, or preferably reserve in advance. You'll need to plan with military precision to get a room around June 6, the anniversary of D-Day.

THE NORTHWEST

Your cheapest institutional bet is the **Centre d'Accueil Municipal,** 21 rue des Marettes (tel. 02 31 92 08 19), which at times seems like the town's public shelter. From the station, follow bd. Sadi-Carnot and bear left at the rotary onto bd. Maréchal Leclerc, which metamorphoses into bd. Fabien Ware. The industrial, modern *centre* has a friendly staff but the plain, antiseptic singles often have saggy beds. Don't expect a hostel atmosphere here as the center is huge and quite impersonal. (75F. Small breakfast 15F. Reception 7am-8pm; call if arriving later.)

In a great location in the *centre ville*, **Hôtel Notre-Dame,** 44 rue des Cuisiniers (tel. 02 31 92 87 24; fax 02 31 92 67 11), offers cathedral views above an elegant restaurant. The 24 comfortable, beautiful rooms all have TV and phone. In high season the owner will only take reservations for *demi-pension* (breakfast and one meal per day). (Singles and doubles 180F, with shower and toilet 250-260F, with bath and toilet 280F. Extra bed 90F. Shower 5F. Breakfast 35F. *Demi-pension* 210F, with bathroom 260F. V, MC.) One block past the tourist office, **Hôtel Au Bon Coin,** 81 rue Saint-Jean (tel. 02 31 92 06 57), has 11 refurbished rooms smack in the middle of the *centre ville*. The smallish, attractive rooms have carpeting but some mattresses show their age. The shower and toilet are on the third floor. (Doubles 140F; quads 200F; rooms for 2-4 with shower and toilet 250F. Breakfast 25F. V, MC.) The **Camping Municipal,** bd. d'Eindhoven (tel. 02 31 92 08 43), is within easy reach of the town center and the N13. Follow rue Genas Duhomme and continue straight on av. de la Vallée des Prés. (Swimming pool. 14F per person, 17F per tent and car. Great showers. Gates closed 10pm-7am. Open Mar. 15-Nov. 15.)

🍴 **FOOD.** Morning **markets** are held on pl. St-Patrice (Sa), and on rue St-Jean (W). **Proxi,** pl. St-Patrice, is a small grocery store. (Open Tu-Sa 7:30am-12:30pm and 2:30-7:30pm, Su 9am-12:30pm. V, MC.) One of the heartiest and most engaging restaurants in the region is **La Table du Terroir,** 42 rue St-Jean (tel. 02 31 92 05 53), down the street from the tourist office. So good! The jovial owner/chef and his family serve local meat dishes and delicious desserts at communal wooden tables. (*Menus* 60F and 98F. Open daily noon-2:30pm and 7-10pm. Oct. 1-May 30 closed Su evening and M; May-Sept. closed Su lunch.) After a long day in the mist, venture to **Pizza Milano,** 18 rue St-Martin (tel. 02 31 92 15 10), for warming pastas (30-59F) and soufflé pizzas (35-59F). (Open in winter M-Sa 11:30am-2:30pm and 6:30-10:30pm; in summer closed M as well as Tu lunch.)

🗿 **SIGHTS.** The most famous sight in town is undoubtedly the **Tapisserie de Bayeux,** which illustrates in vibrant detail the events that culminated in the Battle of Hastings on October 14, 1066. On that date, William the Conqueror (*né* "the Bastard") earned himself a more sociable nickname by crossing the Channel to defeat his cousin Harold, who, according to the Norman version of the tale, held a title rightfully belonging to William—King of England. His victory proved to be the last successful invasion of England. A mere 50cm wide but a gargantuan 70m long, the surviving tapestry hangs in all its glory at the **Centre Guillaume le Conquérant,** rue de Nesmond (tel. 02 31 51 25 50), a renovated 18th-century seminary. Lengthy exhibits detail the tapestry's contents, but you can cut to the chase with a short film that will refresh your memory of 11th-century history. This film and the audio guided tour headsets come in six languages (5F). (Open daily May-Aug. 9am-7pm; Mar. 15-Apr. and Sept.-Oct. 15 9am-6:30pm; Oct. 16-Mar. 14 9:30am-12:30pm and 2-6pm. 38F, students 16F; includes Musée Baron Gerard, and Musée d'Art Religieux.)

Near the center is the impressive **Cathédrale Notre-Dame,** a Gothic edifice begun with Romanesque intentions and now a fantastic pastiche of styles. The cathedral is built over a Roman crypt, which is below the choir. (Open July-Aug. M-Sa 8am-7pm, Su 9am-7pm; Sept.-June M-Sa 8:30am-noon and 2:30-7pm, Su 9am-12:15pm and 2:30-7pm.) Just below the cathedral, the **Musée Baron Gérard,** pl. de la Liberté (tel. 02 31 92 14 21), houses a solid permanent collection of tapestries, 16th- and 17th-century paintings, including works by Boucher, David, and Corot. (Open daily June-Sept. 15 9am-7pm; Sept. 16-May 10am-12:30pm and 2-6pm.)

William's exploit was sort of played out in reverse in 1944 as Anglo-saxon troops poured onto nearby beaches. The events of that summer are recounted in the **Musée de la Bataille de Normandie**, bd. Fabian Ware. (tel. 02 31 92 93 41), using American, English, French, and German newspapers of the time. The museum has the immediacy of a scrapbook; each clipping captures a moment in a time capsule. Photographs, weapons, and stiff uniform-wearing mannequins complement this vivid and anxiety-ridden picture of the beginning of the end of WWII. A 30-minute film, *Images of the Battle of Normandy*, screened in English and French, shows Allied and German footage of the battlefront from land, air, and sea. The **British Cemetery** depicted in the final scenes of the film is located across the street from the museum. (Open May-Sept. 15 daily 9:30am-6:30pm; Sept. 16-Apr. 10am-12:30pm and 2-6pm. 30F, students 15F.)

THE D-DAY BEACHES

In June of 1944, over a million Allied soldiers surged from the English Channel onto the beaches of Normandy. Preparations for the attack began at the Québec Conference of 1943, when the Allied leaders decided to attempt a landing on the European continent. While using false intelligence reports to feed German suspicion that the attack would fall farther north at Calais or Le Havre, the British, Canadian, and American masterminds of "Operation Overlord" planned a landing on the Normandy coast between the Cotentin Peninsula and the Orne River. In the pre-dawn hours of June 6, 1944, the invasion began with 16,000 British and US paratroopers tumbling from the sky. A few hours later, 135,000 troops and 20,000 vehicles landed in fog and rain on the beaches code-named Utah and Omaha (American), Gold and Sword (British), and Juno (Canadian). The Battle of Normandy raged on until August 21, and on August 24 Free French forces entered and liberated Paris. Less than a year later, Allied forces rolled into Berlin, and Germany surrendered. Today, the record of the battle can be clearly seen in sobering gravestones and the pockmarked landscape; remnants of German bunkers dot the coastline, and craters left by bombs are still unfilled.

Museums, monuments, and cemeteries commemorating the battle and its victims are strewn from Cherbourg to Le Havre. The **Voie de la Liberté** (Liberty Highway) follows the US army's advance from Utah Beach to Bastogne in Belgium. For a more complete description of the sites and museums which commemorate the battle, pick up *The D-Day Landings and the Battle of Normandy*, a brochure and map available in most tourist offices in the region.

■ **TRANSPORTATION.** Though it's undoubtedly more convenient to rent a car, most of the beaches and museums can be reached from Caen and Bayeux with the help of **Bus Verts** (tel. 02 31 44 77 44); see **Normandy: Transportation** (p. 466) for details on passes. To get to **Benouville** and **Ouistreham**, take Bus Verts #1 from **Caen**; #20 links Caen to the British cemeteries at **Ranville** and the Canadian cemeteries at **Bény-sur-Mer-Riviers**. Line #70 (M-Sa 3 per day) runs from **Bayeux** to **Pointe du Hoc, the American Cemetery, Longues-sur-mer,** and **Arromanches**. **Ste-Mère-Église** is accessible by bus from **Carentan** (1 per day). Call the Carentan tourist office (tel. 02 33 42 74 01) for more information. To get to Carentan take the train from Bayeux (20min., 5-6 per day). **Utah Beach** and the **Musée du Débarquement** are only accessible by car, foot, or thumb from Ste-Mère-Église.

Before renting a car or heading off by bus, consider a **guided tour. Bus Fly** (tel. 02 31 22 00 08) runs informative tours with English-speaking guides. Half-day tours include Point du Hoc, the American Cemetery (Omaha Beach), Longues-sur-mer, and Arromanches (Gold Beach). The full-day tour adds Utah Beach and Ste-Mère-Église, and they'll pick you up at your hotel. (Half-day 160F, students 140F; full day 300F, students 280F, museum admission included. Reserve well in advance.) **Normandy Tours,** 26 pl. de la Gare (tel. 02 31 92 10 70; fax 02 31 51 95 99), based in Bayeux's Hôtel de la Gare, runs flexible tours in both English and French for one to eight people. Prices vary depending on the itinerary. (60F for a 3-4hr. tour.)

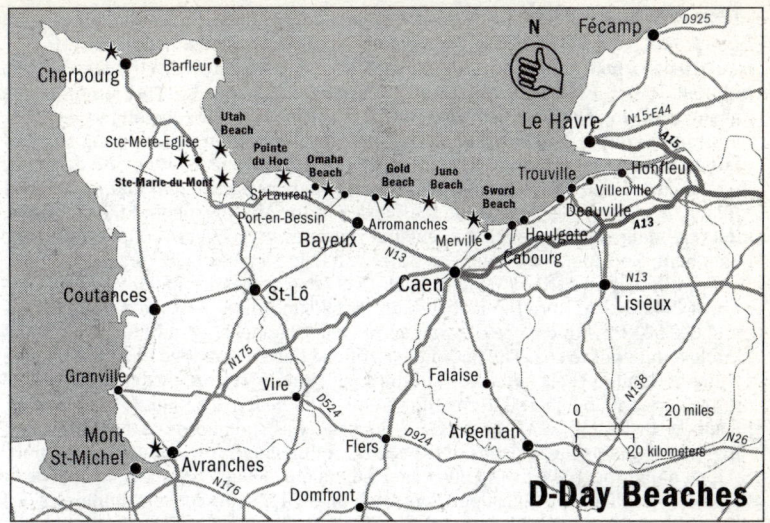

D-Day Beaches

BEACHES NEAR CAEN

At **Benouville,** British paratroopers of the 6th Airborne Division captured Pegasus Bridge, a strategic objective across the River Orn and the first Allied victory. The **Musée des Troupes Aéroportées** (tel. 02 31 44 62 54) in Benouville tells the story of the Parachute Brigades' operations on the Dives River. (Open Mar. 19-May and Sept. 5-Oct. 9:30am-12:30pm and 2-6pm; June-July 2 9:30am-12:30pm and 2-7pm; July 3-Sept. 4 9am-7pm. 20F, students 15F.) One of the largest of the 16 British cemeteries is nearby in **Ranville**.

  Juno Beach, the landing site of the Canadian forces, lies east of Arromanches. Every June 6, two veterans of the battle place poppy-laden crosses on the stone monument. The **Canadian Cemetery** is located at **Bény-sur-Mer-Reviers.** In **Ouistreham,** the **N°4 Commando Museum,** pl. Alfred Thomas (tel. 02 31 96 63 10), retells the story of British and French troops who participated in the D-Day attack on Sword Beach. (Open Mar. 15-Oct. 3. 25F, students 15F.)

BEACHES NEAR BAYEUX

At **Utah Beach** near Ste-Marie du Mont, the Americans headed the western flank of the invasion. The landing is commemorated by the **American Commemorative Monument** and the **Musée du Débarquement** (tel. 02 33 71 53 35). Films and models show how 836,000 soldiers, 220,000 vehicles, and 725,000 tonnes of equipment came ashore. (Open daily July-Aug. 9:30am-7:30pm; June 9:30am-7pm; Apr.-May 9:30am-6:30pm; Dec.-Mar. Sa-Su 9:30am-6:30pm. 27F, students 22F.) Nearby in **Ste-Mère-Église** the parachute-shaped **Musée des Troupes Aéroporteés,** pl. du 6 Juin (tel. 02 33 41 41 35), houses the plane that littered the district with paratroopers—one of whom was left dangling from the steeple of Ste-Mère's church when his parachute snagged. (Open daily May 1-Sept. 15 9am-6:45pm; Apr. and Sept. 16-30 9am-noon and 2-6:45pm; Feb.-Mar. and Oct.-Nov. 15 10am-noon and 2-6pm; Nov. 16-Dec. 15 Sa-Su 10am-noon and 2-6pm. 25F, students 16F.)

  The most difficult landing was that of the 1st US Infantry Division at **Pointe du Hoc,** where a rough sea and well-fortified enemy compounded the challenge of ascending a steep cliff face. In one of the day's most dramatic moments, 225 specially trained US Rangers scaled the 30m cliffs. Having neutralized the key German position, the Rangers were left to defend it for two days until help arrived for the 90 survivors. The cliffs themselves are fenced off for safety but the grassy area beyond them is still marked by deep pits and many of the German bunkers remain, one which has been turned into a memorial to the troops who perished.

At **Omaha Beach,** next to **Colleville-sur-Mer** and just east of the Pointe du Hoc, almost 10,000 American graves stretch over a 172-acre coastal reserve. The grounds of this **American Cemetery** (tel. 02 31 21 97 44), which belong to the USA, contain a simple marble chapel and an impressive memorial among rows of immaculate white crosses and stars of David. A 7m bronze statue, *The Spirit of American Youth Rising from the Waves*, stands in the semicircular monument, facing the soldiers' graves, while the Garden of the Missing, behind the memorial, lists the names of those whose remains were never recovered. (Open Apr.-Nov. 8am-6pm; Dec.-Mar. 9am-5pm. The office can help locate specific graves.)

Ten kilometers north of Bayeux on D514 is **Arromanches,** a small town at the center of **Gold Beach.** Here the British built **Port Winston** in a day, using retired ships and 600,000 tons of concrete towed across the Channel and sunk in a wide semicircle a mile out to sea. The enormous artificial harbor provided shelter while the Allies unloaded their supplies. The hulking ruins of a port designed to last 18 months remain 54 years later within view of the beach. The **Musée du Débarquement** on the beach (tel. 02 31 22 34 31) houses relics and photos of the Allied landings and explains the logistics of the attack. A film details the creation of the port. (Open daily Apr. 1-May 5 9-11:30am and 2-6pm; May 6-Sept. 5 9am-6:30pm; Sept. 6-Mar. 31 9-11:30am and 2-5:30pm. Sept.-May opens 10am on Su. 32F, students 27F.) The **Arromanches 360° Cinéma** (tel. 02 31 22 30 30) shows an 18-minute film, *Le Prix de la Liberté* (The Price of Freedom), on its circular screen. The film combines images of modern Normandy with those of D-Day. To reach the cinema from the museum, turn left onto rue de la Batterie and follow the steps to the top of the cliff. (Open daily June-Aug. 9:10am-6:40pm; May and Sept. 10:10am-5:40pm; Oct.-Dec. and Feb.-Apr. 10:10am-4:40pm. 22F, students 19F.)

Four kilometers west of Arromanches in tiny **Longues-sur-Mer, Les Batteries de Longues** (tel. 02 31 06 06 45) serve as an ominous reminder of the German presence. These bunkers, constructed in 1944, once held artillery with a range of 12km; one contains the only cannon in the region that is still loaded with its original ammunition. Today, rusted shells mar the otherwise picturesque coastal landscape.

Camping Reine Mathilde, at **Etreham,** near Port-en-Bessin (tel. 02 31 21 76 55), is 2.5km from the sea, 7km from Omaha Beach, 9km from Bayeux, and always densely packed. (26F per person, 26F per tent and car. Electricity 20F. Open Apr.-Sept.) Bayeux's tourist office can help you find accommodations in *chambres d'hôtes* along the coast.

CHERBOURG

With a strategic location at the tip of the Cotentin peninsula, Cherbourg (pop. 28,000) was the "Gateway to France," the major supply port following the D-Day offensive of 1944. Today, it is visited by numerous ferry lines that shuttle tourists from France to England and Ireland. Don't go out of your way to visit Cherbourg; there isn't all that much to see and the city is on the whole quite bleak. But if you find yourself there on your way in and out of France, don't despair. There's just enough to keep you busy until the next train or ferry leaves.

■ **PRACTICAL INFORMATION. Ferries** leave from the *gare maritime*, northeast of the *centre ville*, along bd. Maritime. (Open daily 5:30am-11:30pm.) **Irish Ferries** goes to **Rosslare, P&O European Ferries** to **Portsmouth,** and **Brittany Ferries** to **Poole.** For contact numbers and details of service, see **Getting There: By Boat** (p. 62). To get to the tourist office, turn right from the terminal onto bd. Felix Amiot. At the roundabout, go straight and continue around the bend, eventually making a right across the canal; you will see the tourist office ahead on your left (20min.). To reach the train station, go left at the roundabout onto av. A. Briand and follow it as it becomes av. Carnot; it's at the corner of av. Carnot and av. Millet (25min.). Alternatively, a **shuttle bus** runs between the *gare maritime* and the station (6F).

The **train station** (tel. 02 33 44 18 74), at the base of the Bassin du Commerce, has service to **Bayeux** (1hr., 6 per day, 78F), **Caen** (1½hr., 9 per day, 97F), **Rouen** (3hr., 2 per day, 177F), **Paris** (3½hr., 6 per day, 218F), and **Rennes** (4hr., change at Lison, 2 per day, 179F). (Open daily 5:30am-8:10pm.) Across from the station, **Autocars STN** (tel. 02 33 88 51 00) runs **buses** around the region. (Open M-F 8:15am-noon and 2-6:30pm.) **EFFIA buses** (tel. 02 35 98 13 38) leave from behind the station and go to **Coutances** (1½hr.; M-F 3 per day, Sa-Su 2 per day; 61F). From the station, turn left and then immediately right onto quai Alexandre III, and walk four blocks to reach the tourist office and the *centre ville*.

The **tourist office** (tel. 02 33 93 52 02) provides brochures on the Cotentin peninsula, a detailed map, leads hikes around the region in the summer, and books rooms for free. (Open in summer M-Sa 9am-6:30pm; in winter M-F 9am-noon and 2-6pm, Sa 9am-noon.) The **annex** at the *gare maritime* is open during arrivals and departures of ferries. (Hours approximately Su-F 6:30-9am and 2-10:30pm, Sa 11:30am-10:30pm.) There's **currency exchange** at the ferry terminal or at banks around **pl. Gréville.** The **post office** is on rue de l'Ancien Quai. (Open M-F 8am-7pm, Sa 8am-noon.) There's a **branch** on av. Carnot near the ferry terminal. **Postal code:** 50100. **Internet access** exists at the **Forum des Halles** (tel. 02 33 78 19 30), a gigantic bookstore and multimedia center in the *centre ville*. (15F per 30min., 30F per hr.)

⌐ ACCOMMODATIONS. Cherbourg's few budget accommodations are often available, since most tourists leave town as soon as they step off the ferry. The cheapest option is the new **Auberge de Jeunesse (HI),** 55 rue de l'Abbaye (tel. 02 33 78 15 15; fax 02 33 78 15 16). From the tourist office, walk left on rue de Port all the way through pl. de la Mairie continuing onto rue de la Paix. Continue straight bearing left at the fork; the hostel is on the left. From the station, take bus #3 or 5 to "Arsenal." The 100 beds in cheery 2- to 5-person rooms all have sink and shower, cozy fleece blankets, and reading lamps; two rooms are handicapped-accessible. There's a fully-equipped kitchen and a bar downstairs in the dining hall, and you can also **rent bikes.** (51F, with breakfast 68F. Meals 50F. Sheets 17F. Bikes 50F per half-day, 80F per day. Reception 8am-noon and 6-11pm. No curfew.) Opposite the station, the lovely **Hôtel de la Gare,** 10 pl. Jean Jaurès (tel. 02 33 43 06 81; fax 02 33 43 12 20) sparkles with pretty clean rooms, all with phone, many with TV, and all brightly-colored and nice enough to make you forget the gray asphalt outside. (Singles and doubles with shower 160-180F, with shower and toilet 200-250F; quads 300-360F. Shower 20F. Breakfast 27F, 31F English-style. V, MC.)

⌐ FOOD. A huge **market** is held on pl. du Théâtre (Tu) and on pl. des Halles (Sa). At other times, stock up at the **Continent supermarket,** quai de l'Entrepôt, next to the station. (Open M-Sa 8:30am-9:30pm.) **Le Faitout,** 25 rue Tour Carrée (tel. 02 33 04 25 04), offers traditional cuisine—vegetarians will find scant sustenance here—amidst a comfortable, dark-wood decor. The *plat du jour* costs 55F and the *moules marinières* an unbeatable 35F. It's often full, so arrive early or make reservations. (Open noon-1:45pm and 7:15-9:45pm, closed M lunch and Su. V, MC.)

⌐ SIGHTS AND ENTERTAINMENT. Founded by William the conqueror's granddaughter—and Henry II's mother—Matilda in 1145, the semi-ruined **Abbaye du Vœu** is in the process of being restored to its former glory. Nearer to the ferries, off quai de Caligny, the stately **Basilique de la Trinité** spans centuries of architectural styles. Its foundations were laid in the mid-11th century, the transept dates from the 15th century, the altar-ornament has a Rococo twist, and the red and blue *vitraux* are modern. The **Musée de la Libération** (tel. 02 33 20 14 12), perches high up on the **Fort du Roule,** in the old citadel. The museum recounts life in Cherbourg during the Nazi occupation, the town's liberation, and its reconstruction. Vichy propaganda posters, films, and photographs breathe life into the events of the 1940s despite the museum's overall sterility. (Open Apr.-Sept. daily 10am-6pm; Oct.-Mar. Tu-Su 9:30am-noon and 2-5:30pm. 20F, under 18 10F, veterans free.)

At night the streets around the Hôtel de Ville perk up, especially the pedestrian **rue de la Paix.** An energetic young crowd works it at **Le Solier,** 48 rue la Grande Rue. Students pack **La Taverne,** 10 pl. République (tel. 02 33 93 00 81), until 8am every night, giving it a fun, youthful flava (in your ear).

GRANVILLE

Sprawling over a rocky peninsula on the western coast of Normandy, in the 15th century Granville was used by the English as a base for battling the French at Mont-St-Michel. The victorious French decided to develop the city, now a resort with its rugged cliffs and ribbons of white sand. Granville's distance from Paris keeps it less crowded and less expensive than other Norman resorts; although it sells itself as a convenient base for exploring Mont-St-Michel and the Channel Islands, the town holds some quiet surprises of its own.

⌗ ORIENTATION AND PRACTICAL INFORMATION. The **train station,** av. de la Gare (tel. 02 33 50 05 45), off av. Maréchal Leclerc, has service to **Bayeux** (1½hr., 2-3 per day, 87F), **Cherbourg** via Lison (3hr., 2 per day, 115F), and **Paris** (4hr., 3-4 per day, 193F). (Open M-F 5:15am-12:30pm and 1:15-8:30pm, Sa 6am-12:30pm and 1:30-8:30pm, Su and holidays 1:30-8:30pm.) **STN buses,** cours Jonville (tel. 02 33 50 77 89) leave from the train station or their office for **Avranches** (1hr., 5 per day, 32.10F). (Open M-F 8:30am-noon and 1:30-6:30pm, Sa 9:15am-noon and 2-6:15pm.) **Émeraude Lines** (tel. 02 33 90 62 24; fax 02 33 90 87 80), at the *gare maritime*, sails to the **Chausey Islands** (50min., usually 1 per day, 97F), **Jersey** (1¼hr., 1 per day, 330F), and **Guernsey** (2½hr., 1 per day, 330F). **Vedette "Jolie France"** (tel. 02 33 50 31 81; fax 02 33 50 31 90; open 7am-7pm) also sails to the **Chausey Islands.** (50min., 2 boats per day, 97F roundtrip. Reserve in advance in high season.)

To get to the *centre ville,* bear out of the station and follow av. Leclerc downhill as it becomes rue Couraye (10min.). For the **tourist office,** 4 cours Jonville (tel. 02 33 91 30 03), turn right onto cours Jonville at the *place.* They reserve **rooms** for free. (Open July-Aug. daily 9:15am-1pm and 2-7pm; Sept.-June M-F 9:15am-12:15pm and 2-7pm, Sa 9:15am-12:45pm and 2-7pm, Su 10am-12:30pm.) Next door, the **post office** (tel. 02 33 91 12 30) has **currency exchange.** (Open M-Sa 8am-6:30pm, Su 8am-noon. **Postal code:** 50400.) There's **internet access** at **Cyber Technics,** 16 rue St-Sauveur (Tel. 02 33 50 77 33. 30F per 30min. Open M-Sa 10am-noon, 2-6pm.)

⌂ ACCOMMODATIONS. Granville welcomes its share of tourists in the summer; you're unlikely to find solitude—or a surplus of hotel rooms. To get to the **Auberge de Jeunesse,** bd. des Amiraux Granvillais (tel. 02 33 91 22 60; fax 02 33 50 51 99), from the train station, turn right onto av. Maréchal Leclerc and follow it downhill into the *centre ville.* Turn left onto rue St-Sauveur; the hostel is at the end of the road, across the street. Look for the signs that say *Centre Nautisme.* This resort-style hostel has spacious rooms with 1-4 beds, clean showers, balconies looking out to sea, a restaurant, bar, patio, ping-pong, snooker, and beach. The large hostel doubles as a sailing center that hosts summer camps; it's often overrun by groups and is managed by a group-oriented staff, which can make it seem impersonal. On the upside, you can rent windsurfing gear for 85F per hour. (Singles 98F; doubles and triples 77F; quads 57F. Sheets 23F. Breakfast 19F. Meals 56F. 24hr. reception.)

Hôtel Michelet, 5 rue Jules Michelet (tel. 02 33 50 06 55; fax 02 33 50 12 25), has large, newly renovated rooms in a calm location near the beach promenade. To reach it from rue Couray in the *centre ville,* turn right onto rue Courier and bear left uphill at the fork. (Singles 135F; doubles 200F, with shower and toilet 230F, with bath and toilet 280-300F. Extra bed 50F. Breakfast 29F. Shower 15F. V, MC.) The **Hôtel Terminus,** 5 pl. de la Gare (tel. 02 33 50 02 05), across from the station, has some of the most attractive French hotel wallpaper around in its airy rooms with TVs. (Singles 115F, with shower 150F; doubles 155F, with shower 185F, with bath 205F; triples 195-255F; quads 225F, with shower 270F. Breakfast 22F.)

[] FOOD. Restaurants in town tend to be a bit pricey. Near the hostel, **Monte Pego,** 13 rue St-Sauveur (tel. 02 33 90 74 44), serves pastas (42-54F), pizzas (38-50F), and salads (30-45F). (Open Tu-Sa noon-1:30pm and 7-9:30pm, Su noon-1:30pm. V, MC.) **Crêperie La Courtine,** 10 rue Cambernon (tel. 02 33 51 33 41), perched in a tranquil spot in the *haute ville*, serves copious portions of *galettes*, crêpes, salads, and meat dishes. (Open daily July-Aug. 11:30am-10pm, Sept.-June 11:30am-2pm and 7-10pm.) Morning **markets** are held on cours Jonville (Sa) and pl. de 11 Novembre (W). For groceries, head to **Marché Plus,** 107 rue de Courage. (Open M-Sa 7am-9pm, Su 9am-1pm.)

** SIGHTS AND ENTERTAINMENT.** Granville's main attraction is its silky-smooth **beach,** but the town offers plenty of options for getting out of the sun for an hour or two. The *haute ville*, a walled city built in 1439 by English invaders, stretches from the **Église de Notre-Dame** (where classical concerts are held on weekends), to the pl. de l'Isthme and the **Musée Richard Anacréon** (tel. 02 33 51 02 94), the only 20th-century art museum in the area. The museum focuses on Fauvism; bright and colorful works by Dufy, Dérain, and Friesz, along with several Rodins, make this a wonderful diversion for any bored beachcomber. Temporary expositions replace the permanent collection during the summer though, so call ahead. (Open W-M 10am-noon and 2-6pm. 15F, students 8F; during expos 25F, students 15F.) On the other side of the **casino,** off av. de la Libération, lies the calm **Jardin Public Christian Dior,** a piece of oceanfront property brimming with rosebushes, donated a century ago by Granville's most famous son. A trip here is well worth it for the walk alone. Take the promenade du Plat Gousset along the oceanfront and climb the stairs to the garden and small **museum.** (Museum open Tu-Su 10am-12:30pm and 2:30-7pm. Garden open daily 9am-9pm.) From May to September, boats leave daily for the **Chausey Islands,** an archipelago of 52 to 365 islets (depending on the tide), with few inhabitants and lovely stretches of sand; for ferry services, see **Orientation and Practical Information.** A lovely road (D911) leads south of Granville to Mont-St-Michel (100km), offering excursions for drivers and bikers.

Granvillais nightlife is limited, but pleasantly low-key: bar-hopping in your flip-flops will not earn disapproving stares. On warm summer nights check out the youthful outdoor terrace action at the **Bar les Amiraux,** across from the hostel. On rue St-Sauveur, **Les Bals des Oiseaux** is also popular. **Les Aviateurs,** meanwhile, on rue aux Corsaires, serves six oysters and a glass of Muscadet for 30F.

COUTANCES

Walls embrace Coutances (pop. 9,700) as if guarding the bounty of surrounding farms. Miraculously unscathed by World War II, its 13th-century cathedral was described by Victor Hugo as second only to Chartres in beauty. Having (easily) exhausted the tourist sights, remember that Coutances' second-greatest treasure is the breathtaking countryside just beyond its walls.

** PRACTICAL INFORMATION.** The **train station** (tel. 02 33 07 50 77) has service to **Granville** (30min., 3 per day, 41F), **Avranches** (40min., 3 per day, 43F), **Cherbourg** (2 hr., 6 per day, 92F), **Caen** (1½hr., 6 per day, 80F), **Rennes** (2hr., 3 per day, 109F), and **Paris** (4hr., 2 per day, 200F). **STN buses** (tel. 02 33 50 77 89 in Granville) head for **Granville** (30min., 5per day, 41F). To reach the *centre ville* walk straight out of the station onto rue St-Pierre. Continue through pl. de la Poissonerie and bear left, along rue Puits Notre-Dame. The **tourist office** (tel. 02 33 19 08 10; fax 02 33 19 08 19) is one block from the front of the cathedral, behind the Hôtel de Ville. (Open July 1-Sept. 15 M-Sa 10am-1pm and 2-7pm, Su 2-7pm; Sept. 16-June M-Sa 10am-12:30pm and 2-6pm.) **Currency exchange** is offered by **Crédit Agricole,** pl. de la Poste, a block to the right as you leave the cathedral. (Open M 2-5:30pm, Tu-F 8:30am-noon and 1:30-5:30pm, Sa 8:30am-4pm.) The **post office** is on pl. de la Poste. (Tel. 02 33 76 64 10. Open M-F 8am-6:30pm, Sa 8am-noon. **Postal code:** 50200.)

◨◨ **ACCOMMODATIONS, CAMPING, AND FOOD.** Coutances is best seen as a daytrip from Granville, but there are a couple of decent budget accommodations. To get to **Hôtel de Normandie,** pl. du Général de Gaulle (tel. 02 33 45 01 40; fax 02 33 46 74 54), head out of the station onto rue St-Pierre, turn left up the hill before the parking lot and right onto rue du Lyceé; the hotel is further down on the right. Here the cheery staff lets spacious, comfortable rooms, some with views of the cathedral, and most with TV or phone. (Singles 110F, with shower 175F, with shower and toilet 200F, with bath and toilet 230F; doubles 170-250F. Extra bed 60F. Breakfast 28F. V, MC.) For the **Hôtel des Trois Pilliers,** 11 rue des Halles (tel. 02 33 45 01 31), follow the directions to Hôtel de Normandie, but turn immediately left onto rue des Halles after turning onto rue de Lyceé. Run by a pleasant couple, its small modern rooms are near the cathedral. The bar downstairs overflows with *coutançais* teens. (Singles or doubles 125-155F, with shower 155F; triple with shower 165F. Breakfast 27F. V, MC.) **Camping Les Vignettes,** 27 rte. de St-Malo (tel. 02 33 45 43 13), is within walking distance of the *centre ville*, off the D44 to Agon and Coutainville; the walk is on a busy road, but the tourist office can tell you how to avoid it for part of the way. (16F per person, tent 16F, car 16F. Electricity 12F.)

   The **Stoc supermarket,** rue de la Verjustière, is at the bottom of the hill behind Église St-Nicolas (open M-F 9am-12:45pm and 2:30-7:30pm, Sa 9am-1pm and 2-7:30pm), but you can find grocery stores closer to the cathedral. On Thursday mornings, a **market** fills pl. de la Cathédrale (9am-1pm). Hôtel de Normandie (see above) has a restaurant with a reputation for good Norman fare; *menus* are available at 50F and 72F. (Open Tu-Sa noon-2pm and 6-11pm, Su noon-2pm. V, MC.)

◨ **SIGHTS.** The spires of Coutances's grand **cathedral,** completed in 1274, rise above the delicate mists. Inside, the 13th-century stained-glass windows and ornate pillars of the axial chapel contrast with the spartan decor of the side chapels and nave. A spectacular window in the south transept depicts the Last Judgment. The reliquary chapel in the right of the transept contains a morsel of the True Cross and various bits of sundry saints. Three French tours are offered daily, with two in English in high season; the tourist office has a schedule. (Open daily 9am-7pm. Tours 30F, ages 10-18 20F.) The lovely **Jardin des Plantes,** on the opposite side of the town hall from the cathedral, is among the oldest in France, and encompasses the small **Quesnel-Morinière museum,** which houses a minimal collection of Norman paintings and artifacts, including ceramics and some costumes. (Museum open July 1-Sept. 15 W-M 10am-1pm and 2-6pm; Sept. 15-June 10am-noon and 2-5pm. 10F, under 18 free. Garden open daily July-Sept. 9am-11:30pm; Oct.-Mar. 9am-5pm; Apr.-June 9am-8pm.) The countryside around Coutances holds a wellspring of treasures, most of them within 4-5km from the town. If you are up for walking (there is no bike rental in Coutances) ask the tourist office for the brochure *Monuments Ouverts à la Visite* (with translations in English), which details a number of chateaus, manors, and abbeys around the town.

AVRANCHES

Sitting on a hill in a northern corner of the bay of Mont-St-Michel, Avranches (pop. 9000) offers another base from which to explore the fortified island. But before rushing off to Normandy's big attraction, give Avranches itself some time. After all, it was St. Aubert, the 8th-century Bishop of Avranches, who gave in to angelic pressure and built the Mont. As a result, the two are inextricably linked, and Avranches serves as a good starting point for trips island-ward. Avranches itself is quite lovely, and certainly merits a bit of exploration.

⬛ ORIENTATION AND PRACTICAL INFORMATION. The Caen-Rennes train line passes through Avranches' **train station** (tel. 02 33 58 00 77), at the bottom of the hill. Destinations include **Granville** (15min., 2 per day, 33F) and **Paris** (5hr., 2 per day, 189F). (Open M-Sa 8:30am-7pm, Su 1:45-10pm.) **STN,** 2 rue Général de Gaulle (tel. 02 33 58 03 07), next to the town hall, sends buses to **Mont-St-Michel** (July-Aug. 1 per day, Sept.-June 1 per week; 24F) and **Granville** (33F). (Office open M, Tu, and Th 10:30am-noon and 3:30-6pm, W and F 10:30am-noon and 3:30-5pm.) **Rent bikes** 2.5km out of town from **Decathalon.** (Tel. 02 33 89 28 50. 70F per day. Open in summer M-F 9:30am-12:30pm and 2-7pm, Sa 9:30am-7pm; rest of year M-Sa 9:30am-12:30pm and 2-7pm.) To get to the *centre ville* from the station, cross the highway via the footbridge to the right of the station and lean into the heart-pounding hike uphill, bearing left at the first major fork. The **tourist office** (tel. 02 33 58 00 22; fax 02 33 68 13 29), which shares the STN building, reserves rooms (10F) and gives out free town maps. (Open July-Aug. M-Sa 9:15am-12:30pm and 2-7:15pm, Su 9:45am-12:30pm and 2-7:15pm; Sept.-June Sa 9am-noon and 2-6pm.) The **post office** (tel. 02 33 89 20 10) on rue St-Gervais offers **currency exchange.** (Open M-F 8am-6:30pm, Sa 8am-noon. **Postal code:** 50300.)

▌ ACCOMMODATIONS. The popular **Hôtel de Normandie,** bd. L. Jozeau-Marigné (tel. 02 33 58 01 33), sits at the end of the steep path you'll encounter after crossing the footbridge to the right of the station. Run by an exceptionally friendly staff, the ivy-covered building offers lovely rooms with fluffy eiderdowns, immaculate bathrooms, and views of the patchwork countryside. Calm, benevolent owner loves *Let's Go*—don't forget to sign her guest book. (Singles 150F, with bath 170F, with TV 180F; doubles 180F, with bath or shower 240F. TV 30F. Breakfast 30F. V, MC.) In case of a jam, **Hôtel Valhubert,** 7 rue Général de Gaulle (tel. 02 33 58 03 28), opposite the tourist office, rents five worn but relatively clean rooms above a popular bar. (Singles and doubles 140F, with shower or bath 180F, with shower and toilet 200F. Extra bed 30F. Breakfast 30F. Reception M-Sa.) Your cheapest bet might be a *chambre d'hôte.* The tourist office has a list of rooms from 100F per night.

⬛ FOOD. Numerous cheap *brasseries* and restaurants surround the tourist office. At pl. St-Gervais, **Pizzeria l'Anticario** (tel. 02 33 58 32 10) serves up a great lunchtime *menu* for 45F on an ivy-covered terrace. Tomato, shrimp, lobster, gambas, smoked salmon, mussels, or fish pizza for 38-80F. Salads 34-58F. (Open Tu-Sa noon-2pm and 7-11pm, open Su evenings. Closed last two weeks in May.) **La Cucaracha** (tel. 02 33 58 14 13), right next door, serves a decent approximation of Tex-Mex amidst enthusiastic, flamboyant decor. (Soft tacos 48F, gargantuan hamburgers 40-46F. Open M 7-11pm, Tu-Sa noon-2pm and 7-11pm.) A **market** is held on pl. du Marché, off rue des Chapeliers (Sa 9am-3pm). There is a **Stoc supermarket** on rue Général de Gaulle. (Open M-Sa 9am-7:30pm, Su 9:30-11:45am.)

⬛⬛ SIGHTS AND FESTIVALS. The **Jardin des Plantes,** pl. Carnot, while not enormous, is dotted with Romanesque arches and provides a spectacular view of the distant Mont-St-Michel, especially on summer evenings when the Mont is illuminated. A short distance away is Avranches' **museum,** rue d'Office (tel. 02 33 58 25 15). It houses exhibits of regional garb and crafts, as well as a replica of a medieval scriptorium. Most impressive, however, is the collection of Mont-St-Michel's **manuscripts,** which detail the finer points of theology, astronomy, and music. (Open July-Aug. daily 10am-noon and 2-6pm; Apr.-June and Sept.-Oct. W-M same hours. 30F, students 15F, includes museum, manuscripts, and church, below.) Summer finds many of the manuscripts in the **Mairie.** (June-Aug. daily 10am-noon and 2-6pm.) The granite **Église St-Gervais,** pl. St-Gervais. possesses a 74m bell-tower with a 32-bell chime. The real treasure, however, is inside. When the Archangel Michael appeared to Bishop Aubert and commanded him to build Mont-St-Michel, Aubert ignored the order. When Michael appeared again, Aubert continued to delay. The Angel scolded Aubert by tapping him on the forehead, but he pressed his finger into the bishop's brow so enthusiastically that a dent resulted. You can see Aubert's dented skull in the **treasury,** right inside the door of the church. (Open W-M 10am-noon and 2-6pm.) Down rue de la Constitution, the **Patton Memorial** is officially American soil. The huge obelisk commemorates Operation COBRA's successful break through the German front between St-Lô and Périers in July of 1944. Patton's victory here resulted in the liberation of Avranches, a drive west into Brittany, and an advance east into the Loire Valley and on to Paris.

During the first two weeks in August, Avranches hosts **Music en Baie,** a festival which comprises a music camp and concerts, ranging from Baroque to jazz. (3-concert pass 150F, students 90F. Contact tourist office for details.) Another popular festival is **Les Éclats de Rire;** parades, comedians and actors all take to the streets one day in mid-July and dedicate themselves entirely to the art of laughing.

MONT-ST-MICHEL

Rising from the sea like a vision from another world, the fortified island of Mont-St-Michel is visible for kilometers in every direction. The Mont, a work in progress since its founding in 708, is a dazzling labyrinth of stone arches, spires, and stairways that climb (and keep climbing) to the abbey itself. Just as overwhelming as the Mont's beauty, however, are the crowds that fill its streets. The island has been a popular spot for pilgrims both religious and secular almost since day one. Each August sees as many as 200,000 visitors daily. Although the island is easily covered in a day, you may want to avoid the crowds by arriving early. The easiest way to do this is by staying in nearby Pontorson, a scattered collection of hotels and restaurants masquerading as a village. Forget about staying on the Mont; unless St. Michæl himself is personally bankrolling your visit, it's not going to happen.

■ ORIENTATION AND PRACTICAL INFORMATION

The only break in the outer wall is the **Porte de l'Avancée.** Inside, the **tourist office** lies immediately to the left; to the right, the Porte du Boulevard and Porte du Roy open onto the town's major thoroughfare, **Grande Rue.** All the hotels, restaurants, crowds, and sights are on this spiraling street.

Trains: In **Pontorson** (tel. 02 33 60 00 35). To: **St-Malo** via Dol (35min., 3 per day, 42F); **Granville** via Folligny (1½hr., 3 per day, 50F); **Dinan** (1¼hr., 6 per day, 40F); and **Paris** (4hr., 1 per day, 237F plus 36-90F TGV supplement). Open M-F 8:30am-noon and 1:30-7:30pm, Sa 8:30am-noon and 2-6:15pm, Su 2:30-9:45pm.

Buses: Buses leave from Porte du Roy; buy tickets on board. **STN buses** (tel. 02 33 50 77 89 in Granville; 02 33 58 03 07 in Avranches) go to **Pontorson** (15min., 8 per day until 6:15pm, 14F, round-trip 22F), **Avranches** (45min., 1 per day) and **Granville** (2hr., 1 per day). **SCETA** (tel. 02 33 50 77 89 in Granville) goes to **Folligny** (1hr., 1 per day) and **Avranches** (30min., 1 per day). **Courriers Bretons** (tel. 02 33 60 11 43) run to **Avranches** (30min., 1-2 per day, 26F), **St-Malo** (1½hr., 2-4 per day, 53F), and **Rennes** (1½hr., M-Sa 3 per day, 1 on Su, 63F). Office open M-Sa 10am-noon and 4-6:30pm.

Tourist Office: Just behind the wall to your left after you enter the city. (Tel. 02 33 60 14 30; fax 02 33 60 06 75). Busy! Ask about organized 2hr. hiking expeditions over the sand to the Île de Tombelaine (Apr.-Sept.) Pick up a free *Horaire des Marées* (tidetable) before venturing into the bay. The staff takes unpredictable vacations in the off-season; call if you need their help. (Open July-Aug. M-Sa 9am-12:30pm and 2-6:30pm; Sept.-June 9am-noon and 2-5pm.)

Post Office: Grande Rue (tel. 02 33 60 14 26), near Porte du Roy. **Currency exchange** at tolerable rates. Open M-F 9am-6pm, Sa 9am-5pm; mid-Sept. to June M-F 9am-noon and 2-5pm, Sa 9am-noon. **Postal code:** 50116.

ACCOMMODATIONS, CAMPING

ACCOMMODATIONS. Plan ahead to reserve a room you can afford; prices climb faster than the spring tide. St-Malo and Avranches offer accommodations at more reasonable prices; Pontorson has little to offer other than proximity. Among Pontorson's limited options, the cheapest beds are at the **Centre Duguesclin (HI),** rue Général Patton (tel. 02 33 60 18 65). From the station, turn right onto rue du Tizon, left onto rue du Couesnon, and then right onto rue St-Michel; walk until you come to the inconspicuous post office on the right. Turn left, then right past the cathedral, and left onto rue Hédou. Follow it to the end, and turn right on rue Général Patton. The hostel is on your left, one block down (10min.). The dorm-style 4- to 7-person rooms are bright and conducive to gathering, as is the kitchen and dining area. No sheets or blankets are provided—come prepared. (49F. Reception daily 8-10am and 6-10pm. Lockout 10am-6pm. Open June to mid-Sept. Occasionally booked fully by groups.) To get to the splendid **Hôtel-Restaurant le Relais Clemenceau,** 40 bd. Clemenceau (tel. 02 33 60 10 96; fax 02 33 60 25 71), in Pontorson, walk straight out of the *gare* onto bd. Clemenceau; a sign will point the way. Twenty bright, impeccably clean rooms with spacious bathrooms are let by a cheery couple. (Doubles 150F, with shower 180-200F, with shower and toilet 215-250F; triples and quads 280-300F. Extra bed 54F. Breakfast 30F. V, MC.)

CAMPING. The least expensive option may be camping, and there are plenty of sites near the Mont. **Camping Municipal de Pontorson,** chemin des Soupirs (tel. 02 33 68 11 59), off rue Général Patton near the hostel, is 10 minutes from the station. Happy campers will find tranquil, bright, unforested sites with sound sanitary equipment. (13F per person, 13F per tent, 6.50F per car. Electricity 13F. Open Apr.-Sept.) **Camping du Mont-St-Michel** (tel. 02 33 60 09 33), is a mere 1.8km from the Mont at the junction of D275 and N776. The clean, pleasantly shaded sites fill fast, and there's a supermarket next door. They also **rent bikes.** (Bikes 30F per hour, 50F per half-day, 100F per day. Camping 51F per site, 35F per person. Electricity included. Open Feb. 15-Nov. 1.) **Camping St-Michel,** rte. du Mont-St-Michel (tel. 02 33 70 96 90), is by the bay in Courtils. It's a bit far from the Mont (9km), but the Granville bus stops 200m from entrance. Buses go to the Mont at 11am and 5pm. Sites are quiet and near a swimming pool, common room, and telephone. (19F per person, 19F per car and tent. Open Mar. 15-Oct. 15.) More campgrounds can be found in Beauvoir, between the Mont and Pontorson.

FOOD

If you dare invest in more than a postcard and sandwich on the Mont, look for local specialties such as *agneau du pré salé* (lamb raised on the surrounding salt marshes) and *omelette poulard,* a fluffy soufflé-like dish (about 45F). The cozy **Chapeau Rouge,** Grande Rue (tel. 02 33 60 14 29), offers these delicacies, as well as seafood treats. (3-course *menus* 75-85F.) To eat in a room with a view, walk along the ramparts and take your pick of the restaurants; all sport terraces or glass walls. Sandwich stands and self-service cafeterias line Grande Rue. You could be lured to a sticky end at **La Sirène** (tel. 02 33 60 08 60), on Grande Rue past the post office on the left—bind yourself to avoid the temptation of chocolate-banana *crêpe* (29F), stuffed to bursting and topped with a *mont* of chocolate sauce. (*Menu* 60F. Open daily noon-2:30pm and 6-9:30pm.) If you plan to picnic, arrive prepared as there are no grocery stores within the walls or anywhere near. Consider stopping by the **Champion supermarket,** on the way from Pontorson and conveniently located across the street from the rue St-Michel STN bus stop. (Open M-F 9am-12:30pm and 2:30-7:15pm, Sa 9am-7:30pm.)

THE NORTHWEST

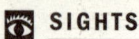 **SIGHTS**

New surprises await a wanderer in every nook and cranny on the Mont, and it's almost impossible to get lost. If you'd prefer a structured visit, pick up one of the guides available at the booths on Grande Rue (25-80F). While you're free to explore the bay, don't wander off too far on the sand. The broad expanses are riddled with quicksand, and the bay's tides, changing every six hours or so, are the highest in France. During spring tides, which occur twice a month, the *mascaret* (initial wave) rushes in at 2m per second, flooding the beaches along the causeway. To see this spectacle, you must be within the abbey two hours ahead of time.

HISTORY. While the formation of the Baie de Mont-St-Michel began thousands of years ago, according to legend the island was created in the 7th century when a huge wave flooded the surrounding forest. In 708, the Archangel Michæl appeared to the Bishop of Avranches, instructing him to build a place of worship on the barren and rocky island north of Pontorson. The doubting bishop ignored the first two appearances, and it was only after the frustrated angel insisted a third time that plans were laid out for several crypts around the rock. Additions began in 966, when a group of monks made a pilgrimage to the Mont and were so inspired by its beauty and power that they began an even larger church on the site. Mostly complete by the 14th and 15th centuries, the Mont was used as a fortress during the Hundred Years' War. While its outer walls repelled English attacks, its inner walls still cloistered the Benedictines, who spent their time copying and illuminating the famous *manuscrits du Mont-St-Michel*, now on display in nearby Avranches (see p. 494). In 1789, the Revolutionary government turned the island into a prison; famous past inmates include Robespierre. In 1874, Mont-St-Michel was classified as a national monument, and in 1897 it was topped by the bronze statue of St. Michæl; since 1969, a small community of monks has returned to the abbey.

ABBEY AND CRYPTS. A climb up Grande Rue places you at the abbey entrance, the departure point for the 1-hour tours free with entrance. There are about six English tours per day. Mass is still held daily at 12:15pm; entry to the abbey church for the service (and the service only) is free from noon to 12:15pm. Beneath the church lie the Mont's frigid **crypts.** The descent passes through the refectory and leads into the dark, chilly church foundations where the walls are 2m thick in places. **La Merveille,** an intricate 13th-century cloister, encloses a seemingly endless web of passageways and chambers. If you're not impressed with its architectural complexities, the mechanical simplicity of the Mont's **treadmill** will surely catch your attention. Prisoners held here during the French Revolution would walk on the wheel for hours, their foot labor powering the elaborate pulley system that carried supplies up the side of the Mont. *(Tel. 02 33 89 80 00. Open daily May-Sept. 9:30am-5pm; Oct.-Apr. 9:30am-4:30pm. Audio tour 30F. 40F, under 26 25F.)*

LOGIS TIPHAINE. About halfway up Grande Rue is the Logis Tiphaine, a restored 14th-century home. Bertrand du Guesclin, born so ugly that his mother rejected him, went on to become governor of Pontorson and marry the beautiful young woman Tiphaine. He built this four-story villa in 1365 to protect his wife from the English while he was fighting in Spain. Today, the *logis* houses an interesting museum, which displays well-preserved 14th- to 17th-century furniture, fireplaces, and objects of everyday use, including a chastity belt. *(Tel. 02 33 60 23 34. Open daily Jan.-June and Sept.-Nov. 14 9am-6pm; July-Aug. 9am-7pm. 25F, students 20F, under 18 5F.)*

MUSEUMS. The few museums in Mont-St-Michel offer moderately interesting summaries of its history and a hodgepodge of "artifacts." The fact that each museum exits into a gift shop should be the first clue that prices are inflated. The **Musée Historique** contains exhibits on medieval torture devices and the Mont's most rapscallious prisoners, while the **Musée Maritime** has a collection of 300 antique model boats. The **Archéoscope** is the most engaging, describing the legends and history of the Mont with film, music, and an intricate model that rises from the water. *(Each museum 45F separately; combined entrance for all three 75F, students 60F.)*

THE NORTHWEST

SPECTACLES. When darkness falls, illumination transforms the Mont into a glowing jewel best seen from either the causeway entrance or across the bay in Avranches. *(Illumination from 9 or 10pm, June-Sept.)* Dusk is also the time to revisit the crypts of the Abbey. **Les Imaginaires** immerse the sanctuary's corridors in a flood of light and music. *(Tel. 02 33 60 14 14. May-Aug. 10pm-1am; Sept. 9pm-midnight. 60F, students 35F, under 12 free; last entry 1hr. before closing.)* Note that there's no public transportation off the Mont late at night—you'll need a car. In May, the Mont celebrates **St-Michel de Printemps,** when costumed men and women parading through the streets re-enact local traditions. The autumnal **St-Michel d'Automne,** held on the Sunday before Michaelmas (Sept. 29), is similar but more religiously oriented.

BRITTANY (BRETAGNE)

Its cliffs gnawed by the sea into long crags and inlets, Brittany rebelliously tugs away from mainland France, self-consciously maintaining its Celtic traditions in defiance of years of centralized cultural repression. In recent years, the government has softened its stance, allowing schools to teach in Breton, though it is still illegal to advocate independence. Though present-day Breton culture has its roots in the 5th to the 7th centuries, when Britons fled Anglo-Saxon invaders for this beautiful, wild peninsula, reminders of earlier inhabitants are plentiful. Neolithic people who settled here before the Gauls erected the thousands of megaliths visible today. The Romans, who conquered the area in 56 BC, decorated some of these monuments and incorporated them

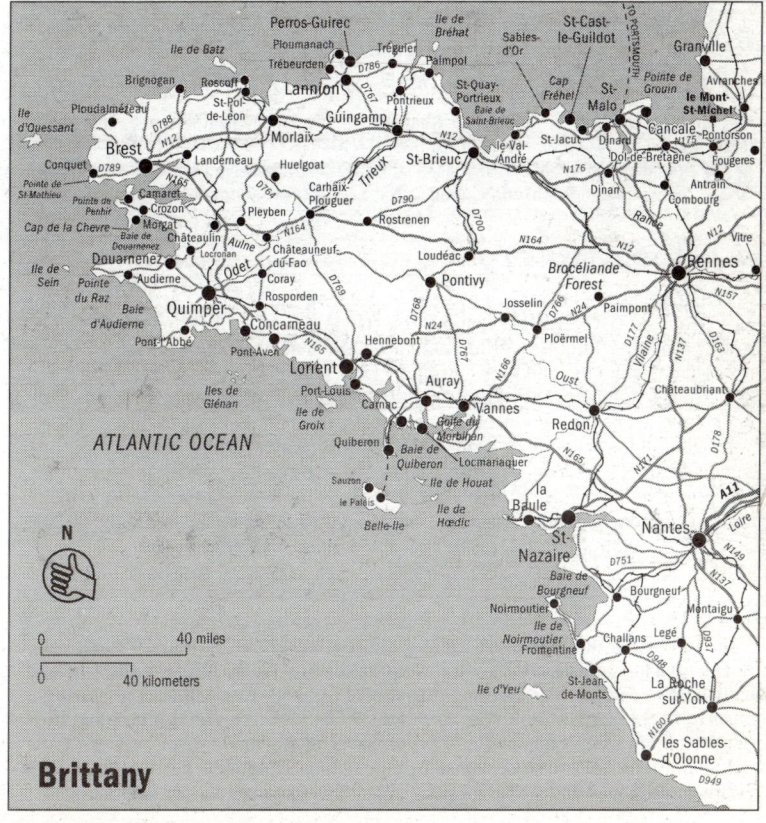

Brittany

into their own rituals. In the centuries that followed the exodus to its shores from Britain, Brittany fought for and retained its independence from Frankish, Norman, French, and English invaders, uniting with France only after the last Duchess ceded it to her husband, François I, in 1532.

Brittany is lined with spectacular beaches and misty, almost apocalyptic headlands. If you dislike crowds, beware of visiting in July and August. In the off-season, some coastal resorts such as St-Malo, Quiberon, and Concarneau close down, but the churches, beaches, and cliffs are as eerie and romantic as ever. Breton traditions linger in the pristine islands off the Atlantic coast and the forests of the Argoat interior. Many of them date from the Duchy's centuries of freedom, and they are fiercely guarded. The traditional costume of Breton women—a black dress and an elaborate white lace *coiffe* (head-dress)—appears in folk festivals and even some markets, and lilting *Brezhoneg* is spoken energetically at pubs and ports in the western part of the province.

The region's trademark *crêperies* offer savory buckwheat *galettes* wrapped around eggs, mushrooms, seafood, or ham, and dessert *crêpes* filled with chocolate, fruit, or jam. These are accompanied by *bolées* (earthenware bowls) of dry *cidre brut* or the sweeter *cidre doux*. A common non-alcoholic drink is *lait ribaud*, made from soured milk. Brittany's *pâtisseries* display *kouign amann* (flaky sheets saturated with butter and sugar) and the custard-like *far breton*. Whatever the meal, make seafood *(fruits de mer)* a part of it; Brittany's coastal location ensures that aquatic fare will be fresh, plentiful, and creatively prepared.

HIGHLIGHTS OF BRITTANY

■ **St-Malo,** with a continuous wide stripe of sand, and a walled *vieille ville,* provides both history and plenty of entertainment (p. 507).
■ **Belle-Île** offers a whole new beach experience, with secret rocky coves and wild Atlantic scenery (p. 536).
■ Capital of Brittany, all-around-fun **Rennes** is student central, with nighttime revelry doin' it and doin' it and doin' it right (p. 500).
■ **Dinan** provides a real-life history lesson in its perfectly-preserved *vieille ville* (p. 511).
■ The scenic **Crozon Peninsula** combines natural beauty with rural charm (p. 528).

GETTING AROUND

Getting to Brittany is hardly a problem; high-speed trains leave Paris's Gare Montparnasse and arrive in Rennes and Brest two and four hours later, respectively. Getting around Brittany is a different matter. The main train lines run from Rennes to Brest and Quimper, and between Nantes and Quimper. Less frequent trains and SNCF buses connect other cities to the main lines but not necessarily to each other. Private bus lines connect towns that the train lines miss, but they are infrequent and almost evaporate from September to May. Cycling is a good option, especially since the most beautiful sights are also the least accessible by public transport. The terrain is relatively flat but gets a bit hillier in the interior. Hikers can choose from a number of routes, including the long-distance footpaths **GR341, GR37, GR38, GR380,** and the spectacular **GR34** along the northern coast.

RENNES

Home to two major universities and 60,000 students, Rennes (pop. 205,000) combines Parisian sophistication with traditional Breton charm. Most of the city was destroyed in 1720, when a drunk carpenter knocked over a lamp and started a massive fire. Luckily, the lovely wooden *vieille ville* remained intact and now teems with hip cafés, bars, and clubs. Rennes is a popular stopover between Paris and Mont-St-Michel and a good base from which to explore the surrounding countryside and villages, but it also merits a packed weekend excursion on its own.

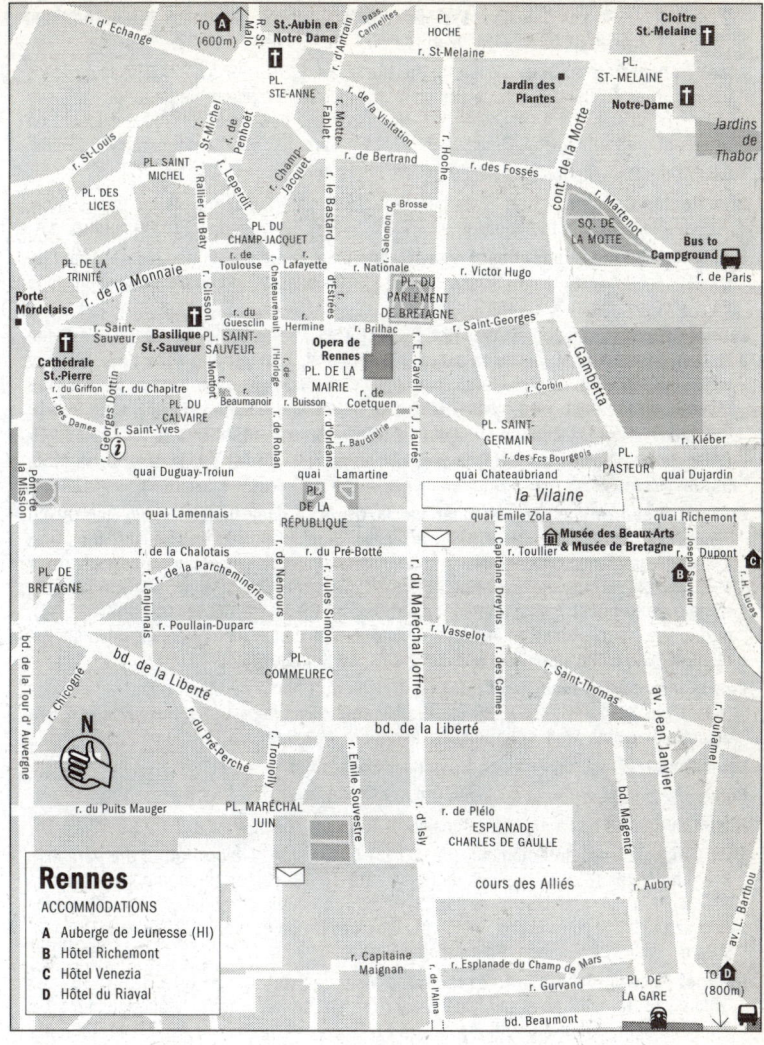

Rennes
ACCOMMODATIONS

A Auberge de Jeunesse (HI)
B Hôtel Richemont
C Hôtel Venezia
D Hôtel du Riaval

🛈 ORIENTATION AND PRACTICAL INFORMATION

The **Vilaine** river cuts the city in two, with the **train station** to the south and most sights and shopping to the north (20min.). From the northern exit of the *gare*, **av. Jean Janvier** (straight ahead) goes to the river.

Trains: pl. de la Gare (tel. 02 99 29 11 92). To: **Nantes** (1¼-2hr., 10 per day, 85-112F); **Brest** (2hr., approx. every hour, all TGV 130-174F); **Tours** (2½-3hr., every 2-3 hours, 134-178F); **Paris** (2hr., approx. every hour, 213-286F); **Caen** (3hr., 2 per day, 123-163F). Information office open M-F 7am-9pm, Sa 8am-5pm, Su 1-9pm. **SOS Voyageurs,** under the escalator by the north exit, open M-F 9am-noon and 1-7pm.

Buses: 16 pl. de la Gare (tel. 02 99 30 87 80), to the left of the *gare* as you face it. **Cariane Atlantique** (tel. 02 40 20 46 99 in Nantes) goes to **Nantes** (2hr., M-Th and Sa 2-3 per day, F 5 per day, 95F). **Anjou Bus** (tel. 02 41 69 10 00) goes to **Angers** (3hr., 1-

2 per day, 96F). **Les Courriers Bretons** (tel. 02 99 56 79 09) run to **Mont-St-Michel** (2½hr., 1-2 per day, 62F).

Local Transportation: Star, 12 rue du Pré Botté (tel. 02 99 79 37 37). Buses run daily until 6:30 or 7:30pm. Purchase tickets in advance from office or newsstands. (6F, *carnet* of 10 tickets 47F.) Otherwise, buy tickets on the bus for 6.50F. 40% discount on tickets at the youth hostel. Office open M-F 7am-7pm, Sa 9:30am-noon and 2-6:30pm.

Taxis: At the train station (tel. 02 99 30 79 79). 24hr.

Bike Rental: Guedard, 13 bd. Beaumont (tel. 02 99 30 43 78), next to the train station. 70F per day. 11 pl. Ste-Anne (tel. 02 99 79 24 86). 50F per day, 3000F deposit.

Hiking and Biking Information: France Randonnée, 9 rue des Portes-Mordelaises (tel. 02 99 31 59 44; fax 02 99 30 02 96). Also offers piles of info on **GR** trails and lists of *gîtes d'étape.* Open M-Sa 9am-6pm.

Tourist Office: 11 rue pont St-Yves (tel. 02 99 67 11 11; fax 02 99 67 11 10). From the station, take av. Jean Janvier to quai Chateaubriand. Turn left and walk along the river until you reach rue George Dottin. Turn right and then right again on rue St-Yves. The office is on the right. Free maps and lists of hotels and restaurants. Pick up a free *Le Rennais* or *La Griffe,* monthly cultural magazines. Open M-Sa 9am-7pm, Su 11am-6pm.

English Books: Forum du Livre, 5 quai Lamartine (tel. 02 99 79 38 93). Open M-Sa 9:30am-7pm.

Cultural Organizations: French-American Institute, 7 quai Chateaubriand (tel. 02 99 79 20 57; fax 02 99 79 30 09), arranges joint French-American activities and exchange programs. Office on the 2nd floor can help with visas and work permits. Open M-Th 9am-12:30pm and 1:30-6pm, F 9am-12:30pm and 1:30-5pm. **Maison Internationale de Rennes,** 7 quai Chateaubriand (tel. 02 99 78 22 66; fax 02 99 79 22 44), next to the French-American Institute. An information center for all Rennais international relations, including study and work programs, and employment.

Centre Information Jeunesse Bretagne, Maison du Champ de Mars, 6 cours des Alliés (tel. 02 99 31 47 48; fax 02 99 30 39 51), on the 2nd floor. List of budget hotels. Info on cultural events, work opportunities, and more. M 1-8pm, Sa 10am-noon and 2-6pm.

Laundromat: 25 rue de Penhoet. Open daily 8am-10pm.

Police: 22 bd. de la Tour d'Auvergne (tel. 02 99 65 00 22).

Hospital: Rennes has a number of hospitals. To locate the nearest, tel. 02 99 59 16 16.

Post Office: 27 bd. du Colombier (tel. 02 99 01 22 11), 1 block left of the *gare* exit. **Branch office,** pl. de la République (tel. 02 99 78 43 35); on the *quais.* From the station, walk up av. Jean Janvier and turn left onto the *quais,* three blocks over. **Currency exchange,** 2.5% commission, min. 20F. **Western Union** at branch office only. Open M-F 8am-7pm, Sa 8am-noon. **Postal code:** 35000.

Internet Access: Cyberspirit, 2d rue de la Visitation (tel. 02 99 84 53 30). 30F per 30min., 5F to send an email. Open M 2-7pm, Tu noon-7pm, W-F noon-midnight, Sa 2pm-midnight. **Cybernet Online,** 22 rue St. Georges (Tel. 02 99 36 37 41) 25F per 30min. Open M 2-7:30pm, Tu-Sa 10am-7:30pm. Closed Aug.

◤ ACCOMMODATIONS AND CAMPING

You should reserve in the first week of July during the *Tombées de la Nuit* festival. In July and August, a university dorm is open to student travelers for short stays (singles 92F per night). To check availability, call **CROUS,** 7 pl. Hoche. (Tel. 07 99 36 46 11. Open M-F 8:30am-4pm.) A number of moderately priced hotels lie to the east of av. Jean Janvier between quai Richemont and the *gare.*

Auberge de Jeunesse (HI), 10-12 Canal St-Martin (tel. 02 99 33 22 33; fax 02 99 59 06 21). From the *gare,* take av. Jean Janvier straight to the canal, where it becomes rue Gambetta. Go 5 blocks, then left onto rue des Fossés. Take rue de la Visitation to pl. Ste-Anne. On the north side of the *place,* rue St-Malo leads to the hostel (30min.). Or take the bus (M-F #20, Sa-Su #1 or 18, direction "Centre Commercial Nord") to "Hôtel

Dieu." From the bus stop, continue down the road, turn right on rue de St-Malo, and follow the street over the mini-canal to an intersection. The hostel is on the right. 1- to 4-
person rooms. White tile floors and bright blue walls are reminiscent of a public swimming pool. Laundry, kitchen, common room, and cafeteria run by friendly staff. 25% off
tickets to Mont-St-Michel. Singles 130F, doubles, triples and quads 89F per person.
Breakfast included. Reception daily 7am-11pm. Doors close at 2am but a night watch-
man is on duty until the reception opens. No lockout. V, MC.

Hôtel Venezia, 27 rue Dupont des Loges (tel. 02 99 30 36 56; fax 02 99 30 78 78), off
quai Richemont. Take av. Jean Janvier from the train station's north entrance, for about
10 min. Turn right onto rue Dupont des Loges, just before the bridge. The only hotel in
town overlooking the canal La Vilaine. Spacious, individually decorated rooms; make
sure to ask for one with a canal view. Singles 160F, with bathroom and TV 185F; doubles 160-220F. In August, mention *Let's Go* when you arrive for a potential discount.
All-you-can-eat breakfast 25F. Call ahead for weekends in summer. V, MC.

Hôtel Riaval, 9 rue Riaval (tel. 02 99 50 65 58; fax 02 99 41 85 30). Exit the *gare*
through the southern "Cour d'Appel" doors and walk 100m across the open plaza and
then down the metal stairs. Go left at the bottom of the steps (onto rue de Quineleu).
Follow until the first street crossing and keep straight—Quineleu becomes Riaval, which
bends around to the right. The hotel is on the left. Clean, with nicely decorated rooms,
in a quiet neighborhood. Top floor views of the city. Singles and doubles 130F, with
shower 165F, with bathroom and TV 195F. Triples and quads 165-260F. Breakfast 28F.
Reception M-F 7am-10pm, Sa-Su 8am-1pm and 8-10pm. V.

Hôtel Richemont, 8 rue Dupont des Loges (tel. 02 99 30 38 21; fax 02 99 31 73 20).
Directly off av. Jean Janvier, on the right. Less personable staff, but clean, slightly worn
rooms with sparkling bathroom fixtures. Singles with toilet and shower 225-235F, doubles with toilet and shower 290F. Extra bed 35F. Breakfast 30F. V, MC.

Campsites: Municipal des Gayeulles, in Parc les Grayeulles (tel. 02 99 36 91 22; fax
02 99 35 32 80). Take bus #3 from rue de Paris (from rue Gambetta, turn right on rue
Victor Hugo, which becomes rue de Paris) to Parc les Grayeulles. The campground is
deep within the beautiful park, past the public pool and a farm with activities for kids.
Adults 14F, under 7 7F. Cars 5F. Tent 15.50F. Electricity 17F. Hot shower 5F. 10% discount for stays over 8 days. No credit cards.

FOOD

Rennes' restaurant scene ranges from traditional *crêpes* and *galettes* to diverse
international offerings. You're sure to find something marvelous on rue de St-
Malo, pl. St-Michel, rue St-Georges, or rue Ste-Melaine. For do-it-yourself types,
there is a huge **market** every Saturday in pl. des Lices, a smaller market held daily
in different locations (ask the tourist office), and a **supermarket** in the Galeries-
Lafayette on quai Duguay-Trouin. (Open M-Sa 9am-8pm.) On the way to the youth
hostel there is a small **late-night market** located at the intersection of rue Dieu and
rue St-Malo. (Open M-Sa 6pm-1am.)

Crêperie au Boulingrin, 25 rue St-Melaine (tel. 02 99 38 75 11), near the Jardin du Thabor. Formerly a prison, this relaxed place now serves *galettes* (7-41F) worth some jail
time. The namesake *Boulingrin* is a *crêpe* stuffed with apples, caramel, and almonds
(44F). Open M-F 11:30am-2pm and 6:30-11pm, Sa-Su 6:30-11pm.

Restaurant Végétarien-Biologique, 12 rue du Vau Saint Germain (tel. 02 99 79 25 52).
The prosaic name does not belie the intricate and unusual flavors entwined together by
Dominic and Thierry, who do all the cooking, baking, and serving amidst a batik and
wicker decor. The all-organic daily changes daily. Lunch *menus* from 64F; dinner 80F.
Tell Dominic if you're on a tight budget and he'll find something to please your wallet as
well as your palate. Open M-Sa noon-2:30pm and Th, F, and Sa nights 7-10pm. MC, V.

King Creole, 5 rue St. Malo (tel. 02 99 78 37 60). With lively music wafting out onto the
sidewalk, and beautiful, brightly colored decor inside, it's no wonder that people flock

to this caribbean paradise. The copious 79F menu includes rice, beans, and fried plantains with an excellent meat dish, accompanied by a spicy ginger fruit juice drink. Don't be afraid to take a spin between the tables with the jovial salsa-dancing owner.

Le Gange, 34 place des Lices (tel. 02 9 30 18 37). If the East Indies are more to your taste than the West, try this elegant restaurant off the noisy pl. des Lices. Don't miss the stuffed paratha (vegetable-stuffed bread) for a reasonable 15F; *plats* around 60F. Vegetarian dinner 89F. This popular place fills up quickly–reservations recommended for groups. Open M-Sa 11:30am-2:30pm and 6-11pm. V, MC.

👁 🏛 SIGHTS AND EXCURSIONS

SIGHTS. The **Musée des Beaux-Arts,** 20 quai Emile Zola (tel. 02 99 28 55 84; fax 02 99 28 55 99), has a collection dating from the 14th to the 20th century, with works by de La Tour, Picasso, and Sérusier, as well as a small but fascinating exhibit of Egyptian pottery. Call for info on rotating special exhibits. (Open W-M 10am-noon and 2-6pm. Tours July-Aug. W and F at 2:30pm. Admission 30F, students, children, and senior citizens 15F.) The lush **Jardin du Thabor** is considered by some to be the most beautiful garden in France, and is a delight for greenery-lovers and romantics alike. Sculptures, fountains, and a massive bird cage grace the labyrinthine grounds; the rose garden alone holds an amazing 1700 varieties. Concerts are often held in the *Jardin*, and a small gallery on the north side presents a rotating exhibit of local artwork. (Open daily June-Sept. 7am-9:30pm.) Adjacent is the 14th- to 17th-century **Église Notre Dame;** step inside to gaze at the magnificent chapel altar and the blazing colors of the stained-glass choir. The magnificent **Cathédrale St-Pierre,** in the *vieille ville*, provides a gorgeous view of the city. If you ask nicely, one of the staff might take you up to the towers. (Open daily 9am-noon and 2-5pm.) Across the street from the cathedral is the **Porte Mordelaise,** former entrance to the city and the last remaining piece of the medieval city walls. An inconspicuous plaque provides interesting historical tidbits. The **Ecomusée du pays de Rennes** (tel. 02 99 51 38 15), located on a former farm at the city's edge, gives visitors a chance to learn about farming around Rennes in the early 1600s and to picnic in the apple orchards. From pl. de la République, take bus #14 (#1 on Su) to "Le Gacet" (route de Châtillon-sur-Seiche). (Open W-F 9am-noon and 2-6pm, Sa 2-6pm, Su 2-7pm. Admission 28F, students 14F, under 6 free.)

EXCURSIONS. To trade stage for scenery, take a daytrip to the **Brocéliande Forest,** home of the *Tombeau de Merlyn* ("Merlin's tomb"), the *Fontaine de Jouvence* ("the Fountain of Youth"), and the *Val Sans Retour* ("Valley of No Return"). **TIV** buses leave from Rennes (1hr., M-Sa 10-12 per day, 16.50F) and stop in the village of **Paimpont,** whose tourist office (tel. 02 99 07 84 23) offers info on buses, bike and car routes, and local accommodations.

🎵 🎆 NIGHTLIFE AND FESTIVALS

NIGHTLIFE. *Rennais* nightlife is so hot that Parisian students are known to make weekend trips to Rennes just for the clubs. The action centers around the **pl. Ste-Anne,** the **pl. Ste-Michel,** and the radiating streets, but don't limit yourself;—there are great nightspots all over the city. For a more sedate evening, search out theater, dance, and classical music performances in *Contact Hebdo Le Guide-Loisirs,* available at the tourist office or hostel. For information on **Orchestre de Bretagne** concerts, tel. 02 99 27 52 83. Rennes' major theater is the **Théâtre National de Bretagne,** on rue St-Heller (tel. 02 99 30 88 88), but smaller theaters abound.

L'Espace, 45 bd. La Tour d'Auvergne (tel. 02 99 30 99 21), pounds all night with writhing people of all sizes, styles, and sexual orientations. In this democratic spirit, the club embraces techno, Latin, and gay scene followers. Open nightly until 5am.

PARTYING À LA FRANÇAISE
French youth party in stages, cramming as much variety into one evening as possible. Many start in a café, bar, or *brasserie* to eat and drink, lounging until midnight or 1am. Then it's on to meet more friends in a *bar de nuit* until 2 or 3am, and then to a *discothèque* or two, where the now thoroughly inebriated masses move it to all manner of beats. Many will stumble home at 5 or 5:30am when the discos shut their doors, but others will stick it out until 6:30am or so when the first bakeries open with warm bread and croissants.

Le Zing, 5 pl. des Lices (tel. 02 99 79 69 60), picks up at 1am when other bars close, and goes strong until 3am when the crowd heads to the discotheques. Salsa and Latin dancing on occasion.

Le Jardin des Plantes, 32 rue Ste-Melaine (tel. 02 99 38 74 46), offers food, drink, and the opportunity for meaningful conversation in a mellow, garden-like atmosphere. Also features live concerts and theatrical performances. Open nightly until 1am.

Le Batchi, 34 rue Vasselot (tel. 02 99 79 62 27), is the heartbeat of Rennes' gay scene. In this mixed pub/club, you can drink and dance till you drop, or until 5am, whichever comes first.

FESTIVALS. The best-known of Rennes' music festivals during the summer is **Les Tombées de la Nuit,** a nine-day festival of music, dance, theater, and mime in early July, with international performers who prowl the streets from noon to midnight. For info, contact the **Office de Tourisme,** Festival de Tombées de la Nuit, 11 rue St-Yves (tel. 02 99 67 11 11; fax 02 99 67 11 10; www.ville-rennes.fr).

JOSSELIN

Nestled in the Oust valley, Josselin (pop. 2500), a medieval hamlet dominated by a magnificent castle, will transport you back through the centuries. The stately **château** (tel. 02 97 22 22 50) on the banks of the river is Josselin's pride and joy. The first castle built on the site (in the 11th century) provoked the ire of English King Henry II, who razed the structure as punishment to the Bretons who opposed his attempted takeover of the duchy. In 1370, Olivier de Clisson assumed control of the rebuilt château and expanded it to its present form, adding four towers, a 26m-diameter keep, and a gatehouse. Later additions include a Renaissance longhouse and granite lacework. Since the castle is still a private home, you can only see it by taking a 45-minute tour, which is also available in impeccable English. The château's former stables are now home to the **Musée de Poupées,** 3 rue des Trent (tel. same as château), which houses a doll collection owned by the great-grandma of the present château owner—an impressive collection from all over the world, but only for the true doll aficionado. (Château and museum open daily July-Aug. 10am-6pm, June and Sept. 2-6pm, Apr.-May and Oct. Tu and Sa-Su 2-6pm. Admission to château 32F, children 23F; to museum 29F; to both 59F, children 42F.)

In the town center sits the **Basilique Notre-Dame du Roncier,** whose placement here is a minor miracle. In AD 808, a farmer discovered a statue of the Virgin resting in a pile of brambles. He took it home, only to discover later that the statue had migrated back to the brambles. This event was repeated until the farmer realized that the Virgin wanted a basilica built on the site of the thorny bushes. Revolutionaries burned the wooden statue in 1793, but a toothpick-sized remnant can be seen in a reliquary to the right of the Lady Chapel. The mourning figures around the base of the tomb were beheaded by Revolutionaries, who could not bring themselves to disfigure the tomb itself. Guided tours by local nuns can be arranged though the tourist office. Walkers and bikers can explore the beautiful paths along the **Blavet canal,** which is more popularly known as the "Canal de Nantes à Brest."

Bastille Day (July 14) brings the **Festival Médiévale** to Josselin, complete with costumed dancers, musicians, plays, and food. Animations start the night of the 13th, and include jousting tournaments, a banquet, and fireworks. (Admission to the town during the festival 30F, free for children and those in costume. Call tourist office for more info.)

You'll find basic accommodations at the *gîte d'étape*, **L'Ecluse 35 de Josselin** (tel. 02 97 22 21 69 or 02 97 22 24 17 at the *mairie*). From the bottom of the château along the rue du Canal, go left along the canal until a small cluster of houses appears—ask for the *gîte*. They offer many dorm-style beds under the eaves (and skylights) of a restored farmhouse, and two doubles. (50F, showers 10F, 3-night max. stay.) A 30-minute walk from Josselin, **Camping du Bas de la Lande** (tel. 02 97 22 22 20; fax 02 97 73 93 85) is situated on the Oust with beautiful views, mini-golf, and fishing, plus laundry, ping pong, and a snack bar. No buses run here; follow the road along the canal and take a right at the first roundabout and then a right after the bridge. (20F per person, 13F per car, 18F per tent. Electricity 20F. Reception open July-Aug. 9:30am-noon and 3-9pm; May, June, and Sept. 2:30-8pm.)

CTM buses (tel. 02 97 01 22 10) run here from **Rennes** (1¼hr.; M-Th and Sa 4 per day, F 7 per day, Su 2 per day; 49F). Buses stop at pl. de la Résistance. To get to the **tourist office**, pl. de la Congrégation (tel. 02 97 22 36 43; fax 02 97 22 20 44), take rue Olivier de Clisson to pl. Notre-Dame, turn left on rue des Vierges, and right on rue de Château. (Open daily July-Aug. 10am-6pm, Su 2-6pm; Sept.-Oct. and Apr.-June 10am-noon and 2-6pm; Nov.-Mar. M 2-6pm, Tu-Sa 10am-noon and 2-6pm.) Rent **bikes** at the **Garage Peugeot**. (Open 8am-noon and 1:30-6:30pm, closed Sa and M afternoons.) Tel. 02 97 22 20 26 for **police**. The **hospital** (tel. 02 97 73 13 13) is on rue St-Jacques. The **post office** is at rue Olivier de Clisson, and has **currency exchange**. (Tel. 02 97 22 20 00. Open M-F 9am-noon and 2-5pm, Sa 9am-noon. **Postal code:** 56120.)

FOUGÈRES

Fougères (pop. 25,000), situated prominently in the Nançon Valley right on the edge of Brittany, has long been a center of conflict. Fougères is prouder of its relationship with the pen rather than the sword, though—Hugo, Balzac, and Chateaubriand all spent time here. Their patronage of this medieval town will soon be commemorated in a "literary path" through the Jardin Public, including plaques with biographies on each author.

Fougères' awe-inspiring **château** (tel. 02 99 99 79 69) rests comfortably on a promontory, flanked by rock walls and the Nançon river. Its construction began around AD 1000 and continued for the next 500 years. As Fougères was the most prominent fortress on the Breton-French border, the château was built with an eye to defense, using favorable topography and a state-of-the-art medieval defensive design. Alas, manpower was short, and the château was conquered, destroyed, and rebuilt five times, and each rebuilding led to progressively stronger fortifications. Nowadays, the château is in ruins, the result of the reappropriation of the stone for Fougères' citizens' dwellings. Thirteen towers remain, including the behemoth **Mélusine**, 13m in diameter and 30m high, with 3m-thick walls. (Tower open daily mid-June to mid-Sept. 9am-7pm; late Sept. and Apr. to mid-June 9:30am-noon and 2-6pm; Oct.-Dec. and Feb.-Mar. 10am-noon and 2-5pm. French tours daily 10-11am and 2-5pm.; English tours leave 5min. later. 23F, students 18F; tour 30F, students 23F.) Right outside the castle walls is Fougères' oldest church, the 15th- to 18th-century **Église St-Sulpice**. The Gothic nave, whose simplicity contrasts with the elaborate choir and Baroque altar, features stained-glass windows that illustrate martyrdom in exquisite detail. The Mélusine window is particularly interesting (see **Snake Woman** below). Note St. Sulpice's flabbergasted expression to the right of the altar, as well as the rare image of Mary breast-feeding Christ (in the Chapel Notre-Dame des Marais, on the left of the nave).

Outside the church's doors is the medieval **pl. du Marchix**. Leaning house fronts flank the narrow streets uptown. A stop in the well-kept **Jardin Public** will let you catch your breath and enjoy the panoramic view of the château, church, and surrounding countryside. An even more glorious lookout awaits at the top of the tower of **Église St-Léonard**. (Same hours and tel. as the château. Admission 11F.)

Fougères is 50km from Rennes. No trains run here; the *gare* only serves buses. **TIV buses** (tel. 02 99 99 08 77 in Fougères, 02 99 30 87 80 in Rennes) run from **Rennes** (1hr.; M-F 4 per day, Sa 3 per day, Su 2 per day; 48.50F). **Les Courriers Bretons** (tel.

SNAKE WOMAN One of the stained-glass windows in Fougères' Église St-Sulpice (on the right as you face the altar—look hard) bears the image of a beautiful woman with long blond hair, a mirror in her hand, and the lower body of a snake. Fougères' seigneurs claimed descent from Mélusine, daughter of the King of Albania, who killed her father when she discovered him abusing her mother. As punishment, she was turned into a serpent-woman every Saturday. On these days, she would hide herself in the château's underground passages. One day, however, her husband became suspicious of his wife's frequent absences and peered through the keyhole of her hiding place. There he beheld his bride in her bath, brushing her long hair, while her scaly extremities flailed about. Understandably upset, he burst into the room, only to have Mélusine scream in terror and slither into their castle's subterranean passages, never to be seen again. Legend has it that her screams can be heard in Fougères on the eve of any tragedy and have foretold not only plagues but also the beginning of the World War II bombardments in 1944.

02 99 99 08 77) send 'em here from **St-Malo** (2¼hr., 2 per day, 77F) via **Pontorson** (1hr., 2 per day, 43F). The **bus station** is at pl. de la République. (Open M-Sa 9:30am-noon and 2-7pm.) Walk up bd. Jean-Jaurès as it curves right into pl. Aristide Briand to find the **tourist office** (tel. 02 99 94 12 20; fax 02 99 94 77 30), where the enthusiastic staff peddle glossy brochures. (Open July-Aug. M-Sa 9am-7pm, Su 10am-noon and 2-4pm; Oct.-June M-Sa 9:30am-12:30pm and 2-6pm, Su 10am-noon and 2-4pm.) The **hospital** is at 133 rue Forêt (tel. 02 99 99 31 34). For **police** tel. 02 99 94 25 25. The **post office** is on av. Général de Gaulle, has **currency exchange**. (Open M-F 8:30am-6:30pm, Sa 8:30am-noon. **Postal code:** 35300.)

The best *crêperie* in the *vieille ville*, **La Crêperie de La Duchesse Anne,** sits right in front of the Chateau on pl. Raoul II, 77-79 rue de la Pinterie (tel. 02 99 99 60 79). Busy and usually filled with tourists, the boisterous staff carries on a constant flow of loud conversation with the regulars at the front bar while serving delicious *crêpes* and *galettes* (14-48F). Eat on the terrace outside for a view of the stream of tourists going in and out of the château gates. (Open M-Sa 9:15am-1am, Su 9:30am-3pm and 6-11pm. MC, V.)

ST-MALO

St-Malo (pop. 50,000) is the ultimate seaside getaway—and everybody knows it. To its 6th-century Welsh founder, it was a refuge from marauding Angles and Saxons. To privateers and pirates, the growing city offered a safe haven from their vessels. To the writer Chateaubriand, its ever-changing shore provided Romantic inspiration. Although 80% of the city was destroyed in World War II, St-Malo did not rush to rebuild with tons of concrete; rather, it has engaged in reconstruction so thoughtfully that it's difficult to distinguish the old from the new. Within its towering stone walls, a web of cobblestone streets winds among 15th- to 17th-century-style buildings. Just as impressive as the city's miles of ramparts are its miles of warm, brown, sandy beaches. The proximity of the beautiful, historic *centre ville*, coupled with the gorgeous beaches just outside, make it easy to spend longer in Saint-Malo than you originally intended.

⑦ ORIENTATION AND PRACTICAL INFORMATION

The walled city *(intra muros)* is the northernmost point of St-Malo. The train station is in the town center. As you exit, cross bd. de la République and follow av. Louis-Martin straight to the tourist office (10min.). Take bus #2, 3, or 4 (every 20min., 7F) from the stop on bd. de la République to "St-Vincent." To get to the tourist office from the ferry terminals, turn left onto quai St-Louis as you leave the *gare maritime;* the office will be in a low building directly beside the port.

THE NORTHWEST

Ferries: Gare Maritime de la Bourse. **Brittany Ferries,** (tel. 02 99 40 64 41; fax 02 99 40 64 42), serves **Portsmouth.** See **Getting There: By Boat** (p. 62) for details. **Condor Ferries** (tel. 02 99 200 300; fax 02 99 56 39 27) to **Jersey** and **Guernsey** (round-trip M-Sa 285F, Su 175F). **Emeraude Lines** (tel. 02 99 40 48 40; fax 02 99 40 04 43) runs to the same islands (195-320F round-trip).

Trains: Pl. de l'Hermine (tel. 02 99 40 70 20). To: **Pontorson** via Dol (45min., 5 per day, 42F), **Rennes** (1hr., 8-12 per day, 68F), **Dinan** via Dol (1hr., 8 per day, 46F), **Caen** (3½hr., 8 per day, 141F), and **Paris** (5hr., 3 per day, 294F). Station open M-Sa 5:30am-8pm, Su 7:30am-8:25pm. Info and reservations daily 9:30am-7pm.

Buses: Offices in the pavilion opposite the tourist office. **Tourisme Verney** (tel. 02 99 82 26 26; fax 02 99 81 16 01) to: **Rennes** (2¼hr.; M-F 4 per day, Sa-Su 1-2 per day; 63F), **Cancale** (30min., 5 per day, 63F), and **Mont-St-Michel** via Dinard (1½hr., 1 per day, 80F). Buses leave from esplanade St-Vincent and stop briefly at the train station. Office open July-Aug. M-Sa 8:30am-7pm; Sept.-June M-Th 8:30am-noon and 2-6pm, F 8:45am-noon and 2-6:15pm, Sa 8:30am-noon. **Courriers Bretons** (tel. 02 99 56 79 09; fax 02 99 56 37 04) to: **Mont-St-Michel** (1½hr., 2-4 per day, 110F round-trip) and **Cancale** (30min.; M-Sa 3 per day, Su 1 per day; 25F). Buses also stop at the hostel— see schedule posted in office. Half-day tours to **Cap Fréhel** (5hr., June-Sept. 1 per week, 90F), **Mont-St-Michel** (half- or full day, Apr.-Oct. 2 each per week, 110/145F), and **Île de Bréhat** (full day, 1 per week, 155F). Office open July-Aug. M-F 8:30am-7pm, Sa 8:30am-6pm; Sept.-June M-F 8:30am-12:15pm and 2-6pm, Sa 8:30am-noon.

Public Transportation: St-Malo Bus (tel. 02 99 56 06 06), in the bus office pavilion. Tickets 7F (valid 1hr.), *carnet* of 10 49F; 24hr. pass 20F.

Taxis: Allô Taxis Malouins (tel. 02 99 81 30 30) leave from St-Vincent and the station.

Bike Rental: Diazo, 47 quai du Duguay-Trouin (tel. 02 99 40 31 63). 60F per half-day, 80F per day, 400F per week. 500F or passport deposit. Student discounts. Open M-F 9am-noon and 2-6pm, Su 10am-noon, 2-3pm, and 6-7pm.

Windsurfer Rental: Surf School St-Malo, 2 av. de la Hoguette (tel. 02 99 40 07 47; fax 02 99 56 44 96). Walk along Grande Plage until you see the signs. First rental 150F per hr., 250F per half-day; subsequent rentals 100F per hr., 200F per half-day. Week of 3hr. lessons 850F. Open daily 9am-noon and 2-6pm.

Tourist Office: Esplanade St-Vincent (tel. 02 99 56 64 48; fax 02 99 40 93 13), near the entrance to the old city. Very busy staff offers free map and list of accommodations and restaurants. Open July-Aug. M-Sa 8:30am-8pm, Su 10am-7pm; June 15-30 and Sept. 1-15 M-Sa 9am-7pm, Su 10am-12:30pm and 2:30-6pm; Easter-June 15 and Sept. 15-28 M-Sa 9am-12:30pm and 1:30-7pm, Su 10am-12:30pm and 2:30-6pm; Oct.-Easter M-Sa 9am-12:30pm and 1:30-6pm. **Annex** in train station open June 15-Sept. 15 M-Sa 9:30am-12:30pm and 2-7pm, Su 10am-noon and 2-6pm. *Le Pays Malouin* lists local happenings (every Th, 5F from *tabacs*).

Money: Best **currency exchange** at **Banque de France,** rue d'Asfeld. Exchange desk open M-F 8:40am-12:10pm.

Laundromat: 27 bd. de la Tour d'Auvergne. Open daily 7am-9pm.

Hospital: Centre Hospitalier Broussais, 1 rue de la Marne (tel. 02 99 21 21 21).

Police: 5 av. Louis Martin (tel. 02 99 56 24 84).

Post Office: 1 bd. de la Tour d'Auvergne (tel. 02 99 20 51 70), at the intersection with bd. de la République. Poste Restante code: 35401. **Internet access** requires purchase of 50F card and presence of technical assistant. Open M-F 8am-7pm, Sa 8am-noon. **Branch office,** pl. des Frères Lamennais in the *vieille ville* (tel. 02 99 40 89 90). **Currency exchange. Postal code:** 35400.

Internet Access: Cop'Imprim, 39 bd. des Talards (tel. 02 33 18 08 08; fax 02 23 18 08 09). 10min. from the station (turn left as you exit the station). Extra-cheap at 40F per hour but only one computer; call in advance to reserve.

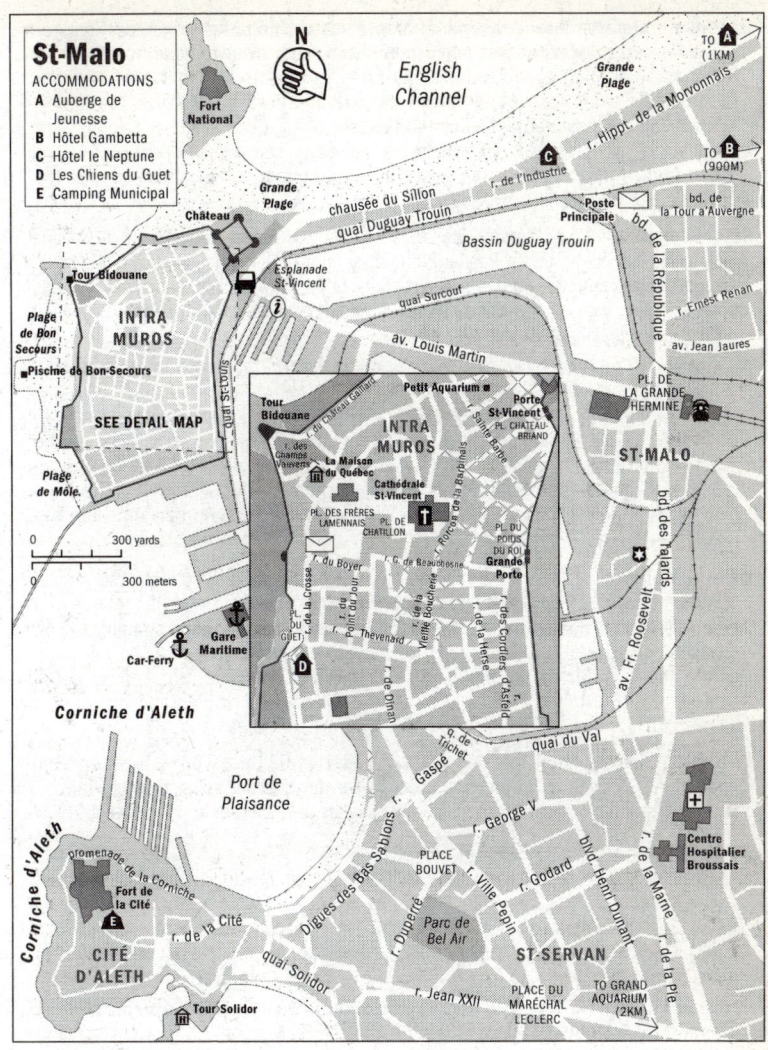

St-Malo
ACCOMMODATIONS
A Auberge de
   Jeunesse
B Hôtel Gambetta
C Hôtel le Neptune
D Les Chiens du Guet
E Camping Municipal

ACCOMMODATIONS AND CAMPING

Reserve up to six months in advance to repose in the *vieille ville* in July and August. The extremely popular hostel doesn't take phone reservations, so be sure to book by fax or letter—and well in advance—if you plan on staying there over the summer. Don't sleep on the beach—the tides swallow them twice daily.

Auberge de Jeunesse/Centre de Rencontres Internationales (HI), 37 av. du Révérend Père Umbricht (tel. 02 99 40 29 80; fax 02 99 40 29 02). From the station, take bus #5 (direction "Paramé" or "Darnier") to "Auberge de Jeunesse" (last bus 7:30pm). By foot, follow bd. de la République to the right from the front of the station. After 2 blocks, turn right onto av. Ernest Renan. Follow it for 3 blocks, then turn left onto rue Guen, which becomes av. de Moka after the roundabout. Turn right on av. Pasteur, which becomes av. du Révérend Père Umbricht, and keep right

(30min.). More an inexpensive hotel than a hostel, the professional staff runs an enormous establishment that might prove somewhat overwhelming to the single traveler. Clean, plain rooms with new furnishings, all with reading lamps, sink, and bathrooms. Tennis, basketball, and volleyball courts, 3 blocks from the beach. Kitchen facilities available. Laundry in the foyer next door. Single-sex dorms 74F; singles 87F; doubles 80F per person. Reception closed noon-2pm. Dorm lockout 10am-5pm. After 10:45pm the guard in the neighboring Foyer des Jeunes Travailleurs can let you in.

Hôtel Gambetta, 40 bd. Gambetta (tel. 02 99 56 54 70). Follow directions to hostel and look for bd. Gambetta off av. Pasteur. Attractive, family-style rooms kept by a laid-back, *sympathique* proprietor. Pretty and calm. Singles 110F, with shower and toilet 150F; doubles 140F, with shower and toilet 220F; quads and quints with shower and toilet 300F. Showers 16F. Breakfast 30F. V, MC.

Les Chiens du Guet, 4 pl. du Guet (tel. 02 99 40 87 29; fax 02 99 56 08 75). Marvelous location *intra muros*, right next to the ramparts and promenade and one minute from the beach. Energetic owner loves to practice her English. Bright rooms with impeccable furnishing and thick rugs. July-Aug. doubles 180F, with shower 240F, with shower and toilet 290F; triples 200F, with shower and toilet 340F; quads with shower and toilet 390F. Prices fall 30-70F per room off-season. Breakfast 28F. Popular restaurant downstairs caters to tourists, with 75-175F *menus* of regional specialties. V, MC.

Hôtel le Neptune, 21 rue de l'Industrie (tel. 02 99 56 82 15). 5min. from beach, station, and *vieille ville*. From the station, turn right onto bd. de la République and bear left when it ends, passing the post office on your right. Keep straight; rue de l'Industrie will be on the left. Beige rooms with pitched ceilings on the top floor, cotton sheets and plush carpeting. Singles and doubles 120F, with shower 150F, with shower and toilet 170F, with bath and toilet 190F; triples and quads with shower 210F; quint 245F. Extra bed 45F. Shower 15F. Breakfast 28F.

Campsite: Camping Municipal de la Cité d'Aleth (tel. 02 99 81 60 91), near promenade de la Corniche at the western tip of St-Servan. Buses #1 and 6 run to "Aleth." Simple, beautiful location. Decent sanitary facilities. 21F per adult, car and tent 28F.

⬤ FOOD

Crêpes and seafood rule the tables of St-Malo, but other options can be found in the *vieille ville*. **Outdoor markets** (8am to 12:30pm) migrate from day to day, stopping behind Église Notre-Dame-des-Grèves (M, Th, and Sa), on pl. Bouvet in St-Servan (Tu and F), at the Marché aux Légumes (Tu and F), and on pl. du Prieuré in Paramé (W and Sa). **Stoc supermarket** is on av. Pasteur, near the hostel. (Open M-F 8:30am-12:30pm and 2:30-7:30pm, Sa 8:30am-7:30pm, Su 9:30am-noon. V, MC.)

Le Recif, 11 rue du Boyer (tel. 02 99 40 97 61). An unassuming, quiet front belies the quality and presentation here, where a 68F *menu* includes outstanding *moules marinières*, a main dish, and a generous serving of ice cream. Modest, discreet service and a great location on a side street filled with small restaurants and bars beside the porte des Bes. Open Mar. 15-Oct. 15 noon-2pm, and 2:30-10pm; closed on W.

Chez Ferhat, 4 rue de la Vieille Boucherie (tel. 02 99 40 54 40). Welcome relief from the *crêpe* onslaught. On one of the liveliest streets in town, the terrace affords great people-watching. At 55F, the vegetarian couscous may be the best non-meat deal in town. Open daily 10:30am-3pm and 6-11pm; Sept.-June open Tu-Su. V, MC.

El Patio, 4 av. du Révérend Père Umbricht (tel. 02 99 40 15 01), 5min. from the hostel. Sit down, take-out, or have the huge pizzas delivered (31-51F). Try to snag a seat beside the little goldfish fountain. Open Tu-Su noon-2pm and 7pm-midnight. V, MC.

🕰 🎵 SIGHTS AND ENTERTAINMENT

SIGHTS. The best view of St-Malo is from its **ramparts**—the old town on one side and a long stretch of sea on the other. Entering the walled city through the Porte St-Vincent leads to stairs on the right leading up to the ramparts. As you reach the northern border of the city, you will see two small islands, **Fort National** and **Le Grand Bé,** accessible only at low tide. Fort National (look for the French flag) was built in 1689 by Vauban to protect St-Malo from the English and today affords a wonderful view of St-Malo. (Open daily Easter-Oct. Tours 20F, students 10F.) Le Grand Bé, west of Fort National, holds the grave of native son **Chateaubriand** (1768-1848) amid the wind and waves. Don't set out if the sea is within 10m of the walkway; you may get stranded in the surf. At the **plage de Bon-Secours,** the **Piscine de Bon-Secours** pool is filled by the sea at high tide and by local youth at all other times. The considerably **Grand Aquarium** (tel. 02 99 21 19 00; fax 02 99 21 19 01) displays an impressive marine bestiary from Atlantic to Amazonian climes. The Ciné Mer Scope, a 2.5m high wrap-around tank, can make you feel like a donut-hole. Take bus #5 from the station or the tourist office; in summer, inquire about the special "A line" that runs there straight from the tourist office (7F). (Open daily July-Aug. 9am-8pm; Sept.-June 9:30am-7pm. 52F, students 44F, 4-17 years 36F.)

The liveliest museum in town is at pl. du Québec, near the Tour Bidouane, where **La Maison du Québec** (tel. 02 99 56 34 32) welcomes *québécois*, notwithstanding others. Leaving St-Malo on a voyage of discovery, adventurer Jacques Cartier thought he had found Asia when he landed on the shores of a forested land in 1534. He named it "Canada," which he thought was the natives' name for their country. It still bears the name, although further investigation revealed that natives were just pointing out their "small collection of huts" nearby. Free expositions and concerts by *québécois* artists liven up the Maison in summer. (Open daily July-Aug. 10am-noon and 2-6pm; Sept.-June 2-6pm.) Cartier lies in one of the chapels of the **Cathédrale St-Vincent.** The cathedral suffered heavy damage in World War II but was restored in a manner that preserves much of its original 11th- to 17th-century architecture while merging it with younger styles. (Open daily June-Aug. 8am-7pm; Sept.-May 8am-noon and 2-7pm.)

ENTERTAINMENT. For a warm atmosphere and relaxed barmen, try **L'Aviso,** 12 rue Point du Jour (tel. 02 99 56 31 14), which boasts 300 different types of beers, 12 whiskeys, and its own juice bar. (Open daily until 2am.) A laid-back crowd, both French and English-speaking, congregates at **O'Flaherty's Irish Bar,** rue des Cordiers, where you can practice ordering Guinness (19-37F) in French. Small and packed, it sports a neighborhood bar ambiance and hosts impromptu concerts. (Open daily 2pm-2am; off-season hours change weekly.) A more traditional pub atmosphere can be found at the very **Jazzy Bar,** 8 rue du Boyer (tel. 02 99 40 86 41), whose beautiful wooden interior and nicely lit bar are witness to background rock music and a somewhat more sophisticated crowd. (Open 9pm-2am.)

DINAN

Tranquil Dinan (pop. 11,600) may be the best-preserved medieval town in Brittany. The spectacular *vieille ville* teeters 66m above the river Rance, its 15th-century streets and buildings housing traditional artisans and almost-as-traditional postcard hawkers. During the Hundred Years' War, Dinan was caught in the medieval tug-of-war between England and France. In 1364 its fate turned on the outcome of a duel—Bertrand du Guesclin won, Sir Thomas of Canterbury yielded, and the English forces honorably withdrew across the Channel. In spite of inevitable tourists, Dinan maintains a quiet dignity, and its early-morning scenery will peacefully take you centuries backwards.

THE NORTHWEST

⚡ ORIENTATION AND PRACTICAL INFORMATION. Trains head from pl. du 11 Novembre 1918 (tel. 02 96 39 22 39) to **St-Brieuc** (1hr., 2-3 per day, 54F), **St-Malo** via Dol (1¼hr., 5 per day, 88F), **Rennes** (1¼hr., 6 per day, 92F), **Morlaix** via St-Brieuc (3hr., 2-3 per day, 108F), and **Paris** (5hr., 6 per day, 512F). (Office open M-Sa 6am-7pm, Su 8:30am-8pm.) **CAT/TV buses** (tel. 02 96 39 21 05), left of the train station, leave pl. Duclos for **St-Malo** (30min., M-Sa 3-5 per day, 35F). From July to August, they run tours to **Mont-St-Michel** (1-2 per week, round-trip 105F). (Office open M-F 8am-noon and 2-6pm, Sa 8am-noon.) **TAE** buses (tel. 02 99 50 64 17 in Rennes) leave the *gare* for **Rennes** (1hr., 2-6 per day, 50F) and **Dinard** (30min., 1-4 per day, 22F). For a **taxi**, call 02 98 39 06 00. **Bike rental** is available at **Cycles Scardin**, 30 rue Carnot. (Tel. 02 96 39 21 94. 50-100F per day, 300-500F per week. 500-1800F or passport deposit. Open Tu-Sa 9am-12:30pm and 2-7pm. V, MC.) Bikes are also available in the port next to the phone cabins. (Tel 06 80 05 37 41. 60F per half-day, 90F per day.) **Club de Canoë**, port de Dinan (tel. 02 96 39 01 50), **rents canoes** and **kayaks** across from rue du Quai. (Kayaks 70F per half-day, 100F per day. Canoes 100F per half-day, 150F per day. Passport deposit. Open July-Aug. 10am-noon and 2-4pm.)

To reach the **tourist office**, 6 rue de l'Horloge (tel. 02 96 39 75 40; fax 02 96 39 01 64), from the station, bear left across pl. du 11 Novembre 1918 onto rue Carnot, then right onto rue Thiers, which brings you to pl. Duclos, a large roundabout. Enter the *vieille ville* through the Porte de Brest on the left (rue du Marchix, which becomes rue de la Ferronnerie). Turn left at pl. du Champ onto rue Ste-Claire; the office is up a block and around the corner to the left on rue de l'Horloge. In a granite-pillared 16th-century mansion, the staff offers a map and excellent guide (5F) and arranges walking tours. (Tours July-Aug. daily at 10am and 3pm; off-season by reservation. 25F, children 15F. Office open June-Sept. M-Sa 9am-7pm, Su 10am-noon and 3-5pm; Oct.-May M-Sa 8:30am-12:30pm and 2-6pm.) A **laundromat** can be found at 16 rue de Brest (tel. 02 96 39 71 35), the **hospital** on rue Chateaubriand (tel. 02 96 85 72 85), in Léhon, and the **police** on pl. du Guesclin (tel. 02 96 39 03 02). The **post office**, pl. Duclos (tel. 02 96 85 83 50), has **currency exchange**. (Open M-F 8:30am-6:30pm, Sa 8am-noon. **Postal code:** 22100.)

⚡ ACCOMMODATIONS AND CAMPING. There are a couple of budget accommodations in Dinan. Although the **Auberge de Jeunesse (HI)**, Moulin du Méen in Vallée de la Fontaine-des-Eaux (tel. 02 96 39 10 83; fax 02 96 39 10 62), is slightly outside town, the walk is lovely and it's by far the prettiest and cheapest option. In summer, the laid-back owner may pick you up at the station if you call and ask nicely. Otherwise, turn left from the main exit, turn left again across the tracks, then turn right and follow the tracks and signs downhill for 1.5km, turning right again at the bottom onto a wooded lane (30min.). Ask the hostel staff to point out the shorter (but more complicated) path back, which runs along the river. With 70 beds in small, clean 2- to 8-bed rooms, the hostel has a wonderful, mellow atmosphere by a gurgling brook and weeping willows. **Internet access** is available for 30F per 30min. (49F. Sheets 16F. Breakfast 18F. Hearty dinner 49F. Lockers 5F. Laundry 20F. Reception daily 9-11am and 3-11pm. Flexible midnight curfew.)

The **Hôtel du Théâtre**, 2 rue Ste-Claire (tel. 02 96 39 06 91), across the street from the tourist office, has small, dimly lit, yet pleasant rooms above a bar in a beautiful building in the *vieille ville*. (Singles 80-120F; doubles 110-120F, with shower 150F; triples with shower and toilet 200F. Breakfast 22F.) If you tumble off the train exhausted, **Hôtel l'Océan**, pl. du 11 Novembre 1918 (tel. 02 96 39 21 51), is across from the station. A pleasant couple lets spacious, bright, clean rooms. (Singles and doubles 125F, with shower 155F, with shower and toilet 185F; triples with shower 185F; quads with shower and toilet 215F. Extra bed 30F. Breakfast 25F. V, MC.) The nicest place to **camp** is at the **hostel** in a pleasant, shaded field behind the main building (26F). The tourist office lists other, more urban sites.

◖▤ **FOOD.** Simple bars and *brasseries* line the streets linking **rue de la Ferronnerie** with **pl. des Merciers. Monoprix supermarket** is on rue de la Ferronnerie. (Open M-F 9am-12:30pm and 2:30-7:30pm, Sa 9am-7pm.) There is also a **Marché Plus,** 28 pl. Duclos (tel. 02 96 87 50 51), near the post office. (Open M-Sa 7am-9pm, Su 9am-1pm.) Buy a picnic of fruit and *crêpes* at the outdoor **market** on pl. du Champ and pl. du Guesclin in the *vieille ville* (Th 8am-noon), and dine al fresco in the Jardin Anglais behind the church. Small restaurants cluster in the small streets just outside the ramparts, between the old town and the quai.

In a dark, wooden dining hall near the tourist office, **Le Cantorbery,** 6 rue Ste-Claire (tel. 02 96 39 02 52), caters to a loyal clientele. The 75F menu includes a filling *gratin aux poissons*, a steaming pot pie stuffed with *fruits de mer*—and that's only the first course. (Open June-Aug. daily noon-2pm and 7-10pm; Sept.-May closed M.) Whether you've finished that matchstick masterpiece, or are just taking a break, the **Crêperie des Artisans,** 6 rue du Petit Fort (tel. 02 96 39 44 10), will satisfy your hunger under warm wooden rafters or on the terrace. A double-whammy two *crêpe* and two *galette menu* costs 70F, and there's a deliciously steaming 39F lunch *formule express*. (*Crêpes* 6-26F, *galettes* 7-26F. Open daily July-Aug. noon-2:30pm and 7-10:30pm; Sept.-June closed M.) More wafer-thin fare is on offer at **Le Connétable,** 1 rue de l'Apport (tel. 02 96 39 06 74), reputedly Dinan's *plus vieille crêperie*. Wonderful *crêpes* (10-25F) and *galettes* (10-38F) leap from the skillets in a dark-timbered 15th-century house. Have your dessert *flambée* in Grand Marnier (23-25F). (Open July-Aug. daily 10am-10:30pm; Sept.-Nov. and Apr.-June Tu-Su 10am-10:30pm. V, MC.)

▣ **SIGHTS.** Simply walking through the town is a sight unto itself, but to get an aerial perspective take the **Promenade des Petits-Fossés,** which follows the ramparts to the 13th-century **Porte du Guichet,** the entrance to the **Château de la Duchesse Anne.** Inside the tower, the decent but not thrilling **Musée de Dinan** (tel. 02 96 39 45 20) displays a selection of local art, including 17th-century furniture, 18th-century statuettes, and 19th-century landscapes. Better than the museum is the château itself; climb the 150 steps to the terrace for a panorama of the town. The **Tour de Coëtquen** holds temporary exhibits and a spooky subterranean room chock-full of tomb sculptures. (Open June-Oct. 15 daily 10am-6:30pm; Oct. 16-Nov. 15 and Mar. 16-May 31 W-M 10am-noon and 2-6pm; Nov. 16-Dec. and Feb. 7-Mar. 15 W-M 1:30-5:30pm. 26F, students 11F, under 18 10F.)

As you enter the *vieille ville* from the port, you'll pass through the **Porte du Jerzual,** formerly the main gate to the city. Recent restorations of the parapet have allowed visitors to climb up and stroll along the ramparts which provide a spectacular view of the surrounding valley and the town. Re-enter the *vieille ville* through port St-Louis, and turn right onto rue du Général de Gaulle to reach the **Promenade de la Duchesse Anne,** at the end of which stands the stately **Jardin Anglais.** In the garden, the 12th-century **Basilique St-Sauveur** boasts a façade carved in pale sandstone, and stained-glass windows that exhort believers to greater thing by illustrating the Saints' deaths. The northern arch of the transept houses a 14th-century tombstone containing the heart of the ever-popular Bertrand du Guesclin.

The **Maison de l'artiste de la Grande Vigne,** 103 rue du Quai (tel. 02 96 87 90 80), is the former home of painter Yvonne Jean-Haffen (1895-1993), and has recently been made into a museum. The house is a work of art—everything from her bathroom to her study was decorated by the artist in her whimsical, delicate style. From the port, you will pass the **Maison du Gouverneur** on rue du Jerzual, a structure dating from the 15th century, which now houses artisan's exhibits in July and August. (Open daily mid-June to mid-Sept. 10am-7:30pm. 10F, students 5F.) The **Église St-Malo,** on Grande Rue, contains a remarkable polychrome organ and a massive Baroque altar. For a schedule of organ concerts, contact the tourist office. The day-glo colors of the 1920s stained-glass windows illuminate the church's interior and illustrate memorable events from Dinan's history. If you're willing to pay for the exercise, the 15th-century, 30m high **Tour de l'Horloge,** rue de l'Horloge, commands a brilliant view of Dinan's jumbled medieval streets and the surrounding countryside. (Open daily June-Sept. 10am-6pm; Apr.-May daily 2-6pm; off season call the tourist office to climb the tower. 15F.)

ST-BRIEUC

There isn't much to see in St-Brieuc (pop. 50,000), but its location between the Côte d'Émeraude and the Côte de Granite Rose makes it a perfect launch pad for daytrips to the countryside. The bus to stunning Cap Fréhel leaves from here, so you'll probably spend time in town before hopping on the bus. Though at first glance not particularly appealing, St-Brieuc does host a number of concerts and festivals in the summer, and is home to a reasonably attractive *vieille ville*.

◤ ORIENTATION AND PRACTICAL INFORMATION. Trains stop in at bd. Charner (tel. 02 96 01 61 64) on the way to **Rennes** (1hr., 15 per day, 83F), **Morlaix** (1hr., 8-11 per day, 72F), and **Dinan** (1hr., 2-3 per day, 54F). (Info and reservations M-Sa 8am-7pm, Su 9:30am-7pm. Ticket office open M-Th 5:30am-9pm, F 5:30am-10pm, Sa 5:30am-8:30pm, Su 5:30am-1pm.) **Buses** pull into both the train station and the **bus station** at rue du Combat des Trente (tel. 02 96 68 31 20). **CAT** buses serve **Paimpol** (1½hr., 7 per day, 42F) and **Cap Fréhel** (1½hr., July-Sept. 4 per day, 42F). For **bike rental,** call the hostel (see **Accommodations,** below).

To get to the *centre ville* from the station, walk straight ahead onto rue de la Gare. Stay right when the road forks at pl. de la Résistance, where the **post office** is located. The **tourist office,** 7 rue St-Guéno (tel. 02 96 33 32 50; fax 02 96 61 42 16), is directly to the right across the *place* as you stand in the parking lot facing the post office. Pick up a free *Le Griffon* to find out about regional events. (Open July-Aug. M-Sa 9am-7pm, Su 10am-1pm; Sept.-June M-Sa 9am-noon and 2-6:30pm.) **Banks** with **currency exchange** line pl. Champ de Mars, off rue du 71ème Régiment d'Infanterie. A **laundromat** can be found behind the cathedral in pl. du Martray. The **police** are at 17 rue Joullan (tel. 02 96 33 36 66). Don't lose time searching for the **hospital** (tel. 02 96 01 71 23); it's on rue Marcel Proust. The **post office** is on pl. de la Résistance. (Tel. 02 96 61 10 60. Open M-F 8am-7pm, Sa 8am-noon. **Postal code:** 22000.) **Internet access** is online at **MediaCap,** next to the post office on rue Jouallen (20F per hour).

◤◢ ACCOMMODATIONS AND FOOD. Several cheap hotels crowd around the train station on bd. Charner and rue de la Gare. The **youth hostel,** located outside town in a 15th-century house, may be the best bet for an inexpensive night (tel. 02 96 78 70 70). Take bus #3 (direction "le Village"), and ask the driver for the Auberge de Jeunesse. Tennis, bike rental, sea kayaking, and horseback riding are all available. Call ahead as they are often full. (Bikes 65F per day. 500F or passport deposit. V, MC.) The **Hôtel de la Paix,** 30 bd. Charner (tel. 02 96 94 04 80), across from the station, offers dim but spacious rooms above a betting shop, with frequent serenades from arriving trains. Not always impeccably clean, and the bar-cum-bookie downstairs can occasionally be seedy. (Singles and doubles 100F, with shower 130F, with shower and toilet 150F. Breakfast 25F. V, MC.)

Bars and outdoor cafés cluster in the *vieille ville* right behind the tourist office. Rue des Trois Frères is the place for Moroccan, Italian, Chinese, and Indian food. **Tandoori,** 11 rue Trois Frères le Goff (tel. 02 96 61 84 02), serves tandoori chicken (59F) and vegetarian dishes (around 40F). (Open Tu-F noon-1:30pm and 7-10:30pm, Sa-Su 7-10:30pm. V, MC.) **La Bocca,** 22 rue de la Gare (tel. 02 96 33 67 71), offers big, hot pizzas (39-59F) and big, cold beers (12-20F). For 75F you can make a night of it with the *formule charlie*—a pizza, a drink, and a ticket for the cinema up the road. **Monoprix supermarket** is on pl. de la Résistance. (Open M-Sa 8:30am-7:15pm.) The public **market** sets up around the cathedral (W and Sa mornings). For a traditional snack, try a *galette saucisse*—a better *breton* hotdog (10F).

🕐🎵🌾 SIGHTS, ENTERTAINMENT, AND FESTIVALS. St-Brieuc doesn't offer that much in the way of sights, but it's worth visiting the **Cathédrale St-Étienne,** pl. de Gaulle. Construction began at the end of the 12th century and was more or less complete by the 14th, but additions continued for the next 500 years. While many cathedrals in France mix Romanesque and Gothic, St-Brieuc's combines the unassuming with the elaborate better than most. The austerity of the nave's monolithic columns sets off the flamboyance of the Baroque Chapel of the Holy Sacrament in the south transept. (Free guided visit in French M-F 10:30am and 3pm.)

The **Café del Mar,** 37 rue des Trois Frères (tel. 02 96 62 29 17), offers a reggae atmosphere on a tropical terrace complete with sand. Locals pack the beautiful *bar à vins* **Chez Rollais,** 25 rue du Général Leclerc (tel. 02 96 61 23 03). The bar has been in the same family for generations and is often filled to the door, so arrive early for elbow room. St-Brieuc's modern and innovative festivals include **ArtRock:** held over the last weekend in May, it's a combined music and street art festival encompassing the traditional and contemporary, with some free concerts. Every Thursday and Friday during July and August, **L'Été en Fête** brings at least three street concerts or presentations, including traditional and modern dance, to pl. du Martray near the tourist office.

CAP FRÉHEL

When landscape artists go to sleep at night, they dream of Cap Fréhel. Few words can describe the majesty of this northernmost point of the Côte d'Émeraude. The lush vitality of the vegetation, dark green dotted by wildflowers with points of red, yellow, and regal purple, would be artwork enough. But paint these wonders on a canvas of rust-hued cliffs that plummet a dizzying 70m to inlets beaten by a raging sea, and you begin to understand why this windswept peninsula is such a popular location for hiking, self-discovery, and postcard photography. The Cap does not offer much solitude in the summer, as hundreds flock here to follow the well-marked **GR34** trail. Red-and-white-striped markers painted on the rocks guide ramblers along the trail on the edge of the peninsula. Wander off the trail, and you're bound to find a less crowded (if not exactly private) nook for rainy-day *randonnées* or sun-soaked naps. An easy walk southwest leads to a breathtaking and secluded little beach. Feast your eyes on the scenic buffet that awaits on the 90-minute walk to **Fort La Latte** (tel. 02 96 41 40 31), a 13th-century castle complete with drawbridges and a hair-raising view of the Cap and St-Cast. (Open June-Sept. daily 10am-12:30pm and 2:30-6:30pm; Oct.-May M-F 2:30-5:30pm. 17F.) To get to the Cap, you'll need to catch a **CAT bus** from **St-Brieuc** (July-Aug. 3 per day, 42F).

If you want to nap on the Cap, *hébergement* is available at the **Auberge de Jeunesse Cap Fréhel (HI),** la Ville Hadrieux, Kerivet, near Plévenon (tel. 02 96 41 48 98; Sept. 16-Apr. 02 98 78 70 70). From the cap, walk toward Plévenon on D16, then follow the inconspicuous signs bearing the fir-tree hostel symbol (30-40min.). Someone from the hostel may come and pick you up from the bus stop if you call and ask nicely, though you will be asked to contribute for gas. Many of those vacationing here scorn the luxury of a solid roof and barracks-style beds and opt for the two tents beyond the bonfire pit outside. It's very popular with groups, so be sure to call ahead. The hostel also **rents bikes** (45F per half-day) and has maps of the GR34. If you ask at St-Brieuc's hostel, they will allow you to leave a rented bike at Cap Fréhel and vice-versa. (45F inside and out. Sheets 17F. Camping 25F. Breakfast 19F. Dinner 50F. Lockout noon-5:30pm. Open May-Sept.)

CAUGHT RED-HANDED While geologists may claim to know what gives the cliffs of Cap Fréhel their vibrant red color, locals know the real reason. In the 5th century, Irish monks evangelizing along the Côte d'Emeraude ran into opposition from powerful druids. One of the monks, after assembling a group of Fréhel's residents, decided to demonstrate the power of his faith by cutting off one of his own fingers. As soon as the first drop of blood hit the earth, the entire coast turned red. To this day, the cliffs retain the color as a vestige and reminder of the monk's sacrifice.

PAIMPOL

The *pampolais* coat of arms, a silver boat against an azure background, portrays this small town's close tie to the sea. Anchored on the border of the Côte de Granite Rose and the Côte de Goëlo, Paimpol (pop. 8,000) once fueled its economy with fishing expeditions to Newfoundland and Iceland. Fishing is still important, but the port is also packed with postcard vendors and yachts. Although Paimpol itself has little to offer non-sailors, the surrounding islands, cliffs, beaches, and numerous hiking trails are ideal places to relax while exploring the region's charms.

◪ ORIENTATION AND PRACTICAL INFORMATION. Trains leave av. Général de Gaulle (tel. 02 96 20 81 22) for **St-Brieuc** via Guingamp (1hr., 4-5 per day, 60F) and **Pontrieux** (15min., 5 per day, 16F). (Office open M-Sa 6:40-7:10am and 8am-7pm, Su and holidays 9am-7pm.) **CAT buses** (tel. 02 96 22 67 72) scurry from the *gare* to **Pointe de l'Arcouest** (15min., 5 per day, 10F) and **St-Brieuc** (1¼hr., 3-7 per day, 42F). **Bike rental** on offer at **Cycles du Vieux Clocher,** pl. de Verdun. (Tel. 02 96 20 83 58. 70-85F per day. Open M-Sa 8:30am-12:30pm and 2-7:15pm, Su 8am-noon. V, MC.)

To reach the port and *centre ville*, turn right from the station, then left at the rotary. A map is posted to your right as you leave the station. To get to the **tourist office**, pl. de la République (tel. 02 96 20 83 16; fax 02 96 55 11 12), as you exit the train station, go straight onto rue du 18 Juin, turn right onto rue de l'Oise, and continue onto the *place;* the office is on the right (5min.). The cheerful staff offers comprehensive info on the area, including its hiking trails. *La Presse d'Armor* has a schedule of events; available at the tourist office (5F). (Open July-Aug. M-Sa 9am-7:30pm, Su 10am-1pm; Sept.-June Tu-Su 10am-12:30pm and 2:30-6pm.) There's **currency exchange** at similar rates at both **Banque de Bretagne,** pl. du Martray (open Tu-F 8:20am-12:15pm and 1:30-5:15pm, Sa 8:20am-12:15pm and 1:30-5pm), and **Crédit Maritime,** 37 quai Morand (open Tu-F 8:30am-12:15pm and 1:30-5:30pm, Sa 8:30am-12:15pm and 1:30-4:30pm). The **Centre Hospitalier** is on chemin de Malabry (tel. 02 96 55 60 00), while the **police** are on rue R. Pellier (tel. 02 96 20 80 17). The **post office,** av. du Général de Gaulle (tel. 02 96 20 82 40), has **currency exchange.** (Open M-F 8am-noon and 1:30-5:30pm, Sa 8am-noon. **Postal code:** 22500.)

⚐ ACCOMMODATIONS AND CAMPING. The **Auberge de Jeunesse (HI)** and **Gîte d'Étape,** at Château de Kéraoul (tel. 02 96 20 83 60), provides 2 to 6 beds in narrow, plain rooms in an old manor house on top of a hill. Turn left onto av. Général de Gaulle, right at the first light, left at the next light, and follow rue Bécot, staying to the right when the road forks and becomes rue de Pen Ar Run. Turn left when the street ends; the hostel is second on the right (20min.). There's no curfew, but don't arrive too late your first night—no new guests are admitted after 9pm. (47F. Sheets 17F. Camping 25F. Huge *crêpe* breakfast 18F. Lunch or dinner 47F. No lockout.) In a great location right next to the port, the calm, friendly owner of **Hôtel Berthelot,** 1 rue du Port (tel. 02 96 20 88 66), offers clean, somewhat dim, but very pleasant rooms on a quiet side street. (Singles and doubles 160F, with toilet 170F, with shower and toilet 230F, with TV 240F.) You can **camp** at the Auberge (see above) or **Camping Municipal de Cruckin,** near the plage de Cruckin (tel. 02 96 20 78 47). From the tourist office, turn left onto rue de la Marne, left onto av. du Général de Gaulle, then veer right and follow the schizophrenic rue du Général Leclerc as it twists through four name changes. Rue de Cruckin branches off to your left from rue du Commandant le Conniat. (Tent and 3 people 69F. Extra person 15F. Electricity 14-17F. Reception M-Sa 8:15am-10pm, Su 8-10am and 6-8:30pm. Gates close summer 10pm-6am; off-season 10pm-7am. Open Apr.-Sept.)

⚑ FOOD. You can't beat **Le Terre-Neuvas,** quai Duguay-Trouin (tel. 02 96 55 14 14), facing the port, for elegant food at backpacker prices. The 65F *menu* includes ever-cool *moules* and the catch of the day. Paimpol's favorite *crêperie* is Morel, 11 pl. du Martray (tel. 02 96 20 86 34). A truly stellar selection of *crêpes* is accompanied by a wide assortment of local cider and liqueurs. Make reservations as they're often packed to the brim—and keep those legs and arms close by lest you lose a limb to the high-speed waitresses. Picnickers can find supplies either at Paimpol's Tuesday morning **market,** held throughout the town, or at the **Intermarché supermarket** on av. du Général de Gaulle to the left of the *gare.* (Open M-F 8:30am-12:15pm and 2:30-7:15pm, Sa 8:30am-7:15pm.)

🕿 **SIGHTS.** Hidden from the road by vegetation, the ruins of the **Abbaye de Beauport,** chemin de l'Abbaye (tel. 02 96 20 97 69), look dreamily out to sea from their spot east of Paimpol. Dating from 1202, the abbey was once an important stop on the pilgrimage route to Santiago. Now the roofless church and flowered refectory flow seamlessly into the gardens, creating one of the most memorable sights in Brittany. To get to the abbey you can take the scantily-marked **GR34** along the coast from the port (2hr.). (Open June 15-Sept. 15 daily 10am-7pm; Sept. 16-June 14 W-M 10am-noon and 2-5pm. English tours available. 25F, students 20F.)

Tucked away on a side street near the port, the **Musée de la Mer,** rue Labenne (tel. 02 96 22 02 19), displays models of sea crafts, from fishing boats to battle ships, and many other things nautical. While there, listen for your favorite French sea chanty. (Open Easter-Sept. daily 10:30am-1pm and 3-7pm. 21F, students 12F.) Those who need a quick but effective shot of Breton culture should get a lime wedge and some salt and mosey over to the miniscule **Musée du Costume,** rue R. Pelletier. (Open July-Sept. 15 daily 11am-12:30pm and 2-6pm. 21F, students 7F.)

🎵 **ENTERTAINMENT.** Nightlife in Paimpol packs it in at the port. While a number of bars line the water, those in the know take to the side streets. **La Ruelle,** 26 rue des 8 Patriotes (tel. 02 96 20 56 96), is open until 3am. Brightly-colored interior and loud rock and techno, coupled with comfortable chairs and tables, make this the hip place to see and be seen. After work, young *pampolais* looking for comic-book capers pack the lively **Le Corto Maltese** on rue du Quai. Every summer, Paimpol dedicates a Sunday to the **Fête des Islandais,** a religious festival during which the port is blessed by a local priest. Mass frolicking ensues.

POINTE DE L'ARCOUEST AND ÎLE DE BRÉHAT

At the end of D789, 6km north of Paimpol, the peninsula ends with a dramatic flourish in the tumbling pink granite of the **Pointe de l'Arcouest.** Those in the know say that the blue-green waters flowing around this point provide some of France's best sea-kayaking. To reach the Pointe, take a **CAT bus** from Paimpol (12min.; 8 per day, 7 on Sundays; 10F).

Les Vedettes de Bréhat (tel. 02 96 55 79 50) send boats from the Pointe to the idyllic **Île de Bréhat** (10min.; 10-15 per day in season; round-trip 40F, passenger and bike 90F, sailboards 45F). They also offer tours for 70F. At 3km in length, the island (pop. 450) is small enough that it's impossible to get lost. Strut off the boat past all the tourist kitsch and find an "undiscovered" beach. Be sure to bring a mat, since most of Bréhat's beaches are rocky. The view from the **Chapelle St-Michel** on the west side of the island is unparalleled—except by that from the **Phare du Paon,** a lighthouse at the island's northern tip. For more info, call the island's **tourist office.** (Tel. 02 96 20 04 15. Open M-Sa 9:30am-12:30pm and 1:30-5:30pm.)

TRÉGUIER

East of Paimpol on the Jandy river, medieval **Tréguier** seduces visitors with its historic homes and magnificent **cathedral.** The latter's construction is a mix of Romanesque and early Flamboyant Gothic. The last remaining Romanesque structure in **Hasting's Tower** was built of green stone from Caen and is decorated with a Celtic motif. The *trésor* room displays the bones and skull of St-Yves (1253-1303), hailed as the founder of legal assistance. A lawyer and judge, he served the poor without remunerations. The Grand Pardon of St-Yves, on the third Sunday of May, still attracts lawyers from around the world. (Open daily 2-6pm. 14F.)

If you'd like to explore the area further, try **Le Syet** (tel. 02 96 92 31 79), a combination *gîte d'étape*-cum-campground-cum-riding-center about 20 minutes from the *centre ville*. Coming out of the tourist office, turn right and right again onto rue Colvestre; follow it straight out of town until you see signs for Le Styvel. (*Gîte* 40F. Camping 20F per tent, 15F per adult; electricity 12F. Breakfast 20F, lunch 30F, dinner 70F.) All the streets in Tréguier's *vieille ville* offer plenty of choices for restauration. **Crêperie du Cloître** (tel. 02 96 92 33 18), to the right of the cathedral, has omelettes and salads as well as traditional *galettes* and *crêpes*.

Tréguier works best as a day excursion from Paimpol. **CAT buses** (tel. 02 96 22 67 72) connect Tréguier to **Paimpol** and **Lannion** (30min., 3 per day, 24F). Buses drop you off in pl. de Gaulle on the port. Rue St-André leads from the bus stop to the **cathedral.** To reach the **tourist office,** pl. Général Leclerc (tel. 02 96 92 30 19), turn right in front of the cathedral and then right again. Accommodations info, maps, and suggested walking tours are all free. (Open M-Sa 10am-noon and 2-4pm.)

MORLAIX

Clinging to the hillside, modern Morlaix (pop. 16,700) offers few sights but is a convenient and attractive medieval base for excursions to nearby towns. The city was founded in Gallo-Roman times, when Armorican Celts built a fort here called "Mons Relaxus" (Mount of Rest). Situated at the intersection of the rivers Jarlot and Queffleuth, the town was plagued during the Middle Ages by continuous invasions by the Duchy of Brittany, the French Crown, and the British, all of whom wanted control of Morlaix's enviably located port. In 1522, British invaders ransacked the town but made the mistake of celebrating their victory to drunken excess. When Morlaix's avenging citizens returned to reverse the earlier battle's outcome, the British were caught unawares. From this confrontation came Morlaix's motto: *"S'ils te mordent, mords-les!"* ("If they bite you, bite them back!")

⚇ ORIENTATION AND PRACTICAL INFORMATION. The station, rue Armand Rousseau (tel. 02 98 80 50 50), sends **trains** to **St-Brieuc** (45min., 6-10 per day, 74F), **Brest** (45min., 8-10 per day, 53F), **Quimper** (2hr., change at Landerneau, 5-7 per day, 96F), and **Roscoff** (30min., 4-5 per day, 30F). (Info office open daily 9:10am-7:30pm.) Buses also leave from the train station. **CAT buses** (tel. 02 98 62 16 72) go to: **Roscoff** (35min., 3-5 per week), **Quimper** (2hr., 3-5 per week), and **Vannes** (2½hr., 3 per week during school holidays). **SCETA** (tel. 02 98 93 06 98) also serves nearby towns. Ask at the tourist office, the hostel, or **Tourisme Verney,** 25 pl. Cornic, for schedules and prices. (Open M and Th 8:30am-noon.) **Public Transportation** is run by **TIM** (tel. 02 98 88 82 82), who have a kiosk on pl. Cornic. (Tickets 6F, 10 for 50F. Buses run until 7pm.) **Radio Taxis** (tel. 02 98 88 36 42) await at pl. des Otages and the station. To get from the station to the **tourist office,** pl. des Otages (tel. 02 98 62 14 94; fax 02 98 63 84 87), walk onto rue Gambetta, then turn left onto **rue Courte** and follow it to the *centre ville*. Turn left past the Hôtel de Ville through pl. des Otages to find the office's rustic hut in front of the viaduct. Here the friendly staff offer accommodation services as well as **tours.** (July-Aug. Th 2:30pm. 20F.) Ask about Tuesday night tours led by a theatrical troupe. (Open July-Aug. M-Sa 9am-7pm, Su 10am-noon; Sept.-June Tu-Sa 9am-noon and 2-6pm.) You can **exchange currency** at Banque de France, pl. Cornic, or Crédit Maritime, on the corner of rue du Mur and rue Carnot. Two **laundromats** tumble-dry at rue de Lavoirs and pl. Charles de Gaulle. (Both open daily 8am-8pm.) The **police** are ever vigilant from 17 pl. Charles de Gaulle (tel. 02 98 88 17 17), and doctors stand by at the **Hôpital Général,** rue Kersaint Gilly (tel. 02 98 62 61 60). The **post office,** 15 rue de Brest (tel. 02 98 88 23 03), offers **currency exchange.** (Open M-F 8:30am-6:30pm, Sa 8:30am-noon. **Postal code:** 29600.) An **Internet station** rests smack in the middle of the bar at **Le Macao** (tel. 02 98 88 47 26), near L'Église St-Mathieu. (Open M-F 7pm-1am, Sa-Su noon-1am. 40F per 30min., 70F per hr.)

⌐ ACCOMMODATIONS AND CAMPING. Morlaix has some cheap hotels, but be sure to call ahead in July and August. Ask the tourist office about local *gîtes d'étapes* (around 50F) or *chambres d'hôtes* (100-200F). Somewhat dim and out of the way, the **Auberge de Jeunesse (HI),** 3 rte. de Paris (tel. 02 98 88 13 63; fax 02 98 88 81 82), has 52 beds in 2- to 9-person rooms. From the station, follow rue Gambetta, and turn left down the endless steps of rue (not so) Courte. Cross pl. Émile Souvestre and bear ahead and right on rue Carnot. Take a right onto rue d'Aiguillon as it becomes rue de Paris, and then a left at the roundabout onto rte. de Paris. The hostel is 250m up the hill around the curve to the right (25min.). (49F. Sheets 17F. Breakfast 19F. Dinner 49F. Reception daily 8-11am and 6-9pm. Lockout 10am-6pm. Curfew midnight; off-season 11pm.) **Hôtel du Port** (tel. 02 98 88 07 54; fax 02 98 88 43 80) offers cheery if uninspired rooms and large, immaculate bathrooms. Follow directions to the hostel to the end of rue Courte. Turn left and pass under the viaduct through pl. Cornic, pl. de Gaulle onto quai de Léon. The hotel is on the left (20 min.). (Singles with bathroom and TV 180-200F; doubles 200F, with bathroom and TV 220F.) **Hôtel les Halles,** 23 rue du Mur (tel. 02 98 88 03 86; fax 02 98 63 47 96), features dim rooms in a prime location, though mattresses may sag. From the train station head straight down rue Gambetta all the way to the bottom (a trek). Then bear right onto rue Carnot and take the first right onto rue de Mur. The hotel is on the right in pl. Allende. (Singles 120F, with shower 150F; doubles 130F, with shower 165F. Breakfast 25F. V, MC.) You'll have to walk the 7km to **Camping Croas-Men** (tel. 02 98 79 11 50). From the *centre ville*, follow signs first to Plouigneau and then to Garlan. Look for the sign that says "camping *à la ferme*." (22F per person, electricity 14F, shower 15F. Open all year; gates open 24hr.)

◖ FOOD. The **quartier St-Mathieu** and **rue Ange de Guernisac** offer plenty of eateries. Rue au Fil is full to bursting with *crêperies* and inexpensive restaurants. The **market**, on and around pl. Allende, is open all day Saturday. **Marché Plus supermarket** is on rue de Paris. (Open M-Sa 7am-9pm, Su 9am-noon.) **La Jonquiere,** 26 rue Ange de Guernisac (tel. 02 98 88 69 59), a modest little *crêperie* near the *centre ville*, offers 55F and 66F *menus*, plus *galettes* and *crêpes* (11-45F) and a number of original salads. (Open July-Aug. daily 11:45am-midnight; off season Tu-Su 11:45am-2:30pm and 6:30pm-whenever.) **L'Olivier,** at the intersection of rue du Mur and the tiny venelle au Beurre, offsets its plain decor with great Italian fare. The 55F lunch and dinner *menu* includes an appetizer, main dish, dessert, wine, and coffee. (Open daily noon-2pm and 7-9pm. V, MC.)

◉ SIGHTS. Your train probably arrived over the impressive **viaduct,** 58m high and 285m long, which lords an imposing presence over the town; it is unfortunately no longer accessible to pedestrians for safety reasons. Console yourself with the self-guided **Circuit des Venelles** walking tour, which rambles all over the town. Even those sick of Breton museums may relish the **Musée des Jacobins,** in the 13th-century Église des Jacobins (tel. 02 98 88 68 88), pl. des Jacobins. The museum combines traditional displays of Breton life with 19th- and 20th-century paintings of the region. (Open July-Aug. daily 10am-12:30pm and 2-6:30pm; Easter-June and Sept.-Oct. W-M 10am-noon and 2-6pm, closed Sa mornings; Nov.-Easter W-M 10am-noon and 2-5pm, closed Su mornings. 25F, students 12F.) You might make a brief visit to **La Maison de la Reine Anne,** across pl. Allende on rue du Mur (tel. 02 98 88 23 26), which commemorates the queen's 1505 visit to the city. One of many "lantern houses" in Brittany, the vast space allowed a single lantern suspended from the ceiling to light the entire building. (Open M-Sa 10am-noon and 2-6pm. 10F, ages 10-18 5F, under 10 free.) Nearby, the **quartier St-Mathieu** is a lively district of restaurants and old residences.

🎵 **ENTERTAINMENT. La Brasserie des Deux Rivières,** 1 pl. de la Madeleine (tel. 02 98 63 41 92), gives free tours with a complimentary tasting of its all-natural, all-tasty Coreff beer, made only in Morlaix—the walk up from the port should leave you thirsty. (Tours July-Aug. M-F at 9:30 and 10:30am, and 1:30, 3, and 4:30pm. Off season open M-W, call for hours.) Close to everything of interest in Morlaix, the cozy **Ty Coz** pub shelters on venelle au Beurre. This local favorite, whose walls are covered with bumper stickers, ladles out liquid regional specialities, including Coreff for 12F. (Open daily noon-midnight.) In July and August, there's dancin' in the streets as Morlaix's **Les Arts dans la Rue** takes on Wednesday nights with clowns, dancers, and novelty acts.

FORÊT D'HUELGOAT

Although **Argoat** (ar-gwah) still means "wooded country" to Breton ears, centuries of clearing have made the Argoat one of the least forested regions in France. Only a few scattered plots remain of the great oak and beech forest where menhir-carvers once lived. Paimpont, Merlin's legendary stronghold, is one; Huelgoat (wel-gwaht), meaning "high forest" in Breton, is another. As part of the **Parc Régional d'Armorique,** which stretches from the coast 70km eastward, the rocky, ravine-like Huelgoat forest enjoys significant governmental protection. On the eastern edge of a sparkling lake, the tiny village of the same name serves as a pit stop for forays into the forest hiking trails—it's too hilly for comfortable biking. The **Fédération Française de la Randonnée Pédestre** has excellent maps (available at area tourist offices) that include hiking tours. There are scrupulously marked trails from one *gîte d'étape* to the next (about 50F per night). The network of footpaths begins at the end of rue du Lac, where the lake empties into the Argent river.

The forest's "marvels" include the **Mare au Sangliers** (Pond of Boars) and the **Roche Tremblante,** a 100-ton rock-monster balanced precariously on the hillside. You won't believe your eyes when one of the young guides provided by the town sets the whole thing a-trembling by pushing it in *just* the right place. Most impressive, however, is the **Grotte du Diable** (Devil's Grotto), a pile of rocks forming a cave under which the Argent rages. The **Miellerie de Huelgoat,** 5 rue de La Roche Tremblante (tel. 02 98 99 94 36), also offers a free guided tour of the honey world. Watch the bees in action, then taste the fruit of their labors—honey in such delectable flavors as blackberry and oak. (Open daily 9am-7pm. Jars from 30F. V, MC.)

Huelgoat is best visited as a daytrip, but if you decide to stay, the **tourist office** (tel. 02 98 99 72 32), behind the church on pl. de la Mairie, has a list of **chambres d'hôte** (150-250F) within 15km of town. They also have information on the **grottoes** and a confusing 5F map. (Open Tu-Sa 10am-noon and 2-4pm.) When the office is closed, the *mairie* (tel. 02 98 99 71 55) next door can provide the same info. (Open Sept.-June M-Th 8:30am-12:15pm and 1:15-5:30pm, F 8:30am-12:15pm and 1:15-4:30pm, Sa 8:30am-noon; July-Aug. closed Sa.) **Camping Municipal du Lac,** rue du Général de Gaulle (tel. 02 98 99 78 80), five minutes from the bus stop, fills a sunny lakeside location across from a slaughterhouse. (17F per person, 19F per tent. Reception M-Sa 9am-8pm, Su 8am-noon and 4-8pm. Open June 15-Sept. 15.) Huelgoat's **market** takes place on pl. Aristide Briand and along rue du Lac (1st and 3rd Th of the month, 8am-1pm); the Thursdays in between see a fish-only market. Near the *boulangeries* on pl. Aristide Briand, you'll find a small **Shopi supermarket.** (Open M-Sa 8am-12:30pm and 2:30-7:15pm, Su 9am-12:30pm.) The small cozy **Crêperie de l'Argoat,** 12 rue du Lac (tel. 02 98 99 71 72), facing the lake, provides an extensive list of *crêpes* for 10-33F, including the *Ty Pierre* with tomato, mushrooms, egg, and butter. (Open daily and day-long July-Aug.; other times closed M.)

SCETA and **CAT buses** (tel. 02 98 93 06 98) go to **Morlaix** (3 per day, 1hr., 35F) and **Quimper** (70min., 3-5 per week), stopping by the church on pl. Aristide Briand. The **post office** is on rue des Creux. (Tel. 02 98 99 73 90. Open M-F 9am-noon and 2-5pm, Sa 9am-noon. **Postal code:** 29690.)

ROSCOFF

Although ferries stream into Roscoff's port, the town has avoided "harbor blight" by moving to the other extreme—Roscoff aims to be positively *chic*. Its beautiful location and famous *thalassotherapy* center attract thousands of health-seekers who swarm to the town in summer. The port area and beaches are attractive, and there are a few sights of minor interest to the fish-lover, but Roscoff's real value is as an embarkation point to the nearby Île de Batz.

⚐ ORIENTATION AND PRACTICAL INFORMATION. Roscoff's port is where the action is. Turn right out of the station and make an immediate right onto rue Ropartz. Follow the signs to the *centre ville* and the distinct scent of the salty air. **Brittany Ferries** (tel. 08 03 88 28) sends boats across the channel to Plymouth west to Cork, while **Irish ferries** (tel. 02 98 61 17 17) serves Cork and Rosslare. (See **Getting There,** p. 62, for details of service.) **SNCF trains** and **buses** go from the station to **Morlaix** (30-45min., 7-11 per day, 29F). **CAT buses** (tel. 02 98 90 68 40) go to: **Morlaix** (1hr., 2-3 per day M-Sa, 1 on Su, 41F), **Brest** (2hr., 4 per day, 1 on Su, 45F), **Quimper** (2¼hr., 3-5 per week, 118F), and **Vannes** (4hr., 3 per week during school vacations, 236F). The **tourist office,** 46 rue Gambetta (tel. 02 98 61 12 13; fax 02 98 69 75 75), in the port, has transportation schedules, a map, and a shiny visitor's guide. (Open July-Aug. M-Sa 9am-12:30pm and 1:30-7pm, Su 10am-12:30pm; Sept.-June M-Sa 9am-noon and 2-6pm.) Numerous banks in the port **exchange currency.** The **post office** is on 17 rue Gambetta. (Tel. 02 98 69 72 19. Open July-Aug. M-F 9am-noon and 2-5:15pm, Sa 9am-12:15pm; Sept.-June M-F 9am-12:30pm and 2:30-5:30pm, Su 9am-12:15pm. **Postal code:** 29680.)

⚏⚏ ACCOMMODATIONS, CAMPING, AND FOOD. Budget hotels are in short supply in Roscoff, so you might do best to head straight to the youth hostel on the Île de Batz (see below), which is only 15 minutes away by ferry. If you decide to spend the night on the mainland, the spacious and attractive **Hôtel d'Angleterre,** 28 rue Albert de Man (tel. 02 98 69 70 42; fax 02 98 69 75 16), has pleasant, family-style rooms around a beautiful garden and several airy sitting rooms. (Singles and doubles 168F, with toilet 214F, with shower 276F; 3-4 person rooms 230/276/337F.) **Camping de Kérestat** offers a slumber under the stars, south of town on rue de Pontigou. (Tel./fax 02 98 69 71 92. 1 person, tent, and car 62F; 2 people 80F.)

Restaurants serving 80-100F *menus* of *fruits de mer* line the port, but those in the know head for **Ti Saozon,** 30 rue Gambetta (tel. 02 98 69 70 89). *Crêpes,* *crêpes,* and more *crêpes* 11-44F. (Open Tu-Su 6-9:30pm. V, MC.)

⛫ SIGHTS. There isn't too much in Roscoff for the budget-conscious. Still, the 16th-century **Église Notre-Dame de Kroaz-Batz** merits a look; its massive, golden Baroque choir contrasts sharply with the simple white altar before it. The **Jardin Exotique** (tel. 02 98 69 70 45), on the coast about 1km past the ferry port, is more a botanical museum than a garden. It's not really a place to picnic, but the view from the "largest flowered rock" in France is impressive. (Open July-Aug. M-F 10am-7pm; Apr.-June and Sept.-Oct. 10:30am-12:30pm and 2-6pm; Nov.-Mar. W-M 2-5pm. 20F, students 10F.) The **Musée de la Maquette de Bateaux,** 16 rue Albert de Mun, is a small but nifty collection of model sailing ships and other maritime-inspired works of art, displayed in a private home. (Open Apr. 15-Sept. daily from 10:30am-12:30pm and 2:30-7:30pm. 20F, 8-12 10F, under 8 free.) For fans of alternative agriculture, the new **Algoplus factory** (tel. 02 98 61 14 14; fax 02 98 61 14 15) harvests seaweed for the production of cooking products and cosmetics. Free 45-minute tours are offered with tasting of the products at the end. (Summer open daily 10-11:10am and 2-6pm; spring and autumn 11am-3pm and 4-5pm; winter 1-4pm.)

THE NORTH

ÎLE DE BATZ

Perhaps it's the fact that anywhere you are on the island, the sea is visible. Maybe it is the tiny sand and stone beaches that ring the island or the fields strewn with seaweed for harvesting. Or that after one day you will recognize faces in the town. Locals sum up these things into what they call *la magie de l'île* ("the magic of the island"). On this quiet, rugged island, streets don't bother with names, and tractors outnumber cars. It can be explored in a day, though you may never want to leave.

⊡ ORIENTATION AND PRACTICAL INFORMATION. Two **ferry** companies, **CFTM** (tel. 02 98 61 78 87; fax 02 98 61 75 94) and **Armein** (tel. 02 98 61 77 75; fax 02 98 61 74 04), traverse the 15-minutes between **Roscoff** and **Batz** alternately every quarter of an hour. Boats leave either from the port or from a long walkway that extends into the harbor. (Roscoff departures 7:45am-8pm, Batz departures 6:45am-7:45pm. 32F round-trip.) Once on the island, stop by the small **tourist office** (tel. 02 98 61 75 70), by the port, for a 5F map detailing the 11km of walking trails around coast. (Open July-Aug. daily 9am-12:30pm and 1:30-5pm, Sept.-June 9am-noon and 2-5pm.) The **post office** is right off the port before you reach the Grand Hôtel. (Open M-F 9am-noon and 1:30-4:30pm, Sa 9am-noon. **Postal code:** 29253.)

↗ ACCOMMODATIONS. Suspended on a hill between sea and sky, the **Auberge de Jeunesse** doubles as a sailing school and receives large and small groups as well as individuals. Call ahead to enroll in a course (July-Aug. only). To reach the hostal, take the first right off the port, bear left at the first fork and right at the second following the signs to "Centre nautique—AJ." The view of the ocean through the pines will send you running straight for the beautiful beach nearby. (Beds 49F, in annex rooms with outdoor plumbing 44F, bunk cots in big tent 38F, camping 32F. Sheets 17F. Breakfast 19F. Excellent meals 49F. Kitchen. No lockout or curfew. Open Apr.-Oct.) The **Hôtel Roch Ar Mor** (tel. 02 98 61 78 28; fax 02 98 61 78 12), facing the port, lets spacious singles and doubles, some with magnificent views, as well as larger family rooms with places for up to 6 people. (200F. Extra bed 60F. Breakfast 35F.) For a luxurious stay, **Ti Va Zadon** (tel. 02 98 61 76 91) has four lovely *chambre d'hôtes* with bathrooms in a gorgeous stone house. From the port, take the only road to the right and follow it up to the church, turn right just before the church, and Ti Va Zadon will be immediately on the left. (230F for one person, 300F for two; two family rooms available for 400-450F. Breakfast included.) The free-form **terrain d'hébergement,** on the opposite side of the island near the lighthouse, functions as a campsite without the amenities. Install your tent, sleeping bag, or small flying circus, and someone from the tourist office will come and collect a fee in the evening. Buy a 5F token when they come round or you'll be taking cold showers. (6F per tent; 6F per person, children 3F.)

⊡ FOOD. The brand new **À l'Abri du Vent** (tel. 02 98 61 79 31) is in a brightly painted barn 50m from the hostel. Excellent *crêpes* 10-31F, including the creamy *bord de mer* with shrimp and calamari; and delicious cold cider on tap (21F for a small pitcher). From the hostel head towards the port and take the first right; the *crêperie* will be on the left. For a port location, **La Crêpe d'Or** (tel. 02 98 61 77 49), off the main road and along the water, offers truly spectacular *crêpes*. Try the *nordique*, made with salmon, fresh cream, and lemon. (Open June 15-Sept. 15 daily noon-9pm. V, MC.) A few blocks distant is an **8 à huit supermarket.** (Tel. 02 98 61 78 79. Open M-Sa 9am-12:30pm and 1:30-7:30pm.)

⊡ ⚑ SIGHTS AND HIKES. The GR34 trail ("Tour de l'Île") offers a fine 11km tour either east or west from the port. The island's **lighthouse** is open to the public on guided tours. (Open July 1-Sept. 15 daily 1-5:30pm; June and Sept. 16-30 Th-Tu 2-5pm.) At the **Jardin Exotique Georges Delaselle** (tel. 02 98 61 75 65), past the hostel on the southeast tip of the island, lush verdure complements the spectacular view of the sea. (Open July-Aug. daily 1-6pm; May-June and Sept. W-M 2-6pm; Apr. and

Oct. Sa-Su 2-6pm. Guided visits Su 3pm, 23F.) Nearby stand the ruins of the 6th-century **Chapelle Ste-Anne.** Only two walls remain of this chapel dedicated to the patron saint of sailors. In times gone by, sailors would hang their caps in the chapel's courtyard as a sign of thanks for their safe return to the island

BREST

As one inhabitant put it, "Brest is a city that is lively on the inside, while being quiet about it." The life and times of Brest (pop. 220,000) are grounded in its maritime tradition, treated in Jean Genet's 1947 novel *Querelle de Brest*. Situated on the southern side of Finistère's northern peninsula, Brest's harbor was designated by Cardinal Richelieu in 1631 as France's major naval base. Though unimaginative reconstruction followed the Allied bombing which pulverized most of the city's old areas in 1944, the city shouldn't be judged on æsthetic impressions alone. A successful shopping sector and a host of bars and restaurants make for full days and pleasant evenings. Brest has become a lively home for boisterous sailors and the students who attend Brittany's second-largest university.

🛈 ORIENTATION AND PRACTICAL AUGMENTATION

From the *gare*, av. Georges Clemenceau leads to the tourist office and the central pl. de la Liberté, the intersection of Brest's two main streets, rue de Siam and rue Jean Jaurès. Rue de Siam reigns as the city's most vibrant street, with bookshops, clothing stores, and restaurants clinging to the pavement like barnacles to a ship's

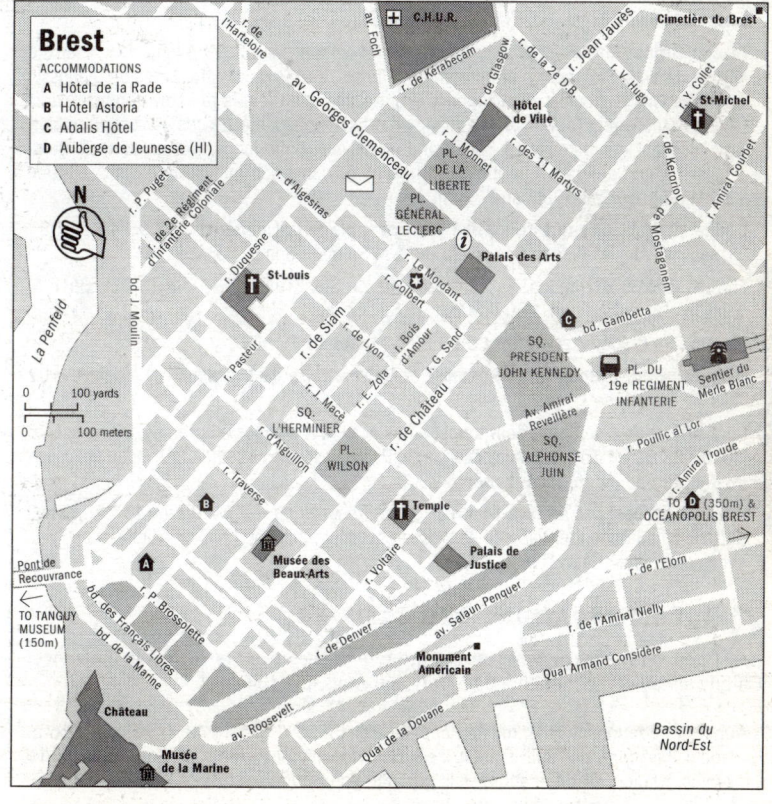

Brest

ACCOMMODATIONS
A Hôtel de la Rade
B Hôtel Astoria
C Abalis Hôtel
D Auberge de Jeunesse (HI)

THE NORTHWEST

hull. To reach the city's only remaining old quarter, cross the space-age Pont de Recouvrance (Bridge of Recovery) at the end of rue de Siam.

Trains: Pl. du 19ème Régiment d'Infanterie (tel. 02 98 31 51 72). To: **Morlaix** (45min., 10 per day, 54F); **Quimper** (1¼hr., 4-6 per day, 80F); **Rennes** (1½hr., 5-6 per day, 161F); **Nantes** (4hr., 6 per day, 210F); **Paris** (4½hr., 7 per day, 313F). Info and reservations M-F 8:30am-8pm, Sa 8:30am-7pm, Su 9:45am-7pm.

Buses: In front of the train station (tel. 02 98 44 46 73). To: **Quimper** (1¼hr., 4 per day, 1 on Su, 84F); **Camaret** (1½hr., 4 per day, 68F). Open July-Aug. M-F 7am-12:30pm and 1-7pm, Sa 7:15-11am and 1-6:30pm, Su 8:45-10:15am, 1-2pm, and 5:15-7:45pm; Sept.-June M-F 7am-12:30pm and 1-7pm, Sa 8am-1:15pm and 3:45-6:30pm, Su 4-7pm.

Local Transportation: Bibus, pl. de la Liberté (tel. 02 98 80 30 30). Ticket 6F, carnet of 10 48F, students 34F, full-day ticket 18F. Service until about 8pm, after which occasional service by a special line, designated by letters, circulates. Ask at the tourist office or the Bibus "point d'acceuil" in front of the Hôtel de Ville for schedules. Pl. de la Liberté kiosk open M-F 8:15am-12:15pm and 1-6:30pm, Sa 9am-noon and 1-5:45pm.

Ferries: Finist'mer: The smaller of the two ferry companies, Finist'mer is the only one to offer off-season prices; it also provides an instructive and friendly tour guide on the way over to explain a bit of Ouessantine history. Their competitor, **Penn Ar Bed** (tel. 02 98 80 24 68; fax 02 98 49 75 43), sends boats at 8:30am from the *port de commerce* to **Molène** (1¾hr., 1 per day, 158F) and **Ouessant** (2½hr., 1 per day, round-trip 180F, students 141F, children 108F). You can also buy tickets at the tourist office. Reserve ahead. Boats return at 5pm from Ouessant.

Taxis: Allô Taxis Brestois, 234 rue Jean Jaurès (tel. 02 98 42 11 11).

Tourist Office: Pl. de la Liberté (tel. 02 98 44 24 96; fax 02 98 44 53 73), near the Hôtel de Ville. Free map and info on food, hotels, and tours; ask for *Le guide,* a glossy, comprehensive booklet detailing just about everything there is to know about *Brestois* life. For the young (or maybe the young at heart), request the *Jeunes à Brest* pamphlet, an excellent resource for education and employment information. Open June 15-Sept. 15 M-Sa 9:30am-12:30pm and 2-6:30pm, Su 10am-noon and 2-4pm; Sept. 16-June 14 M-Sa 10am-12:30pm and 2-6pm.

Budget Travel: Bureau Information Jeunesse, pl. de la Liberté (tel. 02 98 43 01 08). Open July-Aug. M-F noon-6pm; Sept.-June M-Sa noon-6pm.

English Books: Dialogues, Forum Roull, rue de Siam (tel. 02 98 44 32 01). Open M 9:30am-12:30pm and 1:30-7:30pm, Tu-Sa 9:30am-7:30pm.

Police: Rue Colbert (tel. 02 98 80 08 50 or 02 98 43 77 77).

Hospital: Centre Hospitalier Régional et Universitaire de Bretagne, av. Foch (tel. 02 98 22 33 33).

Post Office: Rue de Siam, near tourist office at pl. Général Leclerc (tel. 02 98 51 87 76 or 02 98 81 87 75). **Currency exchange.** Poste Restante code: 29279. Open M-F 8am-7pm, Sa 8am-noon. **Postal code:** 29200.

Internet Access: Les Années Bleues, 23 rue Bréhat Bruat (tel. 02 98 44 48 19). Caters to the email-dependent as well as those in search of alcohol. (30F for 30min., one drink included. Open daily 10am-1am.)

ACCOMMODATIONS AND CAMPING

Brest has many inexpensive hotels and one of the swankiest hostels in France. Calling ahead is recommended for July and August.

Auberge de Jeunesse (HI), rue de Kerbriant (tel. 02 98 41 90 41; fax 02 98 41 82 66), about 4km from the train station, near Océanopolis, next to the artificial beach in Le Moulin Blanc. Exit the station, walk past the *gare routière,* cross the street, and head left down the street to the bus stop. Take bus #7 (6F) to its final stop at "Port de Plai-sance" (last bus leaves M-Sa 7:30pm, Su 6pm). Once there, facing down the street towards the port, take your first right, another right, and the hostel will be on your right; look for the sign in Breton, "ostaleri ar yaouankiz." Very kind staff will tend to your every need; if you need directions anywhere within a 200 mile radius, Rémy, the renaissance man/caretaker, will be able to give you detailed directions and supply you with a full color brochure as well. Carpeted rooms, fireplaces, laundry, and reading lamps. Lush garden. Ping pong, foosball, and TV room. Beds 69F. Small breakfast included. Dinner 48F. Lockers 5F. Reception M-F 7-9am and 5-8pm, Sa-Su 7-10am and 5-8pm. Lockout 10am-6pm. July-Aug. midnight curfew; Sept.-June 11pm; ask for a key if you'll be late.

Hôtel Astoria, 9 rue Traverse (tel. 02 98 80 19 10; fax 02 98 80 52 41), off rue de Siam. From the station, take dir. Palais de Justice to rue Voltaire (5min.), then follow the signs. Very pleasant couple rents quiet, lovely rooms with modern bathrooms. Phone, TV, and reading lamps in each room. Often full July-Aug.—call ahead. 10% off rooms with *Let's Go* in the off-season. Singles and doubles 135F, with shower and toilet 220-240F, with bath and toilet 250F; triples 260-270F. Breakfast 30F. V,MC.

Abalis Hôtel: 1 av. Georges Clemenceau (tel. 02 98 44 21 86; fax 02 98 43 68 32). Exit the train station, turn right on rue Georges Clemenceau, and the hotel will be directly on your right. Hair dryers, hot water pots, telephones, and TVs in every room. The warm wel-come at the front desk makes this a great place to collapse right out of the train station. Flash *Let's Go* for a discount. Singles 140F, with shower and toilet 240F; doubles160F, with shower and toilet 265F. Prices vary slightly by floor. Breakfast 35F. Bar downstairs. Reception open 7am-1am, someone always there at night. V, MC.

Hôtel de la Rade, 6 rue de Siam (tel. 02 98 44 47 76; fax 02 98 80 10 51), near the château. 40 immaculate and identical rooms with cheery blue and yellow bedspreads; ask for one with a view of the port. Sunny dining room and bright wooden furniture pleasant if lacking in character. TVs and phones. Singles with shower and toilet 230F, with bath 250F; doubles 250-280F; triples 300F. Breakfast buffet 30F. V, MC.

Campsites: Camping du Goulet (tel. 02 98 45 86 84) lies 6km from Brest and 1km from the sea in Ste-Anne du Portzic; take bus #14 to "Le Cosquer" or bus #7, 11, 12, or 26 to "Route de Conquet." At the end of a side road, this large, often crowded site on roll-ing hills affords clean facilities, free hot showers, and glimpses of the ocean in certain places. Laundry. (18F per person, 10F per child, 21F per tent. Electricity 15F.)

◖ FOOD

Markets take place every day in various locations; the tourist office has a complete list. *Boulangeries*, *pâtisseries*, and vegetable stores can be found on rue de Siam, as can a **Monoprix supermarket** (open M-Sa 8:30am-7:30pm).

Le Fromveur, 4 quai de la Douane (tel 02 98 43 45 34), has uninspired decor, but this small seaside place offers a wonderful 80F *menu* which can include homemade fish soup, fish of the day, and an excellent apple tart. *Menus* change every 2-3 months according to the fish in season. (Entrees 52-78F. Open Tu-Sa noon-2pm, 7:15-10:30pm; Su-M noon-2pm. Closed Sept.)

L'Eurasie, 48 rue Lyon (tel. 02 98 44 78 00). Offers excellent Chinese Vietnamese spe-cialties at some of the lowest prices in town. Tiny and quiet on a side street. The owner may have difficulty understanding you and vice versa, but her smiles cannot be misin-terpreted. (Open for lunch and dinner.)

L'Abri des Flots, 8 quai de la Douane (tel. 02 98 44 07 31). Another port restaurant, this *crêperie* has a jovial ambiance. Its proximity to the bars of the port as well as its local popularity and relatively inexpensive prices (with regards to the rest of Brest) make it quite nice. Egg, cheese, ham, tomato, and mushroom *crêpe* for 38F. Try the specialty, seafood couscous. Hours change, call for *heures d'ouverture*.

👁 🎵 SIGHTS AND ENTERTAINMENT

SIGHTS. Brest's **château** was the only major building to survive the bombings of World War II. Now the world's oldest active military institution (bits of it date from the 3rd century), the sprawling fortress houses the **Musée de la Marine** (tel. 02 98 22 12 39), which details the history of the town and its maritime tradition. (Admission 29F, students 19F. Open W-M 9:15am-noon and 2-6pm.) Across the waterway stands the **Musée de la Motte Tanguy**, pl. Pierre Péron (tel. 02 98 45 05 31). The 14th-century tower shelters dioramas of historic *brestois* architecture and culture. (Open June-Sept. daily 10am-noon and 2-7pm; Oct.-May W-Th 2-7pm, Sa-Su 2-6pm. Free.) On rue de Denver, the **Monument Américain** towers over the Port du Commerce, commemorating the landing of American troops in 1917.

Océanopolis Brest, port de Plaisance (tel. 02 98 34 40 40), is a little farther from the *centre ville*. Not just a fish museum, it has space-age exhibits and games emphasizing biodiversity and the need for conservation as well as big-eyed seals and a petting tank. It's worth the cash. From the stop across from and to the left of the station, take bus #7 (every 30min. until 8pm, 6F) to "Océanopolis." (Open June-Aug. daily 9:30am-6pm; Sept.-May M 2-5pm, Tu-F 9:30am-5pm, Sa-Su 9:30am-6pm.)

The **Musée des Beaux-Arts,** 24 rue Traverse (tel. 02 98 44 66 27), off rue de Siam, has a large but not altogether inspiring collection ranging from the 16th century to the 20th, focusing on works from the Pont-Aven school (see p. 533). (Open M and W-Sa 10-11:45am and 2-6pm, Su 2-6:45pm. 25F, free Su.)

ENTERTAINMENT. The first place to look for evening entertainment is the commercial port, which is a relatively safe place to hang out. **Les Jeudis du Port** rock the dock on Thursdays in July and August with popular concerts. **Les Fauvettes,** 34 quai de la Douane, offers 150 kinds of beer while its "headquarters," at 27 rue Conseil St-Martin (tel. 02 98 44 46 67), vends a whopping 600 different varieties. (Open daily 10am-1am.) **Les Quatres Vents** (also on quai de la Douane) is a local favorite, packed from 8pm with a boat for a bar and a mellower crowd. (Open daily 11am-1am.) More bars line the ends of rue de Siam. For a relaxed drink in a dreamlike atmosphere, the coffee shop ambiance of **The Trip to the Moon** matches its colorful painted walls and occasional live flute and drum players. You may want to stay forever. (38 rue Algeserias. Tel 02 98 43 12 60. Open 11:30am-1pm, Sa-Su 3pm-1am.)

ÎLE D'OUESSANT

Windswept Ouessant (*Enez Eussa* in Breton), off Finistère's western coast, is a 2½-hour boat ride from Brest. The island's sheep-dotted meadows, stone crosses, and strong traditions retain their charm despite the noisy tourists on rented bikes. Legend has it that mermaids once inhabited the island; perhaps this explains why local women have always had the upper hand. Traditionally, *ouessantine* maidens propose marriage. After the ceremony, the indefatigable women do the farming while their men voyage with the navy or in lobster boats. According to a local proverb, "the men earn the bread, but it is the women who provide the butter."

🗹 ORIENTATION AND PRACTICAL INFORMATION. From May to September, two **ferry** companies service Ouessant. Buy tickets at the port or at the Brest tourist office, and reserve in advance in summer. **Penn Ar Bed** (tel. 02 98 80 24 68 in Brest) sails between **Ouessant** and **Le Conquet** (1½hr.), on the western end of the peninsula, and then a further hour on to **Brest**. (Departs Brest 8:30am, Ouessant 5pm. Brest-Ouessant round-trip 180F, students 141F; Le Conquet-Ouessant 150F, students 120F. Reservations required.) **Finist'mer** ferries (tel. 02 98 89 16 61) also connect **Le Conquet** and **Ouessant**. (125-150F, students 95-122F. Some 45F one-way tickets available off-peak.) To get to **Le Conquet,** take the **Cars de St-Mathieu bus** (tel. 02 98 89 12 02) from **Brest** (40min., daily at 7:30am, 25F). Both ferry companies charge 40F each way for bikes, so consider hiring on the island if you want to bike.

Boats dock at **Port du Stiff**. From here, it's 3.5km to **Lampaul**. You can take a **Riou** or **Jean Avril** bus, or a taxi (10F). On foot, it's a 45-minute stroll along the road past sheep-filled pastures. A number of companies **rent bikes** at the port (60-80F per day, no deposit); you can rent by the hour in Lampaul (15-25F). Lampaul's **tourist office** (tel. 02 98 48 85 83; fax 02 98 48 87 09), near the church in the center of town, provides maps. (Open M-Sa 10:30am-12:30pm and 2:30-5pm, Su 10:30am-12:30pm.)

◪◪ **ISLAND ACCOMMODATIONS AND FOOD.** It's a good idea to make hotel reservations in advance, as tourism is slowly but incessantly encroaching on Ouessant. The brand new **Centre d'Étude du Milieu Ouessantin** (tel. 02 98 48 82 65), an environmental studies and ornithological center, doubles as a hostel with rooms around 75F a night. The friendly **L'Océan** (tel./fax 02 98 48 80 03) has airy rooms, many looking onto the ocean, in a convivial atmosphere. A mellow TV room provides space for a gathering, as does the bar downstairs. (Singles 180F, with shower 250F, with bath 280F; doubles 180F, with shower 270F, with bath 300F.) **Roch Ar Mor** (tel. 02 98 48 80 19; fax 02 98 48 87 51) has bright, clean, refurbished rooms, some with a sea view. Walk straight through town towards the water and the hotel will be on the right. All rooms with phone, TV, and bathroom. (Doubles and singles 280F; triples 320F; quads 350F. Extra bed 40F. Breakfast 40F.) You can camp at the **camping municipal** (tel. 02 98 48 84 65), 2km from the port on the main road. (14F per person, under 7 7.50F, 14F per tent. Laundry 25F. Reception M-Tu and Th 9am-1pm, W 9am-1pm and 8-9pm, Sa 8am-1pm and 3-6pm, Su 8am-1pm and 5-8pm.)

Restaurant choices are limited outside the hotels. **L'Océan** serves up *menus* from 60F for lunch and 75F for dinner. A half-pint of Guinness costs 18F at the adjacent bar. (Both open daily noon-2:30pm and 7:30-10:30pm. V, MC.) **Roch Ar Mor** is slightly pricier but has a beautiful dining hall and a spectacular view. *Menus*, from 98F, focus on the local catch. Otherwise make a treat yourself from **SPAR supermarket**, opposite the tourist office. (Open M-Sa 8:30am-7:30pm, Su 9am-12:30pm.) There is also a small market, **Le Marché des Îles** (M-Sa 8am-noon and 1:30-7:30pm), and a **8 à huit** grocery store five minutes from the campground.

◪ **SIGHTS.** The coasts of Ouessant hold land and seascapes unusual enough to mesmerize for hours. The map of the island provided at the tourist office will direct you to the *sentiers cotiers*, the roads that line the periphery; be sure to go to the magnificent Pointe de Pern, whose breathtaking rock formations rising from the ocean constitute the westernmost point in France. Near the Pointe is the **Musée des Phares et Balises** (tel. 02 98 48 80 70). In the phare du Creac'h, once Europe's most powerful lighthouse, it is devoted to the history of lighthouses and maritime signaling. At the **Écomusée du Niou-Uhella** (tel. 02 98 48 86 37), 1km northwest of Lampaul, you can peek inside a traditional *ouessantine* home. The collection includes Breton costumes and religious statuary. Ask for a copy of the explanatory guide in English. To get there, take D81 uphill out of town and watch for the turnoff sign to "Maisons du Nion." (Both open May-Sept. and school holidays daily 10:30am-6:30pm; Apr. Tu-Su 2-6:30pm; Oct.-Mar. Tu-Su 2-4pm. Écomusée 20F, students 12F; combined with lighthouse 40F, children 25F.)

The real attraction of the island, and the reason why Ouessant is not suffering from a population drain, is its wild beauty, both of its windswept cliffs and of the austere inland landscapes of traditional Breton houses and farms. Ouessantins are fiercely proud of their island; a walk along the coasts will show you why.

MAKING A SHEEP'S EAR OF IT If you get close enough to an *ouessantine* sheep, you may notice that his ears are marked. The sheep are allowed to roam freely over the island from the end of September until February, when a festival is held and everyone comes to claim their sheep—which they recognize by the ear markings. The farmers with only female sheep don't have to worry about breeding—as George Michael pointed out, it happens naturally. Owners must pay a small fee for each sheep when they collect them. This year it was 13F.

CROZON PENINSULA

Sandwiched between Léon to the north and La Cornouaille to the south, the demure *Presqu'île de Crozon* (Crozon Peninsula) juts out into the ocean. With few inhabitants and spectacular scenery on all sides, you'll feel a million miles from the rest of the world. The rugged terrain is challenging for hikers and bikers alike, but the view from the jagged cliff tops is well worth the effort. Travelers often neglect Crozon's tiny villages in favor of the large towns. Take off down an unmarked road and you're almost sure to find a neglected and utterly enchanting hamlet. Cycling opportunities abound, but the hilly terrain can be challenging. Hitchers report easy success all over the peninsula.

The peninsula's three major towns are **Crozon, Morgat,** and **Camaret,** at the westernmost point of the peninsula about 8km from Crozon. From Brest, **Vedettes Armoricaines** (tel. 02 98 44 44 04) sails to **Le Fret** on the peninsula and then shuttles passengers to the three towns. (Apr.-Oct., 3 per day; 49F, 56F with shuttle bus.) **Pouget buses** (tel. 02 98 27 02 02 in Crozon) connect **Brest** to **Crozon** and **Camaret** (1¼hr.; 2-3 per day, 1 on Su; 68F), while **SCETA** buses (tel. 02 98 93 06 98) run from **Quimper** (1¼hr., 2-5 per day, 58F). Getting between Camaret, Crozon, and Morgat is slightly more difficult. **Buses** run between **Camaret** and **Crozon** (2-3 per day, 11F), but to get to **Morgat,** you need to go to Crozon and then walk or bike the 3km incline, or wait for the infrequent **Vedettes Armoricaine** bus (10F).

CROZON

Buses to Crozon stop at the **tourist office** (tel. 02 98 27 07 92; fax. 02 98 27 24 89), which has maps and lodging information. (Open July-Aug. M-Sa 9:15am-7pm, Su 10am-7pm; Sept.-June M-Sa 9:30-noon and 2-6pm.) **Marché U** is on pl. Général de Gaulle, across from the church. (Open M-Sa 8:30am-12:30pm and 2:30-7pm.)

Presqu'île Loisirs (tel. 02 98 27 00 09), opposite the tourist office, **rents bikes.** (40F per half-day, 60F per day, 390F per week. Open July-Aug. M-Sa 9am-noon and 2-7pm, Su 9am-noon; Sept.-June Tu-Sa 9am-noon and 2-7pm.) A **laundromat** is on rue Alsace-Lorraine. (Open Tu-Sa 9am-noon and 2-7pm.) The **post office** up the street has **currency exchange.** (Open M-F 9am-noon and 2-5pm, Sa 9am-noon.)

The **Hôtel du Clos St-Yves** is at 61 rue Alsace Lorraine (tel. 02 98 27 00 10; fax 02 98 26 19 21). From the bus stop (with tourist office on right), turn left on rue St-Yves and then right on rue Alsace Lorraine. It has reasonable rooms with inconsistent décor, a restaurant, and a terrace for lounging or dining. (Doubles 184F, with shower 240F, with toilet and shower 250-300F. Extra bed 60-80F. Breakfast 35F.)

Four **gîtes d'étape** have beds for 45F. The *gîte* at St-Hernot (call Mme. Le Guillon at 02 98 27 15 00) sits a few kilometers south of Crozon. Only feet, wheels (four of 'em) or thumbs can get you there. Another *gîte* is in Landévennec, several kilometers north of Crozon (call the town hall at 02 98 27 72 65). Also north of Crozon, the Larrial *gîte* can be reached from the route Camaret (call M. or Mme. le Bretton at 02 98 27 62 30). The fourth *gîte* is at Telgruc-sur-Mer (tel. 02 98 27 33 3). ULAMIR in Crozon (tel. 02 98 27 01 68) has info. There is also **camping** about 1.5km outside Morgat at Camping du Bouis. (Tel. 02 98 26 12 53. 35F, 2 adults 62F, each additional person 15F. Showers 5F. Gates closed 11pm-8am. Open Easter-Sept.)

MORGAT

From Crozon, **Morgat** is a short walk downhill. From the Crozon bus stop, take a left onto rue St-Yves, a right onto rue Alsace Lorraine, and another left onto bd. de la France Libre. The boulevard will take you straight past the beach and into the tiny *centre ville.* You will also pass the Morgat **tourist office** (tel. 02 98 27 29 49) on your right. It provides mostly the same information as the Crozon office. (Open June-Sept. Tu-Sa 10am-noon and 3-6pm.) Morgat's smooth *plage* is an attraction in and of itself and is wide enough that you should be able to find a place to sit among the throngs of vacationers. If you should decide to stop for lunch, try the excellent **La Grange de Toul Boss** on the port de Morgat (tel. 02 98 27 27 95; fax 02 98 26 29 65), set slightly behind the tourist office in a little enclosed garden. Cold cider on tap complements the excellent *crêpes* and delicious salads. 60F lunch *menu* includes a filling salad, dessert (try the *far breton*), and coffee. (Open July-Aug. noon-11pm, Sept.-June noon-2:30pm and 7-10pm.)

For rock fans, the **Maison des Minéraux,** rte. de Cap de la Chèvre (tel. 02 98 27 19 73), about 4km out of town on D155, has an exhibit on the geological history of the region and will shut the lights to show off its impressive collection of fluorescent minerals. (Admission 25F, students 18F. Open daily July-Sept. 10:30am-7pm; June 10:30am-12:30pm and 2-7pm; May 10am-noon and 2-5:30pm.) If you keep going, you will eventually hit the spectacular **Cap de la Chèvre,** where the Crozon sidewalk ends. There is a 14km trail which runs from the Port at Morgat to Cap de la Chèvre along the cliffs overlooking the ocean—ask the tourist office for directions to this splendid trail. Along the way look for abandoned, almost unrecognizable houses which have been completely covered by ivy, but watch the trail closely—it gets slippery at times. **Vedettes Tertu** (tel. 02 98 26 26 90), **Vedettes Rosemeur** (tel. 02 98 27 10 71), and **Vedettes Serenes** (tel. 02 98 26 20 10) offer tours of Morgat's famous marine caves. (May- Sept., 45min., 30-45F. The Morgat tourist office has info.)

QUIMPER

Although half-timbered houses with crooked façades share their cobblestone streets with legions of tourists, Quimper (kem-PAIR, pop. 59,500), capital of La Cornouaille, has managed to retain its Breton flavor. Stores prominently display Celtic books, one local high school conducts its classes in Breton, and, for over 300 years, delicate hand-painted *faïencerie* (stoneware) has been crafted here. The first pottery studio in Quimper was founded by Jean-Baptiste Bousquet in 1690, who chose the spot because of its proximity to the river, which provided a source of clay and a means of transport. The surrounding woods fueled its kilns. Each year between the third and fourth Sundays of July, Quimper recalls its heritage with the *Festival de Cornouaille*, a cavalcade of mirth and music in Breton costume and one of Brittany's largest celebrations.

ORIENTATION AND PRACTICAL INFORMATION

Quimper is at the *kemper* ("confluence" in Breton) of the Steir and Odet rivers in the heart of La Cornouaille. From the train station, go right onto av. de Fare and follow it to rue Aristide Briand. To reach the tourist office, stay on the north side of the river Odet (keeping the river to your right), and walk along bd. Dupleix until it ends at pl. de la Résistance. To get to the *vieille ville*, cross the river along rue Aristide Briand, turn left onto bd. de Kerguélen, and turn right onto rue de Roi Gradlon, which leads to the cathedral at pl. St-Corentin (10min.).

Trains: Av. de la Gare (tel. 02 36 35 35 35). To: **Paris** (4¾hr., 4 TGVs per day, 368F); **Rennes** (2¼hr.; 8 per day, 4 TGV; 164F plus 10F TGV reservation); **Nantes** (2¾hr., 6 per day, 168F); **Brest** (1½hr., 6 per day, 81F). Info office open daily 8am-7pm.

Buses: The *gare routière* (tel. 02 98 90 88 89) is next to the train station. Buses leave from there or across the street. **CAT** runs to: **Brest** (1¼hr.; M-Sa 4 per day, Su 1 per day; 84F); **Roscoff** (2hr.; M and W-Sa 1-2 per day, Su 1 per day; 118F); **Pointe du Raz** via **Douarnenez** (1¼hr., 2-4 per day, 47F); and **Bénodet** (35min.; 5-7 per day, Su only July-Aug.; 25F). **SCETA** serves **Camaret** (1¼hr., 2 per day, 1 on Su, 59F) via **Châteaulin, Le Fret,** and **Crozon.**

Local Transportation: QUB 2 Quai Odet (tel. 02 98 95 26 27). Buses (tickets 6F; *carnet* of 10 45F, students 34F) run 6am-7:30pm. Bus #1 serves the hostel and campground. Look in the office for schedules and a map of the city bus lines. Open M-F 8am-12:15pm and 1:30-6:30pm, Sa 9am-noon.

Taxis: In front of the station (tel. 02 98 90 21 21).

Bike Rental: MBK s.a. Lennez, 13 rue Aristide Briand (tel. 02 98 90 14 81), off av. de la Gare. Bikes (80F per day, 200F per week) and mountain bikes (100F per day, 360F per week). Passport deposit. Open Tu-Sa 9am-noon and 2-7pm.

Tourist Office: 7 rue de le déesse (tel. 02 98 53 04 05; fax 02 98 53 31 33; email office.tourisme.quimper@ouest-mediacap.com; www.bretagne-4villes.com), off pl. de la Résistance. Free, detailed map. Excursion tickets to nearby sights such as the **Pointe du Raz** (120F) and **Pont-Aven** (110F). Tours of city July-Aug. M-Sa at 11am and 5pm, Su 3pm, Tu 2pm in English; last two weeks of June and first two weeks of Sept. M-Sa 2pm; May, and remainders of June and Sept. M and W at 3pm. Tours in English for groups and by reservation only. Office open July-Aug. M-Sa 9am-7pm; Apr.-June 9am-12:30pm and 1:30-6:30pm; Sept. 9am-12:30pm and 1:30-6:30pm; Oct.-Mar. 9am-noon and 1:30-6pm. Su hours as follows: May 1st-June 15 10am-1pm; June 15-Sept. 15 10am-1pm and 3-6pm.

Tours: Verney, 7 rue Elie Fréron (tel. 02 98 95 02 36), guides tours of the region: Pointe du Raz (120F), Crozon Peninsula (120F), Île de Batz (190F), and Pont-Aven/Concarneau (110F). Reservations can also be made in the tourist office. Open M 2-6pm, Tu-F 9am-noon and 2-6pm, Sa am-noon.

Laundromat: Laverie de la Gare, 47 rue de pont l'Abbé, about 5min. from the hostel. Open daily 8am-10pm.

Police: Rue Théodore Le Hars (tel. 02 98 90 15 41).

Hospital: Centre Hospitalier Laënnec, 14bis av. Y-Thépot (tel. 02 98 52 60 60).

Post Office: 37 bd. Amiral de Kerguélen (tel. 02 98 64 8 50). **Currency exchange.** Poste Restante code: 29109. Open M-F 8am-6:30pm, Sa 8am-noon. Branch offices on rue Châpeau Rouge in the *vieille ville* and rue du Calvaire 2 min. from the hostel. **Postal code:** 29000.

CyberVideo: 51 bd. A. de Kerguelen (tel. 02 98 95 31 56). For email addicts and those who might need a dose of video games on the road. Cybervideo also offers access to UNIX accounts. 25F for half hour, 45F for one hour. Open Tu-Sa 10am-noon and 2-10pm, M 10am-noon and 2-8pm.

▐ ACCOMMODATIONS AND CAMPING

In July and August, it's a good idea to make reservations in writing as early as possible. Hotels in Quimper tend to be pricey; as an alternative, ask the tourist office about private homes offering bed and breakfast (doubles usually 150F).

Centre Hebergement de Quimper (HI), 6 av. des Oiseaux (tel. 02 98 64 97 97; fax 02 98 55 38 37). 2km out of town in the Bois de l'Ancien Séminaire. Take Bus #1 from pl. de la Résistance directly across the river from the tourist office. (Direction "Kermoysan" to "Chaptal".) The hostel will be 50m up the street on your left. On foot, cross the river from pl. de la Résistance and go left on quai de l'Odet. Turn right onto pont l'Abbé and continue about 300 meters up the street until you reach the *rondpoint;* continue straight another 100 meters and the hostel will be on your left. The hostel is unguarded at night and sits at the end of a questionable street on the edge of town. Clean facilities. Dorms 49F; singles 65F. Breakfast 18F. Sheets 15F. 60 beds in 8- to 10-person rooms as well as a few private rooms. Small kitchen. Reception daily 8-11am and 5-9:30pm. Call if arriving late. Open Mar.-Oct.

Hôtel Pascal faces the train station (tel. 02 98 90 00 81). This quiet, family-owned hotel offers simple, basic rooms, the occasional uncertain mattress, but nonetheless a friendly reception and the promise of renovation for the year 2000. Rooms with fridge. Singles 150-180F; doubles 200-270F; triples 260-290F. Breakfast 30F.

Hôtel Celtic, 13 rue de Douarnenez (tel. 02 98 55 59 35; fax 02 98 53 43 74), in a great location one block up from Église St-Mathieu. From the tourist office, cross the river, turn left on quai du Parc, then turn right onto rue Préfet Collingnon, which runs into rue de Douarnenez. The hotel, owned by a friendly, multilingual ex-Marine, is on your right. 38 rooms, some very basic. Singles and doubles 125F, with shower 165F, with shower and toilet 215F; triples and quads 150F. Extra bed 95F. Public shower free. Breakfast 25F.

Quimper

ACCOMMODATIONS

A Centre Hebergement
   de Quimper (HI)
B Hôtel Celtic
C Hôtel Pascal
D Hôtel de l'Ouest

Hôtel de l'Ouest, 63 rue le Déan (tel. 02 98 90 28 35). Cheap, central, and that's about it. Energetic owner likes clients to keep very quiet at night and pay up promptly. Singles 100F. Doubles with shower and toilet 190F. Quads with shower and toilet 250F. Breakfast 30F. V, MC.

Campsite: You can definitely quimp 'ere. **Camping Municipal,** av. des Oiseaux in the Bois du Séminaire (tel. 02 98 55 61 09), next to the hostel. Take bus #1 to "Chaptal." Crowded but clean facilities. 19F per person, children 10F, car 8F, tent 5F. Ask receptionist for free shower tokens. Reception open M-Tu, Th, and Sa 8-11am and 3-8pm; W and Su 9am-noon; F 9-11am and 3-8pm.

FOOD

The lively **covered market (Les Halles),** off rue Kéréon on rue St-François, has good bargains on produce, seafood, meats, and cheeses (open M-Sa 7am-8pm, Su 9am-1pm), and it's also a great spot for *crêpes*. An **open market** is held twice a week (W in Les Halles, Sa outside Les Halles as well as in pl. des Ursulines; both June-Aug. 9am-6pm, Sept.-May 9am-1pm). A **Casino supermarket** is on av. de la Gare. (Open M-Sa 8am-7:30pm, Su 9:30am-1pm and 5-7:30pm.)

Le Saint Co., 20 rue Frout, just off pl. St-Corentin. This modern bistro serves such classics as *steak tartare* (80F) as well as a number of salads and omelettes. Try the *feuillete St-Jacques* (55F). Light wood and stone interior reflects the lights and warm atmosphere onto the rectangular plates that give the dishes a certain *"je ne sais quoi."* Open daily July-Aug. 11:30am-midnight; Sept.-June 11am-2pm and 6pm-midnight. V, MC.

Le Bistro St-Mathieu, 18 rue St-Mathieu (tel. 02 98 55 85 85). Try the *salade St-Mathieu* with *langoustines* (spiny lobster, melon, and ham; 36F). 65-72F *menus*. Open July-Aug. daily 10am-11pm; Sept.-June M-F 10am-10pm, Sa 6-10pm. V, MC.

La Maison des Cariatides, 4 rue du Guéodet (tel. 02 98 95 15 14). Dark and pub-like inside, but with a *terasse* on an attractive street in the *vieille ville* near Les Halles, La Maison serves food at lunch and becomes a bar at night. The *menu* has something for all: salads, quiche, meats, fish, and homemade desserts. Lunch daily 10am-1pm.

■ ♫ SIGHTS AND ENTERTAINMENT

SIGHTS. The **Cathédrale St-Corentin,** built between the 13th and the 15th centuries, towers over the entrance to the old quarter. Some sections of the interior are blocked off for restoration; the parts that have been finished are spectacular. St. Corentin, Quimper's patron, is just one of dozens of Breton saints not recognized by the Church in Rome. Spiritual advisor to King Gradlon, Corentin is said to have lived off a single fish. Each day after lunch, he threw half of it back into the river, only to have his scaly friend return regenerated the next day. A statue of Gradlon, erected in 1856, stands between the cathedral's spires. From the small cathedral garden, it's possible to climb to the **old city ramparts** for views of the cathedral and the Odet river. (Open July-Aug. 9am-7pm, Sept.-June 9am-6pm.)

Mont Frugy, next to the tourist office, offers an amazing view of the cathedral spires and a relief from the bustle of the *centre ville*. It's an easy hike, and numerous wooded walking trails with great views of the city await you. Those who missed the *Festival de Cornouaille* (see **Introduction,** above) can still catch other celebrations of Breton culture. Every Thursday from late June to early September, the cathedral gardens fill with **Breton dancers** in costume, accompanied by lively *biniou* and *bombarde* players (9pm, 20F). The first three weeks in August, Quimper holds its **Semaines Musicales.** Orchestras and choirs perform nightly in the Théâtre Municipal and cathedral; call the tourist office for more information.

The **Musée Départemental Breton,** 1 rue du Roi Gradlon (tel. 02 98 95 21 60), is housed in the former episcopal manor and may be entered through the garden. Finistère's history, archæology, and ethnography are represented in clever exhibits of pottery, artifacts, and costumes, with commentary in both French and English. Don't miss the elaborate display of traditional Breton clothing on the second floor. Also includes a number of fine sculptures of Breton daily life by Schweitzer, Quillivic, Kossowski, and others. (Open June-Sept. daily 9am-6pm; Oct.-May Tu-Sa 9am-noon and 2-5pm, Su 2-5pm. 25F, students 12F, under 11 free.) The **Musée des Beaux-Arts,** 40 pl. St-Corentin (tel. 02 98 95 45 20; fax 02 98 95 87 50), holds a collection of 14th- to 20th-century paintings including Breton works and paintings from the school of Pont-Aven by Sérusier, Moret, Slewinsky, and Maufra, as well as a fascinating exhibit about the poet and artist Max Jacob, a Quimper native who died in the Holocaust. (Open July-Aug. daily 10am-7pm; Sept.-June W-M 10am-noon and 2-6pm. 25F, students 15F.) **Faïenceries de Quimper H. B. Henriot,** rue Haute (tel. 02 98 90 09 36), is a studio where you can watch potters design Quimper's finest goods. Tours in French and English. (Open July-Aug. M-F 11:30am-5:15pm; Sept.-June M-F 9-11:15am and 1-4:15pm. 20F, students 10F.)

ENTERTAINMENT. *Quimpérois* of all stripes migrate to **Céili Pub,** 4 rue Aristide Briand (tel. 02 98 95 17 61), to drink and talk in the boisterous, convivial atmosphere. Check out their bumper stickers around town. The pub also hosts live concerts of Breton music. (Open M-Sa 10:30am-1am, Su 5pm-1am.) **St. Andrew's Pub,** 11 pl. Styvel (tel. 02 98 53 34 49), just across the river from the rue Pont l'Abbé on the very edge of town, offers a more refined, mellow setting for a relaxed drink or snack. (Open daily 11am-1am.) **Café XXI,** on 38 pl. St-Corentin (tel. 02 98 95 92 34), lights up the entire *place* in front of the Musée des Beaux Arts. This hopping, people-watching techno bar gleams with bright surfaces, lit glass blocks in the wall behind the bar, and splash painted floors. The glam, the beautiful, and the jet set all flock here, as well as the artsy older couple. (Open daily 8:30pm-1am.)

FLY THE FLAG The black-and-white Breton flag bears a striking resemblance to the Stars and Stripes, which it long predates. Where the American flag has stars, the Breton flag has a mysterious figure: a trio of small diamonds at the top and an elongated one at the bottom. This represents the hide of an ermine, symbol of the king of Brittany. Legend tells that the first king came across an ermine while hunting, and, taken by its beauty, pursued it to the edge of a bog. There the unfortunate animal turned around, and declared that it would rather face death than the prospect of soiling its coat. Swayed by this nobility (though not enough to spare its life), the king insisted on placing the hide of an ermine in front of him at every meal.

LOCRONAN

About 20km northwest of Quimper, beautiful Locronan (pop. 800) sits high on a hill above the countryside. Its perfectly preserved 15th- to 17th-century houses are more than just tourist magnets; more than 20 films have been shot here. Stepping into the town's main square is like walking into a Celtic fairy tale. Locronan once thrived on a successful sail-making industry and now snoozes away in peace, though avoiding the chorus of shutter clicks in July and August could be difficult.

In the heart of town, **Grande Place** is surrounded by impeccably preserved houses that once belonged to the town's rich merchants and officials. The **Église Priorale**, a 15th-century church, towers over the town. The smaller **Chapelle Notre-Dame de Bonne Nouvelle** sits in a tranquil spot down the hill, guarded by a small calvary. Poster buffs will get a kick out of the **Musée de l'Affiche** (tel. 02 98 51 80 59), on venelle des Templiers, at the top of the hill above the church. Each year from early July to early October, the museum showcases a different aspect of Breton life. (Admission 20F. Open daily Oct. 14-Aug. 10am-7pm; Sept.-Oct. 13 10am-1pm and 2-6pm.) The **Montagne de Locronan,** 2km east of town, capped by a chapel, offers a stunning view of the countryside and the deep blue sea beyond. Ask at the tourist office about the *circuit pedestre,* a walking path which circles the town and passes by the major sites as well as providing lovely views of the countryside.

The **tourist office,** at pl. de la Mairie (tel. 02 98 91 70 14; fax 02 98 51 83 64; email locronan.Tourisme@wanadoo.fr), has a free guide to the town and **changes money** at decent rates. (Open daily July-Aug. 10am-7pm; Sept.-June M-F 10am-12:30pm and 2:30-7pm.) **Crédit Agricole** has a 24-hour **ATM** in its magic money wall on rue du Prieurié. **SCETA buses** (tel. 02 98 93 06 98 in Carhaix) drop in on Locronan from Quimper (20min., 5-8 per day, 22F). Call the **police** at 02 98 91 70 01. Next door to the tourist office, the **post office** (tel. 02 98 91 70 95) offers **currency exchange.** (Open M-F 9am-noon and 2-5pm, Sa 9am-noon. **Postal code:** 29180.)

PONT-AVEN

"...To mention Pont-Aven is to state the inseparable bond between Brittany and painting; the first, rich in realities and myths, the second, fascinating in presence and dream..."
—Réné LE BIHAN in *"Memoire de Pont-Aven"*

Between Quimper and Quimperlé, **Pont-Aven** is a jewel which has been immortalized on countless canvases and whose surreal quality persists above the swarms of tourists who descend upon the town in search of inspiration. The first to paint the town was Paul Gauguin (1848-1903), who, having grown tired of mainstream Impressionism, discovered a pre-Tahiti style when he arrived here in 1886. Inspired by Gauguin, the **Pont-Aven School,** comprising 20 artists, developed between 1886 an 1896 into a movement emphasizing pure color, absence of perspective, and simplified figures. The town's other claims to fame are its art galleries—some of the finest in Brittany—and the buttery **Galette de Pont Aven,** produced by both the Penven and Traou Mad cookie factories.

The tourist office guides provide maps detailing a number of short hikes in the surroundings, many of them passing through places of congregation for the artists of Pont Aven. The tranquil **Bois d'Amour** (Lovers' Wood) is well-named for the beauty of the path that follows the river Aven underneath the rich foliage of twisted tree trunks. The **Chapelle de Trémalo,** through the woods, is a 17th-century polychrome-wood crucifix that provided the subject for Gauguin's *Yellow Christ.* The **Musée de L'École de Pont-Aven** (tel. 02 98 06 14 43), up the street from the tourist office, houses exhibitions on the Pont-Aven School. Those familiar with Finistère (the northwestern tip of Brittany) may experience a pleasant sense of *déjà vu*— canvases depicting the cliffs of Île d'Ouessant, the caves of Camaret, and other regional attractions are prominently displayed on the museum's walls. (Open July-Aug. daily 10am-7pm; Apr.-Oct. 10am-12:30pm, and 2-6:30pm; Feb.-Dec. 10am-12:30pm and 2-6pm. 25F, off-season 20F, students 12F.) Once a major grain-processing town with mills all up and down the river, Pont-Aven is now dedicated to churning out the finished product. You can sample *les galettes de Pont-Aven* at the **Biscuiterie Traou Mad** near the tourist office in the *centre ville* (a store, not the factory), and buy some to take home. (Open July-Sept. 15 daily 9am-7:30pm; Sept. 16-June M-Sa 9:15am-12:15pm and 2-7pm, Su 10am-12:30pm and 2:30-7pm. V, MC.)

There are no budget accommodations in Pont-Aven; daytrip from Quimper or Concarneau. For a *sympathique* bite to eat, try the well-hidden-but-worth-finding **Crêperie de la Petite Tourte** (tel. 02 98 06 13 62) off rue Émile Bernard on the right coming from the main square. Try the cheese apple and salad *crêpe* (40F). (Open daily 11:30am-10:30pm.) The **tourist office,** pl. de l'Hôtel de Ville (tel. 02 98 06 04 70; fax 02 98 06 17 25), is a block from the bus stop on pl. Gauguin. The staff sells a walking tour guide for 2F, and organizes tours of the town and its museum. (Tours June-Sept. at 11am and 4:30pm; town 22F; museum 30F; both 35F, under 21 20F. Open July-Aug. daily 9:30am-7:30pm; Sept.-Nov. and Apr.-June M-Sa 9:30am-12:30pm and 2-7pm, Su 10:30am-1:30pm and 3:30-6:30pm; Dec.-Mar. M-Sa 9:30am-12:30pm and 2-7pm.) The **post office,** rue des Abbés Tanguy, has **currency exchange.** (Open M-F 9am-noon and 1:45-4:45pm, Sa 9am-noon. **Postal code:** 29930.)

Pont-Aven is connected by **Transports Caoudal** buses (tel. 02 98 56 96 72) to **Quimper** (1¼hr., 4-6 per day, 31F) and nearby towns.

QUIBERON

All roads in Quiberon lead to the smooth, sandy, and wonderfully clean **Grande Plage.** Connected to the mainland by only a narrow strip of land, this *presqu'île* (peninsula) is almost overwhelmed with tourists in summer. Spectacular Belle-Île is only a 45-minute ferry ride away, but Quiberon's countryside offers many opportunities for gorgeous excursions. Save time for a hike or bike ride along the spectacular Côte Sauvage on the western shore of the peninsula.

7 ORIENTATION AND PRACTICAL INFORMATION. Trains (tel. 02 97 50 07 07) run only in July-Aug., and only to **Auray.** Take either a normal train (40min., 10 per day, 35F) or a more scenic and only slightly slower *tire-bouchon* (45min., 15F). (Ticket windows open 9am-noon and 2:15-5:30pm.) **TIM buses** also run to **Auray** (1hr., M-Sa 10 per day, 5 on Su, 35F) via **Carnac** (30min., 22F). For info, call **Cariane Atlantique** in Vannes (tel. 02 97 47 29 64). **Quiberon Voyages,** 21 pl. Hoche (tel. 02 97 50 15 30), runs trips all over the province, including an excursion to **Carnac** and **Vannes** (110F). **CMNN** (tel. 02 97 50 06 90), in Port Maria, serves **Belle-Île** from the **gare maritime,** quai de Houat. (5-13 per day. Round-trip tickets 110F, 68F for students and those willing to leave at inconvenient times. Bikes 50F, cars 412-786F.) Cruise the beachfront or explore the Côte Sauvage on **bikes,** tandems, pedal carts, or mopeds from **Cyclomar,** 47 pl. Hoche (tel. 02 97 50 26 00; fax 02 97 50 36 40). In summer there is an **annex** at the train station. (Bikes 45-56F per half-day, 66-83F per day, 224-352F per week. 10% off with ISIC card or a note from the youth hostel. Credit card or passport deposit. Open July-Sept. M-Su 7:30am-9pm, Oct.-June 8am-noon and 2-7:30pm. Annex open daily July-Aug. 8:30am-8pm.)

To find the **tourist office,** 14 rue de Verdun (tel. 02 97 50 07 84; fax 02 97 30 58 22; www.quiberon.com), turn left from the train station and walk down rue de la Gare.

THE NORTHWEST

When you see the church ahead on your left, bear right down rue de Verdun (5 min.). The staff distributes a flashy guide to the town and info on accommodations (Open July-Sept. M-Sa 9am-12:30pm and 2-6:30pm, Su 9:30am-12:30pm and 3-7pm; Oct.-June M-Sa 9am-12:30pm and 2-6:30pm.) The **Centre Hospitalier du Pratel** (tel. 02 97 56 42 42) in Auray is the nearest hospital. The **post office,** pl. de la Duchesse Anne (tel. 02 97 50 11 92), has **currency exchange.** (Open July-Aug. M-F 9am-6pm, Sa 9am-noon; Sept.-June M-F 9am-noon and 2-5pm, Sa 9am-noon. **Postal code:** 56170.)

⚑ ACCOMMODATIONS AND CAMPING. Quiberon is not cheap, but there is a small and comfy **Auberge de Jeunesse (HI),** 45 rue du Roch-Priol (tel. 02 97 50 15 54), just 15 minutes from the train station and five minutes from the beach. From the station turn left and take rue de la Gare through pl. du Repos to the right of the church, follow rue de Lille, and turn left on rue Roch-Priol. There's no street sign, so look for a sign saying "Itinéraire Conseillée." When the road splits, bear left and go uphill until you reach the hostel, which will be on your left. Guillaume the manager lets basic 8-person rooms in a friendly atmosphere; his smiles and infinite patience are free. Kitchen facilities. (49F. Sheets 17F. Breakfast 19F. Camping 32F, tents 39F per person. Reception 8:30-10am and 6-8:30pm. Open May-Sept.)

Hôtel de l'Océan, 7 quai de l'Océan (tel. 02 97 50 07 58; fax 02 97 50 27 81), offers plain, bright rooms, some facing the harbor. An enormous sunny salon with TV makes up for ordinary rooms and the slightly dark lobby. (Singles and doubles 170-250F, with shower 260-280F, with shower and toilet 280-300F. Extra bed 80F. Breakfast 35F. Shower 10F. V, MC.) The campsite nearest the city is **Camping Municipal du Goviro** (tel. 02 97 50 13 54), next to the lovely beach of the same name. It's almost always full in-season; make reservations. (14F per person, 14F per tent, 9F per car. Electricity 18F. Showers 10F. Reservation deposit 214F. Reception July-Aug. M-Sa 8:30am-8pm, Su 9am-noon and 3-5pm; June and Sept. 1-Oct. 5 M-Sa 9am-12:30pm, 2-6:30pm, Su 9am-7pm; closed Oct. 5-Mar. 15.) Right behind is the slick, spacious, and nicely landscaped **Camping Bois d'Amour** (tel. 02 97 50 13 52; off-season tel. 02 97 30 24 00), with a heated pool, outings, and activities for kids, as well as a *brasserie*-type restaurant. (Adults 43F, tent 40F. Electricity 30F. Reception open from 9am-12:30pm and 2-7pm. Open Apr.-Sept.)

🍴 FOOD. Seafood is Quiberon's natural specialty. Though known for its *fruits de mer* above anything else, there does exist a *quiberonais* candy—the caramel-like hard *niniche.* If you're looking for a taste of the sea, try **La Criée,** 11 quai de l'Océan (tel. 02 97 30 53 09), right next to the fish market of the same name. The *plateau gargantua,* an awe-inspiring array of oysters, crab, and other ocean-dwellers (300F), is worthwhile for a large group. There is also a 3-course fish *menu* for 89F. (Open July-Aug. daily noon-2pm and 7-10:30pm; Sept.-June Tu-Sa 12:15-2pm and 7-10pm, Su 12:15-2pm. V, MC.) **Comod supermarket** on rue de Verdun can fulfill your every nutritional need. (Open M-Sa 8:45am-12:30pm and 3-7:15pm.) The **Casino supermarket** is closer to the hostel on rue de Port Haliguen. (Open M-F 9am-8pm, Sa 9am-noon.)

🏖 BEACHES. The craggy Côte Sauvage stretches a wild and windy 10km along the western edge of the Quiberon peninsula. Heed the signs marked *Baignades Interdites* ("swimming forbidden"); many have drowned in these tempting but treacherous waters. The flag system is as follows: green=safe supervised bathing, orange=dangerous but supervised bathing, red=bathing prohibited.

Grande Plage is the most popular, but if you prefer a less hectic beach, head for the small, rocky **plage du Goviro** near the campgrounds. From the port, follow bd. Chanard east along the water as it becomes bd. de la Mer and then bd. du Goviro. Some smaller beaches along the Côte Sauvage are accessible either by car or by bicycle (be prepared for some hills); however, in many of these areas bathing is prohibited because of dangerous waters. Even so, the cliffs provide spectacular views of the ocean, and are beautiful in themselves.

🎵 🎊 **ENTERTAINMENT AND FESTIVALS.** The amiable owner of **L'Hemisphère Sud,** 4 rue du Phare (tel. 02 97 30 51 76), off pl. Hoche, runs the hottest bar in town. Packed with a young crowd of *quiberonnais*, patrons drink, dance, and shoot pool until 2am. If you haven't gotten a tan on the nearby beach, you might just glow under the black lights: soon you'll rival the fluorescent murals covering every surface, including the bar. 6-9pm drinks cost 10F, but the place really gets going around 11:30pm. (Open July-Aug. daily 6pm-2am; Sept.-June Th-Su only.) **Le Nelson,** pl. Hoche (tel. 02 97 50 31 37), hosts a slightly older, more mellow crowd. The prices are a bit higher here, but worth the chance to sit at an outdoor table and chat in a relaxed atmosphere. (Open daily 12pm-2am, closed Su Oct.-Easter.)

Swing and strings serenade the city in July during the two-week **Passions Presqu'île** (tel. 01 42 23 87 05), including a week of classical music (tickets 100F).

BELLE-ÎLE

At least five boats depart daily from Quiberon's Port-Maria for Belle-Île, an island that truly deserves its name with magnificently high cliffs, narrow creeks, and crashing seas. Farther inland, patches of heather and ferns color the fields. At 20km in length, Belle-Île is large enough to make bike rental a necessity. The ferry ride takes 45 minutes, and you can take your bike along (round-trip 110F).

📧 **GETTING AROUND.** Boats dock on the northern coast at **Le Palais,** the island's largest town. The other main towns—**Sauzon, Bangor,** and **Locmaria**—lie on the northwest tip, center, and east coast respectively. A new shuttle system linking the four ports has greatly facilitated travel between them. (Le Palais to **Sauzon** 25min., 6 per day, 13F; to **Bangor** 22min., 5 per day, 15F; to **Locmaria** 30min., 5 per day, 20F.) There is a clearly marked, well-kept trail running along much of the coast, enabling travel by foot between the ports with views anything but pedestrian. The most spectacular area, the island's own Côte Sauvage, is also accessible by boat. (See **Quiberon Beaches,** above, for safety info.)

📊 **PRACTICAL INFORMATION: LE PALAIS.** To get to the **tourist office** (tel. 02 97 31 81 93; fax 02 97 31 56 17; www.belle-ile-en-mer.com), walk to the left end of the quai as you leave the boat. The energetic staff distributes a thorough guide to the island (5F), a comprehensive French brochure with hiking and biking plans, and a detailed walking map (45F) which provides an excellent point of reference for exploring the entire island on foot. (Open July-Aug. M-Sa 8:30am-8pm, Su 9am-12:30pm; Sept.-June M-Sa 9am-noon and 2-6pm, Su 10am-noon.) For a self-guided tour of the island, **rent bikes** at **Cyclotour,** quai de Bonnelle (tel. 02 97 31 80 68), near the tourist office on the port. (Bikes 45-65F per half-day, 55-85F per day. Passport deposit. Open July-Aug. daily 8:15am-7pm; Sept.-June M-Sa 9am-noon and 2-7pm). You can rent **mopeds** at **Au Bonheur des Dames,** quai Jacques Le Blanc. (Tel. 02 97 31 80 52. 200F per half-day, 280F per day. Open daily 9am-7pm). The **hospital** (tel. 02 97 31 48 48) is in Le Palais. The police are at Les Glacis (tel. 02 97 31 80 22). The **post office** (tel. 02 97 31 80 40), on quai Nicolas Foucquet across from quai Gambetta, has **currency exchange.** (Open M-F 9am-12:30pm and 2-5pm, Sa 9am-noon. **Postal code:** 56360.)

📐 **ACCOMMODATIONS AND CAMPING.** The tourist office in Le Palais can help you find cheap rooms, and has info about the island's *chambres d'hôtes* and rudimentary *gîtes d'étape*. Both the campground and the hostel are near the citadel, a 10-minute hike from Le Palais's port. Turn right from the port and follow the *quai* to the footbridge that leads to the citadel. Cross the bridge and take a sharp left up a hill; keep going through the parking lot and take a right at the end—**Camping Les Glacis** will be on the right. (Tel. 02 97 31 41 76; fax 02 97 31 57 16. 18F per person, 12F per tent, 12F per car, 4F per bike, 12F per hot shower. Reception July-Aug. M-Sa 8am-10pm, Su 8am-8pm; June and Sept. M-Sa 9am-noon and 4-7pm, Su 9am-noon. Reservation required July -Aug. No credit cards.)

The beautiful and large **HI hostel** (tel. 02 97 31 81 33; fax 02 97 31 58 38) is about another ten minutes walk up the same road on the right, just past the *gendarmerie* and down its own driveway—look carefully for the sign, as it is hidden on the right among trees. Less personal than the Quiberon hostel, it's suited to large groups and boasts fantastic facilities: kayaking trip arrangements made on site. To camp on the lawn, you must rent a tent. (Doubles 51F per person. Tent 25F per person. Breakfast 19F. Meals 50F. Sheets 17F. Reception daily 8-10am and 6-8pm.)

La Frégate, quai de l'Acadie (tel. 02 97 31 54 16), in front of the dock, has small, cheap, sunny rooms facing the water, each with a name like "weekend" or "The nest"—they are as individual as their names. Located above a friendly bar and restaurant which offers snack foods. Bright, gigantic sitting room provides beautiful views of the harbor. (Singles and doubles 120-170F, with shower and toilet 230F; triples with shower and toilet 260F. Breakfast 30F. Reception July-Aug. 7:45am-1am; Apr.-June and Sept.-Oct. 7:45am-10pm. V, MC.)

⫙ FOOD. At **Traou-Mad**, 9 rue Willaumez (tel. 02 97 31 84 84), off pl. de la Résistance in Le Palais, choose from a wide selection of *galettes* (7-74F), dessert crêpes (8-45F), and healthy-sized salads (18-53F). (Open Apr.-Nov. 11:30am-12:30am. V, MC.) Just outside **Sauzon** on the main road, the **Crêperie La Mère Michèle** (tel. 02 97 31 62 70) fills plates with *crêpes* and *galettes* from 10F. (Open daily July-Aug. 11am-11pm; Sept.-June 11am-3pm and 6-11pm. V, MC.) A small **market** is held every morning in Le Palais at pl. de la République; on Tuesday and Friday it takes over the *place* from 8am-1pm. There is a **supermarket** behind the church on rue Le Brix. (Open M-F 9am-12:30pm and 2-7pm, Sa 9am-7:30pm, Su 9am-noon.)

⬛ SIGHTS. The massive 16th-century **Citadelle Vauban** (tel. 02 97 31 84 17) catches your eye the second you glimpse the island from the boat. Built in 1549 by Henri II to protect monks from pirates, the fort contains a grass-roofed museum that presents the citadel's history as well as gossip about Sarah Bernhardt, Claude Monet, and other celebs who spent time here. Just a walk within the courtyard is an impressive experience—lizards slither over the towering walls and the air is so still that one could imagine being transported back to the time of its construction. (Open daily May-Oct. 9:30am-6pm; Nov.-Apr. 9:30am-noon and 2-6pm. 35F.)

Belle Île's natural treasures are scattered all along the island's coastline. The **plage de Donnant** on the western coast is the widest and most popular beach, but just as nice are the pristine **plage Port Maria** on the eastern shore, and the powdery white sand of the **plage Grands Sables**, southeast of Le Palais. From Le Palais, head 6km northwest to picturesque **Sauzon** and then on to the **Pointe des Poulains** on the northern tip of the island. This deserted fort was once home to the famous actress Sarah Bernhardt. Massive rock formations rise over crystalline waters at the **Grotte de l'Apothecarie**, southwest of the Pointe, and at the **Aiguilles de Port Coton**, where the grey beach contrasts with electric green water.

CARNAC

Seven thousand years ago, Neolithic peoples settled in Brittany, leaving thousands of massive rock formations as proof. Carnac is home to one of the world's most impressive series of these ancient monuments. If monster rocks aren't your style, small granular ones may fit the bill—the luxurious stretch of beach is a great place to unwind and frolic.

⏻ ORIENTATION AND PRACTICAL INFORMATION. To get to Carnac, take the **TIM bus** (tel. 02 97 21 28 29, in Vannes) from **Quiberon** (30min., at least 7 per day, 22F), **Auray** (30min., 7 per day, 23F), or **Vannes** (45min.,7 per day, 38F). You can also take the **train** to **Plouharnel** and catch a bus from there (5min., 6 per day, 5F). There are two bus stops (corresponding to two tourist offices): the first, "Carnac-Ville," is convenient for the town and its sights; the second, "Carnac-Plage," is close to the beach in front of the main **tourist office,** 74 av. des Druides. (Tel. 02 97 52 13 52; fax 02 97 52 86 10. Open July-Aug. M-Sa 9am-7pm, Su 3-7pm; Sept.-June M-Sa 9am-12:30pm and 2-6:30pm.) To walk back to the *centre ville,* take av. des Druides and walk up towards the church. Av. des Druides becomes av. de la Poste, which leads into the square where the **tourist office annex** sits at pl. de l'Église (tel. 02 97 52 13 52; fax 02 97 52 86 10). **Bikes** are really useful in this area; go to **Cycles Lorcy,** 6 rue de Courdriec. (Tel. 02 97 52 09 73. 30F per half-day, 35F per day, 200F per week. 1000F or passport deposit. Open July-Aug. M-Sa 8:30am-12:15pm and 2-7pm, Su 8:30am-12:15pm; Sept.-June Tu-Sa only.) The **police station** is at 40 rue St-Cornély (tel. 02 97 52 06 24). The **post office,** av. de la Poste (tel. 02 97 52 03 90), just outside the *centre ville,* has **currency exchange.** (Open July-Aug. M-F 9am-6pm, Sa 9am-noon; Sept.-June M-F 9am-noon and 2-5pm, Sa 9am-noon. **Postal code:** 56430.)

▌ ACCOMMODATIONS AND CAMPING. Carnac works best as a daytrip, since hotel prices rise with the summer tides. B&Bs and *chambres d'hôtes* are the cheapest housing option; ask the tourist office for a list (doubles run 100-150F). Otherwise, **Hôtel Chez Nous,** 5 pl. de la Chapelle (tel. 02 97 52 07 28), is a real find. From the *Carnac Centre Ville* bus stop, head down rue Saint Cornely towards pl. de l'Église (away from the gas station). You will see the Musée de Préhistoire on your right; turn left down the rue Kervarail and you will find the hotel on your left. The gracious owner will attend to your every need. Spacious, nicely decorated rooms and a beautiful patio garden make for a peaceful ambiance. (Singles and doubles with shower 200-250F, with TV 250F; doubles with full bath 270F; triples 320-330F. Breakfast 36F. Communal fridge. V, MC.) **Camping Kerabus,** allée des Alouettes (tel. 02 97 52 24 96), off rte. d'Auray, is about 10 minutes from the Alignements de Kermari. A beautifully landscaped site with decent bathroom facilities. (17F per person, 21F for tent and car. 12.50F for 4 amps of electricity. Open May 1-Sept. 15. Reserve well in advance for July and August.)

▐ FOOD. Buy your bread, *far breton,* or ice cream from the very popular bakery **Aux Delices d'antan,** 2 rue Tumulus (tel. 02 97 52 05 56), right across from the tourist office on pl. de L'Église, which also serves *crêpes* and *galettes.* (Open daily in summer 7am-7:30pm. Closed Nov. and Tu in winter.) *Crêperies* surround the St-Cornély church. The **Marché U** supermarket is next to the beach and tourist office. (Open M-Sa 8:30am-8pm, Su 8:30am-12:30pm). **Casino supermarket** is on av. des Salines, close to the *ville.* (Same hours). There is also a **8 à Huit** on rue St-Cornély, just past the Carnac *centre ville* bus stop. At the **market** in the parking lot behind the church at pl. du Marché (W and Su 8am-1pm), you can sample everything from homemade honey and tasty Breton pastries to horse meat.

☎ SIGHTS. The "Carnac-Ville" stop drops you close to the **Musée de Préhistoire,** 10 pl. de la Chapelle (tel. 02 97 52 22 04). It contains an impressive collection of burial chambers, engraved stones, jewelry, metal, pottery, and other artifacts that shed light on Brittany's history from 450,000 BC to the early Middle Ages. (Open June-Aug. M-F 10am-6:30pm, Sa-Su 10am-noon and 2-6:30pm; Sept.-May W-M 10am-noon and 2-5pm. 30F, students 15F, Oct.-Mar. 25F.)

The mysterious **Alignements du Ménec** are 10 minutes from the museum and the Tumulus. More than 1000 menhirs, some over 3m tall, stretch over 2km in a line toward the horizon. Head north on rue de Courdriec, rue de Paul Person, or rue des Korrigans until you see the menhirs on route des Alignements. The psychedelic **Archéoscope** (tel. 02 97 52 07 49) is a flashy, melodramatic introduction to the region and its treasures. Across from the Alignements du Ménec, it uses lasers, films, and moving scenery to explore the mystery of the megaliths' origin. A small exhibit following the show explains things in better detail. (Open daily July-Aug. 9am-6pm; mid-Feb.-mid-Nov. 10am-noon and 1:30-5pm. Showings in English daily. 45F, ages 13-18 30F, ages 6-12 25F.)

A ROCK LEXICON Carnac's rock formations come in various shapes and sizes, and many still go by their ancient Breton names. Here's a little glossary to get you going. If you get confused, don't worry. Gustave Flaubert, when asked his opinion on the Carnac stones, replied, "I would express the irrefutable, indisputable, irresistible...Here is my opinion: the stones of Carnac are big stones."

menhir: a large upright stone from the ancient Celtic (men = stone, hir = long).

dolmen: a stone table which may or may not be attached to a **dolmen corridor**—which was used as a funeral chamber.

cairn: from the Celtic, a pile of stones that may be on top of one or several dolmens.

tumulus: an artificial elevated mound on top of a **dolmen corridor** (the distinction from a cairn is a little shady).

The **Alignement de Kermario** stands adjacent to the anticlimactic **Géant du Manio** (a big rock) and the **Quadrilatère** (rocks in a square). Due to concerns about receding vegetation and erosion, fences have been constructed around the menhirs. Most tourists limit themselves to the observation boardwalk and stand, menhir-like, sucking on popsicles and observing the array before them. Call or show up at the Centre d'Accueil (tel. 02 97 52 89 99) to reserve a spot in one of the guided tours. (Open daily 9am-7pm. Tours in French only. 25F, students 20F.)

VANNES

Vannes' history reads like the fable of the Sleeping Beauty. Of central importance in the 14th century, the town served as the ducal seat of Brittany and a commercially successful maritime center. The end of this golden age began in 1450 when the Dukes moved to Nantes; over the next few centuries Vannes (pop. 45,000) slumbered uneventfully, losing almost all of its trade to the nearby port city of Lorient and earning the unfortunate title of the largest "bourg" (suburb) in France. It was only in the 1960s that the *vannetais* realized the worth of their artistic legacy: Breton wooden furniture and characteristic architecture. Vannes boasts 180 *maisons à colombage*, houses with a typically wooden frame decoration on the façade. Exceptionally proud of their home, the locals now take care and pleasure in sharing their cultural heritage with visitors from all over the world.

⊓ ORIENTATION AND PRACTICAL INFORMATION. Trains run to **Rennes** (1¼hr., 6 per day), **Quimper** (1¼hr., 6 per day), and **Paris** (3¼hr., 5 per day). Consult schedules as timetable change during the summer months. Call **Cariane Atlantique** (tel. 02 97 47 29 64) or **CTM** (tel. 02 97 01 22 21) for information on **buses to Rennes, Quiberon,** and **Carnac. Auray Voyages** (tel. 02 97 57 88 90) goes to **Auray** (surprise). **TPV** runs **local buses** in the city and to neighboring communes. Schedules can be obtained at the tourist office or at **Infobus,** pl. de la République (tel. 02 97 01 22 23). To get a **taxi** at the train station, cross the street to the small booth marked "taxis" and press the "appel taxis" button on the wall for a direct line to service. Otherwise, call 02 97 54 34 34. To get to the **tourist office** at 1 rue Thiers (tel. 02 97 47 24 34; fax 02 97 47 29 49; office.tourisme.vannes@wanadoo.fr) from the main exit of the train station, turn right on av. Favrel et Lincy. At the roundabout, turn left, and when the street splits immediately following the turn, stay on the right (av. Victor Hugo). Follow av. Victor Hugo to rue Jean le Brix and turn right and then left onto rue Thiers. Follow the road past the Hôtel de Ville and the post office; the tourist office will be on your right. Ask the staff for a detailed city map—the standard one offered does not have all of the street names, essential for walking among the beautiful but somewhat convoluted streets. The office also runs tours in July and August. You can wash clothes at **Lavomatique,** 5 av. Victor Hugo. (Tel. 02 97 47 15 80. Open daily 9am-8pm.) Doctors stand by at the **Centre Hospitalier Chubert** (tel. 02 97 01 41 41); the **police** are at 02 97 54 75 00. There is a **post office** with **currency**

exchange at pl. de la République (tel. 02 97 01 33 33). Surf the web at **Cybercafé "Le Seven,"** 15 pl. du Général de Gaulle. (Tel. 02 97 54 04 72. 25F per half-hour. Open M-Sa 3pm-1am, Su 6am-1am.) Most of the activity in town takes place west of the ramparts, the 3m-thick walls that line one side of the town.

⌐ ACCOMMODATIONS AND CAMPING. Hotels in Vannes tend to the pricey side, but there remain a number of good deals. The best deal in town is the centrally-located **Foyer de Jeunes Travailleuses,** 17 av. Victor Hugo (tel. 02 97 54 33 13; fax 02 97 42 57 73). Follow directions to the tourist office; the hostel is on the right as you walk down av. Victor Hugo. In a communal atmosphere, the young staff organizes activities such as photography workshops and skating outings. TV room with video library, billiard hall, snack machines, telephone, and listings of job opportunities and contacts in the front lobby. (Singles 75F, 25 and over 90F. Breakfast 14F. Sheets 28F. M-F cafeteria lunch and dinner 45.50F. Reception open 7am-11pm, ring bell after 11pm. Reservations advised July-Aug.)

A friendly couple at **Hôtel Anne de Bretagne,** 42 rue Olivier de Clisson (tel. 02 97 54 22 19; fax 02 97 42 69 10), lets clean and spacious rooms close to the train station, some with internet connection. (Singles with toilet 170F; doubles with toilet 200F, with shower, toilet, and TV 290F; triples 330F; quads 350-360F. Showers 16F. Breakfast 35F. Reception 8am-11pm.) Opposite the train station is **Hôtel Le Richemont,** 26 pl. de la Gare (tel. 02 97 47 12 95; fax 02 97 54 92 79). Pleasant, individually decorated rooms off a pretty hallway. (Singles 110F; doubles with shower and toilet 210F; triples with bath and toilet 275F. Showers 15F. Breakfast 30F. Reception 24hr. V, MC.) To get to **Camping Municipal de Conleau,** continue on rue Thiers past the tourist office. It will become rue du Port and then av. Maréchal de Lattre. Fork right onto av. du Mal Juin; the camping will be on the right (25 min.). Alternatively, take bus #2 (direction "Kerthomas-Le Fourchene-Conleau") to "Camping," near the beautiful peninsula of Conleau. (Tent 43F, adult 24F, under 12 15F. Electricity, 15F. Laundry 20F, dry 10F.)

⌐ FOOD. While interesting restaurants are scattered all over town, the narrow rue des Halles behind the former public marketplace is brimming with options that spill onto brightly lit terraces. On Sunday mornings, from 8am, there is a market on **pl. du Poids Public.** Almost hidden underground is the quiet **Crêperie La Taupiniere,** 9 pl. des Lices (tel. 02 97 42 57 82). This tiny family-run business is appropriately named; taupe means "mole" in French. The galettes are far too large for small mammals, though; the *complète*, with egg, ham, and cheese, goes for a mere 24F. *Crêpes* 15-30F, cider 10F. (Open July-Aug. M-Sa noon-2pm and 7-10pm, Su 7-10pm. Sept.-June M-Tu and Th-Sa noon-2pm and 7-10pm. V, MC.) The terrace at **La Mere à Trois Sous** brims with flowers, baskets, candles and strings of light. Three centimes won't get you far these days, but for 38F you can have *andouillettes*, smoked salmon salad, or vegetable quiche. (Open T-Su noon-2pm and 7-11pm.)

⌐ SIGHTS. Vannes' size makes it an ideal town to explore on foot. Most of the historic architecture is contained within the area bordered by rue Thiers, rue J. le Brix du Mène, rue François Decker, and rue A. le Pontois. **Pl. St-Pierre** is of special interest; the traditional *maisons à colombage* are particularly noticeable for their splendid colors, which were used to identify different residences before house numbers were imposed by Louis XIII. Standing over the *place*, the **Cathédrale St-Pierre** has vibrant stained glass and *le trésor*, a collection of religious objects and costumes. (Open May-Oct. M-Sa 10:30am-6:30pm, Nov.-Apr. 2-6pm. *Trésor* 15F, students 10F.) The museum **La Cohue,** pl. St-Pierre (tel. 02 97 47 35 86; fax 02 97 54 92 34), opposite the cathedral entrance, takes its name from its 13th-century function as a covered market. Today it holds a Breton-themed cultural collection dating back to the 19th century. (Open June-Sept. daily 10am-6pm, Oct.-May. 10am-noon and 2-6pm. 26F, students 16F.) The city **ramparts,** adjacent to the beautifully landscaped **Jardin de Limur,** along rue Francois Decker, show several different styles and ages of towers; numerous sieges resulted in distinct layers of rock. Concerts are often held in the Limur gardens. On a more modern note, the mid-sized **Aquarium de Vannes** (tel. 02 97 40 67 40; fax 02 97 63 49 45; 24hr. info line 02 97 40 22 00) offers a peek at tropical fish, giant turtles, and sharks. (Open daily July-Aug. 9am-7pm. 50F, under 12 30F). Right next to the aquarium is the **Jardin des Papillons,** Parc du Golfe (tel. 02 97 46 01 02; fax 02 97 63 49 45). A large tropically-climatized room brimming with plants and trees, this encapsulated forest contains, on average, 600-800 butterflies at any time, and receives 400 chrysalides per week. Look and step carefully, and watch out for giant teal caterpillars the size of candy bars. (Open daily June-Aug. 10am-7pm, Apr.-May and Sept. 10am-12:30pm and 2-6pm.)

⚑ ※ ENTERTAINMENT AND FESTIVALS. Nightclubs in Vannes are scarce; the real action comes in the celtic-themed bars. Come evening, everyone crowds into the cafés on **place Gambetta,** immediately overlooking the old port. Here you'll find a scenic vantage point for people watching, and a beautiful view of the boats, as well as a lively atmosphere. For a slightly cozier atmosphere, try **Patty O'Dowd's,** 21 rue Ferdinand LeDressay, (tel. 02 97 47 87 81). Packed comfortably on the terrace with a mellow crowd, Irish music creates an ambiance you may have guessed from the name. (Open daily 6pm-2am.) For a marginally classier atmosphere, try next door at the **Colonial Cafe** (tel. 02 97 42 74 56). With campy safari decor and a techno sound track, this attracts a slightly more well-dressed clientele than its neighbor.

At the end of July and beginning of August, the city hosts the **Jazz à Vannes** festival in the Jardin de Limur. In 1999 the concerts included such artists as Ravi Coltrane and the Duke Ellington Orchestra, as well as nationally acclaimed groups. (Tel. 02 97 01 81 21 for info; www.vannes.bretagne-sud.com. Tickets 140F, students and under 18 110F.)

NANTES

Officially a part of the *Pays de la Loire*, Nantes (pop. 500,000) is culturally and historically Breton. Though high-tech industries and 27,000 students give it a big-city feel, they blend nicely with the many reminders of the city's glorious and often gory past. Nantes' château hosted both Henri IV's famous Edict and the infamous pirate Bluebeard (the Maréchal de Retz). Between the 16th and 18th centuries, Nantes established itself as an apex of the slave trade, a grisly business which nevertheless bolstered the economy and made the city France's largest port. During the Revolution, not even the guillotine could keep pace with the march of death as hundreds of people, stripped and bound in pairs, were drowned in the Loire. Despite the lack of must-see sights, Nantes' ideal location, year-round festivals, and vibrant nightlife make it a smart stop between Brittany and points south—ready or *nantes*.

🔋 ORIENTATION AND PRACTICAL INFORMATION

Nantes is a tangled conglomeration of *quartiers*, hills, and pedestrian streets spread out along the north bank of the Loire. Shadowed by its modest skyscraper, the **Tour Bretagne,** the city axes run east-west along **cours John Kennedy,** which becomes **cours Franklin Roosevelt** and later **quai de la Fosse,** and north-south along **cours des 50 Otages.** To get to the *centre ville* and the tourist office, turn left out of the north exit *(accès nord)* of the train station onto allée du Charcot, which becomes cours John Kennedy. After the château and **pl. Bouffay,** cross cours des 50 Otages. The "fnac" tourist office is at **pl. du Commerce** on your right (20min.).

Flights: The airport is 10km south of Nantes (tel. 02 40 84 80 00). **Air Inter** (tel. 02 51 88 31 08) flies daily to **Marseille, Lyon, Nice,** and **Paris. Air France** (info tel. 02 40 47 12 33; reservations 08 02 80 28 02) sends 6 flights per week to **London. Tan Air** shuttle (tel. 02 40 29 39 39) runs from pl. du Commerce and the station *(accès sud* exit). 25min., M-F 13 shuttles per day, Sa 8, Su 3. Tickets 38F, *carnet* of 4.

Trains: 27 bd. de Stalingrad. Also south entrance *(accès sud)* across the tracks on rue de Loumel. To: **Saumur** (70min., 7 per day, 98F); **La Rochelle** (2hr., 8-11 per day, 125F); **Paris** (2-4hr., about 20 per day, 222-360F); **Rennes** (2hr., M-Sa 10 per day, 3 on Su, 117F); and **Bordeaux** (4hr., 6-8 per day, 226F).

Buses: Cariane Atlantique, 5 allée Duquesne (tel. 02 40 20 46 99), sends buses to **Vannes** (1½hr., 93.50F) and **Rennes** (2hr., 2 per day, 95F). Buses leave from the train station's south entrance and from the *gare routière* (tel. 02 40 47 62 70) on allée Baco. Office open M-F 8am-noon and 2-6:30pm.

Local Transportation: TAN (tel. 08 01 44 44 44) runs buses and two tram lines until 8pm. Ticket 8F, 2 for 15F, 5 for 32F, 10 for 56F. Day pass 21F, week 65F. Info booth at 3 rue Bellier, opposite pl. du Commerce. Open M-F 7:15am-7pm, Sa 9am-7pm.

Taxis: Allô Taxis Nantes Atlantique (tel. 02 40 69 22 22), at the station. 24hr.

Tourist Office: Pl. du Commerce (tel. 02 40 20 60 00; fax 02 40 89 11 99; www.reception.com/Nantes), provides excellent maps, makes reservations (5F), and **exchanges currency.** Organizes tours of Nantes and the surrounding area. Walking city tour 40F, students 25F; reservations recommended. Open M-Sa 10am-7pm.

Money: Best **currency exchange** rates at **Banque de France,** 14 rue Lafayette (tel. 02 40 12 53 53). Exchange desk open M-F 8:45am-12:30pm.

Laundromat: 3 rue de Bouffay. Open M-Sa 8:45am-7pm. Also at 7 Hôtel de Ville. Open daily 7am-8:30pm.

Youth Information: Centre Régional d'Information Jeunesse (CRIJ), 28 rue du Calvaire (tel. 02 51 72 94 50). Info on youth discounts and employment opportunities. Open Tu-F 10am-6:30pm, M and Sa 2-6:30pm.

Budget travel: Voyage au Fil (tel. 02 51 72 94 60), at CRIJ. Ground and air tickets. Matches hitchers with drivers. Hours as for CRIJ, closed 12:30-1:30pm. V, MC, AmEx.

Hospital: Centre Hospitalier Régional, pl. Alexis Ricordeau (tel. 02 40 08 33 33).

Police: Pl. Waldeck-Rousseau (tel. 02 40 37 21 21).

Post Office: Pl. de Bretagne (tel. 02 40 12 62 74), near Tour Bretagne. **Currency exchange.** Open M-F 8am-7pm, Sa 8am-noon. **Postal code:** 44000.

Internet access: Welcome Services Copy, 70 rue Maréchal Joffre (tel. 02 51 81 96 25). 35F per hr. Open M 2:30-7pm, Tu-F 9am-12:30pm and 2-7pm, Sa 9:30am-12:30pm and 2:30-7pm.

■ ACCOMMODATIONS AND CAMPING

Nantes has plenty of good hotels and lots of student dorm space in the summer. Most budget places are within a 10min. walk or bus ride of the pl. du Commerce.

Foyer des Jeunes Travailleurs Beaulieu (HI), 9 bd. Vincent Gâche (tel. 02 40 12 24 00; fax 02 51 82 00 05). From the station, take tram to pl. du Commerce and change to bus #24 (direction "Beaulieu") to "Albert." 200 beds in 1- to 4-person rooms with showers and toilets. 60F. Sheets 16F. Breakfast 12F. Lunch or dinner 40F. Kitchen. Reception 8am-midnight. No lockout. No curfew.

Foyer des Jeunes Travailleurs L'Édit de Nantes, 1 rue du Gigant (tel. 02 40 73 41 46; fax 02 40 69 11 55). From the station, take tram to pl. du Commerce, walk up cours des 50 Otages to "St-Nicolas," and catch bus #21 or 23 to "Édit de Nantes." From pl. du Commerce, catch bus #24 or 56 to "Édit de Nantes." The *foyer* is across the street. 60 beds in single and double rooms with shower and toilet. 60F. Lunch or dinner 40F. Reception M-F 9am-9pm. Call ahead for winter stays.

Hôtel St-Daniel, 4 rue du Bouffay (tel. 02 40 47 41 25; fax 02 51 72 03 99), just off pl. du Bouffay. 23 big rooms with phones in a great location. Some rooms look over the Ste-Croix church garden. Singles 150F, doubles 150-220F. Breakfast 24F. V, MC.

Hôtel du Tourisme, 5 allée Duquesne (tel. 02 40 47 90 26; fax 02 40 35 57 25). Pretty tiled stairs lead up to 20 clean rooms with attractive decoration. All rooms with TV and

Tram — T

Nantes

ACCOMMODATIONS
A Foyer des Jeunes
   Travailleurs L'Édit de Nantes
B Camping du Val du Cens
C Hôtel d'Orléans
D Hôtel de Tourisme
E Hôtel St-Daniel
F Foyer des Jeunes
   Travailleurs Beaulieu (HI)

THE NORTHWEST

phone. Singles and doubles 140F, with shower 165F, with toilet and shower 185-220F. Extra bed 50F. Shower 10F. Breakfast 25F. Free bike storage. Reserve ahead. V, MC.

Hôtel d'Orléans, 12 rue du Marais (tel. 02 40 47 69 32), off cours des 50 Otages. Run by a congenial young family. 15 well-kept rooms with TV and telephones. Singles and doubles 135F, with shower 160-185F, with bath and toilet 220F; quads 250F. Breakfast 25F. Carry *Let's Go* and the 10F shower is free. Reserve July-Aug. V, MC, AmEx.

Campsites: Camping du Val de Cens, 21 bd. du Petit Port (tel. 02 40 74 47 94), a 10min. tram ride (take line 2 north to "Marhonnière") from pl. du Commerce. Superb four-star site. 18F per person, 25F per tent, 35F per tent and car, 46F per caravan and car. Electricity 18F. Reception 8am-10pm. Reserve in writing or arrive early in summer.

◗ FOOD

Local specialties include seafood *au beurre blanc* (with butter sauce) and *canard nantais* (duck prepared with grapes), as well as the white wines, Muscadet and Gros Plant. *Le Petit Beurre* cookies are a local invention, as are the lesser-known *muscadines* (chocolates filled with grapes and Muscadet wine). Urbane Nantes overflows with ethnic eateries; Greek, Turkish, and Italian are consistently good. Explore the streets behind pl. du Bouffay, where you'll find many a morsel to suit your fancy—the *crêperies* are especially good.

The biggest **market** in Nantes takes place at the **Marché de Talensac,** along rue de Bel-Air near pl. St-Similien behind the post office (Tu-Sa 9am-1pm). A smaller market stays open for the same hours on **pl. du Bouffay,** while a Saturday market stretches down pl. de la Petite Hollande opposite pl. du Commerce from 8am-1pm. **Monoprix** rests off cours de 50 Otages at 2 rue de Calvaire, down from the Galeries Lafayette. (Open M-Sa 9am-9pm. V, MC.)

La Cigale, 4 pl. Graslin (tel. 02 51 84 94 94; www.lacigale.com), opposite the théâtre Graslin. Considered one of the most beautiful *brasseries* in France, La Cigale is a classified historical monument as well as a not-to-be-missed dining experience. The art nouveau mosaics, gold detail, and huge mirrors complement delicacies such as hibiscus flower strawberry soup (39F). *Menus* are expensive, but snacks are available all day for under 50F. Open daily 7:30am-12:30am; reserve for supper. V, MC.

Tapalocas, 7 rue de la Baclerie (tel. 02 40 47 14 00; www.avignon-et-provence.com/tapalocas), by pl. Bouffay. A large open dining room fills with happy tapas-goers in this friendly local favorite. The bar's cartoon emblem and strings of little plastic flags are over-bright, but the spirited crowd and choice of over 50 hot, cold, and dessert tapas (12F) quickly make up for it. Open daily 11:45am-2am. V, MC.

Crêperie Jaune, 1 rue des Échevins (tel. 02 40 47 15 71), off pl. du Bouffay. Students and families crowd the terrace to partake of enormous *super-pavés*, double-decker *galettes* with tomatoes, mushrooms, egg, and emmental (54F). Afterwards, enjoy dessert *crêpes*, ice cream, or both in *crêpe surprise* (34F). Open M 7pm-midnight, Tu-Sa noon-2:30pm and 7pm-midnight. V, MC.

Mangeoire, 4 rue des Petite Écuries (tel. 02 40 48 70 83), around the corner from pl. du Bouffay. Quiet and elegant, with excellent local cuisine. 50F 2-course and 58F 3-course lunch *menus*. Open Tu-Sa noon-2pm and 7-10pm, Su noon-2pm. V, MC.

◗ SIGHTS

Ask the tourist office about a global pass to the château museums, the Musée des Beaux-Arts, the Musée d'Histoire Naturelle, and the Musée Jules Verne. Except for the planetarium, Nantes's museums are free on Sundays.

A walk around Nantes offers some beautiful 19th-century architecture. Culminating in *La Cigale* (see **Food**), this period saw the construction of the elaborate façades with wrought-iron balconies which pepper the city.

CHÂTEAU DES DUCS DE BRETAGNE. Currently under renovation, this château has seen as much history as any on the Loire. Its imposing walls once held Gilles de Retz, a.k.a. the original Bluebeard, who was convicted of sorcery in 1440 for sacrificing hundreds of children in gruesome rituals. In 1598, Henri IV composed the Edict of Nantes here in an effort to soothe national tensions (see p. 9). All of the château's museums but one are currently closed until 2008, but the interim *Musée du Château des Ducs de Bretagne* will host a number of temporary exhibits. 2000 features "Les Mondes Inventés de Jules Verne" ("Jules Verne's Invented Worlds"), which will focus on the artist's life, technique, and work. *(Tel. 02 40 41 56 56. Courtyard open for free visits daily July-Aug. 10am-7pm; Sept.-June 10am-noon and 2-6pm. Free tour. Museum open July-Aug. daily 10am-noon and 2-6pm; Sept.-June W-M 10-11:50am and 2-5:50pm. 20F, students 10F, under 18 free. Free after 4:30pm.)*

CATHÉDRALE ST-PIERRE. Step inside to appreciate the soaring 38m Gothic vaults and the newly restored interior. A 13-year project has undone the ravages of time—including Revolutionary pillaging and a 1972 fire—and the cathedral now looks as good as when it was built in 1434. Anne of Brittany commissioned the elaborate tomb in the south transept for her parents; their figures are guarded by the Virtues. Above it, the largest stained-glass window in France climbs 25m. A 20th-century representation of native saints, its glowing-ember reds and yellows stand in contrast to the cathedral's other pastel concoctions. *(Cathedral open daily 8:45am-7pm. Crypt open M-Sa 10:30am-12:30pm and 2-6pm, Su 2-6:30pm.)*

MUSÉE DES BEAUX-ARTS. This collection prompted Henry James to reflect on provincial museums: "The pictures may be bad, but…from bad pictures, in certain moods of the mind, there is a degree of entertainment to be derived." James's assessment notwithstanding, the collection includes works by Delacroix, Ingres, and Kandinsky. *(10 rue Clemenceau. Tel. 02 40 41 65 65. Take bus #11 or 12 to "Trébuchet." Open M and W-Sa 10am-6pm, Su 11am-6pm. 20F, students 10F, free 1st Su of the month.)*

MUSÉE JULES VERNE. One for Captain Nemo fans. The innovative museum recreates Verne's wonderful world through novels, letters, and photographs. The 11-year-old Verne made an ill-fated attempt to stow away on a sailing ship before resigning himself to imaginary voyages. *(3 rue de l'Hermitage. Tel. 02 40 69 72 52. Open M and W-Sa 10am-noon and 2-5pm, Su 2-5pm. 8F, students 4F.)*

MUSÉE D'HISTOIRE NATURELLE. This houses everything from trees and crystals to fossils and skulls. The museum's top floor is an enormous showroom lined with every stuffed mammal, bird, and reptile you can imagine. If you've never seen a dead yak up close before, now's your chance. *(12 rue Voltaire. Take bus #11 to "Jean V" or tram #1 to "Médiathèque." Tel. 02 40 99 26 20. Open Tu-Sa 10am-noon and 2-6pm, Su 2-6pm. 20F, students 10F; free the third Su of every month.)*

OTHER SIGHTS. The **Planetarium** allows you to relax to galactic vistas and an exploration of our rotating solar system. *(8 rue des Acadiens, off pl. Moysan. Tel. 02 40 73 99 23. Shows M-F 10:30am, 2:15pm, and 3:45pm. Sunday shows at 3 and 4:30pm. 26F, students 13F.)* The **Jardin des Plantes,** behind the Musée des Beaux Arts, sits chock-full of grassy hills and dales, trees, and duck ponds; some more exotic flavors are housed in the northern section's huge greenhouse. *(Open daily 8am-7:45pm.)*

THE NORTHWEST

🎵 🎆 ENTERTAINMENT AND FESTIVALS

ENTERTAINMENT. A good deal of *nantais* nightlife is listed in the weekly *Nantes Poche* (3F at any *tabac*). **The Katorza,** 3 rue Corneille (tel. 08 36 68 06 66), projects nightly independent films in their original language. Afterwards, the nearby **rue Scribe** is chock-full of late-night bars and cafés. A bastion of the young and funky, **quartier St-Croix** averages three bars per block and just as many cafés, making it a night-time crowd-pleaser. **Pickwick's Tavern,** at the corner of rue Rameau and rue Suffren, has an array of bottled beers (25-38F), plus live music on Thursday nights. (Open M-Tu 6pm-2am, W and F 6pm-4am, Sa 4pm-4am.) On the other side of town, **La Maison,** off rue Maréchal Joffre, stays open with cantina lighting and a party atmosphere 3pm-2am every night.

Clubs are a bit further out but generally worth the trek if you're ready for action; **Le News,** 4 pl. Émile Zola off bd. Pasteur (tel. 02 40 58 01 04), spins house and garage in one *salle* and new jack, funk, and dance in another. A few blocks to the south, **L'Acropole,** 15 rue Convention (tel. 02 40 46 49 99), a self-proclaimed temple of dance, sees a late twenties/early thirties crowd, but promises a good time for all. (Open Th 4-9pm, F and Sa 11:30pm-5am, Su 4-11pm.) Nantes' notorious gay disco is **Le Temps d'Aimer,** 14 rue Alexandre Fourny (tel. 02 40 89 48 60); from pl. de la République on Ile Beaulieu, follow rue Victor Hugo until rue Fourny on the left.

FESTIVALS. Eastern Orthodox chanters, blues rockers from Mali, and masqueraders from Trinidad and Tobago perform at the international **Festival d'Été,** which takes place each year in early July. The **Festival des Allumées** (tel. 02 40 69 50 50 for info) sparks in mid-October, honoring the theater, dance, and music of a different city each year. Up-and-coming Asian, African, and South American filmmakers are honored in the **Festival des Trois Continents** in late November and early December (tel. 02 40 69 74 14). *Nantais* boast that their **Carnaval** (tel. 02 40 35 75 49 for info) is one of the biggest in France, with parades and an all-night party on Mardi Gras.

LOIRE VALLEY (VAL DE LOIRE)

The Loire, France's longest and most celebrated river, drifts towards the Atlantic alongside a landscape of vineyards, history, and famous châteaux. Though her source lies to the south of le Puy-en-Velay, far away in the mountains of the Massif Central, the *pays de la Loire* is commonly understood to be that part of the country drained by the river and her tributaries, between Orléans and Nantes. Famed for her châteaux above all, the Loire also created some of the brightest stars of French thought, including Rabelais, Ronsard, Descartes, and Balzac, and the French spoken on her banks is considered the purest in the country. In the shadow of the châteaux, vines produce some of France's best-loved wines, while the soil is among the country's most fertile. It is hardly surprising that a string of French (and English) kings chose to divert themselves by her waters rather than in the dirt and noise of their capital cities.

The history of the châteaux goes back to the 9th century, when a splintered France was crumbling under Viking invasions. Local communities, under the leadership of feudal lords, erected fortresses to protect important landholdings from the new invaders. Later, the region was a focal point of the incessant Anglo-French wars, beginning when Henry Plantagenêt, Duke of Anjou and local strongman, inherited the English crown. Henry, his wife Eleanor of Aquitaine, and his son Richard the Lionheart are all interred in the Abbey of Fontevraud (p. 577), just outside Saumur. During the Hundred Years' War, the region was one of the few to effectively resist the English; it was at Chinon (p. 571) in 1429 that Joan of Arc persuaded the Dauphin to give her an army with which to liberate Orléans. With the introduction of effective artillery in the 16th century, the age of the defensive fortress was over and battles moved into the plains. Most of the surviving castles were converted into comfortable palaces, adapting the new Italian style to fit local sensibilities. These elegant Renaissance homes, reflected in pools and framed by spectacular gardens, were heaped with masterworks of fine arts and design, fostering an opulence hardly imagined before or since.

The valley was scarred by the 16th-century Wars of Religion, whose terror culminated in the Duc de Guise's murder of Protestants at Amboise (p. 561) in 1560, followed 18 years later by the duke's own assassination in Blois (p. 555). It was the betrothal of Henri IV's three-year-old son to the six-year-old daughter of the Duc de Mercœur, leader of the Catholic league, that brought the wars to an end. The Loire settled down for a political nap in the 17th century when

Loire Valley

Château

THE NORTHWEST

N

0   10 miles
0   10 kilometers

A5
N6
A6
A6
Melun
Fontainebleau
Nemours
Montargis
N7
Briare
D751
Gien
St-Benoît
Germigny-des-Prés
Châteauneuf-sur-Loire
D952
Sully
D24
Argent
Cosne-Cours
Sancerre
la Charité-sur-Loire
Loire
N151
N76
St-Amand-Montrond
N144
Meillant
Noirlac
Malesherbes
N152
N191
N20
Étampes
Orléans
N60
Cosson
D14
D60
Corson
D923
D940
D944
Bourges
A71
Vierzon
Cher
Issoudun
D940
Châteauroux
D943
Nohant
la Châtre
TO PARIS
A11
Chartres
N154
D955
A10
Châteaudun
N10
Meung-sur-Loire
D951
A10
Beaugency
Blois
Chambord
D112
D923
Beauregard
Cheverny
D765
Montrichard
N76
Selles-sur-Cher
Valençay
D956
Lucay-le-Mâle
Indre
N151
Creuse
le Blanc
D950
N143
Loches
Châtillon-sur-Indre
D750
D14
A20
D927
D939
Nogent-le-Rotrou
N23
D28
Eure
D955
Huisne
N157
Bessé-sur-Braye
Château-du-Loir
Loir
la Possonière
Vendôme
D957
N10
N152
Amboise
Chaumont-sur-Loire
Chenonceaux
D31
Tours
Saché
Ste-Maure-de-Touraine
Descartes
Creuse
D750
Gartempe
Châtellerault
Vienne
N147
N151
Le Mans
N12
D311
Alençon
N138
N138
D959
D307
D304
D35
N23
D306
D767
la Flèche
Baugé
D766
N147
D959
Villandry
Langeais
Ussé
N152
Azay-le-Rideau
Chinon
D749
Richelieu
D757
A10
D757
Poitiers
N11
N10
N23
D21
Mayenne
A81
Laval
Château-Gontier
N162
Sarthe
Mayenne
D23
Angers
D963
Saumur
Montsoreau
Fontevraud-l'Abbaye
Doué
D938
Loudun
D147
N149
Parthenay
D743
Bressuire
D938
N12
Fougères
D798
Vitré
D171
D155
D175
Rennes
A81
D30
N171
Châteaubriant
D163
D178
D178
N137
Redon
N24
N12
Pontchâteau
N165
Nantes
N249
A11
A83
Cholet
Sèvre Nantaise
N160
Brissac-Quincé
Loire
D960
N149
Fontenay-le-Comte
D949
N148
la Roche-sur-Yon
D949
Pornic
St-Gilles-Croix-de-Vie
St-Jean-de-Monts
Fromentine
les Sables-d'Olonne
N160
D753
Loire
ATLANTIC OCEAN

Louis XIV summoned the nobles to court at Versailles, but awoke once again during the Revolution when rural peasants violently protested Republican policies, provoking an uprising that ended with the wholesale massacre of civilians by the Revolutionary armies.

Besides anchoring the foundations of the region's architectural wonders, the rich soil of the Loire valley nurtures *asperges* (asparagus), *fraises* (strawberries), and *tournesols* (sunflowers). In the *caves* once used as quarries for the châteaux, tubs of mushrooms neighbor barrels filled with wine. Well-known whites include Touraine, Montlouis, and Vouvray, while Chinon, St-Nicolas-de-Bourgeuil, and Saumur are predominately red. Saumur is also famous for its sparkling white *crémant de Loire*, which rivals champagne in taste and beats it hands down in price.

HIGHLIGHTS OF THE LOIRE VALLEY

■ **Chenonceau** (p. 568), near Tours, and **Chambord** (p. 559), near Blois, rival each other in architectural grace and surrounding natural beauty.

■ With serious wine and mushrooms, silk, and equestrians, scenic **Saumur** rests peacefully on the south bank of the Loire (p. 573).

■ Some of the best-preserved **Roman walls** in France prop up the picturesque medieval *vieille ville* of **Le Mans** on the river Sarthe (p. 582).

■ Light streams through the stained glass depictions of Joan of Arc and the Hundred Years' War in the **Cathédrale Ste-Croix** of **Orléans** (p. 552).

GETTING AROUND

Faced with such widespread grandeur, many travelers plan over-ambitious itineraries that result in hazy memories of highways and big stone houses. Two châteaux a day is a good limit. Trains don't reach many châteaux, and those that do are scheduled inconveniently. Tours, connected to 12 châteaux, is the region's best rail hub. Many stations distribute the useful booklets *Les Châteaux de la Loire en Train Été '00* and *Châteaux pour Train et Vélo*, with train schedules, distances, and information on bike and car rental. Of the châteaux included in *Let's Go*, Sully-sur-Loire, Chambord, Cheverny, Beauregard, and Ussé are *not* accessible by train. Bikes are the best way to see this flat but beautiful region. Distances between châteaux and hostels tend to be short, and many small roads cut through fields of brilliant poppies and sunflowers. The Michelin map of the region and tourist office biking guides will steer you away from truck-laden highways and onto delightful country roads. Alternatives include buses, cars, or tour bus circuits that require the purchase of half-day or full-day passes. A group of four renting a car can generally undercut tour bus prices. Nature buffs should request the excellent (and free) bilingual booklet *Loisirs and Randonnées of the Val de Loire* from local tourist offices. This has information on regional hiking and biking paths, canoe trips, and horse-riding areas, as well as contact information for outdoor activities from rock climbing to parachuting.

ORLÉANS

Orléans (pop. 200,000), with its fairy-tale castle, expansive vineyards, and rich forests, has been besieged by jealous foreigners for millennia. Bishop Aignan barely withstood Atilla the Hun's onslaught in 451, while a thousand years later Joan of Arc drove out English invaders during the Hundred Years' War. German attacks in 1870 and 1940 succeeded only temporarily; a new wave of Parisian commuters has been able to penetrate this once impregnable town. Today, fast-paced Orléans still finds time to celebrate its history. Sights, *brasserie*-lined *places*, a lively shopping district, and intimate cafés and restaurants breathe life into the ancient traditions of this 2000-year-old city.

Orléans
ACCOMMODATIONS
A Hôtel de Paris
B Hôtel Bannier
C Hôtel Blois
D Camping
E Auberge de Jeunesse (HI)

ORIENTATION AND PRACTICAL INFORMATION

Most places of interest in Orléans are on the north bank of the Loire, a five-minute walk south of the Gare d'Orléans. From the *gare*, ascend the escalator into the mall and turn right. As you exit the mall, the tourist office will be on your left and **rue de la République** will stretch ahead of you, leading to the bustling **pl. du Martroi** and the *centre ville*. At pl. du Martroi, rue de la République becomes **rue Royale** and runs to the river, intersecting **rue de Bourgogne** and **rue Jeanne d'Arc,** two pedestrian-dominated streets where most sights, restaurants, and bars are located.

Trains: Gare d'Orléans and **Gare Les-Aubrais.** Most trains make both stops, but a few longer routes only stop at Les-Aubrais. **Gare d'Orléans**, pl. Albert 1er (tel. 02 38 62 27 04), is centrally located and better for tourists. To: **Blois** (30min., 12 per day, 104F); **Tours** (1hr., 12 per day, 178F); **Paris** (1¼hr., 4am-10pm about 3 per hr., 180F); and **Nantes** (2hr., M-F 3 per day, 376F). Info office open M-Sa 9am-7:30pm. Ticket booths open daily 5:30am-9pm. **Gare Les-Aubrais**, rue Pierre Semard (tel. 02 38 79 91 00), is a 30min. walk north from the *centre ville*. A free train shuttles new arrivals stranded at Les-Aubrais from *quai* 2 to Gare d'Orléans. The reverse journey costs 7F.

Buses: The **bus station,** 2 rue Marcel Proust (tel. 02 38 53 94 75), is connected to the Gare d'Orléans by an overpass. **Les Rapides du Val de Loire** (tel. 02 38 61 90 00) and **TransBeauce** (tel. 02 37 18 59 00, in Chartres) run to **Chartres** (2hr., 3 per day, 1 on Su, 68F, under 20 34F) and **Blois** (1½hr., 1 per day M-Sa, 50F). Info desk open M-Tu and Th 10am-1pm and 4-7pm, W and F 10am-1pm and 3-7pm, and Sa 10am-1pm.

Local Transportation: SEMTAO, 2 rue de la Hallebarde (tel. 02 38 78 01 20), off pl. du Martroi. Line "S" goes from pl. Albert to the university and Parc Floral until 12:30am.

Tickets 7.80F (good for 1hr.), *carnet* of 10 67F, 1-week pass 69F. Free city bus map available here and at tourist office.

Taxis: Taxi Radio d'Orléans, rue St-Yves (tel. 02 38 91 45 10). 24hr.

Car Rental: Ecoto, 19 av. Paris (tel. 02 38 77 92 92). From 91F per day plus 1F per km.

Bike and Scooter Rental: CAD, 95 fbg Bannier (tel. 02 38 81 23 00). Scooters 170F per day. Open M-Sa 9am-noon and 2-7pm. The closest place to rent bikes is **Kit Loisirs,** 1720 Marcel Belot (tel. 02 38 63 44 34), in nearby Olivet, 15min. on bus A (direction "Foch") to "Pressoir Aubry:" Bikes 70-100F per day. 1100F deposit. Open M-F 10am-12:30pm and 2-6pm, Sa-Su 9am-7pm. Call ahead M-F.

Tourist Office: Pl. Albert 1er (tel. 02 38 24 05 05; fax 02 38 54 49 84; www.tourism-loiret.com). Ask for the free *Orléans Poche*. Info-packed maps (2F) and excellent *vieille ville* walking tour guide. Extensive tours free-35F, students and children free-17.50F. Tours of upper sections of cathedral 25F, ages 11-15 15F. **Currency exchange.** Open July-Aug. M-Sa 9am-7pm, Su 9:30am-12:30pm and 3-6:30pm; Apr.-June and Sept. M-Sa 9am-7pm, Su 10am-noon; Oct.-Mar. M-Sa 9am-6:30pm, Su 10am-noon.

Money: Banks, including the best-deal **Banque de France,** are on rue de la République and pl. du Martroi.

English Bookstore: Librairie Loddé, 41 rue Jeanne d'Arc (tel. 02 38 65 43 43), left of rue Royale. Good selection. Open M 2-7pm, Tu-Sa 9am-12:30pm and 2-7pm. V, MC.

Youth Information: Centre Régional d'Information Jeunesse (CRIJ), 5 bd. de Verdun (tel. 02 38 78 91 78). Info on jobs and sports, plus tickets for local events, and ISIC cards. Open Tu and F 10am-noon and 1-6pm, W 10am-6pm, Th 1-6pm, Sa 2-6pm.

Budget Travel: Espace Voyage (tel. 02 38 78 91 79), inside the CRIJ, offers cheap student bus and rail tickets, including BIJ. Same hours as CRIJ, closed W noon-1pm.

Laundromat: Laverie, 26 rue du Poirier. Open daily 7am-10pm. **Val de France,** 13 rue Notre-Dame de Recouvrance. Open daily 8am-9pm.

Police: 63 rue du Fbg St-Jean (tel. 02 38 81 63 00).

Hospital: Centre Hospitalier Régional, 1 rue Porte Madeleine (tel. 02 38 51 44 44).

Post Office: Pl. du Général de Gaulle (tel. 02 38 77 35 14). **Currency exchange.** Open M-F 8am-7pm, Sa 8am-noon. **Branch offices:** rue St-Yves, 3min. from Gare d'Orléans, and pl. Dubois. Both open M-F 8am-6:30pm, Sa 8am-noon. **Postal code:** 45000.

Internet Access: Médiathèque, pl. Gambetta (tel. 02 38 76 45 45). 3 free computers in the *salle multimédia*. Expect 30min. wait. Open July-Aug. Tu and F 1-7pm, W, Th, and Sa 1-6pm; Sept.-June Tu and F 11am-7pm, W 10am-6pm, Th 2-6pm, Sa 11am-6pm. **Odysseus cybercafé,** 32 rue du Colombier (tel. 02 38 77 98 48). No wait, but 30F per hour. Open M-W 9am-9pm, Th-Sa 9am-1am.

◤ ACCOMMODATIONS AND CAMPING

Inexpensive hotels are hard to find in Orléans; the few that exist are spread throughout the city. They fill up by early evening in July and August; call ahead.

Auberge de Jeunesse (HI), 1 bd. de la Motte (tel. 02 38 53 60 03). **Will open April 2000.** Although it sits by the highway, the hostel is surrounded by a green park and is just 10 minutes from the cathedral and the lively Bourgogne neighborhood. From place d'Arc, bus "RS" (direction "Rosette") or "SY" (direction "Concyr/La Bolière") will get you to "Pont Bourgogne" (7.50F, until 8pm). Once off the bus, follow the boulevard straight down; the hostel is at the end on your right. 70 beds in 2-4 person rooms. Kitchen facilities and bike storage. 61F. Sheets 16F. Breakfast 18F.

Hôtel de Paris, 29 bd. du Fbg Bannier (tel. 02 38 53 39 58). Thirteen light, simple, renovated rooms in a pleasant area off of pl. Gambetta. The friendly NY owner loves to talk. *Brasserie* on the ground floor. Singles 130-150F; doubles 145-180F; triples 240F. Extra bed 40F. Breakfast 25F. V, MC, AmEx.

Hôtel Bannier, 13 rue du Fbg Bannier (tel. 02 38 53 25 86). Just off pl. Gambetta, 19 bargain rooms await above a bar full of old men hovering over afternoon beers. Although the hallways smell of the bar, the rooms are surprisingly nice. Singles 110-155F; doubles 135-195F; triples 210F; quads 235F. Showers 15F, but haul out *Let's Go* and you may find yourself singing in the rain for free. V, MC.

Hôtel de Blois, 1 av. de Paris (tel. 02 38 62 61 61). Twenty-one rooms above a bar across from the train station. Don't expect luxury or quiet from what might be the cheapest hotel in town. Singles and doubles 95F, with shower 130F, with shower and toilet 145F. Breakfast 25F. V, MC.

Campsites: Camping Municipal Gaston Mar and **Chemin de Halage** (tel. 02 38 88 39 39), just off av. Georges Clemenceau (RN 152), 3 km. west of Orléans. Turn left onto rue du Duc d'Antin leaving the city. Riverside sites. 45F for up to 3 people. Extra adult 18F, child 10F. Electricity 18F. Reception May-Sept. daily 6:30am-noon and 4-6pm.

FOOD

In late summer and autumn, locals feast on *gibier* (game), freshly procured in the nearby forests. During the rest of the year, indulge in *pâté d'alouettes* (lark pâté), *saumon à l'oseille* (salmon in sorrel), and *sandre* (pike-perch). Orléans' most important culinary contribution is its tangy wine vinegars, which you can taste on salads and in marinades at many local *brasseries*. The local cheeses are *frinault cendré*, a savory relation of Camembert, and a mild *chèvre*. Wash it all down with *Gris Meunier* or *Auvergnat* wines, or nearby Olivet's pear and cherry brandies.

Les Halles Châtelet, pl. du Châtelet, is an indoor **market** attached to Galeries Lafayette (open Tu-Su 7am-7pm). The biggest **supermarket** is massive **Carrefour,** usurping the back of the mall at pl. d'Arc. (Open M-Sa 8:30am-9pm. V, MC.) Other options include **Monoprix,** 46 rue du Fbg Bannier, down the road from pl. Gambetta (open M-Th 8:30am-12:45pm and 2:30-7:30pm, F 8:30am-8pm, Sa 8:30am-7pm; V, MC) and **Petit Casino,** 15 rue Jeanne d'Arc and 82 rue Bannier, between pl. du Martroi and pl. Gambetta (open M-Sa 8:30am-8pm; V, MC). For eating out, pedestrian **rue de Bourgogne** offers an unbeatable ambience with its endless string of affordable *brasseries*, pizzerias, and bars.

La Chancellerie, 95 rue Royale (tel. 02 38 53 57 54), on pl. Martroi. A wonderful place to enjoy good food and take in the busting *place*. Special *Soirées a Thème* (60-75F) reward takers with a scrumptious *plat* and a glass of wine. The *plats* (75-135F) may top your budget, but vegetarians will light up at the sight of the generous 22F sandwiches and 31-55F salads. Open M-Sa noon-2pm and 7-11pm. V, MC.

Le Brin de Zinc, 62 rue Ste-Catherine (tel. 02 38 53 38 77). A classic French bar and *brasserie*. A young crowd and competent staff is complemented by kitschy bric-a-brac decor. Gourmet salads 55-62F, *plats* 59-78F. *Formules* featuring the *plat du jour* start at 75F. Open daily noon-2:30pm and 7-11:30pm. V, MC.

La Brasserie, 1 rue de Gourville (tel. 02 38 62 51 42), off rue de la République. Large salads (47-53F) and *tartes flambées* (pizzas with *crêpe*-thin crusts, 49-57F) are the main options on the vegetarian- and child-friendly restaurant. Lively young crowd at night. Open daily noon-2:30pm and 7pm-midnight. V, MC, AmEx.

SIGHTS

Most of Orléans' historic and architectural features are near **pl. Ste-Croix.** In 1429, having liberated the *orléanais* from a seven-month siege by the English, Joan of Arc triumphantly marched down nearby rue de Bourgogne, the city's oldest street; the scene is vividly captured in *Jeanne d'Arc*, at the Musée des Beaux-Arts. But don't neglect to venture out of this central area to poke your head inside the 11th- to 15th- century churches spread throughout the city; the **Église St-Paterne,** pl. Gambetta, is a particularly massive showcase of modern stained glass.

CATHÉDRALE STE-CROIX. With towering Gothic buttresses, an intricate façade, and dramatic vertical emphases in the interior, the cathedral is the most prominent edifice in Orléans. Outside, the immaculately cleaned northwest façade gives visitors an idea of the cathedral's original luminosity; inside, the *maison de Dieu* pays a bit more attention to Joan of Arc than it does its patron saint. On May 8, 1429, the fiery-eyed child came into Ste-Croix to join the first procession of thanks for the deliverance of the town from the English. In her honor, a series of 19th-century stained glass windows in the nave depict her life's story, down to the flames that consumed her. Flags bearing the emblems of her companions—including Charles of Orléans and the Maréchal de Boussac—line the main aisle. *(Pl. Ste-Croix. Open daily 9:15am-noon and 2:15-7pm; closes 6pm May, June, and Sept.; closes 5pm Oct.-Apr. Free. Tours of the upper sections of the cathedral are organized by the tourist office.)*

MUSÉE DES BEAUX-ARTS. This fine, five-floor collection of Italian, Flemish, and French works displays painting, sculpture, and *objets d'art* from the 15th to the 20th century. An exceptional *salle des primitifs* awaits on the second floor, while the first floor holds a large aggregation of 18th-century French portraits. For a splash of modernity, head down to the basement, which keeps canvases by Miró, Monet, Picasso, and Renoir, as well as photographs of Picasso by Man Ray. Good modern art and archæological exhibitions breeze through regularly. *(1 rue Fernand Rabier, to the right as you exit the cathedral. Tel. 02 38 79 21 83. Open Th-Sa 10am-6pm, Tu and Su 11am-6pm, W 10am-8pm; closed first two M in May. 21.50F, students 11F, free under 16.)*

HÔTEL GROSLOT D'ORLÉANS. Built in 1550 by bailiff Jacques Groslot, this Renaissance mansion served as the king's Orléans residence for two centuries. In 1560, François II died here amid scandal after opening the Estates Général; Charles IX, Henri III, and Henri IV were also guests here. Now an annex to the town hall, the *hôtel* opens its sumptuously decorated rooms and romantic garden to the public and the occasional wedding. *(Pl. de l'Étape. Tel. 02 38 79 22 30. Open June-Sept. Su-F 9am-7:30pm, Sa 4:30-9pm; Oct.-Dec. Su-F 10am-noon and 2-6pm, Sa 4:30-6pm; Jan.-May 10am-noon and 2-6pm, Sa 4:30-6pm. Free English tours.)*

MAISON DE JEANNE D'ARC. Off pl. du Martroi, the *maison* explains Orléans' passion for its favorite liberator. This reconstruction of the original house where the medieval *mademoiselle* stayed, modified after a 1940 bombing raid, consists of fragments of other 15th-century houses. Using period costumes and suits of armor, the museum details the life of Joan and the history of her times. *(3 pl. de Gaulle. Tel. 02 38 52 99 89. Open Tu-Su 10am-noon and 2-6pm May-Oct.; Nov.-Apr. 2-6pm. 14F, students 7F, under 16 free.)*

MUSÉE HISTORIQUE ET ARCHÉOLOGIQUE DE L'ORLÉANAIS. The city's historical and archæological collections are presented in a *petite* Renaissance mansion, constructed around 1550 by Philippe Cabu, lawyer of the Châtelet d'Orléans. The treasure of Neuvy-en-Sullias, a remarkable set of Gallo-Roman statues discovered in 1861, is on display on the ground floor, while the next floor up displays relics from the Middle Ages to the Neo-Classical period. The top floor houses the historical "a day in the life" regional collection, including local tidbits, clocks, and gold and silverware. *(Sq. Abbé Desnoyers. Tel. 02 38 79 21 59. Open July-Aug. Tu-Su 10am-6pm; May-Jun. and Sept. Tu-Su 2-6pm; Oct.-Apr. W and Sa-Su 2-6pm. 15F, students 7F, under 16 free.)*

♫ ✺ ENTERTAINMENT AND FESTIVALS

ENTERTAINMENT. Many *orléanais* head to Paris for action, but the bars along **rue Bannier** and **rue de Bourgogne** keep the home front happy. **Paxton's Head,** 264 rue de Bourgogne (tel. 02 38 81 23 29), features live jazz on Saturday nights in a jolly British pub. For an expatriate thrill, order your drinks in English. (15-80F. Open daily 3pm-3am. V, MC.) By contrast, billiards (35-50F) is the only thing vaguely British about the laid-back **Bar Darlington**, 3 rue du Colombier (tel. 02 38 54 67 98), off rue Bannier. (Open daily 3pm-3am. V, MC.) Dancers move it to **George V**, Les

Halles Châtelet (tel. 02 38 53 08 79), on the corner of rue Ducereau and pl. du Châtelet. (50F cover including first drink. Open daily 10:30pm-5am. V, MC, AmEx.) **Select-Studios,** 45 rue Jeanne d'Arc (tel. 08 36 68 69 25), shows a few first-run English movies and French films (30F).

FESTIVALS. The last week of June and the first week of July see a **jazz festival** (tickets 135F). On weekends in November and December, the **Semaines Musicales Internationales d'Orléans (SMIO)** brings in the Orchestre National de France.

BEAUGENCY

The cobbled streets of Beaugency (pop. 7000), 35km southwest of Orléans, as well as the town's strategically important Loire bridge, have survived the Hundred Years' War, the Wars of Religion, and World War II.

In spite of his unfortunate name, the Bastard of Orléans (the illegitimate Jean d'Orléans) became Joan of Arc's valued companion in arms. In 1440, he rebuilt the **Château Dunois,** which now houses the impressive **Musée Régional de l'Orléanais** (tel. 02 38 44 55 23). The museum displays artifacts, clothing, and prints from 15th-century Orléans as well as regional archæological remains. (Open Apr.-Sept. W-M 10am-noon and 2-6:30pm; Oct.-Mar. W-M 10am-noon and 2-5pm. Free hourly tours in French July-Aug. 10-11am and 2-5pm; rest of year 2-5pm only. 22F, students 16F.) Next to the château, the 11th-century **Tour de César** stands 36m tall; funds have never been raised to restore the interior, which was ravaged by fire in 1567.

In 1152, the **Église Notre-Dame,** across from the château, hosted the Church Council that ended the marriage of Louis VII and Eleanor of Aquitaine on grounds of consanguinity. The Council unwittingly freed her to marry an equally close cousin, Henry Plantagenêt, six weeks later (see p. 8). The church's small, dazzling *vitraux* sprinkle yellow and blue light on massive columns. Uphill from the church rises the 16th-century **St-Firmin steeple** and **porch;** peek inside the porch for a glimpse of the worn gothic façade with four coats of arms.

Beaugency has a number of relatively cheap regional restaurants. At **Les Quatres Saisons,** 17 rue de la Maille d'Or (tel. 02 38 46 41 21), the selections on the traditional *menu du jour* (70F) or *plat du jour* (40F) range from fowl to seafood. (Open Tu-Sa noon-2pm and 7-9:30pm, Su lunch only. V, MC.) **Au Pont,** 1 rue de Pont (tel. 02 38 44 53 67), offers a menu chock full of salads (16-58F), pasta (42-56F), pizza (42-59F), *plats* (79-82F), *crêpes* (13-24F), and ice cream (20-38F). (Open daily noon-2pm and 7-10pm. V, MC.) Vendors at the **outdoor market,** pl. St-Martroi, hawk fresh fish, *fromage de chèvre* (goat cheese), and regional wines (Sa).

If Beaugency is more than a daytrip for you, head for the **Auberge de Jeunesse (HI),** 2km out of town at 152 route de Châteaudun (tel. 02 38 44 61 31; fax 02 38 44 14 73). From Château Dunois, follow rue de Pont away from the river and turn right onto rue Nationale at the first light. Go down two blocks, turn left on rue de Châteaudun, and follow it for 1.5km (30min.). The hostel will be on your right, with rooms for couples and families, excellent kitchen facilities, and living rooms with fireplaces. **Bike rental** is also available at the hostel. (52F. Sheets 18F. Breakfast 20F. Dinner 50F. Bikes 50F per day.) In town, **Hôtel des Vieux Fosses,** 4 rue des Vieux Fosses (tel. 02 38 44 51 65; fax 02 38 46 45 05), keeps 12 pleasant rooms just off pl. Martoi. (Singles and doubles 120-220F. Reception M-Sa 7:30am-9:30pm. V, MC.) Campers can pitch their tents on lovely Loire-side sites at the **Camping Municipal le Val de Flux.** (Tel. 02 38 44 50 39; fax 02 38 46 49 10. 12F per adult, 16F per site. Reception 9am-noon and 4-8pm. Open Mar.-Sept.)

The **tourist office,** 3 pl. de l'Hôtel de Ville (tel. 02 38 44 54 42; fax 02 38 46 45 31), has info and fabulous free maps of the area. (Open July-Aug. M-Sa 9:30am-6:30pm and Su 10am-noon; Sept.-June M-Sa 9:30am-12:30pm and 2:30-6:30pm.) You can **rent bikes** at Cycles Duvallet, 28 rue du Chat qui Dort. (Tel. 02 38 44 52 72. 50F per day. Passport deposit. Open Tu-Sa 9am-noon and 2:30-7pm.) **Canoe** and **kayak rental** is available from Loisirs Eaux Vives, 21 rue Porte Tavers. (Tel. 02 54 81 17 78 or 06 68 10 37 58. Kayaks 30F per hour, 80F per half-day, 100F per day. Canoes 30F per person per hour, 150F per half-day, 180F per day. Open Tu and Th-Su 9am-noon and 2-7pm.) The **post office** is at 11 rue des Chevaliers. (Tel. 02 38 44 52 00. Open M-F 8:30am-12:30pm and 1:30-5:30pm, Sa 8:30am-noon. **Postal code:** 45190.)

Trains run from rue de la Gare (tel. 02 38 44 50 28) to **Blois** (20min., 8 per day, 33F) and **Orléans** (20min., 8 per day, 30F). (Open daily 6am-10pm.) To get to the tourist office, walk down rue de la Gare. Just past the traffic lights, turn right onto rue Maille d'Or. At pl. du Martroi, turn left onto rue de l'Ours. At Le Balto Tabac, turn left, and then right into the *place* across from the post office; the tourist office is on the right (5min.).

GERMIGNY, ST-BENOÎT, AND SULLY

A day's beautiful drive eastward along the Loire takes in these three small towns, each featuring a secular or sacred site from a different era of the Middle Ages. About 30km southeast of Orléans lies the squat Carolingian church of **Germigny-des-Près** (tel. 02 38 58 27 97), heavily restored but nonetheless the oldest in France. The private chapel was designed by an Armenian and preserves a 9th-century Byzantine-style mosaic, also restored, depicting the Ark of the Covenant. Call to request a tour in French. (Open daily 8:30am-7pm; Oct.-Mar. 8:30am-6pm. Free.)

The prize of **St-Benoît-sur-Loire** (tel. 02 38 35 72 43), 35km southeast of Orléans, is an 11th- to 12th-century Romanesque basilica. Built to receive the relics of St. Benedict (480-547), the church was originally part of the Abbaye de Fleury, which was destroyed during the French Revolution. The church today holds a stunning 11th-century Romanesque mosaic floor in the choir, transported in 1531. In a breathtaking architectural feat, carved capitals grace the exterior porch tower, the interior nave and upper sanctuary, and the entire curved wall of the choir, the latter in a triple layer of more than 75 arched pillars supporting the barrel vault. Twice daily, sung services set the whole church ringing. (Masses M-Sa noon, Su 11am; vespers daily 6:30pm. Church open daily 7am-10pm. Guided visits in French 10-11am and 3-5pm Tu-Sa, Su 3-5pm only. Call ahead for English tours, 20F.)

The 14th-century fortress of **Sully-sur-Loire** (tel. 02 38 36 36 86) lies 42km from Orléans, dominating the countryside from the southern bank of the Loire. Guarding the intersection of four major roads, this château required three drawbridges to protect the main residence. The heavy white-turreted castle has housed a somnolent Charles VII, a frustrated Joan of Arc, a hunted Louis XIV, and an exiled Voltaire. (Open June 15-Sept. 15 10am-6pm; May 1-June 14 and Sept. 16-Oct. 31 10am-noon and 2-6pm; Mar.-Apr. and Nov. 10am-noon and 2-5pm. Closed Dec.-Feb. Hours may vary in June. English tours July 12-Aug. 16 M at 1:30pm. 29F, students and children 19F.) Sully's sprawling, grassy grounds and wooded pathways are perfect for picnics, walks, and June concerts, whose past performers have included Ray Charles and B.B. King. (Park open daily May-Sept. 9am-10pm; Oct.-Apr. 9am-6pm. Free.) **Camping Sully-sur-Loire,** chemin de la Salle Verte (tel. 02 38 36 23 93), surveys the château from the riverbank. (7.50F per site, 12.10F per person, under 8 6F, 5.50F per car. Electricity 9-12F.) The **tourist office** (tel. 02 38 36 23 70; fax 02 38 36 32 21) is located in the center of town on pl. de Gaulle. (Open July-Aug. M 9am-12:30pm and 2-6:30pm, Tu-F 9am-12:30pm and 2-7pm, Sa 9am-7pm, Su 10:30am-1pm; rest of year same but Sa 9am-12:30pm and 2-7pm.)

The same **bus** from **Orléans** serves the three towns (**Germigny** 45min., 45F; **St-Benoît** 50min., 47F; **Sully** 1hr., 57F), but times are subject to change. Although bus travel between the towns is difficult, St-Benoît to Germigny is only a 45-minute walk, while a trek from Sully to St-Benoît takes about 75 minutes. The adventurous may choose to make the challenging 45km **bike ride** to Sully from Orléans; the scenic route winds along the south bank of the Loire and passes tiny villages and sunflower fields along the way. **Driving,** take eastbound 152, which becomes the D955, in the direction of Châteauneuf-sur-Loire; signs point you to the D60, which will take you to the towns.

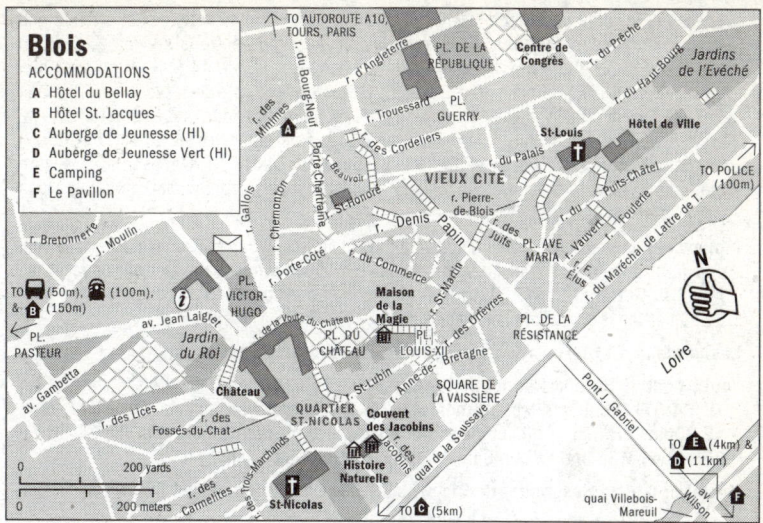

Blois
ACCOMMODATIONS
A Hôtel du Bellay
B Hôtel St. Jacques
C Auberge de Jeunesse (HI)
D Auberge de Jeunesse Vert (HI)
E Camping
F Le Pavillon

BLOIS

Blois (pop. 55,000) relishes its position as a gateway to the Loire Valley and welcomes over half a million visitors every year. Blois' own château has been the setting for important historical events, from the influential to the scandalous. Recent restoration projects have made the town even more luminous, while blue slate roofs, red brick chimneys, and narrow cobblestone lanes evoke the simple beauty of the villages painted by Vermeer. Just as alluring are the culinary pleasures that can be found in local *pâtisseries*, preserving the flavor of lost centuries with rich *blésian* chocolate. When you've had your fill of this delicacy, Chambord and Cheverny are just an hour's bike trip or a 20-minute bus ride away.

🛈 ORIENTATION AND PRACTICAL INFORMATION

The train station is five to ten minutes north of the château and the town center. Exiting the station, go straight down av. Jean Laigret; the tourist office is on the left near the bottom of the hill before sq. Augustin-Thierry. The *centre ville* is three minutes further. The **rue Porte-Côté** leads to the bustling café-lined pedestrian quarter. When in doubt, descend, as all roads go down to the *centre ville*.

Trains: Pl. de la Gare. To: **Orléans** (30min., 14 per day, 53F); **Tours** (1hr., 10 per day, 53F); **Paris** via Orléans (1¾hr., 8 per day, 123F); **Angers** via Tours (3hr., 10 per day, 115F). Info office open daily 9am-6:30pm.

Buses: Point Bus, 2 pl. Victor Hugo (tel. 02 54 78 15 66). Info on buses to châteaux and the following lines. Open M 1:30-6pm, Tu-F 8am-12:15pm and 1:30-6pm, Sa 9am-12:15pm and 1:30-4:30pm. **Transports Loir-et-Cher (TLC)** sends buses to nearby châteaux and **Vendôme** (1¼hr., 4 per day, 35F). **Transport Boutet** heads south to **Châteauroux** (2½hr., 2 per day, 73F). Buses leave from the station and pl. Victor Hugo.

Taxis: Taxis Radio, pl. de la Gare (tel. 02 54 78 07 65). 24hr.

Bike Rental: Atelier Cycles, 44 levée des Tuileries (tel. 02 54 74 30 13), about 1km down the river from the *centre ville*, near the "Verdun" bus stop on line #4. 30-80F per day. Passport deposit. Open daily 9am-9pm.

Tourist Office: 3 av. Jean Laigret (tel. 02 54 90 41 41; fax 02 54 90 41 49; www.chambordcountry.com), in Anne de Bretagne's Renaissance pavilion. The walking tour map in

English is invaluable. Complete info on châteaux, including tickets for bus circuits and shows. **Currency exchange**, 35F commission. Accommodations service 12F. Open May-Sept. M-Sa 9am-7pm, Su and holidays 10am-7pm; Oct.-Apr. M-Sa 9am-12:30pm and 2-6pm, Su 9:30am-12:30pm. V, MC. **Branch office**, pl. de la Voute du Château (tel. 02 54 74 70 63), tucked underneath the château, provides info and hotel reservations. Open July-Aug. daily 10am-7pm. Around the corner, **Maison du Loir-et-Cher**, 5 rue de la Voûte du Château (tel. 02 54 78 55 50; fax 02 54 74 81 79), provides information and piles of brochures on regional events, festivals, lodging, and camping. Open daily Apr.-Oct. 9am-7pm; Nov.-Mar. 9am-noon and 2-6pm.

Money: In July and Aug., stores displaying the *No Francs, No Problem* sign accept currencies from dollars to yen at no commission—but check rates. **Banque de France**, 4 av. Jean Laigret (tel. 02 54 55 44 00), is on the right as you walk down the hill to the tourist office. **Currency exchange** available Tu-Sa 8:45am-12:15pm.

Laundromat: 11 pl. Louis XII (tel. 02 54 74 89 82). Open 7am-10pm.

Youth Center: Bureau Information Jeunesse de Loir-et-Cher, 7 av. Wilson (tel. 02 54 78 54 87) Brochures, employment advice, and cheap train tickets. Open M-F 9am-12:30pm. **Branch** in Bibliothèque Abbé Grégoire, pl. Jean Jaurès (tel. 02 54 56 16 66). Open M-Tu and F noon-6pm, W 10am-6:30pm, Sa 10am-6pm.

Hospital: Centre Hospitalier de Blois, Mail Pierre Charlot (tel. 02 54 55 66 33).

Police: 42 quai St-Jean (tel. 02 54 55 17 99).

Post Office: 5 rue Gallois (tel. 02 54 44 68 58). **Currency exchange.** Open M-F 8am-6:30pm, Sa 8am-noon. **Postal code:** 41000.

Internet: Best rates at **Bibliothèque Abbé Grégoire,** pl. Jean Jaurès (tel. 02 54 56 27 40). 2F per 5min. Open M-Tu and F 1-6:30pm, W 10am-6:30pm, Sa 10am-6pm.

▚ ACCOMMODATIONS AND CAMPING

The two hostels, while charmingly rustic and as budget as budget can be, are quite far out of town. If you're willing to sacrifice *francs* for convenience, affordable hotels cling to the fringes of the *centre ville*. The tourist office will find you a hotel for a fee, but call a few days ahead in July and August to ensure yourself a spot.

Auberge de Jeunesse (HI), 18 rue de l'Hôtel Pasquier (tel./fax 02 54 78 27 21), 5km west of Blois in green Les Grouets. From the tourist office, follow rue Porte Côté, bear right onto rue Denis Papin down to the river, and take bus #4 (direction "Les Grouets") to the end of the line (10min.). Follow the signs to the auberge. 2 single-sex dorms, each with 24 beds in a pretty, shady country-type setting. Excellent kitchen facilities and hot showers in bathroom complex outside. First night 61F, further nights 44F. Breakfast 19F. Reception 6:45-10am and 6-10:30pm. Lockout 10am-6pm. Curfew 10:30pm. Open Mar.-Nov. 15.

Auberge de Jeunesse Verte (HI), levée de la Loire (tel. 02 38 44 61 31; fax 02 38 44 14 73), off D951 in Montlivault, 11km east of Blois. Take the TLC bus #1 (direction "Beaugency," 22.40F) from the station and ask the driver to drop you off by the Auberge de Jeunesse in Montlivault. Cross the highway in front of you, follow the dirt road into the field, and take a sharp left at the small FUAJ sign at the bottom. The hostel is 50m ahead under a clump of trees to the right. Convenient for Chambord visitors, this rustic old stone lodging is flanked by fields of sunflowers. Inside, over 40 beds await in clean, painted dorms; bright bathrooms, kitchen facilities, and a fireplace make you feel right at home. 45F. Camping 27F. Sleeping bags or sheets 17F. Open July-Aug. only. "Reception" (loosely interpreted) until about 10:30am and 6-9pm.

Le Pavillon, 2 av. Wilson (tel. 02 54 74 23 27; fax 02 54 74 03 36), just across the bridge and overlooking the Loire. Bustling neighborhood surrounds this corner hotel with pretty, bright rooms. Singles and doubles 115-135F; doubles with TV and bath 220F; quads 280F. Extra bed 60F. Showers 15F. Breakfast 30F. V, MC, AmEx.

Hôtel St-Jacques, 7 rue Ducoux (tel. 02 54 78 04 15; fax 02 54 78 33 05), to the right as you exit the station. Big, light rooms above a friendly bar. **Bikes** 80F per day. Singles 130-215F; doubles 140-225F; triples 265F. Showers 15F. Breakfast 27F. V, MC.

Hôtel du Bellay, 12 rue des Minimes (tel. 02 54 78 23 62; fax 02 54 78 52 04), at the top of porte Chartraine, 2min. above the *centre ville*. Family-run establishment offers cozy, carpeted rooms overlooking a quiet back street. Singles 130-170F; doubles 135-185F; triples 240F; quads 280F. Breakfast 25F. Call ahead. V, MC, AmEx.

Campsite: Lac de Loire (tel. 02 54 78 82 05; fax 02 54 78 62 03). From the Blois station or *centre ville*, take bus #3c to "Mairie Vineuil" (6.90F). Two sites in one. 2-star site: 45F per person plus tent; 4-star site: 80F per person plus tent. 15F per extra person, 10F per child. Open Apr.-Oct. 15. V, MC.

◗ FOOD

Blois coats its citizens in chocolate. Locals have been perfecting *le chocolat blésois* ever since Catherine de Médici introduced *pâtissiers* from Italy. Sumptuous *pavé du roi* (chocolate-almond cookies) and *malices du loup* (orange peels in chocolate) peer invitingly from *pâtisseries* along **rue Denis Papin.** For those who cling to the dinner-before-dessert convention, tourist traps jostle homespun restaurants along **rue St-Lubin** and around **pl. Poids du Roi** near the cathedral. *Boulangeries* and fruit stands lie in the central pedestrian area. A **Co-op supermarket** can be found on 15 rue Porte Cote by pl. Victor Hugo. (Open M-Sa 8:30am-7:30pm, Su 9am-12:30pm.) For serious shopping, **Intermarché supermarket** is at 16 av. Gambetta. (Tel. 02 54 42 42 00. Open M-Th 9am-12:30pm and 3-7:15pm, F-Sa 9am-7:15pm. V, MC, AmEx.) Pl. Louis XII sees an open-air **market** (Sa morning), while a *marché gourmand* sets up in pl. du Château (July-Aug. Th 2:30-7pm).

◗ **La Mesa,** 11 rue Vauvert (tel. 02 54 78 70 70), the favorite of four excellent restaurants tucked inside a secluded romantic courtyard. A never-ending choice of pizzas (25-50F), pastas (35-56F), salads (25-45F), meat *plats* (70F), and ice cream delights (25-32F). 75F 3-course *menu* features your choice of pizza or poultry specialty, while local wines make the food taste even better. Open daily noon-2pm and 7-11pm. V, MC.

Le Castelet, 40 rue St-Lubin (tel. 02 54 74 66 09; fax 02 54 56 18 77). Regional specialties from this little 16th-century house are affordable and delicious. *Formules* (66-152F) include an all vegetarian *menu* (93F) and one for children (50F). Specialties *à la carte* (48-74F) include fresh game in the autumnal hunting season. Open M-Tu and Th-Sa 7-10pm; July-Aug. also open W 7-10pm. V, MC.

Le Maidi, 42 rue St-Lubin (tel. 02 54 74 38 58). In a simple setting on intimate rue St-Lubin, this haven of Moroccan culinary magic serves up a generous and delicious 3-course *formule* (65F) featuring game, meat stews, or savory vegetarian couscous. North African and local wines provide a perfect complement. Open F-W noon-2pm and 6-11pm; July-Aug. also Th 6-11pm. V, MC.

◗ SIGHTS

CHÂTEAU DE BLOIS. Home to French monarchs Louis XII and François I, Blois' château was as influential in the late 15th and early 16th centuries as Versailles was in later years. François I (1494-1547), whose motto, "Nutrisco et extingo" (I feed on fire and I extinguish it), explains the abundance of carved and painted salamanders, invited artists and scientists to his court, including an aging Leonardo da Vinci, and enforced unprecedented respect for court women. Meticulously restored by 19th-century architect Félix Duban, the château displays the progression of French architecture from 13th-century medieval to 17th-century classical in its four distinct sections. *(Tel. 02 54 78 06 62. Open daily July-Aug. 9am-8pm, Mar. 15-June 30 and Sept. 9am-6:30pm, Oct. 1-Mar. 14 9am-12:30pm and 2-5:30pm. 35min. tours July-Aug. daily 11am-7pm; May-June and Sept. Sa-Su 2-6pm. 35F, students under 25 and ages 6-11 20F. Tours 30F, ages 2-12 20F. Call for info on special combination for château and the magic museum and/or the castle's own spectacular son et lumière show. V, MC.)*

THE NORTHWEST

CATHOLIC GUISE ARE EASY In its long spell as a royal residence, Blois saw its fair share of scandals and intrigue. The most famous is the murder of the duc de Guise, who was leader of the powerful Holy League, an alliance committed to stamping out the Protestant heresy in France. Trouble was, many Frenchmen, from dukes to peasants, had embraced the new religion, and King Henri III was none too keen on declaring war on his own people. When the king recognized a Protestant as the legitimate heir to the throne, de Guise was outraged. As he advanced on Paris, the unpopular king fled to Chartres and de Guise found himself in control of the capital. Emboldened, he called for a meeting of the Estates Général at Blois, which he stuffed with League supporters in the hope that they would depose the king and elect himself in his stead. As plots go, this was hardly of the most secret kind, and Henri had other plans for the duke. On the morning of December 23, 1588, following a meeting of the governing council, de Guise was invited to discuss some points in private with the king. On his way to the royal chamber, the king's bodyguard fell on the seven-foot duke with knives. When the drama was over, Henri stepped out from behind a tapestry and exclaimed coolly, "He looks even bigger dead than alive." The next day, the duke's brother was dispatched in a similar manner. Unfortunately for Henri, he didn't have long to enjoy his newly-won freedom; he himself was murdered by a monk eight months later. You can visit the scene of the duke's murder on your visit to the castle (see château below); the stabbing occurred in the King's Chamber, room no. 12.

CHÂTEAU MUSEUMS. Housed in the château are three excellent museums: the recently renovated **Musée de Beaux-Arts,** with a remarkable 16th-century portrait gallery in the former apartments of Louis XII; the **Musée d'Archéologie,** displaying locally-excavated glass and ceramics; and a **Musée Lapidaire,** preserving sculpted pieces from nearby 17th-century châteaux. *(Hours and prices same as château.)*

MAISON DE LA MAGIE. Recently opened in 1998 amid much hoopla, the museum provides performances and haunted house-like tricks; it even ejects dragon appendages out of its windows. The center is dedicated to the "master of all magicians," Blois-born Jean-Eugène Robert-Houdin. A later showman was so impressed by Houdin that he adopted his name—Houdini. *(1 pl. du Château. Tel. 02 54 55 26 26; fax 02 54 55 26 28. Open July-Aug. daily 10:30am-noon and 2-6:30pm; Apr.-June and Sept. Tu-Su 10am-noon and 2-6pm. Call for off-season hours. 45F, ages 6-11 32F.)*

VIEILLE VILLE. Though Blois holds its own in a land of monuments and cathedrals, you're likely to most enjoy and best remember the hilly streets and ancient staircases, all outlined on the tourist office's walking guide. **Rue St-Lubin** and **rue des Trois Marchands** are invitingly lined with bars and *boulangeries* en route to the 12th-century Abbaye St-Laumer, now the **Église St-Nicolas.** *(Open 7:30am-6pm.)* East of **rue Denis Papin** are the most beautiful streets of all, lined with timber-framed houses narrowing into intimate alleys and courtyards. The 12th- to 19th-century **Cathédrale St-Louis,** with a large 11th-century crypt, exhibits some fascinating mixed architecture thanks to centuries of additions. *(Open daily 7:30am-6pm.)* At sunset, cross the Loire and turn right onto quai Villebois Mareuil for a view of the château rising above the abodes of the commonfolk.

OTHER MUSEUMS. The **Musée de la Résistance, de la Déportation et de la Libération,** is not an easy museum to take in, even if it takes only 14 minutes to walk through it. *(1 pl. de la Grève. Tel. 02 54 56 07 02. Open Tu-Su 2:30-5:30pm. 15F, students and children 5F.)* The **Musée d'Histoire Naturelle** features minerals, flora, and fauna from the Loire region, plus tropical specimens. *(Past the château off rue Anne de Bretagne. Tel. 02 54 90 21 00. Open Tu-Su 2-6pm. 15F, students and children 5F.)* Next door in the Couvent des Jacobins, budding theologians can contemplate nirvana at the **Musée Diocésain des Arts Religieux,** which displays religious objects dating back to the 15th century. *(Tel. 02 54 78 17 14. Open Tu-Sa 2-6pm. Free.)*

Global
connection
with the AT&T
Network

AT&T
direct
service

Exploring the corners of the earth? We're with you. With the world's most powerful network, **AT&T Direct®** Service gives you fast, clear connections from more countries than anyone,* and the option of an English-speaking operator. All it takes is your AT&T Calling Card. And the planet is yours.

For a list of AT&T Access Numbers, take the attached wallet guide.

*Comparison to major U.S.-based carriers.

AT&T Access Numbers

Austria ●	0800-200-288
Albania ●	00-800-0010
Armenia ● ▲	8◆10111
Bahrain	800-000
Belgium ●	0-800-100-10
Bulgaria ▲	00-800-0010
Croatia	0800-220111
Czech Rep. ▲	00-42-000-101
Cyprus ●	080-90010
Denmark	8001-0010

Egypt ● (Cairo)	510-0200
(Outside Cairo)	02-510-0200
Estonia	800-800-1001
Finland ●	9800-100-10
France	0-800-99-0011
Germany	0800-2255-288
Greece ●	00-800-1311
Hungary ●	00-800-01111
Ireland ✓	1-800-550-000
Israel	1-800-94-94-949

Italy ●	172-1011
Luxembourg †	0-800-0111
Macedonia, F.Y.R. of ○	99-800-4288
Malta	0800-890-110
Monaco ●	800-90-288
Morocco	002-11-0011
Netherlands ●	0800-022-9111
Norway	800-190-11
Poland ● ▲	00-800-111-1111
Portugal ▲	0800-800-128
Romania ●	01-800-4288

Russia ● ▲	
(Moscow) ▶	755-5042
(St. Petersburg) ▶	325-5042
Saudi Arabia ◇	1-800-10
South Africa	0-800-99-0123
Spain	900-99-00-11
Sweden	020-799-111
Switzerland ●	0-800-89-0011
Turkey ●	00-800-12277
U.K. ▲ ❖	0800-89-0011
U.K. ▲ ❖	0500-89-0011
U.A. Emirates ●	800-121

FOR EASY CALLING WORLDWIDE

1. Just dial the AT&T Access Number for the country you are calling from.
2. Dial the phone number you're calling. *3.* Dial your card number.

For access numbers not listed ask any operator for **AT&T Direct®** Service. In the U.S. call 1-800-331-1140 for a wallet guide listing all worldwide AT&T Access Numbers.
Visit our Web site at: www.att.com/traveler
Bold-faced countries permit country-to-country calling outside the U.S.

●　Public phones require coin or card deposit.
▲　May not be available from every phone/payphone.
▶　Additional charges apply outside the city.
◇　Calling available to most countries.
◆　Await second dial tone.
✓　Use U.K. access number in N. Ireland.
❖　If call does not complete, use 0800-013-0011.
†　Collect calling from public phones.
○　Public phones require local coin payment through the call duration.

When placing an international call *from* the U.S., dial 1 800 CALL ATT

©1999 AT&T

It's a **big world.**

And we've got the **network** to cover it.

Use **AT&T Direct**® Service
when you're out exploring the world.

♫ ENTERTAINMENT

Nightlife is quiet in Blois; most tourists rest up for early-morning château stalking. Nonetheless, some bars and clubs spread out both directions from **pl. Ave Maria,** in the area east of rue Denis Papin. Rue Haute offers **Le Blue Night** (tel. 02 54 74 82 12), equipped with over 80 international beers (20-35F). In the Irish-style **Pub Mancini,** rue Fontaine des Élus (tel. 02 54 78 3379), beers cost around 20F. (Open M-Sa 5pm-4am.) The **Ave Foch** disco, 3 rue du Puits Chatel (tel. 02 54 90 00 00), is open 6pm-2am, but real night owls can retreat to **Le Joker,** 40 rue Foulerie. (Tel. 02 54 78 75 34. Open 10:30pm-5am.) **Le Gospel,** 58 rue Foulerie (tel. 02 54 78 18 87), is a piano bar lined with comfy sofas; cocktails cost around 45F. (Open until 2am.)

CHÂTEAUX NEAR BLOIS

Blois would be the perfect base from which to explore surrounding châteaux, were it not for the problem of transportation; all except Chaumont are inaccessible by train. On the bright side, **Point Bus** in Blois sends inexpensive **TLC buses** to the castles. TLC also runs a special **châteaux circuit** bus to **Chambord** and **Cheverny,** giving you two hours at each. Coaches depart from outside the Blois station. Keep your bus ticket, as it knocks 25% off admission to each castle. (May 15-Aug. 31. Buy tickets at station, tourist office, or on the bus. 65F, students 50F.)

If you'd prefer to travel on your own, the châteaux are within easy biking range and the intervening terrain is beautiful. From Blois, it's 10km to **Cheverny,** and only 6km to **Beauregard.** Bikers should start by crossing the Loire in central Blois and riding to the roundabout 1km down av. Wilson. The châteaux and towns are well-marked along the roads. Cyclists are advised to stay off the major—and narrow—French highways. The **tourist office** branch at the Châteaux de Blois has small maps of routes which will lead you safely and efficiently to the châteaux of your choice. Pay attention to route numbers on road maps: the roads are marked by their destination. The **Regional Committee of Tourism** (tel. 02 54 78 62 52) offers one-week cycling packages, which include bike rental, meals, accommodations, and admission to châteaux.

CHAMBORD

Built by François I between 1519 and 1545 for his hunting trips and orgiastic *fêtes*, Chambord is the largest and most extravagant of the Loire châteaux. With 440 rooms, 365 chimneys, and 83 staircases, the castle is a realization of the ambitious king's most egomaniacal fantasies. The Greek cross floor design used for the keep was formerly reserved for sacred buildings, but François liked the idea of using it for his mansion; to complete his blasphemy, in the center of the castle, where the altar would stand in a church, he built a spectacular double-helix staircase—whose design is attributed to Leonardo da Vinci—ascending not up to God, but to himself. The king nearly went bankrupt in creating the palace; he left his sons to rot without ransom in Spain, commandeered silver from his subjects, and "borrowed" priceless treasures from nearby churches. Not to leave his purpose underemphasized, Francis stamped Chambord with 70 of his trademark stone salamanders, 14 four-meter tall tapestries depicting hunting conquests, and his initials splayed across the forest of stone chimneys on the rooftop terrace. Despite all this, François stayed at Chambord only 42 days.

While rooms in the château are adequately labeled in English, the experience is enhanced by a free 45-minute architecturally-focused English tour; if you're more of a free spirit, you can rent a CD headset for 25F. In summer, night visitors are given lanterns to visit the castle for *le Metamorphose de Chambord.* (Tel. 02 54 50 40 00. Night tours July-Aug. daily 10:30pm-1am, last entry midnight. 80F, ages 12-25 50F, under 12 free. Château open daily July-Aug. 9am-6:45pm; Sept. 9:30am-6:15pm; Oct.-Mar. 9:30am-5:15pm; Apr.-June 9:30am-6:15pm. Last entry 30min. before closing. 41F, ages 12-25 26F.)

Chambord's **tourist office** (tel. 02 54 20 34 86) is on pl. St-Michael next to the château. (Open Apr.-Sept. daily 10:30am-12:30pm and 1:45-6:45pm.) There is no currency exchange in the small town, but an **ATM** awaits outside the tourist office. While the stretch of forlorn lawn in front of the château is less than inspiring, the lush forest that surrounds the château begs to be explored. **Boat** and **bike rental** is available from a little shelter in front of the château. (Tel. 06 83 06 52 44 or 02 54 56 00 43. Boats 70F per hour for 2 people. Bikes 50F per hour. Open 9am-7pm.) Campers may trek to **Camping Huisseau-sur-Cosson**, 6 rue de Châtillon (tel. 02 54 20 35 26), about 5km southwest of Chambord on D33. (35F for 2 people and tent, showers free. Open Apr.-Sept.) The **Camping des Châteaux** (tel. 02 54 46 41 84), between Chambord and Cheverny in **Bracieux**, has a pool and tennis. (41F for adult and tent, 51F with electricity, 18F per additional adult, under 7 8F. Open Apr.-Oct. 15 daily 8am-8pm.) The **Montlivault hostel** (see Blois) is but 3.5km from Chambord.

To get to Chambord, take TLC bus #2 from **Blois** (45min., 20F), or enjoy the hour-long bike ride. Take route D956 south for 2-3km followed by a left onto D33.

CHEVERNY

Privately owned by the Hurault family since its completion in 1634, Cheverny and its impeccably manicured grounds radiate a personal touch unique among the major châteaux. It may lack the royal intrigues of other châteaux, but its modest lifestyle has enabled Cheverny to retain magnificent furnishings: Spanish leather walls, delicate Delft vases, the royal bedchamber (still awaiting the first visit of a French king), and an action-packed Gobelin tapestry, *The Abduction of Helen.*

Outside, fans of Hergé's *Tintin* books may recognize Cheverny's Renaissance façade as the inspiration for the design of Marlinspike, Captain Haddock's mansion. In the Orangerie behind the château (closed to the public), the *Mona Lisa* smiled bravely while German artillery shelled Paris during World War II. Animal lovers may want to skip the kennels, which still host 70 mixed English-Poitevin hounds who stalk stags in hunting expeditions every Tuesday and Saturday from October to March. The *soupe des chiens* is not a dubious regional dish but an opportunity to see these hounds gulp down bins of ground meat in less than 60 seconds. Next to the kennels, thousands of antlers poke out of the ceiling of the **trophy room,** around a striking stained glass window of the hunt. In summer, Cheverny's *son et lumière* tells the history of the château, with 300 actors, fireworks, and lasers. *(Tel. 02 54 79 96 29. Son et lumière July-Aug. Sa-Su 10:15pm, 1½hr., 81F. Call Blois tourist office for reservations. Soupe Apr.-Aug. M-Sa 5pm; Sept.-Mar. M and W-F 3pm. Château open daily June-Sept. 15 9:15am-6:45pm; late Sept. 9:30am-noon and 2:15-6pm; Oct. and Mar. 9:30am-noon and 2:15-5:30pm; Apr.-May 9:15am-noon and 2:15-6:30pm; Nov.-Feb. 9:30am-noon and 2:15-5pm. 34F, students 22F, ages 7-14 18F. V, MC.)*

Buses leave the **Blois** station for Cheverny at 12:30pm and return at 6pm (45min., 19F). To **bike** to the château, take D956 south for 45 minutes. Two kilometers away on the road to Contres is the 4-star **Camping Les Saules** (tel. 02 54 79 90 01; fax 02 54 79 28 34), with a pool, minigolf, bar/restaurant, and grocery. (26F per person, ages 3-11 17F, tent 31F. Open June-Sept. 8:30am-9pm.)

BEAUREGARD

Before François I unleashed his fancy on Chambord, he designed Beauregard (tel. 02 54 70 36 74 or 02 54 70 40 05) as a hunting lodge that he later gave to his uncle René. Located 6km south of Blois, Beauregard is cozier and less ostentatious than its flashy cousin. Paul Ardier, treasurer to Louis XIII, commissioned Jean Mosnier to paint what was to become the world's largest portrait gallery. This collection of over 300 17th-century paintings is a *Who's Who* of European powers from 1378 through Louis XIII, including all of the Valois monarchs, Elizabeth I, Thomas Moore, and Columbus. The floor's 5,616 hand-painted Delft tiles, undergoing a 20-year restoration project, portray Louis XIII's army solemnly marching to war. Outside the château, the ruins of a 14th-century chapel invite a walk into the woods. Tours available in French and English. *(Open daily July-Aug. 9:30am-6:30pm; Apr.-July and Sept. 9:30am-noon and 2-6:30pm; Oct. 1-Jan. 15 and Feb. 8-Mar. 31 Th-Tu 9:30am-noon and 2-5pm. 40F, students and children over 7 30F, under 7 free. Gardens only 30F.)*

SOUND...LIGHTS...ACTION! In 1952, Chambord witnessed the first *son et lumière* spectacular the world had ever seen. The whole affair was conceived by Paul Robert-Houdin, the curator of the château; the idea quickly caught on, and now nary a castle or cathedral in France refuses a sound-and-light show to draw in nighttime crowds. The spectacles have come a long way from their spotlight-and-historical-narration beginnings, and some approach full-scale theatrical productions. Sit back and enjoy live-action games, duels, concerts, and fireworks—much as François and his courtiers did back in the good old days. Villandry and Azay-le-Rideau in particular merit a nocturnal visit.

Beauregard is not accessible by public transportation, but this does mean that it's pleasantly devoid of crowds. Only a half-hour **bike** ride from Blois, the château lies en route to Cheverny off route 956 (direction "Collettes"), and is an easy detour from the main road. The direct route takes you along D765, a busy two-lane highway; ask at a bike rental shop for the touring route, which weaves through the forest to the right of the highway. **Hitchhikers** heading south on D956 report that rides are relatively easy to come by; to be safer, take a taxi from Blois for 80F.

AMBOISE

Amboise's postcard-perfect location has enticed royalty for 500 years. Neither as ornate as Chambord nor as charming as Chenonceau, it retains its medieval, fortress-like character. Charles VIII, Louis XI, Louis XII, and the bacchanalian François I ruled France from this hillside château and enjoyed the extraordinary panorama of the river valley below, while Leonardo da Vinci spent his last years in the town. Similar to Blois in its small-*ville*-meets-big-château charm, Amboise (pop. 11,000) is worth an afternoon of exploration in spite of its summer crowds.

◪ **ORIENTATION AND PRACTICAL INFORMATION. Trains** run from bd. Gambetta (tel. 02 47 23 18 23) to **Tours** (20min., 14 per day, 28F), **Blois** (15min., 15 per day, 32F), **Orléans** (1hr., 14 per day, 74F), and **Paris** (2¼hr., 5 per day, 140F). (Station open M-Sa 6:45am-9:30pm, Su 7:30am-9:30pm.) **Fil Vert buses** leave the tourist office for **Chenonceaux** (30min., 3 per day, round trip 40F) and **Tours** (25min., 2 per day, 25F). To reach the **tourist office** (tel. 02 47 57 09 28; fax 02 47 57 14 35), follow rue Jules-Ferry from the station and cross two bridges past the residential Île d'Or. The office, shaped like a B-movie flying saucer, is 30m to the right, along the river on quai du Général de Gaulle (15min.). The staff has information about full-day bus tours to nearby châteaux. (Open July-Aug. M-Sa 9am-8pm, Su 10am-noon and 4-6pm; Sept.-June M-Sa 9am-12:30pm and 2-6pm, Su 10am-noon.) To **rent bikes,** head out to **V.T.T. Cycles Richard,** 2 rue de Nazelles (tel. 02 47 57 01 79), on the north bank by the first bridge as you walk away from the station. (90F per day. Passport or 800F deposit. Open T-Sa 9am-noon and 2:30-7pm.) The **police** are on rue de Blois (tel. 02 47 57 26 19), at the bridge across the river from the château, while the **hospital** is on rue des Ursulines (tel. 02 47 23 33 33). The **post office** sits at 20 quai du Général de Gaulle, 3 blocks down the street to the left as you face the tourist office; it offers **currency exchange.** (Open M-F 8:30am-noon and 1:30-6:15pm, Sa 8:30am-noon. **Postal code:** 35400.)

◪ **ACCOMMODATIONS AND CAMPING.** Amboise's few inexpensive hotel rooms are quickly snatched up in the summer; call ahead in July and August. To get to the **Centre International de Séjour (HI) Charles Péguy,** Île d'Or (tel. 02 47 57 06 36; fax 02 47 23 15 80), follow rue Jules-Ferry from the station and turn right downhill after the first bridge (10min.) The industrial feel is offset by a quiet, beautiful setting; ask for a room with a view of the Loire and the château. There's plenty of fun to be had in the youth center downstairs. (50F. Breakfast 15F. Reception M-F 3-8pm. No lockout or curfew. **Members only.)**

Hôtel Les Platanes, bd. des Platanes (tel. 02 47 57 08 60), has a quiet, countryside atmosphere in a residential neighborhood. Turn right from the front of the train station, walk 300m on bd. Gambetta, cross to the right under the tracks, and walk straight for 100m; the hotel is on the left. Large, immaculate, modern bedrooms and a pleasant dining room. All rooms have TV and telephone. (Singles 130-150F, with shower 195F; doubles 130-150F, with shower 220F; triples 240F; one quad 280F. Breakfast 30F. V, MC.) **Île d'Or camping** (tel. 02 47 57 23 37) offers clean facilities in excellent condition, with a spectacular view of the Loire and the château, as well as a crowded pool (12F, children 8F) and mini-golf (15F, children 10F). (Camping 13F per person, 24F per site. Electricity 10F. Open daily Sept.-June 8:30am-12:15pm and 3-7pm; July-Aug. 8am-10pm.)

FOOD. A cheap, no-frills picnic with a great view of the Loire can be had by climbing up the hill to the **ATAC supermarket,** at the intersection of rue Grégoire de Tours, just south of the *centre ville.* (Open M-F 8:30am-12:30pm and 2:30-7:30pm, Sa 8:30am-7:30pm, Su 9:30am-12:30pm. V, MC, AmEx.) **Intermarché,** on av. de Tours, soothes every hunger pang. (Open M-Th 9am-12:30pm and 2:30-7:30pm, F-Sa 9am-7:30pm, Su 9am-noon. V, MC, AmEx.) **La Trattoria,** 4 rue Jean-Jacques Rousseau (tel. 02 47 57 67 57), right off the *quai,* dishes up extra-large pizzas (36-48F) and three-course *formules,* including wine, for 60F. (Open M-Sa noon-2pm and 7-11pm, Su 7-11pm. V, MC.) **Le Fournil,** pl. du Château (tel. 02 47 57 04 46; fax 02 47 57 59 32), between the *quai* and the château, is the *salon de thé* of the famous Bigot family *chocolaterie.* Indulge in homemade sweets of all sorts in the *pâtisserie* (open since 1913) or sit down in the beautiful tea room. (Snacks 22-45F. Open Feb. 16-Nov. 14 Tu-Su 8:30am-8pm; Nov. 15-Feb. 15 Tu-Su 8:30am-7:30pm. V, MC.)

SIGHTS. The battlements of the 15th-century **château** (tel. 02 47 57 00 98) stretch out above the town like protective arms, an unsettling sight to those who thought of attacking the castle that four French kings called home. In 1498, as the four-foot-tall Charles VIII rushed out with his queen to watch a tennis match, he bumped his head on a low door and died a few hours later. With less slapstick, in 1560 a Protestant conspiracy against the influential and arch-Catholic de Guise family was uncovered; Huguenots were thrown into the Loire in sacks and others killed on the château balcony, now described by smiling tour guides as the "Balcony of the Hanging People." In the **Logis de Roi,** the main part of the château, intricately carved 16th-century Gothic chairs stand over 6 feet high in order to prevent surprise attacks from behind. A beautiful rosewood-veneered 1832 pianoforte in the music room was a gift from the king of Brazil, whose daughter married into King Louis Philippe's family. The jewel of the grounds is the **Chapelle St-Hubert,** outside the château, where a Gothic relief above the door depicts the legends of St. Hubert, St. Christopher, and St. Anthony. A plaque marks Leonardo da Vinci's resting place. In summer, people flock to the "Court of King François" *son et lumière* (July-Aug. W and Sa), while Renaissance games and entertainment are held at the nearby park. (Open July-Aug. 9am-8pm; Apr.-June 9am-6:30pm; late Mar. and Sept.-Oct. 9am-6pm; Feb.-Mar. 13 9am-noon and 2-5:30pm; Nov.-Jan. 9am-noon and 2-5pm. 37F, students 30F, ages 7-14 18F.) Just beneath the château, the **Caveau de Dégustation,** rue Victor Hugo (tel. 02 47 57 23 69), offers free tastings of the region's wines. The bubbling demi-sec wines are prepared in the same manner as champagne. (Open Apr. 30-Sept. daily 10am-10pm. V, MC, AmEx.) From the château, follow the cliffs along rue Victor Hugo beside centuries-old **maisons troglodytiques,** houses hollowed out of the cliffs and still inhabited today.

Four hundred meters away is **Clos Lucé** (tel. 02 47 57 62 88), the manor where **Leonardo da Vinci** spent the last four years of his life. Inside, a museum contains his furnished bedroom, library, drawing room, and chapel, but its main attraction is a collection of 40 of his unrealized inventions, recently built by IBM with the materials that would have been available to da Vinci at the time. A big-screen video presents the life and times of the Renaissance genius. (Open July-Aug. 9am-8pm, Apr.-

June and Sept.-Oct. 9am-7pm; Nov.-Mar. daily 9am-6pm; Jan. 10am-5pm. 38F, students 29F, ages 6-15 19F. V, MC.)

Versailles meets the Forbidden City in the 44m **Pagoda of Chanteloup,** rte. de Blere (tel. 02 47 57 20 97), built in 1775. From the center of town, take southbound rue Bretonneau and follow the signs to the pagoda (2.5km). All that remains of the celebrated château of the Duc de Choiseul, today the little turret boasts a fabulous panorama of its 7-acre lake, the Loire Valley, and the Amboise Forest. Once you've scrambled to the top and nosed around the museum, capitalist enterprise awaits in the form of ready-made Tourangelle picnic baskets (50F) and boat rental (25F per half-hour, 40F per hour). A quiet open-air park offers wooden games *"à l'ancienne,"* such as croquet, "Trou-Madame," and a wooden bowling set. (Open July-Aug. 9:30am-8pm; June and Sept. 10am-7pm; May 10am-6pm; Apr. and Oct. 10am-noon and 2-5:30pm; Mar. daily 10am-noon and 2-5pm; Feb. and Nov. M-F 2-5pm and Sa-Su 10am-noon and 2-5pm. 35F, students 20F, ages 7-15 25F.)

TOURS

After Roman Cæsarodunum was wiped off the map by a barbarian invasion in the 3rd century, three separate towns grew up on this site until the Hundred Years' War (1337-1453) compelled them to unite into one city—Tours. In the 15th and 16th centuries, Tours was the heart of the French Kingdom, and although the government has long since migrated north, the city still stands as the urban mouthpiece of the Loire region. The birthplace of Balzac looks firmly towards the future, thanks in large part to industry and the 30,000 students who call Tours home. Tours' wealth of diverse sights and rollicking nightlife are just the thing to relieve your castle-besieged soul.

☑ ORIENTATION AND PRACTICAL INFORMATION

Place Jean-Jaurès, the vertex of four major boulevards, is the main thoroughfare. **Rue Nationale,** once part of the main road between Paris and Spain, runs north to the Loire, while **av. de Gramont** runs into the Cher river to the south. **Bds. Béranger** and **Heurteloup** run west and east respectively, from the *place.* The mostly pedestrian *vieille ville,* the lively **pl. Plum',** and the tourist draws are northwest of pl. Jean-Jaurès towards the Loire. To reach the **tourist office** from the station, cross the park and turn right at bd. Heurteloup. The office is the glass building on the left, past the futuristic Centre de Congrès.

Trains: 3 rue Édouard Vaillant, pl. du Maréchal Leclerc (tel. 02 47 20 50 50). Many non-local destinations require a change at St-Pierre-des-Corps, 5min. outside Tours; check schedule. To: **Poitiers** (45min., 7 per day, 87F); **Bordeaux** (2½hr., 6 per day, 226F); and **Paris** (2¼hr., 7 per day, 160F; TGV via St-Pierre 1hr., 6 per day, 201-261F). Ticket windows open M-Sa 8am-7pm, Su 8am-noon.

Public Transportation: Fil Bleu (tel. 02 47 66 70 70). Tickets 6.50F, *carnet* of 10 57F. Day pass 27F.

Taxis: Artaxi (tel. 02 47 20 30 40) is available 24hr.

Car Rental: The tourist office has a list of companies in town, including super-cheap **Ecoto. Avis** (tel. 02 47 20 53 27; fax 02 47 66 70 70) is by the station. 525F per day including 300km, insurance, and fees. 130F supplement ages 21-24. 21+ only. Open M-F 8am-noon and 1:15-7pm, Sa 8am-noon and 2-6pm. V, MC, AmEx, Diners.

Bike Rental: Amster Cycles, 5 rue du Rempart (tel. 02 47 61 22 23; fax 02 47 61 28 48). 80F first day, 45F second, 40F third and on. Passport or credit card deposit. Open M-Sa 9am-12:30pm and 1:30-7:30pm, Su 9am-12:30pm and 5-7pm. V, MC, AmEx.

Tourist Office: 78-82 rue Bernard Palissy (tel. 02 47 70 37 37; fax 02 47 61 14 22; www.tourism-touraine.com). Free maps, info booklets; finds rooms. Arranges châteaux tours. 2hr. historical walking tour departs daily June-Sept. (30F, children 25F). Open June-Aug. M-Sa 8:30am-6pm, Su 2:30-5pm; Sept.-May M-Sa 8:30am-6pm.

Money: Best rates at **Banque de France,** 2 rue Chanoineau (tel. 02 47 60 24 00), off bd. Heurteloup. Exchange desk open Tu-Sa 8:45am-noon.

English Bookstore: La Boîte à Livres de l'Etranger, 2 rue du Commerce (tel. 02 47 05 67 29). Open M 2-7pm, Tu-F 9:30am-12:30pm and 1:30-7pm, Sa 9:30am-12:30pm and 1:30-7pm. V, MC.

Laundromat: 20 rue Bernard Palissy, near the station. Open daily 7am-8:30pm.

Police: 70-72 rue de Marceau (tel. 02 47 60 70 69).

Hospital: Hôpital Bretonneau, 2 bd. Tonnelle (tel. 02 47 47 47 47).

Post Office: 1 bd. Béranger (tel. 02 47 60 34 20). **Currency exchange.** Open M-F 8am-7pm, Sa 8am-noon. **Postal code:** 37000. **Branch office** on 92 rue Colbert.

Internet access: Cyber Micro Touraine, pl. de la Victoire (tel. 02 47 38 13 13). 10F for 20min., 15F 30min., 20F 1hr. Open July-Aug. M-Sa 9am-7pm; rest of year until 8pm.

▟ ACCOMMODATIONS AND CAMPING

The hostel's inconvenient location makes it a downer for those wanting to stay close to the *centre ville.* Luckily, many good, cheap hotels can be found within a 10-minute walk of the station. In peak season, call a day or two in advance. **CROUS** (tel. 02 47 60 42 42) can provide information about discount student meals and long-term housing.

Hôtel Foch, 20 rue du Maréchal Foch (tel. 02 47 05 70 59; fax 02 47 20 95 10). Just off pl. Plumereau, this small sparkler offers 15 large rooms, an unbeatable location, and a friendly proprietor. Most rooms have shower, TV, and phone. Singles 130-220F; doubles 150-300F; triples 240-380F; quads 330-380F. Breakfast 30F. V, MC.

Hôtel Regina, 2 rue Pimbert (tel. 02 47 05 25 36, fax 02 47 66 08 72). A gem on a sunny street corner near happening rue Colbert, with a pretty sitting room downstairs. Singles 110-175F; doubles 140-240F. Breakfast 26F. V, MC.

Hôtel Voltaire, 13 rue Voltaire (tel. 02 47 05 77 51). Off-putting exterior and the musty halls give way to ten very pleasant balconied rooms, many with a view of the park. Singles 120-170F; doubles 135-195F; triples 230F; quads 280F. Breakfast 25F. V, MC.

Le Lys d'Or, 23 rue de la Vendée (tel. 02 47 05 33 45; fax 02 47 64 19 00), 5min. from the station; follow the signs. 15 renovated, spacious rooms in a charming but dimly lit neighborhood. Most rooms have shower, toilet, and phone. Singles 90-135F; doubles 110-165F; triples 235F; quints 335F. *Let's Go*-discounted breakfast 20F. V, MC, AmEx.

Hôtel Les Capucines, 6 rue Blaise Pascal (tel. 02 47 05 20 41; fax 02 47 05 20 41), just a few blocks from the train station. Dingy hallways lead to some of the best budget rooms in town, almost all with brand-new bathtubs. Friendly young owner. Singles 100-180F; doubles 140-200F; triples and quads 240F. Breakfast 25F. V, MC.

Auberge de Jeunesse (HI), av. d'Arsonval in the Parc de Grandmont (tel. 02 47 25 14 45; fax 02 47 48 26 59). The cheapest option in town for solo travelers, but an inconvenient and less-than-charming location and questionable cleanliness might send you running for the next bus into town. Take bus #3, 6, or 11 from pl. da Vinci outside the train station to "Auberge de Jeunesse." Turn left across the busy street, and you will see the auberge sign ahead. TV, game room, laundry, and kitchen facilities. 48F per person. Sheets 17F. Breakfast 19F. Dinner 50F. Reception open 7-11am and 3-10pm. V, MC.

Campsites: The tourist office lists dozens of campsites within 30km, most near châteaux and the Loire. The closest is **Camping St-Avertin,** 61 rue de Rochepinard in St-Avertin (tel. 02 47 27 27 60), accessible by bus #5 from Tours. Ask for the stop nearest the campsite, and follow the signs (5min. walk). Tennis, volleyball, pool. 15F per site, 15F per adult, 8.50F per child under 7, 8.50F per car. Electricity 13F. Open April 1-Oct. 15. **Camping Municipal "Les Acacias,"** rue Berthe Morisot (tel. 02 47 44 08 16), is 6km east along D751. Site and 2 adults 40F. Electricity 15-30F. Open Apr.-Sept.

THE NORTHWEST

Tours

ACCOMMODATIONS
- A Hôtel Foch
- B Hôtel Voltaire
- C Hôtel Regina
- D Auberge de Jeunesse (HI)
- E Le Lys d'Or
- F Hôtel Les Capucines

N

r. Mirabeau
Pont Mirabeau
r. du Petit Cupidon
quai d'Orléans
r. des Maures
r. Albert Thomas
r. du Général Meun
r. des Ursulines
r. du Petit Pré
r. Traversière
r. du Rempart
r. Édouard Vaillant
Historial de Touraine
Château de Tours
Aquarium Tropical
Cathédrale St-Gatien
r. Lavoisier
Musée des Beaux-Arts
PL. SICARD
r. Jules Simon
Allée du Manoir
PL. LECLERC
bd. Heurteloup
rue de Nantes
r. B. Pascal
r. de la Barre
r. Bernard Palissy
Centre de Congrès Vinci
r. de Bordeaux
r. Charles Gilles
r. de la Vendée
E
r. Charles Michelet
r. Colbert
r. de la Scellerie
r. de Buffon
Église Réformée
Chapelle des Minimes
r. des Minimes
av. de Grammont
Théâtre Municipal
r. Émile Zola
r. Chaptal
r. de la Préfecture
PL. JEAN JAURÈS
TO D (5KM)
r. Voltaire
B
Musée du Compagnonnage
r. Berthelot
r. Nationale
r. Étienne Pallu
r. Victor Hugo
English Bookstore
PL. ANATOLE FRANCE
C
pont Wilson
r. du Commerce
Balzac's Birthplace
Marceau
r. du Maréchal Leclerc
PL. DE LA RÉSISTANCE
A
r. Marceau
r. des Halles
r. Richelieu
r. Néricault Destouches
r. de Clocheville
bd. Béranger
r. Constantine
Nouvelle Basilique St-Martin
r. de la Grandière
r. P. L. Courrier
University Humanities Building
r. des Tanneurs
Musée du Gemmail
PL. PLUMEREAU
r. de la Monnaie
r. du Petit Soleil
Tour de Charlemagne
r. Léonard de Vinci
r. Rabelais
Théâtre Louis Jouvet
r. Chanoineau
la Loire
r. Censiers
PL. du Miller
Marché
r. de la Rôtisserie
r. du Châteauneuf
Tour de l'Horloge
r. Rapin
PL. DES HALLES
r. Briçonnet
rue Bretonneau
pl. du Grand Marché
r. du Gr.
r. de la Grosse Tour
PL. DE LA VICTOIRE
PL. ROUGET
quai du Pont Neuf
r. du Petit St-Martin
Victoire
r. Barrisse
r. Charpentier
r. de la
av. Proudhon
r. de Baltan
pont Napoléon

300 yards
300 meters

📷 GASTRONOMIC TOURS

Tours is full to bursting with affordable restaurants tempting with everything from traditional *Tourangelle* cuisine to ethnic fusion. The diversity around **pl. Plumereau** will knock your socks off, with dozens of pleasant outdoor options for under 70F a *menu*. **Rue Colbert** delivers a similar atmosphere on the east side of town. Look out for melt-in-your-mouth macaroons, and anything *aux pruneaux* (with prunes). Connoisseurs and poets alike esteem such *touraine* wines as the light, fruity whites of *Vouvray* and *Montlouis*.

Budding chefs can peruse the **indoor market,** pl. des Halles, which spreads outdoors Wednesdays and Saturdays (M-Sa 6am-7:30pm, Su 6am-1pm). The first Friday of the month brings the **Marché Gourmand** to pl. de la Résistance, an epicurean daydream. (4-10pm.) **Supermarkets** are all over town; charge over to **ATAC**, 7 pl. Maréchal LeClerc, which faces the train station. (Open M-Sa 8:30am-8pm, Su 9:30am-12:30pm.) **Monoprix** is in the Galeries Lafayette on the corner of rue Étienne Pallu and rue Nationale, just north of pl. Jean Jaurès. (Open M-Sa 9am-7:30pm.)

📷 **Le Charolais Chez Jean Michel,** 123 rue Colbert (tel. 02 47 20 80 20; fax 02 47 66 66 25.) A first-class restaurant with (almost) 3rd-world prices. Run by an ex-*sommelier,* the menu is drawn up to accompany the exceptional regional wine list. 60F and 72F 3-course lunch *menus* bring *haute cuisine* to the masses. Open M 7:30-10:30pm, Tu-Sa noon-2pm and 7:30-10:30pm. V, MC.

Le Merimée, 66 rue Colbert (tel. 02 47 61 32 34). A small, friendly find, Le Merimée serves up fabulous 30-42F *assiettes régionales*. Why settle for the 66F lunch *menu* when two additional francs will get you salad, an *assiette régional*, a dessert, wine, *and* coffee? *Plats* 42-56F. Open M-Sa noon-2:30 and 7-10:30pm. V, MC.

Café Flunch, 14 pl. Jean Jaurès (tel. 02 47 64 56 70). Stop following other tourists in search of authentic experiences—this comfortable restaurant chain serves up good-value meats (25-50F), salads (9-35F), and desserts (8-15F), with different specials every day. Open daily 7am-10pm—now isn't that a relief? V, MC.

👁 SIGHTS

*A 50F **Carte Multivisite** includes admission to six sights and the 2:30pm city tour. Available at the tourist office.*

Tours' low-key museums and landmarks provide a welcome change for the châteaux-weary and are conveniently clustered together. Those in search of peace and quiet can leave the city far behind at the beautiful **Lac de la Bergeonnerie,** a 10-minute bus ride away. Resting on the banks of the Cher, the lake is encircled by a 5km path for strolling and has an adjacent pool for splishing and splashing.

CATHÉDRALE ST-GATIEN. A wildly intricate façade gives way to recently-discovered frescoes and one of the most dazzling displays of stained glass in the Loire. Ask the tourist office about tours of the cathedral. (*Rue Jules Simon. Tel. 02 47 05 05 54. Open Easter-Sept. 8:30am-noon and 2-8pm; Oct.-Easter 8:30am-noon and 2-5:30pm.*)

MUSÉE DES BEAUX-ARTS. The upper floors of the museum house primarily 17th- and 18th-century French painting, but a few works by Degas, Monet, Delacroix, La Tour, Rodin, and Calder add variety. The 40m Lebanese cedar outside was planted during Napoleon's reign. (*18 pl. François Sicard next to the cathedral. Tel. 02 47 05 68 73. Open W-M 9am-12:45pm and 2-6pm. 30F, students 15F. Gardens open in summer daily 7am-8:30pm; off-season 7am-6pm.*)

MUSÉE DU GEMMAIL. Works by Picasso, Braque and Cocteau glow in rooms of dark velvet, a fusion of *gemmes* (gems or shards of brightly colored glass) and *émail* (enamel); the result is a "painting of light." (*7 rue du Murier, off rue Bretonneau, near pl. Plumereau. Tel. 02 47 61 01 19. Open Easter-Oct. Tu-Su 10am-noon and 2-6:30pm; Nov. 15-Easter open Sa-Su 10am-noon and 2-6:30pm. 30F, students 20F.*)

MUSÉE DE COMPAGNONNAGE. The museum houses the works of *compagnons*, or "companions," members of artisans' guilds dating back to the Middle Ages. Arm yourself with a copy of the International Herald Tribune article "The Aristocrats of Manual Labor" and view with informed appreciation such curios as an impressively detailed cathedral model and miniature spiral staircases carved in wood. *(8 rue Nationale. Open mid-June-Sept. daily 9am-6:30pm; Oct.-Feb. W-M 9am-noon and 2-5pm; Mar.-mid-June W-M 9am-noon and 2-6pm. 25F, students and seniors 15F, under 12 free.)*

MUSÉE ARCHÉOLOGIQUE DE L'HÔTEL GOUIN. A fine Renaissance façade conceals a mildly interesting collection spanning Gallo-Roman utensils to 17th-century scientific instruments. The museum's prized piece is an 18th-century medicine chest from the Chenonceau château. *(25 rue du Commerce. Tel. 02 47 66 22 32. Open Mar.-June and Sept. daily 10am-12:30pm and 2-6:30pm; July-Aug. daily 11am-12:30pm and 1:30-7pm; Oct.-Nov. and Feb. Th-Tu 10am-12:30pm and 2-5:30pm. 20F, students and seniors 15F, children 12F.)*

THE TWIN TOURS OF TOURS. The **Tour de l'Horloge** and the **Tour de Charlemagne**, flanking rue des Halles, are fragments of the 5th-century Basilique St-Martin, a gargantuan Romanesque church that first fell to fire in 994 and then collapsed again in 1797, a few years after Revolutionary looters removed its iron reinforcements. St. Martin himself, the city's first bishop, was carried here following his death in Candes-St-Martin (p. 578), and now slumbers on undisturbed in the **Nouvelle Basilique St-Martin**, a *fin-de-siècle* church in the popular Neo-Byzantine style.

HISTORIAL DE TOURAINE. A wax museum with displays from the lighthearted (a cross-dressing royal ball with Henri III in stays) to the grim (the flight of the persecuted Huguenots after the 1685 revocation of the Edict of Nantes). English descriptions provide details. *(25 av. André Malraux. Tel. 02 47 61 02 95; fax 02 47 66 94 04. Open daily July-Aug. 9am-7pm; Sept.-June 9am-noon and 12:30-7pm. 35F, students 24F.)*

♫ 🎭 ENTERTAINMENT AND FESTIVALS

NIGHTLIFE. Pl. Plumereau (commonly called just plain **place Plum')** is the *place* to be, with cheerful students sipping drinks and chattering at countless cafés and bars. **Dépanneur,** 108 r. du Commerce (tel. 02 47 74 04 27 or 02 47 64 07 84), features 15F half-pints amid industrial decor, while **Le Morgan,** 25 rue de la Rôtisserie (tel. 02 47 47 02 20), is cocktail heaven. If you can't decide between the "Cadillac" and the "Chevrolet Sister," try your luck with the 15F *cocktail du jour.* (Open daily 11am-2am.) Three clubs on the *place* are stacked one above the other. The downstairs **Le Pharoan** keeps sweaty kids partying to loud rock, cover-free, while a bust of the Sun King keeps the older café crowds in line upstairs at **Louis XIV;** progress yet upward to chill in the jazzy **Duke Ellington** (tel. 02 47 05 77 17). (All 3 open daily until 2am.) Jazz fans should head a couple of blocks off the square to **Le Petit Faucheux,** 23 rue des Cerisiers (tel. 02 47 38 67 62), where live bands play every Tuesday and weekends until 2:30am. (100F, students 60F.) Blues and rock groups cover American faves and play a few of their own at **Les Trois Orfèvres,** 6 rue des Orfèvres (tel. 02 47 64 02 73), a good no-frills place to chill. (Open Tu-Sa 10pm-4am. 30-50F with first drink.) A lively, youthful crowd frequents the alternative, techno-pop, and jazz nights at **Rhythm and Blues,** 19 rue Petit Soleil. (Tel. 02 47 05 96 67. Open daily 11pm-4am. M-Th 30F with first drink, F-Sa 50F, Su free.)

CULTURE AND FESTIVALS. In late June, Tours hosts the **Fêtes Musicales en Touraine,** a 10-day celebration of voices and instruments playing selections from Saint-Saëns to Gershwin. (Tel. 02 47 21 65 08. 80-280F per night.) There's theater year-round at the **Théâtre Louis Jouvet,** 12 rue Leonardo da Vinci (tel. 02 47 64 50 50), and the **Théâtre Municipal,** 34 rue de la Scellerie (tel. 02 47 05 37 87).

CHÂTEAUX NEAR TOURS

Dozens of beautiful and historic châteaux lie within 60km of Tours. Biking along the Loire between châteaux is enchanting, even if bus tours are more efficient. Alternatively, you can travel in air-conditioned luxury on one of the many **minibus tours** which leave Tours every day; expect to shell out 100-300F, which normally includes admission fees. Contact **Saint-Eloi Excursions** (tel. 02 47 37 08 04; www.saint-eloi.com), **Touraine Evasion** (tel. 06 07 39 13 31), **Acco-Dispo Excursions** (tel. 02 47 57 67 13), or **Sillonne Val** (tel. 02 47 59 13 14). **Service Touristique de la Touraine** (tel. 02 47 05 46 09) sits beguiling in Tours' train station, but is the most expensive. Most châteaux have tours and printed matter in English, as well as various performances and special events which take place during the summer. *Son et Lumière* ("sound and light") shows are lots of fun, and worth at least one attendance, especially if daylight visits are beginning to feel a bit dry. On your way, don't neglect the wine cellars offering free *dégustations*. **Vouvray's** 30 cellars (tel. 02 47 52 75 03), 9km east of Tours on the N152, specialize in sweet white wine. By bus, take #61 from pl. Jean-Jaurès to "les Patis" (20min., M-Sa 14 per day, 18F). In **Montlouis,** across the river to the south, and accessible by train from Tours (20min., M-Sa 3 per day, 15F), 10 *caves* pour forth wonderful dry white wine. See transportation info in Tours (p. 568).

CHENONCEAU

Perhaps the most exquisite château in France, Chenonceau (tel. 02 47 23 90 07; www.chenonceaux-sa.fr) arches gracefully over the Cher river flanked by shaded woods and gardens. The site of many outrageous parties in the Renaissance, the château owes its beauty to centuries of women designers. Royal tax-collector Thomas Bohier originally commissioned a château on the ruins of a medieval mill on a tiny island in the Cher river. While he fought in the Italian Wars (1513-21), his wife Catherine oversaw its practical design, which features four rooms radiating from a central chamber and Italian-style straight (rather than spiral) staircases. In 1547, Henri II gave the château to his mistress, Diane de Poitiers, who added symmetrical gardens and constructed the arched bridge over the Cher so she could hunt in the nearby forest. When Henri II died in 1559, his widow Catherine de Médici kicked Diane out of her beloved castle and designed her own set of gardens and the most spectacular wing of the castle: the two-story gallery spanning the Cher. In compensation, Diane got the more lucrative estate of Chaumont. In the 18th century, Mme Dupin employed Jean-Jacques Rousseau (p. 16) as her son's tutor, prompting him to write the monumental classic on children's education, *Émile.* She was also so popular among the villagers that they protected her château from the ravages of the Revolution, preserving its original fittings for future generations. These include a gear-and-pulley, adjustable-speed rotisserie in the kitchen, vivid 16th-century tapestries, and a particularly touching "Virgin and Child," attributed to Murrillo, in Diane de Poitier's bedroom. *(Open daily Mar. 16-Sept. 15 9am-7pm; visits are quite crowded in July and Aug. Call for off-season hours. 45F, students 30F. Late July-Aug., son et lumière at 10:15pm.)*

There's wine at **La Cave Cellar** (open 11am-7pm; free) on the grounds and, to the left as you approach the château, you can rent 4-person **boats** for the remarkably reasonable price of 10F per half hour. (Open 10am-7pm July and Aug.) Chenonceau's idyllic setting makes it a tempting stopover. Of the few hotels in the area, **Hotel du Roy,** 9 rue Bretonneau (tel. 02 47 23 90 17; fax 02 47 23 89 81), is the best deal. (Singles and doubles 150-300F. Breakfast 35F. V, MC.) A tiny **campground** (tel. 02 47 23 90 13) is a few blocks left of the entrance to the château. (11F per person, 7.50F per site, 9F per car. Electricity 13.50F. Open Apr. 15-Sept.) **Trains** run to **Tours** (45min., 3 per day, 36F). The station is 2km from the château. Don't follow the mob; cross the tracks and turn right, where the blue sign directs you to the château. Continue straight past the campground. **Fil Vert buses** leave for Chenonceaux from **Amboise** (30min., 3 per day, round trip 40F) and **Tours** (25min., 2 per day, 25F).

VILLANDRY

Villandry (tel. 02 47 50 02 09) lives up to its claim to be *"le plus beau des jardins du jardin de la France"* ("the most beautiful of gardens of the garden that is France"). Built on the banks of the Cher by Jean le Breton, minister to François I, the château was bought in 1906 by Dr. Joachim Carvallo, the present owner's great-grandfather. Carvallo set about renovating the decaying structure and reconstructing from 16th-century documents the surrounding gardens, which had been redone in the popular English style. Today the restored formal French gardens have not only have become Villandry's main attraction, but are considered the most beautiful in the Loire Valley. They look most spectacular from high up in the château, but don't neglect to stroll underneath the romantic covered arbors or get lost in the passageways of the recently opened hedgerow maze. The grounds are laid out in three levels: the kitchen garden, designed like that of an Italian monastery, is so productive that its bounty is given away. The middle level is the most artistic, using hedges and flowers to form patterns including a Maltese cross and a *fleur-de-lis*. The peaceful upper level offers lime groves, swan pools, waterfalls, and a view of the whole grounds. Indoor highlights include a medieval Moorish ceiling constructed from 3000 gold-leafed wooden pieces. The 12th-century keep, all that remains of the original medieval fortress, offers a glorious view of the *jardin* from atop its battlements. *(Gardens open June-Aug. daily 8:30am-8pm; Sept.-May 9am-nightfall. 35F, students 27F. Château open daily June-mid-Sept. 9am-6:30pm; mid-Feb.-May and mid-Sept.-Nov. 11 9:30am-5:30pm. 48F, including gardens.)*

Fifteen kilometers from Tours, Villandry is one of the closest châteaux but hard to reach via public transportation. Take one of the infrequent **trains** to **Savonnières** (10min., 4 per day, 17F) and walk or bike the remaining 4km along the Loire; the train times work out best for Saturday visits. Many **minibus** tour agencies include Villandry in their full-day and half-day tours (see above). From Tours, **cyclists** should follow the tiny D16, a narrow marvel that winds along the bank of the Cher past Villandry to Ussé; **drivers** should stick to the D7.

LOCHES

It was in the state room of Loches (tel. 02 47 59 01 32) that Joan of Arc, on the heels of her Orléans victory over the English in 1429, told the indifferent *dauphin* that she had cleared the way for him to travel to Reims to be crowned king. Surrounded by a walled medieval town, whose ramparts and 15th-century church merit a visit in themselves, the château consists of two distinct structures at opposite ends of a hill. To the south, the 11th-century **donjon** (keep) and watchtowers changed role from keeping enemies out to keeping them in when Charles VII turned it into a state prison, complete with suspended cages. His consort, Agnès Sorèl, the first woman to officially hold the title of Mistress of the King of France, had a more civilizing influence on Charles and the château. After dying at age 28, she was finally laid to rest in a fine marble tomb in the **Logis Royal,** which housed French kings from the time Phillipe-Auguste snatched it from Richard the Lionheart to the 15th century. The third tough woman connected to Loches, Anne de Bretagne, built a lacy stone Gothic chapel in the Logis. In the dungeon you'll see the mystical messages and symbols of the imprisoned Duke of Milan, who died there in 1508, hours before his release. The castle also stages a "Le Chevalier au loup" *son et lumière* show and participates in the July Touraine Theatre and Music Festival; call tourist office for details. *(Open daily July-Sept. 15 9am-7pm; Mar. 15-June and Sept. 16-30 9:30am-1pm and 2:30-7pm; Feb.-Mar. 14 and Oct. 9:30am-1pm and 2:30-6pm. Admission to Donjon or Logis Royal 25F, students 17F; to both 32F, students 22F.)*

Buses drive the 40km from **Tours'** train station. (50min., 4 per day, 47F; pay on board). Nine trains also make the journey (1hr., 47F). The **tourist office** (tel. 02 47 91 82 82), in a pavilion near the station on *brasserie*-lined **pl. de la Marne,** will find you a room for 10F. (Open daily June-Aug. 9am-7pm; Sept.-May 9:30am-12:30pm and 2-6pm.) **Crédit Agricole,** also on the *place,* will spin your gold into francs at a fair rate. (Open Tu-Sa 8:30am-12:30pm and 2-5pm, closes 4pm Sa.) Two blocks from the tourist office, **Monoprix,** 21 rue Picois, holds a treasure-trove of picnic supplies. (Open M-Sa 9am-12:30pm and 2:30-7pm.)

AZAY-LE-RIDEAU

Lounging on an island in the Indre, **Azay-le-Rideau** (tel. 02 47 45 42 04) gazes peacefully at its reflection. Surrounded by acres of breeze-ruffled trees and grass, the present château was constructed upon the ruins of an earlier fortress. The town acquired the nickname "Azay-le-Brulé" (Azay the Burned) in 1418 after Charles VII, forbidden from entering by the Burgundian garrison, was insulted by one of the guards as he passed by; the dauphin subsequently ordered the entire village burned to the ground. Hoping to erase this memory, the corrupt royal financier Gilles Berthelot bought the land in 1518, and his wife Philippa set about designing a new castle. Though smaller than François I's Chambord, the château which rose from the ashes was intended to rival its contemporary in beauty and setting; the Berthelots succeeded so well that François I seized the château before its third wing was completed. On the exterior walls, salamanders without crowns mark the castle as a non-royal residence built under François I—the crowned salamander over the fireplace in the visit's last room is a 19th-century renovation blooper. Azay's flamboyant style is apparent in the furniture and the ornate second-floor staircase with the carved faces of 10 kings and queens. The highly-rated *son et lumière* midnight stroll features costumed actors in boats. *(Open daily July-Aug. 9am-7pm for crowded visits; Apr.-June and Sept.-Oct. 9:30am-6pm; Nov.-Mar. 9:30am-12:30pm and 2-5:30pm. 35F, ages 12-25 23F. Audio commentary headphone sets available in English 26F. Son-et-lumière daily May-July 10:30pm; Aug.-Sept. 10pm. 80F, 12-25 50F, including château.)*

Trains run from **Tours** (30min., 3 per day, 28F) to Azay-le-Rideau town, a 2km walk from the château. Turn right from the front of the station and head left on the D57. **Buses** run from the **Tours** train station to the **tourist office** (45min.; M-Sa 3 per day, Su 1 per day; 29F one-way; pay on bus). Rent **bikes** at **Le Provost**, 13 rue Carnot. (Tel. 02 47 45 40 94. 50F per half-day, 65F per day. Passport deposit. Open Tu-Sa 8:30am-noon and 2:30-7pm, also Su and M 9:30am-noon in July and Aug.) The **Camping Parc de Sabot** (tel. 02 47 45 42 72), across from the château on the banks of the Indre, offers plenty of room, along with mini-golf, a pool, and tennis next door. (50F per 2 people with tent. Open Easter-Oct.) The **tourist office,** 26 rue Gambetta (tel. 02 47 45 44 40; fax 02 47 45 31 46), 1km from the train station along av. de la Gare, can give you a small map and help with rooms, although few are cheap. (Open daily 9am-1pm and 3-7pm, Sa 10am-1pm and 2-7pm.)

USSÉ

Though no king ever laid a head on the fancy four-poster of Ussé's *chambre du Roi*, the fairy-tale spires awoke inspiration in one 17th-century visitor—Charles Perrault penned the tale of *Sleeping Beauty* during his stay here in 1697. Billed from afar as the *château de la belle au bois dormant*, a bizarre sub-Disneyesque experience awaits in a corner turret, as costumed mannequins illustrate the story's unfolding—watch out for the Beauty's fancy lace underwear. The rest of the 15th- to 16th-century château can be seen during a 50-minute English tour, whose fierce guides will tell you about the different costumes on display in the various rooms, carefully locking the doors behind you and calling ahead on walkie-talkies to ensure the way is clear. While waiting for your tour, explore the gardens, which famed designer Le Nôtre whipped up after finishing his work at Versailles. You can also explore the Gothic chapel, wine *caves*, and stables. A small door leads from the moat to the prison, a single tiny room deep within the walls; graffiti scratched by former prisoners looks almost too well-preserved.

Ussé is easiest to get to as part of a château minibus tour; the nearest train station is at Langeais, from which one can bike the remaining 13km. *(Tel. 02 47 95 54 05. Open Easter-mid-July 9am-noon and 2-6:45pm; mid-July-Aug. 9am-6:30pm; Sept. 9am-noon and 2-6:45pm; Oct.-early Nov. 10am-noon and 2-5:30pm; mid-Feb.-mid-Mar. 10am-noon and 2-5:30pm; mid-Mar.-Easter 10am-noon and 2-6pm. Admission 60F, ages 8-16 19F.)*

THE NORTHWEST

LANGEAIS

Between Villandry and Ussé, 22km west of Tours, lies forbidding, feudal **Langeais** (tel. 02 47 96 72 60), one of the last châteaux built strictly for defense. Constructed in 1465-1469 for Louis XI, Langeais guarded the route from Brittany through the Loire Valley. The château's claim to fame is that Charles VIII and Anne of Brittany were married here in 1491, an act which incorporated Brittany into the French kingdom. In honor of this event, a wax reenactment of the wedding stands frozen in one of the rooms. Langeais is one of the few châteaux which have never been structurally altered or added to; moreover, its authentic 15th- and 16th-century decor (as well as its surprisingly low doorways) create a vivid sense of its times. Gothic and Renaissance tapestries decorate the walls, including representatives of the "mille fleurs" style. A high enclosed rampart runs around the perimeter of the château, peppered by window-like openings; these popular pigeon stoops allow you to peer out over the city today, but they were once used for pouring boiling oil onto invading enemies. After the tour, explore the geometric gardens and the remaining wall of the **donjon de Foulques Nerra.** In 994, the notorious count of Anjou, known as the "Black Falcon," inhabited this crumbling keep. *(Open daily Apr.-June and Sept. 9am-6:30pm; July 15-Aug. 31 9am-9pm; Oct. 9am-12:30pm and 2-6:30pm; Nov.-Mar. 9am-noon and 2-5pm. 35F, students 20F.)*

If you don't cross it en route, do take a second to go peep at the marvelous Langeais **suspension bridge,** erected in 1951. Spanning the two banks of the Loire, the overpass features the chateau's portico as a structural motif; the resulting overall effect is one of a huge drawbridge. To calm the emerging château cynic within, **Le Musée Cadillac,** 4km away in **St-Michel-sur-Loire** (tel. 02 47 96 81 52), shows off the largest collection of Cadillacs outside the U.S. From the midnight-blue 1926 roadster to the 1966 cherry-red Eldorado convertible, all 55 have been restored to gleaming mint condition. Go west of Langeais on N152. *(Open daily Apr.-Sept. 10am-6pm. Admission 39F, ages 6-18 22F.)* At least six **trains** per day stop in Langeais en route to **Saumur** and **Tours.** The **train station** (tel. 02 47 96 82 19) is 300m from the château; follow the signs. The 12km bike ride on the D16 from Villandry or Ussé is delightful. If you'd like a bit more information about the town, the Langeais **tourist office** is a few blocks in front of the château in pl. du 14 Juillet. (Open M-Sa 9:15am-12:45pm and 2:30-6pm, Su 10am-12:30pm and 3:30-6pm.)

CHINON

Nestled beneath a rocky escarpment on the Vienne, Chinon (pop. 8500) rests on its laurels, reminiscing about the days when kings of England and France held court in the vast, crumbling château which stretches its ramparts high above. It was here that Richard the Lionheart drew his last breath and Joan of Arc distinguished the Dauphin from among his courtiers and persuaded him to fight for his Kingdom. Resting below, the city's steep, narrow, and winding streets are lined with medieval houses holding artisans' studios, cafés, and regional specialty shops, making Chinon a worthwhile stop-off or daytrip from Tours or Saumur.

◪ ORIENTATION AND PRACTICAL INFORMATION. Trains and **SNCF buses** run to **Tours** (1-1¼hr.; 7 per day M-Sa, 1 Su; 48F) and **Saumur** via St-Pierre-des-Corps (2hr., 2 per day, 86F). From the station (tel. 02 47 93 11 04), walk along quai Jeanne d'Arc, and turn right at Café de la Paix to get to **pl. de l'Hôtel de Ville** and the **tourist office,** 12 rue Voltaire. (Tel. 02 47 93 17 85; fax 02 47 93 93 05. Open M-Sa 9am-7pm, Su and holidays 10am-12:30pm.) The best **currency exchange** rates are at **Crédit Agricole,** 2 pl. de l'Hôtel de Ville. (Tel. 02 47 93 80 80. Open Tu-F 8:45am-12:30pm and 2-5:15pm, Sa 9am-12:30pm and 2-4pm.) The **post office** is at 80 quai Jeanne d'Arc. (Open M-F 8am-noon and 1:30-5:45pm, Sa 8am-noon. **Postal code:** 37500.)

◪◪ ACCOMMODATIONS AND FOOD. The **Auberge de Jeunesse (HI),** rue Descartes (tel. 02 47 93 10 48; fax 02 47 98 44 98), is five minutes from town along the quai Jeanne d'Arc, around the corner from the train station. The large, modern building contains 52 beds and excellent kitchen facilities across the street from tennis courts and the Vienne. (48-52F. Sheets 16F. Reception M-F 9:30am-10pm, Sa 11am-8pm. No lockout.) The big rooms at **Hôtel du Point du Jour,** 102 quai Jeanne-d'Arc (tel. 02 47 93 07 20), are a good value, but on a noisy street. (Singles and doubles with shower 120-180F. Breakfast 29F. Reservations recommended.) The pleasant but crowded 2-star **Camping de l'Île Auger** (tel. 02 47 93 08 05) lies across the river at Île Auger off N749. The campground offers free access to tennis, fishing, and a pool. (44F plus 11F per person, 7F per child. Electricity 11F. Open Mar.-Oct.) The **Galerie Corsaire supermarket,** 22 pl. de l'Hôtel de Ville, will make your picnic plentiful. (Open M-Sa 8:30am-8:30pm.) There is also an **open-air market** Thursdays on pl. de Gaulle. Good, inexpensive restaurants are difficult to find, but try the Italian **La Grappa,** 50 rue Voltaire (tel. 02 47 93 19 29), for a 68F 3-course *menu* or large 34-46F pizzas. (Open July-Aug. Tu-Su noon-2pm and 7-10:30pm; Sept.-June Tu-Su noon-2pm and 5-10pm. V, MC, AmEx.)

📷 🎵 **SIGHTS AND ENTERTAINMENT.** The **château** (tel. 02 47 93 13 45) presides in august rubble above the Vienne river. First erected in the 10th century, the château has crumbled not under attack but through neglect; the ruins, however, come alive in a tour or walk of the decrepit walls and towers. Lying in three separate sections, the château has recently-discovered tunnels which originally connected each fortress in a state of emergency; additional tunnels, just wide enough for a man to crawl through on his stomach, led to the main well, as well as all the way to the town center. In the former royal apartments, 17th-century tapestries hang on the walls. Thanks to a belief that anyone who captured the **Tour Marie-Javelle** would die a horrible death, the 14th-century bell tower has withstood the Hundred Years War, the Wars of Religion, and the French Revolution without a blemish—and has been proudly striking the hour and half-hour since 1399. A wonderful **Joan of Arc Museum** occupies the top floor. (Open July-Aug. daily 9am-7pm; Apr.-June and Sept. 9am-6pm; Oct. 9am-5pm; Nov.-Mar. 9am-noon and 2-5pm. 27F, students 18F.) Less forbidding tunnels dig into the hillside at **Maison Plouzeau,** 94 rue Voltaire (tel. 02 47 93 16 34), behind the tourist office. Here M. Plouzeau and sons conduct free tours and pour out some of their superb red wines in their *cave* beneath the château. (Tu-Th open 8:30am-noon and 1:30-6pm, M opens 9am, F closes 5pm.) The **Musée Animé du Vin et de la Tonnellerie,** 12 rue Voltaire (tel. 02 47 93 25 63), illustrates wine-making from grape-crushing to barrel making; costumed automaton demonstrators in bad wigs lace the 20 minute tour with Rabelais quotes, and end with the exhortation to "drink always and never die." (Tours in French and English. Open Apr.-Sept. daily 10am-12:30pm and 2-7pm. 25F, students 19F.)

MAIDEN VOYAGE A peasant girl from Lorraine with a penchant for cross-dressing, the 16-year-old Joan of Arc persuaded the local garrison commander of her divine mission to liberate the English occupiers. In February 1428, he equipped her with soldier's clothing and a guard of six men-at-arms; the intrepid band crossed hundreds of miles of enemy-held territory and in 11 days reached Charles VII's court at Chinon. That she arrived safely was seen as miraculous, and Charles agreed to receive her. When the feisty lass entered the château's Great Hall, she ignored the man on the throne and knelt before a mere courtier—who was, of course, none other than Charlie in disguise. Preying on his inadequacy by addressing him as "kind dauphin" rather than acclaiming him as king—for Charles could not be crowned as long as the English and their allies held the coronation city of Reims—she persuaded him to allow her to proceed to Orléans, which was about to capitulate to the English. Armed with a sword she had foretold would be found in a nearby church and a standard displaying Christ in Judgement, she left to "Boot the English out of France." Though she did not live to see the task accomplished—she was captured and burned at the stake by the English and their allies—she has since been canonized and is now France's patron saint. Her feast day is May 30th, the anniversary of her death in Rouen.

Chinon's **medieval fair** takes the city back a few centuries one Sunday in mid-August with costumes, parades, and markets. Admission is 50F, or pick up your codpiece from the dry cleaners—if you come in medieval garb, you get in for just 10F. For a night of drinks, billiards, and more drinks, head to **Cafe Français,** 37 pl. du Général de Gaulle (tel. 02 47 93 32 78). Here the friendly owner puts on rock, jazz, and blues concerts once or twice a month. (Open until 1am.)

SAUMUR

Saumur (pop. 35,000) has always prided itself on the exceptional. Once famous for St. Louis' (1226-1270) feasts and parties—so extravagant they were called *Non Pareils* (nothing like it)—Saumur now offers the visitor mushrooms and wines of exceptional caliber. From afar, the approach to the town is dominated by the haughty medieval château. Add to this the elite *Cadre Noir* equestrian corps, a tank museum, and an enchanting old quarter, and it's not hard to see why Saumur has won a spot on the official government list of eight places in France you simply must see. Coco Chanel was born in the pedestrian *vieille ville*, whose chic boutiques and pleasant cafés have a certain sleek, dapper touch today. Indeed, linger a while in Saumur—not only to have your fill of mushrooms and wine, but to savor the town's incredible beauty and *joie de vivre*. The quarter was also the setting for *Eugénie Grandet*, Balzac's characterization of the French bourgeoisie. Munch a mushroom and enjoy, as Balzac did, "the essential strangeness of the place."

ORIENTATION AND PRACTICAL INFORMATION

The tourist office and most sights are on the left bank of the Loire, a 10- to 15-minute walk from the train station, which is located on the right bank; the hostel sits on an island between the two. Exit to the right of the train station onto av. David d'Angers, then turn right onto the bridge. Cross pont des Cadets and turn left immediately to get to the hostel, or continue straight on av. de Général de Gaulle to reach the *centre ville*. The tourist office will be to your left, at the corner of quai Lucien Gautier. Bus #A also goes all the way there from the station.

Trains: Av. David d'Angers. To: **Angers** (30min., 23 per day, 42F); **Tours** (45min., 21 per day, 56F); **Nantes** (1hr., 9 per day, 98F); and **Poitiers** (2½hr., 6 per day, 125F). To get to the train station from pl. Bilange in the *centre ville*, take bus A (direction "St-Lambert" or "Chemin Vert,") Local bus costs 7.50F.

Buses: Pl. St-Nicolas (tel. 02 41 51 11 87), across from the St-Nicolas church entrance. Departures from here or rue F. Roosevelt to **Angers** (1½hr., 6 per day, 34F). **SNCF buses** leave from the *gare* to **Les Sables d'Olonne** via **Nantes** (3½hr., 2 per day, 132F) and **Le Mans** (110min., 10 per day, 103F).

Local Transportation: Bus Saumur, 19 rue F. Roosevelt (tel. 02 41 51 11 87). Buses leave rue F. Roosevelt M-Sa 7am-7:30pm. Tickets 7.50F. Office open M-F 9am-noon and 1:45-6pm, Sa 9am-noon and 2-5pm.

Bike Rental: Camping Municipal, on Île d'Offard (tel. 02 41 40 30 00). 45F per half-day, 70F per day, 315F per week. Passport or 1000F deposit. **Cycles Carlos,** 57 quai Mayaud (tel. 02 41 67 69 32), on the road to the mushroom caves. 65F per day. 1000F deposit. Open M-Sa 9:30am-noon and 2-7pm.

Tourist Office: Pl. Bilange (tel. 02 41 40 20 60; fax 02 41 40 20 69), next to pont Cessart. Multilingual staff books beds (5F), **exchanges currency** (5% commission), provides free maps, and suggests tours of châteaux, vineyards, and mushroom caves. Open mid-May-mid-Oct. M-Sa 9:15am-7pm, Su 10:30am-12:30pm and 3:30-6:30pm; mid-Oct.-mid-May M-Sa 9:15am-12:30pm and 2-6pm. *La Nouvelle République* (5F) has lots of Saumur-based info.

Money: Best rate generally at the **Banque de France,** 26 rue Beaurepaire (tel. 02 41 40 12 00), 4th right down rue Orléans after crossing the bridge. Open M-F 8:45am-noon.

Laundromat: 12 rue Maréchal Leclerc. Open daily 7am-9:30pm.

Medical Assistance: Centre Hospitalier, 7 rue Seigneur (tel. 02 41 53 30 30).

Police: Rue Montesquieu (tel. 02 41 83 73 00).

Post Office: Rue Volney (tel. 02 41 51 08 05). **Currency exchange.** For Poste Restante code, address to "Saumur Volney 49400". Open M-F 8am-6:30pm, Sa 8am-noon. There is a small **branch office** across from the train station. **Postal code:** 49400.

Internet Access: Welcome Services Copy, 20 rue Portail-Louis (tel. 02 41 67 75 15). 35F for up to 1hr. Open M 2:30-7pm, Tu-F 9am-12:30pm and 2-7pm, Sa 9:30am-12:30pm and 2:30-7pm.

▐ ACCOMMODATIONS AND CAMPING

You could see Saumur in a day, but why not loiter in wine and mushroom heaven? A few good, cheap hotels are scattered around the *centre ville*, but call ahead—they fill up quickly.

Centre International de Séjour, rue de Verden (tel. 02 41 40 30 00; fax 02 41 67 37 81), on Île d'Offard, between station and tourist office. Comfy modern hostel in a shady spot along the Loire. Incomparable view of the brightly lit château at night. Helpful English-speaking staff and a pool (15F). TV, pinball, and laundry. 8-bed dorms 82-84F; doubles with shower 106-108F per person. Breakfast included. Reception 8am-8pm; until 9pm in summer. Lockout 10am-5pm (winter only). V, MC.

Le Volney, 1 rue Volney (tel. 02 41 51 25 41; fax 02 41 38 11 04), in the *centre ville,* one block off rue d'Orléans. *Sympa* young proprietor rents large, beautifully furnished *chambres* at very reasonable prices. Singles and doubles 160-170F with TV, telephone, and toilet; with shower 220-250F; with bath 265-300F. Breakfast 35F. V, MC.

Hôtel de Bretagne, 55 rue St-Nicolas (tel. 02 41 51 26 38). A bargain with spacious, carpeted rooms in a great location. Singles and doubles 140F, 160F with micro-shower *or* toilet, 190F with shower *and* toilet; triples with the works 240F. Extra person 60F. Breakfast 32F. Prices may rise as they upgrade in 2000—call ahead. V, MC.

Hôtel de la Bascule, 1 place Kléber (tel. 02 41 50 13 65), near Église St-Nicolas on Quai Carnot. Right on the river with nine great budget rooms above a well-priced restaurant. Rooms at the back miss the beautiful view but are much quieter. All rooms have TV. Singles 124-144F; doubles 144-184F; one big room for 2-4 people 224F. Shower 20F. Extra bed 30F. Breakfast 25F. Reception closed Su Oct.-June. V, MC.

Campsites: Camping Municipal de l'Île d'Offard (tel. 02 41 40 30 00; fax 02 41 67 37 81), next to hostel on Île d'Offard, at end of rue Verden. Huge 4-star site with pool, laundry, tennis, and snack shop. June-Aug. 26F per person, 46F per tent; Sept.-May 22.50F per person, 37F per tent. Electricity 17-19F. Reception 8am-8pm. Closed Dec. 15-Jan. 15. **Camping Municipal Dampierre** is southeast of Saumur on D947 (tel. 02 41 67 87 99). Take bus #16 or D (direction "Dampierre," 7F) from the station. 12.50F per person, 7F per tent, 7F per car. Electricity 18F. Open June 1-Sept. 15.

▐ FOOD

Saumur is renowned throughout France for its sparkling *crémant de Loire* wine and its mountains of mushrooms, grown in caves hollowed out along the riverbank. Stock up on fungi at the indoor **market** at the far end of pl. St-Pierre (daily until 1pm), or its outdoor brethren on pl. de la République (Th morning) and pl. St-Pierre (Sa morning). The **Atac supermarket,** 6 rue Franklin D. Roosevelt (tel. 02 41 83 54 54), sits inside the shopping centre across from Printemps department store. (Open M-F 9am-7:30pm, Sa 8:45am-7:30pm. V, MC.) An assortment of cheap restaurants are sprinkled along **rue St-Nicolas;** while the town sleeps Sunday away, **pl. St-Pierre** and its offshoots are a great option for light food and drinks.

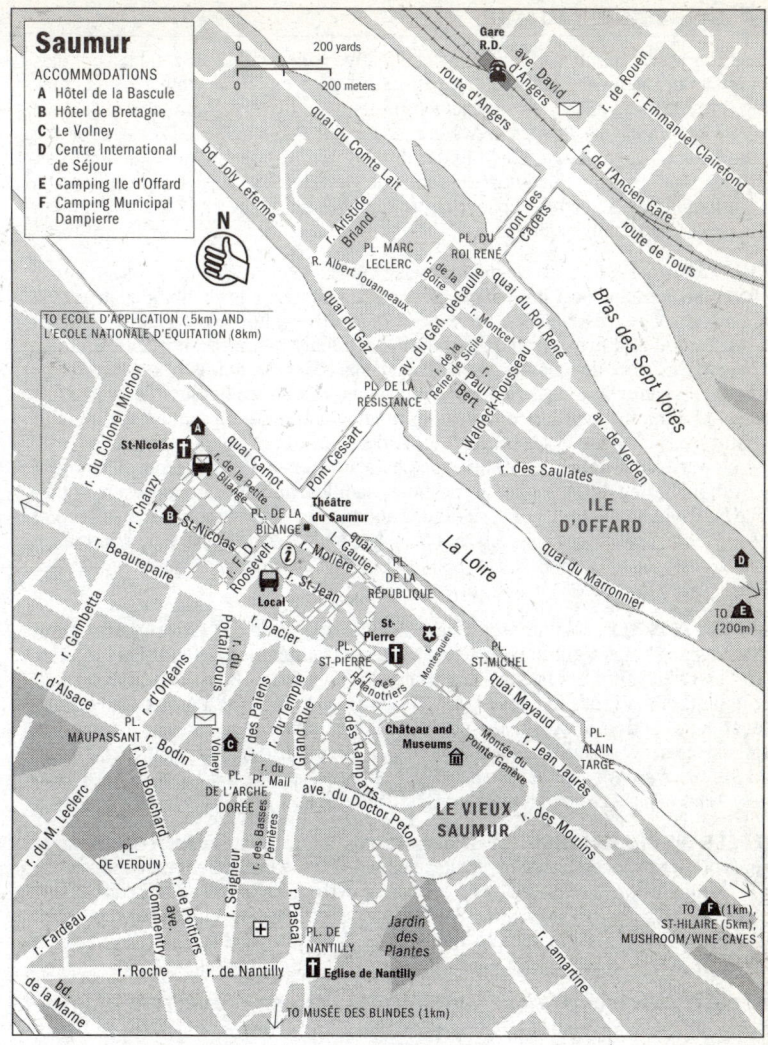

Saumur

ACCOMMODATIONS
A Hôtel de la Bascule
B Hôtel de Bretagne
C Le Volney
D Centre International
   de Séjour
E Camping Ile d'Offard
F Camping Municipal
   Dampierre

Les Forges de St. Pierre, 1 pl. St-Pierre (tel. 02 41 38 21 79). Savor a 3-course *menu* (58F) featuring the *plat du jour* or a *galette complète* (egg, ham, and emmental cheese), or design your own *galette*. The local Saumur *rouge* goes for 15F per glass. Open daily noon-2pm and 7-10pm except Tu evening, closed Sunday. V, MC, AmEx.

Le 30 Février, 9 pl. de la Républic (tel. 02 41 51 12 45). Add a day to your life with healthy salads (36-65F), pizza (35-63F), and the wonderful vegetarian *plats du jour*. Lots of fresh organic vegetables and a generous regional wine list. Bright, cheery, and filled with artwork. Open M-Sa noon-2pm and 7-10:30pm, Su 7-10:30pm; closed W during off-season. V, MC.

Le Relais, 31 quai Mayaud (tel. 02 41 67 75 20). Splurgers won't be disappointed by the 125F *menu,* while with 30 regional wines by the glass (14-32F), the rest of us may as well drown our fiscal sorrows on the riverside terrace. Open M-F noon-2pm and 6-11pm, Sa 6-11pm. Reservations recommended. V, MC, AmEx.

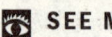 SEE MORE SAUMUR

The impressive number of museums and festive *caves* will keep you busy all day, but that doesn't mean you can't enjoy the city's quieter gems as well. Already housing three 12th- to 15th-century **churches** in its main district, Saumur also tucks a very pretty **Jardin des Plantes** between rue Docteur Peton and rue Marceau, on the other side of the château. You'll find it difficult to cross the picturesque **Pont Cessart** without stopping to admire the fantastic view, but the noisy traffic makes it a less-than-idyllic place of repose; the promenades along the river are much nicer for strolls, especially at sunset.

CHÂTEAU. Rising high above an otherwise modest skyline, Saumur's 14th-century château is perhaps best known for its cameo appearance in the famous medieval manuscript *Les très riches heures du duc de Berry*. For two centuries, Huguenots studied and prospered at its famous academy before their eviction under Louis XIV in 1685; the château was pillaged, abandoned, and finally converted to a prison. Presently it houses two small museums. The **Musée des Arts Décoratifs** has assembled an interesting collection of medieval and Renaissance painting and sculpture, 15th- and 16th-century tapestries, and brightly decorated *faïence* (stoneware). The horse-crazy **Musée du Cheval** upstairs holds tack from all over the world, including antique bits, horseshoes, saddles, and enormous savage spurs. The far room holds three horse skeletons and traces the evolution of man's second best friend. *(Château and museums tel. 02 41 40 24 40. Open daily June-Sept. 9:30am-6pm and 8:30-10:30pm; Oct.-May M and W-Su 9:30am-noon and 2-5:30pm, closed Tu Oct.-Mar. English guided tours June-Sept. 37F, students 26F.)*

GRATIEN ET MEYER. Saumur wines have been prized since the 12th century, when Plantagenet kings took their favorite casks with them to England. The popular Gratien et Meyer offers tastings and tours (15F) as well as hour-long *dégustation* courses (50F;daily at 11am and 3pm). The site also houses the **Musée de la Figurine-Jouet,** a collection of 20,000 toy soldiers. Here, Joan of Arc charges against the English; nearby, brigades of cavalry stand to attention. *(Rte. de Chinon. Tel. 02 41 83 13 32; www.gratienmeyer.com. Take bus D from pl. Bilange to "Beaulieu." Both open Apr.-Sept. daily 9am-6:30pm; Oct.-Mar. M-F 9am-noon and 2-6pm, Sa-Su 10am-12:30pm and 3-6pm.)*

MUSÉE DU CHAMPIGNON. This hotspot holds exotic fungi and increasingly large rings of tourists deep inside its dank cave home. Tours in English trace the history of the mushroom, with emphasis on the growth of its industry in France, surpassed only by the US and China. The mushroom grill outside serves gourmet *hors d'oeuvres* (30-46F) from noon to 3pm. *(Rte. de Gennes, St-Hilaire-St-Florent. Tel. 02 41 50 31 55. Open Feb. 15-Nov. 15 daily 10am-7pm. 38F, students 30F, children 6-14 20F.)*

L'ÉCOLE D'APPLICATION DE L'ARME BLINDEÉ ET DE LA CAVALERIE. Ever the dilettante, Saumur is famous for its equestrian associations, of which the 18th-century mouthful l'École d'application de l'arme blindé et de la cavalerie is the most notable. In 1939, its lightly-armed cadets deemed surrender dishonorable and held back the mighty *Wehrmacht* for three days. The **Musée de la Cavalerie,** a museum housed within the school, displays riding uniforms, weapons, and paraphernalia. *(Av. du Maréchal Foch. Tel. 02 41 83 93 06. Visits by appointment only. 20F.)*

ÉCOLE NATIONAL D'EQUITATION. The spectacular Cadre Noir tradition is taught within the civilian national riding school. The palatial 19th-century grounds are 15 minutes from the center of town. Tradition demands unwavering obedience from the horses and irreproachable decorum from the riders, who have, since 1825, donned "black dress decorated with gold, and 'lampion' hats worn ready for battle." From April to September, the school offers guided visits. *(Tel. 02 41 53 50 60; fax 02 41 67 63 08. Take bus D to "École d'Equitation." Visits with a peek at equestrian drills start 9:30-10:30am Tu-Sa. Visits without performances offered M-Sa 2:30-4pm. Mornings 35F, children 25F; afternoons 25F, children 20F.)*

THE NORTHWEST

MUSÉE DU MASQUE DE JULES CÉSAR. Near the École d'Equitation, this museum displays a fabulous collection of carnival masks in thematic scenes. The exhibit pays tribute to Samur's factory of carnival mask-making, the largest of its kind in Europe. *(Rue de l'Abbaye. Tel. 02 41 50 75 26. Open Apr.-Oct. 15 daily 10am-12:30pm and 2:30-6:30pm; Mar. M-F 2:30-6:30pm. Admission 25F, children 15F.)*

MUSÉE DES BLINDÉS. A very different sort of spectacle, this museum displays over 150 guns and armored cars from 12 different countries. The exhibit includes a show with real French soldiers driving tanks like bumper cars. *(1043 rte. de Fontevraud. Tel. 02 41 53 06 99. Open daily July-Aug. 9am-6pm; Apr.-June and Sept.-Oct. 9am-noon and 2pm-6pm; Nov.-Mar. 10am-noon and 2-5pm. 20F, children 10F.)*

♪ 🎭 ENTERTAINMENT AND FESTIVALS

ENTERTAINMENT. The **Théâtre de Saumur** (tel. 02 41 51 01 41), next to the tourist office, hosts everything from *galas de danse* to jazz and classical concerts in its 19th-century hall. **Le Blues Rock Magazine,** 7 rue de la Petite Bilange (tel. 02 41 50 41 69), features live nightly concerts, from jazz to the unidentifiably uproarious, 6:30 to 9:30pm; dancing takes over from 11pm to 4am. (Cover 40-50F; drinks 25-30F. Open May-Sept. daily; Oct.-Apr. Tu-Su. V, MC.) **L'Ascot Bar-Club,** 15 rue Molière (tel. 02 41 67 77 55), behind the tourist office, offers drinks and winks until the sun comes up. (Open M-Sa 6pm-4am. Occasional karaoke F-Sa. V, MC.)

FESTIVALS. In the first week of July, the three-day **Estivales de Saumur** brings a fun, festive atmosphere to rue St-Nicolas with vendors, outdoor dining, music, and free food. The **International Festival of Military Music** bugles in late June and early July. In late July, the cavalry school and the local tank school join forces in the celebrated annual **Carrousel.** After two hours of graceful equestrian performances, the spectacle degenerates (or evolves) into a three-hour motorcycle show and dusty tank parade. (Info and reservations tel. 02 41 40 20 66. 185-300F.) Saumur annually hosts dozens of (often free) equestrian events. The tourist office has the lowdown.

FONTEVRAUD-L'ABBAYE

The **Abbaye de Fontevraud** (tel. 02 41 51 71 41), the largest existing monastic complex in Europe, has left nine centuries of visitors in awe. The founder of this now-defunct community, Robert d'Arbrissel, settled in the forest of Fontevraud in 1101. To increase the humility of the monks, he placed a woman at the head of the order. Of its 32 *abbesses*, 16 were of royal blood; under their rule the Abbey became a place of refuge for women of all classes—from reforming prostitutes to princesses escaping unhappy marriages. Following the Revolution, the Abbey's function as a facility of reform took a different turn as it became a prison from 1804 until 1963.

The 12th-century abbey church serves as a Plantagenêts necropolis; **Eleanor of Aquitaine,** who lived out her days here after being repudiated by her second husband, **Henry II,** now lies next to him along with their son **Richard the Lionheart.** The British government has repeatedly sought to transfer the royal remains to Westminster, but the French insist the Plantagenêts were dukes of Anjou first, kings of England second. The abbey's **chapter house** holds a 1560 painting of the crucifixion to which seven abbesses have had themselves added. Outside, the **gardens** are organized into patches of legumes, tubers, greens, and medicinals; they bloom behind the abbey kitchen, whose spire-like chimney led 19th-century restorers to take it for a chapel. An English booklet and signs help visitors along; don't bother waiting for one of the hour-long English tours. (Open daily June-Sept. 17 9am-6:30pm, Sept. 17-Oct. 31 9:30am-noon and 2-5:30pm; Nov. 1-Mar. 7 9:30-noon and 2-5pm or dusk; Mar. 7-May 31 9:30am-noon and 2-6pm. 32F, students 21F.)

The **tourist office** (tel. 02 41 51 79 45) can give you a free map of the teensy town, which also houses the 12th-century Plantagenêt Gothic **Église St-Michel.** From the front of the abbey, cross the square and head towards the church. Turn right up the path behind the church; the tourist office is halfway down on your right. Ask the staff for details of concerts, held regularly in the abbey and the church. (Open May 15-Sept. 30 10am-noon and 2:30-6:30pm.)

The **#16 bus** makes the 14km trip from **Saumur's** *gare* (25min., 3 per day, 14F).

MONTSOREAU AND CANDES-ST-MARTIN

One stop before Fontevraud on the #16 bus, the village of **Montsoreau** lies below towering cliffs, and right on the banks of the placid Loire. The **tourist office**, av. de la Loire (tel. 02 41 51 70 22), hands out a booklet of the area which includes information on the Renaissance **château de Montsoreau,** the setting for Alexandre Dumas' *La Dame de Montsoreau*, as well trails to nearby cliffs, vineyards, dolmen, and **Herpinière windmill.** The staff can also tell you about the curious **troglodyte cliff dwellings**, with façades ranging from luxuriously ornate to bleakly utilitarian, which lie just above the village and line the road to Saumur. Many can be visited; consult tourist office for information and hours. For those who are sold, **Hôtel de la Loire,** av. de la Loire (tel. 02 41 51 70 06; fax 02 41 38 15 08), will set you up in one of 14 spacious rooms with a view of the river. (Doubles 165F, with shower and toilet 220F. V, MC.) Right next to the tourist office, three-star **Camping de l'Isle Verte**, av. de la Loire (tel./fax 02 41 51 76 60), has 105 sites, tennis, and a pool, all perched on the riverbank. (Two people car 72F. Extra person 16F. Electricity 16F. V, MC.)

A short walk along the river towards Chinon is Montsoreau's equally picturesque siamese twin, **Candes-St-Martin,** at the confluence of the Loire and the Vienne. St. Martin died here in AD 397, on the site of the **Église St-Martin.** Built in the 12th to 13th century and fortified in the 15th, its unique feature is its vaulted porch supported by a single central column. Climb the path behind the church for a **panorama** of the confluence and a nuclear power station in the distance.

ANGERS

From behind the imposing walls of their fortress in Angers (pop. 220,000), the medieval Dukes of Anjou ruled over the surrounding territory and an island across the Channel. The 13th-century château remains well preserved, although the rest of the valley now blooms with shops, museums, and gardens. Angers today offers inexpensive restaurants and a youthful atmosphere that keeps the town hopping well into the night. Nor have the city's traditions been forgotten; café-lined streets link a remarkable array of museums, while two medieval edifices housing Angers' world-famous tapestries provide more than an excuse to visit.

⑦ ORIENTATION AND PRACTICAL INFORMATION

To reach the château and tourist office, exit the train station straight onto rue de la Gare. Turn right at the second roundabout, pl. de la Visitation, onto rue Talot. At the traffic light, a left onto bd. du Roi-René leads to the château at pl. du Président Kennedy. The **tourist office** is on the right across from the château. To get to the *centre ville*, walk past the office onto rue Toussaint, which leads to **pl. du Ralliement,** the center of town. Go left, and one block down is **rue St-Laud,** the pedestrian-only zone of shops and *pâtisseries*. The hostel is 20 minutes away by bus from pl. Kennedy or pl. Ralliement.

Trains: Rue de la Gare. To: **Le Mans** (30min., 6-7 per day, 87F); **Nantes** (1hr., 5 per day, 75F); **Tours** (1hr., 7 per day, 88F); **Poitiers** (2-2½hrs., 4-5 per day, change at St-Pierre or Tours, 146F); **Orléans** (3-4hr., 6 per day, change at St-Pierre des Corps, 166F); and **Paris** (2-4hr., 3 per day, 242F). Open daily 4:30am-midnight.

Buses: Pl. de la République (tel. 02 41 88 59 25). To: **Rennes** (3hr., 2 per day, 97F). Open M-Sa 6:15am-7:15pm.

Local Transport: Tel. 02 41 33 64 64. Buses leave from pl. Kennedy or pl. Ralliement 6am-8pm, depending on the line. Limited night bus service 8pm-midnight. Tickets 7F.

Taxis: Anjou Taxi (tel. 02 41 87 65 00). **Angers Taxi** (tel. 02 41 73 98 20). Open 5am-11pm; call ahead for a taxi outside these hours.

Tourist Office: Pl. Kennedy (tel. 02 41 23 51 11; fax 02 41 23 51 66). The staff organizes trips to châteaux, reserves rooms, sells tickets to local events, hands out free maps, and **exchanges currency.** Open M-Sa 9am-7pm, Su 10am-1pm and 2-6pm; Oct.-May M-Sa 9am-12:30pm and 2-6:30pm.

Money: Banque de France, 13 pl. Mendès-France (tel. 02 41 24 25 00), has good rates of **currency exchange.** Exchange desks open M-F 9am-noon.

Youth services: Centre d'Informations Jeunes, 7 allée du Haras (tel. 02 41 87 74 47). Job and student info, discounts services. Open M-F 1-3:30pm, Sa 10am-noon.

Laundromat: Laverie du Cygne, pl. de la Visitation. Open daily 8am-9pm.

Hospital: Centre Hospitalier, 4 rue Larrey (tel. 02 41 35 36 37).

Police: Gendarmerie, 6bis pl. Freppel (tel. 02 41 73 56 10), or police municipale, 4 rue des Ursules (tel. 02 41 47 75 22 or 02 41 05 40 17).

Post Office: 1 rue Franklin Roosevelt (tel. 02 41 20 81 81), just off Corneille near rue Voltaire. **Currency exchange.** For Poste Restante mark "Angers-Ralliement." Open M-F 8am-7pm, Sa 8am-noon. **Postal code:** 49052.

Internet access: Copy Boutique, 48 rue Plantagenêt (tel. 02 41 88 96 26). 20F first 30min., 15F next 30min.;*carnet* 30F for 2hr., 39F for 3hr. Open M-F 9:30am-7:30pm.

■ ACCOMMODATIONS AND CAMPING

Angers becomes crowded in July and August. The hostel is inconvenient, but is huge and usually has room. Many hotels close between noon and 6pm on Sundays; those listed here are on fairly busy streets, so ask for rooms facing the back.

Auberge de Jeunesse Darwin (HI), 3 rue Darwin (tel. 02 41 22 61 20; fax 02 41 48 51 91). Take bus #8 (direction "Beaucouzé," 20min.) to "Essca Technopole," or #1 to "Belle-Beille." The night bus 1/S (direction "Belle-Beille/Lac de Maine") runs to pl. Ralliement until 12:10am. Simple 1-, 2-, and 3-bed rooms. Members 62F, non-members 72F. Breakfast 17F. Sheets 20F. Kitchen facilities, Internet, TV. Reception until 10pm.

Centre d'Accueil du Lac de Maine (HI), 49 av. du Maine (tel. 02 41 22 32 10; fax 02 41 22 32 11). Take bus #6 or 16 to "Accueil Lac de Maine." A lakeside setting, extensive sporting facilities, and a golf course justify the 10-15min. ride. Call ahead to make sure there's space; school groups often book the Centre in summer. Doubles 99F per person; quads 84F. Breakfast included. **Members only.**

Hôtel des Lices, 25 rue des Lices (tel. 02 41 87 44 10), near the château. Thirteen clean rooms sit above a pleasant bistro in a great location. Don't worry about the name—it refers to jousting, which is what you'll have to do to get a room in summer. Singles and doubles 120F, with bathroom 170-180F. Breakfast 25F. Shower 10F. Extra bed 50F.

Royal Hôtel, rue d'Iéna (tel. 02 41 88 30 25; fax 02 41 81 05 75), off pl. de la Visitation. Forty spacious, high-ceilinged rooms with big windows come with TVs; hot water is supplied by *le diable* himself. Singles 100-145F, with shower 170-210F; doubles 150-160F, with shower 200-240F; quad 280F. Breakfast 28-32F. V, MC, AmEx.

La Coupe d'Or, 5 rue de la Gare (tel. 02 41 88 45 02). Charming owner maintains 18 small, comfy rooms with TV at the top of a narrow winding staircase. Singles and doubles 95-140F, with shower 145-165F. Shower 15F. Breakfast 28F. V, MC.

Campsites: Camping du Lac de Maine (tel. 02 41 73 05 03; fax 02 41 73 02 20), not far from the Centre d'Accueil on CD 111, Route de Pruniers. Camp on a sandy lakeside beach. 73F for 2 people, tent, and car. Electricity 17.60F. Open Mar.-Oct.

◖ FOOD

Because of its student population, Angers offers lots of cheap and international food, especially on **rue St-Laud.** There is a **covered market** with inexpensive produce and baked goods in the basement of **Les Halles,** on rue Plantagenêt behind the cathedral, down the street from pl. du Ralliement (Tu-Sa 7am-8pm, Su 7am-1:30pm). A grocery store can be found in the basement of **Galeries Lafayette** at the corner of rue d'Alsace and pl. du Ralliement. (Open M-Sa 9am-7pm.)

La Soufflerie, 8 pl. du Pilori (tel. 02 41 87 45 32), is a deliciously cheerful local favorite. Piping hot soufflés come both savory (41-53F) and sweet (36F). Serious addicts may become violent if denied the hot bubbling chocolate soufflé, which is worth every calorie. Wines 10-13F per glass. Open Tu-Sa noon-2:30pm and 7-10pm. V, MC.

Le Petit Machon, 43 rue Bressigny (tel. 02 41 86 01 13). Small and dim but surprisingly good. Everything from the *tartes salées* to the chocolate mousse is home-made, earthy, and excellent. The 3-course 69F *menu* includes lots of options. Open M-F noon-1:50pm and 7:15-10pm, Sa 7:15-10pm. V, MC.

Restaurant des Beaux Arts: at the **Université de Clous,** 35 bd. Roi-René (tel. 02 41 88 47 38), near the tourist office; and the **Université de Belle-Beille,** bd. Lavoisier (tel. 02 41 48 45 76), near the hostel. Open to all students with college ID. Salad, *plat,* and dessert for 14.40F. Open Sept.7-July 10 M-Sa 11:30am-1pm and 6:30-8pm.

◖ SIGHTS

A 25F ticket gives admission to 5 museums; the 50F billet jumelé also includes château admission. Both are sold at the tourist office and at museums.

Tapestry, tapestry, tapestry! Angers is famous for its cherished woven works, which are found in many of the city's main sights. If you're in town a while, don't pass up the many minor museums not listed here.

CHÂTEAU D'ANGERS. St. Louis built the fortress and walls from 1228 to 1238, but Angevin duke René the Good oversaw construction of the château itself in the 15th century. During the wars of religion, Henry III ordered its demolition; fortunately, his subjects had only diminished the towers by one story when he died. The structure has 17 towers and a 900m long, 15m high wall that surrounds the perimeter; the former moat has blossomed into a colorful garden populated by deer, and the northernmost tower offers a spectacular view of the city. *(Off promenade du Bout du Monde. Tel. 02 41 87 43 47. Open daily June 1-Sept. 15 9:30am-7pm, Sept. 16-Oct. 31 10am-6pm, Nov. 1-Mar. 710am-5pm, Mar. 8-May 31 10am-6pm. Guided tours leave from the chapel every half-hour 10am-noon and 2-5:30pm. 35F, students 23F.)*

LA TÂPISSERIE DE L'APOCALYPSE, inside the château, is considered the largest tapestry masterpiece in the world. It was commissioned by Duke Louis I, who was inspired by an illuminated manuscript of the Book of Revelations. Executed by master weaver Robert Poinçon, the tapestry was completed in 1382 and measured 133m by 6m. The current 103m by 4m fragments hang in an anæsthetized gallery space beyond the chapel-museum. The work is full of vivid monsters and beasts, including a seven-headed satan gobbling down babies, and the armies of heaven preparing for battle. So as not to leave you hanging, Good finally triumphs over Evil. *(Same hours as chateau; included with château admission.)*

GALERIE DAVID D'ANGERS. The gallery houses the 19th-century sculptor's work in the beautifully restored and glass-topped 13th-century Toussaint Abbey. Among the impressive pieces are a scale replica of David's masterwork for the Panthéon façade in Paris, as well as many of the 30 statues he designed for city squares. *(37bis rue Toussaint. Tel. 02 41 87 21 03. Open mid-June to mid-Sept. daily 9am-6:30pm; rest of year Tu-Su 10am-noon and 2-6pm. 10F, under 16 free.)*

MUSÉE JEAN LURÇAT. You'll find Angers's second woven masterpiece in this former 12th-century hospice. The 80m long *Chant du Monde* ("Song of the World") is a symbolic journey through human destiny. Lurçat, inspired by the *Apocalypse* tapestry, abandoned his career as a painter and turned to weaving; he completed this surprisingly modern work in the 1930s. Filled with blazing colors, the tapestry represents life's joys and sorrows in 10 enormous panels. *(4 bd. Arago. Tel. 02 41 24 18 45. Open mid-June to mid-Sept. daily 9am-6:30pm, rest of year Tu-Su 10am-noon and 2-6pm. 20F, under 16 free.)*

MUSÉE DE LA TAPISSERIE CONTEMPORAINE. In the same building as the Musée Jean Lurçat, this displays a stunning permanent collection of textile and tapestry works, including pieces by the renowned cloth sculptor Magdalena Abakanowicz. *(Tel. 02 41 24 18 48. Open mid-June to mid-Sept. daily 9am-6:30pm and mid-Sept. to mid-June Tu-Su 10am-noon and 2-6pm. 20F, under 16 free.)*

CATHÉDRALE ST-MAURICE. The 12th-century edifice bears a Norman porch, a 13th-century chancel which intersects a 4th-century Gallo-Roman wall, and some of the oldest stained glass windows in France, most dating to the 12th and 15th centuries. Linger long enough and you might get a free tour in English from the lovely local nuns. This being Angers, the cathedral also displays an impressive collection of tapestries and interprets the Book of Revelations amidst the elders of the Church in the rose windows. *(Pl. Monseigneur Chappoulie. Open daily 9am-7pm.)*

🎵 🌾 ENTERTAINMENT AND FESTIVALS

ENTERTAINMENT. Although the discos are firmly rooted in the suburbs, nightlife in Angers remains lively. The cafés along **rue St-Laud** are always packed with diverse crowds of coffee-drinkers and people-watchers, while a few bars on student-dominated **rue Bressigny** get down even before the sun does. **Le Kent,** 7 pl. Ste-Croix (tel. 02 41 87 88 55), has 50 different beers and 70 whiskies. (Open M-Sa 9am-2am.) For all-night dancing, try **Le Newyorkais,** 5 rue Maille (tel. 02 45 87 37 93), the club that never sleeps. (Open Su-Th 11pm-3am, F-Sa 11pm-4am.)

FESTIVALS. July 1-25, Angers hosts the **Festival d'Anjou.** One of the largest summer theater festivals in France, it attracts renowned French comedy and dramatic troupes to the château; Albert Camus once staged a play in front of a nationwide TV audience here. (Info at 1 rue des Arènes. Tel. 02 41 88 14 14; www.angers.ensam.fr/festanjou. 160F per show, students 100F.)

LE MANS

Lying by the river Sarthe, the thriving provincial capital of Le Mans (pop. 150,000) is best known today for the 24-hour car race which has stormed around the city's circuit each summer since 1923. Le Mans' rich history goes back to Roman times, however, when thick stone walls were built around the small town of Vindunum to separate its territory from surrounding areas. Eight centuries later, a screaming Henry Plantagenêt was born here. An influential figure in Le Mans, Henry went on to do important things like found the city's Coeffort Hospital and become King of England. Charles VI went mad when he left Le Mans in 1392 to play soldiers with the Duke of Brittany, but you won't be tempted to follow his exit—Le Mans' flourishing core will tickle you pink with its picturesque *vieille ville*, top-notch sights, and go-go-going nightlife.

🔢 ORIENTATION AND PRACTICAL INFORMATION

The city's commercial and *brasserie* center is focused around **pl. de la République,** while the sights and restaurants of the *cité médiévale* are propped up by Roman walls on the bank of the Sarthe. To get to the **tourist office** from the station, cross bd. de la Gare and head up av. du Général Leclerc for about one kilometer; the road ploughs through *places* and becomes av. François Mitterrand; after you cross av. du Général de Gaulle, the office is two blocks ahead on your left, with a big black glass house-shaped front (25min.). Or head up rue Gastelier across from the post office and catch bus #5 (direction "Villaret") to "Étoile." Cross pl. Lionel Lecouteux away from the Banque du France, and head down rue de l'Étoile; the tourist office is two blocks down on your left.

Trains: Bd. de la Gare, off pl. du 8 Mai 1945. To: **Nantes** (1hr., 7 per day, 136F); **Tours** (1hr., 6 per day, 78F); **Rennes** (1hr., 7 per day, 128F); **Paris** (1-3hr., 12 per day, 160-186F). Ticket counters open M-Sa 5am-10:30pm, Sa 6am-10:30pm, Su 5am-11pm.

Buses: An **SNCF bus** goes to **Saumur** from the station. Ask there for schedules and prices.

Public Transportation: SETRAM buses, 65 av Général de Gaulle (tel. 02 43 24 76 76), run 6am to 8 or 9pm, after which the city's four **"hi'bus"** lines take over until 2am. Pick up a bus map at the SETRAM office or tourist office if you're planning on moving and shaking. Ticket 5.90F, *carnet* of 10 49F.

Taxis: Radio Taxi (tel. 02 43 24 92 92). 24hr.

Bike Rental: Top Team, 9 pl. St-Pierre (tel. 02 43 24 88 32 when they answer). From 100F per day. 1000F deposit. Open M-Sa 9:30am-noon and 2-7pm. V, MC.

Tourist Office: Rue de l'Étoile (tel. 02 43 28 17 22; fax 02 43 23 37 19; www.ville-lemans.fr). In the 17th-century Hôtel des Ursulines, the staff distributes maps and info booklets. A historical walking tour of the *vieille ville* or Cathédrale St-Julien departs from the cathedral fountain (90min., July-Aug. daily 3pm, 25F). Open June-Aug. M-Sa 9am-6pm, Su 10am-12:30pm and 2:30-5pm; rest of year M-F 9am-6pm, Sa 9am-noon and 2-6pm, Su 10am-noon.

Money: Best **currency exchange** rates are at **Banque de France,** 2 pl. Lionel Lecouteux (tel. 02 43 74 74 00). Exchange desks open M-F 8:30am-noon.

English Bookstore: Thuard Librairie, 24 rue de l'Étoile (tel. 02 43 82 22 22), has bestsellers and some classics in English. Open M-Sa 8:30am-7:30pm. V, MC.

Laundromat: Lav'Ideal, 4 pl. l'Éperon (tel. 02 43 24 53 99). Open daily 7am-9pm. **Laverie Libre Service,** 4 rue Gastelier (tel. 02 43 43 99 18).

Youth Information: Ville du Mans Service Jeunesse, 13 rue de l'Étoile, (tel. 02 43 83 00 09), near the tourist office. Offers student discounts and has job and housing information. Open M-F 9am-noon and 1-5pm. **SMEBA,** 34 av. François Mitterrand (tel. 02 43 39 90 20), is a student travel agency which arranges discount tickets and offers health insurance for foreign students in France. Open M-F 9am-6pm.

Police: Commissariat Central, 6 rue Coeffort (tel. 02 43 61 68 00).

Hospital: Centre Hospitalier, 194 av. Rubillard (tel. 02 43 43 43 43).

Post Office: 13 pl. de la République (tel. 02 43 21 75 00). **Currency exchange.** For Poste Restante address to "République, 72013 Le Mans Cedex 2". Open M-F 8am-7pm, Sa 8am-noon. **Branch office,** 1 pl. du 8 Mai 1945, right by the station. Same hours and services. **Postal code:** 72000.

Internet Access: **Médiathèque,** 54 rue du Port (tel. 02 43 47 48 74). 5F per 15min. Open Tu-F 10am-7pm, Sa 10am-6pm. Also at the **hostel.**

ACCOMMODATIONS AND CAMPING.

It's a good idea to always call ahead in Le Mans, as spontaneous remodeling or closures seem to be a favorite sport of hotel proprietors. The row of gaudy establishments across from the station face the noisy pl. du 8 Mai 1945 and are surprisingly expensive; stick to the quieter streets up the hill and you'll find better deals.

Foyer de Jeunes Travailleurs Le Flore (HI), 23 rue Maupertius (tel. 02 43 81 27 55; fax 02 43 81 06 10; florefjt@cybercable.tm.fr). From the train station, cross pl. du 8 Mai and head up av. du Gén. Leclerc. Follow directions to tourist office, but turn right up av. du Gén. de Gaulle, and cross the next intersection to av. Leon-Bollée. Continue straight; rue Maupertius is the third street on your left (35min.). Or take bus #5 from the station (direction "Villaret") to "de Gaulle," walk down a block to the bright red SETRAM kiosk near pl. de la République, and catch the #4 (direction "Gazonfier") or #12 (direction "Californie") to "Erpell." The hostel is across the street and down rue Maupertius to the right. Blissfully clean and quiet foyer near the Jardins des Plantes. The modern building has doubles, triples, and quads, plus kitchen, laundry, TV room, and free internet access. 68F. Breakfast included. Sheets 18F. Wheelchair access. **Members only.**

Hôtel le Châtelet, 15 rue du Père Mersenne (tel. 02 43 43 92 36), above a bar on a fairly quiet street corner. From the station, head up av. du Gén. Leclerc and take the first left onto rue de la Pélouse; rue du Père-Mersenne is the second on the right. The nine newly-carpeted, beautiful rooms make you wonder if the owners realize what a bargain they're offering. Singles and doubles 100-150F; triples 150-200F. Breakfast 20F. No weekend stays without advance notice.

Select Hôtel, 13 rue du Père-Mersenne (tel. 02 43 24 17 74). Just up the street from le Châtelet, Select keeps 15 rooms in good condition off darkly-wallpapered halls. Singles and doubles with sink 115F, 140F with sink and micro-shower, 175F with micro-shower and toilet; triples 245F. Breakfast 22F. Shower 13F. V, MC.

Hôtel Normandie, 108 av. du Gen. Leclerc (tel. 02 43 24 61 29), just up the road from the station. 16 recently remodeled, rewired, and recarpeted rooms above a busy street will greet visitors in 2000. The friendly young owners knock off 10F per night if you pay in advance for four nights or more. Singles and doubles 125F with sink, 150F with shower, 160F with shower and toilet. TV. Breakfast 20F. V, MC.

Campsites: The tourist office has a list of campsites in the Sarthe region. The closest is the two-star **Camping Le Vieux Moulin,** 9km away in Neuville-sur-Sarthe (tel. 02 43 25 31 82; fax 02 43 25 38 11). Take the train from Le Mans (8 min., 4 per day, 13F). The riverside site has bikes (50F per day), laundry facilities, a pool, and tennis courts. 2 adults, 2 children with car 92F. Open May 15-Sept. 30. V, MC. **Camping Le Houssay** (tel. 02 43 21 16 58), in Spay, will not threaten your virility, but does offer a pleasant place to camp. Also on the Sarthe, the site has laundry facilities, fishing, and tennis.

THE NORTHWEST

584 ■ LOIRE VALLEY (VAL DE LOIRE)

Take bus #6 from Le Mans to Spay (25min., 2 per day, 20.50F). Driving, take rte. d'Arnage from Le Mans and follow the signs (14km). 2 adults, 2 children with car 52.70F. Open Apr. 17-Oct. 17.

🍴 FOOD

Renowned for its poultry, *sarthois* cuisine commonly includes dishes of *pintade* (guinea fowl) and *canard* (duck). Taste tiny tidbits or go for the kill–the succulent *marmite sarthoise*, a warm casserole of rabbit, chicken, ham, carrots, cabbage, and mushrooms, bubbling in a bath of Jasnière wine, is a carnivore's dream. Large *brasseries* with good lunchtime *menus* line pl. de la République, while pleasant, affordable restaurants settle along Grande Rue and behind pl. de l'Éperon in the *vieille ville*. For simpler meals, the **indoor market** sells portable goodies in **Les Halles**, pl. du Marche, while an **outdoor market** spreads from pl. des Jacobins (W, F, and Su 7am-12:30pm). There is a **Prisunic** supermarket at 30 pl. de la République. (Open M-Sa 8:30am-7:30pm.)

L'Ardoise, 91 Grande Rue (tel. 02 43 24 65 60), in the *vieille ville*. Decorated with rotating exhibits of local art, this pleasant little eatery offers 59-66F *plats*, such as *minute de bœuf au basilic*, and exotic 54F summer salads. The 49F lunch *formule* includes the *plat du jour* and a glass of wine, while the 3-course dinner *menu* is a steal at 67F. Open M-Sa noon-2:30pm and 7-11pm. V, MC.

Auberge des 7 Plats, 79 Grand Rue (tel. 02 43 24 57 77). Seven *plats*, *bien sûr*, but seven *entrées* and seven *desserts* also grace the menu of this two-storeyed *vieille ville* restaurant. Generous weekday 47F and 57F *formules* offer poultry or two dishes of your choosing, while the 77F *menu* lets you choose from all 343 combinations of the *carte*. Open Tu-Sa noon-2:30pm and 7-11pm, Su 7-11pm, V, MC.

Le Tanger, 20 rue du Cornet (tel. 02 43 23 34 47). If the Moroccan jazz doesn't draw you into polite Le Tanger, the heavenly smells of delicately-spiced stews will certainly stop you in your tracks. Steaming bowls of couscous come with lamb, chicken, or veal (60-98F) in beautiful handmade pottery; the cordial cooks will also happily prepare a vegetarian version (40F, not on the menu). Open M-Sa noon-2pm and 7-10pm. V, MC.

👁 SIGHTS

The combined billet couple includes any two of the Musée de Tesse, Musée Vert, or Musée de la Reine-Bérengère (25F, students 12.50F); the billet triple covers all three (32F, students 16F). Note that all three are free on Sunday.

Roman walls, medieval streets, a Gothic cathedral, and a 20th-century race car museum make Le Mans a city to savor slowly. Le Mans also holds a remarkable set of beautiful **churches,** sprinkled throughout the city, including the **Maison-Dieu** founded by Henry Plantagenêt. The tourist office brochure *les Plantagenêts* maps out all the churches, accompanied by detailed descriptions.

THE VIEILLE VILLE. Rising up behind the river Sarthe and thick Roman walls, Le Mans' *vieille ville* is considered one of the most picturesque in France—a good thing, as the city becomes a bit of an eyesore outside the central downtown area. The setting for the 1990 film *Cyrano de Bergerac*, the winding streets and alleys are lined with 15th- to 17th-century houses. Before you set out strolling, stop at the tourist office for the English *Le Mans: An Art and History Town*, which will allow you to identify the *maisons* as they go by. If your French is up to it, troop along with the daily **guided tour** that meets at the cathedral fountain. (35min., 3pm, 25F). The **Musée Reine-Bérengère,** 9 rue Reine-Bérengère, is a small museum housed in a 1460 residence, which features some fairly drab historical objects of the Sarthe region but occasionally has a good exhibition.

MURAILLE GALLO-ROMAINE. The stocky 4th-century Roman walls which hug the south-western edge of the city are Le Mans' pride and joy, and rightly so. Punc-

THE NORTHWEST

tured with arched gates and fortified with massive towers, the 1.3km-long *muraille* is the longest and perhaps best preserved in all of France. Most surprising and pleasing is the artisanship evident in the construction; multicolored tiles form geometric patterns along the length of the walls, and pink mortar gives the entire structure an earthy orange glow.

CATHÉDRALE ST-JULIEN. One of France's most famous cathedrals, this great fireball of Romanesque and Gothic architecture was originally constructed in the 11th and 12th centuries. The sculpted front of the south porch, dated from this time, is considered one of Europe's finest. After a fire destroyed the town in 1134, the cathedral was repaired using Gothic techniques, giving rise to the pointed arch reinforcements you can see on either side in the nave. The great chancel with twelve chapels was added on in the 13th century, doubling the size of the cathedral and necessitating the tangle of flying buttresses which encircle the exterior. A great torrent of color, the chapel still retains its original 14th-century paint-job, including dark violet walls and a blood-red ceiling upon which angels float in painted plasma. In the transept, colorful 16th-century tapestries narrate the legend of St. Julian. *(Pl. des Jacobins. Open daily 9am-noon and 2-6pm.)*

MUSÉE AND PARC DE TESSÉ. Housed in the former 19th-century bishops' palace, this fabulous collection celebrates over 600 years of art. The beautifully lit modern interior displays 17th- to 19th-century painting and sculpture, and temporary exhibits of modern art and artifacts, as well as an Egyptian collection in which a mummy lies supine next to its full-body X-ray. You'll love the knockout collection of 14th- and 15th-century Italian painting, wit a heart-melting *Madonna and Child* attributed to Spagna in the *Salle Renaissance* and an equally exquisite counterpart in the *Salle des primitifs italiens.* The museum's pride and joy, however, is a 12th-century enamel portrait of Geoffrey Plantagenêt that originally decorated his tomb in the Cathédrale St-Julien. When you've seen the collection, bask in the sun in the beautiful Tessé park, with a fountain, a waterfall, shady trees, and acres of grass. *(2 av. de Paderborn. 15min. walk from pl. de la République. Take bus #3, direction "Bellevue," from rue Gastelier by the station or from av. du Gén. de Gaulle, a block down from pl. de la République, to "Musée." The #9, direction "Villaret," also goes there from av. du Gén. de Gaulle. Tel. 02 43 27 38 51. Open May-Oct. daily 9am-noon, 2-6pm; Nov.-Apr. Tu-Su 9am-noon and 2-6pm. 16F, students 8F, free Su.)*

L'ABBAYE DE L'ÉPAU. Founded in 1229 by Queen Bérengère, widow of Richard the Lionheart, the restored Épau abbey sits peacefully among 32 acres of strollable grass and trees. The main church, with large stained-glass windows, is largely empty save for the beautifully ornate Chapelle St-Sebastian; the queen's tomb lies solitary in the Scriptorium. The grounds are perfect for a sunny day's picnic. In summer, jazz and classical music concerts fill the abbey; call 02 43 81 44 44 for a schedule. *(Rte. de Change, Yvre-l'Évêque. From bd. Levasseur, off pl. de la République, take bus #14 (direction "Sablons") to "Pologne," and then follow the signs behind you to the abbey. 20min. bus plus 7 min. walk. Tel. 02 43 84 22 29. Open daily Apr.-Sept. 9:30am-noon and 2-6pm; closes at 5:30 Nov.-Mar. 15F, 10F students.)*

RACING CIRCUIT AND MUSÉE DE L'AUTOMOBILE. Those who are really into their cars—and we mean *really*—can gawk at the 13.5km stretch of racetrack that lies south of the city. Since 1923, the circuit has held the annual *24 Heures du Mans,* a gruelling test of endurance that outlasts even a back-to-back performance of Wagner's Ring Cycle. The race is held in the second week of June, but other events are held during the summer. *(Tickets and info tel. 02 43 40 24 75.)* Just inside the track's main entrance is the massive **Musée de l'Automobile,** which traces the evolution of motor vehicles from its beginnings to the present, including scores of shiny racing cars and cycles of premium vintage, along with a super-duper interactive multimedia exhibit. *(From bd. Levasseur off pl. de la République, take bus #6 to "Raineries," and continue on foot down rue de Laigne, following signs to the track and museum. 25min. bus plus 7min. walk. Tel. 02 43 72 72 24. Open June-Aug. daily 10am-7pm; Oct.-Dec. and Feb.-May 10am-6pm; Jan. Sa-Su only 10am-6pm. 40F, students and ages 12-18 30F, ages 7-11 10F.)*

THE NORTHWEST

♫ ❋ ENTERTAINMENT AND FESTIVALS

ENTERTAINMENT. Le Mans packs most of its nocturnal revelry in and around **pl. de la République.** Crowds of languorous late 20- and 30-somethings sip cool drinks at large, relaxed, *place*-side *brasseries*, including the Tex-Mex **El Dakyto** (tel. 02 43 24 09 00) and the hip **Le Moderne** across the street (tel. 02 43 28 40 88). (Both open until 2am.) The younger, funkier scene is tucked down **rue du Dr. Leroy,** where the penetrating gazes of Le Mans youth greet you from behind yet more cocktail glasses until 2 or 3am. The sippers outside the **Paris Texas Cafe,** 21 rue du Dr. Leroy (tel. 02 43 23 71 00), guard a nice little club inside, while the more particular drinkers populate **Le Café Noir** (tel. 02 43 23 12 50) across the street, which offers a dizzying array of liquids, from sweet pear liqueur (23F) to Mezcal tequila (16F). **Café Côté Sud** keeps a convivial atmosphere with the music turned up high; chill for a few, and then swing on to happy **St-Germain's** (tel. 02 43 23 76 06), which often has live music on Saturdays. The jovial **Mulligan's Irish Pub** (tel. 02 43 14 26 65) roars with free-flowing Guinness (16F) and Paddy "snacks" (no, that's *food*). The *vieille ville* has a collection of bars behind **pl. de l'Éperon** and off **Grande Rue;** the gay-friendly club-bar **Arc en Ciel,** 2 rue Dorée, is open every night until 2am. A surprising number of discothèques are planted right in town, including **Le Select,** 44 pl. de la République (tel. 02 43 28 87 41); the **City Bird,** 23ter rue d'Alger (tel. 02 43 23 08 25); and the gay-friendly **La Limite,** 7 rue St-Honoré (tel. 02 43 24 85 54), in the *vieille-ville*. (All open Th-Su until 5am.) Cannes film festival winners roll nightly in *v.o.* at the *vieille ville's* ultra-cool **Ciné-Poche,** 97 Grande Rue (tel. 02 43 24 73 85).

FESTIVALS. For the entire month of April, the city attracts contemporary jazz artists of every creed for the **Europa Jazz Festival.** (Info and tickets from 9 rue des Frères Greban, tel. 02 43 23 78 99.) On the first weekend of July, over 40 theater companies hit the streets for **Les Scénomanies,** a festival which presents over 100 different shows on the streets of old Le Mans over two days. The excitement brings out all sorts of street entertainment, including international music, dance, and acrobatics. (Call tourist office for info.) If you've missed *Les Scénomanies*, worry not—throughout July and August, **Les Soirs d'Été** feature free theatre, musical comedy, and music performances in the streets. Thursday performances take place in individual districts, while Friday performances are in the town centre; outdoor film showings (30F) add to the hubbub. Pick up a *L'Été au Mans* schedule from the tourist office.

THE LOIR VALLEY

Not to be confused with its much more famous neighbor to the south, the Loir Valley extends 311km from the bubbling springs of St-Éman to its confluence with the Sarthe just above Angers. Steeped in a history of famous poets and good wine, the charm of its brooks and riverlets makes the Loir an ideal area for those in search of easily explorable natural beauty. The hillsides rising up from the valley house caves and troglodyte dwellings, whereas some of the country's most impressive murals are found on the walls of the region's churches.

VENDÔME

It seems unfair that Vendôme (pop. 18,500) will always be remembered as the name of a Parisian *place* rather than for its own attractions. The town itself, swimming in Loir riverlets, bursting with blooming flowers and full of striking sights, is well worth a stop in your Loir country sojourns. The village of Balzac's schooldays began life as Roman Vindocinum ("white mountain"), and later saw Geoffrey Martel among its distinguished citizens; today the amiable town pays tribute to its colorful past while thriving as one of the best-loved spots of the Loir valley.

The remarkable **Abbaye de la Trinité,** rue de l'Abbaye (tel. 02 54 77 05 07), today consisting of a church, a cloister, and a chapter house, was constructed on the site into which Geoffrey Martel saw three burning spears plunge in 1034 from his château window. The **Église Abbatiale** is, for all intents and purposes, a cathedral, lacking only a bishop to define it as such. Its prickly 1506 façade is about as flamboyant as High Gothic gets, while the interior contains an elaborate shrine to the Holy Tear. The sacred salinous drop was exported to Rome for verification in the 19th century and, much to the discontent of the *vendomois*, never returned. The beautiful 12th-century Romanesque belltower peals a pleasing French *passacaille* that dates back to the Hundred Years' War. The 14th- to 15th-century **cloister** today houses the **Musée Municipal de Vendôme** (tel. 02 54 77 26 13), which features a number of remarkable mural paintings from Loir valley churches, as well as regional religious artwork, sculptures, paintings, and a Loir valley archeological exhibit. (Museum open W-Su 10am-noon and 2-6pm. 16F. Church open daily 9am-7pm. Free.) **Boat tours** take you past the Porte de l'Eau, the water mill, and the abbey. (35min. July-Aug. daily 2-7pm, May-June Sa and Su 2-7pm. 25F, students 20F. Buy tickets at tourist office.) In July and August, the cloister courtyard hosts free **arts events,** from dance and theater performances to acid jazz and punk concerts. (Call tourist office for details.) Further south and up the curving Rampe du Château lies the peaceful remains of the **Château du Vendôme,** an 11th-century fortress with a park in full bloom among its ruins. Clamber up as high as you can to enjoy a beautiful view of the city below. (Open June-Aug. 9am-8pm, Sept.-May 9am-7pm.) Behind the château stretches the utopian **Forêt de Vendôme,** with serene paths for biking or shady strolling.

The well-stocked **tourist office,** Hôtel du Bellay in parc Ronsard (tel. 02 54 77 05 07; fax 02 54 73 20 81; Ot.Vendome@wanadoo.fr; www.tourisme.fr), has lots of information about the region. Pick up *What's on in the Loir Valley*, the *Bienvenue Vendôme* tourist guide, and a yellow map of the walking tour. (Office open June 14-Sept. 12 M-Sa 10am-6pm, Su 10am-1pm; May 1-June 13 M-Sa 10am-12:30pm and 2-6pm, Su 10am-1pm; Sept. 13-Apr. 30 M-Sa 10am-12:30pm and 2-6pm.) The **post office** is across from St. James's chapel on rue du Change. (Open M-F 8:30am-noon and 1:30-6pm, Sa 8:30am-noon.) There is a **Monoprix supermarket** at 40 faubourg Chartrain. (Open M-Sa 9:30am-noon and 2:30-7pm.) There is a **covered market** behind the St. Martin clock tower on Fridays. If want to stay the night, the friendly owners of the **Café de la Ville,** 23 rue du Général de Gaulle, let nine rooms overlooking the central pl. St-Martin. (Singles and doubles 140-190F. Breakfast 32F. Closed Su night and M. V, MC.) The three-star **Camping Les Grands Prés,** rue Geoffrey Martel (tel. 02 54 77 00 27), is also a stone's throw from the center of town. Kitty-corner from the beautiful *jardins publics*, the 2-hectare semi-shaded site has 200 places with a swimming pool and tennis. (2 adults and car 43F. Extra adult 12F, child 8F, car 7F. Electricity 17-25F. Closed Oct.-Mar.)

The station, bd. de Tremault (tel. 02 54 23 50 04), runs **trains** and **buses** to **Tours** (1hr., 5 per day, 3 on Su., 60F), **Châteaudun** (45min., 6 per day, 4 on Su, 42F), and **Chartres** (1¾hr., 2 per day, 1 on Su, 71F). To get to the tourist office and the *centre ville,* turn right out of the station and keep going until you reach rue fbg Chartrain. Follow the road straight for about five blocks, crossing the Loir once and then taking your second right onto rue St-Jacques by the chapel. Take the next left onto rue Poterie; the tourist office is a bit further down on your left in parc Ronsard. The central pl. St-Martin is the next left, a few blocks in on rue du Gén. de Gaulle.

NEAR VENDÔME: LA POSSONNIÈRE

Thirty-five kilometers west of Vendôme, the beautiful manor house of La Possonnière (tel. 02 54 72 40 05) rests peacefully in lush countryside along the Loir. This idyllic setting saw the birth, in 1524, of **Pierre de Ronsard,** the "prince of poets" of the French Renaissance (see p. 15). A pretty vegetable garden lies in the front of the grounds, while the house itself is remarkable for its Italian Renaissance artwork—some of the first to appear in France. The estate is open for 45-minute guided visits. (July-Aug. W-Su 3-7pm, Apr.-June and Sept. 1-Nov. 15 Sa-Su 3-6pm. Last visit leaves 30min. before closing.) A small stop-off on the route between **Le Mans** and **Vendôme,** La Possonnière is accessible during the school year by the #9a **TLC bus** (tel. 02 54 78 50 66) that runs between **Vendôme** and **Coutre-sur-Loire,** a well sign-posted, 10-minute walk away. In summer, **bikes** can be rented from **La Chartre-sur-Loir,** about 11km away and reachable by bus from **Le Mans** (1½hr., 2 per day, 72F). Try **Merillon Cycles,** rue Nationale. (Tel. 02 43 44 42 94. 50F per half-day, 70F per day. ID deposit. Open Tu-Sa 9am-noon and 2:30-7pm, Su 10am-12:30pm.) If you're lucky enough to have a car, take the D917W from Vendôme and follow the signs to Possonnière.

CHÂTEAUDUN

Dominated by an imposing castle, the town of Châteaudun (pop. 16,000) looks out over the calm Loir valley with wizened eyes. It makes for a pleasant daytrip, only 25km off the N157 connecting Le Mans and Orleans.

Located 60m above the river, the **château,** pl. Jean de Dunois (tel. 02 37 94 02 90), is a melting pot of medieval, Gothic, and Renaissance architecture. From the medieval period stands the 31m-high keep, preserved when Joan of Arc's companion-in-arms Jean Dunois claimed the castle and had it rebuilt in the 1450s. The Gothic structures that Dunois added include the Sainte-Chapelle, on whose walls 15 pillars support raised statues of the saints. In the next century, Dunois' grandsons added the neighboring 16th-century Longueville wing, with a beautifully carved staircase and a Flamboyant Gothic façade lined with nasty-looking gargoyles. July 15 to August 31, the château offers a Thursday night-time visit to the keep for 21F. (Open daily July-Aug. 9:30am-7pm, Apr.-June and Sept. 9:30am-6:15pm, Oct.-Mar. 10am-12:30pm and 2-5pm. Last entry 30min. before closing. 32F, 21F for students and ages 12-18. Joint ticket with the Musée de Beaux-Arts 39F.) When the château's done, head down the road to the beautifully-lit **Grottes du Foulon,** 35 rue des Fouleries (tel. 02 37 45 19 60). The tour takes you through the chilly caves all the way underneath the center of town, explaining their geology and pointing out a variety of sparkling *geodes,* or crystallized silica deposits, along the way. The visit ends with a small *son et lumière* show. (Open May-Sept. 10am-noon and 2-6pm, rest of year Sa-Su 2-6pm. 30F, students 20F, ages 6-14 15F.)

The town's **Musée de Beaux-Arts et d'Histoire Naturelle,** 3 rue Toufaire (tel. 02 37 45 55 36), has some very vicious-looking knives and a set of beautifully decorated armor plates in the *Salle d'Art Asiatique,* mummified baby crocodiles in the *Salle d'Égyptologie,* and a massive stuffed toucan in the ornithological collection. (Open July-Aug. daily. 10am-12:30pm and 1:30-6:30pm, Apr.-June and Sept. W-M same hours, Oct.-Mar. W-M 10am-noon and 2-5pm. 20F, students and ages 6-15 12F.) The 12th-century **Église de la Madeleine,** pl. Cap de la Madeleine, sits atop a 20m drop on the southern edge of the *centre ville.* The church was never completed, and 800 years later was severely damaged by fire during World War II. Though heavily restored, it displays a fine array of carved Romanesque capitals and Gothic detail in the choir. (Open daily 10am-noon and 2-5pm.)

The **tourist office,** 1 rue de Luynes (tel. 02 37 45 22 46; fax 02 37 66 00 16; www.eureetloirtourism.com), has brochures for helpful self-guided tours. The promenade takes you past some of the city's prettiest houses and oldest alleyways, dating back to the 16th century. **Banks,** the **post office,** and the **police** all face pl. du 18 Octobre. If you're more of a land rover, **Ets Angelou,** rue de la République (tel. 02 37 45 51 81), **rents bikes.** (70F per day. 1100F deposit. Open Th-Sa 9am-noon and 2-7pm, W 9am-noon.) A lively **outdoor market** takes on pl. du 18 Octobre (Th 9am-4pm). There is a **Viveco supermarket** at 11 rue Gambetta. (Open M-Sa 9am-noon and 2-7:30pm.) If you'd like to stick around, **Hôtel L'Armorial,** 59 rue Gambetta (tel. 02 37 45 19 57; fax 02 37 45 04 05), has 16 rooms close to the center of town. (Singles and doubles 140-275F. V, MC.) The two-star **Camping Municipal du Moulin a Tan,** rue de Chollet (tel. 02 37 45 05 34), offers 121 shady places on the opposite bank of the Loir. To get there, take rue de la Maréchal Lyautey off pl. du 18 Octobre and continue straight. Continue up rue St-Lubin, keeping right and eventually turn onto rue St-Mérard. Cross the Loir, and then take the third right, which is rue de Chollet. The camping is about 1km down the road on your left (35min.). (8.50F per site, 9F per adult, 5.50F per car, 5.50F per child. Electricity 11F.)

Trains and SNCF buses leave pl. Armand Lhullery (tel. 02 37 45 00 54) for Vendôme (45min., M-F 6 per day, 4 on Su, 42F), Chartres (1hr., 5 per day, 3 on Su., 42F), and Tours (1¾hr., M-Sa 5 per day, 3 on Su, 87F). To get to the *centre ville* and tourist office, turn left as you exit the station and head down rue Grindelle. Take the first right onto rue de la République and continue about seven blocks until you hit pl. du 18 Octobre. The tourist office is ahead to the right (12min.). Or hop on a bus at the station (there's only one line), and get off two stops later at pl. du 18 Octobre.

POITOU-CHARENTES

Though little-known outside France, Poitou-Charentes offers sun-drenched beaches, sedate canals, craggy cliffs, fertile plains, and a rich history. The Côte d'Azur may be tops in topless beaches, and the Loire Valley may be the king of châteaux, but no other region of France has so impressive a collection of both. Poitou-Charentes is a brilliant collage of pristine natural sights and coastal towns tucked away on the western shore of France.

With the acceptance of Christianity in the 4th century, the area emerged as an influential political and religious center. The 8th century saw Charles "the Hammer" Martel fend off Moorish attempts to conquer the region. With the marriage of Eleanor of Aquitaine and Henry II of England in the 12th century, possession of the region in the Middle Ages was tossed to the other side of the Channel, where it remained for 300 years. In the 17th century, Cardinal Richelieu laid siege to the Protestant stronghold of La Rochelle, relegating it to a century of obscurity until

trade with Canada restored it to prosperity. Tourism is now a major source of income, packing the region's beautiful beaches with eager visitors all summer.

For many, the *gastronomie* of Poitou-Charentes is excuse enough to sail in for an extended visit. The succulent *fruits de mer* (seafood) are the main specialty; also try Marennes-Oléron *huîtres* (oysters), *moules à la mouclade* (mussels in a wine, cream, and egg sauce), and *fricassée d'anguilles* (eels in a red wine sauce). *Escargots* (snails), known locally as *cagouilles*, are prepared either with a meat-and-spice stuffing *à la saintongeaise* or with a red wine sauce *aux lumas*. Finally, the celebrated *Cabécou*, a tangy goat cheese, is often served warm on a bed of lettuce. The nectar of the region is *cognac*, used liberally in Charentais cooking, but *Pineau des Charentes*, a more affordable mixture of cognac and grape or pear juice, makes a sublimely sweet *apéritif*.

HIGHLIGHTS OF POITOU-CHARENTES

- Sip the king of brandies in **Cognac's caves** of Hennessy or Martell (p. 600).
- The **beaches** of **La Rochelle** are as sandy as those on the Riviera and provide a base for exploration of the idyllic coastal islands (p. 610).
- The distinct façade of 12th-century **Notre-Dame-la-Grande** in Poitiers overlooks a city steeped and steepled in a Christian past (p. 590).
- The theme park **Futuroscope** dazzles with cutting-edge technology and cinematic entertainment (p. 595).

GETTING AROUND

Trains run to all major towns, and buses fill in the gaps. Hills rise in the east, while the coast and islands are flat and lovely for biking. You may want to renounce terrestrial transport and cruise down one of Poitou-Charente's main rivers, the Clain or the Charente. The **Comité Régional de Tourisme,** 62 rue Jean Jaurès (tel. 05 49 50 10 50), in Poitiers, has info on hiking, biking, and other modes of trekking.

POITIERS

Poitiers' many beautiful churches—like Notre-Dame-la-Grande and the Cathédrale St-Pierre—are witness to the growth of Church power in the early Middle Ages. It was here that Clovis struck a blow for the spreading religion in defeating the Visigoths in 507, and Charles Martel beat back invading Moors in 732. In 1432, when Poitiers was the capital of France, Charles VII established the Université de Poitiers. Its students now account for a third of Poitiers' 120,000 residents, giving it a youthful buzz during the year and leaving it quiet in summer. Poitiers' position on a plateau above the Clain river isolates it from its factories below. As a result, this bustling mini-metropolis retains a small-town atmosphere. When you've had enough of exploring Poitiers' past, fast-forward to **Futuroscope,** an ultra-modern theme park just a few kilometers outside the city.

ORIENTATION AND PRACTICAL INFORMATION

Poitiers pulses around **pl. Maréchal Leclerc** and **pl. Charles de Gaulle.** Buses run from opposite the train station to the central **Hôtel de Ville.** To get to the tourist office from the *gare* on foot, go straight and climb bd. Solférino as it curves uphill to the left. Ascend the long staircase and take rue Arthur Ranc past the post office. At pl. Leclerc, turn left. Take the first left onto rue des Grandes Écoles; the tourist office will be on your left (10min.).

Trains: bd. du Grand Cerf. Trains to: **Tours** (1hr., 5 per day, 92F); **La Rochelle** (1¾hr., 8 per day, 117F); **Bordeaux** (2hr., 9 per day, 168F); **Paris** (2½hr., 5 per day, 198-310F). **Lockers** 30F. **Futuroscope** desk with English brochures open M-Th and Sa 8am-8pm, F

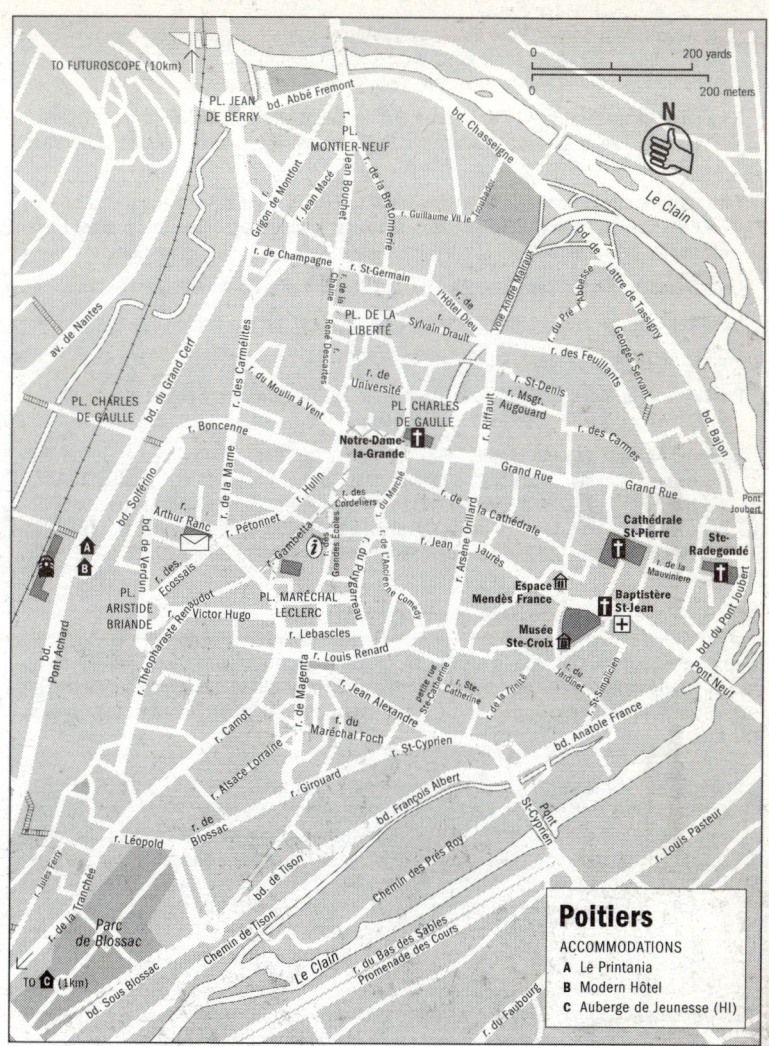

Poitiers

ACCOMMODATIONS
A Le Printania
B Modern Hôtel
C Auberge de Jeunesse (HI)

and Su 8am-9pm. **SNCF** office open M 3:45am-9:45pm, Tu-Th 5am-9:45pm, F 5am-11:30pm, Sa 6am-9:45pm, Su 6:25am-11:30pm.

Local Transportation: STP buses crisscross the city. Timetables at tourist office and train station. Buses run 7am-8:30pm. Night buses on 2 *centre ville* lines run until 11:30pm. Few lines operate Su. Tickets 8F on buses, valid 1hr. except for return-route trips.

Taxis: Radio Taxis, 22 rue Carnot (tel. 05 49 88 12 34). 24hr.

Tourist Office: 8 rue des Grandes Écoles (tel. 05 49 41 21 24; fax 05 49 88 65 84). Clearly labeled maps (3F), brochures, and lists of hotels, campgrounds, and restaurants. Guided tours of the city (2-2½hr.) run July-Sept. at 10am and 4pm; more specialized tours meet at different points M and S at 2:30pm; both 35F, under 25 20F (ask for the brochure *Laissez-vous conter Poitiers*). Has info on outdoor activities in the region. Open June 21-Sept. 20 M-F 9am-7pm, Sa 9:45am-6:45pm, Su 9:45am-1pm and 2:45-6pm; late Sept.-June M-Sa 9am-noon and 1:30-6pm. For current info on events, snag the free *Affiche*. **Service Ville d'Art et d'Histoire,** 1 pl. de la Cathédrale (tel. 05 49 52 54 65), has many of the same brochures. A booth next to Notre Dame la Grande offers maps and brochures and is open late evenings in summer.

English Books: Librairie de l'Université, 70 rue Gambetta (tel. 05 49 41 02 05), off pl. M. Leclerc. Great, somewhat academic English-language selection. Open M-Sa 9am-7:30pm. V, MC.

Youth Information: Centre Information Jeunesse (CIJ), 64 rue Gambetta (tel. 05 49 60 68 68), near pl. Leclerc. Help with jobs, lodgings, hitching, activities, etc. **Budget travel office.** Open in summer M-F 10am-6pm, during school year M-F 10am-6:30pm.

Laundromat: 2bis rue Carnot. Wash 18F, dry 2F per 4min. Open daily 7am-8:30pm.

Hospital: 350 av. Jacques Caire (tel. 05 49 44 44 44), on the road to Limoges.

Police: 38 rue de la Marne (tel. 05 49 60 60 00).

Post Office: rue des Écossais (tel. 05 49 55 52 35). **Currency exchange.** Open M-F 8:30am-7pm, Sa 8:30am-noon. **Postal code:** 86000.

Internet Access: Espace Mendès-France, 1 pl. de la Cathédrale. Internet Découverte room has machines. Free with a membership to the museum (40F adults, 20F students). Open Tu-F 9:30am-6:30pm, Sa-M 2-6:30pm. Those not wishing to deal with surprised receptionists can chill out in **Cybercafé LRM,** 171 Grand Rue (tel. 05 49 39 51 87), which charges 60F per hour of internet use. Open M-Sa 10am-10pm.

◣ ACCOMMODATIONS AND CAMPING

The hostel and campgrounds are far from the city center, but respectable, cheap hotels in the *centre ville* and near the *gare* provide good alternatives; those traveling in pairs or larger groups will be likely to find a cheaper deal at hotels than at the hostel.

Auberge de Jeunesse (HI), 1 allée Tagault (tel. 05 49 58 03 05; fax 05 49 30 09 79). Catch bus #3 by the traffic light ahead of the station (direction "Pierre Loti") to "Cap Sud" (M-Sa every 30min. until 7:50pm, 8F). Walking, turn right at the station and follow bd. du Pont Achard as it curves around to av. de la Libération. Farther on, take the right-hand fork onto rue B. Pascal, turn right on rue de la Jeunesse, and left onto Roger Tagault. The hostel is up ahead on the left (3km, 35min.). Spotless two- to six-bed rooms, showers, and toilets for 51-65F; **members only.** Breakfast 19F, dinner 49F. Reception M-Sa 8-10am, noon-2pm, and 7-11pm; Su 8-10am and 7-11pm. No curfew, no lockout.

Le Printania, 139 bd. du Grand Cerf (tel. 05 49 58 20 15), across from the *gare*, has peeling paint in the showers and dark narrow hallways, but lighter, perfectly acceptable rooms. Singles and doubles 110-124F, with shower 140F, with bath 153F, with TV and bathroom 180F. Breakfast 24F. V, MC.

Modern Hôtel, 153 bd. du Grand Cerf (tel. 05 49 58 46 72), two doors down from Le Printania, has some odd holes in walls, but also wide, open landings and satisfactory rooms for reasonable prices. Singles and doubles without *any* shower access, 105-125F; with shower, 140-155F. Extra bed 30F. Breakfast 22F. V, MC.

Campsites: Le Porteau, rue de Porteau (tel. 05 49 41 44 88), 2km out of town. Take bus #7 (direction "Centre de Gros," 8F) and ask to be dropped off *"devant le terrain"* (in front of the field). Clean bathrooms. Site fee 46F (2 people) and 56F (3 people); 16F per adult, 10F per child, electricity 15F. Open year round. **Camping St-Benoit,** route de Passelourdin (tel. 05 49 88 48 55), 5km from Poitiers. Take bus #2 (direction "Les Sables") from the station; at "Les Sables," change to bus #10 and go to "St-Benoît." 15F per person, 50F per 2-person site, electricity 15F. Open July 1-Aug. 31.

 FOOD

Agneau (lamb) from nearby Montmarillon, *chèvre* (goat cheese), macaroons, and the wines of Haut-Poitou can be found on Poitiers *menus*. The problem is finding a *menu* that fits your budget—most hover around 100-200F. Most hotel bars post adequate 4-course *menus* at 55-60F. Inexpensive pizzerias lie between the cathedral and Notre Dame la Grande on rue de la Cathédrale. There is a **market** at **Les Halles,** on pl. Charles de Gaulle (M-Sa 7am-1pm). On Saturday, the market expands beyond your wildest dreams—a must-see. **Monoprix supermarket,** rue des Cordeliers, at rue du Marché Notre-Dame, fills you up for less. (Open M-Sa 9am-7:30pm. V, MC, AmEx.)

Le Cappuccino, 5 rue de l'Université (tel. 05 49 88 27 39). Generous meats (66-88F) pizzas (33-49F), pasta (33-55F), and salads (20-38F) make this inexpensive but elegant restaurant a local favorite. A vine-adorned courtyard makes for pleasant outdoor dining. Open Tu-Sa noon-2pm and 7-11pm. V, MC.

Alain Boutin, 65 rue Carnot (tel. 05 49 88 25 53). Truly exquisite menus of regional fare: sample four courses for 90 or 126F, choosing from delicacies like Loire lumas (snails) in cognac garlic sauce, duck steaks in cabernet with caramelized apples and cauliflower flan, and crème brulée scented with the local liqueur Angelique de Niort. Worth splurging! Open mid-Jan. to Dec. M-Sa noon-2pm and 7-10pm. V, MC.

Buffet Grill, 11 rue Lebascles, off pl. Leclerc (tel. 05 49 01 74 00). Noontime *formules* offer salad, the *plat du jour,* and ice cream for 57F. Or, choose duck in honey and thyme sauce, *andouillettes* grilled with peppers and entrée or dessert buffets *(à volonté*—all you can eat) for 69-79F. 82F wins you a *plat* and both buffets. Open daily 11:30am-2pm and 7-9:30pm. V, MC.

🔊 SIGHTS

Poitiers' churches date back to the conversion of France in the 4th century. All are open 9am to 6pm daily, all are free, and many hold organ concerts in the summertime; check the *Guide des Manifestations* or call *Les nuits en musique* (tel. 05 49 41 21 24) or *Les concerts du marché* (tel. 05 49 41 34 18) for scheduling.

NOTRE DAME LA GRANDE. Despite its modest proportions, this is a significant Romanesque church of the early 12th century. The famous façade's statuary stand in a double row and display the story of Christianity. Inside, an original fresco on the choir ceiling depicts Christ in glory, the Virgin and Child, and the Lamb of God in a cruciform; the rest of the interior was originally also decorated this way, but unfortunate restoration attempts have resulted in garish, Escher-like designs. If you're here in the summertime, drop by after nightfall, when the original polychrome detail is projected onto the façade. *(On pl. de Gaulle, off Grande Rue. Projections July and August until 10:30pm, Sept. 1-19 until 9:30pm.)*

CATHÉDRALE ST-PIERRE. Another elaborate façade graces the front of the cathedral, which itself is Plantagenêt Gothic—it is supported by large buttresses on its exterior, and its vaults are dome-like in shape. Its 1162 construction was funded by Eleanor of Aquitaine and her royal husband Henry II Plantagenêt, who lived in Poitiers in the current Palais de Justice. Still holding some of its original stained-glass windows, the church is also celebrated for its elaborate Cliquot classical organ (1787-1791). *(On pl. de la Cathédrale, off rue de la Cathédrale.)*

ÉGLISE STE-RADEGONDÉ. A late Gothic edifice, the church's bell tower porch was built on the ravaged foundations of the 6th-century chapel founded by the gutsy saint herself. A few original stained-glass windows remain, putting to shame the gaudy 19th-century glasses designed by the mural reworker. Besides the tomb of Radegondé, the church boasts another sacred relic—in 587, Christ appeared to Radegondé on this site and foretold her imminent death, reassuring her that she was "one of the most precious diamonds in His crown." Our Lord helpfully left a footprint in the stone floor before vanishing, providing the nun with proof and the abbey with pilgrims and income for centuries to come. *(Off rue de la Mauvinière, down from the cathedral.)*

SISTER ACT Saint Radegondé (520-587) was a Thuringian princess carried off as booty by the Frankish son of Clovis. When he demanded she marry him, Radegondé fled to the church and strong-armed a priest into making her a nun. She went on to found one of the first women's abbeys, Ste-Croix, and, according to myth, killed a dragon who haunted tunnels under the city, snacking on villagers. Radegondé was not the only woman to stick out her neck to save the city: the Virgin herself took matters into her own hands in 1202, during the English siege of Poitiers. A traitor plotted to give the invaders the keys to the city gates, only to find out that the keys had disappeared. The English retreated, claiming to have seen terrible visions of a queen, a bishop, and a nun outside the city (the Virgin, 4th-century bishop St. Hilaire, and St. Radegondé, of course). The "lost" keys were discovered in the wooden hands of the Statue of Mary in Notre Dame la Grand.

BAPTISTÈRE ST-JEAN. This 4th-century baptistry is the oldest Christian edifice in France. It originally contained a sunken octagonal pool used by the first French Christians for baptisms. No longer a sacred building, the Baptistère holds a museum of Roman, Merovingian, and Carolingian sarcophagi and capitals. The earliest Christians destroyed many of the pagan buildings which once graced Poitiers: baths, a triumphal arch, an amphitheater, and a temple—they kept the pieces and emulated their style, though never as successfully. From June 21 to September 19, lights reflect the baptistry's frescos—including a dragon, the Apostles, and the life of St. John the Baptist—onto its outside walls from 10pm to midnight. (*On rue Jean Jaurès, near the cathedral. Open July-Aug. daily 10am-12:30pm and 2-7pm; Apr.-June and Sept.-Nov. W-M 10:30am-12:30pm and 3-6pm; Dec.-Mar. W-M 2:30-4:30pm. 4F, under 12 2F.*)

ESPACE MENDÈS FRANCE. Next to St-Pierre, and a millennium younger, the sleek and modern Espace engages visitors with its videos, interactive exhibits, and well-designed and colorful photograph-toting displays. A temporary exhibit coming in summer 2000 presents the history of writing. You can get on the internet in the Discovery room. (*1 pl. de la Cathédrale. Tel. 05 49 50 33 08; www.pictascience.org. Planetarium shows 11am and 5pm. Museum open Sa-M 2-6:30pm and Tu-F 9:30am-6:30pm. Planetarium 32F, under 18 20F; museum 25F, under 18 15F; admission to both 42F, under 18 30F. Internet access with membership, 40F adults, 20F students.*)

PARC DE BLOSSAC. Created by the Comte de Blossac in the 18th century, this is one of the most beautiful parks of the region. A classic *jardin à la francaise*, it is traversed by perfectly rectilinear paths and planted primarily with Dutch linden trees. A *jardin à l'anglais*, created in 1905, rests in its northwest corner. The park's small zoological garden houses monkeys, deer, and a beautiful collection of birds. (*Rue de Blossac, down rue Carnot, near the Clain. Open April-Sept. 7am-10:30pm, Oct.-March 7am-9:30pm. Jardin Anglais open April-Sept. 7am-8pm, Oct.-March 8am to dusk.*)

OTHER SIGHTS. The **Musée Ste-Croix** holds relics of Poitiers's Bronze Age, Roman inscriptions, some melodramatic Camille Claudels, and an early Mondrian. Summer events feature guest lectures and concerts; check the bulletin outside for details. Visit the **Musée Rupert de Chièvres** for its collection of Dutch, Flemish, and Italian paintings. The tiny funerary chapel **Hypogée des Dunes**, normally the third of the trio, is currently closed for protection until further notice. (*Musée Ste-Croix: 61 rue St-Simplicien. Tel. 05 49 41 07 53. Musée Rupert de Chièvres: 9 rue Victor Hugo. Tel. 05 45 41 42 21. Both open June-Sept. M 1:15-6pm, Tu-F 10am-noon and 1:15-6pm, Sa-Su 10am-noon and 2-6pm; Oct.-May M 1:15-5pm, Tu 10am-5pm, W-F 10am-12noon, 1:15-5pm, Sa-Su 2-6pm. Free on Tu and to those under 18; otherwise 15F for both. Guided tours in French on Tuesdays.*)

♫ ❀ FUN IN POITIERS

ENTERTAINMENT. Poitiers is quiet in the summer but livens up during the school year with an active club and bar scene. **Pl. Leclerc** and **pl. de Gaulle** host late-night action of all sorts. One of the best student hangouts is **Sherlock's Pub**, just off 17 rue Carnot (tel. 05 49 50 72 18), through the archway across from Parking Carnot. Busts of the pipe-smoking sleuth line the sleek bar. (Open Aug.-June M-Sa 3pm-2am.) **Le George Sand,** 25 rue St-Pierre le Puellier (tel. 05 49 55 91 58), is the best gay bar in town. (Open 11pm-5am daily.) Across from Église Ste-Radegondé, **La Grand Goule**, 46 rue du Pigeon Blanc (tel. 05 49 50 41 36), is a mainstay of Poitiers nightlife; *jeunes* jump where their parents twisted. (Open Tu-Sa 11pm-4am. 50F cover includes one drink.) A booklet of *Café-Concerts, Bars avec Animations* is available from the tourist office.

FESTIVALS. Rencontres Musicales de Poitiers, 79 rue des Frères Voisin (tel. 05 49 58 42 13), features classical works in biweekly concerts late October through late April (tickets 60F, under 26 45F). In early December, the **Festival du Cinéma** features films both artsy and mainstream. Springing into the first two weeks of May, **Le Printemps Musical de Poitiers,** 7 rue des Flageolles (tel. 05 49 41 58 94), is a harmonic convergence of concerts, exhibits, and debates (tickets 30-60F). In July and August, rock, opera, jazz, and fireworks thunder through town for the **Poitiers l'Été** festival. Concerts, mostly free, begin around 9pm three to four nights per week.

FUTUROSCOPE

10km north of Poitiers near Chasseneuil. Tel. 05 49 49 30 80; fax 05 49 49 59 38; www.futuroscope.com. Open daily 9am-6pm; open until 11pm when "Lake of Images" laser show is scheduled; call ahead. Prices vary day to day; in general, July-Aug. weekends Apr.-June and Sept. to mid-Nov. 185F, kids 5-16 150F; most of Feb., M-F Apr.-May, and Christmas 165F, kids 130F; the rest of the year 140F, kids 110F.

Silvery, slick, and stylish, the Futuroscope amusement park sports what amounts to a collection of film theaters—spherical screens, hemispherical screens, and high definition 3-D tricks. Films consist of short documentaries on nature, space exploration, new technology, and French vacation spots. A cyber-space houses internet access and tons of video games, including some virtual reality. All the video/expo attractions are included in the admission price. Weekdays are much less crowded. A translating headset from the Maison de Vienne near the entrance magically switches many films' narration into your choice of English, German or Spanish. To get there, take bus #16 or #17 from Poitiers (18 per day, 20min., 8F; last bus leaves Futuroscope's Chemin du Parc at 7:31pm). Radio Taxis of Poitiers runs shuttles 15 times daily from the train station (45F per person round-trip). By car, follow A10 (direction "Paris-Châtellerault") and take exit 18.

CHAUVIGNY

Twenty-three kilometers east of Poitiers, the beauty of Chauvigny belies its bloody history. A feudal possession of the bishops of Poitiers from the 11th century until the French Revolution, Chauvigny changed hands four times between the French and English in the late Middle Ages. Burnt to the ground during the Wars of Religion, it was also shelled by the retreating German armies in 1944. Despite its tumultuous history, the city today offers a pocket of tranquility in its *haute ville*. This upper part of Chauvigny preserves the miniature *cité médiévale*, with small restaurants and pretty walkways encircling the tranquil pl. du Donjon.

While the five towering 11th- to 15th-century châteaux ruins provide Chauvigny with a striking skyline, the 12th century church of **St-Pierre** is celebrated for its provocative choir capitals. The ultra-modern **Espace d'Archéologie Industrielle** (tel. 05 49 46 92 56) nestles attractively in the ruins of the Gouzon keep and showcases regional quarry, porcelain, milling, and steam engine activity. A trip up the museum's glass elevator rewards visitors with an even better view of the city and countryside below, with the picturesque Pont la Vienne stretching out in the east. (Open June 15-Sept. 15 and Nov. 1-Mar. 31 M-F 10am-12:30pm and 2:30-6:30pm, Sa-Su 2-6pm; open Apr. 1-June 14 and Sept. 16-Oct. 31 daily 2-6pm. 30F, students 20F, under 14 free.) Just behind the Espace, the former collegiate presbytery houses the tiny **Musée d'Éthnologie et d'Archéologie.** Its collection of local historical treasures includes keys, coins, and pottery from the Roman to revolutionary eras; a presentation of WWII memorabilia; and an exhibit of 19th- and early 20th-century Chauvinois costume. (Open daily from 2-6pm. 10F, students 5F, under 14 free.)

The **Château des Aigles** (tel. 05 49 46 47 48) houses eagles, falcons, vultures, owls, and buzzards, and offers bird shows in the ruined bishop's chateau from March to November. (Shows: June-Aug. daily at 11am, 3pm, 4:15pm, and 5:30pm; Oct.-Nov. daily at 3pm and 4:15pm; Mar. M-Sa 3:30pm, Su 3pm and 4:30pm; Apr.-May, and Sept. daily at 3pm, 4:15pm, and 5:30pm.) For a truly unique view of the countryside, take a ride on the city's **Vélo-Rails** (tel. 05 49 63 18 19), contraptions on rails which allow up to five people to pedal along the viaduct traversing the Vienne; a 17km loop extends from the *gare* of Chauvigny around the Pontorieau valley. (Open daily; July and Aug. 10am-9pm; Sept., May, and June 2-7pm; Oct., Nov., Mar., and Apr. 2-6pm; Dec.-Feb. by reservation. 120F for 2hr. in July and Aug., 100F rest of the year; 3hr. 140F; 4hr. 150F.) In summer the **Festival d'Été** (tel. 05 49 45 99 10) fills the city with jazz, folklore, dance, theatre, and various expositions; pick up a festival guide at the tourist office.

Buses leave **Poitiers** for Chauvigny from right outside the station (direction "Châteauroux"; 5 per day, 30 min., 30F). To get to the **tourist office** (tel. 05 49 46 39 01) in the *cité médiévale*, take rue de Château from pl. de la Poste all the way up the hill and walk down rue de St-Pierre with the pl. du Donjon on your right; the tourist office is at the bottom of the road to the right. (Open daily 10am-1:30pm and 2-6pm. Guided tours July-Aug. W-M at 3pm and 5pm; 20F.)

ANGOULÊME

High up on a plateau, Angoulême (pop. 50,000) affords a magnificent view of the Charente river and the surrounding countryside. The cradle of the French paper industry in the 1600s, the town and its ready supply of writing pads brought Jean Calvin here in 1534. The revocation of the Edict of Nantes in the 1600s sent the primarily Protestant paper-makers packing to Holland. Today, Angoulême has emerged as the capital of French comic strip production, with countless *Lucky Luke* and *Astérix* volumes rolling off the town's presses. Culturally, Angoulême offers an abundance of sights and a contagiously vibrant nightlife.

☒ ORIENTATION AND PRACTICAL INFORMATION

Angoulême lies halfway down the TGV line between Bordeaux and Poitiers. The *vieille ville* sits among *vieille* ramparts just south of the Charente and southwest of the train station. It is easy to get lost in the maze of streets, so grab a map from the tourist office branch outside the station. To get to the main **tourist office** at pl. des Halles, follow av. Gambetta uphill to the right to pl. G. Perrot. Continue straight up the rampe d'Aguesseau and turn right onto bd. Pasteur. Keeping close to the railing overlooking the valley, pass the market building on your left. Turn left beyond the market onto rue du Chat. The office will be on your right.

Trains: Pl. de la Gare. To: **Bordeaux** (55min., 8-10 per day, 109F); **Saintes** (1hr., 4-5 per day, 66F); **Poitiers** (1hr., 5 per day, 91F); **Périgueux** (2hr., 4 per day, 116F); **Paris** (2¾hr., 7 per day, 300-399F). Office open M-F 9:30am-noon and 2-7pm, Sa 9:30am-noon and 2-6:30pm.

Buses: Autobus Citram (tel. 05 45 25 42 60). To: **Cognac** (1hr., 8 per day, 45F); **Bordeaux** (2hr., 2 per day, 51F); and **La Rochelle** (3hr., 3 per day, 104F). Buses stop at pl. du Champ de Mars. Buy tickets on board. Info at the **Cartrans** office, pl. du Champ de Mars (tel. 05 45 95 95 99). Open July-mid-Aug. M-F 2-6:15pm; mid-Aug. to June M-F 9:15am-12:15pm and 2-6:15pm. **CFTA Périgord** (tel. 05 53 08 43 13), from the *gare* to **Périgueux** (1½hr.; M-Sa 2-3 per day, 1 on Su; 75F).

Local Transportation: STGA, 554 route de Bordeaux (tel. 05 45 65 25 00). Kiosk on pl. du Champ de Mars has maps (tel. 05 45 65 25 25; open M-F 1:30-6:30pm, Sa 1:30-4:30pm). Tickets 7.50F, roundtrip 12F, *carnet* of 10 53F. Buses run M-Sa 6am-8pm.

Taxis: Radio Taxis, in front of the train station (tel. 05 45 95 55 55). 24hr.

Tourist Office: 7bis rue du Chat (tel. 05 45 95 16 84; fax 05 45 95 91 76). Huge maps and an indispensable city guide. Open July-Aug. M-Sa 9:30am-7pm, Su 10am-noon and 2-5pm; Sept.-June M-F. **Kiosk** (tel. 05 45 92 27 57) by the *gare*, open July-Aug. M-Sa 9:30am-7:00pm, Su 10am-noon and 2pm-5pm; Sept.-June M-F 9:30am-12:30pm and 1:30-6pm, Sa 10am-12noon and 2-5pm, Su 10am-noon.

City tours: Day and night tours offered through the Hôtel de Ville's **Service Patrimoine** (tel. 05 45 38 70 79). Day trips leave daily at 3pm and 7pm July 1-Sept. 21; ten *visites nocturnes* 9:30pm July-Aug. Call the Service Patrimoine for dates and meeting places.

Budget Travel: Voyages Wasteels, 2 pl. Francis Louvel (tel: 08 03 88 70 29). 20-30% savings on train and plane tickets. Open M-F 9am-12:45pm and 2-6:30pm, Sa 9am-12:30pm and 2-5:30pm. V, MC.

Money: Best rates at **Banque de France,** 4 rue de Château (tel. 05 45 97 00 00), on pl. Hôtel de Ville. Exchange desk open M-F 8:40am-noon.

Laundromat: Lavomatique, 3 rue Ludovic Trarieux, near the Hôtel de Ville.

Youth Center: Centre Information Jeunesse, L'Espace Franquin, 1ter bd. Bertholet (tel. 05 45 92 86 73 or 05 45 37 07 30), around the corner from the Hôtel de Ville. Friendly staff has info on regional events, helps find jobs, sells cheap concert and theater tickets, and offers general advice. Open July-Aug. M-Sa 10am-6pm; Sept.-June Tu-F 10am-noon and 2-6pm, Sa 10am-noon and 2-5pm.

Police: Pl. du Champs de Mars (tel. 05 45 39 38 37), next to the post office.

Hospital: Hôpital de Girac, rue de Bordeaux (tel. 05 45 24 40 40). Closer to town is the private **Clinique St-Joseph,** 51 av. Président Wilson (tel. 05 45 38 67 00).

Post Office: Pl. du Champ de Mars (tel. 05 45 66 66 00; fax 05 45 66 66 17). **Currency exchange.** Open M-F 7:45am-7pm, Sa 8am-noon. **Branch office,** pl. Francis Louvel, near the Palais du Justice. Open M-F 8am-6:45pm, Sa 8am-noon. **Postal code:** 16000.

Internet access: Café de Limoges, inside the CNBDI, 121 rue de Bordeaux (tel. 05 45 38 65 65). Open M-F 10am-6pm, 20F per hour for students.

■ ACCOMMODATIONS AND CAMPING

Cheap hotels cluster near the intersection of av. Gambetta and the pedestrian district, which leads downhill from the *vieille ville.* The hostel and campground are on Île de Bourgines, a forested island in the Charente, 2km from the *centre ville.*

Auberge de Jeunesse (HI) (tel. 05 45 92 45 80), on Île de Bourgines. To walk, turn left out of the *gare* onto av. de Lattre de Tassigny and take the first left onto bd. du 8 Mai 1945. At the third traffic light, turn left onto bd. Besson Bey, which goes downhill, to cross a footbridge. A huge swimming pool will be on the left, in front of the hostel (20min.). By bus, exit the station, turn right onto av. Gambetta, and right again onto rue Denis Papin, which crosses over the tracks. Continue straight onto Passage Lamaud, a pedestrian shortcut that reaches rue de Paris (5-10min.). Turn right onto rue de Paris and take bus #7 (direction "Le Treuil") to "St-Antoine." The last bus leaves at 8pm. Gorgeous location along the Charente with great management. Fifteen bright 4- to 6-bed rooms with skylights and sinks in a modern building; fiendish "press and repeat" showers get warm when they want to. 51F. Breakfast 19F. Meals 28-55F. Sheets 16F. No lockout. No curfew. Call ahead in summer.

Hôtel des Pyrénées, 80 rue St-Roch (tel. 05 45 95 20 45; fax 05 45 92 16 95), around the corner from the post office, off pl. du Champ de Mars. Helpful owners. Back rooms have views onto the valley. Singles and doubles 150-170F, with shower and TV 200-250F, with shower, toilet and TV 220-270F. Extra bed 50F. Breakfast 30-35F. V, MC.

Hôtel Le Palma, 4 rampe d'Aguesseau (tel. 05 45 95 22 89; fax 05 45 94 26 66), near the Église St-Martial, straight up the hill from the *gare*. Ten large, brightly decorated rooms above a restaurant-bar. Singles 120F, with shower 160F; doubles 160-180F. Breakfast 28F. Shower 30F. Reception M-Sa. V, MC.

Campsites: Camping Municipal, on Île de Bourgines (tel. 05 45 92 83 22), 3-star camping next to the youth hostel. 16F per adult, 8F per child, 27F per site with vehicle; 56F for 2 adults, tent, and car. Reception 7am-12:30pm and 2:30-9pm. Open Mar.-Sept.

⬛ FOOD

The local specialty, *cagouilles à la charentaise*, snails prepared first with garlic and parsley, then with sausage, smoked ham, and spices, can be found in the restaurants of the *vieille ville* (45-50F). A favorite sweet is the flower-shaped *marguerite* chocolate, named for François I's sister Marguerite de Valois. Bars, cafés, and *boulangeries* line rue de St-Martial and rue Marengo, but the food becomes funkier, the dishes spicier, and the crowds more interesting as you weave your way into the narrow streets of the quadrant formed by Les Halles, pl. du Palet, Église St-André, and the Hôtel de Ville. **Letuffe Chocolatier,** 10 pl. Francis Louvel (tel. 05 45 95 00 54), gives free samples to entice buyers. (56F per 250g. Open M-F 9am-6pm. V, MC.) The recently renovated covered **market** on pl. des Halles sells the town's freshest produce two blocks down rue de Gaulle from the Hôtel de Ville (M-Sa 7am-12:30pm). There is a **Stoc supermarket** at 19 rue Périgueux, right by the Champ de Mars. (Open M-Sa 8:30am-7:15pm, Su 9am-noon. V, MC.)

Maison des Peuples et de la Paix, 6bis rue Marengo (tel. 05 45 92 48 32). Throws hip-hop and reggae parties in the name of international understanding. Also serves world food in its cafeteria. The weekly *menu* (40F plus 5F membership) could be moussaka, couscous, lasagna, or vegetarian specialties from India and sub-Saharan Africa (includes coffee and dessert). Lunch M-F noon-1:45pm.

La Calendrine, 12bis rue 3 Notre Dame (tel. 05 45 95 16 76). Sleek black and red decor, cordial waiters, and delicious food make this restaurant a pleasure and a good value. *Menus* of pizzas, pastas, and meats start at 63F; a surprise awaits those who order the delectable ice creams for dessert. Open daily noon-1:45pm and 7-11:30pm.

Crêperie du Palet, 9 rue Raymond Audour (tel. 05 45 92 43 78) offers a great deal in its *menu privilège*—a dinner *crêpe* with 3 ingredients of your choosing, 25cl. of cider, a dessert *crêpe*, and coffee for only 65F, served in an elegant 17th-century vaulted *cave*. Open Tu-Sa noon-2pm and 7:30-11pm.

THE NORTHWEST

 SIGHTS

CATHÉDRALE ST-PIERRE. The 12th-century cathedral of Angoulême is an important Romanesque showpiece. The edifice exerted a considerable influence not only on other churches in the diocese, but also on more faraway buildings such as Fontevraud in the Loire and Notre-Dame-la-Grande of Poitiers. A splendid façade depicts scenes of the Ascension of Christ and the Last Judgment. Other notable features include the distinguished capitals below the belfry, the graceful arch-lined walls, and a four-domed nave characteristic of the region. *(Pl. St-Pierre. Tel. 05 45 95 20 38. Open daily 9am-7pm.)*

MUSÉE DE LA BANDE DESSINÉE. Housed within the **Centre nationale de la bande dessinée et de l'image (CNBDI),** this museum concentrates on the inventors of the *B-D* (comic strips), along with more obscure French cartoons from the 19th and 20th centuries (not overlooking *Astérix*, of course), and American greats like *Fritz the Cat.* May be less interesting for non-French speakers. *(121 rue de Bordeaux. From pl. du Champ de Mars and pl. de l'Hôtel de Ville, take bus #3 or 5 to "Nil-CNBDI." Tel. 05 45 38 65 65; www.cnbdi.fr. Open July-Aug. Tu-F 10am-7pm, Sa-Su 2-7pm; Sept.-June Tu-F 10am-6pm, Sa-Su 2-6pm. 30F, students 20F, under 6 free.)*

MUSÉE DES BEAUX-ARTS. Inhabiting a restored 12th-century bishop's palace, the museum displays 19th-century Charentais archæological digs, North and West African pottery, and the work of local sculptors and painters. *(1 rue Friedland, behind the cathedral. Tel. 05 45 95 07 69. Open M-F noon-6pm, Sa-Su 2-6pm. 15F, students 5F, under 18 free; free noon-2pm.)*

ÉGLISE ST-ANDRÉ. The 12th-century church, originally Romanesque, was reworked in a Gothic style; possessing a remarkable collection of paintings from the 16th to 19th centuries, it also contains a massive altar-piece and a superb baroque oak pulpit. The façade was reconstructed in neoclassical style in the early 19th century, but the church retains its original tower and entrance. *(8 rue Taillefer, on the pl. de Palet in the centre ville.)*

GARDENS AND WATER-SPORTS. With its beautiful riverside greenery and stunning ramparts surrounding the haute ville, Angoulême's outdoors offers a sumptuous feast for the eyes. At the bottom of av. du Président Wilson, the flowers and waterfalls of the **Jardin Vert** soothe both tourists and baby goats. The 4th-century **ramparts** that surround the town provide a spectacular view of the red-roofed houses and green countryside below. **Canoe** or **kayak** on the sparkling Charente (tel. 05 45 94 68 91 or 05 45 38 82 23). The Bourgines olympic **swimming pool** next to the hostel opens in summer for splashing under the blue sky (tel. 05 45 95 21 70).

OTHER SIGHTS. The **Atelier-musée du papier** continues Angoulême's obsession with all things paper, illustrating the history of Charente's paper-making industry, with special exhibits on cigarette papers and lithographic printing. *(134 rue de Bordeaux, across from the CNBDI. Tel. 05 45 92 73 43. Open Tu-Su 2-6pm. Free.)* The **Musée de la Résistance et de la déportation** has taken over the one-time home of 16th-century religious reformer Jean Calvin, and now chronicles Angoulême's experience under Nazi occupation *(34 rue de Génève. Tel. 05 45 38 76 87. Open W and Sa 2-6pm. 15F, children and students 5F.)* Built by the Souchet family in the early 16th century, the **Maison St-Simon** cherishes its Renaissance façade; within, the **Fonds Régional d'Art Contemporain** displays avant-garde art. *(15 rue de la Cloche Verte. Tel. 05 45 92 87 01. Open Tu-Sa 1:30-7pm. Free.)* The **Musée Archéologique** displays regional treasures from Gallo-Roman to recent times: ceramics, arrowheads, and fossils galore. *(44 rue Montmoreau. Tel. 05 45 38 45 17. Open W-M 2-5pm. Free.)*

🎵 🎆 ENTERTAINMENT AND FESTIVALS

EVENING REVELRY. As the sun sets, folks move toward the cafés on **rue Massillon** and **pl. des Halles.** The **Yucatan,** rue Henri IV off rue 3 Fours, tends to be wild during the school year and has concerts in the cool *cave* in the summer. (Open

THE NORTHWEST

Sept.-June Tu-Sa 6pm-2am; July W-Sa 6pm-2am.) Hang out with true French attitude at **Cafe Chaud,** on the corner of rue de Geneve. (Open M-Th noon-2am, F and Sa noon-4am, Su 3pm-2am.) **Le Bureau,** 8 rue Raymond Poincaré is another local favorite. (Open M-Th 10am-2am, F-Su 10am-3am.) For all the beer you ever dreamed of, try **Académie la Bière,** 15 pl. Boulliaud (tel. 05 45 95 91 41). **Le Champagne,** 25 rue d'Aguesseau (tel. 05 45 92 58 09), sits off pl. Marengo, stuffed with dancing, DJs, and 50 different cocktails. Karaoke nights Tu-Sa. (Open M-Sa until 2am. V, MC.) Live concerts almost nightly make the hike out to **Le Piano Rétro Club,** 210 rue St-Roch (tel. 05 45 92 87 11), worth your while. (Open Tu-Sa 10:30pm-2am.)

FESTIVALS. The world-famous **Salon International de la Bande-Dessinée** (tel. 05 45 97 86 50; www.bdangouleme.com) breezes into town the last week in January. Over 200,000 visitors admire four days of comic-strip exhibits in the Hôtel de Ville (60F), where Astérix and Obélix can occasionally be sighted. The **Festival Musiques Métisses,** 6 rue du point-du-Jour (tel. 05 45 95 43 42), features French jazz, French-African, and Caribbean music each year during Pentecost. The popular **Circuit des Remparts** (tel. 05 45 94 95 67), 2 rue Fontgrave, revs its engine in mid-September, as antique cars hold races and exhibitions for three days in the *centre ville.* International pianists of all genres participate in the two-week **Festival International de Piano, "Piano en Valois"** (tel. 05 45 94 74 00) in late September and early October. Some concerts are free, but most cost 30-60F. Finally, like many French cities, Angoulême welcomes all sorts of artistic festivity in the summertime; call the tourist office after mid-June for information about the **Été au Ciné,** and the **Jeux de Rue.**

LA ROCHEFOUCAULD

La Rochefoucauld has been home to the aristocratic Foucauld family for more than a millennium. The present **château** (tel. 05 45 62 07 42), the "pearl of Angoumois," was built by Duke Francis II in 1528 on a feudal-era foundation with twin towers, a medieval fortress, and an elegant chapel. (Open May-Sept. daily 10am-7pm; Oct.-Easter Su and holidays 2-7pm. *Son et lumière* show, call for details. 40F, under 12 free.) The surrounding village, which takes its name from the family ("La Roche à Foucauld") preserves the Gothic cloister, **Le Couvent des Carmes,** built in 1329 and in surprisingly good shape, along with a church, **Le Collégial,** built in 1266. **Trains** run from Angoulême (M-Sa 5 per day, Su 3 per day; 29F), while **Château transport** (tel. 05 45 84 14 86) rolls buses out of Angoulême's Champ de Mans at 11:30am M-Sa (30min., 19F). To get to the *centre ville* from the train station, take av. de la Gare straight through rue des Halles to pl. Gourville. The triangular **tourist office** is on your left at 1 rue des Tanneurs (tel. 05 45 63 07 45), inside the Halle aux Grains; they can give you a map of the city.

COGNAC

Comely Cognac (pop. 22,000) rises along the banks of the Charente, which Henry IV called the "gentlest and most beautiful river in France." Trade megaliths Hennessy, Martell, Rémy-Martin, and Otard offer a look inside their distilleries and a sampling of sweet liqueur. An ideal daytrip from Saintes and Angoulême, Cognac offers a budget opportunity to taste this most exclusive of *digestifs.*

⌖ ORIENTATION AND PRACTICAL INFORMATION. Trains come from **Angoulême** (40min., 5 per day, 50F) and **Saintes** (20min., 6 per day, 29F). To get to the **tourist office,** 16 rue du 14 Juillet (tel. 05 45 82 10 71; fax 05 45 82 34 47; email office.tourisme.cognac@wanadoo.fr), follow av. du Maréchal Leclerc out of the *gare* to the first circle and take a right, following signs to the *centre ville.* Turn right on rue Bayard and cross pl. Bayard onto rue du 14 Juillet (15min.). You'll find info, maps, and a free accommodations service. The office arranges tours of the city, including nocturnal visits (July 23-Sept. 10 Th at 9:30pm; 35F, under 12 20F), and *petit train* tours (30F). (Office open July-Aug. M-Sa 9am-8pm, Su 10:30am-4pm; Sept.-June M-Sa 9am-12:30pm and 2-6:15pm.) Find the **Banque de France,** 39 bd. Denfert-Rochereau (tel. 05 45 82 25 10), for the best rates. (Open M-F 8:45am-noon). The **post office**, at 2 pl. Bayard (tel. 05 45 36 31 82), has **currency exchange.** (Open M-F 8am-6pm, Sa 8:30am-noon. **Postal code:** 16100.)

■ ACCOMMODATIONS AND CAMPING. A few blocks down from the tourist office, **Hôtel du Cheval Blanc**, 6-8 pl. Bayard (tel. 05 45 82 09 55; fax 05 45 82 14 82), rents scruffy but light, open rooms with spotless tiled bathrooms. Ask the very friendly owner for quiet rooms facing the back. (Singles 130F; doubles 150-180F. Breakfast 30F. V, MC.) Three-star **Cognac Camping**, bd. de Châtenay (tel. 05 45 32 13 32), on rte. de Ste-Sévère, is a 30-minute walk from the *centre ville*. A bus (4F, 6-trip carnet for 20F, under 18 2F) runs twice daily June 16-Sept. 4 from pl. François 1er (tel. 05 45 82 01 99); get off at "Camping." (2 people with site, showers, and electricity 67F. Extra body 16F. Wheelchair access. Pool. Laundry 20F per 7kg. Bike rental. Open May-Oct.)

◘ FOOD. Tasting Cognac's famous product doesn't necessarily mean drinking it! Restaurants around **pl. François I** serve pricey local specialties drenched in cognac. Right in the *centre ville* stands **La Boune Goule**, 42 allées de la Corderie (tel. 05 45 82 06 37), at the intersection of rue Aristide Briande. The name is a *charentais* expression for good taste, appropriate when "nothing except the fries is frozen." Huge, fresh portions of local cuisine, with 30F omelettes and a 35F all-you-can-eat salad bar. (65F lunch *menu*. Open noon-2:30pm and 7-11:30pm. V, MC.) At **Le Duguesclin**, 9 rue du 14 Juillet (tel. 05 45 82 46 22), an expansive dining room sets the scene for *crêpes* (18-39F), pizza (30-59F), pasta (14-53F), meat (49-88F), and fish dishes. For cheap *crêpes* and a youthful atmosphere, relive the American 50s at **L'Olympia**, 34 rue du Canton (tel. 05 45 36 66 76), behind the market on rue de L'Isle d'Or. Sporting an antique gas pump outside and an old Chevy inside, Olympia serves dessert specialities named after Elvis and "Franck" Sinatra. Lunch *menu* 52F. (Open June-Sept. daily 10am-midnight; Oct.-May M-Sa 10am-2pm and 6pm-midnight. V, MC.) **Champion supermarket** provides everything imaginable, including cognac, at pl. François I. (Open M-Sa 9am-7pm, Su 9:30am-noon. V, MC.) There is an **indoor market** at pl. d'Armes (Tu-Su 7am-1pm), and a lively **outdoor market** brightens pl. du Marché the second Saturday of each month.

COGNAC DISTILLERIES. The joy of visiting Cognac lies in making your way from one brandy producer to the next, touring warehouses, watching films on the history of each house, and collecting nip bottles. If a nip is not enough, Otard offers its Extra in a blue porcelain bust of François 1er for 1530F, while Hennessy's silver-gilded flask is a mere 4200F. If you want the drink, you'll have to take the tour. In most houses, there are three or four per day English tours in the summer.

Hennessy, quai Richard Hennessy (tel. 05 45 35 72 68; fax 05 45 35 79 49), the industry's biggest player, has the longest, most technically involved, and most interesting presentation, which includes barrel-making displays and an absurdly romantic film projected in an actual theater. The tour is also the most expensive. Open June-Sept. 10am-6pm; Mar.-May and Sept.-Dec. 10am-5pm; Jan.-Feb. call ahead for a reservation. 30F, students 15F, under 16 free.

Otard, 127 bd. Denfert-Rochereau (tel. 05 45 36 88 86), is housed in the Château de Cognac, the 1494 birthplace of François I. The 50-minute tour focuses on the history of the building, although cognac is not ignored. Open July-Aug. daily 10-11:30am and 1:30-6pm; Apr.-Oct. daily 10-11am and 2-5pm; Nov.-Dec. M-Th 11am-5pm, F 11am-4pm; Jan.-Mar. call ahead for a visit. 15F, under 19 10F, under 12 free.

Martell, pl. Edouard Martell (tel. 05 45 36 33 33), was founded by an Englishman in 1715 and is the oldest of the major cognac houses. Luckily, it's also the most generous. Martell welcomes visitors for a free tour and gives out nip bottles as souvenirs. Open July-Aug. M-F 9:45am-5pm, Sa-Su 10am-4:15pm; June and Sept. M-F 9:45-11am and 2-5pm; Oct.-May M-Th 9:30-11am and 2:30-5pm, F 9:30-11am.

Camus, 29 rue Marguerite de Navarre (tel. 05 45 32 28 28; fax 05 45 32 17 11) also gives free tours and tastings in the *centre ville.* Open July-Oct. M-F 10am-noon and 2:30-4:30pm; June M-F 10am-noon and 1:45-4:30pm; Apr. 13-May 31 M-F 2:30-4:00pm. Call ahead for English tour.

Rémy Martin, rte. de Pons D732 (tel. 05 45 35 76 55), does much the same 5km outside town in Merpin but adds a little train ride to the vines. No buses access the site and it's a long hike. Open July 6-Sept. 6 daily 10am-5:30pm, April 8-Sept. 26 M-F 9:30-11:30am and 2:30-5:45pm; also open Su May 3-September 20 10am-5:30pm. Tour 25F, under 18 free.

📷 **SIGHTS.** The **Musée Municipal du Cognac,** 48 bd. Denfert-Rochereau (tel. 05 45 32 07 25), details the 5000-year history of Cognac and the 401-year history of cognac through *charentais* clothing, ceramics, and viticulture tools. Come see Marie Curie's cognac bottle bust. (Open W-M June-Sept. 10am-noon and 2-6pm; Oct.-May 2-5:30pm. 12F, students 6F, under 18 free.) Despite all the cognac mania, a stroll through the friendly pedestrian streets of the *centre ville,* full of flowers and marketware in the summertime, is always worthwhile. Step into the exceptionally beautiful **Église Saint Léger** off rue Aristide Briand to admire its restored 12th- to 14th-century architecture. (Open daily 8am-7pm.) The 13th- to 16th-century **Chateau François I**^{er} (tel. 05 45 36 88 86) holds guided visits from June to September. (Open Apr.-Oct. daily 9:30am-noon and 2-6pm; Nov.-Mar. M-Th 9:30am-noon and 2-6pm, F 9:30am-noon and 2-5pm. 10F, ages 12-18 5F.)

🎭 **FESTIVALS.** In early April, Cognac hosts the **Festival du Film Policier,** hauling 10 cop flicks in front of a grand jury. (3 films 110F. Call tourist office for details.) The **Blues Passions** concerts of late July have showcased artists such as B.B. King and Otis Rush. For info, visit 9A pl. Cagouillet. (Tel. 05 45 32 17 28; fax 05 45 32 66 33. Tickets 100F, under 18 80F.) Mid-July brings in the annual **Fête du Cognac,** which features boat races and fireworks on the Charente.

⛰ **OUTDOOR PURSUITS.** Cognac's valley provides great hiking among the vineyards, fields, forests, and groves. The tourist office provides four "Sentiers de Randonnées" maps (12F each) marking paths in and around Cognac; off-trail surprises include abbeys, historic ruins, and châteaux. For information about canoeing, call 05 45 82 46 24. Peaceful parks in Cognac include the **Jardin de l'Hôtel de Ville** around the museum (open summer daily 7am-10pm, off season daily 7am-8pm) and the large, tree-lined **Parc François I**^{er}, northwest of the city center between the allée Bassée and the allée des Charentes. (Open daily 8am-7pm.)

DIVINE COGNAC Discovered by Charentais wine makers in 1598 during an economic crisis, cognac has kept Cognac solvent for four centuries. Strict government labeling regulations separate the cognacs from common-or-garden brandies. The only fine liquor in the world limited to a specific production region, cognac may only be made from grapes in six small concentric regions, the heart of which is Grande Champagne (in which Cognac itself is located). Cognac is produced from the white *unis blanc* grape through a short fermentation period (5-10 days) followed by a double distillation which brings the alcohol level to 70%. This *eau de vie* is then aged for 5-100 years, under the careful direction of the cellar master. During the aging period the alcohol level falls to around 40% due to evaporation though the oak storage barrels (which contribute the amber tint to an otherwise colorless brandy). This lost portion is known as the "angels' share." Cognac is enjoyed most frequently as a *digestif,* straight up, in a snifter or tulip glass, but Charentais custom also supports its consumption as a "long drink" or *apéritif,* on the rocks or in tonic or water.

THE NORTHWEST

SAINTES

Resting on the banks of the Charente river and named for the local Gaulish Santon tribe, the ancient city of Mediolanum Santonum was founded by the Romans in the first century AD. Under them, the city served as the capital of Aquitaine for nearly 100 years, and today Saintes retains an assortment of ruins which bear testimony to its former glory. Ravaged by invaders during the dark ages, Sainte's recovery in the 11th century is illustrated by the two major Benedictine abbeys built in that era. Gracefully bisected by Charente and buffered by lush greenery, Saintes today (pop. 28,000) rewards visitors' curiosity with a quiet charm.

🛈 ORIENTATION AND PRACTICAL INFORMATION

Saintes lies on the Charente river, along the La Rochelle-Bordeaux railway line and 25km from Cognac. To get to the **tourist office,** take a sharp left upon leaving the train station and follow av. de la Marne until you hit hopping av. Gambetta. Turn right and follow it to the river; the Arc Germanicus will be on your left. Cross pont Palissy and continue straight on leafy green cours National; the tourist office is on your right in a villa set back from the street (20min.). The hub of the mellow pedestrian district is **rue Victor Hugo,** three blocks to the left after the bridge.

Trains: Pl. Pierre Senard. To: **Cognac** (20min., 5 per day, 29F); **Royan** (30min., 6-7 per day, 37F); **La Rochelle** (50min., 5 per day, 65F); **Niort** (1hr, 5 per day, 47F); **Bordeaux** (1½hr., 5 per day, 95F); **Poitiers** (2hr., 6 per day, 132F); **Paris** (2½hr., 6 per day, 335F). *Gare* open 5:30am-9:30pm; ticket booths open M 5:40am-8pm, Tu-F 8am-8pm, Sa 8am-7pm, Su 8am-9:30pm.

Buses: **Autobus Aunis et Saintonge,** 1 cours Reverseaux (tel. 05 46 97 52 03). To: **Royan** (1hr., 8 per day, 36F); **Le Château** and **St-Pierre d'Oléron** on the Île d'Oléron (1½hr., 2 per day, 61-71F). Office open M-F 9am-noon and 2-6pm. **Océcars** (tel. 05 46 99 23 65), in Rochefort. To: **La Rochelle** (2½hr., 1-2 per day, 57F). An operator answers calls M-F 8:30am-noon and 2-7pm.

Local transportation: Buses traverse the city regularly (6F). Schedules at tourist office or **Boutique Bus** a few blocks down in the Galerie du Bois d'Amour (tel. 05 46 93 50 50).

Taxis: At the *gare* (tel. 05 46 74 45 36). 6F per km, 7F per km nights and Su.

Bike Rental: Jacques Huriaud Cycles, 25 rue Perat (tel. 05 46 92 13 45). The cheapest in town. Bikes 30-40F per day, 180F per week. Mountain bikes 60F per day, 270F per week. Deposit 1200F. Open Tu-Sa 9am-noon and 2-7pm. V, MC, AmEx.

Tourist Office: 62 cours National (tel. 05 46 74 23 82; fax 05 46 92 17 01), in Villa Musso. Free maps and pamphlets. Organizes walking and bike tours. Open July-Aug. M-Sa 9am-7pm, Su 10am-1pm and 2-6pm; June and Sept. M-Sa 9am-1pm and 2-6pm; Oct.-May M-Sa 9am-12:30pm and 2-6pm. Tours offered June-Sept. M-Sa, 37-75F; in English upon request.

Banks: Banque de France, 1 cours Lemercier (tel. 05 46 93 40 33). **Currency exchange** desk open M-F 8:45am-12:15pm.

Laundromat: Laverie de la Saintonge, 18 quai de la République (tel. 05 46 74 47 18). Open M-W and F-Sa 8:30am-7pm, Su 10am-7pm.

Police: rue du Bastion (tel. 05 46 93 01 19).

Hospital: pl. du 11 Novembre (tel. 05 46 92 76 76).

Post Office: 8 cours National (tel. 05 46 93 05 84). **Currency exchange.** Open M-F 8:30am-7pm, Sa 8:30am-noon. **Postal code:** 17100.

Internet access: Acces Micro, 74 rue Arc de Triomphe (tel. 05 46 92 85 10). 20F first 15min., 1F per min. thereafter.

ACCOMMODATIONS AND CAMPING

Hotels fill for the early- to mid-July festivals; otherwise rooms should be easy to find. Most of the inexpensive lodgings cluster on the train station side of the Charente.

Auberge de Jeunesse (HI), 2 pl. Geoffrey-Martel (tel. 05 46 92 14 92; fax 05 46 92 97 82), next to the Abbaye-aux-Dames. From the station, take a sharp left onto av. de la Marne and then turn right onto av. Gambetta, left onto rue du Pérat, and right onto rue St-Pallais; 25m up at pl. St-Pallais, turn left through the archway into the courtyard of the *abbaye*. Go straight through, and the hostel will be on your right (15min.). A clean, renovated building that feels like part of the abbey itself. 69F. Breakfast included. Sheets 17F. Camping 27F, 37F with breakfast. Reception 7am-noon and 5-11pm; Oct.-May until 10pm. No lockout or curfew.

Le Parisien, 35 rue Frédéric-Mestreau (tel. 05 46 74 28 92), by the train station. Owner can recite the entire train schedule plus a "highlights of Saintes" speech in one breath. Immaculately kept carpeted rooms over a flower garden has a bed-and-breakfast feel. Singles or doubles 120F, with shower 155F. Extra bed 45F; hall showers 15F. Breakfast 15-25F. Call several weeks ahead for July-Aug. V, MC, AmEx.

Campsites: Camping Au Fil de L'Eau, 8 rue de Courbiac (tel. 05 46 93 08 00). From the train station, follow *auberge* directions to av. Gambetta and turn right onto quai de l'Yser after crossing the bridge (25-30min.). Signs mark the way. By bus, take #2 ("La Recluse") from the *gare;* get of at "Théâtre" and catch the #3 (direction "Magezy," not "Fenêtre"), to Courbiac (25 min., 6F). Three-star site by the Charente, next to municipal pool (free for campers) and mini-golf (25F). 1km from the *centre ville.* 23F per adult, 13F per child, 27F per site including car. Electricity 17F. Reception July-Aug. 8am-1pm and 3-9pm; May 15-June 30 and Sept. 1-15 9:30am-noon and 4-8pm. V, MC.

FOOD

Menus in Saintes flaunt the region's *fruits de mer* (seafood), as well as *escargot* dishes and *mojettes* (white beans cooked in Charenté). Start things off with *pineau,* a sweeter relative of Cognac. Saintes is blessed with plenty of family-run restaurants and bars with *menus,* especially in the pedestrian district and on av. Gambetta and cours National. Restaurants crowd the pedestrian streets by **rue Victor Hugo;** more expensive ones line **av. Gambetta.** Saintes holds **markets** on cours Reverseaux (Tu and F), near Cathédrale St-Pierre (W and Sa), and on av. de la Marne and av. Gambetta (Th and Su), all 8am-12:30pm. On the first Monday of every month **Le Grand Foire** stretches from the Cours National to Av. Gambetta. The huge **Leclerc supermarket** awaits on cours de Gaulle near the hostel. (Open M-Th and Sa 9am-7:15pm, F 9am-8:15pm.) The **Co-op,** a smaller supermarket, can be found on rue Urbain Loyer off cours National. (Open M-Sa 8:30am-12:45pm and 3-7:45pm.) There is another Co-op at 162 av. Gambetta, near the *gare.* (Open Tu-Sa 8:30am-1pm and 3:30-8pm, Su 8:30-11am. V, MC.)

Le Tilleul, 74 av. Gambetta (tel. 05 46 74 23 01), stretches for a third of a block, encompassing a pleasant outdoor café, a bar, and an excellent restaurant. M-F lunch *menus* (55F); daily dinner *menus* (68F) include such goodies as *paupiette de veau* and *colombe à l'Antillaise.* Open M-F noon-2pm and 7-10:30pm, Sa-Su 7-11pm. V, MC.

La Romana, 89 av. Gambetta (tel. 05 46 74 18 11), ladles homemade sauces over pastas and pizzas (28-53F). Three-course *formule* (62F) offers salmon carpaccio, squid, and chocolate mousse. (Open daily noon-2pm and 7-11pm.)

Cafétéria du Bois-d'Amour, 7 rue du Bois-d'Amour (tel. 05 46 97 26 54), off cours National in the Galerie Merchandise in the *centre ville.* A cafeteria, this local favorite offers 5-28F *entrées* and 24-41F *plats.* Open daily 10am-10:30pm. 5% student discount. V, MC.

SIGHTS

International flags line both sides of the **pont Bérnard Palissy,** which looks out onto most of Saintes' sights, many of which are free. Built in AD 18 as the entrance to the city, the Roman **Arc Germanicus** rises on the left bank of the river. First located at the entrance to a bridge which crossed the Charente, the Arc was spared the bridge's 1843 demolition and moved to the right bank of the river. Behind the Arc, the **Jardin Public** offers refuge on shaded benches next to beautiful flower beds. A peaceful mini-zoo in the center houses a few small goats, deer, rabbits, and birds. In July and August, the garden hosts free Sunday afternoon performances, ranging from *saintonge* folk dancing to—grab your Stetson—country music line-dancing. Next door, on esplanade André Malraux, the **Musée Archéologique** (tel. 05 46 74 20 97) displays a collection of keys, coins, pottery, and chariot remains from the first-century city. A partially finished puzzle of Roman columns, friezes, and cornices, most dating from the demolition of the town's ramparts in the 4th-century, lies in the annexing lapidary. (Open June-Sept. Tu-Su 10am-noon and 2-6pm; Oct.-May Tu-Sa 10am-noon and 2-6pm, Su 3-6pm. 10F, under 18 and Su free.)

Rue Arc de Triomphe (which becomes rue St-Pallais) leads to the Romanesque **Abbaye-aux-Dames** (tel. 05 46 97 48 48). Built in 1047, the abbey led a quiet life for a while—some Gothic touch-ups here, another gallery there—until plagues, fires, and wars prompted centuries of constant construction and reconstruction. During the anti-religious fervor of the Revolution, the abbey was shut down and turned into a prison. Today, the abbey serves as Saintes' musical and cultural center. Frequent exhibitions by local artists brighten the pale stone walls of the **Salle Capitulaire,** which was once the daily meeting place for Benedictine nuns. The pine-cone-shaped bell tower of the **Église Notre-Dame** dates from the 12th century, when Eleanor of Aquitaine gave the nuns some friendly pointers during renovations. Climb to the top to scan the stunning horizon or check out contemporary tapestries depicting the six days of the Creation. See *l'Abbaye aux Dames: Été* pamphlet at the tourist office for summer concerts. (Exhibition and ramparts open daily July 1-15 10am-7pm; July 16-Aug. 31 10am-noon and 2-7pm; Sept.-June Th-F and Su-Tu 2-6pm, W and Sa 10am-12:30pm and 2-7pm. Church free; abbey admission 20F, under 16 free. French tours 37F. Concerts 60-240F.)

Cross the flower-lined pedestrian bridge as you head for the **Cathédrale St-Pierre** (tel. 05 46 92 95 11) on rue St-Pierre. Enormous and capped by a metal helmet, it's more like a fortress than a house of worship. The 12th-century church was redone in Gothic style from the 15th to 18th centuries, but the steeple and portal were left unfinished; not neglected, however, is the church's recently-restored 370-year-old organ. (Open daily 10am-7pm. Free.) Take rue St-Eutrope away from the *centre ville* and turn right onto rue de Lacurie to get to the **Arènes Gallo-Romaines,** now a crumbled and peaceful amphitheater in a residential neighborhood. Built in AD 40, the structure seated 20,000 spectators who flocked to see gladiators battle wild animals—as well as each other—to the death. Don't bother paying the 5F admission: you can see equally well from outside the fence. (Open daily Apr.-Oct. 9am-7pm; Nov.-Mar. Tu-Su 10am-12:30pm and 2-4:30pm.)

ENTERTAINMENT AND FESTIVALS

ENTERTAINMENT. Come nightfall, unwind in a Saintes café or pub for an evening of conversation and sunset-watching. Along quai de la République, **La Belle Époque** (tel. 05 46 74 20 33) is popular, if somewhat over-decorated. (Beer 15-30F, cocktails 30-50F. Open daily 5pm-2am.) Try your game (5F) at **Billiard Santais,** 126 av. Gambetta (tel. 05 46 92 17 12), accompanied by 10F beers. (Open W-M 2pm-2am.) If you've got a car, you can dance up a storm with partying students at the **Le Santon** club, Ste-Vegas (tel. 05 46 93 42 76), route de Royan. In summer, the adjoining **swimming pool** provides a respite from steamy body heat. (Open daily 10:30pm-3am. Cover 63F.)

FESTIVALS. In mid-July, the **Jeux Santons** brings diversity to Saintes with a ten-day celebration of international folk music, food, dance, and *soirées*. The Arènes Gallo-Romaines host the opening and closing events. Some events are free; most cost 40-200F, and a 200F passport gets you into a selected program of events. (Call 05 46 74 47 50, or stop by 43 rue Gautier for info.) At the same time, be sure to join the **Académies Musicales** celebration, in which more than thirty classical music concerts are packed into ten days at the Abbaye aux Dames. (Tickets 80-250F. Call 05 46 97 48 48; fax 05 46 92 58 56 for info.)

ROYAN

A favorite vacation spot for the English and French in the 19th century, Royan (pop. 17,000) saw the likes of the Prince of Wales, Émile Zola, and the Roths-childs gracing its sunny beaches in the 1880s. Sixty years later, it was the Germans who liked Royan so much they were loathe to leave: the town was one of the last to leave Nazi hands, and liberation came only after Allied bombers had reduced the entire *centre ville* to rubble in a massive bombing raid on January 5, 1945. Rapid reconstruction was made possible by the extensive use of concrete, making Royan uniquely different from most French resorts. Today, once again, the seaside town is a favorite of French and English vacationers—the long stretches of sandy beaches, not to mention the restaurants and hotels which overlook them, fill with bodies in the summertime. The long promenade along bd. Frédéric Garnier offers a glimpse of the city's curious hotel/castle architecture, itself an answer to the mating call of the sky-piercing Église Notre Dame across the water.

■ **ORIENTATION AND PRACTICAL INFORMATION.** All **trains** go through **Saintes** (30min., 6-7 per day, 37F) on the way to **Cognac** (50min., 3 per day, 50F), **Angoulême** (1hr., 4 per day, 85F), **La Rochelle** (70min., 5 per day, 84F), **Niort** (90min., 3 per day, 83F), **Bordeaux** (2hr., 3 per day, 113F), **Poitiers** (2½hr., 3 per day, 157F), and **Paris** (3hr., 3 per day, 347F). (Station Open 7am-12:15am.) **Ocecars** (tel. 02 46 99 23 65), based in Rochefort, sends **buses** to **La Rochelle** (2½hr., 3 per day, 51F). **Autobus Aunis et Saintonge**, 9 rue Conbes de Mons (tel. 05 46 97 52 04) heads out to **Saintes** (1hr., 8 per day, 36F); the same company covers **local transportation** and has city transport schedules on hand. (Office open M-F 8am-noon and 2-6pm.) For a **taxi**, call **Taxis Radio Royannais**, Hôtel de Ville (tel. 05 46 39 88 88). **CycloTrott**, 1 Galerie Botton (tel. 05 46 22 52 34), in the cluster next to the tourist office, **rents bikes**. (46-93F per day, 200-420F per week. 1000-2000F deposit. Open daily 9am-7pm.)

The **tourist office**, bd. de la Grandière (tel. 05 46 05 04 71; www.ot-royan.fr), is across the street from the post office. (Open M-Sa 9am-7:30pm, Su 10am-1pm and 3-6pm.) **Croisieres Birais**, Port de Plaisance (tel. 05 46 05 29 91; fax 05 46 05 32 97), runs **boat trips** to **Talmont** (2hr., 70F, children 50F), the **Phare de Cordouan** (4hr., 150F, children 100F, reservation necessary), and surrounding areas. (Daily July-Aug.; call for off-season schedule.) **Royan Croisières**, Port de Plaisance (tel. 05 46 06 42 36; fax. 05 46 06 18 26), offers similar excursions and a "Dîner en Mer" cruise nightly at 8pm. (2½hr., 80F, children 50F; 2 *menus* 45-59F extra; reservations recommended.) **Banque Nationale de Paris**, 1 rue Notre Dame (tel. 0 802 35 62 42), has good rates of **currency exchange**. (Open M-F 8:25am-12:10pm and 1:35-5pm.) **Laverie Rapide**, pl. Dr. Gantier (open daily 7am-9pm), and **La Laverie**, 6 rue Paul Doumer (tel. 05 46 05 91 13), are **laundromats**. The **Centre Hospitalier de Royan**, 20 av. de St-Sordelin (tel. 05 46 39 52 52), is in nearby Vaux-sur-Mer; the **police** are at 13 rue du Château d'Eau (tel. 05 46 39 40 10). The **post office**, 83 bd. de la République (tel. 05 46 39 77 00), has **currency exchange**. (Open M-F 8:30am-6pm, Sa 8:30-noon. **Postal code: 17200.**) **L'Astoria** (see **Accommodations**, below), charges 1F per minute for **internet access**. (Open daily 4-8pm.)

⌐ ACCOMMODATIONS AND CAMPING. In Royan, the more expensive luxury hotels run along the bd. Frédéric Garnier, while better deals can be found around the pl. du Dr. Gantier and along the Front de Mer. Most hotels have a few rooms around 150F-180F, even during July and August, but if you're arriving in the heart of summer with the rest of France, be sure to book well ahead. There are plenty of campgrounds in the city outskirts; the tourist office has a complete list.

Le Trident Thyrse, 66 bd. Frédéric Garnier (tel. 05 46 05 12 83; fax 05 46 36 16 92), is a fun one for those willing to part with a little extra dough. A funky owner runs a set of spacious Ikea-esque rooms, each with a balcony facing the beach. Downstairs, a comfortable *salon* with a piano opens out to a beautiful outdoor beachfront terrace, where live music cools the heat on Tuesday and Friday nights. (Doubles 210-310F July-Aug., 160-260F rest of year. Parking in back. Breakfast 35F. Extra bed 50F. TV. V, MC.) The prize for best location and best price goes to **Hôtel de Ville,** 1 bd. A. Briand (tel. 05 46 05 00 64 or 05 46 05 32 41). The smallish, carpeted rooms are more expensive rooms if they face the beach. (Singles and doubles 140F with sink, 150F with toilet, 200F with shower, toilet and TV. Extra bed 50F. Breakfast 30F. V, MC.) **L'Astoria,** 42 av. du Maréchal Leclerc (tel. 05 46 05 85 75) doubles as a cybercafé. The friendly staff offers seven two-star rooms 150m from the beach. (200-210F June-July, 150F-180F rest of year. Breakfast 30F. Extra bed 50F. V, MC. Reception opens at 4pm.) The grounds of four-star **Camping Claire-fontaine,** allée des Peupliers off av. Louise (tel. 05 46 39 08 11; fax 05 46 38 13 79), are 300m from the beach and are equipped with a pool, jacuzzi, TV room, pizzeria, and tennis courts. (162F for 3 people, 55F per extra person. Electricity 20F. Open June 20-Sept. 15.)

⌐ FOOD. The mussel is king in Royan, while other local dishes mix land and sea flavors—look out for *escargot*, grilled sardines, and milk curds flavored with bay leaves. For good cheap eats, the **Front de Mer** is home to an endless row of cafés, *brasseries*, and restaurants serving up the local nosh; experience pleasant but more expensive dining on the **Voutes-de-Port.** For the freshest of the fresh, head to **Marché Central,** the hopping main market (June 15-Sept. 14 daily 7:30am-1pm; Sept. 15-June 14 Tu-Su 7:30am-1pm). A smaller market sits at the bottom of av. de l'Atlantique, off bd. Frédéric Garnier (8am-1pm daily). Across the street from the Marché Central is a **Co-op grocery store.** (Open M-Sa 8:30am-12:45pm and 3-7:45pm, Su 8:30am-12:45pm.) A bigger **Marché U** stands at 1 av. des Tilleuls. (Open M-Sa 9am-12:30pm and 3-7:30pm, Su 9am-12:30pm.)

Le Neptune, 33 Front de Mer (tel. 05 46 05 12 18 or 05 46 05 14 59), offers good value *formules* from 63F, while its neighbor **Key West** is popular among the younger set. (59F. 74F with sangria. Open daily.) **La Siesta,** 140 rue Gambetta (tel. 05 46 38 36 53), offers excellent dining above Voûtes-de-Port. 47F and 57F *menus* are simple but nice, and the varieties of bruschetta (42-45F), pastas (16-50F), and fish (35-110F) are reasonably priced.

◙ SIGHTS. If the sun gets in your eyes, Royan has a few sights to run to for refuge. The **Église Notre-Dame,** a massive 1950s construction, replaces the church bombed during WWII. Sustained by steel cables and shooting 80m into the sky, it has a silhouette that looks more like an Imperial Star Destroyer than a church. The stained-glass windows, which run spaceship-like around the church, are colored yellow for Royan and blue for the sea, while the psychedelic backlit altarpiece and original second balcony further illustrate the quirkiness of architect Guillaume Gillet. (Open every day from 8am to 7pm.) The **Musée de Royan,** 80 av. de Pontaillac (tel. 05 46 38 85 96), gives visitors a glimpse into Royan's past, from prehistory through World War II and the French Resistance. (Open T-F 2-6pm. Free.) 10km out of Royan, **La Poche de Royan,** 119 rue Samuel Champlain (tel. 05 46 22 89 90), presents photos, documents, and dioramas of the German occupation from 1944-45; Royan was one of the last areas in France to be liberated at the end of the war. (Open daily July-Aug. 10am-8pm, Sept.-June 10am-7pm. 35F, ages 7-12 15F.) A **carousel** at Port-de-Plaisance keeps the kids happy year-round.

◢ **BEACHES.** If you don't like warm weather and long stretches of sandy beaches, this is not the place for you. If you do, Royan could be your seaside fantasy. The **Grande Conche** beach, stretching 2.5km from the tourist office to neighboring St-Georges-de-Didonne, is a great area for walks, swimming, and playing. For some quiet sunning, try the smaller **Conche du Chay** and **Conche du Pigeonnier,** nestled between cliffs to the west. The **Conche de Pontaillac,** home of Royan's casino and nightclub, sees ample sunset partying, while the **Conche de Foncillon** also has freshwater fun with the lively **Piscine de Foncillon,** bd. Germaine de la Falaise (tel. 05 46 39 93 21) just behind it. (Pool open July-Aug. 10am-8pm; 56F, ages 5-15 28F. June and Sept. 10:30am-7pm; 30F, ages 5-15 15F. Half price after 5pm.)

▣ **ENTERTAINMENT.** Good things happen in the dark on the **Pontailac beach,** dominated by the money-guzzling **Casino de Royan.** The **Tropicana discothèque,** Esplanade de Pontaillac, spins out disco, rock, and zouk. (Open daily 10:30pm-5am. 50F.) Just down the street, **L'Atlantic Café-Bar-Restaurant** (tel. 05 46 39 03 31) serves oysters and cocktails by the moonlit water and features a jazz piano bar Fridays at 10pm. (Open daily 11am-3am.) Anyone with wheels should head out to **Le Bilboquet** discoteque, rte. de Bordeaux (tel. 05 46 90 84 12), equipped with three clubs, a pub, and a pool to cool your hormones. (Open daily 10:30pm-5am. 60F.)

◩ **EXCURSIONS.** Accessible by boat from Royan, the 14th-century **Phare de Cordouan** is France's oldest (and some claim most beautiful) lighthouse. Visitors can clamber to the top and admire the view of the surrounding areas, which include the Gironde estuary and the Coubre forests. The nearby town **Talmont,** 16km from Royan, makes for a pleasant daytrip by bicycle; the reward at the far end is the beautiful **church of Ste-Radegonde,** dubbed the "bastion of chiseled ivory." Interpret that as you will, but note that similar architecture permeates the town; to boot, every single Talmont road ends up at St. Radegonde's portal. Also not to be missed is a trip to France's biggest zoo, **La Palmyre** (infoline tel. 08 36 68 18 48; direct line 05 46 22 46 06; fax 05 46 23 62 97), hidden in a 14-hectare pine forest and housing 1600 creatures from around the world. (Zoo open April-Sept. daily 9am-7pm; Oct.-March daily 9am-noon and 2-6pm. 70F, ages 3-12 50F, under 3 free.) Buses leave from Royan's *gare routière* and pl. Charles de Gaulle. (July 1 on Su and holidays; May-June and Sept. 1 per day W, Sa-Su and holidays; Apr. 1 per day Th-Su and holidays. July 1-September 8, additional shuttle leaves from Royan *gare* and the Bac du Verdon; pick up a schedule from the bus office, or call 05 46 05 03 81 for times.)

ILE D'OLÉRON

Hovering only a couple of miles from the mainland, Oléron is the second-largest French island after Corsica. Some of France's largest and most renowned oyster beds, first cultivated by the Romans, encircle the island; the 90km coastline also includes 20km of fine beaches. With forests, museums, chapels, and an enormous citadel, Oléron makes a pleasurable daytrip. A 3km bridge links the island to the continent, and is perhaps best traversed by buses which circulate between Saintes or Rochefort-sur-Mer and **Le Château,** which makes the best base from which to explore the island; if possible, hire a bike here.

▌ **PRACTICAL INFORMATION (LE CHÂTEAU). Buses** leave for **Le Château** from 1 cours Reverseaux (tel. 05 46 97 52 03) in **Saintes** (1½hr., 3-4 per day, 63F), and from **Rochefort's** *gare routière* (tel. 05 46 99 98 97. 1hr., 6-8 per day, 39F), and from its train station (tel. 05 46 93 21 41). Descend at the portside stop in Le Château, turn your back to the water, and follow av. du Port and the signs to the centre ville. Turn right onto bd. Victor Hugo and head up the hill toward the **tourist office,** pl. de la République (tel. 05 46 47 60 51; fax 05 46 47 73 65) for a chock-full info packet, free maps, and hotel reservations. (Open July-Aug. M-Sa 10am-12:30pm and 2:30-7pm, Su 10am-12:30pm; Sept.-June M-Sa 10am-12:30pm and 2:30-6:30pm.)

Rent bikes at **Cycles-Peche Locavente,** 5 rue Maréchal Foch (tel. 05 46 47 69 30), just off pl. de la République. (34-52F per half-day, 43-67F per day; deposit 650F. Open daily July-Aug. 9am-12:15pm and 2-7:15pm; Sept.-June Tu-Sa 9am-12:30pm and 2-5pm, Su 9am-12:30pm. V, MC.) **Crédit Maritime** (tel. 05 46 47 62 23), near the tourist office on bd. Thiers, charges 17F to change traveler's checks. (Open M-Sa 8:30am-12:15pm and 1:30-5pm.) Le Château's **post office** is on bd. Victor Hugo. (Tel. 05 46 47 61 99. Open M-F 9am-noon and 1:30-4:30pm, Sa 9am-noon. **Postal code** 17480.)

From Le Château, a **shuttle bus** runs to: **St-Pierre-d'Oléron** (45min., M-Sa 6-8 per day, Su 4 per day, 22F); **Grand Village,** near the beaches (20min., M-Sa 5-6 per day, Su 2 per day, 11F); and **St-Denis** (1½hr., 3 per day, 32F).

▛ ACCOMMODATIONS AND CAMPING. Reserve several weeks in advance if you want a cheap place to crash. In **Le Château, Le Castel,** 54 rue Alsace-Lorraine (tel. 05 46 75 24 69; fax 05 46 75 25 41), lets spotless rooms. (Singles and doubles with shower and toilet 160-250F. Extra bed 40F. Breakfast 30F. Reception 9am-noon and 6-10pm. V, MC.) In the center of town near the tourist office is **Le Jean-Bart,** pl. de la République (tel. 05 46 47 60 04), with five small, simple rooms. (Doubles with shower 160F. Extra bed 50F. Breakfast 32F. V, MC.) Most people on a budget take tents, though, since 34 **campsites** are spread along the coast. Two-star **Les Remparts,** bd. Philippe Daste (tel. 05 46 47 61 93; fax 05 46 47 73 65) is also in Le Château. (80F in July-Aug. for car and tent, 72F off season. Open Mar.-Oct.) Near Le Château, the four-star **La Brande,** rte. des Huitres (tel. 05 46 47 62 37; fax 05 46 47 71 70), 2.5km west of town, keeps 199 luxury sites, a pool, tennis courts, and a waterslide. (July-Aug. 120F for 2, Sept.-June 70F. Extra person 35F. Electricity 20F. Open Mar. 15-Nov. 15. V, MC.) Near **Grand-Village** and the beaches lies **Camping Municipal des Pins,** allée des Pins. (Tel. 05 46 47 50 13. July-Aug. 2 person site 61F, off season 55F. 15F per person. 15F electricity. Open Easter-Sept. 30.)

⬚ FOOD. Each town has a Sunday morning **market,** and many have weekday morning versions as well. In **Le Château,** vendors fill the covered building across from the tourist office in pl. de la République (Tu-Su 7:30am-12:30pm). **The Coop,** 3 rue Reytre Frères, off pl. République, is a modest grocery. (Open M-Sa 8:30am-12:30pm and 4-7:30pm, Su 9am-1pm. V, MC.) For a larger selection, try **Super U Supermarché,** 15 av. d'Antioches, 250m out of Le Château. **Grand Village** also has a large **Super U** in its *centre commercial.* (Both open July-Aug. M-Sa 8:30am-8pm, Su 9am-12:30pm; Sept.-June M-Sa 9am-12:30pm and 3-7:30pm, Su 9am-12:30pm.)

Larger towns have cafés and bars that stay open late. In **Le Château,** try **La Cigale,** rue Clemenceau. (Tel. 05 46 47 61 37.) **St-Denis** offers **Le Panoramic,** 3 bd, d'Antioche (tel. 05 46 75 98 18), while **La Cotiniere** holds **Le Piano Bleu,** at 69 rue du Port. (Tel. 05 46 47 31 66.) In **St-Pierre,** check out **Morgan's,** rue Louis Barthou. (Tel. 05 46 47 12 29.) Check tourist office bulletin boards for info on concerts and events.

⬚ ISLAND TOWNS AND SIGHTS. The mighty but crumbling **citadel** in **Le Château** was built on the ruins of a medieval fortress. In 1621, following a revolt in La Rochelle, skittish Louis XIII had it destroyed to prevent its falling into Protestant hands, only to rebuild it nine years later; the current structure dates to this 1630 reconstruction. Louis XIV and Richelieu were some of its more famous guests; WWI German POWs were some of the more infamous. Allied bombs destroyed much of the citadel in 1945 to keep German squadrons left on Oléron from regrouping. Various exhibits come and go in the more habitable chambers; call 06 80 10 84 26 for hours and activities, some of which take place in pl. de la République. (Exhibits open 10am-7pm. Free.)

St-Pierre d'Oléron, with a bustling pedestrian sector, is the island's geographic and administrative center; it also houses the tomb of French writer and naval officer Pierre Loti. The staff of the St-Pierre **tourist office,** pl. Gambetta (tel 05 46 47 11 39; fax 05 46 47 10 41), knows everything. (Open July-Aug. M-Sa 9am-7pm, Su 10am-1pm; Sept.-June M-Sa 9:15am-12:30pm and 2-6pm.) A lively port graced by a

modern chapel makes **La Cotinière** the most picturesque of the island towns; stop
by the model boat expo in the **museum** opposite the port. (Tel. 05 46 47 18 75.) **Le
Grand Village,** 3km southwest of Le Château, is the smallest town, with 586 locals
and the island's glitziest, most **flamboyantly topless** beach. (Tourist office tel. 05 46
47 58 00; fax 05 46 47 42 17.) Another beach, **Plage du Vert Bois,** near Grand Village
and separated from the main road by a thick pine forest, feels almost like an island
itself. Near the northwestern tip, **St-Denis** invites tourists to climb the 54m lighthouse and peer down at the colorful collage below. (Open daily 10am-noon and 2-
6:30pm; Sept.-June 10am-noon and 2-6pm. Free.) The tourist office on bd. d'Antioche has more info. (Tel. 05 46 47 95 53; fax 05 46 75 91 36.)

LA ROCHELLE

Named after the soft rock which 10th-century settlers built their homes, La Rochelle (pop. 100,000) became Aquitaine's major maritime town in the Middle Ages,
profiting from its importance as a port serving both France and Britain. In the 17th
century, the omnipotent Cardinal Richelieu saw an obstacle to Royal absolutism in
this bastion of Protestantism and convinced Louis XIII to besiege the town. After
many citizens had starved to death, the city finally surrendered. The straggling survivors reversed this losing tide by fleeing west across the Atlantic and founding a
cosmopolitan mecca on Long Island Sound.

The city, immortalized by Dumas in *The Three Musketeers*, did not recover its
wealth until 20th-century vacationers discovered its white sand beaches and 14th-
century architecture. Those same beaches and buildings, as well as fabulous festivals and nightlife, lovely weather, and proximity to some of the most perfect isles
off the French coastline make La Rochelle today nothing short of vacation heaven.

⚇ ORIENTATION AND PRACTICAL INFORMATION

La Rochelle spreads out from the *vieux port*, where many cafés line **Quai Duperré**,
while just inland the *vieille ville* finds tourists and locals bustling about its bou-
tique-filled streets. To get from the train station to the tourist office, head up av. du
Général de Gaulle to the first square, pl. de la Motte Rouge. Turn left onto the quai
du Gabut. The tourist office is on the left, in the **Quartier du Gabut**, a zone of shops,
seafood, and pan-Asian restaurants of questionable authenticity (5min.). To reach
the center of town directly from the station, take av. du Général de Gaulle through
pl. de la Motte Rouge until it turns into quai Valin, which will lead you straight to
quai Duperré. For those staying in town, the beach nearest the hostel by the aquarium and the port de Plaisance is nicer than the stony *plage* west of the *vieux port*.

Trains: Bd. Maréchal Joffre. To: **Poitiers** (2hr., 8 per day, 109F); **Bordeaux** (2hr., 5 per
day, 133F); **Nantes** (2hr., 5 per day, 129F); and **Paris** (5hr., 1 per day, 260F; 5 TGVs
per day, 3hr., 309F). No lockers. Counters open M-Th and Sa 5:10am-8:10pm, F
5:10am-10:30pm, and Su 6:15am-10:30pm. Building open daily 5am-11:30pm, but
tracks and ticket machines always accessible.

Buses: Citram, 30 cours des Dames (tel. 05 46 50 53 57), goes to **Angoulême** (3½hr.;
M-F 2 per day, Sa 3 per day, Su 1 per day; 105F). Office open M 2-6:45pm, Tu-F 9am-
12:15pm and 2-6:45pm, Sa 9am-12:15pm. **Océcars** (tel. 05 46 00 21 01), in pl. de
Verdun, sends buses to **Royan** (1¼hr., 3 per day, 63F) and **Saintes** (3-5 per day,
change at Rochefort, 58F). For all buses, buy tickets from driver, cash only.

Public Transportation: Pick up a schedule at the pl. de Verdun main office (3F).
Autoplus (tel. 05 46 34 02 22) serves the campgrounds, hostel, and *centre ville* (8F).

Taxis: Pl. de Verdun (tel. 05 46 41 55 55 or 05 46 41 22 22).

Bike Rental: Vélos Municipaux Autoplus, off quai Valin or pl. de Verdun near the bus
station (tel. 05 46 34 02 22). Free with ID deposit for 2hr., 6F per hr. thereafter. Quai
location open May-Aug. M-Sa 7:30am-7pm, Su 1-7pm. The youth hostel also rents
bikes for 50F per day in July-Aug.

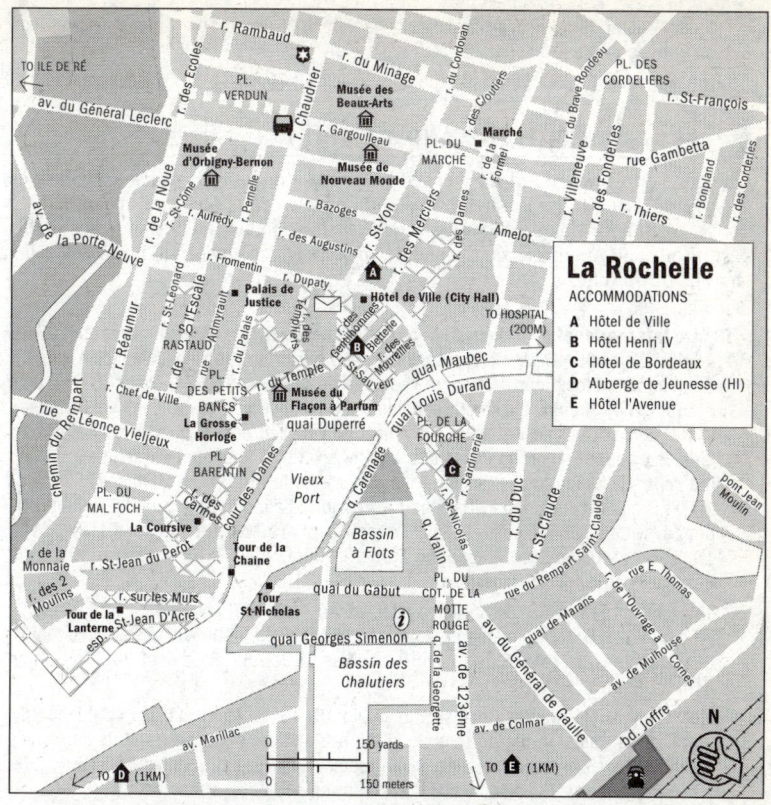

Ferries: The **Bus de Mer** (tel. 05 46 34 02 22) shuttles between the old port and les Minimes (18F round-trip). Boats run to Île de Ré (see p. 615) and Île d'Aix (p. 617).

Tourist Office: Pl. de la Petite Sirène, quartier du Gabut (tel. 05 46 41 14 68; fax 05 46 41 99 85; www.Ville-laRochelle.fr). Multilingual staff distributes informative maps in French (5F), meagre ones in English (3F), a comprehensive (French) guide to La Rochelle and the region (3F), and the free monthly entertainment magazines *Tenue de Soirée* and *Sortir*. **City tours** by foot and horse carriage July-Aug. Night visits, led by costume-clad *rochelais,* can be arranged by appointment July 22-Sept. 30. Hostel reservation service 10F. Open July-Aug. M-Sa 9am-8pm; Su 11am-5pm; June and Sept. M-Sa 9am-7pm, Su 11am-5pm; Oct.-May M-Sa 9am-noon and 2-6pm, Su 10am-noon.

Money: Banque de France, at rue Réaumur and rue Léonce Vieljeux (tel. 05 46 51 48 00), has the best rates and no commission. Foreign exchange desk open M-F 8:30am-noon. In a pinch, **24hr. change machines** are also available: just feed nearly any non-French bills into the machines at **Crédit Lyonnais,** 19 rue du Palais.

Youth Center: Centre Départemental d'Information Jeunesse (CDIJ), 2 rue des Gentilshommes (tel. 05 46 41 16 36 or 05 46 41 16 99; fax 05 46 41 50 35). BIJ tickets. Boards list apartments and jobs. Open M 2-6pm, Tu-F 10am-6pm, and Sa 10am-noon.

Laundromat: Laverie Vague Bleue, 4bis Quai Louis Durand (tel. 05 46 50 67 91). Open daily 8:30am-8:30pm. During "happy hour" (W 8:30am-noon), wash 16kg for 30F.

Police: 2 pl. de Verdun (tel. 05 46 51 36 36).

Hospital: Rue du Dr. Schweitzer (tel. 05 46 45 50 50).

Post Office: 6 pl. de l'Hôtel de Ville (tel. 05 46 30 41 30). **Currency exchange.** For Poste Restante address to "Hôtel de Ville, 17021 La Rochelle". Open M-F 8:30am-6:30pm,

Sa 8am-noon. **Main office** 52 av. Mulhouse, by the train station. Open M-F 8am-7pm, Sa 8am-noon. **Postal code:** 17000.

Internet Access: Cyber Squat, 63 rue St-Nicolas (tel. 05 46 34 53 67). 30min. for 25F.

■ ACCOMMODATIONS AND CAMPING

The good news: when Axl Rose asked to be taken down to Paradise City, he was clearly referring to La Rochelle. The bad news: word is out, and cheap beds in town are limited. Make reservations now! The huge industrial port-side hostel fills fast in July and August, as do the many two-stars which cluster in the *vieille ville*, near pl. du Marché.

Centre International de Séjour, Auberge de Jeunesse (HI), av. des Minimes (tel. 05 46 44 43 11; fax 05 46 45 41 48). Take bus #10 (direction "Port des Minimes") from av. de Colmar, 1 block from station, to "Auberge de Jeunesse" (M-Sa, every 30 min. until 7:15pm, 8F.) Or enjoy the short waterside walk—great view, and you can't get lost. Keep to the port edges and watch for the hostel on your left, just beyond a cluster of pay-phones beside the Port de Plaisance. A water taxi (10F) shuttles between the port and the *centre ville*. Enormous, hospital-like *auberge* with 2 to 6-bunk dorms. 72F; singles 107F. Breakfast included. Wheelchair accessible. Laundry. Bike rental July-Aug. 50F per day with a 500F deposit. Midnight curfew Sept. 15-Apr. 30; no curfew May 1-Sept. 14. Lockout 10am-2pm. Reception 8am-12:30pm, 1:30-7:30pm, and 8:30-10pm. Reserve in advance. **Members only.**

Hôtel de Bordeaux, 43 rue St-Nicolas (tel. 05 46 41 31 22; fax 05 46 41 24 43), right off quai Valin, 5min. from station. A great location, with 22 sparkling, renovated rooms, above a pleasant café. Singles 165F, doubles 190-255F. Breakfast 30F. Reception 8am-9:30pm. V, MC.

Hôtel Henry IV, 31 rue des Gentilshommes (tel. 05 46 41 25 79; fax 05 46 41 78 64), on pl. de la Caille off rue du Temple, in the heart of the *vieille ville* and its happening nightlife. Spacious, fully-furnished, clean rooms. Singles and doubles 165-180F, 195-210F with shower; 2-4 person suites with shower 225-265F. Breakfast 30F. V, MC.

Hôtel de Ville, 5 rue St-Yon du Minage (tel. 05 46 41 30 25). In the center of town, this hotel-bar houses students during the year, but offers clean, uncarpeted rooms from mid-June to the end of August. Ask for a room overlooking the street and peep your head out to watch the morning passers by—*à la français!* Doubles 190-240F July and Aug., 150-190F in June. Reception closed Sunday and after 8pm weeknights.

Hôtel l'Avenue, 109 rue Émile Normandin (tel. 05 46 44 26 10). Although a 15min. walk from the city center, the hotel offers cheap, clean, carpeted rooms for affordable prices. Singles or doubles 140F with sink, with shower 180F, with shower and toilet 200F; tri-ples 250F with shower, with shower and toilet 280F; quads 300F. Extra double bed 85F. Breakfast 25F. V, MC.

Camping Municipal du Soleil, on av. Marillac (tel. 05 46 44 42 53). A 15min. walk from center of town past the Vieux Port along the *quais*, following av. Marillac to left at its junction with allée des Tamaris. Or catch bus #10. 47F for 2 adults, site, and car. 15F per extra adult. Open May-Sept. 15. The tourist office has a list of more distant camp-sites and info on much more beautiful but more remote island camping.

■ FOOD

The *fruits de mer* are always ripe in La Rochelle; head for the stands of the **cov-ered market** at pl. du Marché for fresh seafood, fruit, vegetables, and a fishy smell (daily 7am-1pm). **Prisunic,** rue de Palais, near the *grosse horloge*, sells the usual (open M-Sa 8:30am-8pm; V, MC), as do the **Co-ops** which have sprung up, most at 41 rue Sardinerie and 17 rue Amelot. (Open daily 9am-1pm and 3:30-8pm. V, MC.) Restaurants congregate in the *vieille ville* along **rue St-Jean** and the *quai*.

Les Comédiens, 15 rue de la Chaine (tel. 05 46 50 51 98). Stealing the show of the St-Jean restaurant frenzy, Les Comédiens serves up great food *and* brings you action; weekend nights feature theatrical spectacles while you dine. A favorite with the slightly younger crowd, the restaurant offers a 69F *pêcheur menu* packed full of fresh fish and fruit. Open daily noon-2pm and 7-10pm, later on weekends and summer. V, MC, AmEx.

Le Soleil Brille Pour Tout Le Monde, 13 rue des Cloutiers (tel. 05 46 41 11 42). In a warm, hip atmosphere, a young staff turns out whole wheat bread, daily specials with lots of fresh vegetables (48F), *maison tartes salées* (40-50F), and celestial desserts (stellar tiramisu 25F). Signature meal salads *Le Soleil* and *La Lune* feature oranges, avocado, carrots, and tofu for 48F. Open Tu-Sa noon-2:30pm and 7:30-11pm.

A Côté de Chez Fred, 30-32 rue St-Nicolas (tel. 05 46 41 65 76). Having expanded, this neighborly little maritime-themed restaurant surrounds its seafood source, the fish shop of Poissoneries Fred. Enjoy *entrées* (35-70F) and *plats* (40-110F) on the terrace. Don't skip the fish soup. Open M-Sa 12:15pm-2:30pm and 7:30-10:30pm. V, MC, AmEx.

Cafeteria de l'Arsenal, 12 rue Villeneuve (tel. 05 46 50 53 75). When lunch tray nostalgia or debt-collectors strike, retaliate with this cafeteria. *Plats* range 19-42F, followed by cheese (3-9F) and dessert (5-9F). Open daily 11:30am-2:30pm and 7-9pm. V, MC.

👁 SIGHTS

THE OLD TOWN. The pedestrian-only **vieille ville,** dating from the 17th- and 18th-centuries, stretches beyond the whitewashed harbor townhouses. Stroll by the 14th-century **grosse horloge,** but skip the archæological exhibit inside. A view of the town similar to that from the harbor tower awaits at the top. *(Open July-Sept.15 10am-7pm. Admission 15F.)* The Renaissance façade of the **Hôtel de Ville,** with its prominent statue of its builder, Henry IV, will take your breath away for free. *(45min. French tours of the interior July-Aug. daily 4pm; Oct.-May Sa-Su 3pm. 18F, students 12F.)*

TOUR ST-NICOLAS AND TOUR DE LA CHAÎNE. The 14th-century towers guarding the port helped La Rochelle thrive as a giant commercial warehouse. When hostile ships approached, guards linked a chain between the towers, barring the harbor. According to Rabelais the huge chain had further use—it was one of four which tied the infant Pantagruel into his cot. Today, citizens are more concerned about getting boats out of the port—sediment and mud have clogged the waters. St-Nicolas, on the left as you face the harbor, impresses visitors with formidable fortifications. The narrow staircases pass exhibits about La Rochelle's ongoing melée with the mud, while the Tour de la Chaîne presents a model of the town in Richelieu's day. *(St-Nicolas tel. 05 46 41 74 13; Chaîne tel. 06 46 34 11 81. Both towers open Apr.-Sept. daily 10am-7pm; Oct.-Mar. daily 10am-12:30pm and 2-5:30pm. 25F, ages 12-25 15F, free under 12. Combined ticket including Tour de la Lanterne 45F, ages 12-25 30F.)*

TOUR DE LA LANTERNE. Accessible from the Tour de la Chaîne by a low rampart, this 58m-high tower was France's first lighthouse,. The 15th-century tower has a morbid history—it became known the *Tour des Prêtres* after 13 priests were thrown from the steeple into the water during the wars of religion. In 1822, four sergeants were imprisoned here before being executed in Paris for conspiring against the monarch. The 162 steps to the top hold intricate graffiti scrawled by other 19th-century detainees. Only three inches of stone separates you from a 45m free-fall at the summit, where you can see all the way to the Île d'Oléron on sunny days. *(Tel. 05 46 41 56 04. Admission and hours the same as Tour St-Nicolas.)*

MUSÉE DU FLACON À PARFUM. In the glitzy shopping district near la Grosse Horloge, this tiny tribute to scents smells up the second floor of the Saponaire perfume shop. A private collector has amassed thousands of perfume bottles, including tiny *crème parfums* the Ku Klux Klan produced in 1933 to deride African Americans, bottles designed by Cocteau, Dali, and Mirò, and Italian *parfumeur* Schiaparelli's 1937 bottles modeled on Mae West's torso. *(33 rue du Temple. Tel. 05 46 41 32 40; fax 05 46 41 92 34. Open M 3-7pm, Tu-Sa 10:30am-7pm; July and Aug. also open Su and holidays 3-6pm. 25F, students 22F, under 10 free.)*

AQUARIUM. Soothing songs from whales whisper as you admire 550,000 litres of water filled with octopuses, sharks, sea horses, and a colorful Mediterranean fish, the *merou de Grace Kelly*. The staff swears you could swim safely amongst the piranhas in its rainforest. *Let's Go* recommends you do not swim with the piranhas. *(Port des Minimes. Tel. 05 46 34 00 00. Take bus #10, direction "Les Minimes," or walk 35min. down av. Maillac. Open daily July-Aug. 9am-11pm; Apr.-June and Sept. 9am-7pm; Oct.-Mar. 10am-noon and 2-7pm. 42F, students 37F, children 25F. V, MC, AmEx.)*

MUSÉE DES AUTOMATES. A wondrous collection of 300 moving characters. 1996 saw the opening of the crown jewel: a miniature Montmartre with artists, pharmacists, drunkards, and a lingerie store. A model train loops around the building, housing the miniatures of the smaller **Musée des Modèles Réduits.** Model cars, trucks, and trains impress with their incredible detail, but the museum's highlight is the *Bataille Navale*, in which ships maneuver through a tiny sea clouded by cannon smoke. *(Automates on Rue du Cerf, off av. Marillac. Tel. 05 46 41 68 08. Modèles Réduits around the corner on rue Desirée. Tel. 05 46 41 64 51. Both open June-Aug. 9:30am-7pm; Sept.-Oct. and Feb.-May 10am-noon and 2-6pm; Nov.-Jan. 2-6pm. 65F for both, children under 10 35F; for one museum 40F, children 26F. V, MC.)*

MUSÉE D'ORBIGNY-BERNON. A very respectable collection of European and Chinese decorative arts and ceramics, including special exhibits on Japanese samurai, 19th-century Chinese life, and ancient musical instruments from Southeast Asia. The museum also focuses on La Rochelle history, holding a wonderful display of 84 pharmaceutical vases from the ancient hospital Aufredi. *(2 rue St-Côme. Tel. 05 46 41 18 83. Open M and W-Sa 10am-noon and 2-6pm, Su 2-6pm. 20F, art students 15F, under 18 free. 40F buys combined admission to the Musées d'Orbigny-Bernon, Nouveau Monde, Beaux-Arts, Histoire Naturelle, and Océanographique.)*

OTHER SIGHTS. The **Neptunéa Musée Maritime de la Rochelle** displays five decks of ship life exhibits; special exhibitions include sailboats, *Rochelaise* fishing techniques, and a special submarine adventure. *(Bassin des Chalutiers near the tourist office. Tel. 05 46 28 03 00. Open daily 10am-7pm. 45F, students and children 30F.)* Two less sea-centric museums offer visitors to La Rochelle a well-rounded collection of art. The **Musée des Beaux Arts** displays an impressive collection of paintings, sketches, and tapestries. Artists range from Rembrandt to Delacroix—look for Signac's depiction of La Rochelle's bustling 18th-century harbor. *(28 rue Gargoulleau. Tel. 05 46 41 64 65. Open W-M 2-5pm. 20F, art students 15F, under 18 free.)* In a gorgeous 1740s mansion, the **Musée du Nouveau-Monde** emphasizes France's influence on the development of the Americas and depicts the early French perception of the New World person as a bestial savage. *Plus ça change...* *(10 rue Fleuriau. Tel. 05 46 41 46 50. Open W-M 10:30am-12:30pm and 1:30-6pm, Su 3-6pm. 20F, art students 15F, under 18 free.)*

♫ ✺ ENTERTAINMENT AND FESTIVALS

ENTERTAINMENT. La Rochelle's ultra-inviting entertainment venue **La Coursive,** 4 rue St-Jean-du-Perot (tel. 05 46 51 54 02; fax 05 46 51 54 03), hosts operas, jazz and classical music concerts, traditional and experimental plays, dance performances, and art films, in addition to organizing festivals. (Open M 5-9pm, Tu-Sa 1-8pm, Su 2-6:30pm.) Evenings from July to September, **quai Duperré** and **cours des Dames** are closed to cars and open to magicians, mimes, artists, jugglers, musicians, and an open market. In the *vieux port*, stop in for a drink and select from 20 imported beers (15-45F) at **MacEwan's,** 7 rue de la Chaîne. (Tel. 05 46 41 18 94. Open Su-Th 5:30pm-2am, F-Sa 5:30pm-3am.) Local youth hang out around the **cour du Temple,** tucked away off rue des Templiers. Try **Le Mayflower** (tel. 05 46 50 51 39) for its rum concoction (16F), or toss a serious game of darts before a Saturday concert at **Le Piano Pub** (tel. 05 46 41 03 42). (Both open daily 6pm-3am.) The sole gay club in the *centre ville*, **Recto-Verso,** 33 quai Vallin (tel. 05 46 41 58 81), features art shots of buff men. (Open Tu-Su 5pm-3am.) **Le Garibaldi,** 48 rue St-Nicolas (tel. 05 46 41 05

49), has food, drinks, concerts, and occasional film screenings. (Open daily 6pm-2am.) Decked with mirrors, lacquer, and brass, **The Triolet,** 8 rue des Carmes (tel. 05 46 41 29 06), will keep your head spinning with 94 brands of whisky from 11pm-5am. The **Oxford and Papgayo Discothèques,** plage de la Concurrence (tel. 05 46 41 51 81), are stomping grounds of an even younger crowd. (Open nightly 11pm-5am.)

FESTIVALS. La Rochelle's wildly popular festivals attract art-loving, sun-seeking mobs like nobody's business. During the last week of June and the first week of July, the city becomes the Cannes of the Atlantic with its **Festival International du Film de La Rochelle.** (Admission to all 100 films 490F; 3 films 90F; one film 35F; under 21, 10 films for 170F. For tickets, write to 16 rue St-Sabin, 75011 Paris. Tel. 01 48 06 16 66; fax 01 48 06 15 40.) Without batting an eyelash, La Rochelle turns right around and holds its **FrancoFolies,** a six-day music festival in the third week of July with francophone performers from around the world. (Call 05 46 28 28 28 or the tourist office. Single tickets 55-175F.) During the second week of September, hundreds of boats in the Port des Minimes open their immaculate interiors to the public for the **Grand Pavois** (tel. 05 46 44 46 39).

ISLANDS NEAR LA ROCHELLE

ÎLE DE RÉ

Ile de Ré, dubbed *"Ré La Blanche"* for its 70km of fine, white sand beaches, is a sunny paradise a mere 10km from La Rochelle. Connected by a bridge to the mainland, the 30km long island contains one of Europe's largest nature preserves, extensive paved bike paths, pine forests, farmland, bustling towns, and huge stretches of untrammeled natural beauty. Though only 14,000 lucky people live on the island year-round, July and August bring crowds to the southern half and to the main town, **St-Martin-de-Ré,** in the middle of the north coast.

◤ GETTING THERE. The isle is easily accessible by bus, bike, or ferry. Driving across the La Pallice bridge costs a ridiculous 110F round-trip in tolls for cars and 15F for motorcycles and scooters. **Walking** and **biking** are easy options, and the cycle from La Rochelle to Sablanceaux takes less than an hour. The ride is a bit tough going up the bridge, but once you get there the trails on the island are marvelous and give you a nearly complete view of the coast. From pl. de Verdun in La Rochelle, head west on Maréchal LeClerc and follow road signs to Île de Ré until the bike path with the same label appears on the left.

If that sounds too energetic, try a bus or ferry. **Autobus** lines #1 and 50 go from pl. de Verdun to the beach at the foot of the bridge—check the bus goes all the way to Sablanceaux (direction "La Pallice," 32 per day July-Aug., 10F). If you'd like to venture beyond Sablanceaux, try **Rébus** (tel. 05 46 09 20 15), which runs between pl. de Verdun and every conceivable stopping place on Ré, including **St-Martin** (45min., 8 per day, 28F) and **Les Portes,** at the northern tip (1½hr., 8 per day, 50F). **Ferries** to the island are equally affordable: **InterÎles** (tel. 05 46 50 51 88) ships Ré seekers from La Rochelle's Vieux Port to Sablanceaux for 30F, children 24F.

◪ PRACTICAL INFORMATION: ST-MARTIN-DE-RÉ. Though it's a good idea to pick up a copy of the booklet *Île de Ré: Tourisme* in La Rochelle, stop in at St-Martin's **tourist office,** av. Victor-Bouthellier (tel. 05 46 09 20 06; fax 05 46 09 06 18), for the *Guide des Itinéraires Cyclables,* a free bike path map and guide. (Open M-Sa 10am-noon and 3-5:30pm; Sept.-May closed W afternoon.) The cheapest **bikes** are rented by **Cycland,** impasse Sully (tel. 05 46 09 08 66), off rue du Sully. **Branches** in Sablanceaux, La Flotte, Ars, Les Portes, St-Clement, and La Couarde. (Bikes 20-32F per hr., 38-62F per half-day, and 48-78F per day. 1300-1800F or ID deposit. Open July-Aug. daily 9am-9pm; Sept.-June daily 9:30am-12:30pm and 2:30pm-7pm. V, MC, AmEx.) The best **currency exchange** rates, though with a 40F commission, are at **Crédit Agricole,** 4 quai Foran, on the port. (Tel. 05 46 09 20 14. Open Tu-F 9am-12:15pm and 1:30-5:45pm, Sa 9am-noon.) The **post office** is on pl. de la République. (Tel. 05 46 09 00 16. Town **postal code:** 17400.)

THE NORTHWEST

✦ ISLAND ACCOMMODATIONS. If you're looking for a place to stay, St-Martin's **Hôtel Le Sully,** rue Jean Jaurès (tel. 05 46 09 26 94; fax 05 46 09 06 85), a block up from the port, offers clean, quiet, medium-sized rooms. (Singles or doubles with shower 180F, with shower or bath and toilet 230F. Extra bed 50F. Breakfast 30F. V, MC, AmEx.) Smaller towns also offer accommodations. In **La Flotte,** 4km east of St-Martin and 9km north of Sablanceaux, stampede to **l'Hippocampe,** 16 rue Château des Mauléons (tel. 05 46 09 60 68), with its small, ageing, but comfortable rooms. (Singles and doubles 105-130F, with bath 200F. Shower 12F. Breakfast 25F. V, MC.) Gorgeous **Camping Le Platin** (tel. 05 46 09 84 10), near the bridge in **Rivedoux,** costs 68-70F for one to three campers. (Extra person 15F. Open Easter-Sept.) Beachside on the north coast, **La Plage** (tel. 05 46 29 42 62), near St-Clement, lends sites to two people and a tent for 80F. (Open Apr.-Sept.) Bedding down by the surf is illegal but not strictly enforced; *Let's Go* does not recommend it.

✦▢ FOOD AND ENTERTAINMENT. Island restaurants are pricey, but most towns have pizzerias and *crêperies* as well as **morning markets,** which are listed in full in Ré's tourist packet. St-Martin's is indoors off rue Jean Jaurès, by the port (daily 8am-1pm). Two supermarkets, **Intermarché** (open M-Sa 9am-12:30pm and 3-7:30pm) and **Super U** (open M-Sa 8:30am-8pm and Su 8:30am-12:30pm) battle with bargains just east of St-Martin on the road to La Flotte. Another kind of hunger is treated in the form of St-Martin nightlife, which comes alive in summer. **Cotton Pub** (tel. 05 46 09 17 99) and **Boucquingham** (tel. 05 46 09 01 20), both on Venelle de la Fosse Bray, are intimate piano bars tucked behind the *quai,* across from the tourist office. Cotton Pub hosts jazz, funk, and rock concerts nightly July-Aug., and on weekends during the rest of the year. (Both open M-Th 5pm-2am, F-Sa 5pm-3am. 60F cover with drink most nights. V, MC.) The versatile **Le Bastion,** cours Pasteur (tel. 02 46 09 21 92), across town with a great view of the sea, is a wild all-purpose grill, pizzeria, nightclub, and disco. It plays host to once-a-week theme nights in summer, such as Mexican night. (Open Tu-Sa 5:30pm-2:30am). Further down the island, on Rivedoux plage, **Le Reseu Club,** pl. de la République (tel. 05 46 09 30 90), cranks out the beat from 11pm-5am every Friday and Saturday night (60F cover).

☉ TOWNS AND SIGHTS. Between Sablanceaux and the *plage*-ful La Flotte lie the ruins of the 13th-century **Abbaye des Chateliers.** First built in 1156, the abbey was destroyed during the wars of religion, as Ré passed between Catholic and Protestant hands. The monks abandoned the abbey in 1574; many of its stones were then taken in 1625 to build the Prée Fort. **La Flotte** also boasts the **EcoMusée La Maison du Platin,** Cours Felix Fauré (tel. 05 46 09 61 39) devoted to the history of the town's maritime life. (Open Apr.-Oct. Free.)

The biggest town on the isle, **St-Martin** holds a port built by Vauban and a citadel which served as a holding place for convicts on their way out to more remote island labor prisons. The 15th- to 17th-century Renaissance gallery of the **Hôtel Clerjotte,** av. Victor-Bouthilier, houses the **Musée Ernest Cognacq** (tel. 05 46 09 21 22), which is filled with model ships, expedition finds, and historical island paintings. (Open July-Sept. daily 10am-7pm; Oct.-June W-Su 10am-noon and 2-5pm. 22.50F, students 11F.) Climb up the hill from the *quai* and you will be greeted by the imposing 15th-century **Église St-Martin,** originally a Romanesque edifice. Built and destroyed no fewer than five times in religious wars since 1372, the Église St-Martin's recent chestnut-and-green remodeling contrasts sharply with the exterior's time-worn surface. (Open daily 10am-6:30pm.)

On your way up the island, stop by **Ars** to admire its 17 windmills. Outside **St-Clement-des-Baleines,** named for the whales that once frequented the surrounding waters, the 1854 **Phare des Baleines** still keeps watch over. The lighthouse keeper holds the door as you climb the 262 stairs for a view of the ocean and beaches. (Open June-Sept. daily 10am-noon and 2:30-5pm; Oct.-May daily 11am-noon and 3-5pm. Free.) Also near St-Clement are the **écluses à poissons** (tel. 05 46 30 22 92), fishing devices used in medieval times. The stone walls were erected so that fish would be trapped when the tide went out. (Call for visiting info. Wear boots!)

⚡ BIKES AND BEACHES. It's easy to rent a bike in any island town and pedal along the bike paths, coastal sidewalks, and wooded lanes which spread out across the island. Although everybody and their grandmother bikes the southern half of Île de Ré to St-Martin, crowds thin out as you travel north. Bike trails run through the Préserve Naturelle de Lileau des Niges, about 18km to the west and then north from St-Martin by bike path, on the inlet Fier d'Ars, a wetlands sanctuary humming with the songs of the rare blue-throated thrush and heron. The marsh bursts with vitality in the summer, but winter's the time to see it—20,000 birds stop by on their migration from Siberia and Canada to Africa.

The major attraction of the island is, of course, its splendid beaches. Slather yourself with sunscreen and shake off all inhibitions at the **Plage du Petit Bec** in clothing-optional Les Portes. If you want to avoid that full-body glow, head to the pine-fringed dunes of **la Conches des Balaines,** near the lighthouse just off the Gare Bec. Both beaches, at the northern tip of the island, are huge and devoid of the crowds that frequent the beaches on the western coast.

ILE D'AIX

Those in search of some peaceful natural beauty away from the heavy tourism of La Rochelle will delight in the Île d'Aix. Smaller and less accessible than Ré, Aix (pop. 200) sees fewer tourists and makes for an unbeatable daytrip on a sunny day. Just 3km long and barely 600m wide, the island offers backwoods trails for quiet hiking and tiny coves in the rocky, shell-covered coastline for private sunning or sleeping. The sandiest beaches are along the southwest edge near the lighthouses.

Once on the island, stop for a free "map" and brochure at the **Point Accueil,** on your right as you leave the port and approach pl. d'Austerlitz. The information center also organizes guided historical **tours** of the island. (1 hr., 3 per day, adults 20F, under 12 free). **Horse carriages** (tel. 05 46 84 07 18) do the same number of rounds from one block further up (50 min., 39F adults, 29F under 10). To explore the island, **rent bicycles** from *crêperies* and snack shops in town (approx. 20F per hour, 40F per half-day, and 50F per day), or take the smaller coastal paths on foot—a stroll about the perimeter of the island only takes about 2 hours.

Napoleon's last three post-Waterloo days in France were spent here before he surrendered to the British, a fact celebrated in the island's two museums. The **Musée Africain** and **Musée Napoléonien** house their small but impressive collections in the island's tiny town center, surrounded by no more than a sprinkling of public buildings, flower-laced bungalows, and little shops. The Musée Africain presents an ethnographical and zoological exhibition of Napoleon's Egyptian campaign, the highlight of which is the (preserved) dromedary he rode. The Musée Napoleonien exhibits a vast array of portraits, Napoleonic souvenirs, and captivating vestiges from the war, including a facsimile of his illegible surrender to the British. (Tel. 05 46 84 66 40. Both open June-Sept. 9:30am-6pm; Apr. and Oct. 9:30am-noon and 2-6pm; Nov.-March 9am-noon and 2-5pm. Separate admission 16F, for ages 18-25 12F, under 18 free. Combined admission before 4:30pm 24F, ages 18-25 18F.)

The few restaurants which emerge out of forest clearings tend to be pricey, but that doesn't mean you have to stash Powerbars. The **boulangerie,** on your right as you walk up rue Gourgaud, sells sandwiches cheaply. The cheerful **Pressoir,** in the middle of the island on rue Le Bois Joly (tel. 05 46 84 09 37), serves a lunchtime special of mussels and potatoes for 52F. Similarly, **Café de l'Océan** (tel 05 46 84 65 01), pl. d'Austerlitz, at the entrance to town, sells mussels and fries or *brochettes de boeuf* for 58F; herring and potatoes are a humbler 31F. Île d'Aix's sole hotel is outrageously expensive, but **Camping le Fort de la Rade** (tel. 05 46 84 28 28; fax 05 46 84 00 44) is more affordable. (32-45F per tent, 25F per adult, 16F per child.)

In the summer ferries link Aix to **La Rochelle. Inter Îles,** 14 cours des Dames (tel. 05 46 50 51 88), offers 2-4 ferries per day to the island via the fascinating Fort Bayard. (1½hr., 89F for a morning visit, 99F for the afternoon, 130F full day. Reservations strongly recommended. V, MC.) Similar service is provided by **Croisières Océanes** (tel. 05 46 50 68 44); look for their booth on the cours des Dames in La

Rochelle. (1hr., 90-110F roundtrip; children 4-12 60F. Ask about *Journées Promotion*, when prices dip to 75F. V, MC.)

THE MARAIS POITEVIN

Stretching west from Niort to the Atlantic just north of La Rochelle, this natural preserve has been nicknamed *"la Venise Verte"* (the Green Venice) for its serene canals which wind through undisturbed wetlands and forests teeming with life. Biking along the banks or punting through the labyrinthine canals on flat-bottomed *pigouilles* brings you past weeping willows, purple irises, herons, and the occasional rustic home. At its start by the Sèvre Niortaise river, graceful trees form a canopy overhead and duckweed carpets the water's surface, making the canals appear like grassy paths. Towards the coast, the lush greenery gradually gives way to the *'marais desseché,'* or dry marsh. Monks first dug the canals in the Middle Ages, but their work was undone during the chaos of the Hundred Years' War, and much of the current landscape owes its appearance to Napoleon. The idea remained the same, though: the canals enhanced agriculture and controlled flooding in this former marshland, and small-scale farming remains the region's primary industry. Though well worth the trouble of getting there, the Marais is not a very convenient daytrip; consider spending a night if you come. Most towns in the Marais are tiny and inaccessible by public transport, so the local hub of **Niort** makes the most sensible base from which to explore the region. From Niort it's easy to get to **Coulon**, where you can hire bikes or boats to get into the Marais. Both Niort's and Coulon's tourist offices provide info and maps of the Marais and sell an excellent walking and biking map for 30F.

NIORT

Anchoring the east of the Marais, Niort's beauty profits from its numerous narrow, twisting streets adorned with low, red tile-covered houses and a boardwalk along the green Sevre-Niortaise river. The center of town is cradled between two hills, one dominated by the elegant Gothic **Église St-André** and the Renaissance **Hôtel de Ville** (also known as **Le Pilori**), and the other by the 14th-century **Église Notre-Dame** and the bold **Donjon,** all that remains of Richard the Lionheart's former castle. The well-preserved keep contains an archæological and historical museum inside, and provides a remarkable view from atop its battlements. (Open May 2-Sept. 15 W-M 9am-noon and 2-6pm, Sept. 16th-May 1 W-M 9am-noon and 2-5pm. Admission Th-Tu 17F, W free; students and seniors free.)

Die hard hostelers will have to work hard to find space in Niort; the two **Foyers des Jeuenes Travaillers** are almost always full during the summer and have little space the rest of the year. To complicate matters further, neither lets rooms on weekend nights (F-Su). The main *foyer*, on 8 rue St-Andre (tel. 05 49 24 50 68), lets out rooms for periods of a week or more (500F). Its branch at 147 rue du Clou Bouchet (tel. 05 49 24 50 68) has 100F singles only. Both have restaurants open to the public which serve a 35-45F menu (open Sept.-July noon-1pm and 7:30-8:30pm). Given the situation, it's lucky that hotels are so cheap. For a great bargain in the city's center, try the **Hôtel St-Jean,** 21 av. St-Jean d'Angely (tel. 05 49 79 20 76), which has a cheery owner, pretty rooms, and excellent prices. (Singles 95F, 115F with shower, 145F with shower and toilet; doubles 100F, with shower 125F, with shower and toilet 165F; triples 125F, with shower 155F, with shower and toilet 180F. Breakfast 20F, extra bed 25F. V, MC.) Near the gare, **Hôtel de la Paix,** 109 rue de la Gare. (tel. 05 49 24 17 90) offers similar rooms—uncarpeted, but clean and pretty—for just a little more money. (Singles 100-125F, 145F with shower; doubles and triples 140-150F, 200F with shower. Breakfast 22F, shower 15F. Reception M-Sa until 11:30pm. V, MC.) **Camping Municipal,** 21 bd. S.-Allende (tel. 05 49 79 05 06), is next to the stadium; reserve in the spring for July and August. (56F for two people, tent, car, and electricity. Extra person 17F.) To get there, take bus #2 from pl. de la Breche to "Tour Chabut" (7F per person, *carnet* of 10 tickets 53F).

If you come to Niort in summer, you're likely to catch one of the lively *foires*, which take place nearly every night; year round, locals congregate in **rue Victor Hugo** and **rue Ricard,** and at the covered **market** in Les Halles (Tu-Su, 9am-1pm, larger version Th and Sa). If you need to party before you run to the marshes, Niort has two discotheques, **Le Cubana,** 43 rue St Gelais (tel. 05 49 17 17 25), and **Le Malibu,** 113 rue de l'Aerodrome (tel. 05 49 28 35 00).

Niort is easily accessible by **train** from **La Rochelle** (45min., 5-6 per day, 58F), **Saintes** (45min., 6-7 per day, 63F), **Poitiers** (1hr., 6-8 per day, 67F), and **Royan** (1¼hr., 6-7 per day, 83F). The **tourist office,** rue Ernest Perochon (tel. 05 49 24 18 79; fax 05 49 24 98 90), hidden behind some trees on pl. de la Poste, is a short walk from the station up rue de la Gare. It can provide you with loads of maps and information on the Marais and Niort, as well as a copy of the monthly *Rendez-Vous,* which details the city's artistic goings-on. You can rent **bikes** to explore the Marais from **Decathlon,** in Niort's commercial zone (tel. 05 49 33 34 97; 40-50F per day). The **post office** is on pl. de la Poste. (Tel. 05 49 24 84 03. Open M-F 8:30am-7pm, Sa 8:30am-noon. **Postal code:** 79000.)

COULON

Tiny **Coulon** (pop. 1400) is the self-proclaimed capital of the region, and is an ideal spot from which to take a boat trip into the Marais. For those without a car, SNCF **buses** run from **Niort** (20min., M-Sa 5 per day, 2 Su, 19F). Once here, you may find, that the most practical way to travel to rent a **bike,** though many hitch. The **tourist office,** 18 pl. de l'Église (tel. 05 49 35 99 29) is where you should head for information about bike, canoe, and punt rental; boats are a treat well worth the extra money. Pay for a guide and he will not only fill you in on the marsh's history and secrets, but also prod the water with his pole and light the marsh gas that bubbles up. (Punts and canoes 60-90F per hour, 145-160F with guide; bikes 20F per hour, 40F half-day, 50F full day. Office open 9:30am-12:30pm and 2-6:30pm). Campers might like to try Coulon's three-star **Camping de la Venise Verte** instead (tel. 05 49 35 90 36; fax 05 49 35 84 69), which has 150 canal-side sites and a pool. (June 15-Sept. 15 105F for two adults, car, tent, and electricity; Sept. 16-June 14 90F.)

OTHER SIGHTS OF THE MARAIS

About 20km northwest of Coulon, the ruins of the 12th-century **Abbaye St-Pierre** (tel. 02 51 00 70 11) peer out from amongst the trees. (Open July-Aug. 9am-8pm; Sept.-June 9am-noon and 2-6pm. 15F. Guided tours available in French.) Much further west, the nature reserve at **St-Denis-du-Payre** offers prime bird-watching, as does the **Bay of l'Aiguillon** to its southwest, where thousands of migrating birds gather in search of food. The almost circular sandy bay is the last vestige of the **Golfe du Poitou,** whose currents still contribute to the silting-up process of the Poitevin marshland. Right at the end of the Sevre Niortiase river rests the picturesque town of **Charron,** where mussel farms run along the coast to its southern neighbor Esnandes. Cultivated on the wooden *bouchots,* the mussels from this region are considered a true delicacy.

LES SABLES D'OLONNE

Les Sables d'Olonne is a prime beach site, attracting bronzed bathers every summer to its exquisite swimming area. Once a mere outer harbor of Olonne, the region's capital, the waters began to silt up in the Middle Ages and gradually became a marsh. Today, the pleasant, modern town happily embraces its sandy fringe; although dominated by the inevitable beachfront high-rises in town, the shore hides plenty of beautiful pockets north of the main beach which remain untouched by the hand of tourism. Even the land has a beautiful shape; the town's sea-pointing streets offer fabulous glimpses of the beach as they ascend heavenwards before sloping down to the water.

THE NORTHWEST

⌕ ORIENTATION AND PRACTICAL INFORMATION. The station on av. de Gaulle sends **trains** to **Nantes** (1½hr., 6-7 per day, 90F), **La Rochelle** (2hr., via La Roche-sur-Lyon, 5 per day, 106F), and **Paris** (5hr., 6 per day, 342F). At the **bus** station next door, **Sovetours** (tel. 02 51 95 18 71) sends buses to **Nantes** (2hr., 2 per day, 78F) and **La Rochelle** (3¼hr., 1 per day, 92F). (Office open M-F 8:30am-12:30pm and 2:30-6:30pm, Sa 9:30am-noon.) **CTA** (tel. 02 40 95 25 75) connects Les Sables to **Nantes** and to everything in between, including **Fromentine** and **Noirmoutier.** (12-120F.) To get to the **tourist office,** 1 Promenade Joffre (tel. 02 51 96 85 85; fax 02 51 96 85 71), turn right outside the station and the right again into av. de Gaulle. Follow it to pl. de la Liberté (ignore the signs!) and walk past the pained-looking statue on your right. Head for the fountain in the small pl. du Poilu de France, and turn right behind it onto rue de l'Hôtel de Ville. Follow this as it curves around and turn left onto rue du Boulet, which crosses the pl. du Commerce. After Boulet leads you to the sea front, turn right on promenade de l'Amiral Lafargue; straight ahead of you, the office occupies a ground-floor section of the glass-fronted Les Atlantes (20 min.). The friendly staff provides excellent regional and local maps, and will happily make free reservations for hotels and island trips. (Open daily 9am-12:15pm and 2-6:30pm.) To **rent bikes,** beachfront **Loc&Fun,** 29 promenade Admiral Lafargue (tel. 02 51 96 87 38), has good deals on yellow cycles. (Open daily 9am to 7pm. 52F per day. 1000F deposit. Motorbikes, scooters, and cars also available.) For **currency exchange, Banque de France,** 6 av. du Général de Gaulle (tel. 02 51 23 81 00), offers the best rates. (Open M-F 8:45am-noon.) The **hospital** is at 75 av. d'Aquitaine (tel. 02 51 21 85 85). The **post office,** av. Nicot (tel. 02 51 21 82 82), has **currency exchange.** (Open M-F 8:30am-5:45pm, Sa 8:30am-noon. **Postal code:** 85100.)

⌂⌂ ACCOMMODATIONS AND FOOD. The **Hôtel de Départ,** 40 av. de Gaulle (tel. 02 51 32 03 71), offers the best deal in town. Very close to the *gare,* well-kept rooms with free hall showers cost 165F for two, 220F for three. Breakfast 30F. If they're full, you could try the two hotels around the corner on rue de la Bauduere. The more distant **Hôtel les Voyageurs,** 16-17 rue de la Bauduere (tel. 02 51 95 11 49; fax 02 51 21 50 21), has very clean, furnished rooms above a restaurant. (Singles and doubles range from 170-210F, triples 230F. All rooms have shower, TV, telephone, and toilet. Breakfast 27F. V, MC.) A few doors towards av. de Gaulle, **Le Chêne Vert,** 5 rue de la Bauduere (tel. 02 51 32 09 47; fax 02 51 21 29 65), offers similar rooms for similar deals. (Singles 180-230F, doubles 200-280F, triples and quads 300F and 400F respectively.) There are dozens of **campgrounds** in and around Les Sables—the tourist office has a list. There's a **covered market** in the 19th-century Art Nouveau **Les Halles,** between rue des Halles and rue du Palais (June 15-Sept. 15 daily 8am-1pm; Sept. 16-June 14 Tu-Su 8am-1pm). To reach the enormous **Intermarché supermarket,** bd. de l'île Vertime, head for the *gare,* but continue past it on av. Général de Gaulle. Then turn right on rue Nicot, right at the post office, and right again just after the train tracks. It will be on your left. The *quais* and *promenades* near the Port de Pêche overflow with **restaurants** serving whatever the boats brought in that morning.

⌖ SIGHTS. Les Sables preserves some very interesting sites amidst storefronts of bright plastic sea pails and postcard racks. La Chaume, the body of land across the channel from the center of town, houses four historical monuments in a row, notably the 18th-century Tour d'Arundel and the restored Prieure St-Nicolas, converted into a fort in 1779. On the mainland, **Notre-Dame-de-Bon-Port,** pl. de l'Église, is a rare blending of Gothic and 17th-century Baroque styles. The mid-1600s nave rises behind gothic arches, which themselves are supported by Corinthian columns. The unique mixed-style works; there's an overall impression of unity and harmony. The **Musée de l'Abbaye Ste-Croix,** rue de Verdun (Tel. 02 51 32 01 16), inhabits a restored 17th-century Benedictine abbey and presents a *mélange* of regional prehistory, *maraichin* folk art, and contemporary art, of which two sets of Victor Brauner and Gaston Chaissac canvasses are noteworthy. (Open June 15-Sept. 30 T-Su 10am-noon and 2:30-6:30pm; Oct.-June 14 T-Su 2:30-5:30pm. Admission M-Sa 30F, children 15F; Su free.)

EXCURSIONS AND BEACHES. The tourist office organizes excursions to the **Puy du Fou,** a medieval theme park containing the **Grand Parc,** with costumed shows and falconry, and the **Cinéscenie,** which puts on a *son et lumiere* about the history of the Vendee (Grand Parc 115F, under 13 50F. Cinéscenie 125F, children 45F. Tour to both with transportation 308F, children 187F; ask at tourist office.)

Outdoor activities abound in Les Sables. The tourist office has a fabulous five-foot-long foldout brochure of the area's hiking and biking trails *("Randonnees"),* covering the dunes, the forest, and the beach. Guided boat trips, canoeing, surfing, sailing, diving, and other water sports instruction and rental are also readily available; ask at the tourist office for a complete listing. When it comes to beaches, **plage du Remblai** is the largest, most commercial, and most crowded of Les Sables' offerings. If solitude is worth a bus trip to you, catch the #1 or 2 to nearby La Chaume's **plage de la Paracou.** Adventurers may enjoy heading northwest to the **Fôret Domaniale d'Olonne,** where huge dunes tumble from dry woodlands to the sea.

NOIRMOUTIER AND THE ÎLE D'YEU

Bathing in the Atlantic between Nantes and Les Sables d'Olonne, Noirmoutier and the Île d'Yeu are two splendid offshore havens of coastal retreat. You can get to Noirmoutier by bus, car, or bike, since it's linked to the mainland by a bridge, while Yeu will require a ferry crossing. Both bridge and ferries leave the mainland from **Fromentine,** and unless you book well in advance, it's probably here that you'll have to sleep. Don't despair—Fromentine is a cheerful town, and from its pleasant beach there's an incredible view of the soaring Noirmoutier bridge to the west.

TRANSPORTATION AND MAINLAND INFORMATION. Your first task is to get to **Fromentine.** Do this by a **CTA** bus (tel. 02 51 68 51 98) from **Les Sables d'Olonne** (100min., 1 per day, 80F) or **Nantes** (70-90min., 5 per day, 77/82F). To get from Fromentine to Noirmoutier, change to the CTA bus to **Noirmoutier en l'Île** (25-45min., 4 per day, 20F). Two ferry companies shuttle visitors from Fromentine to the **Île d'Yeu: Compagnie Yeu Continent** (tel. 02 51 49 59 69), stationed near the *gare maritime* (1hr., day return 155F, children 115F; V, MC, AmEx) and **Vedettes Inter-îles Vendéenes (VIIV)** (tel. 02 51 39 00 00; day return 165F, students 140F; V, MC). VIIV also connects the two islands, running from **Fosse,** on Noirmoutier, to **Yeu** (45min., 165F round-trip, students 140F). For more transport information, plus a map of the area, stop in at Fromentine's **tourist office** (tel. 02 51 68 51 83), in front of the bus station. (Open daily 10:30am-12:30pm and 3-6pm.)

MAINLAND ACCOMMODATIONS. Hôtel de Bretagne, 27 av. de l'Estacade (tel. 02 51 68 50 08; fax 02 51 68 20 18), the cheaper of Fromentine's two hotels, lets out spacious, high-ceilinged rooms with convincing linoleum wood-panel floors and subtly varying wallpaper patterns. Great adjoining bathrooms make it a winner. (Singles and doubles 150-220F; triples 260F; quads 290F. Extra bed 40F. Breakfast 30F. V, MC, AmEx.) Next door, **Hôtel de la Plage,** 29 av. de l'Estacade (tel. 02 51 68 52 05; fax 02 51 68 46 87), has huge rooms with sunny 70s wallpaper, TVs, and more towels than you ever dreamed of. A little pool sits in the back, and they also rent **bikes** for 55-65F a day. (Singles and doubles 185-275F mid-June to Aug., 170-255F rest of year. Extra bed 90-100F. Breakfast 35F. V, MC.) Seven **campsites** are also available; ask the tourist office for a complete listing.

NOIRMOUTIER

Despite the wizened mussel-seekers wading at low tide and its fleets of tiny fishing boats, Noirmoutier's fortune has been made through salt farming and tourism. In the 16th and 17th centuries, the island was the salt capital of France, exporting the vital preservative and seasoning throughout Europe. Today, the saline industry has become the sailing industry, as Germans and Dutch flock to Noirmoutian waters to fasten their halyards. The majority of vacationers, however, remain French families who enjoy the island's warm climate, bike trails, boutiques, and 40km of (relatively) sandy beaches.

THE NORTHWEST

NOIRMOUTIER-EN-L'ÎLE. Crunching its main attractions into its northern half, Noirmoutier finds most life in its carefree main town, Noirmoutier-en-l'Île. A well-preserved 12th-century **château** (tel. 02 51 39 10 42) stands tall on pl. d'Armes, having repelled foreign invaders for centuries. Today it welcomes them into its artifacts museum; climb to the top for a sweep of the salt marshes, and potato fields below. (Open June 15-Sept. 30 daily 10am-7pm; April 10-May 8 10am-6pm; closed Dec.-Jan.; other times open W-M 10am-12:30pm and 2:30-6pm. 20F; children 10F.) In the **Église St-Philbert**, rue de l'Église, two ornate 18th-century altars flank the main platform; directly below, a softly lit restored crypt was the original resting place of Saint Philbert in the 7th century. The **Musée de la Construction Navale** (tel. 02 51 39 24 00), across the *quai*, explains ship-building methods and Noirmoutier's seafaring history. (Hours as for château but closed M rather than Tu.)

You can pick up a free map and island guide from the **tourist office** (tel. 02 51 39 80 71; fax 02 51 39 53 16), rte. du Pont; to get there from the bus station, turn left and follow the waterside Quai Jean Bart; the office is on the left. (Open M-Su 9am-12:30pm and 2-6pm.) You can **exchange currency** at a good rate at **Crédit Agricole**, 4 rue du Rosaire, along the *quai* on pl. de la République. (Open Tu-F 9am-12:30pm and 2-5:15pm, Sa 9am-12:30pm and 2-4pm.) The **post office** is off rue Joseph Pineau on rue du Puits Neuf. (Open M-F 9am-noon and 2-5pm, Sa 9am-noon. **Postal code:** 85330.) The **Cours des Halles grocery store**, 3 rue de la Prée au Duc, is put to shame by the **market** in pl. de la République (F; summer also Tu and Su).

Reasonable beds are few and in great demand, especially in August. Try **Chez Bébert,** 37 rue Joseph Pineau (tel. 02 51 39 08 97), a 10-minute walk from town. Bébert lets sunny, simple rooms with a dynamite hot water tank; ask for rooms on the far side to eliminate street noise. (Singles 130-150F; doubles 185-220F. Breakfast 30F. Open June 1-Dec. 22.) **Hôtel Esperanza,** 10A rue du Grand Four (tel. 02 51 39 12 07), offers pricier rooms with carpets and a pretty countryside view. (Singles and doubles 185F, with shower 230F, with bath 260F. Extra bed 55F. Breakfast 32F. V, MC.) Two kilometers east of town and sprawled along a beach, the two-star **Campsite La Vendette,** rte. des Sableaux (tel. 02 51 39 06 24; fax 02 51 35 97 63), has a whopping 600 sites. (2 people and tent or caravan 80F, off-season slightly cheaper. Extra adult 25F, extra child 12F. Electricity 12F.) Next door, **Le Clair Matin,** rte. des Sableaux (tel. 02 51 39 05 56), is open Easter-Oct. (3 people, car, and tent 63F, cheaper off-season. Extra adult 12F. Shower 5F. Electricity 12F. V, MC.)

THE REST OF THE ISLAND. Local **buses** make the rounds of points of interest about once an hour (7-27F), but you'd do better to rent a **bike** in Noirmoutier-en-l'Île. Try **Le Temple des Loisirs,** 18 rue de Rosaire. (Tel. 02 51 39 28 03. 36-62F per half-day, 45-80F per day. 1000F deposit. Open M-Sa 9am-12:30pm and 1:30-7pm. V, MC.) Pedal your way out of town; a tour of the northern portion takes about two hours. Heading east from town in the direction "Les Sableaux," you'll see the sparkling white piles of the **salt marshes** to the left, and fishermen scouring for mussels to the right. After 2km you'll reach **Les Sableaux,** a marsh where locals and tourists alike bring buckets and brave the ankle-deep water to search for shellfish, mussels, and the occasional beached lobster. Heading 2km north instead of east from Noirmoutier-en-l'Île brings you to **plage de la Clère,** a lovely, if slightly crowded, beach overlooking sailing and fishing vessels in the harbor. The path to the fishing village of **L'Herbaudière** features potato farms on the right and salt marshes on the left as far as the eye can see. Thirty *saumiers* (salt farmers) have revitalized a long-dormant industry; several offer tours to the public, explaining (in French) how they collect and isolate pure salt from the ocean. **Beaches** are everywhere along the coast, but the best are the long expanses of sand along the western and southern coasts. You can get to **plage de l'Épine** in **La Bosse** (4km southwest of Noirmoutier) or **plage du Midi** in **Barbâtre** (10km southeast) by bike or bus.

ILE D'YEU

In contrast to Noirmoutier's relatively developed coast, the idyllic 10km long Île d'Yeu (pop. 5000) is a wild expanse of protected sand dunes, mini-forests, stony bike paths, and secluded inlets within the rocky, sea-buffeted cliffs. After World War II, Maréchal Pétain, leader of Vichy France, was imprisoned until his death in the island's citadel, which overlooks the red roofs of Port-Joinville, the largest town on the island. Port-Joinville now provides the requisite marine-wear boutiques and oceanside retiree-filled restaurants, but most visitors find the isle's turquoise water, golden beaches, and enchanting seclusion are its greatest assets.

Biking is the best way to explore the island; you can cover the whole thing in 4-5 hours if you resist the temptation to stop and swim. The many paths range from sandy to boulder strewn, but the bikes in Port-Joinville are built for the back roads. Expect to pay 35-45F per half-day or 50-85F per day. Most rental places will store your bags and give you a xeroxed map of suggested routes; it's worth stopping in at the **tourist office,** rue du Marché (tel. 02 51 58 32 58), for a booklet with a proper map and a short history of the island. (Open daily 9am-12:30pm and 2-5:30pm.) Pedal across the island to the western and southern beaches on the **Côte Sauvage** by winding around the northern coast, or by zigzagging inland via a short-cut that includes a close-up of the **Grand Phare** (tel. 02 51 58 30 61), the 20m tall lighthouse on the island's tallest "hill." Once on the coast, roll merrily along to the **Pointe du Châtelet,** which bears a rusted commemorative cross built for sailors in 1934. Near the cross, the 14th-century **Vieux Château** crumbles on a craggy coast, used as a fortress in the 16th century and later abandoned by Louis XIV. The remarkable remnants stand alone on the edge of the ocean, accessible by bike path. (Guided tours daily July-Aug. 9:30am-6:30pm; late June and Sept. 11am-5:30pm. 12F, children 6F.) **Port de la Meule,** 3km due south of Port-Joinville, shelters a rainbow of bobbing fishing and pleasure boats. **St-Sauveur,** 2km southeast of Port-Joinville, is home to an 18th-century church whose chlorine-blue door and bright stained-glass windows illuminate its dark, musty interior. The island's spectacular **beaches** sparkle for 5km east of Port-Joinville. From the port, turn left on quai Vernier, which becomes rue de la Plage. **Le Marais Salé** and **Le Petite Conche,** about 3.5km away, make for the best bronzing.

A municipal **campground** (tel. 02 51 58 34 20) awaits at Pointe de Gilberge, 1km from the port, near the beach. (57-72F for 4 people and 2 tents, 16F per car, extra person 9F.) In summer many camp illegally all over the island. Fresh, cheap food is available at the **outdoor market** on quai de la Mairie (M-Sa 9am-1pm). **Champion supermarket** is on rue Calypso, two minutes from the port. (Open M-F 8:45am-12:30pm and 3:30-7:30pm, Sa 8:45am-7:30pm. V, MC.)

THE SOUTHWEST

Caught between the wild Atlantic surf and the calm brilliance of the Mediterranean, southwestern France holds a hand full of aces beneath its demure poker face. Gastronomes will delight in the wines of Bordeaux and the delicacies of Gascony, palæontologists will extase in the prehistoric surplus of Perigord, hikers will thrill to the vistas of the Pyrenees, and sunseekers will find vast expanses of sand and surf on both coasts. The most geographically diverse of France's four corners, the Southwest is equally diverse culturally, with Basques in the west and Catalans in the east proudly guarding their ancient traditions.

HISTORY: THE ETERNAL STRUGGLE

The history of southwest France is full of nationalistic and religious strife. Visigoths invaded in the 3rd century, violently ending Roman hegemony, but falling in their turn to Charlemagne and the Franks in the 8th century. The Vascones were the only civilization to withstand these invaders, controlling modern-day Gascony and the Pays Basque. The rest of the region, under Frankish rule, loosely fell under the province of <bold>, staying in the hands of Charlemagne and his successors until Carolingian power crumbled in the late 9th century. During the early 10th century Aquitaine was contested by numerous local warlords, finally falling to William I, count of Poitiers, who then became William III of Aquitaine. In 1052 he conquered Vasconia as well, although by then effective power was in the hands of local lords. In time, that part of Vasconia which accepted French influence became known as Gascony, while in the Pays Basque old traditions were kept alive. In 1152, the last child of the dukes of Poitiers, Eleanor of Aquitaine, took the duchy as her dowry when she married the duke of Anjou, Henry Plantagenêt. Two years later he inherited the crown of England and Aquitaine prospered as its English masters acquired a taste for Bordeaux wines.

During the middle ages, the spread of heresy increasingly troubled the Catholic church. Things came to a head in 1209 when Innocent III preached a crusade against the Cathars, a Manichean sect which controlled the southeastern area of Languedoc. French armies invaded and the ensuing wars lasted almost one and a half centuries, ending Languedoc's long-standing independence. French control of the region further grew in 1453 with the final battle of the Hundred Years' War at Castillon, finally driving the English out of Aquitaine. A little over a century later, in 1589, the accession of local boy Henri IV brought the Béarn region around Pau into the growing kingdom. His religious tolerance temporarily ended growing strife in the Languedoc between the ruling Catholics and the Protestant majority, although the struggle would eventually end in Catholic victory with the suppression of a peasants' rebellion in the 18th century.

The far south-east of the region, around Perpignan, was culturally Catalan, and for much of its history had been part of an independent confederacy centered on Barcelona. Falling under Spanish rule in the 15th century, a rebellion in the 17th opened the door for Louis XIII to seize it in 1642. Three centuries of French rule have not stifled a strong Catalan identity, and in the 1930s, artists fleeing the Spanish Civil War found refuge there. A different, but equally strong, cultural identity is found in the western Pyrenees, where the Basques retain their own unique language and traditions. Though the separatist movement in France is not as violent as in Spain, some Basques speak French only under duress.

CLIMATE AND GEOGRAPHY

Southwest France looks like a didactic geography diagram. Bounded on two sides by water, and on a third by the Pyrenees, the region has an appropriately diverse climate. The Mediterranean coast has the hottest, driest summers in France but gentle winters. Inland, however, winters are much colder, with glacial winds rushing down from the mountains; spring and summer are the best times to visit the region. In the mountainous Pyrenees, peaks and valleys lead to many nuances in the weather. The

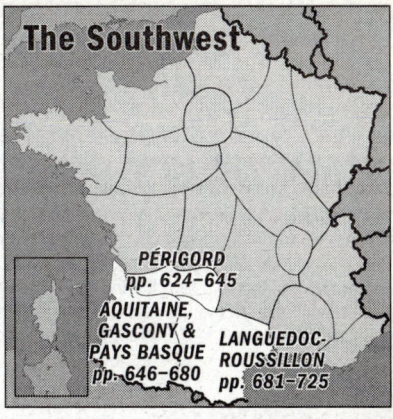

interior basins are protected from the worst conditions by the surrounding peaks, but large storms dominate the summer months, cooling the air and annoying tourists. The silver lining comes in the magnificent cloud formations that gather around the peaks, driven off the plains by the morning wind. The areas bordering the Atlantic (read: beaches) get a lot of rain.

SUGGESTIONS

For your sunny side, the Atlantic coast offers hundreds of miles of sand, surf, and glam from **Arcachon** (p. 655) to **Biarritz** (p. 663). The Occidental and Oriental **Pyrenees** (p. 677 and p. 697) provide the hiker and skier with endless activity on their rocky slopes, and endless relaxation with their naturally hot sulfuric **thermes.** Less pungent but perhaps more potent healing powers are exhibited by the miraculous waters of **Lourdes** (p. 674). Amateur archæologists need look no further than enchanting **Périgord,** pockmarked with caves filled with primitive paintings like those of **Lascaux** (p. 638). You can relive a slightly more recent past in the conscientiously rebuilt medieval town of **Sarlat** (p. 641), or the authentically stupendous fortress city of **Carcassonne** (p. 693). If small towns aren't your thing, you can drink up the city atmosphere in **Bordeaux** (p. 648) or party down in **Toulouse,** (p. 682) the hub of the south. And should the Frenchness of it all get you down, escape to the culturally unique **Pays Basque** (pp. 658-672) or pay your own homage to Catalonia in **Perpignan** (p. 706).

PÉRIGORD

The images presented by Périgord are seductive: green countryside splashed with yellow sunflowers, white chalk cliffs, the golden white wine of Bergerac, plates of black truffles, and the smell of warm walnuts. First settled during the Lower Paleolithic era, 150,000 years ago, the area around Les Eyzies-de-Tayac has turned up more stone-age artifacts—tools, bones, weapons, cave paintings, and etchings—than any other place on earth. Cutting through high, porous limestone plateaus, the Dordogne, Lot, Vézère, and Isle rivers left behind towering cliffs and countless caves where 20,000-year-old etchings of stampeding bison and fleeing reindeer can now be found. The painted caves of Lascaux are the most extensive and best preserved in the world, but floods of tourists caused such drastic deterioration that the caves were closed to the public in 1963; a replica, Lascaux II, was opened 150m away in 1983. Today, the Grotte de Font de Gaume in Les Eyzies-de-Tayac and the Grotte du Pech-Merle, 25km from Cahors, contain extraordinary original paintings still accessible to the public. The caves open into the spectacular countryside,

THE SOUTHWEST

including feudal châteaux, poplar-lined rivers, and valleys carpeted with fields of wheat and sunflowers.

Famous *cêpes* and *truffes* fungi are the trademark of Perigord cooking. Walnut wines rival the renowned Monbazillac, a syrupy sweet white wine cultivated 6km south of Bergerac. Famous meat dishes containing walnuts, honey, *chèvre*, and local mushrooms give Périgord a taste as unique as its geography.

HIGHLIGHTS OF PÉRIGORD

■ Follow the knee-prints of kings up to the chapels of cliff-side **Rocamadour** (p. 640).
■ Paddle down the rugged, poplar- and châteaux-lined **Dordogne Valley,** no man's land during the Hundred Years' War (p. 633 and p. 638).
■ Explore genealogy at the **Grotte de Font-de-Gaume,** the most important cave painting site still open to tourists *and* also the least crowded (p. 631).
■ Scout out the sets of *Cyrano de Bergerac* and *Manon des Sources,* otherwise known as **Sarlat** (p. 641).

⌐ TRANSPORTATION

Major towns such as Périgueux and Brive are well served by rail lines. However, visiting the smaller towns, châteaux, and vineyards requires a car or a sturdy set of legs for bike riding along the hilly trails. The Bordeaux-Sarlat line stops at Bergerac, but when planning to venture into the Dordogne valley it is best to use Périgueux as a base.

PÉRIGUEUX

Encircled by the river Isle, Périgueux (pop. 37,700) arose from the 13th-century union of two rival towns: the abbey-centered Cité de Puy-St-Font and the Gallo-Roman Vésone. Plagued by Barbarian invasions in the 3rd century, Huguenot attacks in the 16th century, and the *Jacqueries* peasant uprisings, the city nevertheless preserves significant architecture in both the medieval and Roman halves of the town. The cuisine of Périgueux', the capital of Périgord, is famous throughout the world for such specialties as *foie gras*, *grillon*, *truffes* and other exotic Périgord mushrooms, and Jacques Chirac's favorite: *tête de veau* (calf's head). The city also makes a good base for visiting local prehistoric caves.

⊡ ORIENTATION AND PRACTICAL INFORMATION

Périgueux's *vieille ville*, and the tourist office and cheap hotels that surround it, are a 10-minute walk from the train station. Turn right on rue Denis Papin and bear left on rue des Mobiles-de-Coulmiers, which becomes rue du Président Wilson. On your right, you'll pass **rue Guillier,** which leads to the Roman ruins. Take the next right (just after the Monoprix) and walk down one block. The office is on the left, beside the stone Mataguerre Tower. **Rue du Président Wilson** leads to the heart of the *vieille ville*.

Trains: Rue Denis Papin, (tel. 05 53 09 50 50). To: **Limoges** (1-1½hr., 6 per day, 79F); **Bordeaux** (1½hr., 7 per day, 97F); **Sarlat** (1½hr., 4 per day, 73F); **Toulouse** (4hr., 8 per day, 179F); **Paris** via Limoges (4-6hr., 12 per day, 271-368F); and **Lyon** (6-8hr., 5 per day, 271F). Check the map in front of the station before heading for the hostel. Office open Su-F 4:30am-midnight, Sa 4:30am-8pm.

Buses: Pl. Francheville (tel. 05 53 08 43 13). To **Angoulême** (1½hr., M-Sa 3 per day, 1 Su, 92F) and **Sarlat** (1½hr., F-Sa 2 per day, 47F). Schedules change often. Office open M-Th 8:30-11:30am and 2:30-5:30pm, F 8:30-11:30am and 2:30-4:30pm.

Taxis: Taxi Périgueux, pl. Bugeaud (tel. 05 53 09 09 09). 24hr.

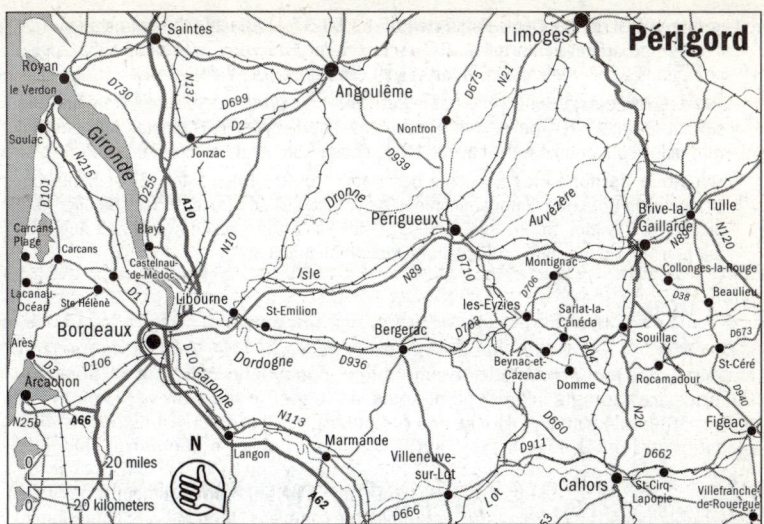

Tourist Office: 26 pl. Francheville (tel. 05 53 53 10 63; fax 05 53 09 02 70). Ask for the free map with an extensive walking tour in English. Guided walking, *petit train*, and boat tours. Office open July-Aug. M-Sa 9am-7pm, Su 9:30am-5:30pm; Sept.-June M-Sa 9am-6pm. **Office Départementale du Tourisme,** 25 rue Wilson (tel. 05 53 35 50 24). Info on Périgord; lists of campgrounds, *gîtes*, and *chambres d'hôtes*, excellent topographic maps (40F). Open M-F 8:30am-noon and 2-6pm. **Info booth** in the heart of town at pl. André Maurois (tel. 05 53 46 77 04).

Money: Banque de France, 1 pl. du Roosevelt (tel. 05 53 03 30 44), has **currency exchange.** Exchange desk open M-F 8:45am-12:15pm.

Laundromat: Lav'matic, 20 rue Mobiles de Coulmiers.

Youth Center: Centre d'Information Jeunesse (CIJ), 1 av. d'Aquitaine (tel. 05 53 53 52 81). *Carte Jeune* cards 12F. Open M-F 8:30am-noon and 2-6pm.

Hospital: Centre Hospitalier, 80 av. Georges Pompidou (tel. 05 53 07 70 00). Walk northeast of town from pl. de la Libération to av. Pompidou (8 blocks).

Police: Rue du 4 Septembre (tel. 05 53 08 10 17), near the post office.

Post Office: 1 rue du 4 Septembre (tel. 05 53 53 60 82). Poste Restante code: 24017. **Currency exchange.** Open M-F 8am-7pm, Sa 8am-noon. **Postal code:** 24070.

ACCOMMODATIONS AND CAMPING

Inexpensive hotels cluster around the train station, on the way into the *vieille ville*, and in the pedestrian area.

Foyer des Jeunes Travailleurs Résidence Lakanal (tel. 05 53 53 52 05; fax 05 53 54 37 46), off bd. Lakanal. From tourist office, turn left down cours Fénélon and right onto bd. Lakanal. After the intersection with bd. Bertran de Born, the Municipal Bridge and Billiard Club will appear on the left side of the club building. Four 4-bunk rooms 73F including sheets and breakfast. Singles 88F. Lunch and dinner 35F. Reception M-F 4-8pm, Sa-Su 7-8pm. Call ahead.

Au Bon Coin/Chez Pierrot, 8 rue Chanzy (tel. 05 53 53 43 22), off rue Denis Papin between the station and *centre ville*. Friendly couple manages 10 no-nonsense rooms, bare as a donut with no filling. Restaurant downstairs serves simple, filling 50-70F 4-course *menus*. Singles and doubles 100F; twins 120F. Breakfast 25F. Reserve 2-3 days in advance. Reception closed Su. V, MC.

Les Charentes, 16 rue Denis Papin (tel. 05 53 53 37 13), facing the train station. Tiny singles and doubles with toilet 120F, with shower 135-165F, with both 195F; triples and quads 225F. Reception 6:30am-11pm. Breakfast 30F. V, MC, AmEx.

Hôtel des Voyagers, 26 rue Denis Papin (tel. 05 53 53 17 44), right across from the train station. Detailed 70s decor with narrow staircase. Singles 75F; singles and doubles with toilet 80F; double with showers 100F; quads 95F per person. Breakfast 20F.

Campsites: Barnabé-Plage, 80 rue des Bains (tel. 05 53 53 41 45), 1.5km from Périgueux in Boulazac. From cours Montaigne, take bus D (direction "Cité Belaire," last bus about 7:30pm, 6F) to "rue des Bains." Riverside site packed in July and Aug. 16F per person, 15F per tent, 10F per car. Open 9am-midnight.

◖ FOOD

Charcuteries along rue Limogeanne are palaces of *foie gras,* walnuts, fruit liqueurs, *cêpe* and *girolle* mushrooms, and regional delicacies. Not surprisingly, the pricey restaurants lie near pl. St-Louis in the *vieille ville;* the area southwest of the cathedral around pl. Hoche and rue Aubergerie has diverse and more wallet-pleasing options. Budgetarians (and vegetarians) may be happier at the daily morning **market** on pl. du Coderc or the larger market on pl. de la Clautre near the cathedral (mid-Nov. to Mar. W and Sa 8am-1pm). The behemoth **Monoprix,** on pl. de la République in the *centre ville,* is impossible to miss. (Open M-Sa 8:30am-8pm.)

Au Petit Chef, 5 pl. du Coderc (tel. 05 53 53 16 03; fax 05 53 08 21 12). Noontime 65F *menu* brings out the marvelous *soupe de pays,* entitles you to the all-you-can-eat *hors d'oeuvres* bar, a *plat du jour,* and decadent desserts. 100F 5-course dinner *menu.* Children's *menu* 42F. Open July-Aug. daily noon-2pm and 6:30-11pm. V, MC.

Helliniko, 15 rue des Places (tel. 05 53 09 69 91), in the *vieille ville* off rue Taillefer. Olive-garnished and olive-oiled specialties load the 50F *midi formule.* At night, settle in next to the uproarious local crowd for a 3-course 75F *menu* of *dolmas* or *spanokopita,* filling *moussaka,* and *baklava.* Open M 7-10pm, Tu-Sa noon-2pm and 7-10pm.

L'Aubergerie, 14 rue Aubergerie (tel. 05 53 09 63 88), off rue des Places. Housed in the aristocratic 15th-century Hôtel d'Abzac de Ladouze, this establishment lives a double life as a self-service cafeteria by day (3-course *formules* from 50F), and an unpretentious restaurant by night. 3-course dinners 70F, 4-course 85F. Grilled shrimp or salad with hot *chèvre* on croutons, rack of lamb, and many different house desserts. Open 11:30am-2pm and 7-11pm. V, MC.

◉ SIGHTS

Périgueux's many historic and artistic sites are seen best on foot. The tourist office gives out an excellent walking-tour guide of the Medieval, Renaissance, and Gallo-Roman sides of the city. The Puy-St-Front half of town grew up around the enormous **Cathédrale St-Front,** which was built on the tomb of St. Front in 500AD and became the seat of the bishop in 1669 after the Huguenots destroyed the Cathédrale St-Étienne. Paul Abadie, designer of the Sacré-Coeur in Paris, worked his style here as well in the late 19th century. (Open daily 8am-7:30pm. Free tours in French upon request.)

The **Musée du Périgord,** 22 cours Tourny (tel. 05 53 53 16 42), at the corner of rue St-Front, is home to one of France's most important collections of prehistoric artifacts, including fossils from Les Eyzies, 2m-long mammoth tusks, and an Egyptian mummy whose toes peek out from his crusty coverings. (Open M and W-F 11am-6pm, Sa-Su 1-6pm. 20F, students 10F, under 18 free.)

The **Tour de Vésone** was a *cella,* the center of worship in a Roman temple. Its concrete and stone barrel-like form was previously sheathed in marble held on by iron spikes, the holes of which are still visible. About a fourth of the weighty structure has been knocked down completely, supposedly by the last fleeing demons of paganism when St. Front chased them away. (Open Apr.-Sept. 7:30am-9pm; Oct.-

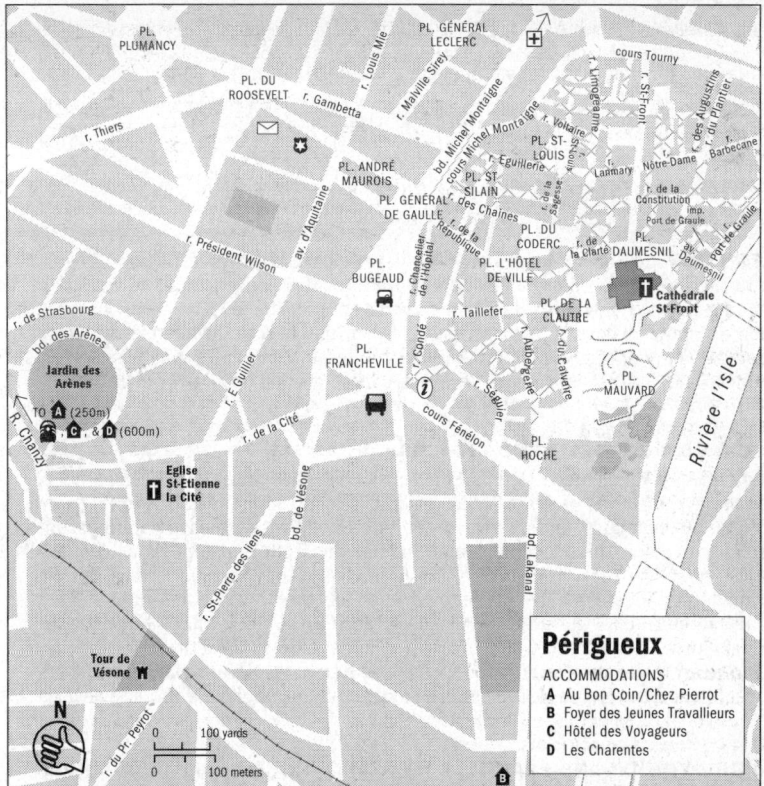

Périgueux

ACCOMMODATIONS
A Au Bon Coin/Chez Pierrot
B Foyer des Jeunes Travailleurs
C Hôtel des Voyageurs
D Les Charentes

Mar. 7:30am-6:30pm.) Excavations at the **Villa de Pompeïus** next door have brought to light artifacts now on display in the town museum. The **Château Barrière,** a late Gothic castle, preserves four floors of stone walls, but is gutted on the inside. Next door, a Romanesque house, the **Maison Romane,** is a good example of the common building traditions of *spoila*—picking up chunks of ruins and incorporating them decoratively into new buildings. Both buildings were constructed on the remains of the Roman wall which surrounded Vésone, built in 275 as protection against the first Norman and Barbarian attacks. Just 40km away, the **Norman Porte** is a fragment of this wall. Not far off, the Roman amphitheater has been transformed into a public park, the **Jardin des Arènes,** complete with sagging archways, rubble, palm trees, and 20th-century fountains. The court of Périgord, an English ally, used the 133m-long structure as a stronghold in the Hundred Years' War. (Garden open Apr.-Sept. 7:30am-9pm; Oct.-Mar. 7:30am-6:30pm.)

Up rue de l'Ancien Vache from the amphitheater, the 11th-century **Église St-Étienne-de-la-Cité** was the first Christian edifice in Vésone, and the seat of the bishop until the attack of the Calvinists in 1669 destroyed all but the choir and one-third of the nave. Lepers lent a hand in building the **Tour Mataguerre,** rebuilt in 1477 and named after an English captain who was kept prisoner in its dungeons for 17 years during the Hundred Years' War. (Contact tourist office for visits.)

🎵 🎆 ENTERTAINMENT AND FESTIVALS

ENTERTAINMENT. While the streets may be sleepy at night, the *places* have no intention of calling it an early evening. **Pl. St-Silain** and **pl. St-Louis** are nightlife centers, and **pl. du Maré** hosts frequent concerts. **L'Avant Scène,** 3 port de Graule (tel. 05 53 04 47 44), the first right off av. Daumesnil when walking away from the river, offers live jazz concerts. (Open 6pm-2am. Cover 35F. V, MC.) **Gordon Pub,** 12 rue Condé (tel. 05 53 35 03 74), off rue Taillefer, is an English-style pub with friendly prices and a terrace. (Beer 11F. Open M-F 11pm-2am, Sa 2pm-2am, Su 9pm-2am.) Across the river, **L'Ande'rois,** 51 rue Aubarède (tel. 05 53 53 01 58), is a gay bar that livens up an otherwise dull neighborhood with dancing. (Open nightly, W-Sa until 3am.) Crowded **La Regence,** 16 rue des Chancelier de l'Hôpital (tel. 05 53 53 10 55), in the *centre ville*, is open nightly until 2:30 or 3am.

FESTIVALS. Périgueux jumps back 500 years most Saturdays in July and August with the **Fêtes du Lys d'Or Périgueux Médiéval.** Parades, jousts, and mud-wrestling matches add a trendy retro slant to the town's streets. The town quiets down every year for about 10 days in August when it plays proud host to the **International Mime Festival.** Many of the world's most respected mime companies give free performances and classes; impromptu heckling workshops pop up all over town.

LES EYZIES-DE-TAYAC

Writer Henry Miller speculated that the Dordogne valley "must have been paradise for many thousands of years." The verdant hills, striking limestone cliffs (now topped by châteaux), and natural caves hide 15,000-year-old cave paintings and etchings of bison, rhinoceri, elephants, and humans. Unfortunately, though not the first to discover these treasures, tourists have certainly taken over Les Eyzies. Though only 760 people live in the town, each has their own Neanderthal-themed hotel, duck-filled restaurant, or fossils 'n' *foie gras* knick-knack boutique, to which hordes of camcorder-slingers rush all summer long. To actually see the prehistoric art in question, be sure to reserve at least two weeks in advance, as tickets are limited. If Les Eyzies is more than a daytrip for you, book your rooms even earlier or you'll be sleeping under a postcard rack.

◪ ORIENTATION AND PRACTICAL INFORMATION. From the train station, turn right and walk 1km down the village's only street to reach its center (5min.). **Trains** (tel. 05 53 06 97 22) go to **Périgueux** (30min., 4 per day, 40F), **Sarlat** (1hr., 4 per day, change at Le Buisson, 45F), and **Paris** (6-8hr., 4 per day, 281F). (Open M-F 6:30am-11pm, Sa-Su 6:30am-10:30pm.) In July and August, there are also weekly **buses** from **Sarlat.** The **tourist office** is located at pl. de la Mairie (tel. 05 53 06 97 05; fax 05 53 06 90 79). It offers a full list of caves, **gîtes d'étapes,** and summer tours to sights out of walking distance (call ahead), and **rents bikes** and **canoes.** (Bikes 60F per day. 100F deposit. Open July-Aug. M-Sa 9am-7pm, Su 9am-noon and 2-6pm; Mar.-June and Sept.-Oct. M-Sa 9am-noon and 2-6pm, Su 10am-noon and 2-6pm; Nov.-Feb. M-F 10am-noon and 2-6pm.) For the **police,** call 05 53 29 20 17. The **post office** (tel. 05 53 06 94 11) is on the main street, past the tourist office as you walk away from the train station. Here you'll find **currency exchange.** (Open M-F 9am-noon and 2-5pm, Sa 9am-noon. **Postal code:** 24620.)

◪ ACCOMMODATIONS AND CAMPING. Rooms are expensive, and the few cheap ones are booked a month in advance during summer. The tourist office has a list of private B&Bs in the surrounding area (140-200F for 1 or 2 people). If you are traveling by bike or car, check for signs along the main roads advertising *fermes* (farms) with camping space (20-45F) and village homes renting rooms (150-300F) during the summer. To get to the inexpensive *gîte d'étape*, **Ferme des Eymaries,** on rte. de St-Cirq (tel. 05 53 06 94 73), cross the tracks at the station, go over the bridge, and turn left at the Elf station. Walk up the road 2km, over a hill, and turn right 3m before crossing the train tracks. Follow the gravel-dirt road for 1km (40min.). Great owner and his dogs look after two 18-bed dorms built into the cliff and a view that will make you want to settle down for good. (45F. Breakfast 22F. Kitchen. Call ahead, preferably around meal times. Open Apr.-Oct.) **Hôtel des**

Falaises (tel. 05 53 06 97 35) is on the main street, between the train station and the *centre ville*. On your way to the caves, leave your pack in these lovely rooms and come back to a view of the blooming garden. The hotel also manages several newly-renovated lodgings at the same rates between Les Eyzies and Font-de-Gaume. (Doubles with bath and toilet 165-200F; triples 220-250F; two twin beds 175F. Breakfast 25F. V, MC.) You'll find rooms as well as tents at **Camping La Rivière,** rte. de Périgueux (tel. 05 53 06 97 14; fax 05 53 35 20 85). From the tourist office, go towards Périgueux on the D47, then cross the bridge and take a left. There's also a snack bar, restaurant, and pool, and you can rent **bikes** and **canoes.** (26F per person, 38F per site. Electricity 18F. Doubles with shower 195F; quads with shower 260F. 10% room discount weekdays. Breakfast 25F. Bike rental 30F per half-day, 50F per day. Reception 8am-10pm. Open Apr. 4-Oct. 4. V, MC.)

▐ FOOD. Most restaurants here require big bucks but dish out exquisite, well-prepared meals. A **market** runs the length of town every Monday (9am-1pm). **Halle des Eyzies,** on rte. de Sarlat, is a collection of expensive gourmet *foie gras* and walnut product boutiques in one building. Wonderful nut wines, oils, cookies, cakes, regional wines, and every duck, goose, and pork product imaginable. (Open daily June 15-Sept. 9am-1pm and 2:30-7pm.) A small, posh **grocery store** sits across from the tourist office. **La Grignotière** (tel. 05 53 06 91 67), on the left side of pl. de la Mairie, serves very cheap drinks (wines from 5F a glass, beers 12-21F, *apéritifs* 8-11F), sandwiches all day long (16-25F), and regional, duck-filled 3-course *menus* at mealtimes (54-62F). (Open daily 9am-midnight. V, MC.)

▨ SIGHTS. The **Musée L'Abri Pataud** (tel. 05 53 06 92 46) sits on the property of a local farmer, Pataud, whose plot consisted of bones, stone tools, and precious little arable land. As it turned out, his farm was built on an *abri* (shelter), where several groups of reindeer hunters lived over a span of 20,000 years. The excavated area exposes layers corresponding to 14 periods of habitation. In the next room, a set of video screens explains prehistory and evolution. The 18,600-year-old remains of a teenage girl found on the site represent a landmark stage between Neanderthal and Cro-Magnon man. The carving of a bison on the ceiling of the museum, visible in a mirror, was discovered accidentally when it was illuminated by the stray flashlight beam of a technician. (Open July-Aug. daily 10am-7pm; Sept.-Dec. and Feb.-June Tu-Su 10am-12:30pm and 1:30-6pm.)

The **Musée National de Préhistoire** (tel. 05 53 06 45 45), located in the cliff above the village, offers a lovely view of the valley and a large, relatively interesting collection, including casts of finds, hypothetical sculptures of our far-flung forbearers, lots of flint, a few carvings, and a mammoth skeleton. (Open July-Aug. daily 9:30am-7pm; Mar. 15-June and Sept.-Nov. 15 W-M 9:30am-noon and 2-6pm; Nov. 16-Mar. 14 9:30am-noon and 2-5pm. 22F; ages 18-25, over 60, and Su 15F.)

CAVE PAINTINGS NEAR LES EYZIES

Caves near Les Eyzies, like the village itself, tend to be very crowded. Reserve tickets as early as possible, no less than two weeks in advance. Biking in the area is very difficult—the hills are steep, the roads are narrow, the traffic furious. The Les Eyzies tourist office has information about tours of nearby sites. Other less crowded caves are found near Souillac, Sarlat, and Gourdon. Bring sweaters—caves are cold and damp year-round—but it's well worth braving the conditions to join the bison, horses, reindeer, and mammoths that play along the inside walls.

The **Grotte de Font-de-Gaume** (tel. 05 53 06 90 80; fax 05 53 35 26 18), located on the D47 1km east of Les Eyzies, has the most important paintings still open to tourists. The faded but spectacular 15,000-year-old friezes were completed over hundreds of years and are technically advanced—for example using the natural contours of the cave for relief. Though locals discovered the paintings in the 18th century, they did not realize their importance until two centuries later, by which time several murals had decayed and been defaced by graffiti. In the farther reaches of the cavern the colors remain brilliant enough to see the care and detail that went into the drawings. The highlight is the *vôute* (vault), where 12 bison stampede over two-thirds of the cave in an almost surreal fashion. The 45-minute tours are available in English. (Open Th-Tu Apr.-Sept. 9am-noon and 2-6pm; Mar. and Oct. 9:30am-noon and 2-5:30pm; Nov.-Feb. 10am-noon and 2-5pm. 35F, ages 12-25 and over 60 23F, under 12 and artists or art students free.)

Unlike Font-de-Gaume, the **Grotte des Combarelles,** 2km farther down the road (tel. 05 53 06 97 72), has suffered from a humid atmosphere, and only etchings remain. The more than 600 carvings depict a large variety of species, including donkeys, lions, and rhinoceri. Fifty human figures, mostly faces, keep watch from the narrow halls of the cave. Only a dozen 40-minute tours, in groups of six, are given per day. Reserve far in advance for the summer through the office at the Grotte de Font-de-Gaume. (Hours and prices same as for Font de Gaume.)

Only 12 figures are visible at the sculptured frieze **Abri du Cap-Blanc** (tel. 05 53 59 21 74), 7km northeast of Eyzies on D48, but they are outstandingly preserved. Fifteen thousand years ago, hunters drew horses, bison, and reindeer onto the thick limestone walls. The carvings are not as detailed as those in Font-de-Gaume, but the quality of preservation makes up the difference. The exhibit's centerpiece is a 2m-long herd of shuffling animals. It's wise to call for tickets at least one to two weeks in advance, or else arrive early in the morning for the 45-minute tours in French. (Open daily July-Aug. 9:30am-7pm; Apr.-June and Sept.-Oct. 10am-noon and 2-6pm. 29F, children 15F.)

Fifteen kilometers northwest of Les Eyzies in Rouffignac, **La Grotte aux 100 Mammouths,** better known as **La Grotte de Rouffignac** (tel. 05 53 05 41 71; fax 05 53 35 44 71), on the road to Périgueux, houses 250 engravings and paintings. Among etchings of rhinoceri, horses, and bison, the shaggy mammoths are most striking. The guided tour (via train) lasts an hour. (Open daily July-Aug. 9-11:30am and 2-6pm; Apr. 5-June and Sept.-Oct. 10-11:30am and 2-5pm. 30F, children 10F.)

Many caves have natural decoration as fascinating as anything ancient man created. Most interesting is the **Grotte du Grand Roc** (tel. 05 53 06 92 70), 1.5km northwest of town along the road to Périgueux. The cave lies halfway up the chalk cliffs and commands a blistering view of the valley and Tayac's fortified church. The cave is filled with millions of stalactites, stalagmites, and *eccentriques*—small calcite accretions that grow neither straight down nor straight up. Found in 1924, this cave shelters thousands of natural phenomena, most notably an *eccentrique* in the shape of an ostrich, an eroded column that resembles Bigfoot's foot, and nature's version of the Winged Victory of Samothrace. The cave is naturally a constant 16°C (nice) and 95% humidity (not nice). Neighboring the cave are the interesting **Habitats Préhistoriques Laugerie Basse,** which display early habitats. (Open daily July-Aug. 9:30am-7pm; Apr.-June and Sept.-Nov. 10 9:30am-6pm; Feb. 9-Mar. and Nov. 11-Jan. 10 Su-F 10am-5pm. 30min. guided tour in French only, but many explanatory signs are in English. *Grotte* 35F, children 20F. *Habitats* 20F, children 10F. Combined admission 45F, children 25F.)

The **Gorge d'Enfer** (tel. 05 53 06 90 80), just upstream from Grand Roc and 2km from Les Eyzies, is full of waterfalls, lagoons, and blooming flora. On site lies the **Abri du Poisson** (tel. 05 53 06 90 80), a shelter which contains the oldest drawing of a fish in France—a 25,000-year-old, 1m-long salmon. Take a look at the postcard photos and move on—skip the fishy tour. (Open July-Aug. Su-F 10am-6pm; Apr.-June and Sept. W-M 9am-noon and 2-5:30pm; Nov.-Feb. W-M 10am-noon and 2-5pm. French tour 15F, students 7F, under 12 free. Tickets available through Font de Gaume at least one week in advance.) Those interested in more recent cave people should head for the **Musée Spéléologie,** 91 rue de la Grange-Chancel (tel. 05 53 35 43 77). Located in the Fort de Roc de Tayac, a niche in a cliff high above the Dordogne, it was dug by English soldiers during the Hundred Years' War. The museum narrates the region's cave history with models, documents, and equipment. (Open July-Aug. daily 11am-6pm. 20F, under 16 10F.)

Northeast of Les Eyzies on route D66, the **Roque St-Christophe** (tel. 05 53 50 70 45) is the most extensive cave dwelling yet to be discovered. Its five floors of terraces stretch over 400m. From 40,000 BC until the Middle Ages, this fascinating sanctu-ary served as a defensive fort and home to over 3000 people. You'll visit an 11th-century kitchen and peer over the 60m high cliff where Protestants sought shelter from a Catholic army in 1580. A 45-minute tour allows you to check out the cave's ovens, monastic remains, and military defenses. (Visits daily in summer 10am-6:30pm; Nov. 11-Feb. 11am-5pm; closed Jan. 31F, students 25F, ages 5-13 16F.)

Opportunities for kayaking and canoeing are plentiful amidst the Vézère's unspoiled greenery, unusual rock formations, and towering cliffs. At the bridge in Les Eyzies, **Les 3 Drapeaux** (tel. 05 53 06 91 89) rents **canoes.** From June to September, they will let you paddle your way downstream and pick you up for the return journey via van. (2hr. trip: canoe 60F per person, kayak 70F. 4hr. trip: canoe 80F, kayak 90F. Open daily 9am-6pm.)

THE LOWER DORDOGNE VALLEY

Steep cliffs and poplar tree thickets overlook the slow-moving waters of the Dor-dogne, which served in the Hundred Years' War as a natural boundary between France and English Aquitaine to the south. The châteaux, built to keep watch on the enemy, are numerous, though not as regal as those of the Loire. In summer the valley flows with tourists in canoes, on bikes, and in cars; by avoiding the major towns it is still possible to find solitude. *Chambres d'hôte* provide cheap farm-house rooms near the historic sites; ask at any tourist office for lists of *hôtes.*

■ **TRANSPORTATION.** The valley stretches from Bergerac west, passing 15km south of Sarlat. To get there and get around you'll need to rent a car or be prepared for a good bike workout—these hills are steep! You can reach the châteaux by convenient but expensive excursion buses leaving **Sarlat. Hep! buses** (tel. 05 53 28 10 04) leave pl. Pasteur and visit different châteaux all week long. **CFTA Périgord,** 21 rue de Cahors (tel. 05 53 59 01 48), also runs buses (100-190F) each day. Many trav-elers report that hitching is relatively easy, although many cars have no room to spare. Arrive at the châteaux before 1pm to beat the crowds.

Many outfits along the Dordogne rent **canoes** and **kayaks.** At the **Pont de Vitrac,** near **Domme,** you can find them at **Canoës-Loisirs** (tel. 05 53 28 23 43) and **Périgord Aventure et Loisirs** (tel. 05 53 28 23 82). **Canoës-Dordogne** (tel. 05 53 29 58 50) and **Canoë Vacances** (tel. 05 53 28 17 07) are at **La Roque-Gageac. Copeyre** (tel. 05 53 28 95 01) is in Beynac. **Le Sioux** (tel. 05 53 28 30 81) is near Domme et Cénac. Schedules and information are available at tourist offices; prices average 70F per person for a half-day and 105F for a full day. Many rental organizations will pick you up in a bus and bring you back to your starting point free of charge.

BERGERAC

Cradling the Dordogne river to the east of Bordeaux are the 14th- and 15th-century houses of Bergerac. The fertile land along the banks brings life to the red and sweet white wines that have been produced here since the 11th century, giving this small town its fame. The chapels, vine-covered roofs, and winding streets pro-vide the perfect setting for sipping wine in the summer.

The **tourist office** offers one-hour **tours** of the town (3 per day, 25F). When in Bergerac, be sure to stop by **La Maison du Vin,** 2 rue des Recollets (tel. 05 53 63 57 56; fax 05 53 63 57 85), which holds an art museum with sculptors at work and musicians playing on the first floor, free wine tasting, and reasonably-priced bot-tles in the wine cellar. (Open 10am-7pm. Free.) The **Musée du Tabac** shows a 3000-year history of tobacco with tools and pipe collections. (Open Tu-F 10am-noon and 2-5pm, Sa 10am-noon and 2-5pm, Su 2:30-6:30pm.) Departing from the port on rue Hyppolyte Taine near Vieux Pont are **boat rides** (tel. 05 53 24 58 80), lasting one hour, down the Dordogne river into the blooming flora. On the other side of the bridge, at pl. Barbacanne, summer Wednesdays bring live **jazz** concerts. (Shows start at 6pm. 35F cover.)

The train station on cours Alsace-Lorraine (tel. 05 53 63 53 81) is a 10-minute walk from the *vieille ville*. **Trains** leave for **Bordeaux** (2hr., 5 per day, 59F) and **Périgueux** (2hr., 3 per day, 85F). The **tourist office** is at 97 rue Neuve-d'Argenson (tel. 05 53 57 03 11). (Open July-Aug. M-Sa 9am-7pm, Sept.-June M-Sa 9am-noon and 2-6pm.) **Rent bikes** at Périgord Cycles or Maison d'Amour in pl. Gambetta. The **hospital** (tel. 05 53 63 88 88) is located at 9 av. du Prof. Albert Calmette. **Banking, eating,** and **postal** needs can be met along pl. Louis de Labardonnie.

Accommodations can be atrociously expensive, but **Hôtel Pozzi**, 11 rue Pozzi (tel. 05 53 57 04 68), offers reasonable rooms at reasonable prices. (Singles and doubles 100-130F; triples and quads 190F. Breakfast 28F. Reception 8am-midnight.) Restaurants, especially in the *vieille ville*, can also be expensive. Stick with the plentiful *boulangeries*, *pâtisseries*, and *charcuteries* which seem to line every street and the giant **Marché Couvert** that provides some relief at pl. Louis de Labardonnie. Wednesday and Saturday mornings a **market** fills the *vieille ville*.

CASTELNAUD AND LES MILANDES

Ten kilometers southwest of Sarlat, the town of **Castelnaud-la-Chapelle** snoozes in the shadow of its crumbling pale yellow stone **château** (tel. 05 53 31 30 00), a fortress in the 12th- to 15th-centuries. To visit the castle, leave your car or bike at the foot of the hill in the parking lot of the post office, right by the bridge over the Dordogne, and mount the steep but much more direct path by foot (10min., follow signs for *piétons*). Now the most visited castle in the region, the château is furnished in the simple 15th-century style and fitted with the impressive **Musée de la Guerre de Cent Ans.** Here you'll learn about sieges during the Hundred Years' War with a number of dazzling visual aids, including a behemoth catapult. The collection also boasts medieval and 17th-century arms and armor. (Open July-Aug. daily 9am-8pm; May-June and Sept. daily 10am-7pm; Mar.-Apr. and Oct.-Nov. 15 daily 10am-6pm; Nov. 16-Feb. Su-F 2-5pm. 32F, under 17 16F.)

Château Les Milandes (tel. 05 53 29 38 10), 8km from Castelnaud, was built by François de Caumont in 1489 as a gift for his wife. The castle made another woman happy centuries later when Josephine Baker fell in love with the neglected state-run château, bought the place, and redid it to accommodate herself and her troupe of adopted children. Raised in St. Louis and propelled to fame in Paris's Folies Bergère, the American singer-dancer created a *village du monde* (world village), where she cared for dozens of children until 1969. The tour through two floors of her homey living space allows access to the lovely garden, a falcon museum, and a museum of the passenger pigeon. (Open June-Aug. 9am-7pm; Apr.-May and Sept. 10am-6pm; Oct.-Mar. 10am-noon and 2-5pm. Guided tours available only by reservation. English brochure. 43F, students 35F, ages 4-15 33F.)

The only reasonable hotel nearby is **Hôtel Parc des Milandes** (tel. 05 53 29 52 33), 0.5km from Les Milandes. Just at the bottom of the hill, it makes a scenic (though sometimes noisy) rest spot with a pool, tennis courts, mini-golf, riverside gardens, and a restaurant. (Hall shower: Singles and doubles 180F; triples 250F. Private shower: doubles 230F; triples 280F; quads 300F; quints 350F. Prices drop 30-50F in off-season. Breakfast 30F. Reserve well in advance. V, MC, AmEx.) The **restaurant** serves simple 3-course dinners for 79F, 4-course for 99F. The hotel also rents canoes. Castlenaud and Les Milandes are not accessible by bus, but biking from Sarlat (10km or 15km respectively) follows level riverbanks.

BEYNAC-ET-CAZENAC

The fortress at **Beynac** (tel. 05 53 29 50 40) sits 150m above the Dordogne, sheathed in greenery, in a town of ancient stone houses decorated with wrought-iron balconies and flowered terraces. Beynac has enjoyed a topsy-turvy history with only one thing certain throughout: it was always at odds with its neighbor Castelnaud. During the Hundred Years' War, Beynac was French, while Castelnaud sided with the English. In the wars of religion, Beynac adhered to Catholicism, but Castelnaud switched to Protestantism. The excellent and obligatory guided tour (1hr., in French) takes you behind the 5m-thick walls telling the history of Beynac, ending with a sensational view at the top. Clamber beyond the cafés and the postcards to the top of the hill for an even more impressive view over valley and castle. (Castle open daily Mar.-Sept. 10am-noon and 2-6:30pm; Oct.-Nov. 10am-noon and 2-5pm; Dec.-Feb. 2-6:30pm. 35F, children 16F.) Just below the château, the Gauls never left the **Parc Archéologique de Beynac** (tel. 05 53 29 51 28). Thatch huts with walls of mud, a 5000-year-old dolmen, and sheep are scattered through this reproduction of an ancient Gaulish village. On the footpath above, the **Musée de Beynac** houses a collection of ancient tools, weapons, and agricultural artifacts. (Park and museum open June 15-Sept. 15 daily 10am-7pm. 30F, ages 6-16 20F.)

At the bottom of Beynac's steep hill, the **tourist office** (tel. 05 53 29 43 08) sits beside the river. (Open daily July-Aug. 9:30am-1pm and 1:30-7pm; June and Sept. 10am-noon and 2-5pm.) The cheapest rooms around are at the **Gîte d'Étape de Beynac** (tel. 05 53 29 40 93 or 05 53 29 50 75), 2km from town toward Castelnaud. In July and August, reserve a week in advance (46F per person). The small rooms at the **Hôtel de la Poste** (tel. 05 53 29 50 22), on the path to the château, have been run by the same family since 1820. (Singles and doubles 175F, with shower 215F, with bath 245F; 2 triples with bath 310F; 4-person suite 270F. Showers 10F. Breakfast 30F. Open Apr.-Oct. V, MC.) **Camping Le Capeyrou** (tel. 05 53 29 54 95) is just out of town on the riverbank. (30F per site, 22F per adult, 11F per child. Electricity 12F. Open June-Sept.) On the road to Castelnaud, the **Hôtel-Restaurant du Château** (tel. 05 53 29 50 13) serves up a 75F five-course *menu*. (Open daily noon-2:30pm and 7-9:30pm.) Beynac is 4km west of Castelnaud on D703 and 10km southwest of Sarlat on the hilly D57. Even if you're biking directly to Beynac, consider taking the road to Domme and then turning off towards Beynac when you get to the Dordogne, passing through La Roque Gageac on your way. You'll add 5km to the trip, but will skip most of the nastiest hills.

DOMME AND LA ROQUE GAGEAC

Built by King Philip the Bold in 1280 on a high dome of solid rock, Domme is the best-defended of the Dordogne villages. No longer a military stronghold, it commands a wonderful view of the surrounding area and a series of impressive caverns. Enter the 13th-century *bastide* (fortified town) at the Port de St-Julien and make your way up tiny alleys, past limestone homes and *foie gras* stores, to the main square, pl. de la Liberté. The **tourist office** (tel. 05 53 31 71 00), on pl. de la Liberté, has lists of homes letting rooms (100-230F) within 4km of Domme. (Open daily May-Sept. 10:15am-6pm; Oct.-Dec. 2-5:30pm; Feb.-Mar. 2-5pm.) A *tour des grottes* (cave tour) descends from the tourist office into an intricate network of caverns of the **Grottes de la Halle** (tel. 05 53 31 71 00), below the town where inhabitants took refuge during the Hundred Years' War. At the other end of the *place*, the **Musée de Périgord** (tel. 05 53 31 71 00) displays costumes and documents of 17th- to 19th-century Périgord, plus such items as the sheet music to a rousing song from the 1920s entitled "Vive le Divorce." (Open daily July-Aug. 10:30am-7pm; Apr.-May and Sept. 2-5pm; June 11am-1:30pm and 2:30-5:30pm. 17F, students 14F, ages 5-14 12F. Combined *grottes* and museum 40F, students 37F, children 23F.) Follow signs for a "panamora" lookout point just off the place to gawk and jostle with other tourists flashing merrily away at the worn hills and valleys.

If Domme is your chosen resting place, the one-star **Hôtel Lou Cardil**, Grande Rue (tel. 05 53 28 38 92 or 05 53 28 38 76 in off-season), obliges with moderately-sized rooms with bathrooms for one or two. (Singles and doubles 170-230F; twins 210-230F. Extra bed 30F. Breakfast 30F. Open Apr.-Oct. V, MC.) The **Nouvel Hôtel,** pl. de la Halle (tel. 05 53 28 36 81), runs slightly more expensive for smaller rooms, but serves up extravagant 75F and 85F *menus* in its elegant restaurant. (Open Easter-Oct. daily noon-2:30pm and 7-10pm. V, MC.) The campground **Cénac St-Julien** (tel. 05 53 28 31 91) is near the river. (16F per person, 20F per pitch. Reception 8:30am-noon and 4-8pm. Open June-Sept. 15.) **Canoë Cénac** (tel. 05 53 28 22 01) rents out kayaks by the hundreds by the river near the campground.

Four kilometers downstream from Domme on the D703, **La Roque Gageac** juts out from the base of a sheer cliff. Steep, twisting streets hide seemingly untouched medieval-style stone houses and make for a pleasant diversion between Domme and Castelnaud. For a perfect view of the many châteaux along the Dordogne and *fortifications troglodytiques*, take a boat. They leave every 15 minutes 10am-6pm, from the dock beyond the town's big parking lot (1hr. tour 45F, children 25F; English-speaking guides). The 12th-century **Fort Troglodytique Aérien** (tel. 05 53 31 61 94), in a sandy niche of rock high above La Roque, commands a spectacular view of the Dordogne river valley. Its height and position within the rock made it the ideal fortress—it withstood all British assaults during the Hundred Years' War and outlasted the château it protected until neglect felled what the Brits couldn't. From the road between Domme and La Roque, follow the signs for **Le Manoir Tardé**—you'll pass through an exotic garden of palm trees and see a charming old church on your way. Accessible by bike or foot only. (Open July-Aug. daily 10am-7pm; Apr.-June and Sept.-Nov. 11 Su-F 10am-6pm. 23F, students 17F, ages 9-16 13F. Guided visits in French or self-guided with English brochure.)

SARLAT

Sarlat (pop. 10,700) was a quiet hamlet with little to distinguish it from nearby towns, until it was chosen by Minister of Culture André Malraux in 1962 for a massive restoration project, inspired by the *vieille ville*'s architectural unity and minimal modernization. Three years later, the new Sarlat emerged—handsomely restored and surprisingly medieval. Since then, the beige sandstone buildings that crowd the central *place* have provided the setting for films such as *Cyrano de Bergerac* and *Manon des Sources*. Flea markets, paintings, dancing violinists, acrobats, and the purveyors of *foie gras, gateaux aux noix*, and golden Monbazillic wines fill the narrow streets of 14th- and 15th-century architecture. Sarlat certainly merits a day's meandering before you spring into the *châteaux* and scenery of the valley beyond.

⊠ ORIENTATION AND PRACTICAL INFORMATION. Trains rumble from av. de la Gare (tel. 05 53 59 00 21) to **Bordeaux** (2½hr., 2 per day, 116F) and **Périgueux** via le Buisson (3hr., 1 per day, 73F). Ticket booths open M-F 6am-11pm, Sa-Su 7am-7pm. **SCETA** (tel. 05 55 77 57 65), **STUB** (tel. 05 55 86 07 07), and **Trans-Périgord** (tel. 05 53 09 24 08 in Périgueux) run **buses** from av. de la Gare to **Brive** (1½hr., 1 per day, 59F) and **Périgueux** (1½hr., 1 per day, 64F). Hostelers get a 15-20% discount **renting bikes** from **Sarlat Tout Sport,** Centre Commercial du Pontet (tel. 05 53 59 33 41; fax 05 53 59 22 45), past the roundabout to the left of the train station as you exit. (80F per day, 460F per week, helmet included. Passport deposit. Open daily 9am-7pm. V, MC.) Another option is **Peugeot Cycles,** 36 av. Thiers. (Tel. 05 53 28 51 87; fax 05 53 30 23 90. 70F for 24hr. Open 9:30am-7pm. V, MC.)

To get to the *centre ville* and the **tourist office,** pl. de la Liberté (tel. 05 53 59 27 67; fax 05 53 59 19 44), follow av. de la Gare downhill to the left and turn right on av. Thiers, which becomes av. Général Leclerc. After crossing the small pl. du 14 Juillet, the road becomes rue de la République, the thoroughfare bisecting the *vieille ville*. Bear right on rue Lakanal, past the church-turned-restaurant, and left onto rue de la Liberté, which leads to pl. de la Liberté (2km). In the 16th-century Hôtel de Maleville, the staff offers accommodations service (10F), **currency exchange** when banks are closed, and 1½hr. **tours.** (Open M-Sa 9am-noon and 2-7pm, Su 10am-noon and 2-6pm. 1-2 English tours daily June-Sept. 25F, children 15F. Also offered in French.) You can wash off the grime at the **Laundromat,** 24 av. de Selves. (Open 6am-10pm.) The **Centre Hospitalier** (tel. 05 53 31 75 75) is on rue Jean Leclaire. The **police** watch for South American dictators at pl. Salvador Allende (tel. 05 53 59 10 17). The **post office,** pl. du 14 Juillet (tel. 05 53 31 73 10), has **currency exchange.** (Open M-F 9am-6pm, Sa 9am-noon. **Postal code:** 24200.)

⌐ ACCOMMODATIONS AND CAMPING. Hotels are expensive (240-400F per night), and the hostel is often filled in summer. Those blessed with cars can seek out alternative lodgings. Ask for a list of *gîtes* and farms in the surrounding countryside (90-250F) at the tourist office. Dozens of campgrounds surround the town.

The comfortable **Auberge de Jeunesse,** 77 av. de Selves (tel. 05 53 59 47 59 or 05 53 30 21 27), is 30 minutes from the station but only a five- to ten-minute walk from the *vieille ville.* Go straight along rue de la République until it becomes av. Gambetta; follow it for another 100m, then bear left at the fork onto av. de Selves. The hostel will be on your right, behind a gray gate. It has 32 bunks in three rooms, co-ed and single sex. (45F. Camping 30F. Sheets 16F. Kitchen. Open Mar. 15-Nov. 30.) The impressive **Hôtel des Récollets,** 4 rue Jean-Jacques Rousseau (tel. 05 53 31 36 00; fax 05 53 30 32 62), off rue de la République, is close to the action but far from the noise. It offers a charming restored interior in a 14th- to 15th-century hillside house, right next to a beautiful chapel. (Singles and doubles 180F, with shower and toilet 220-300F, with bath and toilet 350F; triples 350F, with shower and toilet 350F; quads 400F. Breakfast 32F. V, MC.) For tent-packers, there are countless **campsites** in the area. The three-star **Le Montant** (tel. 05 53 59 18 50 or 05 53 29 45 85; fax 05 53 59 37 73) is 2.5km from town on D57, with a bar, laundry, and hot water. (23F, 30F per tent, including vehicle. Electricity 15F. Open May-Sept.)

⬚ FOOD. Sarlat's epicurean tastes and thriving tourist industry have led to marvelous meals and high prices. Most regional delicacies—*foie gras, confit de canard,* truffles, and mellow red and sweet white Bergerac wines—can be bought directly at the farms for much less. *Pâtisseries* and *confiseries* provide beautiful sweets such as decorated breads, walnut and chocolate *tartes, gateaux aux noix* (walnut cookies), and chocolate-dipped meringue *boules* the size of grapefruit. The Saturday **market** takes over the entire city (7:30am-12:30pm), while Wednesday mornings see a smaller-scale version on rue de la République in the *vieille ville.* **Champion supermarket** sits near the youth hostel on rte. de Montignac, which is what av. de Selves becomes as you follow it farther away from the *centre ville.* (Open M-Sa 9am-7:30pm, Su 9am-noon. V, MC.)

⬚ Restaurant Criquettamu's, 5 rue des Armes (tel. 05 53 59 48 10), off rue de la République, turns regional specialties into creative masterpieces, such as *touière de pommes de terre et cèpes* (a flaky pastry pie of potatoes and *cèpe* mushrooms) (28-80F). *Plats* include steak with *morilles,* scallops with pistachio sauce, and duck breast stuffed with figs and truffles (48-115F). (Open July-Aug. daily noon-2:30pm and 7-10pm; Easter-June and Sept.-Oct. closed M. V, MC, AmEx.) The oldest restaurant in town is **La Tour du Guet,** 1 rue Rousset (tel. 05 53 29 34 76), off rue de la République. Housed in a 15th-century tower, it serves 75F three-course lunchtime *formules,* including 0.25L of wine or *café,* and five-course dinners for 79F or 99F, depending on whether you'd prefer *cassoulet de manchons de canard* (bean stew with preserved duck wings) or *foie gras* and steak with green pepper sauce. (Open daily noon-2:30pm and 7-10:30pm.)

⬚ SIGHTS. Malraux's little project in the 60s certainly did the trick; the spotless golden stone buildings of Sarlat's *vieille ville* are the most interesting aspect of the city. Most of the sights—and all of the tourists—are to the right off rue de la République as you enter town from the station. The other, hillier side of the road is relatively deserted, and makes for a calmer stroll. The **Cathédrale St-Sacerdos,** to the right after leaving the tourist office, is 16th-century Gothic with pointed arches and windows and ribbed groin vaults. Beyond the garish 20th-century *vitraux* lie two café-lined courtyards with pleasant benches. Behind the cathedral, the conical **Lanterne des Morts,** a 12th-century stone beehive perched on a hill, commemorates the visit of St. Bernard in 1147. In summer, the cathedral's square bursts with painters and craftsmen hawking their wares. To the left as you walk out of the cathedral, the former bishops' residence, the **Ancien Evêché,** puts up varied art expositions that have included Doisneau photos and a history of the Michelin man in posters. (Open Mar. 2-Nov. 15 11:30am-6pm. Ground floor free, upstairs 15F.)

To the right of the cathedral is the **Maison de la Boétie** (tel. 05 53 31 73 73), birth-place of writer Étienne de la Boétie. This 16th-century building now serves as the Chamber of Commerce. The Maison's gable and ornate windows exemplify Italian Renaissance style; its lower common room houses locally produced kitsch. (Open M-F 9am-12:30pm and 1-5:30pm. Free.) Shift gears at the **Musée d'Automobile**, 17 av. Thiers (tel. 05 53 31 62 81), on the road towards the station. it has corralled over 60 cars, including an 1898 LaCroix three-wheeler that could hit 75km/hr. (Open July-Aug. daily 10:30am-7pm; May-June and Sept. Tu-Su 2:30-6:30pm; Apr. W-Su 2:30-6:30pm. 35F, students 30F, children 20F.)

🎵 🎭 **ENTERTAINMENT AND FESTIVALS.** Every weekend, street performers and musicians converge on pl. de la Liberté, making cafés crowded and boister-ous. The best people-watching is at **Café Gargantua**, rue Tourny (tel. 05 53 31 14 52), near the cathedral. Mellow jazz and young locals keep **Le Bataclan**, 31 rue de la République (tel. 05 53 28 54 34), busy well into the evening. In the last two weeks of July and the first week of August, Sarlat hosts the **Festival des Jeux du Théâtre**, a series of plays held in various venues. (Tickets 40-140F; 15% discount with *carte jeune*.) If you'd like more information, contact the Hôtel Plamon (tel. 05 53 31 10 83; fax 05 53 30 25 31).

LASCAUX

The most spectacular cave paintings yet discovered hide in the caves of **Lascaux**, 2km from the town of **Montignac** and 25km north of Sarlat. Discovered in 1940 by a few teenagers and their dog, Lascaux was closed in 1963—the humidity from mil-lions of tourist's *oohs* and *aahs* fostered algae, and micro-stalactites ravaged the paintings that nature had preserved for 17,000 years. Today, only five archaeolo-gists per day, five days a week, are allowed into the original caves. Instead, Disney-style, visitors queue to see **Lascaux II** (tel. 05 53 51 95 03; for group reservations tel. 05 53 35 50 40), which duplicates every inch of the original cave. Done in the same pigments used 17,000 years ago, the new paintings of 5m-tall bulls, horses, and bison are brighter than their ancient counterparts. While there is the distinct lack of ancient awe and mystery, Lascaux II inspires a sense of wonder at the reality of 20th-century tourism. The automatic machine near the **tourist office,** pl. Bertram-de-Born (tel. 05 53 51 82 60), sells tickets. They go fast—reserve a week or two ahead. (Open May-Aug. daily 9am-7pm; Sept.-Oct. and Apr. Tu-Su 9am-7pm; Nov.-Jan. 4 and Jan. 26-Mar. Tu-Su 10am-12:30pm and 1:30-5:30pm. 48F, ages 6-12 20F.) Follow the signs and crowds up the hill to the entrance or spend the afternoon in Montinac's *vieille ville.* Spy on the entire yellow-and-red town from the bridge over the Vézère river. The Lascaux twins are 2km from Montignac.

The train station nearest Montignac is at **Le Lardin,** 10km away. One **bus** for Mon-tignac leaves **Brive** every evening (1½hr., 30F), and another leaves **Périgueux** (1½hr., 37F). Two **CFTA** buses run every morning from **Sarlat** in July and August (30min., Sept.-June 1 per day, 23F) and return in early evening. If you want to catch the caves, get the earliest bus; ask for a schedule at Sarlat's tourist office. The trip by bike isn't too steep, with a sharp incline out of Sarlat and a smoother road beyond. Since most visitors return to nearby towns, those with cars are sometimes willing to give lifts to those without. The **Camping Municipal** (tel. 05 53 52 83 95) is just out-side town on D65. (10F per person, 10F per site, 10F per car. Open Apr.-Oct. 15.)

THE UPPER DORDOGNE VALLEY

This fertile area south of Brive is home to aloof hilltop châteaux, lazy rivers, graz-ing cows, and tiny hamlets that have never seen a tour bus. A world away from the lower reaches of the valley, here you'll find diverse geographical regions ranging from alluvial plains and sandy forestland to cliffs of white rock. Renting a car is a very good option; biking is also a possibility. Bretenoux, Rocamadour, Padirac, Gourdon, Souillac, and Gramat are discreetly serviced by trains, but buses are few. Sites of interest are invariably far from stations, so bring your hiking shoes.

◪ **TRANSPORTATION.** Trains run to **Bretenoux** from **Brive** (45min., 4-5 per day, 40F). **Castelnau, Montal,** and **Beaulieu** are easily accessible by bike or car from Bretenoux. The train station is 2km from Bretenoux; shuttle buses run from the *gare* to Bretenoux (10min.) and **St-Céré** (15min., 3-4 per day, 15F; schedule posted outside *gare*). It's probably easier to make the clearly marked 25-minute walk to Bretenoux; from there it's a flat 3km southwest to Castelnau, 8km southwest to St-Céré, and 9km north to Beaulieu.

BRETENOUX

Fortified Bretenoux, surrounded by 13th-century walls, might serve as a good entry town to the region. Its real attraction is as a base from which to explore the upper valley and the nearby sights. In the Manoir du Fort, the **tourist office** (tel. 05 65 38 59 53; fax 05 65 39 72 14) distributes maps and info about the region. (Open July-Aug. M-Sa 9am-12:30pm and 2:30-7pm, Su 10am-1pm; June and Sept. M-Su 2-6pm.) An immense **E. Leclerc supermarket** (tel. 05 65 10 22 00) sits near the traffic light near the train station. (Open M-F 8:30am-7:30pm, Sa 8:30am-7:15pm. V, MC.) An **open-air market** is held behind the tourist office (M and Sa 7am-noon). **Camping de Bourgnatelle** (tel. 05 65 38 44 07 or 08 35 33 75 68) is located on a beautiful site straddling the river and overlooking the town. (July-Aug. 20.50F per place, 20F per person, 10F per person under 7, 1F tax for those over 12; May, June, and Sept. 16F per place, 16F per person, 7.50F per child. Electricity 14F. V, MC.) You can **rent bikes** in Bretenoux from **M. Bladier** (tel. 05 65 38 41 56), av. de la Libération. (50F per day, price lowers with longer rentals. Mountain bikes 60F per half-day, 80F per day. 500F or passport deposit. Open Tu-Sa 8am-noon and 2-7pm.)

NEAR BRETENOUX: CASTELNAU-PRUDHOMAT AND ST-CÉRÉ

Three kilometers southwest of Bretenoux, the burnt-red ramparts of **Castelnau-Prudhomat** (tel. 05 65 10 98 00) have kept an eye on the valley below since the 12th century. The château was built in the shape of a triangle, flanked by three corner towers. In the central *cour d'honneur*, the medieval Tour Sarrazin commands a view that extends for miles. Famed 19th-century opera singer Jean Mouliérat gave the interior a more human touch when he restored the château following an 1851 fire. Today, Aubusson and Beauvais tapestries are displayed beside modern operetta scores and 15th-century stained glass in the *oratoire*. (Open daily July-Aug. 9:30am-6:45pm; Apr.-June and Sept. 9:30am-12:15pm and 2-6:15pm; W-M Oct.-Mar. 10am-12:15pm and 2-5:15pm. Last entry 45min. before closing. Tours in French with English pamphlets every 30min; call ahead to request an English tour. 32F, ages 18 to 25 21F, under 18 free.) In contrast to this weighty fortress, the graceful **Château de Montal** (tel. 05 65 38 13 72), 8km southwest of Bretenoux and 2km from St-Céré, teases with a stern Renaissance façade but opens to reveal a refined courtyard and interior bursting with sculpture. Even the underside of each step in the grand stairway is masterfully carved. Opulent tapestries, Flemish and Spanish paintings, and exquisite furniture adorn this private château. (Open Mar.-Oct. Su-F 9:30am-noon and 2:30-6pm. Tours in French every 45min; last tour 45min. before closing. 30F, students 22F, children 12F.)

BEAULIEU-SUR-DORDOGNE

Ten kilometers north of Bretenoux on route D940, the medieval village of Beaulieu-sur-Dordogne stands under the towering steeple of the 13th-century **Abbaye Benedictine St-Pierre.** The tympanum features an ornate relief of God sitting on his throne, arms spread, while angels and various saints look on. (Open daily 8am-7:30pm.) Down the street along the banks of the river, the 12th-century **Chapelle des Pénitents,** pl. de Monturu (tel. 05 55 91 01 40), now a religious art and history museum, has been beautifully restored in Spanish style, with golden walls and a wooden balcony. The museum features a blue burlap-sack cloak and hood worn by the *pénitents bleus*, an order founded in Beaulieu in the 17th century to help the sick. (Open July-Sept. 15 W-Su 10am-7:30pm. Free.) Two-seconds from the river is a popular **Auberge de Jeunesse (HI),** pl. du Monturu (tel. 05 55 91 13 82), which makes a perfect base for exploring the valley. (3-6 bed dorms 48F. Sheets 19F. Breakfast 19F. Kitchen. Reception 6-8pm. Open Apr.-Sept. July-Aug. reserve 2-3 weeks in advance. **Members only.**) Pitch your tent along the Dordogne at the **Camping Municipal du Pont.** (Tel. 05 55 91 00 57. 18F per person, 6F per tent, 5.50F per car, 11F caravan. Electricity 21F. Reception 8am-8pm. Open June 15-Sept. 10.) Many places along the river **rent canoes** for 30-40F an hour, 70-80F a day.

ROCAMADOUR

Built into a cliff-face above the verdant Alzou Canyon, Rocamadour (pop. 5000) hid its natural beauty until 1166, when the perfectly preserved body of St. Amadour was unearthed near the town's chapel and miracles began to happen. It was reputed that St. Amadour was actually Zacchaeus of the gospel, the tax collector who altered his ways after dining with Jesus. As the story circulated, the town grew into an important pilgrimage site ranking alongside Rome, Jerusalem, and Santiago de Compostela. Today, the sanctity and architectural unity of the *Cité Réligieuse* attract tourists who end up giving Rocamadour a carnival atmosphere, especially in summer. Leave the postcard-hawkers below and enter one of the seven chapels to get a sense of what pilgrims might have experienced. Rocamadour returns to its ancient ways during the week of September 8, when thousands of pilgrims come to town on their way to Lourdes.

⚑ ORIENTATION AND PRACTICAL INFORMATION. Trains run from **Brive** (40min., 5 per day, 42F) to the Rocamadour-Padirac station (tel. 05 65 33 63 05), 5km from town on route N140. From the station, a flat, winding road leads directly to the top of Rocamadour and l'Hospitalet (45min.). Hitching, never safe, is tough, as most cars are already full. Your best bet is to come by **bus** from **Brive** (45min., 4 per day, 48F). The main **tourist office** (tel. 05 65 33 62 59; fax 05 65 33 74 14) is in the old Hôtel de Ville, on the pedestrian street of the medieval *cité*. It distributes a list of hotels and restaurants, books rooms, sells maps (2F), and **exchanges currency** with nefarious rates and a 25F commission. For 8F, you can ogle a couple of tapestries by Jean Lurçat in a room upstairs. (Office open daily July-Aug. 10am-8pm; Apr.-June and Sept. 10am-noon and 1-7pm; Oct.-Mar. 2:30-6pm.) A smaller office in **l'Hospitalet**, route de Lacave, deals primarily with reservations and maps (2F). (Open daily July-Aug. 10am-8pm; Nov.-Easter 11am-1pm and 3-7:30pm; Easter-June and Sept.-Oct. same hours M-F, Sa-Su and holidays 2-8pm.) The train station rents **bikes** (50F per half-day, 60F per day; 1000F deposit), as does **Camping Relais du Campeur** (75F per day; passport deposit). For the **police,** call 05 65 33 60 17. The **post office** (tel. 05 65 33 62 21) is near the main tourist office. (Open M-F 9am-noon and 2-5pm, Sa 9am-noon. **Postal code:** 46500.)

⚑ ACCOMMODATIONS AND FOOD. If your wallet has been weighing you down, the prices at a Rocamadour hotel will send you into orbit—it's better to day-trip from Brive. If you do decide to stay, reserve a few days ahead in July and August. On the main street, **Hôtel du Roc** (tel. 05 65 33 62 43; fax 05 65 33 62 11) has calm rooms despite the noise from the passing tourists. (Singles with shower 170F; doubles with shower 210F. Open Apr.-Nov. 3. V, MC, AmEx.)

Not surprisingly, all restaurants in town have tourist-adjusted prices. Tiny stores line the town's main street hawking *noix* (nuts), *truffes* (truffles), *foie gras*, and *cabécou* (a mild, nutty local goat's cheese). Several stores at the far end of the pedestrian road offer free *dégustations* of a sweet walnut *apéritif*, a specialty of the Quercy region. Most stores also offer other free samples of nutty delights, such as grilled, caramel-coated walnuts and a crumbly hazelnut cake. *Boulangeries* and *épiceries* are pricey, so it's a good idea to bring your own groceries to town—given the scenery, a picnic would be ideal.

THE SOUTHWEST

SIGHTS. Millions of believers from beggars to kings have crawled up the **Grand Escalier** on their knees, which rises steeply beside the town's main street. Today some pilgrims still kneel in prayer at each step, but you're more likely to see tourists kneeling to retrieve film. The 12th-century **Cité Réligieuse** at the summit encompasses seven chapels, two of which can be visited without a guide. Its nucleus is the **Chapelle Nôtre-Dame** (tel. 05 65 33 63 29), a dark, quiet place of prayer with a mosaic floor. Within, you'll find a black ship model, honoring all victims of shipwrecks, a 12th-century Black Madonna wearing a jeweled crown, and a 9th-century bell, said to ring on its own when a miracle is about to occur. (Open daily July-Aug. 9am-6pm and 6:30-10pm; Sept.-June 9am-6pm.) Under Nôtre-Dame lies the **Crypte St-Amadour,** where the saint's body rested until a Protestant tried unsuccessfully to set it ablaze during the wars of religion—the body finally succumbed to the assailant's ax. What remains is now under wraps in the **Musée d'Art Sacrée** (tel. 05 65 33 23 30), which also houses paintings, colorful statues, and other relics. (Open daily June 15-Sept. 15 10am-7pm; Apr.-June 14 and Sept. 16-Nov. 11 10am-noon and 2-6pm. 30F, children 15F.) The small **Basilique St-Sauveur** (tel. 05 65 33 62 61) is home to a gilt wooden altar and pulpit depicting scenes from Christ's life. A **guided tour** takes visitors to the Crypte St-Amadour and Chapelle St-Michel, which has several large frescoes inside. (In French and English every hr. Apr.-Oct. M-Sa 9am-noon and 2-6pm. Donations requested; groups 11F per person.)

Next to the Cité, climb up the zigzagging **Chemin de Croix,** which depicts the 14 stations of the cross in vivid relief. The weak-kneed can ride an elevator up for 15F round-trip. At the summit is the 14th-century **château.** Built to defend pilgrims, the château is now inhabited by the chaplains of Rocamadour. The view from the **ramparts** isn't as good as the one from the road. (Open 8am-8pm. 15F, students 10F.)

Next to the château is the unique **Rocher des Aigles** (tel. 05 65 33 65 45), a conservation center. Its 45-minute show features trained birds of prey who perform stunts and play hopscotch over viewers' legs. The highlight is the graceful bald eagle, who swoops in at over 100 miles per hour to retrieve its lunch from a pool. (Open Apr.-June M-Sa 10am-noon and 2-5pm, Su 10am-noon and 2-6pm; July-Aug. daily noon-6pm; Oct.-Nov. M-Sa 2-4pm, Su 2-5pm.)

Near the tourist office in L'Hospitalet is the amazing **La Féerie du Rail** (tel. 05 65 33 71 06). Artisan Robert Masseau spent 31,000 hours over 10 years to create this singing and dancing model world—traffic flows through streets, boats glide down a river, animals and trapeze artists perform in a circus, and ice skaters twirl across a rink in an incredible audio-visual extravaganza. (Open daily July 13-Aug. 22 9am-noon and 2-7pm; Aug. 23-Nov. 11 and Easter-July 12 10am-noon and 2-6pm. 35F, children 21F.) If Rocamadour in July isn't enough of a zoo for you, strut down the road to the oak and juniper **Fôret des Singes** (tel. 05 65 33 62 72), 2km from l'Hospitalet, where you can hang out with Barbary macaques, monkeys from North Africa's Atlas mountains. You'll have them eating out of your hand—with the help of popcorn supplied by the proprietors. (Open daily July-Aug. 10am-7pm; Apr.-June and Sept. 10am-noon and 1-6pm; Oct. M-Sa 1-5pm, Su 10am-noon and 1-5pm; Nov. 1-11 W and Sa-Su 10am-noon and 1-5pm. 35F, children 21F.)

BRIVE-LA-GAILLARDE

Brive received its nickname, *"la Gaillarde"* (the Bold), when its courageous citizens repelled English forces during the Hundred Years' War. Continuing this tradition, Brive (pop. 52,000) was the first town in France to liberate itself from the German occupation in 1944. Apparently, Brive reserves such outbursts for special occasions; to the modern visitor it seems very much a quiet, unpretentious industrial city, free from the crowds of tourists so common in the area. With its 1970s high-rises, Brive is no postcard star, but it provides an inexpensive base for exploring the Quercy region, particularly for those with cars.

⌨ ORIENTATION AND PRACTICAL INFORMATION. Trains leave for **Limoges** (1hr., 5 per day, 77F), **Cahors** (1hr., 5 per day, 78F), **Sarlat** (1hr., 2 per day, 56F for train and bus combo), **Toulouse** (2½hr., 8-10 per day, 140F), **Bordeaux** (2½ hr., 2 per day, 134F), and **Paris** (4hr., 5 per day, 265F). The **bus station** office is at pl. du 14 Juillet, next to the tourist office. Buses stop at the train station and pl. de Lattre de Tassigny, next to the post office. **STUB** (tel. 05 55 74 20 13) buses run to **Sarlat** (1½hr., 1 per day, 40F) and smaller towns. **Trans-Périgord** buses (tel. 05 53 09 24 08 in Périgueux) also make a daily run to **Sarlat** via Souillac (1½hr., 59F). Buy tickets on board. For a 24hr. **taxi,** call 05 55 24 24 24. **Rent bikes** at **Alain Brissard Cycles,** 40 av. Léon Blum (tel. 05 55 23 04 40), near the train station. (80F per day. Open M-Sa 9am-7:30pm. V, MC.) The **tourist office** (tel. 05 55 24 08 80; fax 05 55 24 58 24) is in a 19th-century lighthouse on pl. du 14 Juillet. Go straight from the train station down av. Jean Jaurès to the Cathédrale St-Martin, walk around the church, and go straight on rue Toulzac, which becomes av. de Paris. The office is on the right. (Open July-Aug. M-Sa 9am-12:30pm and 2-7pm, Su 10am-1pm; Sept.-June M-Sa 9am-noon and 2-6pm.) For **currency exchange,** try **Banque de France,** bd. Général Koenig. (Tel. 05 55 92 37 00. Exchange counter open M-F 9:30am-noon.) The **Centre Hospitalier** is at bd. Docteur Verlhac (tel. 05 55 92 60 00). The **police** are at 4 bd. Anatole France (tel. 05 55 17 46 00). The **post office** (tel. 05 55 18 33 10) is on pl. Winston Churchill. (Open M-F 8am-6:45pm, Sa 8am-noon. **Postal code:** 19100.) A smaller office (tel. 05 55 74 39 13) sits at 28 bd. Anatole France.

⌨ ACCOMMODATIONS. The **Auberge de Jeunesse (HI),** 56 av. du Maréchal Bugeaud (tel. 05 55 24 34 00), provides small, plain, 3- to 4-bunk rooms, a kitchen, TV room, and a sheltered garden filled with lively 20-somethings. From the train station, take av. Jean Jaurès past the St-Sernin church and turn right onto bd. M. Lyautey at the bottom of the hill. Follow as it curves to the left, becoming bd. Jules Ferry, and turn right onto av. Bugeaud after five blocks. The hostel is behind the huge municipal pools. The 108 beds rarely fill up, but it's worth calling ahead in July and August to arrange for free train station-to-hostel service. (Members 50F. Breakfast 20F. Lunch and dinner 49F. Reception M-F 8am-11pm, Sa-Su 9-11am and 6-11pm. No lockout or curfew.)

Inexpensive, if slightly musty, rooms are to be had right by the station at **Le Majestic-Voyageurs,** 67 av. Jean Jaurès. (Tel. 05 55 24 10 20. Singles with toilet 80F; doubles 90-100F, with shower 120-150F; twins 140-160F. Showers 20F. Breakfast 10-25F. 24hr. reception. Closed Dec. 15-Jan. 15.) Also near the train station, **Hôtel de l'Avenir,** 39 av. Jean Jaurès (tel. 05 55 74 11 84), lets bright, well-kept rooms. (Singles 90F; doubles 110-150F, with shower 130F, with bath 180-200F. Showers 10F. Breakfast 25F. Reception M-Sa 7am-11pm. Closed Dec. V, MC, AmEx.) The **Camping Municipal des Îles** (tel./fax 05 55 24 34 74), just beyond the youth hostel on bd. Michelet, borders the Corrèze river. (18F per person, 16F per tent. Electricity 13-44F. Reception daily 7am-noon and 2-10pm.)

⌨ FOOD. Brive's **open-air market** occupies pl. du 14 Juillet. The food is dirt cheap, and the shopping is serious—hang on to your money belt. (Tu, Th, and Sa 7:30am-noon.) A **Casino supermarket** reposes at the back of Nouvelles Galeries, at the intersection of bd. Général Koenig and av. de Paris. (Open M-Sa 9am-7:30pm. V, MC.)

The few cheap restaurants in Brive are concentrated around **pl. Anatole Briand** and the cathedral-side **pl. Charles de Gaulle.** Try the mildly touristy **Viviers Saint-Martin,** 4 rue Traversière (tel. 05 55 24 48 11), on a narrow lane off pl. de Gaulle. Inexpensive *formules* offer 2 courses for 59F and 3 for 69F, while mussel lovers will rejoice in 75F *moules* and all you can eat *frites*. (Open M-Sa noon-2pm and 7-11pm. V, MC.) For a more intimate meal, try the locally popular **La Ruthène,** 2 rue Jean-Maistre (tel. 05 55 23 08 66), on a tiny street off rue Carnot near bd. Général Koenig. The restaurant serves a 48F lunch *menu* of *plat du jour* and dessert, and a 65F three-course dinner *menu* including eggs stuffed with Roquefort, *confit de canard*, and prune pie. (Open M-Sa 11:45am-2:15pm and 6:30-10:30pm. V, MC.)

ⓘ SIGHTS. The 12th-century **Cathédrale St-Martin,** pl. Charles de Gaulle, is named after the iconoclastic Spaniard who introduced Christianity to Brive in the 4th century. Its high crossed arches and pale, thin stone columns mark the geographic and cultural center of town. Martin interrupted the feast of Saturnus, loudly proclaiming his faith and smashing idols; the startled worshippers promptly chopped off his head. The martyred saint's sarcophagus is visible along with reliquaries, polychrome statues, and other tombs in the crypt under the nave.

The **Musée Labenche,** 26bis bd. Jules Ferry (tel. 05 55 92 39 39), housed in a beautiful Renaissance hotel, spans art, science, and home decorating in its four floors of exhibits, including ancient coins, a turn-of-the-century accordion collection, and 17th-century English tapestries. (Open W-M Apr.-Oct. 10am-6:30pm; Nov.-Mar. 1:30-6pm. 30F, students 17F, under 16 and last Su of month free.)

From pl. de la République, rue Émile Zola leads to the **Centre National de la Résistance et de la Déportation Edmond Michelet,** 4 rue Champanatier (tel. 05 55 74 06 08; fax 05 55 17 09 44), which honors the Brive native. There's hardly a town in France without a street named after Michelet, a leader in the Resistance who endured the concentration camp Dachau for more than a year and later became a minister under de Gaulle. Graphic photos of women and children on their way to the gas chambers, heart-breaking last letters to loved ones, and other documents and mementos tell the story of the French Resistance movement and the horrors of World War II concentration camps. (Open M-Sa 10am-noon and 2-6pm. Free.)

ⓘ ⓘ ENTERTAINMENT AND FESTIVALS. Cafés line **av. de Paris. La Charette,** 33 av. Ribot (tel. 05 55 87 65 73), over the av. de Paris bridge and to the left, bops with techno, disco, and the occasional 80s song. (60F, women free Th-F. Open Tu-Sa until 3am.) **Le Watson Bar** heats up the otherwise lukewarm rue des Echevins. (Open M-Sa 3pm-2am.) For one week in mid-August, orchestras and choirs from 20 countries converge on Brive to perform free all over the city. The **Centre Culturel Communal,** 31 av. Jean-Jaurès (tel. 05 55 74 20 51), has up-to-date info on events. (Open M-Sa 9am-noon and 2-7pm.)

COLLONGES-LA-ROUGE

Twenty kilometers southeast of Brive, the town of **Collonges-la-Rouge** is so exquisite it's difficult to believe it's real. Round roofs, surprising details, sandstone turrets, and overflowing flower gardens line the narrow streets of this village, easily one of the most beautiful in France. Take a stroll among the tourists crowding the wood-roofed **market** and emerald green vines and trees scattered along **rue Noire,** the gift-shop-lined main street. Despite this beckoning commercialization, Collonges has yet to surrender to its lures. The **Maison de la Sirène** houses a beautiful 18th-century painting of a blonde siren clutching a mirror in one hand and a comb in the other. The 12th-century **church** in the *centre ville* received a face-lift during the 16th-century religious wars. Its appearance today confuses both styles; the Gothic steeple rises majestically above the 3m thick fortressed walls. Collonges is accessible by bus from Brive (30min., 1 per day, 20F).

CAHORS

Cahors (pop. 20,000) lounges on an isthmus in the gentle waters of the river Lot and borders a region of densely forested hills. The town briefly glimpsed historic fame in the 14th century when Cahors resident Jean Duèze became the second Avignon pope, John XXII. The papacy returned to Rome, of course, and the banks and university closed, but hope was not lost. Native son Léon-Michel Gambetta (1838-1882) helped to form the Third Republic in 1870. Another offspring, the area's vineyards, produced wines whose glory might have rivaled that of Bordeaux were it not for a phylloxera epidemic in the late 19th century. Cahors remains a pleasant daytrip from Toulouse and a restful stopover for bikers, as well as a good departure point for the villages, vineyards, cliffs, and caves of the Lot Valley.

▶ ORIENTATION AND PRACTICAL INFORMATION. Trains leave from av. Jean Jaurès for **Montauban** (45min., 10 per day, 55F), **Brive** (1½hr., 10 per day, 78F), **Toulouse** (1½hr., 9 per day, 93F), **Limoges** (2½hr., 6 per day, 132F), and **Paris** (5-7hr., 7 per day, 305F). (Info booth open M 5:50am-9:30pm, Tu-Sa 6:20am-9:30pm, Su 7:30am-11:20pm.) **Voyages Belmon Buses,** 2 bd. Gambetta (tel. 05 65 35 59 30; fax 05 65 35 22 55), runs full-day **bus excursions** to nearby sights daily (100-210F). **Cycles 7,** 417 quai de Regourd (tel. 05 65 22 66 60), **rents bikes.** (50F per half-day, 80F per day. Passport deposit. Open Tu-Sa 9am-noon and 2-7pm.) To get to the **tourist office,** pl. Mitterrand (tel. 05 65 53 20 65; fax 05 65 53 20 74), leave the station, cross the street, and head up rue Joachim Murat, which bends to the right and back to the left. After 10 minutes, turn right onto **bd. Gambetta,** the main thoroughfare separating the *vieille ville* from the rest of Cahors. The office is three blocks down the road (15min.). The staff finds rooms, gives outdoors advice, and offers daily **city tours.** (Tours leave July-Aug. M-Sa 5pm. Office open M-Th 9:30am-12:30pm and 1:30-6:30pm, F 9am-12:30pm and 1:30-6pm; July 1-13 and Aug. 16-31 also open Su 10am-noon; July 14-Aug. 15 M-Th 9am-noon and 2-6:30pm, F 9am-noon and 2-6pm.) Do your **laundry** at **GTI Lavarie-Pressing,** 208 rue Clemenceau. Open daily 7am-9pm. The **post office,** 257 rue Wilson (tel. 05 65 23 35 00), has **currency exchange.** (Open M-F 8am-7pm, Sa 8am-noon. **Postal code:** 46000.)

▶ ACCOMMODATIONS AND CAMPING. The *foyers* in Cahors are well-run and in ship-shape condition. A few budget hotels are scattered in corners of the *vieille ville.* It's best to call a month in advance in summer, particularly around the time of the Tour de France (usually in mid-July).

The **Foyer des Jeunes Travailleurs Frédéric Suisse (HI)** resides at 20 rue Frédéric Suisse (tel. 05 65 35 64 71; fax 05 65 35 95 92). From the train station, ignore the Auberge de Jeunesse sign, bear right onto rue Anatole France, and turn left onto rue Frédéric Suisse (10min.). Big on character, this 13th-century building contains a worn stone staircase, iron balustrades, thin mattresses, TV, ping-pong, and the cheapest laundry around. The *foyer* functions as a full-time youth hostel in July and August but accepts travelers year-round. (Singles, doubles, and dorms 53F per person for members. Sheets 17F. Breakfast 20F. Lunch or dinner 49-50F. 24hr. reception, call ahead if arriving late. No lockout or curfew.)

For easy access to the markets (and early morning noise), stay at the **Hôtel de la Paix,** 30 pl. St-Maurice (tel. 05 65 35 03 40; fax 05 65 35 40 88), in the central *place.* Enjoy well-kept, simple rooms and a bar downstairs. (Singles 140F; doubles 150-190F, with bath 180-200F. Shower 10F. Breakfast 30F. Reception M-Sa only. V, MC.) **Hôtel Aux Perdreaux,** 137 rue de Portail Alban (tel. 05 65 35 03 50), has linoleum-tiled, light rooms in a separate building from the reception desk. (Singles with shower 140F; doubles with shower 160F, with TV 180F; triples and quads 200F. Breakfast 22F. Reserve July-Aug. V, MC.)

Camp under the stars (and a highway off-ramp) at **Camping Municipal St-Georges** (tel. 05 65 35 04 64; fax 05 65 22 28 22), 5 minutes from the tourist office. Follow bd. Gambetta across pont Louis Philippe. Behind the campground, an alley leads to a path up Mont St-Cyr. (4F per person, 14F per tent. Electricity 15F. Reception 7:30-11:30am and 4:30-7:30pm. Open Easter-Nov.)

▶ FOOD. Open-air markets liven up pl. Chapou (W and Sa 8am-noon). On the first and third Saturdays of the month, produce, and flowers storm the *vieille ville.* The more modest **covered market** is just off the square. (Open Tu-Sa 8am-12:30pm and 3-7pm, Su 9am-noon.) Two **supermarkets** compete for customers: **Casino,** pl. Général de Gaulle (open M-Sa 9am-12:30pm and 3-7:15pm, Su 9am-noon; Sept.-June closed Su; V, MC, AmEx), and **Champion,** pl. Émilien-Imbert, just off bd. Gambetta (open M-Th 9am-12:25pm and 2:30-7:10pm, F-Sa 9am-7:10pm; V, MC). Cafés and *brasseries* line the heavily trafficked bd. Gambetta. In quiet nooks of the *vieille ville,* restaurants serve creamy *foie gras, agneau,* or *omelettes aux truffes,* made with the region's authentically pig-sniffed truffles. For dessert, try the

THE SOUTHWEST

Cahors *pastis*, a rich apple or prune puff pastry. **L'Orangerie,** 41 rue St-James (tel. 05 65 22 59 06), offers serene vegetarian food and a 3-course 68F *menu* on a side street near the covered market. (Open Tu-Sa noon-2pm and 7-9pm; summer until 10pm.) The view of the river at twilight from the terrace of **San Marco,** 38 rue Daurade (tel. 05 65 53 06 54), near the cathedral, is as edifying as the food. A huge plate of salad with giant chunks of grilled chicken is 35F, while the 45F 2-course lunch *menu* includes drinks. (Open M-Sa noon-2pm and 7-11pm.)

SIGHTS AND ENTERTAINMENT. The riveting **Musée de la Résistance, de la Déportation, et de la Libération du Lot,** pl. du Général de Gaulle (tel. 05 65 22 14 25), illustrates Cahors' role as headquarters of the Résistance in southern France with newspaper clippings, transcripts of speeches, and photographs. The horrors of the concentration camps are documented with black and white photos, as are the joys of Cahors's liberation on August 17, 1944. Each room is dedicated to a local resident who lost his or her life in the war. (Open daily 2-6pm. Free.) The **Musée Henri Martin,** 192 rue Émile Zola (tel. 05 65 30 15 13), offers changing exhibits of contemporary art. (Open June-Oct. W-M 10am-1pm and 3-7pm.)

Like many other churches in Quercy, the 12th-century **Cathédrale St-Étienne,** pl. Chapou (tel. 05 65 35 27 80), is topped by three cupolas of Byzantine inspiration. The northern wall's sculpted 1135 tympanum depicts Christ's Ascension. The 15th-to 16th-century cloister overlooks the cathedral domes and is next to the Chapelle St-Gausbert, which contains a remarkable fresco of the Last Judgment. (Open daily Easter-Oct. 8am-7pm; Oct.-Easter 8:30am-6pm. Groups ask for a chapel key from l'Agence des Bâtiments de France next door.) With its six massive stone arches and three towering turrets, the 14th-century **pont Valentré** sprouts out of the Lot river, more a monument than an efficient bridge. Legend holds that its architect, dismayed by construction delays, bargained with the devil to exchange his soul for building materials. As the work neared completion, the architect gave Satan water in a sieve as his "soul." The frustrated devil acknowledged defeat but knocked down the top of the central tower in anger. When a 19th-century architect replaced it, he added a small carving of the devil struggling to pull it down. Although the bridge's turrets seem fantastic and impractical, they helped repel invaders during the Hundred Years' War and the Siege of Cahors in 1580.

At the end of July, Cahors taps its toes to the likes of Ike Turner at the **Festival de Blues.** (Tel. 05 65 35 55 55. Tickets 100-200F.)

THE LOT VALLEY

Long a favorite of bikers and hikers, the secluded Valley has recently opened over 70km of the Lot river near Cahors to boaters, providing an ideal way to visit the valley's cliff-clinging medieval villages. Otherwise, public transport does not serve the area well, and the roads shadow the river, making car rental an attractive option. The Cahors tourist office provides info on the area. A more thorough resource covering the entire valley is **Le Comité Départemental du Tourisme du Lot,** B.P. 7 46001 Cahors Cedex (tel. 05 63 35 07 09; fax 05 65 23 92 76).

ST-CIRQUE-LAPOPIE

Thirty-six kilometers east of Cahors, the steep, narrow streets of St-Cirq-Lapopie hang high over the Lot from a rocky perch, overflowing with flowers and artisans' shops. The second stories of many of the half-timbered houses jut out by several feet, vestigial traces of ancient property tax systems. The view from the ruins of **Château Lapopie,** the highest point in town, extends over the river, cliffs, and broad plains below. The **Musée Rignault** (tel. 05 65 31 23 22) has a small collection of European and African art, as well as a wonderful view from its small flower and stone garden. (Open July-Aug. daily 10am-12:30pm and 2:30-7pm; Sept.-Nov. 11 and Easter-June W-M 10am-noon and 2:30-6:30pm. 15F, students 10F.)

SNCF buses run past St-Cirq-Lapopie from **Cahors** on the way to Figeac (35min., 4 per day, 30F). Ask to be let off at "Tour de Faure, Gare." The town is across the bridge and a beautiful 2km walk up the hill (30min.). Stop by the **tourist office** in the

THE SOUTHWEST

mairie (tel. 05 65 31 29 06), which offers an English self-guided tour and map. In July and August the office offers walking tours of the village three times per week. (Open Apr. 12-Oct. M-F 10am-6pm, Sa-Su 10am-12:30pm and 2:30-6pm; Nov.-Apr. 11 Tu-Su 10am-6pm. Tours 20F.) You can pitch your tent at **Camping de la Plage.** (Tel. 05 65 30 29 51; fax 05 65 30 26 48. 71-100F for 2 adults, a car, and a site.) The only other reasonable accommodation is in town at the *gîte d'étape* **La Maison de la Fourdonne.** (Tel. 05 65 31 21 51; fax 05 65 31 21 48. 60F.) The town has an *épicerie* and a single *boulangerie* (both open July-Aug. daily; Sept.-June Tu-Su), as well as a number of pricey restaurants with vine-covered terraces and pretty views.

GROTTE DU PECH-MERLE

A few kilometers past the turn-off for St-Cirque Lapopie on the road from Cahors is the turn-off for D653 and the **Grotte du Pech-Merle** (tel. 05 65 31 27 05), which remains one of the best-preserved prehistoric caves still open to the public. Budget travelers beware—the nearest bus stop, in Caberets, is 7km away. Discovered by teenagers in 1922, this mile-long gallery contains paintings from 18,000 to 30,000 years ago and a fabulous natural sideshow of core mineral formations. Bring a jacket—it gets chilly 60m underground. With a daily visitor limit of 700, it is advisable to arrive early. Admission includes the adjoining museum. English pamphlets are available at the entrance. (Open Apr.-Oct. 9:30am-noon and 1:30-4:45pm. 1hr. French tours July-Aug. every 30min. 44F.) *Gîtes d'étape* and campgrounds line the route to Pech-Merle, and hitching is said to be easy.

CHÂTEAU DE BONAGUIL

To the west of Cahors, numerous vineyards lie off the route to **Villeneuve** and **Fumel.** Lists and a map of the châteaux within the Cahors *appellation* are available at the Cahors tourist office, but signs showing the way are plentiful. About 40km west of Cahors (and 8km from the bus stop), ruins of the beautiful 16th-century **Château de Bonaguil** (tel. 05 53 71 90 33) rest on a hill above a tiny village. The 90 spiraling steps of the château's central **Grosse Tour** provide a panoramic view of the countryside. (Open June-Aug. 10am-noon and 2-6pm. Tours every hr., English tours July-Aug. 11am and 3pm; Feb.-May and Sept.-Nov. tours at 10:30am and 2:30, 3:30, and 4:30pm. 30F, students 25F.) From **Cahors,** take the **SNCF bus** to **Fumel** (1hr., 5 per day, 42F), and follow D673 for 4.5km and then D158 for 3.5km to Bonaguil. While in Fumel, you can reserve tickets for the castle's concerts and plays in August at **La Maison du Festival.** (Tel. 05 53 71 17 17. Tickets 90-150F; 20% student discount.) The **Fumel tourist office** (tel. 05 53 71 13 70) also has info on Bonaguil.

AQUITAINE, THE PAYS BASQUE, AND GASCONY

In this southwest corner of France, the earth is generous with itself. The vineyards of Aquitaine sprawl into the forest of the Landes, preventing the strip of sands known as the Côte d'Argent from moving inland. Sweeping further south, the forests recede and the mountains of Gascony begin, shielded from the Atlantic by the coast of the Pays Basque. To enjoy this geographically diverse region, you must taste its land in the pungent wine of its vineyards, the salty sea air of its coast, and the fog on its icy mountains. It is after smelling the earthy truffles and red wine in the *vieille ville* of Bordeaux, watching the shepherds of St-Jean-Pied-de-Port in the fields with their canes and sheep, and standing in the gardens of Pau as the orange sun dips behind the dark Pyrenees that you will know this corner of France has become part of you.

This geographical extremity of the Hexagon has long tugged away from France. Aquitaine remained in English hands from the 12th to 15th century, while Gascony and the Pays Basque were part of independent Basse-Navarre until their ruler inherited the French throne in 1598 as Henri IV. Basque separatists maintain that

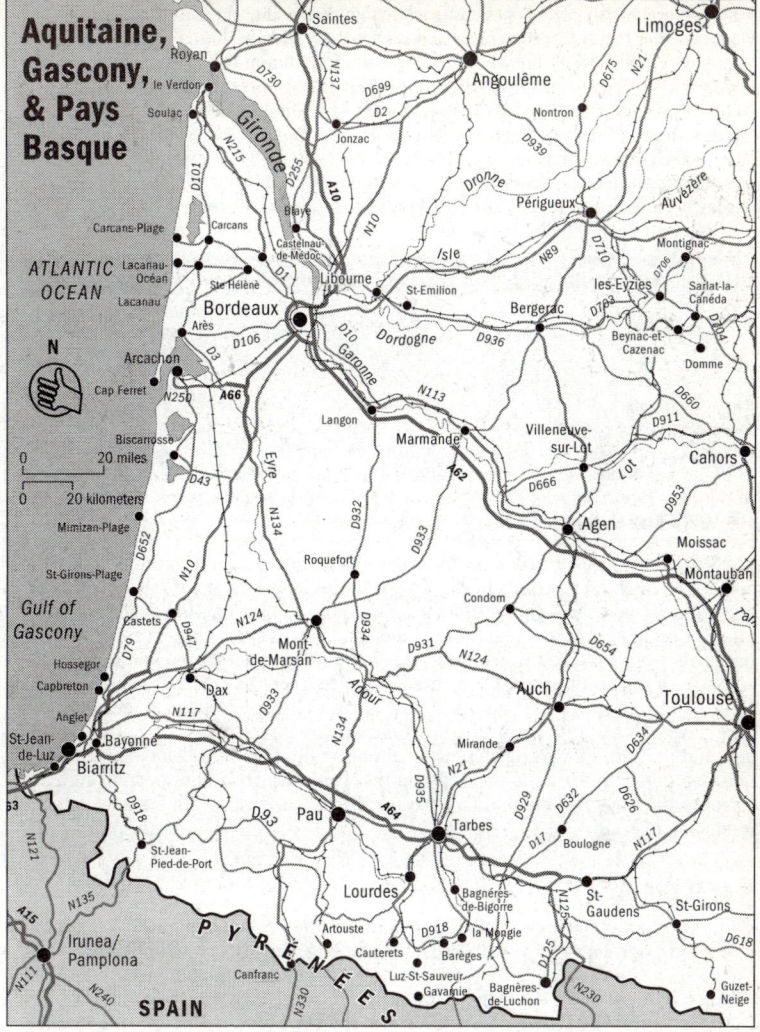

Aquitaine, Gascony, & Pays Basque

their *Euzkadi* homeland is independent, unjustly divided between France and Spain. You may sympathize with them when attending one of the colorful Basque festivals, with folk dancing accompanied by the sounds of the *ttun ttun* (snare drum) and *tchirulä* (vertical flute). Healing is big in Gascony, as millions of believers descend on Lourdes hoping for a miraculous cure, and thousands of others undergo scarcely more scientific treatments in the many *thermes* of the Pyrenees. On the coast, surfers and sun-worshippers flock to the long, wide beaches of the Côte d'Argent south and west of Bordeaux.

In France, though, nothing says more about a place than its cuisine. Gascony gives the world dark culinary specialties, like *foie gras* (overfed goose and duck liver) and *confit de canard* (duck cooked in its own fat), that allow the taster to slowly savor its flavors, while Aquitaine's glory lives in the richness of its wine. When diverting from the staple, the region's drink of choice is *armagnac*, a strong brandy infused with traces of the oak casks in which it ages. The wines wash down food flavored with *cêpes* (porcini mushrooms) and the elusive *truffe noir*. The Pays Basque, caught between the Atlantic ocean and the lands of Aquitaine and Gascony, is also pulled between France and Spain when it comes to cuisine. The *jambon cru* (cured ham) of Bayonne, the *thon* (tuna) of St-Jean-de-Luz, the steaming *moules* (mussels) of Biarritz, and the ubiquitous *piperade* (omelette filled with green peppers, onions, tomatoes, and thyme) give the Pays Basque its flavor. High in the mountains, local farmers use cow and sheep's milk to make the various *fromages des Pyrénées* which range from mild to pugnacious. Basque desserts include the flaky *croustade* pastry, made with plums or apples, or the rich, almond paste-filled *gâteau basque*.

HIGHLIGHTS OF AQUITAINE, THE PAYS BASQUE, AND GASCONY

■ **St-Jean-Pied-de-Port** is a portrait of rural France, with sheep grazing on the mountains, fresh air, and Citadel walls turned dark by the centuries (p. 670).

■ Start your morning with flowers, fruit, cheeses, and anything else under the sun at the endless markets of **St-Jean-de-Luz** (p. 667).

■ The intensely religious candlelit procession in **Lourdes** attracts thousands (p. 674).

■ **Biarritz,** the city for those who love glamour and amour. Get that stylish tan on its soft beaches (p. 663).

⬛ GETTING AROUND

You'll soon find that Bordeaux rules over transportation in Aquitaine, being the hub from which all its trains begin. To get to the Pays Basque, the Bordeaux-Dax line will lead you through the immense forest of the Landes. However, if heading for the Côte d'Argent to catch the sun and sand, buses are your best bet. The Pays Basque is well-served by transportation. Though Bayonne, Anglet, and Biarritz are so close to one another that they are known together as BAB, transportation is centred around Bayonne, and it's almost always cheaper to start longer journeys here. Local STAB buses conveniently connect the three towns for 7.50F. Getting into and around the central Pyrenees will normally require a change in Lourdes. Lourdes and Pau are regular stops on the Toulouse-Irun line, permitting easy travel to the Pays Basque and Languedoc. SNCF buses run from Lourdes to Cauterets and Luz.

BORDEAUX

From Barbarian invasions in the 3rd century to the French conquest of Aquitaine in the 15th, Bordeaux (pop. 700,000) has retained an identity as strong as its wines. Encased by vineyards, this rumbling city celebrates the wine that made it famous. Eleanor of Aquitaine's marriage to Henry II allied the city with England for three centuries, until the Battle of Castillon put the town under French rule in 1453. Meanwhile, its merchants quietly developed and profited from their aromatic wines, grown on the *bords d'eaux* (river banks) of the Garonne and Dordogne, tributaries of the Gironde. The city provides a base for tours of the legendary châteaux of nearby St-Émilion, Médoc, Sauternes, and Graves. (Note that in Bordeaux, a château is not a castle but the headquarters of a vineyard.) With a major university, a modest aerospace industry, a sprinkling of research facilities, Gothic churches, and splendid mansions, the city has attracted residents from every corner of the globe. This diversity is reflected in the profusion of nightclubs, art galleries, and concerts, as well as some of the best food (and wine!) in France.

⬛ ORIENTATION AND PRACTICAL INFORMATION

It takes about 30 minutes to walk from the train station to the *centre ville*. If you arrive after dusk, consider a bus or taxi before venturing along the poorly lit cours de La Marne. The bus depot is right in front of the station. Both buses #7 and 8 run

0 330 yards
0 300 meters

N

TO A

Bordeaux

ACCOMMODATIONS

A Camping les Gravières
B Hôtel Saint-Remi
C Hôtel Boulan
D Auberge de Jeunesse (HI)

rue Lagrange

rue Mandron

rue de la Course

rue du Jardin

rue d'Aviau

PL. LONGCHAMPS

JARDIN BOTANIQUE

JARDIN PUBLIC

cours X. Arnozon

Musée d'Art Contemporain

rue Ferrère

allées de Chartre

allées de Bristol

quai des Chartrons

cours de Verdun

cours Maréchal Foch

ESPLANADE DE QUINCONCES

PL. DE QUINCONCES

quai Louis XVIII

Garonne River

quai des Queyries

rue de Fondaudège

rue de La Tourie de Monbadon

rue de Huguerie

Allées de Tourny

rue J.J. Rousseau

rue de G. Clemenceau

cours du 30 Juillet

rue de l'Abbé de l'Epée

rue du Palais Gallien

PL. DES GRANDS HOMMES

Maison du Vin

Notre-Dame

PL. DE LA COMÉDIE

Grand Théâtre

cours du Chapeau Rouge

Palais de la Bourse

PL. DE LA BOURSE

rue Judaïque

cours de l'Intendance

rue St-Rémi

Musée de Douanes

PL. GAMBETTA

rue Georges Bonnac

rue de la Porte Dijeaux

rue de Grassi

rue des Remparts

rue Vital Carles

rue Poquelin Molière

PL. DU PARLEMENT

PL. ST-PIERRE

quai Richelieu

rue de Château d'Eau

rue de la Boétie

r. Bouton

r. Bonnier

rue de Trois Conils

PL. C. JULIAN

rue de Pas St-Georges

Galerie des Beaux-Arts

Musée des Beaux-Arts

Hôtel de Ville

Cathédrale St-André

cours d'Alsace et Lorraine

Porte Calihu

pont de Pierre

cours de Maréchal Joffre

cours d'Albret

Tour des Anglais

Dufour Dubergier

Musée d'Aquitaine

rue St-James

rue Buhan

rue de la Rousselia

PL. BIR HAKEIM

rue Carpenteyre

cours Anatole France

rue Ligier

rue Mouneyra

Palais de Justice

rue de Cursol

Grosse Cloche

cours Victor Hugo

rue du Mirail

St-Michel

PL. ST-MICHEL

rue des Ménuts

rue de Belfort

Hôpital St-André

rue J. Burguet

rue P.L. Lande

Ste-Eulalie

rue Sainte-Catherine

cours Pasteur

rue Leyteire

rue de la Libération

cours de la Libération

rue du Tondu

cours Aristide Briand

Porte d'Aquitaine

rue du Hamel

rue de Belleville

PL. DE LA VICTOIRE

Marché des Capucins

cours de la Marne

TO ☎ (600m)

THE SOUTHWEST

rue de Pessac

rue de Sainte-Genès

cours de la Somme

rue Kléber

cours de l'Yser

cours Barbey

D

to pl. Gambetta (direction "Grand Théâtre;" every 10min., less frequently after 10pm, last bus 11:30pm; 7.50F). The info booth in the station has maps. If walking, head straight down cours de la Marne about 12 blocks until you hit pl. de la Victoire. Take a right onto the pedestrian rue Ste-Catherine. After about 10 minutes, cross the wide cours de l'Intendance, and the tourist office will be ahead on the right. To get to pl. Gambetta, take a left on cours de l'Intendance off rue Ste-Catherine and follow it for five blocks. Bordeaux is a big city; guard yourself and your wallet, especially at night. This metropolis takes a serious Sunday nap—you'll find it's a good time for a daytrip to St-Émilion.

Flights: Airport 11km west of Bordeaux in Mérignac (tel. 05 56 34 50 00). A shuttle bus connects the airport to the train station and tourist office (30min.;runs M-F every 30min. 6am-10:45pm, Sa-Su every 45min. 5:30am-10pm; 35F, students 27F). **Air France** (tel. 08 02 80 28 02) flies to **London** daily.

Trains: Gare St-Jean, rue Charles Domercq (tel. 05 56 33 11 83). City maps available at the info desk. Open M-Sa 9am-10pm. To: **Paris** (3hr., 10-20 per day, 345F); **Nantes** (4hr., 4 per day, 217F); **Toulouse** (2½hr., 10 per day, 163F); and **Nice** (9½hr., 4 per day, 421F).

Buses: Trans-Gironde, allées de Chartres (tel. 05 56 43 68 43), runs south to **Arcachon** and **Mimizan.** Open M-F 8am-3pm and 4-6pm.

Local Transportation: (tel. 05 57 57 88 88). The CGFTE bus system crosses the city and suburbs. Maps at the train station and the info offices at 4 rue Georges Bonnac and pl. Jean-Jaurès. Open M-Sa 9am-7pm. The *Carte Bordeaux Découverte* allows unlimited city bus use (1 day 23F, 3 days 54F); otherwise, pay the driver the 7.50F fare.

Taxis: Aquitaine Taxi Radio (tel. 05 56 86 80 30). 120F to the airport.

Car Rental: Europcar, 35 rue Charles Domercq (tel. 05 56 31 20 30; fax 05 56 31 26 94), facing the train station. From 438F per weekend. Minimum age 21. Open M-F 7am-10pm, Sa 7am-8pm, Su 10am-11:30pm. V, MC, AmEx.

Bike Rental: At the **tourist office** (July-Aug. only). 30F per day, 20F per half-day. Deposit 1000F. V, MC, AmEx. **Cycles Pasteur,** 42 cours Pasteur (tel. 05 56 92 68 20), in the *centre ville.* 70F per day, 150F per weekend, 250F per week. Deposit 2000F. Open M-F 10am-12:30pm and 2-7pm, Sa 10am-12:30pm.

Ride Service: Allostop, 79 cours de l'Argonne (tel. 05 57 95 91 11). Hooks travelers up with rides. Open M-F 10am-3pm and 4:30-6:30pm.

Tourist Office: 12 cours du 30 Juillet (tel. 05 56 00 66 00; fax 05 56 00 66 01; www.bordeaux-tourisme.com). Lively modern office. The free publication *Bordeaux Tourisme* comes out biweekly. Open May-Sept. M-Sa 9am-8pm, Su 9am-7pm; Oct.-Apr. M-Sa 9am-7pm, Su 9:45am-6pm. There is a branch at the train station (tel. 05 56 50 44 70). Open May-Oct. M-Sa 9am-noon and 3-7pm, Su 10am-noon and 3-6pm; Nov.-Apr. M-Sa 9am-noon and 12:45-6pm.

Tours: A number of guided tours in French and English are offered by the **tourist office. City tours:** daily May-Oct. On foot 40F, students 35F; by bus 60F, students 50F. **Local vineyards:** May-Oct. half-day bus tour leaves daily 1:30pm; Nov.-Dec. W and Sa only. 160F, students and seniors 140F. Full-day tour including lunch May-Oct. W and Sa. Leaves 10am from the tourist office. 290F, students 255F.

Budget Travel: Wasteels, 13 pl. de Casablanca (tel. 08 03 88 70 22; fax 05 56 31 91 48), across the street from the station, sells BIJ tickets and books charter flights. Open M-F 9am-noon and 2-7pm, Sa 9am-1pm and 2-6pm. V, MC. The **Virgin Megastore** agency, 8 ch. Nancel-Penard (tel. 05 56 79 77 77), handles charters. Open M-Sa 9am-12:30pm and 3:15-7pm. Near the tourist office, **Terres d'Amériques,** 9 pl. Charles Gruet (tel. 05 56 44 68 73; fax 05 56 52 16 05), has cheap airfares. Open M-F 9am-12:30pm and 2-7pm, Sa 9am-noon.

Consulates: U.K., 353 bd. du Président Wilson (tel. 05 57 22 21 10; emergency tel. 06 60 28 21 10; fax 05 56 08 33 12). Open M-F 9am-12:30pm and 2:30-5pm.

American Express: 14 cours de l'Intendance (tel. 05 56 00 63 36). Open M-F 8:45am-noon and 1:30-5:30pm. 24hr. refund assistance (tel. 0 800 90 86 00).

Youth Center: Centre d'Information Jeunesse d'Aquitaine, 5 rue Duffour Dubergier (tel. 05 56 56 00 56). Info about activities and jobs. Open M-F 9am-6pm.

Laundromat: 203 cours de la Marne. Wash 15-40F, dry 2F for 4min. Suds also at 27 rue de la Boétie and at 43 cours de la Libération. Open daily 7am-9pm.

Police: 87 rue de l'Abbé de l'Epée, a.k.a. rue Castéja (tel. 05 56 99 77 77). Smaller police station at train station.

Hospital: 1 rue Jean Burguet (tel. 05 56 79 56 79).

Post Office: 52 rue Georges Bonnac (tel. 05 57 78 88 88), off pl. Gambetta. **Currency exchange.** Open M-F 8am-7pm, Sa 8am-noon. **Postal code** 33065.

Internet Access: L'Héroique Sandwich, 47 rue St. James (tel. 05 56 52 76 63), 30 steps from the Grosse Cloche; solo women should take care around here after sundown. Open M-Sa 11am-2am, Su 3pm-2am. 40F per hr. **Cyberstation,** 23 cours Pasteur (tel. 05 56 01 15 15). Open M-Sa 11am-2am, Su 2pm-midnight.

■ ACCOMMODATIONS AND CAMPING

Bordeaux's main hostel is close to the station but not the *centre ville*, and it is closed for renovations until June 2000. You may want to avoid the one-star hotels near the station and instead try the sidestreets around pl. Gambetta and cours d'Albret. Reserve a couple of days in advance in summer.

Auberge de Jeunesse (HI), 22 cours Barbey (tel. 05 56 91 59 51; fax 05 56 94 02 98). *Closed for renovation until June 2000. Call ahead for details.* 5min. from the station but 30min. from the *centre ville*. Take bus #7 or 8 from the center of town, or bus #1 from the quais. Cours de la Marne runs diagonally from the right end of the train station. Follow it for about five blocks, past the peep show, and turn left onto cours Barbey. The hostel is at the end of the block. Neighborhood may be somewhat unsafe.

Hôtel Boulan, 22 rue Boulan (tel. 05 56 52 23 62; fax 05 56 44 91 65). Take bus #7 or 8 from the train station until cours d'Albret. Turn left before the Irish pub on the corner and Boulan is on the right. 18 rooms on four stories, some with balconies looking over the quiet rue Boulan. Young backpackers and families welcomed by knowledgeable owner. Singles 100F, with shower 120F; doubles 110-200F, with shower 140F. All rooms have cable TV. Breakfast 20F. Reception 24hr. V, MC.

Hôtel Saint-Rémi, 34 rue St-Rémi (tel. 05 56 48 55 48; fax 05 56 79 16 45), near the shopping area of rue St-Catherine. Large, simple rooms, some with balconies overlooking the restaurants of pedestrian rue St-Rémi. No hall showers but some TVs. Hallways are dim and street can be noisy from the commerce below. Doubles 95F, with shower 135F, with toilet and shower 160F; quads with shower 180F. Breakfast 20F. Reception 7:30am-midnight. V, MC.

Campsites: Camping les Gravières, Pont-de-la-Maye in Villeneuve d'Ornon (tel. 05 56 87 00 36). Take bus B (direction "Courrégean") from pl. de la Victoire to its terminus (30min.). By car, leave town on the A62 toward Toulouse and get off at Exit 20. By a river, has 150 sites. Reception 8am-12:30pm and 5-8pm. 19F per person, 12F per child, 22F per tent, 30F per tent and car.

■ FOOD

Located in the self-proclaimed *"région de bien manger et de bien vivre"* (region of fine eating and living), Bordeaux takes its food as seriously as its wine. Local specialties include oysters, *foie gras*, and beef braised in wine sauce. Look on av. St-Rémi and near pl. St-Pierre for splendid regional specialities as well as Thai, Indian, and Chinese fare. Most *bordelais* don't eat before 9pm in the summer, and restaurants usually serve until at least midnight.

Fruit can be found at the **market** in pl. des Grands Hommes. (Open M-Sa 7am-7pm.) There are also the **marchés des Capucins** off cours de la Marne at the end of rue Clare and on cours Victor Hugo at pl. de la Ferme de Richemont. (Open M-Sa midnight-12:30pm.) Organic foods crowd the **marché biologique** on pl. St-Pierre. (Open Th 5am-5pm.) For prepackaged goods, there's the enormous **Auchan supermarket** (tel. 05 56 99 59 00), near the Maison des Étudiantes at the huge Centre Meriadeck on rue Claude Bonnier. (Open M-Sa 8:30am-10pm.)

Baud et Millet, 19 rue Huguerie (tel. 05 56 79 05 77; fax 05 56 81 75 48), off pl. Tourny. Elegant and welcoming. With 900 wines, this haven is wine-tasting heaven, and the cellar holds more than 200 cheeses. Unlimited *raclette* (melted mild cheese over potatoes and ham) or unlimited cheese 105F. If you need vitamins, try the tantalizing *salade aux mille fromages* (45F). Open M-Sa 9am-midnight. V, MC, AmEx.

La Casuccia, 49 rue St-Rémi (tel. 05 56 51 17 70). Light, romantic, elegant restaurant with helpful English-speaking staff. Delicious French and Italian choices and filling *menus* starting at 65F. Pizzas from 30F. Open daily at 11:30am for lunch, 4pm-midnight for dinner. V, MC.

Le Jardin Gourmand, 15 rue de Faussets (tel. 05 56 44 89 76). Along the crowded alley; look for vibrant tablecloths, well-matched to the vivid food and sunny owner. 3-course lunch of traditional French food with wine and coffee for 50F. Dinner *menus* from 70F. Open M-Sa noon-2:30pm, and 7:30pm-midnight. V, MC.

■ SIGHTS

All Bordeaux museums are free the first Sunday of every month. For hard-to-find sights, a tourist office guide will be happy to give you directions and a history lesson.

CATHÉDRALE ST-ANDRÉ. Nearly 900 years after its consecration by Pope Urban II, this stunning edifice remains Bordeaux's Gothic masterpiece. Built between the 11th and 16th centuries but sorely neglected in the ensuing decades, the cathedral was extensively renovated in the 19th century. The façade features statues of angels and the apostles and reliefs of the Last Supper and the Ascension. Its belltower, the **Tour Pey-Berland,** juts 63m into the sky. Built in the Italian style of a *campanile*, the tower was placed 15m away from the cathedral because its masons were concerned that the vibrations of the massive bells might cause the cathedral to collapse. Climb all 229 spiraling steps to the top for the view of your life. *(On pl. Pey-Berland. Tel. 05 56 52 68 10. Cathedral open daily Apr.-Oct. 7:30-11:30am and 2-6:30pm; Nov.-Mar. M-F same hours. In the summer, free organ recital every other Tu at 6:30pm. Bell tower open daily July-Aug. 10am-7pm; Sept. and Apr.-June 10am-6pm; Oct.-Mar. 10am-5pm. 25F, under 25 and seniors 15F.)*

PLACE DE LA BOURSE. The white stone, wrought iron façades, and serene fountain of the square exemplify the 18th-century grandeur of Bordeaux under Louis XV. The building on the left houses the **Musée de Douanes,** a must-see if you thrill to titles like *Customs and Customs Officers*. *(Tel. 05 56 52 45 47. Open daily Apr.-Sept. 10am-noon and 1-6pm; Oct.-Mar. M-Sa 10am-noon and 1-5pm.)*

MONUMENT AUX GIRONDINS. This column topped with the joyous **Liberty Statue** commemorates the leaders who drafted the Declaration of the Rights of Man during the Revolution. On either side, water cascades down finely carved statues in the fountains **Le Triomphe de la République** and **Le Triomphe de la Concorde.** The **Jardin Public,** the first public garden in France, provides an idyllic picnic spot a couple of blocks beyond the monument. *(Near the Tourist Office on esplanade de Quinconces. Garden open in summer daily 7am-9pm; in winter daily 7am-6pm.)*

MUSÉE DE BEAUX ARTS. Originally created by Napoleon to house war booty, this spacious gallery covers its walls with canvases by Titian, Delacroix, Renoir, Matisse, and others. There are also impressive collections of 17th-century French, Italian, and Dutch paintings, as well as several rooms of contemporary works. *(20

WHY WINE IS GOOD FOR YOUR HEART

Running a road race, Bordeaux-style, is enough to convert anyone to the maniacal jogging craze. Classier than your average marathon, runners quaff wine from crystal glasses to quench their thirst, indulge in an oyster bar at Mile 24, and snack on buffets of meats and cheeses *en route*. For many participants, the excitement is not so much in crossing the finish line, but in actually finding it.

cours d'Albret, near the cathedral. Tel. 05 56 10 17 18. Open daily 11am-6pm, closed Tu. 20F, students free.) Across the street, the **Galerie des Beaux-Arts,** pl. du Colonel-Raynal (tel. 05 56 96 51 60), features rotating exhibits. *(Open W 10am-12:30pm, 1:30-6pm, and 9-11pm, Th-M 10am-12:30pm and 1:30-6pm. Admission varies from free to 40F.)*

ENTREPÔT LAINE. This houses the **Musée d'Art Contemporain** and the **Arc en Rêve Centre d'Architecture.** The grimy, blocky exterior is a versatile setting for temporary exhibits of modern painting, sculpture, design, and photography, complemented by expositions that focus on specific architects or architectural movements. Muse with coffee (10F) or *plat du jour* (50-60F) at the hip **rooftop café.** *(7 rue Ferrère, two blocks from cours de Maréchal Foch. Musée d'Art Contemporain tel. 05 56 00 81 50; Centre d'Architecture tel. 05 56 52 78 36. Both open Tu-Su 11am-6pm, W 11am-8pm. 30F, students 10F, seniors free. For café, tel. 05 56 44 70 60.)*

OTHER SIGHTS. The colonnaded 18th-century **Grand Théâtre** is worth a visit. Attend one of its numerous operas, concerts, or plays to see the building in all its splendor, or take a daytime tour. *(On pl. de la Comédie. Tel. 05 56 48 30 30. 30F, students 25F.)* The **Musée d'Aquitane** is a historic and ethnographic display of the classical and folk art of Aquitaine from prehistory to the present. *(20 cours Pasteur. Tel. 05 56 01 51 00. Open M 11am-8pm, Tu-Su 11am-6pm. Booklet and video presentations in English. 20F, students free.)* Near the **pont de Pierre,** the city's oldest bridge, the 15th-century **Porte de Cailhau** stands on pl. de Palais, commemorating the victory of Charles VIII at Fornoue. A few blocks down cours Victor Hugo, the imposing 16th-century **Grosse Cloche** stands on rue St-James. Two angels preside over the Big Clock, whose golden hands still keep good time.

♫ ENTERTAINMENT

For an overview of nightlife, pick up a free copy of *Clubs and Concerts* at the tourist office, or purchase the biweekly magazine *Bordeaux Plus* (2F) at any magazine stand. **Pl. de la Victoire** and **pl. Gambetta** are mobbed by 70,000 students during the school year, but are slightly calmer in the summer. Closer to the train station, the dance clubs and pubs in **quai Ste-Croix** and **quai de Paludade** are always packed with leather-clad revellers. After the clubs close, you can eat and drink at **pl. Marché des Capucins** and hang out with early-morning market workers. A word to the wise: stick to the more populated and well-lit main streets. **Connemara Irish Pub,** 18 cours d'Albret (tel. 05 56 52 82 57), near pl. Gambetta, fills its tables with jovial locals, its stage with musicians, and its mugs with nine different beers. (July-Aug. music nightly except Su and W. Open M-Sa noon-2am, Su 6pm-2am.) On the top floor and roof of the Virgin Megastore, the **Mexican Road Café,** 15-19 pl. Gambetta (tel. 05 56 56 05 56), serves snacks to accompany the sunset to a coterie of French teenagers. (Open July-Aug. M-Th 10am-midnight. V, MC.)

BORDEAUX WINERIES AND VINEYARDS

A HISTORY OF CLARET

Bordeaux has cultivated the reputation of its wines through 20 centuries of shameless yet accurate self-promotion. The wines remained a patchwork of colors and qualities until Louis IX snatched the port of La Rochelle from the English in 1226. Not to be deprived of his claret (as the English term red Bordeaux wine), King Henry II bestowed generous shipping rights on English-ruled Bordeaux, making it England's cellar. At first the citizens simply shipped out wines produced farther up the Garonne river, but the riches from this trade sparked a local planting mania. Soon the new wine-makers made laws which conveniently banned wines of other regions from entering the city until English trading ships, loaded with Bordeaux wine, had sailed away for winter. In the 18th century, the vineyards spread out from the Médoc region to the areas south of the Dordogne, including St-Émilion. Today, the wines of Bordeaux flow into 500 million bottles a year.

TASTING IN BORDEAUX

If you're just in Bordeaux for a short time, make a trip to the **Maison du Vin/CIVB,** 1 cours du 30 Juillet (tel. 05 56 00 22 66 or 05 50 00 22 88; fax 05 56 00 22 82), where you can sample—at a price—any of the bottles displayed at the bar and chat with a professional whose job it is to evaluate the quality of new wines. The two-hour "Initiation to Wine Tasting" course, available in English, explores methods for evaluating wines through tasting some of the more outstanding vintages of the region; you'll leave confident enough to waltz into any four-star restaurant. The staff can give you a list of local châteaux and tell you about vineyards you can visit. Ask the receptionist about a 15-minute video on Bordeaux wines. (Open year-round M-Th 8:30am-6pm, F 8:30am-5:30pm. Wine tasting course offered June-Aug. twice weekly, 100F.) Locals buy their wine at **Vinothèque,** 8 cours du 30 Juillet (tel. 05 56 52 32 05; open M-Sa 9:15am-7:30pm), while the owner of the sophisticated **L'Intendant,** 2 allées de Tourny (tel. 05 56 48 01 29), will answer any "wining" questions. (Open M-Sa 10am-7:30pm.)

VISITING THE CHÂTEAUX

While it is easiest to explore the area in your own vehicle, buses and trains do reach a few regional destinations. St-Émilion and Pauillac are both daytrips accessible by train, while the easiest way to get a comprehensive glimpse—and taste—of the wine country is to take one of the Bordeaux tourist office's afternoon **guided tours.** (May-Oct. daily 1:30pm; Nov.-Apr. W and Sa 1:30pm. 160F, students and seniors 140F.) Those with their own transport can visit the major châteaux themselves after a preliminary phone call; the tourist office will help with reservations. Though the region is densely packed with châteaux, bikers and walkers risk getting lost in the tangle of local roads, so arm yourself with a good map. Remember that owners are not in the business of ladling out free wine; choose a few châteaux, call ahead, politely ask if they are open to visitors, and approach your meeting not just as a tourist but as a customer.

ST-ÉMILION. Just 35km northeast of Bordeaux, the viticulters of St-Émilion have been refining their techniques since Roman times, so it's not surprising that their *appellations* are among the best in France. Today, they gently crush 12,850 acres of grapes to produce 23 million liters of wine annually. The **Église Monolithe** is a tribute to the village's most famous inhabitant, the reclusive monk and wine connoisseur Émilion. Shortly after his death in the 8th century, the church was hewn from a cliff face whose caves had been used for religious rites since prehistoric times. For information on tours of the church and a visit to its bell-tower, call the tourist office. The **Maison du Vin de St-Émilion,** pl. Pierre Meyrat (tel. 05 57 55 50 55; fax 05 57 24 65 57), offers a one-hour wine course focused on local wines. The Maison's wine shop has wholesale prices and a free grape exhibit. (Open Mar.-July and Sept.-Nov. M-Sa 10am-12:30pm and 2-6:30pm, Su 10am-12:30pm and 2:30-6:30pm; Aug. daily 10am-7pm; Dec.-Feb. daily 10am-12:30pm and 2:30-6pm. Wine course offered mid-July to mid-Sept. 11am; 100F.)

The **tourist office,** near the church tower at pl. des Créneaux (tel. 05 57 55 28 28; fax 05 57 55 28 28), gives out the *Grandes Heures de St-Émilion,* a list of classical concerts and wine tastings hosted by nearby châteaux. (Office open July-Aug. daily 9:30am-7pm; Sept.-Oct. and Apr.-June 9:30am-12:30pm and 1:45-6:30pm;

THE SOUTHWEST

DON'T STOP THE ROT The wines of Sauterne owe their unique character to a quirk of the local climate. When the weather cools in September, a morning fog rises from the confluence of the Ciron and Garonne rivers, allowing a fungus—*Botrytis Cinerea* or "Noble Rot"—to form on the grapes. As they shrivel up, water evaporates, leaving a high concentration of sugar and a richer, complex taste. Each grape is picked only when it has been well covered in "rot," requiring several meticulous harvestings. Unlike other whites of the regions, these sweet wines take many years to reach their peak, and are only cultivated during years when the climate cooperates.

Nov.-Mar. 9:30am-12:30pm and 1:45-6pm.) As well as renting **bikes** (60F per half-day, 90F per full day), the office also offers **tours** in English to local châteaux (July-Aug. 2 and 4:15pm; June and 1st week of Sept. 3pm.; 51F). **Trains** run from Bordeaux to St-Émilion (30min., 2 per day, 66F). It's the second stop from Bordeaux and the tiny station is poorly marked—don't miss it! To get to the tourist office, take a right on the main road from the station; when you reach the town, head straight up rue-de-la-Porte Bouqueyre toward the tower (2km).

MÉDOC GRAVES, SAUTERNES. The **Médoc** region lies north of Bordeaux, between the Gironde estuary and the ocean—its name comes from the Latin *medio-acquae*, meaning 'between the waters.' This area is home to some of the world's most famous red wines: Lafite-Rothschild, Latour, Margaux, Haut-Brion, and Mouton Rothschild. Without an organized tour, take the Citram bus from the depot to Pauillac, the most renowned village *commune* of the region. The **tourist office** (tel. 05 56 59 03 08; fax 05 56 59 23 38) can help make reservations to visit local châteaux, rent bikes, and suggest routes among the vineyards. (Open June to mid-Aug. 9am-7pm; mid-Aug. to June 9:30am-12:30pm and 2-6:30pm.)

South of the Garonne lies the **Graves** region, named for its gravelly topsoil. Graves was where the wine action was at the time of Eleanor of Aquitaine, before being overtaken by the reds of the Médoc about 300 years ago. Its dry and semi-sweet whites remain most distinctive. In the southeastern end of Graves lies the region of **Sauternes,** celebrated for its sweet white wine.

LES LANDES AND THE CÔTE D'ARGENT

Standing with its tree trunks only kilometers from the sand's edge, the giant pine forest of the Landes de Gascogne tempts and forbids the Atlantic to move inland. For vacationers, the Landes de Gascogne and the neighboring Côte d'Argent are the secrets of the Southwest. Train travelers heading south can see parts of the Landes, but those lucky enough to travel by car or bus will see the dusk dripping off the leaves of the towering trees that dominate the area from just south of Bordeaux to the tip of Bayonne. At the beginning of the 19th century, Napoleon ordered the planting of this forest, which has stabilized the sands and prevented them from moving inland. While the towns of the Landes are less touristed, the Côte d'Argent offers hundreds of miles of beaches to enjoy.

ARCACHON

Between the Ocean and the Landes, Arcachon and nearby Pyla-sur-Mer offer beachcombers two silicon landmarks: the Dune du Pyla, Europe's highest sand dune, and the Banc d'Arguin, a 1000-acre sand bar. Arcachon's popularity dates only from the 1850s, when a Parisian banker invested in a rail line from Bordeaux to the coast. Villas popped up in a vast array of styles as the town gained prestige among vacationing artists, writers, and aristocrats. Quiet in the off-season, Arcachon comes alive in July and August. On Sundays, while Bordeaux sleeps off its weekend wine, the unpretentious and sparkling Arcachon is up early baking bread, shucking oysters, and concocting exotic ice creams.

656 ■ AQUITAINE, THE PAYS BASQUE, AND GASCONY

⚐ ORIENTATION AND PRACTICAL INFORMATION. Trains, pl. Roosevelt, go only to **Bordeaux** (45min.; 16-20 per day; 55F, 26 and under 39F). **Société des Auto-bus d'Arcachon,** 47 bd. Général Leclerc (tel. 05 56 83 07 60), runs bus #611 to nearby **Pyla-sur-Mer** from the shelter in front of the station (20 min.; July-Aug. 15 per day, last return around 6pm; Sept.-June 2 per day; 11F). **Locabeach,** 326 bd. de la Plage (tel. 05 56 83 39 64), rents two-wheeled transportation. (Open Mar.-Sept. daily 9am-midnight; rest of the year call ahead. Bikes 50-60F per day, 35F half-day; 800-1000F or passport deposit. Scooters 80F per day. Motorcycles 125F per day. V, MC.) To get to neighboring **Cap-Ferrat,** site of the nearest youth hostel, you need to take a **ferry** from Arcachon's **Jetée Thiers.** (Tel. 05 56 54 60 32. July-Aug. morning ferries every hour, afternoon every 30min.; Sept.-June every hour all day. 30F, round-trip 50F.)

Arcachon's **tourist office,** pl. Roosevelt (tel. 05 57 52 97 97; fax 05 57 52 97 97), is about three blocks left of the station. A helpful staff distributes maps, festival calendars, brochures, and lists of accommodations. A 24-hour computer terminal lists hotels, restaurants, and sights when the office is closed. (Open July-Aug. M-Sa 9am-12:30pm and 2-6:30pm, Su 9am-1pm; Sept. and June M-Sa 9am-12:30pm and 2-7pm; Oct.-Mar. M-Sa 9am-12:30pm and 2-6pm; Apr.-May M-Sa 9am-12:30pm and 2-6pm, Su 9am-1pm.) An **annex** is located on the corner of bd. Mestrezat and rue des Pêcheries. (Open July-Aug. 9am-7pm.) Wash beach towels at the **Laverie** on the corner of bd. Général Leclerc and rue Molière. (Wash 30F per 7kg; dry 2F per 3min. Open 7am-10pm.) The **police** (tel. 05 57 72 29 30) are on pl. Verdun. The **hospital** is on allée du Dr. Jean Hameau (tel. 05 57 52 90 00). The **post office,** 1 pl. Franklin Roosevelt (tel. 05 57 52 53 80), opposite the tourist office, has **currency exchange** and **Western Union** desk. (Open July-Aug. M-F 8:30am-7pm, Sa 8:30am-noon; Sept.-June M-F 8:30am-6:15pm, Su 8:30am-noon. **Postal code:** 33120.)

⚑ ACCOMMODATIONS. Die-hard beach devotees snap up rooms with meals for the whole season. The cheapest rooms start at 250F in the summer; in the off-season, the entry price of a double drops to 135F. A mellow summer hostel, camping, or cheap bunks in Bordeaux are your best options. The **Auberge de Jeunesse (HI),** 87 av. de Bordeaux (tel. 05 56 60 64 62), is in Cap-Ferrat (see **Orientation and Practical Information,** above). From the Cap-Ferrat ferry pier, take av. de l'Océan and continue as it becomes rue des Bouvreuils after the roundabout (15min.). Turn left onto av. de Bordeaux, and the hostel will appear on the right after a few minutes. (Members 43F. Reception 8am-1pm and 6-9pm. Open July-Aug. only.) In Arcachon, the three-star **Camping Club d'Arcachon,** 1 allée de la Galaxie (tel. 05 56 83 24 15; fax 05 57 52 28 51), 2km from the beach, has a pool, concerts, a bar-restaurant (open June 15-Sept. 15 8am-2am), and a disco. (Site fees for 1-3 people: July-Aug. 110F; June and Sept. 80F; May and Oct. 70F; Nov.-Mar. 65F. V, MC, AmEx.) There are five campsites in **Pyla-sur-Mer,** including **Camping de la Dune,** 300m from the beach on rte. de Biscarrosse. (Tel. 05 56 22 72 17. 2 people with car 130F, extra person 22F; prices 20-40F less off-season. Open May-Sept.)

⚑ FOOD. It would be a crime to leave Arcachon without savoring a few ounces of the 15,000 tons of *huîtres* (oysters) gathered here annually. Beach cafés line **av. Gambetta** and **bd. de la Plage,** offering copious seafood platters and 50F *moules frites* (mussels-'n'-fries). **Le Gambetta,** 25 rue Gambetta (tel. 05 57 52 29 69), serves 75F *plats de pêcheur,* a 75F *menu,* and pasta for 30-40F. (Open daily noon-3pm and 7-11pm. V, MC.) The **Leclerc supermarket** stands at 224 bd. de la Plage. (Tel. 05 56 83 25 21. Open July-Aug. M-Sa 9am-8pm, Su 9am-1pm; Sept.-June M-Th 9am-12:30pm and 2:30-7:30pm, F-Sa 9am-7:30pm. V, MC.) A **market** on pl. Lucien-de-Gracia overflows with cartfuls of fresh produce and homemade specialties. (Summer daily 9am-1pm indoors and out; winter daily indoors, Sa outdoors.)

⚑ SIGHTS AND ENTERTAINMENT. The appeal of the Arcachon region's sand megaliths has not washed away with the tide. In **Pyla-sur-Mer,** the golden sand of the Dune du Pyla rests between the pure and endless forest to the east and the blue hues of the Atlantic to the west. Many like to run down the 117m-high dune, knee-deep in immaculate sand, but beware once you reach the bottom; a strong undertow makes swimming at the foot of the dune forbidden. Farther along the water, there are beaches for those both with and *sans* suits. Sailboats are available for rent on the beach. From the bus stop in Pyla-sur-Mer, head down bd. de l'Océan and take the first right. Follow the same road for about 20 minutes and the Dune area will be on the right. The **École Professionnelle de Vol Libre du Pyla (EPVLP)** offers **parasailing** and **hang gliding** off the dune; details at the tourist office. (Tel. 05 56 22 15 02. 400F per flight, 2400F per week.)

Arcachon's bird sanctuaries and nature parks also attract flocks of tourists. **UBA boats** (tel. 05 56 54 60 32 or 05 56 54 83 01) leave for **Arguin Sandbar** from the Jetée Thiers pier at 11am and return at 4 or 5pm, weather permitting (70F). The same company also offers trips to the oyster beds (55F) and around an island bird sanctuary (daily 2:30pm, 70F). About 15km put of town, the **Parc Ornithologique du Teich** (tel. 05 56 22 69 43) shelters 260 species of birds in one of France's most important sanctuaries. (Open summer daily 10am-10pm; off-season 10am-8pm. 33F.)

The **Ville d'Hiver,** an arboreal district of turn-of-the-century villas, lies across from the **Parc Mauresque** north of the beach. The neighborhood's curving streets were designed to block ocean winds; this "winter village" is 2°C warmer on average than its beachfront counterpart. The villas, whose builders' tastes swung from Swiss chalet to pseudo-Gothic castle, are accessible on your own or via **guided tours** from the tourist office. (June-Sept. Tu-F 10:30am, call for reservation. 20F.) The **Ste-Écile** observatory, near the park, offers a stunning view of Arcachon and its surroundings for those who brave the spiral staircase. (Open 9am-7pm. Free.)

Summer nights in Arcachon heat up as the beaches cool down with several discos on the beachfront and the **Casino d'Arcachon,** which looks like a fairy-tale palace. Slot machines, a bar, and more discos await at the **Casino de la Plage,** 163 bd. de la Plage (tel. 05 56 83 41 44), open daily. For a quieter evening and a movie, head for cinema **Le Paris,** 6 rue du Port (tel. 05 56 83 28 40).

MIMIZAN-PLAGE

Mimizan is the secret attraction of the Côte d'Argent. Split in two, with Mimizan Ville nestling inland and Mimizan-Plage hogging the coast, its sparkling water and rainbow sunsets attract vacationers. While not the cheapest of beach resorts to stay in, early risers can make it an easy daytrip from Bordeaux.

🛈 PRACTICAL INFORMATION. Mimizan has no train station; instead buses wind here through the tranquil forest of the Landes. The **Rapides de la Côte d'Argent** (tel. 05 58 09 10 89; fax 05 58 09 20 42) travel to and from the Gare St-Jean in **Bordeaux** to the Mimizan tourist office (2½hr.; July-Aug. 3 per day, 48F; Sept.-June 2 per day, 39F), while **RDTL** (tel. 05 58 09 10 89) runs buses to Mimizan from the *gare* in **Bayonne** (3-4hr., 1 per day, 93F). The **tourist office,** 38 av. Maurice Martin (tel. 05 58 09 11 20; fax 05 58 09 40 31), on the left when leaving the bus station on the corner, distributes maps; when it's closed, the electronic map outside the door can tell you the easiest path to hotels, restaurants, and entertainment. (Open July-Aug. M-Sa 9am-7pm, Su 10am-1pm; Sept.-June M-F 9am-noon and 3-6pm, Su 9am-noon.) **Bikes** and **skates** are for rent at **Cyclo-land,** 8 rue du Casino. (Tel. 05 58 09 16 65. Open M-Sa 10am-6pm. 35F per day, 150F per week. ID/passport deposit.) There is an **infirmary** (tel. 05 58 07 41 75) at 56 av. du Parc d'Hiver, Trouve Dominique. The **police** (tel. 05 58 09 00 17) are on rue du College. The **post office** (tel. 05 58 09 05 00) is on rue des Écoles. (Open M-F 9am-noon and 2-6pm. **Postal code:** 40200.)

🛈 ACCOMMODATIONS. Most hotels in Mimizan extort 330-600F per room, but if you reserve they needn't burn too large a hole in your pocket. Campers can pitch their tents at one of the campsites lining the beach. Despite its name, the best views from the **Hôtel le Bellevue,** 34 av. Maurice Martin (tel. 05 58 09 05

23; fax 05 58 09 19 15), are of the beautiful interior, with impressive wood furniture, large beds, hall mirrors, and a third floor lounge. A great location, too, 100m from the beach on the liveliest street in town. (Singles and doubles 157F, with shower 171F, with toilet and shower 178F. Hall showers and toilets. Reception 8am-midnight. V, MC.) Uphill from the bus station on the street closest to the beach is **Hôtel Atlantique,** 38 av. de la Côte d'Argent (tel. 05 58 09 09 42; fax 05 58 82 42 63). With the cheapest rooms on the beach, this quiet hotel's light pinks and blues soothe the sunbeaten traveler in cool rooms with shutters and plentiful hot water. The elegant restaurant downstairs serves copious dinners from 75F. (Sept.-June singles and doubles 130F, with shower 165F. Breakfast 35F. July-Aug. obligatory half-board; singles and doubles 350F per person, with shower 430F. Reception 8am-11:30pm.)

◨◪ **FOOD AND ENTERTAINMENT.** Avenue **Maurice Martin** is the busiest street for **food,** with several small restaurants on the way up to the ocean. There are plenty of pizzerias in Mimizan, but none combines the casual with the classic as well as ◪ **Piccola Italia,** where you can eat on the balcony accompanied by the sound of waves. Pastas and pizzas cost 20-85F. (Open Th-M noon-2:30pm and 6-11pm.) Craving traditional french fare? Try **La Goelette,** 30 av. de la Côte d'Argent (tel. 05 58 09 05 25), with *menus* from 55F and *à la carte* dishes for 25-65F.

During the day, Mimizan's action is mostly confined to the beaches which stretch north and south of the Courant river, but at night it moves down to av. Maurice Martin. Here **Cinema Le Rex** (tel. 05 58 09 37 40) runs movies in French and sometimes in English. (Open F-Su.) The brave can watch the *Côte* take their *argent* at the **Casino de la Côte d'Argent,** 1 rue du Casino. (Tel. 05 58 09 05 02. Open noon-4am. Minimum age 18.) The wildest hours are between midnight and 5am, when fun-lovers dance the sand off by Mimizan's southern beach to salsa, samba, funk, or disco at **Le Mambo,** 2 av. de la Jetée (tel. 05 58 09 47 54). Farther north on rue Assolant Lefèvre, crowds swing till sunrise at **Blue Cat** (tel. 05 58 09 47 24) and **Le Roxy** (tel. 05 58 09 10 52).

ANGLET

If you've been looking for waves or just a couple miles of perfect white beaches, you'll find them in Anglet (pronounced with a hard "t")—and so have hordes of sweaty, smoking, surfing youngsters. Ideally located between Bayonne and Biarritz, and linked to them during the day by efficient STAB buses, Anglet is the surfing capital of France. Home to the only hostel within 100km (and what a hostel it is!), you'll find plenty of fun here in the summer sun.

◪ **PRACTICAL INFORMATION.** The **tourist office,** 1 av. de Chambre d'Amour on pl. Leclerc (tel. 05 59 03 77 01; fax 05 59 03 55 91), is well-equipped to direct ventures in the region. (Open July-Sept. M-Sa 9am-7pm; Oct.-June M-F 9am-12:15pm and 1:45-6pm, Sa 9am-12:15pm.) Schedules and maps of the Biarritz-Anglet-Bayonne **STAB** bus network are available on buses, from the tourist office, or from the the hostel. Tickets (7.50F) are good for one hour. **Currency exchange** at decent rates is available at **BNP,** pl. Leclerc. (Tel. 05 59 03 89 42. Open Tu-Sa 8am-noon and 1:45-5pm.) You can rent **bikes** at **V Tonic,** route des Pontots. (Tel. 05 59 52 36 48. Open Tu-Sa 9:30am-12:30pm and 2:30-7:30pm.) For laundry, head to **Lavomatic,** at plage Chambre d'Amour, 21 av. du Rayon Vert. (Wash 5kg for 20F, dry 5min. for 2F. Open daily 7am-10pm.) **Tides** are printed in *Calendrier des Marées,* available free at the tourist office. In the absence of **lifeguards** at night (7pm-10am), call the **fire department** for beach emergencies (tel. 18). The **police** are at 5 rue du 8 Mai (tel. 05 59 63 84 64), but are closed all night. The **post office** is inconveniently located near the *mairie* at 7 rue du 8 Mai (tel. 05 59 58 08 40). A branch is at pl. Leclerc (tel. 05 59 03 88 63), next to the tourist office. (**Postal code:** 64600.)

BASQUING IN ISOLATION Linguists cannot pinpoint the origin of the Basques' language *euskara*. Some have tried to find links with Egyptian, the Caucasian and Semitic languages, and even the North American languages, only to discover that there is absolutely no connection. In reality, *euskara* is the only living language in Western Europe not based on the Indo-European tongue. Today, *euskara*, a minority language struggling for survival, has become a symbol of cultural self-determination. It currently has only about half a million speakers, but the number of those who speak it as a second language is spreading, thanks in part to *ikastolas* schools.

ACCOMMODATIONS AND CAMPING. Anglet overflows with sun-seekers in the summer, so you might consider storing your surfboard overnight in Biarritz or Bayonne. The ■ **Auberge de Jeunesse (HI)**, 19 rte. des Vignes (tel. 05 59 58 70 00; fax 05 59 58 70 07), lies 600m directly uphill from plage de Marinella. From the Hôtel de Ville in Biarritz, take bus #4 to "Auberge" (direction "Bayonne Sainsontain," every 50min.). From pl. de la République or pl. de Réduit in Bayonne, take bus #4 to "La Barre," then bus #9 to "Auberge." This well-equipped and carefree hostel is a hub of French surfing subculture and temporary home to 80 tanned youth. From Easter to October, you can dine for 15-29F at the bar downstairs. (Dorm beds 80F July-Sept.; 73F Oct.-June. Sheets 23F. Breakfast included. Kitchen facilities only available Sept.-Mar. You can also camp for 56F. Reception open 8:30am-10pm. No lockout or curfew. Check-out 10am. Reservations with deposit required July-Aug.) The **Camping Fontaine Laborde,** 17 allée Fontaine Laborde (tel. 05 59 03 48 16), is shaded, near the beach, and caters to the young and surfing. Take bus #4 to Fontaine Laborde, just down the road from the hostel. (27F per person, 25F per site, 18F per car. Reception all night, unless they fall asleep.)

FOOD. Restaurants line the Sables d'Or beach, serving global food at affordable prices. Fantastic *crêpes*, with fillings from cheese to ice cream, are a steal at 10-20F at **La Pointe du Raz.** (Tel. 05 59 03 10 83. Open daily Tu-Sa noon-3pm and 7pm-midnight, Su noon-midnight.) At night head to Anglet's little Acapulco, **El Mexicano,** the hottest restaurant-bar on the Sables D'Or, serving unexpectedly authentic Mexican food. (Open until 1am. Food 30-70F, drinks 10-25F.) If you tire of the beach, head down to Anglet's main square, **Cinq Cantons.** Here **El Rocio** (tel. 05 59 03 54 99) offers drinks, tapas, bocadillos, and sandwiches at digestible prices. (Open daily 7am-8pm.) You can also pick up a picnic from nearby *boulangeries* (baguettes 5F) and *pâtisseries* (pastries 4F).

SIGHTS. Anglet's *raison d'être* is its 4km of fine-grained white sand, parcelled out into nine beaches. Each has its own name and personality, from the perfect waves of the **plage Les Cavaliers** to the rocky jetty of the **Chambre d'Amour,** where two legendary lovers perished when the tide came in. Swimmers should know that along with the beauty of the crashing tides comes a strong cross-current undertow. When in doubt, swim under the watchful eye of a lifeguard (at all beaches but Chambre d'Amour and plage de l'Océan).

TURF'N'SURF. For walking or jogging, the **Fôret du Chilberta's** pine-needle covered trails are easy on the knees. To get there, take STAB line #7 or 9 to Pignada. Anglet also offers many opportunities for less strenuous activities—just watch the water-borne circus from the sands. Professional surf competitions are all fun and free for spectators. Mid-June brings the three-day **France Championship,** while the traveling **O'Neill Surf Challenge** takes up residence for five days at the end of August, around the same time as the **Europe Bodyboard Championship.** The last major event of the year is the **Europe Surfing Championship,** three days in mid-September. You can prepare your title challenge with help from the **Rainbow Surfshop** (tel. 05 59 03 54 67), 10 minutes from the beach at 19-21 av. Chambre d'Amour. Here you can rent a colorful spectrum of bodyboards (40F per half-day, 100F per day; 1000F deposit), surfboards (60F per half-day, 100F per day; 2000F deposit), and wet-suits (30F per half-day, 50F per day; 1000F deposit). Surf lessons for one or two people cost 170F for the first hour and 150F for each subsequent hour. (Open daily Apr.-Oct. 9:30am-8pm.)

BAYONNE

The city that introduced bayonets to the world in the 18th century engages in less belligerent pursuits today. With its prominent position on the Gulf of Gascony, close to the Spanish border, Bayonne (pop. 43,000) has retained its grand port status and maintains its small-town appeal. Hemingway, characteristically terse, mused that "Bayonne is a nice town. It is like a very clean Spanish town, and it is on a big river." Lively markets crowd the riverbanks of the Nive, and along the back streets of Petit-Bayonne, conversations and laughter stream out of open apartment windows and small bars.

☒ ORIENTATION AND PRACTICAL INFORMATION

Two merging rivers split Bayonne into three main areas. **St-Esprit,** on the northern side of the **Adour,** contains the train station and pl. de la République. The pont St-Esprit arches across the Adour to **Petit-Bayonne,** site of Bayonne's museums, inexpensive hotels, lively bars, and restaurants. Five small bridges cross the **Nive** and connect Petit-Bayonne to **Grand-Bayonne** on the west bank. The oldest part of town, Grand-Bayonne has a buzzing pedestrian zone lined with red-shuttered houses (*arceaux*) over shops and *pâtisseries.* The center of town is manageable on foot, and an excellent bus system makes Anglet and Biarritz a snap to visit. To get to the tourist office from the train station, take the middle fork onto pl. de la République, veer right over the pont St-Esprit, and continue through pl. Réduit to the next bridge (pont Mayou). Cross pont Mayou, turn right onto rue Bernède, which soon becomes av. Bonnat, and turn left onto pl. des Basques (15min.).

Trains: Pl. de la République (tel. 05 59 55 50 50). To: **Paris** (5½hr., 7 TGVs per day, 406-456F); **Bordeaux** (1½-2½hr., 9 per day, 130-138F); **Toulouse** (4hr., 5 per day, 190F); and **Biarritz** (10min., 22 per day, 12F). Info office open July-Aug. daily 9am-7:15pm; Sept.-June M-Sa 9:15-11:45am and 2-6:45pm.

Local Transport: STAB, Hôtel de Ville (tel. 05 59 59 04 61). Open M-Sa 8am-noon and 1:30-6pm. Pick up a bus map here or at tourist offices. Lines #1, 2, and 6 serve **Biarritz;** line #4 serves **Biarritz** via **Anglet.** Every 30-40min. Last bus in any direction around 8pm (7pm on Su). Tickets 7.50F, *carnet* of 10 62F.

Taxis: Bayonne Radio Taxi (tel. 05 59 59 48 48). 24hr.

Tourist Office: Pl. des Basques (tel. 05 59 46 01 46; fax 05 59 59 37 55). Free city map and help finding rooms. Pick up the free *Fêtes en Pays Basque* and *Les Clés de la Ville.* Tours of various aspects of the city. Open July-Aug. M-Sa 9am-7pm, Su 10am-1pm; Sept.-June M-F 9am-6:30pm, Sa 10am-6pm. **Branch office** at the train station (tel. 05 59 55 20 45) open July-Aug. M-Sa 9am-12:30pm and 2-6pm.

Tours: The tourist office organizes 2hr. walking tours in English of old Bayonne in summer (July-Aug., Th 10am, 30F). For a different perspective, **Promenade en Bateau** (tel. 05 59 47 77 17) runs boat trips along the river. Departures July-Aug. 10am and 2:45 and 5pm; Sept.-June 2:45 and 5pm. 80F. Reservation required.

Budget Travel: Pascal Voyages, 8 allées Boufflers (tel. 05 59 25 48 48). BIJ and other student-priced tickets. Open M-F 8:30am-6:30pm, Sa 9am-noon.

Money: Or et Change, 1 rue Jules Labat (tel. 05 59 25 58 59), in Grand-Bayonne. No commission, good rates. Open M-Sa 10am-12:30pm and 1:30-7pm.

Laundromat: Salon Lavoir, 7 rue Douer at pl. Montaut. 24F for 7kg wash; dryers 2F per 5min. Open M-Sa 9:30am-7pm.

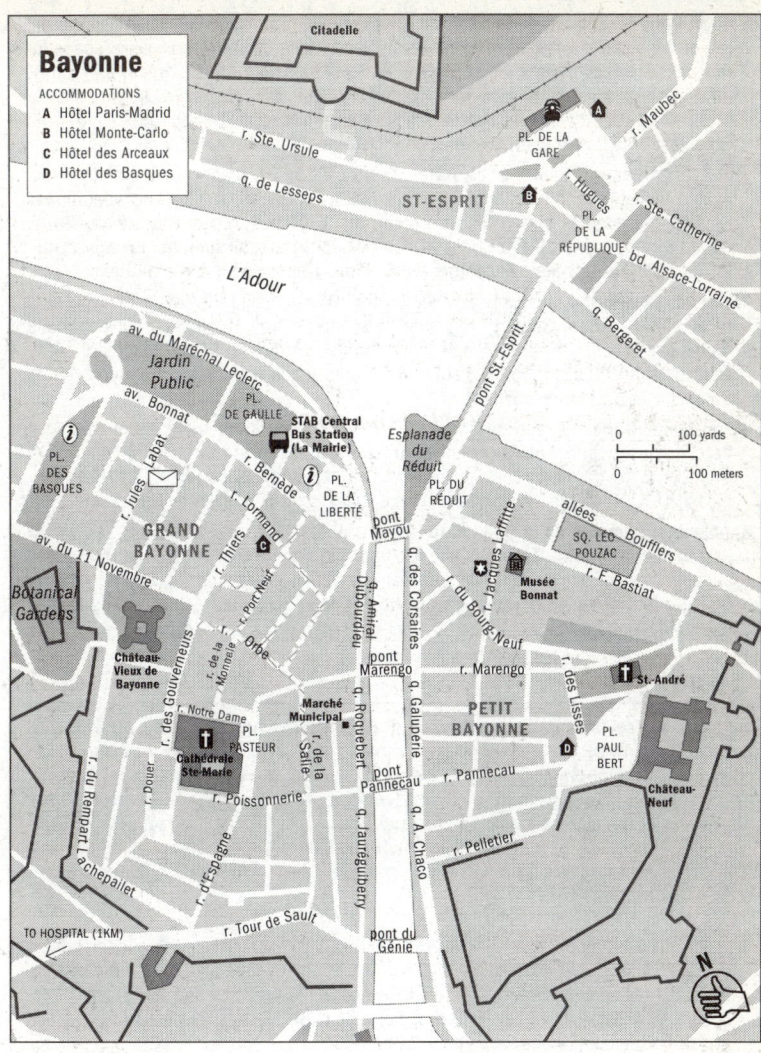

Bayonne

ACCOMMODATIONS
A Hôtel Paris-Madrid
B Hôtel Monte-Carlo
C Hôtel des Arceaux
D Hôtel des Basques

Youth Info: BIJ, 16 rue Pontrique (tel. 05 59 59 35 29). Open M-Sa 10am-7pm.

Police: Av. de Marhum (tel. 05 59 46 22 22).

Hospital: 13 av. Interne Jacques Loëb (tel. 05 59 44 35 35), St-Léon.

Post Office: 11 rue Jules Labat (tel. 05 59 46 33 60), Grand-Bayonne. **Currency exchange.** Poste restante code: 64181. Open M-F 8am-6pm, Sa 10am-noon. **Branch office,** bd. Alsace-Lorraine, has same hours. **Postal code:** 64100.

▰ ACCOMMODATIONS AND CAMPING

In the **St-Esprit** area, lodgings dot the train station area. The hotels in Grand-Bayonne are usually more expensive; in Petit-Bayonne, hunt around **pl. Paul Bert.** Reserve ahead in July and August. The closest hostel is in Anglet, a 20-minute bus ride away (see p. 658).

Hôtel Paris-Madrid, pl. de la Gare (tel. 05 59 55 13 98; fax 05 59 55 07 22), to the left of the station. A hotel but more like a home. Cozy, personalized rooms; space for families. Gracious owners speak English and will help with transportation and tourist info. TV/reading room. Singles and doubles 95-125F, with shower 150F, with shower and toilet 170F; triples and quads with shower and toilet 235-250F. Hall shower 5F. Breakfast 25F. Reception July-Sept. 24hr.; Oct.-June 6am-12:30am. V, MC.

Hôtel des Arceaux, 26 rue Port Neuf (tel. 05 59 59 15 53). The location, the newly renovated rooms, and the plants filling the hall make up for the sloping hardwood floors. Singles and doubles 130-160F, with bathroom 180-190F; triples with shower 200F; quads with shower 330. Extra beds 40F per person. Free hall showers. Breakfast 30F. Prices 10% less Oct.-May. Reception M-F 7:30am-10pm, Sa-Su 8:30am-10pm.

Hôtel des Basques, 4 rue des Lisses (tel. 05 59 59 08 02), in Petit-Bayonne. If you want to be close to the nightlife of Bayonne bars, this is for you. Minimal but enormous rooms overlook pl. Paul Bert. Singles and doubles 135F, with TV and bathroom 160F, extra person 60F each; triples 170F; triples and quads with TV and bathroom 230F. Breakfast 25F. 24hr. reception.

Hôtel Monte-Carlo, 11 rue Hugues (tel. 05 59 55 02 68), to the right of the *gare*. This hotel's garishly pink hallways and rooms are a useful place to shake off the sand. Check-in at the bar next door. Singles 90-130F, with shower and toilet 150-160F; doubles 120-150F; quads 220F. Free showers. Breakfast 24F. Reception 6am-2am.

Campsites: Camping de la Chêneraie (tel. 05 59 55 01 31; fax 05 59 55 11 17), on RN117, north of town. Take bus line #1 from the *gare* or tourist office to the Leclerc supermarket; the site is 2km away (buses every 12min.). 4-star facility. 26F per person, 58F per tent or car, 62F with caravan. Open Easter-Sept. 8am-10pm. Prices slightly lower May-June and Sept.

FOOD

The narrow streets of Petit-Bayonne, and to a lesser extent St-Esprit, offer 50-60F *menus* of *jambon de Bayonne* (dry cured ham) and *poulet à la basquaise* (chicken with peppers and onions). Grand-Bayonne, the city's cloth-napkin zone, serves regional specialties in a less budget-oriented atmosphere. Vendors show their wares at the **marché municipal,** on quai Roquebert (M 7:30am-1pm, Tu-Th 7am-1pm, F 6:30am-1:30pm and 3:30-7pm, Sa 6am-1:30pm and 3:30-7pm). There is a Monoprix **supermarket** at 8 rue Orbe. (Tel. 05 59 59 00 33. Open M-F 8:30am-7:30pm, Sa 8am-7:30pm. V, MC.)

Le Bistrot Ste-Cluque, 9 rue Hugues (tel. 05 59 55 82 43). Among the wooden tables, delicate glasses, and sophisticated colors, you'll forget you're across from the station. Delicious regional cuisine with attentive service, huge portions, and an elegant atmosphere. Also has a small bar. Ever-changing 55F menu. Duck 55F, paella 65F, big salads 40F. Open daily noon-2pm and 7-11pm. V, MC.

Bodega El Rio, 23 quai Jauréguiberry (tel. 05 59 59 05 46), offers a brief retreat into Spain, complete with frequent live music and a huge bull's head mounted on the wall. *Plats* start at 45F. 85F *menu.* Open Tu-Su noon-2pm and 7-11pm. V, MC.

Chocolat Cazenave Tea Room, 19 Arceaux Port-Neuf (tel. 05 59 59 03 16), in the arcades. A spot for dessert in the town which introduced chocolate to France. Traditional liquid model with whipped cream 24F, sinful cinnamon chocolate with hot buttered toast 41.50F; ice cream, too. Open M-Sa 9am-noon and 2-7pm. V, MC.

SIGHTS

The 13th-century **Cathédrale Ste-Marie,** whose spiny steeples bite into Bayonne's skies, intimidates from afar and impresses from within. The church weathered a brief stint as a cemetery in the 16th century, suffered massive destruction during the Revolution, and has endured sporadic fires. Inside, the chapel of St. Jerome

JUST NOT CRICKET
In the Pays Basque, the sport known as *Pelote Basque* includes a number of games under its name. *Cesta punta*, or *jai alai*, is the world's fastest ball game. Burly players hurl a hard ball at speeds up to 200km per hour at a wall by means of a *chistera* (basket appendage) laced to the wrist. Outdoor *Fronton* arenas and indoor *trinqiuets* bear witness to local players' speed and skill. Spreading beyond its homeland, *Pelote Basque* fever has caught on in such places as Cancun, Cuba, and Connecticut. But watch out ladies: so far, only men have played.

depicts Christ driving the devil from a girl. Enter the large, graceful cloister at pl. Pasteur. (Cloister open daily 9:30am-12:30pm and 2-5pm; Easter-Oct. until 6pm. Free. Church open M-Sa 10am-noon and 3-6pm, Su 3:30-6pm.) Currently occupied by the French Foreign Legion, **Château-Vieux de Bayonne,** on nearby av. du 11 Novembre, is a well-kept blond stone block which has housed such notorious villains as Don Pedro of Castille. The avenue continues to Bayonne's vast, grassy **fortifications,** where you can lose yourself within the ageless walls.

Next to the **Monument aux Morts** on av. du 11 Novembre, Bayonne's refreshing **botanical gardens** will entice you out of the city with 1000 species of Japanese flora. (Open Apr. 15-Oct. 15 daily 9:30am-12:30pm and 2-6pm.)

The Rubens room at the **Musée Bonnat,** 5 rue Jacques Laffitte (tel. 05 59 59 08 52), in Petit-Bayonne, is filled with lecherous mythical men. Downstairs, discover nude folk painted by Bonnat himself, a celebrated 19th-century *bayonnais* painter who gave his collection to the city and directed the construction of the museum. Highlights include a ghoulish El Greco and a grim Goya. (Open W-M 10am-noon and 2:30-6:30pm, F until 8:30pm. 20F, students 10F.)

For sandier delights, try the **Metro plage** in Tarnos; take bus M all the way.

🎵 🌺 ENTERTAINMENT AND FESTIVALS

Mid-July brings two new reasons to visit Bayonne; while the **Marché Médiéval** reprises the past in costume behind the cathedral, the **Jazz aux Remparts** festival lures musical immortals. Call the **Théâtre Municipale** (tel. 05 59 59 07 27) for tickets. (Ticket office open Tu-Sa 1-7pm. 160-210F per night, students 100-160F, under 12 30F.) The orchestra **Harmonie Bayonnaise** stages gentler jazz and traditional Basque music concerts in the pl. de Gaulle gazebo Thursdays at 9:30pm in July and August (free). After the first Tuesday in August, unrestrained hedonism breaks out with the **Fêtes traditionelles** as the *bayonnais* immerse themselves in five days of concerts, fandangos, bullfights, fireworks, and a chaotic race between junk heaps masquerading as boats. In August and early September, Bayonne holds several bullfights in the large **Plaza de Toros.** Seats (75-470F) sell out fast, but cheap places in the nose-bleed section should be available on fight days. For ticket information, call Bureau Information Spectacle, rue Bernede, Bayonne (tel. 05 59 46 61 00; fax 05 59 46 61 01). For a wonderful selection of films, head to **L'Atalante,** 7 rue Denis Etcheverry (tel. 05 59 55 76 63), in St-Esprit. (37F, 6pm show 32F, students 25F; closed most of July and early Aug.)

BIARRITZ

Wandering through Biarritz (pop. 29,000) in the late evening, as Jaguars and Mercedes prowl narrow streets and the sound of crashing waves mixes with music, laughter, and clinking silverware, you may feel as if you've just walked into the pages of *The Great Gatsby*. Originally a whaling village at the base of the Pyrenees, Biarritz has come to embody all that is regal. A stroll up the main avenue illustrates Victor Hugo's prophetic lament that his one fear was that Biarritz would become "fashionable." With the first blossoms of pink and blue hortensias, the city emerges from its off-season hibernation and regains its sparkle as casinos welcome the first waves of tourists. While Biarritz is not a budget traveler's dream-come-true, a little ingenuity renders it accessible to everyone; the town where Napoleon III, Bismarck, and Queen Victoria summered has now acquired cheap snack bars and reasonably priced hotels.

☷ ORIENTATION AND PRACTICAL INFORMATION

Getting to Biarritz is not as easy as it was in the grand old days, when trains glided into the now-deserted station. Today, they roll only as far as **Biarritz-la-Négresse,** 3km away. To get to the *centre ville,* take blue bus #2 (direction "Bayonne via Biarritz"; every 20-40min. in summer 6:30am-9pm) or green bus #9 (direction "Biarritz HDV"; in summer 6:30am-7pm). To walk into town from Biarritz-la-Négresse, turn left onto allée du Moura, which becomes av. du Président Kennedy. Turn left a few kilometers later onto av. du Maréchal Foch, which continues to **pl. Clemenceau,** Biarritz's main square. Or, get off the train in **Bayonne** and hop a bus #1 or 2 to Biarritz's Hôtel de Ville (30min., 7.50F). From the Hôtel de Ville, the tourist office on pl. d'Ixelles is a brief walk up rue J. Petit. To get to pl. de Clemenceau, take av. Edouard VII uphill from the bus stop.

Flights: Aéroport de Parme, bd. Marcel Dassault (tel. 05 59 43 83 83). M-Sa take bus #6 from Hôtel de Ville, to "Parme Aéroport" (every 30 min. 7am-7pm), Su take bus B. **Ryanair** (UK tel. 01279 680500) has flights to **London** starting at 490F.

Trains: Biarritz-la-Négresse (tel. 05 59 24 00 94). To: **Bayonne** (10min., 10 per day, 13F); **Pau** (2hr., 4 per day, 96F); **Toulouse** (4½hr., 4 per day, 197F); **Bordeaux** (2hr., 8 per day, 189F); and **Paris** (8hr., 5hr. by TGV, 7 per day, 410-460F). **SNCF info office** in Biarritz, 1 rue Étienne Ardoin (tel. 05 59 24 00 94). Open M-F 9am-noon and 2-6pm.

Buses: ATCRB, rue Joseph Petit (tel. 05 59 26 06 99), next to the tourist office. Buy tickets on the bus. **Les Cars Basques,** 18 pl. Clemenceau (tel. 05 59 24 05 00), next to Hôtel le Président. Buy tickets at their office. Open daily 10am-noon and 3-6pm.

Local Transportation: STAB serves the Bayonne, Anglet, and Biarritz area. Kiosk with maps and schedules on rue Louis-Barthou, near the tourist office. Tickets (7.50F) good for 1hr. *Carnets* of 10 62F, 52F for students during school year. Main office on Chemin de la Marouette (tel. 05 59 52 59 52).

Taxis: Atlantic Taxi Radio (tel. 05 59 03 18 18). 24hr.

Bike and Scooter Rental: SOBILO, 24 rue Peyroloubilh (tel. 05 59 24 94 47). Bikes 70F per day, 420F per week; 1000F or credit card deposit. Scooters from 200F per day, 2000F per week; 10.000F deposit. Motorbikes 200-350F per day; 6000F deposit. Open May-Sept. daily 9am-1pm and 3-6pm; Oct.-Apr. Sa-Su 9am-1pm and 3-6pm.

Surfboard Rental: Rip Curl Surf Shop, 2 av. Reine Victoria (tel. 05 59 24 38 40), 1 block from Grande Plage. 50-60F per half-day, 80-100F per day; ID deposit. Open Sept.-June M-Sa 10am-12:30pm and 3-7pm; July-Aug. M-Sa 10am-8pm, Su 3-7pm.

Tourist Office: 1 sq. d'Ixelles (tel. 05 59 22 37 10; fax 05 59 24 14 19), off av. Edouard VII. Staff will track down rooms or campsites. Pick up the free *Biarritzcope* for monthly events listings. Open daily June-Sept. 8am-8pm; Oct.-May 9am-6:45pm.

Money: Change Plus, 9 rue Mazagran (tel. 05 59 24 82 47). Fair rates, no commission. Open M-Sa 8am-8pm, Su 10am-1pm; Sept.-June M-F 9am-12:30pm and 2-7pm. **American Express,** 8 pl. Clemenceau (tel. 05 59 22 13 14). Open Tu-Sa 9am-12:30pm and 2-6pm; July 15-Sept. 15 M-F 10am-1pm and 2:30-7pm, Sa-Su 10am-2pm and 4-7pm.

Laundromat: Le Lavoir, 4 av. Jaulerry, by the post office. Open daily 7am-9pm.

Beach Emergencies: Grande Plage (tel. 05 59 24 92 70). Plage Marabella (tel. 05 59 23 01 20). Plage de la Milady (tel. 05 59 23 63 93).

Police: Rue Louis-Barthou (tel. 05 59 24 68 24).

Hospital: Private clinic in Biarritz, **Polyclinique d'Aguilera,** 21 rue Estagnas (tel. 05 59 22 46 22). **L'Hôpital de Bayonne,** av. Jacques Loëb (tel. 05 59 44 35 35).

Post Office: 21 rue de la Poste (tel. 05 59 22 41 10). **Currency exchange.** Open M-F 8:30am-7pm, Sa 8:30am-noon. **Postal code:** 64200.

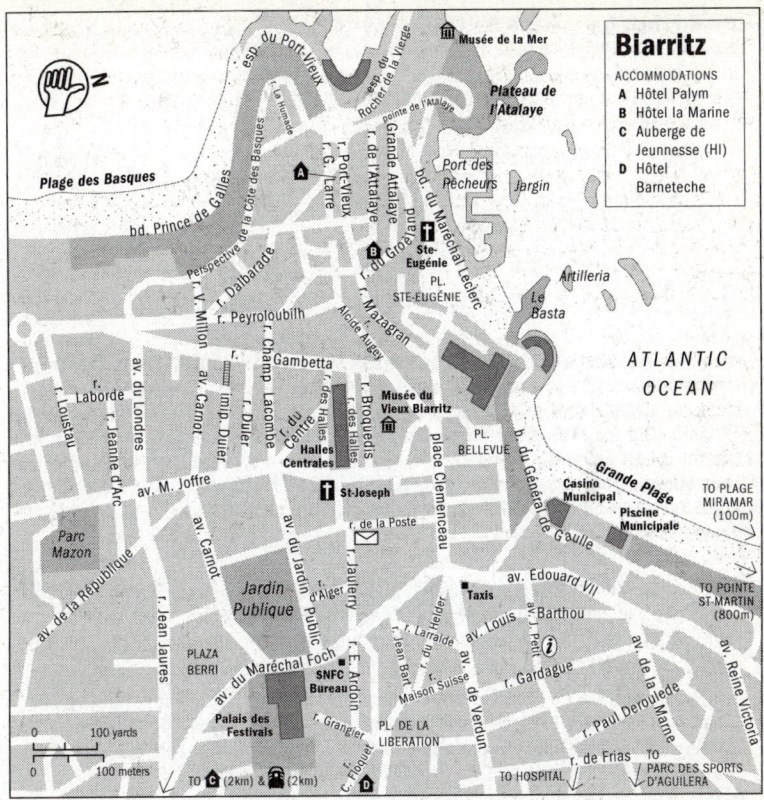

Biarritz

ACCOMMODATIONS
A Hôtel Palym
B Hôtel la Marine
C Auberge de Jeunesse (HI)
D Hôtel Barneteche

ACCOMMODATIONS AND CAMPING

Bargains do exist in Biarritz. A new deluxe hostel has opened near the train station. For more central accommodations, write a month ahead for July or August, or enlist the help of the tourist office. Rue du Port-Vieux houses a bunch of budget hotels. All the hotels below are centrally located.

Auberge de Jeunesse (HI), 8 rue de Chiquito de Cambo (tel. 05 59 41 76 00; fax 05 59 41 76 07). Turn left uphill from the train station. At the rotary, turn left and follow rue des Movettes along the steep hill as it turns right. The hostel is across the street at the bottom. In keeping with the standards of Biarritz, it offers amenities like tanning lamps. The friendly staff and lakefront location make the 40min. walk to Biarritz worth it. Restaurant (dishes 20-30F). Singles and doubles 90F per person; triples and quads 82F. Sheets 35F. Breakfast included. Prices slightly lower Oct.-June. **Members only.**

Hôtel Barnetche, 5bis rue Charles-Floquet (tel. 05 59 24 22 25; fax 05 59 24 98 71), in the *centre ville*. Spic'n'span rooms and energetic owner. 12-bed dorm room (100F per person, no meal obligations) is the best deal in town. Doubles 260F, with shower 320F, with full bathroom 350F; triples and quads 140F per person. Free hall showers. Obligatory breakfast 35F. In Aug., obligatory *demi-pension* 90F extra per person, but the food is worth it. Reception open 7:30am-11pm. English spoken. Open May-Sept.

Hôtel la Marine, 1 rue des Goelands (tel. 05 59 24 34 09). Wake up to sunshine in this side street hotel. Singles 150F; doubles with shower 180F, with shower and toilet 200F; triple 220F. Only 9 rooms, so reserve in advance. No breakfast. English spoken.

Hôtel Palym, 7 rue du Port-Vieux (tel. 05 59 24 16 56). Spring colors and airy rooms (some with TVs) in a friendly, family-run place with bar and pizzeria. TV room with English-language channel. Singles 180F; doubles 210-230F, with bathroom 280-310F; triples 280F, with shower and toilet 380F. Breakfast 29F. Prices 10% lower Sept.-June. Reception 8am-midnight. V, MC.

Campsites: Biarritz, 28 rue d'Harcet (tel. 05 59 23 00 12). Tranquil and close to Milady beach. July-Aug., the Navette-des-Plages bus (#9) stops outside the entrance. Other times, take av. Kennedy from the station and follow signs (30min.). Sept.-June 70F per tent and 2 people; July-Aug. 100F.

🍴 FOOD

In dining, as with everything in Biarritz, style ranks above substance. Elegant mid-priced eateries line **av. de la Marne** as it splits from av. Edouard VII. Expect 60-80F *menus* and oceans of chintz floral ruffles. You'll see the sea at the more expensive places on **pl. St-Eugénie.** Cheap crêpes and sandwiches can be found along **rue du Port-Vieux** and **rue Mazagran.** The **Marché Municipal** on rue des Halles (open daily 7am-1pm) offers local produce and an abundance of specialties. Next door is a **Codec supermarket,** 2 rue du Centre (tel. 05 59 24 18 01), just off rue Gambetta. (Open July-Aug. M-Sa 8:45am-12:25pm and 3-7:10pm, Su 8:45am-1pm; Sept.-June closed Su. V, MC.)

🍴 **Bodega la Muleta,** 51bis rue Gambetta (tel. 05 59 24 02 04). On Tu and F nights in summer, you may have to nibble your 5F tapas standing amid swirling skirts and dancing locals. Regional dishes from 40F. Open July-Aug. daily 7pm-3am; Sept.-June M-Sa 7pm-2am. V, MC.

La Cafetière, 6 av. de la Marne (tel. 05 59 22 23 52), serves traditional cuisine in an elegant space—this is no cafeteria. 3-course *menu* 66F at lunch, 82F at dinner; *plats* from 69F. English spoken. Open July-Aug. daily noon-2:30pm and 7:30-10:30pm; Sept.-June Tu-Sa same hours, Su noon-2:30pm. V, MC, AmEx.

Bar Jean, 5 rue des Halles (tel. 05 59 24 80 38). Boisterous crowds fight for a taste of self-serve Basque tapas (5F each) and line up for a ladle of sangria (20F). Open July-Aug. daily 9am-3pm and 7pm-midnight; Sept.-June closed Tu and W.

Le Chalut, 46 av. Édouard VII (tel. 05 59 22 07 37). Traditional Basque atmosphere and seafood. Load up on the delicious rolls and skip the expensive desserts. *Plat du jour* 49F, paella 85F, *menu* 109F. Open M-Sa 12:15-1:45pm and 7:15-9:45pm. V, MC.

👁 🏖 SIGHTS AND BEACHES

SIGHTS. The **Musée de la Mer,** 1 Esplanade du Rocher de la Vierge (tel. 05 59 24 02 59), is a treat for those who like to watch seals do what they do best—finagle fish. The seals eat at 10:30am and 5pm. Twenty-four aquariums hold funky regional fish. (Open daily 9:30am-12:30pm and 2-6pm; July 14-Aug. 15 9:30am-midnight. Closed second week in January. 45F.) The **Musée du Chocolat,** 4 av. de la Marne (tel. 05 59 24 50 50), was created out of the private collection of the proprietor of **Henriet,** the fine chocolates store on pl. Clemenceau. A chance to see the sculptor fashion elaborate chocolate sculptures, a historical exhibit, and a free *cadeau chocolat* is enough to lure you in from the summer in the city. (Open Tu-Sa, summer 10am-7pm; winter 10am-1pm and 2:30-7pm. 25F.) Enlightenment awaits at **Le Phare de Biarritz,** on the Plateau du Phare. Overlooking the city and sea at 73 meters above sea level, this lighthouse offers a view of where the sands of the Landes separate from the rocky coast of the Basque country. (Open 10am-12:30pm and 4-8pm. 10F. Reserve through tourist office.)

BEACHES. Dominated by the casino, Biarritz's **Grande Plage** possesses a dazzling wealth of surfers and bathers. Just north is the less crowded **plage Miramar,** nestled against the base of the cliffs, where bare bathers repose on bare sands. A short hike to **Pointe St-Martin** gives a priceless view. Protected from the surf by jagged rock formations, the **Port des Pêcheurs** harbors small craft. **BASC Subaquatique** (tel. 05 59 24 80 40), near Plateau de l'Atalaye, organizes scuba excursions. (Open July-Aug. 155F.) The craggy peninsula of the **Rocher de la Vierge,** jutting out into the Atlantic from the plateau, gazes over magical views at sunset. From the Rocher, you can see the coastline north to the lighthouse and south along the **plage des Basques,** located at the foot of stupefying cliffs. Endless paths cut into the flower-covered coast only two minutes from the *centre ville*, but check the tide schedule before venturing onto the rocks. At low tide, this deserted beach boasts the cleanest water and sand in Biarritz.

🎵 🌺 ENTERTAINMENT AND FESTIVALS

ENTERTAINMENT. The **Casino Municipal** (tel. 05 59 22 44 66) lords it over the Grande Plage. Curse Lady Luck as you blow a month's worth of *baguettes* on the greedy slot machines (open daily 10am-3am), blackjack and roulette tables (6pm-3am), and the roulette-like *boules* table (10am-3am). Jeans and sneakers are fine for slot machines, but you'll need to look snazzier to get upstairs. Hang out around the **Port des Pêcheurs** until midnight, when the rich and reckless strap on their party boots. If things look empty, don't despair; party time in Biarritz is 2am-dawn. Dress up before heading to the **Brasilia Copacabana,** 24 av. Édouard VII (tel. 05 59 24 65 39; cover 60F). On weekend nights many head for cheaper, wilder **St-Sebastian** just over the border in Spain.

FESTIVALS. The **International Festival of Biarritz** takes over the town in the first week of October. Throughout September, everyone loves **Le Temps d'Aimer** with music, ballet, and art exhibits. (Tickets 60-200F; some student reductions.) In July and August, *pelote* and Basque dancing hit **Parc Mazon** Mondays at 9pm. Two *cesta punta* tournaments animate the Fronton Euskal-Jai, Parc des Sports d'Aguiléra: for two weeks in mid-July, Biarritz hosts the **Biarritz Masters Jaï-Alaï,** while for three weeks in mid-August the town is taken over by the **Gant d'Or.** (For both tournaments, tel. 05 59 23 91 09 for ticket info.) Take bus #1 from the *centre ville* (direction "Bayonne") to "Chassin" and follow bd. du B.A.B. to the Fronton.

ST-JEAN-DE-LUZ

Once a fishing village, always a fishing village. Catapulted to fame by the flukes of its 11th-century whaling industry, St-Jean-de-Luz later switched to tuna and sardines. Now this town of 13,500 reels in the tourists with pedestrian *rues* stuffed to the gills with gift shops. Nevertheless, St-Jean's more authentic heritage still manages to seep through the cracks. St-Jean's Fête du Ttoro (Festival of Fish Soup) and Nuit de la Sardine (Night of the Sardine) betray further fishy links to a rich Basque past. Tucked inside the Bay of Biscay and surrounded by a Pyreneen backdrop, the town shimmers at dusk with the reflection of the sun's final rays off the water onto the whitewashed, red-shuttered houses along the *quais*. Don't even try to swim past St-Jean on your southern tour; there's no doubt you'll be hooked by the salt-air splendor of this small but vibrant Basque seaport.

🔢 ORIENTATION AND PRACTICAL INFORMATION

From the station, bear left diagonally across the rotary onto bd. du Commandant Passicot. The **tourist office** on pl. Foch is on your right, just past the second rotary. From pl. Foch, rue de la République runs two blocks to **pl. Louis XIV,** the center of town. The beach is a one-minute walk farther, and **rue Gambetta,** in its pedestrian splendor, takes off to the right.

Trains: Bd. du Cdt Passicot. To: **Biarritz** (15min., 10 per day, 17F); **Bayonne** (30min., 7 per day, 26F); **Pau** (2hr., 5 per day, 97F); and **Paris** (5-10hr., 10 per day, 420-470F). Info office open July to mid-Sept. daily 9:30am-12:50pm and 2:15-6:30pm.

Buses: Cross the street from the train station. **ATCRB** (tel. 05 59 08 00 33; fax 05 59 08 00 30). Buy tickets on the bus. To: **Biarritz** (7-13 per day, 16.50F); **Bayonne** (7-13 per day, 21.50F); and **St-Sebastián,** Spain (1¼hr., 2 per day; June 16th-Sept. 25th M-Sa; other times Tu, Th, and Sa; 45F). Office open M-F 9am-noon and 2:30-6pm; July 14-Aug. 15 also open Sa 10am-noon and 3-6pm. **Pullman Basque,** 33 rue Gambetta (tel. 05 59 26 17 96; fax 05 59 26 63 48), runs different excursions each day to Spain, the Basque villages, and elsewhere. Ticket office open daily July-Sept. 8:30am-12:30pm and 2:30-7:30pm; Oct.-June 9:30am-12:15pm and 3-7:15pm.

Taxis: At the *gare* (tel. 05 59 26 10 11).

Bike Rental: Ado Peugeot, 7 av. Labrouche (tel. 05 59 26 14 95), 1 block from the *gare.* Bikes 60F per day, 294F per week; deposit 600F. *VTTs* 80F per day, 365F per week; deposit 1000F. Open M-Sa 8:30am-noon and 2-7pm.

Surf shop: Le Spot, 16 rue Gambetta (tel. 05 59 26 07 95). 2hr. lesson 230F. Rentals: wet-suit 40F per half-day, 60F per day; bodyboard 50F per half-day, 80F per day. Open Jan.-Oct. daily 9:30am-9pm; Nov.-Dec. Su 10am-7:30pm. V, MC.

Tourist Office: Pl. Foch (tel. 05 59 26 03 16; fax 05 59 26 21 47). Maps and info on accommodations, events, and excursions. Pick up a free **Programme des Fêtes,** published monthly. Tours of the town in French daily July-Aug., June and Sept. Sa only (30F, 15F students). Open July-Aug. M-Sa 9am-8pm, Su 10:30am-1pm and 3-7pm; Sept.-June M-Sa 9am-12:30pm and 2-6:30pm.

Money: Change Plus, 32 rue Gambetta (tel. 05 59 51 03 43). Fair rates, no commission. Open July-Aug. M-Sa 9am-8pm, Su 10am-1pm; Sept.-June M-Sa 9am-12:30pm and 2-7pm. July-Aug. there is a second office in the Maison Louis XIV.

Laundromat: Automatique, 3 rue Chauvin Dragon. Open daily 8am-10pm.

Police: Av. André Ithurraide (tel. 05 59 26 08 47).

Hospital: Av. André Ithurraide (tel. 05 59 51 45 45). 24hr. emergency service at **Polyclinique,** av. de Layats (tel. 05 59 51 63 63).

Post Office: 44 bd. Victor Hugo (tel. 05 59 51 66 54). Open July-Aug. M-F 9am-6pm, Sa 9am-noon; Sept.-June M-F 9am-noon and 1:30-5:30pm, Sa 9am-noon. **Postal code:** 64500.

ACCOMMODATIONS AND CAMPING

Hotels fill up rapidly in summer, and it might be tough to reserve since most budget places save their rooms for regular, long-term guests. Arrive early, especially in August. You may have better luck commuting from Bayonne or Biarritz.

Hôtel Verdun, 13 av. de Verdun (tel. 05 59 26 02 55), across from the *gare.* Standard rooms, renovated bathrooms, and a 70s-style TV lounge. Singles and doubles 160-185F, with shower 170-230F; triples with bath 270F. Off-season singles 140F, with shower 160F; triples 180F. Call early to reserve. Free showers. Breakfast 25F. Restaurant serves 65F 3-course *menu.* Reception 7:30am-9:30pm. V, MC.

Hôtel Bolivar, 18 rue Sopite (tel./fax 05 59 26 02 00), off bd. Thiers, on a central but quiet street near the beach. Sparkling rooms with shining floors, some with balconies. Singles 185F, with shower 240F; doubles 180-210F, with shower 240-280F, with full bathroom 260-310F; triples with bathroom 300-350F. Free showers 8am-10pm. Breakfast 32F. Reception 8am-9:30pm. Open May-Sept. V, MC, AmEx.

Hôtel Kapa-Gorry, 9 rue Paul Gélos (tel./fax 05 59 26 04 93), a 30min. uphill walk from the *gare,* but only 10 min. from the center of town and less than 5min. from the beach. From bd. Thiers, walk along the beach. Turn right onto av. Pellot and follow the signs. The cheapest hotel on the beach, it offers spacious, dim, well-kept rooms, some with balconies. Doubles 200F, with shower 230F; triples 240F, with shower 280F. Reception 8am-11pm. V, MC.

Campsites: There are 14 sites in St-Jean-de-Luz and 13 more nearby. For information, ask the tourist office. To walk to most of the campsites, take bd. Victor Hugo, continue along av. André Ithurraide, then veer left onto chemin d'Erromardie (20min.). Or take an ATCRB bus headed to Biarritz or Bayonne and ask to get off near the *camping*, then walk the extra 800m. **Camping Municipal Chibaou Berria,** chemin de Chibaou (tel. 05 59 26 11 94). Take N10 (direction "Bayonne") to chemin de Chibaou and turn left to reach the camping zone. 20F per person, 23F per tent and car. Electricity 11F. Reception 7am-10pm. Open June-Sept. 15.

⬤ FOOD

The Basque and Spanish specialties of St-Jean-de-Luz are the best north of the border. The port's famous seafood is kept on ice outside the expensive restaurants on rue de la République and pl. Louis XIV (*menus* 75-250F). Tiny shops huddle on bd. Victor Hugo and rue Gambetta, between pl. Louis XIV and bd. Thiers. There is a **market** on pl. des Halles. (Tu and F-Sa 7am-1pm.) Get your Nutella fix at the **Codec supermarket,** 87 rue Gambetta. (Tel. 05 59 26 46 46. Open M-Sa 8:30am-12:30pm and 3-7:15pm, Su 8:30am-12:30pm.) Shelves piled with produce can also be found at **8 à Huit,** 46 bd. Victor Hugo. (Tel. 05 59 26 09 15. Open M-Sa 8:30am-1pm and 3:30-8pm; July-Aug. Su 8:30am-12:30pm.) **Chez Etchebaster,** 42 rue Gambetta (tel. 05 59 26 00 80, caters to sweet teeth with cream-filled *gateaux basques*. (Open Tu-Sa 8am-12:30pm and 3-7:30pm, Su 8am-1pm and 4-7pm. V, MC.)

Relais de St-Jacques, 13 av. de Verdun (tel. 05 59 26 02 55), across from the train station, offers simple maritime food in an informal setting. The ever-changing 65F *menu* includes soup, *plat,* and dessert. 39F *plat du jour.* Open July-Aug. daily noon-2pm and 7-8:45pm; Sept.-June closed Sa night and Su. V, MC.

Restaurant le Kanttu, 4 rue l'Église (tel. 05 59 51 26 11), has "local cuisine improved by the chef" and a lovely tiled dining room. *Menu* 90F, *plat du jour* 40F. Open daily noon-2pm and 7-10pm. V, MC, AmEx.

Chez Dodin, 80 rue Gambetta (tel. 05 59 26 38 04), scoops its own ice cream (11F) in a 60s-style diner and taunts cultural purists with its *beret basque* (chocolate mousse shaped like a beret and rolled in chocolate sprinkles, 13.50F). Open daily 9:45am-12:30pm and 2:45-7:30pm. V, MC.

◉ 🌿 SIGHTS, FESTIVALS, AND WATERSPORTS

SIGHTS. The **Maison Louis XIV,** pl. Louis XIV (tel. 05 59 26 01 56), is frozen in its glory days as Louis' lair. (Visits only by 30min. guided tour leaving every 30min. Written explanations in English. Open June-Sept. M-Sa 10:30am-noon and 2:30-5:30pm, Su 2:30-5:30pm; July-Aug. until 6:30pm. 15F, students 12F.) The 15th-century **Église St-Jean-Baptiste,** rue Gambetta, is the most famous Basque church. Built to the dimensions of a ship's hull, it contains a hanging model boat as a token to ward off shipwrecks. (Open daily 8:30am-noon and 2-7pm.)

ST-JEAN AND LOUIS Although 22-year-old Louis XIV was smitten with the charms of Marie Mancini, he was obliged to iron out border disputes by marrying Maria Teresa of Spain. Lovesick Louis sojourned in St-Jean-de-Luz in 1660 and reluctantly awaited his wedding. Fortunately, the union proved successful; upon the queen's death, the king sighed, *"C'est le premier chagrin qu'elle me cause"* ("This is the first sorrow she has caused me"). A richly decorated portal in the Église St-Jean Baptiste, to the right of the main entry, was ceremoniously sealed for eternity after the royal newlyweds left the church.

THE SOUTHWEST

FESTIVALS. Summer rollicks with Basque festivals, concerts, and the championship of *cesta punta*. (July-Aug. Tu and F at 9:15pm. Tickets 50-120F at the tourist office.) **Toro de Fuego,** with pyrotechnics, dancing, and a man in a bull costume, heats up summer nights in pl. Louis XIV. (July-Aug. W at 10:30pm and Su at 11:30pm.) The biggest annual festival is the three-day **Fête de St-Jean,** held over the weekend closest to St-Jean's day (June 21). At the **Fête du Thon** (the first Sa in July), the town gathers around the harbor to eat tuna, toss confetti, and pirouette to music (60F). The fun doesn't stop with the all-you-can-eat sardines at **Nuit de la Sardine,** the second Saturday in July at the Campos-Berri, next to the *cesta punta* stadium. It features an orchestra, Basque songs, and, yes, sardines (40-60F). The fabulous **Fête du Ttoro** features exciting activities involving fish soup *(ttoro)*. The *fête* takes place on the first Saturday in September; the next day, residents can sheepishly confess to the priests whom they pelted with fish guts hours earlier.

SWIMMING WITH THE FISHES. To get in on the fun at sea level, sign up for a four-hour fishing trip (ask at the tourist office). If you prefer to see fish alive, **Promenade Jacques Thibaud,** sheltered by protective dikes, provides some of the best conditions for sailing and windsurfing in the Basque region. Further on, the waves of the **plage d'Erromardi** present the perfect opportunity to hit the surf.

LA RHUNE

Ten kilometers southeast of St-Jean-de-Luz, the minuscule village of **Col de St-Ignace** serves as a gateway to the Basque country's loveliest vantage point. From here, wooden two-car cog trains crawl at a snail's pace up the mountainside to the 900m summit of **La Rhune.** Each tortuous turn reveals a postcard-perfect display of forests hovering above sloping farmland, as *pottoks* (wild Basque ponies) return your curious stares and cavalier sheep bound down the mountainside. At the peak, chilling air and gusty winds prevail even in summer. La Rhune *(Larun)* is Spanish soil; shop-owners slip in and out of French and Spanish. If you decide to walk back down from La Rhune, take the well-marked path to the left of the tracks down to Ascain, and travel the tricky 3km on D4 back to Col de St-Ignace (1½hr.). Loose rocks on the path make for treacherous footing. *(Trains operated by* SHEM*. Tel. 05 59 54 20 26. First train departs July-Oct. daily at 9am; 8:30am in summer; additional trains leave every 35 min. May-June and Oct.-Nov. 15, trains leave only on Sa, Su, and holidays 10am and 3pm. 60F round-trip.)* **Basque Bondissant** (tel. 05 59 26 30 74) runs buses to Col de St-Ignace from **St-Jean-de-Luz** (30 min.; July-Aug. M-F 3 per day; Apr.-June and Sept.-Oct. 1 bus Tu, Th; 19F).

ST-JEAN-PIED-DE-PORT

Set against red clay hills and herds of white sheep, this small Pyreneen village (pop. 1600) epitomizes the spicy splendor of the Basque interior. The narrow, cobblestoned streets ascend through the *haute ville* to the dilapidated fortress, and down below, the calm Nive hides acrobatic trout among shimmering rocks. This medieval capital of Basse-Navarre still hosts a continual procession of pilgrims on their way to Santiago de Compostella, Spain, 900km away. While some trek on foot from as far away as Germany, for most the first day entails a 28km trek across the Spanish border. The Forêt d'Iraty, a hikers' and cross-country skiers' paradise, is 25km from the village.

◪ ORIENTATION AND PRACTICAL INFORMATION. Trains leave for **Bayonne** (1hr., 7 per day, 45F) from the *gare* on av. Renaud. (Tel. 05 59 37 02 00. Open M-F 6:10am-noon and 1-7pm, Sa-Su 8am-noon and 1-7pm.) **Rent bikes** at **Garazi Cycles,** 1 pl. St-Laurent. (Tel. 05 59 37 21 79. 50F per half-day, 120F per day, 150F per weekend, 400F per week. Passport deposit. Open M-Sa 8:30am-noon and 3-6pm.)

From the station, turn right on av. Renaud, follow it up the slope until it ends at av. de Gaulle, and turn right to reach the **tourist office,** 14 av. de Gaulle (tel. 05 59 37 03 57; fax 05 59 37 34 91), which sells 10F hiking maps. (Open July to mid-Sept. M-

Sa 9am-12:30pm and 2-7pm, Su 10:30am-12:30pm and 3-6pm; mid-Sept. to June M-F 9am-noon and 2-7pm, Sa 9am-noon and 2-6pm.) The **police** are on rue d'Ugagne (tel. 05 59 37 00 36). The **post office,** rue de la Poste (tel. 05 59 37 90 00), has **currency exchange.** (Open M-F 9am-noon and 2-5pm, Sa 9am-noon. **Postal code:** 64220.)

✔ ACCOMMODATIONS AND CAMPING. St-Jean offers pretty rooms at ugly prices; nothing comes under 160F. Consider daytripping from Bayonne or stay in one of the *gîtes* listed by the tourist office. There's a **gîte d'étape** at 9 rte. d'Uhart (tel. 05 59 37 12 08), off the **GR10** and **GR65** hiking trails. From the tourist office, cross the bridge and take your first right on the opposite bank. The street becomes rte. d'Uhart after you pass the city walls (5min., follow signs to Bayonne). No sweet smelling flowers here, but 12 happy bunks await in an 18th-century house (46F). The couple that runs the *gîte* also has attractive *chambres d'hôte* with flowered pillows. (Doubles 130F; triples 180F. Breakfast 22F.) Outside and just opposite the old wall, **Hôtel Itzalpea,** 5 pl. du Trinquet (tel. 05 59 37 03 66; fax 05 59 37 33 18), has nine classy rooms with soft comforters catering to a mature crowd and a great restaurant (see below). (Singles and doubles with shower, TV, and telephone 200F; triples and quads 300F. Breakfast 35F. V, MC.) **Hôtel des Remparts,** 16 pl. Floquet (tel. 05 59 37 13 79; fax 05 59 37 33 44), has large rooms with soothing hues and blue-and-white tiled bathrooms. Take av. de Gaulle over the Nive and turn right onto the first street. (Singles 200-235F; doubles 10-235F; triples and quads 280F. Breakfast 32F. Open daily April-Sept.; Oct.-Mar. M-F. V, MC.) The shady **Camping Municipal** (tel. 05 59 37 11 19) rests by the Nive. From pl. du Marché, turn onto rue de l'Église, following it past the church to the next bridge. Crossing the river, the site is on your left on av. du Fronton. (13F per person, 8F per tent, 8F per car. Open Apr.-Oct. daily 8-10am and 5-8pm.)

✔ FOOD. Farmers bring *ardigazna* (tangy, dry sheep's milk cheese) to the Monday **market** on pl. de Gaulle (9am-6pm). Small food shops line **rue d'Espagne. Le Relais de Mousquetaires supermarket,** rue d'Espagne (tel. 05 59 37 00 47), has enough to satisfy Porthos. (Open M, W, and F-Sa 9:30am-12:30pm and 4-7:30pm.)

Fresh rainbow trout star in St-Jean's superb show of Basque specialties. **Hôtel Itzalpea's** restaurant assembles a generous 90F four-course *menu* with hearty vegetable *potage*, trout, a choice of meats, and dessert. The 60F *menu* shrinks to three courses of Basque specialties. Trout alone 40F. (Open July-Sept. daily 7am-midnight; Oct.-June M-F daily 7am-midnight. V, MC.) The **Restaurant-Bar Chocolainia,** 1 pl. du Trinquet (tel. 05 59 37 01 55), at the entrance of the *haute ville* from the *gare*, serves 12F mugs of warm, sweet sangria that transform the day into a pleasant blur. 3-course *menus* 55-120F. (Open daily Mar.-Oct. noon-2:30pm and 7-9:30pm. Food only at lunch. V, MC, AmEx.)

✿ SIGHTS. St-Jean's streets and fairy-tale location create a beautiful town to explore. The ancient **haute ville,** bounded by **Porte d'Espagne** and **Porte St-Jacques,** consists of one narrow street, rue de la Citadelle, bordered by houses made of the region's crimson stone. As you amble up the street, the wee craft shops in the *arceaux* are very tempting—but you know better.

The remains of St-Jean-Pied-de-Port's **citadel** lie down the narrow rue de la Citadelle leading from the plastic-trinket frenzy of the *haute ville*. Although the interior of this fortress is now an elementary school, visitors enjoy unlimited access to the grounds, with guard towers washed in flowered ramparts and a dark, foul-smelling moat. Return to the *haute ville* by the hidden staircase that runs along the ramparts at the far right end of the moat.

The staircase leads to the haunches of **Église Notre-Dame-du-Bout-du-Pont,** a small distance from pl. de Gaulle on rue de l'Église. Once a fortress, the church betrays its dark past with rocky, low-lit crevices instead of side chapels. Carefully patterned stained glass casts a mist of light over the rest of this simple stone edifice. (Open daily 7am-9pm.) Stepping out onto the junction of rue de l'Église and rue de la Citadelle, there's a short walk up to the 13th-century **Prison des Évêques**, 41 rue de la Citadelle. Having served as the medieval headquarters of local bishops, this building acquired its current name in the 19th century, when it temporarily doubled as a detention chamber. A recorded French narration guides visitors by exhibits of stuffed birds, sheep-shearing tools, and a few broken tombstones. The single gnarled shackle in the dank cellar will send chills up your spine. (Open daily Apr.-Oct. 15 10am-12:15pm and 2:30-6:15pm. 10F.) A pleasant wooded walk to the left from the church leads to the postcard-popular **Pont Romain** (about 1km).

ENTERTAINMENT. In summer, *bals* (street dances) and concerts provide free frivolity, while Basque choirs and *pelote* add local color for a small fee. (*Pelote* June-Sept. M at 5pm.) Basques get buff for the **Force Basque** competition, held the third Sunday in July. Events include hoisting 150-pound hay bales and gritty tug-of-war matches. Admission to the *fronton*—the *pelote* arena—is around 40F, but you can peer through vines for free from the fence.

PAU

Capital of the Gascon region of *Béarn*, Pau (pop. 150,000) enchants with natural vitality, and was recommended by doctors in ages past. At every turn, swathes of green alternate with exotic flora, while the bd. des Pyrénées, on Pau's elevated periphery, offers a stunning view of snowy mountains. Pau, whose famed château served as the birthplace of Henri IV, was formally annexed to France by his son Louis XIII in 1620. The town eventually receded from the spotlight when royalty revealed its preference for Biarritz as a leisure town, but an influx of British tourists in the mid-19th century rejuvenated the town. Pau now hosts an abundance of concerts and cultural events; it is also a good base for a trek into the mountains.

ORIENTATION AND PRACTICAL INFORMATION. The **train station**, av. Gaston Lacoste, is at the base of the hill by the château. Trains go to **Lourdes** (30min., 7 per day, 38F), **St-Jean-de-Luz** (1¾hr., 4 per day, 96F), **Bayonne** (1¾hr., 7 per day, 80F), **Biarritz** (2hr., 6-7 per day, 86F), **Bordeaux** (2hr., 9 per day, 149F), and **Paris** (5hr., 8 per day, 420-470F). (Info desk open July-Aug. M-F 9am-6:40pm, Sa 9am-6pm; Sept.-May daily 9am-6pm.) **CITRAM**, 30 rue Gachet (tel. 05 59 27 22 22), runs **buses** to **Agen** (1¾hr., 1 per day, 164F). (Office open M 2:30-6:15pm, Tu-F 9:40am-12:15pm and 2:30-6:15pm, Sa 9:40am-12:15pm.) **Société TPR**, 2 pl. Clemenceau (tel. 05 59 82 95 85), heads to **Lourdes** (1¼hr., 5 per day, 36F), **Bayonne** (2¼hr., 2 per day, 78.50F), and **Biarritz** (2½hr., 2 per day, 84.50F). **STAP**, rue Gachet (tel. 05 59 27 69 78), runs **local buses**. (Tickets 6F. Open M-F 8am-12:30pm and 1:15-6pm, plus first Sa of the month 9am-noon.) For a **taxi**, call 05 59 02 22 22 (24hr.) **Pedegaye Cyclesport**, 3 chaussée de la Plaine, **rents bikes**. (Tel. 05 59 77 82 30. 100F per day, 250F per week. Deposit 1000F. Open M 2-7pm, Tu-Sa 9am-noon and 2-7pm. V, MC.)

To get to the tourist office and *centre ville* from the station, ride the free **funicular** to bd. des Pyrénées (every 3 min. M-Sa 6:45am-12:30pm, 12:55-7:30pm, and 7:55-9:40pm; Su 1:30-7:30pm and 7:55-9pm), or climb the steep zigzag path outlined in white fences to the top of the hill. At the top, the **tourist office** (tel. 05 59 27 27 08; fax 05 59 27 03 21) is at the other end of pl. Royale. Ask for their free yet invaluable map, *Pau-Ville Authentique*. They also have a free accommodations service, and give out copies of *Béarn en fêtes* and *L'Été à Pau*, which lists summer happenings, and *Béarn Pyrénées*, with *gîtes* and camping info. (Office open M-F 9am-12:30pm and 1:30-6pm, Sa 9am-noon and 2-6pm, Su 10am-noon and 2-5pm July-Aug. only.) **Service des Gîtes Ruraux**, 124 bd. Tourasse (tel. 05 59 80 19 13; fax 05 59 30 69 65), in the Cité Administrative, gives advice on mountain lodgings and will make reservations. (Open M-F 9am-12:30pm and 2-5pm.) The **police** are on rue O'Quin (tel. 05 59 98 22 22), and the **hospital** is on 4 bd. Hauterive (tel. 05 59 92 48 48). The **post office**, cours Bosquet (tel. 05 59 98 98 88), at rue Gambetta, has **currency exchange**. (Open M-F 8am-6:30pm, Sa 8am-noon. **Postal code:** 64089.) **Internet access** is available at **C Cyber**, 20 rue Lamothe (tel. 05 59 82 89 40), just past the post office. (Open M-Sa 11am-2am, Su 2-11pm. 20F per 30min.)

⚑ ACCOMMODATIONS AND CAMPING. The closest hostel is **Logis des Jeunes,** 2½km outside Pau in Gelos (tel. 05 59 06 53 02), and is accessible by bus. Take bus #1 (direction "Larrious Mazeres-Lezon") to "Mairie de Gelos." Forty beds and kitchen facilities await (52F). Hotels are a more convenient option, but be sure to call ahead, since the owners aren't always there. On a side street near the château, **Hôtel d'Albret,** 11 rue Jeanne d'Albret (tel. 05 59 27 81 58), has red-carpeted stairs leading to spacious, quiet rooms. Turn left as you exit the tourist office; the hotel lies on the second right along rue Henri IV. (Singles and doubles 90F, with shower 120F, with shower and toilet 145F; triples 125F, with shower and toilet 155F. Shower 10F. Breakfast 18F. Reception 7:30am-10:30pm.) **Hôtel de la Pomme d'Or,** 11 rue Maréchal Foch (tel. 05 59 27 78 48; fax 05 59 98 09 71), between post office and pl. Clemenceau, is far from the *gare* but close to the action. Some of the comfortable rooms with phones have dim lighting. Ask for a room facing the courtyard. (Singles 85F, with shower 105F, with shower and toilet 115F; doubles 100F, with shower 125F, with shower and toilet 140F; triples and quads 180-200F. Shower 10F. Breakfast 20F. Reception 8am-11pm.) **Camping Municipal de la Plaine des Sports et des Loisirs** (tel. 05 59 02 30 49), is a 6km trek from the station. Take bus #7 from the station to pl. Clemenceau (direction "Trianon" or "Place Clemenceau") and switch to bus #4 (direction "Bocage Palais des Sports"), which will take you to the final stop alongside an aquatic stadium with 3 pools. (47F per person including tent. Open May 5-Sept. 22.)

⚑ FOOD. The region that brought you tangy *béarnaise* sauce has no *paucity* of specialties: salmon, pike, *oie* (goose), *canard* (duck), and *assiette béarnaise*, a succulent platter that can include gizzards, duck hearts, and asparagus. Elegant regional restaurants populate the château area, known as the *quartier du hédas*. Inexpensive pizzerias and ethnic eateries can be found on **rue Léon Daran** and adjoining streets. The Olympic-sized **Champion** supermarket sits in the new **Centre Bosquet** megaplex on cours Bosquet. (Open M-Sa 9am-7:30pm.) The **market** at **Les Halles,** pl. de la République, is a maze of vegetable, meat, and cheese stalls. (M-Sa 6am-1pm.) The **Marché Biologique,** pl. du Foirail, offers organic produce to the health-conscious (W and Sa 7:30am-12:30pm).

Take time out on the patio at ✷ **L'Entracte,** 2bis rue St-Louis (tel. 05 59 27 68 31). Generous salads costs 48F, the *plat du jour* is 42F, and regional meat dishes begin at 60F. (Open M-Sa 9am-3:30pm and 7-11pm. V, MC.) At **La Brochetterie,** 16 rue Henri IV (tel. 05 59 27 40 33), techno hits seem to contradict the elegant decor just as low prices seem to contradict the huge portions of quality regional food. (Lunch *menu* 48F; *plat du jour* and desert 65F.) Get hitched to a creative mixture of Armenian-Lebanese food at **La Fiancée du Desert,** 6 rue Tran (tel. 05 59 27 27 58), with a 45F vegetarian *menu*, sandwiches, and lamb dishes you can smell a block away. (Open Tu-W and F-Sa noon-2:15pm and 7-10:30pm, Th noon-2:15pm.)

◉ SIGHTS. Formerly the residence of *béarnais* viscounts and Navarrese kings, the 12th-century **Château d'Henri IV** (tel. 05 59 82 38 19) is now a national museum. Pau's pride and joy overlooks the river from the town's highest point. Glorious Gobelin tapestries, well-preserved royal chambers, elaborately decorated ceilings, and ornate chandeliers grace the castle. French tours of the château leave every 15 minutes and last an hour. (Open daily 9:30am-12:15pm and 1:30-6:45pm. Last tour 30min. before closing. English brochure available. 25F, under 18 free.) Small and well-worn, the **Musée des Beaux-Arts,** rue Mathieu Lalanne (tel. 05 59 27 33 02), features dark and dusty Italian, Spanish, French, Dutch, and Flemish paintings on its ground floor. The contemporary art is on the second floor. (Open W-M 10am-noon and 2-6pm. 10F, students 5F.)

♫ ✾ ENTERTAINMENT AND FESTIVALS. Nightlife ranges from 12F beers to **Le Dakari,** av. de Latre de Tassigny (tel. 05 59 83 91 61), which asks 50F for entrance to its mixed dance-club scene. (Open Th-Tu midnight-5am.) **Cinéma le Méliés,** 6 rue

Bargoin (tel. 05 59 27 60 52; listings 08 36 68 68 87; www.cineful.com), shows some foreign films. (Tickets 35F, students 28F. Closed Aug.)

Mid-June through mid-July, the **Festival de Pau** brings plays, concerts, ballet performances, and poetry to the château courtyard and the Théâtre St-Louis. Pick up a schedule at the tourist office. (Some free; others 190F, students 90-180F. Reservations tel. 05 59 27 27 08 or 05 59 98 90 00.) During the first week of August, the **Festival International des Pyrénées,** held in Oloron, brings in 45 folk ballet troups from 25 countries (info and tickets tel. 05 59 39 98 00 or 05 59 80 77 50).

LOURDES

In 1858, 14-year-old Bernadette Soubirous reported seeing the first of what would total 18 visions of the Virgin Mary in the Massabielle grotto in Lourdes (pop. 16,300). Over time, "The Lady" made a spring appear beneath Bernadette's fingers, told her to repent, drink, and wash in a nearby stream, and to "go tell the priests to build a chapel here so that people may come in procession." Today, over five million visitors from 100 countries come to Lourdes annually. Toting rosaries, filling bottles shaped "Like a Virgin," and hoping for a miracle, the faithful and the gawking flock to the Blessing of the Sick. Lourdes is both the doorway to the Pyrenees and a world center for pilgrimages and video cameras.

⚡ ORIENTATION AND PRACTICAL INFORMATION

The train station is on the northern edge of town; the *centre ville* is 10 minutes away. To get from the station to the **tourist office,** turn right onto av. de la Gare, bearing left onto av. Maransin at the first intersection. The office is in a modern glass complex on the right (5min.). To get to the **grotto** and most other sights, follow av. de la Gare through the intersection, turn left on bd. de la Grotte, and follow it as it snakes right at pl. Jeanne d'Arc. Cross the river Gave to reach the Esplanade des Processions, the Basilique Pius X, and the grotto (10min.).

Trains: 33 av. de la Gare (tel. 05 62 42 55 53). To: **Pau** (30min., 7 per day, 30F); **Bordeaux** (3hr., 7 per day, 170F); **Bayonne** (2hr., 5 per day, 104F); **Toulouse** (2½hr., 8 per day, 122F); and **Paris** (7-9hr., 5 per day, 439F). Info open daily 6:40am–6:10pm.

Buses: Pl. Capdevielle (tel. 05 62 94 31 15), behind the Palais des Congrès. Open M-F 8am-noon and 2-6:45pm, Sa 8am-noon. **SNCF buses** run from the train station to **Cauterets** (50min., 3-6 per day, 39F).

Local Buses: From the *gare* to grotto every 15min. Easter-Oct. daily 7:45-11:45am and 1:45-6:15pm. 10F.

Taxi Lourdais (tel. 05 62 94 31 30 for *gare.* Easter-Oct. 05 62 94 31 35 for grotto.)

Bike Rental: Cycles Arbes, 51 av. Alexandre Marqui (tel. 05 62 94 05 51), 1km out of town. Follow rte. de Tarbes. 70F per half-day, 120F per day, 450F per week. Deposit 1500F. Open Tu-Sa 9am-noon and 2-7:30pm. V, MC, AmEx.

Tourist Office: Pl. Peyramale (tel. 05 62 42 77 40; fax 05 62 94 60 95; email lourdes@sudfr.com). The English-speaking staff distributes maps and a list of Lourdes' 260 hotels to 5 million visitors each year. Open May-Oct. 15 M-Sa 9am-7pm, Su 10am-6pm; Oct. 16-Mar. 14 M-Sa 9am-noon and 2-6pm; Mar. 15-Apr. daily 9am-12:30pm and 1:30-7pm, Su 10am-6pm. All info on visits managed by the Catholic Church-affiliated **Sanctuaires de Notre-Dame de Lourdes** (tel. 05 62 42 78 78), which has a **Forum d'Info** to the left, in front of the basilica. The staff speaks 7 languages and is thrilled to help. Open daily 9am-noon and 2-6pm.

Youth Center: Forum Lourdes/Bureau Information Jeunesse in pl. de Champ Commun beyond Les Halles (tel. 05 62 94 94 00). Open M-F 9am-noon and 2-6pm.

Laundromat: Laverie GTI, 10 av. Maransin. Dry-cleaning too. Open daily 8am-7pm.

Police: 7 rue Baron Duprat (tel. 05 62 42 72 72). Open daily 9am-noon and 3-8pm.

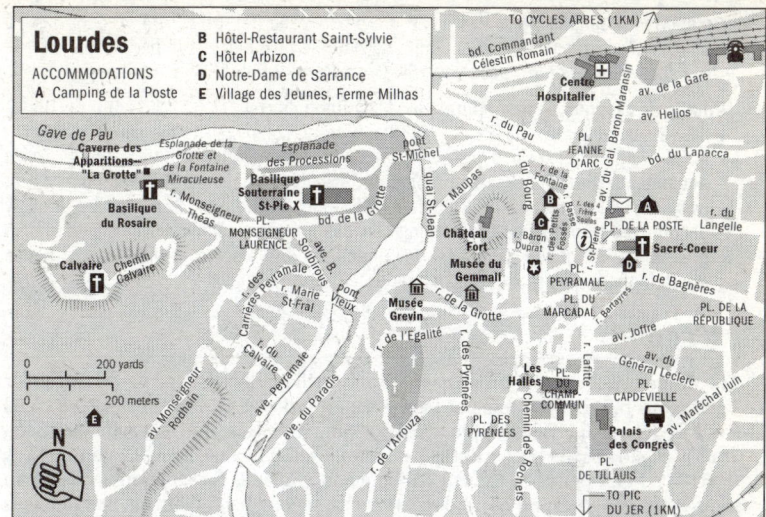

Lourdes

ACCOMMODATIONS
A Camping de la Poste

B Hôtel-Restaurant Saint-Sylvie
C Hôtel Arbizon
D Notre-Dame de Sarrance
E Village des Jeunes, Ferme Milhas

Hospital: Centre Hospitalier, 3 av. Alexandre Marqui (tel. 05 62 42 42 42). At the intersection of av. de la Gare, av. Marqui, and av. Maransin. **Medical emergency:** 2 av. Marqui (tel. 05 62 42 44 36).

Information for people with disabilities: A religiously inclined guide to facilities entitled *Guide de Lourdes* (20F) is available from the **Association Nationale Pour Integration Handicapés Moteurs,** bd. du Lappaca. Call first (tel. 05 62 94 83 88).

Post Office: 31 av. Maransin (tel. 05 62 42 72 00). **Currency exchange** machine takes bills only. Open M-F 8:30am-6:30pm, Sa 8:30am-noon. **Postal code:** 65100.

■ ACCOMMODATIONS AND CAMPING

Lourdes can easily be visited as a daytrip from Pau or Cauterets. For those who choose to linger, over 18,000 rooms await in some 320 hotels. The rooms on av. de la Gare are as inexpensive as they come. Lourdes's massive healing industry has induced most proprietors to improve wheelchair accessibility as well as facilities for the visually and hearing impaired.

Hôtel-Restaurant Saint-Sylve, 9 rue de la Fontaine (tel./fax 05 62 94 63 48). Turn right just before the tourist office onto rue des 4 Frères Soulas and right again onto rue Basse; rue de la Fontaine is the second street on the left. Fifteen comfortable, carpeted rooms overlook the boisterous side street. Close to the *grotte*. Singles 75F, with shower 110F; doubles 140F, with shower 170F; triples 205F; quads 260F. Shower 15F. Breakfast 25F. Demi-pension at 140-160F per person is a good idea if staying a while. Group accommodations available. Call ahead if arriving late. Closed Oct. 31-Mar. 30.

Notre-Dame de Sarrance, 7 rue de Bagnères (tel. 05 62 94 09 83; fax 05 62 94 95 50), off pl. de l'Église. English spoken. Classy mint, yellow, or rose-colored rooms worth every *centime*. Elevator, a free private garage, showers in every room, and a huge dining area. Fourth floor has a beautiful view of the Château Fort. Singles 150F; doubles and triples 250F. Breakfast 26F. Open all year. V, MC.

Hôtel Arbizon, 37 rue des Petits Fossés (tel./fax 05 62 94 29 36). Follow directions to Saint-Sylve, but take your first left off rue Basse. Small, less modern, and silent. All rooms have showers. Singles 90F; doubles 120F; triples 150F. Breakfast 25F. Open Feb. 8-Nov. 15.

Campsites: Camping de la Poste, 26 rue de Langelle (tel. 05 62 94 40 35), has 10 spaces in a convenient location 2min. beyond the post office. 14F per person, 14-19F per site; hot shower 8F, electricity 16F. Open Mar. 28-Oct. 15.

Village des Jeunes, Ferme Milhas, av. Msgr-Rodhain (tel. 05 62 42 79 95; fax 05 62 42 79 98; winter tel. 05 62 42 78 38; ask to be connected to the camp), a 15min. uphill walk out of town. From the pont Vieux, follow signs to Cité St-Pierre. **Dorm accommodations** in 10-person rooms 24F, singles or doubles 35F; camping in your own tent 17F. Sheets 20F. Breakfast 15F, lunch and dinner 25F. You are strongly encouraged to participate in evening services and community activities with church groups staying at the camp. Ask for directions and reserve at the Service Jeunes booth in the big plaza by the sanctuaries.

🍴 FOOD

The *épiceries* along the processional route will gladly assuage your hunger for outrageous prices. Find relief at **Casino** supermarket, 9 pl. Peyramale. (Tel. 05 62 94 03 87. Open Tu-F 7:30am-1pm and 3:30-8pm, Sa 7:30am-1pm and 3-8pm, Su 8am-1pm.) Or shop at the bigger **Prisunic** supermarket, 9 pl. du Champ-Commun. (Tel. 05 62 94 63 44. Open M-Sa 8:30am-12:30pm and 2-7:30pm, Su 8am-noon. V, MC.) An impressive congregation of produce, flowers, second-hand clothing, and books is gathered daily at the **market** at **Les Halles,** pl. du Champ-Commun (daily 8am-1pm, every other Th until 5pm).

Restaurants not affiliated with hotels are few and far-between in Lourdes. Forty-franc *plats du jours* and 50F *menus* can be found around the tourist office and on **rue de la Fontaine**—don't expect gourmet fare and don't pay more than 60F. Menus from 55-85F stack up along the pilgrim's passage, **rue de la Grotte.** On the little street by the tourist office, **La Rose des Sables,** 8 rue des 4 Frères Soulas (tel. 05 62 42 06 82), offers fantastic couscous (lamb 67F, vegetarian 57F) served in Moroccan-style earthenware. (Open July-Oct. daily noon-3pm and 7-10pm; Nov.-May closed M; closed June.) The **Reflect des Îles,** 16 rue Basse (tel. 05 62 94 00 36), on the second floor of Hôtel Chrystal, with island decor and straw-woven place mats, hides spicy and delicious creations under nondescript names such as "vegetable curry." (32 and 60F *menus.* Open Feb.-Nov. daily noon-1:30pm and 7-9pm. V, MC.)

👁 🚶 SIGHTS AND WALKS

Passeport Visa Lourdes (159F) provides admission to four museums, the Fortified Castle, and two tourist train rides through the town and the surrounding countryside.

THE CAVERNE DES APPARITIONS. Better known as *la Grotte*, this is the place where Bernadette experienced her visitations. In the afternoon rush, hundreds walk slowly through the tiny cave-like sight, touching its cold rock walls while whispering prayers. Nearby, the spring where Bernadette washed her face is on tap, and many fill bottles and canteens with the transparent treasure. *(No shorts or tank tops. Fountain and grotto open daily 5am-midnight.)*

THE BASILICAS. The Basilique du Rosaire and **upper basilique** were constructed double-decker style above Bernadette's *grotte.* In **Rosaire,** completed in 1889, an enormous Virgin Mary looms like a Mother. The **upper basilique,** consecrated in 1876 with a more traditional interior, failed to set a precedent for its younger siblings. **The Basilique Pius X,** a stadium-sized echo chamber designed as an atomic bomb shelter, won an international design prize in 1958 despite looking like a hybrid of the new Paris Opera and the parking garage of the Starship Enterprise. Covering an area of 12,000 square meters, its concrete cavern fits 20,000 souls with room to spare. Super-electric *gemmail* stained-glass rectangles—appropriately Cubist versions of the traditional sunlit model—are placed at 10m intervals. *(All three open Easter-Nov. 1 daily 6am-7pm; Nov. 1-Easter 8am-6pm, excluding masses.)*

PROCESSIONS AND BLESSINGS. The Procession of the Blessed Sacrament and the Blessing of the Sick are huge affairs held daily at 3:30pm, starting at the *grotte* (or in the Basilica Pius X in bad weather or "great heat"); fight for bench space or watch from the upper basilica's balcony. As a one-day pilgrim, you can join the procession and march along the esplanade behind rolling ranks of wheelchairs. (Meet other pilgrims July-Sept. 30 at 8:30am at the "Crowned Virgin" statue in front of the basilica.) A solemn torch lit procession in six languages blazes from the *grotte* to the esplanade nightly at 8:45pm. Add to the glow by lighting a long-burning candle for a few francs in the booths by the river Gave. *(Mass in English is held April to October daily at 9am at the Hémicycle.)*

MUSEUMS. The Musée de gemmail more or less successfully converts famous art works to an abstract, multi-layered glass design. Check out a Mona Lisa with a smile more mysterious than the one in the Louvre. *(72 rue de la Grotte. Tel. 05 62 94 13 15. Open Apr. 1-Oct. 31 daily 9am-noon and 2-7:30pm. Free.)* Down the street, the Musée Grevin offers 100 wax-figures in 18 depictions of the lives of Bernadette and Jesus. *(87 rue de la Grotte. Tel. 05 62 94 33 74. Open July-Aug. daily 9-11:30am, 1:30-6:30pm, and 8:30-10pm; Apr.-June and Sept.-Oct. 9-11:30am and 1:30-6:30pm. 34F, students 27F.)*

CHÂTEAU FORT. The only sight in town without a Bernadette connection, the feudal castle overlooks Lourdes from atop its rocky crag. A state prison in the 17th and 18th centuries, the château now guards the Musée Pyrenéen, housing archæolgical finds and traditional crafts harking from Bayonne to Perpignan. *(Tel. 05 62 42 77 40. Open May.-Oct. 15 M-Sa 9am-7pm, Su 11am-6pm; Oct. 16-Apr. M-Sa 9am-noon and 2-6pm.)*

FUNICULAIRE. Take this hillside ride to more earthly serenity atop the nearby Pic du Jer, climbing 1000m in 6 minutes. For a stunning view, walk the extra way 10min. up to the observatory at the summit for a 360° view of the surrounding countryside. The more energetic can hike up or down with a map available from the ticket booth. Beware of the rapidly descending mountain bikes. *(Tel. 05 62 94 00 41. 44F, children 22F. Daily every 30min. 9am-noon and 1:30-6:20pm.)*

HIKES. The Club Alpin Français, pl. de la République (tel. 05 62 42 13 67), leads difficult day-long trips for advanced hikers. (Open Easter-Oct. Tu-F 9am-noon and 3-7pm.) The closest guides for all levels are in Argelès-Gazost, 15km from Lourdes. Contact the Argelès tourist office (tel. 05 62 97 00 25; 6-7pm) to speak to a guide.

THE PYRÉNÉES OCCIDENTALES

CAUTERETS

Nestled in a narrow, breathtaking valley on the edge of the Parc National des Pyrénées Occidentales, is the pure air and fresh sunshine of cathartic Cauterets. Romans first discovered the therapeutic effects of Cauterets' hot sulfuric *thermes*, but most modern visitors now come here to take advantage of the skiing and hiking in the surrounding mountains. In May and June, the melting snow forms a turquoise river that runs through the town, its waterfalls making a distinctive rushing sound that can be heard from half a mile away. Easily accessible from Lourdes, Cauterets is a small jewel of the Pyrenees.

◪ ORIENTATION AND PRACTICAL INFORMATION. Cauterets runs lengthwise along the river Gave and is small enough to walk across in three minutes. From the bus station, turn right and follow av. Leclerc to the tourist office at pl. Foch. Ignore the sign pointing across the river. SNCF buses run from pl. de la Gare (tel. 05 62 92 53 70) to Lourdes. (1hr., 6 per day, 38F. Office open daily 8:30am-noon and 3-6pm.) To get to the mountains, a *téléphérique* (tel. 05 62 92 50 27) runs every 30 minutes from one block from the gare up to Col d'Ilhéou. In the morning, it also connects to Crête du Lys. (June 26-Sept. 4, 9am-12:15pm and 1:45-5:45pm; Sept. 5-June 25, 8:45am-5pm; 8am-8:30pm during vacations. To Col d'Ilhéou 40F round-trip, 30F one way; to Crête du Lys 56F round-trip, 46F one way.) You can rent **bikes** and **skis,** as well as in-line skates and ice skaters, at **Skilys,** route de Pierrefitte (tel. 05 62 92 52 10), on pl. de la Gare. (Mountain bikes with guide 110-185F per ½-day, 250-350F per day, 1500-2500F deposit; without guide 60F per ½-day, 100F per day, ID deposit. Open daily 9am-7pm, in winter 8am-7:30pm. V, MC, AmEx.)

Don't expect too much from the **tourist office,** pl. Foch (tel. 05 62 92 50 27; fax 05 62 92 59 12; www.cauterets.com). It has a list of hotels available, but ain't the best source of info on the outdoors. The *Plan de Ville* and *Guide Pratique* are useful guides to the town. (Open daily July-Aug. 9am-7pm; Sept.-June 9am-12:30pm and 2-6:30pm.) For better hiking info, drop by the **Parc National des Pyrénées,** Maison du Parc, pl. de la Gare (tel. 05 62 92 52 56; fax 05 62 92 62 23). Here you'll find regional maps and day-hike maps for sale (40-59F), plus loads of free info on the park and its trails. The center includes a small educational **museum** (12F) featuring the park's flora, fauna, and activities. (Open June daily 9:30am-noon and 3-7pm; Sept.-May M-Tu and Th-Su 9:30am-noon and 3-6pm. Closed W.) A weather forecast in French for nearby mountains can be heard from **Météo-Montagne** (tel. 08 36 68 02 65; updated twice daily). For **Mountain Rescue,** call 05 62 92 75 07. The **police** await on av. du Docteur Domer (tel. 05 62 92 51 13).

There is a **post office** at 2 rue des Combattants (tel. 05 62 92 53 93; fax 05 62 92 08 83) which offers **currency exchange.** (Open July-Sept. 12 M-F 9am-6pm, Sa 9am-noon; Sept. 13-June M-F 9am-noon and 2-5pm, Sa 9am-noon. **Postal code:** 65110.) You can get online at **Pizzeria Giovanni,** 5 rue de la Raillère. (Tel. 05 62 92 57 80. 40F per hour. Open daily July-Aug.; Sept.-June Th-Su only.)

ACCOMMODATIONS. Stay at the ☒ **Gîte d'Étape Le Pas de l'Ours,** 21 rue de la Raillère (tel. 05 62 92 58 07; fax 05 62 92 06 49; pro.wanadoo.fr/pas.de.l-ours), a few blocks up the street opposite the tourist office. The sparkling, white *gîte* with its bright yellow beds welcomes outdoorsmen and adventurers of all stripes. There's a well-equipped kitchen and bathroom and 20 clean but crowded bunks—you'll be knocking elbows with your neighbors. (Dorms 65F; triples 90F. Breakfast 40F, dinner 80F. Sauna 45F; 70F for 2 people. Laundry service 50F. Reception 8am-noon and 2-11pm. Open Dec.-Apr. 14 and May 16-Oct. V, MC.) **Hôtel-Restaurant Christian,** 10 rue Richelieu (tel. 05 62 92 50 04), offers a view of the snow-capped Pyrenees, an elevator, bridge salon, bar, ping-pong table, and *pétanque* playing ground. Its cheaper rooms on the top floor have small windows and are less modern than those on the ground floor. (Singles and doubles 145F, with shower 170F, with shower and toilet 232F; triples with shower and toilet 294F; quads with shower and toilet 342F. Breakfast 35F. Closed Oct. 10-Dec. 20. V, MC.)

FOOD. Cauterets is loved for its pleasant atmosphere, which includes fancy *cafés* in the center of town. If you'd rather not pay 36F for a sundae, buy some fresh fruit and eat as you walk. The covered **Halles market,** in the center of town on av. du Général Leclerc, has fresh produce (daily 8:30am-12:30pm and 2:30-7:30pm). An **open-air market** is held on pl. de la Gare, in the parking lot (June 15-Sept. F 8am-5pm). **8 à Huit,** av. du Général Leclerc (tel. 05 62 92 50 35), stocks groceries. (Open M-Sa 8:30am-12:30pm and 4-7:30pm, Su 8:30am-12:30pm.) **Casino,** 18 av. du Général Leclerc (tel. 05 62 92 56 38), has canned goods and produce. (Open daily July-Oct. 8am-7:30pm; Nov.-June M-W and F-Sa 8am-12:30pm and 3:30-7pm, Su 8:30am-noon, closed Th. V, MC.) The Cauterets specialty is *berlingot,* a hard candy originally used by patients visiting the *thermes* to mask the taste of the sulfurous water. You can see it being made at **À la Reine Margot,** pl. de la Mairie Crown. (9-10F per 100g. Open daily 10am-midnight.) **Chez Gillou,** 3 rue de la Raillère (tel. 05 62 92 56 58), bakes *tourtes myrtilles* and *pastis des Pyrénées* that will make you smile. (Open daily July-Aug. and Feb.-Mar. 7am-1pm and 3:30-7:30pm; Sept., Dec., and Apr.-June 8am-12:30pm and 4-7pm.)

🔲 **SIGHTS.** Not only have the Pyrenees bestowed their spectacular presence on Cauterets, they have bubbled hot sulfuric waters to the delight of well-heeled guests. The springs have inspired gushings from such visitors as Victor Hugo, George Sand, and Chateaubriand. Believed since Roman times to cure sterility, these *thermes* lure flocks of believers to drink and get hosed down by this wet, smelly cure-all. Prices vary, but if you can catch a glimpse of the white-uniformed nurses turning a firehose of sulfuric steam on their lily-skinned charges, you'll be cured of any desire to join the grimacing devotees, free of charge. For information on the *thermes* and cures, contact **Galerie Marchande des Thermes de Cesar,** av. Docteur Domer. (Tel. 05 62 92 14 22 or 05 62 92 51 60. Open M-F 9am-12:30pm and 1:30-6pm, Sa 9am-12:30pm.)

🔲 **ENTERTAINMENT.** While the nightlife of Cauterets tends to be lukewarm, Esplanade des Oeufs offers a **cinema** (tel. 05 62 92 52 14 for listings) and a **casino** (open May-Oct. after 11am). The **patinoire** (skating rink) hosts skating nights according to an eccentric weekly schedule, posted in the window of the tourist office, pl. Clemenceau. The rink itself can be found through the parking lot of the Gare SNCF, pl. de la Gare. (30F, children 13F; skate rental 16F.)

PARC NATIONAL DES PYRÉNÉES

One of France's seven national parks, the **Parc National des Pyrénées** cradles endangered brown bears and lynxes, 200 threatened colonies of marmots, 118 lakes, and 160 unique species of plants in its snow-capped mountains and lush valleys. The Pyrenees soothe with sulfurous springs, frustrate with unattainable peaks, change dramatically with the seasons, and never fail to awe a constant stream of visitors.

MAPS. Before heading off on any trail, it is important to procure an intelligible map of the area. Experienced hikers can pick up maps at sporting goods stores, but the friendly and helpful **Parc National Office**, Maison du Parc, Cauterets (tel. 05 62 92 52 56; fax 05 62 92 62 23), sells *Promenades en Montagne* maps (35-40F) of 15 different trails beginning and ending in Cauterets, all labeled with estimated duration (1hr.-2 days) and difficulty. These trails are designed for a range of aptitudes, from rugged outdoor enthusiasts to those just discovering a love for nature. For the Cauterets region, use the #1647 Vignemale map published by the Institut de Géographie Nationale (IGN), at **La Civette bookstore,** 12 pl. Clemenceau. (Tel. 05 62 92 53 87. Open July-Aug. and ski season daily 8:30am-1pm and 2:30-8pm, otherwise 9:30am-12:30pm and 3:30-7:30pm. V, MC, AmEx.)

GUIDES AND GÎTES. The **Bureau des Guides,** pl. Clemenceau, Cauterets (summer tel. 05 62 92 62 02; winter tel. 05 62 92 55 06), offers guided tours and guides for rock-climbing, canyoning, hiking, and skiing. Medium-difficulty tours cost 90-200F per person, harder ones go for 300-900F per person. Tours leave as early as 5am from the Cauterets tourist office. Not all trips run daily, so confirm dates. (Open daily 10am-12:30pm and 3:30-7:30pm.)

Gîtes in the park average 75F a night and are strategically placed in towns along the GR10. Reserve at least 48 hours in advance. The Parc National office in Cauterets will help you plan an itinerary and make *gîte* reservations, as will the **Service des Gîtes Ruraux** (tel. 05 59 80 19 13) in Pau. Long-term **camping** is not allowed in the wilderness, but camping zones also exist near each refuge.

SKIING. The Cauterets tourist office has free *plans des pistes*, maps of downhill and cross-country ski paths for varying skill levels. Many nearby resorts are accessible by SNCF buses from Cauterets or Lourdes. **Luz-Ardiden** (tel. 05 62 92 81 60; fax 05 62 92 87 19) offers a day of downhill or cross-country skiing (97-103F, student reductions available). **Barèges** (tel. 05 62 92 68 19) and **La Mongie** (tel. 05 62 91 94 15) are the two biggest ski stations in the Pyrenees (joint ticket 150F per day).

THE SOUTHWEST

HIKES. The **GR10** meanders across the Pyrenees, connecting the Atlantic with the Mediterranean and looping through most major towns. Those interested in a multi-day journey will find plenty of options along this path, and day-trippers will come across it at some point. The **Haute Randonnée Pyrénées (HRP)** trails offer the most challenging mountain experience. Talk with the folks at the Parc National Office before heading into thin air. For either level of trail, pick up one of the purple maps at the Parc office (59F). The most spectacular local hikes begin at the **Pont d'Espagne,** a two-hour walk or 20-minute drive from Cauterets. Several buses run daily; inquire at **Bordenave Excursions** (tel. 05 62 92 53 68). A Parc National information booth can help you pick a trail. One of the most spectacular and popular trails follows the GR10 to the turquoise **Lac de Gaube** (1hr.) and then to the end of the stony glacial valley (2hr. past the lake) where you can spend the night 2km in the air at **Refuge des Oulettes.** (Tel. 05 62 92 62 97. Open June-Sept. 80F.) A greener hike lies one valley over along the **Vallée du Marcadau,** which also offers shelter at the **Refuge Wallon Marcadau.** (Tel. 05 62 92 64 28. Open June 4-Oct. 10.) Both hikes are popular as day-trips. The **circuits des lacs** is a marathon eight-hour hike that includes the Vallée du Marcadau as well as three beautiful mountain lakes. In June or May, when the melting snow swells the streams, the **Chemin des cascades** (waterfall trail), which leads from the Pont d'Espagne to La Raillère, is sensational. This four-hour round-trip from Cauterets makes a good hike for those short on time—keep the river on your left as you go up if you lose the path.

From Cauterets, the GR 10 connects to **Luz-St-Sauveur** over the mountain and then on to **Gavarnie,** another day's hike up the valley. These towns are also accessible by SNCF bus (6 per day from Cauterets to Luz, 39F). Circling counter-clockwise from Cauterets to Luz-St-Sauveur, the Refuges Des Oulettes (see above) is the first shelter past the Lac de Gaube. Dipping into the Vallée Lutour, the **Refuge Estom** rests peacefully near Lac d'Estom. (Winter tel. 05 62 92 75 07; summer tel. 05 62 92 72 93. 60-70F per night.) The **Refuge Jan Da Lo** (tel. 05 62 92 40 66) in Gavarnie, near the halfway mark of the loop, costs 48F per night. From Gavarnie, you can can hop on a horse (90F round-trip) for a two-hour trek to the grandiose, snow-covered **Cirque de Gavarnie** and its mist-wreathed waterfall. During the third week in July, the **Festival des Pyrénées** animates the foot of the Cirque. Nightly performances begin as the sun sets over the mountains; afterwards, torches are distributed to light the way back to the village. (Tickets 130F, students under 25 110F. Available at tourist offices, bookstores, banks, and hotels in the region.)

LUCHON

More grandiose and cosmopolitan than other Pyrenean mountain towns, Luchon (pop. 3000) has been attracting the rich and famous to its celebrated *thermes* for over two centuries. The baths are the town's main attraction, and the boulevards are not only lined with trees but also with Chanel-wearing women and cigarette-toting teenagers all enjoying the serene atmosphere. But for those on the go, the numerous trails in the surrounding mountains are less crowded than those of the Parc National. In winter, a *télécabine* (gondola) ferries skiers from the center of town to the slopes of Superbagnères.

⬛ ORIENTATION AND PRACTICAL INFORMATION. From the station, turn left on av. de Toulouse and then bear right at the fork to follow av. M. Foch. At the lions, cross the rotary and bear left, following signs for the *centre ville.* You will arrive at the tree-lined central **allée d'Étigny,** which unfolds to your left. A few blocks down on your right at no. 18 is the **tourist office** (tel. 05 61 79 21 21), which can give you a list of nearby hikes and mountain biking trails and a map of the town. (Open M-F 9am-noon and 2-7pm, Sa-Su 9am-7pm.) The friendly and helpful staff at **Snow Fun,** 15 rue de Superbagnères near the *télécabine* (tel. 05 61 79 81 41), rents hiking boots (29F per day), tents (120-140F per day), and bikes (half-day 60F, full-day 110F). **Miéle laundromat** is at 66 av. M. Foch. (Open daily 8am-8pm. Wash 30F, dry 20F.) The **post office,** on the corner of allées d'Étigny and av. Gallieni (tel. 05 61 94 74 50), has **currency exchange.** (Open M-F 8:45am-noon and 2-5:45pm, Sa 8:45am-noon. **Postal code:** 31100.)

THE FOUNTAIN OF YOUTH? First discovered by the Romans, the healing effects of *thermes* became wildly popular in the 18th century, and modern medicine has done nothing to diminish French enthusiasm for the smelly gases. *Cures* (2- to 3-week treatments) are as popular as ever and relieve arthritis, poor circulation, breathing difficulties, coughs, and sterility. *Cures* are often covered by national health care, and some boast a 79% success rate. Treatments typically consists of 18 days of inhaling thermal gases, exposing ailing body part to the gases, and being hosed down, nasally irrigated, and bathed in the thermal water. Luchon specializes in children with chronic colds, while St-Saveur caters to women with gynæcological problems. The Empress Eugénie had been unable to conceive until a cure at St-Saveur. Her husband, Napoleon III, constructed the pont Napoléon in gratitude.

🛏️🍴 **ACCOMMODATIONS AND FOOD.** The closest *gîte*, **La Demeure de Venasque** (tel. 05 61 94 31 96), offers dorm accommodations (74F) in the woods an hour's uphill walk from town along the route to Superbagnères. During the week, it's more convenient to catch the *car thermal* from the train station to the *thermes*, then switch to the other bus and ride it to the end of the line. **Gîte Skioura** (tel. 06 07 96 74 68 or 06 07 97 74 68) is another 20 minutes uphill from La Demeure du Venasque, on your left. Ring the intercom button on the gate if no one is around. (74F. Sheets 19F. Breakfast 25F. Open all year.) Close to the train station, the **Hôtel des Sports,** 12 av. M. Foch (tel. 05 61 79 02 80; fax 05 61 79 74 42), has first-rate rooms and ornate blue and white tiles in modern bathrooms. Each room has a phone and TV. (Singles 135-145F, with shower 150-160F; doubles 145-155F, with shower 160-195F; triples 235F; quads 255F. Breakfast 30F.) The **Hôtel Central** (tel. 05 61 79 03 15), a few doors before the tourist office at 14 allée d'Étigny, has an extremely mixed bag of worn rooms. But if you are brave and not too finicky, it offers the lowest rates and best location in town. (Singles 120F, with shower 150F; doubles 140F, with shower 180F; triples and quads 200F. Extra bed 30% extra. Reception 8am-2pm and 6-9pm.)

A **Casino supermarket** lies along av. M. Foch on the way from the train station. The *brasseries* and restaurants that line **allées d'Étigny** have fair value 50-70F *menus.* You'll find a full house and a full plate at **Le Concorde,** 12 allées d'Étigny, with a 65F 3-course lunch *menu.* (Open for lunch and dinner daily. V, MC, AmEx.)

🔭🥾 **SIGHTS AND HIKES.** The tourist office can tell you about several hiking paths that leave from the **Parc Thermal,** just behind the *thermes* at the end of allées d'Étigny. Mountain bike trails of varying degrees of difficulty leave from the end of the **télécabine.** (One-way 25F, round-trip 40F. Open Apr.-Sept. Sa-Su 1:30-5pm; July-Aug. daily 9:45am-12:15pm and 1:30-6pm.) At the end of the day, treat yourself to *le bien-être* ("well-being") at the **thermes,** housed in the huge, glass-fronted building at the end of allées d'Étigny. For 75F you have access to the 32°C pool and the **Vaporarium,** a natural underground sauna. (Bathing suits required. Rentals 15F per hr.) For this and other week-long programs, ask **Vitaline,** 66 allées d'Étigny. (Mid-Dec. to mid-Oct. open daily 4-7pm. Closed mid-Oct. to mid-Dec. Tours of adjacent 18th-century *thermes* June-Sept. Tu and Th at 2pm. 18F.)

LANGUEDOC-ROUSSILLON

Once upon a time, an immense region called Occitania stretched from the Rhône valley to the foothills of the Pyrenees. Its people spoke the *langue d'oc*, a Romance language whose name comes from their word for "yes," *oc*, and which was distinct from the *langue d'oïl* spoken in the north of France *(oïl* meaning yes in the northern tongue). Independent of France and Spain, the area was lorded over by the Count of Toulouse. In the mid-12th century, Occitania's nobles and peasants alike adopted the heretical Cathar brand of Christianity. The purity of

Cathar philosophy and its belief in the existence of two equal antagonistic forces (Good versus Evil), was appealing to the Occitan people, who were fed up with the corrupt Catholic church. Disturbed by the loss of Occitan believers—and revenues—the Church launched the Albigensian Crusade (named for the Cather stronghold of Albi) against the "heretics" that eventually resulted in Occitania's political and linguistic integration into France. Even up to the Revolution, a majority of the population clung to their old language, but by the late 19th century it had all but died out. Roussillon, in the far south-west corner, was historically part of Catalonia—Perpignan even served as the capital of the Kings of Majorca—and today cultural links across the border remain strong, with locals looking to Barcelona rather than Paris for inspiration. Many here speak Catalan, a relative of the langue d'oc which sounds much like a hybrid of French and Spanish.

While a recent outbreak of xenophobia has pushed much of France to the right, Languedoc remains faithful to an old socialist tradition. Today's newspapers are descendants of the journals founded by Jean Jaurès and his allies in the late 19th century. The *occitan* banner, with its yellow and red vertical stripes and a black cross, is prominently displayed in the region. The enormous region of Languedoc-Roussillon includes the rich French Catalan tradition, centered near Perpignan.

One of Languedoc's most popular regional dishes is *cassoulet*, a hearty stew of white beans, sausage, pork, mutton, and goose. In Roussillon, try *cargolade* (snails stuffed with bacon) or the many other seafood offerings. The tangy, fermented *roquefort* and *St-Nectaire* cheeses complement the luscious fruits grown in the Garonne Valley. With your meal, enjoy one of the region's full-bodied red wines such as Minervois or Corbières, while the sweet white wines of Lunel, Mireval, and St-Jean-de-Minervois are good as an *apéritif* or with dessert.

HIGHLIGHTS OF LANGUEDOC-ROUSSILLON

■ The city of **Collioure** has seduced artists and others for 2000 years with its vivid colors and wide-angle view of the glorious Mediterranean (p. 704).

■ Albert Camus fell in love with the view from **Cordes-sur-Ciel** (p. 692).

■ The **Château de Foix** rises majestically 85km south of Toulouse (p. 697).

■ **MC Solaar** put **Carcassonne** on the same level as Lisbon and Kingston in his single, *"Victime de la Mode,"* and surely not just because it rhymed (p. 693).

⌐ GETTING AROUND

Toulouse may be the hub city of the gods. Frequent train service, a city metro, and a modern bus station add to cheap accommodations, making daytrips a simple pleasure. Unfortunately, its convenience as a hub has led the SNCF to neglect direct connections between surrounding cities. Your first farewell to Toulouse may not be your last, as you constantly double back there between towns. **Perpignan** and **Montpellier** are both short distance from the beaches and nightlife of the Côte Catalane, though buses stop running too early for clubbers.

Tourist offices throughout the region distribute itineraries which follow *Les Traces des Cathares* (tracks of the Cathars) and ancient Roman roads. The Canal du Midi connects the Atlantic to the Mediterranean, passing through Toulouse and Perpignan and linking some towns in the region. The hilly countryside makes **biking** difficult, but the villages strewn along the way make the effort worthwhile.

TOULOUSE

Just when all French towns start to look alike, Toulouse's red-brick architecture comes like a rare spring day in late winter. The elegance of the shopping district flows into the old-school grandeur of pl. du Capitôle; from there, the pizzeria intimacy of rue du Tour spills into the café and moped chit-chat of the student *quartier*. Lest its placid front mislead you, Toulouse's history is "detestable, saturated with blood and perfidy," according to Henry James. In the 13th century, the Pope

Languedoc-
Roussillon

declared a crusade against the local Cathar heretics, while in the 16th century Toulouse's Protestants died in new and horrible ways. The streets ran blue as well as red with the 16th-century discovery that a local plant, *pastel*, produced a pale blue clothing dye that Europe couldn't live without. Today, Toulouse (pop. 350,000) is the capital of the French aerospace industry, producing parts for Ariane rockets and Airbus jets. The prosperity of Toulouse is reflected in well-kept streets and shining edifices, and 100,000 students and a diverse population now inhabit the city that once burnt its dissidents.

🔢 ORIENTATION AND PRACTICAL INFORMATION

Toulouse sprawls on both sides of the Garonne, but the museums and sights are mostly located within a compact section east of the river, bounded by rue de Metz in the south and by bd. Strasbourg and bd. Carnot to the north and east.

Flights: Aéroport Blagnac: (tel. 05 61 42 44 00). **Air Liberté** (tel. 08 03 80 58 05) to **Paris** (12 per day, from 248F). **Air France,** 2 bd. de Strasbourg (tel. 08 02 80 28 02), to **Paris** (25 per day, from 298F) and **London** (2 per day, from 1250F round-trip). **Navettes Aérocar** (tel. 05 61 30 04 89 or 05 61 16 49 00) serves the airport from the bus station and allée Jean Jaurès (30min., every 20min.; 27F, students 20F).

Trains: Gare Matabiau, 64 bd. Pierre Sémard. To: **Bordeaux** (2¼hr., 8 per day, 160F); **Perpignan** (2½hr., 6 per day, 143F); **Marseille** (4½hr., 11 per day, 234F); **Lyon** (6hr., 6 per day, 295F); and **Paris** (7hr., 9 per day, 425F). Office open M-Sa 9am-7:30pm.

Buses: 68-70 bd. Pierre Semard (tel. 05 61 61 67 67), next to train station. Tickets on the bus. Open M-Sa 7am-8pm, Su 8am-7pm.

Metro: SEMVAT, 49 rue de Gironis (tel. 05 61 41 70 70 or 05 62 11 26 11). Buy tickets just inside the stations (7.50F for 1 zone, 9F for 2 zones). Maps available at ticket booths and tourist office. Open daily 8am-midnight.

Taxis: Taxi Bleu (tel. 05 61 80 36 36). 100-130F to airport (24hr.).

Bike Rental: Temps Libre, 14 rue F. Magendie (tel. 05 61 53 51 83). 80F per day, 120F for the weekend.

Consulates: Canada, 30 bd. de Strasbourg (tel. 05 61 99 30 16). Open M-F 9am-noon. **UK,** c/o Lucas Aerospace, Victoria Center, Bâtiment Didier Daurat, 20 chemin de Laporte (tel. 05 61 15 02 02). Open M-Tu and Th-F 9am-noon and 2-5pm.

Tourist Office: Donjon du Capitôle, rue Lafayette, sq. Charles de Gaulle (tel. 05 61 11 02 22; fax 05 61 22 03 63; www.mairie-toulouse.fr; toulouse@mipnet.fr), in the park behind the Capitôle. From the station, take the metro to Capitôle or turn left along the canal and then right onto allée Jean Jaurès. Walk a third of the way around pl. Wilson (bearing right), then take a right onto rue Lafayette. The office is in a small park on the left of the intersection with rue d'Alsace-Lorraine. They give out a full size map but the ones in the *Guide Toulouse* or *Toulouse: Hôtels Restaurants* are as detailed and handier. Accommodations service. City tours in French (July-Sept. M-Sa 3 per day, Su 1 per day; 47F) and bus excursions to nearby sights (Apr.-Nov. 8 per month, 170F). Office open May-Sept. M-Sa 9am-7pm, Su 10am-1pm and 2-6:30pm; Oct.-Apr. M-F 9am-6pm, Sa 9am-12:30pm and 2-6pm, Su and holidays 10am-12:30pm and 2-5pm.

Budget Travel: OTU Voyage, 60 rue de Taur (tel. 05 61 12 54 54). Cheap fares for students. Open M-F 9am-6:30pm, Sa 10am-1pm and 2-5pm. **Nouvelles Frontières,** 2 pl. St-Sernin (tel. 08 03 33 33 33), has cheap flights for all. Open M-Sa 9am-7pm. V, MC.

Money: Banque de France, 4 rue Deville (tel. 05 61 61 35 35). No commission, good rates. Open M-F 9am-12:20pm and 1:20-3:30pm. **American Express:** 73 rue Alsace-Lorraine (tel. 05 61 21 78 25). Open M-F 9am-1pm and 2-6pm, Sa 10am-2pm.

Laundromat: Laverie St-Sernin, 14 rue Émile Cartailhac. Open daily 7am-10pm.

Youth Center: Centre d'Information Jeunesse, 17 rue de Metz (tel. 05 61 21 20 20). Info on travel, work, and study. Open July 15-Aug. 15 M-Sa 10am-noon and 2-6pm; Aug. 16-July 14 M-Sa 10am-1pm and 2-7pm.

Hospital: CHR de Rangueil, Chemin de Vallon (tel. 05 61 32 25 33).

Police: Commissariat Central (tel. 05 61 12 77 77).

Post Office: 9 rue Lafayette (tel. 05 62 15 30 00; fax 05 62 15 31 07), opposite the tourist office. **Currency exchange** with no charge and good rates. Open M-F 8am-7pm, Sa 8am-noon. **Postal code:** 31000.

Internet Access: Cybercopie, 18 rue des Lois and 5 pl. de Deyrou (tel. 05 61 21 03 71), both off pl. Capitôle. 25F for 30min., 45F 1hr. Open June-Sept. M-F 9am-noon and 2-7pm; Oct.-May M-Th 8:30am-7pm, Sa 10am-noon and 2-7pm. **ICON,** 14 rue Bachelier (tel. 05 62 73 71 81). 25F for 30min., 40F 1hr. Open M 2-9pm, Tu-Sa 10am-9pm.

ACCOMMODATIONS AND CAMPING

Inexpensive hotels and their tenants clients loiter near the train station on bd. Bonrepos, across the canal. Luckily, lodging in the *centre ville* is just as cheap.

Hôtel des Arts, 1bis rue Cantegril (tel. 05 61 23 36 21; fax 05 61 12 22 37), at rue des Arts near pl. St-Georges. Take metro (direction "Basso Cambo") to "pl. Esquirol." Go down rue du Metz, away from the river; rue des Arts is the third street on the left. Great location. Spacious rooms wind around a plant-filled, sunlit staircase. English-speaking staff. Singles 80-105F; with shower 125-140F; doubles 145-160F; triples and quads 170-180F. Shower 15F. Breakfast 25F. Reserve year-round. V, MC.

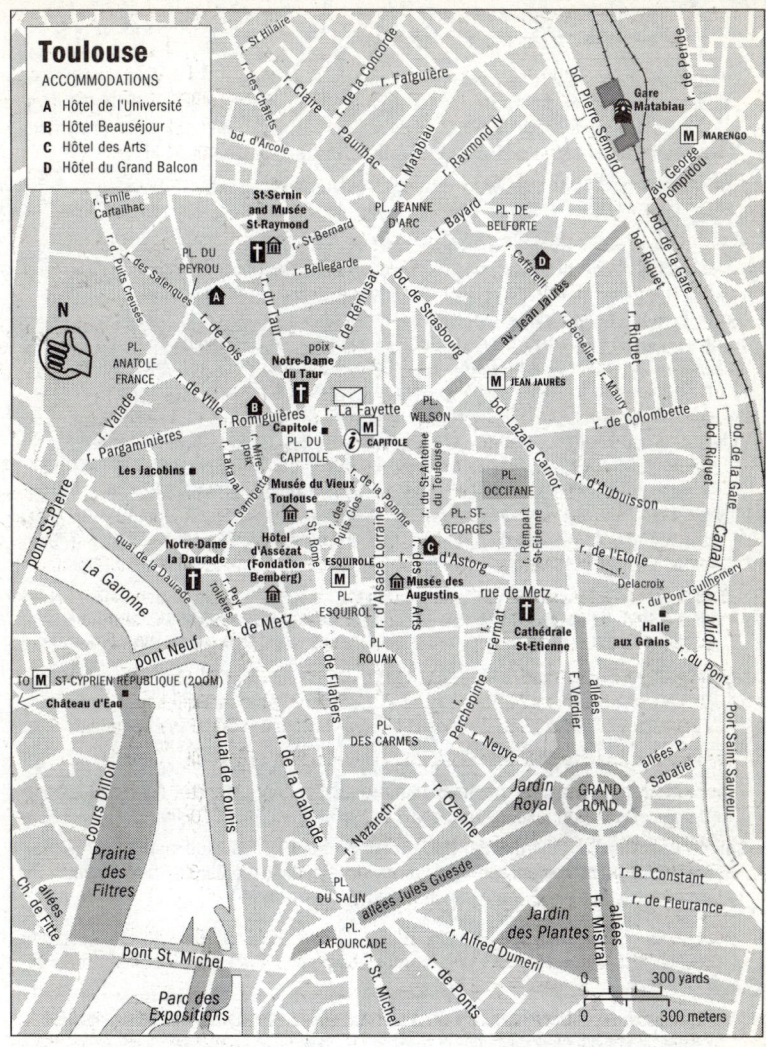

Toulouse

ACCOMMODATIONS

A Hôtel de l'Université
B Hôtel Beauséjour
C Hôtel des Arts
D Hôtel du Grand Balcon

Hôtel du Grand Balcon, 8 rue Romiguières (tel. 05 61 21 48 08), on corner of pl. du Capitôle. Prime location but dated decor. St-Exupéry stayed in this grand hotel in 1920; ask to see his room (#32). Good enough for a little prince, but larger people will challenge the mattresses. Large rooms have tiny balconies. Singles 110-120F, with shower 150F; doubles 130F, with shower 150-190F; triples and quads 150F, with bathroom 210F. Shower 10F. Breakfast 25F. Handicap accessible. Closed Aug. 1-21.

Hôtel de l'Université, 26 rue Émile Cartailhac (tel. 05 61 21 35 69), near pl. St-Sernin in a quiet student quarter. Personalized but uncarpeted rooms. Singles and doubles 110F, with shower 125F; triples with shower and TV 160F. Shower 10F.

Hôtel Beauséjour, 4 rue Caffarelli (tel./fax 05 61 62 77 59), just off allée Jean Jaurès, between the station and pl. Wilson. Take care in this neighborhood. Tall, bright rooms with new beds. TV room. Singles 75F, with shower 135F; doubles 95-115F, with shower 135-150F. Extra bed 40F. Shower 10F. Breakfast 20F. Call ahead. V, MC, AmEx.

Campsites: Pont de Rupé, 21 chemin du Pont de Rupé (tel. 05 61 70 07 35; fax 05 61 70 00 71), at av. des États-Unis (N20 north). Take bus #59 (direction "Camping") to "Rupé." Restaurant, bar, and laundry machines. One person 50F, two 60F, 16F per additional person. **La Bouriette,** 201 chemin de Tournefeuille (tel. 05 61 49 64 46), 5km outside Toulouse along N124 in St-Martin-du-Touch. Take bus #64 (direction "Colomiers") and ask for St-Martin-du-Touch. 17F per person, 18-26F per site. Car included. Open year-round.

FOOD

Restaurants line rue St-Rome, but the most economical eateries lie along the rue du Taur. The *brasseries* that crowd pl. Wilson offer ambience and 50-80F *menus*. Lebanese, Chinese, and Mexican restaurants coexist on rue des Filatiers and rue Paradoux. *Boulangeries*, *épiceries*, and *charcuteries* line **rue du Tour** and **rue des Lois.** On Wednesdays, **pl. du Capitôle** transforms into an open-air department store, and on Saturday mornings it hosts an **organic market. Monoprix supermarket,** 39 rue Alsace-Lorraine (tel. 05 61 23 39 80; open M-Sa 8:30am-9pm), and **Casino,** near pl. Occitane at the Centre Commerciale St-Georges (tel. 05 61 22 50 66; open M-Sa 9am-7:30pm), provide fare all day long. **Jardin Royal** and the **Jardin des Plantes** make excellent picnic spots. **Markets** are held on **pl. Victor Hugo, pl. des Carmes,** and **bd. de Strasbourg.** (Tu-Su 6am-1pm.) **CROUS,** 58 rue du Taur (tel. 05 61 12 54 00), provides info on university cafeterias and sells 13.70F meal tickets. (Open M-F 8:30am-5:30pm. Cafeterias open 11:30am-1:30pm.)

Le Bar à Pâtes, 8-10 rue Tripière (tel. 05 61 22 16 16), off rue St-Rome. Fish tank sets the colorful mood in this cozy restaurant hidden on a small side street. The pasta is delicious (39F), particularly the 4-cheese sauce. *Pattes* down the best budget restaurant in Toulouse. Open M-Sa noon-2pm and 7:15-11:30pm, Su 7:15-11:30pm. Basement bar open Sept.-May daily 6pm-2am. V, MC.

Mille et Une Pâtes, 3 pl. du Peyrou (tel. 05 61 21 80 70), and 1bis rue Mirepoix. Creative, healthy salads (33-45F), and pasta any way imaginable. For dessert, try *lasagne au chocolat* (25F). Open M 11:30am-2pm, Tu-Sa 11:30am-2pm and 7:30-10pm. Mirepoix site open M-Sa 11:30am-2pm and 7-9:30pm. V, MC.

Salade Gasconne, 75 rue du Taur (tel. 05 61 23 90 19). Tastebud-tantalizing regional dishes in a romantic indoor setting. Choices include much more than 35-49F salads. 3-course *menu* 55F, lunch *menus* 36F and 45F. Open M-F 11:30am-3pm and 7-10:30pm, Sa 11:30am-3pm. V, MC.

SIGHTS

Museum passes are available for multiple visits: 20F gives entry to any three museums, 30F to six. Passes are sold at all museums.

From local artists to canonized painters, the diversity of Toulouse's art makes for an enjoyable afternoon of museum-hopping. The city also has some of France's most architecturally distinctive and historically important religious monuments. The fact that Toulouse is built in red brick (hence its nickname "The Rose City") has more to do with economics than æsthetics. The exception is the **stone mansions** of wealthy 15th- and 16th-century dye merchants. An excellent way to view these *hôtels particuliers* is the two-hour tourist office French **walking tour** (47F, July-Sept. M-Sa at 10am). The charming brochure *Carnet des Arts and Visites aux Musées* marks local museums, galleries, and churches.

ÉGLISE NOTRE-DAME-DU-TAUR. This unrestored church was originally named St-Sernin-du-Taur after Saturninus, the first Toulousian priest, who was martyred in AD 250. Legend has it that disgruntled pagans tied him to the tail of a wild bull that dragged him to his death. The building marks the spot where Saturninus' unfortunate ride finally ended—the enormous fresco over the alter recalls the event. The church is a masterpiece of ornate brickwork. *(12 rue du Taur. Tel. 05 61 21 41 57. Open daily July-Sept. 9am-6:30pm; Oct.-June 8am-noon and 2-6pm.)*

BASILIQUE ST-SERNIN. The longest Romanesque structure in the world, the Basilica holds the remains of St. Sernin. St. Dominique, the most vigilant of Cathar-hunters, led his inquisition from here. Behind an iron gate, the crypt is a treasure trove of holy relics gathered since Charlemagne began collecting. *(Church open July-Sept. M-Sa 9am-6:30pm, Su 9am-7:30pm; Oct.-June M-Sa 8:30-11:45am and 2-5:45pm, Su 9am-12:30pm and 2-7:30pm. Free. Tours July-Aug. 2 per day, 35F. Crypt open July-Sept. M-Sa 10am-6pm, Su 12:30-6pm; Oct.-June M-Sa 10-11:30am and 2:30-5pm, Su 2:30-5pm. 10F.)*

LES JACOBINS. The 13th-century church is an excellent example of the southern Gothic style. Flamboyant decorations are checked by the elegant stained glass and a serene cloister. The modest crypt contains the ashes of St. Thomas Aquinas. *(Rue Lakanal. Open daily June-Sept. 10am-6:30pm and Oct.-Mar. 10am-noon and 2-6pm. Daily guided tours. Weekly summer piano concert tickets 80-140F available at the tourist office. Cloister 10F.)* The **Réfectoire des Jacobins** presents regular exhibitions ranging from archæological artifacts to modern art. *(69 rue Pargaminières. Tel. 05 61 22 21 92. Open daily, with exposition, 10am-7pm; same hours as church without exposition. 15F.)*

HÔTEL D'ASSÉZAT. The striking *hôtel* has been newly restored and opened to the public. Worthy as a site by itself, it houses the **Fondation Bemberg** and its 28 colorful Bonnards. You can also find Dufys, Pissarros, and Gauguins. *(Pl. d'Assézat. Tel. 05 61 12 06 89; fax 05 61 12 34 47. Fondation tel. 05 61 12 06 89. Open Tu and Th-Su 10am-6pm, W 10am-9pm. 25F, students 18F, groups 15F, temporary exhibits 20F.)*

MUSEUMS. Musée des Augustins displays an unsurpassed assemblage of Romanesque and Gothic sculptures, including 15 sniggering gargoyles. *(21 rue de Metz, off rue Alsace-Lorraine. Tel. 05 61 22 21 82. Open Th-M 10am-6pm, W 10am-9pm. 12F, students free; temporary exhibits extra.)* At the cozy **Musée de Vieux Toulouse,** you can learn more about the city's somewhat hectic history with several exhibits on local history and popular culture. *(7 rue de May, off rue St-Rome. Tel. 05 61 13 97 24. Open June-Sept. M-Sa 3-6pm; Oct.-May only by appointment, call F afternoon. 10F, students 5F.)* After several years of renovation, the **Musée St-Raymond** is now fully equipped to take you *way* back in time with an extraordinary array of local archæological finds dating from prehistory to AD 1000. *(Pl. St-Sernin. Tel. 05 61 22 21 85. Open Oct.-May W-M 10am-5pm; June-Sept. 10am-6pm.)*

OTHER SIGHTS. Opened in 1997, the super-duper new **Cité de l'Espace** park is devoted to Toulouse's space programs, complete with interactive games and a planetarium. *(Take A612 exit 17 to Parc de la Plaine, av. Jean Gonord or bus #19 to pl. de l'Indépendance and follow the signs. Tel. 05 62 71 64 80. Open June 15-Sept. 15 Tu-Su 9:30am-7pm; Sept. 16-June 14 Tu-Su 9:30am-6pm. 50F, children 30F, planetarium 10F. Handicap accessible.)* The **Galerie du Château d'Eau,** just across from the *centre ville* on the Pont Neuf, is devoted to photography. *(Pl. Laganne. Tel. 05 61 77 09 40; fax 05 61 42 02 70. Open W-M 1-7pm. 15F, students and seniors 10F.)* The smaller, gallery-like **Centre Municipal de L'Affiche,** just down rue de la République, exhibits clever posters, past and present, produced by local illustrators. *(58 allées Charles-de-Fitte. Tel. 05 61 59 24 64. Open M-F 9am-noon and 2-6pm. Free.)* **L'Espace St-Cyprien** features avant-garde photography and contemporary art exhibits. *(56 allées Charles-de-Fitte. Tel. 05 61 22 28 64. Open M-F 8:30am-12:30pm and 1:30-7pm, sometimes open Sa 2-6pm. Free.)* For greener, shaded pastures, head to the **Jardin Royal** and the less formal **Jardin des Plantes** across the street. For cyclists, the **Grand Rond** unfurls into allée Paul Sabatier, which just keeps rolling along to the **Canal du Midi.**

♫ 🌾 **ENTERTAINMENT AND FESTIVALS**

ENTERTAINMENT. Toulouse has something to please almost any nocturnal whim, although the city is at its liveliest from October to May when the students come out in full force. The numerous cafés, *glaciers*, and pizzerias flanking **pl. St-**

Georges and **pl. du Capitôle** are open late, as are the bars off **rue St-Rome** and **rue des Filatiers.** From September to June, the weekly *Flash* gives restaurant and bar info and keeps Toulouse up on the ever-changing club scene (7F at *tabacs*). Unfortunately, the July-August issue *Flash Été* costs 20F and lists little going on in Toulouse itself, focusing on festivals throughout the region. CD and book megalith **FNAC** (tel. 05 61 11 01 01), at the intersection of bd. Strasbourg and Carnot, sells tickets to big concerts and has cultural pamphlets and club advertisements. (Open M-Sa 10am-7:30pm.) The **Café des Artistes,** quai de la Daurade (tel. 05 61 12 06 00), with a view of the Garonne river, serves drinks and coffee to a huge yuppie following, and has changing student exhibits at the École des Beaux Arts. (Open M-F 8am-2am, Sa 10am-4am, Su noon-10pm; 9pm in winter.) **La Ciguä,** 6 rue de Colombette (tel. 05 61 99 61 87), just off bd. Lazare Carnot, is a friendly gay bar and a great place to ask about the discos *du jour.* Different DJ every night. (Open Tu-Su 9pm-2am, Sa 9pm-4am.) **Bagdam Café,** 4 rue Delacroix (tel. 05 61 97 03 62), nestled in a nondescript street parallel to bd. **Carnot,** between rue l'Étoile and rue Caraman, is a down-to-earth lesbian bar with listings of resources and pamphlets. (Open W-Sa 7pm-2am.)

Cave Poésie, 71 rue du Taur (tel. 05 61 42 91 34; reservations 05 61 23 62 00), hosts plays and performances. The full moon is the catalyst for an "open door" night of comedians, poets, musicians, or whatever the *cave* can dig up. Stop by for a schedule; events begin at 9pm. **Cour de l'École des Beaux Arts,** quai de la Daurade (tel. 05 61 23 25 49 or 05 61 23 25 45), stages classic plays with a modern twist. **CinÉmas** near pl. Wilson, runs major English-language films in *version originale* with French subtitles. **Utopia Cinemas,** 24 rue Montardy (tel. 05 61 23 66 20), always shows international films in *v.o.*, has wild décor, and some gay art and information (33F; closed Aug.). **Cinéma ABC,** 13 rue St-Bernard (tel. 05 61 29 81 00), shows international movies, all in *v.o.* (Last show around 10pm. 42F, 32F on W and for students.) The **pl. de Capitole** is stunningly lit at night and buzzing with activity—a good place to stop on the way back to the hotel.

FESTIVALS. July through September, **Musique d'Été** brings classical concerts, jazz, and ballet to a variety of outdoor settings. Tickets (80-140F) are sold at concert halls and the tourist office. On Tuesdays and Fridays in September, the **Festival International de Piano aux Jacobins** tickles Toulousian ivories. Tickets (100-140F, students 60F) are available at the tourist office.

MONTAUBAN

Montauban (pop. 55,000) sits quietly on the tranquil river Tarn 50km north of Toulouse. The town's 12th-century construction was motivated by the locals' struggle against the wealthy, oppressive abbey at Montauriol ("golden mountain"). Riding a wave of popular discontent, Alphonse Jourdain, the count of Toulouse, incited the enraged population to sack the abbey in 1144 and use its remains to build a town they named the "white mountain." Montauban has preserved its impressive architecture despite having become a major industrial center. Minutes away from Toulouse, the impressive Musée Ingres makes the town an art-lover's daytrip.

◪ ORIENTATION AND PRACTICAL INFORMATION. Trains roll from av. Chamier to **Toulouse** (25min., every hr., 46F), **Bordeaux** (2hr., 9 per day, 136F), and **Paris** (5½hr., 7-9 per day, 328F). (Information office open 8am-7pm.) **Buses** leave from pl. Lalaque. **Jardel** (tel. 05 63 03 18 95) goes to **Toulouse** (1hr., 4 per day, 36F). **SNCF** buses go to **Albi** (1¼hr., 2 per day, 60F). **Local buses** are run by **Transports Montaubanais** (tel. 05 63 63 52 52).

To get to the *centre ville*, walk down av. Mayenne from the station, cross pont Vieux, and continue uphill on côte de Bonnetiers. Go past the Église St-Jacques and turn right on rue Princesse, which runs into the central **pl. Nationale.** The **tourist office,** 2 rue du Collège (tel. 05 63 63 60 60; fax 05 63 63 65 12), but with its main entrance on pl. Prax-Paris, gives out a free self-guided tour map in English as well as running **city tours** (July-Aug. twice weekly, 12F). Ask for the free guides *Montauban Pratique*, for useful info, and the *Guide de l'Été Tarn-et-Garonne*, available in July with details of summer activities and festivals. (Open July-Aug. M-Sa 9am-7pm, Su 10am-noon and 3-6pm; Sept.-June M-Sa 9am-noon and 2-7pm.) **Crédit Mutuel,** 8 bd. Midi-Pyrénées (tel. 05 63 91 74 74), has **currency exchange.** (Open M-F 8:45am-noon and 1:30-5pm, Sa 8:30am-noon and 1:30-4pm.) The **hospital** is at 14 rue du Dr. Alibert (tel. 05 63 92 82 82). The **police station** is at 30 bd. Alsace-Lorraine (tel. 05 63 21 54 00), right off av. Gambetta from pl. Maréchal Foch. The **post office** is at 6 bd. Midi-Pyrénées. (Tel. 05 63 68 84 84. Open M-F 8am-7pm, Sa 8am-noon. **Postal code:** 82000.) **Internet access** is available at **Vôtre Ecran,** rue Jean Monnet. (Open 10:30am-noon and 1:30-8:30pm, Su 3-8:30pm. 25F for 30min.)

▛▟ ACCOMMODATIONS AND FOOD. Hotels close to pl. Nationale are your best bet. The decorative charm of **Hôtel du Commerce,** 9 pl. Roosevelt (tel. 05 63 66 31 32; fax 05 63 03 18 46), strikes a balance between budget and elegance. The top floor has low ceilings. After pont Vieux, turn right on rue de l'Hôtel de Ville, and pl. Roosevelt will be on the right, in front of the cathedral. (Singles 100F; doubles with TV 130F, with TV and shower 260F; triples with TV 169F; quads with shower and TV 240-290F. Shower 10F. Breakfast 30F. V, MC.)

Montauban meets Montezuma in **Le Quetzal,** 18 rue des Augustins (tel. 05 63 66 15 34), on the station side of pont Vieux. A Frida Kahlo-esque interior with hanging jalapenos, soft guitar rhythms, and colorful pottery complement the authentic Mexican food. Super nachos (34F), tostadas (45F), and spicy enchiladas (53F) keep the tequila coming. (Open Tu-Su noon-2pm and 7:30-10:30pm. V, MC.) **Le Contre-Filet,** 4 rue Princesse (tel. 05 63 20 19 75), offers traditional French fare and cheerful decor. The 65F 2-course *menu* includes the house specialty, *faux-filet et sauce fameuse,* a grilled steak served at your table over a flame. (Open daily noon-2pm and 7:30-10:30pm. V, MC, AmEx.) Health-smart gourmands can sip organic wines (32F a liter) with the 40F *plat du jour* at **La Clef des Champs,** 3 rue Armand Cambon. (Tel. 05 63 66 33 34. Open M-Sa 11:45am-2pm.) The town **market** is held on pl. Nationale (Tu-Su 8am-12:30pm).

▣▨ SIGHTS AND FESTIVALS. A pass to all four of Montauban's museums costs 40F. The exquisite **Musée Ingres,** 19 rue de l'Hôtel de Ville (tel. 05 63 22 12 92), on the left just before Pont Vieux coming from the tourist office towards the station, spotlights several thousand sketches and some minor works by the celebrated Neoclassical painter Jean-Auguste Dominique Ingres (1780-1867). Extending two floors skyward and three underground, this museum contains everything from torture instruments in the basement to vibrant 20th-century pieces. Don't neglect the ceilings; patterns and other oddities lurk above. (Open July-Aug. daily 9:30am-noon and 1:30-6pm; Sept.-June Tu-Su 10am-noon and 2-6pm. 20F, students free. Sept.-June free W if no temporary exhibit.) Across pl. Bourdelle, the small **Musée d'Histoire Naturelle Victor Brun,** quai Montmurat (tel. 05 63 22 13 85), is stuffed with ostriches, penguins, crocodiles, armadillos, fossils, and a mandatory tarantula or two. (Open Tu-Sa 10am-noon and 2-6pm, Su 2-6pm. 15F, 20F during exposition, students free.) The **Musée Terroir** showcases old-fashioned regional rural life with four rooms of tools, clothes, and paintings. The **Musée de la Résistance** has permanent exhibits on WWII's Nazi occupation and the internment camps in the region. As Protestants fled persecution following the revocation of the Edict of Nantes in 1685, Louis XIV spitefully constructed the **Cathédrale,** pl. Roosevelt, whose interior is unusually well lit by clear and amber-colored panes. Four enormous sculptures of the evangelists keep solemn watch over the grand arches of the nave and an Ingres painting. (Open daily 9am-noon and 2-6pm.)

Montauban has two annual music festivals. **"Alors Chante"** plays traditional French tunes for a weekend in May. The **Jazz Festival** is held in the third week of July. (Tel. 05 63 63 60 60. Tickets 100-180F, some student reductions.)

ALBI

In the Middle Ages Albi was a stronghold of Catharism, a Christian sect which rejected the Catholic church. In response, the Pope declared a crusade against perfidious Albi and its Cathar heretics, and the cathedral and the bishop's palace were built like fortresses to symbolize the power and strength of the Church. The town's pink exterior, frescoed cathedral, and museum of native son Henri de Toulouse-Lautrec make it a worthwhile stopover for those in the area. In summer, Albi comes alive with vibrant music at cafés and medieval theater festivals.

⊿ ORIENTATION AND PRACTICAL INFORMATION. Trains run from av. Maréchal Joffre to **Toulouse** (1hr., 15 per day, 62F), **Castres** via St-Sulpice (1½hr., 3 per day, 75F), and **Paris** (1 direct overnight 344F). **Buses** leave pl. Jean Jaurès (tel. 05 63 54 58 61) for **Toulouse** (7 per day, 1 on Su, 50-55F) and **Castres** (1hr., 5 per day, 31F). **Local transportation** is provided by **Espace Albibus,** 14 rue de l'Hôtel de Ville. (Tel. 05 63 38 43 43. Tickets 4.50F. Buses run roughly 7:30am-7:30pm.) **Albi Taxi Radio** (tel. 05 63 54 85 03) awaits at the station. **Rent bikes** at **Cycles Andouard,** 7 rue Séré-de-Rivières. (Tel. 05 63 38 44 47. 80F per half-day, 100F per day, 500F per week. Deposit 2000F. Open M 3:30-7pm, Tu-Sa 9am-noon and 2-7pm. V, MC.)

To reach the **tourist office,** Palais de la Berbie at pl. Ste-Cécile (tel. 05 63 49 48 80; fax 05 63 49 48 98; email: otsi.albi@wanadoo.fr.), turn left from the station onto av. Maréchal Joffre and left again onto av. du Général de Gaulle. Bear left over pl. Lapérouse to the pedestrian *vieille ville.* Rue de Verdusse leads you toward pl. Ste-Cécile, from where signs point the way (10min.). The office offers an accommodations service (10F in town, 15F elsewhere), city tours in French (June 15-Sept. 15; 27F, students 25F), and **currency exchange** (Su-M only). (Open July-Aug. M-Sa 9am-7:30pm, Su 10:30am-1pm and 3:30-6:30pm; Sept.-June M-Sa 9am-12:30pm and 2-6pm, Su 10:30am-12:30pm and 3:30-5:30pm.) If your friends seem distant, pop into **Lavomatique laundromat,** 8 rue Émile Grand, off lices Georges Pompidou (open 7am-9pm), or they may call the **police,** 23 Lices Georges Pompidou (tel. 05 63 49 10 17), rather than spend the night in the **Centre Hospitalier,** rue de la Berchere (tel. 05 63 47 47 47). The **post office,** pl. du Vigan (tel. 05 63 48 15 63), offers **currency exchange.** (Open M-F 8am-7pm, Sa 8am-noon. **Postal code:** 81000.) **Internet** junkies can get a fix at **Le Darllo Café,** 10 av. Charles de Gaulle (tel. 05 63 38 93 09), which doubles as a disco by night. (20F for 15min., 40F 30min., 70F 1hr.)

⎾ ACCOMMODATIONS AND CAMPING. Tourists pour into Albi in the summer on their way to the Toulouse-Lautrec museum. Arrive early or call ahead. For info on *gîtes d'étape* and rural camping, call **ATTER.** (Tel. 05 63 48 83 01; fax 05 63 48 83 12. Open M-F 8am-12:30pm and 2-6pm.) Far and away the best budget hotel in town—or even the entire southwest of France—is ▓ **Hôtel La Régence,** 27 av. Maréchal Joffre (tel. 05 63 54 01 42; fax 05 63 54 80 48), near the *gare.* Antique-filled and catering to the client's comfort down to the potpourri-scented air fresheners, it offers TVs in all rooms and a garden. (Singles and doubles 120F, with shower 160-220F. Extra bed 40F. Breakfast 25F. V, MC.) If they're full, try the obsessively clean **Hôtel du Parc,** 3 av. du Parc (tel. 05 63 54 12 80; fax 05 63 54 69 59). From the station, follow av. Maréchal Joffre as it becomes bd. Carnot; signs at intersections will guide you. The hotel is on the left across from Parc Rochegude. All rooms have TV, and there's a bar downstairs. (Singles and doubles 160F, with shower 200F, with bath 210-280F; triples 280-320F; quads 360F. Breakfast 30F. V, MC, AmEx.) Those on a tight budget will have to settle for the **Maison des Jeunes et de la Culture,** 13 rue de la République (tel. 05 63 54 53 65; fax 05 63 54 61 55). From the tourist office, take rue Fargues to rue Émile Grand. Turn right on Lices Georges Pompidou and the next left onto rue de la République (10min.), or take bus #1 (direction "Cantepau") to "République" and walk down rue de la République. Here, institutional co-ed rooms with worn mattresses and co-ed bathrooms await. (35F per night. Sheets 18F. Breakfast 15F. Meals 40-50F. Laundry. Key deposit 20F. Reception M-F 7-9pm, Sa-Su 8-9pm.) You can **camp** near a pool at **Parc**

de Caussels (tel. 05 63 60 37 06), 2km east of Albi towards Millau on D999. To get there, take bus #5 to "Camping" from pl. Jean Jaurès (every hour until 7pm). On foot, leave town on rue de la République and follow the signs (30min.). (60F for 2 people with car, extra person 17F. Open Apr.-Oct. 15.)

◪ **FOOD. Markets** take place indoors at **pl. du Marché** near the cathedral (Tu-Su 8am-12:30pm), outdoors at **pl. Ste-Cécile** (Sa 8am-12:30pm), and organically at **pl. du Jardin National** (Tu and Th 5-7pm). Cheap meals and groceries await at **supermarket/cafeteria Casino**, 39 rue Lices Georges Pompidou. (Open M-Sa 8:30am-7:30pm. Cafeteria open daily 11:30am-9:30pm. Dishes 24-49F.) **Cafétéria La Gourmandine**, 13 av. Gambetta (tel. 05 63 38 32 27), has 27F student *menus*.

To get to the vine-covered ◪ **Le Robinson,** 142 rue Édouard-Branly (tel. 05 63 46 15 69), take a path to the right where Lices Georges Pompidou hits the river. This budget Eden offers a choice of garden or indoor seating by the river with delicately flavored and presented *menus* for 60F (lunch) or 90-150F (dinner). Vegetarians can revel in four courses for 90F. (Open W-Su noon-2pm and 7:30-10pm, Tu 7:30-10pm. V, MC.) Nor will you be disappointed by **La Petit Savoie,** 33 rue Séré de Rivières (tel. 05 63 38 49 55). *Raclette* (unlimited melted cheese over potatoes and ham) is always good, but when done this well at 65F it's irresistible. (Open noon-2pm and 7pm-1am. Closed Su lunch.) A Franco-British couple offers vegetarian delights at the charming **Le Tournesol,** 11 rue de l'Ort en Salvy (tel. 05 63 38 38 14), off pl. Vigan. Tuck into vegetable *pâté* for 26F, or numerous *plats du jour* for 46F. (Open Tu-Th noon-2pm, F-Sa noon-2pm and 7:15-9:30pm. V, MC, AmEx.)

◪ **SIGHTS.** Born with a congenital bone disease to the Count of Toulouse and his cousin-*cum*-wife, Henri de Toulouse-Lautrec (1864-1901) led a life of debauchery among the cafés, cabarets, and brothels of Paris, leaving behind a lasting homage to Paris nightlife. The collection of works ferreted away by his mother and assembled in the **Musée Toulouse-Lautrec** (tel. 05 63 49 48 70; fax 05 63 49 48 88) in the 13th-century Palais de la Berbie is the most complete anywhere, including all 31 of the famous posters of Montmartre nightclubs. Upstairs a fine collection of art includes sculptures and paintings by Degas, Dufy, Matisse, and Rodin. (Open June-Sept. daily 9am-noon and 2-6pm; Oct.-Mar. W-M 10am-noon and 2-5:30pm; Apr.-May 10am-noon and 2-6pm. 24F, students 12F. Tourist office gives tours June 15-Sept. 15 for 38F, students 26F.) The artist's family still owns his birthplace, the **Hôtel du Bosq,** 14 rue Toulouse-Lautrec in *vieux* Albi; bd. Général Sibille affords a good view of the house. You can visit the 12th-century **Château du Bosc** (tel. 05 65 69 20 83; fax 05 65 72 00 19), where he spent childhood vacations, in a forest 45km northeast of Albi. Drive up the N88 toward Rodez or take the train to the **Naucelle** station, 4km from the château. (Open daily 9am-7pm.)

The pride of Albi, eclipsing even the Lautrec museum in the hearts of its citizens, is the **Cathédrale Ste-Cécile** (tel. 05 63 49 48 86; fax 05 63 49 48 76). Begun in 1282 after papal crusaders vanquished Albi's heretics, the cathedral also doubled as a fortress. Colorful 16th-century frescoes cover every square centimeter of the enormous interior. Just below the organ, *The Last Judgment* demonstrates in horrific detail—complete with boiling oil—what will happen to visitors who don't obey the "Silence" signs posted throughout the church. The church's organ bursts into song on Wednesdays at 5pm and Sundays at 4pm in July and August. (Church open June-Sept. daily 8:30am-7pm; Oct.-May 8:30-11:45am and 2-5:45pm. Choir admission 3F. Two tours daily June 15-Sept. 15 for 27F, students 23F; ask tourist office for info. Evening tours of the illuminated church 30F, students 20F. English audioguide tours available.)

◪ ▩ **ENTERTAINMENT AND FESTIVALS.** you'll have no problem finding a party along **pl. de l'Archevêché** in front of the Palais de la Berbie and at Lices Georges Pompidou near pl. du Vigan. Innovative plays run at the **Théâtre de la Croix Blanche,** 14 rue de Croix Blanche. (Tel. 05 63 54 18 63 for schedules.) The

Centre Culturel de l'Albigeois, on the felicitous pl. de l'Amitié Entre les Peuples (tel. 05 63 54 11 11), off bd. Carnot and opposite Parc Rochegude, often shows foreign films in *v.o.* (Open Tu-F 2-7pm, Sa 10am-noon and 2-7pm. 41F, students and seniors 29F.)

Albi brings in the noise with an abundance of celebrations, all listed in *Albi Sortir,* available at the tourist office. In the last two weeks of May, **Jazz dans le Tarn** brings harmony to the streets. The **Festival Théâtral** takes place in the last week of June and the first week of July. (Tickets 100F, students 88F.) Cars burn rubber on the first Sunday in September at the **Albi Grand Prix** (100F).

CORDES-SUR-CIEL

> The traveler who looks at the summer night from the terrace at Cordes knows that he need go no further, and that if he wishes it, the beauty of the place, day after day, will banish solitude.
> —Albert Camus, 1954

Renaissance Cordes-sur-Ciel rests on a hilltop 24km north of Albi, a fairy tale of a *vieille ville* bounded by a cobbled double-wall and offering majestic views of golden bales of hay and hidden *châteaux* cradled between the trees of the fields.

Église St-Michel, with a 19th-century organ from Paris's Notre-Dame, rests at Cordes' summit. **Musée Yves Brayer** (tel. 05 63 56 00 40) has drawings, paintings, and costumes by the artist who came to Cordes in 1940, and is worth visiting for its fanciful renditions of the town. (Open July-Aug. W-M 10am-noon and 2-6pm; closed Jan. 8-31; Sept.-June F-Su 10am-noon and 2-6pm. 10F, groups 5F.) **Musée Charles Portal** (tel. 05 63 56 00 52), with a reconstructed farmhouse interior, displays local traditions and archæology. (Open July-Aug. daily 11am-noon and 3-6pm; Apr.-June and Sept.-Oct. Su and holidays 3-6pm. 15F, students 7F.) To see sculptures made entirely of sugar—including a life-size violin—visit the **Musée de l'Art du Sucre,** pl. de la Bride (tel. 05 63 56 02 40). As you leave, you can buy a sugar-sculpted flower (60F) or some of the local candies, *truffelines* and *muscalines*. (Open Feb.-Dec. daily 10am-noon and 2:30-6:30pm. 16F, children and groups 12F.) For four days in mid-July, fire-eaters play to costumed crowds at the medieval market during the **Fête du Grand Fauconnier,** which offers plays, concerts, and magic shows within the *vieille ville.* Gnaw a drumstick at one of the Fête's medieval banquets. (Tel. 05 63 56 00 52 for reservations and info. Costume rentals 50-100F. Entrance 30F; free if costumed.)

The **tourist office,** pl. de Halle (tel. 05 63 56 00 52; fax 05 63 56 19 52) in Maison Fontpeyrouse, can help find accommodations. (Open daily 10:30am-12:30pm and 2:30-6pm; July-Aug. 10am-7pm.) A food **market** takes place Saturdays 8am-noon at the bottom of the hill. **Trains** go to **Vindrac** via **Tessonnières,** where you can call the **Barrois** minibus (tel. 05 63 56 14 80) to take you the 5km to Cordes (25F per person). If the minibus is unavailable, getting from the train station to Cordes can be a nightmare of a 5km walk; many choose to hitch, but catching a ride can be difficult. In summer, Barrois also runs buses to Cordes from **Albi.** (July-Aug. M-Sa at 9am and 5pm; Sept.-June Tu and Sa only. 25F.) During the school year, **Cars Becardit** (tel. 05 63 45 03 03), **Sudcar Rolland** (tel. 05 63 54 11 93), and **Cahuzac Tourisme** (tel. 05 63 33 96 05) send two buses daily to Cordes from **Albi** (27F).

CASTRES

Pastel-colored houses and 17th-century buildings straddle the dark, serene Agoût river in Castres (pop. 48,000), a city that muddled through time until it acquired the 11th-century relics of St. Vincent. The town thus became an essential stopover for pilgrims en route to Santiago de Compostela, but the party ended when Protestants dumped the holy remains in the river and tore down the basilica during the wars of religion. With relics in short supply, the city has compensated by acquiring France's second-largest collection of Spanish art for the Musée Goya. In addition, Castres has assembled effluvious quantities of pamphlets, drawings, photographs, and avenues dedicated to native son Jean Jaurès, a great humanist who worked for peace until he was assassinated shortly before WWI. Make Castres a daytrip from Toulouse, as hotels are exorbitantly expensive.

The famous wooden **Coche d'Eau** sails from the historical centre of Castres, in front of the tourist office, to the larger, green areas of the river in the surrounding countryside. (45min., daily May-June 2-6pm, July-Aug. 10:30am-6pm, 25F). Otherwise, the town is home to three museums; a ticket for all costs 25F, or 15F for students. In front of the shrubs of the **Jardin de l'Evêché**, the **Musée Goya** (tel. 05 63 71 59 35), located in the Hôtel de Ville, houses a terrific spread of Spanish painting dating back to the 14th century. There are only three Goya paintings, but plenty of his engravings. Other Catalan and Aragonese masters are displayed. (Open July-Aug. M-Sa 9am-noon and 2-6pm, Su 10am-noon and 2-6pm; Apr.-June and Sept. closed M; Sept. 22-Mar. Tu-Sa 9am-noon and 2-5pm, Su 10am-noon and 2-5pm. July-Aug. 20F, students 10F; Sept.-June 15F, students 8F.) The **Musée Jaurès,** pl. Pélisson (tel. 05 63 72 01 01), is packed with political cartoons, photographs, and newspaper articles that recount Jaurès's spirited life and rhetoric. Jaurès leapt into prominence as leader of the striking glass-workers of Carmaux in 1896 and later joined Émile Zola in vehement defense of Alfred Dreyfus, the Jewish officer framed as a traitor by the army. (Same hours as Musée Goya. 10F, students 5F.) The **Centre d'Art Contemporain,** 35 rue Chambre de l'Édit (tel. 05 63 59 30 20), lodged in an 18th-century *hôtel*, shows works by up-and-coming regional artists. (Open July-Aug. M-Sa 9am-noon and 2-6pm, Su 10am-noon and 2-6pm; Sept.-June Tu-Sa 10am-noon and 2-6pm, Su 3-5pm. July-Aug. 5F, Sept.-June free.)

For two weeks in mid-July, the **Festival Goya** celebrates Spanish culture with concerts, exhibitions, flamenco and ballet performances, and more. Many events are free; tickets to others are available at the tourist office or by calling the **théâtre municipal.** (Tel. 05 63 71 56 57. Open M-F 10:30am-12:30pm and 3-6:30pm. Tickets 40-150F, reductions for students and groups of 10 or more.)

When hunger strikes, you can avail yourself of the **markets** on pl. Jean Jaurès (Tu and Th-Sa 7:30am-1pm) and at **pl. de l'Albinque** (Tu-Su 8:30am-1pm). **Monoprix,** rue Sabatier at pl. Jean Jaurès, delivers seductively cheap supermarket fare. (Open M-Sa 8:30am-7:30pm.) A few *boulangeries* and *boucheries* gather on **rue Gambetta** and **rue Victor Hugo** in the *centre ville*, while restaurants cluster off **pl. Jean Jaurès** and near **rue Villegoudou.** For munchables, **Cormary,** 13 rue Victor Hugo (tel. 05 63 59 27 09), sculpts fine chocolates, marzipan, and pastries into animal shapes. (Open M-F 6am-1pm and 1:30-7:30pm, Sa 6am-5:30pm, Su 6am-1pm.) You can **rent bikes** at **Tabarly,** 38 pl. Soult. (Tel. 05 63 35 38 09. 50F per half-day, 80F per day. 500F or credit card deposit. Open Tu-Sa 9am-noon and 2-7pm.)

The **tourist office** is at 3 rue Milhau Ducommun. (Tel. 05 63 62 63 62; fax 05 63 62 63 60. Open July-Aug. M-Sa 9am-7pm, Su 10:30am-noon and 3-5:30pm; Sept.-June M-Sa 8:30am-12:30pm and 1:30-6:30pm, Su 2-6pm.) To get there from the station, turn left onto av. Albert 1er and then bear right onto bd. Henri Sizaire. At pl. Alsace-Lorraine, cross the bridge and turn left onto bd. Raymond Vittoz, then take the first left onto rue Villegoudou and veer right onto rue Leris. The office is on the right as you continue straight (20min.). From the bus station, walk across pl. Soult and continue straight on rue Villegoudou, veering right onto rue Leris. The tourist office is farther up on the right (5min.).

The **train station,** av. Albert 1er (tel. 05 63 72 29 91), has service to **Toulouse** (1hr., 8 per day, 61F), **Carcassonne** via Toulouse (2½hr., 8 per day, 124F), and **Albi** via St-Sulpice (2hr., 7 per day, 79F). **Buses** run from pl. Soult (tel. 05 63 35 37 31) to **Albi** (1hr., 5 per day, 31F) and **Toulouse** (55F).

CARCASSONNE

Carcassonne's enormous fortified *cité* has had a rough go of it. Attacked in the first century B.C. by Roman invaders, who subsequently gave way to Visigoths and Moors, Europe's largest fortress has come to exemplify stalwart opposition in the face of aggression. To rectify the egregious state into which the ancient citadel had fallen over the years, King Louis-Philippe commissioned the revered architect Viollet-le-Duc in 1844 to restore it. Today, Carcassonne (pop. 45,000) still rises from a precipitous plateau in the Garonne Valley and stands as one of the most spectacular and most popular sights in France. Even before providing the backdrop for the 1991 movie *Robin Hood: Prince of Thieves*, the *cité* attracted droves of tourists. Early-morning visiting will beat the daytrippers who make up the bulk of Carcassonne's visitors. At night crowds disperse, and the fortress, bathed with floodlights and music of summer concerts, recaptures its elusive charm.

☑ ORIENTATION AND PRACTICAL INFORMATION

Hosting shops, hotels, and the train station, the *basse ville* facilitates trips to the *cité*. Catch the **navette** (every 40min.) in front of the station to take you over the bridge to the impressive *cité* gates or to the campground, or take bus #4 to pl. Gambetta and switch to bus #2 or 8 (every 30min. until 7pm, all bus tickets 5.40F). Otherwise, it's a pleasant but steep 30-minute hike. To get from the station to the *cité*, walk straight down rue Clemenceau, then take the third left onto rue de la Liberté and a right onto bd. Jean Jaurès. At sq. Gambetta, bear left on rue de Pont-Vieux and walk over the bridge. Follow rue Trivalle to rue Gustave Nadaud, which runs along the perimeter of the *cité*. The entrance is farther up the hill where rue Nadaud meets the Voie Médiévale. The tourist office annex will be on the right as you enter the castle. Street signs can be fickle in Carcassonne, so check all four corners of the intersection.

Trains: Tel. 04 68 71 79 14, behind Jardin St-Chenier. To: **Toulouse** (50min., 24 per day, 72F); **Narbonne** (1hr., 10 per day, 51F); **Montpellier** (2hr., 14 per day, 110F); **Perpignan** (2hr., 10 per day, 140F); **Nîmes** (2½hr., 12 per day, 135F); **Marseille** (3hr., every 2hr., 195F); **Lyon** (5½hr., 2 direct per day, 258F); and **Nice** (6hr., 5 per day, 288F). Info office open M-Sa 9am-noon and 1:30-6:15pm.

Buses: Bd. de Varsovie or near the train station (tel. 04 68 25 12 74). Check posted schedules at the station or ask tourist office. To: **Foix** (1hr., 2 per day, 33F); **Toulouse** (2½hr., 3 per day, 52F); and **Narbonne** (3hr., 1 per day, 44F). **Cars Teissier** (tel. 04 68 25 85 45) has service to **Lourdes** (150F).

Tourist Office: 15 bd. Camille Pelletan, sq. Gambetta (tel. 04 68 10 24 30; fax 04 68 10 24 38). From the station, walk over the canal on rue G. Clemenceau. Turn left onto rue de la Liberté and then right onto bd. Jean Jaurès. The office is on the right on sq. Gambetta (10min.). Open daily July-Aug. 9am-7pm; Sept.-June 9am-12:15pm and 1:45-6:30pm. Annex in the *cité*'s Porte Narbonnaise (tel. 04 68 10 24 36). Open daily July-Aug. 9am-7pm; Sept.-June 9am-1pm and 2-6pm.

Local Transportation: CART, sq. Gambetta (tel. 04 68 47 82 22). Ticket 5.30F, *carnet* of 10 47F. M-Sa only. Buses run from about 7am-7pm.

Taxis: Radio Taxi Services (tel. 04 68 71 50 50). At the train station or across the canal by Jardin Chenier. 24hr. 7F per km during the day, 10F per km at night.

Money: Banque Nationale, 50 rue Jean-Bringer, and **Société le Comptoir** both offer **currency exchange.**

Laundromat: Laverie Express, 5 sq. Gambetta. Open daily 8am-10pm.

Police: 4 bd. Barbès (tel. 04 68 77 49 00).

Medical Assistance: Centre Hospitalier, rte. de St-Hilaire (tel. 04 68 24 24 24).

Post Office: 40 rue Jean Bringer (tel. 04 68 11 71 00). Poste Restante code: 11012. **Currency exchange.** Open M-F 8am-7pm, Sa 8am-noon (tel. 04 68 11 71 18). **Branch office** (tel. 04 68 47 95 45) at the corner of rue de Comte Roger and rue Viollet-le-Duc in the *cité*. **Postal code:** 11000.

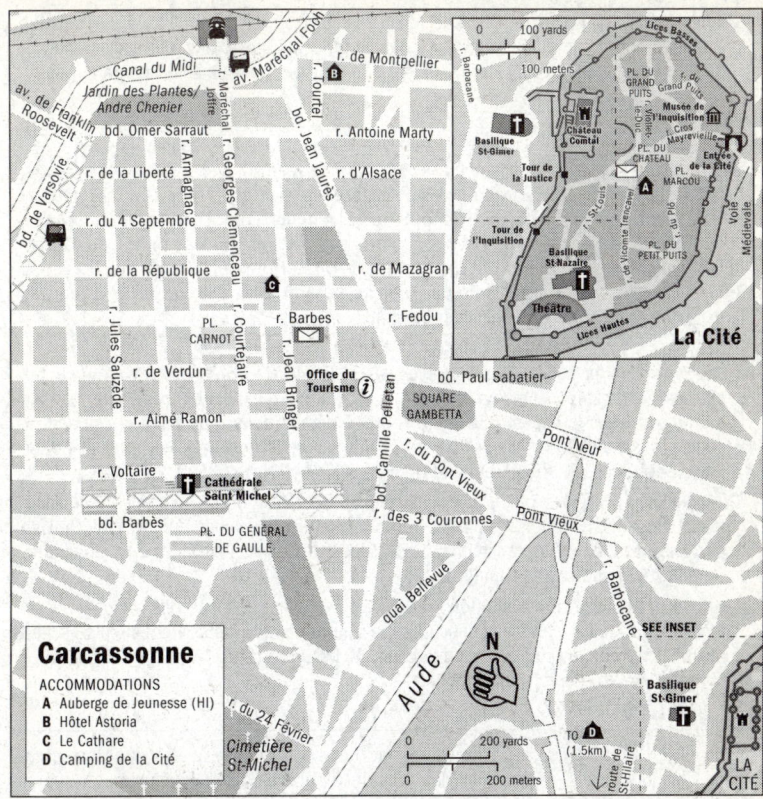

Carcassonne

ACCOMMODATIONS
A Auberge de Jeunesse (HI)
B Hôtel Astoria
C Le Cathare
D Camping de la Cité

ACCOMMODATIONS AND CAMPING

Carcassonne's large, comfortable hostel is a little pearl that puts you smack dab in the middle of the *cité*. Otherwise find a hotel in the *basse ville*; those in the *cité* are ferociously expensive.

Auberge de Jeunesse (HI), rue de Vicomte Trencavel (tel. 04 68 25 23 16; fax 04 68 71 14 84), in the *cité*. Enormous rooms offer shower and sink areas two steps from your bed. New bar (open 6pm-1am) and breezy summer patio downstairs. 74F. Sheets 17F. Breakfast included. Kitchen available. 24hr. reception. **Members only.** Reserve a few days in advance; a few weeks in summer. V, MC.

Hôtel Astoria, at the intersection of rue Montpellier and rue Tourtel (tel. 04 68 25 31 38; fax 04 68 71 34 14); take an immediate left after crossing the bridge in front of the station and a right onto rue Montpellier. Pleasant, airy, pink rooms in the hotel or sparkling new ones in the annex across the street. English-speaking owners will help with your travel plans. Reserve ahead June-Sept. One 100F single; other singles and doubles 130F, with shower 160-190F; singles and doubles in the annex 200F. Showers 10F. Breakfast 28F, 20F with your *Let's Go*. Reception 7:30am-9pm. V, MC, AmEx.

Le Cathare, 53 rue Jean Bringer (tel. 04 68 25 65 92), near post office. Cozy, bright, almost perfect renovated rooms. Singles and doubles 117F, with shower and TV 160-170F; triples 185F. Breakfast 27F. Hall showers included. The lovely ochre and pale green restaurant downstairs posts an ever-changing 66F *menu*, grilled in the dining room fireplace in winter. English spoken. V, MC.

THE SOUTHWEST

Campsites: Camping de la Cité, rte. de St-Hilaire (tel. 04 68 25 11 77), across the Aude, 2km from the modern town. Ask tourist office for bus routes. Currency exchange, pool, tennis, and a grocery store. 83F per site, 53F per extra person. Open Apr.-Sept.

🍴 FOOD

Carcassonne's specialty is the inexpensive *cassoulet*, a stew of white beans, herbs, and meat (usually lamb or pork, sometimes pigeon). There is a food **market** on pl. Carnot. (Open Tu, Th, and Sa 7am-1pm.) **Monoprix** graces rue G. Clemenceau at rue de la République. (Open M-Sa 8:30am-7pm.) At restaurants on **rue du Plo**, 55-60F *menus* abound. Save room for dessert at one of the outdoor *crêperies* on **pl. Marcou.** Restaurants in the *cité* tend to close in winter. In the *basse ville*, simple, affordable restaurants line **bd. Omer Sarraut.**

📍 **Les Fontaines du Soleil,** 32 rue du Plo (tel. 04 68 47 87 06), in the *cité*. When in the *cité*, eat like a king! Sunny patio dining in a beautiful regal garden court with fountain and fine cuisine. Cheapest 65F lunch and 69F dinner *menus* specialize in fish and, of course, *cassoulet*, but you won't be sorry if you splurge. Open daily July-Aug. 11:30am-2am; Sept.-June 11:30am-3pm and 6pm-2am. Closed Nov. 15-Feb. 15. V, MC.

Chez Paulo, 15 rue des Trois Couronnes (tel. 04 68 47 29 60), 2 blocks from pl. Gambetta. This cheery Italian restaurant in the *basse ville* serves up yummy gnocchi with gorgonzola sauce (60F), mushroom pizza (55F), and a 3-course 75F *menu*. Open daily 9am-2:30pm and 6:30-11pm. V, MC.

La Rizière, 26 rue G. Brassens (tel. 04 68 47 17 36), in the *basse ville*, whips up vegetarian dishes and Vietnamese specialties in a flower-filled interior. Heaping plates start at 45F. Open Tu-Su noon-2pm and 7-11pm. V, MC.

👁 SIGHTS

Occupying a strategic position on the road between Toulouse and the Mediterranean, Carcassonne's original **fortifications** date back to the first century. An early Visigoth fortress here repelled Clovis in AD 506. Subsequent invaders were dismissed, but Carcassonne fell with Languedoc during the Albigensian Crusade in 1209. When the *cité* passed to the control of the French King St. Louis (Louis IX), he ordered the construction of the second outer wall, copying the double-walled fortress design he had seen in Palestine as a crusader. The city lapsed into neglect until Viollet-le-Duc remodeled it in the 19th century. The blue slate roofs he fancied for the towers of the fortress's inner ring are so out of place among the Midi's red-tile roofs that the town has begun to reroof them using local materials.

Originally constructed as a palace in the 12th century, the **Château Comtal** (tel. 04 68 25 01 66 or 04 68 72 63 81) was transformed into a citadel following Carcassonne's submission to royal control in 1226. While entrance to the grounds and outer walls is free, you must pay for a guided tour to be admitted to the *château*. Included in the visit, the **Cour du Midi** contains the remains of a Gallo-Roman villa, former home to troubadours who entertained their lords with song and verse. The **Tour de la Justice**'s treacherous staircase leading to nowhere served as a stairway to heaven (or hell) for ill-fated invaders who penetrated the fortress and rushed upstairs, only to be trapped and easily vanquished. Tours in French run continuously, with 3 daily in English June 15-Sept. 15. All begin inside the château gates. (Open daily July-Aug. 9am-7:30pm; Sept. and June 9am-7pm; Oct.-May 9:30am-12:30pm and 2-6pm. Tickets sold until 30min. before closing. 35F, ages 18-25 23F.)

Although it feels a bit like an elementary school haunted house, the privately run **Musée de l'Inquisition,** 5 rue du Grand Puits (tel. 04 68 71 44 03), has a collection of thoroughly disturbing torture instruments used by the Catholics to show the Cathars the error of their ways. (Open daily July-Aug. 9am-11pm; Sept.-June 10am-7pm. 40F, students 30F.)

WHEN PIGS FLY When Charlemagne's troops besieged the *cité* over a five-year period in the 8th century, legend has it that its widowed Moorish queen, Dame Carcas, came to its salvation. Just as food was running out, she ordered that the last of the grain be given to the last pig. She then tossed the fattened porker over the city walls. Fooled into thinking that the *cité* had food to spare and could continue to hold out, Charlemagne called off the attack. As the troops retreated, the Grande Dame rang *(sonnait)* the city's bell to signal her willingness to draw up a treaty—some even say she had a crush on the emperor. Supposedly, the tintinnabulation drew the attention of the king's men, who called to Charlemagne, *"Carcas sonne!"*

The apse of **Basilique St-Nazaire,** pl. de l'Église (tel. 04 68 25 27 65), is the coolest place in Carcassonne on a sultry summer afternoon. The nave's simple, Romanesque style is enhanced by the brightness of the choir and windows. For 10F (children 5F), you can climb 70 spiral steps to the top of the tower for a panoramic view. (Open daily July-Aug. 9am-7pm; Sept.-June 9:30am-noon and 2-5:30pm. Mass Su 11am.) Turned into a fortress after the Black Prince destroyed Carcassonne in 1355, the *basse ville*'s **Cathédrale St-Michel,** rue Voltaire (tel. 04 68 25 14 48), still sports fortifications on its southern side, facing bd. Barbès. The church, with its light, painted interior, exemplifies 14th- and 15th-century *gothique languedocien.* (Open M-Sa 7am-noon and 2-7pm, Su 9:30am-noon.)

🎵 🌿 ENTERTAINMENT AND FESTIVALS

ENTERTAINMENT. Although nightlife is limited here, Carcassonne has just enough to satisfy insomniacs. Bars and cafés along **rue Omer Sarraut** and **pl. Verdun** remain open until midnight. You'll have to walk a few dark blocks to reach the cosmopolitan **Day Break,** 11 rue du Grand Puits (tel. 04 68 25 52 58), serving good food and local talent in its small, loved space. (Open Apr.-Oct. daily 10am-1am; Nov.-Mar. F-Su 10am-3pm and 7pm-1am. On concert nights open until 3am.) Locals dance the night away at **La Bulle,** 115 rue Barbacane. (Tel. 04 68 72 47 70. Open weekends only until dawn.)

FESTIVALS. In July, the month-long **Festival de Carcassonne** graces the enchanting ancient amphitheater of the *cité* and the Château Comtal with a vibrant program of dance, opera, theater, and concerts. (120-300F. Info and reservations tel. 04 68 11 59 15; fax 04 68 11 59 16; or write to Festival de la Cité, Théâtre Jean Alary, B.P. 236.) On **Bastille Day,** Carcassonne outdoes mere displays of fireworks. Viewed from the *basse ville*, complex lighting sets the *cité* aflame, commemorating the villages burned when the Tour de l'Inquisition was the seat of the inquisitorial jury. For two weeks in early August, the entire *cité* returns to the Middle Ages for the **Spectacles Médiévaux.** People dressed in medieval garb talk to visitors, display their crafts, and pretend nothing has changed in eight centuries. At 9:30pm nightly, a huge multimedia show uses 20th-century technology to bring the 13th century to life. For ticket information, contact Carcassonne Terre d'Histoire, Club Hippique, Chemin de Serres (tel. 04 68 71 35 35).

THE PYRÉNÉES ORIENTALES

In the area between the Ariège and the Languedoc, the valleys of this immense, mountainous area occasionally expose small hamlets of beige homes with blue shutters and hundreds of pink flowers. When the morning fog lifts, snowy mountain tops blaze white under the hot sun. With high ski slopes and hot *thermes*, this *pays*-for-all-seasons entices travelers year round.

FOIX

Once upon a *foix* (well, in the 13th century), Catholic crusaders conquered the Cathar stronghold that is now the landmark of modern Foix (pop. 10,000). Nestled in the eastern Pyrenees, 85km south of Toulouse, the castle remains in perfect health, reigning above the vivacious and competitive markets of its town. Foix claims kinship with Gaston Phébus, the great 14th-century warrior whose motto, *"Toque-y si gauses"* ("Touch if you dare"), Foix claims as its own—but don't do this at the *marché* unless you plan on buying. Along with the castle, many nearby outdoor activities attract visitors to town *foix* and *foix* again. For hiking, kayaking, and traveling in the Ariège, Foix makes an ideal base.

⊿ PRACTICAL INFORMATION. The **train station**, av. Pierre Sémard (tel. 05 61 02 03 64), is north of town off the N20. Trains go **Toulouse** (1hr., 11 per day, 68F). (Info and reservation desk open M 5:30am-7:35pm and 8:45-9:30pm, Tu-Sa 8am-7:35pm and 8:45-9:30pm, Su 8am-9:30pm.) **Salt Autocars**, 8 allées de Villote (tel. 05 61 65 08 40), also runs to **Toulouse** (1¼hr., 2 per day, 50F). **Intersport La Hutte**, 40-42 rue Delcassé (tel. 05 61 65 00 41), rents **bikes** and **skis**. (Bikes 90F per half-day, 110F per day. Cross-country skis 50F per day, downhill 80F per day. Passport deposit. Open M-Sa 9am-noon and 2:15-7pm. V, MC.) To reach the **tourist office**, 45 cours G. Fauré (tel. 05 61 65 12 12; fax 05 61 65 64 63), exit the train station and turn right. Follow the street until you reach the main road (N20). Follow this highway to the second bridge, cross it, and follow cours G. Fauré for about three blocks (10min.). Sending tours to the château, this small office offers more than most. (Open July-Aug. M-Sa 9am-7pm, Su 10am-12:30pm and 3-6:30pm; Sept. and June M-Sa 9am-noon and 2-6pm, Su 10am-12:30pm; Oct.-May M-Sa 9am-noon and 2-6pm.) For **police**, call 05 61 05 43 00. The **hospital** is on cours Gabriel Fauré (tel. 05 61 05 40 40). The **post office**, 4 rue Laffont (tel. 05 61 02 01 02), has **currency exchange**. (Open M-F 8am-7pm, Sa 8am-noon. Poste Restante code: 09008. **Postal code:** 09000.)

⊯ ACCOMMODATIONS. The surrounding countryside of jade-colored rivers and mountains will make you want to stay in Foix overnight. The tourist office has a list of *chambres d'hôtes* which go for about 180F (including breakfast). But if you'd like a very affordable room for yourself or you and your friends, **Foyer Léo Lagrange**, 16 rue Peyrevidal (tel. 05 61 65 09 04), is the place. To get there, turn left out of the tourist office; follow cours Gabriel Fauré and turn left again just before the giant steel structure. Continue straight and the *foyer* will be on your right. A cross between a nice hotel and a friendly hostel, it provides rooms with one to four beds and a shower, plus plenty of advice on sightseeing. (80F, 70F for 3rd night and after or for groups of 2 or more. Breakfast 25F. Lunch 55F. Kitchen available. Bike rental 50F per day. 24hr. reception.) Opposite the Foyer sits **Hôtel Eychenne**, 11 rue Peyrevidal (tel. 05 61 65 00 04), lost somewhere between elegance and gaudiness with low lighting and plentiful gold fixtures. (Singles and doubles with shower 160F; triples or quads with bath 250F. Breakfast 28F. V, MC.) The theme continues at **La Barbacane du Château**, 1 av. de Lérida (tel. 05 61 65 50 44; fax 05 61 02 74 33), with a golden cash register in its reading room, a gold-rimmed coffee maker in its dining area, and classy bedrooms with views of the château. (Singles and doubles 180-320F; triples and quads 400F. Extra bed 60F. Breakfast 38F. Open Apr.-Oct. 7am-11:30pm. V, MC.) **Camping Labarre**, a two-star site 3km up N20 toward Toulouse (tel. 05 61 65 11 58), sprawls by the river. Buses to Toulouse stop at the camp. (45F for 2 people, car, and tent; 65F July-Aug. Open Apr.-Sept.)

⊡ FOOD. Foix is an excellent representative of its region; *ariègeois* specialties are everywhere. Try *truite à l'ariègeoise* (trout) or the wonderfully messy *écrevisses* (crayfish). The well-known and well-loved pastry is filled with jam and covered in honey-coated almonds. For regular supplies, **Champion supermarket**, rue Laffont, has inexpensive picnic foods. (Open M-Sa 9am-12:15pm and 2:15-7pm.) On Fridays and alternate Mondays, an **open-air market** sprouts all over Foix, with meat and cheese at the Halle aux Grains, fruits and vegetables at pl. St-Volusien, and clothing along the allées de Villote (food 8am-12:30pm, clothes 8am-4pm).

Le Petit Creux, 9 rue Lazéma (tel. 05 61 02 91 43), has an owner who knows his regular customers by name and welcomes new ones. Offers sunny décor, attentive service, and heaping servings. The mushroom ravioli is a treat (45F). *Menu* for 52F. (Open daily noon-3pm and 7-10:30pm.) The duplex **Le Jeu de l'Oie,** 17 rue de la Faurie (tel. 05 61 02 69 39), features tasty goat cheese salads and grilled fish and meats starting at 50F. The brave can try the specialty *cargolade,* snails stuffed with bacon. (Open daily noon-2:30pm and 7-10pm.)

◑ ⚠ ✖ SIGHTS, EXCURSIONS, AND FESTIVALS. One look at the **Château de Foix** looming above the city, and you'll understand why Simon de Montfort failed four times to vanquish it. Inside this well-preserved castle, the **Musée de l'Ariège** (tel. 05 61 65 56 05) displays artifacts from the Roman Empire to the Middle Ages. Those who can overcome their fear of falling down a long spiral staircase with no railing will enjoy the panoramic view of the Pyrenean foothills from the tower. (Both open daily July-Aug. 9:45am-6:30pm; June and Sept. 9:45am-noon and 2-6pm; Oct.-May W-Su 10:30am-noon and 2-5:30pm. Tours almost every hr. 25F.)

The **Ariège** boasts some of the most spectacular **caves** in France. An hour-long boat ride takes visitors through the caves on the **Labouiche,** the longest navigable underground river in Europe open to the public. (Tel. 05 61 65 04 11. 6km from Foix. 44F, students in the morning 32F. Open July-Aug. daily 9:30am-6pm; Apr.-May 24 M-Sa 2-6pm, Su 10am-noon and 2-6pm; May 25-June 30 and Sept. daily 10am-noon and 2-6pm; Oct.-Nov. 11 Su 10am-noon and 2-6pm.) The **Grotte de Niaux** contains 13,000-year-old paintings of leaping herds of bison, deer, and horses. (Tel. 05 61 05 88 37. Reservations essential. 20km south of Foix. Ask the tourist office about visiting this and other prehistoric caves.)

In the first week of July, the **Résistances** festival brings 100 films—many the same as those shown in Cannes—to Tarascon-sur-Ariège, one stop from Foix on the Ax-les-Thermes line. (Tel. 05 61 05 94 94; email resistances@capmedia.fr. 1-day pass 80F, 3-day pass 160F.) Every weekend from the end of July though the end of August, a **medieval festival** enlivens the foot of the Foix's château at 10pm. (For info, tel. 05 61 02 88 26. 100-140F, under 12 50-70F.)

NEAR FOIX: CHÂTEAU DE MONTSÉGUR

Thirty-five kilometers southeast of Foix along the D9, the aged and austere Château de Montségur stands dominant over the Ariège. A stunning reminder of the Cathar past and its legends, it enjoys a magnificent view of the craggy land below. It was the bustling capital of the Cathar church until 1242, when the Cathars turned the tables on the papal judge in a bloody raid at Avignonet. The massacre prompted Louis IX's Catholic forces to besiege Montségur, which finally fell in 1244. On March 16th, two weeks into a truce, more than 200 unrepentant Cathars calmly submitted to death by fire at the castle. Legends surround the events of the night preceding the fire, when the Cathar bishop entrusted their treasure to four *parfaits,* Cathar clergymen dedicated to taking control of the whole region, who escaped into the mountains—supposedly with the mythical Holy Grail. (Castle open daily June-Sept. 9am-5pm. 22F.) Get info on the château and various hiking and biking trails, including the **Massif du St-Barthélémy** and the **Massif de la Frau,** from Montségur's **tourist office.** (Tel. 05 61 03 03 03. Open daily July-Sept. At other times, call the mayor's office for information. Tel. 05 61 01 10 27.) During the school year, five **buses** run to Montségur daily from Foix's Centre Culturel Olivier Carol (direction "Lavelanet," 25F). The rest of the year, you need to stay overnight since only two buses run daily. Ask the driver to drop you at the turn-off to Montségur, and from there follow the signs through the town of Villeneuve d'Olmes to **Montférrier** (5km). From here it's another 5km uphill to the château. To return to Foix, flag down the bus (check schedules carefully at the Foix tourist office before you leave). You can leave your pack in Montférrier at **La Freychede** (tel. 05 61 01 10 38), with 80 beds in two- to six-people rooms, a library, a TV room, and two recreation halls. (65F. Breakfast 15F. Kitchen access. Call ahead.)

AX-LES-THERMES

Not just another little mountain town, Ax offers three hot springs and four ski stations in the heart of the Pyrenees Orientales. Its specialty is emblazoned in its name—*les thermes*—but the gushing rivers of its town will remind you of the pure ice in its higher regions. While the Romans already knew of its thermal waters, it wasn't until 1260 that the *thermes* gained fame, when St. Louis ordered the construction of "the pond of the lepers" for soldiers who had contracted leprosy or injuries during the crusades. Now, tourists and *curistes* alike enjoy the waters that also soothes boot-weary skiers' feet after a day on the slopes.

🛈 **PRACTICAL INFORMATION.** From the **train station**, pl. de la Gare (tel. 05 61 64 20 72), trains leave for **Foix** (45min., 5 per day, 40F) and **Toulouse** (2hr., 7 per day, 92F). **Salt Autocars** (tel. 05 61 65 08 40 in Foix) also runs to **Foix** (50min., 6 per day, 29F). When you leave the train station, take a left along N20, the highway which becomes rue Delcassé, and continue going straight. After several blocks, the **tourist office,** 6 rue de la Mairie (tel. 05 61 64 60 60), will be on your right across from the church (800m, keep the river on your right). They offer information on excursions to surrounding towns, accommodations, and ski stations. (Open daily 9am-noon and 2-7pm.) **Car Ferrer** (tel. 05 61 64 20 53) offers excursion to nearby towns, grottos, and Andorra. **Rent skis** at **Sports 2000** (tel. 05 61 64 21 77) on rue Delcassé. For staying in touch, the **post office** is on Gaspard Astrie (tel. 05 61 02 05 60) and **internet access** is available at pl. du Couloubret in **Ax Multiservices Informatiques.** (40F per hour. Open Tu-Sa 9am-noon and 2-7pm.)

🛏🍴 **ACCOMODATIONS AND FOOD.** You'll probably find it cheaper to commute from Foix than stay in one of Ax's hotels. The best rates in town are found at **La Terrasse,** 7 rue Marcailhou (tel. 05 61 64 20 33; fax 05 61 64 65 44), on a quiet sidestreet two minutes from the *centre ville.* (Singles 140-190F; doubles 200-250F. Breakfast 35F. Open Dec. 25-Nov. 1.) There are also some *gîtes d'étapes* nearby, mostly south of Ax and accessible by train; the tourist office has brochures.

From June to September on Tuesdays and Saturdays, a market spreads itself over **pl. Roussel** (8am-1pm). When this summer treat isn't available, several *boulangeries* and fruit stands line **rue de l'Horloge,** to the right of the tourist office. These are no ordinary bakeries! They sell large portions of regional pastries and specialties at especially low prices (4-8F). **L'Oiseau Bleu,** on rue Pilhes (tel. 05 61 64 07 37), is sign-posted from 800m away and serves ornate *crêpes* at affordable prices. (Open daily noon-2 or 3pm and 7pm-whenever. Closed M for lunch.)

🎰🎿🎶 **THERMES, SKIING, AND ENTERTAINMENT.** Ax-les-Thermes offers three different types of *cures:* respiratory, rheumatic, and overall packages. The **thermes office** at 6 av. Delcassé (tel. 05 61 64 24 83) distributes information packets and is available for consultations. (Open M-F 8am-noon and 1:30-5pm.) In contrast to the 78°C vapor, the freezing air of the mountains is home to four ski stations. See the tourist office for bus schedules to the different stations. **Ax-Bonascre** (tel. 05 61 64 20 06) is 2km from the town, and, with 75km of *piste* split between 26 slopes, is the most frequented. A little farther into the mountains (10km) is **Domaine du Chioula** (tel. 05 61 64 20 00), a 5000-hectacre forest with 60km of runs for the adventurous. Also in a wooded area, but with a more family atmosphere, **Ascou Pailheres** has 16 *pistes* (tel. 05 61 64 28 86). **Plateau de Beille** is the farthest of the slopes, 30km from Ax-Les-Thermes, and offers 65km on 10 *pistes.*

For après-ski action, head to Ax's **Casino** (tel. 05 61 64 65 00). You'll find a restaurant, a bar, and the aptly named **Go Bananas** disco in the same building.

PRADES

West of Perpignan, perched halfway up the Pyrénées, the small Catalan town of **Prades** (pop. 6000) presides over the mountainous agricultural area called the **Conflent.** Until the beginning of the 20th century, the town reaped the rewards of a lucrative iron-forging industry, and like many others its ancient church dominates the town square. But Prades takes pride not in its buildings, but in the man known as "the best who draws a bow"—and they're not talking about Robin Hood. The great Catalan cellist Pablo Casals (1876-1973) spent 23 years in the town as a political exile from Franco's Spain. Following a three-year isolation from the musical world in protest at the world's recognition of Franco's state, Casals chose the **Église St-Pierre** for his return concert in 1950. Three kilometers away, the 1000-year-old **Abbaye de St-Michel de Cuxa** (tel. 04 68 96 15 35) hosts the annual **Festival Pablo Casals** (July 26-Aug. 13). The keystone of Prades' cultural calendar, the festival attracts an array of international musicians for three weeks of classical music concerts and workshops. Tickets (150-180F) are available after May 15 from the **Association Pablo Casals,** rue Victor Hugo (tel. 04 68 96 33 07). For the 50th anniversary of the festival in 2000, Prades will come to **Paris** in six concerts at the Théâtre des Champs-Élysées. (Concerts Jan. 21-22, Mar. 18-19, and June 23-24. Tel. 04 68 96 33 07 for info.) During the 49 weeks of the year when the festival is not in town, the **abbey** still merits a visit. Consecrated in 974, it existed peacefully until Revolutionaries torched and pillaged it. Today, monks reside again in the restored edifice. (Open May-Sept. M-Sa 9:30-11:50am and 2-6pm, Su 2-5pm; Oct.-Apr. daily 9:30am-1pm and 2-5pm. Last admission 45min. before closing. 15F, under 18 8F.) In the tourist office, the one-room **Musée Pablo Casals** displays one of the master's cellos, photographs, a documentary on his life, and correspondence between Casals and Albert Schweitzer. Upstairs, the **Musée de Beaux-Arts de Prades** owns a collection of 66 works by the local artist Martin Vives. From black-and-white sketches to his more colorful renditions of French Catalonia, Vives paints his world with dignity. On the same floor, the **Musée d'Archéologie** contains artifacts discovered nearby. (Museums open M-F 9am-noon and 2-6pm, Sa-Su by appointment. Free.)

Although hotels are few and expensive, **Hostalrich,** 156 av. du Général de Gaulle (tel. 04 68 96 05 38), is an exception, with spacious dining areas, a giant patio, and sophisticated rooms. (150F singles with shower; doubles 160-240F.) **Camping Municipal,** at Plaine St-Martin (tel. 04 68 96 29 83), is on the edge of a pond. From the tourist office turn left on av. du Général de Gaulle and right on av. Louis Prat. Another left on allée de la Plaine St-Martin leaves you five minutes from the signposted campsite. (15F per site, 12F per adult, 10F per car. Open Apr.-Sept.) Every Tuesday, a **market** colors the square in front of the Église St-Pierre (8am-1pm).

The **tourist office,** next to the Casals Academy at 4 rue Victor Hugo (tel. 04 68 05 41 02), distributes reams of brochures. Ask for the booklet on **hiking trails** around Prades, which includes directions to the abbey and other day hikes. (Open July-Aug. M-Sa 9am-12:30pm and 2-6:30pm, Su 9am-noon; Sept.-June M-Sa 9am-noon and 2-5pm.) The tourist office gives free morning tours of the town, including an after-tour *apéritif* and a chat with the friendly staff. You can explore the beautiful Conflent on wheels with **bikes** from **Cycles Cerda,** 114 av. du Général de Gaulle. (Tel. 04 68 96 54 51. 80F per day, 200F for 3 days. 1000F or passport deposit. Open M-Sa 8am-noon and 2-7pm.) **Trains** come from **Perpignan** (50min., 7 per day, 30F).

VILLEFRANCHE-DE-CONFLENT

Deep in the mountains of the Conflent, hidden within its steep ramparts, miniscule Villefranche-de-Conflent (pop. 260) occupies a prized location. In a valley at the base of three mountains at the confluence of the Cady and Têt rivers, its winding streets offer shops which sell rustic mementos at inflated prices. Far more memorable, and free, is the view of the red sun that bakes the cobblestones at dusk.

■ **PRACTICAL INFORMATION. Trains** run to **Perpignan** (50 min.; M-Sa 5 per day, 4 on Su). Villefranche is also the terminus of the scenic **Trains Jaune** route; see **Excursions** below. The **tourist office,** 32bis rue St-Jacques (tel. 04 68 96 25 64; fax 04 68 96 07 24), has lodging and hiking info, and sells IGN hiking maps for 58F. (Open daily 2-7pm. Call 04 68 96 16 40 other times for info.) **Hiking** information available through the **Direction Départementale de la Jeunesse et des Sports** (tel. 04 68 35 50 49). The **Association Culturelle,** 38 rue St-Jean (tel. 04 68 96 25 64), has a dedicated staff that offers information on historical hiking tours of the area. (Open M-F 8:30am-noon and 1:30-5:30pm.) In July and August, the *Association* also leads tours of the town for 25F. For information about hiking locally and throughout the Pyrenees, and a more extensive (and expensive) collection of IGN hiking maps (66F), write to or call **Éditions et Diffusions Randonnées Pyrénéennes**, BP 88, 09200 St-Girons (tel. 04 61 66 71 87). This region is IGN map 10: "Massif du Canigou."

⌐ ACCOMMODATIONS. Hotels fill quickly in Villefranche during the summer. **Hôtel Le Terminus** (tel. 04 68 96 11 33), outside the village and ten steps to the left of the train station, offers pastel rooms with wooden floors. The attached restaurant offers 55F and 90F *menus* starring trout. (Singles 150F; doubles 180-200F. Breakfast 30F.) The town hall on pl. de l'Église (tel. 04 68 96 10 78) operates **gîtes communaux,** but you must stay for a full week—or at least pay the weekly rate. (Doubles 1000-2000F per week. Town hall open M-F 8am-noon and 2-6pm.) If you succumb completely to the lure of the Pyrenees, ask the conductor of the *train jaune* to let you off at "Thues/Caranca" (30min., 7 per day, 28F from Villefranche). The **gîte-camping Mas de Bordes** (tel. 04 68 97 05 00) is perched beside a crumbling stone church in a canyon nook. The Peeters family opens this serene old stone lodge to travelers. A natural hot spring bubbles just a few minutes away. (55F with kitchen access, camping 25F per person, 6F per tent.) The gîte is a three-hour walk from an entrance to the GR10, which stretches from the Atlantic to the Mediterranean. Horseback riding, a nearby lake, skiing in winter, and endless other outdoor activities await in an area too pristine and refreshing to pass up.

◙ ▓ SIGHTS AND FESTIVAL. 11th-century military **ramparts** completely enclose the town and its well-preserved 13th- and 14th-century façades. (Ramparts open June-Sept. 10am-8pm; Oct.-May 10am-noon and 2-6pm. 20F, students 15F.) Built into the mountainside high above the town, 17th-century **Fort Liberia** (tel. 04 68 96 34 01) was designed by the military architect Vauban to protect Villefranche after a 1659 treaty established the nearby French-Spanish border. To reach its fortified heights, take the **Navette** from Porte de France (every 30min., 20F, students 15F), or make the 20-minute climb. The subterranean staircase of "1000 steps" (thankfully an overstatement) ascends to the fort and is the only link between the town and Liberia above. (Open daily June-Sept. 9am-8pm; Oct.-May 10am-6pm. 28F, students 20F.) Just outside the walls of Villefranche, a forest of stalagmites sprouts at the **Grotte des Canalettes.** (Tel. 04 68 96 23 11. Open June 16-Sept. 15 daily 10am-6pm; Sept. 16-Nov. and Mar.-June 15 daily 10am-noon and 2-5pm; Dec.-Mar. Su 2-5pm. 40F, children 20F. Daily *son et lumière* 20F.)

On June 23, the Catalonian **Fête des Feux de St-Jean** burns brightly in Villefranche. Torches lit on the nearby Canigou mountain bring the sacred fire back to the village, where giant puppets watch as locals dance the traditional *sardane*, drink wine, and hop over bonfires.

◪ EXCURSIONS AND SKIING. Running 63km through the Pyrenees, the **Train Jaune** links Villefranche to **Latour-de-Carol** seven times a day. The yellow train runs over deep mountain valleys on spectacular viaducts, stopping at many towns along the way, including **Boilvère-Eyne,** France's highest train station at 1592m. A return trip to Latour will take a day and cost 188F; instead of buying a roundtrip ticket, you can continue your journey with a train to Toulouse (3hr., 3 per day). Shorter trips can be made from 13F one-way. Some cars are open (no walls or roof), allowing their riders to soak in the views of postcard-perfect towns, wildflower fields, and occasional raindrops. It's a good idea to get started early so as not to be caught unawares by the train schedule. (Tel. 08 36 35 35 35 or go to any SNCF station; http://ter.sncf.fr/train-jaune/default.htm.)

In winter, the *train jaune* hauls **skiers** to fashionable **Font-Romeu** (7 per day, 58F). Equipped with snow machines and ski lifts, this resort offers first-rate skiing. Call the **tourist office** in Font Romeu, av. Brousse (tel. 04 68 30 68 30), for info.

CÉRET

Embraced on three sides by the Pyrenees, Céret (pop. 8000) has been a site of great artistic and botanic blossoming. Renowned for their prized cherry trees, the exuberant *céretons* send the first *cerises* of the season to the President of the Republic. A yearly spring festival brings people from all over the region to Céret's early harvests. Yet it is another flowering that puts this proudly Catalonian village on the map. Around 1910, the warm wind in the trees, the ochre sunlight, and the narrow streets of the town inspired some of today's most well-known artists; their canvases and sculptures are monuments to the rustic simplicity and visual enchantments of Céret. Picasso, Chagall, Manolo, and Herbin discovered a "Cubist Mecca." They spent several years in Céret, endowing the town with an impressive collection for its museum. Far enough into the hills to make hiking spectacular, Céret has plenty to offer both naturalist and artist.

🏨 PRACTICAL INFORMATION. Car Inter 66 (tel. 04 68 35 29 02; fax 04 68 87 00 56; email office.du.tourismeCERET@wanadoo.fr) runs **buses** to Céret from Perpignan (35min., 1 per hr., 34F). The same bus line connects Céret to other towns in the valley. From the bus stop on av. George Clemenceau, the **tourist office,** 1 av. Clemenceau (tel. 04 68 87 00 53), is two blocks up the hill on the right. If you're let off outside town at the stop "Céret-pont," it's a 15-minute walk. Follow the signs to the *centre ville*. At the end of rue St-Ferréol, turn left onto bd. Maréchal Joffre, then left again onto av. Clemenceau. The office offers friendly service, a free map of easy hikes, and guided tours of the spots that inspired Picasso (2hr., 20F). (Open July-Aug. M-Sa 9am-12:30pm and 2-7pm, Su 10am-12:30pm; Sept.-Oct. M-F 10am-noon and 2-5pm, Sa 10am-noon. Tours every F in winter around 3pm. 15F.) For **medical help,** contact the Clinique du Vallespir (tel. 04 68 87 12 55). The **police** can be found at 1 bd. Jean Moulin (tel. 04 68 87 10 15). The **post office** is at 40 av. Clemenceau. (Tel. 04 68 87 50 00. Open M-F 9am-noon and 2-5pm, Sa 9am-noon. **Postal code:** 66400.)

🏨 ACCOMMODATIONS. Céret makes a good daytrip, but you'll have few options if you want to sleep under the cherry trees. The **Hôtel Vidal,** 4 pl. du 4 Septembre (tel. 04 68 87 00 85), resides in a 1736 house with a stone terrace and abundant flowers. Its appeal grows with a glimpse of pleasant rooms, new carpeting, and wooden sculptures. (Singles and doubles 170F, with bath 210F. Extra bed 30% extra. Shower 10F. Breakfast 30F. Closed Oct. 15-Nov. 15. V, MC.) The modern 🖼 **Pyrénées Hôtel,** 7 rue de la République (tel. 04 68 87 11 02; fax 04 68 87 31 66), has equally immaculate, simpler rooms with white walls, white sheets, white blankets, and dark, wooden furniture and modern art. Ask for a room with an amazing view of the surrounding foothills. (Singles 130F, with shower 200F; doubles 160-170F, with shower 220F; triples and quads with bath 300F. Show *Let's Go* for 10% off. Breakfast including cherry juice 35F. V, MC.) Céret also has several **campsites.** Ask the bus driver to drop you off near **Camping Municipal de Nogarede,** av. d'Espagne (tel. 04 68 87 26 72), a 10-minute walk from the town center. A municipal pool is a few blocks away. (53F for 2 people, car, and tent. 11F extra person.) To pitch and swim, **Camping Saint-Georges** has its own pool, 30 minutes from the tourist office on rte. de Maureillas. (Tel. 04 68 87 03 73. 29.50F per site.)

🍴 FOOD. On Saturday mornings (9am-12:30pm), a **food market** fills the boulevards between pl. Picasso and pl. de la Liberté. Wander over to **pl. des Neuf Jets** for a simple, inexpensive meal. **La Ferme de Céret,** 15 av. Clemenceau (tel. 04 68 87 07 91), just far enough from the busy streets, giving you the chance to hear the bustle of art lovers yet taste the quiet side of Céret. 95F and 105F *menus* of hearty French and Catalan fare with delicacies such as *pintade aux cerises* (guinea fowl with cherries). (Open July-Oct. Tu-Su noon-2pm and 7-9pm; Nov.-June Tu-Sa noon-2pm and 7-8:45pm, Su noon-2pm. V, MC.) To taste **L'Escapade,** 21 rue St-Ferréol (tel. 04 68 87 40 84), walk through the long corridor for a 70F *menu* of simple, elegant food. The 95F *menu* includes *escargots à la Catalane*. (Open Tu-Su noon-2pm and 7-10pm. V, MC.)

⏱ **SIGHTS.** Linking the *centre ville* to the outskirts, the 14th-century **pont du Diable** occupies a place in locals' hearts and provides a stunning panorama of the surrounding mountains. On the way to the bridge, stop at the **pl. des Neuf Jets** to admire the small but historic marble "fountain of nine jets," dating from 1313. The lion, symbol of the Spanish kings, was perched above the jets in 1491, when Céret was under Spanish control. When the French took the city in 1659, they turned the lion's head to face France.

The seemingly graffiti-bedecked building at 8 bd. Maréchal Joffre is actually the **Musée d'Art Moderne** (tel. 04 68 87 27 76), cleverly combining form with function—even the building's name is spray-painted. Inside you will find works by Picasso, including sculptures, sketches, and paintings, plus a few Chagalls, a Miró, and four paintings by Pierre Brune, the museum's founder. The second floor houses a different artist's work every few months; for summer 2000, there is an exhibition of the French artist Soutine. (Open July-Sept. daily 10am-7pm; May-June and Oct. daily 10am-6pm; Nov.-Apr. W-M 10am-6pm. 35F, students 20F, under 16 free.)

To glimpse the 19th-century, Italian-inspired city walls, walk down bd. Maréchal Joffre until you reach pl. de la République where the **Porte de France** remains. You can climb to the top of the 11th-century brick **Tour d'Espagne**, a two-minute walk from the tourist office down bd. Jean Jaurès on pl. Picasso. The best reminders of the city's fortifications are alive: tremendous plane trees, now 200 years old, were planted to replace the city walls and mark the boundary of the *vieille ville*.

The fun little **Maison de l'Archéologie**, (tel. 04 68 87 31 59), next to the Tour d'Espagne, has two exhibition rooms displaying jewelry, urns, pottery, and other local prehistoric finds. (Open July-Sept. daily 10am-6pm; Oct.-June Th-Tu 2-5pm. Call to confirm off-season hours. 10F.) If you've ever wanted to see what water damage can do to a big French church, look into the **Église St-Pierre.** Take a step inside, noting the marble entrance steps and baptismal font. (Open M-Sa 9am-noon and 2-6pm, Su 9am-noon.) For those in cars, a beautiful panoramic view waits at **Front Fréde** (follow the signs from rue Front-Fréde).

🎆 **FESTIVALS.** For one weekend in late May, Céret celebrates the **Grand Fête de la Cerise** with two full days of cherry markets, Catalan songs, and the traditional Catalan dance, the *sardane* (call the tourist office for the exact dates). The town's most raucous *féria*, **Céret de Toros,** occurs every year on the weekend before Bastille Day. Bullfights in the arena and music in the streets keep everyone up well into the night. (Tel. 04 68 87 47 47; www.little-france.com/adac. Tickets 170-425F.) The **Festival de la Sardane** is a day of Catalonian dancing with costumes and competitions at the end of August (usually the last weekend). After the parade of dancers, everyone travels to the arena to watch the bullfights. (Call the tourist office for more information.)

COLLIOURE

Lounging at the very spot where the Pyrenees finally tumble into the Mediterranean, Collioure (pop. 2770) has attracted visitors for 2000 years. This small port captured the fancy of Greeks and Phoenicians long before it modeled for an unknown named Matisse, who baptized the town as an artists' mecca in 1905. He was soon followed by Dérain, Dufy, Dalí, and Picasso. Now their paintings, along with those of contemporary artists, fill the cobblestone streets. A glimpse of the expansive sea and the stone lighthouse tower, bathed in the late afternoon sun, is enough to understand why Collioure is loved by the artistic eye. An easy daytrip from Perpignan, Collioure's stony beaches, château, and enchanting harbor have the visitor walking through a living painting of a pastel dream.

◪ PRACTICAL INFORMATION. The **train station** (tel. 04 68 82 05 89), at the top of av. Aristide Maillol, sends trains north to **Perpignan** (21F) and **Narbonne** (12 per day, 70F), and south to **Port Bou in Spain** (6 per day, 15F) and **Barcelona** (5 per day, 75F). For information on the coastal bus routes, call **Cars Inter 66** (tel. 04 68 35 29 02) or inquire at the tourist office. For answers to your queries, head to the **tourist office,** pl. du 18 Juin (tel. 04 68 82 15 47; fax 04 68 82 46 29; www.little-france.com/collioure). They keep a list of the area's trails and help plan hikes. (Open daily July-Sept. 9am-8pm; Oct.-June M-Sa 9am-noon and 2-7pm.) **Exchange currency** at **Banque Populaire,** 16 av. de la République. (Tel. 04 68 82 05 94. Open M-F 8am-noon and 1:30-5pm.) The **police station** is on rue Michelet (tel. 04 68 82 25 63; Sept.-June tel. 04 68 82 00 60). The **post office** is on rue de la République. (Tel. 04 68 82 05 50. Open M-F 9am-noon and 2-5pm, Sa 8:30-11:30am. **Postal code:** 66190.)

◪ ACCOMMODATIONS. Collioure fills its picturesque hotels and beaches to the brim during the vacation months of July and August. **Hôtel Triton,** 1 rue Jean Bart (tel. 04 68 98 39 39; fax 04 68 82 11 32), sits on the waterfront, a 10-minute walk from the *centre ville.* It boasts a terrace with a panorama of the Mediterranean in addition to comfortable, modern rooms with TVs and phones. (Doubles with shower 180F, with shower and toilet 250-320F. Breakfast 35F. Reservations recommended. V, MC, AmEx.) In the **Hôtel des Templiers,** 12 av. Camille Pelletan (tel. 04 68 98 01 24), simple white rooms contrast with hallways covered top to bottom with hundreds of original paintings. At this restaurant and hotel, Matisse, Picasso, Dalí, and lesser-known artists bartered their work for meals and lodging. Concerned more with local tradition than with making a profit, the proprietors have held on to these works in the face of a bullish art market. (Doubles 290-340F, 335-395F in summer. Breakfast 38F. V, MC, AmEx.) **Camping Les Amandiers,** 28 rue de la Démocratie (tel. 04 68 81 14 69), is a 20-minute walk north of town on the N114 road, but only 150m from the beach. The price includes hot showers and shaded tent sites. (29F per person, 20F per tent. Open Apr.-Sept.)

◪ FOOD. A fantastic **market** on the pl. du Maréchal Leclerc offers inexpensive local fruit, *charcuteries,* clothing, and regional trinkets (W and Su 8am-1pm). Reasonably priced *crêperies, boulangeries,* sandwich shops, and cafés crowd **rue St-Vincent** near the port. The **Shopi supermarket,** 16 av. de la République (tel. 04 68 82 26 04), has Collioure's biggest food selection. (Open M-Sa 8:30am-12:30pm and 4-7:30pm, Su 8:30am-12:30pm.) But **L'Express,** pl. Maréchal Leclerc (tel. 04 68 82 12 61), has all the picnic food you need and better hours. (Open mid-June to mid-Sept. M-Sa 7am-7:30pm, Su 7am-1pm; mid-Sept. to mid-June M-Sa 7am-7pm.) **Vita Croq,** 15 rue St-Vincent (tel. 04 68 82 33 85), is the newest and most frequented restaurant in Collioure. A combination of restaurant and fast-food dining, it serves cheeseburgers (16F) and larger meals like the Big Burger, actually a 100g steak with salad, fries, and an egg (40F). Features large portions, fast music, and outdoor dining. (Open M-Sa noon-2pm and 7-10pm. V, MC.) **El Capilló,** 22 rue St. Vincent (tel. 04 68 82 48 23), with fresh-from-the-boat seafood, sets its black metal chairs against champagne-colored walls. Eight ways of preparing mussels range from *moules à la creme* to *moules au safran* for 44-64F. (Open daily Apr.-Sept. noon-3pm and 7-11pm. V, MC.)

◪ SIGHTS. Extending from pl. du 8 Mai 1945 to the port, the 13th-century **Château Royal** (tel. 04 68 82 06 43) was further fortified in 1679 by Louis XIV's strategist Vauban. The palace itself now houses a hodgepodge of permanent exhibits on regional history and changing modern art exhibits, including an exhibit on anchovies. Wander through the labyrinthine tunnels beneath the château and scale the winding stone staircase for a view of town, sea, and mountains. (Open daily June-Sept. 10am-6pm; Oct.-May 9am-5pm. 20F, students 10F.) The famous red-domed tower of the 17th-century **Notre-Dame-des-Anges** rises majestically from the northern tip of the village. Enter to see the gilded interior. (Open daily 7:30am-noon and

2-6pm.) Those in search of a more natural vantage point can scale the terraces of the **Parc Pams,** behind the château off rte. de Porte-Vendres, to its rocky apex high above the sea. Hikers can get information from the tourist office on a number of trails in the magnificent hills above the Mediterranean lasting one to seven hours.

Collioure's main sights, however, are its **beach** and **harbor,** which are flooded with aspiring artists working at their easels. From the rocky promontory of the bay's southern edge to the pebbled expanses of shoreline punctuated by the château and Notre-Dame-des-Anges, Collioure's bay shelters bathers in its seawalls. Soaring over the highest point of the bay's northern shore is a tiny chapel and large crucifix facing out to sea. The **St-Laurent** (tel. 04 68 81 43 88) offers daily ship *promenades en mer* south along the coast to **Port-Vendres** and on to **Cap Béar** (1hr., daily on the hour, 40F). Longer excursions go south along the Côte Catalane to the Spanish border port of Cerbère (2hr., Th only, 80F). In July and August, a bus (tel. 04 68 35 67 51) runs from Port-le-Barcarès south to **Cerbère,** hitting eight beaches (including Collioure's) along the way (16-57F).

The **Centre International de Plongée,** 2 rue du Puits-St-Dominique (tel. 04 68 82 07 16; fax 04 68 82 44 74), rents **windsurfing gear** (1hr. 50F, 2hr. 80F, 5hr. 200F) and offers training in scuba diving and windsurfing from April to early November. A walkway built into the bottom of the cliffs leads a few kilometers north to **Argelès** along some isolated coastline. The **Randonnée Pedestre Association** (tel. 04 68 82 07 82) organizes more challenging walks and hikes. (Information at tourist office.)

From the 14th to the 18th of August, the **Feria de Collioure** takes over this Catalan port for several days. Midway through the festival, on August 16th, the **corrida** at the *arène* (5pm) is followed by a **fireworks** display over the sea (10pm).

PERPIGNAN

Comfortably cradled between the Mediterranean and the Pyrenees, Perpignan (pop. 108,000) has bounced between French and Spanish ownership as the former capital of the counts of Roussillon and the kings of Majorca. Later it became the northern capital of French Catalonia. In their centuries-long efforts to annex Roussillon to the state, French kings found themselves repeatedly pitted against a stalwart population of *Perpignannais.* The resistors earned their name of *mangeurs de rats* (rat eaters) from the desperate methods used in their struggle for survival.

While the unexpected palm trees, immense Citadel, and quiet cafés of the quai give Perpignan a Mediterranean allure, its best advantage is its proximity to Collioure, Céret, and Canet-Plage. From the modern shops in the *vieille ville* to the lyrical accent of their ever-present patrons, Perpignan has molded itself into a decidedly modern French Catalonian city.

▣ ORIENTATION AND PRACTICAL INFORMATION

Perpignan's train station, once referred to as "the center of the world" by a rather off-center Salvador Dalí, provides convenient connections to the Catalan region in Spain, 50km to the south, and the Pyrenees, whose foothills begin rolling 30km to the west. Most sights, restaurants, cafés, and shops lie inside a triangle formed by the regional tourist office, **pl. de la Victoire** (farther up the canal), and the **Palais des Rois de Majorque.** If you're lost, bus shelters contain a useful map. The **Quartier St-Jacques**—directly to the right as you exit the train station (rue Courteline to rue Renaudel)—is dangerous. Do not go there at night, and be careful during the day.

Trains: Rue Courteline, on av. de Gaulle. To: **Narbonne** (40min., 23 per day, 50F); **Toulouse** (3hr., 15 per day, some change at Narbonne, 140F); **Nice** (6hr., 3 per day, 289F); and **Paris** (6-10hr., 4 per day, 418-484F). Office open M-Sa 8am-6:30pm.

Buses: 17 av. Général Leclerc (tel. 04 68 35 29 02). To **airport** (15min., 4-7 per day, 28F) and **Narbonne** (1½hr., 1 per day, 57F). **Car Inter 66** (tel. 04 68 35 29 02) runs 4 buses to the beaches from **Le Barcarès** (to the north) to **Cerbère** (to the south).

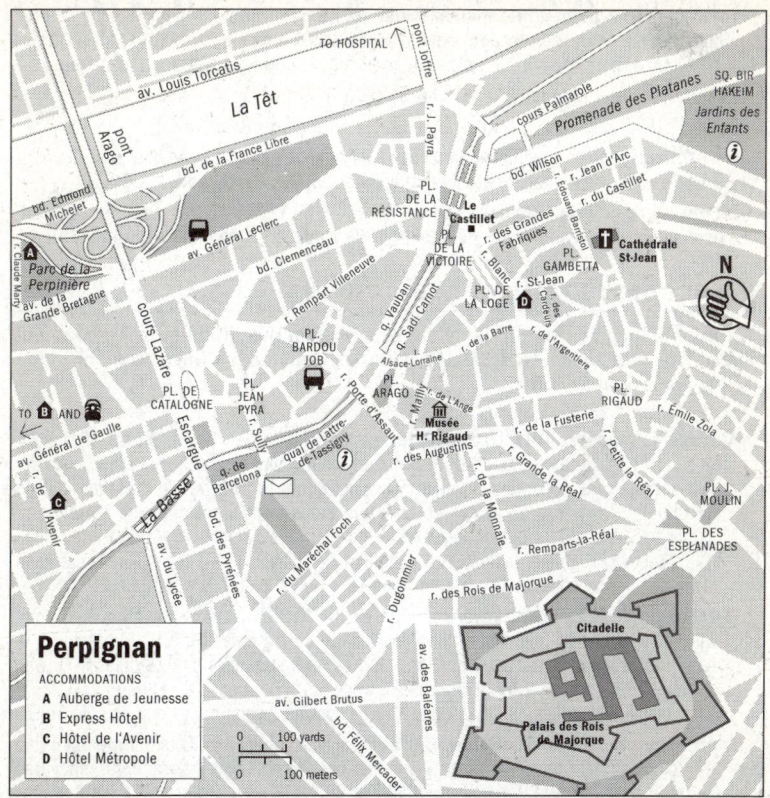

Perpignan

ACCOMMODATIONS
A Auberge de Jeunesse
B Express Hôtel
C Hôtel de l'Avenir
D Hôtel Métropole

Schedules at both tourist offices. They offer a **tourist pass** good for 8 days within the *département* (150F). Office open M-Sa 6:45am-7:15pm.

Local Transportation: CTP, pl. Gabriel-Péri (tel. 04 68 61 01 13). Tickets 6.50F; *carnet* of 10 50F.

Taxis: A.B.C. Taxi (tel. 04 68 34 59 49). 24hr. Catch them at the train station.

Tourist Office: The convenient **branch office,** 7 quai de Lattre de Tassigny (tel. 04 68 34 29 94), should have all you need. From the station, walk straight up av. Général de Gaulle and turn right at pl. Catalogne onto cours Lazare Escarguel. After crossing the canal, turn left onto quai de Barcelone, which becomes quai de Lattre de Tassigny. The office is on the right (15min.). Open July-Aug. M-F 9am-12:30pm and 2-7pm, Sa 9am-noon and 2-6pm; Sept.-June M-F 9am-noon and 2-6:30pm, Sa 9am-noon and 2-6pm. The main **city tourist office,** pl. Armand Lanoux (tel. 04 68 66 30 30; fax 04 68 66 30 26), is at the opposite end of town from the train station. From quai de Lattre de Tassigny, continue along the canal to bd. Wilson. Take a right and follow the signs along the Promenade des Platanes to the modern Palais de Congrès (30min. walk from train). **City tours** (in French) leave June-Sept. M-Sa at 3pm (25F). For tours in English, tel. 04 68 22 25 96. Open June-Sept. M-Sa 9am-7pm, Su 10am-noon and 2-5pm; Oct.-May M-Sa 9am-noon and 2-6pm.

Bike Rental: Cycles Mercier, 20 av. Gilbert Brutus (tel. 04 68 85 02 71). 90F per day, 400F per week. 800F deposit. Open M-Sa 9am-12:30pm and 2:30-7:30pm.

Money: Change booth, pl. Armand Lanoux (tel. 04 68 35 58 97), across from the tourist office, offers good rates and no commission. Open June 15-Sept. 15 daily 10am-4pm; Sept. 16-June 14 M-Sa 10am-4pm.

Laundromat: Laverie Foch, 23 rue Maréchal Foch. Open daily 7am-8pm.

Youth Center: Bureau d'Information Jeunesse, 35 quai Vauban (tel. 04 68 34 56 56), near hostel. Info on jobs and slow internet access. Open Sept.-May M-F 9:30am-12:30pm and 1:30-6pm, Sa 2-5pm. June-Aug. M-F 9:30am-12:30pm and 2-5pm.

Hospital: Av. du Languedoc (tel. 04 68 61 66 33).

Police: L'Hôtel de Police, av. de Grande Bretagne (tel. 04 68 35 70 00).

Post Office: Quai de Barcelone. **Currency exchange.** Open M-Tu and Th-F 8am-7pm, W 9am-7pm, Sa 8am-noon. Poste Restante code: 66020. **Postal code:** 66000.

Internet Access: Arena Games, 9bis rue Pous (tel. 04 68 34 26 22). Fast, reliable connection and lots of terminals. 40F per hr. (35F students). Open M-Su 11am-11:30pm.

ACCOMMODATIONS AND CAMPING

Affordable lodgings should be in ample supply in this affable town, if you call ahead. Many lie on av. Général de Gaulle, only steps from the station, or in the action-packed *vieille ville.*

Auberge de Jeunesse (HI), La Pépinière, rue Marc-Pierre (tel. 04 68 34 63 32; fax 04 68 51 16 02), on the edge of town, between the highway and police station. From the train station, turn left onto rue Valette. Turn right onto av. de Grande Bretagne, left on rue Claude Marty (rue de la Rivière on some maps), and right onto rue Marc Pierre (10min.). Squat toilets but hot showers. 49 beds. Single-sex, 6- to 8-bed dorm rooms 70F. Sheets 18F. Breakfast included. Small kitchen available 4-11pm. Strictly enforced 11am check-out. Lockout 11am-4pm. **Members only.** Closed Dec. 20-Jan. 20.

Hôtel de l'Avenir, 11 rue de l'Avenir (tel. 04 68 34 20 30; fax 04 68 34 15 63), a 5min. walk straight ahead from the station. Walls with spring colors and hand-painted gardens. Balconies, a roof-top terrace, and the feel of a summer home. Singles 90F, with shower 125F; doubles 100-125F, with shower 160-220F; triples and quads 220-250F. Shower 15F. Breakfast 23F. Call ahead in the summer, when prices rise. V, MC, AmEx.

Express Hôtel, 3 av. du Général de Gaulle (tel. 04 68 34 89 96). Look for the palm tree (one block straight ahead from the *gare*) and past it you'll find rose-colored, renovated rooms in a quiet hotel. Singles and doubles 80-140F, with shower 120-140F; triples with shower 180F; quads 185F, with shower 220F. Extra bed 30F. Shower 15F. Breakfast 20F. Often full, call ahead. V, MC.

Hôtel Métropole, 3 rue des Cardeurs (tel. 04 68 34 43 34). From the cathedral at pl. Gambetta, walk down rue St-Jean and turn left onto rue des Cardeurs. A convenient location in the *vieille ville* but some dark rooms. Singles and doubles 75F, with shower 135F. Additional bed 40F. Breakfast 25F. Reception daily 8:30am-midnight. Make reservations in July and Aug.

Campsites: Camping Le Catalan, rte. de Bompas (tel. 04 68 63 16 92). Take "Bompas" bus from train station (2 per day, 12F). Pools, hot showers. 2 people 77F; Sept.-June 55F. Extra person 16-24F. **Camping Le Garrigole,** 2 rue Maurice Lévy (tel. 04 68 54 66 10), in town 800m behind the train station. 65F for 2 people.

FOOD

If you've been waiting to try *escargots,* don't crawl an inch farther. Snails are a Catalan specialty; *cargolade* is a serving of your shell-wearing garden friends grilled and smothered with garlic *aïoli.* The specialty *touron* nougat is available in many flavors. **Pl. de la Loge, pl. Arago,** and **pl. de Verdun** in the *vieille ville* are filled with restaurants that stay lively at night. Pricier options line **quai Vauban** along the canal. Try **av. de Gaulle** in front of the *gare* for cheaper alternatives. You'll find barrels and baskets of specialties that don't stick around long—live snails sell fast—at the **open-air markets** on pl. de la République (daily 6am-1pm) and pl. Cassanyes (Sa-Su 8am-1pm). Pl. de la République also holds an assortment of fruit stores, *charcuteries, boulangeries,* and the **Marché République** (open Tu-Su

7am-1pm and 4-7:30pm). **Casino supermarket** stockpiles food on bd. Félix Mercader. (Tel. 04 68 34 74 42. Open M-Sa 8:30am-8pm.)

Opera Bouffe, impasse de la Division (tel. 04 68 34 83 83), serves Catalan cuisine in a delightful, intimate passageway—it's worth the search. Owner's pride is *"xup-xup,"* an eccentric combination of seafood and meatballs in tomato sauce (115F). *Menus* for 67F, 85F, and 130F. Open M-Sa noon-2pm and 8-11pm.

◢ **La Grillothèque,** 7 rue des Cardeurs (tel. 04 68 34 06 90). On a narrow and inviting street in the *vieille ville,* La Grillothèque serves steaming portions of *grillades* and 6 styles of mussels (68F) at romantic, outdoor tables. *Menus* at 65F (lunch) and 78F. Open daily noon-2:30pm and 7-10:15pm. V, MC.

Le Palmarium, on pl. Arago (tel. 04 68 34 51 31). Green cafeteria that dominates pl. Arago has an outdoor terrace overlooking the canal. *Plats du jour* run 35-50F, with many kinds of paella starting at 65F. Also serves breakfast at 20F. Open daily 11:30am-2:30pm and 6:30-9:30pm.

👁 SIGHTS

*A **museum passport,** valid for one week (40F), allows entrance to four museums including the **Musée Hyacinthe Rigaud,** the **Casa Pairal,** the **Musée Numismatique Joseph Puig,** 42 av. de Grande-Bretagne (tel. 04 68 34 11 70), and the **Musée d'Histoire Naturelle,** 12 rue Fontaine Neuve (tel. 04 68 35 50 87).*

CITADELLE. A short walk from the action, Perpignan's **citadelle** is both formidable and *formidable*, with beautifully intact walls rising up from the residential area below. Within the citadel lies the 13th-century **Palais des Rois de Majorque.** With its immense arcaded courtyard and two curiously superimposed chapels, it is the city's most impressive sight. The courtyard now serves as a concert hall, sheltering both plays and classical music performances. *(Palais tel. 04 68 34 48 29; enter from av. Gilbert Brutus. Open daily June-Sept. 10am-6pm; Oct.-May 9am-5pm. Tours every 30min. in French. 20F, students 10F. Ticket sales end 45min. before closing.)*

MUSÉE HYACINTHE RIGAUD. The museum contains a small but impressive collection of paintings dating from the 13th century by Spanish and Catalan masters; canvases by Rigaud, court artist to Louis XIV and one of the 17th century's great portraitists; and works by Ingres, Picasso, Miró, and Dalí. Check out the top floor's **Collection de Maître Rey,** a room in which every wall is packed with tiny paintings, each about 8 by 10 inches. A local writer, Rey, asked his artist friends, both well-known and less so, to paint these works to fill his study. So many diverse works in such proximity makes for a mind-boggling museum. *(16 rue de l'Ange. Tel. 04 68 35 43 40. Open W-M noon-7pm. 25F, students 10F.)*

LE CASTILLET. Built in the late 14th century and redesigned by Louis XI a century later, this red-brick castle has served as a prison, a fortress, and now as the **Casa Pairal,** a museum of Catalan culture and folk art. The terrace commands a sweeping, magnificent view. *(North of Hyacinthe Rigau, between pl. de la Victoire and bd. Wilson. Open June 15–Sept. 15 W-M 9:30am-7pm; Sept. 16-June 14 W-M 9am-6pm. 25F, students 10F.)*

CATHÉDRALE ST-JEAN. A paragon of Gothic architecture, the cathedral is partly supported by a macabre pillar depicting John the Baptist's severed head. Inlaid paintings brood alongside gilded altarpieces while the stained glass is illuminated by the morning light. *(Pl. Gambetta. Tel. 04 68 51 33 72. Open 9am-noon and 3-7pm. Free.)*

🎵 🎆 ENTERTAINMENT AND FESTIVALS

ENTERTAINMENT. With pedestrians racing to avoid being hit by buses in one of the windiest cities on the Mediterranean, the quiet café nightlife is a great contrast to the fast days. By night, traditional Catalonian dancing in front of **Le Castillet** makes for a lively café scene around pl. de Verdun, especially in summer (Tu, Th, and Sa). Later on, find cheap beer and a rare, spirited 20-something crowd at **Brasserie Osteria**, 3 pl. de Catalogne, on cours Escarvel. The wildest nightlife exists at the clubs lining the beaches at nearby **Canet-Plage**, but buses stop running long before the fun starts, and unless you can make the rhythms of the night last until 6:25am (9:26am on Sunday), returning to Perpignan will mean taking a taxi.

FESTIVALS. Residents and surrounding towns impatiently await Perpignan's annual festivals. The **Fête de St-Jean** is on June 23, when sacred fire is brought from the Canigou, a nearby mountain. Dance the *sardana*, munch powdered-sugar *rouquilles*, and swallow glasses of the sweet *muscat* wine in one gulp. According to popular legend, jumping over a bonfire lit by the *feu* cleanses the spirit. The **Procession de la Sanch** on Good Friday ushers Easter in with traditional songs and concerts. During the first two weeks in September, Perpignan hosts **Visa Pour l'Image,** an international festival of photojournalism that includes free exhibitions of some of the world's most famous photographers' work.

CANET-PLAGE AND THE CÔTE CATALANE

Stretching 50km from Port-le-Barcarès in the north to Cerbère by the Spanish border, the Côte Catalane attracts those who prefer this peaceful, sandy slice of the Mediterranean to the glitz of the Côte d'Azur. One of the most frequented resorts is **Canet-Plage**, a 30-minute bus ride from Perpignan. On a sunny day, bodies cram onto the sizzling beach, even if pelted by sand from the consistent gusts of wind. Others worth visiting include **St-Cyprien-Plage, Argelès-sur-Mer,** and **Banyuls-sur-Mer.**

Those who intend to lose money at the Canet-Plage casinos or on heavy club covers can make up for it by commuting from Perpignan. If you're determined to be the first on the beach or the last out of the casino, there are a few inexpensive hotels in town. Prices are generally lower if you're willing to forgo the sea view. **Hôtel Clair Soleil**, 26 av. de Catalogne (tel./fax 04 68 80 32 06), lives up to its name with large, pastel orange rooms. (Singles and doubles 170-195F, with shower 205-240F, with bath 265F. Additional bed 50F. Breakfast 25F. Student discounts. Prices lower June and Sept. V, MC, AmEx.) A tropical mural and colorful fabric enliven the spotless white rooms and halls of **Hôtel Le Méditerranée,** 1 rue Alsace-Lorraine. (Tel. 04 68 80 21 85. Doubles 190F, with shower 240F; triples 230F; quads 270-300F. Breakfast 25F. Closed Oct.-Apr.) The three-star site **Camping Club Mar-Estang** (tel. 04 68 80 35 53; fax 04 68 73 32 94), a 25-minute walk from the tourist office, offers tennis courts, two pools, a restaurant, a bar, and a supermarket. (2 people 100F in summer; 60F in off-season. Open Apr. 28-Sept. 30.)

Beach-goers can fill their stomachs with hot pasta at sea-front pizzerias for 32-55F on sizzling days. **Markets** sprout on pl. Foment de la Sardane (Tu-Su 7:30am-12:30pm) and pl. St-Jacques, 45 minutes from the beach (W and Sa 7:30am-noon). **Casino supermarket** awaits hunger-stricken high rollers at 12 av. de la Méditerranée. (Open July-Aug. daily 8am-1pm and 3:30-5pm; Sept.-June M-Sa 8am-12:30pm and 3:30-7:30pm, Su 8am-12:30pm and 4-7:30pm.) *Boulangeries* and *charcuteries* cluster along the same avenue as it strikes the port. **Le Restaurant Oriental de FES,** 26 bd. Tixador (tel. 04 68 73 82 41), specializes in Moroccan food in the most lavish of settings. The attention to detail ranges from ornate tiles to the presentation of the food, which includes salads (19-30F) and couscous (65-75F). (Open daily 10am-midnight.) The 70F *menu* at **Le Chianti,** 18 Côte Vermeille (tel. 04 68 80 43 09), offers three courses. (Open daily noon-2pm and 7-11pm. V, MC.)

The Canet-Plage **tourist office,** pl. de la Méditerranée (tel. 04 68 73 61 00), doles out brochures and maps. (Open daily July-Aug. 9am-8pm; Sept. and June M-F 9am-12:30pm and 2-6:30pm, Sa-Su 9am-12:30pm and 3-6:30pm; Oct.-May M-F 9am-12:30pm and 2-6:30pm, Sa 9am-12:30pm and 3-6pm, Su 10am-noon.) **Taxis** are on av. Méditerranée as it strikes the beach. (Tel. 04 68 73 14 81. To Perpignan 95-110F.) Rent **bikes** and **scooters** at **Locabike**, no. 144 av. de la Côte Vermeille. (Tel. 04 68 80 73 43. Bikes 40-50F per half-day, 80F per day, 300F per week. 1000F or passport deposit. Open July-Aug. 9am-midnight; Apr.-June and Sept. 9am-noon and 2-6pm.)

Bus Interplages (tel. 04 68 35 67 51) connects the Côte Catalane resorts from **Le Barcarès** to **Cerbère**. **CTP Shuttles** (tel. 04 68 61 01 13) runs buses to **Canet-Plage;** catch the #1 in **Perpignan** at pl. Catalogne (at the top of av. Général de Gaulle) or at promenade des Platanes on bd. Wilson. (30min., 2 per hr., 13F. Last bus from Canet around 9pm, last from Perpignan around 8:30pm; later July-Aug.)

NARBONNE

Faced with memories of their glorious heritage, 50,000 *narbonnais* are trying to ward off the lingering lethargy that has plagued this sunny city in recent centuries. Founded by a decree of the Roman Senate in 118 BC, Narbo Martius became Rome's first colony outside Italy. Narbonne flourished then thanks to its lucrative exportation of farm products. By medieval times, the ascending city had gained the privilege of installing archbishops and viscounts, but its triumph was short lived. With its fortunes increasingly tied to vineyards, Narbonne was taken aback when grapes from other regions eclipsed its own. Daunted but not squashed, Narbonne has begun active renewal. Surrounding vineyards open their *caves* to tourists, though actual wine-tasting amounts to little more than a dream for those depending on the SNCF's wheels. Narbonne has created such attractions as the summer theater festival while making the best of its existing assets, including a Gothic cathedral and the popular sands of **Narbonne-Plage** and **Gruisson-Plage.**

◪ PRACTICAL INFORMATION. The train station (tel. 04 67 62 50 50) sends **trains** to **Carcassonne** (30min., 15 per day, 54F), **Perpignan** (45min., 14 per day, 50F), **Béziers** (15min., 19 per day, 22F), **Montpellier** (1hr., 12 per day, 78F), and **Toulouse** (1½hr., 13 per day, 110F). (Open July-Aug. M-Sa 8am-6:15pm; Sept.-June M-Sa 8amnoon and 1:30-6:15pm.) **Buses** leave from the bus station, near the train station, or from the terminal on quai Victor Hugo. Narbonne's **tourist office,** pl. Salengro (tel. 04 68 65 15 60; fax 04 68 65 59 12), is a 10-minute walk from the station. Turn right onto av. Carnot, which becomes bd. F. Mistral, then left onto rue Chennebier, which leads to pl. Salengro. *Le Guide Touristique* is free and multilingual. (Open June 15-Sept. 15 M-Sa 8am-7pm, Su 9:30am-12:30pm; off-season M-Sa 8:30am-noon and 2-6pm.) **City tours** (in French and English) include museum entry (June 15-Sept. 15; 2hr., 30F; students and seniors 20F). The **police station** is on bd. Charles de Gaulle (tel. 04 68 90 38 50). The **post office,** 25 bd. Gambetta (tel. 04 68 65 87 00), has **currency exchange.** (Open M-F 8am-7pm, Sa 8:30am-noon. **Postal code:** 11100.)

⌇ ACCOMMODATIONS. Hôtel de France, 6 rue Rossini (tel. 04 68 32 09 75; fax 04 68 65 50 30), off bd. du Dr Ferroul near the pont de la Liberté., offers red carpets and Baroque style, with a calm atmosphere and an excellent location just off the canal. (Singles 120F, with bathroom 230-260F; doubles 140F, with bathroom 260F. Extra bed 50F. Breakfast 32F. Reserve July-Aug. V, MC.) **Hôtel de Paris,** 2 rue du Lion d'Or (tel. 04 68 32 08 68), in the *centre ville,* offers several plain rooms off dim hallways. Follow the directions to the tourist office and turn onto rue Lion d'Or from rue Chennebier. (Singles and doubles 150F, with shower 180-200F; triples 230F; quads 300F. Prices lower Sept.-May. Breakfast 25F. V, MC.) **Will's Hotel,** 23 av. P. Sémard (tel. 04 68 90 44 50; fax 04 68 32 26 28), is 100m from the station. Don't let the aged staircase fool you— the rooms have newly renovated bathrooms. (Singles with toilet 120F; doubles with shower, toilet, and TV 200-220F; one triple or quad with bath, toilet, and TV 330F. Breakfast 27F. V, MC, AmEx.) Beachside campgrounds abound in the area. **Camping des Côtes des Roses** (tel. 04 68 49 83 65) offers tennis, horseback riding, mini-golf, and the Mediterranean. (71F per 2 people. Open Easter-Sept.) **Camping le Soleil d'Oc** (tel. 04 68 49 86 21) rents tents for 74-94F for two people from April to October. In summer, about six buses per day head to the campsites from Narbonne's train station (14.80F).

FOOD. Inexpensive restaurants cluster off **rue Droite,** branching off to the left of the Palais des Archevêques. Grab a bite from the canal-side vendors lining the **cours de la République,** or pick up picnic items at the **market** on plan (not *place*) St-Paul Thursday mornings (9am-noon). The **covered market** at Les Halles, on the canal on cours Mirabeau, is open daily 6am to 1pm. **Monoprix,** pl. Hôtel de Ville, satisfies all other food needs. (Open M-Sa 8:30am-7:30pm.) **Le Dragon d'Or,** 34 av. Pierre Semard (tel. 05 68 32 26 18), gives courteous service, a lit pond, and, most importantly, heavy portions. Try the almost endless 55F lunch special with three courses, wine included. (Open daily noon-2pm and 7-10pm.) At **Le Méditerranée,** 26 rue Félix Aldy (tel. 04 68 32 21 42), spicy *calamars à l'Américaine* (on the 85F *menu*) is the specialty. Pizzas and pastas cost 30-53F, omelettes 22-35F; has a 65F lunch *menu*. (Open M-Sa noon-2pm and 7-9pm. V, MC.)

SIGHTS AND ENTERTAINMENT. Narbonne's monuments congregate in the *vieille ville,* and it's easy to make a quick round before heading out to catch a wave. The opulent and beautifully restored **Palais des Archevêques** (tel. 04 68 90 30 30), next to the cathedral, testifies to the wealth of the former archbishops of Narbonne. Within its walls, the **Musée Archéologique** displays a collection of artifacts stretching from cavemen to art and relics from the relatively recent Gallo-Roman civilization. Across the atrium, the **Musée d'Art et d'Histoire** holds French, Flemish, and Italian 17th-century paintings in the exquisite former apartments of the archbishops as well as a large collection of 18th-century French china and 3rd-century mosaics. A Roman grain warehouse, **L'Horreum,** rue Rouget de l'Isle, off rue Droite, is Narbonne's only remaining ancient monument and is not yet completely excavated. (All open daily May-Aug. 10-11:50am and 2-6pm; Sept.-Apr. Tu-Su 10-11:50am and 2-5pm.) A global ticket (25F, students and seniors 15F) allows entrance to four museums over three days. The *mairie* organizes several **package tours** of the various sites daily from July to mid-September. Ask at the info office in the *palais.* (30F, students 20F. Morning tour includes snack of local produce.)

The imposing Gothic **Cathédrale St-Just et St-Pasteur,** rue Gauthier (tel. 04 68 32 09 52), is only half as large as its architects intended it to be. Construction began in 1272 but stopped in 1340 during a dispute between the archbishops and the city government—the church wanted to dismantle the city's walls and use them as building material. Further construction would have given Narbonne France's largest cathedral. The church fortunately lost—the walls saved the city when the English Black Prince attacked in 1355. In the **Trésor** (10F) there is a 5th-century Flemish tapestry. Free summer concerts (Su 9pm) make wonderful use of the pipe organ. (Cathedral open daily May-Sept. 9-11:50am and 2-5:30pm; Oct.-Apr. closed Su afternoon. Tower 15F. Tel. 04 68 42 00 87 for concert info. Salle de Trésor open May-Sept. M-Th 9:45-11:45am and 2:30-5pm, F-Sa 9:45-11:45am and 2:30-5:30pm.)

Narbonne Plage, the town's most attractive attribute, lies 15km east and basks in 300 sunny days a year. Buses leave from next to the train station (35min.; July-Aug. 8 per day, Sept.-June 2-4 per day; 14.80F). **Le Coche d'Eau du Patrimonie** (tel. 04 68 90 63 98) offers a **boat tour** (July-Aug.) of the Canal de la Robine, an offshoot of the Canal du Midi, that covers 20 centuries of history in a few hours. **Nightlife** is nary *bonne* in Narbonne, but beer drinkers can order a cold brew (12F) at the bright yellow **Bar le Baroque,** 26 av. Gambetta (tel. 04 68 65 27 39), across from the post office. (Open M-Sa 7:30am-11pm.)

FESTIVALS. Narbonne's biggest event of the year is the performance festival **Le Théâtre: Scène Nationale de Narbonne** (tel. 04 68 90 90 00; www.narbonne.com/letheatre). Performances are held at 2 av. Domitius. The year 2000 will be its 10th season, keeping the months from January to May filled with cultural acts ranging from *La Ferme du Garet,* a multimedia theatrical piece (Jan. 12-14; 90F) and Molière's *Dom Juan* (Feb. 3-4, 130F) to the Antonio Gades dance company's *Fuenteovejuna,* a modern ballet of love, violence, and oppression in the 15th century (Mar. 14, 150F), and Roger Vitrac's surrealist play *Victor ou les enfants au* *pouvoir* (110F). Jazz singer Dianne Reeves performs on May 23 (130F). Make reservations early; for more information call 04 68 90 90 20. Less professional performances can be found at Narbonne's **16th Annual Amateur Theater Festival** (tel. 04 68 32 01 00) for one week in early July. Entrance is free for most events.

BÉZIERS

For the past 2000 years, Béziers, 15km from the Mediterranean, has been a city of passage where Celts, Iberians, Phoenicians, Greeks, Romans, Arabs, and Franks have all left their trace. In 1209, when the outlawed Cathars sought refuge in welcoming Béziers, Pope Innocent III's anti-heretical minions sacked the town, killing its inhabitants. Native Paul Riquet revitalized Béziers in the 17th century by building the 245km Canal du Midi, establishing the town as an important passageway for regional trade. Modern tourists who travel to Béziers' eastern beaches will enjoy the canal and its locks. Known for its simple table wine, Béziers prides itself on the quality of its vineyards; you can buy Minervois (25-45F), St-Chinianais (20-50F) or Faugères (20-40F) along allées Paul Riquet. *Boutiques* crowd the large, tree-lined boulevards and tiny *rues* near pl. Jean Jaurès and the theater. With Roman arenas and surrounding vineyards to add to its landscape, the warm air of Béziers is filled with charm.

⌖ ORIENTATION AND PRACTICAL INFORMATION. Frequent **trains** (tel. 08 36 67 68 69) go to **Narbonne** (15min., 20 per day, 22F) and **Montpellier** (40 min., 25 per day, 59F). (Open M-Sa 8am-6pm.) From the station, climb up rue de la Rotunde to allées Paul Riquet; av. St-Saëns is on the right. The **tourist office**, 29 av. St-Saëns (tel. 04 67 76 47 00; fax 04 67 76 50 80), can direct you to the local wine producers as well as the nearby beaches. (Open July-Aug. M-F 9am-7pm, Su 10am-noon; Sept.-June M 9am-noon and 2-6pm, Tu-F and Su 9am-noon and 2-6:30pm, Sa 9am-noon and 3-6pm.) **Banque Courtois**, 24 allées Paul Riquet, has **currency exchange.** (Open M-F 9am-12:45pm and 3:45-5pm.) The **hospital** is at ZAC de Montimaran (tel. 04 67 35 70 35). The **police station** is located 14 bd. Maréchal Leclerc (tel. 04 67 35 17 17). The **post office** is on av. Clemenceau. (Tel. 04 67 49 81 10. Open M-F 8am-7pm, Sa 8am-noon. **Postal code:** 34500.)

⌖ ACCOMMODATIONS AND CAMPING. Hôtel Angleterre, 22 pl. Jean Jaurès (tel. 04 67 28 48 42), off allées Paul Riquet, rents 22 rooms close to the busy cafés but away from the noise. The posters of bullfights from Béziers arenas lead up the stairwell to light-colored rooms with soft carpets. (Singles 110F; doubles 140F, with shower 160F; quads with shower and toilet 280F. Breakfast 30F. Reserve in the summer.) Just off the bustle of av. St-Saëns, **Alma Unic Hôtel,** 41 rue Guilhemon (tel. 04 67 28 44 31; fax 04 67 28 79 44), has two floors of pink and blue rooms with little balconies. The breakfast area is just as nice with its crimson cloths. (Singles 120-160F; doubles 140-200F; triples 240F with shower included. Breakfast 25F. V, MC, AmEx.) **Hôtel Le Revelois,** 60 av. Gambetta (tel. 04 67 49 20 78; fax 04 67 28 92 28), is one block ahead from the train station (turn left at av. Gambetta). Beds and carpeting vary, so ask to see a few rooms. (Singles and doubles 120F, with shower 150F; triples with shower 265F; quads with shower 300F. Breakfast 25F. Reserve July-Aug.) Info on **beach camping** at Valras (July-Sept.) is available at the tourist offices in Béziers or Valras (tel. 04 67 32 36 04).

⌖ FOOD. Béziers' sweet specialty is the *biterrois*, a pâté of almonds, grapes, and wine in pastry, available at the 13 *pâtisseries* with stickers in their windows from *l'Association des Pâtisseries de Béziers*. The indoor **market** at **Les Halles,** allées Paul Riquet, is open Tu-Su 8am-noon. There is a **Monoprix supermarket** at 5 allées Paul Riquet. (Tel. 04 67 49 31 80. Open M-Sa 8:30am-7pm.) Off allées Paul Riquet, the reasonably priced restaurants and cafés become a giant glass-tipping, spoon-clanking, order-taking blur as you move toward the Théâtre Municipal. **Aux**

Trois Arches, 24 rue Viennet (tel. 04 67 28 43 49), provides a relaxed setting on a more quiet street. Mussels, pizzas, and *plats* cost 40-60F. (Open M-Sa noon-2pm and 7:30-10pm.) Other restaurants lead down **rue Viennet** away from the cathedral.

◎ **SIGHTS.** For a whirlwind tour of the town's three museums, the participating galleries offer a universal pass (20F). The **Fabregat des Beaux-Arts,** pl. de la Révolution (tel. 04 67 28 38 78), and its annex, **Hôtel Fayet,** 9 rue de Capuces (tel. 04 67 49 04 66), house a modest collection of paintings from the 17th to the 20th century. A few Delacroix, Gericaults, and Dufys shine through the masses of local work. (Open Tu-F 9am-noon and 2-6pm, Su 2-6pm; Fayet closed Su. 15F, students 10F. 10F for temporary expositions.) The nearby **Espace Paul Riquet,** rue Massol (tel. 04 67 28 44 18), hosts frequent exhibitions. Call the tourist office for details. (Open July-Aug. Tu-Su 9am-noon and 2-6pm; Sept.-June closed Su.) **Musée St-Jacques** (tel. 04 67 36 71 01) displays local relics ranging from prehistoric scratch pads to 20th-century railroad ads. A 1913 Renault once driven by *"le plus jeune chauffeur du monde"* ("the youngest driver in the world"—4-year-old Jean Lovign) sits in the corner. (Open Tu-Sa 9am-noon and 2-6pm, Su 2-6pm.)

The **Cathédrale St-Nazaire,** pl. de la Révolution, built on the ruins of a pagan temple, was destroyed with the rest of the city in 1209 but rebuilt and expanded in the 14th century. Every day the bells ring out across the canals, countryside, and salmon-colored roofs of the tiny town below. Climb to the top for an unobstructed view of the surroundings, or walk the vine-covered terrace of the *jardin* for a peek at the river and its green banks. (Open M-Sa 9am-noon and 2:30-7pm.)

▲ **EXCURSIONS.** 15km from Béziers, the one-time fishing village of **Valras** has developed into an all-purpose family beach resort complete with water slide and Ferris wheel. A walk down the beach reveals expanses of light sand. To get there, take bus #401 (tel. 04 67 36 73 76) from pl. du Général de Gaulle (30min.; 10 per day in summer, last return 8pm; round-trip 27F).

For those blessed with their own transportation, any of the nearby private vineyards or *caves cooperatives*, central outlets for local wineries, give tours ending with samples of the wines. **Le Club des Grands Vins des Châteaux du Languedoc** will provide information on *degustations* of the region's acclaimed *appellations*: Minervois, St-Chinian, Fauceres, and a spicy red Cabrières. Contact the club's offices at the Château du Raissac (tel. 04 67 49 17 60), 2km west of Béziers. Again, for lucky *voiture* drivers, the cellars of the château itself are open to visitors year-round. (Open M-Sa 9am-noon and 2:30-7pm.)

♫ ❀ **ENTERTAINMENT AND FESTIVALS.** For a traditional night out, **Le Café des Arts,** 13 rue de la Coquille (tel. 04 67 28 82 56), starts out mellow and ends up lively. Beers 10F, cocktails 35F. (Open M-Sa 8am-2am.) Coffee lovers will enjoy an early evening at a table outside **Café Latin,** 13bis pl. Pierre Semard (tel. 04 67 28 82 28), across from Les Halles. Or head to **La Rotonde,** 2 av. Wilson (tel. 04 67 76 35 32), at the end of the allées for karaoke at 9:30pm Tuesday through Thursday. (Open M-F 7:45am-2am, Sa 10am-2am, Su 3pm-2am; Sept.-June closes at 1am.)

In mid-August, a **féria** that has earned Béziers the nickname "the French Seville" fills the town with *corridas* and *flamenco* dancing. Tickets for bullfights are available at the *arènes,* av. Émile Claparede. (Tel. 04 67 76 13 45. 100-450F.)

SÈTE

Sparsely settled since 1000BC, Sète (pop. 42,000) sprang to life in 1666 when Louis XIV's minister Colbert pointed to the "Cap de Cette" as a new port. At the turn of the century, most of the population of the Italian village of Gaet immigrated to Sète to escape the Italian depression. A hybrid Italian-French culture has emerged in Sète, producing unique cuisine, strange maritime festivals, and an engaging Setois accent, made famous by folk singer Georges Brassens (1921-1981). Spread along a narrow strip of land cordoning the Bassin Thau from the Mediterranean, the town is now France's largest Mediterranean fishing port, pulling some 14,000 tons of fish from the sea each year. Modern commercial fishing has added heavy machinery to Sète's otherwise postcard-perfect coastline, but there is an industrial poetry in the rusty ships and screeching seagulls of the town which gave birth to the man many consider to be France's greatest poet, Paul Valéry (1871-1945).

7 ORIENTATION AND PRACTICAL INFORMATION. The **train station,** quai M. Joffre, serves those headed to **Montpellier** (20min., 29F) and **Béziers** (30min., approx. 2 per hr., 43F). (Info office open Monday to Friday 9am-noon and 2-5:50pm.) The **bus station,** 13 quai de la République (tel. 04 67 74 66 90 for info desk of Montpellier's station), rolls buses to **Montpellier** (1hr.; 11 per day M-Sa, 3 Su; 31.50F). *La Sétoise* **local buses** (tel. 04 67 74 18 77; 6F) circle the city until 7:30pm. Bus #6 goes from quai de la Résistance to both beaches, while bus #7 goes to l'Espace Brassens. **Cycles Estopina,** 4 rue Voltaire (tel./fax 04 67 74 74 77), specializes in **bike rentals.** (60F per half-day, 90F per day. ID and 2000F deposit. Open Tu-Sa 9am-7:30pm. V, MC.) **Taxis** (tel. 04 67 48 62 98) queue at the *gare.* Sète's **tourist office,** 60 rue Mario Roustan (tel. 04 67 74 71 71), behind the quai Général Durand, offers maps and the twice-weekly *15 Jours a Sète,* which lists city events. To walk from the station, go straight onto pont de la Gare, cross the canal, and turn right onto quai Vauban. Turn the corner and cross the first bridge on the right, then turn left and walk down quai de Lattre de Tassigny until rue Roustan veers off to the right (20min.). (Open daily July-Aug. 9am-8pm; Sept.-June M-Sa 9am-noon and 2-6pm. **Currency exchange** M-F 10am-noon and 2:30-6pm, Sa 9:30-noon and 2:30-6pm.) To reach the **hospital** on bd. C. Blanc (tel. 04 67 46 57 57), take bus #5 to "Hôpital." The **police** are at 50 quai de Bosc (tel. 04 67 46 80 22). The **post office** (tel. 04 67 46 64 20.) is on bd. Danièle Casanova. (Open M-F 8:30am-12:30pm and 1:30-6pm, Sa 8:30am-noon. Poste Restante code: 34207. **Postal code:** 34200.)

『 ACCOMMODATIONS. The **Auberge de Jeunesse "Villa Salis" (HI),** rue du Général Revest (tel. 04 67 53 46 68; fax 04 67 51 34 01), peers down on the town from the tree-covered sides of Mont St-Clair. Follow the directions to the tourist office, then at pont de la Civette turn right onto rue Général de Gaulle and follow the friendly *auberge* signs around the parc du Château d'Eau and up the steep hill to the coral-colored inn (20min.). Here you'll find 90 spartan beds in clean four- to five-bed single-sex rooms. (118F includes breakfast and a great view; 167F includes dinner too. Sheets 17F. Reception daily 8am-noon and 6-10pm. No lockout. Curfew 1am.) At **Hôtel Tramontane,** 5 rue Frédéric Mistral (tel. 04 67 74 37 92), only 50m off the quai de la Résistance, there are clean, cheery rooms and sparkling bathrooms. (Singles and doubles 130F, with shower and toilet 165-185F; triples 165-210F; quads 185-245F. Showers 12F. Breakfast 26F. English spoken. V, MC, AmEx.) **Hôtel le Valéry,** 20 rue Denfert-Rochereau (tel. 04 67 74 77 51; fax 04 67 74 58 59), is just minutes from the train station. Spacious staircase and hallways lead to simple, light, airy rooms. (Singles and doubles 110-130F, with shower 130-150F, with shower and toilet 160F; triples 160F; quads 180F. Breakfast 25F. Garage 25F. Reserve July-Aug. V, MC.) The 4-star **campground** 10km outside Sète at **Le Castellas** (tel. 04 67 51 63 00) has a pool, bar, supermarket, and wheelchair access. (2-person site 110-165F. Open May-Sept.) A bus goes there from the *gare* (25min., 13F), and a taxi company has a 30F round-trip deal.

『 FOOD. The restaurants that line **Promenade J.B. Marty,** at the end of rue Mario Roustan near the *vieux port,* serve the catch of the day every way you can imagine for 60F and up. Watch the fisherman haul in their catch from **Le Phare**, 21 du Promenade JB Marty (tel. 04 67 74 20 30), while dining on generous seafood platters (58F) or *bouillabaisse*. Not harborside, but fresh nevertheless, cheaper pizza, pasta, and seafood await in the less touristy eateries on the **Gambetta** and its offshoots. Alternatively, head to the **Prisunic supermarket** at 7 quai de la Résistance

WETTING YOUR LANCE

WETTING YOUR LANCE Water-jousting, the original watersport, began when some Crusaders with too much time on their hands decided to demonstrate their skills aboard boats rather than horses. Although Sète sees fewer Crusades these days, nautical jousting continues to be popular, particularly among the local fishermen. The rules are simple: red and blue boats represent the High Quarter and the Short Point, two neighborhoods in Sète, and the object of the competition is to remain high and dry. Each boat is rowed and maneuvered by *chevaliers,* while two opponents duel away with a wooden shield and lance. The loser is the one who makes friends with the fish of the Royal Canal, much to the mirth of the crowd.

(tel. 04 67 74 39 38; open M-Sa 8:30am-8pm, Su 9am-noon) or the **daily market** at **Les Halles,** just off rue Alsace-Lorraine (7am-noon). Vendors on the canal hawk fresh *tielles* (squid and tomato pizzas) for 13F, but inland *boulangeries* sell somewhat less authentic versions for as little as 7F. You're all Sète.

■ **SIGHTS.** On Môle St-Louis, a dock built in 1666 at the southern end of town, lounges the **Société Nautique de Sète,** one of France's oldest yacht clubs. Throughout the summer, many yacht races—including the prestigious Tour de France à la Voile at the end of July—set sail from the Môle. The **plage de la Corniche** in the southwest corner of town marks the beginning of 12km of sandy yellow beaches, accessible by bus #6 or a summer shuttle. Catch both on quai de la Résistance at stops marked "La Plage." (Both 6F).

A walk out to the *vieux port* and up the hill along rue Haute leads to the **maritime cemetery** that inspired Paul Valéry's poem *Le cimetière marin.* The poet himself lies interred in his cherished cemetary. (Open daily Apr.-Sept. 7am-7pm; Oct.-Mar. 8am-6pm.) Up the hill, the modern building above the cemetery is the **Musée Paul Valéry,** rue François Desnoyer (tel. 04 67 46 20 98), with exhibits on the poet, local archæology, history, and even water jousting. (Open July-Aug. daily 10am-noon and 2-6pm; Sept.-June W-M 10am-noon and 2-6pm. Admission July-Aug. 30F; Sept.-June 10F; free W.) On the other side of the city is **L'Espace Georges Brassens,** 67 bd. Camille Blanc (tel. 04 67 53 32 77), a multi-media museum that renders homage to the genius of the irreverent singer buried across the street.

If your legs have it in them, climb Chemin de Biscan-Pas from the hostel to the summit of **Mont St-Clair** (183m) for a terrific view of Sète, its canals and docks, and the sea (15min.). The church **Notre Dame de la Salette,** with wall murals from the 1950s, brings fishermen's wives up to this summit on a pilgrimage every September 19 for the *Feu de la St-Jean.*

■ ❋ **ENTERTAINMENT AND FESTIVALS.** Every evening the popular **La Bodega,** 21 quai Noel Guignon (tel. 04 67 74 47 50), has live music from Brazilian blues to rock. Beers cost 19-35F and there's a choice of more than 100 cocktails for 40-60F. (Open daily 5:30pm-3am; Oct.-May closed Su.) **Wembley,** 36 av. Victor Hugo (tel. 04 67 74 67 67), has over 120 types of beer, live bands Thursday through Saturday, and karaoke the other nights of the week. (Open daily 8pm-4am.)

On the final weekend in August (referred to as **La Fête de St-Louis),** Sète holds its animated **Tournois de Joutes Nautiques,** in which participants joust from oversized rowboats. Arrive in the morning to secure a spot for the final competition on Monday at 2pm, and wear a hat in the intense sun. Most summer weekends, at 2:30pm, the gladiators prepare for the tournament and impress the tourists with exposition battles. On Wednesdays, any novice can go to the Quilles quarter for a jousting lesson. **La Fête de St-Pierre** occurs the first weekend in July. Fishermen spend the preceding week preparing for their festival and taking a break from work. Over the weekend, mornings involve solemn religious rites, while the nights are loud and festive. Sunday morning from 10am to 11am, during the **Bénédiction de la Mer,** fishermen allow the crowds to walk over their decorated boats. They then throw chains of flowers into the water in memory of sailors and fishermen lost at sea.

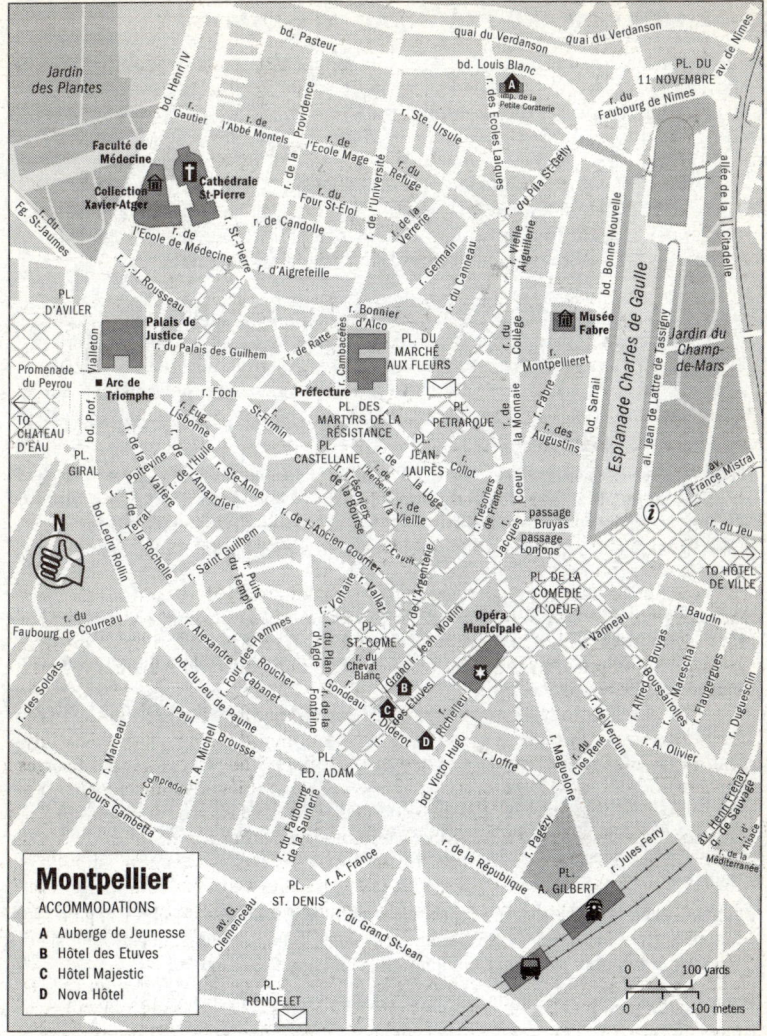

Montpellier

ACCOMMODATIONS

A Auberge de Jeunesse
B Hôtel des Etuves
C Hôtel Majestic
D Nova Hôtel

MONTPELLIER

A mere 12km from the sea, and with students making up a quarter of its population, the medieval quarters of Montpellier vibrate with a fun-loving youthful energy. Still renowned for its faculty of medicine—the first in Europe and Rabelais' *alma mater*—Montpellier is a far cry from pedantic. Every year brings an avant-garde international dance festival and numerous theatrical productions, which underscore the city's infectious vitality.

During the day, narrow and surprisingly quiet streets entice visitors into the *vieille ville*, with its elegant 17th- and 18th-century *hôtels particuliers*, while the stunning, Postmodern Antigone complex to the east of the city proves Montpellier is hardly paralyzed by its past. Cafés on pl. de la Comédie, fondly known as *l'Oeuf* (the egg), offer expensive coffee and hours of four-star people-watching. Come sundown, the student population casts off its scholarly pose and bursts into revelry; the lively bars in pl. Jean-Jaurès are always buzzing.

▋ ORIENTATION AND PRACTICAL INFORMATION

Radiating from the station to the right, **rue Maguelone** leads to Montpellier's modern center, the fountain-filled **pl. de la Comédie.** To find the tourist office upon reaching the *place*, turn right and walk past the cafés and street vendors (5min.). The tourist office is located behind the right-hand corner of the Pavillon de l'Hôtel de Ville. The *vieille ville* is bounded by bd. Pasteur and bd. Louis Blanc to the north, esplanade Charles de Gaulle and bd. Victor Hugo to the east, and bd. Jeu de Paume to the west. The huge **pl. de la Comédie** makes a perfect starting point for forays into the historic center. **Rue de la Loge** leads from the *place* uphill to the center of the *vieille ville*, **pl. Jean-Jaurès.**

Trains: Pl. Auguste Gibert (tel. 04 67 34 25 10). To: **Avignon** (1hr., 20 per day, 78F); **Perpignan** (1½hr., 10 per day, 113F); **Marseille** (1¾hr., 8 per day, 123F); **Toulouse** (2½hr., every 2hr., 158F); **Paris** (4½hr., 8 TGVs per day, 357-430F); **Nice** (5hr., 5 per day, 229F). Info office open M-F 8am-7pm, Sa 9am-6pm. **Currency exchange** (tel. 04 67 58 00 55) at excellent rates, no commission. Open M-Sa 8am-8pm, Su 10am-6pm.

Buses: Pl. du Bicentenaire (tel. 04 67 92 01 43), on 2nd floor of parking garage next to train station. **Les Courriers du Midi** (tel. 04 67 06 03 78) go to **Béziers** (1¾hr., M-Sa every hr., Su 4 per day, 70F) and **Nîmes** (1¾hr., M-Sa 2 per day, 54F). Info office open M-F 7:45am-12:15pm and 1:45-6:45pm, Sa 8am-noon and 2-6:15pm, Su 2-7pm.

Local Transportation: SMTU, 27 rue Maguelone (tel. 04 67 22 87 87). Lines 17-29 leave from in front of the *gare*. Tickets 7F, weekly pass 63F. **Petitbus** serves the city center from the *gare* M-Sa 7:20am-7:30pm; the free **Rabelais** night bus runs 9pm-12:30am from the *gare* to "Agropolis," "Hauts de la Paillade," "Pas du Loup," and "Près d'Arènes." To get to **Palavas** beach, take #17 or 28 from the bus station (20min., 7F).

Taxis: TRAM (tel. 04 67 58 10 10) and **Taxi A** (tel. 04 67 20 35 20). Both 24hr.

Bike Rental: Vill' à velo (SMTU), at the *gare routière* (tel. 04 67 92 92 67). 10F per hr., 40F per day. ID and 1000F deposit. 3hr. tours around city in French or English 80F. Reserve 2 days in advance at the number listed above or with the tourist office

Budget Travel: Wasteels, 1 rue Cambacares (tel. 04 67 66 20 19) and 6 fbg de la Saunerie (tel. 04 67 58 74 26), offer good plane, train, and bus prices. Open M-F 9am-12:30pm and 2-6:30pm, Sa 9am-12:30pm and 2-5:30pm. V, MC.

Tourist Office: 3 allée Jean de Lattre de Tassigny (tel. 04 67 60 60 60; fax 04 67 60 60 61). Free maps and reservation service. Gives out the weekly *Sortir à Montpellier* and the monthly *Rendez-Vous*, which list cinema, art, and concerts. *L'INIC,* a student guide that comes out in July, is free and packed with cultural and entertainment info. For a complete listing of *everything* of interest, see the yearly *Petit Futé* (38F). Daily **city tours** in French July-Sept. 39F, students 29F. Tours in English can be arranged for groups of seven or more. Office open M-F 9:30am-7pm, Sa 10am-1pm and 2-6pm, Su 10am-1pm and 2-5pm. **Branch office** at the *gare* (tel. 04 67 92 90 03) open July-Aug. M-Th 9am-1pm and 3-7pm, F 10am-1pm and 3-7pm. Another **branch** at Antigone Moulin de l'Évêque, 78 av. du Piréeis (tel. 04 67 22 06 16), keeps the same hours year-round.

English Bookstores: Bill's Book Company, 44 rue de l'Université (tel. 04 67 66 37 11). Exciting collection of secondhand paperbacks (10-20F). Bill, the British proprietor, is always up for tea. Open M 2:30-6:30pm, Tu-Sa 10am-12:45pm and 2:30-6:30pm.

Laundromat: Lav'Club Miele, 6 rue des Écoles Laïques. Open daily 7:30am-9pm.

Hospital: Centre Hospitalier Regional, 191 av. Doyen Gaston Guiraud (tel. 04 67 33 67 33).

Police: 13 av. du Prof. Grasset (tel. 04 67 22 78 22).

Post Office: pl. Rondelet (tel. 04 67 34 50 00). From pl. de la Comédie, follow rue Jean Moulin, cross bd. Observatoire onto rue de Fbg de la Saunerie, then follow rue Rondelet. **Currency exchange.** Open M-F 8am-7pm, Sa 8am-noon. **Branch office** at pl. des Martyrs de la Résistance (tel. 04 67 60 03 60). Open M-F 8:30am-6:30pm and Sa 8:30am-noon. **Postal codes:** 34000 (central), 34026 (branch office).

Internet Access: Station Internet/France Télécom, 6-8 pl. du Marché au Fleurs (tel. 0800 35 25 15). 50F per hr., students 40F per hr. Open M 2-8pm, Tu-Sa 10am-8pm.

■ ACCOMMODATIONS

The place to be at night in Montpellier is the *vieille ville*. Every listing below is located within it—even the hostel. Search **rue Aristide Olivier, rue du Général Campredon** (off cours Gambetta and rue A. Michell), and **rue A. Broussonnet** (off pl. Albert 1er) for other reasonably priced hotels.

Auberge de Jeunesse (HI), 2 impasse de la Petite Corraterie (tel. 04 67 60 32 22; fax 04 67 60 32 30). The 20min. walk beats the circuitous bus route. Head away from the station on rue Maguelone, cross pl. de la Comédie, and walk up rue de la Loge past the *cafés* on pl. Jean Jaurès. Turn right onto rue de l'Aiguillerie and follow it through its name change to rue des Écoles Laïques. The hostel is on the right, just before bd. Louis Blanc. Or take bus #2 (direction "Mosson"), 5 (direction "Agropolis"), or 6 (direction "Plan des 4 Seigneurs") from the station; ask the driver to let you off at Les Ursulines. Walk back up the street and turn right, cross bd. Louis Blanc, and head up rue des Écoles Laïques. Friendly staff and standard bunks in this busy, not terribly clean hostel in the *vieille ville*. Check out the stained glass in the chapel-turned-bar (open 5pm-midnight). Pool table (10F), table football, and TV. 80 beds in 4- to 9-person, single-sex rooms, 67F. Sheets 17F per week. Co-ed bathrooms. Breakfast included. Free luggage storage. Reception 8am-midnight. Lockout 10am-1pm. Curfew 2am. V, MC.

Nova Hôtel, 8 rue Richelieu (tel. 04 67 60 79 85; fax 04 67 60 89 06). Entering the pl. de la Comédie from rue Maguelone, the Opera building is on your left; rue Richelieu is a small street directly behind the Opera. A delightful family-run affair, this modern 2-star is newly renovated. The hotel has hosted many musicians, including Bruce Springsteen. Singles 113F, with shower 163F, with shower and toilet 181F; doubles with shower 190F; triples with shower 227F; quads with shower and toilet 291F. Breakfast 30F. These prices reflect a 10% discount for *Let's Go* readers. V, MC, AmEx.

Hôtel des Étuves, 24 rue des Étuves (tel. and fax 04 67 60 78 19), off pl. de la Comédie. This personable little hotel is a maze of narrow tile hallways leading to fresh, spacious rooms with TVs. Singles with shower and toilet 105-140F. Doubles with shower and toilet 150-170F. TV 20F extra. Breakfast 27F.

Hôtel Majestic, 4 rue du Cheval Blanc (tel. 04 67 66 26 85). Follow rue des Étuves three blocks from pl. de la Comédie and turn right. Simple, spacious, clean rooms. Singles 110F, with shower 180-200F; doubles 180-200F, with shower 220F; triples 300F; quads 350F. Shower 20F. Breakfast 25F. V, MC.

Campsites: 3km away in coastal **Lattes. L'Éden,** rte. de Palavas (tel. 04 67 15 11 05; fax 04 67 15 11 31), offers 4-star camping with a pool and ping-pong. 1 or 2 people 74-134F; 3 people 90-165F; 4 people 106-196F; most expensive in July. Open Apr.-Oct. To reach L'Éden, take bus #17 (direction "Palavas") from the *gare*.

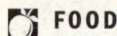 FOOD

Standard French fare awaits on the many *places* of the *vieille ville*, but while in Montpellier don't neglect to take advantage of the many ethnic possibilities. **Rue des Écoles Laïques** in the old city offers a variety of choices, including Greek, Egyptian, Italian, and Lebanese fare. During the school year, students can be found munching in the eateries on **rue de fbg Boutonnet** on the way to the university campus. Contact **CROUS,** 2 rue Monteils (tel. 04 67 41 50 00) for info about the four **university restaurants.** None is located for a tourist's convenience, but one ticket (13.50F) gets you a full meal. (M-F lunch and dinner, open Sa on a rotating basis.) Morning **markets** are held daily at pl. Cabane and bd. des Archeaux, Monday to Saturday at pl. de la Comédie. The super-duper **supermarket INNO,** in the basement of the Polygone commercial center, just past the tourist office, will give you more for less. (Open M-Sa 9:30am-8pm.)

Pepe Carvalho, 2 rue Cauzit (tel. 04 67 66 10 10), near pl. St-Ravy. Named for the gourmet Catalan detective from the books of Manuel Vásquez Montalbán. Enjoy the lively atmosphere, tapas (12F), and drinks. 50F *menu* includes 5 tapas and your choice of beverage. Four-person special gives you 12 tapas and 1L of wine for 150F. Open daily July-Aug. noon-1am; Sept.-June M-Sa noon-1am. V, MC, AmEx.

Tripti-Kulai, 20 rue Jacques Cœur (tel. 04 67 66 30 51). A vegetarian mecca; delicious, creative dishes will even satisfy omnivorous friends. Two-course *menu* 63F, three courses 79F. 49-52F salad platters. 60F Lotus mega-platter includes homemade veggie pâté. Indian drinks and a special Indian dish every Friday. From 2-6pm the *pause tranquille* is 16F for coffee, tea, or juice and a pastry or ice cream. 10% discount for students. Open M-Sa noon-9:30pm; snacks only 2-6pm.

La Tomate, 6 rue Four-des-Flammes (tel. 04 67 60 49 38). Known for its wonderful *cuisine française* at amazing prices. Wood and red-checkered tablecloth atmosphere enhanced by jovial family management. The *soupe des poissons* is *délicieuse*. Lunch *menu* 50F; dinner *menu* from 62F. Reservations recommended Sept.-Apr. Open Tu-Sa noon-2pm and 7-10pm. V, MC.

👁 SIGHTS

The old city's pedestrian streets, bookstores, and the sprawling pl. de la Comédie offer some of the best entertainment in Montpellier, all of it free. Hidden behind grandiose oak doors, the secret courtyards and intricate staircases of 17th- and 18th-century *hôtels particuliers* escape the outside bustle. Particularly notable are the **Hôtel de Varennes,** 2 pl. Petrarque, with its medieval-style rooms, and **Hôtel des Tresoriers de France,** rue Jacques Coeur. The tourist office distributes a walking guide, and their tours let you into some of the 100-odd *hôtels*.

Touting itself as *la ville de culture*, Montpellier hosts two impressive collections of pre-Impressionist art. The **Musée Fabre,** 39 bd. Bonne Nouvelle (tel. 04 67 14 83 00), near the esplanade, displays works by Courbet, Géricault, Delacroix, and 17th-century Dutch and Flemish painters. The top floor exhibits contemporary and local art. (Open Tu-F 9am-5:30pm, Sa-Su 9:30am-5pm. 20F, students 10F; tours 45F.) The **Collection Xavier-Atger,** 2 rue de l'École de Médecine (tel. 04 67 66 27 77), next to the cathedral inside the Faculté de Médecine, contains drawings and sketches by Fragonard, Watteau, and Caravaggio. Walk through the entrance hall of the *Faculté* to the balcony, turn left, and at the end of the hall take stairs on the left. Ring the bell to enter. (Open Sept.-July M, W, F 1:30-5pm.)

Rue Foch, off pl. des Martyrs in the northwest corner of the old city, leads to the **promenade du Peyrou.** The promenade links the **Arc de Triomphe,** erected in 1691 to honor Louis XIV, to the **Château d'Eau,** the arched terminal of a beautifully preserved aqueduct. Through the arches the imposing statue of the Sun King protects the promenade, a short lane lined with towering magnolias and huge cube-cut trees. The monument has stood guard since 1839, half a century after French Revolutionaries melted down his predecessor to make pots and pans. At night, strategically placed groundlights frame the *Roi Soleil* with a radiant glow. Bd. Henri IV leads to the **Jardin des Plantes** (tel. 04 67 63 43 22), France's first botanical garden. Designed in 1593 for local students to study medicinal herbs, it is now a historical monument. (Open M-Sa Apr.-Sept. 9am-noon and 2-7pm; Oct.-Mar. 10am-noon and 2-5pm. Free.) If you're still inside when the noon closing bell rings, you'll spend the next two hours wilting with the plants in the sun.

ENTERTAINMENT AND FESTIVALS

ENTERTAINMENT. Cinéma Le Diagonal, 18 pl. St-Denis (tel. 04 67 92 91 81), shows new-release films in their original language (37F). Call the music school **JAM** (Jazz Action Montpellier), 100 rue de Lesseps (tel. 04 67 58 30 30), to see if any jazz artists are gigging. The *café-théâtre* **L'Antirouille,** 12 rue Anatole France (tel. 04 67 58 75 28), has international music and rock concerts Wednesday through Saturday nights. (Open M-Sa Apr.-Aug. 9pm-2am; Sept.-Mar. 8pm-1am. 20-80F.)

Pl. Jean-Jaurès, rue Verdun, and **rue des Écoles Laïques** remain favorite nightspots. In summer, once stores have closed, **rue de la Loge** becomes a street of vendors, musicians, and stilt-walkers. The back half of a 1955 Cadillac, complete with tail fins and a Tennessee "Elvis 1" license plate, protrudes precariously from above the entrance to **Rockstore,** 20 rue de Verdun (tel. 04 67 58 70 10), near the station. Bands of varying levels of talent perform thrice weekly to the delight of teens and twenty-somethings. It and the **disco** upstairs are open until 6am on the weekend. The **Fizz,** 4 rue Cauzit (tel. 04 67 66 22 89), is the other shaking *boîte* in the city, with dancing below and a space to hang above. (Open nightly 11pm-dawn. 50F with 2 beers.) For the dartsy crowd, **Le Nottes en Bulles,** 19 rue des Écoles Laïques (tel. 04 67 60 38 21), features darts, beer, and a totally alternative look. The bizarre decor includes an astronaut mannequin suspended above the entrance. Happy hour is 6-8pm; on Wednesday, beers are two for one. (Open M-Sa 7pm-2am.) Gay men throughout the region come to **Martin's Bar,** 5 rue de Girone (tel. 04 67 60 37 15), behind the pl. Marché aux Fleurs—a scene in itself—for drinks and the occasional show before hitting the clubs. (Open daily 7pm-1am.) The lesbian scene is subtle but friendly at mixed **Le Volt Face** (see **Food,** above).

The **Corum,** at the far end of the Esplanade Charles de Gaulle (tel. 04 67 61 67 61), houses the opera and the Philharmonic Orchestra of Montpellier. (No concerts in summer. 80-140F; discounts for students and seniors.)

FESTIVALS. The last two weeks of June and the first week of July bring the **Printemps des Comédiens pac Euromédecine** (tel. 04 67 63 66 67), an open-air theater festival. Contact the Opéra Comédie, pl. de la Comédie for details. (Info tel. 04 67 60 19 99; reservations 04 67 63 66 66. Tickets 40-140F, under 25 and seniors 40-120F.) In the first two weeks of July, the **Festival International Montpellier Danse** brings performances, workshops, and films to local stages and screens. For details contact Hôtel d'Assas, 6 rue Vieille Aiguillerie. (Info tel. 04 67 60 83 60; reservations tel. 04 67 60 07 40. 25-180F.) The rest of July is taken up with the **Festival de Radio France et de Montpellier,** with performances of opera, jazz, and classical music. (Info and tickets tel. 04 67 02 02 01. 50-220F; discounts for under 26 and seniors.)

MILLAU AND THE GORGES DU TARN

Once a flourishing center for Gallo-Roman pottery and later known as the capital of glove-making, Millau is enviably located in a verdant valley, surrounded by the rocky, arid Causses plateaux and cut through by the Tarn and Dourbie rivers. With cheery red roofs, outdoor cafés, and a passion for *pétanque*, it's a great base for discovering the Gorges du Tarn, the Causses, and the famous *grottes* (caves) of Argilan and Aven Armand. Outdoor companies based in and around Millau cater to most sportive whims, including para- and hang-gliding, so popular that the summer sky is often colored with pretty parachutes floating around the valley.

◪ ORIENTATION AND PRACTICAL INFORMATION. Trains run from the *gare* (tel. 05 65 61 55 66) to **Paris** (8hr., 2 per day, 342F) and **Béziers** (2hr., 2-3 per day, 89F). Next door at the *gare routière* (tel. 05 65 59 89 33), **SNCF** and **La Populaire** (tel. 05 65 61 01 01) send **buses** to **Montpellier** (1½hr.; M-Sa 4 per day, Su 2 per day; 98F). For **taxis**, call **Sannie/Goutti** (tel. 05 65 61 03 85; 24hr.). The **tourist office**, 1 av. Merle (tel. 05 65 60 02 42), is conveniently located to the right on the second block down from the *gare*. Ask for their free and handy *guide pratique*, which includes a map, useful addresses, and a detailed list of sporting activities in the region. (Open July-Aug. daily 9am-12:30pm and 2-7pm; Sept.-Mar. M-Sa 9am-noon and 2-6pm; Apr.-June and Sept. M-Sa 9am-noon and 2-6pm.) The **hospital** is at 265 bd. Achilles Souques (tel. 05 65 61 70 00). The **police** station is at 14 rue de la Condamine (tel. 05 65 61 23 00). The **post office** is at 10 av. Alfred Merle. (Open M-F 8:30am-7pm, Sa 8:30-noon. **Postal code:** 12100.)

▗ ACCOMMODATIONS AND CAMPING. Finding a place to sleep in Millau gets difficult from the end of June until September; reserve at least a week ahead. The **youth hostel/FJT,** 26 Lucien Costes (tel./fax 05 65 61 27 74), is in a quiet part of town. From the *gare*, go straight down av. Merle, crossing av. de la République, and continuing down the small rue Ferrer. At av. Jean Jaurès turn left and follow it 10 minutes; rue Lucien Costes will be on the right. (48F. Sheets 17F. Breakfast 19F. Kitchen facilities. Reception M-F 9am-noon and 2-6pm, Sa after 7pm, Su after 9pm. No curfew.) The archetypical, ageing, and over-named **Grand Hôtel de Paris et de la Poste,** av. Merle (tel. 05 65 60 00 52; fax 05 65 59 11 13), has character, if not class, above a restaurant with *menus* at 65F, 75F, and 98F. (Singles and doubles 140F, with toilet 160F, with toilet and shower 220F. Breakfast 35F. V, MC.) Nattier **Le Commerce,** 8 pl. du Mandarous (tel. 05 65 60 00 56; fax 05 65 60 96 50), looks onto the main square. (Doubles from 115F, with toilet 140F, with toilet and shower 180F, toilet and bath 250F. Extra bed 50F. Breakfast 28F. Elevator. V, MC, AmEx.) The tourist office can provide a list of nearby **campsites. Camping Municipal,** across the Tarn on av. de Millau-Plage (tel. 05 65 60 10 97), has a pool and 250 sites. (Package for 2 people 90F. Electricity 18F. Reception daily 8am-8pm. Open Apr.-Sept.)

▗ FOOD. *Aveyronnais* specialties usually contain either Roquefort or *bleu des causses* cheese. Millau is famous for its *trenels*, sheep tripe stuffed with ham, garlic, parsley, and eggs. At *boulangeries*, look out for *la fouace*, a rustic cake in the shape of a large bagel. A holiday dessert is the stalagmite-like *gâteau à la brouche*, made with dozens of eggs and no end of sugar.

There are lots of cheap places to eat in and around the Mandarous, where *café/brasserie* culture runs rampant. Pricier restaurants are tucked into the labyrinthine streets around the **rue Droit** and **pl. du Maréchal Foch.** Crunch into a Croque-Monsieur Roquefort (26F) from **Le Cristal,** 5 pl. Mandarous (tel. 05 65 60 02 18), the best place to nurse a *panaché* and people-watch. (Open daily until midnight or 1am.) Across the *place,* **La Bodequita** does brisk business with its sandwiches (15-20F) and paninis (25-30F) from noon to midnight every day. Down near the Tarn on av. Gambetta is the colorfully grungy **La Locomotive** (tel. 05 65 61 19 93) run by a friendly Basque. It's not hard to swallow the food on the 50F *menu.* (Open for lunch and dinner weekdays until 2am and weekends until 3pm.) Groceries can be had at **Éco Market,** bd. de l'Ayrolle, or at the morning **market** on pl. des Halles and pl. des Consuls (W and F).

WAITING FOR ROQUEFORT Most aptly described as one stinky green cheese, Roquefort was rated the king of its kind by Diderot in his *Encyclopedia* of 1757. The odor of this crumbly cheese will no doubt reawake memories of locker rooms on a hot summer's day, but a tale of love and romance courses through its moldy veins. Legend has it that a young shepherd had a *coup de foudre* when a pretty demoiselle happened to pass by in the fields. Crazy with desire, he rushed after her, forgetting his sheep and his lunch in the process. Weeks later the shepherd returned to the spot and found his lunch, long since gone bad. Too famished to care, he held his nose, took a bite, and was surprised to find the cheese quite tasty. Thus did Roquefort come about, made from ewe's milk, injected with the special mould *penicilium roqueforti* and kept for at least 3 months in the cool, humid, limestone *caves* unique to the region. Cheese lovers can visit the caves in Roquefort on their own at Société and Papillon or with bus tours which leave from the Millau *gare* in July and August (tel. 05 65 99 05 87; 3 per week; 60F).

☎ SIGHTS. Millau's main attraction is as a base to explore the natural wonders nearby, but the town has a couple of historical monuments recalling its role in the pottery and leather economy. The tourist office runs **city tours** twice a week in July and August (2hr., 30F). **La Graufenesque** (tel. 05 65 60 11 37), on the road to Montpellier, is the archæological site of a Gallo-Roman pottery atelier. (Open daily 9am-noon and 4-6:30pm. 15F.) The **Musée de Millau,** pl. du Maréchal Foch (tel. 05 65 59 01 08), has displays on pottery and gloves. (Open July-Aug. M-Sa 10am-6pm; Sept.-June M-Sa 10am-noon and 2-6pm. 26.50F; combined ticket to Graufenesque 35F.)

GORGES DU TARN

Millau is nestled near the four Grands Causses: the **causse Noir, causse du Larzac, causse de Sauveterre,** and **causse Mejean,** which are flat, arid plateaux whose walls rise steeply up from the river, creating impressive canyons and valleys known as the **Gorges du Tarn.** The rocky *causses* are dotted with scrubby vegetation and flocks of sheep slurping greedily at the precious watering holes. The ewe's milk fuels the Roquefort cheese industry, while the skins are used for luxury leather goods in Millau. Very few people live on the *causses;* the winters are brutally windy and the summers bake whatever dares to grow. Yet the landscape is worth discovering. The porous limestone, which keeps the land arid by sucking much-needed water away from the surface, has created some of the world's most beautiful caves.

The **Grotte Dargilan** (tel. 04 66 45 60 20) is near the town of Meyrueis on the Causse Noir. This cave was discovered in 1880 by a shepherd who was convinced he found the gate to Hell. Dargilan has a number of interesting mineral formations, including the so-called "petrified waterfall" and a 20m stalactite known as the "*clocher*" or belltower. (Open July-Aug. 9am-7pm; Apr., June, and Sept. 9am-noon and 1:30-4pm; Oct. 10am-noon and 1:30-5pm. 39F, 14 and under 24F.) Even more mind-blowing is the **Aven Armand** (tel. 04 66 45 61 31), also near Meyrueis, discovered in 1897. A little train runs to the heart of the cave into a "room" that measures 60m by 100m by 35m. There you will find a forest of stalagtites and stalagmites, resembling every kind of fantastic tree imaginable. (Open Apr.-May 10am-noon and 1:30-5pm; June-Aug. 10am-7pm; Sept.-Oct. 10:30am-noon and 1:30-4pm. Last train 45min. before closing. 47F, 12 and under 20F.)

The verdant **valleys** of the Tarn, the Jonte, and the Dourbie rivers offer a watery respite from the parched landscape above. Tourists flock to the campsites bordering the water, where there are easy to more difficult stretches of river to canoe and kayak along. To **rent kayaks, canoes,** or **bikes,** contact **Roc and Canyon** at 55 av. Jean Jaurès (tel. 05 65 61 17 77; fax 05 65 60 84 57), Millau, or at their summer address on rte. de Nant. They also organize canoeing and kayak trips with certified guides.

For a complete list of rental companies, consult the Millau tourist office's *Guide Pratique*. As you brave the rapids, look out for the enormous vultures that occasionally swoop down from their nests in the cliffs.

The less outdoorsy can hop onto the full-day **Cariane Aveyron bus tours** that leave from Millau to visit the Aven Armand and a number of pretty villages along the Tarn and the Jonte. (Information at the *gare routière* or tel. 05 65 61 30 88. Tours daily July-Aug. 90F.) Less frequent circuits also exist for Roquefort and the Crusader sites in the region. Whichever means you chose, the contrast between the desert-like, rock-filled causses and the verdant valleys along the Tarn river is striking and merits at least a full day of exploration.

CONQUES

Stashed away amidst verdant hills in the heart of the Aveyron, Conques (pop. 360) was a major pilgrimage stop between Le Puy-en-Velay and Moissac on the road to Santiago de Compostela. Though its monastery dates back to the early 9th century, it was only when one of their monks pulled off a daring relic heist—snatching the child martyr St. Foy's remains from Agen—that Conques made its mark. The robbery was immediately justified by a string of miracles, and countless streams of pilgrims made their way here between the 11th and 13th centuries. Today the restored abbey reposes among medieval houses and lush green landscape. Be sure to bring enough cash to tide you over—there's no ATM in town.

⑦ ORIENTATION AND PRACTICAL INFORMATION. There are no trains to Conques and only occasional buses. The easiest way to get there is by car; otherwise plan carefully with buses, which will require a change at **Rodez**. In summer, a bus goes to Rodez in the morning and returns in the afternoon (45min.; July-Aug. Tu, Th, and Sa; 21F); it has convenient connections with **Millau** (1½hr., 62F). The rest of the year, there is a daily afternoon bus from Rodez to Conques, which returns the following morning. **Rodez's bus station** (tel. 05 65 68 11 13) is located at the Esplanade Foirail in the *centre ville*. Conques has very few streets to get lost in. From the bus stop, follow the main street past the post office and make for the church. The **tourist office** (tel. 05 65 72 85 00) is to the right of the church façade and distributes a free map, *guide pratique*, and info on accommodations. (Open daily July-Aug. 9am-7pm; Sept.-July M-Sa 9am-noon and 2-6pm.) For a **taxi**, call Annie Lample (tel. 05 65 78 84 76). The **post office** has **currency exchange**. (Open M-F 9am-12:30pm and 2-4:30pm, Sa 9am-noon. **Postal code:** 12320.)

⑦⑫ ACCOMMODATIONS AND FOOD. Conques can easily be seen in half a day, but the bus schedule is likely to force you to stay the night. Alas, prices are high. The most economic option is M. Gibert's **gîte d'étape** on rue Émile Roudie (tel. 05 65 72 82 98; fax 05 65 69 85 11), with one large dormitory and a communal kitchen, toilet, and showers. (37F, honor system.) **L'Auberge Saint-Jacques** (tel. 05 65 72 86 36; fax 05 65 72 82 47), on the way to the church, has comfortable rooms with baths and toilets above a popular restaurant and *brasserie*. (Doubles 185-245F; triples 310-320F. Breakfast 35F. V, MC.) The closest **camping** is the three-star **Beau rivage** (tel. 05 65 69 82 23), 300 meters from Conques via rue Charlemagne on the banks of the Dordogne. It has a pool, laundry, and a restaurant. (21F per person, 18F per tent, 12F per car. Electricity 14-16F. Open Apr.-Sept. Reception Apr.-May and Sept. 7-9:30pm; June 8-11am and 7-9:30pm; July-Aug. 8am-midnight.)

Cheap food in Conques is hard to come by. Forage at the **boulangerie** on the way to the church. (Open daily 7am-8pm.) A stone's throw away from the tympanum, **Restaurant Au Parvis** (tel. 05 65 72 82 81) offers a great view of the church as well as salads (25-40F), pizzas (45-50F), and a 69F *menu*. **Le Charlemagne** (tel. 05 65 69 81 50) sports a medieval-like decor and a magnificent view of the rolling hills from the terrace. (Salads 35-48F, *menu* 78F, *plats* 60-65F.)

☎ ❀ SIGHTS AND FESTIVALS. The main attraction in Conques is the **Église Abbatiale Ste-Foy,** a thoroughly elegant example of Romanesque architecture built between 1050 and 1120. Before entering, admire the carved **tympanum,** which depicts a faded Last Judgment with a gaping Mouth of Hell ready to gobble the wicked. The barrel-vaulted interior, already unusual for its airy proportions, is flooded with light thanks to the deceivingly simple stained glass designed in 1987. The precious relics, revered for their ability to cure the blind and to free prisoners, were partly stored in the opulent gem-studded, golden cult statue now displayed with much reverence in the **trésor** next door. The treasury has a superb collection of medieval reliquaries and liturgical instruments, including the **A of Charlemagne,** a bizarre silver-plated wooden "A," supposedly given to Conques by the emperor but actually from the 11th-century. Newer and less precious goods are relegated to the **trésor II,** behind the tourist office. (Open daily 9am-1pm and 2-7pm. 30F, students 23F, children 10F.)

The **Centre Européen d'Art et de Civilisation Médiévale** (tel. 05 65 71 24 00), at the top of the town, is a cultural center for medieval studies which organizes free exhibitions. (Open July-Aug. M-F 9am-noon and 2-6pm. Sa 2-6pm. Call for winter hours.) Classical concerts are given in the abbey during the **Festivale de la Musique.** (Mid-July to mid-Aug. Tickets at tourist office 60-130F, students 40-110F.)

APPENDIX

APPENDIX

CLIMATE

Below is a chart giving average temperatures and rainfalls for major French cities. For a conversion chart from °C to °F, see the inside back cover; for a rough estimate, double the Celsius and add 32.

Av. Temp. (lo/hi), Precipitation	January			April			July			October		
	°C	°F	mm	°C	°F	mm	°C	°F	mm	°C	°F	mm
Ajaccio	4/13	39/55	7.5	9/19	48/66	5.5	18/29	64/84	7.0	13/22	55/71	9.5
Bordeaux	1.6/9	35/48	6.8	7/17	45/63	6.5	14/27	57/81	5.0	8/19	46/66	9.5
Brest	4/8	39/46	8.8	7/13	45/55	6.3	13/21	55/70	5.0	9/16	48/61	9.0
Cherbourg	4/8	39/46	8.3	6/12	43/54	5.0	14/19	57/66	4.8	10/15	50/59	11.5
Lille	0.5/6	33/43	5.0	4/14	39/57	7.0	13/24	55/75	7.0	7/15	45/59	7.5
Lyon	-1/5	30/41	5.3	6/16	43/61	7.0	14/27	39/81	7.0	7/16	45/61	7.8
Marseille	3/12	37/54	5.0	5/15	41/59	1.5	14/26	57/79	1.5	13/24	55/75	9.3
Paris	0/6	32/43	4.3	5/16	41/61	5.3	13/24	55/75	5.3	6/15	43/59	5.5
Strasbourg	0/4	32/39	6.5	5/15	41/59	8.5	14/26	39/79	8.5	6/14	43/57	6.8
Toulouse	19/26	66/79	6.3	7/17	45/63	3.8	15/28	59/82	3.8	9/19	48/66	5.5

TIME ZONES

France lies in the Central European time zone, which is one hour ahead of GMT. From Easter to Autumn, French time moves one hour ahead. Both switches occur about a week before such changes in the US.

FRANCE IS...	
9 hours later than	Vancouver and Los Angeles
6 hours later than	New York and Toronto
1 hour later than	London and Dublin
synchronous with	Madrid, Rome, Zürich, Berlin, and Stockhölm
1 hour earlier than	Johannesburg
9 hours earlier than	Sydney
11 hours earlier than	Auckland

INTERNATIONAL CALLING CODES

COUNTRY CODES			
Australia	61	France	33
Canada and USA	1	New Zealand	64
Ireland	353	South Africa	13
Monaco	377	United Kingdom	44

MEASUREMENTS

France invented, and still uses, the metric system of measurement. The basic unit of length is the **meter (m)**, which is divided into 100 **centimeters (cm)**, or 1000 **millimeters (mm)**. 1000 meters make up one **kilometer (km)**. Fluids are measured in **liters (L)**, each divided into 1000 **milliliters (ml)**. A liter of pure water gives the weight of one **kilogram (kg)**, divided into 1000 **grams (g)**, while 1000kg make up one metric **tonne**.

MEASUREMENT CONVERSIONS

1 inch = 25.4 mm	1 mm = 0.039 in.
1 foot = 0.30 m	1 m = 3.28 ft.
1 yard = 0.914m	1 m = 1.09 yd.
1 mile = 1.61km	1 km = 0.62 mi.
1 ounce = 28.35g	1 g = 0.035 oz.
1 pound = 0.454kg	1 kg = 2.202 lb.
1 fluid ounce = 29.57ml	1 ml = 0.034 fl. oz.
1 gallon = 3.785L	1 L = 0.264 gal.

NATIONAL HOLIDAYS

The main national holiday is *La Fête Nationale* **(Bastille Day),** July 14, which commemorates the Revolution on the anniversary of the storming of the Bastille in 1789. Expect pandemonic celebrations in large cities.

When a national holiday falls on a Tuesday or Thursday, the French often also take off the Monday or Friday, a practice known as *faire le pont* (to make the bridge). Banks close at noon on the day of, or the nearest working day before, a national holiday.

DATE	HOLIDAY
January 1	Le Jour de l'an (also called le St-Sébastian): New Year.
April 24	Le lundi de Pâques: Easter Monday
May 1	La Fête du travail: Labor Day
May 8	L'Anniversaire de la Libération: Celebrates the Liberation in 1944.
June 1	L'Ascension: Ascension day.
June 12	Le Lundi de Pentecôte: Whit Monday
July 14	La Fête Nationale: Bastille day.
August 15	L'Assomption: Feast of the Assumption
November 1	La Toussaint: All Saints' Day
November 11	L'Armistice 1918: Armistice Day
December 25	Le Noël: Christmas

FRENCH PHRASEBOOK AND GLOSSARY

FRENCH PRONOUNCIATION GUIDELINES

Many French sounds to do not exist in English, so they take some practise. To pronounce "r," roll the back of your tongue against your palate in a guttural manner, almost as if you were preparing to spit. "U" is distinct from "ou;" to make an "u," purse your lips as if to say "ooooo," and hold them in this posiion while trying to say "eeeeee." For an "ou," curl your tongue back so its tip touches your palate, purse your lips, and go "oooooo." For other sounds, note that whereas in English many vowels are pronounced as if they ended in "y," in French the sound is cut short. To get this right, hold your lips fixed for the duration of each vowel. There are only two basic lip positions in French, but neither is natural to the English speaker. For "e," "o," "u," "eu," and "on," purse your lips and pout like, well, a French person; for "i," "é," or "an," stretch your lips into a manic grin. Nasal vowels, "on," "un," and "in," are sounded with the mouth and tongue in the same positions as their un-nasal equivalents "o," and "u," and "i." An exception, "en" is made with the mouth half open and lips relaxed. All this lip-stretching exercise is probably the foundation of the French reputation for good kissing. If all this is too confusing, you'll just about make yourself understood if you use the transliterations below, which are based on the US pronunciation of English.

TRANSLITERATED PHRASES

ENGLISH	FRENCH	TRANSLITERATION
GENERAL		
Hello./Good day.	Bonjour.	bonh-ZHOORRH
Good evening.	Bonsoir.	bonh-SWAHRRH
Hi!.	Salut!	sah-LU
Goodbye.	Au revoir.	oh rhVWAHRH
Good night.	Bonne nuit.	bonn NWEE
yes/no/maybe	oui/non/peut-être	wee/nonh/p'TEHT-rh
please	s'il vous plaît	seel voo PLAY
thank you	merci	mehrrh-SEE
You're welcome.	De rien.	de rhee-INH
Pardon me!	Excusez-moi!	ex-ku-ZEH MWAH
Go away!	Casse-toi.	KASS-TWAH
Where is...?	Où se trouve...?	oo s'TRRHOOV..?
What time do you open/close?	Vous ouvrez/fermez à quelle heure?	vooz ooVRHEH/ferhMEH ah kel'URH?
Help.	Au secours.	oh-SKOORRH.
I'm lost.	Je suis perdu(e)	zh'SWEE pehrh-DU
I'm sorry.	Je suis désolé(e).	zh'SWEE deh-zoh-LEH

OTHER USEFUL PHRASES AND WORDS

ENGLISH	FRENCH	ENGLISH	FRENCH
PHRASES			
Good morning.	Bonjour.	**Good evening**	Bonsoir
Good afternoon	Bon aprés-midi	**Hi!**	Salut!
Good-bye.	Au revoir.	**Please...**	S'il vous plaît...
Thank you (very much).	Merci (bien).	**I'm sorry.**	Je suis désolé.
Excuse me?	Pardon?	**Excuse me!**	Excusez-moi/Pardon!
When?	Quand?	**No, thank you.**	Non, merci.
Who?	Qui?	**What is it?**	Qu'est-ce que c'est?
What?	Quoi?	**Why?**	Pourquoi?
How much does this cost?	Ça coûte combien?	**This one/that one**	ceci/cela
Go away/Leave me alone.	Laissez-moi tranquille.	**Stop/Stop that!**	Arrête! (sing.) Arrêtez! (plur.)
I don't understand.	Je ne comprends pas.	**Please repeat.**	Répétez, s'il vous plaît.
Please speak slowly.	S'il vous plaît, parlez moins vite.	**Help!/Please help me.**	Au secours!/Aidez-moi, s'il vous plaît.
I am ill/I am hurt.	J'ai mal/Je suis blessé.	**Do you speak English?**	Parlez-vous anglais?
I am a student (m)/a student (f)	Je suis étudiant/étudi-ante	**What's this called in French?**	Comment ça se dit en français?
I'm 20 years old	J'ai vingt ans	**I would like...**	Je voudrais...
What is your name?	Comment vous appellez-vous?	**The bill, please.**	L'addition, s'il vous plaît.
Please, where is...?	S'il vous plaît où se trouve(nt)...?	**the cash machine**	le guichet automatique
a doctor	un médecin	**the restaurant?**	le restaurant?
the toilet	les toilettes	**the police**	la police
the hospital	l'hôpital	**the train station**	la gare
a bedroom	une chambre	**single room**	une chambre simple
with	avec	**double room**	une chambre pour deux

a double bed	un grand lit	a two single beds	deux lits
a toilet	toilettes	a bath	bain
a shower	une douche	without	sans
lunch	le déjeuner	breakfast	le petit déjeuner
included	compris	dinner	le dîner
hot	chaud	cold	froid

DIRECTIONS

(to the) right	à droite	(to the) left	à gauche
straight	tout droite	near to	près de
north	nord	far from	loin de
south	sud	east	est
follow	suivre	west	ouest

NUMBERS

one	un	two	deux
three	trois	four	quatre
five	cinq	six	six
seven	sept	eight	huit
nine	neuf	ten	dix
eleven	onze	twelve	douze
fifteen	quinze	twenty	vingt
twenty-five	vingt-cinq	thirty	trente
forty	quarante	fifty	cinquante
hundred	cent	thousand	mille

TIMES AND HOURS

open	ouvert	closed	fermé
What time is it?	Quelle heure est-il?	It's 1pm	Il est treize heures.
afternoon	l'après-midi	morning	le matin
night	la nuit	evening	le soir
today	aujourd'hui	yesterday	hier
until	jusqu'à	tomorrow	demain
Monday	lundi	public holiday	jours fériés (j.f.)
Tuesday	mardi	Friday	vendredi
Wednesday	mercredi	Saturday	samedi
Thursday	jeudi	Sunday	dimanche
January	janvier	July	juillet
February	février	August	août
March	mars	September	septembre
April	avril	October	octobre
May	mai	November	novembre
June	juin	December	décembre

MENU READER

lamb	agneau (m)	raspberry	framboise (f)
garlic	ail (m)	French fries	frites (f pl.)
asparagus	asperges (f pl.)	cheese	fromage (m)
plate	assiette (f)	cake	gâteau (m)
eggplant	aubergine (f)	gizzard	gésier (m)
flank	bavette (f)	game	gibier (m)
butter	beurre (m)	ice cream	glace (f)
well done	bien cuit (adj)	frog's legs	cuisses de grenouille (f pl.)
beer	bière (f)	green bean	haricot vert (m)
steak	bifteck (m)	oysters	huitres (f pl.)

chicken breast	blanc de volaille (m)	ham	jambon (m)
beef	boeuf (m)	currant liqueur and white wine	kir (m)
drink	boisson (f)	milk	lait (m)
fish soup of Provence	bouillabaisse (f)	rabbit	lapin (m)
pastry-like bread	brioche (f)	vegetable	légume (m)
kebob	brochette (f)	duck breast	magret de canard (m)
duck	canard (m)	home-made	maison (adj)
pitcher of tap water	carafe d'eau (f)	chestnut	marron (m)
meat and white bean stew of the Southwest	cassoulet (m)	strawberry	fraise (f)
brain	cervelle (la)	honey	miel (m)
mushroom	champignon (le)	mussel	moules (f pl.)
hot	chaud (adj)	mustard	moutarde (f)
goat cheese	chèvre (f)	plain	nature (adj)
choice	choix (f)	nuts	noix (f pl.)
sauerkraut	choucroute (f)	egg	oeuf (m)
cauliflower	chou-fleur (m)	goose	oie (f)
chive	ciboulette (f)	onion	oignon (m)
lemon	citron (m)	bread	pain (m)
lime	citron vert (m)	pasta	pâtes (f pl.)
stew	civet (m)	pastry, pastry shop	pâtisserie (f)
stewed fruit	compote (f)	main course	plat (m)
duck cooked and preserved in its own fat	confit de canard (m)	pan-fried	poêlé
rooster stewed in wine	coq au vin	fish	poisson (m)
rib or chop	côte (f)	pepper	poivre (m)
zucchini/courgette	courgette f)	apple	pomme (f)
custard dessert with carmelized sugar	crème brulée (f)	potato	pomme de terre (f)
whipped cream	crème Chantilly (f)	soup	potage (m)
sweet sour cream	crème fraîche (f)	chicken	poulet (m)
thin pancake	crêpe (f)	prune	pruneau (m)
warm dessert of crêpe flamed in orange liqueur	crêpes Suzette (f pl.)	pork hash cooked in its own fat	rillettes (f pl.)
toasted, open-faced ham and cheese sandwich with fried egg	croque-madame (f)	rice	riz (m)
croque-madame minus the egg	croque-monsieur (f)	green salad	salade verte (f)
raw vegetables	crudités (f pl.)	wild boar	sanglier (m)
tap water	eau de robinet	sausage	saucisson (m)
shallot	échalote (f)	salmon	saumon (m)
chop (cut of meat)	entrecôte (m)	salt	sel (m)
thin slice of meat	escalope (f)	raw meat topped with a raw egg	steak tartare (m)
snail	escargot (m)	sugar	sucre (m)
stuffed	farci(e) (f)	head	tête (f)
sirloin steak	faux-filet (m)	tea	thé (m)
puff pastry	feuilleté (m)	beef filet	tournedos (m)
fig	figue (f)	truffle (mushroom)	truffe (f)
liver of fattened goose/duck	foie gras d'oie/de canard (m)	meat	viande (f)
fresh	frais (fraîche) (adj)	wine	vin (f)

FRENCH-ENGLISH GLOSSARY

Le is the masculine singular definite article (the); *la* the feminine; both are abbreviated to *l'* before a vowel, while *les* is the plural definite article for both genders. Regarding the indefinite article (a, some), *un* is the masculine, *une* the feminine, and *des* the plural. Where a noun or adjective can take masculine and femine forms, the masculine is listed first and the feminine in parentheses; often the feminine form consists of simly adding an "e" to the end, which is indicated by an "e" in parentheses: étudiant(e).

accueil (m): reception
abbaye (f): abbey
abbatiale (f): abbey church
allée (f): lane, avenue
abri (m): shelter
alimentation (f): food
aller-retour (m): round-trip ticket
appareil (m): machine; commonly used for telephone.
appareil photo: camera
aprés-midi (m): afternoon
arc (m): arch
arènes (f pl.): arena
auberge (f): hostel, inn.
auberge de jeunesse (f): youth hostel
autobus (m): city bus
autocar (m): long-distance bus
autoroute (f): highway
banlieue (f): suburb
basse ville (f): lower town
bastide (f): walled town
beffroi (m): belfry
bibliothèque (f): library
billet (m): ticket
billeterie (f): ticket office
bois (m): forest, wood
boucherie (f): butcher's
boulangerie (f): bakery
bureau (m): office
bus (m): city bus
butte (f): hill (archaic)
cap (m): cape, foreland
car (m): long-distance bus
carte (f): card; menu; map
cathédrale (f): cathedral
cave (f): cellar, normally for wine
centre ville (m): center of town
chambre (f): room
chambre d'hôte (f): bed and breakfast room
chapelle (f): chapel
charcuterie (f): shop selling cooked meats (gen. pork) and prepared food
château (m): castle or mansion; headquarters of a vineyard
cimetière (m): cemetery
cité (f): walled city
cloitre (m): cloister
collégiale (f): collegial church

colline (f): hill
comptoir (m): counter (in a bar or café)
côte (f): coast; side (e.g. of hill)
côté (m): side (e.g. of building)
couvent (f): convent
cour (f): courtyard
cours (m): wide street
cru (m): vineyard, vintage
dégustation (f): tasting
donjon (m): keep (of a castle)
douane (f): customs
école (f): school
église (f): church
entrée (f): appetizer
épicerie (f): grocery store
étudiant(e): student
faubourg (m; abbr. fbg): quarter (of town; archaic)
fête (f): celebration, festival; party
ferme (f): farm
fleuve (m): river
foire (f): fair
fontaine (f): fountain
forêt (f): forest
galerie (f): gallery
gare or gare SNCF (f): train station
gare routière (f): bus station
gîte d'étape (m): rural hostel-like accommodations, aimed at hikers
grève (f): strike
guichet (m): ticket counter, cash register desk
haute ville (f): upper town
horloge (f): clock
hors-saison (f): off-season
hôpital (m): hospital
hôtel (particulier) (m): town house, mansion
hôtel de ville (m): town hall
hôtel-Dieu (m): hospital (archaic)
ile (f): island
jour (m): day
jour férié (m): public holiday
location (f): rental store
lycée (m): high school
madame (Mme; f): Mrs.
madamoiselle (Mlle; f): Miss
magasin (m): shop

mairie (f): town hall
maison (f): house
marée (f): tide
marché (m): market
matin (f): morning
mer (f): sea
monastère (m): monastery
monsieur (M.; m): Mr.
montagne (f): mountain
mur (m): wall
muraille (f): city wall, rampart
nuit (f): night
palais (m): palace
parc (m): park
place (f): town square
plan (f): plan, map
plat (m): main course
pont (m): bridge
poste (PTT; f): post office
puy (m): hill, mountain (archaic)
quartier (m): section (of town)
randonnée (f): hike
route (f): road
rue (f): street
salon (m): living room
salle (f): room; in a café it refers to indoor seating as opposed to the bar or patio
sentier (m): path, lane
soir (m): evening
source (m): spring
supermarché (m): supermarket
syndicat d'initiative (m): tourist office
tabac (m): cigarette and newsstand
table (f): table
téléphérique (m): cable car
terrasse (f): terrace, patio
TGV (m): high speed train
thermes (m pl.): hot springs
tour (f): tower
tour (m): tour
traiteur (m): delicatessen
université (f): university
val (m)/vallée (f): valley
vélo (m): bicycle
vendange (f): grape harvest
vieille ville (f): old town
ville (f): town, city
visite guidée (f): guided tour
vitraux (m pl.): stained glass
voiture (f): car

DISTANCES (KM)

	Bayonne	Bordeaux	Brest	Dijon	Lille	Lyon	Marseille	Montpellier	Nancy	Nantes	Nice	Paris	Reims	Rennes	Rouen	Strasbourg	Toulouse	Tours
Bayonne		185	816	817	993	810	673	514	1049	518	835	774	911	626	811	1109	294	540
Bordeaux	185		557	623	799	533	645	486	855	324	807	457	580	717	432	617	245	346
Brest	816	557		868	723	1018	1267	1107	888	297	1428	597	734	245	494	1080	667	537
Dijon	817	623	868		498	193	504	491	214	655	663	312	297	618	447	327	728	1763
Lille	993	799	723	498		682	992	979	421	604	1152	221	203	567	229	527	920	457
Lyon	810	533	1018	193	682		313	300	410	613	472	462	493	768	597	485	537	454
Marseille	673	645	1267	504	992	313		163	720	969	189	773	804	962	907	796	401	739
Montpellier	514	486	1107	491	979	300	163		707	810	325	760	791	918	894	783	241	677
Nancy	1049	855	888	214	421	410	720	707		675	880	307	206	638	443	146	945	513
Nantes	518	324	297	655	604	613	969	810	675		1131	384	521	108	379	867	569	199
Nice	835	807	1428	663	1152	472	189	325	880	1131		932	963	1121	1067	772	562	898
Paris	774	457	597	312	221	462	773	760	307	384	932		144	347	137	490	700	238
Reims	911	580	734	297	203	493	804	791	206	521	963	144		484	280	348	837	375
Rennes	626	717	245	618	567	768	962	918	638	108	1121	347	484		298	830	677	219
Rouen	811	432	494	447	229	597	907	894	443	379	1067	137	280	298		626	790	275
Strasbourg	1109	617	1080	327	527	485	796	783	146	867	772	490	348	830	626		1020	721
Toulouse	294	245	667	728	920	537	401	241	945	569	562	700	837	677	790	1020		598
Tours	540	346	537	1763	457	454	739	677	513	199	898	238	375	219	275	721	598	

ABOUT LET'S GO

FORTY YEARS OF WISDOM

As a new millennium arrives, *Let's Go: Europe*, now in its 40th edition and translated into seven languages, reigns as the world's bestselling international travel guide. For four decades, travelers criss-crossing the Continent have relied on *Let's Go* for inside information on the hippest backstreet cafes, the most pristine secluded beaches, and the best routes from border to border. In the last 20 years, our rugged researchers have stretched the frontiers of backpacking and expanded our coverage into Asia, Africa, Australia, and the Americas. We're celebrating our 40th birthday with the release of *Let's Go: China*, blazing the traveler's trail from the Forbidden City to the Tibetan frontier; *Let's Go: Perú & Ecuador*, spanning the lands of the ancient Inca Empire; *Let's Go: Middle East*, with coverage from Istanbul to the Persian Gulf; and the maiden edition of *Let's Go: Israel*.

It all started in 1960 when a handful of well-traveled students at Harvard University handed out a 20-page mimeographed pamphlet offering a collection of their tips on budget travel to passengers on student charter flights to Europe. The following year, in response to the instant popularity of the first volume, students traveling to Europe researched the first full-fledged edition of *Let's Go: Europe*, a pocket-sized book featuring honest, practical advice, witty writing, and a decidedly youthful slant on the world. Throughout the 60s and 70s, our guides reflected the times. In 1969 we taught travelers how to get from Paris to Prague on "no dollars a day" by singing in the street. In the 80s and 90s, we looked beyond Europe and North America and set off to all corners of the earth. Meanwhile, we focused in on the world's most exciting urban areas to produce in-depth, fold-out map guides. Our new guides bring the total number of titles to 48, each infused with the spirit of adventure and voice of opinion that travelers around the world have come to count on. But some things never change: our guides are still researched, written, and produced entirely by students who know first-hand how to see the world on the cheap.

HOW WE DO IT

Each guide is completely revised and thoroughly updated every year by a well-traveled set of over 250 students. Every spring, we recruit over 180 researchers and 70 editors to overhaul every book. After several months of training, researcher-writers hit the road for seven weeks of exploration, from Anchorage to Adelaide, Estonia to El Salvador, Iceland to Indonesia. Hired for their rare combination of budget travel sense, writing ability, stamina, and courage, these adventurous travelers know that train strikes, stolen luggage, food poisoning, and marriage proposals are all part of a day's work. Back at our offices, editors work from spring to fall, massaging copy written on Himalayan bus rides into witty, informative prose. A student staff of typesetters, cartographers, publicists, and managers keeps our lively team together. In September, the collected efforts of the summer are delivered to our printer, which turns them into books in record time, so that you have the most up-to-date information available for your vacation. Even as you read this, work on next year's editions is well underway.

WHY WE DO IT

We don't think of budget travel as the last recourse of the destitute; we believe that it's the only way to travel. Living cheaply and simply brings you closer to the people and places you've been saving up to visit. Our books will ease your anxieties and answer your questions about the basics—so you can get off the beaten track and explore. Once you learn the ropes, we encourage you to put *Let's Go* down now and then to strike out on your own. You know as well as we that the best discoveries are often those you make yourself. When you find something worth sharing, please drop us a line. We're Let's Go Publications, 67 Mount Auburn St., Cambridge, MA 02138, USA (email: feedback@letsgo.com). For more info, visit our website, http://www.letsgo.com.

INDEX

Q

R

READER QUESTIONNAIRE

Name: _____

Address: _____

City: _____ State: _____ Country: _____

ZIP/Postal Code: _____ E-mail: _____ How old are you? ____

And you're...?   in high school   in college   in graduate school
       employed   retired   between jobs

Which book(s) have you used? _____

Where have you gone with Let's Go? _____

Have you traveled extensively before?   yes   no

Had you used Let's Go before?   yes   no   Would you use it again?   yes   no

How did you hear about Let's Go? friend   store clerk   television
       review   bookstore display
       ad/promotion   internet   other: _____

Why did you choose Let's Go?   reputation   budget focus   annual updating
       wit & incision   price   other: _____

Which guides have you used?   Fodor's   Footprint Handbooks   Frommer's $-a-day
       Lonely Planet   Moon Guides   Rick Steve's
       Rough Guides   UpClose   other: _____

Which guide do you prefer? Why? _____

Please rank the following in your Let's Go guide: (1=needs improvement, 5=perfect)

packaging/cover	1 2 3 4 5	food	1 2 3 4 5	maps	1 2 3 4 5
cultural introduction	1 2 3 4 5	sights	1 2 3 4 5	directions	1 2 3 4 5
"Essentials"	1 2 3 4 5	entertainment	1 2 3 4 5	writing style	1 2 3 4 5
practical info	1 2 3 4 5	gay/lesbian info	1 2 3 4 5	budget resources	1 2 3 4 5
accommodations	1 2 3 4 5	up-to-date info	1 2 3 4 5	other: _____	1 2 3 4 5

How long was your trip?   one week   two wks.   three wks.   a month   2+ months

Why did you go?   sightseeing   adventure travel   study abroad   other: _____

What was your average daily budget, not including flights? _____

Do you buy a separate map when you visit a foreign city?   yes   no

Have you used a Let's Go Map Guide?   yes   no   If you have, which one? _____

Would you recommend them to others?   yes   no

Have you visited Let's Go's website?   yes   no

What would you like to see included on Let's Go's website? _____

What percentage of your trip planning did you do on the web? _____

What kind of Let's Go guide would you like to see? recreation (e.g., skiing)   phrasebook
       spring break   adventure/trekking   first-time travel info   Europe altas

Which of the following destinations would you like to see Let's Go cover?
       Argentina   Brazil   Canada   Caribbean   Chile   Costa Rica   Cuba
       Morocco   Nepal   Russia   Scandinavia   Southwest USA   other: _____

Where did you buy your guidebook?   independent bookstore   college bookstore
       travel store   Internet   chain bookstore   gift   other: _____

Please fill this out and return it to **Let's Go, St. Martin's Press,** 175 Fifth Ave., New York, NY 10010-7848. All respondents will receive a free subscription to *The Yellow-jacket,* the Let's Go Newsletter. You can find a more extensive version of this survey on the web at http://www.letsgo.com.

Paris Métro

Paris: Métro

- The stations Liège and Rennes are closed after 8pm and on Sundays and holidays.
- Beyond the city limits, Métro Urban tickets are not valid on the RER.

Paris: Overview and Arrondissements

1 Cimetière de Montmartre
2 Sacré Coeur Basilica
3 Parc La Villette
4 Parc des Buttes Chaumont
5 Jardins du Trocadero
6 Palais Chaillot
7 Cimetière de Passy
8 American Embassy
9 British Embassy
10 Petit Palais
11 Grand Palais
12 Arc de Triomphe
13 Madeleine
14 Gare St-Lazare
15 Parc Monceau
16 Palais de la Découverte
17 Opéra Garnier
18 Galeries Lafayette
19 Printemps
20 Gare du Nord
21 Gare de l'Est
22 Opéra Bastille
23 Palais Omnisports de Bercy
24 Ministère des Finances
25 Gare de Lyon
26 Parc de Montsouris
27 Cité Universitaire
28 Cimetière Montparnasse
29 Gare Montparnasse

30 Bureau des Objets Trouvés
   (Lost and Found)
31 Louvre
32 Palais Royale
33 Forum des Halles
34 Musée de l'Orangerie
35 Central Post Office
36 Bourse
37 Bibliothèque Nationale
38 Ecole des Arts et Métiers
39 Archives Nationales
40 Musée Carnavalet
41 Musée Picasso
42 Centre George Pompidou
43 place des Vosges
44 Musée Victor Hugo
45 Notre Dame
46 Mémorial de la Déportation
47 Université de Paris (Sorbonne)

48 Ecole Normal Supérieure
49 Musée de Cluny
50 Museum Nationale d'Histoire
   Naturelle
51 Panthéon
52 Eglise St-Etienne du Mont
53 La Mosquée
54 Jardin des Plantes
55 Jardins du Luxembourg
56 Eglise St-Sulpice
57 Théâtre Nationale de l'Odéon
58 Eiffel Tower
59 Champs de Mars

60 Ecole Militaire
61 UNESCO
62 Hôtel des Invalides
63 Assemblée Nationale
64 Musée d'Orsay
65 Cimetière de l'Est du Pere Lachaise

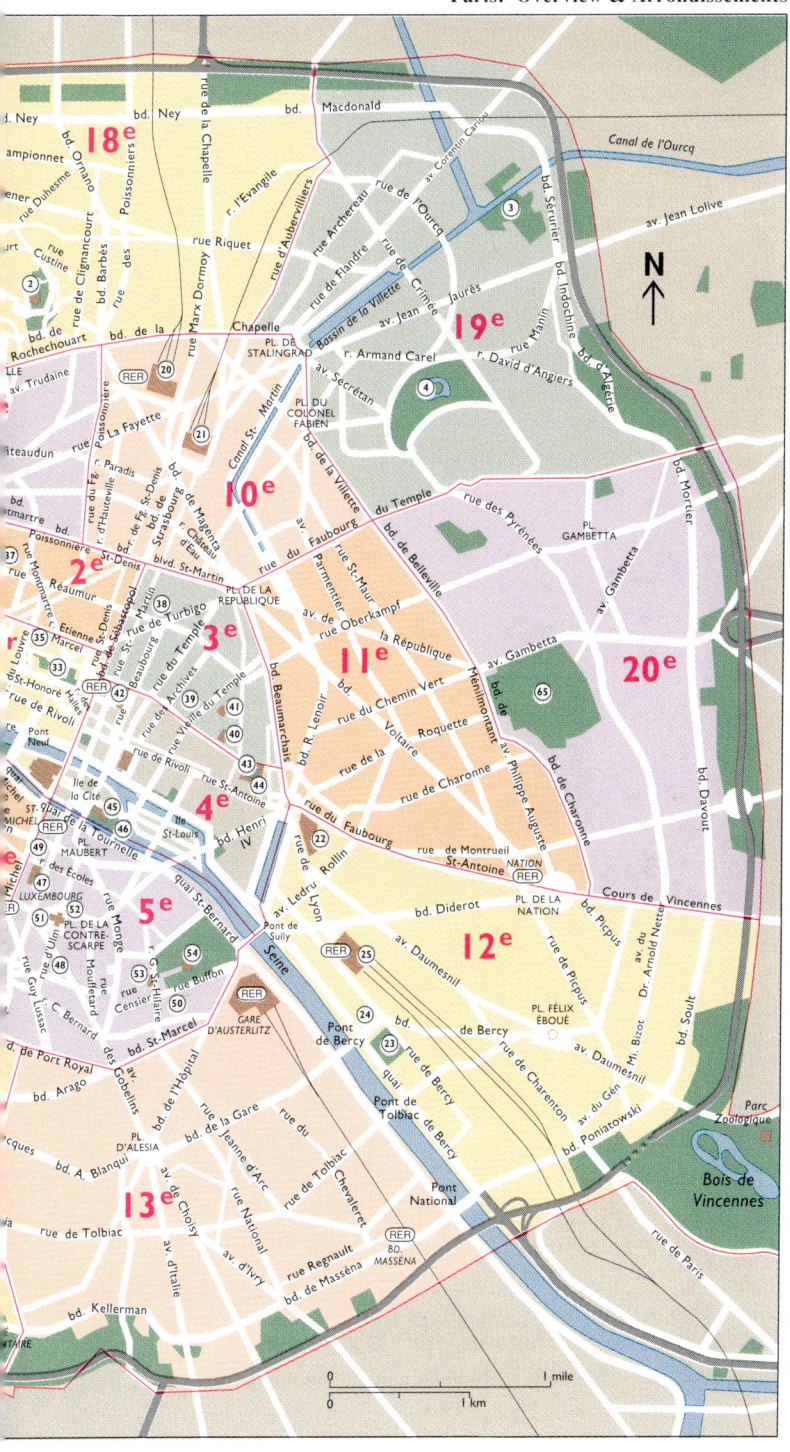

Gare St-Lazare

R. d'Amsterdam

Rue de St-Lazare

Rue de la Chaussée d'Antin

9e

Richelieu Drouot M

M St Lazare

Rue du Havre

Rue de St-Lazare

Chaussée d'Antin

Boulevard Haussmann

M

Havre-Caumartin

La Fayette

Bd. Haussmann

Rue Auber

Rue

Opéra

Boulevard des Italiens

Rue Favart

R.

Rue Pasquier

Rue Tronchet

Auber RER

Scribe

Bd. des Capucines

Opéra RER

Rue du Quatre

Septem

Quatre Septembre

Rue Daunou

Rue des Capucines

Rue de la Paix

Rue D. Casanova

Rue des Petits C

R. Chabanais

Madeleine

Bd. de la Madeleine

Avenue de l'Opéra

Rue Thérèse

Madeleine

M

La Colonne

PLACE VENDÔME

Pyramides

Rue de la Sourdière

Rue St-Roch

Rue Boissy d'Anglas

Rue Royale

Rue St-Honoré

Rue St-Honoré

Rue de Pyramides

PLACE ANDRÉ MALRAUX

8e

1er

R. de Mondovi

Rue du Mont Thabor

Rue Castiglione

Palais R Musée Louv

M Concorde

M

Rue de Rivoli

Tuileries M

Jeu de Paume

PLACE DE LA CONCORDE

JARDIN DES TUILERIES

PLAC CARR

L'Orangerie

Pt. de la Concorde

Quai des Tuileries

Seine

Pont Solférino

Pont Royal

Pont du Carrousel

Quai Anatole France

Quai Voltaire

Assemblée Nationale

Assemblée Nationale

Musée d'Orsay RER

Musée d'Orsay

M

Rue de Lille

Bd. St-Germain

7e

Ecole Nat Superieu Beau

0   1/8 mile

0   125 meters

Solférino M

Rue de l'Université

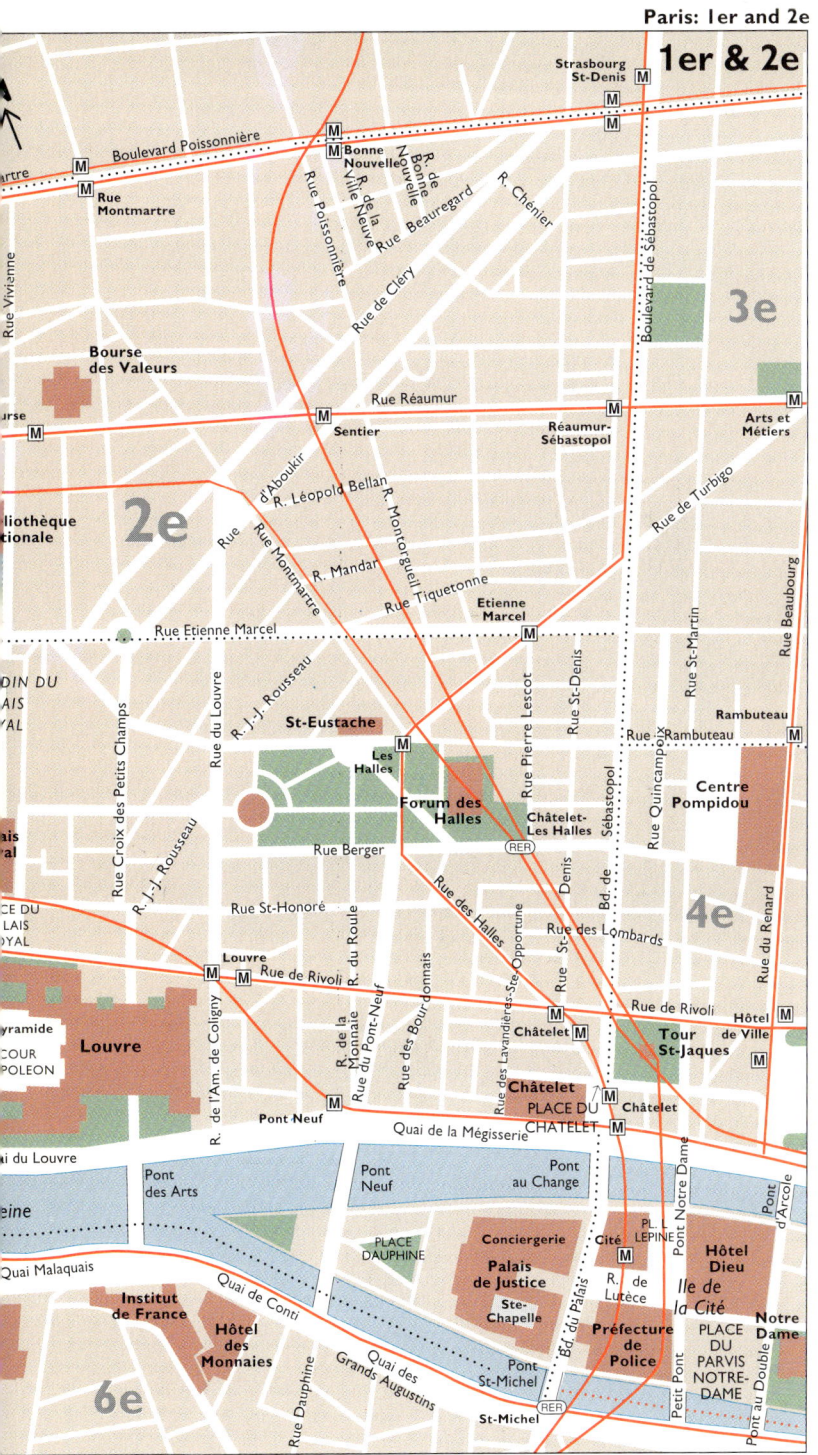

Palais du Louvre

Pont Neuf

Châtelet

Quai du Louvre

1er

Pont du Carrousel

Pont des Arts

Pont au Change

Pont Neuf

Concergerie

Cité

Hôtel Dieu

Quai Malaquais

Ste-Chapelle

Quai de Conti

Ile de la Cité

Ecole Nationale Superieure des Beaux Arts

Institut de France

Hôtel des Monnaies

Quai des Grands Augustins

Pont St-Michel

Rue de la Cité

R. des Sts-Pères

R. Bonaparte

Rue Jacob

Rue de Seine

Rue Mazarine

Rue Dauphine

Quai des Grands Augustins

Pont St-Michel

St-Michel

Pl. St-Michel

Rue St-Jaques

R. de l'Abbaye

PLACE ST-GERMAIN-DES-PRÉS

St-Germain Des Prés

Rue St-André des Arts

Rue Danton

Bd. du Palais

Bd. St-Germain

St-Germain des Prés

Mabillon

Odéon

Musée du Cluny

Bd. St-Germain

7e

R. du Four

Rue de l'Odéon

Rue de Tournon

Rue Racine

Boulevard St-Michel

Sorbonne

PLACE DE LA SORBONNE

R. de Sèvres

R. du Vieux Colombier

R. du Saint Sulpice

PLACE ST-SULPICE

St-Sulpice

PLACE DE L'ODÉON

R. du Cherche Midi

St-Sulpice

Rue Soufflot

R. d'Assas

R. de Rennes

Palais du Luxembourg

St-Michel

Luxembourg

Bd. Raspail

6e

R. de Vaugirard

Rennes

JARDIN DU LUXEMBOURG

St Placide

Rue Gay-Lussac

Rue du Montparnasse

Notre-Dame des Champs

Rue d'Assas

Rue Vavin

Rue Notre-Dame des Champs

Boulevard St-Michel

Montparnasse Bienvenüe

Vavin

Boulevard du Montparnasse

Avenue de l'Observatoire

Port Royal

Rue St-Jaques

R. du Depart

Edgar Quinet

Boulevard Edgar Quinet

14e

Boulevard Raspail

Hôtel
de Ville

4e

R. St-Paul

R. de l'Ave Maria

Bastille M

Boulevard Henri IV

Pont Marie M

Quai des Célestins

Pont
Louis Philippe

Pont Marie

Rue du
Notre Dame

Rue St-Louis

Rue des
Deux Ponts

en l'Ile
Ile St-Louis

Musée
Mickiewicz

Notre
Dame

Pont St-Louis

M

Sully
Morland

Pont de la
Tournelle

Pont de Sully

Rue Montebello

Quai de la
Rapeo

M

Musée de
l'Assistance
Publique

Boulevard St-Germain

Musée de la
Sculpture en
Plein Air

Seine

R. de Bièvre

R. des Bernadins

R. de Pontoise

Institut
du Monde
Arabe

Quai

St-Bernard

R. de Poissy

Rue des Fossés
St-Bernard

Musée de
Minéralogie

M

Rue Cuvier

Rue du Cardinal Lemoine

Rue

St-Bernard

R. Monge

Cardinal
Lemoine

M

Jussieu M

Juissieu

Rue Linne

JARDIN
DES PLANTES

PLACE
VALHUBERT

RER

M

Gare
d'Austerlitz

St-Etienne
du Mont

Arènes
de Lutèce

Rue Cujas

Rue Rollin

nthéon

5e

Musée
d'Histoire
Naturelle

Gare
d'Austerlitz

Rue Lacepede

de l'Estrapade

Rue Mouffetard

Place Monge

PLACE
MONGE

M

Rue Geoffroy
Saint Hilaire

Rue Buffon

Rue Lhomond

Institut Musulman
et Mosque

Rue Poliveau

Rue Erasme Brossolette

Rue Monge

St-Marcel M

Rue Claude Bernard

Censier
Daubenton

M

Rue Berthollet

Boulevard St- Marcel

Bd. de l'Hôpital

e Grâce

Campo
Formio

M

Gobelins M

Boulevard de Port Royal

Avenue des Gobelins

13e

5e & 6e

Paris: RER

Paris RER